MOULD'S MOVIE CAREERS

Actresses

by Paul Mould

First Published in 1999

PUBLISHED BY
PAUL MOULD PUBLISHING

Copyright © Paul Mould 1999

ISBN: 0 9528708 1 9

PRINTED IN GREAT BRITAIN BY
REDWOOD BOOKS

Dedicated to my mother,
who passed her love of the cinema on to me at a very
early age. She never missed a Joan Crawford film
and her rendering of the songs from the films of Jessie
Matthews and Gracie Fields explains my lifelong
interest in musicals.

Best wishes

Paul. Manley

CONTENTS

INTRODUCTION

This book details the careers of over 8,000 actresses; listing their films year by year and naming the director and co-stars. Where known, the former name of the actress is given and any nominations or Academy Awards™. Any known relationship with other members of the movie industry is also included.

Two similar books are planned to give details of both actors and directors.

The period covered is from 1928 to 1998, but some silent films have also been included.

Many films made in Canada, Australia or New Zealand are included and those European films which have been released in either the United Kingdom or the United States.

• • •

The award for Best Song did not start until 1934 and for Best Supporting Actor and Actress until 1936, so the first six years covered in the first index just list the Best Film, Best Actor, Best Actress, Best Director and any Special Awards plus the other nominations.

The following actresses received an Oscar™ for their first film: 1943 Jennifer Jones ("The Song of Bernadette"), 1952 Shirley Booth ("Come Back Little Sheba"), 1964 Julie Andrews ("Mary Poppins"), 1968 Barbra Streisand ("Funny Girl"), 1986 Marlee Matlin ("Children Of A Lesser God").

The following actresses received a nomination for their first film: 1932 Lynn Fontanne ("The Guardsman"), 1939 Greer Garson ("Goodbye Mr Chips"), 1940 Martha Scott ("Our Town"), 1965 Elizabeth Hartman ("A Patch Of Blue"), 1967 Faye Dunnaway ("Bonnie And Clyde"), 1970 Carrie Snodgress ("Diary Of A Mad Housewife"), Jane Alexander ("The Great White Hope"), 1971 Janet Suzman ("Nicolas and Alexandra"), Diana Ross ("Lady Sings The Blues"), 1985 Whoopi Goldberg ("The Color Purple").

The following actresses received a Best Supporting Actress Oscar™ for their first film: 1936 Gale Sondergaard ("Anthony Adverse"), 1943 Katina Paxinou ("For Whom The Bell Tolls"), 1949 Mercedes McCambridge ("All The King's Men"), 1954 Eva Marie Saint ("On The Waterfront"), 1957 Miyoshi Umeka ("Sayonara"), 1967 Estelle Parsons ("Bonnie And Clyde"), 1973 Tatum O;Neal ("Paper Moon"), 1993 Anna Paquin ("Piano").

The following received a Best Supporting Actress Oscar™ in their second film: 1942 Teresa Wright ("Mrs Miniver"), 1966 Sandy Dennis ("Who's Afraid Of Virginia Wolf"), 1969 Goldie Hawn ("Cactus Flower"), 1983 Linda Hunt ("The Year Of Living Dangerously").

The following received a Best Supporting Actress nomination in their first film: 1936 Miliza Korjus ("The Great Waltz"), 1941 Teresa Wright ("The Little Foxes"), Patricia Collinge ("The Little Foxes"), 1944 Angela Lansbury ("Gaslight"), 1951 Lee Grant ("Detective Story"), 1956 Patty McCormack ("The Bad Seed"), Eileen Heckart ("The Bad Seed"), 1957 Diane Varsi ("Peyton Place"), 1962 Mary Badham ("To Kill A Mockingbird"), 1966 Vivian Marchant ("Alfie"), 1968 Sondra Locke ("The Heart Is A Lonely Hunter"), Lynn Carlin ("Faces"), 1969 Dyan Cannon ("Bob And Carol And Ted And Alice"), Cathy Burns ("Last Summer"), 1973 Linda Blair ("The Exorcist"), 1975 Lily Tomlin ("Nashville"), Ronee Blakely ("Nashville"), 1977 Leslie Browne ("The Turning Point"), Quinn Cummings ("The Goodbye Girl"), 1982 Glenn Close ("The World According To Garp"), 1985 Oprah Winfrey ("The Color Purple"), 1996 Marianne Jean-Baptiste ("Secrets And Lies").

Four actresses won both times they were nominated for Best Actress: Luise Rainer, 1936 ("The Great Ziegfeld"), 1937 ("The Good Earth"), Vivien Leigh 1939 ("Gone With The Wind"), 1951 ("Streetcar Named Desire"), Sally Field 1979 ("Norma Rae"), 1984 ("Places In The Heart"), Jodie Foster 1988 ("The Accused"), 1991 ("Silence Of The Lambs").

Actresses with most nominations, either for Best Actress or Best Supporting Actress: Katherine Hepburn - 12, with Oscars™ in 1933 ("Morning Glory"), 1967 ("Guess Who's Coming To Dinner"), 1968 ("The Lion In Winter"), 1981 ("On Golden Pond"). Geraldine Page - 8, finally winning in 1985 ("The Trip To Bountiful"). Greer Garson - 6, five in consecutive years, 1941-45 winning in 1942 ("Mrs Miniver"). Thelma Ritter - 5, between the years 1951-61. Jennifer Jones - 5, four in consecutive years, 1943-46 winning in 1943 ("The Song Of Bernadette"). Irene Dunne - 4. Rosalind Russell - 4.

Until the mid fifties most actresses were contracted to one of the big studios. The second index shows the number of films made by an actress at the individual studios. Some actresses appear on more than one list, as they moved studios, after their contract had expired.

i

Under a contract leading actresses often had to make from four to eight films a year with little chance of complaining about the quality.

It was often when they were loaned out to rival studios that they seized the opportunity to shine in a better role and be considered for an award.

Ann Shirley's career is a good example. She made two films as Dawn O'Day at Fox, before in 1934 she acted in "Anne Of Green Gables" and changed her name to that of the character she portrayed. For this film she moved to R.K.O. and over the next ten years she made twenty more films there but her nomination for Best Supporting Actress came, when she vied with Barbara Stanwyck for the acting honours in "Stella Dallas" at United Artists in 1937.

An even better example is Claire Trevor, who made twenty-three films at Fox Studios between 1933 and 1938 but was nominated for Best Supporting Actress, when loaned to Goldwyn for "Dead End" in 1937. Thereafter she was able to choose roles from any studio and she won the award for Best Supporting Actress in 1948 for "Key Largo" at Warner Brothers and was nominated again in 1954 for "The High And The Mighty" made for John Wayne's own company.

The first chink appeared in the studios' armour, when Olivia De Havilland successfully sued Warner Brothers over "contract slavery", after making sixteen films in four years; many against her better judgement. She proved her point, when she came back after a break of two years to win an Oscar ™ for "To Each His Own" in 1946, followed by a highly-proclaimed performance in "The Snake Pit" in 1948, then a second Oscar ™ in 1949 for "The Heiress".

Other actresses and actors, notably James Cagney, followed her example and by 1956 long contracts were rare. The stars made less films but the quality improved dramatically.

• • •

Dawn O'Day was not the only actress to change her luck by changing her name. Violet Pretty found fame as Anne Heyward. Anna Maria Pierangeli because simply Pier Angeli when she arrived in Hollywood.

Barbara Hershey acted as Barbara Seagall from 1972 to 1975, reverting to Barbara Hershey, after appearing in "Diamonds". Usually, however, actresses keep the name that they chose or that was chosen for them at the start of their career. Susan Weaver read "The Great Gatsby" by F. Scott Fitzgerald, liked the name of one of his characters, and became Sigourney Weaver.

Suzanne Carpentier became Annabella, Ingabor Katrine Klinckerfuss became Karen Verne, Greta Louisa Gustafsson became Greta Garbo, Edda Van Heemsta Hepburn-Ruston became Audrey Hepburn, and Cherilyn Sarkisian became Cher.

Barbara Jo Allen began her career as an ice-skater but, when given the chance to act as a comedienne, she chose the name, Vera Vague, and for several years successfully continued careers under both names.

Over the years some actresses have insisted upon using their title: Mrs Patrick Campbell, Mrs Leslie Carter, Dr Ruth Westheimer, Lady Diana Manners for example. Sandra Lee Henville made nine films between 1939-1942 but was always known as Baby Sandy. Baby Leroy and Baby Bink are also included in this book, although they may have been boys.

If actresses shared a name, the usual procedure was for one to be spelt differently or for an extra initial or christian name to be added, for example: Ann Todd and Ann E. Todd but there are a few cases, where the names are exactly the same. To save confusion they are entered with their country in brackets, for example: Jane Seymour (U.K.), Jane Seymour (U.S.A.) and Mary Morris (U.K.), Mary Morris (U.S.A.).

• • •

Famous pairings are dealt with in the third index. Filmgoers of the thirties and forties would immediately think of Jeanette MacDonald and Nelson Eddy, Ginger Rogers and Fred Astaire, Janet Gaynor and Charles Farrell, Myrna Loy and William Powell, Judy Garland and Mickey Rooney, Greer Garson and Walter Pidgeon or Katherine Hepburn and Spencer Tracey. When more films were made, it was easier to build a sequence between an actress and an actor and the studio system made it more likely but today it would take ten years and is very unlikely, because films are financed by multiple interests and, unless a couple are married or partners, they rarely make more than two or three films together.

This is illustrated by those in the list from the fifties onwards: Elizabeth Taylor and Richard Burton, Joanne Woodward and Paul Newman, Jill Ireland and Charles Bronson, Sondra Locke and Clint Eastwood.

The longest sequence by far was recorded by Penny Singleton and Arthur Lake, who acted together in twenty-seven "Blondie" films.

• • •

When an actress made her first film as a child, the fact is stated, whether she made just the one film or went on to become an adult star, like Elizabeth Taylor, Natalie Wood, Petula Clark, Sally Ann Howes, Pamela Franklyn, Hayley Mills, Brooke Shields, Jodie Foster and Drew Barrymore. Diana Lynn had an extended career, after billed as Dolly Loehr in "There's Magic In Music".

Judy Garland and Deanna Durbin were nearly teenagers, when they began together in a musical short, "Every Sunday" but both of them were soon headlining films.

Shirley Temple on the other hand was only three years old, when she made her debut and she soon received top billing and became the main asset of her studio.

Margaret O'Brien captivated audiences in the forties but her magic faded with her adolescence and Peggy Ann Garner, another favourite of the forties, suffered the same fate but, like many others, she had another bite of the cherry in 1978, appearing in "A Wedding".

Jane Withers had started in 1934, acting with Shirley Temple in "Bright Eyes" and she remained popular until 1947, then had a small role in "Giant" in 1956 and "Captain Newman Mus." in 1963.

Liza Minnelli is included in the list, as she appeared with her mother, Judy Garland, in the last scene of "In The Good Old Summertime"; she was one year old.

Those who found childhood fame include: Edith Fellows, Mitzi Green, Sybil Jason (from South Africa), Gloria Jean, Gigi Perreau, Donna Corcoran and from the U.K.: Binkie Stuart, Joan Dowling, Mandy Miller, Fiona Fullerton, Karen Dotrice and Patsy Kensit. Special Awards were given to: Shirley Temple 1934, Deanna Durbin 1938, Judy Garland 1939, Margaret O'Brien 1944, Peggy Ann Garner 1945 and Hayley Mills 1960. Two child stars won Oscars ™ for Best Supporting Actress: Tatum O'Neal ("Paper Moon") in 1973, Anna Paquin ("The Piano") in 1993. Four others were nominated: Patty McCormack ("The Bad Seed") in 1956, Mary Badham ("To Kill A Mockingbird")) in 1962, Linda Blair ("The Exorcist") in 1973 and Quinn Cummings ("The Goodbye Girl") in 1977.

• • •

Herbert Wilcox directed almost all the films made by his wife, Anna Neagle, even when her co-star, Henry Edwards directed "The Flag Lieutenant" in 1933, Herbert Wilcox was the producer. The fifth index deals initially with wives directed by their husbands or partners. Silent star, Alice Terry, was never directed by anyone but her husband, Rex Ingram.

Elizabeth Bergner had been in silent movies, before Hungarian Paul Czinner directed her talkie debut, "Ariane" in Germany. They then married and made five films together in England, the first being "Catherine The Great".

Marlene Dietrich heads the list of actresses, who had a special affinity with a certain director. Josef von Sternberg made two versions of "The Blue Angel" in 1930; one shot in German and one in English. They were both successful and, when Marlene Dietrich went to America to make "Morocco", he went also as director. He directed six of her next seven films and her performance suffered, when Rouben Mamoulian replaced him for "Song of Songs". The magic returned with a vengeance, when von Sternberg regained the director's chair for "The Scarlet Empress".

No less than five actresses over the years have had their careers inextricably connected with the Swedish director, Ingmar Bergman. They have all been directed by others but their best perfomances have been inspired by Bergman.

Irving Thalberg was not the head of M.G.M. but Louis B. Mayer considered him to be his "boy genius", who turned actors and actresses into superstars. He married one of these, Norma Shearer and, when he died of pneumonia in 1936 at the age of 37, she was devastated and felt unable to make another film, until "Marie Antoinette" in 1938. His reputation was such that today the Irving Thalberg Award is given by the Academy of Motion Picture Arts and Science to honour lifetime achievement in the movie industry. Over a hundred actresses have appeared in films with their husbands or partners. Humphrey Bogart, Laurence Olivier, Ronald Reagan, Tony Curtis, Eddie Fisher, Peter Sellers all acted with two different wives and in Rex Harrison's case it was three. Conversely Paulette Goddard and Elizabeth Taylor acted with two different husbands. When Rex Harrison married Kay Kendall, he knew she was suffering from leukaemia but they made "The Reluctant Debutant" together, then she completed "Once More With Feeling" with Yul Brynner three months before she died.

After they were married Jill Ireland appeared in every film Charles Bronson made and together they fought against the illness that finally separated them.

"No Man Of Her Own" was the only film Carole Lombard and Clark Gable made together. That was in 1932 and in 1942 she was killed in a plane crash in Nevada, returning home with her mother, after selling war bonds in Indianapolis.

Jessica Tandy and Hume Cronyn made several films together and both their names live on in their daughter, Tandy Cronyn, who is also a film actress

Penny Singleton has already been mentioned for making 27 "Blondie" films but other actresses will always be connected with a certain movie character or will be remembered for appearing in a series.

Fay Holden, Cecilia Parker and Sara Haden all acted in 14 "Andy Hardy" films and Ann Rutherford was in twelve.

Ann Sothern made ten "Maisie" pictures and Lois Maxwell was Miss Moneypenny in ten "James Bond" films.

Marjorie Main appeared in nine "Ma and Pa Kettle" films and Glenda Farrell in nine "Torchy Blane" films.

Lupe Velez appeared as "The Mexican Spitfire" eight times and Dorothy Lamour hit the "Road" seven times.

Myrna Loy helped "The Thin Man" walk the dog six times and Spring Byington tried to keep control of "The Jones Family" six times.

Bonita Granville was "Nancy Drew" four times; Margaret Rutherfore solved four "Miss Marple" mysteries, superseded by both Helen Hayes and Joan Hickson, while Edna May Oliver portrayed "Hildegarde Withers" three times with Zasu Pitts giving her version twice.

• • •

It is hoped that this book will be of interest to film buffs and quiz fanatics alike but, althougth every effort has been made to make it definitive, it has proved impossible to include every appearance by every actress. The difficulties will be appreciated when account is made of the fact that the parts taken by some actresses are not included in the credits: for example, Elizabeth Taylor was not on the credit list for "The White Cliffs of Dover" and Linda Darnell was uncredited, when she appeared as the Virgin Mary in "Song of Bernadette". Cameo appearances can easily be missed in some films and characters actresses often play uncredited parts, especially at the start or end of their careers. Twice for example Mary Wickes was spotted in a small part but there was no mention of her in the cast list.

Any errors or omissions are unintentional.

SUZANNE AAREN

1935 STRANGERS ALL
Co-stars: Preston Foster

CAROLINE AARON

1984 THE BROTHER FROM ANOTHER PLANET
Director: John Sayles
Co-stars: Joe Morton Tom Wright Randy Sue Carter

1989 CRIMES AND MISDEMEANORS
Director: Woody Allen
Co-stars: Woody Allen Mia Farrow Claire Bloom

1990 EDWARD SCISSORHANDS
Director: Tim Burton
Co-stars: Johnny Depp Winona Ryder Dianne West Kathy Baker

1991 ALICE
Director: Woody Allen
Co-stars: Mia Farrow Alec Baldwin William Hurt

1993 SLEEPLESS IN SEATTLE
Director: Nora Ephron
Co-stars: Tom Hanks Meg Ryan Ross Malinger

ABBA

1977 ABBA THE MOVIE
Director: Lasse Hallstrom
Co-stars: Abba Robert Hughes Tom Oliver

DIAHANN ABBOTT (*Married Robert De Niro*)

1982 KING OF COMEDY
Director: Martin Scorsese
Co-stars: Robert De Niro Jerry Lewis Sandra Bernhard

1984 LOVE STREAMS
Director: John Cassavetes
Co-stars: Gena Rowlands John Cassavetes Seymour Cassel

MARGARET ABBOTT

1984 LOVE STREAMS
Director: John Cassavetes
Co-stars: Gena Rowlands John Cassavetes Diahann Abbott

SHIRLEY ABICAIR

1954 ONE GOOD TURN
Director: John Paddy Carstairs
Co-stars: Norman Wisdom Joan Rice Thora Hird

ABIGAIL

1973 ALVIN PURPLE
Director: Tim Burstall
Co-stars: Graeme Blundell Lynette Curran Cristine Amor

1974 ALVIN RIDES AGAIN
Director: Robin Copping
Co-stars: Graeme Blundell Alan Finney Chantal Contouri

MICHELE ABRAMS

1991 VICTIM OF BEAUTY
Director: Roger Young
Co-stars: William Devane Jeri Lynn Ryan

1992 BUFFY THE VAMPIRE SLAYER
Director: Fran Rubel Kuzui
Co-stars: Kristy Swanson Donald Sutherland

1992 COOL WORLD
Director: Ralph Bakshi
Co-stars: Kim Basinger Gabriele Bryne Brad Pitt

VICTORIA ABRIL

1981 COMIN' AT YA!
Director: Ferdinando Baldi
Co-stars: Tony Anthony Gene Quintino

1983 THE MOON IN THE GUTTER
Director: Jean-Jacques Beineix
Co-stars: Gerard Depardieu Nastassja Kinski

1983 L'ADDITION
Director: Denis Amar
Co-stars: Richard Berry Richard Bohringer

1985 AFTER DARKNESS
Director: Sergio Guerrez
Co-stars: John Hurt Julian Sands Pamela Salem

1986 MAX, MON AMOUR
Director: Nagisa Oshima
Co-stars: Charlotte Rampling Anthony Higgings Diana Quick

1989 TIE ME UP! TIE ME DOWN!
Director: Pedro Almodovar
Co-stars: Antonio Banderas Francisco Rabal

1991 LOVERS
Director: Vincente Aranda
Co-stars: Jorge Sanz Maribel Verdu

1991 HIGH HEELS
Director: Pedro Almodovar
Co-stars: Marisa Paredes Miguel Bose

1993 KIKA
Director: Pedro Almodovar
Co-stars: Veronica Forque Peter Coyote

1994 JIMMY HOLLYWOOD
Director: Barry Levinson
Co-stars: Joe Pesci Christian Slater

1996 FRENCH TWIST GUILD
Director: Josiane Balasco
Co-stars: Josiane Balasco Alain Chabat

SHARON ACKER

1957 LUCKY JIM
Director: John Boulting
Co-stars: Ian Carmichael Terry-Thomas Hugh Griffith

1967 POINT BLANK
Director: John Boorman
Co-stars: Lee Marvin Angie Dickinson Keenan Wynn

1968 THE FIRST TIME
Director: James Nielson
Co-stars: Jacqueline Bisset Wes Stern Wink Roberts

1970 ACT OF THE HEART
Director: Paul Almond
Co-stars: Genevieve Bujold Donald Sutherland Monique Leyrac

1980 HAPPY BIRTHDAY TO ME
Director: J Lee Thompson
Co-stars: Glenn Ford Melissa Sue Anderson

1980 THE MURDER THAT WOULDN'T DIE
Director: Ron Satlof
Co-stars: William Conrad Jose Ferrer Marji Dusay

1981 THRESHOLD
Director: Richard Pearce
Co-stars: Donald Sutherland Jeff Goldblum Mare Winningham

ACQUANITA

1943 CAPTIVE WILD WOMAN
Director: Edward Dmytryk
Co-stars: Evelyn Ankers John Carradine Martha Vickers

1944 JUNGLE WOMAN
Director: Reginald Le Borg
Co-stars: Evelyn Ankers J. Carrol Naish Lois Collier

1945 JUNGLE CAPTIVE
Director: Harold Young
Co-stars: Otto Kruger Amelita Ward Jerome Cowan

1946 TARZAN AND THE LEOPARD WOMAN
Director: Kurt Neumann
Co-stars: Jonny Weismuller Brenda Joyce

ALICE ADAIR

1988 DESPERADO: AVALANCHE AT DEVIL'S RIDGE
Director: Richard Compton
Co-stars: Alex McArthur Rod Steiger

JEAN ADAIR

1933 ADVICE TO THE LOVELORN
Director: Alfred Werker
Co-stars: Lee Tracy Sally Blane Isabel Jewell

1942 ARSENIC AND OLD LACE
Director: Frank Capra
Co-stars: Cary Grant Josephine Hull Priscilla Lane

NOELLE ADAM

1960 BEAT GIRL
Director: Edmond Greville
Co-stars: Gillian Hills David Farrar Adam Faith

BEVERLEY ADAMS

1966 BIRDS DO IT
Director: Andrew Marton
Co-stars: Tab Hunter Soupy Sales Arthur O' Connell

1966 MURDERERS' ROW
Director: Henry Levin
Co-stars: Dean Martin Ann-Margret Karl Malden

1967 THE AMBUSHERS
Director: Henry Levin
Co-stars: Dean Martin Senta Berger Janice Rule

1967 TORTURE GARDEN
Director: Freddie Francis
Co-stars: Burgess Meredith Jack Palance Peter Cushing

1968 HAMMERHEAD
Director: David Miller
Co-stars: Vince Edwards Judy Geeson Diana Dors

BROOKE ADAMS

1978 DAYS OF HEAVEN
Director: Terence Mallick
Co-stars: Richard Gere Sam Sheperd Linda Manz

1978 INVASION OF THE BODY SNATCHERS
Director: Philip Kaufman
Co-stars: Donald Sutherland Leonard Nimoy

1979 CUBA
Director: Richard Lester
Co-stars: Sean Connery Jack Weston Chris Sarandon

1979 A MAN, A WOMAN AND A BANK
Director: Noel Black
Co-stars: Donald Sutherland Paul Mazursky

1980 TELL ME A RIDDLE
Director: Lee Grant
Co-stars: Lila Kedrova Melvyn Douglas Dolores Dorn

1983 THE DEAD ZONE
Director: David Cronenberg
Co-stars: Christopher Walken Tom Skerritt Herbert Lom

1984 ALMOST YOU
Director: Adam Brooks
Co-stars: Griffin Dunne Karen Young Dana Delany

1984 HUNTED
Director: Michael Roemer
Co-stars: John De Vries Trish Van Devere Ari Meyers

1987 THE LION OF AFRICA
Director: Kevin Connor
Co-stars: Brian Dennehy Josef Shiloa Don Warrington

1987 MAN ON FIRE
Director: Elie Chouraqui
Co-stars: Scott Glen Joe Pesci Danny Aiello

1989 BRIDESMAIDS
Director: Lila Garrett
Co-stars: Shelley Hack Sela Ward Audra Lindley

1991 GAS, FOOD, LODGING
Director: Allison Anders
Co-stars: Ione Skye Fairuza Balk James Brolin

1993 THE LAST HIT
Director: Jan Egelson
Co-stars: Byran Brown Harris Yulin

DOROTHY ADAMS

1944 LAURA
Director: Otto Preminger
Co-stars: Dana Andrews Gene Tierney Clifton Webb

1949 NOT WANTED
Director: Elmer Clifton
Co-stars: Sally Forrest Keefe Brasselle Rita Lupino

1975 PEEPER
Director: Peter Hyams
Co-stars: Michael Caine Natalie Wood Kitty Winn

EDIE ADAMS

1960 THE APARTMENT
Director: Billy Wilder
Co-stars: Jack Lemmon Shirley MacLaine Fred MacMurray

1961 LOVER COME BACK
Director: Delbert Mann
Co-stars: Doris Day Rock Hudson Tony Randall

1962 CALL ME BWANA
Director: Gordon Douglas
Co-stars: Bob Hope Anita Ekberg Lionel Jefferies

1963 UNDER THE YUM YUM TREE
Director: David Swift
Co-stars: Jack Lemmon Carol Lynley Dean Jones

1963 ITS A MAD, MAD, MAD, MAD WORLD
Director: Stanley Kramer
Co-stars: Terry-Thomas Joe E. Brown Ethel Merman

1964 THE BEST MAN
Director: Franklin Schaffner
Co-stars: Henry Fonda Cliff Robertson Margaret Leighton

1964 LOVE WITH THE PROPER STRANGER
Director: Robert Mulligan
Co-stars: Natalie Wood Steve McQueen Tom Bosley

1966   **THE OSCAR**
Director: Russel Rouse
Co-stars: Stephen Boyd Tony Bennett Elke Sommer

1966   **MADE IN PARIS**
Director: Boris Sagal
Co-stars: Ann-Margret Louis Jourdan Richard Crenna

1967   **THE HONEY POT**
Director: Joseph Mankiewicz
Co-stars: Rex Harrison Susan Hayward Cliff Robertson

1973   **UP IN SMOKE**
Director: Lou Adler
Co-stars: Cheech Marin Tommy Chong Tom Skerritt

JANE ADAMS

1945   **HOUSE OF DRACULA**
Director: Erle Kenton
Co-stars: Onslow Stevens John Carradine Lionel Atwill

1946   **BRUTE MAN**
Director: Jean Yarbrough
Co-stars: Rondo Hatton Tom Neal

1946   **LAWLESS BREED**
Co-stars: Kirby Grant Fuzzy Knight

1946   **SMOOTH AS SILK**
Director: Charles Barton
Co-stars: Kent Taylor Virginia Grey

JILL ADAMS

1954   **THE YOUNG LOVERS**
Director: Anthony Asquith
Co-stars: Odile Versois David Knight David Kossoff

1955   **VALUE FOR MONEY**
Director: Ken Annakin
Co-stars: John Gregson Diana Dors Susan Stephen

1955   **ONE JUMP AHEAD**
Director: Charles Saunders
Co-stars: Paul Carpenter Diane Hart Freddie Mills

1956   **PRIVATES PROGRESS**
Director: John Boutling
Co-stars: Ian Carmichael Terry-Thomas Richard Attenborough

1956   **THE GREEN MAN**
Director: Robert Day
Co-stars: Alastair Sim George Cole Terry-Thomas

1957   **BROTHERS-IN-LAW**
Director: Roy Boutling
Co-stars: Ian Carmichael Terry-Thomas Richard Attenborough

1957   **THE SCAMP**
Director: Wolf Rilla
Co-stars: Colin Petersen Richard Attenborough Dorothy Alison

1957   **ONE WAY OUT**
Director: Francis Searle
Co-stars: Eddie Byrne Lyndon Brook

1959   **CARRY ON CONSTABLE**
Director: Gerald Thomas
Co-stars: Sid James Kenneth Connor Kenneth Williams

JOEY LAUREN ADAMS

1997   **CHASING AMY**
Director: Kevin Smith
Co-star: Ben Afflick

JULIE ADAMS

1951   **BRIGHT VICTORY**
Director: Mark Robson
Co-stars: Arthur Kennedy Peggy Dow Will Geer

1951   **HOLLYWOOD STORY**
Director: William Castle
Co-stars: Richard Conte Henry Hull Fred Clark

1952   **HORIZONS WEST**
Director: Budd Boetticher
Co-stars: Rock Hudson Robert Ryan John McIntyre

1952   **THE LAWLESS BREED**
Director: Raoul Walsh
Co-stars: Rock Hudson Hugh O'Brian John McIntyre

1952   **TREASURE OF LOST CANYON**
Director: Ted Tetzlaff
Co-stars: William Powell Charles Drake Henry Hull

1952   **WHERE THE RIVER BENDS**
Director: Anthony Mann
Co-stars: James Stewart Arthur Kennedy Rock Hudson

1953   **WINGS OF THE HAWK**
Director: Budd Boetticher
Co-stars: Van Heflin George Dolenz Rudolfo Acosta

1953   **THE STAND AT APACHE RIVER**
Director: Lee Sholem
Co-stars: Stephen Mc Nally Hugh Marlowe

1953   **MISSISSIPPI GAMBLER**
Director: Rudolph Mate
Co-stars: Tyrone Power Piper Laurie John McIntyre

1953   **THE MAN FROM THE ALAMO**
Director: Budd Boetticher
Co-stars: Glenn Ford Hugh O'Brian Victor Jory

1954   **THE CREATURE FROM THE BLACK LAGOON**
Director: Jack Arnold
Co-stars: Richard Carlson Richard Denning

1955   **THE LOOTERS**
Director: Abner Biberman
Co-stars: Rory Calhoun Ray Danton Thomas Gomez

1955   **THE PRIVATE WAR OF MAJOR BENSON**
Director: Jerry Hopper
Co-stars: Charlton Heston William Demarest

1955   **SIX BRIDGES TO CROSS**
Director: Joseph Pevney
Co-stars: Tony Curtis George Nader Sal Mineo

1956   **ONE DESIRE**
Director: Jerry Hopper
Co-stars: Anne Baxter Rock Hudson Natalie Wood

1956   **FOUR GIRLS IN TOWN**
Director: Jack Sher
Co-stars: George Nader Elsa Martinelli Gia Scala

1956   **AWAY ALL BOATS**
Director: Joseph Pevney
Co-stars: Jeff Chandler George Nader Lex Barker

1957   **SLAUGHTER ON TENTH AVENUE**
Director: Arnold Laven
Co-stars: Richard Egan Jan Sterling Dan Duryea

1957   **SLIM CARTER**
Director: Richard Bartlett
Co-stars: Jock Mahoney Ben Johnson Barbara Hale

1958   **THE GUNFIGHT AT DODGE CITY**
Director: Joseph Newman
Co-stars: Joel McCrea John McIntyre Nancy Gates

1965   **TICKLE ME**
Director: Norman Taurog
Co-stars: Elvis Presley Merry Anders Connie Gilchrist

1967   **VALLEY OF MYSTERY**
Director: Josef Leytes
Co-stars: Richard Egan Peter Graves Lois Nettleton

1971 THE LAST MOVIE
Director: Dennis Hopper
Co-stars: Dennis Hopper Rod Cameron Kris Kristofferson

1974 McQ
Director: John Sturges
Co-stars: John Wayne Eddie Albert Diana Muldaur

1989 CATCHFIRE
Director: Dennis Hopper
Co-stars: Dennis Hopper Jody Foster Dean Stockwell

KATHRYN ADAMS

1939 FIFTH AVENUE GIRL
Director: Gregory La Cava
Co-stars: Ginger Rogers Walter Connolly Tim Holt

1941 BACHELOR DADDY
Director: Harold Young
Co-stars: Donald Woods Baby Sandy Edward Everett Horton

KIM ADAMS

1991 TED AND VENUS
Director: Bud Cort
Co-stars: Bud Cort Jim Brolin Carole Kane

LYNNE ADAMS

1987 NIGHT ZOO
Director: Jean-Claude Lauzon
Co-stars: Roger Le Bel Gilles Maheu

MAUD ADAMS

1971 THE CHRISTIAN LIQUORICE STORE
Director: James Frawley
Co-stars: Beau Bridges Gilbert Roland

1974 THE MAN WITH THE GOLDEN GUN
Director: Guy Hamilton
Co-stars: Roger Moore Christopher Lee Brit Ekland

1975 ROLLERBALL
Director: Norman Jewison
Co-stars: James Caan Ralph Richardson John Houseman

1975 THE DIAMOND MERCENARIES
Director: Val Guest
Co-stars: Telly Savalas Peter Fonda Hugh O'Brian

1980 PLAYING FOR TIME
Director: Daniel Mann
Co-stars: Vanessa Redgrave Jane Alexander Melanie Mayron

1980 TATTOO
Director: Rob Brooks
Co-stars: Bruce Dern Leonard Frey Rikke Borge

1983 OCTOPUSSY
Director: John Glen
Co-stars: Roger Moore Louis Jourdan Vijay Armitraj Lois Maxwell

1987 JANE AND THE LOST CITY
Director: Terry Marcel
Co-stars: Sam Jones Jasper Carrott

1988 ANGEL 3: THE FINAL CHAPTER
Director: Tom De Simone
Co-stars: Mitzi Kapture Richard Roundtree

DAWN ADDAMS

1951 THE UNKNOWN MAN
Director: Richard Thorp
Co-stars: Walter Pidgeon Ann Harding Lewis Stone

1952 PLYMOUTH ADVENTURE
Director: Clarence Brown
Co-stars: Spencer Tracy Gene Tierney Van Johnson

1952 THE HOUR OF THIRTEEN
Director: Harold French
Co-stars: Peter Lawford Roland Culver Derek Bond

1953 THE ROBE
Director: Henry Koster
Co-stars: Richard Burton Jean Simmons Victor Mature

1953 THE MOON IS BLUE
Director: Otto Preminger
Co-stars: David Niven Maggie McNamara William Holden

1953 YOUNG BESS
Director: George Sidney
Co-stars: Jean Simmons Stewart Grainger Charles Laughton

1954 RIDERS TO THE STARS
Director: Richard Carlson
Co-stars: Richard Carlson Herbert Marshall William Lundigan

1957 A KING IN NEW YORK
Director: Charles Chaplin
Co-stars: Charles Chaplin Oliver Johnston Maxine Audley

1958 THE SILENT ENEMY
Director: William Fairchild
Co-stars: Laurence Harvey Michael Craig John Clements

1959 TREASURE OF SAN TERESA
Director: Alvin Rakoff
Co-stars: Eddie Constantine Marius Goring

1960 THE TWO FACES OF DR.JECKYLL
Director: Terence Fisher
Co-stars: Paul Massie Christopher Lee

1963 THE BLACK TULIP
Director: Christian Jacque
Co-stars: Alain Delon Akim Tamiroff Virna Lisi

1964 BALLAD IN BLUE
Director: Paul Henred
Co-stars: Ray Charles Mary Peach Tom Bell

1966 WHERE THE BULLETS FLY
Director: John Gilling
Co-stars: Tom Adams Tim Barratt Mlchael Ripper

1970 THE VAMPIRE LOVERS
Director: Roy Ward Baker
Co-stars: Ingrid Pitt Peter Cushing Pippa Steele

1973 VAULT OF HORROR
Director: Roy Ward Baker
Co-stars: Daniel Massey Terry-Thomas Glynis Johns

NANCY ADDISON

1983 SOMEWHERE TOMORROW
Director: Robert Wiemer
Co-stars: Sarah Jessica Parker Tom Shea Rick Weber

JAN ADELE

1987 HIGH TIDE
Director: Gillian Armstrong
Co-stars: Judy Davis Colin Friels Claudia Karvan

ISABELLE ADJANI

Nominated For Best Actress in 1975 For "The Story of Adele H" and For "Camille Claudel" In 1989

1975 THE STORY OF ADELE H
Director: Francois Truffaut
Co-stars: Bruce Robinson Sylvia Marriott

1976 THE TENANT
Director: Roman Polanski
Co-stars: Roman Polanski Melvyn Douglas Shelley Winters

1978 THE DRIVER
Director: Walter Hill
Co-stars: Ryan O'Neal Bruce Dern Ronee Blakeley

1979 NOSFERATU THE VAMPIRE
Director: Werner Herzog
Co-stars: Klaus Kinski Bruno Ganz Walter Ladengast

1981 POSSESSION
Director: Andrzej Zulawski
Co-stars: Sam Neill Heinz Bennent Michael Hogben

1981 QUARTET
Director: James Ivory
Co-stars: Alan Bates Maggie Smith Suzanne Flon

1983 ONE DEADLY SUMMER
Director: Jean Becker
Co-stars: Alain Souchon Jenny Cleve Suzanne Flon

1983 DEADLY RUN
Director: Claude Miller
Co-stars: Michel Serrault Genevieve Page

1985 SUBWAY
Director: Luc Besson
Co-stars: Christopher Lambert Richard Bohringer

1987 ISHTAR
Director: Elaine May
Co-stars: Dustin Hoffman Warren Beatty Charles Grodin

1988 CAMILLE CLAUDEL
Director: Bruno Nuytten
Co-stars: Gerard Depardieu Laurent Grevill Alain Cuny

1995 LA REINE MARGOT
Director: Patrice Chereau
Co-stars: Vincent Perez Daniel Auteuil Virni Lisi

1996 DIABOLIQUE
Director: Jeremiah Chechik
Co-stars: Sharon Stone Chazz Palminteri

CYNTHIA ADLER

1981 NIGHTRIDERS
Director: George Romero
Co-stars: Ed Harris Gary Lahti Tom Savini

STELLA ADLER

1948 MY GIRL TISA
Director: Elliott Nugent
Co-stars: Lilli Palmer Sam Wanamaker Alan Hale

RENEE ADOREE

1922 DAYDREAMS
Director: Buster Keaton
Co-stars: Buster Keaton

1925 THE BIG PARADE
Director: King Vidor
Co-stars: John Gilbert Hobart Bosworth Claire McDowell

1926 LA BOHEME
Director: King Vidor
Co-stars: Lillian Gish John Gilbert Edward Everett Horton

1926 THE BLACK BIRD
Director: Tod Browning
Co-stars: Lon Chaney Owen Moore Doris Lloyd

1926 THE EXQUISITE SINNER
Director: Josef Von Sternberg
Co-stars: Conrad Nagel

1927 HEAVEN ON EARTH
Director: Phil Rosen
Co-star: Conrad Nagel

1927 MR. WU
Director: William Nigh
Co-stars: Lon Chaney Louise Dresser Anna May Wong

1929 THE PAGAN
Director: W S Van Dyke
Co-stars: Ramon Navarro Dorothy Janis Donald Crisp

1930 REDEMPTION
Director: Fred Niblo
Co-stars: John Gilbert Conrad Nagel Eleanor Boardman

1930 CALL OF THE FLESH
Director: Charles Brabin
Co-stars: Ramon Navarro Dorothy Jordan Nance O'Neil

IRIS ADRIAN

1935 STOLEN HARMONY
Director: Alfred Werker
Co-stars: George Raft Ben Bernie Grace Bradley

1935 RUMBA
Director: Marion Gering
Co-stars: Carole Lombard George Raft Gail Patrick

1936 OUR RELATIONS
Director: Harry Lachman
Co-stars: Laurel & Hardy James Finlayson

1941 SING ANOTHER CHORUS
Co-stars: Johnny Davis George Barbier Walter Catlett

1943 HIS BUTLER'S SISTER
Director: Frank Borzage
Co-stars: Franchot Tone Pat O'Brien Deanna Durbin

1943 LADIES DAY
Co-stars: Patsy Kelly John Barclay Max Baer

1943 LADY OF BURLESQUE
Director: William Wellman
Co-stars: Barbara Stanwyck Michael O'Shea Gloria Dickson

1941 WILD GEESE CALLING
Director: John Brahm
Co-stars: Joan Bennett Henry Fonda Warren William

1944 CAREER GIRL
Director: Wallace Fox
Co-stars: Frances Langford Ariel Heath Edward Norris

1944 BLUEBEARD
Director: Edgar Ulmer
Co-stars: John Carradine Jean Parker Nils Asther

1944 SHAKE HANDS WITH MURDER
Director: Albert Herman
Co-stars: Frank Jenks Douglas Fowley Jack Raymond

1945 BOSTON BLACKIE'S RENDEVOUZ
Co-stars: Chester Morris Nina Foch Steve Cochran

1945 THE STORK CLUB
Director: Hal Walker
Co-stars: Betty Hutton Barry Fitzgerald Robert Benchley

1945 CROSS MY HEART
Director: John Berry
Co-stars: Betty Hutton Sonny Tufts Michael Chekhov

1946 THE BAMBOO BLONDE
Director: Anthony Mann
Co-stars: Frances Langford Ralph Edwards Jane Greer

1948 THE PALEFACE
Director: Norman Z. McLeod
Co-stars: Bob Hope Jane Russell Robert Armstrong

1949 THE SKY DRAGON
Director: Lesley Selander
Co-stars: Roland Winters Keye Luke Lyle Talbot

1950 BLONDIE'S HERO
Director: Edward Bearnds
Co-stars: Penny Singleton Arthur Lake Larry Simms

1961 BLUE HAWAII
Director: Norman Taurog
Co-stars: Elvis Presley Joan Blackman Angela Lansbury

1968 THE ODD COUPLE
Director: Gene Saks
Co-stars: Jack Lemmon Walter Matthau John Fieldler

1975 THE APPLE DUMPLING GANG
Director: Norman Tokar
Co-stars: Bill Bixby Susan Clark Don Knotts

MIMI AGUGLIA

1948 CRY OF THE CITY
Director: Robert Siodmak
Co-stars: Victor Mature Richard Conte Shelley Winters

1949 THAT MIDNIGHT KISS
Director: Norman Taurog
Co-stars: Mario Lanza Kathryn Grayson Keenan Wynn

JENNY AGUTTER (Child)

1964 EAST OF SUDAN
Director: Nathan Juran
Co-stars: Anthony Quayle Sylvia Syms

1969 I START COUNTING
Director: David Greene
Co-stars: Brian Marshall Simon Ward Lana Morris

1970 WALKABOUT
Director: Nicolas Roeg
Co-stars: Lucien John David Gumpilil

1970 THE RAILWAY CHILDREN
Director: Lionel Jeffries
Co-stars: Dinah Sheridan Sally Thomsett Gary Warren

1976 THE MAN IN THE IRON MASK
Director: Mike Newell
Co-stars: Louis Jourdan Richard Chamberlain Patrick McGoohan

1976 LOGAN'S RUN
Director: Michael Anderson
Co-stars: Michael York Richard Jordan Peter Ustinov

1976 THE EAGLE HAS LANDED
Director: John Sturges
Co-stars: Michael Caine Donald Sutherland Robert Duvall

1977 EQUUS
Director: Sidney Lumet
Co-stars: Richard Burton Peter Firth Colin Blakely

1978 DOMINIQUE
Director: Michael Anderson
Co-stars: Jean Simmons Cliff Robertson Simon Ward

1978 CHINA 9, LIBERTY 37
Director: Monte Hellman
Co-stars: Fabio Testi Warren Oates Sam Peckinpah

1978 THE RIDDLE OF THE SANDS
Director: Tony Maylam
Co-stars: Michael York Simon MacCorkindale

1980 THE SURVIVOR
Director: David Hemmings
Co-stars: Robert Powell Joseph Cotten Angela McGregor

1980 SWEET WILLIAM
Director: Claude Whatham
Co-stars: Sam Waterston Anna Massey Arthur Lowe

1981 AMY
Director: Vincent McEveety
Co-stars: Barry Newman Margaret O'Brien Kathleen Nolan

1981 AN AMERICAN WEREWOLF IN LONDON
Director: John Landis
Co-stars: David Naughton Griffin Dunne

1984 SECRET PLACES
Director: Zelda Baron
Co-stars: Marie-Therese Relin Tara MacGowran Claudine Auger

1985 SILAS MARNER
Director: Giles Foster
Co-stars: Ben Kingsley Patsy Kensit Patrick Ryecarte

1989 KING OF THE WIND
Director: Peter Duffell
Co-stars: Frank Finlay Navin Chowdhry Nigel Hawthorne

1990 NOT A PENNY MORE, NOT A PENNY LESS
Director: Clive Donner
Co-stars: Ed Asner Ed Begley Jnr Maryam D'Abo

1990 DARKMAN
Director: Sam Riami
Co-stars: Liam Neeson Frances McDormand Colin Friels

1991 CHIILD'S PLAY 2
Director: John Lafia
Co-stars: Alex Vincent Gerrit Graham Christine Elise

1992 FREDDIE AS FR07 (Voice)
Director: Jon Acevski
Co-stars: Ben Kingsley Phyllis Logan Brian Blessed

MONIQUE AHRENS

1959 A DOG OF FLANDERS
Director: James Clark
Co-stars: David Ladd Donald Crisp Theodore Bikel

ANOUK AIMEE
Nominated For Best Actress in 1966 For "A Man And A Woman"

1948 LOVERS OF VERONA
Director: Andre Cayatte
Co-stars: Pierre Brasseur Serge Reggiani Louis Salou

1949 THE GOLDEN SALAMANDER
Director: Ronald Neame
Co-stars: Trevor Howard Herbert Lom Miles Malleson

1952 CRIMSON CURTAIN
Director: Alexandre Astruc
Co-stars: Jean-Claude Pascal Madeleine Garcia

1952 THE MAN WHO WATCHED TRAINS GO BY
Director: Harold French
Co-stars: Claude Rains Marius Goring Marta Toren

1955 CONTRABAND SPAIN
Director: Lawrence Huntington
Co-stars: Richard Greene Michael Dennison

1958 MONTPARNASSE 19
Director: Jacques Becker
Co-stars: Gerard Philipe Lilli Palmer Lino Ventura

1959 THE JOURNEY
Director: Anatole Litvak
Co-stars: Yul Brynner Deborah Kerr Jason Robards

1960 LOLA
Director: Jacques Demy
Co-stars: Marc Michel Jacques Harden Elina Labourdette

1960 LA DOLCE VITA
Director: Federico Fellini
Co-stars: Marcello Mastroianni Anita Ekberg Alain Cuny

1962 SODOM AND GOMORRAH
Director: Robert Aldrich
Co-stars: Stewart Granger Stanley Baker Pier Angeli

1963 EIGHT AND A HALF
Director: Federico Fellini
Co-stars: Marcello Mastroianni Claudia Cardinale

1966 A MAN AND A WOMAN
Director: Claude Lelouch
Co-stars: Jean-Louis Trintignant Valerie Lagrange

1969 THE MODEL SHOP
Director: Jacques Demy
Co-stars: Gary Lockwood Alexandra Hay Carole Cole

1969 JUSTINE
Director: George Cukor
Co-stars: Dirk Bogarde Michael York John Vernon

1969 THE APPOINTMENT
Director: Sidney Lumet
Co-stars: Omar Sharif Lotte Lenya

1981 THE TRAGEDY OF A RIDICULOUS MAN
Director: Bernardo Bertolucci
Co-stars: Ugo Tognazzi Laura Morante

1984 SUCCESS IS THE BEST REVENGE
Director: Jerzy Skolimowski
Co-stars: Michael York John Hurt

1986 A MAN AND A WOMAN:
TWENTY YEARS LATER
Director: Claude Lelouch
Co-stars: Richard Berry Jean-Louis Trintignant

1990 BETHUNE THE MAKING OF A HERO
Director: Phillip Borsos
Co-stars: Donald Sutherland Helen Mirren

1992 VOICES IN THE GARDEN
Director: Pierre Boutron
Co-stars: Joss Ackland Samuel West Kashia Figura

LYNN AINLEY

1951 THE MAN WITH MY FACE
Director: Edward Nontagne
Co-stars: Barry Nelson Jack Warden

HOLLY AIRD

1987 THE HAPPY VALLEY
Director: Ross Devinish
Co-stars: Denholm Elliott Amanda Hillwood Kathryn Pogson

1989 MOTHER LOVE
Director: Simon Langton
Co-stars: Diana Rigg James Wilby David McCallum

1990 CHAIN
Director: Don Leaver
Co-stars: Peter Capaldi Julia Hills Robert Pugh

1992 CARRY ON COLUMBUS
Director: Gerald Thomas
Co-stars: Jim Dale Bernard Cribbins June Whitfield

MARIA AITKEN

1988 A FISH CALLED WANDA
Director: Charles Crichton
Co-stars: John Cleese Jaime Lee Curtis Kevin Kline

1990 THE FOOL
Director: Christine Edzard
Co-stars: Derek Jacobi Cyril Cusack Ruth Mitchell

MURIEL AKED

1932 ROME EXPRESS
Director: Walter Forde
Co-stars: Conrad Veidt Gordon Harker Esther Ralston

1933 NO FUNNY BUSINESS
Director: John Stafford
Co-stars: Gertrude Lawrence Laurence Olivier Jill Esmond

1934 AUTUMN CROCUS
Director: Carol Reed
Co-stars: Ivor Novello Fay Compton Jack Hawkins

1934 EVENSONG
Director: Victor Saville
Co-stars: Eyelyn Laye Fritz Kortner Emlyn Williams

1939 THE SILENT BATTLE
Director: Herbert Mason
Co-stars: Rex Harrison Valerie Hobson John Loder

1941 COTTAGE TO LET
Director: Anthony Asquith
Co-stars: Leslie Banks John Mills Alastair Sims

1943 THE DEMI-PARADISE
Director: Anthony Asquith
Co-stars: Laurence Olivier Penelope Dudley-Ward Margaret Rutherford

1944 TWO THOUSAND WOMEN
Director: Frank Launder
Co-stars: Phyllis Calvert Flora Robson Jean Kent

1948 SO EVIL MY LOVE
Director: Lewis Allen
Co-stars: Ray Milland Ann Todd Geraldine Fitzgerald

1950 THE HAPPIEST DAYS OF YOUR LIFE
Director: Frank Launder
Co-stars: Alastair Sims Margaret Rutherford Joyce Grenfell

1951 FLESH AND BLOOD
Director: Anthony Kimmins
Co-stars: Richard Todd Glynis Johns Joan Greenwood

1952 THE STORY OF GILBERT AND SULLIVAN
Director: Sidney Gilliat
Co-stars: Robert Morley Maurice Evans Eileen Herlie

ANDRA AKERS

1979 MOMENT BY MOMENT
Director: Jane Wagner
Co-stars: Lily Tomlin John Travolta

1985 DESERT HEARTS
Director: Donna Deitch
Co-stars: Helen Shaver Patricia Charbonneau

DONNA AKERSTEN

1979 MIDDLE AGE SPREAD
Director: John Reid
Co-stars: Grant Tilly Dorothy McKegg

1982 BAD BLOOD
Director: Mike Newell
Co-stars: Jack Thompson Carol Burns Dennis Lill

NELLY ALARD

1990 EATING
Director: Henry Jaglom
Co-stars: Lisa Richards Mary Crosby Gwen Welles

1992 VENICE/VENICE
Director: Henry Jaglom
Co-stars: Melissa Leo Henry Jaglom David Duchovny

MARIA ALBA

1930 HELL'S HEROES
Director: William Wyler
Co-stars: Charles Bickford Raymond Hatton

1931 GOLDIE
Director: Ben Stoloff
Co-stars: Spencer Tracy Jean Harlow Warren Hymer

1932 MR. ROBINSON CRUSOE
Director: Edward Sutherland
Co-stars: Douglas Fairbanks William Farnum

1935 RETURN OF CHANDHU
Co-stars: Bela Lugosi Lucien Prival

ANNA MARIA ALBERGHETTI (Child)

1951   **THE MEDIUM**
Director: Gian-Carlo Menotti
Co-stars: Marie Powers Leo Coleman

1951   **HERE COMES THE GROOM**
Director: Frank Capra
Co-stars: Bing Crosby Jane Wyman Franchot Tone

1952   **STARS AND STRIPES FOREVER**
Director: Henry Koster
Co-stars: Clifton Webb Debra Paget Ruth Hussey

1952   **THE STARS ARE SINGING**
Director: Norman Taurog
Co-stars: Lauritz Melchior Rosemary Clooney

1955   **THE LAST COMMAND**
Director: Frank Lloyd
Co-stars: Sterling Hayden Ernest Borgnine Jim Davis

1956   **TEN THOUSAND BEDROOMS**
Director: Richard Thorpe
Co-stars: Dean Martin Eva Bartok Paul Henreid

1960   **CINDERFELLA**
Director: Frank Tashlin
Co-stars: Jerry Lewis Ed Wynn Robert Hutton

MABEL ALBERTSON

1953   **SO THIS IS LOVE**
Director: Gordon Douglas
Co-stars: Kathryn Grayson Merv Griffin Joan Weldon

1958   **HOME BEFORE DARK**
Director: Mervyn Leroy
Co-stars: Jean Simmons Dan O'Herlihy Rhonda Fleming

1959   **THE GAZEBO**
Director: George Marshall
Co-stars: Glenn Ford Debbie Reynolds John McGiver

1967   **BAREFOOT IN THE PARK**
Director: Gene Saks
Co-stars: Robert Redford Jane Fonda Mildred Natwick

1970   **THE HOUSE THAT WOULD NOT DIE**
Director: John Llewellyn Moxey
Co-stars: Barbara Stanwyck Richard Egan

1972   **WHAT'S UP DOC?**
Director: Peter Bogdanovich
Co-stars: Barbara Streisand Ryan O'Neal Madeline Kahn

ELSIE ALBIIN

1953   **INTIMATE RELATIONS**
Director: Charles Frank
Co-stars: Marian Spencer Ruth Dunning Harold Warrender

1957   **HIDDEN FEAR**
Director: Andre De Toth
Co-stars: John Payne Alexander Knox Anne Neyland

LOLA ALBRIGHT

1949   **CHAMPION**
Director: Mark Robson
Co-stars: Kirk Douglas Arthur Kennedy Marilyn Maxwell

1950   **THE KILLER THAT STALKED NEW YORK**
Director: Earl McEvoy
Co-stars: Charles Korvin Evelyn Keyes

1955   **THE MAGNIFICENT MATADOR**
Director: Budd Boetticher
Co-stars: Anthony Quinn Maureen O'Hara

1955   **THE TENDER TRAP**
Director: Charles Walters
Co-stars: Frank Sinatra Debbie Reynolds Celeste Holm

1957   **THE MONOLITH MURDERS**
Director: John Sherwood
Co-stars: Grant Williams Les Tremayne Phil Harvey

1961   **A COLD WIND IN AUGUST**
Director: Alexander Singer
Co-stars: Scot Marlowe Joe De Santis

1962   **DIAMOND HEAD**
Director: Guy Green
Co-stars: Charlton Heston Yvette Minieux France Nuyen

1962   **KID GALAHAD**
Director: Phil Karlson
Co-stars: Elvis Presley Gig Young Charles Bronson

1964   **THE LOVE CAGE**
Director: Rene Clement
Co-stars: Jane Fonda Alain Delon Sorrell Booke

1966   **LORD LUV A DUCK**
Director: George Axelrod
Co-stars: Roddy McDowall Tuesday Weld Ruth Gordon

1967   **THE HELICOPTER SPIES**
Director: Sam Rolfe
Co-stars: Robert Vaughan David McCallum Carol Lynley

1967   **THE WAY WEST**
Director: Andrew McLaglen
Co-stars: Kirk Douglas Robert Mitchum Richard Widmark

1968   **WHERE WERE YOU WHEN THE LIGHTS WENT OUT**
Director: Hy Averback
Co-stars: Doris Day Terry-Thomas

1968   **THE IMPOSSIBLE YEARS**
Director: Michael Gordon
Co-stars: David Niven Chad Everett Ozzie Nelson

1971   **THE STAR SPANGLED GIRL**
Director: Jerry Paris
Co-stars: Sandy Duncan Tony Roberts Todd Sussman

1977   **DELATA COUNTY U.S.A.**
Director: Glenn Jordan
Co-stars: Jeff Conaway Robert Hays Morgan Brittany

BEATRICE ALDA

1988   **A NEW LIFE**
Director: Alan Alda
Co-stars: Ann-Margret Alan Alda Veronica Hamel

RUTANYA ALDA

1978   **THE FURY**
Director: Brian De Palma
Co-stars: Kirk Douglas John Cassavetes Carrie Snodgress

1978   **THE DEER HUNTER**
Director: Michael Cimino
Co-stars: Robert De Niro Christopher Walken John Savage

1981   **MOMMIE DEAREST**
Director: Frank Perry
Co-stars: Faye Dunaway Diana Scarwid Steve Forrest

1982   **AMITYVILLE 2: THE POSSESSION**
Director: Damiano Damiani
Co-stars: Burt Young James Olson Jack Magner

1984   **RACING WITH THE MOON**
Director: Richard Benjamin
Co-stars: Sean Penn Elizabeth McGovern Nicolas Cage

1987   **APPRENTICE TO MURDER**
Director: R L Thomas
Co-stars: Chad Lowe Mia Sara Donald Sutherland

1989   **PRANCER**
Director: John Hancock
Co-stars: Sam Elliott Rebecca Harrell Cloris Leachman

MARY ALDEN

1914 THE BATTLE OF THE SEXES
Director: D. W. Griffith
Co-stars: Donald Crisp Lillian Gish Owen Moore

MARI ALDON

1951 THE TANKS ARE COMING
Director: Lewis Seiler
Co-stars: Steve Cochran Paul Picerni Philip Carey

1951 DISTANT DRUMS
Director: Raoul Walsh
Co-stars: Gary Cooper Arthur Hunnicutt Ray Teal

1952 THIS WOMAN IS DANGEROUS
Director: Felix Feist
Co-stars: Joan Crawford Dennis Morgan David Brian

1954 MASK OF DUST
Director: Terence Fisher
Co-stars: Richard Conte George Coulouris Alec Mango

1954 THE BAREFOOT CONTESSA
Director: Joseph Mankiewicz
Co-stars: Humphrey Bogart Ava Gardner Rossano Brazzi

1955 SUMMER MADNESS
Director: David Lean
Co-stars: Katherine Hepburn Rossano Brazzi Isa Miranda

LUCETTE ALDOUS

1973 DON QUIXOTE
Director: Rudolf Nureyev
Co-stars: Robert Helpman Rudolf Nureyev

REBECCA ALDRED

1992 THE HUMMINGBIRD TREE
Director: Noella Smith
Co-stars: Patrick Bergin Susan Wooldridge

KATHERINE ALDRIDGE

1940 THE GIRL FROM AVENUE A
Director: Otto Brower
Co-stars: Jane Withers Kent Taylor Elyse Knox

KAY ALDRIDGE

1941 DEAD MEN TELL
Director: Harry Lachman
Co-stars: Sidney Toler Sheila Ryan Sen Yung

1945 PHANTOM OF 42ND. STREET
Director: Albert Herman
Co-stars: Dave O'Brien Alan Mowbray Frank Jenks

1945 THE MAN WHO WALKED ALONE
Co-stars: Dave O'Brien

KITTY ALDRIDGE

1988 AMERICAN ROULETTE
Director: Maurice Hatton
Co-stars: Andy Garcia Robert Stephens Susannah York

1988 AN AFRICAN DREAM
Director: John Smallcombe
Co-stars: John Kani Dominic Jephcott

1989 SLIPSTREAM
Director: Steven Listberger
Co-stars: Mark Hamill Bob Peck Eleanor David

1990 THE WORLD OF EDDIE WEARY
Director: Alan Grint
Co-stars: Ray Brooks Celia Imrie Connie Booth

1993 TO PLAY THE KING
Director: Paul Seed
Co-stars: Ian Richardson Michael Kitchen Diane Fletcher

NORMA ALEANDRO

Nominated For Best Supporting Actress For "Gaby, A True Story" In 1987.

1985 THE OFFICIAL STORY
Director: Luis Puenzo
Co-stars: Hector Alterio Chela Ruiz

1987 GABY - A TRUE STORY
Director: Luis Mandoki
Co-stars: Liv Ullman Rachel Levin Robert Loggia

1989 PASSPORT TO TERROR
Director: Lou Antonio
Co-stars: Lee Remick Roy Thinnes John Standing

1990 VITAL SIGNS
Director: Marisa Silver
Co-stars: Adrian Pasdar Diane Lane Jimmy Smits

1991 ONE MAN'S WAR
Director: Sergio Toledo
Co-stars: Anthony Hopkins Ruben Blades

DOROTHEA ALEXANDER

1989 REUNION
Director: Jerry Schatzberg
Co-stars: Jason Robards Christien Anholt Samuel West

ELIZABETH ALEXANDER

1977 SUMMERFIELD
Director: Ken Hannam
Co-stars: Nick Tate John Walters Charles Tingwell

1978 THE CHANT OF JIMMIE BLACKSMITH
Director: Fred Schepisi
Co-stars: Tommy Lewis Jack Thompson

1981 THE KILLING OF ANGEL STREET
Director: Donald Crombie
Co-stars: John Hargreaves Reg Lye

ERIKA ALEXANDER

1990 THE LONG WALK HOME
Director: Richard Pearce
Co-stars: Sissy Spacek Whoopi Goldberg Dwight Schultz

1990 THE LAST BEST YEAR
Director: John Erman
Co-stars: Bernadette Peters Mary Tyler-Moore

IRENE ALEXANDER

1984 CITY HEAT
Director: Richard Benjamin
Co-stars: Clint Eastwood Burt Reynolds Madeline Kahn

JANE ALEXANDER

Nominated For Best Supporting Actress For "The Great White Hope" In 1970, "All The Presidents Men" In 1976, "Kramer Vs Kramer" In 1979 And "Testament" In 1983

1970 THE GREAT WHITE HOPE
Director: Martin Ritt
Co-stars: James Earl Jones Hal Holbrook Chester Morris

1970 A GUNFIGHT
Director: Lamont Johnson
Co-stars: Kirk Douglas Johnny Cash Karen Black

1972 THE NEW CENTURIONS
Director: Richard Fleischer
Co-stars: George C. Scott Stacy Keach Scott Wilson

1976 ALL THE PRESIDENT'S MEN
Director: Alan J. Pakula
Co-stars: Robert Redford Dustin Hoffman Jason Robards

1977 THE BETSY
Director: Daniel Petrie
Co-stars: Laurence Olivier Robert Duvall Tommy Lee Jones

1978	**A QUESTION OF LOVE**	1934	**OPERATOR 13**

1978 A QUESTION OF LOVE
Director: Jerry Thorpe
Co-stars: Gena Rowlands Ned Beatty Clu Gulagher

1979 KRAMER VS KRAMER
Director: Robert Benton
Co-stars: Dustin Hoffman Meryl Streep Justin Henry

1980 BRUBAKER
Director: Stuart Rosenberg
Co-stars: Robert Redford Yaphet Kotto Morgan Freeman

1980 PLAYING FOR TIME
Director: Daniel Mann
Co-stars: Vanessa Redgrave Melanie Mayron Maud Adams

1982 NIGHT CROSSING
Director: Delbert Mann
Co-stars: Beau Bridges Doug & Frank McKeon Glynnis O'Connor

1983 TESTAMENT
Director: Lynne Litman
Co-stars: William Devane Ross Harris Lukas Haas

1984 CITY HEAT
Director: Richard Benjamin
Co-stars: Clint Eastwood Burt Reynolds Madeline Kahn

1984 CALAMITY JANE
Director: George Sherman
Co-stars: Frederic Forest David Hemmings Ken Kercheval

1985 MALICE IN WONDERLAND
Director: Gus Trikonis
Co-stars: Elizabeth Taylor Richard Dysart Joyce Van Patten

1986 BLOOD AND ORCHIDS
Director: Jerry Thorpe
Co-stars: Kris Kristofferson Sean Young Jose Ferrer

1987 IN LOVE AND WAR
Director: Paul Aaron
Co-star: James Woods

1989 GLORY
Director: Edward Zwik
Co-stars: Matthew Broderick Denzel Washington Cary Elwes

1987 SQUARE DANCE
Director: Daniel Petrie
Co-stars: Jason Robards Winona Ryder Rob Lowe

1992 MISTRESS
Director: Barry Primus
Co-stars: Robert De Niro Martin Landau Eli Wallach

JEAN ALEXANDER

1951 THE MOB
Director: Robert Parrish
Co-stars: Broderick Crawford Betty Buehler Ernest Borgnine

JULIE ALEXANDER

1960 THE PURE HELL OF ST. TRINIANS
Director: Frank Launder
Co-stars: Cecil Parker Joyce Grenfell

KATHERINE ALEXANDER

1933 SHOULD LADIES BEHAVE?
Director: Harry Beaumont
Co-stars: Alice Brady Lionel Barrymore Mary Carlisle

1934 THE BARRETTS OF WIMPOLE STREET
Director: Sidney Franklin
Co-stars: Norma Shearer Charles Laughton Fredric March

1934 DEATH TAKES A HOLIDAY
Director: Mitchell Leisen
Co-stars: Fredric March Evelyn Venable Gail Patrick

1934 OPERATOR 13
Director: Richard Boleslawski
Co-stars: Marion Davies Gary Cooper Jean Parker

1935 CARDINAL RICHELIEU
Director: Rowland Lee
Co-stars: George Arliss Maureen O'Sullivan Edward Arnold

1935 SPLENDOR
Director: Elliott Nugent
Co-stars: Joel McCrea Miriam Hopkins David Niven

1935 ENCHANTED APRIL
Director: Harry Beaumont
Co-stars: Ann Harding Frank Morgan Reginald Owen

1935 AFTER OFFICE HOURS
Director: Robert Z. Leonard
Co-stars: Clark Gable Constance Bennett Billie Burke

1935 SHE MARRIED HER BOSS
Director: Gregory LaCava
Co-stars: Claudette Colbert Melvyn Douglas Jean Dixon

1935 THE GIRL FROM 10TH. AVENUE
Director: Alfred Green
Co-stars: Bette Davis Ian Hunter Colin Clive

1936 MOONLIGHT MURDER
Co-stars: Leo Carrillo Benita Hume

1936 THE DEVIL IS A SISSY
Director: W.S.Van Dyke
Co-stars: Freddie Bartholomew Mickey Rooney Jackie Cooper

1936 SUTTER'S GOLD
Director: James Cruze
Co-stars: Edward Arnold Lee Tracy Binnie Barnes

1937 DOUBLE WEDDING
Director: Richard Thorpe
Co-stars: William Powell Myrna Loy Florence Rice

1937 THE GIRL FROM SCOTLAND YARD
Director: Robert Vignola
Co-stars: Karen Morley Robert Baldwin

1937 THAT CERTAIN WOMAN
Director: Edmund Goulding
Co-stars: Bette Davis Henry Fonda Ian Hunter

1939 BROADWAY SERENADE
Director: Robert Z Leonard
Co-stars: Jeanette MacDonald Lew Ayres Frank Morgan

1942 ON THE SUNNY SIDE
Co-stars: Jane Darwell Roddy McDowall

1945 KISS AND TELL
Co-stars: Shirley Temple Walter Abel Virginia Welles

1949 JOHN LOVES MARY
Director: David Butler
Co-stars: Ronald Reagan Patricia Neal Jack Carson

CHARLOTTE ALEXANDRA

1974 IMMORAL TALES
Director: Walerian Borowczyk
Co-stars: Lise Danvers Paloma Picasso

MARY ALICE

1979 LAWMAN WITHOUT A GUN
Director: Jerrold Freedman
Co-stars: Lou Gossett Jnr Clu Gulager

1989 WOMEN OF BREWSTER PLACE
Director: Donna Deitch
Co-stars: Oprah Winfrey Olivia Cole

1990 TO SLEEP WITH ANGER
Director: Charles Burnett
Co-stars: Danny Glover Paul Butler Vonetta McGee

**1994 FREEDOM ROAD:
THE VERNON JOHNS STORY**
Director: Kenneth Fink
Co-stars: James Earl Jones Joe Seneca

ANA ALICIA

1981 COWARD OF THE COUNTY
Director: Dick Lowry
Co-stars: Kenny Rogers Largo Woodruff

1983 HAPPY ENDINGS
Director: Noel Black
Co-stars: John Schneider Catherine Hicks

1988 MIRACLE LANDING
Director: Dick Lowry
Co-stars: Wayne Rogers Connie Sellecca Nancy Kwan

1989 ROMERO
Director: John Duigan
Co-stars: Raul Julia Richard Jordan Tony Plana

MARTA ALICIA

1991 MINDWARP
Director: Steve Barnett
Co-stars: Angus Scrimm Bruce Campbell

DOROTHY ALISON

1952 MANDY
Director: Alexander MacKendrick
Co-stars: Jack Hawkins Mandy Miller Phyllis Calvert

1953 THE MAGGIE
Director: Alexander MacKendrick
Co-stars: Paul Douglas Hubert Gregg Abe Barker

1953 TURN THE KEY SOFTLY
Director: Jack Lee
Co-stars: Yvonne Mitchell Terence Morgan Joan Collins

1954 CHILD'S PLAY
Director: Margaret Thomson
Co-stars: Mona Washbourne Christopher Beeny

1956 THE LONG ARM
Director: Charles Frend
Co-stars: Jack Hawkins Geoffrey Keen Sidney Tafler

1956 REACH FOR THE SKY
Director: Lewis Gilbert
Co-stars: Kenneth More Muriel Pavlow Lyndon Brook

1957 THE SCAMP
Director: Wolf Rilla
Co-stars: Richard Attenborough Colin Petersen Jill Adams

1958 THE MAN UPSTAIRS
Director: Don Chaffey
Co-stars: Richard Attenborough Bernard Lee Donald Houston

1959 LIFE IN EMERGENCY WARD 10
Director: Robert Day
Co-stars: Michael Craig Glyn Owen Joan Sims

1966 GEORGY GIRL
Director: Silvio Narizzano
Co-stars: Lynn Redgrave James Mason Alan Bates

1967 PRETTY POLLY
Director: Guy Green
Co-stars: Hayley Mills Trevor Howard Shashi Kapoor

1971 DOCTOR JEKYLL AND SISTER HYDE
Director: Roy Ward Baker
Co-stars: Ralph Bates Martine Beswick

1971 BLIND TERROR
Director: Richard Fleischer
Co-stars: Mia Farrow Robin Bailey Paul Nicholas

1972 THE AMAZING MR. BLUNDEN
Director: Lionel Jeffries
Co-stars: Laurence Naismith Lynne Frederick

1988 RIKKI AND PETE
Director: Nadia Tass
Co-stars: Stephen Kearney Nina Landis Bill Hunter

1988 A CRY IN THE DARK
Director: Fred Schepisi
Co-stars: Meryl Streep Sam Neill Dale Reeves

1989 AUSTRALIA
Director: Jean-Jacques Andrien
Co-stars: Jeremy Irons Fanny Ardant Agnes Soral

1989 MALPRACTICE
Director: Bill Bennett
Co-stars: Bob Baines Ian Gilmour

ELIZABETH ALLAN

1931 MICHAEL AND MARY
Director: Victor Saville
Co-stars: Herbert Marshall Edna Best Frank Lawton

1931 ALIBI
Director: Leslie Hiscott
Co-stars: Austin Trevor Franklin Dyall

1932 THE LODGER
Director: John Brahm
Co-stars: Ivor Novello Jack Hawkins Barbara Everest

1932 SERVICE FOR LADIES
Director: Alexander Korda
Co-stars: Leslie Howard Benita Hume Merle Oberon

1933 THE SOLITAIRE MAN
Director: Jack Conway
Co-stars: Herbert Marshall Mary Boland Lionel Atwill

1933 THE SHADOW
Director: George Cooper
Co-stars: Henry Kendall Sam Livesey Cyril Raymond

1933 LOOKING FORWARD
Director: Clarence Brown
Co-stars: Lewis Stone Lionel Barrymore Benita Hume

1933 NO MARRIAGE TIES
Co-star: Richard Dix

1933 ACE OF ACES
Director: Walter Ruben
Co-stars: Richard Dix Ralph Bellamy Frank Conroy

1934 JAVA HEAD
Director: Walter Ruben
Co-stars: John Loder Anna May Wong Ralph Richardson

1934 MEN IN WHITE
Director: Richard Boleslawski
Co-stars: Clark Gable Myrna Loy Jean Hersholt

1934 THE MYSTERY OF MR X
Director: Edgar Selwyn
Co-stars: Robert Montgommery Lewis Stone Ralph Forbes

1934 OUTCAST LADY
Director: Robert Z. Leonard
Co-stars: Constance Bennett Hugh Williams L.G.Caroll

1935 MARK OF THE VAMPIRE
Director: Tod Browning
Co-stars: Lionel Barrymore Jean Hersholt Bela Lugosi

1935 DAVID COPPERFIELD
Director: George Cukor
Co-stars: Freddie Bartholomew Basil Rathbone

1935 A TALE OF TWO CITIES
Director: Jack Conway
Co-stars: Ronald Colman Basil Rathbone

1936   A WOMAN REBELS
Director: Mark Sandrich
Co-stars: Katharine Hepburn Herbert Marshall Van Heflin

1937   THE ADVENTURES OF MICHAEL STROGOFF
Director: George Nicholls
Co-stars: Anton Walbrook Akim Tamiroff

1937   SLAVE SHIP
Director: Tay Garnett
Co-stars: Wallace Berry Warner Baxter Mickey Rooney

1937   CAMILLE
Director: George Cukor
Co-stars: Greta Garbo Robert Taylor Lionel Barrymore

1939   INQUEST
Director: Roy Boulting
Co-stars: Herbert Lom Barbara Everest Hay Petrie

1940   SALOON BAR
Director: Walter Forde
Co-stars: Gordon Harker Mervyn Johns Judy Campbell

1942   THE GREAT MR. HANDEL
Director: Norman Walker
Co-stars: Wilfrid Lawson Malcolm Keen Hay Petrie

1942   WENT THE DAY WELL
Director: Alberto Cavalcanti
Co-stars: Leslie Banks Basil Sydney Mervyn Johns

1944   HE SNOOPS TO CONQUER
Director: Marcel Varnel
Co-stars: George Formby Robertson Hare

1949   THAT DANGEROUS AGE
Director: Gregory Ratoff
Co-stars: Roger Livesey Myrna Loy Richard Greene

1951   NO HIGHWAY
Director: Henry Koster
Co-stars: James Stewart Marlene Dietrich Glynis Johns

1952   FOLLY TO BE WISE
Director: Frank Launder
Co-stars: Alastair Sim Roland Culver Martita Hunt

1953   FRONT PAGE STORY
Director: Gordon Parry
Co-stars: Jack Hawkins Derek Farr Michael Goodliffe

1953   THE HEART OF THE MATTER
Director: George More O'Ferrall
Co-stars: Trevor Howard Maria Schell Peter Finch

1955   THE BRAIN MACHINE
Director: Ken Hughes
Co-stars: Patrick Barr Maxwell Reed Russell Napier

1958   GRIP OF THE STRANGLER
Director: Robert Day
Co-stars: Boris Karloff Jean Kent Vera Day

1960   FROM THE TERRACE
Director: Mark Robson
Co-stars: Paul Newman Joanne Woodward Myrna Loy

1963   DONOVAN'S REEF
Director: John Ford
Co-stars: John Wayne Lee Marvin Dorothy Lamour

1964   CHEYENNE AUTUMN
Director: John Ford
Co-stars: James Stewart Richard Widmark Edward G Robinson

1971   THE STAR SPANGLED GIRL
Director: Jerry Paris
Co-stars: Sandy Duncan Tony Roberts

1972   THE CAREY TREATMENT
Director: Blake Edwards
Co-stars: James Coburn Jennifer O'Neil Pat Hingle

MARGARET ALLAN

1941   BREACH OF PROMISE
Director: Harold Huth
Co-stars: Clive Brook Judy Campbell

MARGUERITE ALLAN

1934   DOCTOR'S ORDERS
Director: Norman Lee
Co-stars: Leslie Fuller John Mills Ronald Shiner

MARISA ALLASIO

1957   THE SEVEN HILLS OF ROME
Director: Roy Rowland
Co-stars: Mario Lanza Renato Rascel Peggie Castle

LOUISE ALLBRITTON

1942   PITTSBURGH
Director: Lewis Seiler
Co-stars: Marlene Dietrich John Wayne Randolph Scott

1942   WHO DONE IT?
Director: Erle Kenton
Co-stars: Abbott & Costello William Gargan William Bendix

1943   THIS IS THE LIFE
Director: Felix Feist
Co-stars: Donald O'Connor Peggy Ryan Susanna Foster

1943   SON OF DRACULA
Director: Robert Siodmak
Co-stars: Lon Chaney Robert Paige Evelyn Ankers

1943   IT COMES UP LOVE
Director: Charles Lamont
Co-stars: Gloria Jean Donald O'Connor Ian Hunter

1943   GOOD MORNING JUDGE
Director: Jean Yarbrough
Co-stars: Dennis O'Keefe Louise Beavers

1943   FIRED WIFE
Director: Charles Lamont
Co-stars: Diana Barrymore Robert Paige Walter Abel

1944   BOWERY TO BROADWAY
Director: Charles Lamont
Co-stars: Maria Montez Turhan Bey Susanna Foster

1944   HER PRIMITIVE MAN
Director: Charles Lamont
Co-stars: Robert Paige Helen Broderick Robert Benchley

1944   SAN DIEGO, I LOVE YOU
Director: Reginald LeBorg
Co-stars: Jon Hall Eric Blore Buster Keaton

1945   THAT NIGHT WITH YOU
Director: William Seitier
Co-stars: Franchot Tone Susanna Foster Buster Keaton

1945   MEN IN HER DIARY
Director: Charles Barton
Co-stars: Peggy Ryan Jon Hall Virginia Grey

1947   THE EGG AND I
Director: Chester Erskine
Co-stars: Claudette Colbert Fred MacMurray Marjorie Main

1948   DON'T TRUST YOUR HUSBAND
Director: Lloyd Bacon
Co-stars: Fred MacMurray Madeleine Carroll

1948   SITTING PRETTY
Director: Walter Lang
Co-stars: Clifton Webb Robert Young Maureen O'Hara

1948   WALK A CROOKED MILE
Director: Gordon Douglas
Co-stars: Dennis O'Keefe Louis Hayward

1949 THE DOOLINS OF OKLAHOMA
Director: Gordon Douglas
Co-stars: Randolph Scott George Macready

CATHERINE ALLEGRET

1965 THE SLEEPING CAR MURDERS
Director: Costa-Gavras
Co-stars: Yves Montand Simone Signoret

1972 LAST TANGO IN PARIS
Director: Bernardo Bertolucci
Co-stars: Marlon Brando Maria Schneider

1973 BURNT BARNS
Director: Jean Chapot
Co-stars: Alain Delon Simone Signoret Miou-Miou

ADRIANNE ALLEN

1947 THE OCTOBER MAN
Director: Roy Baker
Co-stars: John Mills Joan Greenwood Kay Walsh

1948 BOND STREET
Director: Gordon Parry
Co-stars: Roland Young Jean Kent Derek Farr

ADRIENNE ALLEN

1932 THE NIGHT OF JUNE 13TH
Director: Stephen Roberts
Co-stars: Clive Brook Lila Lee Frances Dee

1932 MERRILY WE GO TO HELL
Director: Dorothy Arzner
Co-stars: Sylvia Sidney Fredric March Kent Taylor

1932 SINNERS IN THE SUN
Director: Alexander Hall
Co-stars: Carole Lombard Chester Morris Cary Grant

1936 THE MORALS OF MARCUS
Director: Miles Mander
Co-stars: Lupe Velez Ian Hunter Noel Madison

BARBARA JO ALLEN
(Also Acted As Vera Vague)

1941 THE MAD DOCTOR
Director: Tim Whelan
Co-stars: Basil Rathbone Ellen Drew John Howard

1941 KISS THE BOYS GOODBYE
Director: Victor Schertzinger
Co-stars: Don Ameche Mary Martin Oscar Levant

1941 ICE-CAPADES
Director: Joseph Santly
Co-stars: James Ellison Phil Silvers Jerry Colonna

1942 ICE-CAPADES REVIEW
Director: Bernard Vorhaus
Co-stars: Vera Ralston Richard Denning Ellen Drew

1956 THE OPPOSITE SEX
Director: David Miller
Co-stars: June Allyson Ann Sheridan Joan Collins

1959 SLEEPING BEAUTY *(Voice)*
Director: Clyde Geronimi
Co-stars: Mary Costa Bill Shirley Verna Felton

GRACIE ALLEN *(Married George Burns)*

1932 THE BIG BROADCAST
Director: Frank Tuttle
Co-stars: George Burns Bing Crosby Stuart Erwin

1933 COLLEGE HUMOR
Director: Wesley Ruggles
Co-stars: George Burns Bing Crosby Jack Oakie

1933 INTERNATIONAL HOUSE
Director: Edward Sutherland
Co-stars: George Burns W. C. Fields Stuart Erwin

1934 MANY HAPPY RETURNS
Director: Norman Z. McLeod
Co-stars: George Burns Ray Milland William Demarest

1934 WE'RE NOT DRESSING
Director: Norman Taurog
Co-stars: George Burns Bing Crosby Carole Lombard

1934 SIX OF A KIND
Director: Leo McCarey
Co-stars: George Burns W. C. Fields Charles Ruggles

1935 LOVE IN BLOOM
Director: Elliott Nugent
Co-stars: George Burns Dixie Lee Joe Morrison

1935 HERE COMES COOKIE
Director: Norman Z. McLeod
Co-stars: George Burns George Barbier Betty Furness

1936 COLLEGE HOLIDAY
Director: Frank Tuttle
Co-stars: George Burns Jack Benny Martha Raye

1936 THE BIG BROADCAST OF 1936
Director: Norman Taurog
Co-stars: George Burns Bing Crosby Ethel Merman

1937 THE BIG BROADCAST OF 1937
Director: Mitchell Leisen
Co-stars: George Burns Jack Benny Larry Adler

1937 A DAMSEL IN DISTRESS
Director: George Stevens
Co-stars: George Burns Fred Astaire Joan Fontaine

1938 COLLEGE SWING
Director: Raoul Walsh
Co-stars: George Burns Bob Hope Martha Raye

1938 HONOLULU
Director: Edward Buzzell
Co-stars: George Burns Robert Young Eleanor Powell

1939 THE GRACIE ALLEN MURDER CASE
Director: Alfred Green
Co-stars: Warren William Ellen Drew

1941 MR. & MRS. NORTH
Director: Robert Sinclair
Co-stars: William Post Paul Kelly Rose Hobart

1944 TWO GIRLS AND A SAILOR
Director: Richard Thorpe
Co-stars: Van Johnson June Allyson Gloria De Haven

JOAN ALLEN

1986 MANHUNTER
Director: Michael Mann
Co-stars: William Petersen Kim Greist Brian Cox

1988 TUCKER: THE MAN AND HIS DREAM
Director: Francis Ford Coppola
Co-stars: Jeff Bridges Martin Landau

1989 IN COUNTRY
Director: Norman Jewison
Co-stars: Bruce Willis Emily Lloyd Judith Ivey

1991 WITHOUT WARNING:
THE JAMES BRADY STORY
Director: Michael Uno
Co-stars: Beau Bridges David Strathairn

1993 INNOCENT MOVES
Director: Steven Zaillian
Co-stars: Max Pomeranc Ben Kingsley Joe Mantegna

1993 JOSH AND S. A. M.
Director: Billy Weber
Co-stars: Jacob Tierney Noah Fleiss Chris Penn

1993 ETHAN FROME
Director: John Madden
Co-stars: Liam Neeson Patricia Arquette Tate Donovan

1996 THE CRUCIBLE
Director: Nicolas Hytner
Co-stars: Daniel Day-Lewis Paul Scofield Winona Ryder

1996 NIXON
Director: Oliver Stone
Co-stars: Anthony Hopkins Bob Hoskins Paul Sorvino

1998 THE ICE STORM
Director: Ang Lee
Co-stars: Kevin Kline Sigourney Weaver Christina Ricci

JONELLE ALLEN

1972 COME BACK, CHARLESTON BLUE
Director: Mark Warren
Co-stars: Godfrey Cambridge Raymond St. Jacques

JUDITH ALLEN

1933 THIS DAY AND AGE
Director: Cecil B. Demille
Co-stars: Charles Bickford Richard Cromwell

1933 TOO MUCH HARMONY
Director: Edward Sutherland
Co-stars: Bing Crosby Jack Oakie Lilyan Tashman

1933 HELL AND HIGH WATER
Co-star: Richard Arlen

1933 CAP'N JERICHO
Co-star: Richard Arlen

1934 THE WITCHING HOUR
Director: Henry Hathaway
Co-stars: John Halliday Guy Standing Tom Brown

1934 MEN OF THE NIGHT
Co-star: Bruce Cabot

1934 THE OLD-FASHIONED WAY
Director: William Beaudine
Co-stars: W.C. Fields Joe Morrison Baby Leroy

1934 YOUNG AND BEAUTIFUL
Co-star: William Haines

1934 MARRYING WIDOWS
Co-star: Minna Gombell

1935 RECKLESS ROADS
Co-star: Regis Toomey

1937 BOOTS AND SADDLES
Co-star: Gene Autry

1937 NAVY SPY
Co-star: Roscoe Karns

1937 IT HAPPENED OUT WEST
Co-star: Paul Kelly Leroy Mason

1938 PORT OF MISSING GIRLS
Co-stars: Harry Carey Milburn Stone

KAREN ALLEN

1979 THE WANDERERS
Director: Philip Kaufman
Co-stars: Ken Wahl John Friedrich Toni Kalem

1980 A SMALL CIRCLE OF FRIENDS
Director: Rob Cohen
Co-stars: Brad Davis Jameson Parker Shelley Long

1980 CRUISING
Director: William Friedkin
Co-stars: Al Pacino Paul Sorvino Richard Cox

1981 RAIDERS OF THE LOST ARK
Director: Steven Spielberg
Co-stars: Harrison Ford Ronald Lacey Denholm Elliott

1981 SHOOT THE MOON
Director: Alan Parker
Co-stars: Albert Finney Diane Keaton Peter Weller

1982 SPLIT IMAGE
Director: Ted Kotcheff
Co-stars: Michael O'Keefe James Woods Peter Fonda

1984 STARMAN
Director: John Carpenter
Co-stars: Jeff Bridges Richard Jeckel Robert Phalen

1984 UNTIL SEPTEMBER
Director: Richard Marquand
Co-stars: Thierry L'Hermitte Christopher Cazenove

1987 THE GLASS MENAGERIE
Director: Paul Newman
Co-stars: Joanne Woodward John Malkovich

1987 BACKFIRE
Director: Gilbert Cates
Co-stars: Keith Carradine Jeff Fahey Dean Paul Martin

1989 ANIMAL BEHAVIOUR
Director: Ann Riley
Co-stars: Armand Assante Holly Hunter Josh Mostel

1988 SCROOGED
Director: Richard Donner
Co-stars: Bill Murray Robert Mitchum Lee Majors

1990 CHALLENGER
Director: Glenn Jordan
Co-stars: Brian Kerwin Peter Boyle Lane Smith

1990 SWEET TALKER
Director: Michael Jenkins
Co-stars: Bryan Brown

1993 GHOST IN THE MACHINE
Director: Rachel Talalay
Co-stars: Chris Mulkey Ted Marcoux

1993 KING OF THE HILL
Director: Steven Soderbergh
Co-stars: Jesse Bradford Jeroen Krabbe Lisa Eichhorn

1993 THE VOYAGE
Director: John MacKenzie
Co-stars: Eric Roberts Rutger Hauer Connie Nielson

1994 THE SANDLOT KIDS
Director: David Mickey Evans
Co-stars: Tom Guiry Mike Vitar James Earl Jones

MIKKI ALLEN *(Child)*

1991 REGARDING HENRY
Director: Mike Nicholls
Co-stars: Harrison Ford Annette Bening Donald Moffat

NANCY ALLEN *(Married Brian De Palma)*

1976 CARRIE
Director: Brian De Palma
Co-stars: Sissy Spacek Piper Laurie Amy Irving John Travolta

1978 I WANNA HOLD YOUR HAND
Director: Robert Zemeckis
Co-stars: Bobby DiCicco Marc McClure Will Jordan

1979 HOME MOVIES
Director: Brian De Palma
Co-stars: Kirk Douglas Keith Gordon Vincent Gardenia

1980 DRESSED TO KILL
Director: Brian De Palma
Co-stars: Michael Caine Angie Dickinson Keith Gordon

1981 BLOW OUT
Director: Brian De Palma
Co-stars: John Travolta John Lithgow Dennis Franz

1983 STRANGE INVADERS
Director: Michael Laughlin
Co-stars: Paul Le Mat Louise Fletcher Diana Scarwid

1984 THE PHILADELPHIA EXPERIMENT
Director: Stuart Rafill
Co-stars: Michael Pare Bobby DiCicco

1984 THE BUDDY SISTERS
Director: Glenn Jordan
Co-stars: Richard Dreyfuss Susan Sarandon

1984 TERROR IN THE AISLES
Director: Andrew Kuehn
Co-stars: Donald Pleasence

1986 THE GLADIATOR
Director: Abel Ferrara
Co-stars: Ken Wahl Robert Culp Rosemary Forsyth

1987 ROBOCOP
Director: Paul Verhoeven
Co-stars: Peter Weller Dan O'Herlihy Kurtwood Smith

1988 POLTERGEIST III
Director: Gary Sherman
Co-stars: Tom Skerritt Heather O'Rourke Zelda Rubinstein

1989 LIMIT UP
Director: Richard Martini
Director: Dean Stockwell Brad Hall Sally Kellerman

1990 MEMORIES OF MURDER
Director: Robert Lewis
Co-stars: Robin Thomas Vanity

1990 ROBOCOP 2
Director: Irvin Kerschner
Co-stars: Peter Weller Dan O'Herlihy Tom Noonan

1993 THE MAN WHO WOULDN'T DIE
Director: Bill Condon
Co-stars: Roger Moore Malcolm McDowell

1994 ROBOCOP 3
Director: Fred Dekker
Co-stars: Robert Burke Rip Torn John Castle

ROSALIND ALLEN
1992 TICKS
Director: Tony Randel
Co-stars: Ami Dolenz Seth Green

**1993 CHILDREN OF THE CORN II:
THE FINAL SACRIFICE**
Director: David Price
Co-stars: Terence Knox Ned Romero

SHEILA ALLEN
1964 CHILDREN OF THE DAMNED
Director: Anton Leader
Co-stars: Ian Hendry Alan Badel Barbara Ferris

1987 HEDGEHOG WEDDING
Director: Tim King
Co-stars: Frederick Treves Lynsey Baxter Marsha Fitzalan

1988 PASCALI'S ISLAND
Director: James Dearden
Co-stars: Ben Kingsley Charles Dance Helen Mirren

1991 THE OLD DEVILS
Director: Tristram Powell
Co-stars: John Stride Ray Smith Anna Cropper

1992 SHINING THROUGH
Director: David Seltzer
Co-stars: Melanie Griffith Michael Douglas Joely Richardson

SIAN-BARBARA ALLEN
1972 YOU'LL LIKE MY MOTHER
Director: Lamont Johnson
Co-stars: Rosemary Murphy Patty Duke Richard Thomas

1972 THE FAMILY RICO
Director: Paul Wendkos
Co-stars: Ben Gazzara Sal Mineo Jo Van Fleet

1974 BILLY TWO HATS
Director: Ted Kotcheff
Co-stars: Gregory Peck Desi Arnaz Jnr. Jack Warden

1975 ERIC
Director: James Goldstone
Co-stars: Patricia Neal John Savage Mark Hamill

TANYA ALLEN
1997 REGENERATION
Director: Gilles MacKinnon
Co-stars: Jonathan Pryce James Wilby Jonny Lee Miller

TYRESS ALLEN
1989 TRAPPED
Director: Fred Walton
Co-stars: Kathleen Quinlan Ben Loggins Bruce Abbott

KATHERINE ALLENTUCK
1971 SUMMER OF '42
Director: Robert Mulligan
Co-stars: Jennifer O'Neill Gary Grimes Jerry Hauser

KIRSTIE ALLEY
1984 SINS OF THE PAST
Director: Peter Hunt
Co-stars: Barbara Carrera Kim Cattrall Tracy Reed Debby Boone

1984 RUNAWAY
Director: Michael Crichton
Co-stars: Tom Selleck Cynthia Rhodes Gene L. Simmons

1986 PRINCE OF BEL-AIR
Director: Charles Braverman
Co-stars: Mark Harmon Robert Vaughn Bart Braverman

1986 STARK: MIRROR IMAGE
Director: Noel Nosseck
Co-stars: Nicolas Surovy Dennis Hopper Ben Murphy

1987 SUMMER SCHOOL
Director: Carl Reiner
Co-stars: Mark Harmon Robin Thomas Shawnee Smith

1988 DEADLY PURSUIT
Director: Roger Spottiswoode
Co-stars: Sidney Poitier Tom Berenger Clancy Brown

1989 LOVERBOY
Director: Joan Micklin Silver
Co-stars: Patrick Dempsey Kate Jackson Carrie Fisher

1989 LOOK WHO'S TALKING
Director: Amy Heckerling
Co-stars: John Travolta Olympia Dukakis Bruce Willis

1990 LOOK WHO'S TALKING TOO
Director: Amy Heckerling
Co-stars: John Travolta Roseanne Barr Mel Brooks

1990 MADHOUSE
Director: Tom Ropelewski
Co-stars: John Larroquette Alison LaPlaca John Diehl

1990 SIBLING RIVALRY
Director: Carl Reiner
Co-stars: Bill Pullman Carrie Fisher Scott Bakula

1993 LOOK WHO'S TALKING NOW
Director: Tom Ropelewski
Co-stars: John Travolta Olympia Dukakis Lysette Anthony

1994 DAVID'S MOTHER
Director: Robert Allan Ackerman
Co-stars: Sam Waterson Chris Sarandon

1996 THE VILLAGE OF THE DAMNED
Director: John Carpenter
Co-stars: Christopher Reeve Mark Hamill

1998 DECONSTRUCTING HARRY
Director: Woody Allen
Co-stars: Woody Allen Robin Williams Elizabeth Shue

SARA ALLGOOD
Nominated For Best Supporting Actress For "How Green Was My Valley" In 1941

1929 BLACKMAIL
Director: Alfred Hitchcock
Co-stars: Annie Ondra John Longden Donald Calthrop

1930 JUNO AND THE PAYCOCK
Director: Alfred Hitchcock
Co-stars: Edward Chapman Maire O'Neill John Laurie

1935 LAZYBONES
Director: Michael Powell
Co-stars: Ian Hunter Clare Luce Harold Warrender

1935 THE PASSING OF THE THIRD FLOOR BACK
Director: Berthold Viertel
Co-stars: Conrad Veidt Anna Lee Rene Ray

1936 IT'S LOVE AGAIN
Director: Victor Saville
Co-stars: Jessie Mathews Robert Young Sonnie Hale

1937 STORM IN A TEACUP
Director: Victor Saville
Co-stars: Rex Harrison Vivien Leigh Cecil Parker

1941 LADY HAMILTON
Director: Alexander Korda
Co-stars: Laurence Olivier Vivien Leigh Gladys Cooper

1941 LYDIA
Director: Julian Duvivier
Co-stars: Merle Oberon Joseph Cotten Alan Marshall

1941 DR.JEKYLL AND MR.HYDE
Director: Victor Fleming
Co-stars: Spencer Tracy Ingrid Bergman Lana Turner

1941 HOW GREEN WAS MY VALLEY
Director: John Ford
Co-stars: Walter Pidgeon Maureen O'Hara Roddy McDowall

1942 LIFE BEGINS AT EIGHT THIRTY
Director: Irving Pichel
Co-stars: Monty Woolley Ida Lupino Cornel Wilde

1942 ROXIE HART
Director: William Wellman
Co-stars: Ginger Rogers George Montgomery Adolphe Menjou

1942 THE WAR AGAINST MRS.HADLEY
Director: Harold Bucquet
Co-stars: Fay Bainter Edward Arnold Jean Rogers

1943 FOREVER AND A DAY
Director: Rene Clair
Co-stars: Anna Neagle Ray Milland Jessie Matthews

1943 CITY WITHOUT MEN
Director: Sidney Salkow
Co-stars: Linda Darnell Glenda Farrell Michael Duane

1944 BETWEEN TWO WORLDS
Director: Edward Blatt
Co-stars: John Garfield Edmund Gwenn Paul Henreid

1944 JANE EYRE
Director: Robert Stevenson
Co-stars: Orson Welles Joan Fontaine Margaret O'Brien

1944 THE LODGER
Director: John Brahm
Co-stars: Laird Cregar Merle Oberon George Sanders

1945 KITTY
Director: Mitchell Leisen
Co-stars: Paulette Goddard Ray Milland Eric Blore

1945 THE STRANGE AFFAIR OF UNCLE HARRY
Director: Robert Siodmak
Co-stars: George Sanders Ella Raines

1946 THE SPIRAL STAIRCASE
Director: Robert Siodmak
Co-stars: Dorothy McGuire George Brent Kent Smith

1946 CLUNY BROWN
Director: Ernst Lubitsch
Co-stars: Jennifer Jones Charles Boyer Una O'Connor

1947 MOTHER WORE TIGHTS
Director: Walter Lang
Co-stars: Betty Grable Dan Dailey Mona Freeman

1947 IVY
Director: Sam Wood
Co-stars: Joan Fontaine Herbert Marshall Richard Ney

1948 THE GIRL FROM MANHATTAN
Director: Alfred Green
Co-stars: Dorothy Lamour Charles Laughton

1949 THE ACCUSED
Director: William Dieterle
Co-stars: Loretta Young Robert Cummings Wendell Corey

1950 CHEAPER BY THE DOZEN
Director: Walter Lang
Co-stars: Clifton Webb Myrna Loy Jeanne Crain

WENDY ALLNUT

1972 ALL COPPERS ARE
Director: Sidney Hayers
Co-stars: Nicky Henson Julia Foster Ian Hendry

1980 PALMER
Director: Keith Washington
Co-stars: Ray Winstone Dora Bryan Gerard Moran

ASTRID ALLWYN

1932 LADY WITH A PAST
Director: Edward Griffiths
Co-stars: Constance Bennett Ben Lyon

1932 LOVE AFFAIR
Director: Thornton Freeland
Co-stars: Humphrey Bogart Dorothy MacKail Jack Kennedy

1932 NIGHT MAYOR
Director: Ben Stolof
Co-stars: Lee Tracey Evalyn Knapp Eugene Pallett

1934 SERVANT'S ENTRANCE
Director: Frank Lloyd
Co-stars: Janet Gaynor Lew Ayres Walter Connolly

1934 MYSTERY LINER
Director: William Nigh
Co-stars: Noah Berry Gustav Von Seyffertitz

1934 THE WHITE PARADE
Director: Irving Cummings
Co-stars: Loretta Young John Boles Sara Haden

1935 ACCENT ON YOUTH
Director: Wesley Ruggles
Co-stars: Herbert Marshall Sylvia Sydney

1935 HANDS ACROSS THE TABLE
Director: Mitchell Leisen
Co-stars: Carole Lombard Fred MacMurray Ralph Bellamy

1936 CHARLIE CHAN'S SECRET
Director: Gordon Wiles
Co-stars: Warner Oland Rosina Lawrence Herbert Mundin

1936 FOLLOW THE FLEET
Director: Mark Sandrich
Co-stars: Fred Astaire Ginger Rogers Randolph Scott

1936 STOWAWAY
Director: William Seiter
Co-stars: Shirley Temple Robert Young Alice Faye

1936 DIMPLES
Director: William Seiter
Co-stars: Shirley Temple Frank Morgan Helen Westley

1937 MURDER GOES TO COLLEGE
Director: Charles Reisner
Co-stars: Roscoe Karns Lynne Overman Marsha Hunt

1939 MR SMITH GOES TO WASHINGTON
Director: Frank Capra
Co-stars: James Stewart Jean Arthur Claude Rains

1939 LOVE AFFAIR
Director: Leo McCarey
Co-stars: Irene Dunne Charles Boyer Lee Bowman

1940 THE LONE WOLF STRIKES
Director: Sidney Salkow
Co-stars: Warren William Joan Perry Eric Blore

1941 I'LL SELL MY LIFE
Co-star: John Archer

JUNE ALLYSON

1943 GIRL GRAZY
Director: Norman Taurog
Co-stars: Judy Garland Mickey Rooney Rags Ragland

1943 BEST FOOT FORWARD
Director: Edward Buzzell
Co-stars: Lucille Ball Gloria De Haven William Gaxton

1943 THOUSANDS CHEER
Director: George Sidney
Co-stars: Gene Kelly Kathryn Grayson John Boles

1944 MEET THE PEOPLE
Director: Charles Reisner
Co-stars: Lucille Ball Dick Powell Bert Lahr

1944 MUSIC FOR MILLIONS
Director: Henry Koster
Co-stars: Margaret O'Brien Jose Iturbi Jimmy Durante

1944 TWO GIRLS AND A SAILOR
Director: Richard Thorpe
Co-stars: Van Johnson Gloria DeHaven Jimmy Durante

1945 HER HIGHNESS AND THE BELLBOY
Director: Richard Thorpe
Co-stars: Robert Walker Hedy Lamarr

1945 SAILOR TAKES A WIFE
Director: Richard Whorf
Co-stars: Robert Walker Hume Cronyn Reginald Owen

1946 TWO SISTERS FROM BOSTON
Director: Henry Koster
Co-stars: Kathryn Grayson Peter Lawford Ben Blue

1946 TILL THE CLOUDS ROLL BY
Director: Richard Whorf
Co-stars: Robert Walker Van Heflin Lucille Bremer

1947 GOOD NEWS
Director: Charles Walters
Co-stars: Peter Lawford Mel Torme Joan McCracken

1947 HIGH BARBAREE
Director: Jack Conway
Co-stars: Van Johnson Thomas Mitchell Marilyn Maxwell

1947 THE SECRET HEART
Director: Robert Z. Leonard
Co-stars: Claudette Colbert Walter Pidgeon

1948 WORDS AND MUSIC
Director: Norman Taurog
Co-stars: Mickey Rooney Tom Drake Gene Kelly

1948 THE BRIDE GOES WILD
Director: Norman Taurog
Co-stars: Van Johnson Butch Jenkins Arlene Dahl

1948 THE THREE MUSKETEERS
Director: George Sidney
Co-stars: Gene Kelly Lana Turner Van Heflin

1949 LITTLE WOMEN
Director: Mervyn LeRoy
Co-stars: Elizabeth Taylor Margaret O'Brien Mary Astor

1949 THE STRATTON STORY
Director: Sam Wood
Co-stars: James Stewart Frank Morgan Agnes Moorehead

1950 RIGHT CROSS
Director: John Sturges
Co-stars: Dick Powell Lionel Barrymore Ricardo Montalban

1950 THE REFORMER AND THE REDHEAD
Director: Melvyn Frank
Co-stars: Dick Powell David Wayne Robert Keith

1951 TOO YOUNG TO KISS
Director: Robert Z.Leonard
Co-stars: Van Johnson Gig Young Paula Corday

1952 THE GIRL IN WHITE
Director: John Sturges
Co-stars: Arthur Kennedy Gary Merrill Mildred Dunnock

1952 BATTLE CIRCUS
Director: Richard Brooks
Co-stars: Humphrey Bogart Keenan Wynn Robert Keith

1953 REMAINS TO BE SEEN
Director: Don Weis
Co-stars: Van Johnson Angela Lansbury Louis Calhern

1954 EXECUTIVE SUITE
Director: Robert Wise
Co-stars: Fredrick March William Holden Barbara Stanwyck

1954 WOMAN'S WORLD
Director: Jean Negulesco
Co-stars: Clifton Webb Lauren Bacall Arleen Dahl

1954 THE GLENN MILLER STORY
Director: Anthony Mann
Co-stars: James Stewart Harry Morgan Charles Drake

1955 TIGER IN THE SKY
Director: Gordon Douglas
Co-stars: Alan Ladd James Whitmore Frank Faylen

1955 THE SHRIKE
Director: Jose Ferrer
Co-stars: Jose Ferrer Joy Page Kendall Clark

1955 STRATEGIC AIR COMMAND
Director: Anthony Mann
Co-stars: James Stewart Frank Lovejoy Alex Nicol

1956 YOU CAN'T RUN AWAY FROM IT
Director: Dick Powell
Co-stars: Jack Lemmon Charles Bickford

1956   **THE OPPOSITE SEX**
Director: David Miller
Co-stars: Dolores Gray Joan Collins Ann Sheridan

1957   **MY MAN GODFREY**
Director: Henry Koster
Co-stars: David Niven Martha Hyer Robert Keith

1957   **INTERLUDE**
Director: Douglas Sirk
Co-stars: Rossano Brazzi Keith Andes Jane Wyatt

1958   **A STRANGER IN MY ARMS**
Director: Helmut Kautner
Co-stars: Jeff Chandler Mary Astor Sandra Dee

1972   **THEY ONLY KILL THEIR MASTERS**
Director: James Goldstone
Co-stars: James Garner Katherine Ross

MARIA CONCHITA ALONSO

1984   **MOSCOW ON THE HUDSON**
Director: Paul Mazursky
Co-stars: Robin Williams Cleavant Derricks

1985   **A FINE MESS**
Director: Blake Edwards
Co-stars: Ted Danson Richard Mulligan

1986   **TOUCH AND GO**
Director: Robert Mandel
Co-stars: Michael Keaton Maria Tucci

1986   **BLOOD TIES**
Director: Giacomo Battiato
Co-stars: Brad Davis Tony LoBianco

1987   **EXTREME PREJUDICE**
Director: Walter Hill
Co-stars: Nick Nolte Powers Boothe Rip Torn

1987   **THE RUNNING MAN**
Director: Paul Michael Glaser
Co-stars: Arnold Schwarzenegger Yaphet Kotto Jim Brown

1988   **COLORS**
Director: Dennis Hopper
Co-stars: Sean Penn Robert Duvall Randy Brooks

1988   **VAMPIRE'S KISS**
Director: Robert Bierman
Co-stars: Nicolas Cage Jennifer Beals Elizabeth Ashley

1990   **PREDATOR 2**
Director: Stephen Hopkins
Co-stars: Danny Glover Gary Busey Ruben Blades

1991   **McBAIN**
Director: James Glickenhaus
Co-stars: Christopher Walken Michael Ironside

1992   **TEAMSTER BOSS:**
          THE JACKIE PRESSER STORY
Director: Alastair Reid
Co-stars: Brian Dennehy Jeff Daniels Eli Wallach

1993   **ROOSTERS**
Director: Robert M. Young
Co-stars: Sonia Braga Edward James Olmos

1993   **THE HOUSE OF THE SPIRITS**
Director: Bille August
Co-stars: Jeremy Irons Meryl Streep Glenn Close

CATHERINE ALRIC

1977   **DEAR INSPECTOR**
Director: Philippe De Broca
Co-stars: Annie Girardot Philippe Noiret

ELENA ALTIERI

1948   **BICYCLE THIEVES**
Director: Vittorio De Sica
Co-stars: Lamberto Maggiorani Enzo Staiola

CAROL ALT

1989   **MY FIRST 40 YEARS**
Director: Carlo Vanzina
Co-stars: Elliott Gould Jean Rochefort

ADRIANA ALTARAS

1989   **THREE WOMEN IN LOVE**
Director: Rudolf Thome
Co-stars: Johannes Herrschmann Claudia Matschulla

ANGELA ALVARADO

1988   **SALSA**
Director: Boaz Davidson
Co-stars: Bobby Rosa Rodney Harvey Magali Alvarado

MAGALI ALVARADO

1988   **SALSA**
Director: Boaz Davidson
Co-stars: Bobby Rosa Rodney Harvey Moon Orona

TRINI ALVARADO

1979   **RICH KIDS**
Director: Robert M Young
Co-stars: Jeremy Levy John Lithgow Kathryn Walker

1980   **TIMES SQUARE**
Director: Alan Moyle
Co-stars: Tim Curry Robin Johnson Peter Coffield

1984   **MRS. SOFFEL**
Director: Gillian Armstrong
Co-stars: Diane Keaton Mel Gibson Matthew Modine

1987   **SWEET LORRAINE**
Director: Steve Gomer
Co-stars: Maureen Stapleton Lee Richardson

1988   **SATISFACTION**
Director: Joan Freeman
Co-stars: Justine Bateman Liam Neeson Julia Roberts

1989   **AMERICAN BLUE NOTE**
Director: Ralph Toporoff
Co-stars: Peter MacNicol Tim Guinee Carl Capotorto

1990   **STELLA**
Director: John Erman
Co-stars: Bette Midler John Goodman Marsha Mason

1991   **AMERICAN FRIENDS**
Director: Tristram Powell
Co-stars: Michael Palin Connie Booth Alfred Molina

1992   **THE BABE**
Director: Arthur Hiller
Co-stars: John Goodman Kelly McGillis Bruce Boxleitner

1997   **THE FRIGHTENERS**
Director: Peter Jackson
Co-star: Michael J. Fox

ANICEE ALVINA

1971   **FRIENDS**
Director: Lewis Gilbert
Co-stars: Sean Bury Toby Robbins Ronald Lewis

LIA AMANDA

1955   **THE COUNT OF MONTE CRISTO**
Director: Robert Vernay
Co-stars: Jean Marais Roger Pigant

LEONORA AMAR

1952 CAPTAIN SCARLETT
Director: Thomas Carr
Co-stars: Richard Greene Nedric Young

BETTY AMANN

1929 ASPHALT
Director: Joe May
Co-stars: Gustav Fruhlich Louise Brooks

1931 RICH AND STRANGE
Director: Alfred Hitchcock
Co-stars: Henry Kendall Joan Barry Elsie Randolph

1938 IN OLD MEXICO
Director: Edward Venturini
Co-stars: William Boyd George "Gabby" Hayes

GENEVIEVE AMBAS *(Child)*

1971 THE LITTLE ARK
Director: James Clark
Co-stars: Theodore Bikel Philip Frame

EVE AMBER

1944 THE SUSPECT
Director: Robert Siodmak
Co-stars: Charles Laughton Ella Raines Rosalind Ivan

1945 WOMAN IN GREEN
Director: Roy William Neill
Co-stars: Basil Rathbone Nigel Bruce Hilliary Brooke

AMEDEE

1952 JEUX INTERDITS
Director: Rene Clement
Co-stars: Brigitte Fossey Georges Poujouly

1957 PORTE DES LILAS
Director: Rene Clair
Co-stars: Pierre Brasseur Henri Vidal Dany Carrel

ADRIENNE AMES

1931 24 HOURS
Co-stars: Clive Brook Kay Francis Minor Watson

1932 GUILTY AS HELL
Director: Erle Kenton
Co-stars: Edmond Lowe Victor McLaglen Richard Arlen

1933 FROM HELL TO HEAVEN
Director: Erle Kenton
Co-stars: Carole Lombard Jack Oakie Sidney Blackmer

1933 THE DEATH KISS
Director: Edwin Marin
Co-stars: David Manners Bela Lugosi John Wray

1933 THE AVENGER
Co-star: Ralph Forbes

1933 BROADWAY BAD
Director: Sidney Lanfield
Co-stars: Joan Blondell Ricardo.Cortez Ginger Rogers

1933 A BEDTIME STORY
Director: Norman Taurog
Co-stars: Maurice Chevalier Helen Twelvetrees

1934 GEORGE WHITE'S SCANDALS
Director: George White
Co-stars: George White Rudy Vallee Alice Faye

1934 YOU'RE TELLING ME
Director: Erle Kenton
Co-stars: W C Fields Larry Crabbe Joan Marsh

1935 LADIES LOVE DANGER
Director: Bruce Humberstone
Co-stars: Gilbert Roland Mona Barrie Donald Cook

1935 HARMONY LANE
Director: Joseph Santley
Co-stars: Douglass Montgomery Evelyn Venable

1935 BLACK SHEEP
Director: Allan Dwan
Co-stars: Edmund Lowe Claire Trevor Tom Brown

1935 ABDUL THE DAMNED
Director: Karl Grune
Co-stars: Fritz Kortner Nils Asther Patric Knowles

JOYCE AMES

1969 HELLO DOLLY
Director: Gene Kelly
Co-stars: Barbara Streisand Walter Matthau Michael Crawford

RAMSEY AMES

1944 THE MUMMY'S GHOST
Director: Reginald LeBorg
Co-stars: John Carradine George Zucco

1946 BEAUTY AND THE BANDIT
Director: William Nigh
Co-stars: Gilbert Roland Frank Yaconelli

ROSEMARY AMES

1934 I BELIEVED IN YOU
Director: Irving Cummngs
Co-stars: Victor Jory John Boles Gertrude Michael

1934 THE GREAT HOTEL MURDER
Director: Eugene Forde
Co-stars: Edmund Lowe Victor McLaglen Mary Carlisle

1934 SUCH WOMEN ARE DANGEROUS
Director: James Flood
Co-stars: Warner Baxter Rochelle Hudson Mona Barrie

1935 OUR LITTLE GIRL
Director: John Robertson
Co-stars: Shirley Temple Joel McCrea Lyle Talbot

MADCHEN AMICK

1990 DON'T TELL HER IT'S ME
Director: Malcolm Mowbray
Co-stars: Shelley Long Steve Guttenberg Jamie Gertz

1990 I'M DANGEROUS TONIGHT
Director: Tobe Hunter
Co-stars: Anthony Perkins Dee Wallace Daisy Hall

1992 STEPHEN KING'S SLEEPWALKERS
Director: Mick Garris
Co-stars: Brian Krause Alice Krige Cindy Pickett

1992 TWIN PEAKS: FIRE WALK WITH ME
Director: David Lynch
Co-stars: Sheryl Lee Ray Wise David Bowie

1993 DREAM LOVER
Director: Nicholas Kazan
Co-stars: James Spader Larry Miller Bess Armstrong

1993 LOVE, CHEAT AND STEAL
Director: William Curran
Co-stars: John Lithgow Eric Roberts

1995 COURTYARD
Director: Fred Walton
Co-stars: Andrew McCarthy Cheech Marin

SUZY AMIS

1987 THE BIG TOWN
Director: Ben Bolt
Co-stars: Matt Dillon Diane Lane Bruce Dern Lee Grant

1988 PLAIN CLOTHES
Director: Martha Coolidge
Co-stars: Diane Ladd George Wendt Seymour Cassel

1988 TWISTER
Director: Michael Almereyda
Co-stars: Harry Dean Stanton Crispin Glover Lois Chiles

1990 WHERE THE HEART IS
Director: John Boorman
Co-stars: Dabney Coleman Uma Thurman Joanna Cassidy

1992 RICH IN LOVE
Director: Bruce Beresford
Co-stars: Albert Finney Jill Clayburgh Piper Laurie

1993 WATCH IT
Director: Tom Flynn
Co-stars: Peter Gallagher Lili Taylor Tom Sizemore

1993 THE BALLAD OF LITTLE JOE
Director: Maggie Greenwald
Co-stars: Bo Hopkins Ian McKellen Carrie Snodgress

1994 BLOWN AWAY
Director: Stephen Hopkins
Co-stars: Jeff Bridges Lloyd Bridges Tommy Lee Jones

CHRISTINE AMOR

1973 ALVIN PURPLE
Director: Tim Burstall
Co-stars: Graeme Blundell Lynette Curran Dina Mann

1983 NOW AND FOREVER
Director: Adrian Carr
Co-stars: Cheryl Ladd Robert Coleby Carmen Duncan

EMMA AMOS

1996 SECRETS AND LIES
Director: Mike Leigh
Co-stars: Brenda Blethyn Timothy Spall Marianne Jean-Baptiste

1998 THE TRIBE
Director: Stephen Poliakoff
Co-stars: Joely Richardson Jeremy Northam Trevor Eve

JACQUELINE ANDERE

1962 THE EXTERMINATING ANGEL
Director: Luis Bunuel
Co-stars: Silvia Pinal Enrique Rambal

DONNA ANDERS

1970 COUNT YORGA, VAMPIRE
Director: Bob Keljan
Co-stars: Robert Quarry Roger Perry Judith Lang

LUANA ANDERS

1961 NIGHT TIDE
Director: Curtis Harrington
Co-stars: Dennis Hopper Linda Lawson Gavin Muir

1961 THE PIT AND THE PENDULUM
Director: Roger Corman
Co-stars: Vincent Price Barbara Steele John Kerr

1963 DEMENTIA 13
Director: Francis Ford Coppola
Co-stars: William Campbell Patrick Magee Mary Mitchell

1969 EASY RIDER
Director: Dennis Hopper
Co-stars: Peter Fonda Dennis Hopper Jack Nicholson

1969 THAT COLD DAY IN THE PARK
Director: Robert Altman
Co-stars: Sandy Dennis Michael Burns

1972 WHEN THE LEGENDS DIE
Director: Stuart Millar
Co-stars: Richard Widmark Frederic Forrest

1978 GOIN' SOUTH
Director: Jack Nicholson
Co-stars: Jack Nicholson Mary Steenburgen John Belushi

1982 PERSONAL BEST
Director: Robert Towne
Co-stars: Mariel Hemingway Scott Glenn Patrice Donnelly

1987 BORDER RADIO
Director: Kurt Voss
Co-stars: John Doe Chris D

1991 THE TWO JAKES
Director: Jack Nicholson
Co-stars: Jack Nicholson Harvey Keitel Meg Tilly

MERRY ANDERS

1954 PHFFTT!
Director: Mark Robson
Co-stars: Jack Lemmon Judy Holliday Kim Novak

1957 HEAR ME GOOD
Director: Don McGuire
Co-stars: Hal March Jean Willes Joe E. Ross

1957 DEATH IN SMALL DOSES
Director: Joseph Newman
Co-stars: Peter Graves Mala Powers Chuck Connors

1957 THE DALTON GIRLS
Director: Reginald LeBorg
Co-stars: Penny Edwards Sue George Lisa Davis

1960 THE HYPNOTIC EYE
Director: George Blair
Co-stars: Jacques Bergerac Allison Hayes Marcia Henderson

1963 HOUSE OF THE DAMNED
Director: Maury Dexter
Co-star: Ronald Foster

1964 THE QUICK GUN
Director: Sidney Salkow
Co-stars: Audie Murphy James Best Ted De Corsia

1964 THE TIME TRAVELLERS
Director: Ib Melchior
Co-stars: Preston Foster Phil Carey Joan Woodbury

1965 TICKLE ME
Director: Norman Taurog
Co-stars: Elvis Presley Julia Adams Jocelyn Lane

1967 FLIGHT OF THE COUGAR
Director: Jack Hively
Co-stars: Robert Bray Lee Brown

BRIDGETTE ANDERSEN

1982 SAVANNAH SMILES
Director: Pierre DeMoro
Co-stars: Mark Miller Donovan Scott Peter Graves

1983 NIGHTMARES
Director: Joseph Sargent
Co-stars: Cristina Raines Emilio Estevez Richard Masur

1985 FEVER PITCH
Director: Richard Brooks
Co-stars: Ryan O'Neal Catherine Hicks

1986 PARENT TRAP II
Director: Ronald Maxwell
Co-stars: Hayley Mills Tom Skerritt

BARBARA ANDERSON

1967 IRONSIDE
Director: James Goldstone
Co-stars: Raymond Burr Geraldine Brooks Don Galloway

1973 DON'T BE AFRAID OF THE DARK
Director: John Newland
Co-stars: Kim Darby Jim Hutton William Demarest

1978 DOCTORS' PRIVATE LIVES
Director: Steven Hillard Stern
Co-stars: Donna Mills Ed Nelson John Gavin

1988 BONANZA: THE NEXT GENERATION
Director: William Claxton
Co-stars: John Ireland Robert Fuller

DAPHNE ANDERSON

1952 THE BEGGAR'S OPERA
Director: Peter Brooke
Co-stars: Laurence Olivier Dorothy Tutin Stanley Holloway

1953 HOBSON'S CHOICE
Director: David Lean
Co-stars: Charles Laughton John Mills Brenda De Banzie

1957 NO TIME FOR TEARS
Director: Cyril Frank
Co-stars: Anna Neagle Anthony Quale Sylvia Syms

1957 THE PRINCE AND THE SHOWGIRL
Director: Laurence Olivier
Co-stars: Laurence Olivier Marilyn Monroe Richard Wattis

DONNA ANDERSON

1959 ON THE BEACH
Director: Stanley Kramer
Co-stars: Gregory Peck Ava Gardner Fred Astaire

1960 INHERIT THE WIND
Director: Stanley Kramer
Co-stars: Spencer Tracy Fredric March Gene Kelly

DUSTY ANDERSON

1945 1001 NIGHTS
Director: Alfred Green
Co-stars: Cornel Wilde Evelyn Keyes Phil Silvers

1946 SINGING ON THE TRAIL
Director: Ken Curtis
Co-star: Matt Willis

ELGA ANDERSON

1971 LE MANS
Director: Lee Katzin
Co-stars: Steve McQueen Ronald Leigh-Hunt

ERIKA ANDERSON

1989 A NIGHTMARE ON ELM STREET V
Director: Stephen Hopkins
Co-stars: Robert Englund Lisa Wilcox Nick Mele

1991 SHADOWS OF THE PAST
Director: Gabriel Pelletier
Co-stars: Nicholas Campbell Richard Berry

1991 ZANDALEE
Director: Sam Pillsbury
Co-stars: Nicolas Cage Judge Reinhold Viveca Lindfors

1994 OBJECT OF OBSESSION
Director: Gregory Hippolyte
Co-stars: Scott Valentine

ESTHER ANDERSON

1969 ONE MORE TIME
Director: Jerry Lewis
Co-stars: Peter Lawford Sammy Davis Jnr. Maggie Wright

1969 TWO GENTLEMEN SHARING
Director: Ted Kotcheff
Co-stars: Robin Phillips Judy Geeson Rachel Kempson

1972 A WARM DECEMBER
Director: Sidney Poitier
Co-stars: Sidney Poitier George Baker Earl Cameron

INGRID ANDERSON

1983 HERCULES
Director: Lewis Coates
Co-stars: Lou Ferrigno Mirella D'Angelo Sybil Danning

IVA ANDERSON

1987 REAL MEN
Director: Dennis Feldman
Co-stars: James Belushi John Ritter Barbara Barrie

JEAN ANDERSON

1952 THE BRAVE DON'T CRY
Director: Philip Leacock
Co-stars: John Gregson John Rae Fulton MacKay

1953 THE KIDNAPPERS
Director: Philip Leacock
Co-stars: Duncan MacRae Vincent Winter Jon Whiteley

1954 LEASE OF LIFE
Director: Charles Frend
Co-stars: Robert Donat Kay Walsh Adrienne Corri

1956 A TOWN LIKE ALICE
Director: Jack Lee
Co-stars: Virginia McKenna Peter Finch Maureen Swanson

1957 LUCKY JIM
Director: John Boulting
Co-stars: Ian Carmichael Hugh Griffith Terry-Thomas Sharon Acker

1957 ROBBERY UNDER ARMS
Director: Jack Lee
Co-stars: Peter Finch David McCallum Ronald Lewis

1957 THE BARRETTS OF WIMPOLE STREET
Director: Sidney Franklin
Co-stars: Jennifer Jones Bill Travers John Gielgud

1959 S. O. S. PACIFIC
Director: Guy Green
Co-stars: Eddie Constantine Pier Angelli John Gregson

1964 THE SILENT PLAYGROUND
Director: Stanley Goulden
Co-stars: Roland Curram Ellen McIntosh Bernard Archard

1986 THE GOOD DOCTOR BODKIN ADAMS
Director: Richard Stroud
Co-stars: Timothy West Nigel Davenport

1989 BACK HOME
Director: Piers Haggard
Co-stars: Hayley Mills Hayley Carr Brenda Bruce

1990 CIRCLES OF DECEIT
Director: Stuart Burge
Co-stars: Edward Fox Jane Lapotaire Clare Holman

1990 SURVIVAL OF THE FITTEST
Director: Martyn Friend
Co-stars: Timothy West Nerys Hughes Elizabeth Spriggs

1991 DO NOT DISTURB
Director: Nicholas Renton
Co-stars: Frances Barber Peter Capaldi Stefan Schwartz

1991 THE BLACK VELVET GOWN
Director: Norman Stone
Co-stars: Janet McTeer Bob Peck Geraldine Somerville

1992 THE BOGIE MAN
Director: Charles Gormley
Co-stars: Robbie Coltrane Fiona Fullerton Craig Ferguson

1992 LEON THE PIG FARMER
Director: Vadim Jean
Co-stars: Janet Suzman Brian Clover

1993 INSPECTOR MORSE:
     TWILIGHT OF THE GODS
Director: Herbert Wise
Co-stars: John Thaw John Gielgud Sheila Gish

JUDITH ANDERSON *(Frances Anderson)*
Nominated For Best Supporting Actress In 1940 For "Rebecca"

1933 BLOOD MONEY
Director: Rowland Brown
Co-stars: George Bancroft Frances Dee Chick Chandler

1940 REBECCA
Director: Alfred Hitchcock
Co-stars: Laurence Olivier Joan Fontaine

1940 FORTY LITTLE MOTHERS
Director: Busby Berkeley
Co-stars: Eddie Cantor Bonita Granville Rita Johnson

1941 KING'S ROW
Director: Sam Wood
Co-stars: Ronald Reagan Robert Cummings Ann Sheridan

1941 FREE AND EASY
Director: George Sidney
Co-stars: Nigel Bruce Robert Cummings Ruth Hussey

1941 LADY SCARFACE
Director: Frank Woodruff
Co-stars: Dennis O'Keefe Eric Blore Marc Lawrence

1942 ALL THROUGH THE NIGHT
Director: Vincent Sherman
Co-stars: Humphrey Bogart Conrad Veidt Peter Lorre

1943 EDGE OF DARKNESS
Director: Lewis Milestone
Co-stars: Errol Flynn Ann Sheridan Walter Huston

1944 LAURA
Director: Otto Preminger
Co-stars: Gene Tierney Dana Andrews Clifton Webb

1945 AND THEN THERE WERE NONE
Director: Rene Clair
Co-stars: Walter Huston Barry Fitzgerald Roland Young

1946 THE DIARY OF A CHAMBERMAID
Director: Jean Renoir
Co-stars: Paulette Goddard Burgess Meredith

1946 SPECTRE OF THE ROSE
Director: Ben Hecht
Co-stars: Viola Essen Ivan Kirov Lionel Stander

1946 THE STRANGE LOVE OF MARTHA IVERS
Director: Lewis Milestone
Co-stars: Barbara Stanwyck Van Heflin

1947 TYCOON
Director: Richard Wallace
Co-stars: John Wayne Laraine Day Cedric Hardwicke

1947 THE RED HOUSE
Director: Delmer Daves
Co-stars: Edward G. Robinson Lon McCallister

1947 PURSUED
Director: Raoul Walsh
Co-stars: Robert Mitchum Teresa Wright Dean Jagger

1951 THE FURIES
Director: Anthony Mann
Co-stars: Barbara Stanwyck Walter Huston

1953 SALOME
Director: William Dieterle
Co-stars: Rita Hayworth Stewart Granger

1956 THE TEN COMMANDMENTS
Director: Cecil B. DeMille
Co-stars: Charlton Heston Yul Brynner

1958 CAT ON A HOT TIN ROOF
Director: Richard Brooks
Co-stars: Paul Newman Elizabeth Taylor Burl Ives

1960 CINDERFELLA
Director: Frank Tashlin
Co-stars: Jerry Lewis Anna Maria Alberghetti

1961 DON'T BOTHER TO KNOCK
Director: Cyril Frankel
Co-stars: Richard Todd Elke Sommer June Thorburn

1970 A MAN CALLED HORSE
Director: Elliott Silverstein
Co-stars: Richard Harris Jean Gascon Dub Taylor

KATHERINE ANDERSON
1955 TIGHT SPOT
Director: Phil Karlson
Co-stars: Edward G. Robinson Ginger Rogers Brian Keith

LONI ANDERSON *(Married Burt Reynolds)*
1980 THE JAYNE MANSFIELD STORY
Director: Dick Lowry
Co-stars: Arnold Schwarzenegger Kathleen Lloyd

1982 COUNTRY GOLD
Director: Gilbert Cates
Co-stars: Earl Holliman Linda Hamilton Lee Richardson

1983 A LETTER TO THREE WIVES
Director: Larry Ellikan
Co-stars: Michele Lee Stephanie Zimbalist Ann Sothern

1983 STROKER ACE
Director: Hal Needham
Co-stars: Burt Reynolds Ned Beatty Parker Stevenson

1984 MY MOTHER'S SECRET LIFE
Director: Robert Markowitz
Co-stars: Paul Sorvino Amanda Wyss

1988 TOO GOOD TO BE TRUE
Director: Christian Nyby
Co-stars: Patrick Duffy Julie Harris Glynnis O'Connor

1988 A WHISPER KILLS
Director: Christian Nyby
Co-stars: Joe Penny June Lockhart Jeremy Slate

1989 ALL DOGS GO TO HEAVEN
Director: Gary Goldman
Co-stars: Burt Reynolds Judith Barsi Dom Deluise

1990 COINS IN THE FOUNTAIN
Director: Tony Wharmby
Co-stars: Shanna Reed Stuart Wilson Anthony Newley

1991 WHITE HOT: THE MYSTERIOUS
     MURDER OF THELMA TODD
Director: Paul Wendkos
Co-stars: Robert Davi Lois Smith Scott Paulin

1993 THE FINAL DAYS OF BUTCH
     AND SUNDANCE
Director: Jack Bender
Co-stars: Kenny Rogers Bruce Boxleitner

LYNN ANDERSON
1990 THE WRECK ON THE HIGHWAY
Director: Sandy Johnson
Co-stars: Tam White Ryan Quinn Duncan Duff

MARY ANDERSON
1939 GONE WITH THE WIND
*Director:*s Victor Fleming
Co-stars: Clark Gable Vivien Leigh Leslie Howard

1941   **CHEERS FOR MISS BISHOP**
Director: Tay Garnett
Co-stars: Martha Scott William Gargan Edmund Gwenn

1943   **THE SONG OF BERNADETTE**
Director: Henry King
Co-stars: Jennifer Jones Charles Bickford Vincent Price

1944   **LIFEBOAT**
Director: Alred Hitchcock
Co-stars: John Hodiak William Bendix Tallulah Bankhead

1944   **WILSON**
Director: Henry King
Co-stars: Alexander Knox Charles Coburn Geraldine Fitzgerald

1945   **WITHIN THESE WALLS**
Director: Bruce Hunberstone
Co-stars: Thomas Mitchell Mark Stevens Edward Ryan

1946   **TO EACH HIS OWN**
Director: Mitchell Leisen
Co-stars: Olivia De Havilland John Lund Philip Terry

1946   **BEHIND GREEN LIGHTS**
Director: Otto Brower
Co-stars: William Gargan Carole Landis Richard Crane

1947   **WHISPERING CITY**
Director: Fedor Ozep
Co-stars: Paul Lukas Helmut Dantine John Pratt

1950   **THE UNDERWORLD STORY**
Director: Cy Endfield
Co-stars: Gale Storm Dan Duryea Herbert Marshall

1950   **THE LAST OF THE BUCANEERS**
Director: Lew Landers
Co-stars: Paul Henreid Jack Oakie Karin Booth

1951   **CHICAGO CALLING**
Director: John Reinhardt
Co-stars: Dan Duryea Gordon Gebert Ross Elliott

1953   **DANGEROUS CROSSING**
Director: Joseph Newman
Co-stars: Jeanne Crain Michael Rennie Casey Adams

1958   **JET OVER THE ATLANTIC**
Director: Byron Haskin
Co-stars: Guy Madison Virginia Mayo George Raft

MELISSA SUE ANDERSON

1976   **THE LONLIEST RUNNER**
Director: Michael Landon
Co-stars: Lance Kerwin Michael Landon Brian Keith

1979   **SURVIVAL OF DANA**
Director: Jack Starrett
Co-stars: Robert Carradine Talia Balsam Judge Reinhold

1980   **HAPPY BIRTHDAY TO ME**
Director: J. Lee Thompson
Co-stars: Glenn Ford Sharon Acker Laurence Dane

1983   **FIRST AFFAIR**
Director: Gus Trikonis
Co-stars: Loretta Swit Joel Higgins Kim Delaney

1991   **DEAD MEN DON'T DIE**
Director: Malcolm Marmorstein
Co-stars: Elliott Gould Mark Moses

MELODY ANDERSON

1980   **FLASH GORDON**
Director: Michael Hodges
Co-stars: Sam J. Jones Timothy Dalton Max Von Sydow

1983   **POLICEWOMAN CENTREFOLD**
Director: Reza Bediyi
Co-stars: Ed Marinaro Bert Ramsden David Spielberg

1986   **FIREWALKER**
Director: J. Lee Thompson
Co-stars: Chuck Norris Lou Gossett Jnr. Will Sampson

1986   **BEVERLEY HILLS MADAM**
Director: Harvey Hart
Co-stars: Faye Dunaway Donna Dixon Louis Jourdan

PAMELA ANDERSON

1993   **SNAPDRAGON**
Director: Worth Keeter
Co-stars: Steven Bauer Chelsea Field

1994   **COME DIE WITH ME**
Director: Armand Mastroianni
Co-stars: Rob Estes James Hong

1997   **BARB WIRE**
Co-star: Tenuera Morrison

RONA ANDERSON

1948   **SLEEPING CAR TO TRIESTE**
Director: John Paddy Carstairs
Co-stars: Albert Lieven Jean Kent David Tomlinson

1949   **POET'S PUB**
Director: Frederick Wilson
Co-stars: Derek Bond Barbara Murray Leslie Dwyer

1949   **FLOODTIDE**
Director: Frederick Wilson
Co-stars: Gordon Jackson John Laurie Elizabeth Sellars

1950   **HER FAVOURITE HUSBAND**
Director: Mario Soldati
Co-stars: Jean Kent Robert Beatty Gordon Harker

1950   **THE TWENTY QUESTIONS MURDER MYSTERY**
Director: Paul Stein
Co-stars: Robert Beatty Clifford Evans

1951   **WHISPERING SMITH HITS LONDON**
Director: Francis Searle
Co-stars: Richard Carlson Greta Gynt

1951   **HOME TO DANGER**
Director: Terence Fisher
Co-stars: Guy Rolfe Stanley Baker Alan Wheatley

1954   **DOUBLE EXPOSURE**
Director: John Gilling
Co-stars: John Bentley Garry Marsh Ingeborg Wells

1954   **SHADOW OF A MAN**
Director: Michael McCarthy
Co-stars: Paul Carpenter Jane Griffiths

1954   **THE BLACK RIDER**
Director: Wolf Rilla
Co-stars: Jimmy Hanley Lionel Jeffries Leslie Dwyer

1955   **STOCK CAR**
Director: Wolf Rilla
Co-stars: Paul Carpenter Susan Shaw

1955   **THE FLAW**
Director: Terence Fisher
Co-stars: John Bentley Donald Houston Doris Yorke

1955   **A TIME TO KILL**
Director: Charles Saunders
Co-stars: Jack Watling John Horsley

1955   **LITTLE RED MONKEY**
Director: Ken Hughes
Co-stars: Richard Conte Russell.Napier Colin Gordon

1957   **THE HIDEOUT**
Director: Petra Graham Scott
Co-stars: Dermot Walsh Ronald Howard Sam Kydd

1963	**THE BAY OF SAN MICHEL**	
Director:	John Ainsworth	
Co-stars:	Keenan Wynn Mai Zetterling Ronald Howard	

1964 DEVILS OF DARKNESS
Director: Lance Comfort
Co-stars: Wiliam Sylvester Tracy Reed Diana Decker

VERONICA ANDERSON

1973 SOME CALL IT LOVING
Director: James Harris
Co-stars: Zalman King Carol White Tisa Farrow

BIBI ANDERSSON

1957 THE SEVENTH SEAL
Director: Ingmar Bergman
Co-stars: Max Von Sydow Bengt Ekerot Nils Poppe

1957 WILD STRAWBERRIES
Director: Ingmar Bergman
Co-stars: Victor Sjostrom Ingrid Thulin

1960 THE DEVIL'S EYE
Director: Ingmar Bergman
Co-stars: Jarl Kulle Aexel Duberg

1964 NOW ABOUT THESE WOMEN
Director: Ingmar Bergman
Co-stars: Jarl Kulle Eva Dahlbeck Harriet Andersson

1966 PERSONA
Director: Ingmar Bergman
Co-stars: Liv Ullman Gunnar Bjornstrand

1966 DUEL AT DIABOLO
Director: Ralph Nelson
Co-stars: Sidney Poitier James Garner Bill Travers

1970 STORY OF A WOMAN
Director: Leonardo Bercovici
Co-stars: Robert Stack James Farantino

1970 THE KREMLIN LETTER
Director: John Huston
Co-stars: Richard Boone Orson Welles George Sanders

1971 THE TOUCH
Director: Ingmar Bergman
Co-stars: Elliott Gould Max Von Sydow Sheila Reid

1977 I NEVER PROMISED YOU A ROSE GARDEN
Director: Anthony Page
Co-stars: Kathleen Quinlan Sylvia Sidney

1979 QUINTET
Director: Robert Altman
Co-stars: Paul Newman Vittorio Gassman

1979 AIRPORT '80: THE CONCORDE
Director: David Lowell Rich
Co-stars: Alain Delon Susan Blakely

1983 EXPOSED
Director: James Toback
Co-stars: Nastassja Kinski Rudolf Nureyev Ian McShane

1985 WALLENBERG: A HERO'S STORY
Director: Lamont Johnson
Co-stars: Richard Chamberlain Alice Krige Melanie Mayron

1986 MATADOR
Director: Pedro Almodovar
Co-stars: Antonio Banderas Assumpta Serna Nacho Martinez

1987 BABETTE'S FEAST
Director: Gabiel Axel
Co-stars: Stephane Audran Jarl Kulle Bodil Kjer

1987 LAW OF DESIRE
Director: Pedro Almodovar
Co-stars: Carmen Maura Antonio Banderas

1992 HIGH HEELS
Director: Pedro Almodovar
Co-stars: Victoria Abril Marisa Peredes Miguel Bose

HARRIET ANDERSSON

1952 SUMMER WITH MONIKA
Director: Ingmar Bergman
Co-stars: Lars Ekborg

1953 SAWDUST AND TINSEL
Director: Ingmar Bergman
Co-stars: Ake Gronberg Hasse Ekman Annika Tretow

1953 A LESSON IN LOVE
Director: Ingmar Bergman
Co-stars: Gunnar Bjornstrand Eva Dahlbeck

1955 SMILES OF A SUMMER NIGHT
Director: Ingmar Bergman
Co-stars: Gunnar Bjornstrand Ulla Jacobsson Jarl Kulle

1961 THROUGH A GLASS DARKLY
Director: Ingmar Bergman
Co-stars: Gunnar Bjornstrand Max Von Sydow Lars Passgard

1964 NOW ABOUT THESE WOMEN
Director: Ingmar Bergan
Co-stars: Jarl Kulle Georg Funkquist Eva Dahlbeck

1966 THE DEADLY AFFAIR
Director: Sidney Lumet
Co-stars: James Mason Simone Signoret Harry Andrews

1972 CRIES AND WHISPERS
Director: Ingmar Bergman
Co-stars: Kari Sylwan Ingrid Thulin Liv Ullman

EIKO ANDO

1958 THE BARBARIAN AND THE GEISHA
Director: John Huston
Co-stars: John Wayne Sam Jaffe

GABY ANDRE

1950 HIGHWAY 301
Director: Andrew Stone
Co-stars: Steve Cochran Virginia Grey Richard Egan

1952 THE GREEN GLOVE
Director: Rudolph Mate
Co-stars: Glenn Ford Cedric Hardwicke Geraldine Brooks

1959 THE STRANGE WORLD OF PLANET X
Director: Gilbert Gunn
Co-stars: Martin Benson Forrest Tucker

LONA ANDRE

1933 THE MYSTERIOUS RIDER
Co-stars: Kent Taylor Irving Pichel

1935 BORDER BRIGANDS
Co-star: Buck Jones

1937 TRAILING TROUBLE
Co-star: Ken Maynard

URSULA ANDRESS *(Married John Derek)*

1962 DR. NO
Director: Terence Young
Co-stars: Sean Connery Jack Lord Joseph Wiseman

1963 FOUR FOR TEXAS
Director: Robert Aldrich
Co-stars: Dean Martin Frank Sinatra 3 Stooges

1963 FUN IN ACAPULCO
Director: Richard Thorpe
Co-stars: Elvis Presley Paul Lukas

1963　NIGHTMARE IN THE SUN
Director:　Marc Lawrence
Co-stars:　John Derek Arthur O'Connell Aldo Ray

1965　SHE
Director:　Robert Day
Co-stars:　Peter Cushing John Richardson

1965　THE TENTH VICTIM
Director:　Elio Petri
Co-stars:　Marcello Mastroianni Elsa Martinelli

1965　WHAT'S NEW PUSSYCAT?
Director:　Clive Donner
Co-stars:　Peter O'Toole Peter Sellers Woody Allen

1966　ONCE BEFORE I DIE
Director:　John Derek
Co-stars:　John Derek Richard Jaeckel Rod Lauren

1966　THE BLUE MAX
Director:　John Guillermin
Co-stars:　George Peppard James Mason Jeremy Kemp

1967　AFRICA EXPRESS
Director:　Michele Lupo
Co-stars:　Jack Palance Guiliano Gemma

1967　CASINO ROYALE
Director:　John Huston*
Co-stars:　David Niven Orson Welles Peter Sellers

1968　THE SOUTHERN STAR
Director:　Sidney Hayers
Co-stars:　George Segal Orson Welles Ian Hendry

1970　PERFECT FRIDAY
Director:　Peter Hall
Co-stars:　Stanley Baker David Warner Joan Benham

1971　RED SUN
Director:　Terence Young
Co-stars:　Charles Bronson Alain Delon Capucine

1975　THE LOVES AND TIMES OF SCARAMOUCHE
Director:　Enzo Castellari
Co-stars:　Michael Sarazin Aldo Maccione

1978　THE FIFTH MUSKETEER
Director:　Ken Annakin
Co-stars:　Beau Bridges Sylvia Kristel Rex Harrison

1981　CLASH OF THE TITANS
Director:　Desmond Davis
Co-stars:　Laurence Olivier Claire Bloom Harry Hamlin

SYLVIA ANDREW

1950　THREE CAME HOME
Director:　Jean Negulesco
Co-stars:　Claudette Colbert Patric Knowles Florence Desmond

ANDREWS SISTERS

1940　ARGENTINE NIGHTS
Director:　Albert Rogell
Co-stars:　Ritz Brothers Constance Moore Peggy Moran

1941　BUCK PRIVATES
Director:　Arthur Lubin
Co-stars:　Bud Abbott Lou Costello Lee Bowman

1941　IN THE NAVY
Director:　Arthur Lubin
Co-stars:　Bud Abbott Lou Costello Dick Powell

1941　HOLD THAT GHOST
Director:　Arthur Lubin
Co-stars:　Bud Abbott Lou Costello Richard Carlson

1942　GIVE OUT SISTERS
Director:　Edward Cline
Co-stars:　Grace McDonald Dan Dailey Donald O'Connor

1942　PRIVATE BUCKAROO
Director:　Edward Cline
Co-stars:　Donald O'Connor Peggy Ryan Harry James

1944　FOLLOW THE BOYS
Director:　Edward Sutherland
Co-stars:　Jeanette MacDonald Marlene Dietrich George Raft

1946　MAKE MINE MUSIC *(Voice)*
Director:　Jack Kinney
Co-stars:　Nelson Eddy Dinah Shore Benny Goodman

1947　ROAD TO RIO
Director:　Norman Z. McLeod
Co-stars:　Bing Crosby Bob Hope Dorothy Lamour

CAROL ANDREWS

1945　THE BULLFIGHTERS
Director:　Mal St Clair
Co-stars:　Stan Laurel Oliver Hardy Margo Woode

JULIE ANDREWS *(Married Blake Edwards, Mother of Jennifer Edwards)*
Oscar For Best Actress In 1964 For "Mary Poppins", Nominated For Best Actress For "The Sound Of Music" In 1965 And "Victor/Victoria" In 1982

1964　MARY POPPINS
Director:　Robert Stevenson
Co-stars:　Dick Van Dyke Glynis Johns David Tomlinson

1964　THE AMERICANISATION OF EMILY
Director:　Arthur Hiller
Co-stars:　James Garner James Coburn Liz Fraser

1965　THE SOUND OF MUSIC
Director:　Robert Wise
Co-stars:　Christopher Plummer Richard Haydn Eleanor Parker

1966　HAWAII
Director:　George Roy Hill
Co-stars:　Max Von Sydow Richard Harris Gene Hackman

1966　TORN CURTAIN
Director:　Alfred Hltchcock
Co-stars:　Paul Newman Lila Kedrova Wolfgang Kieling

1967　THOROUGHLY MODERN MILLIE
Director:　George Roy Hill
Co-stars:　Mary Tyler Moore John Gavin James Fox

1968　STAR!
Director:　Robert Wise
Co-stars:　Daniel Massey Michael Craig Richard Crenna

1970　DARLING LILI
Director:　Blake Edwards
Co-stars:　Rock Hudson Jeremy Kemp Lance Percival

1974　THE TAMARIND SEED
Director:　Blake Edwards
Co-stars:　Omar Sharif Sylvia Syms Dan O'Herlihy

1979　10
Director:　Blake Edwards
Co-stars:　Dudley Moore Bo Derek Robert Webber

1980　LITTLE MISS MARKER
Director:　Walter Bernstein
Co-stars:　Walter Matthau Tony Curtis Sara Stimson

1981　S. O. B.
Director:　Blake Edwards
Co-stars:　Robert Preston William Holden Richard Mulligan

1982　VICTOR/VICTORIA
Director:　Blake Edwards
Co-stars:　James Garner Robert Preston Lesley Anne Warren

1983　THE MAN WHO LOVED WOMEN
Director:　Blake Edwards
Co-stars:　Burt Reynolds Kim Basinger

1986　THAT'S LIFE!
Director:　Blake Edwards
Co-stars:　Jack Lemmon Sally Kellerman Jennifer Edwards

1986　DUET FOR ONE
Director:　Andrei Konchalovsky
Co-stars:　Alan Bates Max Von Sydow Rupert Everett

1991　OUR SONS
Director:　John Erman
Co-stars:　Ann-Margret Hugh Grant Zeljko Ivanek

LOIS ANDREWS

1943　DIXIE DUGAN
Director:　Otto Brower
Co-stars:　James Ellison Charles Ruggles Charlotte Greenwood

1944　ROGER TOUHY, GANGSTER
Director:　Robert Florey
Co-stars:　Preston Foster Victor McLaglen Anthony Quinn

1949　RUSTLERS
Co-stars:　Tim Holt Richard Martin

STELLA ANDREWS

1950　THEY WERE NOT DIVIDED
Director:　Terence Young
Co-stars:　Edward Underdown Helen Cherry

TINA ANDREWS

1974　CONRACK
Director:　Martin Ritt
Co-stars:　Jon Voight Paul Winfield Hume Cronyn

CAROL ANDROSKY

1971　FUNNYMAN
Director:　John Korty
Co-stars:　Peter Bonertz Sandra Archer

1973　THE ALL-AMERICAN BOY
Director:　Charles Eastman
Co-stars:　Jon Voight Anne Archer

ANEMONE

1985　DEATH IN A FRENCH GARDEN
Director:　Michel Deville
Co-stars:　Richard Bohringer Michel Piccoli

1988　LE GRAND CHEMIN
Director:　Jean-Loup Hubert
Co-stars:　Christine Pascal Antoine Hubert Richard Bohringer

1992　LE PETIT PRINCE A DIT
Director:　Christine Pascal
Co-stars:　Richard Berry Marie Kleiber Lucie Phan

HEATHER ANGEL

1932　AFTER OFFICE HOURS
Director:　Thomas Bentley
Co-stars:　Frank Lawton Garry Marsh Viola Lyel

1933　PILGRIMAGE
Director:　John Ford
Co-stars:　Henrietta Crossman Norman Foster Charley Grapewin

1933　BERKELEY SQUARE
Director:　Frank Lloyd
Co-stars:　Leslie Howard Valerie Taylor Beryl Mercer

1934　MURDER IN TRINIDAD
Director:　Louis King
Co-stars:　Nigel Bruce Victor Jory J. Carrol Naish

1934　ORIENT EXPRESS
Director:　Paul Martin
Co-stars:　Ralph Morgan Norman Foster Una O'Connor

1934　ROMANCE IN THE RAIN
Director:　Stuart Walker
Co-stars:　Victor Moore Roger Pryor

1935　THE THREE MUSKETEERS
Director:　Rowland Lee
Co-stars:　Walter Abel Paul Lukas Moroni Olson

1935　SPRINGTIME FOR HENRY
Director:　Frank Tuttle
Co-stars:　Otto Kruger Nancy Carroll Nigel Bruce

1935　THE PERFECT GENTLENAN
Director:　Tim Whelan
Co-stars:　Cicely Courtneidge Frank Morgan Herbert Mundin

1935　THE MYSTERY OF EDWIN DROOD
Director:　Stuart Walker
Co-stars:　Claude Rains Douglass Montgomery

1935　THE INFORMER
Director:　John Ford
Co-stars:　Victor McLaglan Wallace Ford Preston Foster

1935　IT HAPPENED IN NEW YORK
Co-star:　Lyle Talbot

1935　THE HEADLINE WOMAN
Co-star:　Roger Pryor

1936　THE BOLD CABALLERO
Co-star:　Bob Livingstone

1936　THE LAST OF THE MOHICANS
Director:　George Seitz
Co-stars:　Randolph Scott Binnie Barnes Bruce Cabot

1937　PORTIA ON TRIAL
Director:　George Nicholls
Co-stars:　Frieda Inescort Walter Abel Ruth Donnelly

1937　WESTERN GOLD
Co-stars:　Leroy Mason Howard Hickman Smith Ballew

1937　BULLDOG DRUMMOND ESCAPES
Co-stars:　Ray Milland Porter Hall.

1938　ARMY GIRL
Director:　George Nicholls
Co-stars:　Madge Evans Preston Foster H. B. Warner

1939　BULLDOG DRUMMOND IN AFRICA
Co-star:　John Howard

1940　PRIDE AND PREJUDICE
Director:　Robert Z.Leonard
Co-stars:　Laurence Olivier Greer Garson Edmund Gwenn

1941　SUSPICION
Director:　Alfred Hitchcock
Co-stars:　Cary Grant Joan Fontaine Cedric Hardwicke

1941　SHADOWS ON THE STAIRS
Director:　Ross Lederman
Co-stars:　Paul Cavanagh Frieda Inescort Turhan Bey

1941　SINGAPORE WOMAN
Director:　Jean Negulesco
Co-stars:　Brenda Marshall David Bruce Rose Hobart

1943　UNDYING MONSTER
Director:　John Brahm
Co-stars:　James Ellison John Howard Halliwell Hobbes

1943　CRY HAVOC
Director:　Richard Thorpe
Co-stars:　Margaret Sullavan Ann Sothern Ella Raines

1944　LIFEBOAT
Director:　Alfred Hitchcock
Co-stars:　Tallulah Bankhead William Bendix Walter Slezak

1948　THE SAXON CHARM
Director:　Claude Binyon
Co-stars:　Robert Montgomery Susan Hayward John Payne

1951 ALICE IN WONDERLAND *(Voice)*
Director: Wilfrid Jackson
Co-stars: Kathryn Beaumont Ed Wynn Richard Haydan

1953 PETER PAN *(Voice)*
Director: Clyde Geronimi
Co-stars: Bobby Driscoll Kathryn Beaumont

1961 THE PREMATURE BURIAL
Director: Roger Corman
Co-stars: Ray Milland Hazel Court Richard Ney

PIER ANGELI *(Anna Maria Pierangeli)* MARRIED: VIC DAMONE

1950 DOMANI E TROPPI TARDI
Director: Leonide Moguy
Co-stars: Lois Maxwell Vittorio De Sica

1951 TERESA
Director: Fred Zinnemann
Co-stars: John Ericson Peggy Ann Garner Ralph Meeker

1951 THE LIGHT TOUCH
Director: Richard Brooks
Co-stars: Stewart Granger George Sanders Kurt Kasznar

1952 THE DEVIL MAKES THREE
Director: Andrew Marton
Co-stars: Gene Kelly Richard Egan Claus Clausen

1953 THE STORY OF THREE LOVES
Director: Gottfried Reinhardt
Co-stars: Kirk Douglas James Mason Moira Shearer

1953 SOMBRERO
Director: Norman Foster
Co-stars: Ricardo Montalban Yvonne De Carlo Cyd Charisse

1954 THE SILVER CHALICE
Director: Victor Saville
Co-stars: Paul Newman Jack Palance Virginia Mayo

1954 THE FLAME AND THE FLESH
Director: Richard Brooks
Co-stars: Lana Turner Carlos Thompson

1956 SOMEBODY UP THERE LIKES ME
Director: Robert Wise
Co-stars: Paul Newman Everett Sloane Sal Mineo

1956 PORT AFRIQUE
Director: Rudolph Mate
Co-stars: Phil Carey Dennis Price Anthony Newley

1957 THE VINTAGE
Director: Jeffrey Hayden
Co-stars: Mel Ferrer John Kerr Michele Morgan

1958 MERRY ANDREW
Director: Michael Kidd
Co-stars: Danny Kaye Noel Purcell Robert Coote

1959 SOS PACIFIC
Director: Guy Green
Co-stars: Eddie Constantine Richard Attenborough John Gregson

1960 THE ANGRY SILENCE
Director: Guy Green
Co-stars: Richard Attenborough Michael Craig Alfred Burke

1962 SODOM AND GOMORRAH
Director: Robert Aldrich
Co-stars: Stewart Granger Stanley Baker

1965 BATTLE OF THE BULGE
Director: Ken Annakin
Co-stars: Henry Fonda Robert Shaw Robert Ryan

GLYNIS ANGELL

1990 AN ANGEL AT MY TABLE
Director: Jane Campion
Co-stars: Kerry Fox Alexia Keogh Karen Fergusson

MURIEL ANGELUS

1931 MY WIFE'S FAMILY
Director: Monte Banks
Co-stars: Gene Gerrard Jimmy Godden Amy Veness

1939 LIGHT THAT FAILED
Director: William Wellman
Co-stars: Ronald Colman Walter Huston Ida Lupino

1940 THE GREAT McGINTY
Director: Preston Sturges
Co-stars: Brian Donlevy Akim Tamiroff William Demarest

1940 SAFARI
Director: Edward Griffith
Co-stars: Douglas Fairbanks Jnr. Madeleine Carroll Tullio Carminati

1940 THE WAY OF ALL FLESH
Director: Louis King
Co-stars: Akim Tamiroff Gladys George Berton Churchill

AVRIL ANGERS

1948 THE BRASS MONKEY
Director: Thornton Freeland
Co-stars: Carroll Levis Carole Landis Herbert Lom

1956 THE GREEN MAN
Director: Robert Day
Co-stars: Alastair Sim George Cole Jill Adams

1956 WOMEN WITHOUT MEN
Director: Elmo Williams
Co-stars: Beverley Michaels Joan Rice Thora Hird

1964 DEVILS OF DARKNESS
Director: Lance Comfort
Co-stars: William Sylvester Tracy Reed Diana Decker

1965 BE MY GUEST
Director: Lance Comfort
Co-stars: David Hemmings Andrea Monet Jerry Lee Lewis

1966 THE FAMILY WAY
Director: Roy Boulting
Co-stars: John Mills Hayley Mills Hywel Bennett

1967 TWO A PENNY
Director: James Collier
Co-stars: Cliff Richard Dora Bryan Ann Holloway

1969 STAIRCASE
Director: Stanley Donen
Co-stars: Richard Burton Rex Harrison Cathleen Nesbitt

1976 CONFESSIONS OF A DRIVING INSTRUCTOR
Director: Norman Cohen
Co-stars: Robin Asquith Anthony Booth

LUCY ANGWIN

1984 MY FIRST WIFE
Director: Paul Cox
Co-stars: John Hargreaves Wendy Hughes Charles Tingwell

EVELYN ANKERS

1938 MURDER IN THE FAMILY
Director: Al Parker
Co-stars: Jessica Tandy Barry Jones Roddy McDowall

1940 THE WOLF MAN
Director: George Waggner
Co-stars: Lou Chaney Warren William Ralph Bellamy

1941 HOLD THAT GHOST
Director: Arthur Lubin
Co-stars: Abbott & Costello Joan Davis Andrews Sisters

1941 HIT THE ROAD
Co-stars: Bowery Boys Gladys George Barton MacLaine

1941	**BURMA CONVOY**
Director:	Noel Smith
Co-stars:	Charles Bickford Cecil Kellaway Turhan Bey

1942	**EAGLE SQUADRON**
Director:	Arthur Lubin
Co-stars:	Robert Stack John Loder Eddie Albert

1942	**THE GHOST OF FRANKENSTEIN**
Director:	Erle Kenton
Co-stars:	Cedric Hardwicke Bela Lugosi Ralph Bellamy

1942	**NORTH TO THE KLONDYKE**
Director:	Erle Kenton
Co-stars:	Broderick Crawford Lon Chaney Andy Devine

1942	**THE GREAT IMPERSONATION**
Director:	John Rawlins
Co-stars:	Ralph Bellamy Aubrey Mather Karen Verne

1942	**PIERRE OF THE PLAINS**
Director:	George Seitz
Co-stars:	John Carroll Ruth Hussey Bruce Cabot

1942	**SHERLOCK HOLMES AND THE VOICE OF TERROR**
Director:	John Rawlins
Co-stars:	Basil Rathbone Nigel Bruce

1943	**YOU'RE A LUCKY FELLOW, MR. SMITH**
Director:	Felix Feist
Co-stars:	Allan Jones Billie Burke David Bruce

1943	**ALL BY MYSELF**
Co-stars:	Rosemary Lane Neal Hamilton

1943	**SON OF DRACULA**
Director:	Robert Siodmak
Co-stars:	Lon Chaney Louise Allbritton Robert Paige

1943	**HERS TO HOLD**
Director:	Frank Ryan
Co-stars:	Deanna Durbin Joseph Cotten Charles Winninger

1943	**THE MAD GHOUL**
Director:	James Hogan
Co-stars:	George Zucco David Bruce Turhan Bey

1943	**HIS BUTLER'S SISTER**
Director:	Frank Borzage
Co-stars:	Deanna Durbin Franchot Tone Pat O'Brien

1943	**CAPTIVE WILD WOMAN**
Director:	Edward Dmytryk
Co-stars:	Acuanetta John Carradine Martha Vickers

1944	**JUNGLE WOMAN**
Director:	Reginald LeBorg
Co-stars:	Acuanetta J. Carrol Naish Milburn Stone

1944	**BOWERY TO BROADWWAY**
Director:	Charles Lamount
Co-stars:	Maria Montez Donald O'Connor Peggy Ryan

1944	**WEIRD WOMAN**
Director:	Reginald LeBorg
Co-stars:	Lon Chaney Ann Gwynne Ralph Morgan

1944	**PARDON MY RHYTHM**
Director:	Felix Feist
Co-stars:	Mel Torme Gloria Jean Patric Knowles

1944	**LADIES COURAGEOUS**
Director:	John Rawlins
Co-stars:	Loretta Young Diana Barrymore Ann Gwynne

1944	**THE INVISIBLE MAN'S REVENGE**
Director:	Ford Beebe
Co-stars:	Jon Hall Leon Errol John Carradine

1945	**THE FROZEN GHOST**
Director:	Harold Young
Co-stars:	Lon Chaney Martin Kosleck Milburn Stone

1946	**THE FRENCH KEY**
Director:	Walter Colmes
Co-stars:	Albert Dekker Mike Mazurki John Eldredge

1946	**QUEEN OF BURLESQUE**
Co-stars:	Carelton Young Rose Larosa

1946	**BLACK BEAUTY**
Director:	Max Nosseck
Co-stars:	Mona Freeman Richard Denning Terry Kilburn

1947	**THE LAST OF THE REDMEN**
Director:	George Sherman
Co-stars:	Jon Hall Michael O'Shea Julie Bishop

1947	**THE LONE WOLF IN LONDON**
Director:	Leslie Goodwins
Co-stars:	Gerald Mohr Eric Blore Alan Napier

1948	**PAROLE INC**
Director:	Albert Zeisler
Co-stars:	Michael O'Shea Turhan Bey Lyle Talbot

1949	**TARZAN'S MAGIC FOUNTAIN**
Director:	Lee Sholem
Co-stars:	Lex Barker Brenda Joyce Albert Dekker

CAMILLE ANKEWICH

1918	**STELLA MARIS**
Director:	Marshall Neilan
Co-stars:	Mary Pickford Conway Tearle

ANNABELLA
(Suzanne Charpentier) Married Tyrone Power

1931	**LE MILLION**
Director:	Rene Clair
Co-stars:	Rene Lefevre Paul Oliver Louis Allibert

1937	**LA CITADELLE DE SILENCE**

1937	**WINGS OF THE MORNING**
Director:	Harold Schuster
Co-stars:	Henry Fonda Leslie Banks John McCormack

1937	**UNDER THE RED ROBE**
Director:	Victor Sjostrom
Co-stars:	Raymond Massey Conrad Veidt

1934	**CARAVAN**
Co-stars:	Charles Boyer Conchita Montenegro

1935	**L'EQUIPAGE**
Director:	Anatole Litvak
Co-stars:	Charles Vanel Jean-Pierre Aumont

1937	**DINNER AT THE RITZ**
Director:	Harold Schuster
Co-stars:	David Niven Paul Lukas Nora Swinburne

1938	**HOTEL DU NORD**
Director:	Marcel Carne
Co-stars:	Louis Jouvet Jean-Pierre Aumont Arletty

1938	**THE BARONESS AND THE BUTLER**
Director:	Walter Lang
Co-stars:	William Powell Nigel Bruce Lynn Bari

1938	**SUEZ**
Director:	Allan Dwan
Co-stars:	Tyrone Power Loretta Young Joseph Schildkraut

1939	**BRIDAL SUITE**
Director:	William Thiele
Co-stars:	Robert Young Walter Connolly Billie Burke

1943	**BOMBER'S MOON**
Director:	Harold Schuster
Co-stars:	George Montgomery Kent Taylor

1943	**TONIGHT WE RAID CALAIS**
Director:	John Brahm
Co-stars:	John Sutton Beulah Bondi Lee J. Cobb

1946   **13, RUE MADELEINE**
Director: Henry Hathaway
Co-stars: James Cagney Richard Conte Sam Jaffe

AMINA ANNABI

1990   **THE SHELTERING SKY**
Director: Bernardo Bertolucci
Co-stars: Debra Winger John Malkovich Campbell Scott

1993   **THE HOUR OF THE PIG**
Director: Leslie Megahy
Co-stars: Colin Firth Ian Holm Lysette Anthony

IMOGEN ANNESLEY

1987   **HOWLING III – THE MARSUPIALS**
Director: Philippe Mora
Co-stars: Barry Otto Max Fairchild Frank Thring

FRANCESCA ANNIS

1960   **HIS AND HERS**
Director: Brian Desmond Hurst
Co-stars: Terry-Thomas Janette Scott Wilfred Hyde White

1963   **CLEOPATRA**
Director: Joseph L. Mankiewicz
Co-stars: Elizabeth Taylor Rex Harrison Richard Burton

1963   **SATURDAY NIGHT OUT**
Director: Robert Hartford-Davis
Co-stars: Bernard Lee Heather Sears Nigel Green

1963   **CROOKS IN CLOISTERS**
Director: Jeremy Summers
Co-stars: Ronald Fraser Barbara Windsor Davy Kaye

1964   **MURDER MOST FOUL**
Director: George Pollock
Co-stars: Margaret Rutherford Ron Moody James Bolam

1965   **THE PLEASURE GIRLS**
Director: Gerry O'Hara
Co-stars: Ian McShane Tony Tanner Mark Eden

1970   **THE WALKING STICK**
Director: Eric Till
Co-stars: David Hemmings Samantha Eggar Phyllis Calvert

1971   **MACBETH**
Director: Roman Polanski
Co-stars: Jon Finch Martin Shaw John Stride

1973   **PENNY GOLD**
Director: Jack Cardiff
Co-stars: James Booth Una Stubbs

1982   **COMING OUT OF THE ICE**
Director: Waris Hussein
Co-stars: John Savage Willie Nelson Ben Cross

1983   **KRULL**
Director: Peter Yates
Co-stars: Ken Marshall Lysette Anthony Freddie Jones

1984   **DUNE**
Director: David Lynch
Co-stars: Jose Ferrer Sian Phillips Dean Stockwell

1986   **UNDER THE CHERRY MOON**
Director: Prince
Co-stars: Kristin Scott-Thomas Prince Jerome Benton

1988   **ONASSIS: THE RICHEST MAN IN THE WORLD**
Director: Waris Hussein
Co-stars: Raul Julia Jane Seymour

1990   **PARNELL AND THE ENGLISHWOMAN**
Director: John Bruce
Co-stars: Trevor Eve David Robb Robert Lang

1991   **THE GRAVY TRAIN GOES EAST**
Director: James Cellan Jones
Co-stars: Ian Richardson Christoph Waltz

JENNIFER ANISTON

1993   **LEPRECHAUN**
Director: Mark Jones
Co-stars: Warwick Davis Ken Olandt Mark Holdon

1997   **SHE'S THE ONE**
Director: Edward Burns
Co-stars: John Mahoney Cameron Diaz Linda Evans ,

1997   **'TIL THERE WAS YOU**
Co-stars: Jeanne Triplehorn Dylan McDermot Sarah Jessica Parker

1998   **PICTURE PERFECT**
Director: Glenn Gordon Caron
Co-stars: Kevin Bacon Kevin Dunn Jay Mohr

1998   **THE OBJECT OF MY AFFECTION**
Director: Nicholas Hytner
Co-stars: Paul Rudd John Pankow Nigel Hawthorne

ANN-MARGRET *(Married Roger Smith)*
Nominated For Best Supporting Actress In 1971 For "Carnal Knowledge" And In 1975 For "Tommy"

1961   **POCKETFUL OF MIRACLES**
Director: Frank Capra
Co-stars: Bette Davis Glenn Ford Hope Lange

1962   **STATE FAIR**
Director: Jose Ferrer
Co-stars: Pat Boone Alice Faye Tom Ewell

1963   **BYE BYE BIRDIE**
Director: George Sidney
Co-stars: Dick Van Dyke Bobby Rydell Janet Leigh

1964   **THE PLEASURE SEEKERS**
Director: Jean Negulesco
Co-stars: Tony Franciosa Carol Lynley Gene Tierney

1964   **KITTEN WITH A WHIP**
Director: Douglas Heyes
Co-stars: John Forsythe Peter Brown Patricia Barry

1964   **VIVA LAS VEGAS**
Director: George Sidney
Co-stars: Elvis Presley Cesare Danova William Demarest

1965   **ONCE A THIEF**
Director: Ralph Nelson
Co-stars: Alain Delon Van Heflin Jack Palance

1965   **THE CINCINNATI KID**
Director: Norman Jewison
Co-stars: Steve McQueen Edward G. Robinson Joan Blondell

1965   **BUS RILEY'S BACK IN TOWN**
Director: Harvey Hart
Co-stars: Michael Parks Jocelyn Brando Kim Darby

1966   **MURDERER'S ROW**
Director: Henry Levin
Co-stars: Dean Martin Karl Malden Camilla Sparv

1966   **MADE IN PARIS**
Director: Boris Sagal
Co-stars: Louis Jordan Richard Crenna Edie Adams

1966   **STAGECOACH**
Director: Gordon Douglas
Co-stars: Alex Cord Bing Crosby Van Heflin

1966   **THE SWINGER**
Director: George Sidney
Co-stars: Tony Franciosa Robert Coote Yvonne Romain

1967   **THE TIGER AND THE PUSSYCAT**
Director: Dino Risi
Co-stars: Vittorio Gassman Eleanor Parker

1970 R.P.M.
Director: Stanley Kramer
Co-stars: Anthony Quinn Gary Lockwood Paul Winfield

1971 C. C. AND COMPANY
Director: Seymour Robbie
Co-stars: Joe Namath William Smith Jennifer Billingsley

1971 CARNAL KNOWLEDGE
Director: Mike Nichols
Co-stars: Jack Nicholson Art Garfunkel Candice Bergen

1973 THE TRAIN ROBBERS
Director: Burt Kennedy
Co-stars: John Wayne Rod Taylor Ben Johnson

1975 TOMMY
Director: Ken Russell
Co-stars: Roger Daltrey Oliver Reed Elton John

1977 THE LAST REMAKE OF BEAU GESTE
Director: Marty Feldman
Co-stars: Marty Feldman Michael York Peter Ustinov

1977 JOSEPH ANDREWS
Director: Tony Richardson
Co-stars: Peter Firth Hugh Griffith John Gielgud

1978 MAGIC
Director: Richard Attenborough
Co-stars: Anthony Hopkins Burgess Meredith Ed Lauter

1978 THE CHEAP DETECTIVE
Director: Robert Moore
Co-stars: Peter Falk John Houseman Dom DeLuise

1979 CACTUS JACK
Director: Hal Needham
Co-stars: Kirk Douglas Arnold Schwarzenegger Paul Lynde

1980 MIDDLE AGE CRAZY
Director: John Trent
Co-stars: Bruce Dern Graham Jarvis Deborah Wakeham

1982 THE RETURN OF THE SOLDIER
Director: Alan Bridges
Co-stars: Alan Bates Julie Christie Glenda Jackson

1982 LOOKIN' TO GET OUT
Director: Hal Ashby
Co-stars: Jon Voight Bert Remsen Burt Young

1982 I OUGHT TO BE IN PICTURES
Director: Herbert Ross
Co-stars: Walter Matthau Dinah Manoff Lance Guest

1983 WHO WILL LOVE MY CHILDREN?
Director: John Erman
Co-stars: Frederic Forrest Cathryn Damon

1984 A STREETCAR NAMED DESIRE
Director: John Erman
Co-stars: Treat Williams Beverly D'Angelo Randy Quaid

1985 TWICE IN A LIFETIME
Director: Bud Yorkin
Co-stars: Gene Hackman Ellen Burstyn Amy Madigan

1986 52 PICK-UP
Director: John Frankenheimer
Co-stars: Roy Scheider John Glover Lonny Chapman

1987 THE TWO MRS.GRENVILLES
Director: John Erman
Co-stars: Claudette Colbert Stephen Collins Sam Wanamaker

1987 A TIGER'S TALE
Director: Peter Douglas
Co-stars: C. Thomas Howell Kelly Preston Charles Durning

1988 A NEW LIFE
Director: Alan Alda
Co-stars: Alan Alda Hal Linden Veronica Hamel

1991 OUR SONS
Director: John Erman
Co-stars: Julie Andrews Hugh Grant Zeljko Ivanek

1992 THE NEWS BOYS
Director: Kenny Ortega
Co-stars: Christian Bale Bill Pullman Robert Duvall

1993 GRUMPY OLD MEN
Director: Donald Petrie
Co-stars: Jack Lemmon Walter Matthau Burgess Meredith

1994 FOLLOWING HER HEART
Director: Lee Grant
Co-star: George Segal Brenda Vaccaro

1996 BLUE RODEO
Director: Peter Werner
Co-star: Kris Kristofferson

ELENI ANOUSAKI

1964 ZORBA THE GREEK
Director: Michael Cacoyannis
Co-stars: Anthony Quinn Alan Bates Irene Papas

SUSAN ANSPACH

1970 FIVE EASY PIECES
Director: Bob Rafelson
Co-stars: Jack Nicholson Karen Black Fannie Flagg

1972 PLAY IT AGAIN SAM
Director: Herbert Ross
Co-stars: Woody Allen Diane Keaton Jerry Lacey

1973 BLUME IN LOVE
Director: Paul Mazursky
Co-stars: George Segal Kris Kristofferson Shelley Winters

1978 THE BIG FIX
Director: Jeremy Paul Kagan
Co-stars: Richard Dreyfuss Bonnie Bedelia John Lithgow

1979 RUNNING
Director: Stephen Hillard Stern
Co-stars: Michael Douglas Lawrence Dane Eugene Levy

1981 MONTENEGRO
Director: Dusan Makavejev
Co-stars: Erland Josephson Per Oscarsson John Zacharias

1981 THE DEVIL AND MAX DEVLIN
Director: Stephen Hillard Stern
Co-stars: Elliott Gould Bill Cosby

1982 DEADLY ENCOUNTER
Director: William Graham
Co-stars: Larry Hagman James Gammon Michael L Gwynne

1984 MISUNDERSTOOD ACCENT
Director: Jerry Schatzberg
Co-stars: Gene Hackman Henry Thomas Rip Torn

1994 CAGNEY AND LACEY: THE RETURN
Director: James Frawley
Co-stars: Tyne Daly Sharon Gless James Naughton

DENISE ANTHONY

1947 DEATH IN HIGH HEELS
Director: Lionel Tomlinson
Co-stars: Don Stannard Veronica Rose Patricia Laffan

JANE ANTHONY

1976 ACES HIGH
Director: Jack Gold
Co-stars: Malcolm McDowell Christopher Plummer Simon Ward

LYSETTE ANTHONY

1982   **IVANHOE**
Director: Douglas Camfield
Co-stars: James Mason Anthony Andrews Sam Neill

1983   **KRULL**
Director: Peter Yates
Co-stars: Ken Marshall Freddie Jones Liam Neeson

1985   **OLIVER TWIST** *(Voice)*
Director: Gareth Davies
Co-stars: Ben Rodska Eric Porter Frank Middlemass

1988   **THE LADY AND THE HIGHWAYMAN**
Director: John Hough
Co-stars: Emma Samms Oliver Reed Hugh Grant

1988   **WITHOUT A CLUE**
Director: Thom Eberhardt
Co-stars: Michael Caine Ben Kingsley Jeffrey Jones

1990   **A GHOST IN MONTE CARLO**
Director: John Hough
Co-stars: Oliver Reed Sarah Miles

1991   **SWITCH**
Director: Blake Edwards
Co-stars: Ellen Barkin Jimmy Smits JoBeth Williams

1991   **THE PLEASURE PRINCIPLE**
Director: David Cohen
Co-stars: Peter Firth Lynsey Baxter Ian Hogg

1992   **HUSBANDS AND WIVES**
Director: Woody Allen
Co-stars: Woody Allen Blythe Danner Judy Davis

1993   **LOOK WHO'S TALKING NOW**
Director: Tom Ropelewski
Co-stars: Kirstie Alley John Travolta

1993   **THE HOUR OF THE PIG**
Director: Lesley Megahey
Co-stars: Colin Firth Ian Holm Nicol Williamson

1995   **DR JEKYLL AND M/S HYDE**
Co-stars: Sean Young Tim Daly

SUSAN ANTON

1983   **CANNONBALL RUN II**
Director: Hal Needham
Co-stars: Burt Reynolds Dom DeLuise Dean Martin

FRANCESCA ANTONELLI

1988   **MIGNON HAS LEFT**
Director: Francesca Archibugi
Co-stars: Stefania Sandelli Jean-Pierre Duriez

LAURA ANTONELLI

1966   **DR. GOLDFOOT AND THE GIRL BOMBS**
Director: Mario Brava
Co-stars: Vincent Price Fabian Forte

1971   **SINK OR SWIM**
Director: Jean-Paul Rappeneau
Co-stars: Jean-Paul Belmondo Marlene Jobert

1972   **DOCTOR POPAUL**
Director: Claude Chabrol
Co-stars: Jean-Paul Belmondo Mia Farrow

1976   **THE INNOCENT**
Director: Luchino Visconti
Co-stars: Giancarlo Giannini Jennifer O'Neill

GABRIELLE ANWAR

1991   **TEEN AGENT**
Director: William Dear
Co-stars: Richard Grieco Linda Hunt Roger Rees

1992   **SCENT OF A WOMAN**
Director: Martin Brest
Co-stars: Al Pacino Chris O'Donnell James Rebhorn

1993   **BODY SNATCHERS**
Director: Abel Ferrara
Co-stars: Billy Wirth Meg Tilly Terry Kinney

1993   **THE CONCIERGE**
Director: Barry Sonnenfeld
Co-stars: Michael J. Fox Anthony Higgins Michael Tucker

1993   **THE THREE MUSKETEERS**
Director: Stephen Herek
Co-stars: Chris O'Donnell Charlie Sheen Kiefer Sutherland

1995   **INNOCENT LIES**
Director: Patrick DeWolf
Co-stars: Stephen Dorff Adrian Dunbar Joanna Lumley

1995   **IN PURSUIT OF HONOR**
Director: Ken Olin
Co-stars: Don Johnson Craig Sheffer

1996   **THINGS TO DO IN DENVER WHEN YOU'RE DEAD**
Director: Gary Leder
Co-stars: Andy Garcia Fairusa Balk

ANNA APFEL

1932   **HEART OF NEW YORK**
Director: Mervyn LeRoy
Co-stars: Joe Smith Charles Dale George Sidney

1932   **SYMPHONY OF SIX MILLION**
Director: Gregory La Cava
Co-stars: Irene Dunne Ricardo Cortez Gregory Ratoff

TINA APICELLA

1951   **BELLISSIMA**
Director: Luchino Visconti
Co-stars: Anna Magnani Walter Chiari

KATHRYN APONOWICZ

1984   **FORDS ON WATER**
Director: Barry Bliss
Co-stars: Elvis Payne Mark Wingett Jason Rose.

CHRISTINA APPLEGATE

1990   **STREETS**
Director: Katt Shea Rubin
Co-stars: David Mendenhall Patrick Richwood

1991   **DON'T TELL MUM THE BABYSITTER'S DEAD**
Director: Stephen Herek
Co-stars: Joanna Cassidy John Getz

ANNABELLE APSION

1990   **THE WIDOWMAKER**
Director: John Madden
Co-stars: David Morrissey Colin Jeavons Alun Armstrong

1991   **ALIVE AND KICKING**
Director: Robert Young
Co-stars: Lenny Henry Robbie Coltrane Jane Horrocks

AMY AQUINO

1995   **BOYS ON THE SIDE**
Director: Herbert Ross
Co-stars: Whoopi Goldberg Drew Barrymore Mary Louise Parker

ANGEL ARANDA

1964   **EL GRECO**
Director: Luciano Salce
Co-stars: Mel Ferrer Rosanna Schiaffino Adolfo Celi

PENNY ARCADE

1991   **I WAS ON MARS**
Director: Dani Levy
Co-stars: Maria Schradar Dani Levy Antonia Rey

ANNE ARCHER
(Daughter Of John Archer And Marjorie Lord)
Nominated For Best Supporting Actress For "Fatal Attraction" In 1987

1971   **THE HONKERS**
Director: Steve Inhat
Co-stars: James Coburn Lois Nettleton Slim Pickens

1972   **CANCEL MY RESERVATION**
Director: Paul Bogart
Co-stars: Bob Hope Eva Marie Saint Ralph Bellamy

1973   **THE ALL-AMERICAN BOY**
Director: Charles Eastman
Co-stars: Jon Voight Carol Androsky

1976   **LIFEGUARD**
Director: Daniel Petrie
Co-stars: Sam Elliott Stephen Young Parker Stevenson

1976   **TRACKDOWN**
Director: Richard Heffron
Co-stars: Jim Mitchum Karen Lamm Erik Estrada

1978   **PARADISE ALLEY**
Director: Sylvester Stallone
Co-stars: Sylvester Stallone Kevin Conway Armand Assante Tom Waits

1980   **RAISE THE TITANIC**
Director: Jerry Jameson
Co-stars: Jason Robards Richard Jordan Alec Guinness

1980   **HERO AT LARGE**
Director: Martin Davidson
Co-stars: John Ritter Kevin McCarthy Kevin Bacon

1981   **GREEN ICE**
Director: Ernest Day
Co-stars: Ryan O'Neal Omar Sharif Philip Stone.

1984   **THE NAKED FACE**
Director: Bryan Forbes
Co-stars: Roger Moore Rod Steiger Elliott Gould

1987   **FATAL ATTRACTION**
Director: Adrian Lyne
Co-stars: Michael Douglas Glenn Close Fred Gwynne

1987   **A DIFFERENT AFFAIR**
Director: Noel Masseck
Co-stars: Tony Roberts Bobby Jacoby Stuart Pankin

1988   **LEAP OF FAITH**
Director: Stephen Gyllenhaal
Co-stars: Sam Neill James Tolkin Elisabeth Ruscio

1990   **NARROW MARGIN**
Director: Peter Hyams
Co-stars: Gene Hackman J. T. Walsh M. Emmet Walsh

1990   **LOVE AT LARGE**
Director: Alan Rudolph
Co-stars: Tom Berenger Elizabeth Perkins Kate Capshaw

1992   **PATRIOT GAMES**
Director: Philip Noyce
Co-stars: Harrison Ford Patrick Bergin Sean Bean

1992   **THE LAST OF HIS TRIBE**
Director: Harry Hook
Co-stars: Jon Voight Graham Greene David Ogden Stiers

1992   **BODY OF EVIDENCE**
Director: Uli Edel
Co-stars: Madonna Willem Dafoe Jurgen Prochnow

1993   **FAMILY PRAYERS**
Director: Scott Rosenfeld
Co-stars: Joe Mantegna Patti Lupone Allen Garfield

1993   **SHORT CUTS**
Director: Robert Altman
Co-stars: Matthew Modine Jack Lemmon Tim Robbins

1994   **CLEAR AND PRESENT DANGER**
Director: Philip Noyce
Co-stars: Harrison Ford Willem Dafoe James Earl Jones

1994   **JANE'S HOUSE**
Director: Glenn Jordan
Co-stars: James Woods Graham Beckel Missy Crider

1994   **BECAUSE MOMMY WORKS**
Director: Robert Markowitz
Co-stars: John Heard Ashley C. Frow

BARBARA ARCHER

1956   **THE FEMININE TOUCH**
Director: Pat Jackson
Co-stars: George Baker Belinda Lee Delphi Lawrence

1957   **STRANGERS' MEETING**
Director: Robert Day
Co-stars: Peter Arne Delphi Lawrence Conrad Phillips

KAREN ARCHER

1982   **GIRO CITY**
Director: Karl Francis
Co-stars: Glenda Jackson Jon Finch Kenneth Colley

1983   **FOREVER YOUNG**
Director: David Drury
Co-stars: James Aubrey Nicholas Gecks Alex McCowen

JUNE ARCHER *(Child)*

1961   **INNOCENT SINNERS**
Director: Philip Leacock
Co-stars: Flora Robson Catherine Lacey David Kossoff

SANDRA ARCHER

1971   **FUNNYMAN**
Director: John Korty
Co-stars: Peter Bonertz Carol Androsky

FANNY ARDANT

1983   **SWANN IN LOVE**
Director: Volker Schlondorff
Co-stars: Jeremy Irons Ornella Muti Alain Delon

1983   **FINALLY, SUNDAY**
Director: Francois Truffaut
Co-stars: Jean-Louis Trintignant Caroline Sihol

1983   **BENVENUTA**
Director: Andre Delvaux
Co-stars: Vittorio Gassman Matthieu Carriere

1983   **LIFE IS A BED OF ROSES**
Director: Alain Resnais
Co-stars: Vittorio Gassman Geraldine Chaplin

1986   **MELO**
Director: Alain Resnais
Co-stars: Sabine Azema Pierre Aditi Andre Dusollier

1987   **THREE SISTERS**
Director: Margarethe Von Trotta
Co-stars: Greta Scacchi Valeria Golino Agnes Soral

1989   **AUSTRALIA**
Director: Jean-Jacques Andrien
Co-stars: Jeremy Irons Agnes Soral Tcheky Karyo

1992   AFRAID OF THE DARK
Director: Mark Peploe
Co-stars: James Fox Paul McGann Clare Holman

1996   SABRINA
Director: Sidney Pollack
Co-stars: Julia Ormond Harrison Ford John Wood

ARIANNE ARDEN

1959   BEYOND THE TIME BARRIER
Director: Edgar Ulmer
Co-stars: Robert Clarke Darlene Tompkins

EVE ARDEN
Nominated For Best Supporting Actress For "Mildred Pierce" In 1945

1937   STAGE DOOR
Director: Gregory La Cava
Co-stars: Katharine Hepburn Ginger Rogers Ann Miller

1937   OH DOCTOR
Director: Edmund Granger
Co-stars: Edward Everett Horton Donrue Leighton William Demarest

1938   LETTER OF INTRODUCTION
Director: John Stahil
Co-stars: Adolphe Menjou Andrea Leeds George Murphy

1938   HAVING WONDERFUL TIME
Director: Alfred Santell
Co-stars: Ginger Rogers Douglas Fairbanks Jnr. Lucille Ball

1938   COCOANUT GROVE
Director: Alfred Santell
Co-stars: Fred MacMurray Harriet Hilliard Ben Blue

1939   A CHILD IS BORN
Director: Lloyd Bacon
Co-stars: Geraldine Fitzgerald Jeffrey Lynn Gladys George

1939   AT THE CIRCUS
Director: Edward Buzzell
Co-stars: Marx Bros. Margaret Dumont Florence Rice

1939   BIG TOWN CZAR
Co-star: Barton MacLaine

1939   ETERNALLY YOURS
Director: Tay Garnett
Co-stars: Loretta Young David Niven Broderick Crawford

1939   THE FORGOTTEN WOMAN
Director: Harold Young
Co-stars: Sigrid Gurie Donald Briggs William Lundigan

1939   WOMEN IN THE WIND
Director: John Farrow
Co-stars: Kay Francis William Gargan Victor Jory

1940   SLIGHTLY HONOURABLE
Director: Tay Garnett
Co-stars: Pat O'Brien Broderick Crawford Edward Arnold

1940   NO, NO NANET
Director: Herbert Wilcox
Co-stars: Anna Neagle Richard Carlson Victor Mature

1940   COMRADE X
Director: King Vidor
Co-stars: Clark Gable Hedy Lamarr Felix Bressart

1941   BEDTIME STORY
Director: Alexander Hall
Co-stars: Loretta Young Fredric March Robert Benchley

1941   MANPOWER
Director: Raoul Walsh
Co-stars: Edward G. Robinson George Raft Marlene Dietrich

1941   THE OBLIGING YOUNG LADY
Director: Richard Wallace
Co-stars: Joan Carroll Ruth Warwick Edmond O'Brien

1941   SHE KNEW ALL THE ANSWERS
Director: Richard Wallace
Co-stars: Joan Bennett Franchot Tone

1941   SHE COULDN'T SAY NO
Co-stars: Roger Pryor Vera Lewis Clem Bevans

1941   WHISTLING IN THE DARK
Director: S. Sylvan Simon
Co-stars: Red Skelton Ann Rutherford Conrad Veidt

1941   ZIEGFELD GIRL
Director: Robert Z. Leonard
Co-stars: Judy Garland Lana Turner Hedy Lamarr

1943   LET'S FACE IT
Director: Sidney Lanfield
Co-stars: Bob Hope Betty Hutton Dona Drake

1943   HIT PARADE OF 1943
Director: Albert Rogell
Co-stars: John Carroll Susan Hayward Gail Patrick

1944   COVER GIRL
Director: Charles Vidor
Co-stars: Rita Hayworth Gene Kelly Phil Silvers

1944   THE DOUGHGIRLS
Co-stars: Alexis Smith Jane Wyman Jack Carson

1944   PATRICK THE GREAT
Director: Frank Ryan
Co-stars: Donald O'Connor Peggy Ryan Frances Dee

1945   MILDRED PIERCE
Director: Michael Curtiz
Co-stars: Joan Crawford Jack Carson Zachary Scott

1945   PAN-AMERICANA
Director: John Auer
Co-stars: Audrey Long Philip Terry Robert Benchley

1945   EARL CARROLL VANITIES
Director: Joseph Santley
Co-stars: Dennis O'Keefe Constance Moore

1946   NIGHT AND DAY
Director: Michael Curtiz
Co-stars: Cary Grant Alexis Smith Monty Woolley

1946   MY REPUTATION
Director: Curtis Bernhardt
Co-stars: Barbara Stanwyck George Brent Lucile Watson

1946   THE KID FROM BROOKLYN
Director: Norman Z. McLeod
Co-stars: Danny Kaye Virginia Mayo Vera-Ellen

1946   THE ARNELO AFFAIR
Director: Arch Oboler
Co-stars: George Murphy Frances Gifford John Hodiak

1947   SONG OF SCHEHERAZADE
Director: Walter Reisch
Co-stars: Yvonne De Carlo Jean-Pierre Aumont Brian Donlevy

1947   THE UNFAITHFUL
Director: Vincent Sherman
Co-stars: Ann Sheridan Zachary Scott Lew Ayres

1948   WHIPLASH
Director: Lewis Seiler
Co-stars: Dane Clark Alexis Smith Zachary Scott

1948   THE VOICE OF THE TURTLE
Director: Irving Rapper
Co-stars: Eleanor Parker Ronald Reagan

1948   ONE TOUCH OF VENUS
Director: William Seiter
Co-stars: Ava Gardner Robert Walker Dick Haymes

1949   MY DREAM IS YOURS
Director: Michael Curtiz
Co-stars: Doris Day Jack Carson Lee Bowman

1949   **THE LADY TAKES A SAILOR**
Director: Michael Curtiz
Co-stars: Jane Wyman Dennis Morgan Allyn Joslyn

1949   **CURTAIN CALL AT CACTUS CREEK**
Director: Charles Lamont
Co-stars: Walter Brennan Donald O'Connor

1950   **PAID IN FULL**
Director: William Dieterle
Co-stars: Lisabeth Scott Diana Lynn Robert Cummings

1950   **TEA FOR TWO**
Director: David Butler
Co-stars: Doris Day Gordon MacRae Gene Nelson

1950   **THREE HUSBANDS**
Director: Irving Reis
Co-stars: Emlyn Williams Ruth Warwick Howard Da Silva

1951   **GOODBYE MY FANCY**
Director: Vincent Sherman
Co-stars: Joan Crawford Robert Young Frank Lovejoy

1952   **WE'RE NOT MARRIED**
Director: Edmund Goulding
Co-stars: Ginger Rogers Marilyn Monroe Mitzi Gaynor

1953   **THE LADY WANTS MINK**
Director: William Seiter
Co-stars: Dennis O'Keefe Ruth Hussey William Demarest

1955   **OUR MISS BROOKS**
Director: Al Lewis
Co-stars: Gale Gordon Robert Rockwell Richard Crenna

1959   **ANATOMY OF A MURDER**
Director: Otto Preminger
Co-stars: James Stewart Lee Remick Arthur O'Connell

1960   **THE DARK AT THE TOP OF THE STAIRS**
Director: Delbert Mann
Co-stars: Robert Preston Dorothy McGuire

1965   **SERGEANT DEADHEAD**
Director: Norman Taurog
Co-stars: Frankie Avalon Deborah Walley Cesar Romero

1972   **A VERY MISSING PERSON**
Director: Russ Mayberry
Co-stars: Julie Newmar James Gregory Ray Danton

1975   **THE STRONGEST MAN IN THE WORLD**
Director: Vincent McEveety
Co-stars: Kurt Russell Cesar Romero

1978   **GREASE**
Director: Randal Kleiser
Co-stars: John Travolta Olivia Newton John Frankie Avalon

1981   **UNDER THE RAINBOW**
Director: Steve Rash
Co-stars: Chevy Chase Carrie Fisher Billy Barty

1982   **GREASE 2**
Director: Patricia Birch
Co-stars: Maxwell Caulfield Michelle Pfeiffer Lorna Luft

MARY ARDEN

1964   **BLOOD AND BLACK LACE**
Director: Mario Bava
Co-stars: Cameron Mitchell Eva Bartok

ASIA ARGENTO

1993   **TRAUMA**
Director: Dario Argento
Co-stars: Christopher Rydell Laura Johnson Brad Dourif

1995   **BITS AND PIECES**
Director: Antonello Grimaldi
Co-stars: Luca Barbareschi Roberto Citran

1996   **B MONKEY**
Director: Michael Radford
Co-stars: Rupert Everett Jared Harris

ALLISON ARGO

1979   **THE GIFT**
Director: Don Taylor
Co-stars: Glenn Ford Julie Harris Maggie Cooper

PEARL ARGYLE

1934   **CHU CHIN CHOW**
Director: Walter Forde
Co-stars: George Robey Fritz Kortner Anna May Wong

1936   **THINGS TO COME**
Director: William Cameron Menzies
Co-stars: Raymond Massey Cedric Hardwicke

BRIGITTE ARIEL

1974   **PIAF – THE EARLY YEARS**
Director: Guy Casaril
Co-stars: Pascale Christophe Pierre Vernier

MARIE-MONIQUE ARKELL

1951   **DIARY OF A COUNTRY PRIEST**
Director: Robert Bresson
Co-stars: Claude Laydu Armand Guibert

ELIZABETH ARLEN

1985   **ST. ELMO'S FIRE**
Director: Joel Schumacher
Co-stars: Demi Moore Rob Lowe Ally Sheedy

1990   **THE FIRST POWER**
Director: Robert Resnikoff
Co-stars: Lou Diamond Phillips Tracy Griffith

ARLETTY *(Leonie Bathiat)*

1938   **HOTEL DU NORD**
Director: Marcel Carne
Co-stars: Annabella Jean-Pierre Aumont Louis Jouvet

1939   **LE JOUR SE LEVE**
Director: Marcel Carne
Co-stars: Jean Gabin Jules Barry Jacqueline Laurent

1939   **FRIC-FRAC**
Director: Maurice Lehman
Co-stars: Michel Simon Fernandel Helene Robert

1939   **CIRCONSTANCES ATTENUANTES**
Director: Jean Boyer
Co-stars: Michel Simon Suzanne Dantes Arnoux

1942   **LES VISITEURS DU SOIR**
Director: Marcel Carne
Co-stars: Jules Berry Marie Dea Alain Cuny

1945   **LES ENFANTS DU PARADIS**
Director: Marcel Carne
Co-stars: Jean-Louis Barrault Pierre Brasseur

1954   **HUIS CLOS**
Director: Jacqueline Audry
Co-stars: Frank Villard Gaby Sylvia

1972   **THE LONGEST DAY**
Director: Ken Annakin
Co-stars: John Wayne Robert Mitchum Henry Fonda

DIMITRA ARLISS

1973   **THE STING**
Director: George Roy Hill
Co-stars: Paul Newman Robert Redford Robert Shaw

1979   A PERFECT COUPLE
Director: Robert Altman
Co-stars: Paul Dooley Marta Heflin Belita Moreno

FLORENCE ARLISS
(Florence Montgomery, Wife Of George Arlis)

1921   DISRAELI
Co-star: George Arliss

1929   DISRAELI
Director: Alfred Green
Co-stars: George Arliss Joan Bennett Anthony Bushell

1931   THE MILLIONAIRE
Director: John Adolfi
Co-stars: George Arliss Evalyn Knapp Noah Beery

1934   THE HOUSE OF ROTHSCHILD
Director: Alfred Werker
Co-stars: George Arliss Loretta Young Boris Karloff

ARMIDA

1930   UNDER A TEXAS MOON
Director: Michael Curtiz
Co-stars: Frank Fay Myrna Loy Raquel Torres

1930   GENERAL CRACK
Director: Alan Crosland
Co-stars: John Barrymore Marian Nixon Lowell Sherman

1937   BORDER CAFE
Co-stars: John Beal Harry Carey

BESS ARMSTRONG

1980   THE ELEVENTH VICTIM
Director: Jonathan Kaplan
Co-stars: Max Gail Eric Burdon Pamela Ludwig

1981   THE FOUR SEASONS
Director: Alan Alda
Co-stars: Carol Burnett Alan Alda Sandy Dennis

1983   HIGH ROAD TO CHINA
Director: Brian Hutton
Co-stars: Tom Sellick Jack Weston Robert Morley

1983   JAWS 3
Director: Joe Alves
Co-stars: Dennis Quaid Simon MacCorkindale Lea Thompson

1986   NOTHING IN COMMON
Director: Gary Marshall
Co-stars: Jackie Gleason Eva Marie Saint Tom Hanks

1993   DREAM LOVER
Director: Nicholas Kazan
Co-stars: James Spader Madchen Amick Larry Miller

1993   THE SKATEBOARD KID
Director: Larry Swerdlove
Co-star: Timothy Busfield

1994   THE LIES BOYS TELL
Director: Tom McLoughlan
Co-stars: Kirk Douglas Richard E. Grant

**1995   SHE STOOD ALONE:
            THE TAILHOOK SCANDAL**
Director: Larry Shaw
Co-star: Gail O'Grady

BRIDGET ARMSTRONG

1977   FOR THE LOVE OF BENJI
Director: Joe Camp
Co-stars: Patsy Garrett Cynthia Smith Peter Bowles

1979   MIDDLE AGE SPREAD
Director: John Reid
Co-stars: Grant Tilly Dorothy McKegg Donna Akersten

JULIA ARNALL

1955   LOST
Director: Guy Green
Co-stars: David Farrar David Knight Thora Hird

1956   HOUSE OF SECRETS
Director: Guy Green
Co-stars: Michael Craig Brenda De Banzie Barbara Bates

1957   THE MAN WITHOUT A BODY
Director: Charles Saunders
Co-stars: Robert Hutton George Coulouris

1958   MARK OF THE PHOENIX
Director: Maclean Rogers
Co-stars: Sheldon Lawrence Anton Diffring Martin Miller

1961   CARRY ON REGARDLESS
Director: Gerald Thomas
Co-stars: Sid James Liz Fraser Kenneth Williams

MARIE-HELENE ARNAULD

1964   FANTOMAS
Director: Andre Hunnebelle
Co-stars: Jean Marais Mylene Demongeot

YVONNE ARNAULD

1930   CANARIES SOMETIME SING
Director: Tom Walls
Co-stars: Tom Walis Cathleen Nesbitt

1930   TONS OF MONEY
Director: Tom Walls
Co-stars: Ralph Lynn Robertson Hare Mary Brough

1933   A CUCKOO IN THE NEST
Director: Tom Walls
Co-stars: Tom Walls Ralph Lynn Gordon James

1934   PRINCESS CHARMING
Director: Maurice Elvy
Co-stars: Evelyn Laye George Crosssmith Max Miller

1935   STORMY WEATHER
Director: Tom Walls
Co-stars: Tom Walls Ralph Lynn Robertson Hare

1940   NEUTRAL PORT
Director: Marcel Varnel
Co-stars: Will Fyffe Phyllis Calvert Leslie Banks

1942   TOMORROW WE LIVE
Director: George King
Co-stars: John Clements Greta Gynt Hugh Sinclair

1947   THE GHOSTS OF BERKELEY SQUARE
Director: Vernon Sewell
Co-stars: Robert Morley Claude Hulbert

1958   MON ONCLE
Director: Jacques Tati
Co-stars: Jacques Tati Jean-Pierre Zola Adrienne Servatie

LUCIE ARNAZ

1975   WHO IS THE BLACK DAHLIA?
Director: Joseph Pevney
Co-stars: Erfrem Zinbalist Jnr. Ronny Cox Tom Bosley

1977   BILLY JACK GOES TO WASHINGTON
Director: Tom Laughlin
Co-stars: Sam Wanamaker Tom Laughlin Lucille Ball

1980   THE JAZZ SINGER
Director: Richard Fleischer
Co-stars: Neil Diamond Laurence Olivier Catlin Adams

1982   SECOND THOUGHTS
Director: Lawrence Turman
Co-stars: Craig Wasson Ken Howard Anne Schedeen

GWEN ARNER

1972 THE TRIAL OF THE CATONSVILLE NINE
Director: Gordon Davidson
Co-stars: Ed Flanders Richard Jordan

JEANETTA ARNETTE

1984 FLIGHT 90: DISASTER ON THE POTOMAC
Director: Robert Lewis
Co-stars: Richard Masur Dinah Manoff

1992 LADYBUGS
Director: Sidney Furie
Co-stars: Rodney Dangerfield Vinessa Shaw Tom Parks

ROSEANNE ARNOLD (*Married Tom Arnold*)

1991 BACKFIELD IN MOTION
Director: Richard Michaels
Co-stars: Tom Arnold Colleen Camp Conchata Ferrell

1992 FREDDY'S DEAD - THE FINAL NIGHTMARE
Director: Rachel Talalay
Co-stars: Robert Englund Lisa Zane Tom Arnold

1993 EVEN COWGIRLS GET THE BLUES
Director: Gus Van Sant
Co-stars: Uma Thurman John Hurt Rain Phoenix

TRACEY ARNOLD

1990 HENRY, PORTRAIT OF A SERIAL KILLER
Director: John McNaughton
Co-stars: Michael Rooker Tom Towles

FRANCOISE ARNOUL

1952 FORBIDDEN FRUIT
Director: Henri Verneuil
Co-stars: Fernandel Claude Nollier Sylvie

1952 THE LOVERS OF TOLEDO
Director: Henri Decoin
Co-stars: Pedro Armendariz Alida Valli

1954 THE LOVERS OF LISBON
Director: Henri Verneuil
Co-stars: Daniel Gelin Trevor Howard Ginette Leclerc

1954 THE SHEEP HAS FIVE LEGS
Director: Henri Verneuil
Co-stars: Fernandel Paulette Dubost Rene Genin

1955 FRENCH CAN-CAN
Director: Jean Renoir
Co-stars: Jean Gabin Maria Felix Edith Piaf

JUDIE ARONSON

1984 FRIDAY THE 13TH.-THE FINAL CHAPTER
Director: Joseph Zito
Co-stars: Kimberley Beck Crispin Glover

1985 WEIRD SCIENCE
Director: John Hughes
Co-stars: Anthony Michael Hall Kelly LeBrock Robert Downey Jnr.

1986 AMERICAN NINJA
Director: Sam Firstenberg
Co-stars: Michael Dudikof Steve James

PATRICIA ARQUETTE (*Married Nicolas Cage*)

1987 A NIGHTMARE ON ELM STREET III: DREAM WARRIORS
Director: Chuck Russell
Co-stars: Robert Englund John Saxon

1987 DADDY
Director: John Herzfeld
Co-stars: Dermot Mulroney Danny Aiello Tess Harper

1988 FAR NORTH
Director: Sam Shepard
Co-stars: Jessica Lange Tess Harper Charles Durning

1990 PRAYER OF THE ROLLERBOYS
Director: Rick King
Co-stars: Corey Haim Christopher Collet

1991 THE INDIAN RUNNER
Director: Sean Penn
Co-stars: David Morse Viggo Mortensen Valeria Golino

1991 WILDFLOWERS
Director: Diane Keaton
Co-stars: Beau Bridges Reese Witherspoon

1992 INSIDE MONKEY ZETTERLAND
Director: Jeffrey Levy
Co-stars: Steven Antin Katherine Helmond Tate Donovan

1993 BETRAYED BY LOVE
Director: John Power
Co-stars: Mare Winningham Steven Weber

1993 TRUE ROMANCE
Director: Tony Scott
Co-stars: Christian Slater Saul Rubinek Brad Pitt

1993 ETHAN FROME
Director: John Madden
Co-stars: Liam Neeson Joan Allen Tate Donovan

1994 HOLY MATRIMONY
Director: Leonard Nimoy
Co-stars: Tate Donovan Armin Muellar-Stahl Lois Smith

1995 BEYOND RANGOON
Director: John Boorman
Co-stars: Frances McDormand Spalding Gray

1996 FLIRTING WITH DISASTER
Director: David Russell
Co-stars: Mary Tyler Moore Lily Tomlin Alan Alda

1996 THE LOST HIGHWAY
Director: David Lynch
Co-stars: Bill Pullman Balthazar Getty

ROSANNA ARQUETTE

1981 S.O.B.
Director: Blake Edwards
Co-stars: Julie Andrews Robert Preston Richard Mulligan

1982 JOHNNY BELINDA
Director: Anthony Harvey
Co-stars: Richard Thomas Dennis Quaid Candy Clark

1982 THE EXECUTIONER'S SONG
Director: Lawrence Schiller
Co-stars: Tommy Lee Jones Christine Lahti Eli Wallach

1982 BABY, IT'S YOU
Director: John Sayles
Co-stars: Vincent Spano Joanna Merlin Jack Davidson

1984 THE PARADE
Director: Peter Hunt
Co-stars: Michael Learned Frederic Forrest Geraldine Page

1985 SILVERADO
Director: Lawrence Kasdan
Co-stars: Kevin Costner Scott Glenn Danny Glover

1985 DESPERATELY SEEKING SUSAN
Director: Susan Seidelman
Co-stars: Madonna Aidan Quinn Mark Blum

1985 THE AVIATOR
Director: George Miller
Co-stars: Christopher Reeve Tyne Daly Sam Wanamaker

1985 **AFTER HOURS**
Director: Martin Scorsese
Co-stars: Griffin Dunne Teri Garr Verna Bloom

1986 **8 MILLION WAYS TO DIE**
Director: Hal Ashby
Co-stars: Jeff Bridges Alexandra Paul Andy Garcia

1986 **NOBODY'S FOOL**
Director: Evelyn Purcell
Co-stars: Eric Roberts Mare Winningham Louise Fletcher

1987 **AMAZON WOMEN ON THE MOON**
Director: John Landis
Co-stars: Ralph Bellamy Carrie Fisher Michelle Pfeiffer

1988 **THE BIG BLUE**
Director: Luc Besson
Co-stars: Jean-Marc Barr Jean Reno Griffin Dunne

1988 **PROMISED A MIRACLE**
Director: Steven Gyllenhall
Co-stars: Judge Reinhold Tom Bower Gary Bayer

1989 **NEW YORK STORIES**
Director: Martin Scorsese
Co-stars: Nick Nolte Patrick O'Neal Talia Shire

1989 **BLACK RAINBOW**
Director: Mike Hodges
Co-stars: Jason Robards Tom Hulce Mark Joy

1990 **SEPARATION**
Director: Barry Davis
Co-star: David Suchet

1990 **SWEET REVENGE**
Director: Charlotte Brandstrom
Co-stars: Carrie Fisher John Sessions Myriam Moszko

1991 **WENDY CRACKS A WALNUT**
Director: Michael Pattison
Co-stars: Bruce Spense. Hugo Weaving

1991 **FLIGHT OF THE INTRUDER**
Director: John Miliius
Co-stars: Willem Dafoe Brad Johnson Danny Glover

1992 **NOWHERE TO RUN**
Director: Robert Harmon
Co-stars: Jean-Claude Van Damme Kieran Culkin Ted Levine

1992 **IN THE DEEP WOODS**
Director: Charles Carrell
Co-stars: Anthony Perkins Chris Rydell Will Patton

1992 **THE LINGUINI INCIDENT**
Director: Richard Shepard
Co-stars: David Bowie Marlee Matlin Buck Henry

1993 **THE WRONG MAN**
Director: Jim McBride
Co-stars: Kevin Anderson John Lithgow

1994 **PULP FICTION**
Director: Quentin Tarantino
Co-stars: John Travolta Bruce Willis Samuel L. Jackson

1996 **CRASH**
Director: David Cronenberg
Co-stars: James Spader Elias Koteas Holly Hunter

JERI ARREDONDO

1993 **SILENT TONGUE**
Director: Sam Shepard
Co-stars: Alan Bates Richard Harris River Phoenix

ROSE ARRICK

1976 **MIKEY AND NICKY**
Director: Elaine May
Co-stars: Peter Falk John Cassavetes Joyce Van Patten

LISA ARRINDELL

1992 **BUYING A LANDSLIDE**
Director: Simon Curtis
Co-stars: Griffin Dunne John Mahoney Peter Gallagher

BEATRICE ARTHUR

1970 **LOVERS AND OTHER STRANGERS**
Director: Cy Howard
Co-stars: Bonnie Bedelia Michael Brandon Robert Dishy

1974 **MAME**
Director: Gene Saks
Co-stars: Lucille Ball Robert Preston Bruce Davison

1988 **MY FIRST LOVE**
Director: Gilbert Cates
Co-stars: Richard Kiley Joan Van Ark Anne Francis

CAROL ARTHUR

1975 **THE SUNSHINE BOYS**
Director: Herbert Ross
Co-stars: Walter Matthau George Burns Richard Benjamin

JEAN ARTHUR *(Gladys Georgianna Greene)*
Nominated For Best Actress For "The More The Merrier" In 1943

1923 **CAMEO KIRBY**
Director: John Ford

1924 **SEVEN CHANCES**
Director: Buster Keaton
Co-Stars Buster Keaton

1925 **DRUG STORE COWBOY**

1926 **THE COWBOY COP**

1927 **THE MASKED MENACE**

1928 **SINS OF THE FATHERS**

1929 **CANARY MURDER CASE**
Director: Malcolm St. Clair
Co-stars: William Powell Louise Brooks

1929 **THE MYSTERIOUS DR. FU MANCHU**
Director: Rowland Lee
Co-stars: Warner Oland Neil Hamilton

1929 **HALFWAY TO HEAVEN**
Co-star: Charles Rogers

1930 **THE RETURN OF DR FU MANCHU**
Director: Rowland Lee
Co-stars: Warner Orland Neil Hamilton O. P. Heggie

1930 **YOUNG EAGLES**
Director: William Wellman
Co-stars: Charles Rogers Paul Lukas Stuart Erwin

1930 **STREET OF CHANCE**
Director: John Cromwell
Co-stars: William Powell Kay Frances

1930 **PARAMOUNT ON PARADE**
Director: Dorothy Arzner
Co-stars: Nancy Carroll Fay Wray Gary Cooper

1930 **DANGER LIGHTS**
Director: George Seitz
Co-stars: Robert Armstrong Louis Wolheim Hugh Herbert

1931 **EX BAD BOY**
Co-stars: Robert Armstrong George Brent

1933 **GANG BUSTER**
Director: Edward Sutherland
Co-stars: Jack Oakie William Boyd Wynne Gibson

1934 **WHIRLPOOL**
Director: Roy William Neill
Co-stars: Jack Holt Donald Cook Lila Lee

1934 THE DEFENSE RESTS
Co-star: Jack Holt

1935 THE PUBLIC MENACE
Co-star: George Murphy

1935 THE WHOLE TOWN'S TALKING
Director: John Ford
Co-stars: Edward G. Robinson Wallace Ford

1935 PARTY WIRE
Director: Erle Kenton
Co-stars: Victor Jory Helen Lowell Robert Allen

1935 DIAMOND JIM
Director: Edward Sutherland
Co-stars: Edward Arnold Cesar Romero

1936 IF YOU COULD ONLY COOK
Director: William Seiter
Co-stars: Herbert Marshall Leo Carrillo

1936 MORE THAN A SECRETARY
Director: Alfred Green
Co-stars: George Brent Lionel Stander

1936 PUBLIC HERO NUMBER ONE
Director: Walter Ruben
Co-stars: Chester Morris Joseph Calleia

1936 THE EX MRS BRADFORD
Director: Stephen Roberts
Co-stars: William Powell Robert Armstrong

1936 ADVENTURE IN MANHATTAN
Director: Edward Ludwig
Co-stars: Joel McCrea Thomas Mitchell

1936 MR. DEEDS GOES TO TOWN
Director: Frank Capra
Co-stars: Gary Cooper Lionel Stander George Bancroft

1936 THE PLAINSMAN
Director: Cecil B. DeMille
Co-stars: Gary Cooper James Ellison Anthony Quinn

1937 EASY LIVING
Director: Mitchell Leisen
Co-stars: Ray Milland Edward Arnold

1937 HISTORY IS MADE AT NIGHT
Director: Frank Borzage
Co-stars: Charles Boyer Leo Carrillo Colin Clive

1938 YOU CAN'T TAKE IT WITH YOU
Director: Frank Capra
Co-stars: James Stewart Ann Miller Lionel Barrymoore

1939 MR. SMITH GOES TO WASHINGTON
Director: Frank Capra
Co-stars: James Stewart Claude Rains Beulah Bondi

1939 ONLY ANGELS HAVE WINGS
Director: Howard Hawks
Co-stars: Cary Grant Rita Hayworth Thomas Mitchell

1940 TOO MANY HUSBANDS
Director: Wesley Ruggles
Co-stars: Melvyn Douglas Fred MacMurray

1940 ARIZONA
Director: Wesley Ruggles
Co-stars: William Holden Warren William

1941 THE DEVIL AND MISS JONES
Director: Sam Wood
Co-stars: Charles Coburn Robert Cummings Edmund Gwenn

1942 THE TALK OF THE TOWN
Director: George Stevens
Co-stars: Ronald Colman Cary Grant Glenda Farrell

1943 THE MORE THE MERRIER
Director: George Stevens
Co-stars: Joel McCrea Charles Coburn

1943 A LADY TAKES A CHANCE
Director: William Seiter
Co-stars: John Wayne Charles Winninger Phil Silvers

1944 THE IMPATIENT YEARS
Director: Irving Cummings
Co-stars: Lee Bowman Charles Coburn

1948 A FOREIGN AFFAIR
Director: Billy Wilder
Co-stars: Marlene Dietrich John Lund

1953 SHANE
Director: George Stevens
Co-stars: Alan Ladd Van Heflin Jack Palance

MAUREEN ARTHUR

1967 HOW TO SUCCEED IN BUSINESS WITHOUT REALLY TRYING
Director: David Swift
Co-stars: Robert Morse Rudy Vallee

1969 HOW TO COMMIT MARRIAGE
Director: Norman Panama
Co-stars: Bob Hope Jane Wyman Tina Louise

ANN-CATHARINE ARTON

1993 WHITE ANGEL
Director: Chris Jones
Co-stars: Peter Firth Harriet Robinson Don Henderson

MONIQUE ARTUR

1951 LES MAIS SALES
Director: Fernand Rivers
Co-stars: Pierre Brasseur Daniel Gelin Claude Hollier

BETTY ARVANITIS

1984 THE NEXT ONE
Director: Nico Mastorakis
Co-stars: Keir Dullea Adrienne Barbeau Peter Hobbs

AMMA ASANTE

1991 THE BEST OF FRIENDS
Director: Alvin Rakoff
Co-stars: John Gielgud Wendy Hiller Patrick McGoohan

LESLIE ASH

1979 QUADROPHENIA
Director: Franc Roddam
Co-stars: Phil Daniels Mark Wingett Toyah Wilcox

1985 SHADEY
Director: Philip Saville
Director: Anthony Sher Billie Whitelaw Patric MacNee

JAYNE ASHBOURNE

1993 MONEY FOR NOTHING
Director: Mike Ockrent
Co-stars: Christien Anholt Julian Glover Paul Reynolds

LORRAINE ASHBOURNE

1988 DISTANT VOICES, STILL LIVES
Director: Terence Davies
Co-stars: Freda Dowie Pete Postlethwaite Angela Walsh

DAPHNE ASHBROOK

1986 THAT SECRET SUNDAY
Director: Richard Colla
Co-stars: James Farantino Parker Stevenson Michael Lerner

1987 CARLY'S WEB
Director: Kevin Luch
Co-stars: Cyril O'Reilly Peter Billingsley Jennifer Dale

1987 **PERRY MASON: THE CASE OF THE MURDERED MADAM**
Director: Ron Satlof
Co-stars: Raymond Burr Barbara Hale

1988 **14 GOING ON 30**
Director: Paul Schneider
Co-stars: Steve Eckholdt Patrick Duffy Loretta Swit

1993 **DEAD MAN'S REVENGE**
Director: Alan Levi
Co-stars: Bruce Dern Michael Ironside

PEGGY ASHCROFT
Oscar For Best Supporting Actress In 1984 For "A Passsage To India"

1925 **RHODES OF AFRICA**
Director: Bertrold Viertel
Co-stars: Walter Huston Oscar Homolka Basil Sydney

1935 **THE WANDERING JEW**
Co-stars: Conrad Veidt Marie Ney Dennis Hoey

1935 **THE 39 STEPS**
Director: Alfred Hitchcock
Co-stars: Robert Donat Madeleine Carroll Godfrey Tearle

1941 **QUIET WEDDING**
Director: Anthony Asquith
Co-stars: Margaret Lockwood Derek Farr Athene Seyler

1959 **THE NUN'S STORY**
Director: Fred Zinnemann
Co-stars: Audrey Hepburn Peter Finch Edith Evans

1969 **SECRET CEREMONY**
Director: Joseph Losey
Co-stars: Elizabeth Taylor Robert Mitchum Mia Farrow

1969 **THREE INTO TWO WONT GO**
Director: Peter Hall
Co-stars: Rod Steiger Claire Bloom Judy Geeson

1971 **SUNDAY, BLOODY SUNDAY**
Director: John Schlesinger
Co-stars: Peter Finch Glenda Jackson Murray Head

1977 **JOSEPH ANDREWS**
Director: Tony Richardson
Co-stars: Peter Firth Ann-Margret Hugh Griffiths

1984 **A PASSAGE TO INDIA**
Director: David Lean
Co-stars: Judy Davis Alec Guinness Victor Banerjee

1987 **WHEN THE WIND BLOWS** *(Voice)*
Co-stars: John Mills David Bowie

1988 **MADAM SOUSATZKA**
Director: John Schlesinger
Co-stars: Shirley MacLaine Twiggy Leigh Lawson

1988 **A PERFECT SPY**
Director: Peter Smith
Co-stars: Alec Guinness Peter Egan Jane Booker

1989 **SHE'S BEEN AWAY**
Director: Peter Hall
Co-stars: Geraldine James James Fox Jackson Kyle

1989 **THE HEAT OF THE DAY**
Director: Christopher Morahan
Co-stars: Michael Gambon Patricia Hodge Michael York

NADENE ASHDOWN *(Child)*

1955 **THE BRIDGES AT TOKO-RI**
Director: Mark Robson
Co-stars: William Holden Grace Kelly Mickey Rooney

JANE ASHER

1961 **THE GREENGAGE SUMMER**
Director: Lewis Gilbert
Co-stars: Kenneth More Susannah York Danielle Darrieux

1964 **THE MASK OF THE RED DEATH**
Director: Roger Corman
Co-stars: Vincent Price Hazel Court Patrick Magee

1966 **ALFIE**
Director: Lewis Gilbert
Co-stars: Michael Caine Vivien Merchant Julia Foster

1970 **THE BUTTERCUP CHAIN**
Director: Robert Ellis Miller
Co-stars: Hywell Bennett Leigh Taylor-Young

1970 **DEEP END**
Director: Jerzy Skolimowsky
Co-stars: John Moulder-Brown Christopher Sandford Diana Dors

1972 **HENRY VIII AND HIS SIX WIVES**
Director: Waris Hussein
Co-stars: Keith Michell Lynne Frederick Frances Cuka

1981 **BRIDESHEAD REVISITED**
Director: Charles Sturridge
Co-stars: Jeremy Irons Anthony Andrews Diana Quick

1983 **RUNNERS**
Director: Charles Sturridge
Co-stars: James Fox Kate Hardie Robert Lang

1985 **DREAMCHILD**
Director: Gavin Miller
Co-stars: Coral Browne Peter Gallagher Ian Holm

1988 **PARIS BY NIGHT**
Director: David Hare
Co-stars: Charlotte Rampling Michael Gambon Robert Hardy

1993 **CLOSING NUMBERS**
Director: Stephen Whittaker
Co-stars: Tim Wooward Patrick Pearson Frank Mills

RENEE ASHERSON

1944 **THE WAY AHEAD**
Director: Carol Reed
Co-stars: David Niven Stanley Holloway Jimmy Hanley

1944 **HENRY V**
Director: Laurence Olivier
Co-stars: Laurence Olivier Robert Newton Esmond Knight

1945 **THE WAY TO THE STARS**
Director: Anthony Asquith
Co-stars: John Mills Michael Redgrave Douglass Montgomery

1948 **ONCE A JOLLY SWAGMAN**
Director: Jack Lee
Co-stars: Dirk Bogarde Bonar Colleano Bill Owen

1949 **THE CURE FOR LOVE**
Director: Robert Donat
Co-stars: Robert Donat Dora Bryan Marjorie Rhodes

1950 **POOL OF LONDON**
Director: Basil Dearden
Co-stars: Bonar Colleano Susan Shaw Earl Cameron

1951 **THE MAGIC BOX**
Director: John Boulting
Co-stars: Robert Donat Margaret Johnston Maria Schell

1953 **THE MALTA STORY**
Director: Brian Desmond Hurst
Co-stars: Alec Guinness Anthony Steel Muriel Pavlow

1961 **THE DAY THE EARTH CAUGHT FIRE**
Director: Val Guest
Co-stars: Edward Judd Janet Munro Leo McKern

1966 **RASPUTIN THE MAD MONK**
Director: Don Sharp
Co-stars: Christopher Lee Barbara Shelley Richard Pasco

1969 THE SMASHING BIRD I USED TO KNOW
Director: Robert Hartford-Davis
Co-stars: Dennis Waterman Maureen Lipman

1973 THEATRE OF BLOOD
Director: Douglas Hickox
Co-stars: Vincent Price Diana Rigg Ian Hendry

1985 ROMANCE ON THE ORIENT EXPRESS
Director: Lawrence Gordon Clark
Co-stars: Cheryl Ladd Stuart Wilson

1992 RUNNING LATE
Director: Udayan Prasad
Co-stars: Peter Bowles Carole Nimmons Ian McNiece

1992 HARNESSING PEACOCKS
Director: James Cellan Jones
Co-stars: Serena Scott-Thomas Peter Davison

1992 MEMENTO TO MORI
Director: Jack Clayton
Co-stars: Maggie Smith Michael Hordern

ELIZABETH ASHLEY

1964 THE CARPETBAGGERS
Director: Edward Dmytryk
Co-stars: George Peppard Alan Ladd Carroll Baker

1965 SHIP OF FOOLS
Director: Stanley Kramer
Co-stars: Vivien Leigh Simone Signoret Oskar Weaner

1965 THE THIRD DAY
Director: Jack Smight
Co-stars: George Peppard Roddy McDowall Arthur O'Connell

1971 THE MARRIAGE OF A YOUNG STOCK BROKER
Director: Lawrence Turman
Co-stars: Richard Benjamin Joanna Shimkus

1972 THE HEIST
Director: Don McDougall
Co-stars: Christopher George Howard Duff Norman Fell

1973 THE MAGICIAN
Director: Marvin Chomsky
Co-stars: Bill Bixby Joan Caulfield Kim Hunter

1974 RANCHO DELUXE
Director: Frank Perry
Co-stars: Jeff Bridges Sam Waterston Harry Dean Stanton

1974 GOLDEN NEEDLES
Director: Robert Clouse
Co-stars: Joe Don Baker Burgess Meredith Ann Sothern

1976 THE GREAT SCOUT AND CATHOUSE THURSDAY
Director: Don Taylor
Co-stars: Lee Marvin Oliver Reed Robert Culp

1978 A FIRE IN THE SKY
Director: Jerry Jameson
Co-stars: Richard Crenna David Dukes Lloyd Bochner

1978 COMA
Director: Michael Crichton
Co-stars: Genevieve Bujold Michael Douglas Richard Widmark

1980 WINDOWS
Director: Gordon Willis
Co-stars: Talia Shire Joseph Cortesa

1981 PATERNITY
Director: David Steinberg
Co-stars: Burt Reynolds Beverley D'Angelo Lauren Hutton

1982 SPLIT IMAGE
Director: Ted Kotcheff
Co-stars: Michael O'Keefe Karen Allen Peter Fonda

1984 HE'S FIRED, SHE'S HIRED
Director: Marc Daniels
Co-stars: Wayne Rogers Karen Valentine Martha Byrne

1987 DRAGNET
Director: Tom Mankiewicz
Co-stars: Dan Aykroyd Tom Hanks Harry Morgan

1988 VAMPIRE'S KISS
Director: Robert Bierman
Co-stars: Nicolas Cage Maria Conchita Alonso Jennifer Beals

1987 THE TWO MRS. GRENVILLES
Director: John Erman
Co-stars: Ann-Margret Claudette Colbert Stephen Collins

1990 BLUE BAYOU
Director: Karen Arthur
Co-stars: Alfre Woodard Roy Thinnes Maxwell Caulfield

1992 IN THE BEST INTEREST OF THE CHILDREN
Director: Michael Ray Rhodes
Co-stars: Sarah Jessica Parker Lexi Randall Jayne Atkinson

IRIS ASHLEY

1936 BLIND MAN'S BUFF
Director: Albert Parker
Co-stars: Basil Sydney James Mason Enid Stamp-Taylor

LYN ASHLEY

1971 QUEST FOR LOVE
Director: Ralph Thomas
Co-stars: Tom Bell Joan Collins Denholm Elliott

MAGDALEN ASQUITH

1987 TESTIMONY
Director: Tony Palmer
Co-stars: Ben Kingsley Sherry Baines Terence Rigby

PAT AST

1976 THE DUCHESS AND THE DIRTWATER FOX
Director: Melvin Frank
Co-stars: Goldie Hawn George Segal

1986 REFORM SCHOOL GIRLS
Director: Tom DeSimone
Co-stars: Linda Carol Sybil Danning

SHAY ASTAR

1993 RIO SHANNON
Director: Mimi Leder
Co-stars: Blair Brown Patrick Van Horn Michael Deluise

ADRIANA ASTI

1961 ACCATONE
Director: Pier Paolo Pasolini
Co-stars: Franco Citti Franca Passut Silvana Corsini

1964 BEFORE THE REVOLUTION
Director: Bernardo Bertolucci
Co-stars: Francesco Barilli Alain Midgette

1973 ZORRO
Director: Duccio Tessari
Co-stars: Frank Latimore Alain Delon Stanley Baker

1976 THE INHERITANCE
Director: Mauro Bolognini
Co-stars: Anthony Quinn Dominique Sanda Fabio Teste

EMMA ASTNER

1990 THE BIG BANG
Director: James Toback
Co-stars: Missy Boyd Polly Frost Charles Lassiter

EMILY ASTON (Child)

1989   ORANGES ARE NOT THE ONLY FRUIT
Director: Beeban Kidron
Co-stars: Geraldine McEwan Charlotte Coleman

GERTRUDE ASTOR

1925   STAGE STRUCK
Director: Allan Dwan
Co-stars: Gloria Swanson Lawrene Gray Ford Sterling

1926   THE STRONG MAN
Director: Frank Capra
Co-stars: Harry Langdon Priscilla Bonner

1926   THE TAXI DANCER
Director: Harry Millarde
Co-stars: Joan Crawford Owen Moore

1927   THE CAT AND THE CANARY
Director: Paul Leni
Co-stars: Creighton Hale Laura La Plante Flora Finch

1931   COME CLEAN
Director: James Horn
Co-stars: Stan Laurel Oliver Hardy Mae Busch

1936   EMPTY SADDLES
Co-star: Buck Jones

MARY ASTOR
Oscar For Best Supporting Actress In 1941 For "The Great Lie"

1924   BEAU BRUMMEL
Director: Harry Beaumont
Co-stars: John Barrymore Carmel Myers Irene Rich

1925   DON Q, SON OF ZORRO
Director: Donald Crisp
Co-stars: Donald Crisp Douglas Fairbanks Jean Hersholt

1926   DON JUAN
Director: Alan Crosland
Co-stars: John Barrymore Warner Oland Myrna Loy

1927   ROSE OF THE GOLDEN WEST
Co-star: Gilbert Roland

1930   THE LASH
Director: Frank Lloyd
Co-stars: Richard Bartlemess James Rennie Marian Nixon

1930   LADIES LOVE BRUTES
Director: Rowland Lee
Co-stars: George Bancroft Fredric March

1930   HOLIDAY
Director: Edward Griffith
Co-stars: Ann Harding Robert Ames Edward Everett Horton

1931   OTHER MEN'S WOMEN
Director: William Wellman
Co-stars: Grant Withers James Cagney Joan Blondell

1931   ROYAL BED
Director: Lowell Sherman
Co-stars: Lowell Sherman Nance O'Neill Anthony Bushell

1931   A SUCCESSFUL CALAMITY
Director: John Adolfi
Co-stars: George Arliss Evalyn Knapp Grant Mitchell

1932   THE LOST SQUADRON
Director: George Archainbaud
Co-stars: Richard Dlx Joel McCrea Dorothy Jordan

1932   RED DUST
Director: Victor Fleming
Co-stars: Clark Gable Jean Harlow Gene Raymond

1933   THE WORLD CHANGES
Director: Mervyn LeRoy
Co-stars: Paul Muni Aline McMahon Jean Muir

1933   CONVENTION CITY
Director: Archie Mayo
Co-stars: Joan Blondell Guy Kibbee Dick Powell

1933   EASY TO LOVE
Director: William Keighley
Co-stars: Adolphe Menjou Genevieve Tobin Guy Kibbee

1933   JENNIE GERHARDT
Director: Marion Gering
Co-stars: Sylvia Sidney Donald Cook Edward Arnold

1933   THE KENNEL MURDER CASE
Director: Michael Curtiz
Co-stars: William Powell Eugene Pallette Jack La Rue

1933   THE LITTLE GIANT
Director: Roy Del Ruth
Co-stars: Edward G. Robinson Helen Vinson Russell Hopton

1934   THE CASE OF THE HOWLING DOG
Director: Alan Crosland
Co-stars: Warren William Allen Jenkins

1934   I AM A THIEF
Director: Robert Florey
Co-stars: Ricardo Cortez Dudley Digges Irving Pichel

1934   THE MAN WITH TWO FACES
Director: Archie Mayo
Co-stars: Edward G. Robinson Ricardo Cortez Mae Clark

1934   RETURN OF THE TERROR
Director: Howard Bretherton
Co-stars: John Halliday Lyle Talbot J. Carrol Naish

1934   UPPERWORLD
Director: Roy Del Ruth
Co-stars: Warren William Ginger Rogers Mickey Rooney

1935   DINKY
Director: Howard Bretherton
Co-stars: Jackie Cooper Roger Pryor Henry O'Neill

1935   MAN OF IRON
Director: William McGann
Co-stars: Barton MacLane John Eldrirge Dorothy Peterson

1935   PAGE MISS GLORY
Director: Mervyn LeRoy
Co-stars: Dick Powell Marion Davies Frank McHugh

1936   AND SO THEY WERE MARRIED
Director: Elliott Nugent
Co-stars: Melvyn Douglas Edith Fellows

1936   DODSWORTH
Director: William Wyler
Co-stars: Walter Huston Ruth Chatterton David Niven Paul Lukas

1936   LADY FROM NOWHERE
Director: Gordon Wiles
Co-stars: Charles Quigley Thurston Hall

1936   THE MURDER OF DR. HARRIGAN
Director: Frank McDonald
Co-stars: Kay Linaker Ricardo Cortez

1937   THE HURRICANE
Co-stars: John Ford
Director: Dorothy Lamour Jon Hall Thomas Mitchell

1937   PARADISE FOR 3
Director: Edward Buzzell
Co-stars: Robert Young Frank Morgan Edna May Oliver

1937   THE PRISONER OF ZENDA
Director: John Cromwell
Co-stars: Ronald Colman Douglas Fairbanks Jnr

1938   THERE'S ALWAYS A WOMAN
Director: Alexander Hall
Co-stars: Joan Blondell Melvyn Douglas Frances Drake

1938　LISTEN DARLING
Director:　Edwin Marin
Co-stars:　Judy Garland Walter Pidgeon Freddie Bartholomew

1939　MIDNIGHT
Director:　Mitchell Leisen
Co-stars:　Claudette Colbert Don Ameche John Barrymore

1940　BRIGHAM YOUNG
Director:　Henry Hathaway
Co-stars:　Tyrone Power Linda Darnell Dean Jagger

1940　TURNABOUT
Director:　Hal Roach
Co-stars:　Adolphe Menjou Carole Landis John Hubbard

1941　THE GREAT LIE
Director:　Edmund Goulding
Co-stars:　Bette Davis George Brent Hattie McDaniel

1941　THE MALTESE FALCON
Director:　John Huston
Co-stars:　Humphrey Bogart Sydney Greenstreet Peter Lorre

1942　ACROSS THE PACIFIC
Director:　John Huston
Co-stars:　Humphrey Bogart Sydney Greenstreet Monte Blue

1942　THE PALM BEACH STORY
Director:　Preston Sturges
Co-stars:　Claudette Colbert Joel McCrea Rudy Vallee

1943　YOUNG IDEAS
Director:　Jules Dassin
Co-stars:　Herbert Marshall Susan Peters Richard Carlson

1943　THOUSANDS CHEER
Director:　George Sidney
Co-stars:　Gene Kelly Kathryn Grayson John Boles

1944　BLONDE FEVER
Director:　Richard Whorf
Co-stars:　Philip Dorn Gloria Grahame Marshall Thompson

1944　MEET ME IN ST. LOUIS
Director:　Vincente Minnelli
Co-stars:　Judy Garland Margaret O'Brien Leon Ames

1946　CLAUDIA AND DAVID
Director:　Walter Lang
Co-stars:　Robert Young Dorothy McGuire Gail Patrick

1947　CASS TIMBERLANE
Director:　George Sidney
Co-stars:　Spencer Tracy Lana Turner Zachary Scott

1947　DESERT FURY
Director:　Lewis Allen
Co-stars:　Burt Lancaster Lisabeth Scott Wendell Corey

1947　FIESTA
Director:　Richard Thorpe
Co-stars:　Esther Williams Ricardo Montalban Cyd Charisse

1948　ACT OF VIOLENCE
Director:　Fred Zinnemann
Co-stars:　Van Heflin Robert Ryan Janet Leigh

1948　ANY NUMBER CAN PLAY
Director:　Mervyn LeRoy
Co-stars:　Clark Gable Alexis Smith Audrey Totter

1949　LITTLE WOMEN
Director:　Mervyn LeRoy
Co-stars:　June Allyson Elizabeth Taylor Margaret O'Brien

1956　THE POWER AND THE PRIZE
Director:　Henry Koster
Co-stars:　Robert Taylor Elizabeth Mueller

1956　A KISS BEFORE DYING
Director:　Gerd Oswald
Co-stars:　Robert Wagner Jeffrey Hunter Virginia Leith

1957　THE DEVIL'S HAIRPIN
Director:　Cornel Wilde
Co-stars:　Cornel Wilde Jean Wallace Arthur Franz Paul Fix

1958　THIS HAPPY FEELING
Director:　Blake Edwards
Co-stars:　Curt Jurgens Debbie Reynolds Alexis Smith

1958　A STRANGER IN MY ARMS
Director:　Helmut Kautner
Co-stars:　June Allyson Jeff Chandler Sandra Dee

1961　RETURN TO PEYTON PLACE
Director:　Jose Ferrer
Co-stars:　Jeff Chandler Carol Lynley Tuesday Weld

1964　HUSH....HUSH SWEET CHARLOTTE
Director:　Robert Aldrich
Co-stars:　Bette Davis Olivia De Havilland

1964　YOUNGBLOOD HAWKE
Director:　Delmer Daves
Co-stars:　James Franciscus Genevieve Page Eva Gabor

NANCY MOORE ATCHISON

1993　PROUDHEART
Director:　Jack Cole
Co-star:　Lorrie Morgan

PEGGY ATCHISON

1984　KNOCKBACK
Director:　Piers Haggard
Co-stars:　Pauline Collins Derrick O'Connor

EILEEN ATKINS

1968　INADMISSABLE EVIDENCE
Director:　Anthony Page
Co-stars:　Nicol Williamson Eleanor Fazan

1975　I DON'T WANT TO BE BORN
Director:　Peter Sasdy
Co-stars:　Joan Collins Ralph Bates Donald Pleasence

1977　EQUUS
Director:　Sidney Lumet
Co-stars:　Richard Burton Peter Firth Jenny Agutter

1978　SHE FELL AMONG THIEVES
Director:　Clive Donner
Co-stars:　Malcolm McDowell Michael Jayston

1982　SMILEY'S PEOPLE
Director:　Simon Langton
Co-stars:　Alec Guinness Curt Jurgens Barry Foster

1982　OLIVER TWIST
Director:　Clive Donner
Co-stars:　George C. Scott Tim Curry Michael Hordern

1983　THE DRESSER
Director:　Peter Yates
Co-stars:　Albert Finney Tom Courtenay Edward Fox

1985　THE BURSTON REBELLION
Director:　Norman Stone
Co-stars:　Bernard Hill John Shrapnell Thelma Whiteley

1987　A HAZARD OF HEARTS
Director:　John Hough
Co-stars:　Diana Rigg Edward Fox Fiona Fullerton

1987　THE VISION
Director:　Norman Stone
Co-stars:　Dirk Bogarde Lee Remick Helena Bonham Carter

1991　THE LOST LANGUAGE OF CRANES
Director:　Nigel Finch
Co-stars:　Brian Cox Angus MacFayden Cathy Tyson

1991 LET HIM HAVE IT
Director: Peter Medak
Co-stars: Chris Eccleston Paul Reynolds Tom Courtenay Tom Bell

1995 JACK AND SARAH
Director: Tim Sullivan
Co-stars: Richard E. Grant Samantha Mathis Judi Dench

JAYNE ATKINSON

1992 IN THE BEST INTEREST OF THE CHILDREN
Director: Michael Ray Rhodes
Co-stars: Sarah Jessica Parker Elizabeth Ashley Lexi Randall

1993 FREE WILLY
Director: Simon Wincer
Co-stars: Jason James Richter Michael Madsen Lori Petty

1995 FREE WILLY 2: THE ADVENTURE HOME
Director: Dwight H. Little
Co-stars: Jason James Ritcher Michael Madsen

ROSALIND ATKINSON

1964 THE PUMPKIN EATER
Director: Jack Clayton
Co-stars: Anne Bancroft Peter Finch James Mason

RUTH ATTAWAY

1959 PORGY AND BESS
Director: Otto Preminger
Co-stars: Sidney Poitier Dorothy Dandridge Pearl Bailey

CHARLOTTE ATTENBOROUGH

1989 THESE FOOLISH THINGS
Director: Charles Gormley
Co-stars: James Fox Lindsay Duncan Alex Kingston

ELSIE ATTENHOF

1952 HEIDI
Director: Luigi Comencini
Co-stars: Elsbeth Sigmund Heinrich Gretler

EDITH ATWATER

1936 WE WENT TO COLLEGE
Co-stars: Walter Abel Una Merkel Hugh Herbert

1945 THE BODY SNATCHER
Director: Robert Wise
Co-stars: Boris Karloff Bela Lugosi Henry Daniell

BRIGITTE AUBER

1949 RENDEZVOUS DE JUILLET
Director: Jacques Becker
Co-stars: Daniel Gelin Maurice Ronet Nicole Courcel

1955 TO CATCH A THIEF
Director: Alfred Hitchcock
Co-stars: Cary Grant Grace Kelly John Williams

LENORE AUBERT

1943 THEY GOT ME COVERED
Director: David Butler
Co-stars: Bob Hope Dorothy Lamour Otto Preminger

1944 ACTION IN ARABIA
Director: Leonide Moguy
Co-stars: George Sanders Virginia Bruce Robert Armstrong

1946 WIFE OF MONTE CRISTO
Director: Edgar Ulmer
Co-stars: John Loder Charles Dingle Fritz Kortner

1947 THE OTHER LOVE
Director: Andre De Toth
Co-stars: Barbara Stanwyck David Niven Richard Conte

1947 I WONDER WHO'S KISSING HER NOW
Director: Lloyd Bacon
Co-stars: Mark Stevens June Haver

1948 CATMAN OF PARIS
Director: Lesley Selander
Co-stars: Carl Esmond Adele Mara Gerald Mohr

1948 ABBOTT AND COSTELLO MEET FRANKENSTEIN
Director: Charles Barton
Co-stars: Bud Abbott Lou Costello Bela Lugosi

ANNE AUBREY

1959 JAZZBOAT
Director: Ken Hughes
Co-stars: Anthony Newley Lionel Jeffries Bernie Winters

1959 THE BANDIT OF ZHOBE
Director: John Gilling
Co-stars: Victor Mature Anthony Newley Norman Woolland

1959 THE KILLERS OF KILIMANJARO
Director: Richard Thorpe
Co-stars: Robert Taylor Anthony Newley

1961 HELLIONS
Director: Ken Annakin
Co-stars: Richard Todd Lionel Jeffries James Booth Marty Wilde

SKYE AUBREY

1972 THE CAREY TREATMENT
Director: Blake Edwards
Co-stars: James Coburn Jennifer O'Neill Elizabeth Allan

CECILE AUBRY

1949 MANON
Director: Henri-Georges Clouzot
Co-stars: Michel Auclair Serge Reggiani Gabrielle Dorziat

1950 THE BLACK ROSE
Director: Henry Hathaway
Co-stars: Tyrone Power Orson Welles Jack Hawkins

DANIELE AUBRY

1965 OPERATION CIA
Director: Christian Nyby
Co-stars: Burt Reynolds John Hoyt

MAXINE AUDLEY

1954 THE SLEEPING TIGER
Director: Joseph Losey
Co-stars: Dirk Bogarde Alexis Smith Alexander Knox

1957 THE PRINCE AND THE SHOWGIRL
Director: Laurence Olivier
Co-stars: Laurence Olivier Marilyn Monroe Richard Wattis

1957 A KING IN NEW YORK
Director: Charles Chaplin
Co-stars: Charles Chaplin Dawn Addams Michael Chaplin

1958 DUNKIRK
Director: Leslie Norman
Co-stars: John Mills Bernard Lee Richard Attenborough

1958 THE VIKINGS
Director: Richard Fleischer
Co-stars: Kirk Douglas Tony Curtis Ernest Borgnine

1959 HELL IS A CITY
Director: Val Guest
Co-stars: Stanley Baker Donald Pleasence Billie Whitelaw

1960 PEEPING TOM
Director: Michael Powell
Co-stars: Carl Boehm Moira Shearer Anna Massey

1960	**BLUEBEARD'S TEN HONEYMOONS**
Director:	Roy Parkinson
Co-stars:	George Sanders Corinne Calvet Patricia Roc

1960	**THE TRIALS OF OSCAR WILDE**
Director:	Ken Hughes
Co-stars:	Peter Finch Yvonne Mitchell James Mason

1961	**PETTICOAT PIRATES**
Director:	David MacDonald
Co-stars:	Charlie Drake Cecil Parker Anne Heywood

1962	**VENGEANCE**
Director:	Freddie Francis
Co-stars:	Anne Heywood Cecil Parker Peter Van Eyck

1964	**THE BATTLE OF THE VILLA FIORITA**
Director:	Delmer Davis
Co-stars:	Maureen O'Hara Rossano Brazzi Richard Todd

1964	**A JOLLY BAD FELLOW**
Director:	Don Chaffey
Co-stars:	Leo McKern Dennis Price Janet Munro

1967	**HERE WE GO ROUND THE MULBERRY BUSH**
Director:	Clive Donner
Co-stars:	Barry Evans Judy Geeson Angela Scoular

1968	**HOUSE OF CARDS**
Director:	John Guillermin
Co-stars:	George Peppard Inger Stevens Orson Welles

1968	**SINFUL DAVEY**
Director:	John Huston
Co-stars:	John Hurt Pamela Franklyn Ronald Fraser

1969	**THE LOOKING GLASS WAR**
Director:	Frank Pierson
Co-stars:	Christopher Jones Pia Degermark Susan George

1969	**FRANKENSTEIN MUST BE DESTROYED**
Director:	Terence Fisher
Co-stars:	Peter Cushing Freddie Jones

1972	**RUNNING SCARED**
Director:	David Hemmings
Co-stars:	Robert Powell Gayle Hunnicutt Georgia Brown

STEPHANE AUDRAN (*Married Claude Chabrol*)

1959	**LES COUSINS**
Director:	Claude Chabrol
Co-stars:	Gerard Blain Jean-Claude Brialy Julliette Mayniel

1960	**LES BONNES FEMMES**
Director:	Claude Chabrol
Co-stars:	Bernadette Lafont Clothilde Joano

1962	**LANDRU**
Director:	Claude Chabrol
Co-stars:	Charles Denner Danielle Darrieux Hildegarde Neff

1968	**LES BICHES**
Director:	Claude Chabrol
Co-stars:	Jacqueline Sassard Jean-Louis Trintignant

1968	**THE CHAMPAGNE MURDERS**
Director:	Claude Chabrol
Co-stars:	Anthony Perkins Maurice Ronet

1968	**LA FEMME INFIDELE**
Director:	Claude Chabrol
Co-stars:	Michel Bouquet Maurice Ronet

1969	**THE LADY IN THE CAR WITH GLASSES AND A GUN**
Director:	Anatole Litvak
Co-star:	Samantha Eggar Oliver Reed

1969	**LE BOUCHER**
Director:	Claude Chabrol
Co-stars:	Jean Yanne Antonio Passalia Mario Beccaria

1971	**JUSTE AVANT LA NUIT**
Director:	Claude Chabrol
Co-stars:	Michel Bouquet Francois Perrier

1972	**THE DISCREET CHARM OF THE BOURGEOISIE**
Director:	Luis Bunuel
Co-stars:	Fernando Rey Bulle Ogier

1974	**VINCENT, FRANCOIS, PAUL AND THE OTHERS**
Director:	Claude Sautet
Co-stars:	Yves Montand Michel Piccoli

1974	**AND THEN THERE WERE NONE**
Director:	Peter Collinson
Co-stars:	Oliver Reed Elke Sommer Charles Aznavour

1975	**THE BLACK BIRD**
Director:	Davld Giler
Co-stars:	George Segal Lee Patrick Elisha Cook

1977	**THE DEVIL'S ADVOCATE**
Director:	Guy Green
Co-stars:	John Mills Timothy West Raf Vallone

1977	**SILVER BEARS**
Director:	Ivan Passer
Co-stars:	Michael Caine Cybill Shepherd Louis Jourdan

1977	**VIOLETTE NOZIERE**
Director:	Claude Chabrol
Co-stars:	Isabelle Huppert Jean Carmier Bernadette Lafont

1978	**BLOOD RELATIVES**
Director:	Claude Chabrol
Co-stars:	Donald Sutherland Donald Pleasence David Hemmings

1979	**EAGLE'S WING**
Director:	Anthony Harvey
Co-stars:	Martin Sheen Sam Waterston Harvey Keitel

1980	**THE BIG RED ONE**
Director:	Samuel Fuller
Co-stars:	Lee Marvin Mark Hamill Robert Carradine

1981	**BRIDESHEAD REVISITED**
Director:	Charles Sturridge
Co-stars:	Jeremy Irons Diana Quick Anthony Andrews

1981	**COUP DE TORCHON**
Director:	Bertrand Tavernier
Co-stars:	Philippe Noiret Isabelle Huppert

1982	**BOULEVARD OF ASSASSINS**
Director:	Boramy Tioulong
Co-stars:	Jean-Louis Trintignant Marie-France Pisier

1982	**SHOCK**
Director:	Sara Robin Davis
Co-stars:	Alain Delon Catherine Deneuve Philippe Leotard

1983	**DEADLY RUN**
Director:	Claude Miller
Co-stars:	Isabelle Adjani Michel Serrault Genevieve Page

1984	**POULET AU VINAIGRE**
Director:	Claude Chabrol
Co-stars:	Jean Poiret Michel Bouquet Pauline Lafont

1985	**THE SUN ALSO RISES**
Director:	James Goldstone
Co-stars:	Jane Seymour Hart Bochner Robert Carradine

1987	**BABETTE'S FEAST**
Director:	Gabriel Axel
Co-stars:	Jean-Philippe Lafont Bibi Andersson Jarl Kulle

1989	**SONS**
Director:	Alexandre Rockwell
Co-stars:	William Forsythe D. B. Sweeny Jennifer Beals

CLAUDINE AUGER

1965 THUNDERBALL
Director: Terence Young
Co-stars: Sean Connery Adolfo Celi Luciana Paluzzi

1967 TRIPLE CROSS
Director: Terence Young
Co-stars: Christopher Plummer Yul Brynner Trevor Howard

1971 LAST HOUSE ON THE LEFT: PART 2
Director: Mario Bava
Co-stars: Claudio Volonte Isa Miranda Laura Betti

1984 SECRET PLACES
Director: Zelda Baron
Co-stars: Marie-Therese Relin Jenny Agutter Tara MacGowran

1993 SALT ON OUR SKIN
Director: Andrew Birkin
Co-stars: Greta Scacchi Vincent D'Onoffrio Petra Berndt

PERNILLA AUGUST

1992 THE BEST INTENTIONS
Director: Bille August
Co-stars: Samuel Froler Max Von Sydow Mona Malm

PHOEBE AUGUSTINE

1992 TWIN PEAKS: FIRE WALK WITH ME
Director: David Lynch
Co-stars: Sheryl Lee Ray Wise Dana Ashbrook

EWA AULIN

1968 CANDY
Director: Christian Marquand
Co-stars: Marlon Brando Charles Aznavour Richard Burton

1969 START THE REVOLUTION WITHOUT ME
Director: Bud Yorkin
Co-stars: Donald Sutherland Gene Wilder

MARIE AULT

1923 WOMAN TO WOMAN
Director: Graham Cutts
Co-stars: Betty Compson Clive Brook

1926 THE LODGER
Director: Alfred Hitchcock
Co-stars: June Ivor Novello Arthur Chesney

1928 KITTY
Director: Victor Saville
Co-stars: John Stuart Estelle Brody Dorothy Cumming

1928 DAWN
Director: Herbert Wilcox
Co-stars: Sybil Thorndike Mary Brough Anna Neagle

1941 MAJOR BARBARA
Director: Gabriel Pascal
Co-stars: Rex Harrison Wendy Hiller Robert Morley

1941 LOVE ON THE DOLE
Director: John Baxter
Co-stars: Deborah Kerr Clifford Evans

TINA AUMONT

1975 ILLUSTRIOUS CORPSES
Director: Francesco Rosi
Co-stars: Lino Ventura Alain Cuny Max Von Sydow

1976 CASANOVA
Director: Federico Fellini
Co-stars: Donald Sutherland Cicely Browne Carmen Scarpitta

1976 A MATTER OF TIME
Director: Vincent Minnelli
Co-stars: Liza Minnelli Ingrid Bergman Charles Boyer

CHARLOTTE AUSTIN

1952 RAINBOW ROUND MY SHOULDER
Director: Richard Quine
Co-stars: Frankie Laine Billy Daniels Arthur Franz

1954 GORILLA AT LARGE
Director: Harmon Jones
Co-stars: Anne Bancroft Lee J. Cobb Cameron Mitchell

1955 DADDY LONG LEGS
Director: Jean Negulesco
Co-stars: Fred Astaire Leslie Caron Thelma Ritter

1957 THE MAN WHO TURNED TO STONE
Director: Leslie Kardos
Co-stars: Victor Jory Ann Doran Paul Cavanagh

KAREN AUSTIN

1985 SUMMER RENTAL
Director: Carl Reiner
Co-stars: John Candy Richard Crenna Rip Torn

1986 ASSASSIN
Director: Sandor Stern
Co-stars: Robert Conrad Robert Webber Richard Young

1988 LAURA LANSING SLEPT HERE
Director: George Schaefer
Co-stars: Katherine Hepburn Joel Higgins

1989 COLUMBO GOES TO THE GUILLOTINE
Director: Leo Penn
Co-stars: Peter Falk Anthony Andrews

1989 THE CASE OF THE HILLSIDE STRANGLERS
Director: Steven Gethers
Co-stars: Richard Crenna Billy Zane

PAM AUSTIN

1964 KISSIN' COUSINS
Director: Gene Nelson
Co-stars: Elvis Presley Arthur O'Connell Glenda Farrell

TERI AUSTIN

1989 FALSE WITNESS
Director: Arthur Alan Seidelman
Co-stars: Phylicia Rashad George Grizzard

TERRY AUSTIN

1947 BORN TO SPEED

1947 PHILO VANCE'S GAMBLE
Co-star: Alan Curtis

1947 PHILO VANCE RETURNS
Co-star: William Wright

VIVIAN AUSTIN

1944 NIGHT CLUB GIRL
Co-stars: Billy Dunn Leon Velasco

1944 TRIGGER TRAIL
Co-stars: Rod Cameron Fuzzy Knight

DOE AVEDON

1954 THE HIGH AND THE MIGHTY
Director: William Wellman
Co-stars: John Wayne Robert Newton Robert Stack

1954 DEEP IN MY HEART
Director: Stanley Donen
Co-stars: Jose Ferrer Merle Oberon Paul Henreid

1956 THE BOSS
Director: Byron Haskin
Co-stars: John Payne William Bishop Gloria McGhee

MARGARET AVERY
Nominated For Best Supporting Actress In 1985 For "The Color Purple"

1973   MAGNUM FORCE
Director: Ted Post
Co-stars: Clint Eastwood Hal Holbrook David Soul

1977   SCOTT JOPLIN
Director: Jeremy Paul Kagan
Co-stars: Billy Dee Williams Clifton Davis Seymour Cassel

1985   THE COLOR PURPLE
Director: Steven Spielberg
Co-stars: Whoopi Goldberg Oprah Winfrey Danny Glover

1988   BLUEBERRY HILL
Director: Strathford Hamilton
Co-stars: Carrie Snodgress Jennifer Rubin

1990   HEAT WAVE
Director: Kevin Hooks
Co-stars: Cicely Tyson James Earl Jones Sally Kirkland

ANGEL AVILES

1992   CHAIN OF DESIRE
Director: Temistocles Lopez
Co-stars: Linda Fiorentino Elias Koteas Grace Zabriskie

1993   MY CRAZY LIFE
Director: Allison Anders
Co-stars: Seidy Lopez Jacob Vargas

MILI AVITAL

1996   DEAD MAN
Director: Jim Jarmusch
Co-stars: Johnny Depp John Hurt Robert Mitchum

NINA AXELROD

1980   MOTEL HELL
Director: Kevin Connor
Co-stars: Rory Calhoun Paul Linke Nancy Parsons

1983   CROSS COUNTRY
Director: Paul Lynch
Co-stars: Richard Beymer Michael Ironside

ANN AYARS

1942   NAZI AGENT
Director: Jules Dassin
Co-stars: Conrad Veidt Dorothy Tree

1942   DR. KILDARE'S VICTORY
Director: W. S. Van Dyke
Co-stars: Lew Ayres Lionel Barrymore Robert Sterling

1943   THE HUMAN COMEDY
Director: Clarence Brown
Co-stars: Mickey Rooney Frank Morgan Marsha Hunt

1943   REUNION IN FRANCE
Director: Jules Dassin
Co-stars: Joan Crawford John Wayne Philip Dorn

1951   THE TALES OF HOFFMAN
Director: Michael Powell
Co-stars: Robert Rounsville Robert Helpman

AGNES AYRES

1921   THE SHEIK
Director: George Melford
Co-stars: Rudolph Valentino Adolphe Menjou Walter Long

1923   HOLLYWOOD
Director: James Cruze
Co-stars: Hope Drown Luke Cosgrove Ruby Lafayette

1926   THE SON OF THE SHEIK
Director: George Fitzmaurice
Co-stars: Rudolph Valentino Vilma Banky

1936   SMALL TOWN GIRL
Director: William Wellman
Co-stars: Janet Gaynor Robert Taylor James Stewart

LEAH AYRES

1983   EDDIE MACON'S RUN
Director: Jeff Kanen
Co-stars: Kirk Douglas John Schneider Lee Purcell

1987   BLOODSPORT
Director: Newt Arnold
Co-stars: Jean-Claude Van Damme Donald Gibb Forest Whitaker

1992   THE PLAYER
Director: Robert Altman
Co-stars: Tim Robbins Greta Scacchi Fred Ward

ROSALIND AYRES

1973   THAT'LL BE THE DAY
Director: Claude Whatham
Co-stars: David Essex Ringo Starr Rosemary Leach

1974   STARDUST
Director: Michael Apted
Co-stars: David Essex Adam Faith Marty Wilde

1974   LITTLE MALCOLM AND HIS STRUGGLE AGAINST THE EUNUCHS
Director: Stuart Cooper
Co-stars: John Hurt John McEnery

1993   EMILY'S GHOST
Director: Colin Finbow
Co-stars: Martin Jarvis Anna Massey Ron Moody

SABINE AZEMA

1983   LIFE IS A BED OF ROSES
Director: Alain Resnais
Co-stars: Vittorio Gassman Geraldine Chaplin

1984   SUNDAY IN THE COUNTRY
Director: Bertrand Tavernier
Co-stars: Louis Ducreux Michel Aumont

1986   MELO
Director: Alain Resnais
Co-stars: Fanny Ardant Pierre Aditi Andre Dusollier

1989   LIFE AND NOTHING BUT
Director: Bertrand Tavernier
Co-stars: Phillippe Noiret Maurice Barrier

1993   SMOKING
Director: Alain Resnais
Co-star: Pierre Arditi

1993   NO SMOKING
Director: Alain Resnais
Co-star: Pierre Arditi

1996   LE BONHEUR
Director: Etienne Chatiliez
Co-star: Michel Serrault Carmen Maura Eric Cantona

SHABANA AZMI

1988   MADAME SOUSATZKA
Director: John Schlesinger
Co-stars: Shirley MacLaine Navin Choudhry Peggy Ashcroft

1992   CITY OF JOY
Director: Roland Joffe
Co-stars: Patrick Swayze Pauline Collins Art Malik

1992   IMMACULATE CONCEPTION
Director: Jamil Dehlavi
Co-stars: James Wilby Melissa Leo James Cossins

CANDICE AZZARA *(Candy)*

1978 **HOUSE CALLS**
Director: Howard Zieff
Co-stars: Walter Matthau Glenda Jackson Art Carney

1980 **FATSO**
Director: Anne Bancroft
Co-stars: Anne Bancroft Dom DeLuise Ron Carey

1982 **MILLION DOLLAR INFIELD**
Director: Hal Cooper
Co-stars: Bonnie Bedelia Robert Costanzo Rob Reiner

1983 **EASY MONEY**
Director: James Signorelli
Co-stars: Rodney Dangerfield Joe Pesci Geraldine Fitzgerald

KARIN BAAL

1968 HANNIBAL BROOKS
Director: Michael Winner
Co-stars: Oliver Reed Michael J. Pollard

BARBARA BABCOCK

1973 BANG THE DRUM SLOWLY
Director: John Hancock
Co-stars: Michael Moriarty Robert De Niro Danny Aiello

1974 CHOSEN SURVIVORS
Director: Sutton Roley
Co-stars: Jackie Cooper Alex Cord Richard Jaeckel

1980 THE BLACK MARBLE
Director: Harold Becker
Co-stars: Robert Foxworth Paula Prentiss James Woods

1982 THE LORDS OF DISCIPLINE
Director: Franc Roddam
Co-stars: David Keith Robert Prosky Michael Biehn

1983 QUARTERBACK PRINCESS
Director: Noel Black
Co-stars: Helen Hunt Don Murray Daphne Zuniga

1984 ATTACK ON FEAR
Director: Mel Damski
Co-stars: Paul Michael Glaser Linda Kelsey Kevin Conway

1985 THAT WAS THEN....THIS IS NOW
Director: Christopher Cain
Co-stars: Emilio Estevez Kim Delaney

1989 HAPPY TOGETHER
Director: Mel Damski
Co-stars: Patrick Dempsey Helen Slater Brad Pitt

1992 FAR AND AWAY
Director: Ron Howard
Co-stars: Tom Cruise Nicole Kidman Robert Prosky

**1993 FUGITIVE NIGHTS:
DANGER IN THE DESERT**
Director: Gary Nelson
Co-stars: Sam Elliott Warren Frost Geno Silva

FABIENNE BABE

1986 FATHERLAND
Director: Kenneth Loach
Co-stars: Gerulf Pannach Cristine Rose

BABY BINK

1994 BABY'S DAY OUT
Director: Patrick Read Johnson
Co-stars: Joe Mantegna Laura Flynn Boyle Brian Haley

BABY LEROY

1933 MISS FANE'S BABY IS STOLEN
Director: Alexander Hall
Co-stars: Dorothy Wieck Alice Brady Jack La Rue

1933 TORCH SINGER
Director: Alexander Hall
Co-stars: Claudette Colbert Ricardo Cortez Lyda Roberti

1933 TILLIE AND GUS
Director: Francis Martin
Co-stars: W.C. Fields Alison Skipworth Jacqueline Wells

1933 A BEDTIME STORY
Director: Norman Taurog
Co-stars: Maurice Chevalier Helen Twelvetrees

1934 IT'S A GIFT
Director: Norman Z. McLeod
Co-stars: W.C. Fields Kathleen Howard Julian Madison

1934 THE OLD-FASHIONED WAY
Director: William Beaudine
Co-stars: W.C. Fields Joe Morison Judith Allen

BABY PEGGY

1923 HOLLYWOOD
Director: James Cruze
Co-stars: Hope Drown Luke Cosgrave Eleanor Lawson

1924 THE LAW FORBIDS
Co-stars: Robert Ellis Elinor Fair

BABY SANDY *(Sandy Lee Henville)*

1939 LITTLE ACCIDENT
Director: Charles Lamont
Co-stars: Hugh Herbert Florence Rice Richard Carlson

1939 UNEXPECTED FATHER
Director: Charles Lamont
Co-stars: Mischa Auer Dennis O'Keefe Shirley Ross

1939 EAST SIDE OF HEAVEN
Director: David Butler
Co-stars: Bing Crosby Joan Blondell Mischa Auer

1940 SANDY IS A LADY
Director: Charles Lamont
Co-stars: Eugene Pallette Mischa Auer Nan Grey

1940 SANDY GETS HER MAN
Director: Otis Garrett
Co-stars: Stuart Erwin Edgar Kennedy Una Merkel

1941 BACHELOR DADDY
Director: Harold Young
Co-stars: Donald Woods Raymond Walburn Edward Everett Horton

LAUREN BACALL

1944 TO HAVE AND HAVE NOT
Director: Howard Hawks
Co-stars: Humphrey Bogart Walter Brennan Hoagy Carmichael

1945 CONFIDENTIAL AGENT
Director: Herman Shumlin
Co-stars: Charles Boyer Katina Paxinou Peter Lorre

1946 THE BIG SLEEP
Director: Howard Hawks
Co-stars: Humphrey Bogart Dorothy Malone Bob Steele

1947 DARK PASSAGE
Director: Delmer Daves
Co-stars: Humphrey Bogart Agnes Moorehead Bruce Bennett

1948 KEY LARGO
Director: John Huston
Co-stars: Humphrey Bogart Edward G. Robinson Claire Trevor

1949 YOUNG MAN OF MUSIC
Director: Michael Curtiz
Co-stars: Kirk Douglas Doris Day Hoagy Carmichael

1950 BRIGHT LEAF
Director: Michael Curtiz
Co-stars: Gary Cooper Patricia Neal Jack Carson

1953   **HOW TO MARRY A MILLIONAIRE**
Director: Jean Negulesco
Co-stars: Marilyn Monroe Betty Grable William Powell

1954   **WOMAN'S WORLD**
Director: Jean Negulesco
Co-stars: Clifton Webb Van Heflin June Allyson

1954   **BLOOD ALLEY**
Director: William Wellman
Co-stars: John Wayne Paul Fix Anita Ekberg

1955   **THE COBWEB**
Director: Vincente Minnelli
Co-stars: Richard Widmark Charles Boyer John Kerr

1956   **WRITTEN ON THE WIND**
Director: Douglas Sirk
Co-stars: Rock Hudson Dorothy Malone Robert Stack

1957   **DESIGNING WOMAN**
Director: Vincente Minnelli
Co-stars: Gregory Peck Dolores Gray Sam Levine

1958   **THE GIFT OF LOVE**
Director: Jean Negulesco
Co-stars: Robert Stack Lorne Greene Evelyn Rudie

1959   **NORTHWEST FRONTIER**
Director: J. Lee-Thompson
Co-stars: Kenneth More Herbert Lom Wilfred Hyde-White

1964   **SEX AND THE SINGLE GIRL**
Director: Richard Quine
Co-stars: Natalie Wood Tony Curtis Henry Fonda

1964   **SHOCK TREATMENT**
Director: Denis Sanders
Co-stars: Roddy McDowall Carol Lynley Stuart Whitman

1966   **THE MOVING TARGET**
Director: Jack Smight
Co-stars: Paul Newman Shelley Winters Janet Leigh

1974   **MURDER ON THE ORIENT EXPRESS**
Director: Sidney Lumet
Co-stars: Albert Finney Ingrid Bergman Wendy Hiller

1976   **THE SHOOTIST**
Director: Don Siegel
Co-stars: John Wayne Ron Howard James Stewart

1978   **PERFECT GENTLEMEN**
Director: Jackie Cooper
Co-stars: Ruth Gordon Sandy Dennis Robert Alda

1979   **HEALTH**
Director: Robert Altman
Co-stars: Glenda Jackson James Garner Carol Burnett

1981   **THE FAN**
Director: Edward Bianchi
Co-stars: James Garner Michael Biehn

1986   **NOT QUITE JERUSALEM**
Director: Lewis Gilbert
Co-stars: Joanna Pacula Sam Robards Todd Graff

1987   **APPOINTMENT WITH DEATH**
Director: Michael Winner
Co-stars: Peter Ustinov John Gielgud Carrie Fisher

1988   **MR NORTH**
Director: Danny Huston
Co-stars: Anthony Edwards Robert Mitchum Anjelica Huston

1988   **TREE OF HANDS**
Director: Giles Foster
Co-stars: Helen Shaver Peter Firth Paul McGann

1990   **MISERY**
Director: Rob Reiner
Co-stars: Kathy Bates James Caan Richard Farnsworth

1990   **DINNER AT EIGHT**
Director: Ron Lago Marsino
Co-stars: John Mahoney Marsha Mason Harry Hamlin

1991   **ALL I WANT FOR CHRISTMAS**
Director: Robert Lieberman
Co-stars: Leslie Nielsen Jamey Sheridan

1992   **THE PORTRAIT**

1993   **A FOREIGN FIELD**
Director: Charles Sturridge
Co-stars: Alec Guinness Leo McKern Jeanne Moreau

1997   **THE MIRROR HAS TWO FACES**
Director: Barbara Streisand
Co-stars: Barbara Streisand Jeff Bridges George Segal

BARBARA BACH *(Married Ringo Starr)*

1977   **THE SPY WHO LOVED ME**
Director: Lewis Gilbert
Co-stars: Roger Moore Curt Jurgens Richard Kiel

1978   **FORCE TEN FROM NAVARONE**
Director: Guy Hamilton
Co-stars: Robert Shaw Edward Fox Harrison Ford

1979   **JAGUAR LIVES!**
Director: Ernest Pintoff
Co-stars: Joe Lewis Christopher Lee Woody Strode

1981   **CAVEMAN**
Director: Carl Gottlieb
Co-stars: Ringo Starr Dennis Quaid Jack Gilford

1984   **GIVE MY REGARDS TO BROAD STREET**
Director: Peter Webb
Co-stars: Paul McCartney Ringo Starr Bryan Brown

CATHERINE BACH

1974   **THUNDERBOLT AND LIGHTFOOT**
Director: Michael Cimino
Co-stars: Clint Eastwood Jeff Bridges

1974   **THE MIDNIGHT MAN**
Director: Burt Lancaster
Co-stars: Burt Lancaster Susan Clark Joan Lorring

1975   **HUSTLE**
Director: Robert Aldrich
Co-stars: Burt Reynolds Catherine Deneuve Ben Johnson

1983   **CANNONBALL RUN II**
Director: Hal Needham
Co-stars: Burt Reynolds Dean Martin Frank Sinatra

1990   **MASTERS OF MENACE**
Director: Daniel Raskov
Co-star: David Rasche

VIVI BACH

1960   **ELECTRA ONE**
Director: Alfonso Balcazel
Co-stars: George Martin Michel Montfort

1963   **DEATH DRUMS ALONG THE RIVER**
Director: Lawrence Huntington
Co-stars: Richard Todd Marianne Koch

STEPHANIE BACHELOR

1944   **EXPERIMENT PERILOUS**
Director: Jacques Tourneur
Co-stars: Hedy Lamarr Paul Lukas George Brent

1944   **SECRETS OF SCOTLAND YARD**
Director: George Blair
Co-stars: C. Aubrey Smith Edgar Barrier Lionel Atwill

1945   **SCOTLAND YARD INVESTIGATOR**
Director: George Blair
Co-stars: C. Aubrey Smith Erich Von Stroheim

1945   **GANGS OF THE WATERFRONT**
Director: George Blair
Co-stars: Robert Armstrong Marion Martin

1945   **EARL CARROLL VANITIES**
Director: Joseph Santley
Co-stars: Constance Moore Dennis O'Keefe Pinky Lee

1947   **BLACKMAIL**
Co-stars: William Marshall Grant Withers

1947   **SPRINGTIME IN THE SIERRAS**
Co-stars: Roy Rogers

OLGA BACLANOVA

1928   **THE DOCKS OF NEW YORK**
Director: Josef Von Sternberg
Co-stars: George Bancroft Betty Compson

1932   **DOWNSTAIRS**
Director: Monta Bell
Co-stars: John Gilbert Virginia Bruce Paul Lukas

1932   **BILLION DOLLAR SCANDAL**
Director: Harry Joe Brown
Co-stars: Robert Armstrong Constance Cummings

1932   **FREAKS** *(Banned In Britain For 30 Years)*
Director: Tod Browning
Co-stars: Wallace Ford Leila Hyams

1943   **CLAUDIA**
Director: Edmund Goulding
Co-stars: Robert Young Dorothy McGuire Ina Clare

ANGELA BADDELEY

1931   **THE GHOST TRAIN**
Director: Walter Forde
Co-stars: Jack Hulbert Cicely Courtneidge Ann Todd

1931   **THE SPECKLED BAND**
Director: Jack Raymond
Co-stars: Raymond Massey Athole Stewart Nancy Price

1932   **ARMS AND THE MAN**
Director: Cecil Lewis
Co-stars: Barry Jones Anne Grey

1934   **THOSE WERE THE DAYS**
Director: Thomas Bentley
Co-stars: Will Hay John Mills Iris Hoey

1948   **QUARTET**
Director: Ken Annakin
Co-stars: Basil Radford Naunton Wayne Dirk Bogarde

HERMIONE BADDELEY
Nominated For Best Supporting Actress In 1959 For "Room At The Top"

1923   **THE GUNS OF LOOS**
Director: Sinclair Hill
Co-stars: Madeline Carroll Henry Victor Bobby Howes

1935   **ROYAL CAVALCADE**
Director: Marcel Varnel
Co-stars: Marie Lohr John Mills Reginald Gardiner

1941   **KIPPS**
Director: Carol Reed
Co-stars: Michael Redgrave Michael Wilding Diana Wynyard

1947   **BRIGHTON ROCK**
Director: John Boulting
Co-stars: Richard Attenborough William Hartnell Carol Marsh

1948   **NO ROOM AT THE INN**
Director: Dan Birt
Co-stars: Freda Jackson Joy Shelton Joan Dowling

1948   **QUARTET**
Director: Arthur Crabtree
Co-stars: George Cole Susan Shaw Mervyn Johns

1948   **THE WOMAN IN QUESTION**
Director: Anthony Asquith
Co-stars: Jean Kent Dirk Bogarde Susan Shaw

1949   **PASSPORT TO PIMLICO**
Director: Henry Cornelius
Co-stars: Stanley Holloway Margaret Rutherford

1949   **DEAR MR. PROHACK**
Director: Thornton Freeland
Co-stars: Cecil Parker Dirk Bogarde Glynis Johns

1951   **SCROOGE**
Director: Brian Desmond Hurst
Co-stars: Alastair Sim Mervyn Johns Jack Warner

1951   **THERE IS ANOTHER SUN**
Director: Lewis Gilbert
Co-stars: Maxwell Reed Susan Shaw Laurence Harvey

1951   **TOM BROWN'S SCHOOLDAYS**
Director: Gordon Parry
Co-stars: John Howard Davies Robert Newton

1952   **TIME GENTLEMEN PLEASE!**
Director: Lewis Gilbert
Co-stars: Eddie Byrne Jane Barrett Dora Bryan

1952   **THE PICKWICK PAPERS**
Director: Noel Langley
Co-stars: James Hayter James Donald Hermione Gingold

1953   **COUNTERSPY**
Director: Vernon Sewell
Co-stars: Dermot Walsh Hazel Court Hugh Latimer

1954   **THE BELLES OF ST. TRINIANS**
Director: Frank Launder
Co-stars: Alastair Sim George Cole Beryl Reid

1956   **WOMEN WITHOUT MEN**
Director: Elmo Williams
Co-stars: Beverley Michaels Joan Rice Avril Angers

1959   **JET STORM**
Director: Cy Endfield
Co-stars: Richard Attenborough Mai Zetterling Diane Cilento

1959   **ROOM AT THE TOP**
Director: Jack Clayton
Co-stars: Laurence Harvey Simone Signoret Heather Sears

1959   **EXPRESSO BONGO**
Director: Val Guest
Co-stars: Laurence Harvey Sylvia Syms Cliff Richard

1960   **MIDNIGHT LACE**
Director: David Miller
Co-stars: Doris Day Rex Harrison Roddy McDowall

1961   **RAG DOLL**
Director: Lance Comfort
Co-stars: Jesse Conrad Kenneth Griffith Patrick MaGee

1961   **INFORMATION RECEIVED**
Director: Robert Lynn
Co-stars: William Sylvester Sabrina Sesselman

1964   **MARY POPPINS**
Director: Robert Stevenson
Co-stars: Julie Andrews Dick Van Dyke Glynis Johns

1964   **THE UNSINKABLE MOLLY BROWN**
Director: Charles Walters
Co-stars: Debbie Reynolds Harve Presnell

1965 DO NOT DISTURB
Director: Ralph Levy
Co-stars: Doris Day Rod Taylor Sergio Fantoni

1965 MARRIAGE ON THE ROCKS
Director: Jack Donohue
Co-stars: Frank Sinatra Dean Martin Deborah Kerr

1966 THE ADVENTURES OF BULLWHIP GRIFFIN
Director: James Neilson
Co-stars: Roddy McDowall Karl Malden

1967 THE HAPPIEST MILLIONAIRE
Director: Norman Tokar
Co-stars: Fred MacMurray Tommy Steele Greer Garson

1970 THE ARISTOCATS *(Voice)*
Director: Wolfgang Reitherman
Co-stars: Eva Gabor Maurice Chevalier

1972 UP THE FRONT
Director: Bob Kellett
Co-stars: Frankie Howerd Bill Fraser Zsa Zsa Gabor

1979 C.H.O.M.P.S.
Director: Don Chaffey
Co-stars: Wesley Eure Jim Backus Regis Toomey

SARAH BADEL
1978 SHE FELL AMONG THIEVES
Director: Clive Donner
Co-stars: Malcolm McDowell Eileen Atkins Karen Dotrice

1988 A PERFECT SPY
Director: Peter Smith
Co-stars: Alec Guinness Peggy Ashcroft Jane Booker

1991 NOT WITHOUT MY DAUGHTER
Director: Brian Gilbert
Co-stars: Sally Field Alfred Molina

NINA BADEN-SEMPER
1973 LOVE THY NEIGHBOUR
Director: John Robins
Co-stars: Jack Smethurst Kate Williams Rudolph Walker

SILVIA BADESCO
1974 STAVISKY
Director: Alain Resnais
Co-stars: Jean-Paul Belnondo Charles Boyer Anny Duperey

MARY BADHAM *(Child)*
Nominated For Best Supporting Actress In 1962 For "To Kill A Mockingbird"
1962 TO KILL A MOCKINGBIRD
Director: Robert Mulligan
Co-stars: Gregory Peck Philip Alford Rosemary Murphy

1966 THIS PROPERTY IS CONDEMNED
Director: Sydney Pollack
Co-stars: Natalie Wood Robert Redford Charles Bronson

1966 LET'S KILL UNCLE
Director: William Castle
Co-stars: Nigel Green Pat Cardi Robert Pickering

ANNETTE BADLAND
1989 CHINESE WHISPERS
Director: Stuart Burge
Co-stars: Niall Buggy Gary Waldhorn

1994 CAPTIVES
Director: Angela Pope
Co-stars: Tim Roth Julia Ormond Peter Capaldi

JANE BADLER
1983 THE FIRST TIME
Director: Charlie Laventhal
Co-stars: Tim Choate Krista Errickson Wendy Fulton

1983 V
Director: Kenneth Johnson
Co-stars: Marc Singer Faye Grant Robert Englund

JOAN BAEZ
1967 DON'T LOOK BACK
Director: D. A. Pennebaker
Co-stars: Bob Dylan Alan Price Donovan

1971 CELEBRATION AT BIG SUR
Director: Baird Bryant
Co-stars: Joni Mitchell Crosby, Stills And Nash

CAROL BAGDASARIAN
1980 THE OCTAGON
Director: Eric Karson
Co-stars: Chuck Norris Karen Carlson Lee Van Cleef

1985 THE AURORA ENCOUNTER
Director: J. McCullogh
Co-stars: Jack Elam Peter Brown

MAXINE BAHNS
1996 SHE'S THE ONE
Director: Edward Burns
Co-stars: John Mahoney Cameron Diaz Jennifer Aniston

1995 THE BROTHERS McMULLEN
Director: Edward Burns
Co-stars: Edward Burns

FRANCESCA BAHRLE
1939 FLYING FIFTY-FIVE
Director: Reginald Denham
Co-stars: Derrick De Marney Marius Goring Ronald Shiner

CYNTHIA BAILEY
1990 WITHOUT YOU I'M NOTHING
Director: John Boskovich
Co-stars: Sandra Bernhard John Doe Steve Antin

MARION BAILEY
1988 COPPERS
Director: Ted Clisby
Co-stars: Tim Roth Reece Dinsdale Sandra Voe

PEARL BAILEY
1948 ISN'T IT ROMANTIC?
Director: Norman Z. McLeod
Co-stars: Veronica Lake Mona Freeman Patric Knowles

1954 CARMEN JONES
Director: Otto Preminger
Co-stars: Dorothy Dandridge Harry Belafonte Diahann Carroll

1956 THAT CERTAIN FEELING
Director: Norman Panama
Co-stars: Bob Hope Eva Marie Saint George Sanders

1958 ST. LOUIS BLUES
Director: Allen Reisner
Co-stars: Nat King Cole Eartha Kit Cab Calloway

1959 PORGY AND BESS
Director: Otto Preminger
Co-stars: Sidney Poitier Dorothy Dandridge Sammy Davis

1960 ALL THE FINE YOUNG CANNIBALS
Director: Michael Anderson
Co-stars: Robert Wagner Natalie Wood

1970 THE LANDLORD
Director: Hal Ashby
Co-stars: Beau Bridges Lee Grant Diana Sands

1976 NORMAN...IS THAT YOU?
Director: George Schlatter
Co-stars: Redd Foxx Michael Warren Dennis Dugan

1977 TUBBY THE TUBA *(Voice)*
Director: Alexander Schure
Co-stars: Dick Van Dyke Jane Powell Ruth Enders

1989 PETER GUNN
Director: Blake Edwards
Co-stars: Peter Strauss Barbara Williams David Rappaport

CHRISTIANE BAILLY

1984 FAVOURITES OF THE MOON
Director: Otar Iosseliani
Co-stars: Katja Rupe Mathieu Amalric

PAULE BAILLARGEON

1987 I'VE HEARD THE MERMAIDS SINGING
Director: Patricia Rozema
Co-stars: Sheila McCarthy John Evans

NATASHA BAIN

1994 ZINKY BOYS GO UNDERGROUND
Director: Paul Tickell
Co-stars: Dmitri Shevchenko Olga Rodina

SHERRY BAINES

1987 TESTIMONY
Director: Tony Palmer
Co-stars: Ben Kingsley Terence Rigby Ronald Pickup

FAY BAINTER
Oscar For Best Supporting Actress In 1938 For "Jezebel"
Nominated For Best Supporting Actress In 1938 For "White Banners"
And In 1961 For "The Children's Hour"

1933 THIS SIDE OF HEAVEN
Director: William Howard
Co-stars: Lionel Barrymore Mae Clarke Una Merkel

1937 MAKE WAY FOR TOMORROW
Director: Leo McCarey
Co-stars: Victor Moore Beulah Bondi Thomas Mitchell

1937 QUALITY STREET
Director: George Stevens
Co-stars: Katherine Hepburn Franchot Tone Joan Fontaine

1938 WHITE BANNERS
Director: Edmund Goulding
Co-stars: Claude Rains Jackie Cooper Bonita Granville

1938 THE SHINING HOUR
Director: Frank Borzage
Co-stars: Joan Crawford Melvyn Douglas Margaret Sullavan

1938 MOTHER CAREY'S CHICKENS
Director: Rowland Lee
Co-stars: Anne Shirley Ruby Keeler Walter Brennan

1938 JEZEBEL
Director: William Wyler
Co-stars: Bette Davis Henry Fonda George Brent

1938 THE ARKANSAS TRAVELLER
Director: Alfred Santell
Co-stars: Bob Burns Jean Parker Irvin S. Cobb

1939 DAUGHTERS COURAGEOUS
Director: Michael Curtiz
Co-stars: Claude Rains John Garfield Lola Lane

1939 THE LADY AND THE MOB
Director: Ben Stoloff
Co-stars: Ida Lupino Lee Bowman Henry Armetta

1939 OUR NEIGHBOURS THE CARTERS
Director: Ralph Murphy
Co-stars: Frank Craven Genevieve Tobin Edmund Lowe

1939 YES, MY DARLING DAUGHTER
Director: William Keighley
Co-stars: Priscilla Lane Roland Yound Jeffrey Lynn

1940 YOUNG TOM EDISON
Director: Norman Taurog
Co-stars: Mickey Rooney Eugene Pallette George Bancroft

1940 A BILL OF DIVORCEMENT
Director: John Farrow
Co-stars: Maureen O'Hara Adolphe Menjou Herbert Marshall

1940 OUR TOWN
Director: Sam Wood
Co-stars: Frank Craven William Holden Martha Scott

1940 MARYLAND
Co-stars: John Payne Walter Brennan

1941 BABES ON BROADWAY
Director: Busby Berkeley
Co-stars: Judy Garland Mickey Rooney Virginia Weidler

1942 JOURNEY FOR MARGARET
Director: W. S. Van Dyke
Co-stars: Margaret O'Brien Robert Young Laraine Day

1942 MRS.WIGGS OF THE CABBAGE PATCH
Director: Ralph Murphy
Co-stars: Hugh Herbert Vera Vague

1942 THE WAR AGAINST MRS HADLEY
Director: Harold Bucquet
Co-stars: Edward Arnold Richard Ney Jean Rogers

1942 WOMAN OF THE YEAR
Director: George Stevens
Co-stars: Spencer Tracy Katherine Hepburn William Bendix

1943 SALUTE TO THE MARINES
Director: S. Sylyan Simon
Co-stars: Wallace Beery Marilyn Maxwell Noah Beery

1943 PRESENTING LILY MARS
Director: Norman Taurog
Co-stars: Judy Garland Van Heflin Richard Carlson

1943 THE HUMAN COMEDY
Director: Clarence Brown
Co-stars: Frank Morgan Mickey Rooney James Craig

1943 THE HEAVENLY BODY
Director: Alexander Hall
Co-stars: William Powell Hedy Lamarr James Craig

1943 CRY HAVOC
Director: Richard Thorpe
Co-stars: Margaret Sullavan Joan Blondell Ann Sothern

1944 DARK WATERS
Director: Andre De Toth
Co-stars: Merle Oberon Franchot Tone Rex Ingram

1944 THREE IS A FAMILY
Director: Edward Ludwig
Co-stars: Charles Ruggles Marjorie Reynolds Helen Broderick

1945 STATE FAIR
Director: Walter Lang
Co-stars: Charles Winninger Dick Haymes Jeanne Crain

1946 THE KID FROM BROOKLYN
Director: Norman Z. McLeod
Co-stars: Danny Kaye Vera-Ellen Virgina Mayo

1946 THE VIRGINIAN
Director: Stuart Gilmore
Co-stars: Joel McCrea Brian Donlevy Sonny Tufts

1947	**DEEP VALLEY**
Director:	Jean Negulesco
Co-stars:	Ida Lupino Dane Clark Wayne Morris

1947	**THE SECRET LIFE OF WALTER MITTY**
Director:	Norman Z. McLeod
Co-stars:	Danny Kaye Virginia Mayo

1948	**JUNE BRIDE**
Director:	Bretaigne Windust
Co-stars:	Bette Davis Robert Montgomery Debbie Reynolds

1948	**GIVE MY REGARDS TO BROADWAY**
Director:	Lloyd Bacon
Co-stars:	Dan Dailey Charles Winninger Nancy Guild

1951	**CLOSE TO MY HEART**
Director:	William Keighley
Co-stars:	Ray Milland Gene Tierney Howard St. John

1953	**THE PRESIDENT'S LADY**
Director:	Henry Levin
Co-stars:	Charlton Heston Susan Hayward John McIntire

1961	**THE CHILDREN'S HOUR**
Director:	William Wyler
Co-stars:	Audrey Hepburn Shirley Maclaine James Garner

BELLE BAKER

1929	**SONG OF LOVE**
Co-star:	Ralph Graves

1944	**ATLANTIC CITY**
Director:	Ray McCarey
Co-stars:	Constance Moore Brad Taylor Jerry Colonna

BETSY BAKER

1982	**THE EVIL DEAD**
Director:	Sam Raimi
Co-stars:	Bruce Campbell Ellen Sandwiss Sarah York

BLANCHE BAKER

1984	**COLD FEET**
Director:	Bruce Van Dusen
Co-stars:	Griffin Dunne Marissa Chibas Joseph Leon

1985	**EMBASSY**
Director:	Robert Lewis
Co-stars:	Nick Mancuso Mimi Rogers Eli Wallach

1986	**RAW DEAL**
Director:	John Irvin
Co-stars:	Arnold Schwarzenneger Kathryn Harrold Sam Wanamaker

1988	**BLUE JEAN COP**
Director:	James Glickenhaus
Co-stars:	Peter Weller Sam Elliott Patricia Charbonneau

1990	**THE HANDMAID'S TALE**
Director:	Volker Schlorndorff
Co-stars:	Natasha Richardson Robert Duvall

CARROLL BAKER
Nominated For Best Actress In 1956 For "Baby Doll"

1953	**EASY TO LOVE**
Director:	Charles Walters
Co-stars:	Esther Williams Van Johnson Tony Martin

1956	**BABY DOLL**
Director:	Elia Kazan
Co-stars:	Karl Malden Eli Wallach Mildred Dunnock

1956	**GIANT**
Director:	George Stevens
Co-stars:	Elizabeth Taylor Rock Hudson James Dean

1958	**THE BIG COUNTRY**
Director:	William Wyler
Co-stars:	Gregory Peck Jean Simmons Burl Ives

1959	**BUT NOT FOR ME**
Director:	Walter Lang
Co-stars:	Clark Gable Lilli Palmer Thomas Gomez

1959	**THE MIRACLE**
Director:	Irving Rapper
Co-stars:	Roger Moore Walter Slezak Vittorio Gassman

1961	**SOMETHING WILD**
Director:	Jack Garfein
Co-stars:	Ralph Meeker Mildred Dunnock Charles Watts

1961	**BRIDGE TO THE SUN**
Director:	Etienne Ferrier
Co-stars:	James Shigeta James Yagi Tetsuro Tamba

1962	**HOW THE WEST WAS WON**
Director:	John Ford
Co-stars:	Debbie Reynolds James Stewart George Peppard

1962	**STATION SIX SAHARA**
Director:	Seth Holt
Co-stars:	Ian Bannen Peter Van Eyck Denholm Elliott

1964	**CHEYENNE AUTUMN**
Director:	John Ford
Co-stars:	Richard Widmark James Stewart Karl Malden

1964	**THE CARPETBAGGERS**
Director:	Edward Dmytryk
Co-stars:	George Peppard Alan Ladd Martha Hyer

1965	**HARLOW**
Director:	Gordon Douglas
Co-stars:	Martin Balsam Red Buttons Angela Lansbury

1965	**SYLVIA**
Director:	Gordon Douglas
Co-stars:	George Maharis Joanne Dru Ann Southern

1965	**MISTER MOSES**
Director:	Ronald Neame
Co-stars:	Robert Mitchum Ian Bannen Alexander Knox

1965	**THE GREATEST STORY EVER TOLD**
Director:	George Stevens
Co-stars:	Max Von Sydow Jose Ferrer Charlton Heston

1967	**JACK OF DIAMONDS**
Director:	Don Taylor
Co-stars:	Joseph Cotten George Hamilton Zsa Zsa Gabor

1971	**CAPTAIN APACHE**
Director:	Alexander Singer
Co-stars:	Lee Van Cleef Stuart Whitmore Percy Herbert

1975	**BLACKMAIL CHASE**
Co-stars:	Arthur Kennedy Curt Jurgens

1975	**JAMES DEAN:** **THE FIRST AMERICAN TEENAGER**
Director:	Ray Connolly
Co-stars:	Natalie Wood Leslie Caron

1977	**ANDY WARHOL'S BAD NEW WORLD**
Director:	Jed Johnson
Co-stars:	Perry King Susan Tyrrell Cyrinda Foxe

1979	**THE WORLD IS FULL OF MARRIED MEN**
Director:	Robert Young
Co-stars:	Anthony Franciosa Paul Nicholas

1980	**THE WATCHER IN THE WOODS**
Director:	John Hough
Co-stars:	Bette Davis David McCallum Ian Bannen

1983	**STAR 80**
Director:	Bob Fosse
Co-stars:	Mariel Hemingway Eric Roberts Cliff Robertson

1986	**NATIVE SON**
Director:	Jerrold Freedman
Co-stars:	Matt Dillon Geraldine Page Art Evans

1987 **IRONWEED**
Director: Hector Babenco
Co-stars: Jack Nicholson Meryl Streep Michael O'Keefe

1990 **KINGERGARTEN COP**
Director: Ivan Reitman
Co-stars: Arnold Schwarzenegger Penelope Ann Miller

1991 **BLONDE FIST**
Director: Frank Clarke
Co-stars: Margi Clarke Ken Hutchison Angela Clarke

1993 **THOSE BEDROOM EYES**
Director: Leon Ichaso
Co-stars: Mimi Rogers William Forsythe Tim Matheson

DIANE BAKER

1959 **THE DIARY OF ANNE FRANK**
Director: George Stevens
Co-stars: Millie Perkins Shelley Winters Ed Wynn

1959 **JOURNEY TO THE CENTER OF THE EARTH**
Director: Henry Levin
Co-stars: James Mason Arleen Dahl Pat Boone

1959 **THE BEST OF EVERYTHING**
Director: Jean Negulesco
Co-stars: Joan Crawford Hope Lange Louis Hayward

1960 **TESS OF THE STORM COUNTRY**
Director: Paul Guilfoyle
Co-stars: Jack Ging Lee Philips Nancy Valentine

1962 **HEMINGWAY'S ADVENTURES OF A YOUNG MAN**
Director: Martin Ritt
Co-stars: Richard Beymer Paul Newman

1962 **NINE HOURS TO RAMA**
Director: Mark Robson
Co-stars: Jose Ferrer Robert Morley Horst Buchholz

1962 **THE 300 SPARTANS**
Director: Rudolph Mate
Co-stars: Richard Egan Ralph Richardson David Farrar

1963 **STRAIT-JACKET**
Director: William Castle
Co-stars: Joan Crawford Leif Erikson Rochelle Hudson

1963 **THE STOLEN HOURS**
Director: Daniel Petrie
Co-stars: Susan Hayward Michael Craig Edward Judd

1963 **THE PRIZE**
Director: Mark Robson
Co-stars: Paul Newman Elke Sommer Edward G. Robinson

1964 **MARNIE**
Director: Alfred Hitchcock
Co-stars: Tippi Hedren Sean Connery Bruce Dern

1965 **MIRAGE**
Director: Edward Dmytryk
Co-stars: Gregory Peck Walter Matthau Walter Abel

1968 **KRAKATOA, EAST OF JAVA**
Director: Bernard Kowalski
Co-stars: Maximillian Schell Rossano Brazzi Brian Keith

1969 **THE HORSE IN THE GREY FLANNEL SUIT**
Director: Norman Tokar
Co-stars: Dean Jones Fred Clark

1969 **THE D.A.:MURDER ONE**
Director: Boris Sagal
Co-stars: Robert Conrad Howard Duff Scott Brady

1970 **THE OLD MAN WHO CRIED WOLF**
Director: Walter Grauman
Co-stars: Edward G. Robinson Ruth Roman Sam Jaffe

1971 **A LITTLE GAME**
Director: Paul Wendkos
Co-stars: Ed Nelson Katy Jurado Howard Duff

1974 **THE LAST SURVIVORS**
Director: Lee Katzin
Co-stars: Martin Sheen Tom Bosley Anne Francis

1976 **BAKER'S HAWK**
Director: Lyman Dayton
Co-stars: Burl Ives Clint Walker Lee Montgomery

1979 **THE PILOT**
Director: Cliff Robertson
Co-stars: Cliff Robertson Gordon MacRae Dana Andrews

1991 **THE SILENCE OF THE LAMBS**
Director: Jonathan Demme
Co-stars: Jodie Foster Anthony Hopkins Scott Glenn

1991 **THE HAUNTED**
Director: Robert Mandel
Co-stars: Jeffrey DeMunn Sally Kirkland Joyce Van Patten

1993 **THE JOY LUCK CLUB**
Director: Wayne Wang
Co-stars: Tsai Chin Lisa Lu France Nuyen

EVADNE BAKER

1965 **THE SOUND OF MUSIC**
Director: Robert Wise
Co-stars: Julie Andrews Christopher Plummer Peggy Wood

FAY BAKER

1950 **THE COMPANY SHE KEEPS**
Director: John Cromwell
Co-stars: Lizabeth Scott Jane Greer Dennis O'Keefe

1951 **THE HOUSE ON TELEGRAPH HILL**
Director: Robert Wise
Co-stars: Richard Basehart Valentina Cortese

HYLDA BAKER

1960 **SATURDAY NIGHT AND SUNDAY MORNING**
Director: Karel Reisz
Co-stars: Albert Finney Rachel Roberts Shirley Ann Field

1967 **UP THE JUNCTION**
Director: Peter Collinson
Co-stars: Suzy Kendall Dennis Waterman Adrienne Posta

1973 **NEAREST AND DEAREST**
Director: John Robins
Co-stars: Jimmy Jewel Madge Hindle Joe Gladwin

JILL BAKER

1987 **HARRY'S KINGDOM**
Director: Robert Young
Co-stars: Timothy West Peter Vaughan Larry Lamb

1989 **BLORE M. P.**
Director: Robert Young
Co-stars: Timothy West Stephen Moore Maggie O'Neill

1989 **TESTIMONY OF A CHILD**
Director: Peter Smith
Co-stars: John Bowe Jonathan Leigh Heather Tobias

JOBY BAKER

1959 **THE LAST ANGRY MAN**
Director: Daniel Mann
Co-stars: Paul Muni David Wayne Betsy Palmer

1960 **THE WACKIEST SHIP IN THE ARMY**
Director: Richard Murphy
Co-stars: Jack Lemmon Ricky Nelson

1967 VALLEY OF MYSTERY
Director: Josef Leytes
Co-stars: Richard Egan Peter Graves Julie Adams

KATHY BAKER

1983 THE RIGHT STUFF
Director: Phillip Kaufman
Co-stars: Sam Shepard Scott Glen Ed Harris

1986 NOBODY'S CHILD
Director: Lee Grant
Co-stars: Marlo Thomas Ray Baker Caroline Kava

1987 STREET SMART
Director: Jerry Schatzberg
Co-stars: Christopher Reeve Mimi Rogers Morgan Freeman

1988 JACKNIFE
Director: David Jones
Co-stars: Robert De Niro Ed Harris Charles Dutton

1988 CLEAN AND SOBER
Director: Glenn Gordon Caron
Co-stars: Michael Keaton Morgan Freeman Tate Donovan

1988 PERMANENT RECORD
Director: Marisa Silver
Co-stars: Alan Boyce Keanu Reeves Jennifer Rubin

1989 DAD
Director: Gary David Goldberg
Co-stars: Jack Lemmon Ted Danson Olympia Dukakis

1990 THE IMAGE
Director: Peter Werner
Co-stars: Albert Finney John Mahoney Marsha Mason

1990 EDWARD SCISSORHANDS
Director: Tim Burton
Co-stars: Johnny Depp Winona Ryder Dianne Wiest

1990 MISTER FROST
Director: Philippe Setbon
Co-stars: Alan Bates Jeff Goldblum Daniel Gelin

1992 ARTICLE 99
Director: Howard Deutch
Co-stars: Ray Liotta Keifer Sutherland Forest Whitaker

1992 JENNIFER EIGHT
Director: Bruce Robinson
Co-stars: Andy Garcia Uma Thurman John Malkovich

1993 MAD DOG AND GLORY
Director: John McNaughton
Co-stars: Robert De Niro Uma Thurman Bill Murray

1994 LUSH LIFE
Director: Michael Elias
Co-stars: Jeff Goldblum Forest Whitaker Lois Chiles

1997 INVENTING THE ABBOTTS
Director: Pat O'Connor
Co-stars: Liv Tyler Jennifer Connelly Billy Crudup

KIRSTEN BAKER

1981 FRIDAY THE 13TH. PART II
Director: Steve Miner
Co-stars: Amy Steel John Furey Adrienne King

LAVERN BAKER

1956 ROCK, ROCK, ROCK!
Director: Michael Schultz
Co-stars: Dyan Cannon Michael Brandon Heather Locklear

JOAN BAKEWELL

1972 THE ADVENTURES OF BARRY MACKENZIE
Director: Bruce Beresford
Co-stars: Barry Crocker Peter Cook

BRENDA BAKKE

1990 I WANT HIM BACK
Director: Catlin Adams
Co-stars: Elliott Gould Brenda Vaccaro Bruce Davison

1993 HOT SHOTS! PART DEUX
Director: Jim Abrahams
Co-stars: Charlie Sheen Lloyd Bridges Valeria Golino

JOSIANNE BALASCO

1981 LE MAITRE D'ECOLE
Director: Claude Berri
Co-stars: Michel Coluche Elaine Mangan

1989 TROP BELLE POUR TOI!
Director: Bertrand Blier
Co-stars: Gerard Depardieu Carole Bouquet

1996 FRENCH TWIST
Director: Josianne Balasco
Co-stars: Victoria Abril Alain Chabat

BELINDA BALASKI

1978 PIRANHA
Director: Joe Dante
Co-stars: Bradford Dillman Heather Menzies Keenan Wynn

1981 THE HOWLING
Director: Joe Dante
Co-stars: Dee Wallace Patrick MacNee Kevin McCarthy

JILL BALCON

1947 NICHOLAS NICKLEBY
Director: Alberto Cavalcanti
Co-stars: Derek Bond Cedric Hardwicke Bernard Miles

1991 EDWARD II
Director: Derek Jarmon
Co-stars: Steven Waddington John Lynch Dudley Sutton

GRETA BALDWIN

1968 PROJECT X
Director: William Castle
Co-stars: Henry Jones Monte Markham

JANIT BALDWIN

1972 PRIME CUT
Director: Michael Ritchie
Co-stars: Gene Hackman Lee Marvin Sissy Spacek

1974 THE CALIFORNIA KID
Director: Richard Heffron
Co-stars: Martin Sheen Vic Morrow Nick Nolte

1977 RUBY
Director: Curtis Harrington
Co-stars: Piper Laurie Stuart Whitman Roger Davis

CARLA BALENDA (A HUGHES INGENUE)

1951 THE WHIP HAND - R.K.O.
Director: William Cameron Menzies
Co-stars: Elliott Reid Edgar Barrier Raymond Burr

1951 SEALED CARGO
Director: Alfred Werker
Co-stars: Dana Andrews Claude Rains Philip Dorn

1953 PRINCE OF PIRATES
Director: Sidney Salkow
Co-stars: John Derek Barbara Rush Edgar Barrier

BETTY BALFOUR

1928 CHAMPAIGNE
Director: Alfred Hitchcock
Co-stars: Gordon Harker Jean Bradin Theodore Von Alten

1930 RAISE THE ROOF
Director: Walter Summers
Co-stars: Maurice Evans Sam Livesey Jack Raine

1934 MY OLD DUTCH
Director: Sinclair Hill
Co-stars: Gordon Harker Florrie Floyd Michael Hogan

1934 EVERGREEN
Director: Victor Saville
Co-stars: Jessie Matthews Sonnie Hale Barry Mackay

1935 SQUIBS
Director: Henry Edwards
Co-stars: Gordon Harker Stanley Holloway Margaret Yarde

1935 FOREVER ENGLAND
Co-star: John Mills

1936 BROWN ON RESOLUTION
Director: Walter Forde
Co-stars: John Mills Barry Mackay Jimmy Hanley

1945 29, ACACIA AVENUE
Director: Henry Cass
Co-stars: Gordon Harker Jimmy Hanley Dinah Sheridan

KATHERINE BALFOUR
1970 LOVE STORY
Director: Arthur Hiller
Co-stars: Ali MacGraw Ryan O'Neal Ray Milland

JENNIFER BALGOBIN
1992 ROADSIDE PROPHETS
Director: Abbe Wool
Co-stars: John Doe Adam Horovitz John Cusack

INA BALIN
Rescued Many Vietnamese Children, Story Told In Her Last Film
1958 THE BLACK ORCHID
Director: Martin Ritt
Co-stars: Sophia Loren Anthony Quinn Frank Puglia

1960 FROM THE TERRACE
Director: Mark Robson
Co-stars: Paul Newman Joanne Woodward Myrna Loy

1961 THE YOUNG DOCTORS
Director: Phil Karlson
Co-stars: Fredric March Ben Gazzara Eddie Albert

1961 THE COMANCHEROS
Director: Michael Curtiz
Co-stars: John Wayne Stuart Whitman Lee Marvin

1964 THE PATSY
Director: Jerry Lewis
Co-stars: Jerry Lewis Everett Sloane Peter Lorre

1965 THE GREATEST STORY EVER TOLD
Director: George Stevens
Co-stars: Max Von Sydow Dorothy McGuire

1969 CHARRO!
Director: Charles Marquis Warren
Co-stars: Elvis Presley Barbara Werle Lynn Kellogg

1969 THE LONELY PROFESSION
Director: Douglas Heyes
Co-stars: Harry Guardino Dean Jagger Joseph Cotten

1980 THE CHILDREN OF AN LAC
Director: John Llewellyn Moxey
Co-stars: Shirley Jones Beulah Quo

MIREILLE BALIN
1937 PEPE LE MOKO
Director: Julien Duvivier
Co-stars: Jean Gabin Line Noro Lucas Gridoux

ESZTER BALINT
1984 STRANGER THAN PARADISE
Director: Jim Jarmusch
Co-stars: John Lurie Richard Edson Cecelia Stark

1992 THE LINGUINI INCIDENT
Director: Richard Shepard
Co-stars: Rosanna Arquette David Bowie Marlee Matlin

FAIRUSA BALK *(Child)*
1985 RETURN TO OZ
Director: Walter Murch
Co-stars: Nicol Williamson Jean Marsh Piper Laurie

1989 VALMONT
Director: Milos Forman
Co-stars: Colin Firth Annette Bening Meg Tilly

1991 GAS, FOOD, LODGING
Director: Allison Anders
Co-stars: Brooke Adams Ione Skye James Brolin

1995 SHADOW OF A DOUBT
Director: Brian Dennehy
Co-stars: Brian Dennehy Bonnie Bedelia

1996 THE CRAFT
Director: Andrew Fleming
Co-stars: Robin Tunney Neve Campbell

**1996 THINGS TO DO IN DENVER
     WHEN YOU'RE DEAD**
Director: Gary Leder
Co-stars: Andy Garcia Treat Williams

KAREN BALKIN *(Child)*
1961 THE CHILDREN'S HOUR
Director: William Wyler
Co-stars: Audrey Hepburn Shirley MacLaine James Garner

ANGELINE BALL
1991 THE COMMITMENTS
Director: Alan Parker
Co-stars: Robert Arkins Michael Aherne Maria Doyle

1998 THE GENERAL
Director: John Boorman
Co-stars: Jon Voight Brendan Gleeson Eamon Owens

JANE BALL
1944 WINGED VICTORY
Director: George Cukor
Co-stars: Lon McCallister Jeanne Crain Edmond O'Brien

1947 FOREVER AMBER
Director: Otto Preminger
Co-stars: Linda Darnell Cornel Wilde George Sanders

LUCILLE BALL
1933 ROMAN SCANDALS
Director: Frank Tuttle
Co-stars: Eddie Cantor Gloria Stuart Ruth Etting

1935 I DREAM TOO MUCH
Director: John Cromwell
Co-stars: Lily Pons Henry Fonda Eric Blore

1935 OLD MAN RHYTHM
Director: Edward Ludwig
Co-stars: Betty Grable Charles Rogers George Barbier

1935 CARNIVAL
Director: Walter Lang
Co-stars: Lee Tracy Jimmy Durante Sally Eilers

1936 BUNKER BEAN
Director: Edward Killy
Co-stars: Owen Davis Louise Latimer Jessie Ralph

1936 KID MILLIONS
Director: Roy Del Ruth
Co-stars: Eddie Cantor Ann Sothern Ethel Merman

1936 FOLLOW THE FLEET
Director: Mark Sandrich
Co-stars: Fred Astaire Ginger Rogers Randolph Scott

1936 THAT GIRL FROM PARIS
Director: Leigh Jason
Co-stars: Lily Pons Gene Raymond Jack Oakie

1937 STAGE DOOR
Director: Gregory La Cava
Co-stars: Katharine Hepburn Ginger Rogers Ann Miller

1937 HITTING A NEW HIGH
Director: Raoul Walsh
Co-stars: Lily Pons Jack Oakie Eric Blore

1938 JOY OF LIVING
Director: Tay Garnett
Co-stars: Irene Dunne Douglas Fairbanks Alice Brady

1938 HAVING WONDERFUL TIME
Director: Alfred Santell
Co-stars: Ginger Rogers Douglas Fairbanks Red Skelton

1938 GO CHASE YOURSELF
Director: Edward Cline
Co-stars: Joe Penner June Travis Jack Carson

1938 THE NEXT TIME I MARRY
Director: Garson Kanin
Co-stars: James Ellison Lee Bowman Granville Bates

1938 ROOM SERVICE
Director: William Seiter
Co-stars: Marx Bros Ann Miller Donald MacBride

1938 THE AFFAIRS OF ANNABEL
Director: Lew Landers
Co-stars: Jack Oakie Ruth Donnelly Bradley Page

1939 ANNABEL TAKES A TOUR
Director: Lew Landers
Co-stars: Jack Oakie Ruth Donnelly Ralph Forbes

1939 BEAUTY FOR THE ASKING
Director: Glenn Tryon
Co-stars: Patric Knowles Donald Woods Frieda Inescourt

1939 FIVE CAME BACK
Director: John Farrow
Co-stars: Chester Morris Patric Knowles Joseph Calleia

1939 THAT'S RIGHT, YOU'RE WRONG
Director: David Butler
Co-stars: Kay Kyser Adolphe Menjou Dennis O'Keefe

1939 TWELVE CROWDED HOURS
Co-stars: Richard Dix Allan Lane

1940 TOO MANY GIRLS
Director: George Abbott
Co-stars: Desi Arnaz Eddie Bracken Ann Miller

1940 THE MARINES FLY HIGH
Director: Ben Stoloff
Co-stars: Richard Dix Chester Morris John Eldredge

1940 DANCE, GIRL, DANCE
Director: Dorothy Arzner
Co-stars: Maureen O'Hara Louis Hayward

1941 THE NAVY STEPS OUT
Director: Richard Wallace
Co-stars: George Murphy Edmond O'Brien Henry Travers

1941 LOOK WHO'S LAUGHING
Director: Allan Dwan
Co-star: Edgar Bergen

1942 SEVEN DAYS LEAVE
Director: Tim Whelan
Co-stars: Victor Mature Ginny Simms Wallace Ford

1942 VALLEY OF THE SUN
Director: George Marshall
Co-stars: James Craig Dean Jagger Cedric Hardwicke

1942 THE BIG STREET
Director: Irving Reis
Co-stars: Henry Fonda Eugene Pallette Barton MacLane

1943 BEST FOOT FORWARD
Director: Edward Buzzell
Co-stars: Nancy Walker William Gaxton Harry James

1943 DUBARRY WAS A LADY
Director: Roy Del Ruth
Co-stars: Red Skelton Gene Kelly Zero Mostel

1943 STAGE DOOR CANTEEN
Director: Frank Borzage
Co-stars: Lon McCallister Cheryl Walker Ethel Merman

1944 ZIEGFELD FOLLIES
Director: Vincente Minnelli
Co-stars: Fred Astaire William Powell Fanny Brice

1944 MEET THE PEOPLE
Director: Charles Reisner
Co-stars: Dick Powell Bert Lahr June Allyson

1944 WITHOUT LOVE
Director: Harold Bucquet
Co-stars: Spencer Tracy Katharine Hepburn Gloria Grahame

1945 ABBOTT & COSTELLO IN HOLLYWOOD
Director: S. Sylvan Simon
Co-stars: Abbott & Costello Dean Stockwell

1946 EASY TO WED
Director: Edward Buzzell
Co-stars: Van Johnson Esther Williams Keenan Wynn

1946 TWO SMART PEOPLE
Director: Jules Dassin
Co-stars: John Hodiak Lloyd Nolan Hugo Haas

1946 THE DARK CORNER
Director: Henry Hathaway
Co-stars: Mark Stevens Clifton Webb William Bendix

1946 LOVER COME BACK
Director: William Seiter
Co-stars: George Brent Charles Winninger Vera Zorina

1947 HER HUSBAND'S AFFAIRS
Director: S. Sylvan Simon
Co-stars: Franchot Tone Gene Lockhart

1947 LURED
Director: Douglas Sirk
Co-stars: Charles Coburn George Sanders Boris Karloff

1949 SORROWFUL JONES
Director: Sidney Lanfield
Co-stars: Bob Hope William Demarest Bruce Cabot

1949 MISS GRANT TAKES RICHMOND
Director: Lloyd Bacon
Co-stars: William Holden Janis Carter

1949 EASY LIVING
Director: Jacques Tourneur
Co-stars: Victor Mature Lisabeth Scott Sonny Tufts

1950 FANCY PANTS
Director: George Marshall
Co-stars: Bob Hope Bruce Cabot Eric Blore

1950 A WONDERFUL DISTINCTION
Director: Edward Buzzell
Co-stars: Rosalind Russell Ray Milland Edmund Gwenn

1950	**THE FULLER BRUSH GIRL**
Director:	Lloyd Bacon
Co-stars:	Eddie Albert Gale Robbins Jeff Donnell

1951	**THE MAGIC CARPET**
Director:	Lew Landers
Co-stars:	Raymond Burr John Agar Patricia Medina

1954	**THE LONG, LONG TRAILER**
Director:	Vincente Minnelli
Co-stars:	Desi Arnaz Marjorie Main Keenan Wynn

1956	**FOREVER DARLING**
Director:	Alexander Hall
Co-stars:	Desi Arnaz James Mason Louis Calhern

1960	**THE FACTS OF LIVE**
Director:	Melvin Frank
Co-stars:	Bob Hope Ruth Hussey Don Defore

1963	**CRITIC'S CHOICE**
Director:	Don Wels
Co-stars:	Bob Hope Marilyn Maxwell Rip Torn

1967	**A GUIDE FOR THE MARRLED MAN**
Director:	Gene Kelly
Co-stars:	Walter Matthau Robert Morse Inger Stevens

1968	**YOURS, MINE AND OURS**
Director:	Mel Shavelson
Co-stars:	Henry Fonda Van Johnson Tim Matheson

1974	**MAME**
Director:	Gene Saks
Co-stars:	Beatrice Arthur Robert Preston Bruce Davison

1977	**BILLY JACK GOES TO WASHINGTON**
Director:	Tom Laughlin
Co-stars:	Tom Laughlin Delores Taylor Sam Wanamaker

1985	**STONE PILLOW**

SUZAN BALL

1952	**UNTAMED FRONTIER**
Director:	Hugo Fregonese
Co-stars:	Joseph Cotten Shelley Winters Scott Brady

1953	**CITY BENEATH THE SEA**
Director:	Budd Boetticher
Co-stars:	Robert Ryan Anthony Quinn Mala Powers

1955	**CHIEF CRAZY HORSE**
Director:	George Sherman
Co-stars:	Victor Mature John Lund Ray Danton

ELSPETH BALLANTYNE

1978	**BLUE FIN**
Director:	Carl Schultz
Co-stars:	Hardy Kruger Greg Rowe Liddy Clark

1982	**BREAKFAST IN PARIS**
Director:	John Lamond
Co-stars:	Barbara Parkins Rod Mullinar Jack Lenoir

KAYE BALLARD

1958	**THE GIRL MOST LIKELY**
Director:	Mitchell Leisen
Co-stars:	Jane Powell Cliff Robertson Keith Andes

1970	**WHICH WAY TO THE FRONT?**
Director:	Jerry Lewis
Co-stars:	Jerry Lewis John Wood Robert Middleton

1976	**THE RITZ**
Director:	Richard Lester
Co-stars:	Jack Weston Rita Moreno Bessie Love

1980	**FALLING IN LOVE AGAIN**
Director:	Steven Paul
Co-stars:	Elliott Gould Susannah York Stuart Paul

1990	**ETERNITY**
Director:	Steven Paul
Co-stars:	Jon Voight Armand Assante Eileen Davidson

GIGI BALLISTA

1965	**THE BIRDS, BEES AND THE ITALIANS**
Director:	Pietro Germi
Co-stars:	Virna Lisi Gastone Mochin

TALIA BALSAM *(Daughter Of Martin Balsam)*

1978	**THE INITIATION OF SARAH**
Director:	Robert Day
Co-stars:	Kay Lenz Shelley Winters Kathryn Crosby

1979	**SURVIVAL OF DANA**
Director:	Jack Starrett
Co-stars:	Melissa Sue Anderson Robert Carradine

1981	**CRAZY TIMES**
Director:	Lee Philips
Co-stars:	Michael Pare David Caruso Ray Liotta

1984	**CALAMITY JANE**
Director:	George Sherman
Co-stars:	Jane Alexander Frederic Forrest David Hemmings

1984	**MASS APPEAL**
Director:	Glenn Jordan
Co-stars:	Jack Lemmon Zeljko Ivanek Charles Durning

1987	**P. I. PRIVATE INVESTIGATIONS**
Director:	Nigel Dick
Co-stars:	Clayton Rohner Ray Sharkey Martin Balsam

1987	**THE WOO WOO KID**
Director:	Phil Alden Robinson
Co-stars:	Patrick Dempsey Beverley D'Angelo

1991	**SINS OF THE MOTHER**
Director:	John Patterson
Co-stars:	Elizabeth Montgomery Dale Midkiff

ALLISON BALSON

1985	**LEGEND OF THE WHITE HORSE**
Director:	Jerzy Domaradski
Co-stars:	Dee Wallace Christopher Lloyd

1987	**BEST SELLER**
Director:	John Flynn
Co-stars:	James Woods Brian Dennehy Victoria Tennant

ANNE BANCROFT *(Married Mel Brooks)*
Oscar For Best Actress In 1962 For "The Miracle Worker", Nominated For Best Actress In 1964 For "The Pumpkin Father", In 1967 For "The Graduate", In 1977 For "The Turning Point", In 1985 For "Agnes Of God"

1952	**DON'T BOTHER TO KNOCK**
Director:	Roy Baker
Co-stars:	Marilyn Monroe Richard Widmark Donna Corcoran

1952	**TREASURE OF THE GOLDEN CONDOR**
Director:	Delmer Daves
Co-stars:	Cornel Wilde Flnlay Currie George Macready

1953	**TONIGHT WE SING**
Director:	Mitchell Leisen
Co-stars:	David Wayne Ezio Pinza Tamara Toumanova

1953	**THE KID FROM LEFT FIELD**
Director:	Harmon Jones
Co-stars:	Dan Dailey Lloyd Bridges Richard Egan

1954	**A LIFE IN THE BALANCE**
Director:	Harry Horner
Co-stars:	Ricardo Montalban Lee Marvin

1954	**THE RAID**
Director:	Hugo Fregonese
Co-stars:	Van Heflin Richard Boone Lee Marvin

1954 GORILLA AT LARGE
Director: Harmon Jones
Co-stars: Cameron Mitchell Raymond Burr Lee Marvin

1954 DEMETRIUS AND THE GLADIAITORS
Director: Delmer Daves
Co-stars: Victor Mature Susan Hayward Michael Rennie

1955 THE NAKED STREET
Director: Maxwell Shane
Co-stars: Anthony Quinn Farley Granger Peter Graves

1955 NEW YORK CONFIDENTIAL
Director: Russel Rouse
Co-stars: Broderick Crawford Richard Conte

1956 NIGHTFALL
Director: Jacques Tourneur
Co-stars: Aldo Ray Brian Keith Jocelyn Brando

1956 SAVAGE WILDERNESS
Director: Anthony Mann
Co-stars: Robert Preston Victor Mature Guy Madison

1956 WALK THE PROUD LAND
Director: Jesse Hibbs
Co-stars: Audle Murphy Charles Drake Tommy Rall

1957 THE RESTLESS BREED
Director: Allan Dwan
Co-stars: Scott Brady Jim Davis Rhys Williams

1957 THE GIRL IN BLACK STOCKINGS
Director: Howard Koch
Co-stars: John Dehner Lex Barker Ron Randell

1962 THE MIRACLE-WORKER
Director: Arthur Penn
Co-stars: Patty Duke Victor Jory Andrew Prine

1964 THE PUMPKIN EATER
Director: Jack Clayton
Co-stars: Peter Finch James Mason Richard Johnson

1966 SEVEN WOMEN
Director: John Ford
Co-stars: Flora Robson Margaret Leighton Sue Lyon

1966 THE SLENDER THREAD
Director: Sydney Pollack
Co-stars: Sidney Poitier Telly Savalas Edward Asner

1967 THE GRADUATE
Director: Mike Nichols
Co-stars: Dustin Hoffman Katharine Ross Murray Hamilton

1972 YOUNG WINSTON
Director: Richard Attenborough
Co-stars: Simon Ward Robert Shaw Anthony Hopkins

1975 THE PRISONER OF SECOND AVENUE
Director: Melvyn Frank
Co-stars: Jack Lemmon Gene Saks Sylvester Stallone

1975 THE HINDENBURG
Director: Robert Wise
Co-stars: George C. Scott Burgess Meredith Roy Thinnes

1976 LIPSTICK
Director: Lamont Johnson
Co-stars: Margaux Hemingway Mariel Hemingway Chris Sarandon

1976 SILENT MOVIE
Director: Mel Brooks
Co-stars: Marty Feldman Dom DeLuise Sid Caesar

1977 THE TURNING POINT
Director: Herbert Ross
Co-stars: Shirley MacLaine Mikhail Baryshnikov Tom Skerritt

1980 FATSO
Director: Anne Bancroft
Co-stars: Dom DeLuise Ron Cary Candice Azzara

1980 THE ELEPHANT MAN
Director: David Lynch
Co-stars: Anthony Hopkins John Hurt John Gielgud

1983 TO BE OR NOT TO BE
Director: Alan Johnson
Co-stars: Mel Brooks Tim Matheson Jose Ferrer

1984 GARBO TALKS
Director: Sidney Lumet
Co-stars: Ron Silver Carrie Fisher Steven Hill

1985 AGNES OF GOD
Director: Norman Jewison
Co-stars: Jane Fonda Meg Tilly Anne Pitoniak

1986 84, CHARING CROSS ROAD
Director: David Jones
Co-stars: Anthony Hopkins Judi Dench Eleanor David

1986 'NIGHT MOTHER
Director: Tom Moore
Co-stars: Sissy Spacek Ed Berke Carol Robbins

1988 TORCH SONG TRILOGY
Director: Paul Bogart
Co-stars: Harvey Fierstein Matthew Broderick Karen Young

1989 BERT RIGBY, YOU'RE A FOOL
Director: Carl Reiner
Co-stars: Robert Lindsay Corbin Bernsen Robbie Coltrane

1992 BROADWAY BOUND
Director: Paul Bogart
Co-stars: Corey Parker Hume Cronyn Jerry Orbach

1992 HONEYMOON IN VEGAS
Director: Andrew Bergman
Co-stars: James Caan Nicolas Cage Jessica Parker

1993 THE ASSASSIN
Director: John Badham
Co-stars: Bridget Fonda Gabriel Byrne Dermot Mulroney

1993 MALICE
Director: Harold Becker
Co-stars: Bill Pullman Nicole Kidman Alec Baldwin

1994 MR JONES
Director: Mike Figgis
Co-stars: Richard Gere Lena Olin

1996 HOME FOR THE HOLIDAYS
Director: Jodie Foster
Co-stars: Holly Hunter Robert Downey Steve Guttenberg

1996 HOW TO MAKE AN AMERICAN QUILT
Director: Jocelyn Moorhouse
Co-stars: Winona Ryder Jean Simmons Ellen Burstyn

1997 DRACULA: DEAD AND LOVING IT
Director: Mel Brooks
Co-stars: Mel Brooks Leslie Neilsen

1997 G.I.JANE
Director: Ridley Scott
Co-stars: Demi Moore Viggo Mortensen

1998 GREAT EXPECTATIONS
Director: Alfonso Cuaron
Co-stars: Ethan Hawke Gwyneth Paltrow Robert De Niro

CLARE BANCROFT

1990 JULIA HAS TWO LOVERS
Director: Bashar Shbib
Co-stars: Daphna Kastner David Duchovny David Charles

HONEY BANE

1982 SCRUBBERS
Director: Mai Zetterling
Co-stars: Amanda York Chrissie Cotterill Kate Ingram

LISA BANES

1985 MARIE
Director: Roger Donaldson
Co-stars: Sissy Spacek Jeff Daniels Morgan Freeman

1986 ONE POLICE PLAZA
Director: Jerry Jameson
Co-stars: Robert Conrad Anthony Zerbe George Dzundza

1988 COCKTAIL
Director: Roger Donaldson
Co-stars: Tom Cruise Bryan Brown Elizabeth Shue

1992 DANGER ISLAND
Director: Lee Wallace
Co-stars: Richard Beymer June Lockhart Gary Graham

1994 TOUCH OF TRUTH
Director: Michael Switzer
Co-stars: Patty Duke Melissa Gilbert

1995 MIAMI RHAPSODY
Director: David Frankel
Co-stars: Sarah Jessica Parker Antonio Banderas Mia Farrow

BEVERLEIGH BANFIELD

1982 BENNY'S PLACE
Director: Michael Schultz
Co-stars: Lou Gossett Jnr. Cicely Tyson David Harris

TALLULAH BANKHEAD

1931 TARNISHED LADY
Director: George Cukor
Co-stars: Clive Brook Phoebe Foster

1931 MY SIN
Director: George Abbott
Co-stars: Fredric March Harry Davenport

1931 THE CHEAT
Director: Irving Pichel

1932 DEVIL AND THE DEEP
Director: Marius Gering
Co-stars: Charles Laughton Cary Grant Gary Cooper

1932 THUNDER BELOW
Director: Richard Wallace
Co-stars: Paul Lukas Charles Bickford

1932 MAKE ME A STAR
Director: William Beaudine
Co-stars: Stuart Erwin Joan Blondell Zasu Pitts

1932 FAITHLESS
Director: Harry Beaumont
Co-stars: Robert Montgomery Hugh Herbert

1944 LIFEBOAT
Director: Alfred Hitchcock
Co-stars: Walter Slezak William Bendix John Hodiak

1945 A ROYAL SCANDAL
Director: Otto Preminger
Co-stars: William Eythe Anne Baxter Charles Coburn

1953 MAIN STREET TO BROADWAY
Director: Tay Garnett
Co-stars: Ethel Barrymore Lionel Barrymore Mary Martin

1964 FANATIC
Director: Silvio Narizanno
Co-stars: Stefanie Powers Peter Vaughan

JENNIFER BANRO

**1988 FRIDAY THE 13TH. PART V11
THE NEW BLOOD**
Director: John Carl Buechler
Co-stars: John Otrin Susan Blu

EMILY BANKS

1967 GUNFIGHT IN ABILENE
Director: William Hale
Co-stars: Bobby Darin Leslie Nielsen Michael Sarrazin

JOAN BANKS

1952 MY PAL GUS
Director: Robert Parrish
Co-stars: Richard Widmark Joanne Dru George Winslow

VILMA BANKY (*Married Rod La Rocque*)

1925 THE EAGLE
Director: Clarénce Brown
Co-stars: Rudolph Valentino Louise Dresser

1925 THE DARK ANGEL
Co-star: Ronald Colman

1926 THE SON OF THE SHEIK
Director: George Fitzmaurice
Co-stars: Rudolph Valentino Agnes Ayres

1926 THE WINNING OF BARBARA WORTH
Director: Henry King
Co-stars: Ronald Colman Gary Cooper

1927 THE NIGHT OF LOVE
Co-star: Ronald Colman

1930 A LADY TO LOVE
Director: Victor Seastrom
Co-stars: Edward G. Robinson Robert Ames

CHANTAL BANLIER

1988 LA PETITE VOLEUSE
Director: Claude Miller
Co-stars: Charlotte Gainsbourg Raoul Billery

CELIA BANNERMAN

1983 BIDDY
Director: Christine Edzard
Co-stars: Sam Ghazoros Patricia Napier John Dalby

JENNIFER BABTIST

1985 THE TOXIC AVENGER
Director: Michael Herz
Co-stars: Andree Marander Mitchell Cohen Mark Torgi

THEDA BARA (*Married Charles Brabin*)
(*The Vamp*) (*Theodosia Goodman*)

1914 A FOOL THERE WAS
Director: Frank Powell
Co-stars: Edward Jose Mabel Frenyer

1916 EAST LYNNE

1916 GOLD AND THE WOMAN

1918 CLEOPATRA

MARLA BARANOVA

1991 THE INNER CIRCLE
Director: Andrei Konchalovsky
Co-stars: Tom Hulce Lolita Davidovich Bob Hoskins

CHRISTINE BARANSKI

1980 PLAYING FOR TIME
Director: Daniel Mann
Co-stars: Vanessa Redgrave Maud Adams Jane Alexander

1986 NINE AND A HALF WEEKS
Director: Adrian Lyne
Co-stars: Mickey Rourke Kim Basinger Karen Young

1990   **REVERSAL OF FORTUNE**
Director: Barbet Schroeder
Co-stars: Glenn Close Jeremy Irons Ron Silver

1993   **THE NIGHT WE NEVER MET**
Director: Warren Leight
Co-stars: Matthew Broderick Annabella Sciorra

OLIVIA BARASH
1984   **REPO MAN**
Director: Alex Cox
Co-stars: Emilio Estevez Harry Dean Stanton Vonetta McGee

1985   **TUFF TURF**
Director: Fritz Kiersch
Co-stars: James Spader Kim Richards Robert Downey Jnr.

RAFFAELE BARBATO
1962   **THE FOUR DAYS OF NAPLES**
Director: Nanni Loy
Co-stars: Lea Massari Frank Wolff

ADRIENNE BARBEAU
1977   **RED ALERT**
Director: William Hale
Co-stars: William Devane Ralph Waite Michael Brandon

1978   **THE CRASH OF FLIGHT 401**
Director: Barry Shear
Co-stars: William Shatner Eddie Albert Lloyd Bridges

1979   **THE FOG**
Director: John Carpenter
Co-stars: Hal Holbrook Janet Leigh Jaimie Lee Curtis

1978   **SOMEONE'S WATCHING ME**
Director: John Carpenter
Co-stars: Lauren Hutton David Birney

1981   **THE CANNONBALL RUN**
Director: Hal Needham
Co-stars: Burt Reynolds Roger Moore Farrah Fawcett

1981   **ESCAPE FROM NEW YORK**
Director: John Carpenter
Co-stars: Kurt Russell Ernest Borgnine Lee Van Cleef

1982   **CREEPSHOW**
Director: George Romero
Co-stars: Carrie Nye Viveca Lindfors Leslie Nielsen

1982   **SWAMP THING**
Director: Wes Craven
Co-stars: Louis Jourdan Ray Wise David Hess

1984   **THE NEXT ONE**
Director: Nico Mastorakis
Co-stars: Keir Dullea Peter Hobbs

1985   **SEDUCED**
Director: Jerrold Freedman
Co-stars: Cybill Shepherd Gregory Harrison Jose Ferrer

1986   **BACK TO SCHOOL**
Director: Alan Metter
Co-stars: Rodney Dangerfield Sally Kellerman Burt Young

1990   **TWO EVIL EYES**
Director: George Romero
Co-stars: Ramy Zada Harvey Keitel Sally Kirkland

ELLEN BARBER
1976   **JUDGE HORTON AND THE SCOTTSBORO BOYS**
Director: Fielder Cook
Co-stars: Arthur Hill Vera Miles

1986   **APOLOGY FOR MURDER**
Director: Robert Bierman
Co-stars: Lesley Ann Warren Peter Weller

FRANCIS BARBER
1985   **A ZED AND TWO NOUGHTS**
Director: Andrea Ferreol
Co-stars: Brian Deacon Eric Deacon Joss Ackland

1987   **SAMMY AND ROSIE GET LAID**
Director: Stephen Frears
Co-stars: Shashi Kapoor Claire Bloom Amanda Donohue

1987   **PRICK UP YOUR EARS**
Director: Stephen Frears
Co-stars: Gary Oldman Alfred Molina Vanessa Redgrave

1988   **WE THINK THE WORLD OF YOU**
Director: Colin Gregg
Co-stars: Alan Bates Max Wall Gary Oldman

1989   **THE GRASSCUTTER**
Director: Ian Mune
Co-stars: Ian McElhinney Martin Maguire Judy McIntosh

1989   **BEHAVING BADLY**
Director: David Tucker
Co-stars: Judi Dench Ronald Pickup Joely Richardson

1990   **THE ORCHID HOUSE**
Director: Horace Ove
Co-stars: Diana Quick Kate Buffery Elizabeth Hurley

1991   **YOUNG SOUL REBELS**
Director: Valentine Nonyela
Co-stars: Mo Sesay Dorian Healy

1991   **INSPECTOR MORSE: THE DEATH OF THE SELF**
Director: Adrlan Shergold
Co-stars: John Thaw Michael Kitchen

1991   **HANCOCK**
Director: Tony Smith
Co-stars: Alfred Molina Mel Martin Malcolm Sinclair

1991   **DO NOT DISTURB**
Director: Nicholas Renton
Co-stars: Peter Capaldi Eva Darlan Stefan Schwartz

1992   **SOFT TOP HARD SHOULDER**
Director: Stefan Schwartz
Co-stars: Peter Capaldi Elaine Collins Simon Callow

1994   **RETURN TO BLOOD RIVER**
Director: Jane Howell
Co-stars: Kevin McNally Warren Clarke Samantha Bond

1994   **IN THE COLD LIGHT OF DAY**
Director: Richard Monks
Co-stars: Jim Carter Stephanie Cole Ronald Pickup

1996   **PHOTOGRAPHING FAIRIES**
Director: Nick Williams
Co-stars: Ben Kingsley Toby Stephens Emily Woof

GLYNIS BARBER
1987   **VISITORS**
Director: Piers Haggard
Co-stars: Michael Brandon John Standing Nicola Paget

1989   **EDGE OF SANITY**
Director: Gerard Kikoine
Co-stars: Anthony Perkins David Lodge Ben Cole

1992   **MISS MARPLE: THE MIRROR CRACK'D SIDE TO SIDE**
Director: Norman Stone
Co-stars: Joan Hickson Claire Bloom

KATIE BARBERI
1989   **NOT QUITE HUMAN 11**
Director: Eric Luke
Co-stars: Alan Thicke Jay Underwood Robyn Lively

BARBETTE
1931   THE BLOOD OF A POET
Director: Jean Cocteau
Co-stars: Lee Miller Enrique Rivero Pauline Carton

JENNIFER BARBOUR
1988   BODY OF EVIDENCE
Director: Roy Campanella
Co-stars: Margot Kidder Barry Bostwick Tony Lobianco

JOYCE BARBOUR
1936   SABOTAGE
Director: Alfred Hitchcock
Co-stars: Sylvia Sidney Oscar Homolka John Loder

1938   HOUSEMASTER
Director: Herbert Brenon
Co-stars: Otto Kruger Diana Churchill Phillips Holmes

1940   SALOON BAR
Director: Walter Forde
Co-stars: Gordon Harker Mervyn Johns Elizabeth Allan

1944   DON'T TAKE IT TO HEART
Director: Jeffrey Dell
Co-stars: Richard Greene Edward Rigby Patricia Medina

1952   IT STARTED IN PARADISE
Director: Compton Bennett
Co-stars: Jane Hylton Ian Hunter Terence Morgan

CAROLINE BARCLAY
1995   WITHIN THE ROCK
Director: Gary J. Tunnicliffe
Co-star: Xander Berkeley

JOAN BARCLAY
1936   MEN OF THE PLAINS
Co-star: Rex Bell

1936   WEST OF NEVADA
Co-star: Rex Bell

1936   RIDING ON
Co-stars: Tom Tyler Roger Williams

1938   THE SINGING OUTLAW
Co-star: Bob Baker

1938   WHIRLWIND HORSEMAN
Co-star: Ken Maynard

1938   TWO GUN JUSTICE
Co-stars: Tim McCoy Betty Compson

1942   BLACK DRAGONS
Co-star: Bela Lugosi

1943   LADIES DAY
Co-stars: Iris Adrian Patsy Kelly Max Baer

1945   THE SHANGHAI COBRA
Co-stars: Sidney Toler Jim Cardwell Benson Fong

1947   DRAGNET
Co-star: Henry Wilcoxon

KATHERINE BARD
1958   THE DECKS RAN RED
Director: Andrew Stone
Co-stars: James Mason Dorothy Dandridge Stuart Whitman

1965   INSIDE DAISY CLOVER
Director: Robert Mulligan
Co-stars: Natalie Wood Robert Redford Ruth Gordon

**1968   HOW TO SAVE A MARRIAGE
            AND RUIN YOUR LIFE**
Director: Fielder Cook
Co-stars: Dean Martin Stella Stevens

MARGARET BARD
1988   THE PRICE OF PASSION
Director: Leonard Nimoy
Co-stars: Diane Keaton Liam Neeson Jason Robards

BRIGITTE BARDOT *(Married Roger Vadim)*
1954   ACT OF LOVE
Director: Anatole Litvak
Co-stars: Kirk Douglas Dany Robin Robert Strauss

1955   THE LIGHT ACROSS THE STREET
Director: Georges Lacombe
Co-stars: Raymond Pellegrin Roger Picaut Claude Romain

1955   HELEN OF TROY
Director: Robert Wise
Co-stars: Rossana Podesta Jacques Sernas Stanley Baker

1955   DOCTOR AT SEA
Director: Ralph Thomas
Co-stars: Dirk Bogarde Brenda De Banzie Michael Medwin

1955   LES GRANDES MANOEUVRES
Director: Rene Clair
Co-stars: Gerard Philipe Michele Morgan Yves Robert

1956   AND GOD CREATED WOMAN
Director: Roger Vadim
Co-stars: Curt Jurgens Jean-Louis Trintignant

1958   HEAVEN FELL THAT NIGHT
Director: Roger Vadim
Co-stars: Stephen Boyd Alida Valli Pepe Nieto

1958   EN CAS DE MALHEUR
Director: Claude Autant-Lara
Co-stars: Jean Gabin Edwige Feuillere Nicole Berger

1958   THE BRIDE IS TOO BEAUTIFUL
Director: Fred Surin
Co-stars: Micheline Presle Louis Jourdan

1959   LOVE IS MY PROFESSION
Director: Henri-Georges Clouzot

1959   BABETTE GOES TO WAR
Director: Christian-Jaque
Co-stars: Jacques Charrier Ronald Howard Yves Vincent

1960   THE WOMAN AND THE PUPPET
Director: Julien Duvivier

1961   THE TRUTH
Director: Henri-Georges Clouzot
Co-stars: Charles Vanel Louis Seignier

1962   A VERY PRIVATE AFFAIR
Director: Louis Malle
Co-stars: Marcello Mastroianni Gregor Von Rezzori

1963   LE MEPRIS
Director: Jean-Luc Godard
Co-stars: Jean-Luc Godard Jack Palance Fritz Lang

1964   LOVE ON A PILLOW
Co-stars: Jean Tuscano

1965   VIVA MARIA!
Director: Louis Malle
Co-stars: Jeanne Moreau George Hamilton Paulette Dubost

1965   DEAR BRIGITTE
Director: Henry Koster
Co-stars: James Stewart Glynis Johns Fabian

1968   SHALAKO
Director: Edward Dmytryk
Co-stars: Sean Connery Jack Hawkins Stephen Boyd

GILLIAN BARGE
1991   CHIMERA
Director: Lawrence Gordon Clark
Co-stars: John Lynch Christine Kavanagh Kenneth Cranham

1993   **A QUESTION OF GUILT**
Director: Stuart Orme
Co-stars: Cherie Lunghi Derrick O'Connor Celia Imrie

LYNN BARI

1938   **THE BARONESS AND THE BUTLER**
Director: Walter Lang
Co-stars: William Powell Annabella Nigel Bruce

1938   **ALWAYS GOODBYE**
Director: Sidney Lanfield
Co-stars: Barbara Stanwyck Herbert Marshall Cesar Romero

1938   **BATTLE OF BROADWAY**
Director: George Marshall
Co-stars: Victor McLaglen Brian Donlevy Gypsy Rose Lee

1938   **JOSETTE**
Director: Allan Dwan
Co-stars: Simone Simon Don Ameche Robert Young

1938   **SHARPSHOOTERS**
Director: James Tinling
Co-stars: Brian Donlevy Wally Vernon Sidney Blackmer

1938   **MR MOTO'S GAMBLE**
Director: Norman Foster
Co-stars: Peter Lorre Keye Luke

1939   **THE RETURN OF THE CISCO KID**
Director: Herbert Leeds
Co-stars: Warner Baxter Cesar Romero

1939   **PACK UP YOUR TROUBLES**
Director: Bruce Humberstone
Co-stars: Ritz Bros. Jane Withers Joseph Schildkraut

1939   **NEWS IS MADE AT NIGHT**
Director: Alfred Werker
Co-stars: Preston Foster Eddie Collins George Barbier

1939   **HOTEL FOR WOMEN**
Director: Gregory Ratoff
Co-stars: Linda Darnell Elsa Maxwell James Ellison

1939   **CHARLIE CHAN IN CITY IN DARKNESS**
Director: Herbert Leeds
Co-stars: Sidney Toler Lon Chaney

1940   **CHARTER PILOT**
Co-star: Lloyd Nolan

1940   **LA CONGA NIGHTS**
Co-stars: Dennis O'Keefe Ferike Boros

1940   **CITY OF CHANCE**
Director: Ricardo Cortez
Co-stars: Donald Woods C. Aubrey Smith June Gale

1940   **PIER 13**
Co-star: Lloyd Nolan

1940   **LILLIAN RUSSELL**
Director: Irving Cummings
Co-stars: Alice Faye Don Ameche Henry Fonda

1941   **SLEEPERS WEST**
Co-stars: Lloyd Nolan Mary Beth Hughes

1941   **PERFECT SNOB**
Director: Ray McCarey
Co-stars: Cornel Wilde Charlotte Greenwood Charles Ruggles

1941   **MOON OVER HER SHOULDER**
Co-stars: Dan Dailey John Sutton Alan Mowbray

1941   **SUN VALLEY SERENADE**
Director: Bruce Humberstone
Co-stars: Sonja Henie John Payne Milton Berle

1941   **BLOOD AND SAND**
Director: Robert Kane
Co-stars: Tyrone Powell Linda Darnell Rita Hayworth

1942   **CHINA GIRL**
Director: Henry Hathaway
Co-stars: Gene Tierney George Montgomery Victor McLaglen

1942   **THE FALCON TAKES OVER**
Director: Irving Reis
Co-stars: George Sanders Ward Bond

1942   **THE NIGHT BEFORE THE DIVORCE**
Co-stars: Joseph Allen Jnr Mary Beth Hughes

1942   **THE MAGNIFICENT DOPE**
Director: Walter Lang
Co-stars: Henry Fonda Don Ameche George Barbier

1942   **ORCHESTRA WIVES**
Director: Archie Mayo
Co-stars: George Montgomery Ann Rutherford Cesar Romero

1942   **SECRET AGENT OF JAPAN**
Director: Irving Pichel
Co-stars: Preston Foster Sen Yung Janis Carter

1943   **HELLO FRISCO, HELLO**
Director: Bruce Humberstone
Co-stars: Alice Faye John Payne Jack Oakie

1944   **THE BRIDGE OF SAN LUIS REY**
Director: Rowland Lee
Co-stars: Akim Tamiroff Louis Calhern Nazimova

1944   **SWEET AND LOWDOWN**
Director: Archie Mayo
Co-stars: Linda Darnell Jack Oakie James Cardwell

1944   **TAMPICO**
Director: Lothar Mendes
Co-stars: Edward G. Robinson Victor McLaglen Mona Maris

1945   **CAPTAIN EDDIE**
Director: Lloyd Bacon
Co-stars: Fred MacMurray Thomas Mitchell Lloyd Nolan

1946   **HOME, SWEET HOMICIDE**
Director: Lloyd Bacon
Co-stars: Randolph Scott Peggy Ann Garner Dean Stockwell

1946   **MARGIE**
Director: Henry King
Co-stars: Jeanne Crain Glenn Langan Alan Young

1946   **NOCTURNE**
Director: Edwin Marin
Co-stars: George Raft Virginia Huston Joseph Pevney

1946   **SHOCK**
Director: Alfred Werker
Co-stars: Vincent Price Frank Latimore Anabel Shaw

1948   **THE MAN FROM TEXAS**
Co-stars: James Craig Reed Hadley

1948   **THE SPIRITUALIST**
Director: Bernard Vorhaus
Co-stars: Richard Carlson Turhan Bey

1951   **I'D CLIMB THE HIGHEST MOUNTAIN**
Director: Henry King
Co-stars: Susan Hayward William Lundigan

1952   **HAS ANYBODY SEEN MY GAL?**
Director: Douglas Sirk
Co-stars: Charles Coburn Piper Laurie Rock Hudson

1954   **ABBOTT & COSTELLO MEET THE KEYSTONE KOPS**
Director: Charles Lamont
Co-stars: Abbott & Costello Fred Clark

NORAH BARING

1929   **A COTTAGE ON DARTMOOR**
Director: Anthony Asquith
Co-stars: Uno Hemming Hans Schlettow

1930 AT THE VILLA ROSE
Director: Leslie Hiscott
Co-stars: Austin Trevor Barbara Gott

1932 STRANGE EVIDENCE
Director: Robert Milton
Co-stars: Leslie Banks Carol Goodner Diana Napier

SOPHIE BARJAC

1981 ALICE
Director: Jerry Gruza
Co-stars: Jean-Pierre Cassel Susannah York Paul Nicholas

1988 THE MAN WHO LIVED AT THE RITZ
Director: Desmond Davis
Co-stars: Perry King Leslie Caron Cherie Lunghi

EVE BARKER

1992 BORN KICKING
Director: Mandie Fletcher
Co-stars: Denis Lawson Sheila Ruskin

PATRICIA BARKER

1986 NUTCRACKER - THE MOTION PICTURE
Director: Carroll Ballard
Co-stars: Hugh Bigney Vanessa Sharp

ELLEN BARKIN *(Married Gabriel Byrne)*

1981 WE'RE FIGHTING BACK
Director: Lou Antonio
Co-stars: Kevin Mahon Paul McCrane Joe Morton

1982 TENDER MERCIES
Director: Bruce Beresford
Co-stars: Robert Duvall Tess Harper Wilford Brimley

1982 DINER
Director: Barry Levinson
Co-stars: Steve Guttenberg Mickey Rourke Kevin Bacon

1983 DANIEL
Director: Sidney Lumet
Co-stars: Timothy Hutton Mandy Patinkin Lindsay Crouse

1983 ENORMOUS CHANGES AT THE LAST MINUTE
Director: Mira Bank
Co-stars: Kevin Bacon Maria Tucci Sudie Bond

1983 EDDIE AND THE CRUISERS
Director: Martin Davidson
Co-stars: Tom Berenger Michael Pare

1984 TERRIBLE JOE MORAN
Director: Joseph Sargent
Co-stars: James Cagney Art Carney Peter Gallagher

1984 HARRY & SON
Director: Paul Newman
Co-stars: Paul Newman Robby Benson Wilford Brimley

1984 THE ADVENTURES OF BUCKAROO BANZAI ACROSS THE EIGHTH DIMENSION
Director: W.D. Richter
Co-stars: Peter Weller John Lithgow Christoper Lloyd

1986 ACT OF VENGEANCE
Director: John MacKenzie
Co-stars: Charles Bronson Wilford Brimley Keanu Reeves

1986 THE BIG EASY
Director: Jim McBrlde
Co-stars: Dennls Quaid Ned Beatty John Goodman

1986 DESERT BLOOM
Director: Eugene Corr
Co-stars: Jon Voight JoBeth Williams Anabeth Gish

1986 DOWN BY LAW
Director: Jim Jarmusch
Co-stars: Tom Waits John Lurie Roberto Benigni

1987 MADE IN HEAVEN
Director: Alan Rudolph
Co-stars: Timothy Hutton Kelly McGillis Maureen Stapleton

1987 SIESTA
Director: Mary Lambert
Co-stars: Gabriel Byrne Isabella Rossellini Jodie Foster

1988 BLOOD MONEY
Director: Jerry Schatzberg
Co-stars: Andy Garcia Morgan Freeman Michael Lombard

1989 SEA OF LOVE
Director: Harold Becker
Co-stars: Al Pacino John Goodman William Hickey

1989 JOHNNY HANDSOME
Director: Walter Hlll
Co-stars: Mickey Rouke Elizabeth McGovern Lance Henriksen

1991 SWITCH
Director: Blake Edwards
Co-stars: Jimmy Smits JoBeth Williams Lorraine Bracco

1992 MAN TROUBLE
Director: Bob Rafelson
Co-stars: Jack Nicholson Beverly D'Angelo Harry Dean Stanton

1992 MAC
Director: John Tuturro
Co-stars: John Tuturro Carl Capotorto Katherine Borowitz

1992 INTO THE WEST
Director: Mike Newell
Co-stars: Gabriel Byrne Ciaran Fitzgerald David Kelly

1993 THIS BOY'S LIFE: A TRUE STORY
Director: Michael Caton-Jones
Co-stars: Leonardo DiCaprio Robert De Niro

1995 BAD COMPANY
Director: Damian Harris
Co-stars: Laurence Fishburne Spalding Gray

1996 WILD BILL
Director: Waltor Hill
Co-stars: Jeff Bridges John Hurt

1997 TRIGGER HAPPY
Director: Larry Bishop
Co-stars: Jeff Goldblum Richard Dreyfuss Gabriel Byrne

MARCIE BARKIN

1976 THE VAN
Director: Sam Grossman
Co-stars: Stuart Getz Danny DeVito Deborah White

1978 SMOKEY AND THE GOOD TIME OUTLAWS
Director: Alex Grasshoff
Co-stars: Jesse Turner Slim Pickens Dianne Sherville

FREDA BARNFORD

1953 HEIGHTS OF DANGER
Director: Peter Bradford
Co-stars: Basil Appleby Annette Cabot

BINNIE BARNES

1931 OUT OF THE BLUE
Director: Gene Gerrard
Co-stars: Gene Gerrard Jessie Matthews Kay Hammond

1933 COUNSEL'S OPINION
Director: Allan Dwan
Co-stars: Henry Kendall Cyril Maude Lawrence Grossmith

1933 THE LADY IS WILLING
Director: Gilbert Miller
Co-stars: Leslie Howard Cedric Hardwicke

1933	**THE PRIVATE LIFE OF HENRY VIII**
Director:	Alexander Korda
Co-stars:	Charles Laughton Robert Donat

1934	**THE PRIVATE LIFE OF DON JUAN**
Director:	Alexander Korda
Co-stars:	Douglas Fairbanks Merle Oberon

1934	**THERE'S ALWAYS TOMORROW**
Director:	Edward Sloman
Co-stars:	Frank Morgan Robert Taylor Alan Hale

1935	**RENDEZVOUS**
Director:	William Howard
Co-stars:	William Powell Rosalind Russel Cesar Romero

1935	**DIAMOND JIM**
Director:	Edward Sutherland
Co-stars:	Edward Arnold Jean Arthur Cesar Romero

1936	**THE LAST OF THE MOHICANS**
Director:	George Seitz
Co-stars:	Randolph Scott Bruce Cabot Heather Angel

1936	**THE MAGNIFICENT BRUTE**
Director:	John Blystone
Co-stars:	Victor McLaglen Jean Dixon Billy Burrud

1936	**SMALL TOWN GIRL**
Director:	William Wellman
Co-stars:	Janet Gaynor Robert Taylor James Stewart

1936	**SUTTER'S GOLD**
Director:	James Cruz
Co-stars:	Edward Arnold Lee Tracy Katharine Alexander

1936	**THREE SMART GIRLS**
Director:	Henry Koster
Co-stars:	Deanna Durbin Charles Winninger Ray Milland

1937	**BROADWAY MELODY OF 1938**
Director:	Roy Del Ruth
Co-stars:	Robert Taylor Eleanor Powell Judy Garland

1938	**THREE BLIND MICE**
Director:	William Seiter
Co-stars:	Loretta Young Joel McCrea David Niven

1938	**GATEWAY**
Director:	Alfred Werker
Co-stars:	Don Ameche Arleen Whelan Raymond Walburn

1938	**THE FIRST HUNDRED YEARS**
Director:	Richard Thorpe
Co-stars:	Robert Montgomery Virginia Bruce

1938	**THE DIVORCE OF LADY X**
Director:	Tim Whelan
Co-stars:	Laurence Olivier Ralph Richardson Merle Oberon

1938	**ALWAYS GOODBYE**
Director:	Sidney Lanfield
Co-stars:	Barbara Stanwyck Herbert Marshall Ian Hunter

1938	**THE ADVENTURES OF MARCO POLO**
Director:	Archie Mayo
Co-stars:	Gary Cooper Sigrid Gurie Basil Rathbone

1939	**HOLIDAY**
Director:	George Cukor
Co-stars:	Katherine Hepburn Cary Grant Doris Nolan

1939	**MAN ABOUT TOWN**
Director:	Mark Sandrich
Co-stars:	Jack Benny Eddie Anderson Dorothy Lamour

1939	**THE THREE MUSKETEERS**
Director:	Allan Dwan
Co-stars:	Don Ameche Ritz Bros Lionel Atwill

1939	**FRONTIER MARSHALL**
Director:	Allan Dwan
Co-stars:	Randolph Scott Cesar Romero Nancy Kelly

1939	**WIFE, HUSBAND AND FRIEND**
Director:	Gregory Ratoff
Co-stars:	Loretta Young Warner Baxter Cesar Romero

1939	**DAYTIME WIFE**
Director:	Gregory Ratoff
Co-stars:	Tyrone Power Linda Darnell Warren William

1941	**NEW WINE**
Director:	Rheinhold Schunzel
Co-stars:	Alan Curtis Ilona Massey Albert Basserman

1941	**SKYLARK**
Director:	Mark Sandrich
Co-stars:	Claudette Colbert Ray Milland Brian Aherne

1941	**ANGELS WITH BROKEN WINGS**
Co-star:	Gilbert Roland

1941	**THIS THING CALLED LOVE**
Director:	Alexander Hall
Co-stars:	Rosalind Russell Melvyn Douglas

1941	**TIGHT SHOES**
Director:	Albert Rogell
Co-stars:	Broderick Crawford John Howard Ann Gwynne

1942	**THREE GIRLS ABOUT TOWN**
Director:	Leigh Jason
Co-stars:	Joan Blondell Janet Blair John Howard

1942	**IN OLD CALIFORNIA**
Director:	William McGann
Co-stars:	John Wayne Albert Dekker Edgar Kennedy

1942	**I MARRIED AN ANGEL**
Director:	W.S. Van Dyke
Co-stars:	Jeanette MacDonald Nelson Eddy Reginald Owen

1942	**CALL OUT THE MARINES**
Director:	Frank Ryan
Co-stars:	Edmund Lowe Victor McLaglen Paul Kelly

1943	**THE MAN FROM DOWN UNDER**
Director:	Robert Z. Leonard
Co-stars:	Charles Laughton Donna Reed

1944	**THE HOUR BEFORE THE DAWN**
Director:	Frank Tuttle
Co-stars:	Franchot Tone Veronica Lake

1944	**UP IN MABEL'S ROOM**
Director:	Allan Dwan
Co-stars:	Dennis O'Keefe Marjorie Reynolds

1944	**BARBARY COAST GENT**
Director:	Roy Del Ruth
Co-stars:	Wallace Beery Chill Wills John Carradine

1945	**IT'S IN THE BAG**
Director:	Richard Wallace
Co-stars:	Fred Allen Jack Benny Don Ameche

1945	**GETTING GERTIE'S GARTER**
Director:	Allan Dwan
Co-stars:	Dennis O'Keefe Marie MacDonald Mischa Auer

1945	**THE SPANISH MAIN**
Director:	Frank Borzage
Co-stars:	Paul Henreid Maureen O'Hara Walter Slezak

1946	**THE TIME OF THEIR LIVES**
Director:	Charles Barton
Co-stars:	Abbott & Costello Marjorie Reynolds

1948	**MY OWN TRUE LOVE**
Director:	Compton Bennett
Co-stars:	Phyllis Calvert Melvyn Douglas

1948	**IF WINTER COMES**
Director:	Victor Saville
Co-stars:	Walter Pidgeon Deborah Kerr Angela Lansbury

1950 SHADOW OF THE EAGLE
Director: Sidney Salkow
Co-stars: Richard Greene Valentina Cortese

1952 DECAMERON NIGHTS
Director: Hugo Fregonese
Co-stars: Louis Jourdan Joan Fontaine Joan Collins

1954 MALAGA
Director: Richard Sale
Co-stars: Maureen O'Hara MacDonald Carey

1966 THE TROUBLE WITH ANGELS
Director: Ida Lupino
Co-stars: Rosalind Russell Hayley Mills

1968 WHERE ANGELS GO, TROUBLE FOLLOWS
Director: James Neilson
Co-stars: Rosalind Russell Van Johnson

1973 FORTY CARATS
Director: Milton Katselas
Co-stars: Liv Ullman Gene Kelly Edward Albert

JOANNA BARNES

1958 AUNTIE MAME
Director: Morton Dacosta
Co-stars: Rosalind Russell Forrest Tucker Coral Browne

1959 TARZAN THE APE MAN
Director: Joseph Newnan
Co-stars: Dennis Miller Cesare Danova Robert Douglas

1961 THE PARENT TRAP
Director: David Swift
Co-stars: Hayley Mills Maureen O'Hara Brian Keith

1964 GOODBYE CHARLIE
Director: Vincent Minnelli
Co-stars: Debbie Reynolds Pat Boone Walter Matthau

1967 DON'T MAKE WAVES
Director: Alexander MacKendrick
Co-stars: Tony Curtis Claudia Cardinale

1970 BS I LOVE YOU
Director: Steven Hilliard Stern
Co-stars: Peter Kastner Joanna Cameron

PRISCILLA BARNES

1988 PERFECT PEOPLE
Director: Bruce Seth Green
Co-stars: Lauren Hutton Perry King June Lockhart

1989 STEPFATHER III: FATHER'S DAY
Director: Guy Magor
Co-stars: Rob Wightman David Tom

SALLY BARNES

1959 MAKE MINE A MILLION
Director: Lance Comfort
Co-stars: Arthur Askey Sid James Dermot Walsh

SUSAN BARNES

1981 SHE'S IN THE ARMY NOW
Director: Hy Averbach
Co-stars: Kathleen Quinlan Melanie Griffith Julie Carmen

1991 MEET THE APPLEGATES
Director: Michael Lehman
Co-stars: Ed Begley Jnr. Stockard Channing Cami Cooper

GERALDINE BARON

1981 CUTTER'S WAY
Director: Ivan Passer
Co-stars: Jeff Bridges John Heard Lisa Eichhorn

1984 CITY GIRL
Director: Martha Coolidge
Co-stars: Laura Harrington Joe Mastroianni Peter Riegert

JOANNE BARON

1994 PET SHOP
Director: Hope Perello
Co-stars: Leigh Ann Orsi Spencer Vrooman

LITA BARON

1948 JUNGLE JIM
Director: Willliam Berke
Co-stars: Johnny Weismuller Virginia Grey George Reeves

IRINA BARONOVA

1940 FLORIAN
Director: Edwin Marin
Co-stars: Robert Young Helen Gilbert Charles Coburn

1949 TRAIN OF EVENTS
Director: Basil Dearden
Co-stars: Valerie Hobson John Clements Jack Warner

JEANNE BARR

1961 LONG DAY'S JOURNEY INTO NIGHT
Director: Sidney Lumet
Co-stars: Katherine Hepburn Ralph Richardson

ROSEANNE BARR

1989 SHE-DEVIL
Director: Susan Seidelman
Co-stars: Meryl Streep Ed Begley Jnr. Sylvia Miles

1990 LOOK WHO'S TALKING TOO
Director: Amy Heckerling
Co-stars: John Travolta Kirstie Alley Olympia Dukakis

1996 BLUE IN THE FACE
Co-stars: Madonna Lily Tomlin Harvey Keitel

SHARON BARR

1981 THE ARCHER AND THE SORCERESS
Director: Nick Corea
Co-stars: Belinda Bauer Kabir Bedi Richard Dix

1993 FUGITIVE NIGHTS:
DANGER IN THE DESERT
Director: Gary Nelson
Co-stars: Sam Elliott Warren Frost Gino Silva

MARIA BARRANCO

1988 WOMEN ON THE VERGE OF
A NERVOUS BREAKDOWN
Director: Pedro Almodovar
Co-stars: Carmen Maura Antonio Banderas

1989 TIE ME UP! TIE ME DOWN!
Director: Pedro Almodovar
Co-stars: Antonio Banderas Victoria Abril

MARIE-CHRISTINE BARRAULT
Nominated For Best Actress In 1976 For "Cousin, Cousine"

1969 MY NIGHT WITH MAUDE
Director: Eric Rohmer
Co-stars: Jean-Louis Trintignant Francoise Fabian

1975 COUSIN, COUSINE
Director: Jean-Charles Tacchella
Co-stars: Marie-France Pisier Guy Marchand

1978 THE MEDUSA TOUCH
Director: Jack Gold
Co-stars: Richard Burton Lee Remick Lino Ventura

1980 STARDUST MEMORIES
Director: Woody Allen
Co-stars: Woody Allen Charlotte Rampling Jessica Harper

1983 SWANN IN LOVE
Director: Volker Schlorndorff
Co-stars: Jeremy Irons Ornella Muti Alain Delon

1983 TABLE FOR FIVE
Director: Robert Lieberman
Co-stars: Jon Voight Richard Crenna Millie Perkins

1989 THE SILENT WOMAN
Director: Joyce Bunuel
Co-stars: Veronique Genest Pierre Clementi

ANNE BARRETT

1943 FOLLIES GIRL
Director: William Rowland
Co-stars: Wendy Barrie Doris Nolan Gordon Oliver

CLAUDIA BARRETT

1953 ROBOT MONSTER
Director: Phil Tucker
Co-stars: George Nader Selena Royle

EDITH BARRETT

L941 LADY FOR A NIGHT
Director: Leigh Jason
Co-stars: Joan Blondell John Wayne Blanche Yurka

1941 LADIES IN RETIREMENT
Director: Charles Vidor
Co-stars: Ida Lupino Louis Hayward Isobel Elsom

1942 GET HEP TO LOVE
Director: Charles Lamont
Co-stars: Gloria Jean Donald O'Connor Peggy Ryan

1943 THE GHOST SHIP
Director: Mark Robson
Co-stars: Richard Dix Russell Wade

1943 ALWAYS A BRIDESMAID
Co-stars: Charles Butterworth Billy Gilbert

1943 I WALKED WITH A ZOMBIE
Director: Jacques Tourneur
Co-stars: Frances Dee James Ellison Tom Conway

1943 THE SONG OF BERNADETTE
Director: Henry King
Co-stars: Jennifer Jones Charles Bickford Vincent Price

1944 JANE EYRE
Director: Robert Stevenson
Co-stars: Joan Fontaine Orson Welles Margaret O'Brien

1945 MOLLY AND ME
Director: Lewis Seiler
Co-stars: Gracie Fields Monty Woolley Reginald Gardiner

1948 RUTHLESS
Director: Edgar Ulmer
Co-stars: Zachary Scott Sydney Greenstreet Diana Lynn

1949 THE LADY GAMBLES
Director: Michael Gordon
Co-stars: Barbara Stanwyck Robert Preston

1952 HOLIDAY FOR SINNERS
Director: Gerald Mayer
Co-stars: Gig Young Keenan Wynn Janice Rule

1956 THE SWAN
Director: Charles Vidor
Co-stars: Grace Kelly Alec Guinness Louis Jourdan

JANE BARRETT

1948 EUREKA STOCKADE
Director: Harry Watt
Co-stars: Chips Rafferty Gordon Jackson Peter Finch

1952 TIME GENTLEMEN PLEASE!
Director: Eddie Byrne
Co-stars: Hermoine Baddeley Dora Bryan

1952 THE SWORD AND THE ROSE
Director: Ken Annakin
Co-stars: Richard Todd Glynis Johns Michael Gough

JUDITH BARRETT

1936 YELLOWSTONE
Co-stars: Mary Gordon Alan Hale

1937 THE GOOD OLD SOAK
Director: Walter Ruben
Co-stars: Wallace Beery Una Merkel Eric Linden

1937 ARMOURED CAR
Co-stars: Robert Wilcox Harry Davenport

1937 LET THEM LIVE
Director: Harold Young
Co-stars: John Howard Nan Grey Robert Wilcox

1939 I'M FROM MISSOURI
Director: Theodore Reed
Co-stars: Bob Burns Gladys George Patricia Morison

1939 DISPUTED PASSAGE
Director: Frank Borzage
Co-stars: Dorothy Lamour John Howard Akim Tamiroff

1939 TELEVISION SPY
Director: Edward Dmytryk
Co-stars: William Henry Anthony Quinn Richard Denning

1940 WOMEN WITHOUT NAMES
Director: Robert Florey
Co-stars: Ellen Drew Robert Paige Fay Helm

1940 ROAD TO SINGAPORE
Director: Victor Schertzinger
Co-stars: Bing Crosby Bob Hope Dorothy Lamour

1940 THOSE WERE THE DAYS
Director: Theodore Reed
Co-stars: William Holden Bonita Granville

LAURINDA BARRETT

1968 THE HEART IS A LONELY HUNTER
Director: Robert Ellis Miller
Co-stars: Alan Arkin Sondra Locke

RONA BARRETT

1978 SEXTETTE
Director: Ken Hughes
Co-stars: Mae West Tony Curtis Ringo Starr

AMBER BARRETTO

1989 LITTLE MONSTERS
Director: Richard Alan Greenberg
Co-stars: Fred Savage Howie Mandel

AMANDA BARRIE

1965 CARRY ON CLEO
Director: Gerald Thomas
Co-stars: Sid James Kenneth Williams Kenneth Connor

BARBARA BARRIE
Nominated For Best Supporting Actress In 1979 For "Breaking Away"

1964 ONE POTATO, TWO POTATO
Director: Larry Peerce
Co-stars: Bernie Hamilton Richard Mulligan

1978   SUMMER OF MY GERMAN SOLDIER
Director: Michael Tuchner
Co-stars: Kristy McNichol Bruce Davison

1979   THE BELL JAR
Director: Larry Peerce
Co-stars: Marilyn Hassett Julie Harris Anne Jackson

1979   BREAKING AWAY
Director: Peter Yates
Co-stars: Dennis Christopher Dennis Quaid Paul Dooley

1980   PRIVATE BENJAMIN
Director: Howard Zieff
Co-stars: Goldie Hawn Eileen Brennan Armand Assante

1982   NOT JUST ANOTHER AFFAIR
Director: Steven Hilliard Stern
Co-stars: Victoria Principal Gil Gerard

1982   TWO OF A KIND
Director: Roger Young
Co-stars: George Burns Robby Benson Cliff Robertson

1985   THE EXECUTION
Director: Paul Wendkos
Co-stars: Loretta Swit Rip Torn Jessica Walter

1986   VITAL SIGNS
Director: Stuart Miller
Co-stars: Edward Asner Gary Cole Kate McNeil

1987   THE PASSAGE
Director: Harry Thompson
Co-stars: Brian Keith Ned Beatty Alexandra Paul

1987   REAL MEN
Director: Dennis Feldman
Co-stars: James Belushi John Ritter Bill Morey

1988   MY FIRST LOVE
Director: Gilbert Cates
Co-stars: Beatrice Arthur Richard Kiley Joan Van Ark

1994   MY BREAST
Director: Betty Thomas
Co-stars: Meredith Baxter Jamey Sheridan Sara Botsford

ELAINE BARRIE

1939   MIDNIGHT
Director: Mitchell Leisen
Co-stars: Claudette Colbert Don Ameche John Barrymore

ELLEN BARRIE

1958   PASSIONATE SUMMER
Director: Rudolph Cartier
Co-stars: Virginia McKenna Bill Travers Yvonne Mitchell

JUDITH BARRIE

1930   PARTY GIRL
Director: Victor Halperin
Co-stars: Douglas Fairbanks Jnr. Jeanette Loff Marie Prevost

1931   EX-FLAME
Co-stars: Neil Hamilton Billie Haggerty

JUNE BARRIE

1990   CLOSE RELATIONS
Director: Adrian Shergold
Co-stars: James Hazeldine Clare Holman Annie Gurney

LISA BARRIE

1959   THE CAREER GIRL
Director: Harold David
Co-stars: June Wilkinson Charles Robert Keane

MONA BARRIE

1934   SUCH WOMEN ARE DANGEROUS
Director: James Flood
Co-stars: Warner Baxter Rosemary Ames Rochelle Hudson

1934   SLEEPERS EAST
Co-star: Wynne Gibson

1934   ALL MEN ARE ENEMIES
Director: George Fitzmaurice
Co-stars: Hugh Williams Helen Twelvetrees

1934   CAROLINA
Director: Henry King
Co-stars: Janet Gaynor Lionel Barrymore Robert Young

1934   CHARLIE CHAN IN LONDON
Director: Eugene Forde
Co-stars: Warner Olanld Alan Mowbray Ray Milland

1934   ONE NIGHT OF LOVE
Director: Victor Schertzinger
Co-stars: Grace Moore Tullio Carminati

1935   STORM OVER THE ANDES
Director: Christy Cabanne
Co-stars: Jack Holt Antonio Moreno Gene Lockhart

1935   MYSTERY WOMAN
Director: Eugene Forde
Co-stars: Gilbert Roland John Halliday Rod La Rocque

1935   LADIES LOVE DANGER
Director: Bruce Humberstone
Co-stars: Gilbert Roland Donald Cook Adrienne Ames

1935   UNWELCOME STRANGER
Co-star: Jack Holt

1935   KING OF BURLESQUE
Director: Sidney Lanfield
Co-stars: Warner Baxter Alice Faye Jack Oakie

1936   LOVE ON THE RUN
Director: W. S. Van Dyke
Co-stars: Clark Gable Joan Crawford Franchot Tone

1936   A MESSAGE TO GARCIA
Director: George Marshall
Co-stars: Wallace Beery Barbara Stanwyck John Boles

1937   SOMETHING TO SING ABOUT
Director: Victor Schertzinger
Co-stars: James Cagney Evelyn Daw Gene Lockhart

1937   MOUNTAIN JUSTICE
Director: Michael Curtiz
Co-stars: Josephine Hutchinson George Brent Guy Kibbee

1937   I MET HIM IN PARIS
Director: Wesley Ruggles
Co-stars: Claudette Colbert Melvyn Douglas

1939   I TAKE THIS WOMAN
Director: W. S. Van Dyke
Co-stars: Spencer Tracy Hedy Lamarr Laraine Day

1940   THE LADY WITH RED HAIR
Director: Curtis Bernhardt
Co-stars: Miriam Hopkins Claude Rains

1941   MURDER AMONG FRIENDS
Director: Ray McCarey
Co-stars: John Hubbard Marjorie Weaver Cobina Wright Jnr

1941   SKYLARK
Director: Mark Sandrich
Co-stars: Claudette Colbert Ray Milland Brian Aherne

1941   NEVER GIVE A SUCKER AN EVEN BREAK
Director: Edward Cline
Co-stars: W.C. Fields Gloria Jean

1941 ELLERY QUEEN AND THE MURDER RING
Director: James Hogan
Co-stars: Ralph Bellamy Margaret Lindsay

1942 STRANGE CASE OF DOCTOR Rx
Director: William Nigh
Co-stars: Lionel Atwill Patric Knowles Ann Gwynne

1942 CAIRO
Director: W. S. Van Dyke
Co-stars: Jeanette MacDonald Robert Young Ethel Waters

1943 ONE DANGEROUS NIGHT
Director: Michael Gordon
Co-stars: Warren William Marguerite Chapman

1944 STORM OVER LISBON
Director: George Sherman
Co-stars: Vera Ralston Erich Von Stronheim Richard Arlen

1946 THE DEVIL'S MASK
Director: Henry Lewis
Co-stars: Jim Bannon Anita Louise Michael Duane

1946 JUST BEFORE DAWN
Director: William Castle
Co-stars: Warner Baxter Adelle Roberts Marion Miller

1952 THE FIRST TIME
Director: Frank Tashlin
Co-stars: Robert Cummings Barbara Hale Jeff Donnell

WENDY BARRIE

1932 WEDDING REHEARSAL
Director: Alexander Korda
Co-stars: Roland Young John Loder Merle Oberon

1933 THE PRIVATE LIFE OF HENRY VIII
Director: Alexander Korda
Co-stars: Charles Laughton Robert Donat Elsa Lancaster

1934 GIVE HER A RING
Director: Arthur Woods
Co-stars: Clifford Mollison Erik Rhodes Stewart Granger

1935 COLLEGE SCANDAL
Director: Elliott Nugent
Co-stars: Arline Judge Kent Taylor Mary Nash

1935 A FEATHER IN HER HAT
Director: Alfred Santell
Co-stars: Basil Rathbone Louis Hayward

1935 SCANDALS OF PARIS
Co-star: Gene Gerrard

1935 IT'S A SMALL WORLD
Director: Irving Cummings
Co-stars: Spencer Tracy Raymond Walburn Irving Bacon

1935 BIG BROADCAST OF 1936
Director: Ben Glason
Co-stars: Jack Oakie Bing Crosby Bill Robinson

1935 MILLIONS IN THE AIR
Director: Ray McCarey
Co-stars: Robert Cummings John Howard Benny Baker

1936 TICKET TO PARADISE
Co-star: Roger Pryor

1937 WINGS OVER HONOLULU
Director: H. C. Potter
Co-stars: Ray Milland William Gargan Kent Taylor

1937 PRESCRIPTION FOR ROMANCE
Co-star: Kent Taylor

1937 VENGEANCE
Director: Del Lord
Co-stars: Lyle Talbot Marc Lawrence Wally Albright

1937 A GIRL WITH IDEAS
Director: S. Sylvan Simon
Co-stars: Walter Pidgeon Kent Taylor George Barbier

1937 DEAD END
Director: William Wyler
Co-stars: Joel McCrea Sylvia Sidney Humphrey Bogart

1938 I AM THE LAW
Director: Alexander Hall
Co-stars: Edward G. Robinson Otto Kruger

1939 DAYTIME WIFE
Director: Gregory Ratoff
Co-stars: Tyrone Power Linda Darnell Warren William

1939 FIVE CAME BACK
Director: John Farrow
Co-stars: Chester Morris Lucille Ball Kent Taylor

1939 THE WITNESS VANISHES
Co-star: Edmund Lowe

1939 THE HOUND OF THE BASKERVILLES
Director: Sidney Lanfield
Co-stars: Basil Rathlone Nigel Bruce

1939 NEWSBOY'S HOME
Director: Harold Young
Co-stars: Jackie Cooper Edmund Lowe Elisha Cook Jnr

1939 PACIFIC LINER
Director: Lew Landers
Co-stars: Victor McLaglen Chester Morris Barry Fitzgerald

1939 THE SAINT STRIKES BACK
Director: John Farrow
Co-stars: George Sanders Barry Fitzgerald Jonathan Hale

1940 THE SAINT TAKES OVER
Director: Jack Hively
Co-stars: George Sanders Jonathan Hale Paul Guilfoyle

1940 MEN AGAINST THE SKY
Director: Leslie Goodwins
Co-stars: Richard Dix Kent Taylor Edmund Lowe

1941 THE SAINT IN PALM SPRINGS
Director: Jack Hively
Co-stars: George Sanders Jonathan Hale Paul Guilfoyle

1941 THE GAY FALCON
Director: Irving Reis
Co-stars: George Sanders Allen Jenkins Turhan Bey

1941 A DATE WITH THE FALCON
Director: Irving Reis
Co-stars: George Sanders Allen Jenkins James Gleason

1942 WOMEN IN WAR
Director: John Auer
Co-stars: Elsie Janis Patric Knowles Mae Clark

1943 FOREVER AND A DAY
Director: Rene Clair
Co-stars: Charles Laughton Jessie Matthews Roland Young

1943 SUBMARINE ALERT
Co-stars: Richard Arlen Abner Biberman

1943 FOLLIES GIRL
Director: William Rowland
Co-stars: Gordon Oliver Doris Nolan Cora Witherspoon

1943 EYES OF THE UNDERWORLD
Director: Roy William Neill
Co-stars: Richard Dix Lon Chaney Don Porter

SYDNEY BIDDLE BARROWS

1987 MAYFLOWER MADAM
Director: Lou Antonio
Co-stars: Candice Bergen Chris Sarandon Chita Rivera

DOROTHY BARRY

1989 SWEETIE
Director: Jane Campion
Co-stars: Genevieve Lemon Karen Colston Tom Lyons

JOAN BARRY

1931 RICH AND STRANGE
Director: Alfred Hitchcock
Co-stars: Henry Kendall Percy Marmont Elsie Randolph

1931 THE OUTSIDER
Director: Harry Lachman
Co-stars: Harold Huth Frank Lawton Mary Clare

1931 MAN OF MAYFAIR
Co-star: Jack Buchanan

1932 ROME EXPRESS
Director: Walter Forde
Co-stars: Conrad Veidt Gordon Harker Esther Ralston

PATRICIA BARRY
(First Appearance As A Baby In "Showboat")

1936 SHOWBOAT
Director: James Whale
Co-stars: Irene Dunne Allan Jones Paul Robeson

1962 SAMMY, THE WAY-OUT SEAL
Director: Norman Tokar
Co-stars: Robert Culp Jack Carson Billy Mumy

1964 DEAR HEART
Director: Delbert Mann
Co-stars: Glenn Ford Geraldine Page Angela Lansbury

1964 KITTEN WITH A WHIP
Director: Douglas Heyes
Co-stars: Ann-Margret John Forsythe Peter Brown

1971 DEAD MEN TELL NO TALES
Director: Walter Grauman
Co-stars: Christopher George Judy Carne

1971 THE MARRIAGE OF A YOUNG STOCKBROKER
Director: Lawrence Turman
Co-stars: Richard Benjamin Joanna Shimkus

1980 BOGIE
Director: Vincent Sherman
Co-stars: Kevin O'Connor Kathryn Harrold

1980 ADDICTION: A CRY FOR LOVE
Director: Paul Wendkos
Co-stars: Susan Blakely Gene Barry Powers Booth

PHYLLIS BARRY

1933 DIPLOMANIACS
Director: William Seiter
Co-stars: Bert Wheeler Robert Woolsey Hugh Herbert

1933 WHAT, NO BEER?
Director: Edward Sedgwick
Co-stars: Buster Keaton Jimmy Durante Rosco Ates

1933 CYNARA
Director: King Vidor
Co-stars: Ronald Colman Kay Francis Henry Stephenson

1934 THE MOONSTONE
Co-star: David Manners

1937 DAMAGED GOODS
Director: Phil Stone
Co-stars: Pedro De Cordoba Arletta Duncan Esther Dale

1937 THE PRINCE AND THE PAUPER
Director: William Keighley
Co-stars: Errol Flynn Billy & Bobby Mauch

1941 UNFINISHED BUSINESS
Director: Gregory La Cava
Co-stars: Irene Dunne Robert Montgomery June Clyde

DEBORAH BARRYMORE
(Daughter Of Roger Moore)

1987 LIONHEART
Director: Franklin Schaffner
Co-stars: Eric Stoltz Gabriel Byrne Nicola Cowper

1900 BULLSEYE!
Director: Michael Winner
Co-stars: Michael Caine Roger Moore Sally Kirkland

DIANA BARRYMORE
(Daughter Of John Barrymore)

1942 BETWEEN US GIRLS
Director: Henry Koster
Co-stars: Kay Francis John Boles Robert Cummings

1942 EAGLE SQUADRON
Director: Arthur Lubin
Co-stars: Robert Stack John Loder Eddie Albert

1942 NIGHTMARE
Director: Tim Whelan
Co-stars: Brian Donlevy Henry Daniell Arthur Shields

1943 FRONTIER BAD MEN
Director: William McGann
Co-stars: Robert Paige Ann Gwynne Lon Chaney

1943 FIRED WIFE
Director: Charles Lamont
Co-stars: Robert Paige Louise Allbritton Watler Abel

1944 LADIES COURAGEOUS
Director: John Rawlins
Co-stars: Loretta Young Geraldine Fitzgerald Evelyn Ankers

DREW BARRYMORE *(Child)*

1980 BOGIE
Director: Vincent Sherman
Co-stars: Kevin O'Connor Kathryn Harold Ann Wedgeworth

1980 ALTERED STATES
Director: Ken Russell
Co-stars: William Hurt Blair Brown Bob Balaban

1982 E.T. THE EXTRA-TERRESTRIAL
Director: Steven Spielberg
Co-stars: Dee Wallace Henry Thomas

1984 FIRESTARTER
Director: Mark Lester
Co-stars: David Keith George C. Scott Martin Sheen

1984 IRRECONCILABLE DIFFERENCES
Director: Charles Shyer
Co-stars: Ryan O'Neal Shelley Long Sharon Stone

1985 CAT'S EYE
Director: Lewis Teague
Co-stars: James Woods Alan King Candy Clark

1986 BABES IN TOYLAND
Director: Clive Donner
Co-stars: Richard Mulligan Eileen Brennan Keanu Reeves

1987 CONSPIRACY OF LOVE
Director: Noel Black
Co-stars: Robert Young Elizabeth Wilson

1988 SEE YOU IN THE MORNING
Director: Alan Pakula
Co-stars: Jeff Bridges Alice Krige Farrah Fawcett

1992 POISON IVY
Director: Katt Shea Ruben
Co-stars: Tom Skerritt Cheryl Ladd Sara Gilbert

1992 DOPPELGANGER: THE EVIL WITHIN
Director: Dennis Christopher
Co-star: George Newbern

1992 GUNCRAZY
Director: Tamra Davis
Co-stars: James LeGros Joe Dallesandro Ione Skye

1993 THE AMY FISHER STORY
Director: Andy Tennant
Co-stars: Anthony John Denison Harley Jane Kozak

1993 WAYNE'S WORLD 2
Director: Stephen Surjik
Co-stars: Mike Myers Dana Carvey Tia Carrere

1993 MOTORAMA
Director: Barry Shils
Co-stars: Jordan Michael Susan Tyrrell

1994 BAD GIRLS
Director: Jonathan Kaplan
Co-stars: Madeleine Stowe Andie MacDowall Dermot Mulroney

1995 MAD LOVE
Director: Antonia Bird
Co-star: Chris O'Donnell

1995 BOYS ON THE SIDE
Director: Herbert Ross
Co-stars: Mary-Louise Parker Whoopi Goldberg

1996 EVERYBODY SAYS I LOVE YOU
Director: Woody Allen
Co-stars: Woody Allen Julia Roberts Goldie Hawn

1997 SCREAM
Director: Wes Craven
Co-star: Henry Winkler

1998 THE WEDDING SINGER
Director: Frank Coraci
Co-stars: Adam Sandler Steve Buscemi Angela Featherstone

ETHEL BARRYMORE
(Sister Of John & Lionel Barrymore)
Oscar For Best Supporting Actress In 1944 For "None But The Lonely Heart", Nominated For Best Supporting Actress In 1946 For "The Spiral Staircase", In 1947 For "The Paradine Case", And In 1949 For "Pinky"

1932 RASPUTLN AND THE EMPRESS
Director: Richard Boleslawski
Co-stars: John & Lionel Barrymore Diana Wynyard

1944 NONE BUT THE LONELY HEART
Director: Clifford Odets
Co-stars: Cary Grant Barry Fitzgerald

1946 THE SPIRAL STAIRCASE
Director: Robert Siodmak
Co-stars: Dorothy MacGuire George Brent Rhonda Fleming

1947 THE PARADINE CASE
Director: Alfred Hitchcock
Co-stars: Gregory Peck Charles Laughton Ann Todd

1947 NIGHT SONG
Director: John Cromwell
Co-stars: Dana Andrews Merle Oberon Hoagy Carmichael

1947 MOSS ROSE
Director: Gregory Ratoff
Co-stars: Victor Mature Peggy Cummings Vincent Price

1947 THE FARMER'S DAUGHTER
Director: H. C. Potter
Co-stars: Loretta Young Joseph Cotten Charles Bickford

1948 MOONRISE
Director: Frank Borzage
Co-stars: Dane Clark Gail Russell Allyn Joslyn

1948 PORTRAIT OF JENNIE
Director: William Dieterle
Co-stars: Jennifer Jones Joseph Cotten David Wayne

1949 PINKY
Director: Elia Kazan
Co-stars: Jeanne Crain Ethel Waters William Lundigan

1949 THE GREAT SINNER
Director: Robert Siodmak
Co-stars: Gregory Peck Ava Gardner Walter Huston

1949 THAT MIDNIGHT KISS
Director: Norman Taurog
Co-stars: Mario Lanza Kathryn Grayson Jose Iturbi

1950 THE RED DANUBE
Director: George Sidney
Co-stars: Walter Pidgeon Peter Lawford Janet Leigh

1951 THE SECRET OF CONVICT LAKE
Director: Michael L Gordon
Co-stars: Glenn Ford Gene Tierney Ann Dvorak

1951 KIND LADY
Director: John Sturges
Co-stars: Maurice Evans Angela Lansbury Betsy Blair

1952 IT'S A BIG COUNTRY
Director: John Sturges
Co-stars: Gene Kelly Van Johnson Janet Leigh

1952 JUST FOR YOU
Director: Elliott Nugent
Co-stars: Bing Crosby Jane Wyman Bob Arthur

1952 DEADLINE USA
Director: Richard Brooks
Co-stars: Humphrey Bogart Kim Hunter Ed Begley

1953 MAIN STREET TO BROADWAY
Director: Tay Garnett
Co-stars: Tom Morton Mary Murphy Lionel Barrymore

1953 THE STORY OF THREE LOVES
Director: Vincente Minnelli
Co-stars: James Mason Moira Shearer Leslie Caron

1954 YOUNG AT HEART
Director: Gordon Douglas
Co-stars: Doris Day Frank Sinatra Gig Young

1956 JOHNNY TROUBLE
Director: John Auer
Co-stars: Stuart Whitman Cecil Kellaway Carolyn Jones

JUDITH BARSI
1987 JAWS - THE REVENGE
Director: Joseph Sargent
Co-stars: Lorraine Gary Karin Young Michael Caine

1987 SLAM DANCE
Director: Wayne Wang
Co-stars: Tom Hulce Mary Elizabeth Mastrantonio Virginia Madsen

1988 THE LAND BEFORE TIME *(Voice)*
Director: Don Bluth
Co-stars: Helen Shaver Pat Hingle Gabriel Damon

1989 ALL DOGS GO TO HEAVEN *(Voice)*
Director: Don Bluth
Co-stars: Burt Reynolds Dom DeLuise Loni Anderson

ISOLDE BARTH
1983 MISCHIEF
Director: Peter Fleischmann
Co-stars: Peter Fleischmann Angelika Stute Baldwin Baas

BONNIE BARTLETT
1982 LOVE LETTERS
Director: Amy Jones
Co-stars: Jaime Lee Curtis James Keach Amy Madigan

1983 DEMPSEY
Director: Gus Trikonis
Co-stars: Treat Williams Sam Waterston Sally Kellerman

1986 THE DELIBERATE STRANGER
Director: Marvin Chomsky
Co-stars: Mark Harmon Frederic Forrest

1987 DEADLY DECEPTION
Director: John Llewellyn Moxey
Co-stars: Matt Salinger Lisa Eilbacher

1988 THE WATCH COMMANDER
Director: Neil Maffeo
Co-stars: Jack Warden Gregg Henry Ben Marley

1988 RIGHT TO DIE
Director: Paul Wendkos
Co-stars: Raquel Welch Michael Gross Joanna Miles

1988 TWINS
Director: Ivan Reitman
Co-stars: Arnold Schwarzenegger Danny DeVito Kelly Preston

MARTINE BARTLETT
1961 SPLENDOUR IN THE GRASS
Director: Elia Kazan
Co-stars: Natalie Wood Warren Beatty Pat Hingle

1975 ALOHA BOBBY AND ROSE
Director: Floyd Mutrux
Co-stars: Paul LeMat Dianne Hull Robert Carradine

ROBIN BARTLETT
1991 REGARDING HENRY
Director: Mike Nichols
Co-stars: Harrison Ford Annette Bening Mikki Allen

1991 TEEN AGENT
Director: William Dear
Co-stars: Richard Grieco Linda Hunt Roger Rees

EVA BARTOK
1951 A TALE OF FIVE CITIES
Director: Montgomery Tully
Co-stars: Bonar Colleano Gina Lollobrigida

1952 THE CRIMSON PIRATE
Director: Robert Siodmak
Co-stars: Burt Lancaster Nick Cravat Noel Purcell

1953 THE ASSASSIN
Director: Ralph Thomas
Co-stars: Richard Todd George Coulouris Sid James

1953 SPACEWAYS
Director: Terence Fisher
Co-stars: Howard Duff Alan Wheatley Michael Medwin

1955 BREAK IN THE CIRCLE
Director: Val Guest
Co-stars: Forrest Tucker Marius Goring Guy Middleton

1956 THE GAMMA PEOPLE
Director: John Gilling
Co-stars: Paul Douglas Leslie Phillips Walter Rilla

1956 TEN THOUSAND BEDROOMS
Director: Richard Thorpe
Co-stars: Dean Martin Walter Slezak Paul Henreid

1958 OPERATION AMSTERDAM
Director: Michael McCarthy
Co-stars: Peter Finch Tony Britton Alexander Knox

1959 SOS PACIFIC
Director: Guy Green
Co-stars: Eddie Constantine Pier Angeli John Gregson

1960 BEYOND THE CURTAIN
Director: Compton Bennett
Co-stars: Richard Greene Marius Goring Lucie Mannheim

1964 BLOOD AND BLACK LACE
Director: Mario Bava
Co-stars: Cameron Mitchell Mary Arden Thomas Reiner

MARGARET BARTON
1947 TEMPTATION HARBOUR
Director: Lance Comfort
Co-stars: Robert Newton Simone Simon William Hartnell

MISCHA BARTON (Child)
1997 LAWN DOGS
Director: John Duigan
Co-star: Sam Rockwell

KIM BASINGER
1978 THE GHOST OF FLIGHT 4OL
Director: Steven Hilliard Stern
Co-stars: Ernest Borgnine Gary Lockwood

1981 HARD COUNTRY
Director: David Greene
Co-stars: Jan-Michael Vincent Michael Parks

1982 MOTHER LODE
Director: Charlton Heston
Co-stars: Charlton Heston Nick Mancuso John Marley

1983 NEVER SAY NEVER AGAIN
Director: Irving Kershner
Co-stars: Sean Connery Barbara Carrera Edward Fox

1983 THE MAN WHO LOVED WOMEN
Director: Blake Edwards
Co-stars: Burt Reynolds Julie Andrews

1984 THE NATURAL
Director: Barry Levinson
Co-stars: Robert Redford Robert Duvall Glenn Close

1985 FOOL FOR LOVE
Director: Robert Altman
Co-stars: Sam Shepard Randy Quaid Harry Dean Stanton

1986 NO MERCY
Director: Richard Pearce
Co-stars: Richard Gere Jeroen Krabbe George Dzundza

1986 NINE AND A HALF WEEKS
Director: Adrian Lyne
Co-stars: Mickey Rourke Margaret Whitton Karen Young

1987 NADINE
Director: Robert Benton
Co-stars: Jeff Bridges Rip Torn Gwen Verdon

1987 BLIND DATE
Director: Blake Edwards
Co-stars: Bruce Willis Alice Hirson Graham Stark

1988 MY STEPMOTHER IS AN ALIEN
Director: Richard Benjamin
Co-stars: Dan Aykroyd Jon Lovitz

1989 BATMAN
Director: Tim Burton
Co-stars: Michael Keaton Jack Nicholson Jack Palance

1991 TOO HOT TO HANDLE
Director: Jerry Rees
Co-stars: Alec Baldwin Robert Loggia Armand Assante

1992 FINAL ANALYSIS
Director: Phil Joanou
Co-stars: Richard Gere Uma Thurman Eric Roberts

1992 COOL WORLD
Director: Ralph Bakshi
Co-stars: Galriel Bryne Brad Pitt Michele Abrams

1993 WAYNE'S WORLD 2
Director: Stephen Surjik
Co-stars: Mike Myers Dana Carvey Tia Carrere

1993 THE REAL McCOY
Director: Russell Mulcahy
Co-stars: Val Kilmer Terence Stamp Zach English

1994 THE GETAWAY
Director: Roger Donaldson
Co-stars: Alec Baldwin Michael Madsen James Woods

1994 PRET-A-PORTER
Director: Robert Altman
Co-stars: Julia Roberts Sophia Loren

1997 L.A.CONFIDENTIAL
Director: Curtis Hanson
Co-stars: Kevin Spacey Guy Pearce Danny DeVito

ELGA BASKIN

1986 COMBAT ACADEMY
Director: Heal Israel
Co-stars: Keith Gordon George Clooney Tina Caspary

1986 THE NAME OF THE ROSE
Director: Jean-Jacques Annaud
Co-stars: Sean Connery Christian Slater

MARIANNE BASLER

1988 A SOLDIER'S TALE
Director: Larry Parr
Co-stars: Gabriel Byrne Judge Reinhold

LINA BASQUETTE

1931 GOLDIE
Director: Ben Stoloff
Co-stars: Spencer Tracey Jean Harlow Warren Hymer

1938 FOUR MEN AND A PRAYER
Director: John Ford
Co-stars: Loretta Young David Niven Richard Greene

HENRIETTA BASS

1990 KEEPING TOM NICE
Director: Louise Panton
Co-stars: John Alderton Gwen Taylor Linus Roach

KIM BASS

1985 THE PROTECTOR
Director: James Clickenhaus
Co-stars: Jackie Chan Danny Aiello Victor Arnold

ELSA BASSERMAN

1943 MADAME CURRIE
Director: Mervyn LeRoy
Co-stars: Greer Garson Walter Pidgeon Robert Walker

GABY BASSET

1953 TOUCHEZ PAS AU GRISBI
Director: Jacques Becker
Co-stars: Jean Gabin Jeanne Moreau Lino Ventura

ANGELA BASSETT

1991 BOYZ N THE HOOD
Director: John Singleton
Co-stars: Larry Fishburne Ice Cube Nia Long

1991 CITY OF HOPE
Director: John Sayles
Co-stars: Vincent Spano Tony Lobianco Barbara Williams

1991 BLIND HATE
Director: John Korty
Co-stars: Corbin Bernsen Sandy Bull Jenny Lewis

1992 MALCOLM X
Director: Spike Lee
Co-stars: Spike Lee Denzel Washington Christopher Plummer

1992 CRITTERS 4: CRITTERS IN SPACE
Director: Rupert Harvey
Co-stars: Don Opper Brad Dourif

1993 PASSION FISH
Director: John Sayles
Co-stars: Mary McDonald Alfre Woodard Leo Burmester

1993 TINA: WHAT'S LOVE GOT TO DO WITH IT?
Director: Brian Gibson
Co-stars: Laurence Fishburne Jennifer Lewis

1996 STRANGE DAYS
Director: Kathryn Bigelow
Co-stars: Ralph Fiennes Juliette Lewis

1996 VAMPIRE IN BROOKLYN
Director: Wes Craven
Co-stars: Eddie Murphy Allen Payne

1997 WAITING TO EXHALE
Director: Forest Whitaker
Co-stars: Whitney Houston Loretta Devine

LINDA BASSETT

1988 PARIS BY NIGHT
Director: David Hare
Co-stars: Charlotte Rampling Michael Gambon Iain Glenn

1990 NEWS HOUNDS
Director: Les Blair
Co-stars: Adrian Edmondson Alison Steadman

1991 A SMALL DANCE
Director: Alan Horrox
Co-stars: Kate Hardie James Hazeldine

SHIRLEY BASSEY

1996 LA PASSIONE
Director: Chris Rea
Co-star: Chris Rea

ALEXANDRA BASTEDO

1975 THE GHOUL
Director: Freddie Francis
Co-stars: Peter Cushing John Hurt Gwen Watford

1976 FIND THE LADY
Director: John Trent
Co-stars: Lawrence Dane John Candy Dick Emery

1984 DRAW!
Director: Steven Hilliard Stern
Co-stars: Kirk Douglas James Coburn

VICTORIA BASTEL

1992 THE BAD LIEUTENANT
Co-stars: Abel Ferrara
Director: Harvey Keitel Frankie Thorn Zoe Lund

FANNY BASTIEN

1987 ANGEL DUST
Director: Edouard Niermans
Co-stars: Bernard Giraudeau Michel Aumont

MICHAL BAT-ADAM

1990 THE IMPOSSIBLE SPY
Director: Jim Goddard
Co-stars: John Shea Eli Wallach

EMMANUELLE BATAILLE

1990 THESE FOOLISH THINGS
Director: Bertrand Tavernier
Co-stars: Dirk Bogarde Jane Birkin

JULIE BATAILLE

1991   C'EST LA VIE
Director: Diane Kurys
Co-stars: Nathalie Baye Richard Berry Zabou

SYLVIE BATAILLE

1936   UNE PARTIE DE CAMPAGNE
Director: Jean Renoir
Co-stars: Georges Darnoul Jane Marken

1938   LES GENS DU VOYAGE
Director: Jacques Feyder
Co-stars: Francoise Rosay Andre Brule Mary Glory

JUSTINE BATEMAN

1985   RIGHT TO KILL?
Director: John Erman
Co-stars: Frederic Forrest Christopher Collet

1986   CAN YOU FEEL ME DANCING?
Director: Michael Miller
Co-stars: Jason Bateman Max Gail

1988   SATISFACTION
Director: Joan Freeman
Co-stars: Liam Neeson Trini Alvarado Julia Roberts

1990   THE FATAL IMAGE
Director: Thomas Wright
Co-stars: Michele Lee Francois Dunoyer

1992   DEADBOLT
Director: Douglas Jackson
Co-stars: Adam Baldwin Michele Scarabelli

1993   THE NIGHT WE NEVER MET
Director: Warren Leight
Co-stars: Matthew Broderick Annabella Sciorra

1993   TERROR IN THE NIGHT
Director: Colin Bucksey
Co-stars: Joe Penny Matt Mulhern

NATALIE BATE

1987   GROUND ZERO
Director: Bruce Myles
Co-stars: Colin Friels Jack Thompson Donald Pleasence

BARBARA BATES

1948   JUNE BRIDE
Director: Bretagne Windust
Co-stars: Bette Davis Robert Montgomery Debbie Reynolds

1949   THE INSPECTOR GENERAL
Director: Henry Koster
Co-stars: Danny Kaye Walter Slezak Alan Hale

1950   ALL ABOUT EVE
Director: Joseph Mankiewicz
Co-stars: Bette Davis Anne Baxter George Sanders

1950   CHEAPER BY THE DOZEN
Director: Walter Lang
Co-stars: Clifton Webb Myrna Loy Jeanne Crain

1950   QUICKSAND
Director: Irving Pichel
Co-stars: Mickey Rooney Jeanne Cagney Peter Lorre

1951   THE SECRET OF CONVICT LAKE
Director: Michael Gordon
Co-stars: Glenn Ford Gene Tierney Ann Dvorak

1951   I'D CLIMB THE HIGHEST MOUNTAIN
Director: Henry King
Co-stars: Susan Hayward William Lundigan

1951   LET'S MAKE IT LEGAL
Director: Richard Sale
Co-stars: Claudette Colbert MacDonald Carey

1952   BELLES ON THEIR TOE
Director: Henry Levin
Co-stars: Myrna Loy Jeanne Crane Hoagy Carmichael

1952   ALL ASHORE
Director: Richard Quine
Co-stars: Mickey Rooney Dick Haymes Ray McDonald

1953   THE CADDY
Director: Norman Taurog
Co-stars: Dean Martin Jerry Lewis Donna Reed

1954   RHAPSODY
Director: Charles Vidor
Co-stars: Elizabeth Taylor Vittorio Gassman

1956   HOUSE OF SECRETS
Director: Guy Green
Co-stars: Michael Craig Julia Arnall Brenda De Banzie

1956   TOWN ON TRIAL
Director: John Guillermin
Co-stars: John Mills Charles Coburn Derek Farr

CHLOE BATES

1991   REDEMPTION
Director: Malcolm McKay
Co-stars: Tom Courtenay Miranda Richardson Lindsay Duncan

FLORENCE BATES

1940   REBECCA
Director: Alfred Hitchcock
Co-stars: Laurence Olivier Joan Fontaine Nigel Bruce

1940   KITTY FOYLE
Director: Sam Wood
Co-stars: Ginger Rogers Dennis Morgan James Graig

1940   THE SON OF MONTE CRISTO
Director: Rowland Lee
Co-stars: Louis Hayward George Sanders Joan Bennett

1941   MEXICAN SPITFIRE AT SEA
Director: Leslie Goodwins
Co-stars: Lupe Velez Leon Errol Charles Rogers

1941   STRANGE ALIBI
Director: Ross Lederman
Co-stars: Arthur Kennedy Joan Perry Howard Da Silva

1941   LOVE CRAZY
Director: Jack Conway
Co-stars: William Powell Myrna Loy Jack Carson

1941   THE CHOCOLATE SOLDIER
Director: Roy Del Ruth
Co-stars: Nelson Eddy Rise Stevens Nigel Bruce

1942   MY HEART BELONGS TO DADDY
Director: Robert Siodmak
Co-stars: Richard Carlson Martha O'Driscoll

1942   WE WERE DANCING
Director: Robert Z. Leonard
Co-stars: Norma Shearer Melvyn Douglas Majorie Man

1942   THE TUTTLES OF TAHITI
Director: Charles Vidor
Co-stars: Charles Laughton Jon Hall Victor Francen

1943   SLIGHTLY DANGEROUS
Director: Wesley Ruggles
Co-stars: Lana Turner Robert Young May Whitty

1943   THEY GOT ME COVERED
Director: David Rutler
Co-stars: Bob Hope Dorothy Lamour Otto Preminger

1943 SARATOGA TRUNK
Director: Sam Wood
Co-stars: Ingrid Bergman Gary Cooper Flora Robson

1943 MR BIG
Director: Charles Lamont
Co-stars: Donald O'Connor Peggy Ryan Glorla Jean

1943 THE MOON AND SIXPENCE
Director: Albert Lewin
Co-stars: George Sanders Herbert Marshall Doris Dudley

1943 HEAVEN CAN WAIT
Director: Ernst Lubitsch
Co-stars: Don Ameche Gene Tierney Charles Coburn

1944 KISMET
Director: William Dieterle
Co-stars: Ronald Colman Marlene Dietrich James Graig

1944 THE MASK OF DEMITRIOS
Director: Jean Negulesco
Co-stars: Zachary Scott Peter Lorre Sydney Greenstreet

1944 BELLE OF THE YUKON
Director: William Seiter
Co-stars: Randolph Scott Gypsy Rose Lee Dinah Shore

1945 OUT OF THIS WORLD
Director: Hal Walker
Co-stars: Eddie Bracken Veronica Lake Diana Lynn

1945 TONIGHT AND EVERY NIGHT
Director: Victor Saville
Co-stars: Rita Hayworth Lee Bowman Janet Blair

1945 SAN ANTONIO
Director: David Butler
Co-stars: Errol Flynn Alexis Smith Paul Kelly

1946 THE DIARY OF A CHAMBERMAID
Director: Jean Renoir
Co-stars: Paulette Goddard Burgess Meredlth

1946 THE TIME, THE PLACE AND THE GIRL
Director: David Butler
Co-stars: Dennis Morgan Jack Carson Martha Vickers

1946 CLAUDIA AND DAVID
Director: Walter Lang
Co-stars: Dorothy McGuire Robert Young Mary Astor

1946 CLUNY BROWN
Director: Ernst Lubitsch
Co-stars: Jennifer Jones Charles Boyer Richard Haydn

1946 THE BRASHER DOUBLOON
Director: John Brahm
Co-stars: George Montgomery Nancy Guild

1947 THE SECRET LIFE OF WALTER MITTY
Director: Norman Z. McLeod
Co-stars: Danny Kaye Virginia Mayo Boris Karloff

1948 WINTER MEETING
Director: Bretaigne Windust
Co-stars: Bette Davis Jim Davis Janis Paige

1948 PORTRAIT OF JENNIE
Director: William Dieterle
Co-stars: Jennifer Jones Joseph Cotten David Wayne

1948 THE INSIDE STORY
Director: Allan Dwan
Co-stars: Marsha Hunt William Lundigan Charles Winninger

1948 MY DEAR SECRETARY
Director: Charles Martin
Co-stars: Kirk Douglas Laraine Day Keenan Wynn

1948 RIVER LADY
Co-stars: Yvonne De Carlo Dan Duryea Rod Cameron

1948 I REMEMBER MAMA
Director: George Stevens
Co-stars: Irene Dunne Barbara Bel Geddes Oscar Homolka

1949 THE GIRL FROM JONE'S BEACH
Director: Peter Godfrey
Co-stars: Ronald Reagan Virginia Mayo

1949 A LETTER TO THREE WIVES
Director: Joseph Mankiewicz
Co-stars: Jeanne Crain Kirk Douglas Ann Sothern

1949 ON THE TOWN
Director: Gene Kelly
Co-stars: Gene Kelly Frank Sinatra Vera-Ellen

1951 LULLABY OF BROADWAY
Director: David Butler
Co-stars: Doris Day Gene Nelson Gladys George

1951 THE TALL TARGET
Director: Anthony Mann
Co-stars: Dick Powell Paula Raymond Adolphe Menjou

1952 THE SAN FRANCISCO STORY
Director: Robert Parrish
Co-stars: Joel McCrea Yvonne De Carlo

JEANNE BATES

1944 THE RACKET MAN
Co-star: Tom Neal

1944 THE SON OF A MONSTER
Director: Will Jason
Co-stars: George Macready Rose Hobart

1944 THE BLACK PARACHUTE
Director: Lew Landers
Co-stars: Larry Parks John Carradine Osa Massen

1945 SERGEANT MIKE
Co-stars: Larry Parks Eddie Acuff

1946 THE MASK OF DIJON
Director: Lew Landers
Co-stars: Erich Von Stroheim William Wright

KATHY BATES *(Married Tony Campisi)*
Oscar For Best Actress In 1990 For "Misery"

1982 COME BACK TO THE FIVE AND DIME, JiMMY DEAN, JIMMY DEAN
Director: Robert Altman
Co-stars: Sandy Dennis Cher Karen Black

1986 THE MORNING AFTER
Director: Sidney Lumet
Co-stars: Jane Fonda Jeff Bridges Raul Julia

1988 ARTHUR II: ON THE ROCKS
Director: Bud Yorkin
Co-stars: Dudley Moore Liza Minnelli John Gielgud

1989 NO PLACE LIKE HOME
Director: Lee Grant
Co-stars: Christine Lahti Jeff Daniels Scott Marlowe

1989 ROE V's WADE
Director: Gregory Hoblit
Co-stars: Holly Hunter Amy Madigan Terry O'Quinn

1990 WHITE PALACE
Director: Luis Mendoki
Co-stars: Susan Sarandon James Spader Eileen Brennan

1990 MEN DON'T LEAVE
Director: Paul Brickman
Co-stars: Jessica Lange Joan Cusack Arliss Howard

1990 MISERY
Director: Rob Reiner
Co-stars: James Caan Richard Farnsworth Lauren Bacall

1991 SHADOWS AND FOG
Director: Woody Allen
Co-stars: Woody Allen Jodie Foster Lily Tomlin

1991	**FRIED GREEN TOMATOES AT THE WHISTLE STOP CAFE**
Director:	Jon Avnet
Co-stars:	Jessica Tandy Mary Stuart Masterson Mary-Louise Parker

1992	**PRELUDE TO A KISS**
Director:	Norman Rene
Co-stars:	Alec Baldwin Meg Ryan Sydney Walker

1992	**AT PLAY IN THE FIELDS OF THE LORD**
Director:	Hector Babenco
Co-stars:	Tom Berenger Daryl Hannah

1992	**HOSTAGES**
Director:	David Wheatley
Co-stars:	Colin Firth Ciaran Hinds Natasha Richardson

1992	**USED PEOPLE**
Director:	Beeban Kidron
Co-stars:	Shirley MacLaine Marcello Mastroianni Jessica Tandy

1993	**A HOME OF OUR OWN**
Director:	Tony Bill
Co-stars:	Edward Furlong Tony Campisi

1994	**NORTH**
Director:	Rob Reiner
Co-stars:	Elijah Wood Bruce Willis Alan Arkin

1995	**DOLORES CLAIBORNE**
Director:	Taylor Hackford
Co-stars:	Jennifer Jason Leigh Christopher Plummer

1996	**ANGUS**
Co-stars:	George C Scott Charlie Talbert

1996	**DIABOLIQUE**
Director:	Jeremiah Chechik
Co-stars:	Sharon Stone Isabelle Adjani

1998	**AMY FOSTER**
Director:	Beeban Kidron
Co-stars:	Rachel Weisz Vincent Perez

1998	**TITANIC**
Director:	James Cameron
Co-stars:	Kate Winslet Leonardo DiCaprio Billy Zane

SUSAN BATSON

1977	**THE INCREDIBLE HULK**
Director:	Kenneth Johnson
Co-stars:	Bill Bixby Lou Ferrigno

VANESSA BAUCHE

1992	**HIGHWAY PATROLMAN**
Director:	Alex Cox
Co-stars:	Robert Sosa Bruno Bichir

KIMBERLEY BAUCOM

1987	**THE ARROGANT**
Director:	Phillippe Blot
Co-stars:	Sylvia Kristel Gary Graham

CLOTHILDE BAUDON

1985	**AN IMPUDENT GIRL**
Director:	Claude Miller
Co-stars:	Charlotte Gainsbourg Bernadette Lafont

BELINDA BAUER

1979	**SUCCESS**
Director:	William Richert
Co-stars:	Jeff Bridges Ned Beatty Bianca Jagger

1983	**FLASHDANCE**
Director:	Adrian Lyne
Co-stars:	Jennifer Beals Michael Nouri Lilia Skala

1987	**THE ROSARY MURDERS**
Director:	Fred Walton
Co-stars:	Donald Sutherland Charles Durning

1988	**ACT OF PIRACY**
Director:	John Cardos
Co-stars:	Gary Busey Ray Sharkey

1990	**ROBOCOP 2**
Director:	Irvin Kershner
Co-stars:	Peter Weller Nancy Allen Dan O'Herlihy

1991	**THE SERVANTS OF TWILIGHT**
Director:	Jeffrey Obrow
Co-stars:	Bruce Greenwood Grace Zabriskie

1993	**NECRONOMICON**
Director:	Brian Yuzna
Co-stars:	Bruce Payne Richard Lynch David Warner

CHARLITA BAUER

1983	**THE CRADLE WILL FALL**
Director:	John Llewellyn Moxey
Co-stars:	Lauren Hutton Ben Murphy

MICHELLE BAUER

1988	**HOLLYWOOD CHAINSAW HOOKERS**
Director:	Fred Olen Ray
Co-stars:	Gunnar Hansen Linnea Quigley

JOANNE BAUMAN

1982	**PURPLE HAZE**
Director:	David Burton Morris
Co-stars:	Peter Nelson Susanne Lack

MICHELE BAUMGARTNER

1981	**THE WOMAN NEXT DOOR**
Director:	Francois Truffaut
Co-stars:	Gerard Depardieu Fanny Ardant

FRANCES BAVIER

1951	**THE DAY THE EARTH STOOD STILL**
Director:	Robert Wise
Co-stars:	Michael Rennie Patricia Neal

1953	**THE MAN IN THE ATTIC**
Director:	Hugo Fregonese
Co-stars:	Jack Palance Constance Smith

HELEN BAXENDALE

1996	**MACBETH**
Co-stars:	Jason Connery Brian Blessed Hildegard Neil

BARBARA BAXLEY

1959	**THE SAVAGE EYE**
Director:	Ben Maddow
Co-stars:	Herschel Bernardi Gary Merrill

1967	**COUNTDOWN**
Director:	Robert Altman
Co-stars:	James Caan Robert Duvall Joanna Moore

1975	**NASHVILLE**
Director:	Robert Altman
Co-stars:	Karen Black Ronee Blakely Lily Tomlin

1979	**NORMA RAE**
Director:	Martin Ritt
Co-stars:	Sally Field Beau Bridges Pat Hingle

ANNE BAXTER

Oscar For Best Supporting Actress In 1946 For " The Razor's Edge"
Nominated For Best Actress In 1950 For "All About Eve"

1940	**20 MULE TEAM**
Director:	Richard Thorpe
Co-stars:	Wallace Beery Leo Carrillo Douglas Fowley

1940	**THE GREAT PROFILE**	1949	**YOU'RE MY EVERYTHING**
Director:	Walter Lang	*Director:*	Walter Lang
Co-stars:	John Barrymore Mary Beth Hughes Lionel Atwill	*Co-stars:*	Dan Dailey Anne Revere Shari Robinson

1941	**CHARLEY'S AUNT**	1950	**A TICKET TO TOMAHAWK**
Director:	Archie Mayo	*Director:*	Richard Sale
Co-stars:	Jack Benny Kay Francis Edmund Gwenn	*Co-stars:*	Dan Dailey Rory Calhoun Walter Brennan

1941	**SWAMP WATER**	1950	**ALL ABOUT EVE**
Director:	Jean Renoir	*Director:*	Joseph Mankiewicz
Co-stars:	Walter Huston Walter Brennan Dana Andrews	*Co-stars:*	Bette Davis George Sanders Celeste Holm

1942	**THE PIED PIPER**	1951	**FOLLOW THE SUN**
Director:	Irving Pichel	*Director:*	Sidney Lanfield
Co-stars:	Monty Woolley Roddy McDowall J. Carrol Naish	*Co-stars:*	Glenn Ford Dennis O'Keefe June Havoc

1942	**THE MAGNIFICENT AMBERSONS**	1952	**MY WIFE'S BEST FRIEND**
Director:	Orson Welles	*Director:*	Richard Sale
Co-stars:	Joseph Cotten Agnes Moorehead Tim Holt	*Co-stars:*	MacDonald Carey Cecil Kellaway Casey Adams

1943	**NORTH STAR**	1952	**O. HENRY'S FULL HOUSE**
Director:	Lewis Milestone	*Director:*	Henry King
Co-stars:	Farley Granger Dana Andrews Walter Brennan	*Co-stars:*	Charles Laughton Gregory Ratoff Marilyn Monroe

1943	**FIVE GRAVES TO CAIRO**	1952	**THE OUTCASTS OF POKER FLATS**
Director:	Billy Wilder	*Director:*	Joseph Newman
Co-stars:	Franchot Tone Erich Von Stroheim	*Co-stars:*	Dale Robertson Cameron Mitchell

1943	**CRASH DIVE**	1953	**I CONFESS**
Director:	Archie Mayo	*Director:*	Alfred Hitchcock
Co-stars:	Tyrone Power Dana Andrews James Gleason	*Co-stars:*	Montgomery Clift Brian Aherne Karl Malden

1944	**THE EVE OF ST. MARK**	1953	**THE BLUE GARDENIA**
Director:	John Stahl	*Director:*	Fritz Lang
Co-stars:	William Eythe Michael O'Shea Vincent Price	*Co-stars:*	Richard Conte Raymond Burr Ann Sothern

1944	**GUEST IN THE HOUSE**	1954	**CARNIVAL STORY**
Director:	John Brahm	*Director:*	Kurt Neuman
Co-stars:	Ralph Bellamy Ruth Warwick Aline McMahon	*Co-stars:*	Steve Cochran Lyle Bettger George Nader

1944	**THE SULLIVANS**	1955	**BEDEVILLED**
Director:	Lloyd Bacon	*Director:*	Mitchell Leisen
Co-stars:	Thomas Mitchell Selena Royle James Cardwell	*Co-stars:*	Steve Forrest Joseph Tomelty

1944	**SUNDAY DINNER FOR A SOLDIER**	1955	**ONE DESIRE**
Director:	Lloyd Bacon	*Director:*	Jerry Hopper
Co-stars:	Charles Winninger John Hodiak Anne Revere	*Co-stars:*	Rock Hudson Julie Adams Natalie Wood

1945	**A ROYAL SCANDAL**	1955	**THE SPOILERS**
Director:	Otto Preminger	*Director:*	Jesse Hibbs
Co-stars:	Tallulah Bankhead William Eythe Charles Coburn	*Co-stars:*	Jeff Chandler Rory Calhoun Barbara Britton

1946	**SMOKY**	1956	**THREE VIOLENT PEOPLE**
Director:	Louis King	*Director:*	Rudolph Mate
Co-stars:	Fred MacMurray Burl Ives Bruce Cabot	*Co-stars:*	Charlton Heston Gilbert Roland

1946	**THE RAZOR'S EDGE**	1956	**THE TEN COMMANDMENTS**
Director:	Edmund Goulding	*Director:*	Cecil B. DeMille
Co-stars:	Tyrone Power Gene Tierney Clifton Webb	*Co-stars:*	Charlton Heston Yul Brynner Nina Foch

1946	**ANGEL ON MY SHOULDER**	1956	**THE COME-ON**
Director:	Archie Mayo	*Director:*	Russell Birdwell
Co-stars:	Paul Muni Claude Rains Hardie Allbright	*Co-stars:*	Sterling Hayden John Hoyt Paul Picerni

1947	**BLAZE OF NOON**	1957	**CHASE A CROOKED SHADOW**
Director:	John Farrow	*Director:*	Michael Anderson
Co-stars:	William Holden Sonny Tufts William Bendix	*Co-stars:*	Richard Todd Herbert Lom Alexander Knox

1947	**THE LUCK OF THE IRISH**	1959	**SUMMER OF THE SEVENTEENTH DOLL**
Director:	Henry Koster	*Director:*	Leslie Norman
Co-stars:	Tyrone Power Cecil Kellaway Lee J. Cobb	*Co-stars:*	Ernest Borgnine John Mills

1948	**HOMECOMING**	1961	**CIMARRON**
Director:	Mervyn LeRoy	*Director:*	Anthony Mann
Co-stars:	Clark Gable Lana Turner John Hodiak	*Co-stars:*	Glenn Ford Maria Schell Russ Tamblyn

1948	**THE WALLS OF JERICHO**	1962	**MIX ME A PERSON**
Director:	John Stahl	*Director:*	Leslie Norman
Co-stars:	Cornel Wilde Kirk Douglas Linda Darnell	*Co-stars:*	Adam Faith Donald Sinden

1949	**YELLOW SKY**	1962	**A WALK ON THE WILD SIDE**
Director:	William Wellman	*Director:*	Edward Dmytryk
Co-stars:	Gregory Peck Richard Widmark Robert Arthur	*Co-stars:*	Jane Fonda Laurence Harvey Capucine

1969 MARCUS WELBY MD.
Director: David Lowell Rich
Co-stars: Robert Young James Brolin

1971 IF TOMORROW COMES
Director: George McCowan
Co-stars: Patty Duke Frank Liu James Whitmore

1971 FOOL'S PARADE
Director: Andrew McLaglen
Co-stars: James Stewart George Kennedy

1980 JANE AUSTIN IN MANHATTAN
Director: James Ivory
Co-stars: Robert Powell Sean Young Michael Wager

BERYL BAXTER

1948 IDOL OF PARIS
Director: Leslie Arliss
Co-stars: Christine Norden Michael Rennie

DEBORAH BAXTER

1965 HIGH WIND IN JAMAICA
Director: Alexander MacKendrick
Co-stars: Anthony Quinn James Coburn

JANE BAXTER

1933 THE CONSTANT NYMPH
Co-star: Victoria Hopper

1934 THE CLAIRVOYANT
Director: Maurice Elvy
Co-stars: Claude Rains Fay Wray Mary Clare

1934 BLOSSOM TIME
Director: Paul Stein
Co-stars: Richard Tauber Carl Esmond Athene Seyler

1934 THE NIGHT OF THE PARTY
Director: Michael Powell
Co-stars: Leslie Banks Viola Keats Ian Hunter

1934 WE LIVE AGAIN
Director: Rouben Mamoulian
Co-stars: Fredric March Anna Sten Sam Jaffe

1935 ENCHANTED APRIL
Director: Harry Beaumont
Co-stars: Ann Harding Frank Morgan Jessie Ralpe

1935 DRAKE OF ENGLAND
Director: Arthur Woods
Co-stars: Matheson Lang Athene Seyler Donald Wolfit

1936 THE MAN BEHIND THE MASK
Director: Michael Powell
Co-stars: Hugh Williams Maurice Schwartz Henry Oscar

1938 SECOND BEST BED
Director: Tom Walls
Co-stars: Tom Walls Veronica Rose Carl Jaffe

1938 HIDEOUT IN THE ALPS
Co-star: Anthony Bushell

1938 THE WARE CASE
Director: Robert Stevenson
Co-stars: Clive Brook Barry K. Barnes Edward Rigby

1938 DUSTY ERMINE
Director: Bernard Vorhaus
Co-stars: Anthony Bushell Margaret Rutherford

1939 THE CHINESE BUNGALOW
Director: George King
Co-stars: Paul Lukas Robert Douglas Kay Walsh

1941 SHIPS WITH WINGS
Director: Sergei Nolbandov
Co-stars: John Clements Leslie Banks Ann Todd

1943 THE FLEMISH FARM
Director: Jeffrey Dell
Co-stars: Clive Brook Clifford Evans Philip Friend

LYNSEY BAXTER

1987 HEDGEHOG WEDDING
Director: Tim King
Co-stars: Frederick Treves Sheila Allen

1988 STARLINGS
Director: David Wheatley
Co-stars: Michael Maloney David Ryall Jane Downs

1988 THE GIRL IN A SWING
Director: Gordon Hessler
Co-stars: Meg Tilly Rupert Frazer

1989 GOLDENEYE
Director: Don Boyd
Co-stars: Charles Dance Phyllis Logan Patrick Ryecart

1989 ACT OF WILL
Director: Don Sharp
Co-stars: Victoria Tennant Elizabeth Hurley Peter Coyote

1991 CLARISSA
Director: Robert Bierman
Co-stars: Saskia Wickham Sean Bean Cathryn Harrison

1991 THE PLEASURE PRINCIPLE
Director: David Cohen
Co-stars: Peter Firth Lysette Anthony

1991 THE GRASS ARENA
Director: Gilles MacKinnon Mark Rylance Peter Postlethwaite

1992 NATURAL LIES
Director: Ben Bolt
Co-stars: Bob Peck Sharon Duce Denis Lawson

MEREDITH BAXTER-BIRNEY *(Married David Birney, until 1978 Meredith Baxter)*

1972 BEN
Director: Phil Karlson
Co-stars: Arthur O'Connell Rosemary Murphy

1973 THE CAT CREATURE
Director: Curtis Harrington
Co-stars: David Hedison Gale Sondergaard

1975 TARGET RISK
Director: Robert Sheerer
Co-stars: Bo Svenson Robert Coote Keenan Wynn

1975 THE NIGHT THAT PANICKED AMERICA
Director: Joseph Sargent
Co-stars: Vic Morrow Eileen Brennan

1976 ALL THE PRESIDENT'S MEN
Director: Alan Pakula
Co-stars: Robert Redford Dustin Hoffman Martin Balsam

1976 BITTERSWEET LOVE
Director: David Miller
Co-stars: Lana Turner Robert Alda Celeste Holm

1978 LITTLE WOMEN
Director: David Lowell
Co-stars: Susan Dey Dorothy McGuire Robert Young

1980 SHE KNOWS TOO MUCH
Director: Paul Lynch
Co-stars: Robert Urich Erik Estrada

1982 TAKE YOUR BEST SHOT
Director: David Greene
Co-stars: Robert Urich Jack Bannon

1985 THE RAPE OF RICHARD BECK
Director: Karen Arthur
Co-stars: Richard Crenna Pat Hingle

1986 KATE'S SECRET
Director: Arthur Allan Seidelman
Co-stars: Edward Asner Ben Masters

1987 THE LONG JOURNEY HOME
Director: Rod Holcomb
Co-stars: David Birney Ray Baker

1990 BURNING BRIDGES
Director: Sheldon Larry
Co-stars: Nick Mancuso Lois Chiles

1991 BUMP IN THE NIGHT
Director: Karen Arthur
Co-stars: Christopher Reeve Shirley Knight

1992 DARKNESS BEFORE DAWN
Director: John Patterson
Co-stars: Stephen Lang

1994 MY BREAST
Director: Betty Thomas
Co-star: Jamey Sheridan Barbara Barrie

1994 FOR THE LOVE OF AARON
Director: John Kent Harrison
Co-stars: Joanna Gleason Keegan MacIntosh

1996 AFTER JIMMY

1997 LET ME CALL YOU SWEETHEART
Director: Bill Corcoran
Co-stars: Victor Garber

FRANCES BAY

1992 SINGLE WHITE FEMALE
Director: Barbet Schroeder
Co-stars: Bridget Fonda Jennifer Jason Leigh

1994 IN THE MOUTH OF MADNESS
Director: John Carpenter
Co-stars: Sam Neill Jorgen Prochnow Charlton Heston

NATHALIE BAYE

1974 THE MOUTH AGAPE
Director: Maurice Pialat
Co-stars: Monique Melinand Hubert Deschamps

1977 THE MAN WHO LOVED WOMEN
Director: Francois Truffaut
Co-stars: Charles Denner Brigitte Fossey

1978 THE GREEN ROOM
Director: Francois Truffaut
Co-stars: Francois Truffaut Jean-Pierre Moulin Jean Daste

1980 THE GIRL FROM LORRAINE
Director: Claude Goretta
Co-stars: Bruno Ganz Angela Winkler

1982 LA BALANCE
Director: Bob Swain
Co-stars: Phillipe Leotard Richard Berry Maurice Ronet

1982 I MARRIED A SHADOW

1982 THE RETURN OF MARTIN GUERRE
Director: Daniel Vigne
Co-stars: Gerard Depardieu Roger Planchon

1985 DETECTIVE
Director: Jean-Luc Godard
Co-stars: Claude Brasseur Johnny Hallyday Alain Cuny

1991 C'EST LA VIE
Director: Diane Kurys
Co-stars: Richard Berry Julie Bataille Zabou

1992 THE LIE
Director: Francois Margolin
Co-stars: Didier Sandre Marc Citti

1993 AND THE BAND PLAYED ON
Director: Roger Spottiswoode
Co-stars: Matthew Modine Lily Tomlin Alan Alda

1997 FOOD OF LOVE
Director: Stephen Poliakoff
Co-stars: Richard E. Grant

HYLDA BAYLEY

1942 MUCH TOO SHY
Director: Marcel Varnel
Co-stars: George Formby Kathleen Harrison Jimmy Clitheroe

EVA MARIA BAYERSWALTES

1984 HEIMAT
Director: Edgar Reitz
Co-stars: Marita Breuer Michael Lesch Dieter Schaad

HETTY BAYNES

1993 LADY CHATTERLEY
Director: Ken Russell
Co-stars: Joely Richardson Sean Bean

BEATRIZ BAZ

1971 HOUSE OF EVIL
Director: Juan Ibanez
Co-stars: Boris Karloff Andres Garcia Julissa

SALLY BAZELY

1969 WHAT'S GOOD FOR THE GOOSE
Director: Menahem Golan
Co-stars: Norman Wisdom Sally Geeson

BRENDA BAZINET

1983 SIEGE
Director: Paul Donovan
Co-stars: Tom Nardini Doug Lennox Terry Despres

1986 ALEX: THE LIFE OF A CHILD
Director: Robert Markowitz
Co-stars: Bonnie Bedelia Craig T. Nelson

BRIGID BAZLEN

1961 THE HONEYMOON MACHINE
Director: Richard Thorpe
Co-stars: Steve McQueen Jim Hutton Paula Prentiss

1961 KING OF KINGS
Director: Nicholas Ray
Co-stars: Jeffrey Hunter Robert Ryan Siobhan McKenna

1962 HOW THE WEST WAS WON
Director: John Ford
Co-stars: Carroll Baker Debbie Reynolds James Stewart

ANN BEACH

1971 UNDER MILK WOOD
Director: Andrew Sinclair
Co-stars: Richard Burton Elizabeth Taylor Peter O'Toole

STEPHANIE BEACHAM

1969 TAM-LIN
Director: Roddy McDowall
Co-stars: Ava Gardner Ian McShane Joanna Lumley

1971 THE NIGHTCOMERS
Director: Michael Winner
Co-stars: Marlon Brando Thora Hird Harry Andrews

1972 DRACULA AD 1972
Director: Alan Gibson
Co-stars: Peter Cushing Christopher Lee Michael Coles

1973 AND NOW THE SCEAMING STARTS
Director: Roy Ward Baker
Co-stars: Peter Cushing Herbert Lom Ian Ogilvy

1988 THE WOLVES OF WILLOUGHBY GRANGE
Director: Stuart Orme
Co-stars: Mel Smith Geraldine James

1989 TROOP BEVERLY HILLS
Director: Jeff Kanew
Co-stars: Shelley Long Graig Nelson Betty Thomas

1990 THE LILAC BUS
Director: Giles Foster
Co-stars: Con O'Neill Dervla Kirwan Beatie Edney

1991 TO BE THE BEST
Director: Tony Wharmby
Co-stars: Anthony Hopkins Lindsay Wagner Stuart Wilson

1993 JILLY COOPER'S RIDERS
Director: Gabrielle Beaumont
Co-stars: Michael Praed Caroline Harker

1992 DANIELLE STEELE'S SECRETS
Director: Peter Hunt
Co-stars: Christopher Plummer Linda Purl Gary Collins

JENNIFER BEALS

1983 FLASHDANCE
Director: Adrian Lyne
Co-stars: Michael Nouri Lilia Skala Belinda Bauer

1985 THE BRIDE
Director: Franc Roddam
Co-stars: Sting Clancy Brown Geraldine Page

1988 VAMPIRE'S KISS
Director: Robert Bierman
Co-stars: Nicolas Cage Maria Conchita Alonso

1989 SONS
Director: Alexandre Rockwell
Co-stars: William Forsythe Stephane Audran Samuel Fuller

1990 DR. M
Director: Claude Chabrol
Co-stars: Alan Bates Jan Niklas

1992 IN THE SOUP
Director: Alexandre Rockwell
Co-stars: Steve Buscemi Seymour Cassel

1992 INDECENCY
Director: Marisa Silver
Co-stars: James Remar Sammi Davis Barbara Williams

1993 NIGHT OWL
Director: Matthew Patrick
Co-star: James Wilder

1994 MRS. PARKER AND THE VICIOUS CIRCLE
Director: Alan Rudolph
Co-stars: Matthew Broderick Campbell Scott Jennifer Jason Leigh

1994 DEAD ON SIGHT
Director: Rueben Preuss
Co-star: Daniel Baldwin

1995 FOUR ROOMS
Director: Allison Anders
Co-stars: Tim Roth Antonio Banderas Ione Skye

1996 DEVIL IN A BLUE DRESS
Director: Carl Franklin
Co-stars: Denzel Washington Tom Sizemore

AMANDA BEARSE

1983 FIRST AFFAIR
Director: Gus Trikonis
Co-stars: Melissa Sue Anderson Loretta Swit Joel Higgins

1985 FREIGHT NIGHT
Director: Tom Holland
Co-stars: Chris Sarandon Roddy McDowall

EMMANUELLE BEART

1986 MANON DES SOURCES
Director: Claude Berri
Co-stars: Yves Montand Daniel Auteuil Margarita Lozano

1991 UN COEUR EN HIVER
Director: Claude Sautet
Co-stars: Daniel Auteuil Andre Dussolliere

1991 J'EMBRASSE PAS
Director: Andre Tachine
Co-stars: Phillipe Noiret Manuel Blanc Ivan Desny

1991 LA BELLE NOISEUSE
Director: Jacques Rivette
Co-stars: Michel Piccoli Jane Birkin

1991 LA BELLE NOISEUSE-DIVERTIMENTO
Director: Jacques Rivette
Co-stars: Michel Piccoli Jane Birkin Gilles Arbona

1993 L'ENFER
Director: Claude Chabrol
Co-stars: Francois Cluzet Andre Wilms Dora Doll

1996 NELLY AND MR ARNAUD
Director: Claude Saudet
Co-star: Michel Serrault

1996 UNE FEMME FRANCAISE
Co-star: Daniel Auteuil

1996 MISSION IMPOSSIBLE
Director: Brian De Palma
Co-stars: Tom Cruise Vanessa Redgrave Kristin Scott-Thomas

ALLYCE BEASLEY

1992 STEPHEN KING'S THE TOMMYKNOCKERS
Director: John Power
Co-stars: Marc Helgenberger Robert Carradine

JENNIFER BEASLEY

1980 COAL MINER'S DAUGHTER
Director: Michael Apted
Co-stars: Sissy Spacek Tommy Lee Jones

MAE BEATTY

1936 SHOW BOAT
Director: James Whale
Co-stars: Irene Dunn Allan Jones Paul Robeson

MAUREEN BEATTY

1992 THE LONG ROADS
Director: Tristram Powell
Co-stars: Edith MacArthur Robert Urquhart

NANCY BEATTY

1988 THE PRICE OF PASSION
Director: Leonard Nimoy
Co-stars: Diane Keaton Liam Neeson Teresa Wright

SUSAN BEAUBIAN

1988 THE NAKED GUN:
FROM THE FILES OF POLICE SQUAD
Director: David Zucker
Co-star: Leslie Nielsen Priscilla Presley Ricardo Montalban

1985 THREE MEN AND A CRADLE
Director: Coline Serreau
Co-stars: Roland Giraud Andre Dussollier

YOLANDE BEAULIEU

1924 MENILMONTANT
Director: Dimitri Kirsanov
Co-stars: Nadia Sibirskaia Guy Belmont

DIANA BEAUMONT

1934 AUTUMN CROCUS
Director: Carol Reed
Co-stars: Ivor Novello Fay Compton Jack Hawkins

KATHRYN BEAUMONT *(Child)*

1948 ON AN ISLAND WITH YOU
Director: Richard Thorpe
Co-stars: Esther Williams Peter Lawford Cyd Charisse

1951 ALICE IN WONDERLAND *(Voice)*
Director: Clyde Geronimi
Co-stars: Ed Wynn Richard Haydn Jerry Colonna

1953 PETER PAN *(Voice)*
Director: Clyde Geronimi
Co-stars: Bobby Driscoll Heather Angel

LUCY BEAUMONT

1927 THE CROWD
Director: King Vidor
Co-stars: Eleanor Boardman James Murray Bert Roach

1931 CAUGHT PLASTERED
Director: William Seiter
Co-stars: Bert Wheeler Robert Woolsey Dorothy Lee

1931 A FREE SOUL
Director: Clarence Brown
Co-stars: Lionel Barrymore Norma Shearer Leslie Howard

1933 HIS DOUBLE LIFE
Director: Arthur Hopkins
Co-stars: Roland Young Lillian Gish

1936 THE DEVIL DOLL
Director: Tod Browning
Co-stars: Lionel Barrymore Maureen O'Sullivan

SUSAN BEAUMONT

1956 EYEWITNESS
Director: Muriel Box
Co-stars: Donald Sinden Muriel Pavlow Belinda Lee

1957 HIGH TIDE AT NOON
Director: Philip Leacock
Co-stars: Betta St. John Michael Craig Flora Robson

1958 THE SPANIARD'S CURSE
Director: Ralph Kemplen
Co-stars: Tony Wright Lee Patterson

1959 THE MAN WHO LIKED FUNERALS
Director: David Eady
Co-stars: Leslie Phillips Bill Fraser

1960 CARRY ON NURSE
Director: Gerald Thomas
Co-stars: Shirley Eaton Hattie Jacques Kenneth Williams

CELINE BEAUVALET

1988 MIGNON HAS LEFT
Director: Francesca Archibugi
Co-stars: Stefania Sandelli Jean-Pierre Duriez

1992 A PRIVATE AFFAIR
Director: Alberto Negrin
Co-star: Rupert Graves

ELLEN BEAVEN

1988 BUSTER
Director: David Green
Co-stars: Phil Collins Julie Walters Larry Lamb

LOUISE BEAVERS

1932 TOO BUSY TO WORK
Director: John Blystone
Co-stars: Will Rogers Marion Nixon Dick Powell

1932 WHAT PRICE HOLLYWOOD?
Director: George Cukor
Co-stars: Constance Bennett Lowell Sherman

1933 BOMBSHELL
Director: Hunt Stromberg
Co-stars: Jean Harlow Lee Tracy Frank Morgan

1934 IMITATION OF LIFE
Director: John Stahl
Co-stars: Claudette Colbert Warren William Rochelle Hudson

1935 ANNAPOLIS FAREWELL
Director: Alexander Hall
Co-stars: Sir Guy Standing Tom Brown

1936 RAINBOW ON THE RIVER
Director: Kurt Neuman
Co-stars: Bobby Breen May Robson Charles Butterworth

1938 MADE FOR EACH OTHER
Director: John Cromwell
Co-stars: Carole Lombard James Stewart Charles Coburn

1939 THE LADY'S FROM KENTUCKY
Director: Alexander Hall
Co-stars: George Raft Ellen Drew Zasu Pitts

1940 I WANT A DIVORCE
Director: Ralph Murphy
Co-stars: Dick Powell Joan Blondell Gloria Dickson

1940 NO TIME FOR COMEDY
Director: William Keighley
Co-stars: James Stewart Rosalind Russell

1940 WOMEN WITHOUT NAMES
Director: Robert Florey
Co-stars: Ellen Drew Robert Paige John Miljan

1941 THE VANISHING VIRGINIAN
Director: Frank Borzage
Co-stars: Frank Morgan Spring Byington

1941 BELLE STAR
Director: Kenneth MacGowan
Co-stars: Gene Tierney Randolph Scott Dana Andrews

1942 REAP THE WILD WIND
Director: Cecil B. DeMille
Co-stars: John Wayne Ray Milland Paulette Goddard

1942 SEVEN SWEETHEARTS
Director: Frank Borzage
Co-stars: Kathryn Grayson Marsha Hunt Van Heflin

1942 HOLIDAY INN
Director: Mark Sandrich
Co-stars: Bing Crosby Fred Astaire Marjorie Reynolds

1943 GOOD MORNING JUDGE
Director: Jean Yarborough
Co-stars: Dennis O'Keefe Louise Alllbritton

1944 BARBARY COAST GENT
Director: Roy Del Ruth
Co-stars: Wallace Beery Binnie Barnes Chill Wills

1948 MR BLANDINGS BUILDS HIS DREAMHOUSE
Director: H. C. Potter
Co-stars: Cary Grant Myrna Loy

1956 TEENAGE REBEL
Director: Edmund Goulding
Co-stars: Ginger Rogers Michael Rennie Mildred Natwick

1956 GOODBYE MY LADY
Director: William Wellman
Co-stars: Brandon De Wilde Walter Brennan Phil Harris

JENNIFER BECK (Jenny)

1984 TIGHTROPE
Director: Richard Tuggle
Co-stars: Clint Eastwood Genevieve Bujold

1986 TROLL
Director: John Carl Beechler
Co-stars: Michael Moriarty Shelley Hack Sonny Bono

KIMBERLY BECK

1984 FRIDAY THE 13TH: THE FINAL CHAPTER
Director: Joseph Zito
Co-stars: Judie Aronson Crispin Glover

DESIREE BECKER

1987 GOOD MORNING BABYLON
Director: Paolo Taviani
Co-stars: Vincent Spano Greta Scacchi Charles Dance

MARIE BECKER

1969 MY NIGHT AT MAUD'S
Director: Eric Rohmer
Co-stars: Jean-Louis Trintignant Francoise Fabian

1990 WINGS OF FAME
Director: Otakar Votocek
Co-stars: Peter O'Toole Colin Firth Andrea Ferreol

KATE BECKINSALE

1991 ONE AGAINST THE WIND
Director: Larry Elikann
Co-stars: Sam Neill Denholm Elliott Judy Davis

1993 MUCH ADO ABOUT NOTHING
Director: Kenneth Branagh
Co-stars: Kenneth Branagh Emma Thompson Richard Briers

1993 ANNA LEE: HEADCASE
Director: Colin Bucksey
Co-stars: Imogen Stubbs Brian Glover Alan Howard

1994 COLD COMFORT FARM
Director: John Schlesinger
Co-star: Rufus Sewell

1996 EMMA
Director: Andrew Davis
Co-stars: Mark Strong Prunella Scales Samantha Bond

1997 SHOOTING FISH
Director: Stefan Schwartz
Co-stars: Stuart Townsend Dan Futterman Dominic Mafham

BONNIE BEDELIA

1969 THEY SHOOT HORSES, DON'T THEY?
Director: Sydney Pollack
Co-stars: Gig Young Jane Fonda Susannah York

1969 THE GYPSY MOTHS
Director: John Frankenheimer
Co-stars: Burt Lancaster Deborah Kerr Gene Hackman

1970 LOVERS AND OTHER STRANGERS
Director: Cy Howard
Co-stars: Gig Young Bea Arthur Anne Jackson

1972 THE STRANGE VENGEANCE OF ROSALIE
Director: Jack Starrett
Co-stars: Ken Howard Anthony Zerbe

1973 HAWKINS ON MURDER
Director: Jud Taylor
Co-stars: James Stewart Strother Martin Margaret Markov

1974 HEAT WAVE!
Director: Jerry Jameson
Co-stars: Ben Murphy Lew Ayres David Huddleston

1978 THE BIG FIX
Director: Jeremy Paul Kagan
Co-stars: Richard Dreyfuss Susan Anspach John Lithgow

1978 A QUESTION OF LOVE
Director: Jerry Thorpe
Co-stars: Gena Rowlands Jane Alexander Ned Beatty

1979 SALEM'S LOT
Director: Tobe Hunter
Co-stars: David Soul James Mason Lew Ayres

1980 FIGHTING BACK
Director: Robert Lieberman
Co-stars: Robert Urich Art Carney Richard Herd

1982 MILLION DOLLAR INFIELD
Director: Hal Cooper
Co-stars: Rob Reiner Robert Costanzo Bruno Kirby

1983 HEART LIKE A WHEEL
Director: Jonathan Kaplan
Co-stars: Beau Bridges Leo Rossi Hoyt Axton

1985 DEATH OF AN ANGEL
Director: Petru Popescu
Co-stars: Nick Mancuso Pamela Ludwig Irma Garcia

1985 LADY FROM YESTERDAY
Director: Robert Day
Co-stars: Wayne Rogers Pat Hingle Tina Chen

1986 VIOLETS ARE BLUE
Director: Jack Fisk
Co-stars: Sissy Spacek Kevin Kline John Kellogg

1986 ALEX: THE LIFE OF A CHILD
Director: Robert Markowitz
Co-stars: Graig T. Nelson Jennie James

1986 THE BOY WHO COULD FLY
Director: Nick Castle
Co-stars: Lucy Deakins Jay Underwood Colleen Dewhurst

1988 DIE HARD
Director: John McTiernan
Co-stars: Bruce Willis Paul Gleason William Atherton

1988 THE PRINCE OF PENNSYLVANLIA
Director: Ron Nyswaner
Co-stars: Fred Ward Keanu Reeves Amy Madigan

1989 SHADOW MAKERS
Director: Roland Joffe
Co-stars: Paul Newman Dwight Schultz John Cusack

1990 PRESUMED INNOCENT
Director: Alan Pakula
Co-stars: Harrison Ford Brian Dennehy Greta Scacchi

1990 DIE HARD 2
Director: Renny Harlin
Co-stars: Bruce Willis William Atherton Franco Nero

1992 SHATTERED SILENCE
Director: Linda Otto
Co-stars: Pam Grier Terence Knox Rip Torn

1993 NEEDFUL THINGS
Director: Fraser Heston
Co-stars: Max Von Sydow Ed Harris Amanda Plummer

1994 SPEECHLESS
Director: Ron Underwood
Co-stars: Geena Davis Michael Keaton Christopher Reeves

1995 JUDICIAL CONSENT
Director: William Bidley
Co-stars: Will Patton Dabney Coleman Lisa Blount

1995 SHADOW OF A DOUBT
Director: Brian Dennehy
Co-stars: Brian Dennehy Fairuza Balk

BARBARA BEDFORD

1925 TUMBLEWEEDS
Director: King Baggott
Co-stars: William S. Hart Lucien Litttlefield

1927 MOCKERY
Director: Benjamin Christensen
Co-stars: Lon Chaney Ricardo Cortez

1934 THE QUITTER
Co-star: William Bakewell

MOLLY BEE

1960 CHARTROOSE CABOOSE
Director: William Reynolds
Co-stars: Ben Cooper Edgar Buchanan

JANET BEECHER

1933 GALLANT LADY
Director: Gregory La Cava
Co-stars: Ann Harding Clive Brook Otto Kruger

1934 THE LAST GENTLEMAN
Director: Sidney Lanfield
Co-stars: George Arliss Ralph Morgan Charlotte Henry

1934 THE MIGHTY BARNUM
Director: Walter Lang
Co-stars: Wallace Beery Virginia Bruce Adolphe Menjou

1934 THE PRESIDENT VANISHES
Director: William Wellman
Co-stars: Arthur Byron Rosalind Russell

1935 SO RED THE ROSE
Director: King Vidor
Co-stars: Margaret Sullavan Randolph Scott Robert Cummings

1935 A VILLAGE TALE
Director: John Cromwell
Co-stars: Randolph Scott Robert Barrat Kay Johnson

1935 LET'S LIVE TONIGHT
Director: Victor Schertzinger
Co-stars: Lillian Harvey Tullio Carminati

1935 THE DARK ANGEL
Director: Sidney Franklin
Co-stars: Merle Oberon Fredric March Herbert Marshall

1936 LOVE BEFORE BREAKFAST
Director: Walter Lang
Co-stars: Carole Lombard Preston Foster Cesar Romero

1937 MY DEAR MISS ALDRICH
Director: George Seitz
Co-stars: Maureen O'Sullivan Walter Pidgeon Rita Johnson

1937 THE GOOD OLD SOAK
Director: Walter Ruben
Co-stars: Wallace Beery Una Merkel Eric Linden

1937 CRIME DOES NOT PAY: GIVE TILL IT HURTS
Director: Felix Feist
Co-stars: Howard Hickman

1937 THE BIG CITY
Director: Frank Borzage
Co-stars: Spencer Tracy Luise Rainer Charley Grapewin

1938 YELLOW JACK
Director: George Seitz
Co-stars: Robert Montgomery Virginia Bruce Lewis Stone

1938 SAY IT IN FRENCH
Director: Andrew Stone
Co-stars: Ray Milland Olympe Bradna Irene Hervey

1939 CAREER
Director: Leigh Jason
Co-stars: Edward Ellis Anne Shirley Leon Errol

1939 MAN OF CONQUEST
Director: George Nicholls
Co-stars: Richard Dix Joan Fontaine

1940 ALL THIS AND HEAVEN TOO
Director: Anatole Litvak
Co-stars: Charles Boyer Bette Davis Jeffrey Lynn

1940 THE MARK OF ZORRO
Director: Rouben Mamoulian
Co-stars: Tyrone Power Linda Darnell Basil Rathbone

1940 THE GAY CABALLERO
Director: Otto Brower
Co-stars: Cesar Romero Sheila Ryan Robert Sterling

1941 THE LADY EVE
Director: Preston Sturges
Co-stars: Barbara Stanwyck Henry Fonda Charles Coburn

1941 A VERY YOUNG LADY
Director: Harold Schuster
Co-stars: Jane Withers John Sutton Nancy Kelly

1941 THE PARSON OF PANAMINT
Director: William McGann
Co-stars: Phillip Terry Ellen Drew Charles Ruggles

1942 SILVER QUEEN
Director: Lloyd Bacon
Co-stars: George Brent Priscilla Lane Bruce Cabot

SYLVIA BEECHER

1929 INNOCENTS OF PARIS
Director: Richard Wallace
Co-stars: Maurice Chevalier Russell Simpson

ERICA BEER

1962 THE COUNTERFEIT TRAITOR
Director: George Seaton
Co-stars: William Holden Lilli Palmer Hugh Griffith

JOY BEHAR

1993 MANHATTAN MURDER MYSTERY
Director: Woody Allen
Co-stars: Woody Allen Diane Keaton Alan Alda

BRIONY BEHETS

1977 THE LONG WEEKEND
Director: Colin Egglestone
Co-stars: John Hargreaves Mike McEwen

DORIS BELACK

1983 SESSIONS
Director: Richard Pearce
Co-stars: Veronica Hamel Jill Eikenberry Jeffrey DeMunn

1985 THE HEARST AND DAVIES AFFAIR
Director: David Lowell Rich
Co-stars: Robert Mitchum Virginia Madsen

1987 BATTERIES NOT INCLUDED
Director: Matthew Robbins
Co-stars: Jessica Tandy Hume Cronyn

1988 HOSTAGE
Director: Peter Levin
Co-stars: Carol Burnett Annette Bening Carrie Hamilton

1990 OPPORTUNITY KNOCKS
Director: Donald Petrie
Co-stars: Dana Carvey Robert Loggia Todd Graff

1991 WHAT ABOUT BOB
Director: Frank Oz
Co-stars: Richard Dreyfuss Bill Murray Julie Hagerty

SHARI BELAFONTE-HARPER

1986 KATE'S SECRET
Director: Arthur Allan Seidelman
Co-stars: Meredith Baxter-Birney Edward Asner

1989 PERRY MASON:
THE CASE OF THE ALL-STAR ASSASSIN
Director: Christian Nyby
Co-stars: Raymond Burr Barbara Hale

1993 FRENCH SILK
Director: Noel Nosseck
Co-stars: Susan Lucci Lee Horsley

BARBARA BELDEN

1944 WHEN THE LIGHTS GO ON AGAIN
Director: William Howard
Co-stars: James Lydon Grant Mitchell

ANA BELEN

1981 THE HOUSE OF BERNARDA ALBA
Director: Mario Camus
Co-stars: Irene Gutierrez Caba Vicky Pena

CHRISTINE BELFORD

1972 THE GROUNDSTAR
Director: Lamont Johnson
Co-stars: George Peppard Michael Sarrazin

1972 BANACEK: DETOUR TO NOWHERE
Director: Jack Smight
Co-stars: George Peppard Ed Nelson

1980 KENNY ROGERS AS THE GAMBLER
Director: Dick Lowry
Co-stars: Kenny Rogers Bruce Boxleitner

1983 CHRISTINE
Director: John Carpenter
Co-stars: Keith Gordon Alexandra Paul Harry Dean Stanton

1986 OUTLAWS
Director: Peter Werner
Co-stars: Rod Taylor Richard Roundtree William Lucking

BARBARA BEL GEDDES
Nominated For Best Supporting Actress In 1948 For "I Remember Mama"

1947 THE LONG NIGHT
Director: Anatole Litvak
Co-stars: Henry Fonda Vincent Price Ann Dvorak

1948 I REMEMBER MAMA
Director: George Stevens
Co-stars: Irene Dunne Oscar Homolka Cedric Hardwicke

1948 BLOOD ON THE MOON
Director: Robert Wise
Co-stars: Robert Mitchum Robert Preston Walter Brennan

1949 CAUGHT
Director: Max Ophuls
Co-stars: James Mason Robert Ryan Natalie Schaefer

1950 PANIC IN THE STREETS
Director: Elia Kazan
Co-stars: Richard Widmark Jack Palance Paul Douglas

1951 FOURTEEN HOURS
Director: Henry Hathaway
Co-stars: Richard Basehart Paul Douglas Grace Kelly

1958 VERTIGO
Director: Alfred Hitchcock
Co-stars: James Stewart Kim Novak Tom Helmore

1959 THE FIVE PENNIES
Director: Melville Shavelson
Co-stars: Danny Kaye Louis Armstrong Bob Crosby

1960 FIVE BRANDED WOMEN
Director: Martin Ritt
Co-stars: Van Heflin Silvana Mangano Jeanne Moreau

1961 BY LOVE POSSESSED
Director: John Sturges
Co-stars: Lana Turner Efrem Zimbalist Jason Robards

1970 THE TODD KILLINGS
Director: Barry Shear
Co-stars: Robert F. Lyons Richard Thomas Belinda Montgomery

1971 SUMMERTREE
Director: Anthony Newley
Co-stars: Michael Douglas Brenda Vaccaro Jack Warden

BELITA

1942 SILVER SKATES
Director: Leslie Goodwins
Co-stars: Kenny Baker Patricia Morison

1943 LADY LET'S DANCE
Director: Frank Woodruff
Co-stars: James Ellison Walter Catlett

1946 SUSPENSE
Director: Frank Tuttle
Co-stars: Barry Sullivan Bonita Granville Albert Dekker

1947 THE GANGSTER
Director: Gordon Wiles
Co-stars: Barry Sullivan Akim Tamiroff John Ireland

1948 THE MAN ON THE EIFFEL TOWER
Director: Burgess Meredith
Co-stars: Burgess Meredith Charles Laughton Franchot Tone

1953 NEVER LET ME GO
Director: Delmer Daves
Co-stars: Clark Gable Gene Tierney Richard Haydn

1954 INVITATION TO THE DANCE
Director: Gene Kelly
Co-stars: Gene Kelly Tommy Rall Tamara Toumanova

ANN BELL
1964 STOPOVER FOREVER
Director: Frederic Goode

1966 THE WITCHES
Director: Cyril Frankel
Co-stars: Joan Fontaine Kay Walsh Alex McGowen

1969 THE RECKONING
Director: Jack Gold
Co-stars: Nicol Williamson Rachel Roberts Zena Walker

1970 THE STATUE
Director: Rod Amateau
Co-stars: David Niven Virna Lisi John Cleese

1977 SPECTRE
Director: Clive Donner
Co-stars: Robert Culp Gig Young John Hurt

1983 CHAMPIONS
Director: John Irvin
Co-stars: John Hurt Edward Woodward Jan Francis

EILEEN BELL
1939 THE FROZEN LIMITS
Director: Marcel Varnel
Co-stars: Bud Flanagan Crazy Gang Moore Marriott

JOY BELL

1989   GRIEVOUS BODILY HARM
Director: Mark Joffe
Co-stars: Colin Friels John Waters

MARIE BELL

1934   LE GRAND JEU
Director: Jacques Feyder
Co-stars: Pierre-Richard Willm Francoise Rosay

1937   UN CARNET DE BAL
Director: Julien Duvivier
Co-stars: Fernandel, Raimu, Francoise Rosay

1963   LA BONNE SOUPE
Director: Robert Thomas
Co-stars: Annie Girardot Bernard Blier Sacha Distel

1965   VAGHE STELLE DELL'ORSA
Director: Luchino Visconti
Co-stars: Claudia Cardinalle Michael Craig

1966   HOTEL PARADISO
Director: Peter Glenville
Co-stars: Alec Guinness Gina Lollobrigida Robert Morley

MAGGIE BELL

1993   DOWN AMONG THE BIG BOYS
Director: Charles Gormley
Co-stars: Billy Connolly Alex Norton

RACHEL BELL

1985   SONG OF EXPERIENCE
Director: Stephen Frears
Co-stars: Alan Bell Shane Merrills Paul Darlow

FLORENCE BELLAMY

1974   IMMORAL TALES
Director: Walerian Borowczyk
Co-stars: Lise Danvers Paloma Picasso

MADGE BELLAMY

1924   THE IRON HORSE
Director: John Ford
Co-stars: George O'Brien J. Farrell MacDonald

1925   HAVOC

1932   WHITE ZOMBIE
Director: Victor Halperin
Co-stars: Bela Lugosi Joseph Cawthorn

1934   CHARLIE CHAN IN LONDON
Director: Eugene Forde
Co-stars: Warner Oland Mona Barrie Ray Milland

DIANE BELLEGO

1988   VIRGIN - 36 FILETTE
Director: Catherine Breillat
Co-stars: Delphine Zentout Etienne Chicot

KATHLEEN BELLER

1977   MARY WHITE
Director: Jud Taylor
Co-stars: Ed Flanders Fionnula Flanagan

1977   THE BETSY
Director: Daniel Petrie
Co-stars: Laurence Olivier Robert Duvall Jane Alexander

1979   PROMISES IN THE DARK
Director: Jerome Helman
Co-stars: Marsha Mason Ned Beatty Susan Clark

1981   NO PLACE TO HIDE
Director: John Llewellyn Moxey
Co-stars: Mariette Hartley

1981   FORT APACHE, THE BRONX
Director: Daniel Petrie
Co-stars: Paul Newman Ed Asner Danny Aiello

1982   THE SWORD AND THE SORCERER
Director: Albert Pyun
Co-stars: Lee Horsley Simon MacCorkindale

1985   DEADLY MESSAGES
Director: Jack Bender
Co-stars: Michael Brandon Scott Paulin

1989   AMY
Director: John Llewellyn Moxey
Co-stars: Gary Graham Mariette Hartley Keir Dullea

AGOSTINA BELLI

1977   HOLOCAUST 200
Director: Alberto De Martino
Co-stars: Kirk Douglas Simon Ward Virginia McKenna

FRANCESCA BELLINI

1961   BACHELOR FLAT
Director: Frank Tashlin
Co-stars: Terry-Thomas Celeste Holm Tuesday Weld

1963   WHO'S MINDING THE STORE
Director: Frank Tashlin
Co-stars: Jerry Lewis Jill St. John Ray Walston

LYNDA BELLINGHAM

1976   CONFESSIONS OF A DRIVING INSTRUCTOR
Director: Norman Cohen
Co-stars: Robin Askwith Anthony Booth

1978   THE WATERLOO BRIDGE HANDICAP
Director: Ross Cramer
Co-stars: Leonard Rossiter Gordon Kaye

1987   THE VISION
Director: Norman Stone
Co-stars: Dirk Bogarde Lee Remick Eileen Atkins

GINA BELMAN

1989   BLACKEYES
Director: Dennis Potter
Co-stars: Michael Gough Carol Royle Nigel Planer

1992   LEON THE PIG FARMER
Director: Gary Sinyor
Co-stars: Mark Frankel Janet Suzman Brian Glover

VIRGINIA BELMONT

1948   SILENT CONFLICT
Director: George Archainbaud
Co-stars: William Boyd Andy Clyde Rand Brooks

BERTHA BELMORE

1934   GIVE HER A RING
Director: Arthur Woods
Co-stars: Clifford Mollison Wendy Barrie Stewart Granger

1934   ARE YOU A MASON?
Director: Henry Edwards
Co-stars: Sonnie Hale Robertson Hare

1936   IN THE SOUP
Director: Henry Edwards
Co-stars: Ralph Lynn Judy Gunn Nelson Keyes

1937   PLEASE TEACHER
Director: Stafford Dickens
Co-stars: Bobby Howes Rene Ray Vera Pearce

1938 YES MADAM
Director: Norman Lee
Co-stars: Bobby Howes Diana Churchill Fred Emney

1938 HOLD MY HAND
Director: Thornton Freeland
Co-stars: Stanley Lupino Barbara Blair Sally Gray

1945 WONDER MAN
Director: Bruce Humberstone
Co-stars: Danny Kaye Vera-Ellen Virginia Mayo

DAISY BELMORE

1929 SEVEN DAYS LEAVE
Director: Richard Wallace
Co-stars: Gary Cooper Beryl Mercer Nora Cecil

PAMELA BELLWOOD

1976 TWO-MINUTE WARNING
Director: Larry Peerce
Co-stars: Charlton Heston John Cassavetes Beau Bridges

1978 DEADMAN'S CURVE
Director: Richard Compton
Co-stars: Richard Hatch Bruce Davison

1980 SERIAL
Director: Bill Persky
Co-stars: Martin Mull Tuesday Weld Sally Kellerman

1983 COCAINE: ONE MAN'S SEDUCTION
Director: Paul Wendkos
Co-stars: Dennis Weaver James Spader

1983 AGATHA CHRISTIE'S SPARKLING CYANIDE
Director: Robert Lewis
Co-stars: Anthony Andrews Deborah Raffin

DAWN BENDER

1953 THE ACTRESS
Director: George Cukor
Co-stars: Jean Simmons Spencer Tracy Teresa Wright

NELLY BENEDETTI

1964 SILKEN SKIN
Director: Francois Truffaut
Co-stars: Jean Desailly Francoise Dorleac

MARIANNE BENET

1960 A TERRIBLE BEAUTY
Director: Tay Garnet
Co-stars: Robert Mitchum Anne Heywood Richard Harris

1961 THE BOY WHO STOLE A MILLION
Director: Charles Crichton
Co-stars: Maurice Reyna Harold Kasket

ADRIANA BENETTI

1942 FOUR STEPS IN THE CLOUDS
Director: Alessandro Blasetti
Co-stars: Gino Cervi Giuditta Rissone

JOAN BENHAM

1954 THE MAN WHO LOVED REDHEADS
Director: Harold French
Co-stars: John Justin Moira Shearer

1963 THE V.I.P.S
Director: Anthony Asquith
Co-stars: Richard Burton Elizabeth Taylor Maggie Smith

1964 MURDER AHOY
Director: George Pollock
Co-stars: Margaret Rutherford Lionel Jeffries Derek Nimmo

1970 PERFECT FRIDAY
Director: Peter Hall
Co-stars: Stanley Baker Ursula Andress David Warner

ANNETTE BENING (Married Warren Beatty)
Nominated For Best Supporting Actress In 1990 For "The Grifters"

1988 THE GREAT OUTDOORS
Director: Howard Deutch
Co-stars: Dan Aykroyd John Candy Lucy Deakins

1988 HOSTAGE
Director: Peter Levin
Co-stars: Carol Burnett Carrie Hamilton Leon Russom

1989 VALMONT
Director: Milos Forman
Co-stars: Colin Firth Meg Tilly Fairuza Balk

1990 THE GRIFTERS
Director: Stephen Frears
Co-stars: Anjelica Huston John Cusack Pat Hingle

1990 POSTCARDS FROM THE EDGE
Director: Mike Nichols
Co-stars: Shirley MacLaine Meryl Streep

1991 REGARDING HENRY
Director: Mike Nichols
Co-stars: Harrison Ford Bill Nunn Mikki Allen

1991 GUILTY BY SUSPICION
Director: Irwin Winkler
Co-stars: Robert De Niro George Wendt Sam Wanamaker

1995 THE AMERICAN PRESIDENT
Director: Rob Reiner
Co-stars: Michael Douglas Richard Dreyfuss Martin Sheen

1995 LOVE AFFAIR
Co-stars: Warren Beatty Garry Shandling

1996 THE GINGER BREAD MAN
Co-stars: Kenneth Branagh

1996 RICHARD III
Director: Ian McKellen
Co-stars: Ian McKellen Maggie Smith Patrick Stewart

1997 MARS ATTACKS!
Director: Tim Burton
Co-stars: Jack Nicholson Glenn Close Warren Beatty Tom Jones

CLAIRE BENITO

1993 BAD BOY BUBBY
Director: Rolf De Heer
Co-stars: Nicholas Hope Carmel Johnson Natalie Carr

FLOELLA BENJAMIN

1975 BLACK JOY
Director: Anthony Simmons
Co-stars: Norman Beaton Trevor Thomas Dawn Hope

ANNE BENNENT

1983 SWANN IN LOVE
Director: Volker Schlondorff
Co-stars: Jeremy Irons Ornella Muti Fanny Ardant

BELLE BENNET

1925 STELLA DALLAS
Director: Henry King
Co-stars: Ronald Colman Alice Joyce Jean Hersholt

1928 THE WAY OF ALL FLESH
Director: Victor Fleming
Co-stars: Emil Jannings Phyllis Haver

1929 THE IRON MASK
Director: Allan Dwan
Co-stars: Douglas Fairbanks Margueritte De La Motte

1930   COURAGE
Director: Archie Mayo
Co-stars: Marian Nixon Rex Bell Blanche Friderici

ALMA BENNETT

1927   LONG PANTS
Director: Frank Capra
Co-stars: Harry Langdon Gladys Brockwell

CONSTANCE BENNETT
(Daughter Of Richard Bennett Sister Of Joan Bennett)

1925   SALLY, IRENE AND MARY
Director: Edmund Goulding
Co-stars: Joan Crawford Sally O'Neil William Haines

1930   COMMON CLAY
Director: Victor Fleming
Co-stars: Lew Ayres Tully Marshall Beryl Mercer

1930   SON OF THE GODS
Director: Frank Lloyd
Co-stars: Richard Barthelmess Geneva Mitchell

1930   THREE FACES EAST
Director: Roy Del Ruth
Co-stars: Erich Von Stroheim Anthony Bushell

1930   RICH PEOPLE
Co-star: John Loder

1931   BORN TO LOVE
Director: Paul Stein
Co-stars: Joel McCrea Paul Cavanagh Anthony Bushell

1931   COMMON LAW
Co-stars: Joel McCrea Lew Cody Hedda Hopper

1931   BOUGHT
Director: Archie Mayo
Co-stars: Ben Lyon Ray Milland Richard Bennett

1931   THE EASIEST WAY
Director: Jack Conway
Co-stars: Robert Montgomery Adolphe Menjou Clark Gable

1932   LADY WITH A PAST
Director: Edward Griffith
Co-stars: Ben Lyon David Manners Astrid Allwyn

1932   ROCKABYE
Director: George Cukor
Co-stars: Joel McCrea Paul Lukas Walter Pidgeon

1932   WHAT PRICE HOLLYWOOD?
Director: George Cukor
Co-stars: Lowell Sherman Neil Hamilton Gregory Ratoff

1932   TWO AGAINST THE WORLD
Director: Archie Mayo
Co-stars: Oscar Apfel Helen Vinson Neil Hamilton

1933   OUR BETTERS
Director: George Cukor
Co-stars: Alan Mowbray Gilbert Roland Charles Starrett

1933   BED OF ROSES
Director: Gregory La Cava
Co-stars: Joel McCrea Pert Kelton

1933   AFTER TONIGHT
Director: George Archainbaud
Co-stars: Gilbert Roland Edward Ellis Mischa Auer

1934   THE AFFAIRS OF CELLINI
Director: Gregory La Cava
Co-stars: Fredric March Frank Morgan Fay Wray

1934   MOULIN ROUGE
Director: Sidney Lanfield
Co-stars: Franchot Tone Tullio Carminati

1934   OUTCAST LADY
Director: Robert Z. Leonard
Co-stars: Hugh Williams Mrs. Patrick Campbell

1935   AFTER OFFICE HOURS
Director: Robert Z. Leonard
Co-stars: Clark Gable Stuart Erwin Billie Burke

1936   EVERYTHING IS THUNDER
Director: Milton Rosmer
Co-stars: Douglass Montgomery Oscar Homolka

1936   LADIES IN LOVE
Director: Edward Griffith
Co-stars: Janet Gaynor Loretta Young Tyrone Power

1937   TOPPER
Director: Norman Z. McLeod
Co-stars: Cary Grant Roland Young Billie Burke

1938   SERVICE DE LUXE
Director: Rowland Lee
Co-stars: Vincent Price Charles Ruggles Helen Broderick

1938   MERRILY WE LIVE
Director: Norman Z. McLeod
Co-stars: Brian Aherne Billie Burke Patsy Kelly

1939   TAIL SPIN
Director: Roy Del Ruth
Co-stars: Alice Faye Joan Davis Nancy Kelly

1939   TOPPER TAKES A TRIP
Director: Norman Z. McLeod
Co-stars: Roland Young Billie Burke Alan Mowbray

1941   TWO-FACED WOMAN
Director: George Cukor
Co-stars: Greta Garbo Melvyn Douglas Roland Young

1941   WILD BILL HICKOK RIDES
Director: Ray Enright
Co-stars: Bruce Cabot Warren William Howard Da Silva

1941   LAW OF THE TROPICS
Director: Ray Enright
Co-stars: Jeffrey Lynn Regis Toomey Craig Stevens

1941   ESCAPE TO GLORY
Director: John Brahm
Co-stars: Pat O'Brien John Halliday Edgar Buchanan

1942   MADAME SPY
Director: Roy William Neill
Co-stars: Don Porter John Litel Edward Brophy

1942   SIN TOWN
Director: Ray Enright
Co-stars: Broderick Crawford Leo Carrillo Patric Knowles

1945   PARIS UNDERGROUND
Director: Gregory Ratoff
Co-stars: Gracie Fields George Rigaud Leslie Vincent

1946   CENTENNIAL SUMMER
Director: Otto Preminger
Co-stars: Jeanne Crain Cornel Wilde Walter Brennan

1947   THE UNSUSPECTED
Director: Michael Curtiz
Co-stars: Claude Rains Joan Caulfield Audrey Totter

1948   SMART WOMAN
Director: Edward Blatt
Co-stars: Brian Aherne Barry Sullivan

1948   ANGEL ON THE AMAZON
Director: John Auer
Co-stars: George Brent Brian Aherne Vera Ralston

1951   AS YOUNG AS YOU FEEL
Director: Harmon Jones
Co-stars: Monty Woolley Thelma Ritter Marilyn Monroe

1965   MADAME X
Director: David Lowell Rich
Co-stars: Lana Turner John Forsythe Burgess Meredith

EILEEN BENNETT

1942   MUCH TOO SHY
Director: Marcel Varnel
Co-stars: George Formby Kathleen Harrison Jimmy Clitheroe

1943   THURSDAY'S CHILD
Director: Rodney Ackland
Co-stars: Sally Ann Howes Wilfrid Lawson Stewart Granger

ENID BENNETT

1918   THE LAW OF MEN

1922   ROBIN HOOD
Director: Allan Dwan
Co-stars: Douglas Fairbanks Wallace Beery Alan Hale

1924   THE SEA HAWK
Director: Frank Lloyd
Co-stars: Milton Sills Wallace Beery

1931   SKIPPY
Director: Norman Taurog
Co-stars: Jackie Cooper Mitzi Green Jackie Searle

1931   WATERLOO BRIDGE
Director: James Whale
Co-stars: Mae Clarke Doris Lloyd Bette Davis

1939   MEET DR CHRISTIAN
Director: Bernard Vorhaus
Co-stars: Jean Hersholt Dorothy Lovett

JILL BENNETT

1954   AUNT CLARA
Director: Anthony Kimmins
Co-stars: Margaret Rutherford Ronald Shiner

1954   HELL BELOW ZERO
Director: Mark Robson
Co-stars: Alan Ladd Stanley Baker Basil Sydney

1956   LUST FOR LIFE
Director: Vincente Minnelli
Co-stars: Kirk Douglas Anthony Quinn James Donald

1960   THE CRIMINAL
Director: Joseph Losey
Co-stars: Stanley Baker Sam Wanamaker Patrick Wymark

1965   THE NANNY
Director: Seth Holt
Co-stars: Bette Davis James Villiers Wendy Craig

1965   THE SKULL
Director: Freddie Francis
Co-stars: Peter Cushing Christopher Lee

1968   INADMISSABLE EVIDENCE
Director: Anthony Page
Co-stars: Nicol Williamson Peter Sallis Eileen Atkins

1968   THE CHARGE OF THE LIGHT BRIGADE
Director: Tony Richardson
Co-stars: David Hemmings Trevor Howard

1969   JULIUS CAESAR
Director: Stuart Burge
Co-stars: John Geilgud Charlton Heston Richard Johnson

1972   I WANT WHAT I WANT
Director: John Dexter
Co-stars: Anne Heywood Paul Rogers Harry Andrews

1975   MR. QUILP
Director: Anthony Newley
Co-stars: David Hemmings David Warner

1976   FULL CIRCLE
Director: Richard Loncraine
Co-stars: Mia Farrow Keir Dullea Tom Conti

1981   FOR YOUR EYES ONLY
Director: John Glen
Co-stars: Roger Moore Julian Glover Topol

1981   COUNTRY
Director: Richard Eyre
Co-stars: Wendy Hiller Leo McKern James Fox

1982   BRITANNIA HOSPITAL
Director: Lindsay Anderson
Co-stars: Leonard Rossiter Malcolm McDowell Joan Plowright

1986   LADY JANE
Director: Trevor Nunn
Co-stars: Helena Bonham Carter John Wood

1988   HAWKS
Director: Robert Ellis
Co-stars: Timothy Dalton Anthony Edwards Janet McTeer

1989   A DAY IN SUMMER
Director: Bob Mahoney
Co-stars: Jack Shepherd Peter Egan Ian Carmichael

1990   THE SHELTERING SKY
Director: Bernardo Bertolucci
Co-stars: Debra Winger John Malkovich

JOAN BENNETT *(Daughter Of Richard Bennett Sister Of Constance Bennett)*

1929   BULLDOG DRUMMOND
Director: Richard Jones
Co-stars: Ronald Colman Lilyan Tashman Montagu Love

1929   DISRAELI
Director: Alfred Green
Co-stars: George Arliss Florence Arliss Anthony Bushel

1930   CRAZY THAT WAY
Co-stars: Jason Robards Kenneth MacKenna

1930   PUTTIN' ON THE RITZ
Director: Edward Sloman
Co-stars: Harry Richman James Gleason Lilyan Tashman

1930   MOBY DICK
Director: Lloyd Bacon
Co-stars: John Barrymore Lloyd Hughes May Boley

1931   HUSH MONEY
Director: Sidney Lanfield
Co-stars: Owen Moore Myrna Loy Hardie Albright

1931   DOCTORS' WIVES
Co-star: Warner Baxter

1931   MANY A SLIP
Co-star: Lew Ayres

1932   CARELESS LADY
Director: Kenneth MacKenna
Co-stars: John Boles Minna Gombell

1932   ME AND MY GAL
Director: Raoul Walsh
Co-stars: Spencer Tracy George Walsh Marion Burns

1932   SHE WANTED A MILLIONAIRE
Director: John Blystone
Co-stars: Spencer Tracy James Kirkwood Una Merkel

1932   THE TRIAL OF VIVIENNE WARE
Director: William Howard
Co-stars: Donald Cook Skeets Gallagher Zasu Pitts

1933   LITTLE WOMEN
Director: George Cukor
Co-stars: Katharine Hepburn Frances Dee Jean Parker

1933 ARIZONA TO BROADWAY
Director: James Tinling
Co-stars: James Dunn Herbert Mundin J. Carrol Naish

1934 THE PURSUIT OF HAPPINESS
Director: Alexander Hall
Co-stars: Francis Lederer Charles Ruggles

1935 THE MAN WHO BROKE THE BANK AT MONTE CARLO
Director: Stephen Roberts
Co-stars: Ronald Colman Montagu Love

1935 THE MAN WHO RECLAIMED HIS HEAD
Director: Edward Ludwig
Co-stars: Claude Rains Henry O'Neill

1935 MISSISSIPPI
Director: Edward Sutherland
Co-stars: Bing Crosby W. C. Fields Gail Patrick

1935 PRIVATE WORLDS
Director: Gregory La Cava
Co-stars: Claudette Colbert Charles Boyer

1935 SHE COULDN'T TAKE IT
Director: Tay Garnett
Co-stars: George Raft Walter Connolly Lloyd Nolan

1935 TWO FOR TONIGHT
Director: Frank Tuttle
Co-stars: Bing Crosby Lynne Overman Mary Boland

1936 BIG BROWN EYES
Director: Raoul Walsh
Co-stars: Cary Grant Walter Pidgeon Lloyd Nolan

1936 WEDDING PRESENT
Director: Richard Wallace
Co-stars: Cary Grant George Bancroft

1936 13 HOURS BY AIR
Director: Mitchell Leisen
Co-stars: Fred MacMurray Brian Donlevy Zasu Pitts

1936 TWO IN A CROWD
Co-star: Joel McCrea

1937 VOGUES OF 1938
Director: Irving Cummings
Co-stars: Warner Baxter Helen Vinson Mischa Auer

1938 ARTISTS AND MODELS ABROAD
Director: Mitchell Leisen
Co-stars: Jack Benny Monty Woolley

1937 I MET MY LOVE AGAIN
Director: Joshua Logan
Co-stars: Henry Fonda Alan Marshall May Whitty

1938 THE TEXANS
Director: James Hogan
Co-stars: Randolph Scott Robert Cummings Walter Brennan

1939 TRADE WINDS
Director: Tay Garnett
Co-stars: Fredric March Ralph Bellamy Thomas Mitchell

1939 THE MAN IN THE IRON MASK
Director: James Whale
Co-stars: Louis Hayward Warren William Alan Hale

1939 THE HOUSEKEEPER'S DAUGHTER
Director: Hal Roach
Co-stars: John Hubbard Adolphe Menjou Victor Mature

1940 GREEN HELL
Director: James Whale
Co-stars: Douglas Fairbanks George Sanders Vincent Price

1940 THE HOUSE ACROSS THE BAY
Director: Archie Mayo
Co-stars: George Raft Walter Pidgeon Lloyd Nolan

1940 THE MAN I MARRIED
Director: Irving Pichel
Co-stars: Francis Lederer Lloyd Nolan Anna Sten

1940 THE SON OF MONTE CRISTO
Director: Rowland Lee
Co-stars: Louis Hayward George Sanders Florence Bates

1941 SHE KNEW ALL THE ANSWERS
Director: Richard Wallace
Co-stars: Franchot Tone John Hubbard

1941 MAN HUNT
Director: Fritz Lang
Co-stars: Walter Pidgeon George Sanders Roddy McDowall

1941 CONFIRM OR DENY
Director: Fritz Lang
Co-stars: Don Ameche Roddy McDowall Arthur Shields

1942 GIRL TROUBLE
Director: Harold Schuster
Co-stars: Don Ameche Billie Burke Alan Dinehart

1942 TWIN BEDS
Director: Tim Whelan
Co-stars: George Brent Mischa Auer Una Merkel

1942 THE WIFE TAKES A FLYER
Director: Richard Wallace
Co-stars: Franchot Tone Allyn Joslyn

1942 WILD GEESE CALLING
Director: John Brahm
Co-stars: Henry Fonda Warren William Ona Munson

1943 MARGIN FOR ERROR
Director: Otto Preminger
Co-stars: Otto Preminger Milton Berle Carl Esmond

1944 THE WOMAN IN THE WINDOW
Director: Fritz Lang
Co-stars: Edward G. Robinson Dan Duryea Raymond Massey

1945 SCARLETT STREET
Director: Fritz Lang
Co-stars: Edward G. Robinson Dan Duryea Margaret Lindsay

1945 NOB HILL
Director: Henry Hathaway
Co-stars: George Raft Vivian Blaine Peggy Ann Garner

1945 COLONEL EFFINGHAM'S RAID
Director: Irving Pichel
Co-stars: Charles Coburn William Eythe Allyn Joslyn

1947 THE MACOMBER AFFAIR
Director: Zoltan Korda
Co-stars: Gregory Peck Robert Preston Reginald Denny

1947 THE WOMAN ON THE BEACH
Director: Jean Renoir
Co-stars: Robert Ryan Charles Bickford Nan Leslie

1948 THE SCAR
Director: Steve Sekeley
Co-stars: Paul Henreid Eduard Franz John Qualen

1948 SECRET BEYOND THE DOOR
Director: Fritz Lang
Co-stars: Michael Redgrave Anne Revere Barbara O'Neill

1948 HOLLOW TRIUMPH
Director: Steve Sekeley
Co-stars: Paul Henreid Eduard Franz Leslie Brooks

1949 THE RECKLESS MOMENT
Director: Max Ophuls
Co-stars: James Mason Geraldine Brooks Henry O'Neill

1950 FOR HEAVEN'S SAKE
Director: George Seaton
Co-stars: Clifton Webb Edmund Gwenn Robert Cummings

1950 FATHER OF THE BRIDE
Director: Vincente Minnelli
Co-stars: Spencer Tracy Elizabeth Taylor Don Taylor

1951 THE GUY WHO CAME BACK
Director: Joseph Newman
Co-stars: Paul Douglas Linda Darnel Don Defore

1952 FATHER'S LITTLE DIVIDEND
Director: Vincente Minnelli
Co-stars: Spencer Tracy Elizabeth Taylor

1954 WE'RE NO ANGELS
Director: Michael Curtiz
Co-stars: Humphrey Bogart Peter Ustinov Aldo Ray

1956 THERE'S ALWAYS TOMORROW
Director: Douglas Sirk
Co-stars: Barbara Stanwyck Fred MacMurray Pat Crowley

1956 NAVY WIFE
Director: Edward Bernds
Co-stars: Gary Merrill Shirley Yagamuchi Judy Nugent

1960 DESIRE IN THE DUST
Director: William Claxton
Co-stars: Raymond Burr Martha Hyer Ken Scott

1970 HOUSE OF THE DARK SHADOWS

1972 THE EYES OF CHARLES SAND
Director: Reza Badigi
Co-stars: Peter Haskell Barbara Rush Sharon Farrell

1976 SUSPIRIA
Director: Dario Argento
Co-stars: Jessica Harper Alida Valli Stefania Casini

LEILA BENNETT

1932 TIGER SHARK
Director: Howard Hawks
Co-stars: Edward G. Robinson J. Carrol Naish Zita Johann

1932 THE FIRST YEAR
Director: William Howard
Co-stars: Janet Gaynor Charles Farrell Minna Gombell

LINDA BENNETT *(Child)*

1955 SEVEN LITTLE FOYS
Director: Melville Shavelson
Co-stars: Bob Hope Milly Vitale James Cagney

MARJORIE BENNETT

1962 WHATEVER HAPPENED TO BABY JANE?
Director: Robert Aldrich
Co-stars: Bette Davis Joan Crawford

1967 GAMES
Director: Curtis Harrington
Co-stars: Simone Signoret James Caan Katherine Ross

1968 COOGAN'S BLUFF
Director: Don Siegel
Co-stars: Clint Eastwood Lee J. Cobb Susan Clark

ROSALIND BENNETT

1989 DEALERS
Director: Colin Bucksey
Co-stars: Paul McGann Rebecca De Mornay Derrick O'Connor

TRACIE BENNETT

1989 SHIRLEY VALENTINE
Director: Lewis Gilbert
Co-stars: Pauline Collins Tom Conti Bernard Hill

HEATHER BENNETTE

1961 THE MISSING NOTE
Director: Michael Passmore
Co-stars: John Moulder-Brown Toke Townley

AMBER BENSON

1993 THB CRUSH
Director: Alan Shapiro
Co-stars: Cary Elwes Alicia Silverstone Jennifer Rubin

ANNETTE BENSON

1928 SHOOTING STARS
Director: Anthony Asquith
Co-stars: Brian Aherne Donald Calthrop Chili Bouchier

DEBORAH BENSON

1977 9/30/55
Director: James Bridges
Co-stars: Richard Thomas Susan Tyrell Lisa Blount

1980 JUST BEFORE DAWN
Director: Jeff Lieberman
Co-stars: George Kennedy Chris Lemmon

ELAINE BENSON

1934 THE OLD CURIOSITY SHOP
Director: Thomas Bentley
Co-stars: Hay Petrie Ben Webster

IVY BENSON

1943 THE DUMMY TALKS
Director: Oswald Mitchell
Co-stars: Jack Warner Claude Hulbert

JODI BENSON

1989 THE LITTLE MERMAID *(Voice)*
Director: Ron Clemente
Co-stars: Buddy Hackett Edie McClurg Pat Carroll

1994 THUMBELINA *(Voice)*
Director: Don Bluth
Co-stars: Carol Channing John Hurt Barbara Cook

LAURA BENSON

1989 I WANT TO GO HOME
Director: Alain Resnais
Co-stars: Adolph Green Gerard Depardieu Linda Lavin

LUCILLE BENSON

1970 YOU CAN'T HAVE EVERYTHING
Director: Martin Zweibach
Co-stars: Richard Thomas Mary Layne

1970 LITTLE FAUSS AND BIG HALSY
Director: Sidney Furie
Co-stars: Robert Redford Michael J. Pollard

1971 DUEL
Director: Steven Spielberg
Co-stars: Dennis Weaver Jacqueline Scott

1972 PRIVATE PARTS
Director: Paul Bartel
Co-stars: Ayn Ruyman John Ventantonio

1973 TOM SAWYER
Director: Don Taylor
Co-stars: Johnny Whitaker Celeste Holm Jodie Foster

1974 THE DAY THE EARTH MOVED
Director: Robert Michael Lewis
Co-stars: Jackie Cooper Stella Stevens

1979 THE CONCRETE COWBOYS
Director: Burt Kennedy
Co-stars: Jerry Reed Tom Selleck Morgan Fairchild

1981 AMY
Director: Vincent McEveety
Co-stars: Jenny Agutter Barry Newman Margaret O'Brien

BEVERLY BENTLEY

1959   SCENT OF MYSTERY
Director: Jack Cardiff
Co-stars: Denholm Elliott Peter Lorre Paul Lukas

IRENE BENTLEY

1933   FRONTIER MARSHALL
Director: Lew Seiler
Co-stars: George O'Brien George E. Stone

BARBI BENTON

1980   FOR THE LOVE OF IT
Director: Hal Kanter
Co-stars: Deborah Raffin Jeff Conaway Tom Bosley

1984   DEATHSTALKER
Director: John Watson
Co-stars: Robert Hill Richard Brooker

1984   AND THE WALLS CAME TUMBLING DOWN
Director: Paul Annett
Co-stars: Peter Wyngarde Gareth Hunt

SUZANNE BENTON

1969   THAT COLD DAY IN THE PARK
Director: Robert Altman
Co-stars: Sandy Dennis Michael Burns

1975   A BOY AND HIS DOG
Director: L. Q. Jones
Co-stars: Don Johnson Jason Robards Charles McGraw

1975   BEST FRIENDS
Director: Noel Nosseck
Co-stars: Richard Hatch Doug Chapin Ann Noland

1976   F. SCOTT FITZGERALD IN HOLLYWOOD
Director: Anthony Page
Co-stars: Jason Miller Tuesday Weld Julia Foster

JEANNE BERETTA

1967   MADEMOISELLE
Director: Tony Richardson
Co-stars: Jeanne Moreau Ettore Manni

BERRY BERENSON

1978 REMEMBER MY NAME
Director: Alan Rudolph
Co-stars: Geraldine Chaplin Anthony Perkins

MARISA BERENSON

1971   DEATH IN VENICE
Director: Luchino Visconti
Co-stars: Dirk Bogarde Bjorn Andresen Silvana Mangano

1972   CABARET
Director: Bob Fosse
Co-stars: Lisa Minnelli Michael York Joel Grey

1975   BARRY LYNDON
Director: Stanley Kubrick
Co-stars: Ryan O'Neal Patrick Magee Leonard Rossiter

1979   KILLER FISH
Director: Antonio Margheriti
Co-stars: Lee Majors Karen Black Margaux Hemingway

1981   S.O.B.
Director: Blake Edwards
Co-stars: Julie Andrews William Holden Robert Preston

1985   ASPHALT WARRIOR
Director: Patrick Millet
Co-stars: Daniel Autenic Marcel Bozzufi

1986   SINS
Director: Douglas Hickox
Co-stars: Joan Collins Jean-Pierre Aumont Gene Kelly

1990   WHITE HUNTER BLACK HEART
Director: Clint Eastwood
Co-stars: Clint Eastwood Jeff Fahey George Dzundza

FRANCOISE BERD

1977   A SPECIAL DAY
Director: Ettore Scola
Co-stars: Sophia Loren Marcello Mastroianni

EVA BERG

1952   THE LONG MEMORY
Director: Robert Hamer
Co-stars: John Mills John McCallum Elizabeth Sellars

GERTRUDE BERG

1951   MOLLY
Co-stars: Philip Loeb Larry Robinson

1953   MAIN STREET TO BROADWAY
Director: Tay Garnett
Co-stars: Tom Morton Ethel Barrymore Henry Fonda

JUDITH-MARIE BERGAN

1975   THE ABDUCTION
Director: Joseph Zito
Co-stars: Gregory Rozakis Dorothy Malone Lawrence Tierney

1988   THE SECRET LIFE OF KATHY McCORMICK
Director: Robert Lewis
Co-stars: Barbara Eden Judy Geeson

FRANCINE BERGE

1963   JUDEX
Director: Georges Franju
Co-stars: Channing Pollock Edith Scob Michel Vitold

1964   LA RONDE
Director: Roger Vadim
Co-stars: Marie Dubois Anna Karina Jane Fonda

1965   LA RELIGIEUSE
Director: Jacques Rivette
Co-stars: Anna Karina Micheline Presle

1966   BENJAMIN
Director: Michel Deville
Co-stars: Pierre Clemente Michele Morgan Catherine Deneuvre

1979   THE GREATEST ATTACK
Director: Pierre Gramier-Deferre
Co-stars: Alain Delon Veronique Jannot

CANDICE BERGEN
Nominated For Best Supporting Actress In 1979 For "Starting Over"

1966   THE GROUP
Director: Sidney Lumet
Co-stars: Joan Hackett Shirley Knight Jessica Walter

1966   THE SAND PEPPLES
Director: Robert Wise
Co-stars: Steve McQueen Richard Attenborough Richard Crenna

1967   LIVE FOR LIFE
Director: Claude Lelouch
Co-stars: Yves Montand Annie Girardo Irene Tunc

1967   THE DAY THE FISH CAME OUT
Director: Michael Cacoyannis
Co-stars: Tom Courtenay Sam Wanamaker

1968   THE MAGUS
Director: Guy Green
Co-stars: Michael Caine Anthony Quinn Anna Karina

1970 THE ADVENTURERS
Director: Lewis Gilbert
Co-stars: Bekim Fehmiu Alan Badel Rossano Brazzi

1970 GETTING STRAIGHT
Director: Richard Rush
Co-stars: Elliott Gould Robert F Lyons Cecil Kellaway

1970 SOLDIER BLUE
Director: Ralph Nelson
Co-stars: Peter Strauss Donald Pleasence Jorge Rivero

1971 T. R. BASKIN
Director: Herbert Ross
Co-stars: Peter Boyle James Caan Marcia Rodd

1971 THE HUNTING PARTY
Director: Don Medford
Co-stars: Gene Hackman Oliver Reed Simon Oakland

1971 CARNAL KNOWLEDGE
Director: Mike Nichols
Co-stars: Jack Nicholson Art Garfunkel Ann-Margret

1974 ELEVEN HARROWHOUSE
Director: Aram Avakian
Co-stars: Charles Grodin James Mason Trevor Howard

1975 THE WIND AND THE LION
Director: John Millius
Co-stars: Sean Connery Brian Keith John Huston

1975 BITE THE BULLET
Director: Richard Brooks
Co-stars: Gene Hackman James Coburn Ben Johnson

1977 THE DOMINO KILLINGS
Director: Stanley Kramer
Co-stars: Gene Hackluan Richard Widmark Mickey Rooney

1978 THE END OF THE WORLD
Director: Lina Wertmuller
Co-stars: Giancarlo Giannini Jill Eikenberry

1978 OLIVER'S STORY
Director: John Korty
Co-stars: Ryan O'Neal Nicola Pagett Ray Milland

1979 STARTING OVER
Director: Alan J. Pakula
Co-stars: Burt Reynolds Jill Clayburgh Charles Durning

1981 RICH AND FAMOUS
Director: George Cukor
Co-stars: Jacqueline Bisset David Selby Meg Ryan

1982 GANDHI
Director: Rlchard Attenborough
Co-stars: Ben Kingsley John Mills Edward Fox

1985 STICK
Director: Burt Reynolds
Co-stars: George Segal Charles Durning Burt Reynolds

1985 MURDER BY REASON OF INSANITY
Director: Anthony Page
Co-stars: Jurgen Prochnow Hector Elizondo

1987 MAYFLOWER MADAM
Director: Lou Antonio
Co-stars: Chris Sarandon Caitlin Clark Chita Rivera

FRANCES BERGEN

1980 AMERICAN GIGOLO
Director: Paul Schrader
Co-stars: Richard Gere Lauren Hutton Nina Van Pallandt

1990 EATING
Director: Henry Jaglom
Co-stars: Lisa Richards Mary Crosby Gwen Welles

POLLY BERGEN

1951 WARPATH
Director: Byron Haskin
Co-stars: Edmond O'Brien Dean Jagger Forrest Tucker

1951 AT WAR WITH THE ARMY
Director: Hal Walker
Co-stars: Martin & Lewis Mike Kellin Jimmie Dundee

1951 THAT'S MY BOY
Director: Hal Walker
Co-stars: Martin & Lewis Eddie Mayehoff Ruth Hussey

1952 THE STOOGE
Director: Norman Taurog
Co-stars: Martin & Lewis Eddie Mayehoff Marie McDonald

1953 FAST COMPANY
Director: John Sturges
Co-stars: Howard Keel Nina Foch Marjorie Main

1953 ESCAPE FROM FORT BRAVO
Director: John Sturges
Co-stars: William Holden Eleanor Parker William Demarest

1953 HALF A HERO
Director: Don Weis
Co-stars: Red Skelton Jean Hagen Charles Dingle

1953 ARENA
Director: Richard Fleischer
Co-stars: Gig Young Jean Hagan Henry Morgan

1962 CAPE FEAR
Director: J. Lee-Thompson
Co-stars: Gregory Peck Robert Mitchum Martin Balsam

1963 THE CARETAKERS
Director: Hall Bartlett
Co-stars: Joan Crawford Robert Stack Herbert Marshall

1963 MOVE OVER DARLING
Director: Michael Gordon
Co-stars: Doris Day James Garner Thelma Ritter

1964 KISSES FOR MY PRESIDENT
Director: Curtis Bernhardt
Co-stars: Fred MacMurray Arlene Dahl

1967 A GUIDE FOR THE MARRIED MAN
Director: Gene Kelly
Co-stars: Walter Matthau Inger Stevens Jack Benny

1967 DON'T MAKE WAVES
Director: Alexander MacKendrick
Co-stars: Tony Curtis Claudia Cardinale

1975 MURDER ON FLIGHT 502
Director: George McCowan
Co-stars: Ralph Bellamy Robert Stack Laraine Day

1987 MAKING MR RIGHT
Director: Susan Seidelman
Co-stars: Ann Magnuson John Malkovich Glenne Headly

1988 ADDICTED TO HIS LOVE
Director: Arthur Seidelman
Co-stars: Barry Bostwick Colleen Camp Rosemary Forsyth

1989 MY BROTHER'S WIFE
Director: Jack Bender
Co-stars: John Ritter Mel Harris David Byron

1990 CRY-BABY
Director: John Waters
Co-stars: Johnny Depp Amy Locane Susan Tyrrell

TUSHKA BERGEN

1988 OUTBACK
Director: Ian Barry
Co-stars: Jeff Fahey Steve Vidler Shane Bryant

1993 **SWING KIDS**
Director: Thomas Carter
Co-stars: Robert Sean Leonard Christian Bale Barbara Hershey

1994 **BARCELONA**
Director: Whit Stillman
Co-stars: Taylor Nichols Chris Eigeman Mira Sorvino

KATIA BERGER

1981 **TALES OF ORDINARY MADNESS**
Director: Marco Ferreri
Co-stars: Ben Gazzara Ornella Muti Susan Tyrrell

NICOLE BERGER

1958 **EN CAS DE MALHEUR**
Director: Claude Autant-Lara
Co-stars: Jean Gabin Brigitte Bardot Edwige Feuiller

1960 **SHOOT THE PIANIST**
Director: Francois Truffaut
Co-stars: Charles Aznavour Marie Dubois

SENTA BERGER

1961 **THE SECRET WAYS**
Director: Phil Karlson
Co-stars: Richard Widmark Sonja Zieman Walter Rillla

1963 **THE VICTORS**
Director: Carl Foreman
Co-stars: George Peppard George Hamilton Albert Finney

1963 **THE WALTZ KING**
Director: Steve Previn
Co-stars: Kerwin Matthews Brian Aherne Peter Kraus

1964 **GOOD NEIGHBOUR SAM**
Director: David Swift
Co-stars: Jack Lemmon Romy Schneider Edward G. Robinson

1965 **THE GLORY GUYS**
Director: Arnold Laven
Co-stars: Tom Tryon Harve Presnell James Caan

1965 **MAJOR DUNDEE**
Director: Sam Peckinpah
Co-stars: Charlton Heston Richard Harris James Coburn

1966 **CAST A GIANT SHADOW**
Director: Melville Shavelson
Co-stars: Kirk Douglas Angie Dickinson Topol

1966 **OUR MAN IN MARRAKESH**
Director: Don Sharp
Co-stars: Tony Randall Terry-Thomas Klaus Kinski

1966 **THE QUILLER MEMORANDUM**
Director: Michael Anderson
Co-stars: George Segal Max Von Sydow Alec Guinness

1966 **THE SPY WITH MY FACE**
Director: John Newland
Co-stars: Robert Vaughn David McCallum Leo G. Carroll

1967 **DIABOLICALLY YOURS**
Director: Julien Duvivier
Co-stars: Alain Delon Sergio Fantoni

1967 **THE AMBUSHERS**
Director: Henry Levin
Co-stars: Dean Martin Janice Rule Kurt Kasznar

1969 **DE SADE**
Director: Cy Endfield
Co-stars: Keir Dullea John Huston Anna Massey

1975 **THE SWISS CONSPIRACY**
Director: Jack Arnold
Co-stars: David Janssen John Ireland Ray Milland

1977 **CROSS OF IRON**
Director: Sam Peckinpah
Co-stars: James Coburn James Mason Maxmillian Schell

SARAH BERGER

1986 **HARD TRAVELLING**
Director: Colin Gregg
Co-stars: Suzanne Burden Tom Bell Jack Shepherd

1987 **STANLEY**
Director: Anna Benson Gyles
Co-stars: Anton Lesser Juliet Stevenson Lesley Dunlop

1990 **THE GREEN MAN**
Director: Elijah Moshinsky
Co-stars: Albert Finney Michael Hordern Josie Lawrence

SARAH BERGHARD

1992 **DEAD ROMANTIC**
Director: Patrick Lau
Co-stars: Janet McTeer Clive Wood Elspet Gray

INGRID BERGMAN
(Mother Of Isabella Rossellini)
**Oscar For Best Actress In 1956 For "Anastasia", In 1964 For "Gaslight"
And Best Supporting Actress In 1974 For "Murder On The Orient Express"
Nominated For Best Actress In 1943 For "For Whom The Bell Tolls", In
1945 For "The Bells Of St. Mary's", Also In 1948 For "Joan Of Arc"And In
1978 For "Autumn Sonata"**

1935 **THE COUNT OF THE OLD TOWN**
Director: Sigurd Wallen
Co-star: Valdemar Dahlquist

1935 **SWEDENHIELMS**
Director: Gustav Molander
Co-stars: Gosta Ekman Tutta Rolf

1935 **WALPURGIS NIGHT**
Director: Gustav Edgren
Co-stars: Lars Hanson Victor Sjostrom Karin Kavli

1936 **INTERMEZZO**
Director: Gustav Molander
Co-stars: Gusta Ekman Bullen Berglund

1937 **A WOMAN'S FACE**
Director: Gustav Molander
Co-stars: Anders Hendrickson Georg Rydeberg

1938 **DOLLAR**
Director: Gustav Molander
Co-stars: Georg Rydeberg Tutta Rolf

1939 **ONE SINGLE NIGHT**
Director: Gustav Molander
Co-stars: Aino Taube Edvin Adolphson

1939 **INTERMEZZO**
Director: Gregory Ratoff
Co-stars: Leslie Howard John Halliday Edna Best

1940 **JUNE NIGHT**
Director: Peter Lindberg
Co-stars: Marianne Lofgren Olaf Widgren

1941 **ADAM HAD FOUR SONS**
Director: Gregory Ratoff
Co-stars: Warner Baxter Susan Hayward Fay Wray

1941 **DR. JECKYLL AND MR HYDE**
Director: Victor Fleming
Co-stars: Spencer Tracy Lana Turner Donald Crisp

1941 **RAGE IN HEAVEN**
Director: W. S. Van Dyke
Co-stars: Robert Montgomery George Sanders Oscar Homolka

1942 CASABLANCA
Director: Michael Curtis
Co-stars: Humphrey Bogart Paul Henreid S. Z. Sakall

1943 FOR WHOM THE BELL TOLLS
Director: Sam Wood
Co-stars: Gary Cooper Katina Paxinou Akim Tamiroff

1944 GASLIGHT
Director: George Cukor
Co-stars: Charles Boyer Joseph Cotten Angela Lansbury

1944 SARATOGA TRUNK
Director: Sam Wood
Co-stars: Gary Cooper Flora Robson Florence Bates

1945 SPELLBOUND
Director: Alfred Hitchcock
Co-stars: Gregory Peck Rhonda Fleming

1945 THE BELLS OF ST MARY'S
Director: Leo McCarey
Co-stars: Bing Crosby Henry Travers William Gargan

1946 NOTORIOUS
Director: Alfred Hitchcock
Co-stars: Cary Grant Claude Rains Louis Calhren

1948 JOAN OF ARK
Director: Victor Fleming
Co-stars: Jose Ferrer John Ireland Hurd Hatfield

1948 ARCH OF TRIUMPH
Director: Lewis Milestone
Co-stars: Charles Boyer Charles Laughton

1949 UNDER CAPRICORN
Director: Alfred Hitchcock
Co-stars: Joseph Cotten Michael Wilding Cecil Parker

1949 STROMBOLI
Director: Roberto Rossellini
Co-stars: Mario Vitali Renzo Cezana

1952 EUROPA 51
Director: Roberto Rossellini
Co-stars: Alexander Knox Ettore Giannini

1952 FEAR
Director: Roberto Rossellini

1953 VOYAGE TO ITALY
Director: Roberto Rossellini
Co-stars: George Sanders Paul Muller Natalia Ray

1956 ELENA AND THE MEN
Director: Jean Renoir
Co-stars: Mel Ferrer Jean Marais Jean Richard

1956 ANASTASIA
Director: Anatole Litvak
Co-stars: Yul Brynner Helen Hayes Martita Hunt

1958 INDISCREET
Director: Stanley Donen
Co-stars: Cary Grant Phyllis Calvet David Kossoff

1958 THE INN OF THE SIXTH HAPPINESS
Director: Mark Robson
Co-stars: Curt Jurgens Robert Donat Athene Seyler

1961 GOODBYE AGAIN
Director: Anatole Litvak
Co-stars: Anthony Perkins Yves Montand Jackie Lane

1964 THE VISIT
Director: Bernard Wicki
Co-stars: Anthony Quinn Paolo Stoppa Irina Demick

1964 THE YELLOW ROLLS ROYCE
Director: Anthony Asquith
Co-stars: Rex Harrison Edmund Purdom Omar Shariff

1969 A WALK IN THE SPRING RAIN
Director: Guy Green
Co-stars: Anthony Quinn Fritz Weaver

1969 CACTUS FLOWER
Director: Gene Saks
Co-stars: Walter Matthau Goldie Hawn Jack Weston

1973 THE HIDEAWAYS
Director: Fielder Cook
Co-stars: Sally Prager Johnny Duran Madeleine Kahn

1974 MURDER ON THE ORIENT EXPRESS
Director: Sidney Lumet
Co-stars: Albert Finney Lauren Bacall Sean Connery

1976 A MATTER OF TIME
Director: Vincente Minnelli
Co-stars: Lisa Minnelli Isabella Rossellini

1978 AUTUMN SONATA
Director: Ingmar Bergman
Co-stars: Liv Ullman Halvar Bjork

1981 A WOMAN CALLED GOLDA

MARY BERGMAN

1989 CHAMELEONS
Director: Glenn Larson
Co-star: Stewart Granger

ELIZABETH BERGNER *(Married Paul Czinner)*

1931 ARIANE
Director: Paul Czinner
Co-stars: Rudolph Forster Annemarie Steinsieck Hertha Guthmar

1934 CATHERINE THE GREAT
Director: Paul Czinner
Co-stars: Douglas Fairbanks Flora Robson Griffith Jones

1935 ESCAPE ME NEVER
Director: Paul Czinner
Co-stars: Hugh Sinclair Griffith Jones Penelope Dudley Ward

1936 DREAMING LIPS
Director: Paul Czinner
Co-stars: Romney Brent Raymond Massey Felix Aylmer

1936 AS YOU LIKE IT
Director: Paul Czinner
Co-stars: Laurence Olivier Richard Ainley Felix Aylmer

1939 A STOLEN LIFE
Director: Paul Czinner
Co-stars: Michael Redgrave Wilfrid Lawson Richard Ainley

1941 PARIS CALLING
Director: Edwin Marin
Co-stars: Basil Rathbone Randolph Scott Gale Sondergaard

1941 49TH PARALLEL
(Defected To Germany During Filming)
Director: Michael Powell
Co-stars: Laurence Olivier Eric Portman

1970 CRY OF THE BANSHEE
Director: Gordon Hessler
Co-stars: Vincent Price Patrick Mower Hugh Griffith

ULLA BERGRYD

1966 THE BIBLE...IN THE BEGINNING
Director: John Huston
Co-stars: John Huston Michael Parks George C. Scott

HELENA BERGSTROM

1989 THE WOMEN ON THE ROOF
Director: Carl-Gustav Nykvist
Co-stars: Amanda Ooms Percy Brandt

1993 HOUSE OF ANGELS
Director: Colin Nutley
Co-stars: Ricard Wolff Sven Wollter

SUSAN BERMAN

1982 SMITHEREENS
Director: Susan Seidelman
Co-stars: Brad Rinn Richard Hell

ELIZABETH BERKLEY

1993 WHITE WOLVES II: LEGEND OF THE WILD
Co-star: Jeremy London

1994 BANDIT GOES COUNTRY
Director: Hal Needham
Co-stars: Brian Bloom Brian Kause

1996 SHOWGIRLS
Director: Paul Verhoeven
Co-stars: Gina Gershon Kyle MacLachlan Gina Ravera

1996 THE FIRST WIVES' CLUB
Director: Hugh Wilson
Co-stars: Goldie Hawn Diane Keaton Bette Midler

1998 THE REAL BLONDE
Director: Tom DeCillo
Co-stars: Matthew Modine Kathleen Turner Buck Henry

JEANNIE BERLIN

1970 THE BABY MAKER
Director: James Bridges
Co-stars: Barbara Hershey Sam Groom Scott Glen

1972 THE HEARTBREAK KID
Director: Elaine May
Co-stars: Charles Grodin Cybill Shepherd Eddie Albert

1972 PORTNOY'S COMPLAINT
Director: Ernest Lehman
Co-stars: Richard Benjamin Karen Black Lee Grant

1990 IN THE SPIRIT
Director: Sandra Seacat
Co-stars: Marlo Thomas Elaine May Peter Falk

CRYSTAL BERNARD

1983 HIGH SCHOOL U.S.A.
Director: Rod Amateau
Co-stars: Michael J. Fox Nancy McKeon Crispin Glover

NICOLETTE BERNARD

1964 IT HAPPENED HERE
Director: Kevin Brownlow
Co-stars: Pauline Murray Sebastian Shaw

MELINA BERNECKER

1990 AN ANGEL AT MY TABLE
Director: Jane Campion
Co-stars: Kerry Fox Iris Churn Alexia Keogh

SANDRA BERNHARD

1982 KING OF COMEDY
Director: Martin Scorsese
Co-stars: Robert De Niro Jerry Lewis Ed Herlihy

1985 FOLLOW THAT BIRD
Director: Ken Kwapis
Co-stars: Carroll Spinney Jim Henson Frank Oz

1987 TRACK 29
Director: Nicolas Roeg
Co-stars: Theresa Russell

1990 WITHOUT YOU I'M NOTHING
Director: John Boskovich
Co-stars: John Doe Steve Antin Ken Foree

1991 HUDSON HAWK
Director: Michael Lehman
Co-stars: Bruce Willis Danny Aiello Andie MacDowell

1991 IN BED WITH MADONNA
Director: Alek Keshishan
Co-stars: Madonna Warren Beatty Kevin Costner

1992 INSIDE MONKEY ZETTERLAND
Director: Jeffrey Levy
Co-stars: Steven Antin Katherine Helmond Patricia Arquette

1994 DALLAS DOLL
Director: Ann Turner
Co-stars: Frank Gallacher Jake Blundell Victoria Longley

1996 UNZIPPED
Director: Douglas Keeve
Co-stars: Naomi Campbell Linda Evangelista Kate Moss

PETRA BERNDT

1993 SALT ON OUR SKIN
Director: Andrew Birkin
Co-stars: Greta Scacchi Vincent D'Onofrio

SARAH BERNHARDT

1912 QUEEN ELIZABETH
Director: Henri Desfontaines
Co-star: Lou Tellegen

OLINKA BEROVA

1968 THE VENGEANCE OF SHE
Director: Cliff Owen
Co-stars: John Richardson Edward Judd Jill Melford

SIMONE BERRIAU

1938 TENDRE ENNEMIE
Director: Max Ophuls
Co-stars: Jacqueline Daix Lucien Nat Georges Vitray

ELIZABETH BERRIDGE

1981 THE FUNHOUSE
Director: Tobe Hunter
Co-stars: Cooper Huckabee Sylvia Miles Kevin Conway

1984 AMADEUS
Director: Milos Forman
Co-stars: Tom Hulce F. Murray Abraham Simon Callow

1987 FIVE CORNERS
Director: Tony Bill
Co-stars: Jodie Foster Tim Robbins John Turturro

1989 HOME FIRES BURNING
Director: Glenn Jordan
Co-stars: Barnard Hughes Sada Thompson Bill Pullman

ELIZABETH BERRINGTON

1996 SECRETS AND LIES
Director: Mike Leigh
Co-stars: Timothy Spall Brenda Blethyn Phyllis Logan

CAROLINE BERRY

1992 FRIDAY ON MY MIND
Director: Marc Evans
Co-stars: Maggie O'Neill Christopher Eccleston

HALLE BERRY

1991 JUNGLE FEVER
Director: Spike Lee
Co-stars: Wesley Snipes Annabella Sciorra Anthony Quinn

1991 THE LAST BOY SCOUT
Director: Tony Scott
Co-stars: Bruce Willis Damon Wayans Chelsea Field

1993 FATHER HOOD
Director: Darrell James Roodt
Co-stars: Patrick Swayze Diane Ladd

1993 THE PROGRAM
Director: David Ward
Co-stars: James Caan Kristy Swanson Craig Sheffer

1994 THE FLINTSTONES
Director: Brian Levant
Co-stars: John Goodman Elizabeth Perkins Elizabeth Taylor

1995 STRICTLY BUSINESS
Co-stars: Joseph Phillips Tommy Davidson

1996 EXECUTIVE DECISION
Director: Stuart Baird
Co-stars: Kurt Russell Steven Seagal David Suchet

1997 B.A.P.S.
Director: Robert Townsend
Co-stars: Martin Landau Ian Richardson Natalie Desselle

MADY BERRY

1932 LA MATERNELLE
Director: Marie Epstein
Co-stars: Madeleine Renaud Paulette Elambert

1937 LE PURITAN
Director: Jeff Musso
Co-stars: Jean-Louis Barrault Pierre Fresnay Viviane Romance

1939 LE JOUR SE LEVE
Director: Marcel Carne
Co-stars: Jean Gabin Jules Berry Arletty

SARAH BERRY

1987 EVIL DEAD 2
Director: Sam Raimi
Co-stars: Bruce Campbell Dan Hicks Kassie Wesley

DOROTHEE BERRYMAN

1986 DECLINE OF THE AMERICAN EMPIRE
Director: Denys Arcand
Co-stars: Dominique Michel Louise Bortal

1989 A PAPER WEDDING
Director: Michel Brault
Co-stars: Genevieve Bujold Manuel Aranguiz

ADELE BERTEI

1983 BORN IN FLAMES
Director: Lizzie Borden
Co-stars: Jeanne Satterfield Kathryn Bigelow

MARINA BERTI

1949 PRINCE OF FOXES
Director: Henry King
Co-stars: Tyrone Power Orson Welles Wanda Hendrix

1950 DEPORTED
Director: Robert Siodmak
Co-stars: Jeff Chandler Marta Toren Claude Dauphin

1951 QUO VADIS
Director: Mervyn LeRoy
Co-stars: Robert Taylor Deborah Kerr Peter Ustinov

1962 MADAME
Director: Christian-Jacque
Co-stars: Sophia Loren Robert Hossein

1963 A FACE IN THE RAIN
Director: Irvin Kirshner
Co-stars: Rory Calhoun Niall MacGinnis

VALERIE BERTINELLI

1979 C.H.O.M.P.S.
Director: Don Chaffey
Co-stars: Wesley Eure Jim Backus Red Buttons

1986 ROCKABYE
Director: Richard Michaels
Co-stars: Rachel Ticotin Jason Alexander

1987 NUMBER ONE WITH A BULLET
Director: Jack Smight
Co-stars: Robert Carradine Billy Dee Williams

1989 TAKEN AWAY
Director: John Patterson
Co-stars: Kevin Dunn Juliet Sorcy

1992 SHADES OF GRAY
Director: Kevin James Dobson
Co-stars: George Dzundza Peter Dobson Micole Mercurio

1993 MURDER OF INNOCENCE
Director: Tom McLoughlin
Co-stars: Stephen Banks Megan Cavanagh

1995 THE HAUNTING OF HELEN WALKER
Director: Tom McLoughlin
Co-stars: Aled Roberts Florence Hoath

JANE BERTISH

1985 DANCE WITH A STRANGER
Director: Mike Newell
Co-stars: Miranda Richardson Rupert Everett

1986 SMART MONEY
Director: Bernard Rose
Co-stars: Bruce Payne Spencer Leigh Alexandra Pigg

1989 SEEING IN THE DARK
Director: Gareth Jones
Co-stars: David Threlfall Sylvestra Le Touzel

SUZANNE BERTISH

1987 HEARTS OF FIRE
Director: Richard Marquand
Co-stars: Fiona Flanagan Bob Dylan Rupert Everett

1989 A DAY IN SUMMER
Director: Bob Mahoney
Co-stars: Jack Shepherd Peter Egan John Sessions

1992 VENICE/VENICE
Director: Henry Jaglom
Co-stars: Henry Jaglomn Nelly Alard Melissa Leo

1993 WALL OF SILENCE
Director: Philip Saville
Co-stars: Bill Patterson Warren Mitchell John Bowe

JULIET BERTO

1967 WEEKEND
Director: Jean-Luc Godard
Co-stars: Mireille Darc Jean Yanne Jean-Pierre Leaud

1974 CELINE AND JULIE GO BOATING
Director: Jacques Rivette
Co-stars: Dominique Labourier Marie-France Pisier

1976 MR. KLEIN
Director: Joseph Losey
Co-stars: Alain Delon Jeanne Moreau Suzanne Flon

BIBI BESCH

1977 THE PACK
Director: Robert Clouse
Co-stars: Joe Don Baker R. G. Armstrong

**1977 PETER LUNDY AND THE
         MEDICINE HAT STALLION**
Director: Michael O'Herlihy
Co-stars: Leif Garrett Mitch Ryan

1979 THE PROMISE
Director: Gilbert Cates
Co-stars: Kathleen Quinlan Stephen Collins

1982 THE BEAST WITHIN
Director: Philippe Mora
Co-stars: Ronny Cox Paul Clemens Don Gordon

1983 THE LONELY LADY
Director: Peter Sasdy
Co-stars: Pia Zadora Lloyd Bochner Ray Liotta

1986 MRS. DELAFIELD WANTS TO MARRY
Director: George Shaefer
Co-stars: Katherine Hepburn Harold Gould

1987 WHO'S THAT GIRL
Director: James Foley
Co-stars: Madonna Griffin Dunne John Mills

1989 STEEL MAGNOLIAS
Director: Herbert Ross
Co-stars: Sally Field Julia Roberts Shirley MacLaine

1989 KILL ME AGAIN
Director: John Dahl
Co-stars: Val Kilmer Joanne Whalley Michael Madsen

1990 TREMORS
Director: Ron Underwood
Co-stars: Kevin Bacon Fred Ward Finn Carter

1995 ABANDONED AND DECEIVED
Director: Joseph Dougherty
Co-stars: Lori Loughlin Brian Kerwin Rosemary Forsythe

ANNE-MARIE BESSE

1986 MAX, MON AMOUR
Director: Nagisa Oshima
Co-stars: Charlotte Rampling Anthony Higgins

EUGENIE BESSERER

1923 ANNA CHRISTIE
Director: John Wray
Co-stars: Blanche Sweet William Russell

1927 THE JAZZ SINGER
Director: Alan Crosland
Co-stars: Al Jolson May McAvoy Myrna Loy

1928 LILAC TIME
Director: George Fitzmaurice
Co-stars: Colleen Moore Gary Cooper

1929 THUNDERBOLT
Director: Josef Von Sternberg
Co-stars: George Bancroft Fay Wray Richard Arlen

ALYSON BEST

1980 HARLEQUIN
Director: Simmon Wincer
Co-stars: Robert Powell David Hemmings Carmen Duncan

1984 MAN OF FLOWERS
Director: Paul Cox
Co-stars: Norman Kaye Chris Haywood

EDNA BEST *(Married Herbert Marshall)*

1930 ESCAPE
Director: Basil Dean
Co-stars: Gordon Harker Gerald Du Maurier Madeleine Carroll

1931 MICHAEL AND MARY
Director: Vlctor Saville
Co-stars: Herbert Marshall Elizabeth Allan Frank Lawton

1931 THE CALENDAR
Co-star: Herbert Marshall

1933 THE MAN WHO KNEW TOO MUCH
Director: Alfred Hitchcock
Co-stars: Leslie Banks Peter Lorre Nova Pilbeam

1934 THE KEY
Director: Michael Curtiz
Co-stars: William Powell Colin Clive Hobart Cavanagh

1937 SOUTH RIDING
Director: Victor Saville
Co-stars: Ralph Richardson Edmund Gwenn Ann Todd

1938 PRISON WITHOUT BARS
Director: Brian Desmond Hurst
Co-stars: Barry K. Barnes Corinne Luchaire

1939 INTERMEZZO
Director: Gregory Ratoff
Co-stars: Leslie Howard Ingrid Bergman John Halliday

1940 THE SWISS FAMILY ROBINSON
Director: Edward Ludwig
Co-stars: Thomas Mitchell Freddie Bartholomew

1940 A DISPATCH FROM REUTERS
Director: William Dieterle
Co-stars: Edward G. Robinson Eddie Albert

1947 THE GHOST AND MRS MUIR
Director: Joseph Mankiewicz
Co-stars: Rex Harrison Gene Tierney Natalie Wood

1947 THE LATE GEORGE APLEY
Director: Joseph Mankiewicz
Co-stars: Ronald Colman Vanessa Brown Richard Haydn

1948 THE IRON CURTAIN
Director: William Wellman
Co-stars: Dana Andrews Gene Tierney Barry Kroeger

DEANNIE BEST

1945 THE SHANGHAI CHEST
Director: William Beaudine
Co-stars: Roland Winters Manton Moreland

MICHELLE BESTBIER

1989 AGENT ORANGE
Director: Robert Davies
Co-star: Phillip Brown

MARTINE BESWICK

1963 FROM RUSSIA WITH LOVE
Director: Terence Young
Co-stars: Sean Connery Robert Shaw Lotte Lenya

1966 ONE MILLION YEARS B.C.
Director: Don Chaffey
Co-stars: John Richardson Raquel Welch

1966 SLAVE GIRLS
Director: Michael Carreras
Co-stars: Michael Latimer Edina Ronay Carol White

1967 BULLET EOR THE GENERAL
Director: Damiano Damiani
Co-stars: Gian-Maria Volonte Klaus Kinski

1967 THE PENTHOUSE
Director: Peter Collinson
Co-stars: Suzy Kendall Terence Morgan Norman Rodway

1971 DOCTOR JEKYLL AND SISTER HYDE
Director: Roy Ward Baker
Co-stars: Ralph Bates Dorothy Alison

1980 THE HAPPY HOOKER GOES TO HOLLYWOOD
Director: Alan Roberts
Co-stars: Chris Lemmon Phil Silvers

1990 MIAMI BLUES
Director: George Armitage
Co-stars: Alec Baldwin Fred Ward Jennifer Jason Leigh

1991 TRANCERS 2: THE RETURN OF JACK DETH
Director: Charles Band
Co-stars: Tim Thomerson Helen Hunt

1992 WIDE SARGASSO SEA
Director: John Duigan
Co-stars: Karina Lombard Rachel Ward Michael York

ZINA BETHUNE

1968 WHO'S THAT KNOCKING AT MY DOOR?
Director: Martin Scorsese
Co-stars: Harvey Keitel Ann Collette

LAURA BETTI

1968 THEOREM
Director: Pier Paolo Pasolini
Co-stars: Terence Stamp Silvana Mangano

1971 THE CANTERBURY TALES
Director: Pier Paolo Pasolini
Co-stars: Pier Paolo Pasolini Hugh Griffith Tom Baker

1971 LAST HOUSE ON THE LEFT PART 2
Director: Mario Bava
Co-stars: Claudine Auger Isa Miranda

1976 1900
Director: Bernardo Bertolucci
Co-stars: Burt Lancaster Robert De Niro Gerard Depardieu

1981 LOIN DE MANHATTAN
Director: Jean-Claude Biette
Co-stars: Jean-Christophe Bouvet Howard Vernon

1989 COURAGE MOUNTAIN
Director: Christopher Leitch
Co-stars: Juliette Caton Charlie Sheen Leslie Caron

ANGELA BETTIS

1995 SPARROW
Director: Franco Zefferelli
Co-stars: Vanessa Redgrave Jonathan Schaech

VALERIE BETTIS

1952 AFFAIR IN TRINIDAD
Director: Vincent Sherman
Co-stars: Rita Hayworth Glenn Ford Torin Thatcher

FRANCA BETTOJA

1964 SANDOKAN AGAINST THE LEOPARD OF SARAWAK
Director: Luigi Capuano
Co-stars: Ray Danton Guy Madison

1965 SANDOKAN FIGHTS BACK
Director: Luigi Capuano
Co-stars: Ray Danton Guy Madison

ALFREDA BEVAN

1932 ON OUR SELECTION
Director: Ken Hall
Co-stars: Bert Bailey Fred McDonald

GILLIAN BEVAN

1988 COPPERS
Director: Ted Gilsby
Co-stars: Tim Roth Reece Dinsdale Sandra Voe

1992 GHOSTWATCH
Director: Lesley Manning
Co-stars: Michael Parkinson Sarah Greene Mike Smith

ISLA BEVAN

1932 THE SIGN OF FOUR
Director: Rowland Lee
Co-stars: Arthur Wontner Ian Hunter Miles Malleson

LESLIE BEVIS

1988 ALIEN NATION
Director: Graham Baker
Co-stars: James Caan Mandy Patinkin Terence Stamp

1993 THE NOVEMBER MEN
Director: Paul Williams
Co-stars: Paul Williams James Andronica Beau Starr

AMBER BEZER

1988 APPOINTMENT WITH DEATH
Director: Michael Winner
Co-stars: Peter Ustinov Lauren Bacall Hayley Mills

HOMI BHABA

1989 TWILIGHT CITY
Director: Reece Auguiste
Co-stars: Andy Coupland Gail Lewis

MAYIM BIALIK (Child)

1988 BEACHES
Director: Garry Marshall
Co-stars: Bette Midler Barbara Hershey John Heard

RACHEL BIANCA

1992 GOLDEN BALLS
Director: Bigas Luna
Co-stars: Javier Bardem Elisa Touati Maribel Verdu

DANIELA BIANCHI

1963 FROM RUSSIA WITH LOVE
Director: Terence Young
Co-stars: Sean Connery Robert Shaw Lotte Lenya

1967 OPERATION KID BROTHER
Director: Alberto De Martino
Co-stars: Neil Connery Adolfo Celi Lois Maxwell

NITA BIEBER

1950 A LADY WITHOUT PASSPORT
Director: Joseph Lewis
Co-stars: Hedy Lamarr John Hodiak James Craig

JESSICA BIELIN

1998 ULEE'S GOLD
Director: Victor Nunez
Co-stars: Peter Fonda Tom Wood Vanessa Zima

MRS. E. BIENVENU

1948 LOUISIANA STORY
Director: Robert Flaherty
Co-stars: Joseph Boudreaux Frank Hardy

KATHRYN BIGELOW

1983   BORN IN FLAMES
Director: Lizzie Borden
Co-stars: Adele Bertei Flo Kennedy Honey

JULIE BIGGS

1964   NOBODY WAVED GOODBYE
Director: Don Owen
Co-stars: Peter Kastner Claude Rae Charmion King

1984   UNFINISHED BUSINESS
Director: Don Owen
Co-stars: Isabelle Mejias Peter Kastner Peter Spence

ROXANN BIGGS

1988   BROKEN ANGEL
Director: Richard Heffron
Co-stars: William Shatner Susan Blakely Millie Perkins

1992   MORTAL SINS
Director: Bradford May
Co-stars: Christopher Reeve Francis Guinan

1994   POINTMAN
Director: Robert Ellis Miller
Co-stars: Jack Scalia Bruce A. Young

LYDIA BILBROOK

1942   MEXICAN SPITFIRE'S ELEPHANT
Director: Leslie Goodwins
Co-stars: Lupe Velez Leon Errol Lyle Talbot

ROSIE BILL

1991   BROKE
Director: Alan Dosser
Co-stars: Timothy Spall Sheila Kelly Larry Lamb

IRENE BILLER

1933   THE MAN WHO DARED
Director: Hamilton McFadden
Co-stars: Preston Foster Zita Johann Joan Marsh

BARBARA BILLINGSLEY

1948   I CHEATED THE LAW
Director: Edward Cahn
Co-stars: Tom Conway Steve Brodie

1987   BAY COVEN
Director: Carl Schenkel
Co-stars: Pamela Sue Martin Tim Matheson Susan Ruttan

JENNIFER BILLINGSLEY

1964   LADY IN A CAGE
Director: Walter Grauman
Co-stars: Olivia De Havilland James Caan Ann Sothern

1971   C .C . AND COMPANY
Director: Seymour Robbie
Co-stars: Joe Namath Ann-Margret William Smith

1972   WELCOME HOME, SOLDIER BOYS
Director: Richard Crompton
Co-stars: Joe Don Baker Billy Green Bush

1973   WHITE LIGHTNING
Director: Joseph Sargent
Co-stars: Burt Reynolds Ned Beatty Diane Ladd

KATE BINCHY

1991   EVENTS AT DRIMAGHLEEN
Director: Robert Cooper
Co-stars: T. P. McKenna Sophie Ward

SYBILLA BINDER

1942   THUNDER ROCK
Director: Roy Boulting
Co-stars: Michael Redgrave Lilli Palmer Barbara Mullen

1942   NIGHT INVADER
Director: Herbert Mason
Co-stars: Anne Crawford David Farrar Marius Goring

1948   BLANCHE FURY
Director: Marc Allegret
Co-stars: Valerie Hobson Stewart Granger Michael Gough

CLARA BINDI

1960   THE MASK OF SATAN
Director: Mario Bava
Co-stars: Barbara Steele John Richardson

CLAIRE BINNEY

1976   DON'S PARTY
Director: Bruce Beresford
Co-stars: Ray Barrett John Hargreaves Graeme Blundell

1983   HOSTAGE
Director: Frank Shields
Co-stars: Ralph Schicha Judy Nunn

JULIETTE BINOCHE

1986   MAUVAIS SONG
Director: Leos Carax
Co-stars: Michel Piccoli Denis Lavant Julie Delpy

1988   THE UNBEARABLE LIGHTNESS OF BEING
Director: Philip Kaufman
Co-stars: Daniel Day-Lewis Lena Olin

1991   WOMEN AND MEN:
IN LOVE THERE ARE NO RULES
Director: Mike Figgis
Co-stars: Scott Glen Andie McDowell

1991   LES AMANTS DU PONT NEUF
Director: Leos Carax
Co-stars: Denis Lavant Klaus-Michael Gruber Daniel Buain

1992   DAMAGE
Director: Louis Malle
Co-stars: Jeremy Irons Rupert Graves Leslie Caron

1993   THREE COLOURS: BLUE
Director: Krzysztof Kieslowski
Co-stars: Benoit Regent Florence Pernel Helene Vincent

1993   WUTHERING HEIGHTS
Director: Peter Kosminsky
Co-stars: Ralph Fiennes Janet McTeer Sophie Ward

1993   THREE COLOURS: WHITE
Director: Krzysztof Kieslowski
Co-stars: Julie Delpy Florence Pernel Jerry Stuhr

1994   THREE COLOURS: RED
Director: Krzysztof Kieslowski
Co-stars: Julie Delpy Irene Jacob

1996   THE HORSEMAN ON THE ROOF
Director: Jean-Paul Rappeneau
Co-stars: Gerard Depardieu Oliver Martinez

THORA BIRCH *(Child)*

1991   PARADISE
Director: Mary Agnes Donoghue
Co-stars: Elijah Wood Melanie Griffith Don Johnson

1991   ALL I WANT FOR CHRISTMAS
Director: Robert Lieberman
Co-stars: Leslie Nielsen Lauren Bacall Harley Jane Kozak

1992 PATRIOT GAMES
Director: Philip Noyce
Co-stars: Harrison Ford Anne Archer Sean Bean

1994 MONKEY TROUBLE
Director: Franco Amurri
Co-stars: Harvey Keitel Mimi Rogers

1996 NOW AND THEN
Co-stars: Demi Moore Melanie Griffith Christina Ricci

1996 ALASKA
Co-stars: Charlton Heston Dirk Benedict Vincent Karthelser

EMMA BIRD

1990 NEEDLE
Director: Gilles MacKinnon
Co-stars: Sean McKee Pete Postlethwaite

LAURIE BIRD

1971 TWO-LANE BACKDROP
Director: Monte Hellman
Co-stars: Warren Oates James Taylor Dennis Wilson

1974 THE COCKFIGHTER
Director: Monte Hellman
Co-stars: Warren Oates Harry Dean Stanton Ed Begley Jnr.

MINAH BIRD

1975 ALFIE DARLING
Director: Ken Hughes
Co-stars: Alan Price Joan Collins Annie Ross

TALA BIRELL *(Natalie Bierl)*

1932 THE DOOMED BATTALION
Director: Cyril Gardner
Co-stars: Luis Trenker Victor Varconi Albert Conti

1933 NAGANA
Director: Ernst Frank
Co-stars: Melvyn Douglas Onslow Stevens

1935 SPRING TONIC
Director: S. Sylvan Simon
Co-stars: Lew Ayres Claire Trevor Zasu Pitts

1935 THE LONE WOLF RETURNS
Director: Roy William Neill
Co-stars: Melvyn Douglas Gail Patrick

1935 LET'S LIVE TONIGHT
Director: Victor Schertzinger
Co-stars: Lilian Harvey Tullio Carminati

1935 CRIME AND PUNISHMENT
Director: Josef Von Sternberg
Co-stars: Peter Lorre Edward Arnold

1935 AIR HAWKS
Director: Albert Rogell
Co-stars: Ralph Bellamy Wiley Post Douglass Dumbrille

1937 SHE'S DANGEROUS
Co-star: Cesar Romero

1942 SEVEN MILES FROM ALCATRAZ
Director: Edward Dmytryk
Co-stars: James Craig Frank Jenks

1943 ONE DANGEROUS NIGHT
Director: Michael Gordon
Co-stars: Warren William Marguerite Chapman

1943 WOMEN IN BONDAGE
Director: Steve Sekely
Co-stars: Gail Patrick Nancy Kelly Anne Nagel

1944 THE PURPLE HEART
Director: Lewis Milestone
Co-stars: Dana Andrews Sam Levine Richard Conte

1944 THE MONSTER MAKER
Director: Sam Newfield
Co-stars: Ralph Morgan J. Carrol Naish Wanda McKay

1945 THE FROZEN GHOST
Director: Harold Young
Co-stars: Lon Chaney Evelyn Ankers Martin Koslek

1946 DANGEROUS MILLIONS
Director: James Tinling
Co-stars: Kent Taylor Dona Drake Leonard Strong

KIM BIRFIELD

1974 THE FLYING SORCERER
Director: Harry Booth
Co-stars: John Bluthal Tim Barrett

JANE BIRKIN

1966 BLOWUP
Director: Michelangelo Antonioni
Co-stars: David Hemmings Vanessa Redgrave Sylvia Miles

1969 THE SWIMMING POOL
Director: Jacques DeRay
Co-stars: Alain Delon Romy Schneider Maurice Ronet

1978 DEATH ON THE NILE
Director: John Guillermin
Co-stars: Peter Ustinov Bette Davis Mia Farrow

1982 EVIL UNDER THE SUN
Director: Guy Hamilton
Co-stars: Peter Ustinov James Mason Diana Rigg

1984 LEAVE ALL FAIR
Director: John Reid
Co-stars: John Gielgud Simon Ward Feodore Atkine

1984 L'AMOUR PAR TERRE
Director: Cecilia Jacques Rivette
Co-stars: Geraldine Chaplin Jean-Pierre Kalfon

1985 DUST
Director: Marion Hansel
Co-stars: Trevor Howard John Matshikiza

1990 THESE FOOLISH THINGS
Director: Bertrand Tavernier
Co-stars: Dirk Bogarde Emmanuelle Bataille

1991 RED FOX
Director: Ian Toynton
Co-stars: Brian Cox John Hurt Didier Flamond

1991 LA BELLE NOISEUSE
Director: Jacques Rivette
Co-stars: Michel Piccoli Emanuelle Beart

1991 LA BELLE NOISEUSE - DIVERTIMENTO
Director: Jagques Rivette
Co-stars: Michel Piccoli David Bursztei

SHELLEY BIRMINGHAM

1966 SLAVE GIRLS
Director: Michael Carreras
Co-stars: Martine Beswick Michael Latimer Carol White

CELIA BIRTWELL

1974 A BIGGER SPLASH
Director: Jack Hazan
Co-stars: David Hockney Peter Schlesinger

DEBBY BISHOP

1986 SID AND NANCY
Director: Alex Cox
Co-stars: Gary Oldman Chloe Webb David Hayman

JULIE BISHOP

1934   **THE BLACK CAT**
Director: Edgar Ulmer
Co-stars: Boris Karloff Bela Lugosi David Manners

1941   **INTERNATIONAL SQUADRON**
Director: Lothar Mendes
Co-stars: Ronald Reagan James Stephenson

1941   **THE NURSE'S SECRET**
Director: Noel Smith
Co-stars: Lee Patrick Regis Toomey Charles Trowbridge

1942   **THE HIDDEN HAND**
Director: Ben Stoloff
Co-stars: Craig Stevens Elizabeth Fraser Willie Best

1942   **BUSSES ROAR**
Director: Ross Lederman
Co-stars: Richard Travis Eleanor Parker Charles Drake

1943   **ACTION IN THE NORTH ATLANTIC**
Director: Lloyd Bacon
Director: Humphrey Bogart Raymond Massey

1943   **NORTHERN PURSUIT**
Director: Raoul Walsh
Co-stars: Errol Flynn Helmut Dantine John Ridgeley

1945   **RHAPSODY IN BLUE**
Director: Irving Rapper
Co-stars: Robert Alda Joan Leslie Alexis Smith

1945   **YOU CAME ALONG**
Director: John Farrow
Co-stars: Lizabeth Scott Robert Cummings Don DeFore

1946   **IDEA GIRL**
Co-stars: Jess Barker Dewey Robinson

1946   **CINDERELLA JONES**
Director: Busby Berkeley
Co-stars: Joan Leslie Robert Alda William Prince

1946   **MURDER IN THE MUSIC HALL**
Director: John English
Co-stars: Vera Ralston Helen Walker Nancy Kelly

1947   **THE LAST OF THE REDMEN**
Director: George Sherman
Co-stars: Jon Hall Michael O'Shea

1949   **SANDS OF IWO JIMA**
Director: Allan Dwan
Co-stars: John Wayne Forrest Tucker Adele Mara

1951   **WESTWARD THE WOMEN**
Director: William Wellman
Co-stars: Robert Taylor Denise Darcell Hope Emerson

1953   **SABRE JET**
Director: Louis King
Co-stars: Robert Stack Coleen Gray Richard Arlen

1957   **THB BIG LAND**
Director: Gordon Douglas
Co-stars: Alan Ladd Virginia Mayo Edmond O'Brien

KELLY BISHOP

1978   **AN UNMARRIED WOMAN**
Director: Paul Mazursky
Co-stars: Jill Clayburgh Alan Bates Michael Murphy

1987   **DIRTY DANCING**
Director: Emile Ardolino
Co-stars: Patrick Swayze Jennifer Grey Cynthia Rhodes

JACQUELINE BISSETT

1966   **CUL-DE-SAC**
Director: Roman Polanski
Co-stars: Donald Pleasence Lionel Stander Francoise Dorleac

1967   **CASINO ROYALE**
Director: John Huston
Co-stars: David Niven Peter Sellers Deborah Kerr

1967   **CAPETOWN AFFAIR**
Director: Robert Webb
Co-stars: James Brolin Claire Trevor Jon Whiteley

1968   **THE DETECTIVE**
Director: Gordon Douglas
Co-stars: Frank Sinatra Lee Remick Ralph Meeker

1968   **BULLITT**
Director: Peter Yates
Co-stars: Steve McQueen Robert Vaughn Robert Duvall

1968   **THE FIRST TIME**
Director: James Nielson
Co-stars: Wes Stern Rick Kelman Wink Roberts

1968   **THE SWEET RIDE**
Director: Harvey Hart
Co-stars: Tony Franciosa Michael Sarazin Bob Denver

1969   **THE GRASSHOPPER**
Director: Jerry Paris
Co-stars: Jim Brown Joseph Cotten

1970   **AIRPORT**
Director: George Seaton
Co-stars: Burt Lancaster Dean Martin George Kennedy

1971   **BELIEVE IN ME**
Director: Stuart Hagmann
Co-stars: Michael Sarazin Jon Cypher Allen Garfield

1971   **THE MEPHISTO WALTZ**
Director: Paul Wendkos
Co-stars: Alan Alda Curt Jurgens Barbara Parkins

1971   **STAND UP AND BE COUNTED**
Director: Jackie Cooper
Co-stars: Stella Stevens Loretta Swit

1972   **THE LIFE AND TIMES OF JUDGE ROY BEAN**
Director: John Huston
Co-stars: Paul Newman Victoria Principal Ava Gardner

1973   **THE THIEF WHO CAME TO DINNER**
Director: Bud Yorkin
Co-stars: Ryan O'Neal Warren Oates Jill Clayburgh

1973   **DAY FOR NIGHT**
Director: Francois Truffaut
Co-stars: Francois Truffaut Valentina Cortese Jean-Pier Aumont

1974   **MURDER ON THE ORIENT EXPRESS**
Director: Sidney Lumet
Co-stars: Albert Finney Ingrid Bergman Lauren Bacall

1975   **THE SPIRAL STAIRCASE**
Director: Peter Collinson
Co-stars: Christopher Plummer Sam Wanamaker

1976   **ST. IVES**
Director: J. Lee-Thompson
Co-stars: Charles Bronson Harry Guardino

1976   **END OF THE GAME**
Director: Maximilian Schell
Co-stars: Jon Voight Robert Shaw Martin Ritt

1977   **THE DEEP**
Director: Peter Yates
Co-stars: Nick Nolte Robert Shaw Lou Gossett

1978   **THE GREEK TYCOON**
Director: J. Lee-Thompson
Co-stars: Anthony Quinn Raf Vallone James Franciscus

1978 **WHO IS KILLING THE GREAT**
CHEFS OF EUROPE?
Director: Ted Kotcheff
Co-stars: George Segal Robert Morley

1980 **WHEN TIME RAN OUT**
Director: James Goldstone
Co-stars: Paul Newman William Holden Ernest Borgnine

1981 **RICH AND FAMOUS**
Director: George Cukor
Co-stars: Candice Bergen David Selby Meg Ryan

1981 **INCHON**
Director: Terence Young
Co-stars: Laurence Olivier David Janssen Ben Gazzara

1983 **CLASS**
Director: Louis John Carlino
Co-stars: Rob Lowe Andrew McCarthy Cliff Robertson

1984 **UNDER THE VOLCANO**
Director: John Huston
Co-stars: Albert Finney Anthony Andrews Katy Jurado

1985 **ANNA KARENINA**
Director: Simon Langton
Co-stars: Christopher Reeve Paul Scolfield Judi Bowker

1986 **CHOICES**
Director: David Lowell Rich
Co-stars: George C. Scott Melissa Gilbert

1987 **HIGH SEASON**
Director: Clare Peplow
Co-stars: James Fox Irene Papas Kenneth Branagh

1989 **SCENES FROM THE CLASS**
STRUGGLE IN BEVERLY HILLS
Director: Paul Bartel
Co-stars: Ed Begley Ray Sharkey Mary Woronov

1989 **WILD ORCHID**
Director: Zalman King
Co-stars: Mickey Rourke Carre Otls Assumpta Serna

1993 **CRIMEBROKER**
Director: Ian Barry
Co-star: Masaya Kato

1994 **LEAVE OF ABSENCE**
Director: Tom McLoughlin
Co-stars: Brian Dennehy Blythe Danner

1996 **LA CEREMONIE**
Director: Claude Charrol
Co-stars: Sandrine Bonnaire Isabelle Huppert Jean-Pierre Cassel

1996 **THE HONEST COURTESAN**
Director: Marshall Herskovitz
Co-stars: Rufus Sewell Catherine McCormack

DENISE BIXLER

1987 **EVIL DEAD 2**
Director: Sam Raimi
Co-stars: Bruce Campbell Sarah Berry Kassie Wesley

ANITA BJORK

1950 **MISS JULIE**
Director: Alf Sjoberg
Co-stars: Ulf Palme Marta Dorff Max Von Sydow

1952 **WAITING WOMEN**
Director: Ingmar Bergman
Co-star: Eva Dahlbeck

1954 **NIGHT PEOPLE**
Director: Nunnally Johnson
Co-stars: Gregory Peck Broderick Crawford Rita Gam

1964 **LOVING COUPLES**
Director: Mai Zetterling
Co-stars: Harriet Andersson Gunnel Lindblom Eva Dahlbeck

1969 **ADALEN 31**
Director: Bo Widerberg
Co-stars: Peter Schildt Kerstin Tidelius

TATJANA BLACHER

1984 **FLIGHT TO BERLIN**
Director: Christopher Petit
Co-stars: Tusse Silberg Eddie Constantine

CILLA BLACK

1968 **WORK IS A FOUR-LETTER WORD**
Director: Peter Hall
Co-stars: David Warner Elizabeth Spriggs

ISOBEL BLACK

1963 **KISS OF THE VAMPIRE**
Director: Don Sharp
Co-stars: Noel Willman Clifford Evans Jennifer Daniel

1967 **THE MAGNIFICENT TWO**
Director: Cliff Owen
Co-stars: Eric Morecambe Ernie Wise Margit Saad

1971 **TWINS OF EVIL**
Director: John Hough
Co-stars: Madeleine Collinson Mary Collinson Peter Cushing

1971 **TEN RILLINGTON PLACE**
Director: Richard Fleischer
Co-stars: Richard Attenborough John Hurt Judy Geeson

KAREN BLACK *(Mother Of Hunter Carson)*
Nominated For Best Supporting Actress In 1970 For "Five Easy Pieces"

1967 **YOU'RE A BIG BOY NOW**
Director: Francis Ford Coppola
Co-stars: Peter Kastner Elizabeth Hartman Geraldine Page

1969 **HARD CONTRACT**
Director: Lee Pogostin
Co-stars: James Coburn Lilli Palmer Lee Remick

1970 **A GUNFIGHT**
Director: Lamont Johnson
Co-stars: Kirk Douglas Johnny Cash Jane Alexander

1970 **FIVE EASY PIECES**
Director: Bob Rafelson
Co-stars: Jack Nicholson Susan Anspach Fannie Flagg

1970 **DRIVE HE SAID**
Director: Jack Nicholson
Co-stars: Bruce Dern William Tepper Michael Margotta

1971 **CISCO PIKE**
Director: Bill Norton
Co-stars: Kris Kristofferson Gene Hackman Harry Dean Stanton

1971 **BORN TO WIN**
Director: Ivan Passer
Co-stars: George Segal Paula Prentiss Robert De Niro

1972 **PORTNOY'S COMPLAINT**
Director: Ernest Lehman
Co-stars: Richard Benjamin Lee Grant Jill Clayburgh

1974 **THE OUTFIT**
Director: John Flynn
Co-stars: Robert Duvall Robert Ryan Joe Don Baker

1974 **LAW AND DISORDER**
Director: Ivan Passer
Co-stars: Carroll O'Connor Ernest Borgnine Anita Dangler

1974	**THE GREAT GATSBY**		1988	**CONFESSIONS OF A LADY COP**

1974 THE GREAT GATSBY
Director: Jack Clayton
Co-stars: Robert Redford Mia Farrow Lois Chiles

1974 AIRPORT 75
Director: Jack Smight
Co-stars: Charlton Heston Gloria Swanson Susan Clark

1975 DAY OF THE LOCUST
Director: John Schlesinger
Co-stars: Donald Sutherland William Atherton

1975 ACE UP MY SLEEVE
Director: Ivan Passel
Co-stars: Omar Sharif Joseph Bottoms

1975 NASHVILLE
Director: Robert Altman
Co-stars: Keith Carradine Shelley Duvall Ned Beatty

1976 FAMILY PLOT
Director: Alfred Hitchcock
Co-stars: Bruce Dern Barbara Harris William Devane

1976 BURNT OFFERINGS
Director: Dan Curtis
Co-stars: Oliver Reed Bette Davis Burgess Meredith

1978 BECAUSE HE'S MY FRIEND
Director: Ralph Nelson
Co-stars: Keir Dullea Jack Thompson Tom Oliver

1978 CAPRICORN ONE
Director: Peter Hyams
Co-stars: Elliott Gould James Brolin Brenda Vaccaro

1978 IN PRAISE OF OLDER WOMEN
Director: George Kaczender
Co-stars: Tom Berenger Susan Strasberg

1979 KILLER FISH
Director: Antonio Margariti
Co-stars: Lee Majors Margaux Hemingway

1979 THE LAST WORD
Director: Roy Boulting
Co-stars: Richard Harris Martin Landau Dennis Christopher

1981 THE GRASS IS SINGING
Director: Michael Raeburn
Co-stars: John Thaw John Kani John Moulder

1982 COME BACK TO THE FIVE AND DIME, JIMMY DEAN, JIMMY DEAN
Director: Robert Altman
Co-stars: Cher Sandy Dennis Kathy Bates

1983 CAN SHE BAKE A CHERRY PIE?
Director: Henry Jaglom
Co-stars: Michael Emil Michael Margotta

1985 MARTIN'S DAY
Director: Alan Gibson
Co-stars: Richard Harris Lindsay Wagner Justin Henry

1986 INVADERS FROM MARS
Director: Tobe Hunter
Co-stars: Timothy Bottoms Louise Fletcher Hunter Carson

1987 IT'S ALIVE III: ISLAND OF THE ALIVE
Director: Larry Cohen
Co-stars: Michael Moriarty James Dixon

1988 THE INVISIBLE KID
Director: Avery Crounse
Co-stars: Jay Underwood Wally Ward Chynna Phillips

1988 OUT OF THE DARK
Director: Michael Schroeder
Co-stars: Cameron Dye Bud Cort Tab Hunter

1988 CONFESSIONS OF A LADY COP
Director: Lee Katzin
Co-stars: Don Murray Frank Sinatra Jnr. James Whitmore

1989 HOMER AND EDDIE
Director: Andrei Konchalovsky
Co-stars: Whoopi Goldberg James Belushi Beah Richards

1990 ZAPPED AGAIN
Director: Douglas Campbell
Co-stars: Todd Eric Andrews Kelli Williams Linda Blair

1990 THE CHILDREN
Director: Tony Palmer
Co-stars: Ben Kingsley Kim Novak Britt Ekland

1992 BOUND AND GAGGED
Director: Daniel Appelby
Co-stars: Chris Denton Elizabeth Saltorelli Ginger Lynn Allen

1997 INVISIBE DAD
Director: Fred Olen Ray
Co-star: Russ Tammblyn

CLARICE BLACKBURN

1968 PRETTY POISON
Director: Noel Black
Co-stars: Anthony Perkins Tuesday Weld Beverly Garland

HONOR BLACKMAN

1947 A BOY, A GIRL AND A BIKE
Director: Ralph Smart
Co-stars: John McCallum Diana Dors Anthony Newley

1948 QUARTET
Director: Harold French
Co-stars: Dirk Bogarde Francoise Rosay Irene Browne

1948 DAUGHTER OF DARKNESS
Director: Max Catto
Co-stars: Siobhan McKenna Anne Crawford Maxwell Reed

1949 CONSPIRATOR
Director: Victor Saville
Co-stars: Robert Taylor Elizabeth Taylor Robert Flemyng

1949 DIAMOND CITY
Director: David MacDonald
Co-stars: David Farrar Diana Dors Niall MacGinnis

1950 SO LONG AT THE FAIR
Director: Terence Fisher
Co-stars: Jean Simmonds Dirk Bogarde David Tomlinson

1951 GREEN GROW THE RUSHES
Director: Derek Twist
Co-stars: Roger Livesey Richard Burton Colin Gordon

1954 THE DELAVINE AFFAIR
Director: Douglas Pierce
Co-stars: Peter Reynolds Gordon Jackson Michael Balfour

1954 THE RAINBOW JACKET
Director: Basil Dearden
Co-stars: Bill Owen Kay Walsh Edward Underdown

1955 THE GLASS CAGE
Director: Montgomery Tully
Co-stars: John Ireland Geoffrey Keen Sid James

1957 ACCOUNT RENDERED
Director: Peter Graham Scott
Co-stars: Griffith Jones Ursula Howells Ewen Solon

1957 YOU PAY YOUR MONEY
Director: MacLean Rogers
Co-stars: Hugh McDermott Jane Hylton Ferdy Mayne

1957 SUSPENDED ALIBI
Director: Alfred Shaughnessy
Co-stars: Patrick Holt Valentine Dyall Andrew Keir

1958 **THE SQUARE PEG**
Director: John Paddy Carstairs
Co-stars: Norman Wisdom Edward Chapman Brian Worth

1958 **A NIGHT TO REMEMBER**
Director: Roy Ward Baker
Co-stars: Kenneth More Ronald Allen Michael Goodliffe

1961 **A MATTER OF W.H.O.**
Director: Don Chaffey
Co-stars: Terry-Thomas Sonja Zieman Alex Nicol

1963 **JASON AND THE ARGONAUTS**
Director: Don Chaffey
Co-stars: Todd Armstrong Niall MacGinnis Andrew Faulds

1964 **GOLDFINGER**
Director: Guy Hamilton
Co-stars: Sean Connery Gert Frobe Shirley Eaton

1965 **LIFE AT THE TOP**
Director: Ted Kotcheff
Co-stars: Laurence Harvey Jean Simmonds Michael Craig

1965 **THE SECRET OF MY SUCCESS**
Director: Andrew Stone
Co-stars: James Booth Lionel Jeffries Shirley Jones

1966 **MOMENT TO MOMENT**
Director: Mervyn LeRoy
Co-stars: Jean Seberg Sean Garrison Arthur Hill

1968 **A TWIST OF SAND**
Director: Don Chaffey
Co-stars: Richard Johnson Roy Dotrice Peter Vaughan

1968 **SHALAKO**
Director: Edward Dmytryk
Co-stars: Sean Connery Brigitte Bardot Jack Hawkins

1969 **TWINKY**
Director: Richard Donner
Co-stars: Charles Bronson Susan George Trevor Howard

1969 **THE LAST GRENADE**
Director: Gordon Flemyng
Co-stars: Stanley Baker Alex Cord Ray Brooks

1970 **THE VIRGIN AND THE GYPSY**
Director: Christopher Miles
Co-stars: Joanna Shimkus Franco Nero Norman Bird

1971 **SOMETHING BIG**
Director: Andrew McLaglen
Co-stars: Dean Martin Brian Keith Ben Johnson

1971 **FRIGHT**
Director: Peter Collinson
Co-stars: Susan George Ian Bannen Dennis Waterman

1976 **TO THE DEVIL A DAUGHTER**
Director: Peter Sykes
Co-stars: Richard Widmark Nastassja Kinski Christopher Lee

1977 **AGE OF INNOCENCE**
Director: Alan Bridges
Co-stars: David Warner Trudy Young Cec Linder

1979 **THE CAT AND THE CANARY**
Director: Radley Metzger
Co-stars: Michael Callan Edward Fox Wendy Hiller

1985 **MINDER ON THE ORIENT EXPRESS**
Director: Francis Megahy
Co-stars: George Cole Dennis Waterman

1989 **VOICE OF THE HEART**
Director: Tony Wharmby
Co-stars: Lindsay Wagner Victoria Tennant James Brolin

JOAN BLACKMAN

1959 **CAREER**
Director: Joseph Anthony
Co-stars: Dean Martin Anthony Franciosa Shirley MacLaine

1959 **GOOD DAY FOR A HANGING**
Director: Nathan Juran
Co-stars: Fred Macmurray Robert Vaughn Maggie Hayes

1960 **VISIT TO A SMALL PLANET**
Director: Norman Taurog
Co-stars: Jerry Lewis Earl Holliman John Willliams

1961 **BLUE HAWAII**
Director: Norman Taurog
Co-stars: Elvis Presley Angela Lansbury Nancy Walters

1962 **KID GALAHAD**
Director: Phil Karlson
Co-stars: Elvis Presley Lola Albright Gig Young

1962 **THE GREAT IMPOSTER**
Director: Robert Mulligan
Co-stars: Tony Curtis Raymond Massey Karl Malden

1963 **TWILIGHT OF HONOR**
Director: Boris Sagal
Co-stars: Richard Chamberlain Claude Rains Nick Adams

1965 **INTIMACY**
Director: Victor Stoloff
Co-stars: Barry Sullivan Nancy Malone

1968 **DARING GAME**
Director: Laslo Benedek
Co-stars: Lloyd Bridges Michael Ansara

1973 **MACON COUNTY LINE**
Director: Richard Compton
Co-stars: Alan Vint Cheryl Waters Geoffrey Lewis

WANDA BLACKMAN

1976 **OBSESSION**
Director: Brian De Palma
Co-stars: Cliff Robertson Genevieve Bujold John Lithgow

NINA BLACKWOOD

1988 **ROCK 'N' ROLL MOM**
Director: Michael Schultz
Co-stars: Dyan Cannon Michael Brandon Heather Locklear

ELLEN BLAIN

1992 **ONCE UPON A FOREST** *(Voice)*
Director: Charles Grosvenor
Co-stars: Michael Crawford Ben Vereen

1992 **CALIFORNIA MAN**
Director: Les Mayfield
Co-stars: Sean Astin Brendan Fraser Megan Ward

1992 **IN MY DAUGHTER'S NAME**
Director: Jud Taylor
Co-stars: John Getz Lee Grant Donna Mills

VIVIEN BLAINE

1942 **GIRL TROUBLE**
Director: Harold Schuster
Co-stars: Don Ameche Joan Bennett Billie Burke

1942 **THROUGH DIFFERENT EYES**
Director: Thomas Loring
Co-stars: Frank Craven Donald Woods Mary Howard

1943 **JITTERBUGS**
Director: Mal St.Clair
Co-stars: Laurel & Hardy Bob Bailey Noel Madison

1944 SOMETHING FOR THE BOYS
Director: Lewis Seiler
Co-stars: Carmen Miranda Michael O'Shea Phil Silvers

1944 GREENWICH VILLAGE
Director: Walter Lang
Co-stars: Carmen Miranda Don Ameche William Bendix

1945 DOLL FACE
Director: Lewis Seiler
Co-stars: Dennis O'Keefe Carmen Miranda Perry Como

1945 NOB HILL
Director: Henry Hathaway
Co-stars: George Raft Joan Bennett Peggy Ann Garner

1945 STATE FAIR
Director: Walter Lang
Co-stars: Dick Haymes Jeanne Crain Charles Winninger

1946 THREE LITTLE GIRLS IN BLUE
Director: Bruce Humberstone
Co-stars: June Haver George Montgomery Vera Ellen

1946 IF I'M LUCKY
Director: Lewis Seiler
Co-stars: Perry Como Carmen Miranda Phil Silvers

1952 SKIRTS AHOY!
Director: Sidney Lanfield
Co-stars: Esther Williams Joan Evans Debbie Reynolds

1955 GUYS AND DOLLS
Director: Joseph Mankiewicz
Co-stars: Marlon Brando Frank Sinatra Jean Simmonds

1979 THE DARK
Director: John Cardos
Co-stars: William Devane Cathy Lee Crosby Richard Jaeckel

1982 PARASITE
Director: Charles Band
Co-stars: Demi Moore Robert Claudini Luca Bercovici

BARBARA BLAIR

1938 HOLD MY HAND
Director: Thornton Freeland
Co-stars: Stanley Lupino Fred Emney Sally Gray

1939 I KILLED THE COUNT
Director: Fred Zelnik
Co-stars: Syd Walker Ben Lyon Terence De Marney

BETSY BLAIR
Nominated For Best Supporting Actress In 1955 For "Marty"

1947 THE GUILT OF JANET AMES
Director: Henry Levin
Co-stars: Rosalind Russell Melvyn Douglas

1951 KIND LADY
Director: John Sturges
Co-stars: Ethel Barrymore Maurice Evans Angela Lansbury

1955 MARTY
Director: Delbert Mann
Co-stars: Ernest Borgnine Esther Minciotti Joe Mantell

1956 THE HALLIDAY BRAND
Director: Joseph Lewis
Co-stars: Joseph Cotten Ward Bond Bill Williams

1956 CALLE MAYOR
Director: Juan Antonio
Co-stars: Rene Blancard Lila Kedrova Yves Massard

1957 IL GRIDO
Director: Michelangelo Antonioni
Co-stars: Steve Cochran Alida Valli Dorian Gray

1961 ALL NIGHT LONG
Director: Basil Dearden
Co-stars: Patrick McGoohan Richard Attenborough

1973 A DELICATE BALANCE
Director: Tony Richardson
Co-stars: Katherine Hepburn Paul Scofield Joseph Cotten

1988 BETRAYED
Director: Constantin Costa-Garvas
Co-stars: Debra Winger Tom Berenger John Heard

ISLA BLAIR
1969 TASTE THE BLOOD OF DRACULA
Director: Peter Sasdy
Co-stars: Christopher Lee Gwen Watford Ralph Bates

1983 REAL LIFE
Director: Francis Megahy
Co-stars: Rupert Everett Cristina Raines Warren Clarke

1984 POPPYLAND
Director: John Madden
Co-stars: Alan Howard Phoebe Nichols Richard Wilson

1989 MOTHER LOVE
Director: Simon Langton
Co-stars: Diana Rigg James Wilby Holly Aird

1991 VALMONT
Director: Milos Forman
Co-stars: Colin Firth Annette Bening Fairuza Balk

1991 THE ADVOCATES
Director: Peter Barber-Fleming
Co-stars: Stella Gonet Ewan Stewart Hugh Ross

1992 THE ADVOCATES: ABOVE THE LAW
Director: Peter Barber-Fleming
Co-stars: Alison Peebles Michael Kitchen

1993 INSPECTOR MORSE:
CHERUBIM AND SERAPHIM
Director: Danny Boyle
Co-stars: John Thaw Kevin Whately

JANET BLAIR
1942 BLONDIE GOES TO COLLEGE
Director: Frank Strayer
Co-stars: Penny Singleton Arthur Lake

1942 BROADWAY
Director: William Seiter
Co-stars: George Raft Pat O'Brien Broderick Crawford

1942 MY SISTER EILEEN
Director: Alexander Hall
Co-stars: Rosalind Russell Brian Aherne June Havoc

1942 THREE GIRLS ABOUT TOWN
Director: Leigh Jason
Co-stars: Joan Blondell Binnie Barnes

1942 TWO YANKS IN TRINIDAD
Director: Gregory Ratoff
Co-stars: Pat O'Brien Brian Donlevy Roger Clark

1943 SOMETHING TO SHOUT ABOUT
Director: Gregory Ratoff
Co-stars: Don Ameche William Gaxton Perry Como

1944 ONCE UPON A TIME
Director: Alexander Hall
Co-stars: Cary Grant James Gleason Wiliam Demarest

1945 TARS AND SPARS
Director: Alfred Green
Co-stars: Alfred Drake Sid Caesar Marc Platt

1945 TONIGHT AND EVERY NIGHT
Director: Victor Saville
Co-stars: Rita Hayworth Lee Bowman Shelley Winters

1946 GALLANT JOURNEY
Director: William Wellman
Co-stars: Glenn Ford Charles Ruggles Henry Travers

1947   **I LOVE TROUBLE**
Director: S. Sylvan Simon
Co-stars: Franchot Tone Janis Carter Adele Jergens

1947   **THE FABULOUS DORSEYS**
Director: Alfred Green
Co-stars: Jimmy Dorsey Tommy Dorsey Arthur Shields

1948   **THE BLACK ARROW**
Director: Gordon Douglas
Co-stars: Louis Hayward George Macready

1948   **THE FULLER BRUSH MAN**
Director: S. Sylvan Simon
Co-stars: Red Skelton Don McGuire Adele Jergens

1962   **BOYS' NIGHT OUT**
Director: Michael Gordon
Co-stars: Kim Novak James Garner Howard Duff

1964   **NIGHT OF THE EAGLE**
Director: Sidney Hayers
Co-stars: Margaret Johnston Peter Wyngarde Kathleen Byron

1968   **THE ONE AND ONLY
GENUINE ORIGINAL FAMILY BAND**
Director: Michael O'Herlihy
Co-stars: Walter Brennan Buddy Ebsen Kurt Russell

1976   **WON TON TON,
THE DOG WHO SAVED HOLLYWOOD**
Director: Michael Winner
Co-stars: Madeleine Kahn Art Carney Bruce Dern

JOYCE BLAIR

1959   **JAZZBOAT**
Director: Ken Hughes
Co-stars: Anthony Newley Anne Aubrey Lionel Jeffries

1965   **BE MY GUEST**
Director: Lance Comfort
Co-stars: David Hemmings Avril Angers Jerry Lee Lewis

JUNE BLAIR

1959   **THE RABBIT TRAP**
Director: Philip Leacock
Co-stars: Ernest Borgnine Bethel Leslie Kevin Corcoran

LINDA BLAIR (Child)
Nominated For Best Supporting Actress In 1973 For "The Exorcist"

1973   **THE EXORCIST**
Director: William Friedking
Co-stars: Max Von Sydow Ellen Burstyn Lee J. Cobb

1974   **AIRPORT '75**
Director: Jack Smight
Co-stars: Charlton Heston Karen Black George Kennedy

1975   **SWEET HOSTAGE**
Director: Lee Philips
Co-stars: Martin Sheen Jeanne Cooper

1977   **EXORCIST II: THE HERETIC**
Director: John Boorman
Co-stars: Richard Burton Louise Fletcher Ned Beatty

1981   **HELL NIGHT**
Director: Tom DeSimone
Co-stars: Vincent Van Patten Peter Barton Kevin Brophy

1983   **CHAINED HEAT**
Director: Paul Nicholas
Co-stars: John Vernon Stella Stevens Sybil Danning

1984   **SAVAGE STREETS**
Director: Danny Steinman
Co-stars: John Vernon Linnea Quigley Robert Dryer

1990   **REPOSSESSED**
Director: Bob Logan
Co-stars: Leslie Nielsen Ned Beatty Anthony Starke

1990   **ZAPPED AGAIN**
Director: Douglas Campbell
Co-stars: Todd Eric Andrews Kelli Williams Karen Black

1991   **FATAL BOND**
Director: Vincent Monton
Co-stars: Jerome Ehlers Joe Bugner

PATRICIA BLAIR

1958   **CITY OF FEAR**
Director: Irving Lerner
Co-stars: Vince Edwards John Archer Lyle Talbot

AMANDA BLAKE

1950   **STARS IN MY CROWN**
Director: Jacques Tourneur
Co-stars: Joel McCrea Ellen Drew Dean Stockwell

1952   **CATTLE TOWN**
Director: Noel Smith
Co-stars: Dennis Morgan Rita Moreno Philip Carey

1952   **SCARLET ANGEL**
Director: Sidney Salkow
Co-stars: Yvonne De Carlo Rock Hudson Richard Denning

1953   **LILI**
Director: Charles Walters
Co-stars: Leslie Caron Mel Ferrer Jean-Pierre Aumont

1953   **SABRE JET**
Director: Louis King
Co-stars: Robert Stack Coleen Gray Julie Bishop

1954   **THE ADVENTURES OF HAJJI BABA**
Director: Don Weis
Co-stars: John Derek Elaine Stewart Thomas Gomez

1954   **A STAR IS BORN**
Director: George Cukor
Co-stars: Judy Garland James Mason Charles Bickford

1987   **GUNSMOKE: RETURN TO DODGE**
Director: Vincent McEveety
Co-stars: James Arness Earl Holliman

1988   **B.O.R.N.**

1988   **THE BOOST**
Director: Harold Becker
Co-stars: James Woods Sean Young Steven Hill

JULIA BLAKE

1977   **THE GETTING OF WISDOM**
Director: Bruce Beresford
Co-stars: Susannah Fowle Barry Humphries

1978   **PATRICK**
Director: Richard Franklin
Co-stars: Susan Penhaligon Robert Helpman

1981   **LONELY HEARTS**
Director: Paul Cox
Co-stars: Wendy Hughes Norman Kaye

1984   **MAN OF FLOWERS**
Director: Paul Cox
Co-stars: Norman Kaye Alyson Best Sarah Walker

1986   **TRAVELLING NORTH**
Director: Carl Schultz
Co-stars: Leo McKern Graham Kennedy

1988   **GEORGIA**
Director: Ben Lewin
Co-stars: Judy Davis John Bach Marshall Napier

1990 FATHER
Director: John Power
Co-stars: Max Von Sydow Carol Drinkwater

JUDITH BLAKE

1936 WANTED: JANE TURNER
Director: Edward Killy Lee Tracy Gloria Stuart

CATHERINE BLAKE

1992 TALE OF A VAMPIRE
Director: Shimako Sato
Co-stars: Julian Sands Suzanna Hamilton

KATHERINE BLAKE

1969 ANNE OF A THOUSAND DAYS
Director: Charles Jarrott
Co-stars: Richard Burton Genevieve Bujold

MADGE BLAKE

1951 THE PROWLER
Director: Joseph Losey
Co-stars: Van Heflin Evelyn Keyes John Maxwell

MARIE BLAKE

1940 DR. KILDARE'S CRISIS
Director: Harold Bucquet
Co-stars: Lew Ayres Lionel Barrymore Robert Young

PAMELA BLAKE

1942 MAISIE GETS HER MAN
Director: Roy Del Ruth
Co-stars: Ann Sothern Red Skelton Leo Gorcey

1942 THE OMAHA TRAIL
Director: Edward Buzzell
Co-stars: James Craig Dean Jagger Chill Wills

1943 UNKNOWN GUEST
Director: Kurt Neumann
Co-stars: Victor Jory Nora Cecil Veda Ann Borg

1945 THREE'S A CROWD
Co-stars: Charles Gordon Virginia Brissac

1945 WHY GIRLS LEAVE HOME
Co-stars: Lola Lane Elisha Cook Jnr.

1946 LIVE WIRES
Co-stars: Leo Gorcey Huntz Hall Bobby Jordan

1948 HIGHWAY 13
Co-stars: Robert Lowery Lyle Talbot Dan Seymour

1949 SKYLINER
Director: William Berke
Co-stars: Richard Travis Rochelle Hudson Steve Geray

1959 GHOST OF ZORRO
Director: Fred Brannon
Co-stars: Clayton Moore Roy Barcroft

PATRICIA BLAKE

1956 THE BLACK SLEEP
Director: Reginald LeBorg
Co-stars: Basil Rathbone Akim Tamiroff Bela Lugosi

SONDRA BLAKE

1989 ROXANNE: THE PRIZE PULITZER
Director: Richard Colla
Co-stars: Perry King Chynna Phillips

SUSAN BLAKELEY

1972 SAVAGES
Director: James Ivory
Co-stars: Louis Stadlen Anne Francine Salome Jens

1974 OPERATION UNDERCOVER
Director: Milton Katselas
Co-stars: Michael Moriarty Yaphet Kotto Richard Gere

1974 THE TOWERING INFERNO
Director: Irving Allen
Co-stars: Paul Newman Steve McQueen William Holden

1974 THE LORDS OF FLATBUSH
Director: Martin Davidson
Co-stars: Perry King Henry Winkler Sylvester Stallone

1975 CAPONE
Director: Steve Carver
Co-stars: Ben Gazzara John Cassavetes Sylvester Stallone

1977 SECRETS
Director: Paul Wendkos
Co-stars: Roy Thinnes John Randolph Melody Thomas

1979 AIRPORT '80: THE CONCORDE
Director: Alain Delon
Co-stars: George Kennedy Sylvia Kristel

1980 MAKE ME AN OFFER
Director: Jerry Paris
Co-star: Patrick O'Neal

1980 ADDICTION: A CRY FOR LOVE
Director: Paul Wendkos
Co-stars: Gene Barry Powers Booth Lainie Kazan

1986 THE TED KENNEDY JR. STORY
Director: Delbert Mann
Co-stars: Craig T. Nelson Kimber Shoop

1986 BLOOD AND ORCHIDS
Director: Jerry Thorpe
Co-stars: Kris Kristofferson Jane Alexander Sean Young

1986 THE ANNIHILATOR
Director: Michael Chapman
Co-stars: Mark Lindsay Chapman Lisa Blount Geoffrey Lewis

1987 OVER THE TOP
Director: Menahem Golan
Co-stars: Sylvester Stallone Robert Loggia

1988 BROKEN ANGEL
Director: Richard Heffron
Co-stars: William Shatner Roxann Biggs Millie Perkins

1989 DREAM A LITTLE DREAM
Director: Marc Rocco
Co-stars: Corey Feldman Jason Robards Piper Laurie

1989 LADYKILLERS
Director: Robert Lewis
Co-stars: Marilu Henner Lesley-Anne Down William Lucking

1990 THE INCIDENT
Director: Joseph Sargent
Co-stars: Walter Matthau Peter Firth Robert Carradine

1990 MURDER TIMES SEVEN
Director: Jud Taylor
Co-stars: Richard Crenna Cliff Gorman

1991 WILDFLOWER
Director: Diane Keaton
Co-stars: Patricia Arquette Beau Bridges Reese Witherspoon

OLIVE BLAKENEY

1934 GIVE HER A RING
Director: Arthur Woods
Co-stars: Clifford Mollison Wendy Barrie Stewart Granger

1935   COME OUT OF THE PANTRY
Director: Jack Raymond
Co-stars: Jack Buchanan Fay Wray Ronald Squire

1941   THAT UNCERTAIN FEELING
Director: Ernst Lubitsch
Co-stars: Merle Oberon Melvyn Douglas Eve Arden

1941   HENRY ALDRICH FOR PRESIDENT
Co-stars: Jimmy Lydon Charles Smith John Litel

1942   HENRY AND DIZZY
Co-stars: Jimmy Lydon Charles Smith John Litel

1942   HENRY ALDRICH EDITOR
Co-stars: Jimmy Lydon Charles Smith John Litel

1943   HENRY ALDRICH GETS GLAMOUR
Co-stars: Jimmy Lydon Charles Smith John Litel

1943   HENRY ALDRICH SWINGS IT
Co-stars: Jimmy Lydon Charles Smith John Litel

1943   HENRY ALDRICH HAUNTS A HOUSE
Co-stars: Jimmy Lydon Charles Smith Mike Mazurki

1944   HENRY ALDRICH BOY SCOUT
Co-stars: Jimmy Lydon Charles Smith Joan Mortimer

1944   HENRY ALDRICH PLAYS CUPID
Director: Hugh Bennett
Co-stars: Jimmy Lydon Diana Lynn Vera Vague

1944   HENRY ALDRICH'S LITTLE SECRET
Co-stars: Jimmy Lydon Charles Smith John Litel

1944   EXPERIMENT PERILOUS
Director: Jacques Tourneur
Co-stars: Hedy Lamarr Paul Lukas George Brent

RONEE BLAKLEY
Nominated For Best Supporting Actress In 1975 For "Nashville"

1975   NASHVILLE
Director: Robert Altman
Co-stars: Keith Carradine Shelley Duvall Karen Black

1978   THE PRIVATE FILES OF J. EDGAR HOOVER
Director: Larry Cohen
Co-stars: Broderick Crawford Jose Ferrer

1978   THE DRIVER
Director: Walter Hill
Co-stars: Ryan O'Neal Bruce Dern Isabel Adjani

1980   THE BALTIMORE BULLET
Director: Robert Ellis Miller
Co-stars: James Coburn Omar Sharif Bruce Boxleitner

1984   A NIGHTMARE ON ELM STREET
Director: Wes Craven
Co-stars: Robert Englund John Saxon Amanda Wyss

1987   A RETURN TO SALEM'S LOT
Director: Larry Cohen
Co-stars: Michael Moriarty Evelyn Keyes June Havoc

ANNE MARIE BLANC

1947   WHITE CRADLE INN
Director: Harold French
Co-stars: Madeleine Carroll Michael Rennie Ian Hunter

DOMINIQUE BLANC

1989   MILOU IN MAY
Director: Louis Malle
Co-stars: Michel Piccoli Miou Miou Harriet Walter

1994   LA REINE MARGOT
Director: Patrice Chereau
Co-stars: Isabelle Adjani Daniel Auteuill Virna Lisi

JENNIFER BLANC

1994   THE COOL AND THE CRAZY
Director: Ralph Bakshi
Co-stars: Alicia Silverstone Jared Leto Matthew Flint

DOMINIQUE BLANCHAR

1960   L'AVVENTURA
Director: Michaelangelo Antonioni
Co-stars: Monica Vitti Gabrielle Ferzetti

MARI BLANCHARD

1951   NO QUESTIONS ASKED
Director: Harold Kress
Co-stars: Barry Sullivan George Murphy Arlene Dahl

1952   BACK AT THE FRONT
Director: George Sherman
Co-stars: Tom Ewell Harvey Lembeck Richard Long

1953   ABBOTT AND COSTELLO GO TO MARS
Director: Charles Lamont
Co-stars: Abbott And Costello Martha Hyer Anita Ekberg

1954   BLACK HORSE CANYON
Director: Jesse Hibbs
Co-stars: Joel McCrea Race Gentry Murvyn Vye

1954   DESTRY
Director: George Marshall
Co-stars: Audie Murphy Lyle Bettger Thomas Mitchell

1954   RAILS INTO LARAMIE
Director: Jesse Hibbs
Co-stars: John Payne Dan Duryea Barton MacLane

1955   SON OF SINBAD
Director: Ted Tetzlaff
Co-stars: Dale Robertson Vincent Price Sally Forrest

1955   THE CROOKED WEB
Director: Nathan Juran
Co-stars: Frank Lovejoy Richard Denning

1956   THE CRUEL TOWER
Director: Lew Landers
Co-stars: Charles McGraw John Ericson Steve Brodie

SUSAN BLANCHARD *(Married Charles Frank)*

1978   THE NEW MAVERICK
Director: Hy Averback
Co-stars: Charles Frank James Garner Jack Kelly

1979   THE YOUNG MAVERICK
Director: Hy Averback
Co-stars: Charles Frank James Woods Harry Dean Stanton

1981   SHE'S IN THE ARMY NOW
Director: Hy Averback
Co-stars: Kathleen Quinlan Melanie Griffith Julie Carmen

1987   RUSSKIES
Director: Rick Rosenthal
Co-stars: Whip Hubley Charles Frank Peter Billingsley

1988   PRINCE OF DARKNESS
Director: John Carpenter
Co-stars: Donald Pleasence Lisa Blount Jameson Parker

JEWEL BLANCHE

1975   AGAINST A CROOKED SKY
Director: Earl Bellamy
Co-stars: Richard Boone Stewart Petersen

CATE BLANCHETTE

1997   PARADISE ROAD
Director: Bruce Beresford
Co-stars: Glenn Close Pauline Collins Jennifer Ehle

1998 OSCAR AND LUCINDA
Director: Gillian Armstrong
Co-star: Ralph Fiennes

DOROTHEE BLANCK
1961 CLEO FROM FIVE TO SEVEN
Director: Agnes Varda
Co-stars: Corinne Marchand Michel Legrand

EVE BLAND
1992 FOOL'S GOLD: THE STORY OF THE BRINKS-MAT ROBBERY
Director: Terry Winsor
Co-stars: Sean Bean Larry Lamb

JOYCE BLAND
1932 THE FLAG LIEUTENANT
Director: Henry Edwards
Co-stars: Henry Edwards Anna Neagle Sam Livesey

1936 DREAMING LIPS
Director: Paul Czinner
Co-stars: Elizabeth Bergner Romney Brent Raymond Massey

CLARA BLANDICK
1930 ONCE A SINNER
Director: John Argyle
Co-stars: Dorothy MacKail Joel McCrea John Halliday

1930 ROMANCE
Director: Clarence Brown
Co-stars: Greta Garbo Lewis Stone Gavin Gordon

1930 TOM SAWYER
Director: John Cromwell
Co-stars: Jackie Coogan Junior Durkin Mitzi Green

1931 I TAKE THIS WOMAN
Director: Marion Gering
Co-stars: Gary Cooper Carole Lombard Helen Ware

1931 THE EASIEST WAY
Director: Jack Conway
Co-stars: Constance Bennett Robert Montgomery Clark Gable

1931 HUCKLEBERRY FINN
Director: Norman Taurog
Co-stars: Jackie Coogan Mitzi Green Junior Durkin

1932 THREE ON A MATCH
Director: Mervyn LeRoy
Co-stars: Joan Blondell Bette Davis Ann Dvorak

1932 SHOPWORN
Director: Nicke Grinde
Co-stars: Barbara Stanwyck Regis Toomey Zasu Pitts

1932 THE BITTER TEA OF GENERAL YEN
Director: Frank Capra
Co-stars: Barbara Stanwyck Nils Asther

1932 THE WET PARADE
Co-stars: Walter Huston Robert Young Jimmy Durante

1932 LIFE BEGINS
Director: James Flood
Co-stars: Loretta Young Eric Linden Preston Foster

1933 CHILD OF MANHATTAN
Director: Edward Buzzell
Co-stars: Nancy Carroll John Boles Betty Grable

1934 THE GIRL FROM MISSOURI
Director: Jack Conway
Co-stars: Jean Harlow Franchot Tone Lionel Barrymore

1934 THE SHOW-OFF
Director: Charles Riesner
Co-stars: Spencer Tracy Madge Evans Henry Wadsworth

1934 SISTERS UNDER THE SKIN
Director: David Burton
Co-stars: Frank Morgan Elissa Landi Doris Lloyd

1936 MAKE WAY FOR A LADY
Director: David Burton
Co-stars: Herbert Marshall Anne Shirley Gertrude Michael

1939 THE WIZARD OF OZ
Director: Victor Fleming
Co-stars: Judy Garland Ray Bolger Jack Haley

1945 PILLOW OF DEATH
Director: Wallace Fox
Co-stars: Lon Chaney Brenda Joyce Rosalind Ivan

1945 FRONTIER GAL
Director: Charles Lamont
Co-stars: Yvonne De Carlo Rod Cameron Sheldon Leonard

1946 SO GOES MY LOVE
Director: Frank Ryan
Co-stars: Myrna Loy Don Ameche Bobby Driscoll

SALLY BLANE
(Sister of Loretta Young and Polly Ann Young)
1929 THE VAGABOND LOVER
Co-stars: Rudy Vallee Marie Dressler Eddie Nugent

1930 LITTLE ACCIDENT
Director: William James Craft
Co-stars: Douglas Fairbanks Anita Page Zasu Pitts

1931 THE STAR WITNESS
Director: William Welllman
Co-stars: Walter Huston Chic Sale Grant Mitchell

1931 TEN CENTS A DANCE
Director: Lionel Barrymore
Co-stars: Barbara Stanwyck Ricardo Cortez

1932 THE RECKONING
Co-star: Richard Tucker

1932 HELLO EVERYBODY
Director: William Seiter
Co-stars: Kate Smith Randolph Scott George Barbier

1932 CROSS EXAMINATION
Co-stars: Richard Tucker H. B. Warner

1933 ADVICE TO THE LOVELORN
Director: Alfred Werker
Co-stars: Lee Tracy Sterling Holloway Isabel Jewell

1934 STOLEN SWEETS
Co-star: Charles Starrett

1934 HALF A SINNER
Director: Kurt Neuman
Co-stars: Berton Churchill Joel McCrea Mickey Rooney

1934 THE SILVER STREAK
Director: Tommy Atkins
Co-stars: Charles Starrett Irving Pichel Arthur Lake

1934 NO MORE WOMEN
Director: Al Rogell
Co-stars: Edmund Lowe Victor McLaglen Minna Gombell

1937 THE GREAT HOSPITAL MYSTERY
Director: James Tinling
Co-stars: Jane Darwell Joan Davis William Demarest

1937 ANGEL'S HOLIDAY
Director: James Tinling
Co-stars: Joan Davis Jane Withers Robert Kent

1937 ONE MILE FROM HEAVEN
Director: Allan Dwan
Co-stars: Claire Trevor Douglas Fowley Bill Robinson

1939 CHARLIE CHAN AT TREASURE ISLAND
Director: Norman Foster
Co-stars: Sidney Toler Cesar Romero Sen Yung

BRENDA BLETHYN
Nominated For Best Supporting Actress In 1996 For "Secrets And Lies"

1989 THE SHAWL
Director: Bill Bryden
Co-stars: Nigel Hawthorne Karl Johnson

1992 A RIVER RUNS THROUGH IT
Director: Robert Redford
Co-stars: Craig Sheffer Brad Pitt Emily Lloyd

1993 THE BULLION BOYS
Director: Christopher Morahan
Co-stars: David Jason Tim Pigott-Smith Gordon Kaye

1996 SECRETS AND LIES
Director: Mike Leigh
Co-stars: Timothy Spall Phyllis Logan Lee Ross

1997 REMEMBER ME?
Director: Nick Hurran
Co-star: James Fleet

1998 GIRLS' NIGHT
Co-stars: Julie Walters Kris Krisofferson

CAROLINE BLISS

1987 THE LIVING DAYLIGHTS
Director: John Glen
Co-stars: Timothy Dalton Maryam D'Abo Jeroen Krabbe

1989 LICENCE TO KILL
Director: John Glen
Co-stars: Timothy Dalton Robert Davi Carey Lowell

LELA BLISS

1946 THE DARK MIRROR
Director: Robert Siodmak
Co-stars: Olivia De Havilland Lew Ayres Thomas Mitchell

GLORIA BLONDELL

1938 ACCIDENTS WILL HAPPEN
Director: William Clemens
Co-stars: Ronald Reagan Dick Purcell

JOAN BLONDELL *(Married Dick Powell)*
Nominated For Best Supporting Actress In 1951 For "The Blue Veil"

1930 SINNER'S HOLIDAY
Director: John Adolfi
Co-stars: Grant Withers Evelyn Knapp James Cagney

1931 OTHER MEN'S WOMEN
Director: William Wellman
Co-stars: Grant Withers Mary Astor James Cagney

1931 NIGHT NURSE
Director: William Wellman
Co-stars: Barbara Stanwyck Ben Lyon Clark Gable

1931 THE PUBLIC ENEMY
Director: William Wellman
Co-stars: James Cagney Jean Harlow Mae Clark

1931 GOD'S GIFT TO WOMEN
Director: Michael Curtiz
Co-stars: Frank Fay Charles Winninger Louise Brooks

1931 ILLICIT
Director: Archie Mayo
Co-stars: Barbara Stanwyck Ricardo Cortez James Rennie

1931 BLONDE CRAZY
Director: Roy Del Ruth
Co-stars: James Cagney Ray Milland Louis Calhern

1931 BIG BUSINESS GIRL
Director: William Seiter
Co-stars: Loretta Young Ricardo Cortez Jack Albertson

1932 CENTRAL PARK
Director: John Adolfi
Co-stars: Wallace Ford Guy Kibbee Patricia Ellis

1932 BIG CITY BLUES
Director: Mervyn LeRoy
Co-stars: Eric Linden Humphrey Bogart Evelyn Knapp

1932 THE CROWD ROARS
Director: Howard Hawks
Co-stars: James Cagney Eric Linden Ann Dvorak

1932 THE FAMOUS FERGUSON CASE
Director: Lloyd Bacon
Co-stars: Tom Brown Adrienne Dore Leslie Fenton

1932 THE GREEKS HAD A WORD FOR THEM
Director: Lowell Sherman
Co-stars: Madge Evans Ina Claire Betty Grable

1932 LAWYER MAN
Director: William Dieterle
Co-stars: William Powell Helen Vinson Alan Dinehart

1932 MAKE ME A STAR
Director: William Beaudine
Co-stars: Stuart Erwin Zasu Pitts Ben Turpin

1932 MISS PINKERTON
Director: Lloyd Bacon
Co-stars: George Brent John Wray Mae Madison

1932 THREE ON A MATCH
Director: Mervyn LeRoy
Co-stars: Bette Davis Ann Dvorak Warren William

1932 UNION DEPOT
Director: Alfred Green
Co-stars: Douglas Fairbanks Alan Hale

1933 HAVANA WIDOWS
Director: Ray Enright
Co-stars: Glenda Farrell Guy Kibbee Lyle Talbot

1933 GOODBYE AGAIN
Director: Michael Curtiz
Co-stars: Warren William Genevieve Tobin Hugh Herbert

1933 GOLD DIGGERS OF 1933
Director: Mervyn LeRoy
Co-stars: Warren William Ruby Keeler Dick Powell

1933 FOOTLIGHT PARADE
Director: Lloyd Bacon
Co-stars: James Cagney Ruby Keeler Dick Powell

1933 CONVENTION CITY
Director: Archie Mayo
Co-stars: Dick Powell Adolphe Menjou Guy Kibbee

1933 BLONDIE JOHNSON
Director: Ray Enright
Co-stars: Chester Morris Allen Jenkins Claire Dodd

1933 BROADWAY BAD
Director: Sidney Lanfield
Co-stars: Ricardo Cordez Ginger Rogers Donald Crisp

1934 DAMES
Director: Ray Enright
Co-stars: Dick Powell Ruby Keeler Hugh Herbert

1934 HE WAS HER MAN
Director: Lloyd Bacon
Co-stars: James Cagney Victor Jory Frank Craven

1934 I'VE GOT YOUR NUMBER
Director: Ray Enright
Co-stars: Pat O'Brien Allen Jenkins Glenda Farrell

1934 KANSAS CITY PRINCESS
Director: William Keighley
Co-stars: Glenda Farrell Hugh Herbert Robert Armstrong

1934 SMARTY
Co-stars: Warren William Edward Everett Horton

1935 TRAVELLING SALESLADY
Director: Ray Enright
Co-stars: Glenda Farrell Hugh Herbert Ruth Donnelly

1935 WE'RE IN THE MONEY
Director: Ray Enright
Co-stars: Glenda Farrell Hugh Herbert Lionel Stander

1935 MISS PACIFIC FLEET
Director: Ray Enright
Co-stars: Glenda Farrell Hugh Herbbrt Allen Jenkins

1935 BROADWAY GONDOLIER
Director: Lloyd Bacon
Co-stars: Dick Powell Adolphe Menjou Judy Canova

1936 BULLETS OR BALLOTS
Director: William Keighley
Co-stars: Edward G. Robinson Humphrey Bogart

1936 COLLEEN
Director: Alfred Green
Co-stars: Dick Powell Ruby Keeler Jack Oakie

1936 GOLD DIGGERS OF 1937
Director: Lloyd Bacon
Co-stars: Dick Powell Victor Moore Glenda Farrell

1936 SONS O' GUNS
Director: Lloyd Bacon
Co-stars: Joe E. Brown Eric Blore Robert Barrat

1936 STAGE STRUCK
Director: Busby Berkeley
Co-stars: Dick Powell Warren William Frank McHugh

1936 THREE MEN ON A HORSE
Director: Mervyn LeRoy
Co-stars: Frank MacHugh Sam Levene Allen Jenkins

1937 STAND-IN
Director: Tay Garnett
Co-stars: Leslie Howard Humphrey Bogart Jack Carson

1937 THE PERFECT SPECIMEN
Director: Michael Curtiz
Co-stars: Errol Flynn May Robson Hugh Herbert

1937 THE KING AND THE CHORUS GIRL
Director: Mervyn LeRoy
Co-stars: Fernand Gravet Jane Wyman

1937 BACK IN CIRCULATION
Director: Ray Enright
Co-stars: Pat O'Brien Margaret Lindsay

1938 THERE'S ALWAYS A WOMAN
Director: Alex Hall
Co-stars: Mervyn Douglas Mary Astor Frances Drake

1939 THE AMAZING MR. WILLIAMS
Director: Alex Hall
Co-stars: Melvyn Douglas Ruth Donnelly

1939 EAST SIDE OF HEAVEN
Director: David Butler
Co-stars: Bing Crosby Mischa Auer Irene Hervey

1939 GOOD GIRLS GO TO PARIS
Director: Alexander Hall
Co-stars: Melvyn Douglas Walter Connelly

1939 THE KID FROM KOKOMO
Director: Lewis Seiler
Co-stars: Pat O'Brien Wayne Morris Jane Wyman

1939 OFF THE RECORD
Director: James Flood
Co-stars: Pat O'Brien Bobby Jordan Alan Baxter

1940 TWO GIRLS ON BROADWAY
Director: S. Sylvan Simon
Co-stars: Lana Turner George Murphy Kent Taylor

1940 I WANT A DIVORCE
Director: Ralph Murphy
Co-stars: Dick Powell Frank Fay Gloria Dickson

1941 LADY FOR A NIGHT
Director: Leigh Jason
Co-stars: John Wayne Ray Middleton Blanche Yurka

1941 MODEL WIFE
Director: Leigh Jason
Co-stars: Dick Powell Charles Ruggles Lee Bowman

1941 TOPPER RETURNS
Director: Roy Del Ruth
Co-stars: Roland Young Eddie Anderson Carole Landis

1942 THREE GIRLS ABOUT TOWN
Director: Leigh Jason
Co-stars: Binnie Barnes Janet Blair John Howard

1943 CRY HAVOC
Director: Richard Thorpe
Co-stars: Margaret Sullavan Ann Sothern Robert Mitchum

1945 ADVENTURE
Director: Victor Fleming
Co-stars: Clark Gable Greer Garson Thomas Mitchell

1945 DON JUAN QUILLIGAN
Director: Frank Tuttle
Co-stars: William Bendix Phil Silvers Ann Revere

1945 A TREE GROWS IN BROOKLYN
Director: Elia Kazan
Co-stars: James Dunn Dohothy McGuire Peggy Ann Garner

1947 NIGHTMARE ALLEY
Director: Edmund Goulding
Co-stars: Tyrone Power Coleen Gray Helen Walker

1947 THE CORPSE CAME C.O.D.
Director: Henry Levin
Co-stars: George Brent Adele Jergens Una O'Connor

1947 CHRISTMAS EVE
Director: Edwin Marin
Co-stars: Ann Harding George Raft Randolph Scott

1950 FOR HEAVEN'S SAKE
Director: George Seaton
Co-stars: Clifton Webb Edmund Gwenn Robert Cummings

1951 THE BLUE VEIL
Director: Curtis Bernhardt
Co-stars: Jane Wyman Charles Laughton Agnes Moorehead

1956 THE OPPOSITE SEX
Director: David Miller
Co-stars: June Allyson Dolores Gray Joan Collins

1957 WILL SUCCESS SPOIL ROCK HUNTER?
Director: Frank Tashlin
Co-stars: Tony Randall Jayne Mansfield

1957 THIS COULD BE THE NIGHT
Director: Robert Wise
Co-stars: Jean Simmons Paul Douglas Tony Franciosa

1957 THE DESK SET
Director: Walter Lang
Co-stars: Spencer Tracy Katharine Hepburn Gig Young

1957 LIZZIE
Director: Hugo Haas
Co-stars: Hugo Haas Eleanor Parker Richard Boone

1960　ANGEL BABY
Director:　Paul Wendkos
Co-stars:　Salome Jens George Hamilton Mercedes McCambridge

1964　ADVANCE TO THE REAR
Director:　George Marshall
Co-stars:　Glenn Ford Melvyn Douglas Stella Stevens

1965　THE CINCINNATI KID
Director:　Norman Jewison
Co-stars:　Steve McQueen Edward G. Robinson Karl Malden

1966　THE SPY IN THE GREEN HAT
Director:　Joseph Sargent
Co-stars:　Robert Vaughn David McCallum Janet Leigh

1966　RIDE BEYOND VENGENCE
Director:　Bernard McEverett
Co-stars:　Chuck Connors Michael Rennie Gloria Grahame

1967　WATERHOLE NO.3
Director:　William Graham
Co-stars:　James Coburn Carroll O'Connor

1968　STAY AWAY JOE
Director:　Peter Tewkesbury
Co-stars:　Elvis Presley Burgess Meredith Katy Jurado

1971　SUPPORT YOUR LOCAL GUNFIGHTER
Director:　Burt Kennedy
Co-stars:　James Garner Suzanne Pleshette

1975　WINNER TAKE ALL
Director:　Paul Bogart
Co-stars:　Shirley Jones Sam Groom Laurence Luckinbill

1975　THE DEAD DON'T DIE
Director:　Curtis Harrington
Co-stars:　George Hamilton Ray Milland Linda Cristal

1978　GREASE
Director:　Randal Kleiser
Co-stars:　John Travolta Olivia Newton-John Eve Arden

1978　OPENING NIGHT
Director:　John Cassavetes
Co-stars:　John Cassavetes Gena Rowlands Ben Gazarra

1979　THE CHAMP
Director:　Franco Zeffirelli
Co-stars:　Jon Voight Faye Dunnaway Ricky Schroeder

ANN BLOOM

1986　THE DIRT BIKE KID
Director:　Hoite Caston
Co-stars:　Peter Billingsley Stuart Pankin Sage Parker

CLAIRE BLOOM

1948　THE BLIND GODDESS
Director:　Harold French
Co-stars:　Eric Portman Michael Dennison Anne Crawford

1952　LIMELIGHT
Director:　Charles Chaplin
Co-stars:　Charles Chaplin Sydney Chaplin Buster Keaton

1953　THE MAN BETWEEN
Director:　Carol Reed
Co-stars:　James Mason Hildegard Neff Geoffrey Toone

1953　INNOCENTS IN PARIS
Director:　Gordon Parry
Co-stars:　Alastair Sim Margaret Rutherford Laurence Harvey

1955　RICHARD III
Director:　Laurence Olivier
Co-stars:　Laurence Olivier Ralph Richardson John Gielgud

1956　ALEXANDER THE GREAT
Director:　Robert Rossen
Co-stars:　Richard Burton Fredric March Danielle Darrieux

1957　THE BROTHERS KARAMAZOV
Director:　Richard Brooks
Co-stars:　Yul Brynner Maria Schell Richard Basehart

1958　THE BUCCANEER
Director:　Anthony Quinn
Co-stars:　Yul Brynner Charlton Heston Charles Boyer

1959　LOOK BACK IN ANGER
Director:　Tony Richardson
Co-stars:　Richard Burton Mary Ure Edith Evans

1962　THE CHAPMAN REPORT
Director:　George Cukor
Co-stars:　Shelley Winters Glynis Johns Jane Fonda

1962　THE WONDERFUL WORLD OF THE BROTHERS GRIMM
Director:　Henry Levin
Co-stars:　Karl Boehm Russ Tamblyn Laurence Harvey

1963　THE HAUNTING
Director:　Robert Wise
Co-stars:　Richard Johnson Russ Tamblyn Julie Harris

1963　EIGHTY THOUSAND SUSPECTS
Director:　Val Guest
Co-stars:　Richard Johnson Yolande Donlan Cyril Cusack

1964　THE OUTRAGE
Director:　Martin Ritt
Co-stars:　Paul Newman Edward G. Robinson Laurence Harvey

1966　THE SPY WHO CAME IN FROM THE COLD
Director:　Martin Ritt
Co-stars:　Richard Burton Sam Wanamaker

1968　CHARLY
Director:　Ralph Nelson
Co-stars:　Cliff Robertson Leon Janney Lilia Skala

1969　THE ILLUSTRATED MAN
Director:　Jack Smight
Co-stars:　Rod Steiger Don Dubbins Robert Drivas

1969　THREE INTO TWO WON'T GO
Director:　Peter Hall
Co-stars:　Rod Steiger Judy Geeson Peggy Ashcroft

1970　RED SKY AT MORNING
Director:　James Goldstone
Co-stars:　Richard Thomas Richard Crenna Catherine Burns

1970　A SEVERED HEAD
Director:　Dick Clement
Co-stars:　Lee Remick Ian Holm Jennie Linden

1973　A DOLL'S HOUSE
Director:　Patrick Garland
Co-stars:　Anthony Hopkins Ralph Richardson Anna Massey

1976　ISLANDS IN THE STREAM
Director:　Franklin Schaffner
Co-stars:　George C. Scott David Hemmings

1981　CLASH OF THE TITANS
Director:　Desmond Davis
Co-stars:　Laurence Olivier Maggie Smith Judi Bowker

1981　BRIDESHEAD REVISITED
Director:　Charles Sturridge
Co-stars:　Jeremy Irons Anthony Andrews Diana Quick

1983　SEPARATE TABLES
Director:　John Schlesinger
Co-stars:　Alan Bates Jullie Christie Brian Deacon

1984　ELLIS ISLAND
Director:　Jerry London
Co-stars:　Richard Burton Kate Burton Faye Dunnaway

1985 DEJA VU
Director: Anthony Richmond
Co-stars: Jaclyn Smith Nigel Terry Shelley Winters

1985 SHADOWLANDS
Director: Norman Stone
Co-stars: Joss Ackland David Waller Philip Stone

1986 ANASTASIA: THE MYSTERY OF ANNA
Director: James Goldman
Co-stars: Amy Irving Olivia De Havilland

1987 SAMMY AND ROSIE GET LAID
Director: Stephen Frears
Co-stars: Shashi Kapoor Frances Barber

1988 THE LADY AND THE HIGHWAYMAN
Director: John Hough
Co-stars: Emma Samms Hugh Grant Oliver Reed

1989 CRIMES AND MISDEMEANORS
Director: Woody Allen
Co-stars: Woody Allen Mia Farrow Angelica Huston

1991 THE CAMOMILE LAWN
Director: Peter Hall
Co-stars: Jennifer Ehle Tara Fitzgerald Oliver Cotton

**1992 MISS MARPLE:
THE MIRROR CRACK'D SIDE TO SIDE**
Director: Norman Stone
Co-stars: Joan Hickson Barry Newman

1992 THE PRINCESS AND THE GOBLIN *(Voice)*
Director: Jozsef Gemes
Co-stars: Joss Ackland Roy Kinnear

1996 DAYLIGHT
Co-star: Sylvester Stallone

LINDSAY BLOOM

1977 ANGELS IN HELL
Director: Larry Buchanan
Co-stars: Victor Holchak Royal Dano Linda Cristal

**1980 THE HAPPY HOOKER GOES
TO HOLLYWOOD**
Director: Alan Roberts
Co-stars: Martine Beswick Chris Lemmon

1984 MORE THAN MURDER
Director: Gary Nelson
Co-stars: Stacey Keach Don Stroud

**1989 MICKEY SPILLANE'S MIKE HAMMER:
MURDER TAKES ALL**
Director: John Nicolella
Co-stars: Stacey Keach Don Stroud

VERNA BLOOM

1969 MEDIUM COOL
Director: Haskell Wexler
Co-stars: Robert Forster Marianna Hill Peter Bonerz

1971 THE HIRED HAND
Director: Peter Fonda
Co-stars: Peter Fonda Warren Oates Severn Darden

1972 HIGH PLAINS DRIFTER
Director: Clint Eastwood
Co-stars: Clint Eastwood Marianna Hill Mitchell Ryan

1973 BADGE 373
Director: Howard Koch
Co-stars: Robert Duvall Eddie Egan Henry Darrow

1978 NATIONAL LAMPOON'S ANIMAL HOUSE
Director: John Landis
Co-stars: John Belushi Tom Hulce John Vernon

1982 HONKYTONK MAN
Director: Clint Eastwood
Co-stars: Clint Eastwood Kyle Eastwood John McIntyre

1985 AFTER HOURS
Director: Martin Scorsese
Co-stars: Griffin Dunne Rosanna Arquette Teri Garr

1985 THE JOURNEY OF NATTY GANN
Director: Jeremy Kagan
Co-stars: Meredith Salenger John Cusack Ray Wise

CATHIANNE BLORE

1986 AN AMERICAN TALE *(Voice)*
Director: Don Bluth
Co-stars: Christopher Plummer Madeline Kahn

LUCIE BLOSSIER

1990 CROSS MY HEART
Director: Jacques Fansten
Co-stars: Sylvain Coppans Nicolas Parodi

LISA BLOUNT

1977 9/30/55
Director: James Bridges
Co-stars: Richard Thomas Susan Tyrrell Dennis Quaid

1982 AN OFFICER AND A GENTLEMAN
Director: Taylor Hackford
Co-stars: Richard Gere Debra Winger David Keith

1983 MURDER ME, MURDER YOU
Director: Gary Nelson
Co-stars: Stacy Keach Don Stroud Tanya Roberts

1984 SECRETS OF THE PHANTOM CAVERNS
Director: Don Sharp
Co-stars: Robert Powell Anne Heywood Richard Johnson

1985 CEASE FIRE
Director: David Nutter
Co-stars: Don Johnson Robert F. Lyons Rick Richards

1985 STORMIN' HOME
Director: Jerry Jameson
Co-stars: Gil Gerard Geoffrey Lewis Pat Corley

1986 THE ANNIHILATOR
Director: Michael Chapman
Co-stars: Mark Lindsay Chapman Susan Blakely

1988 PRINCE OF DARKNESS
Director: John Carpenter
Co-stars: Donald Pleasence Jameson Parker

1989 BLIND FURY
Director: Phillip Noyce
Co-stars: Rutger Hauer Terry O'Quinn Meg Foster

1991 FEMME FATALE
Director: Andre Guttfreund
Co-stars: Colin Firth Liza Zane Billy Zane

1994 MURDER BETWEEN FREINDS
Director: Waris Hussein
Co-stars: Timothy Busfield Stephen Lang

1995 JUDICIAL CONSENT
Director: William Bindley
Co-stars: Will Patton Bonnie Bedelia Dabney Coleman

PEGGY BLOW

1982 PENITENTIARY 2
Director: Jamaa Fanaka
Co-stars: Leon Isaac Kennedy Ernie Hudson

SUSAN BLU

1988 FRIDAY THE 13TH: PART VII: THE NEW BLOOD
Director: John Carl Buechler
Co-stars: Jennifer Banko John Otrin

CORINE BLUE

1992   SAVAGE NIGHTS
Director: Cyril Collard
Co-stars: Cyril Collard Romane Bohringer Carlos Lopez

JEAN BLUE

1946   THE OVERLANDERS
Director: Harry Watt
Co-stars: Chips Rafferty Daphne Campbell John Heyward

1950   BITTER SPRINGS
Director: Ralph Smart
Co-stars: Chips Rafferty Tommy Trinder Gordon Jackson

ABBY BLUESTONE

1980   NIGHT OF THE JUGGLER
Director: Robert Butler
Co-stars: James Brolin Cliff Gorman Julie Carmen

BETIANA BLUM

1993   WE DON'T WANT TO TALK ABOUT IT
Director: Maria Luisa Bemberg
Co-stars: Marcello Mastroianni Alejandra Podesta

INA BLUM

1987   ANITA: DANCES OF VICE
Director: Rosa Von Praunheim
Co-stars: Lotti Huber Mikael Honesseau

1988   VIRGIN MACHINE
Director: Monika Treut
Co-stars: Marcelo Uriona Gad Klein Peter Kern

ERIKA BLUMBERGER

1989   ROSALIE GOES SHOPPING
Director: Percy Adlon
Co-stars: Marianne Sagebrecht Brad Davis Judge Reinhold

TABEA BLUMENSCHEIN

1981   TAXI ZUM KLO
Director: Frank Ripploh
Co-stars: Frank Ripploh Bernd Broaderup Magdelena Montezuma

MARGARET BLYE *(Maggie)*

1967   WATERHOLE NO 3
Director: William Graham
Co-stars: James Coburn Carroll O'Connor Joan Blondell

1968   DIAMONDS FOR BREAKFAST
Director: Christopher Morahan
Co-stars: Marcello Mastroianni Rita Tushingham

1969   THE ITALIAN JOB
Director: Peter Collinson
Co-stars: Michael Caine Noel Coward Benny Hill

1972   EVERY LITTLE CROOK AND NANNY
Director: Cy Howard
Co-stars: Victor Mature Lynn Redgrave Paul Sand

1973   ASH WEDNESDAY
Director: Larry Peerce
Co-stars: Elizabeth Taylor Henry Fonda Helmut Berger

1975   THE STREETFIGHTER
Director: Walter Hill
Co-stars: Charles Bronson James Coburn Jill Ireland

1976   MAYDAY AT 40,000 FEET!
Director: Robert Butler
Co-stars: David Janssen Ray Milland Jane Powell

1977   FINAL CHAPTER: WALKING TALL
Director: Jack Starrett
Co-star: Bo Svenson

1981   GOLDEN GATE
Director: Paul Wendkos
Co-stars: Jean Simmons Richard Kiley Perry King

1981   LIAR'S MOON
Director: David Fisher
Co-stars: Matt Dillon Cindy Fisher Yvonne De Carlo

1982   THE ENTITY
Director: Sidney Furie
Co-stars: Barbara Hershey Ron Silver George Coe

1985   MISCHIEF
Director: Mel Damski
Co-stars: Doug McKeon Chris Nash Kelly Preston

ANN BLYTH

Nominated For Best Supporting Actress In 1945 For "Mildred Pierce"

1944   CHIP OFF THE OLD BLOCK
Director: Charles Lamont
Co-stars: Donald O'Connor Peggy Ryan Patric Knowles

1944   BOWERY TO BROADWAY
Director: Charles Lamont
Co-stars: Jack Oakie Maria Montez Turhan Bey

1944   THE MERRY MONAHANS
Director: Charles Lamont
Co-stars: Jack Oakie Donald O'Connor Peggy Ryan

1945   MILDRED PIERCE
Director: Michael Curtiz
Co-stars: Joan Crawford Jack Carson Zachary Scott

1946   SWELL GUY
Co-star: Sonny Tufts

1947   KILLER McCOY
Director: Roy Rowland
Co-stars: Mickey Rooney Brian Donlevy James Dunn

1947   BRUTE FORCE
Director: Jules Dassin
Co-stars: Burt Lancaster Charles Bickford Hume Cronyn

1948   ANOTHER PART OF THE FOREST
Director: Michael Gordon
Co-stars: Fredric March Edmond O'Brien Dan Duryea

1948   A WOMAN'S VENGEANCE
Director: Zoltan Korda
Co-stars: Charles Boyer Jessica Tandy Cedric Hardwicke

1948   MR. PEABODY AND THE MERMAID
Director: Irving Pichell
Co-stars: William Powell Irene Hervey

1949   FREE FOR ALL
Director: Charles Barton
Co-stars: Robert Cummings Ray Collins Percy Kilbride

1949   ONCE MORE MY DARLING
Director: Robert Montgomery
Co-stars: Robert Montgomery Jane Cowl Charles McGraw

1949   RED CANYON
Director: George Sherman
Co-stars: Howard Duff George Brent Lloyd Bridges

1949   TOP O' THE MORNING
Director: David Miller
Co-stars: Bing Crosby Barry Fitzgerald John McIntyre

1950   OUR VERY OWN
Director: David Miller
Co-stars: Farley Granger Joan Evans Natalie Wood

1951   THUNDER ON THE HILL
Director: Douglas Sirk
Co-stars: Claudette Colbert Anne Crawfoed

1951   KATIE DID IT
Director: Russell Metty
Co-stars: Mark Stevens Cecil Kellaway Craig Stevens

1951   THE HOUSE IN THE SQUARE
Director: Roy Baker
Co-stars: Tyrone Power Michael Rennie Dennis Price

1951   THE GOLDEN HORDE
Director: George Sherman
Co-stars: David Farrar George Macready Richard Egan

1951   THE GREAT CARUSO
Director: Richard Thorpe
Co-stars: Mario Lanza Dorothy Kirsten Eduard Franz

1952   ONE MINUTE TO ZERO
Director: Tay Garnett
Co-stars: Robert Mitchum William Talman Charles McGraw

1952   SALLY AND ST. ANNE
Director: Rudolph Mate
Co-stars: Edmund Gwenn Hugh O'Brian John McIntyre

1952   THE WORLD IN HIS ARMS
Director: Raoul Walsh
Co-stars: Gregory Peck Anthony Quinn John McIntyre

1952   ROSE MARIE
Director: Mervyn LeRoy
Co-stars: Howard Keel Fernando. Lamas Bert Lahr

1953   ALL THE BROTHERS WERE VALIANT
Director: Richard Thorpe
Co-stars: Robert Taylor Stewart Granger

1954   THE STUDENT PRINCE
Director: Richard Thorpe
Co-stars: Edmund Purdom Edmund Gwenn Louis Calhern

1955   KISMET
Director: Vincente Minnelli
Co-stars: Howard Keel Dolores Gray Vic Damone

1956   SLANDER
Director: Roy Rowland
Co-stars: Van Johnson Steve Cochran Marjorie Rambeau

1956   THE KING'S THIEF
Director: Robert Z. Leonard
Co-stars: Edmund Purdom David Niven

1957   THE HELEN MORGAN STORY
Director: Michael Curtiz
Co-stars: Paul Newman Richard Carlson Alan King

1957   THE BUSTER KEATON STORY
Director: Sidney Sheldon
Co-stars: Donald O'Connor Rhonda Fleming

BETTY BLYTHE

1928   GLORIOUS BETSY
Director: Alan Crosland
Co-stars: Conrad Nagel Dolores Gostello John Miljan

1934   GIRL OF THE LIMBERLOST
Director: Christy Cabanne
Co-stars: Louise Dresser Ralph Morgan Marian Marsh

1941   HONKY TONK
Director: Jack Conway
Co-stars: Clark Gable Lana Turner Frank Morgan

1942   DAWN ON THE GREAT DIVIDE
Co-stars: Robert Fraser Raymond Hatton

1943   WHERE ARE YOUR CHILDREN?
Director: William Nigh
Co-stars: Jackie Cooper Gale Storm Patricia Morison

1943   BAR 20
Co-star: William Boyd

1944   THE CHINESE CAT
Director: Phil Rosen
Co-stars: Sidney Toler Benson Fong Joan Woodbury

1951   HOLLYWOOD STORY
Director: William Castle
Co-stars: Richard Conte Julie Adams Richard Egan

PEGGY BLYTHE

1933   THE CONSTANT NYMPH
Director: Basil Dean
Co-stars: Victoria Hopper Brian Aherne Jane Baxter

1934   EVER SINCE EVE
Co-stars: Mary Brian George Meeker

ELEANOR BOARDMAN *(Married King Vidor)*

1918   THE STRANGER'S BANQUET

1924   THE CENTAUR

1925   SINNERS IN SILK

1925   THE CIRCLE
Director: Frank Borzage
Co-stars: Creighton Hale Alec B. Francis

1926   BARDELYS THE MAGNFICENT

1926   TELL IT TO THE MARINES
Director: George Hill
Co-stars: Lon Chaney William Haines Carmel Myers

1927   THE CROWD
Director: King Vidor
Co-stars: James Murray Bert Roach Lucy Beaumont

1929   SHE GOES TO WAR

1930   REDEMPTION
Director: Fred Niblo
Co-stars: John Gilbert Renee Adoree Conrad Nagel

1930   MAMBA
Director: Al Rogell
Co-stars: Jean Hersholt Ralph Forbes

1931   THE FLOOD
Co-star: Monte Blue

1931   WOMEN LOVE ONCE
Co-star: Paul Lukas

1931   THE SQUAW MAN
Director: Cecil B. DeMille
Co-stars: Warner Baxter Lupe Velez Charles Bickford

1931   THE GREAT MEADOW
Director: Charles Brabin
Co-stars: John Mack Brown Lucille La Verne Anita Louise

1933   THE BIG CHANCE

ANNE BOBBY

1989   BORN ON THE FOURTH OF JULY
Director: Oliver Stone
Co-stars: Tom Cruise Bryan Larkin Willem Dafoe

1990   NIGHTBREED
Director: Clive Barker
Co-stars: Craig Sheffer David Cronenberg Hugh Ross

DELIA BOCCARDO

1968   INSPECTOR CLOUSEAU
Director: Bud Yorkin
Co-stars: Alan Arkin Frank Finlay Beryl Reid

1973   MASSACRE IN ROME
Director: George Pan Cosmatos
Co-stars: Richard Burton Marcello Mastroianni

1977　TENTACLES
Director:　Oliver Hellman
Co-stars:　Shelley Winters John Huston Henry Fonda

DOROTHEE BOEUF

1989　PIED PIPER
Director:　Norman Stone
Co-stars:　Peter O'Toole Mare Winningham Susan Wooldridge

SANDRA BOGAN

1989　LIMIT UP
Director:　Richard Martini
Co-stars:　Nancy Allen Dean Stockwell Ray Charles

LUCIENNE BOGEART

1946　LES DAMES DU BOIS DE BOULOGNE
Director:　Robert Bresson
Co-stars:　Maria Casares Paul Bernard

GAIL BOGGS

1990　GHOST
Director:　Jerry Zucker
Co-stars:　Patrick Swayze Demi Moore Whoopi Goldberg

1991　CURLY SUE
Director:　John Hughes
Co-stars:　Kelly Lynch James Belushi Alisan Porter

CHRISTINA BOHM

1979　LADY OSCAR
Director:　Jacques Demy
Co-stars:　Catriona Maccoll Barry Stokes Terence Budd

KATHARINA BOHM

1986　OF PURE BLOOD
Director:　Joseph Sargent
Co-stars:　Lee Remick Patrick McGoohan

CORRINE BOHRER

1988　VICE VERSA
Director:　Brian Gilbert
Co-stars:　Judge Reinhold Fred Savage Swoosie Kurtz

ROMAGNE BOHRINGER

1992　SAVAGE NIGHTS
Director:　Cyril Collard
Co-stars:　Cyril Collard Carlos Lopez Corine Blue

1992　L'ACCOMPAGNATRICE
Director:　Claude Miller
Co-stars:　Richard Bohringer Elane Safanova

1993　MINNA TANNENBAUM
Director:　Martine Dugowson
Co-stars:　Elsa Zylberstein

1997　BURNING UP
Director:　Julian Temple
Co-stars:　James Frain Diana Quick Jim Carter

JEAN BOHT

1988　ESKIMOS DO IT
Director:　Derek Lister
Co-stars:　Liz Fraser Ian Brimble Neil Pearson

1988　MISS MARPLE: 4.50 FROM PADDINGTON
Director:　Martyn Friend
Co-stars:　Joan Hickson Joanna David

CHRISTINE BOISSON

1974　EMMANUELLE
Director:　Just Jaeckin
Co-stars:　Sylvia Kristel Marika Green Alain Cuny

1986　THE PASSAGE
Director:　Rene Manzot
Co-stars:　Alain Delon Alain Musy MacKenzie Phillips

MARY BOLAND

1931　SECRETS OF A SECRETARY
Director:　George Abbott
Co-stars:　Claudette Colbert Herbert Marshall

1932　THE NIGHT OF JUNE 13TH,
Director:　Stephen Roberts
Co-stars:　Clive Brook Lila Lee Frances Dee

1932　IF I HAD A MILLION
Director:　Ernst Lubitsch
Co-stars:　Charles Laughton Gary Cooper George Raft

1932　EVENINGS FOR SALE
Director:　Stuart Walker
Co-stars:　Herbert Marshall Sari Maritza Charles Ruggles

1933　MAMA LOVES PAPA
Director:　Norman Z. McLeod
Co-stars:　Charles Ruggles Lilyan Tashman George Barbier

1933　THE SOLITAIRE MAN
Director:　Jack Conway
Co-stars:　Herbert Marshall Elizabeth Allan May Robson

1933　THREE-CORNERED MOON
Director:　Elliott Nugent
Co-stars:　Claudette Colbert Richard Arlen

1934　STINGAREE
Director:　William Wellman
Co-stars:　Irene Dunne Richard Dix Andy Devine

1934　DOWN TO THEIR LAST YACHT
Co-stars:　Marie Wilson Sterling Holloway

1934　SIX OF A KIND
Director:　Leo McCarey
Co-stars:　Charles Ruggles Burns & Allen W. C. Fields

1934　THE PURSUIT OF HAPPINESS
Director:　Alexander Hall
Co-stars:　Joan Bennett Charles Ruggles

1934　MELODY IN SPRING
Director:　Norman Z. McLeod
Co-stars:　Lanny Ross Charles Ruggles Ann Sothern

1934　FOUR FRIGHTENED PEOPLE
Director:　Cecil B. DeMille
Co-stars:　Claudette Colbert Herbert Marshall

1935　PEOPLE WILL TALK
Director:　Al Santell
Co-stars:　Charles Ruggles Leila Hyams Dean Jagger

1935　THE BIG BROADCAST OF 1936
Director:　Ben Glazer
Co-stars:　Burns & Allen Jack Oakie Bing Crosby

1935　RUGGLES OF RED GAP
Director:　Leo McCarey
Co-stars:　Charles Laughton Charles Ruggles Roland Young

1935　TWO FOR TONIGHT
Director:　Frank Tuttle
Co-stars:　Bing Crosby Joan Bennett Lynne Overman

1936　COLLEGE HOLIDAY
Director:　Frank Tuttle
Co-stars:　Jack Benny Burns & Allen Martha Raye

1936　EARLY TO BED
Co-stars:　Charles Ruggles Gail Patrick

1936　WIVES NEVER KNOW
Co-star:　Charles Ruggles

1937 DANGER-LOVE AT WORK
Director: Otto Preminger
Co-stars: Ann Sothern Jack Haley John Carradine

1937 MARRY THE GIRL
Director: William McGann
Co-stars: Frank Mchugh Hugh Herbert Mischa Auer

1937 THERE GOES THE GROOM
Director: Joseph Santley
Co-stars: Ann Sothern Burgess Meredith Onslow Stevens

1938 LITTLE TOUGH GUYS IN SOCIETY
Director: Erle Kenton
Co-stars: Mischa Auer Helen Parish

1938 ARTISTS AND MODELS ABROAD
Director: Mitchell Leisen
Co-stars: Jack Benny Joan Bennett

1939 BOY TROUBLE
Director: George Archainbaud
Co-stars: Charles Ruggles Donald O'Connor

1939 NIGHT WORK
Co-star: Charles Ruggles

1939 THE MAGNIFICENT FRAUD
Director: Robert Florey
Co-stars: Akim Tamiroff Lloyd Nolan Patricia Morison

1939 THE WOMEN
Director: George Cukor
Co-stars: Norma Shearer Joan Crawford Rosalind Russell

1940 PRIDE AND PREJUDICE
Director: Robert Z. Leonard
Co-stars: Laurence Olivier Greer Garson Edmund Gwenn

1940 NEW MOON
Director: Robert Z. Leonard
Co-stars: Jeanette MacDonald Nelson Eddy George Zucco

1940 HIT PARADE OF 1941
Director: John Auer
Co-stars: Kenny Baker Frances Langford Ann Miller

1940 ONE NIGHT IN THE TROPICS
Director: Edward Sutherland
Co-stars: Allan Jones Nancy Kelly Abbott & Costello

1940 HE MARRIED HIS WIFE
Director: Roy Del Ruth
Co-stars: Joel McCrea Nancy Kelly Roland Young

1944 IN OUR TIME
Director: Vincent Sherman
Co-stars: Ida Lupino Paul Henreid Nancy Coleman

1945 NOTHING BUT TROUBLE
Director: Sam Taylor
Co-stars: Laurel & Hardy Henry O'Neill David Leland

1948 JULIA MISBEHAVES
Director: Jack Conway
Co-stars: Greer Garson Walter Pidgeon Elizabeth Taylor

MAY BOLEY

1930 MOBY DICK
Director: Lloyd Bacon
Co-stars: John Barrymore Joan Bennett Lloyd Hughes

SHANNON BOLIN

1958 DAMN YANKEES
Director: George Abbott
Co-stars: Gwen Verdon Tab Hunter Ray Walston

FLORINDA BOLKAN

1969 THE DAMNED
Director: Luchino Visconti
Co-stars: Dirk Bogarde Ingrid Thulin Helmut Berger

1970 INVESTIGATION OF A CITIZEN ABOVE SUSPICION
Director: Elio Petri
Co-stars: Gian Maria Volonte Salvo Randone

1970 THE LAST VALLEY
Director: James Clavell
Co-stars: Michael Caine Omar Sharif Nigel Davenport

1975 ROYAL FLASH
Director: Richard Lester
Co-stars: Malcolm McDowell Oliver Reed Alan Bates

1988 SISTERS
Director: Michael Hoffman
Co-stars: Patrick Dempsey Jennifer Connelly Lila Kedrova

1988 PRISONER OF RIO
Director: Lech Majewski
Co-stars: Paul Freeman Steven Berkoff Peter Firth

ICIAR BOLLAN

1983 THE SOUTH
Director: Victor Erice
Co-stars: Omero Antonutti Lola Cardona Aurore Clement

TIFFANY BOLLING

1971 THE MARRIAGE OF A YOUNG STOCKBROKER
Director: Lawrence Turman
Co-stars: Richard Benjamin Joanna Shimkus

1975 THE WILD PARTY
Director: James Ivory
Co-stars: James Coco Raquel Welch Perry King

1977 KINGDOM OF THE SPIDERS
Director: John Cardos
Co-stars: William Shatner Woody Strode

EMILY BOLTON

1987 EMPIRE STATE
Director: Ron Peck
Co-stars: Cathryn Harrison Martin Landau Ray McAnally

ANITA BOLSTER
(Listed As Anita Sharp Bolster After 1949)

1942 THE LONDON BLACKOUT MURDERS
Director: George Sherman
Co-stars: John Abbott Mary McLeod

1945 MY NAME IS JULIA ROSS
Director: Joseph Lewis
Co-stars: Nina Foch May Whitty George Macready

1949 THE PERFECT WOMAN
Director: Bernard Knowles
Co-stars: Patricia Roc Nigel Patrick Miles Malleson

1959 THE MAN WHO LIKED FUNERALS
Director: David Eady
Co-stars: Leslie Phillips Susan Beaumont

CYNTHIA BOND

1990 DEF BY TEMPTATION
Director: James Bond III
Co-stars: James Bond III Bill Nunn Samuel L. Jackson

DEANNA BOND

1986 DOGS IN SPACE
Director: Richard Lowenstein
Co-stars: Michael Hutchence Saskia Post

LILLIAN BOND

1931 JUST A GIGOLO
Director: Jack Conway
Co-stars: William Haines Irene Purcell C. Aubrey Smith

1932 MAN ABOUT TOWN
Director: John Francis Dillon
Co-stars: Warner Baxter Karen Morley Alan Mowbray

1932 THE TRIAL OF VIVIENNE WARE
Director: William Howard
Co-stars: Joan Bennett Donald Cook Zasu Pitts

1932 THE OLD DARK HOUSE
Co-stars: Boris Karloff Charles Laughton Raymond Massey

1932 AIR MAIL
Director: John Ford
Co-stars: Pat O'Brien Ralph Bellamy Gloria Stuart

1932 BEAUTY AND THE BOSS
Director: Roy Del Ruth
Co-stars: Warren William Marian Marsh Frederick Kerr

1932 FIREMAN SAVE MY CHILD
Director: Lloyd Bacon
Co-stars: Joe E. Brown Evalyn Knapp

1932 HOT SATURDAY
Director: William Seiter
Co-stars: Nancy Carroll Cary Grant Randolph Scott

1933 DOUBLE HARNESS
Director: John Cromwell
Co-stars: Ann Harding William Powell Kay Hammond

1933 HOT PEPPER
Director: John Blystone
Co-stars: Edmund Lowe Victor McLaglen Lupe Velez

1933 PICK-UP
Director: Marion Gering
Co-stars: Sylvia Sidney George Raft William Harrigan

1934 HELL BENT FOR LOVE
Co-stars: Tim McCoy Lafe McKee

1934 DIRTY WORK
Director: Tom Walls
Co-stars: Ralph Lynn Gordon Harker Robertson Hare

1934 GIRL O' MY DREAMS
Co-stars: Edward Nugent Mary Carlisle

1938 BLONDE CHEAT
Co-stars: Joan Fontaine Derrick De Marney

1939 THE HOUSEKEEPER'S DAUGHTER
Director: Hal Roach
Co-stars: Joan Bennett Adolphe Menjou Victor Mature

1940 THE WESTENER
Director: William Wyler
Co-stars: Gary Cooper Walter Brennan Forrest Tucker

1942 DESPERATE CHANCE FOR ELLERY QUEEN
Director: James Hogan
Co-stars: William Gargan Margaret Lindsay

1953 THE MAZE
Director: William Cameron Menzies
Co-stars: Richard Carlson Veronica Hurst Michael Pate

1955 PIRATES OF TRIPOLI
Director: Felix Feist
Co-stars: Paul Henreid Patricia Medina John Miljan

SAMANTHA BOND

1986 MANSFIELD PARK
Director: David Giles
Co-stars: Sylvestra Le Touzel Anna Massey Bernard Hepton

1989 ONE WAY OUT
Director: Robert Young
Co-stars: Bob Peck Denis Lawson Lesley Nightingale

1989 THE GINGER TREE
Director: Anthony Garner
Co-stars: Daisuke Ryu Joanna McCallum Fumi Dan

1991 THE BLACK CANDLE
Director: Roy Battersby
Co-stars: Denholm Elliott Tara Fitzgerald Sian Phillips

1994 RETURN TO BLOOD RIVER
Director: Jane Howell
Co-stars: Kevin McNally Frances Barber Warren Clarke

1996 EMMA
Director: Andrew Davis
Co-stars: Kate Beckinsale Mark Strong Prunella Scales

1997 TOMORROW NEVER DIES
Co-stars: Pierce Brosnan Teri Hatcher Judi Dench

SHEILA BOND

1952 THE MARRYING KIND
Director: George Cukor
Co-stars: Judy Holliday Aldo Ray Madge Kennedy

SUDIE BOND

1982 COME BACK TO THE FIVE AND DIME, JIMMY DEAN, JIMMY DEAN
Director: Robert Altman
Co-star: Karen Black Cher Sandy Dennis Kathy Bates

1983 ENORMOUS CHANGES AT THE LAST MINUTE
Director: Mirra Bank
Co-stars: Ellen Barkin Kevin Bacon

1984 SWING SHIFT
Director: Jonathon Demme
Co-stars: Goldie Hawn Kurt Russell Christine Lahti

BEULAH BONDI

Nominated For Best Supporting Actress In 1936 For "The Gorgeous Hussy"
Nominated For Best Supporting Actress In 1938 For "Of Human Hearts"

1931 ARROWSMITH
Director: John Ford
Co-stars: Ronald Colman Helen Heyes Myrna Loy

1931 STREET SCENE
Director: King Vidor
Co-stars: Sylvia Sidney Estelle Taylor

1932 RAIN
Director: Lewis Milestone
Co-stars: Joan Crawford Walter Huston Guy Kibbee

1933 THE STRANGER'S RETURN
Director: King Vidor
Co-stars: Lionel Barrymore Miriam Hopkins Stuart Erwin

1933 CHRISTOPHER BEAN
Director: Sam Wood
Co-stars: Marie Dressler Lionel Barrymore Helen Mack

1934 FINISHING SCHOOL
Director: George Nicholls
Co-stars: Frances Dee Ginger Rogers Bruce Cabot

1934 THE PAINTED VEIL
Director: Richard Boleslavski
Co-stars: Greta Garbo Herbert Marshall

1934 TWO ALONE
Director: Elliott Nugent
Co-stars: Jean Parker Tom Brown Zasu Pitts

1935 THE INVISIBLE RAY
Director: Lambert Hillyer
Co-stars: Boris Karloff Bela Lugosi Frank Lawton

1935 THE GOOD FAIRY
Director: William Wyler
Co-stars: Margaret Sullavan Frank Morgan Alan Hale

1936 THE CASE AGAINST MRS. AMES
Director: William Seiter
Co-stars: Madeleine Carroll George Brent

1936 THE GORGEOUS HUSSY
Director: Clarence Brown
Co-stars: Joan Crawford Lionel Barrymore

1936 THE MOON'S OUR HOME
Director: William Seiter
Co-stars: Margaret Sullavan Henry Fonda

1937 MAID OF SALEM
Director: Frank Lloyd
Co-stars: Claudette Colbert Gale Sondergaard

1937 MAKE WAY FOR TOMORROW
Director: Leo McCarey
Co-stars: Victor Moore Thomas Mitchell

1938 OF HUMAN HEARTS
Director: Clarence Brown
Co-stars: Walter Huston James Stewart Guy Kibbee

1938 THE SISTERS
Director: Antole Litvak
Co-stars: Bette Davis Errol Flynn Donald Crisp

1938 THE BUCHANEER
Director: Cecil B. De Mille
Co-stars: Fredric March Franciska Gaal Akim Tamiroff

1938 VIVACIOUS LADY
Director: George Stevens
Co-stars: Ginger Rogers James Stewart Grady Sutton

1939 THE UNDERPUP
Director: Richard Wallace
Co-stars: Gloria Jean Robert Cummings Nan Grey

1939 ON BORROWED TIME
Director: Harold Bucquet
Co-stars: Lionel Barrymore Cedric Hardwicke

1939 MR. SMITH GOES TO WASHINGTON
Director: Frank Capra
Co-stars: James Stewart Jean Arthur

1940 THE CAPTAIN IS A LADY
Director: Robert Sinclair
Co-stars: Charles Coburn Billie Burke Dan Dailey

1940 OUR TOWN
Director: Sam Wood
Co-stars: William Holden Martha Scott Thomas Mitchell

1940 REMEMBER THE NIGHT
Director: Mitchell Leisen
Co-stars: Barbara Stanwyck Fred MacMurray

1941 SHEPHERD OF THE HILLS
Director: Henry Hathaway
Co-stars: John Wayne Betty Field Harry Carey

1941 PENNY SERENADE
Director: George Stevens
Co-stars: Irene Dunne Cary Grant Edgar Buchanan

1941 ONE FOOT IN HEAVEN
Director: Irving Rapper
Co-stars: Fredric March Martha Scott

1943 TONIGHT WE RAID CALAIS
Director: John Brahm
Co-stars: John Sutton Annabella Lee J. Cobb

1943 WATCH ON THE RHINE
Director: Herman Shumlin
Co-stars: Paul Lucas Bette Davis Lucile Watson

1944 THE VERY THOUGHT OF YOU
Director: Delmer Daves
Co-stars: Dennis Morgan Eleanor Parker Dane Clark

1944 OUR HEARTS WERE YOUNG AND GAY
Director: Lewis Allen
Co-stars: Gail Russell Diana Lynn

1944 I LOVE A SOLDIER
Director: Mark Sandrich
Co-stars: Paulette Goddard Sonny Tufts

1944 AND NOW TOMORROW
Director: Irving Pichel
Co-stars: Loretta Young Alan Ladd

1945 BREAKFAST IN HOLLYWOOD
Director: Harold Schuster
Co-stars: Bonita Granville Tom Breneman Zasu Pitts

1945 BACK TO BATAAN
Director: Edward Dmytryk
Co-stars: John Wayne Anthony Quinn Lawrence Tierney

1945 THE SOUTHERNER
Director: Jean Renoir
Co-stars: Zachary Scott Betty Field J. Carrol Naish

1946 SISTER KENNY
Director: Dudley Nichols
Co-stars: Rosalind Russell Alexander Knox

1946 IT'S A WONDERFUL LIFE
Director: Frank Capra
Co-stars: James Stewart Donna Reed Henry Travers

1947 HIGH CONQUEST
Director: Irving Allen
Co-stars: Anna Lee Gilbert Roland C. Aubrey Smith

1948 THE LIFE OF RILEY
Director: Irving Brecher
Co-stars: William Bendix James Gleason John Brown

1948 SO DEAR TO MY HEART
Director: Harold Schuster
Co-stars: Burl Ives Bobby Driscoll Luana Patten

1948 THE SNAKE PIT
Director: Anatole Litvak
Co-stars: Olivia De Havilland Leo Genn Mark Stevens

1948 THE SAINTED SISTERS
Director: William Russell
Co-stars: Veronica Lake Joan Caulfield

1949 MR. SOFT TOUCH
Director: Henry Levin
Co-stars: Glenn Ford Evelyn Keyes John Ireland

1949 THE BLACK BOOK
Director: Anthony Mann
Co-stars: Robert Cummings Arlene Dahl

1950 THE BARON OF ARIZONA
Director: Sam Fuller
Co-stars: Vincent Price Ellen Drew Reed Hadley

1951 THE FURIES
Director: Anthony Mann
Co-stars: Barbara Stanwyck Walter Huston

1952 LONE STAR
Director: Vincent Sherman
Co-stars: Clark Gable Ava Gardner Ed Begley

1953 LATIN LOVERS
Director: Mervyn LeRoy
Co-stars: Lana Turner Ricardo Montalban John Lund

1954 TRACK OF THE CAT
Director: William Wellman
Co-stars: Robert Mitchum Diana Lynn Tab Hunter

1956 BACK FROM ETERNITY
Director: John Farrow
Co-stars: Robert Ryan Rod Steiger Anita Ekberg

1957 THE UNHOLY WIFE
Director: John Farrow
Co-stars: Diana Dors Rod Steiger Marie Windsor

1959 THE BIG FISHERMAN
Director: Rowland Lee
Co-stars: Howard Keel Susan Kohner Martha Hyer

1961 TAMMY TELL ME TRUE
Director: Henry Keller
Co-stars: Sandra Dee John Gavin Cecil Kellaway

1959 A SUMMER PALACE
Director: Delmer Daves
Co-stars: Sandra Dee Dorothy McGuire Richard Egan

1963 TAMMY AND THE DOCTOR
Director: Henry Keller
Co-stars: Sandra Dee Peter Fonda MacDonald Carey

1962 THE WONDERFUL WORLD OF THE BROTHERS GRIM
Director: Henry Levin
Co-stars: Laurence Harvey Karl Boehm Claire Bloom

LISA BONET

1987 ANGEL HEART
Director: Alan Parker
Co-stars: Mickey Rourke Robert De Niro Charlotte Rampling

1994 FINAL COMBINATION
Director: Nigel Dick
Co-stars: Gary Stretch Michael Madsen Tim Russ

1994 NEW EDEN
Director: Alan Metzger
Co-stars: Stephen Baldwin Tobin Bell

HELENA BONHAM CARTER

1985 A ROOM WITH A VIEW
Director: James Ivory
Co-stars: Maggie Smith Denholm Elliott Daniel Day-Lewis

1986 LADY JANE
Director: Trevor Nunn
Co-stars: Cary Elwes John Wood Jill Bennett

1987 A HAZARD OF HEARTS
Director: John Hough
Co-stars: Diana Rigg Edward Fox Fiona Fullerton

1987 THE VISION
Director: Norman Stone
Co-stars: Dirk Bogarde Lee Remick Eileen Atkins

1988 LA MASCHERA
Director: Fiorella Infascelli
Co-stars: Michael Maloney Feodor Chaliapan

1989 GETTING IT RIGHT
Director: Randal Kleiser
Co-stars: Jesse Birdsall John Gielgud Jane Horrocks

1991 HAMLET
Director: Franco Zeffirelli
Co-stars: Mel Gibson Alan Bates Paul Scofield

1991 WHERE ANGELS FEAR TO TREAD
Director: Charles Sturridge
Co-stars: Helen Mirren Judy Davis

1994 A DARK ADAPTED EYE
Director: Tim Fywell
Co-stars: Robin Ellis Sophie Ward Celia Imrie

1992 HOWARDS END
Director: James Ivory
Co-stars: Anthony Hopkins Vanessa Redgrave Emma Thompson

1996 WINGS OF A DOVE
Director: Iain Softley
Co-stars: Linus Roache Alison Elliot

1996 TWELFTH NIGHT
Director: Trvor Nunn
Co-stars: Richard E. Grant Nigel Hawthorne Imogen Stubbs

1996 MIGHTY APHRODITE
Director: Woody Allen
Co-stars: Woody Allen Mira Sorvino

1997 KEEP THE ASPIDISTRA FLYING
Director: Robert Bierman
Co-stars: Richard E. Grant Harriet Walter Liz Smith

1997 MARGARET'S MUSEUM
Co-stars: Kate Nellisan Clive Russell

1997 CHINESE PORTRAITS

SANDRINE BONNAIRE

1985 POLICE
Director: Maurice Pialat
Co-stars: Gerard Depardieu Sophie Marceau Richard Ancanina

1987 UNDER SATAN'S SUN
Director: Maurice Pialat
Co-stars: Gerard Depardieu Maurice Pialat Alain Artur

1989 MONSIEUR HIRE
Director: Patrice Leconte
Co-stars: Michel Blanc Andre Wilms Luc Thuller

1990 CAPTIVE OF THE DESERT
Director: Raymond Depardon
Co-stars: Dobi Kore Isai Kore Fadi Taha

1992 PRAGUE
Director: Ian Sellar
Co-stars: Alan Cumming Brune Ganz Henri Meliss

1995 LA CEREMONIE
Director: Claude Chabrol
Co-stars: Isabelle Huppert Jean-Pierre Cassel

VIVIAN BONNELL

1991 THE JOSEPHINE BAKER STORY
Director: Brian Gibson
Co-stars: Lynn Whitfield Ruben Blades David Duke'

BEVERLEY BONNER

1982 BASKET CASE
Director: Frank Henenlotter
Co-stars: Kevin Van Hentenryck Terri Susan Smith

1990 BASKET CASE 2
Director: Frank Henenlotter
Co-stars: Kevin Van Hentenryck Judy Grafe Annie Ross

PRISCILLA BONNER

1926 THE STRONG MAN
Director: Frank Capra
Co-stars: Harry Langdon Getrude Astor Tay Garnett

1927 LONG PANTS
Director: Frank Capra
Co-stars: Harry Langdon Gladys Brockwell Alma Bennett

MARIA BONNERIE

1992 THE POLAR BEAR KING
Director: Ola Solum
Co-star: Jack Fieldstad

SUSIE BONO

1984 BREAKDANCE 2: ELECTRIC BOOGALOO
Director: Sam Firstenberg
Co-stars: Lucinda Dickey Michael Chambers

JANE BOOKER

1988   **A PERFECT SPY**
Director: Peter Smith
Co-stars: Alec Guinness Peggy Ashcroft Peter Egan

1989   **VIRTUOSO**
Director: Tony Smith
Co-stars: Alfred Molina Alison Steadman John Heard

DEBBY BOONE

1984   **SINS OF THE PAST**
Director: Peter Hunt
Co-stars: Barbara Carrera Kirstie Alley Kim Cattrall

LIBBY BOONE

1977   **FINAL CHAPTER: WALKING TALL**
Director: Jack Starrett
Co-stars: Bo Svenson Margaret Blye

IMOGEN BOORMAN *(Child)*

1985   **DREAMCHILD**
Director: Gavin Miller
Co-stars: Coral Browne Jane Asher Peter Gallagher

1988   **HELLBOUND HELLRAISER II**
Director: Tony Randel
Co-stars: Clare Higgins Kenneth Cranham

1991   **ALIVE AND KICKING**
Director: Robert Young
Co-stars: Lenny Henry Robbie Coltrane Jane Horrocks

KATRINE BOORMAN *(Child)*

1984   **DREAM ONE**
Director: Arnaud Selignac
Co-stars: Jason Connery Charley Boorman

1988   **CAMILLE CLAUDEL**
Director: Bruno Nuytten
Co-stars: Isabelle Adjani Gerard Depardieu Alain Cuny

ADRIAN BOOTH

1946   **LAST FRONTIER UPRISING**
Co-stars: Monte Hale James Taggert

1946   **VALLEY OF THE ZOMBIES**
Co-star: Ian Keith

1949   **THE LAST BANDIT**
Co-stars: Bill Elliott Jack Holt Andy Devine

CONNIE BOOTH *(Married John Cleese)*

1972   **AND NOW FOR SOMETHING COMPLETELY DIFFERENT**
Director: Ian McNaughton
Co-stars: John Cleese Eric Idle Terry Jones

1975   **MONTY PYTHON AND THE HOLY GRAIL**
Director: Terry Jones
Co-stars: Terry Jones Terry Gilliam John Cleese

1986   **PAST CARING**
Director: Richard Eyre
Co-stars: Denholm Elliott Emlyn Williams Joan Greenwood

1987   **THE RETURN OF SHERLOCK HOLMES**
Director: Kevin Connor
Co-stars: Michael Pennington Margaret Colin

1988   **HIGH SPIRITS**
Director: Neil Jordan
Co-stars: Daryl Hannah Peter O'Toole Liam Neeson

1988   **HAWKS**
Director: Robert Ellis Miller
Co-stars: Timothy Dalton Anthony Edwards Janet Mcteer

1990   **THE WORLD OF EDDIE WEARY**
Director: Alan Grint
Co-stars: Ray Brooks Celia Imrie Brian Glover

1991   **AMERICAN FRIENDS**
Director: Tristram Powell
Co-stars: Michael Palin Trini Alvarado

EDWINA BOOTH

1930   **TRADER HORN**
Director: W. S. Van Dyke
Co-stars: Harry Carey Duncan Reynaldo C. Aubrey Smith

KARIN BOOTH

1947   **THE UNFINISHED DANCE**
Director: Henry Koster
Co-stars: Margaret O'Brien Cyd Charisse Danny Thomas

1948   **THE BIG CITY**
Director: Norman Taurog
Co-stars: Margaret O'Brien Danny Thomas George Murphy

1950   **THE CARIBOO TRAIL**
Director: Edwin Marin
Co-stars: Randolph Scott Gabby Hayes Bill Williams

1950   **THE LAST OF THE BUCCANEERS**
Director: Lew Landers
Co-stars: Paul Henreid Jack Oakie Mary Anderson

1952   **CRIPPLE CREEK**
Director: Ray Nazzaro
Co-stars: George Montgomery Jerome Courtland Richard Egan

1953   **CHARGE OF THE LANCERS**
Director: William Castle
Co-stars: Paulette Goddard Jean-Pierre Aumont

1957   **THE CROOKED SKY**
Director: Henry Cass
Co-star: Wayne Morris

1959   **BELOVED INFIDEL**
Director: Henry King
Co-stars: Gregory Peck Deborah Kerr Eddie Albert

SHIRLEY BOOTH
Oscar For Best Actress In 1952 For "Come Back Little Sheba"

1952   **COME BACK, LITTLE SHEBA**
Director: Daniel Mann
Co-stars: Burt Lancaster Terry Moore

1953   **MAIN STREET TO BROADWAY**
Director: Tay Garnett
Co-stars: Tom Morton Mary Murphy Rex Harrison

1954   **ABOUT MRS. LESLIE**
Director: Daniel Mann
Co-stars: Robert Ryan Alex Nicol Marjie Millar

1958   **THE MATCHMAKER**
Director: Joseph Anthony
Co-stars: Anthony Perkins Shirley MacLaine Paul Ford

1958   **HOT SPELL**
Director: Daniel Mann
Co-stars: Anthony Quinn Shirley MacLaine Eileen Heckart

1968   **THE SMUGGLERS**
Director: Norman Lloyd
Co-stars: Kurt Kasznar Charles Drake Carol Lynley

CATERINA BORATTO

1965   **JULIET OF THE SPIRITS**
Director: Federico Fellini
Co-stars: Giulietta Masina Mario Pisu

1975   **SALO OR THE 120 DAYS OF SODOM**
Director: Pier Paolo Pasolini
Co-stars: Paolo Bonacelli Giorgio Cataldi

PAOLA BORBONI

1980 LA CAGE AUX FOLLES II
Director: Edouard Molinaro
Co-stars: Ugo Tognazzi Michel Serrault

1982 YES, GIORGIO
Director: Franklin Schaffner
Co-stars: Luciano Pavarotti Kathryn Harold Eddie Albert

CORNELL BORCHERS

1950 THE BIG LIFT
Director: George Seaton
Co-stars: Montgomery Clift Paul Douglas

1954 THE DIVIDED HEART
Director: Charles Crichton
Co-stars: Yvonne Mitchell Alexander Knox

1956 NEVER SAY GOODBYE
Director: Jerry Hopper
Co-stars: Rock Hudson George Sanders David Janssen

1956 ISTANBUL
Director: Joseph Pevney
Co-stars: Errol Flynn John Bentley Torin Thatcher

1956 OASIS
Director: Yves Allegret
Co-stars: Pierre Brasseur Michele Morgan

1958 FLOODTIDE
Director: Abner Biberman
Co-stars: George Nader Michel Ray Joanna Moore

BRIGITTE BORCHERT

1929 PEOPLE ON SUNDAY
Director: Robert Siodmak
Co-stars: Christl Ehlers Annie Schreyer

LYNN BORDEN

1972 FROGS
Director: George McCowan
Co-stars: Ray Milland Joan Van Ark Judy Pace

1973 AIRPORT S.O.S. HIJACK
Director: Barry Pollack
Co-stars: Adam Roarke Neville Brand

IRENE BORDONI

1929 PARIS
Director: Clarence Badger
Co-stars: Jack Buchanan Jason Robards Louise Closser

1929 SHOW OF SHOWS
Director: John Adolfi
Co-stars: Frank Fay Douglas Fairbanks Jnr. Lupino Lane

1941 LOUISIANA PURCHASE
Director: Irving Cummings
Co-stars: Bob Hope Vera Zorina Victor Moore

CARLA BORELLI

1985 O. C. AND STIGGS
Director: Robert Altman
Co-stars: Paul Dooley Jane Curtin Ray Walston

VEDA ANN BORG

1930 OVER THE WALL
Director: Frank MacDonald
Co-stars: Dick Foran John Litel June Travis

1937 SAN QUENTIN
Director: Lloyd Bacon
Co-stars: Pat O'Brien Humphrey Bogart Ann Sheridan

1940 BITTER SWEET
Director: W. S. Van Dyke
Co-stars: Jeanette MacDonald Nelson Eddy George Sanders

1943 REVENGE OF THE ZOMBIES
Director: Steve Sekeley
Co-stars: John Carradine Gale Storm

1943 UNKNOWN GUEST
Director: Kurt Neuman
Co-stars: Victor Jory Pamela Blake Harry Hayden

1943 MURDER IN TIMES SQUARE

1943 ISLE OF FORGOTTEN SINS
Director: Edgar Ulmer
Co-stars: John Carradine Gale Sondergaard Sidney Toler

1944 THE FALCON IN HOLLYWOOD
Co-stars: Tom Conway Frank Jenks Emory Parnell

1944 THE BIG NOISE
Director: Mal St Clair
Co-stars: Doris Merrick Arthur Space Jack Norton

1944 IRISH EYES ARE SMILING
Director: Gregory Ratoff
Co-stars: Dick Haymes June Haver Monty Woolley

1945 FOG ISLAND
Director: Terry Morse
Co-stars: George Zucco Lionel Atwill Jerome Cowan

1945 ROUGH, TOUGH AND READY
Director: Del Lord
Co-stars: Victor McLaglen Chester Morris Jean Rogers

1945 WHAT A BLONDE
Co-stars: Michael St Angel Elaine Riley

1945 SCARED STIFF
Director: Frank McDonald
Co-stars: Jack Haley Ann Savage Barton MacLaine

1946 THE FABULOUS SUZANNE
Co-stars: Otto Kruger Bill Henry Rudy Vallee

1946 LIFE WITH BLONDIE
Director: Abby Berlin
Co-stars: Penny Slngleton Arthur Lake Marc Lawrence

1947 MOTHER WORE TIGHTS
Director: Walter Lang
Co-stars: Betty Grable Dan Dailey Mona Freeman

1949 MISSISSIPPI RHYTHM
Co-star: Jimmie Davis

1950 RIDER FROM TUCSON
Director: Lesley Selander
Co-stars: Tim Holt Richard Martin Douglas Fowley

1952 AARON SLICK FROM PUNKIN CRICK
Director: Claude Binyon
Co-stars: Alan Young Dinah Shore

1952 BIG JIM McLAIN
Director: Edward Ludwig
Co-stars: John Wayne Nancy Olson James Arness

1953 MR SCOUTMASTER
Director: Henry Levln
Co-stars: Clifton Webb Edmund Gwenn Frances Dee

1953 THREE SAILORS AND A GLRL
Director: Roy Del Ruth
Co-stars: Jane Powell Gordon MacRae Gene Nelson

1955 YOU'RE NEVER TOO YOUNG
Director: Norman Taurog
Co-stars: Martin & Lewis Diana Lynn Nina Foch

NELLY BORGEAUD

1977   THE MAN WHO LOVED WOMEN
Director: Francois Truffaut
Co-stars: Charles Denner Leslie Caron

HILDA BORGSTROM

1921   THY SOUL SHALL BEAR WITNESS
Director: Victor Sjostrom
Co-stars: Victor Sjostrom Astrid Holm

1948   MUSIC IS MY FUTURE
Director: Ingmar Bergman
Co-stars: Mai Zetterling Birger Malmsten

CAROL BORLANLD

1935   MARK OF THE VAMPIRE
Director: Tod Browning
Co-stars: Lionel Barrymore Elizabeth Allan Bela Lugosi

FERIKA BOROS

1940   LA CONGA NIGHTS
Co-stars: Constance Moore Dennis O'Keefe

1942   THE PIED PIPER
Director: Irving Pichel
Co-stars: Monty Woolley Anne Baxter Roddy McDowall

1945   A TREE GROWS IN BROOKLYN
Director: Elia Kazan
Co-stars: Dorothy McGuire James Dunn Joan Blondell

KATHERINE BOROWITZ

1989   FELLOW TRAVELLER
Director: Philip Saville
Co-stars: Ron Silver Imogen Stubbs Hart Bochner

1990   JUST LIKE IN THE MOVIES
Director: Bram Towbin
Co-stars: Jay O. Sanders Alan Ruck

1991   MEN OF RESPECT
Director: William Reilly
Co-stars: John Turturro Rod Steiger Peter Boyle

1992   MAC
Director: John Turturro
Co-stars: John Turturro Michael Badalucco Ellen Barkin

JENNY BOS

1972   HENRY VIII AND HIS SIX WIVES
Director: Waris Hussein
Co-stars: Keith Michell Jane Asher Frances Cuka

LYDIA BOSCH

1987   JARRAPELLEJOS
Director: Antonio Gimenez Rico
Co-stars: Antonio Ferandis Juan Diego

GIULIA BOSCHI

1987   THE SICILIAN
Director: Michael Cimino
Co-stars: Christopher Lambert Terence Stamp Joss Ackland

1988   CHOCOLAT
Director: Claire Denis
Co-stars: Isaach De Bankole Francois Cluzet

LUCIA BOSE

1950   NO PEACE AMONG THE OLIVES
Director: Giuseppe De Santis
Co-stars: Raf Vallone Folco Lulli

1955   DEATH OF A CYCLIST
Director: Juan Antonio Bardem
Co-stars: Alberto Closas Otello Toso

1955   CELA S'APPELLE L'AURORE
Director: Luis Bunuel
Co-stars: Georges Marchal Gianni Esposito

1969   SATYRICON
Director: Federico Fellini
Co-stars: Martin Potter Hiram Keller Capucine

1976   LUMIERE
Director: Jean Moreau
Director: Jean Moreau Francine Racette Bruno Ganz

1987   CHRONICLE OF A DEATH FORTOLD
Director: Francesco Rosi
Co-stars: Rupert Everett Ornella Muti Irene Papas

VIRGINIA BOSLER

1954   BRIGADOON
Director: Vincente Minnelli
Co-stars: Gene Kelly Cyd Charisse Van Johnson

CAITLIN BOSSLEY

1992   CRUSH
Director: Alison MacLean
Co-stars: Marcia Gay Harden William Zappa Donagh Rees

BARBARA BOSSON

1984   THE CALENDAR GIRL MURDERS
Director: William Graham
Co-stars: Sharon Stone Tom Skerritt Robert Culp

1984   THE LAST STARFIGHTER
Director: Nick Castle
Co-stars: Robert Preston Lance Guest Dan O'Herlihy

1985   HOSTAGE FLIGHT
Director: Steven Hilliard Stern
Co-stars: Ned Beatty Jack Gilford John Karlen

CONNEE BOSWELL

1941   KISS THE BOYS GOODBYE
Director: Victor Schwertzinger
Co-stars: Don Ameche Mary Martin Oscar Levant

1942   SYNCOPATION
Director: William Dieterle
Co-stars: Jackie Cooper Adolphe Menjou Bonita Granville

SARA BOTSFORD

1981   BY DESIGN
Director: Claude Jutra
Co-stars: Patty Duke Saul Rubinek Sonia Zimmer

1982   STILL OF THE NIGHT
Director: Robert Benton
Co-stars: Roy Scheider Meryl Streep Jessica Tandy

1986   JUMPIN' JACK FLASH
Director: Penny Marshall
Co-stars: Whoopi Goldberg Stephen Collins Carol Kane

1994   MY BREAST
Director: Betty Thomas
Co-stars: Meredith Baxter Jamey Sheridan Barbara Barrie

SHERRY BOUCHER

1976   LASSIE: THE MIRACLE
Director: Jack Wrather
Co-stars: Skip Burton Larry Wilcox

BARBARA BOUCHET

1966 AGENT FOR H.A.R.M.
Director: Gerd Oswald
Co-stars: Wendell Corey Martin Kosleck Carl Esmond

1967 DANGER ROUTE
Director: Seth Holt
Co-stars: Richard Johnson Diana Dors Carol Lynley

1983 THE SCARLET AND THE BLACK
Director: Jerry London
Co-stars: Gregory Peck John Gielgud Raf Vallone

CHILI BOUCHIER

1928 SHOOTING STARS
Director: Anthony Asquith
Co-stars: Brian Aherne Annette Benson Donald Calthrop

1935 GET OFF MY FOOT
Director: William Beaudine
Co-stars: Max Miller Morland Graham Jane Carr

1937 GYPSY
Director: Roy William Neill
Co-stars: Roland Young Hugh Williams Frederick Burtwell

1939 THE MIND OF MR REEDER
Director: Jack Raymond
Co-stars: Will Fyffe Kay Walsh George Curzon

1945 MURDER IN REVERSE
Director: Montgomery Tully
Co-stars: William Hartnell Jimmy Hanley Dinah Sheridan

1949 OLD MOTHER RILEY'S NEW VENTURE
Director: John Harlow
Co-stars: Arthur Lucan Sebastian Cabot

1949 THE CASE OF CHARLES PEARCE
Director: Norman Lee
Co-stars: Valentine Dyall Bruce Belfrage

DOROTHY BOUCHIER

1931 CARNIVAL
Director: Herbert Wilcox
Co-stars: Matheson Lang Joseph Schildkraut Kay Hammond

EVELYNE BOUIX

1981 BOLERO
Director: Claude Lelouche
Co-stars: James Caan Geraldine Chaplin Nicole Garcia

1986 A MAN AND A WOMAN: 20 YEARS LATER
Director: Claude Lelouche
Co-stars: Anouk Aimee Jean-Louis Trintignant

PATTI BOULAYE

1979 HUSSY
Director: Matthew Chapman
Co-stars: Helen Mirren John Shea Jenny Runacre

ROSALYN BOULTER

1943 RHYTHM SERENADE
Director: Gordon Wellesley
Co-stars: Vera Lynn Jimmy Jewel Ben Warris

1946 GEORGE IN CIVVY STREET
Director: Marcel Varnel
Co-stars: George Formby Ronald Shiner Ian Fleming

1948 FOR THEM THAT TRESPASS
Director: Alberto Cavalcanti
Co-stars: Richard Todd Joan Dowling Patricia Plunkett

INGRID BOULTING

1976 THE LAST TYCOON
Director: Elia Kazan
Co-stars: Robert De Niro Robert Mitchum Tony Curtis

CAROLE BOUQUET
(Partner Of Gerard Depardieu)

1977 THAT OBSCURE OBJECT OF DESIRE
Director: Luis Bunuel
Co-stars: Fernando Rey Angela Molina

1981 FOR YOUR EYES ONLY
Director: John Glen
Co-stars: Roger Moore Topol Julian Glover

1989 TROP BELLE POUR TOI!
Director: Bertrand Blier
Co-stars: Gerard Depardieu Josiane Balasko

1993 TANGO
Director: Patrice Leconte
Co-stars: Thierry L'Hermitte Miou-Miou Philippe Noiret

1994 A BUSINESS AFFAIR
Director: Charlotte Brandstrom
Co-stars: Christopher Walken Jonathan Pryce

1996 LUCIE AUBRAC
Co-star: Daniel Auteuil

LISE BOURDIN

1954 WOMAN OF THE RIVER
Director: Mario Soldati
Co-stars: Sophia Loren Gerard Oury Rik Battaglia

1957 LOVE IN THE AFTERNOON
Director: Billy Wilder
Co-stars: Gary Cooper Audrey Hepburn Maurice Chevalier

CORINNE BOURDON

1992 VAN GOGH
Director: Maurice Pialat
Co-stars: Jacques Dutronc Alexandra London

ELIZABETH BOURGINE

1992 UN COEUR EN HIVER
Director: Claude Sautet
Co-stars: Daniel Auteuill Emmanuelle Beart Myriam Boyer

BETTE BOURNE

1992 A LITTLE BIT OF LIPPY
Director: Chris Bernard
Co-stars: Kenneth Cranham Rachel Davies Tina Earl

HELEN WHITNEY BOURNE

1937 HEAD OVER HEELS
Director: Sonnie Hale
Co-stars: Jessie Matthews Robert Flemyng Romney Brent

WHITNEY BOURNE

1934 CRIME WITHOUT PASSION
Director: Ben Hecht
Co-stars: Claude Rans Stanley Ridge Margo

1936 ONCE IN A BLUE MOON
Director: Ben Hecht
Co-stars: Jimmy Savi Nikita Balieff Cecilia Loftus

1937 FLIGHT FROM GLORY
Director: Lew Landers
Co-stars: Chester Morris Van Heflin Onslow Stevens

1938 THE MAD MISS MANTON
Director: Leigh Jason
Co-stars: Barbara Stanwyck Henry Fonda Sam Levene

JOY BOUSHEL

1981 HUMONGOUS
Director: Paul Lynch
Co-stars: Janet Julian David Wallace Janit Baldwin

1986   **THE FLY**
Director: David Cronenberg
Co-stars: Jeff Goldblum Geena Davis John Getz

ZINA BOUZAIANE

1957   **GOHA**
Director: Jacques Baratier
Co-stars: Omar Sharif Lauro Gozzolo

JULIE BOVASSO

1977   **SATURDAY NIGHT FEVER**
Director: John Badham
Co-stars: John Travolta Karen Lynn Gorney

1978   **THE LAST TENANT**
Director: Jud Taylor
Co-stars: Tony LoBianco Lee Strasberg Christine Lahti

1980   **KING CRAB**
Director: Marvln Chomsky
Co-stars: Barry Newman Gail Strickland Joel Fabian

1980   **WILLIE AND PHIL**
Director: Paul Mazursky
Co-stars: Michael Ontkean Margot Kidder Ray Sharkey

1982   **THE VERDICT**
Director: Sidney Lumet
Co-stars: Paul Newman Charlotte Rampling James Mason

1983   **STAYING ALIVE**
Director: Sylvester Stallone
Co-stars: John Travolta Cynthia Rhodes Finola Hughes

1983   **DANIEL**
Director: Sidney Lumet
Co-stars: Timothy Hutton Mandy Patinkin Lindsay Crouse

1986   **A TIME TO TRIUMPH**
Director: Noel Black
Co-stars: Patty Duke Joseph Bologna

1987   **MOONSTRUCK**
Director: Norman Jewison
Co-stars: Cher Nicolas Cage Danny Aiello

MARIA BOVINO

1993   **BLACK DAISIES FOR THE BRIDE**
Director: Peter Symes
Co-stars: Elaine Hallam Cathryn Bradshaw

BRUNELLA BOVO

1951   **MIRACLE IN MILAN**
Director: Vittorio De Sica
Co-stars: Francesco Golisano Paolo Stoppa

CLARA BOW

1926   **KISS ME AGAIN**
Director: Ernst Lubitsch
Co-stars: Marie Prevost Monte Blare John Roach

1926   **MANTRAP**
Director: William Wellman
Co-stars: Ernest Torrence Eugene Pallette

1927   **WINGS**
Director: William Wellman
Co-stars: Charles Buddy Rogers Richard Arlen

1927   **IT**
Director: Clarence Badger
Co-stars: Antonio Moreno Gary Cooper

1929   **DANGEROUS CURVES**
Director: Lothar Mendes
Co-stars: Richard Arlen Kay Francis

1929   **THE WILD PARTY**
Director: Dorothy Arzner
Co-stars: Fredric March Shirley O'Hara

1930   **PARAMOUNT ON PARADE**
Director: Ernst Lubitsch
Co-stars: Jean Arthur Gary Cooper Jack Oakie

1930   **LOVE AMONG THE MILLIONAIRES**
Director: Frank Tuttle
Co-stars: Stanley Smith Mltzi Green

1930   **HER WEDDING NIGHT**
Director: Frank Tuttle
Co-stars: Charles Ruggles Skeets Gallagher

1930   **TRUE TO THE NAVY**
Director: Frank Tuttle
Co-stars: Fredrlc March Sam Hardy Jed Prouty

1931   **KICK IN**
Co-star: Regis Toomey

1931   **NO LIMIT**
Co-star: Norman Foster

1932   **CALL HER SAVAGE**
Director: John Francis Dillon
Co-stars: Gilbert Roland Thelma Todd

1933   **HOOPLA**
Director: Frank Lloyd
Co-stars: Richard Cromwell Preston Foster

DORIS BOWDON

1939   **DRUMS ALONG THE MOHAWK**
Director: John Ford
Co-stars: Henry Fonda Claudette Colbert Edna May Oliver

1940   **THE GRAPES OF WRATH**
Director: John Ford
Co-stars: Henry Fonda Jane Darwell John Carradine

1943   **THE MOON IS DOWN**
Director: Irving Pichel
Co-stars: Henry Travers Cedric Hardwicke Lee J. Cobb

ROSEMARIE BOWE

1954   **THE GOLDEN MISTRESS**
Director: Joel Judge
Co-stars: John Agar Abner Biberman

1954   **THE ADVENTURES OF HAJJI BABA**
Director: Don Weis
Co-stars: John Derek Elaine Stewart Amanda Blake

JULIE BOWEN

1994   **RUNAWAY DAUGHTERS**
Director: Joe Dante
Co-stars: Dee Wallace Chris Young

LALLY BOWERS

1964   **THE CHALK GARDEN**
Director: Ronald Neame
Co-stars: Edith Evans Deborah Kerr Hayley Mills

1969   **I START COUNTING**
Director: David Greene
Co-stars: Jenny Agutter Brian Marshall Simon Ward

1972   **OUR MISS FRED**
Director: Bob Kellett
Co-stars: Danny La Rue Alfred Marks Lance Percival

1976   **THE SLIPPER AND THE ROSE**
Director: Bryan Forbes
Co-stars: Richard Chamberlain Gemma Craven

JUDI BOWKER

1972 BROTHER SUN, SISTER MOON
Director: Franco Zefferelli
Co-stars: Graham Faulkner Alec Guinness

1975 IN THIS HOUSE OF BREDE
Director: George Schaefer
Co-stars: Diana Rigg Pamela Brown Gwen Watford

1976 EAST OF ELEPHANT ROCK
Director: Don Boyd
Co-stars: Jeremy Kemp John Hurt Anton Rodgers

1977 COUNT DRACULA
Director: Philip Saville
Co-stars: Louis Jourdan Frank Finlay Susan Penhaligon

1981 CLASH OF THE TITANS
Director: Desmond Davis
Co-stars: Laurence Olivier Claire Bloom Maggie Smith

1985 ANNA KARENINA
Director: Simon Langton
Co-stars: Jacqueline Bisset Christopher Reeve Paul Scofield

KARA BOWMAN *(Child)*

1993 HENRI
Director: Simon Shore
Co-stars: John Hewitt Joe McPartland Simon Magill

LISA BOWMAN

1994 RIVER OF GRASS
Director: Kelly Reichardt
Co-stars: Larry Fessenden Dick Russell

TINA BOWMAN

1982 HEY, GOOD LOOKIN' *(Voice)*
Director: Ralph Bakshi
Co-stars: Richard Romanus Jesse Welles

AMANDA BOXER

1991 THE FALLOUT GUY
Director: Paul Tickell
Co-stars: Lou Hirsch Maria Charles Joe Melia

1992 BAD BEHAVIOUR
Director: Les Blalr
Co-stars: Stephen Rea Sinead Cusack Clare Higgins

HELEN BOYCE

1946 ABILENE TOWN
Director: Edwin Marin
Co-stars: Randolph Scott Ann Dvorak Rhonda Fleming

DOROTHY BOYD

1928 THE CONSTANT NYMPH
Director: Adrian Brunel
Co-stars: Mabel Poulton Ivor Novello

1931 THE SPORT OF KINGS
Director: Victor Saville
Co-stars: Leslie Henson Gordon Harker

1933 A SHOT IN THE DARK
Director: George Pearson
Co-stars: Jack Hawkins O. B. Clarence

MISSY BOYD

1990 THE BIG BANG
Director: James Toback
Co-stars: Emma Astner Polly Frost Sheila Kennedy

SARAH BOYD *(Child)*

1984 OLD ENOUGH
Director: Marisa Silver
Co-stars: Rainbow Harvest Danny Aiello Neill Barry

SALLY BOYDEN *(Child)*

1977 BARNABY AND ME
Director: Norman Panama
Co-stars: Sid Caesar Juliet Mills

PHYLLIS BOYENS

1980 COAL MINER'S DAUGHTER
Director: Michael Apted
Co-stars: Slssy Spacek Tommy Lee Jones Levon Helm

KATIE BOYER

1987 LONG GONE

1994 SEE JANE RUN
Director: John Patterson
Co-stars: John Shea Joanna Kerns

MARIANNE BOYER

1980 SPETTERS
Director: Paul Verhoeven
Co-stars: Rutger Hauer Jeroen Krabbe Maarten Spanjer

MARIE-FRANCE BOYER

1965 LE BONHEUR
Director: Agnes Varda
Co-stars: Jean-Claude Drouot Claire Drouot Sandrine Drouot

MYRIAM BOYER

1976 JONAH - WHO WILL BE 25 IN THE YEAR 2000
Director: Alain Tanner
Co-stars: Jean-Luc Bideau Miou-Miou

1991 UN COER EN HIVER
Director: Claude Sautet
Co-stars: Daniel Auteuill Emmanuelle Beart

1991 URANUS
Director: Claude Cerri
Co-stars: Gerald Depardieu Philippe Noiret Michel Blanc

1992 TOUS LES MATINS DU MONDE
Director: Alain Corneau
Co-stars: Gerard Depardieu Anne Brochet Carole Richert

SALLY BOYER

1978 SMOKEY AND THE GOOD-TIME OUTLAWS
Director: Alex Grashoff
Co-stars: Jesse Turner Slim Pickens

KATIE BOYLE

1957 NOT WANTED ON VOYAGE
Director: Brian Rix
Co-stars: Ronald Shiner Griffith Jones

LARA FLYNN BOYLE

1987 AMERIKA
Director: Donald Wrye
Co-stars: Kris Kristofferson Sam Neill Mariel Hemingway

1988 POLTERGEIST III
Director: Gary Sherman
Co-stars: Tom Skerritt Nancy Allen Heather O'Rourke

1989 HOW I GOT INTO COLLEGE
Director: Steve Holland
Co-stars: Corey Parker Anthony Edwards

1989 TERROR ON HIGHWAY 91
Director: Jerry Jameson
Co-stars: Ricky Schroder George Dzundza Matt Clark

1989 THE PREPPIE MURDER
Director: John Herzfeld
Co-stars: William Baldwin Danny Aiello Joanna Kerns

1990 ROOKIE
Director: Clint Eastwood
Co-stars: Clint Eastwood Charlie Sheen Raul Jullia

1990 MAY WINE
Director: Carol Wiseman
Co-stars: Joanna Cassidy Guy Marchand

1991 MOBSTERS
Director: Michael Karbelnikoff
Co-stars: Christian Slater Patrick Dempsey Anthony Quinn

1992 EQUINOX
Director: Alan Rudolph
Co-stars: Matthew Modine Lori Singer Marisa Tomei

1992 WAYNE'S WORLD
Director: Penelope Spheeris
Co-stars: Mike Myers Dana Carvey Rob Lowe

1992 WHERE THE DAY TAKES YOU
Director: Mark Rocco
Co-stars: Dermot Mulroney Balthazar Getty Sean Astin

1993 RED ROCK WEST
Director: John Dahl
Co-stars: Nicolas Cage Dennis Hopper J. T. Walsh

1994 THREESOME
Director: Andrew Fleming
Co-stars: Stephen Baldwin Josh Charles Alexis Arquette

1994 BABY'S DAY OUT
Director: Patrick Read Johnson
Co-stars: Joe Mantegna Joe Pantoliano Baby Bink

1994 PAST TENSE
Director: Graham Clifford
Co-stars: Scott Glenn Anthony LaPaglia

1997 THE TEMP

1998 AFTERGLOW
Director: Alan Rudolph
Co-stars: Julie Christie Nick Nolte Jonny Lee Miller

REIZL BOZYK

1988 CROSSING DELANCY
Director: Joan Micklin Silver
Co-stars: Amy Irving Peter Riegert Sylvia Miles

ELIZABETH BRACCO

1989 MYSTERY TRAIN
Director: Jim Jarmusch
Co-stars: Joe Strummer Cinque Lee Steve Buscemi

LORRAINE BRACCO
(Married Harvey Keitel, Edward James Olmos)
Nominated For Best Supporting Actress In 1990 For "Goodfellas"

1987 SOMEONE TO WATCH OVER ME
Director: Ridley Scott
Co-stars: Tom Berenger Mimi Rogers Jerry Orbach

1989 THE DREAM TEAM
Director: Howard Zieff
Co-stars: Michael Keaton Christopher Lloyd Peter Boyle

1989 SING
Director: Richard Baskin
Co-stars: Peter Dobson Louise Lasser Jessica Steen

1990 GOODFELLAS
Director: Martin Scorsese
Co-stars: Robert De Niro Ray Liotta Joe Pesci

1991 TALENT FOR THE GAME
Director: Robert M. Young
Co-stars: Edward James Olmos Jeff Corbett

1991 SWITCH
Director: Blake Edwards
Co-stars: Ellen Barkin Jimmy Smits JoBeth Williams

1992 RADIO FLYER
Director: Richard Donner
Co-stars: John Heard Adam Baldwin Elijah Wood

1992 MEDICINE MAN
Director: John McTiernan
Co-stars: Sean Connery Jose Wilker

1992 TRACES OF RED
Director: Andy Wolk
Co-stars: James Belushi Tony Goldwyn Faye Grant

1993 EVEN COWGIRLS GET THE BLUES
Director: Gus Van Sant
Co-stars: Uma Thurman John Hurt Rain Phoenix

1993 SCAM
Director: John Flynn
Co-stars: Christopher Walken Miguel Ferrer

1994 BEING HUMAN
Director: Bill Forsyth
Co-stars: Robin Williams John Turturro Anna Galiena

1994 GETTING GOTTI
Director: Roger Young
Co-stars: Anthony John Dennison Ellen Burstyn

1995 THE BASKETBALL DIARIES
Director: D. Scott Kalvert
Co-stars: Leonardo DiCaprio Mark Wahlberg

JANE BRADBURY

1996 WHEN THE CAT'S AWAY
Director: Cedric Klapisch
Co-stars: Garance Claver Estelle Larrivaz

KITTY BRADBURY

1923 THE PILGRIM
Director: Charles Chaplin
Co-stars: Charles Chaplin Edna Purviance Mack Swain

1923 OUR HOSPITALITY
Director: Jack Blystone
Co-stars: Buster Keaton Natalie Talmadge Joe Keaton

KIM BRADEN

1970 TROG
Director: Freddie Francis
Co-stars: Joan Crawford Michael Gough Bernard Kay

CATHRYN BRADSHAW

1989 BERT RIGBY, YOU'RE A FOOL
Director: Carl Reiner
Co-stars: Robert Lindsay Anne Bancroft Corbin Bernsen

1993 BLACK DAISIES FOR THE BRIDE
Director: Peter Symes
Co-stars: Elaine Hallam Maria Bovino

ELIZABETH BRADLEY

1989 A SMALL MOURNING
Director: Chris Bernard
Co-stars: Alison Steadman Stratford Johns Pauline Yates

1992   A LITTLE BIT OF LIPPY
Director: Chris Bernard
Co-stars: Kenneth Cranham Rachel Davies Tina Earl

GRACE BRADLEY

1934   REDHEAD

1935   STOLEN HARMONY
Director: Alfred Werker
Co-stars: George Raft Ben Bernie Iris Adrian

1935   TWO-FISTED
Director: James Cruze
Co-stars: Lee Tracy Roscoe Karns Gail Patrick

1936   ANYTHING GOES
Director: Lewis Milestone
Co-stars: Bing Crosby Ethel Merman Ida Lupino

1936   O.H.M.S.
Director: Raoul Walsh
Co-stars: Wallace Ford John Mills Anna Lee

1936   F. MAN
Co-star: Jack Haley

1936   DON'T TURN 'EM LOOSE
Co-star: Bruce Cabot Harry Jans

1936   THIRTEEN HOURS BY AIR
Director: Mitchell Leisen
Co-stars: Fred MacMurray Joan Bennett Zasu Pitts

1937   IT'S ALL YOURS
Director: Elliott Nugent
Co-stars: Madeleine Carroll Francis Lederer Mischa Auer

1937   LARCENY ON THE AIR
Co-star: Bob Livingstone

1937   ROARING TIMBER
Co-star: Jack Holt

1937   WAKE UP AND LIVE
Director: Sidney Lanfield
Co-stars: Alice Faye Jack Haley Walter Winchell

1941   THERE'S MAGIC IN MUSIC
Director: Andrew Stone
Co-stars: Allan Jones Susannah Foster

1943   TAXI, MISTER
Co-stars: William Bendix Sheldon Leonard Mike Mazurki

OLYMPE BRADNA

1936   COLLEGE HOLIDAY
Director: Frank Tuttle
Co-stars: Jack Benny George Burns Gracie Allen

1937   THE LAST TRAIN FROM MADRID
Director: James Hogan
Co-stars: Dorothy Lamour Lew Ayres Gilbert Roland

1937   SOULS AT SEA
Director: Henry Hathaway
Co-stars: Gary Cooper George Raft Frances Dee

1938   STOLEN HEAVEN
Director: Andrew Stone
Co-stars: Gene Raymond Lewis Stone Glenda Farrell

1938   SAY IT IN FRENCH
Director: Andrew Stone
Co-stars: Ray Milland Irene Hervey Mary Carlisle

1939   THE NIGHT OF NIGHTS
Director: Lewis Milestone
Co-stars: Pat O'Brien Reginald Gardiner Roland Young

1940   SOUTH OF PAGO PAGO
Director: Alfred Green
Co-stars: Victor McLaglen Jon Hall Frances Farmer

1941   INTERNATIONAL SQUADRON
Director: Lothar Mendes
Co-stars: Ronald Reagan Julie Bishop Reginald Denny

ALICE BRADY
Oscar for Best Supporting Actress In 1938 For "In Old Chicago"
Nominated For Best Supporting Actress In 1936 For 'My Man Godfrey'

1933   BROADWAY TO HOLLYWOOD
Director: Willard Mack
Co-stars: Frank Morgan May Robson Mickey Rooney

1933   WHEN LADIES MEET
Director: Harry Beaumont
Co-stars: Ann Harding Robert Mqntgomery Myrna Loy

1933   BEAUTY FOR SALE
Director: Richard Boleslawsky
Co-stars: Madge Evans Una Merkel Otto Kruger

1933   STAGE MOTHER
Director: Charles Brabin
Co-stars: Maureen O'Sullivan Franchot Tone

1933   SHOULD LADIES BEHAVE?
Director: Harry Beaumont
Co-stars: Lionel Barrymore Mary Carlisle

1933   MISS FANE'S BABY IS STOLEN
Director: Alexander Hall
Co-stars: Dorothea Wieck George Barbier

1934   THE GAY DIVORCEE
Director: Mark Sandrich
Co-stars: Fred Astaire Ginger Rogers Eric Blore

1935   LADY TUBBS
Director: Alan Crosland
Co-stars: Douglass Montgomery Anita Louise

1935   LET 'EM HAVE IT
Director: Sam Wood
Co-stars: Rlchard Arlen Virginla Bruce Bruce Cabot

1935   METROPOLITAN
Director: Richard Boleslawsky
Co-stars: Lawrence Tibbett Vlrglnla Bruce

1936   GO WEST, YOUNG MAN
Director: Henry Hathaway
Co-stars: Mae West Randolph Scott Lyle Talbot

1936   MY MAN GODFREY
Director: Gregory La Cava
Co-stars: Carole Lombard William Powell

1937   CALL IT A DAY
Director: Archie Mayo
Co-stars: Olivia De Havilland Ian Hunter

1937   MR DODD TAKES THE AIR
Director: Alfred Green
Co-stars: Kenny Baker Jane Wyman Frank Mchugh

1937   THREE SMART GIRLS
Director: Henry Koster
Co-stars: Deanna Durbin Nan Grey Ray Milland

1937   MERRY GO ROUND OF 1938
Director: Irving Cummings
Co-stars: Bert Lahr Louise Fazenda Jimmy Savo

1937   MIND YOUR OWN BUSINESS
Director: Norman Z. McLeod
Co-stars: Charles Ruggles William Demarest

1937   ONE HUNDRED MEN AND A GIRL
Director: Henry Koster
Co-stars: Deanna Durbin Adolphe Menjou Mlscha Auer

1938   JOY OF LIVING
Director: Tay Garnett
Co-stars: Irene Dunne Douglas Fairbanks Lucllle Ball

1938　IN OLD CHICAGO
Director:　Henry King
Co-stars:　Tyrone Power Alice Faye Don Ameche

1939　YOUNG MR LINCOLN
Director:　John Ford
Co-stars:　Henry Fonda Marjorie Weaver Arleen Whelan

1939　ZENOBIA
Director:　Gordon Douglas
Co-stars:　Oliver Hardy Harry Langdon Jean Parker

JANELLE BRADY

1986　CLASS OF NUKE 'EM HIGH
Director:　Richard Haines
Co-stars:　Gilbert Brenton Robert Pritchard

MOYA BRADY

1987　ROAD
Director:　Alan Clarke
Co-stars:　Jane Horrocks Lesley Sharp Neil Dudgeon

PATTI BRADY

1946　NEVER SAY GOODBYE
Director:　James Kern
Co-stars:　Errol Flynn Eleanor Parker Lucile Watson

1947　STALLION ROAD
Director:　James Kern
Co-stars:　Ronald Reagan Alexis Smith Zachary Scott

RUTH BRADY

1949　CAUGHT
Director:　Max Ophuls
Co-stars:　James Mason Robert Ryan Barbara Bel Geddes

VERONICA BRADY

1934　LOVE, LIFE AND LAUGHTER
Director:　Maurice Elvy
Co-stars:　Gracie Fields John Loder Robb Wilton

SONIA BRAGA

1976　DONA FLOR AND HER TWO HUSBANDS
Director:　Bruno Barreto
Co-stars:　Jose Wilker Mauro Mendonca

1983　GABRIELA
Director:　Bruno Barreta
Co-stars:　Marcello Mastroianni Antonio Cantafora

1985　KISS OF THE SPIDER WOMAN
Director:　Hector Babenco
Co-stars:　William Hurt Raul Julia

1987　THE MAN WHO BROKE A 1000 CHAINS
Director:　Daniel Mann
Co-stars:　Val Kilmer Kyra Sedgewick

1988　THE MILAGRO BEANFIELD WAR
Director:　Robert Redford
Co-stars:　Ruben Blades Richard Bradford

1988　MOON OVER PARADOR
Director:　Paul Mazursky
Co-stars:　Richard Dreyfuss Raul Jullia Polly Holliday

1990　ROOKIE
Director:　Clint Eastwood
Co-stars:　Clint Eastwood Charlie Sheen Raul Julia

1993　ROOSTERS
Director:　Robert Young
Co-stars:　Edward James Olmos Maria Conchita Alonso Danny Nucci

1994　THE BURNING SEASON
Director:　John Frankenheimer
Co-stars:　Raul Julia Edward James Olmos

LILLIAN BRAITHWAITE

1927　DOWNHILL
Director:　Alfred Hitchcock
Co-stars:　Ivor Novello Ben Webster Isabel Jeans

1931　CARNIVAL
Director:　Herbert Wilcox
Co-stars:　Matheson Lang Dorothy Bouchier Kay Hammond

1947　A MAN ABOUT THE HOUSE
Director:　Leslie Arliss
Co-stars:　Margaret Johnston Kieron Moore Dulcie Gray

DOROTHY BRAMHALL

1944　LOVE STORY
Director:　Leslie Arliss
Co-stars:　Margaret Lockwood Stewart Granger Patricia Roc

PAMELA BRANCH

1963　LILLIES OF THE FIELD
Director:　Ralph Nelson
Co-stars:　Sidney Poitier Lillia Skala

SARAH BRANCH

1960　SANDS OF THE DESERT
Director:　John Paddy Carstairs
Co-stars:　Charlie Drake Peter Arne

1960　SWORD OF SHERWOOD FOREST
Director:　Terence Fisher
Co-stars:　Richard Greene Peter Cushing

SIMONA BRANDALISE

1987　LONG LIVE THE LADY!
Director:　Ermanno Olmi
Co-stars:　Marco Esposito Stefania Busarello

JOCELYN BRANDO *(Sister Of Marlon Brando)*

1953　THE BIG HEAT
Director:　Fritz Lang
Co-stars:　Glenn Ford Gloria Grahame Lee Marvin

1953　CHINA VENTURE
Director:　Don Siegel
Co-stars:　Edmond O'Brien Barry Sullivan

1955　TEN WANTED MEN
Director:　Bruce Humberstone
Co-stars:　Randolph Scott Richard Boone

1956　NIGHTFALL
Director:　Jacques Tourneur
Co-stars:　Anne Bancroft Aldo Ray Brian Keith

1959　STEP DOWN TO TERROR
Director:　Harry Keller
Co-stars:　Charles Drake Coleen Miller Rod Taylor

1962　THE UGLY AMERICAN
Director:　George Englund
Co-stars:　Marlon Brando Eiji Okada Pat Hingle

1965　BUS RILEY'S BACK IN TOWN
Director:　Harvey Hart
Co-stars:　Michael Parks Ann-Margret Kim Darby

1978　A QUESTION OF LOVE
Director:　Jerry Thorpe
Co-stars:　Gena Rowlands Jane Alexander Ned Beatty

1981　MOMMIE DEAREST
Director:　Frank Perry
Co-stars:　Faye Dunaway Diana Scarwid Steve Forrest

LUISINA BRANDO

1986 MISS MARY
Director: Maria Luisa Bemberg
Co-stars: Julie Christie Nacha Guevara Iris Marga

1993 WE DON'T WANT TO TALK ABOUT IT
Director: Maria Luisa Bemberg
Co-stars: Marcello Mastroianni Jorge Luz

SHARON H. BRANDON

1988 IRON EAGLE II
Director: Sidney Furie
Co-stars: Lou Gossett Jnr. Stuart Margolin

CAROLYN BRANDT

1964 THE INCREDIBLY STRANGE CREATURES WHO STOPPED LIVING AND BECAME MIXED-UP ZOMBIES
Director: Cash Flagg
Co-stars: Cash Flagg Brett O'Hara

JANET BRANDT

1961 A COLD WIND IN AUGUST
Director: Alexander Singer
Co-stars: Lola Albright Scott Marlowe

1973 HIT
Director: Sidney Furie
Co-stars: Billy Dee Williams Richard Pryor Gwen Welles

LIGIA BRANICE

(Married Walerian Borowczyk)

1971 BLANCHE
Director: Walerian Borowczyk
Co-stars: Michel Simon Lawrence Trimble

BETSY BRANTLEY

1980 THE YOB
Director: Ian Emes
Co-stars: Keith Allen Gary Olsen Lia Williams

1982 FIVE DAYS ONE SUMMER
Director: Fred Zinnemann
Co-stars: Sean Connery Lambert Wilson Anna Massey

1984 ANOTHER COUNTRY
Director: Marek Kanievska
Co-stars: Rupert Everett Colin Firth Anna Massey

1987 THE FOURTH PROTOCOL
Director: John MacKenzie
Co-stars: Michael Caine Pierce Brosnan Joanna Cassidy

1994 SHEPHERD ON THE ROCK
Director: Bob Keen
Co-stars: Bernard Hill John Bowles

NICOLETTA BRASCHI

1986 DOWN BY LAW
Director: Jim Jarmusch
Co-stars: Tom Waits John Lurie Ellen Barkin

1989 MYSTERY TRAIN
Director: Jim Jarmusch
Co-stars: Joe Strummer Elizabeth Bracco Rick Aviles

OLIVE BRASNO

1936 CHARLIE CHAN AT THE CIRCUS
Director: Harry Lachman
Co-stars: Warner Oland Keye Luke George Brasno

JUDITH BRAUN

1952 HORIZONS WEST
Director: Budd Boetticher
Co-stars: Rock Hudson Robert Ryan Julia Adams

1952 RED BALL EXPRESS
Director: Budd Boetticher
Co-stars: Jeff Chandler Sidney Poitier Alex Nicol

LILIA BRAZZI

1966 AFTER THE FOX
Director: Vittorio De Sica
Co-stars: Peter Sellers Victor Mature Britt Ekland

KATHLEEN BRECK

1963 WEST 11
Director: Michael Winner
Co-stars: Alfred Lynch Eric Portman Diana Dors

1966 THE FROZEN DEAD
Director: Herbert Leder
Co-stars: Dana Andrews Anna Palk Philip Gilbert

PATRICIA BREDIN

1959 THE BRIDAL PATH
Director: Frank Launder
Co-stars: Bill Travers Fiona Clyne George Cole

1959 DESERT MICE
Director: Michael Relph
Co-stars: Alfred Marks Sid James Dick Bentley

1959 LEFT, RIGHT AND CENTRE
Director: Sidney Gilliat
Co-stars: Ian Carmichael Alastair Sim Gordon Harker

1960 THE TREASURE OF MONTE CRISTO
Director: Robert Baker
Co-stars: Rory Calhoun John Gregson Sam Kydd

ALICE BREE

1991 TICKETS FOR THE ZOO
Director: Brian Crumlish
Co-stars: Tom Smith Mickey MacPherson

HELEN LLOYD BREED

1992 PASSED AWAY
Director: Charlie Peters
Co-stars: Bob Hoskins Jack Warden Maureen Stapleton

MARGARET BREEN

1930 HEADS UP
Director: Victor Schertzinger
Co-stars: Charles Rogers Helen Kane Victor Moore

HANNA BREJCHOVA

1965 A BLONDE IN LOVE
Director: Milos Forman
Co-stars: Vladimir Pucholt Joseph Sebanek

LUCILLE BREMER

1944 MEET ME IN ST. LOUIS
Director: Vincente Minnelli
Co-stars: Judy Garland Margaret O'Brien Tom Drake

1945 YOLANDA AND THE THIEF
Director: Vincent Minnelli
Co-stars: Fred Astaire Frank Morgan Leon Ames

1946 ZIEGFELD FOLLIES
Director: Vincente Minnelli
Co-stars: Fred Astaire Gene Kelly Judy Garland

1946   TILL THE CLOUDS ROLL BY
Director: Richard Whorf
Co-stars: Robert Walker Van Heflin Judy Garland

1947   DARK DELUSION
Director: Willis Goldbeck
Co-stars: Lionel Barrymore James Craig Edward Arnold

1948   RUTHLESS
Director: Edgar Ulmar
Co-stars: Zachary Scott Sydney Greenstreet Diana Lynn

BELINDA BREMMER

1984   ACT OF PASSION
Director: Simon Langton
Co-stars: Kris Kristofferson Marlo Thomas George Dzundza

AMY BRENNAMAN

1996   HEAT
Director: Michael Mann
Co-stars: Robert De Niro Val Kilmer Al Pacino

EILEEN BRENNAN
Nominated for Best Supporting Actress in 1980 for "Private Benjamin"

1973   THE STING
Director: George Roy Hill
Co-stars: Paul Newman Robert Redford Robert Shaw

1973   SCARECROW
Director: Jerry Schatzberg
Co-stars: Gene Hackman Al Pacino Dorothy Tristan

1974   DAISY MILLER
Director: Peter Bogdanovich
Co-stars: Cybill Shepherd Barry Brown Mildred Natwick

1975   AT LONG LAST LOVE
Director: Peter Bogdanovich
Co-stars: Burt Reynolds Cybill Shepherd Madeline Kahn

1975   HUSTLE
Director: Robert Aldrich
Co-stars: Burt Reynolds Catherine Deneuvre Ben Johnson

1975   THE NIGHT THAT PANICKED AMERICA
Director: Joseph Sargent
Co-stars: Paul Shenar Vic Morrow

1976   MURDER BY DEATH
Director: Robert Moore
Co-stars: Peter Falk Alec Guinness David Niven

1976   THE GREAT SMOKEY ROADBLOCK
Director: John Leone
Co-stars: Henry Fonda Susan Sarandon John Byner

1978   THE CHEAP DETECTIVE
Director: Robert Moore
Co-stars: Peter Falk Louise Fletcher Ann-Margret

1978   FM
Director: John Alonzo
Co-stars: Michael Brandon Martin Mull Alex Karras

1979   WHEN SHE WAS BAD....
Director: Peter Hunt
Co-stars: Cheryl Ladd Robert Urich

1980   PRIVATE BENJAMIN
Director: Howard Zieff
Co-stars: Goldie Hawn Armand Assante Sam Wanamaker

1985   CLUE
Director: Jonathan Lynn
Co-stars: Tim Curry Madeline Kahn Martin Mull

1986   BABES IN TOYLAND
Director: Clive Donner
Co-stars: Drew Barrymore Richard Mulligan Keanu Reeves

1987   BLOOD VOWS
Director: Paul Wendkos
Co-stars: Melissa Gilbert Joe Penny Talia Shire

1988   WEDDING DAY BLUES
Director: Paul Lynch
Co-stars: Cloris Leachman Michelle Green Max Wright

1988   STICKY FINGERS
Director: Catlin Adams
Co-stars: Helen Slater Melanie Mayron Danitra Vance

1990   STELLA
Director: John Erman
Co-stars: Bette Midler John Goodman Trini Alvarado

1990   TEXASVILLE
Director: Peter Bogdanovich
Co-stars: Jeff Bridges Cybill Shepherd Cloris Leachman

1990   WHITE PALACE
Director: Luis Mondoki
Co-stars: Susan Sarandon James Spader Kathy Bates

1992   I DON'T BUY KISSES ANYMORE
Director: Robert Macarelli
Co-stars: Jason Alexander Nia Peeples Lainie Kazan

1994   MY NAME IS KATE
Director: Rod Hardy
Co-stars: Donna Mills Daniel J. Travanti Linda Darlow

SHEILA BRENNAN

1975   THE SPIRAL STAIRCASE
Director: Peter Collinson
Co-stars: Jacqueline Bisset Christopher Plummer

RACHEL BRENNOCK

1971   MR. HORATIO KNIBBLES
Director: Robert Hird
Co-stars: Lesley Roach Gary Smith John Ash

1975   ROBIN HOOD JUNIOR
Director: Matt McCarthy
Co-stars: Keith Chegwin Andrew Sachs Maurice Kaufman

EVE BRENT

1957   FORTY GUNS
Director: Samuel Fuller
Co-stars: Barbara Stanwyck Barry Sullivan Dean Jagger

1958   TARZAN AND THE TRAPPERS
Director: Sandy Howard
Co-stars: Gordon Scott Rickie Sorenson

1958   TARZAN'S FIGHT FOR LIFE
Director: Bruce Humberstone
Co-stars: Gordon Scott Rickie Sorenson

EVELYN BRENT

1927   UNDERWORLD
Director: Josef Von Sternberg
Co-stars: George Bancroft Clive Brook

1928   THE LAST COMMAND
Director: Josef Von Sternberg
Co-stars: Emil Jannings William Powell

1928   INTERFERENCE
Director: Roy Pomeroy
Co-stars: William Powell Clive Brook Doris Kenyon

1928   THE DRAGNET
Director: Josef Von Sternberg
Co-stars: George Bancroft William Powell

1928   BEAU SABREUIR
Director: John Waters
Co-stars: Gary Cooper Noah Beery William Powell

1929   BROADWAY
Director: Paul Fejos
Co-stars: Glenn Tryon Merna Kennedy Robert Ellis

1930   SLIGHTLY SCARLET
Director: Louis Gasnier
Co-stars: Clive Brook Paul Lukas Helen Ware

1931   PAGAN LADY
Director: John Francis Dillon
Co-stars: Conrad Nagel Charles Bickford Roland Young

1931   THE MAD PARADE
Director: William Beaudine
Co-stars: Irene Rich Louise Fazenda Lilyan Tashman

1932   HIGH PRESSURE
Director: Mervyn LeRoy
Co-stars: William Powell George Sidney Frank McHugh

1932   ATTORNEY FOR THE DEFENSE
Director: Irving Cummings
Co-stars: Edmund Lowe Constance Cummings

1935   THE NITWITS
Director: George Stevens
Co-stars: Wheeler & Woolsey Betty Grable

1937   NIGHT CLUB SCANDAL
Director: Ralph Murphy
Co-stars: John Barrymore Charles Bickford

1938   THE LAW WEST OF TOMBSTONE
Director: Glen Tryon
Co-stars: Harry Carey Tim Holt Allan Lane

1941   WIDE OPEN TOWN
Co-stars: William Boyd Russell Hayden Bernice Kay

1941   EMERGENCY LANDING
Co-stars: Forrest Tucker Carol Hughes

1943   THE PAYOFF
Director: Arthur Dreifuss
Co-stars: Lee Tracy Tom Brown Tina Thayer

1943   THE SEVENTH VICTIM
Director: Mark Robson
Co-stars: Kim Hunter Tom Conway Jean Brooks

1944   BOWERY CHAMPS
Director: William Beaudine
Co-stars: Bowery Boys Anne Sterling Ian Keith

1947   ROBIN HOOD OF MONTEREY
Director: Christy Cabanne
Co-star: Gilbert Roland

1948   CHARLIE CHAN AND THE GOLDEN EYE
Director: William Beaudine
Co-stars: Victor Sen Yung Tim Ryan Roland Winters

BOBBIE BRESEE

1983   MAUSOLEUM
Director: Michael Dugan
Co-stars: Marjoe Gortner Norman Burton

1987   SURF NAZIS MUST DIE
Director: Peter George
Co-stars: Barry Brenner Gail Neely

JOAN BRESLAU (Child)

1935   IN PERSON
Director: William Seiter
Co-stars: Ginger Rogers George Brent Alan Mowbray

PATRICIA BRESLIN (Pat)

1954   GO, MAN, GO
Director: James Wong Howe
Co-stars: Dane Clark Sidney Poitier

1958   ANDY HARDY COMES HOME
Director: Howard Koch
Co-stars: Mickey Rooney Fay Holden Cecilia Parker

1961   HOMICIDAL
Director: William Castle
Co-stars: Jean Arless Glenn Corbett Alan Bunce

MICHELE BRETON

1970   PERFORMANCE
Director: Nicolas Roeg
Co-stars: James Fox Mick Jagger Anita Pallenberg

DELIA BRETT

1989   AMERICAN BOYFRIENDS
Director: Sandy Wilson
Co-stars: Margaret Langrick John Wildman

MARITA BREUER

1984   HEIMAT
Director: Edgar Reitz
Co-stars: Michaiil Lesch Dieter Schaad Karin Kienzler

BETTY BREWER (Child)

1942   MRS WIGGS OF THE CABBAGE PATCH
Director: Ralph Murphy
Co-stars: Fay Bainter Vera Vague

CAROL BREWSTER

1953   CAT WOMEN OF THE MOON
Director: Arthur Hilton
Co-stars: Sonny Tufts Marie Windsor Victor Jory

DIANE BREWSTER

1957   BLACK PATCH
Director: Allen Miner
Co-stars: George Montgomery Leo Gordon

1957   COURAGE OF BLACK BEAUTY
Director: Harold Schuster
Co-stars: John Crawford John Bryant

1957   THE INVISIBLE BOY
Director: Herman Hoffman
Co-stars: Richard Eyer Philip Abbott

1958   THE MAN IN THE NET
Director: Michael Curtiz
Co-stars: Alan Ladd Carolyn Jones Charles McGraw

1958   QUANTRILL'S RAIDERS
Director: Edward Bernds
Co-stars: Steve Cochran Leo Gordon Gale Robbins

1958   TORPEDO RUN
Director: Joseph Pevney
Co-stars: Glenn Ford Ernest Borgnine Dean Jones

1959   THE YOUNG PHIILADELPHIANS
Director: Vincent Sherman
Co-stars: Paul Newman Alexis Smith Brian Keith

MAIA BREWTON

1987   ADVENTURES IN BABYSITTING
Director: Chris Columbus
Co-stars: Elizabeth Shue Penelope Ann Miller

MARY BRIAN

1926   BROWN OF HARVARD
Director: Jack Conway
Co-stars: William Haines Jack Pickford

1926   BEAU GESTE
Director: Herbert Brenon
Co-stars: Ronald Colman Neil Hamilton Ralph Forbes

1929	**THE VIRGINIAN**	
Director:	Victor Fleming	
Co-stars:	Gary Cooper Walter Huston Richard Arlen	

1929 THE VIRGINIAN
Director: Victor Fleming
Co-stars: Gary Cooper Walter Huston Richard Arlen

1929 THE MARRIAGE PLAYGROUND
Director: Lothar Mendes
Co-stars: Fredric March Kay Francis Lilyan Tashman

1930 THE ROYAL FAMILY OF BROADWAY
Director: George Cukor
Co-stars: Fredric March Ina Claire

1930 PARAMOUNT ON PARADE
Co-stars: Gary Cooper Clara Bow Jean Arthur

1930 ONLY THE BRAVE
Co-star: Gary Cooper

1930 BURNING UP
Co-stars: Richard Arlen

1930 THE SOCIAL LION
Co-stars: Jack Oakie Skeets Gallagher

1931 THE FRONT PAGE
Director: Lewis Milestone
Co-stars: Adolphe Menjou Pat O'Brien Walter Catlett

1931 GUN SMOKE
Co-stars: Richard Arlen William 'Stage' Boyd

1931 CAPTAIN APPLEJACK
Director: Hobart Henley
Co-stars: John Halliday Kay Strozzi Louise Closser Hale

1932 BLESSED EVENT
Director: Roy Del Ruth
Co-stars: Lee Tracy Ned Sparks Dick Powell

1932 THE UNWRITTEN LAW
Co-star: Theodore Von Eltz

1932 IT'S TOUGH TO BE FAMOUS
Director: Alfred Green
Co-stars: Douglas Fairbanks Walter Catlett

1933 FOG
Director: Albert Rogell
Co-stars: Donald Cook Reginald Denny Maude Eburne

1933 GIRL MISSING
Co-stars: Glenda Farrell Guy Kibbee

1933 HARD TO HANDLE
Director: Mervyn LeRoy
Co-stars: James Cagney Ruth Donnelly Allen Jenkins

1933 MOONLIGHT AND PRETZELS
Co-star: Herbert Rawlinson

1933 SONG OF THE EAGLE
Director: Ralph Murphy
Co-stars: Charles Bickford Richard Arlen Jean Hersholt

1934 EVER SINCE EVE
Co-stars: George Meeker Peggy Blythe

1934 COLLEGE RHYTHM
Director: Norman Taurog
Co-stars: Jack Oakie Joe Penner Lanny Ross

1935 CHARLIE CHAN IN PARIS
Director: Lewis Seiler
Co-stars: Warner Oland Keye Luke John Qualen

1935 THE MAN ON THE FLYING TRAPEZE
Director: Clyde Bruckman
Co-stars: W.C. Fields Kathleen Howard

1936 THE AMAZING QUEST OF ERNEST BLISS
Director: Alfred Zeisler
Co-stars: Cary Grant Ralph Richardson

1936 SPENDTHRIFT
Director: Raoul Walsh
Co-stars: Henry Fonda Pat Paterson George Barbier

1936 TWO'S COMPANY
Director: Tim Whelan
Co-stars: Gordon Harker Patric Knowles Ned Sparks

1943 CALABOOSE
Co-stars: Noah Berry Jnr Jimmy Rogers

1943 I ESCAPED FROM THE GESTAPO
Director: Harold Young
Co-stars: Dean Jagger John Carradine

BRIDGET BRICE

1970 THE TWELVE CHAIRS
Director: Mel Brooks
Co-stars: Mel Brooks Ron Moody Frank Langella

FANNY BRICE

1928 MY MAN
Director: Archie Mayo
Co-stars: Guinn Williams Edna Murphy Andre De Segurova

1934 CRIME WITHOUT PASSION
Director: Ben Hecht
Co-stars: Claude Rains Margo Stanley Ridges

1936 THE GREAT ZIEGFELD
Director: Robert Z Leonard
Co-stars: William Powell Luise Rainer Myrna Loy

1938 EVERYBODY SING
Director: Edwin Marin
Co-stars: Allan Jones Judy Garland Billie Burke

1946 ZIEGFELD FOLLIES
Director: Vincente Minnelli
Co-stars: Fred Astaire Gene Kelly Judy Garland

GENNIE NEVINSON BRICE

1994 MURIEL'S WEDDING
Director: P. J. Hogan
Co-stars: Toni Collette Rachel Griffiths Bill Hunter

BETH BRICKELL

1977 DEATH GAME
Director: Peter Traynor
Co-stars: Sondra Locke Colleen Camp Seymour Cassel

KATHY BRICKMEIER

1983 GETTING IT ON
Director: William Olsen
Co-stars: Martin Yost Heather Kennedy Jeff Edmond

LILLA BRIGNONE

1962 THE ECLIPSE
Director: Michaelangelo Antonioni
Co-stars: Monica Vitti Alain Delon

FRAN BRILL

1980 AMBER WAVES
Director: Joseph Sargent
Co-stars: Dennis Weaver Kurt Russell Mare Winningham

1991 WHAT ABOUT BOB?
Director: Frank Oz
Co-stars: Richard Dreyfuss Bill Murray Julie Hagerty

CYNTHIA BRIMHILL

1987 HARD TICKET TO HAWAII
Director: Andy Sidaris
Co-stars: Dona Spier Hope Marie Carlton Ronn Moss

NANCY BRINKMAN

1945   MR MUGGS RIDES AGAIN
Co-stars: Leo Gorcy Huntz Hall

FRANCOISE BRION

1985   THE FROG PRINCE
Director: Brian Gilbert
Co-stars: Jane Snowden Jean Herivale

DANIELLE BRISEBOIS

1987   BIG BAD MAMA 11
Director: Jim Wynorski
Co-stars: Angie Dickinson Robert Culp

VIRGINIA BRISSAC

1936   TWO AGAINST THE WORLD
Director: William McGann
Co-stars: Humphrey Bogart Beverly Roberts

1937   THE ADVENTUROUS BLONDE
Co-stars: Barton MacLane Glenda Farrell

1940   BLACK FRIDAY
Director: Arthur Lubin
Co-stars: Boris Karloff Bela Lugosi Anne Nagel

1945   THE SCARLET CLUE
Director: Phil Rosen
Co-stars: Sidney Toler Benson Fong Manton Moreland

1945   THREE'S A CROWD
Co-stars: Pamela Blake Charles Gordon

1951   TWO OF A KIND
Director: Henry Levin
Co-stars: Edmond O'Brien Lizabeth Scott Terry Moore

MAI BRITT *(Maj-britt Nilsson In Sweden)*

1949   TO JOY
Director: Ingmar Bergman
Co-star: Stig Olin

1950   SUMMER INTERLUDE
Director: Ingmar Bergman
Co-stars: Birger Malmsten Alf Kjellin

1958   THE HUNTERS
Director: Dick Powell
Co-stars: Robert Mitchum Robert Wagner Richard Egan

1958   THE YOUNG LIONS
Director: Edward Dmytryk
Co-stars: Marlon Brando Montgomery Clift Dean Martin

1959   THE BLUE ANGEL
Director: Edward Dmytryk
Co-stars: Curt Jurgens Theodore Bikel John Banner

1960   MURDER INC.
Director: Burt Balaban
Co-stars: Stuart Whitman Henry Morgan Peter Falk

MORGAN BRITTANY *(Suzanne Cupito)*

1968   YOURS, MINE AND OURS
Director: Mel Shavelson
Co-stars: Lucille Ball Henry Fonda Van Johnson

1976   GABLE AND LOMBARD
Director: Sidney Furie
Co-stars: James Brolin Jill Clayburgh Allen Garfield

1977   DELATA COUNTY U.S.A.
Director: Glen Jordan
Co-stars: Jim Antonio Peter Donat Joanna Miles

1978   THE INITIATION OF SARAH
Director: Robert Day
Co-stars: Kay Lenz Shelley Winters Tony Bill

1991   SUNDOWN: THE VAMPIRE IN RETREAT
Director: Anthony Hickok
Co-stars: David Carradine Bruce Campbell

AILEEN BRITTON

1983   NOW AND FOREVER
Director: Adrian Carr
Co-stars: Cheryl Ladd Robert Coleby Carmen Duncan

BARBARA BRITTON

1942   YOUNG AND WILLING
Director: Edward Griffith
Co-stars: William Holden Susan Hayward Eddie Bracken

1942   WAKE ISLAND
Director: John Farrow
Co-stars: Brian Donlevy Robert Preston William Bendix

1942   MRS WIGGS OF THE CABBAGE PATCH
Director: Ralph Murphy
Co-stars: Fay Bainter Hugh Herbert

1943   SO PROUDLY WE HAIL!
Director: Mark Sandrich
Co-stars: Claudette Colbert Paulette Goddard

1944   TILL WE MEET AGAIN
Director: Frank Borzage
Co-stars: Ray Milland Walter Slezak Lucile Watson

1945   THE GREAT JOHN L
Director: Frank Tuttle
Co-stars: Greg McClure Linda Darnell Otto Kruger

1945   CAPTAIN KIDD
Director: Rowland Lee
Co-stars: Charles Laughton Randolph Scott Gilbert Roland

1946   THE RETURN OF MONTE CRISTO
Director: Henry Levin
Co-stars: Louis Hayward George Macready

1946   THE FABULOUS SUZANNE
Co-stars: Richard Denning Rudy Vallee Veda Ann Borg

1946   THEY MADE ME A KILLER
Director: William Thomas
Co-stars: Robert Lowery Lola Lane Frank Albertson

1946   THE VIRGINIAN
Director: Stuart Gilmore
Co-stars: Joel McCrea Brian Donlevy Sonny Tufts

1947   GUNFIGHTERS
Director: George Waggner
Co-stars: Randolph Scott Dorothy Hart Bruce Cabot

1947   ALBUQUERQUE
Director: Ray Enright
Co-stars: Randolph Scott George "Gabby" Hayes Lon Chaney

1948   COVER-UP
Director: Alfred Green
Co-stars: Dennis O'Keefe William Bendix Art Smith

1948   I SHOT JESSE JAMES
Director: Sam Fuller
Co-stars: Preston Foster John Ireland Tom Tyler

1950   THE BANDIT QUEEN
Director: William Berke
Co-stars: Willard Parker Barton MacLane Thurston Hall

1950   CHAMPAGNE FOR CAESAR
Director: Richard Whorf
Co-stars: Ronald Colman Vincent Price Celeste Holm

1952   BWANA DEVIL
Director: Arch Obeler
Co-stars: Robert Stack Nigel Bruce Ramsey Hill

1952 RIDE THE MAN DOWN
Director: Joe Kane
Co-stars: Brian Donlevy Ella Raines Rod Cameron

1955 THE SPOILERS
Director: Jesse Hibbs
Co-stars: Anne Baxter Jeff Chandler Rory Calhoun

1955 AIN'T MISBEHAVING
Director: Edward Buzzell
Co-stars: Rory Calhoun Piper Laurie Jack Carson

JULIA BRITTON

1988 HARD TIMES
Director: Joao Botelho
Co-stars: Luis Estrela Isabel De Castro Ruy Fortado

1989 BEARSKIN
Director: Ann Guedes
Co-stars: Tom Waits Damon Lowry Charlotte Coleman

PAMELA BRITTON

1945 ANCHORS AWEIGH
Director: George Sidney
Co-stars: Gene Kelly Frank Sinatra Kathryn Grayson

1945 A LETTER FOR EVIE
Director: Jules Dassin
Co-stars: Marsha Hunt John Carroll Hume Cronyn

1950 KEY TO THE CITY
Director: George Sidney
Co-stars: Clark Gable Loretta Young Frank Morgan

1950 D.O.A.
Director: Rudolph Mate
Co-stars: Edmond O'Brien Luther Adler Neville Brand

1950 WATCH THE BIRDIE
Director: Jack Donohue
Co-stars: Red Skelton Arlene Dahl Ann Miller

1969 IF IT'S TUESDAY, THIS MUST BE BELGIUM
Director: Mel Stuart
Co-stars: Suzanne Pleshette Ian Mcshane

EGON BROCHER

1936 ALIBI FOR MURDER
Co-stars: William Gargan Marguerite Churchill

ANNE BROCHET

1990 CYRANO DE BERGERAC
Director: Jean-Paul Rappeneau
Co-stars: Gerard Depardieu Vincent Perez

1992 TOUS LES MATINS DU MONDE
Director: Alain Corneau
Co-stars: Gerard Depardieu Guillaume Depardieu

1997 DRIFTWOOD
Co-star: James Spader

GLADYS BROCKWELL

1916 SINS OF HER PARENT

1923 THE HUNCHBACK OF NOTRE DAME
Director: Wallace Worsley
Co-stars: Lon Chaney Patsy Ruth Miller

1927 SEVENTH HEAVEN
Director: Frank Borzage
Co-stars: Janet Gaynor Charles Farrell David Butler

1927 LONG PANTS
Director: Frank Capra
Co-stars: Harry Longdon Alma Bennett

1928 LIGHTS OF NEW YORK
Director: Bryan Foy
Co-stars: Helene Costello Eugene Pallette Cullen Landis

1929 THE ARGYLE CASE
Co-stars: Thomas Meighan Lila Lee H. B. Warner

HELEN BRODERICK

1931 FIFTY MILLION FRENCHMEN
Director: Lloyd Bacon
Co-stars: Olsen & Johnson William Gaxton

1935 TOP HAT
Director: Mark Sandrich
Co-stars: Fred Astaire Ginger Rogers Eric Blore

1936 SWING TIME
Director: George Stevens
Co-stars: Fred Astaire Ginger Rogers Victor Moore

1937 SHE'S GOT EVERYTHING
Director: Joseph Santley
Co-stars: Ann Sothern Gene Raymond Victor Moore

1937 WE'RE ON THE JURY
Director: Ben Holmes
Co-stars: Victor Moore Philip Huston Louise Latimer

1937 MEET THE MISSUS
Director: Joseph Santley
Co-stars: Victor Moore Anne Shirley Alan Bruce

1937 LIFE OF THE PARTY
Director: William Seiter
Co-stars: Joe Penner Gene Raymond Ann Miller

1938 RADIO CITY REVELS
Director: Ben Stoloff
Co-stars: Bob Burns Jack Oakie Ann Miller Jane Froman

1938 THE RAGE OF PARIS
Director: Henry Koster
Co-stars: Danielle Darrieux Douglas Fairbanks Louis Hayward

1938 ROAD TO RENO
Director: S. Sylvan Simon
Co-stars: Randolph Scott Hope Hampton Glenda Farrell

1938 SERVICE DE LUXE
Director: Rowland Lee
Co-stars: Constance Bennett Vincent Price Charles Ruggles

1938 STAND UP AND FIGHT
Director: W. S. Van Dyke
Co-stars: Wallace Beery Robert Taylor Florence Rice

1939 HONEYMOON IN BALI
Director: Edward Griffith
Co-stars: Madeleine Carroll Fred MacMurray

1940 THE CAPTAIN IS A LADY
Director: Robert Sinclair
Co-stars: Charles Coburn Billie Burke Beulah Bondi

1940 NO, NO NANETTE
Director: Herbert Wilcox
Co-stars: Anna Neagle Richard Carlson Victor Mature

1940 VIRGINIA
Director: Edward Griffith
Co-stars: Madeleine Carroll Fred MacMurray Sterling Hayden

1941 NICE GIRL?
Director: William Seiter
Co-stars: Deanna Durbin Franchot Tone Robert Stack

1941 FATHER TAKES A WIFE
Director: Jack Hively
Co-stars: Gloria Swanson Adolphe Menjou John Howard

1944 CHIP OFF THE OLD BLOCK
Director: Charles Lamont
Co-stars: Donald O'Connor Peggy Ryan Ann Blyth

1944 **HER PRIMITIVE MAN**
Director: Charles Lamont
Co-stars: Robert Paige Louise Allbritton Robert Benchey

1944 **THREE IS A FAMILY**
Director: Edward Ludwig
Co-stars: Charles Ruggles Fay Bainter Marjorie Reynolds

1945 **BECAUSE OF HIM**
Director: Richard Wallace
Co-stars: Deanna Durbin Charles Laughton Franchot Tone

LEA BRODIE

1978 **WARLORDS OF ATLANTIS**
Director: Kevin Connor
Co-stars: Doug McClure Cyd Charisse Peter Gilmore

V. S. BRODIE

1993 **GO FISH**
Director: Rose Troche
Co-stars: Guinevere Turner Anastasia Sharp

ESTELLE BRODY

1928 **KITTY**
Director: Victor Saville
Co-stars: John Stuart Dorothy Cumming Marie Ault

JO ANN BRODY

1973 **THE LONG GOODBYE**
Director: Robert Altman
Co-stars: Elliott Gould Nina Van Pallandt Sterling Hayden

EWA BROK

1984 **SILVER CITY**
Director: Sophia Turkiewicz
Co-stars: Gosia Dobrowolska Ivar Kants Anna Jemison

DOROTHY BROMILEY

1953 **THE GIRLS OF PLEASURE ISLAND**
Director: F. Hugh Herbert
Co-stars: Leo Genn Audrey Dalton Gene Barry

1956 **IT'S GREAT TO BE YOUNG**
Director: Cyril Frankel
Co-stars: John Mills Cecil Parker Jeremy Spenser

1956 **A TOUCH OF THE SUN**
Director: Gordon Parry
Co-stars: Frankie Howerd Ruby Murray Gordon Harker

ELAINE BROMKA

1989 **UNCLE BUCK**
Director: John Hughes
Co-stars: John Candy Amy Madigan Laurie Metcalf

SHEILA BROMLEY

1938 **GIRLS ON PROBATION**
Director: William McGann
Co-stars: Jane Bryan Ronald Reagan Elizabeth Risdon

1938 **ACCIDENTS WILL HAPPEN**
Director: William Clemens
Co-stars: Ronald Reagan Gloria Blondell Dick Purcell

BETTY BRONSON

1926 **BEN HUR**
Director: Fred Niblo
Co-stars: Ramon Novarro Francis X. Bushman May McAvoy

1928 **THE SINGING FOOL**
Director: Lloyd Bacon
Co-stars: Al Jolson Davey Lee Buddy Desylva

1929 **THE LOCKED DOOR**
Director: George Fitzmaurice
Co-stars: Barbara Stanwyck Rod La Rocque

1964 **THE NAKED KISS**
Director: Samuel Fuller
Co-stars: Constance Towers Anthony Eisley Patsy Kelly

LILIAN BRONSON

1946 **SENTIMENTAL JOURNEY**
Director: Walter Lang
Co-stars: Maureen O'Hara John Payne Connie Marshall

1947 **THE SHOCKING MISS PILGRIM**
Director: George Seaton
Co-stars: Betty Grable Dick Haymes Anne Revere

1949 **IN THE GOOD OLD SUMMERTIME**
Director: Robert Z. Leonard
Co-stars: Judy Garland Van Johnson S. Z. Sakall

1950 **THE NEXT VOICE YOU HEAR**
Director: William Wellman
Co-stars: James Whitmore Nancy Davis Jeff Corey

1963 **SPENCER'S MOUNTAIN**
Director: Delmer Daves
Co-stars: Henry Fonda Maureen O'Hara Donald Crisp

ELEANOR BRON

1965 **HELP**
Director: Dick Lester
Co-stars: The Beatles Leo McKern

1966 **ALFIE**
Director: Lewis Gilbert
Co-stars: Michael Caine Vivien Merchant Jane Asher

1967 **BEDAZZLED**
Director: Stanley Donen
Co-stars: Peter Cook Dudley Moore Raquel Welch

1967 **TWO FOR THE ROAD**
Director: Stanley Donen
Co-stars: Albert Finney Audrey Hepburn Claude Dauphin

1969 **WOMEN IN LOVE**
Director: Ken Russell
Co-stars: Glenda Jackson Jennie Linden Alan Bates

1969 **A TOUCH OF LOVE**
Director: Waris Hussein
Co-stars: Sandy Dennis Ian McKellen John Standing

1973 **THE NATIONAL HEALTH**
Director: Jack Gold
Co-stars: Jim Dale Lynn Redgrave Donald Sinden

1980 **THE SECRET POLICEMAN'S BALL**
Director: Roger Graef
Co-stars: John Cleese Peter Cook Michael Palin

1985 **TURTLE DIARY**
Director: John Irvin
Co-stars: Glenda Jackson Ben Kingsley Richard Johnson

1987 **QUARTERMAINE'S TERMS**
Director: Bill Hays
Co-stars: Edward Fox Peter Jeffrey John Gielgud

1987 **LITTLE DORRIT**
Director: Christine Edzard
Co-stars: Derek Jacobi Joan Greenwood Max Wall

1988 **INTRIGUE**
Director: David Drury
Co-stars: Scott Glenn Robert Loggia Martin Shaw

1990 **THE HOUR OF THE LYNX**
Director: Stuart Burge
Co-stars: Simon Donald Sylvestra Le Touzel

1990   **CHANGING STEP**
Director: Richard Wilson
Co-stars: James Convey Susan Wooldridge Anthony Sher

1994   **DEADLY ADVICE**
Director: Mandie Fletcher
Co-stars: Jane Horrocks Imelda Staunton Brenda Fricker

1996   **A LITTLE PRINCESS**
Director: Alphonso Cuaron
Co-stars: Liesel Matthews Vanessa Lee Chester

FAITH BROOK

1948   **UNEASY TERMS**
Director: Vernon Sewell
Co-stars: Michael Rennie Moira Lister Nigel Patrick

1956   **THE INTIMATE STRANGER**
Director: Joseph Losey
Co-stars: Richard Basehart Mary Murphy Mervyn Johns

1957   **CHASE A CROOKED SHADOW**
Director: Michael Anderson
Co-stars: Richard Todd Anne Baxter Herbert Lom

1957   **WICKED AS THEY COME**
Director: Ken Hughes
Co-stars: Arlene Dahl Herbert Marshall Phil Carey

1959   **THE THIRTY-NINE STEPS**
Director: Ralph Thomas
Co-stars: Kenneth More Taina Elg Sid James

1967   **TO SIR, WITH LOVE**
Director: James Clavell
Co-stars: Sidney Poitier Judy Geeson Suzy Kendall

1969   **WALK A CROOKED PATH**
Director: John Brason
Co-stars: Tenniel Evans Christopher Coll Patricia Haynes

1979   **NORTH SEA HIJACK**
Director: Andrew McLaglen
Co-stars: Roger Moore Anthony Perkins James Mason

1980   **THE SEA WOLVES**
Director: Andrew McLaglen
Co-stars: Gregory Peck Roger Moore David Niven

1984   **THE RAZOR'S EDGE**
Director: John Byrum
Co-stars: Bill Murray Denholm Elliott Theresa Russell

1991   **MISS MARPLE:THEY DO IT WITH MIRRORS**
Director: Norman Stone
Co-stars: Joan Hickson Joss Ackland

IRINA BROOK *(Daughter Of Peter Brook)*

1986   **THE GIRL IN THE PICTURE**
Director: Cary Parker
Co-stars: John Gordon Sinclair Gregor Fisher

1986   **CAPTIVE**
Director: Paul Mayersberg
Co-stars: Oliver Reed Xavier Deluc Corinne Decla

1990   **THE FOOL**
Director: Christine Edzard
Co-stars: Derek Jacobi Cyril Cusack Ruth Mitchell

LESLEY BROOK

1938   **DEAD MEN TELL NO TALES**
Director: David MacDonald
Co-stars: Emlyn Williams Hugh Williams

1939   **THE NURSEMAID WHO DISAPPEARED**
Director: Arthur Woods
Co-stars: Arthur Margetson Edward Chapman

1942   **VARIETY JUBILEE**
Director: MacLean Rogers
Co-stars: George Robey Ellis Irving Slim Rhyder

1943   **WHEN WE ARE MARRIED**
Director: Lance Comfort
Co-stars: Raymond Huntley Sydney Howard Marian Spencer

1944   **THE TWILIGHT HOUR**
Director: Paul Stein
Co-stars: Mervyn Johns Basil Radford Marie Lohr

1945   **FOR YOU ALONE**
Director: Geoffrey Faithfull
Co-stars: Jimmy Hanley Dinah Sheridan Irene Handl

HILLARY BROOKE

1942   **COUNTER-ESPIONAGE**
Director: Edward Dmytryk
Co-stars: Warren Willlam Eric Blore Forrest Tucker

1942   **SHERLOCK HOLMES AND THE VOICE OF TERROR**
Director: John Rawlins
Co-stars: Basil Rathbone Nigel Bruce

1943   **SHERLOCK HOLMES FACES DEATH**
Director: Roy William Neill
Co-stars: Dennis Hoey Basil Rathbone Nigel Bruce

1944   **STANDING ROOM ONLY**
Director: Sidney Lanfield
Co-stars: Paulette Goddard Fred MacMurray

1944   **JANE EYRE**
Director: Robert Stevenson
Co-stars: Joan Fontaine Orson Welles Margaret O'Brien

1944   **MINISTRY OF FEAR**
Director: Fritz Lang
Co-stars: Ray Milland Marjorie Reynolds Dan Duryea

1945   **ROAD TO UTOPIA**
Director: Hal Walker
Co-stars: Bing Crosby Bob Hope Dorothy Lamour

1945   **WOMAN IN GREEN**
Director: Roy William Neill
Co-stars: Basil Rathbone Nigel Bruce Henry Daniell

1945   **CRIME DOCTOR'S COURAGE**
Director: George Sherman
Co-stars: Warner Baxter Jerome Cowan

1946   **MONSIEUR BEAUCAIRE**
Director: George Marshall
Co-stars: Bob Hope Joan Caulfield Marjorie Reynolds

1946   **THE STRANGE WOMAN**
Director: Edgar Ulmer
Co-stars: Hedy Lamarr Louis Hayward George Sanders

1947   **I COVER BIG TOWN**
Director: William Thomas
Co-stars: Philip Reed Robert Lowery Byron Barr

1949   **AFRICA SCREAMS**
Director: Charles Barton
Co-stars: Bud Abbott & Lou Costello Max Baer

1950   **THE ADMIRAL WAS A LADY**
Director: Albert Rogell
Co-stars: Edmond O'Brien Wanda Hendrix Rudy Vallee

1950   **VENDETTA**
Director: Mel Ferrer
Co-stars: Faith Domergue George Dolenz Donald Buka Nigel Bruce

1951   **THE LOST CONTINENT**
Director: Samuel Newfield
Co-stars: Cesar Romero John Hoyt Whit Bissell

1952   ABBOTT AND COSTELLO
MEET CAPTAIN KIDD
Director: Charles Lamont
Co-stars: Abbott And Costello Charles Laughton

1953   INVADERS FROM MARS
Director: William Cameron Menzies
Co-stars: Helena Carter Arthur Franz

1953   THE MAZE
Director: William Cameron Menzies
Co-stars: Richard Carlson Veronica Hurst Michael Pate

1953   MEXICAN MANHUNT
Director: Rex Bailey
Co-stars: George Brent Morris Ankrum Karen Sharpe

1955   BENGAZI
Director: Eugene Tevlin
Co-stars: Richard Conte Victor McLaglan Richard Carlson

1956   THE MAN WHO KNEW TOO MUCH
Director: Alfred Hitchcock
Co-stars: James Stewart Doris Day Bernard Miles

AMY BROOKS *(Aimee)*

1989   SAY ANYTHING
Director: Cameron Crowe
Co-stars: John Cusack Ione Skye Lili Taylor

1992   CRITTERS 3
Director: Kristine Peterson
Co-stars: John Calvin Leonardo Dicaprio Katherine Cortez

BEVERLEY BROOKS

1956   FIND THE LADY
Director: Charles Saunders
Co-stars: Donald Houston Mervyn Johns Kay Callard

CARROLL BROOKS

1986   MAUVAIS SONG
Director: Leos Carax
Co-stars: Michel Piccoli Juliette Binoche Julie Delpy

GERALDINE BROOKS

1947   POSSESSED
Director: Curtis Bernhardt
Co-stars: Joan Crawford Raymond Massey Van Heflin

1947   CRY WOLF
Director: Peter Godfrey
Co-stars: Barbara Stanwyck Errol Flynn Richard Basehart

1948   AN ACT OF MURDER
Director: Michael Gordon
Co-stars: Fredric March Florence Eldridge Edmond O'Brien

1948   EMBRACEABLE YOU
Director: Felix Jacoves
Co-stars: Dane Clark Wallace Ford Richard Rober

1949   CHALLENGE TO LASSIE
Director: Richard Thorpe
Co-stars: Edmund Gwenn Donald Crisp Reginald Owen

1949   THE RECKLESS MOMENT
Director: Max Ophuls
Co-stars: James Mason Joan Bennett Henry O'Neill

1949   THE YOUNGER BROTHERS
Director: Edwin Marin
Co-stars: Wayne Morris Bruce Bennett Robert Hutton

1952   THE GREEN GLOVE
Director: Rudolph Mate
Co-stars: Glenn Ford Cedric Hardwicke George Macready

1966   JOHNNY TIGER
Director: Paul Wendkos
Co-stars: Robert Taylor Chad Everett Brenda Scott

1967   IRONSIDE
Director: James Goldstone
Co-stars: Raymond Burr Don Galloway Barbara Anderson

1975   MR. RICCO
Director: Paul Bogart
Co-stars: Dean Martin Eugene Roche Cindy Williams

GLYNIS BROOKS

1990   CLOSE RELATIONS
Director: Adrian Shergold
Co-stars: James Hazeldlne Clare Holman June Barrie

HAZEL BROOKS

1947   BODY AND SOUL
Director:`   Robert Rossen
Co-stars: John Garfield Lilli Palmer Anne Revere

1948   ARCH OF TRIUMPH
Director: Lewis Milestone
Co-stars: Ingrid Bergman Charles Boyer Charles Laughton

1948   SLEEP MY LOVE
Director: Douglas Slrk
Co-stars: Claudette Colbert Don Ameche Robert Cummings

HILDY BROOKS

1981   THE CHOSEN
Director: Jeremy Paul Kagan
Co-stars: Rod Steiger Robby Benson Maximilian Schell

IRIS BROOKS

1972   UP THE SANDBOX
Director: Irwin Kerschner
Co-stars: Barbra Streisand Davld Selby Jane Hoffman

JACQUELINE BROOKS

1975   THE GAMBLER
Director: Karel Reisz
Co-stars: James Caan Paul Sorvino Lauren Hutton

1978   A DEATH IN CANAAN
Director: Tony Richardson
Co-stars: Stefanie Powers Paul Clemens Brian Dennehy

1979   LAST EMBRACE
Director: Jonathon Demme
Co-stars: Roy Scheider Janet Margolin Sam Levene

1980   ACT OF LOVE
Director: Jud Taylor
Co-stars: Ron Howard Mickey Rourke Robert Foxworth

1981   GHOST STORY
Director: John Irvin
Co-stars: Fred Astaire Melvyn Douglas Douglas Fairbanks Jnr

1983   THE ENTITY
Director: Sidney Furie
Co-stars: Barbara Hershey Ron Silver George Coe

1983   WITHOUT A TRACE
Director: Stanley Jaffe
Co-stars: Kate Nelligan Judd Hirsch Stockard Channing

1991   THE NAKED GUN 2 1/2:
THE SMELL OF FEAR
Director: David Zucker
Co-stars: Leslie Nielsen Priscilla Presley

1993   THE GOOD SON
Director: Joseph Rubin
Co-stars: Elijah Wood Macauley Culkin Wendy Crewson

JEAN BROOKS

1943 THE SEVENTH VICTIM
Director: Mark Robson
Co-stars: Kim Hunter Tom Conway Isabel Jewell

1943 THE FALCON IN DANGER
Director: William Clemens
Co-stars: Tom Conway Amelia Ward Elaine Shepard

1943 THE LEOPARD MAN
Director: Jacques Tourneur
Co-stars: Dennis O'Keefe Isabel Jewell Margo

1944 YOUTH RUNS WILD
Director: Mark Robson
Co-stars: Bonita Granville Kent Smith Arthur Shields

LESLIE BROOKS

1942 YOU WERE NEVER LOVELIER
Director: William Smith
Co-stars: Fred Astaire Rita Hayworth Adolphe Menjou

1943 WHAT'S BUZZIN' COUSIN?
Director: Charles Barton
Co-stars: Ann Miller Jeff Donnell John Hubbard

1944 NINE GIRLS
Director: Leigh Jason
Co-stars: Ann Harding Evelyn Keyes Jinx Falkenburg

1946 THE MAN WHO DARED
Co-star: George Macready

1948 THE SCAR
Director: Steve Sekeley
Co-stars: Joan Bennett Paul Henreid Eduard Franz

1948 THE COBRA STRIKES
Co-stars: Richard Fraser Shella Ryan Philip Ahn

1948 ROMANCE ON THE HIGH SEAS
Director: Michael Curtiz
Co-stars: Doris Day Jack Carson Oscar Levant

LOLA BROOKS

1959 ON THE BEACH
Director: Stanley Kramer
Co-stars: Gregory Peck Ava Gardner Fred Astaire

LOUISE BROOKS

1928 A GIRL IN EVERY PORT
Director: Howard Hawkes
Co-stars: Victor McLaglen Robert Armstrong Sally Rand

1928 BEGGARS OF LIFE
Director: William Wellman
Co-stars: Wallace Beery Richard Arlen Rosco Karns

1929 PANDORA'S BOX
Director: G. W. Pabst
Co-stars: Fritz Kortner Franz Lederer Alice Roberts

1929 DIARY OF A LOST GIRL
Director: G. W. Pabst
Co-stars: Fritz Rasp Josef Ravensky

1929 CANARY MURDER CASE
Director: Malcolm St .Clair
Co-stars: William Powell Jean Arthur Eugene Pallette

1929 ASPHALT
Director: Joe May
Co-stars: Gustav Frohlich Betty Amman Else Heller

1931 GOD'S GIFT TO WOMEN
Director: Michael Curtiz
Co-stars: Frank Fay Joan Blondell Laura La Plante

1931 IT PAYS TO ADVERTISE
Director: Frank Tuttle
Co-stars: Norman Foster Carole Lombard Eugene Pallette

1938 OVERLAND STAGE RAIDERS
Director: George Sherman
Co-stars: John Wayne Ray Corrigan Max Terhune

LYN BROOKS

1974 AKENFIELD
Director: Peter Hall
Co-stars: Peggy Cole Garrow Shand Barbara Tilney

MARGARET BROOKS

1967 OUR MOTHER'S HOUSE
Director: Jack Clayton
Co-stars: Dirk Bogarde Pamela Franklin Mark Lester

MARJORIE BROOKS

1935 SHE SHALL HAVE MUSIC
Director: Leslie Hiscott
Co-stars: Jack Hylton Claude Dampier June Clyde

PHYLLIS BROOKS

1935 ANOTHER FACE
Director: Christy Cabanne
Co-stars: Brian Donlevy Wallace Ford Erik Rhodes

1937 DANGEROUSLY YOURS
Director: Mal St. Clair
Co-stars: Cesar Romero Jane Darwell Alan Dinehart

1937 CITY GIRL
Director: Alfred Werker
Co-stars: Ricardo Cortez Robert Wilcox Chick Chandler

1938 CHARLIE CHAN IN HONOLULU
Director: Bruce Humberstone
Co-stars: Sidney Toler Sen Yung Geroge Zucco

1938 REBECCA OF SUNNYBROOK FARM
Director: Allan Dwan
Co-stars: Shirley Temple Gloria Stuart Bill Robinson

1938 IN OLD CHICAGO
Director: Henry King
Co-stars: Tyrone Power Don Ameche Alice Faye

1938 LITTLE MISS BROADWAY
Director: Irving Cummings
Co-stars: Shirley Temple George Murphy Jimmy Durante

1938 STRAIGHT, PLACE AND SHOW
Director: David Butler
Co-stars: Ritz Bros Ethel Merman

1939 CHARLIE CHAN IN RENO
Director: Norman Foster
Co-stars: Sidney Toler Ricardo Cortez Robert Lowery

1941 THE SHANGHAI GESTURE
Director: Josef Von Sternberg
Co-stars: Ona Munson Victor Mature Walter Huston

1943 NO PLACE FOR A LADY
Co-star: Dick Powell

1944 DANGEROUS PASSAGE
Co-stars: Robert Lowery Charles Arnt

SUSAN BROOKS

1985 INVITATION TO THE WEDDING
Director: Joseph Brooks
Co-stars: Ralph Rlchardson John Gielgud Paul Nlcholas

COLETTE BROSSET

1954 FEMMES DE PARIS
Director: Jean Loubignac
Co-stars: Robert Dhery Louis De Funes

1961 **LA BELLE AMERICAINE**
Director: Robert Dhery
Co-stars: Robert Dhery Louls De Funes Annie Ducaux

MARY BROUGH

1928 **DAWN**
Director: Herbert Wilcox
Co-stars: Sybll Thorndike Marie Ault Anna Neagle

1930 **TONS OF MONEY**
Director: Tom Walls
Co-stars: Ralph Lynn Yvonne Arnaud Robertson Hare

1930 **ROOKERY NOOK**
Director: Tom Walls
Co-stars: Ralph Lynn Robertson Hare Tom Walls

1932 **A NIGHT LIKE THIS**
Director: Tom Walls
Co-stars: Tom Walls Ralph Lynn Robertson Hare

1932 **THARK**
Director: Tom Walls
Co-stars: Tom Walls Ralph Lynn Robertson Hare

1933 **A CUCKOO IN THE NEST**
Director: Tom Walls
Co-stars: Ralph Lynn Yvonne Arnaud Gordon James

1933 **TURKEY TIME**
Director: Tom Walls
Co-stars: Tom Walls Robertson Hare Dorothy Hyson

LILIANE BROUSSE

1963 **PARANOIAC**
Director: Freddie Francis
Co-stars: Oliver Reed Janette Scott Maurice Denham

ADA BROWN

1943 **STORMY WEATHER**
Director: Andrew Stone
Co-stars: Bill Robinson Lena Horne Fats Waller

AMELDA BROWN

1987 **LITTLE DORRIT**
Director: Christine Edzard
Co-stars: Derek Jacobi Joan Greenwood Max Wall

1990 **DAKOTA ROAD**
Director: Nick Ward
Co-stars: Charlotte Chatton Jason Carter Alan Howard

1992 **SECONDS OUT**
Director: Bruce MacDonald
Co-stars: Steven Waddington Tom Bell Derek Newark

BARBARA BROWN

1942 **YOU WERE NEVER LOVELIER**
Director: William A. Seiter
Co-stars: Fred Astaire Rita Hayworth Adolphe Menjou

1945 **PILLOW TO POST**
Director: Vincent Sherman
Co-stars: Ida Lupino Sydney Greenstreet Stuart Erwin

1947 **THAT WAY WITH WOMEN**
Director: Frederick De Cordova
Co-stars: Sydney Greenstreet Martha Vickers

1948 **ARTHUR TAKES OVER**
Co-stars: Skip Homeier Howard Freeman

1949 **YES SIR THAT'S MY BABY**
Director: George Sherman
Co-stars: Donald O'Connor Gloria DeHaven

1952 **ABBOTT & COSTELLO:**
JACK AND THE BEANSTALK
Director: Jean Yarbrough
Co-stars: Bud Abbott Lou Costello

BLAIR BROWN

1978 **THE CHOIRBOYS**
Director: Robert Aldrich
Co-stars: Charles Durning Perry King Lou Gossett Jnr.

1978 **AND I ALONE SURVIVED**
Director: William Graham
Co-stars: David Ackroyd Vera Miles

1980 **ALTERED STATES**
Director: Ken Russell
Co-stars: William Hurt Bob Balaban Drew Barrymore

1981 **CONTINENTAL DIVIDE**
Director: Michael Apted
Co-stars: John Belushi Allen Goorwitz Carlin Glynn

1987 **HANDS OF A STRANGER**
Director: Larry Elikan
Co-stars: Armand Assante Beverley D'Angelo

1988 **STRAPLESS**
Director: David Hare
Co-stars: Bruno Ganz Bridget Fonda Alan Howard

1988 **STEALING HOME**
Director: Will Aldis
Co-stars: Mark Harmon Jodie Foster Harold Ramis

1992 **PASSED AWAY**
Director: Charlie Peters
Co-stars: Bob Hoskins Jack Warden Tim Curry

1992 **MAJORITY RULE**
Director: Gwen Arner
Co-stars: John Glover Donald Moffat

1993 **RIO SHANNON**
Director: Mimi Leder
Co-stars: Patrick Van Horn Michael Deluise Shay Astar

1993 **THE GIFT OF LOVE**
Director: Paul Bogart
Co-stars: Andy Griffith Will Friedle

1993 **MISSING PARENTS**
Director: Martin Nicholson
Co-stars: Matt Frewer Bobby Jacoby

1994 **MOMENT OF TRUTH: TO WALK AGAIN**
Director: Randall Zisk
Co-stars: Ken Howard Cameron Bancroft

1994 **THE GOOD POLICEMAN**
Director: Peter Werner
Co-stars: Ron Silver Tony Lobianco Joe Morton

CAITLIN BROWN

1990 **MIAMI BLUES**
Director: George Armitage
Co-stars: Alec Baldwin Fred Ward Jennifer Jason Leigh

ELEONORA BROWN

1960 **TWO WOMEN**
Director: Vittorio De Sica
Co-stars: Sophia Loren Jean-Paul Belmondo Raf Valone

ESTHER BROWN

1956 **THE TEN COMMANDMENTS**
Director: Cecil B. DeMille
Co-stars: Charlton Heston Yul Brynner Anne Baxter

GAYE BROWN

1985   MATA HARI
Director: Curtis Harrington
Co-stars: Sylvia Kristel Christopher Cazanove Oliver Tobias

1993   ROYAL CELEBRATION
Director: Ferdinand Fairfax
Co-stars: Minnie Driver Rupert Graves Peter Howitt

GEORGIA BROWN

1965   A STUDY IN TERROR
Director: James Hill
Co-stars: John Neville Donald Houston Robert Morley

1968   THE FIXER
Director: John Frankenheimer
Co-stars: Alan Bates Dirk Bogarde Hugh Griffith

1969   LOCK UP YOUR DAUGHTERS
Director: Peter Coe
Co-stars: Christopher Plummer Susannah York Tom Bell

1970   THE RAGING MOON
Director: Bryan Forbes
Co-stars: Nanette Newman Malcolm McDowell Bernard Lee

1972   NOTHING BUT THE NIGHT
Director: Peter Sasdy
Co-stars: Christopher Lee Peter Cushing Diana Dors

1972   RUNNING SCARED
Director: David Hemmings
Co-stars: Robert Powell Gayle Hunnicutt Barry Morse

1973   TALES THAT WITNESS MADNESS
Director: Freddie Francis
Co-stars: Jack Hawkins Donald Pleasence

1976   THE SEVEN PERCENT SOLUTION
Director: Herbert Ross
Co-stars: Nicol Williamson Robert Duvall Joel Grey

1976   THE BAWDY ADVENTURES OF TOM JONES
Director: Cliff Owen
Co-stars: Nicky Henson Trevor Howard Joan Collins

1991   VICTIM OF LOVE
Director: Jerry London
Co-stars: Pierce Brosnan JoBeth Williams

JANET BROWN

1965   A HOME OF YOUR OWN
Director: Bob Kellett
Co-stars: Ronnie Barker Richard Briers Bernard Cribbins

1977   WOMBLING FREE
Director: Lionel Jeffries
Co-stars: Lionel Jeffries David Jason Jon Pertwee

1981   FOR YOUR EYES ONLY
Director: John Glen
Co-stars: Roger Moore Carole Bouquet Julian Glover

JUANITA BROWN

1974   CAGED HEAT
Director: Jonathan Demme
Co-stars: Barbara Steele Erica Gavin Rainbeaux Smith

JULIE BROWN

1988   EARTH GIRLS ARE EASY
Director: Julien Temple
Co-stars: Geena Davis Jeff Goldblum Jim Carrey

1993   RAINING STONES
Director: Ken Loach
Co-stars: Bruce Jones Ricky Tomlinson Gemma Phoenix

KAY BROWN

1951   THE STRIP
Director: Leslie Kardos
Co-stars: Mickey Rooney Sally Forrest Louis Armstrong

LINDA BROWN

1993   PLEASURE IN PARADISE
Director: B. Rakeley
Co-stars: Diane Cotton John Paul Lorello

NADIA GAY BROWN

1986   AS SUMMERS DIE
Director: Jean-Claude Tramont
Co-stars: Scott Glenn Jaime Lee Curtis Bette Davis

OLIVIA BROWN

1990   MEMORIES OF MURDER
Director: Robert Lewis
Co-stars: Robin Thomas Nancy Allen Vanity

PAMELA BROWN

1941   ONE OF OUR AIRCRAFT IS MISSING
Director: Michael Powell
Co-stars: Eric Portman Bernard Miles Emrys Jones

1945   I KNOW WHERE I'M GOING
Director:s   Michael Powell
Co-stars: Wendy Hiller Roger Livesey John Laurie

1951   ALICE IN WONDERLAND
Director: Dallas Bower
Co-stars: Carol Marsh Stephen Murray Felix Aylmer

1951   THE TALES OF HOFFMAN
Director: Michael Powell
Co-stars: Moira Shearer Robert Helpman Robert Rounseville

1952   THE SECOND MRS. TANQUERAY
Director: Dallas Bower
Co-stars: Hugh Sinclair Virginia McKenna

1953   PERSONAL AFFAIR
Director: Anthony Pellisier
Co-stars: Leo Genn Glynis Johns Gene Tierney

1955   NOW AND FOREVER
Director: Mario Zampi
Co-stars: Janette Scott Vernon Gray Kay Walsh

1956   LUST FOR LIFE
Director: Vincent Minnelli
Co-stars: Kirk Douglas Anthony Quinn James Donald

1959   THE SCAPEGOAT
Director: Robert Hamer
Co-stars: Alec Guinness Bette Davis Nicole Maurey

1963   CLEOPATRA
Director: Joseph Mankiewicz
Co-stars: Elizabeth Taylor Rlchard Burton Rex Harrison

1964   BECKET
Director: Peter Glenville
Co-stars: Peter O'Toole Richard Burton John Gielgud

1967   HALF A SIXPENCE
Director: George Sidney
Co-stars: Tommy Steele Julia Foster Penelope Horner

1969   SECRET CEREMONY
Director: Joseph Losey
Co-stars: Elizabeth Taylor Robert Mitchum Mia Farrow

1970   WUTHERING HEIGHTS
Director: Robert Fuest
Co-stars: Anna Calder-Marshall Timothy Dalton Ian Ogilvey

1970   **FIGURES IN A LANDSCAPE**
Director: Joseph Losey
Co-stars: Robert Shaw Malcolm McDowell Henry Woolf

1971   **THE NIGHT DIGGER**
Director: Alastair Reid
Co-stars: Patricia Neal Nicholas Clay Yootha Joyce

1972   **LADY CAROLINE LAMB**
Director: Robert Bolt
Co-stars: Sarah Miles Jon Finch Richard Chamberlain John Mills

1973   **DRACULA**
Director: Dan Curtis
Co-stars: Jack Palance Simon Ward Nigel Davenport

1975   **IN THIS HOUSE OF BREDE**
Director: George Schaefer
Co-stars: Diana Rigg Judi Bowker Dennis Quilley

RITZA BROWN

1982   **ATOR, THE FIGHTING EAGLE**
Director: David Hills
Co-stars: Miles O'keefe Edmund Purdom

1985   **THE McGUFFIN**
Director: Colin Bucksey
Co-stars: Charles Dance Brian Glover Phyllis Logan

RUTH BROWN

1988   **HAIRSPRAY**
Director: John Waters
Co-stars: Ricki Lane Sonny Bono Pia Zadora

1991   **TRUE IDENTITY**
Director: Charles Lane
Co-stars: Lenny Henry Frank Langella J.T. Walsh

SHARON BROWN

1988   **MAYBE BABY**
Director: John Avildsen
Co-stars: Molly Ringwald Kenneth Mars Randall Batinkoff

SUSAN BROWN

1987   **ROAD**
Director: Alan Clark
Co-stars: Jane Horrocks Lesley Sharp Neil Dudgeon

1989 LOVING HAZEL
Director: Peter Smith
Co-stars: Hugh Quarshie Gemma Darlington Dona Croll

VANESSA BROWN

1946   **I'VE ALWAYS LOVED YOU**
Director: Frank Borzage
Co-stars: Philip Dorn Catherine McLeod Felix Bressart

1946   **MARGIE**
Director: Henry King
Co-stars: Jeanne Crain Glenn Langan Alan Young

1947   **THE FOXES OF HARROW**
Director: John Stahl
Co-stars: Rex Harrison Maureen O'Hara Victor McLaglen

1947   **THE LATE GEORGE APLEY**
Director: Joseph Mankiewicz
Co-stars: Ronald Colman Edna Best Richard Haydn

1947   **MOTHER WORE TIGHTS**
Director: Walter Lang
Co-stars: Betty Grable Dan Dailey Mona Freeman

1947   **THE GHOST AND MRS. MUIR**
Director: Joseph Mankiewicz
Co-stars: Rex Harrison Gene Tierney Edna Best

1949   **THE HEIRESS**
Director: William Wyler
Co-stars: Olivia De Havilland Montgomery Clift Ralph Richardson

1949   **BIG JACK**
Director: Richard Thorpe
Co-stars: Wallace Beery Marjorie Main Richard Conte

1949   **THE SECRET OF ST. IVES**
Director: Phil Rosen
Co-stars: Richard Ney Henry Daniel Aubrey Mather

1950   **TARZAN AND THE SLAVE GIRL**
Director: Lee Sholem
Co-stars: Lex Barker Robert Alda Hurt Hatfield

1950   **A LETTER TO THREE HUSBANDS**

1952   **THE FIGHTER**
Director: Herbert Kline
Co-stars: Richard Conte Lee J. Cobb Frank Silvera

1952   **THE BAD AND THE BEAUTIFUL**
Director: Vincente Minnelli
Co-stars: Kirk Douglas Lana Turner Dick Powell

1967   **ROSIE!**
Director: David Lowell Rich
Co-stars: Rosalind Russell Brian Aherne Sandra Dee

ANGELA BROWNE

1966   **PRESS FOR TIME**
Director: Robert Asher
Co-stars: Norman Wisdom Derek Bond Peter Jones

1985   **THE ADVENTURES OF SHERLOCK HOLMES: THE COPPER BEACHES**
Director: Paul Annett
Co-stars: Jeremy Brett David Burke

CICELY BROWNE

1976   **CASANOVA**
Director: Federico Fellini
Co-stars: Donald Sutherland Tina Aumont Carmen Scarpitta

CORAL BROWNE

1936   **THE AMATEUR GENTLEMAN**
Director: Thornton Freeland
Co-stars: Douglas Fairbanks Elissa Landi

1938   **BLACK LIMELIGHT**
Co-stars: Raymond Massey Joan Marion Walter Hudd Henry Oscar

1938   **WE'RE GOING TO BE RICH**
Director: Monte Banks
Co-stars: Gracie Fields Victor McLaglen Brian Donlevy

1939   **THE NURSEMAID WHO DISAPPEARED**
Director: Arthur Woods
Co-stars: Arthur Margetson Peter Coke

1940   **LET GEORGE DO IT**
Director: Marcel Varnel
Co-stars: George Formby Phyllis Calvert Garry Marsh

1946   **PICCADILLY INCIDENT**
Director: Herbert Wilcox
Co-stars: Anna Neagle Michael Wilding Edward Rigby

1947   **THE COURTNEYS OF CURZON STREET**
Director: Herbert Wilcox
Co-stars: Anna Neagle Michael Wilding Helen Cherry

1954   **BEAUTIFUL STRANGER**
Director: David Miller
Co-stars: Ginger Rogers Stanley Baker

1958   **AUNTIE MAME**
Director: Morton DaCosta
Co-stars: Rosalind Russell Forrest Tucker Fred Clark

1961 GO TO BLAZES
Director: Michael Truman
Co-stars: Daniel Massey Dave King Robert Morley

1961 THE ROMAN SPRING OF MRS. STONE
Director: Jose Quintero
Co-stars: Vivien Leigh Warren Beatty

1962 TAMAHINE
Director: Philip Leacock
Co-stars: Nancy Kwan John Fraser Dennis Price

1962 DR.CRIPPEN
Director: Robert Lynn
Co-stars: Donald Pleasence Samantha Eggar Donald Wolfit

1967 THE NIGHT OF THE GENERALS
Director: Anatole Litvak
Co-stars: Peter O'Toole Omar Sharif Juliette Greco

1968 THE LEGEND OF LYLAH CLARE
Director: Robert Aldrich
Co-stars: Kim Novak Peter Finch Ernest Borgnine

1969 THE KILLING OF SISTER GEORGE
Director: Robert Aldrich
Co-stars: Beryl Reid Susannah York

1972 THE RULING CLASS
Director: Peter Medak
Co-stars: Peter O'Toole Alastair Sim Arthur Lowe

1973 THEATRE OF BLOOD
Director: Douglas Hickox
Co-stars: Vincent Price Diana Rigg Ian Hendry

1975 THE DROWNING POOL
Director: Stuart Rosenberg
Co-stars: Paul Newman Joanne Woodward Melanie Griffith

1983 AN ENGLISHMAN ABROAD
Director: John Schlesinger
Co-stars: Alan Bates Charles Gray Harold Innocent

1984 AMERICAN DREAMER
Director: Rick Rosenthal
Co-stars: JoBeth Williams Tom Conti Giancarlo Gianinni

1985 DREAMCHILD
Director: Gavin Miller
Co-stars: Peter Gallagher Ian Holm Jane Asher

DIANA BROWNE

1982 BASKET CASE
Director: Frank Henenlotter
Co-stars: Kevin Van Hentenryck Beverley Bonner

IRENE BROWNE

1929 THE LETTER
Director: Jean De Limur
Co-stars: Jeanne Eagels Reginald Owen Herbert Marshall

1933 BERKELEY SQUARE
Director: Frank Lloyd
Co-stars: Leslie Howard Heather Angel Valerie Taylor

1933 CAVALCADE
Director: Frank Lloyd
Co-stars: Clive Brook Diana Wynyard Ursula Jeans

1933 CHRISTOPHER STRONG
Director: Dorothy Arzner
Co-stars: Katherine Hepburn Colin Clive Billie Burke

1933 PEG O' MY HEART
Director: Robert Z. Leonard
Co-stars: Marion Davies Onslow Stevens Alan Mowbray

1936 THE AMATEUR GENTLEMAN
Director: Thornton Freeland
Co-stars: Douglas Fairbanks Jnr. Elissa Landi

1938 PYGMALION
Director: Leslie Howard
Co-stars: Leslie Howard Wendy Hiller Wilfrid Lawson

1946 MEET ME AT DAWN
Director: Thornton Freeland
Co-stars: Hazel Court William Eythe Stanley Holloway

1948 QUARTET
Director: Ken Annakin
Co-stars: Dirk Bogarde Mai Zetterling Basil Radford

1951 THE HOUSE IN THE SQUARE
Director: Roy Baker
Co-stars: Tyrone Power Ann Blyth Michael Rennie

1957 BARNACLE BILL
Director: Charles Frend
Co-stars: Alec Guinness Percy Herbert Harold Goodwin

1959 SERIOUS CHARGE
Director: Terence Young
Co-stars: Anthony Quayle Andrew Ray Cliff Richard

1962 THE WRONG ARM OF THE LAW
Director: Cliff Owen
Co-stars: Peter Sellers Lionel Jeffries Davy Kaye

LESLIE BROWNE
Nominated For Best Supporting Actress In 1977 For "The Turning Point"

1977 THE TURNING POINT
Director: Herbert Ross
Co-stars: Anne Bancroft Shirley MacLaine Tom Skeritt

1980 NIJINSKY
Director: Herbert Ross
Co-stars: Alan Bates George De La Pena Janet Suzman

1987 DANCERS
Director: Herbert Ross
Co-stars: Mikhail Baryshnikov Alessandra Ferri Lynn Seymour

LUCILLE BROWNE

1933 DOUBLE HARNESS
Director: John Cromwell
Co-stars: Ann Harding William Powell Lillian Bond

1935 WESTERN FRONTIER
Co-star: Ken Maynard

1935 TEXAS TERROR
Director: Robert Bradbury
Co-stars: John Wayne George "Gabby" Hayes Yakima Canutt

1937 CHEYENNE RIDES AGAIN
Co-stars: Tom Tyler Lon Chaney

MARJORIE BROWNE

1945 I DIDN'T DO IT
Director: George Formby
Co-stars: George Formby Hilda Mundy Gaston Palmer

PADDY BROWNE

1939 SPY FOR A DAY
Director: Mario Zampi
Co-stars: Duggie Wakefield Albert Lieven Jack Allen

RENO BROWNE

1946 THE GENTLEMAN FROM TEXAS
Co-stars: Johnny Mack Brown Raymond Hatton

SUZANNE BROWNE

1992 KILLER LOOKS
Director: Toby Phillips
Co-stars: Len Donato Janine Lindemoulder

JILL BROWNING

1944 SONG OF THE OPEN ROAD
Director: S. Sylvan Simon
Co-stars: Jane Powell Bonita Granville W. C .Fields

1945 THE TOWN WENT WILD
Director: Ralph Murphy
Co-stars: Freddie Bartholomew Edward Everett Horton

ALISON BRUCE

1990 AN ANGEL AT MY TABLE
Director: Jane Campion
Co-stars: Kerry Fox Alexia Keogh Karen Fergusson

1991 OLD SCORES
Director: Adam Clayton
Co-stars: Robert Pugh Glyn Houston Windsor Davies

BETTY BRUCE

1962 GYPSY
Director: Mervyn LeRoy
Co-stars: Rosalind Russell Natalie Wood Karl Malden

BRENDA BRUCE

1946 PICCADILLY INCIDENT
Director: Herbert Wilcox
Co-stars: Anna Neagle Michael Wilding A. E. Matthews

1946 I SEE A DARK STRANGER
Director: Frank Launder
Co-stars: Deborah Kerr Trevor Howard

1946 WHILE THE SUN SHINES
Director: Anthony Asquith
Co-stars: Ronald Howard Bonar Colleano Barbara White

1947 WHEN THE BOUGH BREAKS
Director: Lawrence Huntington
Co-stars: Patricia Roc Rosamund John Bill Owen

1948 MY MOTHER'S KEEPER
Director: Roy Rich
Co-stars: Jack Warner George Cole Jane Hylton

1958 BEHIND THE MASK
Director: Brian Desmond Hurst
Co-stars: Michael Redgrave Tony Britton Ian Bannen

1960 PEEPING TOM
Director: Michael Powell
Co-stars: Carl Boehm Moira Shearer Anna Massey Esmond Knight

1964 NIGHTMARE
Director: Freddie Francis
Co-stars: Moira Redmond David Knight Jennie Linden

1964 THE UNCLE
Director: Desmond Davis
Co-stars: Rupert Davies Maurice Denham Christopher Ariss

1974 SWALLOWS AND AMAZONS
Director: Claude Watham
Co-stars: Virginia McKenna Ronald Fraser Simon West

1975 ALL CREATURES GREAT AND SMALL
Director: Claude Whatham
Co-stars: Anthony Hopkins Simon Ward

1976 THE MAN IN THE IRON MASK
Director: Mike Newell
Co-stars: Richard Chamberlain Louis Jourdan Jenny Agutter

1985 STEAMING
Director: Joseph Losey
Co-stars: Vanessa Redgrave Diana Dors Sarah Miles

1985 TIME AFTER TIME
Director: Bill Hays
Co-stars: Googie Withers John Gielgud Helen Cherry

1988 THE TENTH MAN
Director: Jack Gold
Co-stars: Anthony Hopkins Kristin Scott Thomas Derek Jacobi

1989 BACK HOME
Director: Piers Haggard
Co-stars: Hayley Mills Jean Anderson Adam Stevenson

1990 ANTONIA AND JANE: A DEFINATIVE REPORT
Director: Beeban Kidron
Co-stars: Imelda Staunton Saskia Reeves

1990 CIRCLES OF DECEIT
Director: Stuart Burge
Co-stars: Edward Fox Jane Lapotaire Clare Holman

1991 DECEMBER BRIDE
Director: Thaddeus O'Sullivan
Co-stars: Saskia Reeves Donal McCann Frank Echlin

1991 GOODBYE CRUEL WORLD
Director: Adrian Shergold
Co-stars: Alun Armstrong Sue Johnston Julian Wadham

1992 HARNESSING PEACOCKS
Director: James Cellan Jones
Co-stars: Serena Scott Thomas John Mills

CAROL BRUCE

1941 KEEP 'EM FLYING
Director: Arthur Lubin
Co-stars: Bud Abbott Lou Costello Martha Raye

1941 THIS WOMAN IS MINE
Director: Frank Lloyd
Co-stars: Franchot Tone John Carroll Walter Brennan

1942 BEHIND THE EIGHT BALL
Director: Edward Cline
Co-stars: Ritz Brothers Dick Foran William Demarest

1980 AMERICAN GIGOLO
Director: Paul Schrader
Co-stars: Richard Gere Lauren Hutton Bill Duke

CHERYL LYNN BRUCE

1989 MUSIC BOX
Director: Costa-Gavras
Co-stars: Jessica Lange Armin Mueller-Stahl Frederic Forrest

JEAN BRUCE

1987 THE DARK ROOM
Director: Guy Slater
Co-stars: Susan Wooldridge Philip Jackson Julie Graham

KATE BRUCE

1919 TRUE HEART SUSIE
Director: D. W. Griffith
Co-stars: Lillian Gish Robert Harron Clarine Seymour

1920 WAY DOWN EAST
Director: D. W. Griffith
Co-stars: Lillian Gish Richard Barthelmess Lowell Sherman

MONA BRUCE

1988 MISS MARPLE: 4.50 FROM PADDINGTON
Director: Martyn Friend
Co-stars: Joan Hickson Joanna David

VIRGINIA BRUCE *(Married John Gilbert)*

1931 PARAMOUNTT ON PARADE
Co-stars: Gary Cooper Richard Arlen Jean Arthur

1930 LILLIES OF THE FIELD
Director: Alexander Korda
Co-stars: Corinne Griffiths Ralph Forbes Patsy Paige

1930 **SLIGHTLY SCARLET**
Director: Edwin Knoff
Co-stars: Clive Brook Evelyn Brent Paul Lukas

1930 **YOUNG EAGLES**
Director: William Wellman
Co-stars: Jean Arthur Charles Rogers Stuart Erwin

1932 **WINNER TAKE ALL**
Director: Roy Del Ruth
Co-stars: James Cagney Marian Nixon Dickie Moore

1932 **THE MIRACLE MAN**
Director: Norman Z. McLeod
Co-stars: Sylvia Sidney Chester Morris Irving Pichell

1932 **SKY BRIDE**
Director: Stephen Roberts
Co-stars: Richard Arlen Jack Oakie Charles Starrett

1932 **DOWNSTAIRS**
Director: Monta Bell
Co-stars: John Gilbert Paul Lukas Hedda Hopper

1932 **KONGO**
Director: William Cowen
Co-stars: Walter Huston Lupe Valez Conrad Nagel

1934 **DANGEROUS CORNER**
Director: Phil Rosen
Co-stars: Melvyn Douglas Conrad Nagel Erin O'Brien Moore

1934 **JANE EYRE**
Director: Christy Cabanne
Co-stars: Colin Clive Beryl Mercer Aileen Pringle

1934 **THE MIGHTY BARNUM**
Director: Walter Lang
Co-stars: Wallace Beery Adolphe Menjou Rochelle Hudson

1935 **THE MURDER MAN**
Director: Tim Whelan
Co-stars: Spencer Tracy Lionel Atwill James Stewart

1935 **METROPOLITAN**
Director: Richard Boleslawski
Co-stars: Lawrence Tibbett Alice Brady Cesar Romero

1935 **LET 'EM HAVE IT**
Director: Sam Wood
Co-stars: Richard Arlen Alice Brady Bruce Cabot

1935 **HERE COMES THE BAND**
Director: Paul Sloane
Co-stars: Ted Lewis Harry Stockwell Ted Healy

1935 **ESCAPADE**
Director: Robert Z. Leonard
Co-stars: William Powell Luise Rainer Frank Morgan

1935 **SHADOW OF DOUBT**
Director: George Seitz
Co-stars: Ricardo Cortez Constance Collier Regis Toomey

1935 **SOCIETY DOCTOR**
Director: George Seitz
Co-stars: Chester Morris Robert Taylor Billie Burke

1935 **TIMES SQUARE LADY**
Director: George Seitz
Co-stars: Robert Taylor Helen Twelvetrees Pinky Tomlin

1936 **THE GREAT ZIEGFELD**
Director: Robert Z. Leonard
Co-stars: William Powell Luise Rainer Myrna Loy

1936 **BORN TO DANCE**
Director: Roy Del Ruth
Co-stars: James Stewart Eleanor Powell Buddy Ebsen

1937 **WOMEN OF GLAMOUR**
Director: Gordon Wiles
Co-stars: Melvyn Douglas Leona Maricle Reginald Denny

1937 **BAD MAN OF BRIMSTONE**
Director: Walter Ruben
Co-stars: Wallace Beery Noah Beery Dennis O'Keefe

1937 **BETWEEN TWO WOMEN**
Director: George Seitz
Co-stars: Franchot Tone Maureen O'Sullivan Edward Norris

1937 **WHEN LOVE IS YOUNG**
Director: Hal Mohr
Co-stars: Walter Brennan Kent Taylor Sterling Holloway

1937 **WIFE, DOCTOR AND NURSE**
Director: Walter Lang
Co-stars: Jane Darwell Loretta Young Warner Baxter

1938 **WOMAN AGAINST WOMAN**
Co-stars: Herbert Marshall Mary Astor

1938 **YELLOW JACK**
Director: George Seitz
Co-stars: Robert Montgomery Lewis Stone Buddy Ebsen

1938 **THERE'S THAT WOMAN AGAIN**
Director: Alexander Hall
Co-stars: Melvyn Douglas Margaret Lindsay

1938 **THERE GOES MY HEART**
Director: Norman Z. McLeod
Co-stars: Fredric March Patsy Kelly Nancy Carroll

1938 **THE FIRST HUNDRED YEARS**
Director: Richard Thorpe
Co-stars: Robert Montgomery Warren William

1938 **ARSENE LUPIN RETURNS**
Director: George Fitzmaurice
Co-stars: Melvyn Douglas Warren William

1939 **LET FREEDOM RING**
Director: Jack Conway
Co-stars: Nelson Eddy Victor McLaglen Lionel Barrymore

1939 **SOCIETY LAWYER**
Director: Edwin Marin
Co-stars: Walter Pidgeon Leo Carrillo Eduardo Ciannelli

1939 **STRONGER THAN DESIRE**
Director: Leslie Fenton
Co-stars: Walter Pidgeon Ann Dvorak Lee Bowman

1940 **THE MAN WHO TALKED TOO MUCH**
Director: Vincent Sherman
Co-stars: George Brent William Lundigan

1940 **HIRED WIFE**
Director: William Seiter
Co-stars: Rosalind Russell Brian Aherne Robert Benchley

1940 **FLIGHT ANGELS**
Director: Lewis Seiler
Co-stars: Dennis Morgan Wayne Morris Jane Wyman

1941 **ADVENTURE IN WASHINGTON**
Director: Alfred Green
Co-stars: Herbert Marshall Gene Reynolds

1941 **THE INVISIBLE WOMAN**
Director: Edward Sutherland
Co-stars: John Barrymore Charles Ruggles

1942 **CAREFUL, SOFT SHOULDER**
Co-stars: James Ellison Sheila Ryan Ralph Byrd

1942 **PARDON MY SARONG**
Director: Erle Kenton
Co-stars: Abbott & Costello Lionel Atwill Robert Paige

1944 **ACTION IN ARABIA**
Director: Leonide Moguy
Co-stars: George Sanders Lenore Aubert Gene Lockhart

1944 **BRAZIL**
Director: Joseph Santley
Co-stars: Tito Guizar Roy Rogers Edward Everett Horton

1945　LOVE, HONOR AND GOODBYE
Co-stars:　Victor McLaglen Edward Ashley

1948　NIGHT HAS A THOUSAND EYES
Director:　John Farrow
Co-stars:　Edward G. Robinson Gail Russell

1949　ASSIGNMENT IN CHINA
Co-star:　William Lundigan

1960　STRANGERS WHEN WE MEET
Director:　Richard Quine
Co-stars:　Kirk Douglas Kim Novak Ernie Kovacs

JANE BRUCKER

1987　DIRTY DANCING
Director:　Emile Ardolino
Co-stars:　Jennifer Grey Patrick Swayze Cynthia Rhodes

HEIDI BRUHL

1963　CAPTAIN SINBAD
Director:　Byron Haskin
Co-stars:　Guy Williams Pedro Armendariz

1975　THE EIGER SANCTION
Director:　Clint Eastwood
Co-stars:　Clint Eastwood George Kennedy Jack Cassidy

PAMELA BRULL

1990　THE GUARDIAN
Director:　William Friedkin
Co-stars:　Jenny Seagrove Dwier Brown Carey Lowell

LENA BRUNDIN

1966　NIGHT GAMES
Director:　Mai Zetterling
Co-stars:　Ingrid Thulin Keve Hjelm Naima Wifstrand

GABRIELLE BRUNE

1952　THE TITFIELD THUNDERBOLT
Director:　Charles Crichton
Co-stars:　George Relph Stanley Holloway

GENEVIEVE BRUNET

1955　THE DIARY OF MAJOR THOMPSON
Director:　Preston Sturges
Co-stars:　Jack Buchanan Martine Carol

BLANCETTE BRUNOY

1938　LA BETE HUMAINE
Director:　Jean Renoir
Co-stars:　Jean Renoir Jean Gabin Simone Simon

1943　GOUPI MAINES ROUGES
Director:　Jacques Becker
Co-stars:　Fernand Ledoux Georges Rollin

GABRIELLE BRUNT

1949　WHISKY GALORE
Director:　Alexander MacKendrick
Co-stars:　Basil Radford Joan Greenwood Gordon Jackson

EILEEN BRY

1980　SPIDERMAN: THE DRAGON'S CHALLENGE
Director:　Don McDougall
Co-stars:　Nicholas Hammond Benson Fong

ELLEN BRY

1986　I-MAN
Director:　Corey Allen
Co-stars:　Scott Bakula Joey Cramer John Anderson

DORA BRYAN

1942　WENT THE DAY WELL?
Director:　Alberto Cavalcanti
Co-stars:　Leslie Banks Elizabeth Allan Basil Sydney

1947　ONCE UPON A DREAM
Director:　Ralph Thomas
Co-stars:　Googie Withers Griffith Jones Guy Middleton

1948　THE FALLEN IDOL
Director:　Carol Reed
Co-stars:　Ralph Richardson Michelle Morgan Bobby Henry

1949　TRAVELLER'S JOY
Director:　Ralph Thomas
Co-stars:　Googie Withers John McCallum Yolande Donlan

1949　THE CURE FOR LOVE
Director:　Robert Donat
Co-stars:　Robert Donat Renee Asherson Gladys Henson

1949　THE BLUE LAMP
Director:　Basil Dearden
Co-stars:　Jack Warner Jimmy Hanley Dirk Bogarde

1950　NO TRACE
Director:　John Gilling
Co-stars:　Hugh Sinclair Dinah Sheridan John Laurie

1950　THE SCARLET THREAD
Director:　Lewis Gilbert
Co-stars:　Laurence Harvey Kathleen Byron

1951　WHISPERING SMITH HITS LONDON
Director:　Francis Searle
Co-stars:　Richard Carlson Greta Gynt

1951　THE QUIET WOMAN
Director:　John Gilling
Co-stars:　Derek Bond Jane Hylton Harry Towb

1951　HIGH TREASON
Director:　Roy Boutling
Co-stars:　Liam Redmond Andre Morrell Mary Morris

1951　LADY GODIVA RIDES AGAIN
Director:　Frank Launder
Co-stars:　Pauline Stroud Dennis Price Diana Dors

1951　CIRCLE OF DANGER
Director:　Jacques Tourneur
Co-stars:　Ray Milland Patricia Roc Marius Goring

1952　THE GIFT HORSE
Director:　Compton Bennett
Co-stars:　Trevor Howard Sonny Tufts James Donald

1952　MADE IN HEAVEN
Director:　John Paddy Carstairs
Co-stars:　David Tomlinson Petula Clark

1952　OLD MOTHER RILEY MEETS THE VAMPIRE
Director:　John Gilling
Co-stars:　Arthur Lucan Bella Lugosi

1952　13, EAST STREET
Director:　Robert Baker
Co-stars:　Patrick Holt Sandra Dorne Sonia Holm

1952　TIME GENTLEMEN PLEASE!
Director:　Lewis Gilbert
Co-stars:　Eddie Byrne Hermione Baddeley Sid James

1952　WOMEN OF TWILIGHT
Director:　Gordon Parry
Co-stars:　Freda Jackson Joan Dowling Lois Maxwell

1952　MISS ROBIN HOOD
Director:　John Guillermin
Co-stars:　Margaret Rutherford Sid James Reg Varney

1953　THE FAKE
Director:　Godfrey Grayson
Co-stars:　Dennis O'Keefe Coleen Gray Hugh Williams

1953   **THE INTRUDER**
Director: Guy Hamilton
Co-stars: Jack Hawkins Michael Medwin Hugh Willliams

1954   **THE CROWDED DAY**
Director: John Guillermin
Co-stars: Joan Rice John Gregson Freda Jackson

1954   **MAD ABOUT MEN**
Director: Ralph Thomas
Co-stars: Glynis Johns Donald Sinden Anne Crawford

1955   **SEE HOW THEY RUN**
Director: Leslie Arliss
Co-stars: Ronald Shiner Greta Gynt James Hayter

1955   **THE COCKLESHELL HEROES**
Director: Jose Ferrer
Co-stars: Jose Ferrer Trevor Howard Anthony Newley

1955   **AS LONG AS THEY'RE HAPPY**
Director: J. Lee Thompson
Co-stars: Jack Buchanan Jean Carson Diana Dors

1956   **CHILD IN THE HOUSE**
Director: Raker Endfield
Co-stars: Eric Portman Phyllis Calvert Mandy Miller

1956   **THE GREEN MAN**
Director: Robert Day
Co-stars: Alastair Sim George Cole Jill Adams

1958   **THE MAN WHO WOULDN'T TALK**
Director: Herbert Wilcox
Co-stars: Anna Neagle Anthony Quayle

1958   **CARRY ON SERGEANT**
Director: Gerald Thomas
Co-stars: Bob Monkhouse William Hartnell Kenneth Williams

1959   **DESERT MICE**
Director: Michael Relph
Co-stars: Alfred Marks Sid James Patricia Bredin

1959   **OPERATION BULLSHINE**
Director: Gilbert Gunn
Co-stars: Donald Sinden Barbara Murray Carole Lesley

1960   **THE NIGHT WE GOT THE BIRD**
Director: Darcy Conyers
Co-stars: Brian Rix Ronald Shiner John Slater

1961   **A TASTE OF HONEY**
Director: Tony Richardson
Co-stars: Rita Tushingham Murray Melvin Robert Stephens

1966   **THE SANDWICH MAN**
Director: Robert Hartford-Davis
Co-stars: Michael Bentine Suzy Kendall Norman Wisdom

1966   **THE GREAT ST. TRINIAN'S TRAIN ROBBERY**
Director: Frank Launder
Co-stars: Frankie Howerd Reg Varney

1967   **TWO A PENNY**
Director: James Collier
Co-stars: Cliff Richard Ann Holloway Aviril Angers

1971   **HANDS OF THE RIPPER**
Director: Peter Sasdy
Co-stars: Eric Porter Angharad Rees Jane Merrow

1972   **UP THE FRONT**
Director: Bob Kellett
Co-stars: Frankie Howerd Bill Fraser Stanley Holloway

1988   **APARTMENT ZERO**
Director: Martin Donovan
Co-stars: Colin Firth Hart Bochner Liz Smith

1990   **PALMER**
Director: Keith Washington
Co-stars: Ray Winstone Louise Plowright Lesley Duff

JANE BRYAN

1936   **THE CAPTAIN'S KID**
Director: Nick Grinde
Co-stars: Guy Kibbee Mary Robson Sybil Jason

1936   **THE CASE OF THE BLACK CAT**
Director: Willliam McGann
Co-stars: Ricardo Cortez June Travis

1937   **CONFESSION**
Director: Joe May
Co-stars: Kay Francis Basil Rathbone Ian Hunter

1937   **KID GALAHAD**
Director: Michael Curtiz
Co-stars: Edward G. Robinson Bette Davis Wayne Morris

1938   **GIRLS ON PROBATION**
Director: Willliam McGann
Co-stars: Ronald Reagan Sheila Bromley Henry O'Neill

1938   **THE SISTERS**
Director: Anatole Litvak
Co-stars: Errol Flynn Bette Davis Anita Louise

1938   **A SLIGHT CASE OF MURDER**
Director: Lloyd Bacon
Co-stars: Edward G. Robinson Willard Parker John Litel

1938   **BROTHER RAT**
Director: William Keighley
Co-stars: Ronald Reagan Wayne Morris Eddie Albert

1938   **BROTHER RAT AND A BABY**
Director: Ray Enright
Co-stars: Jane Wyman Priscilla Lane Wayne Morris

1939   **EACH DAWN I DIE**
Director: William Keighley
Co-stars: James Cagney George Raft George Bancroft

1939   **I AM NOT AFRAID**
Director: Crane Wilbur
Co-stars: Charley Grapewin Henry O'Neill Elizabeth Risdon

1939   **INVISIBLE STRIPES**
Director: Lloyd Bacon
Co-stars: George Raft Humphrey Bogart William Holden

1939   **THE OLD MAID**
Director: Edmund Goulding
Co-stars: Bette Davis Miriam Hopkins George Brent

1939   **WE ARE NOT ALONE**
Director: Edmund Goulding
Co-stars: Paul Muni Flora Robson Una O'Connor

1939   **THOSE GLAMOROUS GIRLS**
Director: S. Sylvan Simon
Co-stars: Lew Ayres Lana Turner Anita Louise

PEGGY BRYAN

1941   **TURNED OUT NICE AGAIN**
Director: Marcel Varnel
Co-stars: George Formby Edward Chapman

BETTY BRYANT

1941   **FORTY THOUSAND HORSEMEN**
Director: Charles Chauvel
Co-stars: Chips Rafferty Grant Taylor

JOYCE BRYANT

1940   **THE EAST SIDE KIDS**
Director: Bob Hill
Co-stars: Leon Ames Dave O'Brien Frankie Burke

KARIS PAIGE BRYANT *(Child)*

1994   **WHILE JUSTICE SLEEPS**
Director: Ivan Passer
Co-stars: Cybill Shepherd Tim Matheson Robyn Stevan

1994 THE SUBSTITUTE WIFE
Director: Peter Werner
Co-stars: Peter Weller Lea Thompson Farrah Fawcett

NANA BRYANT

1935 ONE-WAY TICKET
Director: Herbert Biberman
Co-stars: Lloyd Nolan Walter Connolly Peggy Conklin

1936 THE MAN WHO LIVED TWICE
Director: Harry Lachman
Co-stars: Ralph Bellamy Marian Marsh Isabel Jewell

1936 THE KING STEPS OUT
Director: Joseph Von Sternberg
Co-stars: Grace Moore Franchot Tone Walter Connelly

1936 MEET NERO WOLFE
Director: Herbert Biberman
Co-stars: Edward Arnold Lionel Stander Rita Hayworth

1937 COUNSEL FOR CRIME
Director: John Brahm
Co-stars: Otto Kruger Douglass Montgomery Jacqueline Wells

1937 THE DEVIL IS DRIVING
Director: Harry Lachman
Co-stars: Richard Dix Joan Perry Elisha Cook Jnr.

1937 THE LEAGUE OF FRIGHTENED MEN
Director: Alfred Green
Co-stars: Walter Connolly Lionel Stander

1937 THEODORA GOES WILD
Director: Richard Boleslawski
Co-stars: Irene Dunne Melvyn Douglas Thomas Mitchell

1938 MAN-PROOF
Director: Richard Thorpe
Co-stars: Myrna Loy Franchot Tone Walter Pidgeon

1939 STREET OF MISSING MEN
Co-stars: Charles Bickford Harry Carey

1939 ESPIONAGE AGENT
Director: Lloyd Bacon
Co-stars: Joel McCrea Brenda Marshall Jeffrey Lynn

1940 IF I HAD MY WAY
Director: David Butler
Co-stars: Bing Crosby Charles Winninger Gloria Jean

1941 THE RELUCTANT DRAGON
Director: Alfred Werker
Co-stars: Robert Benchley Frances Gifford Walt Disney

1942 GET HEP TO LOVE
Director: Charles Lamont
Co-stars: Donald O'Connor Gloria Jean Peggy Ryan

1943 HANGMEN ALSO DIE
Director: Fritz Lang
Co-stars: Brian Donlevy Walter Brennan Anna Lee

1945 BREWSTER'S MILLIONS
Director: Allan Dwan
Co-stars: Dennis O'Keefe Helen Walker Eddie Anderson

1946 PERFECT MARRIAGE
Director: Lewis Allen
Co-stars: David Niven Loretta Young Eddie Albert

1947 HER HUSBAND'S AFFAIRS
Director: S. Sylvan Simon
Co-stars: Lucille Ball Franchot Tone Gene Lockhart

1950 HARVEY
Director: Henry Koster
Co-stars: James Stewart Josephine Hull Peggy Dow

1951 FOLLOW THE SUN
Director: Sidney Lanfield
Co-stars: Glenn Ford Anne Baxter Dennis O'Keefe

1955 THE PRIVATE WAR OF MAJOR BENSON
Director: Jerry Hopper
Co-stars: Charlton Heston Julie Adams

PAMELA BRYANT

1981 PRIVATE LESSONS
Director: Alan Myerson
Co-stars: Sylvia Kristel Eric Brown Howard Hesseman

URSALINE BRYANT-YOUNG

1981 ...ALL THE MARBLES
Director: Robert Aldrich
Co-stars: Peter Falk Vicki Frederick Tracy Reed

YVONNE BRYCELAND

1990 FRANKENSTEIN'S BABY
Director: Robert Bierman
Co-stars: Kate Buffery Nigel Planer Gillian Raine

EDITA BRYCHTA

1987 BORDER
Director: Misha Williams
Co-stars: Shaun Scott Daniel Hill Catherine Schell

1989 FLYING IN THE BRANCHES
Director: Eva Kolouchova
Co-stars: Susan Fleetwood Ralph Bates Donald Gee

MARIA BUCELLA

1969 DEAD RUN
Director: Christian-Jacque
Co-stars: Peter Lawford Ira Von Furstenberg Georges Geret

GRAZIA BUCETTA

1968 VILLA RIDES
Director: Buzz Kulik
Co-stars: Yul Brynner Robert Mitchum Charles Bronson

BETH BUCHANAN

1990 THE ROGUE STALLION
Director: Henri Saffron

MEG BUCHANAN

1952 THE BRAVE DON'T CRY
Director: Philip Leacock
Co-stars: John Gregson Fulton Mackay Andrew Keir

SIMONE BUCHANAN

1989 SHAME
Director: Steve Jodrell
Co-stars: Deborra-Lee Furness Tony Barry Gillian Jones

CHRISTINE BUCHEGGER

1980 FROM THE LIFE OF THE MARIONETTES
Director: Ingmar Bergman
Co-stars: Robert Atzorn Martin Benrath

ELIZA BUCKINGHAM

1962 THE WRONG ARM OF THE LAW
Director: Cliff Owen
Co-stars: Peter Sellers Lionel Jeffries Bill Kerr

JAN BUCKINGHAM

1943 AFTER MIDNIGHT WITH BOSTON BLACKIE
Co-stars: Chester Morris Ann Savage George E. Stone

YVONNE BUCKINHHAM

1959 SAPPHIRE
Director: Basil Dearden
Co-stars: Nigel Patrick Michael Craig Yvonne Mitchell

BETTY BUCKLEY

1976   CARRIE
Director: Brian De Palma
Co-stars: Sissy Spacek Piper Laurie Amy Irving

1982   TENDER MERCIES
Director: Bruce Beresford
Co-stars: Robert Duvall Tess Harper Ellen Barkin

1988   ANOTHER WOMAN
Director: Woody Allen
Co-stars: Gena Rowlands Mia Farrow Gene Hackman

1988   FRANTIC
Director: Roman Polanski
Co-stars: Harrison Ford Alexandra Stewart Emmanuelle Seigner

1989   BABYCAKES
Director: Paul Schneider
Co-stars: Ricki Lake Craig Shefffer Paul Benedict

1994   BETRAYAL OF TRUST
Director: George Kaczender
Co-stars: Judd Hirsch Jeff DeMunn Judith Light

SUSAN BUCKNER

1981   DEADLY BLESSING
Director: Wes Craven
Co-stars: Karen Jensen Ernest Borgnine Lois Nettleton

BETTY BUEHLER

1951   THE MOB
Director: Robert Parrish
Co-stars: Broderick Crawford Richard Kiley Ernest Borgnine

KATE BUFFERY

1989   COMEBACK
Director: David Ambrose
Co-stars: Anton Rodgers Stephen Dillon Charles Lamb

1990   FRANKENSTEIN'S BABY
Director: Robert Bierman
Co-stars: Nigel Planer Yvonne Bryceland Sian Thomas

1990   THE ORCHID HOUSE
Director: Horace Ove
Co-stars: Diana Quick Nigel Terry Frances Barber

VALERIE BUHAGIER

1989   ROADKILL
Director: Bruce McDonald
Co-stars: Don McKeller Gary Quigley

1995   ROMANTIC UNDERTAKING
Director: Peter McCubbin
Co-star: William Katt

GENEVIEVE BUJOLD
Nominated For Best Actress In 1969 For "Anne Of A Thousand Days"

1966   LA GUERRE EST FINIE
Director: Alain Resnais
Co-stars: Yves Montand Ingrid Thulin Michel Piccoli

1966   KING OF HEARTS
Director: Philippe De Broca
Co-stars: Alan Bates Pierre Brasseur Micheline Presle

1969   ANNE OF A THOUSAND DAYS
Director: Charles Jarrott
Co-stars: Richard Burton John Colicos Irene Pappas

1970   ACT OF THE HEART
Director: Paul Almond
Co-stars: Donald Sutherland Sharon Acker Monique Leyrac

1971   THE TROJAN WOMEN
Director: Michael Cacoyannis
Co-stars: Katherine Hepburn Irene Papas

1973   EARTHQUAKE
Director: Mark Robson
Co-stars: Charlton Heston Ava Gardner Lorne Greene

1976   ALEX AND THE GYPSY
Director: John Korty
Co-stars: Jack Lemmon James Woods Gino Ardito

1976   SWASHBUCKLER
Director: James Goldstone
Co-stars: Robert Shaw James Earl Jones Beau Bridges

1976   OBSESSION
Director: Brian De Palma
Co-stars: Cliff Robertson John Lithgow Sylvia Willliams

1977   ANOTHER MAN, ANOTHER CHANCE
Director: Claude Lelouch
Co-stars: James Caan Francis Huster Susan Tyrrell

1978   COMA
Director: Michael Crichton
Co-stars: Michael Douglas Richard Widmark Rip Torn

1978   MURDER BY DECREE
Director: Bob Clark
Co-stars: Christopher Plummer James Mason John Gielgud

1980   THE LAST FLIGHT OF NOAH'S ARK
Director: Charles Jarrott
Co-stars: Elliott Gould Ricky Schroder

1981   MISTRESS OF PARADISE
Director: Peter Medak
Co-stars: Chad Everett Anthony Andrews Lelia Goldoni

1982   MONSIGNOR
Director: Frank Perry
Co-stars: Christopher Reeve Fernando Rey Adolfo Celi

1984   TIGHTROPE
Director: Richard Tuggle
Co-stars: Clint Eastwood Dan Hedaya Alison Eastwood

1984   CHOOSE ME
Director: Alan Rudolph
Co-stars: Lesley Ann Warren Keith Carradine Rae Dawn Chong

1985   TROUBLE IN MIND
Director: Alan Rudolph
Co-stars: Keith Carradine Kris Kristofferson Lori Singer

1988   THE MODERNS
Director: Alan Rudolph
Co-stars: Keith Carradine Linda Fiorentino John Lone

1988   DEAD RINGERS
Director: David Cronenberg
Co-stars: Jeremy Irons Barbara Gordon Shirley Douglas

1989   A PAPER WEDDING
Director: Michel Brault
Co-stars: Manuel Aranguiz Dorothee Berryman Monique Lepage

1990   FALSE IDENTITY
Director: James Keach
Co-stars: Stacey Keach Tobin Bell Veronica Cartwright

DIANE BULL

**1993   A TOUCH OF FROST:
NOT WITH KINDNESS**
Director: David Reynolds
Co-stars: David Jason Tony Haygarth

SANDRA BULLOCK

**1989   BIONIC SHOWDOWN: THE SIX MILLION
DOLLAR MAN AND THE BIONIC WOMAN**
Director: Alan Levi
Co-stars: Lee Majors Lindsay Wagner

1992   LOVE POTION NO.9

1992   **WHO SHOT PATAKANGO?**
Director: Robert Brooks
Co-stars: David Knight Brad Randall Kevin Otto

1993   **THE VANISHING**
Director: George Sluizer
Co-stars: Jeff Bridges Kiefer Sutherland Nancy Travis

1993   **THE THING CALLED LOVE**
Director: Peter Bogdanovich
Co-stars: River Phoenix Dermot Mulroney

1993   **WRESTLING ERNEST HEMINGWAY**
Director: Randa Haines
Co-stars: Robert Duvall Richard Harris

1993   **DEMOLITION MAN**
Director: Marco Brambilla
Co-stars: Sylvester Stallone Wesley Snipes Nigel Hawthorne

1994   **SPEED**
Director: Jan De Bont
Co-stars: Keanu Reeves Dennis Hopper Jeff Daniels

1995   **WHILE YOU WERE SLEEPING**
Director: Jon Turteltaub
Co-stars: Bill Pullman Peter Gallagher

1995   **THE NET**
Director: Irwin Winkler
Co-stars: Jeremy Northam Dennis Miller

1995   **STOLEN HEARTS**
Co-stars: Denis Leary

1996   **IN LOVE AND WAR**
Director: Richard Attenborough
Co-stars: Chris O'Donnell

1996   **A TIME TO KILL**
Director: Joel Schumacher
Co-stars: Samuel L. Jackson Kevin Spacey Brenda Fricker

1997   **SPEED 2**
Co-stars: Jason Patric Willem Dafoe

AVIS BUNNAGE

1962   **SPARROWS CAN'T SING**
Director: Joan Littlewood
Co-stars: James Booth Barbara Windsor Roy Kinnear

1962   **THE LONELINESS OF THE LONG DISTANCE RUNNER**
Director: Tony Richardson
Co-stars: Tom Courtenay James Fox

1962   **THE L-SHAPED ROOM**
Director: Bryan Forbes
Co-stars: Leslie Caron Tom Bell Brock Peters

1963   **WHAT A CRAZY WORLD**
Director: Michael Carreras
Co-stars: Joe Brown Susan Maughan Marty Wilde

1965   **ROTTEN TO THE CORE**
Director: John Boulting
Co-stars: Eric Sykes Ian Bannen Dudley Sutton

1966   **THE WHISPERERS**
Director: Bryan Forbes
Co-stars: Edith Evans Eric Portman Nanette Newman

1985   **NO SURRENDER**
Director: Peter Smith
Co-stars: Michael Angelis Bernard Hill Ray McAnally

1990   **THE KRAYS**
Director: Peter Medak
Co-stars: Billie Whitelaw Gary Kemp Martin Kemp

CARA BUONO

1992   **WATERLAND**
Director: Stephen Gyllenhaal
Co-stars: Jeremy Irons Sinead Cusack Ethan Hawke

1994   **THE COWBOY WAY**
Director: Gregg Champion
Co-stars: Woody Harrelson Kiefer Sutherland Dylan McDermot

ANDREA BURCHILL

1987   **HOUSEKEEPING**
Director: Bill Forsyth
Co-stars: Sara Walker Christine Lahti Anne Pitoniak

SUZANNE BURDEN

1986   **HARD TRAVELLING**
Director: Colin Gregg
Co-stars: Tom Bell Nicholas Le Provost Jack Shepherd

MICHELE BURGERS

1993   **FRIENDS**
Director: Elaine Proctor
Co-stars: Kerry Fox Dambisa Kente Marius Weyers

1997   **JUMP**
Director: Les Blair
Co-stars: Lionel Newton Baby Cele

BETTY BURGESS

1935   **CORONADO**
Co-star: Johnny Downs

DOROTHY BURGESS

1929   **IN OLD ARIZONA**
Director: Raoul Walsh
Co-stars: Warner Baxter Edmund Lowe J. Farrell MacDonald

1933   **HOLD YOUR MAN**
Director: Sam Wood
Co-stars: Jean Harlow Clark Gable Stuart Erwin

1933   **LADIES THEY TALK ABOUT**
Director: William Keighley
Co-stars: Barbara Stanwyck Preston Foster

1933   **EASY MILLIONS**
Co-star: Noah Beery

1934   **GAMBLING**
Director: Rowland Lee
Co-stars: George M. Cohan Wynne Gibson

1934   **ORIENT EXPRESS**
Director: Paul Martin
Co-stars: Heather Angel Ralph Morgan Norman Foster

HELEN BURGESS

1937   **THE PLAINSMAN**
Director: Cecil B. DeMille
Co-stars: Gary Cooper Jean Arthur James Ellison

1937   **A DOCTOR'S DIARY**
Director: Charles Vidor
Co-stars: George Bancroft John Trent Ruth Coleman

CAROLINE BURGHARD

1991   **WHO NEEDS A HEART?**
Director: John Akomfrah
Co-stars: Ruth Gemmell Treva Ettiene

VICTORIA BURGOYNE

1990   **ENDING UP**
Director: Peter Sasdy
Co-stars: Wendy Hiller John Mills Googie Withers

BILLIE BURKE (*Married Florenz Ziegfeld*)

1932 A BILL OF DIVORCEMENT
Director: George Cukor
Co-stars: John Barrymore Katherine Hepburn

1933 CHRISTOPHER STRONG
Director: Dorothy Arzner
Co-stars: Katherine Hepburn Colin Clive Ralph Forbes

1933 DINNER AT EIGHT
Director: George Cukor
Co-stars: John Barrymore Lionel Barrymore Jean Harlow

1933 ONLY YESTERDAY
Director: John Stahl
Co-stars: Margaret Sullavan John Boles Reginald Denny

1934 FINISHING SCHOOL
Director: George Nicholls
Co-stars: Frances Dee Ginger Rogers Bruce Cabot

1935 WHERE SINNERS MEET
Director: Walter Ruben
Co-stars: Diana Wynyard Clive Brook Alan Mowbray

1935 SOCIETY DOCTOR
Director: George Seitz
Co-stars: Chester Morris Virginia Bruce Robert Taylor

1935 SPLENDOR
Director: Elliot Nugent
Co-stars: Joel McCrea Miriam Hopkins Helen Westley

1935 SHE COULDN'T TAKE IT
Director: Tay Garnett
Co-stars: George Raft Joan Bennett Walter Connolly

1935 FORSAKING ALL OTHERS
Director: W. S. Van Dyke
Co-stars: Clark Gable Joan Crawford Robert Montgomery

1935 BECKY SHARP
Director: Kenneth McGowan
Co-stars: Miriam Hopkins Francis Dee Cedric Hardwicke

1935 A FEATHER IN HER HAT
Director: Alfred Santell
Co-stars: Pauline Lord Basil Rathbone

1935 DOUBTING THOMAS
Director: David Butler
Co-stars: Will Rogers Alison Skipworth Gail Patrick

1935 AFTER OFFICE HOURS
Director: Robert Z. Leonard
Co-stars: Clark Gable Constance Bennett Stuart Erwin

1936 CRAIG'S WIFE
Director: Dorothy Arzner
Co-stars: Rosalind Russell John Boles

1936 PICCADILLY JIM
Director: Robert Z. Leonard
Co-stars: Robert Montgomery Madge Evans Frank Morgan

1937 NAVY BLUE AND GOLD
Director: Sam Wood
Co-stars: Robert Young James Stewart Florence Rice

1937 PARNELL
Director: John Stahl
Co-stars: Clark Gable Myrna Loy Edmund Gwenn Donald Crisp

1937 TOPPER
Director: Norman Z McLeod
Co-stars: Roland Young Cary Grant Constance Bennett

1938 TOPPER TAKES A TRIP
Director: Norman Z McLeod
Co-stars: Roland Young Constance Bennett

1938 THE YOUNG IN HEART
Director: Richard Wallace
Co-stars: Douglas Fairbanks Janet Gaynor

1938 MERRILY WE LIVE
Director: Norman Z McLeod
Co-stars: Constance Bennett Brian Aherne Ann Dvorak

1938 EVERYBODY SING
Director: Edwin Marin
Co-stars: Judy Garland Fanny Brice Monty Woolley

1939 BRIDAL SUITE
Director: William Thiele
Co-stars: Robert Young Annabella Walter Connolly

1939 ETERNALLY YOURS
Director: Tay Garnett
Co-stars: Loretta Young David Niven Broderick Crawford

1939 REMEMBER?
Director: Norman Z McLeod
Co-stars: Robert Taylor Greer Garson Lew Ayres

1939 THE WIZARD OF OZ
Director: Victor Fleming
Co-stars: Judy Garland Ray Bolger Bert Lahr

1939 ZENOBIA
Director: Gordon Douglas
Co-stars: Oliver Hardy Harry Langdon Jean Parker

1940 IRENE
Director: Herbert Wilcox
Co-stars: Anna Neagle Ray Milland Roland Young

1940 HULLABALOO
Director: Edwin Marin
Co-stars: Frank Morgan Dan Dailey Virginia Grey

1940 THE GHOST COMES HOME
Director: William Thiele
Co-stars: Frank Morgan Ann Rutherford Reginald Owen

1940 THE CAPTAIN IS A LADY
Director: Robert Sinclair
Co-stars: Charles Coburn Dan Dailey Beulah Bondi

1940 AND ONE WAS BEAUTIFUL
Director: Robert Sinclair
Co-stars: Robert Cummings Laraine Day Jean Muir

1941 THE MAN WHO CAME TO DINNER
Director: William Keighley
Co-stars: Monty Woolley Bette Davis Ann Sheridan

1941 ONE NIGHT IN LISBON
Director: Edward Griffith
Co-stars: Fred MacMurray Madeleine Carroll

1941 TOPPER RETURNS
Director: Roy Del Ruth
Co-stars: Roland Young Joan Blondell Carole Landis

1941 THE WILD MAN OF BORNEO
Director: Robert Sinclair
Co-stars: Frank Morgan Mary Howard Dan Dailey

1942 THEY ALL KISSED THE BRIDE
Director: Alexander Hall
Co-stars: Joan Crawford Melvyn Douglas

1942 GIRL TROUBLE
Director: Harold Schuster
Co-stars: Don Ameche Joan Bennett Frank Craven

1943 HI DIDDLE DIDDLE
Director: Andrew Stone
Co-stars: Adolphe Menjou Pola Negri Dennis O'Keefe

1943 YOU'RE A LUCKY FELLOW, MR. SMITH
Director: Felix Feist
Co-stars: Allan Jones Evelyn Ankers

1945 THE CHEATERS
Director: Joseph Kane
Co-stars: Joseph Schildkraut Eugene Pallette Ona Munson

1945 BREAKFAST IN HOLLYWOOD
Director: Harold Schuster
Co-stars: Bonita Granville Tom Breneman Beulah Bondi

1946 THE BACHELOR'S DAUGHTERS
Director: Andrew Stone
Co-stars: Adolphe Menjou Gail Russell Claire Trevor

1949 THE BARKLEYS OF BROADWAY
Director: Charles Walters
Co-stars: Fred Astaire Ginger Rogers Oscar Levant

1950 AND BABY MAKES THREE
Director: Henry Levin
Co-stars: Robert Young Barbara Hale Robert Hutton

1950 FATHER OF THE BRIDE
Director: Vincente Minnelli
Co-stars: Spencer Tracy Elizabeth Taylor Joan Bennett

1951 FATHER'S LITTLE DIVIDEND
Director: Vincente Minnelli
Co-stars: Joan Bennett Elizabeth Taylor Spencer Tracy

1953 SMALL TOWN GIRL
Director: Leslie Kardos
Co-stars: Jane Powell Farley Granger Ann Miller

1959 THE YOUNG PHILADELPHIANS
Director: Vincent Sherman
Co-stars: Paul Newman Barbara Rush Alexis Smith

CHARLOTTE BURKE

1988 PAPERHOUSE
Director: Bernard Rose
Co-stars: Ben Cross Glenne Headley Gemma Jones

DELTA BURKE

1988 WHERE THE HELL'S THAT GOLD
Director: Burt Kennedy
Co-stars: Willie Nelson Gerald McRainey

KATHLEEN BURKE

1933 MURDERS IN THE ZOO
Director: Edward Sutheriand
Co-stars: Lionel Atwill Charles Ruggles John Lodge

**1933 ISLAND OF LOST SOULS
(Banned In Britain Until 1958)**
Director: Erle Kenton
Co-stars: Charles Laughton Bela Lugosi Richard Arlen

1935 THE LAST OUTPOST
Director: Charles Barton
Co-stars: Cary Grant Claude Rains Gertrude Michael

1935 LIVES OF A BENGAL LANCER
Director: Henry Hathaway
Co-stars: Gary Cooper Franchot Tone Guy Standing

1935 NAVY WIFE
Director: Allan Dwan
Co-stars: Claire Trevor Ralph Bellamy Jane Darwell

1935 ROCKY MOUNTAIN MYSTERY
Director: Charles Barton
Co-stars: Randolph Scott Ann Sheridan Chic Sale

1935 AWAKENING OF JIM BURKE
Co-star: Jack Holt

1937 THE SHEIK STEPS OUT
Director: Irving Pichel
Co-stars: Ramon Novarro Lola Lane Gene Lockhart

1937 BOY OF THE STREETS
Director: William Nigh
Co-stars: Jackie Cooper Maureen O'Connor Marjorie Main

KATHY BURKE

1990 AMONGST BARBARIANS
Director: Jane Howell
Co-stars: David Jason Rowena Cooper Anne Carroll

1997 NIL BY MOUTH
Director: Gary Oldman
Co-stars: Ray Winstone Laila Morse

MARIE BURKE

1920 REMODELING HER HUSBAND
Director: Lillian Gish
Co-stars: Dorothy Gish James Rennie

1932 AFTER THE BALL
Co-star: Esther Ralston

1948 WARNING TO WANTONS
Director: Donald Wilson
Co-stars: Harold Warrender Anne Vernon David Tomlinson

1950 ODETTE
Director: Herbert Wilcox
Co-stars: Anna Neagle Trevor Howard Peter Ustinov

1953 THE FLANAGAN BOY
Director: Reginald LeBorg
Co-stars: Tony Wright Barbara Payton Sid James

MICHELLE BURKE

1993 DAZED AND CONFUSED
Director: Richard Linklater
Co-stars: Jason London Wiley Wiggins

PATRICIA BURKE

1946 LISBON STORY
Director: Paul Stein
Co-stars: David Farrar Richard Tauber Walter Rilla

1947 WHILE I LIVE
Director: John Harlow
Co-stars: Tom Walls Sonia Dresdel Carol Raye

1949 FORBIDDEN
Director: George King
Co-stars: Douglass Montgomery Hazel Court Ronald Shiner

1954 THE HAPPINESS OF THREE WOMEN
Director: Maurice Elvy
Co-stars: Brenda De Banzie Eynon Evans

1961 THE IMPERSONATOR
Director: Alfred Shaughnessy
Co-stars: John Crawford Jane Griffith

1967 THE DAY THE FISH CAME OUT
Director: Michael Cacoyannis
Co-stars: Tom Courtenay Sam Wanamaker

NANCY BURNE

1935 DANDY DICK
Director: William Beaudine
Co-stars: Will Hay Esmond Knight

1939 FLYING FIFTY-FIVE
Director: Reginald Denham
Co-stars: Derrick De Marney Marius Goring Amy Veness

AMELIA BURNETTE (Child)

1989 WINTER PEOPLE
Director: Ted Kotcheff
Co-stars: Kurt Russell Kelly McGillis Lloyd Bridges

CAROL BURNETT (Mother Of Carrie Hamilton)

1963 WHO'S BEEN SLEEPING IN MY BED?
Director: Daniel Mann
Co-stars: Dean Martin Elizabeth Montgomery

1972 PETE 'N' TILLIE
Director: Martin Ritt
Co-stars: Walter Matthau Geraldine Page Barry Nelson

1974 THE FRONT PAGE
Director: Billy Wilder
Co-stars: Walter Matthau Jack Lemmon Susan Sarandon

1978 A WEDDING
Director: Robert Altman
Co-stars: Mia Farrow Amy Stryker Lillian Gish

1979 HEALTH
Director: Robert Altman
Co-stars: Lauren Bacall Glenda Jackson James Garner

1980 FRIENDLY FIRE
Director: David Greene
Co-stars: Ned Beatty Sam Waterston Timothy Hutton

1981 THE FOUR SEASONS
Director: Alan Alda
Co-stars: Alan Alda Len Cariou Sandy Dennis

1981 CHU CHU AND THE PHILLY FLASH
Director: David Lowell Rich
Co-stars: Alan Arkin Danny Aiello Ruth Buzzi

1982 ANNIE
Director: John Huston
Co-stars: Albert Finney Aileen Quinn Tim Curry

1983 BETWEEN FRIENDS
Director: Lou Antonio
Co-stars: Elizabeth Taylor Barbara Bush Stephen Young

1983 LIFE OF THE PARTY: THE STORY OF BEATRICE

1988 HOSTAGE
Director: Peter Levin
Co-stars: Carrie Hamilton Annette Bening Leon Russom

1992 NOISES OFF
Director: Peter Bogdanovich
Co-stars: Michael Caine Denholm Elliott Christopher Reeve

1994 SEASONS OF THE HEART
Director: Lee Grant
Co-stars: George Segal Eric Lloyd

OLIVIA BURNETTE (Child)

1992 HARD PROMISES
Director: Martin Davidson
Co-stars: Sissy Spacek William Petersen Mare Winningham

1994 THE GIFT OF LOVE
Director: Paul Bogart
Co-stars: Andy Griffith Blair Brown Penny Fuller

TERRY BURNHAM (Child)

1959 IMITATION OF LIFE
Director: Douglas Sirk
Co-stars: Lana Turner Juanita Moore Susan Kohner

CAROL BURNS

1982 DUSTY
Director: John Richardson
Co-stars: Bill Kerr Noel Trevarthen John Stanton

1982 BAD BLOOD
Director: Mike Newell
Co-stars: Jack Thompson Dennis Lill Donna Akersten

1983 STRIKEBOUND
Director: Richard Lowenstein
Co-stars: Chris Haywood Rob Steele David Kendall

CATHERINE BURNS (Cathy)
Nominated For Best Supporting Actress In 1969 For "Last Summer"

1969 LAST SUMMER
Director: Frank Perry
Co-stars: Barbara Hershey Richard Thomas Bruce Davison

1970 RED SKY AT MORNING
Director: James Goldstone
Co-stars: Richard Thomas Claire Bloom Richard Crenna

1972 NIGHT OF TERROR
Director: Jeannot Szwarc
Co-stars: Donna Mills Martin Balsam Chuck Connors

MARILYN BURNS

1974 THE TEXAS CHAINSAW MASSACRE
Director: Tobe Hooper
Co-stars: Allen Danziger William Vail

1976 EATEN ALIVE
Director: Tobe Hooper
Co-stars: Neville Brand Mel Ferrer Carolyn Jones

MARION BURNS

1932 ME AND MY GAL
Director: Raoul Walsh
Co-stars: Spencer Tracy Joan Bennett George Walsh

1934 DEVIL TIGER
Co-star: Kane Richmond

1935 PARADISE CANYON
Director: Carl Pierson
Co-stars: John Wayne Yakima Canutt

1935 DAWN RIDER
Director: Robert Bradbury
Co-stars: John Wayne Yakima Canutt

MARYEDITH BURRELL

1989 THOSE SHE LEFT BEHIND
Director: Waris Hussein
Co-stars: Gary Cole Joanna Kerns Colleen Dewhurst

SHEILA BURRELL

1950 THE ROSSITER CASE
Director: Francis Searle
Co-stars: Helen Shingler Clement McCallin Stanley Baker

1951 CLOUDBURST
Director: Francis Searle
Co-stars: Robert Preston Elizabeth Sellars Colin Tapley

1954 COLONEL MARCH INVESTIGATES
Director: Cy Endfield
Co-stars: Boris Karloff Ewan Roberts

1963 PARANOIAC
Director: Freddie Francis
Co-stars: Oliver Reed Janette Scott Maurice Denholm

1969 LAUGHTER IN THE DARK
Director: Tony Richardson
Co-stars: Nicol Williamson Anna Karina Sian Phillips

1970 THE SIX WIVES OF HENRY VIII
Director: John Glenister
Co-stars: Keith Michell Annette Crosbie Dorothy Tutin

BONNIE BURROUGHS

1989 HARD TO KILL
Director: Bruce Malmuth
Co-stars: Steven Seagal Kelly Lebrock Bill Sadler

JACKIE BURROUGHS

1982 THE GREY FOX
Director: Philip Borsos
Co-stars: Richard Farnsworth Wayne Robson

1989 A WINTER TAN
Director: John Walker
Co-stars: Erando Gonzales Anita Olanick

SAFFRON BURROWS

1994 WELCOME II THE TERRORDROME
Director: Ngozi Onwurah
Co-stars: Felix Joseph Ben Wynter

1995 CIRCLE OF FRIENDS
Director: Pat O'Connor
Co-stars: Minnie Driver Chris O'Donnell Colin Firth

1996 KARAOKE
Co-stars: Albert Finney Richard E. Grant Roy Hood

1996 COLD LAZARUS
Co-stars: Albert Finney Frances De La Tour

JANET BURSTON

1941 BLONDIE GOES LATIN
Director: Frank Strayer
Co-stars: Penny Singleton Arthur Lake Ruth Terry

ELLEN BURSTYN

Oscar For Best Actress In 1974 For "Alice Dosen't Live Here Anymore"
Nomminated For Best Actress In 1973 For "The Exorcist" And In 1978
For "Same Time, Next Year". Nominated For Best Supporting Actress In
1971 For "The Last Picture Show"

1964 GOODBYE CHARLIE
Director: Vincente Minnelli
Co-stars: Tony Curtis Debbie Reynolds Walter Matthau

1970 ALEX IN WONDERLAND
Director: Paul Mazursky
Co-stars: Donald Sutherland Jeanne Moreau

1971 THE LAST PICTURE SHOW
Director: Peter Bogdanovich
Co-stars: Timothy Bottoms Jeff Bridges Ben Johnson

1972 THE KING OF MARVIN GARDENS
Director: Bob Rafelson
Co-stars: Jack Nicholson Julia Anne Robinson Bruce Dern

1973 THE EXORCIST
Director: William Friedkin
Co-stars: Max Von Sydow Linda Blair Jason Miller

1974 ALICE DOESN'T LIVE HERE ANYMORE
Director: Martin Scorsese
Co-stars: Alfred Lutter Jodie Foster Diane Ladd

1974 HARRY AND TONTO
Director: Paul Mazursky
Co-stars: Art Carney Chief Dan George Geraldine Fitzgerald

1974 THURSDAY'S GAME
Director: Robert Moore
Co-stars: Gene Wilder Bob Newhart Cloris Leachman

1977 PROVIDENCE
Director: Alain Resnais
Co-stars: John Gielgud Dirk Bogarde David Warner

1978 SAME TIME, NEXT YEAR
Director: Robert Mulligan
Co-stars: Alan Alda

1978 A DREAM OF PASSION
Director: Jules Dassin
Co-stars: Melina Mercouri Andreas Voutsinas

1981 RESURRECTION
Director: Daniel Perrie
Co-stars: Sam Shepard Richard Farnsworth Eva Le Galienne

1981 SILENCE OF THE NORTH
Director: Allan Winton King
Co-stars: Tom Skerritt Jennifer McKinney

1984 THE AMBASSADOR
Director: J. Lee Thompson
Co-stars: Robert Mitchum Rock Hudson Donald Pleasence

1985 INTO THIN AIR
Director: Roger Young
Co-stars: Robert Prosky Sam Robards Tate Donovan

1985 SURVIVING
Director: Waris Hussein
Co-stars: Len Cariou Marsha Mason Molly Ringwald

1985 TWICE IN A LIFETIME
Director: Bud Yorkin
Co-stars: Gene Hackman Ann-Margret Amy Madigan

1986 ACT OF VENGEANCE
Director: John MacKenzie
Co-stars: Charles Bronson Wilford Brimley Ellen Barkin

1987 PACK OF LIES
Director: Anthony Page
Co-stars: Alan Bates Teri Garr Sammi Davis

1987 DEAR AMERICA:
LETTERS HOME FROM VIETNAM
Director: Bill Couturie
Co-stars: Robert De Niro Sean Penn

1988 HANNA'S WAR
Director: Menahem Golan
Co-stars: Maruschka Detmers Anthony Andrews David Warner

1991 DYING YOUNG
Director: Joel Schumacher
Co-stars: Julia Roberts Campbell Scott Colleen Dewhurst

1991 GRANDE ISLE
Director: Mary Wambert
Co-stars: Kelly McGillis Jon De Vris Julian Sands

1992 THE CEMETERY CLUB
Director: Bill Duke
Co-stars: Olympia Dukakis Diane Ladd Danny Aiello

1994 GETTING GOTTI
Director: Roger Young
Co-stars: Lorraine Bracco Anthony John Denison

1996 HOW TO MAKE AN AMERICAN QUILT
Director: Jocelyn Moorhouse
Co-stars: Winona Ryder Anne Bancroft Maya Angelou

CLARISSA BURT

1990 THE NEVERENDING STORY II:
THE NEXT CHAPTER
Director: George Miller
Co-stars: Jonathon Brandis Kenny Morrison

DEBRA BURTON

1985 GUNPOWDER
Director: Norman Warren
Co-stars: Gordon Jackson Martin Potter David Gilliam

FLORENCE BURTON

1932 MERRILY WE GO TO HELL
Director: Dorothy Arzner
Co-stars: Sylvia Sidney Fredric March Kent Taylor

KATE BURTON (Daughter Of Richard Burton)

1984   ELLIS ISLAND
Director: Jerry London
Co-stars: Richard Burton Claire Bloom Faye Dunaway

1986   BIG TROUBLE IN LITTLE CHINA
Director: John Carpenter
Co-stars: Kurt Russell Kim Cattrall

1987   UNCLE TOM'S CABIN
Director: Stan Lathan
Co-stars: Bruce Dern Edward Woodward Paula Kelly

1996   AUGUST
Director: Anthony Hopkins
Co-stars: Anthony Hopkins Leslie Phillips

MARGARET BURTON

1933   WHEN LADIES MEET
Director: Harry Beaumont
Co-stars: Ann Harding Myrna Loy Robert Montgomery

STEFANIA BUSARELLO

1987   LONG LIVE THE LADY!
Director: Ermanno Olmi
Co-stars: Marco Esposito Simona Brandalise

MAE BUSCH

1922   FOOLISH WIVES
Director: Erich Von Stroheim
Co-stars: Erich Von Stroheim Rudolph Christians Maude George

1923   THE CHRISTIAN
Director: Maurice Tourneur
Co-stars: Richard Dix Gareth Hughes Phyllis Haver

1925   THE UNHOLY THREE
Director: Tod Browning
Co-stars: Lon Chaney Victor McLaglen Harry Earles

1929   UNACCUSTOMED AS WE ARE
Director: Lewis Foster
Co-stars: Laurel & Hardy Edgar Kennedy Thelma Todd

1929   ALIBI
Director: Roland West
Co-stars: Chester Morris Eleanor Griffith Regis Toomey

1931   CHICKENS COME HOME
Director: James Horne
Co-stars: Laurel & Hardy Thelma Todd James Finlayson

1931   COME CLEAN
Director: James Horne
Co-stars: Laurel & Hardy Charlie Hall Linda Loredo

1932   DOCTOR X
Director: Michael Curtiz
Co-stars: Lee Tracy Lionel Atwill Preston Foster

1932   THEIR FIRST MISTAKE
Director: George Marshall
Co-stars: Laurel & Hardy

1934   THEM THAR HILLS
Director: Charles Rogers
Co-stars: Laurel & Hardy Charlie Hall Billy Gilbert

1934   OLIVER THE EIGHTH
Director: Lloyd French
Co-stars: Laurel & Hardy Jack Barty

1934   GOING BYE BYE
Director: Charles Rogers
Co-stars: Laurel & Hardy Walter Long

1934   FRATERNALLY YOURS
Director: William Seiter
Co-stars: Laurel & Hardy Charley Chase

1935   THE FIXER UPPERS
Director: Charles Rogers
Co-stars: Laurel & Hardy Charles Middleton

1935   TIT FOR TAT
Director: Charles Rogers
Co-stars: Laurel & Hardy Charlie Hall

1936   THE BOHEMIAN GIRL
Director: Charles Rogers
Co-stars: Laurel & Hardy Antonio Moreno Darla Hood

1938   MARIE ANTOINETTE
Director: W. S. Dyke
Co-stars: Norman Shearer Tyrone Power John Barrymore

BARBARA BUSH

1983   BETWEEN FRIENDS
Director: Lou Antonio
Co-stars: Elizabeth Taylor Carol Burnett Henry Ramer

1990   ERNEST GOES TO JAIL
Director: John Cherry
Co-stars: Jim Varney Gailard Sartain

JESSIE BUSLEY

1940   IT ALL CAME TRUE
Director: Lewis Seiler
Co-stars: Humphrey Bogart Ann Sheridan Jeffrey Lynn

PASCALE BUSSIERE

1998   TWILIGHT OF THE ICE NYMPHS
Director: Guy Maddin
Co-star: Shelley Duvall

JUNE BUTHELEZI

1985   KING SOLOMON'S MINES
Director: J. Lee Thompson
Co-stars: Richard Chamberlain Sharon Stone

LOIS BUTLER

1948   MICKEY
Co-stars: John Sutton Skip Homeier

1950   HIGH LONESOME
Director: Alan Le May
Co-stars: John Barrymore Jnr. Chill Wills Kristine Miller

LUCY BUTLER

1993   PROPHET OF EVIL
Director: Jud Taylor
Co-stars: Brian Dennehy Tracy Needham Dee Wallace

SARAH BUTLER

1986   AFTER PILKINGTON
Director: Christopher Morahan
Co-stars: Bob Peck Miranda Richardson Barry Foster

YANCEY BUTLER

1993   HARD TARGET
Director: John Woo
Co-stars: Jean-Claude Van Damme Wilford Brimley Kasi Lemmons

1993   THE HIT LIST
Director: William Webb
Co-stars: Jeff Fahey James Coburn Jeff Kober

1994   DROP ZONE
Director: John Badham
Co-stars: Wesley Snipes Gary Busey Luca Bercovici

DONNA BUTTERWORTH (Child)

1965   THE FAMILY JEWELS
Director: Jerry Lewis
Co-stars: Jerry Lewis Sebastian Cabot Robert Strauss

1965 PARADISE, HAWAIIN STYLE
Director: Michael Moore
Co-stars: Elvis Presley Suzanna Leigh Irene Tsu

RUTH BUZZI

1969 ITS TOUGH TO BE A BIRD *(Voice)*
Director: Ward Kimball
Co-star: Richard Bakalyan

1976 FREAKY FRIDAY
Director: Gary Nelson
Co-stars: Barbara Harris Jodie Foster John Astin

1979 CACTUS JACK
Director: Hal Needham
Co-stars: Kirk Douglas Arnold Schwarzenegger Ann-Margret

**1979 THE APPLE DUMPLING
GANG RIDES AGAIN**
Director: Vincent McEveety
Co-stars: Tim Conway Tim Matheson

1981 CHU CHU AND THE FILLY FLASH
Director: David Lowell Rich
Co-stars: Carol Burnett Alan Arkin

1986 BAD BOYS
Director: Joel Silberg
Co-stars: Adam Baldwin Mike Jolly Michelle Nicastro

SPRING BYINGTON
Nominated For Best Supporting Actress In 1938 For "You Can't Take It With You"

1932 TOO BUSY TO WORK
Director: John Blystone
Co-stars: Will Rogers Marian Nixon Dick Powell

1933 LITTLE WOMEN
Director: George Cukor
Co-stars: Katherine Hepburn Paul Lukas Joan Bennett

1935 AH, WILDERNESS!
Director: Clarence Brown
Co-stars: Wallace Beery Lionel Barrymore Mickey Rooney

1935 THE GREAT IMPERSONATION
Director: Alan Crosland
Co-stars: Edmund Lowe Valerie Hobson

1935 LOVE ME FOREVER
Director: Victor Schertzinger
Co-stars: Grace Moore Leo Carrillo Robert Allen

1935 MUTINY ON THE BOUNTY
Director: Frank Lloyd
Co-stars: Charles Laughton Clark Gable Franchot Tone

1935 ORCHIDS TO YOU
Director: William Seiter
Co-stars: John Boles Jean Muir Charles Butterworth

1935 WAY DOWN EAST
Director: Henry King
Co-stars: Rochelle Hudson Henry Fonda Slim Summerville

1935 WEREWOLF OF LONDON
Director: Stuart Walker
Co-stars: Henry Hull Warner Oland Valerie Hobson

1936 THE VOICE OF BUGLE ANN
Director: Richard Thorpe
Co-stars: Lionel Barrymore Maureen O'Sullivan

1936 THEODORA GOES WILD
Director: Richard Boleslawski
Co-stars: Irene Dunne Melvyn Douglas Thomas Mitchell

1936 PALM SPRINGS
Director: Aubrey Scotto
Co-stars: David Niven Guy Standing Frances Langford

1936 THE GIRL ON THE FRONT PAGE
Director: Harry Beaumont
Co-stars: Edmund Lowe Gloria Stuart

1936 DODSWORTH
Director: William Wyler
Co-stars: Walter Huston Mary Astor David Niven

1936 THE CHARGE OF THE LIGHT BRIGADE
Director: Michael Curtiz
Co-stars: Errol Flynn David Niven

1936 EVERY SATURDAY NIGHT
Director: Frank Strayer
Co-stars: Jed Prouty Florence Roberts June Carlson

1936 EDUCATING FATHER
Director: Frank Strayer
Co-stars: Jed Prouty Florence Roberts June Carlson

1936 BACK TO NATURE
Director: Frank Strayer
Co-stars: Jed Prouty Florence Roberts June Carlson

1937 OFF TO THE RACES
Director: Frank Strayer
Co-stars: Jed Prouty Florence Roberts June Carlson

1937 BORROWING TROUBLE
Director: Frank Strayer
Co-stars: Jed Prouty Florence Roberts June Carlson

1937 BIG BUSINESS
Director: Frank Strayer
Co-stars: Jed Prouty Florence Roberts June Carlson

1937 HOT WATER
Director: Frank Strayer
Co-stars: Jed Prouty Florence Roberts June Carlson

1937 THE ROAD BACK
Director: James Whale
Co-stars: Richard Cromwell John King Louise Fazenda

1937 A FAMILY AFFAIR
Director: George Seitz
Co-stars: Lionel Barrymore Mickey Rooney Cecelia Parker

1937 THE GREEN LIGHT
Director: Frank Borzage
Co-stars: Errol Flynn Anita Louise Margaret Lindsay

1937 HOTEL HAYWIRE
Director: George Archainbaud
Co-stars: Leo Carrillo Lynne Overman Mary Carlisle

1937 IT'S LOVE I'M AFTER
Director: Archie Mayo
Co-stars: Bette Davis Leslie Howard Olivia De Havilland

1937 PENROD AND SAM
Director: William McGann
Co-stars: Frank Craven Billy Mauch Craig Reynolds

1938 PENROD AND HIS TWIN BROTHER
Director: William McGann
Co-stars: Frank Craven Billy Mauch

1938 YOU CAN'T TAKE IT WITH YOU
Director: Frank Capra
Co-stars: Jean Arthur James Stewart Ann Miller

1938 THE ADVENTURES OF TOM SAWYER
Director: Norman Taurog
Co-stars: Tommy Kelly May Robson Walter Brennan

1938 JEZEBEL
Director: William Wyler
Co-stars: Bette Davis Henry Fonda George Brent

1938 THE BUCANEER
Director: Cecil B. DeMille
Co-stars: Fredric March Franciska Gaal Akim Tamiroff

1938	**THE JONES FAMILY IN HOLLYWOOD**	**1942**	**THE AFFAIRS OF MARTHA**
Director:	Frank Strayer	*Director:*	Jules Dassin
Co-stars:	Jed Prouty June Carlson George Ernest	*Co-stars:*	Marsha Hunt Richard Carlson Allyn Joslyn
1938	**LOVE ON A BUDGET**	**1942**	**RINGS ON HER FINGERS**
Director:	Frank Strayer	*Director:*	Rouben Mamoulian
Co-stars:	Jed Prouty June Carlson George Ernest	*Co-stars:*	Gene Tierney Henry Fonda Laird Cregar
1938	**TRIP TO PARIS**	**1943**	**PRESENTING LILY MARS**
Director:	Frank Strayer	*Director:*	Norman Taurog
Co-stars:	Jed Prouty June Carlson George Ernest	*Co-stars:*	Judy Garland Van Heflin Fay Bainter
1938	**DOWN ON THE FARM**	**1943**	**HEAVEN CAN WAIT**
Director:	Frank Strayer	*Director:*	Ernst Lubitsch
Co-stars:	Jed Prouty June Carlson George Ernest	*Co-stars:*	Don Ameche Gene Tierney Charles Coburn
1938	**SAFETY IN NUMBERS**	**1943**	**THE HEAVENLY BODY**
Director:	Frank Strayer	*Director:*	Alexander Hall
Co-stars:	Jed Prouty June Carlson George Ernest	*Co-stars:*	William Powell Hedy Lamarr James Craig
1939	**QUICK MILLIONS**	**1944**	**I'LL BE SEEING YOU**
Director:	Frank Strayer	*Director:*	William Dieterle
Co-stars:	Jed Prouty June Carlson George Ernest	*Co-stars:*	Ginger Rogers Joseph Cotten Shirley Temple
1939	**EVERYBODY'S BABY**	**1945**	**A LETTER FOR EVIE**
Director:	Frank Strayer	*Director:*	Jules Dassin
Co-stars:	Jed Prouty June Carlson George Ernest	*Co-stars:*	Marsha Hunt Hume Cronyn John Carroll
1939	**A CHILD IS BORN**	**1945**	**SALTY O'ROURKE**
Director:	Lloyd Bacon	*Director:*	Raoul Walsh
Co-stars:	Geraldine Fitzgerald Jeffrey Lynn Gladys George	*Co-stars:*	Alan Ladd Gail Russell Bruce Cabot
1939	**THE STORY OF ALEXANDER BELL**	**1945**	**THRILL OF A ROMANCE**
Director:	Irving Cummings	*Director:*	Richard Thorpe
Co-stars:	Don Ameche Henry Fonda Loretta Young	*Co-stars:*	Esther Williams Van Johnson Lauritz Melchior
1939	**THE CHICKEN WAGON FAMILY**	**1946**	**MY BROTHER TALKS TO HORSES**
Director:	Herbert Leeds	*Director:*	Fred Zinnemann
Co-stars:	Jane Withers Leo Carrillo Kane Richmond	*Co-stars:*	Butch Jenkins Peter Lawford Charles Ruggles
1940	**MY LOVE CAME BACK**	**1946**	**MEET ME ON BROADWAY**
Director:	Curtis Bernhardt	*Director:*	Leigh Jason
Co-stars:	Olivia De Havilland Jeffrey Lynn Jane Wyman	*Co-stars:*	Marjorie Reynolds Fred Brady Jinx Falkenburg
1940	**LUCKY PARTNERS**	**1946**	**LITTLE MR. JIM**
Director:	Lewis Milestone	*Director:*	Fred Zinnemann
Co-stars:	Ronald Colman Ginger Rogers Jack Carson	*Co-stars:*	Butch Jenkins James Craig Frances Gifford
1940	**THE BLUE BIRD**	**1946**	**FAITHFUL IN MY FASHION**
Director:	Walter Lang	*Director:*	Sidney Salkow
Co-stars:	Shirley Temple Johnny Russell Nigel Bruce	*Co-stars:*	Tom Drake Donna Reed Harry Davenport
1940	**ON THEIR OWN**	**1946**	**DRAGONWYCK**
Director:	Frank Strayer	*Director:*	Joseph Mankiewicz
Co-stars:	Jed Prouty Florence Roberts June Carlson	*Co-stars:*	Gene Tierney Vincent Price Glenn Langan
1941	**THE DEVIL AND MISS JONES**	**1947**	**CYNTHIA**
Director:	Sam Wood	*Director:*	Robert Z. Leonard
Co-stars:	Charles Coburn Jean Arthur Robert Cummings	*Co-stars:*	Elizabeth Taylor Mary Astor George Murphy
1941	**ELLERY QUEEN AND THE PERFECT CRIME**	**1947**	**IT HAD TO BE YOU**
Director:	James Hogan	*Director:*	Rudolph Mate
Co-stars:	Ralph Bellamy Charles Grapewin	*Co-stars:*	Ginger Rogers Cornel Wilde Percy Waram
1941	**MEET JOHN DOE**	**1947**	**LIVING IN A BIG WAY**
Director:	Frank Capra	*Director:*	Gregory La Cava
Co-stars:	Gary Cooper Barbara Stanwyck Walter Brennan	*Co-stars:*	Gene Kelly Marie McDonald Charles Winninger
1941	**THE VANISHING VIRGINIAN**	**1948**	**BF'S DAUGHTER**
Director:	Frank Borzage	*Director:*	Robert Z Leonard
Co-stars:	Frank Morgan Kathryn Grayson	*Co-stars:*	Barbara Stanwyck Van Heflin Charles Coburn
1941	**WHEN LADIES MEET**	**1949**	**THE BIG WHEEL**
Director:	Robert Z. Leonard	*Director:*	Edward Ludwig
Co-stars:	Joan Crawford Greer Garson Robert Taylor	*Co-stars:*	Mickey Rooney Thomas Mitchell
1942	**THE WAR AGAINST MRS.HADLEY**	**1949**	**IN THE GOOD OLD SUMMERTIME**
Director:	Harold Bucquet	*Director:*	Robert Z Leonard
Co-stars:	Fay Bainter Edward Arnold Richard Ney	*Co-stars:*	Judy Garland Van Johnson Buster Keaton
1942	**ROXIE HART**	**1950**	**LOUISA**
Director:	William Wellman	*Director:*	Alexander Hall
Co-stars:	Ginger Rogers George Montgomery Adolphe Menjou	*Co-stars:*	Charles Coburn Edmund Gwenn Ronald Reagan

1950 DEVIL'S DOORWAY
Director: Anthony Mann
Co-stars: Robert Taylor Louis Calhern Paula Raymond

1950 PLEASE BELIEVE ME
Director: Norman Taurog
Co-stars: Deborah Kerr Robert Walker Mark Stevens

1950 WALK SOFTLY STRANGER
Director: Robert Stevenson
Co-stars: Alida Valli Joseph Cotten Paul Stewart

1951 BANNERLINE
Director: Don Weis
Co-stars: Lionel Barrymore Keefe Brasselle Sally Forrest

1951 ACCORDING TO MRS.HOYLE
Director: Jean Yarborough
Co-stars: Anthony Caruso Brett King Tanis Chandler

1952 ANGELS IN THE OUTFIELD
Director: Clarence Brown
Co-stars: Paul Douglas Janet Leigh Donna Corcoran

1952 BECAUSE YOU'RE MINE
Director: Alexander Hall
Co-stars: Mario Lanza Doretta Morrow James Whitmore

1952 NO ROOM FOR THE GROOM
Director: Douglas Sirk
Co-stars: Tony Curtis Piper Laurie Don Defore

1954 THE ROCKET MAN
Director: Oscar Rudolph
Co-stars: Charles Coburn Anne Francis John Agar

1960 PLEASE DON'T EAT THE DAISIES
Director: Charles Walters
Co-stars: Doris Day David Niven Patsy Kelly

ADRIENNE BYRNE (Child)

1969 MISCHIEF
Director: Ian Shand
Co-stars: Paul Fraser Ian Burton Gerald Sim

ANNE BYRNE

1978 THE END OF THE WORLD
Director: Lina Wertmuller
Co-stars: Candice Bergen Jill Eikenberry

1979 MANHATTAN
Director: Woody Allen
Co-stars: Woody Allen Diane Keaton Meryl Streep

BARBARA BYRNE

1984 THE BOSTONIANS
Director: James Ivory
Co-stars: Christopher Reeve Vanessa Redgrave Jessica Tandy

CATHERINE BYRNE

1986 EAT THE PEACH
Director: Peter Ormrod
Co-stars: Stephen Brennan Eamonn Morrissey Joe Lynch

DEBBIE BYRNE

1985 REBEL
Director: Michael Jenkins
Co-stars: Matt Dillon Bryan Brown Ray Barrett

MARSHA BYRNE (Child)

1982 THE EYES OF THE AMARYLLIS
Director: Frederick King Keller
Co-stars: Ruth Ford Guy Boyd

1983 ANNA TO THE INFINITE POWER
Director: Robert Wiemer
Co-stars: Dina Merril Jack Gilford Mark Patton

1984 HE'S FIRED, SHE'S HIRED
Director: Marc Daniels
Co-stars: Wayne Rogers Karen Valentine

PATSY BYRNE

1972 THE RULING CLASS
Director: Peter Medak
Co-stars: Peter O'Toole Alastair Sim Coral Browne

1993 EMILY'S GHOST
Director: Colin Finbow
Co-stars: Martin Jarvis Anna Massey Ron Moody

JOSEPHINE BYRNES

1991 THE OTHER SIDE OF PARADISE
Director: Renny Rye
Co-stars: Jason Connery Richard Wilson Hywel Bennett

1992 FRAUDS
Director: Stephan Elliott
Co-stars: Phil Collins Hugo Weaving Helen O'Connor

DELMA BYRON

1936 DIMPLES
Director: William Seiter
Co-stars: Shirley Temple Frank Morgan Helen Westley

1937 LAUGHING AT TROUBLE
Director: Frank Strayer
Co-stars: Jane Darwell Sara Haden Lois Wilson

JEAN BYRON

1953 THE MAGNETIC MONSTER
Director: Curt Siodmak
Co-stars: Richard Carlson King Donovan

1953 SERPENT OF THE NILE
Director: William Castle
Co-stars: Rhonda Fleming William Lundigan

KATHLEEN BYRON

1943 SILVER FLEET
Director: Vernon Sewell
Co-stars: Ralph Richardson Esmond Knight Googie Withers

1943 BLACK NARCISSUS
Director: Michael Powell
Co-stars: David Farrar Sabu Jean Simmonds

1949 MADNESS OF THE HEART
Director: Charles Bennett
Co-stars: Margaret Lockwood Paul Dupuis Maxwell Reed

1949 THE SMALL BACK ROOM
Director: Michael Powell
Co-stars: David Farrar Jack Hawkins Leslie Banks

1950 THE SCARLET THREAD
Director: Lewis Gilbert
Co-stars: Laurence Harvey Sidney Tafler Dora Bryan

1950 THE RELUCTANT WIDOW
Director: Bernard Knowles
Co-stars: Jean Kent Guy Rolfe Lana Morris

1950 PRELUDE TO FAME
Director: Fergus McDonnell
Co-stars: Jeremy Spencer Kathleen Ryan Guy Rolfe

1951 TOM BROWN'S SCHOOLDAYS
Director: Gordon Parry
Co-stars: John Howard Davies Robert Newton

1953 YOUNG BESS
Director: George Sidney
Co-stars: Jean Simmons Stewart Granger Charles Laughton

1960 HAND IN HAND
Director: Philip Leacock
Co-stars: Loretta Parry Philip Needs John Gregson

1964 NIGHT OF THE EAGLE
Director: Sidney Hayers
Co-stars: Margaret Johnston Peter Wyngard Janet Blair

1971 TWINS OF EVIL
Director: John Hough
Co-stars: Mary Collinson Peter Cushing Madeline Collinson

1974 CRAZE
Director: Freddie Francis
Co-stars: Jack Palance Diana Dors Julie Ege

1990 PORTRAIT OF A MARRIAGE
Director: Stephen Whittaker
Co-stars: Janet McTeer Cathryn Harrison David Haig

MARION BYRON

1928 STEAMBOAT BILL JNR.
Director: Charles Reisner
Co-stars: Buster Keaton Ernest Torrence

1932 THE HEART OF NEW YORK
Director: Mervyn LeRoy
Co-stars: Joe Smith Charles Dale George Sidney

IRENE GUTIERREZ CABA

1981   THE HOUSE OF BERNARDA ALBA
Director: Mario Camus
Co-stars: Ana Belin Florinda Chico Vicky Pena

FRANCISCA CABALLERO
(Mother Of Pedro Almodovar)

1993   KIKA
Director: Pedro Almodovar
Co-stars: Veronica Forque Peter Coyote Victoria Abril

ANGEL CABAN

1994   HANDGUN
Director: Whitney Ransick
Co-stars: Treat Williams Seymour Cassel Toby Huss

ANNETTE CABOT

1953   HEIGHTS OF DANGER
Director: Peter Bradford
Co-stars: Basil Appleby Freda Barnford

SUSAN CABOT

1951   MURDER INC.
Director: Bretaigne Windust
Co-stars: Humphrey Bogart Zero Mostel Everett Slone

1951   FLAME OF ARABY
Director: Charles Lamont
Co-stars: Maureen O'Hara Jeff Chandler Richard Egan

1952   THE BATTLE AT APACHE PASS
Director: George Sherman
Co-stars: John Lund Jeff Chandler Richard Egan

1952   DUEL AT SILVER CREEK
Director: Don Siegel
Co-stars: Audie Murphy Stephen McNally Faith Domergue

1952   SON OF ALI BABA
Director: Kurt Neumann
Co-stars: Tony Curtis Piper Laurie Victor Jory

1953   GUNSMOKE
Director: Nathan Juran
Co-stars: Audie Murphy Paul Kelly Mary Castle

1954   RIDE CLEAR OF DIABLO
Director: Jesse Hibbs
Co-stars: Audie Murphy Dan Duryea Abbe Lane

1957   SORORITY GIRL

1957   VIKING WOMEN AND THE SEA SERPENT
Director: Roger Corman
Co-stars: Brad Jackson June Kenny Abby Dalton

1958   FORT MASSACRE
Director: Joseph Newman
Co-stars: Joel McCrea Forrest Tucker John Russell

1958   MACHINE GUN KELLY
Director: Roger Corman
Co-stars: Charles Bronson Morey Amsterdam Jack Lambert

JEAN CADELL

1935   DAVID COPPERFIELD
Director: George Cukor
Co-stars: Frank Lawton W. C. Fields Madge Evans

1936   LOVE FROM A STRANGER
Director: Rowland Lee
Co-stars: Ann Harding Basil Rathbone Binnie Hale

1938   PYGMALION
Director: Anthony Asquith
Co-stars: Leslie Howard Wendy Hiller Wilfrid Lawson

1941   QUIET WEDDING
Director: Anthony Asquith
Co-stars: Margaret Lockwood Derek Farr Peggy Ashcroft

1942   THE YOUNG MR. PITT
Director: Carol Reed
Co-stars: Robert Donat Robert Morley Phyllis Calvert

1943   DEAR OCTOPUS
Director: Harold French
Co-stars: Margaret Lockwood Michael Wilding Celia Johnson

1947   JASSY
Director: Bernard Knowles
Co-stars: Margaret Lockwood Patricia Roc Dennis Price

1949   MADELEINE
Director: David Lean
Co-stars: Ann Todd Leslie Banks Elizabeth Sellars

1949   NO PLACE FOR JENNIFER
Director: Henry Cass
Co-stars: Leo Genn Rosamund John Janette Scott

1949   THAT DANGEROUS AGE
Director: Gregory Ratoff
Co-stars: Roger Livesey Myrna Loy Peggy Cummings

1949   WHISKY GALORE
Director: Alexander MacKendrick
Co-stars: Basil Radford Joan Greenwood John Gregson

1949   MARRY ME
Director: Terence Fisher
Co-stars: Derek Bond Susan Shaw Carol Marsh

1951   THE LATE EDWINA BLACK
Director: Maurice Elvy
Co-stars: Geraldine Fitzgerald David Farrar

1953   MEET MR. LUCIFER
Director: Anthony Pellisier
Co-stars: Stanley Holloway Peggy Cummings Kay Kendall

1957   THE LITTLE HUT
Director: Mark Robson
Co-stars: Stewart Granger David Niven Ava Gardner

1957   LET'S BE HAPPY
Director: Henry Levin
Co-stars: Vera-Ellen Tony Martin Robert Flemyng

1958   ROCKETS GALORE
Director: Michael Relph
Co-stars: Jeannie Carson Donald Sinden Roland Culver

SELINA CADELL

1985   NOT QUITE JERUSALEM
Director: Lewis Gilbert
Co-stars: Joanna Pacula Sam Robards Kevin McNally

MARY CADORETTE

PERRY MASON: THE CASE OF THE MUSICAL MURDER
Director: Christian Nyby
Co-stars: Raymond Burr Debbie Reynolds

JEAN CAFFEINE

1992 SLACKER
Director: Richard Linklater
Co-stars: Richard Linklater Rudy Basquet Jan Hockey

JEANNE CAGNEY (Sister Of James Cagney)

1939 GOLDEN GLOVES
Director: Edward Dmytryk
Co-stars: Richard Denning Robert Ryan

1940 QUEEN OF THE MOB
Director: James Hogan
Co-stars: Blanche Yurka Ralph Bellamy Jack Carson

1942 YANKEE DOODLE DANDY
Director: Michael Curtiz
Co-stars: James Cagney Joan Leslie Walter Huston

1948 THE TIME OF YOUR LIFE
Director: H. C. Potter
Co-stars: James Cagney William Bendix Wayne Morris

1950 QUICKSAND
Director: Irving Pichel
Co-stars: Mickey Rooney Barbara Bates Peter Lorre

1952 DON'T BOTHER TO KNOCK
Director: Roy Baker
Co-stars: Marilyn Monroe Richard Widmark Anne Bancroft

1953 A LION IS IN THE STREETS
Director: Raoul Walsh
Co-stars: James Cagney Barbara Hale Anne Francis

GEORGIA CAINE

1933 I AM SUZANNE
Director: Rowland Lee
Co-stars: Lilian Harvey Gene Raymond Leslie Banks

1939 TOWER OF LONDON
Director: Rowland Lee
Co-stars: Basil Rathbone Boris Karloff Barbara O'Neil

1942 THE WIFE TAKES A FLYER
Director: Richard Wallace
Co-stars: Joan Bennett Franchot Tone Allyn Joslyn

1944 HAIL THE CONQUERING HERO
Director: Preston Sturges
Co-stars: Eddie Bracken William DeMarest

SHAKIRA CAINE (Wife Of Michael Caine)

1975 THE MAN WHO WOULD BE KING
Director: John Huston
Co-stars: Sean Connery Michael Caine Saeed Jaffrey

AUDREY CAIRE

1970 JOE
Director: John Avildsen
Co-stars: Dennis Patrick Peter Boyle Susan Sarandon

NEKETA CALAME

1994 THE LION KING (Voice)
Director: Roger Allens
Co-stars: James Earl Jones Jeremy Irons

CLARA CALAMEI

1942 OSSESSIONE
Director: Luchino Visconti
Co-stars: Massimo Girotti Elia Marcuzzo

ALISON CALDER

1990 SOMETIME IN AUGUST
Director: John Glenister
Co-stars: Graig Lorimer Tom Wilkinson Mary Morris

ANNA CALDER-MARSHALL

1970 WUTHERING HEIGHTS
Director: Robert Fuest
Co-stars: Timothy Dalton Harry Andrews Judy Cornwell

1988 INSPECTOR MORSE:
THE SETTLING OF THE SUN
Director: Peter Hammond
Co-stars: John Thaw Robert Stephens

JANE CALDWELL

1993 MANDROID
Director: Jack Ersgard
Co-stars: Brian Cousins Michael Dellafemina

ZOE CALDWELL

1985 THE PURPLE ROSE OF CAIRO
Director: Woody Allen
Co-stars: Mia Farrow Jeff Daniels Danny Aiello

JADE CALEGORY

1988 MAC AND ME
Director: Stewart Raffill
Co-stars: Christine Ebersole Jonathan Ward Tina Caspary

NICOLE CALFIN

1988 DIRTY ROTTEN SCOUNDRELS
Director: Frank Oz
Co-stars: Steve Martin Michael Caine Glenne Headly

MONICA CALHOUN

1988 BAGDAD CAFE
Director: Percy Adlon
Co-stars: Marianne Sagebrecht Jack Palance Christine Kaufman

MARGARET CALLAHAN

1935 HIS FAMILY TREE
Director: Charles Vidor
Co-stars: James Barton Maureen Delany

1935 SEVEN KEYS TO BALDPATE
Director: Edward Killy
Co-stars: Gene Raymond Eric Blore Grant Mitchell

1935 HOT TIP
Co-Star Zasu Pitts

1936 MUSS 'EM UP
Director: Charles Vidor
Co-stars: Preston Foster Ralph Morgan Alan Mowbray

K. CALLAN

1970 JOE
Director: John Avildsen
Co-stars: Dennis Patrick Peter Boyle Susan Sarandon

1989 INCIDENT AT DARK RIVER
Director: Michael Pressman
Co-stars: Mike Farrell Tess Harper Helen Hunt

TRACEY CALLANDER

1984 FUTURE SCHLOCK
Director: Barry Peak
Co-stars: Maryanne Fahey Michael Bishop

KAY CALLARD

1956 FIND THE LADY
Director: Charles Saunders
Co-stars: Donald Houston Mervyn Johns Beverley Brooks

1957   THE FLYING SCOT
Director: Compton Bennett
Co-stars: Lee Patterson Alan Gifford

MARIA CALLAS

1969   MEDEA
Director: Pier Paolo Pasolino
Co-stars: Guiseppe Gentile Massimo Girotti

LIZ CALLAWAY

1995   THE SWAN PRINCESS *(Voice)*
Director: Richard Rich
Co-stars: John Cleese Jack Palance Steven Wright

CECILIA CALEJO

1944   THE CISCO KID RETURNS
Director: John McCarthy
Co-stars: Duncan Reynaldo Roger Pryor

JANESSA BELL CALLOWAY

1993   TINA: WHAT'S LOVE GOT TO DO WITH IT
Director: Brian Gibson
Co-stars: Angela Bassett Laurence Fishburne

CORINNE CALVET

1949   ROPE OF SAND
Director: William Dieterle
Co-stars: Burt Lancaster Paul Henreid Claude Rains

1950   WHEN WILLIE COMES MARCHING HOME
Director: John Ford
Co-stars: Dan Dailey Colleen Townshend Jimmy Lydon

1950   MY FRIEND IRMA GOES WEST
Director: Hal Walker
Co-stars: Martin & Lewis John Lund Marie Wilson

1951   ON THE RIVIERA
Director: Walter Lang
Co-stars: Danny Kaye Gene Tierney Marcel Dalio

1951   THUNDER INTHE EAST
Director: Charles Vidor
Co-stars: Alan Ladd Deborah Kerr Charles Boyer

1951   PEKING EXPRESS
Director: William Dieterle
Co-stars: Joseph Cotten Edmund Gwenn Marvin Miller

1951   QUEBEC
Director: George Templeton
Co-stars: John Barrymore Jnr, Barbara Rush

1952   WHAT PRICE GLORY?
Director: John Ford
Co-stars: James Cagney Dan Dailey William Demarest

1952   SAILOR BEWARE
Director: Hal Walker
Co-stars: Martin & Lewis Robert Strauss Lief Erikson

1953   POWDER RIVER
Director: Louis King
Co-stars: Rory Calhoun Cameron Mitchell Penny Edwards

1953   FLIGHT TO TANGIER
Director: Charles Marquis Warren
Co-stars: Joan Fontaine Jack Palance Robert Douglas

1954   SO THIS IS PARIS
Director: Richard Quine
Co-stars: Tony Curtis Gloria De Haven Gene Nelson

1954   THE FAR COUNTRY
Director: Anthony Mann
Co-stars: James Stewart Walter Brennan Ruth Roman

1960   BLUEBEARD'S TEN HONEYMOONS
Director: Lee Wilder
Co-stars: George Sanders Patricia Roc Jean Kent

1965   APACHE UPRISING
Director: R. G. Springsteen
Co-stars: Rory Calhoun John Russell Lon Chaney

1974   PHANTOM OF HOLLYWOOD
Director: Gene Levitt
Co-stars: Broderick Crawford Peter Lawford John Ireland

JENNIFER CALVERT

1990   COME HOME CHARLIE AND FACE THEM
Director: Robert Bamford
Co-stars: Tom Radcliffe Peter Sallis

PHYLLIS CALVERT

1939   THEY CAME BY NIGHT
Director: Harry Lachman
Co-stars: Will Fyffe Anthony Hulme George Merritt

1940   NEUTRAL PORT
Director: Marcel Varnel
Co-stars: Will Fyffe Leslie Banks Yvonne Arnaud

1940   LET GEORGE DO IT
Director: Marcel Varnel
Co-stars: George Formby Coral Browne Garry Marsh

1940   INSPECTOR HORNLEIGH GOES TO IT
Director: Walter Forde
Co-stars: Gordon Harker Alastair Sim

1940   CHARLEY'S (BIG HEARTED) AUNT
Director: Walter Forde
Co-stars: Arthur Askey Richard Murdoch

1941   KIPPS
Director: Carol Reed
Co-stars: Michael Redgrave Diana Wynyard Max Adrian

1942   THE YOUNG MR. PITT
Director: Carol Reed
Co-stars: Robert Donat John Mills Robert Morley

1942   UNCENSORED
Director: Anthony Asquith
Co-stars: Eric Portman Griffith Jones Irene Handl

1943   THE MAN IN GREY
Director: Leslie Arliss
Co-stars: James Mason Margaret Lockwood Stewart Granger

1944   MADONNA OF THE SEVEN MOONS
Director: Arthur Crabtree
Co-stars: Stewart Granger Patricia Roc Jean Kent

1944   TWO THOUSAND WOMEN
Director: Frank Launder
Co-stars: Flora Robson Patricia Roc Renee Houston

1944   FANNY BY GASLIGHT
Director: Anthony Asquith
Co-stars: James Mason Stewart Granger Wilfrid Lawson

1945   THEY WERE SISTERS
Director: Arthur Crabtree
Co-stars: Dulcie Gray Anne Crawford James Mason

1946   MEN OF TWO WORLDS
Director: Thorold Dickinson
Co-stars: Eric Portman Robert Adams Cathleen Nesbitt

1946   THE MAGIC BOW
Director: Bernard Knowles
Co-stars: Stewart Granger Jean Kent Dennis Price

1947   THE ROOT OF ALL EVIL
Director: Brock Williams
Co-stars: Michael Rennie John McCallum Hubert Gregg

1947 BROKEN JOURNEY
Director: Ken Annakin
Co-stars: James Donald Margot Grahame Guy Rolfe

1947 TIME OUT OF MIND
Director: Robert Siodmak
Co-stars: Robert Hutton Ella Raines Eddie Albert

1948 MY OWN TRUE LOVE
Director: Compton Bennett
Co-stars: Melvyn Douglas Philip Friend Wanda Hendrix

1949 APPOINTMENT WITH DANGER
Director: Lewis Allen
Co-stars: Alan Ladd Paul Stewart Jan Sterling

1949 THE GOLDEN MADONNA
Director: Ladislas Vajda
Co-stars: Michael Rennie Tullio Carminati

1950 THE WOMAN WITH NO NAME
Director: Ladislas Vajda
Co-stars: Edward Underdown Helen Cherry Richard Burton

1951 MR. DENNING DRIVES NORTH
Director: Anthony Kimmins
Co-stars: John Mills Sam Wanamaker Freda Jackson

1952 MANDY
Director: Alexander MacKendrick
Co-stars: Jack Hawkins Terence Morgan Mandy Miller

1953 THE NET
Director: Anthony Asquith
Co-stars: James Donald Robert Beatty Noel Wilman

1956 IT'S NEVER TOO LATE
Director: Michael McCarthy
Co-stars: Guy Rolfe Susan Stephen Sarah Lawson

1956 CHILD IN THE HOUSE
Director: Raker Endfield
Co-stars: Eric Portman Stanley Baker Mandy Miller

1958 A LADY MISLAID
Director: David MacDonald
Co-stars: Gillian Owen Alan White Thorley Walters

1958 INDISCREET
Director: Stanley Donen
Co-stars: Cary Grant Ingrid Bergman Cecil Parker

1959 OSCAR WILDE
Director: Gregory Ratoff
Co-stars: Robert Morley John Neville Ralph Richardson

1964 THE BATTLE OF THE VILLA FIORITA
Director: Delmer Daves
Co-stars: Maureen O'Hara Rossana Brazzi

1968 OH! WHAT A LOVELY WAR
Director: Richard Attenborough
Co-stars: John Gielgud Kenneth More John Mills

1968 TWISTED NERVE
Director: Roy Boulting
Co-stars: Hayley Mills Hywell Bennett Billie Whitelaw

1970 THE WALKING STICK
Director: Eric Till
Co-stars: David Hemmings Samantha Eggar Emlyn Williams

1988 ACROSS THE LAKE
Director: Tony Maylam
Co-stars: Anthony Hopkins Rosemary Leach Dexter Fletcher

1991 JUTE CITY
Director: Stuart Orme
Co-stars: David O'Hara Joanna Roth John Sessions

JOAN CAMDEN

1951 THE CAPTIVE CITY
Director: Robert Wise
Co-stars: John Forsythe Marjorie Crossland

CAMELIA

1949 CAIRO ROAD
Director: David MacDonald
Co-stars: Eric Portman Laurence Harvey Harold Lang

JOANNA CAMERON

1970 B. S. I LOVE YOU
Director: Steven Hilliard Stern
Co-stars: Peter Kastner Louise Sorel Joanna Barnes

1974 NIGHT GAMES
Director: Don Taylor
Co-stars: Barry Newman Susan Howard Anjanette Comer

1976 HIGH RISK
Director: Sam O'Steen
Co-stars: Victor Buono Joseph Sirola Don Stroud

1978 SPIDERMAN STRIKES BACK
Director: Ron Satlof
Co-stars: Nicholas Hammond Chip Fields Robert Alda

MARJORIE CAMERON

1954 KENNETH ANGER, VOL 2: INAUGURATION OF THE PLEASURE DOME
Director: Kenneth Anger
Co-Star Anais Nin

SHIRLEY CAMERON

1983 THE CITY'S EDGE
Director: Ken Quinnell
Co-stars: Hugo Weaving Tommy Lewis Mark Lee

DOMENICA CAMERON-SCORSESE *(Child)*
(Daughter Of Martin Scorsese)

1989 GOD'S WILL
Director: Julia Cameron
Co-stars: Daniel Region Laura Margolis Marge Kotlisky

1992 STRAIGHT TALK
Director: Barnet Kellman
Co-stars: Dolly Parton James Woods Griffin Dunne

MICKI CAMILLERI

1990 RETURN HOME
Director: Ray Argall
Co-stars: Dennis Coard Ben Mendelsohn Rachel Rains

CHINA CAMMEL

1986 WHITE OF THE EYE
Director: Donald Cammell
Co-stars: David Keith Cathy Moriarty Alberta Watson

COLLEEN CAMP

1974 SMILE
Director: Michael Ritchie
Co-stars: Bruce Dern Barbara Feldon Melanie Griffith

1977 CLOUD DANCER
Director: Barry Brown
Co-stars: David Carradine Jennifer O'Neill Salome Jens

1977 DEATH GAME
Director: Peter Traynor
Co-stars: Sondra Locke Seymour Cassel Beth Brickell

1979 APOCALYPSE NOW
Director: Francis Coppola
Co-stars: Martin Sheen Robert Duvall Marlon Brando

1982 THEY ALL LAUGHED
Director: Peter Bogdanovich
Co-stars: Audrey Hepburn Ben Gazzara Dorothy Stratten

1983 SMOKEY AND THE BANDIT 3
Director: Dick Lowry
Co-stars: Jackie Gleason Jerry Reed Mike Henry

1983 VALLEY GIRL
Director: Martha Coolidge
Co-stars: Nicolas Cage Deborah Foreman Elizabeth Daily

1985 CLUE
Director: Jonathan Lynn
Co-stars: Eileen Brennan Tim Curry Madeline Kahn

1985 D. A. R. Y. L.
Director: Simon Wincer
Co-stars: Mary Beth Hurt Michael McKean Kathryn Walker

1987 TRACK 29
Director: Nicolas Roeg
Co-stars: Theresa Russell Gary Oldman Sandra Bernhard

1988 ILLEGALLY YOURS
Director: Peter Bogdanovich
Co-stars: Rob Lowe Kenneth Mars Kim Myers

1988 ADDICTED TO HIS LOVE
Director: Arthur Allan Seidelman
Co-stars: Polly Bergen Erin Gray Linda Purl

1989 THE WICKED STEPMOTHER
Director: Lary Cohen
Co-stars: Bette Davis Babara Carrera Tom Bosley

1991 BACKFIELD IN MOTION
Director: Richard Michaels
Co-stars: Roseanne Arnold Tom Arnold

1992 WAYNE'S WORLD
Director: Penelope Spheeris
Co-stars: Mike Myers Dana Carvey Rob Lowe

1992 UNBECOMING AGE
Director: Alfredo Ringel
Co-stars: Diane Salinger John Calvin George Clooney

1993 SLIVER
Director: Phillip Noyce
Co-stars: Sharon Stone William Baldwin Tom Berenger

HELEN PAGE CAMP
1981 STAND BY YOUR MAN
Director: Jerry Jameson
Co-stars: Annette O'Toole Tim McIntire James Hampton

BEATRICE CAMPBELL
1949 NOW BARABBAS
Director: Gordon Parry
Co-stars: Richard Greene Cedric Hardwicke Richard Burton

1949 NO PLACE FOR JENNIFER
Director: Henry Cass
Co-stars: Leo Genn Rosamund John Janette Scott

1950 THE MUDLARK
Director: Jean Negulesco
Co-stars: Alec Guinness Irene Dunne Andrew Ray

1950 LAST HOLIDAY
Director: Henry Cass
Co-stars: Alec Guinness Kay Walsh Bernard Lee

1951 LAUGHTER IN PARADISE
Director: Mario Zampi
Co-stars: Alastair Sim Joyce Grenfell Hugh Griffith

1951 THE HOUSE IN THE SQUARE
Director: Roy Baker
Co-stars: Tyrone Power Ann Blythe Michael Rennie

1953 GRAND NATIONAL NIGHT
Director: Bob McNaught
Co-stars: Nigel Patrick Moira Lister Noel Purcell

1953 THE MASTER OF BALLANTRAE
Director: William Keighley
Co-stars: Errol Flynn Anthony Steel

1955 THE COCKLESHELL HEROES
Director: Jose Ferrer
Co-stars: Jose Ferrer Trevor Howard Anthony Newley

BEVERLY CAMPBELL
1950 D.O.A.
Director: Rudolph Mate
Co-stars: Edmond O'Brien Pamela Britton Luther Adler

CHERYL CAMPBELL
1980 HAWK THE SLAYER
Director: Terry Marcel
Co-stars: Jack Palance John Terry Bernard Bresslaw

1980 McVICAR
Director: Tom Clegg
Co-stars: Roger Daltrey Adam Faith Georgina Hale

1981 CHARIOTS OF FIRE
Director: Hugh Hudson
Co-stars: Ben Cross Ian Charleson Nigel Havers

1984 THE SHOOTING PARTY
Director: Alan Bridges
Co-stars: James Mason Edward Fox Dorothy Tutin

1984 GREYSTOKE: THE LEGEND OF TARZAN, LORD OF THE APES
Director: Hugh Hudson
Co-stars: Christian Lambert Ralph Richardson Andie MacDowell

1990 CENTREPOINT
Director: Piers Haggard
Co-stars: Jonathan Firth Bob Peck Murray Head

1990 THE CASEBOOK OF SHERLOCK HOLMES: THE DISAPPEARANCE OF LADY CARFAX
Director: John Madden
Co-stars: Jeremy Brett Edward Hardwicke Michael Jayston

1990 INSPECTOR MORSE: THE INFERNAL SERPENT
Director: John Madden
Co-stars: John Thaw Kevin Whately

1991 INSPECTOR WEXFORD: MEANS OF EVIL
Director: Sarah Hellings
Co-stars: George Baker Diane Keen

DAPHNE CAMPBELL
1946 THE OVERLANDERS
Director: Harry Watt
Co-stars: Chips Rafferty John Heywood Jean Blue

ISOBELL CAMPBELL
1950 THE GORBALS STORY
Director: David MacKane
Co-stars: Howard Connell Betty Henderson Russell Hunter

JESICA M.CAMPBELL
1986 IN THE BEST INTEREST OF THE CHILDREN
Director: Michael Ray Rhodes
Co-stars: Sarah Jessica Parker Lexi Randall Elizabeth Ashley

JULIA CAMPBELL
1990 OPPORTUNITY KNOCKS
Director: Donald Petrie
Co-stars: Dana Carvey Robert Loggia Todd Graff

JUDY CAMPBELL
1940 EAST OF PICCADILLY
Director: Harold Huth
Co-stars: Sebastian Shaw Niall Macginnis Martita Hunt

1940 CONVOY
Director: Pen Tennyson
Co-stars: Clive Brook John Clements Albert Lieven

1940 SALOON BAR
Director: Walter Forde
Co-stars: Gordon Harker Elizabeth Allan Mervyn Johns

1941 BREACH OF PROMISE
Director: Harold Huth
Co-stars: Clive Brook Margaret Allan Percy Walsh

1944 THE WORLD OWES ME A LIVING
Director: Vernon Sewell
Co-stars: David Farrar Sonia Dresdel John Laurie

1947 GREEN FOR DANGER
Director: Sidney Gilliat
Co-stars: Alastair Sim Sally Gray Trevor Howard

1948 BONNIE PRINCE CHARLIE
Director: Anthony Kimmins
Co-stars: David Niven Margaret Leighton Jack Hawkins

1970 THERE'S A GIRL IN MY SOUP
Director: Roy Boulting
Co-stars: Peter Sellers Goldie Hawn Tony Britton

1971 MR. FORBUSH AND THE PENGUINS
Director: Roy Boulting
Co-stars: John Hurt Hayley Mills Sally Geeson

L985 ANNA KARENINA
Director: Simon Langton
Co-stars: Jacqueline Bisset Christopher Reeve Paul Scofield

1992 WITCHCRAFT
Director: Peter Sasdy
Co-stars: Peter McEnery Lisa Harrow Alan Howard

KATE CAMPBELL
1933 COME ON TARZAN
Co-Star Ken Maynard

LAURA CAMPBELL
1980 THE LEGEND OF SLEEPY HOLLOW
Director: Henning Schellerup
Co-stars: Jeff Goldblum Meg Foster

LOUISE CAMPBELL
1937 SCANDAL SHEET
Director: James Hogan
Co-stars: Lew Ayres Roscoe Karns Virginia Weidler

1937 NIGHT CLUB SCANDAL
Director: Ralph Murphy
Co-stars: John Barrymore Charles Bickford Evelyn Brent

1938 MEN WITH WINGS
Director: William Wellman
Co-stars: Fred MacMurray Ray Milland Lynne Overman

1938 BULLDOG DRUMMOND'S PERIL
Co-stars: John Howard John Barrymore

1939 THE STAR MAKER
Director: Roy Del Ruth
Co-stars: Bing Crosby Linda Ware Ned Sparks

NAOMI CAMPBELL
1995 MIAMI RHAPSODY
Director: David Frankel
Co-stars: Sarah Jessica Parker Antonio Banderas Mia Farrow

1996 UNZIPPED
Director: Douglas Keeve
Co-stars: Sandra Bernhard Cindy Crawford Kate Moss

NEVE CAMPBELL
1994 WEB OF DECEIT
Director: Bill Corcoran
Co-stars: Corbin Bernsen Amanda Pays Mimi Kuzyk

1996 THE CRAFT
Director: Andrew Fleming
Co-stars: Fairusa Balk Robin Tunney

1996 THE CANTERVILLE GHOST
Director: Syd McCartney
Co-stars: Patrick Stewart Cheri Lunghi Edward Whiley

1997 SCREAM
Director: Wes Craven
Co-stars: Drew Barrymore Henry Winkler

1998 SCREAM 2
Director: Wes Craven
Co-Star Courteney Cox

MRS. PATRICK CAMPBELL
1934 RIPTIDE
Director: Edmund Goulding
Co-stars: Norma Shearer Robert Montgomery Herbert Marshall

1934 OUTCAST LADY
Director: Robert Z. Leonard
Co-stars: Constance Bennett Hugh Williams Elizabeth Allan

1934 ONE MORE RIVER
Director: James Whale
Co-stars: Colin Clive Diana Wynyard Jane Wyatt

1935 CRIME AND PUNISHMENT
Director: Joseph Von Sternberg
Co-stars: Peter Lorre Edward Arnold Tala Birell

TISHA CAMPBELL
1988 SCHOOL DAZE
Director: Spike Lee
Co-stars: Spike Lee Larry Fishburne
Giancarlo Esposito

1989 ROOFTOPS
Director: Robert Wise
Co-stars: Jason Gedrick Troy Beyer Eddie Velez

1990 HOUSE PARTY
Director: Reginald Hudlin
Co-stars: Christopher Reid Robin Harris

1990 ANOTHER 48 HRS.
Director: Walter Hill
Co-stars: Eddie Murphy Nick Nolte Brion James

1992 HOUSE PARTY 2: THE PYJAMA JAM
Director: George Jackson
Co-stars: Christopher Reid Christopher Martin

1994 HOUSE PARTY 3
Director: Eric Meza
Co-stars: Christopher Reid Christopher Martin Angela Means

GIANNA MARIA CANALE
1958 THE WHOLE TRUTH
Director: John Guillermin
Co-stars: Stewart Granger George Sanders Donna Reed

1958 THE SILENT ENEMY
Director: William Fairchild
Co-stars: Laurence Harvey Dawn Addams Michael Craig

1960 QUEEN OF THE PIRATES
Director: Mario Costo
Co-stars: Massimo Serrato Scilla Gabel Paul Muller

1960 THE TREASURE OF MONTE CRISTO
Director: Robert Baker
Co-stars: Rory Calhoun Patricia Bredin

1962 TIGER OF THE SEVEN SEAS
Director: Mario Costo
Co-stars: Massimo Serrato Paul Muller

1963 LION OF ST. MARK
Director: Luigi Capuano
Co-stars: Gordon Scott Rik Battaglia

LINA CANALEJAS
1984 DARK HABITS
Director: Pedro Almodovar
Co-stars: Cristina Pascual Marisa Paredes Carmen Maura

SHEILA CANFIELD
1980 THE FALLS
Director: Peter Greenaway
Co-stars: Colin Cantlie Hilarie Thompson

HEATHER CANNING
1990 MURDER EAST, MURDER WEST
Director: Peter Smith
Co-stars: Jeroen Krabbe Suzanna Hamilton Joanne Pearce

DYAN CANNON
Nominated For Best Supporting Actress In 1969 For "Bob And Carol And Ted And Alice" And In 1978 For "Heaven Can Wait"

1969 BOB AND CAROL AND TED AND ALICE
Director: Paul Mazursky
Co-stars: Natalie Wood Robert Culp Elliott Gould

1970 DOCTORS' WIVES
Director: George Schaefer
Co-stars: Richard Crenna Janice Rule Gene Hackman

1971 THE ANDERSON TAPES
Director: Sidney Lumet
Co-stars: Sean Connery Martin Balsam Ralph Meeker

1971 THE BURGLARS
Director: Henri Verneuil
Co-stars: Omar Sharif Jean-Paul Belmondo

1971 THE LOVE MACHINE
Director: Jack Haley
Co-stars: John Philip Law Robert Ryan David Hemmings

1971 SUCH GOOD FRIENDS
Director: Otto Preminger
Co-stars: James Coco Nina Foch Burgess Meredith

1972 SHAMUS
Director: Buzz Kulik
Co-stars: Burt Reynolds John Ryan Joe Santos

1973 THE LAST OF SHEILA
Director: Herbert Ross
Co-stars: Richard Benjamin James Coburn

1978 HEAVEN CAN WAIT
Director: Warren Beatty
Co-stars: Warren Beatty Buck Henry Julie Christie James Mason

1978 REVENGE OF THE PINK PANTHER
Director: Blake Edwards
Co-stars: Peter Sellers Herbert Lom Robert Webber

1980 HONEYSUCKLE ROSE
Director: Jerry Schatzberg
Co-stars: Willie Nelson Amy Irving Slim Pickins

1980 COAST TO COAST
Director: Joseph Sargent
Co-stars: Robert Blake Michael Lerner

1982 DEATHTRAP
Director: Sidney Lumet
Co-stars: Michael Caine Christopher Reeve Irene Worth

1982 AUTHOR! AUTHOR!
Director: Arthur Hiller
Co-stars: Al Pacino Tuesday Weld Bob Dishey

1988 CADDYSHACK II
Director: Alan Arkush
Co-stars: Jackie Mason Robert Stack Dina Merril

1988 ROCK ' N ' ROLL MOM
Director: Michael Schultz
Co-stars: Michael Brandon Heather Locklear

1992 CHRISTMAS IN CONNECTICUT
Director: Arnold Schwartzenegger
Co-stars: Kris Kristofferson Tony Curtis

1993 THE PICKLE
Director: Paul Mazursky
Co-stars: Danny Aiello Shelley Winters Clotilde Courau

1997 EIGHT HEADS IN A DUFFEL BAG
Co-stars: Joe Pesci Kristy Swanson Andy Comeau

ESME CANNON
1947 HOLIDAY CAMP
Director: Ken Annakin
Co-stars: Jack Warner Kathleen Harrison Hazel Court

1949 THE HUGGETTS ABROAD
Director: Ken Annakin
Co-stars: Jack Warner Susan Shaw Petula Clark

1954 OUT OF THE CLOUDS
Director: Michael Relph
Co-stars: Anthony Steel Robert Beatty Eunice Gayson

1956 SAILOR BEWARE
Director: Gordon Parry
Co-stars: Peggy Mount Shirley Eaton Ronald Lewis

1961 WHAT A CARVE UP!
Director: Pat Jackson
Co-stars: Sid James Kenneth Connor Shirley Eaton

1961 CARRY ON REGARDLESS
Director: Gerald Thomas
Co-stars: Sid James Liz Fraser Bill Owen Joan Sims

1962 CARRY ON CRUISING
Director: Gerald Thomas
Co-stars: Sid James Kenneth Williams Kenneth Connor

1963 CARRY ON CABBY
Director: Gerald Thomas
Co-stars: Sid James Hattie Jacques Charles Hawtrey

WANDA CANNON
1990 THE LAST WINTER
Director: Arron Jim Johnston
Co-stars: Joshua Murray Gerard Parkes

DIANA CANOVA
1976 THE FIRST NUDIE MUSICAL
Director: Mark Haggard
Co-stars: Bruce Kimmel Stephen Nathan Cindy Williams

1983 NIGHT PARTNERS
Director: Noel Nosseck
Co-stars: Yvette Mimieux M. Emmet Walsh Patricia McCormack

JUDY CANOVA

1935   BROADWAY GONDOLIER
Director: Lloyd Bacon
Co-stars: Dick Powell Joan Blondell Adolphe Menjou

1935   GOING HIGHBROW
Director: Robert Florey
Co-stars: Edward Everett Horton Guy Kibbee Zasu Pitts

1935   IN CALIENTE
Director: Lloyd Bacon
Co-stars: Delores Del Rio Pat O'Brien Glenda Farrell

1937   ARTISTS AND MODELS
Director: Raoul Walsh
Co-stars: Jack Benny Ida Lupino Ben Blue

1937   THRILL OF A LIFETIME
Director: George Archainbaud
Co-stars: Betty Grable Johnny Downs Ben Blue

1942   JOAN OF OZARK
Director: Joseph Santley
Co-stars: Joe E. Brown Eddie Foy Jnr. Jerome Cowan

1943   CHATTERBOX
Director: Joseph Santley
Co-stars: Joe E. Brown Rosemary Lane John Hubbard

1944   LOUISIANA HAYRIDE
Co-stars: Matt Willis Minerva Urecal

1945   HIT THE HAY
Co-stars: Ross Hunter Doris Merrick Fortunio Bonanova

1951   HONEYCHILE
Director: R. G. Springsteen
Co-stars: Eddie Foy Jnr Walter Catlett Alan Hale Jnr.

1960   HUCKLEBERRY FINN
Director: Michael Curtiz
Co-stars: Eddie Hodges Tony Randall Archie Moore

1976   CARQUAKE
Director: Paul Bartel
Co-stars: David Carradine Veronica Hamel Bill McKinney

ANNE CANOVAS

1986   MICHIGAN MELODY
Director: Bernard Toublanc-Michel
Co-Star   Edward Meeks

1990   VINCENT AND THEO
Director: Robert Altman
Co-stars: Tim Roth Paul Rhys Johanna Ter Steege

MARIETTA CANTY

1942   THE LADY IS WILLING
Director: Mitchell Leisen
Co-stars: Marlene Dietrich Fred MacMurray Arline Judge

1951   FATHER'S LITTLE DIVIDEND
Director: Vincente Minnelli
Co-stars: Spencer Tracy Elizabeth Taylor Joan Bennett

JAD CAPELJA

1981   PUBERTY BLUES
Director: Bruce Beresford
Co-stars: Nell Schofield Geoff Rhoe Sandy Paul

VIRGINIA CAPERS

1980   WHITE MAMA
Director: Jackie Cooper
Co-stars: Bette Davis Ernest Harden Jnr. Eileen Heckart

1986   THE GEORGE McKENNA STORY
Director: Eric Laneuville
Co-stars: Denzel Washington Lynn Whitfield

1986   FERRIS BUELLER'S DAY OFF
Director: John Hughes
Co-stars: Matthew Broderick Mia Sara Jennifer Grey

1990   PACIFIC PALISADES
Director: Bernard Schmitt
Co-stars: Sophie Marceau Anne Curry Toni Basil

JOOLIA CAPPELMAN

1971   BLEAK MOMENTS
Director: Mike Leigh
Co-stars: Anne Raitt Sarah Stephenson Eric Allan

KATE CAPSHAW (*Married Steven Spielberg*)

1982   A LITTLE SEX
Director: Bruce Paltrow
Co-stars: Tim Matheson Edward Herrman John Glover

1984   DREAMSCAPE
Director: Joseph Ruben
Co-stars: Dennis Quaid Max Von Sidow Christopher Plummer

1984   INDIANA JONES AND THE TEMPLE OF DOOM
Director: Steven Spielberg
Co-stars: Harrison Ford Philip Stone

1984   BEST DEFENSE
Director: Willard Huyck
Co-stars: Dudley Moore Eddie Murphy Helen Shaver

1984   WINDY CITY
Director: Armyan Bernstein
Co-stars: John Shea John Mostel Jim Borrelli

1985   POWER
Director: Sidney Lumet
Co-stars: Richard Gere Julie Christie Gene Hackman

1986   SPACECAMP
Director: Harry Winer
Co-stars: Lea Thompson Leaf Phoenix Tom Skerritt

1987   THE QUICK AND THE DEAD
Director: Robert Day
Co-stars: Sam Elliott Tom Conti Kenny Morrison

1987   CODENAME: DANCER
Director: Buzz Kulik
Co-stars: Jeroen Krabbe Cliff De Young Gregory Sierra

1988   INTERNAL AFFAIRS
Director: Michael Tuchner
Co-stars: Richard Crenna Cliff Gorman Lee Richardson

1989   BLACK RAIN
Director: Ridley Scott
Co-stars: Michael Douglas Andy Garcia Ken Takakura

1990   LOVE AT LARGE
Director: Alan Rudolph
Co-stars: Tom Berenger Elizabeth Perkins Anne Archer

1991   MY HEROES HAVE ALWAYS BEEN COWBOYS
Director: Stuart Rosenberg
Co-stars: Scott Glenn Ben Johnson

1995   NEXT DOOR
Director: Tony Bill
Co-stars: James Woods Randy Quaid

1995   JUST CAUSE
Director: Arne Glimscher
Co-stars: Sean Connery Laurence Fishburne

1996   HOW TO MAKE AN AMERICAN QUILT
Director: Jocelyn Moorhouse
Co-stars: Winona Ryder Rip Torn Anne Bancroft

AHNA CAPRI

1968   **TARGET HARRY**
Director: Roger Corman
Co-stars: Vic Morrow Suzanne Pleshette Victor Buono

1973   **PAYDAY**
Director: Daryl Duke
Co-stars: Rip Torn Elayne Heilveil Michael C. Gwynn

CAPUCINE

1960   **NORTH TO ALASKA**
Director: Henry Hathaway
Co-stars: John Wayne Stewart Granger Fabian

1960   **SONG WITHOUT END**
Director: George Cukor
Co-stars: Dirk Bogarde Genevieve Page Patricia Morison

1962   **A WALK ON THE WILD SIDE**
Director: Edward Dmytryk
Co-stars: Jane Fonda Barbara Stanwyck

1962   **THE LION**
Director: Jack Cardiff
Co-stars: William Holden Pamela Franklin Trevor Howard

1963   **THE PINK PANTHER**
Director: Blake Edwards
Co-stars: David Niven Peter Sellers Claudia Cardinale

1964   **THE SEVENTH DAWN**
Director: Lewis Gilbert
Co-stars: William Holden Susannah York Michael Goodliffe

1965   **WHAT'S NEW PUSSYCAT?**
Director: Clive Donner
Co-stars: Peter O'Toole Peter Sellers Ursula Andress

1967   **THE HONEY POT**
Director: Joseph Mankiewicz
Co-stars: Rex Harrison Susan Hayward Edie Adams

1968   **FRAULEIN DOKTOR**
Director: Alberto Lattuada
Co-stars: Suzy Kendall Kenneth More

1969   **SATYRICON**
Director: Fererico Fellini
Co-stars: Martin Potter Hiram Keller Max Born

1971   **RED SUN**
Director: Terence Young
Co-stars: Charles Bronson Alain Delon Ursula Andress

1977   **THE CON ARTISTS**
Director: Sergio Corbucci
Co-stars: Anthony Quinn Corinne Clery

1979   **ARABIAN ADVENTURE**
Director: Kevin Conner
Co-stars: Christopher Lee Oliver Tobias Micky Rooney

1979   **FROM HELL TO VICTORY**
Director: Hank Milestone
Co-stars: George Peppard Sam Wanamaker Horst Buchholst

1979   **JAGUAR LIVES!**
Director: Ernest Pintoff
Co-stars: Joe Lewis Christopher Lee Barbara Bach

1982   **TRAIL OF THE PINK PANTHER**
Director: Blake Edwards
Co-stars: Peter Sellers Joanna Lumley Herbert Lom

1983   **CURSE OF THE PINK PANTHER**
Director: Blake Edwards
Co-stars: Ted Wass Joanna Lumley David Niven

1989   **MY FIRST 40 YEARS**
Director: Carlo Vanzina
Co-stars: Carol Alt Elliott Gould Pierre Cosso

IRENE CARA

1980   **FAME**
Director: Alan Parker
Co-stars: Lee Curreri Laura Dean Paul McCrane

1984   **CITY HEAT**
Director: Richard Benjamin
Co-stars: Clint Eastwood Burt Reynolds Jane Alexander

1990   **HAPPILY EVER AFTER** *(Voice)*
Director: John Howley
Co-stars: Malcolm McDowell Tracey Ullman Ed Asner

ADA CARASCO

1992   **LIKE WATER FOR CHOCOLATE**
Director: Alfonso Arau
Co-stars: Lumi Cavazos Marco Leonardi

ENRIQUETA CARBALLEIRA

1981   **THE HOUSE OF BERNARDA ALBA**
Director: Mario Camus
Co-stars: Irene Guitierrez Caba Ana Belin

FANNY CARBY

1970   **ONE BRIEF SUMMER**
Director: John MacKenzie
Co-stars: Clifford Evans Felicity Gibson Jennifer Hilary

1977   **LET'S GET LAID**
Director: James Clarke
Co-stars: Fiona Richmond Robin Askwith Anthony Steel

KATHERINE CARD

1947   **THE HUCKSTERS**
Director: Jack Conway
Co-stars: Clark Gable Deborah Kerr Ava Gardner

ANGELA CARDILE

1961   **DIVORCE ITALIAN STYLE**
Director: Pietro Germi
Co-stars: Marcello Mastroianni Daniela Rocca

LORI CARDILE

1982   **PAROLE**
Director: Michael Tuchner
Co-stars: James Naughton Mark Soper Ted Ross

1985   **DAY OF THE DEAD**
Director: George Romero
Co-stars: Terry Alexander Joseph Pilato

MARIA CARDINAL

1967   **MOUCHETTE**
Director: Robert Bresson
Co-stars: Nadine Nortier Jean-Claude Guilbert

TANTOO CARDINAL

1990   **DANCES WITH WOLVES**
Director: Kevin Costner
Co-stars: Kevin Costner Mary McDonnell Graham Greene

1991   **BLACK ROBE**
Director: Bruce Beresford
Co-stars: Lothaire Bluteau Aden Young Sandrine Holt

1994   **LEGENDS OF THE FALL**
Director: Edward Zwick
Co-stars: Brad Pitt Anthony Hopkins Julia Ormond

CLAUDIA CARDINALE

1958   **I SOLITI IGNOTI**
Director: Mario Monicelli
Co-stars: Vittorio Gassman Marcello Mastroianni

1959 UPSTAIRS AND DOWNSTAIRS
Director: Ralph Thomas
Co-stars: Michael Craig Anne Heywood Daniel Massey

1960 ROCCO AND HIS BROTHERS
Director: Luchino Visconti
Co-stars: Alain Delon Renato Salvatori

1960 LA DOLCE VITA
Director: Frederico Fellini
Co-stars: Marcello Mastroianni Anita Ekberg Anouk Aimee

1961 CARTOUCHE
Director: Phillipe De Broca
Co-stars: Jean-Paul Belmondo Odile Versois

1963 EIGHT AND A HALF
Director: Federico Fellini
Co-stars: Marcello Mastroianni Anouk Aimee

1963 THE LEOPARD
Director: Luchino Visconti
Co-stars: Burt Lancaster Alain Delon Paolo Stoppa

1963 THE PINK PANTHER
Director: Blake Edwards
Co-stars: David Niven Peter Sellers Capucine

1964 THE MAGNIFICENT SHOWMAN
Director: Henry Hathaway
Co-stars: John Wayne Rita Hayworth John Smith

1965 BLINDFOLD
Director: Phillip Dunne
Co-stars: Rock Huds0n Jack Warden Guy Stockwell

**1965 VAGHE STELLE DELL'ORSA
(SANDRA OF A THOUSAND DELIGHTS)**
Director: Luchino Visconti
Co-stars: Michael Craig Jean Sorel Marie Bell

1966 THE LOST COMMAND
Director: Mark Robson
Co-stars: Anthony Quinn Alain Delon George Segal

1966 THE PROFESSIONALS
Director: Richard Brooks
Co-stars: Burt Lancaster Lee Marvin Jack Palance

1967 DON'T MAKE WAVES
Director: Alexander McKendrick
Co-stars: Tony Curtis Sharon Tate Jim Backus

1968 A FINE PAIR
Director: Francesco Maselli
Co-stars: Rock Hudson Tomas Milian Ellen Corby

1968 THE HELL WITH HEROES
Director: Joseph Sargent
Co-stars: Rod Taylor Harry Guardino Pete Deuel

1969 ONCE UPON A TIME IN THE WEST
Director: Sergio Leone
Co-stars: Henry Fonda Charles Bronson

1970 THE ADVENTURES OF GERARD
Director: Jerzy Skolimowski
Co-stars: Peter McEnery Eli Wallach Jack Hawkins

1970 RED TENT
Director: Mikhail Kalatoznov
Co-stars: Peter Finch Sean Connery

1975 CONVERSATION PIECE
Director: Luchino Visconti
Co-stars: Burt Lancaster Silvana Mangano Helmut Berger

1979 ESCAPE TO ATHENA
Director: George Cosmatos
Co-stars: Roger Moore David Niven Sonny Bono

1982 FITZCARRALDO
Director: Werner Herzog
Co-stars: Klaus Kinski Jose Lewgoy Paul Hittscher

1987 A MAN IN LOVE
Director: Diane Kurys
Co-stars: Peter Coyote Greta Scacchi Jamie Lee Curtis

1993 SON OF THE PINK PANTHER
Director: Blake Edwards
Co-stars: Roberto Begnini Herbert Lom Jennifer Edwards

ELSA CARDENAS
1956 THE BRAVE ONE
Director: Irving Rapper
Co-stars: Michel Ray Rodolfo Hoyos Carlos Navarro

1963 FUN IN ACAPULCO
Director: Richard Thorpe
Co-stars: Elvis Presley Ursula Andress Paul Lukas

1965 TAGGART
Director: R. G. Springsteen
Co-stars: Tony Young Dan Duryea Dick Foran David Carradine

LOLA CARDONA
1983 THE SOUTH
Director: Victor Erice
Co-stars: Iciar Bollan Omero Antonutti Aurore Clement

NATHALIE CARDONE
1993 L'ENFER
Director: Claude Chabrol
Co-stars: Emmanuelle Beart Francois Cluzet Dora Doll

LAURIE CARDWELL *(Child)*
1961 THE SAND CASTLE
Director: Jerome Hill
Co-stars: Barrie Cardwell Maybelle Nash George Dunham

DANY CAREL
1957 PORTE DES LILAS
Director: Rene Clair
Co-stars: Pierre Brasseur Henri Vidal Amedee

1960 THE HANDS OF ORLAC
Director: Edmond Greville
Co-stars: Mel Ferrer Christopher Lee Donald Wolfit

1960 THE ENEMY GENERAL
Director: George Sherman
Co-stars: Van Johnson Jean-Pierre Aumont

ANNETTE CARELLE
1967 OUR MOTHER'S HOUSE
Director: Jack Clayton
Co-stars: Dirk Bogarde Pamela Franklin Mark Lester

ANNA CARENA
1951 MIRACLE IN MILAN
Director: Vittorio De Sica
Co-stars: Francesco Golisano Brunella Bovo Paolo Stoppa

1970 SUNFLOWER
Director: Vittorio De Sica
Co-stars: Sophia Loren Marcello Mastroianni

CHRISTINE CARERE
1958 MARDI GRAS
Director: Edmund Goulding
Co-stars: Pat Boone Sheree North Tommy Sands

1958 A CERTAIN SMILE
Director: Jean Negulesco
Co-stars: Rossano Brazzi Joan Fontaine Bradford Dillman

1959 A PRIVATE'S AFFAIR
Director: Raoul Walsh
Co-stars: Sal Mineo Barry Coe Gary Crosby

CLARE CAREY
1992 OBSESSED
Director: Jonathan Sanger
Co-stars: William Devane Shannen Doherty Lois Chiles

1995 BETRAYED: A STORY OF THREE WOMEN
Director: William A. Graham
Co-stars: Meredith Baxter Swoozie Kurtz John Terry

JOYCE CAREY
1942 IN WHICH WE SERVE
Director: David Lean
Co-stars: Noel Coward Bernard Miles John Mills

1945 BRIEF ENCOUNTER
Director: David Lean
Co-stars: Celia Johnson Trevor Howard Cyril Raymond

1945 BLITHE SPIRIT
Director: David Lean
Co-stars: Rex Harrison Constance Cummings Kay Hammond

1945 THE WAY TO THE STARS
Director: Anthony Asquith
Co-stars: Michael Redgrave John Mills Rosamund John

1947 THE OCTOBER MAN
Director: Roy Baker
Co-stars: John Mills Joan Greenwood Kay Walsh

1948 LONDON BELONGS TO ME
Director: Sidney Gilliat
Co-stars: Alastair Sim Stephen Murray Susan Shaw

1949 THE CHILTERN HUNDREDS
Director: John Paddy Carstairs
Co-stars: A. E. Matthews Cecil Parker

1949 THE ASTONISHED HEART
Director: Terence Fisher
Co-stars: Noel Coward Margaret Leighton Celia Johnson

1950 HAPPY GO LOVELY
Director: Bruce Humberstone
Co-stars: David Niven Vera-Ellen Cesar Romero

1952 CRY THE BELOVED COUNTRY
Director: Zoltan Korda
Co-stars: Canada Lee Sidney Poitier Geoffrey Keen

1956 LOSER TAKES ALL
Director: Ken Annakin
Co-stars: Glynis Johns Rossano Brazzi Tony Britton

1958 ALIVE AND KICKING
Director: Cyril Frankel
Co-stars: Sybil Thorndyke Kathleen Harrison

1959 THE ROUGH AND THE SMOOTH
Director: Robert Siodmak
Co-stars: Tony Britton Nadja Tiller William Bendix

1961 NEARLY A NASTY ACCIDENT
Director: Don Chaffey
Co-stars: Kenneth Connor Shirley Eaton Jimmy Edwards

1969 A NICE GIRL LIKE ME
Director: Desmond Davis
Co-stars: Barbara Ferris Harry Andrews James Villiers

1988 NUMBER 27
Director: Tristram Powell
Co-stars: Nigel Planer Alun Armstrong Robin Bailey

MICHELE CAREY
1966 EL DORADO
Director: Howard Hawks
Co-stars: John Wayne Robert Mitchum James Caan

1970 DIRTY DINGUS MAGEE
Director: Burt Kennedy
Co-stars: Frank Sinatra George Kennedy Anne Jackson

1971 SCANDALOUS JOHN
Director: Robert Butler
Co-stars: Brian Keith Alfonso Arau Henry Morgan

OLIVE CAREY
1957 RUN OF THE ARROW
Director: Samuel Fuller
Co-stars: Rod Steiger Sarita Montiel Charles Bronson

RICHENDA CAREY
1988 LUCKY SUNIL
Director: Michael Caton-Jones
Co-stars: Kulvinder Ghir Niamh Cusack Benjamin Whitrow

GIA CARIDES
1985 BLISS
Director: Ray Lawrence
Co-stars: Barry Otto Lynette Curran Helen Jones

1991 DAYDREAM BELIEVER
Director: Kathy Mueller
Co-stars: Miranda Otto Martin Kemp Anne Looby

1992 STRICTLY BALLROOM
Director: Baz Luhrmann
Co-stars: Paul Mercurio Tara Morice Bill Hunter

ZOE CARIDES
1988 KADAICHA-THE DEATH STONE
Director: James Bogie
Co-stars: Eric Oldfield Tom Jennings

1990 DEATH IN BRUNSWICK
Director: John Ruane
Co-stars: Sam Neill John Clarke Yvonne Lawley

CARMINE CARIDI
1981 PRINCE OF THE CITY
Director: Sidney Lumet
Co-stars: Treat Williams Jerry Orbach Lindsay Crouse

1985 SUMMER RENTAL
Director: Carl Reiner
Co-stars: John Candy Karen Austin Richard Crenna

1991 FEMME FATALE
Director: Andre Guttfreund
Co-stars: Colin Firth Lisa Zane Billy Zane

CARITA
1967 THE VIKING QUEEN
Director: Don Chaffey
Co-stars: Don Murray Donald Houston Nicola Pagett

CYNTHIA CARLE
1985 ALAMO BAY
Director: Louis Malle
Co-stars: Amy Madigan Ed Harris Donald Moffat

CLAIRE CARLETON
1946 CRIME DOCTOR'S MAN HUNT
Director: William Castle
Co-stars: Warner Baxter Ellen Drew

1951 HONEYCHILE
Director: R. G. Springsteen
Co-stars: Judy Canova Eddie Foy Jnr. Alan Hale Jnr.

1954 WITNESS TO MURDER
Director: Roy Rowland
Co-stars: Barbara Stanwyck George Sanders Gary Merrill

CATHERINE CARLIN

1990 CHOPPER CHICKS IN ZOMBIETOWN
Director: Dan Hoskins
Co-stars: Jamie Rose Kristina Loggia

JEAN CARLIN

1946 WILD WEST
Co-stars: Eddie Dean Louise Currie Roscoe Ates

LYNN CARLIN

Nominated For Best Supporting Actress In 1969 For "Faces"

1969 SILENT NIGHT, LONELY NIGHT
Director: Daniel Petrie
Co-stars: Lloyd Bridges Shirley Jones Carrie Snodgress

1969 FACES
Director: John Cassavetes
Co-stars: Gena Rowlands John Marley Seymour Cassel

1970 ...TICK...TICK...TICK
Director: Ralph Nelson
Co-stars: Fredric March George Kennedy Jim Brown

1971 WILD ROVERS
Director: Blake Edwards
Co-stars: William Holden Ryan O'Neal Karl Malden

1972 BAXTER
Director: Lionel Jeffries
Co-stars: Patricia Neal Scott Jacoby Britt Ekland

1975 THE LIVES OF JENNY DOLAN
Director: Jerry Jameson
Co-stars: Shirley Jones Stephen Boyd Farley Granger

1976 DAWN: PORTRAIT OF A RUNAWAY TEENAGER
Director: Randal Kleiser
Co-stars: Eve Plumb Bo Hopkins

CHRISTINA CARLISI

1993 HEAR NO EVIL
Director: Robert Greenwald
Co-stars: Marlee Matlin Martin Sheen Greg Elam

OLYMPIA CARLISI

1976 CASANOVA
Director: Fererico Fellini
Co-stars: Donald Sutherland Tina Aumont Cicely Browne

1981 THE TRAGEDY OF A RIDICULOUS MAN
Director: Bernardo Bertolucci
Co-stars: Ugo Tognazzi Anouk Aimee

ANNE CARLISLE

1982 LIQUID SKY
Director: Slava Tsukerman
Co-stars: Paula Sheppard Susan Doukas Bob Brady

1984 BLIND ALLEY
Director: Larry Cohen
Co-stars: Brad Rijn Matthew Stockley Ann Magnusan

1985 DESPERATELY SEEKING SUSAN
Director: Susan Seidelman
Co-stars: Madonna Rosanna Arquette Aidan Quinn

DOROTHY CARLISLE

1931 GOLD DUST GERTIE
Director: Lloyd Bacon
Co-stars: Winnie Lightner Chic Johnson Ole Olsen

KITTY CARLISLE

1934 HERE IS MY HEART
Director: Frank Tuttle
Co-stars: Bing Crosby Roland Young Alison Skipworth

1934 MURDER AT THE VANITIES
Director: Mitchell Leisen
Co-stars: Jack Oakie Victor McLaglen Carl Brisson

1934 SHE LOVES ME NOT
Director: Elliott Nugent
Co-stars: Bing Crosby Miriam Hopkins Lynne Overman

1935 A NIGHT AT THE OPERA
Director: Sam Wood
Co-stars: Marx Brothers Allan Jones Margaret Dupont

MARY CARLISLE

1932 HER MAD NIGHT
Co-Star William Davidson

1932 DOWN TO EARTH
Director: David Butler
Co-stars: Will Rogers Dorothy Jordan Irene Rich

1933 COLLEGE HUMOR
Director: Wesley Ruggles
Co-stars: Bing Crosby Burns & Allen Jack Oakie

1933 THE SWEETHEART OF SIGMA CHI
Co-Star Buster Crabbe

1933 SHOULD LADIES BEHAVE?
Director: Harry Beaumont
Co-stars: Alice Brady Lionel Barrymore Conway Tearle

1933 THIS SIDE OF HEAVEN
Director: William Howard
Co-stars: Lionel Barrymore Fay Bainter Mae Clarke

1934 ONCE TO EVERY WOMAN
Director: Lambert Hillyer
Co-stars: Walter Connolly Ralph Bellamy Fay Wray

1934 MURDER IN THE PRIVATE CAR
Director: Harry Beaumont
Co-stars: Russell Hardie Charles Ruggles Una Merker

1934 MILLION DOLLAR RANSOM
Director: Murray Roth
Co-stars: Edward Arnold Phillips Holmes Wini Shaw

1934 GIRL O' MY DREAMS
Co-stars: Edward Nugent Lillian Bond

1934 KENTUCKY KERNELS
Director: George Stevens
Co-stars: Wheeler & Woolsey Spanky McFarland Noah Beery

1934 HANDY ANDY
Director: David Butler
Co-stars: Will Rogers Peggy Wood Robert Taylor

1934 THE GREAT HOTEL MURDER
Director: Eugene Forde
Co-stars: Victor McLaglen Rosemary Ames Edmund Lowe

1935 KIND LADY
Director: George Seitz
Co-stars: Basil Rathbone Aline MacMahon Frank Albertson

1935 SUPERSPEED
Co-stars: Norman Foster Florine McKinney

1935 ONE FRIGHTENED NIGHT
Director: Christy Cabanne
Co-stars: Charles Grapewin Evalyn Knapp

1936 LOVE IN EXILE
Director: Alfred Werker
Co-stars: Clive Brook Helen Vinson Will Fyffe

1937 DOUBLE OR NOTHING
Director: Theodore Reed
Co-stars: Bing Crosby Martha Raye Andy Devine

1937 HOLD 'EM NAVY
Co-Star Lew Ayres

1937 HOTEL HAYWIRE
Director: George Archainbaud
Co-stars: Leo Carrillo Lynne Overman Spring Byington

1938 DOCTOR RHYTHM
Director: Frank Tuttle
Co-stars: Bing Crosby Beatrice Lillie Andy Devine

1938 HUNTED MEN
Director: Louis King
Co-stars: Lloyd Nolan Lynne Overman Anthony Quinn

1938 SAY IT IN FRENCH
Director: Andrew Stone
Co-stars: Ray Milland Olympe Bradna Irene Hervey

1938 TIP-OFF GIRLS
Director: Louis King
Co-stars: Lloyd Nolan Anthony Quinn Roscoe Karns

1938 ILLEGAL TRAFFIC
Director: Louis King
Co-stars: Robert Preston J. Carrol Naish

1939 CALL A MESSENGER
Director: Arthur Lubin
Co-stars: Dead End Kids Robert Armstrong Buster Crabbe

1939 BEWARE, SPOOKS!
Director: Edward Sedgwick
Co-stars: Joe E. Brown Clarence Kolb Marc Lawrence

1940 DANCE, GIRL, DANCE
Director: Dorothy Arzner
Co-stars: Maureen O'Hara Louis Hayward Lucille Ball

1942 BABY FACE MORGAN
Director: Arthur Dreifuss
Co-stars: Richard Cromwell Robert Armstrong Chick Chandler

1943 DEAD MEN WALK
Director: Sam Newfield
Co-stars: George Zucco Dwight Frye

JUNE CARLSON

1936 EVERY SATURDAY NIGHT
Director: Frank Strayer
Co-stars: Spring Byington Jed Prouty George Ernest

1936 EDUCATING FATHER
Director: Frank Strayer
Co-stars: Spring Byington Jed Prouty George Ernest

1936 BACK TO NATURE
Director: Frank Strayer
Co-stars: Spring Byington Jed Prouty George Ernest

1937 OFF TO THE RACES
Director: Frank Strayer
Co-stars: Spring Byington Jed Prouty George Ernest

1937 BORROWING TROUBLE
Director: Frank Strayer
Co-stars: Spring Byington Jed Prouty George Ernest

1937 BIG BUSINESS
Director: Frank Strayer
Co-stars: Spring Byington Jed Prouty George Ernest

1937 HOT WATER
Director: Frank Strayer
Co-stars: Spring Byington Jed Prouty George Ernest

1938 LOVE ON A BUDGET
Director: Frank Strayer
Co-stars: Spring Byington Jed Prouty George Ernest

1938 TRIP TO PARIS
Director: Frank Strayer
Co-stars: Spring Byington Jed Prouty George Ernest

1938 DOWN ON THE FARM
Director: Frank Strayer
Co-stars: Spring Byington Jed Prouty George Ernest

1938 SAFETY IN NUMBERS
Director: Frank Strayer
Co-stars: Spring Byington Jed Prouty George Ernest

1938 THE JONES FAMILY IN HOLLYWOOD
Director: Frank Strayer
Co-stars: Spring Byington Jed Prouty George Ernest

1939 QUICK MILLIONS
Director: Frank Strayer
Co-stars: Spring Byington Jed Prouty George Ernest

1939 EVERYBODY'S BABY
Director: Frank Strayer
Co-stars: Spring Byington Jed Prouty George Ernest

1940 ON THEIR OWN
Director: Frank Strayer
Co-stars: Spring Byington Jed Prouty George Ernest

1945 COME OUT FIGHTING
Director: William Beaudine
Co-stars: Leo Gorcy Huntz Hall Gabriel Dell

KAREN CARLSON

1972 THE CANDIDATE
Director: Michael Ritchie
Co-stars: Robert Redford Peter Boyle Don Porter

1978 MATILDA
Director: Daniel Mann
Co-stars: Elliott Gould Robert Mitchum Harry Guardino

1980 THE OCTAGON
Director: Eric Karson
Co-stars: Chuck Norris Lee Van Cleef Art Hindle

1982 IN LOVE WITH AN OLDER WOMAM
Director: Jack Bender
Co-stars: John Rititer Jamie Ross Jeff Altman

1985 BROTHERLY LOVE
Director: Jeff Bleckner
Co-stars: Judd Hirsch George Dzundza Barry Primus

1985 WILD HORSES
Director: Dick Lowry
Co-stars: Kenny Rogers Pam Dawber Ben Johnson

VERONICA CARLSON

1968 DRACULA HAS RISEN FROM HIS GRAVE
Director: Freddie Francis
Co-stars: Christopher Lee Rupert Davies

1969 FRANKENSTEIN MUST BE DESTROYED
Director: Terence Fisher
Co-stars: Peter Cushing Freddie Jones

1969 CROSSPLOT
Director: Alvin Rakoff
Co-stars: Roger Moore Martha Hyer Alexis Kanner

1970 THE HORROR OF FRANKENSTEIN
Director: Jimmy Sangster
Co-stars: Ralph Bates Kate O'Mara Joan Rice

1974 VAMPIRA
Director: Clive Donner
Co-stars: David Niven Teresa Graves Jennie Linden

1975 THE GHOUL
Director: Freddie Francis
Co-stars: Peter Cushing Alexandra Bastedo John Hurt

ING-MARIE CARLSSON

1985 MY LIFE AS A DOG
Director: Lasse Hallstrom
Co-stars: Anton Glanzelius Anki Liden

KARIN CARLSSON-KAVIL

1937 A WOMAN'S FACE
Director: Gustaf Molander
Co-stars: Ingrid Bergman Anders Henrikson

MARGIT CARLQUIST

1955 SMILES OF A SUMMER NIGHT
Director: Ingmar Bergman
Co-stars: Gunnar Bjornstrand Eva Dahlbeck

HOPE MARIE CARLTON

1987 HARD TICKET TO HAWAII
Director: Andy Sidaris
Co-stars: Dona Spier Harold Diamond

CHRISTINA CARLWIND

1985 MY LIFE AS A DOG
Director: Lasse Hallstrom
Co-stars: Anton Glanzelius Melinda Kinnaman

CARMEN

1972 HICKEY AND BOGGS
Director: Robert Culp
Co-stars: Robert Culp Bill Cosby Rosalind Cash

JEWEL CARMEN

1926 THE RAT
Director: Roland West
Co-stars: Tullio Carminati Louise Fazenda Emily Fitzroy

JULIE CARMEN

1979 CAN YOU HEAR THE LAUGHTER?
Director: Burt Brinkeroff
Co-stars: Ira Angustain Kevin Hooks

1980 GLORIA
Director: John Cassavetes
Co-stars: Gena Rowlands John Adames Buck Henry

1980 NIGHT OF THE JUGGLER
Director: Robert Butler
Co-stars: James Brolin Cliff Gorman Dan Hedaya

1981 SHE'S IN THE ARMY NOW
Director: Hy Averbach
Co-stars: Kathleen Quinlan Melanie Griffith

1988 THE MILAGRO BEANFIELD WAR
Director: Robert Redford
Co-stars: Ruben Blades Sonia Braga John Heard

1989 GORE VIDAL'S BILLY THE KID
Director: William Graham
Co-stars: Val Kilmer Wilford Brimley

1989 THE NEON EMPIRE
Director: Larry Pearce
Co-stars: Ray Sharkey Linda Fiorentino Gary Busey

1989 FRIGHT NIGHT, PART II
Director: Tommy Lee Wallace
Co-stars: Roddy McDowall Traci Lin

1994 IN THE MOUTH OF MADNESS
Director: John Carpenter
Co-stars: Sam Neill Jorgen Prochnow Charlton Heston

LOENE CARMEN

1987 THE YEAR MY VOICE BROKE
Director: John Duigan
Co-stars: Noah Taylor Ben Mendelsohn Lynette Curran

JUDY CARNE
(Married Burt Reynolds, Robert Bergmann)

1969 ALL THE RIGHT NOISES
Director: Gerry O'Hara
Co-stars: Tom Bell Olivia Hussey John Standing

1971 DEAD MEN TELL NO TALES
Director: Walter Grauman
Co-stars: Christopher George Patricia Barry

ANN CAROL

1935 THE GHOST RIDER
Co-stars: Rex Lease Bobby Nelson

CINDY CAROL

1965 DEAR BRIGITTE
Director: Henry Koster
Co-stars: James Stewart Glynis Johns Fabian

LINDA CAROL

1986 REFORM SCHOOL GIRLS
Director: Tom De Simone
Co-stars: Sybil Danning Pat Ast Sherri Stoner

MARTINE CAROL

1952 LES BELLES DE NUIT
Director: Rene Clair
Co-stars: Gerard Philipe Gina Lollobrigida

1952 ADORABLE CREATURES
Director: Christian Jacque
Co-stars: Daniel Gelin Danielle Darrieux

1952 LUCRETIA BORGIA
Director: Christian Jacque
Co-stars: Pedro Armendariz Massimo Serato

1953 LOVE, SOLDIERS AND WOMEN
Director: Christian Jacque
Co-stars: Raf Vallone Paolo Stoppa

1955 LOLA MONTES
Director: Max Ophuls
Co-stars: Anton Walbrook Peter Ustinov Oskar Werner

1955 THE DIARY OF MAJOR THOMPSON
Director: Preston Sturges
Co-stars: Jack Buchanan Noel-Noel

1956 AROUND THE WORLD IN EIGHTY DAYS
Director: Mike Todd
Co-stars: David Niven Robert Newton Cantinflas

1957 ACTION OF THE TIGER
Director: Terence Young
Co-stars: Van Johnson Herbert Lom Sean Connery

1957 AUSTERLITZ
Director: Abel Gance
Co-stars: Pierre Mondy Jack Palance Orson Welles

1959 TEN SECONDS TO HELL
Director: Robert Aldrich
Co-stars: Jack Palance Jeff Chandler

SUE CAROL

1930 CHECK AND DOUBLE CHECK
Director: Melville Brown
Co-stars: Amos And Andy Duke Ellington Irene Rlch

1930 FOX MOVIETONE FOLLIES OF 1929
Director: David Butler
Co-stars: Dixie Lee Lola Lane El Brendel

1930 DANCING SWEETIES
Co-stars: Grant Withers Kate Price

1930 THE GOLDEN CALF
Co-stars: El Brendel Jack Mulhall Marjorie White

1930 THE LONE STAR RANGER
Co-Star George O'Brien

LESLIE CARON (Married Peter Hall)
Nominated For Best Actress In 1953 For "Lili"
And In 1962 For "The L-Shaped Room"

1951 AN AMERICAN IN PARIS
Director: Vincente Minnelli
Co-stars: Gene Kelly Oscar Levant George Guetary

1951 THE MAN WITH A CLOAK
Director: Fletcher Markle
Co-stars: Joseph Cotten Barbara Stanwyck Louis Calhern

1952 GLORY ALLEY
Director: Raoul Walsh
Co-stars: Ralph Meeker Kurt Kasznar Gilbert Roland

1953 LILI
Director: Charles Walters
Co-stars: Jean-Pierre Aumont Mel Ferrer Kurt Kasznar

1953 THE STORY OF THREE LOVES
Director: Vincente Minnelli
Co-stars: Farley Granger Kirk Douglas James Mason

1954 THE GLASS SLIPPER
Director: Charles Walters
Co-stars: Michael Wilding Elsa Lanchester Barry Jones

1955 DADDY LONG LEGS
Director: Jean Negulesco
Co-stars: Fred Astaire Thelma Ritter Terry Moore

1956 GABY
Director: Curtis Bernhardt
Co-stars: John Kerr Taina Elg Cedric Hardwicke

1958 GIGI
Director: Vincente Minnelli
Co-stars: Maurice Chevalier Louis Jourdan Hermoine Gingold

1959 THE MAN WHO UNDERSTOOD WOMEN
Director: Nunnally Johnson
Co-stars: Henry Fonda Cesare Danova

1959 THE DOCTOR'S DILEMMA
Director: Anthony Asquith
Co-stars: Dirk Bogarde Alastair Sim Robert Morley

1960 THE SUBTERRANEANS
Director: Ranald MacDougall
Co-stars: George Peppard Roddy McDowall Janice Rule

1960 FANNY
Director: Joshua Logan
Co-stars: Charles Boyer Maurice Chevalier Horst Buchholz

1962 GUNS OF DARKNESS
Director: Anthony Asquith
Co-stars: David Niven James Robertson Justice

1962 THE L-SHAPED ROOM
Director: Bryan Forbes
Co-stars: Tom Bell Brock Peters Cicely Courtneidge

1964 FATHER GOOSE
Director: Ralph Nelson
Co-stars: Cary Grant Trevor Howard Jack Good

1965 IS PARIS BURNING?
Director: Rene Clement
Co-stars: Charles Boyer Orson Welles Glenn Ford

1965 A VERY SPECIAL FAVOR
Director: Michael Gordon
Co-stars: Charles Boyer Rock Hudson Walter Slezak

1966 PROMISE HER ANYTHING
Director: Arthur Hiller
Co-stars: Warren Beatty Keenan Wynn

1971 CHANDLER
Director: Paul Magwood
Co-stars: Warren Oates Charles McGraw Mitchell Ryan

1975 JAMES DEAN: THE FIRST AMERICAN TEENAGER
Director: Ray Connolly
Co-stars: Natalie Wood Carroll Baker

1977 THE MAN WHO LOVED WOMEN
Director: Francois Truffaut
Co-stars: Charles Denner Brigitte Fossey

1977 VALENTINO
Director: Ken Russell
Co-stars: Rudolf Nureyev Michelle Phillips Felicity Kendall

1983 THE UNAPPROACHABLE
Director: Krzysztof Zanussi
Co-stars: Daniel Webb Leslie Malon

1983 DANGEROUS MOVES
Director: Richard Dembo
Co-stars: Michel Piccoli Alexandre Arbatt

1988 THE MAN WHO LIVED AT THE RITZ
Director: Desmond Davis
Co-stars: Perry King Cheri Lunghi

1989 COURAGE MOUNTAIN
Director: Christopher Leitch
Co-stars: Juliette Caton Charlie Sheen

1992 DAMAGE
Director: Louis Malle
Co-stars: Jeremy Irons Julliette Binoche Miranda Richardson

1996 FUNNY BONES
Director: Peter Chelsom
Co-stars: Lee Evans Jerry Lewis Oliver Platt

BETHANY CARPENTER
1983 TIGER TOWN
Director: Alan Shapiro
Co-stars: Roy Scheider Justin Henry Ron McClarty

BETTY CARR
1954 SEVEN BRIDES FOR SEVEN BROTHERS
Director: Stanley Donen
Co-stars: Jane Powell Howard Keel Russ Tamblyn

1972 CANCEL MY RESERVATION
Director: Paul Bogart
Co-stars: Bob Hope Eva Marie Saint Ralph Bellamy

CAROLE CARR
1952 DOWN AMONG THE Z MEN
Director: Maclean Rogers
Co-stars: Harry Secombe Peter Sellers Spike Milligan

CAROLINE CARR
1992 FRANKIE'S HOUSE
Director: Peter Fisk
Co-stars: Iain Glenn Kevin Dillon Steven Vidler

CHARMIAN CARR
1965 THE SOUND OF MUSIC
Director: Robert Wise
Co-stars: Julie Andrews Christopher Plummer Richard Haydn

DARLEEN CARR
1971 THE BEGUILED
Director: Don Siegel
Co-stars: Clint Eastwood Geraldine Page Elizabeth Hartman

1973 RUNAWAY!
Director: David Lowell Rich
Co-stars: Ben Johnson Ben Murphy Vera Miles

1981 BRET MAVERICK
Director: Stuart Margolin
Co-stars: Stuart Margolin James Garner Ed Bruce

1986 HERO IN THE FAMILY
Director: Mel Damski
Co-stars: Christopher Collet Cliff De Young Annabeth Gish

HAYLEY CARR

1989 BACK HOME
Director: Piers Haggard
Co-stars: Hayley Mills Brenda Bruce Jean Anderson

JANE CARR

1933 DICK TURPIN
Director: John Stafford
Co-stars: Victor McLaglen Frank Vosper Gillian Lind

1933 ORDERS IS ORDERS
Director: Walter Forde
Co-stars: Charlotte Greenwood James Gleason Ray Milland

1934 LORD EDGWARE DIES
Director: Henry Edwards
Co-stars: Austin Trevor Richard Cooper

1934 THOSE WERE THE DAYS
Director: Thomas Bentley
Co-stars: Will Hay John Mills Angela Baddeley

1935 GET OFF MY FOOT
Director: William Beaudine
Co-stars: Max Miller Chili Bouchier

1935 THE LAD
Director: Henry Edwards
Co-stars: Gordon Harker Betty Stockfield

1935 THE TRIUMPH OF SHERLOCK HOLMES
Director: Leslie Hiscott
Co-stars: Arthur Wontner Ian Fleming

1936 MILLIONS
Director: Leslie Hiscott
Co-stars: Gordon Harker Frank Pettingell Richard Hearne

1937 THE LILAC DOMINO
Director: Fred Zelnik
Co-stars: June Knight Michael Bartlett Athene Seyler

1942 LADY FROM LISBON
Director: Leslie Hiscott
Co-stars: Francis L. Sullivan Martita Hunt

1942 ALIBI
Director: Brian Desmond Hurst
Co-stars: Margaret Lockwood Hugh Sinclair James Mason

JANE CARR (Child)

1969 THE PRIME OF MISS JEAN BRODIE
Director: Ronald Neame
Co-stars: Maggie Smith Pamela Franklin

MARIAN CARR

1946 SAN QUENTIN
Director: Gordon Douglas
Co-stars: Lawrence Tierney Raymond Burr

1954 RING OF FEAR
Director: James Edward Grant
Co-stars: Clyde Beatty Pat O'Brien

1954 WORLD FOR RANSOM
Director: Robert Aldrich
Co-stars: Dan Duryea Patric Knowles

1955 CELL 2455, DEATH ROW
Director: Fred Sears
Co-stars: William Campbell Kathryn Grant

1956 GHOST TOWN
Director: Allen Miner
Co-stars: Kent Taylor John Smith

1956 INDESTRUCTABLE MAN
Director: Jack Pollexfen
Co-stars: Lon Chaney Jnr. Casey Adams

MARY CARR

1928 LIGHTS OF NEW YORK
Director: Bryan Foy
Co-stars: Helene Costello Cullen Landis

1931 PACK UP YOUR TROUBLES
Director: George Marshall
Co-stars: Stan Laurel Oliver Hardy

1931 ONE GOOD TURN
Director: James Horne
Co-stars: Stan Laurel Oliver Hardy

NATALIE CARR

1993 BAD BOY BUBBY
Director: Rolf De Heer
Co-stars: Nicholas Hope Claire Benito

NEVA CARR-GLYN

1969 AGE OF CONSENT
Director: Michael Powell
Co-stars: James Mason Helen Mirren

RAFFAELLA CARRA

1965 VON RYAN'S EXPRESS
Director: Mark Robson
Co-stars: Frank Sinatra Trevor Howard John Leyton

LIANELLA CARRELL

1948 BICYCLE THIEVES
Director: Vittorio De Sica
Co-stars: Lamberto Maggiorani Enzo Staiola

BARBARA CARRERA

1975 THE MASTER GUNFIGHTER
Director: Tom Laughlin
Co-stars: Tom Laughlin Ron O'Neal Lincoln Kilpatrick

1976 EMBRYO
Director: Ralph Nelson
Co-stars: Rock Hudson Diane Ladd Roddy McDowall

1977 THE ISLAND OF DR. MOREAU
Director: Don Taylor
Co-stars: Burt Lancaster Michael York Richard Basehart

1981 CONDORMAN
Director: Charles Jarrott
Co-stars: Michael Crawford Oliver Reed James Hampton

1981 THE ANTAGONISTS
Director: Boris Sagal
Co-stars: Peter O'Toole Nigel Davenport Timothy West

1981 MATT HOUSTON
Director: Richard Lang
Co-stars: Lee Horsley Pamela Hensley Jill St. John

1982 I, THE JURY
Director: Richard Heffron
Co-stars: Armand Assante Alan King Luarene London

1983 LONE WOLF McQUADE
Director: Steve Carver
Co-stars: Chuck Norris David Carradine R. G. Armstrong

1983   NEVER SAY NEVER AGAIN
Director: Irving Kerschner
Co-stars: Sean Connery Kim Basinger Pat Roach

1984   SINS OF THE PAST
Director: Peter Hunt
Co-stars: Kim Cattrall Debby Boone Kirstie Alley

1985   WILD GEESE II
Director: Peter Hunt
Co-stars: Scott Glenn Edward Fox Laurence Olivier

1989   THE WICKED STEPMOTHER
Director: Lary Cohen
Co-stars: Bette Davis Richard Moll Tom Bosley

1989   MURDER IN PRADISE
Co-Star   Kevin Kilner

1992   IN TOO DEEP
Director: Bob Misiorowski
Co-stars: Michael Pare Michael Ironside

TIA CARRERE

1988   ALOA SUMMER
Director: Tommy Lee Wallace
Co-stars: Chris Makepeace Yuji Okumoto

1991   SHOWDOWN IN LITTLE TOKYO
Director: Mark Lester
Co-stars: Dolph Lundgren Brandon Lee

**1991   HARLEY DAVIDSON AND
           THE MARLBORO MAN**
Director: Simon Winger
Co-stars: Mickey Rourke Don Johnson Chelsea Field

1992   WAYNE'S WORLD
Director: Penelope Spheeris
Co-stars: Mike Myers Dana Carvey Rob Lowe

1993   WAYNE'S WORLD 2
Director: Stephen Surjik
Co-stars: Mike Myers Dana Carvey Christopher Walken

1993   RISING SUN
Director: Philip Kaufman
Co-stars: Sean Connery Wesley Snipes Harvey Keitel

1993   CROSSFIRE
Director: Rick King
Co-stars: Jeff Fahey Martin Donovan Teri Polo

1997   HIGH SCHOOL HIGH
Director: David Zucker
Co-Star   Jon Lovitz

TONIA CARRERO

**1988   FABLE OF THE BEAUTIFUL
           PIGEON FANCIER**
Director: Ray Guerra
Co-stars: Ney Locarraco Claudia Ohana

FLORENCE CARREZ

1962   LE PROCES DE JEANNE D'ARC
Director: Robert Bresson
Co-stars: Jean-Claude Fourneau Marc Jacquier

MONICA CARRICO

1984   HIGHWAY TO HELL
Director: Mark Griffiths
Co-stars: Eric Stoltz Stuart Margolin

ELPIDIA CARRILLO

1994   MY FAMILY
Director: Gregory Nava
Co-Star   Jimmy Smits

MARI CARRILLO

1984   DARK HABITS
Director: Pedro Almodavar
Co-stars: Carmen Maura Cristina Pascual

ANNE CARROLL

1989   HOME RUN
Director: Nicholas Renton
Co-stars: Michael Kitchen Keith Barron

1989   TAKE ME HOME
Director: Jane Howell
Co-stars: Keith Barron Maggie O'Neill Annette Crosbie

1990   AMONGST BARBARIANS
Director: Jane Howell
Co-stars: David Jason Rowene Cooper

CORINNE CARROLL

1983   POLICEWOMAN CENTREFOLD
Director: Reza Bediyi
Co-stars: Melody Anderson Ed Marinado

DIAHANN CARROLL
Nominated For Best Actress In 1974 For "Claudine"

1954   CARMEN JONES
Director: Otto Preminger
Co-stars: Dorothy Dandridge Harry Belafonte Pearl Bailey

1959   PORGY AND BESS
Director: Otto Preminger
Co-stars: Sidney Poitier Dorothy Dandridge Pearl Bailey

1961   PARIS BLUES
Director: Martin Ritt
Co-stars: Paul Newman Joanne Woodward Sidney Poitier

1967   HURRY SUNDOWN
Director: Otto Preminger
Co-stars: Jane Fonda Michael Caine Rex Ingram

1968   THE SPLIT
Director: Gordon Flemyng
Co-stars: Jim Brown Ernest Borgnine Julie Harris

1974   CLAUDINE
Director: John Berry
Co-stars: James Earl Jones David Kruger Yvette Curtis

1990   MURDER IN BLACK AND WHITE
Director: Robert Iscove
Co-stars: Richard Crenna Cliff Gorman

1991   THE FIVE HEARTBEATS
Director: Robert Townsend
Co-stars: Robert Townsend Michael Wright Tico Wells

GEORGIA CARROLL

1944   CAROLINA BLUES
Co-stars: Kay Kyser Ann Miller Victor Moore

HELENA CARROLL

1987   THE DEAD
Director: John Huston
Co-stars: Anjelica Huston Donal McGann Dan O'Herlihy

1992   THE MAMBO KINGS
Director: Arne Glimcher
Co-stars: Antonio Banderas Armand Assante Cathy Moriarty

JANET CARROLL

1983   RISKY BUSINESS
Director: Paul Brickman
Co-stars: Tom Cruise Rebecca De Mornay

1987 BLUFFING IT
Director: James Sadwith
Co-stars: Dennis Weaver Michelle Little

1987 THE KILLING TIME
Director: Rick King
Co-stars: Beau Bridges Kiefer Sutherland Wayne Rogers

1988 SHARING RICHARD
Director: Peter Bonerz
Co-stars: Ed Marinaro Eileen Davidson

1989 FAMILY BUSINESS
Director: Sidney Lumet
Co-stars: Sean Connery Dustin Hoffman Matthew Broderick

JEAN CARROLL
1968 THE LEGEND OF LYLAH CLARE
Director: Robert Aldrich
Co-stars: Kim Novak Peter Finch Coral Browne

JILL CARROLL
1983 PSYCHO II
Director: Richard Franklin
Co-stars: Anthony Perkins Vera Miles Meg Tilly

1987 THE UNHOLY
Director: Camilio Vilo
Co-stars: Trevor Howard Ben Cross Hal Holbrook

JOAN CARROLL (Child)
1940 LADDIE
Co-Star: Tim Holt

1940 PRIMROSE PATH
Director: Gregory La Cava
Co-stars: Ginger Rogers Joel McCrea

1941 THE OBLIGING YOUNG LADY
Director: Richard Wallace
Co-stars: Ruth Warrick Edmond O'Brien Eve Arden

1944 TOMORROW THE WORLD
Director: Leslie Fenton
Co-stars: Fredric March Betty Field Skip Homeier

1944 MEET ME IN ST. LOUIS
Director: Vincente Minnelli
Co-stars: Judy Garland Margaret O'Brien Leon Ames

1945 THE BELLS OF ST. MARY'S
Director: Leo McCarey
Co-stars: Bing Crosby Ingrid Bergman

1957 ROGUE'S YARN
Director: Vernon Sewell
Co-stars: Nicole Maurey Derek Bond Hugh Latimer

JESSICA RENE CARROLL
1984 SENTIMENTAL JOURNEY
Director: James Goldstone
Co-stars: Jaclyn Smith David Dukes Maureen Stapleton

LISA HART CARROLL
1983 TERMS OF ENDEARMENT
Director: James Brooks
Co-stars: Shirley MacLaine Jack Nicholson Debra Winger

1985 MOVING VIOLATIONS
Director: Neal Israel
Co-stars: Stephen McHattie Jennifer Tilly John Murray

MADELEINE CARROLL
(Married Sterling Hayden, Had a B.A. Degree)
1927 THE GUNS OF LOOS
Director: Sinclair Hill
Co-stars: Henry Victor Bobby Howes Hermione Baddeley

1929 ATLANTIC
Director: E. A. Dupont
Co-stars: Franklin Dyall Monty Banks John Longden

1929 THE CROOKED BILLET
Director: Adrian Brunel
Co-stars: Carlyle Blackwell Gordon Harker

1930 ESCAPE
Director: Basil Dean
Co-stars: Gerald Du Maurier Edna Best Gordon Harker

1930 FRENCH LEAVE
Director: Jack Raymond
Co-stars: Sydney Howard Arthur Chesney Henry Kendal

1930 THE SCHOOL FOR SCANDAL
Director: Maurice Elvey
Co-stars: Basil Gill Henry Hewitt Ian Fleming

1930 YOUNG WOODLEY
Director: Thomas Bentley
Co-stars: Frank Lawton Sam Livesey Billy Milton

1930 THE W PLAN
Director: Victor Saville
Co-stars: Brian Aherne Gordon Harker Gibb McLaughlin

1933 SLEEPING CAR
Director: Anatole Litvak
Co-stars: Ivor Novello Kay Hammond Stanley Holloway

1933 I WAS A SPY
Director: Victor Saville
Co-stars: Conrad Veidt Herbert Marshall Edmund Gwenn

1934 THE WORLD MOVES ON
Director: John Ford
Co-stars: Franchot Tone Reginald Denny Stepin Fetchit

1935 THE THIRTY-NINE STEPS
Director: Alfred Hitchcock
Co-stars: Robert Donat Godfrey Tearle John Laurie

1935 THE DICTATOR
Director: Victor Saville
Co-stars: Clive Brook Emlyn Williams Helen Haye

1936 SECRET AGENT
Director: Alfred Hitchcock
Co-stars: John Gielgud Robert Young Peter Lorre

1936 THE CASE AGAINST MRS. AMES
Director: William Seiter
Co-stars: George Brent Beulah Bondi

1936 THE GENERAL DIED AT DAWN
Director: Lewis Milestone
Co-stars: Gary Cooper Akim Tamiroff

1936 LLOYDS OF LONDON
Director: Henry King
Co-stars: Tyrone Power George Sanders C. Aubrey Smith

1937 ON THE AVENUE
Director: Roy Del Ruth
Co-stars: Dick Powell Alice Faye Joan Davis

1937 IT'S ALL YOURS
Director: Elliott Nugent
Co-stars: Francis Lederer Mlscha Auer

1937 THE PRISONER OF ZENDA
Director: John Cromwell
Co-stars: Ronald Colman Douglas Fairbanks David Niven

1938 BLOCKADE
Director: William Dieterle
Co-stars: Henry Fonda Leo Carrillo John Halliday

1939 CAFE SOCIETY
Director: Edward Griffith
Co-stars: Fred MacMurray Shirley Ross

1939 HONEYMOON IN BALI
Director: Edward Griffith
Co-stars: Fred MacMurray Allan Jones

1940 MY SON, MY SON
Director: Charles Vidor
Co-stars: Brian Aherne Louis Hayward Laraine Day

1940 NORTHWEST MOUNTED POLICE
Director: Cecil B. DeMille
Co-stars: Gary Cooper Robert Preston Preston Foster

1940 SAFARI
Director: Edward Griffith
Co-stars: Douglas Fairbanks Tullio Carminati

1940 VIRGINIA
Director: Edward Griffith
Co-stars: Fred MacMurray Sterling Hayden

1941 BAHAMA PASSAGE
Director: Edward Griffith
Co-stars: Sterling Hayden Flora Robson

1941 ONE NIGHT IN LISBON
Director: Edward Griffith
Co-stars: Fred MacMurray Edmund Gwenn Billie Burke

1942 MY FAVORITE BLONDE
Director: Sidney Lanfield
Co-stars: Bob Hope Gale Sondergaard George Zucco

1947 WHITE CRADLE INN
Director: Harold French
Co-stars: Michael Rennie Ian Hunter Michael McKeag

1948 DON'T TRUST YOUR HUSBAND
Director: Lloyd Bacon
Co-stars: Fred MacMurray Loulse Allbritton

1949 THE FAN
Director: Otto Preminger
Co-stars: Jeanne Crain George Sanders Rlchard Greene

MOON CARROLL

1929 THE LAST OF MRS. CHEYNEY
Director: Sidney Franklin
Co-stars: Norma Shearer Basil Rathbone

NANCY CARROLL *(Ann La Hiff)*
Nominated For Best Actress In 1930 For "The Devil's Holiday"

1928 ABIE'S IRISH ROSE
Director: Victor Fleming
Co-stars: Jean Hersholt Charles Rogers Bernard Gorcey

1928 SHOPWORN ANGEL
Director: Richard Wallace
Co-stars: Gary Cooper Paul Lukas Emmett King

1930 LAUGHTER
Director: Harry D'Abbabie D'Arrast
Co-stars: Fredric March Frank Morgan

1930 HONEY
Director: Wesley Ruggles
Co-stars: Lillian Roth Stanley Smith Mitzi Green

1930 FOLLOW THRU
Director: Lloyd Corrigan
Co-stars: Charles Rogers Jack Haley Zelma O'Neal

1930 DEVIL'S HOLIDAY
Director: Edmund Goulding
Co-stars: Phillips Holmes Paul Lukas Ned Sparks

1930 PARAMOUNT ON PARADE
Director: Lothar Mendes
Co-stars: Jean Arthur Clara Bow Gary Cooper

1930 DANGEROUS PARADISE
Co-Star Richard Arlen

1931 PERSONAL MAID
Co-Star Gene Raymond

1931 THE NIGHT ANGEL
Director: Edmund Goulding
Co-stars: Fredric March Alan Hale Alison Skipworth

1932 UNDERCOVER MAN
Director: James Flood
Co-stars: George Raft Gregory Ratoff Roscoe Karns

1932 SCARLET DAWN
Director: William Dieterle
Co-stars: Douglas Fairbanks Lilyan Tashman

1932 HOT SATURDAY
Director: William Seiter
Co-stars: Cary Grant Randolph Scott Jane Darwell

1932 BROKEN LULLABY
Director: Ernst Lubitsch
Co-stars: Lionel Barrymore Phillips Holmes Zasu Pitts

1932 WAYWARD
Co-stars: Richard Arlen Dorothy Stickney

1933 THE WOMAN ACCUSED
Director: Paul Sloane
Co-stars: Cary Grant John Halliday Louis Calhern

1933 I LOVE THAT MAN
Co-Star Edmund Lowe

1933 THE KISS BEFORE THE MIRROR
Co-Star Charles Grapewin

1933 CHILD OF MANHATTAN
Director: Edward Buzzell
Co-stars: John Boles Charles Jones Jane Darwell

1934 TRANSATLANTIC MERRY GO ROUND
Director: Ben Stoloff
Co-stars: Jack Benny Gene Raymond

1934 JEALOUSY
Director: Roy William Neill
Co-stars: George Murphy Donald Cook

1935 ATLANTIC ADVENTURE
Director: Albert Rogell
Co-stars: Lloyd Nolan Harry Langdon John Wray

1935 SPRINGTIME FOR HENRY
Director: Frank Tuttle
Co-stars: Otto Kruger Nigel Bruce Heather Angel

1935 AFTER THE DANCE
Co-stars: George Murphy Jack Dean

1935 I'LL LOVE YOU ALWAYS
Co-stars: George Murphy Raymond Walburn Jean Dixon

1938 THAT CERTAIN AGE
Director: Edward Ludwig
Co-stars: Deanna Durbin Melvyn Douglas Jackie Cooper

1938 THERE GOES MY HEART
Director: Norman Z McLeod
Co-stars: Fredric March Virginia Bruce Patsy Kelly

VIRGINIA CARROLL
1948 TRIGGERMAN
Co-stars: Johnny Mack Brown Raymond Hatton

FRANCES CARSON
1941 TWO-FACED WOMAN
Director: George Cukor
Co-stars: Greta Garbo Melvyn Douglas Constance Bennett

JEAN CARSON *(Jeannie)*
1955 AS LONG AS THEY'RE HAPPY
Director: J. Lee Thompson
Co-stars: Jack Buchanan Janette Scott Diana Dors

1955 AN ALLIGATOR NAMED DAISY
Director: J. Lee Thompson
Co-stars: Donald Sinden Diana Dors Roland Culver

1958 ROCKETS GALORE
Director: Michael Relph
Co-stars: Donald Sinden Ian Hunter Noel Purcell

RENEE CARSON

1946 DEADLINE FOR MURDER
Director: James Tinling
Co-stars: Paul Kelly Kent Taylor Sheila Ryan

MARGIT CARSTENSEN

1973 TENDERNESS OF WOLVES
Director: Ulli Lommel
Co-stars: Kurt Raab Jeff Roden

1975 THE BITTER TEARS OF PETRA VON KANT
Director: Rainer Werner Fassbinder
Co-stars: Hanna Schygulla Eva Mattes

1976 CHINESE ROULETTE
Director: Rainer Werner Fassbinder
Co-stars: Andrea Schober Anna Karina

1981 POSSESSION
Director: Andrzej Zulawski
Co-stars: Isabelle Adjani Sam Neill

MARCELIA CARTAXO

1985 THE HOUR OF THE STAR
Director: Suzana Amaral
Co-stars: Jose Dumont Tamara Taxman

CARMEN CARTELLIERI

1925 HANDS OF ORLAC
Director: Robert Wiene
Co-stars: Conrad Veidt Alexandra Sorina

ALICE CARTER

1989 GROSS ANATOMY
Director: Thom Eberhardt
Co-stars: Matthew Modine Daphne Zuniga Christine Lahti

ANN CARTER *(Child)*

1943 NORTH STAR
Director: Lewis Milestone
Co-stars: Anne Baxter Farley Granger Dana Andrews

1944 THE CURSE OF THE CAT PEOPLE
Director: Robert Wise
Co-stars: Simone Simon Kent Smith

1949 BLONDIE HITS THE JACKPOT
Director: Edward Bernds
Co-stars: Penny Singleton Arthur Lake

FINN CARTER

1990 TREMORS
Director: Ron Underwood Kevin Bacon Fred Ward

HELENA CARTER

1947 INTRIQUE
Director: Edwin Marin
Co-stars: George Raft June Havoc Tom Tully

1947 SOMETHING IN THE WIND
Director: Irving Pichel
Co-stars: Deanna Durbin Donald O'Connor

1948 RIVER LADY
Co-stars: Yvonne De Carlo Dan Duryea Rod Cameron

1949 THE FIGHTING O'FLYNN
Director: Arthur Pierson
Co-stars: Douglas Fairbanks Jnr. Richard Greene

1949 SOUTH SEA SINNER
Director: Bruce Humberstone
Co-stars: MacDonald Carey Shelley Winters

1950 DOUBLE CROSSBONES
Director: Charles Barton
Co-stars: Donald O'Connor Will Geer John Emery

1950 KISS TOMORROW GOODBYE
Director: Gordon Douglas
Co-stars: James Cagney Barbara Payton Ward Bond

1952 THE GOLDEN HAWK
Director: Sidney Salkow
Co-stars: Sterling Hayden Rhonda Fleming John Sutton

1952 BUGLES IN THE AFTERNOON
Director: Roy Rowland
Co-stars: Ray Milland Hugh Marlowe Forrest Tucker

1953 INVADERS FROM MARS
Director: William Cameron Menzies
Co-stars: Arthur Franz Leif Erickson

JANIS CARTER

1942 GIRL TROUBLE
Director: Harold Schuster
Co-stars: Joan Bennett Billie Burke Don Ameche

1942 JUST OFF BROADWAY
Director: Herbert Leeds
Co-stars: Lloyd Nolan Marjorie Weaver Phil Silvers

1942 SECRET AGENT OF JAPAN
Director: Irving Pichel
Co-stars: Preston Foster Lynn Bari Noel Madison

1943 SWING OUT THE BLUES
Co-Star Bob Haymes

1943 THE GHOST THAT WALKS ALONE
Director: Lew Landers
Co-stars: Arthur Lake Frank Sully Lynne Roberts

1944 THE MISSING JUROR
Director: Budd Boetticher
Co-stars: Jim Bannon George Macready

1945 THE POWER OF THE WHISTLER
Co-Star Richard Dix

1945 ONE WAY TO LOVE
Director: Ray Enright
Co-stars: Willard Parker Marguerite Chapman Chester Morris

1946 THE FIGHTING GUARDSMAN
Director: Henry Levin
Co-stars: Willard Parker Anita Louise George Macready

1946 THE NOTORIOUS LONE WOLF
Director: Ross Lederman
Co-stars: Gerald Mohr Eric Blore Don Beddoe

1946 NIGHT EDITOR
Co-Star William Gargan

1947 I LOVE TROUBLE
Director: S. Sylvan Simon
Co-stars: Franchot Tone Janet Blair Adele Jergens

1947 FRAMED
Director: Richard Wallace
Co-stars: Glenn Ford Barry Sullivan

1948 SLIGHTLY FRENCH
Director: Douglas Sirk
Co-stars: Dorothy Lamour Don Ameche Willard Parker

1949 **THE WOMAN ON PIER 13**
Director: Robert Stevenson
Co-stars: Laraine Day Robert Ryan John Agar

1949 **MISS GRANT TAKES RICHMOND**
Director: Lloyd Bacon
Co-stars: Lucille Ball William Holden Gloria Henry

1950 **A WOMAN OF DISTINCTION**
Director: Edward Buzzell
Co-stars: Rosalind Russell Ray Milland Edmund Gwenn

1950 **AND BABY MAKES THREE**
Director: Henry Levin
Co-stars: Robert Young Barbara Hale Robert Hutton

1951 **FLYING LEATHERNECKS**
Director: Nicholas Ray
Co-stars: John Wayne Robert Ryan Don Taylor

1951 **MY FORBIDDEN PAST**
Director: Robert Stevenson
Co-stars: Ava Gardner Robert Mitchum Melvyn Douglas

1951 **SANTE FE**
Director: Irving Pichel
Co-stars: Randolph Scott Jerome Courtland Warner Anderson

1952 **THE HALF-BREED**
Director: Stuart Gilmore
Co-stars: Robert Young Jack Buetel Barton MacLane

JUNE CARTER CASH (*Wife Of Johnny Cash*)

1978 **THADDEUS ROSE AND EDDIE**
Director: Jack Starrett
Co-stars: Johnny Cash Diane Ladd Bo Hopkins

1983 **MURDER IN COWETA COUNTY**
Director: Gary Nelson
Co-stars: Johnny Cash Andy Griffith Cindi Knight

MRS. LESLIE CARTER

1935 **ROCKY MOUNTAIN MYSTERY**
Director: Charles Barton
Co-stars: Randolph Scott Kathleen Burke Ann Sheridan

LOUISE CARTER

1932 **HELL'S HIGHWAY**
Director: Rowland Brown
Co-stars: Richard Dix Tom Brown Rochelle Hudson

1932 **BROKEN LULLABY**
Director: Ernst Lubitsch
Co-stars: Lionel Barrymore Phillips Holmes Nancy Carroll

1933 **JENNIE GERHARDT**
Director: Marion Gering
Co-stars: Sylvia Sidney Donald Cook Mary Astor

1933 **THE MONKEY'S PAW**
Co-Star Ian Simpson

1934 **YOU'RE TELLING ME**
Director: Erle Renton
Co-stars: W. C. Fields Larry Crabbe Adrienne Ames

LYNDA CARTER

1975 **THE NEW ORIGINAL WONDER WOMAN**
Director: Leonard Horn
Co-stars: Lyle Waggoner Red Buttons

1975 **A MATTER OF WIFE ... AND DEATH**
Director: Marvin Chomsky
Co-stars: Rod Taylor Tom Drake Anita Gillette

1982 **HOTLINE**
Director: Jerry Jameson
Co-stars: Steve Forrest James Booth Monte Markham

1987 **STILLWATCH**
Director: Rod Holcomb
Co-stars: Angie Dickinson Don Murray Stuart Whitman

1989 **MICKEY SPILLANE'S MIKE HAMMER: MURDER TAKES ALL**
Director: John Nicolella
Co-stars: Stacy Keach Don Stroud

1991 **DANIELLE STEEL'S DADDY**
Director: Michael Miller
Co-stars: Patrick Duffy Kate Mulgrew

1991 **I POSED FOR PLAYBOY**
Director: Stephen Stafford
Co-stars: Michelle Green Amanda Peterson

RANDY SUE CARTER

1984 **THE BROTHER FROM ANOTHER PLANET**
Director: John Sayles
Co-stars: Joe Morton Tom Wright

ANNA CARTERET

1965 **DATELINE DIAMONDS**
Director: Jeremy Summers
Director: William Lucas Kenneth Cope

1989 **THE HEAT OF THE DAY**
Director: Christopher Morahan
Co-stars: Michael Gambon Patricia Hodge

KATRIN CARTLIDGE

1993 **NAKED**
Director: Mike Leigh
Co-stars: David Trewlis Lesley Sharp Claire Skinner

1996 **BREAKING THE WAVES**
Director: Lars Von Trier
Co-stars: Emily Watson Stellan Skarsgard

PAULINE CARTON

1931 **THE BLOOD OF A POET**
Director: Jean Cocteau
Co-stars: Lee Miller Enrique Rivero Barbette

ANGELA CARTWRIGHT

1965 **THE SOUND OF MUSIC**
Director: Robert Wise
Co-stars: Julie Andrews Christopher Plummer Peggy Wood

1983 **HIGH SCHOOL U.S.A.**
Director: Rod Amateau
Co-stars: Michael J. Fox Nancy McKeon Todd Bridges

MARYSE CARTWRIGHT

1986 **THE DOG WHO STOPPED THE WAR**
Director: Andre Melancon
Co-stars: Cedric Jourde Julien Elie

NANCY CARTWRIGHT

1985 **NOT MY KID**
Director: Michael Tuchner
Co-stars: George Segal Stockard Channing Tate Donovan

VERONICA CARTWRIGHT

1963 **THE BIRDS**
Director: Alfred Hitchcock
Co-stars: Tippi Hedren Rod Taylor Jessica Tandy

1975 **INSERTS**
Director: John Byrum
Co-stars: Richard Dreyfuss Jessica Harper Bob Hoskins

1978 GOIN' SOUTH
Director: Jack Nicholson
Co-stars: Jack Nicholson Mary Steenburgen Christopher Lloyd

1978 INVASION OP THE BODY SNATCHERS
Director: Philip Kaufman
Co-stars: Donald Sutherland Brooke Adams

1979 ALIEN
Director: Ridley Scott
Co-stars: Sigourney Weaver Tom Skerritt John Hurt

1982 PRIME SUSPECT
Director: Noel Black
Co-stars: Mike Farrell Teri Garr Lane Smith

1983 THE RIGHT STUFF
Director: Philip Kaufman
Co-stars: Sam Shepard Scott Glenn Barbara Hershey

1983 NIGHTMARES
Director: Joseph Sargent
Co-stars: Cristina Raines Timothy James Emilio Estevez

1986 FLIGHT OF THE NAVIGATOR
Director: Randal Kleiser
Co-stars: Joey Cramer Cliff De Young

1987 THE WITCHES OF EASTWICK
Director: George Miller
Co-stars: Jack Nicholson Susan Sarandon Cher

1989 DESPERATE FOR LOVE
Director: Michael Tuchner
Co-stars: Christian Slater Brian Bloom Scott Paulin

1990 FALSE IDENTITY
Director: James Keach
Co-stars: Genevieve Bujold Stacy Keach Tobin Bell

1992 MAN TROUBLE
Director: Bob Rafelson
Co-stars: Jack Nicholson Ellen Barkin Beverly D'angelo

1994 MY BROTHER'S KEEPER
Director: Glenn Jordan
Co-stars: John Lithgow Annette O'Toole

MARGHERITA CARUSO

1964 THE GOSPEL ACCORDING TO MATTHEW
Director: Pier Paolo Pasolini
Co-stars: Enrique Irazoqui Mario Socrate

LYNNE CARVER

1937 MADAME X
Director: Sam Wood
Co-stars: Gladys George John Beal Warren William

1937 THE BRIDE WORE RED
Director: Dorothy Arzner
Co-stars: Joan Crawford Robert Young Franchot Tone

1937 MAYTIME
Director: Robert Z. Leonard
Co-stars: Jeanette MacDonald Nelson Eddy John Barrymore

1938 YOUNG DR. KILDARE
Director: Harold Bucquet
Co-stars: Lionel Barrymore Lew Ayres

1938 EVERYBODY SING
Director: Edwin Marin
Co-stars: Allan Jones Judy Garland Fanny Brice

1938 A CHRISTMAS CAROL
Director: Edwin Marin
Co-stars: Reginald Owen Terry Kilburn June Lockhart

1939 HUCKLEBERRY FINN
Director: Richard Thorpe
Co-stars: Mickey Rooney Walter Connolly Rex Ingram

1940 CRIME DOES NOT PAY: POUND FOOLISH
Director: Felix Feist
Co-Star Neil Hamilton

1941 CRIME DOES NOT PAY: SUCKER LIST
Director: Roy Rowland
Co-Star John Archer

1945 FLAME OF THE WEST
Co-stars: Johnny Mack Brown Raymond Hatton

1946 DRIFTING ALONG
Co-stars: Johnny Mack Brown Raymond Hatton Douglas Fowley

TINA CARVER

1955 INSIDE DETROIT
Director: Fred Sears
Co-stars: Pat O'Brien Dennis O'Keefe Mark Damon

1957 FROM HELL IT CAME
Director: Dan Milner
Co-stars: Tod Andrews Linda Watkins

GISELE CASADESUS

1948 ENTRE ONZE HEURES ET MINUI
Director: Henri Decoin
Co-stars: Louis Jouvet Madeleine Robinson

1974 VERDICT
Director: Andre Cayatte
Co-stars: Sophia Loren Jean Gabin Henri Garcin

MARIA CASAJUANA

1928 A GIRL IN EVERY PORT
Director: Howard Hawks
Co-stars: Victor McLaglen Robert Armstrong Myrna Loy

MARIA CASARES

1945 LES ENFANTS DU PARADIS
Director: Marcel Carne
Co-stars: Arletty Pierre Brasseur Jane Marken

1946 LES DAMES DU BOIS DE BOULOGNE
Director: Robert Bresson
Co-stars: Elina Labourdette Paul Bernard

1950 ORPHEE
Director: Jean Cocteau
Co-stars: Jean Marais Marie Dea Juliette Greco

1960 LE TESTAMENT D'ORPHEE
Director: Jean Cocteau
Co-stars: Jean Cocteau Edouard Dermit Francois Perier

1988 LA LECTRICE
Director: Michel Deville
Co-stars: Miou-Miou Regis Royer Marianne Denicourt

PENNY CASDAGLI

1971 PUPPET ON A CHAIN
Director: Geoffrey Reeve
Co-stars: Barbara Parkins Sven-Bertil Taube

KATHLEEN CASE

1954 HUMAN DESIRE
Director: Fritz Lang
Co-stars: Gloria Grahame Glenn Ford Broderick Crawford

CHIARA CASELLI

1991 MY OWN PRIVATE IDAHO
Director: Gus Van Sant
Co-stars: River Phoenix Keanu Reeves James Russo

1997 BEYOND THE CLOUDS
Director: Michaelangelo Antonioni
Co-stars: John Malkovich Fanny Ardant

ADRIANA CASELOTTI

1937   SNOW WHITE AND THE SEVEN DWARFS (Voice)
Director: David Hand
Co-stars: Lucille La Verne Billy Gilbert

CATHY CASEY

1990   HUSH-A-BYE-BABY
Director: Margo Harker
Co-stars: Emer McCourt Sinead O'Connor

SUE CASEY

1966   THE BEACH GIRLS AND THE MONSTER
Director: Jon Hall
Co-stars: Jon Hall Arnold Lessing

ROSALIND CASH

1971   THE OMEGA MAN
Director: Boris Sagal
Co-stars: Charlton Heston Anthony Zerbe

1972   THE NEW CENTURIONS
Director: Richard Fleischer
Co-stars: George C. Scott Jane Alexander

1972   HICKEY AND BOGGS
Director: Robert Culp
Co-stars: Robert Culp Bill Cosby Michael Moriarty

1974   UPTOWN SATURDAY NIGHT
Director: Sidney Poitier
Co-stars: Sidney Poitier Bill Cosby Harry Belafonte

1978   THE CLASS OF MISS MACMICHAEL
Director: Silvo Narizzano
Co-stars: Glenda Jackson Oliver Reed

1984   ADVENTURES OF BUCKAROO BANZAI ACROSS THE 8TH DIMENSION
Director: W. D. Richter
Co-stars: Peter Weller John Lithgow Ellen Barkin

MARIA PIA CASILIO

1952   UMBERTO D
Director: Vittorio De Sica
Co-stars: Carlo Battista Lina Gennari

GOLDA CASIMIR

1966   THE SPECIALIST
Director: James Hill
Co-stars: Bernard Miles Colin Ellis Sheila Shand

BARBARA CASON

1970   THE HONEYMOON KILLERS
Director: Leonard Kastle
Co-stars: Shirley Stoler Tony Lobianco

TINA CASPARY

1986   COMBAT ACADEMY
Director: Heal Israel
Co-stars: Keith Gordon George Clooney Dana Hill

1987   CAN'T BUY ME LOVE
Director: Steve Rash
Co-stars: Patrick Dempsey Amanda Peterson Seth Green

1988   MAC AND ME
Director: Stewart Raffill
Co-stars: Christine Ebersole Jonathan Ward

MAMA CASS

1970   PUFNSTUF
Director: Hollingsworth Morse
Co-stars: Jack Wild Billie Hayes Martha Raye

PEGGY CASH

Nominated For Best Supporting Actress In 1958 For "Auntie Mame"

1958   AUNTIE MAME
Director: Morton Dacosta
Co-stars: Rosalind Russell Forrest Tucker Coral Browne

1969   IF IT'S TUESDAY, THIS MUST BE BELGIUM
Director: Mel Stuart
Co-stars: Suzanne Pleshette Ian McShane

KATHERINE CASSAVETES

1971   MINNIE AND MOSKOWITZ
Director: John Cassavetes
Co-stars: John Cassavetes Gena Rowlands Seymour Cassel

1974   A WOMAN UNDER THE INFLUENCE
Director: John Cassavetes
Co-stars: Gena Rowlands Peter Falk

SANDRA CASSEL

1972   LAST HOUSE ON THE LEFT
Director: Wes Craven
Co-stars: David Hess Lucy Grantham

CINDY CASSELL

1964   EMIL AND THE DETECTIVES
Director: Peter Tewksbury
Co-stars: Walter Slezak Bryan Russell

JOANNA CASSIDY

1973   THE OUTFIT
Director: John Flynn
Co-stars: Robert Duvall Karen Black Robert Ryan

1973   AN INVESTIGATION OF MURDER
Director: Stuart Rosenberg
Co-stars: Walter Matthau Bruce Dern

1974   THE BANK SHOT
Director: Gower Champion
Co-stars: George C. Scott Sorrell Brooke

1977   THE LATE SHOW
Director: Robert Benton
Co-stars: Art Carney Lily Tomlin Howard Duff

1977   STUNTS
Director: Mark Lester
Co-stars: Robert Forster Fiona Lewis Bruce Glover

1980   NIGHT GAMES
Director: Roger Vadim
Co-stars: Cindy Pickett Barry Primus

1983   UNDER FIRE
Director: Roger Spottiswoode
Co-stars: Gene Hackman Nick Nolte Ed Harris

1984   INVITATION TO HELL
Director: Wes Craven
Co-stars: Robert Urich Susan Lucci Kevin McCarthy

1987   A FATHER'S REVENGE
Director: John Herzfeld
Co-stars: Brian Dennehy Ron Silver Anthony Valentine

1987   THE FOURTH PROTOCOL
Director: John MacKenzie
Co-stars: Michael Caine Pierce Brosnan Ned Beatty

1988   1969
Director: Ernest Thompson
Co-stars: Kiefer Sutherland Robert Downey Jnr. Winona Ryder

1988   NIGHTMARE AT BITTER CREEK
Director: Tim Burstall
Co-stars: Lindsey Wagner Tom Skerritt

1988 WHO FRAMED ROGER RABBIT?
Director: Robert Zemekis
Co-stars: Bob Hoskins Christopher Lloyd

19889 THE PACKAGE
Director: Andrew Davis
Co-stars: Gene Hackman Tommy Lee Jones Pam Grier

1990 WHERE THE HEART IS
Director: John Boorman
Co-stars: Dabney Coleman Uma Thurman Suzy Amis

1990 MAY WINE
Director: Carol Wiseman
Co-stars: Guy Marchand Lara Flynn Boyle

1991 DON'T TELL MUM THE BABYSITTER'S DEAD
Director: Stephen Herek
Co-stars: Christina Applegate John Getz

1992 LIVE! FROM DEATH ROW
Director: Patrick Duncan
Co-stars: Druce Davison Jason Tomlins

1995 SLEEP, BABY SLEEP
Director: Armand Mastroianni
Co-stars: Tracey Gold Kyle Chandler

NADIA CASSINI

1972 PULP
Director: Mike Hodges
Co-stars: Michael Caine Mickey Rooney Lizabeth Scott

STEFANIA CASSINI

1976 SUSPIRIA
Director: Dario Argento
Co-stars: Jessica Harper Alida Valli Joan Bennett

1977 ANDY WARHOL'S BAD
Director: Jed Johnson
Co-stars: Carroll Baker Perry King Susan Tyrrell

ANN CASSON

1932 DANCE PRETTY LADY
Director: Anthony Asquith
Co-stars: Carl Harbord Michael Hogan

1940 GEORGE AND MARGARET
Director: George King
Co-stars: Judy Kelly Marie Lohr Oliver Wakefield

MAXINE CASSON

1976 CONFESSIONS OF A DRIVING INSTRUCTOR
Director: Norman Cohen
Co-stars: Robin Askwith Anthony Booth

ANA CASTELL

1987 MACU, THE POLICEMAN'S WIFE
Director: Solveig Hoogesteijn
Co-stars: Daniel Alvarado Maria Luisa Mosquera

GLORIA CASTILLO

1957 INVASION OF THE SAUCER MEN
Director: Edward Cahn
Co-stars: Steve Terell Frank Gorshin Ed Nelson

JESSICA CASTILLO

1980 GLORIA
Director: John Cassavetes
Co-stars: Gena Rowlands John Adames Buck Henry

ANALIA CASTRO

1985 LA HISTORIA OFICIAL
Director: Luis Puenzo
Co-stars: Hector Alterio Norma Aleandro

MARY CASTLE

1952 THE LAWLESS BREED
Director: Raoul Walsh
Co-stars: Rock Hudson Julie Adams John McIntyre

1953 GUNSMOKE
Director: Nathan Juran
Co-stars: Audie Murphy Paul Kelly Susan Cabot

1956 CRASHING LAS VEGAS
Director: Jean Yarbrough
Co-stars: Leo Gorcy Huntz Hall

1960 THE JAILBREAKERS
Director: Alexander Grasshoff
Co-stars: Robert Hutton Michael O'Connell

PEGGIE CASTLE

1952 HAREM GIRL
Director: Edward Bernds
Co-stars: Joan Davis Arthur Blake

1952 INVASION, U.S.A.
Director: Alfred Green
Co-stars: Dan O'Herlihy Gerald Mohr

1953 I, THE JURY
Director: Harry Essex
Co-stars: Biff Elliott Preston Foster John Qualen

1953 99, RIVER STREET
Director: Phil Karlson
Co-stars: John Payne Evelyn Keyes Brad Dexter

1954 THE LONG WAIT
Director: Victor Saville
Co-stars: Anthony Quinn Charles Coburn Gene Evans

1955 TALL MAN RIDING
Director: Lesley Selander
Co-stars: Randolph Scott Robert Barrat Dorothy Malone

1955 TARGET ZERO
Director: Harmon Jones
Co-stars: Richard Conte Charles Bronson Chuck Connors

1956 THE OKLAHOMA WOMAN
Director: Roger Corman
Co-stars: Richard Denning Cathy Downs Tudor Owen

1957 THE SEVEN HILLS OF ROME
Director: Roy Rowland
Co-stars: Mario Lanza Renato Rascel

1957 THE BEGINNING OF THE END
Director: Bert Gordon
Co-stars: Peter Graves Morris Ankrum

1957 BACK FROM THE DEAD
Director: Charles Marquis Warren
Co-stars: Arthur Franz Marsha Hunt

MURIEL CATALA

1974 VERDICT
Director: Andre Cayatte
Co-stars: Sophia Loren Jean Gabin Henri Garcin

DARLENE CATES

1993 WHAT'S EATING GILBERT GRAPE?
Director: Lasse Hallstrom
Co-stars: Johnny Depp Leonardo DiCaprio

GEORGINA CATES

1994 AN AWFULLY BIG ADVENTURE
Director: Mike Newell
Co-stars: Alan Rickman Hugh Grant

1995　FRANKIE STARLIGHT
Director:　Michael Lindsay-Hogg
Co-stars:　Anne Parillaud Matt Dillon Rudi Davis

1998　STIFF UPPER LIPS
Director:　Gary Sinyor
Co-stars:　Sam West Robert Portal Prunella Scales

PHOEBE CATES
1982　FAST TIMES AT RIDGEMONT HIGH
Director:　Amy Heckerling
Co-stars:　Sean Penn Jennifer Jason Leigh

1984　GREMLINS
Director:　Joe Dante
Co-stars:　Zach Galligan Keye Luke Scott Brady

1988　BRIGHT LIGHTS, BIG CITY
Director:　James Bridges
Co-stars:　Michael J. Fox Kiefer Sutherland Dianne Wiest

1988　SHAG
Director:　Zelda Barron
Co-stars:　Scott Coffey Bridget Fonda Annabeth Gish

1990　GREMLINS 2
Director:　Joe Dante
Co-stars:　Zach Galligan John Glover Robert Prosky

1991　DROP DEAD FRED
Director:　Ate De Jong
Co-stars:　Rik Mayall Marsha Mason Carrie Fisher

1993　BODIES, REST AND MOTION
Director:　Michael Sternberg
Co-stars:　Bridget Fonda Tim Roth Eric Stolz

MARY JO CATLETT
1994　SERIAL MOM
Director:　John Waters
Co-stars:　Kathleen Turner Sam Waterston Ricki Lake

BRIGITTE CATILLON
1988　LA LECTRICE
Director:　Michel Deville
Co-stars:　Miou-Miou Regis Royer Maria Casares

1992　UN COEUR EN HIVER
Director:　Claude Sautet
Co-stars:　Daniel Auteuil Emmanuelle Beart

VICTORIA CATLIN
1989　HOWLING V: THE REBIRTH
Director:　Neal Sundstrom
Co-stars:　Elizabeth Silverstein Mark Faulkner

JULIETTE CATON *(Child)*
1989　COURAGE MOUNTAIN
Director:　Christopher Leitch
Co-stars:　Leslie Caron Charlie Sheen

1993　AN EXCHANGE OF FIRE
Director:　Tony Bicat
Co-stars:　Frank Finlay James Fleet Caroline Langrishe

1993　WALL OF SILENCE
Director:　Philip Saville
Co-stars:　Bill Paterson Warren Mitchell John Bowe

KIM CATTRALL
1975　ROSEBUD
Director:　Otto Preminger
Co-stars:　Peter O'Toole Richard Attenborough Peter Lawford

1981　TRIBUTE
Director:　Bob Clark
Co-stars:　Jack Lemmon Lee Remick Robby Benson

1981　TICKET TO HEAVEN
Director:　Ralph Thomas
Co-stars:　Nick Mancuso Saul Rubinek Meg Foster

1981　PORKY'S
Director:　Bob Clark
Co-stars:　Dan Monahan Mark Herrier Susan Clark

1984　SINS OF THE PAST
Director:　Peter Hunt
Co-stars:　Barbara Carrera Debby Boone Kirstie Alley

1984　POLICE ACADEMY
Director:　Hugh Wilson
Co-stars:　Steve Guttenberg Bubba Smith Donovan Scott

**1985　POLICE ACADEMY 2:
THEIR FIRST ASSIGNMENT**
Director:　Jerry Paris
Co-stars:　Steve Guttenberg Bubba Smith

1985　TURK 182
Director:　Bob Clark
Co-stars:　Timothy Hutton Robert Urich Robert Culp

1985　HOLD-UP
Director:　Alexandre Arcady
Co-stars:　Jean-Paul Belmondo Guy Marchand

1985　CITY LIMITS
Director:　Aaron Lipstadt
Co-stars:　Darrell Larson Robby Benson James Earl Jones

1986　BIG TROUBLE IN LITTLE CHINA
Director:　John Carpenter
Co-stars:　Kurt Russell Dennis Dun Kate Burton

**1987　POLICE ACADEMY 4:
CITIZENS ON PATROL**
Director:　Jim Drake
Co-stars:　Steve Guttenberg Sharon Stone

1987　MANNEQUIN
Director:　Michael Gottlieb
Co-stars:　Andrew McCarthy Estelle Getty James Spader

1988　MASQUERADE
Director:　Bob Swaim
Co-stars:　Rob Lowe Meg Tilly Dana Delany

1988　MIDNIGHT CROSSING
Director:　Roger Holzberg
Co-stars:　Faye Dunaway Daniel J. Travanti Ned Beatty

1989　THE RETURN OF THE MUSKETEERS
Director:　Richard Lester
Co-stars:　Michael York Oliver Reed

1990　BONFIRE OF THE VANITIES
Director:　Brian De Palma
Co-stars:　Tom Hanks Bruce Willis Melanie Griffith

**1991　STAR TREK VI:
THE UNDISCOVERED COUNTRY**
Director:　Nicholas Meyer
Co-stars:　William Shatner Leonard Nimoy

1991　SPLIT SECOND
Director:　Tony Maylam
Co-stars:　Rutger Hauer Michael J. Pollard

1991　MIRACLE IN THE WILDERNESS
Director:　Kevin James Dobson
Co-stars:　Kris Kristofferson Peter Alan Morris

1992　DOUBLE VISION
Director:　Rob Knights
Co-Star:　Gale Hansen

1994　ABOVE SUSPICION
Director:　Steven Schacter
Co-stars:　Christopher Reeve Joe Mantegna

1995 LIVE NUDE GIRLS
Director: Julianna Levin
Co-Star Dana Delaney

1995 THE HEIDI CHRONICLES
Director: Paul Bogart
Co-stars: Tom Hulce Peter Friedman Jamie Lee Curtis

CAROLINE CATZ

1992 THE GUILTY
Director: Colin Gregg
Co-stars: Michael Kitchen Sean Gallagher Eleanor David

1992 UNDER THE SUN
Director: Michael Winterbottom
Co-stars: Kate Hardie Iker Ibanez

JOAN CAULFIELD (*Married Frank Ross*)

1945 DUFFY'S TAVERN
Director: Hal Walker
Co-stars: Victor Moore Bob Hope Bing Crosby

1946 MISS SUSIE SLAGLE'S
Director: John Berry
Co-stars: Lillian Gish Veronica Lake Sonny Tufts

1946 BLUE SKIES
Director: Stuart Heisler
Co-stars: Fred Astaire Bing Crosby Billie De Wolfe

1946 MONSIEUR BEAUCAIRE
Director: George Marshall
Co-stars: Bob Hope Marjorie Reynolds

1947 THE UNSUSPECTED
Director: Michael Curtiz
Co-stars: Claude Rains Constance Bennett

1947 VARIETY GIRL
Director: George Marshall
Co-stars: Mary Hatcher Olga San Juan

1947 WELCOME STRANGER
Director: Elliott Nugent
Co-stars: Bing Crosby Barry Fitzgerald

1947 DEAR RUTH
Director: William Russell
Co-stars: William Holden Mona Freeman

1948 LARCENY
Director: George Sherman
Co-stars: John Payne Dan Duryea Shelley Winters

1948 THE SAINTED SISTERS
Director: William Russell
Co-stars: Veronica Lake Barry Fitzgerald

1949 DEAR WIFE
Director: Richard Haydn
Co-stars: William Holden Edward Arnold

1950 THE PETTY GIRL
Director: Henry Levin
Co-stars: Robert Cummings Elsa Lanchester

1951 DEAR BRAT
Co-stars: Wlliam Holden Mona Freeman Edward Arnold

1951 THE LADY SAYS NO
Director: Frank Ross
Co-stars: David Niven James Robertson Justice Henry Jones

1955 THE RAINS OF RANCHIPUR
Director: Jean Negulesco
Co-stars: Lana Turner Richard Burton Fred MacMurray

1963 CATTLE KING
Director: Tay Garnett
Co-stars: Robert Taylor Robert Midddleton Larry Gates

1967 RED TOMAHAWK
Director: R. G. Springsteen
Co-stars: Howard Keel Broderick Crawford

1968 BUCKSKIN
Director: Michael Moore
Co-stars: Barry Sullivan Wendell Corey Barbara Hale

1973 THE DARING DOBERMANS
Director: Bryon Chudnow
Co-stars: Tim Considine David Moses Charles Robinson

1973 THE MAGICIAN
Director: Marvin Chomsky
Co-stars: Bill Bixby Keene Curtis Kim Hunter

1976 PONY EXPRESS RIDER

MARTINE CAULTIER

1989 MILOU IN MAY
Director: Louis Malle
Co-stars: Michel Piccoli Miou-Miou Harriet Walter

LUMI CAVAJOS

1992 LIKE WATER FOR CHOCOLATE
Director: Alfonso Arau
Co-stars: Marco Leonardi Ada Carrasco

VALERIA CAVALI

1990 EVERYBODY'S FINE
Director: Giuseppe Tornatore
Co-stars: Marcello Mastroianni Michele Morgan

MEGAN CAVANAGH

1992 A LEAGUE OF THEIR OWN
Director: Penny Marshall
Co-stars: Madonna Geena Davis Tom Hanks Lori Petty

1993 MURDER OF INNOCENCE
Director: Tom McLoughlin
Co-stars: Valerie Bertinelli Stephen Banks

GRACE CAVE

1971 FAMILY LIFE
Director: Ken Loach
Co-stars: Sandy Ratcliff Bill Dean Alan McNaughton

INGRID CAVEN

1978 IN A YEAR WITH 13 MOONS
Director: Rainer Werner Fassbinder
Co-stars: Volker Spengler Gottfried John

BRENDA CAVENDISH

1978 TARKA THE OTTER
Director: David Cobham
Co-stars: Peter Bennett Edward Underdown Reg Lye

MIMI CECCHINI

1988 NICKY AND GINO
Director: Robert Young
Co-stars: Tom Hulce Ray Liotta Jamie Lee Curtis

1990 CADILLAC MAN
Director: Roger Donaldson
Co-stars: Robin Williams Tim Robbins Pamela Reed

NORA CECIL

1929 SEVEN DAYS LEAVE
Director: Richard Wallace
Co-stars: Gary Cooper Beryl Mercer

1934 THE OLD-FASHIONED WAY
Director: William Beaudine
Co-stars: W. C. Fields Joe Morrison

1943   UNKNOWN GUEST
Director: Kurt Neuman
Co-stars: Victor Jory Pamela Blake

CLEMENTINE CELARIE
1986   BETTY BLUE
Director: Jean-Jacques Beineix
Co-stars: Beatrix Dalle Jean-Hugues Anglade

1994   LE CRI DU COEUR
Director: Idrissa Ovedraogo
Co-stars: Richard Bohringer Felicite Woassi

1996   LES MISERABLES
Director: Claude Lelouche
Co-stars: Jean-Paul Belmondo Salome Lelouche

TERESA CELLI
1949   BORDER INCIDENT
Director: Anthony Mann
Co-stars: Ricardo Montalban George Murphy

1949   BLACK HAND
Director: Richard Thorpe
Co-stars: Gene Kelly J. Carrol Naish

1950   RIGHT CROSS
Director: John Sturges
Co-stars: Dick Powell June Allyson Lionel Barrymore

1950   THE ASHALT JUNGLE
Director: John Huston
Co-stars: Sterling Hayden Louis Calhern Marilyn Monroe

ANTOINETTE CELLIER
1935   MUSIC HATH CHARMS
Director: Thomas Bentley
Co-stars: Henry Hall Carol Goodner Billy Milton

1936   OURSELVES ALONE
Director: Walter Summers
Co-stars: Niall MacGinnis John Lodge

1936   THE TENTH MAN
Director: Brian Desmond Hurst
Co-stars: John Lodge Clifford Evans

1937   THE GREAT BARRIER
Director: Milton Rosmer
Co-stars: Richard Arlen Lilli Palmer

1939   I KILLED THE COUNT
Director: Fred Zelnik
Co-stars: Syd Walker Ben Lyon Barbara Blair

1943   DEAR OCTOPUS
Director: Harold French
Co-stars: Margaret Lockwood Michael Wilding Celia Johnson

1947   THE END OF THE RIVER
Director: Derek Twist
Co-stars: Sabu Esmond Knight Robert Douglas

CAROLINE CELLIER
1984   POULET AU VINAIGRE
Director: Claude Chabrol
Co-stars: Jean Poiret Stephane Audran

VALENTINA CERVI
1996   THE PORTRAIT OF A LADY
Director: Jane Campion
Co-stars: Nicole Kidman Barbara Hershey John Malkovich

SARAH CHADWICK
1994   THE ADVENTURES OF PRISCILLA, QUEEN OF THE DESERT
Director: Stephan Elliott
Co-stars: Terence Stamp Hugo Weaving

FAY CHALDECOTT
1934   DAVID COPPERFIELD
Director: George Cukor
Co-stars: Frank Lawton W. C. Fields Madge Evans

LEE CHAMBERLAIN
1975   LET'S DO IT AGAIN
Director: Sidney Poitier
Co-stars: Sidney Poitier Bill Cosby Calvin Lockhart

MARILYN CHAMBERS
1971   TOGETHER
Director: Sean Cunningham

1972   BEHIND THE GREEN DOOR
Director: Jim Mitchell
Co-stars: George McDonald Johnny Keyes

1977   RABID
Director: David Cronenberg
Co-stars: Frank Moore Joe Silver Patricia Gage

1981   ANGEL OF HEAT
Director: Meryl Schreibman
Co-stars: Stephen Johnson Mary Woronov

LYNE CHAMPAGNE
1971   MON ONCLE ANTOINE
Director: Claude Jutra
Co-stars: Claude Jutra Jean Duceppe Jacques Gagnon

BETH CHAMPION
1992   SECRETS
Director: Michael Pattinson
Co-stars: Dannii Minogue Malcolm Kennard

MARGE CHAMPION
(Married Gower Champion)

1950   MR. MUSIC
Director: Richard Haydn
Co-stars: Bing Crosby Nancy Olson Gower Champion

1951   SHOWBOAT
Director: George Sidney
Co-stars: Kathryn Grayson Howard Keel Ava Gardner

1952   LOVELY TO LOOK AT
Director: Mervyn Leroy
Co-stars: Kathryn Grayson Howard Keel Ann Miller

1952   EVERYTHING I HAVE IS YOURS
Director: Robert Z Leonard
Co-stars: Dennis O'Keefe Eduard Franz Gower Champion

1953   GIVE A GIRL A BREAK
Director: Stanley Donen
Co-stars: Debbie Reynolds Bob Fosse Gower Champion

1954   JUPITER'S DARLING
Director: George Sidney
Co-stars: Esther Williams Howard Keel George Sanders

1955   THREE FOR THE SHOW
Director: H. C. Potter
Co-stars: Betty Grable Jack Lemmon Gower Champion

1968   THE SWIMMER
Director: Sydney Pollack
Co-stars: Burt Lancaster Janice Rule Kim Hunter

1968   THE PARTY
Director: Blake Edwards
Co-stars: Peter Sellers Claudine Longet Steve Franken

1970   THE COCKEYED COWBOYS OF CALICO COUNTY
Director: Tony Leader
Co-stars: Dan Blocker Nanette Fabray

JACQUI CHAN

1960 THE WORLD OF SUZIE WONG
Director: Richard Quine
Co-stars: William Holden Nancy Kwan Sylvia Syms

MELISSA CHAN

1990 VICTIM OF INNOCENCE
Director: Mel Damski
Co-stars: Cheryl Ladd Julia Nickson-Soul

MICHELE CHAN

1989 AMERICAN NINJA 3: BLOOD HUNT
Director: Cedric Sundstrom
Co-stars: David Bradley Steve James

NAOMI CHANCE

1953 THE SAINT'S RETURN
Director: Seymour Friedman
Co-stars: Louis Hayward Sidney Tafler

1954 THE END OF THE ROAD
Director: Wolf Rilia
Co-stars: Finlay Currie Duncan Lamont

1957 SUSPENDED ALIBI
Director: Alfred Shaughnessy
Co-stars: Patrick Holt Honor Blackman

ANNA CHANCELLOR

1993 CENTURY
Director: Stephen Poliakoff
Co-stars: Charles Dance Clive Owen Miranda Richardson

1994 STAGGERED
Director: Martin Clunes
Co-stars: Martin Clunes Michael Praed Sylvia Syms

1996 KARAOKE
Co-stars: Albert Finney Saffron Burrows Roy Hudd

ESTEE CHANDLER

1985 THE EMERALD FOREST
Director: John Boorman
Co-stars: Charley Boorman Powers Booth Meg Foster

1987 TEEN WOLF TOO
Director: Christopher Leitch
Co-stars: Jason Bateman Kim Darby John Astin

HELEN CHANDLER

1930 OUTWARD BOUND
Director: Robert Milton
Co-stars: Leslie Howard Douglas Fairbanks Jnr. Beryl Mercer

1930 ROUGH ROMANCE
Co-stars: George O'Brien Antonio Moreno

1931 FANNY FOLEY HERSELF
Director: Melville Brown
Co-stars: Edna May Oliver Rochelle Hudson

1931 A HOUSE DIVIDED
Director: William Wyler
Co-stars: Walter Huston Kent Douglass

1931 DAYBREAK
Director: Jacques Feyder
Co-stars: Ramon Navarro C. Aubrey Smith Karen Morley

1931 DRACULA
Director: Tod Browning
Co-stars: Bela Lugosi David Manners Dwight Frye

1931 THE LAST FLIGHT
Director: William Dieterle
Co-stars: Richard Barthelmess David Manners

1931 SALVATION NELL
Director: James Cruze
Co-stars: Ralph Graves Sally O'Neill

1933 THE WORST WOMAN IN PARIS
Director: Monta Bell
Co-stars: Benita Hume Adolphe Menjou

1933 GOODBYE AGAIN
Director: Michael Curtiz
Co-stars: Warren William Joan Blondell Genevieve Tobin

1933 CHRISTOPHER STRONG
Director: Dorothy Arzner
Co-stars: Katharine Hepburn Colin Clive Billie Burke

1934 THE LONG LOST FATHER
Director: Ernest Schoedsack
Co-stars: John Barrymore Donald Cook

1934 RADIO PARADE OF 1935
Director: Arthur Woods
Co-stars: Will Hay Alfred Drayton Ted Ray

1934 THE UNFINISHED SYMPHONY
Director: Anthony Asquith
Co-stars: Marta Eggerth Ronald Squire

1934 LOVER DIVINE
Co-Star: Hans Jaray

1938 MISTER BOGGS STEPS OUT
Co-Star: Stuart Erwin

JOAN CHANDLER *(Child)*

1947 STALLION ROAD
Director: James Kern
Co-stars: Ronald Reagan Alexis Smith Zachary Scott

1947 HUMORESQUE
Director: Jean Negulesco
Co-stars: Joan Crawford John Garfield Oscar Levant

1948 ROPE
Director: Alfred Hitchcock
Co-stars: James Stewart Farley Granger John Dall

MIMI CHANDIER

1943 AND THE ANGELS SING
Director: George Marshall
Co-stars: Dorothy Lamour Betty Hutton Fred MacMurray

SARI CHANG

1987 CHINA GIRL
Director: Abel Ferrara
Co-stars: James Russo David Caruso Russell Wong

SYLVIA CHANG

1989 SOURSWEET
Director: Mike Newell
Co-stars: Danny Dun Jodi Long Wlliam Chow

TISA CHANG

1966 AMUSH BAY
Director: Ron Winston
Co-stars: Hugh O'Brian Mickey Rooney James Mitchum

CAROL CHANNING

1956 THE FIRST TRAVELLING SALESLADY
Director: Arthur Lubin
Co-stars: Ginger Rogers Barry Nelson

1967 THOROUGHLY MODERN MILLIE
Director: George Roy Hill
Co-stars: Julie Andrews Mary Tyler Moore

1968   SKIDOO
Director: Otto Preminger
Co-stars: Jackie Gleason Groucho Marx Mickey Rooney

1978   SGT. PEPPER'S LONELY HEARTS CLUB BAND
Director: Michael Schultz
Co-stars: Peter Frampton Bee Gees

1994   THUMBELINA *(Voice)*
Director: Don Bluth
Co-stars: Jodi Benson John Hurt Barbara Cook

MARGO CHANNING

1972   SLEUTH
Director: Joseph Mankiewicz
Co-stars: Laurence Olivier Michael Caine

RUTH CHANNING

1934   LAZY RIVER
Director: George Seitz
Co-stars: Jean Parker Robert Young Nat Pendleton

STOCKARD CHANNING
Nominated For Best Actress In 1993 For "Six Degrees Of Separation"

1973   THE GIRL MOST LIKELY TO
Director: Lee Phillips
Co-stars: Edward Asner Warren Berlinger

1975   THE FORTUNE
Director: Mike Nichols
Co-stars: Jack Nicholas Warren Beatty Florence Stanley

1976   THE BIG BUS
Director: James Frawley
Co-stars: Joseph Bologna John Beck Jose Ferrer

1977   DANDY THE ALL-AMERICAN GIRL
Director: Jerry Schatzberg
Co-stars: Sam Waterston Richard Doughty

1978   THE CHEAP DETECTIVE
Director: Robert Moore
Co-stars: Peter Falk Ann-Margret James Coco

1978   GREASE
Director: Randall Kleiser
Co-stars: Olivia Newton-John John Travolta Eve Arden

1983   WITHOUT A TRACE
Director: Stanley Jaffe
Co-stars: Kate Nelligan Judd Hirsch David Dukes

1985   NOT MY KID
Director: Michael Tuchner
Co-stars: George Segal Viveka Davis Andrew Robinson Gary Bayer

1986   HEARTBURN
Director: Mike Nichols
Co-stars: Meryl Streep Jack Nicholson Jeff Daniels

1987   THE ROOM UPSTAIRS
Director: Stuart Margolin
Co-stars: Sam Waterston Linda Hunt James Handy

1988   A TIME OF DESTINY
Director: Gregory Nava
Co-stars: William Hurt Timothy Hutton Melissa Leo

1989   STAYING TOGETHER
Director: Lee Grant
Co-stars: Sean Astin Melina Dillon Dermot Mulroney

1989   PERFECT WITNESS
Director: Robert Mandel
Co-stars: Brian Dennehy Aidan Quinn

1991   MEET THE APPLEGATES
Director: Michael Lehmann
Co-stars: Ed Begley Dabney Coleman Bobby Jacoby

1993   SIX DEGREES OF SEPARATION
Director: Fred Schepisi
Co-stars: Will Smith Donald Sutherland Mary Beth Hurt

1993   MARRIED TO IT
Director: Arthur Hiller
Co-stars: Beau Bridges Mary Stuart Masterson Cybil Shepherd

1994   DAVID'S MOTHER
Director: Robert Allan Ackerman
Co-stars: Sam Waterston Chris Sarandon Kirstie Alley

1996   SMOKE
Director: Wayne Wang
Co-stars: Harvey Keitel William Hurt Forest Whitaker

1996   UP CLOSE AND PERSONAL
Director: Jon Avnet
Co-stars: Robert Redford Michelle Pfeiffer

1996   THE FIRST WIVES CLUB
Director: Hugh Wilson
Co-stars: Goldie Hawn Diane Keaton Bette Midler

1997   MOLL FLANDERS
Director: Pen Densham
Co-stars: Robin Wright Morgan Freeman John Lynch

MARCHELLE CHANTAL

1937   ROMANCE IN FLANDERS
Director: Maurice Elvy
Co-stars: Paul Cavanagh Garry Marsh Alastair Sim

ROSALIND CHAO

1980   THE BIG BRAWL
Director: Robert Clous
Co-stars: Jackie Chan Jose Ferrer Mako

1980   SPIDERMAN: THE DRAGON'S CHALLENGE
Director: Don McDougall
Co-stars: Nicholas Hammond Benson Fong

1981   AN EYE FOR AN EYE
Director: Steve Carver
Co-stars: Chuck Norris Christopher Lee Mako

1983   THE TERRY FOX STORY
Director: Ralph Thomas
Co-stars: Eric Fryer Robert Duvall

1988   SHOOTER
Director: Gary Nelson
Co-stars: Jeffery Nordling Alan Rock Helen Hunt

1992   MEMOIRS OF AN INVISIBLE MAN
Director: John Carpenter
Co-stars: Chevy Chase Sam Neill Daryl Hannah

1993   THE JOY LUCK CLUB
Director: Wayne Wang
Co-stars: Kieu Chinh Tsai Chin France Nuyen

1994   WEB OF DECEPTION
Director: Richard Colla
Co-stars: Powers Booth Lisa Collins Pam Dawber

BAIRBRE NI CHAOIMH

1990   AUGUST SATURDAY
Director: Diarmuid Lawrence
Co-stars: Sorcha Cusack Tim McInnerney

GERALDINE CHAPLIN
(Daughter Of Charles Chaplin)

1965   DOCTOR ZHIVAGO
Director: David Lean
Co-stars: Omar Sharif Julie Christie Alec Guinness

1967 I KILLED RASPUTIN
Director: Robert Hossein
Co-stars: Gert Frobe Peter McEnery Ira Furstenberg

1970 THE HAWAIIANS
Director: Tom Gries
Co-stars: Charlton Heston Tina Chen John Phillip Law

1972 ZERO POPULATION GROWTH
Director: Michael Campus
Co-stars: Oliver Reed Diane Cilento

1972 INNOCENT BYSTANDERS
Director: Peter Collinson
Co-stars: Stanley Baker Dana Andrews

**1973 THE THREE MUSKETEERS:
THE QUEEN'S DIAMONDS**
Director: Richard Lester
Co-stars: Michael York Oliver Reed Raquel Welch

1974 THE FOUR MUSKETEERS
Director: Richard Lester
Co-stars: Frank Finlay Richard Chamberlain Raquel Welch

1975 NASHVILLE
Director: Robert Altman
Co-stars: Keith Carradine Karen Black Ned Beatty

1976 BUFFALO BILL AND THE INDIANS
Director: Robert Altman
Co-stars: Paul Newman Burt Lancaster Joel Grey

1976 WELCOME TO L. A.
Director: Alan Rudolph
Co-stars: Keith Carradine Sally Kellerman

1977 ROSELAND
Director: James Ivory
Co-stars: Teresa Wright Lou Jacobi Christopher Walken

1978 REMEMBER MY NAME
Director: Alan Rudolph
Co-stars: Anthony Perkins Moses Gunn Jeff Goldblum

1978 A WEDDING
Director: Rolbrt Altman
Co-stars: Carol Burnett Lillian Gish Amy Stryker

1980 THE MIRROR CRACK'D
Director: Guy Hamilton
Co-stars: Angela Lansbury Elizabeth Taylor Kim Novak

1981 BOLERO
Director: Claude Lelouch
Co-stars: James Caan Robert Hossein

1983 LIFE IS A BED OF ROSES
Director: Alain Resnais
Co-stars: Vittorio Gassman Fanny Ardant

1985 THE CORSICAN BROTHERS
Director: Ian Sharp
Co-stars: Trevor Eve Olivia Hussey Simon Ward

1984 L'AMOUR PAR TERRE
Director: Jacques Rivette
Co-stars: Jane Birkin Jean-Pierre Kalfon

1988 THE MODERNS
Director: Alan Rudolph
Co-stars: Keith Carradine Linda Fiorentino John Lone

1989 I WANT TO GO HOME
Director: Alain Resnais
Co-stars: Adolph Green Gerard Depardieu Linda Lavin

1990 THE CHILDREN
Director: Tony Palmer
Co-stars: Ben Kingsley Kim Novak Britt Ekland

1993 CHAPLIN
Director: Richard Attenborough
Co-stars: Robert Downey Kevin Kline

1993 A FOREIGN FIELD
Director: Charles Sturridge
Co-stars: Alec Guinness Lauren Bacall Leo McKern

1993 THE AGE OF INNOCENCE
Director: Martin Scorsese
Co-stars: Daniel Day-Lewis Michelle Phfeiffer Winona Ryder

1996 HOME FOR THE HOLIDAYS
Director: Jodie Foster
Co-stars: Holly Hunter Robert Downey Ann Bancroft

1996 GULLIVER'S TRAVELLS
Co-stars: Ted Danson Mary Steenburgen John Gielgud

CONSTANCE CHAPMAN

1971 A DAY IN THE DEATH OF JOE EGG
Director: Peter Medak
Co-stars: Alan Bates Janet Susman Sheila Gish

1974 IN CELEBRATION
Director: Lindsay Anderson
Co-stars: Alan Bates James Bolam Brian Cox Bill Owen

1979 LADY OSCAR
Director: Jacques Demy
Co-stars: Catriona MacColl Barry Stokes Christina Bohm

1985 LENT
Director: Peter Barber-Fleming
Co-stars: Harry Andrews Fabia Drake David Langton

1986 CLOCKWISE
Director: Christopher Morahan
Co-stars: John Cleese Penelope Wilton Alison Steadman

1988 RUN FOR THE LIFEBOAT
Director: Douglas Livingstone
Co-stars: Stacey Tendeter David Burke

EDYTHE CHAPMAN

1923 THE TEN COMMANDMENTS
Director: Cecil B. DeMille
Co-stars: Theodore Roberts Estelle Taylor Richard Dix

JANET CHAPMAN

1938 BROADWAY MUSKETEERS
Director: John Farrow
Co-stars: Ann Sheridan Marie Wilson Dick Purcell

1939 ON TRIAL
Co-stars: Margaret Lindsay John Litel

JUDITH CHAPMAN

1981 THE FIVE OF ME
Director: Paul Wendkos
Co-stars: David Birney Dee Wallace Mitchell Ryan

1987 AND GOD CREATED WOMAN
Director: Roger Vadim
Co-stars: Rebecca De Mornay Vincent Spano Frank Langella

MARGUERITE CHAPMAN

1932 MAN HUNT
Director: William Clemens
Co-stars: William Gargan Ricardo Cortez

1940 CHARLIE CHAN AT THE WAX MUSEUM
Director: Lynn Shores
Co-stars: Sidney Toler Sen Yung Marc Lawrence

1942 SUBMARINE RAIDER
Director: Lew Landers
Co-stars: John Howard Bruce Bennett Warren Ashe

1943 ONE DANGEROUS NIGHT
Director: Michael Gordon
Co-stars: Warren William Eric Blore Mona Barrie

1943   MY KINGDOM FOR A COOK
Director: Richard Wallace
Co-stars: Charles Coburn Isobel Elsom

1943   MURDER IN TIME SQUARE
Director: Lew Landers
Co-stars: Edmund Lowe Sidney Blackmer John Litel

1943   DESTROYER
Director: William Seiter
Co-stars: Edward G. Robinson Glenn Ford

1943   APPOINTMENT IN BERLIN
Director: Alfred Green
Co-stars: George Sanders Gale Sondergaard

1945   COUNTER-ATTACK
Director: Zoltan Korda
Co-stars: Paul Muni Larry Parks George Macready

1945   ONE WAY TO LOVE
Director: Ray Enrigrt
Co-stars: Willard Parker Chester Morris Hugh Herbert

1945   PARDON MY PAST
Director: Leslie Fenton
Co-stars: Fred MacMurray Akim Tamiroff Rita Johnson

1946   THE WALLS CAME TUMBLING DOWN
Director: Lothar Mendes
Co-stars: Lee Bowman George Macready

1948   RELENTLESS
Director: George Sherman
Co-stars: Robert Young Willard Parker

1948   GALLANT BLADE
Director: Henry Levin
Co-stars: Larry Parks George Macready Victor Jory

1948   CORONER CREEK
Director: Ray Enright
Co-stars: Randolph Scott George Macready Sally Eilers

1949   GREEN PROMISE
Director: William Russell
Co-stars: Walter Brennan Natalie Wood Robert Paige

1951   KANSAS RAIDERS
Director: Ray Enright
Co-stars: Audie Murphy Brian Donlevy Tony Curtis

1951   FLIGHT TO MARS
Director: Lesley Selander
Co-stars: Cameron Mitchell Arthur Franz

1952   BLOODHOUNDS OF BROADWAY
Director: Harmon Jones
Co-stars: Mitzi Gaynor Scott Brady Michael O'Shea

1952   THE LAST PAGE
Director: Terence Fisher
Co-stars: George Brent Diana Dors Raymond Huntley

1955   THE SEVEN YEAR ITCH
Director: Billy Wilder
Co-stars: Marilyn Monroe Tom Ewell Evelyn Keyes

JANET CHAPPELL

1970   THE VIRGIN AND THE GYPSY
Director: Christopher Miles
Co-stars: Joanna Shimkus Franco Nero

LISA CHAPPELL

1993   DESPERATE REMEDIES
Director: Stewart Main
Co-stars: Jennifer Ward-Lealand Cliff Curtis Kiri Mills

PATRICIA CHARBONNEAU

1985   DESERT HEARTS
Director: Donna Deitch
Co-stars: Helen Shaver Audra Lindley Andra Akers

1986   C. A. T. SQUAD - STALKING DANGER
Director: William Friedkin
Co-stars: Joe Cortese Jack Youngblood

1988   BLUE JEAN COP
Director: James Glickenhaus
Co-stars: Peter Weller Sam Elliott Antonio Fargas

1988   CALL ME
Director: Sollace Mitchell
Co-stars: Patti D'Arbanville Stephen McHattie Sam Freed

1988   DISASTER AT SILO SEVEN
Director: Larry Elikann
Co-stars: Perry King Ray Baker Peter Boyle

1989   DESPERADO: BADLANDS JUSTICE
Director: E. W. Swackhamer
Co-stars: Alex McArthur John Rhys-Davies

1990   ROBOCOP 2
Director: Irvin Kershner
Co-stars: Peter Weller Nancy Allen Dan O'Herlihy

1991   K2
Director: Franc Roddam
Co-stars: Michael Biehn Matt Craven Luca Bercovici

1991   THE OWL
Director: Tom Holland
Co-stars: Adrian Paul Brian Thompson Erika Flores

CYD CHARISSE
(Started Career As Lily Norwood) (Tula Elice Finklea)

1943   SOMETHING TO SHOUT ABOUT
Director: Gregory Ratoff
Co-stars: Don Ameche Janet Blair Perry Como

1944   ZIEGFELD FOLLIES
Director: Vincente Minnelli
Co-stars: William Powell Fred Astaire Gene Kelly

1946   THE HARVEY GIRLS
Director: George Sidney
Co-stars: Judy Garland Ray Bolger John Hodiak

1946   THREE WISE FOOLS
Director: Edward Buzzell
Co-stars: Margaret O'Brien Lionel Barrymore Edward Arnold

1947   THE UNFINISHED DANCE
Director: Henry Koster
Co-stars: Margaret O'Brien Danny Thomas Karin Booth

1947   FIESTA
Director: Richard Thorpe
Co-stars: Esther Williams Ricardo Montalban Mary Astor

1948   ON AN ISLAND WITH YOU
Director: Richard Thorpe
Co-stars: Jimmy Durante Peter Lawford Esther Williams

1948   THE KISSING BANDIT
Director: Laslo Benedek
Co-stars: Frank Sinatra Kathryn Grayson Ann Miller

1949   EAST SIDE, WEST SIDE
Director: Mervyn LeRoy
Co-stars: James Mason Barbara Stanwyck Ava Gardner

1950   TENSION
Director: John Berry
Co-stars: Richard Basehart Audrey Totter Barry Sullivan

1951   MARK OF THE RENEGADE
Director: Hugo Fregonese
Co-stars: Ricardo Montalban Gilbert Roland George Tobias

1951   THE WILD NORTH
Director: Andrew Marton
Co-stars: Stewart Granger Wendell Corey

1952   **SINGIN' IN THE RAIN**
Director: Gene Kelly
Co-stars: Gene Kelly Donald O'Connor Debbie Reynolds

1953   **SOMBRERO**
Director: Norman Foster
Co-stars: Ricardo Montalban Yvonne De Carlo Pier Angeli

1953   **THE BAND WAGON**
Director: Vincente Minnelli
Co-stars: Fred Astaire Jack Buchanan Oscar Levant

1954   **DEEP IN MY HEART**
Director: Stanley Donen
Co-stars: Jose Ferrer Merle Oberon Paul Henreid

1954   **BRIGADOON**
Director: Vincente Minnelli
Co-stars: Gene Kelly Van Johnson Elaine Stewart

1955   **IT'S ALWAYS FAIR WEATHER**
Director: Gene Kelly
Co-stars: Gene Kelly Dan Dailey Michael Kidd

1956   **MEET ME IN LAS VEGAS**
Director: Roy Rowland
Co-stars: Dan Dailey Agnes Moorehead Lena Horne

1957   **SILK STOCKINGS**
Director: Rouben Mamoulian
Co-stars: Fred Astaire Peter Lorre Janis Paige

1958   **PARTY GIRL**
Director: Nicholas Ray
Co-stars: Robert Taylor Lee J. Cobb John Ireland

1958   **TWILIGHT FOR THE GODS**
Director: Joseph Pevney
Co-stars: Rock Hudson Arthur Kennedy Richard Haydn

1960   **FIVE GOLDEN HOURS**
Director: Mario Zampi
Co-stars: Ernie Kovacs Kay Hammond George Sanders

1962   **TWO WEEKS IN ANOTHER TOWN**
Director: Vincente Minnelli
Co-stars: Edward G. Robinson Kirk Douglas

1966   **THE SILENCERS**
Director: Phil Karlson
Co-stars: Dean Martin Stella Stevens Dahlia Lavi

1967   **MAROC 7**
Director: Gerry O'Hara
Co-stars: Gene Barry Elsa Martinelli Leslie Phillips

1976   **WON TON TON THE DOG WHO SAVED HOLLYWOOD**
Director: Michael Winner
Co-stars: Madeline Kahn Art Carney Bruce Dern

1978   **WARLORDS OF ATLANTIS**
Director: Kevin Connor
Co-stars: Doug McClure Peter Gilmore Shane Rimmer

1989   **SWIMSUIT**
Director: Chris Thomson
Co-stars: William Katt Catharine Oxenberg Nia Peeples

JEANETTE CHARLES

1988   **THE NAKED GUN: FROM THE FILES OF POLICE SQUAD**
Director: David Zucker
Co-stars: Leslie Nielsen Priscilia Presley

MARIA CHARLES

1990   **THE FOOL**
Director: Christine Edzard
Co-stars: Derek Jacobi Cyril Cusack Ruth Mitchell

1991   **THE FALLOUT GUY**
Director: Paul Tickell
Co-stars: Lou Hirsch Amanda Boxer Joe Melia

KATE CHARLESON

1983   **TERMS OF ENDEARMENT**
Director: James Brooks
Co-stars: Shirley MacLaine Debra Winger Jack Nicholson

LESLIE CHARLESON

1993   **WOMAN ON THE LEDGE**
Director: Chris Thomson
Co-stars: Colleen Pink Zinter Josh Taylor Deidre Hall

CHARLITA

1953   **RIDE, VAQUERO**
Director: John Farrow
Co-stars: Robert Taylor Ava Gardner Howard Keel

ELSPETH CHARLTON

1990   **SOMETIME IN AUGUST**
Director: John Glenister
Co-stars: Crail Lorimar Tom Wilkinson Mary Morris

MELANIE CHARTOFF

1987   **KENNY ROGERS AS THE GAMBLER - THE LEGEND CONTINUES**
Director: Dick Lowry
Co-stars: Linda Gray Kenny Rogers Bruce Boxleitner

ANNAZETTE CHASE

1979   **GOLDIE AND THE BOXER**
Director: David Miller
Co-stars: O. J. Simpson Melissa Michaelson Phil Silvers

BARRIE CHASE

1958   **MARDI GRAS**
Director: Edmund Goulding
Co-stars: Pat Boone Christine Carere Sheree North

1961   **THE GEORGE RAFT STORY**
Director: Joseph Newman
Co-stars: Ray Danton Julie London Jayne Mansfield

1962   **CAPE FEAR**
Director: J.lee Thompson
Co-stars: Robert Mitchum Gregory Peck Polly Bergen

1965   **THE FLIGHT OF THE PHOENIX**
Director: Robert Aldrich
Co-stars: James Stewart Peter Finch Ian Bannen

ILKA CHASE

1930   **FAST AND LOOSE**
Director: Fred Newmeyer
Co-stars: Miriam Hopkins Carole Lombard Frank Morgan

1930   **THE FLORADORA GIRL**
Director: Harry Beaumont
Co-stars: Marion Davies Lawrence Gray Walter Catlett

1930   **LET'S GO PLACES**
Director: Frank Strayer
Co-stars: Joseph Wagstaff Lola Lane Dixie Lee

1930   **ONCE A SINNER**
Director: John Argyle
Co-stars: Dorothy MacKail Joel McCrea George Brent

1931   **THE GAY DIPLOMAT**
Director: Richard Boleslawski
Co-stars: Ivan Lebedeff Genevieve Tobin

1932   **THE ANIMAL KINGDOM**
Director: Edward Griffith
Co-stars: Leslie Howard Ann Harding Myrna Loy

1935   **SOAK THE RICH**
Director: Ben Hecht
Co-stars: Walter Connolly John Howard Mary Taylor

1936   **THE LADY CONSENTS**
Director: Stephen Roberts
Co-stars: Ann Harding Herbert Marshall Margaret Lindsay

1939   **STRONGER THAN DESIRE**
Director: Leslie Fenton
Co-stars: Walter Pidgeon Virginia Bruce Ann Dvorak

1942   **NOW VOYAGER**
Director: Irving Rapper
Co-stars: Bette Davis Claude Rains Paul Henreid

1943   **NO TIME FOR LOVE**
Director: Mitchell Leisen
Co-stars: Claudette Colbert Fred MacMurray June Havoc

1948   **MISS TATLOCK'S MILLIONS**
Director: Richard Haydn
Co-stars: John Lund Wanda Hendrix Monty Woolley

1954   **JOHNNY DARK**
Director: George Sherman
Co-stars: Tony Curtis Piper Laurie Don Taylor

1955   **THE BIG KNIFE**
Director: Robert Aldrich
Co-stars: Jack Palance Ida Lupino Shelley Winters

1960   **OCEAN'S ELEVEN**
Director: Lewis Milestone
Co-stars: Frank Sinatra Dean Martin Peter Lawford

LIBBIE CHASE
1977   **DRACULA'S DOG**
Director: Albert Band
Co-stars: Jose Ferrer Michael Pataki Jan Shutan

JEAN CHATBURN
1936   **THE GREAT ZIEGFELD**
Director: Ropert Z. Leonard
Co-stars: William Powell Luise Rainer Myrna Loy

1937   **BAD GUY**
Co-stars: Bruce Cabot Virginia Grey

RUTH CHATTERTON (*Married Ralph Forbes*)
Nominated For Best Actress In 1929 For "Madame X"

1929   **CHARMING SINNERS**
Director: Robert Milton
Co-stars: Clive Brook William Powell Florence Eldridge

1929   **MADAME X**
Director: Lionel Barrymore
Co-stars: Raymond Hackett Lewis Stone Sidney Toler

1930   **LADY OF SCANDAL**
Director: Sidney Franklin
Co-stars: Basil Rathbone Ralph Forbes Nance O'Neil

1930   **ANYBODY'S WOMAN**
Director: Dorothy Arzner
Co-stars: Clive Brook Paul Lukas Virginia Hammond

1930   **THE RIGHT TO LOVE**
Director: Richard Wallace
Co-stars: Paul Lukas David Manners Irving Pichel

1930   **SARAH AND SON**
Director: Dorothy Arzner
Co-stars: Fredric March Phillippe De Lacy Doris Lloyd

1930   **PARAMOUNT ON PARADE**
Director: Dorothy Arzner
Co-stars: Jean Arthur Clara Bow Gary Cooper

1931   **THE MAGNIFICENT LIE**
Co-stars: Charles Boyer Sam Hardy

1931   **ONCE A LADY**
Director: Guthrie McClintic
Co-stars: Ivor Novello Jill Esmond Geoffrey Kerr

1932   **THE RICH ARE ALWAYS WITH US**
Director: Alfred Green
Co-stars: George Brent John Miljan Bette Davis

1932   **TOMORROW AND TOMORROW**
Director: Richard Wallace
Co-stars: Paul Lukas Robert Ames Tad Alexander

1932   **THE CRASH**
Director: William Dieterle
Co-stars: George Brent Paul Cavanagh Barbara Leonard

1933   **FEMALE**
Director: Michael Curtiz
Co-stars: George Brent Johnny Mack Brown Ruth Donnelly

1933   **FRISCO JENNY**
Director: William Welllman
Co-stars: Louis Calhern Donald Cook J. Carrol Naish

1933   **LILLY TURNER**
Director: William Wellman
Co-stars: George Brent Frank McHugh Ruth Donnelly

1934   **JOURNAL OF A CRIME**
Director: William Keighley
Co-stars: Adolphe Menjou Claire Dodd George Barbier

1936   **LADY OF SECRETS**
Director: Marion Gering
Co-stars: Otto Kruger Lionel Atwill Lloyd Nolan

1936   **GIRL'S DORMITORY**
Director: Irving Cummings
Co-stars: Herbert Marshall Simone Simon Tyrone Power

1936   **DODSWORTH**
Director: William Wyler
Co-stars: Walter Huston Mary Astor David Niven Paul Lukas

1937   **THE RAT**
Director: Jack Raymond
Co-stars: Anton Walbrook Rene Ray Beatrix Lehman

1938   **A ROYAL DIVORCE**
Director: Jack Raymond
Co-stars: Pierre Blanchar Frank Cellier John Laurie

CHARLOTTE CHATTON
1990   **DAKOTA ROAD**
Director: Nick Ward
Co-stars: Jason Carter Rachel Scott Amelda Brown

EMMANUELLE CHAULET
1987   **MY GIRLFRIEND'S BOYFRIEND**
Director: Eric Rohmer
Co-stars: Sophie Renoir Eric Vieillard

MONIQUE CHAUMETTE
1984   **SUNDAY IN THE COUNTRY**
Director: Bertrand Tavernier
Co-stars: Louis Ducreux Sabine Azema

1987   **MASQUES**
Director: Claude Chabrol
Co-stars: Philippe Noiret Bernadette Lafont Robin Renucci

1988   **BEATRICE**
Director: Bernard Taverier
Co-stars: Bernard Pierre Donnadieu Julie Delphy

JACQUELINE CHAUVEAU
1971 LE SOUFFLE AU COEUR
Director: Louis Malle
Co-stars: Lea Massari Benoit Ferreux Daniel Gelin

INGRID CHAVEZ
1990 GRAFFITI BRIDGE
Director: Prince
Co-stars: Prince Morris Day Jerome Benton

ANDREA CHECCI
1949 BEYOND THE GATES
Director: Rene Clement
Co-stars: Jean Gabin Isa Miranda Vera Talchi

1960 THE MASK OF SATAN
Director: Mario Bava
Co-stars: Barbara Steele John Richardson Ivo Garrani

1961 THE ASSASSIN
Director: Elio Petrie
Co-stars: Marcello Mastroianni Micheline Presle

MOLLY CHEEK
1979 TORN BETWEEN TWO LOVERS
Director: Delbert Mann
Co-stars: Lee Remick Joseph Bologna George Peppard

MICHELEINE CHEIREL
1935 LA KERMESSE HEROIQUE
Director: Jacques Feyder
Co-stars: Francoise Rosay Louis Jouvet Jean Murat

1945 CORNERED
Director: Edward Dmytryk
Co-stars: Dick Powell Walter Slezak Morris Carnovsky

1946 SO DARK THE NIGHT
Director: Joseph Lewis
Co-stars: Steven Geray Ann Codee

1947 CRIME DOCTOR'S GAMBLE
Director: William Castle
Co-stars: Warner Baxter Steven Geray

ALIDA CHELLI
1966 THEY'RE A WEIRD MOB
Director: Michael Powell
Co-stars: Walter Chiari Clare Dunne Chips Rafferty

TSILLA CHELTON
1991 TATIE DANIELLE
Director: Etienne Chatiliez
Co-stars: Catherine Jacob Isabelle Nanty Eric Prat

JOAN CHEN
1986 TAI-PAN
Director: Daryl Duke
Co-stars: Bryan Brown John Stanton Tom Guinee

1987 THE LAST EMPEROR
Director: Bernardo Bertolucci
Co-stars: Peter O'Toole John Lone

1989 SALUTE OF THE JUGGLER
Director: David Peoples
Co-stars: Rutger Hauer Delroy Lindo Anna Katerina

1991 TURTLE BEACH
Director: Stephen Wallace
Co-stars: Greta Scacchi Jack Thompson Art Malik

1991 WEDLOCK
Director: Lewis Teague
Co-stars: Rutger Hauer Mimi Rogers James Remar

1993 HEAVEN AND EARTH
Director: Oliver Stone
Co-stars: Tommy Lee Jones Haing S. Ngor Debbie Reynolds

1994 GOLDEN GATE
Director: John Madden
Co-stars: Matt Dillon Bruno Kirby Teri Polo

1994 ON DEADLY GROUND
Director: Steven Seagal
Co-stars: Steven Seagal Michael Caine John C. McGinley

LILY CHEN
1991 CHILDREN OF THE DRAGON
Director: Peter Smith
Co-stars: Bob Peck Linda Cropper Gary Sweet

TINA CHEN
1969 ALICE'S RESTAURANT
Director: Arthur Penn
Co-stars: Arlo Guthrie Pat Quinn James Broderick

1970 THE HAWAIIANS
Director: Tom Gries
Co-stars: Charlton Heston Geraldine Chaplin Mako

1978 THE GHOST OF FLIGHT 401
Director: Steven Hilliard Stern
Co-stars: Ernest Borgnine Kim Basinger

1985 LADY FROM YESTERDAY
Director: Robert Day
Co-stars: Wayne Rogers Bonnie Bedelia Pat Hingle

CHER *(Cherilyn Sarkisian) (Married Sonny Bono)*
Oscar For Best Actress In 1987 For "Moonstruck"
Nominated For Best Supporting Actress In 1983 For "Silkwood"

1967 GOOD TIMES
Director: William Friedkin
Co-stars: Sonny Bono George Sanders Larry Duran

1982 COME BACK TO THE FIVE AND DIME, JIMMY DEAN JIMMY DEAN
Director: Robert Altman
Co-stars: Sandy Dennis Karen Black

1983 SILKWOOD
Director: Mike Nicholls
Co-stars: Meryl Streep Kurt Russell Fred Ward

1985 MASK
Director: Peter Bogdanovich
Co-stars: Eric Stoltz Richard Dysart Laura Dern

1987 SUSPECT
Director: Peter Yates
Co-stars: Liam Neeson Dennis Quaid John Mahoney

1987 MOONSTRUCK
Director: Norman Jewison
Co-stars: Nicolas Cage Danny Aiello Olympia Dukakis

1987 THE WITCHES OF EASTWICK
Director: George Miller
Co-stars: Susan Sarandon Michelle Pfeiffer Jack Nicholson

1990 MERMAIDS
Director: Richard Benjamin
Co-stars: Bob Hoskins Winona Ryder Christina Ricci

1992 THE PLAYER
Director: Robert Altman
Co-stars: Tim Robbins Greta Scacchi Whoopi Goldberg

1996 IF THESE WALLS COULD TALK
Co-stars: Sissy Spacek Demi Moore

VIRGINIA CHERRILL (MARRIED CARY GRANT)

1931 DELICIOUS
Director: David Butler
Co-stars: Janet Gaynor Charles Farrell El Brendel

1931 CITY LIGHTS
Director: Charles Chaplin
Co-stars: Charles Chaplin Florence Lee Harry Myers

1933 HE COULDN'T TAKE IT
Co-stars: Ray Walter Jane Darwell

HELEN CHERRY (Married Trevor Howard)

1947 THE COURTNEYS OF CURZON STREET
Director: Herbert Wilcox
Co-stars: Anna Neagle Michael Wilding

1950 MORNING DEPARTURE
Director: Roy Baker
Co-stars: John Mills Richard Attenborough Nigel Patrick

1950 LAST HOLIDAY
Director: Henry Cass
Co-stars: Alec Guinness Kay Walsh Beatrice Campbell

1950 THEY WERE NOT DIVIDED
Director: Terence Young
Co-stars: Edward Underdown Ralph Clanton

1950 THE WOMAN WITH NO NAME
Director: George More O'Ferrall
Co-stars: Phyllis Calvert Edward Underdown

1951 HIS EXCELLENCY
Director: Robert Hamer
Co-stars: Eric Portman Cecil Parker Susan Stephen

1951 YOUNG WIVES' TALE
Director: Henry Cass
Co-stars: Joan Greenwood Nigel Patrick Audrey Hepburn

1952 CASTLE IN THE AIR
Director: Henry Cass
Co-stars: David Tomlinson Barbara Kelly Margaret Rutherford

1957 HIGH FLIGHT
Director: John Gilling
Co-stars: Ray Milland Kenneth Haigh Anthony Newley

1962 THE DEVIL'S AGENT
Director: John Paddy Carstairs
Co-stars: Peter Van Eyck Marianne Koch

1969 HARD CONTACT
Director: S. Lee Pogostin
Co-stars: James Coburn Lilli Palmer Lee Remick

1974 ELEVEN HARROWHOUSE
Director: Aram Avakian
Co-stars: Charles Grodin James Mason Trevor Howard

1985 TIME AFTER TIME
Director: Bill Hays
Co-stars: Googie Withers Ursula Howells John Gielgud

ELIZABETH CHESHIRE

1980 MELVIN AND HOWARD
Director: Jonathan Demme
Co-stars: Paul Le Mat Jason Robards Jnr. Mary Steenburgen

1984 THE SEDUCTION OF MISS LEONA
Director: Joseph Hardy
Co-stars: Lynn Redgrave Anthony Zerbe

VANESSA LEE CHESTER (Child)

1996 A LITTLE PRINCESS
Director: Alfonso Cuaron
Co-stars: Liesel Matthews Eleanor Bron Liam Cunningham

1997 THE LOST WORLD: JURASSIC PARK
Director: Steven Spielberg
Co-stars: Jeff Goldblum Julianne Moore

MAGGIE CHEUNG

1986 POLICE STORY
Director: Jackie Chang
Co-stars: Jackie Chang Brigette Lin Bill Tung

ANNA CHEVALIER

1931 TABU
Director: Robert Flaherty
Co-stars: Matahi Hitu Kong Ah

LITA CHEVRET

1932 SYMPHONY OF SIX MILLION
Director: Gregory La Cava
Co-stars: Irene Dunne Ricardo Cortez Anna Appel

1937 SANDFIOW
Co-Star Buck Jones

KIM CHEW

1985 DIM SUM: A LITTLE BIT OF HEART
Director: Wayne Wang
Co-stars: Lauren Chew Victor Wong Cora Miao

LAUREN CHEW

1981 CHAN IS MISSING
Director: Wayne Wang
Co-stars: Wood Moy Marc Hayashi Peter Wang

1985 DIM SUM : A LITTLE BIT OF HEART
Director: Wayne Wang
Co-stars: Kim Chew Victor Wong Cora Miao

SHARON CHEYNE

1991 THE LAUGHTER OF GOD
Director: Tony Bicat
Co-stars: Peter Firth Amanda Donohoe Sylvia Syms

GRETA CHI

1967 FATHOM
Director: Leslie Martinson
Co-stars: Raquel Welch Tony Franciosa Clive Revill

MARISSA CHIBAS

1985 4 COLD FEET
Director: Bruce Van Dusen
Co-stars: Griffin Dunne Blanche Baker Joseph Leon

FLORINDA CHICO

1981 THE HOUSE OF BERNARDA ALBA
Director: Mario Camus
Co-stars: Irene Guiterrrez Cara Ana Belin

BARBARA CHILCOTT

1966 THE TRAP
Director: Sidney Hayers
Co-stars: Oliver Reed Rita Tushingham

1975   LIES MY FATHER TOLD ME
Director: Jan Kadar
Co-stars: Yossi Yadin Len Birman Marilyn Lightstone

KIRSTY CHILD

1975   PICNIC AT HANGING ROCK
Director: Peter Weir
Co-stars: Rachel Roberts Dominic Guard Helen Morse

KIRSTEN CHILDS

1989   SEE NO EVIL - HEAR NO EVIL
Director: Arthur Hiller
Co-stars: Richard Pryor Gene Wilder Kevin Spacey

TRACEY CHILDS

1980   SENSE AND SENSIBILITY
Director: Rodney Bennett
Co-stars: Irene Richard Diana Fairfax

LOIS CHILES

1973   THE WAY WE WERE
Director: Sydney Pollack
Co-stars: Barbra Streisand Robert Redford Patrick O'Neal

1974   THE GREAT GATSBY
Director: Jack Clayton
Co-stars: Robert Redford Mia Farrow Karen Black

1978   COMA
Director: Michael Crichton
Co-stars: Genevieve Bujold Michael Douglas Richard Widmark

1978   DEATH ON THE NILE
Director: John Guillermin
Co-stars: Peter Ustinov Bette Davis Mia Farrow

1979   MOONRAKER
Director: Lewis Gilbert
Co-stars: Roger Moore Michael Lonsdale Richard Kiel

1984   RAW COURAGE
Director: Robert Rosen
Co-stars: Ronny Cox Art Hindle M. Emmet Walsh

1986   SWEET LIBERTY
Director: Alan Aldla
Co-stars: Alan Aldla Michael Caine Michelle Pfeiffer

1987   CREEPSHOW 2
Director: Michael Gornick
Co-stars: George Kennedy Dorothy Lamour Tom Savini

1987   BROADCAST NEWS
Director: James Brooks
Co-stars: William Hurt Holly Hunter Jack Nicholson

1988   TWISTER
Director: Michael Almereyda
Co-stars: Harry Dean Stanton Suzy Amis Crispin Glover

1989   SAY ANYTHING
Director: Cameron Crowe
Co-stars: John Cusack Ione Skye Lili Taylor

1990   BURNING BRIDGES
Director: Sheldon Larry
Co-stars: Nick Mancuso Meredith Baxter

1992   OBSESSED
Director: Jonathon Sanger
Co-stars: William Devane Shannen Doherty Clare Carey

1992   DIARY OF A HIT MAN
Director: Roy London
Co-stars: Forest Whitaker Sherilyn Fenn Sharon Stone

1992   UNTIL THE END OF THE WORLD
Director: Wim Wenders
Co-stars: Solveig Dommartin William Hurt Sam Neill

1994   LUSH LIFE
Director: Michael Elias
Co-stars: Jeff Goldblum Forest Whitaker Kathy Baker

MAY CHIN

1993 THE WEDDING BANQUET
Director: Ang Lee
Co-stars: Winston Chao Mitchell Lichtenstein

TSAI CHIN

1965   INVASION
Director: Alan Bridges
Co-stars: Edward Judd Valerie Gearon Yoko Tani

1965   THE FACE OF FU MANCHU
Director: Don Sharp
Co-stars: Christopher Lee Nigel Green Karin Dor

1966   THE BRIDES OF FU MANCHU
Director: Don Sharp
Co-stars: Christopher Lee Douglas Wilmer

1967   VENGEANCE OF FU MANCHU
Director: Jeremy Summers
Co-stars: Christopher Lee Howard Marion Crawford

1967   YOU ONLY LIVE TWICE
Director: Lewis Gilbert
Co-stars: Sean Connery Tetsuro Tamba Karin Dor

1969   THE VIRGIN SOLIERS
Director: John Dexter
Co-stars: Hywel Bennett Nigel Patrick Lynn Redgrave

1993   THE JOY LUCK CLUB
Director: Wayne Wang
Co-stars: Kieu Chinh Tamlyn Tomita France Nuyen

KIEV CHINH

1990   VIETNAM, TEXAS
Director: Robert Ginty
Co-stars: Robert Ginty Haing S. Ngor Tim Thomerson

1993   THE JOY LUCK CLUB
Director: Wayne Wang
Co-stars: Tsai Chin Tamlyn Tomita France Nuyen

MELISSA CHIMENTI

1973   CHINO
Director: John Sturges
Co-stars: Charles Bronson Jill Ireland Vincent Van Patten

ANNA CHLUMSKY *(Child)*

1991   MY GIRL
Director: Howard Zieff
Co-stars: Dan Aykroyd Jaime Lee Curtis Macauley Culkin

1994   MY GIRL 2
Director: Howard Zieff
Co-stars: Dan Aykroyd Jaime Lee Curtis Christine Ebersole

1994   THE MOMMY MARKET
Director: Tia Brellis
Co-stars: Sissy Spacek Asher Metchick

CAROLYN CHOA

1991   TRULY, MADLY, DEEPLY
Director: Anthony Minghella
Co-stars: Juliet Stevenson Alan Rickman Bill Paterson

RAE DAWN CHONG
(Daughter Of Tommy Chong - Comedian)

1981   QUEST FOR FIRE
Director: Jean-Jacques Annaud
Co-stars: Everett McGill Ron Perlman

1984 BEAT STREET
Director: Stan Lathan
Co-stars: Guy Davis Jon Chardiet Leon W. Grant

1984 CHOOSE ME
Director: Alan Rudolph
Co-stars: Genevieve Bujold Lesley Ann Warren Keith Carradine

1984 FEAR CITY
Director: Abel Ferrara
Co-stars: Melanie Griffith Tom Berenger Rossano Brazzi

1985 AMERICAN FLYERS
Director: John Badham
Co-stars: Kevin Costner David Grant Janice Rule

1985 THE COLOR PURPLE
Director: Steven Spielberg
Co-stars: Whoopi Goldberg Danny Glover Oprah Winfrey

1985 BADGE OF THE ASSASSIN
Director: Mel Damski
Co-stars: James Woods Yaphet Kotto Alex Rocco

1985 CITY LIMITS
Director: Aaron Lipstadt
Co-stars: Darrell Larson John Stockwell Kim Cattrall

1985 COMMANDO
Director: Mark Lester
Co-stars: Arnold Schwarzenegger Dan Hedaya Vernon Wells

1986 SOUL MAN
Director: Steve Miner
Co-stars: C. Thomas Howell Melora Harding Leslie Nielsen

1987 THE SQUEEZE
Director: Roger Young
Co-stars: Michael Keaton Liane Langland John Davidson

1987 THE PRINCIPAL
Director: Christopher Cain
Co-stars: James Belushi Michael Wright Troy Winbush

1990 CURIOSITY KILLS
Director: Colin Bucksey
Co-stars: C. Thomas Howell

1990 TALES FROM THE DARKSIDE
Director: John Harrison
Co-stars: Deborah Harry Christian Slater Steve Buscemi

1991 PRISON STORIES: WOMEN ON THE INSIDE
Director: Donna Deitch
Co-stars: Lolita Davidovich Rachel Ticotin

1991 ON THE STREETS OF L.A.
Director: Georg Stanford Brown
Co-stars: Louis Gossett Jnr. Blair Underwood

1992 AMAZON
Director: Mika Kaurismaki
Co-stars: Kari Vaananen Robert Davi Aili Savio

SARITA CHOUDHURY

1991 MISSISSIPPI MASALA
Director: Mira Nair
Co-stars: Denzel Washington Roshan Seth Joe Seneca

1992 WILD WEST
Director: David Attwood
Co-stars: Naveen Andrews Ronny Jhutti Ravi Kapoor

CAROL CHRISTENSEN

1960 FRECKLES
Director: Andrew McLaglen
Co-stars: Martin West Jack Lambert Ken Curtis

1961 THE BIG SHOW
Director: James Clark
Co-stars: Esther Williams Cliff Robertson Nehemiah Persoff

CLAUDIA CHRISTIAN

1988 CLEAN AND SOBER
Director: Glenn Gordon Caron
Co-stars: Michael Keaton Kathy Baker Morgan Freeman

1988 THE HIDDEN
Director: Jack Sholder
Co-stars: Kyle McLachlan Michael Nouri

1988 POLICE STORY: MONSTER MANOR
Director: Aaron Lipstadt
Co-stars: Brian McNamara Clayton Rohner

1988 ARENA
Director: Peter Manoogian
Co-stars: Paul Satterfield Hamilton Camp

1990 DANIELLE STEEL'S KALEIDOSCOPE
Director: Jud Taylor
Co-stars: Jaclyn Smith Perry Green Donald Moffat

1990 MANIAC COP 2
Co-stars: William Lustig
Co-stars: Robert Davi Michael Lerner Bruce Campbell

1990 THINK BIG
Director: Jon Turteltaub
Co-stars: Peter Paul David Paul David Carradine

1991 LIES OF THE TWINS
Director: Tim Hunter
Co-stars: Aidan Quinn Isabella Rossellini

1993 HEXED
Director: Alan Spencer
Co-stars: Ayre Gross Adrienne Shelly Ray Baker

1993 MIND OF THE KILLER
Director: John Patterson
Co-stars: Tim Matheson Alberta Watson

1993 UPWORLD
Director: Stan Winston
Co-stars: Anthony Michael Hall Jerry Orbach

LINDA CHRISTIAN *(Married Tyrone Power)*

1947 GREEN DOLPHIN STREET
Director: Victor Saville
Co-stars: Lana Turner Van Heflin Donna Reed

1948 TARZAN AND THE MERMAIDS
Director: Robert Florey
Co-stars: Johnny Weismuller Brenda Joyce

1952 THE HAPPY TIME
Director: Richard Fleischer
Co-stars: Charles Boyer Bobby Driscoll Louis Jourdan

1952 BATTLE ZONE
Director: Lesley Selander
Co-stars: John Hodiak Stephen McNally Martin Milner

1954 ATHENA
Director: Richard Thorpe
Co-stars: Jane Powell Edmund Purdom Debbie Reynolds

1956 THUNDERSTORM
Director: John Guillermin
Co-stars: Carlos Thompson Charles Korvin

1959 HOUSE OF THE SEVEN HAWKS
Director: Richard Thorpe
Co-stars: Robert Taylor Nicole Maurey

1963 THE V.I.P. S
Director: Anthony Asquith
Co-stars: Richard Burton Elizabeth Taylor Margaret Rutherford

TINA CHRISTIANA

1973 BADGE 373
Director: Howard Koch
Co-stars: Robert Duvall Eddie Egan Verna Bloom

MADY CHRISTIANS

1934   **A WICKED WOMAN**
Director: Charles Brabin
Co-stars: Charles Bickford Betty Furness Robert Taylor

1935   **SHIP CAFE**
Director: Robert Florey
Co-stars: Carl Brisson Arline Judge William Frawley

1935   **ESCAPADE**
Director: Robert Z. Leonard
Co-stars: William Powell Luise Rainer Virginia Bruce

1936   **COME AND GET IT**
Director: Howard Hawks
Co-stars: Joel McCrea Frances Farmer Edward Arnold

1937   **SEVENTH HEAVEN**
Director: Henry King
Co-stars: James Stewart Simone Simon John Qualen

1937   **THE WOMAN BETWEEN**
Director: Anatole Litvak
Co-stars: Paul Muni Miriam Hopkins Louis Hayward

1937   **HEIDI**
Director: Allan Dwan
Co-stars: Shirley Temple Jean Hersholt Helen Westley

1943   **TENDER COMRADE**
Director: Edward Dmytryk
Co-stars: Ginger Rogers Robert Ryan Ruth Hussey

1944   **ADDRESS UNKNOWN**
Director: William Cameron Menzies
Co-stars: Paul Lukas Carl Esmond

1948   **ALL MY SONS**
Director: Irving Reis
Co-stars: Edward G. Robinson Burt Lancaster Howard Duff

1948   **LETTER FROM AN UNKNOWN WOMAN**
Director: Max Ophuls
Co-stars: Joan Fontaine Louis Jourdan Art Smith

AUDREY CHRISTIE

1942   **KEEPER OF THE FLAME**
Director: George Cukor
Co-stars: Spencer Tracey Katherine Hepburn Richard Whorf

1952   **DEADLINE U.S.A.**
Director: Richard Brooks
Co-stars: Humphrey Bogart Ethel Barrymore Kim Hunter

1956   **CAROUSEL**
Director: Henry King
Co-stars: Gordon MacRae Shirley Jones Cameron Mitchell

1961   **SPLENDOR IN THE GRASS**
Director: Elia Kazan
Co-stars: Natalie Wood Warren Beatty Pat Hingle

1964   **THE UNSINKABLE MOLLY BROWN**
Director: Charles Walters
Co-stars: Debbie Reynolds Harve Presnell Ed Begley

1966   **FRANKIE AND JOHNNY**
Director: Frederick De Cordova
Co-stars: Elvis Presley Donna Douglas Harry Morgan

1967   **THE BALLAD OF JOSIE**
Director: Andrew McLaglen
Co-stars: Doris Day Peter Graves George Kennedy

DOROTHY CHRISTIE

1931   **PARLOR, BEDROOM AND BATH**
Director: Edward Sedgewick
Co-Star   Buster Keaton

1934   **SONS OF THE DESERT**
Director: William Seiter
Co-stars: Stan Laurel Oliver Hardy Mae Busch

1947   **THE FABULOUS JOE**
Co-stars: Walter Abel Margot Grahame John Eldredge

HELEN CHRISTIE

1970   **LUST FOR A VAMPIRE**
Director: Jimmy Sanster
Co-stars: Ralph Bates Suzanna Leigh Barbara Jefford

JULIE CHRISTIE
Oscar For Best Actress In 1965 For "Darling"
Nominated For Best Actress In 1971 For "McCabe And Mrs. Miller"
Nominated For Best Actress In 1997 For "Afterglow"

1962   **CROOKS ANONYMOUS**
Director: Ken Annakin
Co-stars: Leslie Phillips Stanley Baxter Robertson Hare

1962   **THE FAST LADY**
Director: Ken Annakin
Co-stars: Leslie Phillips Stanley Baxter Kathleen Harrison

1963   **BILLY LIAR**
Director: John Schlesinger
Co-stars: Tom Courtenay Wilfred Pickles Leonard Rossiter

1964   **YOUNG CASSIDY**
Director: John Ford
Co-stars: Rod Taylor Maggie Smith Flora Robson

1965   **DARLING**
Director: John Schlesinger
Co-stars: Dirk Bogarde Laurence Harvey Roland Curram

1965   **DOCTOR ZHIVAGO**
Director: David Lean
Co-stars: Omar Sharif Rod Steiger Tom Courtenay

1966   **FAHRENHEIT 451**
Director: Francois Truffaut
Co-stars: Oskar Werner Cyril Cusack Jeremy Spenser

1967   **FAR FROM THE MADDING CROWD**
Director: John Schlesinger
Co-stars: Terence Stamp Peter Finch Alan Bates

1968   **PETULIA**
Director: Richard Lester
Co-stars: George C. Scott Richard Chamberlain Shirley Knight

1969   **IN SEARCH OF GREGORY**
Director: Peter Wood
Co-stars: Michael Sarazin John Hurt Roland Culver

1970   **THE GO-BETWEEN**
Director: Joseph Losey
Co-stars: Alan Bates Michael Redgrave Dominic Guard

1971   **McCABE AND MRS. MILLER**
Director: Robert Altman
Co-stars: Warren Beatty Shelley Duvall William Devane

1973   **DON'T LOOK NOW**
Director: Nicolas Roeg
Co-stars: Donald Sutherland Hilary Mason Massimo Serrato

1975   **SHAMPOO**
Director: Hal Ashby
Co-stars: Warren Beatty Lee Grant Goldie Hawn

1977   **DEMON SEED**
Director: Donald Cammell
Co-stars: Fritz Weaver Gerrit Graham Barry Kroeger

1978   **HEAVEN CAN WAIT**
Director: Warren Beatty
Co-stars: Warren Beatty James Mason Jack Warden

1981　THE ANIMALS FILM
Director:　Victor Schonfeld
Co-Star　Sandy Dennis

1981　MEMOIRS OF A SURVIVOR
Director:　David Gladwell
Co-stars:　Christopher Guard Nigel Hawthorne

1982　THE RETURN OF THE SOLDIER
Director:　Alan Bridges
Co-stars:　Alan Bates Ann-Margret Ian Holm

1982　HEAT AND DUST
Director:　James Ivory
Co-stars:　Greta Scacchi Christopher Cazenove Susan Fleetwood

1983　SEPARATE TABLES
Director:　John Schlesinger
Co-stars:　Alan Bates Claire Bloom Brian Deacon

1983　THE GOLD DIGGERS
Director:　Sally Potter
Co-stars:　Colette Laffont Hilary Westlake Tom Osbourne

1985　POWER
Director:　Sidney Lumet
Co-stars:　Richard Gere Gene Hackman Kate Capshaw

1986　MISS MARY
Director:　Maria Luisa Bemberg
Co-stars:　Nacha Guevara Luisina Brando

1990　FOOLS OF FORTUNE
Director:　Pat O'Connor
Co-stars:　Iain Glenn Niamh Cusack Michael Kitchen

1993　THE RAILWAY STATION MAN
Director:　Michael Whyte
Co-stars:　Donald Sutherland John Lynch Frank Maccusker

1996　DRAGONHEART *(Voice)*
Co-stars:　Dennis Quaid David Thewlis Sean Connery

1997　HAMLET
Director:　Kenneth Branagh
Co-stars:　Kate Winslet Derek Jacobi Richard Briers

1997　AFTERGLOW
Director:　Alan Rudolph
Co-stars:　Nick Nolte Lara Flynn Boyle Jonny Lee Miller

JUNE CHRISTIE

1975　NASHVILLE
Director:　Robert Altman
Co-stars:　Shelley Duvall Lily Tomlin Karen Black

MADELINE CHRISTIE

1987　THE DUNROAMIN' RISING
Director:　Moira Armstrong
Co-stars:　Russell Hunter Elizabeth Sellers

VIRGINIA CHRISTINE

1943　TRUCK BUSTERS
Co-stars:　Richard Travis Ruth Ford

1944　THE MUMMY'S CURSE
Director:　Leslie Goodwins
Co-stars:　Peter Coe Martin Kosleck Lon Chaney Jnr.

1946　THE KILLERS
Director:　Robert Siodmak
Co-stars:　Burt Lancaster Edmond O'Brien Ava Gardner

1948　NIGHT WIND

1955　NOT AS A STRANGER
Director:　Stanley Kramer
Co-stars:　Robert Mitchum Gloria Grahame Frank Sinatra

1956　NIGHTMARE
Director:　Maxwell Shane
Co-stars:　Edward G. Robinson Kevin McCarthy Connie Russell.

1956　INVASION OF THE BODY SNATCHERS
Director:　Don Siegel
Co-stars:　Kevin McCarthy Dana Wynter

1964　ONE MAN'S WAY
Director:　Denis Sanders
Co-stars:　Don Murray Diana Hyland Carol Ohmart

1967　GUESS WHO'S COMING TO DINNER
Director:　Stanley Kramer
Co-stars:　Spencer Tracy Katherine Hepburn

FRANCOISE CHRISTOPHE

1966　KING OF HEARTS
Director:　Philippe De Broca
Co-stars:　Alan Bates Genevieve Bujold Micheline Presle

1970　BORSALINO
Director:　Jacques Deray
Co-stars:　Alain Delon Jean-Paul Belmondo Michel Bouquet

PASCALE CHRISTOPHE

1974　PIAF - THE EARLY YEARS
Director:　Guy Casaril
Co-stars:　Brigitte Ariel Guy Trejean Pierre Vernier

KAY CHRISTOPHER

1947　DICK TRACY'S DILEMMA
Director:　John Rawlins
Co-stars:　Ralph Byrd Jack Lambert Ian Keith

ANN CHRISTY

1928　SPEEDY
Director:　Ted Wilde
Co-stars:　Harold Lloyd Brooks Benedict Babe Ruth

EILEEN CHRISTY

1952　I DREAM OF JEANNIE
Director:　Allan Dwan
Co-stars:　Ray Middleton Bill Shirley Muriel Lawrence

BELLE CHRYSTALL

1932　THE FRIGHTENED LADY
Director:　Hayes Hunter
Co-stars:　Cathleen Nesbit Emlyn Williams Gordon Harker

1933　FRIDAY THE THIRTEENTH
Director:　Victor Saville
Co-stars:　Jessie Matthews Max Miller Edmund Gwenn

1937　EDGE OF THE WORLD
Director:　Michael Powell
Co-stars:　Niall MacGinnis John Laurie Finlay Currie

1938　YELLOW SANDS
Director:　Herbert Brenon
Co-stars:　Marie Tempest Wilfrid Lawson Robert Newton

1939　POISON PEN
Director:　Paul Stein
Co-stars:　Flora Robson Robert Newton Ann Todd

1940　THE HOUSE OF THE ARROW
Director:　Harold French
Co-stars:　Kenneth Kent Diana Churchill Clifford Evans

DRU-ANN CHUKRON

1981　NEIGHBORS
Director:　John Avidsem
Co-stars:　John Belushi Dan Aykroyd Cathy Moriarty

IDA F.O.CHUNG
1985   DIM SUM: A LITTLE BIT OF HEART
Director: Wayne Wang
Co-stars: Lauren Chew Kim Chew Victor Wong

SANDRA CHURCH
1962   THE UGLY AMERICAN
Director: George Englund
Co-stars: Marlon Brando Eiji Okada Jocelyn Brando

DIANA CHURCHILL
1935   FOREIGN AFFAIRS
Director: Tom Walls
Co-stars: Tom Walls Roy Kellino Ralph Lynn

1936   POT LUCK
Director: Tom Walls
Co-stars: Tom Walls Robertson Hare Ralph Lynn

1936   SENSATION
Director: Brian Desmond Hurst
Co-stars: John Lodge Margaret Vyner Athene Seyler

1936   DISHONOUR BRIGHT
Director: Tom Walls
Co-stars: Tom Walls Eugene Pallette Betty Stockfield

1937   THE DOMINANT SEX
Director: Herbert Brenon
Co-stars: Phillips Holmes Carol Goodner Romney Brent

1937   SCHOOL FOR HUSBANDS
Director: Andrew Marton
Co-stars: Rex Harrison Henry Kendall June Clyde

1938   YES MADAM
Director: Norman Lee
Co-stars: Bobby Howes Billy Milton Fred Emney Bertha Belmore

1938   JANE STEPS OUT
Co-Star   Jean Muir

1938   HOUSEMASTER
Director: Herbert Brenon
Co-stars: Otto Kruger Phillips Holmes Rene Ray

1940   THE HOUSE OF THE ARROW
Director: Harold French
Co-stars: Kenneth Kent Clifford Evans Belle Chrystall

1940   LAW AND DISORDER
Director: David MacDonald
Co-stars: Barry K. Barnes Alastair Sim Edward Chapman

1940   THE SPIDER
Director: Maurice Elvey
Co-stars: Derrick De Marney Cecil Parker Jean Gillie

1948   SCOTT OF THE ANTARTIC
Director: Charles Frend
Co-stars: John Mills Derek Bond Kenneth More

MARGUERITE CHURCHILL
1930   THE BIG TRAIL
Director: Raoul Walsh
Co-stars: John Wayne El Brendel Tyrone Power Snr.

1930   BORN RECKLESS
Director: John Ford
Co-stars: Edmund Lowe Lee Tracy Warren Hymer

1930   HARMONY AT HOME
Co-stars: Rex Bell William Collier

1931   AMBASSADOR BILL
Director: Sam Taylor
Co-stars: Will Rogers Greta Missen Ray Milland

1931   CHARLIE CHAN CARRIES ON
Director: Hamilton McFadden
Co-stars: Warner Oland John Garrick Marjorie White

1931   QUICK MILLIONS
Director: Rowland Brown
Co-stars: Spencer Tracy Sally Eilers George Raft

1931   RIDERS OF THE PURPLE SAGE
Director: Hamilton McFadden
Co-stars: George O'Brien Noah Beery

1932   FORGOTTEN COMMANDMENTS
Director: Louis Gasnier
Co-stars: Gene Raymond Sari Maritza

1933   GIRL WITHOUT A ROOM

1936   DRACULA'S DAUGHTER
Director: Lambert Hillyer
Co-stars: Otto Kruger Gloria Holden Edward Van Sloan

1936   THE WALKING DEAD
Director: Michael Curtiz
Co-stars: Boris Karloff Edmund Gwenn Ricardo Cortez

1936   ALIBI FOR MURDER
Co-stars: William Gargan Egon Brocher Gene Morgan

SARAH CHURCHILL
(Daughter Of Winston Churchill, Married Vic Oliver)
1940   SPRING MEETING
Director: Walter Mycroft
Co-stars: Nova Pilbeam Basil Sydney Michael Wilding

1941   HE FOUND A STAR
Director: John Paddy Carstairs
Co-stars: Vic Oliver Joan Greenwood Evelyn Dall

1949   ALL OVER THE TOWN
Director: Derek Twist
Co-stars: Normand Wooland Fabia Drake Cyril Cusack

1950   ROYAL WEDDING
Director: Stanley Donen
Co-stars: Fred Astaire Jane Powell Peter Lawford

1959   SERIOUS CHARGE
Director: Terence Young
Co-stars: Anthony Quayle Andrew Ray Cliff Richard

IRIS CHURN
1990   AN ANGEL AT MY TABLE
Director: Jane Campion
Co-stars: Kerry Fox Alexia Keogh Karen Fergusson

DIANE CILENTO
(Married Sean Connery, Mother Of Jason Connery)
Nominated For Best Supporting Actress In 1963 For "Tom Jones"

1952   WINGS OF DANGER

1954   THE ANGEL WHO PAWNED HER HARP
Director: Alan Bromly
Co-stars: Felix Aylmer Sheila Sweet

1955   PASSAGE HOME
Director: Roy Baker
Co-stars: Peter Finch Anthony Steel Hugh Griffith

1957   THE ADMIRABLE CRIGHTON
Director: Lewis Gilbert
Co-stars: Kenneth More Cecil Parker Sally Ann Howes

1958   THE TRUTH ABOUT WOMEN
Director: Muriel Box
Co-stars: Julie Harris Mai Zetterling Eva Gabor

1959   JET STORM
Director: Cy Endfield
Co-stars: Mai Zetterling Virginia Maskell Stanley Baker

1960   THE FULL TREATMENT
Director: Val Guest
Co-stars: Ronald Lewis Claude Dauphin Bernard Braden

1961   THE NAKED EDGE
Director: Michael Anderson
Co-stars: Gary Cooper Deborah Kerr Michael Wilding

1962   I THANK A FOOL
Director: Robert Stevens
Co-stars: Peter Finch Susan Hayward Kieron Moore

1963   TOM JONES
Director: Tony Richardson
Co-stars: Albert Finney Hugh Griffith Susannah York

1963   THE THIRD SECRET
Director: Charles Crighton
Co-stars: Stephen Boyd Pamela Franklin Jack Hawkins

1964   RATTLE OF A SIMPLE MAN
Director: Muriel Box
Co-stars: Harry H. Corbett Thora Hird Charles Dyer

1965   THE AGONY AND THE ECSTACY
Director: Carol Reed
Co-stars: Rex Harrison Charlton Heston Harry Andrews

1967   HOMBRE
Director: Martin Ritt
Co-stars: Paul Newman Fredric March Richard Boone

1968   NEGATIVES
Director: Peter Medak
Co-stars: Glenda Jackson Peter McEnery Maurice Denham

1972   ZERO POPULATION GROWTH
Director: Michael Campus
Co-stars: Oliver Reed Geraldine Chaplin

1973   THE WICKER MAN
Director: Robin Hardy
Co-stars: Edward Woodward Britt Ekland Christopher Lee

1973   HITLER: THE LAST TEN DAYS
Director: Ennio De Concini
Co-stars: Alec Guinness Simon Ward Adolfo Celi

1984   THE BOY WHO HAD EVERYTHING
Director: Stephen Wallace
Co-stars: Jason Connery Laura Williams

JANA CILLIERS
1989   A PRIVATE LIFE
Director: Francis Gerard
Co-stars: Bill Flynn Kevin Smith Embeth Davidtz

KELLY CINNANTE
1989   TRUE LOVE
Director: Nancy Savoca
Co-stars: Annabella Sciorra Ron Eldard Aida Tutturro

1991   MORTAL THOUGHTS
Director: Alan Rudolph
Co-stars: Demi Moore Bruce Willis Glenne Headly

FLAMINIA CINQUE
1990   THE WIDOWMAKER
Director: John Madden
Co-stars: David Morrissey Annabelle Apsion Alun Armstrong

AUGUSTA CIOLLI
1955   MARTY
Director: Delbert Mann
Co-stars: Ernest Borgnine Betsy Blair Esther Minciotti

PATRICIA CISARANO
1983   SKYLINE
Director: Fernando Colomo
Co-stars: Antonio Resines Beatriz Perez-Porro

MARCELLA CISNEY
1951   HARD, FAST AND BEAUTIFUL
Director: Ida Lupino
Co-stars: Claire Trevor Sally Forrest Carleton Young

GABRIELLE CLAES
1982   ALL NIGHT LONG
Director: Chantal Akerman
Co-stars: Natalia Akerman Aurore Clement Paul Allio

NICOLE CLAFAN
1986   MAX, MON AMOUR
Director: Nagisa Oshima
Co-stars: Charlotte Rampling Anthony Higgins Victoria Abril

BERNICE CLAIRE
1930   NO, NO NANETTE
Co-Star   Alexander Gray

1930   SONG OF THE FLAME
Co-Star   Alexander Gray

1930   SPRING IS HERE
Co-Star   Alexander Gray

1931   KISS ME AGAIN
Director: William Seiter
Co-stars: Walter Pidgeon Frank McHugh Edward Everett Horton

INA CLAIRE
1930   THE ROYAL FAMILY OF BROADWAY
Director: George Cukor
Co-stars: Fredric March Mary Brian Frank Conroy

1931   REBOUND
Director: E. H. Griffith
Co-stars: Robert Williams Myrna Loy Robert Ames

1932   THE GREEKS HAD A WORD FOR THEM
Director: Lowell Sherman
Co-stars: Lowell Sherman Joan Blondell Madge Evans

1939   NINOTCHKA
Director: Ernst Lubitsch
Co-stars: Greta Garbo Melvyn Douglas Felix Bressart

1943   CLAUDIA
Director: Edmund Goulding
Co-stars: Dorothy McGuire Robert Young Reginald Gardiner

JENNIFER CLAIRE
1986   THE GOOD WIFE
Director: Ken Cameron
Co-stars: Rachel Ward Bryan Brown Sam Neill

MARION CLAIRE
1937   MAKE A WISH
Director: Kurt Neuman
Co-stars: Basil Rathbone Bobby Breen Ralph Forbes

AIME CLARIOND
1938   LES DISPARUS DE ST. AGIL
Director: Christian-Jacques
Co-stars: Michel Simon Erich Von Stroheim

1946   L'HOMME AU CHAPEAU ROND
Director: Pierre Billon
Co-stars: Raimu Lucy Valnor

1947   MONSIEUR VINCENT
Director: Maurice Cloche
Co-stars: Pierre Fresnay Lise Delamare

COLLEEN CLARE

1937 WE'RE ON THE JURY
Director: Ben Holmes
Co-stars: Helen Broderick Victor Moore Louise Latimer

DIANE CLARE

1958 ICE COLD IN ALEX
Director: J. Lee Thompson
Co-stars: John Mills Sylvia Syms Anthony Quayle

1958 THE RELUCTANT DEBUTANTE
Director: Vincente Minnelli
Co-stars: Rex Harrison Kay Kendall Sandra Dee

1965 THE PLAGUE OF THE ZOMBIES
Director: John Gilling
Co-stars: Andre Morrell John Carson

1966 THE HAND OF NIGHT
Director: Frederick Goode
Co-stars: William Sylvester Edward Underdown

1967 THE VULTURE
Director: Lawrence Huntingdon
Co-stars: Robert Hutton Akim Tamiroff Broderick Crawford

IMOGEN CLARE

1988 THE LAIR OF THE WHITE WORM
Director: Ken Russell
Co-stars: Amanda Donohoe Hugh Grant Sammi Davis

1990 I HIRED A CONTRACT KILLER
Director: Aki Kaurismaki
Co-stars: Jean-Pierre Leaud Margi Clarke

MARY CLARE

1931 KEEPERS OF YOUTH
Director: Thomas Bentley
Co-stars: Garry Marsh Ann Todd Robin Irvine

1931 THE OUTSIDER
Director: Harry Lachman
Co-stars: Harold Huth Joan Barry Frank Lawton

1933 THE CONSTANT NYMPH
Director: Basil Dean
Co-stars: Victoria Hopper Jane Baxter Brian Aherne

1934 THE CLAIRVOYANT
Director: Maurice Elvey
Co-stars: Claude Rains Fay Wray Jane Baxter

1934 LORNA DOONE
Director: Basil Dean
Co-stars: Victoria Hopper John Loder Margaret Lockwood

1935 THE PASSING OF THE THIRD FLOOR BACK
Director: Berthold Viertel
Co-stars: Conrad Veidt Rene Ray

1935 THE GUV'NOR
Director: Milton Rosmer
Co-stars: George Arliss Gene Gerrard Viola Keats

1937 THE MILL ON THE FLOSS
Director: Tim Whelan
Co-stars: Geraldine Fitzgerald Victoria Hopper James Mason

1937 THE RAT
Director: Jack Raymond
Co-stars: Anton Walbrook Ruth Chatterton Rene Ray

1937 YOUNG AND INNOCENT
Director: Alfred Hitchcock
Co-stars: Nova Pilbeam Derrick De Marney Basil Radford

1938 CLIMBING HIGH
Director: Carol Reed
Co-stars: Jessie Matthews Michael Redgrave Alastair Sim

1938 THE LADY VANISHES
Director: Alfred Hitchcock
Co-stars: Margaret Lockwood Michael Redgrave May Whitty

1938 THE CHALLENGE
Director: Luis Trenker
Co-stars: Luis Trenker Robert Douglas Joan Gardner

1939 MRS. PYM OF SCOTLAND YARD
Director: Fred Elles
Co-stars: Edward Lexy Nigel Patrick Anthony Ireland

1939 A GIRL MUST LIVE
Director: Carol Reed
Co-stars: Margaret Lockwood Lilli Palmer Hugh Sinclair

1939 ON THE NIGHT OF THE FIRE
Director: Brian Desmond Hurst
Co-stars: Ralph Richardson Diana Wynyard

1939 THERE AIN'T NO JUSTICE
Director: Pen Tennyson
Co-stars: Jimmy Hanley Edward Rigby Phyllis Stanley

1940 OLD BILL AND SON
Director: Ian Dalrymple
Co-stars: Morland Graham John Mills Renee Houston

1941 THIS MAN IS DANGEROUS
Director: Lawrence Huntington
Co-stars: James Mason Margaret Vyner

1942 THE NIGHT HAS EYES
Director: Leslie Arliss
Co-stars: James Mason Joyce Howard Wilfrid Lawson

1942 NEXT OF KIN
Director: Thorold Dickinson
Co-stars: Nova Pilbeam Mervyn Johns Basil Radford

1943 THEY MET IN THE DARK
Director: Karel Lamac
Co-stars: James Mason Joyce Howard David Farrar

1943 THE HUNDRED POUND WINDOW
Director: Brian Desmond Hurst
Co-stars: Frederick Leister Anne Crawford

1944 FIDDLERS THREE
Director: Harry Watt
Co-stars: Tommy Trinder Sonnie Hale Diana Decker

1944 ONE EXCITING NIGHT
Director: Walter Forde
Co-stars: Vera Lynn Donald Stewart Frederick Leister

1946 LONDON TOWN
Director: Wesley Ruggles
Co-stars: Sid Field Greta Gynt Kay Kendall

1947 ESTHER WATERS
Director: Ian Dalrymple
Co-stars: Kathleen Ryan Dirk Bogarde Morland Graham

1948 OLIVER TWIST
Director: David Lean
Co-stars: Alec Guinness Robert Newton John Howard Davies

1948 THE THREE WEIRD SISTERS
Director: Dan Birt
Co-stars: Nancy Price Mary Merrall Nova Pilbeam

1949 CARDBOARD CAVALIER
Director: Walter Forde
Co-stars: Sid Field Margaret Lockwood Claude Hulbert

1950 PORTRAIT OF CLARE
Director: Lance Comfort
Co-stars: Margaret Johnston Richard Todd Robin Bailey

1952 THE BEGGAR'S OPERA
Director: Peter Brook
Co-stars: Laurence Olivier Dorothy Tutin Stanley Holloway

1952　PENNY PRINCESS
Director:　Val Guest
Co-stars:　Dirk Bogarde Yolande Donlan Anthony Oliver

1952　MOULIN ROUGE
Director:　John Huston
Co-stars:　Jose Ferrer Colette Marchand Zsa Zsa Gabor

1954　MAMBO
Director:　Robert Rossen
Co-stars:　Silvana Mangano Michael Rennie Shelley Winters

PHYLLIS CLARE

1933　AUNT SALLY
Director:　Tim Whelan
Co-stars:　Cicely Courtneidge Sam Hardy Billy Milton

BETSY CLARK

1993　BOXING HELENA
Director:　Jennifer Chambers Lynch
Co-stars:　Julian Sands Sherilyn Fenn Bill Paxton

CANDY CLARK
Nominated For Best Supporting Actress In 1973 For "American Graffiti"

1972　FAT CITY
Director:　John Huston
Co-stars:　Stacy Keach Jeff Bridges Susan Tyrrell

1973　AMERICAN GRAFFITI
Director:　George Lucas
Co-stars:　Richard Dreyfuss Ron Howard Cindy Williams

1975　I WILL......I WILL......FOR NOW
Director:　Norman Panama
Co-stars:　Elliott Gould Diane Keaton Paul Sorvino

1976　THE MAN WHO FELL TO EARTH
Director:　Nicolas Roeg
Co-stars:　David Bowie Rip Torn Buck Henry

1977　CITIZENS' BAND
Director:　Jonathan Demme
Co-stars:　Paul Lemat Charles Napier Marcia Rodd

1978　THE BIG SLEEP
Director:　Michael Winner
Co-stars:　Robert Mitchum Sarah Miles James Stewart

1979　MORE AMERICAN GRAFFITI
Director:　B. W. Norton
Co-stars:　Bo Hopkins Ron Howard Paul Lemat

1981　NATIONAL LAMPOON'S MOVIE MADNESS
Director:　Henry Jaglom
Co-stars:　Robby Benson Richard Widmark Diane Lane

1982　Q-THE WINGED SERPENT
Director:　Larry Cohen
Co-stars:　Michael Moriarty David Carradine Richard Roundtree

1982　JOHNNY BELINDA
Director:　Anthony Harvey
Co-stars:　Richard Thomas Rosanna Arquette Dennis Quaid

1983　HAMBONE AND HILLIE
Director:　Roy Watts
Co-stars:　Lillian Gish Timothy Bottoms Robert Walker

1983　BLUE THUNDER
Director:　John Badham
Co-stars:　Roy Scheider Warren Oates Malcolm McDowell

1984　AMITYVILLE 3D
Director:　Richard Fleischer
Co-stars:　Tony Roberts Tess Harper Meg Ryan

1985　CAT'S EYE
Director:　Lewis Teague
Co-stars:　Drew Barrymore James Woods Alan King

1986　AT CLOSE RANGE
Director:　James Foley
Co-stars:　Sean Penn Christopher Walken Millie Perkins

1988　THE BLOB
Director:　Chuck Russell
Co-stars:　Shawnee Smith Kevin Dillon Donovan Leitch

CAROLYN ANN CLARK

1983　THE CRADLE WILL FALL
Director:　John Llewellyn Moxey
Co-stars:　Lauren Hutton Ben Murphy

CONNIE CLARK

1995　THE OTHER MOTHER
Director:　Bethany Booney
Co-stars:　Francis Fisher Deborah May

DORAN CLARK

1982　TOO FAR TO GO
Director:　Fielder Cook
Co-stars:　Michael Moriarty Blythe Danner Glenn Close

JUDY CLARK

1944　MINSTREL MAN
Director:　Joseph Lewis
Co-stars:　Benny Fields Gladys George Roscoe Karns

1944　BEAUTIFUL BUT BROKE
Director:　Charles Barton
Co-stars:　Joan Davis Jane Frazee John Hubbard

LIDDY CLARK

1978　BLUE FIN
Director:　Carl Schultz
Co-stars:　Hardy Kruger Greg Rowe John Jarrett

1982　KITTY AND THE BAGMAN
Director:　Donald Crombie
Co-stars:　John Stanton Val Lehman Collette Mann

MAMO CLARK

1940　MAN AND HIS MATE
Director:　Hal Roach
Co-stars:　Victor Mature Carole Landis John Hubbard

MARILYN CLARK

1962　TOO LATE BLUES
Director:　John Cassavetes
Co-stars:　Bobby Darin Stella Stevens Seymour Cassel

MARLENE CLARK

1974　THE BEAST MUST DIE
Director:　Paul Annett
Co-stars:　Calvin Lockhart Peter Cushing Charles Gray

MARY KAI CLARK

1977　9/30/55
Director:　James Bridges
Co-stars:　Richard Thomas Susan Tyrrell Lisa Blount

PETULA CLARK (Child)

1944　MEDAL FOR THE GENERAL
Director:　Maurice Elvey
Co-stars:　Godfrey Tearle Jeanne De Casalais John Laurie

1944　STRAWBERRY ROAN
Director:　Maurice Elvey
Co-stars:　William Hartnell Carol Raye Walter Fitzgerald

1945　I KNOW WHERE I'M GOING
Director:　Michael Powell
Co-stars:　Wendy Hiller Roger Livesey Pamela Browne

1946 LONDON TOWN
Director: Wesley Ruggles
Co-stars: Sid Field Greta Gynt Kay Kendall

1947 VICE VERSA
Director: Peter Ustinov
Co-stars: Roger Livesey Anthony Newley Kay Walsh

1948 HERE COME THE HUGGETTS
Director: Ken Annakin
Co-stars: Jack Warner Kathleen Harrison Susan Shaw

1948 EASY MONEY
Director: Bernard Knowles
Co-stars: Jack Warner Mervyn Johns Dennis Price

1949 VOTE FOR HUGGETT
Director: Ken Annakin
Co-stars: Jack Warner David Tomlinson Diana Dors

1949 THE HUGGETTS ABROAD
Director: Ken Annakin
Co-stars: Jack Warner Dinah Sheridan Jimmy Hanley

1949 DON'T EVER LEAVE ME
Director: Arthur Crabtree
Co-stars: Jimmy Hanley Edward Rigby Hugh Sinclair

1949 THE ROMANTIC AGE
Director: Edmond Greville
Co-stars: Hugh Williams Mai Zetterling Margot Grahame

1950 DANCE HALL
Director: Charles Crighton
Co-stars: Natasha Parry Jane Hylton Bonar Colleano

1951 WHITE CORRIDORS
Director: Pat Jackson
Co-stars: James Donald Googie Withers Godfrey Tearle

1952 MADE IN HEAVEN
Director: John Paddy Carstairs
Co-stars: David Tomlinson Richard Wattis

1952 THE CARD
Director: Ronald Neame
Co-stars: Alec Guinness Glynis Johns Valerie Hobson

1954 THE GAY DOG
Director: Maurice Elvey
Co-stars: Wilfred Pickles Megs Jenkins John Blythe

1954 THE HAPPINESS OF THREE WOMEN
Director: Maurice Elvey
Co-stars: Eynon Evans Brenda De Banzie

1954 THE RUNAWAY BUS
Director: Val Guest
Co-stars: Frankie Howerd Margaret Rutherford Belinda Lee

1957 THAT WOMAN OPPOSITE
Director: Compton Bennett
Co-stars: Dan O'Herlihy Phyllis Kirk Jack Watling

1958 6:5 SPECIAL
Director: Alfred Shaughnessy
Co-stars: Pete Murray Josephine Douglas Diane Todd

1968 FINIAN'S RAINBOW
Director: Francis Ford Coppola
Co-stars: Fred Astaire Tommy Steele Don Francks

1969 GOODBYE, MR. CHIPS
Director: Herbert Ross
Co-stars: Peter O'Toole Michael Bryant Michael Redgrave

SUSAN CLARK

1967 BANNING
Director: Dick Berg
Co-stars: Robert Wagner Anjannette Comer Jill St. John

1968 MADIGAN
Director: Don Siegel
Co-stars: Richard Widmark Henry Fonda Michael Dunne

1968 COOGAN'S BLUFF
Director: Don Siegel
Co-stars: Clint Eastwood Lee J. Cobb Betty Field

1969 THE FORBIN PROJECT
Director: Joseph Sargent
Co-stars: Eric Braeden Gordon Pinsent William Schallert

1969 SKULDUGGERY
Director: Gordon Douglas
Co-stars: Burt Reynolds Chips Rafferty Edward Fox

1969 TELL THEM WILLIE BOY IS HERE
Director: Abraham Polonsky
Co-stars: Robert Redford Robert Blake

1970 VALDEZ IS COMING
Director: Edwin Sherrin
Co-stars: Burt Lancaster Jon Cypher Frank Silvera

1971 THE SKIN GAME
Director: Paul Bogart
Co-stars: James Garner Lou Gossett Brenda Sykes

1973 SHOWDOWN
Director: George Seaton
Co-stars: Rock Hudson Dean Martin Donald Moffat

1973 TRAPPED
Director: Frank DeFilitta
Co-stars: James Brolin Earl Holliman Robert Hooks

1974 AIRPORT 75
Director: Jack Smight
Co-stars: Charlton Heston Karen Black George Kennedy

1974 THE MIDNIGHT MAN
Director: Burt Lancaster
Co-stars: Burt Lancaster Cameron Mitchell Joan Lorring

1975 NIGHT MOVES
Director: Arthur Penn
Co-stars: Gene Hackman Jennifer Warren James Woods

1975 THE APPLE DUMPLING GANG
Director: Norman Tokar
Co-stars: Bill Bixby David Wayne Don Knotts

1978 MURDER BY DECREE
Director: Bob Clark
Co-stars: Christopher Plummer James Mason John Gielgud

1979 THE NORTH AVENUE IRREGULARS
Director: Bruce Bilson
Co-stars: Edward Herrman Patsy Kelly Alan Hale

1979 HILL'S ANGELS
Director: Bruce Bilson
Co-stars: Edward Herrman Babara Harris Michael Constantine

1979 PROMISES IN THE DARK
Director: Jerome Hellman
Co-stars: Marsha Mason Ned Beatty Michael Brandon

1979 CITY ON FIRE
Director: Alvin Rakoff
Co-stars: Barry Newman Henry Fonda Shelley Winters

1980 DOUBLE NEGATIVE
Director: George Bloomfield
Co-stars: Michael Sarrazin Anthony Perkins Howard Duff

1981 PORKY'S
Director: Bob Clark
Co-stars: Dan Monahan Mark Herrier Kim Cattrall

1982 MAID IN AMERICA
Director: Paul Aaron
Co-stars: Alex Karras Fritz Weaver Mildred Natwick

1993   **SNOWBOUND: THE JIM AND JENNIFER STOLPA STORY**
Director: Christian Duguay
Co-stars: Neil Patrick Harris Michael Gross

1995   **BUTTERBOX BABIES**
Director: Don McBrearty
Co-stars: Peter McNeil Catherine Fitch Cedric Smith

TRILBY CLARK

1930   **HARMONY HEAVEN**
Director: Thomas Bentley
Co-stars: Polly Ward Stuart Hall Jack Raine

ANGELA CLARKE (U.S.A.)

1949   **MRS. MIKE**
Director: Louis King
Co-stars: Dick Powell Evelyn Keyes

1950   **CAPTAIN CAREY U.S.A.**
Director: Mitchell Leisen
Co-stars: Alan Ladd Wanda Hendrix Francis Lederer

1952   **THE MIRACLE OF OUR LADY OF FATIMA**
Director: John Brahm
Co-stars: Gilbert Roland Frank Silvera

1953   **HOUDINI**
Director: George Marshall
Co-stars: Tony Curtis Janet Leigh Torin Thatcher

1953   **BENEATH THE 12 MILE REEF**
Director: Robert Webb
Co-stars: Robert Wagner Terry Moore Gilbert Roland

1955   **SEVEN LITTLE FOYS**
Director: Melville Shavelson
Co-stars: Bob Hope George Tobias Milly Vitale

ANGELA CLARKE (U.K.)

1990   **DANCIN' THRU THE DARK**
Director: Mike Ockrent
Co-stars: Claire Hackett Con O'Neill Julia Deakin

1991   **BLONDE FIST**
Director: Frank Clarke
Co-stars: Margi Clarke Carroll Baker Ken Hutchison

1991   **BERNARD AND THE GENIE**
Director: Paul Weitland
Co-stars: Lenny Henry Rowan Atkinson Alan Cummings

CAITLIN CLARKE

1981   **DRAGONSLAYER**
Director: Matthew Robbins
Co-stars: Peter MacNichol Ralph Richardson

1987   **MAYFLOWER MADAM**
Director: Lou Antonio
Co-stars: Candice Bergen Chris Sarandon Chita Rivera

1994   **BLOWN AWAY**
Director: Stephen Hopkins
Co-stars: Jeff Bridges Lloyd Bridges Tommy Lee Jones

HOPE CLARKE

1977   **A PIECE OF THE ACTION**
Director: Sidney Poitier
Co-stars: Sidney Poitier Bill Cosby James Earl Jones

LYDIA CLARKE

1952   **THE ATOMIC CITY**
Director: Jerry Hopper
Co-stars: Gene Barry Lee Aaker Nancy Gates

MAE CLARKE *(Mary Klotz)*

1929   **BIG TIMES**

1929   **NIX ON DAMES**

1930   **THE FALL GUY**
Co-stars: Alan Roscoe Wynne Gibson Pat O'Malley

1931   **SEED**
Director: John Stahl
Co-stars: John Boles Genevieve Tobin Bette Davis

1931   **FRANKENSTEIN**
Director: James Whale
Co-stars: John Boles Colin Clive Boris Karloff

1931   **RECKLESS LIVING**
Co-stars: Ricardo Cortez Matt McHugh

1931   **THE PUBLIC ENEMY**
Director: William Wellman
Co-stars: James Cagney Jean Harlow Joan Blondell

1931   **THE FRONT PAGE**
Director: Lewis Milestone
Co-stars: Adolphe Menjou Pat O'Brien Mary Brian

1931   **WATERLOO BRIDGE**
Director: James Whale
Co-stars: Douglass Montgomery Enid Bennett Bette Davis

1932   **THREE WISE GIRLS**
Director: William Beaudine
Co-stars: Jean Harlow Marie Prevost Andy Devine

1932   **PENGUIN POOL MURDER**
Director: George Archainbaud
Co-stars: Edna May Oliver James Gleason Donald Cook

1932   **NIGHT WORLD**
Director: Hobart Henley
Co-stars: Lew Ayres Boris Karloff George Raft

1932   **THE IMPATIENT MAIDEN**
Director: James Whale
Co-stars: Lew Ayres Una Merkel John Halliday

1932   **THE FINAL EDITION**
Co-Star   Bradley Page

1933   **TURN BACK THE CLOCK**
Co-stars: Lee Tracy Peggy Shannon C. Henry Gordon

1933   **FAST WORKERS**
Director: Todd Browning
Co-stars: John Gilbert Robert Armstrong

1933   **PENTHOUSE**
Director: W. S. Van Dyke
Co-stars: Warner Baxter Myrna Loy Phillips Holmes

1933   **LADY KILLER**
Director: Roy Del Ruth
Co-stars: James Cagney Margaret Lindsay

1934   **THE MAN WITH TWO FACES**
Director: Archie Mayo
Co-stars: Edward G. Robinson Mary Astor Ricardo Cortez

1934   **THIS SIDE OF HEAVEN**
Director: William Howard
Co-stars: Lionel Barrymore Fay Bainter Una Merkel

1934   **NANA**
Director: Dorothy Arzner
Co-stars: Anna Sten Phillips Holmes Lionel Atwill

1934   **FLAMING GOLD**
Co-Star   Pat O'Brien

1935   **THE SILK HAT KID**
Director: Bruce Humberstone
Co-stars: Lew Ayres Paul Kelly Ralf Harolde

1935 HITCH-HIKE LADY
Director: Aubrey Scotto
Co-stars: Alison Skipworth Arthur Treacher

1936 WILD BRIAN KENT
Director: Howard Bretherton
Co-stars: Ralph Bellamy Stanley Andrews Lew Kelly

1936 GREAT GUY
Director: John Blystone
Co-stars: James Cagney James Burke Edward Brophy

1936 HATS OFF
Co-Star John Payne

1936 THE HOUSE OF A THOUSAND CANDLES
Co-stars: Phillips Holmes Irving Pichel

1936 HEARTS IN BONDAGE

1942 FLYING TIGERS
Director: David Miller
Co-stars: John Wayne John Carroll Anna Lee

1942 WOMEN IN WAR
Director: John Auer
Co-stars: Elsie Janis Wendy Barrie Patric Knowles

1944 HERE COME THE WAVES
Director: Mark Sandrich
Co-stars: Bing Crosby Betty Hutton Sonny Tufts

1948 DAREDEVILS OF THE CLOUDS
Co-stars: Robert Livingstone

1950 ANNIE GET YOUR GUN
Director: George Sidney
Co-stars: Betty Hutton Howard Keel Edward Arnold

1951 THE GREAT CARUSO
Director: Richard Thorpe
Co-stars: Mario Lanza Ann Blyth Dorothy Kirsten

1952 SINGIN' IN THE RAIN
Director: Stanley Donen
Co-stars: Gene Kelly Donald O'Connor Debbie Reynolds

1952 BECAUSE OF YOU
Director: Albert Cohen
Co-stars: Loretta Young Jeff Chandler Alex Nicol

1954 MAGNIFICENT OBSESSION
Director: Douglas Sirk
Co-stars: Jane Wyman Rock Hudson Barbara Rush

1955 COME NEXT SPRING
Director: R. G. Springsteen
Co-stars: Ann Sheridan Steve Cochran Walter Brennan

1955 WITCHITA
Director: Jacques Tourneur
Co-stars: Joel McCrea Vera Miles Edgar Buchanan

1956 MOHAWK
Director: Kurt Neumann
Co-stars: Scott Brady Rita Gam Neville Brand

1958 THE VOICE IN THE MIRROR
Director: Harry Keller
Co-stars: Richard Egan Julie London Walter Matthau

1966 BIG DEAL AT DODGE CITY
Director: Fielder Cook
Co-stars: Henry Fonda Joanne Woodward Jason Robards

1967 THOROUGHLY MODERN MILLIE
Director: George Roy Hill
Co-stars: Julie Andrews Mary Tyler Moore John Gavin

1970 WATERMELON MAN
Director: Melvyn Van Peebles
Co-stars: Godfrey Cambridge Estelle Parsons Manton Moreland

MARGI CLARKE

1985 LETTER TO BREZHNEV
Director: Chris Bernard
Co-stars: Alexandra Pigg Peter Firth Alfred Molina

1990 I HIRED A CONTRACT KILLER
Director: Aki Kaurismaki
Co-stars: Jean-Pierre Leaud Kenneth Colley

1991 BLONDE FIST
Director: Frank Clarke
Co-stars: Carroll Baker Ken Hutchison Angela Clarke

MINDY CLARKE

1993 RETURN OF THE LIVING DEAD III
Director: Brian Yuzna
Co-stars: J. Trevor Edmond Kent McCord

1993 RETURN TO TWO-MOON JUNCTION
Director: Farhad Mann
Co-stars: John Clayton Schafer Louise Fletcher

SHIRLEY CLARKE

1969 LIONS LOVE
Director: Agnes Varda
Co-stars: Viva Gerome Ragni James Rado

LANA CLARKSON

1984 DEATHSTALKER
Director: John Watson
Co-stars: Robert Hill Barbi Benton Richard Brooker

PATRICIA CLARKSON

1988 THE DEAD POOL
Director: Buddy Van Horn
Co-stars: Clint Eastwood Liam Neeson David Hunt

1990 AUNT JULIA AND THE SCRIPTWRITER
Director: Jon Amiel
Co-stars: Barbara Hershey Keanu Reeves

1992 LEGACY OF LIES
Director: Bradford May
Co-stars: Michael Ontkean Martin Landau Eli Wallach

1992 FOUR EYES AND SIX GUNS
Director: Piers Haggard
Co-stars: Judge Reinhold Fred Ward

1996 NEIL SIMON'S LONDON SUITE
Director: Jay Sandrich
Co-stars: Kelsey Grammer Madeline Kahn Julie Hagerty

JUANIN CLAY

1982 THE LONG SUMMER OF GEORGE ADAMS
Director: Stuart Margolin
Co-stars: James Garner Joan Hackett

JILL CLAYBURGH
Nominated For Best Actress In 1978 For "An Unmarried Woman"
Nominated For Best Actress In 1979 For "Starting Over"

1969 THE WEDDING PARTY
Director: Brian De Palma
Co-stars: Charles Pflugar Ray McNally Robert De Niro

1972 PORTNOY'S COMPLAINT
Director: Ernest Lehman
Co-stars: Richard Benjamin Karen Black Lee Grant

1973 THE THIEF WHO CAME TO DINNER
Director: Bud Yorkin
Co-stars: Ryan O'Neal Jacqueline Bisset Warren Oates

1976 SILVER STREAK
Director: Arthur Hiller
Co-stars: Gene Wilder Richard Pryor Patrick McGoohan

1976 GABLE AND LOMBARD
Director: Sidney Furie
Co-stars: James Brolin Allen Garfield Red Buttons

1977 SEMI-TOUGH
Director: Michael Ritchie
Co-stars: Burt Reynolds Kris Kristofferson Robert Preston

1978 AN UNMARRIED WOMAN
Director: Paul Mazursky
Co-stars: Alan Bates Michael Murphy Cliff Gorman

1979 STARTING OVER
Director: Alan J. Pakula
Co-stars: Burt Reynolds Candice Bergen Charles Durning

1979 LA LUNA
Director: Bernardo Bertolucci
Co-stars: Matthew Barry Renato Salvatori Fred Gwynne

1980 IT'S MY TURN
Director: Claudia Weill
Co-stars: Michael Douglas Charles Grodin Beverly Garland

1981 FIRST MONDAY IN OCTOBER
Director: Ronald Neame
Co-stars: Walter Matthau James Stephens

1982 I'M DANCING AS FAST AS I CAN
Director: Jack Hofsiss
Co-stars: Nicol Williamson Dianne Wiest

1986 MILES TO GO
Director: David Greene
Co-stars: Tom Skerritt Mimi Kuzyk Rosemary Dunsmore

1987 SHY PEOPLE
Director: Andrei Konchalovsky
Co-stars: Barbara Hershey Martha Plimpton Don Swayze

1989 FEAR STALK
Director: Larry Shaw
Co-stars: Stephen Macht Lorna Luft Sandy McPeak

1990 UNSPEAKABLE ACTS
Director: Linda Otto
Co-stars: Brad Davis Bess Meyer Bebe Neuwirth

1992 RICH IN LOVE
Director: Bruce Beresford
Co-stars: Albert Finney Kathryn Erbe Piper Laurie

1992 WHISPERS IN THE DARK
Director: Christopher Crowe
Co-stars: Annabella Sciorra Alan Alda Anthony LaPaglia

1994 HONOR THY FATHER AND MOTHER: THE MENENDEZ KILLINGS
Director: Paul Schneider
Co-stars: James Farentino Billy Warlock David Beron

1994 FOR THE LOVE OF NANCY
Director: Paul Schneider
Co-stars: William Devane Tracey Gold

JANE CLAYTON

1938 IN OLD MEXICO
Director: Edward Venturini
Co-stars: William Boyd George Hayes Russell Hayden

1940 THE SHOWDOWN
Co-stars: William Boyd George Hayes Russell Hayden

MELISSA CLAYTON

1992 HOUSE IV: THE REPOSSESSION
Director: Lewis Apernathy
Co-stars: Terri Treas Scott Burkholder

JUNE CLAYWORTH

1935 STRANGE WIVES
Co-Star Roger Pryor

1936 TWO-FISTED GENTLEMAN
Co-stars: James Dunn Paul Guilfoyle

1937 MARRIED BEFORE BREAKFAST
Director: Edwin Marin
Co-stars: Robert Young Florence Rice

1939 ALMOST A GENTLEMAN
Co-stars: James Ellison Robert Kent

1946 CRIMINAL COURT
Director: Robert Wise
Co-stars: Tom Conway Martha O'Driscoll Robert Armstrong

1947 BEAT THE BAND
Co-stars: Phillip Terry Donald MacBride

1948 BODYGUARD
Co-Star Lawrence Tierney

1950 THE WHITE TOWER
Director: Ted Tetzlaff
Co-stars: Glenn Ford Claude Rains Alida Valli

1961 THE MARRIAGE-GO-ROUND
Director: Walter Lang
Co-stars: James Mason Susan Hayward Julie Newmar

KATHLEEN CLEAVER

1969 ZABRISKIE POINT
Director: Michaelangelo Antonioni
Co-stars: Mark Frechette Rod Taylor Paul Fix

YVONNE CLECH

1963 LE FEU FOLLET
Director: Louis Malle
Co-stars: Maurice Ronet Lena Skerla Jeanne Moreau

SARA CLEE

1987 SHOOT FOR THE SUN
Director: Ian Knox
Co-stars: Jimmy Naill Brian Cox Billy McColl

MARGHARETH CLEMENTI

1976 CASANOVA
Director: Federico Fellini
Co-stars: Donald Sutherland Tina Aumont Cicely Browne

ANDREE CLEMENT

1946 LA SYMPHONIE PASTORALE
Director: Jean Delannoy
Co-stars: Michele Morgan Pierre Blanchar Line Noro

1950 DIEU A BESOIN DES HOMMES
Director: Jean Delannoy
Co-stars: Pierre Fresnay Madeleine Robinson

AURORE CLEMENT

1974 LACOMBE, LUCIEN
Director: Louis Malle
Co-stars: Pierre Blaise Gilberte Rivet

1982 ALL NIGHT LONG
Director: Chantal Akerman
Co-stars: Veronique Alain Natalia Akerman

1983 THE SOUTH
Director: Victor Erice
Co-stars: Omero Antonutti Lola Cardona Iciar Bollan

1984 PARIS, TEXAS
Director: Wim Wenders
Co-stars: Harry Dean Stanton Nastassja Kinski Dean Stockwell

MARJORIE CLEMENTS

1944 DEAD OR ALIVE
Co-stars: Tex Ritter Dave O'Brien

CORINNE CLERY

1977 THE CON ARTISTS
Director: Sergio Corbucci
Co-stars: Anthony Quinn Capucine Adriano Celentano

1979 MOONRAKER
Director: Lewis Gilbert
Co-stars: Roger Moore Lois Chiles Richard Kiel

CAROL CLEVELAND

1971 AND NOW FOR SOMETHING COMPLETELY DIFFERENT
Director: Ian McNaughton
Co-stars: John Cleese Eric Idle

1983 MONTY PYTHON LIVE AT THE HOLLYWOOD BOWL
Director: Terry Hughes
Co-stars: John Cleese Michael Palin

JENNY CLEVE

1983 ONE DEADLY SUMMER
Director: Jean Becker
Co-stars: Isabelle Adjani Alain Souchon Suzanne Flon

EDITH CLEVER

1976 DIE MARQUISE VON O
Director: Eric Rohmer
Co-stars: Bruno Ganz Peter Luhr

1982 PARSIFAL
Director: Hans Jurgen Syberberg
Co-stars: Michael Kutter Karin Krick

LYNNE CLEVERS

1935 LA KERMESSE HEROIQUE
Director: Jacques Feyder
Co-stars: Francoise Rosay Louis Jouvet Jean Murat

LORRAINE CLEWES

1938 PRISON WITHOUT BARS
Director: Brian Desmond Hurst
Co-stars: Edna Best Barry K. Barnes Mary Morris

CLARE CLIFFORD

1987 WISH YOU WERE HERE
Director: David Leland
Co-stars: Emily Lloyd Tom Bell Barbara Durkin

COLLEEN CLIFFORD

1984 WHERE THE GREEN ANTS DREAM
Director: Werner Herzog
Co-stars: Bruce Spence Ray Barrett Roy Marika

JANE CLIFFORD

1990 MY KINGDOM FOR A HORSE
Director: Barbara Rennie
Co-stars: Sean Bean Sheila Hancock Bryan Pringle

VERONICA CLIFFORD

1987 THE RAGGEDY RAWNEY
Director: Bob Hoskins
Co-stars: Bob Hoskins Dexter Fletcher Zoe Wanamaker

PATRICIA CLIPPER

1990 BLUE HEAT
Director: John MacKenzie
Co-stars: Brian Dennehy Joe Pantoliano Jeff Fahey

KIRSTEN CLOKE

1989 MEGAVILLE
Director: Peter Lehner
Co-stars: Daniel J. Travanti Billy Zane Grace Zabriskie

ROSEMARY CLOONEY *(Aunt of George Clooney)*

1952 THE STARS ARE SINGING
Director: Norman Taurog
Co-stars: Lauritz Melchior Anna Maria Alberghetti Fred Clark

1953 HERE COME THE GIRLS
Director: Claude Binyon
Co-stars: Bob Hope Arlene Dahl Tony Martin

1954 RED GARTERS
Director: George Marshall
Co-stars: Guy Mitchell Gene Barry Jack Carson

1954 WHITE CHRISTMAS
Director: Michael Curtis
Co-stars: Bing Crosby Danny Kaye Vera-Ellen

1954 DEEP IN MY HEART
Director: Stanley Donen
Co-stars: Jose Ferrer Merle Oberon Doe Avedon

1994 RADIOLAND MURDERS
Director: Mel Smith
Co-stars: Brian Benben Mary Stuart Masterston Ned Beatty

GLENN CLOSE

Nominated For Best Supporting Actress In 1982 For "The World According To Garp" And In 1984 For "The Natural"
Nominated For Best Actress In 1987 For "Fatal Attractions" And In 1988 For "Dangerous Liaisons"

1979 TOO FAR TO GO
Director: Fielder Cook
Co-stars: Michael Moriarty Blythe Danner Ken Kercheval

1982 THE WORLD ACCORDING TO GARP
Director: George Roy Hill
Co-stars: Robin Willliams John Lithgow

1983 THE BIG CHILL
Director: Lawrence Kasdan
Co-stars: Tom Berenger Jeff Goldblum Meg Tilly

1984 THE STONE BOY
Director: Christopher Cain
Co-stars: Robert Duvall Jason Presson Frederic Forrest

1984 THE NATURAL
Director: Barry Levinson
Co-stars: Robert Redford Robert Duvall Barbara Hershey

1985 MAXIE
Director: Paul Aaron
Co-stars: Mandy Patinkin Ruth Gordon Barnard Hughes

1985 JAGGED EDGE
Director: Richard Marquand
Co-stars: Jeff Bridges Robert Loggia Peter Coyote

1987 FATAL ATTRACTION
Director: Adrian Lyne
Co-stars: Michael Douglas Anne Archer Fred Gwynne

1988 DANGEROUS LIAISONS
Director: Stephen Frears
Co-stars: John Malkovich Michelle Pfeiffer Swoosie Kurtz

1988 STONES FOR IBARRA
Director: Jack Gold
Co-stars: Keith Carradine Alfonso Arau Trinidad Silver

1989 IMMEDIATE FAMILY
Director: Jonathan Kaplan
Co-stars: James Woods Mary Stuart Masterson

1990 REVERSAL OF FORTUNE
Director: Barbet Schroeder
Co-stars: Jeremy Irons Ron Silver Anabella Sciorra

1991 SARAH, PLAIN AND TALL
Director: Glenn Jordan
Co-stars: Christopher Walken Jon De Vries

1991 MEETING VENUS
Director: Istvan Szabo
Co-stars: Niels Arestrup Marian Labuda Victor Poletti

1991 HAMLET
Director: Franco Zefferelli
Co-stars: Mel Gibson Paul Scofield Alan Bates

1991 101 DALMATIONS
Director: Stephen Herek
Co-stars: Joely Richardson Joan Plowright Jeff Daniells

1992 HOOK
Director: Steven Spielberg
Co-stars: Dustin Hoffman Robin Williams Julia Roberts

1993 SKYLARK
Director: Joseph Sargent
Co-stars: Christopher Walken Lexi Randall

1995 SERVING IN SILENCE:
THE MARGARETHE CAMMERMEYER STORY
Director: Jeff Bleckner
Co-Star Judy Davis

1996 MARY REILLY
Director: Stephen Frears
Co-stars: Julia Roberts John Malkovich

1997 PARADISE ROAD
Director: Bruce Beresford
Co-stars: Jennifer Ehle Pauline Collins

1997 IN AND OUT
Director: Frank Oz
Co-stars: Kevin Kline Joan Cusack Matt Dillon

1997 MARS ATTACKS
Director: Tim Burton
Co-stars: Jack Nicholson Annette Bening Warren Beatty

SUZANNE CLOUTIER

1946 TEMPTATION
Director: Irving Pichel
Co-stars: Merle Oberon George Brent Charles Korvin

1952 OTHELLO
Director: Orson Welles
Co-stars: Orson Welles Michael MacLiammoir Robert Coote

1952 DERBY DAY
Director: Herbert Wilcox
Co-stars: Anna Neagle Michael Wilding Googie Withers

1961 ROMANOFF AND JULIET
Director: Peter Ustinov
Co-stars: Sandra Dee John Gavin Akim Tamiroff

VERA CLOUZOT
(Married Henri-Georges Clouzot)

1953 THE WAGES OF FEAR
Director: Henri-Georges Clouzot
Co-stars: Yves Montand Charles Vanel Peter Van Eyck

1955 LES DIABOLIQUES
Director: Henri-Georges Clouzot
Co-stars: Simone Signoret Charles Vanel

1957 LES ESPIONS
Director: Henri-Georges Clouzot
Co-stars: Martita Hunt Peter Ustinov Sam Jaffe

JUNE CLYDE

1930 THE CUCKOOS
Director: Paul Sloane
Co-stars: Wheeler & Woolsey Jobyna Howland Dorothy Lee

1932 RADIO PATROL
Co-stars: Robert Armstrong Lila Lee Andy Devine

1932 STEADY COMPANY
Co-Star Henry Armetta

1932 TESS OF THE STORM COUNTRY
Director: Alfred Santell
Co-stars: Janet Gaynor Charles Farrell

1932 RACING YOUTH
Co-Star Frank Albertson

1933 A STUDY IN SCARLET
Director: Edwin Marin
Co-stars: Reginald Owen Warburton Gamble Anna May Wong

1934 HOLLYWOOD PARTY
Director: George Stevens
Co-stars: Laurel & Hardy Lupe Velez Eddie Quillan

1935 SHE SHALL HAVE MUSIC
Director: Leslie Hiscott
Co-stars: Jack Hylton Claude Dampier

1935 LET'S MAKE A NIGHT OF IT
Director: Graham Cutts
Co-stars: Buddy Rogers Claire Luce Fred Emney

1935 DANCE BAND
Director: Marcel Varnel
Co-stars: Buddy Rogers Fred Duprez Richard Herne

1935 CHARING CROSS ROAD
Director: Albert De Courville
Co-stars: John Mills Derek Oldham Judy Kelly

1936 LAND WITHOUT MUSIC
Director: Walter Forde
Co-stars: Richard Tauber Jimmy Durante Diana Napier

1937 AREN'T MEN BEASTS
Director: Graham Cutts
Co-stars: Robertson Hare Alfred Drayton Billy Milton

1937 SCHOOL FOR HUSBANDS
Director: Andrew Marton
Co-stars: Rex Harrison Diana Churchill

1941 UNFINISHED BUSINESS
Director: Gregory La Cava
Co-stars: Irene Dunne Robert Montgomery

1941 COUNTRY FAIR
Co-Star Eddie Foy Jnr

1943 HI YA CHUM
Director: Harold Young
Co-stars: Ritz Brothers Jane Frazee Robert Paige

1944 SEVEN DOORS TO DEATH
Director: Elmer Clifton
Co-stars: Chick Chandler George Meeker Gregory Gay

1945 HOLLYWOOD AND VINE
Director: Alexis Thurn-Taxis
Co-stars: James Ellison Wanda McRay Ralph Morgan

1946 BEHIND THE MASK
Co-Star James Cardwell

1952 TREASURE HUNT
Director: John Paddy Carstairs
Co-stars: Jimmy Edwards Martita Hunt Susan Stephen

1957 AFTER THE BALL
Director: Compton Bennett
Co-stars: Pat Kirkwood Laurence Harvey Clive Morton

FIONA CLYNE
1959   THE BRIDAL PATH
Director: Frank Launder
Co-stars: Bill Travers Gordon Jackson Patricia Bredin

KIM COATES
1989   COLD FRONT
Director: Paul Bnarbic
Co-stars: Martin Sheen Beverly D'Angelo Michael Ontkean

1992   THE LAST BOY SCOUT
Director: Tony Scott
Co-stars: Bruce Willis Damon Wayons Chelsea Feilds

1993   DEAD BEFORE DAWN
Director: Charles Correll
Co-stars: Cheryl Ladd Jameson Parker Hope Lange

1993   BLACK FOX: GOOD MEN AND BAD
Director: Steven Hilliard Stern
Co-stars: Christopher Reeve Tony Todd

1994   WEB OF DECEIT
Director: Bill Corcoran
Co-stars: Corbin Bernsen Amanda Pays Mimi Kuzyk

PHYLLIS COATES
1951   CATTLE EMPIRE
Director: Charles Marquis Warren
Co-stars: Joel McCrea Gloria Talbot

1957   I WAS A TEENAGE FRANKENSTEIN
Director: Herbert Strock
Co-stars: Whit Bissell Gary Conway

1958   BLOOD ARROW
Director: Charles Marquis Warren
Co-stars: Scott Brady Don Haggerty

JULIE COBB
1978   STEEL COWBOY
Director: Harvey Laidman
Co-stars: James Brolin Rip Torn Melanie Griffith

1979   SALEM'S LOT
Director: Tobe Hooper
Co-stars: David Soul James Mason Bonnie Bedelia

1983   UNCOMMON VALOR
Director: Rod Amateau
Co-stars: Mitchell Ryan Ben Murphy Barbara Parkins

KACEY COBB
1977   THE CRATER LAKE MONSTER
Co-stars: William Stromberg
Co-stars: Richard Cardella Glenn Roberts

DOROTHY COBURN
1927   FLYING ELEPHANTS
Director: Frank Butler
Co-stars: Stan Laurel Oliver Hardy James Finlayson

1928   THE FINISHING TOUCH
Director: Clyde Bruckman
Co-stars: Stan Laurel Oliver Hardy Edgar Kennedy

NANA COBURN
1991   RETURN TO THE BLUE LAGOON
Director: William Graham
Co-stars: Brian Krause Milla Jovovich Lisa Pelikan

IMOGENE COCA
1963   UNDER THE YUM YUM TREE
Director: David Swift
Co-stars: Jack Lemmon Carol Lynley Dean Jones

1983   NATIONAL LAMPOON'S VACATION
Director: Harold Ramis
Co-stars: Chevy Chase Beverly D'Angelo

1984   NOTHING LASTS FOREVER
Director: Tom Schiller
Co-stars: Zach Galligan Lauren Tom

ANN CODEE
1943   TONIGHT WE RAID CALAIS
Director: John Brahm
Co-stars: Annabella John Sutton Beulah Bondi

1946   SO DARK THE NIGHT
Director: Joseph Lewis
Co-stars: Steven Geray Micheleine Cheirel

1950   UNDER MY SKIN
Director: Jean Negulesco
Co-stars: John Garfield Micheline Presle Luther Adler

1951   THE LADY PAYS OFF
Director: Douglas Sirk
Co-stars: Linda Darnell Stephen McNally Gigi Perreau

1958   KINGS GO FORTH
Director: Delmer Daves
Co-stars: Frank Sinatra Tony Curtis Natalie Wood

CORINNE CODEREY
1973   L'INVITATION
Director: Claude Goretta
Co-stars: Jean-Luc Bideau Jean Champion Pierre Collet

TERESE CODLING
1974   KADOYNG
Director: Ian Shand
Co-stars: Adrian Hall Leo Maguire Bill Owen

CAMILLE CODURI
1988   HAWKS
Director: Robert Ellis
Co-stars: Timothy Dalton Anthony Edwards Janet McTeer

1990   KING RALPH
Director: David Ward
Co-stars: John Goodman Peter O'Toole John Hurt

1990   NUNS ON THE RUN
Director: Jonathan Lynn
Co-stars: Eric Idle Robbie Coltrane Janet Suzman

KATHLEEN CODY
1972   SNOWBALL EXPRESS
Director: Norman Tokar
Co-stars: Dean Jones Nancy Olson Henry Morgan

1973   DOUBLE INDEMNITY
Director: Jack Smight
Co-stars: Richard Crenna Samantha Eggar Lee J. Cobb

1973   CHARLEY AND THE ANGEL
Director: Vincent McEveety
Co-stars: Fred MacMurray Henry Morgan Cloris Leachman

1974   SUPERDAD
Director: Vincent McEveety
Co-stars: Bob Crane Barbara Rush Kurt Russell

DENISE COFFEY
1970   PERCY
Director: Ralph Thomas
Co-stars: Hywell Bennett Denholm Elliott Cyd Hayman

1980   SIR HENRY AT RAWLINSON END
Director: Steve Roberts
Co-stars: Trevor Howard Patrick Magee

1983 ANOTHER TIME, ANOTHER PLACE
Director: Michael Radford
Co-stars: Phyllis Logan Giovanni Mauriello

JESSICA LYNN COHEN

1993 THE NUTCRACKER
Director: Emile Ardolino
Co-stars: Darci Kistler Kyra Nichols Macauley Culkin

CLAUDETTE COLBERT

(Claudette Chauchoin / Married Norman Foster)
Oscar For Best Actress In 1934 For "It Happened One Night"
Nominated For Best Actress In 1935 For "Private Worlds"
Nominated For Best Actress In 1944 For "Since You Went Away"

1927 FOR THE LOVE OF MIKE
Director: Frank Capra
Co-stars: Ben Lyon George Sidney Ford Sterling

1929 THE HOLE IN THE WALL
Director: Robert Florey
Co-stars: Edward G. Robinson Donald Meek

1929 THE LADY LIES
Director: Hobart Henley
Co-stars: Walter Huston Charles Ruggles

1930 THE BIG POND
Director: Hobart Henley
Co-stars: Maurice Chevalier Nat Pendleton

1930 MANSLAUGHTER
Director: George Abbott
Co-stars: Fredric March Emma Dunn

1931 HIS WOMAN
Director: Edward Sloman
Co-stars: Gary Cooper Joseph Calleia

1931 HONOR AMONG LOVERS
Director: Dorothy Arzner
Co-stars: Fredric March Ginger Rogers

1931 SECRETS OF A SECRETARY
Director: George Abbott
Co-stars: Herbert Marshall Mary Bolland

1931 THE SMILING LIEUTENANT
Director: Ernst Lubitsch
Co-stars: Maurice Chevalier Miriam Hopkins

1932 THE SIGN OF THE CROSS
Director: Cecil B. DeMille
Co-stars: Fredric March Charles Laughton

1932 THE WISER SEX
Director: Berthold Viertel
Co-stars: Melvyn Douglas William Boyd

1932 THE PHANTOM PRESIDENT
Director: Norman Taurog
Co-stars: George M. Cohan Jimmy Durante

1932 THE MISLEADING LADY
Director: Stuart Walker
Co-stars: Edmund Lowe Stuart Erwin

1932 MAKE ME A STAR
Director: William Beaudine
Co-stars: Stuart Erwin Joan Blondell Zasu Pitts

1932 THE MAN FROM YESTERDAY
Director: Berthold Viertel
Co-stars: Charles Boyer Clive Brook

1933 I COVER THE WATERFRONT
Director: James Cruze
Co-stars: Ben Lyon Ernest Torrence

1933 THREE-CORNERED MOON
Director: Elliott Nugent
Co-stars: Mary Bolland Richard Arlen Tom Brown

1933 TONIGHT IS OURS
Director: Stuart Walker
Co-stars: Fredric March Alison Skipworth

1933 TORCH SINGER
Director: Alexander Hall
Co-stars: Ricardo Cortez David Manners

1934 IT HAPPENED ONE NIGHT
Director: Frank Capra
Co-stars: Clark Gable Walter Connelly

1934 IMITATION OF LIFE
Director: John Stahl
Co-stars: Warren William Louise Beavers Ned Sparks

1934 FOUR FRIGHTENED PEOPLE
Director: Cecil B. DeMille
Co-stars: Herbert Marshall Mary Bolland

1934 CLEOPATRA
Director: Cecil B. DeMille
Co-stars: Henry Wilcoxon Warren William

1935 THE BRIDE COMES HOME
Director: Wesley Ruggles
Co-stars: Fred MacMurray Robert Young

1935 THE GILDED LILY
Director: Wesley Ruggles
Co-stars: Fred MacMurray Ray Milllnd

1935 PRIVATE WORLDS
Director: Gregory La Cava
Co-stars: Charles Boyer Joel McCrea

1935 SHE MARRIED HER BOSS
Director: Gregory La Cava
Co-stars: Melvyn Douglas Raymond Walburn

1936 UNDER TWO FLAGS
Director: Frank Lloyd
Co-stars: Ronald Colman Victor McLaglen Nigel Bruce

1937 TOVARICH
Director: Anatole Litvak
Co-stars: Charles Boyer Basil Rathbone

1937 MAID OF SALEM
Director: Frank Lloyd
Co-stars: Fred MacMurray Gale Sondergaard

1937 I MET HIM IN PARIS
Director: Wesley Ruggles
Co-stars: Melvyn Douglas Robert Young

1938 BLUEBEARD'S EIGHTH WIFE
Director: Ernst Lubitsch
Co-stars: Gary Cooper David Niven

1939 DRUMS ALONG THE MOHAWK
Director: John Ford
Co-stars: Henry Fonda Edna May Oliver John Carradine

1939 LT'S A WONDERFUL WORLD
Director: W. S. Van Dyke
Co-stars: James Stewart Guy Kibbee Nat Pendleton

1939 MIDNIGHT
Director: Mitchell Leisen
Co-stars: Don Ameche Mary Astor John Barrymore

1939 ZAZA
Director: George Cukor
Co-stars: Herbert Marshall Bert Lahr

1940 BOOM TOWN
Director: Jack Conway
Co-stars: Clark Gable Spencer Tracy Hedy Lamarr

1940 ARISE MY LOVE
Director: Mitchell Leisen
Co-stars: Ray Milland Walter Abel George Zucco

1941   **REMEMBER THE DAY**
Director: Henry King
Co-stars: John Payne Shepperd Strudwick Anne Revere

1941   **SKYLARK**
Director: Mark Sandrich
Co-stars: Ray Milland Brian Aherne Walter Abel

1942   **THE PALM BEACH STORY**
Director: Preston Sturges
Co-stars: Joel McCrea Rudy Vallee Mary Astor

1943   **SO PROUDLY WE HAIL**
Director: Mark Sandrich
Co-stars: Paulette Goddard Veronica Lake

1943   **NO TIME FOR LOVE**
Director: Mitchell Leisen
Co-stars: Fred MacMurray Richard Haydn

1944   **PRACTICALLY YOURS**
Director: Mitchell Leisen
Co-stars: Fred MacMurray Robert Benchley

1944   **SINCE YOU WENT AWAY**
Director: John Cromwell
Co-stars: Joseph Cotten Jennifer Jones Shirley Temple

1945   **TOMORROW IS FOREVER**
Director: Irving Pichel
Co-stars: Orson Welles George Brent Natalie Wood

1945   **GUEST WIFE**
Director: Sam Wood
Co-stars: Don Ameche Dick Foran Grant Mitchell

1946   **WITHOUT RESERVATIONS**
Director: Mervyn LeRoy
Co-stars: John Wayne Don Defore Phil Brown

1946   **THE SECRET HEART**
Director: Robert Z. Leonard
Co-stars: Walter Pidgeon June Allyson

1947   **THE EGG AND I**
Director: Chester Erskine
Co-stars: Fred MacMurray Marjorie Main Ida Moore

1948   **SLEEP, MY LOVE**
Director: Douglas Sirk
Co-stars: Don Ameche Robert Cummings Hazel Brooks

1949   **FAMILY HONEYMOON**
Director: Claude Binyon
Co-stars: Fred MacMurray Rita Johnson Gigi Perreau

1949   **BRIDE FOR SALE**
Director: William Russell
Co-stars: George Brent Robert Young Max Baer

1950   **THE SECRET FURY**
Director: Mel Ferrer
Co-stars: Robert Ryan Paul Kelly Jane Cowl

1950   **THREE CAME HOME**
Director: Jean Negulesco
Co-stars: Patric Knowles Sessue Heyakawa

1951   **THUNDER ON THE HILL**
Director: Douglas Sirk
Co-stars: Ann Blyth Robert Douglas Anne Crawford

1951   **LET'S MAKE IT LEGAL**
Director: Richard Sale
Co-stars: MacDonald Carey Zachary Scott Robert Wagner

1952   **THE PLANTER'S WIFE**
Director: Ken Annakin
Co-stars: Jack Hawkins Jeremy Spenser Ram Gopal

1953   **LOVE, SOLDIERS AND WOMEN**
Director: Jean Delannoy
Co-stars: Michele Morgan Martine Carol

1955   **TEXAS LADY**
Director: Tim Whelan
Co-stars: Barry Sullivan Ray Collins James Bell

1961   **PARRISH**
Director: Delmer Daves
Co-stars: Troy Donahue Karl Malden Connie Stevens

1987   **THE TWO MRS. GRENVILLES**
Director: John Erman
Co-stars: Ann-Margret Sam Wanamaker Elizabeth Ashley

NICOLE COLCHAT

1982   **ALL NIGHT LONG**
Director: Chantal Akerman
Co-stars: Aurore Clement Natalia Akerman Paul Allio

MABEL COLCORD

1933   **LITTLE WOMEN**
Director: George Cukor
Co-stars: Katharine Hepburn Joan Bennett Frances Dee

CAROLE COLE

1969   **THE MODEL SHOP**
Director: Jacques Demy
Co-stars: Anouk Aimee Gary Lockwood Alexandra Hay

1969   **THE MAD ROOM**
Director: Bernard Girard
Co-stars: Shelley Winters Stella Stevens Michael Burns

ELIZABETH COLE

1966   **HAWAII**
Director: George Roy Hill
Co-stars: Max Von Sydow Julie Andrews Richard Harris

JULIE DAWN COLE

1971   **WILLY WONKA AND THE CHOCOLATE FACTORY**
Director: Mel Stuart
Co-stars: Gene Wilder Jack Albertson

KAREN COLE

1984   **ACT OF PASSION**
Director: Simon Langton
Co-stars: Kris Kristofferson Marlo Thomas George Dzundza

NATALIE COLE

1994   **LILY IN WINTER**
Director: Delbert Mann
Co-Star   Brian Bonsall

OLIVIA COLE

1977   **HEROES**
Director: Jeremy Paul Kagan
Co-stars: Henry Winkler Sally Field Harrison Ford

1981   **MISTRESS OF PARADISE**
Director: Peter Medak
Co-stars: Genevieve Bujold Chad Everett Anthony Andrews

1982   **SOME KIND OF HERO**
Director: Michael Pressman
Co-stars: Richard Pryor Margot Kidder Ray Sharkey

1989   **WOMEN OF BREWSTER PLACE**
Director: Donna Deitch
Co-stars: Oprah Winfrey Mary Alice

PEGGY COLE

1974   **AKENFIELD**
Director: Peter Hall
Co-stars: Garrow Shand Barbara Tilney Lyn Brooks

STEPHANIE COLE

1994 IN THE COLD LIGHT OF DAY
Director: Richard Monks
Co-stars: Frances Barber Ronald Pickup

CHARLOTTE COLEMAN

1987 INAPPROPRIATE BEHAVIOUR
Director: Andrew Davies
Co-stars: Jenifer Landor Rosemary Martin

1989 BEARSKIN
Director: Ann Guedes
Co-stars: Tom Waits Damon Lowry Bill Paterson

1989 A VIEW OF HARRY CLARK
Director: Sandy Johnson
Co-stars: Griff Rhys Jones Elaine Page Ian Hart

1989 ORANGES ARE NOT THE ONLY FRUIT
Director: Beeban Kidron
Co-stars: Geraldine McEwan Kenneth Cranham

1990 SWEET NOTHING
Director: Tony Smith
Co-stars: Lee Ross Janet McTeer Victor Maddern

1994 FOUR WEDDINGS AND A FUNERAL
Director: Mike Newell
Co-stars: Hugh Grant Andie MacDowell James Fleet

NANCY COLEMAN

1941 DANGEROUSLY THEY LIVE
Director: Robert Florey
Co-stars: John Garfield Raymond Massey Lee Patrick

1942 DESPERATE JOURNEY
Director: Raoul Walsh
Co-stars: Errol Flynn Ronald Reagan Raymond Massey

1942 THE GAY SISTERS
Director: Irving Rapper
Co-stars: Barbara Stanwyck Geraldine Fitzgerald George Brent

1942 KING'S ROW
Director: Sam Wood
Co-stars: Ronald Reagan Robert Cummings Betty Field

1943 EDGE OF DARKNESS
Director: Lewis Milestone
Co-stars: Errol Flynn Ann Sheridan Walter Huston

1943 DEVOTION
Director: Curtis Bernhardt
Co-stars: Ida Lupino Olivia De Havilland Arthur Kennedy

1944 IN OUR TIME
Director: Vincent Sherman
Co-stars: Ida Lupino Paul Henreid Mary Boland

1946 HER SISTER'S SECRET
Director: Edgar Ulmer
Co-stars: Margaret Lindsay Philip Reed Felix Bressart

1947 MOURNING BECOMES ELECTRA
Director: Dudley Nichols
Co-stars: Michael Redgrave Rosalind Russell Kirk Douglas

1947 VIOLENCE
Director: Jack Bernard
Co-stars: Michael O'Shea Sheldon Leonard Peter Whitney

1969 SLAVES
Director: Herbert Biberman
Co-stars: Stephen Boyd Ossie Davis Dionne Warwick

RENEE COLEMAN

1989 WHO'S HARRY CRUMB?
Director: Paul Flaherty
Co-stars: John Candy Jeffrey Jones Annie Potts

1992 A LEAGUE OF THEIR OWN
Director: Penny Marshall
Co-stars: Tom Hanks Geena Davis Lori Petty Madonna

1993 PENTHALON
Director: Bruce Malmuth
Co-stars: Dolph Lundgren David Soul

RUTH COLEMAN

1937 A DOCTOR'S DIARY
Director: Charles Vidor
Co-stars: George Bancroft Helen Burgess John Trent

1937 THE CRIME NOBODY SAW
Co-stars: Lew Ayres Colin Tapley

1937 WILD MONEY
Co-stars: Lynne Overman Edward Everett Horton

1937 A NIGHT OF MYSTERY
Co-stars: Grant Richards Roscoe Karns

SIDNEY COLEMAN

1994 NECRONOMICON
Director: Brian Yuzna
Co-stars: Jeffrey Combs Bruce Payne David Warner

ETHEL COLERIDGE

1930 PLUNDER
Director: Tom Walls
Co-stars: Tom Walls Ralph Lynn Robertson Hare

1930 ROOKERY NOOK
Director: Tom Walls
Co-stars: Tom Walls Ralph Lynn Robertson Hare

1943 WHEN WE ARE MARRIED
Director: Lance Comfort
Co-stars: Raymond Huntley Marian Spencer Olga Lindo

SYLVIA COLERIDGE

1939 I MET A MURDERER
Director: Roy Kellino
Co-stars: James Mason Pamela Kellino William Devlin

1986 THE GOOD DOCTOR BODKIN ADAMS
Director: Richard Stroud
Co-stars: Timothy West Nigel Davenport

MILDRED COLES

1941 LADY SCARFACE
Director: Frank Woodruff
Co-stars: Judith Anderson Dennis O'Keefe Eric Blore

1948 SONG OF THE DRIFTER
Co-stars: Jimmy Wakely Patsy Moran

EILEEN COLGEN

1970 QUACKSER FORTUNE HAS A COUSIN IN THE BRONX
Director: Waris Hussein
Co-stars: Gene Wilder Margot Kidder

JEAN COLIN

1935 CHARING CROSS ROAD
Director: Albert De Courville
Co-stars: John Mills June Clyde Jude Kelly

1939 THE MIKADO
Director: Victor Schertzinger
Co-stars: Martyn Green Kenny Baker John Barclay

MARGARET COLIN

1986 SOMETHING WILD
Director: Jonathan Demme
Co-stars: Jeff Daniels Melanie Griffith Ray Liotta

1986 PRETTY IN PINK
Director: Howard Deutch
Co-stars: Molly Ringwald Harry Dean Stanton James Spader

1987 THE RETURN OF SHERLOCK HOLMES
Director: Kevin Connor
Co-stars: Michael Pennington Lila Kaye

1987 THREE MEN AND A BABY
Director: Leonard Nimoy
Co-stars: Tom Selleck Steve Guttenberg Ted Danson

1987 LIKE FATHER, LIKE SON
Director: Rod Daniel
Co-stars: Dudley Moore Kirk Cameron Sean Astin

1989 FIGHTING JUSTICE
Director: Joseph Ruben
Co-stars: James Woods Robert Downey Jnr. Kurtwood Smith

1990 GOODNIGHT SWEET WIFE

1991 THE BUTCHER'S WIFE
Director: Terry Hughes
Co-stars: Demi Moore Jeff Daniels Mary Steenburgen

1993 AMOS AND ANDREW
Director: E. Max Frye
Co-stars: Nicolas Cage Samuel L. Jackson Michael Lerner

1996 INDEPENDENCE DAY
Director: Roland Emmbrich
Co-stars: Bill Pullman Jeff Goldblum Mary McDonnell

1997 THE DEVIL'S OWN
Director: Alan J. Pakula
Co-stars: Brad Pitt Harrison Ford Natascha McElhone

DEBORAH COLLARD

1993 THE SECRET ADVENTURES OF TOM THUMB
Director: Dave Borthwick
Co-stars: Nick Upton Frank Passingham

BARBARA COLLENTINE

1978 A DIFFERENT STORY
Director: Paul Aaron
Co-stars: Perry King Meg Foster Valerie Curtin

ANN COLLETTE

1968 WHO'S THAT KNOCKING AT MY DOOR?
Director: Martin Scorsese
Co-stars: Harvey Keitel Zina Bethune

TONI COLLETTE

1992 SPOTSWOOD
Director: Mark Joffe
Co-stars: Anthony Hopkins Ben Mendelson Dan Wyllie

1994 MURIEL'S WEDDING
Director: P. J. Hogan
Co-stars: Bill Hunter Rachel Griffiths Jeanie Drynan

1996 EMMA
Director: Douglas McGrath
Co-stars: Gwyneth Paltrow Greta Scacchi Ewan McGregor

1998 THE JAMES GANG
Director: Mike Barker
Co-stars: Helen McCrory John Hannah

JEANNE COLLETIN

1974 EMMANUELLE
Director: Just Jaeckin
Co-stars: Sylvia Kristel Marika Green Alain Cuny

CRISTINA COLLIER

1986 MR. LOVE
Director: Roy Battersby
Co-stars: Barry Jackson Maurice Denham Margaret Tysack

CONSTANCE COLLIER

1935 SHADOW OF DOUBT
Director: George Seitz
Co-stars: Ricardo Cortez Virginia Bruce Regis Toomey

1936 PROFESSIONAL SOLDIER
Director: Tay Garnett
Co-stars: Victor McLaglen Freddie Bartholomew

1936 GIRLS' DORMITORY
Director: Irving Cummings
Co-stars: Simone Simon Herbert Marshall Tyrone Power

1937 A DAMSEL IN DISTRESS
Director: George Stevens
Co-stars: Fred Astaire Joan Fontaine George Burns & Gracie Allen

1937 WEE WILLIE WINKIE
Director: John Ford
Co-stars: Victor McLaglen June Lang Michael Whalen

1937 STAGE DOOR
Director: Gregory La Cava
Co-stars: Kathleen Hepburn Ginger Rogers Ann Miller Eve Arden

1937 THUNDER IN THE CITY
Director: Marion Gering
Co-stars: Edward G. Robinson Lulu Deste Nigel Bruce

1938 ZAZA
Director: George Cukor
Co-stars: Claudette Colbert Herbert Marshall Bert Lahr

1940 SUSAN AND GOD
Director: George Cukor
Co-stars: Joan Crawford Fredric March Ruth Hussey John Carroll

1943 STAGE DOOR CANTEEN
Director: Frank Borzage
Co-stars: Cheryl Walker Lon McCallister

1945 WEEKEND AT THE WALDORF
Director: Robert Z Leonard
Co-stars: Walter Pidgeon Ginger Rogers Van Johnson

1945 KITTY
Director: Mitchell Leisen
Co-stars: Paulette Goddard Ray Milland Cecil Kellaway

1946 MONSIEUR BEAUCAIRE
Director: George Marshall
Co-stars: Bob Hope Joan Caulfield Marjorie Reynolds

1946 THE DARK CORNER
Director: Henry Hathaway
Co-stars: Mark Stevens Clifton Webb Lucille Ball

1947 THE PERILS OF PAULINE
Director: George Marshall
Co-stars: Betty Hutton John Lund

1948 ROPE
Director: Alfred Hitchcock
Co-stars: James Stewart Farley Granger John Dall

1948 AN IDEAL HUSBAND
Director: Alexander Korda
Co-stars: Paulette Goddard Michael Wilding Hugh Williams

1948 THE GIRL FROM MANHATTAN
Director: Alfred Green
Co-stars: Dorothy Lamour Charles Laughton George Montgomery

1950 WHIRLPOOL
Director: Otto Preminger
Co-stars: Gene Tierney Jose Ferrer Richard Conte Charles Bickford

LESLEY COLLIER

1971 TALES OF BEATRIX POTTER
Director: Reginald Mills
Co-stars: Wayne Sleep Ann Howard Frederick Ashton

LOIS COLLIER

1943 SHE'S FOR ME
Co-stars: David Bruce Grace McDonald

1944 LADIES COURAGEOUS
Director: John Rawlins
Co-stars: Loretta Young Geraldine Fitzgerald Evelyn Ankers

1944 JUNGLE WOMAN
Director: Reginald LeBorg
Co-stars: Acquanetta J. Carrol Naish Evelyn Ankers

1945 THE CRIMSON CANARY
Director: John Hoffman
Co-stars: Noah Beery Jnr. John Litel Steven Geray

1946 THE CAT CREEPS
Director: Erle Kenton
Co-stars: Noah Beery Jnr. Paul Kelly Rose Hobrt

1946 A NIGHT IN CASABLANCA
Director: Archie Mayo
Co-stars: Marx Brothers Charles Drake Sig Ruman

1947 SLAVE GIRL
Director: Charles Lamont
Co-stars: Yvonne De Carlo George Brent Broderick Crawford

1949 MISS MINK OF 1949
Co-stars: Richard Lane June Storey Don Kohler

PATIENCE COLLIER

1968 DECLINE AND FALL
Director: John Krish
Co-stars: Robin Phillips Genevieve Page Donald Wolfit

1968 BABY LOVE
Director: Alastair Reid
Co-stars: Linda Hayden Ann Lynn Keith Barron

1970 EVERY HOME SHOULD HAVE ONE
Director: James Clark
Co-stars: Marty Feldman Judy Cornwell Julie Ege

1970 PERFECT FRIDAY
Director: Peter Hall
Co-stars: Stanley Baker Ursula Andress David Warner

1971 COUNTESS DRACULA
Director: Peter Sasdy
Co-stars: Ingrid Pitt Nigel Green Lesley-Anne Down

1981 THE FRENCH LIEUTENANT'S WOMAN
Director: Karel Reisz
Co-stars: Jeremy Irons Meryl Streep Leo McKern

1985 THE ADVENTURES OF SHERLOCK HOLMES: THE COPPER BEACHES
Director: Paul Annett
Co-stars: Jeremy Brett David Burke Natasha Richardson

PATRICIA COLLINGE
Nominated For Best Supporting Actress In 1941 For "The Little Foxes"

1941 THE LITTLE FOXES
Director: William Wyler
Co-stars: Bette Davis Herbert Marshall Teresa Wright

1943 TENDER COMRADE
Director: Edward Dmytryk
Co-stars: Ginger Rogers Robert Ryan Ruth Hussey

1943 SHADOW OF A DOUBT
Director: Alfred Hitchcock
Co-stars: Joseph Cotten Teresa Wright Hume Cronyn

1944 CASANOVA BROWN
Director: Sam Wood
Co-stars: Gary Cooper Teresa Wright Frank Morgan

1951 TERESA
Director: Fred Zinnemann
Co-stars: Pier Angeli John Ericson Ralph Meeker

1952 WASHINGTON STORY
Director: Robert Pirosh
Co-stars: Van Johnson Patricia Neal Louis Calhern

1959 THE NUN'S STORY
Director: Fred Zinnemann
Co-stars: Audrey Hepburn Peter Finch Edith Evans

CORA SUE COLLINS (Child)

1935 TWO SINNERS
Director: Arthur Lubin
Co-stars: Otto Kruger Martha Sleeper Minna Gombell

1935 LITTLE MEN
Director: Phil Rosen
Co-stars: Ralph Morgan Junior Durkin Frankie Darro

1939 WOMAN DOCTOR
Director: Sidney Salkow
Co-stars: Frieda Inescort Henry Wilcoxon Claire Dodd

1942 GET HEP TO LOVE
Director: Charles Lamont
Co-stars: Gloria Jean Donald O'Connor Peggy Ryan

ELAINE COLLINS

1991 AND THE COW JUMPED OVER THE MOON
Director: Penny Cherns
Co-stars: Phyllis Logan Anne Downie

1992 SOFT TOP, HARD SHOULDER
Director: Stefan Schwartz
Co-stars: Peter Capaldi Frances Barber

JAYNE COLLINS

1976 ONE HOUR TO ZERO
Director: Jeremy Summers
Co-stars: Toby Bridge Dudley Sutton Andrew Ashby

JOAN COLLINS (Married Anthony Newley)

1951 LADY GODIVA RIDES AGAIN
Director: Frank Launder
Co-stars: Pauline Stroud Diana Dors Dennis Price

1952 I BELIEVE IN YOU
Director: Basil Dearden
Co-stars: Celia Johnson Harry Fowler Laurence Harvey

1952 JUDGEMENT DEFERRED
Director: John Baxter
Co-stars: Hugh Sinclair Abraham Sofaer Harry Locke

1952 DECAMERON NIGHTS
Director: Hugo Fregonese
Co-stars: Louis Jourdan Joan Fontaine

1953 OUR GIRL FRIDAY
Director: Noel Langley
Co-stars: Kenneth More George Cole Robertson Hare

1953 THE SQUARE RING
Director: Basil Dearden
Co-stars: Jack Warner Robert Beatty Kay Kendall

1953 TURN THE KEY SOFTLY
Director: Jack Lee
Co-stars: Yvonne Mitchell Terence Morgan Dorothy Alison

1954 THE GOOD DIE YOUNG
Director: Lewis Gilbert
Co-stars: Laurence Harvey Gloria Grahame Rene Ray

1955   THE GIRL IN THE RED VELVET SWING
Director: Richard Fleischer
Co-stars: Ray Milland Farley Granger

1955   THE VIRGIN QUEEN
Director: Henry Koster
Co-stars: Bette Davis Richard Todd Herbert Marshall

1955   LAND OF THE PHAROAHS
Director: Howard Hawks
Co-stars: Jack Hawkins James Robertson Justice

1956   THE OPPOSITE SEX
Director: David Miller
Co-stars: June Allyson Dolores Gray Ann Sheridan

1957   THE WAYWARD BUS
Director: Victor Vicas
Co-stars: Dan Dailey Jayne Mansfield Rick Jason

1957   SEA WIFE
Director: Bob McNaught
Co-stars: Richard Burton Cy Grant Basil Sydney

1957   STOPOVER TOKYO
Director: Richard Breen
Co-stars: Robert Wagner Edmond O'Brien Ken Scott

1957   ISLAND IN THE SUN
Director: Robert Rossen
Co-stars: James Mason Joan Fontaine Harry Belafonte

1958   THE BRAVADOS
Director: Henry King
Co-stars: Gregory Peck Stephen Boyd Lee Van Cleef

1958   RALLY ROUND THE FLAG BOYS
Director: Leo McCarey
Co-stars: Paul Newman Joanne Woodward Jack Carson

1960   SEVEN THIEVES
Director: Henry Hathaway
Co-stars: Edward G. Robinson Rod Steiger Eli Wallace

1960   ESTHER AND THE KING
Director: Raoul Walsh
Co-stars: Richard Egan Dennis O'Day Sergio Fantoni

1962   THE ROAD TO HONG KONG
Director: Norman Panama
Co-stars: Bing Crosby Bob Hope Dorothy Lamour

1967   STAR TREK: ERRAND OF MERCY
Director: John Newland
Co-stars: William Shatner Leonard Nimoy

1967   WARNING SHOT
Director: Buzz Kulik
Co-stars: David Janssen Sam Wanamaker Keenan Wynn

**1969   CAN HIERONYMUS MERKIN EVER
FORGET MERCY HUMMPE AND
FIND TRUE HAPPINESS**
Director: Anthony Newley
Co-stars: Anthony Newley Milton Berle Stubby Kaye

1970   UP IN THE CELLAR
Director: Theodore Flicker
Co-stars: Wes Stern Larry Hagman Judy Pace

1970   THE EXECUTIONER
Director: Sam Wanamaker
Co-stars: George Peppard Nigel Patrick Judy Geeson

1971   QUEST FOR LOVE
Director: Ralph Thomas
Co-stars: Tom Bell Denholm Elliott Simon Ward

1971   REVENGE
Director: Sidney Hayers
Co-stars: Sinead Cusuck James Booth Kenneth Griffiths

1972   TALES FROM THE CRYPT
Director: Freddie Francis
Co-stars: Ralph Richardson Richard Greene

1972   FEAR IN THE NIGHT
Director: Jimmy Sangster
Co-stars: Peter Cushing Judy Geeson Ralph Bates

1973   TALES THAT WITNESS MADNESS
Director: Freddie Francis
Co-stars: Jack Hawkins Donald Houston

1974   FOOTBALL CRAZY
Director: Luigi Filipo D'Amico
Co-stars: Lando Buzzanca Danielle Vargas

1975   ALFIE DARLING
Director: Ken Hughes
Co-stars: Alan Price Sheila White Rula Lenska

1975   I DON'T WANT TO BE BORN
Director: Peter Sasdy
Co-stars: Ralph Bates Eileen Atkins Donald Pleasence

1976   THE BAWDY ADVENTURES OF TOM JONES
Director: Cliff Owen
Co-stars: Nicky Henson Trevor Howard

1977   EMPIRE OF THE ANTS
Director: Bert Gordon
Co-stars: Robert Lansing Albert Salmi Jacqueline Scott

1978   THE BIG SLEEP
Director: Michael Winner
Co-stars: Robert Mitchum Sarah Miles John Mills

1978   THE STUD
Director: Quentin Masters
Co-stars: Oliver Tobias Sue Lloyd Mark Burns

1979   THE BITCH
Director: Gerry O'Hara
Co-stars: Kenneth Haigh Ian Hendry Sue Lloyd

1979   A GAME FOR VULTURES
Director: James Fargo
Co-stars: Richard Harris Richard Rountree Ray Milland

1979   SUNBURN
Director: Richard Serafian
Co-stars: Farrah Fawcett Charles Grodin

1982   NUTCRACKER
Director: Anwar Kawadri
Co-stars: Carol White Paul Nicholas William Franklyn

1984   HER LIFE AS A MAN
Director: Robert Ellis Miller
Co-stars: Robyn Douglass Robert Culp Marc Singer

1984   THE CARTIER AFFAIR
Director: Rod Holcomb
Co-stars: David Hasselhoff Telly Savalas Ed Lauter

1986   MONTE CARLO
Director: Anthony Page
Co-stars: George Hamilton Lauren Hutton Philip Madoc

1986   SINS
Director: Douglas Hickox
Co-stars: Jean-Pierre Aumont Gene Kelly Timothy Dalton

1993   DECADENCE
Director: Steven Berkoff
Co-stars: Christopher Biggins Michael Winner

1995   IN THE BLEAK MIDWINTER
Director: Kenneth Branagh
Co-stars: Michael Maloney Julia Sawalha John Sessions

LISA COLLINS
1994 WEB OF DECEPTION
Director: Richard Colla
Co-stars: Powers Booth Pam Dawber

PATRICIA COLLINS
1980 CIRCLE OF TWO
Director: Jules Dassin
Co-stars: Richard Burton Tatum O'Neal Kate Reid

1989 FINAL JUDGEMENT
Director: David Robertson
Co-stars: Michael Beck Catherine Colvey

1989 SPEAKING PART'S
Director: Atom Egoyan
Co-stars: Michael McManus Arsinee Khanjian Gabrielle Rose

1990 DEEP SLEEP
Director: Patricia Gruben
Co-stars: Stuart Margolin Megan Follows Margot Kane

PAULINE COLLINS
Nominated For Best Actress In 1989 For Shirley Valentine

1984 KNOCKBACK
Director: Piers Haggard
Co-stars: Derrick O'Connor Peggy Atchison Michelle Mulvany

1989 SHIRLEY VALENTINE
Director: Lewis Gilbert
Co-stars: Tom Conti Bernard Hill Julia McKenzie

1992 CITY OF JOY
Director: Roland Joffe
Co-stars: Patrick Swayze Om Puri Shabana Azmi

1997 PARADISE ROAD
Director: Bruce Beresford
Co-stars: Glenn Close Jennifer Ehle Cate Blanchette

ROBERTA COLLINS
1972 THE UNHOLY ROLLERS
Director: Vernon Zimmerman
Co-stars: Claudia Jennings Louis Quinn Alan Vint

1974 CAGED HEAT
Director: Jonathan Demme
Co-stars: Juanita Brown Erica Gavin Rainbeaux Smith

TRACEY COLLINS
1969 ON THE RUN
Director: Pat Jackson
Co-stars: Dennis Conoley Robert Kennedy Gordon Jackson

MADELEINE COLLINSON
(Twin Sister Of Mary Collinson)

1971 TWINS OF EVIL
Director: John Hough
Co-stars: Mary Collinson Peter Cushing Kathleen Byron

MARY COLLINSON
(Twin Sister Of Madeleine Collinson)

1971 TWINS OF EVIL
Director: John Hough
Co-stars: Madeleine Collinson Peter Cushing Dennis Price

JUNE COLLYER
1928 FOUR SONS
Director: John Ford
Co-stars: Margaret Mann James Hall Earle Fox George Meeker

1928 HANGMAN'S HOUSE
Director: John Ford
Co-stars: Victor McLaglen Earle Fox Larry Kent

1930 SWEET KITTY BELLAIRS
Director: Alfred Green
Co-stars: Claudia Dell Ernest Torrence Walter Pidgeon

1930 THE MAN FROM WYOMING
Director: Rowland Lee
Co-stars: Gary Cooper Regis Toomey Morgan Farley

1930 CHARLEY'S AUNT
Director: Al Christie
Co-stars: Charles Ruggles Hugh Williams Doris Lloyd

1931 HONEYMOON LANE
Co-stars: Eddie Dowling Noah Beery

1933 BEFORE MIDNIGHT
Co-Star Ralph Bellamy

1934 LOST IN THE STRATOSPHERE
Co-stars: Eddie Nugent William Cagney

1935 THE GHOST WALKS
Director: Frank Strayer
Co-stars: John Miljan Richard Carle

1935 MURDER BY TELEVISION
Director: Clifford Sanforth
Co-stars: Bela Lugosi George Meeker

PIA COLOMBO
1974 PARADE
Director: Jaques Tati
Co-stars: Jaques Tati Karl Kossmayer

MIRIAM COLON
1971 THE POSSESSION OF JOEL DELANEY
Director: Waris Hussein
Co-stars: Shirley MacLaine Perry King

1981 BACK ROADS
Director: Martin Ritt
Co-stars: Vincent Spano Todd Graff Tony LoBianco

1991 CITY OF HOPE
Director: John Sayler
Co-stars: Michael McManus Arsinee Khanjian Gabrielle Rose

HORTENSIA COLORADO
1982 THE LEGEND OF WALKS FAR WOMAN
Director: Mel Damski
Co-stars: Raquel Welch Bradford Dillman

CLARA COLOSIMO
1972 ALFREDO, ALFREDO
Director: Pietro Germi
Co-stars: Dustin Hoffman Stefania Sandrelli Carla Gravina

KAREN COLSTON
1989 SWEETIE
Director: Jane Campion
Co-stars: Genevieve Lemon Tom Lycos Jon Darling

CATHERINE COLVEY
1989 FINAL JUDGEMENT
Director: David Robertson
Co-stars: Michael Beck Patricia Collins

JESSIE COMBE
1978 THE BILL DOUGLAS TRILOGY
Director: Bill Douglas
Co-stars: Stephen Archibald Paul Kermack Lita Roza

MURIEL COMBEAU
1989 ROMUALD AND JULIETTE
Director: Coline Serreau
Co-stars: Daniel Auteuil Firmine Richard

HOLLY MARIE COMBS

1988 SWEET HEARTS DANCE
Director: Robert Greenwald
Co-stars: Don Johnson Susan Sarandon Jeff Daniels

1992 CHAIN OF DESIRE
Director: Temistocles Lopez
Co-stars: Linda Fiorentina Elias Koteas Angel Aviles

1992 DR. GIGGLES
Director: Manny Coto
Co-stars: Larry Drake Richard Bradford Michelle Johnson

BETTY COMDEN

1944 GREENWICH VILLAGE
Director: Walter Lang
Co-stars: Carmen Miranda Don Ameche Vivian Blaine

ANJANETTE COMER

1965 THE LOVED ONE
Director: Tony Richardson
Co-stars: Robert Morse Rod Steiger James Coburn

1965 QUICK BEFORE IT MELTS
Director: Delbert Mann
Co-stars: George Maharis Robert Morse James Gregory

1966 THE APPALOOSA
Director: Sidney Furie
Co-stars: Marlon Brando John Saxon Frank Silvera

1967 BANNING
Director: Ron Winston
Co-stars: Robert Wagner Jill St. John Guy Stockwell

1967 GUNS FOR SAN SEBASTIAN
Director: Henri Verneuil
Co-stars: Anthony Quinn Charles Bronson Sam Jaffe

1968 IN ENEMY COUNTRY
Director: Harry Keller
Co-stars: Tony Franciosa Guy Stockwell Tom Bell

1970 THE FIRECHASERS
Director: Sidney Havers
Co-stars: Chad Everett Keith Barron Rupert Davies

1970 RABBIT, RUN
Director: Jack Smight
Co-stars: James Caan Carrie Snodgress Jack Albertson

1973 THE BABY
Director: Ted Post
Co-stars: Ruth Roman Marianna Hill

1974 DEATH STALK
Director: Robert Day
Co-stars: Vince Edwards Robert Webber Carol Lynley

1974 LEPKE
Director: Menahem Golan
Co-stars: Tony Curtis Michael Callan Milton Berle

1974 NIGHT GAMES
Director: Don Taylor
Co-stars: Barry Newman Susan Howard Stefanie Powers

1977 FIRE SALE
Director: Alan Arkin
Co-stars: Alan Arkin Vincent Gardenia Kay Medford

DOROTHY COMINGORE

1941 CITIZEN KANE
Director: Orson Welles
Co-stars: Orson Welles Joseph Cotten Everett Sloane

1944 THE HAIRY APE
Director: Alfred Santell
Co-stars: William Bendix Susan Hayward John Loder

1951 THE BIG NIGHT
Director: Joseph Losey
Co-stars: John Barrymore Jnr. Preston Foster Joan Lorring

LILIANA COMOROWSKO

1992 SCANNERS 3: THE TAKEOVER
Director: Christian Duguay
Co-stars: Steve Parrish Colin Fox

BETTY COMPSON
Nominated For Best Actress In 1929 For "The Barker"

1923 HOLLYWOOD
Director: James Cruz
Co-stars: Hope Drown Luke Cossgrove Ruby Lafayette

1923 WOMAN TO WOMAN
Director: Graham Cutts
Co-stars: Clive Brook Josephine Earle Marie Ault

1925 EVE'S SECRET
Co-Star: Jack Holt

1925 THE PONY EXPRESS
Director: James Cruze
Co-stars: Ricardo Cortez Wallace Beery Ernest Torrence

1927 THE BIG CITY
Co-stars: Lon Chaney James Murray Marceline Day

1928 THE BARKER
Co-stars: Douglas Fairbanks Jnr Dorothy MacKaill

1929 ON WITH THE SHOW
Director: Alan Crosland
Co-stars: Louise Fazenda Sally O'Neil Joe E. Brown

1929 THE GREAT GABBO
Director: James Cruze
Co-stars: Erich Von Stroheim Margie Kane

1929 SHOW OF SHOWS
Director: John Adolfi
Co-stars: John Barrymore Chester Morris Patsy Ruth Miller

1930 THE CASE OF SERGEANT GRISCHA
Director: Herbert Brenon
Co-stars: Chester Morris Jean Hersholt

1930 THE SPOILERS
Director: Edward Carewe
Co-stars: Gary Cooper William Boyd Kay Johnson

1931 THE GAY DIPLOMAT
Director: Richard Boleslawski
Co-stars: Ivan Lebedeff Genevieve Tobin Ilka Chase

1933 WEST OF SINGAPORE
Co-stars: Noel Madison Creighton Hale

1933 DESTINATION UNKNOWN
Director: Tay Garnett
Co-stars: Pat O'Brien Ralph Bellamy Alan Hale

1936 THE MILLIONAIRE KID
Co-Star: Bryant Washburn

1938 TWO GUN JUSTICE
Co-stars: Tim McCoy Joan Barclay John Merton

1941 MR. AND MRS. SMITH
Director: Alfred Hitchcock
Co-stars: Carole Lombard Robert Montgomery Jack Carson

FAY COMPTON

1931 TELL ENGLAND
Director: Anthony Asquith
Co-stars: Carl Harbord Dennis Hoey Tony Bruce

1933 WALTZES FROM VIENNA
Director: Alfred Hitchcock
Co-stars: Jessie Matthews Esmond Knight

1934 AUTUMN CROCUS
Director: Basil Dean
Co-stars: Ivor Novello Jack Hawkins Diana Beaumont

1937 THE MILL ON THE FLOSS
Director: Tim Whelan
Co-stars: Geraldine Fitzgerald James Mason Mary Clare

1939 SO THIS IS LONDON
Director: Thornton Freeland
Co-stars: George Sanders Alfred Drayton

1940 THE PRIME MINISTER
Director: Thorold Dickinson
Co-stars: John Gielgud Diana Wynyard Will Fyffe

1946 ODD MAN OUT
Director: Carol Reed
Co-stars: James Mason Robert Newton Kathleen Ryan

1947 NICHOLAS NICKLEBY
Director: Alberto Cavalcanti
Co-stars: Derek Bond Cedric Hardwicke

1947 ESTHER WATERS
Director: Ian Dalrymple
Co-stars: Kathleen Ryan Dirk Bogarde Cyril Cusack

1948 BRITANNIA MEWS
Director: Jean Negulesco
Co-stars: Maureen O'Hara Dana Andrews Sybil Thorndyke

1948 LONDON BELONGS TO ME
Director: Sldney Gilliat
Co-stars: Alastair Sim Stephen Murray

1950 BLACKMAILED
Director: Marc Allegret
Co-stars: Dirk Bogarde Mai Zetterling Michael Gough

1951 LAUGHTER IN PARADISE
Director: Mario Zampi
Co-stars: Alastair Sim Hugh Griffith Joyce Grenville

1952 THE LADY POSSESSED
Director: Roy Kellino
Co-stars: James Mason June Havoc Pamela Kellino

1952 OTHELLO
Director: Orson Welles
Co-stars: Orson Welles Michael MacLiammoir

1954 AUNT CLARA
Director: Anthony Kimmins
Co-stars: Margaret Rutherford Ronald Shiner

1956 DOUBLE CROSS
Director: Anthony Squire
Co-stars: Donald Houston William Hartnell

1956 TOWN ON TRIAL
Director: John Guillermin
Co-stars: John Mills Charles Coburn Barbara Bates

1957 THE STORY OF ESTHER COSTELLO
Director: David Miller
Co-stars: Joan Crawford Heather Sears

1969 I START COUNTING
Director: David Greene
Co-stars: Jenny Agutter Simon Ward Brian Marshall

1970 THE VIRGIN AND THE GYPSY
Director: Christopher Miles
Co-stars: Joanna Shimkus Franco Nero

JOYCE COMPTON

1929 THE WILD PARTY
Director: Dorothy Arzner
Co-stars: Clara Bow Fredric March Shirley O'Hara

1930 WILD COMPANY
Co-stars: Frank Albertson H. B. Warner Sharon Lynn

1930 HIGH SOCIETY BLUES
Director: David Butler
Co-stars: Janet Gaynor Charles Farrell Louise Fazenda

1933 BERKELEY SQUARE
Director: Frank Lloyd
Co-stars: Leslie Howard Heather Angel Valerie Taylor

1935 LET 'EM HAVE IT
Director: Sam Wood
Co-stars: Richard Arlen Virginia Bruce Alice Brady

1935 THE WHITE PARADE
Director: Irving Cummings
Co-stars: Loretta Young John Boles Dorothy Wilson

1936 COUNTRY GENTLEMEN
Director: Ralph Staub
Co-stars: Olsen & Johnson Lila Lee Pierre Watkin

1936 TRAPPED BY TELEVISION
Co-stars: Mary Astor Lyle Talbot Nat Pendleton

1937 THE AWFUL TRUTH
Director: Leo McCarey
Co-stars: Irene Dunne Cary Grant Ralph Bellamy

1937 SMALL TOWN BOY
Co-Star: Stuart Erwin

1938 ARTISTS AND MODELS ABROAD
Director: Mitchell Leisen
Co-stars: Jack Benny Joan Bennett

1938 THE LAST WARNING
Director: Albert Rogell
Co-stars: Preston Foster Frank Jenks

1938 SPRING MADNESS
Director: S. Sylvan Simon
Co-stars: Maureen O'Sullivan Lew Ayres Ruth Hussey

1939 BALALAIKA
Director: Lawrence Weingarten
Co-stars: Nelson Eddy Ilona Massey Charles Ruggles

1939 ROSE OF WASHINGTON SQUARE
Director: Gregory Ratoff
Co-stars: Tyrone Power Alice Faye Al Jolson

1940 SKY MURDER
Director: George Seitz
Co-stars: Walter Pidgeon Karen Verne Donald Meek

1940 TURNABOUT
Director: Hal Roach
Co-stars: Adolphe Menjou John Hubbard Mary Astor

1940 THE VILLAIN STILL PURSUED HER
Director: Edward Cline
Co-stars: Buster Keaton Anita Louise

1940 HONEYMOON DEFERRED
Director: Lew Landers
Co-stars: Edmund Lowe Margaret Lindsay Elizabeth Risdon

1941 MANPOWER
Director: Raoul Walsh
Co-stars: Edward G. Robinson George Raft Marlene Dietrich

1941 BEDTIME STORY
Director: Alexander Hall
Co-stars: Loretta Young Fredric March Eve Arden

1942 TOO MANY WOMEN
Co-stars: Neil Hamilton George Davis

1946 DARK ALIBI
Director: Phil Karlson
Co-stars: Sidney Toller Benson Fong Teala Loring

1948 A SOUTHERN YANKEE
Director: Edward Sedgwick
Co-stars: Red Skelton Arlene Dahl John Ireland

JULIETTE COMPTON

1930 MOROCCO
Director: Josef Von Sternberg
Co-stars: Marlene Dietrich Gary Cooper Adolphe Menjou

1931 RICH MAN'S FOLLY
Director: John Cromwell
Co-stars: George Bancroft Frances Dee Robert Ames

1931 HUSBAND'S HOLIDAY
Director: Robert Milton
Co-stars: Clive Brook Charles Ruggles Charles Winninger

1932 STRANGERS IN LOVE
Director: Lothar Mendes
Co-stars: Fredric March Kay Francis Stuart Erwin

1932 WESTWARD PASSAGE
Director: Robert Milton
Co-stars: Laurence Olivier Ann Harding Zasu Pitts

1933 PEG O' MY HEART
Director: Robert Z .Leonard
Co-stars: Marion Davies Onslow Stevens Alan Mowbray

1933 THE MASQUERADER
Director: Richard Wallace
Co-stars: Ronald Colman Elissa Landi Halliwell Hobbes

1934 GRAND CANARY
Director: Irving Cummings
Co-stars: Warner Baxter Madge Evans H. B. Warner

1934 BEHOLD MY WIFE
Director: Mitchell Leisen
Co-stars: Gene Raymond Sylvia Sidney Laura Hope Crews

VIOLA COMPTON

1936 THE MAN IN THE MIRROR
Director: Maurice Elvy
Co-stars: Edward Everett Horton Genevieve Tobin

CRISTI CONAWAY

1992 BATMAN RETURNS
Director: Tim Burton
Co-stars: Michael Keaton Michelle Pfeiffer Danny Devito

1993 ATTACK OF THE 50FT. WOMAN
Director: Christopher Guest
Co-stars: Daryl Hannah Frances Fisher Daniel Baldwin

LAURA DUKE CONDOMINAS

1974 LANCELOT OF THE LAKE
Director: Robert Bresson
Co-stars: Luc Simon Humbert Balsan

CARMEN CONESA

**1991 HOW TO BE A WOMAN AND
NOT DIE IN THE ATTEMPT**
Director: Ana Belen
Co-stars: Carmen Maura Antonio Resines

PEGGY CONKLIN

1934 THE PRESIDENT VANISHES
Director: William Wellman
Co-stars: Arthur Byron Janet Beecher Paul Kelly

1935 ONE-WAY TICKET
Director: Herbert Biberman
Co-stars: Lloyd Bridges Walter Connolly Edith Fellows

1936 HER MASTER'S VOICE
Director: Joseph Santly
Co-stars: Edward Everett Horton Laura Hope Crews

1936 THE DEVIL IS A SISSY
Director: W. S. Van Dyke
Co-stars: Freddie Bartholomew Mickey Rooney Jackie Cooper

1938 HAVING WONDERFUL TIME
Director: Alfred Santell
Co-stars: Ginger Rogers Douglas Fairbanks Jnr

CORINNE CONLEY

1995 BUTTERBOX BABIES
Director: Don McBrearty
Co-stars: Susan Clark Peter McNeil Shannon Lawson

MARY CONLON

1987 THE PARTY
Director: Sebastian Graham-Jones
Co-stars: Andrew Keir Jack Shepherd Kenneth Cranham

DIDI CONN

1977 YOU LIGHT UP MY LIFE
Director: Joseph Brooks
Co-stars: Joe Silver Michael Zaslow Melanie Mayron

1978 MURDER AT THE MARDI GRAS
Director: Ken Annakin
Co-stars: Bill Daily David Wayne Harry Morgan

JANE CONNELL

1963 LADYBUG LADYBUG
Director: Frank Perry
Co-stars: James Frawley William Daniels

1974 MAME
Director: Gene Saks
Co-stars: Lucille Ball Robert Preston Beatrice Arthur

1977 MAGNIFICENT MAGNET OF SANTA MESA
Director: Hy Averbach
Co-stars: Michael Burns Keene Curtis

MAUREEN CONNELL

1957 THE RISING OF THE MOON
Director: John Ford
Co-stars: Eileen Crowe Cyril Cusack Maureen Delany

1957 LUCKY JIM
Director: John Boulting
Co-stars: Ian Carmichael Terry-Thomas Hugh Griffith

1957 THE ABOMINABLE SNOWMAN
Director: Val Guest
Co-stars: Peter Cushing Forrest Tucker Richard Wattis

1958 ECHO OF BARBARA
Director: Sidney Hayers
Co-stars: Mervyn Johns Ronald Hines Tom Bell

1958 KILL HER GENTLY
Director: Charles Saunders
Co-stars: Griffith Jones Marc Lawrence

1958 THE MAN UPSTAIRS
Director: Don Chaffey
Co-stars: Richard Attenborough Bernard Lee Dorothy Alison

1962 DANGER BY MY SIDE
Director: Charles Saunders
Co-stars: Anthony Oliver Alan Tilvern

JENNIFER CONNELLY

1986 LABYRINTH
Director: Jim Henson
Co-stars: David Bowie Toby Froud Shelley Thompson

1988 SISTERS
Director: Michael Hoffman
Co-stars: Patrick Dempsey Sheila Kelley Florinda Balkan

1990 THE HOT SPOT
Director: Dennis Hopper
Co-stars: Don Johnson Virginia Madsen William Sadler

1991 CAREER OPPORTUNITIES
Director: Bryan Gordon
Co-stars: Frank Whaley Dermot Mulroney Jenny O'Hara

1991 THE ROCKETEER
Director: Joe Johnston
Co-stars: Bill Campbell Alan Arkin Timothy Dalton

1992 THE HEART OF JUSTICE
Director: Bruno Barreto
Co-stars: Eric Stoltz Dermot Mulroney Vincent Price

1994 OF LOVE AND SHADOWS
Director: Betty Kaplan
Co-Star Antonio Banderas

1996 MULHOLLAND FALLS
Director: Lee Tamahori
Co-stars: Nick Nolte John Malkovich Melanie Griffith

1997 INVENTING THE ABBOTTS
Director: Pat O'Connor
Co-stars: Liv Tyler Kathy Baker Billy Crudup

1998 DARK CITY
Director: Alex Proyas
Co-stars: William Hurt Kiefer Sutherland Rufus Sewell

LEONE CONNERY

1990 EFFIE'S BURNING
Director: Nigel Evans
Co-stars: Paula Tilbrook Phyllis Logan Gordon Jackson

NORMA CONNOLLY

1972 THE OTHER
Director: Robert Mulligan
Co-stars: Uta Hagen Diana Muldaur Martin Udvarnoky

PATRICIA CONNOLLY

1969 COLOUR ME DEAD
Director: Eddie Davis
Co-stars: Tom Tryon Carolyn Jones Rick Jason

FRANCES CONROY

1988 ANOTHER WOMAN
Director: Woody Allen
Co-stars: Gena Rowlands Mia Farrow Ian Holm

1988 DIRTY ROTTEN SCOUNDRELS
Director: Frank Oz
Co-stars: Steve Martin Michael Caine Glenne Headly

1992 SCENT OF A WOMAN
Director: Martin Brest
Co-stars: Al Pacino Chris O'Connell Gabrielle Anwar

1995 THE NEON BIBLE
Director: Atom Egoyan
Co-stars: Michael McManus Arsinee Khanjian Gabrielle Rose

SUE CONROY

1931 THE GIRL HABIT
Director: Terence Davis
Co-stars: Gena Rowlands Diana Scarwid Denis Leary

MABEL CONSTANDUROS

1942 SALUTE JOHN CITIZEN
Director: Maurice Elvy
Co-stars: Edward Rigby Stanley Holloway George Robey

1944 MEDAL FOR THE GENERAL
Director: Maurice Elvy
Co-stars: Godfrey Tearle Jeanne De Casalis Petula Clark

1947 WHITE UNICORN
Director: Bernard Knowles
Co-stars: Margaret Lockwood Joan Greenwood Ian Hunter

CATHERINE CONTI

1973 CRY OF THE BLACK WOLVES
Director: Harald Reini
Co-stars: Ron Ely Raymond Harmstorf

MARIE-CHRISTINA CONTI

1984 UNTIL SEPTEMBER
Director: Richard Marquand
Co-stars: Karen Allen Thierry L'Hermitte

CHANTAL CONTURI

1974 ALVIN RIDES AGAIN
Director: Robin Copping
Co-stars: Graeme Blundell Alan Finney Frank Thring

PEGGY CONVERSE

1953 MISS SADIE THOMPSON
Director: Curtis Bernhardt
Co-stars: Rita Hayworth Jose Ferrer Aldo Ray

MICHELE CONWAY

1984 LOVE STREAMS
Director: John Cassavetes
Co-stars: John Cassavetes Gena Rowlands Seymour Cassel

BARBARA COOK

1994 THUMBELINA *(Voice)*
Director: Don Bluth
Co-stars: Jodi Benson Carol Channing John Hurt

MARIANNE COOK

1956 FOUR GIRLS IN TOWN
Director: Jack Sher
Co-stars: George Nader Julie Adams Elsa Martinelli

1957 INTERLUDE
Director: Douglas Sirk
Co-stars: Rossano Brazzi June Allyson Jane Wyatt

TRACEY COOK

1993 BERMUDA GRACE
Director: Mark Sobel
Co-stars: William Sadler Serena Scott-Thomas Leslie Phillips

BERYL COOKE

1989 THE REAL EDDY ENGLISH
Director: David Attwood
Co-stars: Stephen Persaud Frank Windsor Sue Devaney

JENNIFER COOKE

1986 FRIDAY THE 13TH. PART VI: JASON LIVES
Director: Tom McLoughlin
Co-stars: Thom Matthews David Kagen

GEORGINA COOKSON

1957 THE NAKED TRUTH
Director: Mario Zampi
Co-stars: Peter Sellers Terry-Thomas Peggy Mount

1964 CATACOMBS
Director: Gordon Hessler
Co-stars: Gary Merrill Neil McCallum Jane Merrow

MARJORIE COOLEY

1940   THE GREAT COMMANDMENT
Director: Irving Pichel
Co-stars: John Beal Albert Dekker

PAT COOMBS

1971   ON THE BUSES
Director: Harry Booth
Co-stars: Reg Varney Doris Hare Anna Karen

1971   DAD'S ARMY
Director: Norman Cohen
Co-stars: Arthur Lowe Clive Dunn John Laurie

1972   OOH...YOU ARE AWFUL
Director: Cliff Owen
Co-stars: Dick Emery Derren Nesbitt Ronald Fraser

1972   ADOLF HITLER – MY PART IN HIS DOWNFALL
Director: Norman Cohen
Co-stars: Spike Milligan Jim Dale

1973   A COUPLE OF BEAUTIES
Co-stars: Bunny Lewis Tim Barrett

CAROLINE COON

1980   RUDE BOY
Director: Jack Hazan
Co-stars: Ray Grange John Green Barry Baker

CAMI COOPER

1989   SHOCKER
Director: Wes Craven
Co-stars: Michael Murphy Peter Berg Heather Langenkamp

1991   MEET THE APPLEGATES
Director: Michael Lehman
Co-stars: Ed Begley Jnr. Stockard Channing Bobby Jacoby

DERYN COOPER

1978   SKIN DEEP
Director: Geoff Steven
Co-stars: Jim Macfarland Ken Blackburn Alan Jervis

GLADYS COOPER
Nominated For Best Supporting Actress In 1942 For "Now Voyager", In 1943 For "The Song Of Bernadette" And In 1964 For "My Fair Lady"

1935   THE IRON DUKE
Director: Victor Saville
Co-stars: George Arliss Emlyn Williams Ellaline Terriss

1940   KITTY FOYLE
Director: Sam Wood
Co-stars: Ginger Rogers Dennis Morgan James Craig

1940   REBECCA
Director: Alfred Hitchcock
Co-stars: Laurence Olivier Joan Fontaine George Sanders

1941   LADY HAMILTON
Director: Alexander Korda
Co-stars: Laurence Olivier Vivien Leigh Henry Wilcoxon

1941   THE GAY FALCON
Director: Irving Reis
Co-stars: George Sanders Wendy Barrie Allen Jenkins

1941   THE BLACK CAT
Director: Albert Rogell
Co-stars: Basil Rathbone Broderick Crawford Gale Sondergaard

1942   EAGLE SQUADRON
Director: Arthur Lubin
Co-stars: Robert Stack Diana Barrymore Jon Hall

1942   NOW VOYAGER
Director: Irving Rapper
Co-stars: Bette Davis Paul Henreid Claude Rains

1942   THIS ABOVE ALL
Director: Anatole Litvak
Co-stars: Tyrone Power Joan Fontaine Thomas Mitchell

1943   THE SONG OF BERNADETTE
Director: Henry King
Co-stars: Jennifer Jones Charles Bickford William Eythe

1943   MR. LUCKY
Director: H. C. Potter
Co-stars: Cary Grant Laraine Day Charles Bickford Paul Stewart

1943   PRINCESS O'ROURKE
Director: Norman Krasna
Co-stars: Olivia De Havilland Robert Cummings Charles Coburn

1943   FOREVER AND A DAY
Director: Rene Clair
Co-stars: Anna Neagle Ray Milland Charles Laughton

1944   MRS. PARKINGTON
Director: Tay Garnett
Co-stars: Greer Garson Walter Pidgeon Edward Arnold

1944   THE WHITE CLIFFS OF DOVER
Director: Clarence Brown
Co-stars: Irene Dunne Alan Marshall Frank Morgan

1945   THE VALLEY OF DECISION
Director: Tay Garnett
Co-stars: Greer Garson Gregory Peck Lionel Barrymore

1945   LOVE LETTERS
Director: William Dieterle
Co-stars: Jennifer Jones Joseph Cotten Anita Louise

1946   THE GREEN YEARS
Director: Victor Saville
Co-stars: Charles Coburn Dean Stockwell Jessica Tandy

1946   THE COCKEYED MIRACLE
Director: S. Sylvan Simon
Co-stars: Frank Morgan Cecil Kellaway Audrey Totter

1946   BEWARE OF PITY
Director: Maurice Elvey
Co-stars: Lilli Palmer Albert Lieven Cedric Hardwicke

1947   THE BISHOP'S WIFE
Director: Henry Koster
Co-stars: Cary Grant Loretta Young David Niven

1948   HOMECOMING
Director: Mervyn LeRoy
Co-stars: Clark Gable Lana Turner Anne Baxter John Hodiak

1948   THE PIRATE
Director: Vincente Minnelli
Co-stars: Gene Kelly Judy Garland Walter Slezak

1949   THE SECRET GARDEN
Director: Fred Wilcox
Co-stars: Margaret O'Brien Dean Stockwell Herbert Marshall

1949   MADAME BOVARY
Director: Vincente Minnelli
Co-stars: Jennifer Jones Van Heflin Louis Jourdan

1951   SONS OF THE MUSKETEERS
Director: Lewis Allen
Co-stars: Cornel Wilde Maureen O'Hara Dan O'Herlihy

1951   THUNDER ON THE HILL
Director: Douglas Sirk
Co-stars: Claudette Colbert Ann Blyth Robert Douglas

1954   THE MAN WHO LOVED REDHEADS
Director: Harold French
Co-stars: John Justin Moira Shearer

1958 SEPARATE TABLES
Director: Delbert Mann
Co-stars: Burt Lancaster Wendy Hiller David Niven

1963 THE LIST OF ADRIAN MESSINGER
Director: John Huston
Co-stars: George C. Scott Dana Wynter Clive Brook

1964 MY FAIR LADY
Director: George Cukor
Co-stars: Rex Harrison Audrey Hepburn Stanley Holloway

1967 THE HAPPIEST MILLIONAIRE
Director: Norman Tokar
Co-stars: Fred MacMurray Tommy Steele Greer Garson

1969 A NICE GIRL LIKE ME
Director: Desmond Davis
Co-stars: Barbara Ferris Harry Andrews

INEZ COOPER

1943 WINGS OVER THE PACIFIC
Co-stars: Edward Norris Montague Love

JEANNE COOPER

1961 THE INTRUDER
Director: Roger Corman
Co-stars: William Shatner Frank Maxwell Leo Gordon

1962 BLACK ZOO
Director: Robert Gordon
Co-stars: Michael Gough Virginia Grey Jerome Cowan

1972 KANSAS CITY BOMBER
Director: Jerrold Freedman
Co-stars: Raquel Welch Kevin McCarthy Jodie Foster

1975 SWEET HOSTAGE
Director: Lee Philips
Co-stars: Linda Blair Martin Sheen

LOUISE COOPER

1980 BLACK JACK
Director: Kenneth Loach
Co-stars: Jean Franval Stephen Hirst

MAGGIE COOPER

1979 AND BABY MAKES SIX
Director: Waris Hussein
Co-stars: Colleen Dewhurst Warren Oates Timothy Hutton

1981 AN EYE FOR AN EYE
Director: Steve Carver
Co-stars: Chuck Norris Christopher Lee Matt Clark

MAXINE COOPER

1955 KISS ME DEADLY
Director: Robert Aldrich
Co-stars: Ralph Meeker Albert Dekker Cloris Leachman

MIRIAM COOPER

1916 INTOLERANCE
Director: D. W. Griffith
Co-stars: Mae Marsh Lillian Gish Norma Talmadge

ROWENA COOPER

1990 AMONGST BARBARIANS
Director: Jane Howell
Co-stars: David Jason Anne Carroll Lee Ross

1991 TELL ME THAT YOU LOVE ME
Director: Bruce MacDonald
Co-stars: Judith Scott Sean Bean James Wilby

JOAN COPELAND

1958 THE GODDESS
Director: John Cromwell
Co-stars: Kim Stanley Lloyd Bridges Betty Lou Holland

1977 ROSELAND
Director: James Ivory
Co-stars: Geraldine Chaplin Teresa Wright Christopher Walken

1981 CAGNEY AND LACEY
Director: Ted Post
Co-stars: Loretta Swit Tyne Daly Al Waxman

1986 HAPPY NEW YEAR
Director: John Avildsen
Co-stars: Peter Falk Charles Durning Wendy Hughes

1990 LASERMAN
Director: Peter Wang
Co-stars: Peter Wang Marc Hayashi Tony Leung

1990 MURDER IN BLACK AND WHITE
Director: Robert Iscove
Co-stars: Richard Crenna Cliff Gorman

TERI COPLEY

1984 I MARRIED A CENTREFOLD
Director: Peter Werner
Co-stars: Timothy Daly Diane Ladd Bert Remsen

1989 TRANSYLVANIA TWIST
Director: Jim Wynorski
Co-stars: Robert Vaughn Steve Altman

GRACE COPPIN

1949 LOST BOUNDARIES
Director: Alfred Werker
Co-stars: Mel Ferrer Beatrice Pearson Canada Lee

GIA COPPOLA (Child)
(Daughter Of Francis Ford Coppola)

1989 NEW YORK STORIES
Director: Francis Ford Coppola
Co-stars: Giancarlo Giannini Talia Shire

SOPHIA COPPOLA (Child)
(Daughter Of Francis Ford Coppola)

1986 PEGGY SUE GOT MARRIED
Director: Francis Ford Coppola
Co-stars: Kathleen Turner Nicolas Cage

1990 THE GODFATHER, PART III
Director: Francis Ford Coppola
Co-stars: Al Pacino Diane Keaton Andy Garcia

1992 INSIDE MONKEY ZETTERLAND
Director: Jefery Levy
Co-stars: Steven Antin Patricia Arquette Bo Hopkins

NELLY CORRADI

1947 THE BARBER OF SEVILLE
Director: Tito Gobbi
Co-stars: Tito Gobbi Perrucio Tagliavini

CLAIRE CORBETT

1985 ARCHER'S ADVENTURE
Director: Denny Lawrence
Co-stars: Brett Climo Robert Coleby Doreen Warburton

GRETCHEN CORBETT

1971 LET'S SCARE JESSICA TO DEATH
Director: John Hancock
Co-stars: Zohra Lampert Kevin O'Connor

1976 THE SAVAGE BEES
Director: Bruce Geller
Co-stars: Ben Johnson Michael Parks Horst Buchholz

1981 TIMEWARP
Director: Allan Sandler
Co-stars: Peter Kastner Adam West Steven Mond

1982 MILLION DOLLAR INFIELD
Director: Hal Cooper
Co-stars: Bonny Bedelia Robert Costanzo Rob Reiner

1985 NORTH BEACH AND RAWHIDE
Director: Harry Falk
Co-stars: William Shatner Tate Donovan James Olson

LEONORA CORBETT

1932 LOVE ON WHEELS
Director: Victor Saville
Co-stars: Jack Hulbert Edmund Gwenn Gordon Harker

1933 FRIDAY THE THIRTEENTH
Director: Victor Saville
Co-stars: Jessie Matthews Max Miller Sonnie Hale

1933 THE CONSTANT NYMPH
Director: Basil Dean
Co-stars: Victoria Hopper Brian Aherne Jane Baxter

1934 WARN LONDON
Director: Hayes Hunter
Co-stars: Edmund Gwenn John Loder

1935 HEART'S DESIRE
Director: Paul Stein
Co-stars: Richard Tauber Diana Napier Frank Vosper

1936 LIVING DANGEROUSLY
Co-Star Otto Kruger

1937 FAREWELL AGAIN
Director: Tim Whelan
Co-stars: Flora Robson Leslie Banks Robert Newton

1940 UNDER YOUR HAT
Director: Maurice Elvy
Co-stars: Jack Hulbert Cicely Courtneidge Cecil Parker

VIRGINIA LEE CORBIN

1926 HANDS UP
Director: Clarence Badger
Co-stars: Raymond Griffith Marion Nixon Montagu Love

ELLEN CORBY

Nominated For Best Supporting Actress In 1948 For I Remember Mama

1948 I REMEMBER MAMA
Director: George Stevens
Co-stars: Irene Dunne Barbara Bel Geddes Oscar Homolka

1949 CAPTAIN CHINA
Director: Lewis Foster
Co-stars: John Payne Gail Russell Jeffrey Lynn

1950 CAGED
Director: John Cromwell
Co-stars: Eleanor Parker Agnes Moorehead Jan Sterling

1950 THE GUNFIGHTER
Director: Henry King
Co-stars: Gregory Peck Helen Westcott Millard Mitchell

1952 FEARLESS FAGAN
Director: Stanley Donen
Co-stars: Carleton Carpenter Janet Leigh Keenan Wynn

1953 SHANE
Director: George Stevens
Co-stars: Alan Ladd Jean Arthur Van Heflin

1955 ILLEGAL
Director: Lewis Allen
Co-stars: Edward G. Robinson Nina Foch Jayne Mansfield

1958 MACABRE
Director: William Castle
Co-stars: William Prince Jim Backus Jacqueline Scott

1958 VERTIGO
Director: Alfred Hitchcock
Co-stars: James Stewart Kim Novak Barbara Bel Geddes

1963 THE STRANGLER
Director: Burt Topper
Co-stars: Victor Buono David McLean Diane Sayer

1966 THE NIGHT OF THE GRIZZLY
Director: Josepeh Pevney
Co-stars: Clint Walker Martha Hyer Keenan Wynn

1968 A FINE PAIR
Director: Francesco Maselli
Co-stars: Rock Hudson Claudia Cardinale Leon Askin

1971 THE HOMECOMING: A CHRISTMAS STORY
Director: Fielder Cook
Co-stars: Richard Thomas Andrew Duggan Patricia Neal

1982 A DAY FOR THANKS ON WALTON'S MOUNTAIN
Director: Harry Harris
Co-stars: Ralph Waite Jon Walmsley

DONNA CORCORAN (Child)

1952 MILLION DOLLAR MERMAID
Director: Mervyn LeRoy
Co-stars: Esther Williams Victor Mature Walter Pidgeon

1952 YOUNG MAN WITH IDEAS
Director: Mitchell Leisen
Co-stars: Glenn Ford Ruth Roman Nina Foch

1952 DON'T BOTHER TO KNOCK
Director: Roy Baker
Co-stars: Marilyn Monroe Richard Widmark Anne Bancroft

1952 ANGELS IN THE OUTFIELD
Director: Clarence Brown
Co-stars: Paul Douglas Janet Leigh Keenan Wynn

1953 DANGEROUS WHEN WET
Director: Charles Walters
Co-stars: Esther Williams Jack Carson Charlotte Greenwood

1953 I LOVE MELVYN
Director: Don Weis
Co-stars: Donald O'Connor Debbie Reynolds

1953 SCANDAL AT SCOURIE
Director: Jean Negulesco
Co-stars: Greer Garson Walter Pidgeon Agnes Moorehead

1953 GYPSY COLT
Director: Andrew Morton
Co-stars: Ward Bond Frances Dee Lee Van Cleef

MARIA CORDA

1927 THE PRIVATE LIFE OF HELEN OF TROY
Director: Alexander Korda
Co-stars: Lewis Stone Ricardo Cortez

MARA CORDAY

1954 SO THIS IS PARIS
Director: Richard Quine
Co-stars: Tony Curtis Gene Nelson Gloria DeHaven

1954 DRUMS ACROSS THE RIVER
Director: Nathan Juran
Co-stars: Audie Murphy Walter Brennan Lyle Bettger

1955 TARANTULA
Director: Jack Arnold
Co-stars: Leo G. Carroll John Agar Nestor Paiva

1955 MAN WITHOUT A STAR
Director: King Vidor
Co-stars: Kirk Douglas Jeanne Crain Claire Trevor

1955 THE MAN FROM BITTER RIDGE
Director: Jack Arnold
Co-stars: Lex Barker Stephen McNally John Dehner

1956 RAW EDGE
Director: John Sherwood
Co-stars: Rory Calhoun Yvonne De Carlo Rex Reason

1956 A DAY OF FURY
Director: Harmon Jones
Co-stars: Dale Robertson Jock Mahoney Carl Benton Reid

1957 THE BLACK SCORPION
Director: Edward Ludwig
Co-stars: Richard Denning Carlos Rivas

1957 THE GIANT CLAW
Director: Fred Sears
Co-stars: Jeff Morrow Morris Ankrum

1977 THE GAUNTLET
Director: Clint Eastwood
Co-stars: Clint Eastwood Sondra Locke Pat Hingle

1990 ROOKIE
Director: Clint Eastwood
Co-stars: Clint Eastwood Charlie Sheen Raul Julia

MARCELLE CORDAY

1936 THE GREAT ZIEGFELD
Director: Robert Z. Leonard
Co-stars: William Powell Luise Ralner Myrna Loy

PAULA CORDAY

1947 THE EXILE
Director: Max Ophuls
Co-stars: Douglas Fairbanks Jnr. Maria Montez Henry Daniell

1951 THE SWORD OF MONTE CRISTO
Director: Maurice Geraghty
Co-stars: George Montgomery Robert Warwick

1951 TOO YOUNG TO KISS
Director: Robert Z. Leonard
Co-stars: June Allyson Van Johnson Gig Young

1952 YOU FOR ME
Director: Don Weis
Co-stars: Peter Lawford Jane Greer Gig Young

1952 THE BLACK CASTLE
Director: Nathan Juran
Co-stars: Richard Green Stephen McNally Boris Karloff

1955 THE FRENCH LINE
Director: Lloyd Bacon
Co-stars: Jane Russell Gilbert Roland Arthur Hunnicutt

RITA CORDAY

1943 THE FALCON AND THE CO-EDS
Co-Star Tom Conway

1945 THE FALCON IN SAN FRANCISCO
Co-stars: Tom Conway Sharyn Moffett

1946 THE FALCON'S ALIBI
Co-stars: Tom Conway Emory Parnell

CATHLEEN CORDELL

1938 GASLIGHT
Director: Thorold Dickinson
Co-stars: Anton Walbrook Robert Newton Diana Wynyard

HELENE CORDET

1953 THE LIMPING MAN
Director: Charles De Lautour
Co-stars: Lloyd Bridges Moira Lister Leslie Phillips

MICHELE CORDUE

1953 THE PROUD AND THE BEAUTIFUL
Director: Yves Allegret
Co-stars: Michele Morgan Gerard Philipe

ANNIE CORDY

1970 RIDER ON THE RAIN
Director: Rene Clement
Co-stars: Charles Bronson Marlene Jobert Jill Ireland

1971 LE CHAT
Director: Pierre Granier-Deferre
Co-stars: Jean Gabin Simone Signoret

ISABELLE COREY

1955 BOB LE FLAMBEUR
Director: Jean-Pierre Melville
Co-stars: Roger Duchesne Daniel Caucny

1956 IT HAPPENED IN ROME

1956 AND GOD CREATED WOMAN
Director: Roger Vadim
Co-stars: Brigitte Bardot Curt Jurgens Jane Marken

ANN CORIO

1944 CALL OF THE JUNGLE
Co-stars: James Bush Harry Burns

CATHERINE CORKILL

1985 TWO FATHERS' JUSTICE
Director: Rod Holcomb
Co-stars: Robert Conrad George Hamilton Brooke Bundy

CATHERINE CORMAN

1990 FRANKENSTEIN UNBOUND
Director: Roger Corman
Co-stars: John Hurt Bridget Fonda Catherine Rabett

MADDIE CORMAN

1992 MY NEW GUN
Director: Stacy Cochran
Co-stars: Diane Lane Stephen Collins James LeGross

PAMELA CORME

1935 LAZYBONES
Director: Michael Powell
Co-stars: Clare Luce Ian Hunter Sara Allgood

ELLIE CORNELL

1988 HALLOWEEN 4:
THE RETURN OF MICHAEL MYERS
Director: Dwight Little
Co-Star Donald Pleasence

1989 HALLOWEEN 5
Director: Dominique Othenin-Girard
Co-stars: Donald Pleasence Wendy Coplan

1990 CHIPS, THE WAR DOG
Director: Ed Kaplan
Co-stars: Brandon Douglas Ned Vaughn William Devane

KATHERINE CORNELL

1943 STAGE DOOR CANTEEN
Director: Frank Borzage
Co-stars: Cheryl Walker Lon McCallister Judith Anderson

LILIAN CORNELL

1940 NIGHT AT EARL CARROLL'S
Director: Kurt Neuman
Co-stars: J. Carrol Naish Blanche Stewart

AURORE CORNU

1970 CLAIRE'S KNEE
Director: Eric Rohmer
Co-stars: Jean-Claude Brialy Laurence De Monaghan

ANN CORNWALL

1927 COLLEGE
Director: James Horne
Co-stars: Buster Keaton Snitz Edwards Harold Goodwin

CHARLOTTE CORNWALL

1990 THE KRAYS
Director: Peter Medak
Co-stars: Billie Whitelaw Gary Kemp Martin Kemp

JUDY CORNWELL

1969 COUNTRY DANCE
Director: J. Lee Thompson
Co-stars: Peter O'Toole Susannah York Michael Craig

1970 EVERY HOME SHOULD HAVE ONE
Director: James Clark
Co-stars: Marty Feldman Shelley Berman Julie Ege

1970 WUTHERING HEIGHTS
Director: Robert Fuest
Co-stars: Anna Calder-Marshall Timothy Dalton

1985 SANTA CLAUS: THE MOVIE
Director: Jeannot Szwarc
Co-stars: Dudley Moore John Lithgow Burgess Meredith

MADY CORRELL

1937 MIDNIGHT MADONNA
Director: James Flood
Co-stars: Warren William Edward Ellis Jonathan Hale

ADRIENNE CORRI

1951 THE RIVER
Director: Jean Renoir
Co-stars: Nora Swinburne Esmond Knight Arthur Shields

1954 MEET MR. CALLAGHAN
Director: Charles Saunders
Co-stars: Derrick De Marney Delphi Lawrence

1954 MAKE ME AN OFFER
Director: Cyril Frankel
Co-stars: Peter Finch Rosalie Crutchley Wilfrid Lawson

1954 LEASE OF LIFE
Director: Charles Frend
Co-stars: Robert Donat Kay Walsh Denholm Elliott

1954 DEVIL GIRL FROM MARS
Director: David MacDonald
Co-stars: Patricia Laffan Hugh McDermott Hazel Court

1956 BEHIND THE HEADLINES
Director: Charles Saunders
Co-stars: Paul Carpenter Hazel Court

1956 THREE MEN IN A BOAT
Director: Ken Annakin
Co-stars: Laurence Harvey Jimmy Edwards David Tomlinson

1956 THE FEMININE TOUCH
Director: Pat Jackson
Co-stars: George Baker Belinda Lee Delphi Lawrence

1957 THE BIG CHANCE
Director: Peter Graham Scott
Co-stars: Willy Russell Ferdy Mayne Ian Colin

1958 CORRIDORS OF BLOOD
Director: Robert Day
Co-stars: Boris Karloff Chrlstopher Lee Betta St. John

1959 THE ROUGH AND THE SMOOTH
Director: Robert Siodmak
Co-stars: Tony Britton Nadja Tiller William Bendix

1960 THE HELLFIRE CLUB
Director: Robert Baker
Co-stars: Keith Michell Peter Arne Peter Cushing

1965 DOCTOR ZHIVAGO
Director: David Lean
Co-stars: Omar Sharif Julie Christie Tom Courtenay

1965 A STUDY IN TERROR
Director: James Hill
Co-stars: John Neville Anthony Quale Barbara Windsor

1965 BUNNY LAKE IS MISSING
Director: Otto Preminger
Co-stars: Laurence Olivier Carol Lynley Noel Coward

1967 AFRICA - TEXAS STYLE
Director: Andrew Marton
Co-stars: John Mills Hugh O'Brian Nigel Green

1967 THE VIKING QUEEN
Director: Don Chaffey
Co-stars: Carita Don Murray Andrew Keir

1967 WOMAN TIMES SEVEN
Director: Vittorio De Sica
Co-stars: Vittorio De Sica Shirley MacLaine Michael Caine

1969 MOON ZERO TWO
Director: Roy Ward Baker
Co-stars: James Olson Catherina Von Schell Warren Mitchell

1969 THE FILES OF THE GOLDEN GOOSE
Director: Sam Wanamaker
Co-stars: Yul Brynner Edward Woodward

1971 A CLOCKWORK ORANGE
Director: Stanley Kubrick
Co-stars: Malcolm McDowell Michael Bates Warren Clarke

1971 VAMPIRE CIRCUS
Director: Robert Young
Co-stars: Laurence Payne Lynne Frederick Thorley Walters

1973 MADHOUSE
Director: Jim Clark
Co-stars: Vincent Price Peter Cushing Natasha Pyne

1975 ROSEBUD
Director: Otto Preminger
Co-stars: Peter O'Toole Peter Lawford Raf Vallone

ANETA CORSEAULT

1958 THE BLOB
Director: Irvin Yeaworth
Co-stars: Steve McQueen Earl Rowe Olin Howlin

SILVANA CORSINI

1961 ACCATONE
Director: Pier Paolo Pasolini
Co-stars: Franco Citti Franca Pasut Adriana Asti

MARY CORTES

1942 SEVEN DAYS LEAVE
Director: Tim Whelan
Co-stars: Lucille Ball Victor Mature Ginny Sims

VALENTINA CORTESA
Nominated For Best Supporting Actress In 1974 For Day For Night

1949 THE GLASS MOUNTAIN
Director: Henry Cass
Co-stars: Michael Dennison Dulcie Gray Tito Gobbi

1949 THIEVES' HIGHWAY
Director: Jules Dassin
Co-stars: Richard Conte Jack Oakie Millard Mitchell

1949 MALAYA
Director: Richard Thorpe
Co-stars: Spencer Tracy James Stewart John Hodiak

1949 BLACK MAGIC
Director: Gregory Ratoff
Co-stars: Orson Welles Nancy Guild Akim Tamiroff

1950 SHADOW OF THE EAGLE
Director: Sidney Salkow
Co-stars: Richard Greene Greta Gynt Binnie Barnes

1951 THE HOUSE ON TELEGRAPH HILL
Director: Robert Wise
Co-stars: Richard Basehart William Lundigan

1951 THE SECRET PEOPLE
Director: Thorold Dickinson
Co-stars: Audrey Hepburn Charles Goldner Megs Jenkins

1954 THE BAREFOOT CONTESSA
Director: Joseph Mankiewicz
Co-stars: Humphrey Bogart Ava Gardner Rossano Brazzi

1954 MAGIC FIRE
Director: William Dieterle
Co-stars: Alan Badel Yvonne De Carlo Carlos Thompson

1955 LE AMICHE
Director: Michaelangelo Antonioni
Co-stars: Eleanore Rossi Drago Yvonne Furneaux

1956 CALABUCH
Director: Luis Berlanga
Co-stars: Edmund Gwenn Franco Fabrizi

1965 JULIET OF THE SPIRITS
Director: Federico Fellini
Co-stars: Giulietta Masina Mario Pisu Sylva Koscina

1968 THE LEGEND OF LILAH CLARE
Director: Robert Aldrich
Co-stars: Kim Novak Peter Finch Coral Browne

1962 BARABBAS
Director: Dino De Laurentios
Co-stars: Anthony Quinn Silvana Mangano Jack Palance

1972 THE ASSASSINATION OF TROTSKY
Director: Joseph Losey
Co-stars: Richard Burton Alain Delon

1972 BROTHER SUN, SISTER MOON
Director: Franco Zeffirelli
Co-stars: Graham Faulkner Judi Bowker

1973 DAY FOR NIGHT
Director: Francois Truffaut
Co-stars: Jacqueline Bisset Jean-Pierre Aumont

1974 THE FLESH OF THE ORCHID
Director: Patrice Chereau
Co-stars: Charlotte Rampling Simone Signoret

1980 WHEN TIME RAN OUT
Director: James Goldstone
Co-stars: Paul Newman Jacqueline Bisset William Holden

1989 THE ADVENTURES OF BARON MUNCHHAUSEN
Director: Terry Gilliam
Co-stars: John Neville Oliver Reed

KATHARINE CORTEZ
1992 CRITTERS 3
Director: Kristine Peterson
Co-stars: Aimee Brooks John Calvin Leonardo DiCaprio

1992 FINAL ANALYSIS
Director: Phil Joanou
Co-stars: Richard Gere Uma Thurman Kim Basinger

RENEE COSINA
1950 LES ENFANTS TERRIBLES
Director: Jean-Pierre Melville
Co-stars: Nicole Stephane Edouard Dermithe

MARY COSTA
1953 MARRY ME AGAIN
Director: Frank Tashlin
Co-stars: Robert Cummngs Marie Wilson Ray Walker

1959 SLEEPING BEAUTY *(Voice)*
Director: Clyde Geronimi
Co-stars: Bill Shirley Barbara Jo Allen

1972 THE GREAT WALTZ
Director: Andrew Stone
Co-stars: Horst Buchholz Nigel Patrick Rossano Brazzi

SUZANNE COSTALLOS
1991 TRUST
Director: Hal Hartley
Co-stars: Adrienne Shelly Martin Donovan John MacKay

1991 TRUE LOVE
Director: Nancy Savoca
Co-stars: Annabella Sciorra Ron Edward Aida Turturro

CAROL COSTELLO *(Daughter Of Lou Costello)*
1954 ABBOTT AND COSTELLO MEET THE KEYSTONE KOPS
Director: Charles Lamont
Co-stars: Bud Abbott Lou Costello

DOLORES COSTELLO
(Also Credited As Dolores Costello Barrymore)
(Married John Barrymore)

1926 THE SEA BEAST
Director: Millard Webb
Co-stars: John Barrymore George O'Hara Mike Donlin

1927 WHEN A MAN LOVES
Director: Alan Crosland
Co-stars: John Barrymore Warner Oland Stuart Holmes

1928 GLORIOUS BETSY
Director: Alan Crosland
Co-stars: Conrad Nagel John Miljan Betty Blythe

1929 NOAH'S ARK
Director: Michael Curtiz
Co-stars: Noah Beery Louise Fazenda Guinn Williams Myrna Loy

1931 EXPENSIVE WOMAN
Co-stars: Anthony Bushell H. B. Warner

1936 LITTLE LORD FAUNTLEROY
Director: John Cromwell
Co-stars: Freddie Bartholomew Mickey Rooney

1936 YOURS FOR THE ASKING
Co-Star George Raft

1938 BREAKING THE ICE
Director: Edward Cline
Co-stars: Bobby Breen Charles Ruggles Dorothy Peterson

1938 BELOVED BRAT
Co-Star: Bonita Granville

1939 KING OF THE TURF
Director: Alfred Green
Co-stars: Adolphe Menjou Walter Abel Roger Daniel

1942 THE MAGNIFICENT AMBERSONS
Director: Orson Welles
Co-stars: Joseph Cotten Tim Holt Anne Baxter

1943 THIS IS THE ARMY
Director: Michael Curtis
Co-stars: George Murphy Joan Leslie Irving Berlin

GLORIA COSTELLO

1958 TEENAGE MONSTER
Director: Jacques Marquette
Co-stars: Anne Gwynne Gilbert Perkins

HELENE COSTELLO
(Made The First All-Talking Film)

1928 LIGHTS OF NEW YORK
Director: Bryan Foy (Warner)
Co-stars: Cullen Landis Gladys Brockwell Tom Dugan

MARICLARE COSTELLO

1971 LET'S SCARE JESSICA TO DEATH
Director: John Hancock
Co-stars: Zohra Lampert Barton Heyman

1980 ALL GOD'S CHILDREN
Director: Jerry Thorpe
Co-stars: Richard Widmark Ned Beatty Ruby Dee

1981 COWARD OF THE COUNTY
Director: Dick Lowry
Co-stars: Kenny Rogers Fredric Lehne Ana Alicia

1985 HEART OF A CHAMPION: THE RAY MANCINI STORY
Director: Richard Michaels
Co-stars: Robert Blake Doug McKeon

1987 DOUBLE SWITCH
Director: David Greenwalt
Co-stars: George Newbern Elizabeth Shue

1987 AMERICAN HARVEST
Director: Dick Lowry
Co-stars: Wayne Rogers Fredric Lehne Earl Holliman

KAMI COTLER

1971 THE HOMECOMING: A CHRISTMAS STORY
Director: Fielder Cook
Co-stars: Richard Thomas Andrew Duggan Patricia Neal

1982 A WEDDING ON WALTON'S MOUNTAIN
Director: Lee Philips
Co-stars: Ralph Waite Jon Walmsley Judy Norton-Taylor

1982 A DAY FOR THANKS ON WALTON'S MOUNTAIN
Director: Harry Harris
Co-stars: Ralph Waite Jon Walmsley Judy Norton-Taylor

1982 MOTHER'S DAY ON WALTON'S MOUNTAIN
Director: Gwen Arner
Co-stars: Ralph Waite Jon Walmsley Judy Norton-Taylor

FANNY COTTENCON

1982 L'ETOILE DU NORD
Director: Pierre Granier-Deferre
Co-stars: Simone Signoret Philippe Noiret

1987 ANGEL DUST
Director: Edouard Niermans
Co-stars: Bernard Giraudeau Fanny Bastien Michel Aumont

CATHERINE COTTER

1936 OUTLAWS OF THE RANGE
Co-stars: Bill Cody Bill Cody Jnr.

CHRISSIE COTTERILL

1982 SCRUBBERS
Director: Mai Zetterling
Co-stars: Amanda York Kate Ingram Honey Bane

DIANE COTTON

1993 PLEASURE IN PARADISE
Director: B. Rakeley
Co-stars: John Paul Lorello Linda Brown

JOSIE COTTON

1985 NOMADS
Director: Jonn McTiernan
Co-stars: Pierce Brosnan Lesley-Anne Down Adam Ant

PHYLLIS COUGHLAN

1970 THE BROTHERHOOD OF SATAN
Director: Bernard McEveety
Co-stars: Strother Martin Anna Capri Alvy Moore

ALICE COULTEIARD

1993 THE CEMENT GARDEN
Director: Andrew Birkin
Co-stars: Charlotte Gainsbourg Sinead Cusack Ned Birkin

ELIZABETH COUNCIL

1960 I PASSED FOR WHITE
Director: Fred Wilcox
Co-stars: Sonya Wilde James Franciscus Pat Michon

BARBARA COUPER

1948 THE STORY OF SHIRLEY YORKE
Director: Maclean Rogers
Co-stars: Derek Farr Dinah Sheridan

1949 THE LAST DAYS OF DOLWYN
Director: Emlyn Williams
Co-stars: Emlyn Williams Edith Evans Richard Burton

1950 HAPPY GO LOVELY
Director: Bruce Humberstone
Co-stars: David Niven Vera-Ellen Cesar Romero

1951 THE LADY WITH A LAMP
Director: Herbert Wilcox
Co-stars: Anna Neagle Michael Wilding Felix Aylmer

1970 THE ENGAGEMENT
Director: Paul Joyce
Co-stars: David Warner Michael Bates Juliet Harmer

DIANA COUPLAND

1968 CHARLIE BUBBLES
Director: Albert Finney
Co-stars: Albert Finney Liza Minnelli Billie Whitelaw

1970 SPRING AND PORT WINE
Director: Peter Hammond
Co-stars: James Mason Susan George Hannah Gordon

1970 THE TWELVE CHAIRS
Director: Mel Brooks
Co-stars: Mel Brooks Ron Moody Frank Langella

1972 BLESS THIS HOUSE
Director: Gerald Thomas
Co-stars: Sid James Sally Geeson Terry Scott

1975 OPERATION DAYBREAK
Director: Lewis Gilbert
Co-stars: Timothy Bottoms Martin Shaw Nicola Pagett

CLOTILDE COURAU

1992 MAP OF THE HUMAN HEART
Director: Vincent Ward
Co-stars: Jason Scott Lee Anne Parillaud Patrick Bergin

1993 THE PICKLE
Director: Paul Mazursky
Co-stars: Danny Aiello Dyan Cannon Shelley Winters

NICOLE COURCEL

1949 RENDEZVOUS DE JUILLET
Director: Jacques Becker
Co-stars: Daniel Gelin Maurice Ronet Brigitte Auber

1949 LA MARIE DU PORT
Director: Marcel Carne
Co-stars: Jean Gabin Blanchette Brunoy Claude Romain

1962 SUNDAYS AND CYBELE
Director: Serge Bougignon
Co-stars: Hardy Kruger Patricia Gozzi

HAZEL COURT

1944 DREAMING
Director: John Baxter
Co-stars: Flanagan & Allen Dick Francis Philip Wade

1946 CARNIVAL
Director: Stanley Haynes
Co-stars: Sally Gray Michael Wilding Bernard Miles

1946 GAIETY GEORGE
Director: George King
Co-stars: Richard Greene Ann Todd Peter Graves

1946 MEET ME AT DAWN
Director: Thornton Freeland
Co-stars: William Eythe Stanley Holloway Basil Sidney

1947 THE ROOT OF ALL EVIL
Director: Brock Williams
Co-stars: Phyllis Calvert Michael Rennie

1947 HOLIDAY CAMP
Director: Ken Annakin
Co-stars: Jack Warner Kathleen Harrison Dennis Price

1947 DEAR MURDERER
Director: Arthur Crabtree
Co-stars: Eric Portman Greta Gynt Dennis Price

1948 BOND STREET
Director: Gordon Parry
Co-stars: Roland Young Jean Kent Derek Farr

1949 FORBIDDEN
Director: George King
Co-stars: Douglass Montgomery Patricia Burke Ronald Shiner

1952 GHOST SHIP
Director: Vernon Sewell
Co-stars: Dermot Walsh Hugh Burden John Robinson

1953 COUNTERSPY
Director: Vernon Sewell
Co-stars: Dermot Walsh Hermione Baddeley Bill Travers

1954 DEVIL GIRL FROM MARS
Director: David MacDonald
Co-stars: Patricia Laffan Hugh McDermott

1955 THE NARROWING CIRCLE
Director: Charles Saunders
Co-stars: Paul Carpenter Ferdy Mayne Trevor Reid

1956 BEHIND THE HEADLINES
Director: Charles Saunders
Co-stars: Paul Carpenter Adrienne Corri

1957 THE CURSE OF FRANKENSTEIN
Director: Terence Fisher
Co-stars: Peter Cushing Christopher Lee

1957 HOUR OF DECISION
Director: C. Pennington-Richards
Co-stars: Jeff Morrow Lionel Jeffries

1959 THE MAN WHO COULD CHEAT DEATH
Director: Terence Fisher
Co-stars: Anton Diffring Christopher Lee

1959 THE SHAKEDOWN
Director: John Lemont
Co-stars: Donald Pleasence Bill Owen Robert Beatty

1960 DOCTOR BLOOD'S COFFIN
Director: Sidney Furie
Co-stars: Kieron Moore Ian Hunter Kenneth J. Warren

1961 THE PREMATURE BURIAL
Director: Roger Corman
Co-stars: Ray Milland Heather Angel Richard Ney

1963 THE RAVEN
Director: Roger Corman
Co-stars: Vincent Price Peter Lorre Boris Karloff

1964 THE MASQUE OF THE RED DEATH
Director: Roger Corman
Co-stars: Vincent Price Jane Asher Patrick Magee

SUZANNE COURTAL

1952 LES JEUX INDERDITS
Director: Rene Clement
Co-stars: Brigitte Fossey Georges Poujouly Amadee

MARGARET COURTENAY

1986 DUET FOR ONE
Director: Andrei Konchalovsky
Co-stars: Julie Andrews Alan Bates Max Von Sydow

CICELY COURTNEIDGE *(Married Jack Hulbert)*

1930 ELSTREE CALLING
Director: Jack Hulbert
Co-stars: Jack Hulbert Tommy Handley Will Fyffe

1931 THE GHOST TRAIN
Director: Walter Forde
Co-stars: Jack Hulbert Donald Calthrop Ann Todd

1932 HAPPY EVER AFTER
Director: Robert Stevenson
Co-stars: Jack Hulbert Lilian Harvey Sonnie Hale

1932 JACK'S THE BOY
Director: Walter Forde
Co-stars: Jack Hulbert Francis Lister Winifred Shotter

1933 FALLING FOR YOU
Director: Robert Stevenson
Co-stars: Jack Hulbert Tamara Desni Alfred Drayton

1933 AUNT SALLY
Director: Tim Whelan
Co-stars: Sam Hardy Billy Milton Hartley Power

1933 SOLDIERS OF THE KING
Director: Maurice Elvey
Co-stars: Anthony Bushell Dorothy Hyson Edward Everett Horton

1935 THINGS ARE LOOKING UP
Director: Albert De Courville
Co-stars: Max Miller William Gargan

1935   THE PERFECT GENTLEMAN
Director: Tim Whelan
Co-stars: Frank Morgan Henry Stephenson Heather Angel

1935   ME AND MARLBOROUGH
Director: Victor Saville
Co-stars: Tom Walls Barry McKay Alfred Drayton

1936   EVERYBODY DANCE
Director: Charles Riesner
Co-stars: Ernest Truex Percy Parsons Billie De La Volta

1937   TAKE MY TIP
Director: Herbert Mason
Co-stars: Jack Hulbert Frank Cellier Harold Huth

1940   UNDER YOUR HAT
Director: Maurice Elvey
Co-stars: Jack Hulbert Austin Trevor Leonora Corbett

1960   THE SPIDER'S WEB
Director: Godfrey Grayson
Co-stars: Jack Hulbert Glynis Johns John Justin

1962   THE L-SHAPED ROOM
Director: Bryan Forbes
Co-stars: Leslie Caron Tom Bell Brock Peters

**1965   THOSE MAGNIFICENT MEN
          IN THEIR FLYING MACHINES**
Director: Ken Annakin
Co-stars: Benny Hill Tony Hancock Terry-Thomas

1966   THE WRONG BOX
Director: Byran Forbes
Co-stars: Ralph Richardson John Mills Michael Caine

1972   NOT NOW DARLING
Director: Ray Cooney
Co-stars: Ray Cooney Jack Hulbert Leslie Phillips

DAPHNE COURTNEY

1936   MURDER BY ROPE
Director: George Pearson
Co-stars: Constance Godridge Wilfred Hyde White

INEZ COURTNEY.

1932   BIG CITY BLUES
Director: Mervyn LeRoy
Co-stars: Joan Blondell Eric Linden Humphrey Bogart

1935   MILLIONS IN THE AIR
Director: Ray McCarey
Co-stars: Wendy Barrie Willie Howard John Howard

1935   THE RAVEN
Director: Lew Landers
Co-stars: Bela Lugosi Boris Karloff Irene Ware

1937   PARTNERS IN CRIME
Director: Ralph Murphy
Co-stars: Lynne Overman Roscoe Karns Anthony Quinn

1938   FIVE OF A KIND
Director: Herbert Leeds
Co-stars: Jean Hersholt Claire Trevor Cesar Romero

1939   BLONDIE MEETS THE BOSS
Director: Frank Strayer
Co-stars: Penny Singleton Arthur Lake Don Beddoe

1940   THE SHOP AROUND THE CORNER
Director: Ernst Lubitsch
Co-stars: James Stewart Margaret Sullavan

JENI COURTNEY (Child)

1991   THE SECRET OF ROAN INNISH
Director: John Sayles
Co-stars: Richard Sheridan Cillian Byrne

MAGGIE COUSINEAU

1980   RETURN OF THE SECAUCUS SEVEN
Director: John Sayles
Co-stars: John Sayles Mark Arnott Gordon Clapp

MARY COUSTAS

1993   HERCULES RETURNS
Director: David Parker
Co-stars: David Argue Bruce Spence

JULIE COVINGTON

1982   ASCENDANCY
Director: Edward Bennett
Co-stars: Ian Charleson John Phillips Susan Engel

JANE COWL

1943   STAGE DOOR CANTEEN
Director: Frank Borzage
Co-stars: Cheryl Walker Lon McCallister Judith Anderson

1949   ONCE MORE, MY DARLING
Director: Robert Montgomery
Co-stars: Robert Montgomery Ann Blyth Charles McGraw

1949   NO MAN OF HER OWN
Director: Mitchell Leisen
Co-stars: Barbara Stanwyck John Lund Phyllis Thaxter

1950   THE SECRET FURY
Director: Mel Ferrer
Co-stars: Claudette Colbert Robert Ryan Paul Kelly

1951   PAYMENT ON DEMAND
Director: Curtis Bernhardt
Co-stars: Bette Davis Barry Sullivan Kent Taylor

NICOLA COWPER

1985   DREAMCHILD
Director: Gavin Miller
Co-stars: Coral Browne Peter Gallagher Ian Holm

1985   THE BURSTON REBELLION
Director: Norman Stone
Co-stars: Eileen Atkins Bernard Hill John Shrapnel

1987   LIONHEART
Director: Franklin Schaffner
Co-stars: Eric Stoltz Gabriel Byrne Dexter Fletcher

COURTENEY COX

**1987   IF IT'S TUESDAY?
          IT STILL MUST BE BELGIUM**
Director: Bob Sweeney
Co-stars: Claude Akins Bruce Weitz

1987   MASTERS OF THE UNIVERSE
Director: Gary Goddard
Co-stars: Dolph Lundgren Frank Langella Meg Foster

1988   COCOON: THE RETURN
Director: Daniel Petrie
Co-stars: Don Ameche Hume Croyn Jessica Tandy

1989   ROXANNE: THE PRIZE PULITZER
Director: Richard Colla
Co-stars: Perry King Chynna Phillips Sondra Blake

1991   SHAKING THE TREE
Director: Duane Clark
Co-stars: Arye Gross Gale Hansen Christina Haag

1992   BATTLING FOR BEAUTY
Director: Art Wolf
Co-stars: Debbie Reynolds Suzanne Pleshette Doug McClure

1993 ACE VENTURA, PET DETECTIVE
Director: Tom Shadyac
Co-stars: Jim Carrey Sean Young Dan Marino

1995 A FEEL FOR MURDER
Director: Jack Sholder
Co-stars: Jeff Fahey Michael Beach

1997 SCREAM
Director: Wes Craven
Co-stars: Henry Winkler Drew Barrymore Neve Campbell

1997 SCREAM 2
Director: Wes Craven
Co-Star Neve Campbell

RUTH COX
1979 THE ATTIC
Director: George Edwards
Co-stars: Carrie Snodgress Ray Milland Rosemary Murphy

VEANNE COX
1989 MISS FIRECRACKER
Director: Thomas Schlamme
Co-stars: Holly Hunter Mary Steenburgen Tim Robbins

RUTH CRACKNELL
1978 THE NIGHT PROWLER
Director: Jim Sharman
Co-stars: Kerry Walker John Frawley Maggie Kirkpatrick

CAROLYN CRAIG
1958 HOUSE ON HAUNTED HILL
Director: William Castle
Co-stars: Vincent Price Carol Ohmart Richard Long

CATHERINE CRAIG
1942 YOU WERE NEVER LOVELIER
Director: William A. Seiter
Co-stars: Fred Astaire Rita Hayworth Adolphe Menjou

1943 SPY TRAIN
Co-stars: Richard Travis Bill Hunter Thelma White

1944 HERE COME THE WAVES
Director: Mark Sandrich
Co-stars: Bing Crosby Betty Hutton Sonny Tufts

CHARMAINE GRAIG
**1994 WHITE FANG 2:
MYTH OF THE WHITE WOLF**
Director: Ken Olin
Co-stars: Scott Bairstow Victoria Racimo

DAVINA CRAIG
1939 HOOTS MON!
Director: Roy William Neill
Co-stars: Florence Desmond Max Miller Garry Marsh

DIANE CRAIG
1970 NED KELLY
Director: Tony Richardson
Co-stars: Mick Jagger Allen Bickford Mark McManus

1977 THE MANGO TREE
Director: Kevin Dobson
Co-stars: Christopher Pate Geraldine Fitzgerald Robert Helpman

1981 DOUBLE DEAL
Director: Brian Kavanagh
Co-stars: Louis Jourdan Angela Punch McGregor Bruce Spence

1986 TRAVELLING NORTH
Director: Carl Schultz
Co-stars: Leo McKern Julia Blake Graham Kennedy

HELEN CRAIG
1948 THEY LIVE BY NIGHT
Director: Nicholas Ray
Co-stars: Farley Granger Cathy O'Donnell Howard Da Silva

1948 THE SNAKE PIT
Director: Anatole Litvak
Co-stars: Olivia De Havilland Leo Genn Mark Stevens

WENDY CRAIG
1958 ROOM AT THE TOP
Director: Jack Clayton
Co-stars: Laurence Harvey Simone Signoret Heather Sears

1962 THE MIND BENDERS
Director: Basil Dearden
Co-stars: Dirk Bogarde John Clements Mary Ure

1963 THE SERVANT
Director: Joseph Losey
Co-stars: Dirk Bogarde James Fox Sarah Miles

1965 THE NANNY
Director: Seth Holt
Co-stars: Bette Davis Jill Bennett Pamela Franklin

1966 JUST LIKE A WOMAN
Director: Bob Fuest
Co-stars: Francis Matthews John Wood Dennis Price

1967 I'LL NEVER FORGET WHAT'S 'IS NAME
Director: Michael Winner
Co-stars: Oliver Reed Orson Welles

1977 JOSEPH ANDREWS
Director: Tony Richardson
Co-stars: Peter Firth Ann-Margret Hugh Griffith

YVONNE CRAIG
1957 YOUNG LAND
Director: Ted Tetzlaff
Co-stars: Dan O'Herlihy Patrick Wayne Dennis Hopper

1959 THE GENE KUPRA STORY
Director: Don Weis
Co-stars: Sal Mineo Susan Kohner James Darren

1961 BY LOVE POSSESSED
Director: John Sturges
Co-stars: Lana Turner Efrem Zimbalist Jnr. Barbara Bel Geddes

1962 IT HAPPENED AT THE WORLD'S FAIR
Director: Norman Taurog
Co-stars: Elvis Presley Joan O'Brien

1966 ONE SPY TOO MANY
Director: Joseph Sargent
Co-stars: Robert Vaughn David McCallum Dorothy Provine

1966 ONE OF OUR SPIES IS MISSING
Co-stars: Robert Vaughn David McCallum Leo G. Carroll

1967 IN LIKE FLINT
Director: Gordon Douglas
Co-stars: James Coburn Lee J. Cobb Anna Lee

INGRID CRAIGIE
1992 FORCE OF DUTY
Director: Pat O'Connor
Co-stars: Donal McCann Adrian Dunbar Patrick Malahide

1994 A MAN OF NO IMPORTANCE
Director: Suri Krishnamma
Co-stars: Albert Finney Tara Fitzgerald Rufus Sewell

JEANNE CRAIN
Nominated For Best Actress In 1949 For "Pinky"
1944 HOME IN INDIANA
Director: Henry Hathaway
Co-stars: June Haver Lon McCallister Walter Brennan

1944   **IN THE MEANTIME, DARLING**
Director: Otto Preminger
Co-stars: Frank Latimore Eugene Pallette Mary Nash

1944   **WINGED VICTORY**
Director: George Cukor
Co-stars: Lon McCallister Edmund O'Brien Don Taylor

1945   **STATE FAIR**
Director: Walter Lang
Co-stars: Dick Haymes Dana Andrews Vivian Blaine

1945   **LEAVE HER TO HEAVEN**
Director: John Stahl
Co-stars: Gene Tierney Cornel Wilde Vincent Price

1946   **MARGIE**
Director: Henry King
Co-stars: Glenn Langan Alan Young Lynn Bari

1946   **CENTENNIAL SUMMER**
Director: Otto Preminger
Co-stars: Cornel Wilde Linda Darnell Walter Brennan

1948   **YOU WERE MEANT FOR ME**
Director: Lloyd Bacon
Co-stars: Dan Dailey Oscar Levant Barbara Lawrence

1948   **APARTMENT FOR PEGGY**
Director: George Seaton
Co-stars: Edmund Gwenn William Holden Gene Lockhart

1948   **A LETTER TO THREE WIVES**
Director: Joseph Mankiewicz
Co-stars: Ann Sothern Linda Darnell Kirk Douglas

1949   **PINKY**
Director: Elia Kazan
Co-stars: Ethel Barrymore Ethel Waters William Lundigan

1949   **THE FAN**
Director: Otto Preminger
Co-stars: Madeleine Carroll George Sanders Richard Greene

1950   **CHEAPER BY THE DOZEN**
Director: Walter Lang
Co-stars: Clifton Webb Myrna Loy Barbara Bates

1950   **I'LL GET BY**
Director: Richard Sale
Co-stars: June Haver Gloria De Haven William Lundigan

1951   **PEOPLE WILL TALK**
Director: Joseph Mankiewicz
Co-stars: Cary Grant Finlay Currie Walter Slezak

1951   **TAKE CARE OF MY LITTLE GIRL**
Director: Jean Negulesco
Co-stars: Mitzi Gaynor Dale Robertson Jean Peters

1951   **THE MODEL AND THE MARRIAGE BROKER**
Director: George Cukor
Co-stars: Thelma Ritter Scott Brady

1952   **BELLES ON THEIR TOES**
Director: Henry Levin
Co-stars: Myrna Loy Edward Arnold Jeffrey Hunter

1952   **O.HENRY'S FULL HOUSE**
Director: Henry King
Co-stars: Charles Laughton David Wayne Marilyn Monroe

1953   **DANGEROUS CROSSING**
Director: Joseph Newman
Co-stars: Michael Rennie Casey Adams Carl Betz

1953   **CITY OF BAD MEN**
Director: Harmon Jones
Co-stars: Dale Robertson Richard Boone Lloyd Bridges

1953   **VICKI**
Director: Harry Horner
Co-stars: Jean Peters Richard Boone Casey Adams

1954   **DUEL IN THE JUNGLE**
Director: George Marshall
Co-stars: Dana Andrews David Farrar Patrick Barr

1955   **MAN WITHOUT A STAR**
Director: King Vidor
Co-stars: Kirk Douglas Claire Trevor Richard Boone

1955   **THE SECOND GREATEST SEX**
Director: George Marshall
Co-stars: George Nader Bert Lahr Mamie Van Doren

1955   **GENTLEMEN MARRY BRUNETTES**
Director: Richard Sale
Co-stars: Jane Russell Alan Young Rudy Vallee

1956   **THE FASTEST GUN ALIVE**
Director: Russel Rouse
Co-stars: Glenn Ford Broderick Crawford Russ Tamblyn

1957   **THE JOKER IS WILD**
Director: Charles Vidor
Co-stars: Frank Sinatra Mitzi Gaynor Eddie Albert

1957   **THE TATTERED DRESS**
Director: Jack Arnold
Co-stars: Jeff Chandler Jack Carson Gail Russell

1960   **GUNS OF THE TIMBERLAND**
Director: Robert Webb
Co-stars: Alan Ladd Gilbert Roland Frankie Avalon

1961   **NEFERTITE, QUEEN OF THE NILE**

1962   **MADISON AVENUE**
Director: Bruce Humberstone
Co-stars: Dana Andrews Eleanor Parker Eddie Albert

1962   **PONTIUS PILATE**
Director: Irving Rapper
Co-stars: Jean Marais John Drew Barrymore Basil Rathbone

1967   **HOT ROAD TO HELL**

1972   **SKYJACKED**
Director: John Guilermin
Co-stars: Charlton Heston Yvette Mimieux Walter Pidgeon

NORMA CRANE

1956   **TEA AND SYMPATHY**
Director: Vincente Minnelli
Co-stars: Deborah Kerr John Kerr Leif Erickson

1961   **ALL IN A NIGHT'S WORK**
Director: Joseph Anthony
Co-stars: Shirley MacLaine Dean Martin Charles Ruggles

1966   **PENELOPE**
Director: Arthur Hiller
Co-stars: Natalie Wood Ian Bannen Peter Falk

1971   **FIDLER ON THE ROOF**
Director: Norman Jewison
Co-stars: Topol Molly Picon Paul Michael Glaser

BARBARA CRAMPTON

1985   **RE-ANIMATOR**
Director: Stuart Gordon
Co-stars: Jeffrey Combs Bruce Abbott Robert Sampson

1989   **PUPPET MASTER**
Co-stars: David Schmoeller
Co-stars: Paul Lemat Irene Miracle Matt Roe

GEMMA CRAVEN *(Married Fraser Hines)*

1976   **THE SLIPPER AND THE ROSE**
Director: Bryan Forbes
Co-stars: Richard Chamberlain Kenneth More

1983 WAGNER
Director: Tony Palmer
Co-stars: Richard Burton Vanessa Redgrave John Gielgud

1991 DOUBLE X
Director: Shani Grewal
Co-stars: Simon Ward William Katt Norman Wisdom

1993 THE MARSHSAL
Director: Alan Clayton
Co-stars: Alfred Molina Anna Cropper Jude Law

1993 THE MYSTERY OF EDWIN DROOD
Director: Timothy Forder
Co-stars: Robert Powell Nanette Newman Finty Williams

MIMI CRAVEN

1994 MIDNIGHT HEAT
Director: Harvey Frost
Co-stars: Tim Matheson Stephen Mendel

1994 LAST GASP
Director: Scott McGinnis
Co-stars: Joanna Pacula Robert Patrick

ANNE CRAWFORD

1942 NIGHT INVADER
Director: Herbert Mason
Co-stars: David Farrar Carl Jaffe Marius Goring

1942 THE PETERVILLE DIAMOND
Director: Walter Forde
Co-stars: Donald Stewart Renee Houston William Hartnell

1943 MILLIONS LIKE US
Director: Frank Launder
Co-stars: Patricia Roc Gordon Jackson Eric Portman

1943 THE DARK TOWER
Director: John Harlow
Co-stars: Ben Lyon David Farrar Herbert Lom William Hartnell

1943 THE HUNDRED POUND WINDOW
Director: Brian Desmond Hurst
Co-stars: Frederick Leister David Farrar

1944 TWO THOUSAND WOMEN
Director: Frank Launder
Co-stars: Phyllis Calvert Flora Robson Patricia Roc

1945 THEY WERE SISTERS
Director: Arthur Crabtree
Co-stars: James Mason Phyllis Calvert Dulcie Gray

1946 BEDELIA
Director: Lance Comfort
Co-stars: Margaret Lockwood Ian Hunter Barry K. Barnes

1946 CARAVAN
Director: Arthur Crabtree
Co-stars: Stewart Granger Jean Kent Robert Helpman

1947 MASTER OF BANKDAM
Director: Walter Forde
Co-stars: Tom Walls Dennis Price Stephen Murray

1948 NIGHT BEAT
Director: Harold Huth
Co-stars: Maxwell Reed Ronald Howard Christine Norden

1948 IT'S HARD TO BE GOOD
Director: Jeffrey Dell
Co-stars: Jimmy Handley Raymond Huntley

1948 DAUGHTER OF DARKNESS
Director: Lance Comfort
Co-stars: Siobhan McKenna Maxwell Reed Barry Morse

1948 THE BLIND GODDESS
Director: Harold French
Co-stars: Eric Portman Michael Dennison Claire Bloom

1950 TONY DRAWS A HORSE
Director: John Paddy Carstairs
Co-stars: Cecil Parker Derek Bond Barbara Murray

1950 TRIO
Director: Harold French
Co-stars: James Hayter Nigel Patrick Jean Simmons

1951 THUNDER ON THE HILL
Director: Douglas Sirk
Co-stars: Claudette Colbert Ann Blyth Robert Douglas

1953 STREET CORNER
Director: Muriel Box
Co-stars: Rosamund John Peggy Cummings Terence Morgan

1953 KNIGHTS OF THE ROUND TABLE
Director: Richard Thorpe
Co-stars: Robert Taylor Mel Ferrer Ava Gardner

1954 MAD ABOUT MEN
Director: Ralph Thomas
Co-stars: Glynis Johns Donald Sinden Margaret Rutherford

CAROL ANN CRAWFORD

1983 ANOTHER TIME, ANOTHER PLACE
Director: Michael Radford
Co-stars: Phyllis Logan Giovanni Mauriello

CINDY CRAWFORD

1996 FAIR GAME
Director: Andrew Sipes
Co-stars: William Baldwin Steven Berkoff Christopher McDonald

1996 UNZIPPED
Director: Douglas Keeve
Co-stars: Sandra Bernhard Naomi Campbell Kate Moss

GWEN CRAWFORD

1944 HERE COME THE WAVES
Director: Mark Sandrich
Co-stars: Bing Crosby Betty Hutton Sonny Tufts

JOAN CRAWFORD
(Started Career As Lucille De Sueur) (Billie Cassin)
(Married Douglas Fairbanks Jnr / Franchot Tone)
Oscar For Best Actress In 1945 For "Mildred Pierce". Nominated For
Best Actress In 1947 For "Possessed" And In 1952 For "Sudden Fear"

1925 PRETTY LADIES
Director: Monta Bell
Co-stars: Zasu Pitts Tom Moore Norma Shearer

1925 SALLY, IRENE AND MARY
Director: Edmund Goulding
Co-stars: Constance Bennett Sally O'Neil Henry Kolker

1926 THE TAXI DANCER
Director: Harry Millard
Co-stars: Owen Moore Gertrude Astor

1927 THE UNKNOWN
Director: Tod Browning
Co-stars: Lon Chaney Norman Kerry John George

1927 TRAMP, TRAMP, TRAMP
Director: Harry Edwards
Co-stars: Harry Langdon Alec B. Frances

1928 ACROSS TO SINGAPORE
Co-Star Ramon Navarro

1928 OUR DANCING DAUGHTERS
Director: Harry Beaumont
Co-stars: Johnny Mack Brown Anita Page Nils Asther

1929 OUR MODERN MAIDENS
Co-stars: Douglas Fairbanks Jnr. Rod La Rocque Anita Page

1929 UNTAMED
Co-stars: Robert Montgomery Ernest Torrence

1929 THE HOLLYWOOD REVUE OF 1929
Director: Charles Reisner
Co-stars: Jack Benny Laurel & Hardy Buster Keaton

1930 MONTANA MOON
Director: Malcolm St. Clair
Co-stars: Johnny Mack Brown Ricardo Cortez

1930 OUR BLUSHING BRIDE
Co-stars: Robert Montgomery Anita Page Dorothy Sebastian

1931 LAUGHING SINNERS
Director: Harry Beaumont
Co-stars: Clark Gable Neil Hamilton Guy Kibbee

1931 DANCE, FOOLS, DANCE
Director: Harry Beaumont
Co-stars: Lester Vail Clark Gable Cliff Edwards

1931 PAID
Director: Sam Wood
Co-stars: Kent Douglass Robert Armstrong Marie Prevost

1931 POSSESSED
Director: Clarence Brown
Co-stars: Clark Gable Wallace Ford Frank Conroy

1931 THIS MODERN AGE
Director: Nick Grinde
Co-stars: Pauline Frederick Neil Hamilton Emma Dunn

1932 RAIN
Director: Lewis Milestone
Co-stars: Walter Huston Willlam Gargan Beulah Bondi

1932 LETTY LYNTON
Director: Clarence Brown
Co-stars: Robert Montgomery May Robson Lewis Stone

1932 GRAND HOTEL
Director: Edmund Goulding
Co-stars: Greta Garbo John Barrymore Lionel Barrymore

1933 DANCING LADY
Director: Robert Z Leonard
Co-stars: Clark Gable Fred Astaire Nelson Eddy

1933 TODAY WE LIVE
Director: Howard Hawks
Co-stars: Gary Cooper Franchot Tone Robert Young

1934 SADIE McKEE
Director: Clarence Brown
Co-stars: Franchot Tone Edward Arnold Gene Raymond

1934 CHAINED
Director: Clarence Brown
Co-stars: Clark Gable Otto Kruger Stuart Erwin

1935 FORSAKING ALL OTHERS
Director: W. S. Van Dyke
Co-stars: Clark Gable Robert Montgomery Billie Burke

1935 I LIVE MY LIFE
Director: W. S. Van Dyke
Co-stars: Brian Aherne Frank Morgan Aline McMahon

1935 NO MORE LADIES
Director: George Cukor
Co-stars: Robert Montgomery Franchot Tone Joan Fontaine

1936 LOVE ON THE RUN
Director: W. S. Van Dyke
Co-stars: Clark Gable Franchot Tone Reginald Owen

1936 THE GORGEOUS HUSSY
Director: Clarence Brown
Co-stars: Robert Taylor James Stewart Franchot Tone

1937 MANNEQUIN
Director: Frank Borzage
Co-stars: Spencer Tracy Alan Curtis Ralph Morgan

1937 THE LAST OF MRS. CHEYNEY
Director: Richard Boleslawski
Co-stars: Robert Montgomery William Powell

1937 THE BRIDE WORE RED
Director: Dorothy Arzner
Co-stars: Robert Young Franchot Tone Billie Burke

1938 THE SHINING HOUR
Director: Frank Borzage
Co-stars: Robert Young Margaret Sullavan Melvyn Douglas

1939 ICE FOLLIES OF 1939
Director: Reinhold Schunzel
Co-stars: James Stewart Lew Ayres Lionel Stander

1939 THE WOMEN
Director: George Cukor
Co-stars: Norma Shearer Rosalind Russell Joan Fontaine

1940 SUSAN AND GOD
Director: George Cukor
Co-stars: Fredric March Ruth Hussey Rita Hayworth

1940 STRANGE CARGO
Director: Frank Borzage
Co-stars: Clark Gable Ian Hunter Peter Lorre

1941 WHEN LADIES MEET
Director: Robert Z Leonard
Co-stars: Greer Garson Robert Taylor Herbert Marshall

1941 A WOMAN'S FACE
Director: George Cukor
Co-stars: Melvyn Douglas Conrad Veidt Osa Massen

1942 THEY ALL KISSED THE BRIDE
Director: Alexander Hall
Co-Star Melvyn Douglas Roland Young Billie Burke

1943 REUNION IN FRANCE
Director: Jules Dassin
Co-stars: John Wayne Philip Dorn Reginald Owen

1943 ABOVE SUSPICION
Director: Richard Thorpe
Co-stars: Fred MacMurray Conrad Veidt Basil Rathbone

1944 HOLLYWOOD CANTEEN
Director: Delmer Daves
Co-stars: Robert Hutton Joan Leslie Bette Davis

1945 MILDRED PIERCE
Director: Michael Curtiz
Co-stars: Ann Blyth Jack Carson Zachary Scott

1946 HUMORESQUE
Director: Jean Negulesco
Co-stars: John Garfield Oscar Levant Joan Chandler

1947 DAISY KENYON
Director: Otto Preminger
Co-stars: Henry Fonda Dana Andrews Peggy Ann Garner

1947 POSSESSED
Director: Curtis Bernhardt
Co-stars: Raymond Massey Van Heflin Geraldine Brooks

1949 FLAMINGO ROAD
Director: Michael Curtiz
Co-stars: David Brian Sydney Greenstreet Zachary Scott

1949 IT'S A GREAT FEELING
Director: David Butler
Co-stars: Doris Day Dennis Morgan Jack Carson

1950 HARRIET CRAIG
Director: Vincent Sherman
Co-stars: Wendell Corey Allyn Joslyn

1950 THE DAMNED DON'T CRY
Director: Vincent Sherman
Co-stars: Kent Smith David Brian Steve Cochran

1951 GOODBYE MY FANCY
Director: Vincent Sherman
Co-stars: Robert Young Frank Lovejoy Eve Arden

1952 SUDDEN FEAR
Director: David Miller
Co-stars: Joseph Kaufman Jack Palance Gloria Grahame

1952 THIS WOMAN IS DANGEROUS
Director: Felix Feist
Co-stars: David Brian Dennis Morgan Mari Aldon

1953 TORCH SONG
Director: Charles Walters
Co-stars: Michael Wilding Gig Young Henry Morgan

1953 JOHNNY GUITAR
Director: Nicholas Ray
Co-stars: Sterling Hayden Mercedes McCambridge

1955 FEMALE ON THE BEACH
Director: Joseph Pevney
Co-stars: Jeff Chandler Jan Sterling Cecil Kellaway

1955 QUEEN BEE
Director: Ranald MacDougall
Co-stars: Barry Sullivan John Ireland Fay Wray

1956 AUTUMN LEAVES
Director: Robert Aldrich
Co-stars: Cliff Robertson Vera Miles Lorne Green

1957 THE STORY OF ESTHER COSTELLO
Director: David Miller
Co-stars: Heather Sears Rossano Brazzi

1959 THE BEST OF EVERYTHING
Director: Jean Negulesco
Co-stars: Hope Lange Louis Jourdan Brian Aherne

1962 WHATEVER HAPPENED TO BABY JANE?
Director: Robert Aldrich
Co-stars: Bette Davis Victor Buono Anna Lee

1963 THE CARETAKERS
Director: Hall Bartlett
Co-stars: Polly Bergen Robert Stack Herbert Marshall

1964 STRAIGHT-JACKET
Director: William Castle
Co-stars: Diane Baker Rochelle Hudson

1965 I SAW WHAT YOU DID
Director: William Castle
Co-stars: John Ireland Leif Ericson

1967 BERSERK
Director: Jim O'Connolly
Co-stars: Robert Hardy Diana Dors Judy Geeson

1970 TROG
Director: Freddie Frances
Co-stars: Michael Gough Bernard Kay David Griffin

KATHERINE CRAWFORD

1969 A WALK IN THE SPRING RAIN
Director: Guy Green
Co-stars: Ingrid Bergman Anthony Quinn

1976 CODE NAME: MINUS ONE
Director: Alan Levi
Co-stars: Ben Murphy Richard Dysart Dana Elcar

MARTHA CRAWFORD

1985 FOOL FOR LOVE
Director: Robert Altman
Co-stars: Sam Shepard Kim Basinger Randy Quaid

RACHEL CRAWFORD

1996 CAPTIVE HEART: THE JAMES MINK STORY
Director: Bruce Pittman
Co-stars: Lou Gossett Jnr. Kate Nelligan Peter Outerbridge

JOY, LEANNA, MONICA CREEL (*Triplets*)

1989 PARENT TRAP III
Director: Mollie Miller
Co-stars: Hayley Mills Barry Bostwick Jayne Meadows

1989 PARENT TRAP HAWAIIAN HONEYMOON
Director: Mollie Miller
Co-stars: Hayley Mills Barry Bostwick

TERESA CRESPO

1988 OUT OF THE DARK
Director: Michael Schroeder
Co-stars: Karen Black Cameron Dye

LAURA HOPE CREWS

1933 BLIND ADVENTURE
Director: Ernest Schoedsack
Co-stars: Robert Armstrong Roland Young

1933 I LOVED YOU WEDNESDAY
Director: Henry King
Co-stars: Warner Baxter Elissa Landi Victor Jory

1933 IF I WERE FREE
Director: Elliott Nugent
Co-stars: Irene Dunne Clive Brook Henry Stephenson

1933 THE SILVER CHORD
Director: John Cromwell
Co-stars: Irene Dunne Joel McCrea Frances Dee

1934 BEHOLD MY WIFE
Director: Mitchell Leisen
Co-stars: Gene Raymond Sylvia Sidney

1934 AGE OF INNOCENCE
Director: Philip Moeller
Co-stars: Irene Dunne John Boles Lionel Atwill

1936 HER MASTER'S VOICE
Director: Joseph Santley
Co-stars: Edward Everett Horton Peggy Conklin

1937 CONFESSION
Director: Joe May
Co-stars: Kay Frances Basil Rathbone Ian Hunter

1937 THE ROAD BACK
Director: James Whale
Co-stars: Richard Cromwell Slim Summerville Barbara Reed

1937 CAMILLE
Director: George Cukor
Co-stars: Greta Garbo Robert Taylor Lionel Barrymore

1937 ANGEL
Director: Ernst Lubitsch
Co-stars: Marlene Dietrich Melvyn Douglas

1938 DOCTOR RHYTHM
Director: Frank Tuttle
Co-stars: Bing Crosby Mary Carlisle Beatrice Lillie

1938 IDIOT'S DELIGHT
Director: Clarence Brown
Co-stars: Clark Gable Norma Shearer Burgess Meredith

1939 THE RAINS CAME
Director: Clarence Brown
Co-stars: Tyrone Power Myrna Loy George Brent

1939 REMEMBER?
Director: Norman Z McLeod
Co-stars: Robert Taylor Greer Garson Lew Ayres

1939 RENO
Director: John Farrow
Co-stars: Richard Dix Gail Patrick Anita Louise

1939 THE STAR MAKER
Director: Roy Del Ruth
Co-stars: Bing Crosby Louise Cambell Ned Sparks

1939 GONE WITH THE WIND
Director: Victor Fleming
Co-stars: Clark Gable Vivien Leigh Leslie Howard

1940 THE GIRL FROM AVENUE A
Director: Otto Brower
Co-stars: Jane Withers Kent Taylor Jesse Ralph

1940 THE LADY WITH RED HAIR
Director: Curtis Bernhardt
Co-stars: Miriam Hopkins Claude Rains Victor Jory

1941 THE FLAME OF NEW ORLEANS
Director: Rene Clair
Co-stars: Marlene Dietrich Roland Young Bruce Cabot

1941 ONE FOOT IN HEAVEN
Director: Irving Rapper
Co-stars: Fredric March Martha Scott Beulah Bondi

WENDY CREWSON

1984 HEARTSOUNDS
Director: Glenn Jordan
Co-stars: James Garner Mary Tyler Moore Sam Wanamaker

1987 A HOBO'S CHRISTMAS
Director: Will MacKenzie
Co-stars: Barnard Hughes Gerald McRaney William Hickey

1988 SPIES, LIES AND NAKED THIGHS
Director: James Frawley
Co-stars: Harry Anderson Linda Purl Ed Begley Jnr

1989 GETTING MARRIED IN BUFFALO JUNCTION
Director: Eric Till
Co-stars: Paul Gross Victoria Snow

1992 FOLKS!
Director: Ted Kotcheff
Co-stars: Don Ameche Tom Selleck Anne Jackson

1992 THE DOCTOR
Director: Randa Haines
Co-stars: William Hurt Christine Lahti Elizabeth Perkins

1993 THE GOOD SON
Director: Joseph Rubin
Co-stars: Elijah Wood Macauley Culkin David Morse

1993 SPENSER: A SAVAGE PLACE
Director: Joseph S. Scanlan
Co-stars: Robert Ulrich Avery Brooks

1997 AIR FORCE ONE
Director: Wolfgang Petersen
Co-stars: Harrison Ford Gary Oldman Dean Stockwell

MISSY CRIDER

1994 GIRLS IN PRISON
Director: John McNaughton
Co-stars: Ione Skye Anne Heche Nicolette Scorsese

1994 JANE'S HOUSE
Director: Glenn Jordan
Co-stars: James Woods Anne Archer Graham Beckel

1994 VISIONS OF TERROR
Director: Sam Pilsbury
Co-stars: Barbara Eden Ted Marcoux

1995 SEARCH FOR SARAH
Director: Fred Gerber
Co-stars: Patty Duke Richard Crenna

ISA CRINO

1963 LILIES OF THE FIELD
Director: Ralph Nelson
Co-stars: Sidney Poitier Lilia Skala Pamela Branch

TRACEY CRISP

1966 PRESS FOR TIME
Director: Robert Asher
Co-stars: Norman Wisdom Derek Bond Angela Browne

1970 PERCY
Director: Ralph Thomas
Co-stars: Hywel Bennett Denholm Elliott Elke Sommer

LINDA CRISTAL

1958 THE PERFECT FURLOUGH
Director: Blake Edwards
Co-stars: Tony Curtis Janet Leigh Keenan Wynn

1958 THE FIEND WHO WALKED THE WEST
Director: Gordon Douglas
Co-stars: Hugh O'Brian Dolores Michaels

1959 THE LAST OF THE FAST GUNS
Director: George Sherman
Co-stars: Gilbert Roland Jock Mahoney Lorne Greene

1960 THE ALAMO
Director: John Wayne
Co-stars: John Wayne Laurence Harvey Richard Widmark

1961 TWO RODE TOGETHER
Director: John Ford
Co-stars: James Stewart Richard Widmark Shirley Jones

1968 PANIC IN THE CITY
Director: Eddie Davis
Co-stars: Howard Duff Stephen McNally Dennis Hopper

1974 MR. MAJESTYK
Director: Richard Fleischer
Co-stars: Charles Bronson Al Lettieri Lee Purcell

1975 THE DEAD DON'T DIE
Director: Curtis Harrington
Co-stars: George Hamilton Ray Milland Ralph Meeker

1977 ANGELS IN HELL
Director: Larry Buchanan
Co-stars: Victor Holchak Lindsay Bloom Royal Dano

CAROLYN CROFT

1988 EVIL IN CLEAR RIVER
Director: Karen Arthur
Co-stars: Lindsay Wagner Randy Quaid Michael Flynn

EMMA CROFT

1992 AS YOU LIKE IT
Director: Christine Edzard
Co-stars: Griff Rhys Jones Cyril Cusack James Fox

DONA CROLL

1989 LOVING HAZEL
Director: Peter Smith
Co-stars: Hugh Quarshie Susan Brown Gemma Darlington

1989 THE REAL EDDY ENGLISH
Director: David Attwood
Co-stars: Stephen Persaud Frank Windsor Sue Devaney

1991 HALLELUJAH ANYHOW
Director: Matthew Jacobs
Co-stars: Keith David George Harris Clare Perkins

HELEN CROMWELL

1933 THE SILVER CORD
Director: John Cromwell
Co-stars: Irene Dunne Joel McCrea Frances Dee

CLAUDIA CRON

1982 HIT AND RUN
Director: Charles Braverman
Co-stars: Paul Perri Will Lee Bart Braverman

1982 DINER
Director: Barry Levinson
Co-stars: Steve Guttenberk Mickey Rourke Ellen Barkin

1983 RUNNING BRAVE
Director: D. S. Everett
Co-stars: Robby Benson Pat Hingle Jeff McCracken

GAIL CRONAUER

1987 POSITIVE ID.
Director: Andy Anderson
Co-stars: Stephanie Rascoe John Davies Laura Lane

LAUREL CRONIN

1991 HOOK
Director: Steven Spielberg
Co-stars: Dustin Hoffman Robin Williams Julia Roberts

1992 BEETHOVEN
Director: Brian Levant
Co-stars: Charles Grodin Bonnie Hunt Dean Jones

1992 HOUSESITTER
Director: Frank Oz
Co-stars: Goldie Hawn Steve Martin Dana Delany

SHERRIE CRONN

1979 THE WORLD IS FULL OF MARRIED MEN
Director: Robert Young
Co-stars: Carroll Baker Paul Nicholas

TANDY CRONYN
(Daughter Of Jessica Tandy And Hume Cronyn)

1984 THE GUARDIAN
Director: David Greene
Co-stars: Martin Sheen Lou Gossett Jnr. Arthur Hill

1991 A MONTH OF SUNDAYS
Director: Allan Kroeker
Co-stars: Hume Cronyn Vincent Gardenia

1991 THE STORY LADY
Director: Larry Elikann
Co-stars: Jessica Tandy Stephanie Zimbalist Ed Begley Jnr.

ANNA CROPPER

1969 ALL NEAT IN BLACK STOCKINGS
Director: Christopher Morahan
Co-stars: Susan George Victor Henry

1970 CROMWELL
Director: Ken Hughes
Co-stars: Richard Harris Alec Guinness Robert Morley

1989 A DAY IN SUMMER
Director: Bob Mahoney
Co-stars: Jack Shepherd Peter Egan Suzanne Bertish

1990 VAN GOGH
Director: Anna Benson Gyles
Co-stars: Linus Roache Jack Shepherd Jim Broadbent

1991 THE OLD DEVILS
Director: Tristram Powell
Co-stars: John Stride Ray Smith Sheila Allen

1993 THE MARSHSAL
Director: Alan Clayton
Co-stars: Alfred Molina Gemma Craven Jude Law

LINDA CROPPER

1991 CHILDREN OF THE DRAGON
Director: Peter Smith
Co-stars: Bob Peck Lily Chen Gary Sweet

ANNETTE CROSBIE

1959 THE BRIDAL PATH
Director: Frank Launder
Co-stars: Bill Travers Fiona Clyne Patricia Bredin

1965 SKY WEST AND CROOKED
Director: John Mills
Co-stars: Hayley Mills Ian McShane Geoffrey Baildon

1970 THE SIX WIVES OF HENRY VIII
Director: John Glenister
Co-stars: Keith Michel Dorothy Tutin Elvi Hale

1976 THE SLIPPER AND THE ROSE
Director: Bryan Forbes
Co-stars: Richard Chamberlain Gemma Craven

1980 HAWK THE SLAYER
Director: Terry Marcel
Co-stars: Jack Palance Bernard Bresslaw Cheryl Campbell

1985 ORDEAL BY INNOCENCE
Director: Desmond Davis
Co-stars: Donald Sutherland Christopher Plummer

1989 BEYOND THE PALE
Director: Diarmuid Lawrence
Co-stars: Prunella Scales Ronald Hines Jeff Rawle

1989 SUMMER'S LEASE
Director: Colin Rogers
Co-stars: Susan Fleetwood John Gielgud Mel Martin

1989 TAKE ME HOME
Director: Jane Howell
Co-stars: Keith Baron Maggie O'Neill Reece Dinsdale

1991 JUTE CITY
Director: Stuart Orme
Co-stars: David O'Hara Joanna Roth John Sessions

1991 THE POPE MUST DIE
Director: Peter Richardson
Co-stars: Robbie Coltrane Beverly D'Angelo Herbert Lom

1992 LEON THE PIG FARMER
Director: Gary Sinyor
Co-stars: Mark Frankel Janet Suzman Brian Glover

CATHY LEE CROSBY

1973 AN INVESTIGATION OF MURDER
Director: Stuart Rosenberg
Co-stars: Walter Matthau Bruce Dern

1974 WONDER WOMAN
Director: Vincent McEveety
Co-stars: Ricardo Montalban Kaz Garas Andrew Prine

1976 TRACKDOWN
Director: Richard Heffron
Co-stars: Jim Mitchum Karen Lamm Anne Archer

1979 THE DARK
Director: John Cardos
Co-stars: William Devane Richard Jaeckel Vivian Blaine

1986 INTIMATE STRANGERS
Director: Robert Ellis Miller
Co-stars: Stacy Keach Teri Garr Priscilla Lopez

1994 UNTAMED LOVE
Director: Paul Aaron
Co-stars: John Getz Ashlee Lauren

DENISE CROSBY

1985 DESERT HEARTS
Director: Donna Deitch
Co-stars: Patricia Charbonneau Helen Shaver Auora Lindley

1988 ARIZONA HEAT
Director: John G. Thomas
Co-stars: Michael Parks Hugh Farrington

1989 PET SEMATARY
Director: Mary Lambert
Co-stars: Dale Midkiff Fred Gwynne Michael Lombard

1994 MAX
Director: Charles Wilkinson
Co-Star R. H. Thomson

KATHRYN CROSBY *(Married Bing Crosby)*

1978 THE INITIATION OF SARAH
Director: Robert Day
Co-stars: Kay Lenz Shelley Winters Tisa Farrow

KIM CROSBY

1989 TARZAN IN MANHATTAN
Director: Michael Schultz
Co-stars: Joe Lara Tony Curtis Jan-Michael Vincent

MARY CROSBY

1981 GOLDEN GATE
Director: Paul Wendkos
Co-stars: Jean Simmons Richard Kiley Perry King

1983 CONFESSIONS OF A MARRIED MAN
Director: Charles Pratt
Co-stars: Robert Conrad Jennifer Warren

1984 THE ICE PIRATES
Director: Stewart Rafill
Co-stars: Robert Urich Anjelica Huston Ron Perlman

1985 FINAL JEOPARDY
Director: Michael Pressman
Co-stars: Richard Thomas Jeff Corey

1988 QUICKER THAN THE EYE
Director: Nicolas Gessner
Co-stars: Ben Gazzara

1990 EATING
Director: Henry Jaglom
Co-stars: Lisa Richards Gwen Welles Frances Bergen

MARCIA CROSS

1990 BAD INFLUENCE
Director: Curtis Hanson
Co-stars: Rob Lowe James Spader Kathleen Wilhoite

1996 ALL SHE EVER WANTED
Director: Michael Scott
Co-Star James Marshall

MARJORIE CROSSLAND

1951 THE CAPTIVE CITY
Director: Robert Wise
Co-stars: John Forsythe Joan Camden

LAURA CROSSLEY

1993 THE SECRET GARDEN
Director: Agnieszka Holland
Co-stars: Kate Maberly Maggie Smith John Lynch

HENRIETTA CROSSMAN

1930 THE ROYAL FAMILY OF BROADWAY
Director: George Cukor
Co-stars: Fredric March Ina Clare Mary Brian

1933 PILGRIMAGE
Director: John Ford
Co-stars: Heather Angel Norman Foster Marian Nixon

1934 AMONG THE MISSING
Co-stars: Richard Cromwell Billy Seward Paul Hurst

1934 CAROLINA
Director: Henry King
Co-stars: Janet Gaynor Lionel Barrymore Robert Young

1934 MENACE
Director: Ralph Murphy
Co-stars: Gertrude Michael Paul Cavanagh Ray Milland

1934 SUCH WOMEN ARE DANGEROUS
Director: James Flood
Co-stars: Warner Baxter Rosemary Ames Rochelle Hudson

1935 ELINOR NORTON
Director: Hamilton McFadden
Co-stars: Claire Trevor Gilbert Roland Hugh Williams

1935 THE DARK ANGEL
Director: Sidney Franklin
Co-stars: Merle Oberon Fredric March Herbert Marshall

1936 CHARLIE CHAN'S SECRET
Director: Gordon Wiles
Co-stars: Warner Oland Rosina Lawrence Astrid Allwyn

1937 PERSONAL PROPERTY
Director: W. S. Van Dyke
Co-stars: Jean Harlow Robert Taylor Reginald Owen

LINDSAY CROUSE *(Married David Mamet)*
Nominated For Best Supporting Actress In 1984 For "Places In The Heart"

1976 ALL THE PRESIDENT'S MEN
Director: Alan Pakula
Co-stars: Robert Redford Dustin Hoffman Martin Balsam

1977 SLAPSHOT
Director: George Roy Hill
Co-stars: Paul Newman Michael Ontkean Jennifer Warren

1977 BETWEEN THE LINES
Director: Joan Micklin Silver
Co-stars: John Heard Jeff Goldblum Jill Eikenberry

1981 PRINCE OF THE CITY
Director: Sidney Lumet
Co-stars: Treat Williams Jerry Orbach Don Billett

1982 THE VERDICT
Director: Sidney Lumet
Co-stars: Paul Newman James Mason Charlotte Rampling

1983 DANIEL
Director: Sidney Lumet
Co-stars: Timothy Hutton Mandy Patinkin Ed Asner

1984 ICEMAN
Director: Fred Schipisi
Co-stars: Timothy Hutton John Lone Josef Sommer

1984 PLACES IN THE HEART
Director: Robert Benton
Co-stars: Sally Field Ed Harris Amy Madigan

1987 HOUSE OF GAMES
Director: David Mamet
Co-stars: Joe Mantegna Mike Nussbaum Lilia Skala

1989 COLUMBO: SEX AND THE MARRIED DETECTIVE
Director: James Frawley
Co-stars: Peter Falk Julia Montgomery

1990 COMMUNION
Director: Philippe Mora
Co-stars: Christopher Walken Joel Carlson Frances Sternhagen

1990 DESPERATE HOURS
Director: Michael Cimino
Co-stars: Mickey Rourke Anthony Hopkins Mimi Rogers

1993 CHANTILLY LACE
Director: Linda Yellin
Co-Star Jill Eikenberry

1993 OUT OF DARKNESS
Director: Larry Eikann
Co-stars: Diana Ross Ann Weldon Beah Richards

1995 THE INDIAN IN THE CUPBOARD
Director: Frank Oz
Co-stars: Rishi Bhat Hal Scardino Steve Coogan

1996 THE JUROR
Director: Brian Gibbon
Co-stars: Demi Moore Alec Baldwin James Gandolfini

1997 THE ARRIVAL
Director: David Twohy
Co-stars: Charlie Sheen Ron Silver

EILEEN CROWE

1936 THE PLOUGH AND THE STARS
Director: John Ford
Co-stars: Barbara Stanwyck Preston Foster Arthur Shields

1946 HUNGRY HILL
Director: Brian Desmond Hurst
Co-stars: Margaret Lockwood Dennis Price Cecil Parker

1949 TOP O' THE MORNING
Director: David Miller
Co-stars: Bing Crosby Barry Fitzgerald Ann Blyth

1952 THE QUIET MAN
Director: John Ford
Co-stars: John Wayne Maureen O'Hara Victor McLaglen

1957 THE RISING OF THE MOON
Director: John Ford
Co-stars: Maureen Connell Cyril Cusack Dennis O'Dea

SARAH CROWE

1992 CARRY ON COLUMBUS
Director: Gerald Thomas
Co-stars: Jim Dale Leslie Phillips Bernard Cribbins

JOSEPHINE CROWELL

1924 HOT WATER
Director: Sam Taylor
Co-stars: Harold Lloyd Jobyna Ralston

1925 THE MERRY WIDOW
Director: Erich Von Stroheim
Co-stars: Mae Murray John Gilbert Tully Marshall

SHELLEY CROWHURST

1968 THE GREAT PONY RAID
Director: Frederic Goode
Co-stars: Edward Underdown Michael Brennan Patrick Barr

JEANANNE CROWLEY

1983 EDUCATING RITA
Director: Lewis Gilbert
Co-stars: Michael Caine Julie Walters Michael Williams

1987 THE VENUS DE MILO INSTEAD
Director: Danny Boyle
Co-stars: Iain Cuthbertson Ruth McGuigan

1989 STAR TRAP
Director: Tony Bicat
Co-stars: Nicky Henson Frances Tomelty Jim Carter

1989 THE REAL CHARLOTTE
Director: Tony Barry
Co-stars: Patrick Bergin Joanna Roth Jemma Redgrave

KATHLEEN CROWLEY

1956 WESTWARD HO THE WAGONS
Director: William Beaudine
Co-stars: Fess Parker Jeff York George Reeves

1959 CURSE OF THE UNDEAD
Director: Edward Dein
Co-stars: Michael Pate Eric Fleming John Hoyt

1965 SHOWDOWN
Director: R. G. Springsteen
Co-stars: Audie Murphy Charles Drake Skip Homeier

1970 THE LAWYER
Director: Sidney Furie
Co-stars: Barry Newman Diana Muldaur Harold Gould

PAT CROWLEY *(Patricia)*

1954 MONEY FROM HOME
Director: George Marshall
Co-stars: Dean Martin Jerry Lewis Richard Haydn

1954 RED GARTERS
Director: George Marshall
Co-stars: Rosemary Clooney Guy Mitchell Jack Carson

1955 SQUARE JUNGLE
Director: Jerry Hopper
Co-stars: Tony Curtis Ernest Borgnine Jim Backus

1956 WALK THE PROUD LAND
Director: Jesse Hibbs
Co-stars: Audie Murphy Anne Bancroft Charles Drake

1956 THERE'S ALWAYS TOMORROW
Director: Douglas Sirk
Co-stars: Barbara Stanwyck Fred MacMurray Joan Bennett

1956 HOLLYWOOD OR BUST
Director: Frank Tashlin
Co-stars: Dean Martin Jerry Lewis Anita Ekberg

1958 THE SCARFACE MOB
Director: Phil Karlson
Co-stars: Robert Stack Neville Brand Keenan Wynn

1965 TO TRAP A SPY
Director: Don Medford
Co-stars: Robert Vaughn Lucianna Paluzzi Fritz Weaver

1965 THE WILD WOMEN OF WONGO
Director: James Wolcott
Co-Star Jean Hawkshaw

1972 THE BISCUIT EATER
Director: Vincent McEveety
Co-Star Earl Holliman Godfrey Cambridge Lew Ayres

SUZAN CROWLEY

1986 BORN OF FIRE
Director: Jamil Dehlavi
Co-stars: Peter Firth Stefan Kalipha Oh-Tee

SU CRUIKSHANK

1987 THOSE DEAR DEPARTED
Director: Ted Robinson
Co-stars: Gary MacDonald Pamela Stephenson

1988 YOUNG EINSTEIN
Director: Yahoo Serious
Co-stars: Yahoo Serious John Howard Peewee Wilson

BLANCHETTE CRUNOY

1952   **COIFFEUR POUR DAMES**
Director: Jean Boyer
Co-stars: Fernandel Renee Devillers

KATE CRUTCHLEY

1980   **PROSTITUTE**
Director: Tony Garnett
Co-stars: Eleanor Forsythe Kim Lockett Nancy Samuels

ROSALIE CRUTCHLEY

1947   **TAKE MY LIFE**
Director: Ronald Neame
Co-stars: Hugh Williams Greta Gynt Marius Goring

1950   **PRELUDE TO FAME**
Director: Fergus McDonell
Co-stars: Jeremy Spencer Guy Rolfe Kathleen Ryan

1952   **THE SWORD AND THE ROSE**
Director: Ken Annakin
Co-stars: Richard Todd Glynis Johns Michael Gough

1954   **MAKE ME AN OFFER**
Director: Cyril Frankel
Co-stars: Peter Finch Adrienne Corri Wilfrid Lawson

1956   **THE SPANISH GARDENER**
Director: Philip Leacock
Co-stars: Dirk Bogarde Jon Whiteley Michael Hordern

1956   **THE GAMMA PEOPLE**
Director: John Gilling
Co-stars: Paul Douglas Leslie Phillips Eva Bartok

1957   **MIRACLE IN SOHO**
Director: Julian Ames
Co-stars: John Gregson Belinda Lee Billie Whitelaw

1957   **SEVEN THUNDERS**
Director: Hugo Fregonese
Co-stars: Stephen Boyd Kathleen Harrison Tony Wright

1958   **A TALE OF TWO CITIES**
Director: Ralph Thomas
Co-stars: Dirk Bogarde Dorothy Tutin Christopher Lee

1959   **BEYOND THIS PLACE**
Director: Jack Cardiff
Co-stars: Van Johnson Vera Miles Emlyn Williams

1960   **NO LOVE FOR JOHNNIE**
Director: Ralph Thomas
Co-stars: Peter Finch Mary Peach Billie Whitelaw

1960   **SONS AND LOVERS**
Director: Jack Cardiff
Co-stars: Dean Stockwell Trevor Howard Mary Ure

1970   **THE SIX WIVES OF HENRY VIII**
Director: John Glenister
Co-stars: Keith Michel Annette Crosbie Elvi Hale

1970   **CREATURES THE WORLD FORGOT**
Director: Don Chaffey
Co-stars: Julie Ege Brian O'Shaughnessy Marcia Fox

1970   **WUTHERING HEIGHTS**
Director: Robert Fuest
Co-stars: Anna Calder-Marshall Timothy Dalton Harry Andrews

1971   **BLOOD FROM THE MUMMY'S TOMB**
Director: Seth Holt
Co-stars: Andrew Kier Valerie Leon James Villiers

1971   **WHOEVER SLEW AUNTIE ROO?**
Director: Curtis Harrington
Co-stars: Shelley Winters Mark Lester Ralph Richardson

1972   **AU PAIR GIRLS**
Director: Val Guest
Co-stars: Gabrielle Drake Richard O'Sullivan Astrid Frank

1973   **THE HOUSE IN NIGHTMARE PARK**
Director: Peter Sykes
Co-stars: Frankie Howerd Ray Milland Hugh Burden

1973   **MAHLER**
Director: Ken Russell
Co-stars: Robert Powell Georgina Hale Benny Lee

1973   **AND NOW THE SCREAMING STARTS!**
Director: Roy Ward Baker
Co-stars: Peter Cushing Stephanie Beacham

1982   **SMILEY'S PEOPLE**
Director: Simon Langton
Co-stars: Alec Guinness Curt Jurgens Eileen Atkins

1983   **THE ALAMUT AMBUSH**
Director: Ken Grier
Co-stars: Terence Stamp Robin Sachs Richard Wilson

1985   **ELENI**
Director: Peter Yates
Co-stars: Kate Nelligan John Malkovich Linda Hunt

1985   **THE ADVENTURES OF SHERLOCK HOLMES: THE NORWOOD BUILDER**
Director: Ken Grieve
Co-stars: Jeremy Brett David Burke Helen Ryan

1989   **SHE'S BEEN AWAY**
Director: Peter Hall
Co-stars: Peggy Ashcroft Geraldine James James Fox

1992   **GOD ON THE ROCKS**
Director: Ross Cramer
Co-stars: Sinead Cusack Minnie Driver Bill Paterson

ABIGAIL CRUTTENDEN

1982   **P'TANG YANG KIPPERBANG**
Director: Michael Apted
Co-stars: Alison Steadman Garry Cooper John Albasiny

1988   **THE BELL RUN**
Director: Alan Dossor
Co-stars: Amanda Hillwood Bruce Payne Maggie Ollerenshaw

1990   **CENTREPOINT**
Director: Piers Haggard
Co-stars: Jonathan Firth Bob Peck Murray Head

1995   **LOVE ON A BRANCH LINE**
Co-stars: Michael Moloney Leslie Phillips

CELIA CRUZ

1992   **THE MAMBO KINGS**
Director: Arne Glimcher
Co-stars: Antonio Banderas Armand Assante Cathy Moriarty

PENELOPE CRUZ

1992   **JAMON, JAMON**
Director: Bigas Luna
Co-stars: Anna Galiena Stefania Sandrelli Javier Bardem

SYLVIE CUBERTAFONT

1988   **LA VIE EST UN LONG FLEUVE TRANQUILLE**
Director: Etienne Chatilliez
Co-stars: Valerie Lalande Benott Magimel

FRANCES CUKA

1972   **HENRY VIII AND HIS SIX WIVES**
Director: Waris Hussein
Co-stars: Keith Michell Jane Asher Jenny Bos

QUINN CULKIN

1993 THE GOOD SON
Director: Joseph Rubin
Co-stars: Elijah Wood Macauley Culkin Wendy Crewson

LORRAINE CULLEN

1970 DIARY OF A MAD HOUSEWIFE
Director: Frank Perry
Co-stars: Carrie Snodgress Richard Benjamin

KIMBERLY CULUM

1991 THE RAPTURE
Director: Michael Tolkin
Co-stars: Mimi Rogers David Duchovny

CONSTANCE CUMMINGS

1931 THE CRIMINAL CODE
Director: Howard Hawks
Co-stars: Walter Huston Phillips Holmes Boris Karloff

1931 THE LAST PARADE
Director: Erle Kenton
Co-stars: Jack Holt Tom Moore Gaylord Pendleton

1931 THE GUILTY GENERATION
Director: Rowland Lee
Co-stars: Robert Young Leo Carrillo Boris Karloff

1931 TRAVELLING HUSBANDS
Co-stars: Hugh Herbert Dorothy Peterson Frank McHugh

1932 NIGHT AFTER NIGHT
Director: Archie Mayo
Co-stars: George Raft Mae West Wynne Gibson

1932 MOVIE CRAZY
Director: Clyde Bruckman
Co-Star Harold Lloyd

1932 BILLION DOLLAR SCANDAL
Director: Harry Joe Brown
Co-stars: Frank Morgan Robert Armstrong

1932 BEHIND THE MASK
Director: John Francis Dillon
Co-stars: Jack Holt Boris Karloff

1932 AMERICAN MADNESS
Director: Frank Capra
Co-stars: Walter Huston Pat O'Brien Kay Johnson

1932 ATTORNEY FOR THE DEFENSE
Director: Irving Cummings
Co-stars: Edmund Lowe Evelyn Brent

1932 WASHINGTON MERRY-GO-ROUND
Director: James Cruze
Co-stars: Lee Tracy Alan Dinehart Walter Connolly

1933 THE MIND READER
Director: Roy Del Ruth
Co-stars: Warren William Allen Jenkins Mayo Methot

1933 LOOKING FOR TROUBLE
Director: William Wellman
Co-stars: Spencer Tracy Jack Oakie Arline Judge

1933 HEADS WE GO
Co-Star Frank Lawton

1933 THE CHARMING DECEIVER
Co-stars: Frank Lawton Gus McNaughton

1933 CHANNEL CROSSING
Director: Milton Rosmer
Co-stars: Matheson Lang Max Miller Edmund Gwenn

1933 BROADWAY THRU A KEYHOLE
Director: Lowell Sherman
Co-stars: Russ Columbo Paul Kelly Texas Guinan

1934 GLAMOUR
Director: William Wyler
Co-stars: Paul Lukas Philip Reed Joseph Cawthorne

1934 THIS MAN IS MINE
Director: John Cromwell
Co-stars: Irene Dunne Ralph Bellamy Kay Johnson

1935 REMEMBER LAST NIGHT?
Director: James Whale
Co-stars: Edward Arnold Sally Eilers Robert Young

1936 SEVEN SINNERS
Director: Albert De Courville
Co-stars: Edmund Lowe Henry Oscar Felix Aylmer

1937 STRANGERS ON A HONEYMOON
Co-Star Hugh Sinclair

1940 BUSMAN'S HONEYMOON
Director: Arthur Woods
Co-stars: Robert Montgomery Leslie Banks Robert Newton

1941 THIS ENGLAND
Director: David MacDonald
Co-stars: John Clements Emlyn Williams Esmond Knight

1942 THE FOREMAN WENT TO FRANCE
Director: Charles Frend
Co-stars: Tommy Trinder Gordon Jackson

1945 BLITHE SPIRIT
Director: David Lean
Co-stars: Rex Harrison Kay Hammond Margaret Rutherford

1951 INTO THE BLUE
Director: Herbert Wilcox
Co-stars: Michael Wilding Odile Versois Jack Hulbert

1956 THE INTIMATE STRANGER
Director: Joseph Losey
Co-stars: Richard Basehart Roger Livesey Mary Murphy

1960 THE BATTLE OF THE SEXES
Director: Charles Crichton
Co-stars: Peter Sellers Robert Morley Donald Pleasence

1962 IN THE COOL OF THE DAY
Director: Robert Stevens
Co-stars: Jane Fonda Peter Finch Angela Lansbury

1963 SAMMY GOING SOUTH
Director: Alexander McKendrick
Co-stars: Edward G. Robinson Harry H. Corbett

1971 JANE EYRE
Director: Delbert Mann
Co-stars: George C. Scott Susannah York Ian Bannen

1986 DEAD MAN'S FOLLY
Director: Clive Donner
Co-stars: Peter Ustinov Jean Stapleton Jonathan Cecil

DOROTHY CUMMINGS

1927 THE DIVINE WOMAN
Director: Victor Sjostrom
Co-stars: Greta Garbo Lars Hanson Polly Moran

1927 KING OF KINGS
Director: Cecil B. DeMille
Co-stars: H.B. Warner Jacqueline Logan Joseph Schildkraut

1927 THE WIND
Director: Victor Sjostrom
Co-stars: Lillian Gish Lars Hanson Montagu Love

1928 KITTY
Director: Victor Saville
Co-stars: John Stuart Estelle Brody Marie Ault

1929 APPLAUSE
Director: Rouben Mamoulian
Co-stars: Helen Morgan Joan Peers Henry Wadsworth

PEGGY CUMMINGS

1940 DR. O'DOWD
Director: Herbert Mason
Co-stars: Shaun Glenville Mary Merrall Patricia Roc

1942 SALUTE JOHN CITIZEN
Director: Maurice Elvey
Co-stars: Edward Rigby Jimmy Hanley Dinah Sheridan

1943 OLD MOTHER RILEY, DETECTIVE
Director: Lance Comfort
Co-stars: Arthur Lucan Kitty McShane Marjorie Rhodes

1944 ENGLISH WITHOUT TEARS
Director: Harold French
Co-stars: Lili Palmer Michael Wilding Margaret Rutherford

1944 WELCOME MR. WASHINGTON
Director: Leslie Hiscott
Co-stars: Barbara Mullen Donald Stewart Graham Moffatt

1947 MOSS ROSE
Director: Gregory Ratoff
Co-stars: Victure Mature Ethel Barrymore Vincent Price

1947 THE LATE GEORGE APLEY
Director: Joseph Mankiewicz
Co-stars: Ronald Colman Edna Best Richard Haydn

1948 GREEN GRASS OF WYOMING
Director: Louis King
Co-stars: Charles Coburn Burl Ives Robert Arthur

1948 ESCAPE
Director: Joseph Mankiewicz
Co-stars: Rex Harrison William Hartnell Norman Wooland

1949 THAT DANGEROUS AGE
Director: Gregory Ratoff
Co-stars: Myrna Loy Roger Livesey Richard Greene

1950 MY DAUGHTER JOY
Director: Gregory Ratoff
Co-stars: Edward G. Robinson Richard Greene Nora Swinburn

1950 GUN CRAZY
Director: Joseph Lewis
Co-stars: John Dall Barry Kroeger Morris Carnovsky

1952 WHO GOES THERE?
Director: Anthony Kimmins
Co-stars: Valerie Hobson George Cole Nigel Patrick

1953 STREET CORNER
Director: Muriel Box
Co-stars: Rosamund John Anne Crawford Terence Morgan

1953 MEET MR. LUCIFER
Director: Anthony Pellissier
Co-stars: Stanley Holloway Jack Watling Kay Kendall

1953 THE LOVE LOTTERY
Director: Charles Crichton
Co-stars: David Niven Herbert Lom Ann Vernon

1954 ALWAYS A BRIDE

1956 MARCH HARE
Director: George More O'Ferrall
Co-stars: Terence Morgan Martita Hunt Cyril Cusack

1957 NIGHT OF THE DEMON
Director: Jacques Tourneur
Co-stars: Dana Andrews Niall MacGinnis Athene Seyler

1957 HELL DRIVERS
Director: Cy Endfield
Co-stars: Stanley Baker Patrick McGoohan Sid James

1957 CARRY ON ADMIRAL
Director: Val Guest
Co-stars: David Tomlinson Brian Reece Eunice Gayson

1958 THE CAPTAIN'S TABLE
Director: Jack Lee
Co-stars: John Gregson Donald Sinden Nadia Gray

1961 IN THE DOGHOUSE
Director: Darcy Conyers
Co-stars: Leslie Phillips James Booth Fenella Fielding

QUINN CUMMINGS
Nominated For Best Supporting Actress In 1977 For "The Goodbye Girl"

1977 THE GOODBYE GIRL
Director: Herbert Ross
Co-stars: Richard Dreyfuss Marsha Mason Barbara Rhoades

JULIETTE CUMMINS

1985 FRIDAY THE THIRTEENTH: A NEW BEGINNING
Director: Danny Steinmann
Co-stars: John Shepard Shavar Ross

ANNE CUNNINGHAM

1963 BITTER HARVEST
Director: Peter Graham Scott
Co-stars: Janet Munro John Stride Alan Badel

CECIL CUNNINGHAM

1931 SUSAN LENOX, HER FALL AND RISE
Director: Robert Z. Leonard
Co-stars: Greta Garbo Clark Gable

1937 THE AWFUL TRUTH
Director: Leo McCarey
Co-stars: Irene Dunne Cary Grant Ralph Bellamy

1938 COLLEGE SWING
Director: Raoul Walsh
Co-stars: George Burns Gracie Allen Bob Hope

1941 HURRY, CHARLIE, HURRY
Co-Star: Leon Errol

1942 COWBOY SERENADE
Co-stars: Gene Autry Smiley Burnette Fay McKenzie

1942 THE WIFE TAKES A FLYER
Director: Richard Wallace
Co-stars: Joan Bennett Franchot Tone

MARGO CUNNINGHAM

1976 THE SAILOR WHO FELL FROM GRACE WITH THE SEA
Director: Lewis John Carlino
Co-Star: Kris Kristofferson Sarah Miles

SARAH CUNNINGHAM

1972 THE COWBOYS
Director: Mark Rydell
Co-stars: John Wayne Bruce Dern Colleen Dewhurst

ZAHMA CUNNINGHAM

1953 HERE COME THE GIRLS
Director: Claude Binyon
Co-stars: Bob Hope Rosemary Clooney Tony Martin

BARBARA CUPISTI

1989 THE CHURCH
Director: Michele Soavi
Co-stars: Hugh Quarshie Thomas Arana Feodor Chaliapin

LYNETTE CURRAN

1973 ALVIN PURPLE
Director: Tim Burstall
Co-stars: Graeme Blundell Christine Amor Dina Mann

1985   BLISS
Director: Ray Lawrence
Co-stars: Barry Otto Helen Jones Gia Carides

1987   THE YEAR MY VOICE BROKE
Director: John Duigan
Co-stars: Noah Taylor Loene Carmen Graeme Blundell

CHERIE CURRIE

1980   FOXES
Director: Adrian Lyne
Co-stars: Jodie Foster Sally Kellerman Adam Faith

LOUISE CURRIE

1943   THE APE MAN
Director: William Beaudine
Co-stars: Bela Lugosi Wallace Ford Minerva Urecal

1944   FORTY THIEVES
Co-stars: Jimmy Rogers William Boyd

1946   GUN TOWN
Co-Star   Kirby Grant

1946   WILD WEST
Co-stars: Eddie Dean Al "Lash" Larue Roscoe Ates

1947   THE CHINESE RING
Director: William Beaudine
Co-stars: Roland Winters Victor Sen Yung

1947   SECOND CHANCE
Co-stars: Kent Taylor Ann Doran Dennis Hoey

MARY CURRIER

1940   NOBODY'S CHILDREN
Co-stars: Edith Fellows Ben Taggart

1948   JOAN OF ARC
Director: Victor Fleming
Co-stars: Ingrid Bergman Jose Ferrer Francis L. Sullivan

ANNE CURRY

1990   PACIFIC PALISADES
Director: Bernard Schmitt
Co-stars: Sophie Marceau Adam Coleman Howard Toni Basil

ANN CURTHOYS

1989   TESTIMONY OF A CHILD
Director: Peter Smith
Co-stars: Jill Baker John Bowe Heather Tobias

1990   KEEPING TOM NICE
Director: Louise Panton
Co-stars: John Alderton Gwen Taylor Linus Roache

JANE CURTIN

1977   BABY MAKES THREE
Co-Star   Dabney Coleman

1980   HOW TO BEAT THE HIGH COST OF LIVING
Director: Robert Scheerer
Co-stars: Susan St. James Jessica Lang

1985   O.C. AND STIGGS
Director: Robert Altman
Co-stars: Paul Dooley Ray Walston Tina Louise

1993   CONEHEADS
Director: Steve Barron
Co-stars: Dan Aykroyd Michelle Burke Laraine Newman

VALERIE CURTIN

1974   ALICE DOESN'T LIVE HERE ANYMORE
Director: Martin Scorsese
Co-stars: Ellen Burstyn Jodie Foster

1976   THE GREAT SMOKEY ROADBLOCK
Director: John Leone
Co-stars: Henry Fonda Eileen Brennan Susan Sarandon

1978   A DIFFERENT STORY
Director: Paul Aaron
Co-stars: Perry King Meg Foster Peter Donat

1985   MAXIE
Director: Paul Aaron
Co-stars: Glenn Close Mandy Patinkin Ruth Gordon

JAIME LEE CURTIS (Married Christopher Guest)

1978   HALLOWEEN
Director: John Carpenter
Co-stars: Donald Pleasence Nancy Loomis

1979   THE FOG
Director: John Carpenter
Co-stars: Adrienne Barbeau Janet Leigh Hal Holbrook

1980   PROM NIGHT
Director: Paul Lynch
Co-stars: Leslie Nielsen Casey Stevens Eddie Benton

1980   TERROR TRAIN
Director: Roger Spottiswoode
Co-stars: Ben Johnson David Copperfield Hart Bochner

1981   SHE'S IN THE ARMY NOW
Director: Hy Averbach
Co-stars: Kathleen Quinlan Melanie Griffith

1981   HALLOWEEN 2
Director: Rick Rosenthal
Co-stars: Donald Pleasence Charles Cyphers Dick Warlock

1982   LOVE LETTERS
Director: Amy Jones
Co-stars: James Keach Matt Clark Bonnie Bartlett

1983   TRADING PLACES
Director: John Landis
Co-stars: Dan Aykroyd Eddie Murphy Don Ameche

1985   PERFECT
Director: James Bridges
Co-stars: John Travolta Anne De Salvo Marilu Henner

1986   AS SUMMERS DIE
Director: Jean-Claude Tramont
Co-stars: Scott Glen Bette Davis John Randolph

1987   AMAZING GRACE AND CHUCK
Director: Mike Newell
Co-stars: Gregory Peck William I. Petersen

1987   A MAN IN LOVE
Director: Diane Kurys
Co-stars: Peter Coyote Greta Scacchi Claudia Cardinale

1988   A FISH CALLED WANDA
Director: Charles Crichton
Co-stars: John Cleese Kevin Kline Michael Palin

1988   NICKY AND GINO
Director: Robert M. Young
Co-stars: Tom Hulce Ray Liotta Todd Graff

1990   BLUE STEEL
Director: Kathryn Bigelow
Co-stars: Ron Silver Clancy Brown Louise Fletcher

1991   MY GIRL
Director: Howard Zieff
Co-stars: Dan Aykroyd Macauley Culkin Anna Chlumsky

1992   FOREVER YOUNG
Director: Steve Miner
Co-stars: Mel Glbson Elijah Wood

1993　MOTHER'S BOYS
Director:　Yves Simoneau
Co-stars:　Peter Gallagher Joanne Whalley Vanessa Redgrave

1994　MY GIRL 2
Director:　Howard Zieff
Co-stars:　Dan Aykroyd Anna Chlumsky Austin O'Brien

1994　TRUE LIES
Director:　James Cameron
Co-stars:　Arnold Schwarzenegger Tom Arnold Bill Paxton

1995　THE HEIDI CHRONICLES
Director:　Paul Bogart
Co-stars:　Tom Hulce Kim Cattrall Peter Friedman

1996　FIERCE CREATURES
Co-stars:　John Cleese Kevin Kline Michael Palin

LIANE CURTIS

1984　SIXTEEN CANDLES
Director:　John Hughes
Co-stars:　Molly Ringwald Justin Henry Anthony Michael Hall

1988　CRITTERS 2
Director:　Mick Garris
Co-stars:　Scott Grimes Don Opper Barry Corbin

YVETTE CURTIS

1974　CLAUDINE
Director:　John Berry
Co-stars:　Diahann Carroll James Earl Jones David Kruger

JILL CURZON

1966　DALEKS – INVASION EARTH 2150
Director:　Gordon Flemyng
Co-stars:　Peter Cushing Roy Castle Jennie Linden

ANN CUSACK

1992　A LEAGUE OF THEIR OWN
Director:　Penny Marshall
Co-stars:　Madonna Geena Davis Lori Petty Tom Hanks

1992　OVEREXPOSED
Director:　Robert Markovitchi
Co-stars:　Marcy Walker Dan Lauria Terence Knox

1993　MALICE
Director:　Harold Becker
Co-stars:　Nicole Kidman Alec Baldwin Bill Pullman

1994　RENAISSANCE MAN
Director:　Penny Marshall
Co-stars:　Danny Devito Gregory Hines Cliff Robertson

JOAN CUSACK *(Sister Of John Cusack)*
Nominated For Best Supporting Actress In 1988 For "Working Girl" And 1997 For "In And Out"

1983　CLASS
Director:　Lewis John Carlino
Co-stars:　Jacqueline Bisset Rob Lowe

1984　SIXTEEN CANDLES
Director:　John Hughes
Co-stars:　Molly Ringwald Anthony Michael Hall Justin Henry

1987　THE ALLNIGHTER
Director:　Tamar Simon Hoffs
Co-stars:　Susanna Hoffs Dedee Pfeifer

1988　MARRIED TO THE MOB
Director:　Jonathan Demme
Co-stars:　Michelle Pfeiffer Dean Stockwell Matthew Modine

1988　WORKING GIRL
Director:　Mike Nichols
Co-stars:　Harrison Ford Sigourney Weaver Melanie Griffith

1988　STARS AND BARS
Director:　Pat O'Connor
Co-stars:　Daniel Day-Lewis Harry Dean Stanton

1989　SAY ANYTHING
Director:　Cameron Crowe
Co-stars:　John Cusack Ione Skye John Mahoney

1990　MY BLUE HEAVEN
Director:　Herbert Ross
Co-stars:　Steve Martin Rick Moranis Carol Kane

1990　MEN DON'T LEAVE
Director:　Paul Brickman
Co-stars:　Jessica Lange Kathy Bates Chris O'Donnell

1992　TOYS
Director:　Barry Levinson
Co-stars:　Robin Williams Michael Gambon Donald O'Connor

1992　ACCIDENTAL HERO
Director:　Stephen Frears
Co-stars:　Dustin Hoffman Geena Davis Andy Garcia

1993　ADDAMS FAMILY VALUES
Director:　Barry Sonnenfeld
Co-stars:　Angelica Huston Raul Julia Christina Ricci

1997　IN AND OUT
Director:　Frank Oz
Co-stars:　Kevin Kline Glenn Close Matt Dillon

NIAMH CUSACK *(Daughter of Cyril Cusack, Sister Of Sinead And Sorcha Cusack)*

1988　PARIS BY NIGHT
Director:　David Hare
Co-stars:　Charlotte Rampling Michael Gambon Jane Asher

1988　LUCKY SUNIL
Director:　Michael Caton-Jones
Co-stars:　Kulvinder Ghir Tariq Yunus Benjamin Whitrow

1990　FOOLS OF FORTUNE
Director:　Pat O'Connor
Co-stars:　Iain Glen Mary Elizabeth Mastrantonio Julie Christie

1992　ANGELS
Director:　Philip Saville
Co-stars:　Tom Bell Cathy Tyson Louise Lombard

1992　THE PLAYBOYS
Director:　Gilles MacKinnon
Co-stars:　Albert Finney Aidan Quinn Robin Wright

**1994　THE TALE OF MR. TOAD:
THE FURTHER ADVENTURE OF PETER RABBIT AND BENJAMIN BUNNY (VOICE)**
Co-stars:　Dinsdale Landen Don Henderson Enn Reitel

SINEAD CUSACK
(Married Jeremy Irons, Daughter Of Cyril Cusack, Sister Of Niahm And Sorcha Cusack)

1970　HOFFMAN
Director:　Alvin Rakoff
Co-stars:　Peter Sellers Jeremy Bulloch Ruth Dunning

1970　DAVID COPPERFIELD
Director:　Delbert Mann
Co-stars:　Robin Phillips Susan Hampshire Edith Evans

1971　REVENGE
Director:　Sidney Hayers
Co-stars:　Joan Collins James Booth Ray Barrett

1971　TAM-LIN
Director:　Roddy McDowall
Co-stars:　Ava Gardner Ian McShane Cyril Cusack

1989   VENUS PETER
Director: Ian Sellar
Co-stars: Ray McAnally Gordon R. Strachan David Hayman

1989   THE HEN HOUSE
Director: Danny Boyle
Co-stars: Tony Doyle Barry Birch Pat Leary

1992   GOD ON THE ROCKS
Director: Ross Cramer
Co-stars: Bill Paterson Rebecca Edwards Minnie Driver

1992   BAD BEHAVIOUR
Director: Les Blair
Co-stars: Stephen Rea Philip Jackson Clare Higgins

1992   WATERLAND
Director: Stephen Gyllenhaal
Co-stars: Jeremy Irons Ethan Hawke Grant Warnock

1993   SPARROW
Director: Franco Zefferelli
Co-stars: Angela Bettis Jonathan Schaech

1993   THE CEMENT GARDEN
Director: Andrew Birkin
Co-stars: Charlotte Gainsbourg Ned Birkin

1996   STEALING BEAUTY
Director: Bernardo Bertolucci
Co-stars: Liv Tyler Jeremy Irons Donal McCann

SORCHA CUSACK *(Daughter Of Cyril Cusack, Sister Of Niamb And Sinead Cusack)*

1978   A HITCH IN TIME
Director: Jan Darnley Smith
Co-stars: Patrick Troughton Michael McVey Jeff Rawle

1989   THE REAL CHARLOTTE
Director: Tony Barry
Co-stars: Jeananne Crowley Patrick Bergin Joanna Roth

1990   SHOOT THE REVOLUTION
Director: Jane Howell
Co-stars: Bernard Hill Bob Peck Freddie Jones

1990   AUGUST SATURDAY
Director: Diarmuid Lawrence
Co-stars: Tim McInnerny Barry McGovern Peter Caffrey

**1993   INSPECTOR MORSE:
CHERUBIM AND SERAPHIM**
Director: Danny Boyle
Co-stars: John Thaw Isla Blair Kevin Whateley

KATE CUTLER

1932   WEDDING REHEARSAL
Director: Alexander Korda
Co-stars: Roland Yound Wendy Barrie Merle Oberon

1935   MOSCOW NIGHTS
Director: Anthony Asquith
Co-stars: Laurence Olivier Penelope Dudley Ward

1938   PYGMALION
Director: Anthony Asquith
Co-stars: Leslie Howard Wendy Hiller Wilfrid Lawson

LISE CUTTER

**1988   DESPERADO:
AVALANCHE AT DEVIL'S RIDGE**
Director: Richard Compton
Co-stars: Alex McArthur Rod Steiger

PATRICIA CUTTS

1949   THE ADVENTURES OF P.C.49
Director: Godfrey Grayson
Co-stars: Hugh Latimer John Penrose Pat Nye

1950   YOUR WITNESS
Director: Robert Montgomery
Co-stars: Robert Montgomery Leslie Banks Felix Aylmer

1954   THE MAN WHO LOVED REDHEADS
Director: Harold French
Co-stars: John Justin Moira Shearer Roland Culver

1958   MERRY ANDREW
Director: Michael Kidd
Co-stars: Danny Kaye Pier Angeli Robert Coote

1959   THE TINGLER
Director: William Castle
Co-stars: Vincent Price Judith Evelyn Darryl Hickman

1959   BATTLE OF THE CORAL SEA
Director: Paul Wendkos
Co-stars: Cliff Robertson Gia Scala

MIRIAM CYR

1986   GOTHIC
Director: Ken Russell
Co-stars: Gabriel Byrne Natasha Richardson Timothy Spall

ZSUZSA CZINKOCZI

1982   DIARY FOR MY CHILDREN
Director: Marta Meszaros
Co-stars: Anna Polony Jan Nowicki

1987   DIARY FOR MY LOVES
Director: Marta Meszaros
Co-stars: Ana Polony Jan Nowicki Pal Zolnay

FRANCES DABLE

1928 THE CONSTANT NYMPH
Director: Adrian Brunel
Co-stars: Mabel Poulton Ivor Novello Dorothy Boyd

AUGUSTA DABNEY

1957 THAT NIGHT
Director: John Newland
Co-stars: John Beal Shepperd Strudwick Ralph Murphy

1980 F.D.R.: THE LAST YEAR
Director: Anthony Page
Co-stars: Jason Robards Eileen Heckart Kim Hunter

1986 VIOLETS ARE BLUE
Director: Jack Fisk
Co-stars: Sissy Spacek Kevin Kline Bonnie Bedelia

1988 RUNNING ON EMPTY
Director: Sidney Lumet
Co-stars: Christine Lahti River Phoenix Martha Plimpton

MARYAM D'ABO

1987 THE LIVING DAYLIGHTS
Director: Jonn Glen
Co-stars: Timothy Dalton Jeroen Krabbe Joe Don Baker

1990 NOT A PENNY MORE, NOT A PENNY LESS
Director: Clive Donner
Co-stars: Ed Asner Ed Begley Jnr. Jenny Agutter

1992 LEON THE PIG FARMER
Director: Gary Sinyor
Co-stars: Mark Frankel Janet Suzman Connie Booth

1993 SHOOTFIGHTER
Director: Pat Alan
Co-stars: Bolo Yeung Martin Kove

**1993 THE RED SHOE DIARIES:
ANOTHER WOMAN'S LIPSTICK**
Director: Zalman King
Co-Star Christina Fulton

1993 DOUBLE OBSESSION
Director: Eduardo Montes
Co-stars: Margaux Hemingway Frederic Forrest

1993 DANGEROUS DESIRE
Director: Paul Donovan
Co-star: Richard Grieco

OLIVIA D'ABO

1984 CONAN THE DESTROYER
Director: Richard Fleischer
Co-stars: Arnold Schwarzenegger Grace Jones

1989 BEYOND THE STARS
Director: David Saperstein
Co-stars: Christian Slater Martin Sheen Sharon Stone

1992 MIDNIGHT'S CHILD
Director: Colin Bucksey
Co-stars: Marcy Walker Cotter Smith

1993 THE ASSASSIN
Director: John Badham
Co-stars: Bridget Fonda Gabriel Byrne Anne Bancroft

1993 FOR LOVE AND GLORY
Director: Roger Young
Co-stars: Robert Foxworth Kate Mulgrew Tracey Griffith

1993 WAYNE'S WORLD 2
Director: Stephen Surjik
Co-stars: Mike Myers Dana Carvey Tia Carrere

1994 GREEDY
Director: Jonathan Lynn
Co-stars: Kirk Douglas Michael J. Fox Nancy Travis

1994 CLEAN SLATE
Director: Mick Jackson
Co-stars: Dana Carvey Valeria Golino Michael Gambon

CORINNE DACLA

1989 HOME RUN
Director: Nicholas Renton
Co-stars: Michael Kitchen Keith Barron Anne Carroll

FRANCES DADE

1930 GRUMPY
Director: George Cukor
Co-stars: Cyril Maude Phillips Holmes Paul Cavanagh Paul Lukas

1930 RAFFLES
Director: George Fitzmaurice
Co-stars: Ronald Colman Kay Francis David Torrence

1931 DRACULA
Director: Tod Browning
Co-stars: Bela Lugosi Helen Chandler David Manners

1931 THE SEA-WOLF

1933 PHANTOM THUNDERBOLT
Co-Star Ken Maynard

LIL DAGOVER

1919 THE CABINET OF DR. CALIGARI
Director: Robert Wiene
Co-stars: Werner Krause Conrad Veidt

1921 DESTINY
Director: Fritz Lang
Co-stars: Rudolph Klein Rogge Bernhard Gotzke

1922 DOCTOR MABUSE THE GAMBLER
Director: Fritz Lang
Co-stars: Rudolph Klein Rogge Alfred Abel

1931 CONGRESS DANCES
Director: Erik Charrell
Co-stars: Conrad Veidt Lilian Harvey Henri Garat

1931 THE WOMAN FROM MONTE CARLO
Director: Michael Curtiz
Co-stars: Walter Huston Warren William

DIANE D'AGUILA

1989 A WINTER TAN
Director: John Frizzell
Co-stars: Jackie Burroughs Erando Gonzales Anita Olanick

ARLENE DAHL

1947 MY WILD IRISH ROSE
Director: David Butler
Co-stars: Dennis Morgan Alan Hale George Tobias

1948 **THE BRIDE GOES WILD**
Director: Norman Taurog
Co-stars: Van Johnson June Allyson Butch Jenkens

1948 **A SOUTHERN YANKEE**
Director: Edward Sedgwick
Co-stars: Red Skelton Brian Donlevy George Coulouris

1949 **THE BLACK BOOK**
Director: Anthony Mann
Co-stars: Robert Cummings Richard Basehart Beulah Bondi

1949 **AMBUSH**
Director: Sam Wood
Co-stars: Robert Taylor John Hodiak Jean Hagan Leon Ames

1949 **SCENE OF THE CRIME**
Director: Roy Rowland
Co-stars: Van Johnson Gloria DeHaven Tom Drake Leon Ames

1950 **WATCH THE BIRDIE**
Director: Jack Donohue
Co-stars: Red Skelton Ann Miller Leon Ames Pamela Britton

1950 **THREE LITTLE WORDS**
Director: Richard Thorpe
Co-stars: Fred Astaire Red Skelton Vera-Ellen Debbie Reynolds

1950 **THE OUTRIDERS**
Director: Roy Rowland
Co-stars: Joel McCrea Claude Jarman Jnr. Ramon Navarro

1951 **NO QUESTIONS ASKED**
Director: Harold Kress
Co-stars: Barry Sullivan George Murphy Jean Hagan

1951 **INSIDE STRAIGHT**
Director: Gerald Mayer
Co-stars: David Brian Mercedes McCambridge Barry Sullivan

1952 **CARIBBEAN**
Director: Edward Ludwig
Co-stars: Cedric Hardwicke John Payne Dennis Hoey

1953 **DESERT LEGION**
Director: Joseph Pevney
Co-stars: Alan Ladd Richard Conte Akim Tamiroff

1953 **THE DIAMOND QUEEN**
Director: John Brahm
Co-stars: Fernando Lamas Gilbert Roland Sheldon Leonard

1953 **HERE COME THE GIRLS**
Director: Claude Binyon
Co-stars: Bob Hope Rosemary Clooney Tony Martin

1953 **JAMAICA RUN**
Director: Lewis Foster
Co-stars: Ray Milland Wendell Corey Patric Knowles

1953 **SANGAREE**
Director: Edward Ludwig
Co-stars: Fernando Lamas Francis L. Sullivan John Sutton

1954 **BENGAL BRIGADE**
Director: Laslo Benedek
Co-stars: Rock Hudson Dan O'Herlihy Ursula Thiess

1954 **WOMAN'S WORLD**
Director: Jean Negulesco
Co-stars: Clifton Webb Lauren Bacall Van Heflin

1956 **WICKED AS THEY COME**
Director: Ken Hughes
Co-stars: Herbert Marshall Phil Carey Sid James

1956 **SLIGHTLY SCARLET**
Director: Allan Dwan
Co-stars: Rhonda Fleming John Payne Kent Taylor Ted De Corsia

1956 **FORTUNE IS A WOMAN**
Director: Sidney Gilliat
Co-stars: Jack Hawkins Dennis Price Bernard Miles

1959 **JOURNEY TO THE CENTER OF THE EARTH**
Director: Henry Levin
Co-stars: James Mason Pat Boone Diane Baker

1964 **KISSES FOR MY PRESIDENT**
Director: Curtis Bernhardt
Co-stars: Polly Bergen Fred MacMurray

EVA DAHLBECK

1952 **WAITING WOMEN**
Director: Ingmar Bergman
Co-Star Anita Bjork

1953 **A LESSON IN LOVE**
Director: Ingmar Bergman
Co-stars: Gunnar Bjornstrand Harriet Andersson

1954 **JOURNEY INTO AUTUMN**
Director: Ingmar Bergman
Co-stars: Harriet Andersson Naima Wifstrand

1955 **SMILES OF A SUMMER NIGHT**
Director: Ingmar Bergman
Co-stars: Gunnar Bjornstrand Ulla Jacobsson

1962 **THE COUNTERFEIT TRAITOR**
Director: George Seaton
Co-stars: William Holden Lilli Palmer Hugh Griffith

1964 **LOVING COUPLES**
Director: Mai Zetterling
Co-stars: Harriet Andersson Gunnel Lindblom Anita Bjork

1964 **NOW ABOUT THESE WOMEN**
Director: Ingmar Bergman
Co-stars: Jarl Kulle Georg Funkquist Karen Kavli

IRENE DAILEY

1971 **THE GRISSOM GANG**
Director: Robert Aldrich
Co-stars: Kim Darby Scott Wilson Connie Stevens

ELIZABETH DAILY (E.G.Daily)

1982 **THE ESCAPE ARTIST**
Director: Caleb Deschanel
Co-stars: Griffin O'Neal Raul Julia Teri Garr

1983 **FUNNY MONEY**
Director: Gregg Smith
Co-stars: Gregg Henry Gareth Hunt Annie Ross

1983 **VALLEY GIRL**
Director: Martha Coolidge
Co-stars: Nicolas Cage Deborah Foreman Colleen Camp

1984 **NO SMALL AFFAIR**
Director: Jerry Schatzberg
Co-stars: Demi Moore Jon Cryer George Wendt

1985 **PEE-WEE'S BIG ADVENTURE**
Director: Tim Burton
Co-stars: Paul Reubens Diane Salinger Mark Holton

1992 **DRIVING ME CRAZING**
Director: Peter Faiman
Co-stars: Ethan Randall JoBeth Williams Ari Meyers

JOANNE DAINTON

1970 **THE FIRECHASERS**
Director: Sidney Hayers
Co-stars: Chad Everett Anjanette Comer Keith Barron

PATRICIA DAINTON

1950 **THE DANCING YEARS**
Director: Harold French
Co-stars: Dennis Price Giselle Preville Anthony Nicholls

1952　CASTLE IN THE AIR
Director:　Henry Cass
Co-stars:　David Tomlinson Helen Cherry Margaret Rutherford

1956　THE PASSIONATE STRANGER
Director:　Muriel Box
Co-stars:　Ralph Richardson Margaret Leighton

1957　AT THE STROKE OF NINE
Director:　Lance Comfort
Co-stars:　Stephen Murray Patrick Barr Dermot Walsh

1961　THE THIRD ALIBI
Director:　Montgomery Tully
Co-stars:　Laurence Payne Jane Griffiths

JACQUELINE DAIX

1938　TENDRE ENNEMIE
Director:　Max Ophuls
Co-stars:　Simone Berriau Georges Vitray Marc Valbel

VICKI DAKIL

1982　THE PERSONALS
Director:　Peter Markle
Co-stars:　Bill Schoppert Karen Landry Paul Elding

SUZANNE DALBERT

1951　THE LADY AND THE BANDIT
Director:　Ralph Murphy
Co-stars:　Louis Hayward Patricia Medina Tom Tully

1953　THE 49TH. MAN
Director:　Fred Sears
Co-stars:　John Ireland Richard Denning Touch Connors

AMY DALBY

1965　THE SECRET OF MY SUCCESS
Director:　Andrew Stone
Co-stars:　James Booth Lionel Jeffries Shirley Jones

LYNN DALBY

1975　LEGEND OF THE WEREWOLF
Director:　Freddie Francis
Co-stars:　Peter Cushing Ron Moody Hugh Griffith

ESTHER DALE

1934　CRIME WITHOUT PASSION
Director:　Ben Hecht
Co-stars:　Claude Rains Margo Whitney Bourne Stanley Ridges

1935　THE WEDDING NIGHT
Director:　King Vidor
Co-stars:　Gary Cooper Anna Sten Sig Ruman Helen Vinson

1935　PRIVATE WORLDS
Director:　Gregory La Cava
Co-stars:　Claudette Colbert Charles Boyer Joel McCrea

1935　IN OLD KENTUCKY
Director:　George Marshall
Co-stars:　Will Rogers Bill Robinson Dorothy Wilson Louise Henry

1935　I DREAM TOO MUCH
Director:　John Cromwell
Co-stars:　Lily Pons Henry Fonda Eric Blore Lucille Ball

1935　CURLY TOP
Director:　Irving Cummings
Co-stars:　Shirley Temple John Boles Rochelle Hudson

1936　THE CASE AGAINST MRS. AMES
Director:　William Seiter
Co-stars:　Madeleine Carroll George Brent

1936　HOLLYWOOD BOULEVARD
Director:　Robert Florey
Co-stars:　John Halliday Marsha Hunt Robert Cummings

1937　DAMAGED GOODS
Director:　Phil Stone
Co-stars:　Pedro De Cordoba Douglas Walton Arletta Duncan

1937　THE AWFUL TRUTH
Director:　Leo McCarey
Co-stars:　Irene Dunne Cary Grant Ralph Bellamy

1938　MADE FOR EACH OTHER
Director:　John Cromwell
Co-stars:　Carole Lombard James Stewart Charles Coburn

1938　CONDEMMED WOMAN
Director:　Lew Landers
Co-stars:　Sally Eilers Louis Hayward Anne Shirley Lee Patrick

1939　BLACKMAIL
Director:　H.C. Potter
Co-stars:　Edward G. Robinson Ruth Hussey Guinn Williams

1940　AND ONE WAS BEAUTIFUL
Director:　Robert Sinclair
Co-stars:　Robert Cummings Laraine Day Jean Muir

1940　THE MORTAL STORM
Director:　Frank Borzage
Co-stars:　Frank Morgan James Stewart Margaret Sullavan

1940　BLONDIE HAS SERVANT TROUBLE
Director:　Frank Strayer
Co-stars:　Penny Singleton Arthur Lake

1940　UNTAMED
Director:　George Archainbaud
Co-stars:　Ray Milland Akim Tamiroff Jane Darwell

1941　DANGEROUSLY THEY LIVE
Director:　Robert Florey
Co-stars:　John Garfield Raymond Massey Nancy Coleman

1941　UNFINISHED BUSINESS
Director:　Gregory La Cava
Co-stars:　Irenne Dunne Robert Montgomery Preston Foster

1941　BACK STREET
Director:　Robert Stevenson
Co-stars:　Margaret Sullavan Charles Boyer Richard Carlson

1941　ALOMA OF THE SOUTH SEAS
Director:　Alfred Santell
Co-stars:　Dorothy Lamour Jon Hall Dona Drake

1942　BLONDIE GOES TO COLLEGE
Director:　Frank Strayer
Co-stars:　Larry Simms Jonathan Hale.larry Parks

1946　MARGIE
Director:　Henry King
Co-stars:　Jeanne Crain Glenn Langan Alan Young Barbara Lawrence

1946　A STOLEN LIFE
Director:　Curtis Bernhardt
Co-stars:　Bette Davis Glenn Ford Dane Clark Walter Brennan

1946　MY REPUTATION
Director:　Curtis Bernhardt
Co-stars:　Barbara Stanwyck George Brent Warner Anderson

1946　SMOKY
Director:　Louis King
Co-stars:　Fred McMurray Anne Baxter Burl Ives Bruce Cabot

1947　THE UNFINISHED DANCE
Director:　Henry Koster
Co-stars:　Margaret O'Brien Cyd Charisse Danny Thomas

1949　HOLIDAY AFFAIR
Director:　Don Hartman
Co-stars:　Janet Leigh Robert Mitchum Wendell Corey

1952 MONKEY BUSINESS
Director: Howard Hawks
Co-stars: Cary Grant Ginger Rogers Marilyn Monroe Charles Coburn

JANET DALE
1980 NICE WORK
Director: Christopher Menaul
Co-stars: Warren Clarke Hayden Gwynne David Calder

JENNIFER DALE
1987 CARLY'S WEB
Director: Kevin Luch
Co-stars: Daphne Ashbrook Cyril O'Reilly Peter Billingsley

1991 THE ADJUSTER
Director: Atom Egoyan
Co-stars: Elias Koteas Maury Chaykin Gabrielle Rose

1993 CADILLAC GIRLS
Director: Nicholas Kendall
Co-stars: Adam Beach Mia Kershner

VIRGINIA DALE
1939 DEATH OF A CHAMPION
Director: Robert Florey
Co-stars: Lynne Overman Donald O'Connor Robert Paige

1940 LOVE THY NEIGHBOUR
Director: Mark Sandrich
Co-stars: Jack Benny Fred Allen Mary Martin

1940 WORLD PREMIERE
Director: Ted Tetzlaff
Co-stars: John Barrymore Ricardo Cortez Frances Farmer

1941 KISS THE BOYS GOODBYE
Director: Victor Schertzinger
Co-stars: Mary Martin Don Ameche Oscar Levant

1942 HOLIDAY INN
Director: Mark Sandrich
Co-stars: Bing Crosby Fred Astaire Marjorie Reynolds

1948 DOCKS OF NEW ORLEANS
Director: Derwin Abrahams
Co-stars: Roland Winters Victor Sen Yung

CASS DALEY
1942 THE FLEET'S IN
Director: Victor Schertzinger
Co-stars: Dorothy Lamour William Holden Betty Hutton

1942 STAR SPANGLED RHYTHM
Director: George Marshall
Co-stars: Victor Moore Betty Hutton Eddie Bracken

1943 RIDING HIGH
Director: George Marshall
Co-stars: Dorothy Lamour Dick Powell Victor Moore

1943 CRAZY HOUSE
Director: Edward Cline
Co-stars: Ole Olson Chic Johnson Martha O'Driscoll

1945 OUT OF THIS WORLD
Director: Hal Walker
Co-stars: Eddie Bracken Veronica Lake Diana Lynn

1947 LADIES' MAN
Director: William Russell
Co-stars: Eddie Bracken Virginia Wells Spike Jones

1954 RED GARTERS
Director: George Marshall
Co-stars: Rosemary Clooney Guy Mitchell Jack Carson

1967 THE SPIRIT IS WILLING
Director: William Castle
Co-stars: Sid Caesar Vera Miles Mary Wickes

1968 NORWOOD
Director: Jack Haley Jnr.
Co-stars: Glen Campbell Kim Darby Carol Lynley

EVELYN DALL
1938 KICKING THE MOON AROUND
Director: Walter Forde
Co-stars: Hal Thompson Florence Desmond Max Bacon

1941 HE FOUND A STAR
Director: John Paddy Carstairs
Co-stars: Vic Oliver Sarah Churchill Joan Greenwood

1942 KING ARTHUR WAS A GENTLEMAN
Director: Marcel Varnel
Co-stars: Arthur Askey Anne Shelton Jack Train

1944 TIME FLIES
Director: Walter Forde
Co-stars: Tommy Handley Felix Aylmer George Moon

CHARLENE DALLAS
1974 RANCHO DELUXE
Director: Frank Perry
Co-stars: Sam Waterston Jeff Bridges Elizabeth Ashley

BEATRICE DALLE
1986 BETTY BLUE
Director: Jean-Jacques Beineix
Co-stars: Jean-Hughes Anglade

1991 NIGHT ON EARTH
Director: Jim Jarmusch
Co-stars: Winona Ryder Gena Rowlands Rosie Perez

1992 LA FILLE DE L'AIR
Director: Maroun Bagdadi
Co-stars: Thierry Fortineau Hippolyte Girardot

ABBY DALTON
1958 STAKEOUT ON DOPE STREET
Director: Irvin Kershner
Co-stars: Yale Wexler Jonathon Haze Morris Miller

1957 VIKING WOMEN AND THE SEA SERPENT
Director: Roger Corman
Co-stars: Brad Jackson Susan Cabot June Kenny

AUDREY DALTON
1952 MY COUSIN RACHEL
Director: Henry Koster
Co-stars: Olivia De Havilland Richard Burton John Sutton

1953 TITANIC
Director: Jean Negulesco
Co-stars: Clifton Webb Barbara Stanwyck Thelma Ritter

1953 THE GIRLS OF PLEASURE ISLAND
Director: F. Hugh Herbert
Co-stars: Leo Genn Gene Barry Dorothy Bromiley

1954 DRUM BEAT
Director: Delmer Daves
Co-stars: Alan Ladd Marisa Pavan Robert Keith Charles Bronson

1955 CONFESSION
Director: Ken Hughes
Co-stars: Sydney Chaplin John Bentley Peter Hammond

1955 THE PRODIGAL
Director: Richard Thorpe
Co-stars: Lana Turner Edmund Purdom Louis Calhern

1956 HOLD BACK THE NIGHT
Director: Allan Dwan
Co-stars: John Payne Mona Freeman Chuck Connors

1957 THE MONSTER THAT CHALLENGED THE WORLD
Director: Arnold Laver
Co-Star: Tim Holt

1958 SEPARATE TABLES
Director: Delbert Man
Co-stars: Burt Lancaster Rita Hayworth David Niven Deborah Kerr

1959 THE OTHER EDEN
Director: Muriel Box
Co-stars: Leslie Phillips Niall MacGinnis Milo O'Shea

1961 MR. SARDONICUS
Director: William Castle
Co-stars: Ronald Lewis Guy Rolfe Oscar Homolka

KRISTEN DALTON

1994 DIGITAL MAN
Director: Phillip Roth
Co-stars: Matthias Hues Ken Olandt

JANE DALY

1928 WEST OF ZANZIBAR
Director: Tod Browning
Co-stars: Lon Chaney Lionel Barrymore Mary Nolan

TYNE DALY

1969 JOHN AND MARY
Director: Peter Yates
Co-stars: Dustin Hoffman Mia Farrow Michael Tolan Sunny Griffin

1974 LARRY
Director: William Graham
Co-stars: Frederic Forrest Michael McGuire Robert Walden

1975 THE ENTERTAINER
Director: Donald Wrye
Co-stars: Jack Lemmon Ray Bolger Sada Thompson Annette O'Toole

1976 THE ENFORCER
Director: James Fargo
Co-stars: Clint Eastwood Harry Guardino Bradford Dillman

1977 TELEFON
Director: Don Siegel
Co-stars: Charles Bronson Lee Remick Alan Badel Sheree North

1981 CAGNEY AND LACEY
Director: Ted Post
Co-stars: Loretta Swit Al Waxman Joan Copeland Ronald Hunter

1985 THE AVIATOR
Director: George Miller
Co-stars: Christopher Reeve Rosanna Arquette Jack Warden

1985 MOVERS AND SHAKERS
Director: William Asher
Co-stars: Walter Matthau Charles Grodin Vincent Gardenia

1987 KIDS LIKE THESE
Director: Georg Stanford Brown
Co-stars: Richard Crenna Martin Balsam

1989 STUCK WITH EACH OTHER
Director: Georg Stanford Brown
Co-stars: Richard Crenna Eileen Heckart

1991 THE LAST TO GO
Director: John Erman
Co-stars: Terry O'Quinn Annabeth Gish Sarah Trigger

1993 SCATTERED DREAMS
Director: Neema Barnette
Co-star: Gerald McRaney

1994 CAGNEY AND LACEY: THE RETURN
Director: James Frawley
Co-stars: Sharon Gless Al Waxman

JACQUELINE DALYA

1949 THE TREASURE OF SIERRA MADRE
Director: John Huston
Co-stars: Humphrey Bogart Walter Huston Tim Holt

1950 WABASH AVENUE
Director: Henry Koster
Co-stars: Betty Grable Victor Mature Phil Harris

BERTILA DAMAS

1991 FIRES WITHIN
Director: Gillian Armstrong
Co-stars: Greta Scacchi Jimmy Smits Vincent D'Onofrio

1991 NOTHING BUT TROUBLE
Director: Dan Ackroyd
Co-stars: Dan Ackroyd Chevy Chase Demi Moore

ADRIENNE D'AMBICOURT

1933 THE EAGLE AND THE HAWK
Director: Stuart Walker
Co-stars: Fredric March Cary Grant Jack Oakie

CHARLOTTE D'AMBOISE

1989 AMERICAN BLUE NOTE
Director: Ralph Toporoff
Co-stars: Peter MacNichol Trini Alvarado Tim Guinee

DONATELLA DAMIANI

1980 CITY OF WOMEN
Director: Federico Fellini
Co-stars: Marcello Mastroianni Anna Prucnal Ettore Manni

LILI DAMITA (Married Errol Flynn)

1929 THE BRIDGE OF SAN LUIS REY
Co-Star: Don Alvarado

1929 THE COCK-EYED WORLD
Director: Raoul Walsh
Co-stars: Victor McLaglen Edmund Lowe El Brendel

1931 FIGHTING CARAVANS
Director: David Burton
Co-stars: Gary Cooper Ernest Torrence Tully Marshall

1931 FRIENDS AND LOVERS
Director: Victor Schertzinger
Co-stars: Laurence Olivier Adolphe Menjou

1932 THE MATCH KING
Director: Howard Bretherton
Co-stars: Warren William Glenda Farrell Harold Huber

1932 THIS IS THE NIGHT
Director: Frank Tuttle
Co-stars: Charles Ruggles Roland Young Cary Grant

1933 GOLDIE GETS ALONG
Co-Star: Sam Hardy

1935 FRISCO KID
Director: Lloyd Bacon
Co-stars: James Cagney Margaret Lindsay Ricardo Cortez

1935 BREWSTER'S MIILLIONS
Director: Thornton Freeland
Co-stars: Jack Buchanan Nancy O'Neil Amy Veness

CATHRYN DAMON (Child)

1982 NOT IN FRONT OF THE CHILDREN
Director: Joseph Hardy
Co-stars: Linda Gray John Getz John Lithgow

1983 WHO WILL LOVE MY CHILDREN?
Director: John Erman
Co-stars: Ann-Margret Frederic Forrest Donald Moffat

1988 SHE'S HAVING A BABY
Director: John Hughes
Co-stars: Kevin Bacon Elizabeth McGovern Alec Baldwin

EDIE DAMS

1980 ADDICTION: A CRY FOR LOVE
Director: Paul Wendkos
Co-stars: Susan Blakely Gene Barry Lainie Kazan

DANA

1971 FLIGHT OF THE DOVES
Director: Ralph Nelson
Co-stars: Ron Moody Dorothy McGuire Jack Wild

BARBARA DANA

1977 FIRE SALE
Director: Alan Arkin
Co-stars: Alan Arkin Rob Reiner Vincent Gardenia Kay Medford

LEORA DANA

1957 3.10 TO YUMA
Director: Delmer Daves
Co-stars: Glenn Ford Van Heflin Felicia Farr

1958 KINGS GO FORTH
Director: Delmer Davies
Co-stars: Frank Sinatra Tony Curtis Natalie Wood

1958 SOME CAME RUNNING
Director: Vincente Minnelli
Co-stars: Frank Sinatra Dean Martin Shirley MacLaine

1960 POLLYANNA
Director: David Swift
Co-stars: Hayley Mills Jane Wyman Karl Malden Adolphe Menjou

1969 CHANGE OF HABIT
Director: William Graham
Co-stars: Elvis Presley Mary Tyler Moore Ed Asner

1971 WILD ROVERS
Director: Blake Edwards
Co-stars: William Holden Ryan O'Neal Karl Malden Lynn Carlin

1981 SHOOT THE MOON
Director: Alan Parker
Co-stars: Albert Finney Diane Keaton Karen Allen Peter Weller

1982 BABY IT'S YOU
Director: John Sayles
Co-stars: Rosanna Arquette Vincent Spano Joanna Merlin

1984 AMITYVILLE 3D
Director: Richard Fleischer
Co-stars: Tony Roberts Tess Harper Candy Clark Meg Ryan

VIOLA DANA

1923 HOLLYWOOD
Director: James Cruze
Co-stars: Hope Drown Luke Cosgrave Eleanor Lawson

1929 SHOW OF SHOWS
Director: John Adolfi
Co-stars: Frank Fay Douglas Fairbanks Jnr. Lupino Lane

DOROTHY DANDRIDGE

Nominated For An Oscar For Best Actress In 1954 For Carmen Jones

1941 SUN VALLEY SERENADE
Director: Bruce Humberstone
Co-stars: Sonja Henie John Payne Glenn Miller

1941 BAHAMA PASSAGE
Director: Edward Griffith
Co-stars: Madeleine Carroll Sterling Hayden Flora Robson

1941 LADY FROM LOUISIANA
Director: Bernard Vorhaus
Co-stars: John Wayne Ona Munson Ray Middleton

1943 HIT PARADE OF 1943
Director: Albert Rogell
Co-stars: John Carroll Susan Hayward Gail Patrick

1944 ATLANTIC CITY
Director: Ray McCarey
Co-stars: Constance Moore Jerry Colonna Adele Mara

1951 TARZAN'S PERIL
Director: Byron Haskin
Co-stars: Lex Barker Virginia Huston George Macready

1953 REMAINS TO BE SEEN
Director: Don Weis
Co-stars: June Allyson Van Johnson Angela Lansbury John Beal

1953 BRIGHT ROAD
Director: Gerald Mayer
Co-stars: Harry Belafonte Robert Horton

1954 CARMEN JONES
Director: Otto Preminger
Co-stars: Harry Belafonte Olga James Pearl Bailey

1957 ISLAND IN THE SUN
Director: Robert Rossen
Co-stars: Harry Belafonte James Mason Joan Fontaine

1958 THE DECKS RAN RED
Director: Andrew Stone
Co-stars: James Mason Broderick Crawford Stuart Whitman

1959 PORGY AND BESS
Director: Otto Preminger
Co-stars: Sidney Poitier Sammy Davis Pearl Bailey

1960 MOMENT OF DANGER
Director: Laslo Benedek
Co-stars: Trevor Howard Edmund Purdom Michael Hordern

ALEXANDRA DANE

1968 CARRY ON UP THE KHYBER
Director: Gerald Thomas
Co-stars: Sid James Kenneth Willlams Roy Castle

PATRICIA DANE

1942 GRAND CENTRAL MURDER
Director: S. Sylvan Simon
Co-stars: Van Heflin Cecilia Parker Sam Levene

1942 JOHNNY EAGER
Director: Mervyn LeRoy
Co-stars: Robert Taylor Van Heflin Lana Turner

1942 RIO RITA
Director: S. Sylvan Simon
Co-stars: Bud Abbott Lou Costello Kathryn Grayson

1942 SOMEWHERE I'LL FIND YOU
Director: Wesley Ruggles
Co-stars: Clark Gable Lana Turner Robert Sterling

1943 I DOOD IT!
Director: Vincente Minnelli
Co-stars: Red Skelton Eleanor Powell Lena Horne

CLAIRE DANES

1995 LITTLE WOMEN
Director: Gilliam Armstrong
Co-stars: Winona Ryder Susan Sarandon Gabriel Byrne

1998 THE RAINMAKER
Director: Francis Coppola
Co-stars: Matt Damon Jon Voight Danny DeVito

1998   U-TURN
Director: Oliver Stone
Co-stars: Nick Nolte Jon Voight Sean Penn

1995   HOME FOR THE HOLIDAYS
Director: Jodie Foster
Co-stars: Holly Hunter Anne Bancroft Robert Downey Jnr

1997   WILLIAM SHAKESPEARE'S ROMEO AND JULIET
Director: Baz Luhrman
Co-stars: Leonardo DiCaprio Miriam Margoyles

CONNIE DANESE

1989   SOCIETY
Director: Brian Yuzna
Co-stars: Bill Warlock Devin Devasquez Ben Meyerson

BEVERLY D'ANGELO

1977   FIRST LOVE
Director: Joan Darling
Co-stars: William Katt Susan Dey John Heard Robert Loggia

1978   EVERY WHICH WAY BUT LOOSE
Director: James Fargo
Co-stars: Clint Eastwood Sondra Locke Geoffrey Lewis

1979   HAIR
Director: Milos Forman
Co-stars: John Savage Treat Williams Nicholas Ray Annie Golden

1981   HONKY TONK FREEWAY
Director: John Schlesinger
Co-stars: William Devane Beau Bridges Teri Garr

1981   PATERNITY
Director: David Steinberg
Co-stars: Burt Reynolds Norman Fell Elizabeth Ashley

1983   NATIONAL LAMPOON'S VACATION
Director: Harold Ramis
Co-stars: Chevy Chase Randy Quaid Eddie Bracken

1984   A STREETCAR NAMED DESIRE
Director: John Erman
Co-stars: Ann-Margret Treat Williams Randy Quaid

1984   FINDERS KEEPERS
Director: Richard Lester
Co-stars: Michael O'Keefe David Wayne Louis Gossett

1984   HIGHPOINT
Director: Peter Carter
Co-stars: Richard Harris Christopher Plummer Peter Donat

1985   DOUBLETAKE
Director: Jud Taylor
Co-stars: Richard Crenna Cliff Gorman Vincent Baggetta

1985   BIG TROUBLE
Director: John Cassavetes
Co-stars: Peter Falk Alan Arkin Robert Stack

1985   NATIONAL LAMPOON'S EUROPEAN VACATION
Director: Amy Heckerling
Co-stars: Chevy Chase Eric Idle

1986   THE MAN WHO FELL TO EARTH
Director: Robert Roth
Co-star: Lewis Smith

1987   THE WOO WOO KID
Director: Phil Alden Robinson
Co-stars: Patrick Dempsey Talia Balsam Betty Jinnette

1987   MAID TO ORDER
Director: Amy Jones
Co-stars: Ally Sheedy Michael Ontkean Valerie Perrine Dick Shawn

1988   ARIA
Director: Julian Temple
Co-stars: Buck Henry Anita Morris Gary Kasark John Hurt

1987   HANDS OF A STRANGER
Director: Larry Elikann
Co-stars: Armand Assante Blair Brown Michael Lerner

1988   HIGH SPIRITS
Director: Neil Jordan
Co-stars: Daryl Hannah Peter O'Toole Liam Neeson

1989   NATIONAL LAMPOON'S CHRISTMAS VACATION
Director: Jeremiah Chechik
Co-stars: Chevy Chase Diane Ladd

1989   COLD FRONT
Director: Paul Bnarbic
Co-stars: Martin Sheen Michael Ontkean Kim Coates

1990   DADDY'S DYIN': WHO'S GOT THE WILL
Director: Jack Fisk
Co-stars: Beau Bridges Tess Harper

1991   THE MIRACLE
Director: Neil Jordan
Co-stars: Niall Byrne Donal McGann Lorraine Pilkington

1991   THE POPE MUST DIE
Director: Peter Richardson
Co-stars: Robbie Coltrane Herbert Lom Robert Stephens

1992   MAN TROUBLE
Director: Bob Rafelson
Co-stars: Jack Nicholson Ellen Barkin Harry Dean Stanton

1994   LIGHTNING JACK
Director: Simon Wincer
Co-stars: Paul Hogan Cuba Gooding Jnr Pat Hingle

1994   FRAME-UP
Director: Michael Switzer
Co-star: Richard Crenna

1996   EYE FOR AN EYE
Director: John Schlesinger
Co-stars: Sally Field Kiefer Sutherland Ed Harris

MIRELLA D'ANGELO

1983   HERCULES
Director: Luigi Cozzi
Co-stars: Lou Ferrigno Sybil Danning Rossana Podesta

ANITA DANGLER

1974   LAW AND DISORDER
Director: Ivan Passer
Co-stars: Carroll O'Connor Ernest Borgnine Ann Wedgeworth

1978   SLOW DANCING IN THE BIG CITY
Director: John Avildsen
Co-stars: Paul Sorvino Anne Ditchburn

ELSA DANIEL

1957   THE HOUSE OF THE ANGEL
Director: Leopoldo Torre Nilsson
Co-stars: Lautaro Murua Guillermo Battaglia

1958   THE FALL
Director: Leopoldo Torre Nilsson
Co-stars: Duilio Marzia Lydia Lamaison

JENNIFER DANIEL

1963   KISS OF THE VAMPIRE
Director: Don Sharp
Co-stars: Noel Willman Clifford Evans Isobel Black

1966   THE REPTILE
Director: John Gilling
Co-stars: Noel Willman Jaqueline Pearce Ray Barrett

ISA DANIELI

1985   MACARONI
Director: Ettore Scolla
Co-stars: Jack Lemon Marcello Mastroianni Daria Nicolodi

SUZANNE DANIELLE

1978   CARRY ON EMMANUELLE
Director: Gerald Thomas
Co-stars: Kenneth Williams Joan Sims Kenneth Connor

1979   ARABIAN ADVENTURE
Director: Kevin Connor
Co-stars: Christopher Lee Mickey Rooney Capucine

1983   THE BOYS IN BLUE
Director: Val Guest
Co-stars: Tommy Cannon Bobby Ball Roy Kinnear Eric Sykes

ANGELA DANIELS

1978   ADVENTURES OF A PLUMBER'S MATE
Director: Stanley Long
Co-stars: Christopher Neil Elaine Paige

BEBE DANIELS *(Married Ben Lyons)*

1919   MALE AND FEMALE
Director: Cecil B. DeMille
Co-stars: Gloria Swanson Lila Lee

1921   THE AFFAIRS OF ANATOL
Director: Cecil B. DeMille
Co-stars: Wallace Reid Gloria Swanson

1924   ARGENTINE LOVE
Co-stars: James Rennie Ricardo Cortez

1929   RIO RITA
Director: Luther Reed
Co-stars: Wheeler & Woolsey John Boles Dorothy Lee

1930   DIXIANA
Director: Luther Reed
Co-stars: Wheeler & Woolsey Everett Marshall Jobyna Howland

1930   ALIAS FRENCH GERTIE
Director: George Archainbaud
Co-Star   Ben Lyon

1930   A SOUTHERN MAID
Co-Star   Clifford Mollison

1931   THE MALTESE FALCON
Director: Roy Del Ruth
Co-stars: Ricardo Cortez Thelma Todd Dwight Frye

1931   HONOR OF THE FAMILY
Director: Lloyd Bacon
Co-stars: Warren William Frederick Kerr Alan Mowbray

1931   REACHING FOR THE MOON
Director: Edmund Goulding
Co-stars: Douglas Fairbanks Claud Allister Bing Crosby

1932   SILVER DOLLAR
Director: Alfred Green
Co-stars: Edward G. Robinson Aline McMahon Jobyna Howland

1933   FORTY-SECOND STREET
Director: Lloyd Bacon
Co-stars: Warner Baxter Ruby Keeler Dick Powell

1933   COUNSELLOR-AT-LAW
Director: William Wyler
Co-stars: John Barrymore Melvyn Douglas Thelma Todd

1933   COCKTAIL HOUR
Co-stars: Randolph Scott Sidney Blackmer

1935   MUSIC IS MAGIC
Director: George Marshall
Co-stars: Alice Faye Ray Walker Hattie McDaniel

1941   HI GANG
Director: Marcel Varnel
Co-stars: Ben Lyon Vic Oliver Moore Marriott Graham Moffatt

1954   LIFE WITH THE LYONS
Director: Val Guest
Co-stars: Ben, Barbara, Richard Lyon Molly Weir

LYNN DANIELSON

1988   OUT OF THE DARK
Director: Michael Schroeder
Co-stars: Karen Black Cameron Dye Teresa Crespo

LISA DANIELY

1952   HINDLE WAKES
Director: Arthur Crabtree
Co-stars: Leslie Dwyer Brian Worth Sandra Dorne

1953   THE WEDDING OF LILLI MARLENE
Director: Arthur Crabtree
Co-stars: Hugh McDermott Sid James Joan Heal

1955   TIGER BY THE TAIL
Director: John Gilling
Co-stars: Larry Parks Constance Smith Thora Hird

1957   THE VICIOUS CIRCLE
Director: Gerald Thomas
Co-stars: John Mills Derek Farr Noelle Middleton

1957   THE MAN IN THE ROAD
Director: Lance Comfort
Co-stars: Derek Farr Ella Raines Donald Wolfit

1959   A HONOURABLE MURDER
Director: Geoffrey Grayson
Co-stars: Norman Woolland Margaretta Scott

**1983   THE ADVENTURES OF SHERLOCK
          HOLMES: THE CROOKED MAN**
Director: Alan Grint
Co-stars: Jeremy Brett David Burke

1987   SOUVENIR
Director: Geoffrey Reeve
Co-stars: Christopher Plummer Catherine Hicks

JACQUELINE DANKWORTH

1989   1871
Director: Ken McMullen
Co-stars: Roshan Seth Ana Padrao John Lynch Timothy Spall

JUDY DANN

1953   DESTINATION GOBI
Director: Robert Wise
Co-stars: Richard Widmark Don Taylor Casey Adams

BLYTHE DANNER *(Mother of Gwyneth Paltrow)*

1971   TO KILL A CLOWN
Director: George Bloomfield
Co-stars: Alan Alda Heath Lamberts Eric Clavering

1972   1776
Director: Peter Hunt
Co-stars: William Daniels Howard Da Silva Ken Howard

1973   LOVIN' MOLLY
Director: Sidney Lumet
Co-Star   Anthony Perkins Beau Bridges Susan Sarandon

1974	**F.SCOTT FITZGERALD AND "THE LAST OF THE BELLES"**
Director:	George Schaefer
Co-Star	Richard Chamberlain Susan Sarandon

1975	**HEARTS OF THE WEST**
Director:	Howard Zieff
Co-stars:	Jeff Bridges Andy Griffith Donald Pleasence

1976	**FUTUREWORLD**
Director:	Richard Heffron
Co-stars:	Peter Fonda Yul Brynner Arthur Hill Jim Antonio

1977	**THE COURT MARTIAL OF GEORGE ARMSTRONG CUSTER**
Director:	Glen Jordan
Co-stars:	James Olson Brian Keith

1979	**THE GREAT SANTINI**
Director:	Lewis John Carlino
Co-stars:	Robert Duvall Michael O'Keefe Stan Shaw

1979	**TOO FAR TO GO**
Director:	Fielder Cook
Co-stars:	Michael Moriarty Glenn Close Ken Kercheval

1982	**MAN, WOMAN AND CHILD**
Director:	Dick Richards
Co-stars:	Martin Sheen David Hemmings Craig T. Nelson

1983	**IN DEFENSE OF KIDS**
Director:	Gene Reynolds
Co-stars:	Sam Waterston Joyce Van Patten Beth Ehlers

1985	**GUILTY CONSCIENCE**
Director:	David Greene
Co-stars:	Anthony Hopkins Swoosie Kurtz

1986	**BRIGHTON BEACH MEMOIRS**
Director:	Gene Saks
Co-stars:	Bob Dishy Judith Ivey Jonathan Silverman

1988	**ANOTHER WOMAN**
Director:	Woody Allen
Co-stars:	Gena Rowlanda Mia Farrow Ian Holm Gene Hackman

1989	**MONEY, POWER, MURDER**
Director:	Lee Philips
Co-stars:	Kevin Dobson Josef Summer John Cullum

1990	**MR. AND MRS.BRIDGE**
Director:	James Ivory
Co-stars:	Paul Newman Joanne Woodward Simon Callow

1990	**ALICE**
Director:	Woody Allen
Co-stars:	Mia Farrow Joe Mantegna Judy Davis William Hurt

1991	**THE PRINCE OF TIDES**
Director:	Barbra Streisand
Co-stars:	Barbra Streisand Nick Nolte Kate Nelligan Melinda Dillon

1992	**HUSBANDS AND WIVES**
Director:	Woody Allen
Co-stars:	Woody Allen Mia Farrow Judy Davis Liam Neeson

1994	**LEAVE OF ABSENCE**
Director:	Tom McLoughlin
Co-stars:	Brian Denehy Jacquelline Bisset

1995	**TO WONG FOO, THANKS FOR EVERYTHING! JULIE NEWMAR**
Director:	Beeban Kidrow
Co-stars:	Patrick Swayze Wesley Snipes

SYBIL DANNING

1972	**BLUEBEARD**
Director:	Edward Dmytryk
Co-stars:	Richard Burton Raquel Welch Joey Hetherton

1980	**CUBA CROSSING**
Director:	Chuck Workman
Co-stars:	Stuart Whitman Robert Vaughn Woody Strode

1980	**BATTLE BEYOND THE STARS**
Director:	Jimmy Murakami
Co-stars:	Richard Thomas George Peppard John Saxon

1983	**CHAINED HEAT**
Director:	Paul Nicolas
Co-stars:	Linda Blair John Vernon Stella Stevens

1983	**HERCULES**
Director:	Luigi Cozzi
Co-stars:	Lou Ferrigno Mirella D'Angelo Rossana Podesta

1986	**REFORM SCHOOL GIRLS**
Director:	Tom DeSimone
Co-stars:	Linda Carol Pat Ast Charlotte McGinnis

GERALDINE DANON

1991	**COMPANY BUSINESS**
Director:	Nicholas Meyer
Co-stars:	Gene Hackman Mikhail Baryshnikov Terry O'Quinn

1993	**THE OLD WOMAN WHO WALKED IN THE SEA**
Director:	Dominique Roulet
Co-stars:	Jeanne Moreau Michel Serrault

SUZANNE DANTES

1939	**CIRCONSTANCES ATTENUANTES**
Director:	Jean Boyer
Co-stars:	Michel Simon Arletty Mila Parely

LISE DANVERS

1974	**IMMORAL TALES**
Director:	Walerian Borowczyk
Co-stars:	Charlotte Alexandra Paloma Picasso

MAIA DANZIGER

1980	**DR. HECKYL AND MR. HYPE**
Director:	Charles Griffith
Co-stars:	Oliver Reed Sunny Johnson Mel Wells

DIANE D'AQUILA

1994	**JANE'S HOUSE**
Director:	Glenn Jordan
Co-stars:	James Woods Anne Archer Graham Beckel

PATTI D'ARBANVILLE

1969	**FLESH**
Director:	Paul Morrissey
Co-stars:	Joe Dallesandro Geraldine Smith Candy Darling

1974	**RANCHO DELUXE**
Director:	Frank Perry
Co-stars:	Sam Waterston Jeff Bridges Elizabeth Ashley Slim Pickings

1978	**BIG WEDNESDAY**
Director:	John Milius
Co-stars:	Jan-Michael Vincent William Katt Gary Busey Lee Purcell

1979	**THE MAIN EVENT**
Director:	Howard Zieff
Co-stars:	Barbra Streisand Ryan O'Neal Paul Sand

1980	**TIME AFTER TIME**
Director:	Nicholas Meyer
Co-stars:	Malcolm McDowell David Warner Mary Steenburgen

1985	**THE BOYS NEXT DOOR**
Director:	Penelope Spheeris
Co-stars:	Maxwell Caulfield Charlie Sheen Hank Garrett

1985 **REAL GENIUS**
Director: Martha Coolidge
Co-stars: Val Kilmer Gabe Jarrett Michelle Meyrink

1988 **FRESH HORSES**
Director: David Anspaugh
Co-stars: Molly Ringwald Andrew McCarthy Ben Stiller

1988 **CROSSING THE MOB**
Director: Steven Hilliard Stern
Co-stars: Jason Bateman Maura Tierney Frank Stallone

1988 **CALL ME**
Director: Sollace Mitchell
Co-stars: Patricia Charbonneau Sam Freed Stephen McHattie

1989 **WIRED**
Director: Larry Pearce
Co-stars: Michael Chiklist J.T.Walsh Ray Sharkey

1993 **BLIND SPOT**
Director: Michael Uno
Co-stars: Joanne Woodward Laura Linney Fritz Weaver

PATRIKA DARBO

1989 **LEAVING NORMAL**
Director: Edward Zwick
Co-stars: Christine Lahti Meg Tilly Maury Chaykin

1989 **SPACED INVADERS**
Director: Patrick Read Johnson
Director: Douglas Barr Royal Dano Ariana Richards

1994 **ROSEANNE AND TOM:**
       A HOLLYWOOD MARRIAGE
Director: Richard Colla
Co-stars: Stephen Lee Jan Hoag

KIM DARBY

1965 **BUS RILEY'S BACK IN TOWN**
Director: Harvey Hart
Co-stars: Michael Parks Ann-Margret Jocelyn Brando

1968 **NORWOOD**
Director: Jack Haley Jnr.
Co-stars: Carol Lynley Pat Hingle Glen Gampbell

1969 **TRUE GRIT**
Director: Henry Hathaway
Co-stars: John Wayne Glen Campbell Dennis Hopper Robert Duvall

1970 **THE STRAWBERRY STATEMENT**
Director: Stuart Hagman
Co-stars: Bruce Davison Bud Cort Murray MacLeod

1971 **THE GRISSOM GANG**
Director: Robert Aldrich
Co-stars: Scott Wilson Tony Musante Connie Stevens

1973 **DON'T BE AFRAID OF THE DARK**
Director: John Newland
Co-stars: Jim Hutton Pedro Armendariz

1978 **THE ONE AND ONLY**
Director: Carl Reiner
Co-stars: Henry Winkler Gene Saks Polly Holiday

1982 **THE CAPTURE OF GRIZZLY ADAMS**
Director: Don Keeslar
Co-stars: Dan Haggerty Noah Beery Keenan Wynn

1985 **BETTER OFF DEAD**
Director: Michael Jaffe
Co-stars: John Cusack David Ogden Stiers Demian Slade

1985 **EMBASSY**
Director: Robert Lewis
Co-stars: Nick Mancuso Mimi Rogers Eli Wallach Sam Wanamaker

1985 **FIRST STEPS**
Director: Sheldon Larry
Co-stars: Judd Hirsch Amy Steel John Pankow Frances Lee McCain

1987 **TEEN WOLF TOO**
Director: Christopher Leitch
Co-stars: Jason Bateman John Astin Paul Sand

MIREILLE DARC

1967 **WEEKEND**
Director: Jean-Luc Godard
Co-stars: Jean Yanne Jean-Pierre Leaud Juliet Berto

1968 **THE BLONDE FROM PEKING**
Director: Nicolas Gessner
Co-stars: Claudio Brook Edward G. Robinson

1972 **THERE ONCE WAS A COP**
Director: Georges Lautner
Co-stars: Alain Delon Michael Constantine

1974 **SOMEONE IS BLEEDING**
Director: Georges Lautner
Co-stars: Alain Delon Claude Brasseur

DENISE DARCEL

1948 **THUNDER IN THE PINES**
Co-stars: George Reeves Ralph Byrd

1950 **TARZAN AND THE SLAVE GIRL**
Director: Lee Sholem
Co-stars: Lex Barker Vanessa Brown Robert Alda

1951 **WESTWARD THE WOMEN**
Director: William Wellman
Co-stars: Robert Taylor John McIntyre Hope Emerson

1952 **YOUNG MAN WITH IDEAS**
Director: Mitchell Leisen
Co-stars: Glenn Ford Ruth Roman Donna Corcoran

1953 **FLAME OF CALCUTTA**
Director: Seymour Friedman
Co-stars: Patric Knowles Paul Cavanagh George Keymas

1953 **DANGEROUS WHEN WET**
Director: Charles Walters
Co-stars: Esther Williams Fernando Lamas Jack Carson

1953 **VERA CRUZ**
Director: Robert Aldrich
Co-stars: Gary Cooper Burt Lancaster Cesar Romero

JANINE DARCEY

1938 **ENTREE DES ARTISTES**
Director: Marc Allegret
Co-stars: Louis Jouvet Odette Joyeux Claude Dauphin

1939 **FRENCH WITHOUT TEARS**
Director: Anthony Asquith
Co-stars: Ray Miilland Ellen Drew Roland Culver

1955 **RIFIFI**
Director: Jules Dassin
Co-stars: Jean Servais Carl Mohner Marie Sabouret

SHEILA DARCY

1941 **JUNGLE MAN**
Co-Star Buster Crabbe

ADRIENNE DARE

1932 **TWO SECONDS**
Director: Mervyn LeRoy
Co-stars: Edward G. Robinson Preston Foster J. Carrol Naish

DOROTHY DARE

1935 GOLD DIGGERS OF 1935
Director: Busby Berkeley
Co-stars: Dick Powell Adolphe Menjou Gloria Stuart

1935 FRONT PAGE WOMAN
Director: Michael Curtiz
Co-stars: Bette Davis George Brent Wini Shaw

IRENE DARE (Child)

1939 EVERYTHING'S ON ICE
Co-stars: George Meeker Roscoe Karns

ZENA DARE

1937 OVER THE MOON
Director: Thornton Freeland
Co-stars: Merle Oberon Rex Harrlson Ursula Jeans

FLORENCE DAREL

1989 A TALE OF SPRINGTIME
Director: Eric Rohmer
Co-stars: Anne Teyssedre Hughes Quester

1991 URANUS
Director: Claude Berri
Co-stars: Gerard Depardieu Philippe Noiret Michel Blanc

1992 THE STOLEN CHILDREN
Director: Gianni Amelio
Co-stars: Enrico Lo Verso Valentina Scalisi

1992 THE SECRET STEAK
Director: Lazare Iglesis
Co-stars: Daniel Ceccaldi Daniel Lebrun

1993 FAUSTO
Director: Remy Duchemin
Co-stars: Ken Higelin Jean Yanne

COLETTE DARFEUIL

1930 THE END OF THE WORLD
Director: Abel Gance
Co-stars: Abel Gance Sylvia Grenade Victor Francen

EVA DARLAN

1991 DO NOT DISTURB
Director: Nicholas Renton
Co-stars: Frances Barber Peter Capaldi Jean Anderson

CANDY DARLING

1969 FLESH
Director: Paul Morrissey
Co-stars: Joe Dallesandro Geraldine Smith John Christian

JOAN DARLING

1979 THE TWO WORLDS OF JENNIE LOGAN
Director: Frank De Felitta
Co-stars: Lindsay Wagner Marc Singer

GEMMA DARLINGTON (Child)

1989 LOVING HAZEL
Director: Peter Smith
Co-stars: Hugh Quarshie Susan Brown Dona Croll

LINDA DARLOW

1989 IMMEDIATE FAMILY
Director: Jonathan Kaplan
Co-stars: Glenn Close James Woods Mary Stuart Masterson

1994 MY NAME IS KATE
Director: Rod Hardy
Co-stars: Daniel J. Travanti Donna Mills Eileen Brennan

LINDA DARNELL (Monetta Elayse Darnell)
(Killed In Fire At A Friends House)

1939 HOTEL FOR WOMEN
Director: Gregory Ratoff
Co-stars: Elsa Maxwell James Ellison Ann Sothern

1939 DAYTIME WIFE
Director: Gregory Ratoff
Co-stars: Tyrone Power Warren William Wendy Barrie

1940 BRIGHAM YOUNG
Director: Henry Hathaway
Co-stars: Tyrone Power Dean Jagger Brian Donlevy

1940 CHAD HANNA
Director: Henry King
Co-stars: Henry Fonda Dorothy Lamour John Carradine

1940 THE MARK OF ZORRO
Director: Rouben Mamoulian
Co-stars: Tyrone Power Basil Rathbone

1940 STAR DUST
Director: Walter Lang
Co-stars: John Payne Roland Young Charlotte Greenwood

1941 RISE AND SHINE
Director: Allan Dwan
Co-stars: Jack Oakie George Murphy Walter Brennan

1941 BLOOD AND SAND
Director: Rouben Mamoulian
Co-stars: Tyrone Power Rita Hayworth Laird Cregar

1942 THE LOVES OF EDGAR ALAN POE
Director: Harry Lachman
Co-stars: John Shepperd Jane Darwell

1943 SONG OF BERNADETTE
Director: Henry King
Co-stars: Jennifer Jones Charles Bickford Vincent Price

1943 CITY WITHOUT MEN
Director: Sidney Salkow
Co-stars: Glenda Farrell Michael Duane Sara Allgood

1944 IT HAPPENED TOMORROW
Director: Rene Clair
Co-stars: Dick Powell Jack Oakie Edgar Kennedy

1944 SUMMER STORM
Director: Douglas Sirk
Co-stars: George Sanders Anna Lee Hugo Haas

1944 SWEET AND LOWDOWN
Director: Archie Mayo
Co-stars: Jack Oakie Lynn Bari James Cardwell

1944 BUFFALO BILL
Director: William Wellman
Co-stars: Joel McCrea Maureen O'Hara Thomas Mitchell

1945 FALLEN ANGEL
Director: Otto Preminger
Co-stars: Alice Faye Dana Andrews Charles Bickford

1945 THE GREAT JOHN L
Director: Frank Tuttle
Co-stars: Greg McClure Barbara Britton Otto Kruger

1945 HANGOVER SQUARE
Director: John Brahm
Co-stars: Laird Cregar George Sanders Glenn Langan

1946 CENTENNIAL SUMMER
Director: Otto Preminger
Co-stars: Jeanne Crain Cornel Wilde Walter Brennan

1946 ANNA AND THE KING OF SIAM
Director: John Cromwell
Co-stars: Irenne Dunne Rex Harrison Lee J. Cobb

1946 **MY DARLING CLEMENTINE**
Director: John Ford
Co-stars: Henry Fonda Victor Mature Walter Brennan

1947 **FOREVER AMBER**
Director: Otto Preminger
Co-stars: Cornel Wilde George Sanders Richard Greene

1948 **THE WALLS OF JERICHO**
Director: John Stahl
Co-stars: Cornel Wilde Kirk Douglas Anne Baxter

1948 **UNFAITHFULLY YOURS**
Director: Preston Sturges
Co-stars: Rex Harrison Rudy Vallee Barbara Lawrence

1949 **SLATTERY'S HURRICANE**
Director: Andre De Toth
Co-stars: Richard Widmark Veronica Lake Gary Merrill

1949 **A LETTER TO THREE WIVES**
Director: Joseph Mankiewicz
Co-stars: Jeanne Crain Ann Sothern Kirk Douglas

1949 **EVERYBODY DOES IT**
Director: Edmund Goulding
Co-stars: Paul Douglas Celeste Holm Charles Coburn

1950 **NO WAY OUT**
Director: Joseph Mankiewicz
Co-stars: Richard Widmark Sidney Poitier

1950 **TWO FLAGS WEST**
Director: Robert Wise
Co-stars: Joseph Cotten Jeff Chandler Cornel Wilde

1951 **THE 13TH. LETTER**
Director: Otto Preminger
Co-stars: Charles Boyer Constance Smith Michael Rennie

1951 **SATURDAY ISLAND**
Director: Stuart Heisler
Co-stars: Tab Hunter Donald Gray

1951 **THE LADY PAYS OFF**
Director: Douglas Sirk
Co-stars: Stephen McNally Gigi Perreau Virginia Field

1951 **THE GUY WHO CAME BACK**
Director: Joseph Newman
Co-stars: Paul Douglas Joan Bennett Don Defore

1952 **BLACKBEARD THE PIRATE**
Director: Raoul Walsh
Co-stars: Robert Newton William Bendix Keith Andes

1952 **NIGHT WITHOUT SLEEP**
Director: Roy Baker
Co-stars: Gary Merrill Hildegarde Neff Hugh Beaumont

1953 **SECOND CHANCE**
Director: Rudolph Mate
Co-stars: Robert Mitchum Jack Palance Roy Roberts

1954 **THIS IS MY LOVE**
Director: Stuart Heisler
Co-stars: Faith Domergue Dan Duryea Rick Jason

1956 **DAKOTA INCIDENT**
Director: Lewis Foster
Co-stars: Dale Robertson John Lund Regis Toomey

1957 **ZERO HOUR**
Director: Hall Bartlett
Co-stars: Dana Andrews Sterling Hayden

VICKI DARNELL

1988 **BRAIN DAMAGE**
Director: Frank Henenlotter
Co-stars: Rick Herbst Jennifer Lowry Theo Barnes

DANIELLE DARRIEUX

1935 **MAYERLING**
Director: Anatole Litvak
Co-stars: Charles Boyer Marthe Regnier Suzy Prim

1938 **THE RAGE OF PARIS**
Director: Henry Koster
Co-stars: Douglas Fairbanks Louis Hayward Mischa Auer

1940 **KATIA**

1951 **RICH, YOUNG AND PRETTY**
Director: Norman Taurog
Co-stars: Jane Powell Vic Damone Fernando Lamas

1949 **OCCUPE-TOI D'AMELIE**
Director: Claude Autant-Lara
Co-stars: Jean Desailly Bourville Carrette

1952 **FIVE FINGERS**
Director: Joseph Mankiewicz
Co-stars: James Mason Michael Rennie Walter Hampden

1952 **ADORABLE CREATURES**
Director: Christian Jaque
Co-stars: Daniel Gelin Edwige Feuillere Martine Carol

1952 **LE PLAISIR**
Director: Max Ophuls
Co-stars: Claude Dauphin Jean Gabin Simone Simon

1953 **MADAME DE .....**
Director: Max Ophuls
Co-stars: Charles Boyer Vittorio DeSica Lea De Lea

1954 **LE ROUGE ET LE NOIR**
Director: Claude Autant-Lara
Co-stars: Gerard Philipe Antonella Lualdi

1955 **LADY CHATTERLEY'S LOVER**
Director: Marc Allegret
Co-stars: Leo Genn Erno Crisa

1956 **ALEXANDER THE GREAT**
Director: Robert Rossen
Co-stars: Richard Burton Fredric March Claire Bloom

1958 **MARIE OCTOBRE**
Director: Julien Duvivier
Co-stars: Serge Reggiani Bernard Blier Lino Ventura

1961 **THE GREENGAGE SUMMER**
Director: Lewis Gilbert
Co-stars: Kenneth More Susannah York Jane Asher

1962 **LANDRU**
Director: Claude Chabrol
Co-stars: Charles Denner Stephane Audran Hildegarde Neff

1967 **THE YOUNG GIRLS OF ROCHEFORT**
Director: Jacques Demy
Co-stars: Catharine Deneuvre Francois Dorleac George Chakaris

1968 **BIRDS COME TO DIE IN PERU**
Director: Romain Gary
Co-stars: Jean Seberg Maurice Ronet Pierre Brasseur

1986 **SCENE OF THE CRIME**
Director: Andre Techine
Co-stars: Catherine Deneuvre Wadeck Stanczak

SONIA DARRIN

1946 **THE BIG SLEEP**
Director: Howard Hawks
Co-stars: Humphrey Bogart Lauren Bacall Martha Vickers

BARBARA DARROW

1958 **QUEEN OF OUTER SPACE**
Director: Edward Bearnds
Co-stars: Zsa Zsa Gabor Eric Fleming Paul Birch

Bette Davis

Joan Crawford

Greta Garbo

Marlene Dietrich

LILI DARVAS
(Married Ferenc Molnar) (Hungarian Playwright)

1956   MEET ME IN LAS VEGAS
Director: Roy Rowland
Co-stars: Dan Dailey Cyd Charisse Lena Horne

1971   SZERELEM
Director: Karoly Makk
Co-stars: Mari Torocsik Ivan Darvas Tibor Bitskey

BELLA DARVI

1954   THE EGYPTIAN
Director: Michael Curtiz
Co-stars: Edmund Purdom Victor Mature Jean Simmons

1954   HELL AND HIGH WATER
Director: Samuel Fuller
Co-stars: Richard Widmark Cameron Mitchell David Wayne

1955   THE RACERS
Director: Henry Hathaway
Co-stars: Kirk Douglas Gilbert Roland Cesar Romero

JANE DARWELL
Oscar For Best Supporting Actress In 1940 For "The Grapes Of Wrath"

1931   HUCKLEBERRY FINN
Director: Norman Taurog
Co-stars: Jackie Coogan Mitzi Green Junior Durkin

1932   HOT SATURDAY
Director: William Seiter
Co-stars: Nancy Carroll Cary Grant Randolph Scott

1932   HE COULDN'T TAKE IT
Co-stars: Virginia Cherrill Ray Walter

1933   CHILD OF MANHATTAN
Director: Edward Buzzell
Co-stars: Nancy Carroll John Boles Betty Grable

1934   BLIND DATE
Director: Roy William Neill
Co-stars: Ann Sothern Paul Kelly Mickey Rooney

1934   THE MOST PRECIOUS STONE
Director: Lambert Hillyer
Co-stars: Anita Louise Ben Alexander

1934   ONE NIGHT OF LOVE
Director: Victor Schertzinger
Co-stars: Grace Moore Tullio Carminati

1935   PADDY O'DAY
Director: Lewis Seiller
Co-stars: Jane Withers Pinky Tomlin Rita Hayworth Francis Ford

1935   ONE MORE SPRING
Co-stars: Janet Gaynor Warner Baxter Walter Woolf King

1935   NAVY WIFE
Director: Allan Dwan
Co-stars: Claire Trevor Ralph Bellamy Ben Lyons Warren Hymer

1935   McFADDEN'S FLATS
Director: Ralph Murphy
Co-stars: Walter Kelly Andy Clyde Betty Furness

1935   CURLY TOP
Director: Irving Cummings
Co-stars: Shirley Temple John Boles Rochelle Hudson Esther Dale

1936   CRAIG'S WIFE
Director: Dorothy Arzner
Co-stars: Rosalind Russell John Boles Thomas Mitchell

1936   THE FIRST BABY
Co-stars: Johnny Downs Shirley Dean Gene Lockhart

1936   POOR LITTLE RICH GIRL
Director: Irving Cummings
Co-stars: Shirley Temple Jack Haley Alice Faye

1936   CAPTAIN JANUARY
Director: David Butler
Co-stars: Shirley Temple Guy Kibbee Buudy Ebsen June Lang

1936   RAMONA
Director: Henry King
Co-stars: Loretta Young Don Ameche Kent Taylor

1936   STAR FOR A NIGHT
Co-stars: Evelyn Venable J. Edward Bromberg

1936   WE'RE ONLY HUMAN
Director: James Flood
Co-stars: Preston Foster Jane Wyatt James Gleason

1937   SLAVE SHIP
Director: Tay Garnett
Co-stars: Wallace Beery Warner Baxter Mickey Rooney

1937   THE SINGING MARINE
Director: Ray Enright
Co-stars: Dick Powell Doris Weston Hugh Herbert

1937   NANCY STEELE IS MISSING
Director: George Marshall
Co-stars: Victor McLaglen June Lang Peter Lorre

1937   WIFE, DOCTOR AND NURSE
Director: Walter Lang
Co-stars: Loretta Young Warner Baxter Virginia Bruce

1931   LOVE IS NEWS
Director: Tay Garnet
Co-stars: Tyrone Power Loretta Young Don Ameche Dudley Digges

1937   LAUGHING AT TROUBLE
Director: Frank Strayer
Co-stars: Sara Haden Lois Wiilson Allan Lane

1937   THE JURY'S SECRET
Director: Edward Sloman
Co-stars: Kent Taylor Fay Wray Nan Grey Larry Blake

1937   THE GREAT HOSPITAL MYSTERY
Director: James Tinling
Co-stars: Joan Davis Sally Blane William Demarest

1937   FIFTY ROADS TO TOWN
Director: Norman Taurog
Co-stars: Don Ameche Ann Sothern Slim Summerville

1937   DANGEROUSLY YOURS
Director: Mal St. Clair
Co-stars: Cesar Romero Phyllis Brooks Alan Dinehart

193S   BATTLE OF BROADWAY
Director: George Marshall
Co-stars: Victor McLaglen Brian Donlevy Gypsey Rose Lee

1938   CHANGE OF HEART
Director: James Tinling
Co-stars: Gloria Stuart Michael Whalen Lyle Talbot

1938   FIVE OF A KIND
Director: Herbert Leeds
Co-stars: Jean Hersholt Claire Trevor Cesar Romero

1938   LITTLE MISS BROADWAY
Director: Irving Cummings
Co-stars: Shirley Temple George Murphy Jimmy Durante

1938   THREE BLIND MICE
Director: William Seiter
Co-stars: Loretta Young Joel McCrea Binnie Barnes David Niven

1938   UP THE RIVER
Director: Alfred Werker
Co-stars: Preston Foster Arthur Treacher Tony Martin

1939   MIRACLE ON MAIN STREET
Director: Steve Sekely
Co-stars: Margo Walter Abel Lyle Talbot Wynne Gibson

1939	**THE RAINS CAME**
Director:	Clarence Brown
Co-stars:	Tyrone Power Myrna Loy George Brent Brenda Joyce

1939	**GONE WITH THE WIND**
Director:	Victor Fleming
Co-stars:	Clark Gable Vivien Leigh Leslie Howard

1940	**CHAD HANNA**
Director:	Henry King
Co-stars:	Henry Fonda Dorothy Lamour Linda Darnell

1940	**BRIGHAM YOUNG**
Director:	Henry Hathaway
Co-stars:	Dean Jagger Tyrone Power Linda Darnell Mary Astor

1940	**THE GRAPES OF WRATH**
Director:	John Ford
Co-stars:	Henry Fonda John Carradine Dorris Bowden

1940	**UNTAMED**
Director:	George Archainbaud
Co-stars:	Ray Milland Akim Tamiroff Esther Dale

1941	**THIEVES FALL OUT**
Director:	Ray Enright
Co-stars:	Eddie Albert Joan Leslie Anthony Quinn Alan Hale

1941	**SMALL TOWN DEB**
Co-stars:	Jane Withers Jackie Searl

1941	**ALL THAT MONEY CAN BUY**
Director:	William Dieterle
Co-stars:	Walter Huston Edward Arnold Simone Simon

1942	**ALL THROUGH THE NIGHT**
Director:	Vincent Sherman
Co-stars:	Humphrey Bogart Conrad Veidt Peter Lorre

1942	**THE BATTLE OF MIDWAY (VOICE)**
Director:	John Ford
Co-stars:	Henry Fonda Donald Crisp

1942	**THE GREAT GILDERSLEEVE**
Director:	Gordon Douglas
Co-stars:	Harold Peary Nancy Gates Charles Arnt

1942	**HIGHWAYS BY NIGHT**
Director:	Peter Godfrey
Co-stars:	Richard Carlson Jane Randolph Barton MacLane

1942	**ON THE SUNNY SIDE**
Co-stars:	Roddy McDowell Katherine Alexander Freddy Mercer

1942	**THE LOVES OF EDGAR ALAN POE**
Director:	Harry Lachman
Co-stars:	John Shepperd Linda Darnell

1942	**MEN OF TEXAS**
Director:	Ray Enright
Co-stars:	Robert Stack Anne Gwynne Broderick Crawford

1943	**TENDER COMRADE**
Director:	Edward Dmytryk
Co-stars:	Ginger Rogers Robert Ryan Kim Hunter

1943	**THE OX-BOW INCIDENT**
Director:	William Wellman
Co-stars:	Henry Fonda Dana Andrews Anthony Quinn

1943	**GOVERNMENT GIRL**
Director:	Dudley Nichols
Co-stars:	Olivia De Havilland Sonny Tufts Anne Shirley

1944	**THE IMPATIENT YEARS**
Director:	Irving Cummings
Co-stars:	Jean Arthur Lee Bowman Charles Coburn

1945	**SUNDAY DINNER FOR A SOLDIER**
Director:	Lloyd Bacon
Co-stars:	Anne Baxter John Hodiak Charles Wininiger

1945	**I LIVE IN GROSVENER SQUARE**
Director:	Herbert Wilcox
Co-stars:	Anna Neagle Rex Harrison Dean Jagger

1945	**CAPTAIN TUGBOAT ANNIE**
Director:	Phil Rosen
Co-stars:	Edgar Kennedy Charles Gordon

1946	**MY DARLING CLEMENTINE**
Director:	John Ford
Co-stars:	Henry Fonda Victor Mature Cathy Downs Linda Darnell

1946	**THREE WISE FOOLS**
Director:	Edward Buzzell
Co-stars:	Margaret O'Brien Lionel Barrymore Thomas Mitchell

1947	**THE RED STALLION**
Co-stars:	Robert Paige Noreen Nash Pierre Watkin

1948	**THREE GODFATHERS**
Director:	John Ford
Co-stars:	John Wayne Harry Carey Pedro Armendariz Mae Marsh

1950	**THE DAUGHTER OF ROSIE O'GRADY**
Director:	David Butler
Co-stars:	June Haver Gordon MacRae S.Z. Sakall

1950	**WAGONMASTER**
Director:	John Ford
Co-stars:	Ben Johnson Ward Bond Joanne Dru Harry Carey Jnr

1950	**CAGED**
Director:	John Cromwell
Co-stars:	Eleanor Parker Agnes Moorehead Jan Sterling

1951	**JOURNEY INTO LIGHT**
Director:	Stuart Heisler
Co-stars:	Sterling Hayden Viveca Lindfors Thomas Mitchell

1951	**THE LEMON DROP KID**
Director:	Sidney Lanfield
Co-stars:	Bob Hope Marilyn Maxwell Lloyd Nolan

1952	**WE'RE NOT MARRIED?**
Director:	Edmund Goulding
Co-stars:	Victor Moore Ginger Rogers Marilyn Monroe

1953	**IT HAPPENS EVERY THURSDAY**
Director:	Joseph Pevney
Co-stars:	Loretta Young John Forsyth Jim Conlin

1953	**THE SUN SHINES BRIGHT**
Director:	John Ford
Co-stars:	Charles Winninger Arleen Whelan John Russell

1953	**AFFAIR WITH A STRANGER**
Director:	Roy Rowland
Co-stars:	Jean Simmons Victor Mature Mary Jo Tarola

1953	**THE BIGAMIST**
Director:	Collier Young
Co-stars:	Edmond O'Brien Joan Fontaine Ida Lupino

1955	**HIT THE DECK**
Director:	Roy Rowland
Co-stars:	Jane Powell Ann Miller Debbie Reynolds Tony Martin

1958	**THE LAST HURRAH**
Director:	John Ford
Co-stars:	Spencer Tracy Jeffrey Hunter Pat O'Brien Basil Rathbone

1959	**HOUND-DOG MAN**
Director:	Don Siegel
Co-stars:	Fabian Stuart Whitman Carol Lynley Betty Field

1964	**MARY POPPINS**
Director:	Robert Stevenson
Co-stars:	Julie Andrews Dick Van Dyke Glynis Johns

STACEY DASH

1988	**MOVING**
Director:	Allan Metter
Co-stars:	Richard Pryor Beverly Todd Randy Quaid

1992	**MO' MONEY**
Director:	Peter MacDonald
Co-stars:	Damon Wayans Marlon Wayans Joe Santos

1994 RENAISSANCE MAN
Director: Penny Marshall
Co-stars: Danny DeVito Gregory Hines Cliff Robertson

1995 CLUELESS
Director: Amy Heckerling
Co-stars: Alicia Silverstone Paul Rudd Elisa Donovan

STELLA DASSAS
1959 HIROSHIMA MON AMOUR
Director: Alain Resnais
Co-stars: Emmanuelle Riva Eiji Okada Pierre Barbaud

MARIE-HELENE DASTE
1943 LES ANGES DU PECHE
Director: Robert Bresson
Co-stars: Renee Faure Jany Holt Mila Parely Sylvie

SOPHIE DAUMIER
1964 DO YOU LIKE WOMEN?
Director: Jean Leon
Co-stars: Guy Bedos Edwige Feuillere Gregoire Aslan

DOMINIQUE DAVALOS
1987 SALVATION
Director: Beth B
Co-stars: Stephen McHattie Viggo Mortensen Exene Cervenka

ELYSSA DAVALOS
1977 GOOD AGAINST EVIL
Director: Paul Wendkos
Co-stars: Dack Rambo Dan O'Herlihy Jenny O'Hara

1979 THE APPLE DUMPLING GANG RIDES AGAIN
Director: Vincent McEveety
Co-stars: Tim Conway Don Knotts

1987 RIVIERA
Director: John Frankenheimer
Co-stars: Ben Masters Patrick Bauchau Jon Finch

DOROTHY DAVE
1934 HAPPINESS AHEAD
Director: Mervyn LeRoy
Co-stars: Dick Powell Josephine Hutchinson Frank McHugh

CLAIRE DAVONPORT
1978 ADVENTURES OF A PLUMBER'S MATE
Director: Stanley Long
Co-stars: Christopher Neil Elaine Page

1978 CARRY ON EMMANUELLE
Director: Gerald Thomas
Co-stars: Kenneth Williams Suzanne Danielle Joan Sims

DORIS DAVENPORT
1940 THE WESTENER
Director: William Wyler
Co-stars: Gary Cooper Walter Brennan Forrest Tucker

LAURA DAVENPORT
1989 FIRST AND LAST
Director: Alan Dossor
Co-stars: Joss Ackland Pat Heywood Patricia Routledge

1991 TELL ME THAT YOU LOVE ME
Director: Bruce MacDonald
Co-stars: Judith Scott Sean Bean James Wilby

BELINDA DAVEY
1986 DEATH OF A SOLDIER
Director: Philippe Mora
Co-stars: Reb Brown Bill Hunter James Coburn

ELEANOR DAVID
1982 PINK FLOYD - THE WALL
Director: Alan Parker
Co-stars: Bob Geldof Christine Hargreaves Bob Hoskins

1984 COMFORT AND JOY
Director: Bill Forsyth
Co-stars: Bill Paterson Alex Norton C.P. Grogan

1986 84, CHARING CROSS ROAD
Director: David Jones
Co-stars: Anne Bancroft Anthony Hopkins Judi Dench

**1986 THE RETURN OF SHERLOCK HOLMES:
THE MAN WITH THE TWISTED LIP**
Director: Patrick Lau
Co-stars: Jeremy Brett Edward Hardwicke

1988 THE WOLVES OF WILLOUGHBY CHASE
Director: Stuart Orme
Co-stars: Stephanie Beacham Geraldine James

1988 LADDER OF SWORDS
Director: Norman Hull
Co-stars: Martin Shaw Juliet Stevenson Bob Peck

1989 SLIPSTREAM
Director: Steven Listberger
Co-stars: Mark Hamill Bob Peck Ben Kingsley Bill Paxton

1989 THE SPIRIT OF MAN
Director: Peter Barnes
Co-stars: Peter Baylis Dilys Laye Nigel Hawthorne

1991 LONDON KILLS ME
Director: Hanif Kureshi
Co-stars: Justin Chadwick Fiona Shaw Emer McCourt

1992 THE GUILTY
Director: Colin Gregg
Co-stars: Michael Kitchen Sean Gallagher Caroline Catz

JOANNA DAVID
1985 ANNA KARENINA
Director: Simon Langton
Co-stars: Jacqueline Bisset Christopher Reeve Paul Scofield

1988 MISS MARPLE: 4.50 FROM PADDINGTON
Director: Martyn Friend
Co-stars: Joan Hickson David Horovitch

1989 UNEXPLAINED LAUGHTER
Director: Gareth Davies
Co-stars: Diana Rigg Elaine Paige Jon Finch

LILIANE DAVID
1960 BREATHLESS
Director: Jean-Luc Godard
Co-stars: Jean-Luc Godard Jean-Paul Belmondo Jean Seberg

LOLITA DAVIDOVICH *(Married Ron Shelton)*
1985 TWO FATHERS' JUSTICE
Director: Rod Holcomb
Co-stars: Robert Conrad George Hamilton Brooke Bundy

1987 ADVENTURES IN BABYSITTING
Director: Chris Columbus
Co-stars: Elizabeth Shue Maia Brewton

1989 BLAZE
Director: Ron Shelton
Co-stars: Paul Newman Jerry Hardin Garland Bunting

1991 THE INNER CIRCLE
Director: Andrei Konchalovsky
Co-stars: Tom Hulce Bob Hoskins Bess Meyer

1991 OBJECT OF BEAUTY
Director: Michael Lindsay-Hogg
Co-stars: John Malkovich Andie MacDowell Joss Ackland

1991 PRISON STORIES: WOMEN ON THE INSIDE
Director: Donna Deitch
Co-stars: Rae Dawn Chong Rachel Ticotin

1992 RAISING CAIN
Director: Brian De Palma
Co-stars: John Lithgow Steven Bauer Frances Sternhagen

1992 LEAP OF FAITH
Director: Richard Pearce
Co-stars: Steve Martin Debra Winger Liam Neeson

1993 BOILING POINT
Director: James Harris
Co-stars: Wesley Snipes Dennis Hopper Viggo Mortensen

1993 YOUNGER AND YOUNGER
Director: Percy Adlon
Co-stars: Donald Sutherland Julie Delpy Sally Kellerman

1994 INTERSECTION
Director: Mark Rydell
Co-stars: Richard Gere Sharon Stone Jenny Morrison

1994 COBB
Director: Ron Shelton
Co-stars: Tommy Lee Jones Robert Wuhl

1997 JUNGLE 2 JUNGLE
Director: Tim Allen
Co-stars: Sam Huntingdon Martin Short

EILEEN DAVIDSON

1982 HOUSE OF EVIL
Director: Mark Rosman
Co-stars: Kathryn McNeil Christopher Lawrence Janis Zido

1988 SHARING RICHARD
Director: Peter Bonertz
Co-stars: Ed Marinaro Nancy Frangione Janet Carroll

1990 ETERNITY
Director: Steven Paul
Co-stars: Jon Voight Armand Assante Kaye Ballard

EMBETH DAVIDTZ

1989 A PRIVATE LIFE
Director: Francis Gerard
Co-stars: Bill Flynn Jana Cilliers Kevin Smith

1991 TILL DEATH US DO PART
Director: Yves Simoneau
Co-stars: Treat Williams Arliss Howard Rebecca Jenkins

**1992 ARMY OF DARKNESS:
THE MEDIEVAL DEAD**
Director: Sam Raimi
Co-stars: Bruce Campbell Bridget Fonda

1993 SCHINDLER'S LIST
Director: Steven Spielberg
Co-stars: Liam Neeson Ben Kingsley Ralph Fiennes

1996 THE FEAST OF JULY
Director: Christopher Menaul
Co-stars: Tom Bell Ben Chaplin Gemma Jones

1996 ROALD DAHL'S MATILDA
Director: Danny DeVito
Co-stars: Danny DeVito Rhea Perlman Hara Wilson

BETTY ANNE DAVIES

1934 DEATH AT BROADCASTING HOUSE
Director: Reginald Denham
Co-stars: Ian Hunter Austin Trevor Jack Hawkins

1937 MERRY COMES TO TOWN
Director: George King
Co-stars: Zasu Pitts Guy Newall Hermoine Gingold

1949 THE PASSIONATE FRIENDS
Director: David Lean
Co-stars: Anne Todd Claude Rains Trevor Howard

1949 THE HISTORY OF MR. POLLY
Director: Anthony Pelissier
Co-stars: John Mills Sally Ann Howes Meg Jenkins

1949 NOW BARABBAS
Director: Gordon Parry
Co-stars: Richard Greene Cedric Hardwicke Richard Burton

1950 THE WOMAN WITH NO NAME
Director: Ladislas Vajda
Co-stars: Phyllis Calvert Edward Underdown

1950 TRIO
Director: Ken Annakin
Co-stars: James Hayter Anne Crawford Nigel Patrick Michael Rennie

1951 AN OUTCAST OF THE ISLANDS
Director: Carol Reed
Co-stars: Trevor Howard Kerima Ralph Richardson

1952 MEET ME TONIGHT
Director: Anthony Pelissier
Co-stars: Ted Ray Kay Walsh Nigel Patrick Valerie Hobson

1953 GRAND NATIONAL NIGHT
Director: Bob McNaught
Co-stars: Nigel Patrick Moira Lister Beatrice Campbell

1954 CHILDREN GALORE
Director: Terence Fisher
Co-stars: Eddie Byrne Marjorie Rhodes June Thorburn

1954 THE BELLES OF ST. TRINIANS
Director: Frank Launder
Co-stars: Alastair Sim George Cole Joyce Grenfell

CYNTHIA DAVIES

1975 COOLEY HIGH
Director: Michael Schultz
Co-stars: Glynn Turman Garrett Morris

GWENLLIAN DAVIES

1988 OUT OF LOVE
Director: Michael Houldey
Co-stars: Juliet Stevenson Darydd Hywel Emrys James

1992 REBECCA'S DAUGHTERS
Director: Karl Francis
Co-stars: Peter O'Toole Paul Rhys Joely Richardson

LINDY DAVIES

1986 MALCOLM
Director: Nadia Tass
Co-stars: Colin Friels John Hargreaves Chris Haywood

LYNETTE DAVIES

1992 THE CHRISTMAS STALLION
Director: Peter Edwards
Co-stars: Daniel J. Travanti Meredith Edwards

MARION DAVIES *(Marion Douras)* MARRIED to RANDOLPH HEARST

1918 CECILIA OF THE PINK ROSES

1924 JANICE MEREDITH
Director: Mason Hopper
Co-stars: Harrison Ford Macklyn Arbuckle W.C. Fields

1925 LIGHTS OF OLD BROADWAY
Director: Monta Bell
Co-stars: Conrad Nagel Julia Swayne Gordon

1927 THE PATSY
Director: King Vidor
Co-stars: Marie Dressler Del Henderson Lawrence Gray

1927	**QUALITY STREET**
Director: King Vidor

1928 SHOW PEOPLE
Director: King Vidor
Co-stars: William Haines Del Henderson John Gilbert Elinor Glyn

1928 HER CARDBOARD LOVER

1929 THE HOLLYWOOD REVUE OF 1929
Director: Charles Reisner
Co-stars: Jack Benny Laurel & Hardy

1929 NOT SO DUMB
Director: King Vidor
Co-stars: Elliott Nugent Raymond Hackett Franklin Pangborn

1930 THE FLORADORA GIRL
Director: Harry Beaumont
Co-stars: Lawrence Gray Walter Catlett Ilka Chase

1931 FIVE AND TEN
Director: Robert Z Leonard
Co-stars: Leslie Howard Irene Rich Douglass Montgomery

1931 BACHELOR FATHER
Director: Robert Z Leonard
Co-stars: C. Aubrey Smith Ray Milland Ralph Forbes

1931 IT'S A WISE CHILD
Director: Robert Z Leonard
Co-stars: Sidney Blackmer James Gleason Polly Moran

1932 POLLY OF THE CIRCUS
Director: Alfred Santell
Co-stars: Clark Gable C. Aubrey Smith Ray Milland

1932 BLONDIE OF THE FOLLIES
Director: Edmund Goulding
Co-stars: Jimmy Durante Robert Montgomery

1933 GOING HOLLYWOOD
Director: Raoul Walsh
Co-stars: Bing Crosby Patsy Kelly Stuart Erwin

1933 PEG O' MY HEART
Director: Robert Z Leonard
Co-stars: Onslow Stevens Alan Mowbray Robert Creig

1934 OPERATOR 13
Director: Richard Boleslowski
Co-stars: Gary Cooper Jean Parker Ted Healy

1935 PAGE MISS GLORY
Director: Mervyn Leroy
Co-stars: Dick Powell Pat O'Brien Mary Astor Frank McHugh

1936 HEARTS DIVIDED
Director: Frank Borzage
Co-stars: Dick Powell Charles Ruggles Claude Rains

1936 CAIN AND MABEL
Director: Lloyd Bacon
Co-stars: Clark Gable Allen Jenkins Roscoe Karns

1937 EVER SINCE EVE
Director: Lloyd Bacon
Co-stars: Robert Montgomery Frank McHugh Patsy Kelly

NICOLA DAVIES

1972 ALL COPPERS ARE
Director: Sidney Hayers
Co-stars: Nicky Henson Martin Potter Julia Foster

RACHEL DAVIES

1986 KNIGHTS AND EMERALDS
Director: Ian Emes
Co-stars: Christopher Wild Warren Mitchell Beverley Hills

1992 A LITTLE BIT OF LIPPY
Director: Chris Bernard
Co-stars: Kenneth Cranham Alison Swann Bette Bourne Rudi Davies

1989 RESURRECTED
Director: Paul Greengrass
Co-stars: David Thewlis Tom Bell Rita Tushingham

SIAN LEISA DAVIES

1987 HEAVEN ON EARTH
Director: Allan Kroeker
Co-stars: R. H. Thomson Amos Crawley Maureen McRae

SUE JONES DAVIES

1992 ELENYA
Director: Steve Gough
Co-stars: Margaret John Pascale Delafouge Jones Seiriol Tomos

BETTE DAVIS
(Ruth Elizabeth Davis) (Married Harmon Nelson, Arthur Farnsworth, Gary Merrill)
**Oscar For Best Actress In 1935 For "Dangerous" And In 1938 For" Jezebel"
Nominated For Best Actress In 1939 For "Dark Victory", In 1940 For
"The Letter", In 1941 For The Little Foxes, In 1942 For "Now Voyager",
In 1944 For "Mr. Skeffington", In 1950 For "All About Eve", In 1952 For
"The Star" and In 1961 For "Whatever Happened To Baby Jane"**

1931 BAD SISTER
Director: Hobart Henley
Co-stars: Conrad Nagel Sidney Fox Zasu Pitts

1931 SEED
Director: John Stahl
Co-stars: John Boles Genevieve Tobin Zasu Pitts

1931 WATERLOO BRIDGE
Director: James Whale
Co-stars: Douglass Montgomery Mae Clark Doris Lloyd

1932 WAY BACK HOME
Director: William Seiter
Co-stars: Phillips Lord Effie Palmer Frank Albertson

1932 THE MENACE
Director: Roy William Neill
Co-stars: H.B. Warner Walter Byron

1932 HELL'S HOUSE
Director: Howard Higgin
Co-stars: Junior Durkin Pat O'Brien Emma Dunn

1932 THE MAN WHO PLAYED GOD
Director: John Adolfi
Co-stars: George Arliss Donald Cook Ray Milland

1932 SO BIG
Director: William Wellman
Co-stars: Barbara Stanwyck George Brent Alan Hale

1932 THE RICH ARE ALWAYS WITH US
Director: Alfred Green
Co-stars: Ruth Chatterton George Brent

1932 THE DARK HORSE
Director: Alfred Green
Co-stars: Warren William Guy Kibbee Frank McHugh

1932 CABIN IN THE COTTON
Director: Michael Curtiz
Co-stars: Richard Barthelmess Dorothy Jordan

1932 THREE ON A MATCH
Director: Mervyn LeRoy
Co-stars: Ann Dvorak Joan Blondell Humphrey Bogart

1933 20,000 YEARS IN SING SING
Director: Michael Curtiz
Co-stars: Spencer Tracy Lyle Talbot Louis Calhern

1933 PARACHUTE JUMPER
Director: Alfred Green
Co-stars: Douglas Fairbanks Leo Carrillo Frank McHugh

1933	**THE WORKING MAN**
Director:	John Adolfi
Co-stars:	George Arliss Hardie Albright Douglass Dumbrille

1933	**EX-LADY**
Director:	Robert Florey
Co-stars:	Gene Raymond Frank McHugh Claire Dodd

1933	**BUREAU OF MISSING PERSONS**
Director:	Roy Del Ruth
Co-stars:	Lewis Stone Pat O'Brien Glenda Farrell

1934	**FASHIONS OF 1934**
Director:	William Dieterle
Co-stars:	William Powell Frank McHugh

1934	**THE BIG SHAKEDOWN**
Director:	John Francis Dillon
Co-stars:	Charles Farrell Glenda Farrell Richardo Cortez

1934	**JIMMY THE GENT**
Director:	Michael Curtiz
Co-stars:	James Cagney Alice White Mayo Methot

1934	**FOG OVER FRISCO**
Director:	William Dieterle
Co-stars:	Donald Woods Margaret Lindsay Alan Hale

1934	**OF HUMAN BONDAGE**
Director:	John Cromwell
Co-stars:	Leslie Howard Frances Dee Reginald Denny

1934	**HOUSEWIFE**
Director:	Alfred Green
Co-stars:	George Brent Ann Dvorak John Halliday

1935	**BORDERTOWN**
Director:	Archie Mayo
Co-stars:	Paul Muni Margaret Lindsay Eugene Pallette

1935	**THE GIRL FROM 10TH. AVENUE**
Director:	Alfred Green
Co-stars:	Ian Hunter Colin Clive Alison Skipworth

1935	**FRONT PAGE WOMAN**
Director:	Michael Curtiz
Co-stars:	George Brent Wini Shaw J. Carrol Naish

1935	**SPECIAL AGENT**
Director:	William Keighley
Co-stars:	George Brent Ricardo Cortez J. Carrol Naish

1935	**DANGEROUS**
Director:	Alfred Green
Co-stars:	Franchot Tone Margaret Lindsay Dick Foran

1936	**THE PETRIFIED FOREST**
Director:	Archie Mayo
Co-stars:	Leslie Howard Humphrey Bogart Dick Foran

1936	**THE GOLDEN ARROW**
Director:	Alfred Green
Co-stars:	George Brent Eugene Pallette Dick Foran

1936	**SATAN MET A LADY**
Director:	William Dieterle
Co-stars:	Warren William Arthur Treacher

1937	**MARKED WOMAN**
Director:	Lloyd Bacon
Co-stars:	Humphrey Bogart Eduardo Ciannelli Mayo Methot

1937	**KID GALLAHAD**
Director:	Michael Curtiz
Co-stars:	Edward G.robinson Humphrey Bogart Wayne Morris

1937	**THAT CERTAIN WOMAN**
Director:	Edmund Goulding
Co-stars:	Henry Fonda Ian Hunter Anita Louise

1937	**IT'S LOVE I'M AFTER**
Director:	Archie Mayo
Co-stars:	Leslie Howard Olivia De Havilland Patric Knowles

1938	**JEZEBEL**
Director:	William Wyler
Co-stars:	Henry Fonda George Brent Margaret Lindsay

1938	**THE SISTERS**
Director:	Anatole Litvak
Co-stars:	Errol Flynn Donald Crisp Beulah Bondi

1939	**DARK VICTORY**
Director:	Edmund Goulding
Co-stars:	George Brent Humphrey Bogart Geraldine Fitzgerald

1939	**JUAREZ**
Director:	William Dieterle
Co-stars:	Paul Muni John Garfield Brian Aherne

1939	**THE OLD MAID**
Director:	Edmund Goulding
Co-stars:	Miriam Hopkins George Brent Jane Bryan

1939	**THE PRIVATE LIVES OF ELIZABETH AND ESSEX**
Director:	Michael Curtiz
Co-stars:	Errol Flynn Alan Hale

1940	**ALL THIS AND HEAVEN TOO**
Director:	Anatole Litvak
Co-stars:	Charles Boyer Jeffrey Lynn Barbara O'Neill

1940	**THE LETTER**
Director:	William Wyler
Co-stars:	Herbert Marshall Frieda Inescort Sen Yung

1941	**THE GREAT LIE**
Director:	Edmund Goulding
Co-stars:	George Brent Mary Astor Hattie McDaniel

1941	**THE BRIDE CAME C.O.D.**
Director:	William Keighley
Co-stars:	James Cagney Stuart Erwin Jack Carson

1941	**THE LITTLE FOXES**
Director:	William Wyler
Co-stars:	Herbert Marshall Teresa Wright Dan Duryea

1941	**THE MAN WHO CAME TO DINNER**
Director:	William Keighley
Co-stars:	Monty Woolley Jimmy Durante Ann Sheridan

1942	**IN THIS OUR LIFE**
Director:	John Huston
Co-stars:	George Brent Dennis Morgan Olivia De Havilland

1942	**NOW VOYAGER**
Director:	Irving Rapper
Co-stars:	Paul Henreid Claude Rains Gladys Cooper

1943	**WATCH ON THE RHINE**
Director:	Herman Shumlin
Co-stars:	Paul Lukas George Coulouris Geraldine Fitzgerald

1943	**THANK YOUR LUCKY STARS**
Director:	David Butler
Co-stars:	Dennis Morgan Joan Leslie S.Z. Sakall

1943	**OLD ACQUAINTANCE**
Director:	Vincent Sherman
Co-stars:	Miriam Hopkins Gig Young Anne Revere

1944	**MR. SKEFFINGTON**
Director:	Vincent Sherman
Co-stars:	Claude Rains Walter Abel Richard Waring

1944	**HOLLYWOOD CANTEEN**
Director:	Delmer Daves
Co-stars:	Joan Leslie Robert Hutton Dane Clark

1945	**THE CORN IS GREEN**
Director:	Irving Rapper
Co-stars:	John Dall Nigel Bruce Arthur Shields

1946	**A STOLEN LIFE**
Director:	Curtis Bernhardt
Co-stars:	Glenn Ford Dane Clark Walter Brennan

1946 DECEPTION
Director: Irving Rapper
Co-stars: Paul Henreid Claude Rains John Abbott

1948 WINTER MEETING
Director: Bretaigne Windust
Co-stars: James Davis Janis Paige Florence Bates

1948 JUNE BRIDE
Director: Bretaigne Windust
Co-stars: Robert Montgomery Debbie Reynolds

1949 BEYOND THE FOREST
Director: King Vidor
Co-stars: Joseph Cotten David Brian Ruth Roman Dona Drake

1950 ALL ABOUT EVE
Director: Joseph Mankiewicz
Co-stars: Anne Baxter George Sanders Celeste Holm

1951 PAYMENT ON DEMAND
Director: Curtis Bernhardt
Co-stars: Barry Sullivan Kent Taylor Frances Dee

1952 ANOTHER MAN'S POISON
Director: Irving Rapper
Co-stars: Gary Merrill Anthony Steel Emlyn Williams

1952 PHONE CALL FROM A STRANGER
Director: Jean Negulesco
Co-stars: Gary Merrill Shelley Winters Michael Rennie

1952 THE STAR
Director: Stuart Heisler
Co-stars: Sterling Hayden Natalie Wood Barbara Lawrence

1955 THE VIRGIN QUEEN
Director: Henry Koster
Co-stars: Richard Todd Joan Collins Herbert Marshall

1956 STORM CENTER
Director: Daniel Taradash
Co-stars: Brian Keith Kim Hunter Paul Kelly

1956 THE CATERED AFFAIR
Director: Richard Brooks
Co-stars: Ernest Borgnine Debbie Reynolds Barry Fitzgerald

1959 JOHN PAUL JONES
Director: John Farrow
Co-stars: Robert Stack Marisa Pavan Charles Coburn

1959 THE SCAPEGOAT
Director: Robert Hamer
Co-stars: Alec Guinness Nicole Maurey Pamela Brown

1961 POCKETFUL OF MIRACLES
Director: Frank Capra
Co-stars: Glenn Ford Hope Lange Thomas Mitchell

1961 WHATEVER HAPPENED TO BABY JANE
Director: Robert Aldrich
Co-stars: Joan Crawford Barbara Merrill

1964 DEAD RINGER
Director: Paul Henreid
Co-stars: Karl Malden Peter Lawford Jean Hagen

1964 LA NOIA
Director: Damiano Damiani
Co-stars: Horst Buchholz Catherine Spaak Lea Padovani

1964 WHERE LOVE HAS GONE
Director: Edward Dmytryk
Co-stars: Susan Hayward Joey Heatherton Jane Greer

1964 HUSH. . .HUSH, SWEET CHARLOTTE
Director: Robert Aldrich
Co-stars: Olivia De Havilland Joseph Cotten

1965 THE NANNY
Director: Seth Holt
Co-stars: Wendy Craig Williaim Dix Pamela Franklin

1968 THE ANNIVERSARY
Director: Roy Ward Baker
Co-stars: Sheila Hancock Jack Hedley James Cossins

1971 CONNECTING ROOMS
Director: Franklin Gollings
Co-stars: Michael Redgrave Alexis Kanner Leo Genn

1971 BUNNY O'HARE
Director: Gerd Oswald
Co-stars: Ernest Borgnine Jack Cassidy Jay Robinson

1972 MADAME SIN
Director: David Greene
Co-stars: Robert Wagner Denholm Elliott Dudley Sutton

1972 THE JUDGE AND JAKE WYLER
Director: David Lowell Rich
Co-stars: Doug McClure Lou Jacobi Joan Van Ark

1972 LO SCOPONE SCIENTIFICO
Director: Luigi Comencini
Co-stars: Alberto Sordi Silvana Mangano Joseph Cotten

1973 SCREAM PRETTY PEGGY

1976 BURNT OFFERINGS
Director: Dan Curtis
Co-stars: Oliver Reed Karen Black Burgess Meredith

1978 DEATH ON THE NILE
Director: John Guillermin
Co-stars: Peter Ustinov Mia Farrow David Niven

1978 RETURN FROM WITCH MOUNTAIN
Director: John Hough
Co-stars: Christopher Lee Kim Richards Jack Soo

1980 THE WATCHER IN THE WOODS
Director: John Hough
Co-stars: Lynn Holly-Johnson Carroll Baker David McCallum

1980 WHITE MAMA
Director: Jackie Cooper
Co-stars: Ernest Harden Eileen Heckart Anne Ramsey

1981 FAMILY REUNION
Director: Fielder Cook
Co-stars: J. Ashley Hyman Roy Dotrice David Huddelston

1982 A PIANO FOR MRS. CIMINO
Director: George Schaefer
Co-stars: Keenan Wynn Penny Fuller Alexa Kenin

1983 RIGHT OF WAY
Director: George Schaefer
Co-stars: James Stewart Melinda Dillon John Harkins

1983 HOTEL
Director: Jerry London
Co-stars: James Brolin Shirley Jones Mel Torme

1985 MURDER WITH MIRRORS
Director: Dick Lowry
Co-stars: Helen Hayes John Mills Leo McKern Dorothy Tutin

1986 AS SUMMERS DIE
Director: Jean-Claude Tramont
Co-stars: Scott Glen Jamie Lee Curtis Ron O'Neal

1987 THE WHALES OF AUGUST
Director: Lindsay Anderson
Co-stars: Lillian Gish Vincent Price Ann Sothern

1989 THE WICKED STEPMOTHER
Director: Larry Cohen
Co-stars: Barbara Carrera Tom Bosley Evelyn Keyes

CAROLE DAVIS

1987 MANNEQUIN
Director: Michael Gottlieb
Co-stars: Andrew McCarthy Kim Cattrall James Spader

1991 TEEN AGENT
Director: William Dear
Co-stars: Richard Grieco Linda Hunt Roger Rees

DEBBIE DAVIS

1972 THE AMAZING MR. BLUNDEN
Director: Lionel Jeffries
Co-stars: Laurence Naismith Diana Dors David Lodge

DIANE DAVIS

1992 FINAL SHOT: THE HANK GATHERS STORY
Co-Star Victor Lore

DOROTHY DAVIS

**1976 THE LITTLE GIRL WHO LIVES
DOWN THE LANE**
Director: Zev Braun
Co-stars: Jodie Foster Martin Sheen

ELAINE DAVIS

1954 THE ATOMIC KID
Director: Leslie Martinson
Co-stars: Mickey Rooney Robert Strauss Bill Goodwin

ESSIE DAVIS

1993 THE CUSTODIAN
Director: John Dingwall
Co-stars: Anthony LaPaglia Hugo Weaving Barry Otto

GAIL DAVIS

1949 THE FAR FRONTIER
Co-stars: Roy Rogers Andy Devine

1953 ON TOP OF OLD SMOKEY
Director: George Archainbaud

**1977 RACE FOR YOUR LIFE,
CHARLIE BROWN** *(Voice)*
Director: Bill Melendez
Co-stars: Duncan Watson Greg Felton

GEENA DAVIS

(Married Jeff Goldblum, Renny Harlin)
**Oscar For Best Supporting Actress In 1988 For The Accidental Tourist
Nominated For Best Actress In 1991 For Thelma And Louise**

1982 TOOTSIE
Director: Sydney Pollack
Co-stars: Dustin Hoffman Jessica Lange Teri Garr

1985 FLETCH
Director: Michael Ritchie
Co-stars: Chevy Chase Tim Matheson Joe Don Baker

1985 SEXPIONAGE
Director: Don Taylor
Co-stars: Linda Hamilton Sally Kellerman James Franciscus

1986 THE FLY
Director: David Cronenberg
Co-stars: Jeff Goldblum John Getz Joy Boushel

1988 EARTH GIRLS ARE EASY
Director: Julien Temple
Co-stars: Jeff Goldblum Jim Carrey Julie Brown

1988 BEETLEJUICE
Director: Tim Burton
Co-stars: Alec Baldwin Michael Keaton Catherine O'Hara

1988 THE ACCIDENTAL TOURIST
Director: Lawrence Kasdan
Co-stars: William Hurt Kathleen Turner

1990 QUICK CHANGE
Director: Bill Murray
Co-stars: Bill Murray Randy Quaid Jason Robards Philip Bosco

1991 THELMA AND LOUISE
Director: Ridley Scott
Co-stars: Susan Sarandon Harvey Keitel Brad Pitt

1992 A LEAGUE OF THEIR OWN
Director: Penny Marshall
Co-stars: Lori Petty Madonna Tom Hanks

1992 ACCIDENTAL HERO
Director: Stephen Frears
Co-stars: Dustin Hoffman Andy Garcia Joan Cusack

1994 ANGIE
Director: Martha Coolidge
Co-stars: Stephen Rea James Gandolfini Philip Boscoe

1994 SPEECHLESS
Director: Ron Underwood
Co-stars: Michael Keaton Christopher Reeve

1996 THE LONG KISS GOODNIGHT
Director: Renny Harlin
Co-stars: Samuel L. Jackson

1996 CUTTHROAT ISLAND
Director: Renny Harlin
Co-stars: Matthew Modine

GWEN E. DAVIS

1986 UNNATURAL CAUSES
Director: Lamont Johnson
Co-stars: John Ritter Alfre Woodard Patti Labelle

HOPE DAVIS

1990 FLATLINES
Director: Joel Schumacher
Co-stars: Kiefer Sutherland Julia Roberts Kevin Bacon

1998 GUY
Director: Michael Lindsay-Hogg
Co-star: Vincent D'Onofrio

ILAH DAVIS

1978 HARDCORE
Director: Paul Schrader
Co-stars: George C. Scott Peter Boyle Season Hubley

JOAN DAVIS

1932 TOO BUSY TO WORK
Director: John Blystone
Co-stars: Will Rogers Dick Powell Marian Nixon

1935 GEORGE WHITE'S 1935 SCANDALS
Director: George White
Co-stars: George White Alice Faye James Dunn Ned Sparks

1937 ANGEL'S HOLIDAY
Director: James Tinling
Co-stars: Jane Withers Robert Kent John Qualen

1937 THE GREAT HOSPITAL MYSTERY
Director: James Tinling
Co-stars: Jane Darwell Sally Blane Sig Ruman

1937 THE HOLY TERROR
Director: James Tinling
Co-stars: Jane Withers Tony Martin El Brendel Leah Ray

1937 LIFE BEGINS IN COLLEGE
Director: William Seiter
Co-stars: Tony Martin Ritz Bros . Gloria Stuart

1937 LOVE AND HISSES
Director: Sidney Lanfield
Co-stars: Simone Simon Bert Lahr Walter Winchell

1937	**ON THE AVENUE**
Director:	Roy Del Ruth
Co-stars:	Dick Powell Madeleine Carroll Ritz Bros.

1937	**THIN ICE**
Director:	Sidney Lanfield
Co-stars:	Tyrone Power Sonja Henie Sig Ruman Alan Hale

1937	**WAKE UP AND LIVE**
Director:	Sidney Lanfield
Co-stars:	Alice Faye Walter Winchall Ben Bernie Jack Haley

1937	**TIME OUT FOR ROMANCE**
Director:	Malcolm St. Clair
Co-stars:	Claire Trevor Michael Whalen William Demarest

1938	**SALLY, IRENE AND MARY**
Director:	William Seiter
Co-stars:	Alice Faye Tony Martin Jimmy Durante

1938	**MY LUCKY STAR**
Director:	Roy Del Ruth
Co-stars:	Sonja Henie Richard Greene Buddy Ebsen

1938	**JUST AROUND THE CORNER**
Director:	Irving Cummings
Co-stars:	Shirley Temple Charles Farrell Bert Lahr

1938	**JOSETTE**
Director:	Allan Dwan
Co-stars:	Simone Simon Don Ameche Robert Young Lynn Bari

1938	**HOLD THAT CO-ED**
Director:	George Marshall
Co-stars:	John Barrymore George Murphy Jack Haley

1939	**DAYTIME WIFE**
Director:	Gregory Ratoff
Co-stars:	Tyrone Power Linda Darnell Warren William

1939	**TAIL SPIN**
Director:	Roy Del Ruth
Co-stars:	Alice Faye Constance Bennett Jane Wyman

1940	**MANHATTAN HEARTBEAT**
Director:	David Burton
Co-stars:	Robert Sterling Virginia Gilmore Don Beddoe

1941	**SUN VALLEY SERENADE**
Director:	Bruce Humberstone
Co-stars:	Sonja Henie Glenn Miller John Payne

1941	**HOLD THAT GHOST**
Director:	Arthur Lubin
Co-stars:	Abbott & Costello Andrews Sisters Mischa Auer

1942	**YOKEL BOY**
Director:	Joseph Santley
Co-stars:	Eddie Foy Albert Dekker Alan Mowbray

1943	**AROUND THE WORLD**
Director:	Allan Dwan
Co-stars:	Kay Kyser Ginny Sinms Mischa Auer Iss Kabibble

1943	**TWO SENORITAS FROM CHICAGO**
Co-stars:	Jinx Falkenburg Ann Savage Bob Haymes

1944	**BEAUTIFUL BUT BROKE**
Director:	Charles Barton
Co-stars:	Jane Frazee John Hubbard Judy Clark

1944	**SHOW BUSINES**
Director:	Edwin Marin
Co-stars:	Eddie Cantor George Murphy Constance Moore

1945	**GEORGE WHITE'S SCANDALS**
Director:	Felix Feist
Co-stars:	Jack Haley Jane Greer Philip Terry

1945	**SHE GETS HER MAN**
Director:	Eric Kenton
Co-stars:	William Gargan Leon Errol Milburn Stone

1946	**SHE WROTE THE BOOK**
Director:	Charles Lamont
Co-stars:	Jack Oakie Gloria Stuart Mischa Auer

1948	**IF YOU KNEW SUSIE**
Director:	Gordon Douglas
Co-stars:	Eddie Cantor Allyn Joslyn Bobby Driscoll

1949	**MAKE MINE LAUGHS**
Co-Star	Jack Haley

1950	**LOVE THAT BRUTE**
Director:	Alexander Hall
Co-stars:	Paul Douglas Jean Peters Cesar Romero

1951	**THE GROOM WORE SPURS**
Director:	Richard Whorf
Co-stars:	Ginger Rogers Jack Carson Stanley Ridges

1952	**HAREM GIRL**
Director:	Edward Bernds
Co-stars:	Peggie Castle Arthur Blake Paul Marion

JUDY DAVIS *(Married Colin Friels)*
Nominated For Best Actress In 1984 For "A Passage To India" And Best Supporting Actress In 1992 For "Husbands And Wives'

1979	**MY BRILLIANT CAREER**
Director:	Gillian Armstrong
Co-stars:	Sam Neill Wendy Hughes Robert Grubb

1981	**HEATWAVE**
Director:	Philip Noyce
Co-stars:	Richard Noir Chris Haywood Bill Hunter Anna Jemison

1981	**WINTER OF OUR DREAMS**
Director:	John Duigan
Co-stars:	Bryan Brown Cathy Downes Baz Luhrman

1982	**WHO DARES WINS**
Director:	Ian Sharp
Co-stars:	Lewis Collins Ingrid Pitt Richard Widmark

1984	**A PASSAGE TO INDIA**
Director:	David Lean
Co-stars:	Alec Guinness Peggy Ashcroft Art Malik Victor Banerjee

1986	**KANGAROO**
Director:	Tim Burstall
Co-stars:	Colin Friels John Walton Julie Nihill

1987	**HIGH TIDE**
Director:	Gillian Armstrong
Co-stars:	Jan Adele Colin Friels Claudia Karvan John Clayton

1988	**GEORGIA**
Director:	Ben Lewin
Co-stars:	John Bach Marshall Napier Julia Blake

1989	**IMPROMPTU**
Director:	James Lapine
Co-stars:	Hugh Grant Mandy Patinkin Emma Thompson

1990	**ALICE**
Director:	Woody Allen
Co-stars:	Mia Farrow Joe Mantegna Blythe Danner Alec Baldwin

1991	**BARTON FINK**
Director:	Joel Coen
Co-stars:	John Turturro John Goodman Michael Lerner Jon Polito

1991	**THE NAKED LUNCH**
Director:	David Cronenberg
Co-stars:	Peter Weller Ian Holm Julian Sands Roy Scheider

1991	**ABSOLUTE POWER**
Director:	Clint Eastwood
Co-stars:	Clint Eastwood Laura Linney Gene Hackman Scott Glen

1991	**WHERE ANGELS FEAR TO TREAD**
Director:	Charles Sturridge
Co-stars:	Helen Mirren Rupert Graves

1991 ONE AGAINST THE WIND
Director: Larry Elikann
Co-stars: Sam Neill Denholm Elliott Anthony Higgins

1992 ON MY OWN
Director: Antonio Tibaldi
Co-stars: Matthew Ferguson Jan Rubes

1992 HUSBANDS AND WIVES
Director: Woody Allen
Co-stars: Woody Allen Blythe Danner Mia Farrow Liam Neesen

1994 THE NEW AGE
Director: Michael Tolkin
Co-stars: Peter Weller Patrick Bauchau

1994 HOSTILE HOSTAGES
Director: Ted Demme
Co-stars: Kevin Spacey Glynis Johns Denis Leary

1995 SERVING IN SILENCE:THE MARGARETHE CAMERMEYER STORY
Director: Jeff Bleckner
Co-star: Glenn Close

1997 ABSOLUTE POWER
Director: Clint Eastwood
Co-stars: Clint Eastwood Laura Linney Gene Hackman

1998 DECONSTRUCTING HARRY
Director: Woody Allen
Co-stars: Woody Allen Kirstie Alley

LISA DAVIS

1957 THE DALTON GIRLS
Director: Reginald LeBorg
Co-stars: Merry Anders Penny Edwards Sue George

MILDRED DAVIS

1922 DOCTOR JACK
Director: Fred Newmeyer
Co-stars: Harold Lloyd John Prince

1923 SAFETY LAST
Director: Fred Newmeyer
Co-stars: Harold Lloyd Noah Young

NANCY DAVIS *(Married Ronald Reagan)*

1949 SHADOW ON THE WALL
Director: Pat Jackson
Co-stars: Ann Sothern Zachary Scott Gigi Perreau

1949 EAST SIDE, WEST SIDE
Director: Mervyn LeRoy
Co-stars: James Mason Barbara Stanwyck Van Heflin Ava Gardner

1950 THE NEXT VOICE YOU HEAR
Director: William Wellman
Co-stars: James Whitmore Jeff Corey Lillian Bronson

1951 SHADOW IN THE SKY
Director: Fred Wilcox
Co-stars: Ralph Meeker James Whitmore Jean Hagan

1951 NIGHT INTO MORNING
Director: Fletcher Markle
Co-stars: Ray Milland John Hodiak Jean Hagan

1952 IT'S A BIG COUNTRY
Director: Richard Thorpe
Co-stars: Ethel Barrymore Van Johnson Gene Kelly Fredric March

1952 TALK ABOUT A STRANGER
Director: David Bradley
Co-stars: George Murphy Lewis Stone Kurt Kasznar

1953 DONOVAN'S BRAIN
Director: Felix Feist
Co-stars: Lew Ayres Gene Evans Steve Brodie Lisa K. Howard

1957 HELLCATS OF THE NAVY
Director: Nathan Juran
Co-stars: Ronald Reagan Arthur Franz Robert Arthur

PATRICIA DAVIS

1983 NIGHT PARTNERS
Director: Noel Nosseck
Co-stars: Yvette Mimieux Diana Canova Patricia McCormack

PHYLLIS DAVIS

1970 BEYOND THE VALLEY OF THE DOLLS
Director: Russ Meyer
Co-stars: Dolly Read Cynthia Myers Marcia McBroom

ROCHELLE DAVIS

1994 THE CROW
Director: Alex Proyas
Co-stars: Brandon Lee Ernie Hudson Michael Wincott

SALLY DAVIS

1990 CAN YOU HEAR ME THINKING?
Director: Christopher Morahan
Co-stars: Judi Dench Michael Williams

SAMI DAVIS

1986 MONA LISA
Director: Neil Jordan
Co-stars: Bob Hoskins Cathy Tyson Michael Caine Robbie Coltrane

1987 PACK OF LIES
Director: Anthony Page
Co-stars: Ellen Burstyn Teri Garr Alan Bates Ronald Hines

1987 A PRAYER FOR THE DYING
Director: Mike Hodges
Co-stars: Mickey Rourke Bob Hoskins Alan Bates

1987 HOPE AND GLORY
Director: John Boorman
Co-stars: Sarah Miles David Hayman Susan Woolridge Ian Bannen

1988 THE RAINBOW
Director: Ken Russell
Co-stars: Amanda Donohue Paul McGann David Hemmings

1988 THE LAIR OF THE WHITE WORM
Director: Ken Russell
Co-stars: Amanda Donohue Hugh Grant

1988 CONSUMING PASSIONS
Director: Giles Foster
Co-stars: Vanessa Redgrave Jonathan Pryce Freddie Jones

1992 INDECENCY
Director: Marissa Silver
Co-stars: Jennifer Beals James Remar Barbara Williams

1995 FOUR ROOMS
Director: Quentin Tarantino
Co-stars: Tim Roth Madonna Antonio Banderas Ione Skye

SHIRLEY DAVIS

1949 PRINCE OF THE PLAINS
Co-stars: Monte Hale Paul Hurst

VIVEKA DAVIS

1981 SHOOT THE MOON
Director: Alan Parker
Co-stars: Albert Finney Diane Keaton Karen Allen

1985 NOT MY KID
Director: Michael Tuchner
Co-stars: George Segal Stockard Channing Tate Donovan

1991 CURLY SUE
Director: John Hughes
Co-stars: Kelly Lynch James Belushi Alisan Porter

ROSANNA DAVON

1987 THE AVENGER
Director: David Blyth
Co-stars: Scott Feraco Robert Sedgewick Teresa Blake

YOLA D'AVRIL

1930 ALL QUIET ON THE WESTERN FRONT
Director: Lewis Milestone
Co-stars: Lew Ayres Lewis Wolheim John Wray

1935 CAPTAIN BLOOD
Director: Michael Curtiz
Co-stars: Errol Flynn Olivia De Havilland Basil Rathbone

PAMELA ANN DAVY

1968 AMSTERDAM AFFAIR
Director: Gerry O'Hara
Co-stars: Wolfgang Kieling Caterina Von Schell

EVELYN DAW

1937 SOMETHING TO SING ABOUT
Director: Victor Schertzinger
Co-stars: James Cagney Mona Barrie

MARJORIE DAW

1917 REBECCA OF SUNNYBROOK FARM
Director: Marshall Neilan
Co-stars: Mary Pickford Eugene O'Brien

PAM DAWBER

1978 A WEDDING
Director: Robert Altman
Co-stars: Carol Burnett Paul Dooley Mia Farrow Howard Duff

1980 THE GIRL, THE GOLD WATCH AND EVERYTHING
Director: William Wiard
Co-stars: Robert Hays Zohra Lampert

1983 THROUGH NAKED EYES
Director: John Llewellyn Moxey
Co-stars: David Soul Fionnula Flanagan

1985 WILD HORSES
Director: Dick Lowry
Co-stars: Kenny Rogers Ben Johnson Richard Farnsworth

1985 THIS WIFE FOR HIRE
Director: James Drake
Co-stars: Robert Klein Laraine Newman Ann Jillian

1990 DO YOU KNOW THE MUFFIN MAN?
Director: Gilbert Cates
Co-stars: John Shea Brian Bonsall

1990 FACE OF FEAR
Director: Farhad Mann
Co-stars: Lee Horsley Bob Balaban Kevin Conroy

1992 STAYED TUNED
Director: Peter Hyams
Co-stars: John Ritter Jeffrey Jones Heather McComb

1994 A CHILD'S CRY FOR HELP
Director: Sandor Stern
Co-stars: Veronica Hamel Daniel Hugh Kelly

1994 WEB OF DECEPTION
Director: Richard Colla
Co-stars: Powers Booth Lisa Collins

1995 TRAIL OF TEARS
Director: Donald Wrye
Co-stars: Katey Sagal William Russ

1996 A STRANGER TO LOVE
Director: Peter Levin
Co-stars: Beau Bridges Tess Harper

GLORIA DAWN

1977 THE MANGO TREE
Director: Kevin Dobson
Co-stars: Christopher Pate Geraldine Fitzgerald Diane Craig

MARPESSA DAWN

1958 BLACK ORPHEUS
Director: Marcel Camus
Co-stars: Breno Mello Ademar Da Silva

SUGAR DAWN (Child)

1941 LONE STAR LAW MEN
Co-stars: Tom Keene Betty Miles Frank Yaconelli

MICHELINE DAX

1953 RUE DE L'ESTRAPADE
Director: Jacques Becker
Co-stars: Louis Jourdan Anne Vernon Daniel Gelin

ELSPETH DUXBURY

1960 MAKE MINE MINK
Director: Robert Asher
Co-stars: Terry-Thomas Athene Seyler Billie Whitelaw

ALICE DAY

1929 LITTLE JOHNNY JONES
Director: Mervyn LeRoy
Co-stars: Eddie Buzzell Edna Murphy Robert Edeson

1929 IS EVERYBODY HAPPY?
Director: Archie Mayo
Co-stars: Ted Lewis Ann Pennington Lawrence Grant

1932 GOLD
Co-Star Jack Hoxie

ANNETTE DAY

1967 DOUBLE TROUBLE
Director: Norman Taurog
Co-stars: Elvis Presley John Williams Yvonne Romain

BAYBI DAY

1974 THE DRILLER KILLER
Director: Abel Ferrara
Co-stars: Carolyn Marx Jimmy Laine Peter Yellen

CORA LEE DAY

1991 DAUGHTERS OF THE DUST
Director: Julie Dash
Co-stars: Alva Rogers Kaycee Moore Barbara-O

DORIS DAY (Married Marty Melcher)
Nominated For Best Actress In 1959 For "Pillow Talk"

1948 ROMANCE ON THE HIGH SEAS
Director: Michael Curtiz
Co-stars: Jack Carson Oscar Levant

1949 MY DREAM IS YOURS
Director: Michael Curtlz
Co-stars: Jack Carson Adolphe Menjou

1949 IT'S A GREAT FEELING
Director: David Butler
Co-stars: Jack Carson Dennis Morgan

1950 **TEA FOR TWO**
Director: David Butler
Co-stars: Gordon MacRae Gene Nelson

1950 **YOUNG MAN WLTH A HORN**
Director: Michael Curtiz
Co-stars: Kirk Douglas Lauren Bacall

1950 **FINE AND DANDY**
Director: Roy Del Ruth
Co-stars: James Cagney Gordon MacRae

1950 **STORM WARNING**
Director: Stuart Heisler
Co-stars: Ginger Rogers Ronald Reagan

1951 **LULLABY OF BROADWAY**
Director: David Butler
Co-stars: Gene Nelson Gladys George

1951 **STARLIFT**
Director: Roy Del Ruth
Co-stars: Gordon MacRae Virginia Mayo

1952 **I'LL SEE YOU IN MY DREAMS**
Director: Michael Curtlz
Co-stars: Danny Thomas Patrice Wymore

1952 **LUCKY ME**
Director: Jack Donohue
Co-stars: Robert Cummings Phil Silvers

1952 **THE WINNING TEAM**
Director: Lewis Seiler
Co-stars: Ronald Reagan Frank Lovejoy

1952 **APRIL IN PARIS**
Director: David Butler
Co-stars: Ray Bolger Claude Dauphin

1952 **ON MOONLIGHT BAY**
Director: Roy Del Ruth
Co-stars: Gordon MacRae Leon Ames

1953 **BY THE LIGHT OF THE SILVERY MOON**
Director: David Butler
Co-stars: Gordon MacRae Leon Ames

1953 **CALAMITY JANE**
Director: David Butler
Co-stars: Howard Keel Phil Carey Dick Wesson

1954 **YOUNG AT HEART**
Director: Gordon Douglas
Co-stars: Frank Sinatra Gig Young Ethel Barrymore

1955 **LOVE ME OR LEAVE ME**
Director: Charles Vidor
Co-stars: James Cagney Robert Keith Tom Tully

1955 **THE MAN WHO KNEW TOO MUCH**
Director: Alfred Hltchcock
Co-stars: James Stewart Bernard Miles

1956 **JULIE**
Director: Andrew Stone
Co-stars: Louis Jourdan Barry Sullivan

1957 **THE PAJAMA GAME**
Director: Stanley Donen
Co-stars: John Raitt Carol Haney Eddie Foy

1958 **TEACHER'S PET**
Director: George Seaton
Co-stars: Clark Gable Gig Young

1958 **THE TUNNEL OF LOVE**
Director: Gene Kelly
Co-stars: Richard Widmark Gig Young Gia Scala

1959 **IT HAPPENED TO JANE**
Director: Richard Quine
Co-stars: Jack Lemon Ernie Kovacs

1959 **PILLOW TALK**
Director: Michael Gordon
Co-stars: Rock Hudson Tony Randall

1960 **MIDNIGHT LACE**
Director: David Miller
Co-stars: Rex Harrison Myrna Loy

1960 **PLEASE DON'T EAT THE DAISIES**
Director: Charles Walters
Co-stars: David Niven Janis Paige

1961 **LOVER COME BACK**
Director: Delbert Mann
Co-stars: Rock Huds0n Tony Randall

1962 **THAT TOUCH OF MINK**
Director: Delbert Mann
Co-stars: Cary Grant Gig Young John Astin

1962 **JUMBO**
Director: Charles Walters
Co-stars: Jimmy Durante Stephen Boyd

1963 **THE THRILL OF IT ALL**
Director: Norman Jewison
Co-stars: James Garner Reginald Owen

1963 **MOVE OVER DARLING**
Director: Michael Gordon
Co-stars: James Garner Thelma Ritter

1964 **SEND ME NO FLOWERS**
Director: Norman Jewison
Co-stars: Rock Hudson Tony Randall

1965 **DO NOT DISTURB**
Director: Ralph Levy
Co-stars: Rod Taylor Sergio Fantoni Leon Askin

1966 **THE GLASS BOTTOM BOAT**
Director: Frank Tashlin
Co-stars: Rod Taylor John McGiver Dom DeLuise

1967 **THE BALLAD OF JOSIE**
Director: Andrew McLaglen
Co-stars: Peter Graves George Kennedy

1967 **CAPRICE**
Director: Frank Tashlin
Co-stars: Richard Harris Ray Walston Irene Tsu

1968 **WHERE WERE YOU WHEN THE LIGHTS WENT OUT**
Director: Hy Averbach
Co-stars: Terry-Thomas Robert Morse

1968 **WITH SIX YOU GET EGG ROLL**
Director: Howard Morris
Co-stars: Brian Keith Barbara Hershey

FRANCES DAY

1933 **THE GIRL FROM MAXIM'S**
Director: Alexander Korda
Co-stars: Leslie Henson Lady Tree Stanley Holloway

1937 **THE GIRL IN THE TAXI**
Director: Andre Berthomieu
Co-stars: Henri Garat Lawrence Grossmith Jean Gillie

1944 **FIDDLERS THREE**
Director: Harry Watt
Co-stars: Tommy Trinder Sonnie Hale Diana Decker

1957 **THERE'S ALWAYS THURSDAY**
Director: Charles Saunders
Co-stars: Marjorie Rhodes Jill Ireland Charles Victor

JILL DAY

1955 **ALL FOR MARY**
Director: Wendy Toye
Co-stars: Nigel Patrick David Tomlinson Kathleen Harrison

JOSETTE DAY

1946   **LA BELLE ET LA BETE**
Director: Jean Cocteau
Co-stars: Jean Marais Mila Parely Marcel Andre

1946   **LA FILLE DU PUISATIER**
Director: Marcel Pagnol
Co-stars: Raimu Fernandel Charpin

1948   **LES PARENTS TERRIBLES**
Director: Jean Cocteau
Co-stars: Jean Marais Yvonne De Bray Gabrielle Dorziat

LARAINE DAY

1939   **CRIME DOES NOT PAY: THINK FIRST**
Director: Roy Rowland
Co-stars: Marc Lawrence Sara Haden

1939   **TARZAN FINDS A SON**
Director: Richard Thorpe
Co-stars: Johnny Weismuller Maureen O'Sullivan

1939   **SERGEANT MADDEN**
Director: Josef Von Sternberg
Co-stars: Wallace Beery Tom Brown Alan Curtis

1939   **I TAKE THIS WOMAN**
Director: W.S. Van Dyke
Co-stars: Spencer Tracy Hedy Lamarr Jack Carson

1939   **CALLING DR. KILDARE**
Director: Harold Bucquet
Co-stars: Lew Ayres Lionel Barrymore Lana Tuner

1939   **THE SECRET OF DR. KILDARE**
Director: Harold Bucquet
Co-stars: Lew Ayres Lionel Barrymore

1940   **DR. KILDARE'S CRISIS**
Director: Harold Bucquet
Co-stars: Lew Ayres Lionel Barrymore Robert Young

1940   **DR. KILDARE GOES HOME**
Director: Harold Bucquet
Co-stars: Lew Ayres Lionel Barrymore Gene Lockhart

1940   **DR. KILDARE'S STRANGE CASE**
Director: Harold Bucquet
Co-stars: Lew Ayres Lionel Barrymqre

1940   **FOREIGN CORRESPONDENT**
Director: Alfred Hitchcock
Co-stars: Joel McCrea Herbert Marshall Edmund Gwenn

1940   **MY SON, MY SON**
Director: Charles Vidor
Co-stars: Brian Aherne Madeleine Carroll Louis Hayward

1940   **THE TRIAL OF MARY DUGGAN**
Director: Norman Z McLeod
Co-stars: Robert Young Tom Conway Marsha Hunt

1940   **THE BAD MAN**
Director: Richard Thorpe
Co-stars: Wallace Beery Lionel Barrymore Ronald Reagan

1940   **AND ONE WAS BEAUTIFUL**
Director: Robert Sinclair
Co-stars: Robert Cummings Jean Muir Billie Burke

1941   **DR. KILDARE'S WEDDING DAY**
Director: Harold Buquet
Co-stars: Lew Ayres Lionel Barrymore Red Skelton

1941   **KATHLEEN**
Director: Harold Bucquet
Co-stars: Shirley Temple Herbert Marshall Gail Patrick

1941   **UNHOLY PARTNERS**
Director: Mervyn LeRoy
Co-stars: Edward G. Roblnson Edward Arnold Marsha Hunt

1941   **A YANK ON THE BURMA ROAD**
Director: George Seitz
Co-stars: Barry Nelson Stuart Crawford Keye Luke

1942   **JOURNEY FOR MARGARET**
Director: W.S. Van Dyke
Co-stars: Margaret O'Brien Robert Young Fay Bainter

1942   **FINGERS AT THE WINDOW**
Director: Charles Lederer
Co-stars: Basil Rathbone Lew Ayres Miles Mander

1943   **MR. LUCKY**
Director: H.C. Potter
Co-stars: Cary Grant Charles Bickford Gladys Cooper

1944   **THE STORY OF DR. WASSELL**
Director: Cecil B. DeMille
Co-stars: Gary Cooper Signe Hasso Dennis O'Keefe

1944   **BRIDE BY MISTAKE**
Director: Richard Wallace
Co-stars: Marsha Hunt Alan Marshall Allyn Joslyn

1945   **KEEP YOUR POWDER DRY**
Director: Edward Buzzell
Co-stars: Lana Turner Susan Peters Bill Johnson

1945   **THOSE ENDEARING YOUNG CHARMS**
Director: Lewis Allen
Co-stars: Robert Young Ann Harding Bill Williams

1946   **THE LOCKET**
Director: John Brahm
Co-stars: Robert Mitchum Brian Aherne Gene Raymond

1947   **TYCOON**
Director: Richard Wallace
Co-stars: John Wayne Cedric Hardwicke Anthony Quinn

1948   **MY DEAR SECRETARY**
Director: Charles Martin
Co-stars: Kirk Douglas Keenan Wynn Rudy Vallee

1949   **THE WOMAN ON PIER 13**
Director: Robert Stevenson
Co-stars: Robert Ryan John Agar Thomas Gomez

1954   **THE HIGH AND THE MIGHTY**
Director: William Wellman
Co-stars: John Wayne Robert Newton Robert Stack

1956   **THREE FOR JAMIE DAWN**
Director: Thomas Carr
Co-stars: Ricardo Montalban Richard Carlson June Havoc

1956   **TOY TIGER**
Director: Jerry Hopper
Co-stars: Jeff Chandler Cecil Kellaway David Janssen

1959   **THE THIRD VOICE**
Director: Hubert Cornfield
Co-stars: Edmond O'Brien Julie London

1975   **MURDER ON FLIGHT 502**
Director: George McCowan
Co-stars: Robert Stack Ralph Bellamy Polly Bergen

MARCELINE DAY

1926   **THE BARRIER**
Director: George Hill
Co-stars: Lionel Barrymore Norman Kerry Henry B. Walthall

1927   **LONDON AFTER MIDNIGHT**
Director: Tod Browning
Co-stars: Lon Chaney Conrad Nagel Polly Moran

1927   **THE BIG CITY**
Director: Tod Browning
Co-stars: Lon Chaney Betty Compson James Murray

1928 THE CAMERAMAN
Director: Edward Sedgewick
Co-stars: Buster Keaton Harold Goodwin Harry Gribbon

1929 THE WILD PARTY
Director: Dorothy Arzner
Co-stars: Clara Bow Fredric March Shirley O'Hara

1931 THE MAD PARADE
Director: William Beaudine
Co-stars: Evelyn Brent Irene Rich Louise Fazenda

1932 THE CRUSADER
Co-Star Walter Byron

1933 THE FIGHTING PARSON
Director: Hoot Gibson
Co-stars: Bill Robbins Ethel Wales

1933 THE TELEGRAPH TRAIL
Co-Star John Wayne

SUSAN DAY
1967 THE BIG MOUTH
Director: Jerry Lewis
Co-stars: Jerry Lewis Harold S. Stone Buddy Lester

VERA DAY
1955 A KID FOR TWO FARTHINGS
Director: Carol Reed
Co-stars: Celia Johnson Diana Dors David Kossoff

1956 IT'S A GREAT DAY
Director: John Warrington
Co-stars: Ruth Dunning Edward Evans Nancy Roberts

1957 THE PRINCE AND THE SHOWGIRL
Director: Laurence Olivier
Co-stars: Laurence Olivier Marilyn Monroe Sybil Thorndyke

1957 QUARTERMASS II
Director: Val Guest
Co-stars: Brian Donlevy Sid James Bryan Forbes William Franklin

1958 GRIP OF THE STRANGLER
Director: Robert Day
Co-stars: Boris Karloff Elizabeth Allan Jean Kent

1958 TOO MANY CROOKS
Director: Mario Zampi
Co-stars: Terry-Thomas George Cole Sid James

1958 I WAS MONTY'S DOUBLE
Director: John Guillermin
Co-stars: John Mills Cecil Parker Leslie Phillips

1958 UP THE CREEK
Director: Val Guest
Co-stars: David Tomilinson Peter Sellers Lionel Jeffries

1960 TROUBLE WITH EVE
Director: Francis Searle
Co-stars: Robert Urquart Hy Hazell Sally Smith

1960 AND THE SAME TO YOU
Director: George Pollack
Co-stars: Brian Rix Leo Franklyn Tommy Cooper

1961 WATCH IT SAILOR
Director: Wolf Rilla
Co-stars: Dennis Price Liz Fraser Marjorie Rhodes

GABRIELLE DAYE
1975 SUNSET ACROSS THE BAY
Director: Stephen Frears
Co-stars: Harry Markham Bob Peck Peter Wallis

MARIA DEA
1939 PIEGES
Director: Robert Siodmak
Co-stars: Maurice Chevalier Erich Von Stroheim Pierre Renoir

1942 LES VISITEURS DU SOIR
Director: Marcel Carne
Co-stars: Arletty Jules Berry Alain Cuny

1949 ORPHEE
Director: Jean Cocteau
Co-stars: Jean Marais Francois Perier Juliette Greco

JULIA DEAKIN
1990 DANCIN' THRU THE DARK
Director: Mike Ockrent
Co-stars: Claire Hackett Con O'Neill Angela Clarke

LUCY DEAKINS
1986 THE BOY WHO COULD FLY
Director: Nick Castle
Co-stars: Jay Underwood Bonnie Bedelia Fred Gwynne

1988 THE GREAT OUTDOORS
Director: Howard Deutch
Co-stars: Dan Aykroyd John Candy Annette Bening

1989 CHEETAH
Director: Jeff Blyth
Co-stars: Keith Coogan Colin Mothupi Timothy Landfield

ALLISON DEAN
1988 COMING TO AMERICA
Director: John Landis
Co-stars: Eddie Murphy James Earl Jones Don Ameche

1993 RUBY IN PARADISE
Director: Victor Nunez
Co-stars: Ashley Judd Todd Field Dorothy Lyman

1995 ABANDONED AND DECEIVED
Director: Joseph Dougherty
Co-stars: Lori Loughlin Brian Kerwin Rosemary Forsythe

FELICITY DEAN
1985 STEAMING
Director: Joseph Losey
Co-stars: Vanessa Redgrave Sarah Miles Diana Dors

1987 THE WHISTLE BLOWER
Director: Simon Langton
Co-stars: Michael Caine James Fox Nigel Havers

ISABEL DEAN
1949 THE PASSIONATE FRIENDS
Director: David Lean
Co-stars: Ann Todd Trevor Howard Claude Rains

1952 TWENTY-FOUR HOURS OF A WOMAN'S LIFE
Director: Victor Saville
Co-stars: Merle Obern Richard Todd Leo Glenn

1953 THE STORY OF GILBERT AND SULLIVAN
Director: Sidney Gilliat
Co-stars: Robert Morley Maurice Evans

1954 OUT OF THE CLOUDS
Director: Basil Dearden
Co-stars: Anthony Steel Robert Beatty Gordon Harker

1957 DAVY
Director: Michael Relph
Co-stars: Harry Secombe Ron Randell George Relph Susan Shaw

1958 VIRGIN ISLAND
Director: Pat Jackson
Co-stars: Virginia Maskell John Cassavetes Sidney Poitier

1965 HIGH WIND IN JAMAICA
Director: Alexander MacKendrick
Co-stars: Anthony Quinn James Coburn Gert Frobe

1968   INADMISSIBLE EVIDENCE
Director: Anthony Page
Co-stars: Nicol Williamson Jill Bennett

1975   RANSOM
Director: Caspar Wrede
Co-stars: Sean Connery Ian McShane Norman Bristow William Fox

1976   THE BAWDY ADVENTURES OF TOM JONES
Director: Cliff Owen
Co-stars: Nicky Henson Trevor Howard

1982   FIVE DAYS ONE SUMMER
Director: Fred Zinnemann
Co-stars: Sean Connery Betsy Brantly Lambert Wilson

1990   INSPECTOR MORSE: SINS OF THE FATHER
Director: Peter Hammond
Co-stars: John Thaw Lisa Harrow

JULIA DEAN

1944   THE CURSE OF THE CAT PEOPLE
Director: Robert Wise
Co-stars: Simone Simon Kent Smith Jane Randolph

1947   OUT OF THE BLUE
Director: Leigh Jason
Co-stars: George Brent Carole Landis Ann Dvorak

1948   THE EMPEROR WALTZ
Director: Billy Wilder
Co-stars: Bing Crosby Joan Fontaine Richard Haydn

LAURA DEAN

1980   FAME
Director: Alan Parker
Co-stars: Irene Cara Lee Curreri Paul McCrane

1984   ALMOST YOU
Director: Adam Brooks
Co-stars: Brooke Adams Griffin Dunne Karen Young

MARGIA DEAN

1949   RED DESERT
Co-stars: Don Barry Tom Neal Jack Holt

1955   THE QUATERMASS EXPERIMENT
Director: Val Guest
Co-stars: Brian Donlevy Jack Warner Gordon Jackson

1958   AMBUSH AT CIMARRON PASS
Director: Jodie Copeland
Co-stars: Scott Brady Clint Eastwood

SHIRLEY DEAN

1936   THE FIRST BABY
Co-stars: Johnny Downs Jane Darwell Gene Lockhart

1936   CHARLIE CHAN AT THE CIRCUS
Director: Harry Lachman
Co-stars: Warner Oland Keye Luke J. Carrol Naish

LEZLIE DEAN

1988   976-EVIL
Director: Robert Englund
Co-stars: Stephen Geoffreys Sandy Dennis Patrick O'Bryan

1992   FREDDY'S DEAD - THE FINAL NIGHTMARE
Director: Rachel Talalay
Co-stars: Robert Englund Lisa Zane Yaphet Kotto

MARJORIE DEANE

1938   GIRL'S SCHOOL
Co-stars: Martha O'Driscoll Peggy Moran Kenneth Howell

GINA DeANGELIS

1989   COUSINS
Director: Joel Schumacher
Co-stars: Ted Danson Isabelle Rossellini Sean Young

ELIZABETH DEAR

1961   THE GREENGAGE SUMMER
Director: Lewis Gilbert
Co-stars: Kenneth More Susannah York Danielle Darrieux

1964   THE BATTLE OF THE VILLA FIORITA
Director: Delmer Daves
Co-stars: Maureen O'Hara Rossano Brazzi

JEAN DE BAER

1986   84, CHARING CROSS ROAD
Director: David Jones
Co-stars: Anne Bancroft Anthony Hopkins Judi Dench

1993   THE MAN WITHOUT A FACE
Director: Mel Gibson
Co-stars: Mel Gibson Margaret Whitton Geoffrey Lewis

BRENDA DE BANZIE

1951   THE LONG DARK HALL
Director: Anthony Bushell
Co-stars: Rex Harrison Lilli Palmer Patricia Wayne

1952   I BELIEVE IN YOU
Director: Basil Dearden
Co-stars: Celia Johnson Cecil Parker Joan Collins

1953   HOBSON'S CHOICE
Director: David Lean
Co-stars: Charles Laughton John Mills Prunella Scales

1954   THE HAPPINESS OF THREE WOMMEN
Director: Maurice Elvy
Co-stars: Eynon Evans Petula Clark Patricia Burke

1954   THE PURPLE PLAIN
Director: Robert Parrish
Co-stars: Gregory Peck Maurice Denham Lyndon Brook

1955   A KID FOR TWO FARTHINGS
Director: Carol Reed
Co-stars: Celia Johnson Diana Dors David Kossoff

1955   DOCTOR AT SEA
Director: Ralph Thomas
Co-stars: Dirk Bogarde Brigitte Bardot Maurice Denham

1955   AS LONG AS THEY'RE HAPPY
Director: J. Lee Thompson
Co-stars: Jack Buchanan Diana Dors Jean Carson

1956   HOUSE OF SECRETS
Director: Guy Green
Co-stars: Michael Craig Julia Arnall David Kossoff

1956   THE MAN WHO KNEW TOO MUCH
Director: Alfred Hitchcock
Co-stars: James Stewart Doris Day

1958   TOO MANY CROOKS
Director: Mario Zampi
Co-stars: Terry-Thomas George Cole Sid James Joe Melia

1959   THE THIRTY-NINE STEPS
Director: Ralph Thomas
Co-stars: Kenneth More Taina Elg Sid James Barry Jones

1959   PASSPORT TO SHAME
Director: Alvin Rakoff
Co-stars: Eddie Constantine Odile Versois Diana Dors

1960   THE ENTERTAINER
Director: Tony Richardson
Co-stars: Laurence Olivier Joan Plowright Albert Finney

1961   **FLAME IN THE STREETS**
Director: Roy Ward Baker
Co-stars: John Mills Sylvia Syms Johnny Sekka Earl Cameron

1961   **THE MARK**
Director: Guy Green
Co-stars: Stuart Whitman Maria Schell Rod Steiger Maurice Denham

1961   **COME SEPTEMBER**
Director: Robert Mulligan
Co-stars: Rock Hudson Gina Lollobrigida Sandra Dee Bobby Darin

1962   **A PAIR OF BRIEFS**
Director: Ralph Thomas
Co-stars: Michael Craig Mary Peach Liz Fraser Ron Moody

1963   **THE PINK PANTHER**
Director: Blake Edwards
Co-stars: David Niven Peter Sellers Capucine Claudia Cardinale

1967   **PRETTY POLLY**
Director: Guy Green
Co-stars: Hayley Mills Trevor Howard Shashi Kapoor Peter Bayliss

CLOTILDE DE BAYSER

1988   **LA PETIT VOLEUSE**
Director: Claude Miller
Co-stars: Charlotte Gainsbourg Raoul Billery

KRISTINE DE BELL

1979   **MEATBALLS**
Director: Ivan Reitman
Co-stars: Bill Murray Harvey Atkin Ron Barry

1980   **THE BIG BRAWL**
Director: Robert Clouse
Co-stars: Jackie Chan Jose Ferrer Mako

DAISY DE BELLEFEUILLE

1987   **90 DAYS**
Director: Giles Walker
Co-stars: Stefan Wodoslawsky Sam Grana Christine Pak

SHARON DE BORD

1970   **THE CHEYENNE SOCIAL CLUB**
Director: Gene Kelly
Co-stars: James Stewart Henry Fonda Shirley Jones

YVONNE DE BRAY

1943   **LOVE ETERNAL**
Director: Jean Delannoy
Co-stars: Jean Marais Madeleine Sologne Jean Murat

1948   **GIGI**
Director: Jacqueline Audry
Co-stars: Daniele Delorme Gaby Morlay Frank Villard

1948   **LES PARENTS TERRIBLES**
Director: Jean Cocteau
Co-stars: Jean Marais Gabrielle Dorziat Josette Day

CELIA DE BURGH

1977   **SOUND OF LOVE**
Director: John Power
Co-Star   John Jarrett

1983   **PHAR LAP**
Director: Simon Wincer
Co-stars: Tom Burlinson Martin Vaughan Judy Morris

ROSEMARY DE CAMP

1941   **HOLD BACK THE DAWN**
Director: Mitchell Leisen
Co-stars: Charles Boyer Olivia De Havilland Paulette Goddard

1942   **EYES IN THE NIGHT**
Director: Fred Zinnemann
Co-stars: Edward Arnold Ann Harding Donna Reed

1942   **THE COMMANDOS STRIKE AT DAWN**
Director: John Farrow
Co-stars: Paul Muni Anna Lee Lillian Gish

1942   **THE JUNGLE BOOK**
Director: Zoltan Korda
Co-stars: Sabu Joseph Calleia John Qualen Frank Puglia

1942   **YANKEE DOODLE DANDY**
Director: Michael Curtiz
Co-stars: James Cagney Joan Leslie Walter Huston

1943   **THIS IS THE ARMY**
Director: Michael Curtis
Co-stars: George Murphy Joan Leslie Irving Berlin

1944   **PRACTICALLY YOURS**
Director: Mitchell Leisen
Co-stars: Claudette Colbert Fred MacMurray

1944   **BOWERY TO BROADWAY**
Director: Charles Lamont
Co-stars: Maria Montez Turhan Bey Susanna Foster Jack Oakie

1944   **THE MERRY MONAHANS**
Director: Charles Lamont
Co-stars: Donald O'Connor Peggy Ryan Jack Oakie

1945   **BLOOD ON THE SUN**
Director: Frank Lloyd
Co-stars: James Cagney Sylvia Sidney Wallace Ford

1945   **TOO YOUNG TO KNOW**
Co-stars: Joan Leslie Robert Hutton Arthur Shields

1945   **DANGER SIGNAL**
Director: Robert Florey
Co-stars: Faye Emerson Zachary Scott Mona Freeman

1945   **RHAPSODY IN BLUE**
Director: Irving Rapper
Co-stars: Robert Alda Joan Leslie Alexis Smith Osxar Levant

1945   **PRIDE OF THE MARINES**
Director: Delmer Daves
Co-stars: John Garfield Eleanor Parker Dane Clark

1946   **NORA PRENTICE**
Director: Vincent Sherman
Co-stars: Ann Sheridan Kent Smith Robert Alda

1946   **FROM THIS DAY FORWARD**
Director: John Berry
Co-stars: Joan Fontaine Mark Stevens Henry Morgan

1948   **THE LIFE OF RILEY**
Director: Irving Brecher
Co-stars: William Bendix James Gleason Beulah Bondi

1949   **LOOK FOR THE SILVER LINING**
Director: David Butler
Co-stars: June Haver Ray Bolger Gordon MacRae

1949   **NIGHT UNTO NIGHT**
Director: Don Siegel
Co-stars: Ronald Reagan Viveca Lindfors Broderick Crawford

1949   **THE STORY OF SEABISCUIT**
Director: David Butler
Co-stars: Shirley Temple Barry Fitzgerald

1951   **ON MOONLIGHT BAY**
Director: Roy Del Ruth
Co-stars: Doris Day Gordon MacRae Leon Ames Mary Wickes

1951   **NIGHT INTO MORNING**
Director: Fletcher Markle
Co-stars: Ray Milland Nancy Davis John Hodiak Lewis Stone

1952 SCANDAL SHEET
Director: Phil Karlson
Co-stars: Broderick Crawford John Derek Donna Reed

1952 TREASURE OF LOST CANYON
Director: Ted Tetzlaff
Co-stars: William Powell Julia Adams Tommy Ivo

1953 SO THIS IS LOVE
Director: Gordon Douglas
Co-stars: Kathryn Grayson Merv Griffin Walter Abel

1953 BY THE LIGHT OF THE SILVERY MOON
Director: David Butler
Co-stars: Doris Day Gordon Macrae Leon Ames

1960 13 GHOSTS
Director: William Castle
Co-stars: Charles Herbert Donald Woods Jo Morrow

YVONNE DE CARLO

1942 ROAD TO MOROCCO
Director: David Butler
Co-stars: Bing Crosby Bob Hope Dorothy Lamour

1944 HERE COME THE WAVES
Director: Mark Sandrich
Co-stars: Bing Crosby Betty Hutton Sonny Tufts

1945 SALOME, WHERE SHE DANCED
Director: Charles Lamont
Co-stars: Rod Cameron Walter Slezak Albert Dekker

1945 FRONTIER GAL
Director: Charles Lamont
Co-stars: Rod Cameron Sheldon Leonard Andy Devine

1947 BRUTE FORCE
Director: Jules Dassin
Co-stars: Burt Lancaster Ann Blyth Howard Duff

1947 SLAVE GIRL
Director: Charles Lamont
Co-stars: George Brent Broderick Crawford Albert Dekker

1947 SONG OF SCHERERAZADE
Director: Walter Reisch
Co-stars: Jean-Pierre Aumont Brian Donlevy Eve Arden

1948 RIVER LADY
Co-stars: Dan Duryea Rod Cameron Helena Carter Florence Bates

1948 CRISS CROSS
Director: Robert Siodmak
Co-stars: Burt Lancaster Dan Duryea Tony Curtis

1948 CASBAH
Director: John Berry
Co-stars: Tony Martin Marta Toren Peter Lorre Hugo Haas

1948 CALAMITY JANE AND SAM BASS
Director: George Sherman
Co-stars: Howard Duff Dorothy Hart Willard Parker

1948 BLACK BART
Director: George Sherman
Co-stars: Dan Duryea Jeffrey Lynn John McIntyre

1949 BUCCANEER'S GIRL
Director: Frederick De Cordova
Co-stars: Philip Friend Robert Douglas

1949 THE GAL WHO TOOK THE WEST
Director: Frederick De Cordova
Co-stars: Charles Coburn Scott Brady

1950 THE DESERT HAWK
Director: Frederick De Cordova
Co-stars: Richard Green Jackie Gleason

1951 HOTEL SAHARA
Director: Ken Annakin
Co-stars: Peter Ustinov David Tomlinson Albert Lieven

1952 HURRICANE SMITH
Director: Jerry Hopper
Co-stars: John Ireland James Craig Forrest Tucker

1952 SCARLET ANGEL
Director: Sidney Salkow
Co-stars: Rock Hudson Richard Denning Amanda Blake

1952 THE SAN FRANCISCO STORY
Director: Robert Parrish
Co-stars: Joel McCrea Sidney Blackmer Florence Bates

1953 SHOTGUN
Director: Lesley Selander
Co-stars: Sterling Hayden Zachary Scott Robert Wilke

1953 SEA DEVILS
Director: Raoul Walsh
Co-stars: Rock Hudson Maxwell Reed Bryan Forbes

1953 SOMBRERO
Director: Norman Foster
Co-stars: Ricardo Montalban Pier Angeli Cyd Charisse

1953 FORT ALGIERS
Director: Lesley Selander
Co-stars: Carlos Thopmson Raymond Burr Leif Erikson

1953 THE CAPTAIN'S PARADISE
Director: Anthony Kimmins
Co-stars: Alec Guinness Celia Johnson Miles Malleson

1953 BORDER RIVER
Director: George Sherman
Co-stars: Joel McCrea Pedro Armendariz

1954 HAPPY EVER AFTER
Director: Mario Zampi
Co-stars: David Niven Barry Fitzgerald George Cole

1954 PASSION

1954 MAGIC FIRE
Director: William Dieterle
Co-stars: Alan Badel Peter Cushing Carlos Thompson

1955 FLAME OF THE ISLANDS
Director: Edward Ludwig
Co-stars: Howard Duff Zachary Scott Kurt Kasznar

1956 DEATH OF A SCOUNDREL
Director: Charles Martin
Co-stars: George Sanders Zsa Zsa Gabor Tom Conway

1956 RAW EDGE
Director: John Sherwood
Co-stars: Rory Calhoun Mara Corday Neville Brand

1956 THE TEN COMMANDMENTS
Director: Cecil B. De Mille
Co-stars: Charlton Heston Yul Brynner John Derek

1957 BAND OF ANGELS
Director: Raoul Walsh
Co-stars: Clark Gable Sidney Poitier Patric Knowles

1959 TIMBUKTU
Director: Jacques Tourneur
Co-stars: Victor Mature George Dolenz John Dehner

1963 McLINTOCK
Director: Andrew McLaglen
Co-stars: John Wayne Maureen O'Hara Chill Wills

1964 THE LAW OF THE LAWLESS
Director: William Claxton
Co-stars: Dale Robertson William Bendix

1964 A GLOBAL AFFAIR
Director: Jack Arnold
Co-stars: Bob Hope Lilo Pulver Robert Sterling

1967 HOSTILE GUNS
Director: R.G. Springsteen
Co-stars: George Montgomery Tab Hunter

1968 THE POWER
Director: Byron Haskin
Co-stars: Michael Rennie George Hamilton Aldo Ray

1968 ARIZONA BUSHWACKERS
Director: Lesley Selander
Co-stars: Howard Keel Brian Donlevy John Ireland

1971 THE SEVEN MINUTES
Director: Russ Meyer
Co-stars: Phil Carey John Carradine David Brian

1976 WON TON, TON THE DOG WHO SAVED HOLLYWOOD
Director: Michael Winner
Co-stars: Madeline Kahn Art Carney Bruce Dern

1981 LIAR'S MOON
Director: David Fisher
Co-stars: Matt Dillion Cindy Fisher Susan Tyrell

1986 A MASTERPIECE OF MURDER
Director: Bob Hope Don Ameche Stella Stevens Clive Revell

1988 AMERICAN GOTHIC
Director: John Hough
Co-stars: Rod Steiger Michael J. Pollard Sarah Torgov

1991 OSCAR
Director: John Landis
Co-stars: Sylvester Stallone Ornella Muti Vincent Spano

JEANNE DE CASALAIS

1934 NELL GWYN
Director: Herbert Wilcox
Co-stars: Anna Neagle Cedric Hardwicke Miles Malleson

1940 SAILORS THREE
Director: Walter Forde
Co-stars: Tommy Trinder Michael Wilding Claude Hulbert

1940 CHARLEY'S BIG HEARTED AUNT
Director: Walter Forde
Co-stars: Arthur Askey Richard Murdoch Phyllis Calvert

1941 THOSE KIDS FROM TOWN
Director: Lance Comfort
Co-stars: Shirley Lenner Percy Marmont George Cole

1941 COTTAGE TO LET
Director: Anthony Asquith
Co-stars: Leslie Banks Alastair Sim John Mills George Cole

1944 MEDAL FOR THE GENERAL
Director: Maurice Elvey
Co-stars: Godfrey Tearle Petula Clark Mabel Constanduros

1946 THIS MAN IS MINE
Director: Marcel Varnel
Co-stars: Tom Walls Glynis Johns Nova Pilbeam

1947 THE TURNERS OF PROSPECT ROAD
Director: Maurice Wilson
Co-stars: Wilfrid Lawson Maureen Glynne

1948 THE WOMAN HATER
Director: Terence Young
Co-stars: Stewart Granger Edwige Feulliere Ronald Squire

1950 THE TWENTY QUESTION MURDER MYSTERY
Director: Paul Stein
Co-stars: Robert Beatty Rona Anderson

ISABEL DE CASTRO

1988 HARD TIMES
Director: Joao Botelho
Co-stars: Luis Estrela Julia Britton Ruy Furtado

DIANA DECKER

1944 FIDDLERS THREE
Director: Harry Watt
Co-stars: Tommy Trinder Sonnie Hale Prances Day

1949 MURDER AT THE WINDMILL
Director: Val Guest
Co-stars: Garry Marsh Jon Pertwee Jimmy Edwards

1953 WILL ANY GENTLEMAN?
Director: Michael Anderson
Co-stars: George Cole Veronica Hurst Jon Pertwee

1955 A YANK IN ERMINE
Director: Gordon Parry
Co-stars: Peter Thompson Noelle Middleton Jon Pertwee

1961 LOLITA
Director: Stanley Kubrick
Co-stars: James Mason Sue Lyon Shelley Winters

1964 DEVILS OF DARKNESS
Director: Lance Comfort
Co-stars: William Sylvester Hubert Noel Tracy Reed

CORINNE DECLA

1986 CAPTIVE
Director: Paul Mayersberg
Co-stars: Irina Brook Oliver Reed Xavier Deluc

FRANCES DEE *(Married Joel McCrea)*

1930 PLAYBOY OF PARIS
Director: Ludwig Berger
Co-stars: Maurice Chevalier Stuart Erwin

1931 RICH MAN'S FOLLY
Director: John Cromwell
Co-stars: George Bancroft Juliette Compton

1931 ALONG CAME YOUTH
Co-Star Charles 'Buddy' Rogers

1931 CAUGHT!
Director: Edward Sloman
Co-stars: Richard Arlen Louise Dresser

1931 AN AMERICAN TRAGEDY
Director: Josef Von Sternberg
Co-stars: Phillips Holmes Sylvia Sidney

1932 IF I HAD A MILLION
Director: Ernst Lubitsch
Co-stars: Charles Laughton Gary Cooper George Raft

1932 LOVE IS A RACKET
Director: William Wellman
Co-stars: Douglas Fairbanks Ann Dvorak Lee Tracy

1932 THE NIGHT OF JUNE 13TH.
Director: Stephen Roberts
Co-stars: Clive Brook Lila Lee Mary Bolland

1932 THE STRANGE CASE OF CLARA DEANE
Director: Max Marcin
Co-stars: Wynne Gibson Pat O'Brien

1932 THIS RECKLESS AGE
Director: Frank Tuttle
Co-stars: Peggy Shannon Charles Ruggles Charles Rogers

1933 THE HEADLINE SHOOTER
Co-Star William Gargan

1933 TARZAN THE FEARLESS
Co-Star Buster Crabbe

1933 ONE MAN'S JOURNEY
Director: John Robertson
Co-stars: Lionel Barrymore Joel McCrea May Robson

1933 LITTLE WOMEN
Director: George Cukor
Co-stars: Katherine Hepburn Joan Bennett Jean Parker

1933 KING OF THE JUNGLE
Director: Max Marcin
Co-stars: Buster Crabbe Douglass Dumbrille

1933 CRIME OF THE CENTURY
Director: William Beaudine
Co-stars: Jean Hersholt Wynne Gibson Stuart Erwin

1933 BLOOD MONEY
Director: Rowland Brown
Co-stars: George Bancroft Judith Anderson

1933 THE SILVER CHORD
Director: John Cromwell
Co-stars: Irene Dunnne Joel McCrea Eric Linden

1934 OF HUMAN BONDAGE
Director: John Cromwell
Co-stars: Leslie Howard Bette Davis Reginald Owen

1934 FINISHING SCHOOL
Director: George Nicholls
Co-stars: Ginger Rogers Bruce Cabot Beulah Bondi

1934 COMING OUT PARTY

1935 BECKY SHARP
Director: Rouben Mamoulian
Co-stars: Miriam Hopkins Cedric Hardwicke Nigel Bruce

1935 THE GAY DECEPTION
Director: William Wyler
Co-stars: Francis Lederer Benita Hume Akim Tamiroff

1936 HALF ANGEL
Co-Star Brian Donlevy

1937 A MAN BETRAYED
Director: John Auer
Co-stars: John Wayne Wallace Ford Ward Bond

1937 SOULS AT SEA
Director: Henry Hathaway
Co-stars: Gary Cooper George Raft Harry Carey

1937 WELLS FARGO
Director: Frank Lloyd
Co-stars: Joel McCrea Bob Burns Lloyd Nolan

1938 IF I WERE KING
Director: Frank Lloyd
Co-stars: Ronald Colman Basil Rathbone Ellen Drew

1939 COAST GUARD
Co-Star Randolph Scott

1941 SO ENDS OUR NIGHT
Director: John Cromwell
Co-stars: Fredric March Margaret Sullavan Glenn Ford

1942 MEET THE STEWARTS
Director: Alfred Green
Co-stars: William Holden Grant Mitchell

1943 I WALKED WITH A ZOMBIE
Director: Jacques Tourneur
Co-stars: James Ellison Tom Conway

1943 HAPPY LAND
Director: Irving Pichel
Co-stars: Don Ameche Harry Carey Natalie Wood

1944 PATRICK THE GREAT
Director: Frank Ryan
Co-stars: Donald O'Connor Peggy Ryan Donald Cook

1947 THE PRIVATE AFFAIRS OF BEL AMI
Director: Albert Lewin
Co-stars: George Sanders Angela Lansbury

1948 THEY PASSED THIS WAY
Director: Alfred Green
Co-stars: Joel McCrea Joseph Calleia Charles Bickford

1951 PAYMENT ON DEMAND
Director: Curtis Bernhardt
Co-stars: Bette Davis Barry Sullivan John Sutton

1952 BECAUSE OF YOU
Director: Albert Cohen
Co-stars: Loretta Young Jeff Chandler Alex Nicol Mae Clarke

1953 MR. SCOUTMASTER
Director: Henry Levin
Co-stars: Clifton Webb Edmund Gwenn George Wlnslow

1953 GYPSY COLT
Director: Andrew Marton
Co-stars: Donna Corcoran Ward Bond Lee Van Cleef

GEORGETTE DEE

1985 SEDUCTION: THE CRUEL WOMAN
Director: Monika Treut
Co-stars: Mechthild Grossman Udo Kier

KIKI DEE

1965 DATELINE DIAMONDS
Director: Jeremy Summers
Co-stars: William Lucas Kenneth Cope Patsy Rowlands

RUBY DEE

1950 NO WAY OUT
Director: Joseph Mankiewicz
Co-stars: Sidney Poitier Richard Widmark Linda Darnell

1951 THE TALL TARGET
Director: Anthony Mann
Co-stars: Dick Powell Adolphe Menjou Paula Raymond

1957 EDGE OF THE CITY
Director: Martin Ritt
Co-stars: Sidney Poitier John Cassavetes Jack Warden

1958 ST. LOUIS BLUES
Director: Allen Reisner
Co-stars: Nat King Cole Eartha Kitt Pearl Bailey

1958 TAKE A GIANT STEP
Director: Philip Leacock
Co-stars: Johnny Nash Estelle Hemsley

1961 A RAISIN IN THE SUN
Director: Daniel Petrie
Co-stars: Sidney Poitier Claudia McNeil Diana Sands

1963 THE BALCONY
Director: Joseph Strick
Co-stars: Shelley Winters Lee Grant Peter Falk

1965 TAGGART
Director: R. G. Springsteen
Co-stars: Tony Young Dan Duryea Dick Foran

1968 UP TIGHT
Director: Jules Dassin
Co-stars: Raymond St. Jacques Julian Mayfield Frank Silvera

1971 BUCK AND THE PREACHER
Director: Sidney Poitier
Co-stars: Sidney Poitier Harry Belafonte Cameron Mitchell

1980 ALL GOD'S CHILDREN
Director: Jerry Thorpe
Co-stars: Richard Widmark Ned Beatty Ossie Davis

1982 CAT PEOPLE
Director: Paul Schrader
Co-stars: Nastassja Kinski Malcolm McDowell John Heard

1985   THE ATLANTA CHILD MURDERS
Director: John Erman
Co-stars: Jason Robards Rip Torn James Earl Jones

1989   DO THE RIGHT THING
Director: Spike Lee
Co-stars: Spike Lee Danny Aiello Ossie Davis John Savage

**1990   THE COURT MARTIAL OF
JACKIE ROBINSON**
Director: Larry Peerce
Co-stars: Andre Braugher Stan Shaw

1990   DECORATION DAY
Director: Robert Markowitz
Co-stars: James Garner Bill Cobbs

1991   JUNGLE FEVER
Director: Spike Lee
Co-stars: Spike Lee Wesley Snipes Annabella Sciorra John Turturro

1993   COP AND A HALF
Director: Henry Winkler
Co-stars: Burt Reynolds Ray Sharkey Holland Taylor

SANDRA DEE *(Married Bobby Darin)*

1957   UNTIL THEY SAIL
Director: Rolert Wise
Co-stars: Jean Simmons Paul Newman Joan Fontaine Piper Laurie

1958   A STRANGER IN MY ARMS
Director: Helmut Kautner
Co-stars: June Allyson Jeff Chandler Mary Astor

1958   THE RELUCTANT DEBUTANT
Director: Vincente Minnelli
Co-stars: Rex Harrison Kay Kendall John Saxon

1959   THE WILD AND THE INNOCENT
Director: Jack Sher
Co-stars: Audie Murphy Joanne Dru Gilbert Roland

1959   A SUMMER PLACE
Director: Delmer Daves
Co-stars: Dorothy McGuire Richard Egan Arthur Kennedy

1959   THE RESTLESS YEARS
Director: Helmut Kautner
Co-stars: John Saxon Luana Patten Teresa Wright

1959   IMITATION OF LIFE
Director: Douglas Sirk
Co-stars: Lana Turner Juanita Moore John Gavin Robert Alda

1959   GIDGET
Director: Paul Wendkos
Co-stars: James Darren Cliff Robertson Arthur O'Connell

1960   PORTRAIT IN BLACK
Director: Michael Gordon
Co-stars: Lana Turner Anthony Quinn Richard Basehart

1961   ROMANOFF AND JULIET
Director: Peter Ustinov
Co-stars: Peter Ustinov John Gavin Akim Tamiroff John Phillips

1961   COME SEPTEMBER
Director: Robert Mulligan
Co-stars: Rock Hudson Gina Lollobrigida Bobby Darin

1961   TAMMY TELL ME TRUE
Director: Henry Keller
Co-stars: John Gavin Charles Drake Beulah Bondi

1962   IF A MAN ANSWERS
Director: Henry Levin
Co-stars: Bobby Darin Cesar Romero John Lund

1963   TAMMY AND THE DOCTOR
Director: Henry Keller
Co-stars: Peter Fonda Beulah Bondi Margaret Lindsay

1963   TAKE HER, SHE'S MINE
Director: Henry Koster
Co-stars: James Stewart Robert Morley Philippe Forquet

1964   I'D RATHER BE RICH
Director: Jack Smight
Co-stars: Maurice Chevalier Robert Goulet Andy Williams

1965   THAT FUNNY FEELING
Director: Richard Thorpe
Co-stars: Bobby Darin Donald O'Connor Nita Talbot

1966   A MAN COULD GET KILLED
Director: Ronald Neame
Co-stars: James Garner Melina Mercouri Robert Coote

1967   DOCTOR YOU'VE GOT TO BE KIDDING
Director: Peter Tewkesbury
Co-stars: George Hamilton Celeste Holm

1967   ROSIE!
Director: David Lowell Rich
Co-stars: Rosalind Russell Brian Aherne Juanita Morre

1970   THE DUNWICH HORROR
Director: Daniel Haller
Co-stars: Dean Stockwell Ed Begley Sam Jaffe Talia Shire

OLIVE DEERING

1949   SAMSON AND DELILAH
Director: Cecil B. DeMille
Co-stars: Hedy Lamarr Victor Mature George Sanders

1950   CAGED
Director: John Cromwell
Co-stars: Eleanor Parker Agnes Moorehead Jan Sterling

1956   THE TEN COMMANDMENTS
Director: Cecil B. DeMille
Co-stars: Charlton Heston Yul Brynner Anne Baxter

MARY DEES

1937   SARATOGA
Director: Jack Conway
Co-stars: Clark Gable Jean Harlow Lionel Barrymore
(Replaced Jean Harlow, When She Died Just Before The Film Was Completed)

STEPHANIE DEES

1988   EVIL IN CLEAR RIVER
Director: Karen Arthur
Co-stars: Lindsay Wagner Randy Quaid Carolyn Croft

PIA DEGERMAN

1967   ELVIRA MADIGAN
Director: Bo Widerberg
Co-stars: Thommy Berggren Lennart Malmer Nina Widerberg

1970   THE LOOKING GLASS WAR
Director: Frank Pierson
Co-stars: Christopher Jones Anthony Hopkins Susan George

ELSA DE GIORGI

1975   SALO OR THE 120 DAYS OF SODOM
Director: Pier Paolo Pasolini
Co-stars: Paolo Bonacelli Giorgio Cataidi

MARTINA DEGNAN

1990   GHOST
Director: Jerry Zucker
Co-stars: Patrick Swayze Demi Moore Whoopi Goldberg

CONSUELO DE HAIVLAND

1986   BETTY BLUE
Director: Jean-Jacques Beineix
Co-stars: Beatrice Dalle Jean-Hugues Anglade

GLORIA DeHAVEN

1940 SUSAN AND GOD
Director: George Cukor
Co-stars: Joan Crawford Fredric March Rita Hayworth Ruth Hussey

1943 THOUSANDS CHEER
Director: George Sidney
Co-stars: Kathryn Grayson Gene Kelly John Boles Kay Kyser

1943 BEST FOOT FORWARD
Director: Edward Buzzell
Co-stars: Lucille Ball June Allyson Harry James

1943 BROADWAY RHYTHM
Director: Roy Del Ruth
Co-stars: George Murphy Charles Winninger Ginny Simms

1944 TWO GIRLS AND A SAILOR
Director: Richard Thorpe
Co-stars: June Allyson Van Johnson Jimmy Durante

1944 BETWEEN TWO WOMEN
Director: Willis Goldbeck
Co-stars: Van Johnson Lionel Barrymore Marilyn Maxwell

1944 STEP LIVELY
Director: Tim Whelan
Co-stars: Frank Sinatra George Murphy Adolphe Menjou

1944 THE THIN MAN GOES HOME
Director: Richard Thorpe
Co-stars: William Powell Myrna Loy Anne Revere

1948 SUMMER HOLIDAY
Director: Rouben Mamoulian
Co-stars: Walter Huston Mickey Rooney Frank Morgan

1949 SCENE OF THE CRIME
Director: Roy Rowland
Co-stars: Van Johnson Arlene Dahl Tom Drake Leon Ames

1949 YES SIR, THAT'S MY BABY
Director: George Sherman
Co-stars: Donald O'Connor Charles Coburn

1949 THE DOCTOR AND THE GIRL
Director: Curtis Bernhardt
Co-stars: Glenn Ford Charles Coburn Janet Leigh

1950 I'LL GET BY
Director: Richard Sale
Co-stars: June Haver William Lundigan Dennis Day Harry James

1950 SUMMER STOCK
Director: Charles Walters
Co-stars: Judy Garland Gene Kelly Eddie Bracken Phil Silvers

1950 THREE LITTLE WORDS
Director: Richard Thorpe
Co-stars: Fred Astaire Red Skelton Vera-Ellen

1950 THE YELLOW CAB MAN
Director: Jack Donohue
Co-stars: Red Skelton Walter Slezak Edward Arnold

1951 TWO TICKETS TO BROADWAY
Director: James Kern
Co-stars: Janet Leigh Eddie Bracken Tony Martin

1952 DOWN AMONG THE SHELTERING PALMS
Director: Edmund Goulding
Co-stars: Jane Greer Mitzi Gaynor David Wayne

1954 SO THIS IS PARIS
Director: Richard Quine
Co-stars: Tony Curtis Gene Nelson Corinne Calvet

1955 THE GIRL RUSH
Director: Robert Pirosh
Co-stars: Rosalind Russell Eddie Albert Fernando Lamas

1975 WHO IS THE BLACK DAHLIA
Director: Joseph Pevney
Co-stars: Efrem Zimbalist Jnr Lucy Arnaz Rick Jason Tom Bosley

**1976 WON TON TON, THE DOG
WHO SAVED HOLLYWOOD**
Director: Michael Winner
Co-stars: Madeline Kahn Art Carney Bruce Dean

OLIVIA DE HAVILLAND (Sister Joan Fontaine)
Oscar For Best Actress In 1946 For To "Each His Own" And In 1949 For
The Heiress. Nominated For Best Actress In 1948 For "The Snake Pit"
And In 1941 For Hold Back The Dawn

1935 CAPTAIN BLOOD
Director: Michael Curtiz
Co-stars: Errol Flynn Basil Rathbone Guy Kibbee

1935 THE IRISH IN US
Director: Lloyd Bacon
Co-stars: James Cagney Pat O'Brien Frank McHugh

1935 A MIDSUMMER NIGHT'S DREAM
Director: William Dieterle
Co-stars: James Cagney Mickey Rooney

1936 ALIBI IKE
Director: Ray Enright
Co-stars: Joe E. Brown Ruth Donnelly Roscoe Carns

1936 ANTHONY ADVERSE
Director: Mervyn LeRoy
Co-stars: Fredric March Edmund Gwenn Claude Rains

1936 THE CHARGE OF THE LIGHT BRIGADE
Director: Michael Curtiz
Co-stars: Errol Flynn Patric Knowles

1937 IT'S LOVE I'M AFTER
Director: Archie Mayo
Co-stars: Bette Davis Leslie Howard Patric Knowles

1937 THE GREAT GARRICK
Director: James Whale
Co-stars: Brian Aherne Lionel Atwill Lana Turner

1937 CALL IT A DAY
Director: Archie Mayo
Co-stars: Ian Hunter Alice Brady Roland Young

1938 FOUR'S A CROWD
Director: Michael Curtiz
Co-stars: Errol Flynn Rosalind Russell Walter Connelly

1938 GOLD IS WHERE YOU FIND IT
Director: Michael Curtiz
Co-stars: George Brent Claude Rains Tim Holt

1938 HARD TO GET
Director: Ray Enright
Co-stars: Dick Powell Charles Winninger Isabel Jeans

1938 THE ADVENTURES OF ROBIN HOOD
Director: Michael Curtiz
Co-stars: Errol Flynn Basil Rathbone Claude Rains Patric Knowles

1939 DODGE CITY
Director: Michael Curtiz
Co-stars: Errol Flynn Ann Sheridan Alan Hale

**1939 THE PRIVATE LIVES OF
ELIZABETH AND ESSEX**
Director: Michael Curtiz
Co-stars: Errol Flynn Bette Davis

1939 WINGS OF THE NAVY
Director: Lloyd Bacon
Co-stars: George Brent John Payne Frank McHugh

1939 GONE WITH THE WIND
Director: Victor Fleming
Co-stars: Clark Gable Vivien Leigh Leslie Howard

1940 MY LOVE CAME BACK
Director: Curtis Bernhardt
Co-stars: Jeffrey Lynn Charles Winninger

1940 RAFFLES
Director: Sam Wood
Co-stars: David Niven Dudley Digges May Whitty

1940 SANTA FE TRAIL
Director: Michael Curtiz
Co-stars: Errol Flynn Raymond Massey Van Heflin

1941 THEY DIED WITH THEIR BOOTS ON
Director: Raoul Walsh
Co-stars: Errol Fyynn Arthur Kennedy

1941 THE STRAWBERRY BLONDE
Director: Raoul Walsh
Co-stars: James Cagney Rita Hayworth Jack Carson

1941 HOLD BACK THE DAWN
Director: Mitchell Leisen
Co-stars: Charles Boyer Paulette Goddard

1942 THE MALE ANIMAL
Director: Elliott Nugent
Co-stars: Henry Fonda Jack Carson Joan Leslie

1942 IN THIS OUR LIFE
Director: John Huston
Co-stars: Bette Davis Charles Coburn Dennis Morgan

1943 GOVERNMENT GIRL
Director: Dudley Nichols
Co-stars: Sonny Tufts Anne Shirley James Dunn

1943 DEVOTION
Director: Curtis Bernhardt
Co-stars: Ida Lupino Nancy Coleman Arthur Kennedy

1943 PRINCESS O'ROURKE
Director: Norman Krasna
Co-stars: Robert Cummings Charles Coburn Jack Carson

1943 THANK YOUR LUCKY STARS
Director: David Butler
Co-stars: Eddie Cantor Dennis Morgan Joan Leslie

1946 THE WELL-GROOMED BRIDE
Director: Sidney Lanfield
Co-stars: Ray Milland Sonny Tufts James Gleason

1946 TO EACH HIS OWN
Director: Mitchell Leisen
Co-stars: John Lund Roland Culver

1946 THE DARK MIRROR
Director: Robert Siodmak
Co-stars: Lew Ayres Thomas Mitchell Gary Owen

1948 THE SNAKE PIT
Director: Anatole Litvak
Co-stars: Leo Genn Mark Stevens Ceeleste Holm

1949 THE HEIRESS
Director: William Wyler
Co-stars: Montgomery Clift Ralph Richardson

1952 MY COUSIN RACHEL
Director: Henry Koster
Co-stars: Richard Burton John Sutton Audrey Dalton

1955 THAT LADY
Director: Terence Young
Co-stars: Paul Scofield Gilbert Roland Dennis Price

1955 NOT AS A STRANGER
Director: Stanley Kramer
Co-stars: Robert Mitchum Frank Sinatra Gloria Grahame

1956 THE AMBASSADOR'S DAUGHTER
Director: Norman Krasna
Co-stars: John Forsythe Edward Arnold Myrna Loy

1958 THE PROUD REBEL
Director: Michael Curtiz
Co-stars: Alan Ladd David Ladd Dean Jagger Cecil Kellaway

1959 LIBEL
Director: Anthony Asquith
Co-stars: Dirk Bogarde Robert Morley Paul Massie

1962 LIGHT IN THE PIAZZA
Director: Guy Green
Co-stars: Yvette Mimieux George Hamilton Rossano Brazzi

1964 LADY IN A CAGE
Director: Walter Grauman
Co-stars: James Caan Ann Sothern Jeff Corey

1964 HUSH...HUSH SWEET CHARLOTTE
Director: Robert Aldrich
Co-stars: Bette Davis Joseph Cotten Mary Astor

1970 THE ADVENTURERS
Director: Lewis Gilbert
Co-stars: Bekim Fehmiu Alan Badel Candice Bergin

1972 POPE JOAN
Director: Michael Anderson
Co-stars: Liv Ullman Trevor Howard Franco Nero

1977 AIRPORT '77
Director: George Seaton
Co-stars: James Stewart Jack Lemmon Lee Grant

1978 THE FIFTH MUSKETEER
Director: Ken Annakin
Co-stars: Beau Bridges Sylvia Kristel Rex Harrison

1978 THE SWARM
Director: Irwin Allen
Co-stars: Michael Caine Richard Widmark Katharine Ross

1982 MURDER IS EASY
Director: Claude Whatham
Co-stars: Bill Bixby Helen Hayes Lesley-Anne Down

1986 ANASTASIA: THE MYSTERY OF ANNA
Director: James Goldman
Co-stars: Amy Irving Omar Sharif Claire Bloom

FANNIE BELLE DeKNIGHT

1929 HALLELUJAH!
Director: King Vidor
Co-stars: Daniel L. Haynes Nina Mae McKinney Harry Gray

MARG DELAIN

1976 DAWN: PORTRAIT OF A RUNAWAY TEENAGER
Director: Randal Kleiser
Co-stars: Eve Plumb Bo Hopkins

SUZY DELAIR (SUZETTE)

1947 QUAI DES OFREVRES
Director: Henri-Georges Clouzot
Co-stars: Louis Jouvet Bernard Blier

1947 THE MURDERER LIVES AT 21

1949 PATTES BLANCHES

1950 ROBINSON CRUSOELAND
Director: John Berry
Co-stars: Stan Laurel Oliver Hardy

1956 GERVAIS
Director: Rene Clement
Co-stars: Maria Schell Francois Perrier Mathilde Casadeus

1960 ROCCO AND HIS BROTHERS
Director: Luchino Visconti
Co-stars: Alain Delon Renato Salvatori

MARGUERITE DE LA MOTTE

1920 THE MARK OF ZORRO
Director: Fred Niblo
Co-stars: Douglas Fairbanks Noah Beery

1921   **THE THREE MUSKETEERS**
Director: Fred Niblo
Co-stars: Douglas Fairbanks Eugene Pallette Adolphe Menjou

1921   **THE NUT**
Director: Ted Reed
Co-stars: Douglas Fairbanks Gerald Pring William Lowery

1929   **THE IRON MASK**
Director: Allan Dwan
Co-stars: Douglas Fairbanks Belle Bennett

CASSANDRA DELANEY

1984   **ONE NIGHT STAND**
Director: John Duigan
Co-stars: Tyler Coppin Jay Hackett Saskia Post

GLORIA DELANEY

1979   **PENITENTIARY**
Director: Jamaa Fanaka
Co-stars: Leon Isaac Kennedy Thommy Pollard Hazel Spears

JOAN DELANEY

1967   **THE PRESIDENT'S ANALYST**
Director: Theodore Flicker
Co-stars: James Coburn Godfrey Cambridge

1969   **DON'T DRINK THE WATER**
Director: Howard Morris
Co-stars: Jackie Gleason Estelle Parsons Ted Bessell

1971   **BUNNY O'HARE**
Director: Gerd Oswald
Co-stars: Bette Davis Ernest Borgnine Jack Cassidy

KIM DELANEY

1983   **FIRST AFFAIR**
Director: Gus Trikonis
Co-stars: Loretta Swit Melissa Sue Anderson Joel Higgins

1985   **THAT WAS THEN...THIS IS NOW**
Director: Christopher Cain
Co-stars: Emilio Estevez Craig Sheffer

1987   **PERRY MASON: THE CASE OF THE SINISTER SPIRIT**
Director: Richard Lang
Co-stars: Raymond Burr William Katt

1987   **CAMPUS MAN**
Director: Ron Casden
Co-stars: John Dye Steve Lyon Morgan Fairchild

1987   **CHRISTMAS COMES TO WILLOW CREEK**
Director: Richard Lang
Co-stars: John Schneider Tom Wopat Hoyt Axton

1989   **TAKE MY DAUGHTERS, PLEASE**
Director: Larry Elikan
Co-stars: Rue McClanahan Deirdre Hall Susan Rattan

1991   **HANGFIRE**
Director: Peter Maris
Co-stars: Brad Davis Jan-Michael Vincent George Kennedy

1991   **BODY PARTS**
Director: Eric Red
Co-stars: Jeff Fahey Lindsay Duncan Brad Dourif

1993   **THE DISAPPEARANCE OF CHRISTINA**
Director: Karen Arthur
Co-stars: John Stamos Robert Carradine

1994   **DARKMAN 11:THE RETURN OF DURANT**
Director: Bradford May
Co-star: Larry Drake

1995   **TALL, DARK AND DEADLY**
Director: Kenneth Fink
Co-stars: Jack Scalia Todd Allen

1995   **CLOSER AND CLOSER**
Director: Fred Gerber
Co-star: Svott Kraft

PAT DELANEY

1979   **HOMETOWN U.S.A.**
Director: Max Baer
Co-stars: Gary Springer David Wilson Brian Kerwin

CATHLEEN DELANY

1987   **THE DEAD**
Director: John Huston
Co-stars: Anjelica Huston Donal McCann Dan O'Herlihy

1991   **THE MIRACLE**
Director: Neil Jordan
Co-stars: Niall Byrne Donal McCann Beverly D'Angelo

DANA DELANY

1984   **THREESOME**
Director: Lou Antonio
Co-stars: Stephen Collins Deborah Raffin Joel Higgins

1984   **ALMOST YOU**
Director: Adam Brooke
Co-stars: Brooke Adams Griffin Dunne Karen Young

1986   **WHERE THE RIVER RUNS BLACK**
Director: Christopher Cain
Co-stars: Charles Durning Conchata Ferrell

1988   **MASQUERADE**
Director: Bob Swaim
Co-stars: Rob Lowe Meg Tilly Kim Cattrall

1991   **RIGHT SLEEPER**

1992   **HOUSESITTER**
Director: Frank Oz
Co-stars: Steve Martin Goldie Hawn Julie Harris

1993   **TOMBSTONE**
Director: George Pan Cosmatos
Co-stars: Kurt Russell Val Kilmer Sam Elliott

1993   **DONATO AND DAUGHTER**
Director: Charles Bronson

1994   **EXIT TO EDEN**
Director: Garry Marshall
Co-stars: Paul Mercurio Rosie O'Donnell

1994   **THE ENEMY WITHIN**
Director: Jonathan Darby
Co-stars: Sam Waterston Forest Whitaker

1995   **LIVE NUDE GIRLS**
Director: Julianna Levin
Co-star: Kim Cattrall

1997   **FLY AWAY HOME**
Director: Carroll Ballard
Co-stars: Anna Paquin Jeff Daniels

MAUREEN DELANY

1935   **HIS FAMILY TREE**
Director: Charles Vidor
Co-stars: James Barton William Harrigan Margaret Callahan

1946   **ODD MAN OUT**
Director: Carol Reed
Co-stars: James Mason Robert Newton Kathleen Ryan

1952   **THE HOLLY AND THE IVY**
Director: George More O'Ferrall
Co-stars: Ralph Richardson Celia Johnson

1956 JACQUELINE
Director: Roy Baker
Co-stars: John Gregson Kathleen Ryan Jacqueline Ryan

1957 THE RISING OF THE MOON
Director: John Ford
Co-stars: Maureen Connell Eileen Crowe Cyril Cusack

1957 THE STORY OF ESTHER COSTELLO
Director: David Miller
Co-stars: Joan Crawford Heather Sears Rossano Brazzi

1957 THE SCAMP
Director: Wolf Rilla
Co-stars: Richard Attenborough Colin Peterson Dorothy Alison

1958 THE DOCTOR'S DILEMMA
Director: Anthony Asquith
Co-stars: Leslie Caron Dirk Bogarde

PAULINE DELANY

1964 NOTHING BUT THE BEST
Director: Clive Donner
Co-stars: Alan Bates Denholm Elliott Millicent Martin

1970 PERCY
Director: Ralph Thomas
Co-stars: Hywel Bennett Denholm Elliott Cyd Hayman

1983 TRENCHCOAT
Director: Michael Tuchner
Co-stars: Margot Kidder Robert Hays David Suchet

CHRISTINE DELAROCHE

1966 THE DEFECTOR
Director: Raoul Levy
Co-stars: Montgomery Clift Hardy Kruger Roddy McDowall

SOPHIE DE LA ROCHEFOUCAULD

1994 BAMBINO MIO
Director: Edward Bennett
Co-stars: Julie Walters Georges Corraface John McArdle

FRANCES DE LA TOUR

1972 OUR MISS FRED
Director: Bob Kellett
Co-stars: Danny La Rue Alfred Marks Lance Percival

1977 WOMBLING FREE
Director: Lionel Jeffries
Co-stars: Lionel Jeffries David Jason Bonnie Langford Jon Pertwee

1980 RISING DAMP
Director: Joe McGrath
Co Stars Leonard Rossiter Don Warrington Denholm Elliott

1985 MURDER WITH MIRRORS
Director: Dick Lowry
Co-stars: Helen Hayes Bette Davis John Mills Dorothy Tutin

1994 GHENGIS COHN
Director: Elijah Moshinsky
Co-stars: Anthony Sher Robert Lindsay Diana Rigg

1996 COLD LAZURUS
Director: Renny Rye
Co-stars: Albert Finney Diane Ladd Anna Chancelor

LAURA DE LA UZ

1990 HELLO HEMINGWAY
Director: Fernando Perez
Co-stars: Raul Paz Hermina Sanchez Enrique Molina

BILLIE DE LA VOLTA

1936 EVERYBODY DANCE
Director: Charles Riesner
Co-stars: Cicely Courtneidge Ernest Truex Percy Parsons

LISE DELEMERE

1938 LA MARSEILLAISE
Director: Jean Renoir
Co-stars: Pierre Renoir Louis Jouvet Elisa Ruis

1947 MONSIEUR VINCENT
Director: Maurice Cloche
Co-stars: Pierre Fresnay Aime Clairiond

CLAUDIA DELL

1930 BIG BOY
Director: Alan Crosland
Co-stars: Al Jolson Noah Beery Louise Closser Hale

1930 SWEET KITTY BELLAIRS
Director: Alfred Green
Co-stars: Ernest Torrence Walter Pidgeon June Collyer

1931 FIFTY MILLION FRENCHMEN
Director: Lloyd Bacon
Co-stars: Ole Olsen Chic Johnson William Gaxton

1931 BACHELOR APARTMENT
Director: Lowell Sherman
Co-stars: Lowell Sherman Irene Dunne Mae Murray Norman Kerry

1932 DESTRY RIDES AGAIN
Co-Star Tom Mix

1932 MIDNIGHT LADY
Co-Star Theodore Von Eltz

1937 BOOTS OF DESTINY
Co-stars: Ken Maynard Vince Barnett

1944 BLACK MAGIC
Director: Phil Rosen
Co-stars: Sidney Toler Mantan Moreland Jacqueline De Wit

DOROTHY DELL *(Best Friend Of Dorothy Lamour Killed In A Car Crash In 1934.)*

1934 WHARF ANGEL
Director: George Somnes
Co-stars: Victor McLaglen Preston Foster Alison Skipworth

1934 LITTLE MISS MARKER
Director: Alexander Hall
Co-stars: Shirley Temple Adolphe Menjou Charles Bickford

1934 SHOOT THE WORKS
Director: Wesley Ruggles
Co-stars: Jack Oakie Ben Bernie Arline Judge

MYRNA DELL

1946 NOCTURNE
Director: Edwin Marin
Co-stars: George Raft Lynn Bari Virginia Huston

1946 THE FALCON'S ADVENTURE
Director: William Berke
Co-stars: Tom Conway Madge Meredith Robert Warwick

1949 LUST FOR GOLD
Director: S. Sylvan Simon
Co-stars: Ida Lupino Glenn Ford Gig Young

1949 ROUGHSHOD
Director: Mark Robson
Co-stars: Robert Sterling Gloria Grahame Martha Hyer

1949 SEARCH FOR DANGER
Director: Jack Bernhard
Co-stars: John Calvert Albert Dekker Douglas Fowley

1949 THE LOST TRIBE
Co-Star Johnny Weissmuller

1950 DESTINATION MURDER
Director: Edward Cahn
Co-stars: Joyce MacKenzie Stanley Clements Hurd Hatfield

ALICIA DEL LARGO

1984 EL NORTE
Director: Gregory Nava
Co-stars: Zaide Silvia Gutierrez David Villapando

NATHALIE DELON *(Married Alain Delon)*

1967 THE SAMURAI
Director: Jean-Pierre Melville
Co-stars: Alain Delon Francois Perrier Cathy Rosier

1971 TAKE IT EASY
Director: Jacques Deray
Co-stars: Alain Delon Paul Meurisse

1971 WHEN EIGHT BELLS TOLL
Director: Etienne Perrier
Co-stars: Anthony Hopkins Robert Morley Jack Hawkins

1972 BLUEBEARD
Director: Edward Dmytryk
Co-stars: Richard Burton Raquel Welch Joey Hetherton

1975 THE ROMANTIC ENGLISHWOMAN
Director: Joseph Losey
Co-stars: Glenda Jackson Michael Caine Helmut Berger

DANIELE DELORME

1948 GIGI
Director: Jacqueline Audry
Co-stars: Gaby Morlay Yvonne De Bray Frank Villard

1950 L'INGENUE LIBERTINE
Director: Jacqueline Audry
Co-stars: Frank Villard Jean Tissier Claude Nicot

1958 LES MISERABLES
Director: Jean-Paul Le Chanois
Co-stars: Jean Gabin Bernard Blier Bourvil

1976 PARDON MON AFFAIRE
Director: Yves Robert
Co-stars: Jean Rochefort Claude Brasseur Anny Duperey

1984 NOVEMBER MOON
Director: Alexandra Von Grote
Co-stars: Gabrile Osburg Christine Millet Bruno Pradal

PILAR DEL REY

1966 AND NOW MIGUEL
Director: James Clark
Co-stars: Pat Cardi Michael Ansara Guy Stockwell

JULIE DELPY

1986 MAUVAIS SONG
Director: Leos Carax
Co-stars: Michel Piccoli Juliette Binoche Denis Lavant

1988 BEATRICE
Director: Bertrand Tavernier
Co-stars: Bernard Pierre Donnadieu Nils Tavernier

1991 EUROPA, EUROPA
Director: Losange Agniezka
Co-stars: Marco Hofschneider Saloman Perel Andre Wilms

1991 VOYAGER
Director: Volker Schlondorff
Co-stars: Sam Shepard Barbara Sukowa Traci Lind

1993 YOUNGER AND YOUNGER
Director: Percy Adlon
Co-stars: Donald Sutherland Lolita Davidovich Sally Kellerman

1993 THE THREE MUSKETEERS
Director: Stephen Herek
Co-stars: Chris O'Donnell Charlie Sheen Kieffer Sutherland

1993 THREE COLOURS: WHITE
Director: Krzysztof Kiesloski
Co-stars: Zbignien Zamachowski Jerzy Stuhr

1994 KILLING ZOE
Director: Roger Avery
Co-stars: Eric Stolz Gary Kemp Jean-Hugues Anglade

1994 THREE COLOURS; RED
Director: Krzysztof Kiesloski
Co-stars: Irene Jacob Julliette Binoch Jean-Luis Trintingnant

1995 BEFORE SUNRISE
Director: Richard Linklater
Co-stars: Ethan Hawke Erni Mangold

1997 AN AMERICAN WEREWOLF IN PARIS
Director: Anthony Waller
Co-star: Tom Everett Scott

DOLORES DEL RIO *(Lolita Dolores Asunsolo De Martinez)(Married Jaime Del Rio)*

1926 WHAT PRICE GLORY?
Director: Raoul Walsh
Co-stars: Victor McLaglan Edmund Lowe

1928 REVENGE
Co-star: Leroy Mason

1928 EVANGELINE
Co-Star Roland Drew

1930 THE BAD ONE
Director: George Fitztmaurice
Co-stars: Edmund Lowe Don Alvarado Blanche Friderici

1932 BIRD OF PARADISE
Director: King Vidor
Co-stars: Joel McCrea John Halliday Skeets Gallagher

1933 GIRL OF THE RIO
Co-Star Leo Carrillo

1933 FLYING DOWN TO RIO
Director: Thornton Freeland
Co-stars: Gene Raymond Ginger Rogers Fred Astaire

1934 MADAME DUBARRY
Director: William Dieterle
Co-stars: Reginald Owen Anita Louise Verree Teasdale

1934 WONDER BAR
Director: Lloyd Bacon
Co-stars: Al Jolson Kay Francis Dick Powell

1935 IN CALIENTE
Director: Lloyd Bacon
Co-stars: Pat O'Brien Leo Carrillo Wini Shaw

1935 I LIVE FOR LOVE
Director: Busby Berkeley
Co-stars: Allen Jenkins Everett Marshall Guy Kibbee

1936 ACCUSED
Director: Thornton Freeland
Co-stars: Douglas Fairbanks Florence Desmond

1937 LANCER SPY
Director: Gregory Ratoff
Co-stars: George Sanders Peter Lorre Virginia Field

1938 INTERNATIONAL SETTLEMENT
Director: Eugene Forde
Co-stars: George Sanders June Lang John Carradine

1940 THE MAN FROM DAKOTA
Director: Leslie Fenton
Co-stars: Wallace Beery John Howard Donald Meek

1942 JOURNEY INTO FEAR
Director: Orson Welles
Co-stars: Orson Welles Joseph Cotten Jack Moss Ruth Warwick

1943 MARIA CANDELARIA
Director: Emilio Fernandez
Co-stars: Pedro Armendariz Alberto Galan

1946 LA OTRA

1947 THE FUGITIVE
Director: John Ford
Co-stars: Henry Fonda Ward Bond Pedro Armendariz

1960 FLAMING STAR
Director: Don Siegal
Co-stars: Elvis Presley Steve Forrest Barbara Eden

1964 CHEYENNE AUTUMN
Director: John Ford
Co-stars: Richard Widmark James Stewart Carroll Baker

1967 MORE THAN A MIRACLE
Director: Francisco Rosi
Co-stars: Sophia Loren Omar Sharif Leslie French

1978 THE CHILDREN OF SANCHEZ
Director: Hall Bartlett
Co-stars: Anthony Quinn Katy Jurado Lupita Ferrer

VANESSA DEL RIO

1981 AFTERNOON DELIGHTS
Director: Warren Evans
Co-stars: Eric Edwards Merle Michaels Samantha Fox

IRENE DELROY

1930 LIFE OF THE PARTY
Director: Roy Del Ruth
Co-stars: Winnie Lightner Charles Butterworth Jack Whiting

1930 MEN OF THE SKY

LAURA DEL SOL

1983 CARMEN
Director: Carlos Saura
Co-stars: Antonio Gades Paco De Lucia Christina Hoyos

1985 THE HIT
Director: Stephen Frears
Co-stars: Terence Stamp John Hurt Tim Roth

1989 KILLING DAD
Director: Michael Austin
Co-stars: Denholm Elliott Julie Walters Richard E. Grant

GUADALUPE DEL TORO

1986 DONA HERLINDA AND HER SON
Director: Jaime Humberto Hermosillo
Co-stars: Arturo Meza Leticia Lupersio

JACQUELINE DELUBAC

1936 BONNE CHANCE
Director: Sacha Guitry
Co-stars: Sacha Guitry Robert Darthez

LORELLA DE LUCA

1958 THE SIGN OF THE GLADIATOR
Director: Guido Brignone
Co-stars: Anita Ekberg George Marchal Folco Luli

GIUDITTA DEL VECCHIO

1992 LEOLO
Director: Jean-Claude Lauzon
Co-stars: Maxime Collin Ginette Reno Pierre Bourgault

ALICE DELYSIA

1934 EVENSONG
Director: Victor Saville
Co-stars: Evelyn Laye Carl Esmond Emlyn Williams

DONNA DeMARIO

1948 THE WOMAN FROM TANGIER
Co-stars: Adele Jergens Michael Duane

ORANE DEMAZIS

1931 MARIUS
Director: Alexander Korda
Co-stars: Raimu Pierre Fresnay Alida Rouffe

1932 FANNY
Director: Marc Allegret
Co-stars: Raimu Pierre Fresnay Alida Rouffe Charpin

1936 CESAR
Director: Marcel Pagnol
Co-stars: Raimu Pierre Fresnay Alida Rouffe Andre Fouche

1937 HARVEST
Director: Marcel Pagnol
Co-stars: Fernandel Gabriel Gabrio Edouard Delmont

MARIA DE MEDEIROS

1989 1871
Director: Ken McMullen
Co-stars: Roshan Seth Ana Padrao Timothy Spall

1990 HENRY AND JUNE
Director: Philip Kaufman
Co-stars: Fred Ward Uma Thurman Richard E. Grant

1991 MEETING VENUS
Director: Istvan Szabo
Co-stars: Glenn Close Niels Arestrup Erland Josephson

1992 GOLDEN BALLS
Director: Bigas Luna
Co-stars: Javier Bardem Elisa Touati Maribel Verdu

1992 L'HOMME DE MA VIE
Director: Jean-Charles Tacchella
Co-stars: Thierry Fortineau Jean-Pierre Bacri

1994 PULP FICTION
Director: Quentin Tarantino
Co-stars: John Travolta Bruce Willis Uma Thurman

IRINA DEMICK

1962 THE LONGEST DAY
Director: Ken Annakin
Co-stars: John Wayne Robert Mitchum Henry Fonda

1964 THE VISIT
Director: Bernhard Wicki
Co-stars: Ingrid Bergman Anthony Quinn Paolo Stoppa

1965 UP FROM THE BEACH
Director: Robert Parrish
Co-stars: Cliff Robertson Red Buttons Francoise Rosay

1965 THOSE MAGNIFICENT MEN IN THEIR FLYING MACHINES
Director: Ken Annakin
Co-stars: Sarah Miles James Fox Terry-Thomas

1968 THE SICILIAN CLAN
Director: Henri Verneuill
Co-stars: Jean Gabin Alain Delon Lino Ventura

1969 PRUDENCE AND THE PILL
Director: Fielder Cook
Co-stars: David Niven Deborah Kerr Judy Geeson

KATHERINE DeMILLE
(Adopted Daughter Of Cecil B. DeMille)

1934 BELLE OF THE NINETIES
Director: Leo McCarey
Co-stars: Mae West Roger Pryor John Miljan

1934 VIVA VILLA
Director: Jack Conway
Co-stars: Wallace Beery Stuart Erwin

1935 ALL THE KING'S HORSES
Director: Frank Tuttle
Co-stars: Carl Brisson Mary Ellis Eugene Pallette

1935 THE BLACK ROOM
Director: Roy William Neill
Co-stars: Boris Karloff Marian Marsh Thurston Hall

1935 THE CRUSADES
Director: Cecil B. DeMille
Co-stars: Loretta Young Henry Wilcoxon Ian Keith

1936 ROMEO AND JULIET
Director: George Cukor
Co-stars: Leslie Howard Norma Shearer Basil Rathbone

1936 BANJO ON MY KNEE
Director: John Cromwell
Co-stars: Barbara Stanwyck Joel McCrea Walter Brennan

1936 THE SKY PARADE
Co-Star Kent Taylor

1936 LOVE UNDER FIRE
Director: George Marshall
Co-stars: Loretta Young Don Ameche Frances Drake John Carradine

1936 RAMONA
Director: Henry King
Co-stars: Loretta Young Don Ameche Kent Taylor Pauline Frederick

1937 CHARLIE CHAN AT THE OLYMPICS
Director: Bruce Humberstone
Co-stars: Warner Oland Keye Luke Allan Lane

1940 ELLORY QUEEN, MASTER DETECTIVE
Director: Kurt Neuman
Co-stars: Ralph Bellamy Margaret Lindsay

1941 ALOMA OF THE SOUTH SEAS
Director: Alfred Santell
Co-stars: Dorothy Lamour Jon Hall Dona Drake

1947 BLACK GOLD
Director: Phil Karlson
Co-stars: Anthony Quinn Ducky Louie Elyse Knox Raymond Hatton

1947 UNCONQUERED
Director: Cecil B. DeMille
Co-stars: Gary Cooper Paulette Goddard Howard Da Silva

LAURENCE DE MONAGHAN

1970 CLAIRE'S KNEE
Director: Eric Rohmer
Co-stars: Jean-Claude Brialy Aurora Cornu

CATHERINE DEMONGEOT *(Child)*

1960 ZAZIE DANS LE METRO
Director: Louis Malle
Co-stars: Philippe Noiret Vittorio Caprioli

MYLENE DEMONGEOT

1957 BONJOUR TRISTESSE
Director: Otto Preminger
Co-stars: David Niven Deborah Kerr Jean Seberg

1957 THE WITCHES OF SALEM
Director: Raymond Rouleau
Co-stars: Simone Signoret Yves Montand

1959 UPSTAIRS AND DOWNSTARS
Director: Ralph Thomas
Co-stars: Michael Graig Anne Heywood Sid James

1960 UNDER TEN FLAGS
Director: Silvio Narizzano
Co-stars: Van Heflin Charles Laughton Cecil Parker

1960 THE SINGER NOT THE SONG
Director: Roy Baker
Co-stars: Dirk Bogarde John Mills Laurence Naismith

1963 DOCTOR IN DISTRESS
Director: Ralph Thomas
Co-stars: Dirk Bogarde Samantha Eggar Barbara Murray

1964 FANTOMAS
Director: Andre Hunebelle
Co-stars: Jean Marais Louis De Funes Marie-Helene Arnaud

1968 THE PRIVATE NAVY OF SERGEANT O'FARRELL
Director: Frank Tashlin
Co-stars: Bob Hope Gina Lollobrigida Jeffrey Hunter

1970 TWELVE PLUS ONE
Director: Nicholas Gessner
Co-stars: Vittorio Gassman Sharon Tate Orson Welles

1970 FUNGUS
Director: Marc Simenon
Co-stars: Alida Valli Jean-Claude Bouillon Philippe Monnet

REBECCA DE MORNAY

1983 RISKY BUSINESS
Director: Paul Brickman
Co-stars: Tom Cruise Richard Masur Joe Pantoliano

1985 RUNAWAY TRAIN
Director: Andrei Konchalovsky
Co-stars: Jon Voight Eric Roberts

1985 THE TRIP TO BOUNTIFUL
Director: Peter Masterton
Co-stars: Geraldine Page Richard Bradford

1987 AND GOD CREATED WOMAN
Director: Roger Vadim
Co-stars: Vincent Spano Frank Langella Donovan Leitch

1988 FEDS
Director: Dan Goldberg
Co-stars: Mary Gross Ken Marshall Larry Cedar

1989 DEALERS
Director: Colin Bucksey
Co-stars: Paul McGann John Castle Derrick O'Connor

1992 THE HAND THAT ROCKS THE CRADLE
Director: Curtis Hanson
Co-Star Annabella Sciorra

1993 GUILTY AS SIN
Director: Sidney Lumet
Co-stars: Don Johnson Stephen Long Jack Warden

1993 THE THREE MUSKETEERS
Director: Stephen Herek
Co-stars: Chris O'Donnell Charlie Sheen Kieffer Sutherland

1993 GETTING OUT
Director: John Korty
Co-stars: Robert Knepper Carol Mitchell-Leon

CAROL DEMPSTER

1921 DREAM STREET
Director: D.W. Griffith
Co-stars: Ralph Graves Charles Emmett Mack Tyrone Power

1924 AMERICA
Director: D.W. Griffith
Co-stars: Neil Hamilton Lionel Barrymore Frank Walsh

1924 ISN'T LIFE WONDERFUL?
Director: D.W. Griffith
Co-stars: Neil Hamilton Helen Lowell Lupino Lane

1925 SALLY OF THE SAWDUST
Director: D.W. Griffith
Co-stars: W.C. Fields Alfred Lunt Effie Shannon

1926 SORROWS OF SATAN
Director: D.W. Griffith
Co-stars: Adolphe Menjou Ricardo Cortez Lya De Putti

SUSAN DENBERG

1967 FRANKENSTEIN CREATED WOMAN
Director: Terence Fisher
Co-stars: Peter Cushing Thorley Walters

JUDI DENCH *(Married Michael Williams)*
(Mother Of Finty Williams)

1965 FOUR IN THE MORNING
Director: Anthony Simmons
Co-stars: Ann Lynn Norman Rodway Joe Melia

1965 HE WHO RIDES A TIGER
Director: Charles Crichton
Co-stars: Tom Bell Paul Rogers Kay Walsh

1965 A STUDY IN TERROR
Director: James Hill
Co-stars: John Neville Donald Houston Robert Morley

1973 LUTHER
Director: Guy Green
Co-stars: Stacy Keach Patrick McGee Hugh Griffith Robert Stevens

1974 DEAD CERT
Director: Tony Richardson
Co-stars: Scott Antony Michael Williams Julian Clover Nina Thomas

1974 JOHN OSBORNE'S LUTHER
Director: Guy Green
Co-stars: Stacey Keach Hugh Griffith Patrick McGee

1985 A ROOM WITH A VIEW
Director: James Ivory
Co-stars: Maggie Smith Denholm Elliott Daniel Day Lewis

1985 WETHERBY
Director: David Hare
Co-stars: Vanessa Redgrave Ian Holm Tim McInnerny Stuart Wilson

1986 84, CHARING CROSS ROAD
Director: David Jones
Co-stars: Anne Bancroft Anthony Hopkins Maurice Denham

1988 A HANDFUL OF DUST
Director: Charles Sturridge
Co-stars: James Wilby Kristin Scott Thomas

1989 HENRY V
Director: Kenneth Branagh
Co-stars: Kenneth Branagh Derek Jacobi Michael Williams

1989 BEHAVING BADLY
Director: David Tucker
Co-stars: Ronald Pickup Frances Barber Joely Richardson

1990 CAN YOU HEAR ME THINKING?
Director: Christopher Morohan
Co-stars: Michael Williams Richard Henders

1995 JACK AND SARAH
Director: Tim Sullivan
Co-stars: Richard E. Grant Samantha Mathis Ian McKellen

1996 HAMLET
Director: Kenneth Branagh
Co-stars: Kenneth Branagh Derek Jacobi Julie Christie Kate Winslet

1997 TOMORROW NEVER DIES
Co-stars: Pierce Brosnan Teri Hatcher Michelle Yeoh

CATHERINE DENEUVE

1964 LES PARAPLUIES DE CHERBOURG
Director: Jacques Demy
Co-stars: Anne Vernon Nino Castelnuovo

1965 REPULSION
Director: Roland Polanski
Co-stars: Ian Hendry John Fraser Patrick Wymark Renne Houston

1966 BENJAMIN
Director: Michel Deville
Co-stars: Pierre Clementi Michele Morgan Michel Piccoli

1967 BELLE DE JOUR
Director: Luis Bunuel
Co-stars: Jean Sorel Michel Piccoli Genevieve Page

1967 LES DEMOISELLES DE ROCHEFORT
Director: Jacques Demy
Co-stars: Francois Dorleac Gene Kelly

1968 MAYERLING
Director: Terence Young
Co-stars: Omar Sharif James Mason Ava Gardner Genevieve Page

1969 THE APRIL FOOLS
Director: Stuart Rosenberg
Co-stars: Jack Lemon Myrna Loy Charles Boyer

1970 TRISTANA
Director: Luis Bunuel
Co-stars: Fernando Rey Franco Nero Lola Gaos

1970 MISSISSIPPI MERMAID
Director: Francois Truffaut
Co-star: Jean-Paul Belmondo

1971 THE MAGIC DONKEY
Director: Jacques Demy

1972 DIRTY MONEY
Director: Jean-Pierre Melville
Co-stars: Alain Delon Richard Crenna Simone Valere

1975 HUSTLE
Director: Robert Aldrich
Co-stars: Burt Reynolds Ben Johnson Eddie Albert

1977 MARCH OR DIE
Director: Dick Richards
Co-stars: Gene Hackman Terence Hiill Max Von Sydow Ian Holm

1978 LE SAUVAGE
Director: Jean-Paul Rappeneau
Co-stars: Yves Montand Luigi Vannucchi Dana Wynter

1979 COURAGE FUYONS
Director: Yves Robert
Co-stars: Jean Rochefort Robert Webber

1980 THE LAST METRO
Director: Francois Truffaut
Co-stars: Gerard Depardieu Heinz Bennant Jean Poiret

1981 JE VOUS AIME
Director: Claude Berri
Co-stars: Jean-Louis Trintignant Serge Gainsbourg Gerard Depardieu

1981 A CHOICE OF ARMS
Director: Alain Corneau
Co-stars: Yves Montand Gerard Depardieu Michel Galabru

1982 SHOCK
Director: Robin Davis
Co-stars: Alain Delon Philippe Leotard Stephane Audran

1983 THE HUNGER
Director: Tony Scot
Co-stars: Susan Sarandon David Bowie Cliff De Young

1984 FORT SAGANNE
Director: Alain Corneau
Co-stars: Gerard Depardieu Philippe Noiret Sophie Marceau

1985 LOVE SON
Director: Elie Chouraqui
Co-stars: Christopher Lambert Richard Ancinina Jacques Perrin

1986   **SCENE OF THE CRIME**
Director: Andre Techine
Co-stars: Danielle Darrieux Wadeck Stanczak Victor Lanoux

1993   **MA SAISON PREFEREE**
Director: Andre Techine
Co-stars: Daniel Auteuil Marthe Villa Longa

MARIANNE DENICOURT

1988   **LA LECTRICE**
Director: Michel Deville
Co-stars: Miou-Miou Regis Royer Maria Casares

1991   **LA BELLE NOISEUSE**
Director: Jacques Rivette
Co-stars: Michel Piccoli Emmanuelle Beart Jane Birkin

MARIA DENIS

1949   **PRIVATE ANGELO**
Director: Peter Ustinov
Co-stars: Peter Ustinov Godfrey Tearle Marjorie Rhodes

BARBARA DENNECK

1968   **PLAYTIME**
Director: Jacques Tati
Co-stars: Jacques Tati Jacqueline Lecomte Henri Piccoli

EILEEN DENNES

1923   **COMIN' THRO' THE RYE**
Director: Cecil Hepworth
Co-stars: Alma Taylor Shayle Gardner Ralph Forbes

SANDY DENNIS *(Sandra Dale Dennis)*
Oscar For Best Supporting Actress In 1966 For Who's Afraid Of Virginia Woolf

1961   **SPLENDOR IN THE GRASS**
Director: Elia Kazan
Co-stars: Natalie Wood Warren Beatty Pat Hingle

1966   **WHO'S AFRAID OF VIRGINA WOOLF**
Director: Mike Nichols
Co-stars: Elizabeth Taylor Richard Burton George Segal

1968   **SWEET NOVEMBER**
Director: Robert Ellis Miller
Co-stars: Anthony Newley Theodore Bikel

1968   **THE FOX**
Director: Mark Rydell
Co-stars: Anne Heywood Keir Dullea Glyn Morris

1969   **THAT COLD DAY IN THE PARK**
Director: Robert Altman
Co-stars: Michael Burns Luana Anders John Garfield Jnr

1969   **A TOUCH OF LOVE**
Director: Waris Hussein
Co-stars: Ian McKellen Michael Coles John Standing

1970   **THE OUT-OF-TOWNERS**
Director: Arthur Hiller
Co-stars: Jack Lemmon Sandy Baron Billy Dee Williams

1971   **MILLION DOLLAR DUCK**
Director: Vincent McEveety
Co-stars: Dean Jones Joe Flynn

1972   **SOMETHING EVIL**
Director: Steven Spielberg
Co-stars: Darren McGavin Ralph Bellamy Jeff Corey

1974   **MR SYCAMORE**
Director: Pancho Kohner
Co-stars: Jason Robards Jean Simmons

1975   **UP THE DOWN STAIRCASE**
Director: Robert Mulligan
Co-stars: Patrick Bedford Eileen Heckart

1976   **NASTY HABITS**
Director: Michael Lindsay-Hogg
Co-stars: Glenda Jackson Melina Mercouri Geraldine Page

1976   **GOD TOLD ME TO**
Director: Larry Cohen
Co-stars: Tony LoBianco Deborah Raffin Slyvia Sidney

1978   **PERFECT GENTLEMEN**
Director: Jackie Cooper
Co-stars: Lauren Bacall Ruth Gordon Lisa Pelikan

1981   **THE FOUR SEASONS**
Director: Alan Alda
Co-stars: Alan Alda Carol Burnett Len Cariou Rita Moreno

1981   **THE ANIMALS FILM**
Director: Victor Schonfeld
Co-star: Julie Christie

1982   **COME BACK TO THE FIVE AND DIME, JIMMY DEAN, JIMMY DEAN**
Director: Robert Altman
Co-stars: Cher Karen Black Kathy Bates

1985   **THE EXECUTION**
Director: Paul Wendkos
Co-stars: Loretta Swit Jessica Walter Rip Torn Barbara Barrie

1988   **ANOTHER WOMAN**
Director: Woody Allen
Co-stars: Gena Rowlands Mia Farrow Blythe Danner Ian Holm

1988   **976-EVIL**
Director: Robert Englund
Co-stars: Stephen Geoffreys Patrick O'Bryan Jim Metzler

1988   **PARENTS**
Director: Bob Balaban
Co-stars: Randy Quaid Mary Beth Hurt Deborah Rush

1991   **THE INDIAN RUNNER**
Director: Sean Penn
Co-stars: David Morse Viggo Mortensen Patricia Arquette

SABRINA DENNISON

1989   **SANTA SANGRE**
Director: Alejandro Jodorowsky
Co-stars: Axel Jodorowsky Blanca Guerra Guy Stockwell

CHRISTA DENTON

1986   **THE GATE**
Director: Tibor Takacs
Co-stars: Stephen Dorff Louis Tripp Jennifer Irwin

1988   **SCANDAL IN A SMALL TOWN**
Director: Anthony Page
Co-stars: Raquel Welch Ronny Cox Frances Lee McCain

ROSSY DE PALMA

1988   **WOMEN ON THE VERGE OF A NERVOUS BREAKDOWN**
Director: Pedro Almodovar
Co-stars: Carmen Maura Antonio Banderas

1993   **KIKA**
Director: Pedro Almodovar
Co-stars: Veronica Forque Peter Coyote Victoria Abril

ELIZABETH DEPARDIEU

1986   **JEAN DE FLORETTE**
Director: Claude Berri
Co-stars: Yves Montand Gerard Depardieu Daniel Auteuil

1986   **MANON DES SOURCES**
Director: Claude Berri
Co-stars: Yves Montand Emmanuelle Beart Daniel Auteuil

MIRANDA DE PENCIER

1995   HARRISON BERGERON
Director: Bruce Pittman
Co-stars: Sean Astin Christopher Plummer Andrea Martin

DOROTHY DE POLIOLO

1960   L'AVVENTURA
Director: Michaelangelo Antonioni
Co-stars: Gabriele Ferzetti Monica Vitti Lea Massari

LYA DE PUTTI

1925   VARIETY
Director: E.A. Dupont
Co-stars: Emil Jannings Maly Delschaft Warwick Ward

1926   SORROWS OF SATAN
Director: D.W. Griffith
Co-stars: Adolphe Menjou Ricardo Cortez Carol Dempster

BO DEREK *(Married John Derek)*

1977   ORCA
Director: Michael Andrews
Co-stars: Richard Harris Charlotte Rampling Keenan Wynn

1979   10
Director: Blake Edwards
Co-stars: Dudley Moore Julie Andrews Robert Webber Dee Wallace

1980   A CHANGE OF SEASONS
Director: Richard Lang
Co-stars: Anthony Hopkins Shirley MacLaine Michael Brandon

1981   TARZAN THE APE MAN
Director: John Derek
Co-stars: Richard Harris John Phillip Law Miles O'Keefe

1984   BOLERO
Director: John Derek
Co-stars: George Kennedy Andrea Occhipinti Ana Obregon

1990   GHOSTS CAN'T DO IT
Director: John Derek
Co-stars: Anthony Quinn Don Murray Julie Newman

1995   TOMMY BOY
Director: Peter Segal
Co-stars: Chris Farley Brian Dennehy Rob Lowe

LAURA DERN

(Daughter Of Diane Ladd And Bruce Dern)
Nominated For An Oscar For Best Actress In 1991 For Rambling Rose

1983   HAPPY ENDINGS
Director: Jerry Thorpe
Co-stars: Lee Montgomery Jill Schoelen Sarah Nevin

1984   TEACHERS
Director: Arthur Hiller
Co-stars: Nick Nolte JoBeth Williams Lee Grant Judd Hirsch

1985   MASK
Director: Peter Bogdanovich
Co-stars: Cher Sam Elliott Eric Stolz Estelle Getty Richard Dysart

1985   SMOOTH TALK
Director: Joyce Chopra
Co-stars: Treat Williams Levon Helm Mary Kay Place

1986   BLUE VELVET
Director: David Lynch
Co-stars: Kyle MacLachlan Isabella Rossellini Dennis Hopper

1988   HAUNTED SUMMER
Director: Ivan Passer
Co-stars: Philip Anglim Alice Krige Eric Stolz Peter Berling

1989   SHADOW MAKERS
Director: Roland Joffe
Co-stars: Paul Newman Dwight Schultz Bonnie Bedelia

1990   WILD AT HEART
Director: David Lynch
Co-stars: Nicolas Cage Diane Ladd Isabella Rossellini

1991   RAMBLING ROSE
Director: Martha Coolidge
Co-stars: Robert Duvall Diane Ladd Lukas Haas John Heard

1992   AFTERBURN
Director: Robert Markowitz
Co-stars: Vincent Spano Robert Loggia Michael Rooker

1993   A PERFECT WORLD
Director: Clint Eastwood
Co-stars: Clint Eastwood Kevin Costner T.J. Lowther Leo Burmester

1993   JURASSIC PARK
Director: Steven Spielberg
Co-stars: Sam Neill Richard Attenborough Jeff Goldblum

BARBARA DE ROSSI

1986   BLOOD TIES
Director: Giacomo Battiato
Co-stars: Brad Davis Tony LoBianco Vincent Spano

1988   VAMPIRE IN VENICE
Director: Augusto Caminito
Co-stars: Klaus Kinski Donald Pleasence Christopher Plummer

PORTIA DE ROSSI

1994   SIRENS
Director: John Duigan
Co-stars: Hugh Grant Tara Fitzgerald Elle MacPherson

MARCELLE DERRIEN

1947   LE SILENCE EST D'OR
Director: Rene Clair
Co-stars: Maurice Chevalier Francois Perier Dany Robin

CHANTAL DERUAZ

1981 DIVA
Director: Jean-Jacques Beineix
Co-stars: Frederic Andrei Roland Bertin Richard Bohringer

ANA DE SADE

1984   TRIUMPHS OF A MAN CALLED HORSE
Director: John Hough
Co-stars: Richard Harris Michael Beck

ANNE DE SALVO

1982   STREET COP
Director: Sandor Stern
Co-stars: Karen Valentine John Getz Vincent Gardenia

1985   PERFECT
Director: James Bridges
Co-stars: John Travolta Jaime Lee Curtis Marilu Henner

1987   BURGLAR
Director: Hugh Wilson
Co-stars: Whoopi Goldberg Bob Goldthwaite Lesley Ann Warren

1990   TAKING CARE OF BUSINESS
Director: Arthur Hiller
Co-stars: James Belushi Charles Grodin Loryn Locklin

1993   CASUALTIES OF LOVE:
        THE LONG ISLAND LOLITA STORY
Director: John Hertzfield
Co-stars: Jack Scalia Lawrence Tierney Alyssa Milan

FRANCESCA DE SAPIO

1989   TORRENTS OF SPRING
Director: Jerzy Skolimowski
Co-stars: Timothy Hutton Nastassja Kinski Valeria Golino

CHRISTIANE DESBOIS

1992 A WINTER'S TALE
Director: Eric Rohmer
Co-stars: Charlotte Very Michel Voletti

FRANCESCA DE SCAFFA

1956 EDGE OF HELL
Director: Hugo Haas
Co-stars: Hugo Haas Ken Carlton June Hammerstein

SANDY DESCHER *(Child)*

1956 THE OPPOSITE SEX
Director: David Miller
Co-stars: June Allyson Joan Collins Ann Miller

1958 A GIFT FOR HEIDI
Director: George Templeton
Co-stars: Douglas Fowley Van Dyke Parks

CATHERINE DE SEYNES

1986 AMOROSA
Director: Mai Zetterling
Co-stars: Stina Ekblad Erland Josephson Philip Zanden

NANCY DESHON

1935 SILENT VALLEY
Co-stars: Tom Tyler Charles King

KAY DESLYS

1928 THEIR PURPLE MOMENT
Director: James Parrott
Co-stars: Stan Laurel Oliver Hardy Anita Garvin

FLORENCE DESMOND

1931 SALLY IN OUR ALLEY
Director: Maurice Elvy
Co-stars: Gracie Fields Ian Hunter Ivor Barnard

1933 MR SKITCH
Director: James Cruze
Co-stars: Will Rogers Zasu Pitts Rochelle Hudson

1935 NO LIMIT
Director: Monty Banks
Co-stars: George Formby Edward Rigby Jack Hobbs

1936 KEEP YOUR SEATS PLEASE
Director: Monty Banks
Co-stars: George Formby Alastair Sim Harry Tate

1938 KICKING THE MOON AROUND
Director: Walter Forde
Co-stars: Evelyn Dall Hal Thompson Max Bacon

1939 HOOTS MON!
Director: Roy William Neill
Co-stars: Max Miller Hal Walters Davina Craig

1950 THREE CAME HOME
Director: Jean Negulesco
Co-stars: Claudette Colbert Patric Knowles Sylvia Andrew

1956 CHARLEY MOON
Director: Guy Hamilton
Co-stars: Max Bygraves Dennis Price Patricia Driscoll

1969 SOME GIRLS DO
Director: Ralph Thomas
Co-stars: Richard Johnson Daliah Lavi Bebi Loncar

TAMARA DESNI

1933 FALLING FOR YOU
Director: Jack Hulbert
Co-stars: Jack Hulbert Cicely Courtneidge Alfred Drayton

1934 JACK AHOY!
Director: Walter Forde
Co-stars: Jack Hulbert Nancy O'Neil Alfred Drayton

1936 LOVE IN EXILE
Director: Alfred Werker
Co-stars: Clive Brook Helen Vinson Mary Carlisle

1937 FIRE OVER ENGLAND
Director: William Howard
Co-stars: Flora Robson Laurence Olivier Raymond Massey

1937 THE SQUEAKER
Director: William Howard
Co-stars: Edmund Lowe Ann Todd Robert Newton

1944 FLIGHT FROM FOLLY
Director: Herbert Mason
Co-stars: Pat Kirkwood Hugh Sinclair Sydney Howard

1947 THE HILLS OF DONEGAL

1950 DICK BARTON AT BAY
Director: Godfrey Grayson
Co-stars: Don Stannard George Ford Percy Walsh

ROSANA DE SOTO

1987 LA BAMBA
Director: Luis Valdez
Co-stars: Lou Diamond Phillips Elizabeth Pena Joe Pantoliano

1988 STAND AND DELIVER
Director: Ramon Menendez
Co-stars: Edward James Olmos Lou Diamond Phillips Andy Garcia

NADA DESPOTOVICH

1989 TAKEN AWAY
Director: John Patterson
Co-stars: Valerie Bertinelli Kevin Dunn Juliet Sourcey

1989 BABYCAKES
Director: Paul Schneider
Co-stars: Ricki Lake Craig Sheffer Betty Buckley

1991 THE ROCKETEER
Director: Joe Johnston
Co-stars: Bill Campbell Alan Arkin Jennifer Connelly

1992 DON'T TELL HER IT'S ME
Director: Malcolm Mowbray
Co-stars: Steve Guttenberg Jami Gertz Shelley Long

1992 CRIMINAL BEHAVIOUR
Director: Michael Miller
Co-stars: A. Martinez Cliff DeYoung Farrah Fawcett

SUZANNE DESPRES

1935 MARIS CHAPDELAINE
Director: Julien Duvivier
Co-stars: Madeleine Renaud Jean Gabin Jean-Pierre Aumont

NATALIE DESSELLE

1997 B.A.P.S.
Director: Robert Townsend
Co-stars: Halle Berry Martin Landau Ian Richardson

LULU DESTE

1937 THUNDER IN THE CITY
Director: Marion Gering
Co-stars: Edward G. Robinson Ralph Richardson Nigel Bruce

MARUSCHKA DETMERS

1988 HANNA'S WAR
Director: Menahem Golan
Co-stars: Ellen Burstyn Anthony Andrews David Warner

1992 THE MAMBO KINGS
Director: Arne Glimcher
Co-stars: Armand Assante Antonio Banderas Cathy Moriarty

1994 LOVE IN THE STRANGEST WAY
Director: Christopher Frank
Co-stars: Thierry L'Hermitte Nadia Fares

ROSITA DE TRIANA

1962 STRANGERS IN THE CITY
Director: Rick Carrier
Co-stars: Robert Gentile Camilo Delgado Robert Corso

LOREDANA DETTO *(Married Ermanno Olmi)*

1961 THE JOB
Director: Ermanno Olmi
Co-stars: Sandro Panzeri Tullio Kezich

CHARLOTTE DE TURKHEIM

1992 MON PERE, CE HEROS
Director: Gerard Lauzier
Co-stars: Gerard Depardieu Marie Gillain Patrick Mille

SUE DEVANEY

1989 THE REAL EDDY ENGLISH
Director: David Attwood
Co-stars: Stephen Persaud Frank Windsor Dona Croll

DEVIN DEVASQUEZ

1989 SOCIETY
Director: Brian Yuzna
Co-stars: Bill Warlock Ben Meyerson Connie Danese

RENEE DEVILLERS

1948 LES DERNIERES VACANCES
Director: Roger Leenhardt
Co-stars: Roger Leenhardt Michel Francois Odile Versois Pierre Dux

1952 COIFFEUR POUR DAMES
Director: Jean Boyer
Co-stars: Fernandel, Blanchette Crunoy Arlette Poirier

KAMALA DEVI

1962 GERONIMO
Director: Arnold Laven
Co-stars: Chuck Connors Ross Martin Adam West

LORETTA DEVINE

1983 ANNA TO THE INFINITE POWER
Director: Robert Wiemer
Co-stars: Dina Merril Jack Gilford

1988 LITTLE NIKITA
Director: Richard Benjamin
Co-stars: Sidney Poitier River Phoenix Carolina Kava

1988 STICKEY FINGERS
Director: Catlin Adams
Co-stars: Helen Slater Melanie Mayron Eileen Brennan

1996 WAITING TO EXHALE
Director: Forest Whitaker
Co-stars: Whitney Houston Angela Bassett Lela Rochon

PAMELA DEVIS

1949 THE PERFECT WOMAN
Director: Bernard Knowles
Co-stars: Patricia Roc Nigel Patrick Miles Malleson

KARLA DE VITO *(Married Robby Benson)*

1990 MODERN LOVE
Director: Robby Benson
Co-stars: Robby Benson Rue McClanahan Burt Reynolds

KATY DE VOLPI

1987 90 DAYS
Director: Giles Walker
Co-stars: Stefan Wodoslawsky Sam Grana Christine Pak

LAURA DEVON

1965 RED LINE 7000
Director: Howard Hawks
Co-stars: James Caan Charlene Holt Marianna Hill

1966 A COVENANT WITH DEATH
Director: Lamont Johnson
Co-stars: George Maharis Katy Jurado Earl Holliman

1966 CHAMBER OF HORRORS
Director: Hy Averback
Co-stars: Patrick O'Neal Patrice Wymore Wilfrid Hyde White

1967 GUNN
Director: Blake Edwards
Co-stars: Craig Stevens Ed Asner Helen Traubel

MARILYN DEVON

1967 FIRST TO FIGHT
Director: Christian Nyby
Co-stars: Chad Everett Gene Hackman Dean Jagger

EMMANUELLE DEVOS

1997 MA VIE SEXUELLE
Co-Star Mathieu Almeric

ELAINE DEVRY

1970 THE CHEYENNE SOCIAL CLUB
Director: Gene Kelly
Co-stars: James Stewart Henry Fonda Shirley Jones

1973 THE BOY WHO CRIED WEREWOLF
Director: Nathan Juran
Co-stars: Kerwin Matthews Scott Sealey

ADELINE DE WALT REYNOLDS

1941 COME LIVE WITH ME
Director: Clarence Brown
Co-stars: James Stewart Hedy Lamarr Ian Hunter

1945 A TREE GROWS IN BROOKLYN
Director: Elia Kazan
Co-stars: James Dunn Dorothy McGuire Peggy Ann Garner

1948 THE GIRL FROM MANHATTAN
Director: Alfred Green
Co-stars: Dorothy Lamour Charles Laughton George Montgomery

1952 LYDIA BAILEY
Director: Jean Negulesco
Co-stars: Dale Robertson Anne Francis Charles Korvin

1952 PONY SOLDIER
Director: Joseph Newman
Co-stars: Tyrone Power Cameron Mitchell Robert Horton

CATHERINE DEWHURST

1959 THE NUN'S STORY
Director: Fred Zinnemann
Co-stars: Audrey Hepburn Edith Evans Peggy Ashcroft

COLLEEN DEWHURST
(Mother Of Campbell Scott)

1960 MAN ON A STRING
Director: Andre De Toth
Co-stars: Ernest Borgnine Kerwin Mathews

1966 A FINE MADNESS
Director: Irvin Kerschner
Co-stars: Sean Connery Joanne Woodward Jean Seberg

1971 THE LAST RUN
Director: Richard Fleischer
Co-stars: George C. Scott Tony Musante Trish Van Devere

1972 THE COWBOYS
Director: Mark Rydell
Co-stars: John Wayne Bruce Dern Slim Pickins Robert Carradine

1974 McQ
Director: John Sturges
Co-stars: John Wayne Eddie Albert Diana Muldaur Clu Gulager

1977 ANNIE HALL
Director: Woody Allen
Co-stars: Woody Allen Diane Keaton Tony Roberts Carol Kane

1978 ICE CASTLES
Director: Donald Wrye
Co-stars: Robby Benson Lynn-Holly Johnson Tom Skerritt

1979 AND BABY MAKES SIX
Director: Waris Hussein
Co-stars: Warren Oates Mildred Dunnock Timothy Hutton

1979 WHEN A STRANGER CALLS
Director: Fred Walton
Co-stars: Charles Durning Tony Beckley Carol Kane

1980 BABY COMES HOME
Director: Waris Hussein
Co-stars: Warren Oates Mildred Dunnock Devon Erickson

1980 ESCAPE
Director: Robert Michael Lewis
Co-stars: Timothy Bottoms Kay Lenz Antonio Fargas

1981 TRIBUTE
Director: Bob Clark
Co-stars: Jack Lemon Lee Remick Robby Benson Kim Cattrall

1983 THE DEAD ZONE
Director: David Cronenberg
Co-stars: Christopher Walken Brooke Adams Tom Skerritt

1985 ANNE OF GREEN GABLES
Director: Kevin Sullivan
Co-stars: Megan Follows Richard Farnsworth Patricia Hamilton

1986 AS IS
Director: Michael Lindsay-Hogg
Co-stars: Robert Carradine Joanna Miles Jonathan Hadary

1986 BETWEEN TWO WOMEN
Director: Jon Avnet
Co-stars: Farrah Fawcett Michael Nouri

1986 THE BOY WHO COULD FLY
Director: Nick Castle
Co-stars: Lucy Deakins Jay Underwood Bonnie Bedelia

1989 OBSESSED
Director: Robin Spry
Co-stars: Kerrie Keane Daniel Pilon Saul Rubinek Lynne Griffin

1989 THOSE SHE LEFT BEHIND
Director: Waris Hussein
Co-stars: Gary Cole Joanna Kerns George Coe

1990 DANIELLE STEEL'S KALEIDOSCOPE
Director: Jud Taylor
Co-stars: Jaclyn Smith Perry King Donald Moffat

1991 DYING YOUNG
Director: Joel Schumacher
Co-stars: Julia Roberts Campbell Scott Ellen Burstyn

1992 BED AND BREAKFAST
Director: Robert Ellis Miller
Co-stars: Roger Moore Talia Shire Ford Rainey

JACQUELINE DE WIT

1944 BLACK MAGIC
Director: Phil Rosen
Co-stars: Sidney Toler Manton Moreland Frances Chan

1946 LITTLE GIANT
Director: William Seiter
Co-stars: Bud Abbott Lou Costello Brenda Joyce

1947 THE LONE WOLF IN MEXICO
Director: Ross Lederman
Co-stars: Gerald Mohr Sheila Ryan Eric Blore

1950 THE GREAT JEWEL ROBBER
Director: Peter Godfrey
Co-stars: David Brian Marjorie Reynolds John Archer

1955 THE SHRIKE
Director: Jose Ferrer
Co-stars: Jose Ferrer June Allyson Joy Page

PEGGY DEXTER

1943 THEATRE ROYAL
Director: John Baxter
Co-stars: Bud Flanagan Chesney Allen Horace Kenny

SALLY DEXTER

1989 THE ACT
Director: Roy Battersby
Co-stars: Jack Shepherd Barry Jackson Kenneth Haigh

SUSAN DEY

1972 SKYJACKED
Director: John Guillermin
Co-stars: Charlton Heston Yvette Mimieux Jeanne Crain

1977 MARY JANE HARPER CRIED LAST NIGHT
Director: Allen Reisner
Co-stars: John Vernon Tricia O'Neil

1977 FIRST LOVE
Director: Joan Darling
Co-stars: William Katt John Heard Beverly D'Angelo

1978 LITTLE WOMEN
Director: David Lowell
Co-stars: Meredith Baxter Dorothy McGuire Greer Garson

1981 LOOKER
Director: Michael Crighton
Co-stars: Albert Finney James Coburn Leigh Taylor-Young

1982 THE GIFT OF LIFE
Director: Jerry London
Co-stars: Paul LeMat Edward Herrman Cassie Yates

1983 SUNSET LIMOUSINE
Director: Terry Hughes
Co-stars: John Ritter Lainie Kazan Martin Mull

1985 ECHO PARK
Director: Robert Dornhelm
Co-stars: Thomas Hulce Michael Bowen Christopher Walker

1987 THE ANGER IN GREEN

1993 BEYOND BETRAYAL
Director: Carl Schenkel
Co-stars: Richard Dean Anderson

1993 LOVE, LIES AND LULLABIES
Director: Rod Hardy
Co-stars: Piper Laurie Andy Romano Kathleen York

**1993 WHOSE CHILD IS THIS?:
THE WAR FOR BABY JESSICA**
Director: John Kent Harrison
Co-stars: Michael Ontkean Amanda Plummer David Keith

KATE DEZINA

1990 SURE FIRE
Director: Jon Jost
Co-stars: Tom Blair Kristi Hager Robert Ernst

AYESHA DHARKER

1992 CITY OF JOY
Director: Roland Joffe
Co-stars: Patrick Swayze Pauline Collins Art Malik

MARGARET DIAMOND

1948 ESTHER WATERS
Director: Ian Dalrymple
Co-stars: Kathleen Ryan Dirk Bogarde Cyril Cusack

1957 THE HOSTAGE
Director: Harold Huth
Co-stars: Ron Randell Mary Parker Carl Jaffe

MARION DIAMOND

1992 TALE OF A VAMPIRE
Director: Shimato Sato
Co-stars: Julian Sands Suzanna Hamilton Kenneth Cranham

SELMA DIAMOND

1984 ALL OF ME
Director: Carl Reiner
Co-stars: Steve Martin Lily Tomlin Victoria Tennant

DOLORES DIANE

1943 HI BUDDY!
Director: Harold Young
Co-stars: Dick Foran Harriet Hilliard Robert Paige

CAMERON DIAZ

1995 THE MASK
Co-Star Jim Carry

1996 FEELING MINNESOTA
Director: Steven Baigelman
Co-stars: Keanu Reeves Vincent D'Onofrio

1996 A LIFE LESS ORDINARY
Director: Danny Boyle
Co-stars: Ewan McGregor Holly Hunter Delroy Lindo

1996 THE LAST SUPPER
Co-stars: Annabeth Gish Bill Paxton Ron Pearlman

1997 SHE'S THE ONE
Director: Edward Burns
Co-stars: Edward Burns John Mahoney Jennifer Aniston

1997 MY BEST FRIEND'S WEDDING
Director: P.J. Hogan
Co-stars: Julia Roberts Dermot Mulroney Rupert Everett

1997 HEAD ABOVE WATER
Director: Jim Wilson
Co-stars: Harvey Keitel Billy Zane Craig Sheffer

MARIA ISABEL DIAZ

1990 HELLO HEMINGWAY
Director: Fernando Perez
Co-stars: Laura De La Uz, Raul Paz, Enrique Molina

SOPHIA DIAZ

1992 FEMME FATALE
Director: Udayan Prasad
Co-stars: Simon Callow Donald Pleasence Colin Welland

MIRIAM DIAZ-AROCO

1992 BELLE EPOQUE
Director: Fernando Trueba
Co-stars: Gabina Diego Jorge Sanz Penelope Cruz

IDA DI BENEDETTO

1984 NOI TRE
Director: Pupi Avati
Co-stars: Christopher Davidson Lino Capolicchio Dario Parasini

MARY DIBLEY

1919 THE NATURE OF THE BEAST
Director: Cecil Hepworth
Co-stars: Alma Taylor Gerald Ames James Carew

JUDY DICK

1976 STORM BOY
Director: Henri Safran
Co-stars: Greg Rowe Peter Cummins David Gulpilil

LUCINDA DICKEY

1984 BREAKDANCE
Director: Joel Silberg
Co-stars: Adolfo Quinones Michael Chambers Ben Lokey

1984 BREAKDANCE 2: ELECTRIC BOOGALOO
Director: Sam Firstenberg
Co-stars: Adolfo Quinones Susie Bono

1984 NINJA 111: THE DOMINATION
Director: Sam Firstenberg
Co-stars: Sho Kosugi Jordan Bennett David Chung

ANGIE DICKINSON

1955 TENNESSEE'S PARTNER
Director: Allan Dwan
Co-stars: Ronald Reagan John Payne Rhonda Fleming

1955 THE MAN WITH THE GUN
Director: Richard Wilson
Co-stars: Robert Mitchum Jan Sterling Henry Hull

1956 I MARRIED A WOMAN
Director: Hal Kanter
Co-stars: George Gobal Diana Dors Adolphe Menjou

1956 TENSION AT TABLE ROCK
Director: Charles Marquis Warren
Co-stars: Richard Egan Dorothy Malone

1956 THE BLACK WHIP
Director: Charles Marquis Warren
Co-stars: Hugh Marlowe Coleen Gray

1957 CHINA GATE
Director: Samuel Fuller
Co-stars: Gene Barry Nat King Cole Lee Van Cleef

1957 SHOOTOUT AT MEDICINE BEND
Director: Richard Bare
Co-stars: Randolph Scott James Craig James Garner

1958 CRY TERROR
Director: Andrew Stone
Co-stars: James Mason Rod Steiger Inger Stevens

1959 RIO BRAVO
Director: Howard Hawks
Co-stars: John Wayne Dean Martin Walter Brennan

1960 THE SINS OF RACHEL CADE
Director: Gordon Douglas
Co-stars: Roger Moore Peter Finch Errol John

1960 OCEAN'S ELEVEN
Director: Lewis Milestone
Co-stars: Frank Sinatra Dean Martin Sammy Davis

1960 A FEVER IN THE BLOOD
Director: Vincent Sherman
Co-stars: Efrem Zimbalist Don Ameche Jack Kelly

1960 THE BRAMBLE BUSH
Director: Daniel Petrie
Co-stars: Richard Burton Martha Hyer

1962 JESSICA
Director: Jean Negulesco
Co-stars: Maurice Chevalier Noel-Noel Sylva Koscina

1962 ROME ADVENTURE
Director: Delmer Daves
Co-stars: Suzanne Pleshette Rossano Brazzi Troy Donahue

1963 CAPTAIN NEWMAN
Director: David Miller
Co-stars: Gregory Peck Tony Curtis Eddie Albert

1964 THE KILLERS
Director: Don Siegel
Co-stars: John Cassavetes Lee Marvin Ronald Reagan

1965 THE ART OF LOVE
Director: Norman Jewison
Co-stars: James Garner Dick Van Dyke Elke Sommer

1966 CAST A GIANT SHADOW
Director: Melville Shavelson
Co-stars: Kirk Douglas Senta Berger Topol

1966 THE CHASE
Director: Arthur Penn
Co-stars: Marlon Brando Jane Fonda Robert Redford

1967 POINT BLANK
*Director:*s John Boorman
Co-stars: Lee Marvin Keenan Wynn Carroll O'Connor

1969 SAM WHISKEY
Director: Arnold Laven
Co-stars: Burt Reynolds Clint Walker Ossie Davis

1969 SOME KIND OF A NUT
Director: Garson Kanin
Co-stars: Dick Van Dyke Rosemary Forsyth Dennis King

1969 YOUNG BILLY YOUNG
Director: Burt Kennedy
Co-stars: Robert Mitchum Robert Walker Jnr David Carradine

1971 PRETTY MAIDS ALL IN A ROW
Director: Roger Vadim
Co-stars: Rock Hudson Telly Savalas Roddy McDowall

1974 BIG BAD MAMA
Director: Steve Carver
Co-stars: William Shatner Tom Skerritt

**1980 CHARLIE CHAN AND THE CURSE
OF THE DRAGON QUEEN**
Director: Clive Donner
Co-stars: Peter Ustinov Brian Keith

1980 DRESSED TO KILL
Director: Brian De Palmer
Co-stars: Michael Caine Nancy Allen Keith Gordon

1980 KLONDYKE FEVER
Director: Peter Carter
Co-stars: Jeff East Rod Steiger

1981 DEATH HUNT
Director: Peter Hunt
Co-stars: Charles Bronson Lee Marvin Ed Lauter

1984 JEALOUSY
Director: Jeffrey Bloom
Co-stars: Paul Michael Glaser David Carradine France Nuyen

1984 A TOUCH OF SCANDAL

1987 BIG BAD MAMA II
Director: Jim Wynorski
Co-stars: Robert Culp Bruce Glover Julie McCullough

1987 POLICE STORY: THE FREEWAY KILLINGS
Director: William Graham
Co-stars: Richard Crenna Ben Gazzara

1987 STILLWATCH
Director: Rod Holcomb
Co-stars: Lynda Carter Don Murray Stuart Whitman

1988 ONCE UPON A TEXAS TRAIN
Director: Burt Kennedy
Co-stars: Willie Nelson Richard Widmark Stuart Whitman

1993 EVEN COWGIRLS GET THE BLUES
Director: Gus Van Sant
Co-stars: Uma Thurman John Hurt Rain Phoenix

SHEILA DICKINSON

1992 CLAIRE OF THE MOON
Director: Nicole Conn
Co-stars: Trisha Todd Faith McDevitt

BRENDA DICKSON

1973 THE DEATHMASTER
Director: Ray Danton
Co-stars: Robert Quarry Bill Ewing John Fiedler

GLORIA DICKSON

1937 THEY WON'T FORGET
Director: Mervyn LeRoy
Co-stars: Claude Rains Otto Kruger Lana Turner

1938 SECRETS OF AN ACTRESS
Director: William Keighley
Co-stars: Kay Francis George Brent Ian Hunter

1938 RACKET BUSTERS
Director: Lloyd Bacon
Co-stars: George Brent Humphrey Bogart Allen Jenkins

1938 HEART OF THE NORTH
Director: Lew Seiler
Co-stars: Dick Foran Gale Page Patric Knowles

1938 GOLD DIGGERS IN PARIS
Director: Ray Enright
Co-stars: Rudy Vallee Rosemary Lane Hugh Herbert

1939 ON YOUR TOES
Director: Ray Enright
Co-stars: Vera Zorina Eddie Albert Alan Hale Donald O'Connor

1939 WATERFRONT
Co-stars: Dennis Morgan

1939 THEY MADE ME A CRIMINAL
Director: Busby Berkeley
Co-stars: John Garfield Claude Rains Bowery Boys

1940 I WANT A DIVORCE
Director: Ralph Murphy
Co-stars: Dick Powell Joan Blondell Jessie Ralph

1941 THIS THING CALLED LOVE
Director: Alexander Hall
Co-stars: Rosalind Russell Melvyn Douglas

1943 LADY OF BURLESQUE
Director: William Wellman
Co-stars: Barbara Stanwyck Michael O'Shea Iris Adrian

GABINA DIEGO

1992 BELLE EPOQUE
Director: Fernando Trueba
Co-stars: Miriam Diaz-Arco Jorge Sanz Penelope Cruz

MARSHA DIETLEIN

1987 THE RETURN OF THE LIVING DEAD: PART 2
Director: Ken Widerhorn
Co-stars: James Karen Thom Matthews

DENA DIETRICH

1974   THE STRANGE AND DEADLY OCCURRENCE
Director: Charles Frend
Co-stars: Robert Stack Vera Miles

1975   THE WILD PARTY
Director: James Ivory
Co-stars: James Coco Raquel Welch Perry King

1980   BABY COMES HOME
Director: Waris Hussein
Co-stars: Colleen Dewhurst Warren Oates Mildred Dunnock

MARLENE DIETRICH *(Maria Magdalene Dietrich)(Married Rudolph Sieber)*
Nominated For Best Actress In 1930 For Morocco

1923   THE LITTLE NAPOLEON

1925   JOYLESS STREET
Director: G. W. Pabst
Co-stars: Greta Garbo Asia Nielson Werner Kraves

1930   THE BLUE ANGEL
Director: Joseph Von Sternberg
Co-stars: Emil Jannings Rosa Valetta

1930   MOROCCO
Director: Josef Von Sternberg
Co-stars: Gary Cooper Adolphe Menjou

1931   DISHONORED
Director: Josef Von Sternberg
Co-stars: Victor McLaglen Lew Cody

1932   BLONDE VENUS
Director: Josef Von Sternberg
Co-stars: Cary Grant Herbert Marshall

1932   SHANGHAI EXPRESS
Director: Josef Von Sternberg
Co-stars: Clive Brook Anna May Wong

1933   SONG OF SONGS
Director: Rouben Mamoulian
Co-stars: Brian Aherne Lionel Atwill

1934   THE SCARLET EMPRESS
Director: Josef Von Sternberg
Co-stars: John Lodge Sam Jaffe C. Aubrey Smith

1935   THE DEVIL IS A WOMAN
Director: Josef Von Sternberg
Co-stars: Lionel Atwill Cesar Romero

1936   DESIRE
Director: Frank Borzage
Co-stars: Gary Cooper John Halliday Akim Tamiroff

1936   THE GARDEN OF ALLAH
Director: Richard Boleslawski
Co-stars: Charles Boyer Basil Rathbone

1937   KNIGHT WITHOUT ARMOUR
Director: Jacques Feyder
Co-stars: Robert Donat John Clements Herbert Lom

1937   ANGEL
Director: Ernst Lubitsch
Co-stars: Herbert Marshall Melvyn Douglas

1939   DESTRY RIDES AGAIN
Director: George Marshall
Co-stars: James Stewart Charles Winninger Mischa Auer

1940   SEVEN SINNERS
Director: Tay Garnett
Co-stars: John Wayne Albert Dekker Broderick Crawford

1941   MANPOWER
Director: Raoul Walsh
Co-stars: Edward G. Robinson George Raft Alan Hale

1941   THE FLAME OF NEW ORLEANS
Director: Rene Clair
Co-stars: Roland Young Bruce Cabot Andy Devine

1942   THE LADY IS WILLING
Director: Mitchell Leisen
Co-stars: Fred MacMurray Aline MacMahon

1942   PITTSBURG
Director: Lewis Seiler
Co-stars: John Wayne Randolph Scott Louise Allbritton

1942   THE SPOILERS
Director: Ray Enright
Co-stars: John Wayne Randolph Scott Margaret Lindsay

1944   KISMET
Director: William Dieterle
Co-stars: Ronald Colman James Craig Edward Arnold

1944   FOLLOW THE BOYS
Director: Edward Sutherland
Co-stars: Orson Welles George Raft Dinah Shore

1946   MARTIN ROUMAGNAC
Director: Georges Lacombe
Co-stars: Jean Gabin Margo Lion Marcel Herrand

1947   GOLDEN EARRINGS
Director: Mitchell Leisen
Co-stars: Ray Milland Murvyn Vye Dennis Hoey

1948   A FOREIGN AFFAIR
Director: Billy Wilder
Co-stars: Jean Arthur John Lund Millard Mitchell

1949   JIGSAW
Director: Fletcher Markle
Co-stars: Franchot Tone Jean Wallace Henry Fonda

1950   STAGE FRIGHT
Director: Alfred Hitchcock
Co-stars: Richard Todd Jane Wyman Alastair Sim

1951   NO HIGHWAY
Director: Henry Koster
Co-stars: James Stewart Glynis Johns Jack Hawkins

1952   RANCHO NOTORIOUS
Director: Fritz Lang
Co-stars: Arthur Kennedy Mel Ferrer Gloria Henry

1956   AROUND THE WORLD IN EIGHTY DAYS
Director: Michael Anderson
Co-stars: David Niven Robert Newton

1957   THE MONTE CARLO STORY
Director: Samuel Taylor
Co-stars: Vittorio De Sica Arthur O'Connell

1957   WITNESS FOR THE PROSECUTION
Director: Billy Wilder
Co-stars: Tyrone Power Charles Laughton

1958   TOUCH OF EVIL
Director: Orson Welles
Co-stars: Orson Welles Charlton Heston Janet Leigh Joseph Calleia

1961   JUDGEMENT AT NUREMBERG
Director: Stanley Kramer
Co-stars: Spencer Tracy Burt Lancaster Judy Garland

1962   THE BLACK FOX *(Voice)*
Director: Louis Clyde Stoumen

1964   PARIS, WHEN IT SIZZLES
Director: Richard Quine
Co-stars: William Holden Audrey Hepburn

1978   JUST A GIGOLO
Director: David Hemmings
Co-stars: David Hemmings David Bowie Sydne Rome Kim Novak

DALILAH DI LAZZARO

1974   ANDY WARHOL'S FRANKENSTEIN
Director: Paul Morrissey
Co-stars: Udo Kier Joe Dallesandro

1980   THREE MEN TO DESTROY
Director: Jacques Deray
Co-stars: Alain Delon Pierre Dux

VICTORIA DILLARD

1991   RICHOCHET
Director: Russell Mulcahey
Co-stars: Denzel Washington John Lithgow Lindsay Wagner

1992   DEEP COVER
Director: Bill Duke
Co-stars: Larry Fishburne Jeff Goldblum Sydney Lassick

PHYLLIS DILLER

1966   BOY DID I GET A WRONG NUMBER !
Director: George Marshall
Co-stars: Bob Hope Elke Sommer Marjorie Lord

1966   EIGHT ON THE LAM
Director: George Marshall
Co-stars: Bob Hope Shirley Eaton Jill St. John

**1967   DID YOU HEAR THE ONE ABOUT THE
          TRAVELLING SALESLADY?**
Director: Don Weis
Co-Star   Bob Denver Jeanette Nolan

1968   THE ADDING MACHINE
Director: Jerome Epstein
Co-stars: Milo O'Shea Billie Whitelaw Sydney Chaplin

**1968   THE PRIVATE NAVY OF
          SERGEANT O'FARRELL**
Director: Frank Tashlin
Co-stars: Bob Hope Gina Loliobrigida

1990   HAPPILY EVER AFTER (VOICE)
Director: John Howley
Co-stars: Malcolm McDowell Tracey Ullman Ed Asner

MELINDA DILLON
Nominated For Best Supporting Actress In 1997 For "Close Encounters
Of Third Kind" And In 1981 For "Absence Of Malice"

1976   BOUND FOR GLORY
Director: Hal Ashby
Co-stars: David Carradine Ronny Cox Gail Strickland John Lehne

1977   CLOSE ENCOUNTERS OF THE THIRD KIND
Director: Steven Spielberg
Co-stars: Richard Dreyfuss Teri Garr

1978   F.I.S.T.
Director: Norman Jewison
Co-stars: Sylvester Stallone Rod Steiger Peter Boyle Tony LoBianco

1981   HELLINGER'S LAW
Director: Leo Penn
Co-stars: Telly Savalas Morgan Stevens Rod Taylor Janet Dubois

1981   ABSENCE OF MALLICE
Director: Sidney Pollack
Co-stars: Paul Newman Sally Field Bob Balaban

1983   A CHRISTMAS STORY
Director: Bob Clark
Co-stars: Peter Billingsley Darren McGavin Ian Petrella

1983   RIGHT OF WAY
Director: George Schaefer
Co-stars: Bette Davis James Stewart Priscilla Merrill

1984   SONGWRITER
Director: Alan Rudolph
Co-stars: Willy Nelson Kris Kristofferson Lesley Ann Warren

1986   SHATTERED SPIRITS
Director: Robert Greenwald
Co-stars: Martin Sheen Roxana Zal Lukas Haas

1987   BIG FOOT AND THE HENDERSONS
Director: William Dear
Co-stars: John Lithgow David Suchet Don Ameche

1988   SHATTERED INNOCENCE
Director: Sandor Stern
Co-stars: Jonna Lee John Pleshette Kris Kamm Ben Frank

1989   STAYING TOGETHER
Director: Lee Grant
Co-stars: Sean Astin Stockard Channing Jim Haynie Levon Helm

1989   NIGHTBREAKER
Director: Peter Markle
Co-stars: Martin Sheen Emilio Estevez Lea Thompson

1990   CAPTAIN AMERICA
Director: Albert Pyun
Co-stars: Matt Salinger Ronny Cox Ned Beatty Scott Paulin

1991   THE PRINCE OF TIDES
Director: Barbra Streisand
Co-stars: Barbra Streisand Nick Nolte Blythe Danner Kate Nelligan

1994   CONFESSIONS:TWO FACES OF EVIL
Director: Gilbert Cates
Co-stars: James Earl Jones Jason Bateman James Wilder

EMMA D'INVERNO

1985   BLOOD HUNT
Director: Peter Barber-Fleming
Co-stars: Andrew Keir Iain Glen Nigel Stock

SUSAN DIOL

1989   THE ROAD RAIDERS
Director: Richard Lang
Co-stars: Bruce Boxleitner Noble Willingham

ROSE DIONE

1921   LITTLE LORD FAUNTLEROY
Director: Alfred Green
Co-stars: Mary Pickford Claude Gillingwater Kate Price

1923   SALOME
Director: Charles Bryant
Co-stars: Nazimova, Mitchell Lewis Nigel De Brulier

PAOLA DIONISOTTI

1978   THE SAILOR'S RETURN
Director: Jack Gold
Co-stars: Tom Bell Shope Shodeinde George Costigan

1989   INSPECTOR WEXFORD: THE VEILED ONE
Director: Mary McMurray
Co-stars: George Baker Louie Ramsey

DIONNE QUINS

1936   THE COUNTRY DOCTOR
Director: Henry King
Co-stars: Jean Hersholt Dorothy Peterson June Lang

1936   REUNION
Director: Norman Taurog
Co-stars: Jean Hersholt Rochelle Hudson Slim Summerville

1938   FIVE OF A KIND
Director: Herbert Leeds
Co-stars: Jean Hersholt Claire Trevor Cesar Romero

MAMADOU DIOUME

1989   THE MAHABARATA
Director: Peter Brook
Co-stars: Urs Biher Georges Corraface Ryszard Cieslak

NICOLA DI PINTA
1994 UNA PURA FORMALITA
Director: Giuseppe Tornatore
Co-stars: Gerard Depardieu Roman Polanski

MAGGIE DIRANE
1934 MAN OF ARAN
Director: Robert Flaherty
Co-stars: Colman King Michael Dillane

ANNE DITCHBURN
1978 SLOW DANCING IN THE BIG CITY
Director: John Avildsen
Co-stars: Paul Sorvino Anita Dangler

MARY DIVENY
1988 THE HOUSE ON CARROLL STREET
Director: Peter Yates
Co-stars: Kelly McGillis Jeff Daniels Mandy Patinkin

DOROTHY DIX
1931 NEVADA BUCKAROO
Co-Star Bob Steele

RACHEL DIX
1976 ADVENTURES OF A TAXI DRIVER
Director: Stanley Long
Co-stars: Barry Evans Judy Geeson Liz Fraser

PHYLLIS DIXEY
1947 DUAL ALIBI
Director: Alfred Travers
Co-stars: Herbert Lom Ronald Frankau Terence De Marney

ADELE DIXON
1941 BANANA RIDGE
Director: Walter Mycroft
Co-stars: Robertson Hare Alfred Drayton Nova Pilbeam

BETH DIXON
1991 THE BALLAD OF THE SAD CAFE
Director: Simon Callow
Co-stars: Vanessa Redgrave Keith Carradine Rod Steiger

DONNA DIXON *(Married Dan Aykroyd)*
1984 NO MAN'S LAND
Director: Rod Holcomb
Co-stars: Stella Stevens Estelle Getty Janis Paige

1985 SPIES LIKE US
Director: John Landis
Co-stars: Chevy Chase Dan Aykroyd Steve Forrest

1986 BEVERLY HILLS MADAM
Director: Harvey Hart
Co-stars: Faye Dunaway Melody Anderson Robin Givens

1988 THE COUCH TRIP
Director: Michael Ritchie
Co-stars: Dan Aykroyd Charles Grodin Walter Matthau

1992 WAYNE'S WORLD
Director: Penelope Spheeris
Co-stars: Mike Myers Dana Carvey Rob Lowe

JEAN DIXON
1934 SADIE McKEE
Director: Clarence Brown
Co-stars: Joan Crawford Franchot Tone Gene Raymond

1935 SHE MARRIED HER BOSS
Director: Gregory LaCava
Co-stars: Claudette Colbert Melvyn Douglas

1935 I'LL LOVE YOU ALWAYS
Co-stars: George Murphy Nancy Carroll Raymond Walburn

1935 MR. DYNAMITE
Co-stars: Edmund Lowe Esther Ralston

1936 TO MARY - WITH LOVE
Director: John Cromwell
Co-stars: Warner Baxter Myrna Loy Claire Trevor

1936 MY MAN GODFREY
Director: Gregory LaCava
Co-stars: Carole Lombard William Powell Alice Brady

1936 THE MAGNIFICENT BRUTE
Director: John Blystone
Co-stars: Victor McLaglen Binnie Barnes William Hall

1937 SWING HIGH, SWING LOW
Director: Mitchell Leisen
Co-stars: Carole Lombard Fred MacMurray Dorothy Lamour

1937 YOU ONLY LIVE ONCE
Director: Fritz Lang
Co-stars: Sylvia Sidney Henry Fonda Barton MacLane

1938 JOY OF LIVING
Director: Tay Garnett
Co-stars: Irene Dunne Douglas Fairbanks Jnr. Alice Brady

1938 HOLIDAY
Director: George Cukor
Co-stars: Cary Grant Katherine Hepburn Lew Ayres

JILL DIXON
1957 JUST MY LUCK
Director: John Paddy Carstairs
Co-stars: Norman Wisdom Margaret Rutherford

1958 A NIGHT TO REMEMBER
Director: Roy Ward Baker
Co-stars: Kenneth More Ronald Allen Honor Blackman

1964 WITCHCRAFT
Director: Don Sharp
Co-stars: Jack Hedley Lon Chaney Jnr. Marie Ney

JOAN DIXON (H HUGHES DISCOVERY)
1950 BUNCO SQUAD
Director: Norman Taurog
Co-stars: Robert Sterling Ricardo Cortez Elizabeth Risdon

1951 ROADBLOCK - RKO.
Director: Harold Daniels
Co-stars: Charles McGraw Lowell Gilmore Milburn Stone

LAURA DIXON
1991 BROKE
Director: Alan Dossor
Co-stars: Timothy Spall Sheila Kelley Larry Lamb

SHAE D'LYN *(Child)*
1994 SECRETS
Director: Jud Taylor
Co-stars: Richard Kiley Veronica Hamel

KAELA DOBKIN
1997 OVERDRIVE
Co-star: Steve Guttenberg

FRANCES DOBLE
1932 THE WATER GYPSIES
Director: Maurice Elvy
Co-stars: Ann Todd Sari Maritza Ian Hunter

GOSIA DOBROWOLSKA

1984 SILVER CITY
Director: Sophia Turkiewicz
Co-stars: Ivar Kants Anna Jemison Steve Bisley

1990 GOLDEN BRAID
Director: Paul Cox
Co-stars: Chris Haywood Paul Chubb Norman Kaye

1991 A WOMAN'S TALE
Director: Paul Cox
Co-stars: Sheila Florance Norman Kaye Chris Haywood

1992 THE NUN AND THE BANDIT
Director: Paul Cox
Co-stars: Chris Haywood Victoria Eagger Norman Kaye

1992 CAREFUL
Director: Guy Maddin
Co-stars: Kyle McCulloch Sarah Nevile Brent Neal

1993 THE CUSTODIAN
Director: John Dingwall
Co-stars: Anthony LaPaglia Hugo Weaving Kelly Dingwall

ANITA DOBSON

1990 THE WORLD OF EDDIE WEARY
Director: Alan Grint
Co-stars: Ray Brooks Celia Imrie Connie Booth

1994 BEYOND BEDLAM
Director: Vadim Jean
Co-stars: Craig Fairbrass Elizabeth Hurley Georgina Hale

TAMARA DOBSON

1973 CLEOPATRA JONES
Director: Jack Starrett
Co-stars: Shelley Winters Bernie Casey Brenda Sykes

1976 NORMAN....IS THAT YOU?
Director: George Schlatter
Co-stars: Redd Foxx Pearl Bailey Michael Warren

1983 CHAINED HEAT
Director: Paul Nicolas
Co-stars: Linda Blair John Vernon Sybil Danning

1984 AMAZONS
Director: Paul Michael Glaser
Co-stars: Jack Scalia Madeline Stowe Stella Stevens

VIKI DOBSON

1937 CATCH AS CATCH CAN
Director: Roy Kellino
Co-stars: James Mason Eddie Pola Finlay Currie

CLAIRE DODD

1932 PARACHUTE JUMPER
Director: Alfred Green
Co-stars: Douglas Fairbanks Bette Davis Leo Carrillo

1932 HOLLYWOOD SPEAKS
Director: Eddie Buzzell
Co-stars: Pat O'Brien Genevieve Tobin Rita Leroy

1932 LAWYER MAN
Director: William Dieterle
Co-stars: William Powell Joan Blondell Helen Vinson

1933 FOOTLIGHT PARADE
Director: Lloyd Bacon
Co-stars: James Cagney Joan Blondell Dick Powell

1933 BLONDIE JOHNSON
Director: Ray Enright
Co-stars: Joan Blondell Chester Morris Allen Jenkins

1933 ELMER THE GREAT
Director: Mervyn LeRoy
Co-stars: Joe E. Brown Patricia Ellis Frank McHugh

1933 EX-LADY
Director: Robert Florey
Co-stars: Bette Davis Gene Raymond Frank McHugh

1933 HARD TO HANDLE
Director: Mervyn LeRoy
Co-stars: James Cagney Ruth Donnelly Mary Brian

1934 THE PERSONALITY KID
Director: Alan Crosland
Co-stars: Pat O'Brien Glenda Farrell Henry O'Neill

1934 JOURNAL OF A CRIME
Director: William Keighley
Co-stars: Ruth Chatterton Adolphe Menjou

1934 GAMBLING LADY
Director: Archie Mayo
Co-stars: Barbara Stanwyck Pat O'Brien Joel McCrea

1935 THE CASE OF THE CURIOUS BRIDE
Director: Michael Curtiz
Co-stars: Warren William Margaret Lindsay

1935 DON'T BET ON BLONDES
Co-stars: Warren William Guy Kibbee

1935 THE GOOSE AND THE GANDER
Co-stars: Charles Coleman Frank Orth Ralph Forbes

1935 THE PAYOFF
Co-Star: James Dunn

1935 I SELL ANYTHING
Director: Robert Florey
Co-stars: Pat O'Brien Ann Dvorak Roscoe Karns

1935 THE GLASS KEY
Director: Frank Tuttle
Co-stars: George Raft Rosalind Keith Ray Milland

1935 ROBERTA
Director: William Seiter
Co-stars: Fred Astaire Ginger Rogers Irene Dunne Randolph Scott

1936 THE SINGING KID
Director: William Keighley
Co-stars: Al Jolsen Sybil Jason Allen Jenkins

1936 THE CASE OF THE VELVET CLAWS
Director: William Clemens
Co-stars: Warren William Wini Shaw

1938 CHARLIE CHAN IN HONOLULU
Director: Bruce Humberstone
Co-stars: Sidney Toler Sen Yung Phyllis Brooks

1938 FAST COMPANY
Director: Edward Buzzell
Co-stars: Melvyn Douglas Florence Rice Louis Calhern

1938 ROMANCE IN THE DARK
Director: H.C. Potter
Co-stars: Gladys Swarthout John Boles John Barrymore

1938 THREE LOVES HAS NANCY
Director: Richard Thorpe
Co-stars: Janet Gaynor Robert Montgomery Franchot Tone

1939 WOMAN DOCTOR
Director: Sidney Salkow
Co-stars: Frieda Inescort Henry Wilcoxon Cora Witherspoon

1940 SLIGHTLY HONOURABLE
Director: Tay Garnett
Co-stars: Pat O'Brien Broderick Crawford Edward Arnold

1940 IF I HAD MY WAY
Director: David Butler
Co-stars: Bing Crosby El Brendel Gloria Jean Charles Winninger

1941   IN THE NAVY
Director: Arthur Lubin
Co-stars: Bud Abbott & Lou Costello Dick Powell Andrew Sisters

1942   THE MAD DOCTOR OF MARKET STREET
Director: Joseph Lewis
Co-stars: Lionel Atwill Nat Pendleton

NORMA DOGGETT

1954   SEVEN BRIDES FOR SEVEN BROTHERS
Director: Stanley Donen
Co-stars: Jane Powell Howard Keel Russ Tamblyn

SHANNEN DOHERTY
(Married Ashley Hamilton)

1985   GIRLS JUST WANT TO HAVE FUN
Director: Alan Metter
Co-stars: Sara Jessica Parker Helen Hunt Lee Montgomery

1989   HEATHERS
Director: Michael Lehman
Co-stars: Winona Ryder Christian Slater Kim Walker

1992   OBSESSED
Director: Jonathan Sanger
Co-stars: William Devane Clare Carey Lois Chiles

**1992   BEVERLY HILLS 90210:
WALSH FAMILY CHRISTMAS**
Director: Aaron Spelling
Co-stars: Jason Priestley Luke Perry

1993   BLINDFOLD: ACTS OF OBSESSION
Director: Lawrence Simeone
Co-stars: Judd Nelson Kristian Alfonso

1994   JAILBREAKERS
Director: William Friedkin
Co-star: Antonio Sabato Jnr.

1998   NOWHERE
Director: Gregg Araki
Co-stars: Traci Lords Rose McGowan

RAINBOW DOLAN

1987   IN THE AFTERMATH: ANGELS NEVER SLEEP
Director: Carl Colpaert
Co-stars: Tony Markes Kenneth McCabbe

AMI DOLENZ (Daughter Of Mickey Dolenz)

1989   SHE'S OUT OF CONTROL
Director: Stan Dragoti
Co-stars: Tony Danza Catherine Hicks Wallace Shawn

1992   TICKS
Director: Tony Randel
Co-stars: Rosalind Allen Seth Green Virginia Keehne

1995   ADDICTED TO LOVE
Director: Paul Ziller
Co-stars: Jeff Fahey

BIRGIT DOLL

1986   PLEASE, LET THE FLOWERS LIVE
Director: Duccio Tessari
Co-stars: Klausjurgen Wussow Kurt Meisel

1986   THE SECOND VICTORY
Director: Gerald Thomas
Co-stars: Anthony Andrews Max Von Sydow Helmut Griem

DORA DOLL

1953   TOUCHEZ PAS AU GRISBI
Director: Jacques Becker
Co-stars: Jean Gabin Jeanne Moreau Lino Ventura

1958   THE YOUNG LIONS
Director: Edward Dmytryk
Co-stars: Marlon Brando Dean Martin Montgomery Clift

1976   BLACK AND WHITE IN COLOUR
Director: Jean-Jacques Annaud
Co-stars: Jean Carmet Catherine Rouvel

1993   L'ENFER
Director: Claude Chabrol
Co-stars: Emmanuelle Beart Francois Cluzet

SANDRA DOME

1987   EAT THE RICH
Director: Peter Richardson
Co-stars: Nosher Powell Fiona Richmond Dawn French

FAITH DOMERGUE

1946   THE YOUNG WIDOW
Director: Edwin Marin
Co-stars: Jane Russell Louis Hayward Marie Wilson

1950   VENDETTA
Director: Mel Ferrer
Co-stars: George Dolenz Nigel Bruce Hilary Brooke Joseph Calleia

1950   WHERE DANGER LIVES
Director: John Farrow
Co-stars: Robert Mitchum Claude Rains Maureen O'Sullivan

1952   DUEL AT SILVER CREEK
Director: Don Seigel
Co-stars: Audie Murphy Stephen McNally Susan Cabot

1953   THE GREAT SIOUX UPRISING
Director: Lloyd Bacon
Co-stars: Jeff Chandler Lyle Bettger

1954   THIS IS MY LOVE
Director: Stuart Heisler
Co-stars: Linda Darnell Dan Duryea Rick Jason

1954   SANTA FEE PASSAGE
Director: William Whitney
Co-stars: John Payne Rod Cameron Slim Pickins

1955   IT CAME FROM BENEATH THE SEA
Director: Robert Gordon
Co-stars: Kenneth Tobey Donald Curtis Ian Keith

1955   CULT OF THE COBRA
Director: Francis Lyon
Co-stars: Richard Long Marshall Thompson David Janssen

1955   THIS ISLAND EARTH
Director: Joseph Newman
Co-stars: Jeff Morrow Rex Reason Lance Fuller

1956   TIMESLIP
Director: Ken Hughes
Co-stars: Gene Nelson Donald Grey Joseph Tomelty

1959   ESCORT WEST
Director: Francis Lyon
Co-stars: Victor Mature Elaine Stewart Noah Beery Rex Ingram

1963   CALIFORNIA
Co-stars: Jock Mahoney Michael Pate Susan Seaforth

1973   THE HOUSE OF SEVEN CORPSES
Director: Paul Harrison
Co-stars: John Ireland John Carradine

BERTA DOMINGUEZ

1988   VIRGIN - 36 FILLETTE
Director: Catherine Breillat
Co-stars: Delphine Zentout Etienne Chicot

SOLVEIG DOMMARTIN

1987 WINGS OF DESIRE
Director: Wim Wenders
Co-stars: Bruno Ganz Peter Falk Curt Bois

1991 UNTIL THE END OF THE WORLD
Director: Wim Wenders
Co-stars: William Hurt Sam Neill Jeanne Moreau

1993 FARAWAY, SO CLOSE!
Director: Wim Wenders
Co-stars: Bruno Ganz Otto Sander Nastassja Kinski

ELINOR DONAHUE

1983 HIGH SCHOOL U.S.A.
Director: Rod Amateau
Co-stars: Michael J. Fox Nancy McKeon Todd Bridges

1992 FREDDY'S DEAD - THE FINAL NIGHTMARE.
Director: Rachel Talalay
Co-stars: Rachel Englund Lisa Zane

MARY ELINOR DONAHUE *(Child)*

1948 THREE DARING DAUGHTERS
Director: Fred Wilcox
Co-stars: Jeanette MacDonald Jane Powell Jose Iturbi

PATRICIA DONAHUE

1981 CUTTER'S WAY
Director: Ivan Passer
Co-stars: Jeff Bridges John Heard Lisa Eichhorn

JULIANA DONALD

1984 THE MUPPETS TAKE MANHATTAN
Director: Frank Oz
Co-stars: Art Carney Liza Minnelli Brooke Shields

SHEILA DONALD

1990 CHANGING STEP
Director: Richard Wilson
Co-stars: James Convey Susan Wooldridge Eleanor Bron

NORMA DONALDSON

1972 ACROSS 110TH. STREET
Director: Barry Shear
Co-stars: Anthony Quinn Yaphet Kotto Anthony Franciosa

DOROTHY DONEGAN

1944 SENSATIONS OF 1945
Director: Andrew Stone
Co-stars: Eleanor Powell Dennis O'Keefe Sophie Tucker

YOLANDE DONLAN *(Married Val Guest)*

1949 TRAVELLER'S JOY
Director: Ralph Thomas
Co-stars: Googie Withers John McCallum Maurice Denham

1949 MISS PILGRIM'S PROGRESS
Director: Val Guest
Co-stars: Michael Rennie Garry Marsh Jon Pertwee

1950 MISTER DRAKE'S DUCK
Director: Val Guest
Co-stars: Douglas Fairbank's Jnr, Wilfrid Hyde White

1952 PENNY PRINCESS
Director: Val Guest
Co-stars: Dirk Bogarde A.E. Matthews Reginald Beckwith

1957 TARZAN AND THE LOST SAFARI
Director: Bruce Humberstone
Co-stars: Gordon Scott Robert Beatty

1959 EXPRESSO BONGO
Director: Val Guest
Co-stars: Laurence Harvey Cliff Richard Sylvia Syms

1962 JIGSAW
Director: Val Guest
Co-stars: Jack Warner Ronald Lewis Michael Goodliffe

1963 EIGHTY THOUSAND SUSPECTS
Director: Val Guest
Co-stars: Claire Bloom Richard Johnson Cyril Cusack

DOLORES DONLON

1954 THE LONG WAIT
Director: Victor Saville
Co-stars: Anthony Quinn Charles Coburn Peggie Castle

1956 FLIGHT TO HONG KONG
Director: Joseph Newman
Co-stars: Rory Calhoun Barbara Rush Pat Conway

DENISE DONMANT

1988 HEART OF MIDNIGHT
Director: Matthew Chapman
Co-stars: Jennifer Jason Leigh, Peter Coyote Sam Schact

CHRISTINE DONNA

1974 CONFESSIONS OF A WINDOW CLEANER
Director: Val Guest
Co-stars: Robin Asquith Anthony Booth

CAROLE DONNE

1949 AMAZON QUEST
Co-stars: Tom Neal Frank Lacteen

JEFF DONNELL

1942 MY SISTER EILEEN
Director: Alexander Hall
Co-stars: Rosalind Russell Brian Aherne Janet Blair June Havoc

1943 THERE'S SOMETHING ABOUT A SOLDIER
Director: Alfred Green
Co-stars: Tom Neal Evelyn Keyes

1943 WHAT'S BUZZIN' COUSIN
Director: Charles Barton
Co-stars: Ann Miller John Hubbard Eddie Anderson

1943 A NIGHT TO REMEMEBER
Director: Richard Wallace
Co-stars: Loretta Young Brian Aherne Sidney Toler

1944 NINE GIRLS
Director: Leigh Jason
Co-stars: Ann Harding Evelyn Keyes Anita Louise Nina Foch

1944 THREE IS A FAMILY
Director: Edward Ludwig
Co-stars: Charles Ruggles Fay Bainter Arthur Lake

1944 THE BOOGIE MAN WILL GET YOU
Director: Lew Landers
Co-stars: Boris Karloff Peter Lorre

1945 EADIE WAS A LADY
Director: Arthur Dreifuss
Co-stars: Ann Miller Joe Besser William Wright

1945 OVER 21
Director: Alexander Hall
Co-stars: Irene Dunne Alexander Knox Charles Coburn

1945 TARS AND SPARS
Director: Alfred Green
Co-stars: Sid Ceasar Alfred Drake Janet Blair Marc Platt

1946 THE UNKNOWN
Director: Henry Levin
Co-stars: Karen Morley Jim Bannon

1947   **MR. DISTRICT ATTORNEY**
Co-Star   Michael O'Shea

1949   **STAGECOACH KID**
Director: Lew Landers
Co-stars: Tim Holt Richard Martin Joe Sawyer Thurston Hall

1949   **ROUGHSHOD**
Director: Mark Robson
*Co-stars:*r   Robert Sterling Gloria Grahame Claude Jarman Jnr

1949   **EASY LIVING**
Director: Jacques Tourneur
Co-stars: Victor Mature Lucille Ball Lisabeth Scott

1950   **IN A LONELY PLACE**
Director: Nicholas Ray
Co-stars: Humphrey Bogart Gloria Grahame Frank Lovejoy

1950   **WALK SOFTLY STRANGER**
Director: Robert Stevenson
Co-stars: Joseph Cotten Alida Valli Spring Byington

1950   **THE FULLER BRUSH GIRL**
Director: Lloyd Bacon
Co-stars: Lucille Ball Eddie Albert Gale Robbins

1951   **THREE GUYS NAMED MIKE**
Director: Charles Walters
Co-stars: Jane Wyman Van Johnson Barry Sullivan

1952   **THIEF OF DAMASCUS**
Director: Will Jason
Co-stars: Paul Henreid Lon Chaney John Sutton

1952   **BECAUSE YOUR MINE**
Director: Joe Pasternak
Co-stars: Mario Lanza Dorretta Morrow James Whitmore

1952   **THE FIRST TIME**
Director: Frank Tashlin
Co-stars: Robert Cummings Barbara Hale Mona Barrie

1953   **FLIGHT NURSE**
Director: Allan Dwan
Co-stars: Joan Leslie Forrest Tucker Arthur Franz

1953   **SO THIS IS LOVE**
Director: Gordon Douglas
Co-stars: Kathryn Grayson Merv Griffin Walter Abel

1956   **THE GUNS OF FORT PETTICOAT**
Director: George Marshall
Co-stars: Audie Murphy Kathryn Grant

1957   **MY MAN GODFREY**
Director: Henry Koster
Co-stars: David Niven June Alyson Martha Hyer Robert Keith

1962   **THE IRON MAIDEN**
Director: Gerald Thomas
Co-stars: Michael Craig Cecil Parker Alan Hale Noel Purcell

PATRICE DONNELLY

1982   **PERSONAL BEST**
Director: Robert Towne
Co-stars: Mariel Hemingway Scott Glenn Luana Anders

RUTH DONNELLY

1932   **BLESSED EVENT**
Director: Roy Del Ruth
Co-stars: Lee Tracy Ned Sparks Mary Brian Dick Powell

1933   **CONVENTION CITY**
Director: Archie Mayo
Co-stars: Joan Blondell Adolphe Menjou Dick Powell Mary Aster

1933   **EVER IN MY HEART**
Director: Archie Mayo
Co-stars: Barbara Stanwyck Otto Kruger Ralph Bellamy

1933   **FEMALE**
Director: Michael Curtiz
Co-stars: Ruth Chatterton George Brent Johnny Mack Brown

1933   **FOOTLIGHT PARADE**
Director: Lloyd Bacon
Co-stars: James Cagney Joan Blondell Dick Powell Ruby Keeler

1933   **GOODBYE AGAIN**
Director: Michael Curtiz
Co-stars: Warren William Joan Blondell Genevieve Tobin

1933   **HARD TO HANDLE**
Director: Mervyn LeRoy
Co-stars: James Cagney Mary Mary Brian Allen Jenkins

1933   **HAVANNA WIDOWS**
Director: Ray Enright
Co-stars: Joan Blondell Glenda Farrell Guy Kibbee Frank McHugh

1933   **LADIES THEY TALK ABOUT**
Director: William Keighley
Co-stars: Barbara Stanwyck Preston Foster

1933   **LILLY TURNER**
Director: William Wellman
Co-stars: Ruth Chatterton George Brent Frank McHugh

1934   **THE MERRY WIVES OF RENO**
Director: Bruce Humberstone
Co-stars: Margaret Lindsay Donald Woods

1934   **MANDALAY**
Director: Michael Curtiz
Co-stars: Kay Francis Ricardo Cortez Lyle Talbot Warner Orland

1934   **WONDER BAR**
Director: Lloyd Bacon
Co-stars: Al Jolsen Kay Francis Dolores Del Rio Dick Powell

1934   **HOUSEWIFE**
Director: Alfred Green
Co-stars: Bette Davis George Brent Ann Dvorak John Halliday

1934   **HEAT LIGHTNING**
Director: Mervyn LeRoy
Co-stars: Aline MacMahon Ann Dvorak Preston Foster

1935   **HANDS ACROSS THE TABLE**
Director: Mitchell Leisen
Co-stars: Carole Lombard Fred MacMurray

1935   **PERSONAL MAID'S SECRET**
Director: Arthur Greville Collins
Co-stars: Anita Louise Margaret Lindsay

1935   **MAYBE IT'S LOVE**
Co-stars: Gloria Stuart Frank McHugh Henry Travers

1935   **RED SALUTE**
Director: Sidney Lanfield
Co-stars: Barbara Stanwyck Robert Young Hardie Albright

1935   **TRAVELLING SALESLADY**
Director: Ray Enright
Co-stars: Joan Blondell Hugh Herbert Glenda Farrell

1935   **THE WHITE COCKATOO**
Director: Alan Grosland
Co-stars: Ricardo Cortez Jean Muir Minna Gombell

1936   **13 HOURS BY AIR**
Director: Mitchell Leisen
Co-stars: Fred MacMurray Joan Bennett Brian Donlevy

1936   **MR. DEEDS GOES TO TOWN**
Director: Frank Capra
Co-stars: Gary Cooper Jean Arthur Lionel Stander

1936   **THE SONG AND DANCE MAN**
Director: Allan Dwan
Co-stars: Paul Kelly Claire Trevor Michael Whalen

1936   **MORE THAN A SECRETARY**
Director: Alfred Green
Co-stars: Jean Arthur George Brent Reginald Denny

1936   **CAIN AND MABEL**
Director: Lloyd Bacon
Co-stars: Clark Gable Marion Davies Allen Jenkins

1936   **FATAL LADY**
Director: Edward Ludwig
Co-stars: Mary Ellis Walter Pidgeon John Halliday

1936   **ALIBI IKE**
Director: Ray Enright
Co-stars: Joe E. Brown Olivia De Havilland Roscoe Karns

1937   **PORTIA ON TRIAL**
Director: George Nicholls
Co-stars: Frieda Inescort Walter Abel Neil Hamilton

1938   **A SLIGHT CASE OF MURDER**
Director: Lloyd Bacon
Co-stars: Edward G. Robinson Jane Bryan

1938   **HOLIDAY**
Director: George Cukor
Co-stars: Katherine Hepburn Cary Grant Lew Ayres Binnie Barnes

1938   **ARMY GIRL**
Director: George Nicholls
Co-stars: Madge Evans Preston Foster James Gleason

1938   **THE AFFAIRS OF ANNABEL**
Director: Lew Landers
Co-stars: Lucille Ball Jack Oakie Bradley Page

1939   **ANNABEL TAKES A TOUR**
Director: Lew Landers
Co-stars: Lucille Ball Jack Oakie Ralph Forbes

1939   **THE AMAZING MR. WLLLAMS**
Director: Alexander Hall
Co-stars: Melvyn Douglas Joan Blondell

1939   **MR. SMITH GOES TO WASHINGTON**
Director: Frank Capra
Co-stars: James Stewart Jean Arthur Claude Rains

1940   **MY LITTLE CHICKADEE**
Director: Edward Cline
Co-stars: Mae West W.C. Fields Joseph Callelia Dick Foran

1941   **YOU BELONG TO ME**
Director: Wesley Ruggles
Co-stars: Henry Fonda Barbara Stanwyck Edgar Buchanan

1941   **RISE AND SHINE**
Director: Allan Dwan
Co-stars: Linda Darnell Jack Oakie George Murphy Walter Brennan

1943   **THIS IS THE ARMY**
Director: Michael Curtis
Co-stars: George Murphy Joan Leslie Irving Berlin

1945   **PILLOW TO POST**
Director: Vincent Sherman
Co-stars: Ida Lupino Sydney Greenstreet William Prince

1945   **CROSS MY HEART**
Director: John Berry
Co-stars: Betty Hutton Sonny Tufts Michael Chekhov

1945   **THE BELL'S OF ST. MARY'S**
Director: Leo McCarey
Co-stars: Bing Crosby Ingrid Bergman Henry Travers

1946   **CINDERELLA JONES**
Director: Busby Berkeley
Co-stars: Joan Leslie Julie Bishop Robert Alda

1947   **THE FABULOUS TEXAN**
Director: Edward Ludwig
Co-stars: William Elliott John Carroll Andy Devine

1950   **THE EAGLE AND THE HAWK**
Director: Lewis Foster
Co-stars: John Payne Rhonda Fleming Dennis O'Keefe

1950   **WHERE THE SIDEWALK ENDS**
Director: Otto Preminger
Co-stars: Dana Andrews Gene Tierney Gary Merrill

1951   **THE SECRET OF CONVICT LAKE**
Director: Michael Gordon
Co-stars: Glenn Ford Gene Tierney Ethel Barrymore

1951   **I'D CLIMB THE HIGHEST MOUNTAIN**
Director: Henry King
Co-stars: Susan Haywood William Lundigan Rory Calhoun

1952   **THE WILD BLUE YONDER**
Director: Allan Dwan
Co-stars: Wendell Corey Vera Ralston Walter Brennan

1955   **A LAWLESS STREET**
Director: Joseph Lewis
Co-stars: Randolph Scott Angela Lansbury Jean Parker

1956   **AUTUMN LEAVES**
Director: Robert Aldrich
Co-stars: Joan Crawford Cliff Robertson Vera Miles

1957   **THE WAY TO THE GOLD**
Director: Robert Webb
Co-stars: Jeffrey Hunter Sheree North Walter Brennan

JUDITH DONNER

1964   **SEANCE ON A WET AFTERNOON**
Director: Bryan Forbes
Co-stars: Kim Stanley Nanette Newman Patrick Magee

DEIRDRE DONOGHUE

1988   **JOYRIDERS**
Director: Aisling Walsh
Co-stars: Patricia Kerrigan Andrew Connolly Billie Whitelaw

AMANDA DONOHUE

1986   **CASTAWAY**
Director: Nicolas Roeg
Co-stars: Oliver Reed Georglna Hale Frances Barber

1986   **FOREIGN BODY**
Director: Ronald Neame
Co-stars: Victor Banerjee Warren Mitchell Geraldine McEwan

1988   **AN AFFAIR IN MIND**
Director: Colin Luke
Co-stars: Stephen Dillon Richard Hammett Anne Lambton

1988   **THE LAIR OF THE WHITE WORM**
Director: Ken Russell
Co-stars: Hugh Grant Sammi Davis Peter Capaldi

1988   **THE RAINBOW**
Director: Ken Russell
Co-stars: Sammi Davis David Hemmings Paul McGann

1988   **TANK MALLING**
Director: James Marcus
Co-stars: Ray Winstone Jason Connery Marsha Hunt Nick Berry

1989   **DIAMOND SKULLS**
Director: Nicholas Broomfield
Co-stars: Gabriel Byrne Michael Hordern Judy Parfitt

1990   **PAPER MASK**
Director: Christopher Morahan
Co-stars: Paul McGann Tom Wilkinson Jimmy Yuill

1991   **THE LAUGHTER OF GOD**
Director: Tony Bicat
Co-stars: Peter Firth Sylvia Syms Neil Duncan Sharon Cheyne

1993 THE SUBSTITUTE
Director: Martin Donovan

1995 THE MADNESS OF KING GEORGE
Director: Nicholas Hytner
Co-stars: Nigel Hawthorne Helen Mirren Ian Holm

1996 SHAME II: THE SECRET
Director: Dan Lerner
Co-stars: Kay Lenz Geoffrey Blake

1997 LIAR LIAR
Director Ton Shadyac
Co-stars Jim Carrey Maura Tierney Justin Cooper

ELISA DONOVAN

1995 CLUELESS
Director Amy Heckerling
Co-stars Alicia Silverstone Stacey Dash Paul Rudd

ELIZABETH DONOVAN

1967 DR. FAUSTUS
Director: Nevill Coghill
Co-stars: Richard Burton Elizabeth Taylor Ian Marter

ALLISON DOODY

1987 A PRAYER FOR THE DYING
Director: Mike Hodges
Co-stars: Mickey Rourke Bob Hoskins Alan Bates

1988 TAFFIN
Director: Francis Megahy
Co-stars: Pierce Brosnan Ray McAnally

1989 INDIANA JONES AND THE LAST CRUSADE
Director: Steven Spielberg
Co-stars: Harrison Ford Sean Connery Denholm Elliott

1990 DUEL OF HEARTS
Director: John Hough
Co-Star Benedict Taylor

LUCINDA DOOLING

1985 THE ALCHEMIST
Director: James Amante
Co-stars: Robert Ginty John Sanderford

KARIN DOR

1967 YOU ONLY LIVE TWICE
Director: Lewis Gilbert
Co-stars: Sean Connery Charles Gray Lois Maxwell

1969 TOPAZ
Director: Alfred Hitchcock
Co-stars: John Forsythe Dany Robin Michel Piccoli

ANN DORAN

1938 YOU CAN'T TAKE IT WITH YOU
Director: Frank Capra
Co-stars: Jean Arthur James Stewart Ann Miller

1938 EXTORTION
Co-stars: Gene Morgan J. Farrell MacDonald Frank Wilson

1938 BLONDIE
Director: Frank Strayer
Co-stars: Arthur Lake Penny Singleton Larry Simms

1941 DIVE BOMBER
Director: Michael Curtiz
Co-stars: Errol Flynn Fred MacMurray Alexis Smith Ralph Bellamy

1941 PENNY SERENADE
Director: George Stevens
Co-stars: Irene Dunne Cary Grant Edgar Buchanan Beulah Bondi

1941 MEET JOHN DOE
Director: Frank Capra
Co-stars: Gary Cooper Barbara Stanwyck Edward Arnold

1944 HERE COME THE WAVES
Director: Mark Sandrich
Co-stars: Bing Crosby Betty Hutton Sonny Tufts

1944 I LOVE A SOLDIER
Director: Mark Sandrich
Co-stars: Paulette Goddard Sonny Tufts Beulah Bondi

1945 PRIDE OF THE MARINES
Director: Delmer Daves
Co-stars: John Garfield Eleanor Parker Dane Clark

1947 MAGIC TOWN
Director: William Wellman
Co-stars: James Stewart Jane Wyman Kent Smith Wallace Ford

1947 SECOND CHANCE
Co-stars: Kent Taylor Louise Currie Dennis Hoey

1947 FEAR IN THE NIGHT
Director: Maxwell Shane
Co-stars: Paul Kelly DeForrest Kelley Kay Scott

1948 PITFALL
Director: Andre De Toth
Co-stars: Dick Powell Lisabeth Scott Jane Wyatt Raymond Burr

1948 CALAMITY JANE AND SAM BASS
Director: Gearge Sherman
Co-stars: Yvonne De Carlo Howard Duff

1951 LOVE IS BETTER THAN EVER
Director: Stanley Donen
Co-stars: Elizabeth Taylor Larry Parks Tom Tully

1951 THE PAINTED HILLS
Director: Harold Kress
Co-stars: Paul Kelly Bruce Cowling Gary Gray Art Smith

1954 THE BOB MATHIAS STORY
Director: Frances Lyon
Co-stars: Melba Mathias Ward Bond Bob Mathias

1955 REBEL WITHOUT A CAUSE
Director: Nicholas Ray
Co-stars: James Dean Jim Backus Natalie Wood

1957 THE MAN WHO TURNED TO STONE
Director: Leslie Kardos
Co-stars: Victor Jory Charlotte Austin

1958 THE VOICE IN THE MIRROR
Director: Harry Keller
Co-stars: Richard Egan Julie London Walter Matthau

1958 IT! THE TERROR FROM BEYOND SPACE
Director: Edward Cahn
Co-stars: Marshall Thompson Shawn Smith

1964 THE BRASS BOTTLE
Director: Robert Arthur
Co-stars: Tony Randall Burl Ives Barbara Eden Edward Andrews

1981 ALL NIGHT LONG
Director: Jean-Claude Tramont
Co-stars: Barbra Streisand Gene Hackman Diane Ladd

MARY DORAN

1930 THE DIVORCEE
Director: Robert Z. Leonard
Co-stars: Norma Shearer Chester Morris Conrad Nagel

1931 THE CRIMINAL CODE
Director: Howard Hawks
Co-stars: Walter Huston Phillips Holmes Constance Cummings

1932 MISS PINKERTON
Director: Lloyd Bacon
Co-stars: Joan Blondell George Brent Mae Madison

1932   EXPOSURE
Co-stars: Walter Byron Tully Marshall Pat O'Malley

ADRIENNE DORE

1929   THE WILD PARTY
Director: Dorothy Arzner
Co-stars: Clara Bow Fredric March Shirley O'Hara

1932   THE RICH ARE ALWAYS WITH US
Director: Alfred Green
Co-stars: Ruth Chatterton George Brent Bette Davis

1932   THE FAMOUS FERGUSON CASE
Director: Lloyd Bacon
Co-stars: Joan Blondell Tom Brown

EDNA DORE

1988   HIGH HOPES
Director: Mike Leigh
Co-stars: Philip Davis Ruth Sheen David Bamber

1991   GAS AND CANDLES
Director: Alvin Rakoff
Co-stars: Bert Parnaby Leslie Sands Mark Lewis Jones

MARTA DORFF

1950   MISS JULIE
Director: Alf Sjoberg
Co-stars: Anita Bjork Ulf Palme Max Von Sydow

ANGELA DORIAN

1967   CHUKA
Director: Gordon Douglas
Co-stars: Rod Taylor Ernest Borgnine John Mills

1968   ROSEMARY'S BABY
Director: Roman Polanski
Co-stars: Mia Farrow John Cassavetes Ruth Gordon

FRANCOISE DORLEAC

1964   SILKEN SKIN
Director: Francois Truffaut
Co-stars: Jean Desailly Nelly Benedetti

1964   GENGHIS KHAN
Director: Henry Levin
Co-stars: Omar Sharif Stephen Boyd James Mason

1964   THAT MAN FROM RIO
Director: Philippe De Broca
Co-stars: Jean-Paul Belmondo Jean Servais Adolfo Celi

1966   CUL-DE-SAC
Director: Roman Polanski
Co-stars: Lionel Stander Jack MacGowran Donald Pleasence

1966   WHERE THE SPIES ARE
Director: Val Guest
Co-stars: David Niven Cyril Cusack Nigel Davenport

1967   BILLION DOLLAR BRAIN
Director: Ken Russell
Co-stars: Michael Caine Oscar Homolka Karl Malden

1967   THE YOUNG GIRLS OF ROCHEFORT
Director: Jacques Demy
Co-stars: Catherine Deneuvre Gene Kelly

DOLORES DORN

1954   PHANTOM OF THE RUE MORGUE
Director: Roy Del Ruth
Co-stars: Karl Malden Claude Dauphin Steve Forrest

1954   THE BOUNTY HUNTER
Director: Andre De Toth
Co-stars: Randolph Scott Marie Windsor Ernest Borgnine

1958   UNCLE VANYA
Co-Star: Franchot Tone

1961   UNDERWORLD U.S.A.
Director: Samuel Fuller
Co-stars: Cliff Robertson Beatrice Kay Larry Gates

1962   13, WEST STREET
Director: Philip Leacock
Co-stars: Alan Ladd Rod Steiger Michael Callan

1974   TRUCK STOP WOMEN
Director: Mark Lester
Co-stars: Claudia Jennings John Martino

1980   TELL ME A RIDDLE
Director: Lee Grant
Co-stars: Lila Kedrova Melvyn Douglas Brooke Adams

SANDRA DORNE

1950   HAPPY GO LOVELY
Director: Bruce Humberstone
Co-stars: David Niven Vera-Ellen Cesar Romero

1952   HINDLE WAKES
Director: Arthur Crabtree
Co-stars: Lisa Daniely Leslie Dwyer Brian Worth

1952   THE BEGGAR'S OPERA
Director: Peter Brook
Co-stars: Laurence Olivier Stanley Holloway Dorothy Tutin

1952   13, EAST STREET
Director: Robert Baker
Co-stars: Patrick Holt Sonia Holm Dora Bryan

1953   WHEEL OF FATE
Director: Frank Searle
Co-stars: Patric Doonan Bryan Forbes John Horsley

1953   MARILYN
Director: Wolf Rilla
Co-stars: Maxwell Reed Leslie Dwyer

1955   POLICE DOG
Director: Derek Twist
Co-stars: Joan Rice Tim Turner Charles Victor

1956   THE GELIGNITE GANG
Director: Terence Fisher
Co-stars: Wayne Morris James Kenney Patrick Holt

1958   THE BANK RAIDERS
Director: Maxwell Munden
Co-stars: Peter Reynolds Sydney Tafler Rose Hill

1964   DEVIL DOLL
Director   Lindsay Shonteff
Co-stars   Bryant Halliday William Sylvester Yvonne Romain

1972   ALL COPPERS ARE
Director: Sidney Hayers
Co-stars: Nicky Henson Julia Foster Ian Hendry

KATE DORNING

1976   THE COPTER KIDS
Director: Ronnie Spender
Co-stars: Sophie Neville Sophie Ward Paul Chambers

SARAH ROWLAND DOROFF (Child)

1989   THREE FUGITIVES
Director: Francis Veber
Co-stars: Nick Nolte Martin Short James Earl Jones

DOROTHEE

1979   LOVE ON THE RUN
Director: Francois Truffaut
Co-stars: Jean-Pierre Leaud Claude Jade Marie-France Pisier

DIANA DORS

1946 THE SHOP AT SLY CORNER
Director: George King
Co-stars: Oscar Homolka Muriel Pavlow Derek Farr

1947 DANCING WITH CRIME
Director: John Paddy Carstairs
Co-stars: Richard Attenborough Shelia Sim Barry K. Barnes

1947 A BOY, A GIRL AND A BIKE
Director: Ralph Smart
Co-stars: John McCallum Honor Blackman Anthony Newley

1948 GOOD TIME GIRL
Director: David McDonald
Co-stars: Jean Kent Dennis Price Bonar Colleano

1948 HERE COME THE HUGGETTS
Director: Ken Annakin
Co-stars: Jack Warner Kathleen Harrison Susan Shaw

1948 THE CALENDAR
Director: Arthur Crabtree
Co-stars: Greta Gynt Johm McCallum Sonia Holm

1948 OLIVER TWIST
Director: David Lean
Co-stars: Alec Guinness Robert Newton Anthony Newley

1949 VOTE FOR HUGGETT
Director: Ken Annakin
Co-stars: Petula Clark David Tomlinson Jack Warner

1949 DIAMOND CITY
Director: David MacDonald
Co-stars: David Farrar Honor Blackman Ann Crawford

1950 DANCE HALL
Director: Charles Crighton
Co-stars: Natasha Parry Petula Clark Bonar Colleano

1951 LADY GODIVA RIDES AGAIN
Director: Frank Launder
Co-stars: Pauline Stroud Dennis Price Violet Prety

1951 WORM EYE'S VIEW
Director: Jack Raymond
Co-stars: Ronald Shiner Garry Marsh John Blythe

1952 THE LAST PAGE
Director: Terence Fisher
Co-stars: George Brent Marguerite Chapman

1952 THE GREAT GAME
Director: Maurice Elvey
Co-stars: James Hayter Glyn Houston Thora Hird

1953 IT'S A GRAND LIFE
Director: John Blakeley
Co-stars: Frank Randle Jennifer Jayne Dan Young

1953 THE WEAK AND THE WICKED
Director: J. Lee-Thompson
Co-stars: Glynis Johns John Gregson Jane Hylton

1955 VALUE FOR MONEY
Director: Ken Annakin
Co-stars: John Gregson Susan Stephen Derek Farr

1955 A KID FOR TWO FARTHINGS
Director: Carol Reed
Co-stars: Celia Johnson Joe Robinson David Kossoff

1955 AN ALLIGATOR NAMED DAISY
Director: J. Lee-Thompson
Co-stars: Donald Sinden Jean Carson Stanley Holloway

1955 AS LONG AS THEY'RE HAPPY
Director: J. Lee-Thompson
Co-stars: Jack Buchanan Jean Carson Janette Scott

1956 I MARRIED A WOMAN
Director: Hal Kanter
Co-stars: George Gobel Adolphe Menjou Jessie Royce-Landis

1956 YIELD TO THE NIGHT
Director: J. Lee-Thompson
Co-stars: Yvonne Mitchell Michael Craig Athene Seyler

1957 THE UNHOLY WIFE
Director: John Farrow
Co-stars: Rod Steiger Tom Tryon Beulah Bondi Marie Windsor

1958 TREAD SOFTLY STRANGER
Director: Gordon Parry
Co-stars: George Baker Terence Morgan Wilfrid Lawson

1959 PASSPORT TO SHAME
Director: Alvin Rakoff
Co-stars: Eddie Constantine Odile Versois Herbert Lom

1959 SCENT OF MYSTERY
Director: Jack Cardiff
Co-stars: Denholm Elliott Peter Lorre Paul Lukas

1961 KING OF THE ROARING 20S
Director: Joseph Newman
Co-stars: David Janssen Mickey Rooney Jack Carson

1961 ON THE DOUBLE
Director: Melville Shavelson
Co-stars: Danny Kaye Margaret Rutherford

1962 MRS. GIBBON'S BOYS
Director: Max Varnel
Co-stars: Kathleen Harrison Lionel Jeffries Dick Emery

1963 WEST 11
Director: Michael Winner
Co-stars: Alfred Lynch Eric Portman Kathleen Harrison

1966 THE SANDWICH MAN
Director: Robert Hartford-Davis
Co-stars: Michael Bentine Norman Wisdom

1967 BERSERK
Director: Jim O'Connolly
Co-stars: Joan Crawford Robert Hardy Ty Hardin

1967 DANGER ROUTE
Director: Seth Holt
Co-stars: Richard Johnson Sylvia Syms Sam Wanamaker

1968 HAMMERHEAD
Director: David Miller
Co-stars: Vince Edwards Peter Vaughan Judy Geeson

1968 BABY LOVE
Director: Alastair Reid
Co-stars: Linda Hayden Keith Barron Dick Emery

1970 THERE'S A GIRL IN MY SOUP
Director: Roy Boulting
Co-stars: Peter Sellers Goldie Hawn John Comer

1970 DEEP END
Director: Jerzy Skolimowski
Co-stars: Jane Asher John Moulder-Brown

1971 HANNIE CAULDER
Director: Burt Kennedy
Co-stars: Raquel Welch Robert Culp Ernest Borgnine

1972 THE PIED PIPER
Director: Jacques Demy
Co-stars: Donovan Jack Wild Donald Pleasence

1972 THE AMAZING MR.BLUNDEN
Director: Lionel Jeffries
Co-stars: Laurence Naismith Lynne Frederick

1972 NOTHING BUT THE NIGHT
Director: Peter Sasdy
Co-stars: Christopher Lee Peter Cushing Keith Barron

1973 THEATRE OF BLOOD
Director: Douglas Hickox
Co-stars: Vincent Price Jack Hawkins Diana Rigg

1973 STEPTOE AND SON RIDE AGAIN
Director: Peter Sykes
Co-stars: Harry H. Corbett Wilfred Bramble Bill Maynard

1973 FROM BEYOND THE GRAVE
Director: Kevin Connor
Co-stars: Peter Cushing David Warner Ian Bannen

1974 CRAZE
Director: Freddie Francis
Co-stars: Jack Palance Julie Ege Edith Evans

1976 THE AMOROUS MILKMAN
Director: Derren Nesbitt
Co-stars: Julie Ege Brendon Price Roy Kinnear Megs Jenkins

1976 ADVENTURES OF A TAXI DRIVER
Director: Stanley Long
Co-stars: Barry Evans Judy Geeson Adrienne Posta Liz Fraser

1976 KEEP IT UP DOWNSTAIRS

1977 ADVENTURES OF A PRIVATE EYE
Director: Stanley Long
Co-stars: Christopher Neil Suzy Kendall Harry H. Corbett Liz Fraser

1984 STEAMING
Director: Joseph Losey
Co-stars: Vanessa Redgrave Sarah Miles Brenda Bruce

FIFI D'ORSAY

1930 WOMEN EVERYWHERE
Co-Star Harold Murray

1931 YOUNG AS YOU FEEL
Director: Frank Borzage
Co-stars: Will Rogers Lucien Littlefield Donald Dillaway

1931 WOMEN OF ALL NATIONS
Director: Raoul Walsh
Co-stars: Edmund Lowe Victor McLaglen Greta Nissen

1933 THEY JUST HAD TO GET MARRIED
Director: Edward Ludwig
Co-stars: Zasu Pitts Slim Summerville

1933 THE LIFE OF JIMMY DOLAN
Director: Archie Mayo
Co-stars: Douglas Fairbanks Jnr. Loretta Young

1933 GOING HOLLYWOOD
Director: Raoul Walsh
Co-stars: Bing Crosby Marion Davies Patsy Kelly

1934 WONDER BAR
Director: Lloyd Bacon
Co-stars: Al Jolson Kay Francis Dolores Del Rio Dick Powell

SANDRA DORSEY

1980 ANGEL CITY
Director: Philip Leacock
Co-stars: Ralph Waite Jennifer Jason Leigh, Paul Winfield

GLORIA DORSON

1991 DANIELLE STEEL'S DADDY
Director: Michael Miller
Co-stars: Patrick Duffy Lynda Carter Kate Mulgrew

GABRIELLE DORZIAT

1939 LA FIN DU JOUR
Director: Julien Duvivier
Co-stars: Victor Francen Louis Jouvet Michel Simon

1943 LE BARON FANTOME
Director: Serge De Poligny
Co-stars: Jany Holt Odette Joyeux Alain Cuny

1948 LES PARENTS TERRIBLES
Director: Jean Cocteau
Co-stars: Jean Marais Yvonne De Bray Josette Day

1949 MANON
Director: Henri-Georges Clouzot
Co-stars: Cecile Aubry Michel Auclair Serge Reggiani

1950 TOMORROW IS TOO LATE
Director: Leonide Moguy
Co-stars: Vittorio De Sica Lois Maxwell Pier Angeli

1952 SO LITTLE TIME
Director: Compton Bennett
Co-stars: Marius Goring Maria Schell Barbara Mullen

1953 LITTLE BOY LOST
Director: George Seaton
Co-stars: Bing Crosby Claude Dauphin Nicole Maurey

1954 ACT OF LOVE
Director: Anatole Litvak
Co-stars: Kirk Douglas Dany Robin Brigitte Bardot

1957 LES ESPIONS
Director: Henri-Georges Clouzot
Co-stars: Martita Hunt Peter Ustinov Sam Jaffe

1962 GIGOT
Director: Gene Kelly
Co-stars: Jackie Gleason Katherine Kath Jean Lefebvre

1962 A MONKEY IN WINTER
Director: Henri Verneuil
Co-stars: Jean Gabin Jean-Paul Belmondo Suzanne Flon

1965 THOMAS L'IMPOSTEUR
Director: Georges Franju
Co-stars: Emmanuele Riva Jean Servais Edith Scob

KAREN DOTRICE *(Child) (Daughter Of Roy Dotrice Sister Of Michelle Dotrice)*

1963 THE THREE LIVES OF THOMASINA
Director: Don Chaffey
Co-stars: Susan Hampshire Patrick McGoohan

1964 MARY POPPINS
Director: Robert Stevenson
Co-stars: Julie Andrews Dick Van Dyke Glynis Johns

1967 THE GNOME-MOBILE
Director: Robert Stevenson
Co-stars: Walter Brennan Matthew Garber Ed Wynn

1977 JOSEPH ANDREWS
Director: Tony Richardson
Co-stars: Peter Firth Ann-Margret Hugh Griffith

1978 SHE FELL AMONG THIEVES
Director: Clive Donner
Co-stars: Malcolm McDowell Eileen Atkins Sarah Badel

1978 THE THIRTY-NINE STEPS
Director: Don Sharp
Co-stars: Robert Powell John Mills Eric Porter

MICHELE DOTRICE
(Daughter Of Roy Dotrice Sister Of Karen Dotrice)

1966 THE WITCHES
Director: Cyril Frankel
Co-stars: Joan Fontaine Kay Walsh Leonard Rossiter

1970 BLOOD ON SATAN'S CLAW
Director: Piers Haggard
Co-stars: Patrick Wymark Linda Hayden Tamara Ustinov

1970 AND SOON THE DARKNESS
Director: Robert Fuest
Co-stars: Pamela Franklin Sandor Eles Clare Kelly

1977 NOT NOW, COMRADE
Director: Ray Cooney
Co-stars: Leslie Phillips Roy Kinnear Don Estelle

CATHERINE DOUCET

1934 LITTLE MAN, WHAT NOW?
Director: Frank Borzage
Co-stars: Margaret Sullavan Douglass Montgomery

1934 AS HUSBANDS GO
Director: Hamilton McFadden
Co-stars: Warner Baxter Helen Vinson Warner Oland

1934 THE PARTY'S OVER
Co-stars: Ann Sothern Stuart Erwin Henry Travers

1935 RENDEZVOUS AT MIDNIGHT
Director: Christy Cabanne
Co-stars: Ralph Bellamy Valerie Hobson Irene Ware

1936 POPPY
Director: Edward Sutherland
Co-stars: W.C. Fields Rochelle Hudson Richard Cromwell

1936 THESE THREE
Director: William Wyler
Co-stars: Merle Oberon Miriam Hopkins Joel McCrea

1936 THE LUCKIEST GIRL IN THE WORLD
Director: Eddie Buzzell
Co-stars: Jane Wyatt Louis Hayward

1937 WHEN YOU'RE IN LOVE
Director: Robert Riskin
Co-stars: Grace Moore Cary Grant Thomas Mitchell

1937 MAN OF THE PEOPLE
Director: Edwin Marin
Co-stars: Joseph Calleia Thomas Mitchell Florence Rice

1941 NOTHING BUT THE TRUTH
Director: Elliott Nugent
Co-stars: Bob Hope Paulette Goddard Edward Arnold

ANGELA DOUGLAS *(Married Kenneth More)*

1962 SOME PEOPLE
Director: Clive Donner
Co-stars: Kenneth More Ray Brooks David Hemmings

1963 IT'S ALL HAPPENING
Director: Don Sharp
Co-stars: Tommy Steele Michael Medwin Bernard Bresslaw

1964 THE COMEDY MAN
Director: Alvin Rakoff
Co-stars: Kenneth More Cecil Parker Dennis Price

1965 CARRY ON COWBOY
Director: Gerald Thomas
Co-stars: Sid James Jim Dale Kenneth Williams

1966 CARRY ON SCREAMING
Director: Gerald Thomas
Co-stars: Harry H. Corbett Fenella Fielding Jim Dale

1967 MAROC 7
Director: Gerry O'Hara
Co-stars: Gene Barry Elsa Martinelli Cyd Charisse

1967 CARRY ON, FOLLOW THAT CAMEL
Director: Gerald Thomas
Co-stars: Phil Silvers Anita Harris Joan Sims

1968 CARRY ON UP THE KHYBER
Director: Gerald Thomas
Co-stars: Sid James Roy Castle Terry Scott

1973 DIGBY: THE BIGGEST DOG IN THE WORLD
Director: Joseph McGrath
Co-stars: Jim Dale Spike Milligan

1991 MISTERIOSO
Director: John Glenister
Co-stars: Jack Shepherd Suzan Sylvester Sharon Duce

DIANA DOUGLAS *(Married Kirk Douglas Mother Of Michael Douglas)*

1949 HOUSE OF STRANGERS
Director: Joseph Mankiewicz
Co-stars: Edward G. Robinson Susan Hayward Luther Adler

1951 STORM OVER TIBET
Director: Andrew Marton
Co-stars: Rex Reason Myron Healey

1955 THE INDIAN FIGHTER
Director: Andre De Toth
Co-stars: Kirk Douglas Elsa Martinelli Walter Matthau

DONNA DOUGLAS

1966 FRANKIE AND JOHNNIE
Director: Frederick De Cordova
Co-stars: Elvis Presley Harry Morgan Nancy Kovack

HAZEL DOUGLAS

1993 CLOSING NUMBERS
Director: Stephen Whittaker
Co-stars: Jane Asher Tim Woodward Patrick Pearson

ILLEANA DOUGLAS

1991 CAPE FEAR
Director: Martin Scorsese
Co-stars: Robert De Niro Nick Nolte Jessica Lange

1993 GRIEF
Director: Richard Glatzer
Co-stars: Craig Chester Jackie Best Lucy Gutteridge

1995 TO DIE FOR
Director: Gus Van Sant
Co-stars: Nicole Kidman Matt Dillon

1997 GRACE OF MY HEART
Director: Allison Ander
Co-stars: Patsy Kensit Matt Dillon John Turturro

1998 PICTURE PERFECT
Director Glenn Gordon Caron
Co-stars Jennifer Aniston Kevin Bacon Jay Mohr

1998 BELLA MAFIA
Co-star: Vanessa Redgrave Nastassja Kinski Jennifer Tilly

JOSEPHINE DOUGLAS

1958 6:5 SPECIAL
Director: Alfred Shaughnessy
Co-stars: Pete Murray Diane Todd Finlay Currie

SALLY DOUGLAS

1965 CARRY ON COWBOY
Director: Gerald Thomas
Co-stars: Sid James Jim Dale Angela Douglas

SARAH DOUGLAS

1977 THE PEOPLE THAT TIME FORGOT
Director: Kevin Connor
Co-stars: Patrick Wayne Doug McClure

1980 SUPERMAN II
Director: Richard Lester
Co-stars: Christopher Reeve Gene Hackman Margot Kidder

1984 CONAN THE DESTROYER
Director: Richard Fleischer
Co-stars: Arnold Schwarzeneggar Grace Jones

1986 SOLAR WARRIORS
Director: Alan Johnson
Co-stars: Richard Jordan Jami Gertz Jason Patric Lukas Haas

1989 THE RETURN OF SWAMP THING
Director: Jim Wynorski
Co-stars: Louis Jourdan Heather Locklear

1991 BEASTMASTER 2:
THROUGH THE PORTAL OF TIME
Director: Sylvia Tabet
Co-stars: Marc Singer Kari Wuhrer Wings Hauser

1991 PUPPET MASTER 3: TOULON'S REVENGE
Director: David De Cotean
Co-stars: Guy Rolfe Richard Lynch Walter Gotell

1992 MEATBALLS 4
Director: Bob Logan
Co-stars: Corey Feldman Jack Nance

1993 RETURN OF THE LIVING DEAD 3
Director: Brian Yuzna
Co-stars: J. Trevor Edmund Mindy Clarke Kent McCord

SHARON DOUGLAS

1945 FOG ISLAND
Director: Terry Morse
Co-stars: George Zucco Lionel Atwill Jerome Cowan

SHIRLEY DOUGLAS

1961 LOLITA
Director Stanley Kubrick
Co-stars James Mason Sue Lyon Shelley Winters

1988 DEAD RINGERS
Director: David Cronenberg
Co-stars: Jeremy Irons Genevieve Bujold Barbara Gordon

SUSAN DOUGLAS

1947 THE PRIVATE AFFAIRS OF BEL AMI
Director: Albert Lewin
Co-stars: George Sanders Angela Lansbury

1949 LOST BOUNDARIES
Director: Alfred Werker
Co-stars: Mel Ferrer Beatrice Pearson Canada Lee

1951 FIVE
Director: Arch Obeler
Co-stars: William Phipps James Anderson Earl Lee

SUZANNE DOUGLAS

1989 TAP
Director: Nick Castle
Co-stars: Gregory Hines Sammy Davis Jnr. Joe Morton

JUDIE DOUGLASS

1984 CONSTANCE
Director: Bruce Morrison
Co-stars: Donogh Rees Shane Briant Martin Vaughan

1993 ABSENT WITHOUT LEAVE
Director: John Laing
Co-stars: Craig McLachlan Tony Barry Katrina Hobbs

ROBYN DOUGLASS

1979 BREAKING AWAY
Director: Peter Yates
Co-stars: Dennis Christopher Dennis Quaid Barbara Barrie

1981 GOLDEN GATE
Director: Paul Wendkos
Co-stars: Jean Simmons Richard Kiley Melanie Griffith

1982 PARTNERS
Director: James Burrows
Co-stars: Ryan O'Neal John Hurt Kenneth McMillan

1983 ROMANTIC COMEDY
Director: Arthur Hiller
Co-stars: Dudley Moore Mary Steenburgen Frances Sternhagen

1984 HER LIFE AS A MAN
Director: Robert Ellis Miller
Co-stars: Robert Culp Marc Singer Joan Collins

1984 THE LONELY GUY
Director: Arthur Hiller
Co-stars: Steve Martin Charles Grodin Judith Ivey

MARIE-LAURE DOUGNAC

1991 DELCATESSEN
Director: Marc Caro
Co-stars: Dominique Pinon Jean-Claude Dreyfus Karin Ward

SUSAN DOUKAS

1982 LIQUID SKY
Director: Slava Tsukerman
Co-stars: Anne Carlisle Paula Sheppard Bob Brady

ANNA DOUKING

1971 JUSTE AVANT LA NUIT
Director: Claude Chabrol
Co-stars: Stephane Audran Michel Bouquet

BILLIE DOVE (MARRIED HOWARD HUGHES) 2ND HUSBAND

1926 THE BLACK DOVE

1928 ADMIRATION

1930 SWEETHEARTS AND WIVES
Co-Star William Haines

1930 PAINTED ANGEL

1930 THE OTHER TOMORROW
Co-Star Kenneth Thomson

1930 NOTORIOUS AFFAIR

1931 THE AGE FOR LOVE
Director: Frank Lloyd
Co-stars: Adrian Morris Charles Starrett Lois Wilson

1931 THE LADY WHO DARED

1932 BLONDIE OF THE FOLLIES
Director: Edmund Goulding
Co-stars: Marion Davies Robert Montgomery Zasu Pitts

1932 COCK OF THE AIR
Co-stars: Chester Morris Matt Moore

PEGGY DOW

1949 UNDERTOW
Director: William Castle
Co-stars: Scott Brady John Russell Dorothy Hart

1949 WOMAN IN HIDING
Director: Michael Gordon
Co-stars: Ida Lupino Howard Duff Stephen McNally

1950 THE SLEEPING CITY
Director: George Sherman
Co-stars: Richard Conte Coleen Gray Alex Nicol

1950 HARVEY
Director: Henry Koster
Co-stars: James Stewart Josephine Hull Cecil Kellaway

1951 I WANT YOU
Director: Mark Robson
Co-stars: Dorothy McGuire Dana Andrews Farley Granger

1951 BRIGHT VICTORY
Director: Mark Robson
Co-stars: Arthur Kennedy Julie Adams James Edwards

1951 YOU NEVER CAN TELL
Director: Lou Breslow
Co-stars: Dick Powell Charles Drake Joyce Holden

1959 SHAKEDOWN
Director: Joseph Pevney
Co-stars: Howard Duff Brian Donlevy Anne Vernon

FREDA DOWIE

1988 DISTANT VOICES, STILL LIVES
Director: Terence Davies
Co-stars: Pete Postlethwaite Angela Walsh

CONSTANCE DOWLING

1944 KNICKERBOCKER HOLIDAY
Director: Harry Joe Brown
Co-stars: Nelson Eddy Charles Coburn

1944 UP IN ARMS
Director: Elliott Nugent
Co-stars: Danny Kaye Dinah Shore Dana Andrews Louis Calhern

1946 BLACK ANGEL
Director: Roy William Neill
Co-stars: Dan Duryea June Vincent Peter Lorre

1946 THE WELL-GROOMED BRIDE
Director: Sidney Lanfield
Co-stars: Ray Milland Olivia De Havilland Sonny Tufts

1947 THE FLAME
Director: John Auer
Co-stars: Vera Ralston John Carroll Robert Paige Henry Travers

1954 GOG
Director: Herbert Strock
Co-stars: Richard Egan Herbert Marshall

DORIS DOWLING

1945 THE LOST WEEKEND
Director: Billy Wilder
Co-stars: Ray Milland Jane Wyman Howard Da Silva

1946 THE BLUE DAHLIA
Director: George Marshall
Co-stars: Alan Ladd William Bendix Veronica Lake

1949 BITTER RICE
Director: Giuseppe De Santis
Co-stars: Silvana Mangano Raf Vallone Vittorio Gassman

1951 OTHELLO
Co-stars: Orson Welles
Director: Orson Welles Michael MacLiammoir Robert Coote

1966 BIRDS DO IT
Director: Andrew Marton
Co-stars: Soupey Sales Tab Hunter Arthur O'Connell

JOAN DOWLING (Child)

1946 HUE AND CRY
Director: Charles Crichton
Co-stars: Alastair Sim Jack Warner Harry Fowler

1948 NO ROOM AT THE INN
Director: Dan Birt
Co-stars: Freda Jackson Joy Shelton Hermoine Baddeley

1948 FOR THEM THAT TRESPASS
Director: Alberto Cavalcanti
Co-stars: Richard Todd Patricia Plunkett

1949 TRAIN OF EVENTS
Director: Charles Crichton
Co-stars: Valerie Hobson John Clements Susan Shaw

1949 LANDFALL
Director: Ken Annakin
Co-stars: Michael Dennison Patricia Plunkett Kathleen Harrison

1950 POOL OF LONDON
Director: Basil Dearden
Co-stars: Bonar Colleano Susan Shaw Renee Asherson

1950 MURDER WITHOUT CRIME
Director: J. Lee Thompson
Co-stars: Dennis Price Derek Farr Patricia Plunkett

1952 WOMEN OF TWILIGHT
Director: Gordon Parry
Co-stars: Freda Jackson Rene Ray Lois Maxwell

KATHRYN DOWLING

1982 DINER
Director: Barry Levinson
Co-stars: Steve Guttenberg Mickey Rourke Ellen Barkin

RACHEL DOWLING

1987 THE DEAD
Director: John Huston
Co-stars: Anjelica Huston Donal McCann Dan O'Herlihy

ANGELA DOWN

1974 MAHLER
Director Ken Russell
Co-stars Robert Powell Georgina Hale Lee Montague

1989 CLOWNS
Director: David Mahoney
Co-stars: Harry Andrews Stephen Moore Robbie Engels

1996 EMMA
Director Douglas McGrath
Co-stars Gwyneth Paltrow Jeremy Northam Greta Scacchi

LESLEY-ANNE DOWN

1969 THE SMASHING BIRD I USED TO KNOW
Director: Robert Hartford-Davis
Co-stars: Madeline Hinde Maureen Lipman Dennis Waterman

1971 ASSAULT
Director: Sidney Hayers
Co-stars: Frank Finlay Suzy Kendall James Laurenson Freddie Jones

1971 COUNTESS DRACULA
Director: Peter Sasdy
Co-stars: Ingrid Pitt Nigel Green Sandor Eles

1972 POPE JOAN
Director: Michael Anderson
Co-stars: Liv Ullmann Trevor Howard Franco Nero Mario Schel

1973 SCALAWAG
Director: Kirk Douglas
Co-stars: Kirk Douglas Mark Lester Neville Brand David Stroud

1975 BRANNIGAN
Director: Douglas Hickox
Co-stars: John Wayne Judy Geeson Mel Ferrer John Stride

1976 THE PINK PANTHER STRIKES AGAIN
Director: Blake Edwards
Co-stars: Peter Sellers Leonard Rossiter Herbert Lom

1977 A LITTLE NIGHT MUSIC
Director: Hal Prince
Co-stars: Elizabeth Taylor Diana Rigg Len Cariou

1977 THE BETSY
Director: Daniel Petrie
Co-stars: Laurence Olivier Robert Duvall Katharine Ross

1978 THE FIRST GREAT TRAIN ROBBERY
Director: Michael Crighton
Co-stars: Sean Connery Donald Sutherland

1979 HANOVER STREET
Director: Peter Hyams
Co-stars: Harrison Ford Christopher Plummer Patsy Kensit

1980 ROUGH CUT
Director: Don Siegel
Co-stars: Burt Reynolds David Niven Timothy West Joss Ackland

1980 SPHINX
Director: Franklin Schaffner
Co-stars: Frank Langella Maurice Ronet John Gielgud

1982 MURDER IS EASY
Director: Claude Whatham
Co-stars: Bill Bixby Olivia De Havilland Helen Hayes

1985 NOMADS
Director: John McTiernan
Co-stars: Pierce Brosnan Anna Maria Montegelli Adam Ant

1989 NIGHT WALK
Director: Jerold Freedman
Co-stars: Robert Ryan Mark Joy Bert Remsen

1989 LADYKILLERS
Director: Robert Lewis
Co-stars: Marilu Henner Susan Blakely Thomas Calabro

1993 DEATH WISH 5: THE FACE OF DEATH
Director: Allan Goldstein
Co-stars: Charles Bronson Michael Parks Ken Walsh

1995 MUNCHIE STRIKES BACK
Director Jim Wynorski

1996 THE SECRET AGENT CLUB
Co-Star Hulk Hogan

CATHY DOWNES

1981 WINTER OF OUR DREAMS
Director: John Dulgan
Co-stars: Judy Davis Bryan Brown Peter Mochrie

ANNE DOWNIE

1991 AND THE COW JUMPED OVER THE MOON
Director: Penny Cherns
Co-stars: Phyllis Logan Elaine Collins

MOIRA DOWNIE

1986 DEATH IS PART OF THE PROCESS
Director: Bill Hays
Co-stars: Art Malik Jack Klapp Estelle Kohler

PENNY DOWNIE

1991 EX
Director: Paul Seed
Co-stars: Griff Rhys Jones Geraldine James Dermot Crowley

1991 STANLEY AND THE WOMEN
Director: David Tucker
Co-stars: John Thaw Geraldine James Sheila Gish

1991 UNDERBELLY
Director: Nicholas Renton
Co-stars: David Hayman Tom Wilkinson Christine Kavanagh

1993 INSPECTOR MORSE: DEADLY SLUMBER
Director: Stuart Orme
Co-stars: John Thaw Brian Cox Janet Suzman

CATHY DOWNS

1946 MY DARLING CLEMENTINE
Director: John Ford
Co-stars: Henry Fonda Victor Mature Linda Darnell

1946 THE DARK CORNER
Director: Henry Hathaway
Co-stars: Mark Stevens Clifton Webb Lucille Ball

1948 PANHANDLE
Director: Lesley Selander
Co-stars: Rod Cameron Anne Gwynne Blake Edwards

1948 THE NOOSE HANGS HIGH
Director: Charles Barton
Co-stars: Bud Abbott Lou Costello Joseph Calleia

1950 THE SUNDOWNERS
Director: George Templeton
Co-stars: Robert Preston Robert Sterling Chill Wills

1955 THE BIG TIP OFF
Director: Frank McDonald
Co-stars: Richard Conte Constance Smith Bruce Bennett

1956 THE SHE CREATURE
Director: Edward Cahn
Co-stars: Marla English Tom Conway Chester Morris

1956 THE OKLAHOMA WOMEN
Director Roger Corman
Co-stars Richard Denning Peggie Castle Tudor Owen

1957 THE AMAZING COLOSSAL MAN
Director: Bert Gordon
Co-stars: Glenn Langan William Hudson James Seay

1959 MISSILE TO THE MOON
Director: Richard Cunha
Co-stars: Richard Travis k.t. Stevens

JANE DOWNS

1958 A NIGHT TO REMEMBER
Director: Roy Ward Baker
Co-stars: Kenneth More Ronald Allen Honor Blackman

1988 STARLINGS
Director: David Wheatley
Co-stars: Michael Malony Lynsey Baxter David Ryall

MARIA DOYLE

1991 THE COMMITMENTS
Director: Alan Parker
Co-stars: Robert Arkins Michael Arkins Angeline Ball

MAXINE DOYLE

1934 BABBIT
Director: William Keighley
Co-stars: Guy Kibbee Aline MacMahon Minna Gombell

1934 SIX DAY BIKE RIDER
Director: Lloyd Bacon
Co-stars: Joe E. Brown Frank McHugh Gordon Westcott

1934 STUDENT TOUR
Director: Charles Reisner
Co-stars: Jimmy Durante Charles Butterworth Nelson Eddy

SUSANNAH DOYLE

1993 DIRTYSOMETHING
Director: Carl Prechezer
Co-stars: Bernard Hill Paul Reynolds Rachel Weisz

PAMELA D'PELIA

1991 TED AND VENUS
Director: Bud Cort
Co-stars: Bud Cort Jim Brolin Kim Adams Carol Kane

VALDA Z. DRABLA

1991 SWOON
Director: Tom Kalin
Co-stars: Daniel Schlachet Craig Chester Ron Vawter

1991 NORTH OF VORTEX
Director: Constatine Giannaris
Co-stars: Stavros Zalmas Howard Napper

ELEANORA ROSSI DRAGO

1953 LOVE, SOLDIERS AND WOMEN
Director: Jean Delannoy
Co-stars: Michele Morgan Claudette Colbert Martine Carol

1955 LE AMICHE
Director: Michaelangelo Antonioni
Co-stars: Valentina Cortesa Yvonne Furneaux

1963 LOVE AT TWENTY
Director: Francois Truffaut
Co-stars: Jean-Pierre Leaud Marie-France Pisier

BETSY DRAKE *(Married Cary Grant)*

1948 EVERY GIRL SHOULD BE MARRIED
Director: Don Hartman
Co-stars: Cary Grant Franchot Tone Diana Lynn

1949 DANCING IN THE DARK
Director: Irving Reis
Co-stars: William Powell Mark Stevens Adolphe Menjou

1950 PRETTY BABY
Director: Bretaigne Windust
Co-stars: Dennis Morgan Edmund Gwenn Zachary Scott

1952 ROOM FOR ONE MORE
Director: Norman Taurog
Co-stars: Cary Grant Lurene Tuttle George Winslow

1957 WILL SUCCESS SPOIL ROCK HUNTER?
Director: Frank Tashlin
Co-stars: Jayne Mansfield Tony Randall

1958 NEXT TO NO TIME
Director: Henry Cornelius
Co-stars: Kenneth More Roland Culver Bessie Love

1958 INTENT TO KILL
Director: Jack Cardiff
Co-stars: Richard Todd Herbert Lom Alexander Knox

1965 CLARENCE THE CROSS-EYED LION
Director: Andrew Marton
Co-stars: Marshall Thompson Richard Haydn

CLAUDIA DRAKE

1943 BORDER PATROL
Co-stars: William Boyd Andy Clyde Jay Kirby

1945 BEDSIDE MANNER
Director: Andrew Stone
Co-stars: Ruth Hussey John Carroll Charles Ruggles

1945 DETOUR
Director: Edgar Ulmer
Co-stars: Tom Neal Ann Savage Tim Ryan

1946 THE FACE OF MARBLE
Director: William Beaudine
Co-stars: Joan Carradine Robert Shayne Maris Wrixon

DONA DRAKE

1941 ALOMA OF THE SOUTH SEAS
Director: Alfred Santell
Co-stars: Dorothy Lamour Jon Hall Philip Reed

1941 LOUISIANA PURCHASE
Director: Irving Cummings
Co-stars: Bob Hope Vera Zorina Victor Moore

1942 ROAD TO MOROCCO
Director: David Butler
Co-stars: Bob Hope Dorothy Lamour Bing Crosby

1943 LET'S FACE IT
Director: Sidney Lanfield
Co-stars: Bob Hope Betty Hutton Eve Arden Zasu Pitts

1943 SALUTE FOR THREE
Director: Ralph Murphy
Co-stars: MacDonald Carey Betty Jane Rhodes Marty May

1946 DANGEROUS MILLIONS
Director: James Tingling
Co-stars: Kent Taylor Tala Birell Leonard Strong

1946 WITHOUT RESERVATIONS
Director: Mervyn Le Roy
Co-stars: Claudette Colbert John Wayne Don Defore

1948 ANOTHER PART OF THE FOREST
Director: Michael Gordon
Co-stars: Fredric March Florence Eldridge

1948 SO THIS IS NEW YORK
Director: Richard Fleischer
Co-stars: Henry Morgan Rudy Vallee Virginia Grey

1949 BEYOND THE FOREST
Director: King Vidor
Co-stars: Bette Davis Joseph Cotten David Brian Ruth Roman

1949 THE GIRL FROM JONES BEACH
Director: Peter Godfrey
Co-stars: Ronald Reagan Virginia May Eddie Bracken

1950 FORTUNES OF CAPTAIN BLOOD
Director: Gordon Douglas
Co-stars: Louis Hayward Patricia Medina

1951 THE BANDITS OF CORSICA
Director: Ray Nazarro
Co-stars: Richard Greene Paula Raymond Raymond Burr

1951 VALENTINO
Director: Lewis Allen
Co-stars: Anthony Dexter Eleanor Parker Patricia Medina

1952 KANSAS CITY CONFIDENTIAL
Director: Phil Karlson
Co-stars: Preston Foster John Payne Coleen Gray

1954 PRINCESS OF THE NILE
Director: Harmon Jones
Co-stars: Debra Paget Michael Rennie Jeffrey Hunter

FABIA DRAKE

1938 MEET MR. PENNY
Director: David MacDonald
Co-stars: Richard Goolden Vic Oliver Kay Walsh

1949 ALL OVER THE TOWN
Director: Derek Twist
Co-stars: Norman Wooland Sarah Churchill Cyril Cusack

1957 NOT WANTED ON VOYAGE
Director: MacLean Rogers
Co-stars: Ronald Shiner Brian Rix Katie Boyle

1958 GIRLS AT SEA
Director: Gilbert Gunn
Co-stars: Guy Rolfe Ronald Shiner Michael Hordern

1969 A NICE GIRL LIKE ME
Director: Desmond Davis
Co-stars: Barbara Ferris Harry Andrews Gladys Cooper

1971 TAM-LIN
Director: Roddy MacDowall
Co-stars: Ava Gardner Ian McShane Richard Wattis

1985 LENT
Director: Peter Barber-Fleming
Co-stars: Harry Andrews Constance Chapman David Langton

1985 A ROOM WITH A VIEW
Director James Ivory
Co-stars Maggie Smith Denholm Elliott Helena Bonham-Carter

1989 VALMONT
Director: Milos Forman
Co-stars: Colin Firth Annette Bening Meg Tilly

FRANCES DRAKE
1934 BOLERO
Director: Wesley Ruggles
Co-stars: George Raft Carole Lombard Sally Rand Ray Milland

1934 LADIES SHOULD LISTEN
Director: Frank Tuttle
Co-stars: Cary Grant Rosita Moreno George Barbier

1934 THE TRUMPET BLOWS
Director: Stephen Roberts
Co-stars: George Raft Adolphe Menjou Edward Ellis

1935 LES MISERABLES
Director: Richard Boleslawski
Co-stars: Fredric March Charles Laughton Rochelle Hudson

1935 MAD LOVE
Director: Karl Freund
Co-stars: Peter Lorre Colin Clive Ted Healy Isabel Jewell

1935 THE INVISIBLE RAY
Director: Lambert Hillyer
Co-stars: Boris Karloff Bela Lugosi Frank Lawton

1935 FORSAKING ALL OTHERS
Director: W.S. Van Dyke
Co-stars: Clark Gable Joan Crawford Robert Montgomery

1936 TRANSIENT LADY
Co-stars: Edward Ellis Clarke Williams

1936 AND SUDDEN DEATH
Director: Charles Barton
Co-stars: Randolph Scott Tom Brown Billy Lee

1937 LOVE UNDER FIRE
Director: George Marshall
Co-stars: Loretta Young Don Ameche Walter Catlett

1937 MIDNIGHT TAXI
Director: Eugene Forde
Co-stars: Brian Donlevy Alan Dinehart Gilbert Roland Sig Ruman

1938 SHE MARRIED AN ARTIST
Director: Marion Gering
Co-stars: John Boles Albert Dekker

1938 THERE'S ALWAYS A WOMAN
Director: Alex Hall
Co-stars: Joan Blondell Melvyn Douglas Mary Astor

1938 THE LONE WOLF IN PARIS
Director: Albert Rogell
Co-stars: Francis Lederer Albert Dekker

1939 IT'S A WONDERFUL WORLD
Director: W.S. Van Dyke
Co-stars: James Stewart Claudette Colbert Ernest Truex

1942 THE AFFAIRS OF MARTHA
Director: Jules Dassin
Co-stars: Marsha Hunt Richard Carlson Allyn Joslyn

GABRIELLE DRAKE
1969 CONNECTING ROOMS
Director: Franklin Gollings
Co-stars: Bette Davis Michael Redgrave Alexis Kanner

1972 AU PAIR GIRLS
Director: Val Guest
Co-stars: Richard O'Sullivan Astrid Frank John Le Mesurier

POLLY DRAPER
1993 DANIELLE STEEL'S HEARTBEAT
Director: Michael Miller
Co-Star John Ritter

1993 BROKEN PROMISES: TAKING EMILY BACK
Director: Donald Wyre
Co-stars: Cheryl Ladd Robert Desiderio

1995 SCHEMES
Director Derek Westervelt
Co-star: James McCaffrey

NINA DRAXTEN
1988 FAR NORTH
Director: Sam Shepard
Co-stars: Jessica Lange Tess Harper Charles Durning

FRAN DRESCHER
1978 AMERICAN HOT WAX
Director: Floyd Mutrux
Co-stars: Tim McIntire Laraine Newman Chuck Berry

1989 U.H.F.
Director: Jay Levey
Co-stars: Weird Al Yankovic Victoria Jackson Kevin McCarthy

1990 CADILLAC MAN
Director: Roger Donaldson
Co-stars: Robin Williams Tim Robblns Pamela Reed

1994 CAR 54, WHERE ARE YOU ?
Director Bill Fishman
Co-stars David Johansen John C. McGinley

1997 THE BEAUTICIAN AND THE BEAST
Co-star: Timothy Dalton

SONIA DRESDEL
1944 THE WORLD OWES ME A LIVING
Director: Vernon Sewell
Co-stars: David Farrar Judy Campbell John Laurie

1947 WHILE I LIVE
Director: John Harlow
Co-stars: Tom Walls Carol Raye Clifford Evans

1948 THIS WAS A WOMAN
Director: Tim Whelan
Co-stars: Barbara White Walter Fitzgerald Marjorie Rhodes

1948 THE FALLEN IDOL
Director: Carol Reed
Co-stars: Ralph Richardson Michele Morgan Bobby Henrey

1950 THE CLOUDED YELLOW
Director: Ralph Thomas
Co-stars: Trevor Howard Jean Simmons Barry Jones

1955 NOW AND FOREVER
Director: Mario Zampi
Co-stars: Janette Scott Vernon Gray Pamela Brown

1962 THE BREAK
Director: Lance Comfort
Co-stars: Tony Britton William Lucas Eddie Byrne

LOUISE DRESSER
Nominated For Best Actress In 1928 For "A Ship Comes In"
1923 RUGGLES OF REDGAP
Director: James Cruze
Co-stars: Edward Everett Hortin Ernest Torrence Lois Wilson

1925 THE EAGLE
Director: Clarence Brown
Co-stars: Rudolph Valentino Vilma Banky

1927 MR. WU
Director: William Nigh
Co-stars: Lon Chaney Anna May Wong Renee Adoree Ralph Forbes

1930 LIGHTNIN'
Director: Henry King
Co-stars: Wlll Rogers Joel McCrea Sharon Lynn J.M. Kerrigan

1930 MAMMY
Director: Michael Curtiz
Co-stars: Al Jolson Lowell Sherman Hobart Bosworth

1931 CAUGHT!
Director: Edward Sloman
Co-stars: Richard Arlen Francis Dee Tom Kennedy

1933 CRADLE SONG
Director: Mitchell Leisen
Co-stars: Dorothea Wieck Evelyn Venable Kent Taylor

1933 DR. BULL
Director: John Ford
Co-stars: Will Rogers Vera-Ellen Marian Nixon Andy Devine

1933 BROADWAY BAD
Director: Sidney Lanfield
Co-stars: Ginger Rogers Joan Blondell Ricardo Cortez

1933 SONG OF THE EAGLE
Director: Ralph Murphy
Co-stars: Charles Bickford Richard Arlen Jean Hersholt

1933 STATE FAIR
Director: Henry King
Co-stars: Will Rogers Janet Gaynor Lew Ayres Sally Eilers

1934 THE WORLD MOVES ON
Director: John Ford
Co-stars: Madeleine Carroll Franchot Tone Reginald Denny

1934 SERVANT'S ENTRANCE
Director: Frank Lloyd
Co-stars: Janet Gaynor Lew Ayres Walter Connolly Sig Ruman

1934 THE SCARLETT EMPRESS
Director: Josef Von Sternberg
Co-stars: Marlene Dietrich John Lodge

1934 GIRL OF THE LIMBERLOST
Director: Christy Cabanne
Co-stars: Marian Marsh Ralph Morgan Henry B. Walthall

1934 DAVID HARUM
Director: James Cruze
Co-stars: Will Rogers Evelyn Venable Kent Taylor Stepin Fetchit

1934 THE COUNTY CHAIRMAN
Director: John Blystone
Co-stars: Will Rogers Evelyn Venable Kent Taylor Mickey Rooney

1937 MAID OF SALEM
Director: Frank Lloyd
Co-stars: Claudette Colbert Fred MacMurray Bonita Granville

MARIE DRESSLER
Oscar For Best Actress In 1930 For Min And Bill
Nominated For Best Actress In 1932 For Emma

1914 TILLIE'S PUNCTURED ROMANCE
Director: Mack Sennett
Co-stars: Charles Chaplin Mabel Normand

1915 TILLIE'S TOMATO SURPRISE
Director: Mack Senmett

1916 TILLIE WAKES UP
Director: Mack Sennett

1927 THE PATSY
Director: King Vidor
Co-stars: Marion Davies Del Henderson Jane Winton

1928 BRINGING UP FATHER
Director: Jack Conway
Co-stars: J. Farrell MacDonald Polly Moran Grant Withers

1929 THE VAGABOND LOVER
Co-stars: Sally Blane Rudy Vallee Eddie Nugent

1929 CHASING RAINBOWS
Director: Charles Reisner
Co-stars: Bessie Love Charles King Polly Moran

1929 THE DIVINE LADY
Director: Frank Lloyd
Co-stars: Corinne Griffith Montague Love Victor Varconi

1929 HOLLYWOOD REVUE
Director: Charles Reisner
Co-stars: Norma Shearer John Gilbert Laurel & Hardy Bessie Love

1929 DANGEROUS FEMALES
Co-Star Polly Moran

1930 ANNA CHRISTIE
Director: Clarence Brown
Co-stars: Greta Garbo Charles Bickford James T. Mack

1930 CAUGHT SHORT
Director: Charles Reisner
Co-stars: Polly Moran Charles Morton Anita Page

1930 LET US BE GAY
Director: Robert Z. Leonard
Co-stars: Norma Shearer Rod La Rocque Sally Eilers

1930 MIN AND BILL
Director: George Hill
Co-stars: Wallace Beery Dorothy Jordan Marjorie Rambeau

1931 POLITICS
Director: Charles Reisner
Co-stars: Polly Moran Roscoe Ates Karen Morley John Miljan

1931 REDUCING
Director: Charles Reisner
Co-stars: Polly Moran Anita Page Sally Eilers

1932 PROSPERITY
Director: Sam Wood
Co-stars: Polly Moran Anita Page Norman Foster Henry Armetta

1932 EMMA
Director: Clarence Brown
Co-stars: Richard Cromwell Jean Hersholt Myrna Loy

1933 TUGBOAT ANNIE
Director: Mervyn LeRoy
Co-stars: Wallace Beery Robert Young Maureen O'Sullivan

1933 DLNNER AT EIGHT
Director: George Cukor
Co-stars: John Barrymore Lionel Barrymore Walace Beery

1933 CHRISTOPHER BEAN
Director: Sam Wood
Co-stars: Lionel Barrymore Beulah Bondi Helen Mack

ELLEN DREW
1938 SING YOU SINNERS
Director: Wesley Ruggles
Co-stars: Bing Crosby Fred MacMurray Donald O'Connor

1938 IF I WERE KING
Director: Frank Lloyd
Co-stars: Ronald Colman Basil Rathbone Frances Dee

1939 FRENCH WITHOUT TEARS
Director: Anthony Asquith
Co-stars: Ray Milland Guy Middleton Roland Culver

1939 GERONIMO
Director: Paul Sloane
Co-stars: Preston Foster Andy Devine Gene Lockhart

1939 THE GRACIE ALLEN MURDER CASE
Director: Alfred Green
Co-stars: Gracie Allen Warren William

1939 THE LADY'S FROM KENTUCKY
Director: Alexander Hall
Co-stars: George Raft Hugh Herbert Zasu Pitts

1940 WOMEN WITHOUT NAMES
Director: Robert Florey
Co-stars: Robert Paige John Miljan Fay Helm

1940   **TEXAS RANGERS RIDE AGAIN**
Director: James Hogan
Co-stars: John Howard Akim Tamiroff Broderick Crawford

1940   **THE MONSTER AND THE GIRL**
Director: Stuart Heisler
Co-stars: Paul Lukas Robert Paige Joseph Calleia

1940   **CHRISTMAS IN JULY**
Director: Preston Sturges
Co-stars: Dick Powell William Demarest Ernest Truex

1940   **BUCK BENNY RIDES AGAIN**
Director: Mark Sandrich
Co-stars: Jack Benny Eddie Anderson Phil Harris

1941   **THE MAD DOCTOR**
Director: Tim Whelan
Co-stars: Basil Rathbone John Howard Ralph Morgan

1941   **THE NIGHT OF JANUARY 16TH.**
Director: William Clemens
Co-stars: Robert Preston Nils Asther

1941   **OUR WIFE**
Director: John Stahl
Co-stars: Melvyn Douglas Ruth Hussey Charles Coburn

1941   **THE PARSON OF PANAMINT**
Director: William McGann
Co-stars: Charles Ruggles Phillip Terry

1941   **REACHING FOR THE SUN**
Director: William Wellman
Co-stars: Joel McCrea Eddie Bracken Albert Dekker

1942   **THE REMARKABLE ANDREW**
Director: Stuart Heisler
Co-stars: William Holden Brian Donlevy

1942   **NIGHT PLANE FROM CHUNGKING**
Director: Ralph Murphy
Co-stars: Robert Preston Otto Kruger Sen Yung

1942   **MY FAVOURITE SPY**
Director: Tay Garnett
Co-stars: Kay Kyser Ginny Simms Jane Wyman Ish Kabibble

1942   **ICE-CAPADES REVUE**
Director: Bernard Vorhaus
Co-stars: Richard Denning Jerry Collonna Vera Ralston

1944   **THE IMPOSTER**
Director: Julien Duvivier
Co-stars: Jean Gabin Richard Whorf Allyn Joslyn

1945   **MAN ALIVE**
Director: Ray Enright
Co-stars: Pat O'Brien Adolphe Menjou Rudy Vallee Jason Robbard

1945   **CHINA SKY**
Director: Ray Enright
Co-stars: Randolph Scott Ruth Warwick Anthony Quinn

1946   **CRIME DOCTOR'S MAN HUNT**
Director: William Castle
Co-stars: Warner Baxter William Frawley

1946   **ISLE OF THE DEAD**
Director: Mark Robson
Co-stars: Boris Karloff Alan Napier Jason Robards Marc Cramer

1946   **JOHNNY O'CLOCK**
Director: Robert Rossen
Co-stars: Dick Powell Lee J. Cobb Evelyn Keyes

1949   **THE MAN FROM COLORADO**
Director: Henry Levin
Co-stars: Glenn Ford William Holden Ray Collins

1949   **INDIAN SCOUT**
Director: Ford Beebe
Co-stars: George Montgomery Philip Reed Noah Beery Jnr

1949   **THE CROOKED WAY**
Director: Robert Florey
Co-stars: John Payne Sonny Tufts Rhys Williams

1950   **THE BARON OF ARIZONA**
Director: Sam Fuller
Co-stars: Vincent Price Beulah Bondi Vladimir Sokoloff

1950   **CARGO TO CAPETOWN**
Director: Earl McEvoy
Co-stars: John Ireland Broderick Crawford Edgar Buchanan

1950   **THE GREAT MISSOURI RAID**
Director: Gordon Douglas
Co-stars: MacDonald Carey Wendell Corey

1950   **STARS IN MY CROWN**
Director: Jacques Tourneur
Co-stars: Joel McCrea Dean Stockwell Lewis Stone

1951 MAN IN THE SADDLE
Director: Andre De Toth
Co-stars: Randolph Scott Alexander Knox Joan Leslie

LINZI DREW

1988   **ARIA**
Director: Nicolas Roeg
Co-stars: Theresa Russell Elizabeth Hurley Bridget Fonda

NANCY DREXEL.

1929   **FOUR DEVILS**
Co-stars: Janet Gaynor Charles Morton Barry Norton

1932 MAN FROM HELL'S EDGES
Co-stars: Bob Steele

CAROL DRINKWATER ? 1980 CLOCKWORK ORANGE

1983   **ALL CREATURES GREAT AND SMALL: THE HOMECOMING**
Director: Terence Dudley
Co-stars: Christopher Timothy Robert Hardy

1989   **A MASTER OF THE MARIONETTES**
Director: Pedr Jones
Co-stars: Kenneth Cranham John Duttine

1990   **FATHER**
Director: John Power
Co-stars: Max Von Sydow Julie Blake Steve Jacobs

PATRICIA DRISCOLL

1956   **CHARLEY MOON**
Director: Guy Hamilton
Co-stars: Max Bygraves Dennis Price Shirley Eaton

BETTY DRIVER

1938   **PENNY PARADISE**
Director: Carol Reed
Co-stars: Edmund Gwenn Jimmy O'Dea Maire O'Neill

1939   **LET'S BE FAMOUS**
Director: Walter Forde
Co-stars: Jimmy O'Dea Sonnie Hale Patrick Barr

MINNIE DRIVER (Amelia Driver)

1992   **GOD ON THE ROCKS**
Director: Ross Cramer
Co-stars: Sinead Cusack Bill Patterson Rebecca Edwards

1993   **ROYAL CELEBRATION**
Director: Ferdinand Fairfax
Co-stars: Rupert Graves Peter Howitt Caroline Goodall

1995   **GOLDENEYE**
Director: Martin Campbell
Co-stars: Pierce Brosnan Robbie Coltrane Famke Janssen

1996   SLEEPERS
Director: Harry Levinson
Co-stars: Dustin Hoffman Brad Pitt Robert De Niro

1996   CIRCLE OF FRIENDS
Director: Pat O'Connor
Co-stars: Chris O'Donnell Geraldine O'Rawe Colin Firth

1997   THE FLOOD
Co-stars: Christian Slater Morgan Freeman

1997   BIG NIGHT
Co-stars: Tony Shalhoub Isabella Rossellini Ian Holm

1997   GROSSE POINT BLANK
Co-stars: John Cusack Dan Akroyd Alan Arkin

1998   HARD RAIN
Director: Mikael Saloman
Co-stars: Christian Slater Randy Quaid Morgan Freeman

1998   GOOD WILL HUNTING
Director: Gus Van Sant
Co-stars: Matt Damon Ben Affleck Robin Williams

CLAIRE DROUOT

1965   LE BONHEUR
Director: Agnes Varda
Co-stars: Jean-Claude Drouot Marie-France Boyer Sandrine Drouot

SANDRINE DROUOT

1965   LE BONHEUR
Director: Agnes Varda
Co-stars: Jean-Claude Drouot Marie-France Boyer Claire Drouot

DORINE DROW

1972   DOGS TO THE RESCUE
Director: Paul Fritz-Nemeth
Co-stars: Tony Kramreither Gheorges Gima

EVE DRUCE

1971   WHERE DOES IT HURT?
Director: Rod Amateau
Co-stars: Peter Sellers Jo Ann Pflug Rick Lenz

JOANNE DRU

1946   ABIE'S IRISH ROSE
Director: Edward Sutherland
Co-stars: Richard Norris Eric Blore Michael Chekhov

1948   RED RIVER
Director: Howard Hawks
Co-stars: John Wayne Montgomery Clift Walter Brennan

1949   SHE WORE A YELLOW RIBBON
Director: John Ford
Co-stars: John Wayne John Agar Victor McLaglen

1949   ALL THE KING'S MEN
Director: Robert Rossen
Co-stars: Broderick Crawford Mercedes McCambridge John Ireland

1950   711 OCEAN DRIVE
Director: Joseph Newman
Co-stars: Edmond O'Brien Otto Kruger Don Porter

1950   VENGEANCE VALLEY
Director: Richard Thorpe
Co-stars: Burt Lancaster Robert Walker Sally Forrest

1950   WAGONMASTER
Director: John Ford
Co-stars: Ben Johnson Ward Bond Alan Mowbray Harry Carey Jnr

1951   MR. BELVEDERE RINGS THE BELL
Director: Henry Koster
Co-stars: Clifton Webb Hugh Marlowe Zero Mostel

1952   THE PRIDE OF ST. LOUIS
Director: Harmon Jones
Co-stars: Dan Dailey Richard Haydn Richard Crenna

1952   MY PAL GUS
Director: Robert Parrish
Co-stars: Richard Widmark George Winslow Audrey Totter

1953   THUNDER BAY
Director: Anthony Mann
Co-stars: James Stewart Dan Duryea Gilbert Roland

1953   FORBIDDEN
Director: Rudolph Mate
Co-stars: Tony Curtis Lyle Bettger Marvin Miller

1953   DUFFY OF SAN QUENTIN
Director: Walter Doniger
Co-stars: Paul Kelly Louis Hayward Maureen O'Sullivan

1954   THE SIEGE AT RED RIVER
Director: Rudolph Mate
Co-stars: Van Johnson Richard Boone Jeff Morrow

1954   THREE RING CIRCUS
Director: Joseph Pevney
Co-stars: Dean Martin Jerry Lewis Zsa Zsa Gabor Sig Ruman

1955   SINCERELY YOURS
Director: Gordon Douglas
Co-stars: Liberace Dorothy Malone William Demarest

1955   HELL ON FRISCO BAY
Director: Frank Tuttle
Co-stars: Alan Ladd Edward G. Robinson Paul Stewart

1955   THE DARK AVENGER
Director: Henry Levin
Co-stars: Errol Flynn Peter Finch Yvonne Furneaux

1957   DRANGO
Director: Hall Bartlett
Co-stars: Jeff Chandler Ronald Howard Julie London

1958   THE LIGHT IN THE FOREST
Director: Herschel Daugherty
Co-stars: James MacArthur Jessica Tandy

1959   THE WILD AND THE INNOCENT
Director: Jack Sher
Co-stars: Audie Murphy Gilbert Roland Sandra Dee

1960   SEPTEMBER STORM
Director: Byron Haskin
Co-stars: Mark Stevens Robert Strauss

1965   SYLVIA
Director: Gordon Douglas
Co-stars: Carroll Baker George Maharis Edmond O'Brien

ALICE DRUMMOND

1990   AWAKENINGS
Director: Penny Marshall
Co-stars: Robert De Niro Robin Willliams Julie Kavner

1991   TALES FROM THE DARKSIDE:THE MOVIE
Director: John Harrison
Co-stars: Deborah Harry Christian Slater Julianne Moore

1994   NOBODY'S FOOL
Director: Robert Benton
Co-stars: Paul Newman Jessica Tandy Melanie Griffith

1993   BLOODSTREAM
Director: Stephen Tolkin
Co-stars: Cuba Gooding Jnr. Moira Kelly Omar Epps

CLARE DRUMMOND

1989   PIED PIPER
Director: Norman Stone
Co-stars: Peter O'Toole Mare Winningham Susan Wooldridge

REANA E. DRUMMOND

1991 STRAIGHT OUT OF BROOKLYN
Director: Matty Rich
Co-stars: Matty Rich George T. Odom Ann D. Sanders Barbara Sanon

JEANIE DRYNAN

1976 DON'S PARTY
Director: Bruce Beresford
Co-stars: Ray Barrett Claire Binney John Hargreaves

1984 FANTASY MAN
Director: John Meagher
Co-stars: Harold Hopkins Kerry Mack Kate Fitzpatrick

1994 MURIEL'S WEDDING
Director: P.J. Hogan
Co-stars: Toni Collette Bill Hunter Rachel Griffith

DENISE DUBARRY

1978 DEADMAN'S CURVE
Director: Richard Compton
Co-stars: Richard Hatch Bruce Davison Pamela Bellwood

1984 KGB: THE SECRET WAR
Director: Dwight Little
Co-stars: Michael Billington Michael Ansara

JESSICA DUBLIN

1989 THE TOXIC AVENGER PART 11
Director: Michael Herz
Co-stars: Ron Fazio John Altamura Phoebe Legere

1989 THE TOXIC AVENGER PART 111
Director: Michael Herz
Co-stars: Ron Fazio John Altamura Phoebe Legere

JANET DUBOIS

1981 HELLINGER'S LAW
Director: Leo Penn
Co-stars: Telly Savalas Morgan Stevens Melinda Dillon

1988 I'M GONNA GIT YOU, SUCKA
Director: Keenan Ivory Wayans
Co-stars: Keenan Ivory Wayans Bernie Casey Antonio Fargas

1990 HEART CONDITION
Director: James Parrott
Co-stars: Bob Hoskins Denzel Washington Chloe Webb

MARIE DUBOIS

1960 SHOOT THE PIANIST
Director: Francois Truffaut
Co-stars: Charles Aznavour Nicole Berger Michele Mercier

1961 UNE FEMME EST UNE FEMME
Director: Jean-Luc Godard
Co-stars: Jean-Paul Belmondo Anna Karina

1962 JULES AND JIM
Director: Francois Truffaut
Co-stars: Jeanne Moreau Oskar Werner Henri Serre

1964 LA RONDE
Director: Roger Vadim
Co-stars: Anna Karina Jane Fonda Catherine Spaak

1968 THE DAY THE HOT LINE GOT HOT
Director: Etienne Perier
Co-stars: Charles Boyer Robert Taylor

1974 VINCENT, FRANCOIS, PAUL AND THE OTHERS
Director: Claude Sautet
Co-stars: Yves Montand Michel Piccoli

MARTA DU BOIS

1979 BOULEVARD NIGHTS
Director: Michael Pressman
Co-stars: Richard Yniguez Danny De La Paz

1986 JOHNNIE MAE GIBSON: FBI
Director: Bill Duke
Co-stars: Howard E. Robbins Richard Lawson Lynn Whitfield

1989 THE TRIAL OF THE INCREDIBLE HULK
Director: Bill Bixby
Co-stars: Bill Bixby Lou Ferrigno Rex Smith

PAULETTE DUBOST

1939 LA REGLE DU JEU
Director: Jean Renoir
Co-stars: Jean Renoir Marcel Dalio Nora Gregor Mila Parely

1954 THE SHEEP HAS FIVE LEGS
Director: Henri Verneuil
Co-stars: Fernandel Francoise Arnoul Delmont

1965 VIVA MARIA!
Director: Louis Malle
Co-stars: Jeanne Moreau Brigitte Bardot George Hamilton

1980 THE LAST METRO
Director: Francois Truffaut
Co-stars: Catherine Deneuvre Gerard Depardieu Jean Poiret

1989 MILOU IN MAY
Director: Louis Malle
Co-stars: Michel Piccoli Miou Miou Harriet Walter

ANNE DUBOT

1969 MY NIGHT WITH MAUDE
Director: Eric Rohmer
Co-stars: Jean-Louis Trintignant Francoise Fabian

CLAIRE DUBREY

1938 CRIME DOES NOT PAY:MIRACLE MONEY
Director: Leslie Fenton
Co-Star John Miljan

1944 OH,WHAT A NIGHT
Co-stars: Jean Parker Marjorie Rambeau

ANNIE DUCAUX

1961 LA BELLE AMERICAINE
Director: Robert Dhery
Co-stars: Robert Dhery Louis De Funes Colette Brosset Alfred Adam

SHARON DUCE

1978 ABSOLUTION
Director: Anthony Page
Co-stars: Richard Burton Dominic Guard Billy Connolly

1990 SHOOTING STARS
Director: Chris Bernard
Co-stars: Helmut Griem Gary McDonald

1991 MISTERIOSO
Director: John Glenister
Co-stars: Suzan Sylvester Jack Shepherd Hugh Ross

1991 BUDDY'S SONG
Director: Claude Whatham
Co-stars: Roger Daltry Chesney Hawkes Michael Elphick

1992 NATURAL LIES
Director: Ben Holt
Co-stars: Bob Peck Denis Lawson Lynsey Baxter

DEBORAH DUCHENE

1991 PERFECTLY NORMAL
Director: Yves Simoneau
Co-stars: Robbie Coltrane Michael Riley Kenneth Welsh

MARGUERITE DUCOURET

1947   **LA CAGE AUX ROSSIGNOLS**
Director: Jean Dreville
Co-stars: Noel-Noel Micheline Francey Rene Genin

MARY DUDDY

1988   **THE TEMPTATION OF EILEEN HUGHES**
Director: Tristram Powell
Co-stars: Jim Norton Angharard Rees Ethina Roddy

DORIS DUDLEY

1936   **A WOMAN REBELS**
Director: Mark Sandrich
Co-stars: Katherine Hepburn Herbert Marshall Elizabeth Allan

1943   **THE MOON AND SIXPENCE**
Director: Albert Lewin
Co-stars: George Sanders Herbert Marshall Steve Geray

1950   **THE SECRET FURY**
Director: Mel Ferrer
Co-stars: Claudette Colbert Robert Ryan Jane Cowl

LESLIE DUDLEY (Child)

1955   **JOHN AND JULIE**
Director: William Fairchild
Co-stars: Colin Gibson Peter Sellers Moira Lister

PENELOPE DUDLEY WARD

1935   **ESCAPE ME NEVER**
Director: Paul Czinner
Co-stars: Elizabeth Bergner Hugh Sinclair Griffith Jones

1935   **MOSCOW NIGHTS**
Director: Anthony Asquith
Co-stars: Laurence Olivier Harry Baur Athene Seyler

1938   **THE CITADEL**
Director: King Vidor
Co-stars: Robert Donat Rosalind Russell Rex Harrison

1940   **CONVOY**
Director: Pen Tennyson
Co-stars: Clive Brook John Clements Judy Campbell

1940   **THE CASE OF THE FRIGHTENED LADY**
Director: George King
Co-stars: Marius Goring Helen Haye Patrick Barr

1941   **MAJOR BARBARA**
Director: Gabriel Pascal
Co-stars: Wendy Hiller Rex Harrison Robert Newton

1942   **IN WHICH WE SERVE**
Director: David Lean
Co-stars: Noel Coward Bernard Miles John Mills

1943   **THE DEMI-PARADISE**
Director: Anthony Asquith
Co-stars: Laurence Olivier Maragret Rutherford Felix Aylmer

1944   **THE WAY AHEAD**
Director: Carol Reed
Co-stars: David Niven William Hartnell Jimmy Hanley

1944   **ENGLISH WITHOUT TEARS**
Director: Harold French
Co-stars: Lilli Palmer Michael Wilding Roland Culver

LAURA CLAIRE DUERDEN

1989   **A VIEW OF HARRY CLARK**
Director: Alastair Reid
Co-stars: Griff Rhys Jones Elaine Paige Del Henney

AMANDA DUFF

1938   **JUST AROUND THE CORNER**
Director: Irving Cummings
Co-stars: Shirley Temple Bill Robinson Joan Davis

1939   **MR. MOTO IN DANGER ISLAND**
Director: Norman Foster
Co-stars: Peter Lorre Jean Hersholt Warren Hymer

1940   **CITY OF CHANCE**
Director: Ricardo Cortez
Co-stars: Lynn Barri C. Aubrey Smith Donald Woods

1941   **THE DEVIL COMMANDS**
Director: Edward Dmytryk
Co-stars: Boris Karloff Richard Fiske Anne Revere

PATTY DUFFEK

1987   **HARD TICKET TO HAWAII**
Director: Andy Sidaris
Co-stars: Dona Spier Ronn Moss Hope Marie Carlton

BEE DUFFELL

1966   **FAHRENHEIT 451**
Director: Francois Truffaut
Co-stars: Julie Christie Oskar Werner Cyril Cusack

NICOLA DUFFETT

1992   **HOWARDS END**
Director: James Ivory
Co-stars: Anthony Hopkins Vanessa Redgrave Emma Thompson

JULIA DUFFY

1983   **NIGHT WARNING**
Director: William Asher
Co-stars: Jimmy McNichol Susan Tyrrell Bo Svenson

1989   **BEAUTY AND DENISE**
Director   Neal Israel
Co-stars   John Karlen David Carradine Dinah Manoff

1994   **KIDZ IN THE WOOD**
Director: Neal Israel
Co-Star   Dave Thomas

KAREN DUFFY

1994   **BLANK CHECK**
Director: Rupert Wainright
Co-stars: Brian Bonsell Miguel Ferrer James Rebhorn

1994   **DUMB AND DUMBER**
Director   Peter Farrelly
Co-stars   Jim Carrey Jeff Daniels Lauren Holly

NATALIE DUFFY

1987   **BUSINESS AS USUAL**
Director: Lezli-An Barrett
Co-stars: Glenda Jackson John Thaw Cathy Tyson

YVON DUFOUR

1977   **KING SOLOMON'S TREASURE**
Director: Alvin Rakoff
Co-stars: David McCallum Brit Ekland Patrick MacNee

YVETTE DUGAY

1951   **THE CIMARRON KID**
Director: Budd Boetticher
Co-stars: Audie Murphy Beverly Tyler James Best

1952   **HIAWATHA**
Director: Kurt Neumann
Co-stars: Vincent Edwards Keith Larsen Morris Ankrum

FLORRIE DUGGER

1976　BUGSY MALONE
Director:　Alan Parker
Co-stars:　Scott Baio Jodie Foster John Cassisi

OLYMPIA DUKAKIS *(Married Louis Zorich, Cousin Of Michael Dukakis)*
Oscar For Best Supporting Actress In 1987 For "Moonstruck"

1980　THE IDOLMAKER
Director:　Taylor Hackford
Co-stars:　Ray Sharkey Paul Land Peter Gallagher

1985　WALLS OF GLASS
Director:　Scott Goldstein
Co-stars:　Philip Bosco Gelaldine Page Linda Thorson

1987　MOONSTRUCK
Director:　Norman Jewison
Co-stars:　Cher Nicholas Cage Vincent Gardenia Danny Aiello

1988　WORKING GIRL
Director:　Mike Nichols
Co-stars:　Melanie Griffith Harrison Ford Sigourney Weaver

1989　STEEL MAGNOLIAS
Director:　Herbert Ross
Co-stars:　Sally Field Dolly Parton Shirley MacLaine

1989　DAD
Director:　Gary David Goldberg
Co-stars:　Jack Lemmon Ted Danson Kathy Baker Ethan Hawke

1989　LOOK WHO'S TALKING
Director:　Amy Heckerling
Co-stars:　John Travolta Kirstie Alley George Segal

1990　LOOK WHO'S TALKING TOO
Director:　Amy Heckerling
Co-stars:　John Travolta Kirstie Alley Bruce Willis

1990　IN THE SPIRIT
Director:　Sandra Seacat
Co-stars:　Marlo Thomas Elaine May Melanie Griffith Peter Falk

1992　OVER THE HILL
Director:　George Miller
Co-stars:　Sigrid Thornton Derek Fowlds Bill Kerr

1993　LOOK WHO'S TALKING NOW
Director:　Tom Ropelski
Co-stars:　John Travolta Kirstie Alley George Segal

1993　NAKED GUN 33 1/3: THE FINAL INSULT
Director:　Peter Segal
Co-stars:　Leslie Nielsen Priscilla Presley

1993　THE CEMETERY CLUB
Director:　Bill Duke
Co-stars:　Ellen Burnstyn Diane Ladd Danny Aiello

1994　I LOVE TROUBLE
Director:　Charles Shyer
Co-stars:　Julia Roberts Nick Nolte Saul Rubinek

1995　YOUNG AT HEART
Director　Alan Arkush

1996　MR HOLLAND'S OPUS
Director　Stephen Herek
Co-stars　Richard Dreyfuss Jay Thomas Glenne Headley

1998　PICTURE PERFECT
Director　Glenn Gordon Caron
Co-stars　Jennifer Aniston Kevin Bacon Jay Mohr

ANNA DUKASZ

1987　'68
Director:　Steven Kovacks
Co-stars:　Eric Larson Robert Locke Neil Young

PATTY DUKE *(Married John Astin Mother Of Sean And Mackenzie Astin)*
Oscar For Best Supporting Actress In 1962 For "The Miracle Worker"

1958　THE GODDESS
Director:　John Cromwell
Co-stars:　Kim Stanley Lloyd Bridges Steven Hill

1959　HAPPY ANNIVERSARY
Director:　David Miller
Co-stars:　David Niven Mitzi Gaynor Carl Reiner

1962　THE MIRACLE WORKER
Director:　Arthur Penn
Co-stars:　Anne Bancroft Victor Jory Andrew Prine

1965　BILLIE
Director:　Don Weiss
Co-stars:　Jim Backus Jane Greer Warren Berlinger Billy De Wolfe

1967　VALLEY OF THE DOLLS
Director:　Mark Robson
Co-stars:　Barbara Parkins Sharon Tate Susan Hayward

1969　ME, NATALIE
Director:　Fred Coe
Co-stars:　James Farantino Martin Balsam Elsa Lanchester Al Pacino

1971　IF TOMORROW COMES
Director:　Frank Liu
Co-stars:　James Whitmore Anne Baxter Pat Hingle Mako

1972　DEADLY HARVEST
Director:　Michael O'Herlihy
Co-stars:　Richard Boone Michael Constantine

1972　YOU'D LIKE MY MOTHER
Director:　Lamont Johnson
Co-stars:　Rosemary Murphy Richard Thomas

1978　THE SWARM
Director:　Irwin Allen
Co-stars:　Michael Caine Katherine Ross Richard Widmark

1981　THE VIOLATION OF SARAH MCDAVID
Director:　John Llewellyn Moxey
Co-stars:　Ned Beatty Ally Sheedy

1984　BEST KEPT SECRETS
Director:　Jerrold Freedman
Co-stars:　Frederic Forrest Peter Coyote Meg Foster

1986　A TIME TO TRIUMPH
Director:　Noel Black
Co-stars:　Joseph Bologna Julie Bovasso Dara Modglin

1986　WILLY/MILLY
Director:　Paul Schneider
Co-stars:　Pamela Segall Eric Gurry Mary Tanner Seth Green

1987　PERRY MASON: THE CASE OF THE MURDERED MADAM
Director:　Ron Satlof
Co-stars:　Raymond Burr Barbara Hale

1988　FATAL JUDGEMENT
Director:　Gilbert Cates
Co-stars:　Tom Conti Joe Regalbutto

1989　PERRY MASON: CASE OF THE AVENGING ACE
Director:　Christian Nyby
Co-stars:　Raymond Burr Erin Gray

1989　EVERYBODY'S BABY
Director:　Mel Damski
Co-stars:　Pat Hingle Beau Bridges Roxana Zal

1989　AMITYVILLE 4: THE EVIL ESCAPES
Director:　Sandor Stern
Co-stars:　Jane Wyatt Norman Lloyd

1992 PRELUDE TO A KISS
Director: Norman Rene
Co-stars: Alec Baldwin Meg Ryan Kathy Bates

1993 ONE WOMAN'S COURAGE
Director: Charles Robert Carner
Co-stars: James Farantino Margot Kidder

1993 NO CHILD OF MINE
Director: Michael Katleman
Co-stars: Tracey Nelson G.W. Bailey

1993 FAMILY OF STRANGERS
Director: Sheldon Larry
Co-stars: Melissa Gilbert Martha Gibson

1994 TOUCH OF TRUTH
Director: Michael Switzer
Co-stars: Bradley Pearce Melissa Gilbert

1995 SEARCH FOR SARAH
Director Fred Gerber
Co-stars Richard Crenna Missy Crider

1996 TO FACE HER PAST
Co-star: Tracey Gold

SANDRINE DUMAS

1988 THE LEGEND OF THE HOLY DRINKER
Director: Ermanno Olmi
Co-stars: Rutger Hauer Anthony Quinn

1989 VALMONT
Director: Milos Forman
Co-stars: Colin Firth Annette Bening Meg Tilly

DANIELLE DUMONT

1957 THE HUNCHBACK OF NOTRE DAME
Director: Jean Delannoy
Co-stars: Anthony Quinn Gina Lollobrigida Alain Cuny

MARGARET DUMONT

1929 THE COCOANUTS
Director: Robert Florey
Co-stars: Marx Bros Kay Frances Oscar Shaw Mary Eaton

1930 ANIMAL CRACKERS
Director: Victor Herrman
Co-stars: Grouco Chico Harpo Zeppo Marx

1931 THE GIRL HABIT
Director: Eddie Cline
Co-stars: Charles Ruggles Tamara Geva Sue Conroy

1933 DUCK SOUP
Director: Leo McCarey
Co-stars: Marx Bros Louis Calhern Raquel Torres Edgar Kennedy

1935 A NIGHT AT THE OPERA
Director: Sam Wood
Co-stars: Marx Bros Allan Jones Kitty Carlisle Sig Ruman

1937 A DAY AT THE RACES
Director: Sam Wood
Co-stars: Marx Bros Allan Jones Maureen O'Sullivan Sig Ruman

1937 HIGH FLYERS
Director: Edward Cline
Co-stars: Wheeler & Woolsey Lupe Velez Marjorie Lord Jack Carson

1937 LIFE OF THE PARTY
Director: William Seiter
Co-stars: Joe Penner Gene Raymond Ann Miller

1937 WISE GIRL
Director: Leigh Jason
Co-stars: Miriam Hopkins Ray Milland Walter Abel

1938 DRAMATIC SCHOOL
Director: Robert Sinclair
Co-stars: Luise Rainer Paulette Goddard Lana Turner

1939 AT THE CIRCUS
Director: Edward Buzzell
Co-stars: Marx Bros Florence Rice Eve Arden

1941 THE BIG STORE
Director: Charles Reisner
Co-stars: Marx Bros Tony Martin Virginia Grey

1941 NEVER GIVE A SUCKER AN EVEN BREAK
Director: Edward Cline
Co-stars: W.C. Fields Gloria Jean Leon Errol

1941 SING YOUR WORRIES AWAY
Director: Edward Sutherland
Co-stars: Bert Lahr Buddy Ebsen June Havoc

1943 THE DANCING MASTERS
Director: Mal St. Clair
Co-stars: Laurel & Hardy Trudy Marshall Robert Mitchum

1945 THE HORN BLOWS AT MIDNIGHT
Director: Raoul Walsh
Co-stars: Jack Benny Alexis Smith Dolores Moran

1945 DIAMOND HORSESHOE
Director: George Seaton
Co-stars: Betty Grable Dick Haymes William Gaxton Phil Silvers

1946 LITTLE GIANT
Director: Willliam Seiter
Co-stars: Abbott & Costello Brenda Joyce George Cleveland

1952 THREE FOR BEDROOM C
Director: Milton Bren
Co-stars: Gloria Swanson Fred Clark Hans Conreid

1953 STOP YOUR KILLING ME
Director: Roy Del Ruth
Co-stars: Broderick Crawford Claire Trevor Virginia Gibson

1962 ZOTZ!
Director: William Castle
Co-stars: Tom Poston Fred Clark Jim Backus Cecil Kellaway

1964 WHAT A WAY TO GO
Director: J. Lee-Thompson
Co-stars: Shirley McLaine Robert Mitchum Gene Kelly

STEFFI DUNA

1933 MAN OF TWO WORLDS
Director: Walter Ruben
Co-stars: Francis Lederer Elissa Landi Henry Stephenson

1935 ONE NEW YORK NIGHT
Director: Jack Conway
Co-stars: Franchot Tone Una Merkel Conrad Nagel

1936 PAGLIACCI
Director: Karl Grune
Co-stars: Richard Tauber Diana Napier Esmond Knight

1936 ANTHONY ADVERSE
Director: Mervyn LeRoy
Co-stars: Fredric March Olivia De Havilland Edmund Gwenn

1936 DANCING PIRATE
Co-stars: Frank Morgan Victor Varconi

1936 I CONQUER THE SEA
Co-Star Douglas Walton

1936 HI GAUCHO!
Co-Star John Carroll

1938 FLIRTING WITH FATE
Director: Frank McDonald
Co-stars: Joe E. Brown Leo Carrillo Beverly Roberts

1938 RASCALS
Director: Bruce Humberstone
Co-stars: Jane Withers Rochelle Hudson Borrah Minevitch

1940　WATERLOO BRIDGE
Director:　Mervyn LeRoy
Co-stars:　Robert Taylor Vivien Leigh Lucile Watson

1940　THE MARINES FLY HIGH
Director:　Ben Stoloff
Co-stars:　Richard Dix Chester Morris Lucille Ball

1940　THE GREAT MCGINTY
Director:　Preston Sturges
Co-stars:　Brian Donlevy Muriel Angelus Akim Tamiroff

DIXIE DUNBAR

1934　GEORGE WHITE'S SCANDALS
Director:　George White
Co-stars:　George White Alice Faye Rudy Valley Jimmy Durante

1935　KING OF BURLESQUE
Director:　Sidney Lanfield
Co-stars:　Warner Baxter Alice Faye Jack Oakie

1936　GIRL'S DORMITORY
Director:　Irving Cummings
Co-stars:　Simone Simon Herbert Marshall Tyrone Power

1936　ONE IN A MILLION
Director:　Sidney Lanfield
Co-stars:　Sonja Henie Don Ameche Ned Sparks

1936　SING, BABY, SING
Director:　Sidney Lanfield
Co-stars:　Alice Faye Adolphe Menjou Patsy Kelly

1936　EDUCATING FATHER
Co-Star　Kenneth Howell

1937　SING AND BE HAPPY
Co-stars:　Tony Martin Leah Ray

1937　LIFE BEGINS IN COLLEGE
Director:　William Seiter
Co-stars:　Joan Davis Tony Martin Gioria Stuart

ARLETTA DUNCAN

1937　DAMAGED GOODS
Director:　Phil Stone
Co-stars:　Pedro De Cordoba Esther Dale Phyllis Barry

CARMEN DUNCAN

1980　HARLEQUIN
Director:　Simon Wincer
Co-stars:　Robert Powell David Hemmings Broderick Crawford

1983　NOW AND FOREVER
Director:　Adrian Carr
Co-stars:　Cheryl Ladd Robert Coleby Christopher Amor

1984　RUN, CHRISSIE, RUN
Director:　Chris Langman
Co-stars:　Annie Jones Michael Aitkins Shane Briant

JULIE DUNCAN

1943　COWBOY IN THE CLOUDS
Co-stars:　Charles Starrett Jimmy Wakely Dub Taylor

LINDSAY DUNCAN

1983　LOOSE CONNECTIONS
Director:　Richard Eyre
Co-stars:　Stephen Rea Jan Niklas Gary Olsen

1987　PRICK UP YOUR EARS
Director:　Stephen Frears
Co-stars:　Gary Oldman Alfred Molina Vanessa Redgrave

1989　THESE FOOLISH THINGS
Director:　Charles Gormley
Co-stars:　James Fox Ciaran Madden Michael Keating

1990　THE REFLECTING SKIN
Director:　Philip Ridley
Co-stars:　Viggo Mortensen Jeremy Cooper Sheila Moore

1991　REDEMPTION
Director:　Malcolm McKay
Co-stars:　Tom Courtenay Miranda Richardson Nick Moran

1991　BODY PARTS
Director:　Eric Red
Co-stars:　Jeff Fahey Kim Delaney Brad Dourif Peter Murniik

1993　A YEAR IN PROVENCE
Director:　David Tucker
Co-stars:　John Thaw Jean-Pierre Delage Jo Doumerg

1996　A MIDSUMMER'S NIGHT DREAM
Director:　Adrian Noble
Co-stars:　Alex Jennings Desmond Barrit

MARY DUNCAN

1928　THE RIVER
Co-stars:　Charles Farrell

1930　KISMET
Director:　John Francis Dillon
Co-stars:　Otis Skinner Loretta Young David Manners

1930　CITY GIRL
Director:　F.W. Murnau
Co-stars:　Charles Farrell David Torrence Edith Yorke

1930　BOUDOIR DIPLOMAT
Co-Star　Ian Keith

1931　FIVE AND TEN
Co-Star　Leslie Howard

1931　THE AGE FOR LOVE
Director:　Frank Lloyd
Co-stars:　Billie Dove Adrian Morris Lois Wilson

1933　MORNING GLORY
Director:　Lowell Sherman
Co-stars:　Katherine Hepburn Douglas Fairbanks Jnr

PAMELA DUNCAN

1957　ATTACK OF THE CRAB MONSTERS
Director:　Roger Corman
Co-stars:　Richard Garland Russell Johnson

1957　MY GUN IS QUICK
Director:　Phil Victor
Co-stars:　Robert Bray Whitney Blake Pat Donahue

1957　THE UNDEAD
Director:　Roger Corman
Co-stars:　Richard Garland Allison Hayes Billy Barty

PAULA DUNCAN

1985　JENNY KISSED ME
Director:　Brian Trenchard-Smith
Co-stars:　Deborrah-Lee Furness Ivar Kants Tamsin West

SANDY DUNCAN

1971　THE STAR SPANGLED GIRL
Director:　Jerry Paris
Co-stars:　Tony Roberts Elizabeth Allan Todd Susman

1978　THE CAT FROM OUT OF SPACE
Director:　Norman Tokar
Co-stars:　Ken Berry Roddy McDowall Harry Morgan

1991　ROCK-A-DOODLE (Voice)
Director:　Don Bluth
Co-stars:　Glen Campbell Christopher Plummer Phil Harris

JENNIE DUNDAS

1984   **THE HOTEL NEW HAMPSHIRE**
Director: Tony Richardson
Co-stars: Rob Lowe Jodie Foster Beau Bridges

1984   **MRS. SOFFEL**
Director: Gillian Armstrong
Co-stars: Diane Keaton Mel Gibson Matthew Modine

1985   **LEGAL EAGLES**
Director: Ivan Reitman
Co-stars: Robert Redford Debra Winger Daryl Hannah

1986   **ANASTASIA: THE MYSTERY OF ANNA**
Director: Marvin Chomsky
Co-stars: Amy Irving Olivia De Havilland

CHRISTINE DUNFORD

1998   **ULEE'S GOLD**
Director   Victor Nunez
Co-stars   Peter Fonda Tom Wood Vanessa Zima

JOANNA DUNHAM

1961   **DANGEROUS AFTERNOON**
Director: Charles Saunders
Co-stars: Ruth Dunning Nora Nicholson Howard Pays

1970   **THE HOUSE THAT DRIPPED BLOOD**
Director: Peter Duffell
Co-stars: Christopher Lee Peter Cushiing

KATHARINE DUNHAM

1942   **STAR SPANGLED RHYTHM**
Director: George Marshall
Co-stars: Victor Moore Betty Hutton Eddie Bracken

1943   **STORMY WEATHER**
Director: Andrew Stone
Co-stars: Bill Robinson Lena Horne Fats Waller

1954   **MAMBO**
Director: Robbert Rossen
Co-stars: Silvana Mangano Michael Rennie Shelley Winters

STEPHANIE DUNHAM

1992   **A THOUSAND HEROES**
Director   Lamont Johnson
Co-stars   Charlton Heston Richard Thomas James Coburn

LESLEY DUNLOP

1977   **A LITTIE NIGHT MUSIC**
Director: Hal Prince
Co-stars: Elizabeth Taylor Diana Rigg Len Cariou

1987   **STANLEY**
Director: Annia Benson Gyles
Co-stars: Anton Lesser Juliet Stevenson Sarah Berger

CAROLYN DUNN

1985   **BREAKING ALL THE RULES**
Director: James Orr
Co-stars: Carl Marotte Rachel Hayward

EMMA DUNN

1930   **THE TEXAN**
Director: John Cromwell
Co-stars: Gary Gooper Fay Wray Oscar Apfel

1931   **THIS MODERN AGE**
Director: Nick Grinde
Co-stars: Joan Crawford Pauline Frederick Neil Hamilton

1931   **BAD SISTER**
Director: Holart Henley
Co-stars: Conrad Nagel Sidney Fox Bette Davis Humphrey Bogart

1931   **THE GUILTY GENERATION**
Director: Rowland Lee
Co-stars: Leo Carrillo Boris Karloff Robert Young

1932   **BROKEN LULLABY**
Director: Ernst Lubitsch
Co-stars: Lionel Barrymore Phllips Holmes Nancy Carroll

1932   **BLESSED EVENT**
Director: Roy Del Ruth
Co-stars: Lee Tracy Mary Brian Dick Powell

1932   **HELL'S HOUSE**
Director: Howard Higgin
Co-stars: Bette Davis Pat O'Brien Junior Durkin

1933   **HARD TO HANDLE**
Director: Mervyn LeRoy
Co-stars: James Cagney Ruth Donnelly Mary Brian

1933   **ELMER THE GREAT**
Director: Mervyn LeRoy
Co-stars: Joe E. Brown Patricia Ellis Claire Dodd

1934   **DR. MONICA**
Director: William Keighley
Co-stars: Kay Francis Warren William Jean Muir

1935   **KEEPER OF THE BEES**
Director: Christy Cabanne
Co-stars: Neil Hamilton Betty Furness Edith Fellows

1937   **WHEN YOU'RE IN LOVE**
Director: Robert Riskin
Co-stars: Grace Moore Cary Grant Aline MacMahon

1937   **MADAME X**
Director: Sam Wood
Co-stars: Gladys George John Beal Warren William

1937   **HIDEAWAY**
Co-stars: Marjorie Lord J. Carrol Naish Bradley Page

1938   **THREE LOVES HAS NANCY**
Director: Richard Thorpe
Co-stars: Janet Gaynor Robert Montgomery. Claire Dodd

1938   **THE COWBOY AND THE LADY**
Director   H.C. Potter
Co-stars   Gary Cooper Merle Oberon Walter Brennan

1939   **SON OF FRANKENSTEIN**
Director: Rowland Lee
Co-stars: Basil Rathbone Boris Karloff Bela Lugosi

1941   **SCATTERGOOD BAINES**
Director: Christy Cabanne
Co-stars: Guy Kibbee Carol Hughes John Archer

1941   **RISE AND SHINE**
Director: Allan Dwan
Co-stars: Linda Darnell George Murphy Walter Brennan

1941   **LADIES IN RETIREMENT**
Director: Charles Vidor
Co-stars: Ida Lupino Louis Hayward Elsa Lanchester

1942   **THE TALK OF THE TOWN**
Director: George Stevens
Co-stars: Ronald Colman Cary Grant Jean Arthur

1944   **MY BUDDY**
Director: Steve Sekely
Co-stars: Don Barry Ruth Terry Lynne Roberts

1947   **LIFE WITH FATHER**
Director: Michael Curtiz
Co-stars: William Powell Irene Dunne Elizabeth Taylor

JOSEPHINE. DUNN

1928   **THE SINGING FOOL**
Director: Lloyd Bacon
Co-stars: Al Jolson Betty Bronson Buddy DeSylva

NORA DUNN

1988 WORKING GIRL
Director Mike Nichols
Co-stars Melanie Griffith Sigourney Weaver Harrison Ford

1990 MIAMI BLUES
Director: George Armitage
Co-stars: Fred Ward Alec Baldwin Jennifer Jason Leigh

1991 STEPPING OUT
Director Lewis Gilbert
Co-stars Liza Minnelli Shelley Winters Julie Walters

1993 PASSION FISH
Director: John Sayles
Co-stars: Mary McDonnell Alfre Woodard Angela Bassett

STEPHANIE DUNNAM

1987 INDEPENDENCE
Director: John Patterson
Co-stars: John Bennett Perry Isabella Hofman Amanda Wyss

FAYE DUNAWAY

Oscar for Best Actress In 1976 For "Network". Nominated For Best
Actress In 1967 For "Bonnie And Clyde" and In 1974 For "Chinatown"

1967 THE HAPPENING
Director: Elliott Silverstein
Co-stars: Anthony Quinn George Maharis Oscar Homolka

1967 HURRY SUNDOWN
Director: Otto Preminger
Co-stars: Jane Fonda Michael Caine Rex Ingram

1967 BONNIE AND CLYDE
Director: Arthur Penn
Co-stars: Warren Beatty Gene Hackman Estelle Parsons

1968 THE EXTRAORDINARY SEAMAN
Director: John Frankenheimer
Co-stars: David Niven Mickey Rooney Alan Alda

1968 THE THOMAS CROWN AFFAIR
Director: Norman Jewison
Co-stars: Steve McQueen Paul Burke Jack Weston

1969 A PLACE FOR LOVERS
Director: Vittorio De Sica
Co-stars: Marcello Mastroianni Caroline Mortimer

1969 THE ARRANGEMENT
Director: Elia Kazan
Co-stars: Kirk Douglas Deborah Kerr Richard Boone

1970 LITTLE BIG MAN
Director: Arthur Penn
Co-stars: Dustin Hoffman Martin Balsam Richard Mulligan

1970 PUZZLE OF A DOWNFALL CHILD
Director: Jerry Schatzberg
Co-stars: Barry Primus Viveca Lindfors

1971 DOC
Director: Frank Perry
Co-stars: Stacy Keach Harris Yulin Mike Witney Dan Greenburg

1971 THE DEADLY TRAP
Director: Rene Clement
Co-stars: Frank Langella Barbara Parkins

1973 OKLAHOMA CRUDE
Director: Stanley Kramer
Co-stars: George C. Scott John Mills Jack Palance

**1973 THE THREE MUSKETEERS:
THE QUEEN'S DIAMONDS**
Director: Richard Lester
Co-stars: Michael York Oliver Reed Raquel Welch

1974 THE FOUR MUSKETEERS
Director: Richard Lester
Co-stars: Michael York Richard Chamberlain Frank Finlay

1974 CHINATOWN
Director: Roman Polanski
Co-stars: Jack Nicholson John Huston Diane Ladd

1974 THE TOWERING INFERNO
Director: Irwin Allen
Co-stars: Paul Newman Steve McQueen William Holden

1975 THREE DAYS OF THE CONDOR
Director: Sidney Pollack
Co-stars: Robert Redford Cliff Robertson

1976 VOYAGE OF THE DAMNED
Director: Stuart Rosenberg
Co-stars: Max Von Sydow Orson Welles James Mason Lee Grant

1976 NETWORK
Director: Sidney Lumet
Co-stars: William Holden Peter Finch Robert Duvall Ned Beatty

1978 THE EYES OF LAURA MARS
Director: Irvin Kerschner
Co-stars: Tommy Lee Jones Brad Dourif

1979 THE CHAMP
Director: Franco Zeffirella
Co-stars: Jon Voight Ricky Schroeder Jack Warden

1980 THE FIRST DEADLY SIN
Director: Brian Hutton
Co-stars: Frank Sinatra Brenda Vaccaro James Whitmore

1981 MOMMIE DEAREST
Director: Frank Perry
Co-stars: Diana Scarwid Steve Forrest Howard Da Silva

1983 THE WICKED LADY
Director: Michael Winner
Co-stars: Alan Bates John Gielgud Denholm Elliott

1984 ELLIS ISLAND
Director: Jerry London
Co-stars: Claire Bloom Richard Burton Kate Burton Joan Greenwood

1984 SUPERGIRL
Director: Jeannot Szwarc
Co-stars: Helen Slater Peter O'Toole Mia Farrow

1985 ORDEAL BY INNOCENCE
Director: Desmond Davis
Co-stars: Donald Sutherland Christopher Plummer

1986 BEVERLY HILLS MADAM
Director: Harvey Hart
Co-stars: Louis Jourdan Melody Anderson Donna Dixon

1987 BARFLY
Director: Barbet Schroeder
Co-stars: Mickey Rourke Alice Krige Jack Nance

1988 BURNING SECRET
Director: Andrew Birkin
Co-stars: Klaus Maria Brandauer David Eberts

1988 MIDNIGHT CROSSING
Director: Roger Holzberg
Co-stars: Daniel J. Travanti Kim Cattrall Ned Beatty

1988 RASPBERRY RIPPLE
Director: Nigel Finch
Co-stars: John Gordon Sinclair Rosie Kerslake Nabil Shaban

1989 COLD SASSY TREE
Director: Joan Tewkesbury
Co-stars: Richard Widmark Frances Fisher John Jackson

1990 SILHOUETTE
Director: Carl Schenker
Co-stars: David Rasche John Terry Ron Campbell Carlos Gomez

1990	**THE HANDMAID'S TALE**	
Director:	Volker Schlondorff	
Co-stars:	Natasha Richardson Robert Duvall	

1990 **THE HANDMAID'S TALE**
Director: Volker Schlondorff
Co-stars: Natasha Richardson Robert Duvall

1991 **SCORCHERS**
Director: David Beaird
Co-stars: Denholm Elliott Emily Lloyd James Earl Jones

1991 **THE TWO JAKES** *(Voice)*
Director Jack Nicholson
Co-stars Jack Nicholson Harvey Keitel Meg Tilly

1992 **ARIZONA DREAM**
Director: Emir Kusturica
Co-stars: Johnny Depp Jerry Lewis Lili Taylor

1993 **THE TEMP**
Director: Tom Holland
Co-stars: Timothy Hutton Lara Flynn Boyle Dwight Schultz

1994 **A FAMILY DIVIDED**
Director Donald Wrye
Co-stars Stephen Collins Cameron Bancroft

1994 **DON JUAN DE MARCO**
Director Jeremy Leven
Co-stars Johnny Depp Marlon Brando

1997 **ALBINO ALLIGATOR**
Director: Kevin Spacey
Co-Star Matt Dillon

1997 **THE CHAMBER**
Director: James Foley
Co-stars: Gene Hackman Chris O'Donnell

CLARE DUNNE

1966 **THEY'RE A WIERD MOB**
Director: Michael Powell
Co-stars: Walter Chiari Chips Rafferty Alida Chelli

DOMINIQUE DUNNE
(Sister Of Griffin Dunne)(Strangled By Boyfriend
John Sweeney 30th October, 1982)

1981 **THE DAY THE LOVING STOPPED**
Director: Daniel Mann
Co-stars: Dennis Weaver Valerie Harper Ally Sheedy

1982 **POLTERGEIST**
Director: Tobe Hunter
Co-stars: JoBeth Williams Beatrice Straight Heather O'Rourke

1982 **THE SHADOW RIDERS**
Director: Andrew McLaglen
Co-stars: Tom Selleck Sam Elliott Ben Johnson

ELIZABETH DUNNE

1939 **BLONDIE TAKES A VACATION**
Director: Frank Strayer
Co-stars: Penny Singleton Arthur Lake Larry Simms

IRENE DUNNE
Nominated For Best Actress In 1931 For "Cimarron", In 1936 For
"Theodora Goes Wild", In 1937 For "The Awful Truth", In 1939 For
"Love Affair" and also In 1948 For "I Remember Mama"

1930 **LEATHERNECKING**
Director: Edward Cline
Co-stars: Ken Murray Eddie Foy Jnr Louise Fazenda

1931 **CONSOLATION MARRIAGE**
Director: Paul Sloane
Co-stars: Pat O'Brien Myrna Loy Lester Vail

1931 **CIMARRON**
Director: Wesley Ruggles
Co-stars: Richard Dix Estelle Taylor Nance O'Neill

1931 **BACHELOR APARTMENT**
Director: Lowell Sherman
Co-stars: Mae Murray Lowell Sherman Norman Kerry

1932 **BACK STREET**
Director: John Stahl
Co-stars: John Boles June Clyde Zasu Pitts

1932 **SYMPHONY OF SIX MILLION**
Director: Gregory La Cava
Co-stars: Ricardo Cortez Gregory Ratoff

1932 **13 WOMEN**
Director: George Archainbaud
Co-stars: Ricardo Cortez Myrna Loy Jill Esmond

1933 **THE SECRET OF MADAME BLANCHE**
Director: Charles Brabin
Co-stars: Phillips Holmes Jean Parker

1933 **THE SILVER CORD**
Director: John Cromwell
Co-stars: Joel McCrea Frances Dee Eric Linden

1933 **IF I WERE FREE**
Director: Elliott Nugent
Co-stars: Clive Brook Nils Asther Laura Hope Crews

1933 **ANN VICKERS**
Director: John Cromwell
Co-stars: Walter Huston Bruce Cabot Edna May Oliver

1933 **NO OTHER WOMAN**
Co-Star Charles Bickford

1934 **AGE OF INNOCENCE**
Director: Philip Moeller
Co-stars: John Boles Lionel Atwill Helen Westley

1934 **STINGAREE**
Director: William Wellman
Co-stars: Richard Dix Mary Bolland Andy Devine

1934 **THIS MAN IS MINE**
Director: John Cromwell
Co-stars: Ralph Bellamy Constance Cummings

1935 **SWEET ADELINE**
Director: Mervyn LeRoy
Co-stars: Donald Woods Hugh Herbert Winni Shaw

1935 **ROBERTA**
Director: William Seiter
Co-stars: Fred Astaire Ginger Rogers Randolph Scott

1935 **MAGNIFICENT OBSESSION**
Director: John Stahl
Co-stars: Robert Taylor Ralph Morgan Sara Haden

1936 **THEODORA GOES WILD**
Director: Richard Boleslawski
Co-stars: Melvyn Douglas Thomas Mitchell

1936 **SHOWBOAT**
Director: James Whale
Co-stars: Allan Jones Paul Robeson Helen Morgan

1937 **HIGH, WIDE AND HANDSOME**
Director: Rouben Mamoulian
Co-stars: Randolph Scott Dorothy Lamour

1937 **THE AWFUL TRUTH**
Director: Leo McCarey
Co-stars: Cary Grant Ralph Bellamy Molly Lamont

1938 **JOY OF LIVING**
Director: Tay Garnett
Co-stars: Douglas Fairbanks Alice Brady Guy Kibbee

1939 **LOVE AFFAIR**
Director: Leo McCarey
Co-stars: Charles Boyer Maria Ouspenskaya Lee Bowman

1939 INVITATION TO HAPPINESS
Director: Wesley Ruggles
Co-stars: Fred MacMurray Charles Ruggles

1939 WHEN TOMORROW COMES
Director: John Stahl
Co-stars: Charles Boyer Barbara O'Neill Nydia Westman

1940 MY FAVORITE WIFE
Director: Garson Kanin
Co-stars: Cary Grant Randolph Scott Scotty Beckett

1941 PENNY SERENADE
Director: George Stevens
Co-stars: Cary Grant Beulah Bondi Ann Doran

1941 UNFINISHED BUSINESS
Director: Gregory La Cava
Co-stars: Robert Montgomery Preston Foster

1943 A GUY NAMED JOE
Director: Victor Flemming
Co-stars: Spencer Tracy Van Johnson Esther Williams

1944 THE WHITE CLIFFS OF DOVER
Director: Clarence Brown
Co-stars: Alan Marshall Peter Lawford May Whitty

1944 TOGETHER AGAIN
Director: Charles Vidor
Co-stars: Charles Boyer Charles Coburn

1945 OVER 21
Director: Alexander Hall
Co-stars: Alexander Knox Charles Coburn

1946 ANNA AND THE KING OF SIAM
Director: John Cromwell
Co-stars: Rex Harrison Linda Darnell Lee J. Cobb

1947 LIFE WITH FATHER
Director: Michael Curtiz
Co-stars: William Powell Elizabeth Taylor

1948 I REMEMBER MAMA
Director: George Stevens
Co-stars: Barbara Bel Geddes Oscar Homolka

1950 NEVER A DULL MOMENT
Director: George Marshall
Co-stars: Fred MacMurray Natalie Wood Andy Devine

1950 THE MUDLARK
Director: Jean Negulesco
Co-stars: Andrew Ray Alec Guinness Anthony Steel

1952 IT GROWS ON TREES
Director: Arthur Lubin
Co-stars: Dean Jagger Joan Evans Rlchard Crenna

RUTH DUNNING

1953 INTIMATE RELATIONS
Director: Charles Frank
Co-stars: Marian Spencer Russell Enoch Harold Warrender

1956 IT'S A GREAT DAY
Director: John Warrington
Co-stars: Edward Evans Christopher Beeney Vera Day

1961 DANGEROUS AFTERNOON
Director: Charles Saunders
Co-stars: Nora Nicholson Joanna Dunham Howard Pays

1970 HOFFMAN
Director: Alvin Rakoff
Co-stars: Peter Sellers Sinead Cusack Jeremy Bulloch

1973 THE HOUSE IN NIGHTMARE PARK
Director: Peter Sykes
Co-stars: Frankie Howerd Ray Milland Hugh Burden

MIILDRED DUNNOCK
Nominated For Best Supporting Actress In 1951 For "Death Of A Salesman" And In 1956 For "Baby Doll"

1945 THE CORN IS GREEN
Director: Irving Rapper
Co-stars: Bette Davis John Dall Joan Lorring Nigel Bruce

1947 KISS OF DEATH
Director: Henry Hathaway
Co-stars: Victor Mature Brian Donlevy Richard Widmark

1951 DEATH OF A SALESMAN
Director: Laslo Benedick
Co-stars: Fredric March Kevin McCarthy

1951 I WANT YOU
Director: Mark Robson
Co-stars: Dorothy McGuire Dana Andrews Farley Granger

1952 THE GIRL IN WHITE
Director: John Sturges
Co-stars: June Allyson Arthur Kennedy Gary Merrill

1952 VIVA ZAPATA !
Director Elia Kazan
Co-stars Marlon Brando Jean Peters Anthony Quinn

1953 THE JAZZ SINGER
Director: Michael Curtiz
Co-stars: Danny Thomas Peggy Lee Edward Franz

1954 BAD FOR EACH OTHER
Director: William Fadiman
Co-stars: Charlton Heston Lisabeth Scott Dianne Foster

1955 THE TROUBLE WITH HARRY
Director: Alfred Hitchcock
Co-stars: Edmund Gwenn Shirley MacLaine

1956 BABY DOLL
Director: Elia Kazan
Co-stars: Carroll Baker Karl Malden Eli Wallach Lonny Chapman

1956 LOVE ME TENDER
Director Robert Webb
Co-stars Elvis Presley Debra Paget Richard Egan

1957 PEYTON PALACE
Director: Mark Robson
Co-stars: Lana Turner Arthur Kennedy Hope Lange Lloyd Nolan

1959 THE NUN'S STORY
Director: Fred Zinnemann
Co-stars: Audrey Hepburn Edith Evans Peggy Ashcroft

1960 THE STORY ON PAGE ONE
Director: Clifford Odets
Co-stars: Rita Hayworth Gig Young Hugh Griffith

1960 BUTTERFIELD 8
Director: Daniel Mann
Co-stars: Elizabeth Taylor Laurence Harvey Eddie Fisher

1961 SOMETHING WILD
Director: Jack Garfein
Co-stars: Carroll Baker Ralph Meeker Jean Stapleton

1962 SWEET BIRD OF YOUTH
Director: Richard Brooks
Co-stars: Paul Newman Geraldine Page Ed Begley Rip Torn

1964 BEHOLD A PALE HORSE
Director: Fred Zinneman
Co-stars: Gregory Peck Anthony Quinn Omar Sharif

1964 YOUNGBLOOD HAWKE
Director Delmer Daves
Co-stars James Franciscus Genevieve Page Mary Astor

1966 SEVEN WOMEN
Director: John Ford
Co-stars: Anne Bancroft Flora Robson Sue Lyon Betty Field

1969 WHATEVER HAPPENED TO AUNT ALICE
Director: Lee Katzin
Co-stars: Geraldine Page Ruth Gordon

1973 A SUMMER WITHOUT BOYS
Director: Jeannot Szwarc
Co-stars: Barbara Rush Michael Moriarty Kay Lenz

1973 A BRAND NEW LIFE
Director: Sam O'Steen
Co-stars: Cloris Leachman Martin Balsam Gene Nelson

1974 MURDER OR MERCY
Director: Harvey Hart
Co-stars: Melvyn Douglas Bradford Dillman David Birney

1975 THE SPIRAL STAIRCASE
Director: Peter Collinson
Co-stars: Jacqueline Bisset Christopher Plummer Sam Wanamaker

1976 ONE SUMMER LOVE
Director: Gilbert Cates
Co-stars: Beau Bridges Susan Sarandon Michael B. Miller

1979 AND BABY MAKES SIX
Director: Waris Hussein
Co-stars: Colleen Dewhurst Warren Oates Timothy Hutton

1980 BABY COMES HOME
Director: Waris Hussein
Co-stars: Colleen Dewhurst Warren Oates Lee Wallace

1981 ISABEL'S CHOICE
Director: Guy Green
Co-stars: Jean Stapleton Richard Kiley Peter Coyote Betsy Palmer

1987 PICK-UP ARTIST
Director: James Toback
Co-stars: Molly Ringwald Robert Downey Danny Aiello

LISA DUNSHEATH

1983 EDDIE MACON'S RUN
Director: Jeff Kanen
Co-stars: Kirk Douglas John Schneider Lee Purcell

ROSEMARY DUNSMORE

1986 MILES TO GO
Director: David Greene
Co-stars: Jill Clayburgh Tom Skerritt Mimi Kuzyk

1987 AFTER THE PROMISE
Director: David Greene
Co-stars: Mark Harmon Diana Scarwid Trey Ames

1988 GO TO THE LIGHT
Director: Mike Robe
Co-stars: Linda Hamilton Richard Thomas Piper Laurie

KIRSTEN DUNST

1995 LITTLE WOMEN
Director Gillian Armstrong
Co-stars Winona Ryder Susan Sarandon Gabriel Byrne

ANNIE DUPEREUX

1960 LOLA
Director: Jacques Demy
Co-stars: Anouk Aimee Marc Michel Elina Larbourdette

ANNY DUPEREY

1974 STAVISKY
Director: Alain Resnais
Co-stars: Jean-Paul Belmondo Charles Boyer Francois Perier

1976 PARDON MON AFFAIRE
Director: Yves Robert
Co-stars: Jean Rochfort Claude Brasseur Danielle Delorme

1977 PARDON MON AFFAIRE TOO
Director: Yves Robert
Co-stars: Jean Rochfort Danielle Delorme Guy Bedos

1977 BOBBY DEERFIELD
Director: Sydney Pollack
Co-stars: Al Pacino Marthe Keller Walter McGinn

1979 FROM HELL TO VICTORY
Director: Hank Milestone
Co-stars: George Peppard George Hamilton Capucine

STARLETTE DUPOIS

1987 HOLLYWOOD SHUFFLE
Director: Robert Townsend
Co-stars: Robert Townsend Anne-Marie Johnson Helen Martin

ANNE DUPONT

1992 AMERICAN NINJA 5
Director: Bobby Gene Leonard
Co-stars: David Bradley Lee Reyes Pat Morita

MINNIE DUPREE

1938 THE YOUNG IN HEART
Director: Richard Wallace
Co-stars: Douglas Fairbanks Jnr. Janet Gaynor Billie Burke

LOUISE DUPREY

1990 DANCIN' THRU THE DARK
Director: Mike Ockrent
Co-stars: Claire Hackett Con O'Neill Angela Clarke

JUNE DUPREZ

1936 THE CRIMSON CIRCLE
Director: Reginald Denham
Co-stars: Hugh Wakefield Noah Beery Alfred Drayton

1939 THE LION HAS WINGS
Director: Michael Powell
Co-stars: Merle Oberon Ralph Richardson Robert Douglas

1939 THE SPY IN BLACK
Director: Michael Powell
Co-stars: Conrad Veidt Valerie Hobson Sebastian Shaw

1939 THE FOUR FEATHERS
Director: Zoltan Korda
Co-stars: John Clements Ralph Richardson Jack Allen

1942 LITTLE TOKYO, USA
Director: Otto Brower
Co-stars: Preston Foster Brenda Joyce Harold Huber

1943 FOREVER AND A DAY
Director: Rene Clair
Co-stars: Anna Neagle Ray Milland Charles Laughton Eric Blore

1944 NONE BUT THE LONELY HEART
Director: Clifford Odets
Co-stars: Cary Grant Ethel Barrymore Jane Wyatt

1945 THE BRIGHTON STRANGLER
Director: Max Nosseck
Co-stars: John Loder Michael St. Angel

1945 AND THEN THERE WERE NONE
Director: Rene Clair
Co-stars: Walter Huston Barry Fitzgerald Roland Young

1946 CALCUTTA
Director: John Farrow
Co-stars: Alan Ladd Gail Russell William Bendix Lowell Gilmore

1946 THAT BRENNAN GIRL
Director: Alfred Santell
Co-stars: Mona Freeman James Dunn William Marshall

DEANNA DURBIN (Special Award 1938)

1936 EVERY SUNDAY
Director: Felix Feist
Co-Star Judy Garland

1936 THREE SMART GIRLS
Director: Henry Koster
Co-stars: Barbara Reid Nan Grey Charles Winninger Ray Milland

1936 ONE HUNDRED MEN AND A GIRL
Director: Henry Koster
Co-stars: Adolphe Menjou Leopold Stokowski Mischa Auer

1938 MAD ABOUT MUSIC
Director: Norman Taurog
Co-stars: Herbert Marshall Gail Patrick Arthur Treacher

1938 THAT CERTAIN AGE
Director: Edward Ludwig
Co-stars: Melvyn Douglas Jackie Cooper Nancy Carroll

1939 THREE SMART GIRLS GROW UP
Director: Henry Koster
Co-stars: Nan Grey Charles Winninger Robert Cummings

1939 FIRST LOVE
Director: Henry Koster
Co-stars: Robert Stack Eugene Pallette Helen Parrish

1940 IT'S A DATE
Director: William Seiter
Co-stars: Walter Pidgeon Kay Francis Henry Stephenson

1940 SPRING PARADE
Director: Henry Koster
Co-stars: Robert Cummings Henry Stephenson Mischa Auer

1941 NICE GIRL?
Director: William Seiter
Co-stars: Franchot Tone Robert Stack Walter Brennan

1941 IT STARTED WITH EVE
Director: Henry Koster
Co-stars: Charles Laughton Robert Cummings Guy Kibbee

1943 THE AMAZING MRS. HOLLIDAY
Director: Bruce Manning
Co-stars: Edmond O'Brien Barry Fitzgerald

1943 HERS TO HOLD
Director: Frank Ryan
Co-stars: Joseph Cotten Charles Winninger Gus Schilling

1943 HIS BUTLER'S SISTER
Director: Frank Borzage
Co-stars: Franchot Tone Pat O'Brien Evelyn Ankers

1944 CAN'T HELP SINGING
Director: Frank Ryan
Co-stars: David Bruce Robert Paige Akim Tamiroff

1944 CHRISTMAS HOLIDAY
Director: Robert Siodmak
Co-stars: Gene Kelly Gladys George Richard Whorf

1945 LADY ON A TRAIN
Director: Charles David
Co-stars: Ralph Bellamy David Bruce Dan Duryea

1945 BECAUSE OF HIM
Director: Richard Wallace
Co-stars: Charles Laughton Franchot Tone Helen Broderick

1947 SOMETHING IN THE WIND
Director: Irving Pichel
Co-stars: Donald O'Connor Charles Winninger John Dall

1947 I'LL BE YOURS
Director: William Seiter
Co-stars: Tom Drake William Bendix Adolphe Menjou

1948 FOR THE LOVE OF MARY
Director: Frererick De Cordova
Co-stars: Edmond O'Brien Harry Davenport Jeffery Lynn

1948 UP IN CENTRAL PARK
Director: William Seiter
Co-stars: Dick Haymes Vlncent Price Albert Sharpe

MARINA DURELL

1973 BADGE 373
Director: Howard Kock
Co-stars: Robert Duvall Verna Bloom Henry Darrow

ANNE-MARIE DURINGER

1958 COUNT FIVE AND DIE
Director: Victor Vicas
Co-stars: Nigel Patrick Jeffrey Hunter David Kossoff

1977 THE LACE MAKER
Director: Claude Goretta
Co-stars: Isabelle Huppert Yves Beneyton Florence Giorgetti

1982 VERONIKA VOSS
Director: Rainer Werner Fassbinder
Co-stars: Rosel Zech Hilmar Thate Doris Schade

BARBARA DURKIN

1987 WISH YOU WERE HERE
Director: David Leland
Co-stars: Emily Lloyd Tom Bell Clare Clifford

CARMEN DU SAUTOY

1983 THE ALAMUT AMBUSH
Director: Ken Grier
Co-stars: Terence Stamp Robin Sach Richard Wilson

1990 THE ORCHID HOUSE
Director: Horace Ove
Co-stars: Diana Quick Frances Barber Kate Buffery

MARJI DUSAY

1968 SWEET NOVEMBER
Director: Robert Ellls Miller
Co-stars: Anthony Newley Sandy Dennis Theodore Bikel

1977 MacARTHUR
Director: Joseph Sargent
Co-stars: Gregory Peck Ed Flanders Dan O'Herlihy

1980 THE MURDER THAT WOULDN'T DIE
Director: Ron Satlof
Co-stars: Willliam Conrad Jose Ferrer Sharon Acker

1987 MADE IN HEAVEN
Director: Alan Rudolph
Co-stars: Timothy Hutton Kelly McGillis Maureen Stapleton

ANN DUSENBERRY

1977 THE POSSESSED
Director: Jerry Thorpe
Co-stars: James Farantino Joan Hackett Harrison Ford

1978 LITTLE WOMEN
Director: David Lowell
Co-stars: Meredith Baxter Susan Dey Dorothy McGuire

1979 HEART BEAT
Director: John Byrum
Co-stars: Nick Nolte Sissy Spacek John Heard Ray Sharkey

1981 CUTTER'S WAY
Director: Ivan Passer
Co-stars: Jeff Bridges John Heard Lisa Eichhorn

1983 CONFESSIONS OF A MARRIED MAN
Director: Charles Pratt
Co-stars: Robert Conrad Jennifer Warren

1984 HE'S NOT YOUR SON
Director: Don Taylor
Co-stars: Donna Mills Ken Howard George Coe

1986 LONG TIME GONE
Director: Robert Butler
Co-stars: Paul Lemat Wil Wheaton Barbara Stock

ELIZA DUSHKU *(Child)*

1992 THAT NIGHT
Director: Craig Bolotin
Co-stars: C. Thomas Howell Helen Shaver Juliette Lewis

1993 THIS BOY'S LIFE
Director: Michael Caton-Jones
Co-stars: Robert De Niro Leonardo DiCaprio Ellen Barkin

NANCY DUSSAULT

1979 THE IN-LAWS
Director: Arthur Miller
Co-stars: Peter Falk Alan Arkin Penny Peyser

MARIA DUVALL

1982 PERMANENT VACATION
Director Jim Jarmusch
Co-stars Chris Parker Leila Gastol

SHELLEY DUVALL

1970 BREWSTER McCLOUD
Director: Robert Altman
Co-stars: Bud Cort Sally Kellerman Rene Auberjonois

1971 McCABE AND MRS. MILLER
Director: Robert Altman
Co-stars: Warren Beatty Julie Christie Keith Carradine

1974 THIEVES LIKE US
Director: Robert Altman
Co-stars: Keith Carradine Louise Fletcher John Schuck

1975 NASHVILLE
Director: Robert Altman
Co-stars: Keith Carradine David Arkin Karen Black Ned Beatty

1977 3 WOMEN
Director: Robert Altman
Co-stars: Sissy Spacek Janice Rule Robert Fortier John Cromwell

1977 ANNIE HALL
Director: Woody Allen
Co-stars: Woody Allen Diane Keaton Tony Roberts Carol Kane

1980 POPEYE
Director: Robert Altman
Co-stars: Robin Williams Ray Walston Paul Dooley Paul L. Smith

1980 THE SHINING
Director: Stanley Kubrick
Co-stars: Jack Nicholson Danny Lloyd Barry Nelson

1981 TIME BANDITS
Director: Terry Gilliam
Co-stars: John Cleese Sean Connery Ian Holm David Warner

1987 ROXANNE
Director: Fred Schepisi
Co-stars: Steve Martin Daryl Hannah Michael J. Pollard

1991 SUBURBAN COMMANDO
Director: Burt Kennedy
Co-stars: Hulk Hogan Christopher Lloyd Jack Elam

1998 TWILIGHT OF THE ICE NYMPHS
Director: Guy Maddin
Co-star: Pascale Bussiere

ELSPETH DUXBURRY

1960 MAKE MINE MINK
Director: Robert Asher
Co-stars: Terry-Thomas Athene Seyler Billie Whitelaw

ANN DVORAK *(Ann McKim)*
(Daughter Of Silent Actress Anna Lehr)

1931 THE GUARDSMAN
Director: Sidney Franklin
Co-stars: Lynn Fontanne Alfred Lunt Roland Young Zasu Pitts

1931 SKY DEVILS
Director: Edward Sutherland
Co-stars: Spencer Tracy William Boyd

1932 THE STRANGE LOVE OF MOLLY LOUVAIN
Director: Michael Curtiz
Co-stars: Lee Tracy Leslie Fenton

1932 LOVE IS A RACKET
Director: William Wellman
Co-stars: Douglas Fairbanks Frances Dee Lee Tracy

1932 THE CROWD ROARS
Director: Howard Hawks
Co-stars: James Cagney Joan Blondell Eric Linden

1932 CROONER
Director: Lloyd Bacon
Co-stars: David Manners Ken Murray J. Carrol Naish

1932 SCARFACE
Director: Howard Hawks
Co-stars: Paul Muni George Raft Boris Karloff

1932 THREE ON A MATCH
Director: Mervyn LeRoy
Co-stars: Joan Blondell Bette Davis Humphrey Bogart

1933 THE WAY TO LOVE
Director: Norman Taurog
Co-stars: Maurice Chevalier Minna Gombell

1933 COLLEGE COACH
Director: William Wellman
Co-stars: Dick Powell Pat O'Brien Lyle Talbot

1934 THE FRIENDS OF MR. SWEENEY
Director: Edward Ludwig
Co-stars: Charles Ruggles Eugene Pallette

1934 GENTLEMEN ARE BORN
Director: Alfred Green
Co-stars: Franchot Tone Dick Foran Jean Muir

1934 HEAT LIGHTNING
Director: Mervyn LeRoy
Co-stars: Aline McMahon Preston Foster Lyle Talbot

1934 HOUSEWIFE
Director: Alfred Green
Co-stars: Bette Davis George Brent John Halliday

1934 SIDE STREETS
Director: Alfred Green
Co-stars: Aline McMahon Paul Kelly Henry O'Neill

1934 MASSACRE
Co-Star Richard Bathelmess

1935 SWEET MUSIC
Co-stars: Rudy Vallee Helen Morgan Ned Sparks

1935 THANKS A MILLION
Director: Roy Del Ruth
Co-stars: Dick Powell Fred Allen Patsy Kelly

1935 I SELL ANYTHING
Director: Robert Florey
Co-stars: Pat O'Brien Claire Dodd Roscoe Carns

1935 "G" MEN
Director: William Keighley
Co-stars: James Cagney Margaret Lindsay Robert Armstrong

1935 DR. SOCRATES
Director: William Dieterle
Co-stars: Paul Muni Barton MacLane Robert Barrat

1935 BRIGHT LIGHTS
Director: Busby Berkeley
Co-stars: Joe E. Brown Patricia Ellis William Gargan

1936 WE WHO ARE ABOUT TO DIE
Director: Christy Cabanne
Co-stars: Preston Foster John Beal Gordon Jones

1937 MANHATTAN MERRY-GO-ROUND
Director: Charles Reisner
Co-stars: Phil Regan Leo Carrillo James Gleason

1937 THE CASE OF THE STUTTERING BISHOP
Director: William Clemens
Co-stars: Donald Woods Anne Nagel

1937 MIDNIGHT COURT
Co-Star Gordon Elliott

1937 RACING LADY
Co-Star Harry Carey

1937 SHE'S NO LADY
Co-Star Gavin Williams

1938 GANGS OF NEW YORK
Director: James Cruze
Co-stars: Charles Bickford Wynne Gibson

1938 MERRILY WE LIVE
Director: Norman Z McLeod
Co-stars: Constance Bennett Brian Aherne Billie Burke

1939 STRONGER THAN DESIRE
Director: Leslie Fenton
Co-stars: Walter Pidgeon Virginia Bruce Ilka Chase

1939 BLIND ALLEY
Director: Charles Vidor
Co-stars: Chester Morris Ralph Bellamy

1941 THIS WAS PARIS
Director: John Harlow
Co-stars: Ben Lyon Griffith Jones Robert Morley

1942 SQUADRON LEADER X
Director: Lance Comfort
Co-stars: Eric Portman Walter Fitzgerald Henry Oscar

1943 ESCAPE TO DANGER
Director: Lance Comfort
Co-stars: Eric Portman Karel Stepanek Ronald Adam

1945 FLAME OF THE BARBARY COAST
Director: Joseph Kane
Co-stars: John Wayne Joseph Schildkraut

1945 MASQUERADE IN MEXICO
Director: Mitchell Leisen
Co-stars: Dorothy Lamour Arturo De Cordova

1946 THE BACHELOR'S DAUGHTERS
Director: Andrew Stone
Co-stars: Adolphe Menjou Billie Burke Gail Russell

1946 ABILENE TOWN
Director: Edwin Marin
Co-stars: Randolph Scott Rhonda Fleming Lloyd Bridges

1947 THE LONG NIGHT
Director: Anatole Litvak
Co-stars: Henry Fonda Vincent Price Barbara Bel Geddes

1947 OUT OF THE BLUE
Director: Leigh Jason
Co-stars: George Brent Carole Landis Turhan Bey

1947 THE PRIVATE AFFAIRS OF BEL AMI
Director: Albert Lewin
Co-stars: George Sanders Angela Lansbury

1948 THE WALLS OF JERICHO
Director: John Stahl
Co-stars: Cornel Wilde Kirk Douglas Linda Darnell

1950 OUR VERY OWN
Director: David Miller
Co-stars: Ann Blyth Farley Granger Joan Evans

1950 MRS. O'MALLEY AND MR. MALONE
Director: Norman Taurog
Co-stars: Marjorie Main James Whitmore Fred Clark

1950 A LIFE OF HER OWN
Director: George Cukor
Co-stars: Lana Turner Ray Milland Tom Ewell

1951 I WAS AN AMERICAN SPY
Director: Lesley Selander
Co-stars: Gene Evans Philip Ahn Richard Loo

1951 THE SECRET OF CONVICT LAKE
Director: Michael Gordon
Co-stars: Glenn Ford Gene Tierney Ethel Barrymore

HILARY DWYER

1968 WITCHFINDER GENERAL
Director: Michael Reeves
Co-stars: Vincent Price Ian Ogilvy Rupert Davies

1969 THE OBLONG BOX
Director: Gordon Hessler
Co-stars: Vincent Price Christopher Lee Peter Arne

1969 THE BODY SNATCHERS
Director: Gerry Levy
Co-stars: George Sanders Maurice Evans Patrick Allen

1970 CRY OF THE BANSHEE
Director: Gordon Hessler
Co-stars: Vincent Price Elizabeth Bergner Hugh Griffith

1971 WUTHERING HEIGHTS
Director: Robert Fuest
Co-stars: Anna Calder-Marshall Timothy Dalton Ian Ogilvy

RUTH DWYER

1925 SEVEN CHANCES
Director: Buster Keaton
Co-stars: Buster Keaton Ray Barnes Snitz Edwards

AMINTA DYNE

1948 KISS THE BLOOD OFF MY HANDS
Director: Norman Foster
Co-stars: Joan Fontaine Burt Lancaster Robert Newton

1949 SONG OF INDIA
Director: Albert Rogell
Co-stars: Sabu Gail Russell Turhan Bey

NOEL DYSON

1966 PRESS FOR TIME
Director: Robert Asher
Co-stars: Norman Wisdom Derek Bond Angela Browne

JEAN EAGLES
Nominated For Best Actress In 1929 For "The Letter"

1927   MAN, WOMAN AND SIN
Director: Monta Bell
Co-stars: John Gilbert Marc McDermott

1929   THE LETTER
Director: Jean De Limur
Co-stars: O.P. Heggie Reginald Owen Herbert Marshall

1929   JEALOUSY
Co-star: Anthony Bushell

ELIZABETH EARL
1998   FAIRYTALE:A TRUE STORY
Director: Charles Sturridge
Co-stars: Paul McGann Peter O'Toole Harvey Keitel

TINA EARL
1989   A SMALL MOURNING
Director: Chris Bernard
Co-stars: Alison Steadman Stratford Johns Ian Deam

1992   A LITTLE BIT OF LIPPY
Director: Chris Bernard
Co-stars: Kenneth Cranham Rachel Davies Alison Swann

JOSEPHINE EARLE
1923   WOMAN TO WOMAN
Director: Graham Cutts
Co-stars: Betty Compson Clive Brook Marie Ault

DAISY EARLES
1932   FREAKS
Director: Tod Browning
Co-stars: Wallace Ford Olga Baclanova Leila Hyams

LESLIE EASTERBROOK
1986   POLICE ACADEMY 3: BACK IN TRAINING
Director: Jerry Paris
Co-stars: Steve Guttenberg Bubba Smith

1987   POLICE ACADEMY 4: CITIZENS ON PATROL
Director: Jim Drake
Co-stars: Steve Guttenberg Sharon Stone

**1988   POLICE ACADEMY 5:
          ASSIGNMENT MIAMI BEACH**
Director: Alan Myerson
Co-stars: Matt McCoy Janet Jones

1989   POLICE ACADEMY 6: CITY UNDER SEIGE
Director: Peter Bonertz
Co-stars: Michael Winslow Bubba Smith

JOYCE EASTON
1970   THE BROTHERHOOD OF SATAN
Director: Bernard McEveety
Co-stars: Strother Martin Alvy Moore Anna Capri

1978   THE FURY
Director: Brian De Palma
Co-stars: Kirk Douglas John Cassavetes Carrie Snodgress

SHEENA EASTON
1987   SIGN O' THE TIMES
Director: Prince
Co-star: Prince

**1992   FERN GULLY:
          THE LAST RAINFOREST (Voice)**
Director: Bill Kroyer
Co-stars: Tim Curry Samantha Mathis

1993   TEKWAR
Director: William Shatner
Co-stars: William Shatner Greg Evignan

ALISON EASTWOOD
(Daughter Of Clint Eastwood)

1984   TIGHTROPE
Director: Richard Tuggle
Co-stars: Clint Eastwood Genevieve Bujold Dan Hedaya

JAYNE EASTWOOD
1987   THE KIDNAPPING OF BABY JOHN DOE
Director: Peter Gerretsen
Co-stars: Janet-Laine Green Geoffrey Bowes

DORIS EATON
1929   THE VERY IDEA
Co-stars: Frank Craven Olive Tell Theodor Von Eltz

GILLIAN EATON
1989   1996
Director: Karl Francis
Co-stars: Keith Barron Alun Armstrong Dudley Sutton

KATE EATON
1992   RESNICK: LONELY HEARTS
Director: Bruce MacDonald
Co-stars: Fiona Victory Neil Dudgeon Tom Wilkinson

MARJORIE EATON
1979   THE ATTIC
Director: George Edwards
Co-stars: Carrie Snodgress Ray Milland Rosemary Murphy

MARY EATON
1929   THE COCOANUTS
Director: Robert Florey
Co-stars: Marx Brothers Margaret Dumont Kay Francis

1929   GLORIFYING THE AMERICAN GIRL
Director: Millard Webb
Co-stars: Eddie Cantor Helen Morgan Rudy Vallee

SHIRLEY EATON
1954   THE LOVE MATCH
Director: David Paltenghi
Co-stars: Arthur Askey Thora Hird Glenn Mervyn

1956   SAILOR BEWARE
Director: Gordon Parry
Co-stars: Peggy Mount Esma Cannon Roland Lewis Cyril Smith

1956   THREE MEN IN A BOAT
Director: Ken Annakin
Co-stars: Laurence Harvey David Tomlinson Jimmy Edwards

1956   CHARLEY MOON
Director: Guy Hamilton
Co-stars: Max Bygraves Dennis Price Michael Medwin

1957   DOCTOR AT LARGE
Director: Ralph Thomas
Co-stars: Dirk Bogarde Muriel Pavlow Donald Sinden

19557   THE NAKED TRUTH
Director: Mario Zampi
Co-stars: Dennis Price Peter Sellers Terry-Thomas Peggy Mount

1958   FURTHER UP THE CREEK
Director: Val Guest
Co-stars: David Tomlinson Frankie Howerd Thora Hird

1958   CARRY ON SERGEANT
Director: Gerald Thomas
Co-stars: Bob Monkhouse William Hartnell Kenneth Williams

1959   CARRY ON NURSE
Director: Gerald Thomas
Co-stars: Kenneth Williams Charles Hawtrey Bill Owen

1960   CARRY ON CONSTABLE
Director: Gerald Thomas
Co-stars: Sid James Eric Barker Leslie Phillips

1961   DENTIST ON THE JOB
Director: C. Pennington-Richards
Co-stars: Bob Monkhouse Ronnie Stevens

1961   NEARLY A NASTY ACCIDENT
Director: Don Chaffey
Co-stars: Kenneth Connor Richard Wattis Peter Jones

1961   WHAT A CARVE UP!
Director: Pat Jackson
Co-stars: Sid James Dennis Price Donald Pleasence

1963   THE GIRL HUNTERS
Director: Roy Rowland
Co-stars: Mickey Spillane Lloyd Nolan Hy Gardner

1964   GOLDFINGER
Director: Guy Hamilton
Co-stars: Sean Connery Honor Blackman Gert Frobe Harold Sakata

1964   RHINO
Director: Ivan Tors
Co-stars: Harry Guardino Robert Culp

1966   TEN LITTLE INDIANS
Director: George Pollock
Co-stars: Dennis Price Leo Genn Hugh O'Brian

1966   EIGHT ON THE LAM
Director: George Marshall
Co-stars: Bob Hope Phyllis Diller Jill St. John

1966   AROUND THE WORLD UNDER THE SEA
Director: Andrew Marton
Co-stars: Lloyd Bridges David McCallum

1968   THE BLOOD OF FU MANCHU
Director: Jesus Franco
Co-stars: Christopher Lee Richard Greene

HILLARY EAVES

1940   CRIMES AT THE DARK HOUSE
Director: George King
Co-stars: Tod Slaughter Sylvia Marriott Hay Petrie

NORMA EBERHARDT

1958   THE RETURN OF DRACULA
Director: Paul Landres
Co-stars: Francis Lederer Ray Stricklyn Jimmie Baird

CHRISTINE EBERSOLE

1984   AMADEUS
Director: Milos Forman
Co-stars: Tom Hulce F. Murray Abraham Simon Callow

1984   GHOST DAD
Director: Sidney Poitier
Co-stars: Bill Cosby Kimberley Russell Ian Bannen Barry Corbin

1984   THIEF OF HEARTS
Director: Douglas Day Stewart
Co-stars: Steven Bauer Barbara Williams

1986   ACCEPTABLE RISKS
Director: Rick Wallace
Co-stars: Brian Dennehy Kenneth McMillan Beah Richards

1988   MAC AND ME
Director: Stewart Raffill
Co-stars: Jonathan Ward Tina Caspary Lauren Stanley

1991   DEAD AGAIN
Director: Kenneth Branagh
Co-stars: Emma Thompson Andy Garcia

1992   FOLKS!
Director: Ted Kotcheff
Co-stars: Tom Selleck Don Ameche Anne Jackson Robert Pastorelli

1993   DYING TO LOVE YOU
Director: Robert Iscove
Co-stars: Tim Matheson Tracy Pollan Frances Lee McCain

1994   MY GIRL 2
Director: Howard Zief
Co-stars: Dan Aykroyd Jamie Lee Curtis Anna Chlumskey

VILMA EBSEN (Sister Of Buddy Ebsen)

1935   BROADWAY MELODY OF 1936
Director: Roy Del Ruth
Co-stars: Robert Taylor Eleanor Powell Buddy Ebsen

MAUDE EBURNE

1930   THE BAT WHISPERS
Director: Roland West
Co-stars: Chester Morris Una Merkel Spencer Charters

1931   THE GUARDSMAN
Director: Sidney Franklin
Co-stars: Alfred Lunt Lynn Fontainne Roland Young

1931   BLONDE CRAZY
Director: Roy Del Ruth
Co-stars: James Cagney Joan Blondell Ray Milland

1931   BOUGHT
Director: Archie Mayo
Co-stars: Constance Bennett Ben Lyon Ray Milland

1931   INDISCREET
Director: Leo McCarey
Co-stars: Gloria Swanson Ben Lyon Barbara Kent

1932   POLLY OF THE CIRCUS
Director: Alfred Santell
Co-stars: Marion Davies Clark Gable C. Aubrey Smith

1932   THE FIRST YEAR
Director: William Howard
Co-stars: Janet Gaynor Charles Farrell Minna Gombell

1932   THIS RECKLESS AGE
Director: Frank Tuttle
Co-stars: Charles Rogers Peggy Shannon Frances Dee

1932   MAN HUNT
Co-stars: Junior Durkin Charlotte Henry

1933   FOG
Director: Albert Rogell
Co-stars: Donald Cook Mary Brian Reginald Denny

1933   LADIES THEY TALK ABOUT
Director: William Keighley
Co-stars: Barbara Stanwyck Preston Foster

1933 THE VAMPIRE BAT
Director: Frank Strayer
Co-stars: Lionel Atwill Fay Wray Melvyn Douglas

1933 THE WARRIOR'S HUSBAND
Director: Walter Lang
Co-stars: Elissa Landi Marjorie Rambeau David Manners

1934 LAZY RIVER
Director: George Seitz
Co-stars: Jean Parker Robert Young Nat Pendleton

1935 THE LEAVENWORTH CASE
Director: Lewis Collins
Co-stars: Donald Cook Norman Foster Jean Rouverol

1935 RUGGLES OF RED GAP
Director: Leo McCarey
Co-stars: Charles Laughton Mary Boland Charles Ruggles

1936 POPPY
Director: Edward Sutherland
Co-stars: W.C. Fields Rochelle Hudson Richard Cromwell

1937 LIVE, LOVE AND LEARN
Director: George Fitzmaurice
Co-stars: Robert Montgomery Rosalind Russell

1937 WHEN'S YOUR BIRTHDAY
Co-stars: Joe E. Brown Suzanne Karen

1937 HOLLYWOOD COWBOY
Co-star: George O'Brien

1939 MOUNTAIN RHYTHM
Co-stars: Gene Autry Smiley Burnette

1941 YOU BELONG TO ME
Director: Wesley Ruggles
Co-stars: Barbara Stanwyck Henry Fonda

1944 THE SUSPECT
Director: Robert Siodmak
Co-stars: Charles Laughton Rosalind Ivan Ella Raines

1944 THE PRINCESS AND THE PIRATE
Director: David Butler
Co-stars: Bob Hope Virginia Mayo Victor McLaglen

1944 THE BOOGIE MAN WILL GET YOU
Director: Lew Landers
Co-stars: Boris Karloff Peter Lorre Jeff Donnell

AMY ECCLES
1970 LITTLE BIG MAN
Director: Arthur Penn
Co-stars: Dustin Hoffman Martin Balsam Faye Dunaway

AGNETA ECKEMYR
1974 THE ISLAND AT THE TOP OF THE SEA
Director: Robert Stevenson
Co-stars: Donald Sinden David Hartman

BARBARA EDA-YOUNG
1973 SERPICO
Director: Sidney Lumet
Co-stars: Al Pacino John Randolph Tony Roberts

HELEN JEROME EDDY
1917 REBECCA OF SUNNYBROOK FARM
Director: Marshall Neilan
Co-stars: Mary Pickford Marjorie Daw

1931 SOOKY
Co-star: Robert Coogan

1931 MATA HARI
Director: George Fitzmaurice
Co-stars: Greta Garbo Ramon Navarro Lionel Barrymore

1932 MADAME BUTTERFLY
Director: Marion Gering
Co-stars: Sylvia Sidney Cary Grant Charles Ruggles

1933 TORCH SINGER
Director: Alexander Hall
Co-stars: Claudette Colbert Ricardo Cortez Baby Leroy

1934 RIPTIDE
Director: Edmund Goulding
Co-stars: Norma Shearer Robert Montgomery Herbert Marshall

1934 GIRL OF THE LIMBERLOST
Director: Christy Cabanne
Co-stars: Louise Dresser Marian Marsh Ralph Morgan

1934 HELLDORADO
Director: James Cruze
Co-stars: Richard Arlen Madge Evans Ralph Bellamy

1935 RENDEZVOUS AT MIDNIGHT
Director: Christy Cabanne
Co-stars: Ralph Bellamy Valerie Hobson Irene Ware

1936 KLONDYKE ANNIE
Director: Raoul Walsh
Co-stars: Mae West Victor McLaglen Philip Reed

1938 CITY STREETS
Director: Albert Rogell
Co-stars: Edith Fellows Leo Carrillo Mary Gordon

1939 BLONDIE BRINGS UP BABY
Director: Frank Strayer
Co-stars: Penny Singleton Arthur Lake Fay Helm

ALICE EDEN
1939 CAREER
Director: Leigh Jason
Co-stars: Edward Ellis Ann Shirley Janet Beecher

BARBARA EDEN
1959 A PRIVATE'S AFFAIR
Director: Raoul Walsh
Co-stars: Sal Mineo Barry Coe Gary Crosby Terry Moore

1960 FLAMING STAR
Director: Don Seigel
Co-stars: Elvis Presley Dolores Del Rio Steve Forrest

1961 ALL HANDS ON DECK
Director: Norman Taurog
Co-stars: Pat Boone Buddy Hackett Dennis O'Keefe

1961 VOYAGE TO THE BOTTOM OF THE SEA
Director: Irwin Allen
Co-stars: Walter Pidgeon Joan Fontaine

1962 THE WONDERFUL WORLD OF THE BROTHERS GRIMM
Director: George Pal
Co-stars: Laurence Harvey Karl Boehm Claire Bloom

1963 THE YELLOW CANARY
Director: Buzz Kulik
Co-stars: Pat Boone Steve Forrest Jack Klugman Jesse White

1964 7 FACES OF DR. LAO
Director: George Pal
Co-stars: Tony Randall Arthur O'Connell John Erikson

1964 RIDE THE WILD SURF
Director: Don Taylor
Co-stars: Fabian Tab Hunter Shelley Fabares

1964 QUICK, LET'S GET MARRIED
Director: William Dieterle
Co-stars: Ginger Rogers Ray Milland Walter Abel

1964 THE BRASS BOTTLE
Director: Harry Keller
Co-stars: Tony Randall Burl Ives Edward Andrews

1974 THE STRANGER WITHIN
Director: Lee Phillips
Co-stars: George Grizzard Joyce Van Patten

1976 THE AMAZING DOBERMANS
Director: David Chudnow
Co-stars: Fred Astaire James Franciscus Jack Carter

1978 HARPER VALLEY PTA
Director: Richard Bennett
Co-star: Ronny Cox

1985 I DREAM OF JEANIE - FIFTEEN YEARS ON
Director: William Asher
Co-stars: Wayne Rodgers Bill Daley

1988 THE SECRET LIFE OF KATHY McCORMICK
Director: Robert Lewis
Co-stars: Josh Taylor Judy Geeson

1989 BRAND NEW LIFE
Director: Eric Laneuville
Co-stars: Don Murray Shawnee Smith Jenny Garth

1991 HELL HATH NO FURY
Director: Thomas Wright
Co-stars: Loretta Swit David Ackroyd Amanda Petersen

1991 LETHAL CHARM
Director: Richard Michaels
Co-stars: Stuart Wilson Heather Locklear Julie Fulton

1994 VISIONS OF TERROR
Director: Sam Pilsbury
Co-stars: Ted Marcoux Missy Crider

ELANA EDEN

1960 THE STORY OF RUTH
Director: Henry Koster
Co-stars: Peggy Wood Viveca Lindfors Stuart Whitman

LINDA EDMOND

1989 GOD'S WILL
Director: Julia Cameron
Co-stars: Marge Kotlisky Danielo Region

ELIZABETH EDMONDS

1982 SCRUBBERS
Director: Mai Zeterling
Co-stars: Amanda York Chrissie Cotterill Kate Ingram

BEATTY EDNIE *(Daughter Of Sylvia Syms)*

1986 HIGHLANDER
Director: Russell Mulcahy
Co-stars: Christopher Lambert Roxanne Hart Sean Connery

1988 THE DARK ANGEL
Director: Peter Hammond
Co-stars: Peter O'Toole Jane Lapotaire Tim Woodward

1989 WILD FLOWERS
Director: Robert Smith
Co-stars: Alan Bates Colette O'Neil Sheila Keith

1990 MR. JOHNSON
Director: Bruce Beresford
Co-stars: Maynard Eziashi Pierce Brosnan Edward Woodward

1990 THE LILAC BUS
Director: Giles Foster
Co-stars: Stephanie Beacham Con O'Neill Dervla Kirwan

1993 IN THE NAME OF THE FATHER
Director: Jim Sheridan
Co-stars: Daniel Day-Lewis Emma Thompson John Lynch

1993 MacGYVER: TRIAL TO DOOMSDAY
Director: Charlie Correll
Co-stars: Richard Dean Anderson Peter Egan

OLGA EDWARDS

1946 CAESAR AND CLEOPATRA
Director: Gabriel Pascal
Co-stars: Claude Rains Vivien Leigh Stewart Granger

1953 BLACK ORCHID
Director: Charles Saunders
Co-stars: John Bentley Mary Laura Wood Ronald Howard

ELAINE EDWARDS

1958 CURSE OF THE FACELESS MAN
Director: Edward Cahn
Co-stars: Richard Anderson Adele Mara Gar Moore

1960 THE PURPLE GANG
Director: Frank McDonald
Co-stars: Robert Blake Barry Sullivan Jody Lawrance

HENRYETTA EDWARDS

1956 THE FEMININE TOUCH
Director: Pat Jackson
Co-stars: George Baker Belinda Lee Delphi Lawrence

JENNIFER EDWARDS *(Child)*
(Daughter Of Julie Andrews And Blake Edwards)

1968 HEIDI
Director: Delbert Mann
Co-stars: Jean Simmons Maxmillian Schell Michael Redgrave

1983 THE MAN WHO LOVED WOMEN
Director: Blake Edwards
Co-stars: Burt Reynolds Julie Andrews Kim Basinger

1986 THAT'S LIFE
Director: Blake Edwards
Co-stars: Jack Lemmon Julie Andrews Sally Kellerman

1988 SUNSET
Director: Blake Edwards
Co-stars: Bruce Willis James Garner Mariel Hemingway

1989 PETER GUNN
Director: Blake Edwards
Co-stars: Peter Strauss Barbara Williams Pearl Bailey

1989 ALL'S FAIR

1993 SON OF THE PINK PANTHER
Director: Blake Edwards
Co-stars: Roberto Benigni Claudia Cardinale

JOAN EDWARDS

1947 HIT PARADE OF 1947
Director: Frank McDonald
Co-stars: Eddie Albert Constance Moore Gil Lamb

MARION EDWARDS

1981 ROAD GAMES
Director: Richard Franklin
Co-stars: Stacey Keach Grant Page Jamie Lee Curtis

MAUDIE EDWARDS

1943 THE SHIPBUILDERS
Director: John Baxter
Co-stars: Clive Brook Morland Graham Finlay Currie

1943 MY LEARNED FRIEND
Director: Basil Dearden
Co-stars: Will Hay Claude Hulbert Mervyn Johns

1945 I'LL BE YOUR SWEETHEART
Director: Val Guest
Co-stars: Margaret Lockwood Michael Rennie Vic Oliver

1962 BAND OF THIEVES
Director: Peter Bazencenet
Co-stars: Acker Bilk Jimmy Thompson Jennifer Jayne

NORMA EDWARDS
1993 HUSH LITTLE BABY
Director: Jorge Montesi
Co-stars: Diane Ladd Wendel Meldrum Geraint Wyn Davies

PENNY EDWARDS
1948 FEUDIN' FUSSIN' AND A-FIGHTIN'
Director: George Sherman
Co-stars: Donald O'Connor Marjorie Main

1948 TWO GUYS FROM TEXAS
Director: David Butler
Co-stars: Dennis Morgan Jack Carson Dodothy Malone

1952 PONY SOLDIER
Director: Joseph Newman
Co-stars: Tyrone Power Cameron Mitchell Robert Horton

1953 POWDER RIVER
Director: Louis King
Co-stars: Rory Calhoun Cameron Mitchell Corinne Calvert

1957 THE DALTON GIRLS
Director: Reginald LeBorg
Co-stars: Merry Anders Sue George John Russell

REBECCA EDWARDS (Child)
1992 GOD ON THE ROCKS
Director: Ross Cramer
Co-stars: Sinead Cusack Bill Paterson Minnie Driver

RONNIE CLARE EDWARDS
1982 A DAY FOR THANKS ON WALTON'S MOUNTAIN
Director: Harry Harris
Co-stars: Ralph Waite Ellen Corby

1984 FUTURE COP
Director: Charles Band
Co-stars: Ernest Borgnine Tim Thomerson Helen Hunt

1994 8 SECONDS
Director: John Avildsen
Co-stars: Luke Perry Stephen Baldwin James Rebhorn

JENNY EGAN
1960 POLLYANNA
Director: David Swift
Co-stars: Hayley Mills Jane Wyman Karl Malden Richard Egan

AUD EGEDE-NISSEN
1922 DOCTOR MABUSE THE GAMBLER
Director: Fritz Lang
Co-stars: Rudolphe Klein-Rogge Alfred Abel

JULIE EGE
1970 EVERY HOME SHOULD HAVE ONE
Director: James Clark
Co-stars: Marty Feldman Shelley Berman

1970 CREATURES THE WORLD FORGOT
Director: Don Chaffey
Co-stars: Brian O'Shaughnessy Robert John

1971 THE MAGNIFICENT SEVEN DEADLY SINS
Director: Graham Stark
Co-stars: Roy Hudd Joan Sims Harry Secombe

1971 UP POMPEII
Director: Bob Kellett
Co-stars: Frankie Howerd Barbara Murray Patrick Cargill

1972 GO FOR A TAKE
Director: Harry Booth
Co-stars: Reg Varney Norman Rossington Sue Lloyd

1972 NOT NOW DARLING
Director: Ray Cooney
Co-stars: Leslie Phillips Moira Lister Barbara Windsor

1972 RENTADICK
Director: Jim Clark
Co-stars: James Booth Richard Briers Donald Sinden

1973 THE FINAL PROGRAMME
Director: Robert Fuest
Co-stars: Jon Finch Jenny Runacre Hugh Griffith

1974 CRAZE
Director: Freddie Francis
Co-stars: Jack Palance Diana Dors Trevor Howard

1974 THE LEGEND OF THE SEVEN GOLDEN VAMPIRES
Director: Roy Ward Baker
Co-stars: Peter Cushing David Chiang

1974 THE MUTATIONS
Director: Jack Cardiff
Co-stars: Donald Pleasence Tom Baker Brad Harris

1974 PERCY'S PROGRESS
Director: Ralph Thomas
Co-stars: Leigh Lawson Elke Sommer Judy Geeson

1976 THE AMOROUS MILKMAN
Director: Derren Nesbitt
Co-stars: Brendan Price Diana Dors Donna Reading

SAMANTHA EGGAR
Nominated For Best Actress In 1965 For "The Collector"
1962 DR. CRIPPEN
Director: Robert Lynn
Co-stars: Donald Pleasence Coral Browne Donald Wolfit

1962 THE WILD AND THE WILLING
Director: Ralph Thomas
Co-stars: Dirk Bogarde Mylene Demongeot Leo McKern

1963 DOCTOR IN DISTRESS
Director: Ralph Thomas
Co-stars: Dirk Bogarde Leo McKern Mylene Demongeot

1964 PSYCHE 59
Director: Alexander Singer
Co-stars: Patricia Neal Curt Jurgens Ian Bannen

1965 RETURN FROM THE ASHES
Director: J. Lee-Thompson
Co-stars: Maxmillian Schell Ingrid Thulin Herbert Lom

1965 THE COLLECTOR
Director: William Wyler
Co-stars: Terence Stamp Mona Washbourne

1966 WALK DON'T RUN
Director: Charles Walters
Co-stars: Cary Grant Jim Hutton John Standing

1967 DOCTOR DOOLITTLE
Director: Richard Fleischer
Co-stars: Rex Harrison Anthony Newley Richard Attenborough

1969 THE LADY IN THE CAR WITH GLASSES AND A GUN
Director: Anatole Litvak
Co-stars: Oliver Reed John McEnery

1970 THE WALKING STICK
Director: Eric Till
Co-stars: David Hemming Phyllis Calvert Emlyn Williams

1970   THE MOLLY MAGUIRES
Director: Martin Ritt
Co-stars: Sean Connery Richard Harris Frank Finlay

1971   THE LIGHT AT THE EDGE OF THE WORLD
Director: Kevin Billington
Co-stars: Kirk Douglas Yul Brynner

1973   DOUBLE INDEMNITY
Director: Jack Smight
Co-stars: Richard Crenna Robert Webber Kathleen Cody

1974   ALL THE KIND STRANGERS
Director: Burt Kennedy
Co-stars: Stacy Keach John Savage Bobby Benson

1976   WHY SHOOT THE TEACHER?
Director: Silvio Narrizzano
Co-stars: Bud Cort Chris Wiggins Gary Reineke

1976   THE SEVEN PER CENT SOLOUTION
Director: Herbert Ross
Co-stars: Nicol Williamson Robert Duvall Vanessa Redgrave

1977   WELCOME TO BLOOD CITY
Director: Peter Sasdy
Co-stars: Jack Palance Keir Dullea Barry Morse Ken James

1977   THE UNCANNY
Director: Denis Haroux
Co-stars: Ray Milland Peter Cushing Susan Penhaligon

1979   THE BROOD
Director: David Cronenberg
Co-stars: Oliver Reed Art Hindle Cindy Hinds

1980   THE EXTERMINATOR
Director: James Glickenhaus
Co-stars: Robert Ginty Christopher George Sid James

1987   LOVE AMONG THIEVES
Director: Roger Young
Co-stars: Audrey Hepburn Robert Wagner Jerry Orbach

NICOLE EGGERT

1986   THE ANNHILATOR
Director: Michael Chapman
Co-stars: Mark Lindsay Chapman Susan Blakely Lisa Blount

MARTHA EGGBERT

1934   THE UNFINISHED SYMPHONY
Director: Willy Forst
Co-stars: Helen Chandler Beryl Laverick Hans Jaray

1935   MY HEART IS CALLING
Director: Carmine Gallone
Co-stars: Jan Kiepura Sonnie Hale Marie Lohr

1942   FOR ME AND MY GAL
Director: Busby Berkeley
Co-stars: Judy Garland Gene Kelly George Murphy

1943   PRESENTING LILY MARS
Director: Norman Taurog
Co-stars: Judy Garland Van Heflin Fay Bainter

LOUISE EGOLF

1985   FOOL FOR LOVE
Director: Robert Altman
Co-stars: Sam Shepard Kim Basinger Randy Quaid

JENNIFER EHLE
(Daughter Of Rosemary Harris)

1991   THE CAMOMILE LAWN
Director: Peter Hall
Co-stars: Tara Fitzgerald Oliver Cotton Felicity Kendall

1993   BACKBEAT
Director: Ian Softley
Co-stars: Ian Hart Stephen Dorff Sheryl Lee

1995   PRIDE AND PREJUDICE
Co-stars: Colin Firth Alison Steadman Julia Sawalha

1996   PARADISE ROAD
Director: Bruce Beresford
Co-stars: Glenn Close Pauline Collins

1997   WILDE
Director: Brian Gilbert
Co-stars: Stephen Fry Tom Wilkinson Jude Law

BETH EHLERS

1983   IN DEFENSE OF KIDS
Director: Gene Reynolds
Co-stars: Blythe Danner Sam Waterston Joyce Van Patten

1983   THE HUNGER
Director: Tony Scott
Co-stars: Catherine Deneuvre Susan Sarandon David Bowie

BESS EHRHARDT

1939   ICE FOLLIES OF 1939
Director: Reinhold Schunzel
Co-stars: Joan Crawford James Stewart Lew Ayers

LISA EICHHORN

1979   YANKS
Director: John Schlesinger
Co-stars: Richard Gere Vanessa Redgrave Rachel Roberts

1979   THE EUROPEANS
Director: James Ivory
Co-stars: Lee Remick Robin Ellis Tim Woodward

1980   WHY WOULD I LIE?
Director: Larry Peerce
Co-stars: Treat Williams Gabriel Swann Susan Heldfond

1981   CUTTER'S WAY
Director: Ivan Passer
Co-stars: Jeff Bridges John Heard Ann Dusenberry

1986   BLIND JUSTICE
Director: Rod Holcomb
Co-stars: Tim Matheson Mimi Kusyk Tom Atkins

**1986   AGATHA CHRISTIE'S
MURDER IN THREE ACTS**
Director: Gary Nelson
Co-stars: Peter Ustinov Tony Curtis Emma Samms

1989   MOON 44
Director: Roland Emmerich
Co-stars: Michael Pare Malcolm McDowell Dean Devlin

1991   GRIM PRAIRIE TALES
Director: Wayne Coe
Co-stars: James Earl Jones Brad Dourif Will Hare

1993   KING OF THE HILL
Director: Steven Soderberg
Co-stars: Jesse Bradford Jeroen Krabbe Karen Allen

1993   THE VANISHING
Director: George Sluizer
Co-stars: Jeff Bridges Kiefer Sutherland Sandra Bullock

1994   A MODERN AFFAIR
Director: Vern Oakley
Co-star: Stanley Tucci

JILL EIKENBERRY (Married Michael Tucker)
1977   BETWEEN THE LINES
Director: Joan Micklin Silver
Co-stars: John Heard Lindsay Crouse

1978   **THE END OF THE WORLD**
Director: Lina Wertmuller
Co-stars: Candice Bergen Giancarlo Giannini

1979   **BUTCH AND SUNDANCE: THE EARLY YEARS**
Director: Richard Lester
Co-stars: William Katt Tom Berenger Brian Dennehy

1980   **HIDE IN PLAIN SIGHT**
Director: James Caan
Co-stars: James Caan Kenneth McMillan Danny Aiello

1980   **SWAN SONG**
Director: Jerry London
Co-stars: David Soul Bo Brundin Murray Hamilton

1981   **ARTHUR**
Director: Steve Gordon
Co-stars: Dudley Moore John Gielgud Lisa Minnelli

1983   **SESSIONS**
Director: Richard Pearce
Co-stars: Veronica Hamel Jeffrey Demunn George Coe

1986   **THE MANHATTAN PROJECT**
Director: Marshall Brickman
Co-stars: John Lithgow John Mahoney

1987   **ASSAULT AND MATRIMONY**
Director: James Frawley
Co-stars: Michael Tucker Michelle Phillips

1988   **A STONING IN FULHAM COUNTY**
Director: Larry Elikann
Co-stars: Ron Perlman Theodor Bikel Gregg Henry

1989   **CAST THE FIRST STONE**
Director: John Korty
Co-star: Joe Spano

1990   **RUNAWAY HEART**
Director: James Frawley
Co-stars: Michael Tucker Elaine Stritch Ray Wise

1991   **LIVING A LIE**
Director: Larry Shaw
Co-stars: Peter Coyote Roxanne Hart David Andrews

1992   **A TOWN TORN APART**
Director: Daniel Petrie
Co-stars: Michael Tucker Carole Galloway Linda Griffiths

1993   **RUGGED GOLD**
Director: Michael Anderson
Co-star: Art Hindle

1994   **TRAPPED AND DECEIVED**
Director: Robert Iscove
Co-stars: Paul Sorvino Helen Shaver Jennie Garth

1995   **THE OTHER WOMAN**
Director: Gabrielle Beaumont
Co-stars: Lloyd Bridges Laura Leighton

1996   **TAKEN AWAY**
Director: Jerry Jameson
Co-star: Michael Tucker

1996   **MY VERY BEST FRIEND**
Co-star: Jaclyn Smith

CINDY EILBACHER

1970   **CROWHAVEN FARM**
Director: Walter Gauman
Co-stars: Hope Lange Paul Burke John Carradine

LISA EILBACHER

1972   **THE WAR BETWEEN MEN AND WOMEN**
Director: Melville Shavelson
Co-stars: Jack Lemmon Barbara Harris Jason Robards

1977   **SPIDERMAN**
Director: E. Swackhamer
Co-stars: Nicholas Hammond David White Hilly Hicks

1981   **ON THE RIGHT TRACK**
Director: Lee Phillips
Co-stars: Gary Coleman Maureen Stapleton

1982   **AN OFFICER AND A GENTLEMAN**
Director: Taylor Hackford
Co-stars: Richard Gere Debra Winger

1983   **RYAN'S FOUR**
Director: Jeff Bleckner
Co-stars: Tom Skerritt Timothy Daly

1983   **TEN TO MIDNIGHT**
Director: J. Lee-Thompson
Co-stars: Charles Bronson Andrew Stevens

1984   **BEVERLY HILLS COP**
Director: Martin Brest
Co-stars: Eddie Murphy Judge Reinhold

1986   **MONTE CARLO**
Director: Anthony Page
Co-stars: Joan Collins George Hamilton Lauren Hutton

1987   **DEADLY DECEPTION**
Director: John Llewellyn Moxey
Co-stars: Matt Salinger Mildred Natwick

1989   **LEVIATHAN**
Director: George Pan Cosmatos
Co-stars: Peter Welles Richard Crenna Amanda Pays

1990   **JOSHUA'S HEART**
Director: Michael Pressman
Co-stars: Melissa Gilbert Tim Matheson

JANET EILBER

1983   **ROMANTIC COMEDY**
Director: Arthur Hiller
Co-stars: Dudley Moore Mary Steenburgen Frances Sternhagen

1989   **COLUMBO: GRAND DECEPTIONS**
Director: Sam Wanamaker
Co-stars: Peter Falk Robert Foxworth Andy Romano

SALLY EILERS *(Dorothea Eilers)*
(Married Hoot Gibson, Harry Joe Brown)

1928   **THE GOODBYE KISS**

1930   **DOUGH BOYS**
Director: Edward Sedgwick
Co-stars: Buster Keaton Cliff Edwards Edward Brophy

1930   **LET US BE GAY**
Director: Robert Z. Leonard
Co-stars: Norma Shearer Rod La Rocque Marie Dressler

1931   **OVER THE HILL**
Director: Henry King
Co-stars: James Dunn Mae Marsh Edward Crandall

1931   **QUICK MILLIONS**
Director: Rowland Brown
Co-stars: Spencer Tracy Marguerite Churchill George Raft

1931   **REDUCING**
Director: Charles Reisner
Co-stars: Marie Dressler Polly Moran Anita Page

1931　THE BLACK CAMEL
Director:　Hamilton McFadden
Co-stars:　Warner Oland Bela Lugosi Robert Young

1931　BAD GIRL
Director:　Frank Borzage
Co-stars:　James Dunn Minna Gombell William Fawley

1931　A HOLY TERROR

1932　PRIDE OF THE LEGION
Co-stars:　Jason Robards Snr. Glenn Tryon Tom Dugan

1932　HAT CHECK GIRL
Co-stars:　Ginger Rogers Monroe Owsley

1932　DISORDERLY CONDUCT
Director:　John Considine
Co-stars:　Spencer Tracy El Brendel Ralph Bellamy

1932　DANCING TEAM
Director:　Sidney Lanfield
Co-stars:　James Dunn Minna Gombell Ralph Morgan

1932　I SPY

1933　WALLS OF GOLD
Co-star:　Ralph Morgan

1933　HOLD ME TIGHT
Co-stars:　James Dunn Kenneth Thomson

1933　SAILOR'S LUCK
Co-star:　James Dunn

1933　SECOND HAND WIFE
Co-star:　Ralph Bellamy

1933　CENTRAL AIRPORT
Director:　William Wellman
Co-stars:　Richard Barthelmess Tom Brown Glenda Farrell

1933　STATE FAIR
Director:　Henry King
Co-stars:　Will Rogers Janet Gaynor Lew Ayres

1934　SHE MADE HER BED
Co-star:　Richard Arlen

1935　STIKE ME PINK
Director:　Norman Taurog
Co-stars:　Eddie Cantor Ethel Merman Parkyakarkus

1935　PURSUIT
Director:　Edwin Marin
Co-stars:　Chester Morris Scotty Beckett Henry Travers

1935　CARNIVAL
Director:　Walter Lang
Co-stars:　Lee Tracy Jimmy Durante Dickie Walters

1935　ALIAS MARY DOW
Director:　Kurt Neuman
Co-stars:　Ray Milland Henry O'Neill

1936　REMEMBER LAST NIGHT?
Director:　James Whale
Co-stars:　Edward Arnold Constance Cummings Robert Young

1936　FLORIDA SPECIAL
Co-star:　Jack Oakie

1936　DON'T GET PERSONAL
Co-star:　Pinky Tomlin James Dunn

1936　TALK OF THE DEVIL
Director:　Carol Reed
Co-stars:　Ricardo Cortez Basil Sydney Charles Carson

1937　WE HAVE OUR MOMENTS
Director:　Alfred Werker
Co-stars:　James Dunn Mischa Auer David Niven

1938　TARNISHED ANGEL
Director:　Lew Landers
Co-stars:　Ann Miller Paul Guilfoyle

1938　CONDEMMED WOMAN
Director:　Lew Landers
Co-stars:　Louis Hayward Anne Shirley Lee Patrick

1939　FULL CONFESSION
Director:　John Farrow
Co-stars:　Victor McLaglen Barry Fitzgerald

1941　I WAS A PRISONER ON DEVIL'S ISLAND
Director:　Lew Landers
Co-stars:　Donald Woods Eduardo Cianello

1945　STRANGE ILLUSION
Co-stars:　Warren William Jayne Hazard

1948　CORONER CREEK
Director:　Ray Enright
Co-stars:　Randolph Scott Marguerite Chapman Wallace Ford

DEBRA EISENSTADT

1994　OLEANNA
Director:　David Mamet
Co-star:　William H. Macy

ANITA EKBERG

1953　ABBOTT AND COSTELLO GOES TO MARS
Director:　Charles Lamont
Co-stars:　Abbott And Costello Mari Blanchard Martha Hyer

1955　BLOOD ALLEY
Director:　William Wellman
Co-stars:　John Wayne Lauren Bacall Paul Fix Mike Mazurki

1955　ARTISTS AND MODELS
Director:　Frank Tashlin
Co-stars:　Dean Martin Jerry Lewis Shirley MacLaine

1956　BACK FROM ETERNITY
Director:　John Farrow
Co-stars:　Robert Ryan Rod Steiger Phyllis Kirk Beulah Bondi

1956　HOLLYWOOD OR BUST
Director:　Frank Tashlin
Co-stars:　Dean Martin Jerry Lewis Pat Crowley

1956　WAR AND PEACE
Director:　King Vidor
Co-stars:　Audrey Hepburn Henry Fonda Mel Ferrer John Mills

1956　ZARAK
Director:　Terence Young
Co-stars:　Victor Mature Michael Wilding Bonar Colleano

1957　VALERIE
Director:　Gerd Oswald
Co-stars:　Sterling Haden Anthony Steel John Wengraf

1957　PARIS HOLIDAY
Director:　Gerd Oswald
Co-stars:　Bob Hope Fernandel Martha Hyer Andre Morell

1957　INTERPOL
Director:　John Gilling
Co-stars:　Victor Mature Bonar Colleano Trevor Howard Sid James

1958　THE MAN INSIDE
Director:　John Gilling
Co-stars:　Nigel Patrick Jack Palance Donald Pleasence Sid James

1958　THE SCREAMING MIMI
Director:　Gerd Oswald
Co-stars:　Phil Carey Harry Townes Gypsy Rose Lee

1958　THE SIGN OF THE GLADIATOR
Director:　Riccardo Freda
Co-stars:　George Marchal Folco Lulli Jacques Sernas

1960 LA DOLCE VITA
Director: Federico Fellini
Co-stars: Marcel Mastroianni Anouk Aimee Lex Barker

1962 BOCCACCIO 70
Director: Federico Fellini
Co-stars: Sophia Loren Romy Schneider Luigi Giuliani

1962 CALL ME BWANA
Director: Gordon Douglas
Co-stars: Bob Hope Edie Adams Lionel Jeffries Percy Herbert

1963 FOUR FOR TEXAS
Director: Robert Aldrich
Co-stars: Frank Sinatra Dean Martin Ursula Andress

1965 THE ALPHABET MURDERS
Director: Frank Tashlin
Co-stars: Tony Randall Robert Morley Guy Rolfe

1966 WAY.....WAY OUT
Director: Gordon Douglas
Co-stars: Jerry Lewis Connie Stevens Robert Morley Dick Shawn

1967 WOMAN TIMES SEVEN
Director: Vittorio De Sica
Co-stars: Shirley MacLaine Peter Sellers Michael Caine

1968 THE GLASS SPHINX
Director: Fulvio Lucisano
Co-stars: Robert Taylor Gianna Sera Jack Stuart

1987 INTERVISTA
Director: Federico Fellini
Co-stars: Marcel Mastroianno Tonino Delli Colli

STINA EKBLAD
1986 AMOROSA
Director: Mai Zetterling
Co-stars: Erland Josephson Philip Zanden Catherine De Seynes

BRITT EKLAND (*Married Peter Sellers*)
1966 AFTER THE FOX
Director: Vittorio De Sica
Co-stars: Peter Sellers Victor Mature Akim Tamiroff

1967 THE BOBO
Director: Robert Parrish
Co-stars: Rossano Brazzi Adolfo Celi Peter Sellers

1967 THE DOUBLE MAN
Director: Franklin Schaffner
Co-stars: Yul Brynner Clive Revell Moira Lister

1968 THE NIGHT THEY RAIDED MINSKY'S
Director: William Friedkin
Co-stars: Jason Robards Norman Wisdom Bert Lahr

1969 STILETTO
Director: Bernard Kowalski
Co-stars: Alex Cord Barbara McNair Patrick O'Neal

1970 PERCY
Director: Ralph Thomas
Co-stars: Hywel Bennett Elke Sommer Denholm Elliott

1970 MACHINE GUN McCAIN
Director: Giuliano Montadlo
Co-stars: John Cassavetes Peter Falk Gena Rowlands

1970 GET CARTER
Director: Mike Hodges
Co-stars: Michael Caine John Osborne Ian Hendry George Sewell

1971 ENDLESS NIGHT
Director: Sidney Gilliat
Co-stars: Hayley Mills Hywel Bennett George Sanders

1971 NIGHT HAIR CHILD
Director: James Kelly
Co-stars: Mark Lester Harry Kruger Lilli Palmer

1971 A TIME FOR LOVING
Director: Christopher Miles
Co-stars: Joanna Shimkus Mel Ferrer Susan Hampshire

1972 BAXTER
Director: Lionel Jeffries
Co-stars: Patricia Neal Scott Jacoby Paul Eddington Lynn Carlin

1972 ASYLUM
Director: Roy Ward Baker
Co-stars: Patrick Magee Robert Powell Richard Todd

1973 THE WICKER MAN
Director: Robin Hardy
Co-stars: Edward Woodward Christopher Lee Diane Cilento

1974 THE MAN WITH THE GOLDEN GUN
Director: Guy Hamilton
Co-stars: Roger Moore Maud Adams Christopher Lee

1975 ROYAL FLASH
Director: Richard Lester
Co-stars: Malcolm McDowall Oliver Reed Alan Bates Tom Bell

1977 KING SOLOMON'S TREASURE
Director: Alvin Rakoff
Co-stars: David McCallum John Colicos Patrick MacNee

1980 THE MONSTER CLUB
Director: Roy Ward Baker
Co-stars: Vincent Price John Carradine Richard Johnson

1988 SCANDAL
Director: Michael Caton-Jones
Co-stars: John Hurt Joanna Whalley Bridget Fonda

1990 THE CHILDREN
Director: Tony Palmer
Co-stars: Ben Kingsley Kim Novak Joe Don Baker Karen Black

AGNETTA EKMANNER
1966 HUGS AND KISSES
Director: Jonas Cornell
Co-stars: Sven-Bertil Taube Hakan Serner Lina Granhagen

PAULETTE ELAMBERT (*Child*)
1932 LA MATERNELLE
Director: Marie Epstein
Co-stars: Madeleine Renaud Mady Berry Alice Tissot

JOAN ELAN
1953 THE GIRLS OF PLEASURE ISLAND
Director: F. Hugh Herbert
Co-stars: Leo Genn Gene Barry Audrey Dalton

FLORENECE ELDRIDGE
(*Married Fredric March*)
1929 CHARMING SINNERS
Director: Robert Milton
Co-stars: Ruth Chatterton Clive Brook William Powell

1929 THE STUDIO MURDER MYSTERY
Director: Frank Tuttle
Co-stars: Neil Hamilton Warner Oland Fredric March

1930 THE DIVORCEE
Director: Robert Z. Leonard
Co-stars: Norma Shearer Chester Morris Conrad Nagel

1932 13 WOMEN
Director: George Archainbaud
Co-stars: Irene Dunne Myrna Loy Ricardo Cortez

1933 THE STORY OF TEMPLE DRAKE
Director: Stephen Roberts
Co-stars: Miriam Hopkins Jack La Rue

1933	**DANGEROUSLY YOURS**	**1961**	**THE BACCHANTES**

1933 DANGEROUSLY YOURS
Director: Frank Tutle
Co-stars: Warner Baxter Miriam Jordan Herbert Mundin

1934 A MODERN HERO
Director: G. W. Pabst
Co-stars: Richard Bartlemess Jean Muir Marjorie Rambeau

1935 LES MISERABLES
Director: Richard Boleslawski
Co-stars: Fredric March Charles Laughton John Beal

1936 MARY OF SCOTLAND
Director: John Ford
Co-stars: Katherine Hepburn Fredric March Donald Crisp

1948 ANOTHER PART OF THE FOREST
Director: Michael Gordon
Co-stars: Fredric March Ann Blyth Dan Duryea

1949 CHRISTOPHER COLUMBUS
Director: David MacDonald
Co-stars: Fredric March Linden Travers Derek Bond

1960 INHERIT THE WIND
Director: Stanley Kramer
Co-stars: Spencer Tracy Fredric March Gene Kelly

ERIKA ELENIAK

1990 BAYWATCH: NIGHTMARE BAY
Director: Richard Compton
Co-stars: David Hasselhoff Richard Jaeckel

1992 UNDER SEIGE
Director: Andrew Davis
Co-stars: Steven Seagal Tommy Lee Jones Gary Busey

1994 CHASERS
Director: Dennis Hopper
Co-stars: Dennis Hopper Tom Berenger Crispin Clover

1993 THE BEVERLY HILLBILLIES
Director: Penelope Spheeris
Co-stars: Diedrich Bader Dabney Coleman Lily Tomlin

FAVIOLA ELENKA

1989 SANTA SANGRE
Director: Alenjandro Jodorowsky
Co-stars: Axel Jodorowsky Guy Stockwell Blanca Guerra

TANIA ELG

1955 THE PRODIGAL
Director: Richard Thorpe
Co-stars: Lana Turner Edmund Purdom Louis Calhern

1955 DIANE
Director: David Miller
Co-stars: Lana Turner Roger Moore Pedro Armendariz

1956 GABY
Director: Curtis Bernhardt
Co-stars: Leslie Caron John Kerr Cedric Hardwicke

1957 LES GIRLS
Director: George Cukor
Co-stars: Gene Kelly Kay Kendall Mitzi Gaynor

1958 IMITATION GENERAL
Director: George Marshall
Co-stars: Glenn Ford Red Buttons Dean Jones

1959 WATUSI
Director: Kurt Neuman
Co-stars: George Montgomery David Farrar Rex Ingram

1960 THE THIRTY-NINE STEPS
Director: Ralph Thomas
Co-stars: Kenneth More Sid James Brenda De Banzie

1961 THE BACCHANTES
Director: Giorgio Ferrori
Co-stars: Akim Tamiroff Pierre Brice Alberto Lupo

1970 HERCULES IN NEW YORK
Director: Arthur Alan Seidelman
Co-stars: Arnold Stang Arnold Schwarzenegger

AVRIL ELGAR

1986 THE CHILDREN OF DYNMOUTH
Director: Peter Hammond
Co-stars: John Bird Peter Jones Gary Raymond

YONA ELIAN

1983 THE LAST WINTER
Director: Riki Shelach Missimoff
Co-stars: Kathleen Quinlan Stephen Macht

KATHLEEN ELIOT

1938 WEST OF RAINBOW'S END
Co-star: Tim McCoy

CHRISTINE ELISE

1991 CHILD'S PLAY 2
Director: John Lafia
Co-stars: Alex Vincent Jenny Agutter Gerrit Graham

1992 BEVERLY HILLS 90210: WALSH FAMILY CHRISTMAS
Director: Aaron Spelling
Co-stars: Shannen Doherty Luke Perry

1993 BODY SNATCHERS
Director: Abel Ferrara
Co-stars: Gabrielle Anwar Billy Wirth Meg Tilly

1993 BOILING POINT
Director: James Harris
Co-stars: Wesley Snipes Dennis Hopper Valerie Perrine

KIMBERLEY ELISE

1997 SET IT OFF
Director: F. Gary Gray
Co-stars: Viveca Fox Jada Pinkett Queen Latifah

YVONNE ELLIMAN

1973 JESUS CHRIST SUPERSTAR
Director: Norman Jewison
Co-stars: Ted Neeley Carl Anderson Barry Dennen

MARIA ELLINGSEN

1994 D2 THE MIGHTY DUCKS
Director: Sam Weisman
Co-stars: Emilio Estevez Kathryn Erbe Michael Tucker

ALLISON ELLIOT

1996 THE WINGS OF A DOVE
Director: Iain Softly
Co-stars: Helena Bonham-Carter Linus Roche

1996 THE UNDERNEATH
Director: Steven Soderbergh
Co-stars: Peter Gallagher William Fichtner

EDYTHE ELLIOTT

1943 THE GREAT MIKE
Co-stars: Stuart Erwin Carl Switzer Robert Henry

JANE ELLIOTT

1969 CHANGE OF HEART
Director: William Graham
Co-stars: Elvis Presley Mary Tyler Moore Leora Dana

1972 ONE IS A LONLEY NUMBER
Director: Mel Stuart
Co-stars: Trish Van Devere Melvyn Douglas Janet Leigh

LAURA ELLIOTT

1949 SPECIAL AGENT
Director: William Thomas
Co-stars: William Eythe George Reeves Paul Valentine

1951 STRANGERS ON A TRAIN
Director: Alfred Hitchcock
Co-stars: Farley Granger Robert Walker Ruth Roman

1952 DENVER AND RIO GRANDE
Director: Bryon Haskin
Co-stars: Edmond O'Brien Sterling Hayden Dean Jagger

PATRICIA ELLIOTT

1978 SOMEBODY KILLED HER HUSBAND
Director: Lamont Johnson
Co-stars: Farrah Fawcett-Majors Jeff Bridges

ANTONIA ELLIS

1970 PERCY
Director: Ralph Thomas
Co-stars: Hywel Bennett Denholm Elliot Elke Sommer

1971 THE BOY FRIEND
Director: Ken Russell
Co-stars: Twiggy Christopher Gable Tommy Tune

1974 MAHLER
Director: Ken Russell
Co-stars: Robert Powell Georgina Hale Lee Montague

CAROLINE ELLIS

1977 CONFESSIONS FROM A HOLIDAY CAMP
Director: Norman Cohen
Co-stars: Robin Askwith Anthony Booth

DIANE ELLIS

1929 HIGH VOLTAGE
Co-stars: Carole Lombard Owen Moore Bill Boyd

1930 LAUGHTER
Director: Harry D'Abbabie D'Arrast
Co-stars: Fredric March Nancy Carroll Frank Morgan

GWEN ELLIS

1992 HEDD WYN: THE ARMAGEDDON POET
Director: Paul Turner
Co-stars: Huw Garmon Catrin Fychan Lilo Silyn

JACQUELINE ELLIS

1961 THE SINISTER MAN
Director: Clive Donner
Co-stars: Patrick Allen John Bentley Eric Young

1963 THE HIJACKERS
Director: Jim O'Connolly
Co-stars: Anthony Booth Derek Francis Arthur English

MARY ELLIS

1934 BELLADONNA
Director: Robert Milton
Co-stars: Conrad Veidt Cedric Hardwicke John Stuart

1935 ALL THE KING'S HORSES
Director: Frank Tuttle
Co-stars: Carl Brisson Eugene Pallette Katherine DeMille

1935 PARIS IN SPRING
Director: Lewis Milestone
Co-stars: Tullio Carminati Ida Lupino

1936 FATAL LADY
Director: Edward Ludwig
Co-stars: Walter Pidgeon John Halliday Ruth Donnelly

1937 GLAMOROUS NIGHT
Director: Brian Desmond Hurst
Co-stars: Otto Kruger Victor Jory Barry Mackay

1959 THE THREE WORLDS OF GULLIVER
Director: Jack Sher
Co-stars: Kerwin Mattehws Basil Sydney Jo Morrow

PATRICIA ELLIS

1932 CENTRAL PARK
Director: John Adolphi
Co-stars: Joan Blondell Wallace Ford Guy Kibbee

1933 ELMER THE GREAT
Director: Mervyn LeRoy
Co-stars: Joe E. Brown Frank McHugh Claire Dodd

1933 EASY TO LOVE
Director: William Keighley
Co-stars: Adolphe Menjou Genevieve Tobin Mary Astor

1933 THE KING'S VACATION
Co-stars: Dick Powell George Arliss

1933 THE NARROW CORNER
director Alfred Green
Co-stars: Douglas Fairbanks Jnr. Ralph Bellamy Arthur Hohl

1933 THE PICTURE SNATCHER
Director: Lloyd Bacon
Co-stars: James Cagney Ralph Bellamy Alice White

1933 THE WORLD CHANGES
Director: Mervyn LeRoy
Co-stars: Paul Muni Aline MacMahon Mary Astor

1934 THE ST. LOUIS KID
Director: Ray Enright
Co-stars: James Cagney Hobart Cavanagh Allen Jenkins

1934 HAROLD TEEN
Director: Murray Roth
Co-stars: Hal Le Roy Rochelle Hudson Guy Kibbee

1934 BIG-HEARTED HERBERT
Director: William Keighley
Co-stars: Guy Kibbee Aline MacMahon Philip Reed

1934 THE CIRCUS CLOWN
Co-stars: Joe E. Brown Donald Dillaway

1934 DOWN THE STRETCH
Co-star: Mickey Rooney

1935 BRIGHT LIGHTS
Director: Busby Berkeley
Co-stars: Joe E. Brown Ann Dvorak William Gargan

1935 HOLD 'EM YALE
Director: Sidney Lanfield
Co-stars: Cesar Romero Larry Crabbe Andy Devine

1935 WHILE THE PATIENT SLEPT
Director: Ray Enright
Co-stars: Aline MacMahon Guy Kibbee Lyle Talbot

1935 A NIGHT AT THE RITZ
Co-star: William Gargan

1936 SING ME A LOVE SONG
Director: Ray Enright
Co-stars: James Melton Hugh Herbert Zasu Pitts

1936 SNOWED UNDER
Co-stars: George Brent Genevieve Tobin Glenda Farrell

1936 POSTAL INSPECTOR
Co-stars: Bela Lugosi Michael Loring

1936 **STRANDED**
Director: Frank Borzage
Co-stars: George Brent Kay Francis Donald Woods

1936 **FRESHMAN LOVE**
Co-star: Warren Hull

1936 **BOULDER DAM**
Director: Frank McDonald
Co-stars: Ross Alexander Lyle Talbot Eddie Acuff

1937 **MELODY FOR TWO**
Director: Louis King
Co-stars: James Melton Wini Shaw Marie Wilson

1937 **PARADISE FOR 2**
Director: Thornton Freeland
Co-stars: Jack Hulbert Googie Withers Arthur Riscoe

1937 **RHYTHM IN THE CLOUDS**
Co-star: William Hull

1937 **STEP LIVELY, JEEVES**
Co-stars: Arthur Treacher Arthur Housman

1938 **LADY IN THE MORGUE**
Director: Otis Garrett
Co-stars: Preston Foster Frank Jenks Barbara Pepper

1938 **THE CASE OF THE LUCKY LEGS**
Director: Archie Mayo
Co-stars: Warren William Genevieve Tobin Lyle Talbot

1938 **BLOCKHEADS**
Director: John Blystone
Co-stars: Stan Laurel Oliver Hardy Minna Gombell

1939 **FUGITIVE AT LARGE**
Co-stars: Jack Holt Ernie Adams

TRACEY ELLIS

1988 **THE PRINCE OF PENNSYLVANIA**
Director: Ron Nyswaner
Co-stars: Fred Ward Keanu Reeves Bonnie Bedelia

ISOBEL ELSOM

1923 **THE WANDERING JEW**
Director: Maurice Elvey
Co-stars: Matheson Lang Florence Sanders Hutin Britton

1941 **LADIES IN RETIREMENT**
Director: Charles Vidor
Co-stars: Ida Lupino Louis Hayward Elsa Lanchester

1942 **SEVEN SWEETHEARTS**
Director: Frank Borzage
Co-stars: Kathryn Grayson Marsha Hunt Van Heflin

1942 **THE WAR AGAINST MRS. HADLEY**
Director: Harold Bucquet
Co-stars: Fay Bainter Edward Arnold Jean Rogers

1942 **YOU WERE NEVER LOVELIER**
Director: William Seiter
Co-stars: Fred Astaire Rita Hayworth Adele Mara

1943 **FIRST COMES COURAGE**
Director: Dorothy Arzner
Co-stars: Merle Oberon Brian Aherne Carl Esmond

1943 **LAUGH YOUR BLUES AWAY**
Director: Charles Barton
Co-stars: Jinx Falkenberg Bert Gordon Douglass Drake

1943 **MY KINGDOM FOR A COOK**
Director: Richard Wallace
Co-stars: Charles Coburn Marguerite Chapman Ed Gargan

1944 **CASANOVA BROWN**
Director: Sam Wood
Co-stars: Gary Cooper Teresa Wright Frank Morgan

1944 **BETWEEN TWO WORLDS**
Director: Edward Blatt
Co-stars: John Garfield Edmund Gwenn Sydney Greenstreet

1947 **ESCAPE ME NEVER**
Director: Peter Godfrey
Co-stars: Errol Flynn Ida Lupino Eleanor Parker

1947 **THE GHOST AND MRS. MUIR**
Director: Joseph Mankiewicz
Co-stars: Rex Harrison Gene Tierney Anna Lee

1947 **IVY**
Director: Sam Wood
Co-stars: Joan Fontaine Herbert Marshall Patric Knowles

1947 **LOVE FROM A STRANGER**
Director: Richard Whorf
Co-stars: Sylvia Sidney John Hodiak Ann Richards

1947 **MONSIEUR VERDOUX**
Director: Charles Chaplin
Co-stars: Charles Chaplin Martha Raye Marilyn Nash Irving Bacon

1947 **THE TWO MRS. CARROLLS**
Director: Peter Godfrey
Co-stars: Barbara Stanwyck Humphrey Bogart Alexis Smith

1948 **SMART WOMAN**
Director: Edward Blat
Co-stars: Constance Bennett Brian Aherne Barry Sullivan

1954 **DESIREE**
Director: Henry Koster
Co-stars: Jean Simmons Marlon Brando Merle Oberon

1954 **DEEP IN MY HEART**
Director: Stanley Donen
Co-stars: Jose Ferrer Merle Oberon Paul Henreid

1955 **LOVE IS A MANY SPLENDID THING**
Director: Henry King
Co-stars: William Holden Jennifer Jones

1956 **THE GUNS OF FORT PETTICOAT**
Director: George Marshall
Co-stars: Audie Murphy Kathryn Grant Jeff Donnell

1958 **ROCK-A-BYE-BABY**
Director: Frank Tashlin
Co-stars: Jerry Lewis Marilyn Maxwell Reginald Gardiner

1959 **THE MIRACLE**
Director: Irving Rapper
Co-stars: Carroll Baker Roger Moore Walter Sleazak

1961 **SECOND TIME AROUND**
Director: Vincent Sherman
Co-stars: Debbie Reynolds Andy Griffith Steve Forrest

1964 **THE PLEASURE SEEKERS**
Director: Jean Negulesco
Co-stars: Ann-Margret Carol Lynley Gene Tierney

1964 **MY FAIR LADY**
Director: George Cukor
Co-stars: Rex Harrison Audrey Hepburn Stanley Holloway

ANDREA ELSON

1987 **ALF**
Director: Tom Patchett
Co-stars: Max Wright Ann Schedeen Anne Meara

1992 **FRANKENSTEIN - THE COLLEGE YEARS**
Director: Tom Shadyac
Co-stars: William Ragsdale Larry Miller

LOTTIE ELWIN

1949 **C MAN**
Director: Irving Rapper
Co-stars: Dean Jagger John Carradine

AMANDA ELWES
1993   A TOUCH OF FROST: NOT WITH KINDNESS
Director: David Reynolds
Co-stars: David Jason Tony Haygarth

GEORGIA EMELI
1991   DANIELLE STEEL'S DADDY
Director: Douglas Cramer
Co-stars: Patrick Duffy Kate Mulgrew

FAYE EMERSON
1941   NINE LIVES ARE NOT ENOUGH
Director: Edward Sutherland
Co-stars: Ronald Reagan Howard De Silva

1942   MURDER IN THE BIG HOUSE
Director: Reeves Eason
Co-stars: Van Johnson George Meeker Frank Wilcox

1942   THE HARD WAY
Director: Vincent Sherman
Co-stars: Ida Lupino Dennis Morgan Jack Carson Joan Leslie

1942   JUKE GIRL
Director: Curtis Bernhardt
Co-stars: Ann Sheridan Ronald Reagan Richard Whorf

1943   DESTINATION TOKYO
Director: Delmer Daves
Co-stars: Cary Grant John Garfield Dane Clark

1943   FIND THE BLACKMAILER
Director: Ross Lederman
Co-stars: Jerome Cowan Gene Lockhart Robert Kent

1944   THE DESERT SONG
Director: Robert Florey
Co-stars: Dennis Morgan Irene Manning Bruce Cabot

1944   CRIME BY NIGHT
Director: William Clemens
Co-stars: Jerome Cowan Jane Wyman Eleanor Parker

1944   BETWEEN TWO WORLDS
Director: Edward Blatt
Co-stars: John Garfield Edmund Gwenn Sydney Greenstreet

1944   THE MASK OF DIMITRIOS
Director: Jean Negulesco
Co-stars: Zachary Scott Sydney Greenstreet Peter Lorre

1944   UNCERTAIN GLORY
Director: Raoul Walsh
Co-stars: Errol Flynn Paul Lukas Jean Sullivan

1944   THE VERY THOUGHT OF YOU
Director: Delmer Daves
Co-stars: Dennis Morgan Eleanor Parker Dane Clark

1945   DANGER SIGNAL
Director: Robert Florey
Co-stars: Zachary Scott Rosemary De Camp Mona Freeman

1945   HOTEL BERLIN
Director: Peter Godfrey
Co-stars: Raymond Massey Peter Lorre Helmut Dantine

1946   HER KIND OF MAN
Director: Frederick De Cordova
Co-stars: Dane Clark Zachary Scott Janis Page

1946   NOBODY LIVES FOREVER
Director: Jean Negulesco
Co-stars: John Garfield Walter Brennan Geraldine Fitzgerald

HOPE EMERSON
Nominated For Best Supporting Actress In 1950 For Caged
1948   CRY OF THE CITY
Director: Robert Sidomak
Co-stars: Victor Mature Richard Conte Shelley Winters

1949   DANGER IN THE DARK
Director: Irving Reis
Co-stars: William Powell Mark Stevens Betsy Drake

1949   ADAM'S RIB
Director: George Cukor
Co-stars: Spencer Tracy Katherine Hepburn Judy Holiday

1949   HOUSE OF STRANGERS
Director: Joseph Mankiewicz
Co-stars: Edward G. Robinson Susan Hayward Richard Conte

1949   THIEVES' HIGHWAY
Director: Jules Dassin
Co-stars: Richard Conte Valentina Cortesa

1950   CAGED
Director: John Cromwell
Co-stars: Eleanor Parker Agnes Moorehead Ellen Corby

1950   DOUBLE CROSSBONES
Director: Charles Barton
Co-stars: Donald O'Connor Helena Carter Will Geer

1951   BELLE LE GRAND
Director: Allan Dwan
Co-stars: Vera Ralston John Carroll William Ching

1951   WESTWARD THE WOMEN
Director: William Wellman
Co-stars: Robert Taylor Denise Darcel John McIntyre

1955   UNTAMED
Director: Henry King
Co-stars: Tyrone Power Susan Hayward Richard Egan John Justin

1956   THE DAY THEY GAVE BABIES AWAY
Director: Allen Reisner
Co-stars: Glynis Johns Cameron Mitchell

1956   THE GUNS OF FORT PETTICOAT
Director: George Marshall
Co-stars: Audie Murphy Kathryn Grant Jeff Donnell

KATHERINE EMERY
1946   THE LOCKET
Director: John Brahm
Co-stars: Laraine Day Robert Mitchum Brian Aherne

1946   ISLE OF THE DEAD
Director: Mark Robson
Co-stars: Boris Karloff Ellen Drew Helene Thimig

1947   THE PRIVATE AFFAIRS OF BEL AMI
Director: Albert Lewin
Co-stars: George Sanders Angela Lansbury

1949   STRANGE BARGAIN
Director: Will Price
Co-stars: Jeffrey Lynn Henry Morgan Martha Scott

1953   THE MAZE
Director: William Cameron Menzies
Co-stars: Richard Carlson Veronica Hurst Lillian Bond

MARI EMLYN
1986   COMING UP ROSES
Director: Stephen Bayley
Co-stars: Dafydd Hywell Iola Gregory Olive Michael

ALPHONSIA EMMANUEL
1989   MURDER ON THE MOON
Director: Michael Lindsay-Hogg
Co-stars: Brigitte Neilsen Julian Sands Brian Cox

1990   HOUSE OF CARDS
Director: Paul Seed
Co-stars: Ian Richardson Susannah Harker Diane Fletcher

1991 UNDER SUSPICION
Director: Simon Moore
Co-stars: Liam Neeson Laura San Giacomo Kenneth Cranham

1992 PETER'S FRIENDS
Director: Kenneth Branagh
Co-stars: Kenneth Branagh Hugh Laurie Stephen Fry

KATHERINE EMMETT

1922 ORPHANS OF THE STORM
Director: D.W. Griffith
Co-stars: Lillian Gish Lucille La Verne

1931 THE NIGHT ANGEL
Director: Edmund Goulding
Co-stars: Fredric March Nancy Carroll Alan Hale

MARIA EMO

1955 HERR PUNTILA AND HIS SERVANT MATTI
Director: Alberto Cavalcanti
Co-stars: Curt Bois Edith Prager

1961 HITLER
Director: Stuart Heisler
Co-stars: Richard Basehart Martin Kosleck

TAMEKA EMPSON

1996 BEAUTIFUL THING
Director: Hettie MacDonald
Co-stars: Glenn Berry Linda Henry Scott Neal

RUTH ENDERS

1977 TUBBY THE TUBA *(Voice)*
Director: Alexander Schure
Co-stars: Dick Van Dyke Pearl Bailey Jane Powell

LENA ENDRE

1989 ISTANBUL
Director: Mats Arehn
Co-stars: Timothy Bottoms Twiggy Robert Morley

GEORGIA ENGEL

1971 TAKING OFF
Director: Milos Forman
Co-stars: Lynn Carlin Buck Henry Linnea Heacock

1985 THE CARE BEARS MOVIE
Director: Arna Seiznick
Co-stars: Mickey Rooney Harry Dean Stanton

RUTH C. ENGEL

1988 PHANTASM 2
Director: Don Coscarelli
Co-stars: James Le Gros Reggie Bannister Angus Scrimm

SUSAN ENGEL

1971 KING LEAR
Director: Peter Brook
Co-stars: Paul Scofield Irene Worth Cyril Cusack

1973 BUTLEY
Director: Harold Pinter
Co-stars: Alan Bates Jessica Tandy Georgina Hale

1982 ASCENDANCY
Director: Edward Bennett
Co-stars: Julie Covington Ian Charleson John Phillips

WERA ENGELS

1934 FUGITIVE ROAD
Director: Frank Strayer
Co-stars: Erich Von Stroheim Leslie Fenton George Humbert

KARIN ENGH

1969 A PLACE FOR LOVERS
Director: Vittorio De Sica
Co-stars: Faye Dunaway Marcello Mastroianni

OLGA ENGL

1931 EMIL AND THE DETECTIVES
Director: Gerhard Lamprecht
Co-stars: Fritz Rasp Kathe Haack

CAROLINE ENGLAND

1987 CARIANI AAND THE COURTESANS
Director: Leslie Megahy
Co-stars: Paul McGann Lucy Hancock Diana Quick

SUE ENGLAND

1945 THIS LOVE OR OURS
Director: William Dieterle
Co-stars: Merle Oberon Charles Korvin Claude Rains

1948 KIDNAPPED
Director: William Beaudine
Co-stars: Roddy McDowell Dan O'Herlihy Jeff Corey

MARLA ENGLISH

1955 DESERT SANDS
Director: Lesley Selander
Co-stars: John Carradine Ralph Meeker J. Carrol Naish

1956 THE SHE CREATURE
Director: Edward Cahn
Co-stars: Tom Conway Chester Morris Ron Randell

SUE ENGLISH

1955 TEENAGE CRIME WAVE
Director: Fred Sears
Co-stars: Tommy Cook Molly McCart Frank Griffin

PATRICIA ENGLUND

1957 STAGE STRUCK
Director: Sidney Lumet
Co-stars: Susan Strasberg Henry Fonda Joan Greenwood

KATHRYN ERBE

1991 WHAT ABOUT BOB?
Director: Frank Oz
Co-stars: Bill Murray Richard Dreyfuss Julie Haggerty

1992 RICH IN LOVE
Director: Bruce Beresford
Co-stars: Albert Finney Jill Clayburgh Piper Laurie

1994 D2 THE MIGHTY DUCKS
Director: Sam Weisman
Co-stars: Emilio Estevez Michael Tucker Jan Rubes

ELIZABETH ERCY

1961 PHADERA
Director: Juled Dassin
Co-stars: Melina Mercouri Anthony Perkins Raf Vallone

1967 THE SORCERERS
Director: Michael Reeves
Co-stars: Boris Karloff Catherine Lacey Susan George

CYNTHIA ERLAND

1989 RIVER OF DEATH
Director: Steve Carver
Co-stars: Michael Dudikoff Donald Pleasence Herbert Lom

LAURA ERNST

1991 TOO MUCH SUN
Director: Robert Downey
Co-stars: Robert Downey Jnr. Ralph Macchio Eric Idle

KRISTA ERRICKSON

1980 LITTLE DARLINGS
Director: Ronald Maxwell
Co-stars: Tatum O'Neal Kristy McNichol Matt Dillon

1983 THE FIRST TIME
Director: Charlie Loventhal
Co-stars: Tim Choate Wendy Fulton Jane Badler

1989 MORTAL PASSIONS
Director: Andrew Lane
Co-stars: Zach Galligan Michael Bowen Luca Bercovici

EILEEN ERSKINE

1946 GREAT EXPECTATIONS
Director: David Lean
Co-stars: John Mills Alec Guinness Martita Hunt

MARILYN ERSKINE

1951 WESTWARD THE WOMEN
Director: William Wellman
Co-stars: Robert Taylor Denise Darcel Hope Emerson

1952 A SLIGHT CASE OF LARCENCY
Director: Don Weis
Co-stars: Mickey Rooney Eddie Bracken Elaine Stewart

1952 THE GIRL IN WHITE
Director: John Sturges
Co-stars: June Allyson Arthur Kennedy Gary Merrill

1953 THE EDDIE CANTOR STORY
Director: Alfred Green
Co-stars: Keefe Brasselle Aline MacMahon Arthur Franz

FAITH ESHAM

1984 CARMEN
Director: Francesco Rosi
Co-stars: Julia Migenes-Johnson Placido Domingo

JILL ESMOND

1931 ONCE A LADY
Director: Gutherie McClintic
Co-stars: Ruth Chatterton Ivor Novello Doris Lloyd

1931 THE SKIN GAME
Director: Alfred Hitchcock
Co-stars: Edmund Gwenn John Longden Helen Haye

1932 STATE'S ATTORNEY
Director: George Archainbaud
Co-stars: John Barrymore William Boyd Helen Twelvetrees

1932 13 WOMEN
Director: George Archainbaud
Co-stars: Irene Dunne Myrna Loy Florence Eldridge

1932 LADIES OF THE JURY
Director: Lowell Sherman
Co-stars: Edna May Oliver Kitty Kelly Ken Murray

1933 F.P.1
Director: Karl Hartl
Co-stars: Conrad Veidt Leslie Fenton Donald Calthrop

1933 NO FUNNY BUSINESS
Director: John Stafford
Co-stars: Gertrude Lawrence Laurence Olivier Muriel Aked

1942 THE PIED PIPER
Director: Irving Pichel
Co-stars: Monty Woolley Anne Baxter Roddy McDowall

1944 CASANOVA BROWN
Director: Sam Wood
Co-stars: Gary Cooper Teresa Wright Frank Morgan

1946 BEDELIA
Director: Lance Comfort
Co-stars: Margaret Lockwood Ian Hunter Anne Crawford

1946 THE BANDIT OF SHERWOOD FOREST
Director: Henry Levin
Co-stars: Cornel Wilde Anita Louise Henry Daniel

1948 ESCAPE
Director: Joseph Mankiewicz
Co-stars: Rex Harrison William Hartnell Peggy Cummings

1954 NIGHT PEOPLE
Director: Nunnally Johnson
Co-stars: Gregory Peck Broderick Crawford Rita Gam

1955 A MAN CALLED PETER
Director: Henry Koster
Co-stars: Richard Todd Jean Peters Marjorie Rambeau

ANGEL ESPINOSA

1971 HOUSE OF EVIL
Director: Jack Hill
Co-stars: Boris Karloff Julissa Andres Garcia

VIOLA ESSEN

1946 SPECTRE OF THE ROSE
Director: Ben Hecht
Co-stars: Ivan Kirov Michael Chekov Lionel Stander

CHRISTINE ESTABROOK

1984 ALMOST YOU
Director: Adam Brooks
Co-stars: Brooke Adams Griffin Dunne Karen Young

1984 ACT OF PASSION
Director: Simon Langton
Co-stars: Kris Kristofferson Marlo Thomas Linda Thorson

ESTELITA

1953 TROPIC ZONE
Director: Lewis Foster
Co-stars: Ronald Reagan Rhonda Fleming Noah Berry Jnr.

1996 JESSE JAMES MEETS FRANKENSTEIN'S DAUGHTER
Director: William Beaudine
Co-stars: John Lupton Cal Bolder

AGNES ESTERHAZY

1925 JOYLESS STREET
Director: G.W. Pabst
Co-stars: Asta Nielsen Werner Krauss Greta Garbo

RENEE ESTEVEZ *(Daughter Of Martin Sheen)*

1986 SHATTERED SPIRITS
Director: Robert Greenwald
Co-stars: Martin Sheen Melinda Dillon Roxana Zal

1991 DEAD SILENCE
Director: Peter Oafallon
Co-stars: Steven Brill Lisanna Falk Carrie Mitchum

1992 SINGLE WHITE FEMALE
Director: Barbet Schroeder
Co-stars: Bridget Fonda Jennifer Jason Leigh

1993 PAPER HEARTS
Director: Rod McCall
Co-stars: Sally Kirkland James Brolin Kris Kristofferson

ANGELINA ESTRADA

1990 GHOST
Director: Jerry Zucker
Co-stars: Patrick Swayze Demi Moore Whoopi Goldberg

RUTH ETTING

1933 ROMAN SCANDALS
Director: Frank Tuttle
Co-stars: Eddie Cantor Gloria Stuart Edward Arnold

1934 THE GIFT OF GAB
Director: Karl Freund
Co-stars: Gloria Stuart Edmund Lowe Ethel Waters

1934 HIPS, HIPS HOORAY
Director: Mark Sandrich
Co-stars: Bert Wheeler Robert Woolsey Thelma Todd

CHRISTINE EUDES

1958 TWO MEN IN MANHATTAN
Director: Jean-Pierre Melville
Co-stars: Jean-Pierre Melville Pieere Grasset

LINDA EVANGELISTA

1996 UNZIPPED
Co-stars: Cindy Crawford Kate Moss

DALE EVANS *(Married Roy Rogers)*

1943 WAR OF THE WILDCATS
Director: Albert Rogell
Co-stars: John Wayne Martha Scott Albert Dekker

1944 CASANOVA IN BURLESQUE
Director: Leslie Goodwins
Co-stars: Joe E. Brown June Havoc Ian Keith

1944 THE YELLOW ROSE OF TEXAS
Director: Joseph Kane
Co-stars: Roy Rogers Grant Withers Harry Shannon

1944 SAN FERNANDO VALLEY
Co-star: Roy Rogers

1945 UTAH
Co-stars: Roy Rogers George "Gabby" Hayes

1945 THE BIG SHOW-OFF
Co-star: Marjorie Manners

1945 BELLS OF ROSARITA
Co-star: Roy Rogers

1946 MY PAL TRIGGER
Director: Frank McDonald
Co-star: Roy Rogers Jack Holt George "Gabby" Hayes

1946 ROLL ON, TEXAS MOON
Co-stars: Roy Rogers Bob Nolan

DEBBIE EVANS

1982 ANGELO MY LOVE
Director: Robert Duvall
Co-stars: Angelo Evans Michael Evans Ruthie Evans

EDITH EVANS

Nominated For Best Supporting Actress In 1963 For "Tom Jones" And In 1964 For "The Chalk Garden". Nominated For Best Actress In 1966 For "The Whisperers"

1948 THE QUEEN OF SPADES
Director: Thorold Dickinson
Co-stars: Anton Walbrook Ronald Howard Yvonne Mitchell

1949 THE LAST DAYS OF DOLWYN
Director: Emlyn Williams
Co-stars: Emlyn Williams Richard Burton Hugh Griffith

1952 THE IMPORTANCE OF BEING ERNEST
Director: Anthony Asquith
Co-stars: Michael Redgrave Michael Dennison

1959 LOOK BACK IN ANGER
Director: Tony Richardson
Co-stars: Richard Burton Claire Bloom Mary Ure

1959 THE NUN'S STORY
Director: Fred Zinnemann
Co-stars: Audrey Hepburn Peter Finch Peggy Ashcroft

1963 TOM JONES
Director: Tony Richardson
Co-stars: Albert Finney Hugh Griffith Susannah York

1964 YOUNG CASSIDY
Director: John Ford
Co-stars: Rod Taylor Maggie Smith Flora Robson Michael Redgrave

1964 THE CHALK GARDEN
Director: Ronald Neame
Co-stars: Deborah Kerr Hayley Mills John Mills Elizabeth Sellars

1966 THE WHISPERERS
Director: Bryan Forbes
Co-stars: Eric Portman Nanette Newman Ronald Fraser

1967 FITZWILLY
Director: Delbert Mann
Co-stars: Dick Van Dyke Barbara Feldon John McGiver

1969 CROOKS AND CORONETS
Director: Jim O'Connelly
Co-stars: Telly Savalas Warren Oates Nicky Benson

1969 THE MADWOMAN OF CHAILLOT
Director: Bryan Forbes
Co-stars: Katherine Hepburn Danny Kaye Yul Brynner

1969 PRUDENCE AND THE PILL
Director: Fielder Cook
Co-stars: David Niven Deborah Kerr Judy Geeson

1970 SCROOGE
Director: Ronald Neame
Co-stars: Albert Finney Michael Medwin Alec Guinness

1970 DAVID COPPERFIELD
Director: Delbert Mann
Co-stars: Robin Phillips Susan Hampshire Wendy Hiller

1973 A DOLL'S HOUSE
Director: Patrick Garland
Co-stars: Claire Bloom Anthony Hopkins Ralph Richardson

1974 CRAZE
Director: Freddie Francis
Co-stars: Jack Palance Diana Dors Julie Ege Hugh Griffith

1976 THE SLIPPER AND THE ROSE
Director: Bryan Forbes
Co-stars: Richard Chamberlain Gemma Craven

1976 NASTY HABITS
Director: Michael Lindsay-Hogg
Co-stars: Glenda Jackson Melina Mercouri Sandy Dennis

ESTELLE EVANS

1962 TO KILL A MOCKINGBIRD
Director: Robert Mulligan
Co-stars: Gregory Peck Mary Badham Phillip Alford

1969 THE LEARNING TREE
Director: Gordon Parks
Co-stars: Kyle Johnson Alex Clarke Dana Elcar

JILL EVANS

1945 29 ACACIA AVENUE
Director: Henry Cass
Co-stars: Gordon Harker Betty Balfour Carla Lehman

JOAN EVANS

1949   **ROSEANNA McCOY**
Director: Irving Reis
Co-stars: Farley Granger Raymond Massey Charles Bickford

1950   **OUR VERY OWN**
Director: David Miller
Co-stars: Farley Granger Ann Blyth Jane Wyatt Natalie Wood

1950   **EDGE OF DOOM**
Director: Mark Robson
Co-stars: Farley Granger Dana Andrews Robert Keith Mala Powers

1952   **IT GROWS ON TREES**
Director: Arthur Lubin
Co-stars: Irene Dunne Dean Jagger Richard Crenna

1952   **SKIRTS AHOY!**
Director: Sidney Lanfield
Co-stars: Esther Williams Vivian Blaine Debbie Reynolds

1953   **COLUMN SOUTH**
Director: Frederick De Cordova
Co-stars: Audie Murphy Robert Sterling

1954   **THE OUTCAST**
Director: William Witney
Co-stars: John Derek Jim Davis

1958   **NO NAME ON THE BULLET**
Director: Jack Arnold
Co-stars: Audie Murphy Charles Drake

1959   **THE FLYING FONTAINES**
Director: George Sherman
Co-stars: Michael Callan Joe Desantis

LINDA EVANS

1974   **NAKIA**
Director: Leonard Horn
Co-stars: Robert Forster Arthur Kennedy Stephen McNally

1964   **THOSE CALLOWAYS**
Director: Norman Tokar
Co-stars: Brian Keith Vera Miles Walter Brennan

1974   **THE KLANSMAN**
Director: Terence Young
Co-stars: Lee Marvin Richard Burton Cameron Mitchell

1975   **MITCHELL**
Director: Andrew McLaglen
Co-stars: Joe Don Baker Martin Balsam John Saxon

1979   **AVALANCHE EXPRESS**
Director: Mark Robson
Co-stars: Robert Shaw Lee Marvin Maxmilian Schell

1979   **TOM HORN**
Director: William Wiard
Co-stars: Steve McQueen Richard Fairnsworth Slim Pickins

1983   **KENNY ROGERS AS THE GAMBLER: THE ADVENTURE CONTINUES**
Director: Dick Lowry
Co-stars: Bruce Boxleitner Kenny Rogers

1986   **LAST FRONTIER**
Director: Simon Wincer
Co-stars: Jack Thompson Jason Robards Judy Morris

1990   **SHE'LL TAKE ROMANCE**
Co-stars: Tom Skerritt Larry Poindexter

1991   **THE GAMBLER RETURNS: THE LUCK OF THE DRAW**
Director: Dick Lowry
Co-stars: Kenny Rogers Gene Barry

MADGE EVANS *(Child)*

1925   **WINNING THROUGH**
Co-stars: Richard Barthelmess

1931   **HEARTBREAK**
Co-stars: Charles Farrell John Arledge

1931   **SPORTING BLOOD**
Director: Charles Brabin
Co-stars: Clark Gable Ernest Torrence Lew Cody

1931   **SON OF INDIA**
Co-star: Ramon Navarro

1931   **GUILTY HANDS**
Director: W.S. Van Dyke
Co-stars: Lionel Barrymore Kay Francis C. Aubrey Smith

1932   **ARE YOU LISTENING?**
Director: Harry Beaumont
Co-stars: William Haines Karen Morley Wallace Ford

1932   **FAST LIFE**
Director: Harry Pollard
Co-star: William Haines

1932   **THE GREEKS HAD A WORD FOR THEM**
Director: Lowell Sherman
Co-stars: Joan Blondell Ina Claire

1932   **HUDDLE**
Director: Sam Wood
Co-stars: Ramon Navarro Una Merkle Conrad Nagel

1932   **LOVERS COURAGEOUS**
Director: Robert Z Leonard
Co-stars: Robert Montgomery Roland Young

1932   **WEST OF BROADWAY**
Director: Harry Beaumont
Co-stars: John Gilbert El Brendel Ralph Bellamy

1933   **THE NUISANCE**
Director: Jack Conway
Co-stars: Lee Tracy Frank Morgan Charles Butterworth

1933   **THE MAYOR OF HELL**
Director: Archie Mayo
Co-stars: James Cagney Allen Jenkins Frankie Darro

1933   **BROADWAY TO HOLLYWOOD**
Director: William Mack
Co-stars: Frank Morgan Alice Brady Mickey Rooney

1933   **HELL BELOW**
Director: Jack Conway
Co-stars: Robert Montgomery Walter Huston Robert Young

1933   **HALLELUJAH, I'M A BUM**
Director: Lewis Milestone
Co-stars: Al Jolson Frank Morgan Hgarry Landon

1933   **DINNER AT EIGHT**
Director: George Cukor
Co-stars: Lionel Barrymore Marie Dressler Jean Harlow

1933   **BEAUTY FOR SALE**
Director: Richard Boleslawski
Co-stars: Alice Brady Una Merkel Otto Kruger

1934   **DAVID COPPERFIELD**
Director: George Cukor
Co-stars: Freddie Bartholomew W.C. Fields Roland Young

1934   **DEATH ON THE DIAMOND**
Director: Edward Sedgewick
Co-stars: Robert Young Nat Pendleton Mickey Rooney

1934   **EXCLUSIVE STORY**
Director: George Seitz
Co-stars: Franchot Tone Joseph Calleia J. Carrol Naish

1934 FUGITIVE LOVERS
Director: Richard Boleslawski
Co-stars: Robert Montgomery Ted Healy

1934 GRAND CANARY
Director: Irving Cummings
Co-stars: Warner Baxter H.B. Warner Marjorie Rambeau

1934 HELLDORADO
Director: James Cruze
Co-stars: Richard Arlen Ralph Bellamy James Gleason

1934 PARIS INTERLUDE
Director: Edwin Marin
Co-stars: Otto Kruger Robert Young Una Merkel Ted Healy

1934 THE SHOW-OFF
Director: Charles Riesner
Co-stars: Spencer Tracy Clara Blandick

1934 STAND UP AND CHEER
Director: Hamilton McFadden
Co-stars: Warner Baxter Nigel Bruce Shirley Temple

1934 WHAT EVERY WOMAN KNOWS
Director: Gregory La Cava
Co-stars: Helen Hayes Brian Aherne Lucile Watson

1935 THE TUNNEL
Director: Maurice Elvey
Co-stars: Richard Dix Leslie Banks George Arliss

1935 MEN WITHOUT NAMES
Director: Ralph Murray
Co-stars: Fred MacMurray Lynne Overman Dean Jagger

1935 AGE OF INDISCRETION
Director: Edward Ludwig
Co-stars: Paul Lukas Helen Vinson May Robson

1936 CALM YOURSELF
Director: Georg Seitz
Co-stars: Robert Young Nat Pendleton Ralph Morgan

1936 PENNIES FROM HEAVEN
Director: Norman Z McLeod
Co-stars: Bing Crosby Edith Fellows Louis Armstrong

1936 PICCADILLY JIM
Director: Robert Z Leonard
Co-stars: Robert Montgomery Frank Morgan Eric Blore

1937 ESPIONAGE
Director: Kurt Neumann
Co-stars: Edmund Lowe Paul Lukas Ketti Gallian

1938 ARMY GIRL
Director: George Nichols
Co-stars: Preston Foster James Gleason

1938 SINNERS IN PARADISE
Director: James Whale
Co-stars: John Boles Bruce Cabot Gene Lockhart

MARGUERITE EVANS

1925 STAGESTRUCK
Director: Allan Dwan
Co-stars: Gloria Swanson Lawrence Gray Gertrude Astor

MICHELLE EVANS

1993 THE MYSTERY OF EDWIN DROOD
Director: Timothy Forder
Co-stars: Robert Powell Nanette Newman Gemma Craven

MONICA EVANS

1968 THE ODD COUPLE
Director: Gene Saks
Co-stars: Jack Lemmon Walter Matthau Herb Edelman

MURIEL EVANS

1936 MR. DEEDS GOES TO TOWN
Director: Frank Capra
Co-stars: Gary Cooper Jean Arthur Raymond Walburn

1936 THREE ON THE TRAIL
Co-stars: William Boyd James Ellison

1936 CALL OF THE PRAIRIE
Co-stars: William Boyd James Ellison George Hayes

PEGGY EVANS

1949 THE BLUE LAMP
Director: Basil Dearden
Co-stars: Jack Warner Jimmy Hanley Dirk Bogarde

1951 CALLING BULLDOG
Director: Victor Saville
Co-stars: Walter Pidgeon Margaret Leighton

RUTHIE EVANS

1982 ANGELO MY LOVE
Director: Robert Duvall
Co-stars: Angelo Evans Michael Evans Debbie Evans

EDITH EVANSON

1945 THE JADE MASK
Director: Phil Rosen
Co-stars: Sidney Toler Manton Moreland Hardie Albright

1948 ROPE
Director: Alfred Hitchcock
Co-stars: James Stewart John Dall Farley Granger

1950 THE MAGNIFICENT YANKEE
Director: John Sturges
Co-stars: Louis Calhern Ann Harding Philip Ober

JUDITH EVELYN

1951 THE 13TH LETTER
Director: Otto Preminger
Co-stars: Charles Boyer Linda Darnell Constance Smith

1954 REAR WINDOW
Director: Alfred Hitchcock
Co-stars: James Stewart Grace Kelly Thelma Ritter

1954 THE EGYPTIAN
Director: Michael Curtiz
Co-stars: Edmund Purdom Victor Mature Peter Ustinov

1956 GIANT
Director: George Stevens
Co-stars: Rock Hudson Elizabeth Taylor James Dean

1956 HILDA CRANE
Director: Phillip Dunne
Co-stars: Jean Simmons Guy Madison Jean-Pierre Aumont

1957 THE BROTHERS KARAMAZOV
Director: Richard Brooks
Co-stars: Yul Brynner Maria Schell Richard Basehart

1958 TWILIGHT FOR THE GODS
Director: Joseph Pevney
Co-stars: Rock Hudson Cyd Charisse Arthur Kennedy

1959 THE TINGLER
Director: William Castle
Co-stars: Vincent Price Darryl Hickman Patricia Cutts

BARBARA EVEREST

1932 THE LODGER
Director: Maurice Elvey
Co-stars: Ivor Novello Elizabeth Allan Jack Hawkins

1935   SCROOGE
Director: Henry Edwards
Co-stars: Seymour Hicks Donald Calthrop Athene Seyler

1937   JUMP FOR GLORY
Director: Raoul Walsh
Co-stars: Douglas Fairbanks Jnr. Valerie Hobson Alan Hale

1937   OLD MOTHER RILEY
Director: Oswald Mitchell
Co-stars: Arthur Lucan Kitty McShane Patrick Ludlow

1938   OLD MOTHER RILEY M.P.
Director: Oswald Mitchell
Co-stars: Arthur Lucan Kitty McShane Edith Sharpe

1939   INQUEST
Director: Roy Boutling
Co-stars: Elizabeth Allan Herbert Lom Olive Sloane

1943   MISSION TO MOSCOW
Director: Michael Curtis
Co-stars: Walter Huston Ann Harding Oscar Homolka

1944   THE UNINVITED
Director: Lewis Allen
Co-stars: Ray Milland Ruth Hussey Gail Russell

1944   JANE EYRE
Director: Robert Stevenson
Co-stars: Joan Fontaine Orson Welles Margaret O'Brien

1944   GASLIGHT
Director: George Cukor
Co-stars: Charles Boyer Ingrid Bergman Joseph Cotten

1945   THE VALLEY OF DECISION
Director: Tay Garnett
Co-stars: Greer Garson Gregory Peck Lionel Barrymore

1946   WANTED FOR MURDER
Director: Lawrence Huntingdon
Co-stars: Eric Portman Dulcie Gray Derek Farr

1949   MADELEINE
Director: David Lean
Co-stars: Ann Todd Leslie Banks Elizabeth Sellars

1959   TRUNK CRIME
Director: Roy Boutling
Co-stars: Manning Whiley Michael Drake Hay Petrie

1962   THE MAN WHO FINALLY DIED
Director: Quentin Lawrence
Co-stars: Stanley Baker Mai Zetterling

NANCY EVERHARD

1989   THE PUNISHER
Director: Mark Goldblatt
Co-stars: Dolph Lungren Lou Gossett Jnr. Jeroen Krabbe

1989   THE TRIAL OF THE INCREDIBLE HULK
Director: Bill Bixby
Co-stars: Bill Bixby Lou Ferrignol Rex Smith

1991   THIS GUN FOR HIRE
Director: Lou Antonio
Co-stars: Robert Wagner John Harkins Frederick Lehne

ANN EVERS

1939   GUNGA DIN
Director: George Stevens
Co-stars: Cary Grant Victor McLaglen Douglas Fairbanks Jnr.

JANE EVERS

1985   SHE'LL BE WEARING PINK PYJAMAS
Director: John Goldschmidt
Co-stars: Julie Walters Anthony Higgins

CORY EVERSON

1992   DOUBLE IMPACT
Director: Sheldon Lettich
Co-stars: Jean-Claude Van Damme Geoffrey Lewis Alan Scarfe

PAT EVISON

1979   TIM
Director: Michael Pate
Co-stars: Piper Laurie Mel Gibson Alwyn Kurts

1982   STARSTRUCK
Director: Gillian Armstrong
Co-stars: Jo Kennedy Ross O'Donovan Margo Lee

RENATE EWERT

1960   THE RED CIRCLE
Director: Jurgen Roland
Co-stars: Fritz Rasp Karl Saebisch

BARBARA EWING

1967   TORTURE GARDEN
Director: Freddie Francis
Co-stars: Burgess Meredith Jack Palance Peter Cushing

1968   DRACULA HAS RISEN FROM THE GRAVE
Director: Freddie Francis
Co-stars: Christopher Lee Rupert Davies

SUSAN EYTON-JONES

1991   LANA IN LOVE
Director: Basher Shbib
Co-stars: Daphna Kastner Clark Gregg Michael Gillis

NANNETTE FABARES

1939 A CHILD IS BORN
Director: Lloyd Bacon
Co-stars: Geraldine Fitzgerald Jeffrey Lynn Gladys George

SHELLEY FABARES

1956 NEVER SAY GOODBYE
Director: Jerry Hopper
Co-stars: Rock Hudson George Sanders Cornell Borchers

1964 RIDE THE WILD SURF
Director: Don Taylor
Co-stars: Fabian Tab Hunter Barbara Eden

1965 GIRL HAPPY
Director: Boris Sagal
Co-stars: Elvis Presley Gary Crosby Nita Talbot

1966 SPINOUT
Director: Norman Taurog
Co-stars: Elvis Presley Cecil Kellaway Diane McBain

1967 CLAMBAKE
Director: Arthur Nadel
Co-stars: Elvis Presley Bill Bixby Gary Merrill

1971 BRIAN'S SONG
Director: Buzz Kulik
Co-stars: Billy Dee Williams James Caan Judy Pace

1987 HOT PURSUIT
Director: Steven Lisberger
Co-stars: John Cusack Robert Loggia Wendy Gazelle

JULIETTE FABER

1941 LES INCONNUS DANS LA MAISON
Director: Henri Decoin
Co-stars: Raimu Jacques Baumer Jean Tissier

AVA FABIAN

1990 WELCOME HOME, ROXY CARMICHAEL
Director: Jim Abrahams
Co-stars: Winona Ryder Jeff Daniels Laila Robins

FRANCOISE FABIAN

1957 THE FANATICS
Director: Alex Joffe
Co-stars: Pierre Fresnay Michel Auclair Gregoire Aslan

1969 MY NIGHT WITH MAUDE
Director: Eric Rohmer
Co-stars: Jean-Louis Trintignant Antoine Vitez

1973 HAPPY NEW YEAR
Director: Claude Lelouche
Co-stars: Lino Ventura Charles Gerard

1983 BENVENUTA
Director: Andre Delvaux
Co-stars: Fanny Ardant Vittorio Gassman Matthieu Carriere

1989 REUNION
Director: Jerry Schatzberg
Co-stars: Jason Robards Christien Anholt Samuel West

JANICE FABIAN

1988 INVASION EARTH: THE ALIENS ARE HERE
Director: Robert Skotak
Co-stars: Christian Lee Larry Bagby

OLGA FABIAN

1944 WATERFRONT
Co-stars: John Carradine Maris Wrixon

NANNETTE FABRAY

**1939 THE PRIVATE LIVES OF
          ELIZABETH AND ESSEX**
Director: Michael Curtiz
Co-stars: Bette Davis Errol Flynn

1953 THE BAND WAGON
Director: Vincente Minnelli
Co-stars: Fred Astaire Jack Buchanan Oscar Levant

1969 THE HAPPY ENDING
Director: Richard Brooks
Co-stars: Jean Simmons Shirley Jones Bobby Darin

**1970 THE COCKEYED COWBOYS
          OF CALICO COUNTY**
Director: Tony Leader
Co-stars: Dan Blocker Mickey Rooney

1981 AMY
Director: Vincent McEveety
Co-stars: Jenny Agutter Barry Newman Margaret O'Brien

SATURNIN FABRE

1946 LES PORTES DE LA NUIT
Director: Marcel Carne
Co-stars: Pierre Brasseur Yves Montand Serge Reggiani

1948 CLOCHEMERLE
Director: Pierre Chenal
Co-stars: Simone Michels Jane Marken Paul Demange

CHRISTINE FABREGA

1966 SECOND BREATH
Director: Jean-Pierre Melville
Co-stars: Lino Ventura Paul Meurisse

VALERIE FABRIZI

1966 RINGO AND HIS GOLDEN PISTOL
Director: Sergio Corbucci
Co-stars: Mark Damon Ettore Manni

MAYANNE FAHEY

1984 FUTURE SCHLOCK
Director: Barry Peak
Co-stars: Michael Bishop Tracey Callender Peter Cox

1985 THE DUNERA BOYS
Director: Sam Lewin
Co-stars: Joseph Spano Bob Hoskins Warren Mitchell

1988 CELIA
Director: Ann Turner
Co-stars: Rebecca Smart Nicholas Eadie Victoria Longley

MYRNA FAHEY

1960 THE FALL OF THE HOUSE OF USHER
Director: Roger Corman
Co-stars: Vincent Price Mark Damon

FLORBELLE FAIRBANKS

1927 THE LOVES OF SUNYA
Director: Albert Parker
Co-stars: Gloria Swanson John Boles

MORGAN FAIRCHILD

1979 THE CONCRETE COWBOYS
Director: Burt Kennedy
Co-stars: Tom Sellick Jerry Reed Claude Akins

1980 THE MEMORY OF EVA RYKER
Director: Walter Grauman
Co-stars: Natalie Wood Robert Foxworth Mel Ferrer

1983 HOTEL
Director: Jerry London
Co-stars: Bette Davis James Brolin Shirley Jones

1984 THE ZANY ADVENTURES OF ROBIN HOOD
Director: Ray Austin
Co-stars: George Segal Roddy McDowall

1985 PEE-WEE'S BIG ADVENTURE
Director: Tim Burton
Co-stars: Paul Reubins Elizabeth Daily James Brolin

1987 CAMPUS MAN
Director: Ron Casden
Co-stars: John Dye Steve Lyon Kim Delaney

1990 HOW TO MURDER A MILLIONAIRE
Director: Paul Schneider
Co-stars: Joan Rivers Alex Rocco David Ogden Stiers

1995 CRIMINAL HEARTS
Director: David Payne
Co-stars: Kevin Dillon Amy Locane

VIRGINIA BROWN FAIRE

1927 THE TEMPTRESS
Director: Fred Niblo
Co-stars: Greta Garbo Antonio Moreno Lionel Barrymore

1934 WEST OF THE DIVIDE
Director: Robert Bradbury
Co-stars: John Wayne George Hayes Yakima Canutt

DIANA FAIRFAX

1980 SENSE AND SENSIBILITY
Director: Rodney Bennett
Co-stars: Irene Richard Tracey Childs

1990 PORTRAIT OF A MARRIAGE
Director: Stephen Whittaker
Co-stars: Janet McTeer David Haig Cathryn Harrison

HEATHER FAIRFIELD

1989 THE WAR OF THE ROSES
Director: Danny De Vito
Co-stars: Danny De Vito Michael Douglas Kathleen Turner

1989 A DEADLY SILENCE
Director: John Patterson
Co-stars: Mike Farrell Bruce Weitz Charles Haid

1991 SINS OF THE MOTHER
Director: John Patterson
Co-stars: Elizabeth Montgomery Dale Midkiff Talia Balsam

MICHELLE FAIRLEY

1992 FLEA BITES
Director: Alan Dossor
Co-stars: Nigel Hawthorne Anthony Hill Tim Healy

1992 FORCE OF DUTY
Director: Pat O'Connor
Co-stars: Donald McCann Adrian Dunbar Patrick Malahide

1992 THE LONG ROADS
Director: Tristram Powell
Co-stars: Edith MacArthur Robert Urquart Maureen Beattie

1993 COMICS
Director: Diarmuid Lawrence
Co-stars: Danny Webb Frank Grimes

SANDRA FAISON

1969 THE STERILE CUCKOO
Director: Alan J. Pakula
Co-stars: Liza Minnelli Tim McIntyre Wendell Burton

MARIANNE FAITHFUL

1967 I'LL NEVER FORGET WHAT'S 'IS NAME
Director: Michael Winner
Co-stars: Oliver Reed Orson Welles Carol White

1968 GIRL ON A MOTORCYCLE
Director: Jack Cardiff
Co-stars: Alain Delon Roger Mutton

1969 HAMLET
Director: Tony Richardson
Co-stars: Nicol Williamson Anthony Hopkins Gordon Jackson

1975 GHOST STORY
Director: Stephen Weeks
Co-stars: Murray Melvin Leigh Lawson

**1980 KENNETH ANGER VOL. IV:
INVOCATION OF MY DEMON BROTHER**
Director: Kenneth Anger
Co-star: Leslie Huggins

1991 DREAMING
Director: Mike Alexander
Co-stars: Ewen Bremner Billy Connolly

1994 SHOPPING
Director: Paul Anderson
Co-stars: Sadie Frost Sean Pertwee Jonathan Pryce

LOLA FALANA

1970 THE LIBERATION OF L.B.JONES
Director: William Wyler
Co-stars: Lee J. Cobb Lee Majors Barbara Hershey

1974 THE KLANSMAN
Director: Terence Young
Co-stars: Lee Marvin Richard Burton Cameron Mitchell

EDIE FALCO

1992 LAWS OF GRAVITY
Director: Nick Gomez
Co-stars: Peter Greene Adam Trese Arabella Field

MARIA FALCONETTI

1928 THE PASSION OF JOAN OF ARC
Director: Carl Dreyer
Co-stars: Eugene Silvain Michel Simon

LISANNE FALK

1989 HEATHERS
Director: Michael Lehmann
Co-stars: Winona Ryder Christian Slater Shannen Doherty

1991 DEAD SILENCE
Director: Peter O'Fallon
Co-stars: Steven Brill Renee Estevez Carrie Mitchum

ROSSELLA FALK

1956 MODESTY BLAISE
Director: Joseph Losey
Co-stars: Monica Vitti Dirk Bogarde Terence Stamp

1963 EIGHT AND A HALF
Director: Federico Fellini
Co-stars: Marcello Mastroianni Claudia Cardinale

1968 THE LEGEND OF LYLAH CLARE
Director: Robert Aldrich
Co-stars: Kim Novak Peter Finch Ernest Borgnine

JINX FALKENBERG

1943 LAUGH YOUR BLUES AWAY
Director: Charles Barton
Co-stars: Bert Gordon Isobel Elsom Douglass Drake

1943 SHE HAS WHAT IT TAKES
Director: Charles Barton
Co-stars: Tom Neal Constance Worth Joe King

1943 TWO SENORITAS FROM CHICAGO
Co-stars: Ann Savage Joan Davis Bob Haymes

1944 NINE GIRLS
Director: Leigh Jason
Co-stars: Ann Harding Evelyn Keyes Anita Louise

1944 COVER GIRL
Director: Charles Vidor
Co-stars: Rita Hayworth Gene Kelly Phil Silvers

1945 THE GAY SENORITA
Co-star: Jim Bannon

1946 TALK ABOUT A LADY
Director: George Sherman
Co-stars: Forrest Tucker Trudy Marshall Joe Besser

1946 MEET ME ON BROADWAY
Director: Leigh Jason
Co-stars: Marjorie Reynolds Fred Brady Spring Byington

DEBORAH FALLENDER

1977 JABERWOCKY
Director: Terry Gillian
Co-stars: Micharl Palin Max Wall Warren Mitchell

ADRIENNE FANCEY

1950 A WOMAN OF DISTINCTION
Director: Edward Buzzell
Co-stars: Rosalind Russell Ray Milland Edmund Gwenn

ARLENE FARBER

1974 ALL THE KIND STRANGERS
Director: Burt Kennedy
Co-stars: Stacey Keach Samantha Eggar John Savage

VIOLET FAREBROTHER

1927 EASY VIRTUE
Director: Alfred Hitchcock
Co-stars: Isabel Jeans Franklyn Dyall Ian Hunter

1956 FORTUNE IS A WOMAN
Director: Sidney Gilliat
Co-stars: Jack Hawkins Arlene Dahl Dennis Price

DEBRAH FARENTINO

1992 BUGSY
Director: Barry Levinson
Co-stars: Warren Beatty Annette Bening Harvey Keitel

1993 SON OF THE PINK PANTHER
Director: Blake Edwards
Co-stars: Roberto Benigni Claudia Cardinale

1994 XXXS AND OOOS
Director: Alan Arkush
Co-stars: Andrea Parker Nia Peebles

1994 DEAD AIR
Director: Fred Walton
Co-star: Gregory Hines

NADIA FARES

1994 LOVE IN THE STRANGEST WAY
Director: Christopher Frank
Co-stars: Thierry L'Hermitte Maruschka Detmers

CAROLYN FARINA

1989 METROPOLITAN
Director: Whit Stillman
Co-stars: Edward Clements Christopher Eigman

LYNN FARLAIGH

1989 HEARTLAND
Director: Kevin Billington
Co-stars: Anthony Hopkins Glynn Houston Jane Horrocks

FRANCES FARMER

1936 BORDER FLIGHT
Co-star: Grant Withers

1936 TOO MANY PARENTS

1936 RHYTHM ON THE RANGE
Director: Norman Taurog
Co-stars: Bing Crosby Martha Raye Bob Burns

1936 COME AND GET IT
Director: Howard Hawkes
Co-stars: Edward Arnold Joel McCrea Walter Brennan

1937 EBB TIDE
Director: James Hogan
Co-stars: Ray Milland Oscar Homolka Barry Fitzgerald

1937 EXCLUSIVE
Director: Alexander Hall
Co-stars: Charles Ruggles Fred MacMurray Lloyd Nolan

1937 THE TOAST OF NEW YORK
Director: Howard Lee
Co-stars: Edward Arnold Cary Grant Jack Oakie

1938 RIDE A CROOKED MILE
Director: Alfred Green
Co-stars: Akim Tamiroff Leif Erikson Lynne Overman

1940 SOUTH OF PAGO PAGO
Director: Alfred Green
Co-stars: Victor McLaglen Jon Hall Olympe Bradna

1940 WORLD PREMIER
Director: Ted Tetzlaff
Co-stars: John Barrymore Ricardo Cortez Eugene Pallett

1940 FLOWING GOLD
Director: Alfred Green
Co-stars: John Garfield Pat O'Brien Raymond Walburn

1941 BADLANDS OF DAKOTA
Director: Alfred Green
Co-stars: Robert Stack Broderick Crawford Richard Dix

1941 AMONG THE LIVING
Director: Stuart Heisler
Co-stars: Albert Dekker Susan Hayward Harry Carey

1942 SON OF FURY
Director: John Cromwell
Co-stars: Tyrone Power Gene Tierney George Sanders

MIMSY FARMER

1963 SPENCER'S MOUNTAIN
Director: Delmer Daves
Co-stars: Henry Fonda Maureen O'Hara James MacArthur

1965 BUS RILEY'S BACK IN TOWN
Director: Harvey Hart
Co-stars: Michael Parks Ann Margret Jocelyn Brando

1971 ROAD TO SALINA
Director: George Lautner
Co-stars: Rita Hayworth Robert Walker Jnr. Ed Begley

1983 THE GIRL FROM TRIESTE
Director: Pasquale Festa Campanile
Co-stars: Ben Gazzara Ornella Muti

1986 CODENAME: WILDERNESS
Director: Anthony Dawson
Co-stars: Lewis Collins Ernest Borgnine Lee Van Cleef

SUSAN FARMER

1964 THE DEVIL-SHIP PIRATES
Director: Don Sharp
Co-stars: Christopher Lee Andrew Keir John Cairney

1966 RASPUTIN THE MAD MONK
Director: Don Sharp
Co-stars: Christopher Lee Richard Pasco Barbara Shelley

1966 DRACULA, PRINCE OF DARKNESS
Director: Terence Fisher
Co-stars: Christopher Lee Barbara Shelley Richard Pasco

1974 PERSECUTION
Director: Don Chaffey
Co-stars: Lana Turner Ralph Bates Trevor Howard

VIRGINIA FARMER

1950 CYRANO DE BERGERAC
Director: Michael Gordon
Co-stars: Jose Ferrer Mala Powers William Prince

1950 BORN TO BE BAD
Director: Nicholas Ray
Co-stars: Joan Fontaine Robert Ryan Zachary Scott

ELLEN FARNER

1964 LES PARAPLUIES DE CHERBOURG
Director: Jacques Demy
Co-stars: Catherine Deneuvre Anne Vernon

SHANNON FARNON

1975 AGAINST A CROOKED DKY
Director: Earl Bellamy
Co-stars: Richard Boone Stewart Petersen Henry Wilcoxon

FELICIA FARR (Married Jack Lemmon)

1956 TIMETABLE
Director: Mark Stevens
Co-stars: Mark Stevens King Calder Wesley Addy Jack Klugman

1956 THE FIRST TEXAN
Director: Byron Haskin
Co-stars: Joel McCrea Jeff Morrow Wallace Ford

1956 THE LAST WAGON
Director: Delmer Daves
Co-stars: Richard Widmark Tommy Retig Susan Kohner Nick Adams

1956 JUBAL
Director: Delmer Daves
Co-stars: Glenn Ford Ernest Borgnine Rod Steiger

1957 3.10 TO YUMA
Director: Delmer Daves
Co-stars: Glenn Ford Van Heflin Leora Dane Richard Jaeckel

1958 ONIONHEAD
Director: Norman Taurog
Co-stars: Andy Griffiths Walter Matthau Erin O'Brien

1964 KISS ME STUPID
Director: Billy Wilder
Co-stars: Dean Martin Kim Novak Ray Walston Cliff Osmond

1966 THE VENETIAN AFFAIR
Director: Jerry Thorpe
Co-stars: Robert Vaughn Elke Sommer Karl Boehm

1971 KOTCH
Director: Jack Lemmon
Co-stars: Walter Matthau Deborah Winter Charles Aidman

1986 THAT'S LIFE
Director: Blake Edwards
Co-stars: Jack Lemmon Julie Andrews Jennifer Edwards

MICHELLE FARR

1992 SINGLE WHITE FEMALE
Director: Barbet Schroeder
Co-stars: Briget Fonda Jennifer Jason Leigh

PATRICIA FARR

1938 ALL-AMERICAN SWEETHEART
Co-stars: Jaqueline Wells Allen Brook Scott Colton

CHARLOTTE FARRAN

1988 LA LECTRICE
Director: Michel Deville
Co-stars: Miou-Miou Regis Royer Marianne Denicourt

GWENN FARRAR

1935 SHE SHALL HAVE MUSIC
Director: Leslie Hiscott
Co-stars: Jack Hylton Marjorie Brooks June Clyde

JANE FARRAR

1943 PHANTOM OF THE OPERA
Director: Arthur Lubin
Co-stars: Claude Rains Nelson Eddy Susannah Foster

1944 DOUBLE EXPOSURE
Director: William Berke
Co-stars: Chester Morris Nancy Kelly Richard Gaines

GLENDA FARRELL

1930 LITTLE CEASAR
Director: Mervyn LeRoy
Co-stars: Edward G. Robinson Douglas Fairbanks Jnr

1932 I AM A FUGITIVE FROM A CHAIN GANG
Director: Mervyn LeRoy
Co-stars: Paul Muni Preston Foster

1932 THE MATCH KING
Director: Howard Bretherton
Co-stars: Warren William Lili Damita Harold Huber

1932 THREE ON A MATCH
Director: Mervyn LeRoy
Co-stars: Bette Davis Joan Blondell Ann Dvorak Humphrey Bogart

1932 LIFE BEGINS
Director: James Flood
Co-stars: Elliott Nugent Loretta Young Preston Foster

1932 SCANDAL FOR SALE
Co-stars: Pat O'Brien Charles Bickford Walter Brennan

1933 LADY FOR A DAY
Director: Frank Capra
Co-stars: May Robson Warren William Jean Parker

1933 A MAN'S CASTLE
Director: Frank Borzage
Co-stars: Spencer Tracy Loretta Young Walter Connolly

1933 CENTRAL AIRPORT
Director: William Wellman
Co-stars: Richard Barthelmess Sally Eilers Tom Brown

1933 THE KEYHOLE
Director: Michael Curtiz
Co-stars: Kay Francis George Brent Allen Jenkins

1933 GAMBLING SHIP
Director: Max Marcin
Co-stars: Cary Grant Benita Hume Jack La Rue

1933 BUREAU OF MISSING PERSONS
Director: Roy Del Ruth
Co-stars: Pat O'Brien Bette Davis Lewis Stone

1933 GRAND SLAM
Director: William Dieterle
Co-stars: Paul Lukas Loretta Young Frank McHugh

1933 HAVANA WIDOWS
Director: Ray Enright
Co-stars: Joan Blondell Guy Kibbee Lyle Talbot Frank McHugh

1933 MARY STEVENS M.D.
Director: Lloyd Bacon
Co-stars: Kay Francis Lyle Talbot Thelma Todd

1933 MYSTERY OF THE WAX MUSEUM
Director: Michael Curtiz
Co-stars: Lionel Atwill Fay Wray Frank McHugh

1933 GIRL MISSING
Co-stars: Guy Kibbee Mary Brian

1934 I'VE GOT YOUR NUMBER
Director: Ray Enright
Co-stars: Joan Blondell Pat O'Brien Allen Jenkins

1934 DARK HAZARD
Director: Alfred Green
Co-stars: Edward G. Robinson Genevieve Tobin

1934 THE PERSONALITY KID
Director: Alan Crosland
Co-stars: Pat O'Brien Claire Todd Henry O'Neill

1934 THE MERRY WIVES OF RENO
Director: Bruce Humberstone
Co-stars: Margaret Lindsay Donald Woods

1934 KANSAS CITY PRINCESS
Director: William Keighley
Co-stars: Joan Blondell Hugh Herbert Robert Armstrong

1934 HI NELLIE!
Director: Mervyn LeRoy
Co-stars: Paul Muni Ned Sparks Robert Barrat

1934 HEAT LIGHTNING
Director: Mervyn LeRoy
Co-stars: Aline McMahon Ann Dvorak Preston Foster

1934 THE BIG SHAKEDOWN
Director: John Francis Dillon
Co-stars: Bette Davis Charles Farrell Richard Cortez

1935 GOLD DIGGERS OF 1935
Director: Busby Berkeley
Co-stars: Dick Powell Adolphe Menjou Gloria Stuart

1935 WE'RE IN THE MONEY
Director: Ray Enright
Co-stars: Joan Blondell Hugh Herbert Lionel Stander

1935 TRAVELLING SALESLADY
Director: Ray Enright
Co-stars: Joan Blondell Hugh Herbert Ruth Donnelly

1935 GO INTO YOUR DANCE
Director: Archie Mayo
Co-stars: Al Jolson Ruby Keeler Helen Morgan

1935 LITTLE BIG SHOT
Director: Michael Curtiz
Co-stars: Sybill Jason Robert Armstrong J. Carrol Naish

1935 THE SECRET BRIDE
Director: William Dieterle
Co-stars: Barbara Stanwyck Warren William

1935 MISS PACIFIC FLEET
Director: Ray Enright
Co-stars: Joan Blondell Hugh Herbert Allen Jenkins

1935 IN CALIENTE
Director: Lloyd Bacon
Co-stars: Pat O'Brien Dolores Del Rio Leo Carrillo

1936 GOLD DIGGERS OF 1937
Director: Busby Berkeley
Co-stars: Dick Powell Joan Blondell Victor Moore

1936 HIGH TENSION
Director: Allan Dwan
Co-stars: Brian Donlevy Norman Foster Helen Wood

1936 SMART BLONDE
Director: Frank McDonald
Co-stars: Barton MacLane Wini Shaw Jane Wyman

1936 SNOWED UNDER
Co-stars: George Brent Genevieve Tobin Frank McHugh

1937 FLY AWAY BABY
Director: Frank McDonald
Co-stars: Barton MacLane

1937 HOLLYWOOD HOTEL
Director: Busby Berkeley
Co-stars: Dick Powell Rosemary Lane Lola Lane

1937 BREAKFAST FOR TWO
Director: Alfred Santell
Co-stars: Barbara Stanwyck Herbert Marshall Eric Blore

1937 YOU LIVE AND LEARN
Director: Arthur Woods
Co-stars: Claude Hulbert Glen Alyn John Carol

1937 THE ADVENTUROUS BLONDE
Director: Frank McDonald
Co-stars: Barton MacLane Virginia Brissac

1937 BLONDES AT WORK
Director: William Beaudine
Co-stars: Barton MacLane

1938 ROAD TO RENO
Director: S. Sylvan Simon
Co-stars: Randolph Scott Hope Hampton Helen Broderick

1938 TORCHY GETS HER MAN
Director: William Beaudine
Co-stars: Barton MacLane

1939 TORCHY BLANE IN CHINATOWN
Director: William Beaudine
Co-stars: Barton MacLane

1939 TORCHY RUNS FOR MAYOR
Director: William Beaudine
Co-stars: Barton MacLane

1938 STOLEN HEAVEN
Director: Andrew Stone
Co-stars: Gene Raymond Olympe Bradne Lewis Stone

1942 TWIN BEDS
Director: Tim Whelan
Co-stars: George Brent Joan Bennett Una Merkel

1942 JOHNNY EAGER
Director: Mervyn LeRoy
Co-stars: Robert Taylor Van Heflin Lana Turner

1942 THE TALK OF THE TOWN
Director: George Stevens
Co-stars: Ronald Colman Cary Grant Jean Arthur

1943	**KLONDYKE KATE**
Co-stars:	Tom Neal Ann Savage Sheldon Leonard

1943	**CITY WITHOUT MEN**
Director:	Sidney Salkow
Co-stars:	Linda Darnell Michael Duane Sara Allgood

1944	**EVER SINCE VENUS**
Director:	Arthur Dreifuss
Co-stars:	Hugh Herbert Billy Gilbert Ann Savage

1947	**I LOVE TROUBLE**
Director:	S. Sylvan Simon
Co-stars:	Franchot Tone Janet Blair Janis Carter

1952	**APACHE WAR SMOKE**
Director:	Harold Kress
Co-stars:	Gilbert Roland Robert Horton

1953	**GIRLS IN THE NIGHT**
Director:	Jack Arnold
Co-stars:	Harvey Lembeck Joyce Holden Don Gordon

1954	**SUSAN SLEPT HERE**
Director:	Frank Tashlin
Co-stars:	Dick Powell Debbie Reynolds Anne Francis

1954	**SECRET OF THE INCAS**
Director:	Jerry Hopper
Co-stars:	Charlton Heston Robert Young Yma Sumac

1955	**THE GIRL IN THE RED VELVET SWING**
Director:	Richard Fleischer
Co-stars:	Joan Collins Ray Milland

1959	**MIDDLE OF THE NIGHT**
Director:	Delbert Mann
Co-stars:	Fredric March Kim Novak Lee Grant

1963	**KISSIN' COUSINS**
Director:	Gene Nelson
Co-stars:	Elvis Presley Arthur O'Connell Jack Albertson

1964	**THE DISORDERLY ORDERLY**
Director:	Frank Tashlin
Co-stars:	Jerry Lewis Everett Sloane Susan Oliver

JUDY FARRELL

1979	**CHAPTER TWO**
Director:	Robert Moore
Co-stars:	James Caan Marsha Mason Valerie Harper

SHARON FARRELL

1966	**THE SPY WITH MY FACE**
Director:	John Newland
Co-stars:	Robert Vaughn David McCallum Senta Berger

1968	**A LOVELY WAY TO DIE**
Director:	David Lowell Rich
Co-stars:	Kirk Douglas Sylva Koscina Eli Wallach

1969	**THE REIVERS**
Director:	Mark Rydell
Co-stars:	Steve McQueen Will Geer Rupert Crosse

1969	**MARLOWE**
Director:	Paul Bogart
Co-stars:	James Garner Rita Moreno Bruce Lee

1972	**THE EYES OF CHARLES SAND**
Director:	Reza Badiyi
Co-stars:	Peter Haskell Barbara Rush Joan Bennett

1974	**IT'S ALIVE**
Director:	Larry Cohen
Co-stars:	John Ryan Andrew Duggan Guy Stockwell

1979	**THE LAST RIDE OF THE DALTON GANG**
Director:	Dan Curtis
Co-stars:	Cliff Potts Randy Quaid Jack Palance

1979	**THE STUNT MAN**
Director:	Richard Rush
Co-stars:	Peter O'Toole Steve Railsback Barbara Hershey

1980	**OUT OF THE BLUE**
Director:	Dennis Hopper
Co-stars:	Dennis Hopper Linda Manz Raymond Burr

1983	**LONE WOLF McQUADE**
Director:	Steve Carver
Co-stars:	Chuck Norris David Carradine Barbara Carrera

1984	**NIGHT OF THE COMET**
Director:	Tom Eberhardt
Co-stars:	Catherine Mary Stewart Kelli Maroney

TERRY FARRELL

1986	**BEVERLY HILLS MADAM**
Director:	Harvey Hart
Co-stars:	Faye Dunaway Donna Dixon

1992	**HELLRAISER III:HELL ON EARTH**
Director:	Anthony Hickox
Co-stars:	Doug Bradley Paula Marshall

DEBBIE FARRINGTON

1977	**THE BLACK PANTHER**
Director:	Ian Merrick
Co-stars:	Donald Sumpter Marjorie Yates David Swift

JULIA FARRON

1966	**ROMEO AND JULIET**
Director:	Paul Czinner
Co-stars:	Margot Fonteyne Rudolf Nureyev David Blair

MIA FARROW
(Daughter Of Maureen O'Sullivan And John Farrow Married Frank Sinatra, Andre Previn, Woody Allen)

1964	**GUNS AT BATASI**
Director:	John Guillermin
Co-stars:	Richard Attenborough Flora Robson Jack Hawkins

1968	**A DANDY IN ASPIC**
Director:	Anthony Mann
Co-stars:	Laurence Harvey Tom Courteney Peter Cook

1968	**ROSEMARY'S BABY**
Director:	Roman Polanski
Co-stars:	John Cassavetes Ruth Gordon Patsy Kelly

1969	**SECRET CEREMONY**
Director:	Joseph Losey
Co-stars:	Elizabeth Taylor Robert Mitchum Peggy Ashcroft

1969	**JOHN AND MARY**
Director:	Peter Yates
Co-stars:	Dustin Hoffman Michael Tolan Tyne Daly Stanley Beck

1971	**BLIND TERROR**
Director:	Richard Fleischer
Co-stars:	Robin Bailey Dorothy Alison Paul Nicholas

1971	**FOLLOW ME**
Director:	Carol Reed
Co-stars:	Topol Michael Jayston

1972	**DOCTEUR POPAUL**
Director:	Claude Chabrol
Co-stars:	Jean-Paul Belmondo Laura Antonnelli

1974	**THE GREAT GATSBY**
Director:	Jack Clayton
Co-stars:	Robert Redford Karen Black Sam Waterston

1976	**FULL CIRCLE**
Director:	Richard Loncraine
Co-stars:	Keir Dullea Tom Conti Jill Bennett

1978 AVALANCHE
Director: Corey Allen
Co-stars: Rock Hudson Robert Forster Jeannette Nolan

1978 DEATH ON THE NILE
Director: John Guillermin
Co-stars: Peter Ustinov Bette Davis David Niven

1978 A WEDDING
Director: Robert Altman
Co-stars: Carol Burnett Amy Stryker Lauren Hutton

1979 HURRICANE
Director: Jan Troeli
Co-stars: Jason Robards Trevor Howard Max Von Sydow

1982 A MIDSUMMER NIGHT'S SEX COMEDY
Director: Woody Allen
Co-stars: Woody Allen Jose Ferrer Mary Steenburgen

1982 THE LAST UNICORN *(Voice)*
Director: Arthur Rankin
Co-stars: Alan Arkin Christopher Lee Paul Frees

1983 ZELIG
Director: Woody Allen
Co-stars: Woody Allen Stephanie Farrow Garrett Brown Will Holt

1984 SUPERGIRL
Director: Jeannot Szwarc
Co-stars: Helen Slater Faye Dunnaway Peter O'Toole

1984 BROADWAY DANNY ROSE
Director: Woody Allen
Co-stars: Woody Allen Nick Apollo Forte Milton Berle Sandy Baron

1985 THE PURPLE ROSE OF CAIRO
Director: Woody Allen
Co-stars: Jeff Daniels Danny Aiello Dianne Wiest

1986 HANNAH AND HER SISTERS
Director: Woody Allen
Co-stars: Michael Caine Dianne Wiest Maureen O'Sullivan

1987 RADIO DAYS
Director: Woody Allen
Co-stars: Woody Allen Dianne Wiest Seth Green Josh Mostel

1987 SEPTEMBER
Director: Woody Allen
Co-stars: Denholm Elliott Dianne Wiest Elaine Stritch

1988 ANOTHER WOMAN
Director: Woody Allen
Co-stars: Gena Rowlands Ian Holm Blythe Danner Sandy Dennis

1989 CRIMES AND MISDEMEANORS
Director: Woody Allen
Co-stars: Woody Allen Alan Alda Claire Bloom Anjelica Huston

1989 NEW YORK STORIES
Director: Woody Allen
Co-stars: Woody Allen Mae Questell Marvin Chatinover Nick Nolte

1990 ALICE
Director: Woody Allen
Co-stars: Joe Mantegna Alec Baldwin William Hurt Judy Davis

1991 SHADOWS AND FOG
Director: Woody Allen
Co-stars: Woody Allen Kathy Bates Jody Foster Lily Tomlin

1992 HUSBANDS AND WIVES
Director: Woody Allen
Co-stars: Woody Allen Blythe Danner Judy Davis Liam Neelson

1994 WIDOWS' PEAK
Director: John Irvin
Co-stars: Joan Plowright Adrian Dunbar Natasha Richardson

1995 MIAMI RHAPSODY
Director: David Frankel
Co-stars: Sarah Jessica Parker Antonio Banderas

STEPHANIE FARROW

1983 ZELIG
Director: Woody Allen
Co-stars: Woody Allen Mia Farrow Garreth Brown Will Holt

TISA FARROW
(Sister Of Mia Farrow Daughter Of Maureen O'Sullivan And John Farrow)

1972 AND HOPE TO DIE
Director: Rene Clement
Co-stars: Jean-Louis Trintignant Robert Ryan Aldo Ray

1973 SOME CALL IT LOVING
Director: James Harris
Co-stars: Zalman King Carol White Richard Pryor

1976 BLAZING MAGNUM
Director: Martin Herbert
Co-stars: Stuart Whitman John Saxon Gayle Hunnicutt

1977 FINGERS
Director: James Tobak
Co-stars: Harvy Keitel Jim Brown Danny Aiello

1978 THE INITIATION OF SARAH
Director: Robert Day
Co-stars: Kay Lenz Shelley Winters Kathryn Crosby

FRANCOISE FAUCHER

1988 REVOLVING DOORS
Director: Francis Mankiewicz
Co-stars: Monique Spaziani Miou-Miou Gabriel Arcand

LIZA FAULKNER

1992 THE LOVER
Director: Jean-Jacques Annaud
Co-stars: Jane March Tony Leung Frederique Meininger

CONSUELO FAUST

1987 HEAT AND SUNLIGHT
Director: Rob Nilsson
Co-stars: Rob Nilsson Don Bajema Bill Bailey Bill Ackridge

LAURA FAVALI

1991 CLUBLAND
Director: Laura Sims
Co-stars: Paul Bhattacharjee David Morrissey Ruth Sheen

FARRAH FAWCETT
(Fawcett-Majors) Married Lee Majors)

1970 MYRA BECKINRIDGE
Director: Michael Sarnel
Co-stars: Mae West Raquel Welsh John Huston Rex Reed

1975 MURDER ON FLIGHT 502
Director: George McCowan
Co-stars: Robert Stack Sony Bono Dave Clark Laraine Day

1976 LOGAN'S RUN
Director: Michael Anderson
Co-stars: Michael York Richard Jordan Jenny Agutter

1978 SOMEBODY KILLED HER HUSBAND
Director: Lamont Johnson
Co-stars: Jeff Bridges John Wood Tammy Grimes

1979 SUNBURN
Director: Richard Sarafian
Co-stars: Charles Grodin Art Carney Joan Collins

1980 SATURN 3
Director: Stanley Donen
Co-stars: Kirk Douglas Harvey Keitel Douglas Lambert

1981   THE CANNONBALL RUN
Director: Hal Needham
Co-stars: Burt Reynolds Dom DeLuise Dean Martin Sammy Davis

1985   THE BURNING RED
Director: Robert Greenwald
Co-stars: Paul Le Mat Richard Masur Grace Zabriske

1986   EXTREMITIES
Director: Robert M.young
Co-stars: James Russo Diana Scarwid Alfre Woodard

1986   BETWEEN TWO WOMEN
Director: Jon Avnet
Co-stars: Colleen Dewhurst Michael Nouri

1987   THE RICHEST WOMAN IN THE WORLD
Director: Charles Jarrott
Co-stars: Burl Ives Kevin McCarthy Bruce Davison

1988   SEE YOU IN THE MORNING
Director: Alan Pakula
Co-stars: Jeff Bridges Alice Krige Drew Barrymore

1989   SMALL SACRIFICES
Director: David Greene
Co-stars: Ryan O'Neal John Shea Emily Perkins

1989   MARGARET BOURKE-WHITE
Director: Lawrence Schiller
Co-stars: Frederic Forrest Mitchell Ryan

1992   CRIMINAL BEHAVIOUR
Director: Michael Miller
Co-stars: A. Martinez Cliff DeYoung Nada Despotovich

1994   THE SUBSTITUTE WIFE
Director: Peter Werner
Co-stars: Peter Weller Lea Thompson Karis Bryant

1998   THE APOSTLE
Director: Robert Duvall
Co-stars: Robert Duvall Miranda Richardson Billy Bob Thornton

MICHELLE FAWDON
1977   CATHY'S CHILD
Director: Donald Crombie
Co-stars: Alan Cassell Bob Hughes Sophia Haskas

1986   TRAVELLING NORTH
Director: Carl Schultz
Co-stars: Leo McKern Julia Blake Graham Kennedy

DOROTHY FAY
1939   TRIGGER PALS
Co-stars: Art Jarrett Al "Fuzzy" St. John Nina Guilbert

ALICE FAYE
1934   GEORGE WHITE'S SCANDALS
Director: Harry Lachman
Co-stars: George White Rudy Vallee Jimmy Durante

1935   GEORGE WHITE'S 1935 SCANDALS
Director: George White
Co-stars: James Dunn Eleanor Powell Ned Sparks

1934   NOW I'LL TELL
Director: Edwin Burke
Co-stars: Spencer Tracy Helen Twelvetrees Leon Ames

1934   SHE LEARNED ABOUT SAILORS
Director: George Marshall
Co-stars: Lew Ayres Mitchell & Durant

1934   365 NIGHTS IN HOLLYWOOD
Director: George Marshall
Co-stars: James Dunn John Bradford Grant Mitchell

1935   KING OF BURLESQUE
Director: Sidney Lanfield
Co-stars: Warner Baxter Jack Oakie Fats Waller

1935   EVERY NIGHT AT EIGHT
Director: Raoul Walsh
Co-stars: George Raft Frances Langford

1936   POOR LITTLE RICH GIRL
Director: Irving Cummings
Co-stars: Shirley Temple Jack Haley Gloria Stuart

1936   STOWAWAY
Director: William Seiter
Co-stars: Shirley Temple Robert Young Helen Westley

1936   SING, BABY SING
Director: Sidney Lanfield
Co-stars: Adolphe Menjou Patsy Kelly Ritz Bros.

1937   ON THE AVENUE
Director: Roy Del Ruth
Co-stars: Dick Powell Madeleine Carroll Joan Davis

1937   WAKE UP AND LIVE
Director: Sidney Lanfield
Co-stars: Walter Winchell Ben Bernie Jack Haley

1937   YOU'RE A SWEETHEART
Director: David Butler
Co-stars: George Murphy Ken Murray William Gargan

1937   YOU CAN'T HAVE EVERYTHING
Director: Norman Taurog
Co-stars: Don Ameche Charles Winninger Ritz Bros.

1938   SALLY, IRENE AND MARY
Director: William Seiter
Co-stars: Tony Martin Joan Davis Gypsy Rose Lee

1938   IN OLD CHICAGO
Director: Henry King
Co-stars: Tyrone Power Don Ameche Alice Brady

1938   ALEXANDER'S RAGTIME BAND
Director: Henry King
Co-stars: Tyrone Power Don Ameche Ethel Merman

1939   TAIL SPIN
Director: Roy Del Ruth
Co-stars: Constance Bennett Joan Davis Nancy Kelly

1939   ROSE OF WASHINGTON SQUARE
Director: Gregory Ratoff
Co-stars: Tyrone Power Al Jolson Joyce Compton

1939   HOLLYWOOD CAVALCADE
Director: Irving Cummings
Co-stars: Don Ameche Buster Keaton Ben Turpin

1939   BARRICADE
Director: Gregory Ratoff
Co-stars: Warner Baxter Charles Winninger

1940   LILLIAN RUSSELL
Director: Irving Cummings
Co-stars: Don Ameche Henry Fonda Edward Arnold

1940   LITTLE OLD NEW YORK
Director: Henry King
Co-stars: Richard Greene Fred MacMurray Brenda Joyce

1940   TIN PAN ALLEY
Director: Walter Lang
Co-stars: Betty Grable John Payne Jack Oakie

1941   THE GREAT AMERICAN BROADCAST
Director: Archie Mayo
Co-stars: John Payne Jack Oakie Cesar Romero

1941   WEEKEND IN HAVANA
Director: Walter Lang
Co-stars: John Payne Cesar Romero Carmen Miranda

194   THAT NIGHT IN RIO
Director: Irving Cummings
Co-stars: Don Ameche Carmen Miranda S.Z. Sakall

1943 HELLO FRISCO, HELLO
Director: Bruce Humberstone
Co-stars: John Payne Jack Oakie Laird Cregar

1943 THE GANG'S ALL HERE
Director: Busby Berkeley
Co-stars: Carmen Miranda James Ellison Phil Baker

1944 FOUR JILLS IN A JEEP
Director: William Seiter
Co-stars: Kay Francis Martha Ray Carole Landis

1944 TAKE IT OR LEAVE IT
Director: Ben Stoloff
Co-stars: Phil Baker Phil Silvers Marjorie Massow

1945 FALLEN ANGEL
Director: Otto Preminger
Co-stars: Dana Andrews Linda Darnell Anne Revere

1962 STATE FAIR
Director: Jose Ferrer
Co-stars: Pat Boone Tom Ewell Ann-Margret Bobby Darin

1976 WON TON TON, THE DOG WHO SAVED HOLLYWOOD
Director: Michael Winner
Co-stars: Madeline Kahn Art Carney Bruce Dern

1978 THE MAGIC OF LASSIE
Director: Don Chaffey
Co-stars: James Stewart Mickey Rooney Pernell Roberts

FRANCES FAYE

1978 PRETTY BABY
Director: Louis Malle
Co-stars: Susan Sarandon Brooke Sheilds Keith Carradine

JANINA FAYE (Child)

1958 THE ADVENTURES OF HAL 5
Director: Don Sharp
Co-stars: Peter Godsell William Russell Edwin Richfield

1962 DON'T TALK TO STRANGE MEN
Director: Pat Jackson
Co-stars: Christine Gregg Cyril Raymond Gillian Lind

1962 THE DAY OF THE TRIFFIDS
Director: Steve Sekely
Co-stars: Howard Keel Janette Scott Kieron Moore

1964 THE BEAUTY JUNGLE
Director: Val Guest
Co-stars: Janette Scott Ian Hendry Roland Fraser

JULIA FAYE

1929 DYNAMITE
Director: Cecil B. DeMille
Co-stars: Kay Johnson Charles Bickford Conrad Nagel

1929 NOT SO DUMB
Director: King Vidor
Co-stars: Marion Davies Elliott Nugent Franklin Pangborn

1949 SAMSON AND DELILAH
Director: Cecil B. DeMille
Co-stars: Hedy Lamarr Victor Mature George Sanders

1956 THE TEN COMMANDMENTS
Director: Cecil B. DeMille
Co-stars: Charlton Heston Yul Brynner Anne Baxter

ELEANOR FAZAN

1968 INADMISSABLE EVIDENCE
Director: Anthony Page
Co-stars: Nicol Williamson Jill Bennett Peter Sallis

LOUISE FAZENDA

1926 THE BAT
Director: Roland West
Co-stars: Tullio Carminati Jewel Carmen Emily Fitzroy

1928 THE TERROR
Director: Roy Del Ruth
Co-stars: May McAvoy John Miljan Edward Everett Horton

1929 ON WITH THE SHOW
Director: Alan Crosland
Co-stars: Betty Compson Joe E. Brown Ethel Waters

1929 NOAH'S ARK
Director: Michael Curtiz
Co-stars: Dolores Costello Noah Beery Myrna Loy

1929 THE DESERT SONG
Director: Roy Del Ruth
Co-stars: John Boles Carlotta King Johnny Arthur

1930 BRIDE OF THE REGIMENT
Director: John Frances Dillon
Co-stars: Vivienne Segal Allan Prior Walter Pidgeon

1930 LEATHERNECKING
Director: Edward Cline
Co-stars: Irene Dunne Ken Murray Lilyann Tashman

1930 HIGH SOCIETY BLUES
Director: David Butler
Co-stars: Janet Gaynor Charles Farrell Hedda Hopper

1930 LOOSE ANKLES
Director: Ted Wilde
Co-stars: Loretta Young Douglas Fairbanks Daphne Pollard

1930 RAIN OR SHINE
Director: Frank Capra
Co-stars: Joe Cook Joan Peers Dave Chasen Tom Howard

1931 THE MAD PARADE
Director: William Beaudine
Co-stars: Evelyn Brent Irene Rich Lilyan Tashman

1931 CUBAN LOVE SONG
Director: W.S. Van Dyke
Co-stars: Lawrence Tibbett Lupe Valez Jimmy Durante

1933 ALICE IN WONDERLAND
Director: Norman Z McLeod
Co-stars: Cary Grant Gary Cooper W.C. Fields

1933 ONCE IN A LIFETIME
Director: Russell Mack
Co-stars: Jack Oakie Sidney Fox Aline Macmahon

1934 WONDER BAR
Director: Lloyd Bacon
Co-stars: Al Jolson Kay Francis Dolores Del Rio Dick Powell

1934 CARAVAN
Director: Erik Charrel
Co-stars: Loretta Young Charles Boyer Jean Parker

1935 THE CASINO MURDER CASE
Director: Edwin Marin
Co-stars: Paul Lukas Rosalind Russell Eric Blore

1935 BROADWAY GONDELIER
Director: Lloyd Bacon
Co-stars: Dick Powell Joan Blondell Adolphe Menjou

1935 THE WINNING TICKET
Director: Charles Reisner
Co-stars: Leo Carrillo Irene Hervey James Ellison

1936 I MARRIED A DOCTOR
Director: Archie Mayo
Co-stars: Josephine Hutchinson Pat O'Brien Guy Kibbee

1936 COLLEEN
Director: Alfred Green
Co-stars: Dick Powell Ruby Keeler Jack Oakie

1937 EVER SINCE EVE
Director: Lloyd Bacon
Co-stars: Marion Davies Robert Montgomery Patsy Kelly

1937 FIRST LADY
Director: Stanley Logan
Co-stars: Kay Francis Preston Foster Anita Louise Walter Connolly

1937 MERRY GO ROUND OF 1938
Director: Irving Cummings
Co-stars: Jimmy Savo Bert Lahr Mischa Auer

1937 THE ROAD BACK
Director: James Whale
Co-stars: Richard Cromwell John King Andy Devine

1937 SWING YOUR LADY
Director: Ray Enright
Co-stars: Humphrey Bogart Nat Pendleton Ronald Reagan

1939 THE OLD MAID
Director: Edmund Goulding
Co-stars: Bette Davis Jane Bryan Miriam Hopkins

SHEILA FEARN

1976 THE LIKELY LADS
Director: Michael Tuchner
Co-stars: Rodney Bewes James Bolam Brigit Forsyth

1980 GEORGE AND MILDRED
Director: Peter Frazer Jones
Co-stars: Yootha Joyce Brian Murphy Norman Eshley

ANGELA FEATHERSTONE

1994 DARK ANGEL: THE ASCENT
Director: L. Assani
Co-stars: Daniel Markel Michael Genovese

1998 THE WEDDING SINGER
Director: Frank Coraci
Co-stars: Adam Sandler Drew Barrymore Steve Buscemi

BIRGITTE FEDERSPIEL

1966 SULT
Director: Henning Carlsen
Co-stars: Per Oscarsson Gunnel Lindblom Knud Rex

MELINDA FEE

1980 THE ALIENS ARE COMING
Director: Harvey Hart
Co-stars: Tom Mason Ed Harris Caroline McWilliams

CAROLEEN FEENEY

1995 DENISE CALLS UP
Director: Hal Salwen
Co-stars: Timothy Daly Dana Wheeler-Nicholson

HONOR FEHRSON

1963 IT HAPPENED HERE
Director: Andrew Mollo
Co-stars: Sebastian Shaw Pauline Murray Fiona Lekland

ANDREA FELDMAN

1970 TRASH
Director: Paul Morrissey
Co-stars: Joe Dallesandro Geri Miller Holly Woodlawn

BARBARA FELDON

1967 FITZWILLY
Director: Delbert Mann
Co-stars: Dick Van Dyke Edith Evans Sam Waterston

1971 GETTING AWAY FROM IT ALL
Director: Lee Philips
Co-stars: Gary Collins Larry Hagman Burgess Meredith

1974 SMILE
Director: Michael Ritchie
Co-stars: Bruce Dern Geoffrey Lewis Melanie Griffith

1976 NO DEPOSIT, NO RETURN
Director: Norman Tokar
Co-stars: David Niven Darren McGavin John Williams

1980 THE NUDE BOMB
Director: Clive Donner
Co-stars: Don Adams Sylvia Kristel Rhonda Fleming

1989 GET SMART, AGAIN
Director: Gary Nelson
Co-stars: Don Adams Bernie Kopell Dick Gautier

TOVAH FELDSHUH

1977 THE AMAZING HOWARD HUGHES
Director: William Graham
Co-stars: Tommy Lee Jones Ed Flanders Lee Purcell

1978 TERROR OUT OF THE SKY
Director: Lee Katzin
Co-stars: Efrem Zimbalist Jnr. Dan Haggerty Bruce French

1980 THE IDOLMAKER
Director: Taylor Hackford
Co-stars: Ray Sharkey Peter Gallagher Paul Land

1983 DANIEL
Director: Sidney Lumet
Co-stars: Timothy Hutton Mandy Patinkin Ellen Barkin

1985 BREWSTER'S MILLIONS
Director: Walter Hill
Co-stars: Richard Pryor John Candy Lonette McKee

MARIA FELIX

1955 FRENCH CAN-CAN
Director: Jean Renoir
Co-stars: Jean Gabin Francoise Arnoul Edith Piaf

CATHERINE FELLER

1961 THE CURSE OF THE WEREWOLF
Director: Terence Fisher
Co-stars: Oliver Reed Clifford Evans Yvonne Romain

EDITH FELLOWS (Child)

1934 MRS. WIGGS OF THE CABBAGE PATCH
Director: Norman Taurog
Co-stars: Pauline Lord W.C. Fields

1935 ONE-WAY TICKET
Director: Herbert Biberman
Co-stars: Lloyd Nolan Walter Connolly Peggy Conklin

1935 KEEPER OF THE BEES
Director: Christy Cabanne
Co-stars: Neil Hamilton Betty Furness Emma Dunn

1935 SHE MARRIED HER BOSS
Director: Gregory LaCava
Co-stars: Claudette Colbert Mervyn Douglas

1936 AND SO THEY WERE MARRIED
Director: Elliott Nugent
Co-stars: Melvyn Douglas Mary Astor Donald Meek

1936 PENNIES FROM HEAVEN
Director: Norman Z. McLeod
Co-stars: Bing Crosby Madge Evans Louis Armstrong

1938 CITY STREETS
Director: Albert Rogell
Co-stars: Leo Carillo Tommy Bond Mary Gordon

1939   **FIVE LITTLE PEPPERS**
Director: Charles Barton
Co-stars: Clarence Kolb Ronald Sinclair Dorothy Seese

1939   **FIVE LITTLE PEPPERS AND HOW THEY GREW**
Director: Charles Barton
Co-stars: Tommy Bond Jimmy Leake

1939   **OUT WEST WITH THE PEPPERS**
Director: Charles Barton
Co-stars: Clarence Kolb Charles Peck Tommy Bond

1939   **FIVE LITTLE PEPPERS AT HOME**
Director: Charles Barton
Co-stars: Dorothy Seese Jimmy Leake Tommy Bond

1939   **PRIDE OF THE BLUE GRASS**
Co-stars: Granville Bates Arthur Loft

1940   **FIVE LITTLE PENNIES IN TROUBLE**
Director: Charles Barton
Co-stars: Ronald Sinclair Dorothy Seese

1940   **MUSIC IN MY HEART**
Director: Joseph Santley
Co-stars: Rita Hayworth Tony Martin George Tobias

1940   **NOBODY'S CHILDREN**
Co-stars: Ben Taggert Mary Currier

1941   **HER FIRST BEAU**
Director: Theodore Reed
Co-stars: Jane Withers Jackie Cooper William Tracy

VERNA FELTON

1941   **DUMBO (Voice)**
Director: Ben Sharpsteen
Co-stars: Sterling Holloway Ed Brophy Herman Bing

1951   **ALICE IN WONDERLAND (Voice)**
Director: Clyde Geronimi
Co-stars: Kathryn Beaumont Ed Wynn Richard Haydn

1955   **PICNIC**
Director: Joshua Logan
Co-stars: William Holden Kim Novak Rosalind Russell

1959   **SLEEPING BEAUTY (Voice)**
Director: Clyde Geronimi
Co-stars: Mary Costa Bill Shirley Eleanor Audley

HILDA FENEMORE

1957   **THE TOMMY STEEL STORY**
Director: Gerard Bryant
Co-stars: Patrick Westwood Charles Lamb

1978   **ABSOLUTION**
Director: Anthony Page
Co-stars: Richard Burton Dominic Guard Billy Connolly

1990   **KILLING TIME**
Director: David Atwood
Co-stars: Pip Donaghy Aidan Gillen Ivor Roberts

1991   **BROKE**
Director: Alan Dosser
Co-stars: Timothy Spall Sheila Kelley Larry Lamb

SHERILYN FENN

1985   **JUST ONE OF THE GUYS**
Director: Lisa Gottlieb
Co-stars: Joyce Hyser Clayton Rohner Billy Jacoby

1968   **THRASHIN'**
Director: David Winters
Co-stars: Josh Broslin Robert Rusler Brett Marx

1988   **TWO-MOON JUNCTION**
Director: Zalman King
Co-stars: Richard Tyson Louise Fletcher Burl Ives

1990   **PHANTOMS**
Director: Charles Bond

1990   **WILD AT HEART**
Director: David Lynch
Co-stars: Nicolas Cage Laura Dern Diane Ladd

1990   **BACKSTREET DREAMS**
Director: Jason O'Malley
Co-stars: Jason O'Malley Brooke Shields

1992   **RUBY**
Director: John MacKenzie
Co-stars: Danny Aiello Frank Orsatti Jane Hamilton

1992   **DESIRE AND HELL AT SUNSET MOTEL**
Director: Allen Castle
Co-stars: Whip Hubley David Hewlett Paul Bartel

1992   **OF MICE AND MEN**
Director: Gary Sinese
Co-stars: Gary Sinese John Malkovich Ray Walston Casey Siemaszko

1992   **DIARY OF A HIT MAN**
Director: Roy London
Co-stars: Forest Whitaker Sharon Stone James Belushi

1993   **THREE OF HEARTS**
Director: Yurek Bogayevicz
Co-stars: Kelly Lynch William Baldwin Gail Strickland

1993   **BOXING HELENA**
Director: Jennifer Chambers Lynch
Co-stars: Julian Sands Nicolette Scorsese

1993   **FATAL INSTINCT**
Director: Carl Reiner
Co-stars: Armand Assante Kate Nelligan Sean Young

1995   **THE ASSASSINATION FILE**
Director: John Harrison
Co-star: Tom Verica

SYLVIE FENNIC

1988   **THE MUSIC TEACHER**
Director: Gerard Corbiau
Co-stars: Jose Van Dam Anne Roussel Phillipe Volter

JEAN FENNELL

1988   **FURTHER AND PARTICULAR**
Director: Steve Dwoskin
Co-stars: Richard Butler Irene Marot Julia Righton

STEPHANIE FERACY

1986   **CLASSIFIED LOVE**
Director: Don Taylor
Co-stars: Michael McKean Dinah Manoff Paula Trueman

1987   **BLIND DATE**
Director: Blake Edwards
Co-stars: Kim Basinger Bruce Willis Phil Hartman

1988   **THE GREAT OUTDOORS**
Director: Howard Deutch
Co-stars: Dan Aykroyd John Candy Annette Bening

1989   **BRIDESMAIDS**
Director: Lila Garrett
Co-stars: Shelley Hack Sela Ward Brooke Adams

1993   **THE ONLY WAY OUT**
Director: Rod Hardy
Co-stars: John Ritter Henry Winkler

PAMELYN FERDIN

1969   **A BOY NAMED CHARLIE BROWN (Voice)**
Director: Bill Melendez
Co-stars: Peter Robbins Glenn Gilger

1976 LASSIE: THE MIRACLE
Director: Jack Wrather
Co-stars: Skip Burton Larry Wilcox Sherry Boucher

JANET FERGUSON

1971 200 MOTELS
Director: Frank Zappa
Co-stars: Frank Zappa Tony Palmer Theodore Bikel Ringo Star

KAREN FERGUSON

1990 AN ANGEL AT MY TABLE
Director: Jane Campion
Co-stars: Kerry Fox Alexia Keogh Iris Churn

ANOUK FERJAC

1967 LIVE FOR LIFE
Director: Claude Lelouch
Co-stars: Yves Montand Candice Bergen Annie Giradot

1974 PIAF - THE EARLY YEARS
Director: Guy Casaril
Co-stars: Brigitte Ariel Pascale Christophe

1977 PEPPERMINT SODA
Director: Diane Kurys
Co-stars: Eleonore Klarwein Odile Michel Yves Renier

ESTER FERNADEZ

1946 TWO YEARS BEFORE THE MAST
Director: John Farrow
Co-stars: Alan Ladd Brian Donlevy William Bendix

EVELINA FERNANDEZ

1992 AMERICAN ME
Director: Edward James Olmos
Co-stars: Edward James Olmos William Forsythe Pepe Serna

WILHELMENIA WIGGINS FERNANDEZ

1981 DIVA
Director: Jean-Jacques Beineix
Co-stars: Frederic Andrei Roland Bertin Richard Bohringer

LISA FERRADAY

1951 CHINA CORSAIR
Director: Ray Nazarro
Co-stars: Jon Hall Ron Randell Ernest Borgnine

1952 CALIFORNIA CONQUEST
Director: Lew Landers
Co-stars: Cornel Wilde Teresa Wright John Dehner

1952 THE LAST TRAIN FROM BOMBAY
Director: Fred Sears
Co-stars: Jon Hall Christine Larson

NANCY FERRARA *(Married Abel Ferrara)*

1993 DANGEROUS GAME
Director: Abel Ferrara
Co-stars: Madonna Harvey Keitel James Russo

CHRISTINE FERRARE

1968 THE IMPOSSIBLE YEARS
Director: Michael Gordon
Co-stars: David Niven Lola Albright Chad Everett

1971 J.W.COOP
Director: Cliff Robertson
Co-stars: Cliff Robertson Geraldine Page R.G. Armstrong

BIBI FERREIRA

1947 THE END OF THE RIVER
Director: Derek Twist
Co-stars: Sabu Esmond Knight Robert Douglas

CONCHATA FERRELL

1979 HEARTLAND
Director: Richard Pearce
Co-stars: Rip Torn Barry Primus Lilia Skala Amy Wright

1984 THE SEDUCTION OF MISS LEONA
Director: Joseph Hardy
Co-stars: Lynn Redgrave Anthony Zerbe Brian Dennehy

1985 NORTH BEACH AND RAWHIDE
Director: Harry Falk
Co-stars: William Shatner Tate Donovan James Olson

1986 WHERE THE RIVER RUNS BLACK
Director: Christopher Cain
Co-stars: Charles Durning Peter Horton

1987 EYE ON THE SPARROW
Director: John Korty
Co-stars: Mare Winningham Keith Carradine Bianca Rose

1988 MYSTIC PIZZA
Director: Donald Petrie
Co-stars: Julia Roberts Annabeth Gish Lili Taylor

1988 MAYBE BABY
Director: John Avildson
Co-stars: Molly Ringwald Kenneth Mars Randall Batinkoff

1990 EDWARD SCISSORHANDS
Director: Tim Burton
Co-stars: Johnny Depp Winona Ryder Dianne Wiest Alan Arkin

1991 BACKFIELD IN MOTION
Director: Richard Michaels
Co-stars: Roseanne Arnold Tom Arnold Colleen Camp

TYRA FERRELL

1991 BOYZ 'N' THE HOOD
Director: John Singleton
Co-stars: Larry Fishburne Cuba Gooding Jnr. Nia Long

1991 JUNGLE FEVER
Director: Spike Lee
Co-stars: Wesley Snipes Annabella Sciorra Anthony Quinn

1992 EQUINOX
Director: Alan Rudolph
Co-stars: Matthew Modine Fred Ward Lara Flynn Boyle

ANDREA FERREOL

1978 DESPAIR
Director: Rainer Werner Fassbinder
Co-stars: Dirk Bogarde Volker Spengler Klaus Lowitsch

1980 THE LAST METRO
Director: Francois Traffaut
Co-stars: Catherine Deneuvre Gerard Depardieu Jean Poiret

1980 THREE BROTHERS
Director: Francesco Rosi
Co-stars: Philippe Noiret Charles Vanel Michele Placido

1983 THE PRIZE OF PERIL
Director: Yves Boisset
Co-stars: Gerard Lanvin Michel Piccoli Marie-France Pisier

1983 THE MAN FROM TRIESTE
Director: Pasquale Festa Campanile
Co-stars: Ben Gazzara Ornella Muti

1985 A ZED AND TWO NOUGHTS
Director: Peter Greenaway
Co-stars: Eric Deacon Brian Deacon Frances Barber

1989 THE MAESTRO
Director: Marion Hansel
Co-stars: Malcom McDowell Charles Aznavour Francis Lemaire

1990   **THE NIGHT OF THE FOX**
Director: Charles Jarrott
Co-stars: George Peppard Deborah Raffin John Mills

1990   **THE PHANTOM OF THE OPERA**
Director: Tony Richardson
Co-stars: Charles Dance Burt Lancaster Teri Polo

1990   **WINGS OF FAME**
Director: Otakar Votocek
Co-stars: Peter O'Toole Colin Firth Maria Becker

1993   **THE EDGE OF THE HORIZON**
Director: Fernando Lopez
Co-stars: Claude Brasseur Ana Padrao

1996   **ED McBAIN'S 87TH PRECINCT: ICE**
Director: Bradford May
Co-stars: Dale Midkiff Joe Pantoliano Andrea Parker

LUPITA FERRER

1978   **THE CHILDREN OF SANCHEZ**
Director: Hall Bartlett
Co-stars: Anthony Quinn Dolores Del Rio Katy Jurado

ANNA MARIA FERRERO

1955   **THE GOLDEN FALCON**
Co-stars: Ludovici Bragaglia Nadia Gray Frank Latimor

VERONICA FERRES

1992   **SCHTONK!**
Director: Helmut Dietl
Co-stars: Gotz George Christiane Horbiger Rolf Hoppe

EVE FERRET

1985   **BILLY THE KID AND THE GREEN BAIZE VAMPIRE**
Director: Alan Clarke
Co-stars: Phil Daniels Alun Armstrong

1986   **ABSOLUTE BEGINNERS**
Director: Julien Temple
Co-stars: Eddie O'Connell Patsy Kensit David Bowie

ALESSANDRA FERRI

1987   **DANCERS**
Director: Herbert Ross
Co-stars: Mikhail Baryshnikov Leslie Browne Lynn Seymour

AUDREY FERRIS

1929   **HONKY TONK**
Director: Lloyd Bacon
Co-stars: Sophie Tucker Lila Lee George Duryea

BARBARA FERRIS

1962   **SPARROWS CAN'T SING**
Director: Joan Littlewood
Co-stars: James Booth Barbara Windsor Roy Kinnear

1963   **A PLACE TO GO**
Director: Basil Dearden
Co-stars: Rita Tushingham Mike Sarne Doris Hare

1964   **THE SYSTEM**
Director: Michael Winner
Co-stars: Oliver Reed Jane Merrow Julia Foster

1964   **CHILDREN OF THE DAMMED**
Director: Anton Leader
Co-stars: Ian Hendry Alan Badel Sheila Allen

1965   **CATCH US IF YOU CAN**
Director: John Boorman
Co-stars: Dave Clark Five David Lodge Yootha Joyce

1968   **INTERLUDE**
Director: Kevin Billington
Co-stars: Oskar Werner Virginia Maskell John Cleese

1990   **THE KRAYS**
Director: Peter Medak
Co-stars: Billie Whitelaw Gary Kemp Martin Kemp

IRENA FERRIS

1985   **BEVERLY HILLS COP**
Director: Corey Allen
Co-stars: Lisa Hartman James Brolin David Hemmings

PAM FERRIS

1992   **MR. WAKEFIELD'S CRUSADE**
Director: Angela Pope
Co-stars: Peter Capaldi Michael Maloney James Grout

1996   **ROALD DAHL'S MATILDA**
Director: Danny De Vito
Co-stars: Danny De Vito Rhea Perlman Embeth Davidtz Mara Wilson

JOYCE FERRY

1970   **LAWMAN**
Director: Michael Winner
Co-stars: Burt Lancaster Robert Ryan Sheree North

DEBRA FEUER *(Married Mickey Rourke)*

1978   **LACY AND THE MISSISSIPPI QUEEN**
Director: Robert Butler
Co-stars: Kathleen Lloyd Jack Elam James Keach

1981   **RED FLAG: THE ULTIMATE GAME**
Director: Don Taylor
Co-stars: Barry Bostwick William Devane Joan Van Ark

1985   **TO LIVE AND DIE IN L.A.**
Director: William Freidkin
Co-stars: William L. Petersen Willem Dafoe

1988   **HOMEBOY**
Director: Michael Seresin
Co-stars: Mickey Rourke Christopher Walken

EDWIDGE FEULLLERE

1935   **GOLGOTHA**
Director: Julien Duvivier
Co-stars: Robert Le Vigan Harry Baur Jean Gabin

1948   **THE WOMAN HATER**
Director: Terence Young
Co-stars: Stewart Granger Ronald Squire Mary Jerrold

1952   **ADORABLE CREATURES**
Director: Christian Jaque
Co-stars: Daniel Gelin Martine Carol Danielle Darrieux

1958   **EN CAS DE MALHEUR**
Director: Claude Autant-Lara
Co-stars: Jean Gabin Brigitte Bardot

1964   **DO YOU LIKE WOMEN?**
Director: Jean Leon
Co-stars: Sophie Daumier Guy Bedos Gregoire Aslan

1974   **THE FLESH OF THE ORCHID**
Director: Patrice Chereau
Co-stars: Charlotte Rampling Simone Signoret

GWEN FFRANGCON-DAVIES

1966   **THE WITCHES**
Director: Cyril Frankel
Co-stars: Joan Fontaine Kay Walsh Michele Dotrice

1968   **THE DEVIL RIDES OUT**
Director: Terence Fisher
Co-stars: Christopher Lee Charles Gray Patrick Mower

1970 LEO THE LAST
Director: John Boorman
Co-stars: Marcello Mastroianni Billie Whitelaw Calvin Lockhart

MARY FICKETT

1957 MAN ON FIRE
Director: Ranald MacDougall
Co-stars: Bing Crosby Inger Stevens E.G. Marshall

ARABELLA FIELD

1992 LAWS OF GRAVITY
Director: Nick Gomez
Co-stars: Peter Greene Adam Trese Edie Falco

BETTY FIELD

1939 OF MICE AND MEN
Director: Lewis Milestone
Co-stars: Burgess Meredith Lon Chaney Charles Bickford

1939 WHAT A LIFE
Director: Theodore Reed
Co-stars: Jackie Cooper John Howard Lionel Stander

1940 VICTORY
Director: John Cromwell
Co-stars: Fredric March Cedric Hardwicke Sig Ruman

1940 SEVENTEEN
Director: Lewis King
Co-stars: Jackie Cooper Otto Kruger Ann Shoemaker

1941 BLUES IN THE NIGHT
Director: Anatole Litvak
Co-stars: Priscilla Lane Richard Whorf Lloyd Nolan

1941 SHEPHERD OF THE HILLS
Director: Henry Hathaway
Co-stars: John Wayne Harry Carey Beulah Bondi

1942 KING'S ROW
Director: Sam Wood
Co-stars: Ann Sheridan Robert Cummings Ronald Reagan

1942 GREAT WITHOUT GLORY

1942 ARE HUSBANDS NECESSARY?
Director: Norman Taurog
Co-stars: Ray Milland Patricia Morison

1943 FLESH AND FANTASY
Director: Julien Duvivier
Co-stars: Edward G. Robinson Charles Boyer Barbara Stanwyck

1944 THE GREAT MOMENT
Director: Preston Sturges
Co-stars: Joel McCrea William Demarest Harry Carey

1944 TOMORROW THE WORLD
Director: Leslie Fenton
Co-stars: Fredric March Skip Homeier Agnes Moorehead

1945 THE SOUTHERNER
Director: Jean Renoir
Co-stars: Zachary Scott Beulah Bondi J. Carrol Naish

1949 THE GREAT GATSBY
Director: Elliott Nugent
Co-stars: Alan Ladd Howard De Silva Barry Sullivan

1955 PICNIC
Director: Joshua Logan
Co-stars: William Holden Kim Novak Rosalind Russell

1956 BUS STOP
Director: Joshua Logan
Co-stars: Marilyn Monroe Don Murray Arthur O'Connell

1958 PEYTON PLACE
Director: Mark Robson
Co-stars: Lana Turner Hope Lange Lloyd Nolan Arthur Kennedy

1959 HOUND-DOG MAN
Director: Don Siegel
Co-stars: Fabian Stuart Whitman Carol Lynley Royal Dano

1960 BUTTERFIELD 8
Director: Daniel Mann
Co-stars: Elizabeth Taylor Laurence Harvey Eddie Fisher

1961 BIRDMAN OF ALCATRAZ
Director: John Frankenheimer
Co-stars: Burt Lancaster Thelma Ritter Karl Malden

1966 SEVEN WOMEN
Director: John Ford
Co-stars: Anne Bancroft Flora Robson Sue Lyon Anna Lee

**1968 HOW TO SAVE A MARRIAGE...
AND RUIN YOUR LIFE**
Director: Fielder Cook
Co-stars: Dean Martin Stella Stevens

1968 COOGAN'S BLUFF
Director: Don Siegel
Co-stars: Clint Eastwood Lee J. Cobb Susan Clark Don Stroud

CHELSEA FIELD

1987 MASTERS OF THE UNIVERSE
Director: Gary Goddard
Co-stars: Dolph Lungren Frank Langella Meg Foster

1988 PRISON
Director: Renny Harlin
Co-stars: Viggo Mortensen Lane Smith Tom Everett

1989 SKIN DEEP
Director: Blake Edwards
Co-stars: John Ritter Vincent Gardenia Alyson Rees

1990 MURDER C.O.D.
Director: Alan Metzger
Co-stars: William Devane Patrick Duffy Janet Margolin

1991 THE LAST BOY SCOUT
Director: Tony Scott
Co-stars: Bruce Willis Damon Wayans Noble Willingham

**1991 HARLEY DAVIDSON AND
THE MARLBORO MAN**
Director: Simon Wincer
Co-stars: Mickey Rourke Don Johnson

1992 THE DARK HALF
Director: George Romero
Co-stars: Timothy Hutton Amy Madigan Julie Harris

1993 COMPLEX OF FEAR
Director: Brian Grant
Co-stars: Hart Bochner Joe Don Baker

1993 SIS EXTREME JUSTICE
Director: Mark Lester
Co-stars: Lou Diamond Phillips Scott Glenn

1993 SNAPDRAGON
Director: Worth Keeter
Co-stars: Steven Bauer Pamela Anderson

1993 ROYCE
Director: Rob Holcomb
Co-stars: James Belushi Peter Boyle

1993 DUST DEVIL: THE FINAL CUT
Director: Richard Stanley
Co-stars: Robert Burke Zakes Mokae Rufus Swart

MARGARET FIELD

1952 THE MAN FROM PLANET X
Director: Edgar Ulmer
Co-stars: Raymond Bond William Schallert Robert Clarke

1952 FOR MEN ONLY
Director: Paul Henried
Co-stars: Paul Henreid Robert Sherman Russell Johnson Vera Miles

MARY FIELD

1942 MISS ANNIE ROONEY
Director: Edwin Marin
Co-stars: Shirley Temple William Gargan Peggy Ryan

1943 A LADY TAKES A CHANCE
Director: William Seiter
Co-stars: Jean Arthur John Wayne Charles Winninger

1948 A SONG IS BORN
Director: Howard Hawks
Co-stars: Danny Kaye Virginina Mayo Steve Cochran

1948 UP IN CENTRAL PARK
Director: William Seiter
Co-stars: Deanna Durbin Dick Haymes Vincent Price

1955 THE PRIVATE WAR OF MAJOR BENSON
Director: Jerry Hopper
Co-stars: Charlton Heston Julie Adams Sal Mineo

1955 LUCY GALLANT
Director: Robert Parrish
Co-stars: Jane Wyman Charlton Heston William Demarest

SALLY FIELD

Received An Oscar For Best Actress In 1979 For "Norma Rae"
Received An Oscar For Best Actress In 1984 For "Places In The Heart"

1967 THE WAY WEST
Director: Andrew McLaglen
Co-stars: Kirk Douglas Robert Mitchum Richard Widmark

1971 MONGO'S BACK IN TOWN
Director: Marvin Chomsky
Co-stars: Joe Don Baker Telly Savalas Anne Francis

1976 STAY HUNGRY
Director: Bob Rafaelson
Co-stars: Jeff Bridges Arnold Schwarzenegger Robert Englund

1977 SMOKEY AND THE BANDIT
Director: Hal Needham
Co-stars: Burt Reynolds Jackie Gleason Mike Henry

1977 HEROES
Director: Jeremy Paul Kagan
Co-stars: Henry Winkler Harrison Ford Val Avery

1978 HOOPER
Director: Hal Needham
Co-stars: Burt Reynolds Jan-Michael Vincent Brian Keith

1978 THE END
Director: Burt Reynolds
Co-stars: Burt Reynolds Dom DeLuise Joanne Woodward Myrna Loy

1979 NORMA RAE
Director: Martin Ritt
Co-stars: Beau Bridges Ron Leibman Pat Hingle Barbara Baxley

1979 BEYOND THE POSEIDON ADVENTURE
Director: Irwin Allen
Co-stars: Michael Caine Telly Savalas Shirley Jones

1980 SMOKEY AND THE BANDIT II
Director: Hal Needham
Co-stars: Burt Reynolds Jackie Gleason Jerry Reed

1981 BACK ROADS
Director: Martin Ritt
Co-stars: Tommy Lee Jones David Keith Miriam Colon

1981 ABSENCE OF MALICE
Director: Sidney Pollack
Co-stars: Paul Newman Melinda Dillon Bob Balaban

1982 KISS ME GOODBYE
Director: Robert Mulligan
Co-stars: Jeff Bridges James Caan Claire Trevor Mildred Natwick

1984 PLACES IN THE HEART
Director: Robert Benton
Co-stars: Danny Glover John Malkovich Ed Harris

1985 MURPHY'S ROMANCE
Director: Martin Ritt
Co-stars: James Garner Brian Kerwin Corey Haim

1987 PUNCHLINE
Director: David Seltzer
Co-stars: Tom Hanks John Goodman Mark Rydell Kim Greist

1987 SURRENDER
Director: Jerry Belson
Co-stars: Michael Cain Steve Guttenberg Jackie Cooper

1989 STEEL MAGNOLIAS
Director: Herbert Ross
Co-stars: Dolly Parton Shirley MacLaine Julia Roberts

1991 SOAPDISH
Director: Michael Hoffman
Co-stars: Kevin Klein Whoopi Goldberg Carrie Fisher

1991 NOT WITHOUT MY DAUGHTER
Director: Brian Gilbert
Co-stars: Alfred Molina Sheila Rosenthal Sarah Badel

1993 MRS. DOUBTFIRE
Director: Chris Columbus
Co-stars: Robin Williams Pierce Brosnan

1993 HOMEWARD BOUND:
THE INCREDIBLE JOURNEY*(Voice)*
Director: Duwayne Dunham
Co-stars: Don Ameche Michael J. Fox

1994 FORREST GUMP
Director: Robert Zemekis
Co-stars: Tom Hanks Gary Sinise

1996 EYE FOR AN EYE
Director: John Schlesinger
Co-star: Kiefer Sutherland

SHIRLEY ANN FIELD

1959 HORRORS OF THE BLACK MUSEUM
Director: Arthur Crabtree
Co-stars: Michael Gough Geoffrey Keen

1960 SATURDAY NIGHT AND
SUNDAY MORNING
Director: Karel Reisz
Co-stars: Albert Finney Rachel Roberts

1960 PEEPING TOM
Director: Michael Powell
Co-stars: Michael Powell Carl Boehm Moira Shearer Anna Massey

1960 THE MAN IN THE MOON
Director: Basil Dearden
Co-stars: Kenneth More Michael Hordern John Phillips

1960 THE ENTERTAINER
Director: Laurence Olivier
Co-stars: Brenda De Banzie Joan Plowright

1960 BEAT GIRL
Director: Edmond Greville
Co-stars: David Farrar Noelle Adam Gillian Hills

1962 THE DAMNED
Director: Joseph Losey
Co-stars: MacDonald Carey Alexander Knox Oliver Reed

1962 LUNCH HOUR
Director: James Hill
Co-stars: Robert Stephens Kay Walsh Nigel Davenport

1962   **THE WAR LOVER**
Director: Philip Leacock
Co-stars: Steve McQueen Robert Wagner Michael Crawford

1963   **KINGS OF THE SUN**
Director: J. Lee-Thompson
Co-stars: Yul Brynner George Charkiris Richard Basehart

1966   **DOCTOR IN CLOVER**
Director: Ralph Thomas
Co-stars: Leslie Phillips James Robertson Justice Joan Sims

1966   **ALFIE**
Director: Lewis Gilbert
Co-stars: Michael Caine Vivien Merchant Julia Foster

1985   **MY BEAUTIFUL LAUNDERETTE**
Director: Stephen Frears
Co-stars: Saeed Jaffrey Daniel-Day Lewis Rita Wolf

1989   **THE RACHEL PAPERS**
Director: Damien Harris
Co-stars: Dexter Fletcher Ione Skye Michael Gambon

1989   **GETTING IT RIGHT**
Director: Randal Kleiser
Co-stars: Jesse Birdsall John Gielgud Lynn Redgrave

1992   **HEAR MY SONG**
Director: Peter Chelsom
Co-stars: Ned Beatty Adrian Dunbar Tara Fitzgerald

1993   **LADY CHATTERLEY**
Director: Ken Russell
Co-stars: Joely Richardson Sean Bean James Wilby

SYLVIA FIELD

1945   **JUNIOR MISS**
Director: George Seaton
Co-stars: Peggy Ann Garner Allyn Joslyn Mona Freeman

VIRGINIA FIELD (*Margaret Cynthia Field*)

1934   **THE LADY IS WILLING**

1935   **THANK YOU, JEEVES**
Director: Arthur Grenville Collins
Co-stars: David Niven Arthur Treacher Willie Best

1936   **LADIES IN LOVE**
Director: Edward Griffith
Co-stars: Tyrone Power Janet Gaynor Loretta Young Don Ameche

1936   **LLOYDS OF LONDON**
Director: Henry King
Co-stars: Tyrone Power Madeleine Carroll George Sanders

1936   **CAREER WOMAN**
Director: Lewis Seiler
Co-stars: Claire Trevor Michael Whalen Isabel Jewell

1937   **LANCER SPY**
Director: Gregory Ratoff
Co-stars: George Sanders Dolores Del Rio Peter Lorre Sig Ruman

1937   **THINK FAST MR. MOTO**
Director: Norman Foster
Co-stars: Peter Lorre Sig Ruman Thomas Beck

1937   **LONDON BY NIGHT**
Director: William Thiele
Co-stars: George Murphy Rita Johnson George Zucco

1938   **CHARLIE CHAN AT MONTE CARLO**
Director: Eugene Forde
Co-stars: Warner Oland Keye Luke Sidney Blackmer

1939   **ETERNALLY YOURS**
Director: Tay Garnett
Co-stars: Loretta Young David Niven Broderick Crawford

1939   **BRIDAL SUITE**
Director: William Thiele
Co-stars: Robert Young Annabella Billie Burke

1939   **THE SUN NEVER SETS**
Director: Rowland Lee
Co-stars: Basil Rathbone Douglas Fairbanks Lionel Atwill

1940   **WATERLOO BRIDGE**
Director: Mervyn LeRoy
Co-stars: Vivien Leigh Robert Taylor Lucile Watson

1940   **HUDSON'S BAY**
Director: Irving Pichell
Co-stars: Paul Muni Laird Cregar Gene Tierney John Sutton

1940   **DANCE, GIRL, DANCE**
Director: Dorothy Arzner
Co-stars: Maureen O'Hara Louis Hayward Lucile Ball

1941   **SINGAPORE WOMAN**
Director: Jean Negulesco
Co-stars: Brenda Marshall David Bruce Heather Angel

1940   **THE CISCO KID AND THE LADY**
Director: Herbert Leeds
Co-stars: Cesar Romero George Montgomery Ward Bond

1942   **ATLANTIC CONVOY**

1943   **THE CRYSTAL BALL**
Director: Elliott Nugent
Co-stars: Paulette Goddard Ray Milland William Bendix

1946   **THE IMPERFECT LADY**
Director: Lewis Allen
Co-stars: Ray Milland Teresa Wright Cedric Hardwicke

1947   **REPEAT PERFORMANCE**
Director: Alfred Werker
Co-stars: Joan Leslie Louis Hayward Richard Basehart

1947   **DREAM GIRL**
Director: Mitchell Leisen
Co-stars: Betty Hutton MacDonald Carey Peggy Wood

1947   **CHRISTMAS EVE**
Director: Edwin Marin
Co-stars: George Raft Randolph Scott George Brent

1948   **JOHN LOVES MARY**
Director: David Butler
Co-stars: Ronald Reagan Patricia Neal Jack Carson

1949   **A CONNECTICUT YANKEE IN KING ARTHUR'S COURT**
Director: Tay Garnett
Co-stars: Bing Crosby Rhonda Fleming William Bendix

1950   **DIAL 1119**
Director: Gerald Mayer
Co-stars: Marshall Thompson Andrea King Keefe Brasselle

1951   **THE LADY PAYS OFF**
Director: Douglas Sirk
Co-stars: Linda Darnell Stephen McNally Gigi Perreau

1951   **WEEKEND WITH FATHER**
Director: Douglas Sirk
Co-stars: Van Heflin Patricia Neal Gigi Perreau

1946   **PERFECT MARRIAGE**
Director: Lewis Allen
Co-stars: David Niven Loretta Young Eddie Albert

1957   **APPOINTMENT WITH A SHADOW**
Director: Richard Carlson
Co-stars: George Nader Joanna Moore Brian Keith

1961   **THE EXPLOSIVE GENERATION**

1964   **THE EARTH DIES SCREAMING**

DOROTHY FIELDING

1985 FRIGHT NIGHT
Director: Tom Holland
Co-stars: Chris Sarandon Amanda Bearse Roddy McDowall

1989 THE PREPPIE MURDER
Director: John Herzfeld
Co-stars: William Baldwin Danny Aiello Lara Flynn Boyle

EMMA FIELDING

1992 DREAD POETS SOCIETY
Director: Andy Wilson
Co-stars: Benjamin Zephaniah Timothy Spall Alex Jennings

1998 THE SCARLET TUNIC
Director: Stuart St. Paul
Co-stars: Simon Callow Jean Marc Barr

FENELLA FIELDING

1959 FOLLOW A STAR
Director: Robert Asher
Co-stars: Norman Wisdom June Laverick Ron Moody

1960 NO LOVE FOR JOHNNY
Director: Ralph Thomas
Co-stars: Peter Finch Mary Peach Stanley Holloway

1960 FOXHOLE IN CAIRO
Director: John Moxey
Co-stars: James Robertson Justice Albert Lieven

1960 DOCTOR IN LOVE
Director: Ralph Thomas
Co-stars: Michael Craig Leslie Phillips Virginia Maskell

1961 IN THE DOGHOUSE
Director: Darcy Conyers
Co-stars: Leslie Phillips Peggy Cummins James Booth

1962 THE OLD DARK HOUSE
Director: William Castle
Co-stars: Tom Poston Janette Scott Robert Morley

1966 DROP DEAD DARLING
Director: Ken Hughes
Co-stars: Tony Curtis Rosanna Schiaffino Nancy Kwan

1966 DOCTOR IN CLOVER
Director: Ralph Thomas
Co-stars: Leslie Phillips Shirley Anne Field Arthur Haynes

1966 CARRY ON SCREAMING
Director: Gerald Thomas
Co-stars: Harry H. Corbett Angela Douglas Jon Pertwee

1969 LOCK UP YOUR DAUGHTERS
Director: Peter Coe
Co-stars: Christopher Plummer Susannah York Glynis Johns

MARJORIE FIELDING

1941 QUIET WEDDING
Director: Anthony Asquith
Co-stars: Margaret Lockwood Derek Farr Bernard Miles

1943 YELLOW CANARY
Director: Herbert Wilcox
Co-stars: Anna Neagle Nova Pilbeam Richard Greene

1943 THE DEMI-PARADISE
Director: Anthony Asquith
Co-stars: Laurence Olivier Margaret Rutherford

1946 QUIET WEEKEND
Director: Harold French
Co-stars: Derek Farr George Thorpe Edward Rigby

1947 FAME IS THE SPUR
Director: Roy Boutling
Co-stars: Michael Redgrave Rosamund John Bernard Miles

1948 SPRING IN PARK LANE
Director: Herbert Wilcox
Co-stars: Anna Neagle Michael Wilding Tom Walls

1948 EASY MONEY
Director: Bernard Knowles
Co-stars: Jack Warner Edward Rigby Mervyn Johns

1949 THE CHILTERN HUNDREDS
Director: John Paddy Carstairs
Co-stars: A.E. Matthews Cecil Parker Joyce Carey

1950 THE FRANCHISE AFFAIR
Director: Lawrence Huntingdon
Co-stars: Michael Dennison Dulcie Gray Hy Hazell

1950 PORTRAIT OF CLARE
Director: Lance Comfort
Co-stars: Margaret Johnston Richard Todd Robin Bailey

1951 THE LAVENDER HILL MOB
Director: Charles Crighton
Co-stars: Alec Guinness Sid James Alfie Bass

1951 CIRCLE OF DANGER
Director: Jacques Tourneur
Co-stars: Ray Milland Patricia Roc Marius Goring

1952 THE WOMAN'S ANGLE
Director: Leslie Arliss
Co-stars: Edward Underdown Cathy O'Donnell Peter Reynolds

1952 MANDY
Director: Alexander MacKendrick
Co-stars: Jack Hawkins Terence Morgan Phyllis Calvert

GRACIE FIELDS *(Married Monte Banks)*

1931 SALLY IN OUR ALLEY
Director: Maurice Elvey
Co-stars: Ian Hunter Florence Desmond Gibb McLaughlin

1931 LOOKING ON THE BRIGHT SIDE
Director: Basil Dean
Co-stars: Richard Dolman Julian Rose Wyn Richmond

1933 THIS WEEK OF GRACE
Director: Maurice Elvey
Co-stars: Frank Pettingell Douglas Wakefield

1934 SING AS WE GO
Director: Basil Dean
Co-stars: John Loder Frank Pettingell Stanley Holloway

1934 LOVE, LIFE AND LAUGHTER
Director: Maurice Elvey
Co-stars: John Loder Norah Howard Robb Wilton

1936 QUEEN OF HEARTS
Director: Monte Banks
Co-stars: John Loder Enid Stamp Taylor Edward Rigby Hal Gordon

1937 THE SHOW GOES ON
Director: Basil Dean
Co-stars: Owen Nares Arthur Sinclair Edward Rigby

1938 KEEP SMILING
Director: Monte Banks
Co-stars: Roger Livesey Tommy Fields Jack Donohue Edward Rigby

1938 WE'RE GOING TO BE RICH
Director: Monte Banks
Co-stars: Victor McLaglen Brian Donlevy Gus McNaughton

1940 SHIPYARD SALLY
Director: Monte Banks
Co-stars: Sidney Howard Norma Varden Oliver Wakefield

1943 HOLY MATRIMONY
Director: John Stahl
Co-stars: Monty Woolley Laird Cregar Eric Blore Una O'Connor

1943 STAGE DOOOR CANTEEN
Director: Frank Borzage
Co-stars: Cheryl Walker Lon McCallister Judith Anderson

1945 MOLLY AND ME
Director: Lewis Seiler
Co-stars: Monty Woolley Roddy McDowall Reginald Gardiner

1945 PARIS UNDERGROUND
Director: Gregory Ratoff
Co-stars: Constance Bennett George Rigaud Kurt Kreuger

HOLLY FIELDS

1994 RUNAWAY DAUGHTER
Director: Joe Dante
Co-stars: Dee Wallace Chris Young Jenny Lewis

KATHY FIELDS

1971 JOHNNY GOT HIS GUN
Director: Dalton Trumbo
Co-stars: Timothy Bottoms Jason Robards Marsha Hunt

MARIE FIELDS

1983 THE ATLANTIS INTERCEPTORS
Director: Roger Franklin
Co-stars: Christopher Connelly Mike Miller

SUZANNE FIELDS

1974 FLESH GORDON
Director: Howard Ziehm
Co-stars: Jason Williams John Hoyt William Hunt

VANETTA FIELDS

1976 A STAR IS BORN
Director: Frank Pierson
Co-stars: Barbra Streisand Kris Kristofferson Gary Busey

KASHIA FIGURA

1992 VOICES IN THE GARDEN
Director: Pierre Boutron
Co-stars: Anouk Aimee Joss Ackland Samuel West

MAIA FILAR

1992 DECEIVED
Director: Damian Harris
Co-stars: Goldie Hawn John Heard Kate Reid

AUDREY FILDES

1949 KIND HEARTS AND CORONETS
Director: Robert Hamer
Co-stars: Dennis Price Alec Guinness Valerie Hobson

CARMEN FILPI

1985 PEE-WEE'S BIG ADVENTURE
Director: Tim Burton
Co-stars: Paul Reubens Elizabeth Daily Tony Bill

FLORA FINCH

1927 THE CAT AND THE CANARY
Director: Paul Leni
Co-stars: Creighton Hale Laura La Plante Tully Marshall

1930 SWEET KITTY BELLAIRS
Director: Alfred Green
Co-stars: Claudia Dell Walter Pidgeon Ernest Torrence

1936 SHOW BOAT
Director: James Whale
Co-stars: Irene Dunne Allan Jones Paul Robeson

NATALIE FINLAND

1986 LABYRINTH
Director: Jim Henson
Co-stars: David Bowie Jennifer Connelly Shelley Thompson

DEBORAH FINDLAY

1992 ANGLO-SAXON ATTITUDES
Director: Diarmuid Lawrence
Co-stars: Richard Johnson Dorothy Tutin

1992 NATURAL LIES
Director: Ben Bolt
Co-stars: Bob Peck Sharon Duce Lynsey Baxter

MARION FINLAYSON

1963 THE INCREDIBLE JOURNEY
Director: Fletcher Markle
Co-stars: Emile Genest Tommy Tweed Sandra Scott

SYLVIA FINDLEY

1955 ROBBER'S ROOST
Director: Sidney Salkow
Co-stars: George Montgomery Richard Boone Peter Graves

EVELYN FINLEY

1943 COWBOY COMMANDOES
Co-stars: Ray Corrigan Max Terhune Dennis Moore

SHEILA FINN

1963 HALLELUJAH THE HILLS
Director: Adolfas Mekas
Co-stars: Peter H. Beard Martin Greenbaum Peggy Steffans

SIOBHAN FINNERAN

1986 RITA, SUE AND BOB TOO
Director: Alan Clarke
Co-stars: Michelle Holmes George Costigan Lesley Sharp

KATIE FINNERMAN

1990 NIGHT OF THE LIVING DEAD
Director: Tom Savani
Co-stars: Tony Wood Patricia Tallman Tom Towles

MICHELLE FINNEY

1979 HOT MONEY
Co-stars: Orson Welles Michael Murphy Bobby Pickett

SHIRLEY JO FINNEY

1985 ECHO PARK
Director: Robert Dornhelm
Co-stars: Susan Dey Thomas Hulce Michael Bowen

ANGELA FINOCCHIARO

1991 VOLERE VOLARE
Director: Maurizio Nichetti
Co-stars: Maurizio Nichetti Mariella Valentini Remo Remotti

MARIA FIORE

1952 DUE SOLDI DI SPERANZA
Director: Renato Castellani
Co-stars: Vicenzo Musolino Filumina Russo

LINDA FIORENTINO

1985 AFTER HOURS
Director: Martin Scorsese
Co-stars: Griffin Dunne Rosanna Arquette Verna Bloom

1988 THE MODERNS
Director: Alan Rudolph
Co-stars: Keith Carradine Genevieve Bujold John Lone

1989 **THE NEON EMPIRE**
Director: Larry Pearce
Co-stars: Ray Sharkey Gary Busey Julie Carmen

1991 **SHOUT**
Director: Jeffrey Hornaday
Co-stars: John Travolta Heather Graham Richard Jordan

1992 **FIXING THE SHADOW**
Director: Larry Ferguson
Co-stars: Charlie Sheen Michael Madsen Rip Torn

1993 **CHAIN OF DESIRE**
Director: Temistocles Lopez
Co-stars: Grace Zabriske Angel Aviles Assumpta Serna

1994 **THE LAST SEDUCTION**
Director: John Dahl
Co-stars: Peter Berg Bill Pullman Bill Nunn

1994 **BEYOND THE LAW**
Director: Larry Ferguson
Co-star: Charlie Sheen Michael Madsen

1995 **JADE**
Director: William Friedkin
Co-stars: David Caruso Chazz Palminteri

1997 **LARGER THAN LIFE**
Co-stars: Bill Murray Matthew McConaughey Janeanne Garafalo

1997 **UNFORGETTABLE**
Director: John Dahl
Co-star: Ray Liotta

ANN FIRBANK
1958 **BEHIND THE MASK**
Director: Brian Desmond Hurst
Co-stars: Michael Redgrave Vanessa Redgrave Ian Bannen

1960 **CARRY ON NURSE**
Director: Gerald Thomas
Co-stars: Shirley Eaton Kenneth Connor Charles Hawtrey

1967 **ACCIDENT**
Director: Joseph Losey
Co-stars: Dirk Bogarde Stanley Baker Vivien Merchant

1972 **ASYLUM**
Director: Roy Ward Baker
Co-stars: Robert Powell Barbara Parkins Richard Todd

1975 **BRIEF ENCOUNTER**
Director: Alan Bridges
Co-stars: Richard Burton Sophia Loren Jack Hedley

1979 **STORIES FROM A FLYING TRUNK**
Director: Christine Edzard
Co-stars: Murray Melvin Johanna Sonnex

1984 **A PASSAGE TO INDIA**
Director: David Lean
Co-stars: Judy Davis Peggy Ashcroft James Fox

ANN FIRTH
1942 **THE FIRST OF THE FEW**
Director: Leslie Howard
Co-stars: Leslie Howard David Niven Rosamund John

1943 **BELL-BOTTOM GEORGE**
Director: Marcel Varnel
Co-stars: George Formby Reginald Purdell Peter Murray-Hill

1948 **SCOTT OF THE ANTARTIC**
Director: Charles Frend
Co-stars: John Mills James Robertson Justice Derek Bond

KAI FISCHER
1960 **THE HELLFIRE CLUB**
Director: Robert Baker
Co-stars: Keith Michell Adrienne Corri Bill Owen

KATE FISCHER
1994 **SIRENS**
Director: John Duigan
Co-stars: Hugh Grant Tara Fitzgerald Elle MacPherson Sam Neill

MADELEINE FISCHER
1955 **LE AMICHE**
Director: Michaelangelo Antonioni
Co-stars: Eleanora Rossi Drago Valentina Cortesa

NANCY FISH
1990 **THE EXORCIST III**
Director: William Peter Blatty
Co-stars: George C. Scott Ed Flanders Brad Dourif

1991 **SLEEPING WITH THE ENEMY**
Director: Joseph Ruber
Co-stars: Julia Roberts Patrick Bergin Kyle Secor

1992 **DR GIGGLES**
Director: Manny Coto
Co-stars: Larry Drake Michelle Johnson Richard Bradford

1992 **DEATH BECOMES HER**
Director: Robert Zemeckis
Co-stars: Meryl Streep Goldie Hawn Bruce Willis

CARRIE FISHER
(Daughter Of Debbie Reynolds And Eddie Fisher)
1975 **SHAMPOO**
Director: Hal Ashby
Co-stars: Warren Beatty Julie Christie Lee Grant Goldie Hawn

1977 **STAR WARS**
Director: George Lucas
Co-stars: Mark Hamill Harrison Ford Peter Cushing Alec Guinness

1980 **THE BLUES BROTHERS**
Director: John Landis
Co-stars: John Belushi Dan Aykroyd Kathleen Freeman

1980 **THE EMPIRE STRIKES BACK**
Director: Irvin Kershner
Co-stars: Mark Hamill Harrison Ford Billy Dee Williams

1981 **UNDER THE RAINBOW**
Director: Steve Rash
Co-stars: Chevy Chase Billy Barty Eve Arden Joseph Maler

1983 **RETURN OF THE JEDI**
Director: Richard Marquand
Co-stars: Mark Hamill Harrison Ford Billy Dee Williams

1984 **GARBO TALKS**
Director: Sidney Lumet
Co-stars: Anne Bancroft Ron Silver Catherine Hicks Steven Hill

1985 **THE MAN WITH ONE RED SHOE**
Director: Stan Dragoli
Co-stars: Tom Hanks James Belushi Lori Singer

1986 **HANNAH AND HER SISTERS**
Director: Woody Allen
Co-stars: Mia Farrow Diane Wiest Michael Caine

1987 **AMAZON WOMEN ON THE MOON**
Director: Joe Dante
Co-stars: Rosanna Arquette Michelle Pfeiffer Griffin Dunne

1988 **APPPOINTMENT WITH DEATH**
Director: Michael Winner
Co-stars: Peter Ustinov Lauren Bacall Piper Laurie

1989 **THE BURBS**
Director: Joe Dante
Co-stars: Tom Hanks Bruce Dern Rick Ducommun Corey Feldman

1989 **LOVERBOY**
Director: John Micklin Silver
Co-stars: Patrick Dempsey Kate Jackson Kirstie Alley

1989 WHEN HARRY MET SALLY
Director: Rob Reiner
Co-stars: Billy Crystal Meg Ryan Bruno Kirby

1990 SIBLING RIVALRY
Director: Carl Reiner
Co-stars: Kirstie Alley Bill Pulman Jami Gertz Scott Bakula

1990 SWEET REVENGE
Director: Charlotte Brandstom
Co-stars: Rosanna Arquette John Sessions

1991 SOAPDISH
Director: Michael Hoffman
Co-stars: Sally Field Kevin Kline Whoopi Goldberg

1991 DROP DEAD FRED
Director: Ate De Jong
Co-stars: Phoebe Cates Rik Mayall Marsha Mason

1992 THIS IS MY LIFE
Director: Nora Ephron
Co-stars: Julie Kavner Dan Aykroyd Samantha Mathis

CINDY FISHER
1981 LIAR'S MOON
Director: David Fisher
Co-stars: Matt Dillion Christopher Connelly Susan Tyrrell

FRANCES FISHER
1983 CAN SHE BAKE A CHERRY PIE?
Director: Henry Jaglom
Co-stars: Karen Black Michael Emil

1987 TOUGH GUYS DON'T DANCE
Director: Norman Mailer
Co-stars: Ryan O'Neal Isabella Rossellini

1988 PATTY HEARST
Director: Paul Schrader
Co-stars: Natasha Richardson William Forsythe Ving Rhames

1989 COLD SASSY TREE
Director: Joan Tewkesbury
Co-stars: Faye Dunaway Richard Widmark Lee Garlington

1990 WELCOME HOME, ROXY CARMICHAEL
Director: Jim Abrahams
Co-stars: Winona Ryder Jeff Daniels Dinah Manoff

1990 SUDIE AND SIMPSON
Director: Joan Tewkesbury
Co-stars: Lou Gossett Jnr. Sara Gilbert

1992 UNFORGIVEN
Director: Clint Eastwood
Co-stars: Clint Eastwood Gene Hackman Richard Harris

1993 PRAYING MANTIS
Director: James Keach
Co-stars: Jane Seymour Barry Bostwick Anne Schedeen

1993 ATTACK OF THE 50 FT. WOMAN
Director: Christopher Guest
Co-stars: Daryl Hannah Daniel Baldwin William Windom

1994 BABYFEVER
Director: Henry Jaglom
Co-stars: Victoria Foyt Matt Salinger Eric Roberts

1995 THE OTHER MOTHER
Director: Bethany Booney
Co-stars: Deborah May Connie Clark

1998 TITANIC
Director: James Cameron
Co-stars: Leonardo Di Caprio Kate Winslet Billy Zane

TRICIA LEIGH FISHER *(Daughter Of Eddie Fisher)*
1991 BOOK OF LOVE
Director: Robert Shayne
Co-stars: Chris Young Keith Koogan Michael McKean

CATHERINE FITCH
1995 BUTTERBOX BABIES
Director: Don McBrearty
Co-stars: Susan Clark Peter McNeil Shannon Lawson

MARSHA FITZALAN
1989 GOLDENEYE
Director: Don Boyd
Co-stars: Charles Dance Phyllis Logan Lynsey Baxter

ELLA FITZGERALD
1941 RIDE 'EM COWBOY
Director: Arthur Lubin
Co-stars: Abbott & Costello Dick Foran Anne Gwynne

1956 PETE KELLY'S BLUES
Director: Jack Webb
Co-stars: Jack Webb Edmond O'Brien Janet Leigh Peggy Lee

1960 LET NO MAN WRITE MY EPITAPH
Director: Phillip Leacock
Co-stars: James Darren Burl Ives Shelley Winters

1987 SOMEONE TO WATCH OVER ME *(Voice)*
Director: Ridley Scott
Co-stars: Tom Berenger Mimi Rogers Lorraine Bracco

GERALDINE FITZGERALD
(Mother Of Michael Lindsay-Hogg
Great Aunt Of Tara Fitzgerald)
1935 TURN OF THE TIDE
Director: Norman Walker
Co-stars: John Garrick Niall McGinnis Sam Livesey

1937 THE MILL ON THE FLOSS
Director: Tim Whelan
Co-stars: Frank Lawton James Mason Victoria Hopper

1939 A CHILD IS BORN
Director: Lloyd Bacon
Co-stars: Jeffrey Lynn Gladys George Gale Page Eve Arden

1939 DARK VICTORY
Director: Edmund Goulding
Co-stars: Bette Davis George Brent Humphrey Bogart

1939 WUTHERING HEIGHTS
Director: William Wyler
Co-stars: Laurence Olivier Merle Oberon David Niven

1940 TIL WE MEET AGAIN
Director: Edmund Goulding
Co-stars: George Brent Merle Oberon Frank McHugh

1941 SHINING VICTORY
Director: Irving Rapper
Co-stars: James Stephenson Donald Crisp Barbara O'Neill

1941 FLIGHT FROM DESTINY
Director: Vincent Sherman
Co-stars: Thomas Mitchell Jeffrey Lynn Mona Marris

1942 THE GAY SISTERS
Director: Irving Rapper
Co-stars: Barbara Stanwyck Nancy Coleman George Brent

1943 WATCH ON THE RHINE
Director: Herman Shumlin
Co-stars: Bette Davis Paul Lukas Lucile Watson

1944 WILSON
Director: Henry King
Co-stars: Alexander Knox Charles Coburn Thomas Mitchell

1944 LADIES COURAGEOUS
Director: John Rawlins
Co-stars: Loretta Young Diana Barrymore Evelyn Ankers

1945 **THE STRANGE AFFAIR OF UNCLE HARRY**
Director: Robert Siodmak
Co-stars: George Sanders Ella Raines

1946 **THREE STRANGERS**
Director: Jean Negulesco
Co-stars: Sydney Greenstreet Peter Lorre Joan Lorring

1946 **O.S.S.**
Director: Irving Pichel
Co-stars: Alan Ladd Patric Knowles Don Beddoe

1946 **NOBODY LIVES FOREVER**
Director: Jean Negulesco
Co-stars: John Garfield Walter Brennan George Coulouris

1948 **SO EVIL MY LOVE**
Director: Lewis Allen
Co-stars: Ray Milland Ann Todd Moira Lister

1951 **THE LATE EDWINA BLACK**
Director: Maurice Elvey
Co-stars: David Farrar Roland Culver Jean Cadell

1958 **TEN NORTH FREDERICK**
Director: Philip Dunne
Co-stars: Gary Cooper Suzy Parker Diana Varsi

1961 **THE FIERCEST HEART**
Director: George Sherman
Co-stars: Stuart Whitman Juliet Prowse Raymond Massey

1965 **THE PAWNBROKER**
Director: Sidney Lumet
Co-stars: Rod Steiger Brock Peters Baruch Lumet

1968 **RACHEL, RACHEL**
Director: Paul Newman
Co-stars: Joanne Woodward Estelle Parsons James Olson

1973 **THE LAST AMERICAN HERO**
Director: Lamont Johnson
Co-stars: Jeff Bridges Valerie Perrine Ned Beatty

1974 **HARRY AND TONTO**
Director: Paul Mazursky
Co-stars: Art Carney Ellen Burstyn Chief Dan George

1975 **ECHOES OF A SUMMER**
Director: Don Taylor
Co-stars: Jody Foster Richard Harris Lois Nettleton

1977 **THE MANGO TREE**
Director: Kevin Dobson
Co-stars: Christopher Pate Robert Helpman Diane Craig

1981 **ARTHUR**
Director: Steve Gordon
Co-stars: Dudley Moore John Gielgud Liza Minnelli

1983 **EASY MONEY**
Director: James Signorelli
Co-stars: Rodney Dangerfield Joe Pesci Tom Ewell

1983 **DIXIE: CHANGING HABITS**
Director: George Englund
Co-stars: Suzanne Pleshette Cloris Leachman Judith Ivey

1985 **DO YOU REMEMBER LOVE?**
Director: Jeff Bleckner
Co-stars: Joanne Woodward Richard Kiley Susan Ruttan

1986 **NIGHT OF COURAGE**
Director: Elliott Silverstein
Co-stars: Barnard Hughes Daniel Hugh-Kelly

1988 **ARTHUR II: ON THE ROCKS**
Director: Bud Yorkin
Co-stars: Dudley Moore Liza Minnelli John Gielgud

1991 **BUMP IN THE NIGHT**
Director: Karen Arthur
Co-stars: Meredith Baxter Christopher Reeve Shirley Knight

NUALA FITZGERALD

1980 **CIRCLE OF TWO**
Director: Jules Dassin
Co-stars: Richard Burton Tatum O'Neal Kate Read

TARA FITZGERALD
(Great Niece Of Geraldine Fitzgerald
Niece Of Michael Lindsay-Hogg)

1991 **THE CAMOMILE LAWN**
Director: Peter Hall
Co-stars: Jennifer Ehle Felicity Kendall Paul Eddington

1991 **THE BLACK CANDLE**
Director: Roy Battersby
Co-stars: Samantha Bond Denholm Elliott Sian Phillips

1992 **ANGLO-SAXON ATTITUDES**
Director: Diarmuid Lawrence
Co-stars: Richard Johnson Elizabeth Spriggs

1992 **HEAR MY SONG**
Director: Peter Chelsom
Co-stars: Ned Beatty Adrian Dunbar Shirley Ann Field

1993 **THE ENGLISHMAN WHO WENT UP A HILL AND CAME DOWN A MOUNTAIN**
Co-star: Hugh Grant

1994 **A MAN OF NO IMPORTANCE**
Director: Suri Krishnamma
Co-stars: Albert Finney Rufus Sewell Brenda Fricker

1994 **SIRENS**
Director: John Duigan
Co-stars: Hugh Grant Sam Neill Elle MacPherson Kate Fischer

1997 **BRASSED OFF**
Director: Mark Herman
Co-stars: Stephen Tompkinson Pete Postlethwaite Jim Carter

MAGGIE FITZGIBBON

1972 **SUNSTRUCK**
Director: James Gilbert
Co-stars: Harry Secombe John Meillon Dawn Lake

COLLEEN FITZPATRICK

1988 **HAIRSPRAY**
Director: John Waters
Co-stars: Sonny Bono Ruth Brown Pia Zadora Debbie Harry

KATE FITZPATRICK

1982 **THE RETURN OF CAPTAIN INVINCIBLE**
Director: Philippe Mora
Co-stars: Alan Arkin Christopher Lee

1984 **FANTASY MAN**
Director: John Meagher
Co-stars: Harold Hopkins Kerry Mack Jeanie Drynan

EMILY FITZROY

1926 **THE BAT**
Director: Roland West
Co-stars: Tullio Carminati Jewel Carmen Louise Fazenda

1927 **MOCKERY**
Director: Benjamin Christensen
Co-stars: Lon Chaney Barbara Bedford Ricardo Cortez

1927 **LOVE**
Director: Edmund Goulding
Co-stars: Greta Garbo John Gilbert George Fawcett

1929 **SHOWBOAT**
Co-stars: Laura La Plante Joseph Schildkraut Otis Harlan

1930 THE MAN FROM BLANKLEY'S
Director: Alfred Green
Co-stars: John Barrymore Loretta Young William Austin

1933 DON QUIXOTE
Director: G.W. Pabst
Co-stars: Feodor Chaliapan George Robey Sidney Fox

LISA FJELDSTAD

1981 LITTLE IDA
Director: Laila Mikkelsen
Co-stars: Sunniva Lindekliev Howard Halvorsen

FANNIE FLAGG

1970 FIVE EASY PIECES
Director: Bob Rafelson
Co-stars: Jack Nicholson Karen Black Susan Anspach

KIRSTEN FLAGSTAD

1937 THE BIG BROADCAST OF 1938
Director: Mitchell Leisen
Co-stars: W.C. Fields Bob Hope Shirley Ross

FIONA FLANAGAN

1987 HEARTS OF FIRE
Director: Richard Marquand
Co-stars: Bob Dylan Rupert Everett

FIONNULA FLANAGAN

1975 THE LEGEND OF LIZZIE BORDEN
Director: Paul Wendkos
Co-stars: Elizabeth Montgomery Ed Flanders

1977 MARY WHITE
Director: Jud Taylor
Co-stars: Ed Flanders Kathleen Beller Tim Matheson

1983 THROUGH NAKED EYES
Director: John Llewellyn Moxey
Co-stars: David Soul Pam Dawber William Schallert

1985 YOUNGBLOOD
Director: Peter Markle
Co-stars: Rob Lowe Cynthia Gibb Patrick Swayze

1992 MAD AT THE MOON
Director: Martin Donovan
Co-stars: Mary Stuart Masterson Hart Bochner Daphne Zuniga

1996 SOME MOTHER'S SON
Director: Terry George
Co-stars: Helen Mirren John Lynch Tom Hollander

ANNE FLANNERY

1981 SCARECROW
Director: Sam Pilsbury
Co-stars: John Carradine Tracy Mann Jonathan Smith

ERIN FLANNERY

1981 INCUBUS
Director: John Hough
Co-stars: John Cassavetes Kerrie Kean John Ireland

SUSAN FLANNERY

1976 THE GUMBALL RALLY
Director: Chuck Bail
Co-stars: Michael Sarrazin Gary Busey John Durren

1979 ANATOMY OF A SEDUCTION
Director: Steven Hillard Stern
Co-stars: Jameson Parker Rita Moreno

SUSAN FLEETWOOD

1981 THE GOOD SOLDIER
Director: Kevin Billington
Co-stars: Jeremy Brett Robin Ellis Vickery Turner

1982 HEAT AND DUST
Director: James Ivory
Co-stars: Julie Christie Greta Scacchi Christopher Cazenove

1985 YOUNG SHERLOCK HOLMES
Director: Barry Levinson
Co-stars: Nicholas Rowe Alan Cox Sophie Ward

1986 THE SACRIFICE
Director: Andrei Tarkovsky
Co-stars: Erland Josephson Valerie Mairesse

1989 SUMMER'S LEASE
Director: Colin Rogers
Co-stars: John Gielgud Rosemary Leach Mel Martin

1989 FLYING IN THE BRANCHES
Director: Eva Kolouchova
Co-stars: Edita Brychta Ralph Bates Donald Gee

1990 THE KRAYS
Director: Peter Medak
Co-stars: Billie Whitelaw Gary Kemp Martin Kemp

1994 A LANDING IN THE SUN
Director: Nicholas Benton
Co-stars: Robert Glenister Roger Allam Judith Scott

JULIETTE FLEMING

1989 BACK HOME
Director: Piers Haggard
Co-stars: Hayley Mills Hayley Carr Jean Anderson

LUCY FLEMING

1975 THE SURVIVORS
Director: Pennant Roberts
Co-stars: Carolyn Seymour Peter Copley

RHONDA FLEMING

1945 SPELLBOUND
Director: Alfred Hitchcock
Co-stars: Ingrid Bergman Gregory Peck John Emery

1946 THE SPIRAL STAIRCASE
Director: Robert Siodmak
Co-stars: Dorothy McGuire George Brent Kent Smith

1946 ABILENE TOWN
Director: Edwin Marin
Co-stars: Randolph Scott Ann Dvorak Lloyd Bridges

1947 ADVENTURE ISLAND
Director: Peter Stewart
Co-stars: Paul Kelly Rory Calhoun

1947 BUILD MY GALLOWS HIGH
Director: Jacques Tourneur
Co-stars: Robert Mitchum Kirk Douglas Jane Greer

1948 A CONNECTICUT YANKEE IN KING ARTHUR'S COURT
Director: Tay Garnett
Co-star: Bing Crosby William Bendix Cedric Hardwicke

1949 THE GREAT LOVER
Director: Alexander Hall
Co-stars: Bob Hope Roland Young Jim Backus

1950 THE EAGLE AND THE HAWK
Director: Lewis Foster
Co-stars: John Payne Dennis O'Keefe Thomas Gomez

1951 CROSSWINDS
Director: Lewis Foster
Co-stars: John Payne Forrest Tucker Robert Lowery

1951 CRY DANGER
Director: Robert Parrish
Co-stars: Dick Powell Richard Erdman William Conrad

1951 HONG KONG
Director: Lewis Foster
Co-stars: Ronald Reagan Nigel Bruce Marvin Miller

1951 THE LAST OUTPOST
Director: Lewis Foster
Co-stars: Ronald Reagan Bruce Bennett Noah Beery

1951 LITTLE EGYPT
Director: Frederick De Cordova
Co-stars: Mark Stevens Nancy Guild Charles Drake

1952 THE GOLDEN HAWK
Director: Sidney Salkow
Co-stars: Sterling Hayden John Sutton Helena Carter

1953 INFERNO
Director: Roy Baker
Co-stars: Robert Ryan William Lundigan

1953 SERPENT OF THE NILE
Director: William Castle
Co-stars: William Lundigan Raymond Burr Julie Newmar

1953 JIVARO
Director: Edward Ludwig
Co-stars: Fernando Lamas Brian Keith Lon Chaney

1953 TROPIC ZONE
Director: Lewis Foster
Co-stars: Ronald Reagan Noah Beery Estelita

1953 PONY EXPRESS
Director: Jerry Hopper
Co-stars: Charlton Heston Forrest Tucker Jan Sterling

1954 YANKEE PASHA
Director: Joseph Pevney
Co-stars: Jeff Chandler Mamie Van Doren Lee J. Cobb

1955 TENNESSEE'S PARTNER
Director: Allan Dwan
Co-stars: John Payne Ronald Reagan Colleen Gray

1956 WHILE THE CITY SLEEPS
Director: Fritz Lang
Co-stars: Dana Andrews George Sanders Ida Lupino

1956 ODONGO
Director: John Gilling
Co-stars: MacDonald Carey Eleanor Summerfield

1956 THE KILLER IS LOOSE
Director: Budd Boetticher
Co-stars: Joseph Cotten Wendell Corey Alan Hale

1956 SLIGHTLY SCARLET
Director: Allan Dwan
Co-stars: John Payne Arlene Dahl Kent Taylor Ted De Corsia

1957 GUN GLORY
Director: Roy Rowland
Co-stars: Stewart Granger Chill Wills Steve Rowland

1957 GUNFIGHT AT THE O.K. CORAL
Director: John Sturges
Co-stars: Burt Lancaster Kirk Douglas John Ireland

1957 THE BUSTER KEATON STORY
Director: Sidney Sheldon
Co-stars: Donald O'Connor Ann Blyth Peter Lorre

1958 ALIAS JESSE JAMES
Director: Norman Z McLeod
Co-stars: Bob Hope Wendell Corey Jim Davis

1958 BULL-WHIP
Director: Harmon Jones
Co-stars: Guy Madison James Griffith Don Beddoe

1958 HOME BEFORE DARK
Director: Mervyn LeRoy
Co-stars: Jean Simmons Dan O'Herlihy Efrem Zimbalist Jnr.

1959 THE BIG CIRCUS
Director: Joseph Newman
Co-stars: Victor Mature Red Buttons Peter Lorre

1980 THE NUDE BOMB
Director: Clive Donner
Co-stars: Don Adams Sylvia Kristel Vittorio Gassman

SUSAN FLEMING

1931 RANGE FEUD
Director: Ross Lederman
Co-stars: Buck Jones John Wayne

1932 MILLION DOLLAR LEGS
Director: Edward Cline
Co-stars: W.C. Fields Jack Oakie Lyda Roberti

1933 HE LEARNED ABOUT WOMEN
Co-stars: Stuart Erwin Sidney Toller Alison Skipworth

DIANE FLETCHER

1975 AUTOBIOGRAPHY OF A PRINCESS
Director: James Ivory
Co-stars: James Mason Madhur Jaffrey Keith Varnier

1990 HOUSE OF CARDS
Director: Paul Seed
Co-stars: Ian Richardson Susannah Harker Colin Jeavons

1990 INSPECTOR MORSE: MASONIC MYSTERIES
Director: Danny Boyle
Co-stars: John Thaw Kevin Whately

1993 TO PLAY THE KING
Director: Paul Seed
Co-stars: Ian Richardson Michael Kitchen Kitty Aldridge

LOUISE FLETCHER
Oscar For Best Actress In 1975 For One Flew Over The Cuckoo's Nest

1974 THIEVES LIKE US
Director: Robert Altman
Co-stars: Keith Carradine Shelley Duvall Tom Skerritt

1975 RUSSIAN ROULETTE
Director: Lou Lombardo
Co-stars: George Segal Gordon Jackson Denholm Elliott

1975 ONE FLEW OVER THE CUCKOO'S NEST
Director: Milos Forman
Co-stars: Jack Nicholson Will Sampson

1977 EXORCIST II: THE HERETIC
Director: John Boorman
Co-stars: Richard Burton Linda Blair Kitty Winn

1978 THE CHEAP DETECTIVE
Director: Robert Moore
Co-stars: Peter Falk John Houseman Dom DeLuise

1978 THOU SHALL NOT COMMIT ADULTERY
Director: Delbert Mann
Co-stars: Wayne Rogers Bert Convy

1979 THE MAGICIAN OF LUBIN
Director: Menahem Golan
Co-stars: Alan Arkin Valerie Perrine Shelley Winters

1979 THE LADY IN RED
Director: Lewis Teague
Co-stars: Pamela Sue Martin Robert Conrad

1980 THE LUCKY STAR
Director: Max Fischer
Co-stars: Rod Steiger Brett Marx Lou Jacobi Helen Hughes

1983   **STRANGE INVADERS**
Director: Michael Laughlin
Co-stars: Paul Le Mat Nancy Allen Michael Lerner

1983   **BRAINSTORM**
Director: Douglas Trumbull
Co-stars: Natalie Wood Christopherwalken Alan Fudge

1986   **THE BOY WHO COULD FLY**
Director: Nick Castle
Co-stars: Lucy Deakins Jay Underwood Colleen Dewhurst

1986   **INVADERS FROM MARS**
Director: Tobe Hooper
Co-stars: Karen Black Timothy Bottoms Hunter Carson

1986   **NOBODY'S FOOL**
Director: Evelyn Purcell
Co-stars: Rosanna Arquette Eric Roberts Jim Youngs

1987   **FLOWERS IN THE ATTIC**
Director: Jeffrey Bloom
Co-stars: Victoria Tennant Lindsay Parker

1988   **TWO-MOON JUNCTION**
Director: Zalman King
Co-stars: Sherilyn Fenn Richard Tyson Burl Ives

1989   **THE KAREN CARPENTER STORY**
Director: Joseph Sargent
Co-stars: Cynthia Gibb Mitchell Anderson

1989   **BEST OF THE BEST**
Director: Bob Radler
Co-stars: Eric Roberts James Earl Jones Sally Kirkland

1990   **BLUE STEEL**
Director: Kathryn Bigelow
Co-stars: Jamie Lee Curtis Ron Silver Clancy Brown

1992   **BLIND VISION**
Director: Shuki Levy
Co-stars: Deborah Shelton Robert Vaughn Ned Beatty

1993   **RETURN TO TWO-MOON JUNCTION**
Director: Farhard Mann
Co-stars: Mindy Clarke John Clayton Schafer

1994   **THE HAUNTING OF SEACLIFF INN**
Director: Walter Klenhard
Co-stars: Ally Sheedy William R. Moses Lucinda West

1996   **TWO DAYS IN THE VALLEY**
Director: John Herzfeld
Co-stars: Eric Stoltz Jeff Daniels Danny Aiello

FREDA FLIER

1946   **THE SPECTRE OF THE ROSE**
Director: Ben Hecht
Co-stars: Viola Essen Ivan Kirov Michael Chekov

HELEN FLINT

1936   **GIVE ME YOUR HEART**
Director: Archie Mayo
Co-stars: Kay Francis George Brent Patric Knowles

1937   **THE BLACK LEGION**
Director: Archie Mayo
Co-stars: Humphrey Bogart Erin O'Brien Moore Dick Foran

SUZANNE FLON

1952   **MOULIN ROUGE**
Director: John Huston
Co-stars: Jose Ferrer Zsa Zsa Gabor Colette Marchand

1955   **MR. ARKADIN**
Director: Orson Welles
Co-stars: Orson Welles Michael Redgrave Akim Tamiroff

1962   **A MONKEY IN WINTER**
Director: Henri Verneuil
Co-stars: Jean Gabin Jean-Paul Belmondo Gabrielle Dorziat

1962   **THE TRIAL**
Director: Orson Welles
Co-stars: Orson Welles Jeanne Moreau Anthony Perkins

1964   **THE TRAIN**
Director: John Frankenheimer
Co-stars: Burt Lancaster Paul Scofield Jeanne Moreau

1973   **THE SILENT ONE**
Director: Claude Pinoteau
Co-stars: Lino Ventura Leo Genn Robert Hardy

1973   **LOVING IN THE RAIN**
Director: Jean-Claude Brialy
Co-stars: Romy Schneider Nino Castelnuovo Mehdi

1976   **MR. KLEIN**
Director: Joseph Losey
Co-stars: Alain Delon Jeanne Moreau Juliet Berto

1976   **DOCTEUR FRANCOISE GAILLARD**
Director: Jean-Louis Bertucelli
Co-stars: Annie Girardot Isabelle Hupert

1976   **BOOMERANG**
Director: Jose Giovanni
Co-stars: Alain Delon Charles Vanel Carla Gravina

1981   **QUARTET**
Director: James Ivory
Co-stars: Alan Bates Maggie Smith Isabelle Adjani

1983   **ONE DEADLY SUMMER**
Director: Jean Becker
Co-stars: Isabelle Adjani Alain Suchon Jenny Cleve

SHEILA FLORANCE

1991   **A WOMAN'S TALE**
Director: Paul Cox
Co-stars: Gosia Dobrowolska Norman Kaye Chris Hayward

FLORELLE

1933   **LES MISERABLES**
Director: Raymond Bernard
Co-stars: Harry Bauer Charles Vanel Jean Servais

ERIKA FLORES

1991   **THE OWL**
Director: Tom Holland
Co-stars: Adrian Paul Patricia Charbonneau Brian Thompson

BESS FLOWERS

1928   **WE FAW DOWN**
Director: Leo McCarey
Co-stars: Stan Laurel Oliver Hardy Vivien Oakland

FLORRIE FLOYD

1934   **MY OLD DUTCH**
Director: Sinclair Hill
Co-stars: Gordon Harker Betty Balfour Michael Hogan

DARLANNE FLUEGEL

1980   **BATTLE BEYOND THE STARS**
Director: Jimmy Muragami
Co-stars: Richard Thomas Robert Vaughn John Saxon

1984   **CONCRETE BEAT**
Director: Glen Gordon
Co-stars: John Getz Kenneth Mcmillan

1984   **ONCE UPON A TIME IN AMERICA**
Director: Sergio Leone
Co-stars: Robert De Niro James Woods Tuesday Weld

1985   **TO LIVE AND DIE IN L.A.**
Director: William Friedkin
Co-stars: William L. Petersen Willem Dafoe

1986   **TOUGH GUYS**
Director: Jeff Kanew
Co-stars: Burt Lancaster Kirk Douglas Alexis Smith

1986   **RUNNING SCARED**
Director: Peter Hyams
Co-stars: Gregory Hines Billy Crystal Tracy Reed

1987   **BULLETPROOF**
Director: Steve Carver
Co-stars: Gary Busey Henry Silva L.Q. Jones

1989   **LOCK UP**
Director: John Flynn
Co-stars: Sylvester Stallone Donald Sutherland John Amos

1991   **PET SEMATARY TWO**
Director: Mary Lambert
Co-stars: Edward Furlong Anthony Edwards Clancy Brown

1993   **SCANNER COP**
Director: Pierre David
Co-stars: Daniel Quinn Richard Lynch Mark Rolston

1993   **SLAUGHTER OF THE INNOCENTS**
Director: James Glickenhaus
Co-stars: Scott Glenn Jesse Cameron-Glickenhaus

BARBARA FLYNN

1990   **THE JUSTICE GAME 2: THE LADY FROM ROME**
Director: Moira Armstrong
Co-stars: Denis Lawson Anita Zagaria

COLLEEN FLYNN

1991   **LATE FOR DINNER**
Director: W.D. Ritcher
Co-stars: Brian Wimmer Peter Berg Marcia Gay Harden

MIRIAM FLYNN

1982   **NATIONAL LAMPOON'S CLASS REUNION**
Director: Michael Miller
Co-stars: Gerrit Graham Michael Lerner

1984   **HER LIFE AS A MAN**
Director: Robert Ellis Miller
Co-stars: Robyn Douglass Robert Culp Marc Singer

1988   **MAYBE BABY**
Director: John Avildsen
Co-stars: Molly Ringwald Randall Batinkoff Kenneth Mars

1988   **18 AGAIN!**
Director: Paul Flaherty
Co-stars: George Burns Charlie Schlatter Red Buttons

NINA FOCH

Nominated For Best Supporting Actress In 1954 For "Executive Suite"

1943   **RETURN OF THE VAMPIRE**
Director: Lew Landers
Co-stars: Bela Lugosi Frieda Inescort Miles Mander

1944   **CRY OF THE WEREWOLF**
Co-star: Stephen Crane

1944   **SHADOW OF THE NIGHT**
Co-stars: Warner Baxter George Zucco Minor Watson

1944   **SHE'S A SOLDIER TOO**
Co-star: Lloyd Bridges

1944   **NINE GIRLS**
Director: Leigh Jason
Co-stars: Ann Harding Evelyn Keyes Jeff Donnell

1945   **A SONG TO REMEMBER**
Director: Charles Vidor
Co-stars: Paul Muni Cornel Wilde Merle Oberon

1945   **MY NAME IS JULIA ROSS**
Director: Joseph Lewis
Co-stars: Dame May Whitty George Macready

1945   **PRISON SHIP**
Co-star: Moy Wing

1945   **I LOVE A MYSTERY**
Director: Henry Levin
Co-stars: George Macready Jim Bannon

1945   **BOSTON BLACKIE'S RENDEZVOUS**
Co-stars: Chester Morris Iris Adrian Steve Cochran

1945   **ESCAPE IN THE FOG**
Director: Budd Boetocher
Co-stars: Otto Kruger William Wright

1947   **JOHNNY O'CLOCK**
Director: Robert Rossen
Co-stars: Dick Powell Evelyn Keyes Ellen Drew Jeff Chandler

1947   **THE GUILT OF JANET AMES**
Director: Henry Levin
Co-stars: Rosalind Russell Melvyn Douglas Sid Caesar

1948   **THE DARK PAST**
Director: Rudolph Mate
Co-stars: William Holden Lee J. Cobb Adele Jergens

1949   **JOHNNY ALLEGRO**
Director: Ted Tetzlaff
Co-stars: George Raft George Macready Will Geer

1949   **UNDERCOVER MAN**
Director: Joseph Lewis
Co-stars: Glenn Ford James Whitmore Barry Kelley

1951   **ST. BENNY THE DIP**
Director: Edgar Ulmer
Co-stars: Freddie Bartholomew Dick Haymes Lionel Stander

1951   **AN AMERICAN IN PARIS**
Director: Vincente Minnelli
Co-stars: Gene Kelly Leslie Caron Oscar Levant

1952   **SCARAMOUCHE**
Director: George Sidney
Co-stars: Stewart Granger Mel Ferrer Eleanor Parker

1952   **YOUNG MAN WITH IDEAS**
Director: Mitchell Leisen
Co-stars: Glenn Ford Ruth Roman Donna Corcoran

1953   **SOMBRERO**
Director: Norman Foster
Co-stars: Ricardo Montalban Pier Angelli Cyd Charisse

1953   **FAST COMPANY**
Director: John Sturges
Co-stars: Howard Keel Polly Bergen Marjorie Main

1954   **EXECUTIVE SUITE**
Director: Robert Wise
Co-stars: Fredric March William Holden Barbara Stanwyck

1954   **FOUR GUNS TO THE BORDER**
Director: Richard Carlson
Co-stars: Rory Calhoun Walter Brennan John McIntyre

1955   **ILLEGAL**
Director: Lewis Allen
Co-stars: Edward G. Robinson Jayne Mansfield Albert Dekker

1955   **YOU'RE NEVER TOO YOUNG**
Director: Norman Taroug
Co-stars: Dean Martin Jerry Lewis Diana Lynn Raymond Burr

1956   **THREE BRAVE MAN**
Director: Philip Dunne
Co-stars: Ray Milland Ernest Borgnine Dean Jagger

1956 THE TEN COMMANDMENTS
Director: Cecil B. DeMille
Co-stars: Charlton Heston Edward G. Robinson

1960 SPARTACUS
Director: Stanley Kubrick
Co-stars: Kirk Douglas Tony Curtis Charles Laughton

1960 CASH McCALL
Director: Joseph Pevney
Co-stars: James Garner Natalie Wood Dean Jagger

1971 SUCH GOOD FRIENDS
Director: Otto Preminger
Co-stars: Dyan Cannon James Coco Jennifer O'Neil

1975 MAHOGANY
Director: Berry Gordy
Co-stars: Diana Ross Anthony Perkins Beah Richards

1988 OUTBACK BOUND
Director: John Llewellyn Moxey
Co-stars: Donna Mills Andrew Clarke John Meillon

1989 SKIN DEEP
Director: Blake Edwards
Co-stars: John Ritter Vincent Gardenia Alyson Reed

1993 SILVER
Director: Phillip Noyce
Co-stars: Sharon Stone William Baldwin Tom Berenger

1993 MORNING GLORY
Director: Steven Stern
Co-stars: Christopher Reeve Deborah Raffin J.T. Walsh Helen Shaver

JANETTE FOGGO

1989 DREAM BABY
Director: Angela Pope
Co-stars: Jenny McCrindle Kevin McNally Peter Capaldi

FRANCESCA FOLAN

1989 BEHAVING BADLY
Director: David Tucker
Co-stars: Judi Dench Ronald Pickup Frances Barber

CLAIRE FOLEY

1944 JANIE
Director: Michael Curtis
Co-stars: Joyce Reynolds Robert Hutton Ann Harding

1946 JANIE GETS MARRIED
Director: Michael Curtiz
Co-stars: Joan Leslie Robert Hutton Edward Arnold

ELLEN FOLEY

1987 FATAL ATTRACTION
Director: Adrian Lyne
Co-stars: Michael Douglas Glenn Close Anne Archer

MEGAN FOLLOWS

1985 ANNE OF GREEN GABLES
Director: Kevin Sullivan
Co-stars: Colleen Dewhurst Richard Farnsworth

1985 SILVER BULLET
Director: Daniel Attias
Co-stars: Corey Haim Gary Busey Everett McGill

1987 SEASON OF DREAMS
Director: Martin Rosen
Co-stars: Frederic Forrest Christine Lahti Peter Coyote

1988 A TIME OF DESTINY
Director: Gregory Nava
Co-stars: William Hurt Timothy Hutton Stockard Channing

1988 INHERIT THE WIND
Director: David Greene
Co-stars: Kirk Douglas Jean Simmons Jason Robards

1990 DEEP SLEEP
Director: Patricia Gruben
Co-stars: Stuart Margolin Patricia Collins Margot Kane

**1991 CRY IN THE WILD:
THE TAKING OF PEGGY ANN**
Director: Charles Correll
Co-stars: David Morse David Soul

1995 UNDER THE PIANO
Director: Stefan Scaini
Co-stars: Teresa Stratas Amanda Plummer

MEGAN FOLSON

1979 HEARTLAND
Director: Richard Pearce
Co-stars: Rip Torn Conchata Ferrell Lilia Skala

BRIDGET FONDA
(Daughter Of Peter Fonda Granddaughter Of Henry Fonda Niece Of Jane Fonda)

1988 ARIA
Director: Franc Roddam
Co-stars: James Mathers John Hurt

1988 SCANDAL
Director: Michael Caton-Jones
Co-stars: John Hurt Joanne Whalley Britt Ekland Ian McKellen

1988 SHAG
Director: Zelda Barron
Co-stars: Phoebe Cates Scott Coffey Annabeth Gish Page Hannah

1988 STRAPLESS
Director: David Hare
Co-stars: Blair Brown Bruno Ganz Alan Howard Michael Gough

1988 YOU CAN'T HURRY LOVE
Director: Richard Martini
Co-stars: David Packer Scott McGinnis David Leisure

1990 THE GODFATHER, PART III
Director: Francis Coppola
Co-stars: Al Pacino Diane Keaton Talia Shire

1990 FRANKENSTEIN UNBOUND
Director: Roger Corman
Co-stars: John Hurt Raul Julia Catherine Rabett

1991 IRON MAZE
Director: Hiroaki Yoshida
Co-stars: Jeff Fahey J.T. Walsh Gabriel Damon

1991 DROP DEAD FRED
Director: Ate De Jong
Co-stars: Phoebe Cates Rik Mayall Marsha Mason

1991 DOC HOLLYWOOD
Director: Michael Caton Jones
Co-stars: Michael J. Fox Julie Warner Barnard Hughes

**1992 ARMY OF THE DARKNESS:
THE MEDIEVAL DEAD**
Director: Sam Raimi
Co-stars: Bruce Campbell Marcus Gilbert

1992 SINGLE WHITE FEMALE
Director: Barbet Schroeder
Co-stars: Jennifer Jason Leigh Steven Weber

1992 SINGLES
Director: Cameron Crowe
Co-stars: Campbell Scott Kyra Sedgwick Sheila Kelley

1993 THE ASSASSIN
Director: John Badham
Co-stars: Gabriel Byrne Anne Bancroft Harvey Keitel

1993   **LITTLE BUDDHA**
Director: Bernado Bertolucci
Co-stars: Keanu Reaves Ying Ruocheng Chris Isaak

1993   **BODIES, REST AND MOTION**
Director: Michael Steinberg
Co-stars: Phoebe Cates Tim Roth Peter Fonda

1994   **CAMILLA**
Director: Deepa Mehta
Co-stars: Jessica Tandy Maury Chaykin

1994   **THE ROAD TO WELLVILLE**
Director: Alan Parker
Co-stars: Anthony Hopkins Matthew Broderick

1995   **IT COULD HAPPEN TO YOU**
Director::   Andrew Bergman
Co-stars: Nicolas Cage Rosie Perez Seymour Cassel

1996   **ROUGH MAGIC**
Director: Clare Peplow
Co-stars: Russell Crowe Jim Broadbent D.W. Moffet

1997   **GRACE OF MY HEART**
Director: Allison Anders
Co-stars: Illeana Douglas John Turturo Patsy Kensit

1998   **JACKIE BROWN**
Director: Quentin Tarantino
Co-stars: Michael Keaton Robert De Niro Samuel L. Jackson

JANE FONDA

*(Daughter Of Henry Fonda, Sister Of Peter Fonda
Aunt Of Bridget Fonda, Married Roger Vadim Sen.
Tom Hayden Ted Turner)*
**Oscar For Best Actress In 1971 For "Klute" And In 1978 For "Coming
Home". Nominated For Best Actress In 1969 For "They Shoot Horses,
Don't They", In 1977 For "Julia" And In 1979 For "China Syndrome"
Nominated For Best Supporting Actress In 1981 For "On Golden Pond"**

1960   **TALL STORY**
Director: Joshua Logan
Co-stars: Anthony Perkins Ray Walston Anne Jackson

1962   **A WALK ON THE WILD SIDE**
Director: Edward Dmytryk
Co-stars: Laurence Harvey Capucine Barbara Stanwyck

1962   **PERIOD OF ADJUSTMENT**
Director: George Roy Hill
Co-stars: Tony Franciosa Jim Hutton Lois Nettleton

1962   **THE CHAPMAN REPORT**
Director: George Cukor
Co-stars: Claire Bloom Shelley Winters Glynis Johns

1962   **IN THE COOL OF THE DAY**
Director: Robert Stevens
Co-stars: Peter Finch Arthur Hill Angela Lansbury

1963   **SUNDAY IN NEW YORK**
Director: Peter Tewkesbury
Co-stars: Cliff Robertson Rod Taylor Robert Culp

1964   **LA RONDE**
Director: Roger Vadim
Co-stars: Marie Dubois Claude Giraud Anna Karina Maurice Ronet

1964   **THE LOVE CAGE**
Director: Rene Clement
Co-stars: Alain Delon Lola Albright Sorrell Booke

1965   **CAT BALLOU**
Director: Elliott Silverstein
Co-stars: Lee Marvin Michael Callan Reginald Denny

1966   **ANY WEDNESDAY**
Director: Robert Ellis Miller
Co-stars: Jason Robards Dean Jones Rosemary Murphy

1966   **THE GAME IS OVER**
Director: Roger Vadim
Co-stars: Peter McEnery Michel Piccoli Tina Marquand

1966   **THE CHASE**
Director: Arthur Penn
Co-stars: Marlon Brando Robert Redford Angie Dickinson

1967   **BAREFOOT IN THE PARK**
Director: Gene Saks
Co-stars: Robert Redford Mildred Natwick Charles Boyer

1967   **HURRY SUNDOWN**
Director: Otto Preminger
Co-stars: Michael Caine Rex Ingram Diahann Carroll

1968   **BARBARELLA**
Director: Roger Vadim
Co-stars: John Phillip Law David Hemmings Anita Pallenberg

1969   **THEY SHOOT HORSES, DON'T THEY**
Director: Sydney Pollack
Co-stars: Gig Young Michael Sarazin Susannah York

1971   **KLUTE**
Director: Alan J. Pakula
Co-stars: Donald Sutherland Roy Scheider Charles Cioffi

1972   **TOUT VA BIEN**
Director: Jean-Luc Godard
Co-stars: Yves Montand Vittorio Capprioli Jean Pignol

1973   **STEELYARD BLUES**
Director: Alan Myerson
Co-stars: Donald Sutherland Peter Boyle Howard Hesseman

1973   **A DOLL'S HOUSE**
Director: Joseph Losey
Co-stars: David Warner Trevor Howard Edward Fox Anna Wing

1976   **THE BLUE BIRD**
Director: George Cukor
Co-stars: Elizabeth Taylor Ava Gardner Patsy Kensit Will Geer

1976   **FUN WITH DICK AND JANE**
Director: Ted Kocheff
Co-stars: George Segal Ed McMahon Dick Gautier

1977   **JULIA**
Director: Fred Zinnemann
Co-stars: Vanessa Redgrave Jason Robards Maxmilian Schell

1978   **COMING HOME**
Director: Hal Ashby
Co-stars: Jon Voight Bruce Dern Robert Carradine

1978   **COMES A HORSEMAN**
Director: Alan J. Pakula
Co-stars: James Caan Jason Robards Richard Farnsworth

1978   **CALIFORNIA SUITE**
Director: Herbert Ross
Co-stars: Alan Alda Michael Caine Maggie Smith

1979   **THE CHINA SYNDROME**
Director: James Bridges
Co-stars: Jack Lemmon Michael Douglas Scott Brady

1979   **THE ELECTRIC HORSEMAN**
Director: Sydney Pollack
Co-stars: Robert Redford Valerie Perrine

1980   **NINE TO FIVE**
Director: Colin Higgins
Co-stars: Dolly Parton Lily Tomlin Dabney Coleman

1981   **ON GOLDEN POND**
Director: Mark Rydell
Co-stars: Henry Fonda Katharine Hepburn Doug McKeon

1981   **ROLLOVER**
Director: Alan J. Pakula
Co-stars: Kris Krisofferson Hume Cronyn Bob Gunton

1984　THE DOLLMAKER
Director:　Daniel Pertie
Co-stars:　Susan Kingsley Geraldine Page Levon Helm

1985　AGNES OF GOD
Director:　Norman Jewison
Co-stars:　Anne Bancroft Meg Tilly Anne Pitoniak

1986　THE MORNING AFTER
Director:　Sidney Lumet
Co-stars:　Jeff Bridges Raul Julia Kathy Bates

1989　OLD GRINGO
Director:　Luis Puenzo
Co-stars:　Gregory Peck Jimmy Smits Patricio Contreras

1990　STANLEY AND IRIS
Director:　Martin Ritt
Co-stars:　Robert De Niro Swoosie Kurtz Martha Plimpton

BROOKE FONTAINE
1984　GHOST DAD
Director:　Sidney Poitier
Co-stars:　Bill Crosby Kimberley Russell Ian Bannen

JACQUELINE FONTAINE
1954　THE COUNTRY GIRL
Director:　George Seaton
Co-stars:　Bing Crosby Grace Kelly William Holden

JOAN FONTAINE *(Joan Burfield, Married Brian Aherne, Sister Of Olivia De Havilland)*
Oscar For Best Actress In 1941 For "Suspicion"
Nominated For Best Actress In 1940 For "Rebecca" And In 1943 For "The Constant Nymph"

1935　NO MORE LADIES
Director:　George Cukor
Co-stars:　Joan Crawford Robert Montgomery Franchot Tone

1937　QUALITY STREET
Director:　George Stevens
Co-stars:　Katharine Hepburn Franchot Tone Eric Blore

1937　THE MAN WHO FOUND HIMSELF
Director:　Lew Landers
Co-stars:　John Beal Philip Huston George Irving

1937　MAID'S NIGHT OUT
Director:　Ben Holmes
Co-stars:　Allan Lane Billy Gilbert Cecil Kellaway

1937　YOU CAN'T BEAT LOVE
Co-star:　Preston Foster

1937　MUSIC FOR MADAME
Director:　John Blystone
Co-stars:　Nino Martini Alan Hale Billy Gilbert

1937　A DAMSEL IN DISTRESS
Director:　George Stevens
Co-stars:　Fred Astaire George Burns Gracie Allen Reginald Gardner

1938　BLONDE CHEAT
Co-stars:　Derrick De Marney Lillian Bond

1938　THE DUKE OF WEST POINT
Director:　Alfred Green
Co-stars:　Louis Hayward Tom Brown Richard Carlson

1938　SKY GIANT
Director:　Ken Landers
Co-stars:　Richard Dix Chester Morris Harry Carey

1939　THE WOMEN
Director:　George Cukor
Co-stars:　Norma Shearer Joan Crawford Rosalind Russell

1939　MAN OF CONQUEST
Director:　George Nicholls
Co-stars:　Richard Dix Gail Patrick Victor Jory

1939　GUNGA DIN
Director:　George Stevens
Co-stars:　Cary Grant Douglas Fairbanks Victor McLaglen

1940　REBECCCA
Director:　Alfred Hitchcock
Co-stars:　Laurence Olivier George Sanders

1941　SUSPICION
Director:　Alfred Hitchcock
Co-stars:　Cary Grant Nigel Bruce Cedric Hardwick

1943　THE CONSTANT NYMPH
Director:　Edmund Goulding
Co-stars:　Charles Boyer Alexis Smith Peter Lorre

1944　FRENCHMAN'S CREEK
Director:　Mitchell Leisen
Co-stars:　Arturo De Cordova Basil Rathbone

1944　JANE EYRE
Director:　Robert Stevenson
*Co-stars:*r　Orson Welles Peggy Ann Garner Elizabeth Taylor

1945　THE AFFAIRS OF SUSAN
Director:　William Seiter
Co-stars:　George Brent Walter Abel Dennis O'Keefe

1946　FROM THIS DAY FORWARD
Director:　John Berry
Co-stars:　Mark Stevens Rosemary De Camp Bobby Driscoll

1947　IVY
Director:　Sam Wood
Co-stars:　Herbert Marshall Patric Knowles Richard Ney

1948　KISS THE BLOOD OFF MY HANDS
Director:　Norman Foster
Co-stars:　Burt Lancaster Robert Newton

1948　YOU GOTTA STAY HAPPY
Director:　H.C. Potter
Co-stars:　James Stewart Eddie Albert Roland Young

1948　LETTER FROM AN UNKNOWN WOMAN
Director:　Max Ophuls
Co-stars:　Louis Jourdan Mady Christians Art Smith

1948　THE EMPEROR WALTZ
Director:　Billy Wilder
Co-stars:　Bing Crosby Richard Haydn Roland Culver

1950　BORN TO BE BAD
Director:　Nicholas Ray
Co-stars:　Robert Ryan Zachary Scott Joan Leslie

1950　SEPTEMBER AFFAIR
Director:　William Dieterle
Co-stars:　Joseph Cotten Jessica Tandy James Lydon

1952　THIS ABOVE ALL
Director:　Anatole Litvak
Co-stars:　Tyrone Power Thomas Mitchell Gladys Cooper

1951　DARLING, HOW COULD YOU
Director:　Mitchell Leisen
Co-stars:　John Lund Mona Freeman Peter Hanson

1952　DECAMERON NIGHTS
Director:　Hugo Fregonese
Co-stars:　Louis Jordan Binnie Barnes Joan Collins

1952　IVANHOE
Director:　Richard Thorpe
Co-stars:　Robert Taylor Elizabeth Taylor George Sanders

1952　SOMETHING TO LIVE FOR
Director:　George Stevens
Co-stars:　Ray Milland Teresa Wright

1953　FLIGHT TO TANGIER
Director:　Charles Marquis Warren
Co-stars:　Jack Palance Corinne Calvet

1953 **THE BIGAMIST**
Director: Ida Lupino
Co-stars: Ida Lupino Edmund O'Brien Edmund Gwenn

1954 **CASANOVA'S BIG NIGHT**
Director: Norman Z McLeod
Co-stars: Bob Hope Vincent Price Basil Rathbone

1956 **BEYOND REASONABLE DOUBT**
Director: Fritz Lang
Co-stars: Dana Andrews Sidney Blackmer Arthur Franz

1956 **SERENADE**
Director: Anthony Mann
Co-stars: Mario Lanza Sarita Montiel Vincent Price

1957 **UNTIL THEY SAIL**
Director: Robert Wise
Co-stars: Paul Newman Jean Simmons Piper Laurie

1957 **ISLAND IN THE SUN**
Director: Robert Rossen
Co-stars: James Mason Harry Belafonte Joan Collins

1958 **A CERTAIN SMILE**
Director: Jean Negulesco
Co-stars: Rossano Brazzi Christine Carrere Bradford Dillman

1961 **VOYAGE TO THE BOTTOM OF THE SEA**
Director: Irwin Allen
Co-stars: Walter Pidgeon Peter Lorre Frankie Avalon

1962 **TENDER IS THE NIGHT**
Director: Henry King
Co-stars: Jennifer Jones Jason Robards Tom Ewell Paul Lukas

1966 **THE WITCHES**
Director: Cyril Frankel
Co-stars: Kay Walsh Alex McCowen Leonard Rossiter

LILLIAN FONTAINE

1947 **IVY**
Director: Sam Wood
Co-stars: Joan Fontaine Herbert Marshall Patric Knowles

1974 **SUDDENLY IT'S SPRING**
Director: Mitchell Leisen
Co-stars: Paulette Goddard Fred MacMurray

LYNN FONTANNE

Nominated For Best Actress In 1931 For "The Guardsman"

1931 **THE GUARDSMAN**
Director: Sidney Franklin
Co-stars: Alfred Lunt Roland Young Zasu Pitts

1943 **STAGE DOOR CANTEEN**
Director: Frank Borzage
Co-stars: Cheryl Walker Lon McCallister Judith Anderson

MARGOT FONTEYN

1966 **ROMEO AND JULIET**
Director: Paul Czinner
Co-stars: Rudolph Nureyev David Blair Julia Farron

CATHERINE FONTENOY

1932 **POIL DE CAROTTE**
Director: Julien Duvivier
Co-stars: Harry Baur Robert Lynen

BRENDA FORBES

1986 **MRS. DELLAFIELD WANTS TO MARRY**
Director: George Shaefer
Co-stars: Katherine Hepburn Harold Gould

1988 **LAURA LANSING SLEPT HERE**
Director: George Shaefer
Co-stars: Katherine Hepburn Karen Austin

HAZEL FORBES

1936 **THE MARRIAGE OF CORBAL**
Director: Karl Grune
Co-stars: Nils Asther Hugh Sinclair Noah Berry

MARY FORBES

1930 **THE MAN WHO CAME BACK**
Director: Raoul Walsh
Co-stars: Janet Gaynor Charles Farrell William Holden

1930 **EAST IS WEST**
Director: Monta Bell
Co-stars: Edward G. Robinson Lupe Velez Lew Ayres

1931 **BORN TO LOVE**
Director: Paul Stein
Co-stars: Constance Bennett Joel McCrea Paul Cavanagh

1933 **BOMBSHELL**
Director: Victor Fleming
Co-stars: Jean Harlow Lee Tracy Frank Morgan

1933 **CAVALCADE**
Director: Frank Lloyd
Co-stars: Clive Brook Diana Wynyard Ursula Jeans

1934 **THE MOST PRECIOUS THING**
Director: Lambert Hillyer
Co-stars: Anita Louise Jane Darwell Ben Alexander

1934 **YOU CAN'T BUY EVERYTHING**
Director: Charles Reisner
Co-stars: May Robson Jean Parker Lewis Stone

1938 **YOU CAN'T TAKE IT WITH YOU**
Director: Frank Capra
Co-stars: Lionel Barrymore James Stewart Jean Arthur

1939 **YOU CAN'T CHEAT AN HONEST MAN**
Director: George Marshall
Co-stars: W.C. Fields Edgar Bergen

1939 **HOLLYWOOD CAVALCADE**
Director: Irving Cummings
Co-stars: Don Ameche Alice Faye Buster Keaton

1941 **NOTHING BUT THE TRUTH**
Director: Elliott Nugent
Co-stars: Bob Hope Paulette Goddard Edward Arnold

1945 **EARL CARROL VANITIES**
Director: Joseph Santley
Co-stars: Constance Moore Dennis O'Keefe Eve Arden

1946 **TERROR BY NIGHT**
Director: Roy William Neill
Co-stars: Basil Rathbone Nigel Bruce Denis Hoey

MERIEL FORBES (Married Ralph Richardson)

1939 **COME ON GEORGE**
Director: Anthony Kimmins
Co-stars: George Formby Pat Kirkwood Ronald Shiner

1943 **THE BELLS GO DOWN**
Director: Basil Dearden
Co-stars: Tommy Trinder James Mason Mervyn Jones

1946 **THE CAPTIVE HEART**
Director: Basil Dearden
Co-stars: Michael Redgrave Jack Warner Basil Radford

1951 **THE LONG DARK HALL**
Director: Anthony Bushell
Co-stars: Rex Harrison Lilli Palmer Raymond Huntley

1952 **HOME AT SEVEN**
Director: Ralph Richardson
Co-stars: Ralph Richardson Margaret Leighton Jack Hawkins

1968   OH! WHAT A LOVELY WAR
Director: Richard Attenborough
Co-stars: Ralph Richardson John Gielgud Kenneth More

MICHELLE FORBES

1993   KALIFORNIA
Director: Dominic Sena
Co-stars: Brad Pitt Juliette Lewis David Duchovny

1996   SWIMMING WITH SHARKS
Director: George Huang
Co-stars: Kevin Spacey Frank Whaley

ANITRA FORD

1974   WONDER WOMAN
Director: Vincent McEveety
Co-stars: Cathy Lee Crosby Ricardo Montalban Kaz Garas

BETTE FORD

1990   MARKED FOR DEATH
Director: Dwight Little
Co-stars: Steven Seagal Joanna Pacula Basil Wallace

CONSTANCE FORD

1956   THE LAST HUNT
Director: Richard Brooks
Co-stars: Stewart Granger Robert Taylor Debra Paget

1959   HOME FROM THE HILL
Director: Vincent Minnelli
Co-stars: Robert Mitchum George Peppard Eleanor Parker

1959   A SUMMER PLACE
Director: Delmer Daves
Co-stars: Richard Egan Dorothy McGuire Sandra Dee

1961   CLAUDELLE INGLISH
Director: Gordon Douglas
Co-stars: Diane McBain Arthur Kennedy Chad Everett

1962   THE CABINET OF DR. CALIGARI
Director: Roger Kay
Co-stars: Glynis Johns Dan O'Herlihy Dick Davalos

1962   ROME ADVENTURE
Director: Delmer Daves
Co-stars: Suzanne Pleshette Troy Donahue Angie Dickinson

1962   HOUSE OF WOMEN
Director: Walter Doniger
Co-stars: Shirley Knight Andrew Duggan Barbara Nichols

1963   THE CARETAKERS
Director: Hall Bartlett
Co-stars: Polly Bergen Joan Crawford Robert Stack

1974   99 AND 44/100% DEAD
Director: John Frankenheimer
Co-stars: Richard Harris Edmond O'Brien Ann Turkel

DOROTHY FORD

1946   LOVE LAUGHS AT ANDY HARDY
Director: George Seitz
Co-stars: Mickey Rooney Lewis Stone Fay Holden

1952   JACK AND THE BEANSTALK
Director: Jean Yarbrough
Co-stars: Bud Abbott Lou Costello Buddy Baer

ELAINE FORD

1991   THEY NEVER SLEPT
Director: Udayan Prasad
Co-stars: Edward Fox Emily Morgan James Fleet

FAITH FORD

1987   YOU TALKING TO ME?
Director: Charles Winkler
Co-stars: Jim Youngs James Noble Bess Motta

1994   NORTH
Director: Rob Reiner
Co-stars: Elijah Wood Bruce Willis John Ritter

GRACE FORD

1936   THE DEVIL-DOLL
Director: Tod Browning
Co-stars: Lionel Barrymore Maureen O'Sullivan Frank Lawton

JAN FORD *(Child)*

1947   THE DEVIL ON WHEELS
Co-star: Daryll Hickman

JULIA FORD

1992   A FATAL INVERSION
Director: Tim Fywell
Co-stars: Douglas Hodge Saira Todd Jeremy Northam

MARGARET FORD

1989   SHAME
Director: Steve Jordell
Co-stars: Deborra-Lee Furness Tony Barry Simone Buchanan

MELISSA FORD

1984   THE ROOMMATE
Director: Neil Cox
Co-stars: Lance Guest Barry Miller Elaine Wilks

RUTH FORD

1941   SECRETS OF THE LONE WOLF
Director: Edward Dmytryk
Co-stars: Warren William Victor Jory Eric Blore

1942   THE GORILLA MAN
Director: Ross Lederman
Co-stars: John Loder Paul Cavanagh John Abbott

1942   THE HIDDEN HAND
Director: Ben Stoloff
Co-stars: Craig Stevens Elizabeth Fraser Julie Bishop

1943   ADVENTURE IN IRAQ
Director: Ross Lederman
Co-stars: Paul Cavanagh John Loder

1943   TRUCK BUSTERS
Co-stars: Richard Travis Virginia Christine

1944   WILSON
Director: Henry King
Co-stars: Alexander Knox Charles Coburn Geraldine Fitzgerald

1945   THE WOMAN WHO CAME BACK
Director: Walter Colmes
Co-stars: Nancy Kelly John Loder Otto Kruger

1963   ACT ONE
Director: Dore Schary
Co-stars: George Hamilton Jason Robards Jnr. George Segal

1972   PLAY IT AS IT LAYS
Director: Frank Perry
Co-stars: Anthony Perkins Tuesday Weld Tammy Grimes

JESSICA FORD

**1986   FOUR ADVENTURES OF
           REINETTE AND MIRABELLE**
Director: Eric Rohmer
Co-stars: Joelle Miquel Marie Riviere

DEBORAH FOREMAN

1983   **VALLEY GIRL**
Director: Martha Coolidge
Co-stars: Nicholas Cage Elizabeth Daily Colleen Camp

1986   **MY CHAUFFEUR**
Director: David Beaird
Co-stars: Sam J. Jones Sean McClory E.G. Marshall

1986   **APRIL FOOL'S DAY**
Director: Fred Walton
Co-stars: Griffin O'Neal Deborah Goodrich Amy Steel

1987   **THE EXPERTS**
Director: Dave Thomas
Co-stars: John Travolta Arye Gross Kelly Preston

1991   **SUNDOWN: THE VAMPIRE IN RETREAT**
Director: Anthony Hickox
Co-stars: David Carradine Morgan Brittany

SALLY FORLONG (Child)

1975   **HIJACK!**
Director: Michael Forlong
Co-stars: Richard Morant Derek Bond James Forlong

CLAIRE FORLANI

1998   **THE LAST TIME I COMMITTED SUICIDE**
Director: Stephen Kay
Co-stars: Thomas Jane Keanu Reeves

CAROL FORMAN

1946   **SAN QUENTIN**
Director: Gordon Douglas
Co-stars: Lawrence Tierney Barton MacLane Raymond Burr

1948   **SUPERMAN**
Director: Spencer Bennet
Co-stars: Kirk Alyn Noel Neill Tommy Bond

1948   **THE FEATHERED SERPENT**
Director: William Beaudine
Co-stars: Roland Winters Keye Luke Manton Morland

1948   **DOCKS OF NEW ORLEANS**
Director: Derwin Abrahams
Co-stars: Roland Winters Manton Morland Virginia Dale

WIN FORMAN

1973   **SUMMER WISHES, WINTER DREAMS**
Director: Gilbert Cates
Co-stars: Joanne Woodward Martin Balsam Sylvia Sidney

BERYL FORMBY (Married George Formby)

1935   **OFF THE DOLE**
Director: Arthur Mertz
Co-stars: George Formby Constance Shotter Dan Young

VERONICA FORQUE

1984   **WHAT HAVE I DONE TO DESERVE THIS?**
Director: Pedro Almodovar
Co-stars: Carmen Maura Luis Hostalot

1993   **KIKA**
Director: Pedro Almodovar
Co-stars: Peter Coyote Victoria Abril Alex Casanovas

CHRISTINE FORREST

1978   **MARTIN**
Director: George Romero
Co-stars: John Amplas Lincoln Maazel Sarah Venable

1988   **MONKEY SHINES:**
           AN EXPERIMENT IN FEAR
Director: George Romero
Co-stars: Jason Beghe John Pankow

IRENE FORREST

1978   **SITTING DUCKS**
Director: Henry Jaglom
Co-stars: Michael Emil Zack Norman Patrice Townsend

1990   **RE-AMINATOR 2**
Director: Brian Yuzna
Co-stars: Bruce Abbott David Gale Fabiana Udenio

SALLY FORREST

1949   **NOT WANTED**
Co-stars: Keefe Brasselle Anne O'Neal

1950   **THE YOUNG LOVERS**

1950   **MYSTERY STREET**
Director: John Sturges
Co-stars: Ricardo Montalban Elsa Lanchester Jan Sterling

1950   **VENGEANCE VALLEY**
Director: Richard Thorpe
Co-stars: Burt Lancaster Robert Walker Joanne Dru

1951   **THE STRIP**
Director: Leslie Kardos
Co-stars: Mickey Rooney William Demarest Louis Armstrong

1951   **HARD, FAST AND BEAUTIFUL**
Director: Ida Lupino
Co-stars: Claire Trevor Carleton Young Robert Clarke

1951   **THE STRANGE DOOR**
Director: Joseph Pevney
Co-stars: Charles Laughton Boris Karloff Michael Pate

1951   **BANNERLINE**
Director: Don Weiss
Co-stars: Lionel Barrymore Keefe Brasselle Spring Byington

1951   **EXCUSE MY DUST**
Director: Roy Rowland
Co-stars: Red Skelton MacDonald Carey William Demarest

1953   **CODE TWO**
Director: Fred Wilcox
Co-stars: Ralph Meeker Keenan Wynn James Craig

1955   **SON OF SINBAD**
Director: Ted Tetzlaff
Co-stars: Dale Robertson Vincent Price Mari Blanchard

1956   **WHILE THE CITY SLEEPS**
Director: Fritz Lang
Co-stars: Dana Andrews George Sanders Ida Lupino

1957   **RIDE THE HIGH IRON**
Director: Don Weiss
Co-stars: Don Taylor Raymond Burr

KAY FORRESTER

1944   **SONG OF THE RANGE**
Co-stars: Jimmy Wakely Dennis Moore

CONSTANCE FORSLUND

1979   **A SHINING SEASON**
Director: Stuart Margolin
Co-stars: Timothy Bottoms Ed Begley Jnr. Rip Torn

ALLISON FORRESTER

1980   **GREGORY'S GIRL**
Director: Bill Forsyth
Co-stars: John Gordon Sinclair Dee Hepburn Chic Murray

GLENNA FORSTER-JONES

1968   **JOANNA**
Director: Michael Sarne
Co-stars: Genevieve Waite Calvin Lockhart Donald Sutherland

1970 LEO THE LAST
Director: John Boorman
Co-stars: Marcello Mastroianni Billie Whitelaw Calvin Lockhart

BRIGIT FORSYTH

1976 THE LIKELY LADS
Director: Michael Tuchner
Co-stars: Rodney Bewes James Bolan Mary Tamm

ROSEMARY FORSYTH

1965 SHENANDOAH
Director: Andrew McLaglen
Co-stars: James Stewart Doug McClure Glenn Corbett

1965 THE WAR LORD
Director: Franklin Schaffner
Co-stars: Charlton Heston Richard Boone Maurice Evans

1966 TEXAS ACROSS THE RIVER
Director: Michael Gordon
Co-stars: Dean Martin Alain Delon Tina Marquand

1969 WHATEVER HAPPENED TO AUNT ALICE?
Director: Lee Katzin
Co-stars: Geraldine Page Ruth Gordon

1969 WHERE IT'S AT
Director: Garson Kanin
Co-stars: David Janssen Brenda Vaccaro Robert Drivas

1969 SOME KIND OF A NUT
Director: Garson Kanin
Co-stars: Dick Van Dyke Angie Dickinson Zohra Lampert

1970 HOW DO I LOVE THEE?
Director: Michael Gordon
Co-stars: Jackie Gleason Maureen O'Hara Rick Lenz

1970 CITY BENEATH THE SEA
Director: Irwin Allen
Co-stars: Stuart Whitman Robert Wagner Richard Basehart

1971 THE DEATH OF ME YET
Director: John Llewellyn Moxey
Co-stars: Doug McClure Darren McGavin Meg Foster

1978 GRAY LADY DOWN
Director: David Greene
Co-stars: Charlton Heston David Carradine Stacey Keach

1986 THE GLADIATOR
Director: Abel Ferrara
Co-stars: Ken Wahl Nancy Allen Robert Culp

1988 ADDICTED TO HIS LOVE
Director: Arthur Allan Seidelman
Co-stars: Barry Bostwick Polly Bergen Erin Gray

1994 DISCLOSURE
Director: Barry Levinson
Co-stars: Michael Douglas Demi Moore Donald Sutherland

1995 ABANDONED AND DECEIVED
Director: Joseph Dougherty
Co-stars: Lori Loughlin Brian Kerwin

ELEANOR FORSYTHE

1980 PROSTITUTE
Director: Tony Garnett
Co-stars: Kate Crutchley Kim Lockett Nancy Samuels

MIMI FORSYTHE

1943 THREE RUSSIAN GIRLS
Director: Henry Kesler
Co-stars: Anna Sten Kent Smith Kathy Frye

1944 SENSATIONS OF 1945
Director: Andrew Stone
Co-stars: Eleanor Powell Sophie Tucker W.C. Fields

JANE FORTH

1970 TRASH
Director: Paul Morrissey
Co-stars: Joe Dallesandro Geri Miller Holly Woodlawn

BRIGITTE FOSSEY (Child)

1952 JEUX INTERDITS
Director: Rene Clement
Co-stars: Georges Poujouly Jacques Marin Amedee

1956 THE HAPPY ROAD
Director: Gene Kelly
Co-stars: Gene Kelly Barbara Laage Michael Redgrave Bobby Clark

1974 LES VALSEUSES
Director: Bertrand Blier
Co-stars: Gerard Depardieu Miou-Miou Patrick Dewaere

1977 THE MAN WHO LOVED WOMEN
Director: Francois Truffaut
Co-stars: Charles Denner Leslie Caron

1979 QUINTET
Director: Robert Altman
Co-stars: Paul Newman Vittorio Gassman Bibi Andersson

1982 ENIGMA
Director: Jeannot Szwark
Co-stars: Martin Sheen Sam Neill Michael Williams

1988 CINEMA PARADISO
Director: Guiseppe Tornatore
Co-stars: Phillippe Noiret Jacques Perrin Mario Leonardi

1989 THE LAST BUTTERFLY
Director: Karel Kachyna
Co-stars: Tom Courtenay Freddie Jones Ingrid Held

DIANNE FOSTER

1953 THE STEEL KEY
Director: Robert Baker
Co-stars: Terence Morgan Joan Rice Esmond Knight

1954 DRIVE A CROOKED ROAD
Director: Richard Quine
Co-stars: Mickey Rooney Kevin McCarthy

1954 BAD FOR EACH OTHER
Director: Irving Rapper
Co-stars: Charlton Heston Lisabeth Scott Marjorie Rambeau

1954 THREE HOURS TO KILL
Director: Alfred Werker
Co-stars: Dana Andrews Donna Reed Stephen Elliott

1955 THE BAMBOO PRISON
Director: Lewis Seiler
Co-stars: Robert Francis Brian Keith Jerome Courtland

1955 THE KENTUCKIAN
Director: Burt Lancaster
Co-stars: Burt Lancaster Diana Lynn Walter Matthau John McIntyre

1955 THE VIOLENT MEN
Director: Rudolph Mate
Co-stars: Edward G. Robinson Barbara Stanwyck Glenn Ford

1957 NIGHT PASSAGE
Director: James Neilson
Co-stars: James Stewart Audie Murphy Brandon De Wilde

1957 MONKEY ON MY BACK
Director: Andre De Toth
Co-stars: Cameron Mitchell Jack Albertson Paul Richards

1957 THE BROTHERS RICO
Director: Phil Karlson
Co-stars: Richard Conte James Darren Kathryn Grant

1958   THE DEEP SIX
Director: Rudolph Mate
Co-stars: Alan Ladd William Bendix Keenan Wynn

1958   THE LAST HURRAH
Director: John Ford
Co-stars: Spencer Tracey Jeffrey Hunter Basil Rathbone

1961   KING OF THE ROARING TWENTIES
Director: Joseph Newman
Co-stars: David Janssen Mickey Rooney Diana Dors

GLORIA FOSTER

1963   NOTHING BUT A MAN
Director: Michael Roemar
Co-stars: Ivan Dixon Abbey Lincoln Yaphet Kotto

1970   THE ANGEL LEVINE
Director: Jan Kadar
Co-stars: Zero Mostel Harry Belafontte Eli Wallach

1985   THE ATLANTA CHILD MURDERS
Director: John Erman
Co-stars: Jason Robards Rip Torn James Earl Jones

ISA FOSTER

1968   ACE HIGH
Director: Giuseppe Colizzi
Co-stars: Terence Hill Eli Wallach Brock Peters

JODIE FOSTER (Child)
Oscar For Best Actress In 1988 For "The Accused" And In 1991 For
Silence Of The Lambs. Nominated For Best Supporting Actress In 1976
For "Taxi Driver" and Best Actress in 1994 for "Nell"

1972   KANSAS CITY BOMBER
Director: Jerrold Freedman
Co-stars: Raquel Welch Kevin McCarthy Norman Alden

1973   NAPOLEAN AND SAMANTHA
Director: Bernard McEveety
Co-stars: Michael Douglas Will Geer

1973   TOM SAWYER
Director: Don Taylor
Co-stars: Johnny Whitaker Celeste Holm Warren Oates Jeff East

1974   SMILE, JENNY, YOU'RE DEAD
Director: Jerry Thorpe
Co-stars: David Janssen Howard Da Silva

1974   ALICE DOESN'T LIVE HERE ANYMORE
Director: Martin Scorsese
Co-stars: Ellen Burstyn Diane Ladd

1975   ECHOES OF A SUMMER
Director: Don Taylor
Co-stars: Richard Harris Lois Nettleton Geraldine Fitzgerald

1976   BUGSY MALONE
Director: Alan Parker
Co-stars: Scott Baio Florrie Dugger John Cassisi Dexter Fletcher

1976   FREAKY FRIDAY
Director: Gary Nelson
Co-stars: Barbara Harris John Astin Patsy Kelly Marie Windsor

**1976   THE LITTLE GIRL WHO LIVES
DOWN THE LANE**
Director: Zev Braun
Co-stars: Martin Sheen Scott Jacoby Alexis Smith

1976   TAXI DRIVER
Director: Martin Scorsese
Co-stars: Robert De Niro Cybil Shepherd Peter Boyle

1977   CANDLESHOE
Director: Norman Tokar
Co-stars: David Niven Helen Hayes Leo McKern Ian Sharrock

1980   FOXES
Director: Adrian Lyne
Co-stars: Scott Baio Sally Kellerman Adam Faith Randy Quaid

1980   CARNY
Director: Robert Kaylor
Co-stars: Gary Busey Robbie Robertson Meg Foster

1983   O'HARA'S WIFE
Director: William Bartman
Co-stars: Ed Asner Mariette Hartley Ray Walston Perry Lang

1984   THE HOTEL NEW HAMPSHIRE
Director: Tony Richardson
Co-stars: Rob Lowe Beau Bridges Nastassja Kinski

1987   FIVE CORNERS
Director: Tony Bill
Co-stars: Tim Robbins John Turturo Todd Graf Elizabeth Berridge

1987   SIESTA
Director: Mary Lambert
Co-stars: Ellen Barkin Gabriel Byrne Isabella Rossellini Grace Jones

1988   THE ACCUSED
Director: Jonathan Kaplan
Co-stars: Kelly McKillis Bernie Coulson

1988   STEALING HOME
Director: Will Aldis
Co-stars: Mark Harmon Blair Brown William McNamara John Shea

1989   CATCHFIRE
Director: Dennis Hopper
Co-stars: Dennis Hopper Dean Stockwell Vincent Price Joe Pesci

1991   LITTLE MAN TATE
Director: Jodie Foster
Co-stars: Diane Wiest Adam Hann-Byrd Harry Connick

1991   SHADOWS AND FOG
Director: Woody Allen
Co-stars: Mia Farrow Kathy Bates Lily Tomlin John Cusack

1991   THE SILENCE OF THE LAMBS
Director: Jonathan Demme
Co-stars: Anthony Hopkins Scott Glenn

1994   MAVERICK
Director: Richard Donner
Co-stars: Mel Gibson James Garner Graham Greene

1993   SOMMERSBY
Director: Jon Amiel
Co-stars: Richard Gere Bill Pullman James Earl Jones

1994   NELL
Director: Michael Apted
Co-stars: Natasha Richardson Liam Neeson

1997   CONTACT
Director: Robert Zemeckis
Co-stars: Tom Skerritt Matthew McConaughey John Hurt

JULIA FOSTER

1962   THE SMALL WORLD OF SAMMY LEE
Director: Ken Hughes
Co-stars: Anthony Newley Robert Stephens

1963   TWO LEFT FEET
Director: Roy Baker
Co-stars: Michael Crawford Nyree Dawn Porter David Hemmings

1964   THE SYSTEM
Director: Michael Winner
Co-stars: Oliver Reed Jane Merrow Barbara Ferris

1964   ONE WAY PENDULUM
Director: Peter Yates
Co-stars: Eric Sykes George Cole Peggy Mount

1964 THE BARGEE
Director: Duncan Wood
Co-stars: Harry H. Corbett Ronnie Barker Hugh Griffith

1966 ALFIE
Director: Lewis Gilbert
Co-stars: Michael Caine Vivien Merchant Shelley Winters Jane Asher

1967 HALF A SIXPENCE
Director: George Sidney
Co-stars: Tommy Steele Pamela Brown Cyril Richard

1970 PERCY
Director: Ralph Thomas
Co-stars: Hywel Bennett Denholm Elliott Elke Sommer

1972 ALL COPPERS ARE
Director: Sidney Hayers
Co-stars: Nicky Henson Ian Hendry Martin Potter

1974 THE GREAT MCGONAGALL
Director: Joe McGrath
Co-stars: Spike Milligan Peter Sellers Valentine Dyall

1976 F. SCOTT FITZGERALD IN HOLLYWOOD
Director: Anthony Page
Co-stars: Jason Miller Tuesday Weld

KATE FOSTER

1985 THE INNOCENT
Director: John MacKenzie
Co-stars: Andrew Hawley Kika Markham Miranda Richardson

KATUNA FOSTER

1987 THE BIT PART
Director: Brendan Maher
Co-stars: John Wood Nicole Kidman Chris Hayward

MEG FOSTER

1970 ADAM AT 6AM
Director: Robert Scheerer
Co-stars: Michael Douglas Lee Purcell Joe Don Baker

1971 THE DEATH OF ME YET
Director: John Llewellyn Moxey
Co-stars: Doug McClure Richard Basehart

1972 THUMB TRIPPING
Director: Quentin Masters
Co-stars: Michael Burns Bruce Dern Marianna Hill

1973 WELCOME TO ARROW BEACH
Director: Laurence Harvey
Co-stars: Laurence Harvey Joanna Pettet Stuart Whitman

1978 A DIFFERENT STORY
Director: Paul Aaron
Co-stars: Perry King Valerie Curtin Peter Donat

1980 CARNY
Director: Robert Kaylor
Co-stars: Gary Busey Jodie Foster Robbie Robertson

1980 THE LEGEND OF SLEEPY HOLLOW
Director: Henning Schellerup
Co-stars: Jeff Goldblum Dick Butkus

1981 TICKET TO HEAVEN
Director: Ralph L. Thomas
Co-stars: Nick Mancuso Saul Rubinek Kim Cattrall

1983 THE OSTERMAN WEEKEND
Director: Sam Peckinpah
Co-stars: Burt Lancaster Rutger Hauer John Hurt

1984 BEST KEPT SECRETS
Director: Jerrold Freedman
Co-stars: Patty Duke Frederic Forrest Peter Coyote

1985 THE EMERALD FORREST
Director: John Boorman
Co-stars: Powers Boothe Charley Boorman

1987 MASTERS OF THE UNIVERSE
Director: Gary Goddard
Co-stars: Dolph Lundgren Frank Langella

1988 THEY LIVE
Director: John Carpenter
Co-stars: Roddy Piper Keith David Peter Jason Jason Robards

1989 STEPFATHER II MAKE ROOM FOR DADDY
Director: Jeff Burr
Co-stars: Terry O'Quinn Caroline Williams

1989 LEVIATHAN
Director: George Pan Cosmatos
Co-stars: Peter Weller Daniel Stern Amanda Pays

1989 BETRAYAL OF SILENCE
Director: Jeffrey Woolnough
Co-stars: Joanne Vannicola Alex Carter

1989 BLIND FURY
Director: Phillip Noyce
Co-stars: Rutger Hauer Terry O'Quinn Brandon Call

1991 DIPLOMATIC IMMUNITY
Director: Peter Maris
Co-stars: Bruce Boxleitner Billy Drago Fabiana Udenio

PHOEBE FOSTER

1931 TARNISHED LADY
Director: George Cukor
Co-stars: Tallulah Bankhead Clive Brook Elizabeth Patterson

1933 OUR BETTERS
Director: George Cukor
Co-stars: Constance Bennett Alan Mowbray Gilbert Roland

SUSANNAH FOSTER

1938 SWEETHEARTS
Director: W.S. Van Dyke
Co-stars: Jeanette MacDonald Nelson Eddy Frank Morgan

1939 THE GREAT VICTOR HERBERT
Director: Andrew Stone
Co-stars: Allan Jones Mary Martin Walter Connelly

1941 GLAMOUR BOY
Director: Ralph Murphy
Co-stars: Jackie Cooper Walter Abel William Demarest

1941 THERE'S MAGIC IN MUSIC
Director: Andrew Stone
Co-stars: Allan Jones Margaret Lindsay

1943 THIS IS THE LIFE
Director: Felix Feist
Co-stars: Donald O'Connor Peggy Ryan Patric Knowles

1943 TOP MAN
Director: Charles Lamont
Co-stars: Donald O'Connor Peggy Ryan Richard Dix Lillian Gish

1943 PHANTOM OF THE OPERA
Director: Arthur Lubin
Co-stars: Nelson Eddy Claude Rains Leo Carrillo

1944 THE CLIMAX
Director: George Waggner
Co-stars: Boris Karloff Turhan Bey Gale Sondergaard

1944 BOWERY TO BROADWAY
Director: Charles Lamont
Co-stars: Maria Montez Turhan Bey Donald O'Connor

1945 FRISCO SAL
Director: George Waggner
Co-stars: Turhan Bey Alan Curtis Andy Devine Thomas Gomez

1945 THAT NIGHT WITH YOU
Director: William Seiter
Co-stars: Franchot Tone David Bruce Buster Keaton

1993 DETOUR
Director: Wade Williams
Co-stars: Tom Neal Jnr Lea Lavish Erin McGraine Duke Howze

TERREA FOSTER

1983 SCREWBALLS
Director: Rafal Zielinski
Co-stars: Peter Keleghan Linda Shane Kent Deuters

SUSANNAH FOWLE

1977 THE GETTING OF WISDOM
Director: Bruce Beresford
Co-stars: Sheila Helpman John Waters Hilary Ryan

ALEXANDRA FOWLER

1992 FRANKIE'S HOUSE
Director: Peter Fisk
Co-stars: Iain Glen Kevin Dillon Steven Vidler

CATE FOWLER

1987 BORDER
Director: Misha Williams
Co-stars: Shaun Scott Daniel Hill Catherine Schell

CONNIE FOX

1977 AMERICAN RASPBERRY
Director: Brael Swirnoff
Co-stars: Art Fleming Warren Oates David Spielberg

EMELIA FOX

1996 REBECCA
Co-stars: Charles Dance Diana Rigg

KERRY FOX

1990 AN ANGEL AT MY TABLE
Director: Jane Campion
Co-stars: Alexia Keogh Karen Fergusson Iris Churn

1990 THE LAST DAYS OF CHEZ NOUS
Director: Gillian Armstrong
Co-stars: Lisa Harrow Bruno Ganz Miranda Otto

1993 FRIENDS
Director: Elaine Proctor
Co-stars: Dambisa Kente Michelle Burgers Marius Weyers

1994 SHALLOW GRAVE
Director: Danny Boyle
Co-stars: Christopher Ecclestone Ewan McGregor Keith Allen

1997 WELCOME TO SARAJEVO
Director: Michael Winterbottom
Co-stars: Stephen Dillane Woody Harrelson

MARCIA FOX

1970 CREATURES THE WORLD FORGOT
Director: Don Chaffey
Co-stars: Julie Ege Brian O'Shaughnessy Robert John

SAMANTHA FOX

1981 AFTERNOON DELIGHTS
Director: Warren Evans
Co-stars: Eric Edwards Merle Michaels Veronica Hart

1981 BABE
Director: John Christopher
Co-stars: Bobbi Jackson Tiffany Clark Ron Jeremy

SIDNEY FOX

1931 STRICTLY DISHONOURABLE
Co-star: Paul Lukas

1931 BAD SISTER
Director: Hobart Henley
Co-stars: Conrad Nagel Bette Davis Humphrey Bogart Zasu Pitts

1932 THE COHENS AND THE KELLYS IN HOLLYWOOD
Director: Harry Pollard
Co-stars: George Sidney Charles Murray

1932 THE MOUTHPIECE
Director: Elliott Nugent
Co-stars: Warren William Aline MacMahon John Wray

1932 MURDERS IN THE RUE MORGUE
Director: Robert Flory
Co-stars: Bela Lugosi Leon Ames Bert Roach

1932 NICE WOMEN
Co-star: James Durkin

1933 DON QUIXOTE
Director: G.W. Pabst
Co-stars: Feodor Chaliapin George Robey Miles Mander

1933 ONCE IN A LIFETIME
Director: Russell Mack
Co-stars: Jack Oakie Aline MacMahon Louise Fazenda

1934 MIDNIGHT
Director: Chester Erkskine
Co-stars: Humphrey Bogart Henry Hull O.P. Heggie

VIRGINIA FOX

1922 COPS
Director: Buster Keaton
Co-star: Buster Keaton

1922 THE ELECTRIC HOUSE
Director: Buster Keaton
Co-star: Buster Keaton

1923 THE LOVE NEST
Director: Buster Keaton
Co-star: Buster Keaton Joe Roberts

VIVECA FOX

1996 INDEPENDENCE DAY
Director: Roland Emmerich
Co-stars: Bill Pullman Jeff Goldblum Randy Quaid

1997 SET IT OFF
Director: F.gary Gray
Co-stars: Jada Pinkett Queen Latifa Kimberley Elise

1997 BOOTY CALL
Co-stars: Tommy Davidson Tamala Jones Jaimie Fox

1998 SOUL FOOD
Director: George Tillman Jnr.
Co-stars: Vanessa Williams Gina Ravera Nia Long

CYRINDA FOXE

1977 ANDY WARHOL'S BAD
Director: Jed Johnson
Co-stars: Carroll Baker Perry King Susan Tyrrell

MARY FOY

1931 A HOUSE DIVIDED
Director: William Wyler
Co-stars: Walter Huston Helen Chandler Kent Douglass

VICTORIA FOYT

1994 BABYFEVER
Director: Henry Jaglom
Co-stars: Matt Salinger Eric Roberts Dinah Lenney

DAWN FRAME

1971 A TASTE OF EVIL
Director: John Llewellyn Moxey
Co-stars: Barbara Stanwyck Barbara Parkins

CHRISTINA FRAMBACK

1963 RAVEN'S END
Director: Bo Widerberg
Co-stars: Thommy Berggren Keve Hjelm Emy Storm

ROLLA FRANCE

1931 A NOUS LA LIBERTE
Director: Rene Clair
Co-stars: Raymond Cordy Henri Marchand Paul Olivier

VERA FRANCES

1942 BACK ROOM BOY
Director: Herbert Mason
Co-stars: Arthur Askey Googie Withers Moore Marriott

1942 KING ARTHUR WAS A GENTLEMAN
Director: Marcel Varnel
Co-stars: Arthur Askey Anne Shelton Evelyn Dall

MICHELINE FRANCEY

1943 LE CORBEAU
Director: Henri-Georges Clouzot
Co-stars: Pierre Fresnay Pierre Larquey Ginette Leclerc

1947 LA CAGE AU ROSSIGNOLS
Director: Jean Dreville
Co-stars: Noel-Noel Georges Biscot Rene Genin

RINA FRANCHETTI

1974 SOMEWHERE BEYOND LOVE
Director: Luigi Comencini
Co-stars: Giuliano Gemma Stefania Sandrelli

ANNE FRANCINE

1972 SAVAGES
Director: James Ivory
Co-stars: Louis Stadlen Salome Jens Neil Fitzgerald

ANNE FRANCIS

1948 SUMMER HOLIDAY
Director: Rouben Mamoulian
Co-stars: Mickey Rooney Walter Huston Frank Morgan

1951 ELOPEMENT
Director: Henry Koster
Co-stars: Clifton Webb Charles Bickford William Lundigan

1952 DREAMBOAT
Director: Claude Binyon
Co-stars: Clifton Webb Ginger Rogers Elsa Lanchester

1952 LYDIA BAILEY
Director: Jean Negulesco
Co-stars: Dale Robertson Charles Korvin

1953 A LION IS IN THE STREETS
Director: Raoul Walsh
Co-stars: James Cagney Barbara Hale John McIntyre

1954 THE ROCKET MAN
Director: Oscar Rudolph
Co-stars: Charles Coburn John Agar George Winslow

1954 SUSAN SLEPT HERE
Director: Frank Tashlin
Co-stars: Dick Powell Debbie Reynolds Glenda Farrell

1954 ROGUE COP
Director: Roy Rowland
Co-stars: Robert Taylor George Raft Janet Leigh

1955 BATTLE CRY
Director: Raoul Walsh
Co-stars: Van Heflin Aldo Ray Dorothy Malone

1955 THE SCARLET COAT
Director: John Sturges
Co-stars: Cornel Wilde Michael Wilding George Sanders

1955 THE BLACKBOARD JUNGLE
Director: Richard Brooks
Co-stars: Glenn Ford Sidney Poitier Louis Calhern

1956 FORBIDDEN PLANET
Director: Fred Wilcox
Co-stars: Walter Pidgeon Leslie Nielsen Earl Holliman

1957 DON'T GO NEAR THE WATER
Director: Charles Walters
Co-stars: Glenn Ford Fred Clark Gia Scala

1957 HIRED GUN

1960 THE CROWDED SKY
Director: Joseph Pevney
Co-stars: Dana Andrews Rhonda Fleming John Kerr

1965 BRAINSTORM
Director: William Conrad
Co-stars: Dana Andrews Jeffrey Hunter Viveca Lindfors

1965 THE SATAN BUG
Director: John Sturges
Co-stars: Dana Andrews George Maharis Richard Basehart

1968 MORE DEAD THAN ALIVE
Director: Robert Spar
Co-stars: Clint Walker Vincent Price Mike Henry

1968 IMPASSE
Director: Richard Benedict
Co-stars: Burt Reynolds Vic Diaz Lyle Bettger

1968 HOOK, LINE AND SINKER
Director: George Marshall
Co-stars: Jerry Lewis Peter Lawford

1968 FUNNY GIRL
Director: William Wyler
Co-stars: Barbra Streisand Omar Sharif Walter Pidgeon

1969 THE LOVE GOD
Director: Nat Hiken
Co-stars: Don Knotts Edmond O'Brien James Gregory

1970 WILD WOMEN
Director: Don Taylor
Co-stars: Hugh O'Brian Marie Windsor Marilyn Maxwell

1971 MONGO'S BACK IN TOWN
Director: Marvin Chomsky
Co-stars: Joe Don Baker Telly Savalas Sally Field

1972 HAUNTS OF THE VERY RICH
Director: Paul Wendkos
Co-stars: Lloyd Bridges Cloris Leachman Tony Bill

1974 THE LAST SURVIVORS
Director: Lee Katzin
Co-stars: Martin Sheen Diane Baker Christopher George

1974 THE FBI STORY: ALVIN KARPIS
Director: Marvin Chomsky
Co-stars: Robert Foxworth David Wayne Kay Lenz

1978 BORN AGAIN
Director: Irving Rapper
Co-stars: Dean Jones Dana Andrews George Brent

1987 LAGUNA HEAT
Director: Simon Langton
Co-stars: Harry Hamlin Jason Robards Rip Torn

1988 MY FIRST LOVE
Director: Gilbert Cates
Co-stars: Beatrice Arthur Richard Kiley Richard Herd

1992 LOVE CAN BE MURDER
Director: Jack Bender
Co-stars: Jaclyn Smith Corbin Bernsen Cliff DeYoung

ARLENE FRANCIS

1932 MURDERS IN THE RUE MORGUE
Co-stars: Bela Lugosi Sidney Fox Bert Roach

1948 ALL MY SONS
Director: Irving Reis
Co-stars: Edward G. Robinson Burt Lancaster Howard Duff

1961 ONE, TWO, THREE
Director: Billy Wilder
Co-stars: James Cagney Horst Buchholz Pamela Tiffin

1963 THE THRILL OF IT ALL
Director: Norman Jewison
Co-stars: Doris Day James Garner Reginald Owen

CAROL FRANCIS

1977 FINGERS
Director: James Toback
Co-stars: Harvey Keitel Tisa Farrow Jim Brown

CONNIE FRANCIS

1960 WHERE THE BOYS ARE
Director: Henry Levin
Co-stars: George Hamilton Dolores Hart Paula Prentiss

1963 FOLLOW THE BOYS
Director: Richard Thorpe
Co-stars: Paula Prentiss Janis Page Russ Tamblyn

1964 LOOKING FOR LOVE
Director: Don Weis
Co-stars: Jim Hutton Susan Oliver Barbara Nichols Joby Baker

1965 WHEN THE BOYS MEET THE GIRLS
Director: Alvin Ganzer
Co-stars: Harve Presnell Sue Anne Langdon Louis Armstrong

GENIE FRANCIS

1995 TERROR IN THE SHADOWS
Director: William Graham
Co-stars: Marcy Walker Leigh J. McClosky

JAN FRANCIS

1979 DRACULA
Director: John Badham
Co-stars: Frank Langella Laurence Olivier Kate Nelligan

1983 CHAMPIONS
Director: John Irvin
Co-stars: John Hurt Edward Woodward Ben Johnson

KAY FRANCIS *(Married Kenneth McKenna)*

1929 THE COCOANUTS
Director: Robert Florey
Co-stars: Marx Brothers Margaret Dumont

1929 DANGEROUS CURVES
Director: Lothar Mendes
Co-stars: Clara Bow Richard Arlen David Newell

1929 THE MARRIAGE PLAYGROUND
Director: Lothar Mendes
Co-stars: Fredric March Mary Brian Lilyan Tashman

1930 BEHIND THE MAKE-UP
Director: Robert Milton
Co-stars: Hal Skelly William Powell Fay Wray

1930 FOR THE DEFENSE
Director: John Cromwell
Co-stars: William Powell Scott Kolk T.E. Jackson

1930 LET'S GO NATIVE
Director: Leo McCarey
Co-stars: Jeanette MacDonald Jack Oakie James Hall

1930 RAFFLES
Director: Harry D'arrast
Co-stars: Ronald Colman David Terence Frances Dade

1930 THE VIRTUOUS SIN
Director: George Cukor
Co-stars: Walter Huston Kenneth MacKenna

1931 24 HOURS
Director: Marion Gering
Co-stars: Clive Brook Miriam Hopkins Regis Toomey

1931 TRANSGRESSION
Director: Herbert Brennon
Co-stars: Ricardo Cortez Paul Cavanagh Nance O'Neil

1931 SCANDAL SHEET
Director: John Cromwell
Co-stars: George Bancroft Clive Brook Regis Toomey

1931 LADIE'S MAN
Director: Lothar Mendes
Co-stars: William Powell Carole Lombard

1931 GUILTY HANDS
Director: W.S. Van Dyke
Co-stars: Lionel Barrymore Madge Evans C. Aubrey Smith

1931 GIRLS ABOUT TOWN
Director: George Cukor
Co-stars: Lilyan Tashman Joel McCrea Eugene Pallette

1932 JEWELL ROBBERY
Director: William Dieterle
Co-stars: William Powell Helen Vinson Alan Mowbray

1932 MAN WANTED
Director: William Dieterle
Co-stars: David Manners Andy Devine Una Merkel

1932 ONE WAY PASSAGE
Director: Tay Garnett
Co-stars: William Powell Frank McHugh Aline McMahon

1932 STREET OF WOMEN
Director: Archie Mayo
Co-stars: Alan Dinehart Roland Young Gloria Stuart

1932 STRANGERS IN LOVE
Director: Lothar Mendes
Co-stars: Fredric March Stuart Erwin George Barbier

1932 TROUBLE IN PARADISE
Director: Ernst Lubitsch
Co-stars: Herbert Marshall Miriam Hopkins

1932 THE FALSE MADONNA
Co-stars: Conway Tearle William "Stage" Boyd

1933 THE HOUSE ON 56TH. STREET
Co-star: John Halliday

1933 CYNARA
Director: King Vidor
Co-stars: Ronald Colman Phyllis Barry Henry Stephenson

1933 I LOVED A WOMAN
Director: Alfred Green
Co-stars: Edward G. Robinson Genevieve Tobin Robert Barrat

1933 THE KEYHOLE
Director: Michael Curtis
Co-stars: George Brent Glenda Farrell Allen Jenkins

1933 MARY STEVENS M.D.
Director: Lloyd Bacon
Co-stars: Lyle Talbot Glenda Farrell Thelma Todd

1933 STORM AT DAYBREAK
Director: Richard Boleslawski
Co-stars: Walter Huston Nils Asther Jean Parker

1934 WONDER BAR
Director: Lloyd Bacon
Co-stars: Al Jolson Dick Powell Dolores Del Rio

1934 MANDALAY
Director: Michael Curtis
Co-stars: Ricardo Cortez Lyle Talbot Shirley Temple

1934 DR. MONICA
Director: William Keighley
Co-stars: Warren William Jean Muir Philip Reed

1934 BRITISH AGENT
Director: Michael Curtis
Co-stars: Leslie Howard J. Carrol Naish Irving Pichel

1935 I FOUND STELLA PARISH
Director: Mervyn LeRoy
Co-stars: Paul Lukas Ian Hunter Jessie Ralph

1935 LIVING ON VELVET
Director: Frank Borzage
Co-stars: George Brent Warren William Henry O'Neill

1936 THE WHITE ANGEL
Director: William Dieterle
Co-stars: Ian Hunter Donald Woods Donald Crisp

1936 STRANDED
Director: Frank Borzage
Co-stars: George Brent Patricia Ellis Donald Woods

1936 STOLEN HOLIDAY
Director: Michael Curtis
Co-stars: Claude Rains Ian Hunter Alison Skipworth

1936 GIVE ME YOUR HEART
Director: Archie Mayo
Co-stars: George Brent Patric Knowles Roland Young

1967 FIRST LADY
Director: Stanley Logan
Co-stars: Preston Foster Anita Louise Walter Connolly

1937 CONFESSION
Director: Joe May
Co-stars: Basil Rathbone Ian Hunter Jane Bryan Donald Crisp

1937 ANOTHER DAWN
Director: William Dieterle
Co-stars: Errol Flynn Ian Hunter Herbert Mundin

1938 SECRETS OF AN ACTRESS
Director: William Keighley
Co-stars: George Brent Ian Hunter Gloria Dickson

1938 WOMEN ARE LIKE THAT
Director: Stanley Logan
Co-stars: Pat O'Brien Ralph Forbes Melville Cooper

1938 KING OF THE UNDERWORLD
Director: Lewis Seiler
Co-stars: Humphrey Bogart James Stephenson

1938 COMET OVER BROADWAY
Director: Busby Berkeley
Co-stars: Ian Hunter John Litel Donald Crisp

1939 IN NAME ONLY
Director: John Cromwell
Co-stars: Cary Grant Carole Lombard Charles Coburn

1939 WOMEN IN THE WIND
Director: John Farrow
Co-stars: William Gargan Eve Arden Victor Jory

1940 MY BILL

1940 LITTLE MEN
Director: Norman Z McLeod
Co-stars: Jack Oakie Jimmy Lydon George Bancroft

1940 IT'S A DATE
Director: William Seiter
Co-stars: Deanna Durbin Walter Pidgeon S.Z. Sakall

1941 THE MAN WHO LOST HIMSELF
Director: Edward Ludwig
Co-stars: Brian Aherne Nils Asther S.Z. Sakall

1941 THE FEMININE TOUCH
Director: W.S. Van Dyke
Co-stars: Don Ameche Rosalind Russell Van Heflin

1941 CHARLEY'S AUNT
Director: Archie Mayo
Co-stars: Jack Benny Anne Baxter Edmund Gwenn

1942 BETWEEN US GIRLS
Director: Henry Koster
Co-stars: Diana Barrymore John Boles Robert Cummings

1942 ALWAYS IN MY HEART
Director: Joe Graham
Co-stars: Walter Huston Gloria Warren Sidney Blackmer

1944 FOUR JILLS IN A JEEP
Director: William Seiter
Co-stars: Martha Raye Carole Landis Dick Haymes

1945 ALLOTMENT WIVES
Co-star: Paul Kelly

1945 DIVORCE
Director: William Nigh
Co-stars: Bruce Cabot Helen Mack Jonathan Hale

MISSY FRANCIS *(Child)*

1981 A GUN IN THE HOUSE
Director: Ivan Nagy
Co-stars: Sally Struthers David Ackroyd Millie Perkins

1982 MAN, WOMAN AND CHILD
Director: Dick Richards
Co-stars: Martin Sheen Blythe Danner David Hemmings

NOEL FRANCIS

1931 SMART MONEY
Director: Alfred Green
Co-stars: Edward G. Robinson James Cagney Evalyn Knapp

1933 THE IMPORTANT WITNESS
Co-star: Noel Madison

1933 SON OF A SAILOR
Co-stars: Joe E. Brown Jean Muir Johnny Mack Brown

1933 REFORM GIRL
Co-stars: Skeets Gallagher

1934 WHAT'S YOUR RACKET?
Co-stars: J. Carrol Naish Creighton Hale

1934 FIFTEEN WIVES
Co-stars: Conway Tearle Ralf Harolde

1934 LINE UP
Co-stars: William Gargan John Miljan Paul Hurst

VERA FRANCES

1942 BACK ROOM BOY
Director: Herbert Mason
Co-stars: Arthur Askey Googie Withers Moore Marriott

1942 KING ARTHUR WAS A GENTLEMAN
Director: Marcel Varnel
Co-stars: Arthur Askey Anne Shelton Evelyn Dall

NANCY FRANGIONE

1988 SHARING RICHARD
Co-stars: Peter Bonerz
Co-stars: Ed Marinaro Eileen Davidson Janet Carroll

ASTRID FRANK

1972 AU PAIR GIRLS
Director: Val Guest
Co-stars: Gabrielle Drake Richard O'Sullivan Nancie Wait

JOANNA FRANK

1985 ALWAYS
Director: Henry Jaglom
Co-stars: Henry Jaglom Patrice Townsend Michael Emil

ARETHA FRANKLIN

1980 THE BLUES BROTHERS
Director: John Landis
Co-stars: John Belushi Dan Aykroyd Kathleen Freeman

1998 THE BLUES BROTHERS 2000
Co-stars: Dan Aykroyd John Goodman James Brown

DIANE FRANKLYN

1982 AMITYVILLE II: THE POSSESSION
Director: Damiano Damiani
Co-stars: Burt Young Rutanya Alda

1983 DEADLY LESSONS
Director: William Wiard
Co-stars: Donna Reed Larry Wilcox Ally Sheedy

1986 DALLAS: THE EARLY YEARS
Director: Larry Elikann
Co-stars: Larry Hagman Dale Midkiff

GLORIA FRANKLYN

1939 LADY OF THE TROPICS
Director: Jack Conway
Co-stars: Hedy Lamarr Robert Taylor Joseph Schildkraut

PAMELA FRANKLYN *(Child)*

1961 THE INNOCENTS
Director: Jack Clayton
Co-stars: Deborah Kerr Megs Jankins Michael Redgrave

1962 THE LION
Director: Jack Cardiff
Co-stars: William Holden Trevor Howard Capucine

1963 A TIGER WALKS
Director: Norman Tokar
Co-stars: Sabu Brian Keith Vera Miles

1963 THE HORSE WITHOUT A HEAD
Director: Don Chaffey
Co-stars: Leo McKern Jean-Pierre Aumont

1964 THE THIRD SECRET
Director: Charles Crichton
Co-stars: Stephen Boyd Jack Hawkins Diane Cilento

1965 THE NANNY
Director: Seth Holt
Co-stars: Bette Davis Jill Bennett Wendy Craig

1967 OUR MOTHER'S HOUSE
Director: Jack Clayton
Co-stars: Dirk Bogarde Margaret Brooks Mark Lester

1968 SINFUL DAVEY
Director: John Huston
Co-stars: John Hurt Nigel Davenport Robert Morley

1969 THE NIGHT OF THE FOLLOWING DAY
Director: Hubert Cornfield
Co-stars: Marlon Brando Richard Boone

1969 THE PRIME OF MISS JEAN BRODIE
Director: Ronald Neame
Co-stars: Maggie Smith Robert Stephens

1970 AND SOON THE DARKNESS
Director: Robert Fuest
Co-stars: Michele Dotrice Sandor Eles John Nettleton

1973 THE LEGEND OF HELL HOUSE
Director: John Hough
Co-stars: Roddy McDowall Gayle Hunnicutt Clive Revell

1973 ACE ELI AND ROGER OF THE SKIES
Director: John Erman
Co-stars: Cliff Robertson Rosemary Murphy

1973 NECROMANCY
Director: Bert Gordon
Co-stars: Orson Welles Michael Ontkean Lee Purcell

1976 THE FOOD OF THE GODS
Director: Bert Gordon
Co-stars: Ida Lupino Marjoe Gortner Ralph Meeker

PATRICIA FRANKLYN

1975 CARRY ON BEHIND
Director: Gerald Thomas
Co-stars: Elke Sommer Kenneth Williams Liz Fraser

CHLOE FRANKS

1951 AN AMERICAN IN PARIS
Director: Vincent Minnelli
Co-stars: Gene Kelly Leslie Caron Oscar Levant

1971 WHO SLEW AUNTIE ROO?
Director: Curtis Harrington
Co-stars: Shelley Winters Ralph Richardson

ELIZABETH FRANZ

1987 THE SECRET OF MY SUCCESS
Director: Herbert Ross
Co-stars: Michael J Fox Helen Slater Richard Jordan

ALICE FRASER

1987 STARLIGHT HOTEL
Director: Sam Pilsbury
Co-stars: Peter Phelps Greer Robson Marshall Napier

CONSTANCE FRASER

1958 A LADY MISLAID
Director: David MacDonald
Co-stars: Phyllis Calvert Gillian Owen Alan White

ELIZABETH FRASER

1941 THE MAN WHO CAME TO DINNER
Director: William Keighley
Co-stars: Monty Woolley Bette Davis

1941 ONE FOOT IN HEAVEN
Director: Irving Rapper
Co-stars: Fredric March Martha Scott Beulah Bondi

1942 THE HIDDEN HAND
Director: Ben Stoloff
Co-stars: Craig Stevens Julie Bishop Willie Best

1953 SO BIG
Director: Robert Wise
Co-stars: Jane Wyman Sterling Hayden Nancy Olson

1954 YOUNG AT HEART
Director: Gordon Douglas
Co-stars: Doris Day Frank Sinatra Ethel Barrymore

1958 THE TUNNEL OF LOVE
Director: Gene Kelly
Co-stars: Doris Day Richard Widmark Gig Young

1959 ASK ANY GIRL
Director: Charles Walters
Co-stars: David Niven Shirley MacLaine Gig Young

1962 TWO FOR THE SEESAW
Director: Robert Wise
Co-stars: Robert Mitchum Shirley MacLaine Billy Gray

1963 WHO'S BEEN SLEEEPING IN MY BED?
Director: Daniel Mann
Co-stars: Dean Martin Elizabeth Montgomery

1965 A PATCH OF BLUE
Director: Guy Green
Co-stars: Sidney Poitier Shelley Winters Elizabeth Hartman

HELEN FRASER

1963 BILLY LIAR
Director: John Schlessinger
Co-stars: Tom Courtenay Julie Christie Wilfred Pickles

1972 A DAY OUT
Director: Stephen Frears
Co-stars: Anthony Andrews James Cossins Brian Glover

1982 INTENSIVE CARE
Director: Gavin Millar
Co-stars: Alan Bennett Julie Walters Thora Hird

LAURA FRASER

1996 SMALL PACES
Director: Gilles Mackinnon
Co-stars: Joe McFadden Iain Robertson Clare Higgins

1998 THE TRIBE
Director: Stephen Poliakoff
Co-stars: Joely Richardson Jeremy Northam George Costigan

LIZ FRASER

1959 THE NIGHT WE DROPPED A CLANGER
Director: Darcy Conyers
Co-stars: Brian Rix Cecil Parker William Hartnell

1960 PURE HELL AT ST. TRINIANS
Director: Frank Launder
Co-stars: Cecil Parker Joyce Grenfell George Cole

1960 THE NIGHT WE GOT THE BIRD
Director: Darcy Conyers
Co-stars: Brian Rix Dora Bryan Ronald Shiner

1960 I'M ALL RIGHT JACK
Director: John Boulting
Co-stars: Ian Carmichael Peter Sellers Irene Handl

1960 TWO-WAY STRETCH
Director: Robert Day
Co-stars: Peter Sellers Lionel Jeffries Bernard Cribbins

1960 FURY AT SMUGGLERS' BAY
Director: John Gilling
Co-stars: Peter Cushing John Fraser June Thorburn

1960 DOCTOR IN LOVE
Director: Ralph Thomas
Co-stars: Michael Craig Leslie Phillips Virginia Maskell

1960 BULLDOG BREED
Director: Robert Asher
Co-stars: Norman Wisdom Edward Chapman Peter Jones

1961 WATCH IT SAILOR
Director: Wolf Rilla
Co-stars: Dennis Price Marjorie Rhodes Irene Handl

1961 RAISING THE WIND
Director: Gerald Thomas
Co-stars: Leslie Phillips Kenneth Williams Eric Barker

1961 CARRY ON REGARDLESS
Director: Gerald Thomas
Co-stars: Sid James Charles Hawtrey Stanley Unwin

1962 THE AMOROUS PRAWN
Director: Anthony Kimmins
Co-stars: Joan Greenwood Dennis Price Ian Carmichael

1962 LIVE NOW - PAY LATER
Director: Jay Lewis
Co-stars: Ian Hendry June Ritchie John Gregson

1962 THE PAINTED SMILE
Director: Lance Comfort
Co-stars: Kenneth Griffith Nanette Newman

1962 A PAIR OF BRIEFS
Director: Ralph Thomas
Co-stars: Michael Craig Mary Peach Roland Culver

1962 CARRY ON CRUISING
Director: Gerald Thomas
Co-stars: Sid James Kenneth Connor Dilys Laye

1963 CARRY ON CABBY
Director: Gerald Thomas
Co-stars: Sid James Bill Owen Milo O'Shea Hattie Jacques

1964 THE AMERICANISATION OF EMILY
Director: Arthur Hiller
Co-stars: Julie Andrews James Garner James Coburn

1966 THE FAMILY WAY
Director: Roy Boulting
Co-stars: John Mills Hayley Mills Hywel Bennett Marjorie Rhodes

1967 UP THE JUNCTION
Director: Peter Collinson
Co-stars: Suzy Kendall Dennis Waterman Hylda Baker

1971 DAD'S ARMY
Director: Norman Cohen
Co-stars: Arthur Lowe John Le Mesurier Clive Dunn John Laurie

1975 CARRY ON BEHIND
Director: Gerald Thomas
Co-stars: Elke Sommer Kenneth Williams Joan Sims

1976 ADVENTURES OF A TAXI DRIVER
Director: Stanley Long
Co-stars: Barry Evans Judy Geeson Diana Dors Adrienne Posta

1976 CONFESSIONS OF A DRIVING INSTRUCTOR
Director: Norman Cohen
Co-stars: Robin Askwith Anthony Booth Bill Maynard

1977 CONFESSIONS FROM A HOLIDAY CAMP
Director: Norman Cohen
Co-stars: Robin Askwith Anthony Booth Bill Maynard

1977 ADVENTURES OF A PRIVATE EYE
Director: Stanley Long
Co-stars: Christopher Neil Suzy Kendall Irene Handl

1988 ESKIMOS DO IT
Director: Derek Lister
Co-stars: Jean Boht Ian Brimble Neil Pearson Ania Marson

1990 CHICAGO JOE AND THE SHOWGIRL
Director: Bernard Rose
Co-stars: Emily Lloyd Patsy Kensit

MOYRA FRASER

1954 THE MAN WHO LOVED REDHEADS
Director: Harold French
Co-stars: John Justin Moira Shearer Joan Benham

1967 HERE WE GO ROUND THE MULBERRY BUSH
Director: Clive Donner
Co-stars: Barry Evans Judy Geeson

1971 THE BOY FRIEND
Director: Ken Russell
Co-stars: Twiggy Christopher Gable Tommy Tune

SALLY FRASER

1955 IT'S A DOG'S LIFE

1956 IT CONQUERED THE WORLD
Director: Roger Corman
Co-stars: Peter Graves Beverly Garland Lee Van Cleef

SHELAGH FRASER (Child)

1947 MASTER OF BANKDAM
Director: Walter Forde
Co-stars: Tom Walls Anne Crawford Dennis Price

1955 RAISING A RIOT
Director: Wendy Toye
Co-stars: Kenneth More Mandy Miller Ronald Squire

BARBARA FRAWLEY

1982 GREAT EXPECTATIONS (Voice)
Director: Jean Tych
Co-stars: Bill Kerr Philip Hinton Simon Hinton

KATY FRAYSSE

1968 TARGET HARRY
Director: Roger Corman
Co-stars: Vic Morrow Suzanne Pleshette Victor Buono

JANE FRAZEE

1941 BUCK PRIVATES
Director: Arthur Lubin
Co-stars: Bud Abbott Lou Costello Lee Bowman Alan Curtis

1941 MOONLIGHT IN HAWAII
Co-star: Johnny Downs

1942 GET HEP TO LOVE
Director: Charles Lamont
Co-stars: Gloria Jean Donald O'Connor Peggy Ryan

1942 HELLZAPOPPIN
Director: H.C. Potter
Co-stars: Ole Olsen Chic Johnson Robert Paige Martha Raye

1942 DON'T GET PERSONAL
Co-stars: Robert Paige Hugh Herbert Mischa Auer

1942 MOONLIGHT IN HAVANA
Director: Anthony Mann
Co-stars: Allan Jones Marjorie Lord

1943 RHYTHM OF THE ISLANDS
Director: Roy William Neill
Co-stars: Alan Jones Andy Devine Mary Wickes

1943 HI YA CHUM
Director: Harold Young
Co-stars: Robert Paige June Clyde Ritz Brothers

1944 BEAUTIFUL BUT BROKE
Director: Charles Barton
Co-stars: Joan Davis John Hubbard Judy Clark

1944 KANSA CITY KITTY

1944 ROSIE THE RIVETER
Director: Joseph Santly
Co-stars: Frank Albertson Vera Vague Frank Jenks

1944 PRACTICALLY YOURS
Director: Mitchell Leisen
Co-stars: Claudette Colbert Fred MacMurray

1946 A GUY COULD CHANGE

1947 CALENDAR GIRL
Director: Allan Dwan
Co-stars: Kenny Baker Victor McLaglen Irene Rich Gail Patrick

1948 UNDER CALIFORNIA STARS
Director: William Whitney
Co-stars: Roy Rogers Andy Devine

SHELIA FRASIER

1972 SUPERFLY
Director: Gordon Parks
Co-stars: Ron O'Neal Carl Lee

1978 CALIFORNIA SUITE
Director: Herbert Ross
Co-stars: Michael Caine Maggie Smith Walter Matthau

CAROL FRAZER

1984 THE BOX OF DELIGHTS
Director: Renny Rye
Co-stars: Patrick Troughton Devin Stansfield Robert Stephens

LYNNE FREDERICK (Married Peter Sellers)

1970 NO BLADE OF GRASS
Director: Cornel Wilde
Co-stars: Nigel Davenport Jean Wallace Patrick Holt

1971 NICHOLAS AND ALEXANDRA
Director: Franklin Schaffner
Co-stars: Michael Jayston Janet Suzman Tom Baker

1971 VAMPIRE CIRCUS
Director: Robert Young
Co-stars: Adrienne Corri Laurence Payne Elizabeth Seal

1972 THE AMAZING MR. BLUNDEN
Director: Lionel Jeffries
Co-stars: Laurence Naismith Diana Dors David Lodge

1972 HENRY VIII AND HIS SIX WIVES
Director: Waris Hussein
Co-stars: Keith Michell Jane Asher Frances Cuka

1973 PHASE IV
Director: Saul Bass
Co-stars: Nigel Davenport Michael Murphy Alan Gifford

1976 VOYAGE OF THE DAMNED
Director: Stuart Rossenberg
Co-stars: Faye Dunaway Orson Welles James Mason

1979 THE PRISONER OF ZENDA
Director: Richard Quine
Co-stars: Peter Sellers Lionel Jeffries Elke Sommer

PAULINE FREDERICK

1924 MARRIED FLIRTS

1924 THREE WOMEN
Director: Ernst Lubitsch
Co-stars: Lew Cody May McAvoy Marie Prevost

1931 THIS MODERN AGE
Director: Nick Grinde
Co-stars: Joan Crawford Neil Hamilton Monroe Owsley

1932 PHANTOM OF CRESTWOOD
Director: Walter Ruben
Co-stars: Ricardo Cortez Anita Louise H.B. Warner

1934 SOCIAL REGISTER
Director: Marshall Neilan
Co-stars: Colleen Moore Charles Winninger Robert Benchley

1936 RAMONA
Director: Henry King
Co-stars: Loretta Young Don Ameche Katherine DeMille

1936 MY MARRIAGE
Director: George Archinbaud
Co-stars: Claire Trevor Kent Taylor Paul Kelly

1938 THANK YOU MR. MOTO
Director: Norman Foster
Co-stars: Peter Lorre Sidney Blackmer

VICKI FREDERICK

1981 ...ALL THE MARBLES
Director: Robert Aldrich
Co-stars: Peter Falk Laurene Landen Burt Young

1985 A CHORUS LINE
Director: Richard Attenborough
Co-stars: Michael Douglas Terence Mann Alyson Reed

1990 CHOPPER CHICKS IN ZOMBIE TOWN
Director: Dan Hoskins
Co-stars: Jamie Rose Catherine Carlen

PHYLLIS FRELICH (Member Of America's National Theatre Of The Deaf)

1985 LOVE IS NEVER SILENT
Director: Joseph Sargent
Co-stars: Mare Winningham Ed Waterstreet Sid Caesar

DAMITA JO FREEMAN

1981 SHE'S IN THE ARMY NOW
Director: Hy Averbach
Co-stars: Kathleen Quinlan Melanie Griffith Rocky Bauer

DEBORAH FREEMAN

1988 WAXWORKS
Director: Anthony Hickox
Co-stars: Zach Galligan Michelle Johnson Miles O'Keefe

DEENA FREEMAN

1983 DEADLY LESSONS
Director: William Wiard
Co-stars: Donna Reed Larry Wilcox Ally Sheedy

HELEN FREEMAN
(Co-Founder Of The Theatre Guild)

1933 SONG OF SONGS
Director: Rouben Mamoulian
Co-stars: Marlene Dietrich Brian Aherne Lionel Atwill

1934 NANA
Director: Dorothy Arzner
Co-stars: Anna Sten Phillips Holmes Lionel Atwill

1944 MADEMOISELLE FIFI
Director: Robert Wise
Co-stars: Simone Simon Kurt Kreuger John Emery

1946 SO DARK THE NIGHT
Director: Joseph Lewis
Co-stars: Steven Geray Ann Codee Micheleine Cheirel

JOAN FREEMAN

1962 PANIC IN THE YEAR ZERO
Director: Ray Milland
Co-stars: Ray Milland Jean Hagen Frankie Avalon

1962 TOWER OF LONDON
Director: Roger Corman
Co-stars: Vincent Price Michael Pate Sara Salby

1964 ROUSTABOUT
Director: John Rich
Co-stars: Elvis Presley Barbara Stanwyck Sue Ann Langdon

1965 THE ROUNDERS
Director: Burt Kennedy
Co-stars: Henry Fonda Glenn Ford Kathleen Freeman

1967 THE RELUCTANT ASTRONAUT
Director: Edward Montagne
Co-stars: Don Knotts Leslie Nielsen Arthur O'Connell

1967 THE FASTEST GUITAR ALIVE
Director: Michael Moore
Co-stars: Roy Orbison Sammy Jackson Lyle Bettger

KATHLEEN FREEMAN

1950 HOUSE BY THE RIVER
Director: Fritz Lang
Co-stars: Louis Hayward Jane Wyatt Lee Bowman

1958 THE FLY
Director: Kurt Neumann
Co-stars: David Hedison Patricia Owens Vincent Price

1960 NORTH TO ALASKA
Director: Henry Hathaway
Co-stars: John Wayne Stewart Granger Capucine

1962 MADISON AVENUE
Director: Bruce Humberstone
Co-stars: Dana Andrews Eleanor Parker Jeanne Crain

1963 THE NUTTY PROFESSOR
Director: Jerry Lewis
Co-stars: Jerry Lewis Stella Stevens Howard Morris

1964 THE DISORDERLY ORDERLY
Director: Frank Tashlin
Co-stars: Jerry Lewis Glenda Farrell Everett Sloane

1965 THE ROUNDERS
Director: Burt Kennedy
Co-stars: Henry Fonda Glenn Ford Chill Wills

1970 THE BALLAD OF CABLE HOGUE
Director: Sam Peckinpah
Co-stars: Jason Robards David Warner

1980 THE BLUES BROTHERS
Director: John Landis
Co-stars: John Belushi Dan Aykroyd Carrie Fisher

1987 THE WOO WOO KID
Director: Phil Aden Robinson
Co-stars: Patrick Dempsey Talia Balsam Beverly D'Angelo

1993 NAKED GUN 33 1/3 : THE FINAL INSULT
Director: Peter Segal
Co-stars: Leslie Nielsen Fred Ward Priscilla Presley

1993 RECKLESS KELLY
Director: Yahoo Serious
Co-stars: Yahoo Serious Melora Hardin Alexei Sayle

MONA FREEMAN

1944 TILL WE MEET AGAIN
Director: Frank Borzage
Co-stars: Ray Milland Barbara Britton Walter Slezak

1944 TOGETHER AGAIN
Director: Charles Vidor
Co-stars: Irene Dunne Charles Boyer Charles Coburn

1945 JUNIOR MISS
Director: George Seaton
Co-stars: Peggy Ann Garner Allyn Joslyn Michael Dunne

1945 DANGER SIGNAL
Director: Robert Florey
Co-stars: Zachary Scott Faye Emmerson Richard Erdman

1946 BLACK BEAUTY
Director: Max Nosseck
Co-stars: Richard Denning Evelyn Ankers Terry Kilburn

1946 THAT BRENNAN GIRL
Director: Alfred Santell
Co-stars: James Dunn June Duprez William Marshall

1947 DEAR RUTH
Director: William Russell
Co-stars: Joan Caulfield William Holden Billy DeWolfe

1947 MOTHER WORE TIGHTS
Director: Walter Lang
Co-stars: Betty Grable Dan Dailey Connie Marshall

1948 ISN'T IT ROMANTIC
Director: Norman Z McLeod
Co-stars: Veronica Lake Patric Knowles Billy DeWolfe

1949 THE HEIRESS
Director: William Wyler
Co-stars: Olivia De Havilland Montgomery Clift

1949 STREETS OF LAREDO
Director: Leslie Fenton
Co-stars: William Holden William Bendix MacDonald Carey

1949 DEAR WIFE
Director: Richard Haydn
Co-stars: William Holden Joan Caulfield Edward Arnold

1950 COPPER CANYON
Director: John Farrow
Co-stars: Ray Milland Hedy Lamarr MacDonald Carey

1950 BRANDED
Director: Rudolph Mate
Co-stars: Alan Ladd Charles Bickford Robert Keith

1951 DEAR BRAT
Director: William Seiter
Co-stars: Billy De Wolfe Edward Arnold Lyle Bettger

1951 DARLING, HOW COULD YOU
Director: Mitchell Leisen
Co-stars: Joan Fontaine John Lund Peter Hanson

1951 THE LADY FROM TEXAS
Director: Joseph Pevney
Co-stars: Josephine Hull Howard Duff Gene Lockhart

1952 THUNDERBIRDS
Director: John Auer
Co-stars: John Derek John Barrymore Jnr. Gene Evans

1952 JUMPING JACKS
Director: Norman Taurog
Co-stars: Dean Martin Jerry Lewis Robert Strauss Don Defore

1952 FLESH AND FURY
Director: Joseph Pevney
Co-stars: Tony Curtis Jan Sterling Wallace Ford

1952 ANGEL FACE
Director: Otto Preminger
Co-stars: Jean Simmons Robert Mitchum Herbert Marshall

1955 BATTLE CRY
Director: Raoul Walsh
Co-stars: Van Heflin Dorothy Malone Aldo Ray Tab Hunter

1955 ROAD TO DENVER
Director: Joe Kane
Co-stars: John Payne Skip Homeier Lee J. Cobb Lee Van Cleef

1956 HUK!
Director: John Barnwell
Co-stars: George Montgomery John Baer James Bell

1956 HOLD BACK THE NIGHT
Director: Allan Dwan
Co-stars: John Payne Peter Graves Chuck Connors Audrey Dalton

1957 DRAGON WELLES MASACRE
Director: Harold Schuster
Co-stars: Barry Sullivan Dennis O'Keefe Katy Jurado

STEPHANIE FREISS

1990 THE KING'S WHORE
Director: Alex Corti
Co-stars: Timothy Dalton Valeria Golino Margaret Tyzack

DAWN FRENCH

1985 THE SUPERGRASS
Director: Peter Richardson
Co-stars: Peter Richardson Jennifer Saunders Adrian Edmondson

1987 EAT THE RICH
Director: Peter Richardson
Co-stars: Peter Richardson Jennifer Saunders Fiona Richmond

1988 THE STRIKE
Director: Peter Richardson
Co-stars: Peter Richardson Robbie Coltrane Nigel Planer

1993 TENDER LOVING CARE
Director: Dewi Humphreys
Co-stars: Rosemary Leach Joan Sims Peter Jones

1996 THE ADVENTURES OF PINOCHIO
Co-stars: John Sessions Griff Rhys-Jones

VALERIE FRENCH

1955 JUBAL
Director: Delmer Daves
Co-stars: Glenn Ford Ernest Borgnine Felicia Farr Charles Bronson

1957 THE GARMENT JUNGLE
Director: Robert Aldrich
Co-stars: Lee J. Cobb Gia Scala Richard Boone

1957 DECISION AT SUNDOWN
Director: Budd Boetticher
Co-stars: Randolph Scott John Carroll Karen Steele

1959 THE FOUR SKULLS OF JONATHAN DRAKE
Director: Edward Cahn
Co-stars: Henry Daniell Eduard Franz

1968 SHALAKO
Director: Edward Dmytryk
Co-stars: Sean Connery Brigitte Bardot Stephen Boyd

YVONNE FRENCH

1986 HONEST, DECENT AND TRUE
Director: Les Blair
Co-stars: Derrick O'Connor Richard E. Grant Gary Oldman

BRENDA FRICKER *(Married Barry Davies)*
Oscar For Best Supporting Actress In 1989 For My Left Foot

1968 SINFUL DAVY
Director: John Huston
Co-stars: John Hurt Pamela Franklin Ronald Fraser

1985 EXPLOITS AT WEST POLEY
Director: Diarmund Lawrence
Co-star: Anthony Page

1988 THE PICNIC
Director: Paul Seed
Co-stars: Billie Whitelaw Iain Glenn Cassie Stuart

1989 MY LEFT FOOT
Director: Jim Sheridan
Co-stars: Daniel-Day Lewis Ray McAnally Fiona Shaw

1990 THE FIELD
Director: Jim Sheridan
Co-stars: Richard Harris John Hurt Tom Berenger Sean Bean

1992 SEEKERS
Director: Peter Barber-Flemin
Co-stars: Joshette Simon Michael Carter Rachel Wilkinson

1992 UTZ
Director: George Sluizer
Co-stars: Armin Muller-Stahl Peter Riegert Paul Scofield

1992 HOME ALONE 2
Director: Chris Columbus
Co-stars: Macauley Culkin Joe Pesci Catherine O'Hara

1993 SO I MARRIED AN AXE MURDERER
Director: Thomas Schlamme
Co-stars: Mike Myers Nancy Travis

1994 A MAN OF NO IMPORTANCE
Director: Suri Krisnamma
Co-stars: Albert Finney Tara Fitzgerald Rufus Sewell

1994 DEADLY ADVICE
Co-stars: Mandie Fletcher
Co-stars: Jane Horrocks Imelda Staunton Jonathan Pryce

1996 A TIME TO KILL
Director: John Schumacher
Co-stars: Matthew McConaughey Sandra Bullock Kevin Spacey

1997 MOLL FLANDERS
Director: Pen Densham
Co-stars: Robin Wright Morgan Freeman Stockard Channing

1998 RESURRECTION MAN
Director: Marc Evans
Co-star: Stuart Townsend

BLANCHE FRIDERICI

1928 SADIE THOMPSON
Director: Raoul Walsh
Co-stars: Gloria Swanson Lionel Barrymore Charles Lane

1930 COURAGE
Director: Archie Mayo
Co-stars: Belle Bennett Marian Nixon Rex Bell

1930 THE CAT CREEPS
Director: Rupert Julian
Co-stars: Helen Twelvetrees Neil Hamilton Jean Hersholt

1930 THE BAD ONE
Director: George Fitzmaurice
Co-stars: Dolores Del Rio Edmund Lowe Don Alvarado

1930 BILLY THE KID
Director: King Vidor
Co-stars: Johnny Mack Brown Wallace Beery Kay Johnson

1931 MURDER BY THE CLOCK
Director: Edward Sloman
Co-stars: Lilyann Tashman William Boyd Regis Toomey

1931 A LADY WITH A PAST
Director: Edward Griffith
Co-stars: Constance Bennett Ben Lyon David Manners

1931 TEN CENTS A DANCE
Director: Lionel Barrymore
Co-stars: Barbara Stanwyck Ricardo Cortez

1931 MATA HARI
Director: George Fitzmaurice
Co-stars: Greta Garbo Ramon Navarro Lionel Barrymore

1931 HONOR OF THE FAMILY
Director: Lloyd Bacon
Co-stars: Bebe Daniels Warren William Alan Mowbray

1931 NIGHT NURSE
Director: William Wellman
Co-stars: Barbara Stanwyck Ben Lyon Clark Gable Joan Blondell

1932 THE HATCHETT MAN
Director: Fred Zinnemann
Co-stars: Edward G. Robinson Loretta Young Lesley Fenton

1932 A FAREWELL TO ARMS
Director: Frank Borzage
Co-stars: Gary Cooper Helen Hayes Adolphe Menjou

1932 LOVE ME TONIGHT
Director: Rouben Mamoulian
Co-stars: Maurice Chevalier Jeanette MacDonald Myrna Loy

1932 NIGHT CLUB LADY
Director: Irving Cummings
Co-stars: Adolphe Menjou Mayo Methot Skeets Gallagher

1933 ADORABLE
Director: William Dieterle
Co-stars: Janet Gaynor Henri Garat Herbert Mundin

1933 AGGIE APPLEBY, MAKER OF MEN
Director: Mark Sandrich
Co-stars: Wynne Gibson William Gargan

1933 THE WAY TO LOVE
Director: Norman Taurog
Co-stars: Maurice Chevalier Ann Dvorak Edward Everett Horton

1933 FLYING DOWN TO RIO
Director: Thornton Freeland
Co-stars: Ginger Rogers Fred Astaire Dolores Del Rio

1933 SECRETS
Director: Frank Borzage
Co-star: Mary Pickford Leslie Howard Doris Lloyd

1934 ALL OF ME
Director: James Flood
Co-stars: Fredric March Miriam Hopkins George Raft

1934 IT HAPPENED ONE NIGHT
Director: Frank Capra
Co-stars: Clark Gable Claudette Colbert Alan Hale

GERTRUD FRIDH

1964 NOW ABOUT THESE WOMEN
Director: Ingmar Bergman
Co-stars: Jarl Kulle Eva Dahlbeck Harriet Andersson

ALICE FRIEDLAND

1976 THE KILLING OF A CHINESE BOOKIE
Director: John Cassavetes
Co-stars: Ben Gazzara Seymour Cassel

MARIA FRIEDMANN

1993 BLACK DAISIES FOR THE BRIDE
Director: Peter Symes
Co-stars: Elaine Hallam Cathryn Bradshaw

ANNA FRIEL

1997 LAND GIRLS
Director: David Leland
Co-stars: Catherine McCormack Rachel Weisz Maureen O'Brien

1998 THE TRIBE
Director: Stephen Poliakoff
Co-stars: Joely Richardson Jeremy Northam George Costigan

RACHEL FRIEND

1985 FROG DREAMING
Director: Brian Trenchard Smith
Co-stars: Henry Thomas Tony Barry

INGE FRIES

1924 ENTR'ACTE
Director: Rene Clair
Co-stars: Jean Borlin Francis Picabia Georges Auric

TRIXIE FRIGANZA

1930 FREE AND EASY
Director: Edward Sedgwick
Co-stars: Buster Keaton Anita Page Robert Montgomery

REBECCA FRITH

1996 LOVE SERENADE
Director: Shirley Barrett
Co-star: Miranda Otto

MARGARET FRITTS

1919 THE FALL OF BABYLON
Director: D.W. Griffith
Co-stars: Tully Marshall Constance Talmadge

CORNELIA FROBOESS

1982 VERONIKA VOSS
Director: Rainer Werner Fassbinder
Co-stars: Rosel Zech Hilmar Thate Doris Schade

EWA FROLING

1982 FANNY AND ALEXANDER
Director: Ingmar Bergman
Co-stars: Gunn Wallgren Christina Schollin

1992 THE OX
Director: Sven Nykvist
Co-stars: Stellan Skarsgard Max Von Sydow Liv Ullmann

JANE FROMAN

1935 STARS OVER BROADWAY
Director: William Keighley
Co-stars: James Melton Pat O'Brien Jean Muir

1938 RADIO CITY REVELS
Director: Ben Stoloff
Co-stars: Bob Burns Jack Oakie Ann Miller

LAUREN FROST

1974 HESTER STREET
Director: Joan Micklin Silver
Co-stars: Steven Keats Carol Kane Mel Howard

LINDSAY FROST

1991 DANIEL STEELE'S PALOMINO
Director: Michael Miller
Co-stars: Lee Horsley Eva Marie Saint Rod Taylor

1992 IN THE SHADOW OF A KILLER
Director: Alan Metzger
Co-stars: Scott Bakula J.T. Walsh Miguel Ferrer

1993 MONOLITH
Director: John Eyres
Co-stars: Bill Paxton John Hurt

POLLY FROST

1990 THE BIG BANG
Director: James Toback
Co-stars: Missy Boyd Sheila Kennedy Charles Lassiter

SADIE FROST

1989 DIAMOND SKULLS
Director: Nicholas Broomfield
Co-stars: Gabriel Byrne Amanda Donohue Judy Parfitt

1992 SPLITTING HEIRS
Director: Robert Young
Co-stars: Eric Idle Rick Moranis Barbara Hershey

1992 BRAM STOKER'S DRACULA
Director: Francis Coppola
Co-stars: Gary Oldman Winona Ryder Anthony Hopkins

1994 THE CISCO KID
Director: Luis Valdez
Co-stars: Jimmy Smits Cheech Marin Bruce Payne

1994 SHOPPING
Director: Paul Anderson
Co-stars: Jude Law Sean Bean Marianne Faithfull

1996 CRIME TIME
Director: George Sluizer
Co-stars: Pete Postlethwaite Stephen Baldwin

KATHY FRYE

1943 THREE RUSSIAN GIRLS
Director: Henry Kesler
Co-stars: Anna Sten Kent Smith Mimi Forsythe

SOLEIL MOON FRYE

1987 YOU RUINED MY LIFE
Director: David Ashwell
Co-stars: Paul Reiser Mimi Rogers

1994 THE ST. TAMMANY MIRACLE
Director: Joy Houck Jnr.
Co-stars: Mark Paul Gosselaar Jamie Luner

1996 THE KILLING SECRET
Director: Noel Nosseck
Co-stars: Ari Meyers Tess Harper

DOLORES FULLER

1953 GLEN OR GLENDA
Director: Edward Wood
Co-stars: Daniel Davis Lyle Talbot Bela Lugosi

FRANCES FULLER

1933 ONE SUNDAY AFTERNON
Director: Stephen Roberts
Co-stars: Gary Cooper Fay Wray Neil Hamilton

1934 ELMER AND ELSIE
Director: Gilbert Pratt
Co-stars: George Bancroft Roscoe Karns Nella Walker

PENNY FULLER

1972 WOMEN IN CHAINS
Director: Bernard Kowalski
Co-stars: Ida Lupino Lois Nettleton Jessica Walker

1976 ALL THE PRESIDENT'S MEN
Director: Alan J. Pakula
Co-stars: Robert Redford Dustin Hoffman Ned Beatty

1980 AMBER WAVES
Director: Joseph Sargent
Co-stars: Mare Winningham Kurt Russell Dennis Weaver

1982 A PIANO FOR MRS. CIMINO
Director: George Schaefer
Co-stars: Bette Daxis Keenan Wynn George Hearn

1984 LICENCE TO KILL
Director: Jud Taylor
Co-stars: James Farentino Don Murray Millie Perkins

1984 CAT ON A HOT TIN ROOF
Director: Jacky Hofsiss
Co-stars: Jessica Lang Tommy Lee Jones Kim Stanley

1986 AS SUMMERS DIE
Director: Jean-Claude Tramont
Co-stars: Scott Glen Jaimie Lee Curtis Bette Davis

1987 AT MOTHER'S REQUEST
Director: Michael Tuchner
Co-stars: Stefanie Powers Frances Sternhagen John Wood

1987 THE TWO MRS. GRENVILLES
Director: John Erman
Co-stars: Ann-Margret Claudette Colbert Sam Wanamaker

1994 THE GIFT OF LOVE
Director: Paul Bogart
Co-stars: Andy Griffith Blair Brown Olivia Burnette

FIONA FULLERTON (*Child*)

1969 RUN WILD, RUN FREE
Director: Richard Sarafian
Co-stars: John Mills Sylvia Syms Mark Lester

1971　NICHOLAS AND ALEXANDRA
Director: Franklin Schaffner
Co-stars: Michael Jayston Janet Suzman Tom Baker

1972　ALICE'S ADVENTURES IN WONDERLAND
Director: William Sterling
Co-stars: Michael Crawford Dudley Moore

1985　A VIEW TO A KILL
Director: John Glen
Co-stars: Roger Moore Christopher Walken Grace Jones

1987　A HAZARD OF HEARTS
Director: John Hough
Co-stars: Helena Bonham-Carter Diana Rigg Edward Fox

**1990　SPYMAKER: THE SECRET
　　　　LIFE OF IAN FLEMING**
Director: Ferdinand Fairfax
Co-star: Jason Connery Joss Ackland Kristen Scott Thomas

1991　TO BE THE BEST
Director: Tony Wharmby
Co-stars: Anthony Hopkins Lindsay Wagner Stuart Wilson

1992　THE BOGIE MAN
Director: Charles Gormley
Co-stars: Robbie Coltrane Jean Anderson Midge Ure

CHRISTINA FULTON

**1993　THE RED SHOE DIARIES:
　　　　ANOTHER WOMAN'S LIPSTICK**
Director: Zalman King
Co-star: Maryam D'Abo

JESSIE LEE FULTON

1974　BUSTER AND BILLIE
Director: Daniel Petrie
Co-stars: Jan-Michael Vincent Joan Goodfellow

JOAN FULTON

1946　BUCK PRIVATES COME HOME
Director: Charles Barton
Co-stars: Bud Abbott Lou Costello Nat Pendleton

1946　CUBAN PETE
Director: Jean Yarborough
Co-stars: Desi Arnaz Beverly Simmons Don Porter

JULIE FULTON

1991　LETHAL CHARGE
Director: Richard Michaels
Co-stars: Stuart Wilson Barbara Eden Heather Locklear

WENDY FULTON

1983　THE FIRST TIME
Director: Charlie Loventhal
Co-stars: Tim Choate Krista Errickson Jane Badler

ANNETTE FUNICELLO *(Child)*

1959　THE SHAGGY DOG
Director: Fred MacMurray Jean Hagen Tommy Kirk

1961　THE HORSEMASTERS
Director: William Fairchild

1961　BABES IN TOYLAND
Director: Jack Donohue
Co-stars: Ray Bolger Tommy Sands Tommy Kirk

1962　ESCAPADE IN FLORENCE
Director: Steve Previn
Co-stars: Ivan Desny Tommy Kirk Nino Castelnuovo

1963　BEACH PARTY
Director: William Asher
Co-stars: Robert Cummings Frankie Avalon Dorothy Malone

1964　BIKINI BEACH
Director: William Asher
Co-stars: Frankie Avalon Martha Hyer Keenan Wynn

1964　MUSCLE BEACH PARTY
Director: William Asher
Co-stars: Frankie Avalon Don Rickles Luciana Palucci

1965　HOW TO STUFF A WILD BIKINI
Director: William Asher
Co-stars: Frankie Avalon Mickey Rooney

1965　THE MONKEY'S UNCLE
Director: Robert Stevenson
Co-stars: Tommy Kirk Leon Ames Arthur O'Connell

1968　HEAD
Director: Bob Rafaelson
Co-stars: The Monkees Victor Mature Teri Garr Jack Nicholson

1987　BACK TO THE BEACH
Director: Lyndall Hobbs
Co-stars: Frankie Avalon Connie Stevens Lori Loughlin

MIRA FURLAN

1993　BABYLON 5
Director: Richard Compton
Co-stars: Michael O'Hare Tamlyn Tomita Jerry Doyle

YVONNE FURNEAUX

1953　THE MASTER OF BALLANTRAE
Director: William Keighley
Co-stars: Errol Flynn Anthony Steel Roger Livesey

1955　LE AMICHE
Director: Michaelangelo Antonioni
Co-stars: Valentina Cortesa Gabriele Ferzetti

1955　THE DARK AVENGER
Director: Henry Levin
Co-stars: Errol Flynn Peter Finch Joanne Dru

1956　LISBON
Director: Ray Milland
Co-stars: Ray Milland Claude Rains Maureen O'Hara Francis Lederer

1959　THE MUMMY
Director: Terence Fisher
Co-stars: Peter Cushing Christopher Lee Felix Aylmer

1960　LA DOLCE VITA
Director: Frederico Fellini
Co-stars: Marcello Mastroianni Anita Ekberg Nadia Gray

1961　THE COUNT OF MONTE CRISTO
Director: Claude Autant-Lara
Co-stars: Louis Jordan Pierre Mondy

1965　REPULSION
Director: Roman Polanski
Co-stars: Catherine Deneuve Ian Hendry Patrick Wymark

1968　THE CHAMPAGNE MURDERS
Director: Claude Chabrol
Co-stars: Anthony Perkins Maurice Ronet Suzanne Lloyd

BETTY FURNESS

1933　AGGIE APPLEBY, MAKER OF MEN
Director: Mark Sandrich
Co-stars: Wynne Gibson Charles Farrell William Gargan

1933　CROSS FIRE
Director: Otto Brower
Co-stars: Tom Keene Edgar Kennedy

1933　PROFESSIONAL SWEETHEART
Director: William Seiter
Co-stars: Ginger Rogers Gregory Ratoff Zasu Pitts

1934 A WICKED WOMAN
Director: Charles Brabin
Co-stars: Mady Christians Charles Bickford Robert Taylor

1934 THE LIFE OR VERGIE WINTERS
Co-stars: Frank Albertson Ann Harding John Boles

1934 DANGEROUS CORNER
Director: Phil Rossen
Co-stars: Melvyn Douglas Virginia Bruce Conrad Nagel

1934 BEGGARS IN ERMINE
Director: Phil Rosen
Co-stars: Lionel Atwill Henry B. Walthall

1934 THE BAND PLAYED ON
Director: Russell Mack
Co-stars: Robert Young Stuart Erwin Leo Carrillo

1935 HERE COMES COOKIE
Director: Norman Z McLeod
Co-stars: George Burns Gracie Allen George Barbier

1935 KEEPER OF THE BEES
Director: Christy Cabanne
Co-stars: Neil Hamilton Emma Dunn Edith Fellows

1935 MAGNIFICENT OBSESSION
Director: John Stahl
Co-stars: Irene Dunne Robert Taylor Ralph Morgan

1935 McFADDEN'S FLATS
Director: Ralph Murphy
Co-stars: Walter Kelly Andy Clyde Jane Darwell

1936 MISTER CINDERELLA
Director: Edward Sedgwick
Co-stars: Jack Haley Arthur Treacher Raymond Walburn

1936 ALL AMERICAN CHUMP
Co-star: Robert Armstrong

1936 SWING TIME
Director: George Stevens
Co-stars: Fred Astaire Ginger Rogers Victor Moore

1936 THE PRESIDENT'S MYSTERY
Co-star: Henry Wilcoxon

1936 CALM YOURSELF
Director: George Seitz
Co-stars: Robert Young Madge Evans Nat Pendleton Ralph Morgan

1937 THEY WANTED TO MARRY
Co-star: Gordon Jones

1937 FAIR WARNING
Director: Norman Foster
Co-stars: J. Edward Bromberg John Payne Victor Killian

1937 MAMA STEPS OUT
Co-star: Guy Kibbee

1937 THE GOOD OLD SOAK
Director: Walter Ruben
Co-stars: Wallace Beery Una Merkel Eric Linden

DEBORRA-LEE FURNESS

1985 JENNY KISSED ME
Director: Brian Trenchard-Smith
Co-stars: Ivar Kants Tamsin West Paula Duncan

1989 SHAME
Director: Steve Jodrell
Co-stars: Tony Barry Simone Buchanan Gillian Jones

1990 THE LAST OF THE FINEST
Director: John MacKenzie
Co-stars: Brian Dennehy Joe Pantoliano Jeff Fahey

1990 BLUE HEAT
Director: John MacKenzie
Co-stars: Brian Dennehy Joe Pantoliano Jeff Fahey

JUDITH FURSE

1939 GOODBYE, MR. CHIPS
Director: Sam Wood
Co-stars: Robert Donat Greer Garson Paul Henreid John Mills

1945 JOHNNY FRENCHMAN
Director: Charles Frend
Co-stars: Francoise Rosay Tom Walls Patricia Roc

1946 BLACK NARCISSUS
Director: Michael Powell
Co-stars: Deborah Kerr David Farrar Jean Simmons Sabu

1949 DEAR MR. PROHACK
Director: Thornton Freeland
Co-stars: Cecil Parker Hermione Baddeley Dirk Bogarde

1957 BLUE MURDER AT ST. TRINIANS
Director: Frank Launder
Co-stars: Alastair Sim George Cole Terry-Thomas

1963 CARRY ON CABBY
Director: Gerald Thomas
Co-stars: Sid James Hattie Jacques Liz Fraser

1964 CARRY ON SPYING
Director: Gerald Thomas
Co-stars: Kenneth Williams Barbara Windsor Eric Barker

IRA FURSTENBERG

1967 I KILLED RASPUTIN
Director: Robert Hossein
Co-stars: Gert Frobe Peter McEnery Geraldine Chaplin

1968 THE BATTLE OF EL ALAMEIN
Director: Calvin Jackson Padget
Co-stars: Frederick Stafford Michael Rennie

1969 DEAD RUN
Director: Christian-Jacque
Co-stars: Peter Lawford Georges Geret Maria Bucella

1970 HELLO-GOODBYE
Director: Jean Negulesco
Co-stars: Michael Crawford Genevieve Gilles Curt Jurgens

CATRIN FYCHAN

1992 HEDD WYN: THE ARMAGEDDON POET
Director: Paul Turner
Co-stars: Huw Garmon Ceri Cunnington Gwen Ellis

VICTORIA FYODOROVA

1985 TARGET
Director: Arthur Penn
Co-stars: Gene Hackman Matt Dillon Gayle Hunnicutt

FRANCISKA GAAL

1938 THE BUCKANEER
Director: Cecil B DeMille
Co-stars: Fredric March Akim Tamiroff Walter Brennan

1938 PARIS HONEYMOON
Director: Frank Tuttle
Co-stars: Bing Crosby Akim Tamiroff

1938 THE GIRL DOWNSTAIRS
Director: Norman Taurog
Co-stars: Franchot Tone Walter Connolly Rita Johnson

SCILLA GABEL

1956 MODESTY BLAISE
Director: Joseph Losey
Co-stars: Monica Vitti Dirk Bogarde Terence Stamp

1959 TARZAN'S GREATEST ADVENTURE
Director: John Guillermin
Co-stars: Gordon Scott Anthony Quayle Sean Connery

1960 QUEEN OF THE PIRATES
Director: Mario Costa
Co-stars: Gianna Maria Canale Massimo Serato Paul Muller

1961 VILLAGE OF DAUGHTERS
Director: George Pollock
Co-stars: Eric Sykes Warren Mitchell Carol White

1962 SODDOM AND GOMORRAH
Director: Robert Aldrich
Co-stars: Stewart Granger Stanley Baker Pier Angeli

OYANKA GABEZAS

1996 CARLA'S SONG
Director: Ken Loach
Co-stars: Robert Carlyle Scott Glenn

LOUISE GABO

1934 MYSTERY RANCH
Co-stars: Tom Tyler Roberta Gale Jack Perrin

EVA GABOR

1941 FORCED LANDING
Co-star: Richard Arlen

1942 PACIFIC BLACKOUT
Director: Ralph Murphy
Co-stars: Robert Preston Martha O'Driscoll

1953 PARIS MODEL
Director: Alfred Green
Co-stars: Paulette Goddard Marilyn Maxwell Barbara Lawrence

1954 THE MAD MAGICIAN
Director: John Brahm
Co-stars: Vincent Price Mary Murphy John Emery

1954 THE LAST TIME I SAW PARIS
Director: Richards Brooks
Co-stars: Elizabeth Taylor Van Johnson Donna Reed

1954 CAPTAIN KIDD AND THE SLAVE GIRL
Director: Lew Landers
Co-stars: Anthony Dexter Alan Hale James Seay

1955 ARTISTS AND MODELS
Director: Frank Tashlin
Co-stars: Dean Martin Jerry Lewis Shirley MacLaine

1957 DON'T GO NEAR THE WATER
Director: Charles Walters
Co-stars: Glenn Ford Gia Scala Fred Clark

1957 MY MAN GODFREY
Director: Henry Koster
Co-stars: David Niven June Allyson Martha Hyer Robert Keith

1957 THE TRUTH ABOUT WOMEN
Director: Muriel Box
Co-stars: Laurence Harvey Mai Zetterling Julie Harris

1958 GIGI
Director: Vincente Minnelli
Co-stars: Leslie Caron Maurice Chevalier Louis Jordan

1959 IT STARTED WITH A KISS
Director: George Marshall
Co-stars: Glenn Ford Debbie Reynolds Fred Clark

1964 YOUNGBLOOD HAWKE
Director: Delmer Daves
Co-stars: James Franciscus Genevieve Page Mary Astor

1970 THE ARISTOCRATS *(Voice)*
Director: Wolfgang Reitherman
Co-stars: Maurice Chevalier Phil Harris Hermione Baddeley

1977 THE RESCUERS *(Voice)*
Director: Art Stevens
Co-stars: Bob Newhart Geraldine Page John McIntyre

1990 RETURN TO GREEN ACRES
Director: William Asher
Co-star: Eddie Albert

ZSA ZSA GABOR *(Married George Sanders)*

1952 MOULIN ROUGE
Director: John Huston
Co-stars: Jose Ferrer Colette Marchand Katherine Kath

1952 LOVELY TO LOOK AT
Director: Mervyn LeRoy
Co-stars: Howard Keel Kathryn Grayson Ann Miller

1952 WE'RE NOT MARRIED
Director: Edmund Goulding
Co-stars: Victor Moore Ginger Rogers Marilyn Monroe

1953 LILI
Director: Charles Walters
Co-stars: Leslie Caron Mel Ferrer Jean-Pierre Aumont Kurt Kaznar

1953 THE STORY OF THREE LOVES
Director: Vincente Minnelli
Co-stars: Kirk Douglas James Mason Pier Angeli

1954 THREE RING CIRCUS
Director: Joseph Pevney
Co-stars: Dean Martin Jerry Lewis Joanne Dru Elsa Lanchester

1956 DEATH OF A SCOUNDREL
Director: Charles Martin
Co-stars: George Sanders Yvonne De Carlo Coleen Gray

1957 THE GIRL IN THE KREMLIN
Director: Russell Birdwell
Co-stars: Lex Barker Jeffrey Stone

1958 THE MAN WHO WOULDN'T TALK
Director: Herbert Wilcox
Co-stars: Anna Neagle Anthony Quale Dora Bryan

1958 QUEEN OF OUTER SPACE
Director: Edward Bearnds
Co-stars: Eric Fleming Paul Birch Barbara Darrow

1959 FOR THE FIRST TIME
Director: Rudolph Mate
Co-stars: Mario Lanza Johanna Von Kozzian Kurt Kasznar

1960 PEPE
Director: George Sidney
Co-stars: Bing Crosby Judy Garland Frank Sinatra Maurice Chevalier

1966 PICTURE MOMMY DEAD
Director: Bert Gordon
Co-stars: Don Ameche Martha Hyer Susan Gordon

1966 DROP DEAD DARLING
Director: Ken Hughes
Co-stars: Tony Curtis Rosanna Schiaffino Nancy Kwan

1967 JACK OF DIAMONDS
Director: Don Taylor
Co-stars: Joseph Cotten George Hamilton Carroll Baker

1972 UP THE FRONT
Director: Bob Kellett
Co-stars: Frankie Howerd Bill Fraser Stanley Holloway Dora Bryan

1994 THE BEVERLEY HILLBILLIES
Director: Penelope Spheeris
Co-stars: Jim Varney Lily Tomlin Cloris Leachman

MONIQUE GABRIELLE

1987 DEATHSTALKER 2: DUEL OF THE TITANS
Director: Jim Wynorski
Co-stars: John Terlesky Toni Naples Maria Socas

1989 TRANSYLVANIA TWIST
Director: Jim Wynorski
Co-stars: Robert Vaughn Teri Copley

RENEE GADD

1934 HAPPY
Director: Fred Zelnick
Co-stars: Stanley Lupino Laddie Cliff Dorothy Hyson

1934 UNCERTAIN LADY
Director: Karl Freund
Co-stars: Edward Everett Horton Genevieve Tobin Mary Nash

1936 THE MAN IN THE MIRROR
Director: Maurice Elvey
Co-stars: Edward Everett Horton Genevieve Tobin

1944 THEY CAME TO A CITY
Director: Basil Dearden
Co-stars: Googie Withers John Clements Raymond Huntley

JACQUELINE GADSON

1927 IT
Director: Clarence Badger
Co-stars: Clara Bow Antonio Moreno William Austin Gary Cooper

1958 WEST OF ZANZIBAR
Director: Tod Browning
Co-stars: Lon Chaney Lionel Barrymore Mary Nolan

ANNA GAEL

1973 BLUE BLOOD
Director: Andrew Sinclair
Co-stars: Oliver Reed Derek Jacobi Fiona Lewis

1978 THERESE AND ISABELE
Director: Radley Metzger
Co-star: Essy Persson

PATRICIA GAGE

1977 RABID
Director: David Cronenberg
Co-stars: Marilyn Chambers Frank Moore Joe Silver

1990 LOOKING FOR MIRACLES
Director: Kevin Sullivan
Co-stars: Greg Spottiswood Zachary Bennett Joe Flaherty

1995 SILENCE OF ADULTERY
Director: Steven Stern
Co-stars: Kate Jackson Art Hindle

JENNY GAGO

1989 THE OLD GRINGO
Director: Luis Puenzo
Co-stars: Jane Fonda Gregory Peck Jimmy Smits

HELEN GAHAGAN

1935 SHE
Director: Irving Pichel
Co-stars: Randolph Scott Nigel Bruce Helen Mack

PHILLIPA GAIL

1991 DO NOT DISTURB
Director: Nicholas Barton
Co-stars: Frances Barber Peter Capaldi Eva Darlan

ZOE GAIL

1948 NO ORCHIDS FOR MISS BLANDISH
Director: St. John Clowes
Co-stars: Linden Travers Jack La Rue

LYNN GAINES

1989 JOBMAN
Director: Darrell Roodt
Co-stars: Kevin Smith Tertius Meintjies

CHARLOTTE GAINSBOURG

1985 AN IMPUDENT GIRL
Director: Claude Miller
Co-stars: Bernadette Lafont Jean-Claude Brailly

1985 LOVE SONGS
Director: Elie Chouraqui
Co-stars: Catherine Deneuve Christopher Lambert Nick Mancuso

1988 LA PETITE VOLEUSE
Director: Claude Miller
Co-stars: Raoul Billery Chantal Banlier Didier Bezace

1990 NIGHT SUN
Director: Paolo Taviani
Co-stars: Julian Sands Nastassja Kinski Massimo Bonetti

1991 MERCI LA VIE
Director: Anouk Grinberg Gerard Depardieu Annie Girardot

1992 AUTOBUS-AUX YEUX DU MONDE
Director: Eric Rochantay
Co-stars: Yvan Attal Kristin Scott-Thomas Marc Berman

1993 THE CEMENT GARDEN
Director: Andrew Birkin
Co-stars: Sinead Cusack Ned Birkin Andrew Robertson

1996 JANE EYRE
Director: Franco Zefferelli
Co-stars: William Hurt Samuel West Joan Plowright

1998 LOVE, ETC.
Director: Marion Vernoux
Co-stars: Yvan Attal Charles Berling

CRISTINA GAIONI

1963   **LOVE AT TWENTY**
Director: Renzo Rossellini
Co-stars: Marie-France Pisier Jean-Pierre Leaud

1963   **FIRE OVER ROME**
Director: Guido Malatesta
Co-stars: Lang Jeffries Moira Orfei Vladimir Medar

SVETLANA GAITAN

1987   **THE BURGLAR**
Director: Valery Ogorodnikov
Co-stars: Oleg Elykomov Yuri Tsapnik

JUNE GALE

1932   **WIN, LOSE OR DRAW**
Co-star: Jack Dempsey

1939   **CHARLIE CHAN AT TREASURE ISLAND**
Director: Norman Foster
Co-stars: Sidney Toler Cesar Romero Sen Yung

1940   **CITY OF CHANGE**
Director: Ricardo Cortez
Co-stars: Lynn Bari C. Aubrey Smith Donald Woods

ROBERTA GALE

1934   **THE TERROR OF THE PLAINS**
Co-stars: Tom Tyler Charles Whitaker

1934   **MYSTERY RANCH**
Co-stars: Tom Tyler Jack Perrin Louise Gabo

GENEVIEVE GALEA

1963   **LES CARABINIERS**
Director: Jean-Luc Godard
Co-stars: Marino Mase Albert Juros Catherine Ribero

ANNA GALIENA

1990   **THE HAIRDRESSER'S HUSBAND**
Director: Patrice Leconte
Co-star: Jean Rochefort

1992   **JAMON, JAMON**
Director: Bigas Luna
Co-stars: Penelope Cruz Stefania Sandrelli Juan Diego

1994   **BEING HUMAN**
Director: Bill Forsyth
Co-stars: Robin Williams John Turturro Lorraine Bracco

1997   **THE LEADING MAN**
Director: John Duigan
Co-stars: Jon Bon Jovi Patricia Hodge Thandie Newton

DENISE GALIK

1978   **CALIFORNIA SUITE**
Director: Herbert Ross
Co-stars: Michael Caine Maggie Smith Walter Matthau

1980   **HUMANOIDS FROM THE DEEP**
Director: Barbara Peeters
Co-stars: Vic Morrow Doug McClure Ann Turkel

ANNIE GALIPEAU

1992   **MAP OF THE HUMAN HEART**
Director: Vincent Ward
Co-stars: Jason Scott Lee Anne Parillaud Patrick Bergin

HELEN GALLAGHER

1960   **STRANGERS WHEN WE MEET**
Director: Richard Quine
Co-stars: Kirk Douglas Kim Novak Barbara Rush

1977   **ROSELAND**
Director: James Ivory
Co-stars: Geraldine Chaplin Teresa Wright Christopher Walken

LUCY GALLARDO

1962   **THE EXTERMINATING ANGEL**
Director: Luis Bunuel
Co-stars: Silvia Pinal Enrique Rambal Jose Baviera

SILVANA GALLARDO

1981   **PRISON STORIES: WOMEN ON THE INSIDE**
Director: Donna Deitch
Co-stars: Lolita Davidovich Rachel Ticotin Rae Dawn Chong

1984   **THE CALENDAR GIRL MURDERS**
Director: William Graham
Co-stars: Tom Skerritt Sharon Stone Robert Culp

1988   **OUT OF THE DARK**
Director: Michael Schroeder
Co-stars: Karen Black Cameron Dye Tab Hunter

GINA GALLEGO

1984   **LUST IN THE DUST**
Director: Paul Bartel
Co-stars: Tab Hunter Lainie Kazan Cesar Romero

ROSINA GALLI

1939   **FISHERMAN'S WHARF**
Director: Bernard Vorhaus
Co-stars: Bobby Breen Leo Carrillo Lee Patrick

KETTI GALLIAN

1934   **MARIE GALANTE**
Director: Henry King
Co-stars: Spencer Tracy Ned Sparks Helen Morgan

1935   **UNDER THE PAMPAS MOON**
Director: James Tingling
Co-stars: Warner Baxter Rita Hayworth J. Carrol Naish

1937   **ESPIONAGE**
Director: Kurt Neumann
Co-stars: Edmund Lowe Madge Evans Paul Lukas

1937   **SHALL WE DANCE ?**
Director: Mark Sandrich
Co-stars: Fred Astaire Ginger Rogers Eric Blore

CAROLE GALLOWAY

1992   **A TOWN TORN APART**
Director: Daniel Petrie
Co-stars: Michael Tucker Jill Eikenberry Linda Griffiths

GRAZIELLA GALVANI

1965   **PIERROT LE FOU**
Director: Jean-Luc Godard
Co-stars: Jean-Paul Belmondo Anna Karina Dirk Sanders

RITA GAM

1952   **THE THIEF**
Director: Russel Rouse
Co-stars: Ray Milland Martin Gabel Harry Bronson

1953   **SAADIA**
Director: Albert Lewin
Co-stars: Cornel Wilde Mel Ferrer Cyril Cusack

1954   **SIGN OF THE PAGAN**
Director: Douglas Sirk
Co-stars: Jeff Chandler Jack Palance George Dolenz

1954 **NIGHT PEOPLE**	**1925** **THE TORRENT**
Director: Nunnally Johnson	*Director:* Monta Bell
Co-stars: Gregory Peck Broderick Crawford Buddy Ebsen	*Co-stars:* Ricardo Cortez Gertrude Olmsted
1956 **MOHAWK**	**1926** **FLESH AND THE DEVIL**
Director: Kurt Neumann	*Director:* Clarence Brown
Co-stars: Scott Brady Lori Nelson Neville Brand Vera Vague	*Co-stars:* John Gilbert Lars Hanson
1960 **HANNIBAL**	**1927** **THE TEMPTRESS**
Director: Edgar Ulmer	*Director:* Fred Niblo
Co-stars: Victor Mature Gabrielle Ferzetti Milly Vitale	*Co-stars:* Antonio Moreno Lionel Barrymore
1961 **KING OF KINGS**	**1927** **LOVE**
Director: Nicholas Ray	*Director:* Edmund Goulding
Co-stars: Jeffrey Hunter Robert Ryan Siobhan McKenna	*Co-stars:* John Gilbert Brandon Hurst
1971 **KLUTE**	**1927** **THE DIVINE WOMAN**
Director: Alan J. Pakula	*Director:* Victor Sjostrom
Co-stars: Jane Fonda Donald Sutherland Charles Cioffi	*Co-stars:* Lars Hanson John Mack Brown
1971 **SHOOTOUT**	**1928** **A WOMAN OF AFFAIRS**
Director: Henry Hathaway	*Director:* Clarence Brown
Co-stars: Gregory Peck Pat Quinn Susan Tyrrell	*Co-stars:* John Gilbert Lewis Stone
1971 **SUCH GOOD FRIENDS**	**1928** **THE MYSTERIOUS LADY**
Director: Otto Preminger	*Director:* Fred Niblo
Co-stars: Dyan Cannon James Coco Jennifer O'Neil	*Co-stars:* Conrad Nagel Gustav Von Seyffertitz

MARIA GAMBARELLI

1935 **HERE'S TO ROMANCE**	**1929** **THE SINGLE STANDARD**
Director: Albert Green	*Director:* John Robertson
Co-stars: Nino Martini Genevieve Tobin Anita Louise	*Co-stars:* Nils Asther John Mack Brown

JULIA GAMBOLD

1929   **WILD ORCHIDS**

1978 **THE PEREGRINE HUNTERS**	**1929** **KISS**
Director: Cecil Petty	*Director:* Jacques Feyder
Co-stars: Gary Dundavan Alex McCrindle Barrie Cosney	*Co-stars:* Conrad Nagel Lew Ayres

SHARON GANS

1972 **SLAUGHTERHOUSE FIVE**	**1930** **ANNA CHRISTIE**
Director: George Roy Hill	*Director:* Clarence Brown
Co-stars: Michael Saks Ron Leibman Valerie Perrine	*Co-stars:* Charles Bickford Marie Dressler

TERESA GANZEL

1930   **ROMANCE**

1982 **THE TOY**	*Director:* Clarence Brown
Director: Richard Donner	*Co-stars:* Lewis Stone Gavin Gordon
Co-stars: Richard Pryor Jackie Gleason Ned Beatty	**1930** **INSPIRATION**

LOLA GAOS

	Director: Clarence Brown
1970 **TRISTANA**	*Co-stars:* Robert Montgomery Lewis Stone
Director: Luis Bunuel	**1931** **SUSAN LENNOX, HER FALL AND RISE**
Co-stars: Catherine Deneuve Fernando Rey Franco Nero	*Director:* Robert Z. Leonard
	Co-stars: Clark Gable Jean Hersholt

OLIVIDA GARA

1931   **MATA HARI**

1980 **PEPI, LUCY, BOM AND THE OTHER GIRLS**	*Director:* George Fitzmaurice
Director: Pedro Almodoavar	*Co-stars:* Ramon Navarro Lionel Barrymore
Co-stars: Carmen Maura Eva Silva	**1932** **GRAND HOTEL**

TERRI GARBER

	Director: Edmund Goulding
1984 **NO MAN'S LAND**	*Co-stars:* John Barrymore Joan Crawford Wallace Beery
Director: Rod Holcomb	**1931** **AS YOU DESIRE ME**
Co-stars: Stella Stevens Donna Dixon Melissa Michaelsen	*Director:* George Fitzmaurice
	Co-stars: Melvyn Douglas Erich Von Stroheim

GRETA GARBO *(Greta Louisa Gustafsson)*
Nominated For Best Actress In 1930 For "Romance" And "Anne Christie"
And Also In 1937 For "Camille". (Honorary Award In 1954)

	1933 **QUEEN CHRISTINA**
1924 **THE ATONEMENT OF GOSTA BERLING**	*Director:* Rouben Mamoulian
Director: Mauritz Stiller	*Co-stars:* John Gilbert Lewis Stone Ian Keith
Co-stars: Lars Hanson Gerda Lundquist	**1934** **THE PAINTED VEIL**
	Director: Richard Boleslawski
	Co-stars: Herbert Marshall George Brent
1925 **JOYLESS STREET**	**1935** **ANNA KARENINA**
Director: G.W. Pabst	*Director:* Clarence Brown
Co-stars: Asta Nielsen Werner Krauss	*Co-stars:* Fredric March Basil Rathbone
	1937 **CAMILLE**
	Director: George Cukor
	Co-stars: Robert Taylor Lionel Barrymore Henry Daniell

1937 CONQUEST
Director: Clarence Brown
Co-stars: Charles Boyer Reginald Owen

1939 NINOTCHKA
Director: Ernst Lubitsch
Co-stars: Melvyn Douglas Sig Ruman Bela Lugosi

1941 THE TWO-FACED WOMAN
Director: George Cukor
Co-stars: Melvyn Douglas Constance Bennett

DELIA GARCES

1952 EL
Director: Luis Bunuel
Co-stars: Arturo De Cordova Luis Beristain Aurora Walker

AMALIA DUQUE GARCIA

1988 MIRACLE IN ROME
Director: Lisandro Duque Naranjo
Co-stars: Frank Ramirez Gerardo Arellano

IRMA GARCIA

1985 DEATH OF AN ANGEL
Director: Petru Popescu
Co-stars: Bonnie Bedellia Nick Mancuso Pamela Ludwig

MADELEINE GARCIA

1952 CRIMSON CURTAIN
Director: Jean-Claude Pascal
Co-stars: Anouk Aimee Jim Gerald

NICOLE GARCIA

1980 MY AMERICAN UNCLE
Director: Alain Resnais
Co-stars: Gerard Depardieu Roger Pierre Henri Laborit

1981 BOLERO
Director: Claude Lelouche
Co-stars: James Caan Geraldine Chaplin Robert Hossein

1983 ORDER OF DEATH
Director: Robert Faenza
Co-stars: Harvey Keitel John Lydon Sylvia Sidney

1985 DEATH IN A FRENCH GARDEN
Director: Michel Deville
Co-stars: Richard Bohringer Michel Piccoli Anemone

STELLA GARCIA

1971 THE LAST MOVIE
Director: Dennis Hopper
Co-stars: Dennis Hopper Julie Adams Kris Kristofferson

1972 JOE KIDD
Director: John Sturges
Co-stars: Clint Eastwood Robert Duvall John Saxon

GINETTE GARCIN

1975 COUSIN COUSINE
Director: Jean-Charles Tachella
Co-stars: Marie-France Pisier Marie-Christine Barrault

1992 L'HOMME DE MA VIE
Director: Jean-Charles Tachella
Co-stars: Maria De Madeiros Thierry Fortineau

STEPHANIE GARCIN

1984 NOVEMBER MOON
Director: Alexandra Von Grote
Co-stars: Gabrile Osberg Christine Millet Danielle Delorme

BETTY GARDE

1948 CALL NORTHSIDE 777
Director: Henry Hathaway
Co-stars: James Stewart Lee J. Cobb Helen Walker

1948 CRY OF THE CITY
Director: Robert Siodmak
Co-stars: Victor Mature Richard Conte Shelley Winters

1950 CAGED
Director: John Cromwell
Co-stars: Eleanor Parker Agnes Moorehead Hope Emerson

1951 THE PRINCE WHO WAS A THIEF
Director: Rudolph Mate
Co-stars: Tony Curtis Piper Laurie Jeff Corey

AVA GARDNER

(Married Mickey Rooney, Frank Sinatra, Artie Shaw)
Nominated For Best Actress In 1935 For "Mogambo"

1942 WE WERE DANCING
Director: Robert Z Leonard
Co-stars: Norma Shearer Melvyn Douglas Marjorie Main

1942 KID GLOVE KILLER
Director: Fred Zinnemann
Co-stars: Van Heflin Lee Bowman Marsha Hunt

1943 GHOSTS ON THE LOOSE
Director: William Beaudine
Co-stars: East Side Kids Bela Lugosi Rick Vallin

1944 MAISIE GOES TO RENO
Director: Harry Beaumont
Co-stars: Ann Sothern John Hodiak Tom Drake

1945 SHE WENT TO THE RACES
Co-stars: James Craig Edmund Gwenn Sig Ruman

1946 WHISTLE STOP
Director: Leonide Moguy
Co-stars: George Raft Tom Conway Victor McLaglen

1946 THE KILLERS
Director: Robert Siodmak
Co-stars: Burt Lancaster Edmund O'Brien Sam Levene

1947 THE HUCKSTERS
Director: Jack Conway
Co-stars: Clark Gable Deborah Kerr Sydney Greenstreet

1948 ONE TOUCH OF VENUS
Director: William Seiter
Co-stars: Robert Walker Dick Haymes Olga San Juan

1949 EAST SIDE, WEST SIDE
Director: Mervyn LeRoy
Co-stars: James Mason Barbara Stanwyck Van Heflin

1949 THE GREAT SINNER
Director: Robert Siodmak
Co-stars: Gregory Peck Walter Huston Ethel Barrymore

1949 THE BRIBE
Director: Robert Z Leonard
Co-stars: Robert Taylor Charles Laughton Vincent Price

1951 MY FORBIDDEN PAST
Director: Robert Stevenson
Co-stars: Robert Mitchum Melvyn Douglas Janis Carter

1951 PANDORA AND THE FLYING DUTCHMAN
Director: Albert Lewin
Co-stars: James Mason Harold Warrender Nigel Patrick

1951 SHOWBOAT
Director: George Sidney
Co-stars: Kathryn Grayson Howard Keel Joe E. Brown

1952   **LONE STAR**
Director: Vincent Sherman
Co-stars: Clark Gable Lionel Barrymore Beulah Bondi

1952   **THE SNOWS OF KILIMANJARO**
Director: Henry King
Co-stars: Gregory Peck Susan Hayward Hildegard Neff

1953   **MOGAMBO**
Director: John Ford
Co-stars: Clark Gable Grace Kelly Donald Sinden

1953   **KNIGHTS OF THE ROUND TABLE**
Director: Richard Thorpe
Co-stars: Robert Taylor Mel Ferrer Stanley Baker

1953   **RIDE, VAQUERO**
Director: John Farrow
Co-stars: Robert Taylor Howard Keel Anthony Quinn

1954   **THE BAREFOOT CONTESSA**
Director: Joseph Mankiewicz
Co-stars: Humphrey Bogart Edmond O'Brien Rossano Brazzi

1956   **BHOWANI JUNCTION**
Director: George Cukor
Co-stars: Stewart Granger Francis Matthews Bill Travers

1957   **THE LITTLE HUT**
Director: Mark Robson
Co-stars: Stewart Granger David Niven Finlay Currie

1957   **THE SUN ALSO RISES**
Director: Henry King
Co-stars: Tyrone Power Errol Flynn Mel Ferrer

1959   **ON THE BEACH**
Director: Stanley Kramer
Co-stars: Gregory Peck Anthony Perkins Fred Astaire

1959   **THE NAKED MAJA**
Director: Henry Koster
Co-stars: Anthony Franciosa Lea Padovani Gino Cervi

1960   **THE ANGEL WORE RED**
Director: Nunnally Johnson
Co-stars: Dirk Bogarde Joseph Cotten Vittorio De Sica

1962   **55 DAYS AT PEKING**
Director: Nicholas Ray
Co-stars: Charlton Heston David Niven Flora Robson

1964   **THE NIGHT OF THE IGUANA**
Director: John Huston
Co-stars: Richard Burton Deborah Kerr Sue Lyon

1964   **SEVEN DAYS IN MAY**
Director: John Frankenheimer
Co-stars: Burt Lancaster Kirk Douglas Fredric March

1966   **THE BIBLE...IN THE BEGINING**
Director: John Huston
Co-stars: John Huston Michael Parks George C. Scott Peter O'Toole

1968   **MAYERLING**
Director: Terence Young
Co-stars: Omar Sharif Catherine Deneuve James Mason

1971   **TAM-LIN**
Director: Roddy McDowall
Co-stars: Ian McShane Cyril Cusack Richard Wattis

1972   **THE LIFE AND TIMES OF JUDGE ROY BEAN**
Director: John Huston
Co-stars: Paul Newman Victoria Principal

1973   **EARTHQUAKE**
Director: Mark Robson
Co-stars: Charlton Heston Lorne Greene Walter Matthau

1975   **PERMISSION TO KILL**
Director: Cyril Frankel
Co-stars: Dirk Bogarde Bekim Fehmiu Timothy Dalton

1976   **THE BLUE BIRD**
Director: George Cukor
Co-stars: Elizabeth Taylor Patsy Kensit Jane Fonda

1976   **THE SENTINEL**
Director: Michael Winner
Co-stars: Cristina Raines Chris Sarandon Jose Ferrer

1977   **THE CASSANDRA CROSSING**
Director: Brian De Palma
Co-stars: Sophia Loren Richard Harris Burt Lancaster

1979   **CITY ON FIRE**
Director: Alvin Rakoff
Co-stars: Henry Fonda Barry Newman Susan Clark

1980   **THE KIDNAPPING OF THE PRESIDENT**
Director: George Mendeluk
Co-stars: Hal Holbrook William Shatner

1981   **PRIEST OF LOVE**
Director: Christopher Miles
Co-stars: Ian McKellen Janet Suzman

1985   **THE LONG HOT SUMMER**
Director: Stuart Cooper
Co-stars: Don Johnson Judith Ivey Cybil Shepherd

1986   **HAREM**
Director: Billy Hale
Co-stars: Omar Sharif Nancy Travis Cherie Lunghi

HY GARDNER

1963   **THE GIRL HUNTERS**
Director: Roy Rowland
Co-stars: Mickey Spillane Shirley Eaton Lloyd Nolan

JOAN GARDNER

1932   **MEN OF TOMORROW**
Director: Zoltan Korda
Co-stars: Maurice Braddell Merle Oberon Robert Donat

1932   **WEDDING REHEARSAL**
Director: Alexander Korda
Co-stars: Roland Young John Loder Wendy Barrie

1934   **THE SCARLET PIMPERNEL**
Director: Harold Young
Co-stars: Leslie Howard Merle Oberon Raymond Massey

1934   **THE PRIVATE LIFE OF DON JUAN**
Director: Alexander Korda
Co-stars: Douglas Fairbanks Merle Oberon

1934   **CATHERINE THE GREAT**
Director: Paul Czinner
Co-stars: Elizabeth Bergner Douglas Fairbanks Jnr.

1936   **THE MAN WHO COULD WORK MIRACLES**
Director: Lothar Mendes
Co-stars: Roland Young Ralph Richardson

1937   **FORGET-ME-NOT**
Director: Zoltan Korda
Co-stars: Benjamino Gigli Ivan Brandt Hugh Wakefield

1937   **DARK JOURNEY**
Director: Victor Saville
Co-stars: Conrad Veidt Vivien Leigh Anthony Bushell

1938   **THE CHALLENGE**
Director: Milton Rosmer
Co-stars: Luis Trenker Robert Douglas Mary Clare

1939   **REBEL SON**
Director: Adrian Brunel
Co-stars: Harry Baur Patricia Roc Roger Livesey

BEVERLY GARLAND

1954   THE ROCKET MAN
Director: Oscar Rudolph
Co-stars: Charles Coburn Spring Byington George Winslow

1954   THE MIAMI STORY
Director: Fred Sears
Co-stars: Barry Sullivan Luther Adler Adele Jergens

1956   IT CONQUERED THE WORLD
Director: Roger Corman
Co-stars: Peter Graves Lee Van Cleef Sally Fraser

1956   GUNSLINGER
Director: Roger Corman
Co-stars: John Ireland Allison Hayes Martin Kingsley

1956   CURUCCU, BEAST OF THE AMAZON
Director: Curt Siodmak
Co-stars: John Bromfield Tom Payne

1957   CHICAGO CONFIDENTIAL
Director: Sidney Salkow
Co-stars: Brian Keith Dick Foran Elisha Cook Jnr.

1957   THE JOKER IS WILD
Director: Charles Vidor
Co-stars: Frank Sinatra Mitzi Gaynor Jeanne Crain

1957   NOT OF THIS EARTH
Director: Roger Corman
Co-stars: Paul Birch Morgan Jones

1959   THE ALLIGATOR PEOPLE
Director: Roy Del Ruth
Co-stars: George MacReady Frieda Inescort Bruce Bennett

1968   PRETTY POISON
Director: Noel Black
Co-stars: Anthony Perkins Tuesday Weld John Randolph

1974   WHERE THE RED FERN GROWS
Director: Norman Tokar
Co-stars: James Whitmore Lonny Chapman Jack Ging

1974   THE DAY THE EARTH MOVED
Director: Robert Michael Lewis
Co-stars: Jackie Cooper Stella Stevens

1977   SIXTH AND MAIN
Director: Christopher Cain
Co-stars: Leslie Nielsen Roddy McDowall Joe Maross

1979   ABRAHAM'S SACRIFICE
Director: John Hively
Co-stars: Gene Barry Andrew Duggan

1980   IT'S MY TURN
Director: Claudia Weill
Co-stars: Jill Clayburgh Michael Douglas Charles Grodin

JUDY GARLAND *(Frances Ethel Gumm)*
(Married Vincente Minnelli, Sid Luft)
(Mother Of Liza Minnelli, Lorna Luft)
Nominated For Best Actress In 1955 For "A Star Is Born"
Nominated For Best Supporting Actress In 1961 For "Judgement At Nuremberg". (Special Award In 1939)

1936   PIGSKIN PARADE
Director: David Butler
Co-stars: Stuart Erwin Jack Haley Patsy Kelly

1936   EVERY SUNDAY
Director: Felix E. Feist
Co-star: Deanna Durbin

1937   THOROUGHBREDS DON'T CRY
Co-stars: Mickey Rooney Ronald Sinclair

1938   LISTEN DARLING
Director: Edwin Marin
Co-stars: Mary Astor Freddie Bartholomew Walter Pidgeon

1937   BROADWAY MELODY OF 1938
Director: Roy Del Ruth
Co-stars: Robert Taylor Eleanor Powell Sophie Tucker

1938   EVERYBODY SING
Director: Edwin Marin
Co-stars: Allan Jones Fanny Brice Monty Woolley

1938   LOVE FINDS ANDY HARDY
Director: George Seitz
Co-stars: Mickey Rooney Lewis Stone Ann Rutherford

1939   THE WIZARD OF OZ
Director: Victor Fleming
Co-stars: Frank Morgan Jack Haley Ray Bolger

1939   BABES IN ARMS
Director: Busby Berkeley
Co-stars: Mickey Rooney Charles Winninger June Preisser

1940   LITTLE NELLIE KELLY
Director: Norman Taurog
Co-stars: Charles Winninger George Murphy

1940   STRIKE UP THE BAND
Director: Busby Berkeley
Co-stars: Mickey Rooney June Preisser

1940   ANDY HARDY MEETS A DEBUTANTE
Director: George Seitz
Co-stars: Mickey Rooney Lewis Stone Cecelia Parker

1941   ZIEGFELD GIRL
Director: Robert Z Leonard
Co-stars: James Stewart Hedy Lamarr Lana Turner

1941   BABES ON BROADWAY
Director: Busby Berkeley
Co-stars: Mickey Rooney Ray MacDonald Virginia Weilder

1941   LIFE BEGINS FOR ANDY HARDY
Director: George Seitz
Co-stars: Mickey Rooney Lewis Stone Ann Rutherford

1942   FOR ME AND MY GIRL
Director: Busby Berkeley
Co-stars: Gene Kelly George Murphy Ben Blue

1943   GIRL CRAZY
Director: Norman Taurog
Co-stars: Mickey Rooney Rags Ragland June Allyson

1944   MEET ME IN ST. LOUIS
Director: Vincente Minnelli
Co-stars: Mary Astor Margaret O'Brien Leon Ames

1945   UNDER THE CLOCK
Director: Vincente Minnelli
Co-stars: Robert Walker James Gleason

1945   ZIEGFELD FOLLIES
Director: Vincente Minnelli
Co-stars: Fred Astaire William Powell Fanny Brice

1943   PRESENTING LILY MARS
Director: Norman Taurog
Co-stars: Van Heflin Fay Bainter Tommy Dorsey

1946   TILL THE CLOUDS ROLL BY
Director: Richard Whorf
Co-stars: Robert Walker Van Heflin Frank Sinatra

1946   THE HARVEY GIRLS
Director: George Sidney
Co-stars: Ray Bolger John Hodiak Cyd Charisse

1948   EASTER PARADE
Director: Charles Walters
Co-stars: Fred Astaire Ann Miller Peter Lawford

1948   **THE PIRATE**
Director: Vincente Minnelli
Co-stars: Gene Kelly Walter Slezak

1948   **WORDS AND MUSIC**
Director: Norman Taurog
Co-stars: Mickey Rooney Tom Drake Gene Kelly

1949   **IN THE GOOD OLD SUMMERTIME**
Director: Robert Z Leonard
Co-stars: Van Johnson S.Z. Sakall Buster Keaton

1950   **SUMMER STOCK**
Director: Charles Walters
Co-stars: Gene Kelly Eddie Bracken Phil Silvers

1955   **A STAR IS BORN**
Director: George Cukor
Co-stars: James Mason Charles Bickford Jack Carson

1960   **PEPE**
Director: George Sidney
Co-stars: William Demarest Bing Crosby

1961   **JUDGEMENT AT NUREMBERG**
Director: Stanley Kramer
Co-stars: Spencer Tracy Burt Lancaster

1962   **GAY PURR-EE** *(Voice)*
Director: Abe Levitow
Co-stars: Robert Goulet Hermione Gingold Mel Blanc

1963   **A CHILD IS WAITING**
Director: John Cassavetes
Co-stars: Burt Lancaster Gena Rowlands

1963   **I COULD GO ON SINGING**
Director: Ronald Neame
Co-stars: Dirk Bogarde Jack Klugman

LOUISE GARLETTI

1961   **THE HIDEOUT**
Director: Raoul Andre
Co-stars: Marcel Mouloudji Yves Vincent Francis Blanche

LEE GARLINGTON

1983   **PSYCHO II**
Director: Richard Franklin
Co-stars: Anthony Perkins Vera Miles Meg Tilly

1986   **PSYCHO III**
Director: Anthony Perkins
Co-stars: Anthony Perkins Diana Scarwid Jeff Fahey

1989   **COLD SASSY TREE**
Director: Joan Tewkesbury
Co-stars: Faye Dunaway Richard Widmark Frances Fisher

1990   **EVIDENCE OF LOVE**
Director: Stephen Gyllenhaal
Co-stars: Barbara Hershey Brian Dennehy

1993   **DYING TO LOVE YOU**
Director: Robert Iscove
Co-stars: Tim Matheson Tracy Pollan

1995   **SEE JANE RUN**
Director: John Patterson
Co-stars: Joanna Kerns John Shea

MARY GARLINGTON

1981   **POLYESTER**
Director: John Waters
Co-stars: Divine Tab Hunter Edith Massey

AMULETTE GARNEAU

1987   **NIGHT ZOO**
Director: Jean-Claude Lauzon
Co-stars: Roger Le Bel Gilles Maheu Jerry Snell

ALICE GARNER

1983   **MONKEY GRIP**
Director: Ken Cameron
Co-stars: Noni Hazelhurst Colin Friels Candy Raymond

1996   **LOVE AND OTHER CATASTROPHIES**
Director: Emme-Kate Croghan
Co-stars: Frances O'Connor Matt Day

PEGGY ANN GARNER *(Child)*
Special Award 1945

1939   **BLONDIE BRINGS UP BABY**
Director: Frank Strayer
Co-stars: Penny Singleton Arthur Lake

1939   **IN NAME ONLY**
Director: John Cromwell
Co-stars: Cary Grant Carole Lombard Kay Francis

1942   **THE PIED PIPER**
Director: Irving Pichel
Co-stars: Monty Woolley Anne Baxter

1943   **JANE EYRE**
Director: Robert Stevenson
Co-stars: Joan Fontaine Orson Welles Elizabeth Taylor

1944   **KEYS OF THE KINGDOM**
Director: John Stahl
Co-stars: Gregory Peck Thomas Mitchell Ann Revere

1945   **A TREE GROWS IN BROOKLYN**
Director: Elia Kazan
Co-stars: James Dunn Dorothy McGuire Lloyd Nolan

1945   **JUNIOR MISS**
Director: George Seaton
Co-stars: Allyn Joslyn Mona Freeman

1945   **NOB HILL**
Director: Henry Hathaway
Co-stars: George Raft Vivian Blaine

1946   **HOME, SWEET HOMICIDE**
Director: Lloyd Bacon
Co-stars: Lynn Bari Randolph Scott Dean Stockwell

1947   **THUNDER IN THE VALLEY**
Co-star: Lon McCallister

1947   **DAISY KENYON**
Director: Otto Preminger
Co-stars: Joan Crawford Henry Fonda Dana Andrews

1948   **SIGN OF THE RAM**
Director: John Sturges
Co-stars: Susan Peters Alexander Knox

1949   **BOMBA THE JUNGLE BOY**
Director: Ford Beebe
Co-stars: Johnny Sheffield Onslow Stevens

1949   **THE BIG CAT**
Director: Phil Karlson
Co-stars: Lon McCallister Preston Foster

1949   **THE LOVEABLE CHEAT**
Co-stars: Charles Ruggles Minerva Urecal

1951   **TERESA**
Director: Fred Zinnemann
Co-stars: Pier Angeli John Ericson

1954   **BLACK WIDOW**
Director: Nunnally Johnson
Co-stars: Ginger Rogers Van Heflin

1978   **A WEDDING**
Director: Robert Altman
Co-stars: Carol Burnett Mia Farrow Amy Stryker

JANEANE GAROFALO

1994 REALITY BITES
Director: Ben Stiller
Co-stars: Winona Ryder Ethan Hawke Swoosie Kurtz

1996 THE TRUTH ABOUT CATS AND DOGS
Director: Michael Lehmann
Co-stars: Uma Thurman Ben Chaplin Jamie Foxx

1997 LARGER THAN LIFE
Co-stars: Bill Murray Linda Fiorentino Matthew McConaughey

1997 COPLAND
Director: James Mangold
Co-stars: Sylvester Stallone Harvey Keitel Robert De Niro

1997 THE MATCHMAKER
Director: Mark Joffe
Co-stars: Denis Leary David O'Hara

TERI GARR
Nominated For Best Supporting Actress In 1982 For "Tootsie"

1964 ROUSTABOUT
Director: John Rich
Co-stars: Elvis Presley Barbara Stanwyck Leif Erickson Raquel Welch

1968 HEAD
Director: Bob Rafaelson
Co-stars: The Monkees Victor Mature Jack Nicholson

1968 STAR TREK: ASSIGNMENT EARTH
Director: Marc Daniels
Co-stars: William Shatner Leonard Nimoy

1974 YOUNG FRANKENSTEIN
Director: Mel Brooks
Co-stars: Gene Wilder Marty Feldman Madeline Kahn

1974 THE CONVERSATION
Director: Francis Coppola
Co-stars: Gene Hackman Frederic Forrest Cindy Williams

1977 OH GOD!
Director: Carl Reiner
Co-stars: George Burns John Denver Ralph Bellamy

1978 CLOSE ENCOUNTERS OF THE THIRD KIND
Director: Steven Spielberg
Co-stars: Richard Dreyfuss Melinda Dillon

1979 THE BLACK STALLION
Director: Carroll Ballard
Co-stars: Kelly Reno Mickey Rooney Clarence Muse

1981 HONKY TONK FREEWAY
Director: John Schlesinger
Co-stars: William Devane Beau Bridges Jessica Tandy

1982 THE ESCAPE ARTIST
Director: Caleb Deschanel
Co-stars: Raul Julia Joan Hackett Desi Arnaz Griffin O'Neal

1982 ONE FROM THE HEART
Director: Frances Coppola
Co-stars: Frederick Forrest Raul Julia Nastassja Kinski

1982 PRIME SUSPECT
Director: Noel Black
Co-stars: Mike Farrell Veronica Cartwright Lane Smith

1982 TOOTSIE
Director: Sydney Pollack
Co-stars: Dustin Hoffman Jessica Lang Bill Murray

1983 THE STING 2
Director: J. Paul Kagan
Co-stars: Jackie Gleason Karl Malden Oliver Reed Mac Davis

1983 MR. MUM
Director: Stan Dragoti
Co-stars: Michael Keaton Frederick Koekler Martin Mull Ann Jillian

1983 THE BLACK STALLION RETURNS
Director: Robert Dalva
Co-stars: Kelly Reno Ferdy Mayne Woody Strode Vincent Spano

1984 FIRSTBORN
Director: Michael Apted
Co-stars: Peter Weller Corey Haim Christopher Collet

1984 TO CATCH A KING
Director: Clive Donner
Co-stars: Robert Wagner Barbara Parkins John Standing

1985 MIRACLES
Director: Jim Kouf
Co-stars: Tom Conti Paul Rodriguez Christopher Lloyd

1985 AFTER HOURS
Director: Martin Scorsese
Co-stars: Griffin Dunne Rosanna Arquette Verna Bloom

1986 INTIMATE STRANGERS
Director: Robert Ellis Miller
Co-stars: Stacy Keach Cathy Lee Crosby Priscilla Lopez

1987 PACK OF LIES
Director: Anthony Page
Co-stars: Ellen Burstyn Alan Bates Sammi Davis Ronald Hines

1987 SHORT TIME
Director: Gregg Champion
Co-stars: Dabney Coleman Matt Frewer Barry Corbin

1988 FULL MOON IN BLUE WATER
Director: Peter Masterson
Co-stars: Gene Hackman Burgess Meredith

1989 LET IT RIDE
Director: Joe Pykin
Co-stars: Richard Dreyfuss Allen Garfield Michelle Phillips

1990 WAITING FOR THE LIGHT
Director: Christopher Monger
Co-stars: Shirley MacLaine Clancy Brown

1991 OUT COLD
Director: Malcolm Mowbray
Co-stars: John Lithgow Randy Quaid Bruce McGill Fred Coffin

1992 MOM AND DAD SAVE THE WORLD
Director: Greg Beeman
Co-stars: Jeffrey Jones Jon Lovitz Eric Idle

1992 DELIVER THEM FROM EVIL: THE TAKING OF ALTA VIEW
Director: Peter Levin
Co-stars: Harry Hamlin Terry O'Quinn

1996 DUMB AND DUMBER
Director: Peter Farrelly
Co-stars: Jim Carrey Jeff Daniels Lauren Holly

BETTY GARRETT

1948 THE BIG CITY
Director: Joe Pasternak
Co-stars: Margaret O'Brien Robert Preston Danny Thomas

1948 WORDS AND MUSIC
Director: Norman Taurog
Co-stars: Mickey Rooney Tom Drake Gene Kelly Mel Torme

1949 TAKE ME OUT TO THE BALL GAME
Director: Busby Berkeley
Co-stars: Gene Kelly Frank Sinatra Esther Williams

1949 ON THE TOWN
Director: Stanley Donen
Co-stars: Gene Kelly Frank Sinatra Ann Miller

1949 NEPTUNE'S DAUGHTER
Director: Edward Buzzell
Co-stars: Esther Williams Red Skelton Keenan Wynn

1955 MY SISTER EILEEN
Director: Richard Quine
Co-stars: Janet Leigh Jack Lemmon Bob Fosse

1957 THE SHADOW ON THE WINDOW
Director: William Asher
Co-stars: John Barrymor Jnr. Phil Carey

JOY GARRETT

1974 WHO?
Director: Jack Gold
Co-stars: Trevor Howard Elliott Gould Lyndon Brook

PATSY GARRETT

1974 BENJI
Director: Joe Camp
Co-stars: Peter Breck Edgar Buchanan Christopher Connelly

1977 FOR THE LOVE OF BENJI
Director: Joe Camp
Co-stars: Cynthia Smith Peter Bowles Ed Nelson

CYNTHIA GARRIS

1988 CRITTERS 2: THE MAIN COURSE
Director: Mick Garris
Co-stars: Terence Mann Don Opper Scott Grimes

MIRANDA GARRISON

1988 SALSA
Director: Boaz Davidson
Co-stars: Robby Rosa Rodney Harvey Magali Alvarado

KATE GARSIDE

1991 CLOSE MY EYES
Director: Stephen Poliakoff
Co-stars: Saskia Reeves Clive Owen Alan Rickman

GREER GARSON

Oscar For Best Actress In 1942 For Mrs. Miniver
Nominated For Best Actress In 1939 For "Goodbye, Mr. Chips", In 1941
For "Blossoms In The Dust", In 1943 For "Madame Curie", In 1944 For
"Mrs. Parkington", In 1945 For "The Valley Of Decision" and In 1960
For "Sunrise At Campobello"

1939 GOODBYE MR. CHIPS
Director: Sam Wood
Co-stars: Robert Donat Paul Henreid John Mills Lyn Harding

1939 REMEMBER?
Director: Norman Z McLeod
Co-stars: Robert Taylor Lew Ayres Billie Burke

1940 PRIDE AND PREDJUDICE
Director: Robert Z Leonard
Co-stars: Laurence Olivier Edmund Gwenn Marsha Hunt

1941 WHEN LADIES MEET
Director: Robert Z Leonard
Co-stars: John Crawford Robert Taylor Herbert Marshall

1941 BLOSSOMS IN THE DUST
Director: Mervyn LeRoy
Co-stars: Walter Pidgeon Felix Bressart Marsha Hunt

1942 RANDOM HARVEST
Director: Mervyn LeRoy
Co-stars: Ronald Colman Susan Peters Reginald Owen

1942 MRS. MINIVER
Director: William Wyler
Co-stars: Walter Pidgeon Teresa Wright Henry Travers

1943 MADAME CURIE
Director: Mervyn LeRoy
Co-stars: Walter Pidgeon May Whitty Van Johnson

1943 THE YOUNGEST PROFESSION
Director: Edward Buzzell
Co-stars: Virginia Weidler Jean Porter John Carroll

1944 MRS. PARKINGTON
Director: Tay Garnett
Co-stars: Walter Pidgeon Edward Arnold Peter Lawford

1945 ADVENTURE
Director: Victor Fleming
Co-stars: Clark Gable Thomas Mitchell Joan Blondell

1945 THE VALLEY OF DECISION
Director: Tay Garnett
Co-stars: Gregory Pack Lionel Barrymore Donald Crisp

1947 DESIRE ME
Director: George Cukor
Co-stars: Robert Mitchum Richard Hart

1948 JULIA MISBEHAVES
Director: Jack Conway
Co-stars: Walter Pidgeon Elizabeth Taylor Cesar Romero

1949 THAT FORSYTE WOMAN
Director: Compton Bennett
Co-stars: Errol Flynn Walter Pidgeon Robert Young

1950 THE MINIVER STORY
Director: H.C. Potter
Co-stars: Walter Pidgeon Henry Wilcoxon Cathy O'Donnell

1951 THE LAW AND THE LADY
Director: Edwin Knoff
Co-stars: Michael Wilding Fernando Lamas Marjorie Main

1953 SCANDAL AT SCOURIE
Director: Jean Negulesco
Co-stars: Walter Pidgeon Donna Corcoran Arthur Shields

1953 JULIUS CAESAR
Director: Joseph Mankiewicz
Co-stars: Marlon Brando James Mason John Gielgud

1954 HER TWELVE MEN
Director: Robert Z Leonard
Co-stars: Robert Ryan Richard Haydn Barry Sullivan

1955 STRANGE LADY IN TOWN
Director: Mervyn LeRoy
Co-stars: Dana Andrews Cameron Mitchell Lois Smith

1960 SUNRISE AT CAMPOBELLO
Director: Vincent Donohue
Co-stars: Ralph Bellamy Hume Cronyn Jean Hagen

1960 PEPE
Director: George Sidney
Co-stars: William Demarest Bing Crosby Frank Sinatra

1966 THE SINGING NUN
Director: Henry Koster
Co-stars: Debbie Reynolds Ricardo Montalban

1967 THE HAPPIEST MILLIONAIRE
Director: Norman Tokar
Co-stars: Fred MacMurray Tommy Steele

1978 LITTLE WOMEN
Director: David Lowell
Co-stars: Meredith Baxter Susan Dey Dorothy McGuire

JENNIE GARTH

1989 BRAND NEW LIFE
Director: Eric Laneuville
Co-stars: Barbara Eden Don Murray Shawnee Smith

1993 LIES OF THE HEART
Director: Michael Uno
Co-stars: Alexis Arquette Gregory Harrison

1993 DANIELLE STEEL'S STAR
Director: Michael Miller
Co-stars: Craig Bierko Ted Wass Terry Farrel

1994 TRAPPED AND DECEIVED
Director: Robert Iscove
Co-stars: Paul Sorvino Jill Eikenbery Helen Shaver

1996 AN UNFINISHED AFFAIR
Director: Rod Hardy
Co-star:: Tim Matheson

ELIZABETH GARVIE

1980 PRIDE AND PREDJUDICE
Director: Cyril Coke
Co-stars: David Rintoul Judy Parfitt Barbara Shelley

1981 THE GOOD SOLDIER
Director: Kevin Billington
Co-stars: Jeremy Brett Susan Fleetwood Robin Ellis

ANITA GARVIN

1928 THEIR PURPLE MOMENT
Director: James Parrott
Co-stars: Stan Laurel Oliver Hardy Kay Deslys

1928 FROM SOUP TO NUTS
Director: Edgar Kennedy
Co-stars: Stan Laurel Oliver Hardy Tiny Sandford

1930 BLOTTO
Director: James Parrott
Co-stars: Stan Laurel Oliver Hardy

1930 BE BIG
Director: James Parrott
Co-stars: Stan Laurel Oliver Hardy Isabelle Keith

LINDA GARY

1987 PINOCCHIO AND THE EMPEROR OF THE NIGHT*(Voice)*
Director: Hal Sutherland
Co-stars: Ed Asner Tom Bosley

LORRAINE GARY

1973 THE MARCUS-NELSON MURDERS
Director: Joseph Sargent
Co-stars: Telly Savalas Jose Ferrer Chita Rivera

1975 JAWS
Director: Steven Spielberg
Co-stars: Robert Shaw Roy Scheider Richard Dreyfuss

1977 I NEVER PROMISED YOU A ROSE GARDEN
Director: Anthony Page
Co-stars: Kathleen Quinlan Bibi Andersson

1978 JAWS 2
Director: Jeannot Szwarc
Co-stars: Roy Scheider Murray Hamilton Joseph Mascolo

1979 JUST YOU AND ME KID
Director: Leonard Stern
Co-stars: George Burns Brooke Shields Ray Bolger

1979 1941
Director: Steven Spielberg
Co-stars: Dan Aykroyd Robert Stack John Belushi

1987 JAWS: THE REVENGE
Director: Joseph Sargent
Co-stars: Lance Guest Karen Young Michael Caine

ANNA-MARIE GASCOINE

1991 DREAM ON
Director: Kitty Fitzgerald
Co-stars: Maureen Harold Amber Styles Ray Stubbs

JILL GASCOINE

1975 CONFESSIONS OF A POP PERFORMER
Director: Norman Cohen
Co-stars: Robin Askwith Anthony Booth

1989 KING OF THE WILD
Director: Peter Duffell
Co-stars: Frank Finlay Jenny Agutter Navin Chowdhry

MARJORIE GASKELL

1935 LAZYBONES
Director: Michael Powell
Co-stars: Clare Luce Ian Hunter Sara Allgood

DOMINIQUE GASPAR

1988 VIRGIN MACHINE
Director: Monika Treut
Co-stars: Ian Blum Marcelo Uriona Peter Kern

LEILA GASTIL

1982 PERMANENT VACATION
Director: Jim Jarmusch
Co-stars: Chris Parker Maria Duval

LISA GASTONI

1956 THREE MEN IN A BOAT
Director: Ken Annakin
Co-stars: David Tomlinson Laurence Harvey Jimmy Edwards

1956 THE BABY AND THE BATTLESHIP
Director: Jay Lewis
Co-stars: John Mills Bryan Forbes Michael Howard

1957 MAN FROM TANGIER
Director: Lance Comfort
Co-stars: Robert Hutton Martin Benson Leonard Sachs

1958 R.X.MURDER
Director: Derek Twist
Co-stars: Marius Goring Rick Jason Mary Merrall

1958 BLUE MURDER AT ST. TRINIANS
Director: Frank Launder
Co-stars: George Cole Terry-Thomas Joyce Grenfell

1962 EVA
Director: Joseph Losey
Co-stars: Stanley Baker Jeanne Moreau Virna Lisi

JOAN GATES

1943 THE GENTLE SEX
Director: Leslie Howard
Co-stars: Rosamund John Joan Greenwood Lilli Palmer

NANCY GATES

1942 THE GREAT GILDERSLEEVE
Director: Gordon Douglas
Co-stars: Harold Peary Jane Darwell Charles Arnt

1944 THE MASTER RACE
Director: Herbert Biberman
Co-stars: George Coulouris Osa Massen Lloyd Bridges

1945 THE SPANISH MAIN
Director: Frank Borzage
Co-stars: Paul Henreid Maureen O'Hara Walter Sleazak

1951 SONS OF THE MUSKETEERS
Director: Lewis Allen
Co-stars: Cornel Wilde Maureen O'Hara Dan O'Herlihy

1952 THE MEMBER OF THE WEDDING
Director: Fred Zinnemann
Co-stars: Ethel Waters Julie Harris Brandon DeWilde

1952 THE ATOMIC CITY
Director: Jerry Hopper
Co-stars: Gene Barry Lydia Clarke Lee Aaker

1953 HELL'S HALF ACRE
Director: John Auer
Co-stars: Wendell Corey Evelyn Keyes Elsa Lanchester

1954 SUDDENLY
Director: Lewis Allen
Co-stars: Frank Sinatra Sterling Hayden James Gleason

1955 MASTERSON OF KANSAS
Director: William Castle
Co-stars: George Montgomery James Griffith

1956 WORLD WITHOUT END
Director: Edward Bernds
Co-stars: Hugh Marlowe Rod Taylor

1956 SEARCH FOR BRIDEY MURPHY
Director: Noel Langley
Co-stars: Teresa Wright Louis Hayward

1956 DEATH OF A SCOUNDREL
Director: Charles Martin
Co-stars: George Sanders Yvonne De Carlo Zsa Zsa Gabor

1956 THE BRASS LEGEND
Director: Gerd Oswald
Co-stars: Hugh O'Brian Raymond Burr

1958 THE GUNFIGHT AT DODGE CITY
Director: Joseph Newman
Co-stars: Joel McCrea Julie Adams John McIntryre

1958 SOME CAME RUNNING
Director: Vincente Minnelli
Co-stars: Frank Sinatra Shirley MacLaine Dean Martin

1960 COMANCHE STATION
Director: Budd Boetticher
Co-stars: Randolph Scott Skip Homeier Claude Akins

SAMANTHA GATES

1978 THE WATER BABIES
Director: Lionel Jeffries
Co-stars: James Mason Billie Whitelaw Joan Greenwood

MARJORIE GATESON

1932 SOCIETY GIRL
Director: Sidney Lanfield
Co-stars: James Dunn Spencer Tracy Peggy Shannon

1932 STREET OF WOMEN
Director: Archie Mayo
Co-stars: Kay Francis Alan Dinehart Roland Young

1932 13 WOMEN
Director: George Archainbaud
Co-stars: Ricardo Cortez Irene Dunne Myrna Loy

1933 EMPLOYEES' ENTRANCE
Director: Roy Del Ruth
Co-stars: Warren William Loretta Young Alice White

1934 SIDE STREETS
Director: Alfred Green
Co-stars: Alice MacMahon Paul Kelly Ann Dvorak

1935 GOIN' TO TOWN
Director: Alexander Hall
Co-stars: Mae West Paul Cavanagh Ivan Lebedeff

1935 YOUR UNCLE DUDLEY
Co-stars: Edward Everett Horton Rosina Lawrence William Benedict

1936 BIG BROWN EYES
Director: Raoul Walsh
Co-stars: Cary Grant Joan Bennett Walter Pidgeon

1936 PRIVATE NUMBER
Director: Roy Del Ruth
Co-stars: Loretta Young Robert Taylor Basil Rathbone

1937 VOGUES OF 1938
Director: Irving Cummings
Co-stars: Joan Bennett Helen Vinson Alan Mowbray

1937 TURN OFF THE MOON
Director: Lewis Seiler
Co-stars: Charles Ruggles Ben Blue Kenny Baker

1937 ARIZONA MAHONEY
Co-star: Joe Cook

1937 WE HAVE OUR MOMENTS
Director: Alfred Werker
Co-stars: James Dunn Sally Eilers David Niven

1938 STABLEMATES
Director: Sam Wood
Co-stars: Wallace Beery Mickey Rooney Margaret Hamilton

1938 THE DUKE OF WEST POINT
Director: Alfred Green
Co-stars: Louis Hayward Joan Fontaine Tom Brown

1938 MAKING THE HEADLINES
Co-stars: Jack Holt Beverley Roberts Tom Kennedy

1940 PAROLE FIXER
Co-star: Robert Paige

1940 POP ALWAYS PAYS
Director: Leslie Goodwins
Co-stars: Leon Errol Dennis O'Keefe Adele Pearce

1941 INTERNATIONAL LADY
Director: Tim Whelan
Co-stars: Ilona Massey George Brent Basil Rathbone

1941 ESCAPE TO GLORY
Director: John Brahm
Co-stars: Pat O'Brien Constance Bennett

1941 THE OBLIGING YOUNG LADY
Director: Richard Wallace
Co-stars: Joan Carroll Edmond O'Brien Eve Arden

1941 HONOLULU LU
Co-stars: Lupe Velez Leo Carrillo Lloyd Bridges Larry Parks

1942 RINGS ON HER FINGERS
Director: Rouben Mamoulian
Co-stars: Gene Tierney Henry Fonda Laird Cregar

1943 RHYTHM OF THE ISLANDS
Director: Roy William Neill
Co-stars: Allan Jones Jane Frazee Andy Devine

1943 NO TIME FOR LOVE
Director: Mitchell Leisen
Co-stars: Claudette Colbert Fred MacMurray Ilka Chase

1944 EVER SINCE VENUS
Director: Arthur Dreifuss
Co-stars: Hugh Herbert Glenda Farrell Ann Savage

1944 SEVEN DAYS ASHORE
Co-stars: Virginia Mayo Alan Dinehart Amelita Ward

1946 ONE MORE TOMORROW
Director: Peter Godfrey
Co-stars: Ann Sheridan Dennis Morgan Jack Carson

JILL GATSBY

1987 A RETURN TO SALEM'S LOT
Director: Larry Cohen
Co-stars: Michael Moriarty Evelyn Keyes June Havoc

DANIELLE GAUBERT

1963 FLIGHT FROM ASHIYA
Director: Michael Anderson
Co-stars: Yul Brynner Richard Widmark Shirley Knight

1970 UNDERGROUND
Director: Arthur Nader
Co-stars: Robert Goulet Laurence Dobkin Carl Duering

1972 THE SKI RAIDERS
Director: George Englund
Co-stars: Jean-Claude Killy Cliff Potts Vittorio De Sica

MARIE STEFANE GAUDRY

1992 ANGEL SQUARE
Director: Anne Wheeler
Co-stars: Ned Beatty Jeremy Radick

JUDITH GAULT

1976 PARTNERS
Director: Dan Owen
Co-stars: Denholm Elliott Hollis McLaren Lee Broker

VALERIE GAUNT

1957 THE CURSE OF FRANKENSTEIN
Director: Terence Fisher
Co-stars: Peter Cushing Christopher Lee Noel Hood

1958 DRACULA
Director: Terence Fisher
Co-stars: Peter Cushing Christopher Lee Carol Marsh

ERICA GAVIN

1970 BEYOND THE VALLEY OF THE DOLLS
Director: Russ Meyer
Co-stars: Dolly Read Cynthia Myers Edy Williams

1974 CAGED HEAT
Director: Jonathan Demme
Co-stars: Juanita Brown Roberta Collins Rainbeaux Smith

CASSANDRA GAVIOLA

1982 CONAN THE BARBARIAN
Director: John Milius
Co-stars: Arnold Schwarzenegger James Earl Jones Mako

LISA GAYE

1954 DRUMS ACROSS THE RIVER
Director: Nathan Juran
Co-stars: Audie Murphy Walter Brennan Lyle Bettger

1956 ROCK AROUND THE CLOCK
Director: Fred Sears
Co-stars: Bill Haley Little Richard Alan Freed

1956 TEN THOUSAND BEDROOMS
Director: Richard Thorpe
Co-stars: Dean Martin Eva Bartok Paul Henreid

1966 CASTLE OF EVIL
Director: Francis Lyon
Co-stars: Virginia Mayo Scott Brady David Brian

1989 THE TOXIC AVENGER PART II
Director: Michael Herz
Co-stars: Ron Fazio John Altamura Rich Collins

**1991 CLASS OF NUKE 'EM HIGH PART II
SUBHUMANOID MELTDOWN**
Director: Eric Louzil
Co-star: Leesa Rowland

ANNA GAYNOR

1957 SEVEN THUNDERS
Director: Hugo Fregonese
Co-stars: James Robertson Justice Stephen Boyd Tony Wright

1964 LIFE UPSIDE DOWN
Director: Alain Jessua
Co-stars: Charles Denner Nicole Gueden

JANET GAYNOR *(Married Charles Farrell)*
Oscar For Best Actress In 1927 For "Sunrise" And For "Seventh Heaven"
Nominated For Best Actress In 1937 For "A Star Is Born"

1926 THE JOHNSTOWN FLOOD
Director: Irving Cummings
Co-stars: George O'Brien Paul Panzer George Harris

1927 SUNRISE
Director: F.W. Murnau
Co-stars: George O'Brien Margaret Livingston

1927 SEVENTH HEAVEN
Director: Frank Borzage
Co-stars: Charles Farrell David Butler

1928 STREET ANGELS
Director: Frank Borzage
Co-stars: Charles Farrell Henry Armetta Guido Trento

1929 SUNNY SIDE UP
Director: David Butler
Co-stars: Charles Farrell Ed Brendel Marjorie White

1929 FOUR DEVILS
Co-stars: Charles Morton Nancy Drexel Barry Norton

1930 HIGH SOCIETY BLUES
Director: David Butler
Co-stars: Charles Farrell Hedda Hopper Louise Fazenda

1930 HAPPY DAYS
Director: Benjamin Stoloff
Co-stars: Charles Farrell Marjorie White

1930 THE MAN WHO CAME BACK
Director: Raoul Walsh
Co-stars: Charles Farrell Kenneth MacKenna Mary Forbes

1931 MERELY MARY ANN
Director: Henry King
Co-stars: Charles Farrell Beryl Mercer G.P. Huntley

1931 DELICIOUS
Director: David Butler
Co-stars: Charles Farrell El Brendel Mischa Auer

1931 DADDY LONG LEGS
Director: Alfred Santell
Co-stars: Warner Baxter Una Merkel Sheila Manners

1932 THE FIRST YEAR
Director: William Howard
Co-stars: Charles Farrell Minna Gombell Dudley Digges

1932 TESS OF THE STORM COUNTRY
Director: Alfred Santell
Co-stars: Charles Farrell Dudley Digges June Clyde

1933 STATE FAIR
Director: Henry King
Co-stars: Will Rogers Lew Ayres Sally Eilers

1933 PADDY THE NEXT BEST THING
Director: Harry Lachman
Co-stars: Warner Baxter Walter Connolly Margaret Lindsay

1933 ADORABLE
Director: William Dieterle
Co-stars: Henri Garat C. Aubrey Smith Herbert Mundin

1934 CAROLINA
Director: Henry King
Co-stars: Lionel Barrymore Robert Young Mona Barrie

1934 CHANGE OF HEART
Director: John Blystone
Co-stars: Charles Farrell Ginger Rogers James Dunn

1934 SERVANTS' ENTRANCE
Director: Frank Lloyd
Co-stars: Lew Ayres Walter Connolly Ned Sparks

1935 ONE MORE SPRING
Co-stars: Warner Baxter Grant Mitchell Jane Darwell

1935 THE FARMER TAKES A WIFE
Director: Victor Fleming
Co-stars: Henry Fonda Charles Bickford Andy Devine

1936 LADIES IN LOVE
Director: Edward Griffith
Co-stars: Simone Simon Tyrone Power Don Ameche

1936 SMALL TOWN GIRL
Director: William Wellman
Co-stars: Robert Taylor James Stewart Binnie Barnes

1937 A STAR IS BORN
Director: William Wellman
Co-stars: Fredric March Adolphe Menjou Andy Devine

1938 THREE LOVES HAS NANCY
Director: Richard Thorpe
Co-stars: Robert Montgomery Franchot Tone Guy Kibbee

1938 THE YOUNG IN HEART
Director: Richard Wallace
Co-stars: Douglas Fairbanks Roland Young

1957 BERNADINE
Director: Henry Levin
Co-stars: Pat Boone Terry Moore Richard Sargeant

MITZI GAYNOR

1950 MY BLUE HEAVEN
Director: Henry Koster
Co-stars: Betty Grable Dan Dailey David Wayne Jane Wyatt

1951 TAKE CARE OF MY LITTLE GIRL
Director: Jean Negulesco
Co-stars: Jeanne Crain Jean Peters Dale Robertson

1951 GOLDEN GIRL
Director: Lloyd Bacon
Co-stars: Dale Robertson Dennis Day James Barton Una Merkel

1952 BLOODHOUNDS OF BROADWAY
Director: Harmon Jones
Co-stars: Scott Brady Michael O'Shea Marguerite Chapman

1952 WE'RE NOT MARRIED
Director: Edmund Goulding
Co-stars: Victor Moore Ginger Rogers Marilyn Monroe

1952 DOWN AMONG THE SHELTERING PALMS
Director: Edmund Goulding
Co-stars: Gloria DeHaven Jane Greer David Wayne

1953 THE I DON'T CARE GIRL
Director: Lloyd Bacon
Co-stars: David Wayne Oscar Levant George Jessel

1954 THERE'S NO BUSINESS LIKE SHOW BUSINESS
Director: Walter Lang
Co-stars: Ethel Merman Dan Dailey Marilyn Monroe

1956 ANYTHING GOES
Director: Robert Lewis
Co-stars: Bing Crosby Donald O'Connor Zizi Jeanmaire

1956 THE BIRDS AND THE BEES
Director: Preston Sturges
Co-stars: George Gobel David Niven Fred Clark

1957 LES GIRLS
Director: George Cukor
Co-stars: Gene Kelly Kay Kendall Tainia Elg Jacques Bergerac

1957 THE JOKER IS WILD
Director: Charles Vidor
Co-stars: Frank Sinatra Jeanne Crain Eddie Albert

1958 SOUTH PACIFIC
Director: Joshua Logan
Co-stars: Rossano Brazzi John Kerr France Nuyen Juanita Hall

1959 HAPPY ANNIVERSARY
Director: David Miller
Co-stars: David Niven Carl Reiner Patty Duke Loring Smith

1960 SURPRISE PACKAGE
Director: Stanley Donen
Co-stars: Yul Bryner Noel Coward George Coulo, George Couloris

1963 FOR LOVE OR MONEY
Director: Michael Gordon
Co-stars: Kirk Douglas Thelma Ritter Gig Young

EUNICE GAYSON

1951 TO HAVE AND TO HOLD
Director: Godfrey Grayson
Co-stars: Avis Scott Patrick Barr Robert Ayres

1954 OUT OF THE CLOUDS
Director: Basil Dearden
Co-stars: Anthony Steel Robert Beatty Gordon Harker

1954 DANCE LITTLE LADY
Director: Val Guest
Co-stars: Mai Zetterling Terence Morgan Mandy Miller

1956 THE LAST MAN TO HANG?
Director: Terence Fisher
Co-stars: Tom Conway Elizabeth Sellars Anthony Newley

1956 ZARAK
Director: Terence Young
Co-stars: Victor Mature Michael Wilding Anita Ekberg

1957 CARRY ON ADMIRAL
Director: Val Guest
Co-stars: David Tomlinson Peggy Cummings Brian Reece

1958 THE REVENGE OF FRANKENSTEIN
Director: Terence Fisher
Co-stars: Peter Cushing Francis Matthews

1962 DR. NO
Director: Terence Young
Co-stars: Sean Connery Ursula Andress Jack Lord

1963 FROM RUSSIA WITH LOVE
Director: Terence Young
Co-stars: Sean Connery Robert Shaw Lotte Lenya

GWEN GAZE

1937 I COVER THE WAR
Co-star: John Wayne

1937 PARTNERS OF THE PLAINS
Co-stars: William Boyd Russell Hayden John Warburton

1943 TWO-FISTED JUSTICE
Co-star: John King

WENDY GAZELLE

1987 SAMMY AND ROSIE GET LAID
Director: Stephen Frears
Co-stars: Shashi Kapoor Claire Bloom Frances Barber

1987 HOT PURSUIT
Director: Steven Lisberger
Co-stars: John Cusack Robert Loggia Jerry Stiller

1989 TRIUMPH OF THE SPIRIT
Director: Robert Young
Co-stars: Willem Dafoe Robert Loggia Edward James Olmos

LUELLA GEAR

1938 CAREFREE
Director: Mark Sandrich
Co-stars: Fred Astaire Ginger Rogers Ralph Bellamy

1954 PHFFFT!
Director: Mark Robson
Co-stars: Jack Lemon Judy Holliday Kim Novak

VALERIE GEARON

1962   NINE HOURS TO RAMA
Director: Mark Robson
Co-stars: Jose Ferrer Diane Baker Robert Morley

1965   INVASION
Director: Alan Bridges
Co-stars: Edward Judd Yoko Tani Lyndon Brook Tsai Chin

1969   ANNE OF A THOUSAND DAYS
Director: Charles Jarrott
Co-stars: Richard Burton Genevieve Bujold

CYNTHIA GEARY

1994   8 SECONDS
Director: John Avildsen
Co-stars: Luke Perry Stephen Baldwin James Rebhorn

LIZ GEBHARDT

1971   PLEASE SIR
Director: Mark Stuart
Co-stars: John Alderton Deryck Guyler Carol Hawkins

PRUNELLA GEE

1975   THE WILBY CONSPIRACY
Director: Ralph Nelson
Co-stars: Sidney Poitier Michael Caine Nicol Williamson

1989   STORMY MONDAY
Director: Mike Figgis
Co-stars: Melanie Griffith Tommy Lee Jones Sean Bean Sting

ELLEN GEER

1971   HAROLD AND MAUDE
Director: Hal Ashby
Co-stars: Ruth Gordon Bud Cort Cyril Cusack

1979   OVER THE EDGE
Director: Jonathan Kaplan
Co-stars: Michael Kramer Pamela Ludwig Matt Dillon

JUDY GEESON

1967   BESERK
Director: Jim O'Connolly
Co-stars: Joan Crawford Robert Hardy Diana Dors Ty Hardin

1967   TO SIR WITH LOVE
Director: James Clavell
Co-stars: Sidney Poitier Suzy Kendall Patricia Routledge Lulu

1967   HERE WE GO ROUND THE MULBERRY BUSH
Director: Clive Donner
Co-stars: Barry Evans Denholm Elliott Moyra Fraser

1968   HAMMERHEAD
Director: David Miller
Co-stars: Vince Edwards Peter Vaughan Diana Dors

1969   PRUDENCE AND THE PILL
Director: Fielder Cook
Co-stars: David Niven Deborah Kerr Edith Evans

1969   THREE INTO TWO WON'T GO
Director: Peter Hall
Co-stars: Rod Steiger Claire Bloom Peggy Ashcroft

1969   TWO GENTLEMAN SHARING
Director: Ted Kotcheff
Co-stars: Robin Phillips Hal Frederick Rachel Kempson

1970   ONE OF THOSE THINGS
Director: Erik Balling
Co-star::   Roy Dotrice

1970   GOODBYE GEMINI
Director: Alan Gibson
Co-stars: Martin Potter Michael Redgrave Alexis Kanner

1970   THE EXECUTIONER
Director: Sam Wanamaker
Co-stars: George Peppard Nigel Patrick Joan Collins

1971   TEN RILLINGTON PLACE
Director: Richard Fleischer
Co-stars: Richard Attenborough John Hurt

1972   FEAR IN THE NIGHT
Director: Jimmy Sangster
Co-stars: Peter Cushing Joan Collins Ralph Bates

1972   DOOMWATCH
Director: Peter Sasdy
Co-stars: Ian Bannen George Sanders John Paul Simon Oates

1974   DIAGNOSIS: MURDER
Director: Sidney Hayers
Co-stars: Christopher Lee Jon Finch Tony Beckley

1974   PERCY'S PROGRESS
Director: Ralph Thomas
Co-stars: Leigh Lawson Elke Sommer Denholm Elliott

1975   BRANNIGAN
Director: Douglas Hickox
Co-stars: John Wayne Mel Ferrer John Stride James Booth

1976   CARRY ON ENGLAND
Director: Gerald Thomas
Co-stars: Windsor Davies Patrick Mower Diane Langton

1976   ADVENTURES OF A TAXI DRIVER
Director: Stanley Long
Co-stars: Barry Evans Liz Fraser Diana Dors

1976   THE EAGLE HAD LANDED
Director: John Sturges
Co-stars: Michael Caine Robert Duvall Jenny Agutter

1978   DOMINIQUE
Director: Michael Anderson
Co-stars: Jean Simmons Cliff Robertson Jenny Agutter Simon Ward

1982   THE PLAGUE DOGS *(Voice)*
Director: Martin Rosen
Co-stars: John Hurt James Bolam Barbara Leigh-Hunt

1988   THE SECRET LIFE OF KATHY McCORMICK
Director: Robert Lewis
Co-stars: Barbara Eden Josh Taylor

SALLY GEESON

1969   WHAT'S GOOD FOR THE GOOSE
Director: Menahem Golan
Co-stars: Noman Wisdom Terence Alexander

1970   CRY OF THE BANSHEE
Director: Gordon Hessler
Co-stars: Vincent Price Elizabeth Bergner Patrick Mower

1971   MR. FORBUSH AND THE PENGUINS
Director: Roy Boutling
Co-stars: John Hurt Hayley Mills Tony Britton

1972   BLESS THIS HOUSE
Director: Gerald Thomas
Co-stars: Sid James Diana Coupland Terry Scott

1972   CARRY ON ABROAD
Director: Gerald Thomas
Co-stars: Sid James Kenneth Williams Charles Hawtrey

1973   CARRY ON GIRLS
Director: Gerald Thomas
Co-stars: Sid James Barbara Windsor June Whitfield

DEBORAH GEFFNER

1983 LEGS
Director: Jerrold Freedman
Co-stars: Gwen Verdon John Heard Sheree North

1984 EXTERMINATOR 2
Director: Mark Buntzman
Co-stars: Robert Ginty Mario Van Peebles Frankie Faison

DANIELLE GEGAUFF

1975 UNE PARTIE DE PLAISIR
Director: Claude Chabrol
Co-stars: Paul Gegauff Paula Moore Michel Valette

MARTHA GEHMAN

1991 A KISS BEFORE DYING
Director: James Dearden
Co-stars: Matt Dillon Sean Young Max Von Sydow

1994 THREESOME
Director: Andrew Fleming
Co-stars: Lara Flynn Boyle Stephen Baldwin Alexis Arquette

LINDA GEISER

1965 THE PAWNBROKER
Director: Sidney Lumet
Co-stars: Rod Steiger Geraldine Fitzgerald Brock Peters

TONI GELLMAN

1980 BABY COMES HOME
Director: Waris Hussein
Co-stars: Colleen Dewhurst Warren Oates Mildred Dunnock

RHODA GEMIGNANI

1984 CONCRETE HEAT
Director: Jay Daniel
Co-stars: John Getz Darlanne Fluegel Kenneth McMillan

RUTH GEMMELL

1991 WHO NEEDS A HEART?
Director: John Akomfrah
Co-stars: Caroline Burghard Treva Ettiene

1997 FEVER PITCH
Director: David Evans
Co-stars: Colin Firth Luke Aikman Neil Pearson

LAURA GEMSER

1978 THE BUSHIDO BLADE
Director: Tom Katani
Co-stars: Richard Boone Toshiro Mifune Frank Converse

VERONIQUE GENEST

1989 THE SILENT WOMAN
Director: Joyce Bunuel
Co-stars: Marie-Christine Barrault Pierre Clementti

VERONICA GENG

1990 THE BIG BANG
Director: James Toback
Co-stars: Emma Astner Missy Boyd Tony Sirico

MARCELLE GENIAT

1935 CRIME AND PUNISHMENT
Director: Pierre Chenal
Co-stars: Pierre Blanchar Harry Baur

LINA GENNARI

1952 UMBERTO D
Director: Vittorio De Sica
Co-stars: Carlo Battista Pia Casillio

ALICE GENTLE

1930 GOLDEN DAWN
Director: Ray Enright
Co-stars: Walter Woolf Vivienne Segal Lupino Lane

1930 SONG OF THE FLAME
Co-stars: Bernice Claire Alexander Gray

LILI GENTLE

1958 SING, BOY, SING
Director: Henry Ephron
Co-stars: Tommy Sands Edmond O'Brien John McIntyre

MINNY GENTRY

1972 COME BACK, CHARLESTON BLUE
Director: Mark Warren
Co-stars: Godfrey Cambridge Raymond St. Jacques

1992 DEF BY TEMPTATION
Director: James Bond III
Co-stars: James Bond III Cythia Bond Bill Nuxn

FLORENCE GEORGE

1938 COLLEGE SWING
Director: Raoul Walsh
Co-stars: George Burns Gracie Allan Bob Hope

GLADYS GEORGE

Nominated For Best Actress In 1936 For "Valiant Is The Word For Carrie"

1934 STRAIGHT IS THE WAY
Co-star: Franchot Tone

1936 VALLIANT IS THE WORD FOR CARRIE
Director: Wesley Ruggles
Co-stars: John Howard Dudley Digges

1937 THEY GAVE HIM A GUN
Director: W.S. Van Dyke
Co-stars: Spencer Tracy Franchot Tone Mary Treen

1937 MADAME X
Director: Sam Wood
Co-stars: John Beal Warren William Reginald Owen Henry Daniell

1938 MARIE ANTOINETTE
Director: W.S. Van Dyke
Co-stars: Tyrone Power Norma Shearer John Barrymore

1938 LOVE IS A HEADACHE
Director: Richard Thorpe
Co-stars: Franchot Tone Mickey Rooney Jessie Ralph

1939 THE ROARING TWENTIES
Director: Raoul Walsh
Co-stars: James Cagney Humphrey Bogart Priscilla Lane

1939 I'M FROM MISSOURI
Director: Theodore Reed
Co-stars: Bob Burns Gene Lockhart Patricia Morison

1939 HERE I AM A STRANGER
Director: Roy Del Ruth
Co-stars: Richard Dix Richard Greene Roland Young Brenda Joyce

1939 A CHILD IS BORN
Director: Lloyd Bacon
Co-stars: Geraldine Fitzgerald Jeffrey Lynn Gale Page

1940 THE HOUSE ACROSS THE BAY
Director: Archie Mayo
Co-stars: Joan Bennett George Raft Walter Pidgeon

1940 THE WAY OF ALL FLESH
Director: Louis King
Co-stars: Akim Tamiroff Muriel Angelus Fritz Leiber

1941 THE MALTESE FALCON
Director: John Huston
Co-stars: Humphrey Bogart Mary Astor Peter Lorre

1941 HIT THE ROAD
Co-stars: Evelyn Ankers Bowery Boys Barton MacLane

1941 THE LADY FROM CHEYENNE
Director: Vincent Sherman
Co-stars: Ida Lupino Joan Leslie Dennis Morgan Jack Carson

1943 THE CRYSTAL BALL
Director: Elliott Nugent
Co-stars: Paulette Goddard Ray Milland William Bendix

1944 CHRISTMAS HOLIDAY
Director: Robert Siodmak
Co-stars: Deanna Durbin Gene Kelly Gale Sondergaard

1944 MINSTREL MAN
Director: Joseph Lewis
Co-stars: Benny Fields Roscoe Carns

1945 STEPPIN' IN SOCIETY
Director: Alexander Esway
Co-stars: Ruth Terry Lola Lane Jack La Rue

1946 THE BEST YEARS OF OUR LIVES
Director: William Wyler
Co-stars: Myrna Loy Dana Andrews Teresa Wright Fredric March

1947 ALIAS A GENTLEMAN
Director: Harry Beaumont
Co-stars: Wallace Beery Tom Drake Leon Ames

1949 FLAMINGO ROAD
Director: Michael Curtiz
Co-stars: Joan Crawford David Brian Sydney Greenstreet

1950 UNDERCOVER GIRL
Director: Joseph Pevney
Co-stars: Alexis Smith Scott Brady Richard Egan

1950 BRIGHT LEAF
Director: Michael Curtis
Co-stars: Gary Cooper Lauren Bacall Patricia Neal Jack Carson

1951 LULLABY OF BROADWAY
Director: David Butler
Co-stars: Doris Day Gene Nelson Billy De Wolfe

1951 DETECTIVE STORY
Director: William Wyler
Co-stars: Kirk Douglas Eleanor Parker William Bendix

GRACE GEORGE

1943 JOHNNY COME LATELY
Director: William Howard
Co-stars: James Cagney Marjorie Main Marjorie Lord

LYNDA DAY GEORGE

1970 CHISUM
Director: Andrew McLaglen
Co-stars: John Wayne Forrest Tucker Ben Johnson

1973 SHE CRIED MURDER
Director: Herschel Daugherty
Co-stars: Telly Savalas Mike Farrell Kate Reid

1974 THE BARBARY COAST
Director: Bill Bixby
Co-stars: William Shatner Dennis Cole John Vernon

1976 DAY OF THE ANIMALS
Director: William Girdler
Co-stars: Christopher George Leslie Nielsen Ruth Roman

1976 MAYDAY AT 40,000 FEET!
Director: Robert Butler
Co-stars: David Janssen Christopher George

1977 MURDER AT THE WORLD SERIES
Director: Andrew McLaglen
Co-stars: Murray Hamilton Michael Parks

1977 PANIC AT THE LAKEWOOD MANOR
Director: Robert Sheerer
Co-stars: Robert Foxworth Myrna Loy Brian Dennehy

1977 ALIENS FROM SPACESHIP EARTH
Director: Don Como
Co-star: Donovan

1978 THE AMAZING CAPTAIN NERO
Director: Alex March
Co-stars: Jose Ferrer Burgess Meredith

1983 YOUNG WARRIORS
Director: Lawrence Foldes
Co-stars: Ernest Borgnine Richard Roundtree

MAUDE GEORGE

1922 FOOLISH WIVES
Director: Erich Von Stroheim
Co-stars: Erich Von Stroheim Rudolph Christians Mae Busch

1928 THE WEDDING MARCH
Director: Erich Von Stroheim
Co-stars: Erich Von Stroheim Fay Wray Zasu Pitts Matthew Betz

MURIEL GEORGE

1934 NELL GWENN
Director: Herbert Wilcox
Co-stars: Anna Neagle Cedric Hardwicke Miles Malleson

1935 LIMELIGHT
Director: Herbert Wilcox
Co-stars: Anna Neagle Arthur Tracy Tilly Losch

1937 LANCASHIRE LUCK
Director: Henry Cass
Co-stars: Wendy Hiller George Carney Nigel Stock

1937 MERRY COMES TO TOWN
Director: George King
Co-stars: Zasu Pitts Betty Ann Davies Hermione Gingold

1938 CRACKERJACK
Director: Albert De Courville
Co-stars: Tom Walls Lilli Palmer Noel Madison

1941 COTTAGE TO LET
Director: Anthony Asquith
Co-stars: Leslie Banks Alastair Sim John Mills

1942 ALIBI
Director: Brian Desmond Hurst
Co-stars: Margaret Lockwood Hugh Sinclair James Mason

1943 DEAR OCTOPUS
Director: Harold French
Co-stars: Margaret Lockwood Michael Wilding Celia Johnson

1950 THE DANCING YEARS
Director: Harold French
Co-stars: Dennis Price Giselle Preville Patricia Dainton

1950 LAST HOLIDAY
Director: Henry Cass
Co-stars: Alec Guinness Kay Walsh Beatrice Campbell

RITA GEORGE

1976 HOLLYWOOD BOULEVARD
Director: Joe Dante
Co-stars: Candice Rialson Mary Woronov Dick Miller

SUE GEORGE

1957 THE DALTON GIRLS
Director: Reginald LeBorg
Co-stars: Merry Anders Penny Edwards John Russeell

SUSAN GEORGE *(Married Simon MacCorkindale)*

1967 THE SORCERERS
Director: Michael Reeves
Co-stars: Boris Karloff Catherine Lacy Ian Ogilvy

1968 THE STRANGE AFFAIR
Director: David Greene
Co-stars: Michael York Jeremy Kemp Jack Watson

1969 TWINKY
Director: Richard Donner
Co-stars: Charles Bronson Trevor Howard Michael Craig

1969 ALL NEAT IN BLACK STOCKINGS
Director: Christopher Monahan
Co-stars: Victor Henry Jack Shepherd

1970 EYEWITNESS
Director: John Hough
Co-stars: Mark Lester Lionel Jeffries Peter Vaughan

1970 THE LOOKING GLASS WAR
Director: Frank Pierson
Co-stars: Christopher Jones Pia Degermark Ralph Richardson

1970 SPRING AND PORT WINE
Director: Peter Hammond
Co-stars: James Mason Diana Coupland Rodney Bewes

1971 STRAW DOGS
Director: Sam Peckinpah
Co-stars: Dustin Hoffman Peter Vaughan David Warner

1971 FRIGHT
Director: Peter Collinson
Co-stars: Ian Bannen Dennis Waterman George Cole Honor Blackman

1974 DIRTY MARY, CRAZY LARRY
Director: John Hough
Co-stars: Peter Fonda Adam Roarke Vic Morrow

1975 MANDINGO
Director: Richard Fleischer
Co-stars: James Mason Perry King Ken Norton Brenda Sykes

1975 OUT OF SEASON
Director: Alan Bridges
Co-stars: Vanessa Redgrave Cliff Robertson Edward Evans

1976 A SMALL TOWN IN TEXAS
Director: Jack Starrett
Co-stars: Timothy Bottoms Bo Hopkins Art Hindle

1977 TOMORROW NEVER COMES
Director: Peter Collinson
Co-stars: Oliver Reed Stephen McHattie Raymond Burr

1981 VENOM
Director: Piers Haggard
Co-stars: Sterling Hayden Klaus Kinski Oliver Reed Sarah Miles

1982 THE FINAL EYE
Director: Robert Michael Lewis
Co-stars: Joseph Cortese Tom Clancy Donald Pleasence

1982 ENTER THE NINJA
Director: Menahem Golan
Co-stars: Franco Nero Alex Courtney Sho Kosugi

1984 THE JIGSAW MAN
Director: Terence Young
Co-stars: Michael Caine Laurence Olivier Robert Powell

1988 JACK THE RIPPER
Director: David Wickes
Co-stars: Michael Caine Armand Assante Jane Seymour

1990 THAT SUMMER OF WHITE ROSES
Director: Rajko Grlic
Co-stars: Tom Conti Rod Steiger Alun Armstrong

1994 THE HOUSE THAT MARY BOUGHT
Director: Simon MacCorkindale
Co-star: Ben Cross

TRICIA GEORGE

1981 DAYS AT THE BEACH
Director: Malcolm Mowbray
Co-stars: Sam Kelly Mark Aspinall Julie Walters

1982 THE MISSIONARY
Director: Richard Loncraine
Co-stars: Michael Palin Maggie Smith Trevor Howard

OLGA GEORGES-PICOT

1969 CONNECTING ROOMS
Director: Franklin Gollings
Co-stars: Bette Davis Michael Redgrave Gabrielle Drake

1970 THE MAN WHO HAUNTED HIMSELF
Director: Basil Dearden
Co-stars: Roger Moore Hildegarde Neil John Carson

1973 THE DAY OF THE JACKAL
Director: Fred Zinnemann
Co-stars: Edward Fox Alan Badel Eric Porter

1974 PERSECUTION
Director: Don Chaffey
Co-stars: Lana Turner Ralph Bates Trevor Howard

LILLIANA GERACE

1965 FISTS IN THE POCKET
Director: Marco Bellocchio
Co-stars: Lou Castel Paola Pitagora Marino Mase

1980 L'ETOIL DU NORD
Director: Pierre Granier-Deferre
Co-stars: Simone Signorett Philippe Noiret

CARMELITA GERAGHTY

1925 THE PLEASURE GARDEN
Director: Alfred Hitchcock
Co-stars: Virginia Valli John Stuart Miles Mander

1926 THE CANYON OF LIGHT

1927 MY BEST GIRL
Director: Sam Taylor
Co-stars: Mary Pickford Charles Rogers Lucien Littlefield

1927 THE LAST TRAIL
Director: Lewis Seiler
Co-stars: Tom Mix William Davidson Robert Brower

MARITA GERAGHTY

1991 SLEEPING WITH THE ENEMY
Director: Joseph Ruben
Co-stars: Julia Roberts Patrick Bergen Kevin Anderson

1991 A CHILD FOR SATAN
Director: Robert Lieberman
Co-stars: Peter Kowanko Shirley Knight Anthony Zerbe

1993 GROUNDHOG DAY
Director: Harold Ramis
Co-stars: Bill Murray Andie MacDowell Chris Elliott

CLAIRE GERARD

1944 UNE FEMME DISPARAIT
Director: Jacques Feyder
Co-stars: Francoise Rosay Henri Guisol Jean Nohain

MARY GERMAINE

1952 WHERE'S CHARLEY?
Director: David Butler
Co-stars: Ray Bolger Robert Shackleton Margaretta Scott

1952 WOMEN OF TWILIGHT
Director: Gordon Parry
Co-stars: Freda Jackson Rene Ray Lois Maxwell

1953 HOUSE OF BLACKMAIL
Director: Maurice Elvy
Co-stars: William Sylvester John Arnatt Denis Shaw

1953 FLANNELFOOT
Director: MacLean Rogers
Co-stars: Ronald Howard Jack Watling Ronald Adam

1954 THE GREEN BUDDHA
Director: John Lemont
Co-stars: Wayne Morris Walter Rilla Arnold Marle

JOANNE GERRARD

1993 THE SNAPPER
Director: Stephen Frears
Co-stars: Tina Kellegher Colm Meaney Ruth McCabe

LISA GERRITSON

1972 THE WAR BETWEEN MEN AND WOMEN
Director: Melville Shavelson
Co-stars: Jack Lemmon Barbara Harris

1974 MIXED COMPANY
Director: Melville Shavelson
Co-stars: Barbara Harris Joseph Bologna Tom Bosley

PATTY ANN GERRITY

1958 CAT ON A HOT TIN ROOF
Director: Richard Brooks
Co-stars: Paul Newman Elizabeth Taylor Burl Ives

GINA GERSHON

1988 COCKTAIL
Director: Roger Donaldson
Co-stars: Tom Cruise Bryan Brown Elizabeth Shue

1988 RED HEAT
Director: Walter Hill
Co-stars: Arnold Schwarzenegger James Belushi Larry Fishburne

1991 CITY OF HOPE
Director: John Sayles
Co-stars: Vincent Spano Tony LoBianco Barbara Williams

1991 OUT FOR JUSTICE
Director: John Flynn
Co-stars: Steven Seagal William Forsyth

1992 THE PLAYER
Director: Robert Altman
Co-stars: Tim Robins Greta Scacchi Whoppi Goldberg

1996 SHOWGIRLS
Director: Paul Verhoeven
Co-stars: Elizabeth Berkley Kyle MacLachlan Gina Raverna

1996 BOUND
Director: Larry Wachowski
Co-stars: Joe Pantoliano Jennifer Tilly

BETTY LOU GERSON

1958 THE FLY
Director: David Hedison
Co-stars: Patricia Owens Herbert Marshall

1961 ONE HUNDRED AND ONE DALMATIONS *(Voice)*
Director: Clyde Geronimi
Co-stars: Rod Taylor Cate Bauer

BERTA GERSTEN

1955 THE BENNY GOODMAN STORY
Director: Valentine Davies
Co-stars: Steve Allen Donna Reed Harry James

VALESKA GERT

1925 DIE FREUDLOSE GASSE
Director: G.W. Pabst
Co-stars: Greta Garbo Asta Nielsen Werner Kraus

1931 DIE DREIGROSCHENOPER
Director: G.W. Pabst
Co-stars: Rudolph Forster Lotte Lenya Carola Neher

JAMIE GERTZ

1985 MISCHIEF
Director: Mel Damski
Co-stars: Doug McKeon Chris Nash Kelly Preston

1986 SOLAR WARRIORS
Director: Alan Johnson
Co-stars: Richard Jordan Jason Patric Lukas Haas

1986 CROSSROADS
Director: Walter Hill
Co-stars: Ralph MacChio Joe Seneca Robert Judd

1987 LESS THAN ZERO
Director: Marek Kanievska
Co-stars: Andrew McCarthy Robert Downey Jnr. James Spader

1987 THE LOST BOYS
Director: Joel Schumacher
Co-stars: Jason Patric Corey Haim Dianne Wiest

1989 RENEGADES
Director: Jack Sholder
Co-stars: Kiefer Sutherland Lou Diamond Phillips Bob Knepper

1989 SILENCE LIKE GLASS
Director: Carl Schenkel
Co-stars: Martha Plimpton George Peppard Gayle Hunnicutt

1990 DON'T TELL HER IT'S ME
Director: Malcolm Mowbray
Co-stars: Shelley Long Steve Guttenberg

1990 SIBLING RIVALRY
Director: Carl Reiner
Co-stars: Kirstie Alley Bill Pullman Carrie Fisher

1992 JERSEY GIRL
Director: David Burton Morris
Co-stars: Dylan McDermott Joseph Bologna Molly Price

1996 TWISTER
Director: Jan De Bont
Co-stars: Bill Paxton Helen Hunt Cary Elwes

SONIA GESSNER

1982 BLOW TO THE HEART
Director: Gianni Amelio
Co-stars: Jean-Louis Trintignant Laura Morante Fausto Rossi

ESTELLE GETTY

1984 NO MAN'S LAND
Director: Rob Holcomb
Co-stars: Stella Stevens Terri Garber Janis Paige

1985 MASK
Director: Peter Bogdanovich
Co-stars: Cher Sam Elliott Eric Stoltz Laura Dern

1985 COPACABANA
Director: Waris Hussein
Co-stars: Barry Manilow Annette O'Toole Joseph Bologna

1987 MANNEQUIN
Director: Michael Gottlieb
Co-stars: Andrew McCarthy Kim Cattrall James Spader

1992 STOP OR MY MUM WILL SHOOT
Director: Roger Spottiswoode
Co-stars: Sylvester Stallone JoBeth Williams

TAMARA GEVA

1931 THE GIRL HABIT
Director: Eddie Cline
Co-stars: Charles Ruggles Margaret Dumont Sue Conroy

1937 MANHATTAN MERRY-GO-ROUND
Director: Charles Reiner
Co-stars: Phil Regan Ann Dvorak Gene Autry

1942 NIGHT PLANE FROM CHUNGKING
Director: Ralph Murphy
Co-stars: Ellen Drew Robert Preston Otto Kruger

1948 THE GAY INTRUDERS
Director: Ray McCarey
Co-stars: John Emery Leif Erickson Virginia Gregg

CESARINA GHERALDI

1942 WE THE LIVING
Director: Goffredo Alessandrini
Co-stars: Alida Valdi Rossano Brazzi

JULIE GHOLSON

1974 WHERE THE LILIES BLOOM
Director: William A. Graham
Co-stars: Harry Dean Stanton Jan Smithers

ALICE GHOSTLEY

1954 NEW FACES
Director: Harry Horner
Co-stars: Eartha Kitt Ronny Graham Robert Clary

1967 ONE BORN EVERY MINUTE
Director: Irvin Kershner
Co-stars: George C. Scott Michael Sarrazin Sue Lyon

1969 VIVA MAX
Director: Jerry Paris
Co-stars: Peter Ustinov Pamela Tiffin John Astin

1973 ACE ELI AND RODGER OF THE SKIES
Director: John Erman
Co-stars: Cliff Robertson Pamela Franklin

1976 GATOR
Director: Burt Reynolds
Co-stars: Burt Reynolds Jack Weston Lauren Hutton Jerry Reed

1978 GREASE
Director: Randal Kleiser
Co-stars: John Travolta Olivia Newton-John Stockard Channing

CYNTHIA GIBB

1985 YOUNGBLOOD
Director: Peter Markle
Co-stars: Rob Lowe Patrick Swayze Ed Lauter

1987 MALONE
Director: Elliott Nugent
Co-stars: Burt Reynolds Cliff Robertson Lauren Hutton

1988 JACK'S BACK
Director: Rowdy Herrington
Co-stars: James Spader Rod Loomis Chris Mulkey

1988 SHORT CIRCUIT 2
Director: Kenneth Johnson
Co-stars: Fisher Stevens Michael McKean Jack Weston

1989 THE KAREN CARPENTER STORY
Director: Joseph Sargent
Co-stars: Mitchell Anderson Louise Fletcher

1990 THE HOUSE ON SYCAMORE STREET
Director: Christian Nyby
Co-stars: Dick Van Dyke Stephen Caffrey

1990 DEATH WARRANT
Director: Deran Serafian
Co-stars: Jean-Claude Van Damme Robert Guillaume

1991 DIAGNOSIS OF MURDER
Director: Barry Steinberg
Co-stars: Dick Van Dyke Bill Bixby Mariette Hartley

1993 GYPSY
Director: Emile Ardolino
Co-stars: Bette Midler Peter Riegert Ed Asner

1993 A TWIST OF THE KNIFE
Director: Jerry London
Co-star: Dick Van Dyke

ROBYN GIBBES

1979 ALISON'S BIRTHDAY
Director: Ian Coughlan
Co-stars: Joanne Samuel Lou Brown Vincent Ball

MARIA GIBBS

1993 METEOR MAN
Director: Robert Townsend
Co-stars: Robert Townsend Bill Cosby James Earl Jones

BELINDA GIBLIN

1979 ALISON'S BIRTHDAY
Director: Ian Coughlan
Co-stars: Joanne Samuel Lou Brown Bunny Brooke

1985 THE EMPTY BEACH
Director: Chris Thomson
Co-stars: Bryan Brown Ray Barrett John Wood

ALTHEA GIBSON (*Ex Tennis Player*)

1959 THE HORSE SOLDIERS
Director: John Ford
Co-stars: John Wayne William Holden Constance Towers

DIANA GIBSON

1936 DANGEROUS WATERS
Co-star: Jack Holt

1937 BEHIND THE HEADLINES
Co-star: Lee Tracy

1937 ADVENTURE'S END
Co-stars: John Wayne Jimmie Lucas

FELICITY GIBSON

1970 ONE BRIEF SUMMER
Director: John MacKenzie
Co-stars: Clifford Evans Jennifer Hilary Peter Egan

HELEN GIBSON

1951 HOLLYWOOD STORY
Director: William Castle
Co-stars: Richard Conte Julie Adams Henry Hull

JUDITH GIBSON

1985 TRIAL RUN
Director: Melanie Read
Co-stars: Annie Whittle Christopher Brown Lee Grant

JULIE GIBSON

1944 THE CONTENDER
Co-stars: Larry Crabbe Arline Judge Glenn Strange

1949 THE BAD MEN OF TOMBSTONE
Director: Kurt Neumann
Co-stars: Broderick Crawford Barry Sullivan

KATHLEEN GIBSON

1939   THE GOOD OLD DAYS
Director: Roy William Neill
Co-stars: Max Miller Hal Waters Martita Hunt

MARTHA GIBSON

1993   FAMILY OF STRANGERS
Director: Sheldon Larry
Co-stars: Patty Duke Melissa Gilbert

MIMI GIBSON

1958   HOUSEBOAT
Director: Melville Shavelson
Co-stars: Cary Grant Sophia Loren Martha Hyer

VIRGININA GIBSON

1951   PAINTING THE CLOUDS WITH SUNSHINE
Director: David Butler
Co-stars: Virginia Mayo Gene Nelson Dennis Morgan

1952   ABOUT FACE
Director: Roy Del Ruth
Co-stars: Eddie Bracken Gordon MacRae Phyllis Kirk

1953   STOP YOU'RE KILLING ME
Director: Roy Del Ruth
Co-stars: Broderick Crawford Claire Trevor Bill Hayes

1954   SEVEN BRIDES FOR SEVEN BROTHERS
Director: Stanley Donen
Co-stars: Howard Keel Jane Powell Tommy Rall

1957   FUNNY FACE
Director: Stanley Donen
Co-stars: Fred Astaire Audrey Hepburn Kay Thompson

WYNNE GIBSON

1930   OUTSIDE THE LAW
Director: Tod Browning
Co-stars: Edward G. Robinson Mary Nolan Owen Moore

1930   THE FALL GUY
Co-stars: Mae Clark Jack Mulihall Pat O'Malley

1931   LADIES OF THE BIG HOUSE
Director: Marion Gering
Co-stars: Sylvia Sidney Gene Raymond Earle Fox

1931   MAN OF THE WORLD
Director: Richard Wallace
Co-stars: William Powell Carole Lombard

1931   CITY STREETS
Director: Rouben Mamoulian
Co-stars: Sylvia Sidney Gary Cooper Paul Lucas

1932   NIGHT AFTER NIGHT
Director: Archie Mayo
Co-stars: George Raft Constance Cummings Mae West

1932   LADY AND GENT
Co-star: George Bancroft

1932   THE STRANGE CASE OF CLARA DEANE
Director: Max Marcin
Co-stars: Pat O'Brien Frances Dee

1932   IF I HAD A MILLION
Director: Ernst Lubitsch
Co-stars: Charles Laughton Gary Cooper George Raft

1933   AGGIE APPLEBY, MAKER OF MAN
Director: Mark Sandrich
Co-stars: Charles Farrell William Gargan Zasu Pitts

1933   HER BODYGUARD
Co-stars: Edmund Lowe Edward Arnold

1933   CRIME OF THE CENTURY
Director: William Beaudine
Co-stars: Jean Hersholt Frances Dee

1933   GANG BUSTER
Director: Edward Sutherland
Co-stars: Jack Oakie Jean Arthur

1934   THE CAPTAIN HATES THE SEA
Director: Lewis Milestone
Co-stars: John Gilbert Walter Connelly

1934   SLEEPERS EAST
Co-star: Mona Barrie

1934   GAMBLING
Director: Rowland Lee
Co-stars: George M. Cohan Dorothy Burgess Theodore Newton

1934   I GIVE MY LOVE
Director: Karl Freund
Co-stars: Paul Lukas Eric Linden Anita Louise

1935   THE CROUCHING BEAST
Director: Victor Hanbury
Co-stars: Fritz Kortner Richard Bird Isabel Jeans

1938   FLIRTING WITH FATE
Director: Frank McDonald
Co-stars: Joe E. Brown Leo Carrillo Beverly Roberts

1938   GANGS OF NEW YORK
Director: James Cruze
Co-stars: Charles Bickford Ann Dvorak Alan Baxter

1939   MIRACLE ON MAIN STREET
Director: Steve Sekeley
Co-stars: Margo Walter Abel Jane Darwell Lyle Talbot

1940   FORGOTTEN GIRLS
Director: Phil Rosen
Co-stars: Louise Platt Donald Woods Robert Armstrong

1943   MYSTERY BROADCAST
Director: George Sherman
Co-stars: Frank Albertson Ruth Terry Nils Asther

PAMELA GIDLEY

1988   THE BLUE IGUANA
Director: John Lafia
Co-stars: Dylan McDermott Jessica Harper Dean Stockwell

1988   CHERRY 2000
Director: Steve De Jarnatt
Co-stars: Melanie Griffiths David Andrews Ben Johnson

1988   PERMANENT RECORD
Director: Marisa Silver
Co-stars: Alan Boyce Keanu Reeves Michelle Meyrink

1991   LIEBSTRAUM
Director: Mike Figgis
Co-stars: Kevin Anderson Kim Novak Bill Pullman

1992   ANGEL STREET
Director: Rod Holcomb
Co-star::   Robin Givens

1993   PAPER HEARTS
Director: Rod McCall
Co-stars: Sally Kirkland James Brolin Kris Kristofferson

THERESE GIEHSE

1958   MADCHEN IN UNIFORM
Director: Geza Radvanyl
Co-stars: Lilli Palmer Romy Schneider Christine Kaufman

1974   LACOMBE, LUCIEN
Director: Louis Malle
Co-stars: Pierre Blaise Aurore Clement Gilberte Rivet

FRANCES GIFFORD

1941 THE RELUCTANT DRAGON
Director: Alfred Werker
Co-stars: Robert Benchley Nana Bryant

1942 TOMBSTONE
Director: William McGann
Co-stars: Richard Dix Kent Taylor Edgar Buchanan

1942 THE REMARKABLE ANDREW
Director: Stuart Heisler
Co-stars: William Holden Brian Donlevy Ellen Drew

1942 MY HEART BELONGS TO DADDY
Director: Robert Siodmak
Co-stars: Richard Carlson Martha O'Driscoll

1942 AMERICAN EMPIRE
Director: William McGann
Co-stars: Richard Dix Preston Foster Leo Carrillo

1943 CRY HAVOC
Director: Richard Thorpe
Co-stars: Margaret Sullavan Joan Blondell Ann Sothern

1943 TARZAN TRIUMPHS
Director: William Thiele
Co-stars: Johnny Weismuller Johnny Sheffield Sig Ruman

1944 MARRIAGE IS A PRIVATE AFFAIR
Director: Robert Z. Leonard
Co-stars: Lana Turner James Craig John Hodiak

1945 THRILL OF A ROMANCE
Director: Richard Thorpe
Co-stars: Esther Williams Van Johnson Lauritz Melchior

1945 SHE WENT TO THE RACES
Co-stars: Ava Gardner James Craig Sig Ruman

1945 OUR VINES HAVE TENDER GRAPES
Director: Roy Rowland
Co-stars: Edward G. Robinson Margaret O'Brien James Craig

1946 LITTLE MR. JIM
Director: Fred Zinnemann
Co-stars: Jackie Jenkins James Craig Luanna Patten

1946 THE ARNELLO AFFAIR
Director: Arch Obeler
Co-stars: George Murphy John Hodiak Dean Stockwell

1948 LUXURY LINER
Director: Richard Whorf
Co-stars: Jane Powell George Brent Lauritz Melchior

1950 RIDING HIGH
Director: Frank Capra
Co-stars: Bing Crosby Coleen Gray Charles Bickford

GLORIA GIFFORD

1978 CALIFORNIA SUITE
Director: Herbert Ross
Co-stars: Michael Caine Maggie Smith Walter Matthau

1983 D.C.CAB
Director: Joel Schumacher
Co-stars: Max Gail Adam Baldwin Gary Busey

1988 VICE VERSA
Director: Brian Gilbert
Co-stars: Judge Reinhold Fred Savage Swoosie Kurtz

ELAINE GIFTOS

1970 GAS-S-S-S
Director: Roger Corman
Co-stars: Robert Corff Pat Patterson Alex Wilson

1984 ANGEL
Director: Robert Vincent O'Neil
Co-stars: Donna Wilkes Cliff Gorman Rory Calhoun

SANDRA GIGLIO

1952 ASSIGNMENT-PARIS
Director: Robert Parrish
Co-stars: George Sanders Dana Andrews Marta Toren

1953 WAR OF THE WORLDS
Director: Byron Haskin
Co-stars: Gene Barry Ann Robinson Les Tremayne

ARIADNA GIL

1992 BELLE EPOQUE
Director: Fernando Trueba
Co-stars: Jorge Sanz Penelope Cruz Maribel Verdu

YVONNE GILAN

1983 ANOTHER TIME, ANOTHER PLACE
Director: Michael Radford
Co-stars: Phyllis Logan Giovanni Mauriello

1985 BLOOD HUNT
Director: Peter Barber-Fleming
Co-stars: Andrew Keir Iain Glen Nigel Stock

HELEN GILBERT

1939 ANDY HARDY GETS SPRING FEVER
Director: W.S. Van Dyke
Co-stars: Mickey Rooney Lewis Stone Fay Holden

1940 FLORIAN
Director: Edwin Marin
Co-stars: Robert Young Charles Coburn Lee Bowman

1942 BEYOND THE BLUE HORIZON
Director: Alfred Santell
Co-stars: Dorothy Lamour Richard Denning

1942 ISLE OF MISSING MEN
Director: Richard Oswald
Co-stars: Gilbert Roland John Howard

JO GILBERT

1951 HURRICANE ISLAND
Director: Lew Landers
Co-stars: Jon Hall Edgar Barrier Marie Windsor

1953 JULIUS CAESAR
Director: Joseph Mankiewicz
Co-stars: James Mason Marlon Brando John Gielgud

JOANNE GILBERT

1957 THE GREAT MAN
Director: Jose Ferrer
Co-stars: Jose Ferrer Dean Jagger Keenan Wynn

1957 RIDE OUT FOR REVENGE
Director: Bernard Girard
Co-stars: Rory Calhoun Lloyd Bridges Gloria Grahame

JODY GILBERT

1942 THE TUTTLES OF TAHITI
Director: Charles Vidor
Co-stars: Charles Laughton Jon Hall Florence Bates

1950 HOUSE BY THE RIVER
Director: Fritz Lang
Co-stars: Louis Hayward Jane Wyatt Lee Bowman

1971 WILLARD
Director: Daniel Mann
Co-stars: Bruce Davison Ernest Borgnine Elsa Lanchester

MELISSA GILBERT

1984 FAMILY SECRETS
Director: Jack Hofsiss
Co-stars: Maureen Stapleton Stefanie Powers James Spader

1985 SYLVESTER
Director: Tim Hunter
Co-stars: Richard Farnsworth Constance Towers Arliss Howard

1986 CHOICES
Director: David Lowell Rich
Co-stars: George C. Scott Jacqueline Bisset

1987 BLOOD VOWS
Director: Paul Wendkos
Co-stars: Joe Penny Talia Shire Eileen Brennan

1990 FORBIDDEN NIGHTS
Director: Waris Hussein
Co-stars: Robin Shou Victor K Wong

1990 THE LOOKALIKE
Director: Gary Nelson
Co-stars: Diane Ladd Bo Brinkman C.K. Bibby

1990 JOSHUA'S HEART
Director: Michael Pressman
Co-star: Tim Matheson

1992 WITH A VENGEANCE
Director: Michael Switzer
Co-stars: Michael Gross Jack Scalia

1993 DYING TO REMEMBER
Director: Arthur Seidelmann
Co-stars: Christopher Stone Scott Planil

1993 FAMILY OF STRANGERS
Director: Sheldon Larry
Co-stars: Patty Duke Martha Gibson

1994 HOUSE OF SECRETS
Director: Mimi Leder
Co-stars: Bruce Boxleitner Kate Vernon

1994 SEEDS OF DECEPTION
Director: Arlene Stanford
Co-stars: Shanna Reed Tom Verica

1994 TOUCH OF TRUTH
Director: Michael Switzer
Co-stars: Patty Duke Bradley Perce Lisa Banes

OLIVE GILBERT

1950 THE DANCING YEARS
Director: Harold French
Co-stars: Dennis Price Patricia Dainton

SARA GILBERT

1990 SUDIE AND SIMPSON
Director: Joan Tewkesbury
Co-stars: Lou Gossett Jnr. Frances Fisher

1992 POISON IVY
Director: Katt Shea Ruben
Co-stars: Drew Barymore Tom Skerritt Cheryl Ladd

JACQUELINE GILBRIDE

1987 THE DARK ROOM
Director: Guy Slater
Co-stars: Susan Woolridge Philip Jackson Julie Graham

CONNIE GILCHRIST

1934 LET'S FALL IN LOVE
Director: David Burton
Co-stars: Ann Sothern Edmund Lowe Miriam Jordan

1941 BARNACLE BILL
Director: Richard Thorpe
Co-stars: Wallace Beery Marjorie Main Leo Carrillo

1941 A WOMAN'S FACE
Director: George Cukor
Co-stars: Joan Crawford Melvyn Douglas Conrad Veidt

1942 GRAND CENTRAL MURDER
Director: S. Sylvan Simon
Co-stars: Van Heflin Cecelia Parker Sam Levene

1942 TORTILLA FLAT
Director: Victor Fleming
Co-stars: Spencer Tracy John Garfield Hedy Lamarr

1942 THE WAR AGAINST MRS. HAADLEY
Director: Harold Bucquet
Co-stars: Fay Bainter Edward Arnold Richard Ney

1942 WE WERE DANCING
Director: Robert Z. Leonard
Co-stars: Norma Shearer Melvyn Douglas Gail Patrick

1943 CRY HAVOC
Director: Richard Thorpe
Co-stars: Margaret Sullavan Joan Blondell Ann Sothern

1943 THE HEAVENLY BODY
Director: Alexander Hall
Co-stars: William Powell Hedy Lamarr James Craig

1943 RATIONING
Director: Willis Goldbeck
Co-stars: Wallace Beery Marjorie Main Donald Meek

1943 SWING-SHIFT MAISIE
Director: Norman Z. Mcleod
Co-stars: Ann Sothern James Craig Jean Rogers

1944 MUSIC FOR MILLIONS
Director: Henry Koster
Co-stars: Margaret O'Brien June Allyson Jimmy Durante

1944 IT SHOULD HAPPEN TO YOU
Director: George Cukor
Co-stars: Judy Holliday Jack Lemmon Peter Lawford

1946 THE YOUNG WIDOW
Director: Edwin Marin
Co-stars: Jane Russell Louis Hayward Faith Domergue

1948 TENTH AVENUE ANGEL
Director: Roy Rowland
Co-stars: Margaret O'Brien Angela Lansbury George Murphy

1949 A LETTER TO THREE WIVES
Director: Joseph Mankiewicz
Co-stars: Jeanne Crain Kirk Douglas Ann Sothern

1949 THE STORY OF MOLLY X
Director: Crane Wilbur
Co-stars: June Havoc John Russell Dorothy Hart

1950 A TICKET TO TOMAHAWK
Director: Richard Sale
Co-stars: Dan Dailey Anne Baxter Marilyn Monroe

1950 TRIPOLI
Director: Will Price
Co-stars: John Wayne Maureen O'Hara Howard Da Silva

1951 THUNDER ON THE HILL
Director: Douglas Sirk
Co-stars: Claudette Colbert Ann Blyth Robert Douglas

1951 HERE COMES THE GROOM
Director: Frank Capra
Co-stars: Bing Crosby Jane Wyman Alexis Smith

1952 FLESH AND FURY
Director: Joseph Pevney
Co-stars: Tony Curtis Jan Sterling Mona Freeman

1953 LONG JOHN SILVER
Director: Bryon Haskin
Co-stars: Robert Newton Kit Taylor Rod Taylor

1956 THE MAN IN THE GRAY FLANNEL SUIT
Director: Nunnally Johnson
Co-stars: Gregory Peck Jennifer Jones Fredric March

1958 AUNTIE MAME
Director: Morton Dacosta
Co-stars: Rosalind Russell Forrest Tucker Coral Browne

1958 MACHINE GUN KELLY
Director: Roger Corman
Co-stars: Charles Bronson Susan Cabot Morey Amsterdam

1959 SAY ONE FOR ME
Director: Frank Tashlin
Co-stars: Bing Crosby Debbie Reynolds Robert Wagner

1965 TICKLE ME
Director: Norman Taurog
Co-stars: Elvis Presley Julia Adams Jocelyn Lane

1965 TWO ON A GUILLOTINE
Director: Wiliam Conrad
Co-stars: Connie Stevens Dean Jones Cesar Romero

PAMELA GILDAY

1986 THRASHIN'
Director: David Winters
Co-stars: Josh Brolin Robert Rusler Sherilyn Fenn

SANDRA GILES

1981 CRAZY TIMES
Director: Lee Philips
Co-stars: Michael Pare Ray Liotta Talia Balsam

GWYNNE GILFORD

1971 BEWARE! THE BLOB
Director: Larry Hagman
Co-stars: Robert Walker Jnr. Godfrey Cambridge Carol Lynley

ELIZABETH GILL

1974 LARRY
Director: William Graham
Co-stars: Fredric Forest Tyne Daly Michael McGuire

MAUD GILL

1928 THE FARMER'S WIFE
Director: Alfred Hitchcock
Co-stars: Jameson Thomas Gordon Harker

PHILLIPA GILL

1949 THE PERFECT WOMAN
Director: Bernard Knowles
Co-stars: Patricia Roc Nigel Patrick Miles Malleson

MARIE GILLAIN

1992 MON PERE, CE HEROS
Director: Gerard Lauzier
Co-stars: Gerard Depardieu Catherine Jacob Patrick Mille

1995 THE BAIT
Director: Bertrand Tavernier
Co-star:: Olivier Sitruk

GENEVIEVE GILLES

1970 HELLO-GOODBYE
Director: Jean Negulesco
Co-stars: Michael Crawford Curt Jurgens Ira Furstenberg

DANA GILLESPIE

1977 THE PEOPLE THAT TIME FORGOT
Director: Kevin Connor
Co-stars: Patrick Wayne Sarah Douglas Doug McClure

1980 BAD TIMING
Director: Nicolas Roeg
Co-stars: Art Garfunkel Theresa Russell Harvey Keitel

EMER GILLESPIE

1987 THE SHUTTER FALLS
Director: Peter Barber-Fleming
Co-stars: Anthony Higgins Stella Gonet

ANITA GILLETTE

1975 A MATTER OF WIFE....AND DEATH
Director: Marvin Chomsky
Co-stars: Rod Taylor Tom Drake Lynda Carter

1995 BOYS ON THE SIDE
Director: Herbert Ross
Co-stars: Whoopi Goldberg Drew Barrymore Mary Louise Parker

RUTH GILLETTE

1933 FRONTIER MARSHALL
Director: Lew Seiller
Co-stars: George O'Brien Irene Bentley George E. Stone

JENNY GILLIAN

1978 THE ABDUCTION OF LORELEI
Director: Richard Rank
Co-stars: Serena John Galt Charles Neal

JEAN GILLIE

1935 WHILE PARENTS SLEEP
Co-stars: MacKenzie Ward Enid Stamp-Taylor

1936 THIS'LL MAKE YOU WHISTLE
Director: Herbert Wilcox
Co-stars: Jack Buchanan Elsie Randolph

1937 THE GIRL IN THE TAXI
Director: Andre Berthomieu
Co-stars: Frances Day Henri Garat MacKenzie Ward

1940 THE SPIDER
Director: Maurice Elvy
Co-stars: Derrick De Marney Diana Churchill Cecil Parker

1940 TILLY OF BLOOMSBURY
Director: Leslie Hiscott
Co-stars: Sydney Howard Michael Wilding Athene Seyler

1943 THE GENTLE SEX
Director: Leslie Howard
Co-stars: Rosamund John Joan Greenwood Lilli Palmer

1943 THE SAINT MEETS THE TIGER
Director: Paul Stein
Co-stars: Hugh Sinclair Clifford Evans Wylie Watson

1944 FLIGHT FROM FOLLY
Director: Herbert Mason
Co-stars: Pat Kirkwood Hugh Sinclair Sydney Howard

1944 TAWNEY PIPIT
Director: Bernard Miles
Co-stars: Bernard Miles Rosamund John Niall MacGinnis

1947 THE MACOMBER AFFAIR
Director: Zoltan Korda
Co-stars: Gregory Peck Joan Bennett Robert Preston

FIONA GILLIES

**1988 THE ADVENTURES OF SHERLOCK HOLMES,
THE HOUND OF THE BASKERVILLES**
Director: Brian Mills
Co-stars: Jeremy Brett Edward Hardwicke Ronald Pickup

1989 MOTHER LOVE
Director: Simon Langton
Co-stars: Diana Rigg James Wilby Isla Blair Holly Aird

1992 FRANKENSTEIN - THE REAL STORY
Director: David Wickes
Co-stars: Patrick Bergin Randy Quaid John Mills

HELENA GILLIES

1990   CHANGING STEP
Director: Richard Wilson
Co-stars: James Convey Susan Woolridge Eleanor Bron

ISABEL GILLIES

1989   METROPOLITIAN
Director: Whit Stillman
Co-stars: Carolyn Farina Edward Clements Dylan Hundley

REBECCA GILLING

1975   THE MAN FROM HONG KONG
Director: Brian Trenchard-Smith
Co-stars: Jimmy Wang Yu George Lazenby

1986   THE BLUE LIGHTNING
Director: Lee Phillips
Co-stars: Sam Elliott Robert Culp John Meillon

ANN GILLIS

1936   THE GREAT ZIEGFIELD
Director: Robert Z. Leonard
Co-stars: William Powell Luise Rainer Myrna Loy

1938   THE ADVENTURES OF TOM SAWYER
Director: Norman Taurog
Co-stars: Tommy Kelly Walter Brennan May Robson

1939   FIRST LOVE
Director: Henry Koster
Co-stars: Deanna Durbin Robert Stack Eugene Pallette

1940   LITTLE MEN
Director: Norman Z. Mcleod
Co-stars: Kay Francis Jack Oakie Jimmy Lydon

1941   NICE GIRL?
Director: William Seiter
Co-stars: Deanna Durbin Franchot Tone Robert Stack

1941   GLAMOUR BOY
Director: Ralph Murphy
Co-stars: Jackie Cooper Susannah Foster William Demarest

1942   TOUGH AS THEY COME

1944   ABBOTT AND COSTELLO IN SOCIETY
Director: Jean Yarbrough
Co-stars: Bud Abbott Lou Costello Kirby Grant

1946   SWEETHEART OF SIGMA CHI
Co-stars: Elyse Knox Alan Hale Jnr.

CAROLINE GILLMER

1982   FIGHTING BACK
Director: Michael Caulfield
Co-stars: Lewis Fitzgerald Kris McQuade Paul Smith

1995   HOTEL SORRENTO
Co-star: Caroline Goodall

MARGALO GILLMORE

1950   CAUSE FOR ALARM
Director: Tay Garnett
Co-stars: Loretta Young Barry Sullivan Irving Bacon

1950   THE HAPPY YEARS
Director: William Wellman
Co-stars: Dean Stockwell Leo G.carroll Darryl Hickman

1950   PERFECT STRANGERS
Director: Bretaigne Windust
Co-stars: Ginger Rogers Dennis Morgan Thelma Ritter

1951   THE LAW AND THE LADY
Director: Edwin Knoff
Co-stars: Greer Garson Michael Wilding Fernando Lamas

1951   ELOPEMENT
Director: Henry Koster
Co-stars: Clifton Webb Anne Francis William Lundigan

1951   BEHAVE YOURSELF!
Director: George Beck
Co-stars: Farley Granger Shelley Winters William Demarest

1952   SKIRTS AHOY!
Director: Sidney Lanfield
Co-stars: Esther Williams Vivian Blaine Joan Evans

1954   WOMAN'S WORLD
Director: Jean Negulesco
Co-stars: Clifton Webb Lauren Bacall June Allyson

1956   HIGH SOCIETY
Director: Charles Walters
Co-stars: Bing Crosby Frank Sinatra Grace Kelly

1956   GABY
Director: Curtis Bernhardt
Co-stars: Leslie Caron John Kerr Taina Elg

1959   UPSTAIRS AND DOWNSTAIRS
Director: Ralph Thomas
Co-stars: Michael Craig Anne Heywood Sid James

VIRGINIA GILMORE

1939   WINTER CARNIVAL
Director: Charles Reisner
Co-stars: Ann Sheridan Richard Carlson Robert Walker

1940   MANHATTAN HEARTBEAT
Director: David Burton
Co-stars: Robert Sterling Joan Davis Don Beddoe

1941   TALL, DARK AND HANDSOME
Director: Bruce Humberstone
Co-stars: Cesar Romero Charlotte Greenwood

1941   SWAMP WATER
Director: Jean Renoir
Co-stars: Walter Huston Walter Brennan Anne Baxter

1941   WESTERN UNION
Director: Fritz Lang
Co-stars: Randolph Scott Robert Young Dean Jagger

1942   THE PRIDE OF THE YANKEES
Director: Sam Wood
Co-stars: Gary Cooper Teresa Wright Walter Brennan

1942   THE LOVES OF EDGAR ALAN POE
Director: Harry Lachman
Co-stars: John Shepperd Linda Darnell

1942   BERLIN CORRESPONDENT
Director: Eugene Forde
Co-stars: Dana Andrews Mona Maris Sig Ruman

1943   CHETNIKS - THE FIGHTING GUERRILAS
Director: Louis King
Co-stars: Philip Dorn Anna Sten John Shepperd

1952   WALK EAST ON BEACON
Director: Alfred Werker
Co-stars: George Murphy Finlay Currie Louisa Horton

MARION GILSENAN

**1989   GETTING MARRIED IN
          BUFFALO JUNCTION**
Director: Eric Till
Co-stars: Wendy Crewson Paul Gross

ERICA GIMPEL

1988   CASE CLOSED
Director: Dick Lowry
Co-stars: Byron Allen Charles Durning James Greene

1991 HOMICIDE
Director: David Manet
Co-stars: Joe Mantega William H Macy Ving Rhames

TERESA GIMPERA

1973 THE SPIRIT OF THE BEEHIVE
Director: Victor Erice
Co-stars: Ana Torrent Fernando Fernan Gomez

HERMIONE GINGOLD

1936 SOMEONE AT THE DOOR
Director: Herbert Brenon
Co-stars: Billy Milton Aileen Marson Noah Beery

1937 MERRY COMES TO TOWN
Director: George King
Co-stars: Zasu Pitts Guy Newall Betty Ann Davies

1938 MEET MR. PENNY
Director: David MacDonald
Co-stars: Richard Goolden Vic Oliver Kay Walsh Fabia Drake

1943 THE BUTLER'S DILEMMA
Director: Leslie Hiscott
Co-stars: Richard Hearne Ronald Shiner

1952 THE PICKWICK PAPERS
Director: Noel Langley
Co-stars: James Hayter Donald Wolfit Hermione Baddeley

1953 OUR GIRL FRIDAY
Director: Noel Langley
Co-stars: Joan Collins Kenneth More Robertson Hare

1956 AROUND THE WORLD IN EIGHTY DAYS
Director: Michael Anderson
Co-stars: David Niven Cantinflas Robert Newton

1958 BELL, BOOK AND CANDLE
Director: Richard Quine
Co-stars: James Stewart Kim Novak Jack Lemmon

1958 GIGI
Director: Vincente Minnelli
Co-stars: Leslie Caron Louis Jordan Maurice Chevalier Eva Gabor

1961 THE NAKED EDGE
Director: Michael Anderson
Co-stars: Gary Cooper Deborah Kerr Diane Cilento

1962 THE MUSIC MAN
Director: Marion Hargrove
Co-stars: Robert Preston Shirley Jones Buddy Hackett

1962 GAY PURR-EE *(Voice)*
Director: Abe Levitow
Co-stars: Judy Garland Robert Goulet Red Buttons Mel Blanc

1964 I'D RATHER BE RICH
Director: Jack Smight
Co-stars: Maurice Chevalier Sandra Dee Robert Goulet

1965 HARVEY MIDDLEMAN FIREMAN
Director: Ernest Pintoff
Co-stars: Gene Troobnick Pat Harty

1966 PROMISE HER ANYTHING
Director: Arthur Hiller
Co-stars: Warren Beatty Leslie Caron Robert Cummings

1967 JULES VERNE'S ROCKET TO THE MOON
Director: Don Sharp
Co-stars: Burl Ives Lionel Jeffries Troy Donahue

1971 WALK UP AND DIE
Director: Robert Day
Co-stars: Robert Forster Jose Ferrer Darren McGavin

1977 A LITTLE NIGHT MUSIC
Director: Hal Prince
Co-stars: Elizabeth Taylor Len Cariou Diana Rigg

1984 GARBO TALKS
Director: Sidney Lumet
Co-stars: Anne Bancroft Ron Silver Carrie Fisher Catherine Hicks

DOMIZIANA GIORDANO

1990 NOUVELLE VAGUE
Director: Jean-Luc Godard
Co-stars: Alain Delon Roland Amstuttz Laurence Cote

FLORENCE GIORGETTI

1977 THE LACEMAKER
Director: Claude Goretta
Co-stars: Isabelle Huppert Yves Beneyton Anne-Marie Duringer

ELEANORA GIORGI

1980 INFERNO
Director: Dario Argento
Co-stars: Leigh McCloskey Irene Miracle

1982 BEYOND THE DOOR
Director: Liliana Cavani
Co-stars: Marcello Mastroianni Tom Berenger Michel Piccoli

MARLENA GIOVI

1990 EATING
Director: Henry Jaglom
Co-stars: Lisa Richards Mary Crosby Gwen Welles

WENDY GIRARD

1986 OUTLAWS
Director: Peter Werner
Co-stars: Rod Taylor William Lucking Richard Roundtree

ANNIE GIRARDOT

1958 MAIGRET SETS A TRAP
Director: Jean Delannoy
Co-stars: Jean Gabin Jean Desailly Lino Ventura

1960 ROCCO AND HIS BROTHERS
Director: Luchino Visconti
Co-stars: Alain Delon Katina Paxinou Suzy Delair

1963 LA BONNE SOUPE
Director: Robert Thomas
Co-stars: Marie Bell Bernard Blier Claude Dauphin

1967 LIVE FOR LIFE
Director: Claude Lelouch
Co-stars: Yves Montand Candice Bergen Irene Tunc

1970 STORY OF A WOMAN
Director: Leonardo Bercovici
Co-stars: Robert Stack Bibi Andersson James Farentino

1972 SHOCK TREATMENT
Director: Alain Jessua
Co-stars: Alain Delon Robert Hirsch Michel Duchaussoy

1976 DOCTEUR FRANCOISE GAILLARD
Director: Jean-Louis Bertucelli
Co-stars: Jean-Pierre Cassel Suzanne Flon

1977 DEAR INSPECTOR
Director: Philippe De Broca
Co-stars: Catherine Alric Philippe Noiret

1981 ALL NIGHT LONG
Director: Jean-Claude Tramont
Co-stars: Barbra Streisand Gene Hackman Diane Ladd

1991 MERCI LA VIE
Director: Bernard Blier
Co-stars: Charlotte Gainsbourg Anouk Grinberg Gerard Depardieu

MICHELE GIRARDON

1956 EVIL EDEN
Director: Luis Bunuel
Co-stars: Georges Marchal Simone Signoret Michel Piccoli

1962 HATARI!
Director: Howard Hawks
Co-stars: John Wayne Hardy Kruger Elsa Martinelli

CINDY GIRLING

1980 THE KIDNAPPING OF THE PRESIDENT
Director: George Mendaluk
Co-stars: Hal Holbrook Van Johnson Ava Gardner

1994 HEART OF A CHILD
Director: Sandor Stern
Co-stars: Ann Jillian Michele Green Rip Torn

LAURA GIRLING

1990 CONQUEST OF THE SOUTH POLE
Director: Gillies MacKinnon
Co-stars: Stefan Rimkus Ewen Bremner

ANNABETH GISH

1986 DESERT BLOOM
Director: Eugene Corr
Co-stars: Jon Voight JoBeth Williams Ellen Barkin

1986 HERO IN THE FAMILY
Director: Mel Damski
Co-stars: Christopher Collet Cliff De Young Darleen Carr

1987 HIDING OUT
Director: Bob Giraldi
Co-stars: Jon Cryer Keith Coogan Oliver Cotton

1988 MYSTIC PIZZA
Director: Donald Petrie
Co-stars: Vincent D'Onofrio Julia Roberts Lili Taylor

1988 SHAG
Director: Zelda Barron
Co-stars: Phoebe Cates Bridget Fonda Scott Coffey Tyrone Power Jnr.

1989 WHEN HE'S NOT A STRANGER
Director: John Gray
Co-stars: Kevin Dillon John Terlesky

1990 COUP DE VILLE
Director: Joe Roth
Co-stars: Patrick Dempsey Arye Gross Daniel Stern

1991 THE LAST TO GO
Director: John Ermann
Co-stars: Tyne Daly Terry O'Quinn Tim Ranson

1996 BEAUTIFUL GIRLS
Director: Ted Demme
Co-stars: Timothy Hutton Uma Thurman Mira Sorvino

1996 THE LAST SUPPER
Co-stars: Cameron Diaz Bill Paxton Mark Harmon

1996 WHAT LOVE SEES
Director: Michael Switzer
Co-star:: Richard Thomas

DOROTHY GISH *(Sister Of Lillian Gish)*

1912 THE NEW YORK HAT
Director: D.W. Griffith
Co-stars: Mary Pickford Lionel Barrymore Lillian Gish Mae Marsh

1913 JUDITH OF BETHULIA
Director: D.W. Griffith
Co-stars: Blanche Sweet Lionel Barrymore Lillian Gish

1914 HOME SWEET HOME
Director: D.W. Griffith
Co-stars: Donald Crisp Henry B. Walthall Mae Marsh Lillian Gish

1918 HEARTS OF THE WORLD
Director: D.W. Griffith
Co-stars: Erich Von Stroheim Noel Coward Lillian Gish

1920 REMODELLING HER HUSBAND
Director: Lillian Gish
Co-stars: James Rennie Marie Burke Frank Kingdom

1922 ORPHANS OF THE STORM
Director: D.W. Griffith
Co-stars: Lillian Gish Joseph Schildkraut

1923 FURY
Director: Henry King
Co-stars: Richard Barthelmess Tyrone Powers Snr Pat Hartigan

1944 OUR HEARTS WERE YOUNG AND GAY
Director: Lewis Allen
Co-stars: Gail Russell Diana Lynn

1946 CENTENNIAL SUMMER
Director: Otto Preminger
Co-stars: Jeanne Crain Cornel Wilde Linda Darnell

1951 WHISTLE AT EATON FALLS
Director: Robert Siodmak
Co-stars: Lloyd Bridges Carleton Carpenter

1963 THE CARDINAL
Director: Otto Preminger
Co-stars: Tom Tyron John Huston Carol Lynley

LILLIAN GISH *(Sister Of Dorothy Gish)*
Honorary Award 1970
Nominated For Best Supporting Actress In 1946 For "Duel In The Sun"

1912 THE NEW YORK HAT
Director: D.W. Griffith
Co-stars: Mary Pickford Lionel Barrymore Dorothy Gish Mae Marsh

1913 JUDITH OF BETHULIA
Director: D.W. Griffith
Co-stars: Blanche Sweet Lionel Barrymore Dorothy Gish

1914 THE BATTLE OF THE SEXES
Director: D.W. Griffith
Co-stars: Donald Crisp Mary Alden Fay Tincher Owen Moore

1914 HOME SWEET HOME
Director: D.W. Griffith
Co-stars: Dorothy Gish Donald Crisp Henry B. Walthall Mae Marsh

1915 THE LILY AND THE ROSE
Co-star:: Mary Arden

1915 BIRTH OF A NATION
Director: D.W. Griffith
Co-stars: Miriam Cooper Mae Marsh Raoul Walsh

1916 INTOLERANCE
Director: D.W. Griffith
Co-stars: Mae Marsh Constance Talmadge Robert Harron

1918 HEARTS OF THE WORLD
Director: D.W. Griffith
Co-stars: Robert Harron Dorothy Gish Noel Coward

1919 BROKEN BLOSSOMS
Director: D.W. Griffith
Co-stars: Donald Crisp Richard Bartlemess Arthur Howard

1920 TRUE HEART SUSIE
Director: D.W. Griffith
Co-stars: Robert Harron Clarine Seymour

1920 WAY DOWN EAST
Director: D.W. Griffith
Co-stars: Richard Barthelmess Lowell Sherman Creighton Hale

1922 ORPHANS OF THE STORM
Director: D.W. Griffith
Co-stars: Dorothy Gish Joseph Schildkraut Frank Puglia

1926   **THE SCARLET LETTER**
Director: Victor Sjostrom
Co-stars: Lars Hanson Karl Dane Henry B. Walthall

1926   **LA BOHEME**
Director: King Vidor
Co-stars: John Gilbert Renee Adoree Edward Everett Horton

1927   **THE WIND**
Director: Victor Sjostrom
Co-stars: Lars Hanson Montagu Love Dorothy Cummings

1933   **HIS DOUBLE LIFE**
Director: Arthur Hopkins
Co-stars: Roland Young Lumsden Hare Lucy Beaumont

1942   **THE COMMANDOES STRIKE AT DAWN**
Director: John Farrow
Co-stars: Paul Muni Anna Lee Robert Coote

1943   **TOP MAN**
Director: Charles Lamont
Co-stars: Donald O'Connor Richard Dix Peggy Ryan Susanna Foster

1946   **MISS SUSIE SLAGLE'S**
Director: John Berry
Co-stars: Veronica Lake Joan Caulfield Sonny Tufts

1946   **DUEL IN THE SUN**
Director: King Vidor
Co-stars: Jennifer Jones Gregory Peck Joseph Cotten

1948   **PORTRAIT OF JENNIE**
Director: William Dieterle
Co-stars: Jennifer Jones Joseph Cotten David Wayne

1955   **THE COBWEB**
Director: Vincente Minnelli
Co-stars: Richard Widmark Lauren Bacall Charles Boyer

1958   **ORDERS TO KILL**
Director: Anthony Asquith
Co-stars: Paul Massie Irene Worth Eddie Albert

1960   **THE UNFORGIVEN**
Director: John Huston
Co-stars: Burt Lancaster Audrey Hepburn Charles Bickford

1966   **FOLLOW ME, BOYS!**
Director: Norman Tokar
Co-stars: Fred MacMurray Vera Miles Charles Ruggles

1967   **THE COMEDIANS**
Director: Peter Glenfield
Co-stars: Elizabeth Taylor Richard Burton Alec Guinness

1967   **WARNING SHOT**
Director: Buzz Kulik
Co-stars: David Janssen Ed Begley Sam Wanamaker

1978   **A WEDDING**
Director: Robert Altman
Co-stars: Carol Burnett Amy Stryker Mia Farrow Paul Dooley

1981   **THIN ICE**
Director: Paul Aaron
Co-stars: Kate Jackson Gerald Prendergast Mimi Kennedy

1983   **HOBSON'S CHOICE**
Director: Gilbert Cates
Co-stars: Richard Thomas Sharon Gless Jack Warden

1983   **HAMBONE AND HILLIE**
Director: Roy Watts
Co-stars: Timothy Bottoms Candy Clark Robert Walker

1986   **SWEET LIBERTY**
Director: Alan Alda
Co-stars: Alan Alda Michael Caine Bob Hoskins Michelle Pfeiffer

1987   **THE WHALES OF AUGUST**
Director: Lindsay Anderson
Co-stars: Bette Davis Ann Sothern Vincent Price

SHEILA GISH

1971   **A DAY IN THE DEATH OF JOE EGG**
Director: Peter Medak
Co-stars: Alan Bates Janet Suzman Peter Bowles

1986   **HIGHLANDER**
Director: Russell Mulcahey
Co-stars: Christopher Lambert Roxanne Hart Sean Connery

1991   **STANLEY AND THE WOMEN**
Director: David Tucker
Co-stars: John Thaw Geraldine James Penny Downie

1992   **DANIELLE STEEL'S JEWELS**
Director: Roger Young
Co-stars: Annette O'Toole Anthony Andrews

1993   **INSPECTOR MORSE:
TWILIGHT OF THE GODS**
Director: Herbert Wise
Co-stars: John Thaw John Gieldud Robert Hardy

ROBIN GIVENS

1986   **BEVERLY HILLS MADAM**
Director: Harvey Hart
Co-stars: Faye Dunaway Melody Anderson Donna Dixon

1989   **THE PENTHOUSE**
Director: David Greene
Co-stars: Robert Guillaume David Hewlett Cedric Smith

1991   **RAGE IN HARLEM**
Director: Bill Duke
Co-stars: Forest Whitaker Gregory Hines Danny Glover

1992   **BOOMERANG**
Director: Reggie Hudlin
Co-stars: Eddie Murphy Halle Berry Grace Jones Eartha Kitt

1992   **ANGEL STREET**
Director: Rod Holcomb
Co-star::   Pamela Gidley

1994   **FOREIGN STUDENT**
Director: Eva Sereny
Co-stars: Marco Hofschneider Rick Johnson

KATHRYN GIVNEY

1949   **MY FRIEND IRMA**
Director: George Marshall
Co-stars: Marie Wilson John Lund Dean Martin Jerry Lewis

1950   **OPERATION PACIFIC**
Director: George Waggner
Co-stars: John Wayne Patricia Neal Ward Bond

1951   **A PLACE IN THE SUN**
Director: George Stevens
Co-stars: Montgomery Clift Elizabeth Taylor Shelley Winters

1951   **LIGHTNING STRIKES TWICE**
Director: King Vidor
Co-stars: Richard Todd Ruth Roman

1954   **THREE COINS IN THE FOUNTAIN**
Director: Jean Negulesco
Co-stars: Clifton Webb Dorothy McGuire Jean Peters

1958   **A CERTAIN SMILE**
Director: Jean Negulesco
Co-stars: Christine Carere Rossano Brazzi

URSULA GLAS

1971   **BLACK BEAUTY**
Director: James Hill
Co-stars: Mark Lester Walter Slezak Patrick Mower

ISABEL GLASSER

1992   PURE COUNTRY
Director: Christopher Cain
Co-stars: George Strait Lesley Ann Warren Rory Calhoun

1992   FOREVER YOUNG
Director: Steve Miner
Co-stars: Mel Gibson Jamie Lee Curtis Elijah Woods

1995   CIRCUMSTANCES UNKNOWN
Co-star::   Judd Nelson

JOANNA GLEASON

1989   CRIMES AND MISDEMEANORS
Director: Woody Allen
Co-stars: Woody Allen Mia Farrow Claire Bloom Anjelica Huston

1990   THE GUYS
Director: Glenn Jordan
Co-stars: James Woods John Lithgow

1991   F/X2
Director: Richard Franklin
Co-stars: Bryan Brown Brian Dennehy Rachel Ticotin

1992   FATHER, SON AND THE MISTRESS
Director: Jay Sandrich
Co-stars: Jack Lemmon Talia Shire Madeline Kahn

1994   FOR THE LOVE OF AARON
Director: John Kent Harrison
Co-stars: Meredith Baxter Keegan MacIntosh

LUCILLE GLEASON *(Married James Gleason)*

1931   GIRLS ABOUT TOWN
Director: George Cukor
Co-stars: Kay Francis Lilyan Tashman Joel McCrea

1936   KLONDYKE ANNIE
Director: Raoul Walsh
Co-stars: Mae West Victor McLaglen Philip Reed

1938   THE HIGGINS FAMILY
Director: Gus Meins
Co-stars: James Gleason Russell Gleason Lynne Roberts

1945   UNDER THE CLOCK
Director: Vincente Minnelli
Co-stars: Judy Garland Robert Walker James Gleason

MICHELE GLEIZER

1988   BEATRICE
Director: Bertrand Tavernier
Co-stars: Bernard Pierre Donnadieu Julie Dephy Nils Tavernier

CANDACE GLENDENNING

1971   NICHOLAS AND ALEXANDRA
Director: Franklin Schaffner
Co-stars: Michael Jayston Janet Suzman Tom Baker

ETHEL GLENDINNING

1936   THE END OF THE ROAD
Director: Alan Bryce
Co-stars: Harry Lauder Ruth Haven Bruce Seton

SHARON GLESS

1975   SWITCH
Director: Robert Day
Co-stars: Robert Wagner Eddie Albert Charles Durning

1978   THE CRASH OF FLIGHT 401
Director: Barry Shear
Co-stars: William Shatner Eddie Albert Lloyd Bridges

1980   REVENGE OF THE STEPFORD WIVES
Director: Robert Fuest
Co-stars: Julie Kavner Audra Lindley

1983   THE STAR CHAMBER
Director: Peter Hyams
Co-stars: Michael Douglas Hal Holbrook Yaphet Kotto

1983   HOBSON'S CHOICE
Director: Gilbert Cates
Co-stars: Richard Thomas Jack Warden Lillian Gish

1985   LETTING GO
Director: Jack Bender
Co-stars: John Ritter Max Gail Joe Cortese

1994   CAGNEY AND LACEY: THE RETURN
Director: James Frawley
Co-stars: Tyne Daily Al Waxman

1994   SEPARATED BY MURDER
Director: Donald Wrye
Co-stars: Ed Bruce Steve Railsback

STACEY GLICK

1981   THE DAY THE LOVING STOPPED
Director: Daniel Mann
Co-stars: Dennis Weaver Valerie Harper Ally Sheedy

1986   BRIGHTON BEACH MEMOIRS
Director: Gene Saks
Co-stars: Blythe Danner Bob Dishy Jonathan Silverman

HELENA GLOAG

1972   THE BILL DOUGLAS TRILOGY: MY CHILDHOOD
Director: Bill Douglas
Co-stars: Stephen Archibald Paul Kermack

1972   THE BILL DOUGLAS TRILOGY: MY AIN FOLK
Director: Bill Douglas
Co-stars: Stephen Archibald Paul Kermack

LEDA GLORIA

1955   DON CAMILLO'S LAST ROUNDD
Director: Carmine Gallone
Co-stars: Fernandel Gino Cervi Claude Silvain

MARIE GLORY

1935   THE KING OF PARIS
Director: Jack Raymond
Co-stars: Cedric Hardwicke Ralph Richardson Phillis Monkman

1938   LES GENS DU VOYAGE
Director: Jacques Feyder
Co-stars: Francoise Rosay Andre Brule Sylvie Bataille

ELINOR GLYN

1927   IT
Director: Clarence Badger
Co-stars: Clara Bow Antonio Moreno William Austin Gary Cooper

CARLIN GLYNN

1985   THE TRIP TO BOUNTIFUL
Director: Peter Masterson
Co-stars: Geraldine Page John Heard Rebecca De Mornay

MARY GLYNNE

1932   THE GOOD COMPANIONS
Director: Victor Saville
Co-stars: John Gielgud Edmund Gwenn Jessie Matthews

MAUREEN GLYNNE

1947   THE TURNERS OF PROSPECT ROAD
Director: Maurice Wilson
Co-stars: Wilfrid Lawson Jeanne De Casalis

CHERYL GODBER

1994   **CRIMINAL**
Director: Corin Campbell-Hill
Co-stars: Paul Popplewell Leanne Whalley Nicky Evans

PAULETTE GODDARD *(Married Charles Chaplin)*
Nominated For Best Supporting Actress In 1943 For "So Proudly We Hail"

1932   **THE KID FROM SPAIN**
Director: Leo McCarey
Co-stars: Eddie Cantor Lyda Roberti Robert Young

1936   **MODERN TIMES**
Director: Charles Chaplin
Co-stars: Charles Chaplin Henry Bergman Chester Conklin

1938   **DRAMATIC SCHOOL**
Director: Robert Sinclair
Co-stars: Luise Rainer Alan Marshall Lana Turner

1938   **THE YOUNG IN HEART**
Director: Richard Wallace
Co-stars: Douglas Fairbanks Janet Gaynor

1939   **THE WOMEN**
Director: George Cukor
Co-stars: Norma Shearer Joan Crawford Joan Fontaine

1939   **THE CAT AND THE CANARY**
Director: Elliott Nugent
Co-stars: Bob Hope Douglass Montgomery

1940   **THE GHOST BREAKERS**
Director: George Marshall
Co-stars: Bob Hope Paul Lukas Willie Best

1940   **THE GREAT DICTATOR**
Director: Charles Chaplin
Co-stars: Charles Chaplin Jack Oakie Billy Gilbert

1940   **NORTHWEST MOUNTED POLICE**
Director: Cecil B. DeMille
Co-stars: Gary Cooper Robert Preston Preston Foster

1940   **SECOND CHORUS**
Director: H.C. Potter
Co-stars: Fred Astaire Burgess Meredith Artie Shaw

1941   **NOTHING BUT THE TRUTH**
Director: Elliott Nugent
Co-stars: Bob Hope Edward Arnold Helen Vinson

1941   **POT O'GOLD**
Director: George Marshall
Co-stars: James Stewart Charles Winninger

1941   **HOLD BACK THE DAWN**
Director: Mitchell Leisen
Co-stars: Olivia De Havilland Charles Boyer Walter Abel

1942   **REAP THE WILD WIND**
Director: Cecil B. DeMille
Co-stars: Ray Milland Raymond Massey John Wayne

1942   **STAR SPANGLED RHYTHM**
Director: George Marshall
Co-stars: Victor Moore Betty Hutton Eddie Bracken

1942   **THE LADY HAS PLANS**
Director: Sidney Lanfield
Co-stars: Ray Milland Roland Young Albert Dekker

1942   **THE FOREST RANGERS**
Director: George Marshall
Co-stars: Fred MacMurray Susan Hayward

1943   **THE CRYSTAL BALL**
Director: Elliott Nugent
Co-stars: Ray Milland William Bendix Gladys George

1943   **SO PROUDLY WE HAIL**
Director: Mark Sandrich
Co-stars: Claudette Colbert Veronica Lake

1944   **STANDING ROOM ONLY**
Director: Sidney Lanfield
Co-stars: Fred MacMurray Edward Arnold

1944   **I LOVE A SOLDIER**
Director: Mark Sandrich
Co-stars: Sonny Tufts Barry Fitzgerald Belulah Bondi

1945   **KITTY**
Director: Mitchell Leisen
Co-stars: Ray Milland Cecil Kellaway Eric Blore

1946   **THE DIARY OF A CHAMBERMAID**
Director: Jean Renoir
Co-stars: Burgess Meredith Hurd Hatfield

1947   **UNCONQUERED**
Director: Cecil B. DeMille
Co-stars: Gary Cooper Howard Da Silva

1947   **VARIETY GIRL**
Director: Mitchell Leisen
Co-stars: Fred MacMurray MacDonald Carey

1948   **AN IDEAL HUSBAND**
Director: Alexander Korda
Co-stars: Hugh Williams Michael Wilding Glynis Johns

1948   **HAZARD**
Director: George Marshall
Co-stars: MacDonald Carey Fred Clark

1948   **ON OUR MERRY WAY**
Director: King Vidor
Co-stars: Burgess Meredith James Stewart Henry Fonda

1948   **BRIDE OF VENGEANCE**
Director: Mitchell Leisen
Co-stars: John Lund MacDonald Carey

1949   **ANNA LUCASTA**
Director: Irving Rapper
Co-stars: Oscar Homolka Broderick Crawford

1952   **BABES IN BAGDAD**
Director: Edgar Ulmer
Co-stars: Gypsy Rose Lee Richard Ney John Boles

1953   **CHARGE OF THE LANCERS**
Director: William Castle
Co-stars: Jean-Pierre Aumont Karin Booth

1953   **PARIS MODEL**
Director: Alfred Green
Co-stars: Eva Gabor Marilyn Maxwell Tom Conway

1953   **VICE SQUAD**
Director: Arnold Laven
Co-stars: Edward G. Robinson K.T. Stevens Porter Hall

1954   **THE STRANGER CAME HOME**
Director: Terence Fisher
Co-stars: William Sylvester Patrick Holt

RENEE GODFREY

1946   **TERROR BY NIGHT**
Director: Roy William Neill
Co-stars: Basil Rathbone Nigel Bruce Alan Mowbray

JUDITH GODRECHE

1993   **TANGO**
Director: Patrice Leconte
Co-stars: Thierry L'Hermitte Miou-Miou Phillippe Noiret

1998   **THE MAN IN THE IRON MASK**
Director: Randall Wallace
Co-stars: Leonardo Di Caprio John Malkovich Jeremy Irons

CONSTANCE GODRIDGE

1935   **FIRST A GIRL**
Director: Victor Saville
Co-stars: Jessie Matthews Sonnie Hale Anna Lee

1936   MURDER BY ROPE
Director: George Pearson
Co-stars: Wilfred Hyde White Donald Read Daphne Courtney

VANDA GODSELL
1959   HELL IS A CITY
Director: Val Guest
Co-stars: Stanley Baker Maxine Audley Billie Whitelaw

1961   SHADOW OF THE CAT
Director: John Gilling
Co-stars: Andre Morrell William Lucas Barbara Shelley

1963   THIS SPORTING LIFE
Director: Lindsay Anderson
Co-stars: Richard Harris Rachel Roberts Alan Badel

1963   CLASH BY NIGHT
Director: Montgomery Tully
Co-stars: Terence Longden Jennifer Jayne Harry Fowler

1963   BITTER HARVEST
Director: Peter Graham Scott
Co-stars: Janet Munro John Stride Alan Badel

ANGELA GOETHALS
1988   HEARTBREAK HOTEL
Director: Chris Columbus
Co-stars: David Keith Tuesday Weld Charlie Schlatter

1991   TRIPLE BOGIE ON A FIVE PAR HOLE
Director: Amos Poe
Co-stars: Eric Mitchell Daisy Hall Robbie Coltrane

1991   VI WARSHAWSKI
Director: Jeff Kanew
Co-stars: Kathleen Turner Charles Durning Nancy Paul

JOANNA GOING
1997   KEYS TO TULSA
Co-stars: Eric Stoltz James Spader Mary Tyler Moore

1997   INVENTING THE ABBOTTS
Director: Pat O'Connor
Co-stars: Liv Tyler Jennifer Connolly Billy Crudup

GILA GOLAN
1966   OUR MAN FLINT
Director: Daniel Mann
Co-stars: James Coburn Lee J. Cobb Benson Fong

1966   THREE ON A COUCH
Director: Jerry Lewis
Co-stars: Jerry Lewis Janet Leigh James Best Leslie Parrish

1969   VALLEY OF GWANGI
Director: James O'Connelly
Co-stars: Richard Carlson Laurence Naismith Freda Jackson

LOUISE GOLD
**1985   BILLY THE KID AND THE
GREEN BAIZE VAMPIRE**
Director: Alan Clarke
Co-stars: Phil Daniels Alun Armstrong

TRACEY GOLD
1983   ANOTHER WOMAN'S CHILD
Director: John Erman
Co-stars: Linda Lavin Tony LoBianco Joyce Van Patten

1983   THURSDAY'S CHILD
Director: Rodney Ackland
Co-stars: Gena Rowlands Don Murray Jessica Walter

1988   DANCE TILL DAWN
Director: Paul Schneider
Co-stars: Alyssa Milano Brian Bloom Chris Young

1994   FOR THE LOVE OF NANCY
Director: Paul Schneider
Co-stars: Jill Clayburgh William Devane

1995   SLEEP, BABY SLEEP
Director: Armand Mastroianni
Co-star::   Kyle Chandler

1995   MIDWEST OBSESSION
Director: Richard T. Heffron
Co-stars: Richard Crenna Cliff Gorman

1996   FACE OF EVIL
Director: Mary Lambert
Co-stars: Perry King Shawnee Smith

1996   TO FACE HER PAST
Co-star::   Patty Duke

WHOOPI GOLDBERG
Oscar For Best Supporting Actress In 1990 For Ghost
Nominated For Best Supporting Actress In 1985 For The Color Purple
1985   THE COLOR PURPLE
Director: Steven Spielberg
Co-stars: Danny Glover Oprah Winfrey Margaret Avery

1986   JUMPIN' JACK FLASH
Director: Penny Marshall
Co-stars: Stephen Collins John Wood Carol Kane

1987   FATAL BEAUTY
Director: Tom Holland
Co-stars: Sam Elliott Ruben Blades Brad Dourif

1987   BURGLAR
Director: Hugh Wilson
Co-stars: Bob Goldthwait Lesley Ann Warren John Goodman

1988   CLARA'S HEART
Director: Robert Mulligan
Co-stars: Neil Patrick Harris Kathleen Quinlan

**1988   STAR TREK THE NEXT GENERATION:
THE OUTRAGEOUS OKONA**
Director: Robert Becker
Co-star: Patrick Stewart Wil Wheaton

**1989   STAR TREK THE NEXT GENERATION:
BOOBY TRAP**
Director: Gabrielle Beaumont
Co-star: Patrick Stewart

**1989   STAR TREK THE NEXT GENERATION:
EVOLUTION**
Director: Winrich Kolbe
Co-star: Patrick Stewart Levar Burton

1989   STAR TREK THE NEXT GENERATION: Q WHO?
Director: Rob Bowman
Co-stars: Brent Spiner Marina Sirtis

1989   KISS SHOT
Director: Jerry London

1990   STAR TREK THE NEXT GENERATION: DEJA Q
Director: Les Landau
Co-stars: Wil Wheaton Levar Burton

1990   STAR TREK THE NEXT GENERATION: FAMILY
Director: Les Landau
Co-stars: Gate McFadden Michael Dorn

**1990   STAR TREK THE NEXT GENERATION:
HOLLOW PURSUITS**
Director: Cliff Bole
Co-star: Jonathan Frankes Patrick Stewart

**1990   STAR TREK THE NEXT GENERATION:
THE LOSS**
Director: Chip Chalmers
Co-stars: Brent Spiner Michael Dorn

1990 STAR TREK THE NEXT GENERATION: YESTERDAY'S ENTERPRISE
Director: David Carsob
Co-star: Wil Wheaton Patrick Stewart

1990 THE LONG WALK HOME
Director: Richard Pearce
Co-stars: Sissy Spacek Dwight Schultz Ving Rhames

1990 GHOST
Director: Jerry Zucker
Co-stars: Patrick Swayze Demi Moore Tony Goldwyn

1990 STAR TREK THE NEXT GENERATION: THE BEST OF BOTH WORLDS
Director: Cliff Bole
Co-star: Marina Siritis Patrick Stewart

1991 STAR TREK THE NEXT GENERATION: IN THEORY
Director: Patrick Stewart
Co-star: Gates McFadden Levar Burton

1991 SOAPDISH
Director: Michael Hoffman
Co-stars: Sally Field Kevin Kline Elizabeth Shue

1992 SARAFINA!
Director: Darrell James Roodt
Co-stars: Leleti Khumalo Miriam Makeba John Kani

1992 THE PLAYER
Director: Robert Altman
Co-stars: Tim Robbins Greta Scacchi Fred Ward

1992 HOUSE PARTY 2: THE PYJAMA JAM
Director: Doug McHenry
Co-stars: Christopher Reid Christopher Martin

1992 SISTER ACT
Director: Emile Ardolino
Co-stars: Maggie Smith Harvey Keitel Mary Wickes

1993 SISTER ACT 2: BACK IN THE HABIT
Director: Bill Duke
Co-stars: Maggie Smith James Coburn Mary Wickes

1993 NATIONAL LAMPOON'S LOADED WEAPON 1
Director: Gene Quintano
Co-stars: Emilio Estevez Tim Curry

1993 MADE IN AMERICA
Director: Richard Benjamin
Co-stars: Ted Danson Will Smith Nia Long

1994 THE PAGEMASTER
Director: Maurice Hunt
Co-stars: Macauley Culkin Ed Begley Jnr. Mel Harris

1994 CORINA, CORINA
Director: Jessie Nelson
Co-star: Ray Liotta Tina Majorino

1994 THE LION KING *(Voice)*
Director: Roger Allers
Co-stars: Matthew Broderick Jeremy Irons

1995 BOYS ON THE SIDE
Director: Herbert Ross
Co-stars: Mary-Louise Parker Drew Barrymore

1996 MOONLIGHT AND VALENTINO
Director: David Anspaugh
Co-stars: Elizabeth Perkins Kathleen Turner

1997 GHOSTS FROM THE PAST
Director: Rob Reiner
Co-stars: Alec Baldwin James Woods

1997 EDDIE
Co-star: Frank Langella

ANNIE GOLDEN

1979 HAIR
Director: Milos Forman
Co-stars: John Savage Treat Williams Beverly D'Angelo

OLIVE FULLER GOLDEN

1914 TESS OF THE STORM COUNTY
Director: Edwin Porter
Co-stars: Mary Pickford Harold Lockwood

MARCY GOLDMAN

1977 THE KENTUCKY FRIED MOVIE
Director: John Landis
Co-stars: Marilyn Joi Saul Kahan Joe Medalis

SHARON GOLDMAN

1981 EYEWITNESS
Director: Peter Yates
Co-stars: William Hurt Christopher Plummer Sigourney Weaver

LELIA GOLDONI

1961 SHADOWS
Director: John Cassavetes
Co-stars: Ben Carruthers Tony Ray Rupert Crosse

1964 HYSTERIA
Director: Freddie Francis
Co-stars: Robert Webber Jennifer Jayne Maurice Denholm

1966 THEATRE OF DEATH
Director: Sam Gallu
Co-stars: Christopher Lee Jenny Till Julian Glover

1974 ALICE DOESN'T LIVE HERE ANYMORE
Director: Martin Scorsese
Co-stars: Ellen Burstyn Diane Ladd Jodie Foster

1975 DAY OF THE LOCUST
Director: John Schlesinger
Co-stars: William Atherton Karen Black

1977 GOOD AGAINST EVIL
Director: Paul Wendkos
Co-stars: Dack Rambo Dan O'Herlihy Elyssa Davalos

1978 BLOODBROTHERS
Director: Robert Mulligan
Co-stars: Paul Sorvino Tony LoBianco Richard Gere

1978 INVASION OF THE BODYSNATCHERS
Director: Philip Kaufman
Co-stars: Donald Sutherland Brooke Adams

1981 MISTRESS OF PARADISE
Director: Peter Medak
Co-stars: Genevieve Bujold Chad Everett Anthony Andrews

1981 CHOICES
Director: Silvio Narizzano
Co-stars: Paul Carafotes Victor French Demi Moore

1984 ANATOMY OF AN ILLNESS
Director: Richard Heffron
Co-stars: Edward Ashner Eli Wallach Millie Perkins

MIRIAM GOLDSCHMIDT

1989 THE MAHABARATA
Director: Peter Brook
Co-stars: Urs Biher Georges Carraface Mamadou Dioumme

JENETTE GOLDSTEIN

1986 ALIENS
Director: James Cameron
Co-stars: Sigourney Weaver Carrie Henn Michael Biehn

1987 NEAR DARK
Director: Kathryn Bigelow
Co-stars: Adrian Pasdar Jenny Wright Bill Paxton

1988 THE PRESIDIO
Director: Peter Hyams
Co-stars: Sean Connery Mark Harmon Meg Ryan

1991 TERMINATOR 2: JUDGEMENT DAY
Director: James Cameron
Co-stars: Arnold Schwarzenegger Linda Hamilton Robert Patrick

VALERIA GOLINO

1986 DUMB DICKS
Director: Filippo Ottoni
Co-stars: David Landsberg Lorin Dreyfuss Christian De Sica

1987 THREE SISTERS
Director: Margaretha Von Trotta
Co-stars: Greta Scacchi Fanny Ardant Agnes Soral

1988 RAIN MAN
Director: Barry Levinson
Co-stars: Dustin Hoffman Tom Cruise Jerry Molen

1988 BIG TOP PEE-WEE
Director: Randal Kleiser
Co-stars: Paul Reubens Penelope Ann Miller Susan Tyrrell

1989 TORRENTS OF SPRING
Director: Jerzy Skolimowski
Co-stars: Timothy Hutton Nastassja Kinski

1990 THE KING'S WHORE
Director: Alex Corti
Co-stars: Timothy Dalton Stephane Freiss Margaret Tyzack

1991 THE INDIAN RUNNER
Director: Sean Penn
Co-stars: David Morse Viggo Mortensen Patricia Arquette

1991 HOT SHOTS!
Director: Jim Abrahams
Co-stars: Charlie Sheen Cary Elwes Lloyd Bridges

1992 YEAR OF THE GUN
Director: John Frankenheimer
Co-stars: Andrew McCarthy Sharon Stone John Pankow

1993 HOT SHOTS! PART DEUX
Director: Jim Abrahams
Co-stars: Charlie Sheen Lloyd Bridges Richard Crenna

1993 PUERTO ESCONDIDO
Director: Gabrielle Salvatores
Co-stars: Diego Abatantuono Claude Bislo

1994 CLEAN SLATE
Director: Mick Jackson
Co-stars: Dana Carvey Michael Gambon Olivia D'Abo

1995 FOUR ROOMS
Director: Allison Anders
Co-stars: Tim Roth Antonio Banderas Marisa Tomei Madonna

LIZA GOLM

1946 SHADOW OF A WOMAN
Director: Joseph Santley
Co-stars: Andrea King Don McGuire Richard Erdman

1951 THE HOODLUM
Director: Max Nosseck
Co-stars: Lawrence Tierney Allene Roberts

ARLENE GOLONKA

1966 THE BUSY BODY
Director: William Castle
Co-stars: Robert Ryan Sid Caesar Anne Baxter

1967 HANG 'EM HIGH
Director: Ted Post
Co-stars: Clint Eastwood Inger Stevens Ed Begley

1979 THE IN-LAWS
Director: Arthur Hiller
Co-stars: Peter Falk Alan Arkin Richard Libertini

1979 THE LAST MARRIED COUPLE IN AMERICA
Director: Gilbert Cates
Co-stars: Natalie Wood George Segal

1982 MY TUTOR
Director: George Bowers
Co-stars: Matt Lattanzi Caren Kaye Kevin McCarthy

1990 THE GUMSHOE KID
Director: Joseph Manduke
Co-stars: Jay Underwood Tracy Scoggins Vince Edwards

MARINA GOLOVINE

1991 OLIVER, OLIVER
Director: Agniewzka Holland
Co-stars: Francois Cluzet Brigitte Rouan Gregoire Colin

MINNA GOMBELL

1931 BAD GIRL
Director: Frank Borzage
Co-stars: Sally Eillers James Dunn William Pawley Frank Darien

1931 BACHELOR'S AFFAIRS
Director: Alfred Werker
Co-stars: Adolphe Menjou Joan Marsh Alan Dinehart

1932 AFTER TOMORROW
Director: Frank Borzage
Co-stars: Charles Farrell Marian Nixon Josephine Hull

1932 CARELESS LADY
Director: Kenneth MacKenna
Co-stars: Joan Bennett John Boles Weldon Heyburn

1932 DANCE TEAM
Director: Sidney Lanfield
Co-stars: Sally Eillers James Dunn Ralph Morgan

1932 THE FIRST YEAR
Director: William Howard
Co-stars: Janet Gaynor Charles Farrell Dudley Digges

1933 HELLO SISTER
Director: Erich Vom Stroheim
Co-stars: James Dunn Boots Mallory Zasu Pitts

1933 HOOPLA
Director: Frank Lloyd
Co-stars: Clara Bow Richard Cromwell Preston Foster

1933 THE WAY TO LOVE
Director: Norman Taurog
Co-stars: Maurice Chevalier Ann Dvorak Arthur Pierson

1934 THE THIN MAN
Director: W.S. Van Dyke
Co-stars: William Powell Myrna Loy Maureen O'Sullivan

1934 MARRYING WIDOWS
Co-star: Judith Allen

1934 NO MORE WOMEN
Director: Al Rogell
Co-stars: Edmund Lowe Victor McLaglen Sally Blane

1934 THE MERRY WIDOW
Director: Ernst Lubitsch
Co-stars: Maurice Chevalier Jeannette MacDonald Una Merkel

1934 CHEATING CHEATERS
Director: Richard Thorpe
Co-stars: Fay Wray Cesar Romero Henry Armetta

1934 BABBIT
Director: William Keighley
Co-stars: Guy Kibbee Aline MacMahon Maxine Doyle Alan Hale

1935 TWO SINNERS
Director: Arthur Lubin
Co-stars: Otto Kruger Martha Sleeper Cora Sue Collins

1935 WOMEN MUST DRESS
Co-star: Hardie Albright

1935 THE WHITE COCKATOO
Director: Alan Crosland
Co-stars: Richard Cortez Jean Muir Ruth Donnelly

1936 CHAMPAGNE CHARLIE
Co-stars: Helen Wood Paul Cavanagh

1937 WIFE, DOCTOR AND NURSE
Director: Walter Lang
Co-stars: Loretta Young Warner Baxter Virginia Bruce

1938 COMET OVER BROADWAY
Director: Busby Berkeley
Co-stars: Kay Francis Ian Hunter John Litel

1938 GOING PLACES
Director: Ray Enright
Co-stars: Dick Powell Anita Louise Ronald Reagan Louis Armstrong

1938 BLOCKHEADS
Director: John Blystone
Co-stars: Laurel & Hardy Billy Gilbert Patricia Ellis

1938 THE GREAT WALTZ
Director: Julien Duvivier
Co-stars: Fernand Gravet Luise Rainer Miliza Korjus

1940 BOOM TOWN
Director: Jack Conway
Co-stars: Clark Gable Spencer Tracy Claudette Colbert Hedy Lamarr

1941 DOOMED CARAVAN
Co-stars: William Boyd Georgia Hawkins

1944 JOHNNY DOESN'T LIVE HERE ANYMORE
Director: Joe May
Co-stars: Simone Simon James Ellison Robert Mitchum

1945 SUNBONNET SUE
Director: Ralph Murphy
Co-stars: Gale Storm Phil Regan George Cleveland

1945 THE TOWN WENT WILD
Director: Ralph Murphy
Co-stars: Freddie Bartholomew James Lydon

1946 PERILOUS HOLIDAY
Director: Edward Griffith
Co-stars: Pat O'Brien Ruth Warwick Alan Hale

1950 PAGAN LOVE SONG
Director: Robert Alton
Co-stars: Esther Williams Howard Keel Rita Moreno

CONSUELO GOMEZ

1992 EL MARIACHI
Director: Robert Rodrigeuz
Co-star: Carlos Gallardo

MARIE GOMEZ

1970 BARQUERO
Director: Gordon Douglas
Co-stars: Lee Van Cleef Warren Oates Forrest Tucker

ALISON GOMPF

1986 CHILDREN OF A LESSER GOD
Director: Randa Haines
Co-stars: William Hurt Marlee Matlin Piper Laurie

STELLA GONET

1987 DOWN WHERE THE BUFFALO ROAM
Director: Ian Knox
Co-stars: Harvey Keitel Andrew Byatt

1987 THE SHUTTER FALLS
Director: Peter Barber-Fleming
Co-stars: Anthony Higgins Emer Gillespie Joan Scott

1991 HEADING HOME
Director: David Hare
Co-stars: Joely Richardson Gary Oldman Michael Bryant

1991 THE ADVOCATES
Director: Peter Barber-Fleming
Co-stars: Isla Blair Ewen Stewart Alison Peebles

CAROLINE GOODALL

1991 HOOK
Director: Steven Spielberg
Co-stars: Dustin Hoffman Robin Williams Julia Roberts

1993 CLIFFHANGER
Director: Renny Harlin
Co-stars: Sylvester Stallone John Lithgow Michael Rooker

1993 ROYAL CELEBRATION
Director: Ferdinand Fairfax
Co-stars: Minnie Driver Rupert Graves Peter Howitt

1993 SCHINDLER'S LIST
Director: Steven Spielberg
Co-stars: Liam Neeson Ben Kingsley Ralph Fiennes

1995 DISCLOSURE
Director: Michael Crichton
Co-stars: Michael Douglas Demi Moore

1996 WHITE SQUALL
Director: Ridley Scott
Co-stars: Jeff Bridges John Savage Scott Wolf

1996 HOTEL SORRENTO
Co-star:: Caroline Gillmer

JOAN GOODFELLOW

1974 BUSTER AND BILLY
Director: Daniel Petrie
Co-stars: Jan-Michael Vincent Pamela Sue Martin

ANNE GOODING

1970 BRONCO BULLFROG
Director: Barney Platts-Mills
Co-stars: Del Walker Sam Shepard Roy Haywood

DODY GOODMAN

1964 BEDTIME STORY
Director: Ralph Levy
Co-stars: David Niven Marlon Brando Shirley Jones

1983 MAX DUGAN RETURNS
Director: Herbert Ross
Co-stars: Jason Robards Marsha Mason Matthew Broderick

1984 SPLASH!
Director: Ron Howard
Co-stars: Tom Hanks Daryl Hannah John Candy

1988 SPLASH TOO
Director: Greg Antonacci
Co-stars: Todd Waring Amy Yasbeck Rita Taggart

1992 FROZEN ASSETS
Director: George Miller
Co-stars: Shelley Long Corbin Bernsen Larry Miller

CAROL GOODNER

1932 STRANGE EVIDENCE
Director: Robert Milton
Co-stars: Leslie Banks George Curzon Frank Vosper

1935 MUSIC HATH CHARMS
Director: Arthur Woods
Co-stars: Henry Hall Antoinette Cellier Billy Milton

1935 MIMI
Director: Paul Stein
Co-stars: Douglas Fairbanks Jnr. Gertrude Lawrence Diana Napier

1937 THE FROG
Director: Jack Raymond
Co-stars: Gordon Harker Noah Berry Jack Hawkins

1937 THE DOMINANT SEX
Director: Herbert Brenon
Co-stars: Diana Churchill Philip Holmes Romney Brent

1938 A ROYAL DIVORCE
Director: Jack Raymond
Co-stars: Pierre Blanchar Ruth Chatterton John Laurie

DEBORAH GOODRICH

1986 APRIL FOOL'S DAY
Director: Fred Walton
Co-stars: Deborah Foreman Amy Steel Griffin O'Neal

ANGELA GOODWIN

1984 AURORA
Director: Maurizio Ponzi
Co-stars: Sophia Loren Daniel J. Travanti Edoardo Ponti

KIA JOY GOODWIN

1993 STRAPPED
Director: Forest Whitaker
Co-stars: Bokeem Woodbine Michael Biehn

LAUREL GOODWIN

1962 GIRLS! GIRLS! GIRLS!
Director: Noman Taurog
Co-stars: Elvis Presley Stella Stevens Jeremy Slate

1963 PAPA'S DELICATE CONDITION
Director: George Marshall
Co-stars: Jackie Gleason Glynis Johns Charles Ruggles

SUKI GOODWIN

1981 HELL NIGHT
Director: Tom De Simone
Co-stars: Linda Blair Vincent Van Patton Peter Barton

LINDA GORANSON

1966 THE TRAP
Director: Sidney Hayers
Co-stars: Oliver Reed Rita Tushingham Barbara Chilcott

BARBARA GORDON

1974 CHRISTINA
Director: Paul Krasny
Co-stars: Barbara Parkins Peter Haskell Marlyn Mason

1988 DEAD RINGERS
Director: David Cronenberg
Co-stars: Jeremy Irons Genevieve Bujold Shirley Douglas

CHRISTINE GORDON

1943 I WALKED WITH A ZOMBIE
Director: Jacques Tourneur
Co-stars: Frances Dee James Ellison Tom Conway

EVE GORDON

1989 LEAVING NORMAL
Director: Edward Zwick
Co-stars: Christine Lahti Meg Tilly Maury Chaykin

1990 AVALON
Director: Barry Levinson
Co-stars: Armin Mueller-Stahl Elizabeth Perkins Joan Plowright

1991 PARADISE
Director: Mary Agnes Donahue
Co-stars: Melanie Griffith Elijah Wood Thora Birch

GLORIA GORDON

1953 BENEATH THE TWELVE MILE REEF
Director: Robert Webb
Co-stars: Robert Wagner Terry Moore Gilbert Roland

1955 A MAN CALLED PETER
Director: Henry Koster
Co-stars: Richard Todd Jean Peters Jill Esmond

HANNAH GORDON

1970 SPRING AND PORT WINE
Director: Peter Hammond
Co-stars: James Mason Susan George Diana Coupland

1975 ALFIE DARLING
Director: Ken Hughes
Co-stars: Alan Price Jill Townsend Joan Collins

1978 WATERSHIP DOWN (Voice)
Director: Martin Rosen
Co-stars: John Hurt Richard Briers Simon Cadell

1990 THE ELEPHANT MAN
Director: David Lynch
Co-stars: John Hurt Anthony Hopkins Anne Bancroft

HILARY GORDON

1986 MOSQUITO COAST
Director: Peter Weir
Co-stars: Harrison Ford Helen Mirren River Phoenix

1988 THE GREAT OUTDOORS
Director: Howard Deutch
Co-stars: Dan Aykroyd John Candy Annette Bening

JULIA SWAYNE GORDON

1925 LIGHTS OF OLD BROADWAY
Director: Monta Bell
Co-stars: Marion Davies Conrad Nagel

1927 IT
Director: Clarence Badger
Co-stars: Clara Bow Antonio Moreno Gary Cooper

MARY GORDON

1935 THE IRISH IN US
Director: Lloyd Bacon
Co-stars: James Cagney Pat O'Brien Olivia De Havilland

1936 YELLOWSTONE
Co-stars: Judith Barrett Alan Hale

1937 THE GREAT O'MALLEY
Director: William Dieterle
Co-stars: Pat O'Brien Humphrey Bogart Ann Sheridan

1938 CITY STREETS
Director: Albert Rogell
Co-stars: Edith Fellows Leo Carrillo Tommy Bond

1939 THE ADVENTURES OF SHERLOCK HOLMES
Director: Alfred Werker
Co-stars: Basil Rathbone Nigel Bruce

1939　THE HOUND OF THE BASKERVILLES
Director:　Sidney Lanfield
Co-stars:　Basil Rathbone Richard Greene

1939　RULERS OF THE SEA
Director:　Frank Lloyd
Co-stars:　Douglas Fairbanks Jnr. Margaret Lockwood

1941　POT O' GOLD
Director:　George Marshall
Co-stars:　James Stewart Paulette Goddard Charles Winninger

1941　BOMBAY CLIPPER
Director:　John Rawlins
Co-stars:　William Gargan Irene Hervey Maria Montez

1942　SHERLOCK HOLMES AND THE SECRET WEAPON
Director:　Roy William Neill
Co-stars:　Basil Rathbone Nigel Bruce

1943　TWO TICKETS TO LONDON
Director:　Edwin Marin
Co-stars:　Alan Curtis Michele Morgan

1945　CAPTAIN EDDIE
Director:　Lloyd Bacon
Co-stars:　Fred MacMurray Lynn Bari Thomas Mitchell

1946　LITTLE GIANT
Director:　William Seiter
Co-stars:　Bud Abbott Lou Costello Brenda Joyce

MAUDE TURNER GORDON

1929　THE LAST MRS. CHEYNEY
Director:　Sidney Franklin
Co-stars:　Norma Shearer Basil Rathbone

1931　HIGH STAKES
Co-stars:　Mae Murray Lowell Sherman Edward Martindell

MURIEL GORDON

1933　THE LONE AVENGER
Co-star:　Ken Maynard

NOELLE GORDON

1946　LISBON STORY
Director:　Paul Stein
Co-stars:　Patricia Burke David Farrar Richard Tauber

REBECCA GORDON

1986　MOSQUITO COAST
Director:　Peter Weir
Co-stars:　Harrison Ford Helen Mirren River Phoenix

1988　THE GREAT OUTDOORS
Director:　Howard Deutch
Co-stars:　Dan Aykroyd John Candy Annette Bening

RUTH GORDON *(Married Garson Kanin)*
**Oscar For Best Supporting Actress In 1968 For Rosemary's Baby
Nomiated For Best Supporting Actress In 1965 For Inside Daisy Clover**

1940　ABE LINCOLN IN ILLINOIS
Director:　John Cromwell
Co-stars:　Raymond Massey Gene Lockhart Mary Howard

1940　DR. EHRLICH'S MAGIC BULLET
Director:　William Dieterle
Co-stars:　Edward G. Robinson Otto Kruger

1941　TWO-FACED WOMAN
Director:　George Cukor
Co-stars:　Greta Garbo Melvyn Douglas Roland Young

1943　EDGE OF DARKNESS
Director:　Lewis Milestone
Co-stars:　Errol Flynn Ann Sheridan Walter Huston

1943　ACTION IN THE NORTH ATLANTIC
Director:　Lloyd Bacon
Co-stars:　Humphrey Bogart Raymond Massey

1965　INSIDE DAISY CLOVER
Director:　Robert Mulligan
Co-stars:　Natalie Wood Robert Redford Christopher Plummer

1966　LORD LUV A DUCK
Director:　George Axelrod
Co-stars:　Roddy McDowell Tuesday Weld Lola Albright

1968　ROSEMARY'S BABY
Director:　Roman Polanski
Co-stars:　Mia Farrow John Cassavetes

1969　WHATEVER HAPPENED TO AUNT ALICE?
Director:　Lee Katzin
Co-stars:　Geraldine Page Rosemary Forsyth

1970　WHERE'S POPPA?
Director:　Carl Reiner
Co-stars:　George Segal Trish Van Devere Ron Leibman

1971　HAROLD AND MAUDE
Director:　Hal Ashby
Co-stars:　Bud Cort Vivian Pickles Cyril Cusack

1973　ISN'T IT SHOCKING?
Director:　John Badham
Co-stars:　Alan Alda Edmond O'Brien Louise Lasser

1976　THE BIG BUS
Director:　James Frawley
Co-stars:　Joseph Bologna Stockard Channing Jose Ferrer

1977　THE PRINCE OF CENTRAL PARK
Director:　Harvey Hart
Co-star:　T.J. Hargrave

1978　PERFECT GENTLEMEN
Director:　Jackie Cooper
Co-stars:　Lauren Bacall Sandy Dennis Lisa Pelikan

1978　EVERY WHICH WAY BUT LOOSE
Director:　James Fargo
Co-stars:　Clint Eastwood Sondra Locke Geoffrey Lewis

1979　BOARDWALK
Director:　Stephen Verona
Co-stars:　Lee Strasberg Janet Leigh Joe Silver Eddie Barth

1980　ANY WHICH WAY YOU CAN
Director:　Buddy Van Horn
Co-stars:　Clint Eastwood Sondra Locke Geoffrey Lewis

1980　MY BODYGUARD
Director:　Tony Bill
Co-stars:　Chris Makepiece Adam Baldwin Matt Dillon

1985　MAXIE
Director:　Paul Aaron
Co-stars:　Glenn Close Mandy Patinkin Harry Hamlin

SERENA GORDON
1989　A TALE OF TWO CITIES
Director:　Philippe Monier
Co-stars:　James Wilby John Mills Anna Massey

SUSAN GORDON *(Daughter Of Bert Gordon)*
1960　THE BOY AND THE PIRATES
Director:　Bert Gordon
Co-stars:　Charles Herbert Murvyn Vye Paul Guilfoyle

1966　PICTURE MOMMY DEAD
Director:　Bert Gordon
Co-stars:　Don Ameche Martha Hyer Zsa Zsa Gabor

VERA GORDON
1926　THE COHENS AND THE KELLYS
Director:　Harry Pollard
Co-stars:　George Sidney Charles Murray Kate Price

1927 THE COHENS AND THE KELLYS IN NEW YORK
Co-stars: George Sidney Charles Murray Kate Price

1928 THE COHENS AND THE KELLYS IN PARIS
Director: William Beaudine
Co-stars: J. Farrell MacDonald George Sidney

1929 THE COHENS AND THE KELLYS IN ATLANTIC CITY
Co-stars: George Sidney Charles Murray

1930 THE COHENS AND THE KELLYS IN AFRICA
Co-stars: George Sidney Charles Murray Kate Price

1930 THE COHENS AND THE KELLYS IN SCOTLAND
Director: William James Craft
Co-stars: Charles Murray George Sidney

1932 THE COHENS AND THE KELLYS IN HOLLYWOOD
Co-stars: Lew Ayres Boris Karloff Sidney Fox

1933 THE COHENS AND THE KELLYS IN TROUBLE
Co-stars: George Sidney Maureen O'Sullivan

19446 ABIE'S IRISH ROSE
Director: Edward Sutherland
Co-stars: Joanne Dru Richard Norris Eric Blore

LUCINDA GORRELL-BARNES

1970 SCRAMBLE
Director: David Eady
Co-stars: Alfred Marks James Hayter Graham Stark

ANNETTE GORMAN

1962 FIVE FINGER EXERCISE
Director: Daniel Mann
Co-stars: Rosalind Russell Jack Hawkins Richard Beymer

MARI GORMAN

1983 PACKIN' IT IN
Director: Jud Taylor
Co-stars: Richard Benjamin Paula Prentiss Molly Ringwald

KAREN LYNN GORNEY

1977 SATURDAY NIGHT FEVER
Director: John Badham
Co-stars: John Travolta Barry Miller Paul Pape

1991 THE HARD WAY
Director: John Badham
Co-stars: Michael J. Fox James Woods Annabella Sciorra

NORAH GORSEN

1955 GEORDIE
Director: Frank Launder
Co-stars: Bill Travers Alastair Sim Miles Malleson

HELEN GOSS

1952 THE PLANTER'S WIFE
Director: Ken Annakin
Co-stars: Claudette Colbert Jack Hawkins Jeremy Spenser

BARBARA GOTT

1930 AT THE VILLA ROSE
Director: Leslie Hiscott
Co-stars: Austin Trevor Norah Baring Richard Cooper

JETTA GOUDAL

1929 LADY OF THE PAVEMANTS
Director: D.W. Griffiths
Co-stars: Lupe Velez William Boyd Albert Conti

1931 BUSINESS AND PLEASURE
Director: David Butler
Co-stars: Will Rogers Joel McCrea Jed Prouty

DELPHINE GOUTTMAN

1990 CROSS MY HEART
Director: Jacques Fansten
Co-stars: Sylvain Copans Nicholas Parodi Lucie Blossier

MONA GOYA

1937 JUGGERNAUT
Director: Henry Edwards
Co-stars: Boris Karloff Joan Wyndham Anthony Ireland

MARIELLE GOZZI

1961 LEON MARIN, PRIEST
Director: Jean-Pierre Melville
Co-stars: Jean-Paul Belmondo Emmanuelle Riva

PATRICIA GOZZI CHILD

1962 SUNDAYS AND CYBELE
Director: Serge Bourginon
Co-stars: Hardy Kruger Nicole Courcel Daniel Ivernel

1965 RAPTURE
Director: John Guillerman
Co-stars: Dean Stockwell Melvyn Douglas Gunnel Lindblom

JODY GRABER

1990 THE GARDEN
Director: Derek Jarman
Co-stars: Kevin Collins Roger Cook Tilda Swinton

BETTY GRABLE
(Married Jackie Coogan, Harry James)

1930 WHOOPEE
Director: Thornton Freeland
Co-stars: Eddie Cantor Eleanor Hunt

1932 PROBATION

1932 HOLD 'EM JAIL
Co-stars: Bert Wheeler Robert Woolsey Edgar Kennedy

1932 THE GREEKS HAD A WORD FOR THEM
Director: Lowell Sherman
Co-stars: Lowell Sherman Joan Blondell Madge Evans

1932 THE KID FROM SPAIN
Director: Leo McCarey
Co-stars: Eddie Cantor Robert Young J. Carrol Naish

1933 CHILD OF MANHATTAN
Director: Edward Buzzell
Co-stars: Nancy Carroll John Boles Jane Darwell

1934 STUDENT TOUR
Director: Charles Reisner
Co-stars: Charles Butterworth Jimmy Durante Nelson Eddy

1934 THE GAY DIVORCEE
Director: Mark Sandrich
Co-stars: Fred Astaire Ginger Rogers Alice Brady

1935 NITWITS
Director: George Stevens
Co-stars: Bert Wheeler Robert Woolsey Fred Keating Evelyn Brent

1935 OLD MAN RHYTHM
Director: Edward Ludwig
Co-stars: Charles Rogers George Barbier Johnny Mercer

1936 PIGSKIN PARADE
Director: David Butler
Co-stars: Jack Haley Stuart Erwin Judy Garland

1936 **COLLEGIATE**
Director: Ralph Murphy
Co-stars: Jack Oakie Frances Langford Ned Sparks

1936 **FOLLOW THE FLEET**
Director: Mark Sandrich
Co-stars: Fred Astaire Ginger Rogers Randolph Scott

1937 **THRILL OF A LIFETIME**
Director: George Archainbaud
Co-stars: Judy Canova Ben Blue Dorothy Lamour

1937 **THIS WAY PLEASE**
Director: Robert Florey
Co-stars: Charles Rogers Ned Sparks Lee Bowman

1938 **COLLEGE SWING**
Director: Raoul Walsh
Co-stars: Burns & Allen Bob Hope Martha Raye

1938 **GIVE ME A SAILOR**
Director: Elliott Nugent
Co-stars: Bob Hope Martha Raye Clarence Kolb

1939 **MAN ABOUT TOWN**
Director: Mark Sandrich
Co-stars: Jack Benny Dorothy Lamour Edward Arnold

1939 **MILLION DOLLAR LEGS**
Director: Nick Grinde
Co-stars: Donald O'Connor Jackie Coogan

1940 **TIN PAN ALLEY**
Director: Walter Lang
Co-stars: Alice Faye John Payne Jack Oakie

1940 **DOWN ARGINTINE WAY**
Director: Irving Cummings
Co-stars: Don Ameche Carmen Miranda Charlotte Greenwood

1941 **A YANK IN THE R.A.F.**
Director: Henry King
Co-stars: Tyrone Power John Sutton Reginald Gardiner

1941 **I WAKE UP SCREAMING**
Director: Bruce Humberstone
Co-stars: Victor Mature Carole Landis Laird Cregar

1941 **MOON OVER MIAMI**
Director: Walter Lang
Co-stars: Don Ameche Carole Landis Robert Cummings

1942 **SPRINGTIME IN THE ROCKIES**
Director: Irving Cummings
Co-stars: John Payne Carmen Miranda Cesar Romero

1942 **SONG OF THE ISLANDS**
Director: Walter Lang
Co-stars: Victor Mature Jack Oakie Thomas Mitchell

1942 **FOOTLIGHT SERENADE**
Director: Gregory Ratoff
Co-stars: John Payne Victor Mature Jane Wyman

1943 **CONEY ISALND**
Director: Walter Lang
Co-stars: George Montgomery Cesar Romero Phil Silvers

1943 **SWEET ROSIE O'GRADY**
Director: Irving Cummings
Co-stars: Robert Young Adolphe Menjou Reginald Gardiner

1944 **TAKE IT OR LEAVE IT**
Director: Ben Stoloff
Co-stars: Phil Baker Phil Silvers Alice Faye Sonja Henie

1944 **PIN UP GIRL**
Director: Bruce Humberstone
Co-stars: John Harvey Martha Raye Joe E. Brown

1944 **FOUR JILLS IN A JEEP**
Director: William Seiter
Co-stars: Dick Haymes Kay Francis Carole Landis

1945 **DIAMOND HORSESHOE**
Director: George Seaton
Co-stars: Dick Haymes Phil Silvers Margaret Dumont

1945 **THE DOLLY SISTERS**
Director: Irving Cummings
Co-stars: June Haver John Payne S.Z. Sakall

1947 **THE SHOCKING MISS PILGRIM**
Director: George Seaton
Co-stars: Dick Haymes Anne Revere Allyn Joslyn

1948 **THAT LADY IN ERMINE**
Director: Ernst Lubitsch
Co-stars: Douglas Fairbanks Cesar Romero Walter Abel

1948 **WHEN MY BABY SMILES AT ME**
Director: Walter Lang
Co-stars: Dan Dailey Jack Oakie June Havoc

1948 **MOTHER WORE TIGHTS**
Director: Walter Lang
Co-stars: Dan Dailey Mona Freeman Connie Marshall

1949 **THE BEAUTIFUL BLONDE
FROM BASHFUL BEND**
Director: Preston Sturges
Co-stars: Cesar Romero Rudy Vallee

1950 **WABASH AVENUE**
Director: Henry Koster
Co-stars: Victor Mature Phil Harris Reginald Gardiner

1950 **MY BLUE HEAVEN**
Director: Henry Koster
Co-stars: Dan Dailey Mitzi Gaynor David Wayne

1951 **MEET ME AFTER THE SHOW**
Director: Richard Sale
Co-stars: MacDonald Carey Rory Calhoun Eddie Albert

1951 **CALL ME MISTER**
Director: Lloyd Bacon
Co-stars: Dan Dailey Danny Thomas Dale Robertson

1953 **HOW TO MARRY A MILLIONAIRE**
Director: Jean Negulesco
Co-stars: Marilyn Monroe Lauren Bacall David Wayne

1953 **THE FARMER TAKES A WIFE**
Director: Henry Levin
Co-stars: Dale Robertson Thelma Ritter John Carroll

1955 **HOW TO BE VERY, VERY POPULAR**
Director: Nunnally Johnson
Co-stars: Sheree North Robert Cummings

1955 **THREE FOR THE SHOW**
Director: H.C. Potter
Co-stars: Marge & Cower Champion Jack Lemmon

SOFIE GRABOL

1992 **THE SILENT TOUCH**
Director: Krzysztof Zanussi
Co-stars: Max Von Sydow Sarah Miles Lothaire Bluteau

CAROL GRACE

1976 **MIKEY AND NICKY**
Director: Elaine May
Co-stars: Peter Falk John Cassavetes Ned Beatty

ELIZABETH GRACEN

1990 **THE DEATH OF THE INCREDIBLE HULK**
Director: Bill Bixby
Co-stars: Bill Bixby Lou Ferrigno Barbara Tarbuck

1990 **MARKED FOR DEATH**
Director: Dwight Little
Co-stars: Steven Seagal Joanna Pacula Basil Wallace

1990   83 HOURS TILL DAWN
Director: Donald Wrye
Co-stars: Peter Strauss Robert Urich Amantha Mathis

SALLY GRACIE

1990   OPPORTUNITY KNOCKS
Director: Donald Petrie
Co-stars: Dana Carvey Robert Loggia Julia Campbell

GENEVIEVE GRAD

1963   THE HERO OF BABYLON
Director: Siro Marcellini
Co-stars: Gordon Scott Moira Orfei Pierro Lulli

1963   SANDOKAN THE GREAT
Director: Umberto Lenzi
Co-stars: Steve Reeves Rik Battaglia Maurice Foli

1964   SANDIKAN AND THE PIRATES OF MALAYA
Director: Umberto Lenzi
Co-star: Steve Reeves

1964   GENDARME IN ST. TROPEZ
Director: Jean Girault
Co-stars: Louis De Funes Michel Galabru

1965   THE GENDARME IN NEW YORK
Director: Jean Girault
Co-stars: Louis De Funes Jean Lefebvre

1978   THE SPACEMEN OF ST. TROPEZ
Director: Jean Girault
Co-stars: Louis De Funes Michel Galabru

ILENE GRAFF

1992   LADYBUGS
Director: Sidney Furie
Co-stars: Rodney Dangerfield Vinessa Shaw Jonathan Brandis

1995   ABANDONED AND DECIEVED
Director: Joseph Dougherty
Co-stars: Lori Loughlin Brian Kerwin Rosemary Forsythe

JUDY GRAFE

1990   BASKET CASE 2
Director: Frank Henenlotter
Co-stars: Kevin Van Hentenryck Annie Ross Chad Brown

AIMEE GRAHAM

1994   REFORM SCHOOL GIRL
Director: Jonathan Kaplan
Co-stars: Matt Leblanc Carolyn Setmore

ANITA GRAHAM

1974   CONFESSIONS OF A WINDOW CLEANER
Director: Val Guest
Co-stars: Anthony Booth Shelia White Robin Askwith

HEATHER GRAHAM

1988   LICENCE TO DRIVE
Director: Greg Beeman
Co-stars: Corey Haim Corey Feldman Carol Kane

1989   DRUGSTORE COWBOY
Director: Gus Van Sant
Co-stars: Matt Dillon Kelly Lynch Grace Zabriskile

1991   SHOUT
Director: Jeffrey Hornaday
Co-stars: John Travolta Richard Jordan Linda Fiorentino

1992   MIDNIGHT STING
Director: Michael Ritchie
Co-stars: James Woods Lou Gossett Jnr. Bruce Dern

1992   O-PIONEERS !
Director: Glenn Jordan
Co-stars: Jessica Lange David Strathairn Reed Diamond

1993   THE BALLAD OF LITTLE JOE
Director: Maggie Greenwald
Co-stars: Suzy Amis Bo Hopkins Carrie Snodgress

JULIE GRAHAM

1987   THE DARK ROOM
Director: Guy Slater
Co-stars: Susan Woolridge Philip Jackson Edith Ruddick

KIRSTY GRAHAM

1996   LOCH NESS
Director: John Henderson
Co-stars: Ted Danson Joely Richardson Ian Holm

NANCY GRAHAM

1990   VICTIM OF INNOCENCE
Director: Mel Damski
Co-stars: Cheryl Ladd Joe Spano Julia Nickson-Soul

SHEILA GRAHAM

1939   THAT'S RIGHT, YOU'RE WRONG
Director: David Butler
Co-stars: Kay Kyser Adolphe Menjou Lucille Ball

STACY GRAHAM

1959   THE EARTH IS MINE
Director: Henry King
Co-stars: Jean Simmons Claude Rains Rock Hudson

THERESE GRAHAM

1984   COUNTRY
Director: Richard Pearce
Co-stars: Jessica Lang Sam Sheperd Wilford Brimley

GLORIA GRAHAME *(Married Nicholas Ray)*
Best Supporting Actress In 1952 For "The Bad And The Beautiful"
Nominated For Best Supporting Actress In 1947 For "Crossfire"

1944   BLONDE FEVER
Director: Richard Whorf
Co-stars: Philip Dorn Mary Astor Marshall Thompson

1945   WITHOUT LOVE
Director: Harold Bucquet
Co-stars: Spencer Tracy Katharine Hepburn Lucille Ball

1946   IT'S A WONDERFUL LIFE
Director: Frank Capra
Co-stars: James Stewart Donna Reed Henry Travers

1947   MERTON OF THE MOVIES
Director: Robert Alton
Co-stars: Red Skelton Virginia O'Brien Alan Mowbray

1947   SONG OF THE THIN MAN
Director: Edward Buzzell
Co-stars: William Powell Myrna Loy Dean Stockwell

1947   IT HAPPENED IN BROOKLYN
Director: Richard Whorf
Co-stars: Frank Sinatra Kathryn Grayson Jimmy Durante

1947   CROSSFIRE
Director: Edward Dmytryk
Co-stars: Robert Young Robert Mitchum Robert Ryan

1949   ROUGHSHOD
Director: Mark Robson
Co-stars: Robert Sterling John Ireland Claude Jarman Jnr.

1949   A WOMAN'S SECRET
Director: Nicholas Ray
Co-stars: Maureen O'Hara Melvyn Douglas Bill Williams

1950 IN A LONELY PLACE
Director: Nicholas Ray
Co-stars: Humphrey Bogart Frank Lovejoy Jeff Donnell

1952 SUDDEN FEAR
Director: David Miller
Co-stars: Joan Crawford Jack Palance Joseph Kaufman

1952 THE BAD AND THE BEAUTIFUL
Director: Vincente Minnelli
Co-stars: Kirk Douglas Lana Turner Dick Powell

1952 MACAO
Director: Nicholas Ray
Co-stars: Robert Mitchum Jane Russell William Bendix

1953 MAN ON A TIGHTROPE
Director: Elia Kazan
Co-stars: Fredric March Cameron Mitchell Adolphe Menjou

1953 THE GREATEST SHOW ON EARTH
Director: Cecil B. DeMille
Co-stars: Charlton Heston James Stewart Betty Hutton

1953 PRISONERS OF THE CASBAH
Director: Richard Bare
Co-stars: Cesar Romero Turhan Bey Nestor Paiva

1953 THE BIG HEAT
Director: Fritz Lang
Co-stars: Glenn Ford Lee Marvin Alexander Scourby

1954 HUMAN DESIRE
Director: Fritz Lang
Co-stars: Glenn Ford Broderick Crawford Edgar Buchanan

1954 NAKED ALIBI
Director: Jerry Hopper
Co-stars: Sterling Hayden Gene Barry Chuck Connors

1954 THE GOOD DIE YOUNG
Director: Lewis Gilbert
Co-stars: Laurence Harvey Margaret Leighton Rene Ray

1955 THE COBWEB
Director: Vincente Minnelli
Co-stars: Richard Widmark Lauren Bacall Charles Boyer

1955 OKLAHOMA!
Director: Fred Zinnemann
Co-stars: Shirley Jones Gordon MacRae Eddie Albert

1955 NOT AS A STRANGER
Director: Stanley Kramer
Co-stars: Robert Mitchum Frank Sinatra Olivia De Havilland

1955 THE MAN WHO NEVER WAS
Director: Ronald Neame
Co-stars: Clifton Webb Robert Flemyng Stephen Boyd

1957 RIDE OUT FOR REVENGE
Director: Bernard Girard
Co-stars: Rory Calhoun Lloyd Bridges Vince Edwards

1959 ODDS AGAINST TOMORROW
Director: Robert Wise
Co-stars: Robert Ryan Harry Bellafonte Shelley Winters

1966 RIDE BEYOND VENGENCE
Director: Bernard McEveety
Co-stars: Chuck Connors Kathryn Hayes Michael Rennie

1970 ESCAPE
Director: John Llewellyn Moxey
Co-stars: Christopher George John Vernon

1970 THE TODD KILLINGS
Director: Barry Shear
Co-stars: Richard Thomas Barbara Bel Geddes Belinda Montgomery

1974 THE GIRL ON THE LATE, LATE SHOW
Director: Gary Nelson
Co-stars: Don Murray Yvonne De Carlo

1979 A NIGHTINGALE SANG IN BERKELEY SQUARE
Director: Ralph Thomas
Co-stars: Richard Jordan David Niven

1980 MELVYN AND HOWARD
Director: Jonathan Demme
Co-stars: Paul Le Mat Jason Robards Mary Steenburgen

1980 HEAD OVER HEELS
Director: Joan Micklin Silver
Co-stars: John Heard Mary Beth Hurt Peter Riegert

MARGOT GRAHAME

1930 ROOKERY NOOK
Director: Tom Walls
Co-stars: Tom Walls Ralph Lynn Robertson Hare

1933 SORRELL AND SON
Director: Jack Raymond
Co-stars: Hugh Williams Winifred Shotter Louis Hayward

1935 THE INFORMER
Director: John Ford
Co-stars: Victor McLaglen Heather Angel Wallace Ford

1935 THE THREE MUSKETEERS
Director: Rowland Lee
Co-stars: Walter Abel Paul Lukas Heather Angel

1935 THE ARIZONIAN
Director: Charles Vidor
Co-stars: Richard Dix Preston Foster Louis Calhern

1936 CRIME OVER LONDON
Director: Alfred Zeisler
Co-stars: Paul Cavanagh Joseph Cawthorn Rene Ray

1936 MAKE WAY FOR A LADY
Director: David Burton
Co-stars: Herbert Marshall Ann Shirley Gertrude Michael

1936 TWO IN THE DARK
Director: Ben Stoloff
Co-stars: Walter Abel Wallace Ford Gail Patrick Alan Hale

1937 FIGHT FOR YOUR LADY
Director: Ben Stoloff
Co-stars: John Boles Jack Oakie Ida Lupino

1937 CRIMINAL LAWYER
Director: Christy Cabanne
Co-stars: Lee Tracy Eduardo Cianelli Erik Rhodes

1937 THE ADVENTURES OF MICHAEL STROGOFF
Director: George Nicholls
Co-stars: Anton Walbrook Elizabeth Allan

1938 THE BUCCANEER
Director: Cecil B. DeMille
Co-stars: Fredric March Akim Tamiroff Walter Brennan

1947 THE FABULOUS JOE
Co-stars: Walter Abel John Eldredge Dorothy Christie

1948 BROKEN JOURNEY
Director: Ken Annakin
Co-stars: Phyllis Calvert James Donald Guy Rolfe

1949 BLACK MAGIC
Director: Gregory Ratoff
Co-stars: Orson Welles Nancy Guild Akim Tamiraoff

1949 THE ROMANTIC AGE
Director: Edmond Greville
Co-stars: Mai Zetterling Hugh Williams Petula Clark

1952 VENETIAN BIRD
Director: Ralph Thomas
Co-stars: Richard Todd Eva Bartok John Gregson

1952   THE CRIMSON PIRATE
Director: Robert Siodmak
Co-stars: Burt Lancaster Nick Cravat Eva Bartok

1952   THE BEGGAR'S OPERA
Director: Herbert Wilcox
Co-star: Laurence Olivier Dorothy Tuton Hugh Griffith

1954   ORDERS ARE ORDERS
Director: David Palteghi
Co-stars: Peter Sellers Tony Hancock Brian Reece

EMMA GRAMATICA

1951   MIRACLE IN MILAN
Director: Vittorio De Sica
Co-stars: Francesco Golisano Brunella Bovo Paolo Stoppa

DOROTHY GRANGER

1930   HOG WILD
Director: James Parrott
Co-stars: Stan Laurel Oliver Hardy Fay Holderness

1942   NORTH TO THE KLONDYKE
Director: Erle Kenton
Co-stars: Broderick Crawford Andy Devine Evelyn Ankers

1945   UNDER WESTERN SKIES
Co-star: Ian Keith

LINA GRANHAGEN

1966   HUGS AND KISSES
Director: Jonas Cornell
Co-stars: Sven-Bertil Taube Agneta Ekmanner

BETH GRANT

1990   FALL FROM GRACE
Director: Karen Arthur
Co-stars: Kevin Spacey Bernadette Peters Richard Herd

1992   DON'T TELL HER IT'S ME
Director: Malcolm Mowbray
Co-stars: Steve Guttenberg Jami Gertz Shelley Long

1992   LOVE FIELD
Director: Jonathan Kaplan
Co-stars: Michelle Pfeiffer Dennis Haysbert Brian Kerwin

1992   WHITE SANDS
Director: Roger Donaldson
Co-stars: Willem Dafoe Mickey Rourke Mary Elizabeth Mastrantonio

1994   SPEED
Director: Jan De Bont
Co-stars: Keanu Reeves Sandra Bullock Dennis Hopper

1994   CITY SLICKERS 2:
        THE LEGEND OF CURLY'S GOLD
Director: Paul Weiland
Co-stars: Billy Crystal Daniel Stern

FAYE GRANT

1983   V
Director: Kenneth Johnson
Co-stars: Marc Singer Jane Badler Michael Durrell

1988   CROSSING DELANCEY
Director: Joan Micklin Silver
Co-stars: Amy Irving Peter Riegert Jeroen Krabbe

1989   THE JANUARY MAN
Director: Pat O'Connor
Co-stars: Kevin Kline Susan Sarandon Harvey Keitel

1990   INTERNAL AFFAIRS
Director: Mike Figgis
Co-stars: Richard Gere Andy Garcia Nancy Travis

1991   OMEN IV: THE AWAKENING
Director: Jorge Montesi
Co-stars: Michael Woods Michael Lerner Ann Hearn

1992   TRACES OF RED
Director: Andy Wolk
Co-stars: James Belushi Lorraine Bracco Tony Goldwyn

KATHRYN GRANT

1955   THE PHENIX CITY STORY
Director: Phil Karlson
Co-stars: Richard Kiley Edward Andrews John McIntrye

1955   CELL 2455, DEATH ROW
Director: Fred Sears
Co-stars: William Cambpell Marian Carr Vince Edwards

1956   THE GUNS OF FORT PETTICOAT
Director: George Marshall
Co-stars: Audie Murphy Hope Emerson Jeff Donnell

1956   THE WILD PARTY
Director: Harry Horner
Co-stars: Anthony Quinn Carol Chimart Arthur Franz

1957   OPERATION MAD BALL
Director: Richard Quine
Co-stars: Jack Lemmon Mickey Rooney Ernie Kovacs

1957   MISTER CORY
Director: Blake Edwards
Co-stars: Tony Curtis Martha Hyer Charles Bickford

1957   THE BROTHERS RICCO
Director: Phil Karlson
Co-stars: Richard Conte James Darren Dianne Foster

1958   THE GUNMAN'S WALK
Director: Phil Karlson
Co-stars: Van Helfin Tab Hunter James Darren

1958   THE SEVENTH VOYAGE OF SINBAD
Director: Nathan Juran
Co-stars: Kerwin Matthews Torin Thatcher

1959   THE BIG CIRCUS
Director: Joseph Newman
Co-stars: Victor Mature Red Buttons Rhonda Fleming

1959   ANATOMY OF A MURDER
Director: Otto Preminger
Co-stars: James Stewart Lee Remick Arthur O'Connell

LEE GRANT
Oscar For Best Supporting Actress In 1975 For "Shampoo"
Nominated For Best Supporting Actress In 1951 For "Detective Story", In
1970 For "The Landlord" And In 1976 For "Voyage Of The Damned"

1951   DETECTIVE STORY
Director: William Wyler
Co-stars: Kirk Douglas Eleanor Parker William Bendix

1955   STORM FEAR
Director: Cornel Wilde
Co-stars: Cornel Wilde Jean Wallace Dan Duryea Steven Hill

1959   MIDDLE OF THE NIGHT
Director: Delbert Mann
Co-stars: Fredric March Kim Novak Glenda Farrell

1963   THE BALCONY
Director: Joseph Strick
Co-stars: Shelley Winters Peter Falk Leonard Nimoy

1967   DIVORCE AMERICAN STYLE
Director: Bud Yorkin
Co-stars: Dick Van Dyke Jason Robards Jean Simmons

1967   VALLEY OF THE DOLLS
Director: Mark Robson
Co-stars: Barbara Parkins Patty Duke Susan Hayward Sharon Tate

1967 IN THE HEAT OF THE NIGHT
Director: Norman Jewison
Co-stars: Sidney Poitier Rod Steiger Warren Oates

1968 BUONA SERA MRS. CAMPBELL
Director: Melvyn Frank
Co-stars: Gina Lollobrigida Telly Savalas Phil Silvers

1969 THE BIG BOUNCE
Director: Alex March
Co-stars: Ryan O'Neil Leigh Taylor-Young Van Heflin

1969 MAROONED
Director: John Sturges
Co-stars: Gregory Peck Richard Crenna David Janssen

1970 THE LANDLORD
Director: Hal Ashby
Co-stars: Beau Bridges Diana Sands Pearl Bailey Louis Gossett

1970 NIGHT SLAVES
Director: Ted Frost
Co-stars: James Franciscus Scott Marlowe

1971 PLAZA SUITE
Director: Arthur Hiller
Co-stars: Walter Matthau Maureen Stapleton Barbara Harris

1972 PORTNOY'S COMPLAINT
Director: Ernest Lehman
Co-stars: Richard Benjamin Karen Black Jill Clayburgh

1974 THE INTERNECINE PROJECT
Director: Ken Hughes
Co-stars: James Coburn Harry Andrews Keenan Wynn

1975 SHAMPOO
Director: Hal Ashby
Co-stars: Warren Beatty Julie Christie Goldie Hawn

1976 PERILIOUS VOYAGE
Director: William Graham
Co-stars: Michael Parks William Shatner Charles McGraw

1976 VOYAGE OF THE DAMNED
Director: Stuart Rosenberg
Co-stars: Faye Dunaway Orson Welles James Mason

1977 AIRPORT '77
Director: Jerry Jameson
Co-stars: Jack Lemmon James Stewart Brenda Vaccaro

1978 THE SWARM
Director: Irwin Allen
Co-stars: Michael Caine Katherine Ross Richard Widmark

1978 DAMIEN: OMEN II
Director: Don Taylor
Co-stars: William Holden Lew Ayres Sylvia Sidney Robert Foxworth

1980 LITTLE MISS MARKER
Director: Walter Bernstein
Co-stars: Walter Matthau Julie Andrews Tony Curtis

1980 CHARLIE CHAN AND THE CURSE OF THE DRAGON QUEEN
Director: Clive Donner
Co-stars: Peter Ustinov Angie Dickinson

1983 THOU SHALL NOT KILL
Director: I.C. Rappaport
Co-stars: Robert Culp Gary Graham Diana Scarwid

1984 A BILLION FOR BORIS
Director: Alex Grassof
Co-stars: Seth Green Scott Tiler

1984 TEACHERS
Director: Arthur Hiller
Co-stars: Nick Nolte JoBeth Williams Laura Dern Judd Hirsch

1985 TRIAL RUN
Director: Melanie Read
Co-stars: Annie Whittle Judith Gibson Christopher Brown

1987 THE BIG TOWN
Director: Ben Bolt
Co-stars: Matt Dillon Diane Lane Tommy Lee Jones Suzy Amis

1988 THE HIJACKING OF THE ACHILLE LAURO
Director: Robert Collins
Co-stars: Karl Malden Vera Miles

1991 DEFENDING YOUR LIFE
Director: Albert Brooks
Co-stars: Albert Brooks Meryl Streep Rip Torn Shirley MacLaine

1992 IN MY DAUGHTER'S NAME
Director: Jud Taylor
Co-stars: Donna Mills John Getz Ari Meyers

1992 FATAL LOVE
Director: Tom McLoughlin
Co-stars: Molly Ringwald Perry King Kim Myers

1995 IT'S MY PARTY
Co-stars: Eric Roberts George Segal Marlee Matlin

LUCY GRANTHAM
1972 THE LAST HOUSE ON THE LEFT
Director: Wes Craven
Co-stars: Davis Hess Sandra Cassel Marc Sheffler

CHARLOTTE GRANVILLE
1934 NOW AND FOREVER
Director: Henry Hathaway
Co-stars: Gary Cooper Carole Lombard Shirley Temple

1934 BEHOLD MY WIFE
Director: Mitchell Leisen
Co-stars: Gene Raymond Sylvia Sidney Juliette Compton

BONITA GRANVILLE
Nominated For Best Supporting Actress In 1936 For "These Three"
1933 CAVALCADE
Director: Frank Lloyd
Co-stars: Clive Brook Diana Wynward Ursula Jeans Herbert Mundin

1935 AH! WILDERNESS
Director: Clarence Brown
Co-stars: Wallace Beery Lionel Barrymore Mickey Rooney

1936 THE PLOUGH AND THE STARS
Director: John Ford
Co-stars: Barbara Stanwyck Preston Foster Barry Fitzgerald

1936 THESE THREE
Director: William Wyler
Co-stars: Merle Oberon Miriam Hopkins Joel McCrea

1937 IT'S LOVE I'M AFTER
Director: Archie Mayo
Co-stars: Leslie Howards Bette Davis Olivia De Havilland

1937 CALL IT A DAY
Director: Archie Mayo
Co-stars: Olivia De Havilland Ian Hunter Anita Louise

1937 MAID OF SALEM
Director: Frank Lloyd
Co-stars: Claudette Colbert Fred MacMurray Gale Sondergaard

1938 BELOVED BRAT
Co-star: Dolores Costello

1938 NANCY DREW, DETECTIVE
Director: William Clemens
Co-star: Frankie Thomas

1938 NANCY DREW AND THE HIDDEN STAIRCASE
Director: William Clemens
Co-star: Frankie Thomas

1938 MERRILY WE LIVE
Director: Norman Z McLeod
Co-stars: Constance Bennett Brian Aherne Billie Burke

1938 WHITE BANNERS
Director: Edmund Goulding
Co-stars: Fay Bainter Claude Rains Jackie Cooper

1939 NANCY DREW: REPORTER
Director: William Clemens
Co-star: Frankie Thomas John Litel Renie Riano

1939 NANCY DREW: TROUBLE SHOOTER
Director: William Clemens
Co-star: Frankie Thomas

1939 ANGELS WASH THEIR FACES
Director: Ray Enright
Co-stars: Ann Sheridan Ronald Reagan Frankie Thomas

1940 ESCAPE
Director: Mervyn LeRoy
Co-stars: Robert Taylor Norma Shearer Conrad Veidt

1940 GALLANT SONS
Director: George Seitz
Co-stars: Jackie Cooper Gene Reynolds Gail Patrick Ian Hunter

1940 FORTY LITTLE MOTHERS
Director: Busby Berkeley
Co-stars: Eddie Cantor Judith Anderson Rita Johnson

1940 H.M. PULHAM ESQUIRE
Director: King Vidor
Co-stars: Robert Young Ruth Hussey Hedy Lamarr Van Heflin

1940 THIRD FINGER LEFT HAND
Director: Robert Z Leonard
Co-stars: Myrna Loy Melvyn Douglas Lee Bowman

1940 THOSE WERE THE DAYS
Director: Theodore Reed
Co-stars: William Holden Ezra Stone Judith Barrett

1940 THE MORTAL STORM
Director: Frank Borzage
Co-stars: Margaret Sullavan Robert Young James Stewart

1941 THE WILD MAN OF BORNEO
Director: Robert Sinclair
Co-stars: Frank Morgan Dan Dailey Mary Howard

1942 SYNCOPATION
Director: William Dieterle
Co-stars: Jackie Cooper Adolphe Menjou Benny Goodman

1942 SEVEN MILES FROM ALCATRAZ
Director: Edward Dmytryk
Co-stars: James Craig Frank Jenks Cliff Edwards

1942 NOW VOYAGER
Director: Irving Rapper
Co-stars: Bette Davis Paul Henreid Claude Rains

1942 THE GLASS KEY
Director: Stuart Heisler
Co-stars: Alan Ladd Veronica Lake William Bendix

1943 HITLER'S CHILDREN
Director: Edward Dmytryk
Co-stars: Tim Holt Otto Kruger Kent Smith H.B. Warner

1944 ANDY HARDY'S BLONDE TROUBLE
Director: George Seitz
Co-stars: Mickey Rooney Lewis Stone Wilde Twins

1944 SONG OF THE OPEN ROAD
Director: S. Sylvan Simon
Co-stars: Jane Powell W.C. Fields Edgar Bergen

1944 YOUTH RUNS WILD
Director: Mark Robson
Co-stars: Kent Smith Jean Brooks Arthur Shields Glenn Vernon

1945 SENORITA FROM THE WEST
Co-stars: Allan Jones Danny Mummery

1946 SUSPENSE
Director: Frank Tuttle
Co-stars: Belita Barry Sullivan Albert Dekker

1946 LOVE LAUGHS AT ANDY HARDY
Director: Willis Goldbeck
Co-stars: Mickey Rooney Lewis Stone Fay Holden

1947 BREAKFAST IN HOLLYWOOD
Director: Harold Schuster
Co-stars: Tom Breneman Beulah Bondi Billie Burke

1947 THE GUILTY
Co-stars: Don Castle Regis Tooney John Litel

1950 GUILTY OF TREASON
Director: Felix Feist
Co-stars: Charles Bickford Paul Kelly Richard Derr

1955 THE LONE RANGER
Director: Stuart Heisler
Co-stars: Clayton Moore Jay Silverheels Lyle Bettger

KAREN GRASSLE

1979 CRISIS IN MID-AIR
Director: Walter Grauman
Co-stars: George Peppard Desi Arnaz Jnr. Don Murray

1983 COCAINE: ONE MAN'S SEDUCTION
Director: Paul Wendkos
Co-stars: Dennis Weaver Pamela Bellwood James Spader

JUDY GRAUBERT

1980 SIMON
Director: Marshall Brickman
Co-stars: Alan Arkin Madeline Kahn Austin Pendleton

TERESA GRAVES

1973 THAT MAN BOLT
Director: Henry Levin
Co-stars: Fred Williamson Byron Webster Miko Mayama

1974 VAMPIRA
Director: Clive Donner
Co-stars: David Niven Jennie Linden Peter Bayliss

CARLA GRAVINA

1960 FIVE BRANDED WOMEN
Director: Martin Ritt
Co-stars: Van Heflin Silvana Mangano Barbara Bel Geddes

1972 ALFREDO, ALFREDO
Director: Pietro Germi
Co-stars: Dustin Hoffman Stefania Sandrelli Danielle Patella

1976 BOOMERANG
Director: Jose Giovanni
Co-stars: Alain Delon Charles Vanel Suzanne Flon

COLEEN GRAY

1947 KISS OF DEATH
Director: Henry Hathaway
Co-stars: Victor Mature Richard Widmark Brian Donlevy

1947 NIGHTMARE ALLEY
Director: Edmund Goulding
Co-stars: Tyrone Power Joan Blondell Mike Mazurki

1948 RED RIVER
Director: Howard Hawks
Co-stars: John Wayne Montgomery Clift Joanne Dru

1948 FURY AT FURNACE CREEK
Director: Bruce Humberstone
Co-stars: Victor Mature Glenn Langan Reginald Gardiner

1949 SAND
Co-stars: Mark Stevens Charley Grapewin

1950 THE SLEEPING CITY
Director: George Sherman
Co-stars: Richard Conte Peggy Dow Alex Nicol

1950 RIDING HIGH
Director: Frank Capra
Co-stars: Bing Crosby Charles Bickford Oliver Hardy

1950 FATHER IS A BACHELOR
Director: Norman Foster
Co-stars: William Holden Charles Winninger Stuart Erwin

1951 APACHE DRUMS
Director: Hugo Fregonese
Co-stars: Stephen McNally Williard Parker Arthur Shields

1951 I'LL GET YOU FOR THIS
Director: Joseph Newman
Co-stars: George Raft Charles Goldner Greta Gynt

1952 KANSAS CITY CONFIDENTIAL
Director: Phil Karlson
Co-stars: John Payne Preston Foster Dona Drake

1953 THE FAKE
Director: Godfrey Grayson
Co-stars: Dennis O'Keefe Ruth Williams Guy Middleton

1953 SABRE JET
Director: Louis King
Co-stars: Robert Stack Richard Arlen Leon Ames Julie Bishop

1953 THE VANQUISHED
Director: Edward Ludwig
Co-stars: John Payne Lyle Bettger Jan Sterling

1954 ARROW IN THE DUST
Director: Lesley Selander
Co-stars: Sterling Hayden Tom Tully Keith Larsen

1955 TENNESSEE'S PARTNER
Director: Allan Dwan
Co-stars: Ronald Reagan John Payne Rhonda Fleming

1955 THE TWINKLE IN GOD'S EYE
Director: George Blair
Co-stars: Mickey Rooney Hugh O'Brian Don Barry

1956 THE KILLING
Director: Stanley Kubrick
Co-stars: Sterling Hayden Marie Windsor Elisha Cook Jnr.

1956 DEATH OF A SCOUNDREL
Director: Charles Martin
Co-stars: George Sanders Yvonne De Carlo Zsa Zsa Gabor

1956 THE BLACK WHIP
Director: Charles Marquis Warren
Co-stars: Hugh Marlowe Angie Dickinson Sheb Wooley

1957 THE VAMPIRE
Director: Paul Landers
Co-stars: John Beal Dabbs Greer Raymond Greenleaf

1958 JOHNNY ROCCO
Director: Paul Landres
Co-stars: Stephen McNally Richard Eyer Russ Conway

1958 HELL'S FIVE HOURS
Director: Jack Copeland
Co-stars: Stephen McNally Vic Morrow

1967 NEW FACE IN HELL
Director: John Guillermin
Co-stars: George Peppard Gayle Hunnicutt Raymond Burr

1971 ELLERY QUEEN: DON'T LOOK BEHIND YOU
Director: Barry Shear
Co-stars: Peter Lawford Harry Morgan

DOLORES GRAY

1955 KISMET
Director: Vincent Minnelli
Co-stars: Howard Keel Ann Blyth Vic Damone

1955 IT'S ALWAYS FAIR WEATHER
Director: Stanley Donen
Co-stars: Gene Kelly Cyd Charisse Dan Dailey

1956 THE OPPOSITE SEX
Director: David Miller
Co-stars: June Allyson Joan Collins Ann Sheridan

1957 DESIGNING WOMAN
Director: Vincente Minnelli
Co-stars: Gregory Peck Lauren Bacall

DULCIE GRAY (Married Michael Dennison)

1944 A PLACE OF ONE'S OWN
Director: Bernard Knowles
Co-stars: James Mason Barbara Mullen Margaret Lockwood

1944 TWO THOUSAND WOMEN
Director: Frank Launder
Co-stars: Phyllis Calvert Flora Robson Anne Crawford

1945 THEY WERE SISTERS
Director: Arthur Crabtree
Co-stars: James Mason Phyllis Calvert Hugh Sinclair

1946 THE YEARS BETWEEN
Director: Compton Bennett
Co-stars: Michael Redgrave Valerie Hobson Flora Robson

1946 WANTED FOR MURDER
Director: Lawrence Huntingdon
Co-stars: Eric Portman Derek Farr Roland Culver

1947 MY BROTHER JONATHAN
Director: Harold French
Co-stars: Michael Dennison Ronald Howard Stephen Murray

1947 A MAN ABOUT THE HOUSE
Director: Leslie Arliss
Co-stars: Margaret Johnston Kieron Moore Felix Aylmer

1947 MINE OWN EXECUTIONER
Director: Anthony Kimmins
Co-stars: Burgess Meredith Kieron Moore Christine Norden

1949 THE GLASS MOUNTAIN
Director: Henry Cass
Co-stars: Michael Dennison Valentina Cortesa

1950 THE FRANCHISE AFFAIR
Director: Lawrence Huntingdon
Co-stars: Michael Dennison Marjorie Fielding

1952 ANGELS ONE FIVE
Director: George More O'Ferrall
Co-stars: Jack Hawkins John Gregson Michael Dennison

1953 THERE WAS A YOUNG LADY
Director: Lawrence Huntingdon
Co-stars: Michael Dennison Bill Owen

1966 A MAN COULD GET KILLED
Director: Ronald Neame
Co-stars: James Garner Melina Mercouri Sandra Dee

ELSPET GRAY (Married Brian Rix)

1948 THE BLIND GODDESS
Director: Harold French
Co-stars: Eric Portman Anne Crawford Hugh Williams

1983 AGATHA CHRISTIE: IN A GLASS DARKLY
Director: Desmond Davis
Co-stars: Emma Piper Nicholas Clay

**1987 INSPECTOR MORSE:
THE SILENT WORLD OF NICHOLAS QUINN**
Director: Brian Parker
Co-star: John Thaw Kevin Whateley

1988 THE GIRL IN A SWING
Director: Gordon Hessler
Co-stars: Meg Tilly Rupert Frazer Lynsey Baxter

1992 DEAD ROMANTIC
Director: Patrick Lau
Co-stars: Janet McTeer Clive Wood Jonny Lee Miller

ERIN GRAY

1979 BUCK ROGERS IN THE 25TH CENTURY
Director: Daniel Haller
Co-stars: Gil Gerrard Pamela Hensley

1982 SIX PACK
Director: Daniel Petrie
Co-stars: Kenny Rogers Diane Lane Barry Corbin

1987 PERRY MASON:
THE CASE OF THE MURDERD MADAM
Director: Ron Satlof
Co-stars: Raymond Burr Barbara Hale

1988 ADDICTED TO HIS LOVE
Director: Arthur Allen Seidelmann
Co-stars: Barry Bostwick Polly Bergen

1993 JASON GOES TO HELL: THE FINAL FRIDAY
Director: Adam Marcus
Co-stars: Steve Williams Kari Keegan

EVE GRAY

1934 MURDER AT MONTE CARLO
Director: Ralph Ince
Co-stars: Errol Flynn Molly Lamont Paul Graetz

1935 DEATH ON THE SET
Director: Leslie Hiscott
Co-stars: Henry Kendall Jeanne Stuart Garry Marsh

GILDA GRAY

1929 PICCADILLY
Director: E.A. Dupont
Co-stars: Jameson Thomas Anna May Wong Charles Laughton

1936 ROSE MARIE
Director: W.S. Van Dyke
Co-stars: Nelson Eddy Jeannette MacDonald James Stewart

1936 THE GREAT ZIEGFIELD
Director: Robert Z. Leonard
Co-stars: William Powell Luise Rainer Myrna Loy

JANINE GRAY

1964 THE PUMPKIN EATER
Director: Jack Clayton
Co-stars: Anne Bancroft Peter Finch James Mason

1965 QUICK BEFORE IT MELTS
Director: Delbert Mann
Co-stars: George Maharris Robert Morse Anjanette Comer

LINDA GRAY

1938 SHADOWS OVER SHANGHAI
Co-stars: James Dunn Ralph Morgan

LINDA GRAY

1979 THE TWO WORLDS OF JENNY LOGAN
Director: Frank De Felita
Co-stars: Lindsay Wagner Marc Singer

1982 NOT IN FRONT OF THE CHILDREN
Director: Joseph Hardy
Co-stars: John Getz John Lithgow Carol Rossen

1987 KENNY ROGERS AS THE GAMBLER PART
III - THE LEGEND CONTINUES
Director: Dick Lowry
Co-star: Kenny Rogers George Kennedy

1991 OSCAR
Director: John Landis
Co-stars: Sylvester Stallone Ornella Muti Kirk Douglas

1993 BONANZA - THE RETURN
Director: Jerry Jameson
Co-stars: Michael Landon Jnr. Dean Stockwell Ben Johnson

1993 WHY MY DAUGHTER?
Director: Chuck Bowman
Co-stars: Antonio Sabbato Jnr. Jaimie Luner

1993 ACCIDENTAL MEETING
Director: Michael Zinreig
Co-stars: Linda Purl

1994 BROKEN PLEDGES
Director: Jorge Montesi
Co-stars: Barry Bonds David Lipper

LORNA GRAY

1939 THE MAN THEY COULD NOT HANG
Director: Nick Grinde
Co-stars: Boris Karloff Roger Pryor Don Beddoe

19452 RIDIN' DOWN THE CANYON
Co-stars: James Seay Addison Richards

NADIA GRAY

1949 THE SPIDER AND THE FLY
Director: Robert Hamer
Co-stars: Eric Portman Guy Rolfe George Cole

1951 NIGHT WITHOUT STARS
Director: Anthony Pellisier
Co-stars: David Farrar Maurice Teynac

1951 VALLEY OF EAGLES
Director: Terence Young
Co-stars: Jack Warner John McCallum Anthony Dawson

1952 TOP SECRET
Director: Mario Zampi
Co-stars: George Cole Oscar Homolka Wilfrid Hyde White

1954 CROSSED SWORDS
Director: Milton Krims
Co-stars: Errol Flynn Gina Lollobrigida Paola Mori

1955 THE GOLDEN FALCON
Co-stars: Ludovico Bragaglia Massimo Serato

1958 FOLLIES BERGERE
Director: Henri Decoin
Co-stars: Jeanmarie Eddie Constantine Yves Robert

1958 THE CAPTAIN'S TABLE
Director: Jack Lee
Co-stars: John Gregson Peggy Cummings Donald Sinden

1960 CANDIDE
Director: Clemment Duhour
Co-stars: Jean-Piere Cassel Pierre Brasseur Daliah Lavi

1960 LA DOLCE VITA
Director: Federico Fellini
Co-stars: Marcello Mastroianni Anita Ekberg Anouk Aimee

1961 MR. TOPAZ
Director: Peter Sellers
Co-stars: Peter Sellers Herbert Lom Leo McKern Billie Whitelaw

1962 MANIAC
Director: Michael Carreras
Co-stars: Kerwin Matthews Donald Houston Justine Lord

1964 THE CROOKED ROAD
Director: Don Chaffey
Co-stars: Robert Ryan Stewart Granger Marius Goring

1967 THE NAKED RUNNER
Director: Sidney Furie
Co-stars: Frank Sinatra Peter Vaughan Derren Nesbitt

SALLY GRAY

1936 CAFE COLETTE
Director: Paul Stein
Co-stars: Paul Cavanagh Greta Nilsen Bruce Seton

1937 OVER SHE GOES
Director: Graham Cutts
Co-stars: Stanley Lupino Laddie Cliff Gina Malo

1938 HOLD MY HAND
Director: Thornton Freeland
Co-stars: Stanley Lupino Fred Emney Barbara Blair

1939 THE LAMBETH WALK
Director: Albert De Courville
Co-stars: Stanley Lupino Seymour Hicks Norah Howard

1939 THE SAINT IN LONDON
Director: John Paddy Carstairs
Co-stars: George Sanders David Burns Henry Oscar

1939 A WINDOW IN LONDON
Director: Herbert Mason
Co-stars: Michael Redgrave Paul Lukas Patricia Roc

1940 THE SAINT'S VACATION
Director: Leslie Fenton
Co-stars: Hugh Sinclair Cecil Parker Arthur MacRae

1941 DANGEROUS MOONLIGHT
Director: Brian Desmond Hurst
Co-stars: Anton Walbrook Derrick De Marney

1946 CARNIVAL
Director: Stanley Haynes
Co-stars: Michael Wilding Bernard Miles Jean Kent

1946 GREEN FOR DANGER
Director: Sidney Gilliat
Co-stars: Alastair Sim Trevor Howard Rosamund John

1947 MARK OF CAIN
Director: Brian Desmond Hurst
Co-stars: Eric Portman Patrick Holt Dermot Walsh

1947 THEY MADE ME A FUGITIVE
Director: Alberto Cavalcanti
Co-stars: Trevor Howard Griffith Jones Rene Ray

1948 OBSESSION
Director: Edward Dmytryk
Co-stars: Robert Newton Naunton Wayne Phil Brown

1949 SILENT DUST
Director: Lance Comfort
Co-stars: Stephen Murray Nigel Patrick Derek Farr

1953 ESCAPE ROUTE
Director: Peter Graham Scott
Co-stars: George Raft Clifford Evans Reginald Tate

1984 THE KEEPER
Director: Tom Drake
Co-stars: Christopher Lee Tell Schreiber Ian Tracey

VIVEAN GRAY

1975 PICNIC AT HANGING ROCK
Director: Peter Weir
Co-stars: Rachel Roberts Dominic Guard Helen Morse

1977 THE LAST WAVE
Director: Peter Weir
Co-stars: Richard Chamberlain Olivia Hamnett David Gulpilil

DIANE GRAYSON

1971 BLIND TERROR
Director: Richard Fleischer
Co-stars: Mia Farrow Robin Bailey Dorothy Alison

JESSIE GRAYSON

1941 THE LITTLE FOXES
Director: William Wyler
Co-stars: Bette Davis Herbert Marshall Teresa Wright

KATHRYN GRAYSON

1941 ANDY HARDY'S PRIVATE SECRETARY
Director: George Seitz
Co-stars: Mickey Rooney Ian Hunter Lewis Stone

1942 RIO RITA
Director: S. Sylvan Simon
Co-stars: Abbott & Costello John Carroll

1942 THE VANISHING VIRGINIAN
Director: Frank Borzage
Co-stars: Frank Morgan Spring Byington

1942 SEVEN SWEETHEARTS
Director: Frank Borzage
Co-stars: Marsha Hunt Van Heflin S.Z. Sakall

1943 THOUSANDS CHEER
Director: George Sidney
Co-stars: Gene Kelly John Boles Jose Iturbi

1945 ANCHORS AWEIGH
Director: George Sidney
Co-stars: Gene Kelly Frank Sinatra Dean Stockwell

1945 ZIEGFELD FOLLIES
Director: Vincente Minnelli
Co-stars: Fred Astaire William Powell Judy Garland

1946 TWO SISTERS FROM BOSTON
Director: Henry Koster
Co-stars: June Allyson Peter Lawford Ben Blue

1946 TILL THE CLOUDS ROLL BY
Director: Richard Whorf
Co-stars: Robert Walker Van Heflin Dinah Shore

1947 IT HAPPENED IN BROOKLYN
Director: Richard Whorf
Co-stars: Frank Sinatra Jimmy Durante Billy Roy

1948 THE KISSING BANDIT
Director: Laslo Benedek
Co-stars: Frank Sinatra J. Carrol Naish

1949 THAT MIDNIGHT KISS
Director: Norman Taurog
Co-stars: Mario Lanza Ethel Barrymore Jose Iturbi

1950 THE TOAST OF NEW ORLEANS
Director: Norman Taurog
Co-stars: Mario Lanza David Niven J. Carrol Naish

1950 GROUNDS FOR MARRIAGE
Director: Robert Z Leonard
Co-stars: Van Johnson Barry Sullivan Lewis Stone

1951 SHOWBOAT
Director: George Sidney
Co-stars: Howard Keel Ava Gardner Joe E. Brown

1952 LOVELY TO LOOK AT
Director: Mervyn Le Roy
Co-stars: Howard Keel Ann Miller Red Skelton

1953 THE DESERT SONG
Director: Bruce Humberstone
Co-stars: Gordon MacRae Steve Cochran

1953 SO THIS IS LOVE
Director: Gordon Douglas
Co-stars: Merv Griffin Walter Abel Joan Weldon

1953 KISS ME KATE
Director: George Sidney
Co-stars: Howard Keel Ann Miller Keenan Wynn

1956 THE VAGABOND KING
Director: Michael Curtiz
Co-stars: Oreste Rita Moreno

JULIETTE GRECO

1949 ORPHEE
Director: Jean Cocteau
Co-stars: Francois Perrier Maria Casares Jean Marais

1956 ELENA AND THE MEN
Director: Jean Renoir
Co-stars: Ingrid Berman Jean Marais Mel Ferrer

1957 BONJOUR TRISTESSE
Director: Otto Preminger
Co-stars: David Niven Deborah Kerr Jean Serberg

1957 THE SUN ALSO RISES
Director: Henry King
Co-stars: Tyrone Power Ava Gardner Errol Flynn

1958 THE ROOTS OF HEAVEN
Director: John Huston
Co-stars: Errol Flynn Trevor Howard Orson Welles

1958 THE NAKED EARTH
Director: Vincent Sherman
Co-stars: Richard Todd Finlay Currie Laurence Naismith

1959 WHIRPOOL
Director: Lewis Allen
Co-stars: William Sylvester Marius Goring Muriel Pavlow

1960 CRACK IN THE MIRROR
Director: Richard Fleischer
Co-stars: Orson Welles Bradford Dillman William Lucas

1960 THE BIG GAMBLE
Director: Richard Fleischer
Co-stars: Stephen Boyd David Wayne Gregory Ratoff

1967 NIGHT OF THE GENERALS
Director: Anatole Litvak
Co-stars: Peter O'Toole Omar Sharif Tom Courtenay

DOROTHY GREEN

1967 TAMMY AND THE MILLIONAIRE
Director: Sidney Miller
Co-stars: Debbie Watson Donald Woods Denver Pyle

ELIZABETH GREEN

1933 FINAL MISSION
Director: Lee Redmond
Co-star: Billy Worth

JANET LAINE-GREEN

1987 THE KIDNAPPING OF BABY JOHN DOE
Director: Peter Gerritson
Co-stars: Jayne Greenwood Geoffrey Bowes

1987 COWBOYS DON'T CRY
Director: Anne Wheeler
Co-stars: Zachary Ansley Ron White

1993 FAMILY PICTURES
Director: Philliip Saville
Co-stars: Anjelica Huston Sam Neill Kyra Sedgwick

1993 MEDICINE RIVER
Director: Stuart Margolin
Co-stars: Graham Greene Sheila Tousey

KERRI GREEN *(Child)*

1985 SUMMER RENTAL
Director: Carl Reiner
Co-stars: John Candy Karen Austin Richard Crenna

1985 THE GOONIES
Director: Richard Donner
Co-stars: Sean Astin Corey Feldman Martha Plimpton

1986 LUCAS
Director: David Seltzer
Co-stars: Corey Haim Charlie Sheen Winona Ryder

1987 THREE FOR THE ROAD
Director: B.W.L. North
Co-stars: Charlie Sheen Sally Kellerman Alan Ruck

LYNDA MASON GREEN

1988 THE RETURN OF BEN CASEY
Director: Joseph Scanlan
Co-stars: Vince Edwards Al Waxman Harry Landers

**1988 THE WAR OF THE WORLDS:
THE RESURRECTION**
Director: Colin Chivers
Co-stars: Jared Martin Philip Akin

MARIKA GREEN

1959 PICKPOCKET
Director: Robert Bresson
Co-stars: Martin Lassalle Kassagi

1974 EMMANUELLE
Director: Just Jaeckin
Co-stars: Sylvia Kristel Daniel Sarky Alain Cuny

MICHELE GREEN

**1986 PERRY MASON:
THE CASE OF THE NOTORIOUS NUN**
Director: Ron Satlof
Co-stars: Raymond Burr Barbara Hale

1988 WEDDING DAY BLUES
Director: Paul Lynch
Co-stars: Max Wright Cloris Leachman Eileen Brennan

1989 IN THE BEST INTEREST OF THE CHILD
Director: David Greene
Co-stars: Meg Tilly Ed Begley Jnr. Michael O'Keefe

1991 I POSED FOR PLAYBOY
Director: Stephen Stafford
Co-stars: Amanda Peterson Lynda Carter

1993 A CHILD TOO MANY
Director: Jorge Motesi
Co-stars: Connor O'Farrell Nancy Stafford

MITZI GREEN

1930 FINN AND HATTIE
Director: Norman Taurog
Co-stars: Leon Errol Zasu Pitts Regis Toomey

1930 HONEY
Director: Wesley Ruggles
Co-stars: Nancy Carroll Lillian Roth Zasu Pitts

1930 LOVE AMONG THE MILLIONAIRES
Director: Frank Tuttle
Co-stars: Clara Bow Stanley Smith Stuart Erwin

1930 TOM SAWYER
Director: John Cromwell
Co-stars: Jackie Coogan Junior Durkin Tully Marshall

1931 HUCKLEBERRY FINN
Director: Norman Taurog
Co-stars: Jackie Coogan Junior Durkin Eugene Pallette

1931 SKIPPY
Director: Norman Taurog
Co-stars: Jackie Cooper Robert Coogan Jackie Searl

1932 LITTLE ORPHAN ANNIE
Director: John Robertson
Co-stars: Edgar Kennedy May Robson Buster Phelps

1932 GIRL CRAZY
Director: William Seiter
Co-stars: Bert Wheeler Robert Whoolsey Eddie Quillan Dorothy Lee

1952 LOST IN ALASKA
Director: Jean Yarbrough
Co-stars: Bud Abbott Lou Costello Tom Ewell Bruce Cabot

1952 BLOODHOUNDS OF BROADWAY
Director: George Jessel
Co-stars: Mitzi Gaynor Scott Brady Margueritte Chapman

ANGELA GREENE

1946 THE TIME, THE PLACE AND THE GIRL
Director: David Butler
Co-stars: Dennis Morgan Jack Carson Janis Paige

1947 KING OF THE BANDITS
Director: Christy Cabanne
Co-stars: Gilbert Roland Chris-Pin Martin

1951 AT WAR WITH THE ARMY
Director: Hal Walker
Co-stars: Dean Martin Jerry Lewis Polly Bergen

1954 ROYAL AFRICAN RIFLES
Director: Lesley Selander
Co-stars: Louis Hayward Veronica Hurst Michael Pate

1958 THE COSMIC MAN
Director: Herbert Greene
Co-stars: Bruce Bennett John Carradine Paul Langton

BARBARA GREENE

1936 BLIND MAN'S BUFF
Director: Albert Parker
Co-stars: Basil Sydney James Mason Enid Stamp-Taylor

1937 MOONLIGHT SONATA
Director: Lothar Mendes
Co-stars: Ignace Paderewski Eric Portman Marie Tempest

ELLEN GREENE

1975 NEXT STOP, GREENWICH VILLAGE
Director: Paul Mazursky
Co-stars: Lenny Baker Shelley Winters Lois Smith

1986 LITTLE SHOP OF HORRORS
Director: Frank Oz
Co-stars: Rick Moranis Vincent Gardenia Steve Martin

1988 TALK RADIO
Director: Oliver Stone
Co-stars: Eric Bogosian Alec Baldwin Leslie Hope

1989 GLORY! GLORY!
Director: Lindsay Anderson
Co-stars: Richard Thomas James Whitmore Barry Morse

1989 DINNER AT EIGHT
Director: Ron Lago Marsino
Co-stars: Lauren Bacall Marsha Mason John Mahoney

1990 PUMP UP THE VOLUME
Director: Allan Moyle
Co-stars: Christian Slater Samantha Mathis Annie Ross

1991 STEPPING OUT
Director: Lewis Gilbert
Co-stars: Liza Minnelli Shelley Winters Julie Walters

1993 NAKED GUN 33 1/3: THE FINAL INSULT
Director: Peter Segal
Co-stars: Leslie Nielsen Priscilla Presley

1994 WAGONS EAST !
Director: Peter Markle
Co-stars: John Candy Joe Mays

GILLIAN GREENE

1988 BONANZA: THE NEXT GENERATION
Director: William Claxton
Co-stars: John Ireland Robert Fuller John Amos

JACLYNNE GREENE

1959 THE CRIMSON KIMONO
Director: Samuel Fuller
Co-stars: Glenn Corbett James Shigeta Victoria Shaw

LAURA GREENE

1969 PUTNEY SWOPE
Director: Robert Downey
Co-stars: Stanley Gottlieb Allan Garfield Antonio Fargas

SARAH GREENE

1992 GHOSTWATCH
Director: Lesley Manning
Co-stars: Michael Parkinson Mike Smith Gillian Bevan

DAWN GREENHALGH

1986 DOING LIFE
Director: Gene Reynolds
Co-stars: Tony Danza Jon Devries Lisa Langlois

1994 WEB OF DECEIT
Director: Bill Corcoran
Co-stars: Corbin Bernsen Amanda Pays Mimi Kuzyk

1995 DANCING IN THE DARK
Director: Bill Corcoran
Co-stars: Victoria Principal Robert Vaughn

CHARLOTTE GREENWOOD

1930 SO LONG LETTY

1931 STEPPING OUT
Co-star: Leila Hyams

1931 FLYING HIGH
Director: Charles Reisner
Co-stars: Bert Lahr Pat O'Brien Guy Kibbee

1931 THE MAN IN POSSESSION
Director: Sam Wood
Co-stars: Robert Montgomery Irene Purcell

1931 PALMY DAYS
Director: Edward Sutherland
Co-stars: Eddie Cantor George Raft

1933 ORDERS IS ORDERS
Director: Walter Forde
Co-stars: James Gleason Ian Hunter Ray Milland

1940 DOWN ARGENTINE WAY
Director: Irving Cummings
Co-stars: Betty Grable Don Ameche Carmen Miranda

1940 STAR DUST
Director: Walter Lang
Co-stars: Linda Darnell John Payne Roland Young

1940 YOUNG PEOPLE
Director: Allan Dwan
Co-stars: Shirley Temple Jack Oakie Arleen Whelan

1941 PERFECT SNOB
Director: Ray McCarey
Co-stars: Charles Ruggles Lynn Bari Cornel Wilde

1941 TALL, DARK AND HANDSOME
Director: Bruce Humberstone
Co-stars: Cesar Romero Virginia Gilmore

1941   **MOON OVER MIAMI**
Director: Walter Lang
Co-stars: Betty Grable Don Ameche Carole Landis

1942   **SPRINGTIME IN THE ROCKIES**
Director: Irving Cummings
Co-stars: Betty Grable John Payne Carmen Miranda

1943   **THE GANG'S ALL HERE**
Director: Busby Berkeley
Co-stars: Alice Faye Carmen Miranda James Ellison

1943   **DIXIE DUGAN**
Director: Otto Brower
Co-stars: James Ellison Lois Andrews Charles Ruggles

1944   **HOME IN INDIANA**
Director: Henry Hathaway
Co-stars: Jeanne Crain June Haver Walter Brennan

1944   **UP IN MABEL'S ROOM**
Director: Allan Dwan
Co-stars: Dennis O'Keefe Marjorie Reynolds

1946   **WAKE UP AND DREAM**
Director: Lloyd Bacon
Co-stars: June Haver John Payne Connie Marshall

1947   **DRIFTWOOD**
Director: Allan Dwan
Co-stars: Natalie Wood Dean Jagger Ruth Warrick

1949   **THE GREAT DAN PATCH**
Director: Joseph Newman
Co-stars: Dennis O'Keefe Gail Russell Ruth Warrick

1949   **OH YOU BEAUTIFUL DOLL**
Director: John Stahl
Co-stars: S.Z. Sakall June Haver Mark Stevens

1953   **DANGEROUS WHEN WET**
Director: Charles Walters
Co-stars: Esther Williams William Demarest

1955   **GLORY**
Director: David Butler
Co-stars: Margaret O'Brien Walter Brennan

1955   **OKLAHOMA!**
Director: Fred Zinnermann
Co-stars: Gordon MacRae Shirley Jones

1956   **THE OPPOSITE SEX**
Director: David Miller
Co-stars: June Allyson Dolores Gray Joan Collins

JOAN GREENWOOD

1941   **HE FOUND A STAR**
Director: John Paddy Carstairs
Co-stars: Vic Oliver Sarah Churchill

1943   **THE GENTLE SEX**
Director: Leslie Howard
Co-stars: Rosamund John Lilli Palmer John Justin

1945   **LATIN QUARTER**
Director: Vernon Sewell
Co-stars: Derrick De Marney Frederick Valk Lily Kann

1945   **THEY KNEW MR. KNIGHT**
Director: Norman Walker
Co-stars: Mervyn Johns Alfred Drayton Nora Swinburne

1946   **A GIRL IN A MILLION**
Director: Francis Searle
Co-stars: Hugh Williams Basil Radford Naunton Wayne

1947   **THE GIRL WITHIN**
Director: Bernard Knowles
Co-stars: Michael Redgrave Richard Attenborough

1947   **THE OCTOBER MAN**
Director: Roy Baker
Co-stars: John Mills Kay Walsh Edward Chapman Joyce Carey

1947   **WHITE UNICORN**
Director: Bernard Knowles
Co-stars: Margaret Lockwood Ian Hunter Dennis Price

1948   **SARABAND FOR DEAD LOVERS**
Director: Michael Relph
Co-stars: Stewart Granger Flora Robson

1948   **THE BAD LORD BRYON**
Director: David MacDonald
Co-stars: Dennis Price Mai Zetterling Sonia Holm

1949   **WHISKY GALORE**
Director: Alexander MacKendrick
Co-stars: Basil Radford Gordon Jackson Jean Cadell

1949   **KIND HEARTS AND CORONETS**
Director: Robert Hamer
Co-stars: Alec Guiness Dennis Price Valerie Hobson

1951   **FLESH AND BLOOD**
Director: Anthony Kimmins
Co-stars: Richard Todd Glynis Johns George Cole

1951   **MR. PEEK-A-BOO**
Co-star: Bourville

1951   **THE MAN IN THE WHITE SUIT**
Director: Alexander MacKendrick
Co-stars: Alec Guinness Cecil Parker

1951   **YOUNG WIVES' TALE**
Director: Henry Cass
Co-stars: Nigel Patrick Derek Farr Audrey Hepburn

1952   **THE IMPORTANCE OF BEING ERNEST**
Director: Anthony Asquith
Co-stars: Michael Redgrave Edith Evans Margaret Rutherford

1954   **KNAVE OF HEARTS**
Director: Rene Clement
Co-stars: Gerard Philip Margaret Johnston Valerie Hobson

1954   **FATHER BROWN**
Director: Robert Hamer
Co stars: Alec Guinness Peter Finch Cecil Parker

1955   **MOONFLEET**
Director: Fritz Lang
Co-stars: Stewart Granger George Sanders Jon Whitely

1957   **STAGE STRUCK**
Director: Sidney Lumet
Co-stars: Henry Fonda Susan Strasberg Herbert Marshall

1961   **MYSTERIOUS ISLAND**
Director: Cy Endfield
Co-stars: Michael Craig Herbert Lom Gary Merrill

1962   **THE AMOROUS PRAWN**
Director: Anthony Kimmins
Co-stars: Cecil Parker Ian Carmichael Denis Price

1963   **TOM JONES**
Director: Tony Richardson
Co-stars: Albert Finney Hugh Griffith Susannah York

1964   **THE MOON SPINNERS**
Director: James Neilson
Co-stars: Hayley Mills Peter McEnery Eli Wallach

1971   **GIRL STROKE BOY**
Director: Bob Kellett
Co-stars: Michael Hordern Clive Francis Patricia Routledge

1977   **HOUND OF THE BASKERVILLES**
Director: Paul Morrissey
Co-stars: Peter Cook Dudley Moore Max Wall

1977 THE UNCANNY
Director: Dennis Heroux
Co-stars: Peter Cushing Ray Milland Susan Penhaligon

1978 THE WATER BABIES
Director: Lionel Jeffries
Co-stars: James Mason Billie Whitelaw Bernard Cribbins

1979 THE FLAME IS LOVE
Director: Michael O'Herlihy
Co-stars: Linda Purl Timothy Dalton Richard Johnson

1984 ELLIS ISLAND
Director: Jerry London
Co-stars: Claire Bloom Richard Burton Faye Dunaway

1986 PAST CARING
Director: Richard Eyre
Co-stars: Denholm Elliott Emlyn Williams Connie Booth

1987 LITTLE DORIT
Director: Christine Edzard
Co-stars: Derek Jacobi Alec Guinness Max Wall

ROSAMUND GREENWOOD

1957 THE PRINCE AND THE SHOWGIRL
Director: Laurence Olivier
Co-stars: Laurence Olivier Marilyn Monroe Jeremy Spenser

GERMAINE GREER

1972 UNIVERSAL SOLDIER
Director: Cy Endfield
Co-stars: George Lazenby Edward Judd Rudolph Walker

JANE GREER *(Married Rudy Vallee)*

1945 TWO O'CLOCK COURAGE
Director: Anthony Mann
Co-stars: Tom Conway Ann Rutherford Richard Lane

1945 GEORGE WHITE'S SCANDALS
Director: Felix Feist
Co-stars: Joan Davis Jack Haley Philip Terry

1945 DICK TRACY
Director: William Berke
Co-stars: Morgan Conway Mike Mazurki Ann Jeffries

1946 THE BAMBOO BLONDE
Director: Anthony Mann
Co-stars: Frances Langford Ralph Edwards Russell Wade

1946 SUNSET PASS
Co-stars: John Laurenz Robert Clarke Steve Brodie

1947 THEY WON'T BELIEVE ME
Director: Irving Pichel
Co-stars: Robert Young Susan Hayward Rita Johnson

1947 SINBAD THE SAILOR
Director: Richard Wallace
Co-stars: Douglas Fairbanks Maureen O'Hara Walter Slezak

1947 BUILD MY GALLOWS HIGH ✓
Director: Jacques Tourneur
Co-stars: Robert Mitchum Kirk Douglas Rhonda Fleming

1948 STATION WEST
Director: Sidney Lanfield
Co-stars: Dick Powell Burl Ives Agnes Moorehead

1949 THE BIG STEAL
Director: Don Siegel
Co-stars: Robert Mitchum William Bendix Patric Knowles

1950 THE COMPANY SHE KEEPS
Director: John Cromwell
Co-stars: Lisabeth Scott Dennis O'Keefe John Hoyt

1951 YOU'RE IN THE NAVY NOW
Director: Henry Hathaway
Co-stars: Gary Cooper Eddie Albert Millard Mitchell

1952 YOU FOR ME
Director: Don Weis
Co-stars: Peter Lawford Gig Young Paula Corday

1952 THE PRISONER OF ZENDA
Director: Richard Thorpe
Co-stars: Stewart Granger James Mason Deborah Kerr

1952 DOWN AMONG THE SHELTERING PALMS
Director: Edmund Goulding
Co-stars: Mitzi Gaynor Gloria De Haven David Wayne

1952 DESPERATE SEARCH
Director: Joseph Lewis
Co-stars: Howard Keel Patricia Medina Keenan Wynn

1952 THE CLOWN
Director: Robert Z. Leonard
Co-stars: Red Skelton Tim Considine Loring Smith

1956 RUN FOR THE SUN
Director: Roy Boutling
Co-stars: Richard Widmark Trevor Howard Peter Van Eyck

1957 MAN OF A THOUSAND FACES
Director: Joseph Pevney
Co-stars: James Cagney Dorothy Malone Robert Evans

1964 WHERE LOVE HAS GONE
Director: Edward Dmytryk
Co-stars: Susan Hayward Bette Davis Mike Connors

1965 BILLIE
Director: Don Weis
Co-stars: Patty Duke Jim Backus Billy De Wolfe Charles Lane

1974 THE OUTFIT
Director: John Flynn
Co-stars: Robert Duvall Karen Black Robert Ryan

1982 THE SHADOW RIDERS
Director: Andrew McLaglen
Co-stars: Tom Selleck Sam Elliott Ben Johnson

1984 AGAINST ALL ODDS
Director: Taylor Hackford
Co-stars: Jeff Bridges Rachel Ward Richard Widmark

1989 IMMEDIATE FAMILY
Director: Jonathan Kaplan
Co-stars: Glenn Close James Woods Kevin Dillon

CLARE GREET

1929 THE MANXMAN
Director: Alfred Hitchcock
Co-stars: Carl Brisson Anny Ondra Malcolm Keen

1932 LORD CAMBER'S LADIES
Director: Benn Levy
Co-stars: Gerald Du Maurier Gertrude Lawrence Benita Hume

1935 MARIA MARTEN OR THE MURDER IN THE RED BARN
Director: George King
Co-stars: Tod Slaughter Eric Portman

CHRISTINA GREGG

1961 RAG DOLL
Director: Lance Comfort
Co-stars: Jess Conrad Hermoine Baddeley Kenneth Griffith

1962 DON'T TALK TO STRANGE MEN
Director: Pat Jackson
Co-stars: Cyril Raymond Conrad Phillips Gillian Lind

EVERLY GREGG

1933 THE PRIVATE LIFE OF HENRY VIII
Director: Alexandra Korda
Co-stars: Charles Laughton Robert Donat

1938   PYGMALION
Director: Anthony Asquith
Co-stars: Leslie Howard Wendy Hiller Wilfrid Lawson

1943   THE GENTLE SEX
Director: Leslie Howard
Co-stars: Rosamund John Joan Greenwood Lilli Palmer

VIRGINIA GREGG

1948   THE GAY INTRUDERS
Director: Ray McCarey
Co-stars: Tamara Geva John Emery Leif Erickson

1954   DRAGNET
Director: Jack Webb
Co-stars: Jack Webb Ben Alexander Richard Boone Ann Robinson

1955   LOVE IS A MANY SPLENDORED THING
Director: Henry King
Co-stars: William Holden Jennifer Jones

1956   CRIME IN THE STREETS
Director: Don Siegel
Co-stars: John Cassavetes James Whitmore Sal Mineo

1957   THE D.I.
Director: Jack Webb
Co-stars: Don Dubbins Monica Lewis Lin McCarthy

1965   TWO ON A GUILLOTINE
Director: William Conrad
Co-stars: Connie Stevens Dean Jones Cesar Romero

1969   DRAGNET
Director: Jack Webb
Co-stars: Harry Morgan Gene Evans Vic Perrin

1970   THE OTHER MAN
Director: Richard Colla
Co-stars: Joan Hackett Roy Thinnes Tammy Grimes

1970   A WALK IN THE SPRING RAIN
Director: Guy Green
Co-stars: Ingrid Bergman Anthony Quinn Fritz Weaver

NORAH GREGOR

1939   LA REGLE DU JEU
Director: Jean Renoir
Co-stars: Marcel Dalio Mila Parely Julien Carette

ROSE GREGORIO

1978   THE EYES OF LAURA MARS
Director: Irving Kerschner
Co-stars: Faye Dunaway Tommy Lee Jones Raul Julia

1979   DUMMY
Director: Frank Perry
Co-stars: Paul Sorvino Brian Dennehy Levar Burton

1981   TRUE CONFESSIONS
Director: Ulu Grosbard
Co-stars: Robert Duvall Robert De Niro Burgess Meredith

1985   DO YOU REMEMBER LOVE?
Director: Jeff Bleckner
Co-stars: Joanne Woodward Richard Kiley Susan Ruttan

1987   FIVE CORNERS
Director: Tony Bill
Co-stars: Jodie Foster Tim Robbins John Turturro

1987   THE LAST INNOCENT MAN
Director: Roger Spottiswoode
Co-stars: Ed Harris Roxanne Hart David Suchet

1991   CITY OF HOPE
Director: John Sayles
Co-stars: Vincent Spano Todd Graff Tony Lo Bianco

HANA GREGOROVA

1992   PRAGUE
Director: Ian Sellar
Co-stars: Alan Cumming Sandrine Bonnaire Bruno Ganz

NATASHA GREGSON

1994   DRAGSTRIP GIRL
Director: Mary Lambert
Co-star: Mark Dacastos

CELIA GREGORY

1979   AGATHA
Director: Michael Apted
Co-stars: Vanessa Redgrave Dustin Hoffman Timothy Dalton

**1989   INSPECTOR WEXFORD:
NO MORE DYING THEN**
Director: Jan Sargent
Co-stars: George Baker Simon Shepherd

**1990   THE CASEBOOK OF SHERLOCK HOLMES:
THE PROBLEM OF THE BRIDGE**
Director: Michael Simpson
Co-stars: Jeremy Brett Daniel Massey

1993   THE BABY OF MACON
Director: Peter Greenaway
Co-stars: Julia Ormond Ralph Fiennes

IOLA GREGORY

1986   COMING UP ROSES
Director: Stephen Bayley
Co-stars: Dafydd Hywel Olive Michael Mari Emlyn

1990   THE LORELEI
Director: Terry Johnson
Co-stars: Amanda Redman Michael Maloney John Nettleton

MARY GREGORY

1973   SLEEPER
Director: Woody Allen
Co-stars: Woody Allen Diane Keaton John Beck

NATALIE GREGORY

1986   AMAZING STORIES 4
Director: Thomas Carter
Co-stars: Joe Seneca Lane Smith

KIM GREIST

1985   BRAZIL
Director: Terry Gilliam
Co-stars: Jonathan Pryce Robert De Niro Michael Palin

1986   MANHUNTER
Director: Michael Mann
Co-stars: William Petersen Joan Allen Brian Cox

1987   PUNCHLINE
Director: David Seltzer
Co-stars: Sally Field Tom Hanks John Goodman

1987   THROW MOMMA FROM THE TRAIN
Director: Danny Devito
Co-stars: Danny Devito Anne Ramsey Billy Crystal Annie Ross

1989   WHY ME?
Director: Gene Quintano
Co-stars: Christopher Lambert Christopher Lloyd J.T. Walsh

1991   PAYOFF
Director: Stuart Cooper
Co-stars: Keith Carradine John Saxon Harry Dean Stanton

**1993   HOMEWARD BOUND:
THE INCREDIBLE JOURNEY**
Director: Duwayne Dunham
Co-stars: Robert Hayes Jean Smart

1994 ROSWELL
Director: Jeremy Kagan
Co-stars: Kyle MacLachlan Martin Sheen Dwight Yoakam

SYLVIA GRENADE

1930 THE END OF THE WORLD
Director: Abel Gance
Co-stars: Abel Gance Colette Darfeuil Victor Francen

JOYCE GRENFELL

1943 THE LAMP STILL BURNS
Director: Maurice Levy
Co-stars: Rosamund John Stewart Granger Godfrey Tearle

1943 THE DEMI-PARADISE
Director: Anthony Asquith
Co-stars: Laurence Olivier Penelope Dudley Ward George Cole

1949 POET'S PUB
Director: Frederick Wilson
Co-stars: Derek Bond Rona Anderson Barbara Murray

1949 A RUN FOR YOUR MONEY
Director: Charles Frend
Co-stars: Alec Guinness Moira Lister Hugh Griffith

1950 THE HAPPIEST DAYS OF YOUR LIFE
Director: Frank Launder
Co-stars: Alaistair Sim Margaret Rutherford

1951 GALLOPING MAJOR
Director: Henry Cornelius
Co-stars: Basil Radford Janette Scott Hugh Griffith

1951 LAUGHTER IN PARADISE
Director: Mario Zampi
Co-stars: Hugh Griffith Alastair Sim Fay Compton

1951 THE MAGIC BOX
Director: John Boutling
Co-stars: Robert Donat Margaret Johnston Maria Schell

1952 THE PICKWICK PAPERS
Director: Noel Langley
Co-stars: James Hayter Harry Fowler James Donald Nigel Patrick

1953 GENEVEIVE
Director: Henry Cornelius
Co-stars: Kenneth More Kay Kendal Dinah Sheridan

1954 THE MILLION POUND NOTE
Director: Ronald Neame
Co-stars: Gregory Peck Jane Griffiths Ronald Squire

1954 FORBIDDEN CARGO
Director: Harold French
Co-stars: Nigel Patrick Elizabeth Sellars Jack Warner

1954 THE BELLES OF ST. TRINIANS
Director: Frank Launder
Co-stars: Alastair Sim George Cole Beryl Reid

1954 BLUE MURDER AT ST. TRINIANS
Director: Frank Launder
Co-stars: Alastair Sim Terry-Thomas Sabrina

1957 THE GOOD COMPANIANS
Director: J. Lee Thompson
Co-stars: Eric Portman Celia Johnson Janette Scott John Fraser

1957 HAPPY IS THE BRIDE
Director: Roy Boulting
Co-stars: Ian Carmichael Janette Scott Cecil Parker

1961 THE PURE HELL OF ST. TRINIANS
Director: Frank Launder
Co-stars: George Cole Cecil Parker Dennis Price

1962 THE OLD DARK HOUSE
Director: William Castle
Co-stars: Janette Scott Robert Morley Tom Poston

1964 THE YELLOW ROLLS ROYCE
Director: Anthony Asquith
Co-stars: Rex Harrison Shirley MacLaine Ingrid Bergman

1964 THE AMERICANISATION OF EMILY
Director: Arthur Hiller
Co-stars: Julie Andrews James Garner Liz Fraser

VANDA GREVILLE

1931 THE GENTLEMAN OF PARIS
Director: Sinclair Hill
Co-stars: Arthur Wontner Hugh Williams Sybil Thorndike

1931 LE MILLION
Director: Rene Clair
Co-stars: Annabella Rene Lefevre Paul Oliver

ANNE GREY

1932 NUMBER SEVENTEEN
Director: Alfred Hitchcock
Co-stars: Leon M. Lyon John Stuart Barry Jones

1932 ARMS AND THE MAN
Director: Cecil Lewis
Co-stars: Barry Jones Angela Baddeley

1933 THE WANDERING JEW
Director: Maurice Elvy
Co-stars: Conrad Veidt Marie Ney Dennis Hoey

1935 BONNIE SCOTLAND
Director: James Horne
Co-stars: Stan Laurel Oliver Hardy June Lang

CAROLE GREY

1962 THE YOUNG ONES
Director: Sidney Furie
Co-stars: Cliff Richard Robert Morley Richard O'Sullivan

1964 DEVILS OF DARKNESS
Director: Lance Comfort
Co-stars: William Sylvester Tracy Reed Diana Decker

1965 CURSE OF THE FLY
Director: Don Sharp
Co-stars: Brian Donlevy George Baker Rachel Kempson

1966 ISLAND OF TERROR
Director: Terence Fisher
Co-stars: Peter Cushing Edward Judd Sam Kydd

DENISE GREY

1947 LE DIABLE AU CORPS
Director: Claude Autant Lara
Co-stars: Micheline Presle Gerard Philipe

1958 CARVE HER NAME WITH PRIDE
Director: Lewis Gilbert
Co-stars: Virginia McKenna Paul Scofield

JENNIFER GREY *(Daughter Of Joel Grey)*

1984 RED DAWN
Director: John Milius
Co-stars: Patrick Swayze Powers Booth Charlie Sheen

1984 THE COTTON CLUB
Director: Francis Coppola
Co-stars: Richard Gere Gregory Hines Diane Lane

1985 AMERICAN FLYERS
Director: John Badham
Co-stars: Kevin Costner David Grant Rae Dawn Chong

1986 FERRIS BUELLER'S DAY OFF
Director: John Hughes
Co-stars: Matthew Broderick Alan Ruck Mia Sara

1987	**DIRTY DANCING**
Director:	Emile Ardolino
Co-stars:	Patrick Swayze Jerry Orbach Cynthia Rhodes

1989	**BLOODHOUNDS OF BRAODWAY**
Director:	Howard Brookner
Co-stars:	Madonna Rutger Hauer Randy Quaid

1990	**CRIMINAL JUSTICE**
Director:	Andy Wolk
Co-stars:	Forest Whitaker Rosie Perez Anthony LaPaglia

1993	**WIND**
Director:	Carroll Ballard
Co-stars:	Matthew Modine Rebecca Miller Cliff Robertson

1995	**THE WEST SIDE WALTZ**
Director:	Ernest Thompson
Co-stars:	Liza Minnelli Shirley MacLaine

1996	**PORTRAITS OF INNOCENCE**
Director:	Bill Corcoran
Co-stars:	Michael Ironside Costas Mandylor

NAN GREY

1934	**BABBIT**
Director:	William Keighley
Co-stars:	Guy Kibbee Aline MacMahon Minna Gombell

1935	**MARY JANE'S PA**
Director:	William Keighley
Co-stars:	Guy Kibbee Aline MacMahon Tom Brown

1936	**DRACULA'S DAUGHTER**
Director:	Lambert Hillyer
Co-stars:	Otto Kruger Marguerite Churchill Irving Pichel

1936	**CRASH DONOVAN**
Co-stars:	John King Jack Holt

1936	**THREE SMART GIRLS**
Director:	Henry Koster
Co-stars:	Deanna Durbin Barbara Read Charles Winninger

1937	**LET THEM LIVE**
Director:	Harold Young
Co-stars:	John Howard Edward Ellis Judith Barrett

1937	**THE JURY'S SECRET**
Director:	Edward Sloman
Co-stars:	Kent Taylor Fay Wray Jane Darwell

1937	**LOVE IN A BUNGALOW**
Co-star:	Kent Taylor

1937	**THE MAN IN BLUE**
Co-star:	Richard Carle

1938	**THE STORM**
Director:	Harold Young
Co-stars:	Charles Bickford Barton MacLane Preston Foster

1939	**THREE SMART GIRLS GROW UP**
Director:	Henry Koster
Co-stars:	Deanna Durkin Helen Parrish Nella Walker

1939	**TOWER OF LONDON**
Director:	Rowland Lee
Co-stars:	Basil Rathbone Boris Karloff Vincent Price

1939	**THE UNDER PUP**
Director:	Richard Wallace
Co-stars:	Gloria Jean Robert Cummings Beulah Bondi

1939	**EX-CHAMP**
Director:	Phil Rosen
Co-stars:	Victor McLaglen Tom Brown Constance Moore

1940	**THE HOUSE OF SEVEN GABLES**
Director:	Joe May
Co-stars:	George Sanders Margaret Lindsay Vincent Price

1940	**THE INVISIBLE MAN RETURNS**
Director:	Joe May
Co-stars:	Vincent Price Cedric Hardwicke John Sutton

1940	**LITTLE BIT OF HEAVEN**
Director:	Andrew Marton
Co-stars:	Gloria Jean Robert Stack Hugh Herbert

1940	**SANDY IS A LADY**
Director:	Charles Lamont
Co-stars:	Baby Sandy Eugene Pallette Tom Brown

SHIRLEY GREY

1931	**SECRET SERVICE**
Director:	J. Walter Ruben
Co-stars:	Richard Dix William Post Jnr. Gavin Gordon

1932	**BACK STREET**
Director:	John Stahl
Co-stars:	Irene Dunne John Boles June Clyde

1932	**UPTOWN NEW YORK**
Co-star:	Jack Oakie

1932	**TEXAS CYCLONE**
Co-star:	Tim McCoy

1933	**BOMBAY MAIL**
Director:	Edwin Marin
Co-stars:	Edmund Lowe Onslow Stevens Ralph Forbes

1933	**TERROR ABOARD**
Director:	Paul Sloane
Co-stars:	Charles Ruggles John Halliday Neil Hamilton

1934	**GIRL IN DANGER**
Co-star:	Ralph Bellamy

1934	**SPECIAL AGENT**
Co-stars:	Tim McCoy Addison Richards

1935	**THE GIRL WHO CAME BACK**
Co-star:	Sidney Blackmer

1935	**THE MYSTERY OF THE MARY CELESTE**
Director:	Denison Clift
Co-stars:	Bela Lugosi Dennis Hoey

VIRGINIA GREY

1936	**OLD HUTCH**
Director:	Walter Ruben
Co-stars:	Wallace Beery Elizabeth Patterson Eric Linden

1937	**BAD GUY**
Co-stars:	Bruce Cabot Jean Chatburn

1938	**YOUTH TAKES A FLING**
Director:	Archie Mayo
Co-stars:	Joel McCrea Andrea Leeds Isabel Jeans

1938	**DRAMATIC SCHOOL**
Director:	Robert Sinclair
Co-stars:	Luise Rainer Paulette Goddard Lana Turner

1939	**BROADWAY SERENADE**
Director:	Robert Z Leonard
Co-stars:	Jeanette MacDonald Lew Ayres Frank Morgan

1939	**ANOTHER THIN MAN**
Director:	W.S. Van Dyke
Co-stars:	William Powell Myrna Loy Otto Kruger Nat Pendleton

1939	**THUNDER AFLOAT**
Director:	George Seitz
Co-stars:	Wallace Beery Chester Morris Regis Toomey

1939	**THE WOMEN**
Director:	George Cukor
Co-stars:	Norma Shearer Joan Crawford Rosalind Russell

1940	**THREE CHEERS FOR THE IRISH**
Director:	Lloyd Bacon
Co-stars:	Thomas Mitchell Dennis Morgan

1940 HULLABALOO
Director: Edwin Marin
Co-stars: Frank Morgan Dan Dailey Billie Burke Donald Meek

1940 KEEPING COMPANY
Director: S. Sylvan Simon
Co-stars: Frank Morgan Irene Rich Dan Dailey John Shelton

1940 THE GOLDEN FLEECING
Director: Leslie Fenton
Co-stars: Lew Ayres Lloyd Nolan Rita Johnson Leon Errol

1940 THE CAPTAIN IS A LADY
Director: Robert Sinclair
Co-stars: Charles Coburn Billie Burke Beulah Bondi

1941 THE BIG STORE
Director: Charles Reisner
Co-stars: Marx Brothers Tony Martin Margaret Dumont

1941 MR. AND MRS. NORTH
Director: Robert Sinclair
Co-stars: Gracie Allen William Post Jnr. Paul Kelly

1941 WHISTLING IN THE DARK
Director: S. Sylvan Simon
Co-stars: Red Skelton Ann Rutherford Conrad Veidt

1942 TARZAN'S NEW YORK ADVENTURE
Director: Richard Thorpe
Co-stars: Johnny Weismuller Johnny Sheffield Maureen O'Sullivan

1942 GRAND CENTRAL MURDER
Director: S. Sylvan Simon
Co-stars: Van Heflin Cecelia Parker Sam Levene

1943 SECRETS OF THE UNDERGROUND
Director: William Morgan
Co-stars: John Hubbard Lloyd Corrigan

1943 SWEET ROSIE O'GRADY
Director: Irving Cummings
Co-stars: Betty Grable Robert Young Adolphe Menjou

1945 MEN IN HER DIARY
Director: Charles Barton
Co-stars: Peggy Ryan Jon Hall Louise Allbritton

1945 GRISSLY'S MILLIONS
Director: John English
Co-stars: Paul Kelly Don Douglas Elizabeth Risdon

1945 FLAME OF THE BARBARY COAST
Director: Joseph Kane
Co-stars: John Wayne Ann Dvorak Joseph Schildkraut

1946 HOUSE OF HORRORS
Director: Jean Yarborough
Co-stars: Martin Kosleck Rondo Hatton Robert Lowery

1946 SMOOTH AS SILK
Director: Charles Barton
Co-stars: Kent Taylor Jane Adams Milburn Stone John Litel

1946 SWAMP FIRE
Director: William Pine
Co-stars: Johnny Weismuller Buster Crabbe Carol Thurston

1947 UNCONQUERED
Director: Cecil B. De Mille
Co-stars: Gary Cooper Paulette Goddard Howard Da Silva

1948 WHO KILLED DOC ROBIN?
Director: Bernard Carr
Co-stars: George Zucco Don Castle

1948 UNKNOWN ISLAND
Co-stars: Philip Reed Barton MacLane Richard Denning

1948 SO THIS IS NEW YORK
Director: Richard Fleischer
Co-stars: Henry Morgan Rudy Vallee Dona Drake

1948 MEXICAN HAYRIDE
Director: Charles Barton
Co-stars: Bud Abbott Lou Costello John Hubbard

1948 JUNGLE JIM
Director: William Berke
Co-stars: Johnny Weismuller George Reeves Lita Baron

1950 HIGHWAY 301
Director: Andrew Stone
Co-stars: Steve Cochran Gaby Andre Richard Egan

1951 SLAUGHTER TRAIL
Director: Irving Allen
Co-stars: Brian Donlevy Gig Young Andy Devine Robert Hutton

1952 PERILOUS JOURNEY
Director: R.G. Springsteen
Co-stars: Vera Ralston Charles Winninger David Brian

1954 THE FORTY NINERS
Director: Thomas Carr
Co-stars: Bill Elliott Henry Morgan John Doucette

1955 THE ROSE TATTOO
Director: Daniel Mann
Co-stars: Anna Magnani Burt Lancaster Marisa Pavan

1955 THE ETERNAL SEA
Director: John Auer
Co-stars: Sterling Hayden Alexis Smith Dean Jagger

1955 ALL THAT HEAVEN ALLOWS
Director: Douglas Sirk
Co-stars: Jane Wyman Rock Hudson Agnes Moorehead

1956 ACCUSED OF MURDER
Director: Joseph Kane
Co-stars: Vera Ralston David Brian Lee Van Cleef

1956 CRIME OF PASSION
Director: Gerd Oswald
Co-stars: Barbara Stanwyck Sterling Hayden Raymond Burr

1957 JEANNE EAGLES
Director: George Sidney
Co-stars: Kim Novak Jeff Chandler Agnes Moorehead

1959 THE RESTLESS YEARS
Director: Helmut Kautner
Co-stars: John Saxon Sandra Dee Luana Patten

1960 PORTRAIT IN BACK
Director: Michael Gordon
Co-stars: Lana Turner Anthony Quinn Richard Basehart

1961 TAMMY TELL ME TRUE
Director: Henry Keller
Co-stars: Sandra Dee John Gavin Charles Drake

1961 BACK STREET
Director: David Miller
Co-stars: Susan Hayward John Gavin Vera Miles Charles Drake

1962 BLACK ZOO
Director: Robert Gordon
Co-stars: Michael Gough Jeanne Cooper Rod Lauren Jerome Cowan

1964 THE NAKED KISS
Director: Samuel Fuller
Co-stars: Constance Towers Anthony Eisley Patsy Kelly

1964 LOVE HAS MANY FACES
Director: Alexander Singer
Co-stars: Lana Turner Cliff Robertson Ruth Roman

1965 MADAME X
Director: David Lowell Rich
Co-stars: Lana Turner John Forsythe Constance Bennett

1967 ROSIE!
Director: David Lowell Rich
Co-stars: Rosalind Russell Vanessa Brown Sandra Dee Brian Aherne

PAM GRIER

1973 COFFY
Director: Jack Hill
Co-stars: Booker Bradshaw William Elliott Sid Haig

1974 FOXY BROWN
Director: Jack Hill
Co-stars: Antonio Vargas Peter Brown Terry Carter

1974 THE ARENA
Director: Steve Carver
Co-stars: Margaret Markov Lucretta Love Paul Muller

1975 FRIDAY FOSTER
Director: Arthur Marks
Co-stars: Yaphet Kotto Godfrey Cambridge Eartha Kitt

1976 DRUM
Director: Steve Carver
Co-stars: Warren Oates Ken Norton Yaphet Kotto

1977 GREASED LIGHTNING
Director: Michael Schultz
Co-stars: Richard Pryor Beau Bridges Vincent Gardenia

1981 FORT APACHE THE BRONX
Director: Daniel Petrie
Co-stars: Paul Newman Ken Wahl Danny Aiello

1983 SOMETHING WICKED THIS WAY COMES
Director: Jack Clayton
Co-stars: Jason Robards Jonathan Pryce

1983 TOUGH ENOUGH
Director: Richard Fleischer
Co-stars: Dennis Quaid Stan Shaw Warren Oates

1985 STAND ALONE
Director: Alan Beattie
Co-star:: Charles Durning

1985 BADGE OF THE ASSASSIN
Director: Mel Damski
Co-stars: James Woods Yaphet Kotto Rae Dawn Chong

1987 THE ALLNIGHTER
Director: Tamar Simon Hoffs
Co-stars: Susan Hoffs Dedee Pfeiffer Joan Cusack

1988 ABOVE THE LAW
Director: Andrew Davis
Co-stars: Steven Seagal Henry Silva Sharon Stone

1989 THE PACKAGE
Director: Andrew Davis
Co-stars: Gene Hackman Joanna Cassidy Tommy Lee Jones

1991 BILL AND TED'S BOGUS JOURNEY
Director: Pete Hewitt
Co-stars: Alex Winter Keanu Reeves Jeff Miller

1992 SHATTERED SILENCE
Director: Linda Otto
Co-stars: Terence Knox Bonnie Bedelia Rip Torn

1993 POSSE
Director: Mario Van Peebles
Co-stars: Mario Van Peebles Billy Zane Richard Jordan

1998 JACKIE BROWN
Director: Quentin Tarantino
Co-stars: Michael Keaton Robert De Niro Samuel L. Jackson

ROSEY GRIER

1972 THE THING WITH TWO HEADS
Director: Lee Frost
Co-stars: Ray Milland Roger Perry William Smith

1972 SKYJACKED
Director: John Guillerman
Co-stars: Charlton Heston Yvette Mimieux Jeanne Crain

SHEILA GRIER

1987 SHADOW ON THE EARTH
Director: Chris Bernard
Co-stars: Billy Hartman Sam Hickman Craig Smith

SIMONE GRIFFETH

1975 DEATH RACE 2000
Director: Paul Bartel
Co-stars: David Carradine Sylvester Stallone

1980 FIGHTING BACK
Director: Robert Lieberman
Co-stars: Robert Urich Art Carney Bonnie Bedelia

1985 HOT TARGET
Director: Denis Lewiston
Co-stars: Steve Marachuk Bryan Marshall Peter McCauley

ETHEL GRIFFIES

1931 WATERLOO BRIDGE
Director: James Whale
Co-stars: Kent Douglas Mae Clarke Bette Davis

1932 LOVE ME TONIGHT
Director: Rouben Mamoulian
Co-stars: Maurice Chevalier Jeanette MacDonald Myrna Loy

1932 TONIGHT IS OURS
Director: Stuart Walker
Co-stars: Fredric March Claudette Colbert Alison Skipworth

1933 TORCH SINGER
Director: Alexander Hall
Co-stars: Claudette Colbert Ricardo Cortez Baby Leroy

1934 WE LIVE AGAIN
Director: Rouben Mamoulian
Co-stars: Fredric March Anna Sten Jane Baxter

1934 FOUR FRIGHTENED PEOPLE
Director: Cecil B. De Mille
Co-stars: Claudette Colbert Herbert Marshall

1935 WEREWOLF OF LONDON
Director: Stuart Walker
Co-stars: Henry Hull Warner Oland Valerie Hobson

1940 VIGIL IN THE NIGHT
Director: George Stevens
Co-stars: Carole Lombard Brian Aherne Anne Shirely

1940 STRANGER ON THE THIRD FLOOR
Director: Boris Ingster
Co-stars: Margaret Tallichet Peter Lorre

1940 IRENE
Director: Herbert Wilcox
Co-stars: Anna Neagle Ray Milland Roland Young

1941 DEAD MEN TELL
Director: Harry Lachman
Co-stars: Sidney Toler Sheila Ryan George Reeves

1941 BILLY THE KID
Director: David Miller
Co-stars: Robert Taylor Brian Donlevy Ian Hunter

1942 CASTLE IN THE DESERT
Director: Harry Lachman
Co-stars: Sidney Toler Arleen Whelan Henry Daniell

1942 BETWEEN US GIRLS
Director: Henry Koster
Co-stars: Diana Barrymore Kay Francis John Boles

1943 DEVOTION
Director: Curtis Bernhardt
Co-stars: Ida Lupino Olivia De Havillland Nancy Coleman

1943 SARATOGA TRUNK
Director: Sam Wood
Co-stars: Ingrid Bergman Gary Cooper Flora Robson

1944 JANE EYRE
Director: Robert Stevenson
Co-stars: Joan Fontaine Orson Welles Margaret O'Brien

1963 THE BIRDS
Director: Alfred Hitchcock
Co-stars: Tippi Hedren Rod Taylor Jessica Tandy

1963 BILLY LIAR
Director: John Schlesinger
Co-stars: Tom Courtenay Julie Christie Leonard Rossiter

CELINE GRIFFIN

1990 ENCOUNTER AT RAVEN'S GATE
Director: Rolf De Heer
Co-stars: Stephen Vidler Ritchie Singer Vince Gil

JOSEPHINE GRIFFIN

1954 THE CROWDED DAY
Director: John Guillermin
Co-stars: Joan Rice John Gregson Freda Jackson

1955 THE MAN WHO NEVER WAS
Director: Ronald Neame
Co-stars: Clifton Webb Robert Flemying Gloria Grahame

1955 PORTRAIT OF ALISON
Director: Guy Green
Co-stars: Robert Beatty Terry Moore William Sylvester

1956 THE SPANISH GARDNER
Director: Philip Leacock
Co-stars: Dirk Bogarde Michael Hordern Jon Whiteley

1956 THE EXTRA DAY
Director: William Fairchild
Co-stars: Richard Basehart Simone Simon George Baker

LORRIE GRIFFIN

1988 ALOHO SUMMER
Director: Tommy Lee Wallace
Co-stars: Chris Makepeace Tia Carrerre Yuji Okumoto

LYNNE GRIFFIN

1983 STRANGE BREW
Director: Rick Moranis
Co-stars: Rick Moranis Dave Thomas Max Von Sydow Paul Dooley

1989 OBSESSED
Director: Robin Spry
Co-stars: Kerrie Keane Daniel Pilon Saul Rubinek

1991 TRUE IDENTITY
Director: Charles Lane
Co-stars: Lenny Henry Frank Langella J.T. Walsh

STEPHANIE GRIFFIN

1956 THE LAST WAGON
Director: Delmer Daves
Co-stars: Richard Widmark Felicia Farr Tommy Retig

CORINNE GRIFFITH

Nominated For Best Actress In 1929 For "The Divine Lady"

1923 SIX DAYS

1929 THE DIVINE LADY
Director: Frank Lloyd
Co-stars: H.B. Warner Montagu Love Marie Dressler

1930 LILLIES OF THE FIELD
Director: Alexandra Korda
Co-stars: Ralph Forbes John Loder Patsy Paige

1932 LILLY CHRISTINE
Co-star: Colin Clive

ELEANOR GRIFFITH

1929 ALIBI
Director: Roland West
Co-stars: Chester Morris Regis Toomey Mae Busch

EVA GRIFFITH

1976 RIDE A WILD PONY
Director: Don Chaffey
Co-stars: Michael Craig John Meillon Robert Bettles

1987 OUR LADY BLUE
Director: Robin Midgley
Co-stars: Patricia Hayes Doreen Mantle Paul Beringer

KRISTIN GRIFFITH

1992 SWITCHING PARENTS
Director: Linda Otto
Co-stars: Brian Cook Daniel Desanto Kathleen York

MELANIE GRIFFITH
(Daughter Of Tippi Hedren And Noel Marshall Married Don Johnson (Twice), Steve Bauer, Antonio Banderas)
Nominated For Best Actress In 1988 For "Working Girl"

1973 THE HARRARD EXPERIENCE
Director: Ted Post
Co-stars: James Whitmore Tippi Hendren Don Johnson

1974 SMILE
Director: Michael Ritchie
Co-stars: Bruce Dern Barbara Felden Michael Kidd

1975 NIGHT MOVES
Director: Arthur Penn
Co-stars: Gene Hackman Jennifer Warren Kenneth Mars

1975 THE DROWNING POOL
Director: Stuart Rosenberg
Co-stars: Paul Newman Joanne Woodward Richard Derr

1977 JOYRIDE
Director: Joseph Ruben
Co-stars: Desi Arnaz Jnr. Robert Carradine Anne Lockhart

1977 ONE ON ONE
Director: Lamont Johnson
Co-stars: Robbie Benson Annette O'Toole Gail Strickland

1978 STEEL COWBOY
Director: Harvey Laidman
Co-stars: James Brolin Rip Torn Jennifer Warren

1981 ROAR (STARTED 1970)
Director: Noel Marshall
Co-stars: Tippi Hedren John Marshall Jerry Marshall

1981 GOLDEN GATE
Director: Paul Wendkos
Co-stars: Jean Simmons Richard Kiley Perry King

1981 SHE'S IN THE ARMY NOW
Director: Hy Averback
Co-stars: Kathleen Quinlan Jaime Lee Curtis

1984 BODY DOUBLE
Director: Brian De Palma
Co-stars: Craig Wasson Greer Henry Deborah Shelton

1984 FEAR CITY
Director: Abel Ferrara
Co-stars: Tom Berenger Billy Dee Williams Rossano Brazzi

1986 SOMETHING WILD
Director: Jonathan Demme
Co-stars: Jeff Daniels Ray Liotta Margaret Colin

1988 THE MILAGRO BEANFIELD WAR
Director: Robert Redford
Co-stars: Ruben Blades Richard Bradford

1988 CHERRY 2000
Director: Steve De Jarnatt
Co-stars: David Andrews Ben Johnson Pamela Gidley

1988 WORKING GIRL
Director: Mike Nichols
Co-stars: Harrison Ford Sigourney Weaver Joan Cusack

1989 STORMY MONDAY
Director: Mike Figgis
Co-stars: Sting Sean Bean Tommy Lee Jones Prunella Gee

**1990 WOMEN AND MEN:
STORIES OF SEDUCTION**
Director: Tony Richardson
Co-stars: Molly Ringwald Beau Bridges James Woods

1990 PACIFIC HEIGHTS
Director: John Schlesinger
Co-stars: Matthew Modine Michael Keaton Tippi Hedren

1990 IN THE SPIRIT
Director: Sandra Seacat
Co-stars: Marlo Thomas Elaine May Peter Falk

1990 BONFIRE OF THE VANITIES
Director: Brian De Palma
Co-stars: Tom Hanks Bruce Willis Kim Cattrall

1991 PARADISE
Director: Mary Agnes Donoghue
Co-stars: Don Johnson Elijah Wood Thora Birch

1992 SHINING THROUGH
Director: David Seltzer
Co-stars: Michael Douglas Liam Neesen Joely Richardson

1992 CLOSE TO EDEN
Director: Sidney Lumet
Co-stars: Eric Thal John Pankow Mia Sara

1993 BORN YESTERDAY
Director: Luis Mandoki
Co-stars: Don Johnson John Goodman Edward Herrman

1994 NOBODY'S FOOL
Director: Robert Benton
Co-stars: Paul Newman Bruce Willis

1994 MILK MONEY
Director: Richard Benjamin
Co-stars: Ed Harris Malcolm McDowell

1995 BUFFALO GIRLS
Co-stars: Anjelica Huston Gabriel Byrne Jack Palance

1996 MULHOLLAND FALLS
Director: Lee Tamahori
Co-stars: Nick Nolte Chazz Palminteri John Malkovich

1996 NOW AND THEN
Co-stars: Demi Moore Christina Ricci Thora Birch

1996 TOO MUCH
Director: Fernanso Trueba
Co-stars: Antonio Banderas Daryl Hannah

1998 LOLITA
Director: Adrian Lyne
Co-stars: Jeremy Irons Dominique Swain

NONA GRIFFITH (Child)

1945 THE UNSEEN
Director: Lewis Allen
Co-stars: Joel McCrea Gail Russell Herbert Marshall

1946 PERFECT MARRIAGE
Director: Lewis Allen
Co-stars: David Niven Loretta Young Eddie Albert

TRACY GRIFFITH (Sister Of Melanie Griffith)

1990 THE FIRST POWER
Director: Robert Resnikoff
Co-stars: Jeff Kober Elizabeth Arden Dennis Lipscomb

1993 FOR LOVE AND GLORY
Director: Roger Young
Co-stars: Robert Foxworth Kate Mulgrew Olivia D'Abo

1993 THE FINEST HOUR
Director: Simon Dotan
Co-star: Rob Lowe

JANE GRIFFITHS

1954 THE MILLION POUND NOTE
Director: Ronald Neame
Co-stars: Gregory Peck Joyce Grenfell A.E. Matthews

1957 THE TRAITOR
Director: Michael McCarthy
Co-stars: Donald Wolfit Robert Bray Rupert Davies

1958 TREAD SOFTLY STRANGER
Director: Gordon Parry
Co-stars: George Baker Terence Morgan Diana Dors

1961 THE THIRD ALIBI
Director: Montgomery Tully
Co-stars: Laurence Payne Patricia Dainton Cleo Laine

1961 THE IMPERSONATOR
Director: Alfred Shaughnessy
Co-stars: John Crawford Patricia Burke John Salew

LINDA GRIFFITHS

1983 LIANNA
Director: John Sayles
Co-stars: Jane Hallaren Jon De Vries Jo Henderson

1992 A TOWN TORN APART
Director: Daniel Petrie
Co-stars: Michael Tucker Jill Eikenberry Carole Galloway

LUCY GRIFFITHS

1961 THE THIRD ALIBI
Director: Montgomery Tully
Co-stars: Laurence Payne Patricia Dainton Jane Griffiths

RACHEL GRIFFITHS

1994 MURIEL'S WEDDING
Director: P.J. Hogan
Co-stars: Toni Collette Bill Hunter Jeanie Drynan

1995 JUDE
Director: Michael Winterbottom
Co-stars: Kate Winslet Christopher Eccleston

1997 AMONG GIANTS
Director: Mark Evans
Co-star: Pete Postlethwaite

1998 MY SON THE FANATIC
Director: Hanif Kureishi
Co-stars: Om Puri Akbar Kurtha

SUSAN GRIFFITHS

1991 MARILYN AND ME
Director: John Patterson

THELMA GRIGG

1947 BUSH CHRISTMAS
Director: Ralph Smart
Co-stars: Chips Rafferty Pat Penny John McCallum

KAROLYN GRIMES

1947 THE PRIVATE AFFAIRS OF BEL AMI
Director: Albert Lewin
Co-stars: George Sanders Angela Lansbury

TAMMY GRIMES

1966 THREE BITES OF THE APPLE
Director: Alvin Ganzer
Co-stars: David McCallum Sylvia Koscina

1970 THE OTHER MAN
Director: Richard Colla
Co-stars: Joan Hackett Roy Thinnes Arthur Hill

1972 PLAY IT AS IT LAYS
Director: Frank Perry
Co-stars: Anthony Perkins Tuesday Weld Ruth Ford

1972 HORROR AT 37,000 FEET
Director: David Lowell Rich
Co-stars: William Shatner Roy Thinnes Buddy Ebsen

1978 SOMEBODY KILLED HER HUSBAND
Director: Lamont Johnson
Co-stars: Farrah Fawcett Jeff Bridges John Wood

1979 THE RUNNER STUMBLES
Director: Stanley Kramer
Co-stars: Dick Van Dyke Kathleen Quinan Ray Bolger

ANOUK GRINBERG

1991 MERCI LA VIE
Director: Bernard Blier
Co-stars: Charlotte Gainsbourg Gerard Depardieu Annie Girardot

1997 MON HOMME
Director: Richard Blier
Co-star: Gerard Lanvin

CHRISTINA GRISANTI

1974 A WOMAN UNDER THE INFLUENCE
Director: John Cassavetes
Co-stars: Gena Rowlands Katherine Cassavetes

KATHRYN GRODY (Married Mandy Patinkin)

1988 PARENTS
Director: Bob Balaban
Co-stars: Randy Quaid Mary Beth Hurt Sandy Dennis

1990 QUICK CHANGE
Director: Bill Murray
Co-stars: Bill Murray Geena Davis Randy Quaid Jason Robards

1990 THE LEMON SISTERS
Director: Joyce Chopra
Co-stars: Diane Keaton Carol Kane Elliott Gould

CLAIRE GROGAN

1980 GREGORY'S GIRL
Director: Bill Forsyth
Co-stars: John Gordon Sinclair Dee Hepburn Chic Murray

1984 COMFORT AND JOY
Director: Bill Forsyth
Co-stars: Bill Paterson Eleanor David Alex Norton

LORETTA GROSS

1989 THE KILL-OFF
Director: Maggie Greenwald
Co-stars: Steve Monroe Cathy Haase Jackson Sims

MARY GROSS

1987 BABY BOOM
Director: Charles Shyer
Co-stars: Diane Keaton Sam Wanamaker James Spader

1988 CASUAL SEX?
Director: Genevieve Robert
Co-stars: Lea Thompson Victoria Jackson Jerry Levine

1988 THE COUCH TRIP
Director: Michael Ritchie
Co-stars: Dan Aykroyd Walter Matthau Charles Grodin

1989 TROOP BEVERLY HILLS
Director: Jeff Kanew
Co-stars: Shelley Long Craig T. Nelson Stephanie Beacham

1989 FEDS
Director: Dan Goldberg
Co-stars: Rebecca De Mornay Fred Dalton Thompson Ken Marshall

MECHTHILD GROSSMAN

1985 SEDUCTION: THE CRUEL WOMAN
Director: Udo Kier
Co-stars: Sheila McLaughlin Georgette Dee

DEBORAH GROVE

1986 THE GATE
Director: Tibor Takacs
Co-stars: Stephen Dorff Christa Denton Louis Tripp

ELAINE GROVE

1982 LIQUID SKY
Director: Slava Tsukerman
Co-stars: Anne Carlisle Paula Sheppard Susan Doukas

SYBIL GROVE

1931 SUNSHINE SUSIE
Director: Victor Saville
Co-stars: Renate Muller Jack Hulbert Owen Nares

LINDA GROVENOR

1980 DIE LAUGHING
Director: Jeff Werner
Co-stars: Robby Benson Charles Durning Elsa Lanchester

SHIRLEY GRUAR

1980 GOODBYE PORK PIE
Director: Geoff Murphy
Co-stars: Tony Barry Kelly Johnson Claire Oberman

ILKA GRUNING

1941 UNDERGROUND
Director: Vincent Sherman
Co-stars: Jeffry Lynn Philip Dorn Karen Verne

1942 DESPERATE JOURNEY
Director: Raoul Walsh
Co-stars: Errol Flynn Ronald Reagan Raymond Massey

1946 TEMPTATION
Director: Irving Pichel
Co-stars: Merle Oberon George Brent Paul Lukas

1947 DESPERATE
Director: Anthony Mann
Co-stars: Steve Brodie Audrey Long Raymond Burr

AH-LEH GUA

1993 THE WEDDING BANQUET
Director: Ang Lee
Co-stars: Winston Chao May Chin Mitchell Lichtenstein

PIPPA GUARD

1982 AN UNSUITABLE JOB FOR A WOMAN
Director: Christopher Petit
Co-stars: Billie Whitelaw Paul Freeman

BLANCA GUERRA

1982 THE ROBBERS OF THE SACRED MOUNTAIN
Director: Bob Schultz
Co-stars: Simon MacCorkindale John Marley

1989 SANTA SANGRE
Director: Alejandro Jodorowsky
Co-stars: Guy Stockwell Thelma Tixou

1991 DANZON
Director: Maria Novaro
Co-stars: Maria Rojo Carmen Salinas Victor Carpinteiro

ANGELICA GUERRERO

1986 DONA HERLINDA AND HER SON
Director: Jaime Humbetto Hermosillo
Co-stars: Arturo Meza Leticia Lupersio

EVELYN GUERRERO

1980 CHEECH AND CHONG'S NEXT MOVIE
Director: Thomas Chong
Co-stars: Thomas Chong Cheech Marin Betty Kennedy Sy Kramer

CARLA GUGINO

1993 SON IN LAW
Director: Steve Rash
Co-stars: Pauly Shore Lane Smith Cindy Pickett

1994 MOTORCYCLE GANG
Director: John Milius
Co-stars: Gerald McRainey Elan Oberon Jake Busey

1995 MIAMI RHAPSODY
Director: David Frankel
Co-stars: Sarah Jessica Parker Mia Farrow Antonio Banderas

NINA GUILBERT

1939 TRIGGER PALS
Co-stars: Art Jarrett Dorothy Fay Al "Fuzzy" St. John

YVETTE GUILBERT

1926 FAUST
Director: F.W. Murnau
Co-stars: Emil Jannings Camilla Horn Gosta Ekman

NANCY GUILD

1946 THE BRASHER DOUBLOON
Director: John Brahm
Co-stars: George Montgomery Florence Bates

1946 SOMEWHERE IN THE NIGHT
Director: Joseph Mankiewicz
Co-stars: John Hodiak Lloyd Nolan Richard Conte

1948 GIVE MY REGARDS TO BROADWAY
Director: Lloyd Bacon
Co-stars: Dan Dailey Charles Winninger Fay Bainter

1949 BLACK MAGIC
Director: Gregory Ratoff
Co-stars: Orson Welles Akim Tamiroff Valentina Cortesa

1951 ABBOTT AND COSTELLO MEET THE INVISIBLE MAN
Director: Charles Lamont
Co-stars: Bud Abbott Lou Costello Arthur Franz

1951 LITTLE EGYPT
Director: Frederick De Cordova
Co-stars: Rhonda Fleming Mark Stevens Adele Jergens

1971 SUCH GOOD FRIENDS
Director: Otto Preminger
Co-stars: Dyan Cannon James Coco Jennifer O'Neil

TEXAS QUINAN

1929 QUEEN OF THE NIGHTCLUBS
Co-star: William Davidson

1929 GLORIFYING THE AMERICAN GIRL
Director: Millard Webb
Co-stars: Mary Eaton Eddie Cantor Helen Morgan

1933 BROADWAY THRU A KEYHOLE
Director: Lowell Sherman
Co-stars: Constance Cummings Russ Columbo

LARA GUIRAO

1992 L627
Director: Bertrand Tavernier
Co-stars: Didier Bezace Charlotte Kady Nils Tavernier

DOROTHY GULLIVER

1931 IN OLD CHEYENNE
Co-stars: Rex Lease Harry Woods

EISI GULP

1984 IN THE BELLY OF THE WHALE
Director: Doris Dorrie
Co-stars: Janna Marangosoff Peter Saltman

JANET GUNN

1994 NIGHT OF THE RUNNING MAN
Director: Mark L. Lester
Co-stars: Andrew McCarthy Scott Glenn

JUDY GUNN

1935 THE LAST JOURNEY
Director: Bernard Vorhaus
Co-stars: Godfrey Tearle Hugh Williams Olga Lindo

1935 THE LOVE TEST
Director: Michael Powell
Co-stars: Louis Hayward David Hutcheson Googie Withers

1935 THE PRIVATE SECRETARY
Director: Henry Edwards
Co-stars: Edward Everett Horton Barry MacKay

1935 VINTAGE WINE
Director: Henry Edwards
Co-stars: Seymour Hicks Eva Moore Miles Malleson

1936 IN THE SOUP
Director: Henry Edwards
Co-stars: Ralph Lynn Bertha Belmore Nelson Keyes

1937 SILVER BLAZE
Director: Thomas Bentley
Co-stars: Arthur Wontner Ian Fleming Lyn Harding

ALIZIA GUR

1966 THE HAND OF NIGHT
Director: Frederick Goode
Co-stars: William Sylvester Diane Claire

1968 TARZAN AND THE JUNGLE BOY
Director: Robert Day
Co-stars: Mike Henry Ronald Gans Ed Johnson

SIGRID GURIE (*Sigrid Haukelid*)

1938 THE ADVENTURES OF MARCO POLO
Director: Archie Mayo
Co-stars: Gary Cooper Basil Rathbone Alan Hale

1938 ALGIERS
Director: John Cromwell
Co-stars: Charles Boyer Hedy Lamarr Joseph Calleia

1939 THE FORGOTTEN WOMAN
Director: Harold Young
Co-stars: Eve Arden Donald Briggs William Lundigan

1939 RIO
Director: John Brahm
Co-stars: Basil Rathbone Victor McLaglen Robert Cummings

1940 THREE FACES WEST
Director: Bernard Vorhaus
Co-stars: John Wayne Charles Coburn Roland Varno

1940 DARK STREETS OF CAIRO
Co-stars: Ralph Byrd Eddie Quillan Yolande Mallot

1944 A VOICE IN THE WIND
Director: Arthur Ripley
Co-stars: Francis Lederer J. Carrol Naish

JANE GURNETT

1987 LOVEBIRDS
Director: Stephen Whittaker
Co-stars: Stephen Bent Linda Henry Lisa Meredith

1989 MELANCHOLIA
Director: Andi Engel
Co-stars: Jeroen Krabbe Susannah York Kate Hardie

RACHEL GURNEY

1951 TOM BROWN'S SCHOOLDAYS
Director: Gordon Parry
Co-stars: John Howard Davies Robert Newton

1956 PORT AFRIQUE
Director: Rudolph Mate
Co-stars: Phil Carey Pier Angeli Dennis Price

1967 FUNERAL IN BERLIN
Director: Guy Hamilton
Co-stars: Michael Caine Oscar Homolka Eva Renzi

SHARON GURNEY

1972 DEATHLINE
Director: Gary Sherman
Co-stars: Hugh Armstrong David Ladd Donald Pleasence

CAROLINE GUTHRIE

1986 THE GIRL IN THE PICTURE
Director: Cary Parker
Co-stars: John Gordon Sinclair Irina Brook Paul Young

ZAIDE SILVIA GUTIERREZ

1992 HIGHWAY PATROLMAN
Director: Alex Cox
Co-stars: Robert Sosa Vanessa Bauche Bruno Bichir

LUCY GUTTERIDGE

1984 TOP SECRET!
Director: David Zucker
Co-stars: Val Kilmer Peter Cushing Jeremy Kemp

1984 A CHRISTMAS CAROL
Director: Clive Donner
Co-stars: George C. Scott Frank Finlay Susannah York Lacey Guyon

1993 GRIEF
Director: Richard Glatzer
Co-stars: Craig Chester Illeana Douglas Alexis Arquette

LACEY GUYON

1992 IN THE BEST INTEREST OF THE CHILDREN
Director: Michael Ray Rhodes
Co-stars: Sarah Jessica Parker Lexi Randall Elizabeth Ashley

JASMINE GUY

1989 HARLEM NIGHTS
Director: Eddie Murphy
Co-stars: Eddie Murphy Richard Pryor Danny Aiello Redd Fox

ANNE-MARIE GWATKIN

1984 SECRET PLACES
Director: Zelda Baron
Co-stars: Marie Therese Relin Tara MacGowran Jenny Agutter

NAN GWYN

1943 IS EVERYBODY HAPPY?
Director: Charles Barton
Co-stars: Ted Lewis Larry Parks Michael Duane

ANN GWYNNE

1939 LITTLE ACCIDENT
Director: Charles Lamont
Co-stars: Baby Sandy Hugh Herbert Florence Rice Richard Carlsen

1940 SPRING PARADE
Director: Henry Koster
Co-stars: Deanna Durbin Robert Cummings Mischa Auer

1940 HONEYMOON DEFERRED
Director: Lew Landers
Co-stars: Edmund Lowe Margaret Lindsay Chick Chandler

1940 GIVE US WINGS
Director: Charles Lamont
Co-stars: Dead End Kids Wallace Ford Victor Jory

1940 BLACK FRIDAY
Director: Arthur Lubin
Co-stars: Boris Karloff Bela Lugosi Anne Nagel Stanley Ridges

1941 THE BLACK CAT
Director: Albert Rogell
Co-stars: Basil Rathbone Gladys Cooper Broderick Crawford

1941 ROAD AGENT
Co-stars: Leo Carillo Andy Devine Luane Walters

1941 MOB TOWN
Director: William Nigh
Co-stars: Dead End Kids Dick Foran Billy Halop

1941 RIDE 'EM HIGH
Director: Arthur Lubin
Co-stars: Bud Abbott Lou Costello Dick Foran Ella Fitzgerald

1941 TIGHT SHOES
Director: Albert Rogell
Co-stars: Broderick Crawford Binnie Barnes John Howard

1942 STRANGE CASE OF DOCTOR RX
Director: William Nigh
Co-stars: Lionel Atwill Patric Knowles Mona Barrie

1942 SIN TOWN
Director: Ray Enright
Co-stars: Broderick Crawford Constance Bennett Andy Devine

1942 BROADWAY
Director: William Seiter
Co-stars: George Raft Pat O'Brien Broderick Crawford Janet Blair

1942 MEN OF TEXAS
Director: Ray Enright
Co-stars: Robert Stack Broderick Crawford Ralph Bellamy

1943 FRONTIER BADMEN
Director: William McGann
Co-stars: Robert Paige Lon Chaney Noah Beery

1943 TOP MAN
Director: Charles Lamont
Co-stars: Donald O'Connor Richard Dix Peggy Ryan Lillian Gish

1943 **WE'VE NEVER BEEN LICKED**
Director: John Rawlins
Co-stars: Richard Quine Noah Beery Harry Davenport

1944 **WEIRD WOMAN**
Director: Reginald Le Borg
Co-stars: Lon Chaney Evelyn Ankers Ralph Morgan

1944 **MOON OVER VEGAS**
Co-stars: David Bruce Addison Richards

1944 **MURDER IN THE BLUE MOON**
Director: Leslie Goodwins
Co-stars: Donald Cook John Litel Grace McDonald

1944 **SOUTH OF DIXIE**
Co-star: David Bruce

1944 **LADIES COURAGEOUS**
Director: John Rawlins
Co-stars: Loretta Young Geraldine Fitzgerald Evelyn Ankers

1945 **HOUSE OF FRANKENSTEIN**
Director: Erle Kenton
Co-stars: Boris Karloff John Carradine Lon Chaney

1946 **FEAR**
Director: Alfred Zeisler
Co-stars: Warren William Peter Cookson Nestor Paiva

1947 **DICK TRACY MEETS GRUESOME**
Director: John Rawlins
Co-stars: Boris Karloff Ralph Byrd Lyle Latell

1948 **PANHANDLE**
Director: Lesley Selander
Co-stars: Rod Cameron Cathy Downs Reed Hadley Blake Edwards

1949 **ARSON INC.**
Co-stars: Robert Lowery Marcia Mae Jones Douglas Fowley

1958 **TEENAGE MONSTER**
Director: Jacques Marquette
Co-stars: Gloria Costello Gilbert Perkins

HAYDEN GWYNNE

1980 **NICE WORK**
Director: Christopher Menaul
Co-stars: Warren Clarke David Cadler Janet Dale

1991 **THE PLEASURE PRINCIPLE**
Director: David Cohen
Co-stars: Peter Firth Lynsey Baxter Lysette Anthony

DENISE GYNGELL

1973 **THE ZOO ROBBERY**
Director: John Black
Co-stars: Paul Gyngell Karen Lucas Sean Barrett

GRETA GYNT

1938 **SECOND BEST BED**
Director: Tom Walls
Co-stars: Tom Walls Jane Baxter Veronica Rose Carl Jaffe

1938 **SEXTON BLAKE AND THE HOODED TERROR**
Director: George King
Co-stars: George Curzon Tod Slaughter

1939 **THE MIDDLE WATCH**
Director: Thomas Bentley
Co-stars: Jack Buchanan Fred Emney Kay Walsh Leslie Fuller

1939 **DARK EYES OF LONDON**
Director: Walter Summers
Co-stars: Bela Lugosi Hugh Williams Wilfred Walter

1939 **THE ARSENAL STADIUM MYSTERY**
Director: Thorold Dickinson
Co-stars: Leslie Banks Brian Worth Esmond Knight

1940 **CROOKS' TOUR**
Director: John Baxter
Co-stars: Basil Radford Naunton Wayne Abraham Sofaer

1941 **THE COMMON TOUCH**
Director: John Baxter
Co-stars: Geoffrey Hibbert Joyce Howard Edward Rigby

1942 **TOMORROW WE LIVE**
Director: George King
Co-stars: John Clements Hugh Sinclair Godfrey Tearle

1943 **IT'S THAT MAN AGAIN**
Director: Walter Forde
Co-stars: Tommy Handley Jack Train Dorothy Summers

1944 **MR. EMMANUEL**
Director: Harold French
Co-stars: Felix Aylmer Walter Rilla Ursula Jeans

1946 **LONDON TOWN**
Director: Wesley Ruggles
Co-stars: Sid Field Kay Kendall Petula Clark Tessie O'Shea

1947 **DEAR MURDERER**
Director: Arthur Crabtree
Co-stars: Eric Portman Dennis Price Maxwell Reed Jack Warner

1947 **TAKE MY LIFE**
Director: Ronald Neame
Co-stars: Hugh Williams Marius Goring Rosalie Crutchley

1948 **EASY MONEY**
Director: Bernard Knowles
Co-stars: Edward Rigby Dennis Price Mervyn Johns Jack Warner

1948 **MR. PERRIN AND MR. TRAILL**
Director: Lawrence Huntingdon
Co-stars: Marius Goring David Farrar

1948 **THE CALENDER**
Director: Arthur Crabtree
Co-stars: John McCallum Leslie Dwyer Raymond Lovell

1950 **SHADOW OF THE EAGLE**
Director: Sidney Salkow
Co-stars: Richard Greene Valentina Cortesse Binnie Barnes

1951 **SOLDIERS THREE**
Director: Tay Garnett
Co-stars: Stewart Granger David Niven Robert Newton

1951 **I'LL GET YOU FOR THIS**
Director: Joseph Newman
Co-stars: George Raft Coleen Gray Charles Goldner

1951 **WHISPERING SMITH HITS LONDON**
Director: Francis Searle
Co-stars: Richard Carlson Rona Anderson

1952 **THE RINGER**
Director: Guy Hamilton
Co-stars: Donald Wolfitt Mai Zetterling Herbert Lom

1955 **SEE HOW THEY RUN**
Director: Leslie Arliss
Co-stars: Ronald Shiner James Hayter Dora Bryan

1955 **THE BLUE PETER**
Director: Wolf Rilla
Co-stars: Kieron Moore Sarah Lawson Mervyn Johns

1956 **FORTUNE IS A WOMAN**
Director: Sidney Gilliat
Co-stars: Jack Hawkins Arlene Dahl Dennis Price

1960 **BLUEBEARD'S TEN HONEYMOONS**
Director: Roy Parkinson
Co-stars: George Sanders Corinne Calvet Patricia Roc Jean Kent

KATHE HAACK

1931 EMIL AND THE DETECTIVES
Director: Gerhard Lamprecht
Co-stars: Fritz Rasp Olga Engl Rolf Wenkhaus

CHRISTINA HAAG

1991 SHAKING THE TREE
Director: Duane Clark
Co-stars: Ayre Gross Gale Hansen Courteney Cox

DOLLY HAAS

1936 BROKEN BLOSSOMS
Director: John Brahm
Co-stars: Emlyn Williams Arthur Margetson Donald Calthorp

1936 SPY OF NAPOLEON
Director: Maurice Elvey
Co-stars: Richard Barthelmess Frank Vosper Francis L. Sullivan

1953 I CONFESS
Director: Alfred Hitchcock
Co-stars: Montgomery Clift Anne Baxter Brian Aherne

CATHY HAASE

1989 THE KILL-OFF
Director: Maggie Greenwald
Co-stars: Loretta Gross Andrew Lee Barrett Steve Monroe

SHELLEY HACK

1979 DEATH CAR ON THE FREEWAY
Director: Hal Needham
Co-stars: George Hamilton Barbara Rush Dinah Shore

1982 KING OF COMEDY
Director: Martin Scorsese
Co-stars: Robert De Niro Jerry Lewis Diahnne Abbott

1983 FOUND MONEY
Director: Bill Persky
Co-stars: Dick Van Dyke Sid Caesar William Prince

1984 SINGLE BARS, SINGLE WOMEN
Director: Harry Winer
Co-stars: Tony Danza Paul Michael Glaser Christine Lahti

1986 THE STEPFATHER
Director: Joesph Ruben
Co-stars: Terry O'Quinn Jill Schoelen Charles Lanyer

1986 TROLL
Director: John Carl Buechler
Co-stars: Noah Hathaway Michael Moriaty June Lockhart

1989 BRIDESMAIDS
Director: Lila Garrett
Co-stars: Sela Ward Brooke Adams Audra Lindley

1995 FREEFALL:THE FATE OF FLIGHT 174
Director: Jorge Montesi
Co-stars: William Devane Mariette Hartley

CLAIRE HACKETT

1990 DANCIN' THRU THE DARK
Director: Mike Ockrent
Co-stars: Angela Clarke Con O'Neill Julia Deakin

1993 A TOUCH OF FROST: CARE AND PROTECTION
Director: Don Leaver
Co-stars: David Jason Bruce Alexander

1994 MEN OF THE MONTH
Director: Jean Stuart
Co-stars: Douglas Hodge Clare Higgins Sandy Ratcliff

JOAN HACKETT
Nominated For Best Supporting Actress In 1981 For "It Hurts Only When I Laugh"

1966 THE GROUP
Director: Sidney Lumet
Co-stars: Candice Bergen Shirley Knight Elizabeth Hartman

1967 ASSIGNMENT TO KILL
Director: Sheldon Reynolds
Co-stars: Patrick O'Neal John Gielgud Oscar Homolka

1967 WILL PENNY
Director: Tom Gries
Co-stars: Charlton Heston Lee Majors Bruce Dern

1969 SUPPORT YOUR LOCAL SHERIFF
Co-stars: Burt Kennedy
Co-stars: James Garner Walter Brennan Henry Morgan

1970 THE OTHER MAN
Director: Richard Colla
Co-stars: Roy Thinnes Tammy Grimes Arthur Hill

1970 HOW AWFUL ABOUT ALLAN
Director: Curtis Harrington
Co-stars: Anthony Perkins Julie Harris Kent Smith

1973 THE LAST OF SHELIA
Director: Herbert Ross
Co-stars: James Coburn James Mason Raquel Welch

1976 TREASURE OF MATECHUMBA
Director: Vincent McEveety
Co-stars: Peter Ustinov Robert Foxworth Vic Morrow

1977 THE POSSESSED
Director: Jerry Thorpe
Co-stars: James Farentino Harrison Ford Diana Scarwid

1980 THE LONG DAYS OF SUMMER
Director: Dan Curtis
Co-stars: Dean Jones Ronnie Scribner Andrew Duggan

1981 IT HURTS ONLY WHEN I LAUGH
Director: Glenn Jordan
Co-stars: Marsha Mason James Coco Kristy McNichol

1982 THE ESCAPE ARTIST
Director: Caleb Deschanel
Co-stars: Griffin O'Neal Raul Julia Teri Garr

1982 THE LONG SUMMER OF GEORGE ADAMS
Director: Stuart Margolin
Co-stars: James Garner Alex Harvey

VANESSA HADAWAY

1993 THE PUNK
Director: Mike Sarne
Co-stars: Charles Creed-Miles Jess Conrad David Shawyer

AVA HADDAD

1992 THE LONG SHADOW
Director: Vilmos Zsigmond
Co-stars: Michael York Liv Ullmann Oded Teomi

ELLIE HADDINGTON

1990 THE LORELEI
Director: Terry Johnson
Co-stars: Amanda Redman Michael Maloney John Nettleton

JULIE ANNE HADDOCK
1979 THE GREAT SANTINI
Director: Lewis John Carlino
Co-stars: Robert Duvall Blythe Danner Stan Shaw

SARA HADEN

1934 ANNE OF GREEN GABLES
Director: George Nicholls
Co-stars: Anne Shirley Tom Brown Helen Westley

1934 SPITFIRE
Director: John Cromwell
Co-stars: Katherine Hepburn Robert Young Martha Sleeper

1934 THE FOUNTAIN
Director: John Cromwell
Co-stars: Ann Harding Brian Aherne Paul Lukas Jean Hersholt

1934 HAT, COAT AND GLOVES
Director: Worthington Miner
Co-stars: Ricardo Cortez Barbara Robbins John Beal

1934 FINISHING SCHOOL
Director: George Nicholls
Co-stars: Frances Dee Ginger Rogers Billie Burke Bruce Cabot

1934 THE LIFE OF VERGIE WINTERS
Director: Alfred Santell
Co-stars: Ann Harding John Boles Helen Vinson

1934 THE WHITE PARADE
Director: Irving Cummings
Co-stars: Loretta Young John Boles Dorothy Wilson

1935 O'SHAUGHNESSY'S BOY
Director: Richard Boleslawski
Co-stars: Wallace Beery Jackie Cooper Leona Maricle

1935 WAY DOWN EAST
Director: Henry King
Co-stars: Rochelle Hudson Henry Fonda Spring Byington

1935 MAGNIFICENT OBSESSION
Director: John Stahl
Co-stars: Irene Dunne Robert Taylor Ralph Morgan

1935 MAD LOVE
Director: Karl Freund
Co-stars: Peter Lorre Colin Clive Frances Drake Isabel Jewell

1936 CAPTAIN JANUARY
Director: David Butler
Co-stars: Shirley Temple Guy Kibbee Buddy Ebsen June Lang

1936 THE CRIME OF DR. FORBES
Director: George Marshall
Co-stars: Robert Kent Gloria Stuart Henry Armetta

1936 POOR LITTLE RICH GIRL
Director: Irving Cummings
Co-stars: Shirley Temple Jack Haley Alice Faye

1936 CAN THIS BE DIXIE?
Director: George Marshall
Co-stars: Jane Withers Slim Summerville Hattie McDaniel

1936 REUNION
Director: Norman Taurog
Co-stars: Jean Hersholt Rochelle Hudson Helen Vinson

1937 UNDER COVER OF NIGHT
Director: George Seitz
Co-stars: Edmund Lowe Henry Daniel Dean Jagger

1937 LAUGHING AT TROUBLE
Director: Frank Strayer
Co-stars: Jane Darwell Lois Wilson John Carradine

1937 THE LAST OF MRS. CHEYNEY
Director: Richard Boleslawski
Co-stars: Joan Crawford Robert Montgomery

1937 A FAMILY AFFAIR
Director: George Seitz
Co-stars: Lionel Barrymore Mickey Rooney Spring Byington

1938 YOU'RE ONLY YOUNG ONCE
Director: George Seitz
Co-stars: Mickey Rooney Lewis Stone Fay Holden

1938 FOUR GIRLS IN WHITE
Director: S. Sylvan Simon
Co-stars: Florence Rice Alan Marshall Una Merkel

1938 JUDGE HARDY'S CHILDREN
Director: George Seitz
Co-stars: Lewis Stone Fay Holden Mickey Rooney

1938 OUT WEST WITH THE HARDIES
Director: George Seitz
Co-stars: Mickey Rooney Lewis Stone Cecelia Parker

1938 LOVE FINDS ANDY HARDY
Director: George Seitz
Co-stars: Mickey Rooney Ann Rutherford Fay Holden

1938 CRIME DOES NOT PAY: THINK IT OVER
Director: Jacques Tourneur
Co-star: Lester Matthews

1939 CRIME DOES NOT PAY: THINK FIRST
Director: Roy Rowland
Co-stars: Laraine Day Marc Lawrence

1939 ANDY HARDY GETS SPRING FEVER
Director: W.S. Van Dyke
Co-stars: Mickey Rooney Helen Gilbert Lewis Stone

1939 THE HARDIES RIDE HIGH
Director: George Seitz
Co-stars: Mickey Rooney Lewis Stone Cecelia Parker

1939 JUDGE HARDY AND SON
Director: George Seitz
Co-stars: Mickey Rooney Lewis Stone June Preisser

1940 THE SHOP AROUND THE CORNER
Director: Ernst Lubitsch
Co-stars: James Stewart Margaret Sullavan

1940 ANDY HARDY MEETS A DEBUTANTE
Director: George Seitz
Co-stars: Mickey Rooney Judy Garland Tom Neal

1941 ANDY HARDY'S PRIVATE SECRETARY
Director: George Seitz
Co-stars: Kathryn Grayson Ian Hunter Mickey Rooney

1941 LOVE CRAZY
Director: Jack Cummings
Co-stars: William Powell Myrna Loy Jack Carson Gail Patrick

1941 LIFE BEGINS FOR ANDY HARDY
Director: George Seitz
Co-stars: Mickey Rooney Judy Garland Lewis Stone

1941 BARNACLE BILL
Director: Richard Thorpe
Co-stars: Wallace Beery Marjorie Main Virginia Weidler

1942 THE COURTSHIP OF ANDY HARDY
Ddirector George Seitz
Co-stars: Mickey Rooney Ann Rutherford Fay Holden

1942 ANDY HARDY'S DOUBLE LIFE
Director: George Seitz
Co-stars: Esther Williams Susan Peters Mickey Rooney

1943 BEST FOOT FORWARD
Director: Edward Buzzell
Co-stars: Lucille Ball June Allyson Gloria De Havilland

1944 ANDY HARDY'S BLONDE TROUBLE
Director: George Seitz
Co-stars: Bonita Granville Jean Porter Mickey Rooney

454

1945 OUR HEARTS WERE GROWING UP
Director: William Russell
Co-stars: Gail Russell Diana Lynn

1945 OUR VINES HAVE TENDER GRAPES
Director: Roy Rowland
Co-stars: Edward G. Robinson Margaret O'Brien James Craig

1946 SHE-WOLF OF LONDON
Director: Jean Yarborough
Co-stars: June Lockhart Don Porter Dennis Hoey

1946 SO GOES MY LOVE
Director: Frank Ryan
Co-stars: Myrna Loy Don Ameche Bobby Driscoll

1946 MR. ACE
Director: Edwin Marin
Co-stars: George Raft Sylvia Sidney Stanley Ridges Jerome Cowan

1946 LOVE LAUGHS AT ANDY HARDY
Director: Willis Goldbeck
Co-stars: Bonita Granville Lina Romay Mickey Rooney Lewis Stone

1947 THE BISHOP'S WIFE
Director: Henry Koster
Co-stars: Cary Grant Loretta Young David Niven

1948 RACHEL AND THE STRANGER
Director: Norman Foster
Co-stars: Loretta Young Robert Mitchum William Holden

1949 THE BIG CAT
Director: Phil Karlson
Co-stars: Peggy Ann Garner Lon McCallister Preston Foster

1950 THE GREAT RUPERT
Director: Irving Pichel
Co-stars: Jimmy Durante Terry Moore Tom Drake Frank Orth

1953 A LION IS IN THE STREETS
Director: Raoul Walsh
Co-stars: James Cagney Barbara Hale Anne Francis

1958 ANDY HARDY COMES HOME
Director: Howard Koch
Co-stars: Mickey Rooney Fay Holden Patricia Breslin

JEAN HAGRAFT

1989 SWEETIE
Director: Jane Campion
Co-stars: Genevieve Lemon Karen Colston Jon Darling

ANNA HAGAN

1967 THE OUTSIDER
Director: Michael Ritchie
Co-stars: Darren McGavin Edmond O'Brien Ann Sothern

MARIANNE HAGAN

1995 HALLOWEEN 6: THE CURSE
Director: Joe Chappelle
Co-stars: Donald Pleasence Paul Rudd

MOLLY HAGAN

1985 CODE OF SILENCE
Director: Andy Davis
Co-stars: Chuck Norris Henry Silva Bert Remsen

1986 DALLAS: THE EARLY YEARS
Director: Larry Ellikan
Co-stars: Larry Hagman David Grant

1987 SOME KIND OF WONDERFUL
Director: Howard Deutch
Co-stars: Mary Stuart Masterson Eric Stoltz

1988 SHOOTDOWN
Director: Michael Pressman
Co-stars: Angela Landsbury George Coe Kyle Secor

1988 JUSTIN CASE
Director: Blake Edwards
Co-stars: George Carlin Douglas Sill Gordon Jump

1988 FRESH HORSES
Director: David Anspaugh
Co-stars: Molly Ringwald Andrew McCarthy Viggo Mortensen

**1988 COLUMBO:
MURDER, SMOKE AND SHADOWS**
Director: James Frawley
Co-stars: Peter Falk Fisher Stevens

JEAN HAGEN
Nominated For Best Supporting Actress In 1952 For "Singin' In The Rain"

1949 ADAM'S RIB
Director: George Cukor
Co-stars: Spencer Tracy Katharine Hepburn Tom Ewell

1949 AMBUSH
Director: Sam Wood
Co-stars: Robert Taylor John Hodiak Arlene Dahl Leon Ames

1949 SIDE STREET
Director: Anthony Mann
Co-stars: Farley Granger Cathy O'Donnell James Craig Paul Kelly

1950 A LIFE OF HER OWN
Director: George Cukor
Co-stars: Lana Turner Ray Milland Tom Ewell Ann Dvorak

1950 THE ASPHALT JUNGLE
Director: John Huston
Co-stars: Louis Calhern Sterling Hayden Marilyn Monroe

1951 NIGHT INTO MORNING
Director: Fletcher Markle
Co-stars: Ray Milland Nancy Davis John Hodiak

1951 NO QUESTION ASKED
Director: Harold Kress
Co-stars: Barry Sullivan George Murphy Arlene Dahl

1951 SHADOW IN THE SKY
Director: Fred Wilcox
Co-stars: Ralph Meeker Nancy Davis James Whitmore

1952 SINGIN' IN THE RAIN
Director: Stanley Donen
Co-stars: Gene Kelly Donald O'Connor Debbie Reynolds

1952 CARBINE WILLIAMS
Director: Richard Thorpe
Co-stars: Jame Stewart Wendell Corey Paul Stewart

1953 ARENA
Director: Richard Fleischer
Co-stars: Gig Young Polly Bergen Henry Morgan Barbara Lawrence

1953 HALF A HERO
Director: Don Weis
Co-stars: Red Skelton Charles Dingle Polly Bergen Mary Wickes

1953 LATIN LOVERS
Director: Mervyn LeRoy
Co-stars: Lana Turner Ricardo Montalban John Lund Rita Moreno

1955 THE BIG KNIFE
Director: Robert Aldrich
Co-stars: Jack Palance Rod Steiger Ida Lupino Shelley Winters

1956 SPRING REUNION
Director: Robert Pirosh
Co-stars: Betty Hutton Dana Andrews James Gleason Irene Ryan

1959 THE SHAGGY DOG
Director: Charles Barton
Co-stars: Fred MacMurray Tommy Kirk Cecil Kellaway

1960 SUNRISE AT CAMPOBELLO
Director: Vincent Donehue
Co-stars: Ralph Bellamy Greer Garson Hume Cronyn

1962   PANIC IN THE YEAR ZERO
Director: Ray Milland
Co-stars: Ray Milland Frankie Avalon Mary Mitchel Joan Freeman

1964   DEAD RINGER
Director: Paul Henreid
Co-stars: Bette Davis Karl Malden Peter Lawford Philip Carey

JENNY HAGEN

1973   ALVIN PURPLE
Director: Tim Burstall
Co-stars: Grame Blundell George Whaley Penne Hackforth

ERICA HAGEN

1973   COFFEE, TEA OR ME
Director: Norman Panama
Co-stars: Karen Valentine John Davidson Lou Jacobi

UTA HAGEN

1972   THE OTHER
Director: Robert Mulligan
Co-stars: Diana Muldaur Chris Udvarnoky Martin Udvarnoky

1978   THE BOYS FROM BRAZIL
Director: Franklin Schaffner
Co-stars: Gregory Peck Laurence Olivier James Mason

1990   REVERSAL OF FORTUNE
Director: Barbet Schroeder
Co-stars: Jeremy Irons Glenn Close Ron Silver

KRISTIE HAGER

1990   SURE FIRE
Director: Jon Jost
Co-stars: Tom Blair Robert Ernst Kate Dezina

JULIE HAGERTY

1980   AIRPLANE!
Director: Jerry Zucker
Co-stars: Robert Stack Lloyd Bridges Ethel Merman

1982   AIRPLANE II: THE SEQUEL
Director: Ken Finkleman
Co-stars: Robert Hays Lloyd Bridges Sonny Bono

1982   A MIDSUMMER NIGHT'S SEX COMEDY
Director: Woody Allen
Co-stars: Woody Allen Mia Farrow Jose Ferrer Tony Roberts

1984   GOODBYE, NEW YORK
Director: Amos Kollek
Co-stars: Amos Kollek David Topaz Shmuel Shiloh

1985   BAD MEDICINE
Director: Harvey Miller
Co-stars: Steve Guttenberg Alan Arkin Bill Macy Julie Kavner

1985   LOST IN AMERICA
Director: Albert Brooks
Co-stars: Albert Brooks Michael Greene Tom Tarpey

1986   BEYOND THERAPY
Director: Robert Altman
Co-stars: Glenda Jackson Tom Conti Jeff Goldblum Genevieve Page

1988   ARIA
Director: Nicholas Roeg
Co-stars: Theresa Russell Bridget Fonda John Hurt Sophie Ward

1989   BLOODHOUNDS OF BROADWAY
Director: Howard Brookner
Co-stars: Madonna Jennifer Grey Rutger Hauer

1989   RUDE AWAKENING
Director: Arron Russo
Co-stars: Aaron Russo Cheech Martin Eric Roberts Robert Carradine

1991   WHAT ABOUT BOB?
Director: Frank Oz
Co-stars: Richard Dreyfuss Charlie Korsmo

1992   NOISES OFF
Director: Peter Bogdanovich
Co-stars: Carol Burnett Michael Caine Denholm Elliott

1996   NEIL SIMON'S LONDON SUITE
Director: Jay Sandrich
Co-stars: Kelsey Grammer Madeline Kahn Patricia Clarkson

MERLE HAGGARD

1975   HUCKLEBERRY FINN
Director: Robert Totten
Co-stars: Ron Howard Donny Most Jack Elam

BRITT HAGMAN

1936   INTERMEZZO
Director: Gustav Molander
Co-stars: Gosta Ekman Ingrid Bergman Inga Tidblad

PAULINE HAHN

1959   TOO YOUNG TO LOVE
Director: Muriel Box
Co-stars: Thomas Mitchell Joan Miller Jess Conrad

MARION HAILEY

1969   LOVERS AND OTHER STRANGERS
Director: Cy Howard
Co-stars: Gig Young Anne Jackson Diane Keaton

PATRICIA HAINES

1965   THE NIGHT CALLER
Director: John Giling
Co-stars: John Saxon Maurice Denham Warren Mitchell

1969   WALK A CROOKED PATH
Director: John Brason
Co-stars: Tenniel Evans Faith Brook Christopher Coll

1970   THE LAST SHOT YOU HEAR
Director: Gordon Hessler
Co-stars: Hugh Marlowe Zena Walker Thorley Walters

MARCELLE HAINIA

1932   BOUDO SAUVE DES EAUX
Director: Jean Renoir
Co-stars: Michael Simon Charles Grandval

KHRYSTYNE HAJE

1987   BATES MOTEL
Director: Richard Rothstein
Co-stars: Bud Cort Jason Bateman Gregg Henry

GABRILLE HAKER

1986   ROUND MIDNIGHT
Director: Bertrand Tavernier
Co-stars: Dexter Gordon Francois Cluzet Martin Scorsese

SARAH HOLCOMB

1980   CADDYSHACK
Director: Harold Ramis
Co-stars: Chevy Chase Rodney Dangerfield Bill Murray

BARBARA HALE *(Mother Of William Katt)*

1940   THE BOY WITH GREEN HAIR
Director: Joseph Losey
Co-stars: Dean Stockwell Robert Ryan Pat O'Brien

1943   **HIGHER AND HIGHER**
Director: Tim Whelan
Co-stars: Frank Sinatra Michelle Morgan Jack Haley

1994   **HEAVENLY DAYS**
Director: Howard Estabrook
Co-stars: Jim Jordan Eugene Pallette Gordon Oliver Marion Jordan

1945   **FIRST YANK INTO TOKYO**
Director: Gordon Douglas
Co-stars: Tom Neal Richard Loo Marc Cramer Keye Luke

1945   **WEST OF THE PECOS**
Director: Phil Rosen
Co-stars: Robert Mitchum Richard Martin Thurston Hall

1946   **LADY LUCK**
Director: Edwin Marin
Co-stars: Robert Young Frank Morgan James Gleason

1947   **A LIKELY STORY**
Director: H.C. Potter
Co-stars: Bill Williams Lanny Rees Sam Levene Nestor Paiva

1949   **THE CLAY PIGEON**
Director: Richard Fleischer
Co-stars: Bill Williams Richard Quine Frank Fenton

1949   **JOLSON SINGS AGAIN**
Director: Henry Levin
Co-stars: Larry Parks William Demarest Tamara Shayne

1949   **THE WINDOW**
Director: Ted Tetzlaff
Co-stars: Bobby Driscoll Arthur Kennedy Ruth Roman Paul Stewart

1950   **THE JACKPOT**
Director: Walter Lang
Co-stars: James Stewart Natalie Wood James Gleason Fred Clark

1950   **AND BABY MAKES THREE**
Director: Henry Levin
Co-stars: Robert Young Robert Hutton Billie Burke

1951   **LORNA DOONE**
Director: Phil Karlson
Co-stars: Richard Greene Anne Howard William Bishop

1952   **LAST OF THE COMANCHES**
Director: Andre De Toth
Co-stars: Broderick Crawford Lloyd Bridges

1952   **THE FIRST TIME**
Director: Frank Tashlin
Co-stars: Robert Cummings Jeff Donnell Mona Barrie

1953   **A LION IS IN THE STREETS**
Director: Raoul Walsh
Co-stars: James Cagney Jeanne Cagney Anne Francis

1953   **THE LONE HAND**
Director: George Sherman
Co-stars: Joel McCrea Alex Nicol Charles Drake James Arness

1953   **SEMINOLE**
Director: Budd Boetticher
Co-stars: Rock Hudson Anthony Quinn Richard Carlson Lee Marvin

1955   **UNCHAINED**
Director: Hall Bartlett
Co-stars: Chester Morris Elroy Hirsch Peggy Knudson

1955   **THE FAR HORIZONS**
Director: Rudolph Mate
Co-stars: Fred MacMurray Charlton Heston Donna Reed

1956   **THE HOUSTON STORY**
Director: William Castle
Co-stars: Gene Barry Edward Arnold Frank Jenks

1956   **THE OKLAHOMAN**
Director: Francis Lyon
Co-stars: Joel McCrea Brad Dexter Gloria Talbot Michael Pate

1956   **7TH CAVALRY**
Director: Joseph Lewis
Co-stars: Randolph Scott Jeannettte Nolan Frank Faylen

1957   **SLIM CARTER**
Director: Richard Bartlett
Co-stars: Jock Mahoney Julie Adams Tim Hovey Ben Johnson

1968   **BUCKSKIN**
Director: Michael Moore
Co-stars: Barry Sullivan Wendell Corey Joan Caulfield

1970   **AIRPORT**
Director: George Seaton
Co-stars: Burt Lancaster Dean Martin George Kennedy Jean Seberg

1975   **THE GIANT SPIDER INVASION**
Director: Bill Rebane
Co-stars: Steve Brodie Leslie Parrish

1978   **BIG WEDNESDAY**
Director: John Millius
Co-stars: Jan-Michael Vincent William Katt Gary Busey

1985   **PERRY MASON RETURNS**
Director: Ron Satlof
Co-stars: Raymond Burr William Katt Patrick O'Neal

1986   **PERRY MASON.:**
THE CASE OF THE NOTORIOUS NUN
Director: Ron Satlof
Co-stars: Timothy Bottoms Michele Greene

1986   **PERRY MASON:**
THE CASE OF THE SHOOTING STAR
Director: Ron Satlof
Co-stars: William Katt Joe Penny Ron Glass

1987   **PERRY MASON:**
THE CASE OF THE LOST LOVE
Director: Ron Satlof
Co-stars: Jean Simmons Gene Barry

1987   **PERRY MASON:**
THE CASE OF THE MURDERED MADAM
Director: Ron Satlof
Co-stars: Patty Duke Erin Gray Ann Jillian

1987   **PERRY MASON: THE CASE OF THE**
SCANDALOUS SCOUNDREL
Director: Christian Nyby
Co-stars: Robert Guillaum Raymond Burr

1987   **PERRY MASON:**
THE CASE OF THE SINISTER SPIRIT
Director: Richard Lang
Co-stars: Dwight Schultz Robert Stack

1989   **PERRY MASON:**
THE CASE OF THE ALL-STAR ASSASSIN
Director: Christian Nyby
Co-stars: Alexander Paul Pernell Roberts

1989   **PERRY MASON:**
THE CASE OF THE AVENGING AGE
Director: Christian Nyby
Co-stars: Patty Duke Erin Gray Larry Wilcox

1989   **PERRY MASON:**
THE CASE OF THE MUSICAL MURDER
Director: Christian Nyby
Co-stars: William R. Moses Debbie Reynolds

1989   **PERRY MASON:**
THE CASE OF THE POISONED PEN
Director: Christian Nyby
Co-stars: Tony LoBianco Cindy Williams David Warner

1990   **PERRY MASON: THE CASE OF THE DESPERATE DECEPTION**
Director: Christian Nyby
Co-stars: Ian McShane Ian Bannen Yvette Mimieux

1990   **PERRY MASON: THE CASE OF THE SILENCED SINGER**
Director: Ron Satlof
Co-stars: Vanessa Williams Tim Reid

1992   **PERRY MASON: THE CASE OF THE POSTHUMOUS PAINTER**
Director: Christian Nyby
Co-stars: David Soul William R. Moses

BINNIE HALE *(Sister Of Sonnie Hale)*

1934   **THE PHANTOM LIGHT**
Director: Michael Powell
Co-stars: Gordon Harker Ian Hunter Donald Calthrop

1935   **HYDE PARK CORNER**
Director: Sinclair Hill
Co-stars: Gordon Harker Eric Portman Donald Wolfit

1936   **LOVE FROM A STRANGER**
Director: Rowland Lee
Co-stars: Ann Harding Basil Rathbone Bruce Seton

DIANA HALE *(Child)*

1943   **THE GOOD FELLOWS**
Director: Jo Graham
Co-stars: Cecil Kellaway Helen Walker James Brown

1945   **THUNDER, SON OF FLICKA**
Director: Louis King
Co-stars: Roddy McDowall Preston Foster Rita Johnson

DOROTHY HALE

1930   **THE LAUGHING LADY**
Co-star: Raymond Walburn

ELVI HALE

1957   **TRUE AS A TURTLE**
Director: Wendy Toye
Co-stars: John Gregson June Thorburn Cecil Parker

1959   **THE NAVY LARK**
Director: Gordon Parry
Co-stars: Cecil Parker Leslie Phillips Ronald Shiner

1970   **THE SIX WIVES OF HENRY VIII**
Director: John Glenister
Co-stars: Keith Michel Annette Crosbie Dorothy Tutin

GEORGIA HALE

1925   **THE GOLD RUSH**
Director: Charles Chaplin
Co-stars: Charles Chaplin Mack Swain Tom Murray

1925   **THE SALVATION HUNTERS**
Director: Josef Von Sternberg
Co-stars: George K. Arthur Bruce Guerin

GEORGINA HALE

1973   **MAHLER**
Director: Ken Russell
Co-stars: Robert Powell Lee Montague Rosalie Crutchley

1973   **BUTLEY**
Director: Harold Pinter
Co-stars: Alan Bates Jessica Tandy Susan Engel

1978   **SWEENEY 2**
Director: Tom Clegg
Co-stars: John Thaw Dennis Waterman Denholm Elliott

1979   **THE WORLD IS FULL OF MARRIED MEN**
Director: Robert Young
Co-stars: Carroll Baker Paul Nicholas

1980   **McVICAR**
Director: Tom Clegg
Co-stars: Roger Daltrey Adam Fatih Cheryl Campbell

1986   **CASTAWAY**
Director: Nicholas Roeg
Co-stars: Oliver Reed Amanda Donohue Frances Barber

1989   **MURDER ON THE MOON**
Director: Michael Lindsay-Hogg
Co-stars: Brigitte Nielsen Julian Sands Brian Cox

1994   **BEYOND BEDLAM**
Director: Vadim Jean
Co-stars: Craig Fairbrass Elizabeth Hurley

JEAN HALE

1964   **PSYCHOMANIA**
Director: Richard Hilliard
Co-stars: Lee Philips Shepperd Strudwick James Farantino

1965   **TAGGART**
Director: R.G. Springsteen
Co-stars: Tony Young Dan Duryea David Carradine

1967   **THE ST. VALENTINE'S DAY MASSACRE**
Director: Roger Corman
Co-stars: Jason Robards George Segal

1967   **IN LIKE FLINT**
Director: Gordon Douglas
Co-stars: James Coburn Lee J. Cobb Anna Lee

LOUISE CLOSSER HALE

1929   **PARIS**
Director: Clarence Badger
Co-stars: Jack Buchanan Irene Bordoni Jason Robards

1929   **THE HOLE IN THE WALL**
Director: Robert Florey
Co-stars: Edward G. Robinson Claudette Colbert

1930   **BIG BOY**
Director: Alan Crosland
Co-stars: Al Jolson Noah Beery Claudia Dell

1931   **DEVOTION**
Director: Robert Milton
Co-stars: Leslie Howard Ann Harding Robert Williams

1931   **DADDY LONG LEGS**
Director: Alfred Santell
Co-stars: Janet Gaynor Warner Baxter Una Merkel

1931   **CAPTAIN APPLEJACK**
Director: Hobart Henley
Co-stars: John Halliday Kay Strozzi Mary Brian

1931   **BORN TO LOVE**
Director: Paul Stein
Co-stars: Constance Bennett Joel McCrea Paul Cavanagh

1931   **PLATINUM BLONDE**
Director: Frank Capra
Co-stars: Robert Williams Jean Harlow Loretta Young

1931   **REBOUND**
Director: E.H. Griffith
Co-stars: Robert Williams Ina Claire Myrna Loy

1932   **SHANGHAI EXPRESS**
Director: Josef Von Sternberg
Co-stars: Marlene Dietrich Clive Brook Anna May Wong

1932   **THE SON-DAUGHTER**
Director: Clarence Brown
Co-stars: Ramon Navarro Helen Hayes Lewis Stone

1932 REBECCA OF SUNNYBROOK FARM
Director: Alfred Santell
Co-stars: Marion Nixon Ralph Bellamy Mae Marsh

1932 THE MAN WHO PLAYED GOD
Director: John Adolphi
Co-stars: George Arliss Violet Hemming Bette Davis

1932 FAITHLESS
Director: Harry Beaumont
Co-stars: Tallulah Bankhead Robert Montgomery Hugh Herbert

1933 THE BARBARIAN
Director: Sam Wood
Co-stars: Ramon Navarro Myrna Loy Reginald Denny

1933 ANOTHER LANGUAGE
Director: Edward Griffith
Co-stars: Helen Haayes Robert Montgomery John Beal

1933 DINNER AT EIGHT
Director: George Cukor
Co-stars: Wallace Beery Marie Dressler Jean Harlow

1933 TODAY WE LIVE
Director: Howard Hawks
Co-stars: Joan Crawford Gary Cooper Robert Young

1933 THE WHITE SISTER
Director: Victor Fleming
Co-stars: Clark Gable Helen Hayes Lewis Stone

ALAINA REED HALL

1992 DEATH BECOMES HER
Director: Robert Zemeckis
Co-stars: Meryl Streep Goldie Hawn Bruce Willis

ANGELA HALL

1992 THE PLAYER
Director: Robert Altman
Co-stars: Tim Robbins Greta Scacchi Whoopi Goldberg

DAISY HALL

1990 I'M DANGEROUS TONIGHT
Director: Tobe Hooper
Co-stars: Anthony Perkins Dee Wallace

1991 TRIPLE BOGIE ON A FIVE PAR HOLE
Director: Amos Poe
Co-stars: Eric Mitchell Robbie Coltrane

DEIDRE HALL

1989 TAKE MY DAUGHTERS, PLEASE
Director: Larry Elikann
Co-stars: Rue McClanahan Kim Delaney Susan Ruttan

1989 PERRY MASON:
THE CASE OF THE ALL-STAR ASSASSIN
Director: Christian Nyby
Co-star: Raymond Burr Pernell Roberts

1993 WOMAN ON THE LEDGE
Director: Chris Thomson
Co-stars: Colleen Zink Pinter Josh Taylor

DELORES HALL

1992 LEAP OF FAITH
Director: Richard Pearce
Co-stars: Steve Martin Debra Winger Lolita Davidovitch

EVELYN HALL

1930 THE RETURN OF DR. FU MANCHU
Director: Rowland Lee
Co-stars: Warner Oland Neil Hamilton Jean Arthur

GITA HALL

1958 WOLF LARSEN
Director: Harmon Jones
Co-stars: Barry Sullivan Peter Graves Thayer David

GRAYSON HALL
Nominated For Best Supporting Actress In 1964 For "The Night Of The Iguana"

1964 THE NIGHT OF THE IGUANA
Director: John Huston
Co-stars: Richard Burton Ava Gardner Sue Lyon

IRMA P. HALL

1998 SOUL FOOD
Director: George Tillman Jnr.
Co-stars: Vanessa Williams Gina Ravera Nia Long

HARRIET HALL

1987 FOXFIRE
Director: Jud Taylor
Co-stars: Jessica Tandy Hume Cronyn John Denver

1987 THE WITCHING OF BEN WAGNER
Director: Paul Emmett
Co-star: Sam Bottoms

JERRY HALL

1980 WILLIE AND PHIL
Director: Paul Mazursky
Co-stars: Michael Ontkean Margot Kidder Ray Sharkey

1989 BATMAN
Director: Tim Burton
Co-stars: Michael Keaton Jack Nicholson Kim Basinger

1992 FREEJACK
Director: Geoff Murray
Co-stars: Emilio Estevez Mick Jagger Rene Russo

JUANITA HALL

1958 SOUTH PACIFIC
Director: Joshua Logan
Co-stars: Mitzi Gaynor Rossano Brazzi John Kerr

1961 FLOWER DRUM SONG
Director: Henry Koster
Co-stars: Nancy Kwan James Shigeta Benson Fong

LOIS HALL

1991 DEAD AGAIN
Director: Kenneth Branagh
Co-stars: Andy Garcia Emma Thompson Richard Easton

MARIAN HALL

1942 THE GORILLA MAN
Director: Ross Lederman
Co-stars: John Loder Ruth Ford Paul Cavanagh

1942 THE HIDDEN HAND
Director: Ben Stoloff
Co-stars: Craig Stevens Elizabeth Fraser Julie Bishop

REBECCA HALL *(Daughter Of Peter Hall)*

1991 THE CAMOMILE LAWN
Director: Peter Hall
Co-stars: Felicity Kendall Jennifer Ehle Tara Fitzgerald

RUTH HALL

1932 THE KID FROM SPAIN
Director: Leo McCarey
Co-stars: Eddie Cantor Lyda Roberti Robert Young

1932   MISS PINKERTON
Director: Lloyd Bacon
Co-stars: Joan Blondell George Brent Mae Madison

1932   RIDE HIM COWBOY
Director: Fred Allen
Co-stars: John Wayne Otis Harlan Henry B. Walthall

1932   BETWEEN FIGHTING MEN
Co-star: Ken Maynard

1938   MEET THE MAYOR
Director: Ralph Ceder
Co-stars: Frank Fay George Meeker Berton Churchill

LILLIAN HALL-DAVIES

1927   THE RING
Director: Alfred Hitchcock
Co-stars: Carl Brisson Ian Hunter Gordon Harker

1928   THE FARMER'S WIFE
Director: Alfred Hitchcock
Co-stars: Jameson Thomas Gordon Harker Maud Gill

ELAINE HALLAM

1993   BLACK DAISIES FOR THE BRIDE
Director: Peter Symes
Co-stars: Cathryn Bradshaw Maria Bovino

JANE HALLAREN

1981   MODERN ROMANCE
Director: Albert Brooks
Co-stars: Albert Brooks Kathryn Harrold Bruno Kirby

1983   LIANNA
Director: John Sayles
Co-stars: Linda Griffiths Jon De Vries Jo Henderson

1988   A NIGHT IN THE LIFE OF JIMMY REARDON
Director: William Richert
Co-stars: River Phoenix Ann Magnusson

1992   MY GIRL
Director: Howard Zieff
Co-stars: Anna Chlumsky Macauley Culkin Dan Ackroyd

MAY HALLATT

1945   PAINTED BOATS
Director: Charles Crighton
Co-stars: Jenny Laird Bill Blewitt Robert Griffith

1946   SEPARATE TABLES
Director: Delbert Mann
Co-stars: Burt Lancaster David Niven Rita Hayworth

1955   THE GOLD EXPRESS
Director: Guy Fergusson
Co-stars: Vernon Gray Ann Walford Delphi Lawrence

1958   BLACK NARCISSUS
Director: Michael Powell
Co-stars: Deborah Kerr David Farrar Jean Simmons Sabu

DARIA HALPRIN

1969   ZABRISKIE POINT
Director: Michaelangelo Antonioni
Co-stars: Mark Frechette Rod Taylor Paul Fix

1971   THE JERUSALEM FILE
Director: John Flynn
Co-stars: Bruce Davison Nicol Williamson Ian Hendry

MARGARET HALSTAN

1952   THE HOLLY AND THE IVY
Director: George More O'Ferrall
Co-stars: Ralph Richardson Celia Johnson

MIE HAMA

1967   YOU ONLY LIVE TWICE
Director: Lewis Gilbert
Co-stars: Sean Connery Charles Gray Lois Maxwell

FATEN HAMAMA

1963   CAIRO
Director: Wolf Rilla
Co-stars: George Sanders Richard Johnson Walter Rilla

VERONICA HAMEL

1976   CARQUAKE
Director: Paul Bartel
Co-stars: David Carradine Bill McKinney Judy Canova

1979   BEYOND THE POSEIDON ADVENTURE
Director: Irwin Allen
Co-stars: Michael Caine Sally Field Telly Savalas

1983   SESSIONS
Director: Richard Pearce
Co-stars: Jill Eikenberry Jefrey DeMunn George Coe

1988   A NEW LIFE
Director: Alan Alda
Co-stars: Alan Alda Ann-Margret John Shea

1991   FILOFAX
Director: Arthur Hiller
Co-stars: James Belushi Charles Grodin Anne De Salvo

1994   A CHILD'S CRY FOR HELP
Director: Sandor Stern
Co-stars: Pam Dawber Daniel Hugh Kelly

1994   SECRETS
Director: Jud Taylor
Co-stars: Richard Kiley Shae D'lyn

1996   TALK TO ME

BETTY HAMILTON

1934   THE PRIVATE LIFE OF DON JUAN
Director: Alexander Korda
Co-stars: Douglas Fairbanks Merle Oberon

CARRIE HAMILTON *(Daughter Of Carol Burnett)*

1988   HOSTAGE
Director: Peter Levin
Co-stars: Carol Burnett Annette Bening Leon Russom

1988   TOKYO POP
Director: Fran Rubel Kazui
Co-stars: Yutaka Tadokoro Tetsuro Tamba

1992   COOL WORLD
Director: Ralph Bakshi
Co-stars: Kim Basinger Gabriel Byrne Brad Pitt

GAY HAMILTON

1967   A CHALLENGE FOR ROBIN HOOD
Director: Pennington Richards
Co-stars: Barrie Ingham James Hayter

JANE HAMILTON

1992   RUBY
Director: John MacKenzie
Co-stars: Danny Aiello Sherilyn Fenn Frank Orsatti

KIPP HAMILTON

1960   THE UNFORGIVEN
Director: John Huston
Co-stars: Burt Lancaster Audrey Hepburn Audie Murphy

LILLIAN HAMILTON

1950   OUTRAGE
Director: Ida Lupino
Co-stars: Mala Powers Tod Andrews Robert Clarke

LINDA HAMILTON

1982   COUNTRY GOLD
Director: Gilbert Cates
Co-stars: Loni Anderson Earl Holliman Dennis Dugan

1984   CHILDREN OF THE CORN
Director: Fritz Kiersch
Co-stars: Peter Horton R.G. Armstrong

1984   THE TERMINATOR
Director: James Cameron
Co-stars: Arnold Schwarzeneger Michael Biehn Paul Winfield

1985   BLACK MOON RISING
Director: Harley Cokliss
Co-stars: Tommy Lee Jones Robert Vaughn Keenan Wynn

1985   SEXPIONAGE
Director: Don Taylor
Co-stars: Sally Kellerman Hunt Block Viveca Lindfors Geena Davis

1986   KING KONG LIVES!
Director: John Guillermin
Co-stars: Peter Elliott George Yiasomi

1988   GO TO THE LIGHT
Director: Mike Robe
Co-stars: Richard Thomas Piper Laurie Ned Beatty Joshua Harris

1990   MR. DESTINY
Director: James Orr
Co-stars: James Belushi Michael Caine Jon Lovitz Rene Russo

1991   TERMINATOR 2: JUDGEMENT DAY
Director: James Cameron
Co-stars: Arnold Schwarzeneger Edward Furlong

1994   SILENT FALL
Director: Bruce Beresford
Co-stars: Richard Dreyfuss John Lithgow Ben Faulkner

1994   SEPARATE LIVES
Director: David Madden
Co-star: James Belushi

1997   DANTE'S PEAK
Director: Roger Donaldson
Co-star: Pierce Brosnan Charles Hallahan

1997   SHADOW CONSPIRACY
Co-stars: Charlie Sheen Donald Sutherland

LOIS HAMILTON

1985   SUMMER RENTAL
Director: Carl Reiner
Co-stars: John Candy Karen Austin Richard Crenna

1986   ARMED RESCUE
Director: Fred Olen Ray
Co-stars: David Carradine Lee Van Cleef Mako

MARGARET HAMILTON

1933   ANOTHER LANGUAGE
Director: Edward Griffith
Co-stars: Helen Hayes Robert Montgomery John Beal

1934   BROADWAY BILL
Director: Frank Capra
Co-stars: Warner Baxter Walter Connolly Myrna Loy

1934   HAT, COAT AND GLOVES
Director: Worthington Miner
Co-stars: Ricardo Cortez Barbara Robbins John Beal

1935   CHATTERBOX
Director: George Nicholls
Co-stars: Anne Shirley Phillips Holmes Edward Ellis

1935   THE FARMER TAKES A WIFE
Director: Victor Fleming
Co-stars: Henry Fonda Janet Gaynor Charles Bickford

1935   WAY DOWN EAST
Director: Henry King
Co-stars: Henry Fonda Rochelle Hudson Slim Summerville

1936   THE MOON'S OUR HOME
Director: William Seiter
Co-stars: Henry Fonda Margaret Sullavan Beulah Bondi

1936   THESE THREE
Director: William Wyler
Co-stars: Merle Oberon Miriam Hopkins Joel McCrea

1936   THE WITNESS CHAIR
Director: George Nicholls
Co-stars: Ann Harding Walter Abel Douglass Dumbrille

1937   THE GOOD OLD SOAK
Director: Walter Ruben
Co-stars: Wallace Beery Una Merkel Janet Beecher

1937   I'LL TAKE ROMANCE
Director: Edward Griffith
Co-stars: Grace Moore Melvyn Douglas Helen Westley

1937   LAUGHING AT TROUBLE
Director: Frank Strayer
Co-stars: Jane Darwell Sara Haden John Carradine

1937   SARATOGA
Director: Jack Conway
Co-stars: Clark Gable Jean Harlow Walter Pidgeon

1937   MOUNTAIN JUSTICE
Director: Michael Curtiz
Co-stars: Josephine Hutchinson George Brent Mona Barrie

1937   NOTHING SACRED
Director: William Wellman
Co-stars: Fredric March Carole Lombard Charles Winninger

1937   YOU ONLY LIVE ONCE
Director: Fritz Lang
Co-stars: Henry Fonda Sylvia Sidney Barton MacLane

1938   THE ADVENTURES OF TOM SAYWER
Director: Norman Taurog
Co-stars: Tommy Kelly Walter Brennan May Robson

1938   BREAKING THE ICE
Director: Edward Cline
Co-stars: Bobby Breen Charles Ruggles Dolores Costello

1938   FOUR'S A CROWD
Director: Michael Curtiz
Co-stars: Errol Flynn Rosalind Russell Olivia De Havilland

1938   MOTHER CAREY'S CHICKENS
Director: Rowland Lee
Co-stars: Anne Shirley Ruby Keeler Fay Bainter

1938   STABLEMATES
Director: Sam Wood
Co-stars: Wallace Beery Mickey Rooney Marjorie Gateson

1939   ANGELS WASH THEIR FACES
Director: Ray Enright
Co-stars: Ann Sheridan Ronald Reagan Dead End Kids

1939   THE WIZARD OF OZ
Director: Victor Fleming
Co-stars: Judy Garland Ray Bolger Jack Haley Bert Lahr

1940   MY LITTLE CHICKADEE
Director: Edward Cline
Co-stars: Mae West W.C. Fields Dick Foran

1940 **THE VILLAIN STILL PURSUED HER**
Director: Edward Cline
Co-stars: Buster Keaton Alan Mowbray Anita Louise

1941 **THE INVISIBLE WOMAN**
Director: Edward Sutherland
Co-stars: John Barrymore Charles Ruggles Virginia Bruce

1942 **THE AFFAIRS OF MARTHA**
Director: Jules Dassin
Co-stars: Marsha Hunt Richard Carlson Spring Byington

1942 **TWIN BEDS**
Director: Tim Whelan
Co-stars: George Brent Joan Bennett Mischa Auer

1943 **CITY WITHOUT MEN**
Director: Sidney Salkow
Co-stars: Linda Darnell Sara Allgood Glenda Farrell

1943 **JOHNNY COME LATELY**
Director: William Howard
Co-stars: James Cagney Grace George Marjorie Main

1944 **GUEST IN THE HOUSE**
Director: John Brahm
Co-stars: Anne Baxter Ralph Bellamy Aline MacMahon

1945 **GEORGE WHITE'S SCANDALS**
Director: Felix Feist
Co-stars: Joan Davis Jack Haley Jane Greer

1947 **DISHONOURED LADY**
Director: Robert Stevenson
Co-stars: Hedy Lamarr John Loder Dennis O'Keefe

1947 **DRIFTWOOD**
Director: Allan Dwan
Co-stars: Natalie Wood Dean Jagger Walter Brennan

1947 **MAD WEDNESDAY**
Director: Preston Sturges
Co-stars: Harold Lloyd Jimmy Conklin Franklin Pangborn

1949 **THE BEAUTIFUL BLOND FROM BASHFUL BEND**
Director: Preston Sturges
Co-stars: Betty Grable Cesar Romero

1949 **THE RED PONY**
Director: Lewis Milestone
Co-stars: Peter Miles Robert Mitchum Myrna Loy

1950 **RIDING HIGH**
Director: Frank Capra
Co-stars: Bing Crosby Coleen Gray Charles Bickford

1950 **WABASH AVENUE**
Director: Henry Koster
Co-stars: Betty Grable Victor Mature Phil Harris

1960 **13 GHOSTS**
Director: William Castle
Co-stars: Charles Herbert Jo Morrow Rosemary De Camp

1967 **ROSIE!**
Director: David Lowell Rich
Co-stars: Rosalind Russell Brian Aherne Sandra Dee

1969 **ANGEL IN MY POCKET**
Director: Alan Rafkin
Co-stars: Andy Griffith Kay Medford Edgar Buchanan

1970 **BREWSTER McCLOUD**
Director: Robert Altman
Co-stars: Bud Cort Sally Kellerman Shelley Duvall

1971 **THE ANDERSON TAPES**
Director: Sidney Lumet
Co-stars: Sean Connery Martin Balsam Dyan Cannon

1972 **THE NIGHT STRANGLER**
Director: Dan Curtis
Co-stars: Darren McGavin Simon Oakland Jo Ann Pflug

1974 **JOURNEY BACK TO OZ** *(Voice) Made In 1964*
Director: Hal Sutherland
Co-stars: Liza Minnelli Mickey Rooney

PATRICIA HAMILTON

1985 **ANNE OF GREEN GABLES**
Director: Kevin Sullivan
Co-stars: Megan Follows Colleen Dewhurst Richard Farnsworth

SUZANNA HAMILTON *(Zanna) (Child)*

1974 **SWALLOWS AND AMAZONS**
Director: Claude Watham
Co-stars: Virginia McKenna Ronald Fraser Simon West

1982 **BRIMSTONE AND TREACLE**
Director: Richard Lochraine
Co-stars: Sting Denholm Elliott Joan Plowright

1984 **1984**
Director: Michael Radford
Co-stars: Richard Burton John Hurt Gregor Fisher

1985 **WETHERBY**
Director: David Hare
Co-stars: Vanessa Redgrave Ian Holm Judi Dench

1985 **OUT OF AFRICA**
Director: Sydney Pollack
Co-stars: Meryl Streep Robert Redford Michael Kitchen

1990 **NEVER COME BACK**
Director: Ben Bolt
Co-stars: Nathaniel Parker James Fox Martin Clunes

1990 **MURDER EAST, MURDER WEST**
Director: Peter Smith
Co-stars: Jeroen Krabbe Joanne Pearce Alexandra Pigg

1990 **SMALL ZONES**
Director: Michael Whyte
Co-stars: Catherine Neilson Sean Bean Stephanie Turner

1992 **TALES OF A VAMPIRE**
Director: Shimako Sato
Co-stars: Julian Sands Kenneth Cranham Marian Diamond

1992 **INSPECTOR MORSE: ABSOLUTE CONVICTION**
Director: Antonia Bird
Co-stars: John Thaw Diana Quick Sean Bean

DILYS HAMLETT

1971 **ASSAULT**
Director: Sidney Hayers
Co-stars: Frank Finlay Suzy Kendall Freddie Jones

1974 **DIAGNOSIS: MURDER**
Director: Sidney Hayers
Co-stars: Christopher Lee Judy Geeson Jon Finch

1975 **WHAT CHANGED CHARLEY FARTHING?**
Director: Sidney Hayers
Co-stars: Doug McClure Hayley Mills

JUNE HAMMERSMITH

1956 **EDGE OF HELL**
Director: Hugo Haas
Co-stars: Hugo Haas Francesca De Scaffa Ken Carlton

ELLEN HAMMILL

1985 **JOEY**
Director: Joseph Ellison
Co-stars: Neill Barry James Quinn Elisa Heinsohn

GABRIELLE HAMMOND

1992 THE END OF THE GOLDEN WEATHER
Director: Ian Mune
Co-stars: Stephen Fulford Stephen Papps Paul Gittins

KAY HAMMOND *(Daughter Of Sir Guy Standing)*

1930 ABRAHAM LINCOLN
Director: D.W. Griffith
Co-stars: Walter Huston Una Merkel Russell Simpson

1931 OUT OF THE BLUE
Director: Gene Gerard
Co-stars: Jessie Matthews Binnie Barnes Gene Gerard

1931 CARNIVAL
Director: Herbert Wilcox
Co-stars: Matheson Lang Dorothy Bouchier Joseph Schildkraut

1933 DOUBLE HARNESS
Director: John Cromwell
Co-stars: Ann Harding William Powell Henry Stephenson

1933 BITTER SWEET
Director: Herbert Wilcox
Co-stars: Anna Neagle Fernand Gravet Hugh Williams

1933 SLEEPING CAR
Director: Anatole Litvak
Co-stars: Madeleine Carroll Ivor Novello

1941 JEANNIE
Director: Harold French
Co-stars: Barbara Mullen Michael Redgrave Wilfrid Lawson

1945 BLITHE SPIRIT
Director: David Lean
Co-stars: Rex Harrison Constance Cummings Margaret Rutherford

1947 CALL OF THE BLOOD
Director: John Clements
Co-stars: John Clements John Justin Lea Padovani Robert Ritti

1960 FIVE GOLDEN HOURS
Director: Mario Zampi
Co-stars: Ernie Kovacs Cyd Charisse George Sanders

NORAH HAMMOND

1957 HOUSE IN THE WOODS
Director: Maxwell Munden
Co-stars: Ronald Howard Patricia Roc Michael Gough

VIRGINIA HAMMOND

1930 ANYBODY'S WOMAN
Director: Dorothy Arzner
Co-stars: Ruth Chatterton Clive Brook Paul Lukas

1932 CABIN IN THE COTTON
Director: Michael Curtiz
Co-stars: Richard Barthelmess Bette Davis Dorothy Jordan

1936 ROMEO AND JULIET
Director: George Cukor
Co-stars: Leslie Howard Norma Shearer John Barrymore

OLIVIA HAMNETT

1977 THE LAST WAVE
Director: Peter Weir
Co-stars: Richard Chamberlain David Gulpil Vivean Gray

1977 PLUNGE INTO DARKNESS
Director: Peter Maxwell
Co-stars: Bruce Barry Tom Richards Wallace Eaton

1980 THE EARTHLING
Director: Peter Collinson
Co-stars: William Holden Ricky Schroder Jack Thompson

SUSAN HAMPSHIRE *(Child)*

1947 THE WOMAN IN THE HALL
Director: Jack Lee
Co-stars: Jean Simmons Ursula Jeans Cecil Parker

1961 DURING ONE NIGHT
Director: Sidney Furie
Co-stars: Don Borisenko Sean Sullivan Joy Webster

1963 THE THREE LIVES OF THOMASINA
Director: Don Chaffey
Co-stars: Patrick McGoohan Karen Dotrice

1964 WONDERFUL LIFE
Director: Sidney Furie
Co-stars: Cliff Richard Walter Slezak Una Stubbs Melvyn Hayes

1964 NIGHT MUST FALL
Director: Karel Reisz
Co-stars: Albert Finney Mona Washbourne Sheila Hancock

1966 THE TRYGON FACTOR
Director: Cyril Frankel
Co-stars: Stewart Granger Cathleen Nesbitt Robert Morley

1966 THE FIGHTING PRINCE OF DONEGAL
Director: Michael O'Herlihy
Co-stars: Peter McEnery Tom Adams

1969 THE VIOLENT ENEMY
Director: Don Sharp
Co-stars: Tom Bell Ed Begley Noel Purcell Michael Standing

1969 MONTE CARLO OR BUST
Director: Ken Annakin
Co-stars: Peter Cook Dudley Moore Tony Curtis Terry-Thomas

1970 DAVID COPPERFIELD
Director: Delbert Mann
Co-stars: Robin Phillips Edith Evans Laurence Olivier

1971 A TIME FOR LOVING
Director: Christopher Miles
Co-stars: Mel Ferrer Joanna Shimkus Britt Ekland

1972 NEITHER THE SEA NOR THE SAND
Director: Fred Burnley
Co-stars: Michael Petrovitch Frank Finlay

1972 LIVING FREE
Director: Jack Couffer
Co-stars: Nigel Davenport Geoffrey Keen

GRAYCE HAMPTON

1930 THE BAT WHISPERS
Director: Roland West
Co-stars: Chester Morris Una Merkel Maude Eburne

HOPE HAMPTON

1923 HOLLYWOOD
Director: James Cruze
Co-stars: Hope Drown Luke Cosgrave Eleanor Lawson

1938 ROAD TO RENO
Director: S. Sylvan Simon
Co-stars: Randolph Scott Glenda Farrell Helen Broderick

RUTH HAMPTON

1954 RICHOCHET ROMANCE
Director: Charles Lamont
Co-stars: Marjorie Main Chill Wills Rudy Vallee

TERRI HANAUER

1990 COMMUNION
Director: Philippe Mora
Co-stars: Christopher Walken Lindsay Crouse Frances Sternhagen

BARBARA HANCOCK

1968   FINIAN'S RAINBOW
Director: Francis Coppola
Co-stars: Fred Astaire Petula Clark Tommy Steele

LUCY HANCOCK

1987   CARIANI AND THE COURTESANS
Director: Leslie Megahy
Co-stars: Paul McGann Michael Gough Diana Quick

SHEILA HANCOCK (*Married John Thaw*)

1960   LIGHT UP THE SKY
Director: Lewis Gilbert
Co-stars: Ian Carmichael Tommy Steel Benny Hill

1962   TWICE ROUND THE DAFFODILS
Director: Gerald Thomas
Co-stars: Juliet Mills Donald Sinden Jill Ireland

1962   THE GIRL ON THE BOAT
Director: Henry Kaplan
Co-stars: Norman Wisdom Richard Briers Millicent Martin

1964   THE MOON SPINERS
Director: James Neilson
Co-stars: Hayley Mills Peter McEnery Eli Wallach Pola Negri

1964   NIGHT MUST FALL
Director: Karl Reisz
Co-stars: Albert Finney Susan Hampshire Mona Washbourne

1968   THE ANNIVERSARY
Director: Roy Ward Baker
Co-stars: Bette Davis Jack Hedley James Cossins

1970   TAKE A GIRL LIKE YOU
Director: Jonathan Miller
Co-stars: Hayley Mills Oliver Reed Noel Harrison

1980   THE WILDCATS OF ST. TRINIANS
Director: Frank Launder
Co-stars: Michael Hordern Rodney Bewes

1987   THE LOVE CHILD
Director: Robert Smith
Co-stars: Peter Capaldi Percy Herbert Lesley Sharp

1988   HAWKS
Director: Robert Ellis
Co-stars: Timothy Dalton Anthony Edwards Janet McTeer

1988   BUSTER
Director: David Green
Co-stars: Phil Collins Julie Walters Larry Lamb Anthony Quayle

1989   ASTERIX AND THE BIG FIGHT
Director: Phillipe Grimond
Co-stars: Ron Moody Bernard Bresslaw Bill Oddie

1994   A BUSINESS AFFAIR
Director: Charlotte Brandstrom
Co-stars: Christopher Walken Jonathan Price

1990   MY KINGDOM FOR A HORSE
Director: Barbara Rennie
Co-stars: Sean Bean Bryan Pringle Jane Clifford

1990   THREE MEN AND A LITTLE LADY
Director: Emile Ardolino
Co-stars: Tom Selleck Ted Danson Nancy Travis

1996   LOVE AND DEATH ON LONG ISLAND
Director: Richard Kwietniowski
Co-stars: John Hurt Jason Priestley

IRENE HANDL

1938   STRANGE BORDERS
Director: Herbert Mason
Co-stars: Tom Walls Renee Saint-Cyr Googie Withers

1939   MRS. PYM OF SCOTLAND YARD
Director: Fred Elles
Co-stars: Mary Clare Edward Lexy Nigel Patrick

1940   DR. O'DOWD
Director: Herbert Mason
Co-stars: Shaun Glenville Peggy Cummings Patricia Roc

1940   GASBAGS
Director: Marcel Varnel
Co-stars: Crazy Gang Moore Marriott Wally Patch

1940   GEORGE AND MARGARET
Director: George King
Co-stars: Judy Kelly Marie Lohr Oliver Wakefield

1940   THE GIRL IN THE NEWS
Director: Carol Reed
Co-stars: Margaret Lockwood Barry K. Barnes Emlyn Williams

1942   UNCENSORED
Director: Anthony Asquith
Co-stars: Eric Portman Phyllis Calvert Griffith Jones

1943   RHYTHM SERENADE
Director: Gordon Wellesley
Co-stars: Vera Lynn Jewell & Warris Jimmy Clitheroe

1943   GET CRACKING
Director: Marcel Varnel
Co-stars: George Formby Dinah Sheridan Edward Rigby

1945   BRIEF ENCOUNTER
Director: David Lean
Co-stars: Trevor Howard Celia Johnson Joyce Carey

1945   FOR YOU ALONE
Director: Geoffrey Faithful
Co-stars: Jimmy Hanley Dinah Sheridan Lesley Brook

1946   THE SHOP AT SLY CORNER
Director: George King
Co-stars: Oscar Homolka Kenneth Griffith Muriel Pavlow

1949   CARDBOARD CAVALIER
Director: Walter Forde
Co-stars: Sid Field Margaret Lockwood Mary Clare

1949   THE PERFECT WOMAN
Director: Bernard Knowles
Co-stars: Patricia Roc Nigel Patrick Stanley Holloway

1951   ONE WILD OAT
Director: Charles Saunders
Co-stars: Robertson Hare Stanley Holloway Sam Costa

1951   YOUNG WIVES' TALE
Director: Henry Cass
Co-stars: Joan Greenwood Nigel Patrick Helen Cherry

1953   THE WEDDING OF LILLI MARLENE
Director: Arthur Crabtree
Co-stars: Lisa Daniely Hugh McDermott

1954   MAD ABOUT MEN
Director: Ralph Thomas
Co-stars: Glynis Johns Donald Sinden Anne Crawford

1954   THE BELLES OF ST. TRINIANS
Director: Frank Launder
Co-stars: Alastair Sim George Cole Joyce Grenfell

1955   A KID FOR TWO FARTHINGS
Director: Carol Reed
Co-stars: Celia Johnson Diana Dors David Kossoff

1957   BROTHERS IN LAW
Director: Roy Boutling
Co-stars: Ian Carmichael Terry-Thomas Miles Malleson

1957   SMALL HOTEL
Director: David MacDonald
Co-stars: Gordon Harker Marie Lohr Janet Munro

1959 CARRY ON NURSE
Director: Gerald Thomas
Co-stars: Shirley Eaton Bill Owen Kenneth Connor

1959 CARRY ON CONSTABLE
Director: Gerald Thomas
Co-stars: Sid James Eric Barker Leslie Phillips Joan Sims

1959 DESERT MICE
Director: Michael Relph
Co-stars: Alfred Marks Sid James Patricia Bredin Dora Bryan

1959 I'M ALL RIGHT JACK
Director: John Boulting
Co-stars: Peter Sellers Ian Carmichael Terry-Thomas

1960 TWO-WAY STRETCH
Director: Robert Day
Co-stars: Peter Sellers Lionel Jeffries Bernard Cribbins

1960 THE REBEL
Director: Robert Day
Co-stars: Tony Hancock George Sanders Paul Massie Dennis Price

1960 THE PURE HELL OF ST. TRINIANS
Director: Frank Launder
Co-stars: Cecil Parker George Cole Joyce Grenfell

1960 THE NIGHT WE GOT THE BIRD
Director: Darcy Conyers
Co-stars: Brian Rix Ronald Shiner Liz Fraser

1960 MAKE MINE MINK
Director: Robert Asher
Co-stars: Terry-Thomas Athene Seyler Billie Whitelaw

1960 INN FOR TROUBLE
Director: C.M. Pennington-Richards
Co-stars: Peggy Mount David Kossoff Leslie Phillips

1960 DOCTOR IN LOVE
Director: Ralph Thomas
Co-stars: Michael Craig Leslie Phillips Virginia Maskell

1960 CARRY ON CONSTABLE
Director: Gerald Thomas
Co-stars: Sid James Eric Barker Joan Sims

1961 DOUBLE BUNK
Director: C.M. Pennington-Richards
Co-stars: Ian Carmichael Janette Scott Liz Fraser

1961 WATCH IT SAILOR!
Director: Wolf Rilla
Co-stars: Dennis Price Liz Fraser Marjorie Rhodes

1963 HEAVENS ABOVE!
Director: John Boulting
Co-stars: Peter Sellers Isabel Jeans Eric Sykes Cecil Parker

1966 MORGAN - A SUITABLE CASE FOR TREATMENT
Director: Karel Reisz
Co-stars: David Warner Vanessa Redgrave

1966 THE WRONG BOX
Director: Bryan Forbes
Co-stars: Ralph Richardson John Mills Michael Caine

1967 SMASHING TIME
Director: Desmond Davis
Co-stars: Rita Tushingham Lynn Redgrave Ian Carmichael

1969 THE ITALIAN JOB
Director: Peter Collinson
Co-stars: Michael Caine Noel Coward Benny Hill

1970 DOCTOR IN TROUBLE
Director: Ralph Thomas
Co-stars: Leslie Phillips Harry Secombe Angela Scoular

1970 THE PRIVATE LIFE OF SHERLOCK HOLMES
Director: Billy Wilder
Co-stars: Robert Stephens Colin Blakely

1972 FOR THE LOVE OF ADA
Director: Ronnie Baxter
Co-stars: Wilfred Pickles Barbara Mitchell Arthur English

1976 CONFESSIONS OF A DRIVING INSTRUCTOR
Director: Norman Cohen
Co-stars: Robin Askwith Anthony Booth Bill Maynard

1977 THE HOUND OF THE BASKERVILLES
Director: Paul Morrissey
Co-stars: Peter Cook Dudley Moore Max Wall

1977 THE LAST REMAKE OF BEAU GESTE
Director: Marty Feldman
Co-stars: Marty Feldman Michael York Ann-Margret Peter Ustinov

1977 STAND UP VIRGIN SOLDIERS
Director: Norman Cohen
Co-stars: Nigel Davenport Robin Askwith

1977 ADVENTURES OF A PRIVATE EYE
Director: Stanley Long
Co-stars: Christopher Neil Suzy Kendall Liz Fraser

1986 HOTEL DU LAC
Director: Giles Foster
Co-stars: Anna Massey Denholm Elliott Googie Withers

DINAH HANDLEY

1989 A SMALL MOURNING
Director: Chris Bernard
Co-stars: Alison Steadman Stratford Johns Pauline Yates

1993 WIDE EYED AND LEGLESS
Director: Richard Loncraine
Co-stars: Julie Walters Jim Broadbent Thora Hird

CAROL HANEY

1956 INVITATION TO DANCE
Director: Gene Kelly
Co-stars: Gene Kelly Belita Tommy Rall Tamara Toumanova

1957 THE PAJAMA GAME
Director: Stanley Donen
Co-stars: Doris Day John Raitt Reta Shaw

HELEN HANFT

1988 COMING TO AMERICA
Director: John Landis
Co-stars: Eddie Murphy Arsenio Hall James Earl Jones

JENNY HANLEY

1970 THE SCARS OF DRACULA
Director: Roy Ward Baker
Co-stars: Christopher Lee Dennis Waterman Bob Todd

1971 TAM-LIN
Director: Roddy McDowell
Co-stars: Ava Gardner Ian McShane Stephanie Beacham

1973 SOFT BEDS, HARD BATTLES
Director: Roy Boulting
Co-stars: Peter Sellers Lila Kedrova Curt Jurgens

1975 ALFIE DARLING
Director: Ken Hughes
Co-stars: Alan Price Jill Townsend Joan Collins

KATIE HANLEY

1973 GODSPELL
Director: David Greene
Co-stars: Victor Garber David Haskell Lynne Thigpen

DARYL HANNAH *(Sister Of Page Hannah)*

1978 THE FURY
Director: Brian De Palma
Co-stars: Kirk Douglas John Cassavetes Carrie Snodgress

1979   **THE FINAL TERROR**
Co-star: Rachel Ward

1981   **HARD COUNTRY**
Director: David Greene
Co-stars: Jan-Michael Vincent Kim Basinger Michael Parks

1982   **SUMMER LOVERS**
Director: Randal Kleiser
Co-stars: Peter Gallacher Valerie Quennessen

1982   **BLADE RUNNER**
Director: Ridley Scott
Co-stars: Harrison Ford Rutger Hauer Sean Young Joe Turkel

1983   **CAMPSITE MASSACRE**
Director: Andrew Davis
Co-stars: John Friedrich Adrian Zmed Rachel Ward

1984   **THE POPE OF GREENWICH VILLAGE**
Director: Stuart Rosenberg
Co-stars: Eric Roberts Mickey Rourke

1984   **RECKLESS**
Director: James Foley
Co-star: Aidan Quinn

1984   **SPLASH!**
Director: Ron Howard
Co-stars: Tom Hanks Eugene Levy John Candy Dody Goodman

1985   **LEGAL EAGLES**
Director: Ivan Reitman
Co-stars: Robert Redford Debra Winger Brian Dennehy

1985   **CLAN OF THE CAVE BEAR**
Director: Michael Chapman
Co-stars: Pamela Reed James Remar Thomas G. Waites

1987   **ROXANNE**
Director: Fred Schepisi
Co-stars: Steve Martin Shelley Duvall Michael J. Pollard

1987   **WALL STREET**
Director: Oliver Stone
Co-stars: Michael Douglas Charlie Sheen Martin Sheen

1988   **HIGH SPIRITS**
Director: Neil Jordan
Co-stars: Peter O'Toole Steve Guttenberg Liam Neeson

1989   **STEEL MAGNOLIAS**
Director: Herbert Ross
Co-stars: Sally Field Dolly Parton Shirley MacLaine

1990   **CRAZY PEOPLE**
Director: Tony Bill
Co-stars: Dudley Moore Paul Reiser Bill Smitrovich

1992   **AT PLAY IN THE FIELDS OF THE LORD**
Director: Hector Babenco
Co-stars: Tom Berenger Kathy Bates

1992   **MEMOIRS OF AN INVISIBLE MAN**
Director: John Carpenter
Co-stars: Chevy Chase Sam Neill Jim Norton

1993   **GRUMPY OLD MEN**
Director: Donald Petrie
Co-stars: Jack Lemmon Walter Matthau Ann-Margaret

1994   **ATTACK OF THE SOFT WOMAN**
Director: Christopher Guest
Co-star: Daniel Baldwin

1995   **THE TIE THAT BINDS**
Director: Wesley Stick
Co-stars: Keith Carradine Vincent Spano Moira Kelly

1996   **TOO MUCH**
Director: Fernando Trueba
Co-stars: Antonio Banderas Melanie Griffith

1996   **THE LAST DAYS OF FRANKIE THE FLY**
Director: Peter Markle
Co-stars: Dennis Hopper Michael Madsen Kiefer Sutherland

1998   **THE REAL BLONDE**
Director: Tom DeCillo
Co-stars: Matthew Modine Kathleen Turner Buck Henry

PAGE HANNAH *(Sister Of Daryl Hannah)*

1987   **CREEPSHOW 2**
Director: Michael Gornick
Co-stars: Lois Chiles George Kennedy Dorothy Lamour

1988   **SHAG**
Director: Zelda Barron
Co-stars: Phoebe Cates Bridget Fonda Annabeth Gish

ALYSON HANNIGAN

1988   **MY STEPMOTHER IS AN ALIEN**
Director: Richard Benjamin
Co-stars: Dan Aykroyd Kim Basinger Jon Lovitz

JANET HANNINGTON

1964   **DAYLIGHT ROBBERY**
Director: Michael Truman
Co-stars: Trudy Moors Gordon Jackson Kirk Martin

BRITTNEY HANSEN

1991   **SHAKING THE TREE**
Director: Duane Clark
Co-stars: Ayre Gross Doug Savant Courteney Cox

GALE HANSEN

1989   **DEAD POETS SOCIETY**
Director: Peter Weir
Co-stars: Robin Williams Ethan Hawke Robert Sean Leonard

1992   **DOUBLE VISION**
Director: Rob Knights
Co-star: Kim Cattrall

PATTI HANSEN

1982   **THEY ALL LAUGHED**
Director: Peter Bogdanovich
Co-stars: Audrey Hepburn Ben Gazzara Dorothy Stratten

VALDA HANSEN

1960   **NIGHT OF THE GHOULS**
Director: Edward Wood
Co-stars: Duke Moore Kenne Duncan Paul Marco

ANN HANSLIP

1955   **WHERE THERE'S A WAY**
Director: Vernon Sewell
Co-stars: Kathleen Harrison George Cole Leslie Dwyer

KRISTINA HANSON

1960   **DINOSAURUS!**
Director: Irvin Yeaworth
Co-stars: Ward Ramsey Paul Lukather Alan Roberts

HAYA HARAREET

1954   **HILL 24 DOESN'T ANSWER**
Director: Thorold Dickinson
Co-stars: Michael Wagner Edward Mulhare Arie Lavi

1958   **BEN HUR**
Director: William Wyler
Co-stars: Charlton Heston Stephen Boyd Hugh Griffith

1961   **THE SECRET PARTNER**
Director: Basil Dearden
Co-stars: Stewart Granger Bernard Lee Hugh Burden

CHRISTINE HARBORT

1981   MESPHISTO
Director: Istavan Szabo
Co-stars: Klaus Maria Brandauer Krystyna Janda

VICTORIA HARDCASTLE

1987   PERSONAL SERVICES
Director: Terry Jones
Co-stars: Julie Walters Alec McCowan Tim Woodward

MARCIA GAY HARDEN

1990   MILLER'S CROSSING
Director: Joel Coen
Co-stars: Albert Finney Gabriel Byrne John Turturro

1991   LATE FOR DINNER
Director: W.D. Ritcher
Co-stars: Brian Wimmer Peter Berg Colleen Flynn

1991   FEVER
Director: Larry Elikan
Co-stars: Armand Assante Sam Neill Greg Henry

1992   CRUSH
Director: Alison McLean
Co-stars: William Zappa Donogh Rees Caitlin Bossley

1992   USED PEOPLE
Director: Beeban Idron
Co-stars: Shirley MacLaine Marcello Mastroianni Kathy Bates

1996   THE FIRST WIVES' CLUB
Director: Hugh Wilson
Co-stars: Goldie Hawn Diane Keaton Bette Midler

1998   FLUBBER
Co-star: Robin Williams

KATE HARDIE (Child)

1983   RUNNERS
Director: Charles Sturridge
Co-stars: James Fox Jane Asher Eileen O'Brien

1985   WINGS OF DEATH
Director: Nicholas Bruce
Co-stars: Dexter Fletcher Tony Haygarth Paula Jacobs

1986   MONA LISA
Director: Neil Jordan
Co-stars: Bob Hoskins Cathy Tyson Michael Caine

1988   TREE OF HANDS
Director: Giles Foster
Co-stars: Helen Shaver Lauren Bacall Peter Firth

1989   MELANCHOLIA
Director: Andi Engel
Co-stars: Jeroen Krabbe Susannah York Jane Gurnett

1989   CONSPIRACY
Director: Christopher Barnard
Co-stars: James Wilby Glyn Houston Tony Caunter

1990   THE KRAYS
Director: Peter Medak
Co-stars: Billie Whitelaw Tom Bell Gary Kemp Martin Kemp

1991   A SMALL DANCE
Director: Alan Horrox
Co-stars: James Hazeldine Linda Bassett Mark Aiken

1992   UNDER THE SUN
Director: Michael Winterbottom
Co-stars: Caroline Catz Iker Ibanez

1993   SAFE
Director: Antonia Bird
Co-stars: Aiden Gillen George Costigan Andrew Tiernan

MELORA HARDIN

1986   SOUL MAN
Director: Steve Miner
Co-stars: C. Thomas Howell Rae Dawn Chong Leslie Nielsen

1990   LAMBADA
Director: Joel Silberg
Co-stars: J. Eddie Peck Keene Curtis Basil Hoffman

1993   RECKLESS KELLY
Director: Yahoo Serious
Co-stars: Yahoo Serious Alexei Sayle Hugo Weaving

1997   ABSOLUTE POWER
Director: Clint Eastwood
Co-stars: Clint Eastwood Gene Hackman Judy Davis Ed Harris

ANN HARDING (Dorothy Gatley)
Nominated For An Oscar For Best Actress In 1930 For "Holiday"

1929   PARIS BOUND

1930   CONDEMMED
Director: Wesley Ruggles
Co-stars: Ronald Colman Dudley Digges

1931   DEVOTION
Director: Robert Milton
Co-stars: Leslie Howard Robert Williams O.P. Heggie

1930   THE GIRL OF THE GOLDEN WEST
Director: John Francis Dillon
Co-stars: James Rennie Harry Bannister

1930   HOLIDAY
Director: Edward Griffith
Co-stars: Robert Ames Mary Astor Hedda Hopper

1931   EAST LYNNE
Director: Frank Lloyd
Co-stars: Clive Brook Conrad Nagel O.P. Heggie

1932   THE ANIMAL KINGDOM
Director: Edward Griffith
Co-stars: Leslie Howard Myrna Loy Neil Hamilton

1932   THE CONQUERORS
Director: William Wellman
Co-stars: Richard Dix Guy Kibbee Donald Cook

1932   PRESTIGE
Director: Tay Garnett
Co-stars: Melvyn Douglas Adolphe Menjou Clarence Muse

1932   WESTWARD PASSAGE
Director: Robert Milton
Co-stars: Laurence Olivier Zasu Pitts Irving Pichel

1933   WHEN LADIES MEET
Director: Harry Beaumont
Co-stars: Robert Montgomery Myrna Loy Frank Morgan

1933   THE RIGHT TO ROMANCE
Co-stars: Robert Young Nils Asther

1933   GALLANT LADY
Director: Gregory La Cava
Co-stars: Clive Brook Otto Kruger Tullio Carminati

1933   DOUBLE HARNESS
Director: John Cromwll
Co-stars: William Powell Reginald Owen Kay Hammond

1934   THE FOUNTAIN
Director: John Cromwell
Co-stars: Brian Aherne Paul Lukas Jean Hersholt

1934   THE LIFE OF VERGIE WINTERS
Director: Alfred Santell
Co-stars: John Boles Helen Vinson Lon Chaney

1934 THEIR BIG MOMENT
Director: James Cruze
Co-stars: Ralph Morgan Zasu Pitts Slim Summerville

1935 THE FLAME WITHIN
Director: Edmund Goulding
Co-stars: Maureen O'Sullivan Louis Hayward Herbert Marshall

1935 PETER IBBETSON
Director: Henry Hathaway
Co-stars: Gary Cooper John Halliday Ida Lupino

1935 ENCHANTED APRIL
Director: Harry Beaumont
Co-stars: Frank Morgan Katherine Alexander Jane Baxter

1935 BIOGRAPHY OF A BACHELOR GIRL
Director: Edward Griffith
Co-stars: Robert Montgomery Edward Arnold

1936 THE LADY CONSENTS
Director: Stephen Roberts
Co-stars: Herbert Marshall Margaret Lindsay Walter Abel

1936 THE WITNESS CHAIR
Director: George Marshall
Co-stars: Walter Abel Moroni Olsen Douglass Dumbrille

1936 LOVE FROM A STRANGER
Director: Rowland Lee
Co-stars: Basil Rathbone Binnie Hale Joan Hickson

1942 EYES IN THE NIGHT
Director: Fred Zinnemann
Co-stars: Edward Arnold Donna Reed Stephen McNally

1943 MISSION TO MOSCOW
Director: Michael Curtiz
Co-stars: Walter Huston Oscar Homolka Eleanor Parker

1943 NORTH STAR
Director: Lewis Milestone
Co-stars: Anne Baxter Farley Granger Dana Andrews

1944 NINE GIRLS
Director: Leigh Jason
Co-stars: Evelyn Keyes Anita Louise Nina Foch

1944 JANIE
Director: Michael Curtiz
Co-stars: Joyce Reynolds Robert Hutton Edward Arnold

1945 THOSE ENDEARING YOUNG CHARMS
Director: Lewis Allen
Co-stars: Robert Young Laraine Day Bill Williams

1946 JANIE GETS MARRIED
Director: Michael Curtiz
Co-stars: Joan Leslie Robert Hutton Edward Arnold

1947 IT HAPPENED ON 5TH AVENUE
Director: Roy Del Ruth
Co-stars: Gale Storm Victor Moore Charles Ruggles

1947 CHRISTMAS EVE
Director: Edwin Marin
Co-stars: George Raft Randolph Scott George Brent

1950 THE MAGNIFICENT YANKEE
Director: John Sturges
Co-stars: Louis Calhern Eduard Franz Philip Ober

1951 THE UNKNOWN MAN
Director: Richard Thorpe
Co-stars: Walter Pidgeon Lewis Stone Barry Sullivan

1956 THE MAN IN THE GREY FLANNEL SUIT
Director: Nunnally Johnson
Co-stars: Gregory Peck Jennifer Jones Fredric March

1956 I'VE LIVED BEFORE
Director: Richard Bartlett
Co-stars: Jock Mahoney Leigh Snowden John McIntyre

1957 STRANGE INTRUDER
Director: Irving Rapper
Co-stars: Edmund Purdom Ida Lupino Jacques Bergerac

JUNE HARDING

1966 THE TROUBLE WITH ANGELS
Director: Ida Lupino
Co-stars: Rosalind Russell Hayley Mills Binnie Barnes

KAY HARDING

1944 THE SCARLET CLAW
Director: Roy William Neill
Co-stars: Basil Rathbone Nigel Bruce Miles Mander

1944 THE MUMMY'S CURSE
Director: Leslie Goodwins
Co-stars: Peter Coe Virginia Christine Martin Kosleck

LUCY HARDING

1993 MONEY FOR NOTHING
Director: Mike Ockrent
Co-stars: Christien Anholt Jayne Ashbourne Julian Glover

FRANCOISE HARDY

1966 GRAND PRIX
Director: John Frankenheimer
Co-stars: James Garner Brian Bedford Eva Marie Saint

SOPHIE HARDY

1965 THREE HATS FOR LISA
Director: Sidney Hayers
Co-stars: Joe Brown Sid James Una Stubbs

1966 THE TRYGON FACTOR
Director: Cyril Franklin
Co-stars: Stewart Granger Susan Hampshire Robert Morley

1968 A TASTE OF EXCITEMENT
Director: Don Sharp
Co-stars: Eva Renzi David Buck Peter Vaughn

ELOISE HARDT

1947 CRIME DOES NOT PAY:
LUCKIEST GUY IN THE WORLD
Director: Joe Newman
Co-star: Barry Nelson

DORIS HARE

1963 A PLACE TO GO
Director: Basil Dearden
Co-stars: Rita Tushingham Mike Sarne John Slater

1971 ON THE BUSES
Director: Harry Booth
Co-stars: Reg Varney Stephen Lewis Anna Karen

1973 MUTINY ON THE BUSES
Director: Harry Booth
Co-stars: Reg Varney Bob Grant Michael Robbins

1973 HOLIDAY ON THE BUSES
Director: Byran Izzard
Co-stars: Reg Varney Anna Karen Stephen Lewis

1975 CONFESSIONS OF A POP PERFORMER
Director: Norman Cohen
Co-stars: Robin Askwith Bill Maynard

1976 CONFESSIONS OF A DRIVING INSTRUCTOR
Director: Norman Cohen
Co-stars: Anthony Booth Sheila White

1977 CONFESSIONS FROM A HOLIDAY CAMP
Director: Norman Cohen
Co-stars: Liz Frazer Lance Percival

1990　NUNS ON THE RUN
Director:　Jonathan Lynn
Co-stars:　Eric Idle Robbie Coltrane Janet Suzman

MARISKA HARGITAY

1989　THE FINISH LINE
Director:　John Nicolella
Co-stars:　James Brolin Josh Brolin John Finnegan

AMY HARGREAVES

1994　BRAINSCAN
Director:　John Flynn
Co-stars:　Edward Furlong Frank Langella T. Ryder Smith

CHRISTINE HARGREAVES

1982　PINK FLOYD-THE WALL
Director:　Alan Parker
Co-stars:　Bob Geldof James Laurenson Eleanor David

CAROLINE HARKER

1993　JILLY COOPER'S RIDERS
Director:　Gabrielle Beaumont
Co-stars:　Marcus Gilbert Michael Praed

SUSANNAH HARKER

1990　HOUSE OF CARDS
Director:　Paul Seed
Co-stars:　Ian Richardson Diane Fletcher Colin Jeavons

1991　CRUCIFER OF BLOOD
Director:　Fraser Heston
Co-stars:　Charlton Heston Richard Johnson Edward Fox

1991　ADAM BEDE
Director:　Giles Foster
Co-stars:　Iain Glen Patsy Kensit James Wilby

JEAN HARLOW *(Harlean Carpenter)*
(Married Charles McGrew, Paul Bern & Harold Rosson. Engaged To William Powell When She Died)

1929　DOUBLE WHOOPEE
Director:　Lewis Foster
Co-stars:　Laurel & Hardy Charlie Hall

1929　THE BACON GRABBERS
Director:　Lewis Foster
Co-stars:　Laurel & Hardy Charlie Hall Edgar Kennedy

1930　HELL'S ANGELS
Director:　Howard Hughes
Co-stars:　Ben Lyon James Hall John Darrow

1931　THE SECRET SIX
Director:　George Hill
Co-stars:　Wallace Beery Lewis Stone Clark Gable

1931　THE PUBLIC ENEMY
Director:　William Wellman
Co-stars:　James Cagney Joan Blondell Mae Clark

1931　THE IRON MAN
Director:　Tod Browning
Co-stars:　Lew Ayres Robert Armstrong Ned Sparks

1931　GOLDIE
Director:　Ben Stoloff
Co-stars:　Spencer Tracy Warren Hymer Lina Basquette

1931　PLATINUM BLONDE
Director:　Frank Capra
Co-stars:　Robert Williams Loretta Young Richard Owen

1932　BEAST OF THE CITY
Director:　Charles Brabin
Co-stars:　Walter Huston Wallace Ford Mickey Rooney

1932　RED DUST
Director:　Victor Fleming
Co-stars:　Clark Gable Mary Astor Gene Raymond

1932　RED-HEADED WOMAN
Director:　Jack Conway
Co-stars:　Chester Morris Lewis Stone Leila Hyams

1932　THREE WISE GIRLS
Director:　William Beaudine
Co-stars:　Mae Clarke Marie Prevost Andy Devine

1933　HOLD YOUR MAN
Director:　Sam Wood
Co-stars:　Clark Gable Stuart Erwin Dorothy Burgess

1933　DINNER AT EIGHT
Director:　George Cukor
Co-stars:　Marie Dressler John Barrymore Lionel Barrymore

1933　BOMBSHELL
Director:　Victor Fleming
Co-stars:　Lee Tracy Pat O'Brien Franchot Tone

1934　THE GIRL FROM MISSOURI
Director:　Jack Conway
Co-stars:　Franchot Tone Lewis Stone Patsy Kelly

1935　CHINA SEAS
Director:　Tay Garnett
Co-stars:　Clark Gable Wallace Beery Rosalind Russell

1935　RECKLESS
Director:　Victor Fleming
Co-stars:　William Powell Franchot Tone Allan Jones

1935　RIFF RAFF
Director:　Walter Ruben
Co-stars:　Spencer Tracy Joseph Calleia Mickey Rooney

1936　WIFE VS SECRETARY
Director:　Clarence Brown
Co-stars:　Clark Gable Myrna Loy James Stewart

1936　SUZY
Director:　George Fitzmaurice
Co-stars:　Cary Grant Franchot Tone Benita Hume

1936　LIBELED LADY
Director:　Jack Conway
Co-stars:　William Powell Myrna Loy Spencer Tracy

1937　PERSONAL PROPERTY
Director:　W.S. Van Dyke
Co-stars:　Robert Taylor Reginald Owen Una O'Connor

1937　SARATOGA
Director:　Jack Conway
Co-stars:　Clark Gable Lionel Barrymore (Mary Dees)

SHALON HARLOW

1998　IN AND OUT
Director:　Frank Oz
Co-stars:　Kevin Kline Matt Dillon Joan Cusack

JULIET HARMER

1970　THE ENGAGEMENT
Director:　Paul Joyce
Co-stars:　David Warner Michael Bates George Innes

1971　QUEST FOR LOVE
Director:　Ralph Thomas
Co-stars:　Tom Bell Joan Collins Denholm Elliott

DEBORAH HARMON

1980　USED CARS
Director:　Robert Zemeckis
Co-stars:　Kurt Russell Jack Warden Gerrit Graham

1985 MY WICKED WICKED WAYS....
THE LEGEND OF ERROL FYLNN
Director: Don Taylor
Co-stars: Duncan Regehr Lee Purcell

1986 PRINCE OF BEL-AIR
Director: Charles Braverman
Co-stars: Mark Harmon Kirstie Alley

MARIE HARMON

1946 THE EL PASO KID
Director: Sunset Carson

ELIZABETH HARNOIS *(Child)*

1985 ONE MAGIC CHRISTMAS
Director: Philip Borsos
Co-stars: Mary Steenburgen Harry Dean Stanton

CHRISTINE HARNOS

1989 COLD DOG SOUP
Director: Alan Metter
Co-stars: Randy Quaid Frank Whaley Sheree North

1994 THE COOL AND THE CRAZY
Director: Ralph Bakshi
Co-stars: Alicia Silverstone Jared Leto Tuesday Knight

MAUREEN HAROLD

1991 DREAM ON
Director: Kitty Fitzgerald
Co-stars: Amber Styles Brian Hogg Ray Stubbs

HARRIET HARPER

1970 THE VIRGIN AND THE GYPSY
Director: Joanna Shimkus
Co-stars: Franco Nero Honor Blackman

JESSICA HARPER

1974 PHANTOM OF THE PARADISE
Director: Brian De Palma
Co-stars: Paul Williams William Finley

1975 INSERTS
Director: John Byrum
Co-stars: Richard Dreyfuss Veronica Cartwright Bob Hoskins

1976 SUSPIRIA
Director: Dario Argento
Co-stars: Alida Valli Joan Bennett Stefania Casini

1979 THE EVICTORS
Director: Charles Pierce
Co-stars: Michael Parks Vic Morrow Sue Anne Langdon

1980 STARDUST MEMOIRS
Director: Woody Allen
Co-stars: Woody Allen Charlotte Rampling Amy Wright Tony Roberts

1981 SHOCK TREATMENT
Director: Jim Sharman
Co-stars: Cliff De Young Richard O'Brien Ruby Wax

1981 PENNIES FROM HEAVEN
Director: Herbert Ross
Co-stars: Steve Martin Bernadette Peters Tommy Rall

1982 MY FAVOURITE YEAR
Director: Richard Benjamin
Co-stars: Peter O'Toole Joseph Bologna Lainie Kazan

1985 WHEN DREAMS COME TRUE
Director: John Llewelyn Moxey
Co-stars: Cindy Williams David Morse Lee Horsley

1988 THE BLUE IGUANA
Director: John Lafia
Co-stars: Dylan McDermott Pamela Gidley Dean Stockwell

1993 MR. WONDERFUL
Director: Anthony Minghella
Co-stars: Matt Dillon Annabelle Sciorra William Hurt

MARJORIE HARPER

1976 THE LIFE AND TIMES OF GRIZZLY ADAMS
Director: Richard Friedenberg
Co-stars: Dan Haggetty Don Shanks

TESS HARPER
Nominated For Best Supporting Actress In 1986 For "Crimes Of The Heart"

1982 TENDER MERCIES
Director: Bruce Beresford
Co-stars: Robert Duvall Betty Buckley Wilford Brimley

1984 AMITYVILLE 3D
Director: Richard Fleischer
Co-stars: Tony Roberts Meg Ryan Candy Clark

1986 CRIMES OF THE HEART
Director: Bruce Beresford
Co-stars: Diane Keaton Jessica Lange Sissy Spacek

1987 DADDY
Director: John Herzfeld
Co-stars: Dermot Mulroney Patricia Arquette Danny Aiello

1987 ISHTAR
Director: Elaine May
Co-stars: Dustin Hoffman Warren Beatty Isabelle Adjani

1988 LITTLE GIRL LOST
Director: Sharron Miller
Co-stars: Frederic Forrest Patricia Kalember Marie Martin

1988 FAR NORTH
Director: Sam Sheppard
Co-stars: Jessica Lange Charles Durning Patricia Arquette

1989 CRIMINAL LAW
Director: Martin Campbell
Co-stars: Gary Oldman Kevin Bacon Joe Don Baker

1989 HER ALIBI
Director: Bruce Beresford
Co-stars: Tom Selleck Paulina Porizkova Hurd Hatfield

1989 INCIDENT AT DARK RIVER
Director: Michael Pressman
Co-stars: Mike Farrell Helen Hunt Arthur Rosenberg

1989 UNCONQUERED
Director: Dick Lowry
Co-stars: Peter Coyote Dermot Mulroney Jenny Robertson

1990 DADDY'S DYIN': WHO'S GOT THE WILL
Director: Jack Fisk
Co-stars: Beau Bridges Beverly D'Angelo

1991 THE MAN IN THE MOON
Director: Robert Mulligan
Co-stars: Sam Waterson Gail Strickland Jason London

1991 MY HEROES HAVE ALWAYS BEEN COWBOYS
Director: Stuart Rosenberg
Co-stars: Scott Glen Ben Johnson

1992 MY NEW GUN
Director: Stacy Cochran
Co-stars: Diane Lane Stephen Collins James LeGros

1992 IN THE LINE OF DUTY: SIEGE OF MARION
Director: Charles Hade
Co-stars: Ed Begley Jnr. Paul LeMat

1995 DEATH IN SMALL DOSES
Director: Sondra Locke
Co-stars: Richard Thomas Glynnis O'Connor Ann Hearn

1996 THE KILLING SECRET
Director: Noel Nosseck
Co-stars: Ari Meyers Soleil Moon Frye

1996 A STRANGER TO LOVE
Director: Peter Levin
Co-stars: Beau Bridges Pam Dawber

VALERIE HARPER

1974 FREEBIE AND THE BEAN
Director: Richard Rush
Co-stars: Alan Arkin James Caan Loretta Swit

1974 THURSDAY'S GAME
Director: Robert Moore
Co-stars: Gene Wilder Bob Newhart Ellen Burnstyn Martha Scott

1979 THE LAST MARRIED COUPLE IN AMERICA
Director: Gilbert Cates
Co-stars: Natalie Wood George Segal

1979 CHAPTER TWO
Director: Robert Moore
Co-stars: James Caan Marsha Mason Joseph Bologna Alan Fudge

1981 THE DAY THE LOVING STOPPED
Director: Daniel Mann
Co-stars: Dennis Weaver Dominique Dunne Ally Sheedy

1984 BLAME IT ON RIO
Director: Stanley Donen
Co-stars: Michael Caine Joseph Bologna Michelle Johnson

1985 THE EXECUTION
Director: Paul Wendkos
Co-stars: Loretta Swit Jessica Walter Sandy Dennis Rip Torn

1987 STRANGE VOICES
Director: Arthur Seidelman
Co-stars: Nancy McKeon Stephen Macht Millie Perkins

1988 THE PEOPLE ACROSS THE LAKE
Director: Arthur Seidelman
Co-stars: Gerald McRaney Barry Corbin

1990 I WANT HIM BACK
Director: Catlin Adams
Co-stars: Elliott Gould Brenda Vaccaro Bruce Davison

1994 DEATH OF A CHEERLEADER
Director: Billy Graham
Co-stars: Kellie Martin Teri Spelling

REBECCA HARRELL *(Child)*

1989 PRANCER
Director: John Hancock
Co-stars: Sam Elliott Cloris Leachman Rutanya Alda

NEDDA HARRIGAN

1936 CHARLIE CHAN AT THE OPERA
Director: Bruce Humberstone
Co-stars: Warner Oland Boris Karloff Keye Luke

1940 DEVIL'S ISLAND
Director: William Clemens
Co-stars: Boris Karloff James Stephenson Robert Warwick

FAWNE HARRIMAN

1980 THE ALIENS ARE COMING
Director: Harvey Hart
Co-stars: Tom Mason Melinda Fee Ed Harris

JOY HARRINGTON

1945 MY NAME IS JULIA ROSS
Director: Joseph Lewis
Co-stars: Nina Foch May Whitty George Macready

KATE HARRINGTON

1968 RACHEL, RACHEL
Director: Paul Newman
Co-stars: Joanne Woodward Estelle Parsons James Olson

LAURA HARRINGTON

1984 CITY GIRL
Director: Martha Coolidge
Co-stars: Joe Mastroianni Carol McGill Peter Riegert

1986 MAXIMUM OVERDIVE
Director: Stephen King
Co-stars: Emillio Estevez Pat Hingle Yeardley Smith

1989 L.A. TAKEDOWN
Director: Michael Mann
Co-stars: Scott Plank Alex McArthur Ely Pouget

1993 LUST FOR MURDER
Director: Nathaniel Gutman
Co-stars: Richard Thomas Virginia Madsen Ted McGinley

1993 WHAT'S EATING GILBERT GRAPE?
Director: Lasse Hallstrom
Co-stars: Johnny Depp Darlene Cates

AMANDA HARRIS

1985 OLIVER TWIST *(Voice)*
Director: Gareth Davies
Co-stars: Eric Porter Frank Middlemass Lysette Anthony

ANITA HARRIS

1967 CARRY ON, FOLLOW THAT CAMEL
Director: Gerald Thomas
Co-stars: Phil Silvers Jim Dale Kenneth Williams

1968 CARRY ON DOCTOR
Director: Gerald Thomas
Co-stars: Frankie Howard Barbara Windsor Sid James

BARBARA HARRIS

Nominated For Best Supporting Actress In 1971 For "Who Is Harry Kellerman And Why Is He Saying Those Terrible Things About Me ?"

1965 A THOUSAND CLOWNS
Director: Fred Coe
Co-stars: Jason Robards Martin Balsam Barry Gordon Gene Saks

1967 OH DAD, POOR DAD, MAMA'S HUNG YOU IN THE CLOSET AND I'M SO SAD
Director: Richard Quine
Co-stars: Rosalind Russell Robert Morse Hugh Griffith

1971 WHO IS HARRY KELLERMAN AND WHY IS HE SAYING THESE TERRIBLE THINGS ABOUT ME?
Director: Ulu Gosbard
Co-stars: Dustin Hoffman Jack Warden Gabriel Dell

1971 PLAZA SUITE
Director: Arthur Hiller
Co-stars: Walter Matthau Maureen Stapleton Lee Grant

1972 THE WAR BETWEEN MEN AND WOMEN
Director: Melville Shavelson
Co-stars: Jack Lemmon Jason Robards

1974 MIXED COMPANY
Director: Melville Shavelson
Co-stars: Joseph Bologna Tom Bosley Lisa Gerritson

1976 FREAKY FRIDAY
Director: Gary Nelson
Co-stars: Jodie Foster John Astin Patsy Kelly Marie Windsor

1976 FAMILY PLOT
Director: Alfred Hitchcock
Co-stars: Karen Black Bruce Dern William Devane Ed Lauter

1978   **MOVIE MOVIE**
Director: Stanley Donen
Co-stars: George C. Scott Trish Van Devere Red Buttons Eli Wallach

1979   **THE NORTH AVENUE IRREGULARS**
Director: Bruce Bilson
Co-stars: Edward Herrman Susan Clark

1979   **THE SEDUCTION OF JOE TYNAN**
Director: Jerry Schatzberg
Co-stars: Alan Alda Meryl Streep Rip Torn

1986   **PEGGY SUE GOT MARRIED**
Director: Francis Coppola
Co-stars: Kathleen Turner Nicholas Cage Leon Ames

1987   **NICE GIRLS DON'T EXPLODE**
Director: Chuck Matinez
Co-stars: Michelle Meyrink Wallace Shawn

1988   **DIRTY ROTTEN SCOUNDRELS**
Director: Frank Oz
Co-stars: Michael Caine Steve Martin Glenne Headly

CASSANDRA HARRIS
1981   **FOR YOUR EYES ONLY**
Director: John Glen
Co-stars: Roger Moore Carole Bouquet Julian Glover

CRYSTAL HARRIS
1976   **AFFAIRS OF JANICE**
Director: Zebedy Colt
Co-stars: Zebedy Colt C.J. Laing Annie Sprinkles

CYNTHIA HARRIS
1982   **RUEBEN, RUEBEN**
Director: Robert Ellis Miller
Co-stars: Tom Conti Kelly McGillis

1985   **IZZY AND MOE**
Director: Jackie Cooper
Co-stars: Jackie Gleason Art Carney Zohra Lampert

1989   **ASK ME AGAIN**
Director: Deborah Reinisch
Co-stars: Robert Bruce Leslie Hope Kathryn Hayes

DANIELLE HARRIS
1988   **HALLOWEEN 4:**
THE RETURN OF MICHAEL MYERS
Director: Dwight Little
Co-stars: Donald Pleasence Beau Starr

1989   **HALLOWEEN 5:**
THE REVENGE OF MICHAEL MYERS
Director: Dominique Othenin-Girard
Co-stars: Donald Pleasence Ellie Cornell

1990   **MARKED FOR DEATH**
Director: Dwight Little
Co-stars: Steven Seagal Joana Pacula

1991   **THE LAST BOY SCOUT**
Director: Tony Scott
Co-stars: Bruce Willis Damon Wayans

1991   **DON'T TELL MOM THE BABYSITTER'S DEAD**
Director: Stephen Herek
Co-stars: Christina Applegate John Getz

1991   **CITY SLICKERS**
Director: Ron Underwood
Co-stars: Billy Crystal Daniel Stern

EDNA MAE HARRIS
1936   **THE GREEN PASTURES**
Director: William Keighley
Co-stars: Rex Ingram Eddie Anderson Oscar Polk

1937   **SPIRIT OF YOUTH**
Co-star: Joe Louis

JO ANN HARRIS
1971   **THE BEGUILED**
Director: Don Siegel
Co-stars: Clint Eastwood Geraldine Page Elizabeth Hartman

1974   **ACT OF VENGENCE**
Director: Bob Kelljan
Co-stars: Peter Brown Jennifer Lee Steve Kanaly

1979   **THE WILD WEST REVISITED**
Director: Burt Kennedy
Co-stars: Robert Conrad Henry Morgan Ross Martin

JULIE HARRIS
Nominated For Best Actress In 1952 For "The Member Of The Wedding"

1952   **THE MEMBER OF THE WEDDING**
Director: Fred Zinnemann
Co-stars: Ethel Waters Brandon De Wilde Nancy Gates

1955   **I AM A CAMERA**
Director: Henry Cornelius
Co-stars: Laurence Harvey Shelley Winters Ron Randell

1955   **EAST OF EDEN**
Director: Elia Kazan
Director: Raymond Massey James Dean Jo Van Fleet Burl Ives

1957   **THE TRUTH ABOUT WOMEN**
Director: Muriel Box
Co-stars: Laurence Harvey Mai Zetterling Diane Cilento

1961   **THE POWER AND THE GLORY**
Co-star: Laurence Olivier

1962   **REQUIEM FOR A HEAVYWEIGHT**
Director: Raplh Nelson
Co-stars: Anthony Quinn Mickey Rooney

1963   **THE HAUNTING**
Director: Robert Wise
Co-stars: Richard Johnson Claire Bloom Russ Tamblyn Lois Maxwell

1966   **THE MOVING TARGET**
Director: Jack Smight
Co-stars: Paul Newman Lauren Bacall Shelley Winters

1967   **REFLECTIONS IN A GOLDEN EYE**
Director: John Huston
Co-stars: Elizabeth Taylor Marlon Brando

1967   **YOU'RE A BIG BOY NOW**
Director: Francis Ford Coppola
Co-stars: Peter Kastner Elizabeth Hartman

1968   **THE SPLIT**
Director: Gordon Flemying
Co-stars: Jim Brown Diahann Carroll Ernest Borgnine

1970   **THE PEOPLE NEXT DOOR**
Director: David Greene
Co-stars: Eli Wallach Cloris Leachman Hal Holbrook

1970   **HOW AWFUL ABOUT ALLAN**
Director: Curtis Harrington
Co-stars: Anthony Perkins Joan Hackett Kent Smith

1975   **JAMES DEAN:**
THE FIRST AMERICAN TEENAGE
Director: Ray Connolly
Co-stars: Natalie Wood Elizabeth Taylor

1976   **VOYAGE OF THE DARKNESS**
Director: George Romero
Co-stars: Timothy Hutton Amy Madison Michael Rooker

1976   **VOYAGE OF THE DAMNED**
Director: Stuart Rosenberg
Co-stars: Faye Dunaway James Mason Orson Welles

1979　THE GIFT
Director:　Don Taylor
Co-stars:　Glenn Ford Maggie Cooper Tom Clancy

1979　THE BELL JAR
Director:　Larry Peerce
Co-stars:　Marilyn Hassett Anne Jackson Barbara Barrie

1988　GORILLAS IN THE MIST
Director:　Michael Apted
Co-stars:　Sigourney Weaver Bryan Brown Iain Glenn

1988　TOO GOOD TO BE TRUE
Director:　Christian Nyby
Co-stars:　Loni Anderson Patrick Duffy Glynnis O'Connor

1992　THE DARK HALF
Director:　George Romero
Co-stars:　Timothy Hutton Amy Madigan Michael Rooker

1992　HOUSESITTER
Director:　Frank Oz
Co-stars:　Goldie Hawn Steve Martin Dana Delaney Donald Moffat

1994　ONE CHRISTMAS
Director:　Tony Bill
Co-stars:　Katherine Hepburn Swoozie Kurtz Henry Winkler

KAY HARRIS

1942　SABOTAGE SQUAD
Co-stars:　Edward Norris George McKay

1943　ROBIN HOOD OF THE RANGE
Co-stars:　Charles Starrett Kenneth MacDonald

LARA HARRIS

1987　NO MAN'S LAND
Director:　Peter Werner
Co-stars:　D.B. Sweeney Charlie Sheen

1988　BLOOD RED
Director:　Peter Masterson
Co-stars:　Eric Roberts Dennis Hopper

1990　THE FOURTH WAR
Director:　John Frankenheimer
Co-stars:　Roy Scheider Jurgen Prochnow

1991　THE FISHER KING
Director:　Terry Gilliam
Co-stars:　Jeff Bridges Robin Williams

LEONORE HARRIS

1987　LENA - MY 100 CHILDREN
Director:　Ed Sherin
Co-stars:　Linda Lavin Cynthia Wilde

MARCIA HARRIS

1924　ISN'T LIFE WONDERFUL ?
Director:　D.W. Griffith
Co-stars:　Carol Dempster Lupino Lane

MARION HARRIS

1929　DEVIL MAY CARE
Co-stars:　Ramon Navarro Dorothy Jordan

MEL HARRIS

1988　K9
Director:　Rod Daniel
Co-stars:　James Belushi Kevvin Tighe James Hardy

1989　MY BROTHER'S WIFE
Director:　Jack Bender
Co-stars:　John Ritter David Byron Polly Bergen

1992　RAISING CAIN
Director:　Brian De Palma
Co-stars:　John Lithgow Steven Bauer Lolita Davidovich

1992　CHILD OF RAGE
Director:　Larry Peerce
Co-stars:　Dwight Schultz

1993　WIND DANCER
Director:　Craig Clyde
Co-stars:　Matt McCoy Raenin Simpson

1993　SUTURE
Director:　David Siegel
Co-stars:　Dennis Haysbert Michael Harris Dina Merrill

1994　THE PAGEMASTER
Director:　Maurice Hunt
Co-stars:　Macauley Culkin Ed Begley Jnr Whoopi Goldberg

1994　THE SPIDER AND THE FLY
Director:　Michael Katleman
Co-stars:　Ted Shackleford

1996　WHAT KIND OF MOTHER ARE YOU?
Director:　Noel Nosseck

MILDRED HARRIS

1928　POWER OF THE PRESS
Director:　Frank Capra
Co-stars:　Douglas Fairbanks Jnr. Jobyna Ralston

1931　NIGHT NURSE
Director:　William Wellman
Co-stars:　Barbara Stanwyck Ben Lyon Joan Blondell

NESTA HARRIS

1998　ON THE BLACK HILL
Director:　Andrew Grieve
Co-stars:　Bob Peck Gemma Jones Jack Walters

ROSALIND HARRIS

1971　FIDDLER ON THE ROOF
Director:　Norman Jewison
Co-stars:　Topol Norma Crane Leonard Frey

ROSEMARY HARRIS *(Mother Of Jennifer Eble)*

Nominated For Best Supporting Actress In 1994 For Tom & Viv

1954　BEAU BRUMMEL
Director:　Curtis Bernhardt
Co-stars:　Stewart Granger Elizabeth Taylor Peter Ustinov

1968　A FLEA IN HER EAR
Director:　Jacques Charon
Co-stars:　Rex Harrison Rachel Roberts Louis Jourdan

1978　THE BOYS FROM BRAZIL
Director:　Franklin Schaffner
Co-stars:　Gregory Peck Laurence Olivier James Mason

1983　THE PLOUGHMAN'S LUNCH
Director:　Richard Eyre
Co-stars:　Ann Scott Jonathan Pryce Tim Curry

1988 CROSSING DELANCEY
Director: Joan Micklin Silver
Co-stars: Amy Irving Peter Riegert Jeroen Krabbe

1990 THE BRIDGE
Director: Syd MacArtney
Co-stars: Saskia Reeves David O'Hara Anthony Higgins

1991 THE CAMOMILE LAWN
Director: Peter Hall
Co-stars: Jennifer Ehle Tara Fitzgerald Felicity Kendall

1993 TOM AND VIV
Director: Brian Gilbert
Co-stars: Willem Dafoe Miranda Richardson Tim Dutton

WINIFRED HARRIS

1930 FAST AND LOOSE
Director: Fred Newmeyer
Co-stars: Miriam Hopkins Carole Lombard Frank Morgan

WYN BOWEN HARRIS

1993 LEAVING LENIN
Director: Endaf Emlyn
Co-stars: Sharon Morgan Shelley Rees Richard Harrington

ZELDA HARRIS

1994 CROOKLYN
Director: Spike Lee
Co-stars: Alfre Wooodward Delroy Lindo Carlton Williams

CAROLE HARRISON

1983 LOOSE CONNECTIONS
Director: Lindsay Duncan
Co-stars: Stephen Rea Gary Olsen

CATHRYN HARRISON *(Daughter Of Noel Harrison, Granddaughter Of Rex Harrison)*

1972 IMAGES
Director: Robert Altman
Co-stars: Susannah York Rene Auberjonois Marcel Bozzuffi

1977 BLUE FIRE LADY
Director: Ross Dimsey

1986 DUET FOR ONE
Director: Andrei Konchalovsky
Co-stars: Julie Andrews Alan Bates Max Von Sydow

1987 EMPIRE STATE
Director: Ron Peck
Co-stars: Martin Landau Ray McAnally Jason Hoganson

1987 THE HAPPY VALLEY
Director: Ross Devenish
Co-stars: Denholm Elliott Holly Aird Amanda Hillwood

1990 PORTRAIT OF A MARRIAGE
Director: Stephen Whittaker
Co-stars: Janet McTeer David Haig Diana Fairfax

1991 CLARISSA
Director: Robert Bierman
Co-stars: Saskia Wickam Sean Bean Lynsey Baxter

IRMA HARRISON

1929 ALIBI
Director: Roland West
Co-stars: Chester Morris Eleanor Griffith Regis Toomey

JENILEE HARRISON

1984 TANK
Director: Martin Chomsky
Co-stars: James Garner Shirley Jones C. Thomas Howell

KATHLEEN HARRISON

1933 THE GOUL
Director: Hayes Hunter
Co-stars: Boris Karloff Cedric Hardwicke Ralph Richardson

1936 BROKEN BLOSSOMS
Director: John Brahm
Co-stars: Dolly Haas Arthur Margetson Emlyn Williams

1937 NIGHT MUST FALL
Director: Richard Thorpe
Co-stars: Robert Montgomery Rosalind Russell May Whitty

1938 BANK HOLIDAY
Director: Carol Reed
Co-stars: Margaret Lockwood Hugh Williams Wally Patch

1938 CONVICT 99
Director: Marcel Varnel
Co-stars: Will Hay Moore Marriott Graham Moffatt Googie Withers

1939 I KILLED THE COUNT
Director: Fred Zelnik
Co-stars: Syd Walker Terence De Marney Ben Lyon

1939 A GIRL MUST LIVE
Director: Carol Reed
Co-stars: Margaret Lockwood Renee Houston Lilli Palmer

1939 THE OUTSIDER
Director: Paul Stein
Co-stars: George Sanders Mary Maguire Peter Murray Hill

1940 THE GIRL IN THE NEWS
Director: Carol Reed
Co-stars: Margaret Lockwood Barry K. Barnes Emlyn Williams

1940 TILLY OF BLOOMSBURY
Director: Leslie Hiscott
Co-stars: Sydney Howard Jean Gillie Michael Wilding

1941 ONCE A CROOK
Director: Herbert Mason
Co-stars: Gordon Harker Sydney Howard Frank Pettingell

1941 KIPPS
Director: Carol Reed
Co-stars: Michael Redgrave Phyllis Calvert Diana Wynyard

1941 THE GHOST TRAIN
Director: Walter Forde
Co-stars: Arthur Askey Richard Murdoch Herbert Lom

1941 I THANK YOU
Director: Marcel Varnel
Co-stars: Arthur Askey Richard Murdoch Moore Marriott

1942 IN WHICH WE SERVE
Director: Noel Coward
Co-stars: Noel Coward Bernard Miles John Mills Celia Johnson

1942 MUCH TOO SHY
Director: Marcel Varnel
Co-stars: George Formby Jimmy Clitheroe Eileen Bennett

1943 DEAR OCTOPUS
Director: Harold French
Co-stars: Margaret Lockwood Michael Wilding Celia Johnson

1946 THE SHOP AT SLY CORNER
Director: George King
Co-stars: Oscar Homolka Muriel Pavlow Derek Farr

1946 WANTED FOR MURDER
Director: Lawrence Huntingdon
Co-stars: Eric Portman Dulcie Gray Derek Farr

1947 HOLIDAY CAMP
Director: Ken Annakin
Co-stars: Jack Warner Flora Robson Dennis Price Hazel Court

1947 TEMPTATION HARBOUR
Director: Lance Comfort
Co-stars: Robert Newton Simone Simon William Hartnell

1948   **THE WINSLOW BOY**
Director: Anthony Asquith
Co-stars: Robert Donat Cedric Hardwicke Jack Watling

1948   **HERE COME THE HUGGETTS**
Director: Ken Annakin
Co-stars: Jack Warner Jane Hylton Susan Shaw

1948   **BOND STREET**
Director: Gordon Parry
Co-stars: Roland Young Jean Kent Derek Farr Ronald Howard

1948   **THE HUGGETTS ABROAD**
Director: Ken Annakin
Co-stars: Jack Warner Dinah Sheridan Jimmy Hanley

1949   **LANDFALL**
Director: Ken Annakin
Co-stars: Michael Dennison Patricia Plunkett David Tomlinson

1949   **NOW BARABBAS**
Director: Gordon Parry
Co-stars: Cedric Hardwicke Richard Greene Kenneth More

1948   **VOTE FOR HUGGETT**
Director: Ken Annakin
Co-stars: Jack Warner Susan Shaw Diana Dors Anthony Newley

1950   **WATEFRONT**
Director: Michael Anderson
Co-stars: Robert Newton Richard Burton Susan Shaw

1950   **DOUBLE CONFESSION**
Director: Ken Annakin
Co-stars: Derek Farr Peter Lorre Joan Hopkins

1950   **TRIO**
Director: Ken Annakin
Co-stars: James Hayter Nigel Patrick Jean Simmons A. Crawford

1951   **SCROOGE**
Director: Brian Desmond Hurst
Co-stars: Alastair Sim Mervyn Johns Jack Warner

1952   **THE PICKWICK PAPERS**
Director: Noel Langley
Co-stars: James Hayter James Donald Hermione Baddeley

1952   **THE HAPPY FAMILY**
Director: Muriel Box
Co-stars: Stanley Holloway Naunton Wayne George Cole

1952   **GOLDEN ARROW**
Director: Gordon Parry
Co-stars: Jean-Pierre Aumont Paula Valenska Burgess Meredith

1953   **THE DOG AND THE DIAMONDS**
Director: Ralph Thomas
Co-stars: George Coulouris Geoffrey Summer

1953   **TURN THE KEY SOFTLY**
Director: Jack Lee
Co-stars: Yvonne Mitchell Joan Collins Terence Morgan

1954   **LILACS IN THE SPRING**
Director: Herbert Wilcox
Co-stars: Anna Neagle Errol Flynn David Farrar

1955   **ALL FOR MARY**
Director: Wendy Toye
Co-stars: Nigel Patrick David Tomlinson Jill Day Leo McKern

1955   **CAST A DARK SHADOW**
Director: Lewis Gilbert
Co-stars: Dirk Bogarde Margaret Lockwood Kay Walsh

1955   **WHERE THERE'S A WILL**
Director: Vernon Sewell
Co-stars: Edward Lexy George Cole Leslie Dwyer

1956   **HOME AND AWAY**
Director: Vernon Sewell
Co-stars: Jack Warner Lana Morris Charles Victor Thora Hird

1956   **IT'S A WONDERFUL WORLD**
Director: Val Guest
Co-stars: George Cole Terence Morgan Mylene Nicole

1956   **THE BIG MONEY**
Director: John Paddy Carstairs
Co-stars: Ian Carmichael Belinda Lee James Hayter

1957   **SEVEN THUNDERS**
Director: Hugo Fregonese
Co-stars: Stephen Boyd Tony Wright Anna Gaylor

1958   **A CRY FROM THE STREETS**
Director: Lewis Gilbert
Co-stars: Max Bygraves Barbara Murray Colin Peterson

1958   **ALIVE AND KICKING**
Director: Cyril Frankel
Co-stars: Sybil Thorndyke Estelle Winwood Stanley Holloway

1961   **ON THE FIDDLE**
Director: Cyril Frankel
Co-stars: Alfred Lynch Sean Connery Cecil Parker Alan King

1962   **MRS. GIBBON'S BOYS**
Director: Max Varnel
Co-stars: Lionel Jeffries Diana Dors Dick Emery

1962   **THE FAST LADY**
Director: Ken Annakin
Co-stars: Stanley Baxter Leslie Phillips Julie Christie

1963   **WEST II**
Director: Michael Winner
Co-stars: Alfred Lynch Eric Portman Diana Dors Freda Jackson

1969   **LOCK UP YOUR DAUGHTERS**
Director: Peter Coe
Co-stars: Susannah York Glynis Johns Ian Bannen Jim Dale

LINDA HARRISON

1967   **A GUIDE FOR THE MARRIED MAN**
Director: Gene Kelly
Co-stars: Walter Matthau Inger Stevens Robert Morse

1968   **PLANET OF THE APES**
Director: Franklin Schaffner
Co-stars: Charlton Heston Roddy McDowall

1969   **BENEATH THE PLANET OF THE APES**
Director: Ted Post
Co-stars: Charlton Heston James Franciscus

SALLY HARRISON

1973   **AND NOW THE SCREAMING STARTS**
Director: Roy Ward Baker
Co-stars: Peter Cushing Stephanie Beacham

SUSAN HARRISON

1957   **SWEET SMELL OF SUCCESS**
Director: Alexander MacKendrick
Co-stars: Burt Lancaster Tony Curtis Sam Levine

KATHRYN HAROLD

1979   **NIGHTWING**
Director: Arthur Hiller
Co-stars: David Warner Stephen Macht Strother Martin

1980   **THE HUNTER**
Director: Buzz Kulik
Co-stars: Steve McQueen Eli Wallach Ben Johnson

1980   **BOGIE**
Director: Vincent Sherman
Co-stars: Kevin O'Connor Ann Wedgeworth Drew Barrymore

1981   **MODERN ROMANCE**
Director: Albert Brooks
Co-stars: Albert Brooks Bruno Kirby Jane Hallaren George Kennedy

1981 **THE PURSUIT OF D.B. COOPER**
Director: Roger Spottiswoode
Co-stars: Robert Duvall Treat Williams

1982 **THE SENDER**
Director: Roger Christian
Co-stars: Zeljko Ivanek Shirley Knight Paul Freeman

1982 **YES, GIORGIO**
Director: Franklin Schaffner
Co-stars: Luciano Pavorotti Eddie Albert Paola Borboni

1984 **HEARTBREAKERS**
Director: Bobby Roth
Co-stars: Peter Coyoye Nick Mancuso Carole Laure

1986 **RAW DEAL**
Director: John Irvin
Co-stars: Arnold Schwarzenegger Sam Wanamaker Robert Davi

LISA HARROW

1975 **ALL CREATURES GREAT AND SMALL**
Director: Claude Whatham
Co-stars: Anthony Hopkins Simon Ward

1976 **IT SHOULDN'T HAPPEN TO A VET**
Director: Eric Till
Co-stars: John Alderton Colin Blakely Bill Maynard

1981 **THE FINAL CONFLICT: OMEN III**
Director: Graham Baker
Co-stars: Sam Neill Rossano Brazzi Don Gordon

1985 **SHAKER RUN**
Director: Bruce Morrison
Co-stars: Cliff Robertson Leif Garnett Shane Briant

1990 **THE LAST DAYS OF CHEZ NOUS**
Director: Gillian Armstrong
Co-stars: Bruno Ganz Kerry Fox Miranda Otto

1990 **INSPECTOR MORSE: SINS OF THE FATHER**
Director: Peter Hammond
Co-stars: John Thaw Kevin Whately

1992 **WITCHCRAFT**
Director: Peter Sasdy
Co-stars: Peter McEnery Alan Howard Clive Wood

1997 **SUNDAY**
Director: Jonathan Nossiter
Co-star: David Suchet

ELIZABETH HARROWER

1969 **THE STERILE CUCKOO**
Director: Alan J. Pakula
Co-stars: Liza Minnelli Wendell Burton Tim McIntyre

DEBBI HARRY *(Deborah)*

1980 **UNION CITY**
Director: Mark Reichert
Co-stars: Dennis Lipscomb Irina Maleeva Everett McGill

1980 **ROADIE**
Director: Alan Rudolph
Co-stars: Meatloaf Kaki Hunter Art Carney Roy Orbison

1983 **VIDEODROME**
Director: David Cronenberg
Co-stars: James Woods Sonja Smits Peter Dvorsky

1987 **FOREVER LULU**
Director: Amos Kollek
Co-stars: Hanna Schygulla Alec Baldwin

1988 **SATISFACTION**
Director: Joan Freeman
Co-stars: Justine Bateman Liam Neeson Trini Alvarado

1988 **HAIRSPRAY**
Director: John Waters
Co-stars: Sonny Bono Ruth Brown Pia Zadora

1990 **TALES FROM THE DARK SIDE**
Director: John Harrison
Co-stars: Matthew Lawrence Christian Slater

DIANE HART

1948 **BRITTANIA MEWS**
Director: Jean Negulesco
Co-stars: Maureen O'Hara Dana Andrews Wilfred Hyde White

1950 **HAPPY GO LOVELY**
Director: Bruce Humberstone
Co-stars: David Niven Vera-Ellen Cesar Romero

1952 **SOMETHING MONEY CAN'T BUY**
Director: Pat Jackson
Co-stars: Patricia Roc Anthony Steel Moira Lister

1952 **YOU'RE ONLY YOUNG TWICE**
Director: Terry Bishop
Co-stars: Duncan MacRae Charles Hawtrey Patrick Barr

1955 **ONE JUMP AHEAD**
Director: Charles Saunders
Co-stars: Paul Carpenter Jill Adams Freddie Mills

1961 **ENTER INSPECTOR DUVAL**
Director: Max Varnel
Co-stars: Anton Diffring Mark Singleton

DOLORES HART

1957 **LOVING YOU**
Director: Hal Kanter
Co-stars: Elvis Presley Lisabeth Scott Wendell Corey

1957 **WILD IS THE WIND**
Director: George Cukor
Co-stars: Anna Magnani Anthony Quinn Tony Franciosa

1958 **LONELY HEARTS**
Director: Vincent Donehue
Co-stars: Montgomery Clift Robert Ryan Myrna Loy

1958 **KING CREOLE**
Director: Michael Curtiz
Co-stars: Elvis Presley Carolyn Jones Walter Matthau

1960 **THE PLUNDERERS**
Director: Joseph Pevney
Co-stars: Jeff Chandler John Saxon Marsha Hunt

1960 **WHERE THE BOYS ARE**
Director: Henry Levin
Co-stars: George Hamilton Paula Prentiss Connie Francis

1961 **FRANCIS OF ASSISI**
Director: Michael Curtiz
Co-stars: Bradford Dillman Stuart Whitman Eduard Franz

1961 **SAIL A CROOKED SHIP**
Director: Irving Brecher
Co-stars: Robert Wagner Ernie Kovacs Carolyn Jones

1962 **COME FLY WITH ME**
Director: Henry Levin
Co-stars: Pamela Tiffin Lois Nettleton Karl Malden

1962 **THE INSPECTOR**
Director: Phillip Dunne
Co-stars: Stephen Boyd Hugh Griffith Leo McKern

1964 **RIDE THE WILD SURF**
Director: Don Taylor
Co-stars: Fabian Shelley Fabares Tab Hunter

DOROTHY HART

1947 **GUNFIGHTERS**
Director: George Waggner
Co-stars: Randolph Scott Barbara Britton Bruce Cabot

1948   **THE COUNTESS OF MONTE CRISTO**
Director: Frederick De Cordova
Co-stars: Sonja Henie Olga San Juan Michael Kirby

1948   **CALAMITY JANE AND SAM BASS**
Director: George Sherman
Co-stars: Yvonne De Carlo Howard Duff Ann Doran

1948   **LARCENCY**
Director: George Sherman
Co-stars: John Payne Joan Caulfield Dan Duryea

1948   **THE NAKED CITY**
Director: Jules Dassin
Co-stars: Barry Fittzgerald Don Taylor Howard Duff

1949   **THE STORY OF MOLLY X**
Director: Crane Wilbur
Co-stars: June Havoc John Russell Connie Gilchrist

1949   **TAKE ONE FALSE STEP**
Director: Chester Erskine
Co-stars: William Powell Shelley Winters Marsha Hunt

1949   **UNDERTOW**
Director: William Castle
Co-stars: Scott Brady John Russell Peggy Dow

1951   **RATON PASS**
Director: Edwin Marin
Co-stars: Dennis Morgan Patricia Neal Steve Cochran

1951   **I WAS A COMMUNIST FOR THE F.B.I.**
Director: Gordon Douglas
Co-stars: Frank Lovejoy Phil Carey Paul Picerni

1952   **LOAN SHARK**
Director: Seymour Friedman
Co-stars: George Raft Paul Stewart Helen Westcott

1952   **TARZAN'S SAVAGE FURY**
Director: Cy Endfield
Co-stars: Lex Barker Patric Knowles Charles Korvin

LINDA HART

1996   **TIN CUP**
Director: Ron Shelton
Co-stars: Kevin Costner Cheech Marin Don Johnson Rene Russo

MARIA HART

1951   **CATTLE QUEEN**
Director: John Carpenter
Co-stars: John Carpenter William Fawcett Emile Meyer

MARY HART

1938   **SHINE ON HARVEST MOON**
Co-stars: Roy Rogers Stanley Andrews

1939   **ROUGH RIDERS ROUND-UP**
Co-stars: Roy Rogers Raymond Hatton George Meeker

MELISSA JOAN HART

1995   **FAMILY REUNION - A RELATIVE NIGHTMARE**
Director: Neal Israel
Co-stars: Jason Marsden Peter Billingsley

ROXANNE HART

1982   **THE VERDICT**
Director: Sidney Lumet
Co-stars: Paul Newman Charlotte Rampling James Mason

1984   **OH GOD! YOU DEVIL**
Director: Paul Bogart
Co-stars: George Burns Suzanne Pleshette David Birney

1984   **OLD ENOUGH**
Director: Marisa Silver
Co-stars: Sarah Boyd Rainbow Harvest Danny Aiello

1986   **HIGHLANDER**
Director: Russell Mulcahey
Co-stars: Christopher Lambert Sean Connery Beattie Edney

1986   **VENGEANCE: THE STORY OF TONY CIMO**
Director: Marc Daniels
Co-stars: Brad Davis Brad Dourif

1987   **THE LAST INNOCENT MAN**
Director: Roger Spottiswoode
Co-stars: Ed Harris David Suchet Rose Gregorio

1988   **PULSE**
Director: Paul Golding
Co-stars: Cliff De Young Joey Lawrence

1991   **LIVING A LIE**
Director: Larry Shaw
Co-stars: Peter Coyote David Andrews Jill Eikenberry

1991   **ONCE AROUND**
Director: Lasse Hallstrom
Co-stars: Richard Dreyfuss Holly Hunter Danny Aiello

SUSAN HART

1965   **CITY UNDER THE SEA**
Director: Jacques Tourneur
Co-stars: Vincent Price David Tomlinson Tab Hunter

1965   **DR. GOLDFOOT AND THE BIKINI MACHINE**
Director: Norman Taurog
Co-stars: Vincent Price Frankie Avalon

TRACIE HART

1989   **THE ACCOUNTANT**
Director: Les Blair
Co-stars: Alfred Molina Georgia Mitchell Clive Panto

VERONICA HART

1981   **AFTERNOON DELIGHTS**
Director: Warren Evans
Co-stars: Eric Edwards Merle Michaels Samantha Fox

MARIETTE HARTLEY

1962   **RIDE THE HIGH COUNTRY**
Director: Sam Peckinpah
Co-stars: Randolph Scott Joel McCrea Edgar Buchanan

1969   **MAROONED**
Director: John Sturges
Co-stars: Gregory Peck Gene Hackman Lee Grant

1970   **BARQUERO**
Director: Gordan Douglas
Co-stars: Lee Van Cleef Warren Oates Forrest Tucker

1971   **THE RETURN OF COUNT YORGA**
Director: Bob Kelljan
Co-stars: Robert Quarry George Macready Roger Perry

1972   **GENESIS II**
Director: John Llewellyn Moxey
Co-star: Kathleen Beller

1982   **DROP-OUT FATHER**
Director: Don Taylor
Co-stars: Dick Van Dyke George Coe Rhea Perlman

1983   **MADD: MOTHERS AGAINST DRUNK DRIVERS**
Director: William A. Graham

1983   **O'HARA'S WIFE**
Director: William Bartman
Co-stars: Ed Asner Jodie Foster Ray Walston

1986   **ONE TERRIFIC GUY**
Director: Lou Antonio
Co-stars: Wayne Rogers Susan Rinell Brian Robbins

1988   1969
Director: Ernest Thompson
Co-stars: Robert Downey Jnr. Kieffer Sutherland Winona Ryder

1989   AMY
Director: John Llewellyn Moxey
Co-stars: Kathleen Beller Gary Graham Keir Dullea

1990   MURDER C.O.D.
Director: Alan Metzger
Co-stars: William Devane Patrick Duffy Chelsea Field

1991   DIAGNOSIS OF MURDER
Director: Barry Steinberg
Co-stars: Dick Van Dyke Cynthia Gibb Bill Bixby

1992   CALIFORNIA MAN
Director: Les Mayfield
Co-stars: Sean Astin Pauly Shore Brendan Fraser

1995   FREEFALL: THE FATE OF FLIGHT 174
Director: Jorge Montesi
Co-stars: William Devane Shelley Hack

ELIZABETH HARTMAN
Nominated For Best Actress In 1965 For "A Patch Of Blue"

1965   A PATCH OF BLUE
Director: Guy Green
Co-stars: Sidney Poitier Shelley Winters Wallace Ford

1966   THE GROUP
Director: Sidney Lumet
Co-stars: Candice Bergen Joan Hackett Shirley Knight

1967   YOU'RE A BIG BOY NOW
Director: Francis Coppola
Co-stars: Peter Kastner Geraldine Page Julie Harris

1968   THE FIXER
Director: John Frankenheimer
Co-stars: Alan Bates Dirk Bogarde Georgia Brown

1971   THE BEGUILED
Director: Don Seigel
Co-stars: Clint Eastwood Geraldine Page Darleen Carr

1973   WALKING TALL
Director: Phil Karlson
Co-stars: Joe Don Baker Gene Evans Rosemary Murphy

1981   FULL MOON HIGH
Director: Larry Cohen
Co-stars: Adam Arkin Ed McMahon Kenneth Mars

1982   THE SECRET OF NIHM *(Voice)*
Director: Don Bluth
Co-stars: Peter Strauss Dom Deluise John Carradine

GRACE HARTMAN

1937   FORTY FIVE FATHERS
Director: James Tingling
Co-stars: Jane Withers Thomas Beck Paul Hartman

1941   SUNNY
Director: Herbert Wilcox
Co-stars: Anna Neagle Ray Bolger Paul Hartman

1943   HIGHER AND HIGHER
Director: Tim Whelman
Co-stars: Frank Sinatra Michele Morgan Jack Haley

LISA HARTMAN

1981   DEADLY BLESSING
Director: Wes Craven
Co-stars: Karen Jensen Ernest Borgnine Lois Nettleton

1984   WHERE THE BOYS ARE
Director: Hy Averback
Co-stars: Lorna Luft Wendy Schaal Russell Todd

1985   BEVERLY HILLS CONNECTION
Director: Corey Allen
Co-stars: James Brolin David Hemmings Irena Ferris

1987   ROSES ARE FOR THE RICH
Director: Michael Miller
Co-star: Bruce Dern

1987   STUDENT EXCHANGE
Director: Mollie Miller
Co-stars: Lindsay Wagner O.J. Simpson

1989   FULL EXPOSURE: THE SEX TAPES SCANDAL
Director: Noel Noseck
Co-stars: Anthony Denison Vanessa Williams

1990   THE OPERATION
Director: Thomas Wright
Co-stars: Joe Penny Kathleen Quinan Jason Beghe

1991   BARE ESSENTIALS

1991   THE RETURN OF ELLIOTT NESS
Director: James Contner
Co-stars: Robert Stack Jack Coleman Philip Bosco

1993   FALSELY ACCUSED
Director: Noel Nosseck
Co-stars: Christopher Meloni Peter Jurasik

1994   SOMEONE ELSE'S CHILD
Director: John Power
Co-stars: Bruce Davison Whip Hubley

RAINBOW HARVEST

1984   OLD ENOUGH
Director: Marisa Silver
Co-stars: Sarah Boyd Danny Aiello Roxanne Hart

JEAN HARVEY

1955   GUNS DON'T ARGUE
Director: Bill Karn
Co-stars: Myron Healy Richard Crane

1963   IT'S ALL HAPPENING
Director: Don Sharp
Co-stars: Tommy Steele Angela Douglas Michael Medwin

JOAN HARVEY

1960   PRETTY BOY FLOYD
Director: Herbert Leder
Co-stars: John Ericson Barry Newman Carl York

LILLIAN HARVEY

1930   THE LOVE WALTZ
Director: Wilhelm Thiele
Co-stars: Joan Batten George Alexander

1931   CONGRESS DANCES
Director: Erik Charrell
Co-stars: Conrad Veidt Henri Garat Willy Fritsch

1932   HAPPY EVER AFTER
Director: Robert Stevenson
Co-stars: Jack Hulbert Edward Chapman

1933   MY LIPS BETRAY
Co-stars: John Boles

1933   MY WEAKNESS

1933   I AM SUZANNE
Director: Rowland Lee
Co-stars: Gene Raymond Leslie Banks Georgia Caine

1935   LET'S LIVE TONIGHT
Director: Victor Schertzinger
Co-stars: Tullio Carminati Hugh Williams

1935   INVITAION TO THE WALTZ

MARILYN HARVEY
1958   THE ASTOUNDING SEA-MONSTER
Director: Ronnie Ashcroft
Co-stars: Robert Clarke Ken Duncan Jeanne Tatum

VERNA HARVEY
1971   THE NIGHTCOMERS
Director: Michael Winner
Co-stars: Stephanie Beacham Marlon Brando Thora Hird

1973   THE ASSASSIN
Director: Peter Crane
Co-stars: Ian Hendry Edward Judd Ray Brooks

SOPHIA HASKAS
1977   CATHY'S CHILD
Director: Donald Crombie
Co-stars: Michelle Fawdon Alan Cassell Bob Hughes

IMOGEN HASSALL
1969   WHEN DINOSAURS RULED THE EARTH
Director: Val Guest
Co-stars: Victoria Vetri Patrick Allen Patrick Holt

1970   INCENSE FOR THE DAMNED
Director: Michael Burrowes
Co-stars: Peter Cushing Patrick Mower

1970   CARRY ON LOVING
Director: Gerald Thomas
Co-stars: Sid James Hattie Jacques Terry Scott

1974   WHITE CARGO
Director: Ray Selfe
Co-stars: David Jason Hugh Lloyd David Prowse

MARILYN HASSETT
1975   THE OTHER SIDE OF THE MOUNTAIN
Director: Larry Peerce
Co-stars: Beau Bridges Belinda Montgomery

1975   THE OTHER SIDE OF THE MOUNTAIN PART 2
Director: Larry Peerce
Co-stars: Timothy Bottoms Nan Martin

1979   THE BELL JAR
Director: Larry Peerce
Co-stars: Julie Haris Anne Jackson Barbara Barrie

SIGNE HASSO
1942   JOURNEY FOR MARGARET
Director: W.S. Van Dyke
Co-stars: Margaret O'Brien Robert Young Laraine Day

1943   ASSIGNMENT IN BRITTANNY
Director: Jack Conway
Co-stars: Jean Pierre Aumont Susan Peters Richard Whorf

1944   THE SEVENTH CROSS
Director: Fred Zinnemann
Co-stars: Spency Tracy Hume Cronyn Jessica Tandy

1944   THE STORY OF DR. WASSELL
Director: Cecil B. DeMille
Co-stars: Gary Cooper Laraine Day Dennis O'Keefe

1945   JOHNNY ANGEL
Director: Edwin Marin
Co-stars: George Raft Claire Trevor Hoagy Carmichael

1945   THE HOUSE ON 92ND. STREET
Director: Henry Hathaway
Co-stars: William Eythe Lloyd Nolan Gene Lockhart

1946   STRANGE TRIANGLE
Co-stars: Preston Foster Annabel Shaw John Shepperd

1946   A SCANDAL IN PARIS
Director: Douglas Sirk
Co-stars: George Sanders Akim Tamiroff Carole Landis

1947   WHERE THER'S LIFE
Director: Sidney Lanfield
Co-stars: Bob Hope William Bendix George Coulouis

1947   A DOUBLE LIFE
Director: George Cukor
Co-stars: Ronald Coleman Shelley Winters Edmond O'Brien

1948   TO THE ENDS OF THE EARTH
Director: Robert Stevenson
Co-stars: Dick Powell Vladimir Sokoloff

1950   CRISIS
Director: Richard Brooks
Co-stars: Cary Grant Jose Ferrer Ramon Navarro Paula Raymond

1965   CARRY ON CLEO
Director: Gerald Thomas
Co-stars: Amanda Barrie Sid James Charles Hawtrey

1966   PICTURE MOMMY DEAD
Director: Bert Gordon
Co-stars: Don Ameche Susan Gordon Martha Hyer

1971   A REFLECTION OF FEAR
Director: William Fraker
Co-stars: Robert Shaw Mary Ure Sondra Locke

1973   THE MAGICIAN
Director: Marvin Chomsky
Co-stars: Bill Bixby Joan Caulfield Kim Hunter

1975   SHELL GAME
Director: Glenn Jordan
Co-stars: John Davidson Tommy Atkins Marie O'Brien Jack Kehoe

1975   THE BLACK BIRD
Director: David Giler
Co-stars: George Segal Stephane Audran Lee Patrick

1977   I NEVER PROMISED YOU A ROSE GARDEN
Director: Anthony Page
Co-stars: Kathleen Quinlan Bibi Andersson Sylvia Sidney

1985   MIRRORS
Director: Harry Winer
Co-stars: Timothy Daly Shanna Reed Anthony Hamilton Keenan Wynn

ANN HASSON
1987   THE VENUS DE MILO INSTEAD
Director: Danny Boyle
Co-stars: Jeanne Crowley Iain Cuthberson

MARY HATCHER
1947   VARIETY GIRL
Director: George Marshall
Co-stars: Olga San Juan Glenn Tryon DeForrest Kelly

1948   ISN'T IT ROMANTIC
Director: Norman Z. McLeod
Co-stars: Veronica Lake Mona Freeman Billy De Wolfe

1949   THE BIG WHEEL
Director: Edward Ludwig
Co-stars: Mickey Rooney Spring Blyington Thomas Mitchell

TERI HATCHER
1988   THE BIG PICTURE
Director: Christopher Guest
Co-stars: Kevin Bacon Jennifer Jason Leigh John Cleese

1989   TANGO AND CASH
Director: Andrei Konchalovsky
Co-stars: Sylvester Stallone Kurt Russell Jack Palance

1991 SOAPDISH
Director: Michael Hoffman
Co-stars: Sally Field Kevin Kline Whoopi Goldberg

1992 STRAIGHT TALK
Director: Barnet Kellman
Co-stars: Dolly Parton James Woods Griffin Dunne

1993 THE NEW ADVENTURES OF SUPERMAN
Director: Robert Butler
Co-stars: Dean Cain John Shea Lane Smith

1994 HEAVEN'S PRISONERS
Director: Phil Joanou
Co-stars: Alec Baldwin Eric Roberts Mary Stuart Masterson

1996 TWO DAYS IN THE VALLEY
Director: John Herzfeld
Co-stars: Eric Stoltz Jeff Daniels James Spader

1997 TOMORROW NEVER DIES
Co-stars: Pierce Brosnan Jonathan Pryce Judi Dench

BRIT HATHAWAY *(Child)*

1991 FIRES WITHIN
Director: Gillian Armstrong
Co-stars: Greta Scacchi Jimmy Smits Vincent D'Onofrio

ROHINI HATTANGADY

1982 GHANDI
Director: Richard Attenborough
Co-stars: Ben Kingsley Candice Bergen John Gielgud

HILO HATTIE

1942 SONG OF THE ISLAND
Director: Walter Lang
Co-stars: Betty Grable Victor Mature Jack Oakie

JEAN HATTON

1939 MR. CHEDWORTH STEPS OUT
Director: Ken Hall
Co-stars: Cecil Kellaway James Raglan Peter Finch

SABINE HAUDEPIN

1962 JULES AND JIM
Director: Francois Truffaut
Co-stars: Jeanne Moreau Oskar Werner Henri Serre

1986 MAX, MON AMOUR
Director: Nagise Oshima
Co-stars: Charlotte Rampling Anthony Higgins Victoria Abril

1989 FORCE MAJEUR
Director: Pierre Jolivet
Co-stars: Patrick Buel Francois Cluzet Alan Bates

YASMINE HAURY

1986 FOUR ADVENTURES OF REINETTE AND MIRABELLE
Director: Eric Rohmer
Co-stars: Joelle Miquel Jessica Forde

RUTH HAVEN

1936 THE END OF THE ROAD
Director: Alan Bryce
Co-stars: Harry Lauder Ethel Glendinning Bruce Seton

JUNE HAVER *(Married Fred MacMurray)*

1944 HOME IN INDIANA
Director: Henry Hathaway
Co-stars: Jeanne Crain Lon McCallister Walter Brennan

1944 IRISH EYES ARE SMILING
Director: Gregory Ratoff
Co-stars: Dick Haymes Monty Wooley Anthony Quinn

1945 WHERE DO WE GO FROM HERE
Director: Gregory Ratoff
Co-stars: Fred MacMurray Joan Leslie Anthony Quinn

1945 THE DOLLY SISTERS
Director: Irving Cummings
Co-stars: Betty Grable John Payne Gene Sheldon

1946 THREE LITTLE GIRLS IN BLUE
Director: Bruce Humberstone
Co-stars: Vivian Blaine Vera-Ellen Celeste Holm

1946 WAKE UP AND DREAM
Director: Lloyd Bacon
Co-stars: John Payne Connie Marshall Charlotte Greenwood

1947 I WONDER WHO'S KISSING HER NOW
Director: Lloyd Bacon
Co-stars: Mark Stevens Martha Stewart Reginald Gardner

1948 SCUDDA HOO, SCUDDA HEY
Director: Hugh Herbert
Co-stars: Lon McCallister Walter Brennan Natalie Wood

1948 SUMMER LIGHTNING
Co-star: Lon McCallister

1949 OH YOU BEAUTIFUL DOLL
Director: John Stahl
Co-stars: S.Z. Sakall Mark Stevens Charlotte Greenwood

1949 LOOK FOR THE SILVER LINING
Director: David Butler
Co-stars: Ray Bolger Gordon MacRae S.Z. Sakall

1950 I'LL GET BY
Director: Richard Sale
Co-stars: Gloria De Haven William Lundigan Dennis Day

1950 THE DAUGHTER OF ROSIE O'GRADY
Director: David Butler
Co-stars: Gordon MacRae Gene Nelson S.Z. Sakall

1951 LOVE NEST
Director: Joseph Newman
Co-stars: William Lundigan Marilyn Monroe Frank Fey

1953 THE GIRL NEXT DOOR
Director: Richard Sale
Co-stars: Dan Dailey Dennis Day Cara Williams

PHYLLIS HAVER

1923 THE CHRISTIAN
Director: Maurice Tourneur
Co-stars: Richard Dix Mae Busch

1926 DON JUAN
Director: Alan Crosland
Co-stars: John Barrymore Mary Astor

1926 WHAT PRICE GLORY ?
Director: Raoul Walsh
Co-stars: Victor McLaglen Edmund Lowe Dolores Del Rio

1927 THE WAY OF ALL FLESH
Director: Victor Fleming
Co-stars: Emil Jannings Belle Bennett

1929 THUNDER
Director: William Nigh
Co-stars: Lon Chaney James Murray

JUNE HAVOC *(Sister Of Gypsy Rose Lee)*

1941 SING YOUR WORRIES AWAY
Director: Edward Sutherland
Co-stars: Bert Lahr Buddy Ebsen Patsy Kelly

1942 POWDER TOWN
Director: Rowland Lee
Co-stars: Victor McLaglen Edmond O'Brien

1942　**MY SISTER EILEEN**
Director:　Alexander Hall
Co-stars:　Rosalind Russell Brian Aherne Janet Blair

1942　**FOUR JACKS AND JILL**
Director:　Jack Hively
Co-stars:　Anne Shirley Ray Bolger Desi Arnaz Eddie Foy

1943　**HELLO FRISCO, HELLO**
Director:　Bruce Humberstone
Co-stars:　Alice Faye John Payne Jack Oakie Lynn Bari

1943　**HI DIDDLE DIDDLE**
Director:　Andrew Stone
Co-stars:　Adolphe Menjou Pola Negri Dennis O'Keefe

1943　**NO TIME FOR LOVE**
Director:　Mitchell Leisen
Co-stars:　Claudette Colbert Fred MacMurray Ilka Chase

1944　**CASANOVA IN BURLESQUE**
Director:　Leslie Goodwins
Co-stars:　Joe E. Brown Dale Evans Ian Keith

1945　**BREWSTER'S MILLIONS**
Director:　Allan Dwan
Co-stars:　Dennis O'Keefe Eddie Anderson Helen Walker

1947　**INTRIQUE**
Director:　Edwin Marin
Co-stars:　George Raft Tom Tully Helena Carter

1947　**GENTLEMEN'S AGREEMENT**
Director:　Elia Kazan
Co-stars:　Gregory Peck Dorothy McGuire John Garfield Celeste Holm

1948　**THE IRON CURTAIN**
Director:　William Wellman
Co-stars:　Dana Andrews Gene Tierney Edna Best

1948　**WHEN MY BABY SMILES AT ME**
Director:　Walter Lang
Co-stars:　Betty Grable Dan Dailey Jack Oakie

1949　**THE STORY OF MOLLY X**
Director:　Crane Wilbur
Co-stars:　John Russell Dorothy Hart Connie Gilchrist

1949　**CHICAGO DEADLINE**
Director:　Lewis Allen
Co-stars:　Alan Ladd Donna Reed Arthur Kennedy

1950　**MOTHER DIDN'T TELL ME**
Director:　Claude Binyon
Co-stars:　Dorothy McGuire William Lundigan Gary Merrill

1951　**FOLLOW THE SUN**
Director:　Sidney Lanfield
Co-stars:　Glenn Ford Anne Baxter Dennis O'Keefe

1952　**THE LADY POSSESSED**
Director:　Roy Kellino
Co-stars:　James Mason Pamela Kellino Fay Compton

1956　**THREE FOR JAMIE DAWN**
Director:　Thomas Carr
Co-stars:　Laraine Day Ricardo Montalban Richard Carlson

1978　**THE PRIVATE FILES OF J.EDGAR HOOVER**
Director:　Larry Cohen
Co-stars:　Broderick Crawford Jose Ferrer Dan Dailey

1980　**CAN'T STOP THE MUSIC**
Director:　Nancy Walker
Co-stars:　Village People Valerie Perrine Barbara Rush

1987　**A RETURN TO SALEM'S LOT**
Director:　Larry Cohen
Co-stars:　Michael Moriarty Samuel Fuller Evelyn Keyes

CAROL HAWKINS

1971　**PLEASE SIR!**
Director:　Mark Stuart
Co-stars:　John Alderton Noel Howlett Joan Sanderson

1972　**CARRY ON ABROAD**
Director:　Gerald Thomas
Co-stars:　Sid James Barbara Windsor Sally Geeson

1975　**CARRY ON BEHIND**
Director:　Gerald Thomas
Co-stars:　Elke Sommer Kenneth Williams Liz Fraser

1975　**CONFESSIONS OF A POP PERFORMER**
Director:　Norman Cohen
Co-stars:　Robin Askwith Anthony Booth

GEORGIA HAWKINS

1941　**DOOMED CARAVAN**
Co-stars:　William Boyd Minna Gombell

JENNIFER HAWKINS

1976　**HAWMPS!**
Director:　Joe Camp
Co-stars:　Christopher Connelly Denver Pyle Slim Pickins

YVETTE HAWKINS

1981　**CAGNEY AND LACEY**
Director:　Ted Post
Co-stars:　Loretta Swit Tyne Daly Al Waxman

1992　**MISSISSIPPI MASALA**
Director:　Mira Nair
Co-stars:　Denzel Washington Sarita Choudbury Roshan Seth

JEAN HAWKSHAW

1965　**THE WILD WOMEN OF WONGO**
Director:　James Wolcott
Co-star:　Pat Crowley

GOLDIE HAWN *(Married Kurt Russell)*
Oscar For Best Supporting Actress In 1969 For "Cactus Flower"
Nominated For Best Actress In 1980 For "Private Benjamin"

1968　**THE ONE AND ONLY GENUINE ORIGINAL FAMILY BAND**
Director:　Michael O'Herlihy
Co-stars:　Walter Brennan Buddy Ebsen Janet Blair Kurt Russell

1969　**CACTUS FLOWER**
Director:　Gene Saks
Co-stars:　Ingrid Bergman Walter Matthau Jack Weston

1970　**THERE'S A GIRL IN MY SOUP**
Director:　Roy Boulting
Co-stars:　Peter Sellers Tony Britton Diana Dors

1971　**THE HEIST**
Director:　Richard Brooks
Co-stars:　Warren Beatty Gert Frobe Robert Webber

1972　**BUTTERFLIES ARE FREE**
Director:　Milton Katselas
Co-stars:　Edward Albert Eileen Heckart

1974　**THE GIRL FROM PETROVKA**
Director:　Robert Ellis Miller
Co-stars:　Hal Holbrook Anthony Hopkins

1974　**SUGARLAND EXPRESS**
Director:　Steven Spielberg
Co-stars:　William Atherton Ben Johnson Michael Saks

1975　**SHAMPOO**
Director:　Hal Ashby
Co-stars:　Warren Beatty Julie Christie Lee Grant

1976 THE DUCHESS AND THE DIRTWATER FOX
Director: Melvin Frank
Co-stars: George Segal Conrad Janis Bob Hoy

1978 FOUL PLAY
Director: Colin Higgins
Co-stars: Chevy Chase Dudley Moore Burgess Meredith

1980 PRIVATE BENJAMIN
Director: Howard Zieff
Co-stars: Eileen Brennan Armand Assante Sam Wanamaker

1980 SEEMS LIKE OLD TIMES
Director: Jay Sandrich
Co-stars: Chevy Chase Charles Grodin Robert Guillaume

1982 BEST FRIENDS
Director: Norman Jewison
Co-stars: Burt Reynolds Jessica Tandy Keenan Wynn

1984 PROTOCOL
Director: Herbert Ross
Co-stars: Chris Sarandon Gail Strickland Cliff De Young

1984 SWING SHIFT
Director: Jonathon Demme
Co-stars: Kurt Russell Christine Lahti Ed Harris

1986 WILDCATS
Director: Michael Ritchie
Co-stars: Swoosie Kurtz James Keach Robyn Lively

1987 OVERBOARD
Director: Garry Marshall
Co-stars: Kurt Russell Edward Herrman Roddy McDowall

1990 BIRD ON A WIRE
Director: John Badham
Co-stars: Mel Gibson David Carradine Bill Duke Jeff Corey

1992 DEATH BECOMES HER
Director: Robert Zemeckis
Co-stars: Meryl Streep Bruce Willis Isabella Rossellini

1992 DECEIVED
Director: Damian Harris
Co-stars: John Heard Robin Bartlett Ashley Peldon

1993 CRISSCROSS
Director: Chris Mengers
Co-stars: Arliss Howard Keith Carradine David Arnott

1993 HOUSESITTER
Director: Frank Oz
Co-stars: Steve Martin Dana Delaney Julie Harris Donald Moffat

1996 EVERYBODY SAYS I LOVE YOU
Director: Woody Allen
Co-stars: Julia Roberts Drew Barrymore Edward Norton

1996 THE FIRST WIVES CLUB
Director: Hugh Wilson
Co-stars: Diane Keaton Bette Midler Stockard Channing

JILL HAWORTH

1960 EXODUS
Director: Otto Preminger
Co-stars: Paul Newman Sal Mineo Eva Marie Saint John Derek

1963 THE CARDINAL
Director: Otto Preminger
Co-stars: Tom Tryon Carol Lynley Dorothy Gish

1965 IN HARM'S WAY
Director: Otto Preminger
Co-stars: John Wayne Kirk Douglas Patricia Neal

1972 TOWER OF EVIL
Director: Jim O'Connolly
Co-stars: Bryant Halliday Anna Palk Anthony Valentine

1974 THE MUTATIONS
Director: Jack Cardiff
Co-stars: Donald Pleasence Tom Baker Julie Ege

ALEXANDRA HAY

1969 THE MODEL SHOP
Director: Jacques Demy
Co-stars: Anouk Aimee Gary Lockwood Carole Cole

LINDA HAYDEN

1968 BABY LOVE
Director: Alastair Reid
Co-stars: Ann Lynn Keith Barron Diana Dors

1970 BLOOD ON SATAN'S CLAW
Director: Piers Haggard
Co-stars: Patrick Wymark Simon Williams Tamara Ustinov

1970 TASTE THE BLOOD OF DRACULA
Director: Peter Sasdy
Co-stars: Christopher Lee Gwen Watford Peter Sallis

1971 SOMETHING TO HIDE
Director: Alastair Reid
Co-stars: Peter Finch Shelley Winters John Stride

1973 MADHOUSE
Director: Jim Clark
Co-stars: Vincent Price Peter Cushing Robert Quarry

1974 VAMPIRA
Director: Clive Donner
Co-stars: David Niven Teresa Graves Peter Bayliss

1974 CONFESSIONS OF A WINDOW CLEANER
Director: Norman Cohen
Co-stars: Robin Askwith Anthony Booth

1977 CONFESSIONS FROM A HOLIDAY CAMP
Director: Norman Cohen
Co-stars: Robin Askwith Bill Maynard

JULIE HAYDON

1932 THE CONQUERORS
Director: William Wellman
Co-stars: Richard Dix Ann Harding Edna May Oliver

1933 13 WOMEN
Director: George Archainbaud
Co-stars: Ricardo Cortez Irene Dunne Myrna Loy

1932 SYMPHONY OF SIX MILLION
Director: Gregory La Cava
Co-stars: Irene Dunne Ricardo Cortez Noel Madison

1934 THEIR BIG MOMENT
Director: James Cruze
Co-stars: Zasu Pitts Slim Summerville Ralph Morgan

1935 THE SCOUNDREL
Director: Ben Hecht
Co-stars: Noel Coward Alexander Woolcott Stanley Ridges

1937 A FAMILY AFFAIR
Director: George Seitz
Co-stars: Lionel Barrymore Spring Byington Mickey Rooney

HELEN HAYE

1931 THE SKIN GAME
Director: Alfred Hitchcock
Co-stars: Edmund Gwenn Jill Esmond John Longden

1935 THE 39 STEPS
Director: Alfred Hitchcock
Co-stars: Robert Donat Madeleine Carroll Peggy Ashcroft

1935 THE DICTATOR
Director: Victor Saville
Co-stars: Clive Brook Madeleine Carroll Emlyn Williams

1937   COTTON QUEEN
Director: Bernhard Vorhaus
Co-stars: Stanley Holloway Will Fyffe Mary Lawson

1937   WINGS OF THE MORNING
Director: Harold Schuster
Co-stars: Henry Fonda Annabella Leslie Banks

1937   THE GIRL IN THE TAXI
Director: Andre Berthomieu
Co-stars: Frances Day Jean Gillie Albert Whelan

1939   A GIRL MUST LIVE
Director: Carol Reed
Co-stars: Margaret Lockwood Lilli Palmer Hugh Sinclair

1939   THE SPY IN BLACK
Director: Michael Powell
Co-stars: Conrad Veidt Valerie Hobson Hay Petrie

1940   THE CASE OF THE FRIGHTENED LADY
Director: George King
Co-stars: Marius Goring Penelope Dudley Ward

1941   KIPPS
Director: Carol Reed
Co-stars: Michael Redgrave Phyllis Calvert Diana Wynyard

1943   DEAR OCTOPUS
Director: Harold French
Co-stars: Margaret Lockwood Michael Wilding Celia Johnson

1943   THE MAN IN GREY
Director: Leslie Arliss
Co-stars: James Mason Margaret Lockwood Stewart Granger

1944   A PLACE OF OWN'S OWN
Director: Bernard Knowles
Co-stars: James Mason Barbara Mullen Margaret Lockwood

1948   ANNA KARENINA
Director: Julien Duvivier
Co-stars: Vivien Leigh Kierron Moore Ralph Richardson

1949   THIRD TIME LUCKY
Director: Gordon Parry
Co-stars: Glynis Johns Dermot Walsh Yvonne Owen

1953   HOBSON'S CHOICE
Director: David Lean
Co-stars: Charles Laughton John Mills Brenda De Banzie

1955   RICHARD III
Director: Laurence Olivier
Co-stars: Laurence Olivier Claire Bloom John Gielgud

1956   MY TEENAGE DAUGHTER
Director: Herbert Wilcox
Co-stars: Anna Neagle Sylvia Syms Kenneth Haigh

1957   ACTION OF THE TIGER
Director: Terence Young
Co-stars: Van Johnson Martine Carol Herbert Lom

1958   THE GYPSY AND THE GENTLEMEN
Director: Joseph Losey
Co-stars: Melina Mercouri Keith Michell Flora Robson

SALMA HAYEK

1994   ROADRACERS
Director: Robert Rodriguez
Co-stars: David Arquette Helen Shaver

1996   DESPERADO
Director: Robert Rodriquez
Co-stars: Antonio Banderas Steve Buscemi

1996   FROM DUSK UNTIL DAWN
Director: Robert Rodriquez
Co-stars: Harvey Keitel George Clooney Juliette Lewis

1996   MY LFE AND TIMES WITH ANTONIN ARTAUD
Co-stars: Sam Frey Marc Bebe

1997   FOOLS RUSH IN
Co-star: Matthew Perry

ALLISON HAYES

1954   SO THIS IS PARIS
Director: Richard Quine
Co-stars: Tony Curtis Gloria De Haven Gene Nelson

1955   CHICAGO SYNDICATE
Director: Fred Sears
Co-stars: Dennis O'Keefe Paul Stewart Abba Lane

1955   COUNT THREE AND PRAY
Director: George Sherman
Co-stars: Van Heflin Joanne Woodward Phil Carey

1956   MOHAWK
Director: Kurt Neuman
Co-stars: Scott Brady Rita Gam Neville Brand Lori Nelson

1956   THE GUNSLINGER
Director: Roger Corman
Co-stars: John Ireland Beverly Garland Martin Kingsley

1957   THE DISEMBODIED
Director: Walter Grauman
Co-stars: Paul Burke John Wengraf

1957   THE UNDEAD
Director: Roger Corman
Co-stars: Richard Garland Pamela Duncan Mel Welles

1957   THE ZOMBIES OF MORA TAU
Director: Edward Cahn
Co-stars: Gregg Palmer Morris Ankrum Autumn Russell

1958   ATTACK OF THE 50FT. WOMAN
Director: Nathan Hertz
Co-stars: William Hudson Roy Gordon Yvette Vickers

1960   THE HYPNOTIC EYE
Director: George Blair
Co-stars: Jacques Bergerac Merry Anders Marcia Henderson

BERNADINE HAYES

1935   THE JUDGEMENT BOOK
Co-star: Conway Tearle

1936   THE ACCUSING FINGER
Co-stas   Paul Kelly Marsha Hunt

1940   SANTE FE MARSHAL
Co-star: Russell Hayden

1944   MR. WINKLE GOES TO WAR
Director: Alfred Green
Co-stars: Edward G. Robinson Ruth Warrick Bob Haymes

1947   DICK TRACY'S DILEMMA
Director: John Rawlins
Co-stars: Ralph Byrd Kay Christopher Jack Lambert

BILLIE HAYES

1970   PUFNSTUF
Director: Hollingsworth Morse
Co-stars: Jack Wild Martha Raye Mama Cass

GLORIA HAYES

1989   HAPPY TOGETHER
Director: Mel Damski
Co-stars: Patrick Dempsey Helen Slater Brad Pitt

GRACE HAYES

1939   BABES IN ARMS
Director: Busby Berkeley
Co-stars: Judy Garland Mickey Rooney Charles Winninger

HELEN HAYES *(Married Charles MacArthur, Mother Of James MacArthur)*
Oscar For Best Actress In 1931 For "The Sin Of Madelon Caudet" And For Best Supporting Actress In 1970 For "Airport"

1931 ARROWSMITH
Director: John Ford
Co-stars: Ronald Colman Myrna Loy Beulah Bondi Richard Bennett

1931 THE SIN OF MADELON CLAUDET
Director: Edgar Selwyn
Co-stars: Robert Young Neil Hamilton Marie Prevost

1932 THE SON-DAUGHTER
Director: Clarence Brown
Co-stars: Ramon Navarro Lewis Stone Warner Oland

1932 A FAREWELL TO ARMS
Director: Frank Borzage
Co-stars: Gary Cooper Adolphe Menjou Henry Armetta

1933 ANOTHER LANGUAGE
Director: Edward Griffith
Co-stars: Robert Montgomery John Beal Henry Travers

1933 NIGHT FLIGHT
Director: Clarence Brown
Co-stars: John Barrymore Lionel Barrymore Clark Gable Myrna Loy

1933 THE WHITE SISTER
Director: Victor Fleming
Co-stars: Clark Gable Lewis Stone Edward Arnold

1934 WHAT EVERBODY KNOWS
Director: Gregory La Cava
Co-stars: Brain Aherne Madge Evans Lucile Watson

1934 CRIME WITHOUT PASSION
Director: Charles MacArthur
Co-stars: Claude Rains Margo Stanley Ridges

1935 VANESSA, HER LOVE STORY
Director: William Howard
Co-stars: Robert Montgomery May Robson Otto Kruger

1943 STAGE DOOR CANTEEN
Director: Frank Borzage
Co-stars: Cheryl Walker Lon McCallister Judith Anderson

1952 MY SON JOHN
Director: Leo McCarey
Co-stars: Robert Walker Dean Jagger Van Heflin

1953 MAIN STREET TO BROADWAY
Director: Tay Garnett
Co-stars: Tom Morton Mary Murphy Ethel Barrymore

1956 ANASTASIA
Director: Antole Litvak
Co-stars: Ingrid Bergman Yul Brynner Martita Hunt

1959 THIRD MAN ON THE MOUNTAIN
Director: Ken Annakin
Co-stars: James MacArthur Michael Rennie Janet Munro

1969 AIRPORT
Director: George Seaton
Co-stars: Burt Lancaster Dean Martin Jean Seberg

1971 DO NOT FOLD, SPINDLE OR MUTILATE
Director: Ted Post
Co-stars: Myrna Loy Sylvia Sidney Mildred Natwick

1974 HERBIE RIDES AGAIN
Director: Robert Stevenson
Co-stars: Keenan Wynn Ken Berry Stephanie Powers

1975 ONE OF OUR DINOSAURS IS MISSING
Director: Robert Stevenson
Co-stars: Peter Ustinov Derek Nimo

1977 CANDLESHOE
Director: Norman Tokar
Co-stars: David Niven Jody Foster Leo McKern

1982 MURDER IS EASY
Director: Claude Whatham
Co-stars: Olivia De Havilland Bill Bixby Lesley-Ann Down

1983 A CARIBBEAN MYSTERY
Director: Robert Lewis
Co-stars: Barnard Hughes Jameson Parker Swoosie Kurtz

1985 MURDER WITH MIRRORS
Director: Dick Lowry
Co-stars: Bette Davis Leo McKern John Mills Dorothy Tutin

LINDA HAYES

1939 THE GIRL FROM MEXICO
Director: Leslie Goodwins
Co-stars: Lupe Velez Donald Woods Leon Errol

1938 THE SPELLBINDER
Director: Jack Hively
Co-stars: Lee Tracey Barbara Read Patric Knowles

1939 CONSPIRACY
Co-star: Allan Lane

1941 RAIDERS OF THE DESERT
Co-stars: Richard Arlen Andy Devine

1941 THE SAINT IN PALM SPRINGS
Co-star: George Sanders

1942 SOUTH OF SANTE FE
Co-stars: Roy Rogers George "Gabby" Hayes

MARGARET HAYES *(Maggie)*

1941 THE NIGHT OF JANUARY 16TH.
Director: William Clemens
Co-stars: Robert Preston Ellen Drew Nils Astner

1941 SULLIVAN'S TRAVELS
Director: Preston Sturges
Co-stars: Joel McCrea Veronica Lake William Demarest

1942 THE LADY HAS PLANS
Director: Sidney Lanfield
Co-stars: Paulette Goddard Ray Milland Roland Young

1943 ONE DANGEROUS NIGHT
Director: Michael Gordon
Co-stars: Warren William Marguerite Chapman Eric Blore

1955 VIOLENT SATURDAY
Director: Richard Fleischer
Co-stars: Richard Egan Victor Mature Sylvia Sidney

1955 THE BLACKBOARD JUNGLE
Director: Richard Brooks
Co-stars: Glenn Ford Anne Francis Louis Calhern

1956 THE BOTTOM OF THE BOTTLE
Director: Henry Hathaway
Co-stars: Van Johnson Joseph Cotten Ruth Roman

1958 FRAULEIN
Director: Henry Koster
Co-stars: Dana Wynter Mel Ferrer Dolores Michaels

1958 THE CASE AGAINST BROOKLYN
Director: Paul Wendkos
Co-stars: Darren McGavin Warren Stevens Emile Meyer

1959 GOOD DAY FOR A HANGING
Director: Nathan Juran
Co-stars: Fred MacMurray Robert Vaughn Joan Blackman

1959 THE BEAT GENERATION
Director: Charles Haas
Co-stars: Ray Danton Steve Cochran Fay Spain

1962 HOUSE OF WOMEN
Director: Walter Doniger
Co-stars: Shirley Knight Constance Ford Barbara Nichols

1962 13, WEST STREET
Director: Philip Leacock
Co-stars: Alan Ladd Rod Steiger Dolores Dawn

PATRICIA HAYES

1942 WENT THE DAY WELL ?
Director: Alberto Cavalcanti
Co-stars: Lesley Banks Elizabeth Allan Frank Lawton

1963 SATURDAY NIGHT OUT
Director: Robert Hartford-Davis
Co-stars: Bernard Lee Heather Sears Nigel Green

1964 THE SICILLIANS
Director: Ernest Morris
Co-stars: Robert Hutton Ursula Howells Reginald Marsh

1967 A GHOST OF A CHANCE
Director: Jan Darnley-Smith
Co-stars: Jimmy Edwards Bernard Cribbins Terry Scott

1969 CARRY ON AGAIN DOCTOR
Director: Gerald Thomas
Co-stars: Sid James Jim Dale Barbara Windsor

1969 CAN HIERONYMUS MERKIN EVER FORGET MERCY HUMPPE AND FIND TRUE HAPPINESS
Director: Anthony Newley
Co-stars: Anthony Newley Joan Collins Milton Berle Stubby Kaye

1971 EDNA, THE INEBRIATE WOMAN
Director: Ted Kotcheff
Co-stars: Barbara Jefford Pat Nye

1973 LOVE THY NEIGHBOUR
Director: John Robins
Co-stars: Jack Smethurst Rudolph Walker Kate Williams

1974 THE BEST OF BENNY HILL
Director: John Robins
Co-stars: Benny Hill Bob Todd Henry McGee

1978 THE CORN IS GREEN
Director: George Cukor
Co-stars: Katherine Hepburn Ian Saynor Bill Fraser

1979 FILM
Director: David Rayner Clark
Co-star: Max Wall

1984 AND THE WALL CAME TUMBLING DOWN
Director: Paul Annett
Co-stars: Peter Wyngarde Gareth Hunt Carol Royle

1984 THE NEVERENDING STORY
Director: Wolfgang Petersen
Co-stars: Barret Oliver Gerald McRaney Moses Gunn

1987 OUR LADY BLUE
Director: Robin Midgley
Co-stars: Doreen Mantle Eva Griffith Paul Beringer

1987 LITTLE DORRIT
Director: Christine Edzard
Co-stars: Derk Jacobi Joan Greenwood Max Wall

1988 A FISH CALLED WANDA
Director: Charles Crighton
Co-stars: John Cleese Kevin Kline Jaimie Lee Curtis

1988 WILLOW
Director: Ron Howard
Co-stars: Val Kilmer Joanne Whalley Jean Marsh

1988 WAR REQUIEM
Director: Derek Jarman
Co-stars: Laurence Olivier Nathaniel Parker Tilda Swinton

1992 BLUE ICE
Director: Russell Mulcahey
Co-stars: Michael Caine Sean Young Ian Holm

CAROLE HAYMAN

1977 CONFESSIONS OF A SEX MANIAC
Director: Alan Birkinshaw
Co-stars: Roger Lloyd-Pack Vicki Hodge

1992 BORN KICKING
Director: Mandie Fletcher
Co-stars: Eve Barker Denis Lawson Sheila Ruskin

CYD HAYMAN

1970 PERCY
Director: Ralph Thomas
Co-stars: Hywel Bennett Elke Sommer Britt Ekland

1976 ROGUE MALE
Director: Clive Donner
Co-stars: Peter O'Toole John Standing Alastair Sim

LINDA HAYNES

1975 THE DROWNING POOL
Director: Stuart Rosenberg
Co-stars: Paul Newman Joanne Woodward Melanie Griffith

1975 THE NICKEL RIDE
Director: Robert Mulligan
Co-stars: Jason Miller Victor French Bo Hopkins

1977 ROLLING THUNDER
Director: John Flynn
Co-stars: William Devane Tommy Lee Jones Lisa Richards

1980 BRUBAKER
Director: Stuart Rosenberg
Co-stars: Robert Redford Yaphet Kotto Jane Alexander

ROBERTA HAYNES

1953 RETURN TO PARADISE
Director: Mark Robson
Co-stars: Gary Cooper Barry Jones Moira MacDonald

1953 THE NEBRASKAN
Director: Fread Sears
Co-stars: Phil Carey Wallace Ford Lee Van Cleef

1953 GUN FURY
Director: Raoul Walsh
Co-stars: Rock Hudson Donna Reed Lee Marvin

KATHRYN HAYS

1966 RIDE BEYOND VENGEANCE
Director: Bernard McEveety
Co-stars: Chuck Connors Michael Rennie Bill Bixby

1967 COUNTERPOINT
Director: Ralph Nelson
Co-stars: Charlton Heston Maximilian Schell Anton Diffring

1989 ASK ME AGAIN
Director: Deborah Reinisch
Co-stars: Robert Bruce Leslie Hope Cynthia Harris

JOAN HAYTHORNE

1956 DRY ROT
Director: Maurice Elvy
Co-stars: Ronald Shiner Brian Rix Peggy Mount

CARMEN HAYWARD

1992 FATHER OF THE BRIDE
Director: Charles Shyer
Co-stars: Steve Martin Diane Keaton Kimberley Williams

RACHEL HAYWARD

1985 BREAKING ALL THE RULES
Director: James Orr
Co-stars: Carl Marotte Carolyn Dunn

SUSAN HAYWARD

Oscar For Best Actress In 1958 For "I Want To Live"
Nominated For Best Actress In 1947 For "Smash-up-the Story Of A Woman", In 1949 For "My Foolish Heart", In 1952 For "With A Song In My Heart" And In 1955 For "I'll Cry Tomorrow"

1939 BEAU GESTE
Director: William Wellman
Co-stars: Gary Cooper Ray Milland Robert Preston

1939 OUR LEADING CITIZEN
Director: Alfred Santell
Co-stars: Bob Burns Charles Bickford Elizabeth Patterson

1941 ADAM HAD FOUR SONS
Director: Gregory Ratoff
Co-stars: Warner Baxter Ingrid Bergman Richard Denning

1941 AMONG THE LIVING
Director: Stuart Heisler
Co-stars: Albert Dekker Frances Farmer Harry Carey

1941 SIS HOPKINS
Co-stars: Bob Crosby Judy Canova

1942 THE FOREST RANGERS
Director: George Marshall
Co-stars: Fred MacMurray Paulette Goddard

1942 STAR SPANGLED RHYTHM
Director: George Marshall
Co-stars: Betty Hutton Eddie Bracken Victor Moore

1942 I MARRIED A WITCH
Director: Rene Clair
Co-stars: Fredric March Veronica Lake Cecil Kellaway

1942 REAP THE WILD WIND
Director: Cecil B. DeMille
Co-stars: John Wayne Ray Milland Robert Preston

1943 JACK LONDON
Director: Alfred Santell
Co-stars: Michael O'Shea Virginia Mayo Osa Massen

1943 CHANGE OF HEART
Director: Albert Rogell
Co-stars: John Carroll Gail Patrick Dorothy Dandridge

1943 YOUNG AND WILLING
Director: Edward Griffith
Co-stars: William Holden Eddie Bracken Robert Benchley

1944 THE HAIRY APE
Director: Alfred Santell
Co-stars: William Bendix John Loder Alan Napier Roman Bohnen

1944 THE FIGHTING SEEBEES
Director: Edward Ludwig
Co-stars: John Wayne Dennis O'Keefe Duncan Renaldo

1944 AND NOW TOMORROW
Director: Irving Pichel
Co-stars: Loretta Young Alan Ladd Beulah Bondi

1946 CANYON PASSAGE
Director: Jacques Tourneur
Co-stars: Dana Andrews Patricia Roc Hoagy Carmichael

1946 DEADLINE AT DAWN
Director: Harold Clurman
Co-stars: Paul Lukas Bill Williams Osa Massen Lola Lane

1947 THE LOST MOMENT
Director: Martin Gabel
Co-stars: Robert Cummings Agnes Moorehead Eduardo Ciannelli

1947 SMASH-UP-THE STORY OF A WOMAN
Director: Stuart Heisler
Co-stars: Lee Bowman Eddie Albert Marsha Hunt

1947 THEY WON'T BELIEVE ME
Director: Irving Pichel
Co-stars: Robert Young Rita Johnson Jane Greer

1948 TAP ROOTS
Director: George Marshall
Co-stars: Van Heflin Boris Karloff Julie London

1948 THE SAXON CHARM
Director: Claude Binyon
Co-stars: Robert Montgomery John Payne Audrey Totter

1949 TULSA
Director: Stuart Heisler
Co-stars: Robert Preston Pedro Armendarittz Chill Wills

1949 MY FOOLISH HEART
Director: Mark Robson
Co-stars: Dana Andrews Kent Smith Robert Keith

1949 HOUSE OF STRANGERS
Director: Joseph Mankiewicz
Co-stars: Edward G. Robinson Richard Conte Luther Adler

1950 RAWHIDE
Director: Henry Hathaway
Co-stars: Tyrone Power Hugh Marlowe Dean Jagger Jack Elam

1951 DAVID AND BATHSHEBA
Director: Henry King
Co-stars: Gregory Peck Raymond Massey Kieron More

1951 I CAN GET IT FOR YOU WHOLESALE
Director: Michael Gordon
Co-stars: Dan Dailey George Sanders Sam Jaffe

1951 I'D CLIMB THE HIGHEST MOUNTAIN
Director: Henry King
Co-stars: William Lundigan Rory Calhoun Barbara Bates

1952 THE LUSTY MEN
Director: Nicholas Ray
Co-stars: Robert Mitchum Arthur Kennedy Arthur Hunnicutt

1952 THE SNOWS OF KILLIMANJARO
Director: Henry King
Co-stars: Gregory Peck Ava Gardner Hildegard Neff

1952 WITH A SONG IN MY HEART
Director: Walter Lang
Co-stars: David Wayne Rory Calhoun Thelma Ritter

1953 WHITE WITCH DOCTOR
Director: Henry Hathaway
Co-stars: Robert Mittchum Walter Sleazak Timothy Carey

1953 THE PRESIDENT'S LADY
Director: Henry Levin
Co-stars: Charlton Heston John McIntyre Fay Bainter

1954 GARDEN OF EVIL
Director: Henry Hathaway
Co-stars: Gary Cooper Richard Widmark Cameron Mitchell

1954 DEMETRIUS AND THE GLADIATORS
Director: Delmer Daves
Co-stars: Victor Mature Michael Rennie Debra Paget

1955 THE CONQUEROR
Director: Dick Powell
Co-stars: John Wayne Pedro Armendariz Agnes Moorehead

1955 I'LL CRY TOMORROW
Director: Daniel Mann
Co-stars: Richard Conte Eddie Albert Jo Van Fleet

1955 SOLDIER OF FORTUNE
Director: Edward Dmytryk
Co-stars: Clark Gable Gene Barry Michael Rennie

1955 UNTAMED
Director: Henry King
Co-stars: Tyrone Power Richard Egan John Justin Agnes Moorehead

1956 TOP SECRET AFFAIR
Director: H.C.Potter
Co-stars: Kirk Douglas Jim Backus Paul Stewart

1958 I WANT TO LIVE
Director: Robert Wise
Co-stars: Simon Oakland Virginia Vincent Theodore Bikel

1958 THUNDER IN THE SUN
Director: Russel Rouse
Co-stars: Jeff Chandler Jacques Bergerac Blanche Yurka

1959 WOMAN OBSESSED
Director: Henry Hathaway
Co-stars: Stephen Boyd Theodore Bikel Dennis Holmes

1961 ADA
Director: Daniel Mann
Co-stars: Dean Martin Ralph Meeker Martin Balsam

1961 BACK STREET
Director: David Miller
Co-stars: John Gavin Vera Miles Charles Drake Virginia Grey

1961 THE MARRIAGE-GO-ROUND
Director: Walter Lang
Co-stars: James Mason Julie Newmar Robert Paige

1962 I THANK A FOOL
Director: Robert Stevens
Co-stars: Peter Finch Diane Cilento Cyril Cusack

1963 THE STOLEN HOURS
Director: Daniel Petrie
Co-stars: Michael Craig Diane Baker Edward Judd Paul Rogers

1964 WHERE LOVE HAS GONE
Director: Edward Dmytryk
Co-stars: Bette Davis Mike Connors Jane Greer

1967 VALLEY OF THE DOLLS
Director: Mark Robson
Co-stars: Barbara Parkins Patty Duke Sharon Tate

1967 THE HONEY POT
Director: Joseph Mankiewicz
Co-stars: Rex Harrison Capucine Maggie Smith

1972 THE REVENGERS
Director: Daniel Mann
Co-stars: William Holden Ernest Borgnine Woody Strode

CHARLOTTE HUGHES HAYWOOD (Child)
(Daughter Of Wendy Hughes And Chris Haywood)

1992 THE NUN AND THE BANDIT
Director: Paul Cox
Co-stars: Gosia Dobrowolska Chris Haywood Norman Kaye

RITA HAYWORTH (Cousin Of Ginger Rogers)
(Married Dick Haymes, Aly Khan) (Margarita Cansino)

1935 CHARLIE CHAN IN EGYPT
Director: Louis King
Co-stars: Warner Oland Pat Paterson Stepin Fetchit

1935 UNDER THE PAMPAS MON
Director: James Tingling
Co-stars: Warner Baxter J. Carrol Naish Jack La Rue

1935 PADDY O'DAY
Director: Lewis Seiler
Co-stars: Jane Withers Pinky Tomlin Jane Darwell

1935 DANTE'S INFERNO
Director: Harry Lachman
Co-stars: Spencer Tracy Claire Trevor Scot Beckett

1936 REBELLION
Co-stars: Tom Keene Duncan Renaldo

1936 HUMAN CARGO
Director: Allan Dwan
Co-stars: Claire Trevor Brian Donlevy Alan Dinehart Ralph Morgan

1936 MEET NERO WOLFE
Director: Herbert Biberman
Co-stars: Lionel Stander Edward Arnold

1937 HIT THE SADDLE
Co-stars: Bob Livingston Ray Corrigan Max Terhune

1937 THE GAME THAT KILLS
Co-stars: Charles Quigley Harry Strang Arthur Loft

1937 TROUBLE IN TEXAS
Co-star: Tex Ritter

1938 CONVICTED
Co-star: Charles Quigley

1938 HOMICIDE BUREAU
Director: C.C.Coleman
Co-stars: Bruce Cabot Marc Lawrence Moroni Olsen

1939 THE LONE WOLF SPY HUNT
Director: Peter Godfrey
Co-stars: Warren William Ida Lupino Eric Blore

1939 THE RENEGADE RANGER
Director: David Howard
Co-stars: George O'Brien Tim Holt Ray Whitley

1939 ONLY ANGELS HAVE WINGS
Director: Howard Hawks
Co-stars: Cary Grant Jean Arthur Thomas Mitchell

1940 BLONDIE ON A BUDGET
Director: Frank Strayer
Co-stars: Penny Singleton Arthur Lake

1940 ANGELS OVER BROADWAY
Director: Ben Hecht
Co-stars: Douglas Fairbanks Thomas Mitchell

1940 MUSIC IN MY HEART
Director: Joseph Santly
Co-stars: Tony Martin George Tobias Eric Blore

1940 THE LADY IN QUESTION
Director: Charles Vidor
Co-stars: Brian Aherne Glenn Ford Irene Rich

1940 SUSAN AND GOD
Director: George Cukor
Co-stars: Joan Crawford Fredric March Ruth Hussey

1941 AFFECTIONATELY YOURS
Director: Lloyd Bacon
Co-stars: Merle Oberon Dennis Morgan Ralph Bellamy

1941 THE STRAWBERRY BLONDE
Director: Raoul Walsh
Co-stars: James Cagney Olivia De Havilland Jack Carson

1941 BLOOD AND SAND
Director: Rouben Mamoulian
Co-stars: Tyrone Power Linda Darnell Nazimova

1941 YOU'LL NEVER GET RICH
Director: Sidney Lanfield
Co-stars: Fred Astaire Robert Benchley

1942 YOU WERE NEVER LOVIER
Director: William Seiter
Co-stars: Fred Astaire Adolphe Menjou Larry Parks

1942 TALES OF MANHATTAN
Director: Julien Duvivier
Co-stars: Charles Boyer Henry Fonda Paul Robeson

1942 MY GAL SAL
Director: Irving Cummings
Co-stars: Victor Mature Carole Landis John Sutton

1944 COVER GIRL
Director: Charles Vidor
Co-stars: Gene Kelly Phil Silvers Eve Arden

1945　TONIGHT AND EVERY NIGHT
Director:　Victor Saville
Co-stars:　Janet Blair Lee Bowman Marc Platt

1946　GILDA
Director:　Charles Vidor
Co-stars:　Glenn Ford George Macready

1947　DOWN TO EARTH
Director:　Alexander Hall
Co-stars:　Larry Parkes Roland Culver

1948　THE LADY FROM SHANGHAI
Director:　Orson Welles
Co-stars:　Orson Welles Everett Sloane

1948　THE LOVES OF CARMEN
Director:　Charles Vidor
Co-stars:　Glenn Ford Victor Jory Ron Randell

1952　AFFAIR IN TRINIDAD
Director:　Vincent Sherman
Co-stars:　Glenn Ford Alexander Scourby

1953　SALOME
Director:　William Dieterle
Co-stars:　Stewart Grainger Charles Laughton

1953　MISS SADIE THOMPSON
Director:　Curtis Bernhardt
Co-stars:　Jose Ferrer Aldo Ray

1957　FIRE DOWN BELOW
Director:　Robert Parrish
Co-stars:　Robert Mitchum Jack Lemmon

1957　PAL JOEY
Director:　George Sidney
Co-stars:　Frank Sinatra Kim Novak

1958　SEPARATE TABLES
Director:　Delbert Mann
Co-stars:　Burt Lancaster David Niven Deborah Kerr

1959　THEY CAME TO CORDURA
Director:　Robert Rossen
Co-stars:　Gary Cooper Ven Heflin Tab Hunter

1960　THE STORY ON PAGE ONE
Director:　Clifford Odets
Co-stars:　Tony Franciosa Gig Young Hugh Griffith

1962　THE HAPPY THIEVES
Director:　George Marshall
Co-stars:　Rex Harrison Joseph Wiseman Alida Valli

1964　THE MAGNIFICENT SHOWMAN
Director:　Henry Hathaway
Co-stars:　John Wayne Claudia Cardinale

1966　THE MONEY TRAP
Director:　Burt Kennedy
Co-stars:　Glenn Ford Elke Sommer Ricardo Montalban

1971　ROAD TO SALINA
Director:　George Lautner
Co-stars:　Mimsy Farmer Robert Walker Jnr.

1972　THE WRATH OF GOD
Director:　Ralph Nelson
Co-stars:　Robert Mitchum Frank Langella Victor Buono

JANE HAZARD
1944　STRANGE ILLUSION
Co-stars:　Warren William Sally Eilers Regis Toomey

1944　CRAZY KNIGHTS
Co-stars:　Bernie Sell John Hamilton Maxie Rosenbloom

HY HAZELL *(Hyacinth Hazel O'Higgins)*
1949　PAPER ORCHID
Director:　Roy Baker
Co-stars:　Hugh Williams Sid James Garry Marsh

1950　DANCE HALL
Director:　Charles Crichton
Co-stars:　Natasha Parry Petula Clark Bonar Colleano

1950　THE FRANCHISE AFFAIR
Director:　Lawrence Huntingdon
Co-stars:　Michael Dennison Dulcie Gray Kenneth More

1950　THE LADY CRAVED EXCITEMENT
Director:　Francis Searle
Co-stars:　Michael Medwin Sid James

1951　AN AMERICAN IN PARIS
Director:　Vincent Minnelli
Co-stars:　Gene Kelly Leslie Caron Oscar Levant

1953　FORCES' SWEETHEART
Director:　MacLean Rogers
Co-stars:　Harry Secombe Michael Bentine Freddie Frinton

1960　TROUBLE WITH EVE
Director:　Frances Searle
Co-stars:　Robert Urquhart Vera Day Sally Smith

NONI HAZLEHURST
1983　MONKEY GRIP
Director:　Ken Cameron
Co-stars:　Colin Friels Alice Garner Candy Raymond

1990　WAITING
Director:　Jackie McKimmie
Co-stars:　Deborra-Lee Furness Helen Jones Fiona Press

LINNEA HEACOCK
1971　TAKING OFF
Director:　Milos Forman
Co-stars:　Lynn Carlin Buck Henry Ike & Tina Turner

EDITH HEAD
1966　THE OSCAR
Director:　Russel Rouse
Co-stars:　Stephen Boyd Elke Sommer Tony Bennett

LENA HEADEY
1992　THE CLOTHES IN THE WARDROBE
Director:　Waris Hussein
Co-stars:　Jeanne Moreau Joan Plowright Julie Walters

1992　WATERLAND
Director:　Stephen Gyllenhall
Co-stars:　Jeremy Irons Sinead Cusack Ethan Hawke

1993　CENTURY
Director:　Stephen Poliakoff
Co-stars:　Charles Dance Clive Owen Miranda Richardson

1994　RUDYARD KIPLING'S THE JUNGLE BOOK
Director:　Stephen Sommers
Co-stars:　Jason Scott Lee Cary Elwes John Cleese

1997　FACE
Director:　Antonia Bird
Co-stars:　Ray Winstone Robert Carlyle Damon Albarn

SHARI HEADLEY
1988　COMING TO AMERICA
Director:　John Landis
Co-stars:　Eddie Murphy Don Ameche Ralph Bellamy

GLENNE HEADLY *(Married John Malkovich)*
1986　SEIZE THE DAY
Director:　Fielder Cook
Co-stars:　Robin Williams Joseph Wiseman Tony Roberts

1987　NADINE
Director:　Robert Benton
Co-stars:　Jeff Bridges Kim Basinger Gwen Verdon

1987 MAKING MR. WRIGHT
Director: Susan Seidelman
Co-stars: Ann Magnuson John Malkovich Laurie Metcalf

1988 PAPERHOUSE
Director: Bernard Rose
Co-stars: Charlotte Burke Ben Cross Gemma Jones

1988 LONESOME DOVE
Director: Simon Wincer
Co-stars: Robert Duvall Tommy Lee Jones Anjelica Huston

1988 DIRTY ROTTEN SCOUNDRELS
Director: Frank Oz
Co-stars: Steve Martin Michael Caine Anton Rogers

1990 DICK TRACY
Director: Warren Beatty
Co-stars: Warren Beatty Madonna Charlie Korsmo Dustin Hoffman

1991 GRAND ISLE
Director: Mary Lambert
Co-stars: Kelly McGillis Jon Devries Ellen Burstyn

1991 MORTAL THOUGHTS
Director: Alan Rudolph
Co-stars: Demi Moore Bruce Willis Harvey Keitel

1993 AND THE BAND PLAYED ON
Director: Roger Spottiswoode
Co-stars: Matthew Modine Alan Alda Richard Gere

1994 GETTING EVEN WITH DAD
Director: Howard Deutsch
Co-stars: Macauley Culkin Ted Danson Saul Rubinek

1996 MR. HOLLAND'S OPUS
Director: Stephen Herek
Co-stars: Richard Dreyfuss Jean Louisa Kelly

1996 TWO DAYS IN THE VALLEY
Director: John Herzfeld
Co-stars: Eric Stoltz Jeff Daniels James Spader

1996 SGT. BILKO
Director: Jonathan Lynn
Co-star: Steve Martin

JOAN HEAL

1953 THE WEDDING OF LILLI MARLENE
Director: Arthur Crabtree
Co-stars: Lisa Daniely Hugh McDermott

1961 IN THE DOGHOUSE
Director: Darcy Coyers
Co-stars: Leslie Phillips Peggy Cummins James Booth

MARY HEALEY

1997 BRASSED OFF
Director: Mark Herman
Co-stars: Tara Fitzgerald Ewen McGregor

CHRISTINE HEALY

1989 SHATTERED
Director: Lamont Johnson
Co-stars: Shelley Long Tom Conti Alan Fudge

**1991 WITHOUT WARNING:
THE JAMES BRADY STORY**
Director: Michael Uno
Co-stars: Beau Bridges Joan Allen David Strathairn

KATHERINE HEALY

1982 SIX WEEKS
Director: Tony Bill
Co-stars: Dudley Moore Mary Tyler Moore Shannon Wilcox

MARY HEALY

1939 SECOND FIDDLE
Director: Sidney Lanfield
Co-stars: Sonja Henie Tyrone Power Rudy Vallee

1939 20,000 MEN A YEAR
Director: Alfred Green
Co-stars: Randolph Scott Preston Foster Margaret Lindsay

1952 THE 5,000 FINGERS OF DR. T
Director: Roy Rowland
Co-stars: Peter Lind Hayes Tommy Rettig Hans Conreid

PATRICIA HEALY

1994 CHINA MOON
Director: John Bailey
Co-stars: Ed Harris Madeleine Stowe Charles Dance

ANN HEARN

1988 THE ACCUSED
Director: Jonathan Kaplan
Co-stars: Jodie Foster Kelly McGillis Bernie Coulson

1991 OMEN IV: THE AWAKENING
Director: Jorge Montesi
Co-stars: Faye Grant Michael Woods

1992 LORENZO'S OIL
Director: George Miller
Co-stars: Nick Nolte Susan Sarandon Peter Ustinov

1995 DEATH IN SMALL DOSES
Director: Sondra Locke
Co-stars: Richard Thomas Tess Harper Shawn Elliott

PATRICIA HEARST

1990 CRY-BABY
Director: John Waters
Co-stars: Johnny Depp Amy Locane Susan Tyrrell

1994 SERIAL MOM
Director: John Waters
Co-stars: Kathleen Turner Sam Waterson Ricki Lake

MARLA HEASLEY

1988 BORN TO RACE
Director: James Fargo
Co-stars: Joseph Bottoms Marc Singer George Kennedy

ARIEL HEATH

1943 THE BLACK HILLS EXPRESS
Co-star: Don Barry

EIRA HEATH

1962 GANG WAR
Director: Frank Marshall
Co-stars: Sean Kelly David Davies Sean Sullivan

JEAN HEATHER

1944 DOUBLE INDEMNITY
Director: Billy Wilder
Co-stars: Fred MacMurray Barbara Stanwyck Edward G. Robinson

1944 GOING MY WAY
Director: Leo McCarey
Co-stars: Bing Crosby Barry Fitzgerald Rise Stevens

1944 OUR HEARTS WERE YOUNG AND GAY
Director: Lewis Allen
Co-stars: Gail Russell Diana Lynn Dorothy Gish

1945 MURDER HE SAYS
Director: George Marshall
Co-stars: Fred MacMurray Marjorie Main Helen Walker

1946   THE WELL-GROOMED BRIDE
Director: Sidney Lanfield
Co-stars: Ray Milland Olivia De Havilland Sonny Tufts

DIANNE HEATHERINGTON

1993   ZERO PATIENCE
Director: John Greyson
Co-stars: John Robinson Norman Fauteux Bernard Behrens

JOEY HEATHERTON
1963   TWILIGHT OF HONOUR
Director: Boris Sagal
Co-stars: Richard Chamberlain Claude Rains Joan Blackman

1964   WHERE LOVE HAS GONE
Director: Edward Dmytryk
Co-stars: Susan Hayward Bette Davis Jane Greer

1965   MY BLOOD RUNS COLD
Director: William Conrad
Co-stars: Troy Donahue Barry Sullivan Jeanette Nolan

1972   BLUEBEARD
Director: Edward Dmytyrk
Co-stars: Richard Burton Raquel Welch Verna Lisi

**1977   THE HAPPY HOOKER GOES
          TO WASHINGTON**
Director: William Levey
Co-stars: George Hamilton Ray Walston

MARION HEATHFIELD
1990   GOLDEN BRAID
Director: Paul Cox
Co-stars: Chris Haywood Gosia Dobrowolski Norman Kaye

ANNE HECHE
1992   O-PIONEERS !
Director: Glenn Jordan
Co-stars: Jessica Lange David Strathairn Deborah May

1994   GIRLS IN PRISON
Director: John McNaughton
Co-stars: Ione Skye Nicolette Scorsese Missy Crider

1996   PIE IN THE SKY
Director: Bryan Gordon
Co-stars: Josh Charles John Goodman

1997   WALKING AND TALKING
Director: Nicole Holafcener
Co-star: Catherine Keener

1997   DONNIE BRASCO
Director: Mike Newell
Co-stars: Johnny Depp Michael Madsen Al Pacino

1997   VOLCANO
Director: Mick Jackson
Co-stars: Tommy Lee Jones Gaby Hoffman

GINA HECHT
1982   NIGHT SHIFT
Director: Ron Howard
Co-stars: Henry Winkler Michael Keaton Shelley Long

1985   ST. ELMO'S FIRE
Director: Joel Schumacher
Co-stars: Demi Moore Rob Lowe Emilio Estevez

1989   BAYWATCH: PANIC AT MALIBU PIER
Director: Richard Compton
Co-stars: David Hasselhoff Parker Stevenson

JENNY HECHT *(Child) (Daughter Of Ben Hecht)*
1952   ACTORS AND SIN
Director: Ben Hecht
Co-stars: Edward G. Robinson Marsha Hunt Eddie Albert

EILEEN HECKART
Nominated For Best Supporting Actress In 1956 For "The Bad Seed"
Oscar For Best Supporting Actress In 1972 For "Butterflies Are Free"

1956   THE BAD SEED
Director: Mervyn LeRoy
Co-stars: Nancy Kelly Patty McCormack Henry Jones

1956   BUS STOP
Director: Joshua Logan
Co-stars: Marilyn Monroe Don Murray Betty Field

1956   MIRACLE IN THE RAIN
Director: Rudolph Mate
Co-stars: Jane Wyman Van Johnson William Gargan

1956   SOMEBODY UP THERE LIKES ME
Director: Robert Wise
Co-stars: Paul Newman Pier Angeli Everett Sloane

1958   HOT SPELL
Director: Daniel Mann
Co-stars: Anthony Quinn Shirley Booth Shirley MacLaine

1960   HELLER IN PINK TIGHTS
Director: George Cukor
Co-stars: Anthony Quinn Sophia Loren Ramon Navarro

1963   MY SIX LOVES
Director: Gower Champion
Co-stars: Debbie Reynolds David Janssen

1968   NO WAY TO TREAT A LADY
Director: Jack Smight
Co-stars: Rod Steiger George Segal Lee Remick

1972   THE VICTIM
Director: Herschel Daugherty
Co-stars: Elizabeth Montgomery George Maharis

1972   BUTTERFLIES ARE FREE
Director: Milton Katselas
Co-stars: Goldie Hawn Edward Albert

1974   ZANDY'S BRIDE
Director: Joan Troell
Co-stars: Gene Hackman Liv Ullman Harry Dean Stanton

1974   THE F.B.I. STORY: ALVIN KARPIS
Director: Marvin Chomsky
Co-stars: Daid Wayne Kay Lenz Anne Francis

1975   UP THE DOWN STAIRCASE
Director: Robert Mulligan
Co-stars: Sandy Dennis Patrick Bedford Sorrel Booke

1976   BURNT OFFERINGS
Director: Dan Curtis
Co-stars: Oliver Reed Bette Davis Karen Black

1980   F.D.R.: THE LAST YEAR
Director: Anthony Page
Co-stars: Jason Robards Kim Hunter Augusta Dabney

1980   WHITE MAMA
Director: Jackie Cooper
Co-stars: Bette Davis Ernest Harden Anne Ramsey

1986   SEIZE THE DAY
Director: Fielder Cook
Co-stars: Robin Williams Joseph Wiseman Jo Van Fleet

1986   HEARTBREAK RIDGE
Director: Clint Eastwood
Co-stars: Clint Eastwood Marsha Mason Moses Gunn Bo Svenson

1989   STUCK WITH EACH OTHER
Director: Georg Stanford Brown
Co-stars: Tyne Daly Richard Crenna Michael J. Pollard

1996   THE FIRST WIVES CLUB
Director: Hugh Wilson
Co-stars: Goldie Hawn Bette Midler Diane Keaton

JUNE HEDIN

1948 I REMEMBER MAMA
Director: George Stevens
Co-stars: Irene Dunne Barbara Bel Geddes Oscar Homolka

TIPPI HEDREN (Married Noel Marshall
Mother Of Melanie Griffith And Tracey Griffith)

1963 THE BIRDS
Director: Alfred Hitchcock
Co-stars: Rod Taylor Jessica Tandy Suzanne Pleshette

1964 MARINE
Director: Alfred Hitchcock
Co-stars: Sean Connery Diane Baker Bruce Dern

1967 A COUNTESS FROM HONG KONG
Director: Charles Chaplin
Co-stars: Marlon Brando Sophia Loren Sydney Chaplin

1970 MR KINGSTREET'S WAR
Director: Percival Rubens
Co-stars: John Saxon Rossano Brazzi

1973 THE HARRARD EXPERIMENT
Director: Ted Post
Co-stars: James Whitmore Don Johnson Laurie Walters

1981 ROAR
Director: Noel Marshall
Co-stars: Noel Marshall Melanie Griffith

1990 PACIFIC HEIGHTS
Director: John Schlesinger
Co-stars: Melanie Griffith Michael Keaton Matthew Modine

1992 THROUGH THE EYES OF A KILLER
Director: Peter Markle
Co-stars: Marg Helgenberger Richard Dean Anderson

DEBORAH HEDWALL

1982 ALONE IN THE DARK
Director: Jack Sholder
Co-stars: Donald Pleasence Jack Palance Dwight Schultz

ASTRIS HEEREN

1969 CASTLE KEEP
Director: Sydney Pollack
Co-stars: Burt Lancaster Peter Falk Jean-Pierre Aumont

HONOR HEFFERNAN

1982 ANGEL
Director: Neil Jordan
Co-stars: Stephen Rea Veronica Quilligan Alan Devlin

KATY HEFLIN

1975 THE KILLER ELITE
Director: Sam Peckinpah
Co-stars: James Caan Robert Duvall Gig Young

MARTA HEFLIN

1976 A STAR IS BORN
Director: Frank Pierson
Co-stars: Barbra Streisand Kris Kristofferson Clydie King

1979 A PERFECT COUPLE
Director: Robert Altman
Co-stars: Paul Dooley Belita Moreno Henry Gibson

1982 COME BACK TO THE FIVE AND DIME, JIMMY DEAN JIMMY DEAN
Director: Robert Altman
Co-stars: Cher Sandy Dennis Karen Black

NORA HEFLIN

1978 THE INITIATION OF SARAH
Director: Robert Day
Co-stars: Kay Lenz Shelley Winters Kathryn Crosby

GEORGINA HEGEDOS

1982 BIG MEAT EATER
Director: Chris Windsor
Co-stars: George Dawson Andrew Gilles

ANNE HEGIRA

1969 THE ARRANGEMENT
Director: Elia Kazan
Co-stars: Kirk Douglas Faye Dunaway Deborah Kerr

KATHERINE HEIGL (Child)

1992 THAT NIGHT
Director: Craig Bolotin
Co-stars: C.Thomas Howell Helen Shaver Juliette Lewis

1994 MY FATHER, THE HERO
Director: Steve Miner
Co-stars: Gerard Depardieu Lauren Hutton Emma Thompson

1995 UNDER SEIGE 2: DARK TERRITORY
Director: Geoff Murphy
Co-stars: Steven Seagal Eric Bogosian

LORNA HEILBRON

1973 THE CREEPING FLESH
Director: Freddie Francis
Co-stars: Peter Cushing Christopher Lee George Benson

1988 THE GIRL IN THE SWING
Director: Gordon Heissler
Co-stars: Meg Tilly Rupert Frazer Lynsey Baxter

VIVIEN HEILBRON

1971 KIDNAPPED
Director: Delbert Mann
Co-stars: Michael Caine Trevor Howard Jack Hawkins

ELAYNE HEILVEIL

1973 PAYDAY
Director: Daryl Duke
Co-stars: Rip Torn Ahna Capri Michael C. Gwynne

1975 A CRY FOR HELP
Director: Daryl Duke
Co-stars: Robert Culp Ken Swofford Chuck McCann

1981 THE ADVENTURES OF NELLIE BLY
Director: Henning Schellerup
Co-stars: Linda Purl Gene Barry J.D. Cannon

CARRIE KEI HEIM

1986 PARENT TRAP II
Director: Ronald Maxwell
Co-stars: Hayley Mills Tom Skerritt Bridget Anderson

LAURIE HEINEMAN

1973 SAVE THE TIGER
Director: John Avildsen
Co-stars: Jack Lemmon Jack Gilford Patricia Smith

ELISA HEINSOHN

1985 JOEY
Director: Joesph Ellison
Co-stars: Neill Barry James Quinn Linda Thorson

CAROL HEISS

1961 SNOW WHITE AND THE THREE STOOGES
Director: Walter Lang
Co-stars: Moe Howard Larry Fine Joe De Rita

INGRID HELD

1986 SKY BANDITS
Director: Zoran Peresic
Co-stars: Scott McGinnis Ronald Lacey Jeff Osterhagge

1989 THE LAST BUTTERFLY
Director: Karel Kachyna
Co-stars: Tom Courtenay Brigitte Fossey Freddie Jones

SUSAN HELDFOND

1980 WHY SHOULD I LIE?
Director: Larry Peerce
Co-stars: Treat Williams Lisa Eichhorn Gabrielle Swann

1980 LOVE AND MONEY
Director: James Toback
Co-stars: Ray Sharkey Ornella Muti Armand Assante

BRIT HELFER

1984 ALLEY CAT
Director: Edward Victor
Co-stars: Robert Torti Michael Wayne Karin Mani

MARG HELGENBERGER

1989 ALWAYS
Director: Steven Spielberg
Co-stars: Richard Dreyfuss Holly Hunter Audrey Hepburn

1989 AFTER MIDNIGHT
Director: Jim Wheat
Co-stars: Jullian McWhirter Pamela Segall Marc McClure

1992 STEPHEN KING'S THE TOMMYKNOCKERS
Director: John Power
Co-stars: Robert Carradine E.G. Marshall

1992 HEARTS OF FIRE
Director: Jeff Bleckner
Co-stars: Tom Skerritt Lesley Ann Warren

1992 THROUGH THE EYES OF A KILLER

1994 WHERE ARE MY CHILDREN
Director: George Kaczender
Co-stars: Corbin Bersen Christopher Noth

1994 KEYS
Director: John Sacred Young
Co-star: Gary Dourdan

1994 SPECIES
Co-stars: Michael Madsen Ben Kingsley Alfred Molina

1995 CONUNDRUM
Director: Douglas Barr
Co-stars: Michael Biehn Ron White Peter McNeill

JENNY HELIA

1935 TONI
Director: Jean Renoir
Co-stars: Charles Blavette Celia Montalvan Max Dalban

ARIANE HELLER

1972 UP THE SANDBOX
Director: Irwin Kerschner
Co-stars: Barbra Streisand David Selby Jane Hoffman

1974 MIXED COMPANY
Director: Melville Shavelson
Co-stars: Barbara Harris Joseph Bologna Tom Bosley

ELSE HELLER

1929 ASPHALT
Director: Joe May
Co-stars: Gustav Frohlich Betty Amann Louise Brooks

RANDEE HELLER

**1979 CAN YOU HEAR THE LAUGHTER?
THE STORY OF FREDDIE PRINZE**
Director: Burt Brinckerhoff
Co-star: Kevin Hooks Julie Carmen

1987 THE LAST FLING
Director: Corey Allen
Co-stars: John Ritter Connie Selleca Paul Sand

ANNE HELM

1960 DESIRE IN THE DUST
Director: William Claxton
Co-stars: Raymond Burr Martha Hyer Joan Bennett

1962 FOLLOW THAT DREAM
Director: Gordon Douglas
Co-stars: Elvis Presley Arthur O'Connell Joanne Moore

1962 THE IRON MAIDEN
Director: Gerald Thomas
Co-stars: Michael Craig Jeff Donnell Cecil Parker

1962 THE MAGIC SWORD
Director: Bert Gordon
Co-stars: Basil Rathbone Estelle Winwood Gary Lockwood

BRIGITTE HELM

1926 METROPOLIS
Director: Fritz Lang
Co-stars: Alfred Abel Gustav Frohlich Fritz Rasp

1927 THE LOVE OF JEANNE NEY
Director: G.W. Pabst
Co-stars: Edith Jehane Uno Henning Fritz Rasp

1934 GOLD
Director: Karl Hartl
Co-stars: Hans Albers Michael Bohnen Lien Deyers

FAY HELM

1939 LIGHT THAT FAILED
Director: William Wellman
Co-stars: Ronald Colman Walter Huston Ida Lupino

1939 BLONDIE BRINGS UP BABY
Director: Frank Strayer
Co-stars: Penny Singleton Arthur Lake Larry Sims

1940 BLONDIE ON A BUDGET
Director: Frank Strayer
Co-stars: Penny Singleton Arthur Lake Rita Hayworth

1940 BLONDIE HAS SERVANT TROUBLE
Director: Frank Strayer
Co-stars: Penny Singleton Arthur Lake Esther Dale

1940 WOMEN WITHOUT NAMES
Director: Robert Florey
Co-stars: Ellen Drew Robert Paige Judith Barrett

1940 THE WOLF MAN
Director: George Waggner
Co-stars: Lon Chaney Jnr. Claude Rains Evelyn Ankers

1943 CALLING DOCTOR DEATH
Director: Reginald LeBorg
Co-stars: Lon Chaney Jnr. Patricia Morison David Bruce

1944 MADEMOISELLE FIFI
Director: Robert Wise
Co-stars: Simone Simon John Emery Alan Napier

1944　**PHANTOM LADY**
Director:　Robert Siodmak
Co-stars:　Franchot Tone Ella Raines Aurora Miranda

1945　**SON OF LASSIE**
Director:　S. Sylvan Simon
Co-stars:　Peter Lawford Donald Crisp June Lockhart

FRANCES HELM

1957　**REVOLT AT FORT LARAMIE**
Director:　Lesley Selander
Co-stars:　John Dehner Gregg Palmer

CHARLOTTE HELMKAMP

1990　**FRANKENHOOKER**
Director:　Frank Henenlotter
Co-stars:　James Lorinz Patty Mullen Shirley Stoller

KATHERINE HELMOND

1974　**DR.MAX**
Director:　James Goldstone
Co-stars:　Lee J.Cobb Janet Ward Robert Lipton

1974　**LARRY**
Director:　William Graham
Co-stars:　Frederic Forrest Tyne Daly Michael McGuire

1975　**THE LEGEND OF LIZZIE BORDEN**
Director:　Paul Wendkos
Co-stars:　Elizabeth Montgomery Ed Flanders

1976　**THE FAMILY PLOT**
Director:　Alfred Hitchcock
Co-stars:　Karen Black Bruce Dern Barbara Harris

1976　**BABY BLUE MARINE**
Director:　John Hancock
Co-stars:　Jan-Michael Vincent Glynnis O'Connor Richard Gere

1981　**TIME BANDITS**
Director:　Terry Gilliam
Co-stars:　John Cleese Sean Connery Ralph Richardson

1985　**SHADEY**
Director:　Philip Saville
Co-stars:　Anthony Sher Billie Whitelaw Leslie Ash

1985　**BRAZIL**
Director:　Terry Gilliam
Co-stars:　Jonathan Pryce Robert De Niro Michael Palin

1987　**OVERBOARD**
Director:　Garry Marshall
Co-stars:　Goldie Hawn Kurt Russell Roddy McDowall

1988　**SAVE THE DOG!**
Director:　Paul Aaron
Co-stars:　Cindy Williams Tony Randall Tom Poston

1989　**THE LADY IN WHITE**
Director:　Frank La Loggia
Co-stars:　Lukas Haas Len Cariou Alex Rocco

1992　**INSIDE MONKEY ZETTERLAND**
Director:　Jefery Levy
Co-stars:　Steven Antin Patricia Arquette Bo Hopkins

1993　**AMORE !**
Director:　Lorenzo Doumani
Co-stars:　Jack Scalia George Hamilton Elliott Gould

SHEILA HELPMAN

1977　**THE GETTING OF WISDOM**
Director:　Bruce Beresford
Co-stars:　Susannah Fowle Patricia Kennedy

VIOLET HEMMING

1932　**ALMOST MARRIED**
Director:　William Cameron Menzies
Co-stars:　Ralph Bellamy Alexander Kirkland

1932　**THE MAN WHO PLAYED GOD**
Director:　John Adolphi
Co-stars:　George Arliss Bette Davis Ray Milland

CAROLE HEMINGWAY

1983　**RETURN ENGAGEMENT**
Director:　Alan Rudolph
Co-stars:　Timothy Leary G. Gordon Liddy

MARGAUX HEMINGWAY

1976　**LIPSTICK**
Director:　Lamont Johnson
Co-stars:　Chris Sarandon Mariel Hemingway Perry King

1979　**KILLER FISH**
Director:　Antonio Margheriti
Co-stars:　Lee Majors Karen Black Gary Collins

1983　**OVER THE BROOKLYN BRIDGE**
Director:　Menahem Golan
Co-stars:　Elliott Gould Shelley Winters Sid Caesar

1986　**KILLING MACHINE**
Director:　Antonio De La Loma
Co-stars:　Jorge Rivero Lee Van Cleef Richard Jaeckel

　　　INNER SANCTUM

　　　DEADLY RIVALS

1993　**DOUBLE OBSESSION**
Director:　Eduardo Montes
Co-stars:　Frederic Forrest Maryam D'Abo

MARIEL HEMINGWAY
Nominated For Best Supporting Actress In 1979 For "Manhattan"

1976　**LIPSTICK**
Director:　Lamont Johnson
Co-stars:　Margaux Hemingway Anne Bancroft Chris Sarandon

1979　**MANHATTAN**
Director:　Woody Allen
Co-stars:　Woody Allen Diane Keaton Meryl Streep Michael Murphy

1982　**PERSONAL BEST**
Director:　Robert Towne
Co-stars:　Scott Glenn Patrice Donnelly Kenny Moore

1983　**STAR 80**
Director:　Bob Fosse
Co-stars:　Eric Roberts Cliff Robertson Carroll Baker Roger Rees

1985　**THE MEAN SEASON**
Director:　Phillip Borsos
Co-stars:　Kurt Russell Richard Jordan Richard Bradford

1985　**CREATOR**
Director:　Ivan Passer
Co-stars:　Peter O'Toole Virginia Madsen Vincent Spano

1987　**AMERICA**
Director:　Donald Wrye
Co-stars:　Kris Kristofferson Sam Neill Christine Lahti Cindy Pickett

1987　**SUPERMAN IV: THE QUEST FOR PEACE**
Director:　Sidney Furie
Co-stars:　Christopher Reeve Gene Hackman

1988　**SUNSET**
Director:　Blake Edwards
Co-stars:　Bruce Willis James Garner Malcolm McDowall

1988　**STEAL THE SKY**
Director:　John Hancock
Co-stars:　Ben Cross Sasson Gabei Mark Rolston Ronald Guttman

1991 DELIRIOUS
Director: Tom Mankiewicz
Co-stars: John Candy Emma Samms Raymond Burr Robert Wagner

1991 INTO THE BADLANDS
Director: Sam Pillsbury
Co-stars: Bruce Dern Dylan McDermott Helen Hunt

1991 FALLING FROM GRACE
Director: John Mellencamp
Co-stars: John Mellencamp Kay Lenz Claude Akins Dub Taylor

1994 EDGE OF DECEPTION
Director: George Mihalka

POLLY HEMINGWAY

1990 OBITUARIES
Director: David Blair
Co-stars: Ian Carmichael Ronald Fraser

1992 A VERY POLISH PRACTICE
Director: David Tucker
Co-stars: Peter Davidson Joanna Kanska Alfred Molina

HELEN HEMINWAY

1978 PATRICK
Director: Richard Franklin
Co-stars: Susan Penhaligon Robert Helpman Bruce Barry

ANOUSKA HEMPEL

1970 THE SCARS OF DRACULA
Director: Roy Ward Baker
Co-stars: Christopher Lee Dennis Waterman Bob Todd

1972 GO FOR A TAKE
Director: Harry Booth
Co-stars: Reg Varney Sue Lloyd Dennis Price

ESTELLE HEMSLEY

1958 TAKE A GIANT STEP
Director: Philip Leacock
Co-stars: Johnny Nash Ruby Dee

1963 AMERICA, AMERICA
Director: Elia Kazan
Co-stars: Stathis Giallelis Frank Wolff Lou Antonio

1965 TAGGART
Director: R.G. Springsteen
Co-stars: Tony Young Dan Duryea Johnny Nash

LISA HEMSLEY

1988 THE THIRTEENTH FLOOR
Director: Chris Roach
Co-stars: Miranda Otto Tim McKenzie

BETTY HENDERSON

1950 THE GORBALS STORY
Director: David MacKane
Co-stars: Howard Connell Russell Hunter Roddy McMillan

FLORENCE HENDERSON

1970 SONG OF NORWAY
Director: Andrew Stone
Co-stars: Toralv Maurstad Harry Secombe Edward G. Robinson

JO HENDERSON

1983 LIANNA
Director: John Sayles
Co-stars: Linda Griffiths Jane Hallaren Jon De Vries

1986 ROCKABYE
Director: Richard Michaels
Co-stars: Valerie Bertinelli Rachel Ticotin Jason Alexander

1987 RACHEL RIVER
Director: Sandy Smolan
Co-stars: Zeljko Ivanek Pamela Reed Craig T. Nelson

MARCIA HENDERSON

1953 THUNDER BAY
Director: Anthony Mann
Co-stars: James Stewart Joanne Dru Dan Duryea

1953 THE GLASS WEB
Director: Jack Arnold
Co-stars: Edward G. Robinson John Forsythe Richard Denning

1953 BACK TO GOD'S COUNTY
Director: Joseph Pevney
Co-stars: Rock Hudson Steve Cochran

1953 ALL I DESIRE
Director: Douglas Sirk
Co-stars: Barbara Stanwyck Richard Carlson Maureen O'Sullivan

1954 NAKED ALIBI
Director: Jerry Hopper
Co-stars: Sterling Hayden Gene Barry Gloria Grahame

1955 THE NAKED HILLS
Director: Josef Shaftel
Co-stars: David Wayne Keenan Wynn James Barton

1956 CANYON RIVER
Director: Harmon Jones
Co-stars: George Montgomery Peter Graves Richard Eyer

1959 TIMBUKTU
Director: Jacques Tourneur
Co-stars: Yvonne De Carlo Victor Mature George Dolenz

1960 THE HYPNOTIC EYE
Director: George Blair
Co-stars: Jacques Bergerac Allison Hayes Merry Anders

SARAH HENDERSON

1996 KIDS
Director: Larry Clark
Co-stars: Leo Fitzpatrick Justin Pierce Chloe Sivigny

SHIRLEY HENDERSON

1991 DREAMING
Director: Mike Alexander
Co-stars: Ewen Bremner Mary McCusker Billy Connolly

LAURI HENDLER

1983 HIGH SCHOOL U.S.A.
Director: Rod Amateau
Co-stars: Michael J. Fox Nancy McKeon Todd Bridges

SANDY HENDRICKSE

1990 DANCIN' THRU THE DARK
Director: Mike Ockrent
Co-stars: Claire Hackett Con O'Neill Angela Clarke

WANDA HENDRIX *(Married Audie Murphy)*

1945 CONFIDENTIAL AGENT
Director: Herman Shumlin
Co-stars: Charles Boyer Lauren Bacall Katina Paxinou

1946 NORA PRENTISS
Director: Vincent Sherman
Co-stars: Ann Sheridan Kent Smith Robert Alda

1947 RIDE THE PINK HORSE
Director: Robert Montgomery
Co-stars: Robert Montgomery Andrea King Thomas Gomez Fred Clark

1947 WELCOME STRANGER
Director: Elliott Nugent
Co-stars: Bing Crosby Joan Caulfield Barry Fitzgerald

1948 MY OWN TRUE LOVE
Director: Compton Bennett
Co-stars: Phyllis Calvert Melvyn Douglas Binnie Barnes

1948 MISS TATLOCK'S MILLIONS
Director: Richard Haydn
Co-stars: John Lund Monty Wooley Robert Stack

1949 PRINCE OF FOXES
Director: Henry King
Co-stars: Tyrone Power Orson Welles Katina Paxinou

1949 SONG OF SURRENDER
Director: Mitchell Leisen
Co-stars: Claude Rains MacDonald Carey Andrea King

1950 SIERRA
Director: Alfred E. Green
Co-stars: Audie Murphy Burl Ives Dean Jagger

1950 SADDLE TRAMP
Director: Hugo Fregonese
Co-stars: Joel McCrea John Russell John McIntyre

1950 THE ADMIRAL WAS A LADY
Director: Albert Rogell
Co-stars: Edmond O'Brien Rudy Vallee Steve Brodie

1951 MY OUTLAW BROTHER
Director: Elliott Nugent
Co-stars: Mickey Rooney Robert Preston Robert Stack

1952 SOUTH OF ALGIERS
Director: Jack Lee
Co-stars: Van Heflin Eric Portman Charles Goldner

1952 THE HIGHWAYMAN
Director: Lesley Selander
Co-stars: Philip Friend Charles Coburn Victor Jory

1953 SEA OF LOST SHIPS
Director: Joe Kane
Co-stars: Walter Brennan John Derek Richard Jaeckel

1953 THE LAST POSSE
Director: Alfred Werker
Co-stars: Broderick Crawford John Derek Charles Bickford

1964 STAGE TO THUNDER ROCK
Director: William Claxton
Co-stars: Barry Sullivan Marilyn Maxwell Allan Jones

GLORIA HENDRY

1973 BLACK BELT JONES
Director: Robert Clouse
Co-stars: Jim Kelly Scatman Crothers Alan Weeks

JANET HENFRY

1985 SHE'LL BE WEARING PINK PAJAMAS
Director: John Goldschmidt
Co-stars: Julie Walters Anthony Higgins

1990 ARTISTS IN CRIME
Director: Silvio Narizzano
Co-stars: Simon Williams Belinda Lang Ursula Howells

SONJA HENIE (Champion Ice Skater)

1936 ONE IN A MILLION
Director: Sidney Lanfield
Co-stars: Don Ameche Ritz Bros Jean Hersholt Ned Sparks

1937 THIN ICE
Director: Sidney Lanfield
Co-stars: Tyrone Power Arthur Treacher Joan Davis Alan Hale

1938 MY LUCKY STAR
Director: Roy Del Ruth
Co-stars: Richard Greene Joan Davis Buddy Ebsen Cesar Romero

1938 HAPPY LANDING
Director: Roy Del Ruth
Co-stars: Don Ameche Cesar Romero Ethel Merman Jean Hersholt

1939 SECOND FIDDLE
Director: Sidney Lanfield
O-stars: Tyrone Power Rudy Vallee Lyle Talbot

1939 EVERYTHING HAPPENS AT NIGHT
Director: Irving Cummings
Co-stars: Ray Milland Robert Cummings

1941 SUN VALLEY SERENADE
Director: Bruce Humberstone
Co-stars: John Payne Jack Oakie Glenn Miller

1942 ICELAND
Director: Bruce Humberstone
Co-stars: John Payne Jack Oakie Osa Massen

1943 WINTERTIME
Director: John Brahm
Co-stars: Cesar Romero Jack Oakie Carole Landis Cornel Wilde

1945 IT'S A PLEASURE
Director: William Seiter
Co-stars: Michael O'Shea Marie McDonald

1948 THE COUNTESS OF MONTE CRISTO
Director: Frederick De Cordova
Co-stars: Olga San Juan Arthur Treacher

CARRIE HENN

1986 ALIENS
Director: James Cameron
Co-stars: Sigourney Weaver Michael Biehn Paul Reiser

MARILU HENNER

1982 HAMMETT
Director: Wim Wenders
Co-stars: Fredric Forrest Peter Boyle Roy Kinnear

1983 THE MAN WHO LOVED WOMEN
Director: Blake Edwards
Co-stars: Burt Reynolds Julie Andrews Kim Bassinger

1984 JOHNNY DANGEROUSLY
Director: Amy Heckerling
Co-stars: Michael Keaton Maureen Stapleton Peter Boyle

1985 PERFECT
Director: James Bridges
Co-stars: John Travolta Jaime Lee Curtis Laraine Newman

1985 RUSTLERS' RHAPSODY
Director: Hugh Wilson
Co-stars: Tom Berenger Andy Griffith Fernando Rey

1985 STARK
Director: Rod Holcomb
Co-stars: Nicholas Surovy Seth Jaffe Dennis Hopper

1989 LADYKILLERS
Director: Robert Lewis
Co-stars: Susan Blakely Lesley-Anne Down William Lucking

1989 CHAINS OF GOLD
Director: Rod Holcomb
Co-stars: John Travolta Hector Elizondo

1991 L.A.STORY
Director: Mike Jackson
Co-stars: Steve Martin Victoria Tennant Richard E. Grant

1992 NOISES OFF
Director: Peter Bogdanovich
Co-stars: Carol Burnett Michael Caine Denholm Elliott

1994 CHASERS
Director: Dennis Hopper
Co-stars: Tom Berenger Erika Eleniak William McNamara

1995 **FIGHT FOR JUSTICE:**
THE NANCY CONN STORY
Director: Bradford May
Co-star: Doug Savant

JILL HENNESSY

1994 **THE PAPER**
Director: Ron Howard
Co-stars: Michael Keaton Marisa Tomei Robert Duvall

1994 **ROBOCOP 3**
Director: Fred Dekker
Co-stars: Robert Burke Nancy Allen Rip Torn

EVA HENNING

1949 **THE DEVIL'S WANTON**
Director: Ingmar Bergman
Co-stars: Doris Svedlund Birger Malmsten Hasse Ekman

CHARLOTTE HENRY

1931 **ARROWSMITH**
Director: John Ford
Co-stars: Ronald Colman Helen Hayes Myrna Loy

1931 **FORBIDDEN**
Director: Frank Capra
Co-stars: Barbara Stanwyck Adolphe Menjou Ralph Bellamy

1932 **LENA RIVERS**

1932 **REBECCA OF SUNNYBROOK FARM**
Director: Alfred Santell
Co-stars: Marian Nixon Ralph Bellamy Mae Marsh

1933 **ALICE IN WONDERLAND**
Director: Norman Z. Mcleod
Co-stars: W.C. Fields Cary Grant Gary Cooper

1933 **MAN HUNT**
Co-star: Junior Durkin

1934 **BABES IN TOYLAND**
Director: Charles Rogers
Co-stars: Stan Laurel Oliver Hardy Johnny Downs

1934 **THE HUMAN SIDE**
Director: Eddie Buzzell
Co-stars: Adolphe Menjou Doris Kenyon Dickie Moore

1934 **THE LAST GENTLEMAN**
Director: Sidney Lanfield
Co-stars: George Arliss Edna May Oliver Ralph Morgan

1935 **THREE KIDS AND A QUEEN**
Director: Edward Ludwig
Co-stars: May Robson Frankie Darro Hedda Hopper

1935 **THE HOOSIER SCHOOLMASTER**
Co-stars: Norman Foster Fred Kohler

1936 **CHARLIE CHAN AT THE OPERA**
Director: Bruce Humberstone
Co-stars: Warner Oland Boris Karloff Keye Luke

1937 **THE MANDARIN MYSTERY**
Director: Ralph Staub
Co-stars: Eddie Quillan Rita LeRoy Franklin Pangborn

DARNITA HENRY

1991 **PARIS TROUT**
Director: Stephen Gyllenhaal
Co-stars: Dennis Hopper Barbara Hershey Ed Harris

GLORIA HENRY

1949 **MISS GRANT TAKES RICHMOND**
Director: Lloyd Bacon
Co-stars: Lucille Ball William Holden Janis Carter

1949 **JOHNNY ALLEGRO**
Director: Ted Tetzlaff
Co-stars: George Raft George Macready Nina Foch

1950 **AL JENNINGS OF OKLAHOMA**
Director: Ray Nazarro
Co-stars: Dan Duryea Gale Storm Dick Foran

1952 **RANCHO NOTORIOUS**
Director: Fritz Lang
Co-stars: Marlene Dietrich Arthur Kennedy Mel Ferrer

1958 **GANG WAR**
Director: Gene Fowler
Co-stars: Charles Bronson Kent Taylor Jennifer Holden

JUDITH HENRY

1996 **THE APPRENTICES**
Director: Pierre Salvadori
Co-stars: Guilliaume Depardieu Francois Cluzet

LINDA HENRY

1987 **LOVEBIRDS**
Director: Stephen Whittaker
Co-stars: Paul Bhattacharjee Stephen Bent Jane Gurnett

1989 **THE YOB**
Director: Ian Emes
Co-stars: Keith Allen Gary Olsen Lia Williams

1996 **BEAUTIFUL THING**
Director: Hettie MacDonald
Co-stars: Glenn Berry Scott Neal Ben Daniels

LOUISE HENRY

1934 **PARIS INTERLUDE**
Director: Edwin Marin
Co-stars: Madge Evans Robert Young Otto Kruger

1935 **IN OLD KENTUCKY**
Director: George Marshall
Co-stars: Will Rogers Bill Robinson Dorothy Wilson

1935 **KING SOLOMAN OF BROADWAY**
Director: Alan Crosland
Co-stars: Edmund Lowe Dorothy Page Pinky Tomlin

1935 **THE CASINO MURDER CASE**
Director: Edwin Marin
Co-stars: Paul Lukas Rosalind Russell Eric Blore

1936 **EXCLUSIVE STORY**
Co-stars: Franchot Tone Madge Evans Stuart Erwin

1936 **END OF THE TRAIL**
Co-stars: Jack Holt Guinn Williams Douglass Dumbrille

1937 **CHARLIE CHAN ON BROADWAY**
Director: Eugene Forde
Co-stars: Warner Oland Keye Luke Leon Ames

1937 **FORTY FIVE FATHERS**
Director: James Tinling
Co-stars: Jane Withers Grace Hartman Paul Hartman

1937 **THE HIT PARADE**
Director: Gus Meins
Co-stars: Frances Langford Phil Regan Pert Kelton

1937 **THERE GOES THE GROOM**
Director: Joseph Santley
Co-stars: Ann Sothern Burgess Meredith Mary Bolland

1938 **THE GAUNT STRANGER**
Director: Walter Forde
Co-stars: Sonnie Hale Wilfrid Lawson Patricia Roc

PAMELA HENSLEY

1975 DOC SAVAGE, MAN OF BRONZE
Director: Michael Anderson
Co-stars: Ron Ely Paul Gleason Bill Lucking

1975 ROLLERBALL
Director: Norman Jewison
Co-stars: James Caan John Houseman Maud Adams

1979 BUCK ROGERS IN THE 25TH CENTURY
Director: Daniel Haller
Co-stars: Gil Gerard Erin Gray Tim O'Connor

1980 THE NUDE BOMB
Director: Clive Bomber
Co-stars: Don Adams Sylvia Kristel Rhonda Fleming

1981 MATT HOUSTON
Director: Richard Lang
Co-stars: Lee Horsley Barbara Carrera Jill St. John

ELIZABETH HENSON

1950 THE GIRL WHO COULDN'T QUITE
Director: Norman Lee
Co-stars: Bill Owen Iris Hoey Betty Stockfield

GLADYS HENSON

1946 THE CAPTIVE HEART
Director: Basil Dearden
Co-stars: Michael Redgrave Jack Warner Basil Radford

1947 FRIEDA
Director: Basil Dearden
Co-stars: Mai Zetterling David Farrar Glynis Johns

1948 LONDON BELONGS TO ME
Director: Sidney Gilliat
Co-stars: Alastair Sim Stephen Murray Susan Shaw

1949 THE HISTORY OF MR. POLLY
Director: Anthony Pellisier
Co-stars: John Mills Sally Ann Howes Megs Jenkins

1949 THE CURE FOR LOVE
Director: Robert Donat
Co-stars: Robert Donat Renee Asherson Dora Bryan Thora Hird

1949 TRAIN OF EVENTS
Director: Basil Dearden
Co-stars: Valerie Hobson John Clements Peter Finch

1949 THE BLUE LAMP
Director: Basil Dearden
Co-stars: Jack Warner Jimmy Hanley Dirk Bogarde

1950 HAPPY GO LOVELY
Director: Bruce Humberstone
Co-stars: David Niven Vera-Ellen Cesar Romero

1950 HIGHLY DANGEROUS
Director: Roy Baker
Co-stars: Margaret Lockwood Dane Clark Marius Goring

1950 CAGE OF GOLD
Director: Basil Dearden
Co-stars: Jean Simmons David Farrar James Donald

1950 THE MAGNET
Director: Charles Frend
Co-stars: Stephen Murray Kay Walsh William Fox

1950 DANCE HALL
Director: Charles Crichton
Co-stars: Natasha Parry Petula Clark Bonar Colleano

1951 LADY GODIVA RIDES AGAIN
Director: Frank Launder
Co-stars: Pauline Stroud Dennis Price Diana Dors

1952 DERBY DAY
Director: Herbert Wilcox
Co-stars: Anna Neagle Michael Wilding Googie Withers

1953 THOSE PEOPLE NEXT DOOR
Director: John Harlow
Co-stars: Jack Warner Charles Victor Marjorie Rhodes

1957 THE PRINCE AND THE SHOWGIRL
Director: Laurence Olivier
Co-stars: Laurence Olivier Marilyn Monroe Jeremy Spencer

1957 DOCTOR AT LARGE
Director: Ralph Thomas
Co-stars: Dirk Bogarde Muriel Pavlow Donald Sinden

1957 DAVY
Director: Michael Relph
Co-stars: Harry Secombe Ron Randell Susan Shaw

1960 NO LOVE FOR JOHNNIE
Director: Ralph Thomas
Co-stars: Peter Finch Mary Peach Stanley Holloway

1963 THE LEATHER BOYS
Director: Sidney Furie
Co-stars: Rita Tushingham Colin Campbell Dudley Sutton

NATASHA HENSTRIDGE

1994 SPECIES
Co-stars: Michael Madsen Ben Kingsley Alfred Molina

1997 MAXIMUM RISK
Director: Ringo Lam
Co-star: Jean-Claude Van Damme

AUDREY HEPBURN *(Edda Van Heem Sta Hepburn-Rushton) (Married Mel Ferrer, Andrew Dotti, Partner Robert Wolders)*
Oscar For Best Actress In 1953 For "Roman Holiday" Nominated For Best Actress In 1954 For "Sabrina", In 1961 For "Breakfast At Tiffany's", In 1959 For "The Nun's Story" And In 1967 For "Wait Until Dark"

1951 LAUGHTER IN PARADISE
Director: Mario Zampi
Co-stars: Alastair Sim Joyce Grenfell Fay Compton George Cole

1951 YOUNG WIVES' TALE
Director: Henry Cass
Co-stars: Joan Greenwood Derek Farr Nigel Patrick

1951 THE SECRET PEOPLE
Director: Thorold Dickinson
Co-stars: Valentina Cortese Charles Goldner

1953 ROMAN HOLIDAY
Director: William Wyler
Co-stars: Gregory Peck Eddie Albert Hartley Power

1954 SABRINA
Director: Billy Wilder
Co-stars: Humphrey Bogart William Holden Martha Hyer

1956 WAR AND PEACE
Director: King Vidor
Co-stars: Henry Fonda Mel Ferrer John Mills Herbert Lom

1957 LOVE IN THE AFTERNOON
Director: Billy Wilder
Co-stars: Gary Cooper Maurice Chevalier John McGiver

1957 FUNNY FACE
Director: Stanley Donen
Co-stars: Fred Astaire Kay Thompson Suzy Parker

1959 GREEN MANSIONS
Director: Mel Ferrer
Co-stars: Anthony Perkins Lee J. Cobb Henry Silva

1959 THE NUN'S STORY
Director: Fred Zinnemann
Co-stars: Peter Finch Edith Evans Peggy Ashcroft

1960 THE UNFORGIVEN
Director: John Huston
Co-stars: Burt Lancaster Audie Murphy John Saxon

1961 BREAKFAST AT TIFFANY'S
Director: Blake Edwards
Co-stars: George Peppard Mickey Rooney Patricia Neal

1962 THE CHILDREN'S HOUR
Director: William Wyler
Co-stars: Shirley MacLaine Miriam Hopkins James Garner

1963 CHARADE
Director: Stanley Donen
Co-stars: Cary Grant Walter Matthau James Coburn

1963 PARIS WHEN IT SIZZLES
Director: Richard Quine
Co-stars: William Holden Noel Coward

1964 MY FAIR LADY
Director: George Cukor
Co-stars: Rex Harrison Stanley Holloway Jeremy Brett

1966 HOW TO STEAL A MILLION
Director: William Wyler
Co-stars: Peter O'Toole Hugh Griffith Eli Wallach

1967 TWO FOR THE ROAD
Director: Stanley Donen
Co-stars: Albert Finney Eleanor Bron Claude Dauphin

1967 WAIT UNTIL DARK
Director: Terence Young
Co-stars: Efrem Zimbalist Alan Arkin Richard Crenna

1976 ROBIN AND MARIAN
Director: Richard Lester
Co-stars: Sean Connery Robert Shaw Ian Holm

1979 BLOODLINE
Director: Terence Young
Co-stars: Ben Gazzara James Mason Omar Sharif

1981 THEY ALL LAUGHED
Director: Peter Bogdanovich
Co-stars: Ben Gazzara John Ritter Colleen Camp

1987 LOVE AMONG THIEVES
Director: Roger Young
Co-stars: Robert Wagner Samantha Eggar Jerry Orbach

1989 ALWAYS
Director: Steven Spielberg
Co-stars: Richard Dreyfuss Holly Hunter Brad Johnson

DEE HEPBURN

1980 GREGORY'S GIRL
Director: Bill Forsyth
Co-stars: John Gordon Sinclair Claire Grogan Chic Murray

DOREEN HEPBURN

1988 DA
Director: Matt Clark
Co-stars: Barnard Hughes Martin Sheen William Hickey

1989 BEYOND THE PALE
Director: Diarmuid Lawrence
Co-stars: Prunella Scales Annette Crosbie Jeff Rawle

KATHERINE HEPBURN
Oscar For Best Actress In 1933 For "Morning Glory", In 1967 For "Guess Who's Coming To Dinner", In 1968 For "The Lion In Winter" and In 1981 For "On Golden Pond"
Nominated For Best Actress In 1935 For "Alice Adams", In 1940 For "The Philadelphia Story", In 1942 For "Woman Of The Year", In 1951 For "African Queen", In 1955 For "Summer Madness", In 1956 For "The Rainmaker", In 1959 For "Suddenly Last Summer" and In 1961 For "Long Day's Journey Into Night"

1932 A BILL OF DIVORCEMENT
Director: George Cukor
Co-stars: John Barrymore Billie Burke David Manners

1933 CHRISTOPHER STRONG
Director: Dorothy Arzner
Co-stars: Colin Clive Billie Burke Ralph Forbes

1933 LITTLE WOMEN
Director: George Cukor
Co-stars: Joan Bennett Frances Dee Jean Parker

1933 MORNING GLORY
Director: Lowell Sherman
Co-stars: Douglas Fairbanks Adolphe Menjou

1934 SPITFIRE
Director: John Cromwell
Co-stars: Robert Young Ralph Bellamy Martha Sleeper

1934 THE LITTLE MINISTER
Director: Richard Wallace
Co-stars: John Beal Alan Hale Donald Crisp

1935 BREAK OF HEARTS
Director: Philip Moeller
Co-stars: Charles Boyer John Beal Jean Hersholt

1935 ALICE ADAMS
Director: George Stevens
Co-stars: Fred MacMurray Hattie McDaniel Fred Stone

1935 SYLVIA SCARLETT
Director: George Cukor
Co-stars: Cary Grant Edmund Gwenn Brian Aherne

1936 MARY OF SCOTLAND
Director: John Ford
Co-stars: Fredric March Florence Eldridge Donald Crisp

1936 A WOMAN REBELS
Director: Mark Sandrich
Co-stars: Herbert Marshall Elizabeth Allan Van Heflin

1937 STAGE DOOR
Director: Gregory La Cava
Co-stars: Ginger Rogers Lucille Ball Ann Miller

1937 QUALITY STREET
Director: George Stevens
Co-stars: Franchot Tone Fay Bainter Joan Fontaine

1938 HOLIDAY
Director: George Cukor
Co-stars: Cary Grant Lew Ayres Doris Nolan

1938 BRINGING UP BABY
Director: Howard Hawkes
Co-stars: Cary Grant Charles Ruggles Barry Fitzgerald

1940 THE PHILADELPHIA STORY
Director: George Cukor
Co-stars: Cary Grant James Stewart Roland Young

1942 WOMAN OF THE YEAR
Director: George Stevens
Co-stars: Spencer Tracy Fay Bainter William Bendix

1942 KEEPER OF THE FLAME
Director: George Cukor
Co-stars: Spencer Tracy Richard Whorf Margaret Wycherley

1943 STAGE DOOR CANTEEN
Director: Frank Borzage
Co-stars: Lon McCallister Cheryl Walker Harpo Marx

1944 THE DRAGON SEED
Director: Jack Conway
Co-stars: Walter Huston Turhan Bey Aline MacMahon

1945 WITHOUT LOVE
Director: Harold Bucquet
Co-stars: Spencer Tracy Keenan Wynn Lucille Ball

1946 UNDERCURRENT
Director: Vincente Minnelli
Co-stars: Robert Taylor Robert Mitchum Edmund Gwenn

1947 SONG OF LOVE
Director: Clarence Brown
Co-stars: Paul Henreid Robert Walker Henry Daniell

1947 THE SEA OF GRASS
Director: Elia Kazan
Co-stars: Spencer Tracy Melvyn Douglas Robert Walker

1948 THE STATE OF THE UNION
Director: Frank Capra
Co-stars: Spencer Tracy Adolphe Menjou Van Johnson

1949 ADAM'S RIB
Director: George Cukor
Co-stars: Spencer Tracy Judy Holliday David Wayne

1951 THE AFRICAN QUEEN
Director: John Huston
Co-stars: Humphrey Bogart Robert Morley Theodore Bikel

1952 PAT AND MIKE
Director: George Cukor
Co-stars: Spencer Tracy Aldo Ray Charles Bronson

1955 SUMMER MADNESS
Director: David Lean
Co-stars: Rossano Brazzi Isa Miranda Darren McGavin

1956 THE RAINMAKER
Director: Joseph Anthony
Co-stars: Burt Lancaster Lloyd Bridges Wendell Corey

1956 THE IRON PETTICOAT
Director: Ralph Thomas
Co-stars: Bob Hope Robert Helpman David Kossoff

1957 THE DESK SET
Director: Walter Lang
Co-stars: Spencer Tracy Gig Young Joan Blondell

1959 SUDDENLY LAST SUMMER
Director: Joseph Mankiewicz
Co-stars: Elizabeth Taylor Montgomery Clift

1961 LONG DAY'S JOURNEY INTO NIGHT
Director: Sidney Lumet
Co-stars: Ralph Richardson Dean Stockwell

1967 GUESS WHO'S COMING TO DINNER
Director: Stanley Kramer
Co-stars: Spencer Tracy Sidney Poitier

1968 THE LION IN WINTER
Director: Anthony Harvey
Co-stars: Peter O'Toole Anthony Hopkins Timothy Dalton

1969 THE MADWOMAN OF CHAILLOT
Director: Bryan Forbes
Co-stars: Yul Brynner Danny Kaye Charles Boyer

1971 THE TROJAN WOMEN
Director: Michael Cacoyannis
Co-stars: Genevieve Bujold Vanessa Redgrave

1973 THE GLASS MENAGERIE
Director: Anthony Harvey
Co-stars: Sam Waterston Joanna Miles Michael Moriarty

1973 A DELICATE BALANCE
Director: Tony Richardson
Co-stars: Paul Scofield Joseph Cotten Lee Remick

1975 ROOSTER COGBURN
Director: Stuart Miller
Co-stars: John Wayne Richard Jordan Anthony Zerbe

1978 THE GREAT BALLOON ADVENTURE
Director: Richard Colla
Co-stars: George Kennedy Vera Miles Dennis Demster

1979 THE CORN IS GREEN
Director: George Cukor
Co-stars: Ian Saynor Bill Fraser Patricia Hayes

1981 ON GOLDEN POND
Director: Mark Rydell
Co-stars: Henry Fonda Jane Fonda Doug McKeon Dabney Coleman

1984 GRACE QUIGLEY
Director: Anthony Harvey
Co-stars: Nick Nolte Walter Abel Elizabeth Wilson

**1984 GEORGE STEVENS -
A FILM MAKER'S JOURNEY**
Director: George Stevens
Co-stars: Cary Grant Fred Astaire

1986 MRS. DELAFIELD WANTS TO MARRY
Director: George Shaefer
Co-stars: Harold Gould Denholm Elliott

1988 LAURA LANSING SLEPT HERE
Director: George Shaefer
Co-stars: Karen Austin Joel Higgins

1991 THE MAN UPSTAIRS
Director: George Shaefer
Co-stars: Ryan O'Neal

1993 THIS CAN'T BE LOVE

1994 LOVE AFFAIR
Director: Glenn Gordon Caron
Co-stars: Warren Beatty Annette Bening

1994 ONE CHRISTMAS
Director: Tony Bill
Co-stars: Henry Winkler Swoozie Kurtz Julie Harris

CARLA HERD
1989 DEATHSTALKER 3
Director: Alfonso Corona
Co-stars: John Allen Nelson Terri Treas Aaron Hernan

LISA HEREDIA
1986 THE GREEN RAY
Director: Eric Rohmer
Co-stars: Marie Riviere Vincent Gautier Eric Hamm

EILEEN HERLIE
1946 HUNGRY HILL
Director: Brian Desmond Hurst
Co-stars: Margaret Lockwood Dennis Price Jean Simmons

1948 HAMLET
Director: Laurence Olivier
Co-stars: Laurence Olivier Basil Sydney Jean Simmons Terence Morgan

1949 THE ANGEL WITH THE TRUMPET
Director: Anthony Bushell
Co-stars: Anthony Bushell Basil Sydney Norman Wooland

1952 ISN'T LIFE WONDERFUL
Director: Harold French
Co-stars: Donald Wolfit Cecil Parker Robert Urquhart

1953 THE STORY OF GILBERT AND SULLIVAN
Director: Sidney Gilliat
Co-stars: Robert Morley Maurice Evans

1958 SHE DIDN'T SAY NO
Director: Cyril Frankel
Co-stars: Jack MacGowran Perlita Neilson Ian Bannen

1962 FREUD
Director: John Huston
Co-stars: Montgomery Clift Larry Parks Susannah York

1968 THE SEA GULL
Director: Sidney Lumet
Co-stars: James Mason Simone Signoret Vanessa Redgrave

IRM HERMANN

1975 THE BITTER TEARS OF PETRA VON KANT
Director: Rainer Werner Fassbinder
Co-star: Margit Carstensen Hanna Schygulla

JOYCE HERON

1942 WOMEN AREN'T ANGELS
Director: Laurence Huntingdon
Co-stars: Robertson Hare Alfred Drayton Polly Ward

1950 SHE SHALL HAVE MURDER
Director: Daniel Birt
Co-stars: Rosamund John Derrick De Marney Felix Aylmer

1975 RUMPOLE OF THE BAILEY
Director: John Gorrie
Co-stars: Leo McKern David Yelland Noel William

CINDY HERRON

1992 JUICE
Director: Ernest Dickerson
Co-stars: Omar Peeps Vermaine Hopkins Khalil Kain

BARBARA HERSHEY (Barbara Herzstein)
From 1973-1975 Acted As Barbara Seagall)
(Partner David Carradine)
Nominated For Best Actress In 1996 For "Portrait Of A Lady"

1968 WITH SIX YOU GET EGG ROLL
Director: Howard Morris
Co-stars: Doris Day Brian Keith Pat Carroll

1969 LAST SUMMER
Director: Frank Perry
Co-stars: Richard Thomas Bruce Davison Cathy Burns

1969 HEAVEN WITH A GUN
Director: Lee Katzin
Co-stars: Glenn Ford Carolyn Jones David Carradine

1970 THE PURSUIT OF HAPPINESS
Director: Robert Mulligan
Co-stars: Michael Sarrazin E.G. Marshall

1970 THE LIBERATION OF L.B.JONES
Director: William Wyler
Co-stars: Lee J.Cobb Lee Majors

1970 THE BABY MAKER
Director: James Bridges
Co-stars: Sam Groom Scott Glen Jeannie Berlin

1972 BOXCAR BERTHA
Director: Martin Scorsese
Co-stars: David Carradine John Carradine Barry Primus

1973 AMERICANA
Director: David Carradine
Co-stars: Bruce Carradine Michael Greene Fran Ryan

1974 THE CRAZY WORLD OF JULIUS VROODER
Director: Arthur Hiller
Co-stars: Timothy Bottoms Albert Salmi

1975 DIAMONDS
Director: Menahem Golan
Co-stars: Robert Shaw Richard Roundtree Shelley Winters

1976 TRIAL BY COMBAT
Co-stars: Kevin Connor
Co-stars: John Mills Peter Cushing Margaret Leighton

1976 THE LAST HARD MAN
Director: Andrew McLaglen
Co-stars: Charlton Heston James Coburn Michael Parks

1976 FLOOD
Director: Earl Bellamy
Co-stars: Robert Culp Carol Lynley Richard Basehart

1977 IN THE GLITTER PALACE
Director: Robert Butler
Co-stars: Chad Everett Howard Duff David Wayne

1979 THE STUNT MAN
Director: Richard Rush
Co-stars: Peter O'Toole Steve Railsbach Alex Rocco

1980 ANGEL ON MY SHOULDER
Director: John Berry
Co-stars: Peter Strauss Richard Kiley Janis Paige Billy Jacoby

1981 TAKE THIS JOB AND SHOVE IT
Director: Gus Trikonis
Co-stars: Robert Hayes Art Carney Eddie Albert

1983 THE RIGHT STUFF
Director: Philip Kaufman
Co-stars: Sam Shepard Scott Glenn Dennis Quaid

1983 THE ENTITY
Director: Sidney Furie
Co-stars: Ron Silver David Labioso Jacqueline Brookes

1984 THE NATURAL
Director: Barry Levinson
Co-stars: Robert Redford Glenn Close Robert Duvall

**1985 MY WICKED, WICKED WAYS
...THE LEGEND OF ERROL FLYNN**
Director: Don Taylor
Co-star: Duncan Regehr Darren McGavin George Coe

1986 HOOSIERS
Director: David Anspaugh
Co-stars: Gene Hackman Dennis Hopper Brad Boyle

1986 HANNAH AND HER SISTERS
Director: Woody Allen
Co-stars: Woody Allen Mia Farrow Michael Caine Carrie Fisher

1986 PASSION FLOWER
Director: Joseph Sargent
Co-stars: Bruce Boxleitner Nicol Williamson

1987 TIN MEN
Director: Barry Levinson
Co-stars: Richard Dreyfuss Danny Devito

1987 SHY PEOPLE
Director: Andrei Konchalowsky
Co-stars: Jill Clayburgh Martha Plimpton

1988 A WORLD APART
Director: Chris Menges
Co-stars: Jodhi May David Suchet Tim Roth

1988 THE LAST TEMPTATION OF CHRIST
Director: Martin Scorsese
Co-stars: Willem Dafoe Harvey Keitel

1988 BEACHES
Director: Garry Marshall
Co-stars: Bette Midler John Heard Spalding Gray

1990 EVIDENCE OF LOVE
Director: Stephen Gyllenhaal
Co-stars: Brian Dennehy Hal Holbrook Matthew Posey

1990 AUNT JULIA AND THE SCRIPTWRITER
Director: Jon Amiel
Co-stars: Keanu Reeves Peter Falk

1990 A KILLING IN A SMALL TOWN

1991 PARIS TROUT
Director: Stephen Gyllenhaal
Co-stars: Dennis Hopper Ed Harris Tina Lifford

1992 SPLITTING HEIRS
Director: Robert Young
Co-stars: Eric Idle Rick Moranis Catherine Zeta Jones

1992 **THE PUBLIC EYE**
Director: Howard Franklin
Co-stars: Joe Pesci Stanley Tucci Jerry Adler

1992 **FALLING DOWN**
Director: Joel Schumacher
Co-stars: Michael Douglas Robert Duvall Tuesday Weld

1992 **DEFENSELESS**
Director: Martin Campbell
Co-stars: Sam Shepard Mary Beth Hurt Sherree North

1993 **SWING KIDS**
Director: Thomas Carter
Co-stars: Robert Sean Leonard Christian Bale Kenneth Branagh

1993 **A DANGEROUS WOMAN**
Director: Stephen Gyllenhaal
Co-stars: Debra Winger Gabriel Byrne Laurie Metcalf

1995 **LAST OF THE DOGMEN**
Co-stars: Tom Berenger

1996 **PORTRAIT OF A LADY**
Director: Jane Campion
Co-stars: Nicole Kidman John Malkovich John Gielgud

IRENE HERVEY

1933 **THE STRANGER'S RETURN**
Director: King Vidor
Co-stars: Lionel Barrymore Miriam Hopkins Belulah Bondi

1934 **LET'S TRY AGAIN**
Director: Worthington Miner
Co-stars: Diana Wynyard Clive Brook Helen Vinson

1934 **THE COUNT OF MONTE CRISTO**
Director: Rowland Lee
Co-stars: Robert Donat Elissa Landi Louis Calhern

1935 **CRIME DOES NOT PAY:
A THRILL FOR THELMA**
Director: Edward Cahn
Co-star: Robert Warwick

1935 **CHARLIE CHAN IN SHANGHAI**
Director: James Tinling
Co-stars: Warner Oland Keye Luke Jon Hall

1935 **HIS NIGHT OUT**
Director: William Nigh
Co-stars: Edward Everett Horton Jack La Rue Robert McWade

1935 **THE WINNING TICKET**
Director: Charles Reisner
Co-stars: Leo Carrillo Louise Fazenda James Ellison

1936 **ABSOLUTE QUITE**
Director: George Seitz
Co-stars: Lionel Atwill Louis Hayward Stuart Erwin

1937 **THE LADY FIGHTS BACK**
Co-stars: William Lundigan Kent Taylor

1937 **THE GIRL SAID NO**
Co-star: Robert Armstrong

1937 **THE LEAGUE OF FRIGHTENED MEN**
Director: Alfred Green
Co-stars: Walter Connolly Lionel Stander

1938 **SAY IT IN FRENCH**
Director: Andrew Stone
Co-stars: Ray Milland Olympe Bradna Mary Carlisle

1939 **HOUSE OF FEAR**
Director: Joe May
Co-star: William Gargan

1939 **SOCIETY SMUGGLERS**
Co-star: Preston Foster

1939 **DESTRY RIDES AGAIN**
Director: George Marshall
Co-stars: James Stewart Marlene Dietrich Charles Winninger

1939 **MISSING EVIDENCE**
Co-star: Preston Foster

1940 **THREE CHEERS FOR THE IRISH**
Director: Lloyd Bacon
Co-stars: Thomas Mitchell Priscilla Lane Alan Hale

1940 **THE BOYS FROM SYRACUSE**
Director: Edward Sutherland
Co-stars: Allan Jones Martha Raye Rosemary Lane

1940 **THE CROOKED ROAD**
Co-stars: Henry Wilcoxon Edmund Lowe

1941 **SAN FRANCISCO DOCKS**
Director: Arthur Lubin
Co-stars: Burgess Meredith Barry Fitzgerald Robert Armstrong

1941 **MR. DYNAMITE**
Director: John Rawlins
Co-stars: Lloyd Nolan J. Carrol Naish Robert Armstrong

1941 **BOMBAY CLIPPER**
Director: John Rawlins
Co-stars: William Gargan Maria Montez Turhan Bey

1942 **FRISCO LIL**
Director: Erle Kenton
Co-stars: Kent Taylor Minor Watson Jerome Cowan

1942 **HALFWAY TO SHANGHAI**
Director: John Rawlins
Co-stars: Kent Taylor Henry Stephenson J. Edward Bromberg

1942 **UNSEEN ENEMY**
Co-stars: Don Terry Leo Carrillo Turhan Bey

1942 **NIGHT MONSTER**
Director: Ford Beebe
Co-stars: Ralph Morgan Bela Lugosi Don Porter Lionel Atwill

1948 **THE LUCKY STIFF**
Director: Lewis Foster
Co-stars: Dorothy Lamour Brian Donlevy Claire Trevor

1948 **MR. PEABODY AND THE MERMAID**
Director: Nunnally Johnson
Co-stars: William Powell Ann Blyth

1949 **MANHANDLED**
Director: Lewis Foster
Co-stars: Dorothy Lamour Dan Duryea Sterling Hayden

1956 **A CRY IN THE NIGHT**
Director: Frank Tuttle
Co-stars: Edmond O'Brien Brian Donlevy Natalie Wood

1956 **TEENAGE REBEL**
Director: Edmund Goulding
Co-stars: Ginger Rogers Michael Rennie Betty Lou Keim

1969 **CACTUS FLOWER**
Director: Gene Saks
Co-stars: Ingrid Bergman Goldie Hawn Walter Matthau

1971 **PLAY MISTY FOR ME**
Director: Clint Eastwood
Co-stars: Clint Eastwood Jessica Walter Donna Mills John Larch

SUSAN HESS
1984 **THREESOME**
Director: Lou Antonio
Co-stars: Stephen Collins Deborah Raffin Joel Higgins

JENNI HETRICK
1980 **SQUEEZE PLAY**
Director: Samuel Well
Co-stars: Jim Harris

LOVE HEWITT

1992   LITTLE MISS MILLIONS
Director: Jim Wynorski
Co-stars: Howard Hesseman Anita Morris

ALMA HEWLETT

1992   BLACK DEATH
Director: Sheldon Larry
Co-stars: Kate Jackson Jerry Orbach David Hewlett

JULIE HEWLETT

1992   BORN KICKING
Director: Mandie Fletcher
Co-stars: Eve Barker Denis Lawson Sheila Ruskin

PHYLLIDA HEWAT

1986   EAST OF IPSWICH
Director: Tristram Powell
Co-stars: John Nettleton Pat Heywood Graham Crowden

SHEREE HEWSON

1976   THE SLIPPER AND THE ROSE
Director: Bryan Forbes
Co-stars: Richard Chamberlain Gemma Craven Kenneth More

VIRGINIA HEY

1981   MAD MAX 2
Director: George Miller
Co-stars: Mel Gibson Bruce Spence Mike Preston

ANNE HEYWOOD *(Started Career As Violet Pretty)*

1951   LADY GODIVA RIDES AGAIN
Director: Frank Launder
Co-stars: Pauline Stroud Dennis Price Kay Kendall

1957   DANGEROUS EXILE
Director: Brian Desmond Hurst
Co-stars: Belinda Lee Keith Michell Martita Hunt

1957   THE DEPRAVED
Director: Paul Dickson
Co-stars: Robert Arden Carroll Levis Basil Dignam

1958   FLOODS OF FEAR
Director: Charles Crichton
Co-stars: Howard Keel Harry H. Corbett Cyril Cusack

1958   VIOLENT PLAYGROUND
Director: Basil Dearden
Co-stars: Stanley Baker David McCallum Peter Cushing

1959   UPSTAIRS AND DOWNSTAIRS
Director: Ralph Thomas
Co-stars: Michael Craig Mylene Demongeot Sid James

1960   A TERRIBLE BEAUTY
Director: Tay Garnett
Co-stars: Robert Mitchum Dan O'Herlihy Richard Harris

1961   PETTICOAT PIRATES
Director: David MacDonald
Co-stars: Charlie Drake Cecil Parker John Turner

1962   VENGEANCE
Director: Freddie Francis
Co-stars: Peter Van Eyck Cecil Parker Jeremy Spenser

1963   THE VERY EDGE
Director: Cyril Frankel
Co-stars: Richard Todd Jeremy Brett Nicole Maurey

1968   THE FOX
Director: Mark Rydell
Co-stars: Sandy Dennis Keir Dullea Glyn Morris

1969   THE CHAIRMAN
Director: J. Lee Thompson
Co-stars: Gregory Peck Arthur Hill Alan Dobie

1969   MIDAS RUN
Director: Alf Kjellin
Co-stars: Fred Astaire Richard Crenna Ralph Richardson

1972   I WANT WHAT I WANT
Director: John Dexter
Co-stars: Paul Rogers Harry Andrews Jill Bennett

1973   TRADER HORN
Director: Reza Badiyi
Co-stars: Rod Taylor Jean Sorel

THE AWFUL STORY OF THE NUN OF MONZA

THE NUNS OF SAINT ARCHANGEL

1984   SECRETS OF THE PHANTOM CAVERNS
Director: Don Sharp
Co-stars: Robert Powell Richard Johnson Lisa Blount

JEAN HEYWOOD

1990   MISSING PERSONS
Director: Derek Bennett
Co-stars: Patricia Routledge Jimmy Jewel Gary Waldhorn

ORIN HEYWOOD

1937   SHE ASKED FOR IT
Co-star: Wiliam Gargan

PAT HEYWOOD

1968   ROMEO AND JULIET
Director: Franco Zefferelli
Co-stars: Olivia Hussey Leonard Whiting Michael York

1970   MUMSY, NANNY, SONNY AND GIRLY
Director: Freddie Francis
Co-stars: Michael Bryant Ursula Howells

1970   ALL THE WAY UP
Director: James McTaggart
Co-stars: Warren Mitchell Kenneth Cranham Richard Briers

1971   TEN RILLINGTON PLACE
Director: Richard Fleischer
Co-stars: Richard Attenborough John Hurt Judy Geeson

1971   WHO EVER SLEW AUNTIE ROO?
Director: Curtis Harrington
Co-stars: Shelley Winters Mark Lester Hugh Griffith

1986   EAST OF IPSWICH
Director: Tristram Powell
Co-stars: John Nettleton Phyllida Hewat

1989   FIRST AND LAST
Director: Alan Dosser
Co-stars: Joss Ackland Lionel Jeffries Patricia Routledge

1989   GETTING IT RIGHT
Director: Randal Kleiser
Co-stars: Jesse Birdsall Jane Horrocks Lynn Redgrave

MARGUERITE HICKEY

1985   MIRRORS
Director: Harry Winer
Co-stars: Anthony Hamilton Keenan Winn Signe Hasso

CATHERINE HICKLAND

1988   GHOST TOWN
Director: Richard Govenor
Co-stars: Franc Luz Penelope Windust Bruce Glover

ELIZABETH HICKLING

1987   **EMPIRE STATE**
Director: Ron Peck
Co-stars: Cathryn Harrison Martin Landau Ray McAnally

BARBARA HICKS

1953   **CONFLICT OF WINGS**
Director: John Eldridge
Co-stars: John Gregson Muriel Pavlow Kierron Moore

1982   **EVIL UNDER THE SUN**
Director: Guy Hamilton
Co-stars: Peter Ustinov Jane Birkin James Mason

1992   **HOWARDS END**
Director: James Ivory
Co-stars: Anthony Hopkins Emma Thompson Vanessa Redgrave

CATHERINE HICKS

1980   **MARILYN : THE UNTOLD STORY**
Director: John Flynn
Co-stars: Richard Basehart John Ireland Sheree North

1982   **DEATH VALLEY**
Director: Dick Richards
Co-stars: Paul Le Mat Stephen McHattie Wilford Brimley

1982   **BETTER LATE THAN NEVER**
Director: Bryan Forbes
Co-stars: David Niven Art Carney Maggie Smith

1983   **HAPPY ENDINGS**
Director: Noel Black
Co-stars: John Schneider Ana Alicia Bibi Osterwald

1984   **GARBO TALKS**
Director: Sidney Lumet
Co-stars: Anne Bancroft Ron Silver Carrie Fisher

1984   **THE RAZOR'S EDGE**
Director: John Byrum
Co-stars: Bill Murray Denholm Elliott Theresa Russell

1985   **FEVER PITCH**
Director: Richard Brooks
Co-stars: Ryan O'Neal Giancarlo Giannini Bridgette Andersson

1986   **PEGGY SUE GOT MARRIED**
Director: Francis Coppola
Co-stars: Kathleen Turner Nicolas Cage Helen Hunt

1986   **STAR TREK IV: THE VOYAGE HOME**
Director: Leonard Nimoy
Co-stars: Leonard Nimoy William Shatner DeForest Kelly

1987   **SOUVENIR**
Director: Geoffrey Reeve
Co-stars: Christopher Plummer Christopher Cazenove Lisa Daniely

1987   **LAGUNA HEAT**
Director: Simon Langton
Co-stars: Harry Hamlin Jason Robards Rip Torn

1989   **CHILD'S PLAY**
Director: Tom Holland
Co-stars: Chris Sarandon Brad Dourif Dinah Manoff

1989   **SHE'S OUT OF CONTROL**
Director: Stan Dragoti
Co-stars: Tony Danza Ami Dolenz Wallace Shawn

1992   **LIEBESTRAUM**
Director: Mike Figgis
Co-stars: Kevin Anderson Pamela Gidley Kim Novak

PATRICIA HICKS

1948   **THE DARK ROAD**
Director: Alfred Goulding
Co-stars: Charles Stuart Joyce Linden Anthony Hollies

TARAL HICKS

1993   **A BRONX TALE**
Director: Robert De Niro
Co-stars: Robert De Niro Chazz Palminteri Lillo Brancato Francis Capra

JOAN HICKSON

1936   **LOVE FROM A STRANGER**
Director: Rowland Lee
Co-stars: Ann Harding Basil Rathbone Binnie Hale

1944   **DON'T TAKE IT TO HEART**
Director: Jeffrey Dell
Co-stars: Richard Greene Patricia Medina Edward Rigby

1948   **THE GUINEA PIG**
Director: Roy Boulting
Co-stars: Richard Attenborough Shelia Sim Robert Flemyng

1950   **SEVEN DAYS TO NOON**
Director: John Boulting
Co-stars: Andre Morrell Barry Jones Olive Sloane Kenneth Griffith

1951   **HIGH TREASON**
Director: Roy Boulting
Co-stars: Liam Redmond Andre Morrell Kenneth Griffith

1952   **THE CARD**
Director: Ronald Neame
Co-stars: Alec Guinness Petula Clark Glynis Johns

1953   **DEADLY NIGHTSHADE**
Director: John Gilling
Co-stars: Emrys Jones Zena Marshall John Horsley

1955   **JUMPING FOR JOY**
Director: John Paddy Carstairs
Co-stars: Frankie Howerd Stanley Holloway

1955   **VALUE FOR MONEY**
Director: Ken Annakin
Co-stars: John Gregson Diana Dors Susan Stephen Jill Adams

1956   **THE EXTRA DAY**
Director: William Fairchild
Co-stars: Richard Basehart Simone Simon George Baker

1956   **CHILD IN THE HOUSE**
Director: Raker Endfield
Co-stars: Mandy Miller Eric Portman Phyllis Calvert

1957   **NO TIME FOR TEARS**
Director: Cyril Frankel
Co-stars: Anna Neagle Anthony Quayle Slyvia Syms

1958   **LAW AND DISORDER**
Director: Charles Crighton
Co-stars: Michael Redgrave Robert Morley Lionel Jeffries

1959   **THE THIRTY-NINE STEPS**
Director: Ralph Thomas
Co-stars: Kenneth More Talna Elg Sid James Barry Jones

1959   **CARRY ON NURSE**
Director: Gerald Thomas
Co-stars: Shirley Eaton Bill Owen Leslie Phillips Joan Sims

1959   **CARRY ON CONSTABLE**
Director: Gerald Thomas
Co-stars: Sid James Eric Barker Kenneth Connor

1959   **UPSTAIRS AND DOWNSTAIRS**
Director: Ralph Thomas
Co-stars: Michael Craig Anne Heyward Sid James

1960   **HIS AND HERS**
Director: Brian Desmond Hurst
Co-stars: Terry-Thomas Janette Scott Oliver Reed

1961   **IN THE DOGHOUSE**
Director: Darcy Conyers
Co-stars: Leslie Phillips Peggy Cummins James Booth

1961 MURDER, SHE SAID
Director: George Pollock
Co-stars: Margaret Rutherford Muriel Pavlow Arthur Kennedy

1965 THE SECRET OF MY SUCCESS
Director: Andrew Stone
Co-stars: James Booth Shirley Jones Stella Stevens

1970 CARRY ON LOVING
Director: Gerald Thomas
Co-stars: Sid James Hattie Jacques Kenneth Williams

1971 A DAY IN THE DEATH OF JOE EGG
Director: Peter Medak
Co-stars: Alan Bates Janet Suzman

1973 THEATRE OF BLOOD
Director: Douglas Hickox
Co-stars: Vincent Price Diana Rigg Diana Dors Ian Hendry

1974 CONFESSIONS OF A WINDOW CLEANER
Director: Val Guest
Co-stars: Robin Askwith Anthony Booth Bill Maynard

1979 YANKS
Director: John Schlesinger
Co-stars: Richard Gere Vanessa Redgrave Lisa Eichhorn

1986 CLOCKWISE
Director: Christopher Morahan
Co-stars: John Cleese Alison Steadman Penelope Wilton

1988 MISS MARPLE: 4.50 FROM PADDINGTON
Director: Martyn Friend
Co-stars: David Horovitch Joanna David

1989 KING OF THE WIND
Director: Peter Duffell
Co-stars: Frank Finlay Jenny Agutter Navin Chowdray

1991 MISS MARPLE:
THEY DO IT WITH MIRRORS
Director: Norman Stone
Co-stars: Jean Simmons Joss Ackland

1992 MISS MARPLE: THE MIRROR CRACK'D
SIDE TO SIDE
Director: Norman Stone
Co-star: Claire Bloom Barry Newman Gwen Watford

1993 CENTURY
Director: Stephen Poliakoff
Co-stars: Charles Dance Clive Owen Miranda Richardson

CONCHA HIDALGO

1988 A TIME OF DESTINY
Director: Gregory Nava
Co-stars: William Hurt Melissa Leo Timothy Hutton

JEAN HIDEY

1959 THE SAVAGE EYE
Director: Ben Maddow
Co-stars: Barbara Baxley Gary Merrill Herschell Bernardi

MARY JANE HIGBY

1970 THE HONEYMOON KILLERS
Director: Leonard Kastle
Co-stars: Shirley Stoler Tony LoBianco Doris Roberts

CLAIRE HIGGINS

1985 19/19
Director: Hugh Brody
Co-stars: Paul Scofield Maria Schell Colin Firth

1987 HELLRAISER
Director: Clive Barker
Co-stars: Andrew Robinson Sean Chapman Robert Hines

1988 HELLBOUND: HELLRAISER II
Director: Tony Randell
Co-stars: Ashley Laurence Kenneth Cranham Doug Bradley

1988 THE FRUIT MACHINE
Director: Philip Saville
Co-stars: Emile Charles Tony Forsyth Robert Stephens

1992 BAD BEHAVIOUR
Director: Les Blair
Co-stars: Stephen Rea Sinead Cusack Philip Jackson

1994 MEN OF THE MONTH
Director: Jean Stuart
Co-stars: Dougals Hodge Claire Hackett Sandy Ratcliffe

1996 SMALL FACES
Director: Gillies MacKinnon
Co-stars: Joe McFadden Laura Fraser Iain Robertson

FRAN HIGGINS

1976 SQUIRM
Director: Jeff Lieberman
Co-stars: John Scardino Patricia Pearcy Jean Sullivan

CHRISTINA HIGUERAS

1992 HOSTAGE
Director: Robert Young
Co-stars: Sam Neill Talisa Sotto James Fox

JENNIFER HILARY

1966 THE IDOL
Director: Daniel Petrie
Co-stars: Jennifer Jones Michael Parks John Leyton

1970 ONE BRIEF SUMMER
Director: John MacKenzie
Co-stars: Clifford Evans Felicity Gibson Peter Egan

1982 FIVE DAYS ONE SUMMER
Director: Fred Zinnemann
Co-stars: Sean Connery Betsy Brantley Lambert Wilson

TINA LOUISE HILBERT

1991 BASKET CASE 3: THE PROGENY
Director: Frank Hennenlotter
Co-stars: Kevin Van Hentenryck Annie Ross

LISE HILBOLDT

1985 NOON WINE
Director: Michael Fields
Co-stars: Fred Ward Pat Hingle Enrique Brown

1986 SWEET LIBERTY
Director: Alan Alda
Co-stars: Alan Alda Michael Caine Michelle Pfeiffer Bob Hoskins

1989 THE KAREN CARPENTER STORY
Director: Joseph Sargent
Co-stars: Cynthia Gibb Mitchell Anderson Louise Fletcher

HILDE HILDEBRAND

1933 VIKTOR UND VIKTORIA
Director: Reinhold Schunzel
Co-stars: Renate Muller Hermann Thimig Fritz Odemar

DANA HILL

1981 SHOOT THE MOON
Director: Alan Parker
Co-stars: Albert Finney Diane Keaton Karen Allen

1983 CROSS CREEK
Director: Martin Ritt
Co-stars: Mary Steenburgen Rip Torn Peter Coyote

1985   NATIONAL LAMPOON'S
EUROPEAN VACATION
Director: Amy Heckerling
Co-stars: Chevy Chase Beverly D'Angelo

1986   COMBAT ACCADEMY
Director: Heal Israel
Co-stars: Keith Gordon Wally Ward George Clooney

1993   TOM AND JERRY: THE MOVIE *(Voice)*
Director: Phil Roman
Co-star: Richard Kind

DORIS HILL

1926   THE BETTER 'OLE
Director: Charles Reisner
Co-stars: Syd Chaplin Harold Goodwin Edgar Kennedy

1931   ONE WAY TRAIL
Director: Ray Taylor
Co-star: Tim McCoy

1933   TRAILING NORTH
Co-star: Bob Steele

LAURA HILL

1990   THE ENGLISHMAN'S WIFE
Director: Robert Cooper
Co-stars: Imelda Staunton Adrian Dunbar Trevor Moore

MARIANNA HILL

1962   BLACK ZOO
Director: Robert Gordon
Co-stars: Michael Gough Jeanne Cooper Virginia Grey

1965   RED LINE 7000
Director: Howard Hawks
Co-stars: James Caan Laura Devon Charlene Holt

1965   PARADISE HAWAIIAN STYLE
Director: Michael Moore
Co-stars: Elvis Presley Suzanna Leigh Irene Tsu

1969   MEDIUM COOL
Director: Haskell Wexler
Co-stars: Robert Forster Verna Bloom Peter Boyle

1970   THE TRAVELLING EXECUTIONER
Director: Jack Smight
Co-stars: Stacy Keach Bud Cort Graham Jarvis

1970   EL CONDOR
Director: John Guillermin
Co-stars: Jim Brown Lee Van Cleef Patrick O'Neal

1972   HIGH PLAINS DRIFTER
Director: Clint Eastwood
Co-stars: Clint Eastwood Verna Bloom Mitchell Ryan Jack Ging

1972   THUMB TRIPPING
Director: Quentin Masters
Co-stars: Michael Burns Meg Foster Bruce Dern

1973   THE BABY
Director: Ted Post
Co-stars: Anjanette Comer Ruth Roman

1977   RELENTLESS
Director: Lee Katzin
Co-stars: Will Sampson Monte Markham John Hillerman

1981   BLOOD BEACH
Director: Jeffrey Bloom
Co-stars: John Saxon David Huffman Burt Young

MELANIE HILL

1989   A NIGHT ON THE TYNE
Director: Corbin Campbell-Hill
Co-stars: Bryan Pringle Alun Armstrong Robson Green

1993   THE HAWK
Director: David Hayman
Co-stars: Helen Mirren George Costigan Rosemary Leach

1996   BRASSED OFF
Director: Mark Harmon
Co-stars: Tara Fitzgerald Ewan McGregor Jim Carter

ROSE HILL

1958   THE BANK RAIDERS
Director: Maxwell Munden
Co-stars: Peter Reynolds Sandra Dorne Sydney Tafler

1958   MR SKEETER
Director: Colin Finbow
Co-stars: Peter Bayliss Orlando Wells Susannah York

1986   PAST CARING
Director: Richard Eyre
Co-stars: Denholm Elliott Emlyn Williams Joan Greenwood

STEPHANIE HILL

1966   ALVAREZ KELLY
Director: Edward Dmytryk
Co-stars: William Holden Richard Widmark Janice Rule

TERESA HILL

1993   PUPPET MASTER 4
Director: Jeff Burr
Co-stars: Guy Rolfe Gordon Currie Chandra West

WENDY HILLER
Oscar For Best Supporting Actress In 1958 For "Separate Tables"
Nominated For Best Actress In 1933 For "Pygmalion" Nominated For
Best Supporting Actress In 1966 For "A Man For All Seasons"

1937   LANCASHIRE LUCK
Director: Henry Cass
Co-stars: George Carney Muriel George Nigel Stock

1938   PYGMALION
Director: Leslie Howard
Co-stars: Leslie Howard Wilfrid Lawson Marie Lohr David Tree

1941   MAJOR BARBARA
Director: David Lean
Co-stars: Rex Harrison Robert Morley Robert Newton

1945   I KNOW WHERE I'M GOING
Director: Michael Powell
Co-stars: Roger Livesey Pamela Brown George Carney

1951   AN OUTCAST OF THE ISLANDS
Director: Carol Reed
Co-stars: Trevor Howard Robert Morley Kerima

1957   SOMETHING OF VALUE
Director: Richard Brooks
Co-stars: Rock Hudson Sidney Poitier Dana Wynter

1957   HOW TO MURDER A RICH UNCLE
Director: Nigel Patrick
Co-stars: Nigel Patrick Charles Coburn Katie Johnson

1958   SEPARATE TABLES
Director: Delbert Mann
Co-stars: Burt Lancaster David Niven Rita Hayworth

1960   SONS AND LOVERS
Director: Jack Cardiff
Co-stars: Dean Stockwell Trevor Howard Mary Ure

1963   TOYS IN THE ATTIC
Director: George Roy Hill
Co-stars: Geraldine Page Dean Martin Gene Tierney

1966   A MAN FOR ALL SEASONS
Director: Fred Zinnemann
Co-stars: Paul Schofield Orson Wells Susannah York

1970 DAVID COPPERFIELD
Director: Delbert Mann
Co-stars: Michael Redgrave Laurence Olivier Ralph Richardson

1974 MURDER ON THE ORIENT EXPRESS
Director: Sidney Lumet
Co-stars: Albert Finney Ingrid Bergman Sean Connery

1976 VOYAGE OF THE DAMNED
Director: Stuart Rosenberg
Co-stars: Faye Dunaway Lee Grant James Mason Orson Welles

1979 THE CAT AND THE CANARY
Director: Radley Metzger
Co-stars: Honor Blackman Olivia Hussey Edward Fox

1980 THE ELEPHANT MAN
Director: David Lynch
Co-stars: John Hurt Anthony Hopkins Anne Bancroft

1981 COUNTRY
Director: Richard Eyre
Co-stars: Leo McKern James Fox Jill Bennett

1982 MAKING LOVE
Director: Arthur Hiller
Co-stars: Michael Onttkean Kate Jackson Harry Hamlin

1987 THE LONELY PASSION OF JUDITH HEARNE
Director: Jack Clayton
Co-stars: Maggie Smith Bob Hoskins

1990 ENDING UP
Director: Peter Sasdy
Co-stars: John Mills Googie Withers Lionel Jeffries

1991 THE BEST OF FRIENDS
Director: Alvin Rakoff
Co-stars: John Gielgud Patrick McGoohan Paul Keown

HARRIET HILLIARD (Married Ozzie Nelson Mother Of Ricky And David Nelson)

1936 FOLLOW THE FLEET
Director: Mark Sandrich
Co-stars: Fred Astaire Ginger Rogers Randolph Scott

1937 LIFE OF THE PARTY
Director: William Seiter
Co-stars: Joe Penner Gene Raymond Ann Miller

1937 NEW FACES OF 1937
Director: Leigh Jason
Co-stars: Joe Penner Milton Berle Ann Miller

1938 COCOANUT GROVE
Director: Alfred Santell
Co-stars: Fred MacMurray Eve Arden Ben Blue

1941 SWEETHEART OF THE CAMPUS
Director: Edward Dmytryk
Co-stars: Ruby Keeler Ozzie Nelson Don Beddoe

1943 HI BUDDY
Director: Harold Young
Co-stars: Dick Foran Robert Paige Marjorie Lord

1943 HONEYMOON LODGE
Co-star: David Bruce

1943 THE FALCON STRIKES BACK
Co-star: Tom Conway

1944 HI GOOD LOOKING
Co-star: Kirby Grant

1944 TAKE IT BIG
Co-star: Ozzie Nelson

1951 HERE COMES THE NELSONS
Director: Frederick De Cordova
Co-stars: Ozzie Nelson Ricky Nelson

PATRICIA HILLIARD

1934 THE PRIVATE LIVE OF DON JUAN
Director: Alexander Korda
Co-stars: Douglas Fairbanks Merle Oberon

1936 THE GHOST GOES WEST
Director: Rene Clair
Co-stars: Robert Donat Jean Parker Eugene Pallette

1937 FAREWELL AGAIN
Director: Tim Whelan
Co-stars: Flora Robson Leslie Banks Robert Newton

VERNA HILLIE

1934 THE STAR PACKER
Director: Robert Bradbury
Co-stars: John Wayne Yakima Cannutt George "Gabby " Hayes

1934 THE TRAIL BEYOND
Director: Robert Bradbury
Co-stars: John Wayne Noah Beery Iris Lancaster

CANDACE HILLIGOSS

1962 CARNIVAL OF SOULS
Director: Herk Harvey
Co-stars: Herk Harvey Francis Feist Sidney Berger

1964 THE CURSE OF THE LIVING CORPSE
Director: Del Tenney
Co-star: Roy Scheider

BEVERLEY HILLS

1986 KNIGHTS AND EMERALDS
Director: Ian Emes
Co-stars: Christopher Wild Warren Mitchell Rachel Davies

GILLIAN HILLS

1960 BEAT GIRL
Director: Edmond Greville
Co-stars: David Farrar Noelle Adam Oliver Reed Adam Faith

1966 BLOWUP
Director: Michaelangelo Antonioni
Co-stars: David Hemmings Sarah Miles Vanessa Redgrave

AMANDA HILLWOOD

1987 SUNDAY PREMIERE
Director: Ross Devenish
Co-stars: Denholm Elliott Holly Aird Kathryn Pogson

1988 THE BELL RUN
Director: Alan Dosser
Co-stars: Bruce Payne Abigail Cruttenden Neil Pearson

1988 INSPECTOR MORSE: THE GHOST IN THE MACHINE
Director: Herbert Wise
Co-stars: John Thaw Patricia Hodge

1989 INSPECTOR MORSE: THE SECRET OF BAY 5B
Director: Jim Goddard
Co-stars: John Thaw Mel Martin

1991 INSPECTOR MORSE: THE LAST ENEMY
Director: James Scott
Co-stars: John Thaw Barry Foster Kevin Whately

1991 INSPECTOR MORSE: DECEIVED BY FLIGHT
Director: Anthony Simmons
Co-stars: John Thaw Norman Rodway

PIPPA HINCHLEY

1989 THE DRESSMAKER
Director: Jim O'Brien
Co-stars: Joan Plowright Billie Whitelaw Jane Horrocks

1989   AND A NIGHTINGALE SANG
Director: Robert Knights
Co-stars: Phyllis Logan Tom Watt Joan Plowright

MADELINE HINDE

1969   THE SMASHING BIRD I USED TO KNOW
Director: Robert Hartford-Davis
Co-stars: Dennis Waterman Maureen Lipman

1970   INCENCE FOR THE DAMNED
Director: Michael Burrows
Co-stars: Peter Cushing Patrick Mower

MADGE HINDLE

1973   NEAREST AND DEAREST
Director: John Robins
Co-stars: Hylda Baker Jimmy Jewel Joe Gladwin

1982   INTENSIVE CARE
Director: Gavin Millar
Co-stars: Alan Bennett Thora Hird Julie Walters

CINDY HINDS

1979   THE BROOD
Director: David Cronenberg
Co-stars: Oliver Reed Samantha Eggar Art Hindle

CONNIE HINES

1950   DUCHESS OF IDAHO
Director: Robert Z. Leonard
Co-stars: Esther Williams Van Johnson John Lund

1960   THUNDER IN CAROLINA
Director: Paul Helmick
Co-stars: Rory Calhoun Alan Hale

MARY HINTON

1942   WOMEN AREN'T ANGELS
Director: Laurence Huntingdon
Co-stars: Robertson Hare Alfred Drayton Polly Ward

BARBARA HINTZ

1947   GERMANY, YEAR ZERO
Director: Roberto Rossellini
Co-stars: Edmund Meschke Ernest Pittschau

INGETRAUD HINTZE

1947   GERMANY, YEAR ZERO
Director: Roberto Rossellini
Co-stars: Edmund Meschke Ernest Pittschau

LAURA HIPPE

1983   MAUSOLEUM
Director: Michael Dugan
Co-stars: Marjoe Gortner Bobbie Bresee Norman Burton

THORA HIRD *(Mother Of Janette Scott)*

1941   THE BLACK SHEEP OF WHITEHALL
Director: Will Hay
Co-stars: Will Hay Basil Sydney Felix Aylmer Ronald Shiner

1942   WENT THE DAY WELL ?
Director: Alberto Cavalcanti
Co-stars: Leslie Banks Elizabeth Allan Frank Lawton

1942   THE FOREMAN WENT TO FRANCE
Director: Charles Frend
Co-stars: Tommy Trinder Constance Cummings

1944   TWO THOUSAND WOMEN
Director: Frank Launder
Co-stars: Phyllis Calvert Flora Robson Patricia Roc

1947   A BOY, A GIRL AND A BIKE
Director: Ralph Smart
Co-stars: Honor Blackman John McCallum Diana Dors

1948   ONCE A JOLLY SWAGMAN
Director: Jack Lee
Co-stars: Dirk Bogarde Bonar Colleano Rennee Asherson

1948   PORTRAIT FROM LIFE
Director: Terence Fisher
Co-stars: Mai Zetterling Robert Beatty Guy Rolfe

1948   THE WEAKER SEX
Director: Roy Baker
Co-stars: Ursula Jeans Cecil Parker Lana Morris

1949   MADNESS OF THE HEART
Director: Charles Bennett
Co-stars: Margaret Lockwood Paul Dupuis Maxwell Reed

1949   FOOLS RUSH IN
Director: John Paddy Carstairs
Co-stars: Sally Anne Howes Guy Rolfe Nora Swinburne

1949   CONSPIRATOR
Director: Victor Saville
Co-stars: Robert Taylor Elizabeth Taylor Honor Blackman

1949   THE CURE FOR LOVE
Director: Robert Donat
Co-stars: Robert Donat Renee Asherson Dora Bryan

1949   BOYS IN BROWN
Director: Montgomery Tully
Co-stars: Dirk Bogarde Jack Warner Michael Medwin

1950   THE MAGNET
Director: Charles Frend
Co-stars: William Fox Stephen Murray Kay Walsh Gladys Henson

1950   ONCE A SINNER
Director: Lewis Gilbert
Co-stars: Pat Kirkwood Jack Watling Joy Shelton

1952   TIME GENTLEMEN PLEASE!
Director: Lewis Gilbert
Co-stars: Eddie Byrne Dora Bryan Hermione Baddeley

1952   THE GREAT GAME
Director: Maurice Elvey
Co-stars: James Hayter Diana Dors Glyn Houston

1952   THE FRIGHTENED MAN
Director: John Gilling
Co-stars: Dermot Walsh Charles Victor Barbara Murray

1952   EMERGENCY CALL
Director: Lewis Gilbert
Co-stars: Jack Warner Joy Shelton Anthony Steel

1953   A DAY TO REMEMBER
Director: Ralph Thomas
Co-stars: Stanley Holloway Donald Sinden Joan Rice

1953   BACKGROUND
Director: Daniel Birt
Co-stars: Valerie Hobson Philip Frend Janette Scott

1953   TURN THE KEY SOFTLY
Director: Jack Lee
Co-stars: Yvonne Mitchell Joan Collins Terence Morgan

1954   ONE GOOD TURN
Director: John Paddy Carstairs
Co-stars: Norman Wisdom Joan Collins Shirley Abicair

1954   THE LOVE MATCH
Director: David Paltenghi
Co-stars: Arthur Askey Shirley Eaton James Kenney

1954   FOR BETTER FOR WORSE
Director: J. Lee Thompson
Co-stars: Dirk Bogarde Susan Stephen Dennis Price

1954   **THE CROWDED DAY**
Director: John Guillerman
Co-stars: Joan Rice John Gregson Dora Bryan

1955   **LOST**
Director: Guy Green
Co-stars: David Farrar Julia Arnall Eleanor Summerfield Joan Sims

1955   **SIMON AND LAURA**
Director: Muriel Box
Co-stars: Peter Finch Kay Kendall Ian Carmichael

1955   **THE QUATERMASS EXPERIMENT**
Director: Val Guest
Co-stars: Brian Donlevy Jack Warner

1955   **TIGER BY THE TALE**
Director: John Gilling
Co-stars: Larry Parks Constance Smith Lisa Daniely

1956   **THE GOOD COMPANIONS**
Director: J. Lee Thompson
Co-stars: Eric Portman Celia Johnson Janette Scott

1956   **WOMEN WITHOUT MEN**
Director: Elmo Williams
Co-stars: Beverly Michaels Joan Rice Avril Angers

1956   **SAILOR BEWARE**
Director: Gordon Parry
Co-stars: Peggy Mount Shirley Eaton Ronald Lewis

1956   **HOME AND AWAY**
Director: Vernon Sewell
Co-stars: Jack Warner Kathleen Harrison Lana Morris

1958   **FURTHER UP THE CREEK**
Director: Val Guest
Co-stars: David Tomlinson Frankie Howerd Shirley Eaton

1960   **THE ENTERTAINER**
Director: Tony Richardson
Co-stars: Laurence Olivier Albert Finney Alan Bates

1962   **A KIND OF LOVING**
Director: John Schlesinger
Co-stars: Alan Bates June Ritchie James Bolam Gwen Nelson

1962   **TERM OF TRIAL**
Director: Peter Glenville
Co-stars: Laurence Olivier Sarah Miles Simone Signoret

1963   **BITTER HARVEST**
Director: Peter Graham Scott
Co-stars: Janet Munro John Stride Alan Badel

1964   **RATTLE OF A SIMPLE MAN**
Director: Muriel Box
Co-stars: Harry H. Corbett Diane Cilento Charles Dyer

1970   **SOME WILL, SOME WON'T**
Director: Duncan Wood
Co-stars: Ronnie Corbett Leslie Phillips Arthur Lowe

1971   **THE NIGHTCOMERS**
Director: Michael Winner
Co-stars: Marlon Brando Stephanie Beacham Harry Andrews

1982   **INTENSIVE CARE**
Director: Gavin Millar
Co-stars: Alan Bennett Julie Walters Helen Fraser

1988   **CONSUMING PASSIONS**
Director: Giles Foster
Co-stars: Vanessa Redgrave Freddie Jones Sami Davis

1993   **WIDE EYED AND LEGLESS**
Director: Richard Loncraine
Co-stars: Julie Walters Jim Broadbent Sian Thomas

GAIL HIRE

1965   **RED LINE 7000**
Director: Howard Hawks
Co-stars: James Caan Laura Devon Charlene Holt

ALICE HIRSON

1982   **MISS ALL-AMERICAN BEAUTY**
Director: Gus Trikonis
Co-stars: Diane Lane Cloris Leachman Jayne Meadows

1986   **DIARY OF A PERFECT MURDER**
Director: Robert Day
Co-stars: Andy Griffith Lori Lethin Kene Holliday

1987   **BLIND DATE**
Director: Blake Edwards
Co-stars: Kim Basinger Bruce Willis George Coe

ELEONORE HIRT

1976   **SEVEN NIGHTS IN JAPAN**
Director: Lewis Gilbert
Co-stars: Michael York Hidemi Aoki Peter Jones

1977   **PREPAREZ VOS MOUCHOIRS**
Director: Bertrand Blier
Co-stars: Gerard Depardieu Carole Laure Riton

GERALDINE HISLOP

1937   **SUNSET IN VIENNA**
Co-stars: Lilli Palmer Tullio Carminati John Garrick

JANE HITCHCOCK

1976   **NICKELODEON**
Director: Peter Bogdanovitch
Co-stars: Ryan O'Neal Tatum O'Neal Burt Reynolds

PATRICIA HITCHCOCK
(Daughter Of Alfred Hitchcock)

1950   **STAGE FRIGHT**
Director: Alfred Hitchcock
Co-stars: Marlene Dietrich Jane Wyman Richard Todd

1951   **STRANGERS ON A TRAIN**
Director: Alfred Hitchcock
Co-stars: Robert Walker Farley Granger Ruth Roman

1960   **PSYCHO**
Director: Alfred Hitchcock
Co-stars: Anthony Perkins Janet Leigh Vera Miles

LINDA HO

1962   **CONFESSIONS OF AN OPIUM EATER**
Director: Albert Zugsmith
Co-stars: Vincent Price Philip Ahn June Kim

JUDITH HOAG

1990   **TEENAGE MUTANT NINJA TURTLES**
Director: Steve Barron
Co-stars: Elias Koteas Josh Pais James Sato

1990   **CADILLAC MAN**
Director: Roger Donaldson
Co-stars: Robin Williams Tim Robbins Pamela Reed

MITZI HOAG

1977   **DEADLY GAME**
Director: Lane Slate
Co-stars: Andy Griffin Dan O'Herlihy Sharon Spellman

FLORENCE HOATH (Child)

1994   **A PIN FOR THE BUTTERFLY**
Director: Hannah Kodicek
Co-stars: Imogen Stubbs Hugh Laurie Joan Plowright

1995   **THE HAUNTING OF HELEN WALKER**
Director: Tom McLoughlin
Co-stars: Alex Roberts Valerie Bertinelli

1998 FAIRYTALE: A TRUE STORY
Director: Charles Sturridge
Co-stars: Paul McGann Peter O'Toole Harvey Keitel

ROSE HOBART

1930 A LADY SURRENDERS
Director: John Stahl
Co-stars: Conrad Nagel Genevieve Tobin Basil Rathbone

1930 LILIOM
Director: Frank Borzage
Co-stars: Charles Farrell Estelle Taylor Dawn O'Day

1931 CHANCES
Director: Allan Dwan
Co-stars: Douglas Fairbanks Jnr. Anthony Bushell

1931 EAST OF BORNEO
Co-stars: George Renavent

1932 DR JEYKLL AND MR HYDE
Director: Rouben Mamoulian
Co-stars: Fredric March Miriam Hopkins

1940 SUSAN AND GOD
Director: George Cukor
Co-stars: Joan Crawford Fredric March Rita Hayworth

1941 SINGAPORE WOMAN
Director: Jean Negulesco
Co-stars: Brenda Marshall David Bruce Virginia Field

1941 ZIEGFELD GIRL
Director: Robert Z. Leonard
Co-stars: James Stewart Judy Garland Lana Turner

1941 NOTHING BUT THE TRUTH
Director: Elliott Nugent
Co-stars: Bob Hope Paulette Goddard Edward Arnold

1941 MR. AND MRS. NORTH
Director: Robert Sinclair
Co-stars: Gracie Allen William Post Jnr. Paul Kelly

1941 NO HANDS ON THE CLOCK
Director: Frank McDonald
Co-stars: Chester Morris Jean Parker Rod Cameron

1943 CRIME DOCTOR'S STRANGEST CASE
Director: Eugene Forde
Co-stars: Warner Baxter Lynn Merrick

1944 THE SOUL OF A MONSTER
Director: Will Jason
Co-stars: George Macready Jim Bannon Jeanne Bates

1945 CONFLICT
Director: Curtis Bernhardt
Co-stars: Humphrey Bogart Alexis Smith Sydney Greenstreet

1946 THE CAT CREEPS
Director: Erle Kenton
Co-stars: Noah Beery Jnr. Lois Collier Paul Kelly

1947 THE FARMER'S DAUGHTER
Director: H.C. Potter
Co-stars: Loretta Young Joseph Cotten Ethel Barrymore

1947 THE TROUBLE WITH WOMEN
Director: Sidney Lanfield
Co-stars: Ray Milland Teresa Wright Brian Donlevy

KATRINA HOBBS

1993 ABSENT WITHOUT LEAVE
Director: John Laing
Co-stars: Craig McLachlan Tony Barry Judie Douglass

MARA HOBEL (Child)

1981 MOMMIE DEAREST
Director: Frank Perry
Co-stars: Faye Dunnaway Diana Scarwid Steve Forrest

1981 THE HAND
Director: Oliver Stone
Co-stars: Michael Caine Andrea Marcovici Rosemary Murphy

VALERIE HOBSON (Married John Profumo)

1934 LIFE RETURNS
Director: Eugene Frenke
Co-stars: Onslow Stevens Lois Wilson

1935 THE BRIDE OF FRANKENSTEIN
Director: James Whale
Co-stars: Boris Karloff Colin Clive Elsa Lanchester

1935 THE GREAT IMPERSONATION
Director: Alan Crosland
Co-stars: Edmund Lowe Lumsden Hare Spring Byington

1935 CHINATOWN SQUAD

1935 RENDEZVOUS AT MIDNIGHT
Director: Christy Cabanne
Co-stars: Ralph Bellamy Irene Ware Catherine Doucet

1935 THE MYSTERY OF EDWIN DROOD
Director: Stuart Walker
Co-stars: Claude Rains Douglass Montgomery

1935 WEREWOLF OF LONDON
Director: Stuart Walker
Co-stars: Henry Hull Warner Oland Spring Byington

1936 THE SECRET OF STAMBOUL
Director: Andrew Marton
Co-stars: James Mason Frank Vosper Kay Walsh

1936 NO ESCAPE
Director: Norman Lee
Co-stars: Billy Milton Henry Oscar Leslie Perrins

1937 JUMP FOR GLORY
Director: Raoul Walsh
Co-stars: Douglas Fairbanks Alan Hale Edward Rigby

1938 THE DRUM
Director: Zoltan Korda
Co-stars: Sabu Roger Livesey Raymond Massey David Tree

1938 THIS MAN IS NEWS
Director: David MacDonald
Co-stars: Barry K. Barnes Alastair Sim Garry Marsh

1939 THIS MAN IN PARIS
Director: David MacDonald
Co-stars: Barry K. Barnes Alastair Sim Garry Marsh

1939 THE SILENT BATTLE
Director: Herbert Mason
Co-stars: Rex Harrison John Loder Muriel Aked

1939 THE SPY IN BLACK
Director: Michael Powell
Co-stars: Conrad Veidt Hay Petrie Marius Goring

1939 Q PLANES
Director: Tim Whelan
Co-stars: Laurence Olivier Ralph Richardson

1940 CONTRABAND
Director: Michael Powell
Co-stars: Conrad Veidt Hay Petrie Esmond Knight

1941 ATLANTIC FERRY
Director: Walter Forde
Co-stars: Michael Redgrave Griffith Jones

1943 THE ADVENTURES OF TARTU
Director: Harold Bucquet
Co-stars: Robert Donat Glynis Johns Walter Rilla

1946 GREAT EXPECTATIONS
Director: David Lean
Co-stars: John Mills Jean Simmons Alec Guinness

1946   **THE YEARS BETWEEN**
Director: Compton Bennett
Co-stars: Michael Redgrave Flora Robson Dulcie Gray

1948   **THE SMALL VOICE**
Director: Fergus McDowell
Co-stars: James Donald Howard Keel Michael Balfour

1948   **BLANCHE FURY**
Director: Marc Allegret
Co-stars: Stewart Granger Michael Gough Maurice Denham

1949   **THE INTERRUPTED JOURNEY**
Director: Daniel Birt
Co-stars: Richard Todd Christine Norden Tom Walls

1949   **KIND HEARTS AND CORONETS**
Director: Robert Hamer
Co-stars: Alec Guinness Dennis Price Joan Greenwood

1949   **TRAIN OF EVENTS**
Director: Basil Dearden
Co-stars: John Clements Peter Finch Susan Shaw

1942   **UNPUBLISHED STORY**
Director: Harold French
Co-stars: Richard Greene Basil Radford Roland Culver

1950   **THE ROCKING HORSE WINNER**
Director: Anthony Pelissier
Co-stars: John Mills Hugh Sinclair Ronald Squire

1952   **WHO GOES THERE?**
Director: Anthony Kimmins
Co-stars: Peggy Cummins George Cole Nigel Patrick

1952   **THE VOICE OF MERRILL**
Director: John Gilling
Co-stars: James Robertson Justice Edward Underdown

1952   **MEET ME TONIGHT**
Director: Anthony Pelissier
Co-stars: Nigel Patrick Ted Ray Kay Walsh

1952   **THE CARD**
Director: Ronald Neame
Co-stars: Alec Guinness Petula Clark Edward Chapman

1953   **BACKGROUND**
Director: Daniel Birt
Co-stars: Philip Friend Janette Scott Mandy Miller

1954   **KNAVE OF HEARTS**
Director: Rene Clement
Co-stars: Gerard Phillipe Margaret Johnston Natasha Parry

KIRSTEN HOCKING

1994   **BITTER VENGEANCE**
Director: Stuart Cooper
Co-stars: Virginia Madsen Gordon Jump

HARRIET HOCTOR

1936   **THE GREAT ZIEGFELD**
Director: Robert Z. Leonard
Co-stars: William Powell Luise Rainer Myrna Loy

1937   **SHALL WE DANCE?**
Director: Mark Sandrich
Co-stars: Fred Astaire Ginger Rogers Edward Everett Horton

KATE HODGE

1990   **THE TEXAS CHAINSHAW**
         MASSACRE III: LEATHERFACE
Director: Jeff Burr
Co-stars: Ken Foree Viggo Mortensen

1992   **RAPID FIRE**
Director: Dwight Little
Co-stars: Brandon Lee Powers Booth Nick Mancuso

1993   **THE HIDDEN II**
Director: Seth Pinsker
Co-star: Raphael Sbarge

PATRICIA HODGE

1975   **THE NAKED CIVIL SERVANT**
Director: Jack Gold
Co-stars: John Hurt Katherine Schofield Quentin Crisp

1983   **BETRAYAL**
Director: David Jones
Co-stars: Jeremy Irons Ben Kingsley

1986   **HOTEL DU LAC**
Director: Giles Foster
Co-stars: Anna Massey Denholm Elliott Googie Withers

1986   **THE RETURN OF SHERLOCK HOLMES:**
         THE SECOND STAIN
Director: John Bruce
Co-stars: Jeremy Brett Edward Hardwicke Harry Andrews

1988   **SUNSET**
Director: Blake Edwards
Co-stars: Bruce Willis James Garner Malcolm McDowell

1988   **JUST ASK FOR DIAMOND**
Director: Stephen Bayly
Co-stars: Susannah York Roy Kinnear Jimmy Nail

1988   **INSPECTOR MORSE:**
         THE GHOST IN THE MACHINE
Director: Herbert Wise
Co-stars: John Thaw Kevin Whateley

1989   **THE HEAT OF THE DAY**
Director: Christopher Morahan
Co-stars: Michael Gambon Michael York

1990   **SPYMAKER:**
         THE SECRET LIFE OF IAN FLEMING
Director: Ferdinand Fairfax
Co-star: Jason Connery Kristen Scott-Thomas

1996   **THE LEADING MAN**
Director: John Duigan
Co-stars: Jon Bon Jovi Anna Galiena Barry Humphries

VICKI HODGE

1975   **CONFESSIONS OF A SEX MANIAC**
Director: Alan Birkinshaw
Co-stars: Roger Lloyd-Pack Candy Baker

JOY HODGES

1935   **PERSONAL SECRETARY**
Co-star: William Gargan

1939   **LITTLE ACCIDENT**
Co-stars: Florence Rice Richard Carlson Peggy Moran

1939   **THE FAMILY NEXT DOOR**
Co-star: Thomas Beck

KATRINA HODIAK

1980   **JANE AUSTEN IN MANHATTAN**
Director: James Ivory
Co-stars: Robert Powell Anne Baxter Tim Choate

ANITA HOEFER

1965   **SITUATION HOPELESS - BUT NOT SERIOUS**
Director: Gottfried Reinhardt
Co-stars: Alec Guinness Robert Redford

IRIS HOEY

1934   **THOSE WERE THE DAYS**
Director: Thomas Bentley
Co-stars: Will Hay John Mills Angela Baddeley

1935 LET'S MAKE A NIGHT OF IT
Director: Graham Cutts
Co-stars: Buddy Rogers June Clyde Fred Emney

1950 THE GIRL WHO COULDN'T QUITE
Director: Norman Lee
Co-stars: Bill Owen Elizabeth Henson Betty Stockfield

BRENDA HOGAN

1948 THE FATAL NIGHT
Director: Mario Zampi
Co-stars: Lester Ferguson Jean Short Patrick MacNee

SUSAN HOGAN

1979 AN AMERICAN CHRISTMAS CAROL
Director: Eric Till
Co-stars: Henry Winkler David Wayne Chris Wiggins

1980 PHOBIA
Director: John Huston
Co-stars: Paul Michael Glaser John Colicos Alexandra Stewart

1986 EASY PREY
Director: Sandor Stern
Co-stars: Gerald McRaney Shawnee Smith Sean McCann

1990 NARROW MARGIN
Director: Peter Hyams
Co-stars: Gene Hackman Anne Archer J.T. Walsh

1991 WHITE FANG
Director: Randal Kleiser
Co-stars: Klaus Maria Branddauer Ethan Hawke Seymour Cassel

DENICE HOFF

1993 BLOODLUST: SUBSPECIES II
Director: Ted Nicolaou
Co-stars: Anders Hove Kevin Blair

ELIZABETH HOFFMAN

1981 FEAR NO EVIL
Director: Frank Loggia
Co-stars: Frank Birney Kathleen Rowe McAllen Daniel Eden

1994 THE RIVER WILD
Director: Curtis Hanson
Co-stars: Meryl Streep Kevin Bacon Joseph Mazzello

GABY HOFFMAN *(Child)*

1989 UNCLE BUCK
Director: John Hughes
Co-stars: John Candy Amy Madigan Macauley Culkin

1992 THIS IS MY LIFE
Director: Nora Ephron
Co-stars: Julie Kavner Samantha Mathis Carrie Fisher

1993 SLEEPLESS IN SEATTLE
Director: Nora Ephron
Co-stars: Tom Hanks Meg Ryan Bill Pullman

1993 THE MAN WITHOUT A FACE
Director: Mel Gibson
Co-stars: Mel Gibson Margaret Whitton Geoffrey Lewis

1996 NOW AND THEN
Co-stars: Demi Moore Melanie Griffith Rita Wilson

1997 VOLCANO
Director: Mick Jackson
Co-stars: Tommy Lee Jones Ann Heche

GERTRUDE HOFFMAN

1940 THE APE
Director: William Nigh
Co-stars: Boris Karloff Maris Wrixon Henry Hall

ISABELLA HOFFMAN

1987 INDEPENDENCE
Director: John Patterson
Co-stars: John Bennett Perry Amanda Wyss Anthony Zerbe

1994 RENAISSANCE MAN
Director: Penny Marshall
Co-stars: Danny DeVito Gregory Hines Cliff Robertson

1995 SHE FOUGHT ALONE
Director: Christopher Leitch
Co-stars: Brian Austin Green Tiffani-Amber Thiessen

JANE HOFFMAN

1972 UP THE SADDLE BOX
Director: Irwin Kershner
Co-stars: Barbra Streisand David Selby Ariane Heller

1987 BATTERIES NOT INCLUDED
Director: Matthew Robbins
Co-stars: Hume Cronyn Jessica Tandy Elizabeth Pena

SUSAN LEE HOFFMAN

1995 OUTBREAK
Director: Wolfgang Petersen
Co-stars: Dustin Hoffman Rene Russo Morgan Freeman

SUSANNAH HOFFS
(Daughter Of Tamar Simon Hoffs)

1987 THE ALLNIGHTER
Director: Tamar Simon Hoffs
Co-stars: Debbie Pfeiffer Joan Cusack Pam Grier

HANNELORE HOGER

1992 THE SECOND HEIMAT
Director: Edgar Reitz
Co-stars: Henry Arnold Salome Kammer Gisela Muller

KRISTIN HOLBY

1983 TRADING PLACES
Director: John Landis
Co-stars: Dan Aykroyd Eddie Murphy Don Ameche

CINDY HOLDEN *(Child)*

1987 LILY MY LOVE
Director: Adrian Shergold
Co-stars: Bill Paterson David Horovitch Ian Sharp

1989 UNEXPLAINED LAUGHTER
Director: Gareth Davies
Co-stars: Diana Rigg Elaine Paige Joanna David

FAY HOLDEN

1937 SOULS AT SEA
Director: Henry Hathaway
Co-stars: Gary Cooper George Raft Frances Dee

1938 SWEETHEARTS
Director: W.S. Van Dyke
Co-stars: Jeanette MacDonald Nelson Eddy Ray Bolger

1938 HOLD THAT KISS
Director: Edwin Marin
Co-stars: Maureen O'Sullivan Dennis O'Keefe Mickey Rooney

1938 YOU'RE ONLY YOUNG ONCE
Director: George Seitz
Co-stars: Lewis Stone Mickey Rooney Ann Rutherford

1938 JUDGE HARDY'S CHILDREN
Director: George Seitz
Co-stars: Lewis Stone Cecilia Parker Ruth Hussey

1938 **LOVE FINDS ANDY HARDY**
Director: George Seitz
Co-stars: Mickey Rooney Judy Garland Lana Turner

1938 **OUT WEST WITH THE HARDYS**
Director: George Seitz
Co-stars: Lewis Stone Mickey Rooney Sara Haden

1939 **THE HARDYS RIDE HIGH**
Director: George Seitz
Co-stars: Lewis Stone Mickey Rooney Cecilia Parker

1939 **ANDY HARDY GETS SPRING FEVER**
Director: W.S. Van Dyke
Co-stars: Mickey Rooney Sara Haden Ann Rutherford

1939 **JUDGE HARDY AND SON**
Director: George Seitz
Co-stars: Lewis Stone June Preisser Maria Ouspenskaya

1939 **SERGEANT MADDEN**
Director: Josef Von Sternberg
Co-stars: Wallace Beery Tom Brown Laraine Day

1940 **ANDY HARDY MEETS A DEBUTANT**
Director: George Seitz
Co-stars: Lewis Stone Mickey Rooney Judy Garland

1941 **ANDY HARDY'S PRIVATE SECRETARY**
Director: George Seitz
Co-stars: Kathryn Grayson Ian Hunter Sara Haden

1941 **LIFE BEGINS FOR ANDY HARDY**
Director: George Seitz
Co-stars: Mickey Rooney Judy Garland Cecilia Parker

1941 **H.M.PULHAM ESQUIRE**
Director: King Vidor
Co-stars: Hedy Lamarr Robert Young Charles Coburn

1941 **I'LL WAIT FOR YOU**
Co-stars: Marsha Hunt Robert Sterling Henry Travers

1941 **ZIEGFELD GIRL**
Director: Robert Z. Leonard
Co-stars: James Stewart Judy Garland Lana Turner

1942 **THE COURTSHIP OF ANDY HARDY**
Director: George Seitz
Co-stars: Lewis Stone Mickey Rooney Donna Reed

1942 **ANDY HARDY'S DOUBLE LIFE**
Director: George Seitz
Co-stars: Mickey Rooney Esther Williams Susan Peters

1944 **ANDY HARDY'S BLONDE TROUBLE**
Director: George Seitz
Co-stars: Bonita Granville Herbert Marshall

1946 **LOVE LAUGHS AT ANDY HARDY**
Director: Willis Goldbeck
Co-stars: Bonita Granville Mickey Rooney Lewis Stone

1946 **LITLE MISS BIG**
Co-stars: Beverley Simmons Frank McHugh Dorothy Morris

1948 **WHISPERING SMITH**
Director: Leslie Fenton
Co-stars: Alan Ladd Robert Preston Brenda Marshall

1949 **SAMSON AND DELILAH**
Director: Cecil B. DeMille
Co-stars: Hedy Lamarr Victor Mature George Sanders

1950 **THE BIG HANGOVER**
Director: Norman Krasna
Co-stars: Van Johnson Elizabeth Taylor Leon Ames

1958 **ANDY HARDY COMES HOME**
Director: Howard Koch
Co-stars: Mickey Rooney Cecilia Parker Sara Haden

GLORIA HOLDEN

1936 **DRACULA'S DAUGHTER**
Director: Lambert Hillyer
Co-stars: Otto Kruger Marguerite Churchill Nan Grey

1937 **THE LIFE OF EMIL ZOLA**
Director: William Dieterle
Co-stars: Paul Muni Joseph Schildkraut Donald Crisp

1938 **HAWAII CALLS**
Director: Edward Cline
Co-stars: Bobby Breen Ned Sparks Warren Hull

1938 **TEST PILOT**
Director: Victor Fleming
Co-stars: Clark Gable Myrna Loy Spencer Tracy

1939 **DODGE CITY**
Director: Michael Curtiz
Co-stars: Errol Flynn Olivia De Havilland Ann Sheridan

1939 **A CHILD IS BORN**
Director: Lloyd Bacon
Co-stars: Geraldine Fitzgerald Gladys George Jeffrey Lynn

1941 **THIS THING CALLED LOVE**
Director: Alexander Hall
Co-stars: Rosalind Russell Melvyn Douglas Lee J. Cobb

1942 **MISS ANNIE ROONEY**
Director: Edwin Marin
Co-stars: Shirley Temple William Gargan Peggy Ryan

1942 **A GENTLEMAN AFTER DARK**
Director: Edwin Marin
Co-stars: Brian Donlevy Miriam Hopkins Preston Foster

1943 **BEHIND THE RISING SUN**
Director: Edward Dmytryk
Co-stars: J. Carrol Naish Tom Neal Robert Ryan

1945 **STRANGE HOLIDAY**
Director: Arch Obeler
Co-stars: Claude Rains Milton Kibbee

1947 **THE HUCKSTERS**
Director: Jack Conway
Co-stars: Clark Gable Debrah Kerr Ava Gardner

1956 **THE EDDY DUCHIN STORY**
Director: George Sidney
Co-stars: Tyrone Power Kim Novak Victoria Shaw

JAN HOLDEN

1956 **ASSIGNMENT REDHEAD**
Director: MacLean Rogers
Co-stars: Richard Denning Carole Matthews Brian Worth

1959 **THE STRANGERS OF BOMBAY**
Director: Terence Fisher
Co-stars: Guy Rolfe Allan Cuthbertson

JENNIFER HOLDEN

1957 **JAILHOUSE ROCK**
Director: Richard Thorpe
Co-stars: Elvis Presley Judy Tyler Dean Jones

1958 **GANG WAR**
Director: Gene Fowler
Co-stars: Charles Bronson Kent Taylor Gloria Henry

JOYCE HOLDEN

1950 **THE MILKMAN**
Director: Charles Barton
Co-stars: Donald O'Connor Jimmy Durante Piper Laurie

1951 **YOU NEVER CALL TELL**
Director: Lou Breslow
Co-stars: Dick Powell Peggy Dow Charles Drake

1951 IRON MAN
Director: Joseph Pevney
Co-stars: Jeff Chandler Evelyn Keyes Rock Hudson

1952 BRONCO BUSTER
Director: Budd Boettocher
Co-stars: John Lund Scott Brady Chill Wills

1953 GIRLS IN THE NIGHT
Director: Jack Arnold
Co-stars: Glenda Farrell Harvey Lembeck Don Gordon

1956 WEREWOLF
Director: Fred Sears
Co-stars: Steven Ritch Don McGowan

MARJEAN HOLDEN

1993 THE PHILADELPHIA EXPERIMENT 2
Director: Stephen Cornwall
Co-star: Brad Johnson

1993 FIST OF JUSTICE
Director: Kim Bass
Co-star: Corey Everson

RUTH HOLDEN

1990 HAPPY FEET
Director: Mike Bradwell
Co-stars: Phyllis Logan Stephen Hancock Marjie Lawrence

FAY HOLDERNESS

1930 HOG WILD
Director: James Parrott
Co-stars: Stan Laurel Oliver Hardy Dorothy Granger

BILLIE HOLLIDAY

1947 NEW ORLEANS
Director: Arthur Lubin
Co-stars: Louis Armstrong Woody Herman Dorothy Patrick

HOPE HOLLIDAY

1963 IRMA LA DOUCE
Director: Billy Wilder
Co-stars: Shirley MacLaine Jack Lemmon Lou Jacobi

1965 THE ROUNDERS
Director: Burt Kennedy
Co-stars: Henry Fonda Glenn Ford Chill Wills

BETTY LOU HOLLAND

1958 THE GODDESS
Director: John Cromwell
Co-stars: Kim Stanley Lloyd Bridges Steven Hill

DIANE HOLLAND

1986 THE CHILDREN OF DYNMOUTH
Director: Peter Hammond
Co-stars: John Bird Peter Jones Avril Elgar

EDNA HOLLAND

1945 KISS AND TELL
Co-stars: Shirley Temple Jerome Courtland Walter Abel

JUDY HOLLIDAY

1944 GREENWICH VILLAGE
Director: Walter Lang
Co-stars: Vivian Blaine Carmen Miranda Don Ameche

1944 WINGED VICTORY
Director: George Cukor
Co-stars: Lon McCallister Jeanne Crain Edmond O'Brien

1949 ADAM'S RIB
Director: George Cukor
Co-stars: Spencer Tracy Katherine Hepburn David Wayne

1950 BORN YESTERDAY
Director: George Cukor
Co-stars: Broderick Crawford William Holden

1953 THE MARRYING KIND
Director: George Cukor
Co-stars: Aldo Ray Mickey Shaughnessy Madge Kennedy

1954 IT SHOULD HAPPEN TO YOU
Director: George Cukor
Co-stars: Jack Lemmon Peter Lawford Michael O'Shea

1954 PHFFFT!
Director: Mark Robson
Co-stars: Jack Lemmon Kim Novak Jack Carson

1956 THE SOLID GOLD CADILLAC
Director: Richard Quine
Co-stars: Paul Douglas John Williams Fred Clark

1956 FULL OF LIFE
Director: Richard Quine
Co-stars: Richard Conte Salvatore Baccaloni

1960 BELLS ARE RINGING
Director: Vincente Minnelli
Co-stars: Dean Martin Fred Clark Jean Stapleton

KENE HOLLIDAY

1984 THE PHILADELPHIA EXPERIMENT
Director: Stewart Raffill
Co-stars: Michael Pare Nancy Allen

1986 DIARY OF A PERFECT MURDER
Director: Robert Day
Co-stars: Andy Griffith Lori Lethin Alice Hirson

1987 IF IT'S TUESDAY, IT STILL MUST BE BELGIUM
Director: Bob Sweeny
Co-stars: Claude Akins Courteney Cox

1991 THE JOSEPHINE BAKER STORY
Director: Brian Gibson
Co-stars: Lynn Whitfield Ruben Blades David Dukes

MARTHA HOLLIDAY

1945 GEORGE WHITE'S SCANDALS
Director: Felix Feist
Co-stars: Joan Davis Jack Haley Jane Greer

POLLY HOLLIDAY

1976 ALL THE PRESIDENT'S MEN
Director: Alan J. Pakula
Co-stars: Robert Redford Dustin Hoffman Jason Robards

1978 THE ONE AND ONLY
Director: Carl Reiner
Co-stars: Henry Winkler Kim Darby Gene Saks

1984 GREMLINS
Director: Joe Dante
Co-stars: Zach Galligan Phoebe Cates Hoyt Axton

1985 AMAZING STORIES 8
Director: Bob Balaban
Co-stars: June Lockhart Milton Berle J.A. Preston

1987 KONRAD
Director: Nell Cox
Co-star: Max Wright

1988 MOON OVER PARADOR
Director: Paul Mazursky
Co-stars: Richard Dreyfuss Raul Julia Sonia Braga

1993 MRS. DOUBTFIRE
Director: Chris Columbus
Co-stars: Robin Williams Sally Field Pierce Brosnan

ANN HOLLOWAY

1967 TWO A PENNY
Director: James Collier
Co-stars: Cliff Richard Dora Bryan Avril Angers

SUSAN HOLLOWAY

1965 WHEN THE BOYS MEET THE GIRLS
Director: Alvin Ganzer
Co-stars: Connie Frances Harve Presnell Herman's Hermits

ELLEN HOLLY

1973 COPS AND ROBBERS
Director: Aram Avakian
Co-stars: Cliff Gorman Joe Bologna Dick Ward

LAUREN HOLLY (Married Jim Carrey)

1990 THE ADVENTURS OF FORD FAIRLANE
Director: Renny Harlin
Co-stars: Andrew Dice Clay Priscilla Presley

1993 DANGEROUS HEART
Director: Michael Scott
Co-stars: Tim Daly Jeffrey Nordling

1993 DRAGON: THE BRUCE LEE STORY
Director: Rob Cohen
Co-stars: Jason Scott Lee Robert Wagner Nancy Kwan

1996 DUMB AND DUMBER
Director: Peter Farrelly
Co-stars: Jim Carrey Jeff Daniels Teri Garr

1997 TURBULENCE
Co-stars: Ray Liotta Ben Cross Rachel Ticotin

ASTRID HOLM

1921 THY SOUL SHALL BEAR WITNESS
Director: Victor Sjostrom
Co-stars: Victor Sjostrom Hilda Borgstrom

CELESTE HOLM

Oscar For Best Supporting Actress In 1947 For "Gentleman's Agreement"
Nominated For Best Supporting Actress In 1949 For "Come To The Stable"
And In 1950 For "All About Eve"

1946 THREE LITTLE GIRLS IN BLUE
Director: Bruce Humberstone
Co-stars: June Haver Vivian Blaine Vera-Ellen

1947 GENTLEMAN'S AGREEMENT
Director: Elia Kazan
Co-stars: Gregory Peck Dorothy McGuire John Garfield

1947 CARNIVAL IN COSTA RICA
Director: Gregory Ratoff
Co-stars: Dick Haymes Vera-Ellen Cesar Romero

1948 ROAD HOUSE
Director: Jean Negulesco
Co-stars: Ida Lupino Richard Widmark Cornel Wilde

1948 THE SNAKE PIT
Director: Anatole Litvak
Co-stars: Olivia De Havilland Leo Genn Mark Stevens

1949 EVERYBODY DOES IT
Director: Edmund Goulding
Co-stars: Paul Douglas Linda Darnell Charles Coburn

1949 A LETTER TO THREE WIVES (Voice)
Director: Joseph Mankiewicz
Co-stars: Jeanne Crain Ann Sothern Linda Darnell

1949 COME TO THE STABLE
Director: Henry Koster
Co-stars: Loretta Young Hugh Marlowe Elsa Lanchester

1949 CHICKEN EVERY SUNDAY
Director: George Seaton
Co-stars: Dan Dailey Natalie Wood Colleen Townsend

1950 ALL ABOUT EVE
Director: Joseph Mankiewicz
Co-stars: Bette Davis George Sanders Ann Baxter

1950 CHAMPAGNE FOR CAESAR
Director: Richard Whorf
Co-stars: Ronald Colman Vincent Price Barbara Britton

1955 THE TENDER TRAP
Director: Charles Walters
Co-stars: Frank Sinatra Debbie Reynolds David Wayne

1956 HIGH SOCIETY
Director: Charles Walters
Co-stars: Frank Sinatra Bing Crosby Grace Kelly

1961 BACHELOR FLAT
Director: Frank Tashlin
Co-stars: Terry-Thomas Tuesday Weld Richard Beymer

1964 CINDERELLA
Director: Charles Dubin
Co-stars: Ginger Rogers Walter Pidgeon

1967 DOCTOR YOU'VE GOT TO BE KIDDING
Director: Peter Tewkesbury
Co-stars: Sandra Dee George Hamilton

1973 TOM SAWYER
Director: Don Taylor
Co-stars: Johnny Whitaker Jodie Foster Warren Oates

1976 BITTERSWEET LOVE
Director: David Miller
Co-stars: Lana Turner Robert Alda Meredith Baxter

1978 THE PRIVATE FILES OF J.EDGAR HOOVER
Director: Larry Cohen
Co-stars: Jose Ferrer Dan Dailey Rip Torn

1987 3 MEN AND A BABY
Director: Leonard Nimoy
Co-stars: Tom Selleck Steve Guttenberg Ted Danson

1989 POLLY
Director: Debbie Allen
Co-stars: Phylicia Rashad Butterfly McQueen

1989 THINGS THAT GO BUMP IN THE NIGHT
Director: E. W. Swackhammer
Co-stars: Ralph Bellamy

ELEANOR HOLM (Champion Swimmer)

1938 TARZAN'S REVENGE
Director: Ross Lederman
Co-stars: Glenn Morris George Barbier Hedda Hopper

SARAH-JANE HOLM

1988 THE PICNIC
Director: Paul Seed
Co-stars: Billie Whitelaw Iain Glen Cassie Stuart Brenda Fricker

SHARON HOLM

1989 STAR TRAP
Director: Tony Bicat
Co-stars: Nicky Henson Frances Tomelty Jeananne Crowley

SONIA HOLM

1947 A BOY, A GIRL AND A BIKE
Director: Ralph Smart
Co-stars: Honor Blackman Diana Dors John McCallum

1947 MIRANDA
Director: Ken Annakin
Co-stars: Glynis Johns Griffith Jones Googie Withers

1947 **THE LOVES OF JOANNA GODDEN**
Director: Charles Frend
Co-stars: Googie Withers John McCallum Jean Kent

1948 **WARNING TO WANTONS**
Director: Donald Wilson
Co-stars: Harold Warrender Anne Vernon David Tomlinson

1948 **THE CALENDAR**
Director: Arthur Crabtree
Co-stars: Greta Gynt John McCallum Leslie Dwyer

1948 **THE BAD LORD BYRON**
Director: David MacDonald
Co-stars: Dennis Price Mai Zetterling Linden Travers

1949 **STOP PRESS GIRL**
Director: Michael Barry
Co-stars: Sally Ann Howes Gordon Jackson Basil Radford

1952 **13, EAST STREET**
Director: Robert Baker
Co-stars: Patrick Holt Sandra Dorne Dora Bryan

1954 **RADIO CAB MURDER**
Director: Vernon Sewell
Co-stars: Jimmy Hanley Lana Morris Sam Kydd

1954 **THE CROWDED DAY**
Director: John Guillermin
Co-stars: Joan Rice John Gregson Rachel Roberts

CLARE HOLMAN

1989 **THE FIFTEEN STREETS**
Director: David Wheatley
Co-stars: Owen Teale Sean Bean Jane Horrocks

1989 **THE WOMAN IN BLACK**
Director: Herbert Wise
Co-stars: Adrian Rawlins Bernard Hepton Pauline Moran

1990 **CIRCLES OF DECEIT**
Director: Stuart Burge
Co-stars: Edward Fox Jane Lapotaire Brenda Bruce

1990 **CLOSE RELATIONS**
Director: Adrian Shergold
Co-stars: James Hazeldine Rosalind March June Barrie

1991 **LET HIM HAVE IT**
Director: Peter Medak
Co-stars: Chris Eccleston Tom Courtenay Eileen Atkins

1992 **AFRAID OF THE DARK**
Director: Mark Peploe
Co-stars: James Fox Fanny Ardant Paul McGann

1993 **TOM AND VIV**
Director: Brian Gilbert
Co-stars: Willem Dafoe Miranda Richardson Rosemary Harris

BRITTANY ASHTON HOLMES

1994 **THE LITTLE RASCALS**
Director: Penelope Spheeris
Co-stars: Travis Tedford Bug Hall

JANE HOLMES

1990 **HAPPY FEET**
Director: Mike Bradwell
Co-stars: Phyllis Logan Mandy More Stephen Hancock

MICHELLE HOLMES

1986 **RITA, SUE AND BOB TOO**
Director: Alan Clarke
Co-stars: Siobhan Finneran George Costigan Lesley Sharp

CHARLENE HOLT

1965 **RED LINE 7000**
Director: Howard Hawks
Co-stars: James Caan Laura Devon Marianna Hill

1966 **EL DORADO**
Director: Howard Hawks
Co-stars: John Wayne Robert Mitchum James Caan

1974 **WONDER WOMAN**
Director: Vincent McEveety
Co-stars: Cathy Lee Crosby Ricardo Montalban Kaz Garas

JENNIFER HOLT

1948 **THE TIOGA KID**
Co-stars: Eddie Dean Lee Bennett

PENELOPE HOLT

1971 **BLOOD FROM THE MUMMY'S TOMB**
Director: Seth Holt
Co-stars: Andrew Kier Valerie Leon James Villiers

SANDRINE HOLT

1990 **BLACK ROBE**
Director: Bruce Beresford
Co-stars: Lothaire Bluteau Aden Young August Schellenberg

1994 **RAPA NUI**
Director: Kevin Reynolds
Co-stars: Jason Scott Lee Esai Morales Zac Wallace

ULA HOLT

1935 **THE NEW ADVENTURES OF TARZAN**
Director: Edward Kull
Co-stars: Bruce Bennett Frank Baker Dale Walsh

1935 **TARZAN AND THE GREEN GODDESS**
Director: Edward Kull
Co-stars: Bruce Bennett Don Catello Lewis Sargent

ARABELLA HOLZBOG

1991 **STONE COLD**
Director: Craig Baxley
Co-stars: Brian Bosworth Lance Henriksen William Forsythe

DARLA HOOD

1936 **THE BOHEMIAN GIRL**
Director: James Horne
Co-stars: Stan Laurel Oliver Hardy Mae Busch

1959 **THE BAT**
Director: Crane Wilbur
Co-stars: Vincent Price Agnes Moorehead John Sutton

MIKI HOOD

1938 **INSPECTOR HORNLEIGH**
Director: Eugene Forde
Co-stars: Gordon Harker Alastair Sim Hugh Williams

NOEL HOOD

1957 **HOW TO MURDER A RICH UNCLE**
Director: Nigel Patrick
Co-stars: Nigel Patrick Charles Coburn Katie Johnson Wendy Hiller

1958 **THE INN OF THE SIXTH HAPPINESS**
Director: Mark Robson
Co-stars: Ingrid Bergman Curt Jurgens

1958 **THE DUKE WORE JEANS**
Director: Gerald Thomas
Co-stars: Tommy Steele June Laverick Michael Medwin

SARAH HOOPER

1990 **THE LAST CROP**
Director: Sue Clayton
Co-stars: Kerry Walker Noah Taylor Les Foxcroft

ELVA MAE HOOVER

1983 THE TERRY FOX STORY
Director: Ralph L. Thomas
Co-stars: Eric Fryer Robert Duvall Rosalind Chao

1986 ALEX: THE LIFE OF A CHILD
Director: Robert Markowitz
Co-stars: Bonnie Bedelia Craig T. Nelson

DAWN HOPE

1975 BLACK JOY
Director: Anthony Simmons
Co-stars: Norman Beaton Floella Benjamin Trevor Thomas

GLORIA HOPE

1922 TESS OF THE STORM COUNTRY
Director: John Robertson
Co-stars: Mary Pickford Jean Hersholt Lloyd Hughes

LESLIE HOPE

1988 TALK RADIO
Director: Oliver Stone
Co-stars: Eric Bogosian Alec Baldwin Ellen Greene

1989 ASK ME AGAIN
Director: Deborah Reinisch
Co-stars: Robert Bruce Cynthia Harris Kathryn Hays

1990 MEN AT WORK
Director: Emilio Estevez
Co-stars: Emilio Estevez Charlie Sheen John Getz Cameron Dye

1993 PARIS, FRANCE
Director: Gerard Ciccoritti
Co-stars: Peter Outerbridge Dan Lett Victor Ertmanis

VIDA HOPE

1945 THE WAY TO THE STARS
Director: Anthony Asquith
Co-stars: Michael Redgrave John Mills Rosamund John

1947 THEY MADE A FUGITIVE
Director: Alberto Cavalcanti
Co-stars: Trevor Howard Sally Gray Rene Ray

1948 THE WOMAN IN QUESTION
Director: Anthony Asquith
Co-stars: Jean Kent Dirk Bogarde Susan Shaw

1949 THE INTERRUPTED JOURNEY
Director: Daniel Birt
Co-stars: Richard Todd Valerie Hobson Christine Norden

1951 GREEN GROW THE RUSHES
Director: Derek Twist
Co-stars: Roger Livesey Richard Burton Honor Blackman

1951 THE MAN IN A WHITE SUIT
Director: Alexander MacKendrick
Co-stars: Alec Guinness Joan Greenwood

1952 WOMEN OF TWILIGHT
Director: Gordon Parry
Co-stars: Freda Jackson Rene Ray Joan Dowling

1954 LEASE OF LIFE
Director: Charles Frend
Co-stars: Robert Donat Kay Walsh Adrienne Corri

1958 RX MURDER
Director: Derek Twist
Co-stars: Marius Goring Rick Jason Lisa Gastoni

1961 IN THE DOGHOUSE
Director: Darcy Conyers
Co-stars: Leslie Phillips Peggy Cummins James Booth

JOAN HOPKINS

1943 WE DIVE AT DAWN
Director: Anthony Asquith
Co-stars: John Mills Eric Portman Jack Watling

1947 TEMPTATION HARBOUR
Director: Lance Comfort
Co-stars: Robert Newton Simone Simon William Hartnell

1948 THE WEAKER SEX
Director: Roy Baker
Co-stars: Ursula Jeans Cecil Parker Lana Morris

1948 THE FIRST GENTLEMAN
Director: Cavalcanti
Co-stars: Cecil Parker Jean-Pierre Aumont Hugh Griffith

1949 MAN ON THE RUN
Director: Lawrence Huntingdon
Co-stars: Derek Farr Peter Lorre Naunton Wayne

JULIE HOPKINS

1959 LIFE IN DANGER
Director: Terry Bishop
Co-stars: Derren Nesbitt Bruce Seton Mary Manson

MIRIAM HOPKINS
Nominated For Best Actress In 1935 For "Becky Sharp"

1930 FAST AND LOOSE
Director: Fred Newmeyer
Co-stars: Charles Starrett Frank Morgan Carole Lombard

1931 THE SMILING LIEUTENANT
Director: Ernst Lubitsch
Co-stars: Maurice Chevalier Claudette Colbert

1931 24 HOURS
Director: Marion Gering
Co-stars: Clive Brook Kay Francis Regis Toomey

1932 TROUBLE IN PARADISE
Director: Ernst Lubitsch
Co-stars: Herbert Marshall Kay Francis

1932 DR. JEKYLL AND MR. HYDE
Director: Rouben Mamoulian
Co-stars: Fredric March Rose Hobart

1932 DANCERS IN THE DARK
Director: David Burton
Co-stars: Jack Oakie George Raft Eugene Pallette

1932 TWO KINDS OF WOMEN
Co-star: Phillips Holmes

1933 DESIGN FOR LIVING
Director: Ernst Lubitsch
Co-stars: Fredric March Gary Cooper

1933 THE STORY OF TEMPLE DRAKE
Director: Stephen Roberts
Co-stars: Jack La Rue William Gargan

1933 THE STRANGER'S RETURN
Director: King Vidor
Co-stars: Lionel Barrymore Franchot Tone Beulah Bondi

1934 SHE LOVES ME NOT
Director: Elliott Nugent
Co-stars: Bing Crosby Kitty Carlisle Lynne Overman

1934 THE RICHEST GIRL IN THE WORLD
Director: William Seiter
Co-stars: Joel McCrea Fay Wray Beryl Mercer

1934 ALL OF ME
Director: James Flood
Co-stars: Fredric March George Raft Helen Mack

1935 BARBARY COAST
Director: Howard Hawks
Co-stars: Edward G. Robinson Joel McCrea Walter Brennan

1935 BECKY SHARP
Director: Rouben Mamoulian
Co-stars: Cedric Hardwicke Nigel Bruce Alan Mowbray

1935 SPLENDOR
Director: Elliott Nugent
Co-stars: Joel McCrea Helen Wesley David Niven

1936 THESE THREE
Director: William Wyler
Co-stars: Merle Oberon Joel McCrea Bonita Granville

1936 MEN ARE NOT GODS
Director: Walter Reisch
Co-stars: Sebastian Shaw Gertrude Lawrence Rex Harrison

1937 WISE GIRL
Director: Leigh Jason
Co-stars: Ray Milland Walter Abel Henry Stephenson

1937 WOMAN CHASES MAN
Director: John Blystone
Co-stars: Joel McCrea Charles Winninger Broderick Crawford

1937 THE WOMAN BETWEEN
Director: Anatole Litvak
Co-stars: Paul Muni Louis Hayward Mady Christians

1939 THE OLD MAID
Director: Edmund Goulding
Co-stars: Bette Davis George Brent Jane Bryan

1940 VIRGINIA CITY
Director: Michael Curtiz
Co-stars: Errol Flynn Randolph Scott Humphrey Bogart

1940 THE LADY WITH RED HAIR
Director: Curtis Bernhardt
Co-stars: Claude Rains Helen Westley Victor Jory

1942 A GENTLEMAN AFTER DARK
Director: Edwin Marin
Co-stars: Brian Donlevy Preston Foster Philip Reed

1943 OLD ACQUAINTANCE
Director: Vincent Sherman
Co-stars: Bette Davis Gig Young John Loder

1949 THE HEIRESS
Director: William Wyler
Co-stars: Olivia De Havilland Ralph Richardson

1951 THE MATING SEASON
Director: Mitchell Leisen
Co-stars: Gene Tierney John Lund Thelma Ritter

1952 THE OUTCASTS OF POKER FLAT
Director: Joseph Newman
Co-stars: Dale Robertson Anne Baxter Cameron Mitchell

1952 CARRIE
Director: William Wyler
Co-stars: Laurence Olivier Jennifer Jones

1961 THE CHILDREN'S HOUR
Director: William Wyler
Co-stars: Audrey Hepburn Shirley MacLaine James Garner

1965 FANNY HILL
Director: Russ Meyer
Co-stars: Laetitia Roman Walter Giller Alex D'Arcy

1966 THE CHASE
Director: Arthur Penn
Co-stars: Marlon Brando Jane Fonda Robert Redford

THELMA HOPKINS

1988 ROCK 'N' ROLL MOM
Director: Michael Schultz
Co-stars: Dyan Cannon Michael Brandon Heather Locklear

VERMAINE HOPKINS

1992 JUICE
Director: Ernest Dickerson
Co-stars: Omar Epps Cindy Herron Khalil Kain

MARIANNE HOPPE

1966 TEN LITTLE INDIANS
Director: George Pollack
Co-stars: Wilfrid Hyde White Dennis Price Shirley Eaton

HEDDA HOPPER *(Became Gossip Columnist)*

1926 THE CAVE MAN
Director: Lewis Milestone
Co-stars: Marie Prevost Matt Moore Myrna Loy

1926 DON JUAN
Director: Alan Crosland
Co-stars: John Barrymore Mary Astor Warner Oland Myrna Loy

1929 HIS GLORIOUS NIGHT
Director: Lionel Barrymore
Co-stars: John Gilbert Catherine Dale Owen Nance O'Neill

1929 THE LAST OF MRS. CHEYNEY
Director: Sidney Franklin
Co-stars: Norma Shearer Basil Rathbone Moon Carroll

1930 HOLIDAY
Director: Edward Griffith
Co-stars: Ann Harding Robert Ames Mary Astor William Holden

1930 HIGH SOCIETY BLUES
Director: David Butler
Co-stars: Janet Gaynor Charles Farrell Joyce Compton

1930 LET US BE GAY
Director: Robert Z Leonard
Co-stars: Norma Shearer Rod La Rocque Marie Dressler

1930 SUCH MEN ARE DANGEROUS
Director: Kenneth Hawks
Co-stars: Warner Baxter Catherine Dale Owen Bela Lugosi

1931 REBOUND
Director: Edward Griffith
Co-stars: Ina Claire Robert Williams Myrna Loy

1931 COMMON LAW
Co-stars: Joel McCrea Constance Bennett Lew Cody

1931 THE PRODIGAL
Director: Harry Pollard
Co-stars: Lawrence Tibbett Esther Ralston Roland Young

1931 FLYING HIGH
Director: Charles Riesner
Co-stars: Bert Lahr Charlotte Greenwood Pat O'Brien

1931 AS YOU DESIRE ME
Director: George Fittzmaurice
Co-stars: Greta Garbo Melvyn Douglas Erich Von Stroheim

1932 DOWNSTAIRS
Director: Monta Bell
Co-stars: John Gilbert Virginia Bruce Paul Lukas Reginald Owen

1932 NIGHT WORLD
Director: Hobart Henley
Co-stars: Lew Ayres Boris Karloff Mae Clarke George Raft

1932 SKYSCRAPER SOULS
Director: Edgar Selwyn
Co-stars: Warren William Maureen O'Sullivan Verree Teasdale

1932	**SPEAK EASILY**		**1939**	**LAUGH IT OFF**

1932 **SPEAK EASILY**
Director: Edward Sedgwick
Co-stars: Buster Keaton Jimmy Durante Thelma Todd

1932 **WEST OF BROADWAY**
Director: Harry Beaumont
Co-stars: John Gilbert Lois Moran El Brendel Ralph Bellamy

1933 **BOMBAY MAIL**
Director: Edwin Marin
Co-stars: Edmund Lowe Shirley Grey Onslow Stevens Ralph Forbes

1933 **BEAUTY FOR SALE**
Director: Richard Boleslawsky
Co-stars: Madge Evans Alice Brady Una Merkel

1935 **ALICE ADAMS**
Director: George Stevens
Co-stars: Katherine Hepburn Fred MacMurray Evelyn Venable

1935 **I LIVE MY LIFE**
Director: W.S. Van Dyke
Co-stars: Joan Crawford Brian Aherne Frank Morgan Eric Blore

1935 **LADY TUBBS**
Director: Alan Crosland
Co-stars: Alice Brady Douglass Montgomery Anita Louise

1935 **ONE FRIGHTENED NIGHT**
Director: Christy Cabanne
Co-stars: Charles Grapewin Mary Carlisle

1935 **THREE KIDS AND A QUEEN**
Director: Edward Ludwig
Co-stars: May Robson Frankie Darro Billy Benedict

1936 **DRACULA'S DAUGHTER**
Director: Lambert Hillyer
Co-stars: Otto Kruger Gloria Holden Marguerite Churchhill

1936 **BUNKER BEAN**
Director: Edward Killy
Co-stars: Owen Davis Lucille Ball Jessie Ralph Louise Latimer

1937 **ARTISTS AND MODELS**
Director: Raoul Walsh
Co-stars: Jack Benny Ida Lupino Ben Blue Martha Raye

1937 **YOU CAN'T BUY LUCK**
Co-star: Onslow Stevens

1937 **MAID'S NIGHT OUT**
Director: Ben Holmes
Co-stars: Joan Fontaine Allan Lane Cecil Kellaway

1937 **NOTHING SACRED**
Director: William Wellman
Co-stars: Carole Lombard Fredric March Charles Winninger

1937 **TOPPER**
Director: Norman Z. McLeod
Co-stars: Roland Young Cary Grant Constance Bennett Billie Burke

1937 **VOGUES OF 1938**
Director: Irving Cummings
Co-stars: Joan Bennett Helen Vinson Mischa Auer

1938 **TARZAN'S REVENGE**
Director: Ross Lederman
Co-stars: Glenn Morris Eleanor Holm George Barbier

1938 **DANGEROUS TO KNOW**
Director: Robert Florey
Co-stars: Akim Tamiroff Anna May Wong Gail Patrick

1939 **THE WOMEN**
Director: George Cukor
Co-stars: Norma Shearer Joan Crawford Rosalind Russell

1939 **MIDNIGHT**
Director: Mitchell Leisen
Co-stars: Claudette Colbert Don Ameche John Barrymore

1939 **LAUGH IT OFF**

1939 **WHAT A LIFE**
Director: Theodore Reed
Co-stars: Jackie Cooper Betty Field John Howard

1939 **THAT'S RIGHT YOU'RE WRONG**
Director: David Butler
Co-stars: Kay Kyser Adolphe Menjou Lucille Ball

1940 **QUEEN OF THE MOB**
Director: James Hogan
Co-stars: Blanche Yurka Ralph Bellamy Jack Carson

1942 **REAP THE WILD WIND**
Director: Cecil B. DeMille
Co-stars: John Wayne Ray Milland Paulette Goddard

1945 **BREAKFAST IN HOLLYWOOD**
Director: Harold Schuster
Co-stars: Tom Breneman Bonita Granville Beulah Bondi

1950 **SUNSET BOULEVARD**
Director: Billy Wilder
Co-stars: Gloria Swanson William Holden Erich Von Stroheim

1960 **PEPE**
Director: George Sidney
Co-stars: William Demarest Maurice Chevalier Judy Garland

1966 **THE OSCAR**
Director: Russel Rouse
Co-stars: Stephen Boyd Elke Sommer Joseph Cotten

VICTORIA HOPPER

1933 **THE CONSTANT NYMPH**
Director: Basil Dean
Co-stars: Brian Aherne Jane Baxter Peggy Blythe

1934 **LORNA DOONE**
Director: Basil Dean
Co-stars: John Loder Margaret Lockwood Roger Livesey Mary Clare

1936 **LABURNUM GROVE**
Director: Carol Reed
Co-stars: Cedric Hardwicke Edmund Gwenn Katie Johnson

1936 **THE MILL ON THE FLOSS**
Director: Tim Whelan
Co-stars: Geraldine Fitzgerald Frank Lawton James Mason

CAMILLA HORN

1926 **FAUST**
Director: F.W. Murnau
Co-stars: Gosta Ekman Emil Jannings Wilhelm Dieterle

1928 **TEMPEST**
Director: Sam Taylor
Co-stars: John Barrymore Louis Wolheim George Fawcett

1929 **ETERNAL LOVE**
Director: Ernst Lubitsch
Co-stars: John Barrymore Victor Varconi Hobart Bosworth

LENA HORNE

1942 **PANAMA HATTIE**

1943 **THOUSANDS CHEER**
Director: George Sidney
Co-stars: Kathryn Grayson Gene Kelly Jose Iturbi John Boles

1943 **STORMY WEATHER**
Director: Andrew Stone
Co-stars: Bill Robinson Fats Waller Cab Calloway

1943 **I DOOD IT**
Director: Vincente Minnelli
Co-stars: Red Skelton Eleanor Powell John Hodiak

1943 CABIN IN THE SKY
Director: Vincente Minnelli
Co-stars: Eddie Anderson Ethel Waters Rex Ingram

1943 BROADWAY RHYTHM
Director: Roy Del Ruth
Co-stars: George Murphy Ginny Simms Charles Winninger

1944 SWING FEVER
Director: Tim Whelan
Co-stars: Kay Kyser Marilyn Maxwell Nat Pendleton William Gargan

1944 ZIEGFELD FOLLIES
Director: Vincente Minnelli
Co-stars: William Powell Fred Astaire Gene Kelly

1945 SENSATIONS OF 1945
Director: Andrew Stone
Co-stars: Eleanor Powell W.C. Fields Sophie Tucker

1946 TILL THE CLOUDS ROLL BY
Director: Richard Whorf
Co-stars: Robert Walker Van Heflin Judy Garland

1948 WORDS AND MUSIC
Director: Norman Taurog
Co-stars: Mickey Rooney Tom Drake Gene Kelly Perry Como

1950 DUCHESS OF IDAHO
Director: Robert Z. Leonard
Co-stars: Esther Williams Van Johnson John Lund Mel Torme

1956 MEET ME IN LAS VEGAS
Director: Roy Rowland
Co-stars: Dan Dailey Cyd Charisse Paul Henreid

1969 DEATH OF A GUNFIGHTER
Director: Don Siegel
Co-stars: Richard Widmark Caroll O'Connor Kent Smith

1978 THE WIZ
Director: Sidney Lumet
Co-stars: Diana Ross Michael Jackson Richard Pryor Ted Ross

LIZ HORNE

1982 GREAT EXPECTATIONS (Voice)
Director: Jean Tych
Co-stars: Bill Kerr Philip Hinton Barbara Frawley

VICTORA HORNE

1946 BLUE SKIES
Director: Stuart Heisler
Co-stars: Bing Crosby Fred Astaire Joan Caulfield

1946 TO EACH HIS OWN
Director: Mitchell Leisen
Co-stars: Olivia De Havilland John Lund Roland Culver

1947 SUDDENLY IT'S SPRING
Director: Mitchell Leisen
Co-stars: Paulette Goddard Fred MacMurray MacDonald Carey

1947 THE GHOST AND MRS. MUIR
Director: Joseph Mankiewicz
Co-stars: Rex Harrison Gene Tierney Edna Best

1950 HARVEY
Director: Henry Koster
Co-stars: James Stewart Peggy Dow Josephine Hull

PENELOPE HORNER

1960 THE ANGRY SILENCE
Director: Guy Green
Co-stars: Richard Attenborough Michael Craig Pier Angeli

1967 HALF A SIXPENCE
Director: George Sidney
Co-stars: Tommy Steele Julia Foster Pamela Brown

1970 THE MAN WHO HAD POWER OVER WOMEN
Director: John Krish
Co-stars: Rod Taylor Carol White James Booth

1973 DRACULA
Director: Dan Curtis
Co-stars: Jack Palance Simon Ward Pamela Brown

BRIGITTE HORNEY

1943 BARON MUNCHHAUSEN
Director: Josef Von Baky
Co-stars: Hans Albers Wilheim Bendow Leo Slezak

1966 THE TRYGON FACTOR
Director: Cyril Frankel
Co-stars: Stewart Grainger Susan Hampshire Robert Morley

JANE HORROCKS

1987 ROAD
Director: Alan Clarke
Co-stars: Mossie Smith Lesley Sharp David Thewlis

1988 THE WOLVES OF WILLOUGHBY CHASE
Director: Stuart Orme
Co-stars: Stephanie Beacham Mel Smith

**1988 INSPECTOR WEXFORD:
NO CRYING HE MAKES**
Director: Mary McMurray
Co-stars: George Baker Louie Ramsay

1988 THE DRESSMAKER
Director: Jim O'Brien
Co-stars: Joan Plowright Billie Whitelaw Tim Ransom

1989 GETTING IT RIGHT
Director: Randal Kleiser
Co-stars: Jessie Birdsall Lynn Redgrave John Gielgud

1989 HEARTLAND
Director: Kevin Billington
Co-stars: Anthony Hopkins Lynn Farleigh Glyn Houston

1989 THE FIFTEEN STREETS
Director: David Wheatley
Co-stars: Owen Teale Sean Bean Billie Whitelaw

1990 THE WITCHES
Director: Nicolas Roeg
Co-stars: Anjelica Huston Mai Zetterling Bill Paterson

1990 LIFE IS SWEET
Director: Mike Leigh
Co-stars: Alison Steadman Jim Broadbent Timothy Spall

1990 MEMPHIS BELLE
Director: Michael Caton-Jones
Co-stars: Matthew Modine John Lithgow Sean Astin

1991 ALIVE AND KICKING
Director: Robert Young
Co-stars: Lenny Henry Robbie Coltrane Annabelle Apsion

1992 BAD GIRL
Director: George Case
Co-stars: Lesley Manville Tom Beard Nicholas Woodeson

1994 DEADLY ADVICE
Director: Mandie Fletcher
Co-stars: Imelda Staunton Brenda Fricker Jonathan Pryce

1997 BRING ME THE HEAD OF MAVIS DAVIS
Co-star: Rik Mayall Danny Aiello

KATY HORSCH

1982 PURPLE HAZE
Director: David Burton Morris
Co-stars: Peter Nelson Chuck McQuary Bernard Badlan

ANNA MARIA HORSFORD

1981   THE FAN
Director: Edward Bianchi
Co-stars: Lauren Bacall James Garner Maureen Stapleton

1982   BENNY'S PLACE
Director: Michael Schultz
Co-stars: Lou Gossett Jnr. Cicely Tyson David Harris

1985   ST. ELMO'S FIRE
Director: Joel Schumacher
Co-stars: Demi Moore Rob Lowe Emilio Estevez

1986   A CASE OF DEADLY FORCE
Director: Michael Miller
Co-stars: Richard Crenna John Shea Tate Donovan

1986   NOBODY'S CHILD
Director: Lee Grant
Co-stars: Marlo Thomas Ray Baker Kathy Baker

**1987   IF IT'S TUESDAY,
IT STILL MUST BE BELGIUM**
Director: Bob Sweeny
Co-stars: Claude Akins Peter Graves

1989   TAKEN AWAY
Director: John Patterson
Co-stars: Valerie Bertinelli Kevin Dunn Juliet Sorcey

1990   PRESUMED INNOCENT
Director: Alan J. Pakula
Co-stars: Harrison Ford Brian Dennehy Bonnie Bedelia

HELEN HORTON

1973   PHASE IV
Director: Saul Bass
Co-stars: Nigel Davenport Lynne Frederick Michael Murphy

LOUISA HORTON

1948   ALL MY SONS
Director: Irving Reis
Co-stars: Edward G. Robinson Burt Lancaster Howard Duff

1952   WALK EAST ON BEACON
Director: Alfred Werker
Co-stars: George Murphy Finlay Currie Virginia Gilmore

DOMINIQUE HORWITZ

1993   STALINGRAD
Director: Joseph Vilsmaier
Co-stars: Thomas Kretchman Sebastian Rudolph

MARJORIE HOSHELLE

1943   FIND THE BLACKMAILER
Director: Ross Lederman
Co-stars: Jerome Cowan Faye Emerson Gene Lockhart

SHIZUKO HOSHI

1990   COME SEE THE PARADISE
Director: Alan Parker
Co-stars: Dennis Quaid Tamlyn Tomita Sab Shimono

ALLISON HOSSACK

1993   NIGHT OWL
Director: Matthew Patrick
Co-stars: Jennifer Beals James Wilder Justin Louis

1994   DANGEROUS INTENTIONS
Director: Michael Uno
Co-stars: Corbin Bernsen Donna Mills

JOAN HOTCHKIS

1973   BREEZY
Director: Clint Eastwood
Co-stars: William Holden Kay Lenz Marj Dusay

1976   ODE TO BILLY JOE
Director: Max Baer
Co-stars: Robby Benson Glynis O'Connor James Best

KATHERINE HOUGHTON
(Niece Of Katherine Hepburn)

1967   GUESS WHO'S COMING TO DINNER
Director: Stanley Kramer
Co-stars: Spencer Tracy Katherine Hepburn Sidney Poitier

1982   THE EYES OF THE AMARYLLIS
Director: Frederick King Keller
Co-stars: Ruth Ford Guy Boyd Martha Byrne

1993   ETHAN FROME
Director: John Madden
Co-stars: Liam Neeson Patricia Arquette Joan Allen

1992   BILLY BATHGATE
Director: Robert Benton
Co-stars: Dustin Hoffman Nicole Kidman Loren Dean

CANDICE HOUSTON

1988   THE LAND BEFORE TIME *(Voice)*
Director: Don Bluth
Co-stars: Helen Shaver Pat Hingle Gabriel Damon

RENEE HOUSTON

1939   A GIRL MUST LIVE
Director: Carol Reed
Co-stars: Margaret Lockwood Lilli Palmer Hugh Sinclair

1940   OLD BILL AND SON
Director: Ian Dalrymple
Co-stars: John Mills Morland Graham Mary Clare

1942   THE PETERVILLE DIAMOND
Director: Walter Forde
Co-stars: Anne Crawford Donald Stewart William Hartnell

1944   TWO THOUSAND WOMEN
Director: Frank Launder
Co-stars: Phyllis Calvert Flora Robson Patricia Roc

1951   LADY GODIVA RIDES AGAIN
Director: Frank Launder
Co-stars: Pauline Stroud Dennis Price Diana Dors

1954   THE BELLES OF ST. TRINIANS
Director: Frank Launder
Co-stars: Alastair Sim George Cole Joyce Grenfell

1956   THE BIG MONEY
Director: John Paddy Carstairs
Co-stars: Ian Carmichael Belinda Lee Jill Ireland

1956   A TOWN LIKE ALICE
Director: Jack Lee
Co-stars: Virginia McKenna Peter Finch Maureen Swanson

1957   TIME WITHOUT PITY
Director: Joseph Losey
Co-stars: Michael Redgrave Alex McCowern Ann Todd

1958   THE HORSE'S MOUTH
Director: Ronald Neame
Co-stars: Alec Guinness Kay Walsh Robert Coote

1959   THE FLESH AND THE FIENDS
Director: John Gilling
Co-stars: Peter Cushing June Laverick Billie Whitelaw

1961   NO MY DARLING DAUGHTER
Director: Ralph Thomas
Co-stars: Juliet Mills Michael Redgrave

1963   CARRY ON CABBY
Director: Gerald Thomas
Co-stars: Kenneth Connor Sid James Hattie Jacques

1964   CARRY ON SPYING
Director: Gerald Thomas
Co-stars: Barbara Windsor Bernard Cribbins Eric Barker

1965   REPULSION
Director: Roman Polanski
Co-stars: Catherine Deneuvre Ian Hendry Patrick Wymark

1966   CUL DE SAC
Director: Roman Polanski
Co-stars: Donald Pleasence Lionel Stander William Franklin

1971   CARRY ON AT YOUR CONVENIENCE
Director: Gerald Thomas
Co-stars: Sid James Kenneth Williams Joan Sims

1975   LEGEND OF THE WEREWOLF
Director: Freddie Francis
Co-stars: Peter Cushing Ron Moody Hugh Griffith

WHITNEY HOUSTON
(God Daughter Of Aretha Franklin, Cousin Of Dionne Warwick, Married Bobby Brown)

1992   THE BODYGUARD
Director: Mick Jackson
Co-stars: Kevin Costner Gary Kemp Ralph Waite

1996   WAITING TO EXHALE
Director: Forest Whitaker
Co-stars: Loretta Devine Angela Bassett Lela Rochon

1997   THE PREACHER'S WIFE
Director: Penny Marshall
Co-stars: Denzil Washington Gregory Hines

ANN HOWARD
1971   TALES OF BEATRIX POTTER
Director: Reginald Mills
Co-stars: Wayne Sleep Lesley Collier

ANNE HOWARD
1951   LORNA DOONE
Director: Phil Karlson
Co-stars: Barbara Hale Richard Greene Ron Randell

BARBARA HOWARD
1984   FRIDAY THE 13TH.: THE FINAL CHAPTER
Director: Joseph Zito
Co-stars: Crispin Glover Corey Feldman

DE DE HOWARD
1981   MATT HOUSTON
Director: Richard Lang
Co-stars: Lee Horsley Pamela Hensley Barbara Carrera

ESTHER HOWARD
1932   MERRILY WE GO TO HELL
Director: Dorothy Arzner
Co-stars: Sylvia Sydney Fredric March Adrienne Allen

1936   KLONDYKE ANNIE
Director: Raoul Walsh
Co-stars: Mae West Victor McLaglen Philip Reed

1942   JACKASS MAIL
Director: Norman Z. Mcleod
Co-stars: Wallace Beery Marjorie Main J. Carrol Naish

1942   MY FAVOURITE BLONDE
Director: Sidney Lanfield
Co-stars: Bob Hope Madeleine Carroll George Zucco

1945   FAREWELL MY LOVELY
Director: Edward Dmytryk
Co-stars: Dick Powell Claire Trevor Anne Shirley

1945   DETOUR
Director: Edgar Ulmer
Co-stars: Tom Neal Ann Savage Claudia Drake

1947   LADY OF DECEIT
Director: Robert Wise
Co-stars: Lawrence Tierney Claire Trevor Walter Slezak

1949   THE BEAUTIFUL BLONDE FROM BASHFUL BEND
Director: Preston Sturges
Co-stars: Betty Grable Cesar Romero

JEAN HOWARD
1936   THE FINAL HOUR
Co-stars: Ralph Bellamy John Dilson

1943   CLAUDIA
Director: Edmund Goulding
Co-stars: Robert Young Dorothy McGuire Ina Clare

1944   THE BERMUDA MYSTERY
Director: Ben Stoloff
Co-stars: Preston Foster Ann Rutherford Charles Butterworth

JOYCE HOWARD
1941   THE COMMON TOUCH
Director: John Baxter
Co-stars: Geoffrey Hibbert Greta Gynt Edward Rigby

1941   FREEDOM RADIO
Director: Anthony Asquith
Co-stars: Diana Wynyard Clive Crooks Derek Farr

1941   LOVE ON THE DOLE
Director: John Baxter
Co-stars: Deborah Kerr Clifford Evans Geoffrey Hibbert

1942   BACK ROOM BOY
Director: Herbert Mason
Co-stars: Arthur Askey Googie Withers Moore Marriott

1942   THE NIGHT HAS EYES
Director: Leslie Arliss
Co-stars: James Mason Wilfrid Lawson Mary Clare

1942   TALK ABOUT JACQUELINE
Director: Harold French
Co-stars: Hugh Williams Carla Lehman Roland Culver

1943   THEY MET IN THE DARK
Director: Karel Lamac
Co-stars: Tom Walls James Mason David Farrar

1943   THE GENTLE SEX
Director: Leslie Howard
Co-stars: Rosamund John Lilli Palmer Joan Greenwood

1945   APPOINTMENT WITH CRIME
Director: John Harlow
Co-stars: William Hartnell Robert Beatty Herbert Lom

1945   THEY KNEW MR. KNIGHT
Director: Norman Walker
Co-stars: Mervyn Johns Alfred Drayton Joan Greenwood

1947   MRS. FITZHERBERT
Director: Montgomery Tully
Co-stars: Peter Graves Leslie Banks Margaretta Scott

KATHLEEN HOWARD
1934   DEATH TAKES A HOLIDAY
Director: Mitchell Leisen
Co-stars: Fredric March Evelyn Venable Guy Standing

1934   IT'S A GIFT
Director: Norman Z. McLeod
Co-stars: W.C. Fields Jean Rouverol Baby LeRoy

1934 ONE MORE RIVER
Director: James Whale
Co-stars: Colin Clive Diana Wynyard Jane Wyatt

1935 THE MAN ON THE FLYING TRAPEZE
Director: Clyde Bruckman
Co-stars: W.C. Fields Mary Brian Vera Lewis

1939 LITTLE ACCIDENT
Director: Charles Lamont
Co-stars: Baby Sandy Florence Rice Richard Carlson

1940 MYSTERY SEA RAIDER
Director: Edward Dmytryk
Co-stars: Carole Landis Henry Wilcoxon Onslow Stevens

1940 YOUNG PEOPLE
Director: Allan Dwan
Co-stars: Shirley Temple Jack Oakie Charlotte Greenwood

1941 SWEETHEART OF THE CAMPUS
Director: Edward Dmytryk
Co-stars: Ruby Keeker Ozzie Nelson Harriet Hilliard

1941 BLOSSOMS IN THE DUST
Director: Mervyn LeRoy
Co-stars: Greer Garson Walter Pidgeon Marsha Hunt

1941 TAKE A LETTER, DARLING
Director: Mitchell Leisen
Co-stars: Rosalind Russell Fred MacMurray

1946 CENTENNIAL SUMMER
Director: Otto Preminger
Co-stars: Jeanne Crain Cornel Wilde Walter Brennan

LISA K. HOWARD

1953 DONOVAN'S BRAIN
Director: Felix Feist
Co-stars: Lew Ayres Gene Evans Nancy Davis

1996 THE BOUNTY HUNTERS
Director: George Ersch Bamer
Co-star: Michael Dudikoff

MARY HOWARD

1937 ALL OVER TOWN
Director: James Horne
Co-stars: Ole Olsen Chic Johnson Harry Stockwell

1938 FOUR GIRLS IN WHITE
Director: S. Sylvan Simon
Co-stars: Florence Rice Ann Rutherford Una Merkel

1940 SPIRIT OF THE PEOPLE
Director: John Cromwell
Co-stars: Raymond Massey Ruth Gordon Gene Lockhart

1941 SWAMP WATER
Director: Jean Renoir
Co-stars: Walter Huston Walter Brennan Anne Baxter

1941 THE WILD MAN OF BORNEO
Director: Robert Sinclair
Co-stars: Frank Morgan Dan Dailey Ian Hunter

1941 BILLY THE KID
Director: David Miller
Co-stars: Robert Taylor Brian Donlevy Ian Hunter

1942 THROUGH DIFFERENT EYES
Director: Thomas Loring
Co-stars: Frank Craven Donald Woods Vivian Blaine

NORAH HOWARD

1934 LOVE, LIFE AND LAUGHTER
Director: Maurice Elvy
Co-stars: Gracie Fields John Loder Robb Wilton

1935 CAR OF DREAMS
Director: Graham Cutts
Co-stars: John Mills Robertson Hare Mark Lester

1939 THE LAMBETH WALK
Director: Albert De Courville
Co-stars: Lupino Lane Sally Gray Wilfrid Hyde White

1939 THE SAINT IN LONDON
Director: John Paddy Carstairs
Co-stars: George Sanders Sally Gray Henry Oscar

1961 TWO LOVES
Director: Charles Walters
Co-stars: Shirley MacLaine Laurence Harvey Jack Hawkins

RANCE HOWARD

1976 EAT MY DUST
Director: Charles Griffith
Co-stars: Ron Howard Corbin Bernsen Christopher Norris

1989 LIMIT UP
Director: Richard Martini
Co-stars: Nancy Allen Dean Stockwell Sally Kellerman

1992 FAR AND AWAY
Director: Ron Howard
Co-stars: Tom Cruise Nicole Kidman Michelle Johnson

RITA HOWARD

1972 THE RAGMAN'S DAUGHTER
Director: Harold Becker
Co-stars: Simon Rouse Victoria Tennant Leslie Sands

1985 THE ADVENTURES OF SHERLOCK HOLMES: THE GREEK INTERPRETER
Director: Derek Marlowe
Co-star: Jeremy Brett David Burke Charles Gray

SUSAN HOWARD

1969 THE SILENT GUN
Director: Michael Caffey
Co-stars: Lloyd Bridges John Beck Ed Begley

1974 NIGHT GAMES
Director: Don Taylor
Co-stars: Barry Newman Stefanie Powers Anjanette Comer

VANESSA HOWARD

1967 HERE WE GO ROUND THE MULBERRY BUSH
Director: Clive Donner
Co-stars: Barry Evans Judy Geeson Moyra Fraser

1967 THE BLOOD BEAST TERROR
Director: Vernon Sewell
Co-stars: Robert Flemyng Wanda Ventham Peter Cushing

1969 LOCK UP YOUR DAUGHTERS
Director: Peter Coe
Co-stars: Christopher Plummer Susannah York Glynis Johns

1970 MUMSY, NANNY, SONNY AND GIRLY
Director: Freddie Francis
Co-stars: Michael Bryant Pat Heywood

1970 THE RISE AND RISE OF MICHAEL RIMMER
Director: Kevin Billington
Co-stars: Peter Cook John Cleese

1971 WHAT BECAME OF JACK AND JILL?
Director: Bill Bain
Co-stars: Paul Nicholas Peter Copley Peter Jeffrey

DOROTHY HOWE

1938 HER JUNGLE LOVE
Director: George Archainbaud
Co-stars: Dorothy Lamour Ray Milland Lynne Overman

JENNY HOWE
1991 TRULY, MADLY, DEEPLY
Director: Anthony Minghella
Co-stars: Juliet Stevenson Alan Rickman Michael Maloney

LETTICE HOWELL
1930 IN GAY MADRID
Director: Robert Z. Leonard
Co-stars: Ramon Navarro Dorothy Jordan Eugenie Besserer

URSULA HOWELLS
1951 FLESH AND BLOOD
Director: Anthony Kimmins
Co-stars: Richard Todd Glynis Johns Joan Greenwood

1952 I BELIEVE IN YOU
Director: Basil Dearden
Co-stars: Celia Johnson Joan Collins Laurence Harvey

1953 THE WEAK AND THE WICKED
Director: J. Lee-Thompson
Co-stars: Glynis Johns Diana Dors John Gregson

1955 THE GILDED CAGE
Director: John Gilling
Co-stars: Alex Nichol Veronica Hurst Clifford Evans

1956 THE LONG ARM
Director: Charles Frend
Co-stars: Jack Hawkins Dorothy Alison Sidney Tafler

1964 THE SICILIANS
Director: Ernest Morris
Co-stars: Robert Hutton Reginald Marsh Warren Mitchell

1965 DR. TERROR'S HOUSE OF HORRORS
Director: Freddie Francis
Co-stars: Peter Cushing Roy Castle Max Adrian

1969 CROSSPLOT
Director: Alvin Rakoff
Co-stars: Roger Moore Martha Hyer Alexis Kanner

1970 MUMSY, NANNY, SONNY AND GIRLY
Director: Freddie Francis
Co-stars: Michael Bryant Pat Heywood

1984 THE COLD ROOM
Director: James Dearden
Co-stars: George Segal Amanda Pays Warren Clarke

1985 TIME AFTER TIME
Director: Bill Hays
Co-stars: John Gielgud Googie Withers Helen Cherry

1990 ARTISTS IN CRIME
Director: Silvio Narizzano
Co-stars: Simon Williams Belinda Lang Edward Judd

SALLY ANN HOWES (Child)
(Daughter Of Bobby Howes)
1943 THURSDAY'S CHILD
Director: Rodney Ackland
Co-stars: Wilfrid Lawson Stewart Granger Eileen Bennett

1944 THE HALFWAY HOUSE
Director: Basil Dearden
Co-stars: Mervyn Johns Glynis Johns Michael Redgrave

1945 DEAD OF NIGHT
Director: Basil Dearden
Co-stars: Mervyn Johns Googie Withers Michael Redgrave

1945 PINK STRING AND SEALING WAX
Director: Robert Hamer
Co-stars: Googie Withers Mervyn Johns Garry Marsh

1947 NICHOLAS NICKLEBY
Director: Cavalcanti
Director: Derek Bond Cedric Hardwicke Bernard Miles

1948 ANNA KARENINA
Director: Julien Duvivier
Co-stars: Vivien Leigh Kieron Moore Ralph Richardson

1949 FOOLS RUSH IN
Director: John Paddy Carstairs
Co-stars: Guy Rolfe Nora Swinburne Thora Hird

1949 STOP PRESS GIRL
Director: Michael Barry
Co-stars: Gordon Jackson Sonia Holm Basil Radford

1951 HONEYMOON DEFERRED
Director: Mario Camerini
Co-stars: Griffith Jones Kieron Moore Lea Padovani

1957 THE ADMIRABLE CRICHTON
Director: Lewis Gilbert
Co-stars: Kenneth Moore Cecil Parker Diane Cilento

1968 CHITTY CHITTY BANG BANG
Director: Ken Hughes
Co-stars: Dick Van Dyke Lionel Jeffries Benny Hill

1980 DEATH SHIP
Director: Alvin Rakoff
Co-stars: George Kennedy Richard Crenna Kate Reid

LOUISE HOWILL
1983 AIR HAWK
Director: David Baker
Co-stars: Eric Oldfield Ellie MacLure

BETH HOWLAND
1983 A CARIBBEAN MYSTERY
Director: Robert Lewis
Co-stars: Helen Hayes Barnard Hughes Season Hubley

JOBYNA HOWLAND
1930 DIXIANA
Director: Luther Reed
Co-stars: Bebe Daniels Robert Woolsey Bert Wheeler

1930 THE CUCKOOS
Director: Paul Sloane
Co-stars: Robert Woolsey Bert Wheeler Dorothy Lee

1930 HOOK. LINE AND SINKER
Director: Eddie Cline
Co-stars: Robert Woolsey Bert Wheeler Dorothy Lee

1930 A LADY'S MORALS
Director: Sidney Franklin
Co-stars: Grace Moore Reginald Denny Wallace Beery

1932 ROCKABYE
Director: George Cukor
Co-stars: Constance Bennett Joel McCrea Walter Pidgeon

1932 SILVER DOLLAR
Director: Alfred Green
Co-stars: Edward G. Robinson Bebe Daniels Aline MacMahon

1933 TOPAZE
Director: Harry D'Abbabie D'Arrast
Co-stars: John Barrymore Myrna Loy Jackie Searl

CHRISTINA HOYOS
1983 CARMEN
Director: Carlos Saura
Co-stars: Antonio Gades Laura Del Sol Paco De Lucia

CAROL HOYT
1993 MIDNIGHT CONFESSIONS
Director: Allan Shusstak
Co-stars: David Milbern Julie Strain

TIFFANY HOYFELD

1968 ACE HIGH
Director: Guiseppe Colizzi
Co-stars: Terence Hill Eli Wallach Bud Spencer

ANNA HRUBY

1979 CATHY'S CHILD
Director: Donald Crombie
Co-stars: Michele Fawdon Alan Cassell Bryan Brown

NANCY HSUEH

1968 TARGETS
Director: Peter Bogdanovich
Co-stars: Boris Karloff Tim O'Kelly James Brown

KELLY HU

1993 SURF NINJAS
Director: Neal Israel
Co-stars: Nicholas Cowan Leslie Nielsen Ernie Reyes Jnr.

LI LI HUA

1958 CHINA GIRL
Director: Frank Borzage
Co-stars: Victor Mature Ward Bond Stuart Whitman

SEASON HUBLEY

1973 THE LOLLY MADONNA WAR
Director: Richard Sarafan
Co-stars: Rod Steiger Robert Ryan Jeff Bridges

1978 HARDCORE
Director: Paul Schrader
Co-stars: George C. Scott Peter Boyle Leonard Gaines

1981 ESCAPE FROM NEW YORK
Director: John Carpenter
Co-stars: Kurt Russell Lee Van Cleef

1983 A CARIBBEAN MYSTERY
Director: Robert Lewis
Co-stars: Helen Hayes Barnard Hughes

1986 UNDER THE INFLUENCE
Director: Thomas Carter
Co-stars: Andy Griffith Keanu Reeves Joyce Van Patten

ELIZABETH HUDDLE

1985 DEADLY MESSAGES
Director: Jack Bender
Co-stars: Kathleen Beller Michael Brandon Scott Paulin

EMILY HUDSON

1988 THE WOLVES OF WILLOUGHBY GRANGE
Director: Stuart Orme
Co-stars: Stephanie Beacham Geraldine James

ROCHELLE HUDSON

1931 ARE THESE OUR CHIDREN?
Director: Wesley Ruggles
Co-stars: Eric Linden Arline Judge Ben Alexander

1931 FANNY FOLEY HERSELF
Director: Melville Brown
Co-stars: Edna May Oliver Helen Chandler

1932 HELL'S HIGHWAY
Director: Rowland Brown
Co-stars: Richard Dix Tom Brown Louise Carter

1933 WILD BOYS OF THE ROAD
Director: William Wellman
Co-stars: Frankie Darro Edwin Philips Arthur Hohl

1933 SHE DONE HIM WRONG
Director: Lowell Sherman
Co-stars: Mae West Cary Grant Gilbert Roland

1933 MR. SKITCH
Director: James Cruze
Co-stars: Will Rogers Zasu Pitts Florence Desmond

1934 THE MIGHTY BARNUM
Director: Walter Lang
Co-stars: Wallace Berry Adolphe Menjou Virginia Bruce

1934 SUCH WOMEN ARE DANGEROUS
Director: James Flood
Co-stars: Warner Baxter Rosemary Ames Mona Barrie

1934 JUDGE PREIST
Director: John Ford
Co-stars: Will Rogers Tom Brown Anita Louise David Landau

1934 IMITATION OF LIFE
Director: John Stahl
Co-stars: Claudette Colbert Louise Beavers Warren William

1934 HAROLD TEEN
Director: Murray Roth
Co-stars: Hal LeRoy Patricia Ellis Hobert Cavanagh

1934 BACHELOR BAIT
Director: George Stevens
Co-stars: Stuart Erwin Grady Sutton Pert Kelton

1934 LES MISERABLES
Director: Richard Boleslawski
Co-stars: Fredric March Charles Laughton John Beal

1935 SHOW THEM NO MERCY
Director: George Marshall
Co-stars: Cesar Romero Bruce Cabot Edward Norris

1935 WAY DOWN EAST
Director: Henry King
Co-stars: Henry Fonda Slim Summerville Andy Devine

1935 CURLY TOP
Director: Irving Cummings
Co-stars: Shirley Temple John Boles Jane Darwell

1935 I'VE BEEN AROUND
Co-star: Chester Morris

1935 LIFE BEGINS AT 40
Co-stars: Will Rogers Richard Cromwell

1936 THE COUNTRY ABROAD
Co-stars: Paul Kelly Alan Hale

1936 EVERBODY'S OLD MAN
Co-stars: Johnny Downs Irwin S. Cobb

1936 THE MUSIC GOES ROUND
Co-stars: Irvin Bacon Harry Richman Jack Pennick

1936 POPPY
Director: Edward Sutherland
Co-stars: W.C. Fields Richard Cromwell

1936 REUNION
Director: Norman Taurog
Co-stars: Jean Hersholt Helen Vinson J. Edward Bromberg

1937 BORN RECKLESS
Director: Malcolm St. Clair
Co-stars: Brian Donlevy Barton MacLane

1937 SHE HAD TO EAT
Co-stars: Jack Haley Franklin Pangborn

1937 THAT I MAY LIVE
Co-star: Robert Kent

1938 MR. MOTO TAKES A CHANCE
Director: Norman Foster
Co-stars: Peter Lorre J. Edward Bromberg

1938 STORM OVER BENGAL
Co-stars: Patric Knowles Richard Cromwell

1938 RASCALLS
Director: Bruce Humberstone
Co-stars: Jane Withers Borrah Minevitch Steffi Duna

1942 QUEEN OF BROADWAY
Co-stars: Buster Crabbe Donald Mayo Vince Barnett

1949 SLYLINER
Director: William Berke
Co-stars: Richard Travis Pamela Blake Steve Geray

1963 STRAIGHT-JACKET
Director: William Castle
Co-stars: Joan Crawford Diane Baker Leif Erikson

1964 THE NIGHT WALKER
Director: William Castle
Co-stars: Robert Taylor Barbara Stanwyck

TONI HUDSON

1985 JUST ONE OF THE GUYS
Director: Lisa Gottleib
Co-stars: Joyce Hyser Clayton Rohner Billy Jacoby

KYMBERLEY HUFFMAN

1994 SLEEPING WITH STRANGERS
Director: William Bolson
Co-stars: Adrienne Shelley Neil Duncan

ANNABELLE HUGGINS

1964 BACK DOOR TO HELL
Director: Monte Hellman
Co-stars: Jack Nicholson Jimmie Rogers

CAROL HUGHES

1936 STAGE STRUCK
Director: Busby Berkeley
Co-stars: Dick Powell Joan Blondell Warren William

1936 THREE MEN ON A HORSE
Director: Mervyn LeRoy
Co-stars: Frank McHugh Joan Blondell Sam Levene

1937 MARRY THE GIRL
Director: William McGann
Co-stars: Mary Boland Frank McHugh Hugh Herbert

1937 MEET THE BOY FRIEND
Co-star: David Carlyle

1937 THE WESTLAND CASE
Co-stars: George Meeker Thomas E. Jackson

1937 RENFREW OF THE ROYAL MOUNTED
Co-star: James Newill

1941 EMERGENCY LANDING
Co-stars: Forrest Tucker Evelyn Brent

1941 UNDER FIESTA STARS
Co-star: Gene Autry Smiley Burnett

1941 SCATTERGOOD BAINES
Director: Christy Cabanne
Co-stars: Guy Kibbee John Archer Emma Dunn

1945 CHARLIE CHAN AND THE RED DRAGON
Director: Phil Rosen
Co-stars: Sidney Toller Fortunio Bonanova

FINOLA HUGHES

1982 NUTCRACKER
Director: Anwar Kawadri
Co-stars: Joan Collins Carol White Paul Nicholas

1983 STAYING ALIVE
Director: Sylvester Stallone
Co-stars: John Travolta Cynthia Rhodes Julie Bovasso

1993 ASPEN EXTREME
Director: Patrick Hasburgh
Co-stars: Paul Gross Peter Berg Teri Polo

HAZEL HUGHES

1962 LUNCH HOUR
Director: James Hill
Co-stars: Shirley Ann Field Robert Stephens Kay Walsh

HELEN HUGHES

1980 THE LUCKY STAR
Director: Max Fischer
Co-stars: Rod Steiger Louise Fletcher Brett Marx

1980 MIDDLE AGE CRAZY
Director: John Trent
Co-stars: Bruce Dern Ann-Margret Deborah Wakeman

1981 INCUBUS
Director: John Hugh
Co-stars: John Cassavetes Kerrie Keane John Ireland

KATHLEEN HUGHES

1949 MR. BELVEDERE GOES TO COLLEGE
Director: Elliott Nugent
Co-stars: Clifton Webb Shirley Temple

1953 IT CAME FROM OUTER SPACE
Director: Jack Arnold
Co-stars: Richard Carlson Barbara Rush

1953 THE GOLDEN BLADE
Director: Nathan Juran
Co-stars: Rock Hudson Piper Laurie George Macready

1953 THE GLASS WEBB
Director: Jack Arnold
Co-stars: Edward G. Robinson John Forsythe Marcia Henderson

1955 CULT OF THE COBRA
Director: Francis Lyon
Co-stars: Faith Domergue Richard Long Jack Kelly

MARI ROWLAND HUGHES

1990 SNOW
Director: Gareth Rowlands
Co-stars: Michael Maloney Rachel Joyce Rupert Frazer

MARY BETH HUGHES

1939 THE WOMEN
Director: George Cukor
Co-stars: Norma Shearer Joan Crawford Rosalind Russell

1940 FREE, BLONDE AND 21
Co-star: Robert Lowery

1940 FOUR SONS
Director: Archie Mayo
Co-stars: Don Ameche Alan Curtis Robert Lowery

1940 THE GREAT PROFILE
Director: Walter Lang
Co-stars: John Barrymore Anne Baxter

1940 STAR DUST
Director: Walter Lang
Co-stars: Linda Darnell John Payne Roland Young

1941 SLEEPERS WEST
Co-stars: Lloyd Nolan Lynn Bari

1941 DESIGN FOR SCANDAL
Director: Norman Taurog
Co-stars: Rosalind Russell Walter Pidgeon Edward Arnold

1941 CHARLIE CHAN IN RIO
Director: Harry Lachman
Co-stars: Sidney Toler Cobina Wright Jnr. Victor Jory

1942 THE NIGHT BEFORE THE DIVORCE
Co-stars: Lynn Bari Joseph Allen

1942 OVER MY DEAD BODY
Director: Mal St. Clair
Co-stars: Milton Berle Reginald Denny Frank Orth

1943 THE OX-BOW INCIDENT
Director: William Wellman
Co-stars: Henry Fonda Dana Andrews Anthony Quinn

1943 NEVER A DULL MOMENT
Director: Edward Lilley
Co-stars: Ritz Brothers Frances Langford George Zucco

1943 MELODY PARADE

1943 GOOD MORNING JUDGE
Director: Jean Yarborough
Co-stars: Eddie Quillan Frances Langford Robert Mitchum

1944 MEN ON HER MIND
Co-star: Edward Norris

1945 THE GREAT FLAMARION
Director: Anthony Mann
Co-stars: Eric Von Stroheim Dan Duryea

1948 CAGED FURY
Co-stars: Richard Denning Sheila Ryan Larry Crabbe

1948 WATERFRONT AT MIDNIGHT
Co-stars: Richard Crane William Gargan Richard Travis

1950 YOUNG MAN OF MUSIC
Director: Michael Curtiz
Co-stars: Kirk Douglas Doris Day Lauren Bacall

1951 CLOSE TO MY HEART
Director: William Keighley
Co-stars: Ray Milland Gene Tierney Fay Bainter

NERYS HUGHES

1990 SURVIVAL OF THE FITTEST
Director: Martyn Frend
Co-stars: Jean Anderson Timothy West Elizabeth Spriggs

RHETTA HUGHES

1973 DON'T PLAY US CHEAP
Director: Melvin Van Peebles
Co-stars: Esther Rolle Avon Long George McCurn

TRESA HUGHES

1973 THE LOLLY MADONNA WAR
Director: Richard Sarafian
Co-stars: Rod Steiger Robert Ryan Jeff Bridges

1986 INTIMATE STRANGERS
Director: Robert Ellis Miller
Co-stars: Teri Garr Stacy Keach Cathy Lee Crosby

WENDY HUGHES (Married Chris Haywood, Mother Of Charlotte Hughes Haywood)

1978 PUZZLE
Director: Gordon Hessler
Co-stars: James Franciscus Robert Helpman Peter Gwynne

1979 MY BRILLIANT CAREER
Director: Gillian Armstrong
Co-stars: Judy Davis Sam Neill Robert Grubb

1979 NEWSFRONT
Director: Phillip Noyce
Co-stars: Bill Hunter Gerard Kennedy Chris Haywood

1981 LONELY HEARTS
Director: Paul Cox
Co-stars: Norman Kaye John Finlayson Julia Blake

1982 A DANGEROUS SUMMER
Director: Quentin Masters
Co-stars: James Mason Tom Skerritt Ian Gilmour

1983 CAREFUL, HE MIGHT HEAR YOU
Director: Carl Schultz
Co-stars: Robyn Nevin Nicholas Gledhill

1984 MY FIRST WIFE
Director: Paul Cox
Co-stars: John Hargreaves Lucy Angwin David Cameron

1986 HAPPY NEW YEAR
Director: John Avildsen
Co-stars: Peter Falk Charles Durning Tom Courtenay

1987 AMERIKA
Director: Donald Wrye
Co-stars: Kris Kristofferson Sam Neill Mariel Hemingway

1987 SHADOWS OF THE PEACOCK
Director: Phillip Noyce
Co-stars: John Lone Steven Jacobs Peta Toppano

1988 BOUNDARIES OF THE HEART
Director: Lex Marinos
Co-stars: John Hargreaves Norman Kaye Julie Nihill

1989 WARM NIGHTS ON A SLOW-MOVING TRAIN
Director: Bob Ellis
Co-stars: Colin Friels Norman Kaye

1991 WILD ORCHID
Director: Zalman King
Co-stars: Tom Skerritt Robert Davi

SHARON HUGUENY

1961 PARRISH
Director: Delmer Daves
Co-stars: Troy Donahue Claudette Colbert Karl Malden

1964 THE YOUNG LOVERS
Director: Samuel Goldwyn Jnr.
Co-stars: Peter Fonda Nick Adams Deborah Walley

GLADYS HULETTE

1921 TOL'ABLE DAVID
Director: Henry King
Co-stars: Richard Bartelmess Ernest Torrence Warner Richmond

DIANE HULL

1969 THE ARRANGEMENT
Director: Elia Kazan
Co-stars: Kirk Douglas Faye Dunaway Deborah Kerr

1975 ALOHA BOBBY AND ROSE
Director: Floyd Mutrux
Co-stars: Paul LeMat Tim McIntrye Robert Carradine

JOSEPHINE HULL
Oscar For Best Supporting Actress In 1950 For "Harvey"

1932 AFTER TOMORROW
Director: Frank Borzage
Co-stars: Charles Farrell Marian Nixon Minna Gombell

1942 ARSENIC AND OLD LACE
Director: Frank Capra
Co-stars: Cary Grant Jean Adair Priscilla Lane

1950 HARVEY
Director: Henry Koster
Co-stars: James Stewart Peggy Dow Charles Drake Cecil Kellaway

1951   **THE LADY FROM TEXAS**
Director: Joseph Pevney
Co-stars: Mona Freeman Howard Duff Ed Begley Craig Stevens

MARY HULL

1942   **SWAMP WOMAN**
Co-stars: Jack La Rue Richard Deane

ANNIE HULLEY

1991   **SLEEPERS**
Director: Geoffrey Sax
Co-stars: Nigel Havers Warren Clarke Michael Gough

HELENA HUMANN

1982   **HANDGUN**
Director: Tony Garnett
Co-stars: Karen Young Clayton Day Suzie Humphries

CATHERINE HUMBLE

1993   **ROYAL CELEBRATION**
Director: Ferdinand Fairfax
Co-stars: Minnie Driver Rupert Graves Peter Howitt

BENITA HUME

1929   **HIGH TREASON**
Director: Maurice Elvy
Co-stars: Jameson Thomas Raymond Massey

1931   **THE FLYING FOOL**
Co-star: Henry Kendall

1932   **LORD CAMBER'S LADIES**
Director: Benn Levy
Co-stars: Gerald Du Maurier Gertrude Lawrence Nigel Bruce

1932   **SERVICE FOR THE LADIES**
Director: Alexander Korda
Co-stars: Leslie Howard Elizabeth Allan Merle Oberon

1933   **THE WORST WOMAN IN PARIS**
Director: Monta Bell
Co-stars: Adolphe Menjou Helen Chandler Harvey Stevens

1933   **ONLY YESTERDAY**
Director: John Stahl
Co-stars: Margaret Sullavan John Boles Billie Burke

1933   **THE LITTLE DAMOZEL**
Director: Herbert Wilcox
Co-stars: Anna Neagle James Rennie Alfred Drayton

1933   **LOOKING FORWARD**
Director: Clarence Brown
Co-stars: Lewis Stone Lionel Barrymore Elizabeth Allan

1933   **GAMBLING SHIP**
Director: Max Marcin
Co-stars: Cary Grant Glenda Farrell Jack La Rue

1934   **JEW SUSS**
Director: Lothar Mendes
Co-stars: Conrad Veidt Cedric Hardwicke Frank Vosper

1934   **THE PRIVATE LIFE OF DON JUAN**
Director: Alexander Korda
Co-stars: Douglas Fairbanks Merle Oberon

1935   **THE GAY DECEPTION**
Director: William Wyler
Co-stars: Francis Lederer Frances Dee Alan Mowbray

1935   **THIS WOMAN IS MINE**
Co-star: Gregory Ratoff

1935   **EIGHTEEN MINUTES**
Co-stars: John Loder Hugh Wakefield Katherine Segarva

1936   **RAINBOW ON THE RIVER**
Director: Kurt Neumann
Co-stars: Bobby Breen May Robson Louise Beavers

1936   **SUZY**
Director: George Fitzmaurice
Co-stars: Jean Harlow Cary Grant Franchot Tone

1936   **TARZAN ESCAPES**
Director: Richard Thorpe
Co-stars: Johnny Weismuller Maureen O'Sullivan Herbert Mundin

1936   **MOONLIGHT MURDER**
Co-stars: Leo Carrillo Katherine Alexander

1936   **THE GARDEN MURDER CASE**
Co-stars: Edmund Lowe Freida Inescort Kent Smith

1937   **THE LAST OF MRS. CHEYNEY**
Director: Richard Boleslawski
Co-stars: Joan Crawford Robert Montgomery

MARJORIE HUME

1954   **CHILDREN GALORE**
Director: Terence Fisher
Co-stars: Eddie Byrne Marjorie Rhodes June Thorburn

MARY-MARGARET HUMES

1995   **LETHAL INTENT**
Director: Bradford May
Co-stars: Andy Griffith John Ritter Mitchell Ryan

RENEE HUMPHREY

1994   **FUN**
Director: Rafal Zielinski
Co-stars: Alicia Witt Leslie Hope William R. Moses

JUDITH HUMPHREYS

1992   **HEDD WYN: THE ARMEGEDDON POET**
Director: Huw Garmon
Co-stars: Catrin Fychan Ceri Cunnington

SUZIE HUMPHREYS

1982   **HANDGUN**
Director: Tony Garnett
Co-stars: Karen Young Clayton Day Helena Humann

GAYLE HUNNICUTT

1966   **THE WILD ANGELS**
Director: Roger Corman
Co-stars: Peter Fonda Nancy Sinatra Michael J. Pollard

1967   **NEW FACE IN HELL**
Director: John Guillerman
Co-stars: George Peppard Raymond Burr Coleen Gray

1968   **THE SMUGGLERS**
Director: Norman Lloyd
Co-stars: Kurt Kasznar Charles Drake Shirley Booth

1969   **MARLOWE**
Director: Paul Bogart
Co-stars: James Garner Rita Moreno Bruce Lee

1969   **EYE OF THE CAT**
Director: David Lowell Rich
Co-stars: Eleanor Powell Michael Sarrazin

1970   **FRAGMENT OF FEAR**
Director: Richard Sarafian
Co-stars: David Hemmings Flora Robson Daniel Massey

1972   **SCORPIO**
Director: Michael Winer
Co-stars: Burt Lancaster Alain Delon Paul Scofield

1972 RUNNING SCARED
Director: David Hemmings
Co-stars: Robert Powell Barry Morse Edward Underdown

1973 VOICES
Director: Kevin Billington
Co-star: David Hemmings

1973 THE LEGEND OF HELL HOUSE
Director: John Hough
Co-stars: Clive Revell Pamela Franklin Roddy McDowall

1975 THE SELLOUT
Director: Peter Collinson
Co-stars: Richard Widmark Oliver Reed Sam Wanamaker

1975 THE SPIRAL STAIRCASE
Director: Peter Collinson
Co-stars: Jacqueline Bisset Christopher Plummer

1976 BLAZING MAGNUM
Director: Martin Herbert
Co-stars: Stuart Whitman John Saxon Martin Landau

1978 ONCE IN PARIS
Director: Frank Gilroy
Co-stars: Wayne Rogers Jack Lenoir Phillippe Hart

1983 THE RETURN OF THE MAN FROM UNCLE
Director: Ray Austin
Co-stars: Robert Vaughn David McCallum

1984 THE ADVENTURES OF SHERLOCK HOLMES: A SCANDAL IN BOHEMIA
Director: Paul Annett
Co-star: Jeremy Brett David Burke Rosalie Williams

1985 TARGET
Director: Arthur Penn
Co-stars: Gene Hackman Matt Dillon Josef Sommer Guy Boyd

1986 DREAM LOVER
Director: Alan J. Pakula
Co-stars: Kristy McNichol Ben Masters Paul Shenar

1989 SILENCE LIKE GLASS
Director: Carl Schenkel
Co-stars: Jami Gertz Martha Plimpton George Peppard

1992 VOICES IN THE GARDEN
Director: Pierre Boutron
Co-stars: Joss Ackland Anouk Aimee Samuel West

AMANDA HUNT

1974 PETERSEN
Director: Tim Burstall
Co-stars: Jack Thompson Jacki Weaver Joey Hohenfels

BONNIE HUNT

1988 RAIN MAN
Director: Barry Levinson
Co-stars: Dustin Hoffman Tom Cruise Valeria Golino

1992 BEETHOVEN
Director: Brian Levant
Co-stars: Charles Grodin Dean Jones Christopher Castile

1993 BEETHOVEN'S 2ND.
Director: Rod Daniel
Co-stars: Charles Grodin Nicholle Tom Debi Mazar

1994 ONLY YOU
Director: Norman Jewison
Co-stars: Robert Downey Jnr. Marisa Tomei

1996 JUMANJI
Director: Joe Johnston
Co-star: Robin Williams

ELEANOR HUNT

1930 WHOOPEE
Director: Thornton Freeland
Co-stars: Eddie Cantor Paul Gregory Betty Grable

1934 BLUE STEEL
Director: Robert Bradbury
Co-stars: John Wayne George Hayes Yakima Canutt

1937 THE GOLD RACKET
Co-star: Conrad Nagel

1937 BANK ALARM
Co-star: Conrad Nagel

ELIZABETH HUNT

1941 GERT AND DAISY'S WEEKEND
Director: MacLean Rogers
Co-stars: Elsie Waters Doris Waters John Slater

1942 GERT AND DAISY CLEAN UP
Director: MacLean Rogers
Co-stars: Elsie Waters Doris Waters Joss Ambler

FRANCES HUNT

1937 YOU'RE A SWEETHEART
Director: David Butler
Co-stars: Alice Faye George Murphy William Gargan

HELEN HUNT

1983 QUARTERBACK PRINCESS
Director: Noel Black
Co-stars: Don Murray Barbara Babcock Dapne Zuniga

1984 TRANCERS
Director: Charles Band
Co-stars: Tim Thomerson Anne Seymour Richard Erdman

1985 GIRLS JUST WANT TO HAVE FUN
Director: Alan Metter
Co-stars: Sarah Jessica Parker Shannon Doherty

1986 PEGGY SUE GOT MARRIED
Director: Francis Coppola
Co-stars: Kathleen Turner Nicolas Cage Leon Ames

1987 PROJECT X
Director: Jonathan Kaplan
Co-stars: Christopher George Matthew Broderick Bill Sadler

1988 STEALING HOME
Director: Will Aldis
Co-stars: Mark Harmon Jody Foster Blair Brown

1988 SHOOTER
Director: Gary Nelson
Co-stars: Jeffrey Nordling Alan Rock Carol Huston

1988 MILES FROM HOME
Director: Gary Sinise
Co-stars: Richard Gere Kevin Anderson Brian Dennehy

1989 NEXT OF KIN
Director: John Irvin
Co-stars: Patrick Swayze Liam Neeson Adam Baldwin

1989 INCIDENT AT DARK RIVER
Director: Michael Pressman
Co-stars: Mike Farrell Tess Harper K. Callan

1991 INTO THE BADLANDS
Director: Sam Pillsbury
Co-stars: Bruce Dern Mariel Hemingway Dylan McDermott

1991 MURDER IN NEW HAMPSHIRE
Director: Joyce Chopra
Co-stars: Chad Allen Michael Learned Ken Howard

1991 **THE WATERDANCE**
Director: Michael Steinberg
Co-stars: Eric Stoltz Wesley Snipes Eizabeth Pena

1991 **TRANCERS 2: THE RETURN OF JACK DETH**
Director: Charles Band
Co-stars: Tim Thomerson Martine Beswick

1992 **IN THE COMPANY OF DARKNESS**
Director: David Anspaugh
Co-stars: Jeff Fahey Steven Weber

1992 **TRANCERS 3: DETH LIVES**
Director: Courtney Joyner
Co-stars: Tim Thomerson Megan Ward Melanie Smith

1992 **ONLY YOU**
Director: Betty Thomas
Co-stars: Andrew McCarthy Kelly Preston Daniel Roebuck

1992 **MR. SATURDAY NIGHT**
Director: Billy Crystal
Co-stars: Billy Crystal David Paymer Julie Warner Jerry Lewis

1996 **NO WAY BACK**
Co-star: Russell Crowe

1996 **TWISTER**
Director: Jan De Bont
Co-stars: Bill Paxton Jami Gertz Cary Elwes

1998 **AS GOOD AS IT GETS**
Director: James Brooks
Co-stars: Jack Nicholson Greg Kinnear Shirley Knight

LINDA HUNT
Best Supporting Actress In 1982 For "The Year Of Living Dangerously"

1980 **POPEYE**
Director: Robert Altman
Co-stars: Robin Wiliams Shelley Duval Ray Walston Paul Dooley

1982 **THE YEAR OF LIVING DANGEROUSLY**
Director: Peter Weir
Co-stars: Mel Gibson Sigourney Weaver

1984 **THE BOSTONIANS**
Director: James Ivory
Co-stars: Christopher Reeve Vanessa Redgrave Madeleine Potter

1984 **DUNE**
Director: David Lynch
Co-stars: Francesca Annis Jose Ferrer Sting

1985 **ELENI**
Director: Peter Yates
Co-stars: Kate Nelligan John Malkovich Oliver Cotton Ronald Pickup

1985 **SILVERADO**
Director: Lawrence Kasdan
Co-stars: Kevin Kostner Scott Glenn John Cleese

1987 **THE ROOM UPSTAIRS**
Director: Stuart Margolin
Co-stars: Stockard Channing Sam Waterston

1989 **SHE-DEVIL**
Director: Susan Seidelman
Co-stars: Meryl Streep Roseanne Barr Ed Begley Jnr. Sylvia Miles

1990 **KINDERGARTEN COP**
Director: Ivan Reitman
Co-stars: Arnold Schwarzenegger Penelope Ann Miller

1991 **TEEN AGENT**
Director: William Dear
Co-stars: Robert Grieco Roger Rees Geraldine James Roger Daltrey

1993 **TWENTY BUCKS**
Director: Keva Rosenfeld
Co-stars: Brendan Fraser Elizabeth Shue

1993 **YOUNGER AND YOUNGER**
Director: Percy Adlom
Co-stars: Donald Sutherland Lolita Davidovich Sally Kellerman

1996 **THE RELIK**
Director: Peter Hyams
Co-stars: Penelope Ann Miller Tom Sizemore

MADGE HUNT

1928 **QUEEN KELLY**
Director: Erich Von Stroheim
Co-stars: Gloria Swanson Seena Owen Walter Byron

MARSHA HUNT

1935 **THE VIRGINIA JUDGE**
Director: Edward Sedgewick
Co-stars: Walter Kelly Johnny Downs Robert Cummings

1936 **COLLEGE HOLIDAY**
Director: Frank Tuttle
Co-stars: Jack Benny George Burns Gracie Allen Martha Raye

1936 **HOLLYWOOD BOULEVARD**
Director: Robert Florey
Co-stars: John Halliday Robert Cummings Esther Dale

1936 **DESERT GOLD**
Co-stars: Robert Cummings Larry Crabbe Tom Keene

1936 **THE ACCUSING FINGER**
Co-stars: Paul Kelly Bernadine Hayes

1937 **EASY TO TAKE**
Co-star: John Howard

1937 **MURDER GOES TO COLLEGE**
Director: Charles Reisner
Co-star: Roscoe Carns Lynne Overman

1938 **COME ON LEATHERNECKS**
Co-star: Richard Cromwell

1939 **THOSE GLAMOROUS GIRLS**
Director: S. Sylvan Simon
Co-stars: Lew Ayres Lana Turner Jane Bryan

1939 **STAR REPORTER**

1940 **THE TRIAL OF MARY DUGAN**
Director: Norman Z McLeod
Co-stars: Laraine Day Robert Young Tom Conway

1940 **CRIME DOES NOT PAY: WOMEN IN HIDING**
Director: Joe Newman
Co-stars: C. Henry Gordon

1940 **IRENE**
Director: Herbert Wilcox
Co-stars: Anna Neagle Ray Milland Roland Young

1940 **ELLERY QUEEN, MASTER DETECTIVE**
Director: Kurt Neuman
Co-stars: Ralph Bellamy Margaret Lindsay

1940 **PRIDE AND PREJUDICE**
Director: Robert Z. Leonard
Co-stars: Laurence Olivier Greer Garson Edmund Gwenn

1941 **UNHOLY PARTNERS**
Director: Mervyn LeRoy
Co-stars: Edward G. Robinson Edward Arnold Laraine Day

1941 **I'LL WAIT FOR YOU**
Co-stars: Robert Sterling Paul Kelly Henry Travers

1941 **BLOSSOMS IN THE DUST**
Director: Mervyn LeRoy
Co-stars: Greer Garson Walter Pidgeon Felix Bressart

1941 **THE PENALTY**
Director: Harold Bucquet
Co-stars: Edward Arnold Lionel Barrymore Robert Sterling

1942	**THE AFFAIRS OF MARTHA**
Director:	Jules Dassin
Co-stars:	Richard Carlson Spring Byington Allyn Joslyn
1942	**JOE SMITH, AMERICAN**
Director:	Richard Thorpe
Co-stars:	Robert Young Darryl Hickman Noel Madison
1942	**KID GLOVE KILLER**
Director:	Fred Zinnemann
Co-stars:	Van Heflin Lee Bowman Ava Gardner
1942	**SEVEN SWEETHEARTS**
Director:	Frank Borzage
Co-stars:	Kathryn Grayson Van Heflin Cecilia Parker
1943	**PILOT NUMBER FIVE**
Director:	George Sidney
Co-stars:	Franchot Tone Gene Kelly Van Johnson
1943	**THE HUMAN COMEDY**
Director:	Clarence Brown
Co-stars:	Mickey Rooney Frank Morgan James Craig
1943	**CRY HAVOC**
Director:	Richard Thorpe
Co-stars:	Margaret Sullavan Joan Blondell Ann Sothern
1944	**BRIDE BY MISTAKE**
Director:	Richard Wallace
Co-stars:	Laraine Day Alan Marshall Allyn Joslyn
1944	**LOST ANGEL**
Director:	Roy Rowland
Co-stars:	Margaret O'Brien James Craig Keenan Wynn Henry O'Neill
1944	**MUSIC FOR MILLIONS**
Director:	Henry Koster
Co-stars:	Margaret O'Brien June Allyson Jose Iturbi
1944	**NONE SHALL ESCAPE**
Director:	Andre De Toth
Co-stars:	Alexander Knox Henry Travers Richard Crane
1945	**THE VALLEY OF DECISION**
Director:	Tay Garnett
Co-stars:	Greer Garson Gregory Peck Lionel Barrymore
1945	**A LETTER FOR EVIE**
Director:	Jules Dassin
Co-stars:	Hume Cronyn John Carroll Spring Byington
1947	**CARNEGIE HALL**
Director:	Edgar Ulmer
Co-stars:	William Prince Frank McHugh Martha O'Driscoll
1947	**SMASH-UP - THE STORY OF A WOMAN**
Director:	Stuart Heisler
Co-stars:	Susan Hayward Lee Bowman
1948	**RAW DEAL**
Director:	Anthony Mann
Co-stars:	Dennis O'Keefe Claire Trevor John Ireland
1948	**THE INSIDE STORY**
Director:	Allan Dwan
Co-stars:	William Lundigan Charles Winninger Gale Patrick
1949	**JIGSAW**
Director:	Fletcher Markle
Co-stars:	Franchot Tone Jean Wallace Marc Lawrence
1949	**TAKE ONE FALSE STEP**
Director:	Chester Erskine
Co-stars:	William Powell Shelley Winters James Gleason
1952	**THE HAPPY TIME**
Director:	Richard Fleischer
Co-stars:	Charles Boyer Bobby Driscoll Louis Jourdan
1952	**ACTORS AND SIN**
Director:	Ben Hecht
Co-stars:	Edward G. Robinson Dan O'Herlihy Jenny Hecht

1957	**BACK FROM THE DEAD**
Director:	Charles Marquis Warren
Co-stars:	Peggie Castle Arthur Franz Dan Haggerty
1957	**BOMBER B52**
Director:	Gordon Douglas
Co-stars:	Karl Malden Natalie Wood Efrem Zimbazlist
1959	**BLUE DENIM**
Director:	Philip Dunne
Co-stars:	Carol Lynley Brandon De Wilde MacDonald Carey
1960	**THE PLUNDERERS**
Director:	Joseph Pevney
Co-stars:	Jeff Chandler John Saxon Forrest Tucker
1971	**JOHNNY GOT HIS GUN**
Director:	Dalton Trumbo
Co-stars:	Timothy Bottoms Jason Robards Donald Sutherland
1987	**UNREPORTED INCIDENT**
Director:	Christopher Baker
Co-stars:	T. P. McKenna Maurice Roeves Tim Brierley
1988	**TANK MALLING**
Director:	James Marcus
Co-stars:	Ray Winstone Jason Connery Amanda Donohue

MARTITA HUNT

1932	**SERVICE FOR LADIES**
Director:	Alexander Korda
Co-stars:	Leslie Howard Elizabeth Allan Merle Oberon
1933	**FRIDAY THE THIRTEENTH**
Director:	Victor Saville
Co-stars:	Sonnie Hale Jessie Matthews Edmund Gwenn
1933	**I WAS A SPY**
Director:	Victor Saville
Co-stars:	Madeleine Carroll Conrad Veidt Herbert Marshall
1936	**TUDOR ROSE**
Director:	Robert Stephenson
Co-stars:	Cedric Hardwicke Nova Pilbeam John Mills
1936	**POT LUCK**
Director:	Tom Walls
Co-stars:	Tom Walls Ralph Lynn Robertson Hare Diana Churchill
1937	**FAREWELL AGAIN**
Director:	Tim Whelan
Co-stars:	Flora Robson Leslie Banks Robert Newton
1937	**GOOD MORNING BOYS**
Director:	Marcel Varnel
Co-stars:	Wil Hay Graham Moffett Lilli Palmer
1938	**STRANGE BORDERS**
Director:	Herbert Mason
Co-stars:	Tom Walls Googie Withers Renee St. Cyr
1939	**THE GOOD OLD DAYS**
Director:	Roy William Neill
Co-stars:	Max Miller Hal Walters Kathleen Gibson
1939	**THE NURSEMAID WHO DISAPPEARED**
Director:	Arthur Woods
Co-stars:	Arthur Margetson Coral Browne
1939	**OLD MOTHER RILEY JOINS UP**
Director:	MacLean Rogers
Co-stars:	Arthur Lucan Kitty McShane Garry Marsh
1939	**TROUBLE BREWING**
Director:	Anthony Kimmins
Co-stars:	George Formby Googie Withers Ronald Shiner
1940	**EAST OF PICCADILLY**
Director:	Harold Huth
Co-stars:	Sebastian Shaw Judy Campbell Niall MacGinnis

1941   **THE SEVENTH SURVIVOR**
Director: Leslie Hiscott
Co-stars: Linden Travers Austin Trevor

1942   **LADY FROM LISBON**
Director: Leslie Arliss
Co-stars: Jane Carr Francis L. Sullivan Charles Victor

1942   **PANAMA HATTIE**
Director: Norman Z McLeod
Co-stars: Ann Sothern Dan Dailey Red Skelton

1943   **THE MAN IN GREY**
Director: Leslie Arliss
Co-stars: Margaret Lockwood James Mason Stewart Granger

1944   **WELCOME MR WASHINGTON**
Director: Leslie Hiscott
Co-stars: Barbara Mullen Donald Stewart Peggy Cummings

1945   **THE WICKED LADY**
Director: Leslie Arliss
Co-stars: Margaret Lockwood James Mason Patricia Roc

1946   **GREAT EXPECTATIONS**
Director: David Lean
Co-stars: John Mills Jean Simmons Alec Guinness

1947   **ANNA KARENINA**
Director: Julien Duvivier
Co-stars: Vivien Leigh Ralph Richardson Kieron Moore

1948   **SO EVIL MY LOVE**
Director: Lewis Allen
Co-stars: Ray Milland Ann Todd Geraldine Fitzgerald

1949   **THE GHOSTS OF BERKELEY SQUARE**
Director: Vernon Sewell
Co-stars: Robert Morley Claude Hulbert Yvonne Arnaud

1949   **THE FAN**
Director: Otto Preminger
Co-stars: Jeanne Crain Madeleine Carroll George Sanders

1952   **FOLLY TO BE WISE**
Director: Frank Launder
Co-stars: Alastair Sim Elizabeth Allan Roland Culver

1952   **IT STARTED IN PARADISE**
Director: Compton Bennett
Co-stars: Jane Hylton Ian Hunter Terence Morgan

1952   **THE STORY OF ROBIN HOOD
AND HIS MERRIE MEN**
Director: Ken Annakin
Co-stars: Richard Todd Joan Rice James Hayter

1952   **TREASURE HUNT**
Director: John Paddy Carstairs
Co-stars: Jimmy Edwards Athene Seyler Susan Stephen

1953   **MELBA**
Director: Lewis Milestone
Co-stars: Patrice Munsel Robert Morley Alec Clunes John McCallum

1955   **KING'S RHAPSODY**
Director: Herbert Wilcox
Co-stars: Anna Neagle Errol Flynn Patrice Wymore

1956   **ANASTASIA**
Director: Antole Litvak
Co-stars: Ingrid Bergman Yul Brynner Helen Hayes Akim Tamiroff

1956   **MARCH HARE**
Director: George More O'Ferrall
Co-stars: Peggy Cummings Terence Morgan Cyril Cusack

1956   **THREE MEN IN A BOAT**
Director: Ken Annakin
Co-stars: Laurence Harvey Jimmy Edwards David Tomlinson

1957   **LES ESPIONS**
Director: Henri-Georges Clouzot
Co-stars: Vera Clouzot Peter Ustinov Sam Jaffe

1957   **DANGEROUS EXILE**
Director: Brian Desmond Hurst
Co-stars: Belinda Lee Keith Michell Richard O'Sullivan

1957   **BONJOUR TRISTESSE**
Director: Otto Preminger
Co-stars: Jean Seberg David Niven Deborah Kerr

1957   **THE ADMIRAL CRICHTON**
Director: Lewis Gilbert
Co-stars: Kenneth More Daine Cilento Cecil Parker

1958   **ME AND THE COLONEL**
Director: Peter Grenville
Co-stars: Danny Kaye Curt Jurgens Nicole Maurey

1960   **BRIDES OF DRACULA**
Director: Terence Fisher
Co-stars: Peter Cushing David Peel Freda Jackson

1960   **SONG WITHOUT END**
Director: George Cukor
Co-stars: Dirk Bogarde Capucine Genevieve Page

1961   **MR. TOPAZE**
Director: Peter Sellers
Co-stars: Peter Sellers Herbert Lom Leo McKern Nadia Gray

1962   **THE WONDERFUL WORLD OF THE
BROTHERS GRIMM**
Director: Henry Levin
Co-stars: Laurence Harvey Karl Boehm Claire Bloom

1964   **THE UNSINKABLE MOLLY BROWN**
Director: Charles Walters
Co-stars: Debbie Reynolds Harve Presnell

1964   **BECKET**
Director: Peter Grenville
Co-stars: Peter O'Toole Richard Burton John Gielgud

1965   **BUNNY LAKE IS MISSING**
Director: Otto Preminger
Co-stars: Laurence Olivier Carol Lynley Noel Coward

ANNE HUNTER

1941   **THE GAY FALCON**
Director: Irving Reis
Co-stars: George Sanders Wendy Barrie Allen Jenkins

HOLLY HUNTER
(Married Janusz Kaminski, Cinematographer)
Oscar For Best Actress In 1993 "For The Piano"
Nominated For Best Actress In 1987 For "Broadcast News"
Nominated For Best Supporting Actress In 1993 For "The Firm"

1984   **SWING SHIFT**
Director: Jonathan Demme
Co-stars: Goldie Hawn Kurt Russell Christine Lahti

1987   **A GATHERING OF OLD MEN**
Director: Volker Schlondorf
Co-stars: Louis Gossett Richard Widmark

1987   **RAISING ARIZONA**
Director: Joel Coen
Co-stars: Nicholas Cage Trey Wilson John Goodman

1987   **BROADCAST NEWS**
Director: James Brooks
Co-stars: William Hurt Albert Brooks Jack Nicholson

1989   **MISS FIRECRACKER**
Director: Thomas Schlamme
Co-stars: Mary Steenburgen Tim Robbins Scott Glen

1989   **ANIMAL BEHAVIOUR**
Director: H. Anne Riley
Co-stars: Karen Allen Armand Assante Josh Mostel

1989	**ROE VS WADE**
Director:	Gregory Hobit
Co-stars:	Amy Madigan Terry O'Quinn Kathy Bates James Gammon

1989	**ALWAYS**
Director:	Steven Spielberg
Co-stars:	Richard Dreyfuss John Goodman Audrey Hepburn

1991	**ONCE AROUND**
Director:	Lasse Hellstrom
Co-stars:	Richard Dreyfuss Danny Aiello Gena Rowlands

1992	**CRAZY IN LOVE**
Director:	Martha Coolridge
Co-stars:	Bill Pullman Julian Sands Gena Rowlands

1993	**THE POSITIVELY TRUE ADVENTURES OF THE ALLEGED TEXAS CHEERLEADER-MURDERING MOM**
Director:	Michael Ritchie
Co-stars:	Beau Bridges Matt Frewer Swoozie Kurtz

1993	**THE PIANO**
Director:	Jane Campion
Co-stars:	Sam Neill Harvey Keitel Anna Paquin Genevieve Lemon

1993	**THE FIRM**
Director:	Sydney Pollack
Co-stars:	Tom Cruise Gene Hackman Jeanne Tripplehorn

1996	**A LIFE LESS ORDINARY**
Director:	Danny Boyle
Co-stars:	Cameron Diaz Ewan McGregor Delroy Lindo

1996	**HOME FOR THE HOLIDAYS**
Director:	Jodie Foster
Co-stars:	Robert Downey Anne Bancroft Charles Durning

1997	**CRASH**
Director:	David Cronenberg
Co-stars:	James Spader Elias Koteas Rosanna Arquette

KAKI HUNTER

1980	**ROADIE**
Director:	Alan Rudolph
Co-stars:	Meatloaf Art Carney Alice Cooper Debbi Harry

1980	**WILLIE AND PHIL**
Director:	Paul Mazursky
Co-stars:	Michael Ontkean Ray Sharkey Margot Kidder

1981	**WHOSE LIFE IS IT ANYWAY?**
Director:	John Badham
Co-stars:	Richard Dreyfuss John Cassavetes Bob Balaban

1984	**JUST THE WAY YOU ARE**
Director:	Edouard Molinaro
Co-stars:	Kristy McNicol Michael Ontkean

1985	**PORKY'S REVENGE**
Director:	James Komack
Co-stars:	Dan Monahan Wyatt Knight Tony Ganios

KATHRYN HUNTER

1992	**MARIA'S CHILD**
Director:	Malcolm McKay
Co-stars:	Yolanda Vasquez David O'Hara Fiona Shaw

1993	**THE BABY OF MACON**
Director:	Peter Greenaway
Co-stars:	Julia Ormond Ralph Fiennes Celia Gregory

KIM HUNTER
Oscar for Best Supporting Actress In 1951 For "A Streetcar Called Desire"

1943	**TENDER COMRADE**
Director:	Edward Dmytryk
Co-stars:	Ginger Rogers Robert Ryan Ruth Hussey

1943	**THE SEVENTH VICTIM**
Director:	Mark Robson
Co-stars:	Tom Conway Jean Brooks Isabel Jewell Evelyn Brent

1944	**WHEN STRANGERS MARRY**
Director:	William Castle
Co-stars:	Robert Mitchum Dean Jagger Neil Hamilton

1945	**YOU CAME ALONG**
Director:	John Farrow
Co-stars:	Lizabeth Scott Robert Cummings Don Defore

1946	**A MATTER OF LIFE AND DEATH**
Director:	Michael Powell
Co-stars:	David Niven Roger Livesey Marius Goring

1951	**A STREETCAR NAMED DESIRE**
Director:	Elia Kazan
Co-stars:	Marlon Brando Vivien Leigh Karl Malden

1952	**DEADLINE U.S.A.**
Director:	Richard Brooks
Co-stars:	Humphrey Bogart Ethel Barrymore Ed Begley

1952	**ANYTHING CAN HAPPEN**
Director:	George Seaton
Co-stars:	Jose Ferrer Kurt Kasznar Oscar Beregi

1956	**BERMUDA AFFAIR**
Director:	Edward Sutherland
Co-stars:	Gary Merrill Ron Randell Zena Marshall

1956	**STORM CENTER**
Director:	Daniel Taradash
Co-stars:	Bette Davis Brian Keith Paul Kelly

1957	**THE YOUNG STRANGER**
Director:	John Frankenheimer
Co-stars:	James MacArthur James Daly James Gregory

1959	**MONEY, WOMEN AND GUNS**
Director:	Richard Bartlett
Co-stars:	Jock Mahoney William Campbell Gene Evans

1964	**LILITH**
Director:	Robert Rossen
Co-stars:	Warren Beatty Jean Seberg Peter Fonda

1968	**THE SWIMMER**
Director:	Sydney Pollack
Co-stars:	Burt Lancaster Janice Rule Marge Champion

1968	**PLANET OF THE APES**
Director:	Franklyn Schaffner
Co-stars:	Charlton Heston Roddy McDowall

1969	**BENEATH THE PLANET OF THE APES**
Director:	Ted Post
Co-stars:	James Franciscus Linda Harrison

1971	**ESCAPE FROM THE PLANET OF THE APES**
Director:	Don Taylor
Co-stars:	Bradford Dillman Ricardo Montablan

1973	**THE MAGICIAN**
Director:	Marvin Chomsky
Co-stars:	Bill Bixby Joan Caulfield Elizabeth Ashley

1975	**TOO MANY SUSPECTS**
Director:	David Greene
Co-stars:	Jim Hutton David Wayne Ray Milland Tim O'Connor

1979	**THE GOLDEN GATE MURDERS**
Director:	Walter Grauman
Co-stars:	David Janssen Susannah York Tim O'Connor

1980	**F.D.R. THE LAST YEAR**
Director:	Anthony Page
Co-stars:	Jason Robards Eileen Heckart Augusta Dabney

NITA HUNTER

1946	**SUSIE STEPS OUT**
Co-star:	Harry Barris

VIRGINIA HUNTER

1944 THE ZIEGFELD FOLLIES
Director: Vincente Minnelli
Co-stars: Judy Garland Fred Astaire Gene Kelly

LOUISE HUNTINGDON

1931 FAIR WARNING
Co-star: George O'Brien

ISABELLE HUPPERT

1974 LES VALSEUSES
Director: Bertrand Blier
Co-stars: Gerard Depardieu Jeanne Moreau Miou-Miou

1975 ROSEBUD
Director: Otto Preminger
Co-stars: Peter O'Toole Richard Attenborough Peter Lawford

1976 DOCTEUR FRANCOISE GAILLARD
Director: Jean-Louis Bertocelli
Co-stars: Annie Girardo Jean-Pierre Cassel

1977 THE LACEMAKER
Director: Claude Goretta
Co-stars: Yves Beneyton Florence Giorgetti Anne Marie Duringer

1977 VIOLETTE NOZIERE
Co-stars: Claude Chabrol
Co-stars: Jean Carmier Stephane Audran

1980 LOULOU
Director: Maurice Pialat
Co-stars: Gerard Depardieu Guy Marchand Humbert Balsan

1980 HEAVEN'S GATE
Director: Michael Cimino
Co-stars: Kris Kristofferson Christopher Walken John Hurt

1981 COUP DE TORCHON
Director: Bertrand Tavernier
Co-stars: Philippe Noiret Stephane Audran

1983 COUP DE FOURDE
Director: Diane Kurys
Co-stars: Miou-Miou Guy Marchand Jean Pierre Bacri

1983 MY BEST FRIEND'S GIRL
Director: Bertrand Blier
Co-stars: Coluche Thierry Lhermitte Daniel Colas

1986 THE BEDROOM WINDOW
Director: Curtis Hanson
Co-stars: Steve Guttenberg Elizabeth McGovern

1991 MADAME BOVARY
Director: Claude Chabrol
Co-stars: Jean-Francois Balmer Christophe Malavoy Jean Yanne

1992 APRES L'AMOUR
Director: Diane Kurys
Co-stars: Bernand Girardeau Hippolyte Girrardot Lio

1994 AMATEUR
Director: Hal Hartley
Co-stars: Martin Donovan Elina Lowensohn Damian Young

1995 LA SEPARATION
Co-star: Daniel Auteuill

1996 LA CEREMONIE
Director: Claude Chabrol
Co-stars: Sandrine Bonnaire Jacqueline Bisset Jean-Pierre Cassel

ELIZABETH HURLEY

1987 ROWING WITH THE WIND
Director: Gonzalo Suarez
Co-stars: Hugh Grant Valentine Pelka Lizzy McInnerny

1988 ARIA
Director: Nicolas Roeg
Co-stars: Theresa Russsell Bridget Fonda John Hurt

1989 ACT OF WILL
Director: Don Sharp
Co-stars: Victoria Tennant Peter Coyote Lynsey Baxter

1990 THE ORCHID HOUSE
Director: Horace Ove
Co-stars: Diana Quick Frances Barber Kate Buffery

1992 PASSENGER 57
Director: Kevin Hooks
Co-stars: Wesley Snipes Bruce Payne Tom Sizemore

1994 BEYOND BEDLAM
Director: Vadim Jean
Co-stars: Craig Fairbrass Keith Allen Jesse Birdsall

1995 MAD DOGS AND ENGLISHMEN
Director: Henry Cole
Co-stars: C. Thomas Howell Joss Ackland Jeremy Brett

VERONICA HURST

1951 LAUGHTER IN PARADISE
Director: Mario Zampi
Co-stars: Alastair Sim George Cole Joyce Grenfell

1952 ANGELS ONE FIVE
Director: George More O'Ferrall
Co-stars: Jack Hawkins John Gregson Dulcie Gray

1952 THE YELLOW BALLOON
Director: J. Lee-Thompson
Co-stars: Kenneth More Andrew Ray William Sylvester

1953 WILL ANY GENTLEMAN?
Director: Michael Anderson
Co-stars: George Cole Jon Pertwee Diana Decker

1953 THE MAZE
Director: William Cameron Menzies
Co-stars: Richard Carlson Michael Pate Lillian Bond

1954 ROYAL AFRICAN RIFLES
Director: Lesley Selander
Co-stars: Louis Hayward Michael Pate Angela Greene

1954 BANG YOU'RE DEAD
Director: Lance Comfort
Co-stars: Jack Warner Derek Farr Gordon Harker

1955 THE GILDED CAGE
Director: John Gilling
Co-stars: Alex Nichol Ursula Howells Clifford Evans

1963 LIVE IT UP
Director: Lance Comfort
Co-stars: David Hemmings Joan Newell Jennifer Moss

1965 LICENSED TO KILL
Director: Lindsay Shonteff
Co-stars: Tom Adams Karel Stepanek Peter Bull

1965 THE BOY CRIED MURDER
Director: George Breakston
Co-stars: Frazer MacIntosh Phil Brown

MARY BETH HURT

1978 INTERIORS
Director: Woody Allen
Co-stars: Kristin Griffith Richard Jordan Geraldine Page

1980 HEAD OVER HEELS
Director: Joan Micklin Silver
Co-stars: John Heard Peter Riegert Gloria Grahame

1980 A CHANGE OF SEASONS
Director: Richard Lang
Co-stars: Anthony Hopkins Shirley MacLaine Bo Derek

1982   **THE WORLD ACCORDING TO GARP**
Director: George Roy Hill
Co-stars: Robin Williams Glenn Close

1985   **COMPROMISING POSITIONS**
Director: Frank Perry
Co-stars: Susan Sarandon Raul Julia Judith Ivey

1985   **D.A.R.Y.L.**
Director: Simon Wincer
Co-stars: Barret Oliver Michael McKean Colleen Camp

1988   **PARENTS**
Director: Bob Balaban
Co-stars: Randy Quaid Sandy Dennis Bryan Madorsky

1989   **SLAVES OF NEW YORK**
Director: James Ivory
Co-stars: Bernadette Peters Madeleine Potter Adam Colman

1991   **NIGHT SLEEPER**
Director: Paul Schrader
Co-stars: Willem Dafoe Susan Sarandon Dana Delany

1992   **DEFENSELESS**
Director: Martin Campbell
Co-stars: Barbara Hershey Sam Shepard Sheree North

1993   **MY BOYFRIEND'S BACK**
Director: Bob Balaban
Co-stars: Andrew Lowery Traci Lind Edward Herrmann

1993   **SIX DEGREES OF SEPARATION**
Director: Fred Schepisi
Co-stars: Stockard Channing Will Smith Ian McKellen

1993   **THE AGE OF INNOCENCE**
Director: Martin Scorsese
Co-stars: Michelle Pfeiffer Daniel Day-Lewis Winona Ryder

OLIVIA HUSSEY

1964   **THE BATTLE OF THE VILLA FIORITA**
Director: Delmer Daves
Co-stars: Maureen O'Hara Rossana Brazzi

1968   **ROMEO AND JULIET**
Director: Franco Zefferelli
Co-stars: Leonard Whiting Milo O'Shea Michael York

1969   **ALL THE RIGHT NOISES**
Director: Gerry O'Hara
Co-stars: Tom Bell Judy Carne John Standing

1972   **LOST HORIZON**
Director: Charles Jarrott
Co-stars: Peter Finch Liv Ullman George Kennedy

1974   **BLACK CHRISTMAS**
Director: Robert Clark
Co-stars: Kier Dullea Margot Kidder John Saxon Andre Martin

1978   **DEATH ON THE NILE**
Director: John Guillermin
Co-stars: Peter Ustinov Bette Davis Mia Farrow David Niven

1979   **THE CAT AND THE CANARY**
Director: Radley Metzger
Co-stars: Honor Blackman Edward Fox Wendy Hiller

1980   **THE MAN WITH BOGART'S FACE**
Director: Robert Day
Co-stars: Robert Sacchi Franco Nero Michelle Phillips

1982   **IVANHOE**
Director: Douglas Camfield
Co-stars: James Mason Anthony Andrews Lysette Anthony

1985   **THE CORSICAN BROTHERS**
Director: Ian Sharp
Co-stars: Trevor Eve Geraldine Chaplin Nicholas Clay

1987   **DISTORTIONS**
Director: Armand Mastroianni

1990   **IT**
Director: Tommy Lee Wallace
Co-stars: Tim Curry John Ritter Annette O'Toole

1990   **PSYCHO IV: THE BEGINNING**
Director: Mick Garris
Co-stars: Anthony Perkins Henry Thomas Dona Mitchell

RUTH HUSSEY
Nominated For Best Supporting Actress In 1940 For "The Philadelphia Story"

1937   **MADAME X**
Director: Sam Wood
Co-stars: Gladys George John Beal Warren William Reginald Owen

1938   **HONOLULU**
Director: Edward Buzzell
Co-stars: Robert Young Eleanor Powell Burns & Allen

1938   **MAN-PROOF**
Director: Richard Thorpe
Co-stars: Myrna Loy Franchot Tone Walter Pidgeon

1938   **JUDGE HARDY'S CHILDREN**
Director: George Seitz
Co-stars: Lewis Stone Mickey Rooney Cecilia Parker

1938   **RICH MAN, POOR MAN**
Director: Reinhold Schunzel
Co-stars: Lew Ayres Lana Turner Robert Young

1938   **SPRING MADNESS**
Director: S. Sylvan Simon
Co-stars: Maureen O'Sullivan Lew Ayres Burgess Meredith

1939   **WITHIN THE LAW**
Director: Gustav Machaty
Co-stars: Tom Neal Paul Kelly Rita Johnson William Gargan

1939   **THE WOMEN**
Director: George Cukor
Co-stars: Norma Shearer Joan Crawford Paulette Goddard

1939   **MAISIE**
Director: Edwn Marin
Co-stars: Ann Sothern Robert Young Ian Hunter Anthony Allan

1939   **BLACKMAIL**
Director: H.C. Potter
Co-stars: Edward G. Robinson Gene Lockhart Guinn Williams

1940   **FIGHT COMMAND**
Director: Frank Borzage
Co-stars: Robert Taylor Walter Pidgeon Red Skelton

1940   **NORTHWEST PASSAGE**
Director: King Vidor
Co-stars: Spencer Tracy Robert Young Walter Brennan

1940   **THE PHILADELPHIA STORY**
Director: George Cukor
Co-stars: Cary Grant Katharine Hepburn James Stewart

1940   **SUSAN AND GOD**
Director: George Cukor
Co-stars: Joan Crawford Fredric March Rita Hayworth

1941   **OUR WIFE**
Director: John Stahl
Co-stars: Melvyn Douglas Ellen Drew Charles Coburn

1941   **H.M.PULHAM ESQUIRE**
Director: King Vidor
Co-stars: Robert Young Hedy Lamarr Van Helfin Charles Coburn

1941   **FREE AND EASY**
Director: George Sidney
Co-stars: Nigel Bruce Robert Cummings Judith Anderson

1942   **PIERRE OF THE PLAINS**
Director: George Seitz
Co-stars: John Carroll Bruce Cabot Reginald Owen

1943   **TENDER COMRADE**
Director: Edward Dmytryk
Co-stars: Ginger Rogers Robert Ryan Kim Hunter

1943   **TENNESSEE JOHNSON**
Director: William Dieterle
Co-stars: Van Heflin Lionel Barrymore Marjorie Main

1944   **THE UNINVITED**
Director: Lewis Allen
Co-stars: Ray Milland Gail Russell Donald Crisp

1944   **MARINE RAIDERS**
Director: Harold Schuster
Co-stars: Pat O'Brien Robert Ryan Frank McHugh

1945   **BEDSIDE MANNER**
Director: Andrew Stone
Co-stars: John Carroll Charles Ruggles Ann Rutherford

1948   **I, JANE DOE**
Director: John Auer
Co-stars: John Carroll Vera Ralston Gene Lockhart

1949   **THE GREAT GATSBY**
Director: Elliott Nugent
Co-stars: Alan Ladd Betty Field Shelley Winters

1950   **MR. MUSIC**
Director: Richard Haydn
Co-stars: Bing Crosby Nancy Olson Marge & Gower Champion

1950   **LOUISA**
Director: Alexander Hall
Co-stars: Spring Byington Ronald Reagan Edmund Gwenn

1951   **THAT'S MY BOY**
Director: Hal Walker
Co-stars: Martin & Lewis Eddie Mayehoff Polly Bergen

1952   **WOMEN OF THE NORTH COUNTRY**
Director: Joseph Kane
Co-stars: Rod Cameron Gale Storm John Agar

1952   **STARS AND STRIPES FOREVER**
Director: Henry Koster
Co-stars: Clifton Webb Debra Paget Robert Wagner

1953   **THE LADY WANTS MINK**
Director: William Seiter
Co-stars: Dennis O'Keefe Eve Arden William Demarest

1960   **THE FACTS OF LIVE**
Director: Melvin Frank
Co-stars: Bob Hope Lucille Ball Don Defore Philip Ober

ANJELICA HUSTON *(Daughter Of John Huston Granddaughter Of Walter Huston)*

Oscar For Best Supporting Actress In 1985 For "Prizzi's Honour". Nominated For Best Supporting Actress In 1989 For "Enemies, A Love Story". Nominated For Best Actress In 1990 For "The Grifters"

1968   **SINFUL DAVEY**
Director: John Huston
Co-stars: John Hurt Pamela Franklin Nigel Davenport

1969   **A WALK WITH LOVE AND DEATH**
Director: John Huston
Co-stars: Assaf Dayan John Hallam Michael Gough

1976   **SWASHBUCKLER**
Director: James Goldstone
Co-stars: Robert Shaw Genevieve Bujold James Earl Jones

1981   **THE POSTMAN ALWAYS RINGS TWICE**
Director: Bob Rafelson
Co-stars: Jack Nicholson Jessica Lange

1984   **THE ICE PIRATES**
Director: Stewart Raffill
Co-stars: Robert Urich Mary Crosby John Carradine

1985   **PRIZZI'S HONOR**
Director: John Huston
Co-stars: Jack Nicholson Kathleen Turner William Hickey

1987   **GARDENS OF STONE**
Director: Francis Coppola
Co-stars: James Caan Dean Stockwell James Earl Jones

1987   **THE DEAD**
Director: John Huston
Co-stars: Donal McCann Rachel Dowling Dan O'Herlihy

1988   **MR. NORTH**
Director: Danny Huston
Co-stars: Anthony Edwards Robert Mitchum Lauren Bacall

1988   **A HANDFUL OF DUST**
Director: Charles Sturridge
Co-stars: James Wilby Rupert Graves Alec Guinness

1988   **LONESOME DOVE**
Director: Simon Wincer
Co-stars: Robert Duvall Tommy Lee Jones Danny Glover

1989   **ENEMIES, A LOVE STORY**
Director: Paul Mazursky
Co-stars: Ron Silver Lena Olin Judith Malina

1989   **CRIMES AND MISDEMEANORS**
Director: Woody Allen
Co-stars: Woody Allen Mia Farrow Alan Alda Claire Bloom

1990   **THR GRIFTERS**
Director: Stephen Frears
Co-stars: John Cusack Annette Bening Pat Hingle

1990   **THE WITCHES**
Director: Nicholas Roeg
Co-stars: Mai Zetterling Bill Paterson Jane Horrocks

1991   **THE ADDAMS FAMILY**
Director: Barry Sonnenfeld
Co-stars: Raul Julia Christopher Lloyd Dan Hedaya

1992   **THE PLAYER**
Director: Robert Altman
Co-stars: Tim Robbins Greta Scacchi Whoopi Goldberg

1993   **ADDAMS FAMILY VALUES**
Director: Barry Sonnenfeld
Co-stars: Raul Julia Joan Cusack Christopher Lloyd

1993   **AND THE BAND PLAYED ON**
Director: Roger Spottiswoode
Co-stars: Mathew Modine Alan Alda Lily Tomlin

1993   **FAMILY PICTURES**
Director: Phillipe Saville
Co-stars: Sam Neill Kyra Sedgwick Dermot Mulroney

1993   **MANHATTAN MURDER MYSTERY**
Director: Woody Allen
Co-stars: Woody Allen Diane Keaton Alan Alda Jerry Adler

1995   **BUFFALO GIRLS**
Co-star: Melanie Griffiths Gabriel Byrne Jack Palance

1996   **THE PEREZ FAMILY**
Co-stars: Marisa Tomei Alfred Molina Chazz Palminteri

1996   **THE CROSSING GUARD**
Director: Sean Penn
Co-stars: Jack Nicholson David Morse Robin Wright

CAROL HUSTON

1988   **SHOOTER**
Director: Gary Nelson
Co-stars: Jeffrey Nordling Helen Hunt Rosalind Chao

KAREN HUSTON

1971 VON RICHTOFEN AND BROWN
Director: Roger Corman
Co-stars: John Phillip Law Don Stroud Hurd Hatfield

VIRGINIA HUSTON

1946 NOCTURNE
Director: Edwin Marin
Co-stars: George Raft Lynn Bari Joseph Pevney

1947 BUILD MY GALLOWS HIGH
Director: Jacques Tourneur
Co-stars: Robert Mitchum Jane Greer Kirk Douglas

1949 FLAMINGO ROAD
Director: Michael Curtiz
Co-stars: Joan Crawford David Brian Sydney Greenstreet

1951 TARZAN'S PERIL
Director: Byron Haskin
Co-stars: Lex Barker George Macready Dorothy Dandridge

1951 FLIGHT TO MARS
Director: Lesley Selander
Co-stars: Cameron Mitchell Arthur Franz Marguerite Chapman

1952 SUDDEN FEAR
Director: David Miller
Co-stars: Joan Crawford Jack Palance Gloria Grahame

1952 THE HIGHWAYMAN
Director: Lesley Selander
Co-stars: Philip Friend Charles Coburn Wanda Hendrix

DEBBIE HUTCHINGS

1981 MEMOIRS OF A SURVIVOR
Director: David Gladwell
Co-stars: Julie Christie Christopher Guard

LINDA HUTCHINS

1961 MARINES LETS GO
Director: Raoul Walsh
Co-stars: Tom Tyron David Hedison Tom Reese

FIONA HUTCHINSON

1986 BIGGLES
Director: John Hough
Co-stars: Neil Dickinson Peter Cushing Alex Hyde-White

1988 AMERICAN GOTHIC
Director: John Hough
Co-stars: Rod Steiger Yvonne De Carlo Michael J. Pollard

JOSEPHINE HUTCHINSON

1934 HAPPINESS AHEAD
Director: Mervyn LeRoy
Co-stars: Dick Powell John Halliday Frank McHugh Allen Jenkins

1935 OIL FOR THE LAMPS OF CHINA
Director: Mervyn LeRoy
Co-stars: Pat O'Brien Jean Muir Donald Crisp

1935 THE MELODY LINGERS ON
Co-star: Helen Westley

1935 RIGHT TO LIVE
Director: William Keighley
Co-stars: George Brent Colin Clive Peggy Wood

1936 THE STORY OF LOUIS PASTEUR
Director: William Dieterle
Co-stars: Paul Muni Anita Louise Donald Woods

1936 I MARRIED A DOCTOR
Director: Archie Mayo
Co-stars: Pat O'Brien Ross Alexander Louise Fazenda

1937 THE WOMEN MEN MARRY
Co-star: George Murphy

1937 MOUNTAIN JUSTICE
Director: Michael Curtiz
Co-stars: George Brent Robert Barrat Mona Barrie

1938 THE CRIME OF DR. HALLET
Director: S. Sylvan Simon
Co-stars: Ralph Bellamy William Gargan Barbara Read

1939 THE SON OF FRANKENSTEIN
Director: Rowland Lee
Co-stars: Basil Rathbone Boris Karloff Bela Lugosi

1940 TOM BROWN'S SCHOOLDAYS
Director: Robert Stevenson
Co-stars: Freddie Bartholomew James Lydon Cedric Hardwicke

1941 HER FIRST BEAU
Director: Theodore Reed
Co-stars: Jane Withers Jackie Cooper Edith Fellows

1946 SOMEWHERE IN THE NIGHT
Director: Joseph Mankiewicz
Co-stars: John Hodiak Nancy Guild Lloyd Nolan

1947 THE TENDER YEARS
Director: Harold Schuster
Co-stars: Joe E. Brown Richard Lyon Noreen Nash

1947 CASS TIMBERLANE
Director: George Sidney
Co-stars: Spencer Tracy Lana Turner Zachary Scott Tom Drake

1949 ADVENTURE IN BALTIMORE
Director: Richard Wallace
Co-stars: Shirley Temple Robert Young John Agar

1951 LOVE IS BETTER THAN EVER
Director: Stanley Donen
Co-stars: Elizabeth Taylor Larry Parks Tom Tully

1952 RUBY GENTRY
Director: King Vidor
Co-stars: Jennifer Jones Charlton Heston Karl Malden

1955 MANY RIVERS TO CROSS
Director: Roy Rowland
Co-stars: Robert Taylor Eleanor Parker Victor McLaglen

1958 SING, BOY, SING
Director: Henry Ephron
Co-stars: Tommy Sands Edmond O'Brien John McIntyre

1959 NORTH BY NORTHWEST
Director: Alfred Hitchcock
Co-stars: Cary Grant Eva Marie Saint James Masonli

1959 STEP DOWN TO TERROR
Director: Harry Keller
Co-stars: Charles Drake Coleen Miller Rod Taylor

1964 BABY THE RAIN MUST FALL
Director: Robert Mulligan
Co-stars: Steve McQueen Lee Remick Don Murray

MURIEL HUTCHINSON

1937 PARTNERS IN CRIME
Director: Ralph Murphy
Co-stars: Lynne Overman Roscoe Karns Anthony Quinn

BETTY HUTTON

1942 THE FLEET'S IN
Director: Victor Schertzinger
Co-stars: Dorothy Lamour William Holden

1942 HAPPY GO LUCKY
Director: Curtis Bernhardt
Co-stars: Mary Martin Dick Powell Eddie Bracken

1942   STAR SPANGLED RHYTHM
Director: George Marshall
Co-stars: Victor Moore Eddie Bracken Bob Hope

1943   LET'S FACE IT
Director: Sidney Lanfield
Co-stars: Bob Hope Dona Drake Eve Arden

1944   HERE COMES THE WAVES
Director: Mark Sandrich
Co-stars: Bing Crosby Sonny Tufts Mae Clark

1943   AND THE ANGEL'S SING
Director: George Marshall
Co-stars: Dorothy Lamour Fred MacMurray

1943   THE MIRACLE OF MORGAN'S CREEK
Director: Preston Sturges
Co-stars: Eddie Bracken Diana Lynn

1945   INCENDIARY BLOND
Director: George Marshall
Co-stars: Arturo De Cordova Charles Ruggles

1945   CROSS MY HEART
Director: John Berry
Co-stars: Sonny Tufts Rhys Williams Ruth Donnelly

1945   DUFFY'S TAVERN
Director: Hal Walker
Co-stars: Ed Gardner Victor Moore Bing Crosby

1945   THE STORK CLUB
Director: Hal Walker
Co-stars: Barry Fitzgerald Don Defore Robert Benchley

1947   THE PERILS OF PAULINE
Director: George Marshall
Co-stars: John Lund William Demarest

1947   DREAM GIRL
Director: Mitchell Leisen
Co-stars: MacDonald Carey Patric Knowles

1950   ANNIE GET YOUR GUN
Director: George Sidney
Co-stars: Howard Keel Edward Arnold J. Carrol Naish

1950   LET'S DANCE
Director: Norman Z. McLeod
Co-stars: Fred Astaire Roland Young George Zucco

1952   SOMEBODY LOVES ME
Director: Irving Brecher
Co-stars: Ralph Meeker Robert Keith Adele Jergens

1952   THE GREATEST SHOW ON EARTH
Director: Cecil B.DeMille
Co-stars: Charlton Heston James Stewart Cornel Wilde

1956   SPRING REUNION
Director: Robert Pirosh
Co-stars: Dana Andrews Jean Hagen James Gleason

LAUREN HUTTON

1968   PAPER LION
Director: Alec March
Co-stars: Alan Alda David Doyle Sugar Ray Robinson

1970   LITTLE FAUSS AND BIG HALSY
Director: Sidney Furie
Co-stars: Robert Redford Michael J. Pollard

1975   THE GAMBLER
Director: Karel Reisz
Co-stars: James Caan Paul Sorvino Burt Young James Woods

1976   GATOR
Director: Burt Reynolds
Co-stars: Burt Reynolds Jack Weston Jerry Reed Mike Douglas

1976   WELCOME TO L.A.
Director: Alan Rudolph
Co-stars: Keith Carradine Sally Kellerman Sissy Spacek

1977   VIVA KNIEVEL!
Director: Gordon Douglas
Co-stars: Evel Knievel Gene Kelly Red Buttons

1978   A WEDDING
Director: Robert Alrman
Co-stars: Carol Burnett Amy Stryker Mia Farrow

1978   SOMEBODY'S WATCHING ME
Director: John Carpenter
Co-stars: David Birney Adrienne Barbeau

1980   AMERICAN GIGOLO
Director: Paul Schrader
Co-stars: Richard Gere Hector Elizondo Nina Van Pallandt

1981   PATERNITY
Director: David Steinberg
Co-stars: Burt Reynolds Beverly D'Angelo Norman Fell

1981   ZORRO, THE GAY BLADE
Director: Peter Medak
Co-stars: George Hamilton Brenda Vacarro James Booth

1983   THE CRADLE WILL FALL
Director: John Llewellyn Moxey
Co-stars: Ben Murphy James Farantino

1983   STARLIGHT:
      THE PLANE THAT COULDN'T LAND
Director: Jerry Jameson
Co-stars: Lee Majors Ray Milland

1984   LASSITER
Director: Roger Young
Co-stars: Tom Selleck Jane Seymour Bob Hoskins Warren Clarke

1985   ONCE BITTEN
Director: Howard Storm
Co-stars: Jim Carrey Karen Kopins Cleavon Little

1985   SCANDAL SHEET
Director: David Lowell Rich
Co-stars: Burt Lancaster Pamela Reed Robert Ulrich

1986   MONTE CARLO
Director: Anthony Page
Co-stars: Joan Collins George Hamilton Malcolm McDowell

1986   SINS
Director: Douglas Hickox
Co-stars: Joan Collins Jean-Pierre Aumont Gene Kelly

1987   TIMESTALKERS
Director: Michael Schultz
Co-stars: William Devane Klaus Kinski Forrest Tucker

1987   MALONE
Director: Elliott Nugent
Co-stars: Burt Reynolds Cliff Robertson Cynthia Gibb

1988   PERFECT PEOPLE
Director: Bruce Seth Green
Co-stars: Perry King Cheryl Pollack June Lockhart

1989   FEAR
Director: Rockne O'Bannon
Co-stars: Ally Sheedy Pruit Taylor Vince John Agar

1992   MISSING PIECES
Director: Leonard Stein
Co-stars: Eric Idle Robert Wuhl

1994   MY FATHER, THE HERO
Director: Steve Miner
Co-stars: Gerard Depardieu Katherine Heigl Dalton James

MARION HUTTON
1944 IN SOCIETY
Director: Jean Yarbrough
Co-stars: Bud Abbott Lou Costello Kirby Grant

JUDY HUXTABLE
1966 THE PSYCHOPATH
Director: Freddie Francis
Co-stars: Patrick Wymark Margaret Johnston John Standing

1969 LES BICYCLETTES DE BELSIZE
Director: Douglas Hickox
Co-star: Anthony May

LEILA HYAMS
1929 SPITE MARRIAGE
Director: Edward Sedgwick
Co-stars: Buster Keaton Dorothy Sebastian Edward Earle

1929 THE 13TH. CHAIR
Director: Tod Browning
Co-stars: Margaret Wycherley Bela Lugosi Conrad Nagel

1930 WAY FOR A SAILOR
Director: Sam Wood
Co-stars: John Gilbert Wallace Beery Polly Moran

1930 THE BIG HOUSE
Director: George Hill
Co-stars: Chester Morris Wallace Beery Robert Montgomery

1930 THE BISHOP MURDER CASE
Director: David Burton
Co-stars: Basil Rathbone Roland Young Alec B. Francis

1931 GENTLEMAN'S FATE
Director: Mervyn LeRoy
Co-stars: John Gilbert Anita Page Marie Prevost

1931 MEN CALL IT LOVE
Co-stars: Adolphe Menjou Norman Foster

1931 THE NEW ADVENTURES OF GET-RICH-QUICK WALLINGFORD
Director: Sam Wood
Co-stars: Jimmy Durante William Haines

1931 PHANTOM OF PARIS
Director: John Robertson
Co-stars: John Gilbert Lewis Stone Ian Keith

1931 SURRENDER
Director: William Howard
Co-stars: Warner Baxter Ralph Bellamy C. Aubrey Smith

1931 STEPPING OUT
Co-star: Charlotte Greenwood

1932 RED-HEADED WOMAN
Director: Jack Conway
Co-stars: Jean Harlow Chester Morris Lewis Stone

1932 FREAKS
Director: Tod Browning
Co-stars: Wallace Ford Olga Baclanova Roscoe Ates

1932 THE BIG BROADCAST
Director: Frank Tuttle
Co-stars: Bing Crosby Gracie Allen George Burns

1933 ISLAND OF LOST SOULS
Director: Erle Kenton
Co-stars: Charles Laughton Bela Lugosi Richard Arlen

1935 PEOPLE WILL TALK
Director: Al Santell
Co-stars: Charles Ruggles Mary Boland Dean Jagger

1935 RUGGLES OF RED GAP
Director: Leo McCarey
Co-stars: Charles Laughton Mary Boland Charles Ruggles

1935 THOUSAND DOLLARS A MINUTE
Co-star: Roger Pryor

PAM HYATT
1986 THE CARE BEARS MOVIE II: A NEW GENERATION
Director: Dale Schott
Co-stars: Maxine Miller Hadley Kay

1988 THE ANN JILLIAN STORY
Director: Corey Allen
Co-stars: Ann Jillian Tony LoBianca Viveca Lindfors

PHILLIPA HYATT
1943 THE BELLS GO DOWN
Director: Basil Dearden
Co-stars: Tommy Trinder James Mason Mervyn Johns

JACQUELINE HYDE
1969 TAKE THE MONEY AND RUN
Director: Woody Allen
Co-stars: Woody Allen Janet Margolin Lonny Chapman

TRACY HYDE
1971 MELODY
Director: Waris Hussein
Co-stars: Jack Wild Mark Lester Roy Kinnear

MARTHA HYER *(Married Hal Wallis)*
Nominated For Best Supporting Actress In 1959 For "Some Come Running"

1949 ROUGHSHOD
Director: Mark Robson
Co-stars: Robert Sterling Gloria Grahame Claude Jarman Jnr

1952 LUCKY ME
Director: Jack Donohue
Co-stars: Doris Day Robert Cummings Phil Silvers

1953 SO BIG
Director: Robert Wise
Co-stars: Jane Wyman Sterling Hayden Richard Beymer

1953 ABBOTT & COSTELLO GO TO MARS
Director: Charles Lamont
Co-stars: Mari Blanchard Anita Ekberg Abbott & Costello

1954 CRY VENGEANCE
Director: Mark Stevens
Co-stars: Mark Stevens Skip Homeier Joan Vohs Dorothy Kennedy

1954 DOWN THREE DARK STREETS
Director: Arnold Laven
Co-stars: Broderick Crawford Ruth Roman Casey Adams

1954 RIDERS TO THE STARS
Director: Richard Carlson
Co-stars: Richard Carlson Herbert Marshall Dawn Addams

1954 SABRINA
Director: Billy Wilder
Co-stars: Audrey Hepburn Humphrey Bogart

1956 SHOWDOWN AT ABILENE
Director: Charles Haas
Co-stars: Jock Mahoney David Janssen Lyle Bettger

1956 RED SUNDOWN
Director: Jack Arnold
Co-stars: Rory Calhoun Dean Jagger Robert Middleton

1956 KELLY AND ME
Director: Robert Z. Leonard
Co-stars: Van Johnson Piper Laurie Onslow Stevens

1956 THE BATTLE OF ROGUE RIVER
Director: William Castle
Co-stars: George Montgomery Richard Denning

1957	**MY MAN GODFREY**	**1965**	**THE SONS OF KATIE ELDER**
Director:	Henry Koster	*Director:*	Henry Hathaway
Co-stars:	June Allyson David Niven Robert Keith	*Co-stars:*	John Wayne Dean Martin Earl Holliman

1957 MY MAN GODFREY
Director: Henry Koster
Co-stars: June Allyson David Niven Robert Keith

1957 PARIS HOLIDAY
Director: Gerd Oswald
Co-stars: Bob Hope Anita Ekberg Frenandel Jean Murat

1957 THE DELICATE DELINQUENT
Director: Don McGuire
Co-stars: Jerry Lewis Darren McGavin

1957 BATTLE HYMN
Director: Douglas Sirk
Co-stars: Rock Hudson Anna Kashfi Dan Duryea

1957 MISTER CORY
Director: Blake Edwards
Co-stars: Tony Curtis Charles Bickford Kathryn Grant

1958 ONCE UPON A HORSE
Director: Hal Kanter
Co-stars: Rowan & Martin Leif Erikson James Gleason

1958 HOUSEBOAT
Director: Melville Shavelson
Co-stars: Cary Grant Sophia Loren Harry Guardino

1959 THE BEST OF EVERYTHING
Director: Jean Negulesco
Co-stars: Joan Crawford Hope Lange Brian Aherne

1959 THE BIG FISHERMAN
Director: Frank Borzage
Co-stars: Howard Keel Susan Kohner John Saxon

1959 SOME CAME RUNNING
Director: Vincente Minnelli
Co-stars: Frank Sinatra Dean Martin Shirley MacLaine

1960 ICE PALACE
Director: Vincent Sherman
Co-stars: Richard Burton Robert Ryan Carolyn Jones

1960 DESIRE IN THE DUST
Director: William Claxton
Co-stars: Raymond Burr Joan Bennett Ken Scott

1961 THE LAST TIME I SAW ARCHIE
Director: Jack Webb
Co-stars: Jack Webb Robert Mitchum France Nuyen Richard Arlen

1961 THE RIGHT APPROACH
Director: David Butler
Co-stars: Frankie Vaughan Juliet Prowse Gary Crosby

1962 A GIRL NAMED TAMIKO
Director: John Sturges
Co-stars: Laurence Harvey France Nuyen Michael Wilding

1963 THE MAN FROM THE DINERS CLUB
Director: Frank Tashlin
Co-stars: Danny Kaye Telly Savalas

1963 WIVES AND LOVERS
Director: John Rich
Co-stars: Janet Leigh Van Johnson Shelley Winters

1964 THE CARPETBAGGERS
Director: Edward Dmytryk
Co-stars: George Peppard Alan Ladd Carroll Baker

1964 FIRST MEN IN THE MOON
Director: Nathan Juran
Co-stars: Lionel Jeffries Edward Judd

1964 BLOOD ON THE ARROW
Director: Sidney Salkow
Co-stars: Dale Robertson Wendell Corey Elisha Cook

1964 BIKINI BEACH
Director: William Asher
Co-stars: Frankie Avalon Annette Funicello Keenan Wynn

1965 THE SONS OF KATIE ELDER
Director: Henry Hathaway
Co-stars: John Wayne Dean Martin Earl Holliman

1966 PICTURE MOMMY DEAD
Director: Burt Gordon
Co-stars: Don Ameche Zsa Zsa Gabor Maxwell Reed

1966 THE NIGHT OF THE GRIZZLY
Director: Joseph Pevney
Co-stars: Clint Walker Keenan Wynn Jack Elam

1966 THE CHASE
Director: Arthur Penn
Co-stars: Marlon Brando Jane Fonda Robert Redford

1967 THE HAPPENING
Director: Elliott Silverstein
Co-stars: Anthony Quinn George Maharis Faye Dunnaway

1969 CROSSPLOT
Director: Alvin Rakoff
Co-stars: Roger Moore Alexis Kanner Dudley Sutton

1973 DAY OF THE WOLVES
Director: Key Ferde Grofe
Co-stars: Richard Egan Rick Jason Jan Murray

DIANA HYLAND

1964 ONE MAN'S WAY
Director: Denis Sanders
Co-stars: Don Murray William Windom Carol Ohmart

1966 SMOKY
Director: George Sherman
Co-stars: Fess Parker Katy Jurado Hoyt Axton

FRANCES HYLAND

1980 HAPPY BIRTHDAY TO ME
Director: J. Lee Thompson
Co-stars: Glenn Ford Melissa Sue Anderson Sharon Acker

JANE HYLTON

1946 DAYBREAK
Director: Compton Bennett
Co-stars: Ann Todd Eric Portman Maxwell Reed

1947 DEAR MURDERER
Director: Arthur Crabtree
Co-stars: Eric Portman Greta Gynt Dennis Price

1947 WHEN THE BOUGH BREAKS
Director: Lawrence Huntingdon
Co-stars: Patric Roc Rosamund John Bill Owen

1948 MY BROTHER'S KEEPER
Director: Roy Rich
Co-stars: Jack Warner George Cole David Tomlinson

1948 HERE COME THE HUGGETS
Director: Ken Annakin
Co-stars: Jack Warner Kathleen Harrison Susan Shaw

1949 PASSPORT TO PIMILCO
Director: Henry Cornelius
Co-stars: Stanley Holloway Margaret Rutherford

1950 DANCE HALL
Director: Charles Crichton
Co-stars: Natasha Parry Petula Clark Diana Dors

1951 THE QUIET WOMAN
Director: John Gilling
Co-stars: Derek Bond Dora Byran Michael Balfour

1952 THE TALL HEADLINES
Director: Terence Young
Co-stars: Flora Robson Mai Zetterling Michael Dennison

1952   IT STARTED IN PARADISE
Director: Compton Bennett
Co-stars: Ian Hunter Terence Morgan Muriel Pavlow

1953   THE WEAK AND THE WICKED
Director: J. Lee Thompson
Co-stars: Glynis Johns John Gregson Diana Dors

1957   YOU PAY YOUR MONEY
Director: MacLean Rogers
Co-stars: Hugh Dermott Honor Blackman

1959   DEVIL'S BAIT
Director: Peter Graham Scott
Co-stars: Geoffrey Keen Gordon Jackson Dermot Kelly

1960   CIRCUS OF HORRORS
Director: Sidney Hayers
Co-stars: Anton Diffring Erika Remberg Donald Pleasence

1961   HOUSE OF MYSTERY
Director: Vernon Sewell
Co-stars: Peter Dyneley Nanette Newman Maurice Kaufman

1978   THE WILD GEESE
Director: Andrew McLaglen
Co-stars: Roger Moore Richard Burton Richard Harris

JOYCE HYSER

1985   JUST ONE OF THE GUYS
Director: Lisa Gottlieb
Co-stars: Clayton Rohner Billy Jacoby Sherilyn Fenn

DOROTHY HYSON *(Daughter Of Dorothy Dickson Married Robert Douglas, Anthony Quayle)*

1933   SOLDIERS OF THE KING
Director: Maurice Elvy
Co-stars: Cicely Courtneidge Edward Everett Horton

1933   TURKEY TIME
Director: Tom Walls
Co-stars: Tom Walls Robertson Hare Mary Brough

1933   THAT'S A GOOD GIRL
Director: Jack Buchanan
Co-stars: Jack Buchanan Elsie Randolph Garry Marsh

1933   THE GHOUL
Director: Hayes Hunter
Co-stars: Boris Karloff Cedric Hardwicke Ralph Richardson

1934   HAPPY
Director: Fred Zelnick
Co-stars: Stanley Lupino Laddie Cliff Will Fyffe

1934   A CUP OF KINDNESS
Director: Tom Walls
Co-stars: Tom Walls Ralph Lynn Claude Hulbert

1934   SING AS WE GO !
Director: Basil Dean
Co-stars: Gracie Fields John Loder Stanley Holloway

1940   SPARE A COPPER
Director: John Paddy Carstairs
Co-stars: George Formby Bernard Lee John Turnbull

1941   YOU WILL REMEMBER
Director: Jack Raymond
Robert Morley Emlyn Williams Roddy McDowall

POLA ILLERY

1930　SOUS LES TOITS DE PARIS
Director:　Rene Clair
Co-stars:　Albert Prejean Gaston Modot

CELIA IMRIE

1989　MURDER ON THE MOON
Director:　Michael Lindsay-Hogg
Co-stars:　Brigitte Nielsen Julien Sands Brian Cox

1990　THE WORLD OF EDDIE WEARY
Director:　Alan Grint
Co-stars:　Ray Brooks Connie Booth Brian Glover

1992　BLUE BLACK PERMANENT
Director:　Margaret Tait
Co-stars:　Jack Shepherd James Fleet Gerda Stevenson

1993　A QUESTION OF GUILT
Director:　Stuart Orme
Co-stars:　Cherie Lunghi Derrick O'Connor Gillian Barge

1994　A DARK ADAPTED EYE
Director:　Tim Fywell
Co-stars:　Helena Bonham Carter Sophie Ward Robin Ellis

1995　IN THE BLEAK MIDWINTER
Director:　Kenneth Branagh
Co-stars:　Michael Malony Julia Sawahla John Sessions

1996　THE BORROWERS
Director:　Peter Hewitt
Co-stars:　John Goodman Jim Broadbent Hugh Laurie

KATHY IMRIE

1992　SHAFT'S BIG SCORE!
Director:　Gordon Parks
Co-stars:　Richard Roundtree Moses Gunn Joseph Mascolo

CLAUDIA INCHAURREGUI

1989　DEATHSTALKER 3
Director:　Alfonso Corona
Co-stars:　John Allen Nelson Carla Herd Terri Treas

ESTELLA INDA

1951　LOS OLIVIDADOS
Director:　Luis Bunuel
Co-stars:　Alfonso Mejia Miguel Inclan Roberto Cobo

FREIDA INESCORT

1935　THE DARK ANGEL
Director:　Sidney Franklin
Co-stars:　Merle Oberan Fredric March Herbert Marshall

1936　GIVE ME YOUR HEART
Director:　Archie Mayo
Co-stars:　Kay Frances George Brent Patric Knowles

1936　THE GARDEN MURDER CASE
Co-stars:　Edmund Lowe Benita Hume Kent Smith

1936　HOLLYWOOD BOULEVARD
Director:　Robert Florey
Co-stars:　John Halliday Marsha Hunt Robert Cummings

1936　IF YOU COULD ONLY COOK
Director:　William Seiter
Co-stars:　Herbert Marshall Leo Carrillo

1936　THE KING STEPS OUT
Director:　Joseph Von Sternberg
Co-stars:　Grace Moore Franchot Tone Victor Jory

1936　MARY OF SCOTLAND
Director:　John Ford
Co-stars:　Katherine Hepburn Fredric March Donald Crisp

1937　PORTIA ON TRIAL
Director:　George Nicholls
Co-stars:　Walter Abel Neil Hamilton Heather Angel

1937　THE GREAT O'MALLEY
Director:　William Dieterle
Co-stars:　Pat O'Brien Humphrey Bogart Ann Sheridan

1937　CALL IT A DAY
Director:　Archie Mayo
Co-stars:　Olivia De Havilland Ian Hunter Anita Louise

1937　ANOTHER DAWN
Director:　William Dieterle
Co-stars:　Errol Fylnn Kay Francis Ian Hunter

1939　BEAUTY FOR THE ASKING
Director:　Glenn Tryon
Co-stars:　Lucille Ball Patric Knowles Donald Woods

1939　TARZAN FINDS A SON
Director:　Richard Thorpe
Co-stars:　Johnny Wiesmuller Johnny Sheffield Maureen O'Sullivan

1939　WOMAN DOCTOR
Director:　Sidney Salkow
Co-stars:　Henry Wilcoxon Claire Dodd Cora Witherspoon

1940　THE TRIAL OF MARY DUGAN
Director:　Norman Z. Mcleod
Co-stars:　Laraine Day Robert Young Tom Conway

1940　PRIDE AND PREJUDICE
Director:　Robert Z. Leonard
Co-stars:　Laurence Olivier Greer Garson Edmund Gwenn

1940　THE LETTER
Director:　William Wyler
Co-stars:　Bette Davis Herbert Marshall Gale Sondergaard

1941　REMEMBER THE DAY
Director:　Henry King
Co-stars:　Claudette Colbert John Payne Shepperd Strudwick

1941　SHADOWS ON THE STAIRS
Director:　Ross Lederman
Co-stars:　Paul Cavanagh Turhan Bey Heather Angel

1941　SUNNY
Director:　Herbert Wilcox
Co-stars:　Anna Neagle John Carroll Ray Bolger Grace Hartman

1941　YOU'LL NEVER GET RICH
Director:　Sidney Lanfield
Co-stars:　Fred Astaire Rita Hayworth Robert Benchley

1942　STREET OF CHANCE
Director:　Jack Hively
Co-stars:　Burgess Meredith Claire Trevor Sheldon Leonard

1943　RETURN OF THE VAMPIRE
Director:　Lew Landers
Co-stars:　Bela Lugosi Nina Foch Miles Mander

1943　IT COMES UP LOVE
Director:　Charles Lamont
Co-stars:　Gloria Jean Donald O'Connor Ian Hunter

1943 THE AMAZING MRS. HOLLIDAY
Director: Bruce Manning
Co-stars: Deana Durbin Edmond O'Brien Barry Fitzgerald

1944 HEAVENLY DAYS
Director: Howard Estabrook
Co-stars: Jim Jordan Marion Jordan Eugene Palette Barbara Hale

1949 THE JUDGE STEPS OUT
Director: Boris Ingster
Co-stars: Alexander Knox Ann Sothern Sharyn Moffett

1951 A PLACE IN THE SUN
Director: George Stevens
Co-stars: Montgomery Clift Elizabeth Tayor Shelly Winters

1955 FOXFIRE
Director: Joseph Pevney
Co-stars: Jane Russell Jeff Chandler Dan Duryea Barton Maclane

1955 FLAME OF THE ISLANDS
Director: Edward Ludwig
Co-stars: Yvonne De Carlo Howard Duff Zachary Scott

1956 THE EDDY DUCHIN STORY
Director: George Sidney
Co-stars: Tyrone Power Kim Novak Victoria Shaw

1956 THE SHE CREATURE
Director: Edward Cahn
Co-stars: Marla English Tom Conway Chester Morris

1957 DARBY'S RANGERS
Director: William Wellman
Co-stars: James Garner Jack Warden Edward Byrnes

1959 THE ALLIGATOR PEOPLE
Director: Roy Del Ruth
Co-stars: George Macready Beverly Garland Bruce Bennett

JOYCE INGALLS

1983 DEADLY FORCE
Director: Paul Aaron
Co-stars: Wings Hauser Paul Shenar Al Ruscio

FELICE INGERSOLL

1948 HE WALKED BY NIGHT
Director: Alfred Walker
Co-stars: Richard Basehart Scott Brady Roy Roberts

KATE INGRAM

1982 SCRUBBERS
Director: Mai Zetterling
Co-stars: Amanda York Chrissie Cotterill Honey Bane

ANTONELLA INTERLENGHI

1985 LA CAGE AUX FOLLIES III
Director: Georges Lautner
Co-stars: Ugo Tognazzi Michel Serrault

INGE IPENBURG

1988 THE NIGHTWATCH
Director: Danny Boyle
Co-stars: Leslie Grantham Michael Feast James Cosmo

JILL IRELAND
(Married David McCullum, Charles Bronson)

1956 THE BIG MONEY
Director: John Paddy Carstairs
Co-stars: Ian Carmichael Belinda Lee

1956 THREE MEN IN A BOAT
Director: Ken Annakin
Co-stars: Jimmy Edwards Laurence Harvey

1957 THERE'S ALWAY THURSDAY
Director: Charles Saunders
Co-stars: Charles Victor Marjorie Rhodes

1957 ROBBERY UNDER ARMS
Director: Jack Lee
Co-stars: Peter Finch David McCallum Maureen Swanson

1957 HELL DRIVERS
Director: Cy Endfield
Co-stars: Stanley Baker Patrick McGoohan Herbert Lom

1962 TWICE ROUND THE DAFFODILLS
Director: Gerald Thomas
Co-stars: Juliet Mills Donald Sinden Joan Sims

1963 JUNGLE STREET
Director: Charles Saunders
Co-stars: David McCallum Kenneth Cope

1968 VILLA RIDES
Director: Buzz Kulik
Co-stars: Yul Brynner Robert Mitchum Charles Bronson

1970 RIDER ON THE RAIN
Director: Rene Clement
Co-stars: Charles Bronson Marlene Jobert Jean Piat

1971 SOMEONE BEHIND THE DOOR
Co-stars: Charles Bronson Anthony Perkins Henri Garcia

1971 COLD SWEAT
Director: Terence Young
Co-stars: James Mason Liv Ullman Jean Topart

1972 THE VALACHI PAPERS
Director: Terence Young
Co-stars: Charles Bronson Joseph Wiseman

1972 THE MECHANIC
Director: Michael Winner
Co-stars: Charles Bronson Jan-Michael Vincent

1973 THE VALDEZ HORSES
Director: John Sturges
Co-stars: Charles Bronson Vincent Van Patten

1975 THE STREETFIGHTER
Director: Walter Hill
Co-stars: Charles Bronson James Coburn Maggie Blye

1975 BRAKEOUT
Director: Tom Gries
Co-stars: Charles Bronson Robert Duvall John Huston

1975 BREAKHEART PASS
Director: Tom Gries
Co-stars: Charles Bronson Ben Johnson Richard Crenna

1976 FROM NOON TILL THREE
Director: Frank Gilroy
Co-stars: Charles Bronson Douglas Fowley Stan Haze

1978 LOVE AND BULLETS
Director: Stuart Rosenberg
Co-stars: Charles Bronson Rod Steiger Henry Silva

1980 THE GIRL, THE GOLD WATCH AND EVERYTHING
Director: William Wiard
Co-stars: Robert Hayes Ed Nelson

1981 DEATH WISH 2
Director: Michael Winner
Co-stars: Charles Bronson Anthony Franciosa

1986 ASSASSINATION
Director: Peter Hunt
Co-stars: Charles Bronson Stephen Elliott Randy Brooks

KATHY IRELAND

1988 ALIEN FROM L.A.
Director: Albert Pyun
Co-stars: Thom Matthews Linda Kerridge

1991 NECESSARY ROUGHNESS
Director: Stan Dragoti
Co-stars: Scott Bakula Hector Elizondo Robert Loggia

1992 DANGER ISLAND
Director: Lee Wallace
Co-stars: Richard Beymer June Lockhart Gary Graham

1993 NATIONAL LAMPOON'S LOADED WEAPON 1
Director: Gene Quintano
Co-stars: Emillio Estevez Whoopi Goldberg

1993 AMORE!
Director: Lorenzo Doumani
Co-stars: Jack Scalia George Hamilton Elliott Gould

PAULA IRVINE

1988 PHANTASM 2
Director: Don Coscarelli
Co-stars: James Le Gros Reggie Bannister Angus Scrimm

AMY IRVING
Nominated for Best Supporting Actress in 1983 for "Yentl"

1976 CARRIE
Director: Brian De Palma
Co-stars: Sissy Spacek Piper Laurie John Travolta

1976 PANACHE
Director: Gary Nelson
Co-stars: Rene Auberjonois David Healy Charles Frank

1978 THE FURY
Director: Brian De Palma
Co-stars: Kirk Douglas John Cassavetes Fiona Lewis

1979 VOICES
Director: Robert Markowitz
Co-stars: Michael Ontkean Alex Rocco Vivecca Lindfors

1980 THE COMPETITION
Director: Joel Oliansky
Co-stars: Richard Dreyfuss Lee Remick

1980 HONEYSUCKLE ROSE
Director: Jerry Schatzberg
Co-stars: Willie Nelson Dyan Cannon Slim Pickins

1983 YENTL
Director: Barbra Streisand
Co-stars: Barbra Streisand Mandy Patinkin

1984 MICKI AND MAUDE
Director: Blake Edwards
Co-stars: Dudley Moore Ann Reinking

1986 ANASTASIA: THE MYSTERY OF ANNA
Director: James Goldman
Co-stars: Olivia De Havilland Omar Sharif

1988 CROSSING DELANCY
Director: Joan Micklin Silver
Co-stars: Peter Riegart Syvlia Miles

1988 WHO FRAMED ROGER RABBIT?
Director: Robert Zemeckis
Co-stars: Bob Hoskins Christopher Lloyd

1990 A SHOW OF FORCE
Director: Bruno Barretto
Co-stars: Robert Duvall Andy Garcia Erik Estrada

1991 AN AMERICAN TAIL: FIEVEL GOES WEST *(Voice)*
Director: Simon Wells
Co-stars: James Stewart Phillip Glasser Dom Deluise

1993 BENEFIT OF THE DOUBT
Director: Jonathan Heap
Co-stars: Donald Sutherland Theodore Bikel Rider Strong

1995 ACTS OF LOVE
Co-star: Dennis Hopper

1998 DECONSTRUCTING HARRY
Director: Woody Allen
Co-stars: Woody Allen Robin Williams Demi Moore

MARGARET IRVING

1930 ANIMAL CRACKERS
Director: Victor Herman
Co-stars: Marx Brothers Margaret Dumont Lillian Roth

1935 THANKS A MILLION
Director: Roy Del Ruth
Co-stars: Dick Powell Ann Dvorak Fred Allen

1936 CHARLIE CHAN AT THE OPERA
Director: Bruce Humberstone
Co-stars: Warner Oland Boris Karloff

1936 EXCLUSIVE STORY
Co-stars: Franchot Tone Madge Evans Stuart Irwin

1937 MEN IN EXILE
Co-stars: Alan Baxter Dick Purcell

1939 MR. MOTO'S LAST WARNING
Director: Norman Foster
Co-stars: Peter Lorre Ricardo Cortez George Sanders

1944 IN SOCIETY
Director: Jean Yarborough
Co-stars: Bud Abbott Lou Costello Marion Hutton

MARY JANE IRVING

1932 WITHOUT HONORS
Co-stars: Harry Carey Gibson Gowland

JENNIFER IRWIN

1986 THE GATE
Director: Tibor Takacs
Co-stars: Stephen Dorff Christa Denton Louis Tripp

MARGARITA ISABEL

1991 DANZON
Director: Maria Novaro
Co-stars: Maria Rojo Carmen Salinas Tito Vasconcelos

ISABELITA

1946 CLUB HAVANA
Director: Edgar Ulmer
Co-stars: Tom Neal Margaret Lindsay Ernest Truex

1946 HIGH SCHOOL HERO
Co-star: Freddie Stewart

PHYLLIS ISLEY

1939 NEW FRONTIER
Co-stars: John Wayne Ray Corrigan

KATHERINE ISOBEL

1991 YES VIRGINIA, THERE IS A SANTA CLAUS
Director: Charles Jarrott
Co-stars: Charles Bronson Richard Thomas

1992 KNIGHT MOVES
Director: Carl Schenkel
Co-stars: Christopher Lambert Diane Lane Tom Skerritt

MARTHE ITTIMANGNAQ

1983 NEVER CRY WOLF
Director: Carroll Ballard
Co-stars: Eugene Corr Brian Dennehy Charles Martin Smith

ROASLIND IVAN

1944 THE SUSPECT
Director: Robert Siodmak
Co-stars: Charles Laughton Ella Raines Henry Daniell

1945 SCARLET STREET
Director: Fritz Lang
Co-stars: Edward G. Robinson Joan Bennett Dan Duryea

1945 PURSUIT TO ALGIERS
Director: Roy William Neill
Co-stars: Basil Rathbone Nigel Bruce Marjorie Riordan

1945 PILLOW OF DEATH
Director: Wallace Fox
Co-stars: Lon Chaney Jnr. Brenda Joyce Clara Blandick

1945 THE CORN IS GREEN
Director: Irving Rapper
Co-stars: Bette Davis John Dall Arthur Shields

1946 THE VERDICT
Director: Don Siegel
Co-stars: Sydney Greenstreet Peter Lorre Joan Lorring

1947 IVY
Director: Sam Wood
Co-stars: Joan Fontaine Herbert Marshall Patric Knowles

1948 JOHNNY BELINDA
Director: Jean Negulesco
Co-stars: Jane Wyman Lew Ayres Charles Bickford

DANA IVEY

1985 THE COLOR PURPLE
Director: Steven Spielberg
Co-stars: Whoopi Goldberg Danny Glover Oprah Winfrey

1988 DIRTY ROTTEN SCOUNDRELS
Director: Frank Oz
Co-stars: Steve Martin Michael Caine Glenne Headly

1990 POSTCARDS FROM THE EDGE
Director: Mike Nichols
Co-stars: Meryl Streep Shirley MacLaine Richard Dreyfuss

1991 THE ADDAMS FAMILY
Director: Barry Sonnenfield
Co-stars: Anjelica Huston Raul Julia Christopher Lloyd

1993 THE ADVENTURES OF HUCK FINN
Director: Stephen Sommers
Co-stars: Elijah Wood Jason Robards Ron Perlman

1993 GUILTY AS SIN
Director: Sidney Lumet
Co-stars: Rebecca De Mornay Don Johnson Jack Warden

1993 SLEEPLESS IN SEATTLE
Director: Nora Ephron
Co-stars: Tom Hanks Meg Ryan Ross Malinger

JUDITH IVEY

1983 DIXIE: CHANGING HABITS
Director: George Englund
Co-stars: Suzanne Pleshette Cloris Leachman

1984 HARRY AND SON
Director: Paul Newman
Co-stars: Paul Newman Robby Benson Ellen Barkin Joanne Woodward

1984 THE WOMAN IN RED
Director: Gene Wilder
Co-stars: Kelly LeBrock Charles Grodin Gene Wilder

1984 THE LONELY GUY
Director: Arthur Hiller
Co-stars: Steve Martin Charles Grodin Robyn Douglas Merv Griffin

1985 THE LONG HOT SUMMER
Director: Stuart Cooper
Co-stars: Ava Gardner Don Johnson Jason Robards

1985 COMPROMISING POSITIONS
Director: Frank Perry
Co-stars: Susan Sarandon Raul Julia Edward Herrmann

1986 BRIGHTON BEACH MEMOIRS
Director: Gene Saks
Co-stars: Blythe Danner Bob Dishy Jonathan Silverman

1987 HELLO AGAIN
Director: Frank Perry
Co-stars: Shelley Long Thor Fields Corbin Bernsen Gabriel Byrne

1989 IN COUNTRY
Director: Norman Jewison
Co-stars: Bruce Willis Emily Lloyd Joan Allen Kevin Anderson

1990 EVERYBODY WINS
Director: Karel Reisz
Co-stars: Debra Winger Nick Nolte Kathleen Wilhoite

1990 LOVE HURTS
Director: Bud Yorkin
Co-stars: Jeff Daniels John Mahoney Cloris Leachman Amy Wright

1991 ALICE
Director: Woody Allen
Co-stars: Mia Farrow Alec Baldwin William Hurt

CATHERINE IVIE

1989 A SMALL MOURNING
Director: Chris Bernard
Co-stars: Alison Steadman Stratford Johns Pauline Yates

SHARON IWAI

1986 A GREAT WALL
Director: Peter Wang
Co-stars: Peter Wang Lin Qinqin Wang Xiao

LINDA JABLONSKA

1989　THE LAST BUTTERFLY
Director:　Karel Kachyna
Co-stars:　Tom Courtenay Brigitte Fossey Freddie Jones

JACKEE

1989　THE RELUCTANT AGENT
Director:　Paul Lynch
Co-stars:　Richard Lawson Dan Hedaya Harold Sylvester

1992　LADYBUGS
Director:　Sidney Furie
Co-stars:　Rodney Dangerfield Jonathan Brandis Vinessa Shaw

ANNE JACKSON *(Married Eli Wallach)*

1959　THE JOURNEY
Director:　Anatole Litvak
Co-stars:　Yul Brynner Deborah Kerr Anouk Aimee

1960　TALL STORY
Director:　Joshua Logan
Co-stars:　Jane Fonda Anthony Perkins Ray Walston

1968　THE TIGER MAKES OUT
Director:　Arthur Hiller
Co-stars:　Eli Wallach Bob Dishy Ruth White

1968　THE SECRET LIFE OF AN AMERICAN WIFE
Director:　George Axelrod
Co-stars:　Walter Matthau Patrick O'Neal

**1968　HOW TO SAVE A MARRIAGE...
　　　　AND RUIN YOUR LIFE**
Director:　Fielder Cook
Co-stars:　Dean Martin Eli Wallach

1970　THE ANGEL LEVINE
Director:　Jan Kadar
Co-stars:　Zero Mostel Harry Belafonte Eli Wallach

1970　DIRTY DINGUS MAGEE
Director:　Burt Kennedy
Co-stars:　Frank Sinatra George Kennedy Lois Nettleton

1970　LOVERS AND OTHER STRANGERS
Director:　Cy Howard
Co-stars:　Bonnie Bedelia Michael Brandon Gig Young

1970　ZIGZAG
Director:　Richard Colla
Co-stars:　George Kennedy Eli Wallach William Marshall

1976　NASTY HABITS
Director:　Michael Lindsay-Hogg
Co-stars:　Glenda Jackson Melina Mercouri Sandy Dennis

1979　THE BELL JAR
Director:　Larry Peerce
Co-stars:　Marilyn Hassett Julie Harris Barbara Barrie

1980　THE SHINING
Director:　Stanley Kubrick
Co-stars:　Jack Nicholson Shelley Duvall Danny Lloyd

1988　OUT ON A LIMB
Director:　Robert Butler
Co-stars:　Shirley MacLaine Charles Dance John Heard

1988　BABY M
Director:　James Steven Sandwith
Co-stars:　JoBeth Williams John Shea Dabney Coleman

1990　FUNNY ABOUT LOVE
Director:　Leonard Nimoy
Co-stars:　Gene Wilder Christine Lahti Mary Stuart Masterson

1992　FOLKS!
Director:　Ted Kotcheff
Co-stars:　Don Ameche Tom Selleck Christine Ebersole

CHEQUITA JACKSON

1992　JUST ANOTHER GIRL ON THE IRT
Director:　Leslie Harris
Co-stars:　Ariyan Johnson Kevin Thigpen

FREDA JACKSON

1944　A CANTERBURY TALE
Director:　Michael Powell
Co-stars:　Eric Portman Sheila Sim Dennis Price

1946　GREAT EXPECTATIONS
Director:　David Lean
Co-stars:　John Mills Alec Guinness Bernard Miles

1946　HENRY V
Director:　Laurence Olivier
Co-stars:　Laurence Olivier Robert Newton Renee Asherson Leo Genn

1948　NO ROOM AT THE INN
Director:　Dan Birt
Co-stars:　Joy Shelton Joan Dowling Sydney Tafler

1951　MR. DENNING DRIVES NORTH
Director:　Anthony Kimmins
Co-stars:　John Mills Phyllis Calvert Sam Wanamaker

1951　FLESH AND BLOOD
Director:　Anthony Kimmins
Co-stars:　Richard Todd Glynis Johns Joan Greenwood

1952　WOMEN OF TWILIGHT
Director:　Gordon Parry
Co-stars:　Rene Ray Lois Maxwell Joan Dowling

1954　THE CROWDED DAY
Director:　John Guillermin
Co-stars:　Joan Rice John Gregson Rachel Roberts

1956　THE LAST MAN TO HANG?
Director:　Terence Fisher
Co-stars:　Tom Conway Elizabeth Sellars Eunice Gayson

1956　BHOWANI JUNCTION
Director:　George Cukor
Co-stars:　Ava Gardner Stewart Granger Francis Matthews

1958　THE FLESH IS WEEK
Director:　Don Chaffey
Co-stars:　John Derek Milly Vitale William Franklyn

1960　BRIDES OF DRACULA
Director:　Terence Fisher
Co-stars:　Peter Cushing David Peel Martita Hunt

1961　SHADOW OF THE CAT
Director:　John Gilling
Co-stars:　Andre Morrell William Lucas Barbara Shelley

1961　ATTEMPT TO KILL
Director:　Royston Morley
Co-stars:　Derek Farr Tony Wright Richard Pearson

1963　TOM JONES
Director:　Tony Richardson
Co-stars:　Albert Finney Susannah York Hugh Griffith

1963 WEST II
Director: Michael Winner
Co-stars: Alfred Lynch Eric Portman Diana Dors

1964 THE THIRD SECRET
Director: Charles Crichton
Co-stars: Stephen Boyd Pamela Franklyn Diane Cilento

1969 VALLEY OF GWANGI
Director: James O'Connelly
Co-stars: Richard Carlson James Franciscus Gila Golan

1978 SHE FELL AMONG THIEVES
Director: Clive Donner
Co-stars: Malcolm McDowell Eileen Atkins Sarah Badel

1981 CLASH OF THE TITANS
Director: Desmond Davis
Co-stars: Laurence Olivier Claire Bloom Maggie Smith

GLENDA JACKSON

Oscar For Best Actress In 1969 For "Women In Love"
Oscar For Best Actress In 1973 For "A Touch Of Class"
Oscar For Best Actress In 1971 For "Sunday, Bloody Sunday"
Nominated For Best Actress In 1975 For "Hedda"

1966 THE MARAT/SADE
Director: Peter Brook
Co-stars: Patrick Magee Ian Richardson Michael Williams

1968 NEGATIVES
Director: Peter Medak
Co-stars: Peter McEnery Diane Cilento Maurice Denham

1968 TELL ME LIES
Director: Peter Brook
Co-stars: Kingsley Amis Paul Scofield Stokely Carmichael

1969 WOMEN IN LOVE
Director: Ken Russell
Director: Jennie Linden Oliver Reed Alan Bates Michael Gough

1970 THE MUSIC LOVERS
Director: Ken Russell
Co-stars: Richard Chamberlain Christopher Gable Max Adrian

1971 MARY QUEEN OF SCOTS
Director: Charles Jarrott
Co-stars: Vanessa Redgrave Trevor Howard Patrick McGoohan

1971 SUNDAY, BLOODY SUNDAY
Director: John Schlesinger
Co-stars: Peter Finch Murray Head Peggy Ashcroft

1971 THE BOY FRIEND
Director: Ken Russell
Co-stars: Twiggy Tommy Tune Christopher Gable

1972 TRIPLE ECHO
Director: Michael Apted
Co-stars: Brian Deacon Oliver Reed Jenny Lee Wright

1973 A TOUCH OF CLASS
Director: Melvin Frank
Co-stars: George Segal Paul Sorvino Hildgarde Neil

1973 BEQUEST TO THE NATION
Director: James Cellan Jones
Co-stars: Peter Finch Michael Jayston Anthony Quayle

1974 THE MAIDS
Director: Christopher Miles
Co-stars: Susannah York Vivien Merchant Mark Burns

1975 THE ROMANTIC ENGLISHWOMAN
Director: Joseph Losey
Co-stars: Michael Caine Helmut Berger

1975 HEDDA
Director: Trevor Nunn
Co-stars: Timothy West Peter Eyre Jennie Linden Patrick Stewart

1976 THE INCREDIBLE SARAH
Director: Richard Fleischer
Co-stars: Daniel Massey Yvonne Mitchell Simon Williams

1976 NASTY HABITS
Director: Michael Lindsay-Hogg
Co-stars: Edith Evans Melina Mercouri Sandy Dennis

1978 THE CLASS OF MISS MacMICHAEL
Director: Silvio Narizzano
Co-stars: Oliver Reed John Standing

1978 STEVIE
Director: Robert Enders
Co-stars: Mona Washbourne Trevor Howard

1978 HOUSE CALLS
Director: Howard Zieff
Co-stars: Walter Matthau Art Carney Richard Benjamin

1979 HEALTH
Director: Robert Altman
Co-stars: Lauren Bacall James Garner Dick Cavett Carol Burnett

1979 LOST AND FOUND
Director: Melvin Frank
Co-stars: George Segal Paul Sorvino Maureen Stapleton

1980 HOPSCOTCH
Director: Ronald Neame
Co-stars: Walter Matthau Sam Waterston George Baker

**1981 THE PATRICIA NEAL STORY:
AN ACT OF LOVE**
Director: Anthony Harvey
Co-star: Dirk Bogarde

1982 GIRO CITY
Director: Karl Francis
Co-stars: Jon Finch Kenneth Colley James Donnelly

1982 THE RETURN OF THE SOLDIER
Director: Alan Bridges
Co-stars: Alan Bates Ann-Margret Julie Christie

1985 TURTLE DIARY
Director: John Irving
Co-stars: Ben Kingsley Richard Johnson Michael Gambon

1986 BEYOND THERAPY
Director: Robert Altman
Co-stars: Tom Conti Julie Hagerty Jeff Goldblum

1988 BUSINESS AS USUAL
Director: Lezli-An Barrett
Co-stars: John Thaw Cathy Tyson Stephen McGann

1988 THE RAINBOW
Director: Ken Russell
Co-stars: Sammi Davis Amanda Donohue Paul McGann

1988 SALOME'S LAST DANCE
Director: Ken Russell
Co-stars: Ken Russell Stratford Johns Nikolas Grace

1989 KING OF THE WIND
Director: Peter Duffell
Co-stars: Frank Finlay Jenny Agutter Richard Harris

1991 A MURDER OF QUALITY
Director: Gavin Miller
Co-stars: Denholm Elliott Joss Ackland Billlie Whitelaw

JANET JACKSON

1993 POETIC JUSTICE
Director: John Singleton
Co-stars: Tupac Shaker Regina King Joe Torry

KATE JACKSON

1972   **LIMBO**
Director: Mark Robson
Co-stars: Katherine Justice Stuart Margolin Hazel Medina

1978   **THUNDER AND LIGHTNING**
Director: Corey Allen
Co-stars: David Carradine Sterling Holloway Ed Barth

1981   **THIN ICE**
Director: Paul Aaron
Co-stars: Gerald Prendergast Lillian Gish Louise Latham

1982   **MAKING LOVE**
Director: Arthur Hiller
Co-stars: Michael Ontkean Harry Hamlin Wendy Hiller

1983   **LISTEN TO YOUR HEART**
Director: Don Taylor
Co-stars: Tim Matheson Cassie Yates George Coe

1989   **LOVERBOY**
Director: Joan Micklin Silver
Co-stars: Patrick Dempsey Kirstie Alley Carrie Fisher

1990   **THE STRANGER WITHIN**
Director: Tom Holland
Co-star: Rick Schroder

1992   **BLACK DEATH**
Director: Sheldon Larry
Co-stars: Jerry Orbach Howard Hesseman Al Waxman

1994   **HARD EVIDENCE**
Director: Jan Egleson
Co-stars: John Shea Dean Stockwell

1994   **ARMED AND INNOCENT**
Director: Jack Bender
Co-star: Gerald McRaney

1995   **SILENCE OF ADULTERY**
Director: Steven Stern
Co-stars: Art Hindle Patricia Gage

1996   **MURDER ON THE IDITAROD TRAIL**

KATHRYN JACKSON

1976   **THE BLACK RIDER**
Director: Larry Spangler
Co-stars: Fred Williamson Isela Vega Brenda Venus

LYNNE JACKSON

1975   **ADIOS AMIGO**
Director: Fred Williamson
Co-stars: Fred Williamson Richard Pryor James Brown Mike Henry

MAHALIA JACKSON

1958   **ST. LOUIS BLUES**
Director: Allen Reisner
Co-stars: Nat King Cole Eartha Kittt Pearl Bailey

1959   **JAZZ ON A SUMMER'S DAY**
Director: Bert Stern
Co-stars: Louis Armstrong Thelonius Monk Chuck Berry

1959   **IMITATION OF LIFE**
Director: Douglas Sirk
Co-stars: Lana Turner Juanita Moore Susan Kohner

1964   **THE BEST MAN**
Director: Franklin Schaffner
Co-stars: Henry Fonda Cliff Robertson Margaret Leighton

MARY JACKSON

1983   **HARDCASTLE AND McCORMICK**
Co-stars: Brian Keith Daniel Hugh-Kelly

SALLY ANNE JACKSON

1982   **REMEMBRANCE**
Director: Colin Gregg
Co-stars: John Altman Martin Barrass Nick Dunning

SHERRY JACKSON (Child)

1953   **TROUBLE ALONG THE WAY**
Director: Michael Curtiz
Co-stars: John Wayne Donna Reed Charles Coburn

1955   **COME NEXT SPRING**
Director: R.G. Springsteen
Co-stars: Ann Sheridan Steve Cochran Walter Brennan

1968   **GUNN**
Director: Blake Edwards
Co-stars: Craig Stevens Laura Devon Helen Traubel

1970   **WILD WOMEN**
Director: Don Taylor
Co-stars: Hugh O'Brian Anne Francis Marilyn Maxwell

1974   **THE GIRL ON THE LATE, LATE SHOW**
Director: Gary Nelson
Co-stars: Gloria Grahame Don Murray Van Johnson

1978   **ABIGAIL WANTED**
Director: Richard Taylor
Co-stars: Christopher Mitchum Bill Watson Bert Hinchman

VICTORIA JACKSON

1988   **BABY BOOM**
Director: Charles Shyer
Co-stars: Diane Keaton Sam Wanamaker Sam Shepard

1988   **CASUAL SEX?**
Director: Genevieve Robert
Co-stars: Lea Thompson Jerry Levine Mary Gross

1989   **DREAM A LITTLE DREAM**
Director: Marc Rocco
Co-stars: Corey Feldman Corey Haim Jason Robards

1989   **U.H.F.**
Director: Jay Levey
Co-stars: Al Yankovic Kevin McCarthy David Bowe

1989   **FAMILY BUSINESS**
Director: Sidney Lumet
Co-stars: Sean Connery Dustin Hoffman Matthew Broderick

1990   **I LOVE YOU TO DEATH**
Director: Lawrence Kasdan
Co-stars: Kevin Kline Tracey Ullman Joan Plowright

CATHERINE JACOB

1991   **TATIE DANIELLE**
Director: Etienne Chatillier
Co-stars: Tsilla Chelton Isabelle Nanty Eric Prat

1992   **MON PERE, CE HEROS**
Director: Gerard Lauzier
Co-stars: Gerard Depardieu Marie Gillian Patrick Mille

1992   **LA FILLE DE L'AIR**
Director: Maroun Bagdadi
Co-stars: Beatrice Dalle Thierry Fortineau

1992   **MERCI LA VIE**
Director: Bertrand Blier
Co-stars: Charlotte Gainsbourg Anouk Grinberg Gerard Depardieu

IRENE JACOB

1991   **THE DOUBLE LIFE OF VERONIQUE**
Director: Krzysztof Kieslowski
Co-stars: Kalina Jedrusik Sandrine Dumas

1993 THE SECRET GARDEN
Director: Agnieszka Holland
Co-stars: Kate Maberly Maggie Smith Hayden Prowse

1994 THREE COLOURS: RED
Director: Krzysztof Kieslowski
Co-stars: Jean-Louis Trintignant Jean-Pierre Lorit

1995 OTHELLO
Director: Oliver Parker
Co-stars: Laurence Fishburne Kenneth Branagh Anna Patrick

1996 ALL MEN ARE MORTAL
Director: Ate De Jong
Co-star: Stephen Rea

1998 INCOGNITO
Director: John Badham
Co-stars: Jason Patric Rod Steiger Ian Richardson

1998 U.S. MARSHALLS
Director: Stuart Baird
Co-stars: Tommy Lee Jones Wesley Snipes Kate Nelligan

JOELLE JACOBI

1989 THE LADY IN WHITE
Director: Frank La Loggia
Co-stars: Lukas Haas Len Cariou Katherine Helmond

EMMA JACOBS

1978 THE STUD
Director: Quentin Masters
Co-stars: Joan Collins Oliver Tobias Sue Lloyd

PAULA JACOBS

1985 SHE'LL BE WEARING PINK PYJAMAS
Director: John Goldschmidt
Co-stars: Julie Walters Anthony Higgins

1985 WINGS OF DEATH
Director: Nicholas Bruce
Co-stars: Dexter Fletcher Kate Hardie Tony Haygarth

ULLA JACOBSSON

1955 SMILES OF A SUMMER NIGHT
Director: Ingmar Bergman
Co-stars: Gunnar Bjornstrand Eva Dahlbeck

1955 ONE SUMMER IN HAPPINESS
Co-star: Folk Sundquist

1962 LOVE IS A BALL
Director: David Swift
Co-stars: Glenn Ford Charles Boyer Hope Lange

1964 ZULU
Director: Cyril Endfield
Co-stars: Stanley Baker Michael Caine Jack Hawkins

1965 THE HEROES OF TELEMARK
Director: Anthony Mann
Co-stars: Kirk Douglas Richard Harris Roy Dotrice

1975 FOX
Director: Rainer Werner Fassbinder
Co-stars: Rainer Werner Fassbinder Karl-Heinz Boehm Peter Chatel

HATTIE JACQUES

1949 TROTTIE TRUE
Director: Brian Desmond Hurst
Co-stars: Jean Kent James Donald Bill Owen

1950 CHANCE OF A LIFETIME
Director: Bernard Miles
Co-stars: Basil Radford Kenneth More Bernard Miles

1952 THE PICKWICK PAPERS
Director: Noel Langley
Co-stars: James Hayter James Donald Nigel Patrick

1952 OLD MOTHER RILEY MEETS THE VAMPIRE
Director: John Gilling
Co-stars: Arthur Lucan Bela Lugosi

1953 OUR GIRL FRIDAY
Director: Noel Langley
Co-stars: Joan Collins Kenneth More Robertson Hare

1958 THE SQUARE PEG
Director: John Paddy Carstairs
Co-stars: Norman Wisdom Edward Chapman Brian Worth

1958 CARRY ON SERGEANT
Director: Gerald Thomas
Co-stars: Bob Monkhouse William Hartnell Shirley Eaton

1959 CARRY ON NURSE
Director: Gerald Thomas
Co-stars: Kenneth Williams Charles Hawtrey Bill Owen

1959 CARRY ON TEACHER
Director: Gerald Thomas
Co-stars: Leslie Phillips Ted Ray Kenneth Connor

1959 FOLLOW A STAR
Director: Robert Asher
Co-stars: Norman Wisdom Jerry Desmonde June Laverick

1960 MAKE MINE MINK
Director: Robert Asher
Co-stars: Terry-Thomas Athene Seyler Billie Whitelaw

1960 CARRY ON CONSTABLE
Director: Gerald Thomas
Co-stars: Sid James Eric Barker Kenneth Connor

1961 CARRY ON REGARDLESS
Director: Gerald Thomas
Co-stars: Sid James Liz Fraser Joan Sims

1961 IN THE DOGHOUSE
Director: Darcy Conyers
Co-stars: Leslie Phillips Peggy Cummins James Booth

1961 WATCH YOUR STERN
Director: Gerald Thomas
Co-stars: Leslie Phillips Eric Barker Joan Sims

1963 CARRY ON CABBY
Director: Gerald Thomas
Co-stars: Sid James Esma Cannon Liz Fraser

1967 THE BOBO
Director: Robert Parrish
Co-stars: Peter Sellers Britt Ekland Rossano Brazzi

1967 THE PLANK
Director: Eric Sykes
Co-stars: Eric Sykes Tommy Cooper Roy Castle

1968 CARRY ON DOCTOR
Director: Gerald Thomas
Co-stars: Frankie Howerd Bernard Bresslaw Anita Harris

1969 RHUBARB
Director: Eric Sykes
Co-stars: Eric Sykes Harry Secombe Jimmy Edwards

1969 CROOKS AND CORONETS
Director: Jim O'Connelly
Co-stars: Telly Savalas Edith Evans Warren Oates

1969 CARRY ON AGAIN DOCTOR
Director: Gerald Thomas
Co-stars: Sid James Barbara Windsor Jim Dales

1969 CARRY ON CAMPING
Director: Gerald Thomas
Co-stars: Sid James Barbara Windsor Bernard Bresslaw

1970 CARRY ON LOVING
Director: Gerald Thomas
Co-stars: Sid James Charles Hawtrey Kenneth Williams

1971 CARRY ON AT YOUR CONVENIENCE
Director: Gerald Thomas
Co-stars: Joan Sims Kenneth Cope Bernard Bresslaw

1972 CARRY ON ABROAD
Director: Gerald Thomas
Co-stars: Sid James June Whitfield Sally Geeson

1972 CARRY ON MATRON
Director: Gerald Thomas
Co-stars: Kenneth Williams Wendy Richards Bill Maynard

1974 CARRY ON DICK
Director: Gerald Thomas
Co-stars: Sid James Jack Douglas Barbara Windsor

CLAUDE JADE

1968 STOLEN KISSES
Director: Francois Truffaut
Co-stars: Jean-Pierre Leaud Delphine Seyrig Michel Lonsdale

MELISSA JAFFA

1974 THE CARS THAT ATE PARIS
Director: Peter Weir
Co-stars: Terry Camillierei John Meillon Kevin Miles

1978 CADDIE
Director: Donald Crombie
Co-stars: Helen Morse Jack Thompson Takis Emmanuel

1989 THE DELINQUENTS
Director: Chris Thompson
Co-stars: Kylie Minogue Charlie Schlatter Desiree Smith

NICOLE JAFFE

1969 THE TOUBLE WITH GIRLS
Director: Peter Tewkesbury
Co-stars: Elvis Presley Marlyn Mason Sheree North

MADHUR JAFFREY

1965 SHAKESPEARE WALLAH
Director: James Ivory
Co-stars: Felicity Kendall Shashi Kapoor Geoffrey Kendall

1969 THE GURU
Director: James Ivory
Co-stars: Michael York Rita Tushingham Barry Foster

1976 AUTOBIOGRAPHY OF A PRINCESS
Director: James Ivory
Co-stars: James Mason Diane Fletcher Keith Varnier

1982 HEAT AND DUST
Director: James Ivory
Co-stars: Julie Christie Greta Scacchi Christopher Cazenove

BIANCA JAGGER

1979 SUCCESS
Director: William Richert
Co-stars: Jeff Bridges Belinda Bauer Ned Beatty

1981 THE CANNONBALL RUN
Director: Hal Needham
Co-stars: Burt Reynolds Roger Moore Dean Martin

JUNE JAGO

1981 DOUBLE DEAL

Director: Brian Kavanagh
Co-stars: Louis Jourdan Angela Punch McGregor Diane Craig

MARINE JAHAN

1983 FLASHDANCE (Uncredited)
Director: Adrian Lyne
Co-stars: Jennifer Beals Michael Nouri (Danced For Beals)

1985 STREETS OF FIRE
Director: Walter Hill
Co-stars: Michael Pare Diane Lane Willem Dafoe

MAGGIE JAKOBSON

1989 NEW YEAR'S DAY
Director: Henry Jaglom
Co-stars: Henry Jaglom Gwen Welles Melanie Winter Milos Forman

LISA JAKUB

1991 RAMBLING ROSE
Director: Martha Coolidge
Co-stars: Laura Dern Robert Duvall Lukas Haas

1991 THE STORY LADY
Director: Larry Elikann
Co-stars: Jessica Tandy Tandy Cronyn Ed Begley Jnr

1993 MATINEE
Director: Joe Dante
Co-stars: John Goodman Cathy Moriarty Simon Fenton

1993 MRS DOUBTFIRE
Director: Chris Columbus
Co-stars: Robin Williams Sally Field Pierce Brosnan

1994 A CHILD'S CRY FOR HELP
Director: Sandor Stern
Co-stars: Veronica Hamel Pam Dawber

1995 BERMUDA TRIANGLE
Director: Ian Toynton
Co-stars: Sam Behrens Susanna Thompson

ANNE JAMES

1952 SOUND OFF
Director: Richard Quine
Co-stars: Mickey Rooney Sammy White Gordon Jones

EILIZABETH JAMES

1968 BORN LOSERS
Director: Tom Laughlin
Co-stars: Tom Laughlin Jane Russell Jeremy Slate

ETTA JAMES

1988 HAIL! HAIL! ROCK 'N' ROLL
Director: Taylor Hackford
Co-stars: Chuck Berry Eric Clapton

GENNIE JAMES (Child)

1984 PLACES IN THE HEART
Director: Robert Benton
Co-stars: Sally Field Danny Glover John Malkovich

1986 THE CHRISTMAS GIFT
Director: Michael Pressman
Co-stars: John Denver Jane Kaczmarek Mary Wickes

1986 ALEX: THE LIFE OF A CHILD
Director: Robert Markowitz
Co-stars: Bonnie Bedelia Craig T. Nelson

GERALDINE JAMES

1980 SWEET WILLIAM
Director: Claude Whatham
Co-stars: Sam Waterston Jenny Agutter Anna Massey

1982　GANDHI
Director:　Richard Attenborough
Co-stars:　Ben Kingsley Candice Bergen Martin Sheen

1988　THE WOLVES OF WILLOUGHBY CHASE
Director:　Stuart Orme
Co-stars:　Stephanie Beacham Mel Smith

1989　SHE'S BEEN AWAY
Director:　Peter Hall
Co-stars:　Peggy Ashcroft James Fox Rachel Kempson Hugh Lloyd

1989　THE TALL GUY
Director:　Mel Smith
Co-stars:　Jeff Goldblum Emma Thompson Rowan Atkinson

1990　THE BRIDGE
Director:　Syd Macartney
Co-stars:　Saskia Reeves David O'Hara Anthony Higgins

1991　PRINCE OF SHADOWS
Director:　Pilar Miro
Co-stars:　Terence Stamp Patsy Kensit Simon Andrew

1991　EX
Director:　Paul Seed
Co-stars:　Griff Rhys Jones Penny Downie Jonathan Hackett

1991　STANLEY AND THE WOMEN
Director:　David Tucker
Co-stars:　John Thaw Sam West Penny Downie

1991　TEEN AGENT
Director:　William Dear
Co-stars:　Richard Griego Linda Hunt Roger Rees Roger Daltrey

1993　NO WORRIES
Director:　David Elfick
Co-stars:　Amy Terelinck Ray Barrett Susan Lyons

JESSICA JAMES

1982　DINER
Director:　Barry Levinson
Co-stars:　Steve Guttenberg Mickey Rourke Ellen Barkin

1989　IMMEDIATE FAMILY
Director:　Jonathan Kaplan
Co-stars:　Glenn Close James Woods Mary Stuart Masterson

NITA JAMES

1938　THE GREAT WALTTZ
Director:　Julien Duvivier
Co-stars:　Fernand Gravet Luise Rainer Miliza Korjus

OLGA JAMES

1954　CARMEN JONES
Director:　Otto Preminger
Co-stars:　Dorothy Dandridge Harry Belafonte Pearl Bailey

REINA JAMES

1986　AFTER PILKINGTON
Co-stars:　Christopher Morahan
Co-stars:　Bob Peck Miranda Richardson Barry Foster

SALLY JAMES

1978　NEVER TOO YOUNG TO ROCK
Director:　Dennis Abey
Co-stars:　Peter Denyer Freddie Jones Peter Noone

ANNE JAMESON

1991　A QUESTION OF ATTRIBUTION
Director:　John Schlesinger
Co-stars:　James Fox Prunella Scales John Carter

JOYCE JAMESON

1963　THE COMEDY OF TERRORS
Director:　Jacques Tourneur
Co-stars:　Vincent Price Peter Lorre Basil Rathbone

1976　THE OUTLAW JOSEY WALES
Director:　Clint Eastwood
Co-stars:　Clint Eastwood Sondra Locke John Vernon

PAULINE JAMESON

1929　THE FLYING SCOTSMAN
Director:　Castleton Knight
Co-stars:　Ray Milland Moore Marriott Alec Hurley

SUSAN JAMESON

1992　THE COUNT OF SOLAR
Director:　Tristram Powell
Co-stars:　David Calder Tyron Woolfe Georgina Hale

MIKKI JAMISON-OLSEN

1978　SHIPWRECK
Director:　Stewart Raffill
Co-stars:　Robert Logan Heather Rattray Sharron Saylor

KRYSTYNA JANDA

1979　THE CONDUCTOR
Director:　Andrzej Wadja
Co-stars:　John Gielgud Andrzej Seweryn

1981　MEPHISTO
Director:　Istavn Szabo
Co-stars:　Klaus Maria Brandauer Karin Boyd Ildiko Bansagi

LOUISA JANES

1989　MOTHER LOVE
Director:　Simon Langton
Co-stars:　Diana Rigg James Wilby David McCallum

DOROTHY JANIS

1929　THE PAGAN
Director:　W.S. Van Dyke
Co-stars:　Ramon Navarro Renee Adoree Donald Crisp

ELSIE JANIS

1942　WOMEN IN WAR
Director:　John Auer
Co-stars:　Wendy Barrie Patric Knowles Mae Clarke

ALLISON JANNEY

1998　BIG NIGHT
Co-stars:　Minnie Driver Isabella Rossellini Ian Holm

1998　THE OBJECT OF MY AFFECTION
Director:　Nicholas Hytner
Co-stars:　Jennifer Aniston Peter Rudd John Pankow

VERONIQUE JANNOT

1979　THE GREATEST ATTACK
Director:　Pierre Gramier-Deferre
Co-stars:　Alain Delon Francine Berge

EILEEN JANSSEN

1948　THE ADVENTURES OF CURLEY AND HIS GANG
Director:　Bernard Carr
Co-stars:　Larry Olsen Frances Rafferty

1948　CURLEY AND HIS GANG IN THE HAUNTED MANSION
Director:　Bernard Carr
Co-stars:　Larry Olsen Don Castle

1948 WHO KILLED DOC ROBIN?
Director: Bernard Carr
Co-stars: Larry Olsen Virginia Grey George Zucco

1954 ABOUT MRS. LESLIE
Director: Daniel Mann
Co-stars: Shirley Booth Robert Ryan Alex Nicol

ELSA JANSSEN

1942 THE PRIDE OF THE YANKEES
Director: Sam Wood
Co-stars: Gary Cooper Teresa Wright Walter Brennan

1943 HIS BUTLER'S SISTER
Director: Frank Borzage
Co-stars: Deanna Durbin Franchot Tone Pat O'Brien

1943 CLAUDIA
Director: Edmund Goulding
Co-stars: Robert Young Dorothy McGuire Ina Clare

1945 DILLINGER
Director: Max Nosseck
Co-stars: Lawrence Tierney Edmund Lowe Anne Jeffreys

1946 CLAUDIA AND DAVID
Director: Walter Lang
Co-stars: Robert Young Dorothy McGuire Mary Astor

1948 SONG OF LOVE
Director: Clarence Brown
Co-stars: Katherine Hepburn Paul Henreid Robert Walker

FAMKE JANSSEN

1992 FATHERS AND SONS

1993 MODEL BY DAY
Director: Christian Duguey
Co-star: Stephen Shellen

1995 GOLDENEYE
Director: Martin Campbell
Co-stars: Pierce Brosnan Robbie Coltrane Minnie Driver

LOIS JANUARY

1938 MOONLIGHT ON THE RANGE
Co-star: Fred Scott

BETY JARDINE

1940 THE GIRL IN THE NEWS
Director: Carol Reed
Co-stars: Margaret Lockwood Barry K. Barnes Emlyn Williams

1943 RHYTHM SERENADE
Director: Gordon Wellesley
Co-stars: Vera Lynn Jimmy Jewel Ben Warriss

JIL JARMYN

1958 TARZAN'S FIGHT FOR LIFE
Director: Bruce Humberstone
Co-stars: Gordon Scott Eve Brent Woody Strode

FRANCESCA JARVIS

1963 LILIES OF THE FIELD
Director: Ralph Nelson
Co-stars: Sidney Poitier Lilia Skala Pamela Branch

SYBIL JASON (Child)

1935 LITTLE BIG SHOT
Director: Michael Curtiz
Co-stars: Glenda Farrell Robert Armstrong J. Carroll Naish

1935 I FOUND STELLA PARISH
Director: Mervyn LeRoy
Co-stars: Kay Francis Paul Lukas Ian Hunter

1936 THE CAPTAIN'S KID
Director: Nick Grinde
Co-stars: Guy Kibbee Jane Bryan Dick Purcell

1936 THE SINGING KID
Director: William Keighley
Co-stars: Al Jolson Allen Jenkins Wini Shaw

1938 THE GREAT O'MALLEY
Director: William Dieterle
Co-stars: Pat O'Brien Humphrey Bogart Ann Sheridan

1938 COMET OVER BROADWAY
Director: Busby Berkeley
Co-stars: Kay Francis Ian Hunter Donald Crisp

1939 THE LITTLE PRINCESS
Director: Walter Lang
Co-stars: Shirley Temple Richard Greene Arthur Treacher

1939 WOMAN DOCTOR
Director: Sidney Salkow
Co-stars: Frieda Inescort Henry Wilcoxon Claire Dodd

1940 THE BLUE BIRD
Director: Walter Lang
Co-stars: Shirley Temple Gale Sondergaard Jessie Ralph

STAR JASPER

1992 JERSEY GIRL
Director: David Burton Morris
Co-stars: Jami Gertz Joseph Bologna Dylan McDermott

JENNIFER JAYNE

1953 IT'S A GRAND LIFE
Director: John Blakley
Co-stars: Frank Randle Diana Dors Dan Young

1958 MARK OF THE PHOENIX
Director: MacLean Rogers
Co-stars: Julia Arnall Sheldon Lawrence Anton Diffring

1958 THE TROLLENBERG TERROR
Director: Quentin Lawrence
Co-stars: Forrest Tucker Janet Munro

1962 BAND OF THIEVES
Director: Peter Bazencenet
Co-stars: Acker Bilk Jimmie Thompson Maudie Edwards

1962 ON THE BEAT
Director: Robert Asher
Co-stars: Norman Wisdom Huntley David Lodge Raymond Huntley

1963 CLASH BY NIGHT
Director: Montgomery Tully
Co-stars: Terence Longden Harry Fowler Peter Sallis

1964 HYSTERIA
Director: Freddie Francis
Co-stars: Robert Webber Lelia Goldoni Maurice Denham

1968 THEY CAME FROM BEYOND SPACE
Director: Freddie Francis
Co-stars: Robert Hutton Michael Gough

GLORIA JEAN

1939 THE UNDERPUP
Director: Richard Wallace
Co-stars: Robert Cummings Nan Grey Beulah Bondi

1940 LITTLE BIT OF HEAVEN
Director: Andrew Marton
Co-stars: Robert Stack Stuart Erwin Nan Grey

1940 IF I HAD MY WAY
Director: David Butler
Co-stars: Bing Crosby Charles Winninger El Brendel

1941   **NEVER GIVE A SUCKER AN EVEN BREAK**
Director: Edward Cline
Co-stars: W.C. Fields Ann Miller Leon Errol

1942   **WHEN JOHNNY COMES MARCHING HOME**
Director: Charles Lamont
Co-stars: Donald O'Connor Allan Jones

1942   **GET HEP TO LOVE**
Director: Charles Lamont
Co-stars: Donald O'Connor Peggy Ryan Jane Frazee

1943   **IT COMES UP LOVE**
Director: Charles Lamont
Co-stars: Donald O'Connor Ian Hunter

1943   **MR. BIG**
Director: Charles Lamont
Co-stars: Donald O'Connor Robert Paige Peggy Ryan

1944   **PARDON MY RHYTHM**
Director: Felix Feist
Co-stars: Mel Torme Patric Knowles Evelyn Ankers

1944   **RECKLESS AGE**

1944   **THE GHOST CATCHERS**
Director: Edward Cline
Co-stars: Olsen & Johnson Leo Carillo Andy Devine

1944   **DESTINY**
Director: Reginald Le Borg
Co-stars: Alan Curtis Frank Craven

1945   **I'LL REMEMBER APRIL**
Co-star: Kirby Grant

1945   **RIVER GANG**
Co-star: Keefe Brasselle

1948   **COPACABANA**
Director: Alfred Green
Co-stars: Groucho Marx Carmen Miranda Steve Cochran

1948   **AN OLD FASHIONED GIRL**

1949   **THERE'S A GIRL IN MY HEART**
Director: Arthur Dreyfuss
Co-stars: Lon Chaney Lee Bowman Peggy Ryan

1961   **LADIES' MAN**
Director: Jerry Lewis
Co-stars: Jerry Lewis Helen Traubel George Raft

MARIANNE JEAN-BAPTISTE

1996   **SECRETS AND LIES**
Director: Mike Leigh
Co-stars: Timothy Spall Brenda Blethyn Phyllis Logan

1998   **MR. JEALOUSY**
Co-star: Eric Stoltz

ZIZI JEANMAIRE *(Married Roland Petit)*

1952   **HANS CHRISTIAN ANDERSON**
Director: Charles Vidor
Co-stars: Danny Kaye Farley Granger John Qualen

1956   **ANYTHING GOES**
Director: Robert Lewis
Co-stars: Bing Crosby Donald O'Connor Mitzi Gaynor

1958   **FOLLIES BERGERE**
Director: Henri Decoin
Co-stars: Eddie Constantine Nadia Gray Yves Robert

ISABEL JEANS

1928   **DOWNHILL**
Director: Alfred Hitchcock
Co-stars: Ivor Novello Ben Webster Sybil Rhoda Ian Hunter

1928   **EASY VIRTUE**
Director: Alfred Hitchcock
Co-stars: Franklyn Dyall Ian Hunter Robin Irvine

1935   **THE DICTATOR**
Director: Victor Saville
Co-stars: Clive Brook Madeleine Carroll Emlyn Williams

1935   **THE CROUCHING BEAST**
Director: Victor Hansbury
Co-stars: Fritz Kortner Wynne Gibson Richard Bird

1938   **TOVARICH**
Director: Anatole Litvak
Co-stars: Claudette Colbert Charles Boyer Basil Rathbone

1938   **YOUTH TAKES A FLING**
Director: Archie Mayo
Co-stars: Joel McCrea Andrea Leeds Virginia Grey

1938   **SECRETS OF AN ACTRESS**
Director: William Keighley
Co-stars: Kay Francis George Brent Ian Hunter

1938   **HARD TO GET**
Director: Ray Enright
Co-stars: Dick Powell Charles Winninger Olivia De Havilland

1938   **GARDEN OF THE MOON**
Director: Busby Berkeley
Co-stars: Pat O'Brien John Payne Margaret Lindsay

1938   **FOOLS FOR SCANDAL**
Director: Mervyn Leroy
Co-stars: Carole Lombard Fernand Gravet Ralph Bellamy

1939   **MAN ABOUT TOWN**
Director: Mark Sandrich
Co-stars: Jack Benny Dorothy Lamour Binnie Barnes

1939   **GOOD GIRLS GO TO PARIS**
Director: Alexander Hall
Co-stars: Mervyn Douglas Joan Blondell Alan Curtis

1941   **SUSPICION**
Director: Alfred Hitchcock
Co-stars: Cary Grant Joan Fontaine Nigel Bruce

1941   **BANANA RIDGE**
Director: Walter Mycroft
Co-stars: Robertson Hare Alfred Drayton Nova Pilbeam

1945   **GREAT DAY**
Director: Lance Comfort
Co-stars: Flora Robson Eric Portman Shelia Sim Philip Friend

1948   **ELIZABETH OF LADYMEAD**
Director: Herbert Wilcox
Co-stars: Anna Neagle Hugh Williams Bernard Lee

1958   **GIGI**
Director: Vincente Minnelli
Co-stars: Leslie Caron Maurice Chevalier Louis Jourdan Eva Gabor

1960   **A BREATH OF SCANDAL**
Director: Michael Curtiz
Co-stars: Sophia Loren Maurice Chevalier John Gavin

1963   **HEAVENS ABOVE!**
Director: John Boutling
Co-stars: Peter Sellers Cecil Parker Ian Carmichael

URSULA JEANS

1933   **FRIDAY THE THIRTEENTH**
Director: Victor Saville
Co-stars: Jessie Matthews Edmund Gwenn Frank Lawton

1933   **CAVALCADE**
Director: Frank Lloyd
Co-stars: Clive Brook Diana Wynyard Herbert Mundin

1933   **I LIVED WITH YOU**
Director: Maurice Elvy
Co-stars: Ivor Novello Ida Lupino Jack Hawkins

1936   **THE MAN IN THE MIRROR**
Director: Maurice Elvy
Co-stars: Alastair Sim Genevieve Tobin Garry Marsh

1938   **DARK JOURNEY**
Director: Victor Saville
Co-stars: Conrad Veidt Vivien Leigh Joan Gardner

1938   **OVER THE MOON**
Director: Thornton Freeland
Co-stars: Rex Harrison Merle Oberon Robert Douglas

1938   **STORM IN A TEACUP**
Director: Victor Saville
Co-stars: Rex Harrison Vivien Leigh Cecil Parker

1943   **THE LIFE AND DEATH OF COLONEL BLIMP**
Director: Michael Powell
Co-stars: Roger Livesey Deborah Kerr

1944   **MR. EMMANUEL**
Director: Harold French
Co-stars: Felix Aylmer Greta Gynt Walter Rilla

1946   **GAIETY GEORGE**
Director: George King
Co-stars: Richard Greene Ann Todd Peter Graves Hazel Court

1948   **THE WOMAN IN THE HALL**
Director: Jack Lee
Co-stars: Jean Simmons Cecil Parker Edward Underdown

1948   **THE WEAKER SEX**
Director: Roy Baker
Co-stars: Cecil Parker Joan Hopkins Lana Morris

1954   **THE NIGHT MY NUMBER CAME UP**
Director: Leslie Norman
Co-stars: Michael Redgrave Sheila Sim

1954   **THE DAM BUSTERS**
Director: Michael Anderson
Co-stars: Richard Todd Michael Redgrave Basil Sydney

1959   **NORTHWEST FRONTIER**
Director: J. Lee Thompson
Co-stars: Kenneth More Lauren Bacall Herbert Lom

1961   **THE QUEEN'S GUARDS**
Director: Michael Powell
Co-stars: Raymond Massey Daniel Massey Robert Stephens

1961   **THE GREEN HELMET**
Director: Michael Furlong
Co-stars: Bill Travers Ed Begley Sid James Meg Jenkins

VICTORIA JEE

1975   **ADIOS AMIGO**
Director: Fred Williamson
Co-stars: Fred Williamson Richard Pyror James Brown Mike Henry

BARBARA JEFFORD

1968   **ULYSSES**
Director: Joseph Strick
Co-stars: Maurice Roeves Milo O'Shea T.P. McKenna

1968   **THE SHOES OF THE FISHERMAN**
Director: Michael Anderson
Co-stars: Anthony Quinn Laurence Olivier

1968   **THE BOFORS GUN**
Director: Jack Gold
Co-stars: Nicol Williamson John Thaw David Warner

1970   **LUST FOR A VAMPIRE**
Director: Jimmy Sangster
Co-stars: Ralph Bates Suzannah Leigh Michael Johnson

1983   **AND THE SHIP SAILS ON**
Director: Federico Fellini
Co-stars: Freddie Jones Peter Cellier Janet Suzman

1989   **REUNION**
Director: Jerry Schatzberg
Co-stars: Jason Robards Christien Anholt Samuel West

1991   **WHERE ANGELS FEAR TO TREAD**
Director: Charles Sturridge
Co-stars: Helen Mirren Helena Bonham Carter

1994   **RETURN TO BLOOD RIVER**
Director: Jane Howell
Co-stars: Kevin McNally Samantha Bond Frances Barber

ANNE JEFFREYS

1944   **STEP LIVELY**
Director: Tim Whelan
Co-stars: Frank Sinatra George Murphy Gloria De Haven

1945   **SING YOUR WAY HOME**
Co-star: Jack Haley

1945   **THOSE ENDEARING YOUNG CHARMS**
Director: Lewis Allen
Co-stars: Robert Young Laraine Day Bill Williams

1945   **ZOMBIES ON BROADWAY**
Director: Gordon Douglas
Co-stars: Wally Brown Alan Carney Bela Lugosi

1945   **DICK TRACY**
Director: William Berke
Co-stars: Morgan Conway Mike Mazurki Jane Greer

1945   **DILLINGER**
Director: Max Nosseck
Co-stars: Lawrence Tierney Edmund Lowe Eduardo Cianelli

1946   **DICK TRACY VERSUS CUEBALL**
Director: Gordon Douglas
Co-stars: Morgan Conway Rita Corday Lyle Latell

1946   **DING DONG WILLIAMS**
Co-star: Glenn Vernon

1946   **GENIUS AT WORK**
Director: Leslie Goodwins
Co-stars: Wally Brown Alan Carney Bela Lugosi

1946   **STEP BY STEP**
Director: Phil Rosen
Co-stars: Lawrence Tierney George Cleveland Lowell Gilmore

1948   **TRAIL STREET**
Director: Ray Enright
Co-stars: Randolph Scott Robert Ryan George "Gabby" Hayes

1948   **RIFFRAFF**
Director: Ted Tetzlaff
Co-stars: Pat O'Brien Walter Slezak Percy Kilbride

1948   **RETURN OF THE BAD MEN**
Director: Ray Enright
Co-stars: Randolph Scott Robert Ryan Steve Brodie

1962   **BOYS' NIGHT OUT**
Director: Michael Gordon
Co-stars: James Garner Kim Novak Tony Randall

1968   **PANIC IN THE CITY**
Director: Eddie Davis
Co-stars: Howard Duff Linda Cristal Dennis Hopper

FRAN JEFFRIES

1964   **SEX AND THE SINGLE GIRL**
Director: Richard Quine
Co-stars: Natalie Wood Tony Curtis Henry Fonda

1965 HARUM SCARUM
Director: Gene Nelson
Co-stars: Elvis Presley Mary Ann Mobley Michael Ansara

EDITH JEHANE
1927 THE LOVE OF JEANNE NEY
Director: G. W. Pabst
Co-stars: Uno Henning Fritz Rasp Brigitte Helm

ANNA JEMISON
1981 HEATWAVE
Director: Philip Noyce
Co-stars: Judy Davis Richard Moir Chris Hayward

1981 SMASH PALACE
Director: Roger Donaldson
Co-stars: Bruno Lawrence Greer Robson Les Kelly

1984 SILVER CITY
Director: Sophia Turkewicz
Co-stars: Gosia Dobrowolska Ivar Kants Steve Bisley

1984 MY FIRST WIFE
Director: Paul Cox
Co-stars: John Hargreaves Wendy Hughes Lucy Angwin

VIRGINIA JENCKS
1953 SALT OF THE EARTH
Director: Herbert Biberman
Co-stars: Juan Chacon Will Geer Mervin Williams

CAROL MAYO JENKINS
1983 HAPPY ENDINGS
Director: Jerry Thorpe
Co-stars: Lee Montgomery Jill Schoelen Laura Dern

MEGS JENKINS
1943 MILLIONS LIKE US
Director: Sidney Gilliat
Co-stars: Patricia Roc Gordon Jackson Eric Portman

1946 GREEN FOR DANGER
Director: Sidney Gilliat
Co-stars: Alastair Sim Sally Gray Trevor Howard

1948 A BOY, A GIRL AND A BIKE
Director: Ralph Smart
Co-stars: Honor Blackman John McCallum Diana Dors

1949 THE HISTORY OF MR. POLLY
Director: Anthony Pelissier
Co-stars: John Mills Sally Ann Howes Finlay Currie

1950 THE MONKEY'S PAW

1951 THE SECRET PEOPLE
Director: Thorold Dickinson
Co-stars: Valentina Cortesa Audrey Hepburn Athene Seyler

1951 WHITE CORRIDORS
Director: Pat Jackson
Co-stars: James Donald Googie Withers Petula Clark

1952 ROUGH SHOOT
Director: Robert Parrish
Co-stars: Joel McCrea Evelyn Keyes Herbert Lom

1953 TROUBLE IN STORE
Director: John Paddy Carstairs
Co-stars: Norman Wisdom Lana Morris Jerry Desmonde

1954 THE GAY DOG
Director: Maurice Elvy
Co-stars: Wilfred Pickles Petula Clark John Blythe

1958 INDISCREET
Director: Stanley Donen
Co-stars: Cary Grant Ingrid Bergman Phyllis Calvert

1959 TIGER BAY
Director: J. Lee Thompson
Co-stars: Hayley Mills John Mills Horst Buchholz

1960 CONSPIRACY OF HEARTS
Director: Ralph Thomas
Co-stars: Lilli Palmer Sylvia Syms Yvonne Mitchell

1961 THE GREEN HELMET
Director: Michael Forlong
Co-stars: Bill Travers Ed Begley Nancy Walters

1961 THE INNOCENTS
Director: Jack Clayton
Co-stars: Deborah Kerr Pamela Franklin Michael Redgrave

1962 LIFE FOR RUTH
Director: Basil Dearden
Co-stars: Michael Craig Janet Munro Patrick McGoohan

1964 MURDER MOST FOUL
Director: George Pollock
Co-stars: Margaret Rutherford Ron Moody James Bolam

1965 BUNNY LAKE IS MISSING
Director: Otto Preminger
Co-stars: Laurence Olivier Carol Lynley Noel Coward

1968 OLIVER !
Director: Carol Reed
Co-stars: Mark Lester Ron Moody Oliver Reed

1972 ASYLUM
Director: Roy Ward Baker
Co-stars: Robert Powell Richard Todd Charlotte Rampling

1976 THE AMOROUS MILKMAN
Director: Derren Nesbitt
Co-stars: Brendan Price Julie Ege Diana Dors

REBECCA JENKINS
1989 BYE BYE BLUES
Director: Anne Wheeler
Co-stars: Michael Ontkean Stuart Margolin Luke Reilly

1991 TILL DEATH US DO PART
Director: Yves Simoneau
Co-stars: Treat Williams Arliss Howard Embeth Davidtz

1992 BOB ROBERTS
Director: Tim Robbins
Co-stars: Tim Robbins Giancarlo Esposito Ray Wise Alan Rickman

ANAIS JEANNERET
1985 DEATH IN A FRENCH GARDEN
Director: Michel Deville
Co-stars: Richard Bohringer Nicole Garcia Anemone

1993 SALT ON OUR SKIN
Director: Andrew Birkin
Co-stars: Greta Scacchi Vincent D'Onofrio Claudine Auger

LUCINDA JENNEY
1988 RAIN MAN
Director: Barry Levinson
Co-stars: Dustin Hoffman Tom Cruise Valeria Golino

1989 WIRED
Director: Larry Pearce
Co-stars: Michael Chiklist Patti D'Arbanville Ray Sharkey

1991 VIGILANTE COP
Director: Mel Damski
Co-stars: Alex McArthur Dale Midkiff Terry O'Quinn

1991 THELMA AND LOUISE
Director: Ridley Scott
Co-stars: Geena Davis Susan Sarandon Harvey Keitel

1992   THE HABITATION OF DRAGONS
Director: Michael Lindsay Hogg
Co-stars: Brad Davis Maureen O'Sullivan

1993   AMERICAN HEART
Director: Martin Bell
Co-stars: Jeff Bridges Edward Furlong Don Harvey

1993   MATINEE
Director: Joe Dante
Co-stars: John Goodman Cathy Moriarty Simon Fenton

CLAUDIA JENNINGS

1972   THE UNHOLY ROLLERS
Director: Vernon Zimmerman
Co-stars: Louis Quinn Roberta Collins Alan Vint

1974   TRUCK STOP WOMEN
Director: Mark Lester
Co-stars: Lieux Dressler John Martino Dolores Dorn

1976   THE GREAT TEXAS DYNAMITE CHASE
Director: Michael Pressman
Co-stars: Jocelyn Jones Johnny Crawford

1978   DEATHSPORT
Director: Henry Suso
Co-stars: David Carradine Richard Lynch William Smithers

PATRICE JENNINGS

1989   SOCIETY
Director: Brian Yuzna
Co-stars: Bill Warlock Devin Devasquez Evan Richards

SALOME JENS

1960   ANGEL BABY
Director: Paul Wendkos
Co-stars: George Hamilton Joan Blondell Mercedes McCambridge

1965   THE FOOL KILLER
Director: Servando Gonzales
Co-stars: Anthony Perkins Edward Albert Henry Hull

1966   SECONDS
Director: John Frankenheimer
Co-stars: Rock Hudson John Randolph Will Geer

1969   ME, NATALIE
Director: Fred Coe
Co-stars: Patty Duke James Farantino Elsa Lanchester

1972   SAVAGES
Director: James Ivory
Co-stars: Louis Stadlen Anne Francine Susan Blakely

1978   CLOUD DANCER
Director: Barry Brown
Co-stars: David Carradine Jennifer O'Neill Joseph Bottoms

1983   UNCOMMON VALOUR
Director: Rod Amateau
Co-stars: Mitchell Ryan Ben Murphy Barbara Parkins

1986   JUST BETWEEN FRIENDS
Director: Allan Burns
Co-stars: Mary Tyler Moore Ted Danson Christine Lahti

CLEO JENSEN

1968   ELVIRA MADIGAN
Director: Bo Widerberg
Co-stars: Thommy Berggren Pia Degermark Lennart Malmer

EULALIE JENSEN

1925   THE THUNDERING HERD
Director: William Howard
Co-stars: Jack Holt Lois Wilson Tim McCoy

MAREN JENSEN

1972   THE SALZBURG CONNECTION
Director: Lee Katzin
Co-stars: Barry Newman Anna Karina Klaus Maria Brandauer

1981   DEADLY BLESSING
Director: Wes Craven
Co-stars: Susan Buckner Ernest Borgnine Lois Nettleton

HELEN JEPSON

1938   THE GOLDWYN FOLLIES
Director: George Marshall
Co-stars: Kenny Baker Vera Zorina Adolphe Menjou

ADELE JERGENS

1945   1001 NIGHTS
Director: Alfred Green
Co-stars: Cornell Wilde Phil Silvers Evelyn Keyes

1946   SHE WOULDN'T SAY YES
Director: Alexander Hall
Co-stars: Rosalind Russell Lee Bowman Charles Winninger

1948   I LOVE TROUBLE
Director: S. Sylvan Simon
Co-stars: Franchot Tone Janet Blair Janis Carter

1948   DOWN TO EARTH
Director: Alexander Hall
Co-stars: Rita Hayworth Larry Parks Roland Culver

1948   THE CORPSE CAME C.O.D.
Director: Henry Levin
Co-stars: George Brent Joan Blondell Jim Bannon

1948   BLONDIE'S ANNIVERSARY
Director: Abby Berlin
Co-stars: Penny Singleton Arthur Lake Larry Simms

1948   THE DARK PAST
Director: Rudolph Mate
Co-stars: William Holden Lee J. Cobb Nina Foch

1948   THE WOMAN FROM TANGIER
Co-stars: Michael Duane Donna Demario

1948   THE FULLER BRUSH MAN
Director: S. Sylvan Simon
Co-stars: Red Skelton Janet Blair Don McGuire

1948   THE PRINCE OF THIEVES
Director: Howard Bretherton
Co-stars: Jon Hall Patricia Morison

1949   TREASURE OF MONTE CRISTO
Director: William Berke
Co-stars: Glenn Langan Steve Brodie Michael Whalen

1949   LADIES OF THE CHORUS
Director: Phil Karlson
Co-stars: Marilyn Monroe Rand Brooks

1949   CRIME DOCTOR'S DIARY
Director: Seymour Friedman
Co-stars: Warner Baxter Lois Maxwell

1950   ARMOURED CAR ROBBERY
Director: Richard Fleischer
Co-stars: Charles McGraw William Talman

1950   BEWARE OF BLONDIE
Director: Edward Bernds
Co-stars: Penny Singleton Arthur Lake Dick Wessel

1950   EDGE OF DOOM
Director: Mark Robson
Co-stars: Dana Andrews Farley Granger Joan Evans Robert Keith

1951   SHOW BOAT
Director: George Sidney
Co-stars: Howard Keel Kathryn Grayson Ava Gardner

1951 SUGARFOOT
Director: Edwin Marin
Co-stars: Randolph Scott Raymond Massey Arthur Hunnicutt

1951 TRY AND GET ME
Director: Cyril Endfield
Co-stars: Frank Lovejoy Kathleen Ryan Lloyd Bridges

1951 ABBOTT AND COSTELLO MEET THE INVISIBLE MAN
Director: Charles Lamont
Co-stars: Abbott & Costello Nancy Guild Arthur Franz

1952 AARON SLICK FROM PUMPKIN CREEK
Director: Claude Binyon
Co-stars: Alan Young Dinah Shore

1952 SOMEBODY LOVES ME
Director: Irving Brecher
Co-stars: Betty Hutton Ralph Meeker Robert Keith

1954 FIREMAN SAVE MY CHILD
Director: Leslie Goodwins
Co-stars: Buddy Hackett Hugh O'Brian Spike Jones

1954 THE MIAMI STORY
Director: Fred Sears
Co-stars: Barry Sullivan Luther Adler Beverly Garland

1955 THE COBWEB
Director: Vincente Minnelli
Co-stars: Richard Widmark Lauren Bacall Charles Boyer John Kerr

1956 THE DAY THE WORLD ENDED
Director: Roger Corman
Co-stars: Richard Denning Lori Nelson Mike Connors

DIANE JERGENS
1959 THE F.B.I. STORY
Director: Mervyn LeRoy
Co-stars: James Stewart Vera Miles Murray Hamilton

MARY JERROLD
1930 THE W PLAN
Director: Victor Saville
Co-stars: Brian Aherne Madeleine Carroll Gordon Harker

1933 FRIDAY THE THIRTEENTH
Director: Victor Saville
Co-stars: Jessie Matthews Edmund Gwenn Sonnie Hale

1934 DOCTOR'S ORDERS
Director: Norman Lee
Co-stars: Leslie Fuller John Mills Ronald Shiner

1942 TALK ABOUT JACQUELINE
Director: Harold French
Co-stars: Hugh Williams Carla Lehman Joyce Howard

1943 THE GENTLE SEX
Director: Leslie Howard
Co-stars: Rosamund John Joan Greenwood Lilli Palmer

1944 THE WAY AHEAD
Director: Carol Reed
Co-stars: David Niven Stanley Holloway William Hartnell

1946 THE MAGIC BOW
Director: Bernard Knowles
Co-stars: Stewart Granger Phyllis Calvert Jean Kent

1947 THE GHOSTS OF BERKELEY SQUARE
Director: Vernon Sewell
Co-stars: Robert Morley Claude Hulbert

1948 MR. PERRIN AND MR. TRAILL
Director: Lawrence Huntington
Co-stars: Marius Goring David Farrar Greta Gynt

1948 THE QUEEN OF SPADES
Director: Thorold Dickinson
Co-stars: Edith Evans Anton Walbrook Yvonne Mitchell

1948 THE WOMAN HATER
Director: Terence Young
Co-stars: Stewart Granger Edwige Feuillere Ronald Squire

1949 MARRY ME
Director: Terence Fisher
Co-stars: Derek Bond Susan Shaw Carol Marsh

1950 SHE SHALL HAVE MURDER
Director: Daniel Birt
Co-stars: Rosamund John Derrick De Marney Felix Aylmer

PATRICIA JESSEL
1958 THE FLESH IS WEAK
Director: Don Chaffey
Co-stars: John Derek Milly Vitale William Franklyn

1958 THE MAN UPSTAIRS
Director: Don Chaffey
Co-stars: Richard Attenborough Donald Houston Bernard Lee

1960 CITY OF THE DEAD
Director: John Moxey
Co-stars: Betta St. John Christopher Lee Dennis Lotis

1966 A FUNNY THING HAPPENED ON THE WAY TO THE FORUM
Director: Richard Lester
Co-stars: Zero Mostel Phil Silvers Buster Keaton

JOAN JETT
1988 LIGHT OF DAY
Director: Paul Schrader
Co-stars: Michael J. Fox Gena Rowlands Michael McKean

GERI JEWELL
1982 TWO OF A KIND
Director: Roger Young
Co-stars: George Burns Robby Benson Cliff Robertson

ISABEL JEWELL
1933 BOMBSHELL
Director: Hunt Stromberg
Co-stars: Jean Harlow Lee Tracy Frank Morgan

1933 COUNSELLOR-AT-LAW
Director: William Wyler
Co-stars: John Barrymore Bebe Daniels Melvyn Douglas

1933 DESIGN FOR LIVING
Director: Ernst Lubitsch
Co-stars: Fredric March Gary Cooper Miriam Hopkins

1933 ADVICE TO THE LOVELORN
Director: Alfred Werker
Co-stars: Lee Tracy Sally Blane Sterling Holloway

1934 MANHATTAN MELODRAMA
Director: W.S. Van Dyke
Co-stars: Clark Gable William Powell Myrna Loy

1934 LET'S BE RITZY
Co-stars: Lew Ayres Frank McHugh

1934 EVELYN PRENTICE
Director: William Howard
Co-stars: Myrna Loy William Powell Rosalind Russell

1935 THE CASINO MURDER CASE
Director: Edwin Marin
Co-stars: Paul Lukas Rosalind Russell Eric Blore

1935 CEILING ZERO
Director: Howard Hawks
Co-stars: James Cagney Pat O'Brien June Travis

1935 MAD LOVE
Director: Karl Freund
Co-stars: Peter Lorre Frances Drake Colin Clive

1935   **SHADOW OF DOUBT**
Director: George Seitz
Co-stars: Ricardo Cortez Virginia Bruce Constance Collier

1935   **TIMES SQUARE LADY**
Director: George Seitz
Co-stars: Robert Taylor Virginia Bruce Pinky Tomlin

1936   **SMALL TOWN GIRL**
Director: William Wellman
Co-stars: Janet Gaynor Robert Taylor James Stewart

1936   **VALLIANT IS THE WORD FOR CARRIE**
Director: Wesley Ruggles
Co-stars: Gladys George John Howard

1936   **GO WEST YOUNG MAN**
Director: Henry Hathaway
Co-stars: Mae West Randolph Scott Warren William

1936   **CAREER WOMAN**
Director: Lewis Seiler
Co-stars: Claire Trevor Michael Whalen Eric Linden

1936   **BIG BROWN EYES**
Director: Walter Wanger
Co-stars: Cary Grant Joan Bennett Walter Pidgeon

1936   **THE MAN WHO LIVED TWICE**
Director: Harry Lachman
Co-stars: Ralph Bellamy Marian Marsh Nan Bryant

1938   **LOST HORIZON**
Director: Frank Capra
Co-stars: Ronald Colman Jane Wyatt Thomas Mitchell

1938   **MARKED WOMAN**
Director: Lloyd Bacon
Co-stars: Bette Davis Humphrey Bogart Jane Bryan

1938   **SWING IT SAILOR**
Co-star: Wallace Ford

1939   **GONE WITH THE WIND**
Director: Victor Fleming
Co-stars: Clark Gable Vivien Leigh Leslie Howard

1940   **IRENE**
Director: Herbert Wilcox
Co-stars: Anna Neagle Ray Milland Roland Young

1943   **THE SEVENTH VICTIM**
Director: Mark Robson
Co-stars: Kim Hunter Tom Conway Hugh Beaumont

1943   **THE LEOPARD MAN**
Director: Jacques Tourneur
Co-stars: Dennis O'Keefe Jean Brooks Margo

1944   **THE MERRY MONAHANS**
Director: Charles Lamont
Co-stars: Donald O'Connor Peggy Ryan Jack Oakie

1948   **THE LADY OF DECEIT**
Director: Robert Wise
Co-stars: Lawrence Tierney Claire Trevor Walter Slezak

1973   **CIAO MANHATTAN**
Director: John Palmer
Co-stars: Edie Sedgwick Wesley Hayes Paul America

JULIE JEZEQUEL

1982   **L'ETOILE DU NORD**
Director: Pierre Granier-Deferre
Co-stars: Simone Signoret Philippe Noiret

ANN JILLIAN (Child)

1962   **GYPSY**
Director: Mervyn LeRoy
Co-stars: Rosalind Russell Natalie Wood Karl Malden

1982   **MAE WEST**
Director: Lee Philips
Co-stars: James Brolin Roddy McDowall Piper Laurie

1983   **DEATH RIDE TO OSAKA**
Director: Jonathan Kaplan
Co-stars: Jennifer Jason Leigh Carolyn Seymour Mako

1983   **MR.MUM**
Director: Stan Dragoti
Co-stars: Michael Keaton Teri Garr Martin Mull

1985   **THIS WIFE FOR HIRE**
Director: James Drake
Co-stars: Pam Dawber Robert Klein Laraine Newman

1988   **PERRY MASON:**
       THE CASE OF THE MURDERED MADAM
Director: Ron Satloff
Co-stars: Raymond Burr William Katt

1988   **THE ANN JILLIAN STORY**
Director: Corey Allen
Co-stars: Tony Lo Bianco Viveca Lindfors Pam Hyatt

1989   **LITTLE WHITE LIES**
Director: Anson Williams
Co-stars: Tim Matheson Amy Yasbeck Marc McClure

1989   **ORIGINAL SIN**
Director: Ron Satlof
Co-stars: Charlton Heston Robert Desiderio Louis Guss

1994   **HEART OF A CHILD**
Director: Sandor Stern
Co-stars: Bruce Greenwood Michele Green

1994   **THE DISAPPEARANCE OF VONNIE**
Director: Graeme Campbell
Co-star: Joe Penny

1995   **IT WAS HIM OR US**
Director: Robert Iscove
Co-stars: Richard Grieco Monique Lanier

1995   **FAST COMPANY**
Director: Gary Nelson
Co-star: Tim Matheson

YOLANDA JILOT

1993   **J.F.K.: RECKLESS YOUTH**
Director: Harry Winer
Co-stars: Patrick Dempsey Terry Kenney

BETTY JINETTE

1988   **THE WOO WOO KID**
Director: Phil Alden Robinson
Co-stars: Patrick Dempsey Talia Balsam Beverly D'Angelo

CLOTHILDE JOANO

1960   **LES BONNES FEMMES**
Director: Claude Chabrol
Co-stars: Stephane Audran Bernadette Lafont Claude Berri

MARLENE JOBART

1970   **THE RIDER ON THE RAIN**
Director: Rene Clement
Co-stars: Charles Bronson Jill Ireland Annie Cordy

1971   **SINK OR SWIM**
Director: Jean-Paul Rappeneau
Co-stars: Jean-Paul Belmondo Laura Antonelli

1971   **CATCH ME A SPY**
Director: Dick Clement
Co-stars: Kirk Douglas Trevor Howard Tom Courtenay

1975 THE EVIL TRAP
Director: Yves Boissett
Co-stars: Tomas Millian Michel Lonsdale Jean Bouise

1979 THE POLICE WAR
Director: Robin Davis
Co-star: Claude Brasseur

ZITA JOHANN

1931 THE STRUGGLE
Director: D.W. Griffith
Co-stars: Hal Skelly Charlotte Wynters Jackson Halliday

1932 TIGER SHARK
Director: Howard Hawks
Co-stars: Edward G. Robinson J. Carrol Naish Richard Arlen

1932 THE MUMMY
Director: Karl Freund
Co-stars: Boris Karloff David Manners Arthur Byron

1933 THE MAN WHO DARED
Director: Hamilton McFadden
Co-stars: Preston Foster Joan Marsh Irene Biller

1933 LUXURY LINER
Director: Lothar Mendes
Co-stars: George Brent Vivienne Osborne Alice White

1933 THE SIN OF NORMA MORAN
Co-star: Paul Cavanagh

1934 GRAND CANARY
Director: Irving Cummings
Co-stars: Warner Baxter Madge Evans Marjorie Rambeau

AZIZI JOHARI

1976 THE KILLING OF A CHINESE BOOKIE
Director: John Cassavetes
Co-stars: Ben Gazzara Seymour Cassel

MARGARET JOHN

1992 ELENYA
Director: Steve Gough
Co-stars: Pascale Delafouge Jones Seiriol Tomos

ROSAMUND JOHN

1934 THE SECRET OF THE LOCH
Director: Milton Rosmer
Co-stars: Seymour Hicks Nancy O'Neil Gibson Gowland

1942 THE FIRST OF THE FEW
Director: Leslie Howard
Co-stars: Leslie Howard David Niven Roland Culver David Horne

1943 THE GENTLE SEX
Director: Leslie Howard
Co-stars: Joan Greenwood Lilli Palmer John Justin

1943 THE LAMP STILL BURNS
Director: Maurice Elvy
Co-stars: Stewart Granger Godfrey Tearle John Laurie

1944 TAWNY PIPIT
Director: Bernard Miles
Co-stars: Bernard Miles Niall McGinnis Jean Gillie Lucie Mannheim

1945 THE WAY TO THE STARS
Director: Anthony Asquith
Co-stars: Michael Redgrave John Mills Renee Asherson

1946 GREEN FOR DANGER
Director: Sidney Gilliatt
Co-stars: Alastair Sim Sally Gray Trevor Howard

1948 THE UPTURNED GLASS
Co-stars: Lawrence Huntingdon
Co-stars: James Mason Pamela Kellino Henry Oscar

1948 FAME IS THE SPUR
Director: Roy Boutling
Co-stars: Michael Redgrave Bernard Miles Carla Lehman

1948 WHEN THE BOUGH BREAKS
Director: Lawrence Huntington
Co-stars: Patricia Roc Bill Owen Patrick Holt

1949 NO PLACE FOR JENNIFER
Director: Henry Cass
Co-stars: Leo Genn Janette Scott Beatrice Campbell

1950 SHE SHALL HAVE MURDER
Director: Daniel Birt
Co-stars: Derrick De Marney Mary Jerrold Joyce Heron

1952 NEVER LOOK BACK
Director: Francis Searle
Co-stars: Hugh Sinclair Guy Middleton Terence Longden

1953 STREET CORNER
Director: Muriel Box
Co-stars: Anne Crawford Peggy Cummins Barbara Murray

ALEXANDRA JOHNES

1990 THE NEVERENDING STORY II: THE NEXT CHAPTER
Director: George Miller
Co-stars: Jonathan Brandis Kenny Morrison

GLYNIS JOHNS *(Daughter Of Mervyn Johns)*
Nominated For Best Supporting Actress In 1960 For "The Sundowners"

1938 MURDER IN THE FAMILY
Director: Al Parker
Co-stars: Barry Jones Jessica Tandy Evelyn Ankers

1938 SOUTH RIDING
Director: Victor Saville
Co-stars: Edna Best Ralph Richardson Edmund Gwenn

1940 UNDER YOUR HAT
Director: Maurice Elvy
Co-stars: Jack Hulbert Cicely Courtneidge Cecil Parker

1941 FORTY-NINTH PARALLEL
Director: Michael Powell
Co-stars: Laurence Olivier Eric Portman Leslie Howard

1943 THE ADVENTURES OF TARTU
Director: Harold Bucquet
Co-stars: Robert Donat Valerie Hobson Walter Rilla

1944 THE HALFWAY HOUSE
Director: Basil Dearden
Co-stars: Mervyn Johns Tom Walls Sally Ann Howes

1945 PERFECT STRANGERS
Director: Alexander Korda
Co-stars: Robert Donat Deborah Kerr Ann Todd

1946 THIS MAN IS MINE
Director: Marcel Varnel
Co-stars: Tom Walls Hugh McDermott Nova Pilbeam

1948 FRIEDA
Director: Basil Dearden
Co-stars: Mai Zetterling David Farrar Flora Robson

1948 MIRANDA
Director: Ken Annakin
Co-stars: Griffith Jones Googie Withers David Tomlinson

1948 AN IDEAL HUSBAND
Director: Alexander Korda
Co-stars: Paulette Goddard Michael Wilding Hugh Williams

1949 DEAR MR. PROHACK
Director: Thornton Freeland
Co-stars: Cecil Parker Hermione Baddely Dirk Bogarde

1949 THIRD TIME LUCKY
Director: Gordon Parry
Co-stars: Dermot Walsh Charles Goldner Yvonne Owen

1950 STATE SECRET
Director: Sidney Gilliatt
Co-stars: Douglas Fairbanks Jack Hawkins Herbert Lom

1951 FLESH AND BLOOD
Director: Anthony Kimmins
Co-stars: Richard Todd Joan Greenwood Andre Morell

1951 ENCORE
Director: Pat Jackson
Co-stars: Nigel Patrick Roland Culver Kay Walsh

1951 APPOINTMENT WITH VENUS
Director: Ralph Thomas
Co-stars: David Niven Kenneth More Noel Purcell

1951 THE MAGIC BOX
Director: John Boulting
Co-stars: Robert Donat Maria Schell Emlyn Williams

1951 NO HIGHWAY
Director: Henry Koster
Co-stars: James Stewart Marlene Dietrich Jack Hawkins

1952 THE CARD
Director: Ronald Neame
Co-stars: Alec Guinness Petula Clark Valerie Hobson

1952 THE SWORD AND THE ROSE
Director: Ken Annakin
Co-stars: Richard Todd James Robertson Justice

1953 ROB ROY, THE HIGHLAND ROGUE
Director: Harold French
Co-stars: Richard Todd Michael Gough Finlay Currie

1953 THE WEAK AND THE WICKED
Director: J. Lee Thompson
Co-stars: Diana Dors Jane Hyton John Gregson

1953 PERSONAL AFFAIR
Director: Anthony Pelissier
Co-stars: Leo Genn Gene Tierney Pamela Brown

1954 THE SEEKERS
Director: Ken Annakin
Co-stars: Jack Hawkins Noel Purcell Laya Raki

1954 MAD ABOUT MEN
Director: Ralph Thomas
Co-stars: Donald Sinden Margaret Rutherford Anne Crawford

1955 JOSEPHINE AND MEN
Director: Roy Boulting
Co-stars: Jack Buchanan Donald Sinden Peter Finch

1955 THE BEACHCOMBER
Director: Muriel Box
Co-stars: Robert Newton Donald Sinden Donald Pleasence

1955 THE COURT JESTER
Director: Melvyn Frank
Co-stars: Danny Kaye Basil Rathbone Cecil Parker

1956 AROUND THE WORLD IN EIGHTY DAYS
Director: Michael Anderson
Co-stars: David Niven Robert Newton Cantinflas

1956 LOSER TAKES ALL
Director: Ken Annakin
Co-stars: Rossano Brazzi Robert Morley Tony Britton

1958 THE DAY THEY GAVE BABIES AWAY
Director: Allen Reisner
Co-stars: Cameron Mitchell Ernest Truex

1958 ANOTHER TIME, ANOTHER PLACE
Director: Lewis Allen
Co-stars: Sean Connery Lana Turner Barry Sullivan

1959 SHALE HANDS WITH THE DEVIL
Director: Michael Anderson
Co-stars: James Cagney Don Murray Richard Harris

1960 THE SPIDER'S WEB
Director: Godfrey Grayson
Co-stars: John Justin Jack Hulbert

1960 THE SUNDOWNERS
Director: Fred Zinnemann
Co-stars: Robert Mitchum Deborah Kerr Peter Ustinov

1962 THE CHAPMAN REPORT
Director: George Cukor
Co-stars: Shelley Winters Claire Bloom Jane Fonda

1962 THE CABINET OF DR. CALIGARI
Director: Roger Kay
Co-stars: Dan O'Herlihy Dick Cavalos Constance Ford

1963 PAPA'S DELICATE CONDITION
Director: George Marshall
Co-stars: Jackie Gleason Charles Ruggles

1964 MARY POPPINS
Director: Robert Stevenson
Co-stars: Julie Andrews David Tomlinson Dick Van Dyke

1965 DEAR BRIGITTE
Director: Henry Koster
Co-stars: James Stewart Fabian Brigitte Bardot

1968 DON'T JUST STAND THERE
Director: Ron Winston
Co-stars: Mary Tyler Moore Robert Wagner Harvey Korman

1969 LOCK UP YOUR DAUGHTERS
Director: Peter Coe
Co-stars: Christopher Plummer Susannah York Tom Bell

1971 UNDER MILK WOOD
Director: Andrew Sinclair
Co-stars: Richard Burton Elizabeth Taylor

1973 VAULT OF HORROR
Director: Roy Ward Baker
Co-stars: Daniel Massey Anna Massey Curt Jurgens

1984 MURDER FOR TWO
Director: Larry Elikan
Co-stars: Michael Nouri James Cromwell

1988 ZELLY AND ME
Director: Tina Rathbone
Co-stars: Isabella Rossellini David Lynch

1994 HOSTILE HOSTAGES
Director: Ted Demme
Co-stars: Judy Davis Kevin Spacey Denis Leary

HARIETTE JOHNS

1948 AN IDEAL HUSBAND
Director: Alexander Korda
Co-stars: Paulette Goddard Michael Wilding Hugh Williams

1954 MEET MR. CALLAGHAN
Director: Charles Saunders
Co-stars: Derrick De Marney Adrienne Corri Belinda Lee

MARION JOHNS

1979 ALISON'S BIRTHDAY
Director: Ian Coughlan
Co-stars: Joanne Samuel Lou Brown Vincent Ball

TRACY CAMILLA JOHNS

1986 SHE'S GOTTA HAVE IT
Director: Spike Lee
Co-stars: Spike Lee Tommy Redmond Hicks Joie Lee

1991 NEW JACK CITY
Director: Mario Van Peebles
Co-stars: Wesley Snipes Bill Nunn Judd Nelson

A. J. JOHNSON

1990 HOUSE PARTY
Director: Reginald Hudlin
Co-stars: Christopher Reid Robin Harris Tisha Campbell

1991 DYING YOUNG
Director: Joel Schumacher
Co-stars: Julia Roberts Campbell Scott Colleen Dewhurst

ANNE-MARIE JOHNSON

1988 HOLLYWOOD SHUFFLE
Director: Robert Townsend
Co-stars: Robert Townsend Starletta Dupois Helen Martin

1991 TRUE IDENTITY
Director: Charles Lane
Co-stars: Charles Lane Lenny Henry Frank Langella J.T. Walsh

1992 THE FIVE HEARTBEATS
Director: Robert Townsend
Co-stars: Michael Wright Leon

ARIYAN JOHNSON

1992 JUST ANOTHER GIRL ON THE IRT
Director: Leslie Harris
Co-stars: Kevin Thigpen Ebony Jerido

BEVERLY JOHNSON

1979 ASHANTI
Director: Richard Fleischer
Co-stars: Michael Caine Peter Ustinov Rex Harrison

CARMEL JOHNSON

1993 BAD BOY BUBBY
Director: Rolf De Heer
Co-stars: Nicholas Hope Claire Benito Natalie Carr

CAROLINE LEE JOHNSON

1991 WHO NEEDS A HEART?
Director: John Akomfrah
Co-stars: Caroline Burghard Treva Etienne Ruth Gemmell

CELIA JOHNSON
Nominated For Best Actress In 1945 For "Brief Encounter"

1942 IN WHICH WE SERVE
Director: David Lean
Co-stars: Noel Coward Bernard Miles John Mills

1943 DEAR OCTOPUS
Director: Harold French
Co-stars: Margaret Lockwood Michael Wilding Roland Culver

1944 THIS HAPPY BREED
Director: David Lean
Co-stars: Robert Newton Stanley Holoway John Mils

1945 BRIEF ENCOUNTER
Director: David Lean
Co-stars: Trevor Howard Stanley Holoway Joyce Carey

1949 THE ASTONISHED HEART
Director: Terence Fisher
Co-stars: Noel Coward Margaret Leighton Joyce Carey

1952 THE HOLLY AND THE IVY
Director: George More O'Ferrall
Co-stars: Ralph Richardson Margaret Leighton

1952 I BELIEVE IN YOU
Director: Basil Dearden
Co-stars: Cecil Parker Laurence Harvey Joan Collins

1953 THE CAPTAIN'S PARADISE
Director: Anthony Kimmins
Co-stars: Alec Guinness Yvonne De Carlo Bill Fraser

1955 A KID FOR TWO FARTHINGS
Director: Carol Reed
Co-stars: Diana Dors David Kossoff Brenda De Banzie

1958 THE GOOD COMPANIONS
Director: J. Lee Thompson
Co-stars: Eric Portman Janette Scott Hugh Griffith

1969 THE PRIME OF MISS JEAN BRODIE
Director: Ronald Neame
Co-stars: Maggie Smith Pamela Franklin Robert Stephens

1978 LES MISERABLES
Director: Glenn Jordan
Co-stars: Richard Jordan Anthony Perkins Cyril Cusack

1980 STAYING ON
Director: Silvio Narizzano
Co-star: Trevor Howard

EDNA JOHNSON

1942 THE LIVING GHOST
Co-stars: James Dunn George Eldredge Jan Whiley

GEORGANN JOHNSON

1958 SHORT CUT TO HELL
Director: James Cagney
Co-stars: Robert Ivers Murvin Vye William Bishop

1986 KATE'S SECRET
Director: Arthur Allan Seidelman
Co-stars: Meredith Baxter-Birney Ben Masters Ed Asner

1992 A HOUSE OF SECRETS AND LIES
Director: Paul Schneider
Co-stars: Connie Selleca Kevin Dobson

HELEN JOHNSON

1930 CHILDREN OF PLEASURE
Co-stars: Kenneth Thompson Lawrence Gray

JUNE JOHNSON

1938 DOUBLE DANGER
Co-stars: Preston Foster Arthur Lake

1941 GANGS OF SONORA
Co-stars: Robert Livinstone Bob Steele

KATIE JOHNSON

1936 LABURNUM GROVE
Director: Carol Reed
Co-stars: Cedric Hardwicke Edmund Gwenn Victoria Hopper

1938 THE LAST ADVENTURERS
Director: Roy Kellino
Co-stars: Niall MacGinnis Linden Travers Kay Walsh

1938 DUSTY ERMINE
Director: Bernard Vorhaus
Co-stars: Jane Baxter Anthony Bushell Margaret Rutherford

1952 I BELIEVE IN YOU
Director: Basil Dearden
Co-stars: Celia Johnson Joan Collins Cecil Parker

1954 THE DELAVINE AFFAIR
Director: Douglas Pierce
Co-stars: Honor Blackman Peter Reynolds Gordon Jackson

1955 THE LADYKILLERS
Director: Alexander MacKendrick
Co-stars: Alec Guinness Peter Sellers Herbert Lom

1958 HOW TO MURDER A RICH UNCLE
Director: Nigel Patrick
Co-stars: Nigel Patrick Charles Coburn Wendy Hiller

KAY JOHNSON

1929 DYNAMITE
Director: Cecil B. DeMille
Co-stars: Charles Bickford Conrad Nagel Joel McCrea

1930 BILLY THE KID
Director: King Vidor
Co-stars: Johnny MacK Brown Wallace Beery Roscoe Ates

1930 THE SPOILERS
Director: Edward Carewe
Co-stars: Gary Cooper William Boyd Betty Compson

1930 MADAME SATAN
Director: Cecil B. DeMille
Co-stars: Reginald Denny Lillian Roth Roland Young

1930 THIS MAD WORLD
Co-star: Basil Rathbone

1931 THE SPY
Co-stars: Neil Hamilton Henry Kolker

1932 AMERICAN MADNESS
Director: Frank Capra
Co-stars: Walter Huston Pat O'Brien Constance Cummins

1934 OF HUMAN BONDAGE
Director: John Cromwell
Co-stars: Leslie Howard Bette Davis Frances Dee

1934 THIS MAN IS MINE
Director: John Cromwell
Co-stars: Irene Dunne Ralph Bellamy Constance Cummings

1934 A VILLAGE TALE
Director: John Cromwell
Co-stars: Randolph Scott Robert Barrat Arthur Hohl

1935 JALNA
Director: John Cromwell
Co-stars: Ian Hunter Nigel Bruce Peggy Wood

1938 WHITE BANNERS
Director: Edmund Goulding
Co-stars: Fay Bainter Claude Rains Bonita Granville

1939 THE REAL GLORY
Director: Henry Hathaway
Co-stars: Gary Cooper David Niven Broderick Crawford

1942 SON OF FURY
Director: John Cromwell
Co-stars: Tyrone Pwer Gene Tierney Frances Farmer

LARAINE JOHNSON

1938 THE PAINTED DESERT
Director: David Howard
Co-stars: George O'Brien Ray Whitley Harry Cording

1938 ARIZONA LEGION
Director: Roy Webb
Co-stars: George O'Brien Chill Wills Glenn Strange

LAURA JOHNSON

1978 OPENING NIGHT
Director: John Cassavetes
Co-stars: John Cassavetes Ben Gazzara Gena Rowlands Joan Blondell

1985 CHILLER
Director: Wes Craven
Co-stars: Michael Beck Beatrice Straight Paul Sorvino

1988 RED RIVER
Director: Richard Michaels
Co-stars: James Arness Ray Walston Bruce Boxleitner

1989 NICK NIGHT
Director: Farhad Mann
Co-stars: Rick Springfield Michael Nader Richard Fancy

1993 PAPER HEARTS
Director: Rod McCall
Co-stars: Sally Kirkland James Brolin Pamela Gidley

1993 TRAUMA
Director: Dario Argento
Co-stars: Christopher Rydell Asia Argento Piper Laurie

1995 AWAKE TO DANGER
Director: Michael Tuchner
Co-stars: Tori Spelling Michael Gross John Getz

LYNN-HOLLY JOHNSON

1978 ICE CASTLES
Director: Donald Wrye
Co-stars: Robby Benson Colleen Dewhusrt Jennifer Warren

1980 THE WATCHER IN THE WOODS
Director: John Hough
Co-stars: Bette Davis Carroll Baker Ian Bannen

1981 FOR YOUR EYES ONLY
Director: John Glen
Co-stars: Roger Moore Carol Bouquet Julian Glover Topol

1984 WHERE THE BOYS ARE
Director: Hy Averback
Co-stars: Lisa Hartman Lorna Luft Wendy Schaal

MAUREEN JOHNSON

1954 ORDERS ARE ORDERS
Director: David Paltenghi
Co-stars: Peter Sellers Brian Reece Tony Hancock

MELODY JOHNSON

1968 RIDE TO HANGMAN'S TREE
Director: Alan Rafkin
Co-stars: Jack Lord James Farentino Don Galloway

1968 COOGAN'S BLUFF
Director: Don Siegel
Co-stars: Clint Eastwood Susan Clark Lee J. Cobb

1968 GAILY, GAILY
Director: Norman Jewison
Co-stars: Beau Bridges Melina Mercouri Brian Keith

1970 THE MOONSHINE WAR
Director: Richard Quine
Co-stars: Patrick McGoohan Richard Widmark Alan Alda

MICHELLE JOHNSON

1984 BLAME IT ON RIO
Director: Stanley Donen
Co-stars: Michael Caine Joseph Bologna Demi Moore

1988 WAXWORK
Director: Anthony Hickox
Co-stars: Zach Galligan Deborah Freeman Miles O'Keefe

1992 DEATH BECOMES HER
Director: Robert Zemeckis
Co-stars: Meryl Streep Goldie Hawn Bruce Willis

1992 FAR AND AWAY
Director: Ron Howard
Co-stars: Tom Cruise Nicole Kidman Thomas Gibson

1992 DR GIGGLES
Director: Manny Coto
Co-stars: Larry Drake Richard Bradford Nancy Fish

1993 BODY SHOT
Director: Dimitri Logothetis
Co-star: Robert Patrick

RITA JOHNSON

1938 MAN-PROOF
Director: Richard Thorpe
Co-stars: Myrna Loy Rosalind Russell Franchot Tone

1938 MY DEAR MISS ALDRICH
Director: George Seitz
Co-stars: Maureen O'Sullivan Walter Pidgeon

1938 LONDON BY NIGHT
Director: William Thiele
Co-stars: George Murphy Virginia Field Leo G. Carroll

1938 LETTER OF INTRODUCTION
Director: John Stahl
Co-stars: Adolphe Menjou Andrea Leeds George Murphy

1938 HONOLULU
Director: Edward Buzzell
Co-stars: Eleanor Powell Robert Young George Burns Gracie Allen

1938 THE GIRL DOWNSTAIRS
Director: Norman Taurog
Co-stars: Franchot Tone Franciska Gaal Walter Connolly

1939 BROADWAY SERENADE
Director: Robert Z. Leonard
Co-stars: Jeanette MacDonald Lew Ayres Frank Morgan

1939 NICK CARTER-MASTER DETECTIVE
Director: Jacques Tourneur
Co-stars: Walter Pidgeon Stanley Ridges

1939 6000 ENEMIES
Director: George Seitz
Co-stars: Walter Pidgeon Paul Kelly Nat Pendleton

1939 STRONGER THAN DESIRE
Director: Leslie Fenton
Co-stars: Walter Pidgeon Ann Dvorak Virginia Bruce

1939 WITHIN THE LAW
Director: Gustav Machaty
Co-stars: Ruth Hussey Tom Neal Paul Kelly

1940 THE GOLDEN FLEECING
Director: Leslie Fenton
Co-stars: Lew Ayres Lloyd Nolan Virginia Grey

1940 FORTY LITTLE MOTHERS
Director: Busby Berkeley
Co-stars: Eddie Cantor Judith Anderson Bonita Granville

1940 EDISON, THE MAN
Director: Clarence Brown
Co-stars: Spencer Tracy Charles Coburn Lynne Overman

1940 CONGO MAISIE
Director: H.C. Potter
Co-stars: Ann Sothern John Carroll Shepperd Strudwick

1941 APPOINTMENT FOR LOVE
Director: William Seiter
Co-stars: Charles Boyer Margaret Sullavan Reginald Denny

1941 HERE COMES MR. JORDAN
Director: Alexander Hall
Co-stars: Robert Montgomery Claude Rains

1942 THE MAJOR AND THE MINOR
Director: Billy Wilder
Co-stars: Ginger Rogers Ray Milland Diana Lynn

1943 MY FRIEND FLICKER
Director: Harold Schuster
Co-stars: Roddy McDowall Preston Foster James Bell

1945 THUNDER, SON OF FLICKER
Director: Louis King
Co-stars: Roddy McDowall Preston Foster James Bell

1945 PARDON MY PAST
Director: Leslie Fenton
Co-stars: Fred MacMurray Marguerite Chapman

1945 THE AFFAIRS OF SUSAN
Director: William Seiter
Co-stars: Joan Fontaine George Brent Dennis O'Keefe

1945 THE NAUGHTY NINETIES
Director: Jean Yarborough
Co-stars: Abbott & Costello Henry Travers

1946 THE PERFECT MARRIAGE
Director: Lewis Allen
Co-stars: David Niven Loretta Young Eddie Albert

1948 THE BIG CLOCK
Director: John Farrow
Co-stars: Charles Laughton Maureen O'Sullivan

1948 MICHIGAN KID
Director: Ray Taylor
Co-stars: Jon Hall Victor McLaglen Andy Devine

1948 THEY WON'T BELIEVE ME
Director: Irving Pichel
Co-stars: Robert Young Susan Hayward Jane Greer

1948 SLEEP, MY LOVE
Director: Douglas Sirk
Co-stars: Claudette Colbert Don Ameche Robert Cummings

1949 FAMILY HONEYMOON
Director: Claude Binyon
Co-stars: Claudette Colbert Fred MacMurray

ROBIN JOHNSON

1980 TIMES SQUARE
Director: Alan Moyle
Co-stars: Tim Curry Trini Alvarado Peter Coffield

VICTORIA JOHNSON

1978 ALIEN ENCOUNTERS
Director: Ed Hunt
Co-stars: Robert Vaughn Christopher Lee Helen Shaver

AMY JOHNSTON

1978 THE BUDDY HOLLY STORY
Director: Steve Rash
Co-stars: Gary Busey Don Stroud Maria Richwine

1988 ARIA
Director: Robert Altman
Co-stars: John Hurt Bridget Fonda Elizabeth Hurley

BECKY JOHNSTON

1983 BORN IN FLAMES
Director: Lizzie Borden
Co-stars: Honey Adele Bertei Jeanne Satterfield

GRACE JOHNSTON

1988 BEACHES
Director: Garry Marshall
Co-stars: Bette Midler Barbara Hershey John Heard

1988 GOD BLESS THE CHILD
Director: Larry Elikann
Co-stars: Mare Winningham Dorian Harewood

JULANNE JOHNSTON

1924 THE THIEF OF BAGDAD
Director: Raoul Walsh
Co-stars: Douglas Fairbanks Snitz Edwards Anna May Wong

MARGARET JOHNSTON

1945 THE RAKE'S PROGRESS
Director: Sidney Gilliat
Co-stars: Rex Harrison Lilli Palmer Guy Middleton

1948 **A MAN ABOUT THE HOUSE**
Director: Leslie Arliss
Co-stars: Kieron Moore Dulcie Gray Felix Aylmer

1949 **PORTRAIT OF CLARE**
Director: Lance Comfort
Co-stars: Richard Todd Robin Bailey Ronald Howard

1951 **THE MAGIC BOX**
Director: John Boutling
Co-stars: Robert Donat Maria Schell Renee Asherson

1954 **KNAVE OF HEARTS**
Director: Rene Clement
Co-stars: Gerard Philipe Joan Greenwood Valerie Hobson

1955 **TOUCH AND GO**
Director: Michael Truman
Co-stars: Jack Hawkins Roland Culver June Thorburn

1963 **GIRL IN THE HEADLINES**
Director: Michael Truman
Co-stars: Ian Hendry Ronald Fraser Natasha Parry

1964 **NIGHT OF THE EAGLE**
Director: Sidney Hayers
Co-stars: Janet Blair Peter Wyngarde Kathleen Byron

1965 **LIFE AT THE TOP**
Director: Ted Kotcheff
Co-stars: Laurence Harvey Jean Simmons Honor Blackman

1966 **THE PSYCHOPATH**
Director: Freddie Frances
Co-stars: Patrick Wymark John Standing Alexander Knox

1968 **SEBASTIAN**
Director: David Greene
Co-stars: Dirk Bogarde John Gielgud Susannah York

SUE JOHNSTONE

1991 **GOODBYE CRUEL WORLD**
Director: Adrian Shergold
Co-stars: Alun Armstrong Brenda Bruce Julian Wadham

1992 **BITTER HARVEST**
Director: Simon Cellan Jones
Co-stars: Josette Simon Rudolph Walker Tomas Milian

1993 **A TOUCH OF FROST: CONCLUSIONS**
Director: Anthony Simmons
Co-stars: David Jason Bruce Alexander

1998 **BRASSED OFF**
Director: Mark Herman
Co-stars: Tara Fitzgerald Stephen Tompkinson Pete Postlewaite

KIM JOHNSTON-ULRICH

1993 **BLOOD TIES**
Director: Jim McBride
Co-stars: Harley Denton Patrick Banchan Bo Hopkins

MARILYN JOI

1978 **THE KENTUCKY FRIED MOVIE**
Director: John Landis
Co-stars: Saul Kahan Marcy Goldman Joe Medalis

MICHELLE JOINER

1992 **TRACES OF RED**
Director: Andt Wolk
Co-stars: James Belushi Lorraine Bracco Tony Goldwyn

MIRJANA JOKOVIC

1989 **EVERSMILE, NEW JERSEY**
Director: Carlos Sorin
Co-star: Daniel Day-Lewis

ANGELINA JOLIE *(Daughter Of Jon Voight)*

1993 **CYBORG 2**
Director: Michael Schroeder
Co-stars: Elias Koteas Billy Drago Jack Palance

1995 **HACKERS**
Co-star: Jonny Lee Miller Fisher Stevens

1998 **GIA**
Director: Michael Cristofer
Co-stars: Mercedes Ruehl Faye Dunaway Elizabeth Mitchell

ANNA JONES

1993 **EMILY'S GHOST**
Director: Colin Finbow
Co-stars: Martin Jarvis Anna Massey Ron Moody

ANNIE JONES

1984 **RUN, CHRISSIE, RUN**
Director: Chris Langman
Co-stars: Carmen Duncan Michael Aitkins Shane Briant

BEULAH HALL JONES

1939 **DRUMS ALONG THE MOHAWK**
Director: John Ford
Co-stars: Henry Fonda Claudette Colbert Edna May Oliver

CAROLYN JONES
Nominated For Best Supporting Actress In 1958 For "The Bachelor Party"

1953 **HOUSE OF WAX**
Director: Andre De Toth
Co-stars: Vincent Price Phyllis Kirk Frank Lovejoy

1954 **THE SARACEN BLADE**
Director: William Castle
Co-stars: Ricardo Montalban Betta St. John Rick Jason

1955 **THE TENDER TRAP**
Director: Charles Walters
Co-stars: Frank Sinatra Debbie Reynolds David Wayne

1956 **JOHNNY TROUBLE**
Director: John Auer
Co-stars: Ethel Barrymore Stuart Whitman Cecil Kellaway

1956 **THE OPPOSITE SEX**
Director: David Miller
Co-stars: June Allyson Douglas Grey Joan Collins Ann Sheridan

1956 **INVASION OF THE BODY SNATCHERS**
Director: Don Siegel
Co-stars: Kevin McCarthy Dana Wynter

1958 **BABY FACE NELSON**
Director: Don Siegel
Co-stars: Mickey Rooney Cedric Hardwicke Anthony Caruso

1958 **THE BACHELOR PARTY**
Director: Delbert Mann
Co-stars: Don Murray E.G. Marshall Jack Warden

1958 **KING CREOLE**
Director: Michael Curtiz
Co-stars: Elvis Presley Walter Matthau Dean Jagger

1958 **THE MAN IN THE NET**
Director: Michael Curtiz
Co-stars: Alan Ladd Diane Brewster Charles McGraw

1958 **MARJORIE MORNINGSTAR**
Director: Irving Rapper
Co-stars: Natalie Wood Gene Kelly Ed Wynn

1959 **LAST TRAIN FROM GUN HILL**
Director: John Sturges
Co-stars: Kirk Douglas Anthony Quinn Earl Holliman

1959 HOLE IN THE HEAD
Director: Frank Capra
Co-stars: Frank Sinatra Edward G. Robinson Eleanor Parker

1959 CAREER
Director: Joseph Anthony
Co-stars: Tony Franciosa Dean Martin Shirley MacLaine

1960 ICE PALACE
Director: Vincent Sherman
Co-stars: Richard Burton Robert Ryan Martha Hyer

1961 SAIL A CROOKED SHIP
Director: Irving Brecher
Co-stars: Robert Wagner Ernie Kovacs Dolores Hart

1963 A TICKLISH AFFAIR
Director: George Sidney
Co-stars: Shirley Jones Gig Young Red Buttons

1969 HEAVEN WITH A GUN
Director: Lee Katzin
Co-stars: Glenn Ford David Carradine Barbara Hershey

1969 THE DANCE OF DEATH
Director: David Giles
Co-stars: Laurence Olivier Geraldine McEwan Robert Lang

1969 COLOUR ME DEAD
Director: Eddie Davis
Co-stars: Tom Tryon Rick Jason Patricia Connolly

1976 DEATH TRAP
Director: Tobe Hooper
Co-stars: Neville Brand Mel Ferrer Marilyn Burns William Finley

CATHERINE ZETA JONES

1991 OUT OF THE BLUE
Director: Nick Hamm
Co-stars: Colin Firth John Lynch Cathy Tyson

1992 CHRISTOPHER COLUMBUS:THE DISCOVERY
Director: John Glenn
Co-stars: Marlon Brando Tom Selleck

1992 SPLITTING HEIRS
Director: Robert Young
Co-stars: Eric Idle Rick Morannis Barbara Hershey

1995 BLUE JUICE
Co-stars: Sean Pertwee Ewan McGregor

1997 THE PHANTOM
Co-stars: Billy Zane Kristy Swanson Treat Williams

CHERRY JONES

1986 ALEX: THE LIFE OF A CHILD
Director: Robert Markowitz
Co-stars: Bonnie Bedelia Craig T. Nelson

1988 LIGHT OF DAY
Director: Paul Schrader
Co-stars: Michael J. Fox Gena Rowlands Joan Jett

1992 HOUSESITTER
Director: Frank Oz
Co-stars: Goldie Hawn Steve Martin Dana Delany

ELIZABETH JONES

1939 DRUMS ALONG THE MOWHAWK
Director: John Ford
Co-stars: Henry Fonda Claudette Colbert Edna May Oliver

GEMMA JONES

1971 THE DEVILS
Director: Ken Russell
Co-stars: Vanessa Redgrave Oliver Reed Dudley Sutton

1988 ON THE BLACK HILL
Director: Andrew Grieve
Co-stars: Bob Peck Mike Gwilym Robert Gwilym

1988 PAPERHOUSE
Director: Bernard Rose
Co-stars: Charlotte Burke Ben Cross Glenne Headley

**1989 INSPECTOR MORSE:
THE DEAD OF JERICHO**
Director: Alastair Reed
Co-stars: John Thaw Patrick Troughton

**1990 INSPECTOR WEXFORD:
SOME LIE AND SOME DIE**
Director: Sandy Johnson
Co-stars: George Baker Diane Keen

1996 THE FEAST OF JULY
Director: Christopher Menaul
Co-stars: Tom Bell Ben Chaplin Embeth Davidtz

1997 WILDE
Director: Brian Gilbert
Co-stars: Stephen Fry Jude Law Vanessa Redgrave

GILLIAN JONES

1988 SHADOWS OF THE PEACOCK
Director: Philip Noyce
Co-stars: Wendy Hughes John Lone Steven Jacobs

1989 SHAME
Director: Steve Jodrell
Co-stars: Deborra-Lee Furness Tony Barry Simone Buchanan

GRACE JONES

1984 CONAN THE DESTROYER
Director: Richard Fleischer
Co-stars: Arnold Schwarzenegger Sarah Douglas Mako

1985 A VIEW TO A KILL
Director: John Glen
Co-stars: Roger Moore Christopher Walken Tanya Roberts

1988 SIESTA
Director: Mary Lambert
Co-stars: Ellen Barkin Gabriel Byrne Isabella Rossellini

1992 BOOMERANG
Director: Reggie Hudlin
Co-stars: Eddie Murphy Robin Givens Halle Berry

HELEN JONES

1985 BLISS
Director: Ray Lawrence
Co-stars: Barry Otto Lynette Curran Gia Carides

1990 WAITING
Director: Jackie McKimmie
Co-stars: Noni Hazlehurst Deborra-Lee Furness Denis Moore

IVY JONES

1973 TRAPPED
Director: Frank DeFelitta
Co-stars: James Brolin Susan Clark Earl Holliman

JANET JONES

1984 THE FLAMINGO KID
Director: Garry Marshall
Co-stars: Matt Dillon Richard Crenna Jessica Walter

1986 AMERICAN ANTHEM
Director: Albert Magnoli
Co-stars: Mitch Gaylord Michelle Phillips Maria Anz

1988 POLICE ACADEMY 5: ASSIGNMENT MIAMI BEACH
Director: Alan Myerson
Co-stars: Matt McCoy Bubba Smith

JENNIFER JONES (Phyllis Isley)
(Married Robert Walker, David O. Selznick)
Oscar For Best Actress In 1943 For "The Song of Bernadette"
Nominated For Best Supporting Actress In 1944 For "Since You Went Away"
Nominated For Best Actress In 1945 For "Love Letters"
Nominated For Best Actress In 1946 For "Duel In The Sun"
Nominated For Best Actress In 1955 For "Love Is A Many-Splendored Thing"

1939 DICK TRACY (Serial)

1943 THE SONG OF BERNADETTE
Director: Henry King
Co-stars: William Eythe Charles Bickford

1944 SINCE YOU WENT AWAY
Director: John Cromwell
Co-stars: Claudette Colbert Shirley Temple Robert Walker

1945 LOVE LETTERS
Director: William Dieterle
Co-stars: Joseph Cotten Cecil Kellaway

1946 CLUNY BROWN
Director: Ernst Lubitsch
Co-stars: Charles Boyer Richard Haydn Una O'Connor

1946 DUEL IN THE SUN
Director: King Vidor
Co-stars: Gregory Peck Joseph Cotten Lillian Gish

1948 PORTRAIT OF JENNIE
Director: William Dieterle
Co-stars: Joseph Cotten Ethel Barrymore

1949 MADAME BOVARY
Director: Vincente Minnelli
Co-stars: Van Heflin James Mason Louis Jourdan

1949 WE WERE STRANGERS
Director: John Huston
Co-stars: John Garfield Pedro Aremendariz

1950 GONE TO EARTH
Director: Michael Powell
Co-stars: David Farrar Cyril Cusack

1952 CARRIE
Director: William Wyler
Co-stars: Laurence Olivier Miriam Hopkins

1952 RUBY GENTRY
Director: King Vidor
Co-stars: Charlton Heston Karl Malden Tom Tully

1954 INDISCRETION OF AN AMERICAN WIFE
Director: Vittorio De Sica
Co-star: Montgomery Clift Richard Beymer

1953 BEAT THE DEVIL
Director: John Huston
Co-stars: Humphrey Bogart Gina Lollobrigida

1955 GOOD MORNING MISS DOVE
Director: Henry Koster
Co-stars: Robert Stack Robert Douglas Chuck Connors

1955 LOVE IS A MANY-SPLENDORED THING
Director: Henry King
Co-stars: William Holden Torin Thatcher

1956 THE MAN IN THE GREY FLANNEL SUIT
Director: Nunnally Johnson
Co-stars: Gregory Peck Fredric March Ann Harding

1958 THE BARRATTS OF WIMPOLE STREET
Director: Sidney Franklin
Co-stars: John Gielgud Bill Travers

1958 A FAREWELL TO ARMS
Director: Charles Vidor
Co-stars: Rock Hudson Vittorio De Sica Kurt Kasznar

1962 TENDER IS THE NIGHT
Director: Henry King
Co-stars: Jason Robards Joan Fontaine Tom Ewell

1966 THE IDOL
Director: Daniel Petrie
Co-stars: Michael Parks John Leyton

1969 ANGEL, ANGEL, DOWN WE GO
Director: Robert Thom
Co-stars: Roddy McDowall Jordan Christopher

1974 THE TOWERING INFERNO
Director: Irwin Allen
Co-stars: Paul Newman William Holden Steve McQueen

JOCELYN JONES

1976 THE GREAT TEXAS DYNAMITE CHASE
Director: Michael Presman
Co-stars: Claudia Jennings Johnny Crawford

LAUREN JONES

1976 CAR WASH
Director: Michael Schultz
Co-stars: Franklin Ajaye Sully Boyar Richard Pryor

LISA JONES

1976 THE LIFE AND TIMES OF GRIZZLY ADAMS
Director: Richard Friedenberg
Co-stars: Dan Haggerty Don Shanks

LUCINDA JONES (Child)

1983 THE WILD DUCK
Director: Henri Safran
Co-stars: Liv Ullman Jeremy Irons John Meillon

MARCIA MAE JONES (Child)

1936 THESE THREE
Director: William Wyler
Co-stars: Merle Oberon Miriam Hopkins Bonita Cranville

1938 HEIDI
Director: Allan Dwan
Co-stars: Shirley Temple Jean Hersholt Arthur Treacher

1938 THE ADVENTURES OF TOM SAWYER
Director: Norman Taurog
Co-stars: Tommy Kelly May Robson Walter Brennan

1938 MAD ABOUT MUSIC
Director: Norman Taurog
Co-stars: Deanna Durbin Herbert Marshall Gail Patrick

1939 THE LITTLE PRINCESS
Director: Walter Lang
Co-stars: Shirley Temple Richard Greene Anita Louise

1939 MEET DR. CHRISTIAN
Director: Bernard Vorhaus
Co-stars: Jean Hersholt Dorothy Lovett Enid Bennett

1940 TOMBOY
Co-stars: Jackie Moran Grant Withers George Cleveland

1944 NINE GIRLS
Director: Leigh Jason
Co-stars: Ann Harding Evelyn Keyes Jinx Falkenberg

1948 STREET CORNER

1949 ARSON INC.
Co-stars: Robert Lowry Douglas Fowley Edward Brophy

1973 THE WAY WE WERE
Director: Sydney Pollack
Co-stars: Barbra Streisand Robert Redford Lois Chiles

MARY JONES

1969 THE PROMISE
Director: Michael Hayes
Co-stars: Ian McKellen John Castle Susan Macready

NANCY JONES

1934 THE PRIVATE LIFE OF DON JUAN
Director: Alexander Korda
Co-stars: Douglas Fairbanks Merle Oberon

NINA JONES

1993 THOSE BEDROOM EYES
Director: Leon Ichaso
Co-stars: Tim Matheson Mimi Rogers Carroll Baker

O-LAN JONES

1990 EDWARD SCISSORHANDS
Director: Tim Burton
Co-stars: Johnny Depp Winona Ryder Dianne Wiest

1993 SHELF LIFE
Director: Paul Bartel
Co-stars: Paul Bartel Andrea Stein Jim Turner Justin Houchin

PEGGY ANN JONES

1968 THE MIKADO
Director: Stuart Burge
Co-stars: Donald Adams Philip Potter Valerie Masterton

RENEE JONES

FRIDAY THE 13TH PART IV: JASON LIVES
Director: Tom McLoughlin
Co-stars: Thom Mathews Jennifer Cooke

SAMANTHA JONES

1968 WAIT UNTIL DARK
Director: Terence Young
Co-stars: Audrey Hepburn Efrem Zimbzlist Jnr. Alan Arkin

1972 GET TO KNOW YOUR RABBIT
Director: Brian De Palma
Co-stars: Tom Smothers John Astin Orson Welles

SAMMEE LEE JONES (Child)

1971 WHAT'S THE MATTER WITH HELEN?
Director: Curtis Harrington
Co-stars: Debbie Reynolds Shelley Winters

SHIRLEY JONES
(Married Jack Cassidy Mother Of David Cassidy)
Oscar For Best Supporting Actress In 1960 For "Elmer Gantry"

1955 OKLAHOMA
Director: Fred Zinnemann
Co-stars: Gordon MacRae Rod Steiger Gene Nelson

1956 CAROUSEL
Director: Henry King
Co-stars: Gordon MacRae Cameron Mitchell Barbara Ruick

1958 APRIL LOVE
Director: Henry Levin
Co-stars: Pat Boone Arthur O'Connell Dolores Michaels

1958 NEVER STEAL ANYTHING SMALL
Director: Charles Lederer
Co-stars: James Cagney Roger Smith Royal Dano

1959 BOBBIKINS
Director: Robert Day
Co-stars: Max Bygraves Billie Whitelaw Lionel Jeffries

1960 ELMER GANTRY
Director: Richard Brooks
Co-stars: Burt Lancaster Jean Simmons Dean Jagger

1961 TWO RODE TOGETHER
Director: John Ford
Co-stars: James Stewart Richard Widmark Anna Lee

1962 THE MUSIC MAN
Director: Marion Hargrove
Co-stars: Robert Preston Hermione Gingold Paul Ford

1963 A TICKLISH AFFAIR
Director: George Sidney
Co-stars: Gig Young Red Buttons Carolyn Jones

1963 THE COURTSHIP OF EDDIE'S FATHER
Director: Vincente Minnelli
Co-stars: Glenn Ford Ronny Howard

1964 BEDTIME STORY
Director: Ralph Levy
Co-stars: David Niven Marlon Brando Dodie Goodman

1964 FLUFFY
Director: Earl Bellamy
Co-stars: Tony Randall Jim Backus Edward Andrews

1965 THE SECRET OF MY SUCCESS
Director: Andrew Stone
Co-stars: James Booth Lionel Jeffries Stella Stevens

1969 THE HAPPY ENDING
Director: Richard Brooks
Co-stars: Jean Simmons Lloyd Bridges Bobby Darin

1969 SILENT NIGHT, LONELY NIGHT
Director: Daniel Petrie
Co-stars: Lloyd Bridges Carrie Snodgress Cloris Leachman

1970 THE CHEYENNE SOCIAL CLUB
Director: Gene Kelly
Co-stars: James Stewart Henry Fonda Robert Middleton

1975 THE LIVES OF JENNY DOLAN
Director: Jerry Jameson
Co-stars: Stephen Boyd Farley Granger James Darren

1975 WINNER TAKE ALL
Director: Paul Bogart
Co-stars: Sam Groom Joan Blondell Sylvia Sidney

1979 BEYOND THE POSEIDON ADVENTURE
Director: Irwin Allen
Co-stars: Michael Caine Sally Field Telly Savalas

1980 THE CHILDREN OF AN LAC
Director: John Llewellyn Moxey
Co-stars: Ina Balin Beulah Quo Alan Fudge

1983 HOTEL
Director: Jerry London
Co-stars: Bette Davis James Brolin Mel Torme

1984 TANK
Director: Martin Chomsky
Co-stars: James Garner Mark Herrier Dorian Harewood

TAMALA JONES

1998 BOOTY CALL
Co-stars: Tommy Davidson Jaimie Fox Vivica Fox

TRACY CHERELLE JONES

1995 DON'T BE A MENACE TO SOUTH CENTRAL WHILE DRINKING YOUR JUICE IN THE HOOD
Director: Paris Barclay
Co-stars: Shawn Wayans Marlon Wayans

URSULA JONES

1988   **HOME FRONT**
Director: Penny Cherns
Co-stars: Stephen McGann Jason Cunliffe Cathy Sandford

1991   **TELL ME THAT YOU LOVE ME**
Director: Bruce MacDonald
Co-stars: Judith Scott Sean Bean James Wilby

NINE-CHRISTINE JONSSON

1948   **PORT OF CALL**
Director: Ingmar Bergman
Co-stars: Bengt Ekund Mini Nelson

DOROTHY JORDAN *(Married Merion Cooper)*

1929   **THE TAMING OF THE SHREW**
Director: Sam Taylor
Co-stars: Douglas Fairbanks Mary Pickford Clyde Cook

1929   **DEVIL MAY CARE**
Co-stars: Ramon Navarro Marion Harris

1930   **MIN AND BILL**
Director: George Hill
Co-stars: Marie Dressler Wallace Beery Marjorie Rambeau

1930   **IN GAY MADRID**
Director: Robert Z. Leonard
Co-stars: Ramon Navarro Lettice Howell Claude King

1930   **CALL OF THE FLESH**
Director: Charles Brabin
Co-stars: Ramon Navarro Ernest Torrence Renee Adoree

1930   **LOVE IN THE ROUGH**
Co-star: Robert Montgomery

1931   **THE BELOVERED BACHELOR**
Director: Lloyd Corrigan
Co-stars: Paul Lukas Charles Ruggles Betty Van Allen

1931   **HELL DIVERS**
Director: George Hill
Co-stars: Wallace Beery Clark Gable Conrad Nagel

1931   **YOUNG SINNERS**
Co-star: Hardie Albright

1932   **THE LOST SQUADRON**
Director: George Archainbaud
Co-stars: Richard Dix Mary Astor Joel McCrea

1932   **CABIN IN THE COTTON**
Director: Michael Curtiz
Co-stars: Richard Barthelmess Bette Davis Tully Marshall

1932   **DOWN TO EARTH**
Director: David Butler
Co-stars: Will Rogers Irene Rich Mary Carlisle

1932   **THE WET PARADE**
Director: Victor Fleming
Co-stars: Walter Huston Myrna Loy Neil Hamilton

1932   **THAT'S MY BOY**
Co-star: Richard Cromwell

1932   **70,000 WITNESSES**
Director: Allen Rivkin
Co-stars: Phillips Holmes Johnny Mack Brown Charles Ruggles

1933   **ONE MAN'S JOURNEY**
Director: John Robertson
Co-stars: Lionel Barrymore May Robson Joel McCrea

1933   **BONDAGE**
Co-star: Alexander Kirkland

MARIAN JORDAN *(Married Jim Jordan)*
(USA Radio Show Fibber McGee And Molly)

1938   **THIS WAY PLEASE**
Director: Robert Florey
Co-stars: Charles Rogers Betty Grable Ned Sparks

1941   **LOOK WHO'S LAUGHING**
Director: Allan Dwan
Co-stars: Lucille Ball Edgar Bergen Jim Jordan

1942   **HERE WE GO AGAIN**
Director: Allan Dwan
Co-stars: Jim Jordan Edgar Bergen Ginny Simms

1944   **HEAVENLY DAYS**
Director: Howard Estabrook
Co-stars: Jim Jordan Eugene Pallette Barbara Hale

MIRIAM JORDAN

1932   **SHERLOCK HOLMES**
Director: William Howard
Co-stars: Clive Brook Reginald Owen Alan Mowbray

1932   **SIX HOURS TO LIVE**
Director: William Dieterle
Co-stars: Warner Baxter John Boles Irene Ware

1933   **DANGEROUSLY YOURS**
Director: Frank Tuttle
Co-stars: Warner Baxter Herbert Mundin Florence Eldredge

1934   **LET'S FALL IN LOVE**
Director: David Burton
Co-stars: Edmund Lowe Ann Sothern Gregory Ratoff

DESIREE JOSEPH

1985   **DESERT BLOOM**
Director: Eugene Corr
Co-stars: Annabeth Gish Jon Voight JoBeth Williams

JACKI JOSEPH

1986   **LITTLE SHOP OF HORRORS**
Director: Frank Oz
Co-stars: Rick Moranis Ellen Greene Steve Martin

1970   **THE CHEYENNE SOCIAL CLUB**
Director: Gene Kelly
Co-stars: Henry Fonda James Stewart Shirley Jones

ELVA JOSEPHSON *(Child)*

1980   **THE BLUE LAGOON**
Director: Randal Kleiser
Co-stars: Brooke Shields Christopher Atkins Leo McKern

INDIRA JOSHI

1986   **LOVE MATCH**
Director: Alan Dossor
Co-stars: Saeed Jaffrey Madhur Jaffrey Rosemary Martin

1988   **THE DIARY OF RITA PATEL**
Director: Michael Jackley
Co-stars: Cheryl Miller Tony Wreddin Ian Arthur

CATHERINE JOURDAN

1968   **A GIRL ON A MOTORCYCLE**
Director: Jack Cardiff
Co-stars: Marianne Faithfull Alain Delon Roger Mutton

MILLA JOVOVICH

1991   **KUFFS**
Director: Bruce Evans
Co-stars: Christian Slater Tony Goldwyn Bruce Boxleitner

1991　RETURN TO THE BLUE LAGOON
Director:　William Graham
Co-stars:　Brian Krause Lisa Pelikan Nana Coburn

1993　DAZED AND CONFUSED
Director:　Richard Linklater
Co-stars:　Jason London Wiley Wiggins Michelle Burke

1996　THE FIFTH ELEMENT
Director:　Luc Besson
Co-stars:　Bruce Willis Gary Oldman Ian Holm

LEATRICE JOY

1921　THE MARRIAGE CHEAT
Co-star:　Peggy Mormont

1922　MANSLAUGHTER
Director:　Cecil B. DeMille
Co-stars:　Thomas Meighan Lois Wilson John Miltern

1923　THE TEN COMMANDMENTS
Director:　Cecil B. DeMille
Co-stars:　Theoder Roberts Richard Dix Nita Naldi

1923　HOLLYWOOD
Director:　James Cruze
Co-stars:　Hope Drown Luke Cosgrave Ruby Lafayette

1926　CLINGING VINE
Director:　Paul Sloane
Co-stars:　Tom Moore Robert Edeson

1939　FIRST LOVE
Director:　Henry Koster
Co-stars:　Deana Durbin Robert Stack Eugene Pallette

1951　LOVE NEST
Director:　Joseph Newman
Co-stars:　William Lundigan June Haver Marilyn Monroe

ALICE JOYCE

1925　STELLA DALLAS
Director:　Henry King
Co-stars:　Ronald Colman Belle Bennett Lois Moran

1926　SO'S YOUR OLD MAN
Director:　Gregory La Cava
Co-stars:　W.C. Fields Charles Rogers

1926　BEAU GESTE
Director:　Herbert Brenon
Co-stars:　Ronald Colman Neil Hamilton Ralph Forbes

1929　THE SQUALL
Director:　Alexander Korda
Co-stars:　Myrna Loy Loretta Young Richard Ticker

1930　THE GREEN GODDESS
Director:　Alfred Green
Co-stars:　George Arliss Ralph Forbes H.B. Warner

1930　SONG O' MY HEART
Director:　Frank Borzage
Co-stars:　John McCormack Maureen O'Sullivan John Garrick

BRENDA JOYCE

1939　HERE I AM A STRANGER
Director:　Roy Del Ruth
Co-stars:　Richard Dix Gladys George Richard Greene

1939　THE RAINS CAME
Director:　Clarence Brown
Co-stars:　Tyrone Power Myrna Loy George Brent

1940　PUBLIC DEB NUMBER ONE
Director:　Gregory Ratoff
Co-stars:　George Murphy Ralph Bellamy Mischa Auer

1940　MARYLAND
Director:　Henry King
Co-stars:　John Payne Walter Brennan Fay Bainter

1940　LITTLE OLD NEW YORK
Director:　Henry King
Co-stars:　Alice Faye Richard Greene Fred MacMurray

1941　MARRY THE BOSS'S DAUGHTER
Co-stars:　Hardie Albright George Barbier

1942　WHISPERING GHOSTS
Director:　Alfred Werker
Co-stars:　Milton Berle John Carradine Willie Best

1942　LITTLE TOYKO, U.S.A.
Director:　Otto Brower
Co-stars:　Preston Foster June Duprez Harold Huber

1943　THUMBS UP
Director:　Joseph Santly
Co-stars:　Richard Fraser Elsa Lanchester

1945　PILLOW OF DEATH
Director:　Wallace Fox
Co-stars:　Lon Chaney J. Edward Bromberg Rosalind Ivan

1945　STRANGE CONFESSION
Co-stars:　Lon Chaney J. Carrol Naish

1945　I'LL TELL THE WORLD
Director:　Leslie Goodwins
Co-stars:　Lee Tracy Raymond Walburn June Preisser

1945　THE ENCHANTED FORREST
Director:　Lew Landers
Co-stars:　Harry Davenport Edmund Lowe Billy Severn

1945　TARZAN AND THE AMAZONS
Director:　Kurt Neuman
Co-stars:　Johnny Weismuller Johnny Sheffield

1946　LITTLE GIANT
Director:　William Sieter
Co-stars:　Bud Abbott Lou Costello Margaret Dumont

1946　THE SPIDER WOMAN STRIKES BACK
Director:　Arthur Lubin
Co-stars:　Gale Sondergaard Rondo Hatton

1946　TARZAN AND THE LEOPARD WOMAN
Director:　Kurt Neuman
Co-stars:　Johnny Weismuller Johnny Sheffield

1948　STEPCHILD
Co-star:　Donald Woods

1948　TARZAN AND THE HUNTRESS
Director:　Kurt Neuman
Co-stars:　Johnny Weismuller Johnny Sheffield

1948　SHAGGY
Co-stars:　Robert Shayne George Noakes

1948　TARZAN AND THE MERMAIDS
Director:　Robert Florey
Co-stars:　Johnny Weismuller Linda Christian

1949　TARZAN'S MAGIC FOUNTAIN
Director:　Lee Sholam
Co-stars:　Lex Barker Evelyn Ankers Albert Dekker

EILEEN JOYCE *(Pianist)*

1943　BATTLE FOR MUSIC
Director:　Donald Taylor
Co-stars:　Hay Petrie Joss Ambler Sir Malcolm Sargent

1945　THE SEVENTH VEIL *(Piano)*
Director:　Compton Bennett
Co-stars:　Ann Todd James Mason Yvonne Owen

JEAN JOYCE

1938　OUTLAWS OF SONORA
Co-stars:　Bob Livingstone Ray Corrigan Max Terhune

NATALIE JOYCE

1928   A GIRL IN EVERY PORT
Director: Howard Hawks
Co-stars: Victor McLaglen Robert Armstrong Louise Brooks

PATRICIA JOYCE

1972   THE VISITORS
Director: Elia Kazan
Co-stars: James Woods Patrick McVey Chico Martinez

PEGGY HOPKINS JOYCE

1932   INTERNATIONAL HOUSE
Director: Edward Sutherland
Co-stars: W.C. Fields George Burns Gracie Allen

RACHEL JOYCE

1990   SNOW
Director: Gareth Rowlands
Co-stars: Michael Maloney Rupert Frazer Ian McNeice

1990   CHILDREN CROSSING
Director: Angela Pope
Co-stars: Peter Firth Saskia Reeves Bob Peck

1992   A FATAL INVERSION
Director: Tim Fywell
Co-stars: Douglas Hodge Jeremy Northam Saira Todd

YOOTHA JOYCE

1964   FANATIC
Director: Silvio Narizzano
Co-stars: Tallulah Bankhead Stephanie Powers Peter Vaughan

1965   CATCH US IF YOU CAN
Director: John Boorman
Co-stars: Dave Clark Five Barbara Ferris David Lodge

1968   OUR MOTHER'S HOUSE
Director: Jack Clayton
Co-stars: Dirk Bogarde Pamela Franklin Mark Lester

1968   CHARLIE BUBBLES
Director: Albert Finney
Co-stars: Albert Finney Liza Minnelli Billie Whitelaw

1971   BURKE AND HARE
Director: Vernon Sewell
Co-stars: Harry Andrews Derren Nesbitt Glynn Edwards

1971   THE NIGHT DIGGER
Director: Alastair Reid
Co-stars: Patricia Neal Nicholas Clay Pamela Browne

1974   A MAN ABOUT THE HOUSE
Director: John Robins
Co-stars: Richard O'Sullivan Paula Wilcox Sally Thomsett

1980   GEORGE AND MILDRED
Director: Peter Frazer Jones
Co-stars: Brian Murphy Norman Eshley Sheila Fearn

ODETTE JOYEUX
(Married Philippe Agnosti) (Cinematographer)

1938   ENTREE DES ARTISTES
Director: Marc Allegret
Co-stars: Louis Jouvet Claude Dauphin Bernard Blier

1943   DOUCE
Director: Claude Autant-Lara
Co-stars: Jean Debucourt Madeleine Robinson Roger Pigaut

1943   LE BARON FANTOME
Director: Serge De Poligny
Co-stars: Jany Holt Alain Cuny Gabrielle Dorziat

1944   SYLVIA AND THE GHOST
Director: Claude Autant-Lara
Co-stars: Francois Perier Jacques Tati Louis Salou

1950   LA RONDE
Director: Max Ophuls
Co-stars: Anton Walbrook Simone Signoret Simone Simon

MICHELLE JOYNER

1991   GRIM PRAIRIE TALES
Director: Wayne Coe
Co-stars: James Earl Jones Brad Dourif Lisa Eichhorn

1995   SHADOWS OF THE PAST
Director: Terry Benedict
Co-star: Dwight Yoakam

1992   BONNIE AND CLYDE: THE TRUE STORY
Director: Gary Hoffman
Co-stars: Dana Ashbrook Tracey Needham

1993   CLIFFHANGER
Director: Renny Harlin
Co-stars: Sylvester Stallone John Lithgow Janine Turner

ASHLEY JUDD

1993   RUBY IN PARADISE
Director: Victor Nunez
Co-stars: Todd Field Bentley Mitchum Alison Dean

1996   SMOKE
Director: Wayne Wang
Co-stars: Harvey Keitel William Hurt Stockard Channing

1996   THE PASSION OF DARKLY NOON
Director: Philip Ridley
Co-stars: Brendan Fraser Viggo Mortensen

1996   HEAT
Director: Michael Mann
Co-stars: Robert De Niro Val Kilmer Jon Voight

1998   KISS THE GIRLS
Director: Gary Fleder
Co-star: Cary Elwes

ARLINE JUDGE

1931   ARE THESE OUR CHILDREN?
Director: Wesley Ruggles
Co-stars: Eric Linden Rochelle Hudson Ben Alexander

1932   GIRL CRAZY
Director: William Seiter
Co-stars: Wheeler & Woolsey Mitzi Green Dorothy Lee

1932   AGE OF CONSENT
Director: Gregory La Cava
Co-stars: Dorothy Wilson Richard Cromwell Eric Linden

1932   ROAR OF THE DRAGON
Director: Wesley Ruggles
Co-stars: Richard Dix Gwili Andre Zasu Pitts

1933   LOOKING FOR TROUBLE
Director: William Wellman
Co-stars: Spencer Tracy Jack Oakie Constance Cummings

1933   FLYING DEVILS
Director: Russell Birdwell
Co-stars: Bruce Cabot Eric Linden Ralph Bellamy

1934   SHOOT THE WORKS
Director: Wesley Ruggles
Co-stars: Jack Oakie Ben Bernie Dorothy Dell

1934   THE PARTY'S OVER
Co-stars: Ann Sothern Stuart Irwin Henry Travers

1935   SHIP CAFE
Director: Robert Florey
Co-stars: Carl Brisson Mady Christians William Frawley

1935	**GEORGE WHITE'S 1935 SCANDALS**	
Director:	George White	
Co-stars:	Alice Faye James Dunn Eleanor Powell	

1935 GEORGE WHITE'S 1935 SCANDALS
Director: George White
Co-stars: Alice Faye James Dunn Eleanor Powell

1935 THE MYSTERIOUS MR. WONG
Director: William Nigh
Co-stars: Bela Lugosi Wallace Ford Fred Warren

1935 WELCOME HOME
Co-stars: James Dunn Rosina Lawrence

1935 KING OF BURLESQUE
Director: Sidney Lanfield
Co-stars: Warner Baxter Alice Faye Jack Oakie

1935 MILLION DOLLAR BABY
Co-star: Ray Walker

1935 COLLEGE SCANDAL
Director: Elliott Nugent
Co-stars: Kent Taylor Wendy Barrie Mary Nash

1936 IT HAD TO HAPPEN
Director: Roy Del Ruth
Co-stars: George Raft Rosalind Russell Leo Carrillo

1936 HERE COMES TROUBLE
Co-star: Paul Kelly

1936 ONE IN A MILLION
Director: Sidney Lanfield
Co-stars: Sonja Henie Don Ameche Ritz Bros

1936 PIGSKIN PARADE
Director: David Butler
Co-stars: Stuart Erwin Patsy Kelly Judy Garland

1936 VALLIANT IS THE WORD FOR CARRIE
Director: Wesley Ruggles
Co-stars: Gladys George John Howard Harry Carey

1942 WILDCAT
Co-stars: Richard Arlen Arthur Hunnicutt

1942 THE LADY IS WILLING
Director: Mitchell Leisen
Co-stars: Marlene Dietrich Fred MacMurray

19452 LAW OF THE JUNGLE
Co-star: John King

1943 SONG OF TEXAS
Co-stars: Roy Rogers Sheila Ryan

1944 THE CONTENDER
Co-stars: Buster Crabbe Julie Gibbon Milton Kibbee

1946 FROM THIS DAY FORWARD
Director: John Berry
Co-stars: Joan Fontaine Mark Stevens Henry Morgan

JANET JULIAN

1981 HUMONGOUS
Director: Paul Lynch
Co-stars: David Wallace Janit Baldwin John Widman

1986 ON DANGEROUS GROUND
Director: Chuck Bail
Co-stars: Stephen Collins Bo Svenson Nicholas Pryor

1990 KING OF NEW YORK
Director: Abel Ferrara
Co-stars: Christopher Walken David Caruso Wesley Snipes

JULISSA

1971 HOUSE OF EVIL
Director: Jack Hill
Co-stars: Boris Karloff Andres Garcia Beatriz Baz

JUNE

1926 THE LODGER
Director: Alfred Hitchcock
Co-stars: Ivor Novello Marie Holt Arthur Chesney

BETTY JUMEL

1944 DEMOBBED
Director: John Blakeley
Co-stars: Norman Evans Dan Young Nat Jackley

KATY JURADO
Nominated For Best Supporting Actress In 1954 For "Broken Lance"

1950 THE BULLFIGHTER AND THE LADY
Director: Budd Boetticher
Co-stars: Robert Stack Gilbert Roland

1952 HIGH NOON
Director: Fred Zinnemann
Co-stars: Gary Cooper Grace Kelly Thomas Mitchell Lloyd Bridges

1952 SAN ANTONE
Director: Joe Kane
Co-stars: Rod Cameron Forrest Tucker Arleen Whelan

1952 THE BRUTE
Director: Luis Bunuel
Co-stars: Pedro Armendariz Rosita Arenas Andres Soler

1953 ARROWHEAD
Director: Charles Marquis Warren
Co-stars: Charlton Heston Jack Palance Brian Keith

1954 BROKEN LANCE
Director: Edward Dmytryk
Co-stars: Spencer Tracy Richard Widmark Jean Peters

1955 THE RACERS
Director: Henry Hathaway
Co-stars: Kirk Douglas Bella Darvi Gilbert Roland Cesar Romera

1955 TRIAL
Director: Mark Robson
Co-stars: Glenn Ford Dorothy McGuire Arthur Kennedy

1956 TRAPEZE
Director: Carol Reed
Co-stars: Burt Lancaster Tony Curtis Gina Lollobrigida

1956 THE MAN FROM DEL RIO
Director: Harry Horner
Co-stars: Anthony Quinn Peter Whitney Whit Bissell

1958 DRAGOON WELLS MASSACRE
Director: Harold Schuster
Co-stars: Barry Sullivan Dennis O'Keefe Mona Freeman

1958 THE BADLANDERS
Director: Delmer Daves
Co-stars: Alan Ladd Ernest Borgnine Claire Kelly Kent Smith

1961 ONE-EYED JACKS
Director: Marlon Brando
Co-stars: Marlon Brando Karl Malden Pina Pellicer Ben Johnson

1962 BARABBAS
Director: Richard Fleischer
Co-stars: Anthony Quinn Silvana Mangano Vittorio Gassman

1966 A COVENANT WITH DEATH
Director: Lamont Johnson
Co-stars: George Maharis Earl Holliman Gene Hackman

1966 SMOKY
Director: George Sherman
Co-stars: Fess Parker Diana Hyland Chuck Roberson Hoyt Axton

1968 STAY AWAY JOE
Director: Peter Tewkesbury
Co-stars: Elvis Presley Burgess Meredith Joan Blondell

1971 A LITTLE GAME
Director: Paul Wendkos
Co-stars: Ed Nelson Howard Duff Diane Baker Mark Gruner

1973 PAT GARRETT AND BILLY THE KID
Director: Sam Peckinpah
Co-stars: James Coburn Kris Kristofferson

1978 THE CHILDREN OF SANCHEZ
Director: Hall Bartlett
Co-stars: Anthony Quinn Dolores Del Rio

1984 UNDER THE VOLCANO
Director: John Huston
Co-stars: Albert Finney Jacqueline Bisset Anthony Andrews

KATHERINE JUSTICE

1968 FIVE CARD STUD
Director: Henry Hathaway
Co-stars: Dean Martin Robert Mitchum Inger Stevens

1972 LIMBO
Director: Mark Robson
Co-stars: Kate Jackson Stuart Margolin Hazel Medina

SUZANNE KAAREN

1936   WHEN'S YOUR BIRTHDAY
Co-stars: Joe E. Brown Maude Eburne

1936   THE GREAT ZIEGFIELD
Director: Robert Z. Leonard
Co-stars: William Powell Luise Rainer Myrna Loy

1942   THE DEVIL BAT
Director: Jean Yarbrough
Co-stars: Bela Lugosi Dave O'Brien

JANE KACZMAREK

1984   FALLING IN LOVE
Director: Ulu Grosbard
Co-stars: Robert De Niro Meyrl Streep Harvey Keitel

1984   FLIGHT 90: DISASTER ON THE POTOMAC
Director: Michael Lewis
Co-stars: Richard Masur Dinah Manoff

1986   THE CHRISTMAS GIFT
Director: Michael Pressman
Co-stars: John Denver Gennie James Mary Wickes

1988   D.O.A.
Director: Rocky Morton
Co-stars: Dennis Quaid Meg Ryan Charlotte Rampling

1988   VICE VERSA
Director: Brain Gilbert
Co-stars: Judge Reinhold Fred Savage Swoosie Kurtz

1989   SPOONER
Director: George Miller
Co-stars: Robert Urich Paul Gleason Barry Corbin

1989   ALL'S FAIR
Director: Rocky Lang
Co-stars: George Segal Sally Kellerman Jennifer Edwards

KAREN KADLER

1962   THE DEVIL'S MESSENGER
Director: Curt Siodmak
Co-stars: Lon Chaney Jnr. John Crawford

CHARLOTTE KADY

1992   L627
Director: Bertrand Tavernier
Co-stars: Didier Bezace Nils Tavernier Philippe Torreton

1990   THESE FOOLISH THINGS
Director: Bertrand Tavernier
Co-stars: Dirk Bogarde Jane Birkin Odette Laure

ELAINE KAGAN

1992   BY THE SWORD
Director: Jeremy Paul Kagan
Co-stars: Eric Roberts Mia Sara

MARILYN KAGAN

1980   FOXES
Director: Adrian Lyne
Co-stars: Jodie Foster Sally Kellerman Adam Faith Scott Baio

FLORENCE KAHN

1936   SECRET AGENT
Director: Alfred Hitchcock
Co-stars: John Gielgud Robert Young Madeleine Carroll

MADELINE KAHN
Nominated For Best Supporting Actress In 1973 For Paper Moon

1972   WHAT'S UP DOC?
Director: Peter Bogdanovich
Co-stars: Barbra Streisand Ryan O'Neal Kenneth Mars

1973   PAPER MOON
Director: Peter Bogdanovich
Co-stars: Ryan O'Neal Tatum O'Neal John Hillerman

1973   THE HIDEAWAYS
Director: Fielder Cook
Co-stars: Ingrid Bergman Sally Prager Johnny Duran

1974   YOUNG FRANKENSTEIN
Director: Mel Brooks
Co-stars: Gene Wilder Marty Feldman Peter Boyle

1974   BLAZING SADDLES
Director: Mel Brooks
Co-stars: Mel Brooks Cleavon Little Gene Wilder Slim Pickins

1975   THE ADVENTURES OF SHERLOCK HOLMES' SMARTER BROTHER
Director: Gene Wilder
Co-stars: Gene Wilder Marty Feldman

1975   AT LONG LAST LOVE
Director: Peter Bogdanovich
Co-stars: Burt Reynolds Cybill Shepherd Eileen Brennan

1976   WON TON TON, THE DOG WHO SAVED HOLLYWOOD
Director: Michel Winnner
Co-stars: Art Carney Bruce Dern

1977   HIGH ANXIETY
Director: Mel Brooks
Co-stars: Mel Brooks Cloris Leachman Harvey Korman Ron Carey

1978   THE CHEAP DECTECTIVE
Director: Robert Moore
Co-stars: Peter Falk Ann-Margret John Houseman

1980   WHOLLY MOSES
Director: Gary Weis
Co-stars: Dudley Moore James Coco Paul Sand

1980   SIMON
Director: Marshall Brickman
Co-stars: Alan Arkin Austin Pendleton Fred Gwynne

1981   HISTORY OF THE WORLD – PART ONE
Director: Mel Brooks
Co-stars: Mel Brooks Dom Deluise Cloris Leachman Sid Caesar

1983   YELLOWBEARD
Director: Mel Damski
Co-stars: Graham Chapman Peter Cook Marty Feldman

1984   SLAPSTICK (OF ANOTHER KIND)
Director: Steven Paul
Co-stars: Jerry Lewis Marty Feldman Jim Backus

1984   CITY HEAT
Director: Richard Benjamin
Co-stars: Clint Eastwood Burt Reynolds Jane Alexander

1985   CLUE
Director: Johnathan Lynn
Co-stars: Eileen Brennan Tim Curry Christopher Lloyd

1986   AN AMERICAN TALE *(Voice)*
Director: Don Bluth
Co-stars: Cathianne Blore Christopher Plummer

Claudette Colbert

Carole Lombard

Ann Sheridan

Ginger Rogers

1986 MY LITTLE PONY *(Voice)*
Director: Michael Joens
Co-stars: Danny DeVito Rhea Pearlman Tony Randall

1990 BETSY'S WEDDING
Director: Alan Alda
Co-stars: Alan Alda Joey Bishop Molly Ringwald Catherine O'Hara

1992 FATHER, SON AND THE MISTRESS
Director: Jay Sandrich
Co-stars: Jack Lemmon Talia Shire Joanne Gleason

1994 MIXED NUTS
Director: Norah Ephron
Co-star: Steve Martin

1996 NEIL SIMON'S LONDON SUITE
Director: Jay Sandrich
Co-stars: Kelsey Grammar Julie Hagerty Patricia Clarkson

JEANNE KAIRNS

1985 WHEN DREAMS COME TRUE
Director: John Llewellyn Moxey
Co-stars: Cindy Williams David Morse Jessica Harper

ELIZABETH KAITAN

1988 ASSAULT OF THE KILLER BIMBOS
Director: Anita Rosenberg
Co-stars: Christina Whitaker Griffin O'Neal

1988 FRIDAY THE THIRTEENTH
PART VII: THE NEW BLOOD
Director: John Carl Buechler
Co-stars: Susan Blu Terry Kiser

1989 AFTERSHOCK
Director: Frank Harris
Co-stars: Christopher Mitchum John Saxon Russ Tamblyn

TONI KALEM

1979 THE WANDERERS
Director: Philip Kaufman
Co-stars: Ken Wahl John Friedrich Karen Allen

1982 SILENT RAGE
Director: Michael Miller
Co-stars: Chuck Norris Ron Silver Steven Keats

1983 RUNNING OUT
Director: Robert Day
Co-stars: Deborah Raffin Tony Bill Paul Hecht

1986 BILLY GALVIN
Director: John Gray
Co-stars: Karl Malden Lenny Von Dahlen Joyce Van Patten

PATRICIA KALEMBER

1988 LITTLE GIRL LOST
Director: Sharron Miller
Co-stars: Tess Harper Frederic Forrest Marie Martin

1990 DANIELLE STEEL'S KALEIDOSCOPE
Director: Jud Taylor
Co-stars: Jaclyn Smith Perry King Donald Moffat

1992 STEPKIDS
Director: Joan Micklin Silver
Co-stars: Griffin Dunne Jenny Lewis Dan Putterman

1995 UNSPOKEN TRUTH
Director: Peter Werner
Co-stars: Lea Thompson Robert Englund

1996 ANGEL FLIGHT DOWN
Director: Charles Wilkinson
Co-star: David Charvet

KITTY KALLEN

1955 THE SECOND GREATEST SEX
Director: George Marshall
Co-stars: Jeanne Crain George Nader Bert Lahr

HELENA KALLIANIOTIS

1970 FIVE EASY PIECES
Director: Bob Rafelson
Co-stars: Jack Nicholson Karen Black Susan Anspach

1972 KANSAS CITY BOMBER
Director: Jerrold Freedman
Co-stars: Raquel Welch Kevin McCarthy Jodie Foster

1976 STAY HUNGRY
Director: Bob Rafelson
Co-stars: Jeff Bridges Sally Field Arnold Schwarzenegger

SALOME KAMMER

1992 THE SECOND HEIMAT
Director: Edgar Reitz
Co-stars: Henry Arnold Noemi Steuer Gisela Muller

IDA KAMINSKA

Nominated For Best Actress In 1965 For "The Shop on the Main Street"

1965 THE SHOP ON MAIN STREET
Director: Jan Kadar
Co-stars: Jozef Kroner Martin Holly

1970 THE ANGEL LEVINE
Director: Jan Kadar
Co-stars: Zero Mostel Harry Belafonte Eli Wallach

ANNA KANAKIS

1983 AFTER THE FALL OF NEW YORK
Director: Martin Dolman
Co-stars: Michael Sopkiw Edmund Purdom Roman Geer

KIRI TE KANAWA

1979 DON GIOVANNI
Director: Joseph Losey
Co-stars: Ruggero Raimondi John Macurdy Edda Moser

CAROL KANE

Nominated For Best Actress In 1975 For "Hester Street"

1971 CARNAL KNOWLEDGE
Director: Mike Nichols
Co-stars: Jack Nicholson Art Arfunkel Candice Bergen

1973 THE LAST DETAIL
Director: Hal Ashby
Co-stars: Jack Nicholson Otis Young Randy Quaid

1974 HESTER STREET
Director: Joan Micklin Silver
Co-stars: Steven Keats Mel Howard Dorrie Kavanaugh

1977 ANNIE HALL
Director: Woody Allen
Co-stars: Woody Allen Diane Keaton Tony Roberts Paul Simon

1977 VALENTINO
Director: Ken Russell
Co-stars: Rudolf Nureyev Leslie Caron Michelle Phillips

1977 THE WORLD'S GREATEST LOVER
Director: Gene Wilder
Co-stars: Gene Wilder Dom DeLuise Fritz Feld

1979 WHEN A STRANGER CALLS
Director: Fred Walton
Co-stars: Charles Durning Tony Beckley Colleen Dewhurst

1983   OVER THE BROOKLYN BRIDGE
Director: Menahem Golan
Co-stars: Elliott Gould Margaux Hemingway

1986   JUMPIN' JACK FLASH
Director: Penny Marshall
Co-stars: Whoopi Goldberg Stephen Collins John Wood

1988   LICENCE TO DRIVE
Director: Greg Beeman
Co-stars: Corey Haim Corey Feldman Richard Masur Heather Graham

1988   STICKY FINGERS
Director: Catlin Adams
Co-stars: Helen Slater Melanie Mayron Eileen Brennan

1988   SCROOGED
Director: Richard Donner
Co-stars: Bill Murray Karen Allen Robert Mitchum Lee Majors

1990   FLASHBACK
Director: Franco Ammuri
Co-stars: Dennis Hopper Kiefer Sutherland Cliff De Young

1990   MY BLUE HEAVEN
Director: Herbert Ross
Co-stars: Steve Martin Rick Moranis Joan Cusack

1990   THE LEMON SISTERS
Director: Joyce Chopra
Co-stars: Diane Keaton Kathryn Grody Elliott Gould

1991   TED AND VENUS
Director: Bud Cort
Co-stars: Jim Brolin Kim Adams Brian Thompson

1992   BABY ON BOARD
Co-stars: Judge Reinhold Alex Stapley Holly Stapley

1992   IN THE SOUP
Director: Alexandre Rockell
Co-stars: Steve Buscemi Jennifer Beals Will Patton

1993   WHEN A STRANGER CALLS BACK
Director: Fred Walton
Co-stars: Charles Durning

1993   ADDAMS FAMILY VALUES
Director: Barry Sonnenfeld
Co-stars: Angelica Huston Raul Julia Joan Cusack

HELEN KANE

1929   POINTED HEELS
Director: Edward Sutherland
Co-stars: William Powell Fay Wray Phillips Holmes

1930   HEADS UP!
Co-stars: Charles Rogers Margaret Breen

1930   DANGEROUS NAN MCGREW
Co-stars: Frank Morgan

IRENE KANE

1955   KILLER'S KISS
Director: Stanley Kubrick
Co-stars: Frank Silvera Jamie Smith Jerry Jarrett

MARGIE KANE

1929   THE GREAT GABBO
Director: James Cruz
Co-stars: Erich Von Stroheim Betty Compson

MARGO KANE

1988   POWWOW HIGHWAY
Director: Jonathan Wacks
Co-stars: A. Martinez Gary Farmer Amanda Wyss

1988   DEEP SLEEP
Director: Praticia Gruben
Co-stars: Stuart Margolin Megan Follows Patricia Collins

CAROL KANEM

1993   EVEN COWGIRLS GET THE BLUES
Director: Gus Van Sant
Co-stars: Uma Thurman John Hurt River Phoenix

LILY KANN

1943   ESCAPE TO DANGER
Director: Lance Comfort
Co-stars: Eric Portman Ann Dvorak Ronald Adam

1945   LATIN QUARTER
Director: Vernon Sewell
Co-stars: Derrick De Marney Joan Greenwood Martin Miller

1953   BACKGROUND
Director: Daniel Birt
Co-stars: Valerie Hobson Philip Friend Janette Scott

1959   NO TREES IN THE STREET
Director: J. Lee Thompson
Co-stars: Sylvia Syms Herbert Lom Carole Lesley

JOANNA KANSKA

1991   SLEEPERS
Director: Geoffrey Sax
Co-stars: Nigel Havers Warren Clarke David Calder

1992   A VERY POLISH PRACTISE
Director: David Tucker
Co-stars: Peter Davidson Alfred Molina Trevor Peacock

NOELLE KAO

1970   HUSBANDS
Director: John Cassavetes
Co-stars: John Cassavetes Peter Falk Ben Gazzara Jenny Runacre

TRACEY KAPINSKY

1992   AMERICAN HEART
Director: Martin Bell
Co-stars: Jeff Bridges Edward Furlong Lucinda Jenny

WENDY KAPLAN

1989   HALLOWEEN 5:
THE REVENGE OF MICHAEL MYERS
Director: Dominique Othenin-Girard
Co-stars: Danielle Harris Donald Pleasence

VALERIE KAPRINSKY

1983   BREATHLESS
Director: James McBride
Co-stars: Richard Gere William Tepper Art Metrano

MITZI KAPTURE

1988   ANGEL 3: THE FINAL CHAPTER
Director: Tom De Simone
Co-stars: Maud Adams Richard Roundtree Kim Shriner

ELENA KARAM

1963   AMERICA AMERICA
Director: Elia Kazan
Co-star: Stathis Giallelis Frank Wolf Linda Marsh

MAY KARASUN

1992   LAKE CONSEQUENCE
Director: Rafael Eisenman
Co-star: Billy Zane Joan Severance Whip Hubley

KYM KARATH
1965 THE SOUND OF MUSIC
Director: Robert Wise
Co-star: Julie Andrews Christopher Plummer Peggy Wood

ANNA KAREN
1971 ON THE BUSES
Director: Harry Booth
Co-star: Reg Varney Doris Hare Stephen Lewis

1972 MUTINY ON THE BUSES
Director: Harry Booth
Co-star: Reg Varney Michael Robbins Pat Coombs

1973 HOLIDAY ON THE BUSES
Director: Bryan Izzard
Co-star: Reg Varney Bob Grant Doris Hare

1973 THE AFFAIR
Director: Gilbert Cates
Co-stars: Natalie Wood Robert Wagner Bruce Davidson

RITA KARIN
1982 SOPHIE'S CHOICE
Director: Alan J. Pakula
Co-stars: Meryl Streep Kevin Kline Peter MacNicol

1989 ENEMIES, A LOVE STORY
Director: Paul Mazursky
Co-stars: Angelica Huston Ron Silver Lena Olin

ANNA KARINA *(Married Jean-Luc Godard)*
1961 UNE FEMME EST UNE FEMME
Director: Jean-Luc Godard
Co-stars: Jean-Paul Belmondo Jean-Claude Brialy

1961 CLEO FROM FIVE TO SEVEN
Director: Agnes Varda
Co-stars: Corinne Marchand Michel Legrand

1963 LE PETIT SOLDAT
Director: Jean-Luc Godard
Co-stars: Michel Subor Henri-Jacques Huet Laszlo Szabo

1964 LA RONDE
Director: Roger Vadim
Co-stars: Marie Dubois Claude Giraud Jane Fonda

1964 BANDE A PART
Director: Jean-Luc Godard
Co-stars: Claude Brasseur Sami Frey

1965 ALPHAVILLE
Director: Jean-Luc Godard
Co-stars: Eddie Constantine Akim Tamiroff Laszlo Szabo

1965 PIERROT LE FOU
Director: Jean-Luc Godard
Co-stars: Jean-Paul Belmondo Dirk Sanders Raymond Devos

1965 LA RELIGIEUSE
Director: Jacques Rivette
Co-stars: Liselotte Pulver Micheline Presle Christine Lenier

1967 LO STRANIERO
Director: Luchino Visconti
Co-stars: Marcello Mastroianni Bernard Blier Georges Wilson

1967 THE OLDEST PROFESSION
Director: Jean-Luc Godard
Co-stars: Jeanne Moreau Raquel Welch Martin Held

1968 THE MAGUS
Director: Guy Green
Co-stars: Michael Caine Anthony Quinn Candice Bergen

1968 BEFORE WINTER COMES
Director: J. Lee-Thompson
Co-stars: David Niven Topol Ori Levi John Hurt

1969 JUSTINE
Director: George Cukor
Co-stars: Anouk Aimee Dirk Bogarde John Vernon Michael York

1969 LAUGHTER IN THE DARK
Director: Tony Richardson
Co-stars: Nicol Williamson Jean-Claude Drouot

1972 THE SALZBERG CONNECTION
Director: Lee Katzin
Co-stars: Barry Newman Klaus Maria Brandauer

1973 BREAD AND CHOCOLATE
Director: Franco Brusati
Co-stars: Nino Manfredi Johnny Dorelli Paulo Turco

1976 CHINESE ROULETTE
Director: Rainer Werner Fassbinder
Co-stars: Andrea Schober Margit Carstensen

OLGA KARLATOS
1983 THE SCARLET AND THE BLACK
Director: Jerry London
Co-stars: Gregory Peck Christopher Plummer

1984 PURPLE RAIN
Director: Albert Magnoli
Co-stars: Prince, Morris Day Jerome Benton

MIRIAM KARLIN
1952 DOWN AMONG THE Z MEN
Director: MacLean Rogers
Co-stars: Harry Secombe Peter Sellers Spike Milligan

1955 THE DEEP BLUE SEA
Director: Anatole Litvak
Co-stars: Vivien Leigh Kenneth More Eric Portman

1960 HAND IN HAND
Director: Philip Leacock
Co-stars: Loretta Parry Philip Needs John Gregson

1960 THE MILLIONAIRESS
Director: Anthony Asquith
Co-stars: Peter Sellers Sophia Loren Alastair Sim

1962 PHANTOM OF THE OPERA
Director: Terence Fisher
Co-stars: Herbert Lom Heather Sears Michael Gough

1962 THE SMALL WORLD OF SAMMY LEE
Director: Ken Hughes
Co-stars: Anthony Newley Julia Foster Robert Stephens

1963 LADIES WHO DO
Director: C. M. Pennington-Richards
Co-stars: Peggy Mount Dandy Nichols

1963 HEAVENS ABOVE!
Director: John Boulting
Co-stars: Peter Sellers Ian Carmichael Isabel Jeans

1964 THE BARGEE
Director: Duncan Wood
Co-stars: Harry H. Corbett Ronnie Barker Hugh Griffith

1966 JUST LIKE A WOMAN
Director: Bob Fuest
Co-stars: Wendy Craig Francis Matthews Dennis Price

1971 A CLOCKWORK ORANGE
Director: Stanley Kubrick
Co-stars: Malcolm McDowell Michael Bates Adrienne Corri

1974 MAHLER
Director: Ken Russell
Co-stars: Robert Powell Georgina Hale Angela Down

1975 DICK DEADEYE, OR DUTY DONE *(Voice)*
Director: Dick Horn
Co-stars: Victor Spinetti Peter Gilmore

1992 UTZ
Director: George Sluizer
Co-stars: Armin Mueller-Stahl Brenda Fricker Paul Scofield

LELIA KARNELLY

1929 THE COCKEYED WORLD
Director: Raoul Walsh
Co-stars: Victor McLaglen Edmund Lowe Lili Damita

SARAH ROSE KARR (Child)

1992 BEETHOVEN
Director: Brian Levant
Co-stars: Charles Grodin Bonnie Hunt Dean Jones

1992 BEETHOVEN'S 2ND
Director: Rod Daniel
Co-stars: Charles Grodin Bonnie Hunt Christopher Castle

TARA KARSIAN

1992 SINGLE WHITE FEMALE
Director: Barbet Schroeder
Co-stars: Bridget Fonda Jennifer Jason Leigh

CLAUDIA KARVAN

1987 HIGH TIDE
Director: Gillian Armstrong
Co-stars: Judy Davis Jan Adele Colin Friels

1990 THE BIG STEAL
Director: Nadia Tass
Co-stars: Ben Mendlesohn Steve Bisley Marshall Napier

1992 REDHEADS
Director: Danny Vendramini
Co-stars: Catherine McClements Alexander Petersons Sally McKenzie

1993 THE HEARTBREAK KID
Director: Michael Jenkins
Co-stars: Alex Dimitriades Steve Bastoni Nico Lathouris

SHARON L. KASE

1991 DIPLOMATIC IMMUNITY
Director: Bruce Boxleitner
Co-stars: Billy Drago Tom Breznahan

RENATE KASCHE

1969 A BLACK VEIL FOR LISA
Director: Massimo Dellamano
Co-stars: John Mills Luciana Paluzzi Robert Hoffman

ROXANNE KASDAN

1992 GRAND CANYON
Director: Lawrence Kasdan
Co-stars: Kevin Kline Danny Glover Mary McDonnell

LENORE KASDORF

1984 MISSING IN ACTION
Director: Joseph Zito
Co-stars: Chuck Norris M. Emmet Walsh James Hong

1990 KID
Director: John Mark Robinson
Co-stars: C. Thomas Howell Sarah Trigger Dale Dye

ANNA KASHFI

1957 BATTLE HYMN
Director: Douglas Sirk
Co-stars: Rock Hudson Dan Duryea Martha Hyer

1958 COWBOY
Director: Delmer Daves
Co-stars: Glenn Ford Jack Lemmon Brian Donlevy

DAPHNA KASTNER

1990 JULIE HAS TWO LOVERS
Director: Bashar Shbib
Co-stars: David Duchovny David Charles Clare Bancroft

1990 EATING
Director: Henry Jaglom
Co-stars: Lisa Richards Mary Crosby Gwen Welles

1991 LANA IN LOVE
Director: Bashar Shbib
Co-stars: Clark Gregg Michael Gilles Cheryl Platt

1992 VENICE/VENICE
Director: Henry Jaglom
Co-stars: Henry Jaglom Nelly Alard Melissa Leo David Duchovny

ANNA KATERINA

1989 SALUTE OF THE JUGGER
Director: David Peoples
Co-stars: Rutger Hauer Delroy Lindo Joan Chen

1990 THE DEATH OF THE INCREDIBLE HULK
Director: Bill Bixby
Co-stars: Bill Bixby Lou Ferrigno Elizabeth Gracen

CAMELIA KATH

1987 THE KILLING TIME
Director: Rick King
Co-stars: Beau Bridges Kiefer Sutherland Wayne Rogers

KATHERINE KATH

1952 MOULIN ROUGE
Director: John Huston
Co-stars: Jose Ferrer Zsa Zsa Gabor Colette Marchand

1957 THESE DANGEROUS YEARS
Director: Herbert Wilcox
Co-stars: Frankie Vaughan Carole Lesley Jackie Lane

1957 LET'S BE HAPPY
Director: Henry Levin
Co-stars: Vera-Ellen Tony Martin Zena Marshall

1958 THE MAN WHO WOULDN'T TALK
Director: Herbert Wilcox
Co-stars: Anna Neagle Anthony Quayle Zsa Zsa Gabor

1959 SUBWAY IN THE SKY
Director: Muriel Box
Co-stars: Van Johnson Hildergarde Neff Albert Lieven

1962 GIGOT
Director: Gene Kelly
Co-stars: Jackie Gleason Gabrielle Dorziat Jacques Marin

1965 THE HIGH BRIGHT SUN
Director: Ralph Thomas
Co-stars: Dirk Bogarde Susan Strasberg Denholm Elliott

DIANA KATIS

1982 PRIVILEGED
Director: Michael Hoffman
Co-stars: Robert Woolley Hugh Grant James Wilby

ANTONIA KATSAROS

1969 AGE OF CONSENT
Director: Michael Powell
Co-stars: James Mason Helen Mirren Jack McGowran

CHRISTINE KAUFMAN (Married Tony Curtis)

1958 MADCHEN IN UNIFORM
Director: Geza Radvanyl
Co-stars: Lilli Palmer Romy Schneider Therese Giehse

1961 TOWN WITHOUT PITY
Director: Gottfried Reinhardt
Co-stars: Kirk Douglas E. G. Marshall Robert Blake

1962 TARAS BULBA
Director: J. Lee Thompson
Co-stars: Yul Brynner Tony Curtis Sam Wanamaker

1962 THE SWORDSMAN OF SIENNA
Director: Etienne Perrier
Co-stars: Stewart Granger Sylvia Koscina

1962 ESCAPE FROM EAST BERLIN
Director: Robert Siodmak
Co-stars: Don Murray Werner Klemperer

1963 WILD AND WONDERFUL
Director: Michael Anderson
Co-stars: Tony Curtis Jules Munshin Marty Ingels

1971 MURDERS IN THE RUE MORGUE
Director: Gordon Hessler
Co-stars: Jason Robards Herbert Lom Lilli Palmer

1988 BAGDAD CAFE
Director: Percy Adlon
Co-stars: Marianne Sagebrecht Jack Palance Monica Calhoun

ELAINE KAUFMAN

1990 THE BIG BANG
Director: James Toback
Co-stars: Emma Astner Polly Frost Tony Sirico

CAROLINE KAVA

1985 THE YEAR OF THE DRAGON
Director: Michael Cimino
Co-stars: Mickey Rourke John Lone Ray Barry

1986 NOBODY'S CHILD
Director: Lee Grant
Co-stars: Marlo Thomas Ray Baker Cathy Baker

1988 LITTLE NIKITA
Director: Richard Benjamin
Co-stars: Sidney Poitier River Phoenix Richard Jenkins

1988 BODY OF EVIDENCE
Director: Roy Campanella
Co-stars: Margot Kidder Barry Bostwick Tony LoBianco

1989 BORN ON THE FOURTH OF JULY
Director: Oliver Stone
Co-stars: Tom Cruise Bryan Larkin Seth Allen

1990 MURDER TIMES SEVEN
Director: Jud Taylor
Co-stars: Richard Crenna Cliff Gorman

CHRISTINE KAVANAGH

1991 CHIMERA
Director: Lawrence Gordon Clark
Co-stars: John Lynch Kenneth Cranham George Costigan

1991 UNDERBELLY
Director: Nicholas Renton
Co-stars: David Hayman Tom Wilkinson Ray Winstone

KAREN KAVLI

1935 WALPURGIS NIGHT
Director: Gustav Edgren
Co-stars: Lars Hanson Victor Sjostrom

1964 NOW ABOUT THESE WOMEN
Director: Ingmar Bergman
Co-stars: Jarl Kulle Eva Dahlbeck Bibi Andersson

JULIE KAVNER

1980 REVENGE OF THE STEPFORD WIVES
Director: Robert Furst
Co-stars: Sharon Gless Audra Lindley

1985 BAD MEDICINE
Director: Harvey Miller
Co-stars: Steve Guttenberg Alan Arkin Julie Haggerty

1987 RADIO DAYS
Director: Woody Allen
Co-stars: Woody Allen Mia Farrow Dianne Wiest Seth Green

1987 SURRENDER
Director: Jerry Belson
Co-stars: Sally Field Michael Caine Peter Boyle

1990 ALICE
Director: Woody Allen
Co-stars: Mia Farrow Joe Mantegna William Hurt

1990 AWAKENINGS
Director: Penny Marshall
Co-stars: Robin Williams Robert De Niro Ruth Nelson

1991 SHADOWS AND FOG
Director: Woody Allen
Co-stars: Woody Allen Mia Farrow Jodie Foster Lily Tomlin

1992 THIS IS MY LIFE
Director: Nora Ephron
Co-stars: Samantha Mathis Gaby Hoffman Carrie Fisher

1994 I'LL DO ANYTHING
Director: James Brooks
Co-stars: Nick Nolte Albert Brooks Joely Richardson

1995 FORGET PARIS
Director: Billy Crystal
Co-stars: Billy Crystal Debra Winger Joe Mantegna

BEATRICE KAY

1945 DIAMOND HORSESHOE
Director: George Seaton
Co-stars: Betty Grable Dick Haymes Phil Silvers

1961 UNDERWORLD U.S.A.
Director: Samuel Fuller
Co-stars: Cliff Robertson Larry Gates Dolores Dorn

BERNICE KAY

1941 WIDE OPEN TOWN
Co-stars: William Boyd Russell Hayden Evelyn Brent

DIANNE KAY

1988 ANDY COLBY'S INCREDIBLE ADVENTURE
Director: Randy Josselyn
Co-stars: Vince Edwards Richard Thomas

FIONA KAY *(Child)*

1984 VIGIL
Director: Vincent Ward
Co-stars: Bill Kerr Penelope Stewart Gordon Shields

JOYCE KAY

1936 THE PRISONER OF SHARK ISLAND
Director: John Ford
Co-stars: Warner Baxter Gloria Stuart Harry Carey

MARY ELLEN KAY

1953 VICE SQUAD
Director: Arnold Laven
Co-stars: Edward G. Robinson Paulette Goddard K. T. Stevens

SYLVIA KAY

1982 COMING OUT OF THE ICE
Director: Waris Hussein
Co-stars: John Savage Francesca Annis Ben Cross

1990 COME HOME CHARLIE AND FACE THEM
Director: Robert Bamford
Co-stars: Tom Radcliffe Jennifer Calvert

CAREN KAYE

1980 CUBA CROSSING
Director: Chuck Workman
Co-stars: Stuart Whitman Robert Vaughn Woody Strode

1982 MY TUTOR
Director: George Bowers
Co-stars: Matt Lattanzi Kevin McCarthy Crispin Glover

1984 POISON IVY
Director: Larry Elikann
Co-stars: Michael J. Fox Nancy McKeon Robert Klein

CELIA KAYE

1964 ISLAND OF THE BLUE DOLPHINS
Director: James Clark
Co-stars: Larry Dornasin George Kennedy

1965 WILD SEED
Director: Brian Hutton
Co-stars: Michael Parks Ross Elliott Eva Novak

CLARISSA KAYE *(Married James Mason)*

1970 NED KELLY
Director: Tony Richardson
Co-stars: Mick Jagger Mark McManus Allen Bickford

1983 DR. FISCHER OF GENEVA
Director: Michael Lindsay-Hogg
Co-stars: James Mason Alan Bates Greta Scacchi

LILA KAYE

1971 BLIND TERROR
Director: Richard Fleischer
Co-stars: Mia Farrow Robin Bailey Dorothy Alison

1981 AN AMERICAN WEREWOLF IN LONDON
Director: John Landis
Co-stars: David Naughton Griffin Dunne Jenny Agutter

1987 THE RETURN OF SHERLOCK HOLMES
Director: Kevin Connor
Co-stars: Michael Pennington Margaret Colin

1990 NUNS ON THE RUN
Director: Jonathan Lynn
Co-stars: Eric Idle Robbie Coltrane Janet Suzman

LUCIE KAYE

1937 JIM HANVEY – DETECTIVE
Co-stars: Tom Brown Guy Kibbee

LAINIE KAZAN

1968 DAYTON'S DEVILS
Director: Jack Shea
Co-stars: Leslie Nielsen Rory Calhoun Hams Gudegast

1968 LADY IN CEMENT
Director: Gordon Douglas
Co-stars: Frank Sinatra Raquel Welch Richard Conte

1980 ADDICTION: A CRY FOR LOVE
Director: Paul Wendkos
Co-stars: Susan Blakely Gene Barry Powers Booth

1982 MY FAVOURITE YEAR
Director: Richard Benjamin
Co-stars: Peter O'Toole Jessica Harper Joseph Bologna

1982 ONE FROM THE HEART
Director: Francis Coppola
Co-stars: Frederic Forrest Teri Garr Nastassja Kinski

1983 SUNSET LIMOUSINE
Director: Terry Hughes
Co-stars: John Ritter Susan Dey Martin Mull

1984 OBSESSIVE LOVE
Director: Steven Hillard Stern
Co-stars: Yvette Mimieux Simon MacCorkindale

1984 LUST IN THE DUST
Director: Paul Bartel
Co-stars: Tab Hunter Geoffrey Lewis Cesar Romero

1985 THE JOURNEY OF NATTY GANN
Director: Jeremy Kagan
Co-stars: Meredith Salenger John Cusack Ray Wise

1986 DELTA FORCE
Director: Menaham Golan
Co-stars: Chuck Norris Lee Marvin Martin Balsam

1988 BEACHES
Director: Garry Marshall
Co-stars: Bette Midler Barbara Hershey John Heard

1991 29TH STREET
Director: George Gallo
Co-stars: Danny Aiello Anthony LaPaglia

1992 I DON'T BUY KISSES ANYMORE
Director: Robert Marcarelli
Co-stars: Jason Alexander Nia Peeples Eileen Brennan

BETTY KEAN

1944 MURDER IN THE BLUE ROOM
Director: Leslie Goodwins
Co-stars: Anne Gwynne Donald Cook June Preisser

1944 MY GAL LOVES MUSIC
Co-stars: Bob Crosby Grace McDonald Walter Catlett

MARIE KEAN

1956 JACQUELINE
Director: Roy Baker
Co-stars: John Gregson Kathleen Ryan Jacqueline Ryan

1958 BROTH OF A BOY
Director: George Pollock
Co-stars: Barry Fitzgerald June Thorburn Tony Wright

1958 ROONEY
Director: George Pollock
Co-stars: John Gregson Barry Fitzgerald Muriel Pavlow

1963 THE QUARE FELLOW
Director: Arthur Dreifuss
Co-stars: Patrick McGoohan Sylvia Syms Dermot Kelly

1963 GIRL WITH GREEN EYES
Director: Desmond Davis
Co-stars: Peter Finch Rita Tushington Lynn Redgrave

1965 I WAS HAPPY HERE
Director: Desmond Davis
Co-stars: Sarah Miles Cyril Cusack Julian Glover

1968 GREAT CATHERINE
Director: Gordon Flemyng
Co-stars: Jeanne Moreau Peter O'Toole Zero Mostel

1970 RYAN'S DAUGHTER
Director: David Lean
Co-stars: Robert Mitchum Sarah Miles John Mills

1975 BARRY LYNDON
Director: Stanley Kubrick
Co-stars: Ryan O'Neal Marisa Berenson Hardy Kruger

1982 ANGEL
Director: Neil Jordan
Co-stars: Stephen Rea Veronica Quilligan Alan Devlin

1987 THE ROCKINGHAM SHOOT
Director: Kieran Hickey
Co-stars: Bosco Hogan Niall Tobin Oliver Maguire

1987 THE LONELY PASSION OF JUDITH HEARNE
Director: Jack Clayton
Co-stars: Maggie Smith Bob Hoskins

KERRIE KEANE

1981 INCUBUS
Director: John Hough
Co-stars: John Cassavetes Helen Hughes John Ireland

1983 SPASMS
Director: William Fruet
Co-stars: Peter Fonda Oliver Reed Al Waxman

1985 A DEATH IN CALIFORNIA
Director: Delbert Mann
Co-stars: Cheryl Ladd Sam Elliott Alexis Smith

1986 KUNG FU: THE MOVIE
Director: Richard Lang
Co-stars: David Carradine Keye Luke Brandon Lee

1986 SECOND SERVE
Director: Anthony Page
Co-stars: Vanessa Redgrave Martin Balsam Louise Fletcher

1988 DISTANT THUNDER
Director: Rick Rosenberg
Co-stars: John Lithgow Reb Brown Janet Margolin

1989 OBSESSED
Director: Robin Spry
Co-stars: Daniel Pilon Saul Rubinek Colleen Dewhurst

CAMILLE KEATON *(Grandniece Of Buster Keaton)*

1977 I SPIT ON YOUR GRAVE
Director: Meir Zarchi

DIANE KEATON
Received Oscar For Best Actress In 1977 For "Annie Hall" Nominated For Best Actress In 1981 For "Reds" And In 1997 For "Marvin's Room",

1970 LOVERS AND OTHER STRANGERS
Director: Cy Howard
Co-stars: Gig Young Bonnie Bedelia Michael Brandon

1972 PLAY IT AGAIN SAM
Director: Herbert Ross
Co-stars: Woody Allen Susan Anspach Jerry Lacy

1972 THE GODFATHER
Director: Francis Coppola
Co-stars: Al Pacino Robert De Niro James Caan

1973 SLEEPER
Director: Woody Allen
Co-stars: Woody Allen John Beck Mary Gregory

1974 THE GODFATHER PART II
Director: Francis Coppola
Co-stars: Al Pacino Robert De Niro Robert Duvall

1975 I WILL … I WILL … FOR NOW
Director: Norman Panama
Co-stars: Elliott Gould Paul Sorvino Victoria Principal

1975 LOVE AND DEATH
Director: Woody Allen
Co-stars: Woody Allen Georges Adel Frank Adu

1976 HARRY AND WALTER GO TO NEW YORK
Director: Mark Rydell
Co-stars: James Caan Elliott Gould

1977 ANNIE HALL
Director: Woody Allen
Co-stars: Woody Allen Tony Roberts Carol Kane Shelly Duvall

1977 LOOKING FOR MR. GOODBAR
Director: Richard Brooks
Co-stars: Richard Gere Tuesday Weld Tom Berenger

1978 INTERIORS
Director: Woody Allen
Co-stars: Woody Allen Richard Jordan Kristin Griffith Marybeth Hurt

1979 MANHATTAN
Director: Woody Allen
Co-stars: Woody Allen Meryl Streep Mariel Hemingway

1981 REDS
Director: Warren Beatty
Co-stars: Warren Beatty Edward Herrman Jack Nicholson

1981 SHOOT THE MOON
Director: Alan Parker
Co-stars: Albert Finney Karen Allen Peter Weller

1984 MRS. SOFFEL
Director: Gillian Armstrong
Co-stars: Mel Gibson Matthew Modine Edward Herrman

1984 THE LITTLE DRUMMER GIRL
Director: George Roy Hill
Co-stars: Yorgo Voragis Klaus Kinski Sami Frey

1986 CRIMES OF THE HEART
Director: Bruce Beresford
Co-stars: Jessica Lange Sissy Spacek Sam Shepard

1987 BABY BOOM
Director: Charles Shyer
Co-stars: Sam Wanamaker Sam Shepard Harold Ramis

1987 RADIO DAYS
Director: Woody Allen
Co-stars: Woody Allen Mia Farrow Diane Wiest Seth Green

1988 THE PRICE OF PASSION
Director: Leonard Nimoy
Co-stars: Liam Neeson Jason Robards Teresa Wright

1990 THE LEMON SISTERS
Director: Joyce Chopra
Co-stars: Carol Kane Elliott Gould Anthony Quinn

1990 THE GODFATHER PART III
Director: Francis Coppola
Co-stars: Al Pacino Talia Shire Andy Garcia

1992 FATHER OF THE BRIDE
Director: Charles Shyer
Co-stars: Steve Martin Kimberley Williams Martin Short

1993 MANHATTAN MURDER MYSTERY
Director: Woody Allen
Co-stars: Alan Alda Anjelica Huston Jerry Adler

1993 LOOK WHO'S TALKING NOW! *(Voice)*
Director: Tom Ropelewski
Co-stars: John Travolta Kirstie Alley

1994 AMELIA EARHART: THE FINAL FLIGHT
Director: Yves Simoneau
Co-stars: Bruce Dern Rutger Hauer

1996 THE FIRST WIVES CLUB
Director: Hugh Wilson
Co-stars: Goldie Hawn Bette Midler Sara Jessica Parker

1997 MARVIN'S ROOM
Co-stars: Meryl Streep Leonardo DiCaprio Gwen Verdon

ELE KEATS

1992 THE NEWS BOYS
Director: Kenny Ortega
Co-stars: Christian Bale Bill Pullman Ann-Margret

1992 FRANKIE AND JOHNNY
Director: Garry Marshall
Co-stars: Al Pacino Michelle Pfeiffer Kate Nelligan

VIOLA KEATS

1934 THE NIGHT OF THE PARTY
Director: Michael Powell
Co-stars: Leslie Banks Jane Baxter Ian Hunter

1935 THE GUV'NOR
Director: Milton Rosmer
Co-stars: George Arliss Patric Knowles Mary Clare

1936 A WOMAN ALONE
Director: Eugene Frenke
Co-stars: Anna Sten Henry Wilcoxon John Garrick

ANNA KEAVENEY

1989 SHIRLEY VALENTINE
Director: Lewis Gilbert
Co-stars: Pauline Collins Tom Conti Alison Steadman

1990 NEEDLE
Director: Gilles MacKinnon
Co-stars: Sean McKee Emma Bird Pete Postlethwaite

LILA KEDROVA
Oscar For Best Supporting Actress In 1964 For "Zorba The Greek"

1956 CALLE MAYOR
Director: Juan Antonio
Co-stars: Betsy Blair Yves Massard Rene Blancard

1958 MONTPARNASSE 19
Director: Jacques Becker
Co-stars: Gerard Phillipe Lilli Palmer Anouk Aimee

1964 ZORBA THE GREEK
Director: Michael Cacoyannis
Co-stars: Anthony Quinn Alan Bates Irene Papas

1965 HIGH WIND IN JAMAICA
Director: Alexander MacKendrick
Co-stars: Anthony Quinn Deborah Baxter James Coburn

1966 TORN CURTAIN
Director: Alfred Hitchcock
Co-stars: Paul Newman Julie Andrews

1966 PENELOPE
Director: Arthur Hiller
Co-stars: Natalie Wood Ian Bannen Peter Falk

1968 THE GIRL WHO COULDN'T SAY NO
Director: Franco Brusati
Co-stars: George Segal Virna Lisi

1970 THE KREMLIN LETTER
Director: John Huston
Co-stars: Richard Boone Orson Welles Bibi Andersson

1971 A TIME FOR LOVING
Director: Christopher Miles
Co-stars: Joanna Shimkus Mel Ferrer Britt Ekland

1973 SOFT BEDS, HARD BATTLES
Director: Roy Boulting
Co-stars: Peter Sellers Curt Jurgens Jenny Hanley

1976 THE TENANT
Director: Roman Polanski
Co-stars: Melvyn Douglas Isabelle Adjani Shelley Winters

1980 TELL ME A RIDDLE
Director: Lee Grant
Co-stars: Melvyn Douglas Brooke Adams Dolores Dorn

1988 SISTERS
Director: Michael Hoffman
Co-stars: Patrick Dempsey Jennifer Connelly Sheila Kelley

KARI KEEGAN

1993 JASON GOES TO HELL: THE FINAL FRIDAY
Director: Adam Marcus
Co-stars: Steve Williams Erin Gray

VIRGINIA KEEHNE

1992 TRICKS
Director: Tony Randel
Co-stars: Rosalind Allen Ami Dolenz Seth Green

RUBY KEELER *(Married Al Jolson)*

1933 FOOTLIGHT PARADE
Director: Lloyd Bacon
Co-stars: James Cagney Joan Blondell Dick Powell

1933 GOLD DIGGERS OF 1933
Director: Mervyn LeRoy
Co-stars: Warren William Joan Blondell Dick Powell

1933 FORTY-SECOND STREET
Director: Lloyd Bacon
Co-stars: Warner Baxter Dick Powell Ginger Rogers

1934 FLIRTATION WALK
Director: Frank Borzage
Co-stars: Dick Powell Pat O'Brien Ross Alexander

1934 DAMES
Director: Ray Enright
Co-stars: Dick Powell Joan Blondell Hugh Herbert Zasu Pitts

1935 SHIPMATES FOREVER
Director: Frank Borzage
Co-stars: Dick Powell Lewis Stone Dick Foran

1935 GO INTO YOUR DANCE
Director: Archie Mayo
Co-stars: Al Jolson Helen Morgan Glenda Farrell

1936 COLLEEN
Director: Alfred Green
Co-stars: Dick Powell Jack Oakie Joan Blondell

1937 READY WILLING AND ABLE
Director: Ray Enright
Co-stars: Ross Alexander Wini Shaw Jane Wyman

1938 MOTHER CAREY'S CHICKENS
Director: Rowland Lee
Co-stars: Fay Bainter Anne Shirley Walter Brennan

1941 SWEETHEART OF THE CAMPUS
Director: Edward Dmytryk
Co-stars: Ozzie Nelson Harriet Hilliard

DIANE KEEN

1976 SWEENEY!
Director: David Wickes
Co-stars: John Thaw Dennis Waterman Colin Welland

1980 SILVER DREAM RACER
Director: David Wickes
Co-stars: David Essex Beau Bridges Christina Raines

**1990 INSPECTOR WEXFORD:
SOME LIE AND SOME DIE**
Director: Sandy Johnson
Co-stars: George Baker Gemma Jones

1990 INSPECTOR WEXFORD:
THE BEST MAN TO DIE
Director: Herbert Wise
Co-stars: George Baker Louie Ramsay

1991 INSPECTOR WEXFORD:
A NEW LEASE OF DEATH
Director: Herbert Wise
Co-stars: George Baker Dorothy Tutin

1991 INSPECTOR WEXFORD:
FROM DOON WITH DEATH
Director: Mary McMurray
Co-stars: George Baker Amanda Redman

1991 INSPECTOR WEXFORD:
MURDER BEING ONCE DONE
Director: John Gorrie
Co-stars: George Baker Louie Ramsay

1991 INSPECTOR WEXFORD: MEANS OF EVIL
Director: Sarah Hellings
Co-stars: George Baker Cheryl Campbell

1991 INSPECTOR WEXFORD:
PUT ON BY CUNNING
Director: Sandy Johnson
Co-stars: George Baker Cherie Lunghi

1991 INSPECTOR WEXFORD:
AN UNKINDNESS OF RAVENS
Director: John Gorrie
Co-star: Christopher Ravenscroft George Baker

MONICA KEENA

1997 SNOW WHITE: A TALE OF TERROR
Director: Michael Cohn
Co-star: Sigourney Weaver

CATHERINE KEENER

1991 SWITCH
Director: Blake Edwards
Co-stars: Ellen Barkin Jimmy Smits JoBeth Williams

1992 JOHNNY SUEDE
Director: Tom DiCillo
Co-stars: Brad Pitt Alison Moir Tina Louise

1997 WALKING AND TALKING
Director: Nicole Holafcener
Co-stars: Anne Heche

1998 THE REAL BLONDE
Director: Tom DeCillo
Co-stars: Matthew Modine Kathleen Turner Daryl Hannah

KISHI KEIKO

1975 THE YAKUZA
Director: Sydney Pollack
Co-stars: Robert Mitchum Brian Keith Takakura Ken

ELIZABETH KEIFER

1992 LADYKILLER
Director: Michael Scott
Co-stars: Mimi Rogers Alice Krige John Shea

VIRGINIA KEILEY

1944 FANNY BY GASLIGHT
Director: Anthony Asquith
Co-stars: Phyllis Calvert James Mason Stewart Granger

BETTY LOU KEIM *(Child)*

1956 TEENAGE REBEL
Director: Edmund Goulding
Co-stars: Ginger Rogers Michael Rennie Mildred Natwick

1956 THESE WILDER YEARS
Director: Roy Rowland
Co-stars: James Cagney Barbara Stanwyck Walter Pidgeon

1957 THE WAYWARD BUS
Director: Victor Vicas
Co-stars: Dan Dailey Jayne Mansfield Joan Collins

ISABELLE KEITH

1930 BE BIG
Director: James Parrott
Co-stars: Stan Laurel Oliver Hardy Anita Garvin

JANE KEITH

1930 THE SEA WOLF
Co-stars: Raymond Hackett Milton Sills

PENELOPE KEITH

1970 EVERY HOME SHOULD HAVE ONE
Director: James Clark
Co-stars: Marty Feldman Julie Ege Judy Cornwell

1975 GHOST STORY
Director: Stephen Weeks
Co-stars: Murray Melvin Marianne Faithfull Barbara Shelley

1977 THE HOUND OF THE BASKERVILLES
Director: Paul Morrissey
Co-stars: Peter Cook Dudley Moore Denholm Elliott

1981 PRIEST OF LOVE
Director: Christopher Miles
Co-stars: Ian McKellen Janet Suzman Ava Gardner

ROSALIND KEITH

1935 ANNAPOLIS FAREWELL
Director: Alexander Hall
Co-stars: Sir Guy Standing Tom Brown Richard Cromwell

1935 THE GLASS KEY
Co-stars: George Raft Claire Dodd

1936 THEODORA GOES WILD
Director: Richard Boleslawski
Co-stars: Irene Dunne Melvyn Douglas Thomas Mitchell

1937 FIND THE WITNESS
Co-stars: John Tyrell Harry Tyler

1937 CRIMINALS OF THE AIR
Co-stars: Charles Quigley Matty Kemp

1937 A FIGHT TO THE FINISH
Co-star: Don Terry

SHEILA KEITH

1978 THE COMEBACK
Director: Peter Walker
Co-stars: Jack Jones Bill Owen Richard Johnson

1983 THE HOUSE OF THE LONG SHADOWS
Director: Peter Walker
Co-stars: Peter Cushing Vincent Price Richard Todd

1989 WILD FLOWERS
Director: Robert Smith
Co-stars: Alan Bates Beatie Edney Colette O'Neil

SELMA KEKLIKIAN

1988 FAMILY VIEWING
Director: Atom Egoyan
Co-stars: David Hemblen Aiden Tierney Gabrielle Rose

TINA KELLEGHER

1993   **THE SNAPPER**
Director: Stephen Frears
Co-stars: Colm Meaney Ruth McCabe Peter Rowen

MARTHE KELLER

1976   **MARATHON MAN**
Director: John Schlesinger
Co-stars: Dustin Hoffman Laurence Olivier Roy Schneider

1977   **BLACK SUNDAY**
Director: John Frankenheimer
Co-stars: Robert Shaw Bruce Dern Fritz Weaver

1977   **BOBBY DEERFIELD**
Director: Sydney Pollack
Co-stars: Al Pacino Anny Duperay Walter McGinn

1978   **FEDORA**
Director: Billy Wilder
Co-stars: William Holden Henry Fonda Hildegarde Neff

1980   **THE FORMULA**
Director: John Avildsen
Co-stars: George C. Scott Marlon Brando John Gielgud

1982   **THE AMATEUR**
Director: Charles Jarrott
Co-stars: John Savage Christopher Plummer Arthur Hill

1983   **WAGNER**
Director: Tony Palmer
Co-stars: Richard Burton Vanessa Redgrave Gemma Craven

1985   **ROUGE BAISER**
Director: Vera Belmont
Co-stars: Lambert Wilson Charlotte Valandrey Isabelle Nanty

1987   **BLACK EYES**
Director: Nikita Mikhalkov
Co-stars: Marcello Mastroianni Silvana Mangano Elena Sofanova

1992   **LAPSE OF MEMORY**
Director: Patrick DeWolf
Co-stars: John Hurt Kathleen Robertson

MARY PAGE KELLER

1989   **THOSE SHE LEFT BEHIND**
Director: Waris Hussein
Co-stars: Gary Cole Joanne Kerns Colleen Dewhurst

1994   **ULTERIOR MOTIVES**
Director: James Becket
Co-stars: Thomas Ian Griffith

ANNETTE KELLERMAN

1916   **A DAUGHTER OF THE GODS**

BARBARA KELLERMAN

1980   **THE SEA WOLVES**
Director: Andrew McLaglen
Co-stars: Gregory Peck Roger Moore David Niven

1989   **THE CHRONICLES OF NARNIA: THE LION, THE WITCH AND THE WARDROBE**
Director: Marilyn Fox
Co-stars: Richard Dempsey Sophie Cook Jonathan Scott

1989   **THE CHRONICLES OF NARNIA: PRINCE CASPIAN**
Director: Marilyn Fox
Co-stars: Richard Dempsey Sophie Cook Jonathan Scott

1989   **THE CHRONICLES OF NARNIA: VOYAGE OF THE DAWN TREADER**
Director: Alex Kirby
Co-stars: Richard Dempsey Sophie Cook Jonathan Scott

1990   **THE CHRONICLES OF NARNIA: THE SILVER CHAIR**
Director: Alex Kirby
Co-stars: David Thwaites Camilla Power

SALLY KELLERMAN
Nominated For Best Supporting Actress In 1970 For "M.A.S.H."

1965   **THE THIRD DAY**
Director: Jack Smight
Co-stars: George Peppard Elizabeth Ashley Roddy McDowall

1968   **THE BOSTON STRANGLER**
Director: Richard Fleischer
Co-stars: Tony Curtis Henry Fonda George Kennedy

1969   **THE APRIL FOOLS**
Director: Stuart Rosenberg
Co-stars: Jack Lemmon Catherine Deneuve Myrna Loy

1970   **BREWSTER McCLOUD**
Director: Robert Altman
Co-stars: Bud Cort Shelley Duvall Rene Auberjonois

1970   **M.A.S.H.**
Director: Robert Altman
Co-stars: Donald Sutherland Elliott Gould Robert Duvall

1971   **A REFLECTION OF FEAR**
Director: William Fraker
Co-stars: Robert Shaw Mary Ure Sondra Locke

1972   **SLITHER**
Director: Howard Zieff
Co-stars: James Caan Peter Boyle Louise Lasser

1972   **LAST OF THE RED HOT LOVERS**
Director: Gene Saks
Co-stars: Alan Arkin Paula Prentiss Renee Taylor

1972   **LOST HORIZON**
Director: Charles Jarrott
Co-stars: Peter Finch Liv Ullman Michael York Bobby Van

1975   **RAFFETY AND THE GOLD DUST TWINS**
Director: Dick Richards
Co-stars: Alan Arkin MacKenzie Phillips Alex Rocco

1976   **WELCOME TO L.A.**
Director: Alan Rudolph
Co-stars: Keith Carradine Sissy Spacek Lauren Hutton

1976   **THE BIG BUS**
Director: James Frawley
Co-stars: Joseph Bologna Stockard Channing John Beck

1978   **MAGEE AND THE LADY**
Director: Gene Levitt
Co-stars: Tony LoBianco Anne Sempler Kevin Leslie

1979   **A LITTLE ROMANCE**
Director: George Roy Hill
Co-stars: Laurence Olivier Diane Lane Arthur Hill

1980   **FOXES**
Director: Adrian Lyne
Co-stars: Jodie Foster Scott Baio Adam Faith Randy Quaid

1980   **HEAD ON**
Director: Michael Grant
Co-stars: Stephen Lack John Huston Lawrence Dane

1980   **LOVING COUPLES**
Director: Jack Smight
Co-stars: Shirley MacLaine James Coburn Susan Sarandon

1980   **SERIAL**
Director: Bill Persky
Co-stars: Martin Mull Tuesday Weld Nita Talbot Christopher Lee

1983   **DEMPSEY**
Director: Gus Trikonis
Co-stars: Treat Williams Sam Waterston Victoria Tennant Jesse Vint

1984   K.G.B.: THE SECRET WAR
Director: Dwight Little
Co-stars: Michael Billington Michael Ansara Denise Dubarry

1985   MOVING VIOLATIONS
Director: Neal Israel
Co-stars: Stephen McHattie Jennifer Tilly John Murray

1985   SEXPIONAGE
Director: Don Taylor
Co-stars: Linda Hamilton Viveca Lindfors Geena Davis

1986   THAT'S LIFE
Director: Blake Edwards
Co-stars: Jack Lemon Julie Andrews Robert Logia Felicia Farr

1986   BACK TO SCHOOL
Director: Alan Metter
Co-stars: Rodney Dangerfield Burt Young Robert Downey

1987   SOMEONE TO LOVE
Director: Henry Jaglom
Co-stars: Henry Jaglom Orson Welles Michael Emil

1987   THREE FOR THE ROAD
Director: B.W.L. North
Co-stars: Charlie Sheen Alan Ruck

1989   ALL'S FAIR
Director: Rocky Lang
Co-stars: George Segal Jennifer Edwards Robert Carradine

1989   LIMIT UP
Director: Richard Martini
Co-stars: Nancy Allen Dean Stockwell Brad Hall Ray Charles

1991   VICTIM OF BEAUTY
Director: Paul Lynch
Co-stars: Jennifer Rubin Peter Outbridge

1992   THE PLAYER
Director: Robert Altman
Co-stars: Tim Robbins Greta Sacchi Whoopi Goldberg

1993   YOUNGER AND YOUNGER
Director: Percy Adlon
Co-stars: Donald Sutherland Lolita Davidovich Linda Hunt

1994   MEATBALLS 3
Director: George Mendeluk
Co-stars: Patrick Dempsey Al Waxman Shannon Tweed

SUSAN KELLERMAN

1987   THE SECRET OF MY SUCCESS
Director: Herbert Ross
Co-stars: Michael J. Fox Helen Slater Richard Jordan

1989   ELVIRA, MISTRESS OF THE DARK
Director: James Signorelli
Co-stars: Cassandra Peterson Daniel Greene

SHEILA KELLEY

1988   SISTERS
Director: Michael Hoffman
Co-stars: Patrick Dempsey Jennifer Connelly Lila Kedrova

1989   MORTAL PASSIONS
Director: Andrew Lane
Co-stars: Zach Galligan Michael Bowen David Warner

1989   LOVING HAZEL
Director: Peter Smith
Co-stars: Hugh Quarshie Susan Brown Gemma Darlington

1989   BREAKING IN
Director: Bill Forsyth
Co-stars: Burt Reynolds Casey Siemaszko Albert Salmi

1991   BROKE
Director: Alan Dosser
Co-stars: Tomothy Spall Larry Lamb Susan Woolridge

1991   PURE LUCK
Director: Nadia Tass
Co-stars: Martin Short Danny Glover Sam Wanamaker

1991   SOAPDISH
Director: Michael Hoffman
Co-stars: Sally Field Whoopi Goldberg Kevin Kline

1992   SINGLES
Director: Cameron Crowe
Co-stars: Bridget Fonda Matt Dillon Campbell Scott

1993   PASSION FISH
Director: John Sayles
Co-stars: Mary McDonnell Alfre Woodard Angela Bassett

SISSY KELLING

1986   FEEL THE MOTION
Director: Wolfgang Buld
Co-stars: Ingrid Locke Frank Meyer-Brockman Meatloaf

PAMELA KELLINO
(Married Roy Kellino, James Mason)

1939   I MET A MURDERER
Director: Roy Kellino
Co-stars: James Mason Sylvia Coleridge William Devlin

1945   THEY WERE SISTERS
Director: Arthur Crabtree
Co-stars: James Mason Phyllis Calvert Dulcie Gray

1947   THE UPTURNED GLASS
Director: Lawrence Huntingdon
Co-stars: James Mason Rosamund John Ann Stephens

1951   PANDORA AND THE FLYING DUTCHMAN
Director: Albert Lewin
Co-stars: James Mason Ava Gardner Nigel Patrick

1952   THE LADY POSSESSED
Director: Roy Kellino
Co-stars: James Mason June Havoc Fay Compton

1952   CHARADE
Director: Roy Kellino
Co-stars: James Mason Scott Forbes Paul Kavanagh

LYNN KELLOGG

1969   CHARRO!
Director: Charles Marquis Warren
Co-stars: Elvis Presley Ina Balin Barbara Werle

BARBARA KELLY (Married Bernard Braden)

1951   A TALE OF FIVE CITIES
Director: Montgomery Tully
Co-stars: Bonar Colleano Gina Lollobrigida

1952   CASTLE IN THE AIR
Director: Henry Cass
Co-stars: David Tomlinson Helen Cherry Margaret Rutherford

1959   JET STORM
Director: Cy Endfield
Co-stars: Richard Attenborough Mai Zetterling Diane Cilento

CAROL KELLY

1958   TERROR IN A TEXAS TOWN
Director: Joseph Lewis
Co-stars: Sterling Hayden Sebastian Cabot Ned Young

CLAIRE KELLY

1958   UNDERWATER WARRIOR
Director: Andrew Marton
Co-stars: Dan Dailey Ross Martin James Gregory

1958 PARTY GIRL
Director: Nicholas Ray
Co-stars: Robert Taylor Cyd Charisse Lee J. Cobb

1958 THE BADLANDERS
Director: Delmer Daves
Co-stars: Alan Ladd Ernest Borgnine Katy Jurado

1959 ASK ANY GIRL
Director: Charles Walters
Co-stars: David Niven Shirley MacLaine Gig Young

1967 A GUIDE FOR THE MARRIED MAN
Director: Gene Kelly
Co-stars: Walter Matthau Inger Stevens Lucille Ball

CLARE KELLY

1966 GEORGY GIRL
Director: Silvio Narizzano
Co-stars: James Mason Lynn Redgrave Charlotte Rampling

1969 ALL NEAT IN BLACK STOCKINGS
Director: Christopher Morahan
Co-stars: Victor Henry Susan George

1970 AND SOON THE DARKNESS
Director: Robert Fuest
Co-stars: Pamela Franklin Michele Dotrice Sandor Eles

GRACE KELLY *(Married Prince Rainier Of Monaco)*
Best Actress in 1954 for "The Country Girl", Nominated for Best
Supporting Actress in 1953 for "Mogambo"

1951 FOURTEEN HOURS
Director: Henry Hathaway
Co-stars: Richard Basehart Paul Douglas Debra Paget

1952 HIGH NOON
Director: Fred Zinnemann
Co-stars: Gary Cooper Thomas Mitchell Lloyd Bridges

1953 MOGAMBO
Director: John Ford
Co-stars: Clark Gable Ava Gardner Donald Sinden

1954 DIAL M FOR MURDER
Director: Alfred Hitchcock
Co-stars: Ray Milland John Williams Robert Cummings

1954 THE BRIDGES AT TOKO-RI
Director: Mark Robson
Co-stars: William Holden Mickey Rooney Fredric March

1054 REAR WINDOW
Director: Alfred Hitchcock
Co-stars: James Stewart Raymond Burr Thelma Ritter

1954 THE COUNTRY GIRL
Director: George Seaton
Co-stars: Bing Crosby William Holden

1955 GREEN FIRE
Director: Andrew Marton
Co-stars: Stewart Granger Paul Douglas

1955 TO CATCH A THIEF
Director: Alfred Hitchcock
Co-stars: Cary Grant John Williams

1956 THE SWAN
Director: Charles Vidor
Co-stars: Alec Guinness Louis Jourdan Brian Aherne

1956 HIGH SOCIETY
Director: Charles Walters
Co-stars: Bing Crosby Frank Sinatra Celeste Holm

JEAN LOUISE KELLY

1989 UNCLE BUCK
Director: John Hughes
Co-stars: John Candy Gabby Hoffman Macauley Culkin

1996 MR. HOLLAND'S OPUS
Director: Stephen Herek
Co-stars: Richard Drefuss Glenne Headley

JEANNE KELLY

1941 A DANGEROUS GAME
Director: John Rawlins
Co-stars: Richard Arlen Andy Devine Marc Lawrence

JUDY KELLY

1933 THE PRIVATE LIFE OF HENRY VIII
Director: Alexander Korda
Co-stars: Charles Laughton Merle Oberon

1934 FOUR MASKED MEN
Director: George Pearson
Co-stars: John Stuart Miles Mander Sebastian Shaw

1934 THE BLACK ABBOT
Director: George Cooper
Co-stars: John Stuart Richard Cooper

1935 CAPTAIN BILL
Director: Ralph Ceder
Co-stars: Leslie Fuller Georgie Harris Hal Gordon

1935 CHARING CROSS ROAD
Director: Albert De Courville
Co-stars: John Mills June Clyde Jean Colin

1935 THINGS ARE LOOKING UP
Director: Albert De Courville
Co-stars: Cicely Courtneidge Max Miller Vivien Leigh

1937 AREN'T MEN BEASTS?
Director: Graham Cutts
Co-stars: Robertson Hare Alfred Drayon June Clyde

1938 PREMIERE
Director: Walter Summers
Co-stars: John Lodge Hugh Williams Edward Chapman

1939 DEAD MAN'S SHOES
Director: Thomas Bentley
Co-stars: Leslie Banks Joan Marion Wilfrid Lawson

1939 AT THE VILLA ROSE
Director: Walter Summers
Co-stars: Kenneth Kent Walter Rilla Peter Murray-Hill

1940 GEORGE AND MARGARET
Director: George King
Co-stars: Marie Lohr Oliver Wakefield Noel Howlett

1942 TOMORROW WE LIVE
Director: George King
Co-stars: John Clements Greta Gynt Hugh Sinclair

1944 IT HAPPENED ONE SUNDAY
Director: Karel Lamac
Co-stars: Robert Beatty Barbara White Marjorie Rhodes

1945 DEAD OF NIGHT
Director: Basil Dearden
Co-stars: Mervyn Johns Googie Withers Michael Redgrave

KATHLEEN KELLY

1936 THE AVENGING HAND
Director: Victor Hanbury
Co-stars: Noah Beery James Harcourt Louis Borell

1937 THE MUTINY OF THE ELSINORE
Director: Roy Lockwood
Co-stars: Paul Lukas Lyn Harding Clifford Evans

KAROLEE KELLY

1955 THE GIRL IN THE RED VELVET SWING
Director: Richard Fleischer
Co-stars: Ray Milland Joan Collins

KITTY KELLY

1932 LADIES OF THE JURY
Director: Lowell Sherman
Co-stars: Edna May Oliver Cora Witherspoon Jill Esmond

MOIRA KELLY

1990 JACOB'S LADDER
Director: Adrian Lyne
Co-stars: Tim Robbins Elizabeth Pena Danny Aiello

1992 THE CUTTING EDGE
Director: Paul Michael Glaser
Co-stars: D. B. Sweeney Roy Dotrice Terry O'Quinn

1992 BILLY BATHGATE
Director: Robert Benton
Co-stars: Dustin Hoffman Nicole Kidman Loren Dean

1992 TWIN PEAKS: FIRE WALK WITH ME
Director: David Lynch
Co-stars: Sheryl Lee Ray Wise Dana Ashbrook

1993 CHAPLIN
Director: Richard Attenborough
Co-stars: Robert Downey Jnr. Geraldine Chaplin Kevin Kline

1993 BLOODSTREAM
Director: Stephen Tolkin
Co-stars: Cuba Gooding Jnr. Omar Epps Alice Drummond

1994 WITH HONORS
Director: Alek Keshisian
Co-stars: Joe Pesci Brendan Fraser Patrick Dempsey

1995 THE TIE THAT BINDS
Director: Wesley Stick
Co-stars: Daryl Hannah Keith Carradine Vincent Spano

MONIKA KELLY

1971 THE CORPSE GRINDERS
Director: Ted Mikels
Co-stars: Sean Kenney Warren Ball Ann Noble

NANCY KELLY

Nominated for Best Actress in 1956 for "The Bad Seed"

1938 SUBMARINE PATROL
Director: John Ford
Co-stars: Richard Greene Preston Foster George Bancroft

1939 TAIL SPIN
Director: Roy Del Ruth
Co-stars: Alice Faye Constance Bennett Joan Davis Jane Wyman

1939 STANLEY AND LIVINGSTONE
Director: Henry King
Co-stars: Spencer Tracy Walter Brennan Richard Greene

1939 JESSE JAMES
Director: Henry King
Co-stars: Tyrone Power Henry Fonda Randolph Scott Brian Donlevy

1939 FRONTIER MARSHALL
Director: Allan Dwan
Co-stars: Randolph Scott Cesar Romero Binnie Barnes Ward Bond

1940 HE MARRIED HIS WIFE
Director: Roy Del Ruth
Co-stars: Joel McCrea Cesar Romero Roland Young

1940 ONE NIGHT IN THE TROPICS
Director: Edward Sutherland
Co-stars: Allan Jones Bud Abbott Lou Costello

1940 PRIVATE AFFAIRS
Director: Albert Rogell
Co-stars: Robert Cummings Roland Young Hugh Herbert

1941 SCOTLAND YARD
Director: Norman Foster
Co-stars: Edmund Gwenn Henry Wilcoxon John Loder

1941 A VERY YOUNG LADY
Director: Harold Schuster
Co-stars: Jane Withers John Sutton Cecil Kellaway

1941 PARACHUTE BATTALION
Director: Leslie Goodwins
Co-stars: Robert Preston Edmond O'Brien Buddy Ebson

1941 FRIENDLY ENEMIES
Director: Allan Dwan
Co-stars: Charles Winninger Charles Ruggles Otto Kruger

1942 TO THE SHORES OF TRIPOLI
Director: Bruce Humberstone
Co-stars: John Payne Maureen O'Hara Randolph Scott

1942 FLY BY NIGHT
Director: Robert Siodmak
Co-stars: Richard Carlson Albert Basserman

1943 TARZAN'S DESERT MYSTERY
Director: William Thiele
Co-stars: Johnny Weismuller Johnny Sheffield Otto Kruger

1943 WOMEN IN BONDAGE
Director: Steve Sekeley
Co-stars: Gail Patrick Gertrude Michael Anne Nagel

1944 SHOW BUSINESS
Director: Edwin Marin
Co-stars: Eddie Cantor Joan Davis George Murphy

1944 DOUBLE EXPOSURE
Director: William Berke
Co-stars: Chester Morris Jane Farrar Richard Gaines

1945 BETRAYAL FROM THE EAST
Director: William Berke
Co-stars: Lee Tracy Richard Loo Abner Biberman

1945 THE WOMAN WHO CAME BACK
Director: Walter Colmes
Co-stars: John Loder Otto Kruger Ruth Ford

1946 MURDER IN THE MUSIC HALL
Director: John English
Co-stars: Vera Ralston William Marshall

1956 THE BAD SEED
Director: Mervyn LeRoy
Co-stars: Patty McCormack Eileen Heckart Henry Jones

PATSY KELLY

1933 THE COUNTESS OF MONTE CRISTO
Director: Karl Freund
Co-stars: Fay Wray Paul Lukas Reginald Owen

1933 GOING TO HOLLYWOOD
Director: Raoul Walsh
Co-stars: Bing Crosby Marion Davies Stuart Erwin

1934 THE GIRL FROM MISSOURI
Director: Jack Conway
Co-stars: Jean Harlow Franchot Tone Lionel Barrymore

1935 EVERY NIGHT AT EIGHT
Director: Raoul Walsh
Co-stars: George Raft Alice Faye Frances Langford

1935 GO INTO YOUR DANCE
Director: Archie Mayo
Co-stars: Al Jolson Ruby Keeler Glenda Farrell Helen Morgan

1935 PAGE MISS GLORY
Director: Mervyn LeRoy
Co-stars: Dick Powell Marion Davies Pat O'Brien

1935 THANKS A MILLION
Director: Roy Del Ruth
Co-stars: Dick Powell Ann Dvorak Fred Allen

1936 SING, BABY, SING
Director: Sidney Lanfield
Co-stars: Alice Faye Adolphe Menjou Ritz Bros.

1936 PRIVATE NUMBER
Director: Roy Del Ruth
Co-stars: Loretta Young Robert Taylor Basil Rathbone

1936 PIGSKIN PARADE
Director: David Butler
Co-stars: Jack Haley Betty Grable Judy Garland

1936 KELLY THE SECOND
Director: Hal Roach
Co-stars: Guinn Williams Charley Chase Pert Kelton

1937 EVER SINCE EVE
Director: Lloyd Bacon
Co-stars: Marion Davies Robert Montgomery Frank McHugh

1937 NOBODY'S BABY
Director: Gus Meins
Co-stars: Lyda Roberti Lynne Overman Robert Armstrong

1937 PICK A STAR
Director: Edward Sedgwick
Co-stars: Jack Haley Rosina Lawrence Stan Laurel Oliver Hardy

1937 WAKE UP AND LIVE
Director: Sidney Lanfield
Co-stars: Jack Haley Alice Faye Walter Winchell

1938 THERE GOES MY HEART
Director: Norman Z. McLeod
Co-stars: Fredric March Virginia Bruce Nancy Carroll

1938 MERRILY WE LIVE
Director: Norman Z. Mcleod
Co-stars: Constance Bennett Brian Aherne Ann Dvorak

1938 THE COWBOY AND THE LADY
Director: H. C. Potter
Co-stars: Gary Cooper Merle Oberon Walter Brennan

1939 THE GORILLA
Director: Allan Dwan
Co-stars: Ritz Bros. Bela Lugosi Lionel Atwill

1941 BROADWAY LIMITED
Director: Gordon Douglas
Co-stars: Marjorie Woodworth Victor McLaglen

1941 PLAYMATES
Director: David Butler
Co-stars: Kay Kyser John Barrymore Lupe Velez

1941 ROAD SHOW
Director: Gordon Douglas
Co-stars: John Hubbard Carole Landis Adolphe Menjou

1941 SING YOUR WORRIES AWAY
Director: Edward Sutherland
Co-stars: Bert Lahr Buddy Ebsen June Havoc

1942 IN OLD CALIFORNIA
Director: William McGann
Co-stars: John Wayne Binnie Barnes Albert Decker

1943 LADIES DAY
Co-stars: Joan Barclay Max Baer Iris Adrian

1960 PLEASE DON'T EAT THE DAISIES
Director: Charles Walters
Co-stars: Doris Day David Niven Janis Page

1960 THE CROWDED SKIES
Director: Joseph Pevney
Co-stars: Dana Andrews Rhonda Fleming Anne Francis

1964 THE NAKED KISS
Director: Samuel Fuller
Co-stars: Constance Towers Anthony Eisley

1966 THE GHOST IN THE INVISIBLE BIKINI
Director: Don Weis
Co-stars: Boris Karloff Basil Rathbone

1968 ROSEMARY'S BABY
Director: Roman Polanski
Co-stars: Mia Farrow John Cassavettes Ralph Bellamy

1976 FREAKY FRIDAY
Director: Gary Nelson
Co-stars: Jodie Foster Barbara Harris John Astin

1979 THE NORTH AVENUE IRREGULARS
Director: Bruce Bilson
Co-stars: Edward Herrman Barbara Harris

PAULA KELLY

1969 SWEET CHARITY
Director: Bob Fosse
Co-stars: Shirley MacLaine Ricardo Montalban Chita Rivera

1970 THE ANDROMEDA STRAIN
Director: Robert Wise
Co-stars: Arthur Hill David Wayne Kate Reid

1974 UPTOWN SATURDAY NIGHT
Director: Sidney Poitier
Co-stars: Sidney Poitier Bill Cosby Harry Belafonte Richard Pryor

1976 DRUM
Director: Steve Carver
Co-stars: Warren Oates Ken Norton Pam Grier

1987 UNCLE TOM'S CABIN
Director: Stan Lathan
Co-stars: Avery Brooks Kate Burton Bruce Dern

RACHEL KELLY

1984 SCREAM FOR HELP
Director: Michael Winner
Co-stars: David Brooks Marie Masters Rocco Sisto

ROZ KELLY

1970 THE OWL AND THE PUSSYCAT
Director: Herbert Ross
Co-stars: George Segal Barbra Streisand Robert Klein

1981 FULL MOON HIGH
Director: Larry Cohen
Co-stars: Adam Arkin Elizabeth Hartman Ed McMahon

TRUDY KELLY

1987 THE VENUS DE MILO INSTEAD
Director: Danny Boyle
Co-stars: Jeananne Crowley Lorcan Cranitch Ann Hasson

LINDA KELSEY

1984 HIS MISTRESS
Director: David Lowell Rich
Co-stars: Robert Urich Julianne Phillips Cynthia Silkes

1984 ATTACK ON FEAR
Director: Mel Damski
Co-stars: Paul Michael Glaser Kevin Conway Barbara Babcock

1993 SUDDEN FURY
Director: Craig Baxley
Co-stars: Neil Patrick Harris John M. Jackson Johnny Galeck

1993 SHATTERED FAMILY
Director: Sandy Smolan
Co-stars: Richard Crenna Rhea Perlman Tom Guiry

1995 IF SOMEONE HAD KNOWN
Director: Eric Laneuville
Co-stars: Kellie Martin Kevin Dobson

TAMSIN KELSEY

1991   YES VIRGINIA, THERE IS A SANTA CLAUS
Director: Charles Jarrott
Co-stars: Charles Bronson Richard Thomas

PERT KELTON

1933   THE BOWERY
Director: Raoul Walsh
Co-stars: Wallace Beery George Raft Fay Wray

1933   BED OF ROSES
Director: Gregory La Cava
Co-stars: Constance Bennett Joel McCrea

1934   BACHELOR BAIT
Director: George Stevens
Co-stars: Stuart Erwin Rochelle Hudson Grady Sutton

1934   THE MEANEST GAL IN TOWN
Co-star: James Gleason

1935   HOORAY FOR LOVE
Director: Walter Lang
Co-stars: Ann Sothern Gene Raymond Bill Robinson

1935   MARY BURNS FUGITIVE
Director: William Howard
Co-stars: Sylvia Sidney Melvyn Douglas Wallace Ford

1935   LIGHTNING STRIKE TWICE
Co-star: Walter Catlett

1936   KELLY THE SECOND
Director: Hal Roach
Co-stars: Patsy Kelly Guinn Williams Charley Chase

1936   CAIN AND MABEL
Director: Lloyd Bacon
Co-stars: Clark Gable Marion Davies Allen Jenkins

1937   THE HIT PARADE
Director: Gus Meins
Co-stars: Frances Langford Phil Regan Louise Henry

1937   WOMEN OF GLAMOUR
Director: Gordon Wiles
Co-stars: Melvyn Douglas Virginia Bruce Reginald Denny

1938   RHYTHM OF THE SADDLE
Co-stars: Gene Autry Smiley Burnette Peggy Moran

1962   THE MUSIC MAN
Director: Marion Hargrove
Co-stars: Robert Preston Shirley Jones Buddy Hackett

1969   THE COMIC
Director: Carl Reiner
Co-stars: Dick Van Dyke Mickey Rooney Cornel Wilde

STELLA KEMBALL

1964   IT HAPPENED HERE
Director: Andrew Mollo
Co-stars: Pauline Murray Sebastian Shaw Nicolette Bernard

LILLIAN KEMBLE-COOPER

1939   GONE WITH THE WIND
Director: Victor Fleming
Co-stars: Clark Gable Vivien Leigh Leslie Howard

VIOLET KEMBLE-COOPER

1933   OUR BETTERS
Director: George Cukor
Co-stars: Constance Bennett Alan Mowbray Gilbert Roland

1934   THE FOUNTAIN
Director: John Cromwell
Co-stars: Ann Harding Brian Aherne Paul Lukas

1935   THE INVISIBLE RAY
Director: Lambert Hillyer
Co-stars: Boris Karloff Bela Lugosi Frances Drake

1935   DAVID COPPERFIELD
Director: George Cukor
Co-stars: Freddie Bartholomew W. C. Fields Roland Young

1935   CARDINAL RICHELIEU
Director: Rowland Lee
Co-stars: George Arliss Maureen O'Sullivan Edward Arnold

1935   VANESSA, HER LOVE STORY
Director: William Howard
Co-stars: Helen Hayes Robert Montgomery May Robson

1936   ROMEO AND JULIET
Director: George Cukor
Co-stars: Leslie Howard Norma Shearer John Barrymore

ELIZABETH KEMP

1980   HE KNOWS YOU'RE ALONE
Director: Armand Mastroianni
Co-stars: Don Scardino Tom Hanks Caitlin O'Heaney

VALLI KEMP

1972   DR. PHIBES RIDES AGAIN
Director: Robert Fuest
Co-stars: Vincent Price Robert Quarry Fiona Lewis

JOAN KEMP-WELCH

1940   BUSMAN'S HONEYMOON
Director: Arthur Woods
Co-stars: Robert Montgomery Constance Cummings Leslie Banks

1941   PIMPERNEL SMITH
Director: Leslie Howard
Co-stars: Leslie Howard Mary Morris Hugh McDermott

1941   THEY FLEW ALONE
Director: Herbert Wilcox
Co-stars: Anna Neagle Robert Newton Edward Chapman

BRENDA KEMPNER

1989   BACK HOME
Director: Piers Haggard
Co-stars: Hayley Mills Hayley Carr Brenda Bruce

RACHEL KEMPSON
(Married Michael Redgrave, Mother Of Vanessa,
Lynn, Corin Regrave Grandmother Of Natasha,
Miranda, Joely Richardson And Jemma Redgrave)

1946   THE CAPTIVE HEART
Director: Basil Dearden
Co-stars: Michael Redgrave Jack Warner Basil Radford

1948   A WOMAN'S VENGEANCE
Director: Zoltan Korda
Co-stars: Charles Boyer Jessica Tandy Ann Blyth

1963   TOM JONES
Director: Tony Richardson
Co-stars: Albert Finney Susannah York Hugh Griffith

1963   THE THIRD SECRET
Director: Charles Crichton
Co-stars: Stephen Boyd Pamela Franklyn Diane Cilento

1965   CURSE OF THE FLY
Director: Don Sharp
Co-stars: Brian Donlevy George Baker Carole Gray

1966   GEORGY GIRL
Director: Silvio Narizzano
Co-stars: Lynn Redgrave James Mason Charlotte Rampling

1967   **THE JOKERS**
Director: Michael Winner
Co-stars: Michael Crawford Oliver Reed Harry Andrews

1969   **TWO GENTLEMEN SHARING**
Director: Ted Kotcheff
Co-stars: Robin Phillips Hal Frederick Judy Geeson

1969   **THE VIRGIN SOLDIERS**
Director: John Dexter
Co-stars: Hywel Bennett Lynn Redgrave Nigel Patrick

1971   **JANE EYRE**
Director: Delbert Mann
Co-stars: George C. Scott Susannah York Ian Bannen

1985   **OUT OF AFRICA**
Director: Sydney Pollack
Co-stars: Meryl Streep Robert Redford Michael Kitchen

1989   **SHE'S BEEN AWAY**
Director: Peter Hall
Co-stars: Peggy Ashcroft Geraldine James Rosalie Crutchley

1989   **STEALING HEAVEN**
Director: Clive Donner
Co-stars: Derek De Lint Kim Thompson Denholm Elliott

1990   **LORNA DOONE**
Director: Andrew Grieve
Co-stars: Clive Owen Sean Bean Polly Walker

FELICITY KENDAL (Daughter Of Geoffrey Kendal, Sister Of Jennifer Kendal)

1965   **SHAKESPEARE WALLAH**
Director: James Ivory
Co-stars: Sashi Kapoor Geoffrey Kendal Madhur Jaffrey

1977   **VALENTINO**
Director: Ken Russell
Co-stars: Rudolph Nureyev Leslie Caron Michelle Phillips

1991   **THE CAMOMILE LAWN**
Director: Peter Hall
Co-stars: Jennifer Ehle Tara Fitzgerald Paul Eddington

JENNIFER KENDAL (Daughter Of Geoffrey Kendal, Sister Of Felicity Kendal)

1970   **BOMBAY TALKIE**
Director: James Ivory
Co-stars: Sashi Kapoor Zia Mohyeddin

1981   **36, CHOWRINGHEE LANE**
Director: Aparna Sen
Co-stars: Dhritiman Chatterjee Geoffrey Kendal Soni Razdan

BRENDA KENDALL

1992   **BRAIN DEAD**
Director: Peter Jackson
Co-stars: Timothy Balme Diana Penalver Elizabeth Moody

KAY KENDALL (Married Rex Harrison)

1946   **LONDON TOWN**
Director: Wesley Ruggles
Co-stars: Sid Field Greta Gynt Tessie O'Shea Petula Clark

1950   **DANCE HALL**
Director: Charles Crichton
Co-stars: Natasha Parry Jane Hylton Diana Dors

1951   **LADY GODIVA RIDES AGIAN**
Director: Frank Launder
Co-stars: Pauline Stroud Dennis Price George Cole

1952   **WINGS OF DANGER**

1952   **IT STARTED IN PARADISE**
Director: Compton Bennett
Co-stars: Jane Hylton Ian Hunter Terence Morgan

1952   **CURTAIN UP**
Director: Ralph Smart
Co-stars: Margaret Rutherford Robert Morley Joan Rice

1953   **STREET OF SHADOWS**
Director: Richard Vernon
Co-stars: Cesar Romero

1953   **MANTRAP**
Director: Terence Fisher
Co-stars: Paul Henreid Kieron Moore Lois Maxwell

1953   **MEET MR. LUCIFER**
Director: Anthony Pellisier
Co-stars: Stanley Holloway Peggy Cummings Jack Watling

1953   **THE SQUARE RING**
Director: Michael Relph
Co-stars: Jack Warner Robert Beatty Joan Collins

1953   **GENEVIEVE**
Director: Henry Cornelius
Co-stars: Kenneth Moore Dinah Sheridan John Gregson

1954   **ABDULLA THE GREAT**
Director: Gregory Ratoff
Co-stars: Gregory Ratoff Sydney Chaplin

1954   **DOCTOR IN THE HOUSE**
Director: Ralph Thomas
Co-stars: Dirk Bogarde Kenneth More Donald Sinden

1954   **FAST AND LOOSE**
Director: Gordon Parry
Co-stars: Brian Reece Stanley Holloway June Thorburn

1955   **THE ADVENTURES OF QUENTIN DURWARD**
Director: Richard Thorpe
Co-stars: Robert Taylor Robert Morley

1955   **SIMON AND LAURA**
Director: Muriel Box
Co-stars: Peter Finch Muriel Pavlow Ian Carmichael Hubert Gregg

1955   **THE CONSTANT HUSBAND**
Co-stars: Sidney Gilliat
Co-stars: Rex Harrison Margaret Leighton Cecil Parker

1957   **LES GIRLS**
Director: George Cukor
Co-stars: Gene Kelly Mitzi Gaynor Tania Elg Leslie Phillips

1958   **THE RELUCTANT DEBUTANTE**
Director: Vincente Minnelli
Co-stars: Rex Harrison Sandra Dee John Saxon

1959   **ONCE MORE WITH FEELING**
Director: Stanley Donen
Co-stars: Yul Brynner Geoffrey Toone Mervyn Johns

SUZY KENDALL

1966   **THE SANDWICH MAN**
Director: Robert Hartford Davis
Co-stars: Michael Bentine Norman Wisdom Dora Bryan

1967   **30 IS A DANGEROUS AGE, CYNTHIA**
Director: Joe McGrath
Co-stars: Dudley Moore Eddie Foy John Bird

1967   **UP THE JUNCTION**
Director: Peter Collinson
Co-stars: Dennis Waterman Adrienne Posta Hylda Baker

1967   **CIRCUS OF FEAR**
Director: John Moxey
Co-stars: Christopher Lee Leo Genn Klaus Kinski

1967   **THE PENTHOUSE**
Director: Peter Collinson
Co-stars: Terence Morgan Norman Rodway Tony Beckley

1967 TO SIR WITH LOVE
Director: James Clavell
Co-stars: Sidney Poitier Judy Geeson Lulu

1968 FRAULEIN DOKTOR
Director: Alberto Lattuada
Co-stars: Kenneth More James Booth Capucine

1969 THE BIRD WITH THE CRYSTAL PLUMMAGE
Director: Dario Argento
Co-stars: Tony Musante Eva Ranzi

1970 DARKER THAN AMBER
Director: Robert Clouse
Co-stars: Rod Taylor Theodore Bikel Jane Russell

1971 ASSAULT
Director: Sidney Hayers
Co-stars: Frank Finlay James Laurenson David Essex

1972 FEAR IS THE KEY
Director: Michael Tuchner
Co-stars: Barry Newman John Vernon Ben Kingsley

1973 TALES THAT WITNESS MADNESS
Director: Freddie Francis
Co-stars: Kim Novak Jack Hawkins Joan Collins

1974 CRAZE
Director: Freddie Francis
Co-stars: Jack Palance Diana Dors Julie Ege Edith Evans

1977 ADVENTURES OF A PRIVATE EYE
Director: Stanley Lang
Co-stars: Christopher Neil Diana Dors Liz Fraser

ALEXA KENIN

1982 HONKYTONK MAN
Director: Clint Eastwood
Co-stars: Clint Eastwood Kyle Eastwood John McIntyre

1982 A PIANO FOR MRS. CIMINO
Director: George Schafer
Co-stars: Bette Davis Penny Fuller Keenan Wynn

1986 PRETTY IN PINK
Director: Howard Deutch
Co-stars: Molly Ringwald Andrew McCarthy Jon Cryer

BETTY KENNEDY

1980 CHEECH AND CHONG'S NEXT MOVIE
Director: Thomas Chong
Co-stars: Thomas Chong Cheech Marin Evelyn Guerrero

DEBORAH KENNEDY

1979 TIM
Director: Michael Pate
Co-stars: Mel Gibson Piper Laurie Pat Evison

FLO KENNEDY

1983 BORN IN FLAMES
Director: Lizzie Borden
Co-stars: Adele Bertei Jeanne Satterfield Pat Murphy

GRACE KENNEDY

1980 THE APPLE
Director: Menahem Golan
Co-stars: Catherine Mary Stewart Joss Ackland Allan Love

HEATHER KENNEDY

1983 GETTING IT ON
Director: William Olsen
Co-stars: Martin Yost Jeff Edmond Kim Saunders

JAYNE KENNEDY

1981 BODY AND SOUL
Director: George Bowers
Co-stars: Leon Isaac Kennedy Muhammed Ali Margo Lee

JO KENNEDY

1982 STARSTRUCK
Director: Gillian Armstrong
Co-stars: Ross O'Donnovan Margo Lee Pat Evison

JOYCE KENNEDY

1934 THE RETURN OF BULLDOG DRUMMOND
Director: Walter Summers
Co-stars: Ralph Richardson Ann Todd

1936 TWELVE GOOD MEN
Director: Ralph Ince
Co-stars: Henry Kendall Nancy O'Neil Percy Parsons

MADGE KENNEDY

1952 THE MARRYING KIND
Director: George Cukor
Co-stars: Judy Holliday Aldo Ray Micky Shaughnessy

1956 THE CATERED AFFAIR
Director: Richard Brooks
Co-stars: Bette Davis Ernest Borgnine Debbie Reynolds

1956 LUST FOR LIFE
Director: Vincente Minnelli
Co-stars: Kirk Douglas Anthony Quinn James Donald

MARIA DOYLE KENNEDY

1997 A FURTHER GESTURE
Director: Robert Dornhelm
Co-star: Stephen Rea

1998 THE GENERAL
Director: John Boorman
Co-star: Jon Voight Brendan Gleeson Eamon Owens

MERNA KENNEDY

1928 THE CIRCUS
Director: Charles Chaplin
Co-stars: Charles Chaplin Allan Garcia Harry Crocker

1929 BROADWAY
Director: Paul Fejos
Co-stars: Glenn Tryon Evelyn Brent Robert Ellis

1932 LADY WITH A PAST
Co-stars: Constance Bennett David Manners

MIMI KENNEDY

1981 THIN ICE
Director: Paul Aaron
Co-stars: Kate Jackson Gerald Prendergast Lilian Gish

1989 IMMEDIATE FAMILY
Director: Jonathan Kaplan
Co-stars: Glenn Close James Woods Mary Stuart Masterson

1991 SINS OF THE MOTHER
Director: John Patterson
Co-stars: Elizabeth Montgomery Talia Balsam Dale Midkiff

1991 PUMP UP THE VOLUME
Director: Allan Moyle
Co-stars: Christian Slater Samatha Mathis Annie Ross

PATRICIA KENNEDY

1977 THE GETTING OF WISDOM
Director: Bruce Beresford
Co-stars: Susannah Fowle Shelia Helpman John Waters

SHEILA KENNEDY

1985   **NATIONAL LAMPOON'S EUROPEAN VACATION**
Director: Amy Heckerling
Co-stars: Beverly D'Angelo Chevy Chase Dana Hill

1990   **THE BIG BANG**
Director: James Toback
Co-stars: Missy Boyd Polly Frost Charles Lassiter

JILL KENNINGTON

1966   **BLOWUP**
Director: Michaelangelo Antonioni
Co-stars: David Hemmings Sarah Miles Vanessa Redgrave

JUNE KENNY

1957   **ATTACK OF THE PUPPET PEOPLE**
Director: Bert Gordon
Co-stars: John Hoyt John Agar

1957   **VIKING WOMEN AND THE SEA SERPENT**
Director: Roger Corman
Co-stars: Brad Johnson Susan Cabot

1958   **EARTH VERSUS THE SPIDER**
Director: Bert Gordon
Co-stars: Edward Kremer Gene Royh Mickey Finn

PATSY KENSIT (Child)
(Married Dan Donovan, Jim Kerr and Noel Gallagher)

1974   **THE GREAT GATSBY**
Director: Jack Clayton
Co-stars: Robert Redford Mia Farrow Bruce Dern

1976   **THE BLUE BIRD**
Director: George Cukor
Co-stars: Elizabeth Taylor Ava Gardner Jane Fonda Cicely Tyson

1979   **HANOVER STREET**
Director: Peter Hyams
Co-stars: Harrison Ford Lesley-Ann Down

1985   **SILAS MARNER**
Director: Giles Foster
Co-stars: Ben Kingsley Jenny Agutter Patrick Ryecart

1986   **ABSOLUTE BEGINNERS**
Director: Julien Temple
Co-stars: Eddie O'Connell David Bowie Lionel Blair

1988   **A CHORUS OF DISAPPROVAL**
Director: Michael Winner
Co-stars: Jeremy Irons Anthony Hopkins Prunella Scales

1989   **LETHAL WEAPON 2**
Director: Richard Donner
Co-stars: Mel Gibson Danny Glover Joe Pesci

1990   **CHICAGO JOE AND THE SHOWGIRL**
Director: Bernard Rose
Co-stars: Emily Lloyd Kiefer Sutherland

1990   **BULLSEYE!**
Director: Michael Winner
Co-stars: Michael Caine Roger Moore Sally Kirkland

1991   **ADAM BEDE**
Director: Giles Foster
Co-stars: Iain Glen James Wilby Sussanah Harker Julia McKenzie

1991   **BLAME IT ON THE BELLBOY**
Director: Mark Herman
Co-stars: Dudley Moore Bryan Brown Alison Steadman

1991   **PRINCE OF SHADOWS**
Director: Pilar Milo
Co-stars: Terence Stamp Geraldine James Simon Andrew

1991   **TWENTY-ONE**
Director: Don Boyd
Co-stars: Patrick Ryecart Rufus Sewell Jack Shepherd

1993   **FULL ECLIPSE**
Director: Anthony Hickox
Co-stars: Mario Van Peebles Bruce Payne

1993   **BITTER HARVEST**
Director: Duane Clark
Co-stars: Stephen Baldwin Jennifer Rubin

1995   **ANGELS AND INSECTS**
Director: Philip Haas
Co-stars: Kristin Scott Thomas Mark Rylance

1996   **GRACE OF MY HEART**
Director: Alison Anders
Co-stars: Ileana Douglass Matt Dillon John Turturro

1996   **LOVE AND BETRAYAL**
Co-stars: Dennis Boutsikaris

APRIL KENT

1956   **I'VE LIVED BEFORE**
Director: Richard Bartlett
Co-stars: Jock Mahoney Ann Harding John McIntyre

1957   **THE INCREDIBLE SHRINKING MAN**
Director: Jack Arnold
Co-stars: Grant Williams Randy Stuart Paul Langton

ANNE KENT

1994   **WIDOWS' PEAK**
Director: John Irving
Co-stars: Joan Plowright Mia Farrow Natasha Richardson

BARBARA KENT

1926   **FLESH AND THE DEVIL**
Director: Clarence Brown
Co-stars: John Gilbert Greta Garbo Lars Hanson

1928   **LONESOME**
Director: Paul Fejos
Co-star: Glenn Tryon

1929   **WELCOME DANGER**
Director: Clyde Bruckman
Co-stars: Harold Lloyd Noah Young Charles Middleton

1930   **FEET FIRST**
Director: Clyde Bruckman
Co-stars: Harold Lloyd Robert McWade

1930   **DUMBBELLS IN ERMINE**
Co-stars: Beryl Mercer Arthur Hoyt Julia Swayne-Gordon

1931   **INDISCREET**
Director: Leo McCarey
Co-stars: Gloria Swanson Ben Lyon Arthur Lake

1932   **VANITY FAIR**
Director: Chester Franklin
Co-stars: Myrna Loy Conway Tearle Anthony Bushell

1932   **EXPOSED**
Co-star: William Collier

1932   **EMMA**
Director: Clarence Brown
Co-stars: Marie Dressler Richard Cromwell Myrna Loy

DIANA KENT

1990   **PALMER**
Director: Keith Washington
Co-stars: Ray Winstone Dora Bryan Lesley Duff

1994   **HEAVENLY CREATURES**
Director: Peter Jackson
Co-stars: Kate Winslet Melanie Lynskey Sarah Peirse

DOROTHEA KENT

1936 **MORE THAN A SECRETARY**
Director: Alfred Green
Co-stars: Jean Arthur George Brent Lionel Stander

1937 **CARNIVAL QUEEN**
Co-star: Robert Wilcox

1937 **SOME BLONDES ARE DANGEROUS**
Co-star: Noah Beery Jnr.

1937 **A GIRL WITH IDEAS**
Director: S. Sylvan Simon
Co-stars: Wendy Barrie Walter Pidgeon Kent Taylor

1938 **YOUTH TAKES A FLING**
Director: Archie Mayo
Co-stars: Joel McCrea Andrea Leeds Isabel Jeans

1938 **GOODBYE BROADWAY**
Co-stars: Tom Brown Frank Jenks

1939 **RISKY BUSINESS**
Director: Arthur Lubin
Co-stars: George Murphy Leon Ames John Wray

1943 **STAGE DOOR CANTEEN**
Director: Frank Borzage
Co-stars: Cheryl Walker Lon McCallister Judith Anderson

1944 **PIN UP GIRL**
Director: Bruce Humberstone
Co-stars: Betty Grable Martha Raye Joe E.Brown

1947 **IT HAPPENED ON FIFTH AVENUE**
Director: Roy Del Ruth
Co-stars: Don Defore Gale Storm Victor Moore

JEAN KENT

1943 **BEES IN PARADISE**
Director: Val Guest
Co-stars: Arthur Askey Max Bacon Anne Shelton

1943 **MISS LONDON LTD.**
Director: Val Guest
Co-stars: Arthur Askey Anne Shelton Jack Train

1943 **WARN THAT MAN**
Director: Lawrence Huntington
Co-stars: Gordon Harker Philip Friend

1944 **CHAMPAGNE CHARLIE**
Director: Alberto Cavalcanti
Co-stars: Tommy Trinder Stanley Holloway

1944 **WATERLOO ROAD**
Director: Sidney Gilliat
Co-stars: John Mills Stewart Granger Joy Shelton

1944 **FANNY BY GASLIGHT**
Director: Anthony Asquith
Co-stars: James Mason Phyllis Calvert Wilfrid Lawson

1944 **TWO THOUSAND WOMEN**
Director: Frank Launder
Co-stars: Flora Robson Patricia Roc Thora Hird

1944 **MADONNA OF THE SEVEN MOONS**
Director: Arthue Crabtree
Co-stars: Phyllis Calvert Stewart Granger

1945 **THE RAKE'S PROGRESS**
Director: Sidney Gilliat
Co-stars: Rex Harrison Lilli Palmer Guy Middleton

1946 **CARAVAN**
Director: Arthur Crabtree
Co-stars: Stewart Granger Anne Crawford

1946 **CARNIVAL**
Director: Stanley Haines
Co-stars: Sally Gray Michael Wilding Bernard Miles

1946 **THE MAGIC BOW**
Director: Bernard Knowles
Co-stars: Stewart Granger Phyllis Calvert

1947 **THE MAN WITHIN**
Director: Bernard Knowles
Co-stars: Michael Redgrave Joan Greenwood

1947 **THE LOVES OF JOANNA GODDEN**
Director: Charles Frend
Co-stars: Googie Withers John McCallum

1948 **GOOD TIME GIRL**
Director: David MacDonald
Co-stars: Dennis Price Flora Robson Diana Dors

1948 **BOND STREET**
Director: Gordon Parry
Co-stars: Roland Young Ronald Howard Patricia Plunkett

1948 **SLEEPING CAR TO TRIESTE**
Director: John Paddy Carstairs
Co-stars: Albert Lieven Finlay Curie

1949 **TROTTIE TRUE**
Director: Brian Desmond Hurst
Co-stars: James Donald Hugh Sinclair Bill Owen

1949 **THE WOMAN IN QUESTION**
Director: Anthony Asquith
Co-stars: Dirk Bogarde Susan Shaw John McCallum

1950 **THE RELUCTANT WIDOW**
Director: Bernard Knowles
Co-stars: Guy Rolfe Kathleen Byron Paul Dupuis

1950 **HER FAVOURITE HUSBAND**
Director: Mario Soldati
Co-stars: Robert Beatty Margaret Rutherford

1951 **THE BROWNING VERSION**
Director: Anthony Asquith
Co-stars: Michael Redgrave Nigel Patrick Bill Travers

1957 **BONJOUR TRISTESSE**
Director: Otto Preminger
Co-stars: David Niven Deborah Kerr Jean Seberg

1957 **THE PRINCE AND THE SHOWGIRL**
Director: Laurence Olivier
Co-stars: Laurence Olivier Marilyn Monroe Sybil Thorndyke

1958 **GRIP OF THE STRANGLER**
Director: Robert Day
Co-stars: Boris Karloff Elizabeth Allan Vera Day

1959 **PLEASE TURN OVER**
Director: Gerald Thomas
Co-stars: Ted Ray Julia Lockwood Leslie Phillips

1959 **BEYOND THIS PLACE**
Director: Jack Cardiff
Co-stars: Van Johnson Vera Miles Emlyn Williams

1960 **BLUEBEARD'S TEN HONEYMOONS**
Director: Lee Wilder
Co-stars: George Sanders Corinne Calvet Patricia Roc

1976 **SHOUT AT THE DEVIL**
Director: Peter Hunt
Co-stars: Lee Marvin Roger Moore Barbara Parkins

1990 **MISSING PERSONS**
Director: Derek Bennett
Co-stars: Patrica Routledge Jimmy Jewel Jean Haywood

MARJORIE KENT *(Child)*

1945 **LEAVE IT TO BLONDIE**
Director: Abby Berlin
Co-stars: Penny Singleton Arthur Lake Larry Simms

1946 BLONDIE KNOWS BEST
Director: Abby Berlin
Co-stars: Penny Singleton Arthur Lake Jerome Cowan

1946 BLONDIE'S BIG MOMENT
Director: Abby Berlin
Co-stars: Penny Singleton Arthur Lake Anita Louise

1946 BLONDIE'S HOLLIDAY
Director: Abby Berlin
Co-stars: Penny Singleton Arthur Lake Grant Mitchell

1946 BLONDIE'S LUCKY DAY
Director: Abby Berlin
Co-stars: Penny Singleton Arthur Lake Larry Simms

1946 LIFE WITH BLONDIE
Director: Abby Berlin
Co-stars: Penny Singleton Arthur Lake Marc Lawrence

1947 BLONDIE'S ANNIVERSARY
Director: Abby Berlin
Co-stars: Penny Singleton Arthur Lake Adele Jurgens

1947 BLONDIE IN THE DOUGH
Director: Abby Berlin
Co-stars: Penny Singleton Arthur Lake Hugh Herbert

1948 BLONDIE'S REWARD
Director: Abby Berlin
Co-stars: Penny Singleton Arthur Lake Chick Chandler

1948 BLONDIE'S SECRET
Director: Edward Berns
Co-stars: Penny Singleton Arthur Lake Danny Mummert

1949 BLONDIE'S BIG DEAL
Director: Edward Berns
Co-stars: Penny Singleton Arthur Lake Ray Walker

1950 BLONDIE'S HERO
Director: Edward Berns
Co-stars: Penny Singleton Arthur Lake Joe Sawyer

1950 BEWARE OF BLONDIE
Director: Edward Berns
Co-stars: Penny Singleton Arthur Lake Dick Wessel

DAMBISA KENTE

1993 FRIENDS
Director: Elaine Proctor
Co-stars: Kerry Fox Michelle Burgers Marius Weyers

DORIS KENYON

1928 THE HOME TOWNERS
Director: Bryan Foy
Co-stars: Richard Bennett Robert McWade Stanley Taylor

1928 INTERFERENCE
Director: Roy Pomeroy
Co-stars: William Powell Evelyn Brent Clive Brook

1931 ALEXANDER HAMILTON
Director: John Adolfi
Co-stars: George Arliss Montagu Love Alan Mowbray

1932 YOUNG AMERICA
Director: Frank Borzage
Co-stars: Spencer Tracy Ralph Bellamy Beryl Mercer

1933 VOLTAIRE
Director: John Adolfi
Co-stars: George Arliss Margaret Lindsay Alan Mowbray

1933 COUNSELLOR-AT-LAW
Director: William Wyler
Co-stars: John Barrymore Bebe Daniels Melvyn Douglas

1934 THE HUMAN SIDE
Director: Eddie Buzzell
Co-stars: Adolphe Menjou Charlotte Henry Dickie Moore

ETHEL KENYON

1932 BY WHOSE HAND?
Director: Ben Stoloff
Co-stars: Ben Lyon Barbara Weeks Tom Dugan

GWEN KENYON

1944 CHARLIE CHAN IN THE SECRET SERVICE
Director: Phil Rosen
Co-stars: Sidney Toler Mantan Moreland

1945 THE CISCO KID IN OLD NEW MEXICO
Director: Phil Rosen
Co-stars: Duncan Renaldo Martin Garralga

ALEXIA KEOGH

1990 AN ANGEL AT MY TABLE
Director: Jane Campion
Co-stars: Kerry Fox Karen Fergusson Iris Churn

DOREEN KEOGH

1970 DARLING LILI
Director: Blake Edwards
Co-stars: Julie Andrews Rock Hudson Jeremy Kemp

JESSIE KEOSIAN

1991 GREEN CARD
Director: Peter Weir
Co-stars: Gerard Depardieu Andie MacDowell Bebe Neuwirth

KERIMA

1951 AN OUTCAST OF THE ISLANDS
Director: Carol Reed
Co-stars: Trevor Howard Robert Morley Wendy Hiller

1958 THE QUIET AMERICAN
Director: Joseph Mankiewicz
Co-stars: Audie Murphy Michael Redgrave Giorgia Moll

JACKIE KERIN

1982 NEXT OF KIN
Director: Tony Williams
Co-stars: John Jarratt Alex Scott Gerda Nicolson

ROXANNE KERNOHAN

1988 CRITTERS 2: THE MAIN COURSE
Director: Mick Garris
Co-stars: Terence Mann Don Opper Cynthia Garris

JOANNA KERNS

1985 THE RAPE OF RICHARD BECK
Director: Karen Arthur
Co-stars: Richard Crenna Meredith Baxter-Birney

1985 STORMIN' HOME
Director: Jerry Jameson
Co-stars: Gil Gerard Lisa Blount Geoffrey Lewis

1987 CROSS MY HEART
Director: Armyan Bernstein
Co-stars: Martin Short Annette O'Toole Paul Reiser

1989 THE PREPPIE MURDER
Director: John Herzfeld
Co-stars: William Baldwin Danny Aiello Lara Flynn Boyle

1989 THOSE SHE LEFT BEHIND
Director: Waris Hussein
Co-stars: Gary Cole Colleen Dewhurst George Coe

1991 CAPTIVE
Director: Michael Tuchner
Co-star: Barry Bostwick

1992   **THE NIGHTMAN**
Director: Charles Baird
Co-stars: Lou Walker Ted Marcoux

1994   **ROBIN COOK'S MORTAL FEAR**
Director: Larry Shaw
Co-stars: Gregory Harrison Robert Englund

1994   **SEE JANE RUN**
Director: John Patterson
Co-stars: John Shea Katie Boyer

1995   **NO ONE COULD PROTECT HER**
Director: Larry Shaw
Co-stars: Anthony John Dennison Peter Macneil

1996   **TERROR IN THE FAMILY**
Director: Gregory Goodell
Co-star: Dan Lauria

DEBORAH KERR (Received Honorary Award In 1993)
Nominated For Best Actress In 1949 For "Edward, My Son", In 1953 For
"From Here To Eternity", In 1956 For "The King And I", In 1957 For
"Heaven Knows Mr. Allison" And In 1960 For "The Sundowners"

1941   **MAJOR BARBARA**
Director: David Lean
Co-stars: Wendy Hiller Rex Harrison Robert Morley

1941   **HATTER'S CASTLE**
Director: Lance Comfort
Co-stars: Robert Newton Emlyn Williams

1941   **PENN OF PENNSYLVANIA**
Director: Lance Comfort
Co-stars: Clifford Evans Henry Oscar Max Adrain

1941   **LOVE ON THE DOLE**
Director: John Baxter
Co-stars: Clifford Evans Joyce Howard Frank Pettingell

1942   **THE DAY WILL DAWN**
Director: Harold French
Co-stars: Hugh Williams Ralph Richardson

1943   **THE LIFE AND DEATH OF COLONEL BLIMP**
Director: Michael Powell
Co-stars: Roger Livesey Anton Walbrook

1945   **PERFECT STRANGERS**
Director: Alexander Korda
Co-stars: Robert Donat Glynis Johns Ann Todd

1946   **I SEE A DARK STRANGER**
Director: Frank Lauder
Co-stars: Trevor Howard Raymond Huntley Brenda Bruce

1946   **BLACK NARCISSUS**
Director: Michael Powell
Co-stars: David Farrar Jean Simmons Kathleen Byron

1947   **THE HUCKSTERS**
Director: Jack Conway
Co-stars: Clark Gable Ava Gardner Sydney Greenstreet

1948   **IF WINTER COMES**
Director: Victor Saville
Co-stars: Walter Pidgeon Janet Leigh Angela Lansbury

1949   **EDWARD MY SON**
Director: George Cukor
Co-stars: Spencer Tracy Ian Hunter James Donald

1950   **PLEASE BELIEVE ME**
Director: Norman Taurog
Co-stars: Robert Walker Mark Stevens Peter Lawford

1951   **QUO VADIS**
Director: Mervyn LeRoy
Co-stars: Robert Taylor Peter Ustinov Finlay Currie

1951   **THUNDER IN THE EAST**
Director: Charles Vidor
Co-stars: Alan Ladd Charles Boyer Corrinne Calvet

1952   **THE PRISONER OF ZENDA**
Director: Richard Thorpe
Co-stars: Stewart Granger James Mason Robert Coote

1953   **JULIUS CAESAR**
Director: Joseph Mankiewicz
Co-stars: John Gielgud James Mason Marlon Brando

1953   **YOUNG BESS**
Director: George Sidney
Co-stars: Jean Simmons Stewart Granger Kathleen Byron

1953   **DREAM WIFE**
Director: Sidney Sheldon
Co-stars: Gary Grant Walter Pidgeon Betta St. John

1953   **FROM HERE TO ETERNITY**
Director: Fred Zinnemann
Co-stars: Burt Lancaster Frank Sinatra Donna Reed

1954   **THE END OF THE AFFAIR**
Director: Edward Dmytyk
Co-stars: Van Johnson Peter Cushing John Mills

1956   **THE PROUD AND PROFANE**
Director: George Seaton
Co-stars: William Holden Thelma Ritter

1956   **TEA AND SYMPATHY**
Director: Vincente Minnelli
Co-stars: John Kerr Leif Erikson Darryl Hickman

1953   **THE KING AND I**
Director: Walter Lang
Co-stars: Yul Brynner Rita Moreno Martin Benson

1957   **AN AFFAIR TO REMEMEBER**
Director: Leo McCarey
Co-stars: Cary Grant Cathleen Nesbitt Richard Denning

1957   **HEAVEN KNOWS MR. ALLISON**
Director: John Huston
Co-star: Robert Mitchum Georgina Hale

1957   **BONJOUR TRISTESSE**
Director: Otto Preminger
Co-stars: David Niven Jean Seberg Juliette Greco

1958   **SEPARATE TABLES**
Director: Delbert Mann
Co-stars: Burt Lancaster David Niven Rita Hayworth

1959   **BELOVED INFIDEL**
Director: Henry King
Co-stars: Gregory Peck Eddie Albert Karin Booth Ken Scott

1959   **THE JOURNEY**
Director: Anatole Litvak
Co-stars: Yul Brynner Anouk Aimee Jason Robards

1959   **COUNT YOUR BLESSINGS**
Director: Jean Negulesco
Co-stars: Rossano Brazzi Maurice Chevalier

1950   **KING SOLOMAN'S MINES**
Director: Compton Bennett
Co-stars: Stewart Granger Richard Carlson Hugo Haas

1960   **THE GRASS IS GREENER**
Director: Stanley Donen
Co-stars: Robert Mitchum Jean Simmons Cary Grant

1960   **THE SUNDOWNERS**
Director: Fred Zinnemann
Co-stars: Robert Mitchum Peter Ustinov Glynis Johns

1961   **THE NAKED EDGE**
Director: Michael Anderson
Co-stars: Gary Cooper Peter Cushing Diane Cilento

1961   **THE INNOCENTS**
Director: Jack Clayton
Co-stars: Megs Jenkins Michael Redgrave Pamela Franklin

1964 THE NIGHT OF THE IGUANA
Director: John Huston
Co-stars: Richard Burton Ava Gardner Sue Lyon

1964 THE CHALK GARDEN
Director: Ronald Neame
Co-stars: Edith Evans Hayley Mills John Mills

1965 MARRIAGE ON THE ROCKS
Director: Jack Donohue
Co-stars: Frank Sinatra Dean Martin Cesar Romero

1967 CASINO ROYALE
Director: John Huston
Co-stars: David Niven Peter Sellers Woody Allen

1966 EYE OF THE DEVIL
Director: J. Lee-Thompson
Co-stars: David Niven Emlyn Williams Flora Robson

1969 THE ARRANGEMENT
Director: Elia Kazan
Co-stars: Kirk Douglas Faye Dunaway Richard Bonne

1969 THE GYPSY MOTHS
Director: John Frankenheimer
Co-stars: Burt Lancaster Gene Hackman

1969 PRUDENCE AND THE PILL
Director: Fielder Cook
Co-stars: David Niven Edith Evans Keith Mitchell

1985 THE ASSAM GARDEN
Director: Mary McMurray
Co-stars: Madhur Jaffrey Alex McCowen

E. KATHERINE KERR

1982 REUBEN, REUBEN
Director: Robert Ellis Miller
Co-stars: Tom Conti Kelly McGillis Roberts Blossom

MARCIA KERR

1986 AEROBICIDE
Director: David Prior
Co-stars: Fritz Matthews David Campbell Ted Prior

MAMAENGOROA KERR-BELL

1994 ONCE WERE WARRIORS
Director: Lee Tamahori
Co-stars: Rena Owen Temuera Morrison

LINDA KERRIDGE

1983 FADE TO BLACK
Director: Vernon Zimmerman
Co-stars: Dennis Christopher Tim Thomerson Mickey Rourke

1983 STRANGER'S KISS
Director: Matthew Chapman
Co-stars: Peter Coyote Victoria Tennant Blaine Novak

1984 MIXED BLOOD
Director: Paul Morrissey
Co-stars: Marilia Pera Richard Ulacia Geraldine Smith

1988 ALIEN FROM L.A.
Director: Albert Pyun
Co-stars: Kathy Ireland Thom Mathews

MARY KERRIDGE

1948 ANNA KARENINA
Director: Julien Duvivier
Co-stars: Vivien Leigh Kieron Moore Ralph Richardson

1955 RICHARD III
Director: Laurence Olivier
Co-stars: Laurence Olivier Claire Bloom John Gielgud

PATRICIA KERRIGAN

1988 JOYRIDERS
Director: Aisling Walsh
Co-stars: Andrew Connolly Billie Whitelaw David Kelly

1992 A FATAL INVERSION
Director: Tim Fywell
Co-stars: Douglas Hodge Jeremy Northam Saira Todd

GILLIAN KERROD

1986 GOOD AS GOLD
Director: John Glenister
Co-stars: David Calder Richard Moore Jane Wood

ROSIE KERSLAKE

1986 BLUNT
Director: John Glenister
Co-stars: Ian Richardson Anthony Hopkins Michael Williams

1988 RASBERRY RIPPLE
Director: Nigel Finch
Co-stars: Faye Dunaway John Gordon Sinclair Shelia Reid

SARA KESTELMAN

1974 ZARDOZ
Director: John Boorman
Co-stars: Sean Connery Charlotte Rampling John Alderton

1975 LISZTOMANIA
Director: Ken Russell
Co-stars: Roger Daltrey Paul Nicholas Ringo Starr

1976 BREAK OF DAY
Director: Ken Hannam
Co-star: Andrew McFarlane

1986 LADY JANE
Director: Trevor Nunn
Co-stars: Helena Bonham Carter Cary Elwes Jane Lapotaire

1992 THE LAST ROMANTICS
Director: Jack Gold
Co-stars: Ian Holm Leo McKern

JANET KEY

1970 PERCY
Director: Ralph Thomas
Co-stars: Hywell Bennett Denholm Elliott Cyd Hayman

1973 AND NOW THE SCREAMING STARTS
Director: Roy Ward Baker
Co-stars: Peter Cushing Stephanie Beacham

KATHLEEN KEY

1926 BEN HUR
Director: Fred Niblo
Co-stars: Ramon Navarro Carmel Myers May McAvoy

ANNE MARIE KEYES

1990 THE BIG BANG
Director: James Toback
Co-stars: Emma Astner Veronica Geng Julius Hemphill

EVELYN KEYES *(Married Artie Shaw)*

1939 UNION PACIFIC
Director: Cecil B. Demille
Co-stars: Barbara Stanwyck Joel McCrea Robert Preston

1939 GONE WITH THE WIND
Director: Victor Fleming
Co-stars: Clark Gable Vivien Leigh Leslie Howard

1940 THE LADY IN QUESTION
Director: Charles Vidor
Co-stars: Rita Hayworth Brian Aherne Glenn Ford

1940	**BEFORE I HANG**		**1951**	**THE PROWLER**
Director:	Nick Grinde		*Director:*	Joseph Losey
Co-stars:	Boris Karloff Bruce Bennett Pedro De Cordoba		*Co-stars:*	Van Heflin John Maxwell Katharine Warren

1940   **BEFORE I HANG**
Director: Nick Grinde
Co-stars: Boris Karloff Bruce Bennett Pedro De Cordoba

1941   **THE FACE BEHIND THE MASK**
Director: Robert Florey
Co-stars: Peter Lorre Don Beddoe George Stone

1941   **HERE COMES MR. JORDAN**
Director: Alexander Hall
Co-stars: Robert Montgomery Claude Rains

1941   **LADIES IN RETIREMENT**
Director: Charles Vidor
Co-stars: Ida Lupino Louis Hayward Elsa Lanchester

1942   **FLIGHT LIEUTENANT**
Director: Sidney Salkow
Co-stars: Glenn Ford Pat O'Brien Johnathan Hale

1942   **THE ADVENTURES OF MARTIN EDEN**
Director: Sidney Salkow
Co-stars: Glenn Ford Claire Trevor Stuart Erwin Dickie Moore

1943   **DANGEROUS BLONDES**
Director: Leigh Jason
Co-stars: Allyn Joslyn Edmund Lowe John Hubbard

1943   **THERE'S SOMETHING ABOUT A SOLDIER**
Director: Alfred Green
Co-stars: Tom Neal Bruce Bennett

1944   **STRANGE AFFAIR**
Co-star: Allyn Joslyn

1944   **NINE GIRLS**
Director: Leigh Jason
Co-stars: Ann Harding Jinx Falkenberg Nina Foch Anita Louise

1945   **1001 NIGHTS**
Director: Alfred Green
Co-stars: Cornel Wilde Phil Silvers Adele Jergens

1946   **THE THRILL OF BRAZIL**
Director: S. Sylvan Simon
Co-stars: Keenan Wynn Ann Miller Allyn Joslyn

1946   **RENEGADES**
Director: George Sherman
Co-stars: Larry Parks William Parker Edgar Buchanan

1946   **THE JOLSON STORY**
Director: Alfred Green
Co-stars: Larry Parks William Demarest Scotty Beckett

1946   **JOHNNY O'CLOCK**
Director: Robert Rossen
Co-stars: Dick Powell Ellen Drew Jeff Chandler

1948   **THE MATING OF MILLIE**
Director: Henry Levin
Co-stars: Glenn Ford Willard Parker Ron Randell

1948   **ENCHANTMENT**
Director: Irving Reis
Co-stars: David Niven Teresa Wright Farley Granger

1949   **MR. SOFT TOUCH**
Director: Henry Levin
Co-stars: Glenn Ford John Ireland Beulah Bondi

1949   **MRS. MIKE**
Director: Louis King
Co-stars: Dick Powell J.M. Kerrigan Angela Clarke

1950   **THE KILLER THAT STALKED NEW YORK**
Director: Earl McEvoy
Co-stars: Charles Korvin Dorothy Malone

1951   **IRON MAN**
Director: Joseph Pevney
Co-stars: Jeff Chandler Stephen McNally Rock Hudson James Arness

1951   **THE PROWLER**
Director: Joseph Losey
Co-stars: Van Heflin John Maxwell Katharine Warren

1952   **ROUGH SHOOT**
Director: Robert Parish
Co-stars: Joel McCrea Marius Goring Roland Culver

1953   **HELL'S HALF ACRE**
Director: John Auer
Co-stars: Wendell Corey Elsa Lanchester Nancy Gates

1953   **SHOOT FIRST**
Director: Robert Parrish
Co-stars: Joel McCrea Herbert Lom Marius Goring

1953   **99, RIVER STREET**
Director: Phil Karlson
Co-stars: John Payne Frank Faylen Peggie Castle Brad Dexter

1955   **THE SEVEN YEAR ITCH**
Director: Billy Wilder
Co-stars: Marilyn Monroe Tom Ewell Victor Moore

1956   **AROUND THE WORLD IN EIGHTY DAYS**
Director: Michael Anderson
Co-stars: David Niven Robert Newton

1984   **ARTIE SHAW: TIME IS ALL YOU'VE GOT**
Director: Brigitte Berman
Co-stars: Artie Shaw Helen Forrest

1987   **A RETURN TO SALEM'S LOT**
Director: Larry Cohen
Co-stars: Michael Moriarty Samuel Fuller June Havoc

1989   **THE WICKED STEPMOTHER**
Director: Larry Cohen
Co-stars: Bette Davis Barbara Carrera Tom Bosley

PERSIS KHAMBATTA

1975   **THE WILBY CONSPIRACY**
Director: Ralph Nelson
Co-stars: Sidney Poitier Michael Caine Prunella Gee

1979   **STAR TREK: THE MOTION PICTURE**
Director: Robert Wise
Co-stars: William Shatner Leonard Nimoy

1981   **NIGHTHAWKS**
Director: Bruce Malmuth
Co-stars: Sylvester Stallone Billy Dee Williams Rutger Hauer

1992   **MEGAFORCE**
Director: Hal Needham
Co-stars: Barry Bostwick Michael Beck Henry Silva

SHAHEEN KHAN

1986   **LOVE MATCH**
Director: Alan Dosser
Co-stars: Saeed Jaffrey Madhur Jaffrey Mick Ford

ARSINEE KHANJIAN

1988   **FAMILY VIEWING**
Director: Atom Egoyan
Co-stars: David Hemblen Aidan Tierney Gabriele Rose

1989   **SPEAKING PARTS**
Director: Atom Egoyan
Co-stars: Michael McManus Gabriele Rose David Hemblen

1991   **THE ADJUSTER**
Director: Atom Egoyan
Co-stars: Elias Koteas Gabrielle Rose Jennifer Dale

LELEI KHUMALO

1992   **SARAFINA!**
Director: Darrell James Roodt
Co-stars: Whoopi Goldberg Miriam Makeba John Kani

MARGOT KIDDER

1969 GAILY, GAILY
Director: Norman Jewison
Co-stars: Beau Bridges Melina Mercouri Brian Keith Hume Cronyn

1970 QUACKSER FORTUNE HAS A COUSIN IN THE BRONX
Director: Waris Hussein
Co-stars: Gene Wilder Seamus Ford

1973 SISTERS
Director: Brian De Palma
Co-stars: Jennifer Salt Charles Durning Bill Finley

1974 THE REINCARNATION OF PETER PROUD
Director: J. Lee Thompson
Co-stars: Michael Sarrazin Jennifer O'Neill

1974 HARRY O
Director: Jerry Thorpe
Co-stars: David Janssen Martin Sheen Sal Mineo Will Geer

1974 BLACK CHRISTMAS
Director: Robert Clark
Co-stars: Olivia Hussey Keir Dullea John Saxon Andre Martin

1975 THE GREAT WALDO PEPPER
Director: George Roy Hill
Co-stars: Robert Redford Bo Svenson

1975 92 IN THE SHADE
Director: Thomas McGuane
Co-stars: Peter Fonda Warren Oates

1978 SUPERMAN
Director: Richard Donner
Co-stars: Christopher Reeve Marlon Brando Glenn Ford

1979 THE AMITYVILLE HORROR
Director: Stuart Rosenberg
Co-stars: James Brolin Rod Steiger Don Stroud

1980 SUPERMAN II
Director: Richard Lester
Co-stars: Christopher Reeve Gene Hackman Ned Beatty

1980 WILLIE AND PHIL
Director: Paul Mazursky
Co-stars: Michael Onkean Ray Sharkey

1981 HEARTACHES
Director: Donald Shebib
Co-stars: Annie Potts Robert Carradine Winston Rekert

1982 SOME KIND OF HERO
Director: Michael Pressman
Co-stars: Richard Pryor Ray Sharkey Lynne Moody

1983 SUPERMAN III
Director: Richard Lester
Co-stars: Christopher Reeve Richard Pryor Annie Ross

1983 TRENCHCOAT
Director: Michael Turner
Co-stars: Robert Hayes David Suchet Ronald Lacey

1985 PICKING UP THE PIECES
Director: Paul Wendkos
Co-stars: David Ackroyd James Farantino Joyce Van Patten

1986 VANISHING ACT
Director: David Greene
Co-stars: Mike Farrell Elliott Gould Fred Gwynne Graham Jarvis

1987 SUPERMAN IV: THE QUEST FOR PEACE
Director: Sidney Furie
Co-stars: Christopher Reeve San Wanamaker Mariel Hemingway

1988 BODY OF EVIDENCE
Director: Roy Campanella
Co-stars: Barry Bostwick Tony LoBianco David Hayward

1990 WHITE ROOM
Director: Patricia Rozema
Co-stars: Kate Nelligan Maurice Godin Sheila McCarthy

1990 WINDRUNNER
Co-star: Jason Wiler

1993 ONE WOMAN'S COURAGE
Director: Charles Robert Carner
Co-stars: Patty Duke James Farantino

1994 YOUNG IVANHOE
Director: Ralph Thomas
Co-stars: Stacy Keach Nick Mancuso

1995 BLOODKNOT
Director: Jorge Montesi
Co-stars: Stacy Keach Nick Mancuso

NICOLE KIDMAN *(Married Tom Cruise)*

1983 BUSH CHRISTMAS
Director: Henri Safran
Co-stars: John Ewart John Howard Mark Spain

1983 BMX BANDITS
Director: Brian Trenchard-Smith
Co-stars: David Argue Bryan Marshall John Ley

1987 THE BIT PART
Director: Brendan Maher
Co-stars: Chris Hayward John Wood Katuna Foster

1988 DEAD CALM
Director: Phillip Noyce
Co-stars: Sam Neill Billy Zane Rod Mulloiner

1989 BANGKOK HILTON
Director: Ken Cameron
Co-stars: Denholm Elliott Hugo Weaving Jerome Ehlers

1990 DAYS OF THUNDER
Director: Tony Scott
Co-stars: Tom Cruise Robert Duvall Randy Quaid

1991 BILLY BATHGATE
Director: Robert Benton
Co-stars: Dustin Hoffman Loren Dean Bruce Willis

1991 FLIRTING
Director: John Duigan
Co-stars: Noah Taylor Thandie Newton Bartholomew Rose

1992 FAR AND AWAY
Director: Ron Howard
Co-stars: Tom Cruise Thomas Gibson Michelle Johnson

1993 MY LIFE
Director: Bruce Joel Rubin
Co-stars: Michael Keaton Michael Constantin Haing S. Ngor

1993 MALICE
Director: Harold Becker
Co-stars: Bill Pullman Alec Baldwin Anne Bancroft

1994 BATMAN FOREVER
Co-star: Val Kilmer

1995 TO DIE FOR
Director: Gus Van Sant
Co-stars: Illeana Douglas

1996 THE PORTRAIT OF A LADY
Director: Jane Campion
Co-stars: John Malkovitch Barbara Hershey Richard E. Grant

1997 EYES WIDE SHUT
Director: Stanley Kubrick
Co-stars: Tom Cruise Harvey Keitel

1997 THE PEACEMAKER
Director: Mimi Leder
Co-star: George Clooney

KARIN KIENZLER

1984 HEIMAT
Director: Edgar Reitz
Co-stars: Marita Breuer Michael Lesch Dieter Schaad

EMMA KILBERG *(Child)*

1989 ISTANBUL
Director: Mats Arehn
Co-stars: Timothy Bottoms Twiggy Robert Morley

WENDY KILBOURNE

1984 THE CALENDER GIRL MURDERS
Director: William Graham
Co-stars: Tom Skerritt Sharon Stone Robert Morse

1989 TURN BACK THE CLOCK
Director: Larry Elikan
Co-stars: Connie Sellecca Dina Merril Gene Barry

MELANIE KILBURN

1990 THE WORLD OF EDDIE WEARY
Director: Alan Grint
Co-stars: Ray Brooks Celia Imrie Connie Booth

NANCY KILGAS

1954 SEVEN BRIDES FOR SEVEN BROTHERS
Director: Stanley Donen
Co-stars: Jane Powell Howard Keel

1956 ROCK AROUND THE CLOCK
Director: Fred Sears
Co-stars: Bill Haley Little Richard Lisa Gaye

1957 HIGH SCHOOL HELLCATS

RUTA KILMONIS

1954 SEVEN BRIDES FOR SEVEN BROTHERS
Director: Stanley Donen
Co-stars: Jane Powell Howard Keel Russ Tamblyn

SHIRLEY KILPATRICK

1958 THE ASTOUNDING SHE-MONSTER
Director: Ronnie Ashcroft
Co-stars: Robert Clarke Ken Duncan Jeanne Tatum

JACQUELINE KIM

1994 DISCLOSURE
Director: Barry Levinson
Co-stars: Michael Douglas Demi Moore Donald Sutherland

JOY KIM

1955 BLOOD ALLEY
Director: William Wellman
Co-stars: John Wayne Lauren Bacall Anita Ekberg

JUNE KIM

1962 CONFESSIONS OF AN OPIUM EATER
Director: Albert Zugsmith
Co-stars: Vincent Price Linda Ho Philip Ahn

ANNE KIMBELL

1954 MONSTER FOM THE OCEAN FLOOR
Director: Wyott Ordung
Co-stars: Wyott Ordung Stuart Wade

1958 GIRLS AT SEA
Director: Gilbert Gunn
Co-stars: Guy Rolfe Ronald Shiner Lionel Jeffries

KAY KIMBERLEY

1970 THE WATERMELON MAN
Director: Melvin Van Peebles
Co-stars: Godfrey Cambridge Estelle Parsons Manton Moreland

MAGGIE KIMBERLEY

1967 THE MUMMY'S SHROUD
Director: John Gilling
Co-stars: John Phillips Andre Morell Elizabeth Sellars

DANA KIMMELL

1982 FRIDAY THE 13TH PART III
Director: Steve Miner
Co-stars: Richard Brooker Catharine Parks

MARKETA KIMBRELL

1965 THE PAWNBROKER
Director: Sidney Lumet
Co-stars: Rod Steiger Geraldine Fitzgerald Brock Peters

MITSUKO KIMURA

1955 THREE STRIPES IN THE SUN
Director: Richard Murphy
Co-stars: Aldo Ray Phil Carey Dick York

ADRIENNE KING

1980 FRIDAY THE 13TH.
Director: Sean Cunningham
Co-stars: Betsy Palmer Jeannine Taylor Robbi Morgan

1981 FRIDAY THE 13TH., PART II
Director: Steve Miner
Co-stars: Amy Steel John Furey Kirsten Baker

ANDREA KING

1944 THE VERY THOUGHT OF YOU
Director: Delmer Daves
Co-stars: Dennis Morgan Eleanor Parker Dane Clark

1945 GOD IS MY CO-PILOT
Director: Robert Florey
Co-stars: Dennis Morgan Dane Clark Raymond Massey

1945 ROUGHLY SPEAKING
Director: Michael Curtiz
Co-stars: Rosalind Russell Jack Carson Robert Hutton

1945 HOTEL BERLIN
Director: Peter Godfrey
Co-stars: Raymond Massey Peter Lorre Faye Emerson

1946 THE BEAST WITH FIVE FINGERS
Director: Robert Florey
Co-stars: Peter Lorre Robert Alda J. Carrol Naish

1946 THE MAN I LOVE
Director: Raoul Walsh
Co-stars: Ida Lupino Robert Alda Martha Vickers

1946 SHADOW OF A WOMAN
Director: Joseph Santly
Co-stars: Don McGuire Richard Erdman William Prince

1947 RIDE THE PINK HORSE
Director: Robert Montgomery
Co-stars: Robert Montgomery Wanda Hendrix Thomas Gomez

1948 MR. PEABODY AND THE MERMAID
Director: Irving Pichel
Co-stars: William Powell Ann Blyth Irene Hervey

1949 SONG OF SURRENDER
Director: Mitchell Leisen
Co-stars: Wanda Hendrix Claude Rains MacDonald Carey

1950   **DIAL 1119**
Director: Gerald Mayer
Co-stars: Marshall Thompson Virginia Field Leon Ames

1951   **THE LEMON DROP KID**
Director: Sidney Lanfield
Co-stars: Bob Hope Marilyn Maxwell Lloyd Nolan

1952   **RED PLANET MARS**
Director: Harry Horner
Co-stars: Herbert Berghof Peter Graves Marvin Miller

1952   **THE WORLD IN HIS ARMS**
Director: Raoul Walsh
Co-stars: Gregory Peck Ann Blyth Anthony Quinn

1957   **DARBY'S RANGERS**
Director: William Wellman
Co-stars: James Garner Jack Warden Stuart Whitman

1957   **BAND OF ANGELS**
Director: Raoul Walsh
Co-stars: Clarke Gable Yvonne De Carlo Patric Knowles

1969   **DADDY'S GONE A-HUNTING**
Director: Mark Robson
Co-stars: Carol White Paul Burke Mala Powers

CAMMI KING

1939   **GONE WITH THE WIND**
Director: Victor Fleming
Co-stars: Clarke Gable Vivien Leigh Leslie Howard

CARLOTTA KING

1929   **THE DESERT SONG**
Director: Roy Del Ruth
Co-stars: John Boles Louise Fazenda Myrna Loy

CAROLE KING

1987   **RUSSKIES**
Director: Rick Rosenthal
Co-stars: Whip Hubley Peter Bilingsley Susan Walters

CAROLINE JUNKO KING

1994   **3 NINJAS FIGHT BACK**
Director: Charles Kanganis
Co-stars: Victor Wong Sean Fox Evan Bonifant

CHARMION KING

1964   **NOBODY WAVED GOODBYE**
Director: Don Owen
Co-stars: Peter Kastner Julie Briggs Claude Rae

1985   **ANNE OF GREEN GABLES**
Director: Kevin Sulllivan
Co-stars: Megan Follows Colleen Dewhurst Richard Farnsworth

CLYDIE KING

1976   **A STAR IS BORN**
Director: Frank Pierson
Co-stars: Barbra Streisand Kris Kristofferson Marta Heflin

DIANA KING

1940   **SPELLBOUND**
Director: John Harlow
Co-stars: Derek Farr Vera Lindsay Hay Petrie

HEIDI KING

1992   **OUT ON A LIMB**
Director: Francis Veber
Co-stars: Matthew Broderick Jeffrey Jones Marian Mercer

1992   **THE MIGHTY DUCKS ARE THE CHAMPIONS**
Director: Stephen Herek
Co-stars: Emilio Estevez Joss Ackland

LORELEI KING

1994   **INTIMATE WITH A STRANGER**
Director: Mel Woods
Co-stars: Roderick Mangin-Turner Janis Lee Amy Tolsky

LORETTA KING

1953   **BRIDE OF THE MONSTER**
Director: Edward Wood
Co-stars: Bela Lugosi Tor Johnson

MABEL KING

1978   **THE WIZ**
Director: Sidney Lumet
Co-stars: Diana Ross Michael Jackson Lena Horne

1979   **THE JERK**
Director: Carl Reiner
Co-stars: Steve Martin Bernadette Peters Catlin Adams

1980   **THE GONG SHOW MOVIE**
Director: Chuck Barris
Co-stars: Chuck Barris Robin Altman Murray Langston Jamie Farr

1991   **DEAD MAN DON'T DIE**
Director: Malcolm Marmorstein
Co-stars: Elliott Gould Melissa Anderson Mark Moses

MAGGIE KING

1990   **THE BIG STEAL**
Director: Nadia Tass
Co-stars: Ben Mendelson Claudia Karvan Steve Bisley

MIKI KING

1988   **BRADDOCK: MISSING IN ACTION III**
Director: Aaron Norris
Co-stars: Chuck Norris Aki Aleong

MORGANA KING

1985   **DEADLY INTENTIONS**
Director: Noel Black
Co-stars: Michael Biehn Madolyn Smith Cloris Leachman

REGINA KING

1993   **POETIC JUSTICE**
Director: John Singleton
Co-stars: Janet Jackson Tupac Shakur Joe Torry

ROWENA KING

1992   **BLACK AND BLUE**
Director: David Hayman
Co-stars: Christopher John Hall Linus Roache Martin Shaw

1993   **TO PLAY THE KING**
Director: Paul Seed
Co-stars: Ian Richardson Michael Kitchen Kitty Aldridge

DANITZA KINGSLEY

1988   **JACK'S BACK**
Director: Rowdy Herrington
Co-stars: James Spader Cynthia Gibb Rod Loomis

SUSAN KINGSLEY

1984   **THE DOLLMAKER**
Director: Daniel Petrie
Co-stars: Geraldine Page Jane Fonda Levon Helm

1984   **OLD ENOUGH**
Director: Marisa Silver
Co-stars: Sarah Boyd Rainbow Harvest Danny Aiello

ALEX KINGSTON

1989 THESE FOOLISH THINGS
Director: Charles Gormley
Co-stars: James Fox Lindsay Duncan Ciaran Madden

1996 MOLL FLANDERS
Director: David Attwood
Co-stars: Daniel Craig James Fleet Ronald Fraiser

NATALIE KINGSTON

1928 STREET ANGELS
Director: Frank Borzage
Co-stars: Janet Gaynor Charles Farrell Henry Armetta

1929 TARZAN THE TIGER
Director: Henry McRae
Co-stars: Frank Merrill Lillian Worth

WINIFRED KINGSTON

1914 THE SQUAW MAN
Director: Cecil B. DeMille
Co-stars: Dustin Farnum Red Wing

1931 THE SQUAW MAN
Director: Cecil B. DeMille
Co-stars: Warner Baxter Lupe Velez Charles Bickford

KATHLEEN KINMONT

1988 HALLOWEEN 4:
THE RETURN OF MICHAEL MYERS
Director: Dwight Little
Co-stars: Donald Pleasence Beau Starr

1990 RE-ANIMATOR 2
Director: Brian Yuzna
Co-stars: Jeffrey Combs Bruce Abbott David Gale

1990 BRIDE OF RE-ANIMATOR
Director: Brian Yuzna
Co-stars: Jeffrey Combs Bruce Abbott Fabiana Udenio

MELANIE KINNAMON

1985 FRIDAY THE 13TH. A NEW BEGINNING
Director: Danny Steinman
Co-stars: John Shepard Richard Young

MELINDA KINNAMON

1985 MY LIFE AS A DOG
Director: Lasse Hallstrom
Co-stars: Anton Glanzelius Anki Liden Manfred Serner

NASTASSJA KINSKI

(Partner of Roman Polanski, Married Ibrahim Moussa, Partner of Quincy Jones)
(Daughter Of Klaus Kinski and Ruth Bridgette)

1975 WRONG MOVE
Director: Wim Wenders

1976 TO THE DEVIL A DAUGHTER
Director: Peter Sykes
Co-stars: Richard Widmark Christopher Lee Denholm Elliott

1979 TESS
Director: Roman Polanski
Co-stars: Leigh Lawson Peter Firth John Collin Richard Pearson

1982 ONE FROM THE HEART
Director: Francis Coppola
Co-stars: Fredric Forrest Teri Garr Raul Julia

1982 CAT PEOPLE
Director: Paul Schrader
Co-stars: Malcolm McDowell John Heard Ruby Dee Ed Begley Jnr.

1983 EXPOSED
Director: James Toback
Co-stars: Rudolf Nureyev Harvey Keitel Ian McShane

1983 THE MOON IN THE GUTTER
Director: Jean-Jacques Beineix
Co-stars: Gerard Depardieu Victoria Abril

1984 MARIA'S LOVERS
Director: Andrei Konchalovsky
Co-stars: John Savage Robert Mitchum Keith Carradine

1984 THE HOTEL NEW HAMPSHIRE
Director: Tony Richardson
Co-stars: Rob Lowe Jodie Foster Beau Bridges

1984 PARIS, TEXAS
Director: Wim Wenders
Co-stars: Harry Dean Stanton Dean Stockwell Aurore Clement

1984 UNFAITHFULLY YOURS
Director: Howard Zieff
Co-stars: Dudley Moore Armand Assante Albert Brooks

1985 HAREM
Director: Arthur Joffe
Co-stars: Ben Kingsley Dennis Goldston Zohra Segal

1986 REVOLUTION
Director: Hugh Hudson
Co-stars: Al Pacino Donald Sutherland Joan Plowright

1989 TORRENTS OF SPRING
Director: Jerzy Skolimowski
Co-stars: Timothy Hutton Valeria Golino William Forsythe

1990 NIGHT SUN
Director: Paolo Taviani
Co-stars: Julian Sands Charlotte Gainsbourg Massimo Bonetti

1993 FARAWAY, SO CLOSE
Director: Wim Wenders
Co-stars: Otto Sander Bruno Ganz Willem Dafoe

1994 TERMINAL VELOCITY
Director: Deran Serafian
Co-stars: Charlie Sheen Garry Bullock James Gandolfini

1997 FATHER'S DAY
Director: Ivan Reitman
Co-stars: Robin Williams Billy Crystal Julia Louis-Dreyfuss

1997 ONE NIGHT STAND
Director: Mike Figgis
Co-stars: Wesley Snipes Robert Downey Jnr. Ming-Na Wen

1998 SAVIOR
Director: Peter Antonijevec
Co-stars: Dennis Quaid Natasa Ninkovic

1998 BELLA MAFIA
Co-stars: Vanessa Redgrave Jennifer Tilly Ileana Douglas

KENDRA KIRCHNER

1982 ANDROID
Director: Aaron Lipstadt
Co-stars: Klaus Kinski Brie Howard Don Opper

PHYLLIS KIRK

1950 OUR VERY OWN
Director: David Miller
Co-stars: Ann Blyth Farley Granger Joan Evans

1950 TWO WEEKS WITH LOVE
Director: Roy Rowland
Co-stars: Jane Powell Ricardo Montalban Debbie Reynolds

1950 MRS. O'MALLEY AND MR. MALONE
Director: Norman Taurog
Co-stars: Marjorie Main James Whitmore Ann Dvorak

1951 THREE GUYS NAMED MIKE
Director: Charles Walters
Co-stars: Jane Wyman Van Johnson Howard Keel

1952 THE IRON MISTRESS
Director: Gordon Douglass
Co-stars: Alan Ladd Virginia Mayo Joseph Calleia

1953 HOUSE OF WAX
Director: Andre De Toth
Co-stars: Vincent Price Frank Lovejoy Carolyn Jones

1953 THUNDER OVER THE PLAINS
Director: Andre De Toth
Co-stars: Randolph Scott Lex Barker Charles McGraw

1954 RIVER BEAT
Director: Guy Green
Co-stars: John Bentley Robert Ayres Glyn Houston

1954 CRIME WAVE
Director: Andre De Toth
Co-stars: Sterling Hayden Gene Nelson Charles Bronson

1954 CANYON CROSSROADS
Director: Alfred Werker
Co-stars: Richard Basehart Stephen Elliott Russell Collins

1956 BACK FROM ETERNITY
Director: John Farrow
Co-stars: Robert Ryan Rod Steiger Anita Ekberg

1957 THE SAD SACK
Director: George Marshall
Co-stars: Jerry Lewis David Wayne Peter Lorre

1957 THAT WOMAN OPPOSITE
Director: Compton Bennett
Co-stars: Dan O'Herlihy Petula Clark William Franklyn

1959 JOHNNY CONCHO
Director: Don McGuire
Co-stars: Frank Sinatra William Conrad Wallace Ford

LOUISE KIRKLAND

1977 ROSELAND
Director: James Ivory
Co-stars: Geraldine Chaplin Teresa Wright Joan Copeland

MURIEL KIRKLAND

1933 HOLD YOUR MAN
Director: Sam Wood
Co-stars: Jean Harlow Clark Gable Stuart Erwin

1934 LITTLE MAN, WHAT NOW?
Director: Frank Borzage
Co-stars: Margaret Sullavan Douglass Montgomery

1934 NANA
Director: Dorothy Arzner
Co-stars: Anna Sten Phillips Holmes Mae Clarke

1934 THE WHITE PARADE
Director: Irving Cummings
Co-stars: Loretta Young John Boles Dorothy Wilson

SALLY KIRKLAND

1971 GOING HOME
Director: Herbert Leonard
Co-stars: Robert Mitchell Brenda Vaccaro Jan-Michel Vincent

1973 THE WAY WE WERE
Director: Sydney Pollack
Co-stars: Barbra Streisand Robert Redford Viveca Lindfors

1975 THE KANSAS CITY MASSACRE
Director: Dan Curtis
Co-stars: Dale Robertson Bo Hopkins Scott Brady

1979 HOMETOWN U.S.A.
Director: Max Baer
Co-stars: Gary Springer David Wilson Julie Parsons

1987 ANNA
Director: Yurek Bogayevicz
Co-stars: Robert Fields Paulina Porizkova

1989 BEST OF THE REST
Director: Bob Radler
Co-stars: James Earl Jones Eric Roberts Louise Fletcher

1989 COLD FEET
Director: Robert Dornheim
Co-stars: Keith Carradine Tom Waits Bill Pullman

1989 REVENGEE
Director: Tony Scott
Co-stars: Kevin Costner Anthony Quinn Madeleine Stowe

1990 HEAT WAVE
Director: Kevin Hooks
Co-stars: Cicely Tyson James Earl Jones Margaret Avery

1990 TWO EVIL EYES
Director: Dario Argento
Co-stars: Harvey Keitel Madeline Potter John Amos

1990 BULLSEYE!
Director: Michael Winner
Co-stars: Michael Caine Roger Moore Patsy Kensit

1991 THE HAUNTED
Director: Robert Mandel
Co-stars: Jeffrey DeMunn Joyce Van Patten Diane Baker

1992 J.F.K.
Director: Oliver Stone
Co-stars: Kevin Costner Joe Pesci Gary Oldman

1992 DOUBLE JEOPARDY
Director: Lawrence Schiller
Co-stars: Rachel Ward Bruce Boxleitner Sela Ward

1992 DOUBLE THREAT
Director: David Prior
Co-stars: Andrew Stevens Sherrie Rose Anthony Franciosa

1992 HIT THE DUTCHMAN
Director: Menahem Golan
Co-stars: Bruce Nozick Eddie Bowz Will Kempe

1994 GUNMEN
Director: Deran Serafian
Co-stars: Christopher Lambert Mario Van Peebles Patrick Stewart

1993 PAPER HEARTS
Director: Rod McCall
Co-stars: James Brolin Pamela Gidley Kris Kristofferson

MAGGIE KIRKPATRICK

1978 THE NIGHT PROWLER

1982 THE PRIVATE MOVIE
Director: Ken Annakin
Co-stars: Kristy McNichol Christopher Atkins Bill Kerr

PAT KIRKWOOD

1939 COME ON GEORGE
Director: Anthony Kimmins
Co-stars: George Formby Joss Ambler Ronald Shiner

1939 BAND WAGON
Director: Marcel Varnel
Co-stars: Arthur Askey Richard Murdoch Moore Marriott

1944 FLIGHT FROM FOLLY
Director: Herbert Mason
Co-stars: Hugh Sinclair Sydney Howard Tamara Desni

1946   **NO LEAVE, NO LOVE**
Director: Charles Martin
Co-stars: Van Johnson Keenan Wynn Edward Arnold

1950   **ONCE A SINNER**
Director: Lewis Gilbert
Co-stars: Jack Watling Joy Shelton Sidney Tafler

1957   **AFTER THE BALL**
Director: Compton Bennett
Co-stars: Laurence Harvey Clive Morton June Clyde

MIA KIRSHNER

1993   **LOVE AND HUMAN REMAINS**
Director: Denys Arcand
Co-stars: Thomas Gibson Ruth Marshall Rich Roberts

1993   **CADILLAC GIRLS**
Director: Nicholas Kendall
Co-stars: Jennifer Dale Adam Beach

1995   **EXOTICA**
Director: Atom Egoyam
Co-stars: Bruce Greenwood Don Mckeller

1995   **JOHNNY'S GIRL**
Director: John Kent Harrison
Co-star: Treat Williams

1996   **THE CROW: CITY OF ANGELS**
Director: Tim Pope
Co-star: Vincent Perez

1997   **ANNA KAENINA**
Director: Bernard Rose
Co-stars: Sophie Marceau Sean Bean James Fox

DOROTHY KIRSTEN

1951   **THE GREAT CARUSO**
Director: Richard Thorpe
Co-stars: Mario Lanza Ann Blyth Eduard Franz

DERVLA KIRWAN

1990   **THE LILAC BUS**
Director: Giles Foster
Co-stars: Stephanie Beacham Con O'Neill Beatie Edney

1991   **DECEMBER BRIDE**
Director: Thaddeus O'Sullivan
Co-stars: Donal McCann Saskia Reeves Patrick Malahide

1991   **A TIME TO DANCE**
Director: Kevin Billington
Co-stars: Ronald Pickup Rosemary McHale Annie Raitt

MAUREEN KIRWIN

1984   **MISUNDERSTOOD**
Director: Jerry Schatzberg
Co-stars: Gene Hackman Henry Thomas Rip Torn

1989   **REUNION**
Director: Jerry Schatzberg
Co-stars: Jason Robards Christien Anholt Samuel West

VIRGINIA KISER

1977   **KILL ME IF YOU CAN**
Director: Buzz Kulik
Co-stars: Alan Alda Talia Shire Barnard Hughes

EARTHA KITT

1954   **NEW FACES**
Director: Harry Horner
Co-stars: Ronny Graham Alice Ghostly Robert Clary Paul Lynde

1958   **MARK OF THE HAWK**
Director: Michael Audley
Co-stars: Sidney Poitier Juano Hernandez John McIntyre

1958   **ST. LOUIS BLUES**
Director: Allen Reisner
Co-stars: Nat King Cole Pearl Bailey Ella Fitzgerald

1958   **ANNA LUCASTA**
Director: Arnold Laven
Co-stars: Frederick O'Neal Sammy Davis Rex Ingram Henry Scott

1965   **SYNANON**
Director: Richard Quine
Co-stars: Edmond O'Brien Chuck Connors Stella Stevens

1971   **UP THE CHASTITY BELT**
Director: Bob Kellett
Co-stars: Frankie Howerd Graham Crowden Roy Hudd

1975   **FRIDAY FOSTER**
Director: Arthur Marks
Co-stars: Pam Grier Yaphet Koto Godfrey Cambridge

1991   **ERNEST SCARED STUPID**
Director: John R. Cherry
Co-stars: Jim Varney Gailard Sartain

1989   **ERIK THE VIKING**
Director: Terry Jones
Co-stars: Tim Robbins Mickey Rooney

1992   **BOOMERANG**
Director: Reggie Hudlin
Co-stars: Eddie Murphy Robin Givens Grace Jones

ELEONORE KLARWEIN *(Child)*

1977   **PEPPERMINT SODA**
Director: Diane Kurys
Co-stars: Odile Michel Anouk Ferjac Yves Renier

MARIE KLEIBER

1992   **LE PETIT PRINCE A DIT**
Director: Christine Pascal
Co-stars: Richard Berry Lucie Phan Anemone

ADELAIDE KLEIN

1948   **THE NAKED CITY**
Director: Jules Dassin
Co-stars: Barry Fitzgerald Don Taylor Howard Duff

1952   **MURDER INC.**
Director: Bretaigne Windust
Co-stars: Humphrey Bogart Zero Mostel Everett Sloane

NITA KLEIN

1963   **MURIEL**
Director: Alain Resnais
Co-stars: Delphine Seyrig Jean-Pierre Kerien Claude Seinval

ALEXANDRA KLUGE *(Sister Of Alexander Kluge)*

1966   **YESTERDAY GIRL**
Director: Alexander Kluge
Co-stars: Gunther Mack Hans Korte Eva Marie Meinecke

JUDY KNAIZ

1969   **HELLO DOLLY**
Director: Gene Kelly
Co-stars: Barbra Streisand Walter Matthau Michael Crawford

EVALYN KNAPP

1930   **RIVER'S END**
Director: Michael Curtiz
Co-stars: Charles Bickford Zasu Pitts J. Farrell Macdonald

1930   **SINNER'S HOLIDAY**
Director: John Adolfi
Co-stars: Grant Withers James Cagney Joan Blondell

1931   **THE MILLIONAIRE**
Director: John Adolfi
Co-stars: George Arliss Florence Arliss James Cagney

1931   **SMART MONEY**
Director: Alfred Green
Co-stars: Edward G. Robinson James Cagney Boris Karloff

1931   **A SUCCESSFUL CALAMITY**
Director: John Adolfi
Co-stars: George Arliss Mary Astor Grant Mitchell

1932   **NIGHT MAYOR**
Director: Ben Stoloff
Co-stars: Lee Tracy Eugene Pallette Warren Hymer

1932   **MADAME RACKETEER**
Director: Alexander Hall
Co-stars: Alison Skipworth Richard Bennett George Raft

1932   **FIREMAN SAVE MY CHILD**
Director: Leslie Goodwins
Co-stars: Joe E. Brown Lillian Bond Guy Kibbee

1932   **BIG CITY BLUES**
Director: Mervyn LeRoy
Co-stars: Joan Blondell Humphrey Bogart Eric Linden

1932   **HIGH PRESSURE**
Director: Mervyn LeRoy
Co-stars: William Powell Evelyn Brent Frank McHugh

1932   **THE VANISHING FRONTIER**
Co-stars: Johnny Mack Brown J. Farrell Macdonald

1933   **HIS PRIVATE SECRETARY**
Co-star: Reginald Barlow

1933   **POLICE CAR 17**
Co-star: Tim McCoy

1934   **A MAN'S GAME**
Co-star: Tim McCoy

1934   **IN OLD SANTE FE**
Co-star: Ken Maynard Kenneth Thomson

1935   **CONFIDENTIAL**
Co-star: Warren Hymer

1935   **ONE FRIGHTENED NIGHT**
Director: Christy Cabanne
Co-stars: Charles Grapewin Mary Carlisle Arthur Hohl

1936   **BULLDOG EDITION**
Co-stars: Ray Walker Regis Toomey

1938   **RAWHIDE**
Co-star: Smith Ballew

1941   **THE LONE WOLF TAKES A CHANCE**
Director: Sidney Salkow
Co-stars: Warren William Henry Wilcoxon

ANNE KNIGHT

1988   **VAMPIRE IN VENICE**
Director: Augusto Caminito
Co-stars: Klaus Kinski Christopher Plummer

ANN KNIGHT

1970   **THE HAWAIINS**
Director: Tom Gries
Co-stars: Charlton Heston Tina Chen Geraldine Chaplin

CINDI KNIGHT

1983   **MURDER IN COWETA COUNTY**
Director: Gary Nelson
Co-stars: Johnny Cash Andy Griffith Earl Hindman

GLADYS KNIGHT

1987   **DESPERADO**
Director: Virgel Vogel
Co-stars: Alex McArthur David Warner Robert Vaughn

JUNE KNIGHT

1935   **BROADWAY MELODY OF 1936**
Director: Roy Del Ruth
Co-stars: Robert Taylor Eleanor Powell Buddy Ebson

1937   **THE LILAC DOMINO**
Director: Fred Zelnik
Co-stars: Michael Bartlett Athene Seyler S.Z. Sakall

1938   **BREAK THE NEWS**
Director: Rene Clair
Co-stars: Jack Buchanan Maurice Chevalier Robb Wilton

1940   **THE HOUSE ACROSS THE BAY**
Director: Archie Mayo
Co-stars: Joan Bennett George Raft Lloyd Nolan

KESHIA KNIGHT

1985   **THE LAST DRAGON**
Director: Michael Schulz
Co-stars: Vanity Chris Murney Faith Prince

PATRICIA KNIGHT *(Married Cornel Wilde)*

1949   **SHOCKPROOF**
Director: Douglas Sirk
Co-stars: Cornel Wilde Esther Minciotti John Baragrey

1951   **THE MAGIC FACE**
Director: Frank Tuttle
Director: Luther Adler Ilka Windish

ROSALIND KNIGHT

1959   **CARRY ON TEACHER**
Director: Gerald Thomas
Co-stars: Ted Ray Hattie Jacques Kenneth Williams

1984   **THE ADVENTURES OF SHERLOCK HOLMES: THE BLUE CARBUNCLE**
Director: David Carson
Co-star: Jeremy Brett David Burke

1993   **ROYAL CELEBRATION**
Director: Ferdinand Fairfax
Co-stars: Minnie Driver Rupert Graves Peter Howitt

SANDRA KNIGHT

1963   **THE TERROR**
Director: Monte Helman
Co-stars: Boris Karloff Jack Nicholson Dorothy Neuman

SHIRLEY KNIGHT *(Married Gene Persson)*
Nominated For Best Supporting Actress In 1960 For "The Dark At The Top Of The Stairs" And In 1962 For "Sweet Bird Of Youth"

1960   **ICE PALACE**
Director: Vincent Sherman
Co-stars: Richard Burton Robert Ryan Carolyn James Martha Hyer

1960   **THE DARK AT THE TOP OF THE STAIRS**
Director: Delbert Mann
Co-stars: Robert Preston Dorothy McGuire

1962   **THE COUCH**
Director: Owen Crump
Co-stars: Grant Williams Onslow Stevens

1962   **HOUSE OF WOMEN**
Director: Walter Doniger
Co-stars: Andrew Duggan Constance Ford Barbara Nichols

1962 SWEET BIRD OF YOUTH
Director: Richard Brooks
Co-stars: Paul Newman Geraldine Page Ed Begley

1963 FLIGHT FROM ASHIYA
Director: Michael Anderson
Co-stars: Yul Brynner Richard Widmark George Chakiris

1966 THE GROUP
Director: Sidney Lumet
Co-stars: Candice Bergen Joan Hackett Joanna Pettit Jessica Walter

1966 DUTCHMAN
Director: Anthony Harvey
Co-stars: Al Freeman Jnr.

1967 THE OUTSIDER
Director: Michael Ritchie
Co-stars: Darren McGavin Anna Hagan Edmond O'Brien

1968 PETULIA
Director: Richard Lester
Co-stars: Julie Christie George C. Scott Richard Chamberlain

1969 THE RAIN PEOPLE
Director: Francis Coppola
Co-stars: James Caan Robert Duvall Marya Zimmet

1974 JUGGERNAUT
Director: Richard Lester
Co-stars: Richard Harris Omar Sharif David Hemmings

1978 THE DEFECTION OF SIMAS DUKIRKA
Director: David Lowell Rich
Co-stars: Alan Arkin Richard Jordan

1979 BEYOND THE POSEIDON ADVENTURE
Director: Irwin Allen
Co-stars: Michael Caine Sally Field Telly Savalas

1981 ENDLESS LOVE
Director: Franco Zeffirelli
Co-stars: Brooke Shields Don Murray Martin Hewitt

1982 THE SENDER
Director: Roger Christian
Co-stars: Kathryn Harold Paul Freeman Zeliko Ivanek

1991 BUMP IN THE NIGHT
Director: Karen Arthur
Co-stars: Meredith Baxter Christopher Reeve

1991 A CHILD FOR SATAN
Director: Robert Lieberman
Co-stars: Peter Kowanko Anthony Zerbe Spalding Gray

1995 FORBIDDEN MEMORIES
Director: Bob Clark
Co-stars: Mary Tyler Moore Linda Lavin

1998 AS GOOD AS IT GETS
Director: James Brooks
Co-stars: Jack Nicholson Greg Kinnear Helen Hunt

TUESDAY KNIGHT
1988 A NIGHTMARE ON ELM STREET IV
Director: Renny Harlin
Co-stars: Robert Englund Rodney Eastman

1994 THE COOL AND THE CRAZY
Director: Ralph Bakshi
Co-stars: Alicia Silverstone Jared Leto Matthew Flint

LYDIA KNOTT
1923 A WOMAN OF PARIS
Director: Charles Chaplin
Co-stars: Edna Purviance Adolphe Menjou Carl Miller

MARILYN KNOWLDEN (Child)
1934 DAVID COPPERFIELD
Director: George Cukor
Co-stars: Frank Lawton John Barrymore Maureen O'Sullivan

1935 LES MISERABLES
Director: Richard Boleslawski
Co-stars: Fredric March Charles Laughton Frances Drake

1936 SHOW BOAT
Director: James Whale
Co-stars: Irene Dunne Allan Jones Charles Winninger

1938 MARIE ANTOINETTE
Director: W.S. Van Dyke
Co-stars: Norma Shearer Tyrone Power Robert Morley

POLLY KNOWLES
1937 WINGS OVER HONOLULU
Director: H.C. Potter
Co-stars: Ray Milland Wendie Barrie William Gargan

ELYSE KNOX
1939 FIGHTING MAD

1940 THE GIRL FROM AVENUE A
Director: Otto Brower
Co-stars: Jane Withers Kent Taylor Jessie Ralph

1941 TANKS A MILLION
Director: Fred Guiol
Co-stars: William Tracy James Gleason Joe Sawyer

1941 SHERIFF OF TOMBSTONE
Co-stars: Roy Rogers Sally Payne

1942 TOP SERGEANT
Co-star: Don Terry

1942 HAY FOOT
Co-stars: William Tracy James Gleason Joe Sawyer

1943 HIT THE ICE
Director: Charles Lamont
Co-stars: Bud Abbott Lou Costello Ginny Simms

1943 MR. BIG
Director: Charles Lamont
Co-stars: Donald O'Connor Gloria Jean Peggy Ryan

1944 ARMY WIVES
Co-stars: Rick Vallin Sam Flint Oscar O'Shea

1946 JOE PALOOKA, CHAMP
Director: Reginald Le Borg
Co-stars: Leon Errol Joe Kirkwood Joe Sawyer

1946 GENTLEMAN JOE PALOOKA
Director: Reginald Le Borg
Co-stars: Leon Errol Joe Kirkwood Guy Kibbee

1946 SWEETHEART OF SIGMA CHI
Co-stars: Ann Gilles Alan Hale Jnr.

1947 BLACK GOLD
Director: Phil Karlson
Co-stars: Anthony Quinn Katherine DeMille Ducky Louie

1948 I WOULDN'T BE IN YOUR SHOES
Co-star: Don Castle

1949 THERE'S A GIRL IN MY HEART
Director: Arthur Dreifuss
Co-stars: Lee Bowman Gloria Jean Lon Chaney Jnr.

PATRICIA KNOX
1946 GENTLEMAN WITH GUNS
Co-stars: Buster Crabbe Al 'Fuzzy' St. John

1946 PRAIRIE BADMEN
Co-stars: Buster Crabbe Al 'Fuzzy' St. John

PEGGY KNUDSEN
1946 THE BIG SLEEP
Director: Howard Hawks
Co-stars: Humphrey Bogart Lauren Bacall Martha Vickers

1946 NEVER SAY GOODBYE
Director: James Kern
Co-stars: Errol Flynn Eleanor Parker Lucile Watson

1946 A STOLEN LIFE
Director: Curtis Bernhardt
Co-stars: Bette Davis Glenn Ford Dane Clark

1947 STALLION ROAD
Director: James Kern
Co-stars: Ronald Reagan Alexis Smith Zachary Scott

1948 PERILOUS WATERS
Co-stars: Don Castle Audrey Long John Miljan

1955 UNCHAINED
Director: Hall Bartlett
Co-stars: Chester Morris Barbara Hale Todd Duncan

1955 GOOD MORNING, MISS DOVE
Director: Henry Koster
Co-stars: Jennifer Jones Robert Stack Robert Douglas

1956 HILDA CRANE
Director: Philip Dunne
Co-stars: Jean Simmons Guy Madison Jean-Pierre Aumont

1956 ISTANBUL
Director: Joseph Pevney
Co-stars: Errol Flynn Cornell Borchers John Bently

MARIANNE KOCH

1962 THE DEVIL'S AGENT
Director: John Paddy Carstairs
Co-stars: Peter Van Eyck MacDonald Carey Billie Whitelaw

1963 DEATH DRUMS ALONG THE RIVER
Director: Lawrence Huntington
Co-stars: Richard Todd Vivi Bach

1964 A FISTFULL OF DOLLARS
Director: Sergio Leone
Co-stars: Clint Eastwood Gian Maria Volonte

LISA KOHANE

1986 DEATH IS PART OF THE PROCESS
Director: Bill Hays
Co-stars: Art Malik John Mathshikiza Eric Flynn

SUSAN KOHNER

Nominated For Best Supporting Actress In 1959 For "Imitation Of Life"

1955 TO HELL AND BACK
Director: Jesse Hibbs
Co-stars: Audie Murphy Marshall Thompson Charles Drake

1956 THE LAST WAGON
Director: Delmer Daves
Co-stars: Richard Widmark Felicia Farr Tommy Rettig

1957 DINO
Director: Thomas Carr
Co-stars: Sal Mineo Brain Keith Frank Faylen

1957 TROOPER HOOK
Co-stars: Charles Marquis Warren
Co-stars: Barbara Stanwyck Joel McCrea Earl Holliman

1959 THE GENE KRUPA STORY
Director: Don Weis
Co-stars: Sal Mineo James Darren Susan Oliver

1959 IMITATION OF LIFE
Director: Douglas Sirk
Co-stars: Lana Turner Juanita Moore Sandra Dee

1959 THE BIG FISHERMAN
Director: Frank Borzage
Co-stars: Howard Keel John Saxon Martha Hyer

1960 ALL THE FINE YOUNG CANNIBALS
Director: Michael Anderson
Co-stars: Natalie Wood Robert Wagner

1961 BY LOVE POSSESSED
Director: John Sturges
Co-stars: Lana Turner Jason Robards Barbara Bel Geddes

1962 FREUD
Director: John Huston
Co-stars: Montgomery Clift Larry Parks Susannah York

MAGDA KONOPKA

1969 WHEN DINOSAURS RULED THE EARTH
Director: Val Guest
Co-stars: Victoria Vetri Patrick Allen Patrick Holt

ANNA KONSTAM

1938 THEY DRIVE BY NIGHT
Director: Arthur Woods
Co-stars: Emlyn Williams Ernest Thesiger Ronald Shiner

1940 SALOON BAR
Director: Walter Forde
Co-stars: Gordon Harker Elizabeth Allan Mervyn Johns

PHYLLIS KONSTAM

1930 MURDER
Director: Alfred Hitchcock
Co-stars: Herbert Marshall Norah Baring Edward Chapman

1931 THE GENTLEMAN OF PARIS
Director: Sinclair Hill
Co-stars: Arthur Wontner Hugh Williams Sybil Thorndyke

LEOPOLDINE KONSTANTIN

1946 NOTORIOUS
Director: Alfred Hitchcock
Co-stars: Cary Grant Ingrid Bergman Claude Rains

SIMONIE KOPAPIK

1976 THE WHITE DAWN
Director: Philip Kaufman
Co-stars: Warren Oates Timothy Bottoms Lou Gossett

KAREN KOPINS

1985 ONCE BITTEN
Director: Howard Storm
Co-stars: Lauren Hutton Jim Carrey Cleavon Little

1986 JAKE SPEED
Director: Andrew Lane
Co-stars: Wayne Crawford John Hurt Leon Ames

SUSANN KORDA

1970 THE DEVIL CAME FROM ARKANSAS
Director: Jesus Franco
Co-stars: Fred Williams Horst Tappert

VERA KORENE

1939 CRIME IN THE MAGINOT LINE
Co-star: Victor Francen

MILIZA KORJUS

Nominated For Best Supporting Actress In 1938 For "The Great Waltz"

1938 THE GREAT WALTZ
Director: Julien Duvivier
Co-stars: Luise Rainer Fernand Gravet Hugh Herbert

MARY KORNMAN

1935 DESERT TRAIL
Co-stars: John Wayne Paul Fix Henry Hull

SYLVA KOSCINA

1957 HERCULES
Director: Pietro Francisci
Co-stars: Steve Reeves Fabrizio Meone Gena Rovere

1960 THE SIEGE OF SYRACUSE
Director: Pietro Francisci
Co-stars: Rossano Brazzi Tina Louise Gino Cervi

1962 THE SWORDSMAN OF SIENNA
Director: Etienne Perier
Co-stars: Stewart Granger Christine Kaufman

1962 JESSICA
Director: Jean Negulesco
Co-stars: Angie Dickinson Maurice Chevalier Noel-Noel

1963 JUDEX
Director: Georges Franju
Co-stars: Channing Pollock Francine Berge Edith Scob

1963 HOT ENOUGH FOR JUNE
Director: Ralph Thomas
Co-stars: Dirk Bogarde Robert Morley Leo McKern

1965 JULIET OF THE SPIRITS
Director: Federico Fellini
Co-stars: Giulietta Masina Alba Cancellieri

1966 THREE BITES AT THE APPLE
Director: Alvin Gazner
Co-stars: David McCallum Tammy Grimes Harvey Korman

1967 THE SECRET WAR OF HARRY FRIGG
Director: Jack Smight
Co-stars: Paul Newman John Williams Tom Bosley

1967 DEADLIER THAN THE MALE
Director: Ralph Thomas
Co-stars: Richard Johnson Elke Sommer Nigel Green

1968 A LOVELY WAY TO DIE
Director: David Lowell Rich
Co-stars: Kirk Douglas Eli Wallach Kenneth Haigh

1969 HORNET'S NEST
Director: Phil Karlson
Co-stars: Rock Hudson Sergio Fantoni Jacques Sernas

1969 THE BATTLE OF NERETVA
Director: Veljko Bulajic
Co-stars: Yul Brynner Curt Jurgens Orson Welles

1972 LISA AND THE DEVIL
Director: Mario Bava
Co-stars: Elke Sommer Telly Savalas Alida Valli

MARINA KOSHETZ

1948 LUXURY LINER
Director: Richard Whorf
Co-stars: Jane Powell George Brent Lauritz Melchior

APOLLONIA KOTERO

1984 PURPLE RAIN
Director: Albert Magnoli
Co-stars: Prince Morris Day Jerome Benton

MARGE KOTLISKY

1989 GOD'S WILL
Director: Julia Cameron
Co-stars: Daniel Region Laura Margolis Linda Edmond

1991 HOMICIDE
Director: David Mamet
Co-stars: Joe Mantegna William H. Macy Ving Rhames

MAYA KOUMANI

1958 THE DIPLOMATIC CORPSE
Director: Montgomery Tully
Co-stars: Robin Bailey Susan Shaw Harry Fowler

KISSA KOUPRINE

1931 THE MYSTERY OF THE YELLOW ROOM
Director: Marcel L'Herbier
Co-stars: Huguette Duflos Roland Toutain

NANCY KOVAK

1962 THE DIARY OF A MADMAN
Director: Reginald Le Borg
Co-stars: Vincent Price Chris Warfield

1963 JASON AND THE ARGONAUTS
Director: Don Chaffey
Co-stars: Todd Armstrong Honor Blackman Andrew Faulds

1965 THE GREAT SIOUX MASSACRE
Director: Sidney Salkow
Co-stars: Joseph Cotten Darren McGavin Phil Carey

1966 FRANKIE AND JOHNNY
Director: Frederick De Cordova
Co-stars: Elvis Presley Donna Douglas Harry Morgan

1966 THE SILENCERS
Director: Phil Karlson
Co-stars: Dean Martin Stella Stevens Cyd Charisse

1966 TARZAN AND THE VALLEY OF GOLD
Director: Robert Day
Co-stars: Mike Henry David Opatoshu

1969 MAROONED
Director: John Sturges
Co-stars: Gregory Peck Richard Crenna David Janssen

HARLEY JANE KOZAK

1989 PARENTHOOD
Director: Ron Howard
Co-stars: Steve Martin Jason Robards Dianne Wiest

1990 ARACHNOPHOBIA
Director: Frank Marshall
Co-stars: Jeff Daniels John Goodman Julian Sands

1991 NECESSARY ROUGHNESS
Director: Stan Dragoti
Co-stars: Scott Bakula Hector Elizondo Robert Loggia

1991 ALL I WANT FOR CHRISTMAS
Director: Robert Lieberman
Co-stars: Jamey Sheridan Leslie Nielsen Lauren Bacall

1993 THE AMY FISHER STORY
Director: Andy Tennant
Co-stars: Drew Barrymore Tom Mason Ken Pogue

1994 THE FAVOR
Director: Donald Petrie
Co-stars: Elizabeth McGovern Bill Pullman

1995 THE ANDROID AFFAIR
Director: Richard Kletter
Co-stars: Saul Rubinek

LINDA KOZLAWSKI

1986 CROCODILE DUNDEE
Director: Peter Falman
Co-stars: Paul Hogan John Meillon Mark Blum

1986 CROCODILE DUNDEE II
Director: John Cornell
Co-stars: Paul Hogan John Meillon Juan Fernandez

1988 FAVOURITE SON
Director: Jeff Bleckner
Co-stars: Robert Loggia Harry Hamlin James Whitmore

1990 ALMOST AN ANGEL
Director: John Cornell
Co-stars: Paul Hogan Charlton Heston Elias Koteas

SUSANNE KRAGE

1970 QUIET DAYS IN CLINCHY
Director: Jens-Jorgen Thorsen
Co-stars: Paul Valjean Louise White

JANE KRAKOWSKI

1991 STEPPING OUT
Director: Lewis Gilbert
Co-stars: Liza Minnelli Shelley Winters Julie Walters

HOPE KRAMER

1945 THE FLYING SERPENT
Director: Sherman Scott
Co-stars: George Zucco Ralph Lewis Eddie Acuff

STEPHANIE KRAMER

1989 TAKE MY DAUGHTERS, PLEASE
Director: Larry Elikann
Co-stars: Rue McClanahan Kim Delaney Susan Ruttan

1990 COINS IN THE FOUNTAIN
Director: Tony Wharmby
Co-stars: Loni Anderson Shanna Reed Anthony Newley

1993 BEYOND SUSPICION
Director: Paul Ziller
Co-star: Jack Scalia

1995 DECEIVED BY TRUST
Director: Chuck Bowman
Co-star: Michael Gross

RAQUEL KRELLE

1993 GHOULIES 4
Director: Jim Wynorski
Co-stars: Pete Liapis Stacie Randall Bobby Di Cicco

CONNIE KRESKI

1969 CAN HIERONYMUS MERKIN EVER FORGET MERCY HUMPPE AND FIND TRUE HAPPINESS?
Director: Anthony Newley
Co-stars: Anthony Newley Joan Collins Milton Berle Stubby Kaye

LISA KREUZER

1974 ALICE IN THE CITIES
Director: Wim Wenders
Co-stars: Rudiger Volger Yella Rotttlander Edda Kochel

1975 KINGS OF THE ROAD
Director: Wim Wenders
Co-stars: Rudiger Volger Hanns Zischler Rudolf Schundler

1977 THE AMERICAN FRIEND
Director: Wim Wenders
Co-stars: Dennis Hopper Bruno Ganz Gerard Blain

1984 FLIGHT TO BERLIN
Director: Christopher Petit
Co-stars: Tusse Silberg Paul Freeman Eddie Constantine

KARIN KRICK

1982 PARSIFAL
Director: Hans Jurgen Syberberg
Co-stars: Michael Kutter Edith Clever Robert Lloyd

KATHIE KRIEGEL

1989 A TALE OF TWO CITIES
Director: Philippe Monnier
Co-stars: James Wilby Serena Gordon John Mills

ALICE KRIGE

1981 GHOST STORY
Director: John Irvin
Co-stars: Fred Astaire Douglas Fairbanks Melvyn Douglas

1981 CHARIOTS OF FIRE
Director: Hugh Hudson
Co-stars: Ben Cross Nigel Havers Ian Charleson Ian Holm

1985 KING DAVID
Director: Bruce Beresford
Co-stars: Richard Gere Edward Woodward Hurd Hatfield

1985 WALLENBERG: A HERO'S STORY
Director: Lamont Johnson
Co-stars: Richard Chamberlain Bibi Andersson

1986 SECOND SERVE
Director: Anthony Page
Co-stars: Vanessa Redgrave Martin Balsam Louise Fletcher

1987 BARFLY
Director: Barbet Schroeder
Co-stars: Mickey Rourke Faye Dunaway Jack Nance

1988 HAUNTED SUMMER
Director: Ivan Passer
Co-stars: Eric Stolz Laura Dern Philip Anglim Don Hodson

1988 SEE YOU IN THE MORNING
Director: Alan J. Pakula
Co-stars: Jeff Bridges Farrah Fawcett Drew Barrymore

1990 MAX AND HELEN
Director: Philip Saville
Co-stars: Treat Williams Martin Landau Jodhi May

1992 STEPHEN KING'S SLEEPWALKERS
Director: Mick Garris
Co-stars: Brian Krause Madchen Amick

1992 LADYKILLER
Director: Michael Scott
Co-stars: Mimi Rogers John Shea Tom Irwin

1995 INSTITUTE BENJAMENTA
Directors Brothers Quay
Co-stars: Mark Rylance Gottfried John Daniel Smith

1995 JOSEPH IN EGYPT
Director: Roger Young
Co-stars: Paul Mercurio Ben Kingsley Lesley Ann Warren

1996 STAR TREK: FIRST CONTACT
Director: Jonathan Frakes
Co-stars: Patrick Stewart Brent Spiner James Cromwell

SLYVIA KRISTEL

1974 EMMANUELLE
Director: Just Jaeckin
Co-stars: Marika Green Daniel Sarky Alain Cuny

1975 EMMANUELLE 2
Director: Francis Giacobetti
Co-stars: Umberto Orsini Catherine Rivet Marion Womble

1978 THE FIFTH MUSKETEER
Director: Ken Annakin
Co-stars: Beau Bridges Lloyd Bridges Rex Harrison

1979 AIRPORT '80: THE CONCORDE
Director: David Lowell Rich
Co-stars: Alain Delon Robert Wagner Susan Blakely

1980 THE NUDE BOMB
Director: Clive Donner
Co-stars: Don Adams Pamela Hensley Rhonda Fleming

1981 PRIVATE LESSONS
Director: Alan Myerson
Co-stars: Eric Brown Ron Foster Pamela Bryant Howard Hesseman

1981 LADY CHATTERLEY'S LOVER
Director: Just Jaeckin
Co-stars: Nicholas Clay Shane Briant Elizabeth Spriggs

1984 EMMANUELLE 4
Director: Francis Giacobetti
Co-stars: Mia Nygren Deborah Power Sophie Berger

1985 MATA HARI
Director: Curtis Harrington
Co-stars: Christopher Casenove Oliver Tobias Gaye Brown

1987 THE ARROGANT
Director: Philippe Blot
Co-stars: Gary Graham Kimberley Baucom

KATHY KRISTOFFERSON

1992 GUYVER: DARK HERO
Director: Steve Wang
Co-stars: David Kyter Christopher Mirendel

NINA KRONJAEGER

1992 MAKING UP
Director: Katja Von Garnier
Co-stars: Katja Riemann Gedeon Burkhard

MARGARETHA KROOK

1966 PERSONNA
Director: Ingmar Bergman
Co-stars: Liv Ullmann Bibi Andersson Gunnar Bjornstrand

CHRISTIANE KRUEGER

1985 ANNE OF GREEN GABLES
Director: Kevin Sullivan
Co-stars: Megan Follows Colleen Dewhurst Richard Farnsworth

ALMA KRUGER

1936 CRAIG'S WIFE
Director: Dorothy Arzner
Co-stars: Rosalind Russell John Boles Billie Burke

1936 THESE THREE
Director: William Wyler
Co-stars: Merle Oberon Miriam Hopkins Joel McCrea

1937 VOGUES OF 1938
Director: Irving Cummings
Co-stars: Joan Bennett Helen Vinson Alan Mowbray

1937 ONE HUNDRED MEN AND A GIRL
Director: Henry Koster
Co-stars: Deanna Durbin Adolphe Menjou Alice Brady

1938 THE GREAT WALTZ
Director: Julien Duvivier
Co-stars: Fernand Gravet Luise Rainer Miliza Korjus

1938 MOTHER CAREY'S CHICKENS
Director: Rowland Lee
Co-stars: Anne Shirley Ruby Keeler Fay Bainter

1938 THE TOY WIFE
Director: Richard Thorpe
Co-stars: Luise Rainer Melvyn Douglas Robert Young

1939 CALLING DR. KILDARE
Director: Harold Bucquet
Co-stars: Lew Ayres Lionel Barrymore Lana Turner

1940 HIS GIRL FRIDAY
Director: Howard Hawks
Co-stars: Cary Garnt Rosalind Russell Ralph Bellamy

1940 YOU'LL FIND OUT
Director: David Butler
Co-stars: Kay Kyser Dennis O'Keefe Ginny Simms

1942 SABOTEUR
Director: Alfred Hitchcock
Co-stars: Robert Cummings Priscilla Lane Otto Kruger

1942 CALLING DR. GILLESPIE
Director: Harold Bucquet
Co-stars: Lionel Barrymore Philip Dorn Dona Reed

1947 DARK DELUSION
Director: Willis Goldbeck
Co-stars: Lionel Barrymore James Craig Lucille Bremer

1947 FOREVER AMBER
Director: Otto Preminger
Co-stars: Linda Darnell George Sanders Cornel Wilde

CHRISTINE KRUGER

1974 THE INTERNECINE PROJECT
Director: Ken Hughes
Co-stars: James Coburn Lee Grant Harry Andrews

SONIA KRUGER

1992 STRICTLY BALLROOM
Director: Baz Luhrmann
Co-stars: Paul Mercurio Tara Morice Bill Hunter

KENDRA KRULL

1995 UNSTRUNG HEROES
Director: Diane Keaton
Co-stars: Andie MacDowell John Turturro Nathan Watt

MARA KRUP

1965 FOR A FEW DOLLARS MORE
Director: Sergio Leone
Co-stars: Clint Eastwood Lee Van Cleef Klaus Kinski

SOBOTKA KUBRICK *(Married Stanley Kubrick)*

1955 KILLER'S KISS
Director: Stanley Kubrick
Co-stars: Frank Silvera Irene Kane Jamie Smith

VIVIAN KUBRICK *(Child)*
(Daughter Of Stanley Kubrick)

1968 2001:A SPACE ODYSSEY
Director: Stanley Kubrick
Co-stars: Keir Dullea Gary Lockwood William Sylvester

YOUKI KUDON

1989 MYSTERY TRAIN
Director: Jim Jarmusch
Co-stars: Steve Buscemi Elizabeth Bracco Rick Aviles

LISA KUDROW

**1997 ROMY AND MICHELE'S
HIGH SCHOOL REUNION**
Co-star: Mira Sorvino

SOPHIE KULLMAN

1991 WHERE ANGELS FEAR TO TREAD
Director: Charles Sturridge
Co-stars: Helen Mirren Helena Bonham-Carter

NANCY KULP

1951 THE MODEL AND THE MARRIAGE BROKER
Director: George Cukor
Co-stars: Thelma Ritter Jeanne Crain

1952 STEEL TOWN
Director: George Sherman
Co-stars: Ann Sheridan John Lund Howard Duff

1955 COUNT THREE AND PRAY
Director: George Sherman
Co-stars: Van Heflin Joanne Woodward Phil Carey

1957 THE THREE FACES OF EVE
Director: Nunnally Johnson
Co-stars: Joanne Woodward David Wayne Lee J. Cobb

1959 FIVE GATES TO HELL
Director: James Clavell
Co-stars: Dolores Michaels Patricia Owens Neville Brand

1961 THE PARENT TRAP
Director: David Swift
Co-stars: Hayley Mills Maureen O'Hara Brian Keith

1963 WHO'S MINDING THE STORE
Director: Frank Tashlin
Co-stars: Jerry Lewis Jill St. John Ray Walston

1964 THE PATSY
Director: Jerry Lewis
Co-stars: Jerry Lewis Everett Sloane Peter Lorre Phil Harris

1966 THE NIGHT OF THE GRIZZLY
Director: Joseph Pevney
Co-stars: Clint Walker Martha Hyer Keenan Wynn

MAGDA KUN

1935 DANCE BAND
Director: Marcel Varnel
Co-stars: Charles Rogers June Clyde Richard Hearne

1938 OLD MOTHER REILLY IN PARIS
Director: Oswald Mitchell
Co-stars: Arthur Lucan Kitty McShane Jerry Verno

1943 HEAVEN IS ROUND THE CORNER
Director: MacLean Rogers
Co-stars: Will Fyffe Leni Lynn Austin Trevor

MARCIA JEAN KURTZ

1974 THE STOOLIE
Director: John Avildsen
Co-stars: Jackie Mason Dan Frazer Anne Marie

1984 COLD FEET
Director: Bruce Van Ducen
Co-stars: Griffin Dunne Marissa Chibas Blanche Baker

SWOOZIE KURTZ

1977 FIRST LOVE
Director: Joan Darling
Co-stars: William Katt Susan Dey John Heard Beverly D'Angelo

1982 THE WORLD ACCORDING TO GARP
Director: George Roy Hill
Co-stars: Robin Williams Glenn Close

1983 A CARIBBEAN MYSTERY
Director: Robert Lewis
Co-stars: Helen Hayes Jameson Parker Brock Peters

1984 AGAINST ALL ODDS
Director: Taylor Hackford
Co-stars: Jeff Bridges Rachel Ward Richard Widmark

1985 A TIME TO LIVE
Director: Rick Wallace
Co-stars: Jeffrey DeMunn Liza Minnelli Corey Haim

1985 GUILTY CONSCIENCE
Director: David Greene
Co-stars: Anthony Hopkins Blythe Danner

1986 TRUE STORIES: A FILM ABOUT A BUNCH OF PEOPLE IN VIRGIL TEXAS
Director: David Byrne
Co-stars: David Byrne John Goodman Spalding Grey

1986 WILDCATS
Director: Michael Ritchie
Co-stars: Goldie Hawn Robyn Lively Brandy Gold James Keach

1988 VICE VERSA
Director: Brian Gilbert
Co-stars: Judge Reinhold Fred Savage Corinne Bohrer

1988 DANGEROUS LIAISONS
Director: Stephen Frears
Co-stars: Glenn Close John Malkovich Michelle Pfeiffer

1988 BRIGHT LIGHTS, BIG CITY
Director: James Bridges
Co-stars: Michael J. Fox Kiefer Sutherland Phoebe Cates

1989 STANLEY AND IRIS
Director: Martin Ritt
Co-stars: Jane Fonda Robert De Niro Martha Plimpton

1990 THE IMAGE
Director: Peter Werner
Co-stars: Albert Finney John Mahoney Kathy Baker Marsha Mason

1990 A SHOCK TO THE SYSTEM
Director: Jan Egleson
Co-stars: Michael Caine Elizabeth McGovern

1992 TERROR ON TRACK NINE
Director: Robert Iscove
Co-stars: Richard Crenna Cliff Gorman

1993 THE POSITIVELY TRUE ADVENTURES OF THE ALLEGED TEXAS CHEERLEADER-MURDERING MOM
Director: Michael Ritchie
Co-stars: Holly Hunter Beau Bridges Matt Frewer

1993 AND THE BAND PLAYED ON
Director: Roger Spottiswoode
Co-stars: Matthew Modine Ian McKellan Alan Alda

1994 REALITY BITES
Director: Ben Stiller
Co-stars: Winona Ryder Ethan Hawke Steve Zahn Joe Don Baker

1994 ONE CHRISTMAS
Director: Tony Bill
Co-stars: Katharine Hepburn Henry Winkler Julie Harris

1995 BETRAYED - A STORY OF THREE WOMEN
Director: William Gargan
Co-stars: Meredith Baxter John Terry

KATY KURTZMAN

1974 HUNTERS OF THE REEF
Director: Alex Singer
Co-stars: Michael Parks Mary Louise Weller William Windom

1978 WHEN EVERY DAY WAS THE FOURTH OF JULY
Director: Dan Curtis
Co-stars: Dean Jones Louise Sorel

MIMI KUZYK

1973 STRIKER'S MOUNTAIN
Director: Allen Simmonds
Co-stars: Leslie Nielsen Bruce Greenwood

1986 MILES TO GO
Director: David Greene
Co-stars: Jill Clayburgh Tom Skerritt Cyndy Preston

1986 BLIND JUSTICE
Director: Rod Holcomb
Co-stars: Tim Matheson Tom Atkins Lisa Eichhorn

1988 THE KISS
Director: Pen Densham
Co-stars: Joanna Pacula Nicholas Kilbertus Meredith Salenger

1993 THE BREAKTHROUGH
Director: Piers Haggard
Co-star: Donald Sutherland

1994 WEB OF DECEIT
Director: Bill Corcoran
Co-stars: Corbin Bernsen Amanda Pays Neve Campbell

ADIA KUZNEYZOFF

1940 DEVIL'S ISLAND
Director: William Clemens
Co-stars: Boris Karloff James Stephenson Nedda Harrigan

NANCY KWAN

1960 THE WORLD OF SUSIE WONG
Director: Richard Quine
Co-stars: William Holden Sylvia Syms Michael Wilding

1961 FLOWER DRUM SONG
Director: Henry Koster
Co-stars: James Shigeta Juanita Hall James Soo Benson Fong

1962 THE MAIN ATTRACTION
Director: Daniel Petrie
Co-stars: Pat Boone Mai Zetterling Yvonne Mitchell

1962 TAMAHINE
Director: Phillip Leacock
Co-stars: John Fraser Dennis Price Derek Nimo Justine Lord

1964 HONEYMOON HOTEL
Director: Henry Levine
Co-stars: Robert Goulet Robert Morse Jill St. John Elsa Lanchester

1964 FATE IS THE HUNTER
Director: Ralph Nelson
Co-stars: Glenn Ford Rod Taylor Suzanne Pleshette

1965 THE WILD AFFAIR
Director: John Krish
Co-stars: Terry-Thomas Jimmy Logan Bud Flanangan

1966 LT. ROBINSON CRUSOE
Director: Byron Paul
Co-stars: Dick Van Dyke Akim Tamiroff

1966 DROP DEAD DARLING
Director: Ken Hughes
Co-stars: Tony Curtis Rosanna Schiaffino Zsa Zsa Gabor

1966 THE CORRUPT ONES
Director: James Hill
Co-stars: Robert Stack Elke Sommer Christian Marquand

1968 HAWAII FIVE-O
Director: Paul Wendkos
Co-stars: Jack Lord Leslie Nielsen Lew Ayres Andrew Duggan

1968 NOBODY'S PERFECT
Director: Alan Rafkin
Co-stars: Doug McClure James Whitmore Steve Carlson

1968 THE WRECKING CREW
Director: Phil Karlson
Co-stars: Dean Martin Elke Sommer Sharon Tate

1969 THE McMASTERS
Director: Alf Kjellin
Co-stars: Brock Peters Burl Ives John Carradine

1983 THE LAST NINJA
Director: William Graham
Co-stars: Michael Beck John McMartin Richard Lynch

1988 MIRACLE LANDING
Director: Dick Lowry
Co-stars: Wayne Rogers Connie Sellecca Ana Alicia James Cromwell

1989 COLD DOG SOUP
Director: Alan Metter
Co-stars: Randy Quaid Frank Whaley Sheree North

1993 DRAGON: THE BRUCE LEE STORY
Director: Rob Cohen
Co-stars: Jason Scott Lee Lauren Holly Robert Wagner

MACHIKO KYO

1950 ROSHO-MON

1953 GATE OF HELL
Director: Teinosuke Kinugasa
Co-stars: Kazuo Hasegawa Isao Yamagata

1956 THE TEAHOUSE OF THE AUGUST MOON
Director: Daniell Mann
Co-stars: Marlon Brando Glenn Ford Paul Ford

L

BARBARA LAARGE

1954 ACT OF LOVE
Director: Anatole Litvak
Co-stars: Kirk Douglas Dany Robin Brigitte Bardot

1956 GUILTY?
Director: Edmond Greville
Co-stars: John Justin Donald Wolfit Stephen Murray

1956 THE HAPPY ROAD
Director: Gene Kelly
Co-stars: Gene Kelly Michael Redgrave Bobby Clark Brigitte Fossey

1961 PARIS BLUES
Director: Martin Ritt
Co-stars: Paul Newman Joanne Woodward Sidney Poitier

1970 DOMICILE CONJUGALE

MARTA LABARR

1938 BREAK THE NEWS
Director: Rene Clair
Co-stars: Jack Buchanan Maurice Chevalier Garry Marsh

1947 TEHERAN
Director: William Freshman
Co-stars: Derk Farr Manning Whiley John Slater

PATTI LaBELLE

1986 UNNATURAL CAUSES
Director: Lamont Johnson
Co-stars: John Ritter Alfre Woodard John Sayles

1989 SING
Director: Richard Baskin
Co-stars: Lorraine Bracco Peter Dobson Louise Lasser

CATERINA SYLOS LABINI

1989 THE ICICLE THIEF
Director: Maurizio Nichetti
Co-stars: Maurizio Nichetti Fererici Rizzo Carlina Torta

HANNA LABORNASKA

1991 EUROPA, EUROPA
Director: Agnieszka Holland
Co-stars: Marco Hofscheneider Julie Delpy Andre Wilms

HILARY LABOUR

1975 THE ROCKY HORROR PICTURE SHOW
Director: Jim Sharman
Co-stars: Tim Curry Susan Sarandon

ELINA LABOURDETTE

1946 LES DAMES DU BOIS DE BOULOGNE
Director: Robert Bresson
Co-stars: Maria Casares Lucienne Bogaert

1951 EDOUARD ET CAROLINE
Director: Jacques Becker
Co-stars: Daniel Gelin Ane Vernon William Tubbs

1954 TO PARIS WITH LOVE
Director: Robert Hamer
Co-stars: Alec Guinness Odile Versios Vernon Gray

1960 LOLA
Director: Jacques Demy
Co-stars: Anouk Aimee Marc Michel Annie Dupereux

KATIE LA BOURDETTE

1985 DESERT HEARTS
Director: Donna Dietch
Co-stars: Helen Shaver Patricia Charbonneau Audra Lindley

DOMINIQUE LABOURIER

1974 CELINE AND JULIE GO BOATING
Director: Jacques Rivette
Co-stars: Juliet Berto Marie-France Pisier

1976 JONAH - WHO WILL BE 25 IN THE YEAR 2000
Director: Alain Tanner
Co-stars: Jean-Luc Bideau Miou-Miou

MARIAN LABUDA

1989 THE LAST OF THE GOOD OLD DAYS
Director: Jiri Menzel
Co-stars: Josef Abraham Barbara Leichnerova

1991 MEETING VENUS
Director: Istvan Szabo
Co-stars: Glenn Close Niels Arestrup Victor Poletti

CAROL LACATELL

1985 FRIDAY THE 13TH., PART V: A NEW BEGINNING
Director: Danny Steinmann
Co-stars: John Shepard Richard Young

CATHERINE LACEY

1938 THE LADY VANISHES
Director: Alfred Hitchcock
Co-stars: Margaret Lockwood Michael Redgrave May Whitty

1940 THE HOUSE OF THE ARROW
Director: Harold French
Co-stars: Kenneth Kent Diana Churchill Clifford Evans

1941 COTTAGE TO LET
Director: Anthony Asquith
Co-stars: Leslie Banks Alastair Sim John Mills

1945 PINK SPRING AND SEALING WAX
Director: Robert Hamer
Co-stars: Googie Withers Mervyn Johns Garry Marsh

1947 THE OCTOBER MAN
Director: Roy Baker
Co-stars: John Mills Joan Greenwood Kay Walsh

1947 WHITE UNICORN
Director: Bernard Knowles
Co-stars: Margaret Lockwood Joan Greenwood Ian Hunter

1949 WHISKEY GALORE!
Director: Alexander MacKendrick
Co-stars: Basil Radford Joan Greenwood Jean Cadell

1958 ROCKETS GALORE
Director: Michael Relph
Co-stars: Jeannie Carson Donald Sinden Gordon Jackson

1958 INNOCENT SINNERS
Director: Philip Leacock
Co-stars: Flora Robson David Kossoff Barbara Mullen

1960 CRACK IN THE MIRROR
Director: Richard Fleischer
Co-stars: Orson Welles Juliette Greco William Lucas

1963   THE SERVANT
Director: Joseph Losey
Co-stars: Dirk Bogarde James Fox Sarah Miles

1967   THE SOCERERS
Director: Michael Reeves
Co-stars: Boris Karloff Ian Ogolvy Susan George

1967   THE MUMMY'S SHROUD
Director: John Gilling
Co-stars: John Phillips Andre Morell Elizabeth Sellars

INGRID LACEY

1990   NEVER COME BACK
Director: Ben Bolt
Co-stars: Nathaniel Parker James Fox Suzanna Hamilton

ANDREE LACHAPELLE

1992   LEOLO
Director: Jean-Claude Lauzon
Co-stars: Maxime Collin Ginette Reno Julien Guiomar

SUSANNE LACK

1982   PURPLE HAZE
Director: David Burton Morris
Co-stars: Peter Nelson Chuck McQuary Bernard Baldan

KATYA LADAN

**1993   THIRTY TWO SHORT FILMS
           ABOUT GLENN GOULD**
Director: Francois Girard
Co-stars: Colm Feore Derek Keurvorst

ALANA LADD *(Daughter Of Alan Ladd)*

1962   YOUNG GUNS OF TEXAS
Director: Maury Dexter
Co-stars: James Mitchum Jody McCrea Chill Wills

CHERYL LADD

1979   WHEN SHE WAS BAD
Director: Peter Hunt
Co-star: Robert Urich

1983   NOW AND FOREVER
Director: Adrian Carr
Co-stars: Robert Coleby Carmen Duncan Christine Amor

1985   ROMANCE ON THE ORIENT EXPRESS
Director: Lawrence Gordon Clark
Co-stars: Stuart Wilson John Gielgud

1985   A DEATH IN CALIFORNIA
Director: Delbert Mann
Co-stars: Sam Elliott Alexis Smith Fritz Weaver

1986   THE MONEY PIT
Director: Richard Benjamin
Co-stars: Tom Hanks Alexander Godunov Maureen Stapleton

1989   THE FULFILLMENT OF MARY GRAY
Director: Piers Haggard
Co-Stars: Ted Levine Lewis Smith

1989   MILLENNIUM
Director: Michael Anderson
Co-stars: Kris Kristofferson Daniel J. Travanti

1990   CRASH: THE MYSTERY OF FLIGHT 1501
Director: Philip Saville
Co-Stars: Jeffrey DeMunn Doug Sheehan

1990   JEKYLL AND HYDE
Director: David Wickes
Co-stars: Michael Caine Joss Ackland Ronald Pickup

1990   VICTIM OF INNOCENCE
Director: Mel Damski
Co-stars: Joe Spano Anthony John Denison Melissa Chan

1991   CHANGES
Director: Charles Jarrett
Co-stars: Michael Nouri Christopher Gartin

1992   POISON IVY
Director: Katt Shea Ruben
Co-stars: Drew Barrymore Tom Skerritt Sarah Gilbert

1992   FATAL MEMORIES
Co-star: Daryl Duke

1993   BROKEN PROMISES! TAKING EMILY BACK
Director: Donald Wrye
Co-stars: Polly Draper Robert Desiderio

1993   DEAD BEFORE DAWN
Director: Charles Correll
Co-stars: Jameson Parker Hope Lange Kim Coates

1995   THE HAUNTING OF LISA
Director: Don McBrearty
Co-Stars: Amelia Robinson Duncan Regehr

DIANNE LADD ~~DAUGHTER OF ALAN LADD~~
(Married Bruce Dern) (Mother of Laura Dern)
**Nominated for Best Supporting Actress In 1974 For "Alice Dosn't Live Here
Anymore", In 1990 For "Wild At Heart", And In 1991 For "Rambling Rose"**

1966   THE WILD ANGELS
Director: Roger Corman
Co-stars: Bruce Dern Peter Fonda Nancy Sinatra Gayle Hunnicutt

1970   W.U.S.A
Director: Stuart Rosenberg
Co-stars: Paul Newman Joanne Woodward Laurence Harvey

1970   REBEL ROUSERS
Co-stars: Martin Cohen
              Cameron Mitchell Jack Nicholson Bruce Dern

1972   THE DEVIL'S DAUGHTER
Director: Jeannot Szwarc
Co-stars: Belinda Montgomery Shelley Winters

1973   WHITE LIGHTNING
Director: Joseph Sargent
Co-stars: Burt Reynolds Jennifer Billingsley Ned Beatty

1974   CHINATOWN
Director: Roman Polanski
Co-stars: Jack Nicholson Faye Dunnaway John Huston

1974   ALICE DOESN'T LIVE HERE ANYMORE
Director: Martin Scorsesse
Co-stars: Ellen Burnstyn Kris Kristofferson

1976   EMBRYO
Director: Ralph Nelson
Co-stars: Rock Hudson Barbara Carrera Roddy McDowall

1978   THADDEUS ROSE AND EDDIE
Director: Jack Starrett
Co-stars: Johnny Cash Bo Hopkins June Carter Cash

1981   ALL NIGHT LONG
Director: Jean-Claude Tramont
Co-stars: Barbra Streisand Gene Hackman Kevin Dobson

1983   SOMETHING WICKED THIS WAY COMES
Director: Jack Clayton
Co-stars: Jason Robards Jonathan Pryce

1984   PURPLE HEARTS
Director: Sidney Furie
Co-stars: Ken Wahl Stephen Lee Lane Smith David Harris

1984   I MARRIED A CENTREFOLD
Director: Peter Werner
Co-stars: Teri Copley Timothy Daly Anson Williams

1985   CRIME OF INNOCENCE
Director: Michael Miller
Co-stars: Andy Griffith Ralph Waite Shawnee Smith

1986   BLACK WIDOW
Director: Bob Rafelson
Co-stars: Debra Winger Theresa Russell Sami Frey Dennis Hopper

1988   PLAIN CLOTHES
Director: Martha Coolidge
Co-stars: George Wendt Arliss Howard Robert Stack Suzy Amis

**1989   NATIONAL LAMPOON'S
          CHRISTMAS VACATION**
Director: Jeremiah Checkik
Co-stars: Chevy Chase Randy Quaid

1990   WILD AT HEART
Director: David Lynch
Co-stars: Laura Dern Nicholas Cage Willem Dafoe

1990   THE LOOKALIKE
Director: Gary Nelson
Co-stars: Bo Brinkman C.K. Bibby

1991   RAMBLING ROSE
Director: Martha Coolidge
Co-stars: Laura Dern Robert Duvall Lukas Haas John Heard

1991   A KISS BEFORE DYING
Director: James Dearden
Co-stars: Matt Dillon Sean Young Max Von Sydow

1993   THE CEMETARY CLUB
Director: Bill Duke
Co-stars: Ellyn Burstyn Olympia Dukakis Danny Aiello

1993   CARNOSAUR
Director: Adam Simon
Co-stars: Raphael Sbarge Jennifer Runyan

1993   FATHER HOOD
Director: Darrell Roodt
Co-stars: Patrick Swayze Halle Berry

1993   HUSH LITTLE BABY
Director: Jorge Montesi
Co-stars: Wendel Meldrum Geraint Wyn Davies Ingrid Veniger

1996   COLD LAZURUS
Director: Renny Rye
Co-stars: Albert Finney Frances De La Tour Saffron Burrows

NICOLE LADMIRAL

1950   DIARY OF A COUNTRY PRIEST
Director: Robert Bresson
Co-stars: Claude Laydu Jean Riveyre Nicole Maurey

RUBY LAFAYETTE

1923   HOLLYWOOD
Director: James Cruze
Co-stars: Hope Drown Luke Cosgrave Eleanor Lawson

PATRICIA LAFFAN

1947   DEATH IN HIGH HEELS
Director: Lionel Tomlinson
Co-stars: Don Stannard Bill Hodge Veronica Rose

1951   QUO VADIS
Director: Mervyn LeRoy
Co-stars: Robert Taylor Deborah Kerr Peter Ustinov

1952   ROUGH SHOOT
Director: Robert Parrish
Co-stars: Joel McCrea Evelyn Keyes Herbert Loy

1954   DEVIL GIRLS FROM MARS
Director: David MacDonald
Co-stars: Hugh McDermott Adrienne Corri Hazel Court

1956   23 PACES TO BAKER STREET
Director: Henry Hathaway
Co-stars: Van Johnson Vera Miles Cecil Parker

1959   HIDDEN HOMICIDE
Director: Tony Young
Co-stars: Griffith Jones James Kenney Bruce Seton

1963   CROOKS IN CLOISTERS
Director: Jeremy Summers
Co-stars: Ronald Fraser Barbara Windsor Bernard Cribbins

YOLANDE LAFFON

1935   MAYERLING
Director: Anatole Litvak
Co-stars: Charles Boyer Danielle Darrieux Suzy Prim

BERNADETTE LAFONT

1958   LE BEAU SERGE
Director: Claude Chabrol
Co-stars: Gerard Blain Michele Meritz Jean-Claude Brialy

1959   A DOUBLE TOUR
Director: Claude Chabrol
Co-stars: Antonelle Lualdi Madeleine Robinson Jean-Claude Brialy

1960   LES BONNES FEMMES
Director: Claude Chabrol
Co-stars: Stephane Audran Clothilde Joano

1971   CATCH ME A SPY
Director: Dick Clement
Co-stars: Kirk Douglas Trevor Howard Tom Courtenay

1972   UNE BELLE FILLE COMME MOI
Director: Francois Truffaut
Co-stars: Claude Brasseur Charles Denner

1973   FORBIDDEN TO KNOW
Director: Nadine Trintignant
Co-stars: Jean-Louis Trintignant Charles Denner

1977   VIOLETTE NOZIERE
Director: Claude Chabrol
Co-stars: Isabelle Huppert Stephane Audran Jean Carmier

1983   DOG DAY
Director: Yves Boisset
Co-stars: Miou Miou Lee Marvin Tina Louise

1985   AN IMPUDENT GIRL
Director: Claude Miller
Co-stars: Charlotte Gainsbourg Jean-Claude Brialy

1986   INSPECTEUR LAVARDIN
Director: Claude Chabrol
Co-stars: Jean Poiret Jean-Claude Brialy Jean-Luc Bideau

1987   MASQUES
Director: Claude Chabrol
Co-stars: Philippe Noiret Robin Renucci Monique Chaumette

COLETTE LAFONT

1983   THE GOLD DIGGERS
Director: Sally Potter
Co-stars: Julie Christie Hilary Westlake David Gale

PAULINE LAFONT

1984   POULET AU VINAIGRE
Director: Claude Chabrol
Co-stars: Jean Poiret Stephane Audran Michel Bouquet

MARIE LAFORET

1967   JACK OF DIAMONDS
Director: Don Taylor
Co-stars: George Hamilton Joseph Cotten Carroll Baker

1985 TANGOS, THE EXILE OF GARDEL
Director: Fernando Solanas
Co-stars: Philippe Leotard Marina Vlady

JOCELYN LA GARDE
Nominated For Best Supporting Actress In 1966 For "Hawaii"

1966 HAWAII
Director: George Roy Hill
Co-stars: Max Von Sydow Julie Andrews Richard Harris

CAROLINE LAGERFELT

1986 IRON EAGLE
Director: Sidney Furie
Co-stars: Lou Gossett Jnr. David Suchet Tim Thomerson

VALERIE LAGRANGE

1966 A MAN AND A WOMAN
Director: Claude Lelouch
Co-stars: Anouk Aimee Jean-Louis Trintignant

CHRISTINE LAHTI (*Married Thomas Schlamme*)
Nominated for Best Supporting Actress In 1984 For "Swing Shift"

1978 THE LAST TENANT
Director: Jud Taylor
Co-stars: Tony LoBianco Lee Strasberg Danny Aiello

1979 AND JUSTICE FOR ALL
Director: Norman Jewison
Co-stars: Al Pacino Jack Warden Lee Strasberg

1981 WHOSE LIFE IS IT ANYWAY?
Director: John Badham
Co-stars: Richard Dreyfuss John Cassavetes Bob Balaban

1982 THE EXECUTIONER'S SONG
Director: Lawrence Schiller
Co-stars: Tommy Lee Jones Rosanna Arquette

1984 SINGLE BARS, SINGLE WOMEN
Director: Harry Winer
Co-stars: Tony Danza Paul Michael Glaser Shelley Hack

1984 SWING SHIFT
Director: Jonathan Demme
Co-stars: Goldie Hawn Kurt Russell Fred Ward Ed Harris

1986 JUST BETWEEN FRIENDS
Director: Allan Burns
Co-stars: Mary Tyler Moore Ted Danson Sam Waterston

1987 SEASON OF DREAMS
Director: Martin Rosen
Co-stars: Frederick Forrest Megan Follows Peter Coyote Roy Baker

1987 HOUSEKEEPING
Director: Bill Forsyth
Co-stars: Sara Walker Andrea Burchill Anne Pitoniak

1987 AMERIKA
Director: Donald Wrye
Co-stars: Kris Kristofferson San Neill Mariel Hemingway

1988 RUNNING ON EMPTY
Director: Sidney Lumet
Co-stars: River Phoenix Judd Hirsch Martha Plimpton

1989 GROSS ANATOMY
Director: Thom Eberhardt
Co-stars: Matthew Modine Daphne Zuniga Todd Field

1989 LEAVING NORMAL
Director: Edward Zwick
Co-stars: Meg Tilly Lenny Von Dohlen Maury Chaykin

1989 NO PLACE LIKE HOME
Director: Lee Grant
Co-stars: Jeff Daniels Scott Marlowe Kathy Bates Lantz Landrey

1990 FUNNY ABOUT LOVE
Director: Leonard Nimoy
Co-stars: Gene Wilder Mary Stuart Masterson Susan Ruttan

1992 THE DOCTOR
Director: Randa Haines
Co-stars: William Hurt Elizabeth Perkins Mandy Patinkin

CLEO LAINE

1961 THE THIRD ALIBI
Director: Montgomery Tully
Co-stars: Laurence Payne Patricia Dainton Jane Griffiths

JENNY LAIRD

1945 PAINTED BOATS
Director: Charles Crichton
Co-stars: Bill Blewitt Robert Griffith May Hallatt

1946 BLACK NARCISSUS
Director: Michael Powell
Co-stars: Deborah Kerr David Farrar Jean Simmons

1950 YOUR WITNESS
Director: Robert Montgomery
Co-stars: Robert Montgomery Leslie Banks Felix Aylmer

1960 VILLAGE OF THE DAMNED
Director: Wolf Rilla
Co-stars: George Sanders Barbara Shelley Charlotte Mitchell

1989 INSPECTOR MORSE: SECOND TIME AROUND
Director: Adrian Shergold
Co-stars: John Thaw Kevin Whately

DAWN LAKE

1972 SUNSTRUCK
Director: James Gilbert
Co-stars: Harry Secombe Maggie Fitzgibbon John Mellon

FLORENCE LAKE

1930 THE ROGUE SONG
Director: Lionel Barrymore
Co-stars: Laurence Tibbett Stan Laurel Oliver Hardy

1930 ROMANCE
Director: Clarence Brown
Co-stars: Greta Garbo Lewis Stone Elliott Nugent

1937 QUALITY STREET
Director: George Stevens
Co-stars: Katherine Hepburn Franchot Tone Fay Bainter

1937 I MET MY LOVE AGAIN
Director: Joshua Logan
Co-stars: Henry Fonda Joan Bennett May Whitty

RICKI LAKE

1988 HAIRSPRAY
Director: John Waters
Co-stars: Debbie Harry Pia Zadora Sonny Bono Divine

1989 COOKIE
Director: Susan Seidelman
Co-stars: Peter Falk Dianne Wiest Emily Lloyd

1989 BABYCAKES
Director: Paul Schneider
Co-stars: Craig Scheffer Paul Benedict Betty Buckley

1990 CRY-BABY
Director: John Waters
Co-stars: Johnny Depp Amy Locane Susan Tyrell

1994 SERIAL MOM
Director: John Waters
Co-stars: Kathleen Turner Sam Waterston Matthew Lillard

VERONICA LAKE

1940   FORTY LITTLE MOTHERS
Director: Busby Berkeley
Co-stars: Eddie Cantor Judith Anderson Rita Johnson

1941   I WANTED WINGS
Director: Mitchell Leisen
Co-stars: Ray Milland William Holden Wayne Morris

1941   SULLIVAN'S TRAVEL
Director: Preston Sturges
Co-stars: Joel McCrea William Demarest Eric Blore

1942   THIS GUN FOR HIRE
Director: Frank Tuttle
Co-stars: Alan Ladd Robert Preston Laird Cregar

1942   THE GLASS KEY
Director: Stuart Heisler
Co-stars: Alan Ladd William Bendix Brian Donlevy

1942   STAR SPANGLED RHYTHM
Director: George Marshall
Co-stars: Victor Moore Betty Hutton Eddie Bracken

1942   I MARRIED A WITCH
Director: Rene Clair
Co-stars: Fredric March Cecil Kellaway Susan Hayward

1943   SO PROUDLY WE HAIL
Director: Mark Sandrich
Co-stars: Claudette Colbert Paulette Goddard

1944   THE HOUR BEFORE THE DAWN
Director: Frank Tuttle
Co-stars: Franchot Tone John Sutton Binnie Barnes

1945   OUT OF THIS WORLD
Director: Hal Walker
Co-stars: Eddie Bracken Diana Lynn Cass Daley

1945   HOLD THAT BLONDE
Director: George Marshall
Co-stars: Eddie Bracken Albert Dekker George Zucco

1945   DUFFY'S TAVERN
Director: Hal Walker
Co-stars: Ed Gardner Victor Moore Betty Hutton

1945   BRING ON THE GIRLS
Director: Sidney Lanfield
Co-stars: Eddie Bracken Sonny Tufts

1946   MISS SUSIE SLAGLE'S
Director: John Berry
Co-stars: Lillian Gish Joan Caulfield Sonny Tufts

1946   THE BLUE DAHLIA
Director: George Marshall
Co-stars: Alan Ladd William Bendix Howard Da Silva

1947   RAMROD
Director: Andre De Toth
Co-stars: Joel McCrea Preston Foster Charles Ruggles

1947   VARIETY GIRL
Director: George Marshall
Co-stars: Mary Hatcher Olga San Juan Glenn Tryon

1948   SAIGON
Director: Leslie Fenton
Co-stars: Alan Ladd Douglas Dick Luther Adler

1948   THE SAINTED SISTERS
Director: William Russell
Co-stars: Joan Caulfield Barry Fitzgerald

1948   ISN'T IT ROMANTIC
Director: Norman Z. McLeod
Co-stars: Patric Knowles Mona Freeman Billy De Wolfe

1949   SLATTERY'S HURRICANE
Director: Andre De Toth
Co-stars: Richard Widmark Linda Darnell Gary Merrill

VALERIE LALANDE

1988   LA VIE EST UN LONG FLEUVE TRANQUILLE
Director: Etienne Chatille
Co-stars: Benott Magimel Tara Romer

TERI LALLY

1985   RESTLESS NATIVES
Director: Michael Hoffman
Co-stars: Vincent Friell Joe Mullaney Ned Beatty

LYDIA LAMAISON

1958   THE FALL
Director: Leopoldo Torre-Nilsson
Co-stars: Elsa Daniel Duilio Marzia Carlos Lopez Monet

BARBARA LA MARR

1921   THE NUT
Director: Ted Reed
Co-stars: Douglas Fairbanks Marguerite De La Mott Gerald Pring

1922   THE PRISONER OF ZENDA
Director: Rex Ingram
Co-stars: Lewis Stone Alice Terry Stuart Holmes

HEDY LAMARR (HEDY KIESLER)

1933   ECSTASE (CZECHOSLOVAKIA)
Director: Gustav Machaty
Co-stars: Andre Nox Pierre Nay Rogoz

1938   ALGIERS
Director: John Cromwell
Co-stars: Charles Boyer Sigrid Gurie Joseph Calleia

1939   I TAKE THIS WOMAN
Director: W. S. Van Dyke
Co-stars: Spencer Tracy Clark Gable Claudette Colbert

1939   LADY OF THE TROPICS
Director: Jack Conway
Co-stars: Robert Taylor Joseph Schildkraut

1940   BOOM TOWN
Director: Jack Conway
Co-stars: Spencer Tracy Clark Gable Claudette Colbert

1940   COMRADE X
Director: King Vidor
Co-stars: Clark Gable Oscar Homolka Felix Bressart

1941   COME LIVE WITH ME
Director: Clarence Brown
Co-stars: James Stewart Ian Hunter Verree Teasdale

1941   H. M. PULHAM ESQUIRE
Director: King Vidor
Co-stars: Robert Young Ruth Hussey Van Heflin

1941   ZIEGFELD GIRL
Director: Robert Z. Leonard
Co-stars: James Stewart Judy Garland Lana Turner

1942   WHITE CARGO
Director: Richard Thorpe
Co-stars: Walter Pidgeon Richard Carlson Frank Morgan

1942   TORTILLA FLAT
Director: Victor Fleming
Co-stars: Spencer Tracy John Garfield Frank Morgan

1942   CROSSROADS
Director: Jack Conway
Co-stars: William Powell Basil Rathbone Claire Trevor

1943 THE HEAVENLY BODY
Director: Alexander Hall
Co-stars: William Powell James Craig Fay Bainter

1944 THE CONSPIRATORS
Director: Jean Negulesco
Co-stars: Paul Henreid Sydney Greenstreet Peter Lorre

1944 EXPERIMENT PERILOUS
Director: Jacques Tourneur
Co-stars: Paul Lukas George Brent Albert Dekker

1945 HER HIGHNESS AND THE BELLBOY
Director: Richard Thorpe
Co-stars: Robert Walker June Allyson Rags Ragland

1946 THE STRANGE WOMAN
Director: Edgar Ulmer
Co-stars: Louis Hayward George Sanders Gene Lockhart

1947 DISHONOURED LADY
Director: Robert Stevenson
Co-stars: John Loder Dennis O'Keefe William Lundigan

1948 LET'S LIVE A LITTLE
Director: Richard Wallace
Co-stars: Robert Cummings Anna Sten Robert Shayne

1949 SAMSON AND DELILAH
Director: Ceille B. DeMille
Co-stars: Victor Mature George Sanders

1950 A LADY WITHOUT A PASSPORT
Director: Joseph Lewis
Co-stars: John Hodiak James Craig George Macready

1950 COPPER CANYON
Director: John Farrow
Co-stars: Ray Milland MacDonald Carey Mona Freeman

1951 MY FAVOURITE SPY
Director: Norman Z. McLeod
Co-stars: Bob Hope Francis L. Sullivan Mike Mazurki

1957 THE STORY OF MANKIND
Director: Irwin Allen
Co-stars: Ronald Colman Marx Bros. Virginia Mayo

1957 THE FEMALE ANIMAL
Director: Harry Keller
Co-stars: Jan Sterling Jane Powell George Nader

ANNE LOUISE LAMBERT

1975 PICNIC AT HANGING ROCK
Director: Peter Weir
Co-stars: Rachel Roberts Dominic Guard Helen Morse

1983 THE DRAUGHTMAN'S CONTRACT
Director: Peter Greenway
Co-stars: Anthony Higgins Janet Suzman Dave Hill

1990 HEROES II - THE RETURN
Director: Donald Crombie
Co-stars: John Bach Nathaniel Parker Craig McLachlan

JANET LAMBERT

1944 UP IN MABEL'S ROOM
Director: Allan Dwan
Co-stars: Dennis O'Keefe Mischa Auer Marjorie Reynolds

ELLE LAMBETTI

1955 THE GIRL IN BLACK
Director: Michael Cacoyannis
Co-stars: George Foundas Dimitri Horna

1957 A MATTER OF DIGNITY
Director: Michael Cacoyannis
Co-stars: Georges Pappas Athena Michaelidou

PENNY LAMBIRTH

1963 LIVE IT UP
Director: Lance Comfort
Co-stars: David Hemmings Joan Newell Jennifer Moss

ANNE LAMBTON

1988 AN AFFAIR IN MIND
Director: Colin Luke
Co-stars: Stephen Dillon Amanda Donohoe Richard Hammatt

1993 UNNATURAL CAUSES
Director: John Davies
Co-stars: Roy Marsden Mel Martin Simon Chandler

KAREN LAMM

1976 TRACKDOWN
Director: Richard Heffron
Co-stars: Jim Mitchum Anne Archer Cathy Lee Crosby

MOLLY LAMONT

1934 MURDER AT MONTE CRISTO
Director: Ralph Nice
Co-stars: Errol Flynn Eve Gray Ellis Irving

1935 ANOTHER FACE
Director: Christy Cabanne
Co-stars: Brian Donlevy Wallace Ford Phyllis Brooks

1936 THE JUNGLE PRINCESS
Director: William Thiele
Co-stars: Dorothy Lamour Ray Milland Akim Tamiroff

1937 A DOCTOR'S DIARY
Director: Charles Vidor
Co-stars: George Bancroft John Trent Helen Burgess

1937 THE AWFUL TRUTH
Director: Leo McCarey
Co-stars: Irene Dunne Cary Grant Ralph Bellamy

1944 THE SUSPECT
Director: Robert Siodmak
Co-stars: Charles Laughton Rosalind Ivan Ella Raines

1946 DEVIL BAT'S DAUGHTER
Director: Frank Wisbar
Co-stars: Rosemary Le Planche John James Michael Hale

1946 SO GOES MY LOVE
Director: Frank Ryan
Co-stars: Myrna Loy Don Ameche Bobby Driscoll

MICHELLE LAMOTHE

1993 STRIKE A POSE
Director: Dean Hamilton
Co-star: Robert Eastwick

DOROTHY LAMOUR
(Mary Leta Dorothy Kaumeyer)
(Married Herbie Kay, William Ross Howard)

1936 THE JUNGLE PRINCESS
Director: William Thiele
Co-stars: Ray Milland Akim Tamiroff

1937 HIGH, WIDE AND HANSOME
Director: Rouben Mamoulian
Co-stars: Irene Dunne Randolph Scott

1937 THE HURRICANE
Director: John Ford
Co-stars: Jon Hall Raymond Massey Mary Astor

1937 THE LAST TRAIN FROM MADRID
Director: James Hogan
Co-stars: Lew Ayres Gilbert Roland Olympe Bradna

1937	**THRILL OF A LIFETIME**
Director:	George Archinbaud
Co-stars:	Betty Grable Judy Cavona Ben Blue

1938	**HER JUNGLE LOVE**
Director:	George Archinbaud
Co-stars:	Ray Milland Lynne Overman

1937	**SWING HIGH, SWING LOW**
Director:	Mitchell Leisen
Co-stars:	Carole Lombard Fred MacMurray

1938	**THE BIG BROADCAST OF 1938**
Director:	Mitchell Leisen
Co-stars:	Bob Hope Shirley Ross W. C. Fields

1938	**SPAWN OF THE NORTH**
Director:	Henry Hathaway
Co-stars:	George Raft Henry Fonda John Barrymore

1939	**ST. LOUIS BLUES**
Director:	Raoul Walsh
Co-stars:	Lloyd Nolan Jerome Cowan Jessie Ralph

1939	**TROPIC HOLIDAY**
Director:	Theodore Reed
Co-stars:	Ray Milland Martha Raye Bob Burns

1939	**MAN ABOUT TOWN**
Director:	Mark Sandrich
Co-stars:	Jack Benny Edward Arnold Phil Harris

1939	**DISPUTED PASSAGE**
Director:	Frank Borzage
Co-stars:	John Howard Akim Tamiroff Keye Luke

1940	**CHAD HANNAH**
Director:	Henry King
Co-stars:	Henry Fonda Linda Darnell John Carradine

1940	**JOHNNY APOLLO**
Director:	Henry Hathaway
Co-stars:	Tyrone Power Edward Arnold Lloyd Nolan

1940	**MOON OVER BURMA**
Director:	Louis King
Co-stars:	Robert Preston Preston Foster Doris Nolan

1940	**ROAD TO SINGAPORE**
Director:	Victor Schertzinger
Co-stars:	Bing Crosby Bob Hope

1940	**TYPHOON**
Director:	Louis King
Co-stars:	Robert Preston Lynne Overman J. Carrol Naish

1941	**ROAD TO ZANZIBAR**
Director:	Victor Schertzinger
Co-stars:	Bing Crosby Bob Hope Una Merkel

1941	**CAUGHT IN THE DRAFT**
Director:	David Butler
Co-stars:	Bing Crosby Lynne Overman Eddie Bracken

1941	**ALOMA OF THE SOUTH SEAS**
Director:	Alfred Santell
Co-stars:	Jon Hall Lynne Overman Dona Drake

1942	**ROAD TO MORROCO**
Director:	David Butler
Co-stars:	Bing Crosby Bob Hope Dona Drake

1942	**STAR SPANGLED RHYTHM**
Director:	George Marshall
Co-stars:	Victor Moore Betty Hutton Eddie Bracken

1942	**THE FLEET'S IN**
Director:	Victor Schertzinger
Co-stars:	William Holden Betty Hutton Eddie Bracken

1942	**BEYOND THE BLUE HORIZON**
Director:	Alfred Santell
Co-stars:	Richard Denning Jack Haley Walter Abel

1943	**AND THE ANGELS SING**
Director:	George Marshall
Co-stars:	Fred MacMurray Diana Lynn Betty Hutton

1943	**DIXIE**
Director:	Edward Sutherland
Co-stars:	Bing Crosby Billy De Wolfe

1943	**RIDING HIGH**
Director:	George Marshall
Co-stars:	Dick Powell Victor Moore Cass Daley

1944	**RAINBOW ISLAND**
Director:	Ralph Murphy
Co-stars:	Eddie Bracken Gil Lamb Barry Sullivan

1945	**ROAD TO UTOPIA**
Director:	Hal Walker
Co-stars:	Bing Crosby Bob Hope Robert Benchley

1945	**A MEDAL FOR BENNY**
Director:	Irving Pichel
Co-stars:	Arturo De Cordova J. Carrol Naish

1945	**MASQUERADE IN MEXICO**
Director:	Mitchell Leisen
Co-stars:	Arturo De Cordova Ann Dvorak

1945	**DUFFY'S TAVERN**
Director:	Hal Walker
Co-stars:	Ed Gardner Victor Moore Bing Crosby

1947	**MY FAVOURITE BRUNETTE**
Director:	Elliott Nugent
Co-stars:	Bob Hope Peter Lorre Lon Chaney

1947	**ROAD TO RIO**
Director:	Norman Z. McLeod
Co-stars:	Bing Crosby Bob Hope Andrews Sisters

1947	**VARIETY GIRL**
Director:	George Marshall
Co-stars:	Mary Hatcher Olga San Juan Glenn Tryon

1947	**WILD HARVEST**
Director:	Tay Garnett
Co-stars:	Alan Ladd Robert Preston Lloyd Nolan

1948	**LULU BELLE**
Director:	Leslie Fenton
Co-stars:	George Montgomery Greg McClure

1948	**THE GIRL FROM MANHATTAN**
Director:	Alfred Green
Co-stars:	Charles Laughton George Montgomery

1948	**THE LUCKY STIFF**
Director:	Lewis Foster
Co-stars:	Brian Donlevy Claire Trevor Irene Hervey

1948	**ON OUR MERRY WAY**
Director:	King Vidor
Co-stars:	Burgess Meredith James Stewart Henry Fonda

1948	**SLIGHTLY FRENCH**
Director:	Douglas Sirk
Co-stars:	Don Ameche Janis Carter Willard Parker

1949	**MANHANDLED**
Director:	Lewis Foster
Co-stars:	Dan Duryea Sterling Hayden Irene Hervey

1952	**ROAD TO BALI**
Director:	Hal Walker
Co-stars:	Bing Crosby Bob Hope Murvyn Vye Jane Russell

1952	**THE GREATEST SHOW ON EARTH**
Director:	Cecil B. DeMille
Co-stars:	Charlton Heston James Stewart

1962	**THE ROAD TO HONG KONG**
Director:	Norman Panama
Co-stars:	Bing Crosby Bob Hope Joan Collins

1963 DONOVAN'S REEF
Director: John Ford
Co-stars: John Wayne Lee Marvin Elizabeth Allan

1964 PAJAMA PARTY
Director: Don Weiss
Co-stars: Tommy Kirk Annette Funicello Buster Keaton

1976 WON TON TON THE DOG WHO SAVED HOLLYWOOD
Director: Michael Winner
Co-stars: Madeline Kahn Art Carney Bruce Dern

1987 CREEPSHOW 2
Director: Michael Gornick
Co-stars: George Kennedy Lois Chiles

JUTTE LAMPE
1981 THE GERMAN SISTERS
Director: Margarethe Von Trotta
Co-stars: Barbara Sukow Rudiger Vogler

ZOHRA LAMPERT
1960 PAY OR DIE
Director: Richard Wilson
Co-stars: Ernest Borgnine Alan Austin Renata Vanni

1961 POSSE FROM HELL
Director: Herbert Coleman
Co-stars: Audie Murphy John Saxon Vic Morrow

1961 SPLENDOR IN THE GRASS
Director: Elia Kazan
Co-stars: Natalie Wood Warren Beatty Pat Hingle

1969 SOME KIND OF NUT
Director: Garson Kanin
Co-stars: Dick Van Dyke Angie Dickinson Rosemary Forsyth

1971 LET'S SCARE JESSICA TO DEATH
Director: John Hancock
Co-stars: Barton Heyman Kevin O'Connor

1978 OPENING NIGHT
Director: John Cassavetes
Co-stars: John Cassavetes Gena Rowlands Ben Gazzara

1980 THE GIRL, THE GOLD WATCH AND EVERYTHING
Director: William Wiard
Co-stars: Robert Hays Pam Dawber

1984 ALPHABET CITY
Director: Amos Poe
Co-stars: Victor Spano Kate Vernon Michael Winslow

1989 AMERICAN BLUE NOTE
Director: Ralph Toporoff
Co-stars: Peter MacNicol Tim Guinee Trini Alvarado

1989 STANLEY AND IRIS
Director: Martin Ritt
Co-stars: Jane Fonda Robert De Niro Swoosie Kurtz

ANN LANCASTER
1968 HOT MILLIONS
Co-stars: Peter Ustinov Maggie Smith Karl Malden

IRIS LANCASTER
1934 THE TRAIL BEYOND
Director: Robert Bradbury
Co-stars: John Wayne Noah Beery Noah Beery Jnr.

ELSA LANCHESTER *(Married Charles Laughton)*
Nominated For Best Supporting Actress In 1949 For "Come To The Stable" And In 1957 For "Witness For The Prosecution"

1933 THE PRIVATE LIFE OF HENRY VIII
Director: Alexander Korda
Co-stars: Charles Laughton Robert Donat

1934 THE PRIVATE LIFE OF DON JUAN
Director: Alexander Korda
Co-stars: Douglas Fairbanks Merle Oberon

1934 DAVID COPPERFIELD
Director: George Cukor
Co-stars: Freddie Bartholomew W. C. Fields Madge Evans

1935 NAUGHTY MARIETTA
Director: W. S. Van Dyke
Co-stars: Jeannette MacDonald Nelson Eddy Frank Morgan

1935 THE BRIDE OF FRANKENSTEIN
Director: James Whale
Co-stars: Boris Karloff Colin Clive Ernest Thesiger

1936 THE GHOST GOES WEST
Director: Rene Clair
Co-stars: Robert Donat Jean Parker Eugene Pallette

1936 REMBRANDT
Director: Alexander Korda
Co-stars: Charles Laughton Gertrude Lawrence

1938 VESSEL OF WRATH
Director: Erich Pommer
Co-stars: Charles Laughton Robert Newton

1941 LADIES IN RETIREMENT
Director: Charles Vidor
Co-stars: Ida Lupino Louis Hayward Isobel Elsom

1942 SONG OF FURY
Director: John Cromwell
Co-stars: Tyrone Power Gene Tierney George Sanders

1942 TALES OF MANHATTAN
Director: Julien Duvivier
Co-stars: Charles Boyer Henry Fonda Charles Laughton

1943 THUMBS UP
Director: Joseph Santley
Co-stars: Brenda Joyce Richard Fraser

1943 LASSIE COME HOME
Director: Fred Wilcox
Co-stars: Elizabeth Taylor Roddy McDowall Donald Crisp

1943 FOREVER AND A DAY
Director: Rene Clair
Co-stars: Charles Laughton Jessie Mathews Edmund Gwenn

1946 THE RAZOR'S EDGE
Director: Edmund Goulding
Co-stars: Tyrone Power Gene Tierney Anne Baxter

1946 THE SPIRAL STAIRCASE
Director: Robert Siodmak
Co-stars: Dorothy McGuire George Brent Ethel Barrymore

1947 NORTHWEST OUTPOST
Director: Allan Dwan
Co-stars: Nelson Eddy Ilona Massey Hugo Haas

1947 THE BISHOP'S WIFE
Director: Henry Koster
Co-stars: Cary Grant Loretta Young David Niven

1947 THE BIG CLOCK
Director: John Farrow
Co-stars: Charles Laughton Ray Milland Maureen O'Sullivan

1949 BUCANEER'S GIRL
Director: Frererick De Cordova
Co-stars: Yvonne De Carlo Philip Friend

1949 COME TO THE STABLE
Director: Henry Koster
Co-stars: Loretta Young Celeste Holm Hugh Marlowe

1949 THE INSPECTOR GENERAL
Director: Henry Koster
Co-stars: Dany Kaye Walter Slezak Barbara Bates

1949 MADAME BOVARY
Director: Vincente Minnelli
Co-stars: Jennifer Jones Van Heflin Louis Jourdan

1949 THE SECRET GARDEN
Director: Fred Wilcox
Co-stars: Margaret O'Brien Herbert Marshall Dean Stockwell

1950 THE PETTY GIRL
Director: Henry Levin
Co-stars: Joan Caulfield Robert Cummings Audrey Long

1950 MYSTERY STREET
Director: John Sturges
Co-stars: Ricardo Montalban Sally Forrest Jan Sterling

1950 FRENCHIE
Director: Louis King
Co-stars: Shelley Winters Joel McCrea Marie Windsor

1952 LES MISERABLES
Director: Lewis Milestone
Co-stars: Michael Rennie Robert Newton Debra Paget

1952 DREAMBOAT
Director: Claude Binyon
Co-stars: Clifton Webb Ginger Rogers Anne Francis

1952 ANDROCLES AND THE LION
Director: Chester Erskine
Co-stars: Alan Young Jean Simmons Robert Newton

1953 HELL'S HALF ACRE
Director: John Auer
Co-stars: Wendell Corey Evelyn Keyes Nancy Gates

1953 THE GIRLS OF PLEASURE ISLAND
Director: F. Hugh Herbert
Co-stars: Leo Genn Gene Barry Audrey Dalton

1954 THE GLASS SLIPPER
Director: Charles Walters
Co-stars: Leslie Caron Michael Wilding Barry Jones

1954 THREE RING CIRCUS
Director: Joseph Pevney
Co-stars: Dean Martin Jerry Lewis Joanne Dru Zsa Zsa Gabor

1957 WITNESS FOR THE PROSECUTION
Director: Billy Wilder
Co-stars: Charles Laughton Tyrone Power Marlene Dietrich

1958 BELL, BOOK AND CANDLE
Director: Richard Quine
Co-stars: James Stewart Kim Novak Jack Lemmon

1964 HONEYMOON HOTEL
Director: Henry Levin
Co-stars: Nancy Kwan Robert Goulet Robert Morse

1964 PAJAMA PARTY
Director: Don Weis
Co-stars: Tommy Kirk Annette Funicello Buster Keaton

1964 MARY POPPINS
Director: Robert Stevenson
Co-stars: Julie Andrews Dick Van Dyke Glynis Johns

1965 THAT DARN CAT
Director: Robert Stevenson
Co-stars: Hayley Mills Dean Jones Dorothy Provine

1967 EASY COME, EASY GO
Director: John Rich
Co-stars: Elvis Presley Dodie Marshall Frank McHugh

1968 BLACKBEARD'S GHOST
Director: Robert Stevenson
Co-stars: Peter Ustinov Dean Jones Suzanne Pleshette

1969 ME, NATALIE
Director: Fred Coe
Co-stars: Patty Duke James Farentino Al Pacino Salome Jens

1971 WILLARD
Director: Daniel Mann
Co-stars: Bruce Davison Ernest Borgnine Sondra Locke

1973 TERROR IN THE WAX MUSEUM
Director: George Fenady
Co-stars: Ray Milland Broderick Crawford Louis Hayward

1973 ARNOLD
Director: George Fenady
Co-stars: Stella Stevens Roddy McDowall Shani Wallis

1976 MURDER BY DEATH
Director: Robert Moore
Co-stars: Peter Falk Peter Sellers Alec Guinness David Niven

1980 DIE LAUGHING
Director: Jeff Werner
Co-stars: Robby Benson Linda Grovenor Peter Coyote

MICHELINE LANCTOT

1974 THE APPRENTICESHIP OF DUDDY KRAVITZ
Director: Ted Kotcheff
Co-stars: Richard Dreyfuss Denholm Elliott

1978 BLOOD RELATIVES
Director: Claude Chabrol
Co-stars: Donald Sutherland Stephane Audran David Hemmings

AUDREY LANDERS

1985 A CHORUS LINE
Director: Richard Attenborough
Co-stars: Michael Douglas Terence Mann Vicki Frederick

MURIEL LANDERS

1967 DOCTOR DOOLITTLE
Director: Richard Fleischer
Co-stars: Rex Harrison Anthony Newley Samantha Eggar

JANET LANDGARD

1968 THE SWIMMER
Director: Sydney Pollack
Co-stars: Burt Lancaster Janice Rule Kim Hunter

INGA LANDGRE

1954 JOURNEY INTO AUTUMN
Director: Ingmar Bergman
Co-stars: Eva Dahlbeck Harriet Andersson Ulf Palme

1964 LOVING COUPLES
Director: Mai Zetterling
Co-stars: Harriet Andersson Gunnar Bjornstrand Anita Bjork

ELISSA LANDI
(Granddaughter of the Empress of Austria)

1931 BODY AND SOUL
Director: Alfred Santell
Co-stars: Charles Farrell Humphrey Bogart Myrna Loy

1931 ALWAYS GOODBYE
Co-stars: Lewis Stone Paul Cavanagh

1931 WICKED
Director: Allan Dwan
Co-stars: Victor McLaglen Una Merkel Theodore Von Eltz

1931 THE YELLOW TICKET
Director: Raoul Walsh
Co-stars: Laurence Olivier Lionel Barrymore Mischa Auer

1932   **THE WOMAN IN ROOM 13**
Director: Henry King
Co-stars: Ralph Bellamy Neil Hamilton Myrna Loy

1932   **THE SIGN OF THE CROSS**
Director: Cecil B. DeMille
Co-stars: Fredric March Charles Laughton

1932   **PASSPORT TO HELL**
Director: Frank Lloyd
Co-stars: Paul Lukas Warner Oland Donald Crisp

1933   **MAN OF TWO WORLDS**
Director: Walter Ruben
Co-stars: Francis Lederer Henry Stephenson Walter Byron

1933   **THE WARRIOR'S HUSBAND**
Director: Walter Lang
Co-stars: Marjorie Rambeau Ernest Truex David Manners

1933   **I LOVED YOU WEDNESDAY**
Director: Henry King
Co-stars: Warner Baxter Victor Jory Laura Hope Crews

1933   **THE MASQUERADER**
Director: Richard Wallace
Co-stars: Ronald Colman Halliwell Hobbes

1934   **SISTERS UNDER THE SKIN**
Director: David Burton
Co-stars: Frank Morgan Joseph Schildkraut

1934   **THE GREAT FLIRTATION**
Director: Ralph Murphy
Co-stars: Adolphe Menjou David Manners Akim Tamiroff

1934   **ENTER MADAME**
Director: Elliott Nugent
Co-stars: Cary Grant Lynne Overman Paul Porcasi

1934   **THE COUNT OF MONTE CRISTO**
Director: Rowland Lee
Co-stars: Robert Donat Louis Calhern Sidney Blackmer

1934   **BY CANDELIGHT**
Director: James Whale
Co-stars: Paul Lukas Nils Asther Esther Ralston

1935   **KOENIGSMARK**
Director: Maurice Tourneur
Co-stars: Pierre Fresnay John Lodge

1935   **WITHOUT REGRET**
Co-star: Paul Cavanagh

1936   **THE AMATEUR GENTLEMAN**
Director: Thornton Freeland
Co-stars: Douglas Fairbanks Gordon Harker

1936   **AFTER THE THIN MAN**
Director: W.S. Van Dyke
Co-stars: William Powell Myrna Loy James Stewart

1936   **MAD HOLLIDAY**
Director: George Seitz
Co-stars: Edmund Lowe Edmund Gwenn Zasu Pitts

1943   **CORREGIDOR**
Director: William Nigh
Co-stars: Otto Kruger Donald Woods Frank Jenks

MARLA LANDI

1955   **THE HORNET'S NEST**
Director: Charles Saunders
Co-stars: Paul Carpenter June Thorburn Nora Nicholson

1957   **ACROSS THE BRIDGE**
Director: Ken Annakin
Co-stars: Rod Steiger David Knight Bernard Lee

1958   **DUBLIN NIGHTMARE**
Director: John Pomeroy
Co-stars: William Sylvester Richard Leech William Sherwood

1958   **FIRST MAN INTO SPACE**
Director: Robert Day
Co-stars: Marshall Thompson Bill Edwards

1959   **THE HOUND OF THE BASKERVILLES**
Director: Terence Fisher
Co-stars: Peter Cushing Andre Morrell Ewen Solon

1961   **PIRATES OF BLOOD RIVER**
Director: John Gilling
Co-stars: Christopher Lee Kerwin Matthews Oliver Reed

CAROLE LANDIS

1940   **MYSTERY SEA RAIDER**
Director: Edward Dmytryk
Co-stars: Henry Wilcoxon Onslow Stevens

1940   **TURNABOUT**
Director: Hal Roach
Co-stars: Adolphe Menjou John Hubbard Mary Astor

1940   **MAN AND HIS MATE**
Director: Hal Roach
Co-stars: Victor Mature John Hubbard Lon Chaney

1941   **TOPPER RETURNS**
Director: Roy Del Ruth
Co-stars: Roland Young Joan Blondell Eddie Anderson

1941   **ROAD SHOW**
Director: Gordon Douglas
Co-stars: John Hubbard Adolphe Menjou Patsy Kelly

1941   **I WAKE UP SCREAMING**
Director: Bruce Humberstone
Co-stars: Betty Grable Victor Mature Laird Cregar

1941   **MOON OVER MIAMI**
Director: Walter Lang
Co-stars: Betty Grable Don Ameche Robert Cummings Jack Haley

1941   **DANCE HALL**
Director: Irving Pichel
Co-stars: Cesar Romero J. Edward Bromberg William Henry

1941   **CADET GIRL**
Co-stars: George Montgomery Shepperd Strudwick

1942   **MANILA CALLING**
Director: Herbert Leeds
Co-stars: Lloyd Nolan Cornel Wilde James Gleason Ralph Byrd

1942   **MY GAL SAL**
Director: Irving Cummings
Co-stars: Rita Hayworth Victor Mature John Sutton Phil Silvers

1942   **THE POWERS GIRL**
Director: Norman Z. McLeod
Co-stars: George Murphy Ann Shirley Dennis Day Alan Mowbray

1942   **ORCHESTRA WIVES**
Director: Archie Mayo
Co-stars: George Montgomery Ann Rutherford Cesar Romero

1943   **WINTERTIME**
Director: John Brahm
Co-stars: Sonja Henie Jack Oakie Cesar Romero

1944   **SECRET COMMAND**
Director: Edward Sutherland
Co-stars: Pat O'Brien Chester Morris Ruth Warrick

1944   **FOUR JILLS IN A JEEP**
Director: William Seiter
Co-stars: Kay Francis Martha Raye Dick Haymes

1945   **HAVING WONDERFUL CRIME**
Director: Eddie Sutherland
Co-stars: George Murphy Pat O'Brien

1946   **IT SHOULDN'T HAPPEN TO A DOG**
Director: Herbert Leeds
Co-stars: Allyn Joslyn Henry Morgan Reed Hadley

1946 A SCANDAL IN PARIS
Director: Douglas Sirk
Co-stars: George Sanders Signe Hasso Akim Tamiroff

1946 BEHIND GREEN LIGHTS
Director: Otto Brower
Co-stars: William Gargan Mary Anderson Richard Crane

1947 OUT OF THE BLUE
Director: Leigh Jason
Co-stars: George Brent Ann Dvorak Turhan Bey Virginia Mayo

1948 NOOSE
Director: Edmond Greville
Co-stars: Nigel Patrick Derek Farr Stanley Holloway

1948 THE BRASS MONKEY
Director: Thornton Freeland
Co-stars: Carroll Levis Herbert Lom Avril Angers

JESSIE ROYCE LANDIS

1930 DERELICT
Director: Rowland Lee
Co-stars: George Bancroft William Boyd Donald Stuart

1949 MR. BELVEDERE GOES TO COLLEGE
Director: Elliott Nugent
Co-stars: Clifton Webb Shirley Temple Alan Young

1950 MOTHER DIDN'T TELL ME
Director: Claude Binyon
Co-stars: Dorothy McGuire William Lundigan June Havoc

1955 TO CATCH A THIEF
Director: Alfred Hitchcock
Co-stars: Cary Grant Grace Kelly John Williams

1956 THE SWAN
Director: Charles Vidor
Co-stars: Alec Guinness Grace Kelly Louis Jourdan Agnes Moorehead

1956 THE GIRL HE LEFT BEHIND
Director: David Butler
Co-stars: Tab Hunter Natalie Wood Jim Backus

1956 I MARRIED A WOMAN
Director: Hal Kanter
Co-stars: George Gobel Diana Dors Adolphe Menjou Nita Talbot

1957 MY MAN GODFREY
Director: Henry Koster
Co-stars: David Niven June Allyson Jay Robinson Martha Hyer

1959 NORTH BY NORTHWEST
Director: Alfred Hitchcock
Co-stars: Cary Grant Eva Marie Saint James Mason

1959 A PRIVATE'S AFFAIR
Director: Raoul Walsh
Co-stars: Sal Mineo Christine Carere Barry Coe Barbara Eden

1961 GOODBYE AGAIN
Director: Anatole Litvak
Co-stars: Ingrid Bergman Anthony Perkins Yves Montand

1962 BON VOYAGE!
Director: James Neilson
Co-stars: Fred MacMurray Jane Wyman Tommy Kirk

1962 BOY'S NIGHT OUT
Director: Martin Ransohoff
Co-stars: James Garner Kim Novak Tony Randall Oscar Homolka

1963 CRITIC'S CHOICE
Director: Don Weis
Co-stars: Bob Hope Lucille Ball Marilyn Maxwell Rip Torn

NINA LANDIS

1988 RIKKI AND PETE
Director: Nadia Tass
Co-stars: Stephen Kearney Bill Hunter Bruce Spence

LAUREEN LANDON

1981 THE CALIFORNIA DOLLS
Director: Robert Aldrich
Co-stars: Peter Falk Vicki Frederick Burt Young

1982 I, THE JURY
Director: Richard Heffron
Co-stars: Armand Assante Barbara Carrera Geoffrey Lewis

1985 AMERICA 3000
Director: David Engelbach
Co-star: Chuck Wagner

1987 IT'S ALIVE III: ISLAND OF THE ALIVE
Director: Larry Cohen
Co-stars: Michael Moriarty Karen Black

AVICE LANDONE

1950 GUILT IS MY SHADOW
Director: Roy Kellino
Co-stars: Patrick Holt Elizabeth Sellars Lana Morris

1951 AN AMERICAN IN PARIS
Director: Vincent Minnelli
Co-stars: Gene Kelly Leslie Caron George Guetary

1953 ESCAPE BY NIGHT
Director: John Gilling
Co-stars: Bonar Colleano Andrew Ray Ted Ray

1954 THE EMBEZZLER
Director: John Gilling
Co-stars: Charles Victor Zena Marshall Peggy Mount

1955 AN ALLIGATOR NAMED DAISY
Director: J. Lee Thompson
Co-stars: Donald Sinden Diana Dors Jean Carson

1957 TRUE AS A TURTLE
Director: Wendy Toye
Co-stars: John Gregson June Thorburn Cecil Parker

1960 FIVE GOLDEN HOURS
Director: Mario Zampi
Co-stars: Enrie Kovacs Cyd Charisse George Sanders

1962 GAOLBREAK
Director: Francis Searle
Co-stars: Peter Reynolds Carol White David Kernan

1963 THE LEATHER BOYS
Director: Sidney Furie
Co-stars: Rita Tushingham Colin Campbell Dudley Sutton

1963 THIS IS MY STREET
Director: Sidney Hayers
Co-stars: June Ritchie Ian Hendry Madge Ryan

1970 BLOOD ON SATAN'S CLAW
Director: Piers Haggard
Co-stars: Patrick Wymark Linda Hayden Tamara Ustinov

1972 THE ADVENTURES OF BARRY MACKENZIE
Director: Bruce Beresford
Co-stars: Barry Crocker Peter Cook

JENNIFER LANDOR

1987 INAPPROPRIATE BEHAVIOUR
Director: Andrew Davies
Co-stars: Charlotte Coleman Rosemary Martin

ROSALYN LANDOR

1972 THE AMAZING MR. BLUNDEN
Director: Lionel Jeffries
Co-stars: Laurence Naismith Lynne Frederick Diana Dors

1984 THE ADVENTURES OF SHERLOCK HOLMES: THE SPECKLED BAND
Director: John Bruce
Co-star: Jeremy Brett David Burke Jeremy Kemp

AUDE LANDRY

1978 BLOOD RELATIVES
Director: Claude Chabrol
Co-stars: Donald Sutherland Stephane Audran David Hemmings

KAREN LANDRY

1982 THE PERSONALS
Director: Peter Markle
Co-stars: Bill Schoppert Paul Elding Vicki Dakil

1987 PATTI ROCKS
Director: David Burton Morris
Co-stars: Chris Mulkey John Jenkins Stephen Loakam

MARGARET LANDRY

1943 GILDERSLEEVE ON BROADWAY
Co-stars: Richard Le Grand Michael Road

VALERIE LANDSBURG

1978 THANK GOD IT'S FRIDAY
Director: Robert Klane
Co-stars: Terri Nunn Jeff Goldblum Debra Winger

1988 THE RYAN WHITE STORY
Director: John Herzfeld
Co-stars: Lukas Haas Judith Light George C. Scott

ABBE LANE *(Married Xavier Cugat)*

1953 WINGS OF THE HAWK
Director: Budd Boetticher
Co-stars: Van Heflin Julie Adams George Dolenz

1954 RIDE CLEAR OF DIABLO
Director: Jesse Hibs
Co-stars: Audie Murphy Dan Duryea Susan Cabot

1955 CHICAGO SYNDICATE
Director: Fred Sears
Co-stars: Dennis O'Keefe Paul Stewart Alison Haynes

1955 THE AMERICANO
Director: William Castle
Co-stars: Glenn Ford Frank Lovejoy Cesar Romero

1958 MARACAIBO
Director: Cornel Wilde
Co-stars: Cornel Wilde Jean Wallace Francis Lederer

DIANE LANE *(Married Christopher Lambert)*

1979 A LITTLE ROMANCE
Director: George Roy Hill
Co-stars: Laurence Olivier Arthur Hill Sally Kellerman

1980 TOUCHED BY LOVE
Director: Gus Trikonis
Co-stars: Deborah Raffin Michael Learned Cristina Rains

1981 NATIONAL LAMPOON'S MOVIE MADNESS
Director: Henry Jaglom
Co-stars: Robby Benson Richard Widmark

1981 CATTLE ANNIE AND LITTLE BRITCHES
Director: Lamont Johnson
Co-stars: Burt Lancaster Rod Steiger

1982 MISS ALL-AMERICAN BEAUTY
Director: Gus Trikonis
Co-stars: Cloris Leachman Jayne Meadows David Dukes

1982 SIX PACK
Director: Daniel Petrie
Co-stars: Kenny Rogers Erin Gray Barry Corbin

1983 RUMBLE FISH
Director: Francis Coppola
Co-stars: Matt Dillon Mickey Rourke Dennis Hopper

1983 THE OUTSIDERS
Director: Francis Coppola
Co-stars: Matt Dillon Rob Lowe Tom Cruise Patrick Swayze

1984 THE COTTON CLUB
Director: Francis Coppola
Co-stars: Richard Gere Nicolas Cage Gregory Hines

1985 STREETS OF FIRE
Director: Walter Hill
Co-stars: Michael Pare Rick Moranis Willem Dafoe Amy Madigan

1987 THE BIG TOWN
Director: Ben Bolt
Co-stars: Matt Dillon Bruce Dern Lee Grant

1988 LONESOME DOVE
Director: Simon Wincer
Co-stars: Robert Duvall Tommy Lee Jones Danny Glover

1990 VITAL SIGNS
Director: Marise Silver
Co-stars: Adrian Pasdar Jimmy Smits Laura San Giacomo

1990 DESCENDING ANGEL
Director: Jeremy Paul Kagan
Co-stars: Eric Roberts George C. Scott Elsa Raven

1992 KNIGHT MOVES
Director: Carl Schenkel
Co-stars: Christopher Lambert Tom Skerritt Daniel Baldwin

1992 MY NEW GUN
Director: Stacy Cochran
Co-stars: Stephen Collins Tess Harper James LeGros Bill Raymond

1993 CHAPLIN
Director: Richard Attenborough
Co-stars: Robert Downey Kevin Kline Anthony Hopkins

1993 INDIAN SUMMER
Director: Mike Binden
Co-stars: Alan Arkin Elizabeth Perkins Vincent Spano

1997 MURDER AT 1600
Co-star: Wesley Snipes

JACKIE LANE (Sister MARA LANE)

1957 THESE DANGEROUS YEARS
Director: Herbert Wilcox
Co-stars: Frankie Vaughn George Baker Carole Lesley

1961 GOODBYE AGAIN
Director: Antole Litvak
Co-stars: Ingrid Bergman Anthony Perkins Yves Montand

JOCELYN LANE

1965 TICKLE ME
Director: Norman Taurog
Co-stars: Elvis Presley Julia Adams Merry Anders

1966 INCIDENT AT PHANTOM HILL
Director: Earl Bellamy
Co-stars: Robert Fuller Dan Duryea Claude Akins

LAURA LANE

1987 POSITIVE ID
Director: Andy Anderson
Co-stars: Stephanie Rascoe John Davis Steve Fromholtz

LOLA LANE *(Sister Of Priscilla & Rosemary Lane)*

1929 FOX MOVIETONE FOLLIES OF 1929
Director: David Butler
Co-stars: El Brendel Sue Carol Dixie Lee

1930 THE BIG FIGHT
Co-star: Guinn Williams

1930 GOOD NEWS
Director: Nick Grinde
Co-stars: Bessie Love Gus Shy Penny Singleton Stanley Smith

1930 COSTELLO CASE
Co-star: Tom Moore

1930 LET'S GO PLACES
Director: Frank Stayer
Co-stars: Joseph Wagstaff Sharon Lynn Ilka Chase Dixie Lee

1935 MURDER ON A HONEYMOON
Director: George Archainbaud
Co-stars: James Gleason Edna May Oliver

1936 DEATH FROM A DISTANCE
Director: Frank Strayer
Co-stars: Russell Hopton George Marion

1937 MARKED WOMAN
Director: Lloyd Bacon
Co-stars: Bette Davis Humphrey Bogart Eduardo Ciannelli

1937 THE SHEIK STEPS OUT
Director: Irving Pichel
Co-stars: Ramon Navarro Gene Lockhart Stanley Field

1937 HOLLYWOOD HOTEL
Director: Busby Berkeley
Co-stars: Rosemary Lane Dick Powell Frances Langford

1938 TORCHY BLANE IN PANAMA
Director: William Beaudine
Co-star: Paul Kelly

1938 FOUR DAUGHTERS
Director: Michael Curtiz
Co-stars: Rosemary Lane Priscilla Lane John Garfield Claude Rains

1939 DAUGHTERS COURAGEOUS
Director: Michael Curtiz
Co-stars: Rosemary Lane Gale Page May Robson Jeffrey Lynn

1939 FOUR WIVES
Director: Michael Curtiz
Co-stars: Rosemary Lane Eddie Albert Claude Rains Gale Page

1940 ZANZIBAR
Director: Harold Schuster
Co-stars: James Craig Eduardo Ciannelli Samuel S.Hinds

1941 FOUR MOTHERS
Director: William Keighley
Co-stars: Frank McHugh Dick Foran Priscilla Lane

1943 MISS V FROM MOSCOW
Director: Albert Herman
Co-stars: Noel Madison Howard Banks

1945 STEPPIN' IN SOCIETY
Director: Alexandre Esway
Co-stars: Gladys George Ruth Terry Jack La Rue

1945 WHY GIRLS LEAVE HOME
Co-stars: Pamela Blake Elisha Cook

1945 IDENTITY UNKNOWN
Director: Walter Colmes
Co-stars: Richard Arlen Bobby Driscoll Cheryl Walker

1946 DEADLINE AT DAWN
Director: Harold Clurman
Co-stars: Bill Williams Susan Hayward Paul Lukas

1946 THEY MADE ME A KILLER
Director: William Thomas
Co-stars: Robert Lowery Barbara Britton

MARA LANE (Sister Jackie Lane)

1955 ANGELA
Director: Dennis O'Keefe
Co-stars: Dennis O'Keefe Rossano Brazzi Arnold Foa

NORA LANE

1931 THE CISCO LANE
Director: Irving Cummings
Co-stars: Warner Baxter Edmund Lowe Conchita Montenegro

PRISCILLA LANE
(Sister of Lola and Rosemary Lane)

1937 VARSITY SHOW
Director: William Keighley
Co-stars: Rosemary Lane Dick Powell Walter Catlett

1938 COWBOY FROM BROOKLYN
Director: Lloyd Bacon
Co-stars: Dick Powell Pat O'Brien Dick Foran Ronald Reagan

1938 MEN ARE SUCH FOOLS
Director: Busby Berkeley
Co-stars: Wayne Morris Humphrey Bogart Hugh Herbert

1938 LOVE, HONOR AND BEHAVE
Co-stars: Wayne Morris

1938 FOUR DAUGHTERS
Director: Michael Curtiz
Co-stars: Lola Lane Rosemary Lane John Garfield Claude Rains

1938 BROTHER RAT
Director: William Keighley
Co-stars: Ronald Reagan Wayne Morris Eddie Albert

1939 BROTHER RAT AND A BABY
Director: Ray Enright
Co-stars: Jane Wyman Jane Bryan Wayne Morris Eddie Albert

1939 DAUGHTERS COURAGEOUS
Director: Michael Curtiz
Co-stars: Lola Lane Rosemary Lane Gale Page May Robson

1939 FOUR WIVES
Director: Michael Curtiz
Co-stars: Jeffrey Lynn Eddie Albert Gale Page

1939 YES, MY DARLING DAUGHTER
Director: William Keighley
Co-stars: Jeffrey Lynn Roland Young Fay Bainter

1939 THE ROARING TWENTIES
Director: Raoul Walsh
Co-stars: James Cagney Humphrey Bogart Jeffrey Lynn

1939 DUST BE MY DESTINY
Director: Lewis Seiler
Co-stars: John Garfield Alan Hale Frank McHugh John Litel

1940 THREE CHEERS FOR THE IRISH
Director: Lloyd Bacon
Co-stars: Thomas Mitchell Dennis Morgan Alan Hale

1941 MILLION DOLLAR BABY
Director: Curtis Bernhardt
Co-stars: Jeffrey Lynn Ronald Reagan May Robson

1941 BLUES IN THE NIGHT
Director: Anatole Litvak
Co-stars: Richard Whorf Lloyd Nolan Jack Carson

1941 FOUR MOTHERS
Director: William Keighley
Co-stars: Lola Lane Rosemary Lane Dick Foran Frank McHugh

1942 SABOTEUR
Director: Alfred Hitchcock
Co-stars: Robert Cummings Otto Kruger Alan Baxter

1942 SILVER QUEEN
Director: Lloyd Bacon
Co-stars: George Brent Bruce Cabot Lynne Overman

1943 THE MEANEST MAN IN THE WORLD
Director: Sidney Lanfield
Co-stars: Jack Benny Eddie Anderson Edmund Gwenn

1944 ARSENIC AND OLD LACE
Director: Frank Capra
Co-stars: Cary Grant Raymond Massey Peter Lorre

1946　FUN ON A WEEKEND
Director:　Andrew Stone
Co-stars:　Eddie Bracken Tom Conway Allen Jenkins

ROSEMARY LANE
(Sister of Lola and Rosemary Lane)

1937　HOLLYWOOD HOTEL
Director:　Busby Berkeley
Co-stars:　Lola Lane Dick Powell Hugh Herbert Ted Healy

1937　VARSITY SHOW
Director:　William Keighley
Co-stars:　Priscilla Lane Dick Powell Walter Catlett Ted Healy

1938　GOLD DIGGERS IN PARIS
Director:　Ray Enright
Co-stars:　Rudy Vallee Hugh Herbert Gloria Dickson

1938　FOUR DAUGHTERS
Director:　Michael Curtiz
Co-stars:　Priscilla Lane Lola Lane Gale Page John Garfield

1939　DAUGHTERS COURAGEOUS
Director:　Michael Curtiz
Co-stars:　Claude Rains May Robson John Garfield

1939　FOUR WIVES
Director:　Michael Curtiz
Co-stars:　Jeffrey Lynn Eddie Albert Claude Rains

1939　BLACKWELL'S ISLAND
Director:　William McGann
Co-stars:　John Garfield Stanley Fields Victor Jory

1939　THE OKLOHOMA KID
Director:　Lloyd Bacon
Co-stars:　James Cagney Humphrey Bogart Donald Crisp

1939　THE RETURN OF DR. X
Director:　Vincent Sherman
Co-stars:　Humphrey Bogart Dennis Morgan John Litel

1940　THE BOYS FROM SYRACUSE
Director:　Edward Sutherland
Co-stars:　Allan Jones Joe Penner Martha Raye

1940　AN ANGEL FROM TEXAS
Director:　Ray Enright
Co-stars:　Eddie Albert Wayne Morris Ronald Reagan

1941　FOUR MOTHERS
Director:　William Keighley
Co-stars:　Lola Lane Priscilla Lane Dick Foran Frank McHugh

1943　CHATTERBOX
Director:　Joseph Santley
Co-stars:　Joe E. Brown Judy Canova John Hubbard

1943　ALL BY MYSELF
Co-stars:　Evelyn Ankers Neil Hamilton

STEPHANIE LANE

1988　ARIA
Director:　Nicolas Roeg
Co-stars:　John Hurt Elizabeth Hurley Bridget Fonda

BARBARA LANG (Married Jack Palance)

1957　HOUSE OF NUMBERS
Director:　Russel Rouse
Co-stars:　Jack Palance Edward Platt Harold J. Stone

BELINDA LANG

1990　ARTISTS IN CRIME
Director:　Silvio Narizzano
Co-stars:　Simon Williams Ursula Howells Edward Judd

CHRISTA LANG (Married Sam Fuller)

1972　DEAD PIGEON ON BEETHOVEN STREET
Director:　Sam Fuller
Co-stars:　Glenn Corbett Anton Diffring

DOREEN LANG

1970　THE HOUSE THAT WOULD NOT DIE
Director:　John Llewellyn Moxey
Co-stars:　Barbara Stanwyck Richard Egan

1990　ALMOST AN ANGEL
Director:　John Cornell
Co-stars:　Paul Hogan Elias Koteas Linda Kozlowski

EVELYN LANG

1970　THE OWL AND THE PUSSYCAT
Director:　Herbert Ross
Co-stars:　Barbra Streisand George Segal Robert Klein

JUDITH LANG

1970　COUNT YORGA, VAMPIRE
Director:　Bob Kelljan
Co-stars:　Robert Quarry Roger Perry Michael Murphy

JULIA LANG

1949　DR. MORELLE AND THE CASE OF THE MISSING HEIRESS
Director:　Godfrey Grayson
Co-star:　Valentine Dyall Jean Lodge

JUNE LANG

1934　MUSIC IN THE AIR
Director:　Joe May
Co-stars:　Gloria Swanson John Boles Douglass Montgomery

1935　BONNIE SCOTLAND
Director:　James Horne
Co-stars:　Stan Laurel Oliver Hardy James Finlayson

1936　THE COUNTRY DOCTOR
Director:　Henry King
Co-stars:　Jean Hersholt Dorothy Peterson Slim Summerville

1936　CAPTAIN JANUARY
Director:　David Butler
Co-stars:　Shirley Temple Guy Kibbee Buddy Ebsen

1936　EVERY SATURDAY NIGHT
Director:　Frank Strayer
Co-stars:　Jed Prouty Spring Byington Florence Roberts

1936　EDUCATING FATHER
Director:　Frank Strayer
Co-stars:　Jed Prouty Spring Byington Kenneth Lake

1936　BACK TO NATURE
Director:　Frank Strayer
Co-stars:　Jed Prouty Spring Byington George Ernest

1936　THE ROAD TO GLORY
Director:　Howard Hawks
Co-stars:　Fredric March Warner Baxter Lionel Barrymore

1936　WHITE HUNTER
Director:　Irving Cummings
Co-stars:　Warner Baxter Wilfrid Lawson Gail Patrick

1937　WEE WILLIE WINKIE
Director:　John Ford
Co-stars:　Shirley Temple Victor McLaglen Cesar Romero

1937　NANCY STEELE IS MISSING
Director:　George Marshall
Co-stars:　Victor McLaglen Peter Lorre Jane Darwell

1937	**ALI BABA GOES TO TOWN**
Director:	David Butler
Co-stars:	Eddie Cantor Tony Martin Roland Young

1937	**OFF TO THE RACES**
Director:	Frank Strayer
Co-stars:	Jed Prouty Spring Byington June Carlson

1937	**BORROWING TROUBLE**
Director:	Frank Strayer
Co-stars:	Jed Prouty Spring Byington Billy Mahan

1937	**BIG BUSINESS**
Director:	Frank Strayer
Co-stars:	Jed Prouty Spring Byington Florence Roberts

1937	**HOT WATER**
Director:	Frank Strayer
Co-stars:	Jed Prouty Spring Byington Kenneth Lake

1938	**INTERNATIONAL SETTLEMENT**
Director:	Eugene Forde
Co-stars:	George Sanders Dolores Del Rio Ruth Terry

1938	**ONE WILD NIGHT**
Director:	Eugene Forde
Co-stars:	Dick Baldwin Lyle Talbot William Demarest

1938	**LOVE ON A BUDGET**
Director:	Frank Strayer
Co-stars:	Jed Prouty Spring Byington George Ernest

1938	**TRIP TO PARIS**
Director:	Frank Strayer
Co-stars:	Jed Prouty Spring Byington June Carlson

1938	**SAFETY IN NUMBERS**
Director:	Frank Strayer
Co-stars:	Jed Prouty Spring Byington Billy Mahan

1938	**DOWN ON THE FARM**
Director:	Frank Strayer
Co-stars:	Jed Prouty Spring Byington Florence Roberts

1939	**EVERYBODY'S BABY**
Director:	Frank Strayer
Co-stars:	Jed Prouty Spring Byington George Ernest

1939	**QUICK MILLIONS**
Director:	Frank Strayer
Co-stars:	Jed Prouty Spring Byington June Carlson

1939	**THE JONES FAMILY IN HOLLYWOOD**
Director:	Frank Strayer
Co-stars:	Jed Prouty Billy Mahan George Ernest

1939	**TOO BUSY TO WORK**
Director:	Frank Strayer
Co-stars:	Jed Prouty Spring Byington Florence Roberts

1939	**CAPTAIN FURY**
Director:	Hal Roach
Co-stars:	Brian Aherne Victor McLaglen Paul Lukas

1939	**INSIDE INFORMATION**
Co-stars:	Dick Foran Harry Carey

1940	**ON THEIR OWN**
Director:	Frank Strayer
Co-stars:	Jed Prouty Spring Byington Kenneth Lake

1942	**FOOTLIGHT SERENADE**
Director:	Gregory Ratoff
Co-stars:	Betty Gable John Payne Victor Mature

1942	**CITY OF SILENT MEN**
Director:	William Nigh
Co-stars:	Frank Albertson Jan Whiley Richard Clarke

k.d. lang

1991	**SALMONBERRIES**
Director:	Percy Adlon
Co-stars:	Rosel Zech Chuck Connors Jane Lind

VERONICA LANG

1976	**DON'S PARTY**
Director:	Bruce Beresford
Co-stars:	Ray Barrett Claire Binney Graeme Blundell

LIBBY LANGDON

1994	**FEDERAL HILL**
Director:	Michael Corrente
Co-stars:	Nicholas Turturro Anthony Desando Michael Raynor

SUE ANN LANGDON

1964	**ROUSTABOUT**
Director:	John Rich
Co-stars:	Elvis Presley Barbara Stanwyck Raquel Welch

1965	**THE ROUNDERS**
Director:	Burt Kennedy
Co-stars:	Henry Fonda Glenn Ford Chill Wills

1965	**WHEN THE BOYS MEET THE GIRLS**
Director:	Alvin Ganzer
Co-stars:	Connie Francis Harve Pressnell

1966	**FRANKIE AND JOHNNY**
Director:	Frederick De Cordova
Co-stars:	Elvis Presley Donna Douglas Nancy Kovak

1967	**A GUIDE FOR THE MARRIED MAN**
Director:	Gene Kelly
Co-stars:	Walter Matthau Inger Stevens Jack Benny

1970	**THE CHEYENNE SOCIAL CLUB**
Director:	Gene Kelly
Co-stars:	Henry Fonda James Stewart Shirley Jones

1972	**THE VICTIM**
Director:	Herschel Daugherty
Co-stars:	Elizabeth Montgomery George Maharis Eileen Heckhart

1979	**THE EVICTORS**
Director:	Charles Pierce
Co-stars:	Michael Parks Jessica Harper Vic Morrow

1980	**WITHOUT WARNING**
Director:	Greydon Clark
Co-stars:	Jack Palance Martin Landau Cameron Mitchell

ANN LANGE

1981	**FAMILY REUNION**
Director:	Fielder Cook
Co-stars:	Bette Davis Roy Doltrice John Shea

1991	**SHADOWS AND FOG**
Director:	Woody Allen
Co-stars:	Woody Allen Mia Farrow Jodie Foster Kathy Bates

1992	**LIEBSTRAUM**
Director:	Mike Figgis
Co-stars:	Kevin Anderson Pamela Gidley Kim Novak

CLAUDIE LANGE

1969	**CROSSPLOT**
Director:	Alvin Rakoff
Co-stars:	Roger Moore Martha Hyer Alexis Kanner

HOPE LANGE

Nominated For Best Supporting Actress In 1957 For Peyton Place

1956	**BUS STOP**
Director:	Joshua Logan
Co-stars:	Marilyn Monroe Don Murray Betty Field

1956	**THE TRUE STORY OF JESSE JAMES**
Director:	Nicholas Ray
Co-stars:	Robert Wagner Jeffrey Hunter Alan Hale

1957 PEYTON PLACE
Director: Mark Robson
Co-stars: Lana Turner Lloyd Nolan Russ Tamblyn

1958 IN LOVE AND WAR
Director: Phillip Dunne
Co-stars: Robert Wagner Jeffrey Hunter Bradford Dilman

1958 THE YOUNG LIONS
Director: Edward Dmytryk
Co-stars: Marlon Brando Dean Martin Mai Britt

1959 THE BEST OF EVERYTHING
Director: Jean Negulesco
Co-stars: Joan Crawford Louis Jourdan Brian Aherne

1961 POCKETFUL OF MIRACLES
Director: Frank Capra
Co-stars: Bette Davis Glenn Ford Thomas Mitchell

1961 WILD IN THE COUNTRY
Director: Phillip Dunne
Co-stars: Elvis Presley Tuesday Weld Millie Perkins

1962 LOVE IS A BALL
Director: David Swift
Co-stars: Glenn Ford Charles Boyer Ricardo Montalban

1970 CROWHAVEN FARM
Director: Walter Grauman
Co-stars: Paul Burke John Carradine Lloyd Bochner

1974 DEATH WISH
Director: Michael Winner
Co-stars: Charles Bronson Vincent Gardenia

1985 A NIGHTMARE ON ELM STREET II: FREDDY'S REVENGE
Director: Jack Sholder
Co-star: Robert Englund Mark Patton Kim Myers

1985 PRIVATE SESSIONS
Director: Michael Pressman
Co-Stars Mike Farrell Maureen Stapleton Kelly McGillis

1986 BLUE VELVET
Director: David Lynch
Co-stars: Kyle MacLachlan Laura Dern Dean Stockwell

1990 AUNT JULIA AND THE SCRIPTWRITER
Director: Jon Amiel
Co-stars: Barbara Hershey Keanu Reeves Peter Falk

1993 DEAD BEFORE DAWN
Director: Charles Correll
Co-stars: Cheryl Ladd Jameson Parker Kim Coates

JESSICA LANGE

(Married Paco Grande Partner of Bob Fosse Mikhail Barysnikov Sam Shepard)

Best Supporting Actress In 1982 For "Tootsie" And In 1994 For "Blue Sky". Nominated For Best Actress In 1982 For "Frances", In 1984 For "Country", In 1985 For "Sweet Dreams" And In 1989 For "Music Box"

1976 KING KONG
Director: John Guillermin
Co-stars: Jeff Bridges Charles Grodin

1979 ALL THAT JAZZ
Director: Bob Fosse
Co-stars: Roy Scheider Ann Reinking Ben Vereen

1980 HOW TO BEAT THE HIGH COST OF LIVING
Director: Robert Scheerer
Co-stars: Susan St. James Jane Curtin

1981 THE POSTMAN ALWAYS RINGS TWICE
Director: Bob Rafelson
Co-stars: Jack Nicholson Anjelica Huston

1982 TOOTSIE
Director: Sydney Pollack
Co-stars: Dustin Hoffman Teri Garr Bill Murray

1982 FRANCES
Director: Graeme Clifford
Co-stars: Kim Stanley Sam Shepard Lane Smith

1984 CAT ON A HOT TIN ROOF
Director: Jacky Hofsiss
Co-stars: Tommy Lee Jones Rip Torn Kim Stanley

1984 COUNTRY
Director: Richard Pearce
Co-stars: Sam Shepard Wilford Brimley

1985 SWEET DREAMS
Director: Karel Reisz
Co-stars: Ed Harris Ann Wedgeworth James Staley

1986 CRIMES OF THE HEART
Director: Bruce Beresford
Co-stars: Diane Kenton Sissy Spacek Sam Shepard

1988 FAR NORTH
Director: Sam Shepard
Co-stars: Tess Harper Charles Durning Patricia Arquette

1988 EVERYBODY'S ALL-AMERICAN
Director: Taylor Hackford
Co-stars: Dennis Quaid Timothy Hutton John Goodman

1989 MUSIC BOX
Director: Costa-Gravas
Co-stars: Armin Mueller-Stahl Frederick Forrest

1990 MEN DON'T LEAVE
Director: Paul Brickman
Co-stars: Joan Cusack Kathy Bates Arliss Howard

1991 CAPE FEAR
Director: Martin Scorsese
Co-stars: Robert De Niro Nick Nolte Martin Balsam

1992 NIGHT AND THE CITY
Director: Irwin Winkler
Co-stars: Robert De Niro Alan King Jack Warden

1992 O-PIONEERS!
Director: Glenn Jordan
Co-Stars David Strathairn Anne Heche Heather Graham

1994 BLUE SKY
Director: Tony Richardson
Co-star: Tommy Lee Jones

1995 ROB ROY
Director: Michael Caton-Jones
Co-stars: Liam Neeson Tim Roth Eric Stoltz

1996 COUSIN BETTE
Director: Des McAnver
Co-stars: Bob Hoskins Elizabeth Shue Kelly MacDonald

1996 A THOUSAND ACRES
Director: Jocelyn Moorhouse
Co-stars: Michelle Pfeiffer Jennifer Jason Leigh

A.J. LANGER

1991 THE PEOPLE UNDER THE STAIRS
Director: Wes Craven
Co-stars: Brandon Adams Everett McGill Wendy Robie

1996 ESCAPE FROM L. A.
Director: John Carpenter
Co-stars: Kurt Russell George Corraface Steve Buscemi

HEATHER LANGENKAMP

1984 A NIGHTMARE ON ELM STREET
Director: Wes Craven
Co-stars: Robert Englund John Saxon Ronee Blakley

**1987 A NIGHTMARE ON ELM STREET III:
DREAM WARRIORS**
Director: Chuck Russell
Co-stars: Robert Englund Patricia Arquette

1989 SHOCKER
Director: Wes Craven
Co-stars: Michael Murphy Peter Berg Cami Cooper

1994 WES CRAVEN'S NEW NIGHTMARE

BONNIE LANGFORD

1977 WOMBLING FREE
Director: Lionel Jeffries
Co-stars: Lionel Jeffries David Jason Janet Brown Jon Pertwee

FRANCES LANGFORD

1935 EVERY NIGHT AT EIGHT
Director: Raoul Walsh
Co-stars: George Raft Alice Faye Patsy Kelly

1936 COLLEGIATE
Director: Ralph Murphy
Co-stars: Jack Oakie Joe Penner Betty Grable Ned Sparks

1936 BORN TO DANCE
Director: Roy Del Ruth
Co-stars: James Stewart Eleanor Powell Buddy Ebsen Una Merkel

1936 PALM SPRINGS
Director: Aubrey Scotto
Co-stars: David Niven Sir Guy Standing Spring Byington

1937 THE HIT PARADE
Director: Gus Meins
Co-stars: Phil Regan Pert Kelton Louise Henry Max Terhune

1937 HOLLYWOOD HOTEL
Director: Busby Berkeley
Co-stars: Dick Powell Rosemary Lane Lola Lane Hugh Herbert

1940 TOO MANY GIRLS
Director: George Abbott
Co-stars: Lucille Ball Desi Arnaz Ann Miller Eddie Bracken

1942 YANKEE DOODLE DANDY
Director: Michael Curtiz
Co-stars: James Cagney Joan Leslie Walter Huston

1940 THE HIT PARADE OF 1941
Director: John Auer
Co-stars: Kenny Baker Ann Miller Phil Silvers

1941 SWING IT, SOLDIER
Co-stars: Ken Murray Hanley Stafford

1943 FOLLOW THE BAND
Director: Jean Yarborough
Co-stars: Eddie Quillan Leon Errol Robert Mitchum

1943 COWBOY IN MANHATTAN
Co-stars: Walter Catlett

1943 NEVER A DULL MOMENT
Director: Edward Lilley
Co-stars: Ritz Bros. George Zucco Franklin Pangborn

1943 THIS IS THE ARMY
Director: Michael Curtiz
Co-stars: George Murphy Joan Leslie Irving Berlin

1944 DIXIE JAMBOREE
Co-stars: Lyle Talbot Eddie Quillan

1944 CAREER GIRL
Director: Wallace Fox
Co-stars: Iris Adrian Ariel Heath Edward Norris Craig Woods

1945 RADIO STARS ON PARADE
Director: Leslie Goodwins
Co-stars: Wally Brown Alan Carney Sheldon Leonard

1946 THE BAMBOO BLONDE
Director: Anthony Mann
Co-stars: Russell Wade Ralph Edwards Jane Greer Iris Adrian

1951 PURPLE HEART DIARY
Director: Richard Quine
Co-stars: Ben Lessy Tony Romano Judd Holdren

1954 THE GLENN MILLER STORY
Director: Anthony Mann
Co-stars: James Stewart June Allyson Harry Morgan

LIANE LANGLAND

1985 MURDER WITH MIRRORS
Director: Dick Lowry
Co-stars: Helen Hayes Bette Davis John Mills

1987 THE SQUEEZE
Director: Roger Young
Co-stars: Michael Keaton Rae Dawn Chong John Davidson

AMANDA LANGLET

1996 A SUMMER'S TALE
Director: Eric Rohmer
Co-stars: Melvil Poupaud Aurelia Nolin Gwenaelle Simons

LISA LANGLOIS

1978 BLOOD RELATIVES
Director: Claude Chabrol
Co-stars: Donald Sutherland Stephane Audran Aude Landry

1982 HARD FEELINGS
Director: Daryl Duke
Co-stars: Carl Marotte Chaelaine Woodward Vincent Bufano

1986 DOING LIFE
Director: Gene Reynolds
Co-stars: Tony Danza Jon Devries Alvin Epstein

SYLVIA LANGOVA

1955 LITTLE RED MOINKEY
Director: Ken Hughes
Co-stars: Richard Conte Rona Anderson Russell Napier

MARGARET LANGRICK

1986 MY AMERICAN COUSIN
Director: Sandy Wilson
Co-stars: John Wildman Richard Donat Jane Mortifee

1987 BIG FOOT AND THE HENDERSONS
Director: William Dear
Co-stars: John Lithgow Melinda Dillon Don Ameche

1989 AMERICAN BOYFRIENDS
Director: Sandy Wilson
Co-stars: John Wildman Jason Blicker Delia Brett

1989 COLD COMFORT
Director: Vic Sarin
Co-stars: Maury Chaykin Paul Gross

CAROLINE LANGRISHE

1979 EAGLE'S WING
Director: Anthony Harvey
Co-stars: Martin Sheen Sam Waterston Harvey Keitel

1980 DEATH WISH
Director: Bertrand Tavernier
Co-stars: Romy Schneider Harvey Keitel Harry Dean Stanton

1988 HAWKS
Director: Robert Ellis Miller
Co-stars: Timothy Dalton Anthony Edwards Janet McTeer

1993 AN EXCHANGE OF FIRE
Director: Tony Bicat
Co-stars: Frank Finlay James Fleet Juliette Caton

DIANE LANGTON

1975 CONFESSIONS OF A POP PERFORMER
Director: Norman Cohen
Co-stars: Robin Askwith Anthony Booth

1976 CARRY ON ENGLAND
Director: Gerald Thomas
Co-stars: Kenneth Connor Patrick Mower Judy Geeson

SARA LANGTON

1987 HOPE AND GLORY
Director: John Boorman
Co-stars: Sarah Miles Susan Wooldridge Ian Bannen

MONIQUE LANIER

1995 IT WAS HIM OR US
Director: Robert Iscove
Co-Stars Richard Grieco Ann Jillian

SUSAN LANIER

1978 THE HILLS HAVE EYES
Director: Wes Craven
Co-stars: Robert Houston Dee Wallace Virginia Vincent

KIM LANKFORD

1978 MALIBU BEACH
Director: Robert Rosenthal
Co-stars: James Draughton Stephen Oliver Michael Luther

1989 CAMERON'S CLOSET
Director: Armand Mastroianni
Co-stars: Cotter Smith Mel Harris Tab Hunter

1991 MISSING PIECES
Director: Leonard Stern
Co-stars: Lauren Hutton Eric Idle Robert Wuhl

1994 NIGHT OF THE RUNNING MAN
Director: Maric Lester
Co-stars: Andrew McCarthy Scott Glenn Janet Gunn

ANGELA LANSBURY

**Nominated For Best Supporting Actress In 1944 For "Gaslight",
In 1945 For "The Picture Of Dorian Gray" And In 1962 For
"The Manchurian Candidate"**

1944 GASLIGHT
Director: George Cukor
Co-stars: Charles Boyer Ingrid Bergman Joseph Cotten May Whitty

1944 NATIONAL VELVET
Director: Clarence Brown
Co-stars: Elizabeth Taylor Mickey Rooney Ann Revere Donald Crisp

1944 THE PICTURE OF DORIAN GRAY
Director: Albert Lewin
Co-stars: Hurd Hatfield George Sanders Donna Reed

1946 TILL THE CLOUDS ROLL BY
Director: Richard Whorf
Co-stars: Robert Walker Van Heflin Mary Nash Lena Horne

1946 THE HOODLUM SAINT
Director: Norman Taurog
Co-stars: William Powell Esther Williams James Gleason

1946 THE HARVEY GIRLS
Director: George Sidney
Co-stars: Judy Garland Ray Bolger John Hodiak Chill Wills

1947 THE PRIVATE AFFAIRS OF BEL AMI
Director: Albert Lewin
Co-stars: George Sanders Ann Dvorak Hugo Haas

1948 IF WINTER COMES
Director: Victor Saville
Co-stars: Walter Pidgeon Deborah Kerr Janet Leigh

1948 STATE OF THE UNION
Director: Frank Capra
Co-stars: Spencer Tracy Katharine Hepburn Adolphe Menjou

1948 TENTH AVENUE ANGEL
Director: Roy Rowland
Co-stars: Margaret O'Brien George Murphy Phyllis Thaxter

1948 THE THREE MUSKETEERS
Director: George Sidney
Co-stars: Gene Kelly Lana Turner Gig Young Van Heflin

1949 SAMSON AND DELILAH
Director: Cecil B. DeMille
Co-stars: Hedy Lamarr Victor Mature George Sanders

1950 THE RED DANUBE
Director: George Sidney
Co-stars: Walter Pidgeon Janet Leigh Ethel Barrymore

1951 KIND LADY
Director: John Sturges
Co-stars: Ethel Barrymore Maurice Evans Betsy Blair Keenan Wynn

1952 MUTINY
Director: Edward Dmytryk
Co-stars: Mark Stevens Patric Knowles Gene Evans Rhys Williams

1953 REMAINS TO BE SEEN
Director: Don Weis
Co-stars: June Allyson Van Johnson Louis Calhern John Beal

1955 THE PURPLE MASK
Director: Bruce Humberstone
Co-stars: Tony Curtis Dan O'Herlihy Gene Barry

1955 A LAWLESS STREET
Director: Joseph Lewis
Co-stars: Randolph Scott Warner Anderson Jean Parker

1955 THE COURT JESTER
Director: Melvin Frank
Co-stars: Danny Kaye Glynis Johns Basil Rathbone

1956 PLEASE MURDER ME
Director: Peter Godfrey
Co-stars: Raymond Burr Dick Foran John Dehner Denver Pyle

1958 THE RELUCTANT DEBUTANT
Director: Vincent Minnelli
Co-stars: Rex Harrison Kay Kendall Sandra Dee

1958 THE LONG HOT SUMMER
Director: Martin Ritt
Co-stars: Orson Welles Paul Newman Joanne Woodward

1959 SUMMER OF THE SEVENTEENTH DOLL
Director: Leslie Norman
Co-stars: Ernest Borgnine John Mills Anne Baxter

1960 THE DARK AT THE TOP OF THE STAIRS
Director: Delbert Mann
Co-stars: Robert Preston Dorothy McGuire

1960 A BREATH OF SCANDAL
Director: Michael Curtiz
Co-stars: Sophia Loren John Gavin Maurice Chevalier

1961 BLUE HAWAII
Director: Norman Taurog
Co-stars: Elvis Presley Joan Blackman John Archer

1962 ALL FALL DOWN
Director: John Frankenheimer
Co-stars: Warren Beatty Brandon De Wilde Karl Malden

1962 THE MANCHURAIN CANDIDATE
Director: John Frankenheimer
Co-stars: Laurence Harvey Frank Sinatra Janet Leigh

1962 IN THE COOL OF THE DAY
Director: Robert Stevens
Co-stars: Jane Fonda Peter Finch Arthur Hill

1964   **THE WORLD OF HENRY ORIENT**
Director: George Roy Hill
Co-stars: Peter Sellers Paula Prentiss Phyllis Thaxter

1964   **DEAR HEART**
Director: Delbert Mann
Co-stars: Glenn Ford Geraldine Page Alice Pearce

1965   **HARLOW**
Director: Gordon Douglas
Co-stars: Carroll Baker Martin Balsam Red Buttons

1965   **THE GREATEST STORY EVER TOLD**
Director: George Stevens
Co-stars: Max Von Sydow Dorothy McGuire Ed Wynn

1965   **THE AMOROUS ADVENTURES
OF MOLL FLANDERS**
Director: Terence Young
Co-stars: Kim Novak Richard Johnson George Sanders

1966   **MISTER BUDDWING**
Director: Delbert Mann
Co-stars: James Garner Jean Simmons Suzanne Pleshette

1970   **SOMETHING FOR EVERYONE**
Director: Harold Prince
Co-stars: Michael York Anthony Corlan Heidelind Weis

1971   **BEDKNOBS AND BROOMSTICKS**
Director: Robert Stevenson
Co-stars: David Tomlinson Sam Jaffe Roy Smart

1978   **DEATH ON THE NILE**
Director: John Guillermin
Co-stars: Peter Ustinov Bette Davis Mia Farrow David Niven

1979   **THE LADY VANISHES**
Director: Anthony Page
Co-stars: Elliott Gould Cybill Shepherd Herbert Lom

1980   **THE MIRROR CRACK'D**
Director: Guy Hamilton
Co-stars: Elizabeth Taylor Kim Novak Rock Hudson Tony Curtis

1983   **THE PIRATES OF PENZANCE**
Director: Wilford Leach
Co-stars: Douglas Slocombe Kevin Kline Linda Ronstadt

1984   **THE COMPANY OF WOLVES**
Director: Neil Jordan
Co-stars: David Warner Graham Crowden Brian Glover

1988   **SHOOTDOWN**
Director: Michael Pressman
Co-stars: George Coe Kyle Secor Molly Hagan John Cullum

1992   **BEAUTY AND THE BEAST** *(Voice)*
Director: Kirk Wise
Co-stars: Paige O'Hara Bobby Benson Jerry Orbach

1998   **ANASTASIA** *(Voice)*
Co-Stars   Meg Ryan John Cusack Christopher Lloyd

JOI LANSING

1965   **HOT SHOTS**
Director: Jean Yarborough
Co-stars: Huntz Hall Stanley Clements Jimmy Murphy

LUCIA LANZARINI

1989   **PLAY ME SOMETHING**
Director: Timothy Neat
Co-stars: Charlie Barron John Berger Tilda Swinton

LILY LAPIDUS

1959   **THE MAN WHO LIKED FUNERALS**
Director: David Eady
Co-stars: Leslie Phillips Susan Beaumont Bill Fraser

ALISON LaPLACA

1990   **MADHOUSE**
Director: Tom Ropelewski
Co-stars: Kirstie Alley John Laroquette Jessica Lundy

ROSEMARY LA PLANCHE *(Miss America 1941)*

1943   **AROUND THE WORLD**
Director: Allan Dwan
Co-stars: Kay Kyser Ginny Simms Joan Davis

1946   **DEVIL BAT'S DAUGHTER**
Director: Frank Wisbar
Co-stars: John James Michael Hale Molly Lamont

LAURA LA PLANTE

1927   **THE CAT AND THE CANARY**
Director: Paul Leni
Co-stars: Creighton Hale Tully Marshall Flora Finch

1929   **THE LAST WARNING**
Director: Paul Leni
Co-stars: Montagu Love John Boles Slim Summerville

1929   **SHOW BOAT**
Co-stars: Joseph Schildkraut Otis Harland Emily Fitzroy

1930   **KING OF JAZZ**
Director: J. Murray Anderson
Co-stars: Paul Whiteman John Boles Jeanette Loff

1930   **CAPTAIN OF THE GUARD**
Director: Paul Fejos
Co-stars: John Boles Lionel Belmore Otis Harlan

1931   **GOD'S GIFT TO WOMEN**
Director: Michael Curtiz
Co-stars: Frank Fay Joan Blondell Charles Winninger

1931   **MEET THE WIFE**
Co-stars: Lew Cody Claude Allister Harry Myers

1932   **ALIAS THE DOCTOR**
Director: Michael Curtiz
Co-stars: Richard Bartelmess Norman Foster Marion Marsh

1935   **MAN OF THE MOMENT**
Director: Monty Banks
Co-stars: Douglas Fairbanks Jnr. Margaret Lockwood

1935   **THE CHURCH MOUSE**
Co-stars: John Batten Clifford Heatherley

1956   **SPRING REUNION**
Director: Robert Pirosh
Co-stars: Betty Hutton Dana Andrews Jean Hagen

HELENE LAPLOVER

1992   **MENSONGE**
Director: Francois Margolin
Co-stars: Natalie Baye Didier Sendre

JANE LAPOTAIRE

1969   **CRESCENDO**
Director: Alan Gibson
Co-stars: Stephanie Powers James Olsen Margaretta Scott

1973   **THE ASPHYX**
Director: Peter Newbrook
Co-stars: Robert Stephens Robert Powell Fiona Walker

1982   **EUREKA**
Director: Nicolas Roeg
Co-stars: Gene Hackman Theresa Russell Rutger Hauer

1984   **TO CATCH A KING**
Director: Clive Donner
Co-stars: Robert Wagner Teri Garr Barbara Parkins

1986 LADY JANE
Director: Trevor Nunn
Co-stars: Helena Bonham Cater Cary Elwes Michael Hordern

1988 THE DARK ANGEL
Director: Peter Hammond
Co-stars: Peter O'Toole Beatie Edney Tim Woodward

1989 MURDER ON THE MOON
Director: Michael Lindsay-Hogg
Co-stars: Brigitte Nielson Julian Sands Brian Cox

1990 CIRCLES OF DECEIT
Director: Stuart Burge
Co-stars: Edward Fox Clare Holman Brenda Bruce

LINDA LARKIN

1992 ALADDIN *(Voice)*
Director: Ron Clements
Co-stars: Scott Weinger Robin Williams Jonathan Freeman

MARY LARKIN

1971 ZEE AND CO.
Director: Brian Hutton
Co-stars: Elizabeth Taylor Susannah York Michael Caine

SHEILA LARKIN

1987 DOWNPAYMENT ON MURDER
Director: Waris Hussein
Co-stars: Connie Sellecca Ben Gazzara David Morse

ELIZABETH LARNER

1970 SONG OF NORWAY
Director: Andrew Stone
Co-stars: Toralv Maurstad Harry Secombe Edward G. Robinson

CARMEN LARNY

1935 DESERT TRAIL
Co-stars: John Wayne Paul Fix Henry Hull

MARY LAROCHE

1958 THE LINEUP
Director: Don Siegel
Co-stars: Warner Anderson Robert Keith Eli Wallach

1959 GIDGET
Director: Paul Wendkos
Co-stars: Sandra Dee James Darren Cliff Robertson

ROSE LA ROSE

1946 QUEEN OF BURLESQUE
Co-stars: Evelyn Ankers Carleton Young

CARMEN LAROUX

1932 SON OF OKLAHOMA
Co-star: Bob Steele

1938 STARLIGHT OVER TEXAS
Co-star: Tex Ritter

FRANCINE LARRIMORE

1937 JOHN MEADE'S WOMEN
Director: Richard Wallace
Co-stars: Edward Arnold Gail Patrick George Bancroft

TITO LARRIVA *(Child)*

1992 THE TENDER
Director: Robert Harmon
Co-stars: John Travolta Jeffrey DeMunn

ESTELLE LARRIVAZ

1996 WHEN THE CAT'S AWAY
Director: Cedric Klapisch
Co-stars: Garence Claver Jane Bradbury

ANNABELLE LARSEN

1990 ALLIGATOR EYES
Director: John Feldman
Co-stars: Roger Kabler Mary McLain John MacKay

CHRISTINE LARSON

1951 THE WELL
Director: Russel Rouse
Co-stars: Richard Rober Henry Morgan Barry Kelley

1952 THE LAST TRAIN FROM BOMBAY
Director: Fred Sears
Co-stars: Jon Hall Lisa Ferraday Douglas Kennedy

1952 BRAVE WARRIOR
Director: Spencer Bennet
Co-stars: Jon Hall Michael Ansara Jay Silverheels

CAROLINE LARTIER

1976 LUMIERE
Director: Jeanne Moreau
Co-stars: Jeanne Moreau Francine Racette Lucia Bose Bruno Ganz

GRACE LA RUE

1933 SHE DONE HIM WRONG
Director: Lowell Sherman
Co-stars: Mae West Cary Grant Gilbert Roland

KATHLEEN LASKEY

1993 HOSTAGES FOR A DAY
Director: John Candy
Co-stars: John Candy George Wendt Peter Torokvei

BARBARA LASS

1963 LOVE AT TWENTY
Director: Marcel Ophuls
Co-stars: Jean-Pierre Leaud Marie-France Pisier

LOUISE LASSER

1969 TAKE THE MONEY AND RUN
Director: Woody Allen
Co-stars: Woody Allen Janet Margolin Marcel Hillaire

1971 BANANAS
Director: Woody Allen
Co-stars: Woody Allen Carlos Montalban Sylvester Stallone

1971 SUCH GOOD FRIENDS
Director: Otto Preminger
Co-stars: Dyan Cannon James Coco Jennifer O'Neil Nina Foch

1972 EVERYTHING YOU ALWAYS WANTED TO KNOW ABOUT SEX
Director: Woody Allen
Co-stars: Woody Allen Lynn Redgrave Anthony Quayle

1972 SLITHER
Director: Howard Zieff
Co-stars: James Caan Peter Boyle Sally Kellerman

1973 ISN'T IT SHOCKING
Director: John Badham
Co-stars: Alan Alda Edmond O'Brien Ruth Gordon Lloyd Nolan

1973 COFFEE, TEA OR ME?
Director: Norman Panama
Co-stars: Karen Valentine John Davidson Lou Jacobi

1980 IN GOD WE TRUST
Director: Marty Feldman
Co-stars: Marty Feldman Peter Boyle Richard Pryor

1985 CRIMEWAVE
Director: Sam Raimi
Co-stars: Paul L. Smith Brian James Sheree Wilson Bruce Campbell

1987 SURRENDER
Director: Jerry Belson
Co-stars: Michael Caine Sally Field Steve Guttenburg Peter Boyle

1989 SING
Director: Richard Baskin
Co-stars: Lorraine Bracco Peter Dobson Jessica Steen Patti Labelle

1989 RUDE AWAKENING
Director: Aaron Russo
Co-stars: Cheech Marin Eric Roberts Julie Haggerty

1990 FRANKENHOOKER
Director: Frank Henenlotter
Co-stars: James Lorinz Patty Mullen Shirley Stoller

1990 MODERN LOVE
Director: Robby Benson
Co-stars: Robby Benson Karlo De Vito Burt Reynolds

SARAH LASSEZ

1993 ROOSTERS
Director: Robert Young
Co-stars: Edward James Olmos Sonia Braga Danny Nucci

CLARISSA LASSIG

1993 A HOME OF OUR OWN
Director: Tony Bill
Co-stars: Kathy Bates Edward Furlong

PAM LATESTA

1990 SUFFERING BASTARDS
Director: Bernard McWilliams
Co-stars: John C. McGinley David Warshofsky

LOUISE LATHAM

1964 MARNIE
Director: Alfred Hitchcock
Co-stars: Tippi Hendren Sean Connery Diane Baker

1971 THE FIRST KILLER
Director: Richard Colla
Co-stars: Raymond Burr George Kennedy Don Galloway

1973 WHITE LIGHTNING
Director: Joseph Sargent
Co-stars: Burt Reynolds Jennifer Billingsley Ned Beatty

1973 DYING ROOM ONLY
Director: Phillip Leacock
Co-stars: Cloris Leachman Ross Martin Ned Beatty

1974 SUGARLAND EXPRESS
Director: Steven Spielberg
Co-stars: Goldie Hawn William Atherton Ben Johnson

1981 THIN ICE
Director: Paul Aaron
Co-stars: Kate Jackson Gerald Prendergast Lillian Gish

1984 THE PHILADELPHIA EXPERIMENT
Director: Stewart Raffill
Co-stars: Michael Pare Nancy Allen Bobby Di Cicco

1984 MASS APPEAL
Director: Glenn Jordan
Co-stars: Jack Lemmon Zeljko Ivanek Charles Durning

1987 STILLWATCH
Co-stars: Rod Holcomb
Co-stars: Lynda Carter Angie Dickinson Don Murray

1989 SETTLE THE SCORE
Director: Edwin Sherin
Co-stars: Jaclyn Smith Jeffrey DeMunn Howard Duff

1991 PARADISE
Director: Mary Agnes Donoghue
Co-stars: Melanie Griffith Don Johnson Thora Birch

1991 THE HAUNTED
Director: Robert Mandel
Co-Stars: Jeffrey DeMunn Joyce Van Patten Diane Baker

1992 LOVE FIELD
Director: Jonathan Kaplan
Co-stars: Michelle Pfeiffer Dennis Haysbert Stephanie McFadden

QUEEN LATIFA

1992 HOUSE PARTY 2: THE PAJAMA JAM
Director: Doug McHenry
Co-stars: Christopher Reid Christopher Martin

1993 MY LIFE
Director: Bruce Joel Rubin
Co-stars: Michael Keaton Nicole Kidman Haing S. Ngor

1997 SET IT OFF
Director: F. Gary Gray
Co-stars: Viveca Fox Jada Pinkett Kimberley Elise

LOUISE LATIMER

1934 THERE'S ALWAYS TOMORROW
Director: Edward Sloman
Co-stars: Frank Morgan Binnie Barnes Robert Taylor

1936 THE PLOT THICKENS
Director: Ben Holmes
Co-stars: Zasu Pitts James Gleason Owen Davis Jnr.

1936 BUNKER BEAN
Director: William Hamilton
Co-stars: Owen Davis Jnr. Lucille Ball Jessie Ralph

1937 WE'RE ON THE JURY
Director: Ben Holmes
Co-stars: Helen Broderick Victor Moore Philip Huston

1938 CALIFORNIA STRAIGHT AHEAD
Director: Arthur Lubin
Co-stars: John Wayne Tully Marshall Robert McWade

CHLOE LATTANZI

1994 A CHRISTMAS ROMANCE
Director: Sheldon Larry
Co-stars: Olivia Newton-John Gregory Harrison

ELLEN HAMILTON LATZEN

1987 FATAL ATTRACTION
Director: Adrian Lyne
Co-stars: Michael Douglas Glenn Close Anne Archer

AGNES LAUCHLAN

1937 OH MR. PORTER
Director: Marcel Varnel
Co-stars: Will Hay Moore Marriott Graham Moffat

1942 THE YOUNG MR. PITT
Director: Carol Reed
Co-stars: Robert Donat Robert Morley Phyllis Calvert

AMANDA LAUGHLIN

**1992 IN THE BEST INTEREST
OF THE CHILDREN**
Director: Michael Ray Rhodes
Co-Stars: Sarah Jessica Parker Lexi Randall

TERESA LAUGHLIN

1974 THE TRIAL OF BILLY JACK
Director: Tom Laughlin
Co-stars: Tom Laughln Delores Taylor Victor Izay Russell Lane

1977 BILLY JACK GOES TO WASHINGTON
Director: Tom Laughlin
Co-stars: Tom Laughlin Delores Taylor Sam Wanamaker

CYNDI LAUPER

1991 OFF AND RUNNING
Director: Edward Bianchi
Co-stars: David Keith Johnny Pinto Jose Perez

1993 GIVE ME A BREAK
Director: James Lapine
Co-stars: Michael J. Fox Christina Vidal Nathan Lane

CAROLE LAURE

1977 PREPAREZ VOS MOUCHOIRS
Director: Bertrand Blier
Co-stars: Gerard Depardieu Patrick Dewaere Riton

1974 SWEET MOVIE
Director: Dusan Makevejev
Co-stars: Pierre Clementi Anna Pruchnal Jane Mallet

1976 BLAZING MAGNUM
Director: Martin Herbert
Co-stars: Stuart Whitman John Saxon Tisa Farrow

1981 ESCAPE TO VICTORY
Director: John Huston
Co-stars: Sylvester Stallone Michael Caine Daniel Massey

1984 HEARTBREAKERS
Director: Bobby Roth
Co-stars: Peter Coyote Nick Mancuso James Laurenson

1993 FLIGHT FROM JUSTICE
Director: Don Kent
Co-stars: Bruce Boxleitner Jean Reno

ODETTE LAURE

1990 THESE FOOLISH THINGS
Director: Bertrand Tavernier
Co-stars: Dick Bogarde Jane Birkin Charlotte Kady

ASHLEE LAUREN

1994 UNTAMED LOVE
Director: Paul Aaron
Co-stars: Cathy Lee Crosby John Getz

TAMMY LAUREN

1980 THE LAST FLIGHT OF NOAH'S ARK
Director: Charles Jarrott
Co-stars: Elliott Gould Genevieve Bujold

1988 THE PEOPLE ACROSS THE LAKE
Director: Arthur Allan Seidelman
Co-stars: Valerie Harper Gerald McRaney

1989 BEAUTY AND DENISE
Director: Neal Israel
Co-stars: David Carradine John Karlen Amy O'Neill

VERONICA LAUREN

1992 FOREVER YOUNG
Director: Steve Miner
Co-stars: Mel Gibson Jamie Lee Curtis Elijah Wood

**1993 HOMEWARD BOUND:
THE INCREDIBLE JOURNEY**
Director: Duwayne Dunham
Co-stars: Robert Hayes Kim Griest

ASHLEY LAURENCE

1987 HELLRAISER
Director: Clive Barker
Co-stars: Andrew Robinson Clare Higgins Sean Chapman

1988 HELLBOUND: HELLRAISER II
Director: Tony Randel
Co-stars: Clare Higgins Kenneth Cranham Doug Bradley

1992 HELLRAISER III: HELL ON EARTH
Director: Anthony Hickox
Co-stars: Terry Farrell Doug Bradley

1995 TRIPLE CROSS
Director: Jeno Hodie
Co-stars: Patrick Bergin Michael Pare Billy Dee Williams

AGNES LAURENT

1960 A FRENCH MISTRESS
Director: Roy Boutling
Co-stars: James Robertson Justice Cecil Parker Ian Bannen

JACQUELINE LAURENT

1939 LE JOUR SE LEVE
Director: Marcel Carne
Co-stars: Jean Gabin Jules Berry Arletty

PIPER LAURIE

Nominated For Best Actress In 1961 For "The Hustler". Nominated For Best Supporting Actress In 1976 For "Carrie" And In 1986 For "Children Of A Lesser God".

1950 LOUISA
Director: Alexander Hall
Co-stars: Spring Byington Ronald Reagan Edmund Gwenn

1950 THE MILKMAN
Director: Charles Barton
Co-stars: Donald O'Connor Jimmy Durante William Conrad

1951 THE PRINCE WHO WAS A THIEF
Director: Rudolph Mate
Co-stars: Tony Curtis Everett Sloane Jeff Corey

1951 SON OF ALI BABA
Director: Kurt Neuman
Co-stars: Tony Curtis Susan Cabot Victor Jory

1952 NO ROOM FOR THE GROOM
Director: Douglas Sirk
Co-stars: Tony Curtis Don Defore Spring Byington

1952 HAS ANYBODY SEEN MY GAL?
Director: Douglas Sirk
Co-stars: Charles Coburn Rock Hudson Gigi Perreau

1953 THE GOLDEN BLADE
Director: Nathan Juran
Co-stars: Rock Hudson George Macready Gene Evans

1953 MISSISSIPPI GAMBLER
Director: Rudolph Mate
Co-stars: Tyrone Power John McIntrye Julia Adams

1954 JOHNNY DARK
Director: George Sherman
Co-stars: Tony Curtis Don Taylor Paul Kelly

1954 DAWN AT SOCORRO
Director: George Sherman
Co-stars: Rory Calhoun David Brien Alex Nicol

1954 DANGEROUS MISSION
Director: Louis King
Co-stars: Victor Mature William Bendix Vincent Price

1955 AIN'T MISBEHAVING
Director: Edward Buzzell
Co-stars: Rory Calhoun Jack Carson Mamie Van Doren

1956   **KELLY AND ME**
Director: Robert Z. Leonard
Co-stars: Van Johnson Martha Hyer Onslow Stevens

1957   **UNTIL THEY SAIL**
Director: Robert Wise
Co-stars: Paul Newman Jean Simmons Joan Fontaine

1961   **THE HUSTLER**
Director: Robert Rossen
Co-stars: Paul Newman Jackie Gleason George C. Scott

1976   **CARRIE**
Director: Brian De Palma
Co-stars: Sissy Spacek Amy Irving John Travolta

1977   **RUBY**
Director: Curtis Harrington
Co-stars: Stuart Whitman Roger Davis Janit Baldwin

1978   **RAINBOW**
Director: Jackie Cooper
Co-stars: Andrea McArdle Don Murray Martin Balsam

1979   **TIM**
Director: Michael Pate
Co-stars: Mel Gibson Alwyn Kurts Pat Evison

1982   **MAE WEST**
Director: Lee Phillips
Co-stars: Ann Jillian James Brolin Roddy McDowall

1985   **LOVE, MARY**
Director: Robert Day
Co-stars: Kristy McNichol Matt Clark David Paymer

1985   **RETURN TO OZ**
Director: Walter Murch
Co-stars: Faruza Balk Nicol Williamson Jean Marsh

1986   **PROMISE**
Director: Glenn Jordan
Co-stars: James Garner James Woods Michael Aldredge

1986   **CHILDREN OF A LESSER GOD**
Director: Randa Haines
Co-stars: William Hurt Marlee Matlin

1988   **APPOINTMENT WITH DEATH**
Director: Michael Winner
Co-stars: Peter Ustinov Lauren Bacall John Gielgud

1988   **GO TO THE LIGHT**
Director: Mike Robe
Co-stars: Linda Hamilton Richard Thomas Ned Beatty

1988   **TIGER WARSAW**
Director: Amin Chaudri
Co-stars: Patrick Swayze Barbara Williams

1989   **DREAM A LITTLE DREAM**
Director: Marc Rocco
Co-stars: Jason Robards Corey Feldman Corey Haim

1990   **RISING SUN**
Director: John David Coles
Co-Star   Brian Dennehy

1991   **OTHER PEOPLE'S MONEY**
Director: Norman Jewison
Co-stars: Danny DeVito Gregory Peck Dean Jones

1992   **RICH IN LOVE**
Director: Bruce Beresford
Co-stars: Albert Finney Jill Clayburgh Kyle MacLachlan

1993   **WRESTLING ERNEST HEMINGWAY**
Director: Randa Haines
Co-stars: Robert Duvall Richard Harris Shirley MacLaine

1993   **TRAUMA**
Director: Dario Argento
Co-stars: Asia Argentio Christopher Rydell Brad Dourif

1993   **LOVE, LIES AND LULLABIES**
Director: Rod Hardy
Co-stars: Susan Dey Lorraine Toussaint Kathleen York

1994   **FIGHTING FOR MY DAUGHTER**
Director: Peter Levin
Co-Stars   Lindsay Wagner Chad Lowe

1998   **THE GRASS HARP**
Director: Charles Matthau
Co-Stars   Sissy Spacek Edward Furlong Walter Matthau

CHARLOTTE LAURIER

1990   **UNE HISTOIRE INVENTEE**
Director: Andre Forcier
Co-stars: Jean Lapointe Louise Marleau

FANNY LAUZIER *(Child)*

1988   **THE TADPOLE AND THE WHALE**
Director: Jean-Claude Lord
Co-stars: Denis Forest Marina Orsini

DOMINIQUE LAVANANT

1985   **THREE MEN AND A CRADLE**
Director: Coline Serreau
Co-stars: Roland Giroud Michel Boujenah Andre Dussollier

1986   **KAMIKAZE**
Director: Didier Grousset
Co-stars: Richard Bohringer Michel Galabru Kim Massee

SANDIE LAVELLE

1994   **LADYBIRD LADYBIRD**
Director: Ken Loach
Co-stars: Crissy Rock Vladimir Vega Ray Winstone

BERYL LAVERICK

1934   **THE UNFINISHED SYMPHONY**
Director: Anthony Asquith
Co-stars: Helen Chandler Marta Eggerth Hans Jaray

JUNE LAVERICK

1956   **IT HAPPENED IN ROME**
Co-star: Vittorio De Sica

1958   **THE DUKE WORE JEANS**
Director: Gerald Thomas
Co-stars: Tommy Steel Michael Medwin Alan Wheatley

1958   **THE GYPSY AND THE GENTLEMAN**
Director: Joseph Losey
Co-stars: Melina Mercouri Keith Michell Flora Robson

1958   **SON OF ROBIN HOOD**
Director: George Sherman
Co-stars: David Hedison David Farrar Philip Friend

1959   **FOLLOW A STAR**
Director: Robert Asher
Co-stars: Norman Wisdom Jerry Desmonde Hattie Jacques

1959   **THE FLESH AND THE FIENDS**
Director: John Giling
Co-stars: Peter Cushing Donald Pleasence George Rose

LUCILLE LA VERNE

1922   **ORPHANS OF THE STORM**
Director: D. W. Griffith
Co-stars: Lillian Gish Dorothy Gish Joseph Schildkraut

1931   **THE GREAT MEADOW**
Director: Charles Brabin
Co-stars: John Mack Brown Eleanor Boardman Anita Louise

1933 PILGRIMAGE
Director: John Ford
Co-stars: Henrietta Crossman Heather Angel Norman Foster

1935 A TALE OF TWO CITIES
Director: Jack Conway
Co-stars: Ronald Colman Elizabeth Allan Basil Rathbone

**1937 SNOW WHITE AND THE
SEVEN DWARFS (Voice)**
Director: David Hand
Co-stars: Adriana Caselotti Billy Gilbert

DALIAH LAVI

1960 CANDIDE
Director: Clement Duhour
Co-stars: Jean-Pierre Cassel Pierre Brasseur Nadia Gray

1962 TWO WEEKS IN ANOTHER TOWN
Director: Vincente Minnelli
Co-stars: Kirk Douglas Cyd Charisse Edward G. Robinson

1964 LORD JIM
Director: Richard Brooks
Co-stars: Peter O'Toole James Mason Curt Jurgens

1966 THE SILENCERS
Director: Phil Karlson
Co-stars: Dean Martin Stella Stevens Cyd Charisse

1966 THE SPY WITH A COLD NOSE
Director: Daniel Petrie
Co-stars: Lionel Jeffries Laurence Harvey Eric Sykes

1966 TEN LITTLE INDIANS
Director: George Pollack
Co-stars: Dennis Price Shirley Eaton Leo Genn

1967 JULES VERNE'S ROCKET TO THE MOON
Director: Don Sharp
Co-Stars Burl Ives Troy Donahue Lionel Jeffries

1967 CASINO ROYALE
Director: John Huston
Co-stars: David Niven Deborah Kerr Orson Welles

1968 NOBODY RUNS FOREVER
Director: Ralph Thomas
Co-stars: Rod Taylor Christopher Plummer Lilli Palmer

1969 SOME GIRLS DO
Director: Ralph Thomas
Co-stars: Richard Johnson Robert Morley Sydney Rome

1971 CATLOW
Director: Sam Wanamaker
Co-stars: Yul Brynner Richard Crenna Leonard Nimoy

LINDA LAVIN

1978 LIKE MOM, LIKE ME
Director: Michael Pressman
Co-stars: Kristy McNichol Patrick O'Neal Max Gail

1983 ANOTHER WOMAN'S CHILD
Director: John Erman
Co-stars: Tony LoBianco Joyce Van Patten Doris Roberts

1984 THE MUPPETS TAKE MANHATTAN
Director: Frank Oz
Co-stars: Liza Minnelli Art Carney Brooke Sheilds

1987 LENA: MY 100 CHILDREN
Director: Ed Sherin
Co-stars: Lenore Harris Cynthia Wilde Torquil Campbell

1989 I WANT TO GO HOME
Director: Alain Resnais
Co-stars: Adolph Green Gerard Depardieu Micheline Presle

1995 FORBIDDEN MEMORIES
Director: Bob Clarke
Co-stars: Mary Tyler Moore Shirley Knight

LEA LAVISH

1993 DETOUR
Director: Wade Williams
Co-stars: Tom Neal Jnr. Erin McGrane Susannah Foster

DEE LAW

1987 THE PASSAGE
Director: Harry Thompson
Co-stars: Brian Keith Ned Beatty Alexandra Paul

PHYLLIDA LAW (Mother Of Emma Thompson)

1988 TREE OF HANDS
Director: Giles Foster
Co-stars: Helen Shaver Lauren Bacall Peter Firth

1992 PETER'S FRIENDS
Director: Kenneth Branagh
Co-stars: Kenneth Branagh Imelda Staunton Emma Thompson

1993 MUCH ADO ABOUT NOTHING
Director: Kenneth Branagh
Co-stars: Kenneth Branagh Richard Briers Keanu Reeves

1997 THE WINTER GUEST
Director: Alan Rickman
Co-star: Emma Thompson

JOAN LAWES

1930 UP THE RIVER
Director: John Ford
Co-stars: Spencer Tracy Warren Hymer Humphrey Bogart

BETTY LAWFORD

1930 OLD ENGLISH
Director: Alfred Green
Co-stars: George Arliss Leon Janney Doris Lloyd

1936 LOVE BEFORE BREAKFAST
Co-stars: Preston Foster Carole Lombard Cesar Romero

1947 THE DEVIL THUMBS A RIDE
Director: Felix Feist
Co-stars: Lawrence Tierney Ted North Nan Leslie

YVONNE LAWLEY

1990 DEATH IN BRUNSWICK
Director: John Ruane
Co-stars: Sam Neill Zoe Caride John Clarke

MARY LAWLOR

1930 GOOD NEWS
Director: Nick Grinde
Co-stars: Bessie Love Stanley Smith Lola Lane

DEBRA LAWRANCE

1984 SILVER CITY
Director: Sophia Turkiewicz
Co-stars: Gosia Dobrowolska Ivar Kants Anna Jemison

JODY LAWRANCE

1951 THE FAMILY SECRET
Director: Henry Levin
Co-stars: John Derek Lee J. Cobb Erin O'Brien-Moore

1951 SON OF DR. JEKYLL
Director: Seymour Friedman
Co-stars: Louis Hayward Alexandrer Knox Gavin Muir

1951 THE MASK OF THE AVENGER
Director: Phil Karlson
Co-stars: John Derek Anthony Quinn Arnold Moss

1951 TEN TALL MEN
Director: Willis Goldbeck
Co-stars: Burt Lancaster Gilbert Roland Kieran Moore

1952 THE BRIGAND
Director: Phil Karlson
Co-stars: Anthony Dexter Anthony Quinn Gale Robbins

1952 ALL ASHORE
Director: Richard Quine
Co-stars: Mickey Rooney Dick Haymes Barbara Bates

1955 THE SCARLET HOUR
Director: Michael Curtiz
Co-stars: Carol Ohmart Tom Tyron Elaine Stritch

1956 THE LEATHER SAINT
Director: Alvin Ganzer
Co-stars: Paul Douglas John Derek Cesar Romero

1960 THE PURPLE GANG
Director: Frank McDonald
Co-stars: Robert Blake Barry Sullivan Marc Cavell

BARBARA LAWRENCE

1946 MARGIE
Director: Henry King
Co-stars: Jeanne Crain Glenn Langan Alan Young

1948 YOU WERE MEANT FOR ME
Director: Lloyd Bacon
Co-stars: Jeanne Crain Dan Dailey Oscar Levant

1948 UNFAITHFULLY YOURS
Director: Preston Sturges
Co-stars: Rex Harrison Linda Darnell Rudy Vallee

1948 THE STREET WITH NO NAME
Director: William Keighley
Co-stars: Richard Widmark Mark Stevens Lloyd Nolan

1948 MOTHER IS A FRESHMAN
Director: Lloyd Bacon
Co-stars: Loretta Young Van Johnson Rudy Vallee

1948 GIVE MY REGARDS TO BROADWAY
Director: Lloyd Bacon
Co-stars: Dan Dailey Charles Winninger Nancy Guild

1949 A LETTER TO THREE WIVES
Director: Joseph Mankiewicz
Co-stars: Kirk Douglas Ann Sothern Linda Darnell

1949 THIEVES' HIGHWAY
Director: Jules Dassin
Co-stars: Richard Conte Valentina Cortesa Lee J. Cobb

1951 TWO TICKETS TO BROADWAY
Director: James Kern
Co-stars: Janet Leigh Eddie Bracken Gloria De Haven

1951 HERE COME THE NELSONS
Director: Frederick De Cordova
Co-stars: Ozzie Nelson Harriet Hilliard

1953 PARIS MODEL
Director: Alfred Green
Co-stars: Paulette Goddard Eva Gabor Marilyn Maxwell

1953 ARENA
Director: Richard Fleischer
Co-stars: Gig Young Jean Hagen Polly Bergen

1955 OKLAHOMA !
Director: Fred Zinnemann
Co-Stars: Gordon MacRae Shirley Jones Rod Steiger

1957 JOE DAKOTA
Director: Richard Bartlett
Co-stars: Jock Mahoney Luana Patten Charles McGraw

1957 KRONOS
Director: Kurt Newman
Co-stars: Jeff Morrow John Emery Morris Ankrum

CAROL LAWRENCE

1961 A VIEW FROM THE BRIDGE
Director: Sidney Lumet
Co-stars: Raf Vallone Maureen Stapleton Jean Sorel

DELPHI LAWRENCE

1954 MEET MR. CALLAGHAN
Director: Charles Saunders
Co-stars: Derrick De Marney Adrienne Corri Belinda Lee

1955 THE GOLD EXPRESS
Director: Guy Fergusson
Co-stars: Vernon Gray Ann Walford May Hallatt

1956 THE FEMININE TOUCH
Director: Pat Jackson
Co-stars: George Baker Belinda Lee Adrienne Corri

1956 DOUBLE CROSS
Director: Anthony Squire
Co-stars: Donald Houston William Hartnell Anton Diffring

1956 IT'S NEVER TOO LATE
Director: Michael McCarthy
Co-stars: Phyllis Calvert Guy Rolfe Susan Stephen

1957 JUST MY LUCK
Director: John Paddy Carstairs
Co-stars: Norman Wisdom Margaret Rutherford Jill Dixon

1957 STRANGERS' MEETING
Director: Robert Day
Co-stars: Peter Arne Conrad Phillips Barbara Archer

1958 SON OF ROBIN HOOD
Director: George Sherman
Co-stars: David Hedison June Laverick David Farrar

1959 THE MAN WHO COULD CHEAT DEATH
Director: Terence Fisher
Co-stars: Anton Diffring Hazel Court

1960 CONE OF SILENCE
Director: Charles Frend
Co-stars: Michael Craig George Sanders Elizabeth Seal

ELIZABETH LAWRENCE

1991 SLEEPING WITH THE ENEMY
Director: Joseph Ruben
Co-stars: Julia Roberts Patrick Bergin Kyle Secor

GERTRUDE LAWRENCE

1929 INNOCENT

1929 THE BATTLE OF PARIS
Director: Robert Florey
Co-stars: Charles Ruggles Walter Petrie Arthur Treacher

1932 ARN'T WE ALL?
Director: Rudolph Mate
Co-stars: Hugh Wakefield Owen Nares Harold Huth

1932 LORD CAMBER'S LADIES
Director: Benn Levy
Co-stars: Gerald Du Maurier Benita Hume Nigle Bruce

1933 NO FUNNY BUSINESS
Director: Victor Hanbury
Co-stars: Laurence Olivier Jill Esmond Gibb Mclaughlin

1935 MIMI
Director: Paul Stein
Co-stars: Douglas Fairbanks Diana Napier Harold Warrender

1936 MEN ARE NOT GODS
Director: Walter Reich
Co-stars: Miriam Hopkins Sebastian Shaw Rex Harrison

1936 REMBRANDT
Director: Alexander Korda
Co-stars: Charles Laughton Elsa Lanchester Roger Livesey

1943 STAGE DOOR CANTEEN
Director: Frank Borzage
Co-stars: Cheryl Walker Lon McCallister Judith Anderson

1950 THE GLASS MENAGERIE
Director: Irving Rapper
Co-stars: Kirk Douglas Jane Wyman Arthur Kennedy

JOSIE LAWRENCE

1990 THE GREEN MAN
Director: Elijah Moshinsky
Co-stars: Albert Finney Michael Hordern Linda Marlowe

1991 ENCHANTED APRIL
Director: Mike Newell
Co-stars: Miranda Richardson Polly Walker Joan Plowright

MADY LAWRENCE

1945 LIGHTNING RAIDERS
Co-stars: Larry Crabbe Al "Fuzzy" St. John Ray Brent

MARJIE LAWRENCE

1990 HAPPY FEET
Director: Mike Bradwell
Co-stars: Phyllis Logan Stephen Hancock Derrick O'Connor

MURIEL LAWRENCE

1952 I DREAM OF JEANNIE
Director: Allan Dwan
Co-stars: Ray Middleton Bill Shirley Rex Allen

PATRICIA LAWRENCE

1973 THE HIRELING
Director: Alan Bridges
Co-stars: Robert Shaw Sarah Miles Peter Egan

1991 THEY NEVER SLEPT
Director: Udayan Prasad
Co-stars: Edward Fox James Fleet Harriet Walter

ROSINA LAWRENCE

1935 WELCOME HOME
Co-stars: James Dunn Arline Judge

1935 YOUR UNCLE DUDLEY
Co-stars: Edward Everett Horton Marjorie Gateson

1936 CHARLIE CHAN'S SECRET
Director: Gordon Wiles
Co-stars: Warner Oland Henriette Crossman Astrid Allwyn

1937 NOBODY'S BABY
Director: Gus Meins
Co-stars: Lyda Roberti Patsy Kelly Robert Armstrong

1937 PICK A STAR
Director: Edward Sedgwick
Co-stars: Jack Haley Patsy Kelly Stan Laurel Oliver Hardy

1937 WAY OUT WEST
Director: James Horne
Co-stars: Stan Laurel Oliver Hardy James Finlayson

SHARON LAWRENCE

1994 SOMEONE SHE KNOWS
Director: Eric Laneauville
Co-stars: Markie Post Gerald McRaney

1995 THE FACE ON THE MILK CARTON
Director: Waris Hussein
Co-star: Kellie Martin

STEPHANIE LAWRENCE

1988 BUSTER
Director: David Green
Co-stars: Phil Collins Julie Walters Larry Lamb

1989 PHANTOM OF THE OPERA
Director: Dwight Little
Co-stars: Robert Englund Jill Schoelen Bill Nighy

CHRISTINA LAWSON

1993 AMERICAN YAKUSI
Director: Frank Cappello
Co-stars: Viggo Mortensen Robert Forster Michael Nouri

LINDA LAWSON

1961 NIGHT TIDE
Director: Curtis Harrington
Co-stars: Dennis Hopper Gavin Muir Luana Anders

1964 APACHE RIFLES
Director: William Witney
Co-stars: Audie Murphy Michael Dante L. Q. Jones

1971 NEVER GIVE AN INCH
Director: Paul Newman
Co-stars: Paul Newman Henry Fonda Lee Remick Michael Sarrazin

MARY LAWSON

1935 THINGS ARE LOOKING UP
Director: Albert De Courville
Co-stars: Cicely Courtneidge Max Miller

1935 A FIRE HAS BEEN ARRANGED
Director: Leslie Hiscott
Co-stars: Bud Flanagan Chesney Allen Alastair Sim

1936 HOUSE BROKEN
Director: Michael Hankinson
Co-stars: Louis Borell Jack Lambert Enid Stamp-Taylor

1937 COTTON QUEEN
Director: Bernard Vorhaus
Co-stars: Stanley Holloway Will Fyffe Jimmy Hanley

SARAH LAWSON

1953 STREET CORNER
Director: Muriel Box
Co-stars: Rosamund John Anne Crawford Peggy Cummins

1954 YOU KNOW WHAT SAILORS ARE
Director: Ken Annakin
Co-stars: Donald Sinden Akim Tamirov Naunton Wayne

1955 THE BLUE PETER
Director: Wolf Rilla
Co-stars: Kieron Moore Greta Gynt Mervyn Johns

1956 IT'S NEVER TOO LATE
Director: Michael McCarthy
Co-stars: Phyllis Calvert Guy Rolfe Susan Stephen

1967 NIGHT OF THE BIG HEAT
Director: Terence Fisher
Co-stars: Christopher Lee Peter Cushing Jane Merrow

1968 THE DEVIL RIDES OUT
Director: Terence Fisher
Co-stars: Christopher Lee Charles Gray Patrick Mower

SHANNON LAWSON

1993 APRIL ONE
Director: Murray Battle
Co-stars: Stephen Shellen Djanet Sears David Strathairn

1995 BUTTERBOX BABIES
Director: Don McBrearty
Co-stars: Susan Clark Peter McNeil Catherine Fitch

ME ME LAY

1972 AU PAIR GIRLS
Director: Val Guest
Co-stars: Gabrielle Drake Richard O'Sullivan Nancie Wait

DILYS LAYE

1949 TROTTIE TRUE
Director: Brain Desmond Hurst
Co-stars: Jean Kent James Donald Bill Owen

1957 BLUE MURDER AT ST. TRINIANS
Director: Frank Launder
Co-stars: Terry-Thomas George Cole Alastair Sim

1959 THE BRIDAL PATH
Director: Frank Launder
Co-stars: Bill Travers Fiona Clyne George Cole

1961 PETTICOAT PIRATES
Director: David MacDonald
Co-stars: Charlie Drake Cecil Parker Anne Heywood

1962 CARRY ON CRUISING
Director: Gerald Thomas
Co-stars: Sid James Kenneth Williams Liz Fraser

1968 CARRY ON DOCTOR
Director: Gerald Thomas
Co-stars: Frankie Howerd Jim Dale Barbara Windsor

1969 CARRY ON CAMPING
Director: Gerald Thomas
Co-stars: Sid James Barbara Windsor Bernard Bresslaw

1989 THE SPIRIT OF MAN
Director: Peter Barnes
Co-stars: Peter Bayliss Eleanor David Nigel Hawthorne

EVELYN LAYE

1930 ONE HEAVENLY NIGHT
Director: George Fitzmaurice
Co-stars: John Boles Leon Errol Lilyan Tashman

1933 WALTZ TIME
Director: William Thiele
Co-stars: Fritz Schultz Gina Malo Jay Laurier

1934 THE NIGHT IS YOUNG
Director: Dudley Murphy
Co-stars: Ramon Navarro Una Merkel Rosalind Russell

1934 PRINCESS CHARMING
Director: Maurice Elvey
Co-stars: Yvonne Arnaud Henry Wilcoxon Max Miller

1934 EVENSONG
Director: Victor Saville
Co-stars: Fritz Kortner Carl Esmond Emlyn Williams Muriel Aked

1970 SAY HELLO TO YESTERDAY
Director: Alvin Rakoff
Co-stars: Jean Simmons Leonard Whiting John Lee

MARY LAYNE

1970 YOU CAN'T HAVE EVERYTHING
Director: Martin Zweibach
Co-stars: Richard Thomas Lucille Benson

LORENA LAYSON

1932 HOLLYWOOD SPEAKS
Director: Eddie Buzzell
Co-stars: Pat O'Brien Genevieve Tobin Rita LeRoy

VERONICA LAZAR

1979 LA LUNA
Director: Bernardo Bertolucci
Co-stars: Jill Clayburgh Matthew Barry Fred Gwynne

CAROL LAZARE

1986 THE FLY
Director: David Cronenberg
Co-stars: Jeff Goldblum Geena Davis John Getz

GABRIELLE LAZURE

1989 HONOUR BOUND
Director: Jennot Szwarc
Co-stars: John Philbin Tom Skerritt George Dzundza

THUY THU LE

1989 CASUALTIES OF WAR
Director: Brian De Palma
Co-stars: Michael J. Fox Sean Penn Don Harvey

HIEP THI LE

1993 HEAVEN AND EARTH
Director: Oliver Stone
Co-stars: Tommy Lee Jones Joan Chen Debbie Reynolds

LEA DI LEA

1953 MADAME DE....
Director: Max Ophuls
Co-stars: Charles Boyer Danielle Darrieux Vittorio De Sica

TRACEY LEA

1985 LETTER TO BREZHNEV
Director: Chris Bernard
Co-stars: Margi Clarke Alexandra Pigg Peter Firth

BRITT LEACH

1983 NIGHT WARNING
Director: William Asher
Co-stars: Jimmy McNichol Susan Tyrrell Bo Svenson

1987 BABY BOOM
Director: Charles Shyer
Co-stars: Diane Keaton Harold Ramis Sam Wanamaker

ROSEMARY LEACH

1971 CIDER WITH ROSIE
Director: Claude Whatham
Co-star: Peter Chandler

1973 THAT'LL BE THE DAY
Director: Claude Whatham
Co-stars: David Essex Ringo Starr James Booth

1975 BRIEF ENCOUNTER
Director: Alan Bridges
Co-stars: Richard Burton Sophia Loren Jack Hedley Ann Firbank

1985 A ROOM WITH A VIEW
Director: James Ivory
Co-stars: Helena Bonham Carter Daniel Day Lewis Maggie Smith

1985 TURTLE DIARY
Director: John Irvin
Co-stars: Glenda Jackson Ben Kingsley Eleanor Bron

1988 ACROSS THE LAKE
Director: Tony Maylam
Co-stars: Anthony Hopkins Mark Stratton Phyllis Calvert

1989 SUMMER'S LEASE
Director: John Mortimer
Co-stars: John Gielgud Susan Fleetwood Mel Martin

1991	**TITMUSS REGAINED**
Director:	Martin Friend
Co-stars:	David Threlfall Kristin Scott Thomas

1992	**AN UNGENTLEMANLY ACT**
Director:	Stuart Urban
Co-stars:	Ian Richardson Bob Peck Ian McNeice

1993	**THE MYSTERY OF EDWIN DROOD**
Director:	Timothy Forder
Co-stars:	Robert Powell Nanette Newman Gemma Craven

1993	**THE HAWK**
Director:	David Hayman
Co-stars:	Helen Mirren George Costigan John Duttine

1993	**TENDER LOVING CARE**
Director:	Dewi Humphreys
Co-stars:	Dawn French Joan Sims Peter Jones Robert Pugh

CLORIS LEACHMAN
(Married George Englund, Director)
Oscar For Best Supporting Actress In 1971 For "The Last Picture Show"

1955	**KISS ME DEADLY**
Director:	Robert Aldrich
Co-stars:	Ralph Meeker Albert Dekker Paul Stuart

1956	**THE RACK**
Director:	Arnold Laven
Co-stars:	Paul Newman Walter Pidgeon Edmond O'Brien

1969	**SILENT NIGHT, LONELY NIGHT**
Director:	Daniel Petrie
Co-Stars	Lloyd Bridges Shirley Jones Lynn Carlin

1969	**BUTCH CASSIDY AND THE SUNDANCE KID**
Director:	George Roy Hill
Co-stars:	Paul Newman Robert Redford Katherine Ross

1970	**W. U. S. A.**
Director:	Stuart Rosenberg
Co-stars:	Paul Newman Joanne Woodward Laurence Harvey

1970	**THE PEOPLE NEXT DOOR**
Director:	David Greene
Co-stars:	Eli Wallach Julie Harris Hal Holbrook

1971	**THE LAST PICTURE SHOW**
Director:	Peter Bogdanovich
Co-stars:	Timothy Bottoms Ben Johnson

1972	**HAUNTS OF THE VERY RICH**
Director:	Paul Wendkos
Co-stars:	Lloyd Bridges Ed Asner Anne Francis

1973	**DYING ROOM ONLY**
Director:	Phillip Leacock
Co-stars:	Ross Martin Ned Beatty Dabney Coleman

1973	**DILLINGER**
Director:	John Milius
Co-stars:	Warren Oates Ben Johnson Michelle Philips

1973	**CRIME CLUB**
Director:	David Lowell Rich
Co-stars:	Lloyd Bridges Martin Sheen Victor Buono Barbara Rush

1973	**CHARLIE AND THE ANGEL**
Director:	Vincent McEveety
Co-stars:	Fred MacMurray Harry Morgan Kurt Russell

1973	**A BRAND NEW LIFE**
Director:	Sam O'Steen
Co-stars:	Martin Balsam Mildred Dunnock Gene Nelson

1974	**DAISY MILLER**
Director:	Peter Bogdanovich
Co-stars:	Cybill Shepherd Barry Brown Mildred Natwick

1974	**DEATH SENTENCE**
Director:	E. W. Swackhamer
Co-stars:	Laurence Lukinbill Nick Nolte Yvonne Wilder

1974	**HITCHHIKE!**
Director:	Gordon Hessler
Co-stars:	Michael Brandon Henry Darrow Cameron Mitchell

1974	**THE MIGRANTS**
Director:	Tom Gries
Co-stars:	Ron Howard Sissy Spacek Cindy Williams

1974	**THURSDAY'S GAME**
Director:	Robert Moore
Co-stars:	Gene Wilder Bob Newhart Ellen Burstyn

1974	**YOUNG FRANKENSTEIN**
Director:	Mel Brooks
Co-stars:	Gene Wilder Marty Feldman Madeline Kahn

1975	**THE NEW ORIGINAL WONDER WOMAN**
Director:	Leonard Horn
Co-stars:	Lynda Carter Lyle Waggoner Red Buttons

1975	**CRAZY MAMA**
Director:	Jonathan Demme
Co-stars:	Ann Sothern Linda Purl Stuart Whitman Jim Backus

1977	**HIGH ANXIETY**
Director:	Mel Brooks
Co-stars:	Mel Brooks Madeline Kahn Harvey Korman

1979	**THE MUPPET MOVIE**
Director:	James Frawley
Co-stars:	Charles Durning Bob Hope Orson Welles James Coburn

1979	**S.O.S. TITANIC**
Director:	William Hale
Co-star:	David Janssen

1979	**THE NORTH AVENUE IRREGULARS**
Director:	Bruce Bilson
Co-stars:	Edward Herrman Barbara Harris Susan Clark

1979	**SCAVENGER HUNT**
Director:	Michael Schultz
Co-stars:	Vincent Price Richard Benjamin James Coco

1980	**HERBIE GOES BANANAS!**
Director:	Vincent McEveety
Co-stars:	Charles Martin Smith John Vernon

1980	**FOOLIN' AROUND**
Director:	Richard Heffron
Co-stars:	Gary Busey Annette O'Toole Eddie Albert

1981	**HISTORY OF THE WORLD - PART ONE**
Director:	Mel Brooks
Co-stars:	Mel Brooks Dom Deluise Madeline Kahn Gregory Hines

1982	**MISS ALL-AMERICAN BEAUTY**
Director:	Gus Trikonis
Co-stars:	Diane Lane David Dukes Jayne Meadows

1983	**DIXIE: CHANGING HABITS**
Director:	George Englund
Co-stars:	Suzanne Pleshette Geraldine Fitzgerald

1985	**DEADLY INTENTIONS**
Director:	Noel Black
Co-stars:	Michael Biehn Madolyn Smith Morgana King

1985	**LOVE IS NEVER SILENT**
Director:	Joseph Sargent
Co-stars:	Mare Winningham Phyllis Frelich Ed Waterstreet

1986	**MY LITTLE PONY** *(Voice)*
Director:	Michael Joens
Co-stars:	Danny DeVito Rhea Pearlman Tony Randall

1988	**WEDDING DAY BLUES**
Director:	Paul Lynch
Co-stars:	Michelle Green Max Wright Eileen Brennan

1989	**PRANCER**
Director:	John Hancock
Co-stars:	Sam Elliott Rebecca Harrell Rutanya Alda Abe Vigoda

1990   **TEXASVILLE**
Director: Peter Bogdanovich
Co-stars: Jeff Bridges Cybill Shepherd Annie Potts Timothy Bottoms

1990   **LOVE HURTS**
Director: Bud Yorkin
Co-stars: Jeff Daniels Judith Ivey John Mahoney Amy Wright

1993   **DOUBLE, DOUBLE TOIL AND TROUBLE**
Director: Stuart Margolin
Co-stars: Mary-Kate Olsen Ashley Olsen

1993   **FALSELY ACCUSED**
Director: Noel Nosseck
Co-Stars   Lisa Hartman Christopher Meloni

1994   **THE BEVERLEY HILLBILLIES**
Director: Penelope Spheeris
Co-stars: Jim Varney Lily Tomlin Dabney Coleman Zsa Zsa Gabor

JENNIFER LEAK

1968   **YOURS, MINE AND OURS**
Director: Mel Shavelson
Co-stars: Lucille Ball Henry Fonda Van Johnson

1969   **EYE OF THE CAT**
Director: David Lowell Rich
Co-stars: Eleanor Parker Michael Sarrazin Gayle Hunnicutt

MICHAEL LEARNED

1980   **TOUCHED BY LOVE**
Director: Gus Trikonis
Co-stars: Deborah Raffin Diane Lane Clu Gulager

1982   **MOTHER'S DAY ON WALTON MOUNTAIN**
Director: Gwen Arner
Co-stars: Ralph Waite Eric Scott Kami Cotler

1984   **THE PARADE**
Director: Peter Hunt
Co-stars: Frederick Forrest Rosanna Arquette

1985   **POWER**
Director: Sidney Lumet
Co-stars: Richard Gere Julie Christie Gene Hackman

1986   **A DEADLY BUSINESS**
Director: John Korty
Co-stars: Alan Arkin Armand Assante Jon Polito

1988   **MERCY ON MURDER?**
Director: Steve Gethers
Co-stars: Robert Young Eddie Albert Frances Reid

1990   **THE WALTON'S CRISIS AN EASTER STORY**
Director: Harry Harris
Co-star: Ralph Waite Kami Cotler

1991   **MURDER IN NEW HAMPSHIRE**
Director: Joyce Chopra
Co-Stars   Chad Allen Ken Howard Helen Hunt

1993   **DRAGON: THE BRUCE LEE STORY**
Director: Rob Cohen
Co-stars: Jason Scott Lee Lauren Holly Robert Wagner

MADELEINE LeBEAU

1942   **GENTLEMAN JIM**
Director: Raoul Walsh
Co-stars: Errol Flynn Alexis Smith Jack Carson

1943   **PARIS AFTER DARK**
Director: Leonide Moguy
Co-stars: George Sanders Philip Dorn Brenda Marshall

1950   **CAGE OF GOLD**
Director: Basil Dearden
Co-stars: Jean Simmons David Farrar James Donald

1963   **EIGHT AND A HALF**
Director: Federico Fellini
Co-stars: Marcello Mastroianni Claudia Cardinale Anouk Aimee

MAYA LEBENZON

1989   **OUT ON THE EDGE**
Director: John Pasquin
Co-stars: Rick Schroder Richard Jenkins Mary Kay Place

KELLY LeBROCK *(Married Steven Seagal)*

1984   **THE WOMAN IN RED**
Director: Gene Wilder
Co-stars: Gene Wilder Charles Grodin Joseph Bologna Judith Ivey

1985   **WEIRD SCIENCE**
Director: John Hughes
Co-stars: Anthony Michael Hall Bill Paxton Robert Downey Jnr.

1989   **HARD TO KILL**
Director: Bruce Malmuth
Co-stars: Steven Seagal Bill Sadler Bonnie Burroughs

1992   **BETRAYAL OF THE DOVE**
Director: Strathford Hamilton
Co-stars: Helen Slater Billy Zane

DANIELLE LeBRUN

1988   **CAMILLE CLAUDEL**
Director: Bruno Nuytten
Co-stars: Isabelle Adjani Gerard Depardieu Alain Cuny

1991   **URANUS**
Director: Claude Beri
Co-stars: Gerard Depardiu Phiippe Noiret Michel Blanc

GINETTE LeCLERC

1938   **LA FEMME DU BOULANGER**
Director: Marcel Pagnol
Co-stars: Raimu Charles Moulin Charpin

1943   **LE CORBEAU**
Director: Henri-Georges Clouzot
Co-stars: Pierre Fresnay Helene Manson Pierre Larquey

1952   **LE PLAISIR**
Director: Max Ophuls
Co-stars: Claude Dauphin Danielle Darrieux Simone Simon

1954   **LES AMANTS DU TAGE**
Director: Henri Verneuill
Co-stars: Daniel Gelin Francois Arnoul Trevor Howard

ODILE LE CLEZIOT

1988   **YOUNG EINSTEIN**
Director: Yahoo Serious
Co-stars: Yahoo Serious John Howard Peewee Wilson

JACQUELINE LECOMTE

1968   **PLAYTIME**
Director: Jacques Tati
Co-stars: Jacques Tati Barbara Denek Henri Piccoli

SUZANNE LEDERER

1976   **JUDGE HORTON AND THE SCOTTSBORO BOYS**
Director: Fielder Cook
Co-stars: Arthur Hill Vera Miles

1986   **WOMEN OF VALOR**
Director: Buzz Kulik
Co-stars: Susan Sarandon Kristy McNichol Alberta Watson

CAZ LEDERMAN

1984   **TAIL OF THE TIGER**
Director: Rolf De Heer
Co-stars: Grant Navin Gordon Poole Dylan Lyle

1989 MALPRACTISE
Director: Bill Bennett
Co-stars: Bob Baines Ian Gilmour Dorothy Alison

LOTTE LEDI

1965 HEIDI
Director: Werner Jacobs
Co-stars: Eva Marie Singhammer Gertraud Mittermayr Gustav Knuth

ANN MARIE LEE

1989 THE FLY II
Director: Chris Walas
Co-stars: Eric Stoltz Daphne Zuniga Lee Richardson

ANNA LEE

1934 THE CAMELS ARE COMING
Director: Tim Whelan
Co-stars: Jack Hulbert Hartley Power Harold Huth

1935 THE PASSING OF THE THIRD FLOOR BACK
Director: Berthold Viertel
Co-stars: Conrad Veidt Rene Ray Beatrix Lehman

1935 FIRST A GIRL
Director: Victor Saville
Co-stars: Jessie Matthews Sonnie Hale Griffith Jones

1936 THE MAN WHO CHANGED HIS MIND
Director: Robert Stevenson
Co-stars: Boris Karloff Donald Calthrop

1936 O.H.M.S.
Director: Raoul Walsh
Co-stars: John Mills Wallace Ford Grace Bradley Frank Cellier

1937 NON-STOP NEW YORK
Director: Robert Stevenson
Co-stars: John Loder Francis L. Sullivan Frank Cellier

1937 KING SOLOMON'S MINES
Director: Robert Stevenson
Co-stars: Cedric Hardwicke Paul Robeson Roland Young

1939 THE FOUR JUST MEN
Director: Walter Forde
Co-stars: Hugh Sinclair Griffith Jones Frank Lawton

1939 YOUNG MAN'S FANCY
Director: Robert Stevenson
Co-stars: Griffith Jones Seymour Hicks Edward Rigby

1940 RETURN TO YESTERDAY
Director: Robert Stevenson
Co-stars: Clive Brook May Whitty Hartley Power

1941 HOW GREEN WAS MY VALLEY
Director: John Ford
Co-stars: Walter Pidgeon Maureen O'Hara Donald Crisp

1941 MY LIFE WITH CAROLINE
Director: Lewis Milestone
Co-stars: Ronald Colman Reginald Gardiner Charles Winninger

1942 FLYING TIGERS
Director: David Miller
Co-stars: John Wayne John Carroll Paul Kelly Mae Clarke

1942 THE COMMANDOS STRIKE AT DAWN
Director: John Farrow
Co-stars: Paul Muni Lillian Gish Robert Coote

1943 HANGMEN ALSO DIE
Director: Fritz Lang
Co-stars: Brian Donlevy Walter Brennan Dennis O'Keefe

1944 SUMMER STORM
Director: Douglas Sirk
Co-stars: George Sanders Linda Darnell Hugo Haas Sig Ruman

1946 BEDLAM
Director: Mark Robson
Co-stars: Boris Karloff Billy House Richard Fraser

1947 THE GHOST AND MRS. MUIR
Director: Joseph Mankiewicz
Co-stars: Rex Harrison Gene Tierney Natalie Wood

1947 HIGH CONQUEST
Director: Irving Allen
Co-stars: Gilbert Roland Beulah Bondi John Qualen

1948 FORT APACHE
Director: John Ford
Co-stars: Henry Fonda John Wayne Shirley Temple

1948 THE BEST MAN WINS
Director: John Sturges
Co-stars: Edgar Buchanan Robert Shayne Hobart Cavanagh

1958 GIDEON OF SCOTLAND YARD
Director: John Ford
Co-stars: Jack Hawkins Dianne Foster Andrew Ray

1958 THE LAST HURRAH
Director: John Ford
Co-stars: Spencer Tracy Jeffrey Hunter Pat O'Brien Basil Rathbone

1958 JET OVER THE ATLANTIC
Director: Byron Haskin
Co-stars: Guy Madison Virginia Mayo George Raft

1959 THE CRIMSON KIMONO
Director: Samuel Fuller
Co-stars: Glenn Corbett James Shigeta Victoria Shaw

1959 THE HORSE SOLDIERS
Director: John Ford
Co-stars: John Wayne William Holden Constance Towers

1959 THIS EARTH IS MINE
Director: Henry King
Co-stars: Jean Simmons Claude Rains Rock Hudson

1961 TWO RODE TOGETHER
Director: John Ford
Co-stars: James Stewart Richard Widmark Shirley Jones

1962 WHATEVER HAPPENED TO BABY JANE?
Director: Robert Aldrich
Co-stars: Bette Davis Joan Crawford

1965 THE SOUND OF MUSIC
Director: Robert Wise
Co-stars: Julie Andrews Christopher Plummer Eleanor Parker

1966 SEVEN WOMEN
Director: John Ford
Co-stars: Anne Bancroft Flora Robson Sue Lyon Betty Field

1967 IN LIKE FLINT
Director: Gordon Douglas
Co-stars: James Coburn Lee J. Cobb Jean Hale Andrew Duggan

BELINDA LEE

1954 THE BELLES OF ST. TRINIANS
Director: Frank Launder
Co-stars: Alastair Sim George Cole Joyce Grenfell

1954 MEET MR. CALLAGHAN
Director: Charles Saunders
Co-stars: Derrick De Marney Harriet Johns Peter Neil

1954 THE RUNAWAY BUS
Director: Val Guest
Co-stars: Frankie Howerd Margaret Rutherford Petula Clark

1955 FOOTSTEPS IN THE FOG
Director: Arthur Lubin
Co-stars: Stewart Granger Jean Simmons Bill Travers

1955 MAN OF THE MOMENT
Director: John Paddy Carstairs
Co-stars: Norman Wisdom Lana Morris Jerry Desmonde

1955 NO SMOKING
Director: Henry Cass
Co-stars: Reg Dixon Lionel Jeffries Myrtle Rowe

1956 WHO DONE IT?
Director: Basil Dearden
Co-stars: Benny Hill David Kossoff Garry Marsh

1956 THE FEMININE TOUCH
Director: Pat Jackson
Co-stars: George Baker Delphi Lawrence Adrienne Corri

1956 EYEWITNESS
Director: Muriel Box
Co-stars: Donald Sinden Muriel Pavlow Michael Craig

1956 THE BIG MONEY
Director: John Paddy Carstairs
Co-stars: Ian Carmichael Robert Helpman Jill Ireland

1957 DANGEROUS EXILE
Director: Brian Desmonde Hurst
Co-stars: Keith Michell Martita Hunt Finlay Currie

1957 MIRACLE IN SOHO
Director: Julian Amyes
Co-stars: John Gregson Cyril Cusack Billie Whitelaw

CANDACE LEE

1955 LOVE IS A MANY SPLENDORED THING
Director: Henry King
Co-stars: William Holden Jennifer Jones

1958 SOUTH PACIFIC
Director: Joshua Logan
Co-stars: Mitzi Gaynor Rossano Brazzi John Kerr

CAROLYN LEE

1942 MRS. WIGGS OF THE CABBAGE PATCH
Director: Ralph Murphy
Co-stars: Fay Bainter Hugh Herbert Vera Vague

CYNTHIA LEE

1985 NEW YORK NIGHTS
Director: Simon Nuchtern
Co-stars: Corinne Alphen Nicholas Cortland Bobbi Burns

DIXIE LEE *(Married Bing Crosby)*

1930 LET'S GO PLACES
Director: Frank Strayer
Co-stars: Joseph Wagstaff Lola Lane Sharon Lynn

1930 CHEER UP AND SMILE
Co-star: Arthur Lake

1930 THE BIG PARTY
Co-star: Frank Albertson

1934 MANHATTAN LOVE SONG
Co-star: Robert Armstrong

1935 REDHEADS ON PARADE
Co-star: John Boles

1935 LOVE IN BLOOM
Director: Elliott Nugent
Co-stars: Burns & Allen Joe Morrison

DOROTHY LEE

1929 RIO RITA
Director: Luther Reed
Co-stars: Bebe Daniels Bert Wheeler Robert Woolsey

1930 THE CUCKOOS
Director: Paul Sloane
Co-stars: Bert Wheeler Robert Woolsey June Clyde

1930 HALF SHOT AT SUNRISE
Director: Paul Sloane
Co-stars: Bert Wheeler Robert Woolsey Edna May Oliver

1930 HOOK, LINE AND SINKER
Director: Edward Cline
Co-stars: Bert Wheeler Robert Woolsey Jobyna Howland

1931 CAUGHT PLASTERED
Director: William Seiter
Co-stars: Bert Wheeler Robert Woolsey Lucy Beaumont

1931 CRACKED NUTS
Director: Edward Cline
Co-stars: Bert Wheeler Robert Woolsey Edna May Oliver

1931 LAUGH AND GET RICH
Director: Gregory La Cava
Co-stars: Hugh Herbert Edna May Oliver

1931 PEACH O'RENO
Director: William Seiter
Co-stars: Bert Wheeler Robert Woolsey Cora Witherspoon

1932 GIRL CRAZY
Director: William Seiter
Co-stars: Bert Wheeler Robert Woolsey Mitzi Green

1934 HIPS, HIPS HOORAY
Director: Mark Sandrich
Co-stars: Bert Wheeler Robert Woolsey Ruth Etting

1934 COCKEYED CAVALIERS
Director: Mark Sandrich
Co-stars: Bert Wheeler Robert Woolsey Thelma Todd

1935 THE RAINMAKERS
Director: Fred Guiol
Co-stars: Bert Wheeler Robert Woolsey George Meeker

ETTA LEE

1924 THE THIEF OF BAGDAD
Director: Raoul Walsh
Co-stars: Douglas Fairbanks Anna May Wong Snitz Edwards

FLORENCE LEE

1931 CITY LIGHTS
Director: Charles Chaplin
Co-stars: Charles Chaplin Virginia Cherrill Harry Myers

GWENN LEE

1931 TRAVELLING HUSBANDS
Co-stars: Constance Cummings Frank McHugh Dorothy Peterson

GYPSY ROSE LEE *(Louise Hovick)*
(Sister Of June Havoc)

1937 YOU CAN'T HAVE EVERYTHING
Director: Norman Taurog
Co-stars: Alice Faye Tony Martin Don Ameche

1937 ALI BABA GOES TO TOWN
Director: David Butler
Co-stars: Eddie Cantor Tony Martin Roland Young

1938 MY LUCKY STAR
Director: Roy Del Ruth
Co-stars: Sonja Henie Richard Greene Cesar Romero Buddy Ebsen

1938 SALLY, IRENE AND MARY
Director: William Seiter
Co-stars: Alice Faye Joan Davis Tony Martin

1938 BATTLE OF BROADWAY
Director: George Marshall
Co-stars: Victor McLaglen Brian Donlevy Lynn Bari

1943   **STAGE DOOR CANTEEN**
Director: Frank Borzage
Co-stars: Cheryl Walker Lon McCallister Judith Anderson

1945   **BELLE OF THE YUKON**
Director: William Seiter
Co-stars: Randolph Scott Dianh Shore Charles Winninger

1952   **BABES IN BAGDAD**
Director: Edgar Ulmer
Co-stars: Paulette Goddard Richard Ney John Boles

1958   **THE SCREAMING MIMI**
Director: Gerd Oswald
Co-stars: Anita Ekberg Phil Carey Harry Townes

1958   **WIND ACROSS THE EVERGLADES**
Director: Nicholas Ray
Co-stars: Burl Ives Christopher Plummer Peter Falk

1963   **THE STRIPPER**
Director: Franklin Schaffner
Co-stars: Joanne Woodward Richard Beymer Carol Lynley

1966   **THE TROUBLE WITH ANGELS**
Director: Ida Lupino
Co-stars: Rosalind Russell Hayley Mills Binnie Barnes

JANIS LEE

1994   **INTIMATE WITH A STRANGER**
Director: Mel Woods
Co-stars: Roderick Mangin-Turner Daphne Nayar

JENNIFER LEE

1974   **ACT OF VENGEANCE**
Director: Bob Kelljan
Co-stars: Jo Ann Harris Peter Brown Steve Kanaly

1994   **THE DUCHESS AND THE DIRTWATER FOX**
Director: Melvyn Frank
Co-stars: Goldie Hawn George Segal

JOANNA LEE

1958   **THE BRAIN EATERS**
Director: Bruno De Sota
Co-stars: Jody Fair Leonard Nimoy Alan Frost

JOIE LEE *(Sister Of Spike Lee)*

1990   **MO'BETTER BLUES**
Director: Spike Lee
Co-Stars   Spike Lee Wesley Snipes Denzel Washington

JONNA LEE

1988   **SHATTERED INNOCENCE**
Director: Sandor Stern
Co-stars: John Pleshette Melinda Dillon Ben Frank

KAAREN LEE

1984   **ROADHOUSE 66**
Director: John Mark Robinson
Co-stars: Willem Dafoe Judge Reinhold Kate Vernon

1985   **ST. ELMO'S FIRE**
Director: Joel Schumacher
Co-stars: Demi Moore Rob Lowe Emilio Estevez

KAIULANI LEE

1983   **CUJO**
Director: Lewis Teague
Co-stars: Dee Wallace Ed Lauter Dany Pintauro

LAURA LEE

1931   **GOING WILD**
Co-stars: Joe E. Brown Frank McHugh Ona Munson

LILA LEE

1919   **MALE AND FEMALE**
Director: Cecil B. DeMille
Co-stars: Gloria Swanson Bebe Daniels Thomas Meighan

1922   **BLOOD AND SAND**
Director: Fred Niblo
Co-stars: Rudolph Valentino Nita Naldi George Field

1923   **HOLLYWOOD**
Director: James Cruze
Co-stars: Hope Drown Luke Cosgrave Eleanor Lawson

1929   **HONKY TONK**
Director: Lloyd Bacon
Co-stars: Sophie Tucker Audrey Ferris George Duyrea

1929   **FLIGHT**
Director: Frank Capra
Co-stars: Jack Holt Ralph Graves Alan Roscoe

1929   **SHOW OF SHOWS**
Director: John Adolphi
Co-stars: Frank Fay Lupino Lane Douglas Fairbanks Jnr.

1929   **THE ARGYLE CASE**
Co-stars: Thomas Meighan H. B. Warner Gladys Brockwell

1930   **THE UNHOLY THREE**
Director: Jack Conway
Co-stars: Lon Chaney Elliott Nugent John Miljan

1932   **THE NIGHT OF JUNE 13TH.**
Director: Stephen Roberts
Co-stars: Clive Brook Gene Raymond Frances Dee

1932   **RADIO PATROL**
Co-stars: Robert Armstrong June Clyde Andy Devine

1933   **FACE IN THE SKY**
Director: Harry Lachman
Co-stars: Spencer Tracy Marian Nixon Stuart Erwin

1934   **STAND UP AND CHEER**
Director: Hamilton McFadden
Co-stars: Warner Baxter Madge Evans Shirley Temple

1934   **WHIRLPOOL**
Director: Roy William Neill
Co-stars: Jack Holt Jean Arthur Allen Jenkins

1934   **I CAN'T ESCAPE**
Co-stars: Onslow Stevens Russell Gleason

1936   **THE EX-MRS. BRADFORD**
Director: Stephen Roberts
Co-stars: William Powell Jean Arthur James Gleason

1936   **COUNTRY GENTLEMEN**
Director: Ralph Staub
Co-stars: Ole Olsen Chic Johnson Joyce Compton

LISA LEE

1951   **LADY GODIVA RIDES AGIN**
Director: Frank Launder
Co-stars: Pauline Stroud Dennis Price Diana Dors

LOIS LEE

1922   **THE PRISONER OF ZENDA**
Director: Rex Ingram
Co-stars: Lewis Stone Alice Terry Stuart Holmes

MARGARET LEE

1965   **FIVE GOLDEN DRAGONS**
Director: Jeremy Summers
Co-stars: Robert Cummings Rupert Davies Klaus Kinski

1967   **CIRCUS OF FEAR**
Director: John Moxey
Co-stars: Christopher Lee Leo Genn Klaus Kinski

MARGO LEE

1982 STARSTUCK
Director: Gillian Armstrong
Co-stars: Jo Kennedy Pat Evison Max Cullen

MARY LEE

1939 SOUTH OF THE BORDER
Director: George Sherman
Co-stars: Gene Autry Smiley Burnette Duncan Renaldo

MICHELE LEE

1967 HOW TO SUCCEED IN BUSINESS WITHOUT REALLY TRYING
Director: David Swift
Co-stars: Robert Morse Rudy Vallee

1968 THE LOVE BUG
Director: Rodert Stevenson
Co-stars: David Tomlinson Dean Jones Joe Flynn

1969 THE COMIC
Director: Carl Reiner
Co-stars: Dick Van Dyke Mickey Rooney Cornel Wilde

1983 A LETTER TO THREE WIVES
Director: Larry Elikann
Co-stars: Loni Anderson Stephanie Zimbalist Charles Frank

1989 SINGLE WOMEN, MARRIED MEN
Director: Nick Havinga
Co-Stars: Lee Horsley

1990 THE FATAL IMAGE
Director: Thomas Wright
Co-stars: Justine Bateman Francois Dunoyer

1992 BROADWAY BOUND
Director: Paul Bogart
Co-stars: Corey Parker Anne Bancroft Hume Cronyn

1993 BIG DREAMS AND BROKEN HEARTS: THE DOTTY WEST STORY
Director: Bill D'Elia
Co-stars: Kenny Rogers Larry Gatlin

NANCY LEE

1959 TEN SECONDS TO HELL
Director: Robert Aldrich
Co-stars: Jack Palance Jeff Chandler Martine Carol

PEGGY LEE

Nominated For Best Supporting Actress In 1956 For "Pete Kelly's Blues"

1950 MR. MUSIC
Director: Richard Haydn
Co-stars: Bing Crosby Nancy Olson Charles Coburn

1953 THE JAZZ SINGER
Director: Michael Curtiz
Co-stars: Danny Thomas Mildred Dunnock Eduard Franz

1955 ABBOTT & COSTELLO MEET THE MUMMY
Director: Charles Lamont
Co-stars: Bud Abbott Lou Costello Marie Windsor

1955 LADY AND THE TRAMP *(Voice)*
Director: Clyde Geronimi
Co-stars: Barbara Luddy Stan Freburg

1956 PETE KELLY'S BLUES
Director: Jack Webb
Co-stars: Jack Webb Edmond O'Brien Janet Leigh Lee Marvin

PINKY LEE

1945 EARL CARROLL VANITIES
Director: Joseph Santley
Co-stars: Constance Moore Dennis O'Keefe Eve Arden

RENATA LEE

1988 ARIZONA HEAT
Director: John Thomas
Co-stars: Michael Parks Denise Crosby Hugh Farrington

RUTA LEE

1954 SEVEN BRIDES FOR SEVEN BROTHERS
Director: Stanley Donen
Co-stars: Jane Powell Howard Keel Russ Tamblyn

1956 GABY
Director: Curtis Bernhardt
Co-stars: Leslie Caron John Kerr Taina Elg

1957 FUNNY FACE
Director: Stanley Donen
Co-stars: Fred Astaire Audrey Hepburn Kay Thompson

1959 ESCAPE FROM PLANET EARTH

1961 SERGEANTS THREE
Director: John Sturges
Co-stars: Frank Sinatra Dean Martin Peter Lawford

1961 OPERATION EICHMAN
Director: R. G. Springsteen
Co-stars: Werner Klemperer Donald Buka John Banner

1964 BULLET FOR A MADMAN
Director: R. G. Springsteen
Co-stars: Audie Murphy Darren McGavin George Tobias

1989 SWEET BIRD OF YOUTH
Director: Nicolas Roeg
Co-stars: Elizabeth Taylor Mark Harmon Rip Torn

1995 FUNNY BONES
Director: Peter Chiselm
Co-stars: Lee Evans Jerry Lewis Leslie Caron

RUTH LEE

1950 WHIRLPOOL
Director: Otto Preminger
Co-stars: Gene Tierney Jose Ferrer Richard Conte

SHERYL LEE

1992 TWIN PEAKS: FIRE WALK WITH ME
Director: David Lynch
Co-stars: Ray Wise Madchen Amick David Bowie

1992 JERSEY GIRL
Director: David Burton Morris
Co-stars: Jami Gertz Joseph Bologna Dylan McDermott

1994 BACKBEAT
Director: Iain Softly
Co-stars: Stephen Dorff Ian Hart Chris O'Neill

1995 FOLLOW THE RIVER
Director: Martin Davidson

VIRGINIA LEE

1948 PAROLE, INC.
Director: Alfred Zeisler
Co-stars: Michael O'Shea Turhan Bey Evelyn Ankers

DEBORRA LEE-FURNESS

1990 WAITING
Director: Jackie McKimmie
Co-stars: Noni Hazelhurst Helen Jones Fiona Press

1991 VOYAGER
Director: Volker Schlondoff
Co-stars: Sam Shepard Julie Delpy Barbara Sukowa

ANDREA LEEDS
Nominated For Best Supporting Actress in 1937 For "Stage Door"

1936   COME AND GET IT
Director: William Wyler
Co-stars: Edward Arnold Joel McCrea Frances Farmer

1937   STAGE DOOR
Director: Gregory La Cava
Co-stars: Katharine Hepburn Ginger Rogers Lucille Ball

1938   YOUTH TAKES A FLING
Director: Archie Mayo
Co-stars: Joel McCrea Isabel Jeans Virginia Grey

1938   LETTER OF INTRODUCTION
Director: John Stahl
Co-stars: Adolphe Menjou George Murphy Eve Arden

1938   THE GOLDWYN FOLLIES
Director: George Marshall
Co-stars: Kenny Baker Vera Zorina Adolphe Menjou

1939   THE REAL GLORY
Director: Henry Hathaway
Co-stars: Gary Cooper David Niven Broderick Crawford

1939   SWANEE RIVER
Director: Sidney Lanfield
Co-stars: Don Ameche Al Jolson Russell Hicks

1939   THEY SHALL HAVE MUSIC
Director: Archie Mayo
Co-stars: Joel McCrea Walter Brennan Gene Reynolds

1940   EARTHBOUND
Co-star: Warner Baxter

ELISSA LEEDS

1981   EARTHBOUND
Director: James Conway
Co-stars: Burl Ives Christopher Connelly Joseph Campanella

MARCIE LEEDS *(Child)*

1987   NEAR DARK
Director: Kathryn Bigelow
Co-Stars   Adrian Pasdar Jenny Wright Bill Paxton

1988   BEACHES
Director: Garry Marshall
Co-stars: Bette Midler Barbara Hershey John Heard

THELMA LEEDS

1937   THE TOAST OF NEW YORK
Director: Rowland Lee
Co-stars: Edward Arnold Cary Grant Frances Farmer

JANE LEEVES

1996   JAMES AND THE GIANT PEACH *(Voice)*
Director: Henry Selig
Co-stars: Paul Terry Joanna Lumley Miriam Margoyles

KIT LE FEVER

1984   GRACE QUIGLEY
Director: Anthony Harvey
Co-stars: Katherine Hepburn Nick Nolte Walter Abel

LAUREL LEFKOW

1992   SMALL METAL JACKET
Director: Steve Hilliker
Co-stars: Debora Weston Marie Theodore Jana Shelden

CANDICE LEFRANC

1991   C'EST LA VIE
Director: Diane Kurys
Co-stars: Nathalie Baye Julie Bataille Richard Berry

EVA LE GALLIENNE
Nominated For Best Supporting Actress In 1981 For "Resurrection"

1955   PRINCE OF PLAYERS
Director: Philip Dunne
Co-stars: Richard Burton Maggie McNamara John Derek

1959   THE DEVIL'S DISCIPLE
Director: Guy Hamilton
Co-stars: Burt Lancaster Kirk Douglas Laurence Olivier

1981   RESURRECTION
Director: Daniel Petrie
Co-stars: Ellen Burstyn Sam Shepard Richard Farnsworth

PHOEBE LEGERE

1989   THE TOXIC AVENGER PART II
Director: Michael Hertz
Co-stars: Ron Fazio John Altamura Lisa Gaye

**1989   THE TOXIC AVENGER PART III:
THE LAST TEMPTATION OF TOXIE**
Director: Michael Hertz
Co-stars: Ron Fazio John Altamura Lisa Gaye

ALISON LEGGATT

1944   THIS HAPPY BREED
Director: David Lean
Co-stars: Robert Newton Celia Johnson John Mills

1945   WATERLOO ROAD
Director: Sidney Gilliat
Co-stars: John Mills Stewart Granger Joy Shelton

1947   A BOY, A GIRL AND A BIKE
Director: Ralph Smart
Co-stars: Honor Blackman John McCallum Diana Dors

1955   TOUCH AND GO
Director: Michael Truman
Co-stars: Jack Hawkins Margaret Johnston June Thorburn

1960   NEVER TAKE SWEETS FROM A STRANGER
Director: Cyril Frankel
Co-stars: Gwen Watford Felix Aylmer

1962   THE DAY OF THE TRIFFIDS
Director: Steve Sekely
Co-Stars   Howard Keel Janette Scott Kieron Moore

1964   ONE WAY PENDULUM
Director: Peter Yates
Co-stars: Eric Sykes George Cole Julia Foster

1967   FAR FROM THE MADDING CROWD
Director: John Schlesinger
Co-Stars   Julie Christie Peter Finch Alan Bates

1969   GOODBYE MR. CHIPS
Director: Herbert Ross
Co-stars: Peter O'Toole Petula Clark Michael Redgrave

DARLING LEGITIMUS

1983   RUE CASES NEGRES
Director: Euzhan Palcy
Co-stars: Garry Cadenat Douta Seck Joby Bernabe

BEATRIX LEHMAN

1935   THE PASSING OF THE THIRD FLOOR BACK
Director: Berthold Viertel
Co-stars: Conrad Veidt Rene Ray Anna Lee

1937   THE RAT
Director: Jack Raymond
Co-stars: Anton Walbrook Ruth Chatterton Rene Ray

1944   CANDLES AT NINE
Director: John Harlow
Co-stars: Jessie Matthews John Stuart Winifred Shotter

1964 PSYCHE 59
Director: Alexander Singer
Co-stars: Patricia Neal Curt Jurgens Samantha Eggar

1966 THE SPY WHO CAME IN FROM THE COLD
Director: Martin Ritt
Co-stars: Richard Burton Claire Bloom

1966 A FUNNY THING HAPPENED ON THE WAY TO THE FORUM
Director: Richard Lester
Co-stars: Zero Mostel Phil Silvers

1969 STAIRCASE
Director: Stanley Donen
Co-stars: Richard Burton Rex Harrison Avril Angers

1979 THE CAT AND THE CANARY
Director: Radley Metzger
Co-stars: Honor Blackman Edward Fox Wendy Hiller

CARLA LEHMAN

1939 SO THIS IS LONDON
Director: Thornton Freeland
Co-stars: Alfred Drayton Berton Churchill Fay Compton

1940 SAILORS THREE
Director: Walter Forde
Co-stars: Tommy Trinder Claude Hulbert Michael Wilding

1941 ONCE A CROOK
Director: Herbert Mason
Co-stars: Gordon Harker Sydney Howard Bernard Lee

1941 COTTAGE TO LET
Director: Anthony Asquith
Co-stars: Alastair Sim John Mills George Cole

1942 FLYING FORTRESS
Director: Walter Forde
Co-stars: Richard Greene Betty Stockfield Donald Stewart

1942 SECRET MISSION
Director: Harold French
Co-stars: Hugh Williams James Mason Michael Wilding

1942 TALK ABOUT JACQUELINE
Director: Harold French
Co-stars: Hugh Williams Joyce Howard Roland Culver

1943 CANDLELIGHT IN ALGERIA
Director: George King
Co-stars: James Mason Walter Rilla Raymond Lovell

1945 29, ACACIA AVENUE
Director: Henry Cass
Co-stars: Gordon Harker Betty Balfour Dinah Sheridan

1947 FAME IS THE SPUR
Director: Roy Boulting
Co-stars: Michael Redgrave Rosamund John Bernard Miles

LILLIAN LEHMAN

1972 TENAFLY
Director: Richard Colla
Co-stars: James McEachin Mel Ferrer Ed Nelson

1992 BODY OF EVIDENCE
Director: Uli Edil
Co-stars: Madonna Willem Dafoe Anne Archer

LOTTE LEHMAN

1948 THE BIG CITY
Director: Norman Taurog
Co-stars: Margaret O'Brien Robert Preston Danny Thomas

LYDIA LEI

1982 HAMMETT
Director: Wim Wenders
Co-stars: Frederic Forrest Marilu Henner Roy Kinnear

BARBARA LEICHNEROVA

1989 THE LAST OF THE GOOD OLD DAYS
Director: Jiri Menzel
Co-stars: Josef Abraham Marian Labuda

AIMEE LEIGH

1992 HELLRAISER III: HELL ON EARTH
Director: Anthony Hickox
Co-stars: Terry Farrell Doug Bradley Paula Marshall

BARBARA LEIGH

1972 JUNIOR BONNER
Director: Sam Peckinpah
Co-stars: Steve McQueen Robert Preston Ida Lupino

JANET LEIGH
(Married Tony Curtis Mother Of Jamie Lee Curtis)
Nominated For Best Supporting Actress In 1960 For "Psycho"

1947 THE ROMANCE OF ROSY RIDGE
Director: Roy Rowland
Co-stars: Van Johnson Thomas Mitchell Dean Stockwell

1948 IF WINTER COMES
Director: Victor Saville
Co-stars: Walter Pidgeon Deborah Kerr Angela Lansbury

1948 THE HILLS OF HOME
Director: Fred Wilcox
Co-stars: Edmund Gwenn Tom Drake Donald Crisp

1948 WORDS AND MUSIC
Director: Norman Taurog
Co-stars: Mickey Rooney Tom Drake Gene Kelly

1948 LITTLE WOMEN
Director: Mervyn LeRoy
Co-stars: June Allyson Elizabeth Taylor Peter Lawford

1949 THAT FORSYTE WOMAN
Director: Compton Bennett
Co-stars: Greer Garson Errol Flynn Robert Young

1950 THE RED DANUBE
Director: George Sidney
Co-stars: Walter Pidgeon Ethel Barrymore Angela Lansbury

1949 THE DOCTOR AND THE GIRL
Director: Curtis Bernhardt
Co-stars: Glenn Ford Gloria DeHaven Charles Coburn

1949 ACT OF VIOLENCE
Director: Fred Zinnemann
Co-stars: Van Heflin Robert Ryan Mary Astor

1949 HOLIDAY AFFAIR
Director: Don Hartman
Co-stars: Robert Mitchum Wendell Corey Esther Dale

1950 JET PILOT
Director: Josef Von Sternberg
Co-stars: John Wayne Jay C. Flippen Paul Fix

1951 TWO TICKETS TO BROADWAY
Director: James Kern
Co-stars: Eddie Bracken Gloria DeHaven Smith & Dale

1951 STRICTLY DISHONOURABLE
Director: Melvin Frank
Co-stars: Ezio Pinza Maria Palma Millard Mitchell

1952 IT'S A BIG COUNTRY
Director: Don Weis
Co-stars: Van Johnson Gene Kelly Ethel Barrymore

1952 FEARLESS FAGAN
Director: Stanley Donen
Co-stars: Carleton Carpenter Keenan Wynn Ellen Corby

1952   **CONFIDENTIALLY CONNIE**
Director: Edward Buzzell
Co-stars: Louis Calhern Van Johnson Walter Sleazak

1952   **ANGELS IN THE OUTFIELD**
Director: Clarence Brown
Co-stars: Paul Douglas Keenan Wynn Donna Corcoran

1952   **SCARAMOUCHE**
Director: George Sidney
Co-stars: Stewart Granger Mel Ferrer Eleanor Parker

1953   **WALKING MY BABY BACK HOME**
Director: Lloyd Bacon
Co-stars: Donald O'Connor Buddy Hackett Lori Nelson

1953   **THE NAKED SPUR**
Director: Anthony Mann
Co-stars: James Stewart Robert Ryan Ralph Meeker

1953   **HOUDINI**
Director: George Marshall
Co-stars: Tony Curtis Torin Thatcher Sig Ruman

1954   **LIVING IT UP**
Director: Norman Taurog
Co-stars: Martin & Lewis Edward Arnold Sheree North

1954   **PRINCE VALIANT**
Director: Henry Hathaway
Co-stars: Robert Wagner James Mason Debra Paget

1954   **ROGUE COP**
Director: Roy Rowland
Co-stars: Robert Taylor George Raft Anne Francis

1955   **MY SISTER EILEEN**
Director: Richard Quine
Co-stars: Bob Fosse Betty Garrett Jack Lemmon

1956   **PETE KELLY'S BLUES**
Director: Jack Webb
Co-stars: Jack Webb Lee Marvin Edmond O'Brien Ella Fitzgerald

1956   **SAFARI**
Director: Terence Young
Co-stars: Victor Mature John Justin Roland Culver

1958   **TOUCH OF EVIL**
Director: Orson Welles
Co-stars: Orson Welles Charlton Heston Akim Tamiroff

1958   **THE VIKINGS**
Director: Richard Fleischer
Co-stars: Kirk Douglas Tony Curtis Ernert Borgnine

1958   **THE PERFECT FURLOUGH**
Director: Blake Edwards
Co-stars: Tony Curtis Elaine Strich Troy Donahue

1960   **PSYCHO**
Director: Alfred Hitchcock
Co-stars: Anthony Perkins Vera Miles John Gavin

1960   **WHO WAS THAT LADY?**
Director: George Sidney
Co-stars: Tony Curtis Dean Martin James Whitmore

1962   **THE MANCHURIAN CANDIDATE**
Director: John Frankenheimer
Co-stars: Frank Sinatra Laurence Harvey Henry Silva

1963   **WIVES AND LOVERS**
Director: John Rich
Co-stars: Van Johnson Shelley Winters Martha Hyer

1966   **AN AMERICAN DREAM**
Director: Robert Gist
Co-stars: Stuart Whitman Eleanor Parker Lloyd Nolan

1966   **KID RODELLO**
Director: Richard Carlson
Co-stars: Richard Carlson Don Murray Broderick Crawford

1966   **THE MOVING TARGET**
Director: Jack Smight
Co-stars: Paul Newman Lauren Bacall Shelley Winters

1966   **THE SPY IN THE GREEN HAT**
Director: Joseph Sargent
Co-stars: Robert Vaughn David McCallum Jack Palance

1966   **THREE ON A COUCH**
Director: Jerry Lewis
Co-stars: Jerry Lewis James Best Mary Ann Mobley Leslie Parrish

1967   **GRAND SLAM**
Director: Guilliano Montaldo
Co-stars: Edward G. Robinson Klaus Kinski

1969   **HELLO DOWN THERE**
Director: Jack Arnold
Co-stars: Tony Randall Jim Backus Roddy McDowall

1972   **NIGHT OF THE LEPUS**
Director: William Claxton
Co-stars: Stuart Whitman Rory Calhoun Paul Fix

1972   **ONE IS A LONELY NUMBER**
Director: Mel Stuart
Co-stars: Trish Van Devere Monte Markham Melvyn Douglas

1977   **MURDER AT THE WORLD SERIES**
Director: Andrew McLaglen
Co-stars: Murray Hamilton Lynda Day George

1979   **BOARDWALK**
Director: Stephen Verona
Co-stars: Ruth Gordon Lee Strasberg Joe Silver

1980   **THE FOG**
Director: John Carpenter
Co-stars: Adrienne Barbeau Hal Holbrook Jamie Lee Curtis

JENNIFER JASON LEIGH
(Daughter Of Vic Morrow) (Jennifer Leigh Morrow)

1980   **ANGEL CITY**
Director: Philip Leacock
Co-stars: Ralph White Paul Winfield Jennifer Warren

1981   **THE KILLING OF RANDY WEBSTER**
Director: Sam Wanamaker
Co-stars: Hal Holbrook James Whitmore Sean Penn

1982   **FAST TIMES AT RIDGEMONT HIGH**
Director: Amy Heckerling
Co-stars: Sean Penn Judge Reinhold Ray Walston

1983   **EASY MONEY**
Director: James Signorelli
Co-stars: Rodney Dangerfield Geraldine Fitzgerald

1983   **DEATH RIDE TO OSAKA**
Director: Jonathan Kaplan
Co-stars: Ann Jillian Carolyn Seymour Mako

1985   **FLESH AND BLOOD**
Director: Paul Verhoeven
Co-stars: Ruter Hauer Jack Thompson Ronald Lacey

1987   **UNDER COVER**
Director: John Stockwell
Co-stars: David Neidorf Barry Corbin Kathleen Wilhoite

1988   **HEART OF MIDNIGHT**
Director: Matthew Chapman
Co-stars: Peter Coyote Gale Mayron Sam Schacht

1988   **THE BIG PICTURE**
Director: Christopher Guest
Co-stars: Kevin Bacon Teri Hatcher John Cleese

1989   **THE LAST EXIT TO BROOKLYN**
Director: Uli Edel
Co-stars: Stephen Lang Burt Young Peter Dobson

1990   MIAMI BLUES
Director: George Armitage
Co-stars: Fred Ward Alec Baldwin Edward Saxon

1991   CROOKED HEARTS
Director: Michael Bortman
Co-stars: Peter Coyote Vincent D'Onofrio Cindy Pickett

1991   BACKDRAFT
Director: Ron Howard
Co-stars: Kurt Russell Rebecca DeMornay Robert De Niro

1992   RUSH
Director: Lili Fini Zanuck
Co-stars: Jason Patric Sam Elliott Max Perlich

1992   SINGLE WHITE FEMALE
Director: Barbet Schroeder
Co-stars: Bridget Fonda Steven Weber Frances Bay

1993   SHORT CUTS
Director: Robert Altman
Co-stars: Anne Archer Andie MacDowell Frances McDormand

1994   MRS. PARKER AND THE VICIOUS CIRCLE
Director: Alan Rudolph
Co-stars: Matthew Broderick Campbell Scott

1994   THE HUDSUCKER PROXY
Director: Joel Coen
Co-stars: Tim Robbins Paul Newman Charles Durning

1995   DOLORES CLAIBORNE
Director: Taylor Hackford
Co-star: Kathy Bates Christopher Plummer

1996   A THOUSAND ACRES
Director: Jocelyn Moorhouse
Co-stars: Michelle Pfeiffer Jessica Lange Jason Robards

1996   WASHINGTON SQUARE
Director: Agnieska Holland
Co-star: Ben Chaplin Albert Finney Maggie Smith

1996   KANSAS CITY
Director: Robert Altman
Co-stars: Miranda Richardson Dermot Mulroney Harry Belafonte

SUZANNA LEIGH

1965   BOEING BOEING
Director: John Rich
Co-stars: Tony Curtis Jerry Lewis Thelma Ritter

1965   THE PLEASURE GIRLS
Director: Gerry O'Hara
Co-stars: Ian McShane Francesca Annis Tony Tanner

1965   PARADISE HAWAIIAN STYLE
Director: Michael Moore
Co-stars: Elvis Presley James Sigeta Irene Tsu

1966   THE DEADLY BEES
Director: Freddie Francis
Co-stars: Frank Finlay Guy Doleman Catherine Finn

1967   DEADLIER THAN THE MALE
Director: Ralph Thomas
Co-stars: Richard Johnson Elke Sommer Sylva Koscina

1968   THE LOST CONTINENT
Director: Michael Carreras
Co-stars: Eric Porter Hildgegard Neff Nigel Stock

1970   LUST FOR A VAMPIRE
Director: Jimmy Sangster
Co-stars: Ralph Bates Barbara Jefford Michael Johnson

VIVIEN LEIGH *(Married Laurence Olivier)*
Oscar For Best Actress In 1939 For "Gone With The Wind"
And In 1951 For "A Streetcar Named Desire"

1935   THINGS ARE LOOKING UP
Director: Albert De Courville
Co-stars: Cicely Courtnedge William Gargan Max Miller

1935   LOOK UP AND LAUGH
Director: Basil Dean
Co-stars: Gracie Fields Duggie Wakefield Harry Tate

1937   FIRE OVER ENGLAND
Director: William Howard
Co-stars: Flora Robson Raymond Massey Laurence Olivier

1937   DARK JOURNEY
Director: Victor Saville
Co-stars: Conrad Veidt Joan Gardner Ursula Jeans

1937   STORM IN A TEACUP
Director: Victor Saville
Co-stars: Rex Harrison Cecil Parker Sara Allgood

1938   A YANK AT OXFORD
Director: Jack Conway
Co-stars: Robert Taylor Maureen O'Sullivan Edmund Gwenn

1937   21 DAYS
Director: Basil Dean
Co-stars: Laurence Olivier Leslie Banks Hay Petrie

1938   ST. MARTIN'S LANE
Director: Tim Whelan
Co-stars: Charles Laughton Rex Harrison Larry Adler

1939   GONE WITH THE WIND
Director: Victor Fleming
Co-stars: Clark Gable Leslie Howard Thomas Mitchell

1940   WATERLOO BRIDGE
Director: Mervyn LeRoy
Co-stars: Robert Taylor Lucile Watson C. Aubrey Smith

1941   THAT HAMILTON WOMAN
Director: Alexander Korda
Co-stars: Laurence Olivier Gladys Cooper

1945   CAESAR AND CLEOPATRA
Director: Gabriel Pascal
Co-stars: Claude Rains Stewart Granger Flora Robson

1947   ANNA KARENINA
Director: Julien Duvivier
Co-stars: Kieron Moore Ralph Richardson

1951   A STREETCAR NAMED DESIRE
Director: Elia Kazan
Co-stars: Marlon Brando Kim Hunter Karl Malden

1955   THE DEEP BLUE SEA
Director: Anatole Litvak
Co-stars: Kenneth More Emlyn Williams Eric Portman

1961   THE ROMAN SPRING OF MRS. STONE
Director: Jose Quintro
Co-stars: Warren Beatty Lotte Lenya

1965   SHIP OF FOOLS
Director: Stanley Kramer
Co-stars: Simone Signoret Jose Ferrer Lee Marvin

BARBARA LEIGH-HUNT

1970   THE SIX WIVES OF HENRY VIII
Director: John Glenister
Co-stars: Keith Michell Annette Crosbie Elvi Hale

1972   HENRY VIII AND HIS SIX WIVES
Director: Waris Hussein
Co-stars: Keith Michell Frances Cuka Jane Asher

1972   FRENZY
Director: Alfred Hitchcock
Co-stars: Jon Finch Barry Foster Anna Massey

1982   THE PLAGUE DOGS *(Voice)*
Director: Martin Rosen
Co-stars: John Hurt James Bolam Judy Geeson

1988   **TUMBLEDOWN**
Director: Richard Eyre
Co-stars: Colin Firth David Calder Paul Rhys

1990   **PAPER MASK**
Director: Christopher Morahan
Co-stars: Paul McGann Amanda Donohue Tom Wilkinson

1990   **INSPECTOR WEXFORD: THE BEST MAN TO DIE**
Director: Herbert Wise
Co-stars: George Baker Julia Ormond

1990   **INSPECTOR MORSE:
THE INFERNAL SERPENT**
Director: John Madden
Co-stars: John Thaw Geoffrey Palmer

1993   **ANNA LEE: HEADCASE**
Director: Colin Bucksey
Co-stars: Imogen Stubbs Brian Glover Alan Howard

KATHRYN LEIGH-SCOTT

1977   **PROVIDENCE**
Director: Alain Resnais
Co-stars: John Gielgud Dirk Bogarde Ellen Burstyn

1989   **VOICE OF THE HEART**
Director: Tony Wharmby
Co-stars: Lindsay Wagner Victoria Tennant James Brolin

LAURA LEIGHTON

1994   **THE OTHER WOMAN**
Director: Gabrielle Beaumont

MARGARET LEIGHTON
Nominated For Best Supporting Actress In 1970 For "The Go-Between"

1948   **THE WINSLOW BOY**
Director: Anthony Asquith
Co-stars: Robert Donat Cedric Hardwicke Basil Radford

1948   **BONNIE PRINCE CHARLIE**
Director: Anthony Kimmins
Co-stars: David Niven Jack Hawkins Finlay Currie

1949   **THE ASTONISHED HEART**
Director: Terence Fisher
Co-stars: Noel Coward Celia Johnson Joyce Carey

1949   **UNDER CAPRICORN**
Director: Alfred Hitchcock
Co-stars: Ingrid Bergman Joseph Cotten Cecil Parker

1950   **THE ELUSIVE PIMPERNEL**
Director: Michael Powell
Co-stars: David Niven Jack Hawkins Robert Coote

1951   **CALLING BULLDOG DRUMMOND**
Director: Victor Saville
Co-stars: Walter Pidgeon David Tomlinson Robert Beatty

1952   **HOME AT SEVEN**
Director: Ralph Richardson
Co-stars: Ralph Richardson Jack Hawkins Campbell Singer

1952   **THE HOLLY AND THE IVY**
Director: George More O'Ferrall
Co-stars: Ralph Richardson Celia Johnson

1954   **THE GOOD DIE YOUNG**
Director: Lewis Gilbert
Co-stars: Laurence Harvey Gloria Grahame Joan Collins

1954   **CARRINGTON V. C.**
Director: Anthony Asquith
Co-stars: David Niven Noelle Middleton Raymond Francis

1954   **THE TECKMAN MYSTERY**
Director: Wendy Toye
Co-stars: John Justin Michael Medwin Roland Culver

1955   **THE CONSTANT HUSBAND**
Director: Sidney Gilliatt
Co-stars: Rex Harrison Kay Kendall Nicole Maurey

1956   **THE PASSIONATE STRANGER**
Director: Muriel Box
Co-stars: Ralph Richardson Carlo Justini Patricia Dainton

1959   **THE SOUND AND THE FURY**
Director: Martin Ritt
Co-stars: Yul Brynner Joanne Woodward Stuart Whitman

1962   **WALTZ OF THE TOREADORS**
Director: John Guillermin
Co-stars: Peter Sellers Dany Robin Cyril Cusack

1964   **THE BEST MAN**
Director: Franklin Schaffner
Co-stars: Henry Fonda Cliff Robertson Ann Sothern

1965   **THE LOVED ONE**
Director: Tony Richardson
Co-stars: Robert Morse John Gielgud Rod Steiger

1966   **SEVEN WOMAN**
Director: John Ford
Co-stars: Anne Bancroft Flora Robson Sue Lyon Anna Lee

1969   **THE MADWOMAN OF CHAILLOT**
Director: Bryan Forbes
Co-stars: Katharine Hepburn Yul Brynner Danny Kaye

1970   **THE GO-BETWEEN**
Director: Joseph Losey
Co-stars: Alan Bates Julie Christie Michael Redgrave

1971   **ZEE AND CO.**
Director: Brian Hutton
Co-stars: Elizabeth Taylor Michael Caine Suzannah York

1972   **LADY CAROLINE LAMB**
Director: Robert Bolt
Co-stars: Sarah Miles Richard Chamberlain Jon Finch

1973   **FROM BEYOND THE GRAVE**
Director: Kevin Connor
Co-stars: Peter Cushing David Warner Diana Dors

1973   **BEQUEST TO THE NATION**
Director: James Cellan Jones
Co-stars: Glenda Jackson Peter Finch Anthony Quale

1974   **GREAT EXPECTATIONS**
Director: Joseph Hardy
Co-stars: Michael York Sarah Miles James Mason Anthony Quale

1976   **TRIAL BY COMBAT**
Director: Kevin Connor
Co-stars: John Mills Barbara Hershey Peter Cushing

VIRGINIA LEITH

1953   **FEAR AND DESIRE**
Director: Stanley Kubrick
Co-stars: Frank Silvera Paul Mazursky Kenneth Harp

1954   **BLACK WIDOW**
Director: Nunnally Johnson
Co-stars: Ginger Rogers Van Heflin Gene Tierney

1955   **WHITE FEATHER**
Director: Robert Webb
Co-stars: Robert Wagner Debra Paget Jeffrey Hunter

1955   **VIOLENT SATURDAY**
Director: Richard Fleischer
Co-stars: Richard Egan Victor Mature Sylvia Sidney

1956   **TOWARD THE UNKNOWN**
Director: Mervyn LeRoy
Co-stars: William Holden Lloyd Nolan James Garner

1956 **ON THE THRESHOLD OF SPACE**
Director: Robert Webb
Co-stars: Guy Madison John Hodiak Dean Jagger

1956 **A KISS BEFORE DYING**
Director: Gerd Oswald
Co-stars: Robert Wagner Jeffrey Hunter Joanne Woodward

FIONA LEKLAND

1963 **IT HAPPENED HERE**
Director: Andrew Mollo
Co-stars: Sebastian Shaw Pauline Murray Honor Fehrson

SALOME LeLOUCHE

1996 **LES MISERABLES**
Director: Claude Lelouche
Co-stars: Jean-Paul Belmondo Michel Boujenais

VALERIE LEMERCIER

1993 **LES VISITEURS**
Director: Jean-Marc Poire
Co-stars: Jean Reno Christian Clavier Marie-Anne Chazel

KASI LEMMONS

1988 **VAMPIRE'S KISS**
Director: Robert Bierman
Co-stars: Nicolas Cage Jennifer Beals Elizabeth Ashley

1990 **THE COURT-MARTIAL OF JACKIE ROBINSON**
Director: Larry Peerce
Co-Stars Andre Brauger Ruby Dee Bruce Dern

1991 **THE SILENCE OF THE LAMBS**
Director: Jonathan Demme
Co-Stars Jody Foster Anthony Hopkins Scott Glenn

1992 **FEAR OF A BLACK HAT**
Director: Rusty Cundieff
Co-stars: Rusty Cundieff Larry B. Scott Mark Christopher

1993 **HARD TARGET**
Director: John Woo
Co-stars: Jean-Claude Van Damme Yancy Butler Lance Henriksen

LISA LEMOLE

1976 **DRIVE-IN**
Director: Rod Amateau
Co-stars: Glen Morshower Gary Cavagnaro Billy Milliken

GENEVIEVE LEMON

1989 **SWEETIE**
Director: Jane Campion
Co-stars: Karen Colston Tom Lycos Dorothy Barry

1993 **THE PIANO**
Director: Jane Campion
Co-stars: Holly Hunter Sam Neill Harvey Keitel Anna Paquin

PRALINE LE MOULT

1988 **LA VIE EST UN LONG FLEUVE TRANQUILLE**
Director: Etienne Chatilliez
Co-stars: Benott Magimel Valerie Lalande

ULLA LEMVIGH-MULLER

1970 **QUIET DAYS IN CLICHY**
Director: Jens-Jorgen Thorsen
Co-stars: Louise White Paul Valjean Susanne Krage

NANCY LENEHAN

1986 **ASSASSIN**
Director: Sandor Stern
Co-stars: Robert Conrad Karen Austin Robert Webber

1988 **ROCK 'N' ROLL MOM**
Director: Michael Schultz
Co-stars: Dyan Cannon Michael Brandon Heather Locklear

1992 **OUT ON A LIMB**
Director: Francis Veba
Co-stars: Matthew Broderick Jeffrey Jones

CHRISTINE LENIER

1965 **LA RELIGIEUSE**
Director: Jacques Rivette
Co-stars: Anna Karina Liselotte Pulver Micheline Presle

SHIRLEY LENNER

1941 **THOSE KIDS FROM TOWN**
Director: Lance Comfort
Co-stars: Jeanne De Casalis Percy Marmont George Cole

DIANH LENNEY

1994 **BABYFEVER**
Director: Henry Jaglom
Co-stars: Victoria Foyt Matt Salinger Eric Roberts

ANNIE LENNOX

1986 **REVOLUTION**
Director: Hugh Hudson
Co-Stars Al Pacino Nastassja Kinski Donald Sutherland

ROSETTA LE NOIRE

1975 **THE SUNSHINE BOYS**
Director: Herbert Ross
Co-stars: Walter Matthau George Burns Richard Benjamin

1987 **THE FATHER CLEMENTS STORY**
Director: Ed Sherin
Co-stars: Lou Gossett Jnr. Carroll O'Connor

RULA LENSKA

1975 **ALFIE DARLING**
Director: Ken Hughes
Co-stars: Alan Price Jill Townsend Joan Collins

LOTTIE LENYA *(Married Bertold Brecht, Musician)*
Nominated For Best Supporting Actress In 1962 For "The Roman Spring of Mrs. Stone"

1931 **DIE DREIGROSCHENOPER**
Director: Don Weis
Co-stars: Rudolph Forster Vladimir Sokoloff Fritz Rasp

1961 **THE ROMAN SPRING OF MRS. STONE**
Director: Jose Quintero
Co-stars: Vivien Leigh Warren Beatty

1963 **FROM RUSSIA WITH LOVE**
Director: Terence Young
Co-stars: Sean Connery Robert Shaw Pedro Armendariz

1969 **THE APPOINTMENT**
Director: Sidney Lumet
Co-stars: Omar Sharif Anouk Aimee

1977 **SEMI-TOUGH**
Director: Michael Ritchie
Co-stars: Burt Reynolds Kris Kristofferson Robert Preston

DONA KEI LENZ

1982 **THE CHALLENGE**
Director: John Frankenheimer
Co-stars: Scott Glenn Toshiro Mifune Calvin Young

KAY LENZ

1968 **BREEZY**
Director: Clint Eastwood
Co-stars: William Holden Marj Dusay Joan Hotchkiss

1973 A SUMMER WITHOUT THE BOYS
Director: Jeannot Szwarc
Co-stars: Barbara Rush Michael Moriarty Mildred Dunnock

1974 THE FBI STORY: ALVIN KARPIS
Director: Martin Chomsky
Co-stars: Robert Foxworth David Wayne

1975 WHITE LINE FEVER
Director: Jonathan Kaplan
Co-stars: Jan-Michael Vincent Slim Pickins Don Porter

1976 MOVING VIOLATION
Director: Charles Dubin
Co-stars: Stephen McHattie Eddie Albert Lonnie Chapman

1976 THE GREAT SCOUT AND CATHOUSE THURSDAY
Director: Don Taylor
Co-stars: Lee Marvin Oliver Reed Robert Culp

1978 THE PASSAGE
Director: J. Lee Thompson
Co-stars: Anthony Quinn James Mason Patricia Neal

1978 THE INITIATION OF SARAH
Director: Robert Day
Co-stars: Shelley Winters Kathryn Crosby Tony Bill

1980 ESCAPE
Director: Robert Michael Lewis
Co-stars: Timothy Bottoms Colleen Dewhurst Antonio Fargas

1981 FAST WALKING
Director: James Harris
Co-stars: James Woods Tim McIntyre Robert Hooks

1986 HOUSE
Director: Steve Miner
Co-stars: William Katt George Wendt Richard Moll

1988 DEATH WISH 4: THE CRACKDOWN
Director: J. Lee Thompson
Co-stars: Charles Bronson Perry Lopez

1989 PHYSICAL EVIDENCE
Director: Michael Crighton
Co-stars: Burt Reynolds Theresa Russell Ned Beatty

1991 FALLING FROM GRACE
Director: John Mellencamp
Co-stars: John Mellencamp Mariel Hemingway Claude Akins Larry Crane

1994 TRAPPED IN SPACE
Director: Arthur Allan Seidelman
Co-Stars Jack Wagner Jack Coleman Sigrid Thornton

1994 AGAINST THEIR WILL
Director: Karen Arthur
Co-Stars Judith Light Stacy Keach Chelcie Ross

1996 SHAME II: THE SECRET
Director: Dan Lerner
Co-stars: Amanda Donohue Gregory Blake

MELISSA LEO

1985 ALWAYS
Director: Henry Jaglom
Co-stars: Henry Jaglom Patrice Townsend Allan Rachins

1988 A TIME OF DESTINY
Director: Gregory Nava
Co-stars: William Hurt Timothy Hutton Stockard Channing

1991 IMMACULATE CONCEPTION
Director: Jamil Dehlavi
Co-stars: James Wilby Tim Choate Shabana Azmi

1991 CAROLINA SKELETON
Director: John Erman
Co-Stars Lou Gossett Jnr. Bruce Dern

1992 VENICE/VENICE
Director: Henry Jaglom
Co-stars: Nelly Alard Suzanne Bertish David Duchovny

ANNE LEON

1952 APPOINTMENT IN LONDON
Director: Philip Leacock
Co-stars: Dirk Bogarde Dinah Sheridan Ian Hunter

1958 CARVE HER NAME WITH PRIDE
Director: Lewis Gilbert
Co-stars: Virginia McKenna Paul Scofield Bill Owen

1987 HOPE AND GLORY
Director: John Boorman
Co-stars: Sarah Miles Sammi Davies Ian Bannen

VALERIE LEON

1969 CARRY ON AGAIN DOCTOR
Director: Gerald Thomas
Co-stars: Sid James Jim Dale Barbara Windsor

1970 CARRY ON UP THE JUNGLE
Director: Gerald Thomas
Co-stars: Sid James Frankie Howerd Terry Scott

1971 BLOOD FROM THE MUMMY'S TOMB
Director: Seth Holt
Co-stars: Andrew Keir James Villiers Tamara Ustinov

1973 CARRY ON GIRLS
Director: Gerald Thomas
Co-stars: Sid James Joan Sims June Whitfield

1975 CONFESSIONS OF AN ODD-JOB MAN
Director: John Sealey
Co-stars: Barry Stokes Gary Soper Sue Lloyd

1983 NEVER SAY NEVER AGAIN
Director: Irving Kershner
Co-stars: Sean Connery Barbara Carrera Kim Basinger

BARBARA LEONARD

1932 THE CRASH
Director: William Dieterle
Co-stars: Ruth Chatterton George Brent Paul Cavanagh

1932 LOVE AFFAIR
Director: Thornton Freeland
Co-stars: Humphrey Bogart Dorothy MacKail Astrid Allwyn

JACQUELINE LEONARD

1991 A TIME TO DANCE
Director: Kevin Billington
Co-stars: Donald Pickup Dervla Kirwan Rosemary McHale

QUEENIE LEONARD

1942 EAGLE SQUADRON
Director: Arthur Lubin
Co-stars: Robert Stack Diana Barrymore Eddie Albert

1944 THE LODGER
Director: John Brahm
Co-stars: Laird Cregar Merle Oberon George Sanders

1945 AND THEN THERE WERE NONE
Director: Rene Clair
Co-stars: Walter Huston Barry Fitzgerald Roland Young

1947 THE LONE WOLF IN LONDON
Director: Leslie Goodwins
Co-stars: Gerald Moir Evelyn Ankers Eric Blore

1951 ALICE IN WONDERLAND *(Voice)*
Director: Clyde Geronimi
Co-stars: Kathryn Beaumont Richard Haydn Ed Winn

1952 THE NARROW MARGIN
Director: Richard Fleischer
Co-stars: Charles McGraw Marie Windsor Jacqueline White

TEA LEONI *(Married David Duchovny)*

1991 SWITCH
Director: Blake Edwards
Co-Stars Ellen Barkin Jimmy Smits JoBeth Williams

1994 THE COUNTERFEIT CONTESSA
Director: Ron Lagomarsino
Co-stars: David Beecroft D. W. Moffat

1995 BAD BOYS
Director: Michael Bay
Co-Stars Will Smith Martin Lawrence

1997 FLIRTING WITH DISASTER
Director: David Russell
Co-stars: Alan Alda Mary Tyler Moore Lily Tomlin

1998 DEEP IMPACT
Director: Mimi Leder
Co-Stars Robert Duvall Morgan Freeman Vanessa Redgrave

EUGENIE LEONTOVITCH

1940 FOUR SONS
Director: Archie Mayo
Co-stars: Don Ameche Alan Curtis Mary Beth Hughes

1941 THE MEN IN HER LIFE
Director: Gregory Ratoff
Co-stars: Loretta Young Conrad Veidt Dean Jagger

1952 THE WORLD IN HIS ARMS
Director: Raoul Walsh
Co-stars: Gregory Peck Ann Blyth Anthony Quinn

1952 ANYTHING CAN HAPPEN
Director: George Seaton
Co-stars: Jose Ferrer Kim Hunter Kurt Kaznar

1955 THE RAINS OF RANCHIPUR
Director: Jean Negulesco
Co-stars: Richard Burton Lana Turner Fred MacMurray

MONIQUE LEPAGE

1989 A PAPER WEDDING
Director: Michel Brault
Co-stars: Genevieve Bujold Manuel Aranguiz Dorothee Berryman

CATHERINE LEPRINCE

1985 ESCALIER C
Director: Jean-Charles Tacchella
Co-stars: Robin Renucci Jean-Pierre Bacri Jacques Weber

RITA LEROY

1932 AMATEUR DADDY
Director: John Blystone
Co-stars: Warner Baxter Marian Nixon William Pawley

1932 HOLLYWOOD SPEAKS
Director: Eddie Buzzell
Co-stars: Pat O'Brien Genevieve Tobin Claire Dodd

1937 FLIGHT FROM GLORY
Director: Lew Landers
Co-stars: Chester Morris Van Heflin Whitney Bourne

1937 THE MANDARIN MYSTERY
Director: Ralph Staub
Co-stars: Eddie Quillan Charlotte Henry George Irving

MAXIME LEROUX

1989 ROMUALD AND JULIETTE
Director: Coline Serreau
Co-stars: Daniel Auteuil Pierre Vernier

1990 MISTER FROST
Director: Phillipe Setbon
Co-stars: Jeff Goldblum Alan Bates Kathy Baker

CAROLE LESLEY

1957 THESE DANGEROUS YEARS
Director: Herbert Wilcox
Co-stars: Frankie Vaughan George Baker Jackie Lane

1957 WOMAN IN A DRESSING GOWN
Director: J. Lee-Thompson
Co-stars: Yvonne Mitchell Anthony Quale

1959 OPERATION BULLSHINE
Director: Gilbert Gunn
Co-stars: Donald Sinden Barbara Murray Ronald Shiner

1959 NO TREES IN THE STREET
Director: J. Lee-Thompson
Co-stars: Sylvia Syms Herbert Lom Melvyn Hayes

1962 THE POT CARRIERS
Director: Peter Graham Scott
Co-stars: Paul Massie Ronald Fraser Dennis Price

LORNA LESLEY

1982 THE SETTLEMENT
Director: Howard Rubie
Co-stars: Bill Kerr John Jarratt Tony Barry

AVRIL LESLIE

1958 6:5 SPECIAL
Director: Alfred Shaughnessy
Co-Stars Diane Todd Pete Murray Josephine Douglas

BETHEL LESLIE

1959 THE RABBIT TRAP
Director: Philip Leacock
Co-stars: Ernest Borgnine David Bryan June Blair

1963 CAPTAIN NEWMAN M. D.
Director: David Miller
Co-stars: Gregory Peck Tony Curtis Angie Dickinson

1965 A RAGE TO LIVE
Director: Walter Grauman
Co-stars: Suzanne Pleshette Bradford Dillman Ben Gazzara

1970 THE MOLLY MAGUIRES
Director: Martin Ritt
Co-stars: Sean Connery Richard Harris Samantha Eggar

1978 OLD BOYFRIENDS
Director: Joan Tewkesbury
Co-stars: Talia Shire Richard Jordan John Belushi

JEAN LESLIE

1969 THE PLOT AGAINST HARRY *(Released 1989)*
Director: Michael Roemer
Co-stars: Martin Priest Maxine Woods

JOAN LESLIE

1939 TWO THOROUGHBREDS
Co-star: James Lydon

1941 THE WAGONS ROLL AT NIGHT
Director: Ray Enright
Co-stars: Humphrey Bogart Sylvia Sidney Eddie Albert

1941 HIGH SIERRA
Director: Raoul Walsh
Co-stars: Humphrey Bogart Ida Lupino Arthur Kennedy

1941 SERGEANT YORK
Director: Howard Hawks
Co-stars: Gary Cooper Walter Brennan George Tobias

1941   **THIEVES FALL OUT**
Director: Ray Enright
Co-stars: Jane Darwell Eddie Albert Anthony Quinn

1942   **THE MALE ANIMAL**
Director: Elliott Nugent
Co-stars: Henry Fonda Olivia De Havilland Jack Carson

1942   **THE HARD WAY**
Director: Vincent Sherman
Co-stars: Ida Lupino Dennis Morgan Jack Carson

1942   **YANKEE DOODLE DANDY**
Director: Michael Curtiz
Co-stars: James Cagney Walter Huston S. Z. Sakall

1943   **THIS IS THE ARMY**
Director: Michael Curtiz
Co-stars: George Murphy Irving Berlin Ronald Reagan

1943   **THANK YOUR LUCKY STARS**
Director: David Butler
Co-stars: Eddie Cantor Dennis Morgan Errol Flynn

1943   **THE SKY'S THE LIMIT**
Director: Edward Griffith
Co-stars: Fred Astaire Robert Ryan Robert Benchley

1944   **HOLLYWOOD CANTEEN**
Director: Delmer Daves
Co-stars: Robert Hutton Bette Davis John Garfield

1945   **RHAPSODY IN BLUE**
Director: Irving Rapper
Co-stars: Robert Alda Alexis Smith Oscar Levant

1945   **WHERE DO WE GO FROM HERE?**
Director: Gregory Ratoff
Co-stars: Fred MacMurray June Haver Anthony Quinn

1945   **TOO YOUNG TO KNOW**
Co-stars: Robert Hutton Rosemary De Camp Arthur Shields

1946   **TWO GUYS FROM MILWAUKEE**
Director: David Butler
Co-stars: Dennis Morgan Jack Carson S. Z. Sakall

1946   **JANIE GETS MARRIED**
Director: Michael Curtiz
Co-stars: Robert Hutton Ann Harding Edward Arnold

1946   **CINDERELLA JONES**
Director: Busby Berkeley
Co-stars: Robert Alda Julie Bishop S. Z. Sakall

1947   **REPEAT PERFORMANCE**
Director: Alfred Werker
Co-stars: Louis Hayward Tom Conway Richard Basehart

1948   **NORTHWEST STAMPEDE**
Director: Albert Rogell
Co-stars: James Craig Jack Oakie

1951   **MAN IN THE SADDLE**
Director: Andre De Toth
Co-stars: Randolph Scott Ellen Drew Alexander Knox

1952   **HELLGATE**
Director: Charles Marquis Warren
Co-stars: Sterling Hayden Jim Arness

1952   **TOUGHEST MAN IN ARIZONA**
Director: R. G. Springsteen
Co-stars: Vaughan Monroe Jean Parker Victor Jory

1952   **THE WOMAN THEY ALMOST LYNCHED**
Director: Allan Dwan
Co-stars: Audrey Totter John Lund Brian Donlevy

1950   **BORN TO BE BAD**
Director: Nicholas Ray
Co-stars: Joan Fontaine Robert Ryan Zachary Scot

1953   **FLIGHT NURSE**
Director: Allan Dwan
Co-stars: Forrest Tucker Arthur Franz Jeff Donnell

1954   **JUBILEE TRAIL**
Director: Joseph Kane
Co-stars: Vera Ralston Forrest Tucker Pat O'Brien

1956   **THE REVOLT OF MAMIE STOVER**
Director: Raoul Walsh
Co-stars: Jane Russell Richard Egan Agnes Moorehead

1986   **CHARLEY HANNAH**
Director: Peter Hunt
Co-stars: Robert Conrad Shane Conrad Christian Conrad

NAN LESLIE

1947   **THE DEVIL THUMBS A RIDE**
Director: Felix Feist
Co-stars: Lawrence Tierney Ted North Betty Lawford

1947   **THE WOMAN ON THE BEACH**
Director: Jean Renoir
Co-stars: Joan Bennett Robert Ryan Charles Bickford

1948   **INDIAN AGENT**
Director: Lesley Selander
Co-stars: Tim Holt George Montgomery Noah Beery Jnr.

1948   **GUNS OF HATE**
Director: Lesley Selander
Co-stars: Tim Holt Richard Martin Steve Brodie

1948   **WESTERN HERITAGE**
Director: Lesley Selander
Co-stars: Tim Holt Richard Martin Jason Robards Snr.

KATE LESTER

1923   **THE HUNCHBACK OF NOTRE DAME**
Director: Wallace Worsley
Co-stars: Lon Chaney Patsy Ruth Miller

KATHY LESTER

1979   **PHANTASM**
Director: Don Coscarelli
Co-stars: Michael Baldwin Bill Thornberry Reggie Bannister

KETTY LESTER

1974   **UPTOWN SATURDAY NIGHT**
Director: Sidney Poitier
Co-stars: Sidney Poitier Bill Cosby Harry Belafonte Richard Pryor

RITA LESTER

1986   **GOOD AS GOLD**
Director: John Glenister
Co-stars: David Calder Jane Wood Jane Morris

VICKI LESTER

1938   **THE MAD MISS MANTON**
Director: Leigh Jason
Co-stars: Barbara Stanwyck Henry Fonda Sam Levene

1938   **THIS MARRIAGE BUSINESS**
Co-stars: Allan Lane Victor Moore

SHELLI LETHER

1993   **BORN TO RUN**
Director: Albert Magnoli
Co-stars: Richard Grieco Jay Acovone

ANNE LE TOURNEAU

1992   **L'HOMME DE MA VIE**
Director: Jean-Charles Tacchella
Co-stars: Maria De Medeiros Thierry Fortineau

SYLVESTRA LE TOUZEL

1986   MANSFIELD PARK
Director: David Giles
Co-stars: Anna Massey Bernard Hepton Samantha Bond

1989   SEEING IN THE DARK
Director: Gareth Jones
Co-stars: David Threlfall Jane Bertish Maurice Denham

AMY LETTERMAN

1977   YOU LIGHT UP MY LIFE
Director: Joseph Brooks
Co-stars: Didi Conn Joe Silver Melanie Mayron

PAULINE LETTS

1963   THE GIRL ON APPROVAL
Director: Charles Frend
Co-stars: Rachel Roberts James Maxwell Annette Whitley

1971   THE TROJAN WOMEN
Director: Michael Cacoyannis
Co-stars: Katherine Hepburn Genevieve Bujold Vanessa Redgrave

1975   CONFESSIONS OF AN ODD-JOB MAN
Director: John Sealey
Co-stars: Barry Stokes Sue Lloyd

ANABELLE LEVENTON

1985   DEFENSE OF THE REALM
Director: David Drury
Co-stars: Gabriel Byrne Greta Scacchi Denholm Elliott

1993   M BUTTERFLY
Director: David Cronenberg
Co-stars: Jeremy Irons John Lone Barbara Sukowa

1993   A TOUCH OF FROST: NOT WITH KINDNESS
Director: David Reynolds
Co-stars: David Jason Tony Haygarth

RACHEL LEVIN

1987   GABY-A TRUE STORY
Director: Luis Mandoki
Co-stars: Liv Ullman Norma Aleandro Robert Loggia

MARSHA LEVINE

1987   NIGHMARE CITY
Director: David Mitchell
Co-stars: Paul Cufos Damian Le

ASHLEE LEVITCH

1998   STAR KID
Co-Stars Joseph Mazello Richard Gilliland

UTA LEVKA

1968   THE BLONDE FROM PEKING
Director: Nicolas Gessner
Co-stars: Mireille Darc Claudio Brook Edward G. Robinson

1969   DE SADE
Director: Cy Endfield
Co-stars: Keir Dullea John Huston Lilli Palmer

CHARLOTTE LEWIS

1986   THE GOLDEN CHILD
Director: Michael Ritchie
Co-stars: Eddie Murphy Charles Dance Victor Wong

1986   PIRATES
Director: Roman Polanski
Co-stars: Walter Matthau Richard Pearson Roy Kinnear

1991   BARE ESSENTIALS

1992   STORYVILLE
Director: Mark Frost
Co-stars: James Spader Jason Robards Joanne Whalley

1993   EXCESSIVE FORCE
Director: Jon Hess
Co-stars: Thomas Ian Griffith Burt Young James Earl Jones

DIANA LEWIS

1940   FORTY LITTLE MOTHERS
Director: Busby Berkeley
Co-stars: Eddie Cantor Bonita Granville Rita Johnson

1940   GO WEST
Director: Edward Buzzell
Co-stars: Marx Brothers John Carroll Walter Woolf King

1940   ANDY HARDY MEETS A DEBUTANTE
Director: George Seitz
Co-stars: Mickey Rooney Lewis Stone Fay Holden

1942   WHISTLING IN DIXIE
Director: S. Sylvan Simon
Co-stars: Red Skelton Ann Rutherford George Bancroft

1942   SEVEN SWEETHEARTS
Director: Frank Borzage
Co-stars: Kathryn Grayson Marsha Hunt S. Z. Sakall

1943   CRY HAVOC
Director: Richard Thorpe
Co-stars: Margaret Sullavan Joan Blondell Ann Sothern

DOROTHY LEWIS

1941   ICE-CAPADES
Director: Joseph Santley
Co-stars: Barbara Jo Allen James Ellison Phil Silvers

FIONA LEWIS

1968   OTLEY
Director: Dick Clement
Co-stars: Tom Courtenay Romy Schneider Leonard Rossiter

1968   WHERE'S JACK
Director: James Clavell
Co-stars: Tommy Steele Stanley Baker Alan Badel

1971   VILLIAN
Director: Michael Tuckner
Co-stars: Richard Burton Ian McShane Nigel Davenport

1972   DR. PHIBES RISES AGAIN
Director: Robert Fuest
Co-stars: Vincent Price Robert Quarry Beryl Reid

1973   DRACULA
Director: Dan Curtis
Co-stars: Jack Palance Simon Ward Pamela Brown

1973   BLUE BLOOD
Director: Andrew Sinclair
Co-stars: Oliver Reed Derek Jacobi Anna Gael

1975   LISZTOMANIA
Director: Ken Russell
Co-stars: Roger Daltrey Paul Nicholas Ringo Starr

1976   DRUM
Director: Steve Carver
Co-stars: Warren Oates Ken Norton Pam Grier

1977   STUNTS
Director: Mark Lester
Co-stars: Robert Forster Joanna Cassidy Bruce Glover

1978   THE FURY
Director: Brian De Palma
Co-stars: Kirk Douglas John Cassavetes Carrie Snodgress

1979 WANDA NEVADA
Director: Peter Fonda
Co-Stars Peter Fonda Brooke Shields Henry Fonda

1983 STRANGE INVADERS
Director: Michael Laughlin
Co-stars: Paul LeMat Nancy Allen Diana Scarwid

1987 INNERSPACE
Director: Joe Dante
Co-Stars: Dennis Quaid Martin Short Meg Ryan

GAIL LEWIS

1989 TWILIGHT CITY
Director: Reece Auguiste
Co-stars: Homi Bhaba Andy Coupland Paul Gilroy

JARMA LEWIS

1955 THE MARAUDERS
Director: Gerald Mayer
Co-stars: Dan Duryea Jeff Richards Keenan Wynn

1955 THE BAR SINISTER
Director: Herman Hoffman
Co-stars: Edmund Gwenn Jeff Richards Dean Jagger

1957 RAINTREE COUNTY
Director: Edward Dmytryk
Co-stars: Elizabeth Taylor Montgomery Clift Lee Marvin

JENNY LEWIS

1988 BABY M
Director: James Steven Sadwith
Co-stars: JoBeth Williams John Shea Anne Jackson

1989 SHANNON'S DEAL
Director: Lewis Teague
Co-stars: Jamey Sheridan Elizabeth Pena Alberta Watson

1991 RUNAWAY FATHER
Director: John Nicolella
Co-stars: Donna Mills Jack Scalia Chris Mulkey

1991 BLIND HATE
Director: John Korty
Co-stars: Corbin Bernsen Angela Bassett Sandy Bull

1992 STEPKIDS
Director: Joan Micklin Silver
Co-stars: Griffin Dunne Dan Futterman Patricia Kalember

1994 RUNAWAY DAUGHTERS
Director: Joe Dante
Co-Stars Dee Wallace Chris Young Julie Bowen

1994 RENAISSANCE MAN
Director: Penny Marshall
Co-Stars Danny DeVito Gregory Hines Cliff Robertson

JULIETTE LEWIS *(Daughter Of Geoffrey Lewis)*
Nominated For Best Supporting Actress In 1991 For "Cape Fear"

1989 NATIONAL LAMPOON'S CHRISTMAS VACATION
Director: Jeremiah Chechik
Co-stars: Chevy Chase Randy Quaid

1990 TOO YOUNG TO DIE
Director: Robert Markovitz
Co-star: Brad Pitt

1991 CROOKED HEARTS
Director: Michael Bortman
Co-stars: Vincent D'Onofrio Peter Coyote Cindy Pickett

1991 CAPE FEAR
Director: Martin Scorsese
Co-stars: Robert De Niro Nick Nolte Jessica Lange

1992 HUSBANDS AND WIVES
Director: Woody Allen
Co-stars: Woody Allen Mia Farrow Blythe Danner Judy Davis

1992 THAT NIGHT
Director: Craig Bolotin
Co-stars: C. Thomas Howell Helen Shaver Eliza Dushku

1993 ROMEO IS BLEEDING
Director: Peter Medak
Co-stars: Gary Oldman Lena Olin Annabella Sciorra

1993 WHAT'S EATING GILBERT GRAPE?
Director: Lasse Hallstrom
Co-stars: Johnny Depp Darlene Cates Leonardo DiCaprio

1993 KALIFORNIA
Director: Dominic Sena
Co-stars: Brad Pitt David Duchovny Michelle Forbes

1994 NATURAL BORN KILLERS
Director: Oliver Stone
Co-stars: Woody Harrelson Robert Downey Jnr. Tommy Lee Jones

1996 STRANGE DAYS
Director: Kathryn Bigelow
Co-stars: Ralph Fiennes Michael Wincott Angela Bassett

1996 FROM DUSK TO DAWN
Director: Robert Rodriquez
Co-stars: George Clooney Harvey Keitel Quentin Tarantino

LINDA LEWIS

1975 DICK DEADEYE, OR DUTY DONE *(Voice)*
Director: Dick Horn
Co-stars: Victor Spinetti Miriam Karlin Barry Cryer

MARCIA LEWIS

1983 NIGHT WARNING
Director: William Asher
Co-stars: Jimmy McNichol Susan Tyrrell Bo Svenson

MONICA LEWIS

1952 EVERYTHING I HAVE IS YOURS
Director: Robert Z. Leonard
Co-stars: Marge Champion Gower Champion Dennis O'Keefe

1953 AFFAIR WITH A STRANGER
Director: Roy Rowland
Co-stars: Jean Simmons Victor Mature Jane Darwell

1957 THE D. I.
Director: Jack Webb
Co-stars: Jack Webb Don Dubbins Jackie Loughery Virginia Gregg

1974 EARTHQUAKE
Director: Mark Robson
Co-Stars Charlton Heston Ava Gardner Lorne Greene

SYLVIA LEWIS

1954 DRUMS OF TAHITI
Director: William Castle
Co-stars: Dennis O'Keefe Patricia Medina Francis L. Sullivan

VERA LEWIS

1931 NIGHT NURSE
Director: William Wellman
Co-stars: Barbara Stanwyck Ben Lyon Clark Gable

1935 THE MAN ON THE FLYING TRAPEZE
Director: Clyde Bruckman
Co-stars: W. C. Fields Kathleen Howard Mary Brian

1941 FOUR MOTHERS
Director: William Keighley
Co-stars: Claude Rains Lolo Lane Priscilla Lane

1941 SHE COULDN'T SAY NO
Co-stars: Roger Pryor Eve Arden Clem Bevans

MONIQUE LEYRAC

1970 ACT OF THE HEART
Director: Paul Almond
Co-stars: Genevieve Bujold Donald Sutherland Sharon Acker

TINA L'HOTSKY

1983 THE LOVELESS
Director: Kathryn Bigelow
Co-stars: Willem Dafoe Robert Gordon J. Don Ferguson

GONG LI

1993 FAREWELL TO THE CONCUBINE
Director: Chen Kaige
Co-stars: Leslie Cheung Zhang Fengyi

1997 TEMPTRESS MOON
Director: Chen Kaige

LILLY LI

1974 SHATTER
Director: Michael Carreras
Co-stars: Stuart Whitman Peter Cushing Ti Lung

ANNE LIBERT

DRACULA, PRISONER OF FRANKENSTEIN
Director: Jesus Franco
Co-stars: Dennis Price Howard Vernon Britt Nichols

GABRIELLA LICUDI

1963 UNEARTHLY STRANGER
Director: John Krish
Co-stars: John Neville Jean Marsh Warren Mitchell

1965 YOU MUST BE JOKING
Director: Michael Winner
Co-stars: Terry-Thomas Lionel Jeffries Denholm Elliott

1967 THE LAST SAFARI
Director: Henry Hathaway
Co-stars: Stewart Granger Kaz Garas Liam Redmond

1967 THE JOKERS
Director: Michael Winner
Co-stars: Michael Crawford Oliver Reed Harry Andrews

1973 SOFT BEDS, HARD BATTLES
Director: Roy Boutling
Co-stars: Peter Sellers Curt Jurgens Jenny Hanley

LAURA LIDDELL

1965 SHAKESPEARE WALLAH
Director: James Ivory
Co-stars: Felicity Kendall Shashi Kapoor Geoffrey Kendall

MIMI LIEBER

1993 WILDER NAPALM
Director: Glenn Gordon Caron
Co-stars: Debra Winger Dennis Quaid Arliss Howard

LO LIEH

1974 BLOOD MONEY
Director: Anthony Dawson
Co-stars: Lee Van Cleef Patty Shepard Karen Yeh

TINA LIFFORD

1991 GRAND CANYON
Director: Lawrence Kasdan
Co-stars: Danny Glover Kevin Kline Steve Martin

1991 PARIS TROUT
Director: Stephen Gyllenhaal
Co-stars: Dennis Hopper Barbara Hershey Ed Harris

JUDITH LIGHT

1988 THE RYAN WHITE STORY
Director: John Herzfeld
Co-stars: Lukas Haas George C. Scott Sarah Jessica Parker

1993 MEN DON'T TELL
Director: Harry Winer
Co-star: Peter Strauss

1994 AGAINST THEIR WILL
Director: Karen Arthur
Co-Stars Kay Lenz Stacy Keach Chelcie Ross

1994 BETRAYAL OF TRUST
Director: George Kaczender
Co-Stars Judd Hirsch Jeffrey DeMunn Betty Buckley

1996 MURDER AT MY DOOR
Co-Star R.H. Thomson

WINNIE LIGHTNER

1929 GOLD DIGGERS OF BROADWAY
Director: Roy Del Ruth
Co-stars: Nancy Welford Conway Tearle Lilyan Tashman

1929 SHOW OF SHOWS
Director: John Adolfi
Co-stars: Frank Fay Monte Blue Lupino Lane

1930 LIFE OF THE PARTY
Director: Roy Del Ruth
Co-stars: Irene Delroy Charles Butterworth Jack Whiting

1930 HOLD EVERYTHING
Director: Roy Del Ruth
Co-stars: Joe E. Brown Georges Carpentier Sally O'Neil

1931 GOLD DUST GERTIE
Director: Lloyd Bacon
Co-stars: Chic Johnson Ole Olsen Dorothy Carlisle

1931 MANHATTAN PARADE
Director: Lloyd Bacon
Co-stars: Joe Smith Charles Dale Charles Butterworth

1933 DANCING LADY
Director: Robert Z. Leonard
Co-stars: Joan Crawford Clark Gable Fred Astaire

MARILYN LIGHTSTONE

1975 LIES MY FATHER TOLD ME
Director: Jan Kadar
Co-stars: Yossi Yadin Len Birman Jeffrey Lymas

1983 SPASMS
Director: William Fruet
Co-stars: Peter Fonda Oliver Reed Kerrie Keane

1985 ANNE OF GREEN GABLES
Director: Kevin Sullivan
Co-stars: Megan Follows Colleen Dewhurst Charmion King

VALERIE LILLEY

1989 LOVING HAZEL
Director: Peter Smith
Co-stars: Hugh Quarshie Susan Brown Gemma Darlington

BEATRICE LILLIE

1926 EXIT SMILING
Director: Sam Taylor
Co-stars: Jack Pickford Doris Lloyd Franklyn Pangborn

1929 SHOW OF SHOWS
Director: John Adolfi
Co-stars: Frank Fay Douglas Fairbanks Jnr. Monte Blue

1938 DOCTOR RHYTHM
Director: Frank Tuttle
Co-stars: Bing Crosby Mary Carlisle Andy Devine

1943 ON APPROVAL
Director: Clive Brook
Co-stars: Clive Brook Googie Withers Roland Culver Hay Petrie

1956 AROUND THE WORLD IN EIGHTY DAYS
Director: Michael Anderson
Co-stars: David Niven Robert Newton

1967 THOROUGHLY MODERN MILLIE
Director: George Roy Hill
Co-stars: Julie Andrews Mary Tyler Moore James Fox

KAY TONG LIM

1988 SAIGON
Director: Christopher Crowe
Co-stars: Willem Dafoe Gregory Hines Amanda Pays

1993 DRAGON: THE BRUCE LEE STORY
Director: Rob Cohen
Co-stars: Jason Scott Lee Lauren Holly Nancy Kwan

YVONNE LIME

1957 I WAS A TEENAGE WEREWOLF
Director: Gene Fowler
Co-stars: Michael Landon Whit Bissell Dawn Richard

BRIGETTE LIN

1986 POLICE STORY
Director: Jackie Chan
Co-stars: Jackie Chan Maggie Cheung Bill Tung Kenneth Tong

KAY LINAKER

1936 EASY MONEY
Co-stars: Onslow Stevens Noel Madison Robert Homans

1936 THE MURDER OF DR. HARRIGAN
Director: Frank McDonald
Co-stars: Ricardo Cortez Mary Astor John Eldridge

1936 ROAD GANG
Director: Louis King
Co-stars: Donald Woods Harry Cording Marc Lawrence

1937 BLACK ACES
Co-star: Buck Jones

1938 CHARLIE CHAN AT MONTE CARLO
Director: Eugene Forde
Co-stars: Warner Oland Keye Luke Virginia Field

1938 THE LAST WARNING
Director: Albert Rogell
Co-stars: Preston Foster Joyce Compton Frank Jenks

1939 DRUMS ALONG THE MOHAWK
Director: John Ford
Co-stars: Henry Fonda Claudette Colbert Edna May Oliver

1939 CHARLIE CHAN IN RENO
Director: Norman Foster
Co-stars: Sidney Toler Ricardo Cortez Phyllis Brooks

1940 CHARLIE CHAN'S MURDER CRUISE
Director: Eugene Forde
Co-stars: Sidney Toler Majorie Weaver Sen Yung

1941 CHARLIE CHAN'S IN RIO
Director: Harry Lachman
Co-stars: Sidney Toler Victor Jory Mary Beth Hughes

1942 CLOSE CALL FOR ELLORY QUEEN
Director: James Hogan
Co-stars: William Gargan Margaret Lindsay

AIDA LINARES

1991 REGARDING HENRY
Director: Mike Nichols
Co-stars: Harrison Ford Annette Bening Bill Nunn

ABBEY LINCOLN

1963 NOTHING BUT A MAN
Director: Michael Roemer
Co-stars: Ivan Dixon Gloria Foster Yaphet Kotto

1968 FOR LOVE OF IVY
Director: Daniel Mann
Co-stars: Sidney Poiteir Beau Bridges Laurie Peters

1972 A SHORT WALK TO DAYLIGHT
Director: Barry Shear
Co-stars: James Brolin Don Mitchell Brooke Bundy

LAR PARK LINCOLN

1988 FRIDAY THE 13TH; PART V: THE NEW BLOOD
Director: John Carl Buechler
Co-stars: Jennifer Banko Susan Blu

CIPE LINCOVSKY

1988 LA AMIGA
Director: Jeannie Meerapfel
Co-stars: Liv Ullman Federico Luppi Victor Laplace

1990 NAKED TANGO
Director: Leonard Schrader
Co-stars: Mathilda May Vincent D'Onofrio Fernando Rey

DELLA LIND

1938 SWISS MISS
Director: John Blystone
Co-stars: Stan Laurel Oliver Hardy Eric Blore

GILLIAN LIND

1932 CONDEMMED TO DEATH
Director: Walter Forde
Co-stars: Arthur Wontner Edmund Gwenn Gordon Harker

1933 DICK TURPIN
Director: Victor Hanbury
Co-stars: Victor McLaglen Jane Carr Frank Vosper

1934 OPEN ALL NIGHT
Director: George Pearson
Co-stars: Frank Vosper Margaret Vines Leslie Perrins

1962 DON'T TALK TO STRANGE MEN
Director: Pat Jackson
Co-stars: Christine Gregg Cyril Raymond Janina Faye

JANE LIND

1991 SALMONBERRRIES
Director: Percy Adlon
Co-stars: k. d. lang Rosel Zech Chuck Connors

TRACI LIND

1989 FRIGHT NIGHT, PART II
Director: Tommy Lee Wallace
Co-stars: Roddy McDowall William Ragsdale Julie Carmen

1989 CLASS OF 1999
Director: Mark Lester
Co-stars: Stacy Keach Malcolm McDowell Pam Grier

1990 THE HANDMAID'S TALE
Director: Volker Schlondorff
Co-stars: Natasha Richardson Robert Duvall Faye Dunaway

1991 VOYAGER
Director: Volker Schlondorff
Co-stars: Sam Shepard Julie Delpy Barbara Sukowa

1992 BUGSY
Director: Barry Levinson
Co-Stars: Warren Beatty Annette Bening Harvey Keitel

1993 MY BOYFRIEND'S BACK
Director: Bob Balaban
Co-stars: Andrew Lowery Edward Herrmann Mary Beth Hurt

1996 CODE NAME: WOLVERINE
Director: David Jackson
Co-Star Antonio Sabato Jnr.

GUNNEL LINDBLOM

1963 THE SILENCE
Director: Ingmar Bergman
Co-stars: Ingrid Thulin Haken Johnherb Birger Malmsten

1966 SULT
Director: Henning Carlsen
Co-stars: Per Oscarsson Birgette Federspiel Knud Rex

JENNIE LINDEN

1964 NIGHTMARE
Director: Freddie Francis
Co-stars: Moira Redmond David Knight Brenda Bruce

1965 DR. WHO AND THE DALEKS
Director: Gordon Flemyng
Co-stars: Peter Cushing Roy Castle Roberta Tovey

1969 WOMEN IN LOVE
Director: Ken Russell
Co-stars: Glenda Jackson Oliver Reed Alan Bates

1970 A SEVERED HEAD
Director: Dick Clement
Co-stars: Lee Remick Ian Holm Claire Bloom

1974 VAMPIRA
Director: Clive Donner
Co-stars: David Niven Teresa Graves Peter Bayliss

1975 HEDDA
Director: Trevor Nunn
Co-stars: Glenda Jackson Timothy West Patrick Stewart

1977 VALENTINO
Director: Ken Russell
Co-stars: Rudolph Nureyev Leslie Caron Michelle Phillips

1985 THE CORSICAN BROTHERS
Director: Ian Sharp
Co-stars: Trevor Eve Geraldine Chaplin Olivia Hussey

JOYCE LINDEN

1948 THE DARK ROAD
Director: Alfred Goulding
Co-stars: Charles Stuart Anthony Hollies Roddy Hayes

1950 DICK BARTON AT BAY
Director: Godfrey Grayson
Co-stars: Don Stannard Tamara Desni George Ford

MARTA LINDEN

1942 A YANK AT ETON
Director: Norman Taurog
Co-stars: Mickey Rooney Freddie Bartholomew Ian Hunter

1943 THE YOUNGEST PROFESSION
Director: Edwar Buzzell
Co-stars: Virginia Weidler Jean Porter Edward Arnold

1943 SWING-SHIFT MAISIE
Director: Norman Z. Leonard
Co-stars: Ann Sothern James Craig Jean Rogers

1944 MAISIE GOES TO RENO
Director: Harry Beaumont
Co-stars: Ann Sothern John Hodiak Ava Gardner

SUNNIVA LINDEKLIEV (Child)

1981 LITTLE IDA
Director: Laila Mikkelsen
Co-stars: Howard Halvorsen Lise Fjeldstad Ellen Westerfjell

JANINE LINDEMOULDER

1992 KILLER LOOKS
Director: Toby Phillips
Co-stars: Suzanne Browne Len Donato

MAGGIE LINDERMAN

1993 THE VANISHING
Director: George Sluizer
Co-stars: Jeff Bridges Kiefer Sutherland Nancy Travis

VIVECA LINDFORS (Married Errol Flynn)

1948 THE ADVENTURES OF DON JUAN
Director: Vincent Sherman
Co-stars: Errol Flynn Robert Douglas Alan Hale

1948 TO THE VICTOR
Director: Delmer Davis
Co-stars: Dennis Morgan Bruce Bennett Dorothy Malone

1949 NIGHT UNTO NIGHT
Director: Don Siegel
Co-stars: Ronald Reagan Rosemary De Camp Broderick Crawford

1949 BACKFIRE
Director: Vincent Sherman
Co-stars: Gordon MacRae Virginia Mayo Edmund O'Brien

1950 DARK CITY
Director: William Dieterle
Co-stars: Charlton Heston Lisabeth Scott Ed Begley

1950 THE FLYING MISSILE
Director: Henry Levin
Co-stars: Glenn Ford Henry O'Neill John Qualen

1950 NO SAD SONGS FOR ME
Director: Rudolph Mate
Co-stars: Margaret Sullavan Wendell Corey Natalie Wood

1951 JOURNEY INTO LIGHT
Director: Stuart Heisler
Co-stars: Sterling Hayden Thomas Mitchell H. B. Warner

1951 FOUR IN A JEEP
Director: Leopold Linberg
Co-stars: Ralph Meeker Michael Medwin Yoseph Yadin

1955 RUN FOR COVER
Director: Nicholas Ray
Co-stars: James Cagney John Derek Ernest Borgnine

1955 MOONFLEET
Director: Fritz Lang
Co-stars: Stewart Granger George Sanders Joan Greenwood

1956 THE HALLIDAY BRAND
Director: Joseph Lewis
Co-stars: Joseph Cotten Ward Bond Bill Wiliams Betsy Blair

1958 I ACCUSE
Director: Jose Ferrer
Co-stars: Jose Ferrer Anton Walbrook Emlyn Williams

1958 TEMPEST
Director: Alberto Lattuada
Co-stars: Van Heflin Silvana Mangano Oscar Homolka

1960 THE STORY OF RUTH
Director: Henry Koster
Co-stars: Elana Eden Peggy Wood Stuart Whitman Tom Tyron

1961 KING OF KINGS
Director: Nicholas Ray
Co-stars: Jeffrey Hunter Robert Ryan Siobhan McKenna Rip Torn

1962 THE DAMNED
Director: Joseph Losey
Co-stars: MacDonald Carey Shirley Ann Field Oliver Reed

1965 BRAINSTORM
Director: William Conrad
Co-stars: Jeffrey Hunter Anne Francis Dana Andrews

1965 SYLVIA
Director: Gordon Douglas
Co-stars: Carroll Baker Peter Lawford Joanne Dru

1970 PUZZLE OF A DOWNFALL CHILD
Director: Jerry Schatzberg
Co-stars: Faye Dunaway Barry Primus Barry Morse

1973 THE WAY WE WERE
Director: Sydney Pollack
Co-stars: Barbra Streisand Robert Redford Lois Chiles

1976 WELCOME TO L. A.
Director: Alan Rudolph
Co-stars: Keith Carradine Sally Kellerman Harvey Keitel

1978 GIRLFRIENDS
Director: Claudia Weill
Co-stars: Melanie Mayron Eli Wallach Bob Balaban Anita Skinner

1978 A WEDDING
Director: Robert Altman
Co-stars: Carol Burnett Vittorio Gassman Amy Stryker

1979 VOICES
Director: Robert Markovitz
Co-stars: Michael Ontkean Amy Irving Alex Roco Barry Miller

1980 MARILYN: THE UNTOLD STORY
Director: Jack Arnold
Co-stars: Catherine Hicks Richard Basehart Sheree North

1981 THE HAND
Director: Oliver Stone
Co-stars: Michael Caine Andrea Marcovicci Rosemary Murphy

1982 CREEPSHOW
Director: George Romero
Co-stars: Stephen King Leslie Nielsen Hal Holbrook Carrie Nye

1984 GOING UNDERCOVER
Director: James Kenelm Clarke
Co-stars: Lea Thompson Chris Lemmon Jean Simmons

1985 SEXPIONAGE
Director: Don Taylor
Co-stars: Sally Kellerman Geena Davis Christopher Atkins

1985 THE SURE THING
Director: Rob Reiner
Co-stars: John Cusack Daphne Zunega Tim Robbins Boyd Gaines

1987 RACHEL RIVER
Director: Sandy Smolan
Co-stars: Pamela Reed Zeljko Ivanek James Olsen

1988 THE ANN JILLIAN STORY
Director: Corey Allen
Co-stars: Ann Jillian Tony LoBianco Tim Webber Pam Hyatt

1991 ZANDALEE
Director: Sam Pillsbury
Co-stars: Nicholas Cage Judge Reinhold Erika Anderson

1992 THE LINGUINI INCIDENT
Director: Richard Shepard
Co-stars: Rosanna Arquette David Bowie Marlee Matlin

1995 STARGATE
Director: Ronald Emmerich
Co-stars: Kurt Russell James Spader Jaye Davidson

1997 TRIAL AND ERROR
Director: Jonathan Lynn
Co-stars: Jeff Daniels Charlize Theron Michael Richards

NATACHA LINDINGER

1998 DOUBLE TEAM
Co-Stars: Jean-Claude Van Damme Mickey Rourke Dennis Rodman

AUDRA LINDLEY

1971 TAKING OFF
Director: Milos Forman
Co-stars: Lynn Carlin Buck Henry Linnea Heacock

1972 THE HEARTBREAK KID
Director: Elaine May
Co-stars: Charles Grodin Cybill Shepherd Jeannie Berlin

1980 REVENGE OF THE STEPFORD WIVES
Director: Robert Fuest
Co-stars: Sharon Gless Julie Kavner

1982 CANNERY ROW
Director: David Ward
Co-stars: Nick Nolte Debra Winger John Huston

1982 BEST FRIENDS
Co-stars: Norman Jewison
Co-stars: Burt Reynolds Goldie Hawn Jessica Tandy

1985 DESERT HEARTS
Director: Donna Deitch
Co-stars: Helen Shaver Patricia Charbonneau Andra Akers

1989 BRIDESMAIDS
Director: Lila Garrett
Co-stars: Shelley Hack Sela Ward Brooke Adams

1989 TAKE MY DAUGHTERS, PLEASE
Director: Larry Elikann
Co-stars: Rue McClanahan Kim Delaney Susan Ruttan

1997 THE RELIC
Co-stars: Penelope Anne Miller Tom Sizemore

SHELBY LINDLEY

1993 SHELF LIFE
Director: Paul Bartel
Co-stars: O-Lan Jones Andrea Stein Jim Turner

OLGA LINDO

1935 THE LAST JOURNEY
Director: Bernard Vorhaus
Co-stars: Godfrey Tearle Hugh Williams Judy Gunn

1937 ROMANCE IN FLANDERS
Director: Maurice Elvey
Co-stars: Paul Cavanagh Marcelle Chantal Garry Marsh

1942 ALIBI
Director: Brian Desmond Hurst
Director: Margaret Lockwood Hugh Sinclair James Mason

1943 WHEN WE ARE MARRIED
Director: Lance Comfort
Co-stars: Raymond Huntley Marian Spencer Sydney Howard

1944 TIME FLIES
Director: Walter Forde
Co-stars: Tommy Handley George Moon Evelyn Dall

1944 GIVE ME THE STARS
Director: Maclean Rogers
Co-stars: Will Fyffe Leni Lynn Ronald Chesney

1950 THE TWENTY QUESTIONS MURDER MYSTERY
Director: Paul Stein
Co-stars: Robert Beatty Rona Anderson Jack Train

1954 AN INSPECTOR CALLS
Director: Guy Hamilton
Co-stars: Alastair Sim Brian Worth Bryan Forbes

1956 THE EXTRA DAY
Director: William Fairchild
Co-stars: Richard Basehart Simone Simon George Baker

1959 MAKE MINE A MILLION
Director: Lance Comfort
Co-stars: Arthur Askey Sid James Dermot Walsh

1959 SAPPHIRE
Director: Basil Dearden
Co-stars: Nigel Patrick Michael Craig Yvonne Mitchell

HELEN LINDSAY

1986 PLAYING AWAY
Director: Horace Ove
Co-stars: Norman Beaton Robert Urquart Nicholas Farrell

MARGARET LINDSAY

1932 THE FOURTH HORSEMAN

1933 PRIVATE DETECTIVE 62
Co-star: William Powell

1933 PADDY THE NEXT BEST THING
Director: Harry Lachman
Co-stars: Janet Gaynor Warner Baxter Walter Connolly

1933 LADY KILLER
Director: Roy Del Ruth
Co-stars: James Cagney Mae Clarke Leslie Fenton Henry O'Neill

1933 CAVALCADE
Director: Frank Lloyd
Co-stars: Clive Brook Diana Wynyard Una O'Connor

1933 BABY FACE
Director: Alfred Green
Co-stars: Barbara Stanwyck George Brent Donald Cook John Wayne

1933 THE WORLD CHANGES
Director: Mervyn LeRoy
Co-stars: Paul Muni Aline McMahon Mary Astor Jean Muir

1933 THE HOUSE ON 56TH STREET

1933 VOLTAIRE
Director: John Adolfi
Co-stars: George Arliss Doris Kenyon Reginald Owen Alan Mowbray

1933 CAPTURED
Director: Roy Del Ruth
Co-stars: Douglas Fairbanks Paul Lukas Leslie Howard

1933 FROM HEADQUATERS
Director: William Dieterle
Co-stars: George Brent Eugene Pallette Hugh Herbert

1934 FOG OVER FRISCO
Director: William Dieterle
Co-stars: Bette Davis Donald Woods Lyle Talbot

1934 BORDERTOWN
Director: Archie Mayo
Co-stars: Paul Muni Bette Davis Eugene Pallette

1934 GENTLEMEN ARE BORN
Director: Alfred Green
Co-stars: Franchot Tone Ross Alexander Dick Foran Jean Muir

1934 THE MERRY WIVES OF RENO
Director: Bruce Humberstone
Co-stars: Donald Woods Glenda Farrell Guy Kibbee

1935 PERSONAL MAID'S SECRET
Director: Arthur Collins
Co-stars: Ruth Donnelly Anita Louise Warren Hull

1935 G MEN
Director: Willaim Keighley
Co-stars: James Cagney Ann Dvorak Robert Armstrong Lloyd Nolan

1935 FRISCO KID
Director: Lloyd Bacon
Co-stars: James Cagney Ricardo Cortez Donald Woods Lili Damita

1935 THE FLORENTINE DAGGER
Director: Robert Florey
Co-stars: Donald Woods Robert Barrat Henry O'Neill

1935 DEVIL DOGS OF THE AIR
Director: Lloyd Bacon
Co-stars: James Cagney Pat O'Brien Frank McHugh

1935 DANGEROUS
Director: Alfred Green
Co-stars: Bette Davis Franchot Tone Alison Skipworth Dick Foran

1935 THE CASE OF THE CURIOUS BRIDE
Director: Michael Curtiz
Co-stars: Warren William Claire Dodd Errol Flynn

1936 ISLE OF FURY
Director: Frank McDonald
Co-stars: Humphrey Bogart Donald Woods

1936 THE LAW IN HER HANDS
Co-star: Warren Hull

1936 THE LADY CONSENTS
Director: Stephen Roberts
Co-stars: Ann Harding Herbert Marshall Walter Abel

1936 PUBLIC ENEMY'S WIFE
Director: Nick Grinde
Co-stars: Pat O'Brien Robert Armstrong Cesar Romero

1937 SONG OF THE CITY
Director: Errol Taggart
Co-stars: Jeffrey Dean Nat Pendleton Edward Norris

1937 SLIM
Director: Ray Enright
Co-stars: Pat O'Brien Henry Fonda Stuart Erwin Jane Wyman

1937 SINNER TAKE ALL
Director: Errol Tagart
Co-stars: Bruce Cabot Joseph Calleia Stanley Ridges

1937 THE GREEN LIGHT
Director: Frank Borzage
Co-stars: Errol Flynn Anita Louise Cedric Hardwicke

1937 BACK IN CIRCULATION
Director: Ray Enright
Co-stars: Pat O'Brien Joan Blondell

1938 BROADWAY MUSKETEERS
Director: John Farrow
Co-stars: Ann Sheridan Marie Wilson John Litel

1938 GARDEN OF THE MOON
Director: Busby Berkeley
Co-stars: Pat O'Brien John Payne Penny Singleton

1938 JEZEBEL
Director: William Wyler
Co-stars: Bette Davis Henry Foster George Brent

1938 THERE'S THAT WOMAN AGAIN
Director: Alexander Hall
Co-stars: Melvyn Douglas Virginia Bruce

1939 20,000 MEN A YEAR
Director: Alfred Green
Co-stars: Randolph Scott Preston Foster Mary Healy

1939 ON TRIAL
Director: Terry Morse
Co-stars: John Litel Edward Norris James Stephenson

1939 **THE UNDERPUP**
Director: Richard Wallace
Co-stars: Gloria Jean Nan Grey Robert Cummings Belauh Bondi

1939 **GOLD IS WHERE YOU FIND IT**
Director: Michael Curtiz
Co-stars: George Brent Olivia De Havilland

1940 **BRITISH INTELLIGENCE**
Director: Terry Morse
Co-stars: Boris Karloff Maris Wrixon Bruce Lester

1940 **HONEYMOON DEFERRED**
Director: Lew Landers
Co-stars: Edmund Lowe Elizabeth Risdon Chick Chandler

1940 **THE HOUSE OF SEVEN GABLES**
Director: Joe May
Co-stars: George Sanders Vincent Price Alan Napier

1940 **ELLERY QUEEN, MASTER DETECTIVE**
Director: Kurt Newman
Co-stars: Ralph Bellamy Charley Grapewin

1941 **THE HARDBOILED CANARY**
Director: Andrew Stone
Co-stars: Susanna Foster Allan Jones Lynne Overman

1940 **ELLERY QUEEN'S PENTHOUSE MYSTERY**
Director: Kurt Newman
Co-stars: Anna May Wong Eduardo Ciannelli

1941 **ELLERY QUEEN AND THE PERFECT CRIME**
Director: James Hogan
Co-stars: Spring Byington James Burke

1941 **ELLERY QUEEN AND THE MURDER RING**
Director: James Hogan
Co-stars: Mona Barrie George Zucco Leon Ames

1941 **THERE'S MAGIC IN MUSIC**
Director: Andrew Stone
Co-stars: Allan Jones Susanna Foster Lynne Overman

1941 **CLOSE CALL FOR ELLERY QUEEN**
Director: James Hogan
Co-stars: William Gargan Ralph Morgan Edward Norris

1942 **DESPERATE CHANCE FOR ELLERY QUEEN**
Director: James Hogan
Co-stars: Lillian Bond Jack La Rue

1942 **ENEMY AGENTS MEET ELLERY QUEEN**
Director: James Hogan
Co-stars: Gilbert Roland Gale Sondergaard

VERA LINDSAY

1940 **SPELLBOUND**
Director: John Harlow
Co-stars: Derek Farr Frederick Leister Hay Petrie

HELFA LINE

1982 **LABYRINTH OF PASSION**
Director: Pedro Almodovar
Co-stars: Celia Roth Imanol Arias Antonio Banderas

STEPHI LINEBURG

1994 **DAD, THE ANGEL AND ME**
Director: Rick Wallace
Co-Stars Judge Reinhold Alan King

SOPHIE LINFIELD

1994 **HOPE IN THE YEAR TWO**
Director: Elijah Moskinsky
Co-stars: Jack Shepherd Tom Bowles

BARBARA YU LING

1986 **PING PONG**
Director: Po Chih Leong
Co-stars: David Yip Lucy Sheen Robert Lee

BAMBI LINN

1955 **OKLAHOMA!**
Director: Fred Zimmemann
Co-Stars: Gordon MacRae Shirley Jones Rod Steiger

LAURA LINNEY

193 **BLIND SPOT**
Director: Michael Toshiuki
Co-stars: Joanne Woodward Fritz Weaver Reed Diamond

1995 **CONGO**

1996 **PRIMAL FEAR**
Director: Gregory Hoblit
Co-stars: Richard Gere Edward Norton Alfre Woodard

1997 **ABSOLUTE FEAR**
Director: Clint Eastwood
Co-stars: Clint Eastwood Gene Hackman Ed Harris Judy Davis

JOANNE LINVILLE

1976 **GABLE AND LOMBARD**
Director: Sidney Furie
Co-stars: James Brolin Jill Clayburgh Allen Garfield

1977 **SECRETS**
Director: Paul Wendkos
Co-stars: Susan Blakely Roy Thinnes Melody Thomas

LIO

1996 **MADRE MUERTA**
Director: Juanma Bajo Ulloa
Co-stars: Ana Alarez Karra Elijalde

MARGO LION

1946 **MARTIN ROUMAGNAC**
Director: Georges Lacombe
Co-stars: Jean Gabin Marlene Dietrich Marcel Herrand

1960 **LOLA**
Director: Jacques Demy
Co-stars: Anouk Aimee Marc Michel Elina Labourdette

THERESE LIOTARD

1980 **DEATH WATCH**
Director: Bertrand Tavernier
Co-stars: Romy Schneider Harvey Keitel Harry Dean Stanton

1990 **LE CHATEAU DE MA MERE**
Director: Yves Robert
Co-stars: Julien Ciamaca Julie Timmerman Joris Molinas

1991 **LA GLOIRE DE MON PERE**

MAUREEN LIPMAN *(Married Jack Rosenthal)*

1967 **UP THE JUNCTION**
Director: Peter Collinson
Co-stars: Suzy Kendall Dennis Waterman Liz Fraser

1969 **THE SMASHING BIRD I USED TO KNOW**
Director: Robert Hartford-Davis
Co-stars: Dennis Waterman Madeleine Hinde

1974 **REGAN**
Director: Tom Clegg
Co-stars: John Thaw Dennis Waterman Lee Montague

1980 **THE WILDCATS OF ST. TRINIANS**
Director: Frank Lauder
Co-stars: Sheila Hancock Michael Hordern

1982 **SMILEY'S PEOPLE**
Director: Simon Langton
Co-stars: Alec Guinness Curt Jurgens Eileen Atkins

1983 EDUCATING RITA
Director: Lewis Gilbert
Co-stars: Michael Caine Julie Walters Michael Williams

1985 WATER
Director: Dick Clement
Co-stars: Michael Caine Valerie Perrine Leonard Rossiter

1985 NATIONAL LAMPOON'S EUROPEAN VACATION
Director: Amy Heckerling
Co-Stars Chevy Chase Beverly D'Angelo Dana Hill

1986 SHIFT WORK
Director: Angela Pope
Co-stars: Stephen Dillon Jeffrey Chiswick Tony Alleff

1992 CARRY ON COLUMBUS
Director: Gerald Thomas
Co-stars: Jim Dale Bernard Cribbins Leslie Phillips

RENNEE LIPPERT

1987 RADIO DAYS
Director: Woody Allen
Co-stars: Woody Allen Mia Farrow Dianne Wiest Julie Kavner

DOREEN LIPSON

1977 ALIEN ENCOUNTERS
Director: Ed Hunt
Co-stars: Robert Vaughn Christopher Lee Helen Shaver

PEGGY LIPTON

1988 ADDICTED TO LOVE
Director: Arthur Allan Seidelman
Co-stars: Barry Bostwick Polly Bergen Colleen Camp

1991 TRUE IDENTITY
Director: Charles Lane
Co-stars: Charles Lane Lenny Henry Frank Langella

1994 DEADLY VOWS
Director: Alan Metzger
Co-stars: Gerald McRaney

ANNA LISA

1959 HAVE ROCKET, WILL TRAVEL
Director: David Lowell Rich
Co-stars: Three Stooges Jerome Cowan Bob Colbert

VIRNA LISI

1961 DUEL OF THE TITANS
Director: Sergio Cabucci
Co-stars: Steve Reeves Gordon Scott Massimo Girotti

1962 EVA
Director: Joseph Losey
Co-stars: Stanley Baker Jeanne Moreau James Villiers

1963 THE BLACK TULIP
Director: Christian Jaque
Co-stars: Alain Delon Akim Tamiroff Dawn Addams

1964 HOW TO MURDER YOUR WIFE
Director: Richard Quine
Co-stars: Jack Lemmon Terry-Thomas Eddie Mayehof

1965 THE BIRDS, BEES AND THE ITALIANS
Director: Pietro Germi
Co-stars: Gastone Mochin Alberto Lionello

1966 ASSAULT ON A QUEEN
Director: Jack Donohue
Co-stars: Frank Sinatra Tony Franciosa Richard Conte

1966 NOT WITH MY WIFE YOU DON'T
Director: Norman Panama
Co-stars: Tony Curtis George C. Scott Carroll O'Connor

1967 THE TWENTY-FIFTH HOUR
Director: Henri Verneuil
Co-stars: Anthony Quinn Michael Redgrave

1967 THE GIRL AND THE GENERAL
Director: Pasquale Festa Campanile
Co-stars: Rod Steiger Umberto Orsini

1968 THE GIRL WHO COULDN'T SAY NO
Director: Franco Brusati
Co-stars: George Segal Lila Kedrova

1969 THE LAST SHOT
Director: Sergio Gobbi
Co-stars: Robert Hossein Charles Aznavour Albert Minsk

1969 THE SECRET OF SANTA VITTORIA
Director: Stanley Kramer
Co-stars: Anthony Quinn Anna Magnani Hardy Kruger

1969 THE CHRISTMAS TREE
Director: Terence Young
Co-stars: William Holden Brook Fuller Bourvil

1969 ARABELLA
Director: Mauro Bolognini
Co-stars: James Fox Terry-Thomas Margaret Rutherford

1970 THE STATUE
Director: Rod Amateau
Co-stars: David Niven Robert Vaughn Ann Bell John Cleese

1972 BLUEBEARD
Director: Edward Dmytryk
Co-stars: Richard Burton Raquel Welch Joey Heatherton

1974 LE SERPENT
Director: Henri Verneuil
Co-stars: Henry Fonda Yul Brynner Dirk Bogarde Farley Granger

1994 LA REINE MARGOT
Director: Patrice Chereau
Co-stars: Isabelle Adjani Daniel Auteuil Vincent Perez

LUCILE LISLE

1936 MIDNIGHT AT MADAME TUSSAUD'S
Director: George Pearson
Co-stars: Charles Oliver Bernard Miles Patrick Barr

EVE LISTER

1935 THE CITY OF BEAUTIFUL NONSENSE
Director: Adrian Brunel
Co-stars: Emlyn Williams Sophie Stewart

1936 SWEENY TODD, THE DEMON BARBER OF FLEET STREET
Director: George King
Co-stars: Tod Slaughter Bruce Seton

MOIRA LISTER

1944 THE AGITATOR
Director: John Harlow
Co-stars: William Hartnell Mary Morris Moore Marriott John Laurie

1944 LOVE STORY
Director: Leslie Arliss
Co-stars: Margaret Lockwood Stewart Granger Patricia Roc

1948 ANOTHER SHORE
Director: Charles Crighton
Co-stars: Robert Beatty Stanley Holloway Michael Medwin

1948 ONCE A JOLLY SWAGMAN
Director: Jack Lee
Co-stars: Dirk Bogarde Renee Asherson Bonar Colleano

1948 SO EVIL MY LOVE
Director: Lewis Allen
Co-stars: Ray Milland Ann Todd Geraldine Fitzgerald

1948   UNEASY TERMS
Director: Vernon Sewell
Co-stars: Michael Rennie Nigel Patrick Faith Brook Joy Shelton

1949   A RUN FOR YOUR MONEY
Director: Charles Frend
Co-stars: Meredith Edwards Donald Houston Alec Guinness

1950   POOL OF LONDON
Director: Basil Dearden
Co-stars: Bonar Colleano Susan Shaw Renee Asherson

1951   WHITE CORRIDORS
Director: Pat Jackson
Co-stars: James Donald Googie Withers Petula Clark Barry Jones

1952   SOMETHING MONEY CAN'T BUY
Director: Pat Jackson
Co-stars: Patricia Roc Anthony Steel A. E. Matthews

1953   TROUBLE IN STORE
Director: John Paddy Carstairs
Co-stars: Norman Wisdom Margaret Rutherford Lana Morris

1953   THE LIMPING MAN
Director: Charles De Latour
Co-stars: Lloyd Bridges Alan Wheatley Leslie Phillips

1953   GRAND NATIONAL NIGHT
Director: Bob McNaught
Co-stars: Nigel Patrick Beatrice Campbell Noel Purcell

1955   THE DEEP BLUE SEA
Director: Anatole Litvak
Co-stars: Vivien Leigh Kenneth More Eric Portman

1955   JOHN AND JULIE
Director: Wiliam Fairchild
Co-stars: Peter Sellers Sid James Andrew Cruikshank

1956   SEVEN WAVES AWAY
Director: Richard Sale
Co-stars: Tyrone Power Mai Zetterling Lloyd Nolan

1964   THE YELLOW ROLLS ROYCE
Director: Anthony Asquith
Co-stars: Rex Harrison Ingrid Bergman Omar Sharif

1967   THE DOUBLE MAN
Director: Franklin Schaffner
Co-stars: Yul Brynner Britt Ekland Clive Revill

1972   NOT NOW DARLING
Director: Ray Cooney
Co-stars: Ray Cooney Leslie Phillips Julie Ege

1989   TEN LITTLE INDIANS
Director: Alan Birkinshaw
Co-stars: Donald Pleasence Brenda Vaccaro Herbert Lom

LITTLE NELL (Nell Campbell)

1975   THE ROCKY HORROR PICTURE SHOW
Director: Jim Sharman
Co-stars: Tim Curray Susan Sarandon Koo Stark

1978   JUBILEE
Director: Derek Jarman
Co-stars: Jenny Runacre Toyah Wilcox Ian Charleson

MICHELLE LITTLE

1987   BLUFFING IT
Director: James Sadwith
Co-stars: Dennis Weaver Janet Carroll Vicki Wauchope

1990   BLUE HEAT
Director: John McKenzie
Co-stars: Brian Dennehy Jeff Fahey Joe Pantoliano

GWEN LITTLEFIELD

1944   SINCE YOU WENT AWAY
Director: John Cromwell
Co-stars: Claudette Colbert Jennfer Jones Shirley Temple

SUSAN LITTLER

1972   THE LOVERS
Director: Herbert Wise
Co-stars: Richard Beckindale Paula Wilcox Joan Scott

ROBYN LIVELEY

1986   WILDCATS
Director: Michael Ritchie
Co-stars: Goldie Hawn Swoosie Kurtz James Keach

1987   NOT QUITE HUMAN
Director: Steven Hilliard Stern
Co-stars: Alan Thicke Jay Underwood Joseph Bologna

1989   NOT QUITE HUMAN II
Director: Eric Luke
Co-stars: Alan Thicke Jay Underwood Greg Mullavey

1989   TEEN WITCH
Director: Dorian Walker
Co-stars: Joshua Miller Dan Gauthier Shelley Berman

1989   THE KARATE KID, PART III
Director: John Avildsen
Co-stars: Richard Macchio Pat Morita Martin L. Kove

MARGARET LIVINGSTON

1927   SUNRISE
Director: F. W. Munrau
Co-stars: Janet Gaynor George O'Brien J. Farrell MacDonald

1929   THE LAST WARNING
Director: Paul Leni
Co-stars: Laura La Plante Montague Love John Boles

1929   THE CHARLATAN

1931   KIKI
Director: Sam Taylor
Co-stars: Mary Pickford Reginald Denny Joseph Cawthorn

1931   SMART MONEY
Director: Alfred Green
Co-stars: Edward G. Robinson James Cagney Evalyn Knapp

SUZETTE LLEWELLYN

1987   SAMMY AND ROSIE GET LAID
Director: Stephen Frears
Co-stars: Claire Bloom Shashi Kapoor Frances Barber

1987   PLAYING AWAY
Director: Horace Ove
Co-stars: Norman Beaton Nicholas Farrell Helen Lindsay

1992   RUNNING LATE
Director: Udayan Prasad
Co-stars: Peter Bowles Carole Nimmons Renee Asherson

1994   WELCOME II THE TERROR DOME
Director: Ngozi Onwurah
Co-stars: Felix Joseph Saffron Burrows Ben Wynter

ALMA LLOYD

1936   THE BIG NOISE
Co-star: Warren Hull

DORIS LLOYD

1926   EXIT SMILING
Director: Sam Taylor
Co-stars: Beatrice Lillie Jack Pickford Harry Myers

1926 THE BLACK BIRD
Director: Tod Browning
Co-stars: Lon Chaney Renee Adoree Owen Moore

1929 DISRAELI
Director: Alfred Green
Co-stars: George Arliss Joan Bennett Florence Arliss

1930 CHARLEY'S AUNT
Director: Al Christie
Co-stars: Charles Ruggles June Collyer Hugh Williams

1930 OLD ENGLISH
Director: Alfred Green
Co-stars: George Arliss Leon Janney Betty Lawford

1930 SARAH AND SON
Director: Dorothy Arzner
Co-stars: Ruth Chatterton Fredric March Philippe De Lacy

1930 WAY FOR A SAILOR
Director: Sam Wood
Co-stars: John Gilbert Wallace Beery Leila Hyams

1931 WATERLOO BRIDGE
Director: James Whale
Co-stars: Mae Clarke Kent Douglass Bette Davis

1931 ONCE A LADY
Director: Guthrie McLintoc
Co-stars: Ruth Chatterton Ivor Novello Jill Esmond

1931 BOUGHT
Director: Archie Mayo
Co-stars: Constance Bennett Ben Lyon Ray Milland

1932 BACK STREET
Director: John Stahl
Co-stars: Irene Dunne John Boles June Clyde

1932 TARZAN THE APE MAN
Director: W. S. Van Dyke
Co-stars: Johnny Weismuller Maureen O'Sullivan

1933 SECRETS
Director: Frank Borzage
Co-stars: Mary Pickford Leslie Howard C. Aubrey Smith

1934 SISTERS UNDER THE SKIN
Director: David Burton
Co-stars: Frank Morgan Elissa Landi Joseph Schildkraut

1934 GLAMOUR
Director: William Wyler
Co-stars: Constance Cummings Paul Lukas Philip Reed

1935 KIND LADY
Director: George Seitz
Co-stars: Basil Rathbone Aline MacMahon Mary Carlisle

1935 MUTINY ON THE BOUNTY
Director: Frank Lloyd
Co-stars: Charles Laughton Clark Gable Franchot Tone

1935 PETER IBBETSON
Director: Henry Hathaway
Co-stars: Gary Cooper Ann Harding Ida Lupino

1938 THE BLACK DOLL
Co-star: William Lundigan

1939 BARRICADE
Director: Gregory Ratoff
Co-stars: Warner Baxter Alice Faye Charles Winninger

1945 MY NAME IS JULIA ROSS
Director: Joseph Lewis
Co-stars: Nina Foch May Whitty George Macready

1946 THE IMPERFECT LADY
Director: Lewis Allen
Co-stars: Ray Milland Teresa Wright Cedric Hardwicke

1951 ALICE IN WONDERLAND (Voice)
Director: Clyde Geronimi
Co-stars: Kathryn Beaumont Jerry Colonna Ed Wynn

1956 THE SWAN
Director: Charles Vidor
Co-Stars Grace Kelly Alec Guinness Louis Jourdan

1960 MIDNIGHT LACE
Director: David Miller
Co-stars: Doris Day Rex Harrison Myrna Loy

1960 THE TIME MACHINE
Director: George Pal
Co-stars: Rod Taylor Yvette Mimieux Alan Young

1965 THE SOUND OF MUSIC
Director: Robert Wise
Co-stars: Julie Andrews Christopher Plummer Richard Haydn

EMILY LLOYD *(Daughter Of Roger Lloyd-Pack)*

1987 WISH YOU WERE HERE
Director: David Leland
Co-stars: Tom Bell Claire Clifford Barbara Durkin

1989 COOKIE
Director: Susan Seidelman
Co-stars: Petr Falk Dianne Wiest Brenda Vaccaro

1989 IN COUNTRY
Director: Norman Jewison
Co-stars: Bruce Willis Joan Allen Kevin Anderson

1990 CHICAGO JOE AND THE SHOWGIRL
Director: Bernard Rose
Co-stars: Kiefer Sutherland Patsy Kensit

1991 SCORCHERS
Director: David Beard
Co-stars: Faye Dunaway Denholm Elliott

1992 A RIVER RUNS THROUGH IT
Director: Robert Redford
Co-stars: Craig Sheffer Brad Pitt Brenda Blethyn

1996 WHEN SATURDAY COMES
Director: Maria Giese
Co-star: Sean Bean

GWYNETH LLOYD

1934 ARE YOU A MASON?
Director: Henry Edwards
Co-stars: Sonnie Hale Robertson Hare Bertha Belmore

KATHLEEN LLOYD

1977 THE CAR
Director: Elliott Silverstein
Co-stars: James Brolin John Marley R. G. Armstrong

1976 THE MISSOURI BREAKS
Director: Arthur Penn
Co-stars: Marlon Brando Jack Nicholson Randy Quaid

1977 SKATEBOARD
Director: George Cage
Co-stars: Allen Garfield Leif Garrett Richard Van Der Wyk

1978 LACY AND THE MISSISSIPPI QUEEN
Director: Robert Butler
Co-stars: Debra Feuer Edward Andrews Jack Elam

1978 IT LIVES AGAIN
Director: Larry Cohen
Co-stars: Frederic Forrest Andrew Duggan

1980 THE JAYNE MANSFIELD STORY
Director: Dick Lowry
Co-stars: Loni Anderson Arnold Schwarzenegger

IVEY LLOYD

1993 RIGOLETTO
Director: Leo Paur
Co-stars: Joseph Paur John Huntingdon

MARIE LLOYD JNR.

1942 VARIETY JUBILEE
Director: Maclean Rogers
Co-stars: Lesley Brook Ellis Irving George Robey

SABRINA LLOYD

1993 FATHER HOOD
Director: Darrell James Roodt
Co-stars: Patrick Swayze Halle Berry Diane Ladd

SUE LLOYD

1965 THE IPCRESS FILE
Director: Sidney Furie
Co-stars: Michael Caine Nigel Green Gordon Jackson

1967 ATTACK ON THE IRON COAST
Director: Paul Wendkos
Co-stars: Lloyd Bridges Andrew Kier Mark Eden

1967 CORRUPTION
Director: Robert Hartford Davis
Co-stars: Peter Cushing Kate O'Mara David Lodge

1968 WHERE'S JACK?
Director: James Clavell
Co-stars: Tommy Steele Stanley Baker Fiona Lewis

1970 PERCY
Director: Ralph Thomas
Co-Stars Hywel Bennett Denholm Elliott Cyd Hayman

1972 GO FOR A TAKE
Director: Harry Booth
Co-stars: Reg Varney Dennis Price Julie Ege

1972 INNOCENT BYSTANDERS
Director: Peter Collinson
Co-stars: Stanley Baker Dana Andrews Geraldine Chaplin

1972 THAT'S YOUR FUNERAL
Director: John Robins
Co-stars: Bill Fraser Raymond Huntley Roy Kinnear

1975 SPANISH FLY
Director: Bob Kellett
Co-stars: Terry-Thomas Leslie Phillips Frank Thornton

1975 CONFESSIONS OF AN ODD-JOB MAN
Director: John Sealey
Co-stars: Barry Stokes Gary Soper Valerie Leon

1978 THE STUD
Director: Quentin Masters
Co-stars: Joan Collins Oliver Tobias Doug Fisher

1979 THE BITCH
Director: Gerry O'Hara
Co-stars: Joan Collins Kenneth Haigh Ian Hendry

SUZANNE LLOYD

1966 THAT RIVIERA TOUCH
Director: Cliff Owen
Co-stars: Eric Morecambe Ernie Wise Paul Stassino

1968 THE CHAMPAGNE MURDERS
Director: Claude Chabrol
Co-stars: Anthony Perkins Staphane Audran Maurice Ronet

ROBYN LOAU

1997 THE IDIOT BOX
Director: David Caesar
Co-stars: Ben Mendelson Jeremy Sims Susie Porter

AMY LOCANE

1989 THE ROAD HOME
Director: Hugh Hudson
Co-stars: Donald Sutherland Adam Horovitz Celia Weston

1990 CRY-BABY
Director: John Waters
Co-stars: Johnny Depp Susan Tyrrell Polly Bergen

1992 SCHOOL TIES
Director: Robert Mandel
Co-stars: Brendon Fraser Matt Damon Chris O'Donnell

1995 ACTS OF LOVE
Co-Stars Dennis Hopper Amy Irving

1995 CRIMINAL HEARTS
Director: Dave Payne
Co-Stars Kevin Dillon Morgan Fairchild

INGRID LOCKE

1986 FEEL THE MOTION
Director: Wolfgang Buld
Co-stars: Sissy Kelling Meatloaf Falco

KATHERINE LOCKE

1951 TRY AND GET ME
Director: Cyril Endfield
Co-stars: Frank Lovejoy Lloyd Bridges Richard Carlson

NANCY LOCKE

1987 THE HOSTAGE
Director: Hanro Mohr
Co-stars: Wings Hauser Karen Black Kevin McCarthy

SHARYL LOCKE

1964 FATHER GOOSE
Director: Ralph Nelson
Co-stars: Cary Grant Leslie Caron Trevor Howard

SONDRA LOCKE

Nominated For Best Supporting Actress in 1968 for "The Heart is a Lonely Hunter"

1968 THE HEART IS A LONELY HUNTER
Director: Robert Ellis Miller
Co-stars: Alan Arkin Stacy Keach

1971 A REFLECTION OF FEAR
Director: William Fraker
Co-stars: Robert Shaw Mary Ure Signe Hasso

1971 WILLARD
Director: Daniel Mann
Co-stars: Bruce Davison Ernest Borgnine Elsa Lanchester

1973 THE SECOND COMING OF SUZANNE
Director: Michael Barry
Co-stars: Richard Dreyfuss Gene Barry

1976 THE OUTLAW JOSEY WALES
Director: Clint Eastwood
Co-stars: Clint Eastwood John Vernon Chief Dan George

1977 DEATH GAME
Director: Peter Traynor
Co-stars: Colleen Camp Seymour Cassell Ruth Warshawsky

1977 THE GAUNTLET
Director: Clint Eastwood
Co-stars: Clint Eastwood Pat Hingle Bill McKinney William Prince

1978 EVERY WHICH WAY BUT LOOSE
Director: James Fargo
Co-stars: Clint Eastwood Ruth Gordon Geoffrey Lewis

1980 ANY WHICH WAY YOU CAN
Director: Buddy Van Horn
Co-stars: Clint Eastwood Ruth Gordon Glen Campbell

1980 BRONCO BILLY
Director: Clint Eastwood
Co-stars: Clint Eastwood Geoffrey Lewis Scat Man Crothers

1983 SUDDEN IMPACT
Director: Clint Eastwood
Co-stars: Clint Eastwood Pat Hingle Bradford Dillman Paul Drake

1986 RATBOY
Director: Sondra Locke
Co-stars: Robert Townsend Christopher Hewett

KIM LOCKETT

1980 PROSTITUTE
Director: Tony Garnett
Co-stars: Eleanor Forsythe Kate Crutchley Nancy Samuels

ANNE LOCKHART

1973 THE MAGICIAN
Director: Marvin Chomsky
Co-stars: Bill Bixby Joan Caulfield Kim Hunter

1977 JOYRIDE
Director: Joseph Ruben
Co-stars: Desi Arnaz Jnr. Robert Carradine Melanie Griffith

1983 YOUNG WARRIORS
Director: Lawrence Foldes
Co-stars: Ernest Borgnine Richard Roundtree Lynda Day George

1983 HAMBONE AND HILLIE
Director: Roy Watts
Co-stars: Lillian Gish Timothy Bottoms Candy Clark

JUNE LOCKHART

1938 A CHRISTMAS CAROL
Director: Edwin Marin
Co-stars: Reginald Owen Terry Kilburn Gene Lockhart

1940 ALL THIS AND HEAVEN TOO
Director: Anatole Litvak
Co-stars: Bette Davis Charles Boyer Jeremy Lynn Barbara O'Neill

1941 SERGEANT YORK
Director: Howard Hawks
Co-stars: Gary Cooper Walter Brennan Joan Leslie Ward Bond

1944 MEET ME IN ST. LOUIS
Director: Vincente Minnelli
Co-stars: Judy Garland Margartet O'Brien Leon Ames

1945 KEEP YOUR POWDER DRY
Director: Edward Buzzell
Co-stars: Lana Turner Laraine Day Susan Peters

1945 SON OF LASSIE
Director: S. Sylvan Simon
Co-stars: Peter Lawford Donald Crisp Nigel Bruce Leon Ames

1946 THE YEARLING
Director: Clarence Brown
Co-stars: Gregory Peck Jane Wyman Claude Jarman Jnr.

1946 SHE-WOLF OF LONDON
Director: Jean Yarborough
Co-stars: Don Porter Sara Haden Lloyd Corrigan

1946 EASY TO WED
Director: Edward Buzzell
Co-stars: Esther Williams Lucille Ball Van Johnson

1947 T-MEN
Director: Anthony Mann
Co-stars: Dennis O'Keefe Charles McGraw Wallace Ford

1947 BURY ME DEAD
Director: Bernard Vorhaus
Co-stars: Cathy O'Donnell Hugh Beaumont Mark Daniels

1957 TIME LIMIT
Director: Karl Malden
Co-stars: Richard Widmark Dolores Michaels Rip Torn

1964 LASSIE'S GREAT ADVENTURE
Director: William Beaudine
Co-stars: Jon Provost Hugh Reilly Richard Kiel

1973 THE BAIT
Director: Leonard Horn
Co-stars: Donna Mills William Devane Michael Constantine

1975 WHO IS THE BLACK DAHLIA?
Director: Joseph Pevney
Co-stars: Efrem Zimbalist Ronny Cox Lucy Arnaz

1981 BUTTERFLY
Director: Matt Cimber
Co-stars: Pia Zadora Stacy Keach Orson Welles Lois Nettleton

1982 THE CAPTURE OF GRIZZLY ADAMS
Director: Don Keeslar
Co-stars: Kim Darby Chuck Connors Dan Haggerty

1983 STRANGE INVADER
Director: Michael Laughlin
Co-Stars: Paul LeMat Nancy Allen Diana Scarwid

1984 THE NIGHT THEY SAVED CHRISTMAS
Director: Jackie Cooper
Co-stars: Jaclyn Smith Art Carney Paul LeMat

1985 AMAZING STORIES 8
Director: Norman Reynolds
Co-stars: Milton Berle Polly Holliday J. A. Preston

1986 TROLL
Director: John Carl Buechler
Co-stars: Michael Moriarty Noah Hathaway Shelly Hack Sonny Bono

1988 A WHISPER KILLS
Director: Christian Nyby
Co-stars: Loni Anderson Joe Penny Jaremy Slate

1988 PERFECT PEOPLE
Director: Bruce Seth Green
Co-stars: Lauren Hutton Perry King Cheryl Pollock

1992 DANGER ISLAND
Director: Tommy Lee Walllace
Co-stars: Richard Beymer Gary Graham Lisa Banes Kathy Ireland

KATHLEEN LOCKHART

1936 TIMES SQUARE PLAYBOY
Co-stars: Warren William Barton MacLane Gene Lockhart

1938 A CHRISTMAS CAROL
Director: Edwin Marin
Co-stars: Reginald Owen Terry Kilburn June Lockhart

1938 BLONDIE
Director: Frank Strayer
Co-stars: Arthur Lake Penny Singleton Gene Lockhart

1941 LOVE CRAZY
Director: Jack Conway
Co-stars: William Powell Myrna Loy Jack Carson

1945 ROUGHLY SPEAKING
Director: Michael Curtiz
Co-stars: Rosalind Russell Jack Carson Robert Hutton

1945 BEWITCHED
Director: Arch Obeler
Co-stars: Phyllis Thaxter Edmund Gwenn Addison Richards

1953 WALKING MY BABY BACK HOME
Director: Lloyd Bacon
Co-stars: Donald O'Connor Janet Leigh Buddy Hackett

HEATHER LOCKLEAR

1984 FIRESTARTER
Director: Mark Lester
Co-stars: David Keith Drew Barrymore George C. Scott

1988 ROCK 'N' ROLL MOM
Director: Michael Schultz
Co-stars: Dyan Cannon Michael Brandon Telma Hopkins

1989 THE RETURN OF THE SWAMP THING
Director: Jim Wynorski
Co-stars: Louis Jourdan Sarah Douglas Dick Durock

1991 LETHAL CHARM
Director: Richard Michaels
Co-Stars Stuart Wilson Barbara Eden Julie Fulton

1992 BODY LANGUAGE
Co-stars: Arthur Allan Seidelman
Co-stars: Linda Purl James Acheson Edward Albert

1993 WAYNE'S WORLD 2
Director: Stephen Surjik
Co-stars: Mike Myers Tia Carrere Kim Basinger

LORYN LOCKLIN

1990 TAKING CARE OF BUSINESS
Director: Arthur Hiller
Co-stars: James Belushi Charles Grodin Anne De Salvo

1991 VIGILANTE COP
Director: Mel Damski
Co-stars: Alex McArthur Dale Midkiff Lucinda Jenny

1993 FORTRESS
Director: Stuart Gordon
Co-stars: Christopher Lambert Kurtwood Smith Jeffrey Combs

JULIA LOCKWOOD *(Child)*
(Daughter Of Margaret Lockwood)

1955 THE FLYING EYE
Director: William Hammond
Co-stars: David Hannaford Harcourt Williams Ivan Craig

1956 MY TEENAGE DAUGHTER
Director: Herbert Wilcox
Co-stars: Anna Neagle Sylvia Syms Kenneth Haigh

1959 PLEASE TURN OVER
Director: Gerald Thomas
Co-stars: Ted Ray Jean Kent Leslie Phillips

MARGARET LOCKWOOD

1934 LORNA DOONE
Director: Basil Dean
Co-stars: Victoria Hopper John Loder Roger Livesey

1935 JURY'S EVIDENCE
Director: Ralph Ince
Co-stars: Hartley Power Nora Swinburne Sebastian Shaw

1935 MAN OF THE MOMENT
Director: Monte Banks
Co-stars: Douglas Fairbanks Laura La Plante Claude Hulbert

1935 MIDSHIPMAN EASY
Director: Carol Reed
Co-stars: Hughie Green Harry Tate Roger Livesey

1936 THE AMATEUR GENTLEMAN
Director: Thornton Freeland
Co-stars: Douglas Fairbanks Elissa Landi

1936 THE BELOVED VAGABOND
Director: Cutis Bernhardt
Co-stars: Maurice Chevalier Betty Stockfield

1937 THE STREET SINGER
Director: Jean De Marguenat
Co-stars: Arthur Tracy Arthur Riscoe Hugh Wakefield

1937 DR. SYN
Director: Roy William Neill
Co-stars: George Arliss John Loder Graham Moffatt

1938 OWD BOB
Director: Robert Stevenson
Co-stars: Will Fyffe John Loder Moore Marriott

1938 BANK HOLIDAY
Director: Carol Reed
Co-stars: Hugh Williams Kathleen Harrison Wally Patch

1938 THE LADY VANISHES
Director: Alfred Hitchcock
Co-stars: Michael Redgrave Paul Lukas May Whitty

1939 A GIRL MUST LIVE
Director: Carol Reed
Co-stars: Renee Houston Lilli Palmer Hugh Sinclair

1939 THE STARS LOOK DOWN
Director: Carol Reed
Co-stars: Michael Redgrave Emlyn Williams Edward Rigby

1939 SUSANNAH OF THE MOUNTIES
Director: William Seiter
Co-stars: Shirley Temple Randolph Scott Victor Jory

1939 RULERS OF THE SEA
Director: Frank Lloyd
Co-stars: Douglas Fairbanks Will Fyffe Alan Ladd

1940 NIGHT TRAIN TO MUNICH
Director: Carol Reed
Co-stars: Rex Harrison Naunton & Wayne Paul Henreid

1940 THE GIRL IN THE NEWS
Director: Carol Reed
Co-stars: Barry K. Barnes Emlyn Williams Mervyn Johns

1941 QUIET WEDDING
Director: Anthony Asquith
Co-stars: Derek Farr A. E. Matthews Peggy Ashcroft

1942 ALIBI
Director: Brain Desmond Hurst
Co-stars: Hugh Sinclair James Mason Raymond Lovell

1943 DEAR OCTOPUS
Director: Harold French
Co-stars: Michael Wilding Celia Johnson Basil Radford

1943 THE MAN IN GREY
Director: Leslie Arliss
Co-stars: James Mason Phyllis Calvert Stewart Granger

1944 A PLACE OF OWN'S OWN
Director: Bernard Knowles
Co-stars: James Mason Barbara Mullen Dennis Price

1944 LOVE STORY
Director: Leslie Arliss
Co-stars: Stewart Granger Patricia Roc Moira Lister

1944 GIVE US THE MOON
Director: Val Guest
Co-stars: Vic Oliver Max Bacon Jean Simmons Peter Graves

1945 I'LL BE YOUR SWEETHEART
Director: Val Guest
Co-stars: Vic Oliver Michael Rennie Maudie Edwards

1945 THE WICKED LADY
Director: Leslie Arliss
Co-stars: James Mason Griffith Jones Patricia Roc

1946 BEDELIA
Director: Lance Comfort
Co-stars: Ian Hunter Barry K. Barnes Anne Crawford

1946 HUNGRY HILL
Director: Brian Desmond Hurst
Co-stars: Dennis Price Jean Simmons Cecil Parker

1947   **JASSY**
Director: Bernard Knowles
Co-stars: Dennis Price Patricia Roc Dermot Walsh

1947   **WHITE UNICORN**
Director: Bernard Knowles
Co-stars: Joan Greenwood Ian Hunter Dennis Price

1948   **LOOK BEFORE YOU LOVE**
Co-stars: Griffith Jones Norman Wooland Michael Medwin

1949   **MADNESS OF THE HEART**
Director: Charles Bennett
Co-stars: Paul Dupuis Kathleen Byron Maxwell Reed

1949   **CARDBOARD CAVALIER**
Director: Walter Forde
Co-stars: Sid Field Jerry Desmonde Claude Hulbert

1950   **HIGHLY DANGEROUS**
Director: Roy Baker
Co-stars: Dane Clark Marius Goring Naunton Wayne

1952   **TRENT'S LAST CASE**
Director: Herbert Wilcox
Co-stars: Michael Wilding Orson Welles John McCallum

1953   **LAUGHING ANNE**
Director: Herbert Wilcox
Co-stars: Forrest Tucker Ronald Shiner Wendell Corey

1954   **TROUBLE IN THE GLEN**
Director: Herbert Wilcox
Co-stars: Forrest Tucker Orson Welles Victor McLaglen

1955   **CAST A DARK SHADOW**
Director: Lewis Gilbert
Co-stars: Dirk Bogarde Kay Walsh Robert Flemyng

1976   **THE SLIPPER AND THE ROSE**
Director: Bryan Forbes
Co-stars: Richard Chamberlain Gemma Craven

BARBARA LODEN

1960   **WILD RIVER**
Director: Elia Kazan
Co-stars: Montgomery Clift Jo Van Fleet Lee Remick

1961   **SPLENDOR IN THE GRASS**
Director: Elia Kazan
Co-stars: Natalie Wood Warren Beatty Pat Hingle

1970   **WANDA**
Director: Barbara Loden
Co-star: Michael Higgins

KATHRYN LODER

1974   **FOXY BROWN**
Director: Jack Hill
Co-stars: Pam Grier Antonio Vargas Peter Brown

JEAN LODGE

1949   **DR. MORELLE AND THE CASE OF THE MISSING HEIRESS**
Director: Godfrey Grayson
Co-stars: Valentine Dyall Julia Lang

1952   **BRANDY FOR THE PARSON**
Director: John Eldridge
Co-stars: James Donald Kenneth More

1954   **THE BLACK KNIGHT**
Director: Tay Garnett
Co-stars: Alan Ladd Peter Cushing Patricia Medina

JEANETEE LOFF

1930   **KING OF JAZZ**
Director: J. Murray Anderson
Co-stars: Paul Whiteman John Boles Laura La Plante

1930   **PARTY GIRL**
Co-star: Marie Prevost

1935   **ST. LOUIS WOMAN**
Co-star: Johnny Mack Brown

CECILIA LOFTUS

1931   **EAST LYNNE**
Director: Frank Lloyd
Co-stars: Ann Harding Clive Brook Conrad Nagel

1936   **ONCE IN A BLUE MOON**
Director: Ben Hecht
Co-stars: Jimmy Savo Whitney Bourne Nikita Balieff

1940   **THE BLUE BIRD**
Director: Walter Lang
Co-stars: Shirley Temple Nigel Bruce Johnny Russell

1940   **LUCKY PARTNERS**
Director: Lewis Milestone
Co-stars: Ronald Colman Ginger Rogers Jack Carson

1941   **THE BLACK CAT**
Director: Albert Rogell
Co-stars: Basil Rathbone Gladys Cooper Broderick Crawford

ELLA LOGAN

1937   **52ND. STREET**
Director: Harold Young
Co-stars: Kenny Baker Ian Hunter Zasu Pitts

1937   **TOP OF THE TOWN**
Director: Ralph Murphy
Co-stars: George Murphy Doris Nolan Hugh Herbert

1938   **THE GOLDWYN FOLLIES**
Director: George Marshall
Co-stars: Kenny Baker Vera Zorina Andrea Leeds

JACQUELINE LOGAN

1923   **HOLLYWOOD**
Director: James Cruze
Co-stars: Hope Drown Luke Cosgrove Eleanor Lawson

1927   **KING OF KINGS**
Director: Cecil B. DeMille
Co-stars: H. B. Warner Joseph Schildkraut Ernest Torrence

1930   **THE MIDDLE WATCH**
Director: Norman Walker
Co-stars: Owen Nares Jack Raines Dodo Watts

JANICE LOGAN

1939   **WHAT A LIFE**
Director: Theodore Reed
Co-stars: Jackie Cooper Betty Field John Howard

1940   **DR. CYCLOPS**
Director: Ernest Schoedsack
Co-stars: Albert Dekker Victor Kilian Thomas Coley

PHYLLIS LOGAN

1983   **ANOTHER TIME, ANOTHER PLACE**
Director: Michael Radford
Co-stars: Giovanni Mauriello Denise Coffey

1985   **THE DOCTOR AND THE DEVILS**
Director: Freddie Francis
Co-stars: Timothy Dalton Jonathan Pryce Twiggy

1985   **THE McGUFFIN**
Director: Colin Bucksey
Co-stars: Charles Dance Brian Glover Francis Matthews

1987   **THE KITCHEN TOTO**
Director: Harry Hook
Co-stars: Bob Peck Edwin Mahinda Robert Urquhart

1988 DEFROSTING THE FRIDGE
Director: Sandy Johnson
Co-stars: Joe Don Baker Maggie O'Neill Emma Wray

1989 AND A NIGHTINGALE SANG
Director: Robert Knights
Co-stars: Tom Watt Joan Plowright John Woodvine

1989 GOLDENEYE
Director: Don Boyd
Co-stars: Charles Dance Lynsey Baxter Richard Griffiths

1989 SITTING TARGETS
Director: Jenny Wilkes
Co-stars: Leslee Udwin Jonathan Hyde Mary Wimbush

1990 HAPPY FEET
Director: Mike Bradwell
Co-stars: Marjie Lawrence Stephen Hancock Jane Holmes

1990 EFFIE'S BURNING
Director: Nigel Evans
Co-stars: Paula Tilbrook Gordon Jackson Ian Sexton

1991 AND THE COW JUMPED OVER THE MOON
Director: Penny Cherns
Co-stars: Elaine Collins Anne Downie Ida Schuster

1992 FREDDIE AS FRO7 (Voice)
Director: Jon Acevski
Co-stars: Ben Kingsley Jenny Agutter

1992 SOFT TOP, HARD SHOULDER
Director: Stefan Schwarttz
Co-stars: Peter Capaldi Elaine Collins Frances Barber

1996 SECRETS AND LIES
Director: Mike Leigh
Co-stars: Timothy Spall Brenda Blethyn Lee Ross

KRISTINA LOGGIA

1990 CHOPPER CHICKS IN ZOMBIETOWN
Director: Dan Hoskins
Co-stars: Jamie Rose Catherine Carlen Lycia Naff

1991 NEW YEAR'S DAY
Director: Henry Jaglom
Co-stars: Maggie Jakobson Gwen Welles David Duchovny

MARIE LOHR

1932 AREN'T WE ALL
Director: Rudolph Mate
Co-stars: Gertrude Lawrence Hugh Wakefield Owen Nares

1934 ROAD HOUSE
Director: Maurice Levy
Co-stars: Gordon Harker Emlyn Williams Violet Loraine

1935 ROYAL CAVALCADE
Director: Marcel Varnel
Co-stars: Hermione Baddeley Esme Percy John Mills

1935 MY HEART IS CALLING
Director: Carmine Gallone
Co-stars: Jan Kiepura Marta Eggerth Sonnie Hale

1935 FOREIGN AFFAIRS
Director: Tom Walls
Co-stars: Tom Walls Roy Kellino Ralph Lynn

1935 FIGHTING STOCK
Director: Tom Walls
Co-stars: Tom Walls Robertson Hare Ralph Lynn

1937 SOUTH RIDING
Director: Victor Saville
Co-stars: Ralph Richardson Edna Best Edmund Gwenn

1938 PYGMALION
Director: Leslie Howard
Co-stars: Leslie Howard Wendy Hiller Wilfrid Lawson

1939 A GENTLEMAN'S GENTLEMAN
Director: Roy William Neill
Co-stars: Eric Blore Peter Coke David Hutcheson

1940 GEORGE AND MARGARET
Director: George King
Co-stars: Judy Kelly Oliver Wakefield Noel Howlett

1941 MAJOR BARBARA
Director: David Lean
Co-stars: Wendy Hiller Rex Harrison Robert Morley

1942 WENT THE DAY WELL
Director: Alberto Cavalcanti
Co-stars: Leslie Banks Elizabeth Allan Mervyn Johns

1944 THE TWIGHLIGHT HOUR
Director: Paul Stein
Co-stars: Mervyn Johns Basil Radford Lesley Brook

1945 THE RAKE'S PROGRESS
Director: Sidney Gilliat
Co-stars: Rex Harrison Lilli Palmer Margaret Johnston

1946 THE MAGIC BOW
Director: Bernard Knowles
Co-stars: Stewart Granger Jean Kent Phyllis Calvert

1947 THE GHOSTS OF BERKELEY SQUARE
Director: Vernon Sewell
Co-stars: Robert Morley Claude Hulbert A E Matthews

1948 ANNA KARENINA
Director: Julien Duvivier
Co-stars: Vivien Leigh Ralph Richardson Kieron Moore

1948 COUNTERBLAST
Director: Paul Stein
Co-stars: Robert Beatty Mervyn Johns Nova Pilbeam

1948 THE WINSLOW BOY
Director: Anthony Asquith
Co-stars: Robert Donat Cedric Hardwicke Margaret Leighton

1954 OUT OF THE CLOUDS
Director: Michael Relph
Co-stars: Anthony Steel Robert Beatty Eunice Gayson

1955 ESCAPADE
Director: Philip Leacock
Co-stars: John Mills Alastair Sim Yvonne Mitchell

1956 SEVEN WAVES AWAY
Director: Richard Sale
Co-stars: Tyrone Power Mai Zetterling Lloyd Nolan

1956 A TOWN LIKE ALICE
Director: Jack Lee
Co-stars: Virginia McKenna Peter Finch Maureen Swanson

1957 SMALL HOTEL
Director: David MacDonald
Co-stars: Gordon Harker Irene Handl Janet Munro

1958 CARLTON - BROWNE OF THE F. O.
Director: John Boutling
Co-stars: Terry-Thomas Peter Sellers Ian Bannen

1968 GREAT CATHERINE
Director: Gordon Flemyng
Co-stars: Jeanne Moreau Peter O'Toole Jack Hawkins

HELENE LOISEUE

1971 MON ONCLE ANTOINE
Director: Claude Jutra
Co-stars: Claude Jutra Jean Duceppe Lyne Champagne

GINA LOLLOBRIGIDA

1948 PAGLIACCI
Co-stars: Tito Gobi

1951   **FANFAN LA TULIPE**
Director: Christian-Jacque
Co-stars: Gerard Philipe Genevieve Page

1951   **A TALE OF FIVE CITIES**
Director: Montgomery Tully
Co-stars: Bonar Colleano Barbara Kelly Lana Morris

1952   **LES BELLES DE NUIT**
Director: Rene Clair
Co-stars: Gerard Philipe Martine Carol

1953   **BREAD LOVE AND DREAMS**
Director: Luigi Comencini
Co-stars: Vittorio De Sica Marisa Merlini

1953   **BEAT THE DEVIL**
Director: John Huston
Co-stars: Humphrey Bogart Jennifer Jones Peter Lorre

1954   **CROSSED SWORDS**
Director: Milton Krims
Co-stars: Errol Flynn Nadia Gray Cesare Danova

1955   **FRISKY**
Co-star: Roberto Risso

1956   **TRAPEZE**
Director: Carol Reed
Co-stars: Burt Lancaster Tony Curtis Katy Jurado

1957   **THE HUNCHBACK OF NOTRE DAME**
Director: Jean Delannoy
Co-stars: Anthony Quinn Jean Dannet Alain Cuny Danielle Dumant

1958   **ANNA OF BROOKLYN**
Director: Reginald Denham
Co-stars: Dale Robertson Vittorio De Sica

1959   **SOLOMAN AND SHEBA**
Director: King Vidor
Co-stars: Yul Brynner George Sanders David Farrar

1959   **NEVER SO FEW**
Director: John Sturges
Co-stars: Frank Sinatra Steve McQueen Peter Lawford

1961   **COME SEPTEMBER**
Director: Robert Mulligan
Co-stars: Rock Hudson Sandra Dee Bobby Darin

1961   **GO NAKED IN THE WORLD**
Director: Ranald MacDougall
Co-stars: Tony Franciosa Ernest Borgnine Luana Patten

1964   **WOMAN OF STRAW**
Director: Basil Dearden
Co-stars: Sean Connery Ralph Richardson Alexander Knox

1965   **STRANGE BEDFELLOWS**
Director: Melvyn Frank
Co-stars: Rock Hudson Gig Young Dave King Edward Judd

1966   **HOTEL PARADISO**
Director: Peter Glenville
Co-stars: Alec Guinness Robert Morley Peggy Mount

1968   **BUONA SERRA MRS. CAMPBELL**
Director: Melvyn Frank
Co-stars: Telly Savalas Phil Silvers Peter Lawford

1968   **CERVANTES**
Director: Vincent Sherman
Co-stars: Horst Buchholz Louis Jourdan Jose Ferrer

1968   **THE PRIVATE NAVY OF SERGEANT O'FARRELL**
Director: Frank Tashlin
Co-stars: Bob Hope Phyllis Diller

1971   **BAD MAN'S RIVER**
Director: Eugenio Martin
Co-stars: Lee Van Cleef James Mason Diana Lorys

1972   **KING, QUEEN, KNAVE**
Director: Jerry Skolimowsky
Co-stars: David Niven John Moulder-Brown

1985   **DECEPTIONS**
Director: Melville Shavelson
Co-stars: Stephanie Powers Sam Wanamaker Jeremy Brett

CAROLE LOMBARD *(Jane Alice Peters)*
(Married William Powell, Clark Gable)
(Disfigured in car accident when 17, died in plane crash in 1942)
Nominated For Best Actress In 1936 For "My Man Godfrey"

1929   **HIGH VOLTAGE**
Co-stars: Owen Moore Bill Boyd Diane Ellis William Revan

1930   **THE ARIZONA KID**
Director: Alfred Santell
Co-stars: Warner Baxter Mona Maris Theodore Von Eltz

1930   **FAST AND LOOSE**
Director: Fred Newmeyer
Co-stars: Miriam Hopkins Frank Morgan Charles Starrett

1931   **IT PAYS TO ADVERTISE**
Director: Frank Tuttle
Co-stars: Norman Foster Louise Brooks Eugene Pallette

1931   **I TAKE THIS WOMAN**
Director: Marion Gering
Co-stars: Cary Cooper Helen Ware Lester Vail

1931   **LADIES' MAN**
Director: Lothar Mendes
Co-stars: William Powell Kay Francis Olive Tell

1931   **MAN OF THE WORLD**
Director: Richard Wallace
Co-stars: William Powell Wynne Gibson

1931   **UP POPS THE DEVIL**
Director: Edward Sutherland
Co-stars: Norman Foster Skeets Gallagher

1932   **VIRTUE**
Director: Eddie Buzzell
Co-stars: Pat O'Brien Mayo Methot Ward Bond

1932   **SINNERS IN THE SUN**
Director: Alexander Hall
Co-stars: Chester Morris Cary Grant Alison Skipworth

1932   **NO MAN OF HER OWN**
Director: Wesley Ruggles
Co-stars: Clark Gable Dorothy MacKaill

1933   **WHITE WOMAN**
Director: Stuart Walker
Co-stars: Charles Laughton Charles Bickford

1933   **SUPERNATURAL**
Director: Victor Halperin
Co-stars: Randolph Scott H. B. Warner Alan Dinehart

1933   **FROM HELL TO HEAVEN**
Director: Erle Kenton
Co-stars: Jack Oakie Sidney Blackmer David Manners

1933   **THE EAGLE AND THE HAWK**
Director: Stuart Walker
Co-stars: Fredric March Cary Grant Jack Oakie

1933   **BRIEF MOMENT**
Co-star: Donald Cook

1934   **BOLERO**
Director: Wesley Ruggles
Co-stars: George Raft Sally Rand Ray Milland

1934   **THE GAY BRIDE**
Director: Jack Conway
Co-stars: Chester Morris Zasu Pitts Nat Pendleton

1934 LADY BY CHOICE
Director: David Burton
Co-stars: May Robson Walter Connolly Roger Pryor

1934 NOW AND FOREVER
Director: Henry Hathaway
Co-stars: Gary Cooper Shirley Temple

1934 TWENTIETH CENTURY
Director: Howard Hawks
Co-stars: John Barrymore Roscoe Karns Walter Connolly

1934 WE'RE NOT DRESSING
Director: Norman Taurog
Co-stars: Bing Crosby Burns & Allen Ethel Merman

1935 RUMBA
Director: Marion Gering
Co-stars: George Raft Lynne Overman Margo

1935 HANDS ACROSS THE TABLE
Director: Mitchell Leisen
Co-stars: Fred MacMurray Ralph Bellamy

1936 LOVE BEFORE BREAKFAST
Director: Walter Lang
Co-stars: Preston Foster Cesar Romero Janet Beecher

1936 MY MAN GODFREY
Director: Gregory La Cava
Co-stars: William Powell Alice Brady Mischa Auer

1936 THE PRINCESS COMES ACROSS
Director: William Howard
Co-stars: Fred MacMurray Alison Skipworth

1937 SWING HIGH, SWING LOW
Director: Mitchell Leisen
Co-stars: Fred MacMurray Dorothy Lamour

1937 TRUE CONFESSION
Director: Wesley Ruggles
Co-stars: Fred MacMurray John Barrymore

1937 NOTHING SACRED
Director: William Wellman
Co-stars: Fredric March Walter Connolly

1938 FOOLS FOR SCANDAL
Director: Mervyn LeRoy
Co-stars: Fernand Gravet Ralph Bellamy Marie Wilson

1939 IN NAME ONLY
Director: John Cromwell
Co-stars: Cary Grant Kay Francis Charles Coburn

1939 MADE FOR EACH OTHER
Director: John Cromwell
Co-stars: James Stewart Charles Coburn Lucile Watson

1940 THEY KNEW WHAT THEY WANTED
Director: Garson Kanin
Co-stars: Charles Laughton William Gargan Frank Fay

1940 VIGIL IN THE NIGHT
Director: George Stevens
Co-stars: Alfred Newman Ann Shirley Brian Aherne

1941 MR. & MRS. SMITH
Director: Alfred Hitchcock
Co-stars: Robert Montgomery Gene Raymond Jack Carson

1942 TO BE OR NOT TO BE
Director: Ernst Lubitsch
Co-stars: Jack Benny Robert Stack Lionel Atwill

KARINA LOMBARD

1992 WIDE SARGASSO SEA
Director: John Duigan
Co-stars: Nathaniel Parker Rachel Ward Michael York

1994 LEGENDS OF THE FALL
Director: Edward Zwick
Co-stars: Brad Pitt Anthony Hopkins Julia Ormond

LOUISE LOMBARD

1992 ANGELS
Director: Philip Saville
Co-stars: Tom Bell Alfred Molina Cathy Tyson

CELINE LOMEZ

1978 THE SILENT PARTNER
Director: Daryl Duke
Co-stars: Christopher Plummer Elliott Gould Susannah York

BEBI LONCAR

1963 THE LONG SHIPS
Director: Jack Cardiff
Co-stars: Richard Widmark Sidney Poitier Russ Tamblyn

1969 SOME GIRLS DO
Director: Ralph Thomas
Co-stars: Richard Johnson Daliah Lavi Sydne Rome

ALEXANDRA LONDON

1992 VAN GOGH
Director: Maurice Pialat
Co-stars: Jacques Dutronc Gerard Sety Corinne Bourdon

JEAN LONDON

1931 OUR WIVE
Director: James Horne
Co-stars: Stan Laurel Oliver Hardy James Finlayson

JULIE LONDON

1945 ON STAGE EVERYBODY
Director: Jean Yarborough
Co-stars: Jack Oakie Peggy Ryan Johnny Coy Otto Kruger

1947 THE RED HOUSE
Director: Delmer Daves
Co-stars: Edward G. Robinson Lon McCallister Rory Calhoun

1948 TAP ROOTS
Director: George Marshall
Co-stars: Susan Hayward Ven Heflin Boris Karloff

1949 TASK FORCE
Director: Delmer Daves
Co-stars: Gary Cooper Walter Brennan Jane Wyatt Wayne Morris

1950 THE FAT MAN
Director: William Castle
Co-stars: J. Scott Smart Rock Hudson Clinton Sundberg

1950 THE RETURN OF THE FRONTIERSMAN
Director: Richard Bare
Co-stars: Gordon MacRae Rory Calhoun Fred Clark

1957 DRANGO
Director: Hall Bartlett
Co-stars: Jeff Chandler Ronald Howard Joanne Dru Donald Crisp

1957 THE GREAT MAN
Director: Jose Ferrer
Co-stars: Jose Ferrer Kennan Wynn Ed Wynn

1958 MAN OF THE WEST
Director: Anthony Mann
Co-stars: Gary Cooper Arthur O'Connell Jack Lord John Denher

1958 A QUESTION OF ADULTERY
Director: Don Chaffey
Co-stars: Anthony Steel Basil Sidney Donald Houston

1958 SADDLE THE WIND
Director: Robert Parrish
Co-stars: Robert Taylor John Cassavetes Donald Crisp

1958 THE VOICE IN THE MIRROR
Director: Harry Keller
Co-stars: Richard Egan Walter Matthau Troy Donohue

1959 THE WONDERFUL COUNTRY
Director: Robert Parrish
Co-stars: Robert Mitchum Gary Merrill Jack Oakie

1959 THE THIRD VOICE
Director: Hubert Cornfield
Co-stars: Edmond O'Brien Laraine Day

1961 THE GEORGE RAFT STORY
Director: Joseph Newman
Co-stars: Ray Danton Jayne Mansfield Frank Gorshin

1967 THE HELICOPTER SPIES
Director: Sam Rolfe
Co-stars: Robert Vaughn David McCallum Carol Lynley

LENORE LONERGAN

1941 TOM, DICK AND HARRY
Director: Garson Kanin
Co-stars: Ginger Rogers George Murphy Burgess Meredith

1951 WESTWARD THE WOMEN
Director: William Wellman
Co-stars: Robert Taylor Denise Darcel Hope Emerson

1951 WHISTLE AT EATON FALLS
Director: Robert Siodmak
Co-stars: Lloyd Bridges Dorothy Gish Carleton Carpenter

1951 THE LADY SAYS NO
Director: Frank Ross
Co-stars: Joan Caulfield David Niven Henry Jones

AUDREY LONG

1944 TALL IN THE SADDLE
Director: Edwin Marin
Co-stars: John Wayne Ella Raines Ward Bond

1945 WANDERER OF THE WASTELAND
Co-stars: Richard Martin James Warren

1945 PAN-AMERICANA
Director: John Auer
Co-stars: Phillip Terry Robert Benchley Eve Arden

1945 A GAME OF DEATH
Director: Robert Wise
Co-stars: John Loder Edgar Barrier Russell Wade

1947 DESPERATE
Director: Anthony Mann
Co-stars: Steve Brodie Raymond Burr Douglas Fowley

1947 LADY OF DECEIT
Director: Robert Wise
Co-stars: Lawrence Tierney Claire Trevor Walter Slezak

1948 THE ADVENTURES OF GALLANT BESS
Director: Lew Landers
Co-stars: Cameron Mitchell Fuzzy Knight

1948 PERILOUS WATERS
Co-star: Don Castle

1950 THE PETTY GIRL
Director: Henry Levin
Co-stars: Joan Caulfield Robert Cummings Elsa Lanchester

JODI LONG

1981 ROLLOVER
Director: Alan J. Pakula
Co-stars: Jane Fonda Kris Kristofferson Hume Cronyn

1988 PATTY HEARST
Director: Paul Schrader
Co-stars: Natasha Richardson William Forsythe Frances Fisher

1989 SOURSWEET
Director: Mike Newell
Co-stars: Sylvia Chang Danny Dun William Chow

1991 ALICE
Director: Woody Allen
Co-stars: Mia Farrow Alec Baldwin William Hurt

NIA LONG

1986 THE B.R.A.T. PATROL
Director: Mollie Miller
Co-stars: Sean Astin Tim Thomerson Brian Keith

1991 BOYZ 'N' THE HOOD
Director: John Singleton
Co-stars: Larry Fishburne Cuba Gooding Jnr. Morris Chestnut

1993 MADE IN AMERICA
Director: Richard Benjamin
Co-stars: Whoopi Goldberg Ted Danson Jennifer Tilly

1995 FRIDAY
Director: Gary Gray
Co-Stars Ice Cube Chris Tucker

1997 LOVE JONES
Director: Theodore Witcher
Co-stars: Larenz Tate

1998 SOUL FOOD
Director: George Tillman Jnr.
Co-Stars Vanessa Williams Gena Ravera Vivica Fox

SHELLEY LONG

1980 A SMALL CIRCLE OF FRIENDS
Director: Rob Cohen
Co-stars: Brad Davis Karen Allen Jameson Parker

1981 CAVEMAN
Director: Carl Gottlieb
Co-stars: Ringo Starr Barbara Bach Dennis Quaid

1982 NIGHT SHIFT
Director: Ron Howard
Co-stars: Henry Winkler Michael Keaton Gina Hecht

1983 LOSIN' IT
Director: Curis Hanson
Co-stars: Tom Cruise John Stockwell John P. Navin

1984 IRRECONCILIABLE DIFFERENCES
Director: Charles Shyer
Co-stars: Ryan O'Neal Drew Barrymore Sharon Stone

1985 THE MONEY PIT
Director: Richard Benjamin
Co-Stars Tom Hanks Maureen Stapleton Alexander Godonov

1986 OUTRAGEOUS FORTUNE
Director: Arthur Hiller
Co-stars: Bette Midler Peter Coyote

1987 HELLO AGAIN
Director: Frank Perry
Co-stars: Judith Ivey Corbin Bernsen Gabriel Byrne

1989 SHATTERED
Director: Lamont Johnson
Co-stars: Tom Conti John Rubenstein Alan Fudge

1989 TROOP BEVERLY HILLS
Director: Jeff Kanew
Co-stars: Stephanie Beacham Craig Nelson Mary Goss

1990 VOICES WITHIN
Director: Lamont Johnson
Co-stars: Tom Conti John Rubenstein Jaimie Rose

1990 DON'T TELL HER IT'S ME
Director: Malcolm Mowbray
Co-stars: Steve Guttenberg Jamie Gertz Kyle MacLaclan

1992 FATAL MEMORIES
Director: Daryl Duke
Co-stars: Helen Shaver Dean Stockwell

1992 A MESSAGE FROM HOLLY
Director: Rod Holcomb
Co-star: Lindsay Wagner

1992 FROZEN ASSETS
Director: George Miller
Co-stars: Corbin Bernsen Larry Miller Paul Sand

1995 THE BRADY BUNCH MOVIE
Director: Betty Thomas
Co-Stars Gary Cole Michael McKean

1997 A VERY BRADY SEQUEL
Co-Star Gary Cole Tim Matheson

CLAUDINE LONGET (*Married Andy Williams*)

1968 THE PARTY
Director: Blake Edwards
Co-stars: Peter Sellers Marge Champion Fay McKenzie

VICTORIA LONGLEY

1986 THE MORE THINGS CHANGE
Director: Robyn Nevin
Co-stars: Judy Morris Barry Otto Peter Carroll

1989 CELIA
Director: Ann Turner
Co-stars: Rebecca Smart Nicholas Eadie Maryanne Fahey

1991 TURTLE BEACH
Director: Stephen Wallace
Co-stars: Greta Scacchi Joan Chen Jack Thompson

1994 DALLAS DOLL
Director: Ann Turner
Co-stars: Frank Gallagher Sandra Bernhard Jake Blundell

ADELE LONGMIRE

1942 BULLET SCARS
Director: Ross Lederman
Co-stars: Regis Toomey Howard Da Silva

MARISA LONGO

1972 THE WAY OF THE DRAGON
Director: Bruce Lee
Co-stars: Bruce Lee Chuck Norris Nora Miao Robert Wall

EMILY LONGSTRETH

1988 THE BIG PICTURE
Director: Christopher Guest
Co-stars: Kevin Bacon J. T. Walsh Jennifer Jason Leigh

ANITA LOO

1962 EXPERIMENT IN TERROR
Director: Blake Edwards
Co-stars: Glenn Ford Lee Remick Stephanie Powers

ANNE LOOBY

1991 DAYDREAM BELIEVER
Director: Kathy Mueller
Co-stars: Miranda Otto Martin Kemp Gia Carides

DEBORAH LOOMIS

1970 HERCULES IN NEW YORK
Director: Arthur Allan Seidelman
Co-stars: Arnold Stang Arnold Strong Tania Elg

NANCY LOOMIS

1976 ASSAULT ON PRECINCT 13
Director: John Carpenter
Co-stars: Austin Stoker Martin West Tony Burton

1978 HALLOWEEN
Director: John Carpenter
Co-stars: Jaimie Lee Curtis Donald Pleasence P. J. Soles

TANYA LOPERT

1978 ONCE IN PARIS
Director: Russell Mack
Co-stars: Wayne Rogers Gayle Hunnicutt Jack Lenoir

1981 TALES OF ORDINARY MADNESS
Director: Marco Ferreri
Co-stars: Ben Gazzara Ornella Muti Susan Tyrrell

JENNIFER LOPEZ

1996 MONEY TRAIN
Co-stars: Woody Harrelson Wesley Snipes

1996 BLOOD AND WINE
Director: Bob Rafaelson
Co-Stars Jack Nicholson Michael Caine

1998 U-TURN
Director: Oliver Stone
Co-Stars Nick Nolte Sean Penn Jon Voight

KAMALA LOPEZ

1987 BORN IN EAST L. A.
Director: Cheech Marin
Co-stars: Cheech Marin Daniel Stern Jan-Michael Vincent

1988 BREAK OF DAWN

MARGA LOPEZ

1958 NAZARIN
Director: Luis Bunuel
Co-stars: Francisco Rabal Rita Macedo

NELIDA LOPEZ

1993 MI VIDA LOCA
Director: Allison Anders
Co-stars: Angel Aviles Jacob Vargas Seidy Lopez

PRISCILLA LOPEZ

1986 INTIMATE STRANGERS
Director: Robert Ellis Miller
Co-Stars Stacy Keach Teri Garr Cathy Lee Crosby

SEIDY LOPEZ

1993 MI VIDA LOCA
Director: Allison Anders
Co-Stars Angel Aviles Jacob Vargas Nelida Lopez

VIOLET LORAINE

1934 ROAD HOUSE
Director: Maurice Elvy
Co-stars: Gordon Harker Emlyn Williams Marie Lohr

JANE LORANGER

1991 THE DARK WIND
Director: Errol Morris
Co-stars: Lou Diamond Phillips Fred Ward Gary Farmer

ISABEL LORCA

1988 SHE'S HAVING A BABY
Director: John Hughes
Co-stars: Kevin Bacon Elizabeth McGovern Alec Baldwin

LAURA GARCIA LORCA

1986 DRAGON RAPIDE
Director: Jaime Camino
Co-stars: Juan Diego Victoria Pena Manuel De Blas

JUSTINE LORD

1962 MANIAC
Director: Michael Carreras
Co-stars: Kerwin Matthews Donald Houston Nadia Gray

1962 TAMAHINE
Director: Philip Leacock
Co-stars: John Fraser Nancy Kwan Dennis Price

1964 ACT OF MURDER
Director: Alan Bridges
Co-stars: John Carson Anthony Bate Dandy Nichols

MARJORIE LORD (MOTHER OF ANNE ARCHER)

1937 FORTY NAUGHTY GIRLS
Director: Edward Cline
Co-stars: Zasu Pitts James Gleason Joan Woodbury

1937 HIDEAWAY
Co-stars: J. Carrol Naish Bradley Page Emma Dunn

1942 MOONLIGHT IN HAVANA
Director: Anthony Mann
Co-stars: Allan Jones Jane Frazee William Frawley

1942 ESCAPE FROM HONG KONG
Co-stars: Don Terry Andy Devine Leo Carrillo

1942 TIMBER
Co-stars: Dan Dailey Leo Carrillo Andy Devine

1943 SHERLOCK HOLMES IN WASHINGTON
Director: Roy William Neill
Co-stars: Basil Rathbone Nigel Bruce

1943 JOHNNY COME LATELY
Director: William Howard
Co-stars: James Cagney Grace George Marjorie Main

1943 HI BUDDY
Director: Harold Young
Co-stars: Dick Foran Harriet Hilliard Robert Paige

1947 NEW ORLEANS
Director: Arthur Lubin
Co-stars: Louis Armstrong Billie Holiday Woody Herman

1953 MEXICAN MANHUNT
Director: Rex Bailey
Co-stars: George Brent Hillary Brooke Morris Ankrum

1966 BOY, DID I GET A WRONG NUMBER
Director: George Marshall
Co-stars: Bob Hope Elke Sommer Phyllis Diller

PAULINE LORD

1934 MRS. WIGGS OF THE CABBAGE PATCH
Director: Norman Taurog
Co-stars: Zasu Pitts W. C. Fields Edith Fellows

1935 A FEATHER IN HER HAT
Director: Alfred Santell
Co-stars: Basil Rathbone Louis Hayward Billie Burke

TRACI LORDS

1988 NOT OF THIS EARTH
Director: Jim Wynorski
Co-stars: Arthur Roberts Lenny Juliano Roger Lodge

1990 CRY-BABY
Director: John Waters
Co-stars: Johnny Depp Amy Locane Susan Tyrrell

1994 SERIAL MOM
Director: John Waters
Co-stars: Kathleen Turner Sam Waterston Ricki Lake

1994 DRAGSTRIP GIRL
Director: Mary Lambert
Co-Stars Mark Decascos Natasha Wagner

1994 BANDIT'S SILVER ANGEL
Director: Hal Needham
Co-Stars Brian Bloom Brian Krause

1998 NOWHERE
Director: Gregg Araki
Co-Stars Shannen Doherty Rose McGowan

LINDA LOREDO

1931 COME CLEAN
Director: James Horne
Co-stars: Stan Laurel Oliver Hardy Mae Busch

SOPHIA LOREN *(Married Carlo Ponti)*
Oscar For Best Actress In 1960 For "Two Women"
Nominated For Best Actress In 1964 For "Marriage-Italian Style"
Received An Honorary Award In 1990

1953 AIDA
Director: Clemente Fracassi
Co-stars: Lois Maxwell Luciano Della Marra

1955 ATTILA THE HUN
Director: Pietro Francisci
Co-stars: Anthony Quinn Irene Papas Henri Vidal

1955 GOLD OF NAPLES
Director: Vittorio De Sica
Co-stars: Eduardo De Felippo Silvana Mangano

1957 BOY ON A DOLPHIN
Director: Jean Negulesco
Co-stars: Alan Ladd Clifton Webb Jorge Mistral

1957 LEGEND OF THE LOST
Director: Henry Hathaway
Co-stars: John Wayne Rossano Brazzi

1957 THE PRIDE AND THE PASSION
Director: Stanley Kramer
Co-stars: Cary Grant Frank Sinatra

1958 HOUSEBOAT
Director: Melville Shavelson
Co-stars: Cary Grant Martha Hyer Harry Guardino

1958 THE BLACK ORCHID
Director: Martin Ritt
Co-stars: Anthony Quinn Ina Balin Jimmy Baird

1958 DESIRE UNDER THE ELMS
Director: Delbert Mann
Co-stars: Anthony Perkins Burl Ives

1958 THE KEY
Director: Carol Reed
Co-stars: William Holden Trevor Howard Bernard Lee

1959 THAT KIND OF WOMAN
Director: Sidney Lumet
Co-stars: Tab Hunter George Sanders Keenan Wynn

1960 HELLER IN PINK TIGHTS
Director: George Cukor
Co-stars: Anthony Quinn Ramon Navarro

1960 A BREATH OF SCANDAL
Director: Michael Curtiz
Co-stars: Maurice Chevalier John Gavin

1960 IT STARTED IN NAPLES
Director: Melville Shavelson
Co-stars: Clark Gable Vittorio De Sica

1960 THE MILLONAIRESS
Director: Anthony Asquith
Co-stars: Peter Sellers Alastair Sim Dennis Price

1960 TWO WOMEN
Director: Vittorio De Sica
Co-stars: Eleanora Brown Jean-Paul Belmondo

1961 EL CID
Director: Anthony Mann
Co-stars: Charlton Heston Raf Vallone Herbert Lom

1962 THE CONDEMNED OF ALTONA
Director: Vittorio De Sica
Co-stars: Fredric March Maximilian Schell

1962 FIVE MILES TO MIDNIGHT
Director: Anatole Litvak
Co-stars: Anthony Perkins Gig Young Yolande Turner

1962 BOCCACCIO 70
Director: Vittorio De Sica
Co-stars: Romy Schneider Anita Ekberg

1962 MADAME
Director: Christian-Jacque
Co-stars: Robert Hossein Julien Bertheau

1963 YESTERDAY, TODAY AND TOMORROW
Director: Vittorio De Sica
Co-star: Marcello Mastroianni

1964 MARRIAGE-ITALIAN STYLE
Director: Vittorio De Sica
Co-stars: Marcello Mastroianni

1964 THE FALL OF THE ROMAN EMPIRE
Director: Anthony Mann
Co-stars: Alec Guinness James Mason

1965 JUDITH
Director: Daniel Mann
Co-stars: Peter Finch Jack Hawkins Hans Verner

1965 LADY L
Director: Peter Ustinov
Co-stars: David Niven Paul Newman Peter Ustinov

1965 OPERATION CROSSBOW
Director: Michael Anderson
Co-stars: George Peppard Tom Courtenay John Mills

1966 ARABESQUE
Director: Stanley Donen
Co-stars: Gregory Peck Alan Badel Kieron Moore

1967 MORE THAN A MIRACLE
]*Director:* Francesco Rosi
Co-stars: Omar Sharif Dolores Del Rio Leslie French

1967 A COUNTESS FROM HONG KONG
Director: Charles Chaplin
Co-stars: Marlon Brando Margaret Rutherford

1968 THE BEST HOUSE IN NAPLES
Co-star: Vittorio Gassman

1970 SUNFLOWER
Director: Vittorio De Sica
Co-star: Marcello Mastroianni

1972 MAN OF LA MANCHA
Director: Arthur Hiller
Co-stars: Peter O'Toole James Coco Harry Andrews

1974 VERDICT
Director: Andre Cayatte
Co-stars: Jean Gabin Michel Albertini Henri Garcin

1975 BRIEF ENCOUNTER
Director: Alan Bridges
Co-stars: Richard Burton Jack Hedley Rosemary Leach

1976 ANGELA
Director: Boris Sagal
Co-stars: Steve Railsback John Huston John Vernon

1976 THE CASSANDRA CROSSING
Director: Brian De Palma
Co-stars: Richard Harris Ava Gardner Burt Lancaster

1977 A SPECIAL DAY
Director: Ettore Scola
Co-stars: Marcello Mastroianni John Vernon

1978 BRASS TARGET
Director: John Hough
Co-stars: George Kennedy Max Von Sydow John Cassavetes

1979 BLOOD FEUD
Director: Lina Wertmuller
Co-stars: Marcello Mastroianni Giancarlo Giannini

1979 FIREPOWER
Director: Michael Winner
Co-stars: James Coburn Eli Wallach O. J. Simpson

1980 SOPHIA LOREN: HER OWN STORY
Director: Mel Stuart
Co-stars: John Gavin Rip Torn Edmund Purdom

1984 AURORA
Director: Maurizo Ponzi
Co-stars: Daniel J. Travanti Edoardo Ponti (Son) Philippe Noiret

1986 COURAGE
Director: Jeremy Kagan
Co-stars: Hector Elizondo Val Avert Ron Rifkin

1994 PRET-A-PORTER
Director: Robert Altman
Co-Star Julia Roberts

TRINITY LOREN

1991 CLASS OF NUKE 'EM HIGH PART II: SUBHUMAN MELTDOWN
Director: Eric Louzil
Co-stars: Lisa Gaye Brick Bronsky

MARGO LORENZ

1954 OUT OF THE CLOUDS
Director: Basil Dearden
Co-stars: Anthony Steel Robert Beatty David Knight

MARA LORENZIO

1933 EL TOPO
Director: Alexandro Jodorowsky
Co-stars: Alexandro Jodorowsky Brontis Jodorowsky David Silva

GLENNIS LORIMER

1938 ASK A POLICEMAN
Director: Marcel Varnel
Co-stars: Will Hay Moore Marriott Graham Moffatt

LOUISE LORIMER

1938 GANGSTER'S BOY
Co-stars: Jackie Cooper Robert Warwick

1952 JAPANESE WAR BRIDE
Director: King Vidor
Co-stars: Shirley Yamaguchi Don Taylor Cameron Mitchell

1952 THE PEOPLE AGAINST O'HARA
Director: John Sturges
Co-stars: Spencer Tracy Diana Lynn Pat O'Brien

ANN LORING

1936 ABSOLUTE QUIET
Director: George Seitz
Co-stars: Lionel Atwill Louis Hayward Irene Hervey

1936 THE ROBIN HOOD OF EL DORADO
Director: William Wellman
Co-stars: Warner Baxter Bruce Cabot Margo

LYNN LORING

1969   JOURNEY TO THE FAR SIDE OF THE SUN
Director: Robert Parrish
Co-stars: Ian Hendry Roy Thinnes Herbert Lom

1972   HORROR AT 37,000 FEET
Director: David Lowell Rich
Co-stars: William Shatner Roy Thinnes

TEALA LORING

1946   DARK ALIBI
Director: Phil Karlson
Co-stars: Sidney Toller Benson Fong Joyce Compton

1946   BLACK MARKET BABIES
Director: William Beaudine
Co-stars: Ralph Morgan Kane Richmonds George Meeker

1946   GAS HOUSE KIDS
Co-star: Billy Halop

1946   BOWERY BOMBSHELL
Director: William Beaudine
Co-stars: Leo Gorcy Huntz Hall Sheldon Leonard

MARION LORNE

1951   STRANGERS ON A TRAIN
Director: Alfred Hitchcock
Co-stars: Robert Walker Farley Granger Ruth Roman

1955   THE GIRL RUSH
Director: Robert Pirosh
Co-stars: Rosalind Russell Eddie Albert Gloria De Haven

LOUISE LORRAINE

1926   EXIT SMILING
Director: Sam Taylor
Co-stars: Beatrice Lillie Jack Pickford Doris Lloyd

LOLITA LORRE

1984   SCREAM FOR HELP
Director: Michael Winner
Co-stars: Rachel Kelly David Brooks Marie Masters

JOAN LORING
Nominated For Best Supporting Actress In 1945 For "The Corn Is Green"

1944   THE BRIDGE OF SAN LUIS REY
Director: Rowland Lee
Co-stars: Lynn Bari Akim Tamiroff Louis Calhern

1945   THE CORN IS GREEN
Director: Irving Rapper
Co-stars: Bette Davis John Dall Nigel Bruce

1946   THREE STRANGERS
Director: Jean Negulesco
Co-stars: Sydney Greenstreet Peter Lorre Geraldine Fitzgerald

1946   THE VERDICT
Director: Don Seigel
Co-stars: Sydney Greenstreet Peter Lorre Rosalind Ivan

1947   THE OTHER LOVE
Director: Andre De Toth
Co-stars: David Niven Barbara Stanwyck Richard Conte

1947   THE GANGSTER
Director: Gordon Wiles
Co-stars: Barry Sullivan Akim Tamiroff Belita

1947   THE LOST MOMENT
Director: Martin Gabel
Co-stars: Robert Cummings Susan Hayward Agnes Moorehead

1948   GOOD SAM
Director: Leo McCarey
Co-stars: Gary Cooper Ann Sheridan Edmund Lowe

1951   THE BIG NIGHT
Director: Joseph Losey
Co-stars: John Barrymore Jnr. Preston Foster Dorothy Comingore

1974   THE MIDNIGHT MAN
Director: Roland Kibbee
Co-stars: Burt Lancaster Susan Clark Cameron Mitchell

DIANA LORYS

1972   BAD MAN'S RIVER
Director: Eugenio Martin
Co-stars: Lee Van Cleef James Mason Gina Lollobrigida

TILLY LOSCH

1935   LIMELIGHT
Director: Herbert Wilcox
Co-stars: Anna Neagle Arthur Tracy Ellis Jeffries

1936   THE GOOD EARTH
Director: Sidney Franklin
Co-stars: Paul Muni Luise Rainer Walter Connolly

1936   THE GARDEN OF ALLAH
Director: Richard Boleslawski
Co-stars: Marlene Dietrich Charles Boyer Basil Rathbone

1946   DUEL IN THE SUN
Director: King Vidor
Co-stars: Gregory Peck Jennifer Jones Joseph Cotten

LOUANNE

1980   THE LONG DAYS OF SUMMER
Director: Dan Curtis
Co-stars: Dean Jones Joan Hackett Donald Moffat

1980   OH GOD! BOOK II
Director: Gilbert Cates
Co-stars: George Burns Suzanne Pleshette Howard Duff

1983   MISSING PIECES
Director: Mike Hodges
Co-stars: Elizabeth Montgomery John Reilly Robin Gammell

DOROTHY LOUDEN

1984   GARBO TALKS
Director: Sidney Lumet
Co-stars: Anne Bancroft Ron Silver Carrie Fisher

LORI LOUGHLIN

1984   AMITYVILLE 3D
Director: Richard Fleischer
Co-stars: Tony Roberts Tess Harper Meg Ryan

1985   NORTH BEACH AND RAWHIDE
Director: Harry Falk
Co-stars: William Shatner Tate Donovan James Olson

1986   BROTHERHOOD OF JUSTICE
Director: Charles Braverman
Co-stars: Keanu Reeves Kiefer Sutherland Joe Spano

1994   ONE OF HER OWN
Director: Armand Mastroianni
Co-stars: Martin Sheen Greg Evigan

1995   ABANDONED AND DECEIVED
Director: Joseph Dougherty
Co-Stars: Brian Kerwin Gordon Clapp Bibi Besch

1996   IN THE LINE OF DUTY: BLAZE OF GLORY
Director: Dick Lowry
Co-Star   Bruce Campbell

JULIA LOUIS-DREYFUSS

1989   NATIONAL LAMPOON'S CHRISTMAS VACATION
Director: Jeremiah Chetchik
Co-stars: Chevy Chase Randy Quaid

1993   **JACK THE BEAR**
Director: Marshall Herskovitz
Co-stars: Danny De Vito Gary Sinese Miko Hughes

1996   **NEIL SIMON'S LONDON SUITE**
Director: Jay Sandrich
Co-Stars   Kelsey Grammer Madeline Kahn Julie Hagerty

1997   **FATHER'S DAY**
Co-stars: Ivan Reitman
Co-stars: Robin Williams Nastassja Kinski Billy Crystal

ANITA LOUISE

1929   **THE MARRIAGE PLAYGROUND**
Director: Lothar Mendes
Co-stars: Fredric March Mary Brian Kay Francis

1931   **THE GREAT MEADOW**
Director: Charles Brabin
Co-stars: Johnny Mack Brown Guinn Williams Eleanor Broadman

1931   **HEAVEN ON EARTH**
Director: Russell Mack
Co-stars: Lew Ayres Harry Beresford Slim Summerville

1931   **EVERTHING'S ROSIE**
Co-stars: Wheeler & Woolsey John Darrow

1932   **PHANTOM OF CRESTWOOD**
Director: Walter Ruben
Co-stars: Ricardo Cortez H. B. Warner Pauline Frederick

1933   **OUR BETTERS**
Director: George Cukor
Co-stars: Constance Bennett Alan Mowbray Gilbert Roland

1934   **THE MOST PRECIOUS THING**
Director: Lambert Hillyer
Co-stars: Jane Darwell Ben Alexander Ward Bond

1934   **MADAME DUBARRY**
Director: William Dieterle
Co-stars: Dolores Del Rio Reginald Owen Victor Jory

1934   **I GIVE MY LOVE**
Director: Karl Freund
Co-stars: Paul Lukas Wynne Gibson Eric Linden

1934   **THE FIREBALL**
Director: William Dieterle
Co-stars: Verree Teasdale Ricardo Cortez Lionel Atwill

1934   **JUDGE PRIEST**
Director: John Ford
Co-stars: Will Rogers Tom Brown Rochelle Hudson David Landau

1934   **BACHELOR OF ARTS**
Co-star: Tom Brown

1934   **ARE WE CIVILISED?**
Co-star: William Farnum

1935   **HERE'S TO ROMANCE**
Director: Alfred Green
Co-stars: Nino Martini Genevieve Tobin Reginald Denny

1935   **LADY TUBBS**
Director: Alan Crosland
Co-stars: Alice Brady Douglass Montgomery Alan Mowbray

1935   **A MIDSUMMER NIGHT'S DREAM**
Director: William Dieterle
Co-stars: James Cagney Dick Powell Mickey Rooney

1936   **ANTHONY ADVERSE**
Director: Mervyn LeRoy
Co-stars: Fredric March Olivia De Havilland Edmond Gwenn

1936   **PERSONAL MAID'S SECRET**
Director: Arthur Greville Collins
Co-stars: Ruth Donnelly Margaret Lindsay

1936   **BRIDES ARE LIKE THAT**
Co-stars: Ross Alexander Dick Purcell

1936   **THE STORY OF LOUIS PASTEUR**
Director: William Dieterle
Co-stars: Paul Muni Josephine Hutchinson

1937   **TOVARICH**
Director: Anatole Litvak
Co-stars: Claudette Colbert Charles Boyer Basil Rathbone

1937   **THE GREEN LIGHT**
Director: Frank Borzage
Co-stars: Errol Flynn Margaret Lindsay Cedric Hardwicke

1937   **THE GO-GETTER**
Director: Busby Berkeley
Co-stars: George Brent Charles Winninger Henry O'Neill

1937   **FIRST LADY**
Director: Stanley Logan
Co-stars: Kay Francis Preston Foster Walter Connolly

1937   **CALL IT A DAY**
Director: Archie Mayo
Co-stars: Olivia De Havilland Ian Hunter Roland Young

1937   **THAT CERTAIN WOMAN**
Director: Edmund Goulding
Co-stars: Bette Davis Henry Fonda Ian Hunter

1938   **THE SISTERS**
Director: Anatole Litvak
Co-stars: Bette Davis Errol Flynn Beulah Bondi Ian Hunter

1938   **MARIE ANTOINETTE**
Director: W. S. Van Dyke
Co-stars: Tyrone Power Norma Shearer John Barrymore

1939   **RENO**
Director: John Farrow
Co-stars: Richard Dix Gail Patrick Paul Cavanagh

1939   **THE LITTLE PRINCESS**
Director: Walter Lang
Co-stars: Shirley Temple Richard Greene Cesar Romero

1939   **MAIN STREET LAWYER**
Co-star: Willard Robertson

1939   **THOSE GLAMOROUS GIRLS**
Director: S. Sylvan Simon
Co-stars: Lew Ayres Lana Turner Jane Bryan Tom Brown

1939   **GOING PLACES**
Director: Ray Enright
Co-stars: Dick Powell Ronald Reagan Louis Armstrong

1939   **THE GORILLA**
Director: Allan Dwan
Co-stars: Ritz Bros. Bela Lugosi Lionel Atwill Patsy Kelly

1940   **THE VILLAIN STILL PURSUED HER**
Director: Edward Cline
Co-stars: Buster Keaton Alan Mowbray Hugh Herbert

1941   **HARMON OF MICHIGAN**
Co-stars: Tom Harmon Larry Parkes

1943   **DANGEROUS BLONDES**
Director: Leigh Jason
Co-stars: Allyn Joslyn Evelyn Keyes Edmund Lowe

1944   **NINE GIRLS**
Director: Leigh Jason
Co-stars: Ann Harding Evelyn Keyes Nina Foch

1944   **CASANOVA BROWN**
Director: Sam Wood
Co-stars: Gary Cooper Teresa Wright Frank Morgan Jill Esmond

1945   **THE FIGHTING GUARDSMAN**
Director: Henry Levin
Co-stars: Williard Parker George Macready John Loder

1945 LOVE LETTERS
Director: William Dieterle
Co-stars: Jennifer Jones Joseph Cotten

1946 SHADOWED
Co-star: Michael Duane

1946 THE DEVIL'S MASK
Director: Henry Levin
Co-stars: Jim Bannon Michael Duane Wendy Barrie

1946 BLONDIE'S BIG MOMENT
Director: Abby Berlin
Co-stars: Penny Singleton Arthur Lake Jerome Cowan

1946 THE BANDIT OF SHERWOOD FOREST
Director: Henry Levin
Co-stars: Cornel Wilde George Macready

1952 RETREAT, HELL!
Director: Joseph Lewis
Co-stars: Frank Lovejoy Richard Carlson Russ Tamblyn

TINA LOUISE

1957 GOD'S LITTLE ACRE
Director: Anthony Mann
Co-Stars Robert Ryan Aldo Ray Jack Lord

1958 THE TRAP
Director: Norman Panama
Co-Stars Richard Widmark Lee J. Cobb Earl Holliman

1958 DAY OF THE OUTLAW
Director: Andre De Toth
Co-Stars Robert Ryan Burl Ives David Nelson

1959 THE HANGMAN
Director: Michael Curtiz
Co-Stars Robert Taylor Jack Lord Fess Parker

1960 THE SIEGE OF SYRACUSE
Director: Pietro Francisci
Co-Stars Rossano Brazzi Gino Cervi Sylva Koscina

1961 ARMORED COMMAND
Director: Byron Haskin
Co-Stars Howard Keel Burt Reynolds Earl Holliman

1964 FOR THOSE WHO THINK YOUNG
Director: Leslie Martinson
Co-Stars James Darren Pamela Tiffin Nancy Sinatra

1968 THE WRECKING CREW
Director: Phil Karlson
Co-Stars Dean Martin Elke Sommer Sharon Tate

1969 HOW TO COMMIT MARRIAGE
Director: Norman Panama
Co-Stars Bob Hope Jane Wyman Jackie Gleason

1969 THE HAPPY ENDING
Director: Richard Brooks
Co-Stars Jean Simmons Shirley Jones Bobby Darin

1969 THE GOOD GUYS AND THE BAD GUYS
Director: Burt Kennedy
Co-Stars Robert Mitchum George Kennedy David Carradine

1974 THE STEPFORD WIVES
Director: Bryan Forbes
Co-Stars Katherine Ross Paula Prentiss Nanette Newman

1983 DOG DAY
Director: Yves Boisset
Co-Stars Miou Miou Lee Marvin Jean Carmet

1985 O.C. AND STIGGS
Director: Robert Altman
Co-Stars Paul Dooley Ray Walston Dennis Hopper

1992 JOHNNY SUEDE
Director: Tom DiCillo
Co-Stars Brad Pitt Alison Moir Catherine Keener

BESSIE LOVE
Nominated For Best Actress In 1929 For "Broadway Melody"

1929 BROADWAY MELODY
Director: Harry Beaumont
Co-stars: Anita Paige Charles King Jed Prouty

1929 CHASING RAINBOWS
Director: Charles Reisner
Co-stars: Charles King Marie Dressler Polly Moran

1929 HOLLYWOOD REVUE
Director: Charles Reisner
Co-stars: Jack Benny Joan Crawford Norma Shearer

1930 GOOD NEWS
Director: Nick Grinde
Co-stars: Stanley Smith Lola Lane Penny Singlelton

1930 SEE AMERICA THIRST
Director: W. J. Craft
Co-stars: Harry Langdon Slim Summerville Stanley Fields

1930 GIRL IN THE SHOW
Co-stars: Raymond Hackett Jed Prouty Nancy Price

1941 ATLANTIC FERRY
Director: Walter Forde
Co-stars: Michael Redgrave Valerie Hobson Griffith Jones

1944 JOURNEY TOGETHER
Director: John Boutling
Co-stars: Richard Attenborough Edward G. Robinson Jack Watling

1958 NOWHERE TO GO
Director: Seth Holt
Co-Stars George Nader Maggie Smith Bernard Lee

1958 NEXT TO NO TIME
Director: Henry Cornelius
Co-stars: Kenneth More Betsy Drake

1959 TOO YOUNG TO LOVE
Director: Muriel Box
Co-stars: Thomas Mitchell Pauline Hahn Jess Conrad

1966 PROMISE HER ANYTHING
Director: Arthur Hiller
Co-stars: Warren Beatty Leslie Caron Lionel Stander

1969 ISADORA
Director: Karel Reisz
Co-stars: Vanessa Redgrave Jason Robards James Fox

1971 CATLOW
Director: Sam Wanamaker
Co-stars: Yul Brynner Richard Crenna Daliah Lavi

1976 GULLIVER'S TRAVELS
Director: Peter Hunt
Co-stars: Richard Harris Catherine Schell Julian Glover

1976 THE RITZ
Director: Richard Lester
Co-stars: Jack Weston Rita Moreno Kaye Ballard

COURTNEY LOVE

1997 THE PEOPLE VS LARRY FLYNT
Director: Milod Forman
Co-star: Woody Harrelson

1997 BASQUIAT
Director: Julian Schnabel
Co-stars: Jeffrey Wright Dennis Hopper Tatum O'Neal

DARLENE LOVE

1987 LETHAL WEAPON
Director: Richard Donner
Co-stars: Mel Gibson Danny Glover Gary Busey

1989 LETHAL WEAPON 2
Director: Richard Donner
Co-Stars Mel Gibson Danny Glover Joe Pesci

1992 LETHAL WEAPON 3
Director: Richard Donner
Co-Stars Mel Gibson Danny Glover Rene Russo

JUNE LOVE

1935 COURAGE OF THE NORTH
Co-stars: John Preston Tom London

LUCRETIA LOVE

1974 THE ARENA
Director: Steve Carver
Co-stars: Pam Grier Margaret Markov Paul Muller

PATTI LOVE

1985 STEAMING
Director: Joseph Losey
Co-stars: Vanessa Redgrave Sarah Miles Diana Dors

1990 THE KRAYS
Director: Peter Medak
Co-stars: Billie Whitelaw Martin Kemp Gary Kemp

PHYLLIS LOVE

1961 THE YOUNG DOCTORS
Director: Phil Karlson
Co-stars: Fredric March Ben Gazzara Eddie Albert

SUZANNE LOVE

1982 BRAINWAVES
Director: Ulli Lommel
Co-stars: Tony Curtis Keir Dulllea Vera Miles

DOROTHY LOVETT

1939 MEET DR. CHRISTIAN
Director: Bernard Vorhaus
Co-stars: Jean Hersholt Robert Baldwin Paul Harvey

1941 SING YOUR WORRIES AWAY
Director: Edward Sutherland
Co-stars: Bert Lahr Buddy Ebson June Havoc

1943 MANTRAP
Director: George Sherman
Co-stars: Henry Stephenson Lloyd Corrigan Joseph Allen

CELIA LOVSKY

1950 CAPTAIN CAREY U. S. A.
Director: Mitchell Leison
Co-stars: Alan Ladd Wanda Hendrix Francis Lederer

1954 RHAPSODY
Director: Charles Vidor
Co-stars: Elizabeth Taylor Vittorio Gassman Louis Calhern

1955 NEW YORK CONFIDENTIAL
Director: Russel Rouse
Co-stars: Broderick Crawford Richard Conte Anne Bancroft

1957 MAN OF A THOUSAND FACES
Director: Joseph Pevney
Co-stars: James Cagney Dorothy Malone Robert Evans

1958 TWILIGHT FOR THE GODS
Director: Joseph Pevney
Co-stars: Rock Hudson Cyd Charisse Arthur Kennedy

1958 I, MOBSTER
Director: Roger Corman
Co-stars: Steve Cochran Lita Milan Robert Strauss

1959 THE GENE KUPRA STORY
Director: Don Weis
Co-stars: Sal Mineo Susan Kohner James Darren

1965 HARLOW
Director: Gordon Douglas
Co-stars: Carroll Baker Martin Balsam Red Buttons

1968 THE POWER
Director: Byron Haskin
Co-stars: Michael Rennie George Hamilton Suzanne Pleshette

FRANCES LOW

1983 LOOSE CONNECTIONS
Director: Richard Eyre
Co-stars: Stephen Rea Lindsay Duncan Carole Harrison

1991 DECEMBER BRIDE
Director: Thaddeus O'Sulliavn
Co-stars: Donal McCann Saskia Reeves Dervla Kirwan

CAREY LOWELL

1989 LICENCE TO KILL
Director: John Glenn
Co-stars: Timothy Dalton Robert Davi Talisa Soto

1990 THE GUARDIAN
Director: William Friedkin
Co-stars: Jenny Seagrove Dwier Brown Brad Hall

1993 SLEEPLESS IN SEATTLE
Director: Nora Ephron
Co-stars: Tom Hanks Meg Ryan Ross Malinger

HELEN LOWELL

1924 ISN'T LIFE WONDERFUL
Director: D. W. Griffith
Co-stars: Carol Dempster Neil Hamilton Lupino Lane

1935 LIVING ON VELVET
Director: Frank Borzage
Co-stars: George Brent Kay Francis Warren William

1935 DEVIL DOGS OF THE AIR
Director: Lloyd Bacon
Co-stars: James Cagney Pat O'Brien Margaret Lindsay

1935 MAYBE IT'S LOVE
Co-stars: Gloria Stuart Ross Alexander Frank McHugh

1936 WILD BRIAN KENT
Director: Howard Bretherton
Co-stars: Ralph Bellamy Mae Clarke Stanley Andrews

1936 PARTY WIRE
Director: Erle Kenton
Co-stars: Jean Arthur Victor Jory Robert Allen

ELINA LOWENSOHN

1992 SIMPLE MEN
Director: Hal Hartley
Co-stars: Robert Burke William Sage Karen Sillas

1994 AMATEUR
Director: Hal Hartley
Co-stars: Isabelle Huppert Martin Donovan Damion Young

1995 NADJA
Co-stars: Peter Fonda

EMILY LOWRY

1934 AS THE EARTH TURNS
Director: Alfred Green
Co-stars: Jean Muir Donald Woods Dorothy Peterson

JENNIFER LOWRY

1988 BRAIN DAMAGE
Director: Frank Hennenlotter
Co-stars: Rick Herbst Theo Barnes Vicki Darnell

JUDITH LOWRY

1972   THE EFFECT OF GAMMA RAYS ON THE MAN IN THE MOON MARIGOLDS
Director: Paul Newman
Co-stars: Joanne Woodward Nell Potts Roberta Wallach

LYNN LOWRY

1975   SHIVERS
Director: David Cronenberg
Co-stars: Paul Hampton Joe Silver Susan Petrie

1976   FIGHTING MAD
Director: Jonathan Demme
Co-stars: Peter Fonda John Doucette Philip Carey

MYRNA LOY (Received An Honorary Award In 1990)

1925   WHAT PRICE BEAUTY?

1925   PRETTY LADIES
Director: Monta Bell
Co-stars: Zasu Pitts Norma Shearer Tom Moore

1926   DON JUAN
Director: Alan Crosland
Co-stars: John Barrymore Mary Astor Warner Oland

1926   SO THIS IS PARIS
Director: Ernst Lubitsch
Co-stars: Monte Blue Patsy Ruth Miller Lilyan Tashman

1926   THE CAVE MAN
Director: Lewis Milestone
Co-stars: Marie Prevost Matt Moore Hedda Hopper

1927   THE JAZZ SINGER
Director: Alan Crosland
Co-stars: Al Jolson May McAvoy William Demarest

1928   A GIRL IN EVERY PORT
Director: Howard Hawkes
Co-stars: Victor McLaglen Robert Armstrong Louise Brooks

1929   THE BLACK WITCH
Director: John Ford
Co-stars: Victor McLaglen David Rollins Walter Lang

1929   NOAH'S ARK
Director: Michael Curtiz
Co-stars: Noah Beery Dolores Costello Louise Fazenda

1929   SHOW OF SHOWS
Director: John Adolfi
Co-stars: Ben Turpin Lupino Lane Alice White Lila Lee

1929   THE SQUALL
Director: Alexander Korda
Co-stars: Loretta Young Zasu Pitts Richard Ticker

1929   THE DESERT SONG
Director: Roy Del Ruth
Co-stars: John Boles Carlotta King Louise Fazenda

1930   UNDER A TEXAS MOON
Director: Michael Curtiz
Co-stars: Frank Fay Raquel Torres Noah Beery

1930   RENEGADES
Director: Victor Fleming
Co-stars: Warner Baxter Bela Lugosi Noah Beery

1930   COCK O' THE WALK
Co-star: Joseph Schildkraut

1931   TRANSATLANTIC
Director: William Howard
Co-stars: Edmund Lowe John Halliday Jean Hersholt

1931   REBOUND
Director: Edward Griffith
Co-stars: Ina Claire Robert Williams Hedda Hopper

1931   HUSH MONEY
Director: Sidney Lanfield
Co-stars: Joan Bennett Owen Moore George Raft

1931   THE DEVIL TO PAY
Director: George Fitzmaurice
Co-stars: Ronald Colman Loretta Young Paul Cavanagh

1931   CONSOLATION MARRIAGE
Director: Paul Sloane
Co-stars: Irene Dunn Pat O'Brien John Halliday

1931   A CONNECTICUT YANKEE
Director: David Butler
Co-stars: Will Rogers Maureen O'Sullivan William Farnum

1931   BODY AND SOUL
Director: Alfred Santell
Co-stars: Charles Farrell Elisa Landi Humphrey Bogart

1931   ARROWSMITH
Director: John Ford
Co-stars: Ronald Colman Helen Hayes Beulah Bondi

1932   THE ANIMAL KINGDOM
Director: Edward Griffith
Co-stars: Leslie Howard Ann Harding William Gargan

1932   EMMA
Director: Clarence Brown
Co-stars: Marie Dressler Jean Hersholt Richard Cromwell

1932   THE MASK OF FU MANCHU
Director: Charles Brabin
Co-stars: Boris Karloff Lewis Stone Charles Starrett

1932   NEW MORALS FOR OLD
Director: Charles Brabin
Co-stars: Robert Young Jean Hersholt Lewis Stone

1932   LOVE ME TONIGHT
Director: Rouben Mamoulian
Co-stars: Maurice Chevalier Jeanette MacDonald

1932   13 WOMEN
Director: George Archainbaud
Co-stars: Ricardo Cortez Irene Dunne Florence Eldridge

1932   VANITY FAIR
Director: Chester Franklin
Co-stars: Conway Tearle Barbara Kent

1932   THE WET PARADE
Director: Victor Fleming
Co-stars: Walter Huston Neil Hamilton Jimmy Durante

1932   THE WOMAN IN ROOM 13
Director: Henry King
Co-stars: Elissa Landi Ralph Bellamy Gilbert Roland

1933   WHEN LADIES MEET
Director: Harry Beaumont
Co-stars: Ann Harding Robert Montgomery Alice Brady

1933   TOPAZE
Director: Harry D'Abbabie D'Arrast
Co-stars: John Barrymore Jackie Searle

1933   THE PRIZEFIGHTER AND THE LADY
Director: W. S. Van Dyke
Co-stars: Max Baer Walter Huston Otto Kruger

1933   NIGHT FLIGHT
Director: Clarence Brown
Co-stars: John Barrymore Lionel Barrymore Clark Gable

1933   THE BARBARIAN
Director: Sam Wood
Co-stars: Ramon Navarro Edward Arnold Reginald Denny

1934   BROADWAY BILL
Director: Frank Capra
Co-stars: Warner Baxter Walter Connolly Ward Bond

1934	**EVELYN PRENTICE**	1940	**I LOVE YOU AGAIN**
Director:	William Howard	*Director:*	W. S. Van Dyke
Co-stars:	William Powell Una Merkel Rosalind Russell	*Co-stars:*	William Powell Frank McHugh Edmund Lowe

1934 EVELYN PRENTICE
Director: William Howard
Co-stars: William Powell Una Merkel Rosalind Russell

1934 MANHATTAN MELODRAMA
Director: W. S. Van Dyke
Co-stars: William Powell Clark Gable Nat Pendleton

1934 MEN IN WHITE
Director: Richard Boleslawski
Co-stars: Clark Gable Elizabeth Allan Otto Kruger

1934 THE THIN MAN
Director: W. S. Van Dyke
Co-stars: William Powell Maureen O'Sullivan

1934 STAMBOUL QUEST
Director: Sam Wood
Co-stars: George Brent Lionel Atwill C. Henry Gordon

1935 WINGS IN THE DARK
Director: James Flood
Co-stars: Cary Grant Dean Jagger Roscoe Karns

1936 AFTER THE THIN MAN
Director: W. S. Van Dyke
Co-stars: William Powell James Stewart Elissa Landi

1936 LIBELED LADY
Director: Jack Conway
Co-stars: William Powell Jean Harlow Spencer Tracy

1936 THE GREAT ZIEGFELD
Director: Robert Z. Leonard
Co-stars: William Powell Luise Rainer Frank Morgan

1936 PETTICOAT FEVER
Director: George Fitzmaurice
Co-stars: Robert Montgomery Reginald Owen

1936 TO MARY - WITH LOVE
Director: John Cromwell
Co-stars: Warner Baxter Ian Hunter Claire Trevor

1936 WHIPSAW
Director: Sam Wood
Co-stars: Spencer Tracy Harvey Stephens Clay Clements

1936 WIFE VS SECRETARY
Director: Clarence Brown
Co-stars: Clark Gable Jean Harlow James Stewart

1937 PARNELL
Director: John Stahl
Co-stars: Clark Gable Edmund Gwenn Donald Crisp

1937 DOUBLE WEDDING
Director: Richard Thorpe
Co-stars: William Powell John Beal Florence Rice

1938 MAN-PROOF
Director: Richard Thorpe
Co-stars: Franchot Tone Walter Pidgeon Rosalind Russell

1938 TEST PILOT
Director: Victor Fleming
Co-stars: Clark Gable Spencer Tracy Lionel Barrymore

1938 TOO HOT TO HANDLE
Director: Jack Conway
Co-stars: Clark Gable Walter Pidgeon Walter Connolly

1939 THE RAINS CAME
Director: Clarence Brown
Co-stars: Tyrone Power George Brent Brenda Joyce

1939 ANOTHER THIN MAN
Director: W. S. Van Dyke
Co-stars: William Powell Otto Kruger Virginia Gray

1939 LUCKY NIGHT
Director: Norman Taurog
Co-stars: Robert Taylor Henry O'Neill Marjorie Main

1940 I LOVE YOU AGAIN
Director: W. S. Van Dyke
Co-stars: William Powell Frank McHugh Edmund Lowe

1940 THIRD FINGER LEFT HAND
Director: Robert Z. Leonard
Co-stars: Melvyn Douglas Lee Bowman Donna Reed Sam Levene

1941 LOVE CRAZY
Director: Jack Conway
Co-stars: William Powell Jack Carson Gail Patrick

1944 THE THIN MAN GOES HOME
Director: Richard Thorpe
Co-stars: William Powell Gloria DeHaven Ann Revere

1946 SO GOES MY LOVE
Director: Frank Ryan
Co-stars: Don Ameche Bobby Driscoll Rhys Williams

1946 THE BEST YEARS OF OUR LIVES
Director: William Wyler
Co-stars: Fredric March Teresa Wright Dana Andrews

1947 BACHELOR KNIGHT
Director: Irving Reis
Co-stars: Cary Grant Shirley Temple Rudy Vallee

1947 THE SENATOR WAS INDISCREET
Director: George Kaufman
Co-stars: William Powell Ella Raines Arleen Whelan

1947 SONG OF THE THIN MAN
Director: Edward Buzzell
Co-stars: William Powell Dean Stockwell Gloria Grahame

1948 MR. BLANDINGS BUILDS HIS DREAM HOUSE
Director: H. C. Potter
Co-stars: Cary Grant Melvyn Douglas Reginald Denny

1949 THE RED PONY
Director: Lewis Milestone
Co-stars: Robert Mitchum Peter Miles Louis Calhern

1949 THAT DANGEROUS AGE
Director: Gregory Ratoff
Co-stars: Roger Livesey Peggy Cummings Richard Greene

1950 CHEAPER BY THE DOZEN
Director: Walter Lang
Co-stars: Clifton Webb Jeanne Carin Barbara Bates

1952 BELLES ON THEIR TOES
Director: Henry Levin
Co-stars: Jeanne Crain Edward Arnold Debra Paget

1956 THE AMBASSADOR'S DAUGHTER
Director: Norman Krasna
Co-stars: Olivia De Havilland John Forsythe

1958 LONELYHEARTS
Director: Vincent Donehue
Co-stars: Montgomery Clift Maureen Stapleton Robert Ryan

1960 MIDNIGHT LACE
Director: David Miller
Co-stars: Doris Day Rex Harrison Roddy McDowall

1960 FROM THE TERRACE
Director: Mark Robson
Co-stars: Paul Newman Joanne Woodward Leon Ames

1969 THE APRIL FOOLS
Director: Stuart Rosenberg
Co-stars: Jack Lemmon Catherine Deneuvre Charles Boyer

1971 DO NOT FOLD, SPINDLE OR MUTILATE
Director: Ted Post
Co-stars: Helen Hayes Sylvia Sidney Vince Edwards

1974 AIRPORT '75
Director: Jack Smight
Co-stars: Charlton Heston Karen Black George Kennedy

1974 INDICT AND CONVICT
Director: Boris Sagal
Co-Stars William Shatner George Grizzard Eli Wallach

1977 PANIC AT LAKEWOOD MANOR
Director: Robert Sheerer
Co-stars: Robert Foxworth Lynda Day George

1978 THE END
Director: Burt Reynolds
Co-stars: Burt Reynolds Sally Field Joanne Woodward Pat O'Brien

1980 JUST TELL ME WHAT YOU WANT
Director: Sidney Lumet
Co-stars: Ali MacGraw Alan King Keenan Wynn

MARGARITA LOZANO

1961 VIRIDIANA
Director: Luis Bunel
Co-stars: Slivia Pinal Francisco Rabal Fernando Rey

1981 THE NIGHT OF SAN LORENZO
Director: Paolo Taviani
Co-stars: Omero Antonutti Claudio Bigagli

1984 KAOS
Director: Paolo Taviani
Co-stars: Claudio Bigagli Ciccio Ingrassia Franco Franchi

1986 MANON DES SOURCES
Director: Claude Berri
Co-stars: Yves Montand Emmanuelle Beart Daniel Auteuill

1990 NIGHT SUN
Director: Paolo Taviani
Co-stars: Julian Sands Charlotte Gainsbourg Nastassja Kinski

LISA LU

1960 THE MOUNTAIN ROAD
Director: Daniel Mann
Co-stars: James Stewart Glenn Corbett Henry Morgan

1962 RIDER ON A DEAD HORSE
Director: Herbert Strock
Co-stars: Bruce Gordon Kevin Hagen John Vyvyan

1977 DEMON SEED
Director: Donald Cammell
Co-stars: Julie Christie Fritz Weaver Gerrit Graham

1979 SAINT JACK
Director: Peter Bogdanovich
Co-stars: Ben Gazzara Denholm Elliott George Lazenby

1993 THE JOY LUCK CLUB
Director: Wayne Lang
Co-stars: Tsai Chin Tamlyn Tomita France Nuyen

ANTONELLA LUALDI

1954 LE ROUGE ET LE NOIR
Director: Claude Autant-Lara
Co-stars: Gerard Philipe Danielle Darrieux

1959 A DOUBLE TOUR
Director: Claude Chabrol
Co-stars: Jacques Dacqmine Madeleine Robinson Bernadette Lafont

**1947 VINCENT, FRANCOIS, PAUL
AND THE OTHERS**
Co-stars: Claude Sautet
Co-stars: Yves Montand Michel Piccoli

PAULA LUBELSKA

1939 TEVYA THE MILKMAN
Director: Maurice Schwartz
Co-stars: Maurice Schwartz Miriam Riselle Rebecca Weintraub

BETTY LUCAS

1984 MY FIRST WIFE
Director: Paul Cox
Co-stars: John Hargreaves Wendy Hughes Lucy Angwin

1991 WENDY CRACKS A WALNUT
Director: Michael Patterson
Co-stars: Rosanna Arquette Hugo Weaving Bruce Spence

KAREN LUCAS (Child)

1973 THE ZOO ROBBERY
Director: John Black
Co-stars: Paul Gyngell Denise Gyngell Richard Willis

LISA LUCAS

1974 THE MIGRANTS
Director: Tom Gries
Co-stars: Cloris Leachman Ron Howard Sissy Spacek

1978 AN UNMARRIED WOMAN
Director: Paul Mazursky
Co-stars: Jill Clayburgh Alan Bates Michael Murphy

1993 HEART AND SOULS
Director: Ron Underwood
Co-stars: Charles Grodin Robert Downey Jnr Kyra Sedgewick

SUSAN LUCCI

1984 INVITATION TO HELL
Director: Wes Craven
Co-stars: Robert Urich Joanna Cassidy Kevin McCarthy

1986 MAFIA BUSINESS
Director: Robert Collins
Co-stars: Tony Curtis Kathleen Widdoes Chuck Shamata

1986 ANASTASIA: THE MYSTERY OF ANNA
Director: Marvin Chomsky
Co-stars: Amy Irving Olivia De Havilland

1988 LADY MOBSTER
Director: John Llewellyn Moxey
Co-stars: Michael Nader Joseph Wiseman Al Ruscio

1991 THE WOMAN WHO SINNED
Director: Michael Switzer
Co-star: Tim Matheson

1992 DOUBLE EDGE
Director: Stephen Stafford
Co-Stars Robert Urich Robert Prosky

1993 FRENCH SILK
Director: Noel Nosseck
Co-stars: Lee Horsley Shari Bellafonte

1995 SEDUCED AND BETRAYED
Director: Felix Enriques Alla
Co-Star David Charvet

ANGELA LUCE

1996 L'AMORE MOLESTO
Co-star: Anna Bonaiuto

CLAIRE LUCE

1930 UP THE RIVER
Director: John Ford
Co-stars: Spencer Tracy Warren Hymer Humphrey Bogart

1935 VINTAGE WINE
Director: Henry Edwards
Co-stars: Seymour Hicks Judy Gunn Miles Malleson

1935 LET'S MAKE A NIGHT OF IT
Director: Graham Cutts
Co-stars: Charles Rogers June Clyde Fred Emney

1935 LAZYBONES
Director: Michael Powell
Co-stars: Ian Hunter Sara Allgood Harold Warrender

1937 OVER SHE GOES
Co-stars: Graham Cutts
Co-stars: Stanley Lupino Laddie Cliff Gina Malo

1937 MADEMOISELLE DOCTEUR
Director: Edmond Greville
Co-stars: Dita Parlo John Loder Erich Von Stroheim

CORINNE LUCHAIRE

1938 PRISON WITHOUT BARS
Director: Brain Desmond Hurst
Co-stars: Edna Best Barry K. Barnes Mary Morris

1939 LE DERNIER TOURNANT
Director: Pierre Chenal
Co-stars: Michel Simon Fernand Gravet Florence Marley

FABRICE LUCHINI

1970 CLAIRE'S KNEE
Director: Eric Rohmer
Co-stars: Jean-Claude Brialy Aurora Cornu Beatrice Romand

1974 IMMORAL TALES
Director: Walerian Borowczyk
Co-stars: Lise Danvers Charlotte Alexandra Paloma Picasso

1985 HOTEL DU PARADIS
Director: Jana Bokova
Co-star: Fernando Rey

JEAN LUCIUS

1938 GIRL'S SCHOOL
Co-stars: Martha O'Driscoll Peggy Moran Kenneth Howell

BARBARA LUDDY

1955 LADY AND THE TRAMP *(Voice)*
Director: Clyde Geronomi
Co-stars: Peggy Lee Bill Thompson Stan Freberg

1959 SLEEPING BEAUTY *(Voice)*
Director: Clyde Geronomi
Co-stars: Mary Costa Bill Shirley Barbara Jo Allen

PAMELA LUDWIG

1979 OVER THE EDGE
Director: Jonathan Kaplan
Co-stars: Michael Kramer Matt Dillon Vincent Spano

1980 THE ELEVENTH VICTIM
Director: Jonathan Kaplan
Co-stars: Bess Armstrong Max Gail Eric Burden

1985 DEATH OF AN ANGEL
Director: Petru Popescu
Co-stars: Bonnie Bedelia Nick Mancuso Irma Garcia

LORNA LUFT
(Daughter Of Judy Garland And Sid Luft)

1982 GREASE 2
Director: Patricia Birch
Co-stars: Michelle Pfeiffer Maxwell Caulfield Eve Arden

1984 WHERE THE BOYS ARE
Director: Hy Averback
Co-stars: Lisa Hartman Wendy Schall Russel Todd

1989 FEAR STALK
Director: Larry Shaw
Co-stars: Jill Clayburgh Stephen Macht Lynne Thigpen

FRANCOISE LUGAGNE

1964 THE DIARY OF A CHAMBERMAID
Director: Luis Bunel
Co-stars: Jeanne Moreau Georges Geret Michel Piccoli

ROSINE LUGUET

1954 FEMMES DE PARIS
Director: Jean Loubignac
Co-stars: Robert Dhery Colette Brosset Louis De Funes

LULU

1967 TO SIR WITH LOVE
Director: James Clavell
Co-stars: Sidney Poitier Judy Geeson Suzy Kendall

LULUBELLE

1943 SWING YOUR PARTNER
Co-star: Vera Vague

JENNY LUMET

1990 Q & A
Director: Sidney Lumet
Co-stars: Nick Nolte Timothy Hutton Patrick O'Neal

JOANNA LUMLEY

1969 SOME GIRLS DO
Director: Ralph Thomas
Co-stars: Richard Johnson Daliah Lavi Robert Morley

1973 SATANIC RITES OF DRACULA
Director: Alan Gibson
Co-stars: Peter Cushing Christopher Lee Freddie Jones

1973 DON'T JUST LIE THERE, SAY SOMETHING
Director: Bob Kellett
Co-stars: Brain Rix Leslie Phillips

1982 TRAIL OF THE PINK PANTHER
Director: Blake Edwards
Co-stars: Peter Sellers Herbert Lom David Niven

1982 CURSE OF THE PINK PANTHER
Director: Blake Edwards
Co-stars: Ted Wass Herbert Lom Capucine

1989 SHIRLEY VALENTINE
Director: Lewis Gilbert
Co-stars: Pauline Collins Tom Conti Bernard Hill

1995 INNOCENT LIES
Director: Patrick DeWolf
Co-Stars: Stephen Dorff Gabrielle Anwar Adrian Dunbar

1996 PRINCE VALLIANT
Co-stars: Stephen Moyer Edward Fox

1996 JAMES AND THE GIANT PEACH
Director: Henry Selig
Co-stars: Paul Terry Pete Postlethwaite Jane Leeves

1996 ABSOLUTELY FABULOUS
Co-stars: Jennifer Saunders Julia Sawahla Jane Horrocks

BARBARA LUNA

1961 THE DEVIL AT FOUR O'CLOCK
Director: Mervyn LeRoy
Co-stars: Spencer Tracy Frank Sinatra Gregoire Aslan

1962 FIVE WEEKS IN A BALOON
Director: Irwin Allen
Co-stars: Cedric Hardwicke Peter Lorre Richard Haydn

1968 FIRECREEK
Director: Bernard McEveety
Co-stars: James Stewart Henry Fonda Inger Stevens

1969 CHE!
Director: Richard Fleischer
Co-stars: Omar Sharif Jack Palance Robert Loggia

JANA LUND

1958 FRANKENSTEIN - 1970
Director: Howard Koch
Co-stars: Boris Karloff Tom Duggan Mike Lane

LUCILLE LUND

1937 VENGEANCE
Director: Del Lord
Co-stars: Lyle Talbot Wendy Barrie Marc Lawrence

ZOE LUND

1992 THE BAD LIEUTENANT
Director: Abel Ferrara
Co-stars: Harvey Keitel Frankie Thorn Victoria Bastel

JESSICA LUNDY

1988 CADDYSHACK II
Director: Alan Arkush
Co-stars: Jackie Mason Dyan Cannon Robert Stack

1990 MADHOUSE
Director: Tom Ropelewski
Co-stars: John Larroquette Kirstie Alley John Diehl

1992 SINGLE WHITE FEMALE
Director: Barbet Schroeder
Co-stars: Bridget Fonda Jennifer Jason Leigh Steve Webber

1996 THE STUPIDS
Director: John Landis
Co-Stars Tom Arnold Christopher Lee

JAIMIE LUNDY

1993 WHY MY DAUGHTER?
Director: Chuck Bowman
Co-stars: Linda Gray Antonio Sabato Jnr.

CHERIE LUNGHI

1981 EXCALIBUR
Director: John Borman
Co-stars: Nigel Terry Helen Mirren Nicol Williamson Nicolas Clay

1982 OLIVER TWIST
Director: Clive Donner
Co-stars: George C. Scott Tim Curry Timothy West Lysette Anthony

1984 PARKER
Director: Jim Goddard
Co-stars: Bryan Brown Bob Peck Kurt Raab

1984 THE SIGN OF FOUR
Director: Desmond Davis
Co-stars: Ian Richardson David Healy Terence Rigby

1985 KING DAVID
Director: Bruce Beresford
Co-stars: Richard Gere Edward Woodward Hurd Hatfield

1986 HAREM
Director: Billy Hale
Co-stars: Nancy Travis Art Malik Sarah Miles Omar Sharif

1986 COAST TO COAST
Director: Sandy Johnson
Co-stars: Lenny Henry John Shea George Baker Peter Vaughan

1986 THE MISSION
Director: Roland Joffe
Co-stars: Robert De Niro Jeremy Irons Ray McInally Liam Neeson

1988 THE MAN WHO LIVED AT THE RITZ
Director: Desmond Davis
Co-stars: Perry King Leslie Caron David Robb

1988 INTRIQUE
Director: David Drury
Co-stars: Scott Glen Robert Loggia Willaim Atherton Martin Shaw

1991 INSPECTOR WEXFORD:
PUT ON BY CUNNING
Director: George Baker
Co-stars: Rossano Brazzi Diane Keen

1993 A QUESTION OF GUILT
Director: Stuart Orme
Co-stars: Derrick O'Connor Peter Jeffrey Celia Imrie

1996 THE CANTERVILLE GHOST
Director: Syd Macartney
Co-Stars Patrick Stewart Neve Campbell Edward Whiley

BEVERLY LUNSFORD

1961 THE INTRUDER
Director: Roger Corman
Co-stars: William Shatner Frank Maxwell Jeanne Cooper

LETICIA LUPERSIO

1986 DONA HERLINDA AND HER SON
Director: Jaime Humberto Hermosillo
Co-stars: Arturo Meza Guadalupe Del Toro

TABITHA LUPIEN *(Child)*

1993 LOOK WHO'S TALKING NOW
Director: Tom Ropelewski
Co-stars: John Travolta Kirstie Alley Lysette Anthony

IDA LUPINO *(Daughter Of Stanley Lupino)*

1932 THE LOVE RACE

1932 HER FIRST AFFAIR
Co-stars: Diana Napier Arnold Riches

1933 I LIVED WITH YOU
Director: Maurice Elvey
Co-stars: Ivor Novello Ursula Jeans Jack Hawkins

1933 THE GHOST CAMERA
Director: Bernard Vorhaus
Co-stars: John Mills Henry Kendall Felix Aylmer

1934 COME ON MARINES
Co-stars: Richard Arlen Toby Wing

1934 SEARCH FOR BEAUTY
Director: Erle Kenton
Co-stars: Buster Crabbe Toby Wing James Gleason

1935 ONE RAINY AFTERNOON
Director: Rowland Lee
Co-stars: Francis Lederer Roland Young Mischa Auer

1935 THE MILKY WAY

1935 PARIS IN SPRING
Director: Lewis Milestone
Co-stars: Mary Ellis Tullio Carminati

1935 PETER IBBETSON
Director: Henry Hathaway
Co-stars: Gary Cooper Ann Harding John Halliday

1935 SMART GIRL
Director: Aubrey Scotto
Co-stars: Gail Patrick Kent Taylor Sidney Blackmer

1936 THE GAY DESPERADO
Director: Rouben Mamoulian
Co-stars: Nino Martini Leo Carrillo Mischa Auer

1936 ANYTHING GOES
Director: Lewis Milestone
Co-stars: Bing Crosby Ethel Merman Charles Ruggles

1937	**ARTISTS AND MODELS**
Director:	Raoul Walsh
Co-stars:	Jack Benny Richard Arlen Gail Patrick

1937	**FIGHT FOR YOUR LADY**
Director:	Ben Stoloff
Co-stars:	John Boles Jack Oakie Erik Rhodes

1937	**LET'S GET MARRIED**
Director:	Alfred Green
Co-stars:	Walter Connolly Ralph Bellamy Reginald Denny

1937	**SEA DEVILS**
Director:	Ben Stoloff
Co-stars:	Victor McLaglen Preston Foster Donald Woods

1939	**THE LADY AND THE MOB**
Director:	Ben Stoloff
Co-stars:	Fay Bainter Lee Bowman Warren Hymer

1939	**LIGHT THAT FAILED**
Director:	William Wellman
Co-stars:	Ronald Colman Walter Huston

1939	**THE LONE WOLF SPY HUNT**
Director:	Peter Godfrey
Co-stars:	Warren William Rita Hayworth Eric Blore

1939	**THE ADVENTURES OF SHERLOCK HOLMES**
Director:	Alfred Werker
Co-stars:	Basil Rathbone Nigel Bruce

1940	**THEY DRIVE BY NIGHT**
Director:	Raoul Walsh
Co-stars:	George Raft Humphrey Bogart Ann Sheridan

1941	**THE SEA WOLF**
Director:	Michael Curtiz
Co-stars:	Edward G. Robinson John Garfield Alexander Knox

1941	**OUT OF THE FOG**
Director:	Anatole Litvak
Co-stars:	John Garfield Thomas Mitchell Eddie Albert

1941	**LADIES IN RETIREMENT**
Director:	Charles Vidor
Co-stars:	Louis Hayward Elsa Lanchester

1941	**HIGH SIERRA**
Director:	Raoul Walsh
Co-stars:	Humphrey Bogart Joan Leslie Arthur Kennedy

1942	**LIFE BEGINS AT EIGHT-THIRTY**
Director:	Irving Pichel
Co-stars:	Monty Wooley Cornel Wilde Sara Allgood

1942	**MOONTIDE**
Director:	Archie Mayo
Co-stars:	Jean Gabin Claude Rains Thomas Mitchell

1942	**THE HARD WAY**
Director:	Vincent Sherman
Co-stars:	Dennis Morgan Jack Carson Joan Leslie

1943	**DEVOTION**
Director:	Curtis Bernhardt
Co-stars:	Olivia De Havilland Arthur Kennedy

1943	**THANK YOUR LUCKY STARS**
Director:	David Butler
Co-stars:	Eddie Cantor Dennis Morgan Errol Flynn

1943	**FOREVER AND A DAY**
Director:	Rene Clair
Co-stars:	Anna Neagle Ray Milland Charles Laughton

1944	**IN OUR TIME**
Director:	Vincent Sherman
Co-stars:	Paul Henreid Nazimova Nancy Coleman

1944	**HOLLYWOOD CANTEEN**
Director:	Delmer Daves
Co-stars:	Joan Leslie Robert Hutton Janis Paige Dane Clark

1945	**PILLOW TO POST**
Director:	Vincent Sherman
Co-stars:	Sydney Greenstreet William Prince

1946	**THE MAN I LOVE**
Director:	Raoul Walsh
Co-stars:	Robert Alda Andrea King Martha Vickers

1947	**ESCAPE ME NEVER**
Director:	Peter Godfrey
Co-stars:	Errol Flynn Eleanor Parker Gig Young

1947	**DEEP VALLEY**
Director:	Jean Negulesco
Co-stars:	Dane Clark Wayne Morris Henry Hull

1948	**ROAD HOUSE**
Director:	Jean Negulesco
Co-stars:	Richard Widmark Cornel Wilde Celeste Holm

1949	**WOMAN IN HIDING**
Director:	Michael Gordon
Co-stars:	Howard Duff Stephen McNally Peggy Dow

1949	**LUST FOR GOLD**
Director:	S. Sylvan Simon
Co-stars:	Glenn Ford Gig Young William Prince

1951	**ON DANGEROUS GROUND**
Director:	Nicholas Ray
Co-stars:	Robert Ryan Ward Bond Ed Begley Cleo Moore

1952	**BEWARE MY LOVELY**
Director:	Harry Horner
Co-stars:	Robert Ryan Taylor Holmes Barbara Whiting

1953	**THE BIGAMIST**
Director:	Ida Lupino
Co-stars:	Edmond O'Brien Joan Fontaine Edmund Gwenn

1953	**JENNIFER**
Director:	Joel Newton
Co-stars:	Howard Duff Robert Nicholas Mary Shipp

1954	**PRIVATE HELL 36**
Director:	Don Siegel
Co-stars:	Steve Cochran Howard Duff Dean Jagger

1955	**THE BIG KNIFE**
Director:	Robert Aldrich
Co-stars:	Jack Palance Rod Steiger Shelley Winters

1955	**WOMEN'S PRISON**

1956	**WHILE THE CITY SLEEPS**
Director:	Fritz Lang
Co-stars:	Vincent Price George Sanders Rhonda Fleming

1957	**STRANGE INTRUDER**
Director:	Irving Rapper
Co-stars:	Edmund Purdom Ann Harding Jacques Bergerac

1971	**WOMEN IN CHAINS**
Director:	Bernard Kowalski
Co-stars:	Lois Nettleton Belinda Montgomery

1972	**JUNIOR BONNER**
Director:	Sam Peckinpah
Co-stars:	Steve McQueen Robert Preston Ben Johnson

1975	**THE DEVIL'S RAIN**
Director:	Robert Fuest
Co-stars:	Ernest Borgnine Eddie Albert Keenan Wynn

1976	**THE FOOD OF THE GODS**
Director:	Bert Gordon
Co-stars:	Marjoe Gortner Ralph Meeker Pamela Franklin

RITA LUPINO *(Daughter of Ida Lupino)*

1949	**NOT WANTED**
Director:	Elmer Clifton
Co-stars:	Sally Forrest Keefe Brasselle Leo Penn

1950 OUTRAGE
Director: Ida Lupino
Co-stars: Mala Powers Todd Andrews Robert Clarke

PATTI LUPONE

1982 FIGHTING BACK
Director: Lewis Teague
Co-stars: Tom Skerritt Michael Sarrazin Yaphet Kotto

1986 WISE GUYS
Director: Brian De Palma
Co-stars: Danny DeVito Harvey Keitel Ray Sharkey

1989 DRIVING MISS DAISY
Director: Bruce Beresford
Co-stars: Jessica Tandy Morgan Freeman Dan Aykroyd

1993 FAMILY PRAYERS
Director: Scott Rosenfelt
Co-stars: Joe Mantegna Anne Archer Allen Garfield

VALERIE LUSH

1981 FRIEND OR FOE
Director: John Krish
Co-stars: Mark Luxford John Holmes Stacey Trendetter

1985 ANNA KARENINA
Director: Simon Langton
Co-stars: Jacqueline Bisset Christopher Reeve Paul Scofield

1987 STANLEY
Director: Anna Benson Gyles
Co-stars: Anton Lesser Juliet Stevenson Lesley Dunlop

THUY AN LU

1981 DIVA
Director: Jean-Jacques Beineix
Co-stars: Frederic Andrei Richard Bohringer Roland Bertin

DORA LUZ

1945 THE THREE CABALLEROS
Director: Norman Ferguson
Co-stars: Aurora Miranda Carmen Molina

VIOLA LYEL

1932 AFTER OFFICE HOURS
Director: Thomas Bentley
Co-stars: Frank Lawton Heather Angel Garry Marsh

1955 SEE HOW THEY RUN
Director: Leslie Arliss
Co-stars: Ronald Shiner Greta Gynt James Hayter

DOROTHY LYMAN

1988 THE PEOPLE ACROSS THE LAKE
Director: Arthur Allan Seidelman
Co-stars: Valerie Harper Gerald McRaney

1993 RUBY IN PARADISE
Director: Victor Nunez
Co-stars: Ashley Judd Todd Field Alison Dean

JACQUIE LYN

1931 PACK UP YOUR TROUBLES
Director: George Marshall
Co-stars: Stan Laurel Oliver Hardy Mary Carr

BECKY JO LYNCH

1984 THE RIVER
Director: Mark Rydell
Co-stars: Mel Gibson Sissy Spacek Scott Glenn

JACKIE LYNCH

1961 TWO AND TWO MAKE SIX
Director: Freddie Francis
Co-stars: George Chakiris Janette Scott Alfred Lynch

KATE LYNCH

1979 MEATBALLS
Director: Ivan Reitman
Co-stars: Bill Murray Harvey Atkin Ron Barry

1986 EASY PREY
Director: Sandor Stern
Co-stars: Gerald McRaney Shawnee Smith Susan Hogan

1992 LETHAL LOLITA
Director: Bradford May
Co-Stars: Ed Marinaro Noelle Parker Lawrence Dane

KELLY LYNCH

1989 DRUGSTORE COWBOY
Director: Gus Van Sant
Co-stars: Matt Dillon James Remar Grace Zabriskie

1989 ROAD HOUSE
Director: Rowdy Herrington
Co-stars: Patrick Swayze Ben Gazzara Sam Elliott

1990 DESPERATE HOURS
Director: Michael Cimino
Co-stars: Mickey Rourke Anthony Hopkins Mimi Rogers

1991 CURLEY SUE
Director: John Hughes
Co-stars: James Belushi Alisan Porter John Getz

1994 FORBIDDEN CHOICES
Director: Jennifer Warren
Co-Stars: Martha Plimpton Rutger Hauer

1994 HEAVEN'S PRISONERS
Director: Phil Joanou
Co-stars: Alec Baldwin Eric Roberts Teri Hatcher

1997 PERSONS UNKNOWN
Director: George Hickenlooper
Co-stars: Joe Mantegna J. T. Walsh Naomi Watts

SUSAN LYNCH

1994 THE SECRET OF ROAN INISH
Director: John Sayles
Co-stars: Mick Lalley Eileen Colgan John Lynch

1996 DOWNTIME
Director: Bharat Malluri
Co-star: Paul McGann

CAROL LYNLEY

1958 THE LIGHT IN THE FOREST
Director: Herschel Daugherty
Co-stars: James MacArthur Jessica Tandy

1959 BLUE DEMIN
Director: Philip Dunne
Co-stars: Brandon De Wilde MacDonald Carey Marsha Hunt

1959 HOLIDAY FOR LOVERS
Director: Henry Levin
Co-stars: Clifton Webb Jane Wyman Paul Henreid Jill St. John

1959 HOUND-DOG MAN
Director: Don Siegel
Co-stars: Fabian Stuart Whitman Arthur O'Connell Betty Field

1961 THE LAST SUNSET
Director: Robert Aldrich
Co-stars: Kirk Douglas Rock Hudson Dorothy Malone

1961 RETURN TO PEYTON PLACE
Director: Jose Ferrer
Co-stars: Jeff Chandler Eleanor Parker Mary Astor

1963   **UNDER THE YUM YUM TREE**
Director: David Swift
Co-stars: Jack Lemmon Dean Jones Imogene Coca

1963   **THE CARDINAL**
Director: Otto Preminger
Co-stars: Tom Tyron Dorothy Gish Maggie MacNamara

1963   **THE STRIPPER**
Director: Franklin Schaffner
Co-stars: Joanne Woodward Claire Trevor Richard Beymer

1964   **SHOCK TREATMENT**
Director: Denis Sanders
Co-stars: Lauren Bacall Stuart Whitman Roddy McDowell

1964   **THE PLEASURE SEEKERS**
Director: Jean Negulesco
Co-stars: Pamela Tiffin Tony Franciosa Gene Tierney

1965   **HARLOW**
Director: Alex Segal
Co-stars: Ginger Rogers Efrem Zimbalist Hurd Hatfield

1965   **BUNNY LAKE IS MISSING**
Director: Otto Preminger
Co-stars: Laurence Olivier Noel Coward Keir Dullea

1967   **DANGER ROUTE**
Director: Seth Holt
Co-stars: Richard Johnson Diana Dors Sylvia Syms Sam Wanamaker

1967   **THE HELICOPTER SPIES**
Director: Sam Rolfe
Co-stars: Robert Vaughn David McCallum Julie London

1967   **THE SHUTTERED ROOM**
Director: David Greene
Co-stars: Gig Young Flora Robson Oliver Reed

1968   **THE SMUGGLERS**
Director: Norman Lloyd
Co-Stars   Kurt Kasznar Charles Drake Shirley Booth

1968   **NORWOOD**
Director: Jack Haley
Co-stars: Glen Campbell Kim Darby Pat Hingle

1969   **THE MALTESE BIPPY**
Director: Norman Panama
Co-stars: Rowan & Martin Julie Newmar Mildred Natwick

1970   **WEEKEND OF TERROR**
Director: Jud Taylor
Co-stars: Robert Walker Gwynne Gilford Godfrey Cambridge

1972   **THE POSEIDON ADVENTURE**
Director: Ronald Neame
Co-stars: Gene Hackman Shelley Winters Ernest Borgnine

1974   **DEATH STALK**
Director: Robert Day
Co-stars: Vince Edwards Robert Webber Vic Morrow

1976   **FLOOD**
Director: Earl Bellamy
Co-stars: Robert Culp Barbara Hershey Roddy McDowell

1979   **THE CAT AND THE CANARY**
Director: Radley Metzger
Co-stars: Honor Blackman Edward Fox Wendy Hiller

1988   **THE ATTIC**
Director: Doug Adams
Co-stars: Gail O'Grady Joanna Miles Michael Hallkey Joseph Gian

ANN LYNN

1959   **NAKED FURY**
Director: Charles Saunders
Co-stars: Reed De Rouen Kenneth Cope Leigh Madison

1960   **PICCADILLY THIRD STOP**
Director: Wolf Rilla
Co-stars: Terence Morgan Yoko Tani Mai Zetterling

1961   **STRONGROOM**
Director: Vernon Sewell
Co-stars: Colin Gordon Derren Nesbitt Keith Faulkner

1961   **FLAME IN THE STREETS**
Director: Roy Ward Baker
Co-stars: John Mills Sylvia Syms Earl Cameron

1963   **THE PARTY'S OVER**
Director: Guy Hamilton
Co-stars: Oliver Reed Eddie Albert Louise Sorel

1964   **THE SYSTEM**
Director: Michael Winner
Co-stars: Oliver Reed Jane Merrow Barbara Ferris

1964   **THE BLACK TORMENT**
Director: Robert Hartford Davis
Co-stars: John Turner Heather Sears Peter Arne

1965   **FOUR IN THE MORNING**
Director: Anthony Simmons
Co-stars: Judi Dench Norman Rodway Joe Melia

1965   **THE UNCLE**
Director: Desmond Davis
Co-stars: Rupert Davies Brenda Bruce Maurice Denham

1968   **BABY LOVE**
Director: Alastair Reid
Co-stars: Linda Hayden Keith Barron Diana Dors

BETTY LYNN

1948   **JUNE BRIDE**
Director: Bretaigne Windust
Co-stars: Bette Davis Robert Montgomery Fay Bainter

1948   **MOTHER IS A FRESHMAN**
Director: Lloyd Bacon
Co-stars: Loretta Young Van Johnson Rudy Vallee

1949   **FATHER WAS A FULLBACK**
Director: John Stahl
Co-stars: Fred MacMurray Maureen O'Hara Natalie Wood

1950   **CHEAPER BY THE DOZEN**
Director: Walter Lang
Co-stars: Clifton Webb Myrna Loy Jeanne Carin

1951   **PAYMENT ON DEMAND**
Director: Curtis Bernhadt
Co-stars: Bette Davis Barry Sullivan Jane Cowl

1956   **BEHIND THE HIGH WALL**
Director: Abner Biberman
Co-stars: Tom Tully Sylvia Sidney John Gavin

BETTY LYNNE

1938   **DEAD MEN ARE DANGEROUS**
Director: Harold French
Co-stars: Robert Newton John Warwick Peter Cawthorne

1937   **DANGEROUS FINGERS**
Co-star: James Stephenson

CHERYL LYNN *(Child)*

1954   **THE BRIDGES AT TOKO-RI**
Director: Mark Robson
Co-stars: William Holden Grace Kelly Mickey Rooney

1986   **THUNDER RUN**
Director: Gary Hudson
Co-Stars   Forrest Tucker John Ireland Jill Whitlow

DIANA LYNN *(Dolly Loehr)*

1938 THEY SHALL HAVE MUSIC
Director: Archie Mayo
Co-stars: Joel McCrea Walter Brennan Jascha Heifetz

1941 THERE'S MAGIC IN MUSIC
Director: Andrew Stone
Co-stars: Allan Jones Susanna Foster Margaret Lindsay

1942 THE MAJOR AND THE MINOR
Director: Billy Wilder
Co-stars: Ginger Rogers Ray Milland Robert Benchley

1943 AND THE ANGELS SING
Director: George Marshall
Co-stars: Fred MacMurray Dorothy Lamour

1943 THE MIRACLE OF MORGAN'S CREEK
Director: Preston Sturges
Co-stars: Betty Hutton Eddie Bracken

1944 OUR HEARTS WERE YOUNG AND GAY
Director: Lewis Allen
Co-stars: Gail Russell Beulah Bondi

1944 HENRY ALDRICH PLAYS CUPID
Director: Hugh Bennett
Co-stars: Jimmy Lydon Charles Smith John Litel Vera Vague

1945 OUR HEARTS WERE GROWING UP
Director: William Russell
Co-stars: Gail Russell Billy De Wolfe

1945 OUT OF THIS WORLD
Director: Hal Walker
Co-stars: Eddie Bracken Veronica Lake Cass Daley

1946 THE BRIDE WORE BOOTS
Director: Irving Pichel
Co-stars: Barbara Stanwyck Robert Cummings

1947 EASY COME, EASY GO
Director: John Farrow
Co-stars: Barry Fitzgerald Sonny Tufts Dick Foran

1947 VARIETY GIRL
Director: George Marshall
Co-stars: Mary Hatcher Olga San Juan Glenn Tryon

1948 EVERY GIRL SHOULD BE MARRIED
Director: Don Hartman
Co-stars: Cary Grant Betsy Darke Franchot Tone

1948 RUTHLESS
Director: Edgar Ulmer
Co-stars: Zachary Scott Sydney Greenstreet Louis Hayward

1948 TEXAS, BROOKLYN AND HEAVEN
Director: William Castle
Co-stars: Guy Madison James Dunn Lionel Stander

1949 MY FRIEND IRMA
Director: George Marshall
Co-stars: Martin & Lewis Marie Wilson John Lund

1950 MY FRIEND IRMA GOES WEST
Director: Hal Walker
Co-stars: Martin & Lewis Marie Wilson Corinne Calvet

1950 PAID IN FULL
Director: William Dieterle
Co-stars: Lisabeth Scott Robert Cummings

1950 ROGUES OF SHERWOOD FOREST
Director: Gordon Douglas
Co-stars: John Derek George Macready Alan Hale

1951 PEOPLE AGAINST O'HARA
Director: John Sturges
Co-stars: Spencer Tracy Pat O'Brien John Hodiak

1951 BEDTIME FOR BONZO
Director: Frederick De Cordova
Co-stars: Ronald Reagan Walter Slezak

1952 MEET ME AT THE FAIR
Director: Douglas Sirk
Co-stars: Dan Dailey Hugh O'Brian Chet Allen

1953 AN ANNAPOLIS STORY
Director: Don Siegel
Co-stars: John Derek Kevin McCarthy Pat Dooley

1953 PLUNDER OF THE SUN
Director: John Farrow
Co-stars: Glenn Ford Francis L. Sullivan Patricia Medina

1954 TRACK OF THE CAT
Director: William Wellman
Co-stars: Robert Mitchum Beulah Bondi Teresa Wright

1955 THE KENTUCKIAN
Co-stars: Burt Lancaster
Co-stars: Burt Lancaster Walter Matthau Dianne Foster

1955 YOU'RE NEVER TOO OLD
Director: Norman Taurog
Co-stars: Martin & Lewis Nina Foch Raymond Burr

ELEANOR LYNN

1938 YOU'RE ONLY YOUNG ONCE
Director: George Seitz
Co-stars: Mickey Rooney Lewis Stone Fay Holden

LENI LYNN

1939 BABES IN ARMS
Director: Busby Berkeley
Co-stars: Judy Garland Mickey Rooney Charles Winninger

1943 HEAVEN IS ROUND THE CORNER
Director: Maclean Rogers
Co-stars: Will Fyffe Austin Trevor Magda Kun

1944 GIVE ME THE STARS
Director: Maclean Rogers
Co-stars: Will Fyffe Olga Lindo Ronald Chesney

1946 GAIETY GEORGE
Director: George King
Co-stars: Richard Greene Ann Todd Hazel Court

SHARON LYNN

1929 SUNNY SIDE UP
Director: David Butler
Co-stars: Janet Gaynor Charles Farrell El Brendel

1930 LIGHTNIN'
Director: Henry King
Co-stars: Will Rogers Louise Dresser Joel McCrea

1930 LET'S GO PLACES
Director: Frank Strayer
Co-stars: Joseph Wagstaff Lola Lane Ilka Chase

1930 FOX MOVIETONE FOLLIES OF 1929
Director: David Butler
Co-stars: Sue Carol Lola Lane Dixie Lee

1930 WILD COMPANY
Co-stars: Frank Alberton H. B. Warner Joyce Compton

1933 BIG EXECUTIVE
Director: Erle Kenton
Co-stars: Ricardo Cortez Richard Bennett Elizabeth Young

1934 ENTER MADAME
Director: Elliott Nugent
Co-stars: Elissa Landi Cary Grant Lynne Overman

1935 GO INTO YOUR DANCE
Director: Archie Mayo
Co-stars: Al Jolson Ruby Keeler Helen Morgan

1937 WAY OUT WEST
Director: James Horne
Co-stars: Stan Laurel Oliver Hardy Rosina Lawrence

VERA LYNN

1942   **WE'LL MEET AGAIN**
Director: Phil Brandon
Co-stars: Patricai Roc Donald Gray Geraldo

1943   **RHYTHM SERENADE**
Director: Gordon Wellesley
Co-stars: Jimmy Jewel Ben Warriss Jimmy Clitheroe

1944   **ONE EXCITING NIGHT**
Director: Walter Forde
Co-stars: Donald Stewart Mary Clare Richard Murdoch

CAROLE LYNNE

1941   **ASKING FOR TROUBLE**
Director: Oswald Mitchell
Co-stars: Max Miller Mark Lester Wilfrid Hyde White

MELANIE LYNSKEY

1995   **HEAVENLY CREATURES**
Director: Peter Jackson
Co-star: Kate Winslet Diana Kent Sarah Peirse

BARBARA LYON

1954   **LIFE WITH THE LYONS**
Director: Val Guest
Co-stars: Bebe Daniels Ben Lyon Richard Lyon

SUE LYON

1962   **LOLITA**
Director: Stanley Kubrick
Co-stars: James Mason Shelley Winters Peter Sellers

1964   **THE NIGHT OF THE IGUANA**
Director: John Huston
Co-stars: Richard Burton Deborah Kerr Ava Gardner

1966   **SEVEN WOMEN**
Director: John Ford
Co-stars: Anne Bancroft Flora Robson Margaret Leighton

1967   **TONY ROME**
Director: Gordon Douglas
Co-stars: Frank Sinatra Jill St. John Gena Rowlands

1967   **ONE BORN EVERY MINUTE**
Director: Irvin Kershner
Co-stars: George C. Scott Michael Sarrazin Harry Morgan

1971   **EVEL KNIEVEL**
Director: Marvin Chomsky
Co-stars: George Hamilton Bert Freed Rod Cameron

1977   **THE END OF THE WORLD**
Director: John Hayes
Co-stars: Christopher Lee Lew Ayres Dean Jagger

1977   **CRASH!**
Director: Charles Band
Co-stars: Jose Ferrer Leslie Parrish John Carradine

COLETTE LYONS

1949   **BLONDIE'S BIG DEAL**
Director: Edward Bernds
Co-stars: Penny Singleton Arthur Lake Larry Simms

1949   **THE LONE WOLF AND HIS LADY**
Director: John Hoffman
Co-stars: Ron Randell June Vincent Alan Mowbray

PHYLLIS LYONS

1993   **CASUALTIES OF LOVE:**
         THE LONG ISLAND LOLITA STORY
Director: John Herzfeld
Co-Stars   Jack Scalia Lawrence Tierney Anne De Salvo

SUSAN LYONS

1983   **THE WINDS OF JARRAH**
Director: Marl Egerton
Co-stars: Terence Donovan Emil Minty Steve Bisley

1991   **WENDY CRACKS A WALNUT**
Director: Michael Pattison
Co-stars: Rosanna Arquette Bruce Spence Kerry Walker

1993   **NO WORRIES**
Director: David Elfick
Co-stars: Amy Terelinck Geraldine James Ray Barrett

1994   **EBBTIDE**

LYA LYS

1930   **L'AGE D'OR**
Director: Luis Bunuel
Co-stars: Gaston Modot Max Ernst Pierre Prevert

1939   **CONFESSIONS OF A NAZI SPY**
Director: Anatole Litvak
Co-stars: Edward G. Robinson Paul Lukas George Sanders

NATASSA LYTESS

1940   **COMRADE X**
Director: King Vidor
Co-stars: Clark Gable Hedy Lamarr Oscar Homolka

DANIELLE LYTTLETON

1989   **AUSTRALIA**
Director: Jean-Jacques Andrien
Co-stars: Jeremy Irons Fanny Ardant Agnes Soral

SYBIL MAAS

1975　COUSIN COUSINE
Director:　Jean-Charles Tacchela
Co-stars:　Marie-France Pisier Marie-Christine Barrault

KATE MABERLY (Child)

1993　THE SECRET GARDEN
Director:　Agniezka Holland
Co-stars:　Maggie Smith John Lynch Haydon Prowse

1997　MOTHER-TIME
Director:　Matthew Jacobs
Co-stars:　Gina McKee Imogen Stubbs Anthony Andrews

MARIANNE MacANDREW

1971　THE SEVEN MINUTES
Director:　Russ Meyer
Co-stars:　Yvonne De Carlo Phil Carey John Carradine

EDITH MacARTHUR

1992　THE LONG ROADS
Director:　Tristram Powell
Co-stars:　Robert Urqhuart Michelle Fairley John McGlynn

JUNE MacCLOY

1931　JUNE MOON
Co-star:　Jack Oakie

CATRIONA MacCOLL

1979　LADY OSCAR
Director:　Jacques Demy
Co-stars:　Barry Stokes Christina Bohm

AIMI MacDONALD

1970　TAKE A GIRL LIKE YOU
Director:　Jonathan Miller
Co-stars:　Hayley Mills Oliver Reed Noel Harrison

GRACE MacDONALD

1942　GIVE OUT SISTERS
Director:　Edward Cline
Co-stars:　Andrews Sisters Dan Dailey Donald O'Connor

1943　GUNG HO!
Director:　Ray Enright
Co-stars:　Randolph Scott Alan Curtis J.Carrol Naish

1943　IT AIN'T HAY
Director:　Erle Kenton
Co-stars:　Budd Abbott Lou Costello Cecil Kellaway

1943　MUG TOWN
Director:　Ray Taylor
Co-stars:　Billy Halop Huntz Hall Jed Prouty

1943　SHE'S FOR ME
Co-stars:　David Bruce Lois Collier

1944　MURDER IN THE BLUE ROOM
Director:　Leslie Goodwins
Co-stars:　Anne Gwynne Donald Cook June Preisser

1944　HAT CHECK HONEY
Director:　Edward Cline
Co-stars:　Leon Errol Walter Catlett Richard Davis

1944　FOLLOW THE BOYS
Director:　Edward Sutherland
Co-stars:　Orson Welles Marlene Dietrich George Raft

1944　DESTINY
Director:　Reginald LeBorg
Co-stars:　Gloria Jean Alan Curtis Frank Craven

1944　MY GAL LOVES MUSIC
Co-stars:　Bob Crosby Betty Keen Walter Catlett

1945　SEE MY LAWYER
Director:　Edward Cline
Co-stars:　Ole Olsen Chic Johnson Alan Curtis

1945　HONEYMOON AHEAD
Co-stars:　Eddie Acuff Allan Jones

JEANNETTE MacDONALD
(Married Gene Raymond)

1929　THE LOVE PARADE
Director:　Ernst Lubitsch
Co-stars:　Maurice Chevalier Lupino Lane

1930　THE VAGABOND KING
Director:　Ludwig Berger
Co-stars:　Dennis King Lillian Roth

1930　THE LOTTERY BRIDE
Director:　Paul Stein
Co-stars:　Joe E.Brown Zasu Pitts John Garrick

1930　MONTE CARLO
Director:　Ernst Lubitsch
Co-stars:　Jack Buchanan Zasu Pitts

1930　OH FOR A MAN!
Co-star:　Reginald Denny

1930　LET'S GO NATIVE
Director:　Leo McCarey
Co-stars:　Jack Oakie James Hall Kay Francis

1931　DON'T BET ON A WOMAN
Co-star:　Edmond Lowe

1931　ANNABELLE'S AFFAIRS
Director:　Alfred Werker
Co-stars:　Victor McLaglen Roland Young Sam Hardy

1932　ONE HOUR WITH YOU
Director:　Ernst Lubitsch
Co-stars:　Maurice Chevalier Genevieve Tobin

1932　LOVE ME TONIGHT
Director:　Rouben Mamoulian
Co-stars:　Maurice Chevalier Myrna Loy

1933　THE CAT AND THE FIDDLE
Director:　William Howard
Co-stars:　Ramon Navarro Frank Morgan Jean Hersholt

1934　THE MERRY WIDOW
Director:　Ernst Lubitsch
Co-stars:　Maurice Chevalier Edward Everett Horton

1935　NAUGHTY MARIETTA
Director:　W.S.Van Dyke
Co-stars:　Nelson Eddy Frank Morgan Elsa Lanchester

1936　ROSE MARIE
Director:　W.S.Van Dyke
Co-stars:　Nelson Eddy James Stewart Allan Jones

1936   SAN FRANCISCO
Director: W.S.Van Dyke
Co-stars: Clark Gable Spencer Tracy Jack Holt

1937   MAYTIME
Director: Robert Z. Leonard
Co-stars: Nelson Eddy John Barrymore Lynne Carver

1937   THE FIRE FLY
Director: Robert Z. Leonard
Co-stars: Allan Jones Warren William Billy Gilbert

1938   SWEETHEARTS
Director: W.S.Van Dyke
Co-stars: Nelson Eddy Frank Morgan Ray Bolger

1938   THE GIRL OF THE GOLDEN WEST
Director: Robert Z. Leonard
Co-stars: Nelson Eddy Walter Pidgeon Buddy Ebsen

1939   BROADWAY SERENADE
Director: Robert Z. Leonard
Co-stars: Lew Ayres Frank Morgan Ian Hunter

1940   BITTER SWEET
Director: W.S.Van Dyke
Co-stars: Nelson Eddy George Sanders Ian Hunter

1940   NEW MOON
Director: Robert Z. Leonard
Co-stars: Nelson Eddy Mary Boland H.B.Warner

1941   SMILIN' THROUGH
Director: Frank Borzage
Co-stars: Gene Raymond Brian Aherne Ian Hunter

1942   I MARRIED AN ANGEL
Director: W.S.Van Dyke
Co-stars: Nelson Eddy Binnie Barnes Reginald Owen

1942   CAIRO
Director: W.S.Van Dyke
Co-stars: Robert Young Ethel Waters Reginald Owen

1944   FOLLOW THE BOYS
Director: Edward Sutherland
Co-stars: George Raft Orson Welles

1948   THREE DARLING DAUGHTERS
Director: Fred Wilcox
Co-stars: Jane Powell Jose Iturbi Edward Arnold

1949   THE SUN COMES UP
Director: Richard Thorpe
Co-stars: Lloyd Nolan Claude Jarman Lewis Tone

KELLY MacDONALD

1996   TRAINSPOTTING
Director: Danny Boyle
Co-stars: Ewan McGregor Robert Carlyle Ewan Bremner

1996   STELLA DOES TRICKS
Director: Cocky Gledroye
Co-star: James Bolam

1996   COUSIN BETTE
Director: Des McAnuff
Co-stars: Jessica Lange Bob Hoskins Elizabeth Shue

MOIRA MacDONALD

1953   RETURN TO PARADISE
Director: Mark Robson
Co-stars: Gary Cooper Roberta Haynes Barry Jones

ANDIE MacDOWALL

**1984   GREYSTOKE: THE LEGEND OF
        TARZAN, LORD OF THE APES**
Director: Hugh Hudson
Co-star: Christopher Lambert Ralph Richardson Ian Holm

1985   ST. ELMO'S FIRE
Director: Joel Schumacher
Co-stars: Rob Lowe Demi Moore Ally Sheedy

1989   SEX. LIES AND VIDEOTAPE
Director: Steve Soderbergh
Co-stars: James Spader Peter Gallagher Laura San Giacomo

1991   HUDSON HAWK
Director: Michael Lehman
Co-stars: Bruce Willis James Coburn Richard E.Grant

**1991   WOMEN AND MEN:
        IN LOVE THERE ARE NO RULES**
Director: Mike Figgis
Co-stars: Scott Glenn Matt Dillon

1991   OBJECT OF BEAUTY
Director: Michael Lindsay-Hogg
Co-stars: John Malkovich Lolita Davidovich

1992   THE PLAYER
Director: Robert Altman
Co-stars: Tim Robbins Greta Scacchi Whoopi Goldberg

1992   RUBY CAIRO
Director: Graeme Clifford
Co-stars: Liam Neesen Viggo Mortensen Jack Thompson

1993   SHORT CUTS
Director: Robert Altman
Co-stars: Matthew Modine Anne Archer Tim Robbins

1993   GROUNDHOG DAY
Director: Harold Ramis
Co-stars: Bill Murray Chris Elliott Stephen Tobolowsky

1994   BAD GIRLS
Director: Jonathan Kaplan
Co-stars: Madeleine Stowe Mary Stuart Masterson Drew Barrymore

1994   FOUR WEDDINGS AND A FUNERAL
Director: Mike Newell
Co-stars: Hugh Grant James Fleet Simon Callow

1995   UNSUNG HEROES
Director: Diane Keaton
Co-stars: John Turturro Michael Richards Nathan Watt

1996   MULTIPLICITY
Director: Harold Ramis
Co-stars: Michael Keaton Harris Yulin

1997   MICHAEL
Director: Nora Ephron
Co-stars: John Travolta William Hurt Bob Hoskins

1998   THE END OF VIOLENCE
Director: Wim Wenders
Co-stars: Gabriel Byrne Bill Pullman Daniel Benzali

RITA MACEDO

**1955   THE CRIMINAL LIFE OF
        ARCHIBALDO DE LA CRUZ**
Director: Luis Bunuel
Co-stars: Ernesto Alonso Ariadna Welter

1958   NAZARIN
Director: Luis Bunuel
Co-stars: Francisco Rabal Marga Lopez

MOYNA MacGILL

1948   THREE DARLING DAUGHTER
Director: Fred Wilcox
Co-stars: Jeannette MacDonald Jane Powell Jose Iturbi

TARA MacGOWRAN

1984   SECRET PLACES
Director: Zelda Baron
Co-stars: Marie-Therese Relin Claudine Auger Jenny Agutter

1988　THE DAWNING
Director:　Robert Knights
Co-stars:　Anthony Hopkins Hugh Grant Rebecca Pidgeon

1991　MURDER IN EDEN
Director:　Nicholas Renton
Co-stars:　Peter Firth Tony Doyle Ian Bannen

ALI MacGRAW (Married Steve McQueen)
Nominated For Best Actress In 1970 For "Love Story"

1968　A LOVELY WAY TO DIE
Director:　David Lowell Rich
Co-stars:　Kirk Douglas Sylva Koscina

1969　GOODBYE COLUMBUS
Director:　Larry Peerce
Co-stars:　Richard Benjamin Jack Klugman

1970　LOVE STORY
Director:　Arthur Hiller
Co-stars:　Ryan O'Neal Ray Milland John Marley

1972　THE GETAWAY
Director:　Sam Peckinpah
Co-stars:　Steve McQueen Ben Johnson Sally Struthers

1978　CONVOY
Director:　Sam Peckinpah
Co-stars:　Kris Kristofferson Ernest Borgnine

1979　PLAYERS
Director:　Anthony Harvey
Co-stars:　Dean-Paul Martin Maxmillian Schell

1980　JUST TELL ME WHAT YOU WANT
Director:　Sidney Lumet
Co-stars:　Alan King Myrna Loy Keenan Wynn

1983　CHINA ROSE
Director:　Robert Day
Co-stars:　George C.Scott Michael Biehn Denis Lill

1992　SURVIVE THE SAVAGE SEA
Director:　Kevin James Dobson
Co-stars:　Robert Urich Danielle Von Zerneck Mark Ballou

MARIA MACHADO

1993　ONE DEADLY SUMMER
Director:　Jean Becker
Co-stars:　Isabelle Adjani Alain Souchon Suzanne Flon

NICOLETTA MACHIAVELLI

1967　DEAD OR ALIVE
Director:　Franco Giraldi
Co-stars:　Robert Ryan Arthur Kennedy Alex Cord

MIMI MACHU

1967　HELL'S ANGELS ON WHEELS
Director:　Richard Rush
Co-stars:　Adam Roarke Jack Nicholson Jana Taylor

BETTY MACK

1932　GALLOPING THRU
Co-stars:　Tom Tyler John Elliott

HELEN MACK

1932　SILENT WITNESS
Director:　Marcel Varnell
Co-stars:　Lionel Atwill Greta Nissen Alan Mowbray

1933　THE SON OF KONG
Director:　Ernest Schoedsack
Co-stars:　Robert Armstrong Frank Reicher John Marston

1933　MELODY CRUISE
Director:　Mark Sandrich
Co-stars:　Phil Harris Charles Ruggles Greta Nissen

1933　CHRISTOPHER BEAN
Director:　Sam Wood
Co-stars:　Marie Dressler Lionel Barrymore Beulah Bondi

1933　CALIFORNIA TRAIL
Director:　Lambert Hillyer
Co-star:　Buck Jones

1933　BLIND ADVENTURE
Director:　Ernest Schoedsack
Co-stars:　Robert Armstrong Roland Young Ralph Bellamy

1934　ALL OF ME
Director:　James Flood
Co-stars:　Fredric March Miriam Hopkins George Raft

1934　COLLEGE RHYTHM
Director:　Norman Taurog
Co-stars:　Jack Oakie Joe Penner Mary Brian

1934　KISS AND MAKE UP
Director:　Harlan Thompson
Co-stars:　Cary Grant Genevieve Tobin Mona Maris

1934　YOU BELONG TO ME
Director:　Alfred Werker
Co-stars:　Lee Tracy Helen Morgan Lynne Overman

1935　SHE
Director:　Irving Pichel
Co-stars:　Randolph Scott Nigel Bruce Helen Gahagan

1935　THE RETURN OF PETER GRIMM
Director:　George Nicholls
Co-stars:　Lionel Barrymore Edward Ellis

1935　FOUR HOURS TO KILL
Director:　Mitchell Leisen
Co-stars:　Richard Barthelmess Ray Milland Dorothy Tree

1935　CAPTAIN HURRICANE
Director:　John Robertson
Co-stars:　James Barton Helen Westley Henry Travers

1936　THE MILKY WAY
Director:　Leo McCarey
Co-stars:　Harold Lloyd Adolphe Menjou Verree Teasdale

1937　FIT FOR A KING
Director:　Edward Sedgewick
Co-stars:　Joe E.Brown Harry Davenport Paul Kelly

1937　SECRETS OF A NURSE
Co-stars:　Edmund Lowe Dick Foran

1937　I PROMISE TO PAY
Director:　Ross Lederman
Co-stars:　Chester Morris Leo Carrillo Thomas Mitchell

1937　THE LAST TRAIN FROM MADRID
Director:　James Hogan
Co-stars:　Dorothy Lamour Lew Ayres Gilbert Roland

1938　GAMBLING SHIP
Co-stars:　Joe Sawyer Robert Wilcox

1939　MYSTERY OF THE WHITE ROOM
Co-stars:　Bruce Cabot Thomas Jackson

1939　CALLING ALL MARINES
Co-star:　Donald Barry

1940　HIS GIRL FRIDAY
Director:　Howard Hawks
Co-stars:　Cary Grant Rosalind Russell Ralph Bellamy

1945　DIVORCE
Director:　William Nigh
Co-stars:　Kay Francis Bruce Cabot Jerome Cowan

JUNE MACK

1979   **BENEATH THE VALLEY OF THE ULTRA VIXENS**
Director: Russ Meyer
Co-stars: Ann Marie Ken Kerr

KERRY MACK

1984   **FANTASY MAN**
Director: John Meagher
Co-stars: Harold Hopkins Jeanie Drynan Kate Fitzpartick

MARION MACK

1926   **THE GENERAL**
Director: Clyde Bruckman
Co-stars: Buster Keaton Glen Cavander

DOROTHY MACKAIL

1921   **THE FACE AT THE WINDOW**

1928   **THE BARKER**

1930   **ONCE A SINNER**
Director: John Argyle
Co-stars: Joel McCrea John Halliday Ilka Chase

1930   **MAN TROUBLE**
Co-star: Kenneth McKenna

1930   **THE OFFICE WIFE**

1930   **STRICTLY MODERN**
Co-star: William Haines

1931   **BRIGHT LIGHTS**
Co-star: Frank Fay

1931   **THE RECKLESS HOUR**
Co-star: Walter Byron

1931   **KEPT HUSBANDS**
Co-star: Joel McCrea

1932   **LOVE AFFAIR**
Director: Thornton Freeland
Co-stars: Humphrey Bogart Astrid Allwyn Barbara Leonard

1932   **NO MAN OF HER OWN**
Director: Wesley Ruggles
Co-stars: Clark Gable Carole Lombard Grant Mitchell

1933   **NEIGHBOURS' WIVES**
Co-star: Tom Moore

1933   **THE CHIEF**
Director: Charles Reisner
Co-stars: Ed Wynn Charles Sale William Boyd

PHOEBE MacKAY

1957   **THE BURGULAR**
Director: Paul Wendkos
Co-stars: Dan Duryea Jayne Mansfield Martha Vickers

BRONWYN MacKAY-PAYNE

1979   **DAWN!**
Director: En Hannam
Co-star: Tom Richards

HELEN MacKELLER

1933   **THE PAST OF MARY HOLMES**
Co-star: Eric Linden

1936   **TWO AGAINST THE WORLD**
Director: William McGann
Co-stars: Humphrey Bogart Beverly Roberts Linda Perry

1937   **DRAEGERMAN COURAGE**
Co-stars: Jean Muir Henry O'Neill Joe Crehan

JAN MacKENZIE

1989   **AMERICAN ANGELS**
Director: Fred Sebastien

JOYCE MacKENZIE

1950   **DESTINATION MURDER**
Director: Edward Cahn
Co-stars: Stanley Clements Hurd Hatfield Albert Dekker

1950   **BROKEN ARROW**
Director: Delmer Daves
Co-stars: James Stewart Jeff Chandler Debra Paget

1951   **THE RACKET**
Director: John Cromwell
Co-stars: Robert Ryan Robert Mitchum Lisazeth Scott

1952   **WAIT TIL THE SUN SHINES NELLIE**
Director: Henry King
Co-stars: David Wayne Jean Peters Hugh Marlowe

1955   **THE FRENCH LINE**
Director: Lloyd Bacon
Co-stars: Jane Russell Gilbert Roland Arthur Hunnicutt

MARY MacKENZIE

1952   **A STOLEN FACE**
Director: Terence Fisher
Co-stars: Paul Henreid Lisabeth Scott Susan Stephen

1954   **THE MASTER PLAN**
Director: Hugh Baker
Co-stars: Wayne Morris Tilda Thamar Norman Wooland

1957   **CLOAK WITHOUT DAGGER**
Director: Michael Anderson
Co-stars: Philip Friend Leslie Dwyer Alan Cuthbertson

1959   **THE MAN WHO LIKED FUNERALS**
Director: David Eady
Co-stars: Leslie Phillips Susan Beaumont Bill Fraser

LOUISE MacKINTOSH

1932   **THE PHANTOM PRESIDENT**
Director: Norman Taurog
Co-stars: Geoge M.Cohan Claudette Colbert Jimmy Durante

JANET MacLACHLAN

1969   **CHANGE OF MIND**
Director: Robert Stevens
Co-stars: Raymond St. Jacques Susan Oliver Leslie Nielsen

1969   **HALLS OF ANGER**
Director: Paul Bogart
Co-stars: Jeff Bridges Calvin Lockhart

1970   **DARKER THAN AMBER**
Director: Robert Clouse
Co-stars: Rod Taylor Suzy Kendall James Booth

1972   **SOUNDER**
Director: Martin Ritt
Co-stars: Paul Winfield Cicely Tyson James Best

1976   **DARK VICTORY**
Director: Robert Butler
Co-stars: Elizabeth Montgomery Anhony Hopkins Michele Lee

1981   **SHE'S IN THE ARMY NOW**
Director: Hy Averbach
Co-stars: Kathleen Quinlan Melanie Griffith Julie Carmen

1993   **HEART AND SOULS**
Director: Ron Underwood
Co-stars: Robert Downey Jnr Charles Grodin Kyra Sedgwick

SHIRLEY MacLAINE *(Sister Of Warren Beatty)*

Nominated For Best Actress In 1958 For "Some Came Running", In 1960 For "The Apartment", In 1963 For "Irma La Douce" And In 1977 For "The Turning Point". Received an Oscar For Best Actress In 1983 For "Terms Of Endearment"

1955 THE TROUBLE WITH HARRY
Director: Alfred Hitchcock
Co-stars: Edmund Gwenn Mildred Natwick

1955 ARTISTS AND MODELS
Director: Frank Tashlin
Co-stars: Dean Martin Jerry Lewis Dorothy Malone

1956 AROUND THE WORLD IN EIGHTY DAYS
Director: Michael Anderson
Co-stars: David Niven Robert Newton

1958 THE MATCHMAKER
Director: Joseph Anthony
Co-stars: Shirley Booth Paul Ford Anthony Perkins

1958 SOME CAME RUNNING
Director: Vincent Minnelli
Co-stars: Frank Sinatra Dean Martin Martha Hyer

1958 THE SHEEPMAN
Director: George Marshall
Co-stars: Glenn Ford Leslie Nielsen Edgar Buchanan

1958 HOT SPELL
Director: Daniel Mann
Co-stars: Shirley Booth Anthony Quinn Earl Holliman

1959 ASK ANY GIRL
Director: Charles Walters
Co-stars: David Niven Gig Young Rod Taylor

1959 CAREER
Director: Joseph Anthony
Co-stars: Anthony Franciosa Dean Martin

1960 THE APARTMENT
Director: Billy Wilder
Co-stars: Jack Lemmon Fred MacMurray Ray Walston

1960 OCEAN'S ELEVEN
Director: Lewis Milestone
Co-stars: Frank Sinatra Dean Martin Sammy Davis

1960 CAN CAN
Director: Walter Lang
Co-stars: Frank Sinatra Maurice Chevalier Louis Jourdan

1961 TWO LOVES
Director: Charles Walters
Co-stars: Jack Hawkins Laurence Harvey Nobu McCarthy

1961 ALL IN A NIGHT'S WORK
Director: Joseph Anthony
Co-stars: Dean Martin Charles Ruggles Jack Weston

1961 THE CHILDREN'S HOUR
Director: William Wyler
Co-stars: Audrey Hepburn James Garner Miriam Hopkins

1962 MY GEISHA
Director: Jack Cardiff
Co-stars: Yves Montand Edward G.Robinson

1962 TWO FOR THE SEESAW
Director: Robert Wise
Co-star: Robert Mitchum

1963 IRMA LA DOUCE
Director: Billy Wilder
Co-stars: Jack Lemmon Lou Jacobi Joan Shawlie

1964 THE YELLOW ROLLS ROYCE
Director: Anthony Asquith
Co-stars: Rex Harrison Ingrid Bergman Omar Sharif

1964 WHAT A WAY TO GO
Director: J.Lee Thompson
Co-stars: Gene Kelly Dean Martin Robert Mitchum

1965 JOHN GOLDFARB PLEASE COME HOME
Director: J.Lee Thompson
Co-stars: Richard Crenna Peter Ustinov

1966 GAMBIT
Director: Ronald Neame
Co-stars: Michael Caine Herbert Lom John Abbott

1967 WOMAN TIMES SEVEN
Director: Vittorio De Sica
Co-stars: Vittorio De Sica Peter Sellers Michael Caine

1968 THE BLISS OF MR. BLOSSOM
Director: Joseph McGrath
Co-stars: Richard Attenborough James Booth

1969 SWEET CHARITY
Director: Bob Fosse
Co-stars: Ricardo Montalban Sammy Davis Stubby Kaye

1969 TWO MULES FOR SISTER SARA
Director: Don Siegel
Co-stars: Clint Eastwood Alberto Morin

1971 THE POSSESSION OF JOEL DELANEY
Director: Waris Hussein
Co-stars: Perry King Lisa Kohane Michael Hordern

1971 DESPERATE CHARACTERS
Director: Frank Gilroy
Co-stars: Kenneth Mars Gerald S.O'Loughlin Jack Somack

1977 THE TURNING POINT
Director: Herbert Ross
Co-stars: Anne Bancroft Mikhail Baryshinkov Tom Skerritt

1979 BEING THERE
Director: Hal Ashby
Co-stars: Peter Sellers Melvyn Douglas Jack Warden

1980 LOVING COUPLES
Director: Jack Smight
Co-stars: James Coburn Susan Sarandon Sally Kellerman

1980 A CHANGE OF SEASONS
Director: Richard Lang
Co-stars: Anthony Hopkins Bo Derek Michael Brandon

1983 TERMS OF ENDEARMENT
Director: James Brooks
Co-stars: Debra Winger Jack Nicholson

1983 CANNONBALL RUN II
Director: Hal Needham
Co-stars: Burt Reynolds Dean Martin Frank Sinatra

1987 OUT ON A LIMB
Director: Robert Butler
Co-stars: Charles Dance John Heard Anne Jackson

1988 MADAME SOUSATZKA
Director: John Schlesinger
Co-stars: Peggy Ashcroft Twiggy Navin Chowdhry

1989 STEEL MAGNOLIAS
Director: Herbert Ross
Co-stars: Sally Field Dolly Parton Julia Roberts

1990 WAITING FOR THE LIGHT
Director: Christopher Monger
Co-stars: Teri Garr Clancy Brown Jeff McCracken

1990 POSTCARDS FOM THE EDGE
Director: Mike Nichols
Co-stars: Meryl Streep Dennis Quaid Gene Hackman

1991 DEPENDING ON YOUR LIFE
Director: Albert Brooks
Co-stars: Albert Brooks Meryl Streep Rip Torn Lee Grant

1992 **USED PEOPLE**
Director: Beeban Kidron
Co-stars: Marcello Mastroianni Kathy Bates Jessica Tandy

1993 **WRESTLING ERNEST HEMINGWAY**
Director: Randa Hains
Co-stars: Robert Duvall Richard Harris Piper Laurie

1994 **GUARDING TESS**
Director: Hugh Wilson
Co-stars: Nicolas Cage Richard Griffiths Edward Albert

1995 **WEST SIDE WATLZ**
Director: Ernest Thompson
Co-stars: Liza Minnelli Jennifer Grey

1996 **EVENING STAR**
Co-star: Miranda Richardson

HILARY MacLEAN

1992 **BLUE BLACK PERMANENT**
Director: Margaret Tait
Co-stars: Celia Imrie Jack Shepherd James Fleet

MARY MacLEOD

1942 **THE LONDON BLACKOUT MURDERS**
Director: George Sherman
Co-stars: John Abbott Lloyd Corrigan Billy Bevan

1982 **BRIMSTONE AND TREACLE**
Director: Richard Loncrane
Co-stars: Sting Denholm Elliott Joan Plowright

ELIZABETH MacLEAN

1990 **PUPPET MASTER II**
Director: David Allen
Co-stars: Corbin Bernsen Gregory Webb

EANNA MacLIAM

1989 **MY LEFT FOOT**
Director: Jim Sheridan
Co-stars: Daniel Day-Lewis Ray McAnanlly Brenda Fricker

1993 **THE SNAPPER**
Director: Stephen Frears
Co-stars: Tina Kellegher Colm Meaney Ruth McCabe

ELLIE MacLURE

1983 **AIR HAWK**
Director: David Baker
Co-stars: Eric Oldfield Louise Howill

CAROL MACREADY

1992 **BAD GIRL**
Director: George Case
Co-stars: Jane Horrocks Lesley Manville Tom Beard

SUSAN MACREADY

1969 **THE PROMISE**
Director: Michael Hayes
Co-stars: Ian McKellen John Castle Mary Jones

1972 **THE DARWIN ADVENTURE**
Director: Jack Couffer
Co-stars: Nicholas Clay Ian Richardson Robert Flemyng

ALINE MACMAHON
Nominated For Best Supporting Actress In 1944 For "Dragon Seed"

1931 **FIVE STAR FINAL**
Director: Mervyn LeRoy
Co-stars: Edward G.Robinson Marian Marsh Boris Karloff

1932 **HEART OF NEW YORK**
Director: Mervyn LeRoy
Co-stars: Joe Smith Charles Dale George Sidney Anna Apfel

1932 **ONE WAY PASSAGE**
Director: Tay Garnett
Co-stars: William Powel Kay Francis Frank McHugh

1932 **LIFE BEGINS**
Director: James Flood
Co-stars: Loretta Young Elliott Nugent Glenda Farrell

1932 **THE MOUTHPIECE**
Director: Elliott Nugent
Co-stars: Warren William Sidney Fox John Wray

1932 **SILVER DOLLAR**
Director: Alfred Green
Co-stars: Edward G.Robinson Bebe Daniels Jobyna Howland

1932 **WEEKEND MARRIAGE**
Director: Thornton Freeland
Co-stars: Loretta Young Norman Foster George Brent

1933 **ONCE IN A LIFETIME**
Director: Russell MacK
Co-stars: Jack Oakie Sidney Fox Zasu Pitts Louise Fazenda

1933 **THE LIFE OF JIMMY DOLAN**
Director: Archie Mayo
Co-stars: Douglas Fairbanks Loretta Young Guy Kibbee

1933 **HEROES FOR SALE**
Director: William Wellman
Co-stars: Richard Barthelmess Loretta Young Robert Barrat

1933 **GOLD DIGGERS OF 1933**
Director: Mervyn LeRoy
Co-stars: Warren William Joan Blondell Dick Powell

1933 **THE WORLD CHANGES**
Director: Mervyn LeRoy
Co-stars: Paul Muni Mary Astor Jean Muir Donald Cook

1934 **SIDE STREETS**
Director: Alfred Green
Co-stars: Paul Kelly Ann Dvorak Henry O'Neill

1934 **THE MERRY FRINKS**
Director: Alfred Green
Co-stars: Guy Kibbee Allen Jenkins Hugh Herbert

1934 **HEAT LIGHTNING**
Director: Mervyn LeRoy
Co-stars: Preston Foster Ann Dvorak Lyle Talbot

1934 **BIG HEARTED HERBERT**
Director: William Keighley
Co-stars: Guy Kibbee Patricia Ellis Philip Reed

1934 **BABBIT**
Director: William Keighley
Co-stars: Guy Kibbee Minna Gombell Alan Hale

1935 **AH, WILDERNESS!**
Director: Clarence Brown
Co-stars: Wallace Beery Mickey Rooney Lionel Barrymore

1935 **I LIVE MY LIFE**
Director: W.S.Van Dyke
Co-stars: Joan Crawford Brian Aherne Frank Morgan

1935 **KIND LADY**
Director: George Seitz
Co-stars: Basil Rathbone Mary Carlisle Frank Albertson

1935 **MARY JANE'S PA**
Director: William Keighley
Co-stars: Guy Kibbee Nan Grey Tom Brown

1935 **WHILE THE PATIENT SLEPT**
Director: Ray Enright
Co-stars: Guy Kibbee Lyle Talbot Patricia Ellis

1937 WHEN YOU'RE IN LOVE
Director: Robert Riskin
Co-stars: Grace Moore Cary Grant Thomas Mitchell

1939 BACK DOOR TO HEAVEN
Director: William Howard
Co-stars: Wallace Ford Stuart Erwin Jimmy Lydon

1941 OUT OF THE FOG
Director: Anatole Litvak
Co-stars: John Garfield Ida Lupino Thomas Mitchell

1942 THE LADY IS WILLING
Director: Mitchell Leisen
Co-stars: Marlene Dietrich Fred MacMurray

1942 TISH
Director: S.Sylvan Simon
Co-stars: Marjorie Main Zasu Pitts Guy Kibbee

1944 GUEST IN THE HOUSE
Director: John Brahm
Co-stars: Anne Baxter Ralph Bellamy Ruth Warwick

1944 DRAGON SEED
Director: Jack Conway
Co-stars: Katharine Hepburn Turhan Bey Walter Huston

1946 THE MIGHTY McGURK
Director: John Waters
Co-stars: Wallace Beery Dean Stockwell Edward Arnold

1948 THE SEARCH
Director: Fred Zinnemann
Co-stars: Montgomery Clift Ivan Jandl Wendell Corey

1949 ROSEANNA McCOY
Director: Irving Reis
Co-stars: Farley Granger Joan Evans Raymond Massey

1950 THE FLAME AND THE ARROW
Director: Jacques Tourneur
Co-stars: Burt Lancaster Virginia Mayo Nick Cravat

1953 THE EDDIE CANTOR STORY
Director: Alfred Green
Co-stars: Keefe Brasselle Marilyn Erskine Arthur Franz

1955 THE MAN FROM LARAMIE
Director: Anthony Mann
Co-stars: James Stewart Arthur Kennedy Donald Crisp

1960 CIMARRON
Director: Anthony Mann
Co-stars: Glenn Ford Maria Schell Anne Baxter

1961 THE YOUNG DOCTORS
Director: Phil Carlson
Co-stars: Fredric March Ben Gazzara George Segal Ina Balin

1962 DIAMOND HEAD
Director: Guy Green
Co-stars: Charlton Heston Yvette Mimieux France Nuyen

1963 ALL THE WAY HOME
Director: Alex Segal
Co-stars: Jean Simmons Robert Preston Pat Hingle

1963 I COULD GO ON SINGING
Director: Ronald Neame
Co-stars: Judy Garland Dirk Bogarde Jack Klugman

DIANA MacNAMARA

1966 CARRY ON; DON'T LOSE YOU'RE HEAD
Director: Gerald Thomas
Co-stars: Sid James Joan Sims Dany Robin

ELLE MacPHERSON

1991 ALICE
Director: Woody Allen
Co-stars: Mia Farrow Alec Baldwin William Hurt

1994 SIRENS
Director: John Duigan
Co-stars: Hugh Grant Tara Fitzgerald Sam Neill

1996 JANE EYRE
Director: Franco Zefferelli
Co-stars: Charlotte Gainsbourg William Hurt Anna Paquin

1996 BOOKWORM
Co-stars: Anthony Hopkins Alec Baldwin

1996 BATMAN AND ROBIN
Director: Joel Schumacher
Co-stars: George Clooney Chris O'Donnell Uma Thurman

SHELIA MacRAE

**1981 GOLDIE AND THE BOXER
GO TO HOLLYWOOD**
Director: David Miller
Co-stars: O.J.Simpson Melissa Michaelson

JEANNE MADDEN

1936 STAGE STRUCK
Director: Busby Berkeley
Co-stars: Dick Powell Joan Blondell Warren William

1937 TALENT SCOUT
Co-star: Donald Woods

AMY MADIGAN

Nominated For Best Supporting Actress In 1985 For "Twice in a Lifetime"

1982 THE AMBUSH MURDERS
Director: Steven Hillard Stern
Co-stars: James Brown Dorian Harewood Alfre Woodard

1982 LOVE LETTERS
Director: Amy Jones
Co-stars: Jamie Lee Curtis James Keach Bud Cort

1982 LOVE CHILD
Director: Larry Peerce

1984 PLACES IN THE HEART
Director: Robert Benton
Co-stars: Sally Field Danny Glover John Malkovich

1985 TWICE IN A LIFETIME
Director: Bud Yorkin
Co-stars: Gene Hackman Ellen Burstyn Ann-Margret

1985 STREETS OF FIRE
Director: Walter Hill
Co-stars: Michael Pare Rick Moranis Willem Dafoe

1985 ALAMO BAY
Director: Louis Malle
Co-stars: Ed Harris Donald Moffat Rudy Young

1988 THE PRINCE OF PENNSYLVANIA
Director: Ron Nyswaner
Co-stars: Fred Ward Keanu Reeves Bonnie Bedelia

1989 ROE VS WADE
Director: Gregory Hoblit
Co-stars: Holly Hunter Kathy Bates Terry O'Quinn

1989 UNCLE BUCK
Director: John Hughes
Co-stars: John Candy Macauley Culkin Laurie Metcalf

1989 FIELD OF DREAMS
Director: Phil Alden Robinson
Co-stars: Kevin Costner Burt Lancaster Ray Liotta

1992 THE DARK HALF
Director: George Romero
Co-stars: Timothy Hutton Julie Harris Michael Rooker

1994　**AND THEN THERE WAS ONE**
Director:　David Jones
Co-stars:　Jane Daly Dennis Boutsikaris

1996　**RIDERS OF THE PURPLE SAGE**
Director:　Charles Haid
Co-stars:　Ed Harris Henry Thomas

1997　**FEMALE PERVERSIONS**
Co-stars:　Tilda Swinton

LEIGH MADISON

1959　**NAKED FURY**
Director:　Charles Saunders
Co-stars:　Reed De Rouen Kenneth Cope Ann Lynn

1959　**THE GIANT BEHEMOTH**
Director:　Douglas Hickox
Co-stars:　Gene Evans Andre Morell John Turner

MAE MADISON

1932　**MISS PINKERTON**
Director:　Lloyd Bacon
Co-stars:　Joan Blondell George Brent John Wray

1932　**THE RICH ARE ALWAYS WITH US**
Director:　Alfred Green
Co-stars:　George Brent Ruth Chatterton Bette Davis

MADONNA

1985　**DESPERATELY SEEKING SUSAN**
Director:　Susan Seidelman
Co-stars:　Rosanna Arquette Aidan Quinn Mark Blum

1986　**SHANGHAI SURPRISE**
Director:　Jim Goddard
Co-stars:　Sean Penn Paul Freeman Richard Griffiths

1987　**WHO'S THAT GIRL?**
Director:　James Foley
Co-stars:　Griffin Dune John Mills Haviland Morris

1989　**BLOODHOUNDS OF BROADWAY**
Director:　Howard Brookner
Co-stars:　Matt Dillon Jennifer Grey Rutger Hauer

1990　**DICK TRACY**
Director:　Warren Beatty
Co-stars:　Warren Beatty Al Pacino Dustin Hoffman Mandy Patinkin

1992　**A LEAGUE OF THEIR OWN**
Director:　Penny Marshall
Co-stars:　Geena Davis Tom Hanks Lori Petty

1992　**BODY OF EVIDENCE**
Director:　Uli Edel
Co-stars:　Willem Dafoe Anne Archer Frank Langella

1992　**SHADOWS AND FOG**
Director:　Woody Allen
Co-stars:　Woody Allen Mia Farrow Jody Foster Lily Tomlin

1993　**DANGEROUS GAME**
Director:　Abel Ferrara
Co-stars:　Harvey Keitel James Russo Nancy Ferrara

1995　**FOUR ROOMS**
Director:　Allison Anders
Co-stars:　Tim Roth Antonio Banderas Jennifer Beals

1996　**BLUE IN THE FACE**
Co-stars:　Roseanne Barr Harvey Keitel Lily Tomlin

1997　**EVITA**
Director:　Alan Parker
Co-stars:　Jonathan Pryce Antonio Banderas Jimmy Nail

VIRGINIA MADSEN (*Married Danny Huston*)

1984　**ELECTRIC DREAMS**
Director:　Steve Barron
Co-stars:　Lenny Von Dohlen Maxwell Caulfield Bud Cort

1984　**DUNE**
Director:　David Lynch
Co-stars:　Francesca Annis Jose Ferrer Sting

1985　**CREATOR**
Director:　Ivan Passer
Co-stars:　Peter O'Toole Mariel Hemingway Vincent Spano

1985　**THE HEARST AND DAVIES AFFAIR**
Director:　David Lowell Rich
Co-stars:　Robert Mitchum Fritz Weaver

1986　**FIRE WITH FIRE**
Director:　Duncan Gibbins
Co-stars:　Craig Sheffer Kate Reid Jon Polito

1987　**LONG GONE**
Director:　Martin Davidson
Co-stars:　William Petersen Dermot Mulroney Katy Boyer

1987　**SLAMDANCE**
Director:　Wayne Wang
Co-stars:　Tom Hulce Mary Elizabeth Mastrantonio Millie Perkins

1988　**THE DEAD CAN'T LIE**
Director:　Lloyd Fonvielle
Co-stars:　Tommy Lee Jones Frederick Forrest

1990　**THE HOT SPOT**
Director:　Dennis Hopper
Co-stars:　Don Johnson Jennifer Connelly

1990　**HIGHLANDER 2: THE QUICKENING**
Director:　Russell Mulcahy
Co-stars:　Christopher Lambert Sean Connery

1991　**IRONCLADS**
Director:　Delbert Mann
Co-star:　Alex Hyde-White

1991　**VICTIM OF LOVE**
Director:　Jerry London
Co-stars:　Pierce Brosnan JoBeth Williams Georgia Brown

1992　**BECOMING COLETTE**
Director:　Danny Huston
Co-stars:　Klaus Maria Brandauer Mathilda May Paul Rhys

1993　**CANDYMAN**
Director:　Bernard Rose
Co-stars:　Kasi Lemmons Tony Todd Vanessa Williams

1993　**LINDA**
Director:　Nathaniel Gutman
Co-stars:　Richard Thomas Ted McGinley

1994　**BLUE TIGER**
Director:　Norberto Barba
Co-stars:　Tornu Nakamura Dean Hallo Harry Dean Stanton

1994　**BITTER VENGEANCE**
Director:　Stuart Cooper
Co-stars:　Gordon Jump Kirsten Hocking

1995　**APOCOLYPSE WATCH**
Director:　Kevin Connor
Co-stars:　Patrick Bergin John Shea

CLARE MAFFEI

1947　**ANTOINE AND ANTOINETTE**
Director:　Jacques Becker
Co-stars:　Roger Pigaut Noell Roquevert

ANNA MAGNANI
Oscar For Best Actress In 1955 For "The Rose Tattoo"
Nominated For Best Actress In 1957 For "Wild Is The Wind"

1945   ROME OPEN CITY
Director: Roberto Rossellini
Co-stars: Aldo Fabrizi Marcel Pagliero Maria Michi

1947   ANGELINA
Director: Luigi Zampa
Co-stars: Nando Bruno Gianni Glori Franco Zeffirelli

1948   THE MIRACLE
Director: Roberto Rossellini
Co-star: Federico Fellini

1948   THE HUMAN VOICE
Director: Roberto Rossellini

1951   BELLISSIMA
Director: Luchino Visconti
Co-stars: Walter Chiari Tian Apicella Gustone Renzelli

1953   THE GOLDEN COACH
Director: Jean Renoir
Co-stars: Duncan Lamont Paul Campbell Ricardo Rioli

1955   THE ROSE TATTOO
Director: Daniel Mann
Co-stars: Burt Lancaster Marisa Pavan Jo Van Fleet

1957   WILD IS THE WIND
Director: George Cukor
Co-stars: Anthony Quinn Tony Franciosa Dolores Hart

1960   THE FUGITIVE KIND
Director: Sidney Lumet
Co-stars: Marlon Brando Joanne Woodward Victor Jory

1969   THE SECRET OF SANTA VITTORIA
Director: Stanley Kramer
Co-stars: Anthony Quinn Virna Lisi Hardy Kruger

ANN MAGNUSON

1984   BLIND ALLEY
Director: Larry Cohen
Co-stars: Anne Carlisle Brad Rijn Matthew Stockley

1987   MAKING MR. RIGHT
Director: Susan Seidelman
Co-stars: John Malkovich Glenne Headly Laurie Metcalf

1988   A NIGHT IN THE LIFE OF JIMMY REARDON
Director: William Richert
Co-stars: River Phoenix Ione Skye

1988   CHECKING OFF
Director: David Leland
Co-stars: Jeff Daniels Melanie Mayron Michael Tucker

1990   LOVE AT LARGE
Director: Alan Rudolph
Co-stars: Tom Berenger Elizabeth Perkins Anne Archer

1994   CABIN BOY
Director: Adam Resnick
Co-stars: Chris Elliott James Gammon Russ Tamblyn

TOVA MAGNUSSON

1993   THE PREMONITION
Director: Rumle Hammerich
Co-stars: Figge Norling Bjorn Kjellman

NICOLE MAGNY

1977   A SPECIAL DAY
Director: Ettore Scola
Co-stars: Sophia Loren Marcello Mastroianni John Vernon

JUDITH MAGRE

1958   THE LOVERS
Director: Louis Malle
Co-stars: Jeanne Moreau Alain Cluny Jean-Marc Bory

KATHLEEN MAGUIRE

1957   EDGE OF THE CITY
Director: Martin Ritt
Co-stars: Sidney Poitier John Cassavetes Jack Warden

1963   FLIPPER
Director: James Clark
Co-stars: Chuck Connors Luke Halpin Connie Scott

1980   WILLIE AND PHIL
Director: Paul Mazursky
Co-stars: Michael Ontkean Ray Sharkey Margot Kidder

MARY MAGUIRE

1937   CONFESSION
Director: Joe May
Co-stars: Kay Francis Ian Hunter Basil Rathbone

1937   ALCATRAZ ISLAND
Director: William McGann
Co-stars: Ann Sheridan Dick Purcell John Litel

1938   KEEP SMILING
Director: Monte Banks
Co-stars: Gracie Fields Roger Livesey Jack Donohue

1939   AN ENGLISHMAN'S HOME
Director: Albert Rodney
Co-stars: Edmund Gwenn Paul Henreid Geoffrey Toone

1939   BLACK EYES
Director: Herbert Brenon
Co-stars: Otto Kruger Walter Rilla John Wood

1939   THE OUTSIDER
Director: Paul Stein
Co-stars: George Sanders Frederick Leister Kathleen Harrison

1941   THIS WAS PARIS
Director: John Harlow
Co-stars: Ben Lyon Ann Dvorak Griffith Jones

VALERIE MAHAFFEY

1986   WOMEN OF VALOR
Director: Buzz Kulik
Co-stars: Susan Sarandon Kristy McNichol Alberta Watson

1987   CODENAME: DANCER
Director: Buzz Kulik
Co-stars: Kate Capshaw Jeroen Krabbe Cliff De Young

SHARON MAHARAJ

1990   EFFIE'S BURNING
Director: Nigel Evans
Co-stars: Paula Tilsbrook Phyllis Logan Gordon Jackson

JANET MAHONEY
Director: Gerald Thomas
Co-stars: Sid James Hattie Jacques Charles Hawtrey

MAGGIE MAHONEY

1956   BLACKJACK KETCHUM, DESPERADO
Director: Earl Bellamy
Co-stars: Howard Duff Victor Jory Angela Stevens

CATRIN MAI

1993   LEAVING LENIN
Director: Endaf Emlyn
Co-stars: Sharon Morgan Shelley Rees Richard Harrington

SHARON MAIDEN

1986 CLOCKWISE
Director: Christopher Morahan
Co-stars: John Cleese Alison Steadman Penelope Wilton

1992 FOOL'S GOLD: THE STORY OF THE BRINK'S-MAT ROBBERY
Director: Terry Windsor
Co-stars: Sean Bean Larry Lamb

CHERYL MAIKER

1989 THE REAL EDDY ENGLISH
Director: David Attwood
Co-stars: Stephen Persaud Sue Devaney Frank Windsor

KATE MAILER

1987 KING LEAR
Director: Jean-Luc Godard
Co-stars: Burgess Meredith Peter Sellers Molly Ringwald

CLAUDETTE MAILLE

1992 LIKE WATER FOR CHOCOLATE
Director: Alfonso Arau
Co-stars: Lumi Cavajos Regina Torne Ada Carrasco

MARJORIE MAIN
Nominated For Best Supporting Actress In 1947 For "The Egg And I"

1937 BOY OF THE STREETS
Director: William Nigh
Co-stars: Jackie Cooper Maureen O'Connor

1937 DEAD END
Director: William Wyler
Co-stars: Joel McCrea Sylvia Sidney Humphrey Bogart

1937 THE MAN WHO CRIED WOLF
Director: Lewis Foster
Co-stars: Lewis Stone Tom Brown Barbara Reed

1937 STELLA DALLAS
Director: King Vidor
Co-stars: Barbara Stanwyck John Boles Ann Shirley Tim Holt

1937 CITY GIRL
Director: Alfred Werker
Co-stars: Ricardo Cortez Phyllis Brooks Robert Wilcox

1938 LITTLE TOUGH GUYS
Director: Harold Young
Co-stars: Billy Halop Helen Parrish Huntz Hall

1938 THE PILOT
Director: Victor Fleming
Co-stars: Clark Gable Myrna Loy Spencer Tracy

1938 TOO HOT TO HANDLE
Director: Jack Conway
Co-stars: Clark Gable Myrna Loy Walter Pidgeon

1939 THEY SHALL HAVE MUSIC
Director: Archie Mayo
Co-stars: Joel McCrea Walter Brennan Jascha Heifetz

1939 LUCKY NIGHT
Director: Norman Taurog
Co-stars: Myrna Loy Robert Taylor Henry O'Neill

1939 THE WOMEN
Director: George Cukor
Co-stars: Norma Shearer Joan Crawford Rosalind Russell

1939 I TAKE THIS WOMAN
Director: W.S.Van Dyke
Co-stars: Spencer Tracy Hedy Lamarr Jack Carson

1939 ANGELS WASH THEIR FACES
Director: Ray Enright
Co-stars: Ann Sheridan Ronald Reagan Dead End Kids

1940 DARK COMMAND
Director: Raoul Walsh
Co-stars: John Wayne Claire Trevor Walter Pidgeon

1940 SUSAN AND GOD
Director: George Cukor
Co-stars: Joan Crawford Fredric March Rita Hayworth

1940 THE TRIAL OF MARY DUGGAN
Director: Norman Z. McLeod
Co-stars: Laraine Day Robert Young Marsha Hunt

1940 WYOMING
Director: Richard Thorpe
Co-stars: Wallace Beery Leo Carrillo Joseph Calleia

1941 BARNACLE BILL
Director: Richard Thorpe
Co-stars: Wallace Beery Leo Carrillo Virginia Weidler

1941 A WOMAN'S FACE
Director: George Cukor
Co-stars: Joan Crawford Melvyn Douglas Conrad Veidt

1941 THE BUGLE SOUNDS
Director: S. Sylvan Simon
Co-stars: Wallace Beery William Lundigan Donna Reed

1941 SHEPHERD OF THE HILLS
Director: Henry Hathaway
Co-stars: John Wayne Betty Field Beulah Bondi

1941 HONKY TONK
Director: Jack Conway
Co-stars: Clark Gable Lana Turner Frank Morgan

1942 THE AFFAIRS OF MARTHA
Director: Jules Dassin
Co-stars: Marsha Hunt Richard Carlson Spring Byington

1942 JACKASS MAIL
Director: Norman Z. McLeod
Co-stars: Wallace Beery J.Carrol Naish Darryl Hickman

1942 WE WERE DANCING
Director: Robert Z. Leonard
Co-stars: Norma Shearer Melvyn Douglas Gail Patrick

1942 TISH
Director: S.Sylvan Simon
Co-stars: Zasu Pitts Aline McMahon Susan Peters

1943 RATIONING
Director: Willis Goldbeck
Co-stars: Wallace Berry Donald Meek Connie Gilchrist

1943 TENNESSEE JOHNSON
Director: William Dieterle
Co-stars: Lionel Barrymore Van Heflin Ruth Hussey

1943 JOHNNY COME LATELY
Director: William Howard
Co-stars: James Cagney Grace George Robert Barrat

1943 HEAVEN CAN WAIT
Director: Ernst Lubitsch
Co-stars: Gene Tierney Don Ameche Laird Cregar

1944 GENTLE ANNIE
Director: Andrew Marton
Co-stars: James Craig Donna Reed Henry Morgan

1944 MEET ME IN ST. LOUIS
Director: Vincente Minnelli
Co-stars: Judy Garland Margaret O'Brien Tom Drake

1945 MURDER HE SAYS
Director: George Marshall
Co-stars: Fred MacMurray Helen Walker Porter Hall

1946 **UNDERCURRENT**
Director: Vincente Minnelli
Co-stars: Katharine Hepburn Robert Taylor Robert Mitchum

1946 **THE HARVEY GIRLS**
Director: George Sidney
Co-stars: Judy Garland Ray Bolger John Hodiak

1946 **BAD BASCOMB**
Director: S.Sylvan Simon
Co-stars: Wallace Beery Margaret O'Brien J.Carrol Naish

1947 **THE EGG AND I**
Director: Chester Erskine
Co-stars: Claudette Colbert Fred MacMurray Percy Kilbride

1947 **THE WISTFUL WIDOW OF WAGON GAP**
Director: John Grant
Co-stars: Bud Abbott Lou Costello George Cleveland

1948 **FEUDING, FUSSIN' AND A-FIGHTING**
Director: George Sherman
Co-stars: Donald O'Connor Percy Kilbride

1949 **MA AND PA KETTLE**
Director: Charles Lamont
Co-star: Percy Kilbride Richard Long Meg Randall

1949 **BIG JACK**
Director: Richard Thorpe
Co-stars: Wallace Beery Richard Conte Edward Arnold

1950 **MRS O'MALLEY AND MR. MALONE**
Director: Norman Taurog
Co-stars: James Whitmore Ann Dvorak Phyllis Kirk

1950 **SUMMER STOCK**
Director: Charles Walters
Co-stars: Judy Garland Gene Kelly Gloria De Haven

1950 **MA AND PA KETTLE GO TO TOWN**
Director: Charles Lamont
Co-star: Percy Kilbride

1951 **MA AND PA KETTLE BACK ON THE FARM**
Director: Edward Sedgewick
Co-star: Percy Kilbride

1951 **YOU BELONG TO MY HEART**
Director: Don Hartman
Co-stars: Ezio Pinza Lana Turner Debbie Reynolds

1951 **THE LAW AND THE LADY**
Director: Edwin Knopf
Co-stars: Greer Garson Michael Wilding Fernando Lamas

1952 **THE BELLE OF NEW YORK**
Director: Charles Walters
Co-stars: Fred Astaire Vera-Ellen Keenan Wynn

1952 **IT'S A BIG COUNTRY**
Director: Richard Thorpe
Co-stars: Ethel Barrymore Van Johnson Gene Kelly

1952 **MA AND PA KETTLE AT THE FAIR**
Director: Charles Barton
Co-star: Percy Kilbride

1953 **FAST COMPANY**
Director: John Sturges
Co-stars: Howard Keel Nina Foch Polly Bergen

1953 **MA AND PA KETTLE ON VACATION**
Director: Charles Barton
Co-star: Percy Kilbride

1954 **MA AND PA KETTLE AT HOME**
Director: Charles Barton
Co-star: Percy Kilbride

1954 **THE LONG, LONG TRAILER**
Director: Vincente Minnelli
Co-stars: Lucille Ball Desi Arnaz Keenan Wynn

1955 **MA AND PA KETTLE AT WAIKIKI**
Director: Lee Sholem
Co-star: Percy Kilbride

1956 **THE KETTLES IN THE OZARKS**
Director: Charles Lamont
Co-star: Arthur Hunnicutt

1956 **FRIENDLY PERSUASION**
Director: William Wyler
Co-stars: Gary Cooper Dorothy McGuire Anthony Perkins

1957 **THE KETTLES ON OLD MACDONALD'S FARM**
Director: Virgil Vogel
Co-star: Parker Fennelly

1965 **THE WORLD OF ABBOTT AND COSTELLO**
Director: Jack Leonard
Co-stars: Bela Lugosi Tom Ewell Bud Abbott Lou Costello

SARA MAIR-THOMAS
1991 **THE PLEASURE PRINCIPLE**
Director: David Cohen
Co-stars: Peter Firth Lynsey Baxter Lysette Anthony

VALERIE MAIRESSE
1986 **THE SACRIFICE**
Director: Andrei Tarkovsky
Co-stars: Erland Josephson Susan Fleetwood Allan Edwall

SANDRA MAJANI
1994 **LE PARFUM D'YVONNE**
Director: Patrice Leconte
Co-stars: Hippolyte Girardot Jean-Pierre Marielle

TINA MAJORINO *(Child)*
1994 **WHEN A MAN LOVES A WOMAN**
Director: Luis Mandoki
Co-stars: Andy Garcia Meg Ryan Ellen Burnstyn

1994 **CORRINA, CORRINA**
Director: Jessie Nelson
Co-stars: Whoopi Goldberg Ray Liotta

MIRIAM MAKEBA
1989 **VOICES OF SARAFINA!**
Director: Nigel Noble
Co-star: Mbongeni Ngema

1992 **SARAFINA!**
Director: Darrell James Roodt
Co-stars: Whoopi Goldberg Leleti Khumalo John Kani

WENDY MAKKENA
1992 **SISTER ACT**
Director: Emile Ardolino
Co-stars: Whoopi Goldberg Maggie Smith Harvey Keitel

1993 **SISTER ACT II: BACK IN THE HABIT**
Co-stars: Whoopi Goldberg Mary Wickes James Coburn

GINA MALCOLM
1969 **MISCHIEF**
Director: Ian Shand
Co-stars: Paul Fraser Ian Burton Adrienne Byrne

PETRA MALAKOVA
1986 **OTELLO**
Director: Franco Zefferelli
Co-stars: Placido Domingo Kaita Ricciarelli Justino Diaz

IRINA MALVEEVA
1980 **UNION CITY**
Director: Mark Reichert
Co-stars: Dennis Lipscomb Deborah Harry Sam McMurray

PEGGY MALEY

1954 HUMAN DESIRE
Director: Fritz Lang
Co-stars: Glenn Ford Gloria Grahame Broderick Crawford

ANNET MALHERBE

1992 THE NORTHENERS
Director: Alex Van Warmerdam
Co-stars: Alex Van Warmerdam Leonard Lucieer Jack Wouterse

JUDITH MALINA

1989 ENEMIES, A LOVE STORY
Director: Paul Mazursky
Co-stars: Anjelica Huston Ron Silver Lena Olin

1990 AWAKENINGS
Director: Penny Marshall
Co-stars: Robert De Niro Robin Williams Julie Kavner

1991 THE ADDAMS FAMILY
Director: Barry Sonnenfeld
Co-stars: Anjelica Huston Raul Julia Christopher Lloyd

LUBA MALINA

1948 MEXICAN HAYRIDE
Director: Charles Barton
Co-stars: Bud Abbott Lou Costello Virginia Gray

JADE MALLE

1987 MAN ON FIRE
Director: Elie Chouraqui
Co-stars: Scott Glenn Joe Pesci Danny Aiello

JANE MALLETT

1974 SWEET MOVIE
Director: Susan Makevejev
Co-stars: Carole Laure Pierre Clementi Sami Frey

TANIA MALLETT

1964 GOLDFINGER
Director: Guy Hamilton
Co-stars: Sean Connery Honor Blackman Gert Frobe

BOOTS MALLORY (*Married William Cagney*)

1932 WALKING DOWN BROADWAY

1932 HANDLE WITH CARE
Co-star: James Dunn

1933 HUMANITY
Co-stars: Alexander Kirkland Ralph Morgan

1933 HELLO SISTER
Director: Alfred Werker
Co-stars: James Dunn Zasu Pitts Minna Gombell

1934 THE BIG RACE
Co-star: John Darrow

PATRICIA MALLORY

1935 POWDERSOME RANGE
Director: Wallace Fox
Co-stars: Harry Carey Bob Steele Tom Tyler

YOLANDE MALLOT

1940 DARK STREETS OF CAIRO
Co-stars: Sigrid Gurie Ralph Byrd Eddie Quillan

MONA MALM

1992 THE BEST INTENTIONS
Director: Billie August
Co-stars: Samuel Froler Pernilla August Max Von Sydow

GINA MALO

1932 GOODNIGHT VIENNA
Director: Herbert Wilcox
Co-stars: Jack Buchanan Anna Neagle Clive Currie

1933 WALTZ TIME
Director: William Thiele
Co-stars: Evelyn Lane Fritz Schultz Jay Laurier

1934 MY SONG FOR YOU
Director: Maurice Elvy
Co-stars: Jan Kiepura Aileen Marson Sonnie Hale

1936 WHERE THERE'S A WILL
Director: William Beaudine
Co-stars: Will Hay Graham Moffat Hartley Power

1936 SOUTHERN ROSES
Director: Fred Zelnick
Co-stars: George Robey Neil Hamilton

1936 JACK OF ALL TRADES
Director: Robert Stevenson
Co-stars: Jack Hulbert Robertson Hare Felix Aylmer

1936 ALL IN
Director: Val Guest
Co-stars: Ralph Lynn Claude Dampier Garry Marsh

1937 OVER SHE GOES
Director: Graham Cutts
Co-stars: Stanley Lupino Laddie Cliff Sally Gray

1940 THE DOOR WITH SEVEN LOCKS
Director: Norman Lee
Co-stars: Leslie Banks Lilli Palmer David Horne

DOROTHY MALONE
Oscar For Best Supporting Actress In 1956 For "Written On The Wind"

1946 JANIE GETS MARRIED
Director: Michael Curtiz
Co-stars: Joan Leslie Robert Hutton Ann Harding

1946 NIGHT AND DAY
Director: Michael Curtiz
Co-stars: Cary Grant Alexis Smith Monty Wooley

1946 THE BIG SLEEP
Director: Howard Hawks
Co-stars: Humphrey Bogart Lauren Bacall John Ridgeley

1948 FLAXEY MARTIN
Director: Richard Bare
Co-stars: Zachary Scott Virginia Mayo Elisha Cook Jnr.

1948 ONE SUNDAY AFTERNOON
Director: Raoul Walsh
Co-stars: Dennis Morgan Janis Paige Don Defore

1948 TO THE VICTOR
Director: Delmer Daves
Co-stars: Dennis Morgan Viveca Lindfors Bruce Bennett

1948 TWO GUYS FROM TEXAS
Director: David Butler
Co-stars: Dennis Morgan Jack Carson Penny Edwards

1948 SOUTH OF ST. LOUIS
Director: Ray Enright
Co-stars: Joel McCrea Zachary Scott Alexis Smith

1949 COLORADO TERRITORY
Director: Raoul Walsh
Co-stars: Joel McCrea Virginia Mayo James Mitchell

1950 CONVICTED
Director: Henry Levin
Co-stars: Glenn Ford Broderick Crawford Millard Mitchell

1950 THE KILLER THAT STALKED NEW YORK
Director: Earl McEvoy
Co-stars: Charles Korvin Evelyn Keyes

1950   **MRS. O'MALLEY AND MR. MALLONE**
Director: Norman Taurog
Co-stars: Marjorie Main James Whitmore Phyllis Kirk

1950   **THE NEVADAN**
Director: Gordon Douglas
Co-stars: Randolph Scott Forrest Tucker George Macready

1953   **SCARED STIFF**
Director: George Marshall
Co-stars: Dean Martin Jerry Lewis Lisabeth Scott

1953   **LAW AND ORDER**
Director: Nathan Juran
Co-stars: Ronald Reagan Preston Foster Alex Nicol

1953   **JACK SLADE**
Director: Harold Schuster
Co-stars: Mark Stevens Barton MacLaine John Litel

1954   **PUSHOVER**
Director: Richard Quine
Co-stars: Fred MacMurray Kim Novak Phil Carey

1954   **YOUNG AT HEART**
Director: Gordon Douglas
Co-stars: Doris Day Frank Sinatra Ethel Barrymore

1954   **PRIVATE HELL 36**
Director: Don Siegel
Co-stars: Ida Lupino Steve Cochran Howard Duff

1955   **TALL MAN RIDING**
Director: Lesley Selander
Co-stars: Randolph Scott Robert Barrat Peggie Castle

1955   **SINCERELY YOURS**
Director: Gordon Douglas
Co-stars: Liberace Joanne Dru Alex Nicol

1955   **FIVE GUNS WEST**
Director: Roger Corman
Co-stars: John Lund Chuck Connors Paul Birch

1955   **BATTLE CRY**
Director: Raoul Walsh
Co-stars: Van Heflin Aldo Ray Mona Freeman Tab Hunter

1955   **ARTISTS AND MODELS**
Director: Frank Tashlin
Co-stars: Dean Martin Jerry Lewis Shirley MacLaine

1955   **AT GUNPOINT**
Director: Alfred Werker
Co-stars: Fred MacMurray Walter Brennan John Qualen

1956   **WRITTEN ON THE WIND**
Director: Douglas Sirk
Co-stars: Rock Hudson Robert Stack Lauren Bacall

1956   **TENSION AT TABLE ROCK**
Director: Charles Marquis Warren
Co-stars: Richard Egan Angie Dickinson

1956   **PILLARS OF THE SKY**
Director: George Marshall
Co-stars: Jeff Chandler Lee Marvin Ward Bond

1957   **TARNISHED ANGELS**
Director: Douglas Sirk
Co-stars: Rock Hudson Robert Stack Jack Carson

1957   **TIP ON A DEAD JOCKEY**
Director: Richard Thorpe
Co-stars: Robert Taylor Gia Scala Martin Gabel

1957   **QUANTEZ**
Director: Harry Keller
Co-stars: Fred MacMurray Sydney Chaplin Michael Ansara

1957   **MAN OF A THOUSAND FACES**
Director: Joseph Pevney
Co-stars: James Cagney Robert Evans Jane Greer

1958   **TOO MUCH, TOO SOON**
Director: Art Napoleon
Co-stars: Errol Flynn Efrem Zimbalist Ray Danton

1959   **WARLOCK**
Director: Edward Dmytryk
Co-stars: Henry Fonda Richard Widmark Anthony Quinn

1960   **THE LAST VOYAGE**
Director: Andrew Stone
Co-stars: Robert Stack George Sanders Edmond O'Brien

1961   **THE LAST SUNSET**
Director: Robert Aldrich
Co-stars: Kirk Douglas Rock Hudson Carol Lynley

1963   **BEACH PARTY**
Director: William Asher
Co-stars: Robert Cummings Annette Funicello Frankie Avalon

1975   **THE ABDUCTION**
Director: Joseph Zito
Co-stars: Gregory Rozakis Judith-Marie Bergan Lawrence Tierney

1977   **GOLDEN RENDEZVOUS**
Director: Ashley Lazarus
Co-stars: Richard Harris Ann Turkel David Janssen

1979   **WINTER KILLS**
Director: William Richert
Co-stars: Jeff Bridges John Huston Elizabeth Taylor

1985   **PEYTON PLACE: THE NEXT GENERATION**
Director: Larry Elikan
Co-stars: Barbara Parkins Tim O'Connor

1992   **BASIC INTINCT**
Director: Paul Verhoeven
Co-stars: Michael Douglas Sharon Stone George Dzundza

NANCY MALONE

1965   **INTIMACY**
Director: Victor Stoloff
Co-stars: Barry Sullivan Jack Ging Joan Blackman

1967   **THE OUTSIDER**
Director: Michael Ritchie
Co-stars: Darren McGavin Edmond O'Brien Ann Sothern

1972   **THE TRIAL OF THE CATONSVILLE NINE**
Director: Gordon Davidson
Co-stars: Richard Jordan Ed Flanders

1974   **SKYWAY TO DEATH**
Director: Gordon Hessler
Co-stars: Ross Martin Stefanie Powers Bobby Sherman

1981   **THE KILLING OF RANDY WEBSTER**
Director: Sam Wanamaker
Co-stars: Hal Holbrook James Whitmore Sean Penn

TINA MALONE

1992   **THE LONG DAY CLOSES**
Director: Terence Davies
Co-stars: Marjorie Yates Leigh McCormack Nicholas Lamont

EVI MALTAGLIATI

1963   **FIRE OVER ROME**
Director: Guido Malatesta
Co-stars: Lang Jeffries Cristina Gaioni Moira Orfei

EILY MALYON

1934   **ROMANCE IN MANHATTAN**
Director: Stephen Roberts
Co-stars: Ginger Rogers Francis Lederer Donald Meek

1936   **A WOMAN REBELS**
Director: Mark Sandrich
Co-stars: Katherine Hepburn Herbert Marshall Elizabeth Allan

1936 ONE RAINY AFTERNOON
Director: Rowland Lee
Co-stars: Francis Lederer Ida Lupino Roland Young

1937 NIGHT MUST FALL
Director: Richard Thorpe
Co-stars: Robert Montgomery Rosalind Russell May Whitty

1939 ON BORROWED TIME
Director: Harold Bucquet
Co-stars: Lionel Barrymore Beulah Bondi Cedric Hardwicke

1939 THE HOUND OF THE BASKERVILLES
Director: Sidney Lanfield
Co-stars: Basil Rathbone Nigel Bruce

1940 UNTAMED
Director: George Archainbaud
Co-stars: Ray Milland Patricia Morison

1943 DEVOTION
Director: Curtis Bernhardt
Co-stars: Ida Lupino Olivia De Havilland Nancy Coleman

1943 THE UNDYING MONSTER
Director: John Brahm
Co-stars: James Ellison John Howard Heather Angel

MAMO

1935 MUTINY ON THE BOUNTY
Director: Frank Lloyd
Co-stars: Charles Laughton Clark Gabnle Franchot Tone

MANARA

1952 THE LITTLE WORLD OF DON CAMILLO
Director: Julien Duvivier
Co-stars: Fernandel Gino Cervi Sylvie

ANNA MANAHAN

1967 ULYSSES
Director: Joseph Strick
Co-stars: Maurice Roeves Barbara Jefford Milo O'Shea

1994 A BUSINESS AFFAIR
Director: Charlotte Brandstrom
Co-stars: Christopher Walken Carole Bucquet

1994 A MAN OF NO IMPORTANCE
Director: Suri Krishnamma
Co-stars: Albert Finney Tara Fitzgerald Rufus Sewell

SHELIA MANAHAN

1948 SAINTS AND SINNERS
Director: Leslie Arliss
Co-stars: Kieron Moore Christine Norden Maire O'Neill

1950 SEVEN DAYS TO NOON
Director: John Boutling
Co-stars: Barry Jones Olive Sloane Andre Morell

SUZY MANDEL

1976 CONFESSIONS OF A DRIVING INSTRUCTOR
Director: Norman Cohen
Co-stars: Robin Askwith Bill Maynard

GINA MANES

1927 NAPOLEAN
Director: Abel Gance
Co-stars: Alber Dieudonne Nicholas Koline Janis Carter

JEANNE MANET

1948 SLIGHTLY FRENCH
Director: Douglas Sirk
Co-stars: Dorothy Lamour Don Ameche Janis Carter

ELAINE MANGAN

1980 MANGANINNIE
Director: John Honey
Co-stars: Mawuyul Yanthalawuy Anna Ralph Phillip Hinton

1981 LE MAITRE D'ECOLE
Director: Claude Berri
Co-stars: Michel Coluche Phillip Hinton Jacques Debary

SILVANA MANGANO

1949 BITTER RICE
Director: Guiseppe De Santis
Co-stars: Raf Vallone Doris Dowling Vittorio Gassman

1951 ANNA
Director: Alberto Lattuada
Co-stars: Raf Vallone Vittorio Gassman Gaby Morlay

1954 MAMBO
Director: Robert Rossen
Co-stars: Michael Rennie Shelley Winters Vittorio Gassman

1954 ULYSSES
Director: Mario Camerini
Co-stars: Kirk Douglas Anthony Quinn Rosanna Podesta

1955 GOLD OF NAPLES
Director: Vittorio De Sica
Co-stars: Sophia Loren Paolo Stoppa Toto

1958 TEMPEST
Director: Alberto Lattuada
Co-stars: Van Heflin Oscar Homolka Viveca Lindfors

1960 FIVE BRANDED WOMEN
Director: Martin Ritt
Co-stars: Van Heflin Vera Miles Barbara Bel Geddes

1962 BARABBAS
Director: Richard Fleischer
Co-stars: Anthony Quinn Jack Palance Ernest Borgnine

1967 OEDIPUS REX
Director: Pier Paolo Pasalini
Co-stars: Franco Citti Alida Valli Carmelo Bene

1968 THEOREM
Director: Pier Paolo Pasalini
Co-stars: Terence Stamp Massimo Girotti Laura Betti

1971 DEATH IN VENICE
Director: Luchino Visconti
Co-stars: Dirk Bogarde Marisa Berenson Bjorn Andresen

1972 LUDWIG
Director: Luchino Visconti
Co-stars: Helmut Berger Romy Schneider Trevor Howard

1974 CONVERSATION BRIDE
Director: Luchino Visconti
Co-stars: Burt Lancaster Helmut Berger Claudia Marsani

1984 DUNE
Director: David Lynch
Co-stars: Francesca Annis Jose Ferrer Sting

1987 BLACK EYES
Director: Nikita Mikhalkov
Co-stars: Marcello Mastroianni Marthe Keller Elena Sofonova

KARIN MANI

1984 ALLEY CAT
Director: Edward Victor
Co-stars: Robert Torti Michael Wayne Brit Helfer

CINDY MANION

1985 THE TOXIC AVENGER
Director: Michael Herz
Co-stars: Andree Marander Mark Torgi Pat Ryan

BERTHA MANN

1930 ALL QUIET ON THE WESTERN FRONT
Director: Lewis Milestone
Co-stars: Lew Ayres Slim Summerville

1930 FREE LOVE
Co-stars: Conrad Nagel Genevieve Tobin Reginald Pasch

COLLETTE MANN

1982 KITTY AND THE BAGMAN
Director: Donald Crombie
Co-stars: Liddy Clark John Stanton Val Lehman

1988 OUTBACK BOUND
Director: John Llewellyn Moxey
Co-stars: Donna Mills John Meillon Nina Foch

LESLIE MANN

1997 GEORGE OF THE JUNGLE
Co-stars: Brendan Fraser John Cleese

LISA MANN

1963 LILLIES OF THE FIELD
Director: Ralph Nelson
Co-stars: Sidney Poitier Lilia Skala Dan Frazer

MARGARET MANN

1928 FOUR SONS
Director: John Ford
Co-stars: James Hall June Collyer George Meeker

TRACEY MANN

1981 SCARECROW
Director: Sam Pilsbury
Co-stars: John Carradine Jonathan Smith Daniel McLaren

1988 THE FOUR MINUTE MILE
Director: Jim Goddard
Co-stars: Richard Huw Nique Needles Michael York

LADY DIANA MANNERS

1922 THE GLORIOUS ADVENTURE
Director: Felix Orman
Co-stars: Victor McLaglen Gerald Lawrence William Luff

MARJORIE MANNERS

1942 TUMBLEWEED TRAIL
Co-stars: Bill Boyd George Cheesbro

1945 THE BIG SHOW-OFF
Co-star: Dale Evans

LUCIE MANNHEIM

1935 THE 39 STEPS
Director: Alfred Hitchcock
Co-stars: Robert Donat Madeleine Carroll Peggy Ashcroft

1936 THE HIGH COMMAND
Director: Thorold Dickinson
Co-stars: James Mason Lionel Atwill Steve Geray

1936 EAST MEETS WEST
Director: Herbert Mason
Co-stars: George Arliss Godfrey Tearle John Laurie

1943 THE YELLOW CANARY
Director: Herbert Wilcox
Co-stars: Anna Neagle Richard Greene Nova Pilbeam

1944 TAWNY PIPIT
Director: Charles Saunders
Co-stars: Bernard Miles Rosamund John Jean Gillie

1944 HOTEL RESERVE
Director: Lance Comfort
Co-stars: James Mason Raymond Lovell Herbert Lom

1960 BEYOND THE CURTAIN
Director: Compton Bennett
Co-stars: Richard Greene Eva Bartok Marius Goring

1965 BUNNY LAKE IS MISSING
Director: Otto Preminger
Co-stars: Laurence Olivier Carol Lynley Noel Coward

HOPE MANNING

1937 THE OLD CORRAL
Co-star: Gene Autry

IRENE MANNING

1942 THE BIG SHOT
Director: Lewis Seiler
Co-stars: Humphrey Bogart Donald Crisp Susan Peters

1942 YANKEE DOODLE DANDY
Director: Michael Curtiz
Co-stars: James Cagney Joan Leslie Walter Huston

1944 SHINE ON HARVEST MOON
Director: David Butler
Co-stars: Dennis Morgan Jack Carson Ann Sheridan

1944 THE DESERT SONG
Director: Robery Florey
Co-stars: Dennis Morgan Bruce Cabot Gene Lockhart

1944 THE DOUGHGIRLS
Director: James Kern
Co-stars: Alexis Smith Jane Wyman Ann Sheridan

1944 MAKE YOUR OWN BED
Director: Peter Godfrey
Co-stars: Jack Carson Jane Wyman Ricardo Cortez

1945 ESCAPE IN THE DESERT
Director: Edward Blatt
Co-stars: Philip Dorn Helmut Dantine Alan Hale

PATRICIA MANNING

1959 THE HIDEOUS SUN DEMON
Director: Robert Clarke
Co-star: Robert Clarke

RUTH MANNING

1979 AND YOUR NAME IS JONAH
Director: Richard Michaels
Co-stars: Sally Struthers James Woods Penny Santon

ANN MANNION

1975 AVALANCHE
Director: Frederic Goode
Co-stars: Michael Portman David Ponder David Dundas

SHELIA MANNORS

1931 DADDY LONG LEGS
Director: Alfred Santell
Co-stars: Janet Gaynor Warner Baxter Una Merkel

1932 LAND OF WANTED MEN
Co-stars: Bill Cody Andy Shuford Gibson Gowland

1932 TEXAS PIONEERS
Co-stars: Bill Cody Leroy Mason

1935 LAWLESS RANGE
Co-star: John Wayne

1935 TOGETHER WE LIVE
Co-star: William Bakewell

1935　BEHIND THE EVIDENCE
Co-star:　Donald Cook

1936　DESERT PHANTOM
Co-star:　Johnny Mack Brown

DINAH MANOFF

1977　THE POSSESSED
Director:　Jerry Thorpe
Co-stars:　James Farentino Joan Hackett Harrison Ford

1980　ORDINARY PEOPLE
Director:　Robert Redford
Co-stars:　Donald Sutherland Mary Tyler Moore Timothy Hutton

1982　I OUGHT TO BE IN PICTURES
Director:　Herbert Ross
Co-stars:　Walter Matthau Ann-Margret Lance Guest

1984　FLIGHT 90: DISASTER ON THE POTOMAC
Director:　Robert Lewis
Co-stars:　Richard Masur Jamie Rose Ken Olin

1986　CLASSIFIED LOVE
Director:　Don Taylor
Co-stars:　Michael McKean Stephanie Feracy Franc Luz

1988　CHILD'S PLAY
Director:　Tom Holland
Co-stars:　Catherine Hicks Chris Sarandon Brad Dourif

1989　BEAUTY AND DENISE
Director:　Neal Israel
Co-stars:　John Karlen David Carradine

1989　STAYING TOGETHER
Director:　Lee Grant
Co-stars:　Sean Astin Stockard Channing Melinda Dillon

1990　WELCOME HOME, ROXY CARMICHAEL
Director:　Jim Abrahams
Co-stars:　Winona Ryder Jeff Daniels Laila Robins

MARIE MANSART

1971　ANNE AND MURIEL
Director:　Francois Truffaut
Co-stars:　Jean-Pierre Leaud Kika Markham Stacey Tendeter

JAYNE MANSFIELD *(Vera Jayne Palmer)*
(Married Mickey Hargitay)

1955　ILLEGAL
Director:　Lewis Allen
Co-stars:　Edwrad G.Robinson Nina Foch

1956　THE GIRL CAN'T HELP IT
Director:　Frank Tashlin
Co-stars:　Tom Ewell Edmond O'Brien Henry Jones

1957　THE BURGLAR
Director:　Paul Wendkos
Co-stars:　Dan Duryea Martha Vickers

1957　KISS THEM FOR ME
Director:　Stanley Donen
Co-stars:　Cary Grant Ray Walston Suzy Parker

1957　THE WAYWARD BUS
Director:　Victor Vicas
Co-stars:　Dan Dailey Joan Collins Rick Jason

1957　WILL SUCCESS SPOIL ROCK HUNTER
Director:　Frank Tashlin
Co-stars:　Tony Randall Betsy Drake Joan Blondell

1958　THE SHERRIFF OF FRACTURED JAW
Director:　Raoul Walsh
Co-stars:　Kenneth More Robert Morley Henry Hull

1960　TOO HOT TO HANDLE
Director:　Terence Young
Co-stars:　Leo Genn Karl Boehm Christopher Lee

1960　THE CHALLENGE
Director:　John Gilling
Co-stars:　Anthony Quayle Dermot Walsh

1961　THE GEORGE RAFT STORY
Director:　Joseph M. Newman
Co-stars:　Ray Danton Julie London

1962　IT HAPPEND IN ATHENS
Director:　Andrew Marton
Co-stars:　Trax Colton Bob Mathias

1964　PANIC BUTTON
Director:　George Sherman
Co-stars:　Maurice Chevalier Eleanor Parker

1967　A GUIDE FOR THE MARRIED MAN
Director:　Gene Kelly
Co-stars:　Walter Matthau Lucille Ball Inger Stevens

MARTHA MANSFIELD

1920　DR. JEKYLL AND MR. HYDE
Director:　John Robertson
Co-stars:　John Barrymore Nita Naldi Louis Wolheim

HELENE MANSON

1943　LE CORBEAU
Director:　Henri-Georges Clouzot
Co-stars:　Pierre Fresnay Pierre Larquey Ginette LeClerc

MARY MANSON

1959　LIFE IN DANGER
Director:　Terry Bishop
Co-stars:　Derren Nesbitt Julie Hopkins Victor Brooks

DOREEN MANTLE

1974　ALL CREATURES GREAT AND SMALL
Director:　Claude Whatham
Co-stars:　Simon West Anthony Hopkins Lisa Harrow

1987　OUR LADY BLUE
Director:　Robin Midgley
Co-stars:　Patricia Hayes Eva Griffith Paul Beringer

1992　MR. WAKEFIELD'S CRUSADE
Director:　Angela Pope
Co-stars:　Peter Capaldi Michael Maloney Richard Griffiths

KITI MANVER

**1988　WOMEN ON THE VERGE
OF A NERVOUS BREAKDOWN**
Director:　Pedro Almodovar
Co-stars:　Carmen Maura Antonio Banderas

LESLEY MANVILLE

1988　HIGH HOPES
Director:　Mike Leigh
Co-stars:　Philip Davis Ruth Sheen David Bamber

1989　THE FIRM
Director:　Alan Clarke
Co-stars:　Gary Oldman Philip Davis Andrew Wilde

1992　BAD GIRL
Director:　George Case
Co-stars:　Jane Horrocks Tom Beard David Bradley

1994　O MARY THIS LONDON
Director:　Suri Krishnamma
Co-stars:　Jason Barry Oba Seagrave Dylan Tighe

1996　SECRETS AND LIES
Director:　Mike Leigh
Co-stars:　Brenda Blethyn Timothy Spall Phyllis Logan

KATE MANX (Married Leslie Stevens)

1962   HERO'S ISLAND
Director: Leslie Stevens
Co-stars: James Mason Neville Brand Rip Torn

LINDA MANZ (child)

1978   DAYS OF HEAVEN
Director: Terence Malik
Co-stars: Richard Gere Brooke Adams Sam Shepard

1979   THE WANDERERS
Director: Philip Kaufman
Co-stars: Ken Wahl Karen Allen Toni Kalem

1980   OUT OF THE BLUE
Director: Dennis Hopper
Co-stars: Dennis Hopper Sharon Farrell Raymond Burr

DAGMAR MANZEL

1990   COMING OUT
Director: Heiner Carow
Co-stars: Matthias Freihof Dirk Kummer Alex Wandtke

1992   SCHTONK!
Director: Helmut Dietl
Co-stars: Gotz George Uwe Ochsenknecht Rolfe Hoppe

ANGELA MAO

1973   ENTER THE DRAGON
Director: Robert Clouse
Co-stars: Bruce Lee John Saxon Jim Kelly

JOANNE MAPP

1987   CHRISTINE
Director: Alan Clarke
Co-stars: Vicky Murdoch Kelly George Mark Harvey

ADELE MARA

1942   ALIAS BOSTON BLACKIE
Director: Lew Landers
Co-stars: Chester Morris George E.Stone Paul Fix

1942   BLONDIE GOES TO COLLEGE
Director: Frank Strayer
Co-stars: Penny Singleton Arthur Lake Janet Blair

1942   YOU WERE NEVER LOVLIER
Director: William Seiter
Co-stars: Fred Astaire Rita Hayworth Adolphe Menjou

1943   REVEILLE WITH BEVERLY
Director: Charles Barton
Co-stars: Ann Miller William Wright Dick Purcell

1944   THROUGHBREDS

1944   ATLANTIC CITY
Director: Ray McCarey
Co-stars: Constance Moore Brad Taylor Jerry Colonna

1946   CATMAN OF PARIS
Director: Lesley Selander
Co-stars: Carl Esmond Lenore Aubert Gerald Mohr

1946   THE INNER CIRCLE
Co-star: Warren Douglas

1946   THE TIGER WOMAN

1947   WEB OF DANGER

1948   WAKE OF THE RED WITCH
Director: Edward Ludwig
Co-stars: John Wayne Gail Russell Gig Young

1948   GALLANT LEGION
Director: Joseph Kane
Co-stars: Bruce Cabot Andy Devine Jack Holt

1948   ANGEL IN EXILE
Director: Allan Dwan
Co-stars: John Carroll Thomas Gomez Barton MacLane

1949   SANDS OF IWO JIMA
Director: Allan Dwan
Co-stars: John Wayne John Agar Forrest Tucker

1952   COUNT THE HOURS
Director: Don Siegel
Co-stars: Teresa Wright MacDonald Carey Dolores Moran

1958   CURSE OF THE FACELESS MAN
Director: Edward Cahn
Co-stars: Richard Anderson Elaine Edwards Gar Moore

1959   THE BIG CIRCUS
Director: Joseph Newman
Co-stars: Victor Mature Red Buttons Rhonda Fleming

MARY MARA

1991   THE HARD WAY
Director: John Badham
Co-stars: Michael J.Fox James Woods Annabella Sciorra

1992   MR. SATURDAY NIGHT
Director: Billy Crystal
Co-stars: Billy Crystal David Paymer Helen Hunt Ron Silver

1992   LOVE POTION NO. 9
Director: Dale Launer
Co-stars: Tate Donovan Sandra Bullock Dale Midkiff

JULIE MARBOEUF

1992   PETAIN
Director: Jean Marboeuf
Co-stars: Jacques Dufilho Jean Yanne Jean-Pierre Cassel

SOPHIE MARCEAU

1984   FORT SAGANNE
Director: Alain Corneau
Co-stars: Gerard Depardieu Catherine Deneuve Phillipe Noiret

1985   POLICE
Director: Maurice Pialat
Co-stars: Gerard Depardieu Richard Ancanini Sandrine Bonnaire

1990   PACIFIC PALISADES
Director: Bernard Schmitt
Co-stars: Adam Coleman Howard Anne Curry Toni Basil

1995   BRAVEHEART
Director: Mel Gibson
Co-stars: Mel Gibson Patrick Mcgoohan

1997   BEYOND THE CLOUDS
Director: Michaelangelo Antonioni
Co-stars: John Malkovich Fanny Ardant Jean Reno

1997   ANNA KARENINA
Director: Bernard Rose
Co-stars: Sean Bean James Fox Alfred Molina

ELSPETH MARCH

1944   MR. EMMANUEL
Director: Harold French
Co-stars: Felix Aylmer Greta Gynt Ursula Jeans

1969   CARRY ON AGAIN DOCTOR
Director: Gerald Thomas
Co-stars: Sid James Barbara Windsor Jim Dale

EVE MARCH

1944   THE CURSE OF THE CAT PEOPLE
Director: Robert Wise
Co-stars: Simone Simon Kent Smith Jane Randolph

JANE MARCH

1992   **THE LOVER**
Director: Jean-Jacques Annaud
Co-stars: Tony Leung Frederique Meininger Lisa Faulkner

1994   **COLOR OF NIGHT**
Director: Richard Rush
Co-stars: Bruce Willis Ruben Blades

MELISSA TORME MARCH

1972   **THE CAREY TREATMENT**
Director: Blake Edwards
Co-stars: James Coburn Jennifer O'Neill Pat Hingle

ROSALIND MARCH

1990   **CLOSE RELATIONS**
Director: Adrian Shergold
Co-stars: James Hazeldine Clare Holman Annie Gurney

COLETTE MARCHAND

Nominated For Best Supporting Actress In 1952 For "Moulin Rouge"

1952   **MOULIN ROUGE**
Director: John Huston
Co-stars: Jose Ferrer Zsa Zsa Gabor Katherine Kath

CORINNE MARCHAND

1961   **CLEO FROM FIVE TO SEVEN**
Director: Agnes Varda
Co-stars: Antoine Bourseiller Michel Legrand Anna Karina

1970   **BORSALINO**
Director: Jacques Deray
Co-stars: Alain Delon Jean-Paul Belmondo Michel Bouquet

1970   **RIDER ON THE RAIN**
Director: Renee Clement
Co-stars: Charles Bronson Jill Ireland Marlene Jobert

NANCY MARCHANT

1957   **THE BACHELOR PARTY**
Director: Delbert Mann
Co-stars: Don Murray E.G. Marshall Jack Warden

1969   **ME, NATALIE**
Director: Fred Coe
Co-stars: Patty Duke James Farantino Elsa Lanchester

1971   **THE HOSPITAL**
Director: Arthur Hiller
Co-stars: George C.Scott Diana Rigg Barnard Hughes

1983   **AGATHA CHRISTIE'S SPARKLING CYANIDE**
Director: Robert Lewis
Co-stars: Anthony Andrews Deborah Raffin

1984   **THE BOSTONIANS**
Director: James Ivory
Co-stars: Christopher Reeves Vanessa Redgrave Jessica Tandy

1987   **FROM THE HIP**
Director: Bob Clark
Co-stars: Judd Nelson Elizabeth Perkins John Hurt

1988   **THE NAKED GUN:**
FROM THE FILES OF POLICE SQUAD
Director: David Zucker
Co-stars: Leslie Nielsen George Kennedy

1992   **BRAIN DONORS**
Director: Dennis Dugan
Co-stars: John Turturro Bob Nelson Mel Smith

CRETA MARGOS

1962   **STRANGERS IN THE CITY**
Director: Rick Carrier
Co-stars: Robert Gentile Camilo Delgardo Robert Corso

ANDREA MARCOVICI

1976   **THE FRONT**
Director: Martin Ritt
Co-stars: Woody Allen Zero Mostel Michael Murphy

1981   **THE HAND**
Director: Oliver Stone
Co-stars: Michael Caine Viveca Lindfors Rosemary Murphy

1983   **PACKIN' IT IN**
Director: Jud Taylor
Co-stars: Richard Benjamin Paula Prentiss Molly Ringwald

1983   **SPACEHUNTER: ADVENTURES**
IN THE FORBIDDEN ZONE
Director: Lamont Johnson
Co-stars: Peter Strauss Molly Ringwald

1985   **THE STUFF**
Director: Larry Cohen
Co-stars: Michael Moriarty Paul Sorvino Danny Aiello

1987   **SOMEONE TO LOVE**
Director: Henry Jaglom
Co-stars: Orson Welles Michael Emil Sally Kellerman

1993   **JACK THE BEAR**
Director: Marshall Herskovitch
Co-stars: Danny DeVito Gary Sinese Miko Hughes

SIMONE MAREUILL

1928   **UN CHIEN ANDALOU**
Director: Luis Bunuel
Co-stars: Luis Bunuel Pierre Batcheff Salvador Dali

JANIE MAREZE

1931   **LA CHIENNE**
Director: Jean Renoir
Co-stars: Michel Simon Georges Flament Jean Gehret

IRIS MARGA

1986   **MISS MARY**
Director: Maria Luisa Bemberg
Co-stars: Julie Christie Nacha Guevara Luisina Brando

MARGO

1934   **CRIME WITHOUT PASSION**
Director: Ben Hecht
Co-stars: Claude Rains Whitney Bourne Stanley Ridges

1935   **RUMBA**
Director: Marion Gering
Co-stars: George Raft Carole Lombard Lynne Overman

1936   **THE ROBIN HOOD OF EL DORADO**
Director: William Wellman
Co-stars: Warner Baxter Bruce Cabot Eric Linden

1936   **WINTERSET**
Director: Alfred Santell
Co-stars: Burgess Meredith John Carradine Paul Guilfoyle

1937   **LOST HORIZON**
Director: Frank Capra
Co-stars: Ronald Colman Jane Wyatt Thomas Mitchell

1939   **MIRACLE ON MAIN STREET**
Director: Steve Sekely
Co-stars: Walter Abel Jane Darwell Lyle Talbot

1943   **GANGWAY FOR TOMORROW**
Director: John Auer
Co-stars: Robert Ryan John Carradine Amelita Ward

1943   **BEHIND THE RISING SUN**
Director: Edward Dmytryk
Co-stars: J.Carrol Naish Robert Ryan Tom Neal

1943 THE LEOPARD MAN
Director: Jacques Tourneur
Co-stars: Dennis O'Keefe Isabel Jewell Jean Brooks

1952 VIVA ZAPATA!
Director: Elia Kazan
Co-stars: Marlon Brando Jean Peters Anthony Quinn

1955 I'LL CRY TOMOROW
Director: Daniel Mann
Co-stars: Susan Hayward Richard Conte Eddie Albert

1958 FROM HELL TO TEXAS
Director: Henry Hathaway
Co-stars: Don Murray Diane Varsi Dennis Hopper

1962 WHO'S GOT THE ACTION
Director: Daniel Mann
Co-stars: Dean Martin Lana Turner Walter Matthau

JANET MARGOLIN

1962 DAVID AND LISA
Director: Frank Perry
Co-stars: Keir Dullea Howard Da Silva Neva Patterson

1965 BUS RILEY'S BACK IN TOWN
Director: Harvey Hart
Co-stars: Michael Parks Ann-Margret Jocelyn Brando

1965 THE SABOTEUR, CODE NAME MORITURI
Director: Bernard Wicki
Co-stars: Yul Brynner Marlon Brando Trevor Howard

1966 NEVADA SMITH
Director: Henry Hathaway
Co-stars: Steve McQueen Karl Malden Brian Keith

1967 ENTER LAUGHING
Director: Carl Reiner
Co-stars: Reni Santoni Jose Ferrer Shelley Winters

1968 BUONA SERA MRS. CAMPBELL
Director: Melvin Frank
Co-stars: Gina Lollobrigida Telly Savalas Peter Lawford

1971 THE LAST CHILD
Director: John Llewellyn Moxey
Co-stars: Van Heflin Michael Cole

1972 FAMILY FLIGHT
Director: Marvin Chomsky
Co-stars: Rod Taylor Kristoffer Tabori Dina Merril

1974 PLANET EARTH
Director: Marc Daniels
Co-stars: John Saxon Ted Cassidy Diana Muldaur

1977 ANNIE HALL
Director: Woody Allen
Co-stars: Woody Allen Diane Keaton Tony Roberts Carol Kane

1979 LAST EMBRACE
Director: Jonathan Demme
Co-stars: Roy Scheider Sam Levene John Glover

1988 DISTANT THUNDER
Director: Rick Rosenberg
Co-stars: John Lithgow Ralph Macchio Kerrie Keane

1990 MURDER C.O.D.
Director: Alan Metzger
Co-stars: William Devane Patrick Duffy Chelsea Field

LAURA MARGOLIS

1989 GOD'S WILL
Director: Julia Cameron
Co-stars: Marge Kotlisky Daniel Region Linda Edmond

MIRIAM MARGOYLES

1980 THE AWAKENING
Director: Mike Newell
Co-stars: Charlton Heston Susannah York Jill Townsend

1983 YENTL
Director: Barbra Streisand
Co-stars: Barbra Streisand Mandy Patinkin Amy Irving Steven Hill

1987 LITTLE DORRIT
Director: Christine Edzard
Co-stars: Derek Jacobi Joan Greenwood Alec Guinness

1990 I LOVE YOU TO DEATH
Director: Lawrence Kasdan
Co-stars: Kevin Kline Tracey Ulman Joan Plowright

1990 ORPHEUS DESCENDING
Director: Peter Hall
Co-stars: Vanessa Redgrave Kevin Anderson

1990 OLD FLAMES
Director: Christopher Morahan
Co-stars: Stephen Fry Simon Callow Clive Francis

1990 PACIFIC HEIGHTS
Director: John Schlesinger
Co-stars: Melanie Griffith Matthew Modine Michael Keaton

1993 THE AGE OF INNOCENCE
Director: Martin Scorsese
Co-stars: Daniel-Day Lewis Michelle Pfeiffer Winona Ryder

1995 BABE *(Voice)*
Director: Chris Noonan
Co-stars: James Cromwell Magna Szubanski

1996 JAMES AND THE GIANT PEACH
Director: Henry Selig
Co-stars: Paul Terry Joanna Lumley Pete Postlethwaite

1997 WILLIAM SHAKESPEARE'S ROMEO AND JULIET
Director: Baz Luhrman
Co-stars: Leonardo DiCaprio Claire Danes

JULIANNA MARGULIES

1997 PARADISE ROAD
Director: Bruce Beresford
Co-stars: Jennifer Ehle Glenn Close Pauline Collins

LYNNE MARGULIES

1979 THE AFTERMATH
Director: Steve Barkett
Co-stars: Steve Barkett Dayle Kerry Larry Latham Sid Haig

MARCELLA MARIANI

1953 SENSO
Director: Luchino Visconti
Co-stars: Alida Valli Farley Granger Massimo Girotti

LEONA MARICLE

1935 O'SHAUGHNESSY'S BOY
Director: Richard Boleslawski
Co-stars: Wallace Beery Jackie Cooper Sara Haden

1937 WOMEN OF GLAMOUR
Director: Gordon Wiles
Co-stars: Melvyn Douglas Virginia Bruce Pert Kelton

1937 WOMAN CHASES MAN
Director: John Blystone
Co-stars: Miriam Hopkins Joel McCrea Charles Winninger

1937 THE FRAME-UP
Co-star: Paul Kelly

1938 THE LONE WOLF IN PARIS
Director: Albert Rogell
Co-stars: Francis Lederer Frances Drake Olaf Hytton

ANNE MARIE

1974 THE STOOLIE
Director: John Avildsen
Co-stars: Jackie Mason Dan Frazer Marcia Jean Kurtz

**1979 BENEATH THE VALLEY
OF THE ULTRA VIXENS**
Director: Russ Meyer
Co-stars: Francesca Natividad June Mack

CONSTANCE MARIE

1993 ISLAND CITY
Director: Jorge Montesi
Co-stars: Kevin Conroy Brenda Strong Pete Koch

1993 12.01
Director: Jack Sholder
Co-stars: Jonathan Silverman Helen Slater Martin Landau

ROSE MARIE

1932 INTERNATIONAL HOUSE
Director: Edward Sutherland
Co-stars: W.C.Fields George Burns Gracie Allen

1953 TOP BANANA
Director: Alfred Greene
Co-stars: Phil Silvers Danny Scholl Jack Albertson

1966 DEAD HEAT ON A MERRY-GO-ROUND
Director: Bernard Girard
Co-stars: James Coburn Camilla Sparv Aldo Ray

ELISA MARINARDI

1983 AND THE SHIPS SAIL ON
Director: Federico Fellini
Co-stars: Freddie Jones Barbara Jefford Peter Cellier

BETH MARION

1936 THE FUGITIVE SHERIFF
Co-star: Ken Maynard

1938 PHANTOM GOLD
Co-stars: Jack Lunden Jimmy Robinson Marin Sais

JOAN MARION

1936 SENSATION
Director: Brian Desmond Hurst
Co-stars: John Lodge Diana Churchill Richard Bird

1937 FOR VALOUR
Director: Tom Walls
Co-stars: Tom Walls Ralph Lynn Veronica Rose Hubert Harben

1938 PREMIERE
Director: Walter Summers
Co-stars: John Lodge Judy Kelly Hugh Williams

1938 BLACK LIMELIGHT
Director: Walter Mycroft
Co-stars: Raymond Massey Coral Browne Henry Oscar

1939 DEAD MAN'S SHOES
Director: Thomas Bentley
Co-stars: Leslie Banks Wilfred Lawson Judy Kelly

1939 TEN DAYS IN PARIS
Director: Tim Whelan
Co-stars: Rex Harrison Karen Verne Leo Genn

1939 SPIES OF THE AIR
Director: David MacDonald
Co-stars: Barry K.Barnes Roger Livesey Basil Radford

MONA MARIS

1930 THE ARIZONA KID
Director: Alfred Santell
Co-stars: Warner Baxter Carole Lombard Theodore Von Eltz

1930 A DEVIL WITH WOMEN
Director: Irving Cummings
Co-stars: Victor McLaglen Humphrey Bogart

1932 THE PASSIONATE PLUMBER
Director: Edward Segdwick
Co-stars: Buster Keaton Jimmy Durante Polly Moran

1934 KISS AND MAKE UP
Director: Harlan Thompson
Co-stars: Cary Grant Genevieve Tobin Helen Mack

1941 FLIGHT FROM DESTINY
Director: Vincent Sherman
Co-stars: Thomas Mitchell Geraldine Fitzgerald

1941 A DATE WITH THE FALCON
Director: Irving Reis
Co-stars: George Sanders James Gleason Wendy Barrie

1941 LAW OF THE TROPICS
Director: Ray Enright
Co-stars: Constance Bennett Jeffrey Lynn Regis Toomey

1941 UNDERGROUND
Director: Vincent Sherman
Co-stars: Jeffrey Lynn Philip Dorn Karen Verne

1942 PACIFIC RENDEZVOUS
Director: George Sidney
Co-stars: Lee Bowman Jean Rogers Carl Esmond

1942 MY GAL SAL
Director: Irving Cummings
Co-stars: Rita Hayworth Victor Mature Carole Landis

1942 BERLIN CORRESPONDENT
Director: Eugene Forde
Co-stars: Dana Andrews Virginia Gilmore Sig Ruman

1944 THE FALCON IN MEXICO
Director: William Clemens
Co-stars: Tom Conway Joseph Vitale

1944 TAMPICO
Director: Lothar Mendes
Co-stars: Edward G.Robinson Lynn Bari Victor McLaglen

1946 HEARTBEAT
Director: Sam Wood
Co-stars: Ginger Rogers Jean-Pierre Aumont Basil Rathbone

STELLA MARIS

1991 TRULY, MADLY, DEEPLY
Director: Anthony Minghella
Co-stars: Juliet Stevenson Alan Rickman Michael Maloney

SARI MARITZA

1932 INTERNATIONAL HOUSE
Director: Edward Sutherland
Co-stars: W.C.Fields George Burns Gracie Allen

1932 EVENINGS FOR SALE
Director: Stuart Walker
Co-stars: Herbert Marshall Mary Boland Charles Ruggles

1932 THE WATER GYPSIES
Director: Maurice Elvy
Co-stars: Ann Todd Ian Hunter Richard Bird

1932 FORGOTTEN COMMANDMENTS
Director: Louis Gasnier
Co-stars: Gene Raymond Irving Pichel Harry Beresford

1933 A LADY'S PROFESSION
Director: Norman Z. McLeod
Co-stars: Alison Skipworth Roland Young Kent Taylor

1934 CRIMSON ROMANCE
Director: David Howard
Co-stars: Ben Lyon James Bush Erich Von Stroheim

JANE MARKEN

1936   UNE PARTIE DE CAMPAGNE
Director: Jean Renoir
Co-stars: Sylvie Bataille Georges Darnoul Paul Temps

1938   HOTEL DU NORD
Director: Marcel Carne
Co-stars: Annabella Louis Jouvet Jean-Pierre Aumont

1943   LUMIERE D'ETE
Director: Jean Gremillion
Co-stars: Madeleine Renaud Pierre Brasseur Madeleine Robinson

1945   LES ENFANTS DU PARADIS
Director: Marcel Carne
Co-stars: Arletty Jean-Louis Barrault Pierre Brasseur

1948   CLOCHEMERLE
Director: Pierre Chenal
Co-stars: Brochard Simone Michels Paul Demange

1948   DEDEE D'ANVERS
Director: Yves Allegret
Co-stars: Simon Signoret Marcel Pagliero Bernard Blier

1948   SUCH A PRETTY LITTLE BEACH
Director: Yves Allegret
Co-stars: Gerard Philipe Jean Servais Carette

1949   LA MARIE DU PORT
Director: Marcel Carne
Co-stars: Jean Gabin Blanchette Brunoy Nicole Courcel

1950   MANEGES
Director: Yves Allegret
Co-stars: Simone Signoret Bernard Blier Frank Villard

1956   AND GOD CREATED WOMAN
Director: Roger Vadim
Co-stars: Brigitte Bardot Curt Jurgens Christian Marquand

ENID MARKEY

1916   CIVILLISATION
Director: Thomas Ince
Co-stars: Howard Hickman J.Barney Sherry

KIKA MARKHAM *(Sister Of Petra Markham)*

1969   FUTTOCK'S END
Director: Bob Kellett
Co-stars: Ronnie Barker Michael Hordern Roger Livesey

1971   ANNE AND MURIEL
Director: Francois Truffaut
Co-stars: Jean-Pierre Leaud Stacey Tendeter Marie Mansart

1981   OUTLAND
Director: Peter Hyams
Co-stars: Sean Connery Peter Boyle Francis Sternhagen

1985   THE INNOCENT
Director: John MacKenzie
Co-stars: Andrew Hawley Tom Bell Miranda Richardson

PETRA MARKHAM *(Sister Of Kika Markham)*

1970   GET CARTER
Director: Mike Hodges
Co-stars: Michael Caine Britt Ekland John Osborne

1973   THE HIRELING
Director: Alan Bridges
Co-stars: Robert Shaw Sarah Miles Peter Egan

MARGARET MARKOV

1973   HAWKINS ON MURDER
Director: Jud Taylor
Co-stars: James Stewart Bonnie Bedelia Kate Reid

1974   THE ARENA
Director: Steve Carver
Co-stars: Pam Grier Lucretia Love Paul Muller

CARLA MARLIER

1960   ZAZIE DANS LA METRO
Director: Louis Malle
Co-stars: Catherine Demongeot Philippe Noiret

LUCY MARLOW

1954   A STAR IS BORN
Director: George Cukor
Co-stars: Judy Garland James Mason Charles Bickford

1955   QUEEN BEE
Director: Ranald MacDougall
Co-stars: Joan Crawford Barry Sullivan John Ireland

1955   TIGHT SPOT
Director: Phil Karlson
Co-stars: Edward G.Robinson Ginger Rogers Brian Keith

1955   MY SISTER EILEEN
Director: Richard Quine
Co-stars: Betty Garrett Janet Leigh Bob Fosse

1955   BRING YOUR SMILE ALONE
Director: Blake Edwards
Co-stars: Constance Towers Frankie Laine Keefe Brasselle

1956   HE LAUGHED LAST
Director: Blake Edwards
Co-stars: Frankie Laine Anthony Dexter Jesse White

FAYE MARLOWE

1945   JUNIOR MISS
Director: George Seaton
Co-stars: Peggy Ann Garner Allyn Joslyn Mona Freeman

1945   HANGOVER SQUARE
Director: John Brahm
Co-stars: Laird Cregar Linda Darnell George Sanders

1946   RENDEZVOUS WITH ANNIE
Director: Allan Dwan
Co-stars: Eddie Albert C.Aubrey Smith

JUNE MARLOWE

1931   PARDON US
Director: James Parrott
Co-stars: Stan Laurel Oliver Hardy Walter Long

LINDA MARLOWE

1986   MR. LOVE
Director: Roy Battersby
Co-stars: Barry Jackson Maurice Denham Margaret Tyzack

1990   THE GREEN MAN
Director: Elijah Moshinsky
Co-stars: Albert Finney Michael Hordern Josie Lawrence

1991   LET HIM HAVE IT
Director: Peter Medak
Co-stars: Christine Ecclestone Paul Reynolds Tom Bell

SALLY ANNE MARLOWE *(child)*

1972   WRECK RAISERS
Director: Harold Orton
Co-stars: Paul Hennen Martin Reynolds Robin Baldwin

FLORENCE MARLY

1939   LE DERNIER TOURNANT
Director: Pierre Chenal
Co-stars: Michel Simon Fernand Gravet Corrine Luchaire

1947 LES MAUDITS
Director: Rene Clement
Co-stars: Paul Bernard Henri Vidal Marcel Dalio

1948 SEALED VERDICT
Director: Lewis Allen
Co-stars: Ray Milland Broderick Crawford John Hoyt

1949 TOKYO JOE
Director: Stuart Heisler
Co-stars: Humphrey Bogart Alexander Knox Jerome Courtland

PATRICIA MARMONT

1954 THE CROWDED DAY
Director: John Guillermin
Co-stars: Joan Rice John Gregson Freda Jackson

KELLI MARONEY

1984 NIGHT OF THE COMET
Director: Tom Eberhardt
Co-stars: Catherine Mary Stewart Geoffrey Lewis Mary Woronov

IRENE MAROT

1988 FURTHER AND PARTICULAR
Director: Steve Dwoskin
Co-stars: Richard Butler Carola Regnier Jean Fennell

TINA MARQUAND

1956 MODESTY BLAISE
Director: Joseph Losey
Co-stars: Monica Vitti Dirk Bogarde Terence Stamp

1966 TEXAS ACROSS THE RIVER
Director: Michael Gordon
Co-stars: Dean Martin Alain Delon Rosemary Forsyth

1966 THE GAME IS OVER
Director: Roger Vadim
Co-stars: Jane Fonda Peter McEnery Michel Piccoli

MARIA ELENA MARQUES

1948 THE PEARL
Director: Emilio Fernandez
Co-stars: Pedro Armendariz Alfonso Bedova

1951 ACROSS THE WILD MISSOURI
Director: William Wellman
Co-stars: Clark Gable Adolphe Menjou John Hodiak

1953 AMBUSH AT TOMAHAWK GAP
Director: Fred Sears
Co-stars: John Hodiak John Derek David Brian

SYLVIA MARRIOTT

1940 CRIMES AT THE DARK HOUSE
Director: George King
Co-stars: Tod Slaughter Hilary Eaves Hay Petrie

1966 THE HAND OF NIGHT
Director: Frederick Goode
Co-stars: William Sylvester Alicia Gur Edward Underdown

1971 ANNE AND MURIEL
Director: Francois Truffaut
Co-stars: Jean-Pierre Leaud Kika Markham Stacey Tendeter

1975 THE STORY OF ADELE H
Director: Francois Truffaut
Co-stars: Isabelle Adjani Bruce Robinson

MARLO MARRON

1993 MI VIDA LOCA
Director: Allison Anders
Co-stars: Angel Aviles Seidy Lopez Jacob Vargas

MARJORIE MARS

1947 TAKE MY LIFE
Director: Ronald Neame
Co-stars: Hugh Williams Greta Gynt Marius Goring

TRACEY MARROW

1984 BREAKDANCE
Director: Joel Silberg
Co-stars: Lucinda Dickey Adolfo Quinones Michael Chambers

CLAUDIA MARSANI

1974 CONVERSATION PIECE
Director: Luchino Visconti
Co-stars: Burt Lancaster Silvana Mangano Helmut Berger

BETTY MARSDEN

1963 THE LEATHER BOYS
Director: Sidney Furie
Co-stars: Rita Tushingham Colin Campbell Dudley Sutton

1965 THE WILD AFFAIR
Director: John Krish
Co-stars: Nancy Kwan Terry-Thomas Bud Flanagan

1968 CARRY ON CAMPING
Director: Gerald Thomas
Co-stars: Sid James Barbara Windsor Bernard Bresslaw

1970 EYEWITNESS
Director: John Hough
Co-stars: Mark Lester Susan George Lionel Jeffries

1983 THE DRESSER
Director: Peter Yates
Co-stars: Albert Finney Tom Courtenay Edward Fox

CAROL MARSH

1947 BRIGHTON ROCK
Director: John Boutling
Co-stars: Richard Attenborough William Hartnell Nigel Stock

1949 HELTER SKELTER
Director: Ralph Thomas
Co-stars: David Tomlinson Mervyn Johns Peter Hammond

1949 MARRY ME
Director: Terence Fisher
Co-stars: Derek Bond Susan Shaw Zena Marshall

1949 THE ROMANTIC AGE
Director: Edmond Greville
Co-stars: Mai Zetterling Hugh Williams Petula Clark

1951 SCROOGE
Director: Brian Desmond Hurst
Co-stars: Alastair Sim Jack Warner Mervyn Johns

1951 ALICE IN WONDERLAND
Director: Dallas Bower
Co-stars: Stephen Murray Pamela Brown Felix Aylmer

1958 DRACULA
Director: Terence Fisher
Co-stars: Peter Cushing Christopher Lee Melissa Stribling

JEAN MARSH *(Married Jon Pertwee)*

1963 UNEARTHLY STRANGER
Director: John Krish
Co-stars: John Neville Gabriella Licudi Warren Mitchell

1976 THE EAGLE HAS LANDED
Director: John Sturges
Co-stars: Michael Caine Donald Sutherland Jenny Agutter

1979 THE CHANGELING
Director: Peter Medak
Co-stars: George C.Scott Melvyn Douglas Trish Van Devere

1981 **GOLIATH AWAITS**	**1944** **FOLLOW THE LEADER**
Director: Kevin Connor	*Director:* William Beaudine
Co-stars: Mark Harmon Christopher Lee Eddie Albert	*Co-stars:* Leo Gorcey Huntz Hall Gabriel Dell

1981   **GOLIATH AWAITS**
Director: Kevin Connor
Co-stars: Mark Harmon Christopher Lee Eddie Albert

1985   **THE CORSICAN BROTHERS**
Director: Ian Sharp
Co-stars: Trevor Eve Geraldine Chaplin Olivia Hussey

1985   **RETURN TO OZ**
Director: Walter Murch
Co-stars: Fairuza Balk Piper Laurie Nicol Williamson

1988   **WILLOW**
Director: Ron Howard
Co-stars: Val Kilmer Joanne Whalley Warwick Davis

1989   **DANNY THE CHAMPION OF THE WORLD**
Director: Gavin Millar
Co-stars: Jeremy Irons Samuel Irons Robbie Coltrane

1989   **A CONNECTICUT YANKEE IN KING ARTHUR'S COURT**
Director: Mel Damski
Co-star: Emma Samms Keshia Knight Pulliam

1989   **ACT OF WILL**
Director: Don Sharp
Co-stars: Victoria Tennant Elizabeth Hurley Lynsey Baxter

1991   **ADAM BEDE**
Director: Giles Foster
Co-stars: Patsy Kensit Iain Glen Susannah Harker

1994   **FATHERLAND**
Director: Christopher Menaul
Co-stars: Rutger Hauer Miranda Richardson Peter Vaughan

JOAN MARSH *(Nancy Ann Rosher) (Child)*

1930   **ALL QUIET ON THE WESTERN FRONT**
Director: Lewis Milestone
Co-stars: Lew Ayres Slim Summerville

1930   **LITTLE ACCIDENT**
Director: William James Craft
Co-stars: Douglas Fairbanks Jnr. Anita Page Sally Blane

1931   **DANCE, FOOLS, DANCE**
Director: Harry Beaumont
Co-stars: Joan Crawford Lester Vail Clark Gable

1931   **BACHELOR'S AFFAIRS**
Director: Alfred Werker
Co-stars: Adolphe Menjou Minna Gombell Alan Dinehart

1933   **THE MAN WHO DARED**
Director: Hamilton McFadden
Co-stars: Preston Foster Zita Johann Irene Biller

1934   **MANY HAPPY RETURNS**
Director: Norman Z. McLeod
Co-stars: George Burns Gracie Allen Ray Milland

1934   **YOU'RE TELLING ME**
Director: Erle Kenton
Co-stars: W.C.Fields Larry Crabbe Adrienne Ames

1936   **DANCING FEET**
Co-star: Eddie Nugent

1937   **LIFE BEGINS IN COLLEGE**
Director: William Seiter
Co-stars: Joan Davis Tony Martin Gloria Stuart

1937   **CHARLIE CHAN ON BROADWAY**
Director: Eugene Forde
Co-stars: Warner Oland Keye Luke Leon Ames

1943   **MR. MUGGS STEPS OUT**
Director: William Beaudine
Co-stars: Leo Gorcey Huntz Hall Billy Benedict

1944   **FOLLOW THE LEADER**
Director: William Beaudine
Co-stars: Leo Gorcey Huntz Hall Gabriel Dell

LINDA MARSH

1963   **AMERICA, AMERICA**
Director: Elia Kazan
Co-stars: Stathis Giallelis Frank Wolff Lou Antonio

LUCILLE MARSH

1944   **COVER GIRL**
Director: Charles Vidor
Co-stars: Rita Hayworth Gene Kelly Phil Silvers

MAE MARSH

1912   **THE NEW YORK HAT**
Director: D.W.Griffith
Co-stars: Mary Pickford Lionel Barrymore Lillian Gish

1913   **JUDITH OF BETHULIA**
Director: D.W.Griffith
Co-stars: Blanche Sweet Lillian Gish Dorothy Gish

1914   **HOME, SWEET HOME**
Director: D.W.Griffith
Co-stars: Henry B.Walthall Lillian Gish Donald Crisp

1915   **THE BIRTH OF A NATION**
Director: D.W.Griffith
Co-stars: Henry B.Walthall Miriam Cooper Lillian Gish

1916   **THE WHARF RAT**
Director: D.W.Griffith

1916   **INTOLERANCE**
Director: D.W.Griffith
Co-stars: Lillian Gish Robert Harron Miriam Cooper

1931   **OVER THE HILL**
Director: Henry King
Co-stars: James Dunn Sally Eilers Edward Crandall

1932   **REBECCA OF SUNNYBROOK FARM**
Director: Alfred Santell
Co-stars: Marian Nixon Ralph Bellamy Alan Hale

1934   **LITTLE MAN, WHAT NOW?**
Director: Frank Borzage
Co-stars: Margaret Sullavan Douglass Montgomery Alan Hale

1936   **HOLLYWOOD BOULEVARD**
Director: Robert Florey
Co-stars: John Halliday Marsha Hunt Robert Cummings

1940   **THE MAN WHO WOULD NOT TALK**
Director: David Burton
Co-stars: Lloyd Nolan Jean Rogers Eric Blore

1940   **YOUNG PEOPLE**
Director: Allan Dwan
Co-stars: Shirley Temple Jack Oakie Charlotte Greenwood

1941   **GREAT GUNS**
Director: Monty Banks
Co-stars: Stan Laurel Oliver Hardy Shelia Ryan

1948   **THREE GODFATHERS**
Director: John Ford
Co-stars: John Wayne Harry Carey Pedro Armendariz

1949   **WHEN WILLIE COMES MARCHING HOME**
Director: John Ford
Co-stars: Dan Dailey Corinne Calvet Colleen Townsend

1949   **THE FIGHTING KENTUCKIAN**
Director: George Waggner
Co-stars: John Wayne Vera Ralston Oliver Hardy

1950   **THE GUNFIGHTER**
Director: Henry King
Director: Gregory Peck Millard Mitchell Karl Malden

1952 NIGHT WITHOUT SLEEP
Director: Roy Baker
Co-stars: Gary Merrill Linda Darnell Hildegarde Neff

1953 THE ROBE
Director: Henry Koster
Co-stars: Richard Burton Jean Simmons Victor Mature

1955 HELL ON FRISCO BAY
Director: Frank Tuttle
Co-stars: Alan Ladd Edward G.Robinson Joanne Dru

1960 SERGEANT RUTLEDGE
Director: John Ford
Co-stars: Jeffrey Hunter Woody Strode Constance Towers

1961 TWO RODE TOGETHER
Director: John Ford
Co-stars: James Stewart Richard Widmark Shirley Jones

MARIAN MARSH

1931 SVENGALLI
Director: Archie Mayo
Co-stars: John Barrymore Donald Crisp Bramwell Fletcher

1931 FIVE STAR FINAL
Director: Mervyn LeRoy
Co-stars: Edward G.Robinson H.B.Warner Boris Karloff

1932 BEAUTY AND THE BOSS
Director: Roy Del Ruth
Co-stars: Warren William Charles Butterworth Lillian Bond

1932 ALIAS THE DOCTOR
Director: Michael Curtizz
Co-stars: Richard Barthelmess Norman Foster Laura LaPlante

1932 UNDER EIGHTEEN
Co-star: Warren William

1933 NOTORIUS BUT NICE
Co-star: J.Carrol Naish

1933 A MAN OF SENTIMENT
Co-star: William Bakewell

1934 GIRL OF THE LIMBERLOST
Director: Christy Cabanne
Co-stars: Louise Dresser Ralph Morgan Henry B.Walthall

1935 THE BLACK ROOM
Director: Roy William Neill
Co-stars: Boris Karloff Katherine DeMille Thurston Hall

1935 CRIME AND PUNISHMENT
Director: Josef Von Sternberg
Co-stars: Peter Lorre Edward Arnold Tala Birell

1935 UNKNOWN WOMAN
Co-stars: Richard Cromwell Henry Armetta

1936 THE MAN WHO LIVED TWICE
Director: Harry Lachman
Co-stars: Ralph Bellamy Ward Bond Isabel Jewell

1936 LADY OF SECRETS
Director: Marion Gering
Co-stars: Ruth Chatterton Otto Kruger Lloyd Nolan

1937 THE GREAT GAMBINI
Director: Charles Vidor
Co-stars: Akim Tamiroff John Trent Genevieve Tobin

1937 SATURDAY'S HEROES
Co-star: Van Heflin

1937 YOUTH ON PAROLE
Co-star: Gordon Oliver

MICHELE MARSH

1971 FIDDLER ON THE ROOF
Director: Norman Jewison
Co-stars: Topol Leonard Frey Molly Picon

1981 THE ADVENTURES OF HUCKLEBERRY FINN
Director: Jack Hiveley
Co-stars: Brock Peters Forrest Tucker

SALLY ANN MARSH

1992 THE PRINCESS AND THE GOBLIN *(Voice)*
Director: Jozsef Gemes
Co-stars: Joss Ackland Claire Bloom Roy Kinnear

ALEXANDRA MARSHALL

1992 THE END OF THE GOLDEN WEATHER
Director: Ian Mune
Co-stars: Stephen Fulford Paul Gittins Stephen Papps

BRENDA MARSHALL *(Married William Holden)*

1939 ESPIONAGE AGENT
Director: Lloyd Bacon
Co-stars: Joel McCrea Jeffrey Lynn George Bancroft

1940 EAST OF THE RIVER
Director: Alfred Green
Co-stars: John Garfield William Lundigan George Tobias

1940 THE MAN WHO TALKED TOO MUCH
Director: Vincent Sherman
Co-stars: George Brent Virginia Bruce Richard Barthelmess

1940 SOUTH OF SUEZ
Director: Lewis Seiler
Co-stars: George Brent Lee Patrick George Tobias

1940 THE SEA HAWK
Director: Michael Curtiz
Co-stars: Errol Flynn Flora Robson Claude Rains

1940 MONEY AND THE WOMAN
Director: William Howard
Co-stars: Jeffrey Lynn Lee Patrick John Litel

1941 THE SMILING GHOST
Director: Lewis Seiler
Co-stars: Alexis Smith Wayne Morris Willie Best

1941 SINGAPORE WOMAN
Director: Jean Negulesco
Co-stars: David Bruce Virginia Field Rose Hobart

1941 FOOTSTEPS IN THE RAIN
Director: Lloyd Bacon
Co-stars: Errol Flynn Ralph Bellamy Lee Patrick

1942 CAPTAINS OF THE CLOUDS
Director: Michael Curtiz
Co-stars: James Cagney Dennis Morgan George Tobias

1942 YOU CAN'T ESCAPE FOREVER
Director: Jo Graham
Co-stars: George Brent Gene Lockhart Roscoe Karns

1943 PARIS AFTER DARK
Director: Leonide Moguy
Co-stars: George Sanders Phillip Dorn Marcel Dalio

1943 BACKGROUND TO DANGER
Director: Raoul Walsh
Co-stars: George Raft Sydney Greenstreet Peter Lorre

1948 WHISPERING SMITH
Director: Leslie Fenton
Co-stars: Alan Ladd Robert Preston Donald Crisp

CONNIE MARSHALL *(child)*

1944 SUNDAY DINNER FOR A SOLDIER
Director: Lloyd Bacon
Co-stars: Anne Baxter Charles Winninger John Hodiak

1946 DRAGONWYCK
Director: Joseph Mankiewicz
Co-stars: Gene Tierney Vincent Price Walter Huston

1946   **HOME SWEET HOMICIDE**
Director: Loyyd Bacon
Co-stars: Lynn Bari Randolph Scott Dean Stockwell

1946   **WAKE UP AND DREAM**
Director: Lloyd Bacon
Co-stars: John Payne June Haver Clem Bevans

1946   **SENTIMENTAL JOURNEY**
Director: Walter Lang
Co-stars: Maureen O'Hara John Payne William Bendix

1947   **MOTHER WORE TIGHTS**
Director: Walter Lang
Co-stars: Betty Grable Dan Dailey Mona Freeman

1947   **DAISY KENTON**
Director: Otto Preminger
Co-stars: Joan Crawford Henry Fonda Dana Andrews

1948   **MR. BLANDINGS BUILDS HIS DREAM HOUSE**
Director: H.C.Potter
Co-stars: Cary Grant Myrna Loy Melvyn Douglas

1949   **GREEN PROMISE**
Director: William Russell
Co-stars: Walter Brennan Natalie Wood

DODIE MARSHALL

1967   **EASY COME, EASY GO**
Director: John Rich
Co-stars: Elvis Presley Frank McHugh Elsa Lanchester

MARION MARSHALL

1949   **I WAS A MALE WAR BRIDE**
Director: Howard Hawks
Co-stars: Cary Grant Ann Sheridan Randy Stuart

1950   **HALLS OF MONTEZUMA**
Director: Lewis Milestone
Co-stars: Richard Widmark Karl Malden Jack Palance

1952   **SAILOR BEWARE**
Director: Hal Walker
Co-stars: Dean Martin Jerry Lewis Corinne Calvet

1952   **THE STOOGE**
Director: Norman Taurog
Co-stars: Dean Martin Jerry Lewis Eddie Mayehoff

MARITA MARSHALL

1986   **WITNESS IN THE WAR ZONE**
Director: Nathaniel Gutman
Co-star: Christopher Walken

PATRICIA MARSHALL

1947   **GOOD NEWS**
Director: Charles Walters
Co-stars: June Allyson Peter Lawford Mel Torme

PAULA MARSHALL

1992   **HELLRAISER III: HELL ON EARTH**
Director: Anthony Hickox
Co-stars: Terry Farrell Doug Bradley

1993   **WARLOCK: THE ARMAGEDDON**
Director: Anthony Hickox
Co-stars: Julian Sands Chris Young Joanna Pacula

1996   **THAT OLD FEELING**
Co-stars: Dennis Farina Bette Midler

PENNY MARSHALL

1991   **THE HARD WAY**
Director: John Badham
Co-stars: Michael J.Fox James Woods Annabella Sciorra

RUTH MARSHALL

1993   **LOVE AND HUMAN REMAINS**
Director: Denys Arcand
Co-stars: Thomas Gibson Cameron Bancroft Mia Kirshner

TRUDY MARSHALL

1943   **THE DANCING MASTERS**
Director: Mal St. Clair
Co-stars: Stan Laurel Oliver Hardy Margaret Dumont

1944   **THE FIGHTING SULLIVANS**
Director: Lloyd Bacon
Co-stars: Anne Baxter Thomas Mitchell Selena Royle

1945   **THE DOLLY SISTERS**
Director: Irving Cummings
Co-stars: Betty Grable June Haver John Payne

1946   **TALK ABOUT A LADY**
Director: George Sherman
Co-stars: Jink Falkenburg Forrest Tucker Joe Besser

ZENA MARSHALL

1949   **MEET SIMON CHERRY**
Director: Godfrey Grayson
Co-stars: Hugh Moxey John Bailey Ernest Butcher

1949   **MARRY ME**
Director: Terence Fisher
Co-stars: Derek Bond Susan Shaw Carol Marsh

1953   **DEADLY NIGHTSHADE**
Director: John Gilling
Co-stars: Emrys Jones John Horsley Joan Hickson

1954   **THE EMBEZZLER**
Director: John Gilling
Co-stars: Charles Victor Peggy Mount Avice Landon

1956   **BERMUDA AFFAIR**
Director: Edward Sutherland
Co-stars: Kim Hunter Gary Merrill Ron Randell

1957   **LET'S BE HAPPY**
Director: Henry Levin
Co-stars: Vera-Ellen Tony Martin Robert Flemyng

1961   **BACKFIRES**
Director: Paul Almond
Co-stars: Alfred Burke Oliver Johnston

1962   **DR. NO**
Director: Terence Young
Co-stars: Sean Connery Ursula Andress Jack Lord

CRISTINA MARSILLACH

1986   **EVERY TIME WE SAY GOODBYE**
Director: Moshe Mizrahi
Co-stars: Tom Hanks Benedict Taylor Anat Atzmen

AILEEN MARSON

1934   **MY SONG FOR YOU**
Director: Maurice Elvy
Co-stars: Jan Kiepura Sonnie Hale Emyln Williams

1934   **ROAD HOUSE**
Director: Maurice Elvy
Co-stars: Gordon Harker Violet Loraine Emlyn Williams

1936   **SOMEONE AT THE DOOR**
Director: Herbert Brenon
Co-stars: Billy Milton Noah Berry Hermione Gingold

1936   **THE TENTH MAN**
Director: Brian Desmond Hurst
Director: John Lodge Antoinette Cellier Clifford Evans

**1987 ALLAN QUARTERMAIN AND
THE LOST CITY OF GOLD**
Director: Gary Nelson
Co-stars: Richard Chamberlain Sharon Stone

ANIA MARSON (child)

1971 NICHOLAS AND ALEXANDRA
Director: Franklin Schaffner
Co-stars: Michael Jayston Janet Suzman Tom Baker

1988 ESKIMOS DO IT
Director: Derek Lister
Co-stars: Jean Boht Liz Fraser Neil Pearson

LYNN MARTA

1972 GENESIS II
Director: John Llewellyn Moxey
Co-stars: Alex Cord Mariette Hartley Harvey Jason

JEANNE MARTEL

1937 TWO MINUTES TO PLAY
Co-stars: Edward Nugent Grady Sutton

JUNE MARTEL

1935 FRONT PAGE WOMAN
Director: Michael Curtiz
Co-stars: Bette Davis George Brent Winni Shaw

1937 FORLORN RIVER
Co-stars: Larry Crabbe Harvey Stephens

DONNA MARTELL

1953 GIVE A GIRL A BREAK
Director: Stanley Donen
Co-stars: Marge Champion Gower Champion Debbie Reynolds

1955 TEN WANTED MEN
Director: Bruce Humberstone
Co-stars: Randolph Scott Jocelyn Brando Richard Boone

GILLIAN MARTELL

1991 102, BOULEVARD HAUSSMANN
Director: Udayan Prasad
Co-stars: Paul Rhys Janet McTeer Alan Bates

NORMA MARTELLI

1981 THE NIGHT OF SAN LORENZO
Director: Paolo Taviani
Co-stars: Omero Antonutti Margarita Lozano

1990 EVERYBODY'S FINE
Director: Guiseppe Tornatore
Co-stars: Marcello Mastroianni Michele Morgan Marino Cenna

CYNTHIA MARTELLS

1991 REGARDING HENRY
Director: Mike Nichols
Co-stars: Harrison Ford Anette Benning Mikki Allen

1993 BLIND SPOT
Director: Michael Toshiuki
Co-stars: Joanne Woodward Laura Linney Fritz Weaver

ANA MARTIN

1967 RETURN OF THE GUNFIGHTER
Director: James Neilson
Co-stars: Robert Taylor Chad Everett Lyle Bettger

ANDRA MARTIN

1958 THE THING THAT COULDN'T DIE
Director: Will Cowan
Co-star: William Reynolds

1958 THE LADY TAKES A FLYER
Director: Jack Arnold
Co-stars: Lana Turner Jeff Chandler Richard Denning

1959 YELLOWSTONE KELLY
Director: Gordon Douglas
Co-stars: Clint Walker Edd Byrnes John Russell

ANDREA MARTIN

1974 BLACK CHRISTMAS
Director: Robert Clark
Co-stars: Olivia Hussey Margot Kidder Keir Dullea

1989 RUDE AWAKENING
Director: Aaron Russo
Co-stars: Cheech Marin Eric Roberts Julie Hagerty

1991 TOO MUCH SUN
Director: Robert Downey
Co-stars: Robert Downey Jnr. Ralph Macchio Eric Idle

1991 STEPPING OUT
Director: Lewis Gilbert
Co-stars: Liza Minelli Shelley Winters Julie Walters

1995 HARRISON BERGERIN
Director: Bruce Pittman
Co-stars: Sean Astin Christopher Plummer Miranda De Pencier

BEVERLEY MARTIN

1981 BURNING AN ILLUSION
Director: Menelik Shabazz
Co-stars: Victor Romero Angela Wynter Pat Williams

EDIE MARTIN

1940 OLD MOTHER RILEY IN BUSINESS
Director: John Baxter
Co-stars: Arthur Lucan Kitty McShane Charles Victor

1943 THE DEMI-PARADISE
Director: Anthony Asquith
Co-stars: Laurence Olivier Margaret Rutherford

1951 THE LAVENDER HILL MOB
Director: Charles Crighton
Co-stars: Alec Guinness Stanley Holloway Alfie Bass

1951 THE MAN IN THE WHITE SUIT
Director: Alexander MacKendrick
Co-stars: Alec Guinness Joan Greenwood Vida Hope

1952 TIME GENTLEMEN PLEASE!
Director: Lewis Gilbert
Co-stars: Eddie Byrne Jane Barrett Dora Bryan

1953 THE TITFIELD THUNDERBOLT
Director: Charles Crichton
Co-stars: George Relph John Gregson Hugh Griffith

1953 GENEVIEVE
Director: Henry Cornelius
Co-stars: Kenneth More Dinah Sheridan Kay Kendall

HELEN MARTIN

**1977 A HERO AIN'T NOTHING
BUT A SANDWICH**
Director: Ralph Nelson
Co-stars: Cicely Tyson Paul Winfield

1987 HOLLYWOOD SHUFFLE
Director: Robert Townsend
Co-stars: Robert Townsend Anne-Marie Johnson Starletta Dupois

1991 A RAGE IN HARLEM
Director: Bill Duke
Co-stars: Forest Whitaker Robin Givens Danny Glover

JEAN MARTIN

1965 ADIOS GRINGOS
Director: George Finlay
Co-stars: Montgomery Wood Evelyn Stewart Peter Cross

JESSICA MARTIN

1987 WHITE LADY
Director: David Rudkin
Co-stars: Cornelius Garrett Sophie Thompson Meg Wynn Owen

KELLIE MARTIN

1986 JUMPIN' JACK FLASH
Director: Penny Marshall
Co-stars: Whoopi Goldberg Stephen Collins Carol Kane

1988 SECRET WITNESS
Director: Eric Laneuville
Co-stars: Paul LeMat David Rasche Leaf Phoenix

1993 MATINEE
Director: Joe Dante
Co-stars: John Goodman Cathy Moriarty Simon Fenton

1994 DEATH OF A CHEERLEADER
Director: Billy Graham
Co-stars: Valerie Harper Tori Spelling

1995 IF SOMEONE HAD KNOWN
Director: Eric Laneuville
Co-stars: Kevin Dobson Linda Kelsey

1995 THE FACE ON THE MILK CARTON
Director: Waris Hussein
Co-star: Sharon Lawrence

LORI MARTIN

1962 CAPE FEAR
Director: J.Lee Thompson
Co-stars: Gregory Peck Robert Mitchum Polly Bergen

1969 THE ANGRY BREED
Director: David Commons
Co-stars: Jan Sterling James MacArthur William Windom

MARCELLA MARTIN

1939 GONE WITH THE WIND
Director: Victor Fleming
Co-stars: Clark Gable Vivien Leigh Leslie Howard

MARIA MARTIN

1965 DOCTOR ZHIVAGO
Director: David Lean
Co-stars: Omar Sharif Julie Christie Rod Steiger

MARIE MARTIN *(child)*

1988 LITTLE GIRL LOST
Director: Sharron Miller
Co-stars: Tess Harper Frederic Forrest Patricia Kalember

MARION MARTIN

1938 SINNERS IN PARADISE
Director: James Whale
Co-stars: Madge Evans John Boles Bruce Cabot

1939 SERGEANT MADDEN
Director: Josef Von Sternberg
Co-stars: Wallace Beery Tom Brown Laraine Day

1939 THE MAN IN THE IRON MASK
Director: James Whale
Co-stars: Louis Hayward Warren William Joan Bennett

1939 INVITATION TO HAPPINESS
Director: Wesley Ruggles
Co-stars: Irene Dunne Fred MacMurray Charles Ruggles

1941 MEXICAN SPITFIRE AT SEA
Director: Leslie Goodwins
Co-stars: Lupe Velez Leon Errol Charles Rogers

1942 MEXICAN SPITFIRE'S ELEPHANT
Director: Leslie Goodwins
Co-stars: Lupe Velez Leon Errol Lyle Talbot

1942 CALL OUT THE MARINES
Director: Frank Ryan
Co-stars: Edmund Lowe Victor McLaglen Binnie Barnes

1942 THE BIG STREET
Director: Irving Reis
Co-stars: Henry Fonda Lucille Ball Eugene Pallette

1943 THEY GOT ME COVERED
Director: David Butler
Co-stars: Bob Hope Dorothy Lamour Lenore Aubert

1943 THE WOMAN OF THE TOWN
Director: George Archainbaud
Co-stars: Albert Dekker Claire Trevor Henry Hull

1945 GANGS OF THE WATERFRONT
Director: George Blair
Co-stars: Robert Armstrong Stephanie Batchelor

1950 DAKOTA LIL
Director: Leslie Selander
Co-stars: Marie Windsor George Montgomery Rod Cameron

MARY MARTIN

1939 THE GREAT VICTOR HERBERT
Director: Andrew Stone
Co-stars: Walter Connolly Allan Jones Susanna Foster

1940 RHYTHM ON THE RIVER
Director: Victor Schertzinger
Co-stars: Bing Crosby Basil Rathbone Oscar Levant

1940 LOVE THY NEIGHBOUR
Director: Mark Sandrich
Co-stars: Jack Benny Fred Allen Eddie Anderson

1941 NEW YORK TOWN
Director: Charles Vidor
Co-stars: Fred MacMurray Robert Preston Akim Tamiroff

1941 THE BIRTH OF THE BLUES
Director: Victor Schertzinger
Co-stars: Bing Crosby Brian Donlevy Carolyn Lee

1941 KISS THE BOYS GOODBYE
Director: Victor Schertzinger
Co-stars: Don Ameche Oscar Levant Connie Boswell

1942 STAR SPANGLED RHYTHM
Director: George Marshall
Co-stars: Eddie Bracken Betty Hutton Victor Moore

1943 TRUE TO LIFE
Director: George Marshall
Co-stars: Dick Powell Franchot Tone Victor Moore

1943 HAPPY GO LUCKY
Director: Curtis Bernhardt
Co-stars: Dick Powell Betty Hutton Eddie Bracken

1946 NIGHT AND DAY
Director: Michael Curtiz
Co-stars: Cary Grant Alexis Smith Monty Woolley

1953 MAIN STREET TO BROADWAY
Director: Tay Garnett
Co-stars: Tom Morton Mary Murphy Lilli Palmer

1959 ACTION STATIONS
Director: Cecil Williamson
Co-stars: Paul Carpenter Joe Robinson

MEL MARTIN

1987 BUSINESS AS USUAL
Director: Lezli-An Barrett
Co-stars: Glenda Jackson John Thaw Cathy Tyson

1989 INSPECTOR MORSE: THE SECRET OF BAY 5B
Director: Jim Goddard
Co-stars: John Thaw Kevin Whately

1989 SUMMER'S LEASE
Director: Colin Rogers
Co-stars: John Gielgud Susan Fleetwood Leslie Phillips

1991 HANCOCK
Director: Tony Smith
Co-stars: Alfred Molina Frances Barber Malcolm Sinclair

MILLICENT MARTIN

1959 LIBEL
Director: Anthony Asquith
Co-stars: Dirk Bogarde Olivia De Havilland Robert Morley

1961 INVASION QUARTET
Director: Jay Lewis
Co-stars: Bill Travers Spike Milligan John Le Mesurier

1962 THE GIRL ON THE BOAT
Director: Henry Kaplan
Co-stars: Norman Wisdom Richard Briers Shelia Hancock

1964 NOTHING BUT THE BEST
Director: Clive Donner
Co-stars: Alan Bates Denholm Elliott Harry Andrews

1966 ALFIE
Director: Lewis Gilbert
Co-stars: Michael Caine Shelley Winters Julia Foster

NAN MARTIN

1968 FOR LOVE OF IVY
Director: Daniel Mann
Co-stars: Sidney Poitier Abby Lincoln Beau Bridges

1968 THREE IN THE ATTIC
Director: Richard Wilson
Co-stars: Yvette Mimieux Judy Pace Chris Jones

1969 GOODBYE COLUMBUS
Director: Larry Peerce
Co-stars: Richard Benjamin Ali MacGraw Jack Klugman

1975 THE OTHER SIDE OF THE MOUNTAIN
Director: Larry Peerce
Co-stars: Marilyn Hassett Beau Bridges

1975 THE OTHER SIDE OF THE MOUNTAIN PART 2
Director: Larry Peerce
Co-stars: Marilyn Hassett Timothy Bottoms

1988 COLUMBO: MURDER, SMOKE AND SHADOWS
Director: James Frawley
Co-stars: Peter Falk Molly Hagan

PAMELA SUE MARTIN *(Married Manuel Rojas)*

1972 TO FIND A MAN
Director: Buzz Kuilik
Co-stars: Darrell O'Connor Lloyd Bridges Tom Ewell

1972 THE POSEIDON ADVENTURE
Director: Ronald Neame
Co-stars: Gene Hackman Ernest Borgnine Shelley Winters

1974 BUSTER AND BILLIE
Director: Daniel Petrie
Co-stars: Jan-Michael Vincent Joan Goodfellow Clifton James

1979 THE LADY IN RED
Director: Lewis Teague
Co-stars: Robert Conrad Louise Fletcher Robert Hogan

1984 TORCHLIGHT
Director: Tom Wright
Co-stars: Steve Railsback Ian McShane Rita Taggart

1987 BAY COVEN
Director: Carl Schenkel
Co-stars: Tim Matheson Woody Harrelson Susan Ruttan

ROSEMARY MARTIN

1984 LAUGHTERHOUSE
Director: Richard Eyre
Co-stars: Ian Holm Penelope Wilton Bill Owen

1986 LOVE MATCH
Director: Alan Dossor
Co-stars: Saeed Jaffrey Madhur Jaffrey Shaheen Khan

1987 INAPPROPRIATE BEHAVIOUR
Director: Andrew Davies
Co-stars: Charlotte Coleman Jenifer Landor Rudi Davies

1988 THE DRESSMAKER
Director: Jim O'Brien
Co-stars: Joan Plowright Jane Horrocks Tim Ransom

1991 THE OBJECT OF BEAUTY
Director: Michael Lindsey-Hogg
Co-stars: Andie McDowell Lolita Davidovich John Malkovich

MARGO MARTINDALE

1991 ROCKETEER
Director: Joe Johnston
Co-stars: Bill Campbell Jennifer Connelly Alan Arkin

1992 LORENZO'S OIL
Director: George Miller
Co-stars: Nick Nolte Susan Sarandon Peter Ustinov

ELSA MARTINELLI

1955 THE INDIAN FIGHTER
Director: Andre De Toth
Co-stars: Kirk Douglas Walter Abel Walter Matthau

1956 FOUR GIRLS IN TOWN
Director: Jack Sher
Co-stars: George Nader Julie Adams Gia Scala

1957 MANUELLA
Director: Guy Hamilton
Co-stars: Trevor Howard Pedro Armendariz Donald Pleasence

1960 BLOOD AND ROSES
Director: Roger Vadim
Co-stars: Mel Ferrer Annette Vadim Marc Allegret

1962 HATARI!
Director: Howard Hawks
Co-stars: John Wayne Hardy Kruger Red Buttons

1962 THE PIGEON THAT TOOK ROME
Director: Melville Savelson
Co-stars: Charlton Heston Harry Guardino

1962 THE TRIAL
Director: Orson Welles
Co-stars: Orson Welles Jeanne Moreau Madeleine Robinson

1963 THE V.I.P.S
Director: Anthony Asquith
Co-stars: Richard Burton Elizabeth Taylor Margaret Rutherford

1963 RAMPAGE
Director: Phil Karlson
Co-stars: Robert Mitchum Jack Hawkins Sabu

1964 THE FABULOUS ADVENTURES OF MARCO POLO
Director: Noel Howard
Co-stars: Horst Buchholz Orson Welles Omar Sharif

1965 THE TENTH VICTIM
Director: Elio Petri
Co-stars: Ursula Andress Marcello Mastroianni

1967 WOMAN TIMES SEVEN
Director: Vittorio De Sica
Co-stars: Vittorio De Sica Shirley MacLaine Peter Sellers

1967 THE OLDEST PROFESSION
Director: Jean-Luc Godard
Co-stars: Jeanne Moreau Raquel Welch Anna Karina

1967 MAROC 7
Director: Gerry O'Hara
Co-stars: Gene Barry Cyd Charisse Denholm Elliott

1968 CANDY
Director: Christian Marquand
Co-stars: Ewa Aulin Marlon Brando Richard Burton

1992 ONCE UPON A CRIME
Director: Eugene Levy
Co-stars: Cybil Sheperd John Candy James Belushi

JEEAN MARTINELLI

1954 LE ROUGE ET LE NOIR
Director: Claude Autant-Lara
Co-stars: Gerard Philipe Danielle Darrieux

ALMA MARTINEZ

1982 BARBAROSA
Director: Fred Schepisi
Co-stars: Willie Nelson Gary Busey Gilbert Roland

1987 BORN IN EAST L.A.
Director: Cheech Marin
Co-stars: Cheech Marin Daniel Stern Jan-Michael Vincent

PATRICE MARTINEZ

1986 THREE AMIGOS!
Director: John Landis
Co-stars: Steve Martin Chevy Chase Martin Short

ALESSANDRA MARTINI

1996 LES MISERABLES
Director: Claude Lelouche
Co-stars: Jean-Paul Belmondo Salome Lelouche Michel Boujenais

MIA MARVIN

1931 THE PUBLIC ENEMY
Director: William Wellman
Co-stars: James Cagney Jean Harlow Joan Blondell

KAY MARVIS

1944 BLOCK BUSTERS
Director: Wallace Fox
Co-stars: Leo Gorcy Huntz Hall Gabriel Dell

CAROLYN MARZ

1974 THE DRILLER KILLER
Director: Abel Ferrara
Co-stars: Jimmy Laine Baybi Day Peter Yellen

FRANCA MARZI

1957 NIGHTS OF CABIRIA
Director: Federico Fellini
Co-stars: Giulietta Masina Francois Perrier Dorian Gray

EMMANUELLE MASIGNAC

1987 THE DIRTY DOZEN: THE DEADLY MISSION
Director: Lee Katzin
Co-stars: Telly Savalas Ernest Borgnine

GIULIETTA MASINA *(Married Federico Fellini)*

1950 LIGHTS OF VARIETY
Director: Federico Fellini
Co-stars: Peppino De Felippo Carla Del Poggio Folco Lulli

1952 EUROPA 51
Director: Roberto Rossellini
Co-stars: Ingrid Bergman Alexander Knox Ettore Giannini

1954 LA STRADA
Director: Federico Fellini
Co-stars: Anthony Quinn Richard Basehart Lidia Venturini

1955 IL BIDONE
Director: Federico Fellini
Co-stars: Broderick Crawford Richard Basehart Franco Fabrizi

1957 NIGHTS OF CABIRIA
Director: Federico Fellini
Co-stars: Francois Perrier Amedeo Nazzari Dorian Gray

1965 JULIET OF THE SPIRITS
Director: Federico Fellini
Co-stars: Mario Pisu Sylva Koscina Alba Cancellieri

1969 THE MADWOMAN OF CHAILLOT
Director: Bryan Forbes
Co-stars: Katherine Hepburn Yul Brynner Danny Kaye

1985 GINGER AND FRED
Director: Federico Fellini
Co-stars: Marcello Mastroianni Franco Fabrizi

VIRGINIA MASKELL

1958 VIRGIN ISLAND
Director: Pat Jackson
Co-stars: John Cassavetes Sidney Poitier Isabel Dean

1958 THE MAN UPSTAIRS
Director: Don Chaffey
Co-stars: Richard Attenborough Bernard Lee Donald Houston

1959 JET STORM
Director: Cy Endfield
Co-stars: Richard Attenborough Mai Zetterling Diane Cilento

1960 DOCTOR IN LOVE
Director: Ralph Thomas
Co-stars: Michael Craig Leslie Phillips James Robertson Justice

1960 SUSPECT
Director: Roy Boutling
Co-stars: Tony Britton Peter Cushing Ian Bannen

1962 ONLY TWO CAN PLAY
Director: Sidney Gilliat
Co-stars: Mai Zetterling Peter Sellers Raymond Huntley

1962 THE WILD AND THE WILLING
Director: Ralph Thomas
Co-stars: Paul Rogers Ian McShane Samantha Eggar

1968 INTERLUDE
Director: Kevin Billington
Co-stars: Barbara Ferris Oskar Werner John Cleese

CILLA MASON

1983 LOOKS AND SMILES
Director: Ken Loach
Co-stars: Graham Green Tony Pitts Carolyn Nicholson

HILARY MASON

1973 DON'T LOOK NOW
Director: Nicolas Roeg
Co-stars: Donald Sutherland Julie Christie Clelia Matania

1975 I DON'T WANT TO BE BORN
Director: Peter Sasdy
Co-stars: Joan Collins Ralph Bates Eileen Atkins

1978 ABSOLUTION
Director: Anthony Page
Co-stars: Richard Burton Dominic Guard Billy Connolly

1990 PHANTOMS
Director: Charles Band
Co-stars: Sherilyn Fenn Malcolm Jamieson

INGRID MASON

1978 SHIMMERING LIGHT
Director: Don Chaffey
Co-stars: Beau Bridges Lloyd Bridges Victoria Shaw

MARGERY MASON

1969 WALK A CROOKED PATH
Director: John Brason
Co-stars: Tenniel Evans Faith Brook Patricia Haines

**1988 INSPECTOR WEXFORD:
SHAKE HANDS FOREVER**
Director: Don Leaver
Co-stars: George Baker Tom Wilkinson

MARSHA MASON (*Married Neil Simon*)
Nominated For Best Actress in 1974 For "Cinderella Liberty", In 1977
For "The Goodbye Girl", In 1979 For "Chapter Two" And In 1981 For
"It Hurts Only When I Laugh"

1973 BLUME IN LOVE
Director: Paul Mazursky
Co-stars: George Segal Susan Anspach Kris Kristofferson

1974 CINDERELLA LIBERTY
Director: Mark Rydell
Co-stars: James Caan Eli Wallach Kirk Calloway

1977 AUDREY ROSE
Director: Robert Wise
Co-stars: Anthony Hopkins John Beck Susan Swift Norman Lloyd

1977 THE GOODBYE GIRL
Director: Herbert Ross
Co-stars: Richard Dreyfuss Quinn Cummings Paul Benedict

1978 THE CHEAP DETECTIVE
Director: Robert Moore
Co-stars: Peter Falk John Houseman Dom DeLuise

1979 CHAPTER TWO
Director: Robert Moore
Co-stars: James Caan Joseph Bologna Valerie Harper

1979 PROMISES IN THE DARK
Director: Jerome Hellman
Co-stars: Ned Beatty Susan Clark Michael Brandon

1981 IT HURTS ONLY WHEN I LAUGH
Director: Glenn Jordan
Co-stars: Kristy McNichol James Coco Joan Hackett

1983 MAX DUGAN RETURNS
Director: Herbert Ross
Co-stars: Jason Robards Matthew Broderick Donald Sutherland

1985 SURVIVING
Director: Waris Hussein
Co-stars: Ellen Burstyn Len Cariou Molly Ringwald River Phoenix

1986 TRAPPED IN SILENCE
Director: Michael Tuchner
Co-stars: Keifer Sutherland Ron Silver John Mahoney

1986 HEARTBREAK RIGDE
Director: Clint Eastwood
Co-stars: Clint Eastwood Moses Gunn Eileen Heckart Everett McGill

1989 DINNER AT EIGHT
Director: Ron Lago Marsino
Co-stars: Lauren Bacall John Mahoney Harry Hamlin

1990 THE IMAGE
Director: Peter Werner
Co-stars: Albert Finney John Mahoney Swoozie Kurtz Kathy Baker

1990 STELLA
Director: John Erman
Co-stars: Bette Midler John Goodman Trini Alvarado

1991 DROP DEAD FRED
Director: Ate De Jong
Co-stars: Phoebe Cates Rik Mayall Carrie Fisher

1996 TWO DAYS IN THE VALLEY
Director: John Herzfeld
Co-stars: Eric Stoltz Jeff Daniels Danny Aiello

PET MASON

1966 MISS MacTAGGART WON'T LIE DOWN
Director: Francis Searle
Co-stars: Barbara Mullen Jack Lambert

PORTLAND MASON
(*Daughter Of Pamela Kellino And James Mason*)

1958 CRY TERROR
Director: Andrew Stone
Co-stars: James Mason Rod Steiger Inger Stevens

STEFANIE MASON

1991 BUGSY
Director: Barry Levinson
Co-stars: Warren Beatty Annette Bening Harvey Keitel

LEA MASSARI

1960 L'AVVENTURA
Director: Michaelangelo Antonioni
Co-stars: Monica Vitti Gabrielle Ferzetti James Addams

1960 THE COLOSSUS OF RHODES
Director: Sergio Leone
Co-stars: Rory Calhoun Georges Marchal

1962 THE FOUR DAYS OF NAPLES
Director: Nanni Loy
Co-stars: Frank Wolff Domenico Formato Raffaele Barbato

1963 CAPTIVE CITY
Director: Joseph Anthony
Co-stars: David Niven Ben Gazzara Michael Craig

1969 LES CHOSES DE MA VIE
Director: Claude Sautet
Co-stars: Michel Piccoli Romy Schneider Jean Bouise

1971 LE SOUFFLE AU COEUR
Director: Louis Malle
Co-stars: Benoit Ferreux Daniel Gelin Fabien Ferreux

1972 AND HOPE TO DIE
Director: Rene Clement
Co-stars: Jean-Louis Trintignant Robert Ryan Tisa Farrow

1973 IMPOSSIBLE OBJECT
Director: John Frankenheimer
Co-stars: Alan Bates Dominique Sanda Michel Auclair

1973 THE SILENT ONE
Director: Claude Pinoteau
Co-stars: Lino Ventura Leo Genn Robert Hardy

1979 CHRIST STOPPED AT EBOLI
Director: Francesca Rosi
Co-stars: Gian Maria Volonte Alain Cuny Irene Papas

GINA MASSAY

1983 THRILLKILL
Director: Anthony D'Andrea
Co-stars: Robin Ward Laura Robinson Eugene Clerk

KIM MASSEE

1986 KAMIKAZE
Director: Didier Grousset
Co-stars: Richard Bohringer Michel Galabru Dominique Lavenant

OSA MASSEN

1939 HONEYMOON IN BALI
Director: Edward Griffith
Co-stars: Madeleine Carroll Fred MacMurray Allan Jones

1941 HONEYMOON FOR THREE
Director: Lloyd Bacon
Co-stars: George Brent Ann Sheridan Charles Ruggles

1941 ACCENT ON LOVE
Director: Ray McCarey
Co-stars: George Montgomery J.Carrol Naish Cobina Wright Jnr.

1941 A WOMAN'S FACE
Director: George Cukor
Co-stars: Joan Crawford Melvyn Douglas Conrad Veidt

1941 YOU'LL NEVER GET RICH
Director: Sidney Lanfield
Co-stars: Fred Astaire Rita Hayworth Robert Benchley

1942 ICELAND
Director: Bruce Humberstone
Co-stars: Sonja Henie John Payne Jack Oakie

1943 JACK LONDON
Director: Alfred Santell
Co-stars: Michael O'Shea Susan Hayward Virginia Mayo

1943 BACKGROUND TO DANGER
Director: Raoul Walsh
Co-stars: George Raft Sydney Greenstreet Peter Lorre

1944 THE BLACK PARACHUTE
Director: Lew Landers
Co-stars: Larry Parks John Carradine Jeanne Bates

1944 THE MASTER RACE
Director: Herbert Biberman
Co-stars: George Coulouris Stanley Ridges Nancy Gates

1946 STRANGE JOURNEY
Co-stars: Paul Kelly Bruce Lester Kurt Katch

1946 DEADLINE AT DAWN
Director: Harold Clurman
Co-stars: Paul Lukas Bill Williams Susan Hayward

1948 MILLION DOLLAR WEEKEND
Co-stars: Gene Raymond Francis Lederer

1949 NIGHT UNTO NIGHT
Director: Don Siegel
Co-stars: Ronald Reagan Viveca Lindfors Broderick Crawford

1950 ROCKETSHIP XM
Director: Kurt Neumann
Co-stars: Lloyd Bridges John Emery Hugh O'Brian

ANNA MASSEY

1958 GIDEON OF SCOTLAND YARD
Director: John Ford
Co-stars: Jack Hawkins Dianne Foster Anna Lee

1960 PEEPING TOM
Director: Michael Powell
Co-stars: Carl Boehm Moira Shearer Shirley Ann Field

1965 BUNNY LAKE IS MISSING
Director: Otto Preminger
Co-stars: Laurence Olivier Carol Lynley Noel Coward

1969 THE LOOKING GLASS WAR
Director: Frank Pierson
Co-stars: Christopher Jones Pia Degermark Susan George

1969 DE SADE
Director: Cy Endfield
Co-stars: Keir Dullea John Huston Lilli Palmer Senta Berger

1972 FRENZY
Director: Alfred Hitchcock
Co-stars: Jon Finch Barry Foster Vivien Merchant

1973 A DOLL'S HOUSE
Director: Patrick Garland
Co-stars: Claire Bloom Anthony Hopkins Denholm Elliott

1973 VAULT OF HORROR
Director: Roy Ward Baker
Co-stars: Daniel Massey Terry-Thomas Glynis Johns

1978 THE MAYOR OF CASTERBRIDGE
Director: David Giles
Co-stars: Alan Bates Ann Stallybrass Jack Galloway

1978 THE CORN IS GREEN
Director: George Cukor
Co-stars: Katharine Hepburn Ian Saynor Bill Fraser

1980 SWEET WILLIAM
Director: Claude Watham
Co-stars: Jenny Agutter Sam Waterston Geraldine James

1982 FIVE DAYS ONE SUMMER
Director: Fred Zinnemann
Co-stars: Sean Connery Betsy Brantley Lambert Wilson

1984 THE CHAIN
Director: Jack Gold
Co-stars: Denis Lawson Maurice Denham Billie Whitelaw

1984 THE LITTLE DRUMMER GIRL
Director: George Roy Hill
Co-stars: Diane Keaton Klaus Kinski David Suchet

1984 ANOTHER COUNTRY
Director: Marek Kanievska
Co-stars: Rupert Everett Colin Firth Betsy Brantley

1985 ANNA KARENINA
Director: Simon Langton
Co-stars: Jacqueline Bisset Paul Scofield Christopher Reeve

1986 FOREIGN BODY
Director: Ronald Neame
Co-stars: Victor Banerjee Warren Mitchell Amanda Donohue

1986 HOTEL DU LAC
Director: Giles Foster
Co-stars: Denholm Elliott Googie Withers Patricia Hodge

1986 MANSFIELD PARK
Director: David Giles
Co-stars: Sylvestra Le Touzel Bernard Hepton Angela Pleasence

1987 A HAZARD OF HEARTS
Director: John Hough
Co-stars: Helena Bonham-Carter Diana Rigg Edward Fox

1989 IMPROMPTU
Director: James Lapine
Co-stars: Judy Davies Hugh Grant Mandy Patinkin

1989 INSPECTOR MORSE: HAPPY FAMILIES
Director: Adrian Shergold
Co-stars: John Thaw Kevin Whateley

1989 MOUNTAINS OF THE MOON
Director: Bob Rafelson
Co-stars: Patrick Bergin Iain Glen Fiona Shaw

1989 KILLING DAD
Director: Michael Dustin
Co-stars: Denholm Elliott Julie Walters Richard E.Grant

1989 A TALE OF TWO CITIES
Director: Philippe Monnier
Co-stars: James Wilby John Mills Jean-Pierre Aumont

1989 **THE TALL GUY**
Director: Mel Smith
Co-stars: Jeff Goldblum Emma Thompson Rowan Atkinson

1990 **THE MAN FROM THE PRU**
Director: Rob Rohrer
Co-stars: Jonathan Pryce Susannah York Richard Pasco

1993 **EMILY'S GHOST**
Director: Colin Finbow
Co-stars: Martin Jarvis Ron Moody Rosalind Ayres

EDITH MASSEY

1973 **PINK FLAMINGOS**
Director: John Waters
Co-stars: Divine David Lochary Mink Stole

1975 **FEMALE TROUBLE**
Director: John Waters
Co-stars: Divine Mary Vivien Pearce Mink Stole

1981 **POLYESTER**
Director: John Waters
Co-stars: Divine Tab Hunter David Samson

ILONA MASSEY (Married Alan Curtis)

1930 **ONE ROMANTIC NIGHT**
Co-star: Alan Curtis

1937 **ROSALIE**
Director: W.S.Van Dyke
Co-stars: Nelson Eddy Eleanor Powell Ray Bolger

1939 **BALALAIKA**
Director: Reinhold Schunzel
Co-stars: Nelson Eddy Frank Morgan Charles Ruggles

1941 **INTERNATIONAL LADY**
Director: Tim Whelan
Co-stars: George Brent Basil Rathbone Gene Lockhart

1941 **NEW WINE**
Director: Reinhold Schunzel
Co-stars: Alan Curtis Albert Basserman Binnie Barnes

1942 **INVISIBLE AGENT**
Director: Edwin Marin
Co-stars: Jon Hall Cedric Hardwicke Peter Lorre

1943 **FRANKENSTEIN MEETS THE WOLF MAN**
Director: Roy William Neill
Co-stars: Lon Chaney Bela Lugosi

1946 **HOLIDAY IN MEXICO**
Director: George Sidney
Co-stars: Jane Powell Walter Pidgeon Jose Iturbi

1947 **NORTHWEST OUTPOST**
Director: Allan Dwan
Co-stars: Nelson Eddy Hugo Haas Elsa Lanchester

1947 **THE PLUNDERERS**
Director: Joseph Kane
Co-stars: Forrest Tucker Rod Cameron Adrian Booth

1949 **LOVE HAPPY**
Director: David Miller
Co-stars: Marx Brothers Vera-Ellen Marilyn Monroe

1958 **JET OVER THE ATLANTIC**
Director: Byron Haskin
Co-stars: Guy Madison Virginia Mayo George Raft

MARIE MASTERS

1984 **SCREAM FOR HELP**
Director: Michael Winner
Co-stars: Rachel Kelly David Brooks Lolita Lorre

FAY MASTERSON

1991 **THE POWER OF ONE**
Director: John Avildsen
Co-stars: Stephen Dorff Morgan Freeman John Gielgud

1993 **THE MAN WITHOUT A FACE**
Director: Mel Gibson
Co-stars: Mel Gibson Nick Stahl Margaret Whitton Geoffrey Lewis

MARY STUART MASTERSON

1985 **AMAZING STORIES**
Director: Steven Spielberg
Co-stars: Kevin Costner Kiefer Sutherland Scot Coffey

1985 **CATHOLIC BOYS**
Director: Michael Dinner
Co-stars: Donald Sutherland Andrew McCarthy Kevin Dillon

1986 **MY LITTLE GIRL**
Director: Connie Kaiserman
Co-stars: James Earl Jones Geraldine Page Anne Meare

1986 **AT CLOSE RANGE**
Director: James Foley
Co-stars: Christopher Walken Sean Penn Christopher Penn

1987 **GARDENS OF STONE**
Director: Francis Coppola
Co-stars: James Caan James Earl Jones Anjelica Huston

1987 **SOME KIND OF WONDERFUL**
Director: Howard Deutch
Co-stars: Eric Stoltz Lea Thompson John Ashton

1988 **MR. NORTH**
Director: Danny Huston
Co-stars: Anthony Edwards Robert Mitchum Lauren Bacall

1989 **IMMEDIATE FAMILY**
Director: Jonathan Kaplan
Co-stars: Glenn Close James Woods Kevin Dillon

1989 **CHANCES ARE**
Director: Emile Ardolino
Co-stars: Cybill Shepherd Robert Downey Jnr. Ryan O'Neal

1990 **FUNNY ABOUT LOVE**
Director: Leonard Nimoy
Co-stars: Gene Wilder Christine Lahti Anne Jackson

1991 **FRIED GREEN TOMATOES**
Director: Jon Avnet
Co-stars: Jessica Tandy Mary-Louise Parker Kathy Bates

1992 **MAD AT THE MOON**
Director: Martin Donovan
Co-stars: Hart Bochner Fionnula Flanagan Daphne Zuniga

1992 **MARRIED TO IT**
Director: Arthur Hiller
Co-stars: Robert Sean Leonard Beau Bridges Stockard Channing

1993 **BENNY & JOON**
Director: Jeremiah Chetchik
Co-stars: Johnny Depp Aidan Quinn Julianne Moore

1994 **BAD GIRLS**
Director: Jonathan Kaplan
Co-stars: Madeleine Stowe Andie MacDowell Drew Barrymore

1994 **HEAVEN'S PRISONERS**
Director: Phil Joanou
Co-stars: Alec Baldwin Eric Roberts Kelly Lynch

1994 **RADIOLAND MURDERS**
Director: Mel Smith
Co-stars: Ned Beatty Brian Benben Anita Morris

1996 **BED OF ROSES**
Director: Michael Goldenberg
Co-star: Christian Slater

VALERIE MASTERSON

1967 THE MIKADO
Director: Stuart Burge
Co-stars: Donald Adams Philip Potter John Reed

MARY ELIZABETH MASTRANTONIO
Nominated For Best Supporting Actress In 1986 For "The Color Of Money"

1983 SCARFACE
Director: Brian De Palma
Co-stars: Al Pacino Michelle Pfeiffer Robert Loggia

1986 THE COLOR OF MONEY
Director: Martin Scorsese
Co-stars: Paul Newman Tom Cruise Helen Shaver

1987 SLAMDANCE
Director: Wayne Wang
Co-stars: Tom Hulce Virginia Madsen Millie Perkins

1989 THE JANUARY MAN
Director: Pat O'Connor
Co-stars: Kevin Kline Susan Sarandon Rod Steiger

1989 THE ABYSS
Director: James Cameron
Co-stars: Ed Harris Michael Biehn Kimberley Scott

1990 CLASS ACTION
Director: Michael Apted
Co-stars: Gene Hackman Colin Friels Larry Fishburne

1990 FOOLS OF FORTUNE
Director: Pat O'Connor
Co-stars: Iain Glen Julie Christie Michael Kitchen

1991 ROBIN HOOD, PRINCE OF THIEVES
Director: Kevin Reynolds
Co-stars: Kevin Costner Morgan Freeman Alan Rickman

1992 WHITE SANDS
Director: Roger Donaldson
Co-stars: Willem Dafoe Mickey Rourke Mimi Rogers

1995 THREE WISHES
Director: Martha Coolridge
Co-stars: Patrick Swayze Michael O'Keefe Joseph Mazzello

CLELIA MATANIA

1960 FIVE GOLDEN HOURS
Director: Mario Zampi
Co-stars: Ernie Kovacs Cyd Charisse George Sanders

1973 DON'T LOOK NOW
Director: Nicolas Roeg
Co-stars: Donald Sutherland Julie Christie Hilary Mason

HEATHER MATARAZZO

1997 WELCOME TO THE DOLL HOUSE
Director: Todd Solondz

MICHELLE MATHESON

1991 THE HOWLING VI: THE FREAKS
Director: Hope Perello
Co-stars: Brendan Hughes Jered Barclay Antonio Fargas

MELBA MATHIAS

1954 THE BOB MATHIAS STORY
Director: Francis Lyon
Co-stars: Bob Mathias Ward Bond Ann Doran

ALEXANDRA MATHIE

1990 PAPER MASK
Director: Christopher Morahan
Co-stars: Paul McGann Amanda Donohue Tom Wilkinson

GINETTE MATHIEU

1992 L'HOMME DE MA VIE
Director: Jean-Charles Tacchella
Co-stars: Lino Ventura Francoise Fabian Charles Gerard

SAMANTHA MATHIS

1989 COLD SASSY TREE
Director: Joan Tewkesbury
Co-stars: Faye Dunaway Richard Widmark Frances Fisher

1990 83 HOURS TILL DAWN
Director: Donald Wrye
Co-stars: Peter Strauss Robert Urich Elizabeth Gracen

1990 PUMP UP THE VOLUME
Director: Allan Moyle
Co-stars: Ellen Greene Annie Ross

1992 THIS IS MY LIFE
Director: Nora Ephron
Co-stars: Julie Kavner Gaby Hoffman Carrie Fisher

1992 FERNGULLY THE LAST RAINFOREST (Voice)
Director: Bill Kroyer
Co-stars: Robin Williams Tim Curry Elton John

1993 THE THING CALLED LOVE
Director: Peter Bogdanovich
Co-stars: River Phoenix Dermot Mulroney Sandra Bullock

1993 THE MUSIC OF CHANCE
Director: Philip Haas
Co-stars: James Spader Mandy Patinkin Joel Grey

1993 SUPER MARIO BROTHERS
Director: Rocky Morton
Co-stars: Bob Hoskins Dennis Hopper Fiona Shaw

1995 JACK AND SARAH
Director: Tim Sullivan
Co-stars: Richard E.Grant Judi Dench Eileen Atkins

1995 LITTLE WOMEN
Director: Gilliam Armstrong
Co-stars: Winona Ryder Susan Sarandon Gabriel Byrne

1996 BROKEN ARROW
Director: John Woo
Co-stars: John Travolta Christian Slater

1996 HOW TO MAKE AN AMERICAN QUILT
Director: Jocelyn Moorhouse
Co-stars: Winona Ryder Anne Bancroft Jean Simmons

MARLEE MATLIN
Oscar For Best Actress In 1986 For "Children Of A Lesser God"

1986 CHILDREN OF A LESSER GOD
Director: Randa Haines
Co-stars: William Hurt Piper Laurie

1987 WALKER
Director: Alex Cox
Co-stars: Ed Harris Peter Boyle Richard Masur

1992 THE LINGUINI INCIDENT
Director: Richard Shepard
Co-stars: Rosanna Arquette David Bowie Buck Henry

1993 HEAR NO EVIL
Director: Robert Greenwood
Co-stars: Martin Sheen D.B.Sweeney Greg Elam

1995 IT'S MY PARTY
Co-stars: Eric Roberts George Segal

CLAUDIA MATSCHULLA

1989 THREE WOMEN IN LOVE
Director: Rudolph Tome
Co-stars: Johannes Herrschmann Adriana Altaras

EVA MATTES

1975 THE BITTER TEARS OF PETRA VON KANT
Director: Rainer Werner Fassbinder
Co-stars: Margit Carstenson Hanna Schygulla

1978 WOYZECK
Director: Werner Herzog
Co-stars: Klaus Kinski Wolfgang Reichman

1978 IN A YEAR WITH 13   MOONS
Director: Rainer Werner Fassbinder
Co-stars: Volker Spengler Gottfried John

1981 CELESTE
Director: Percy Adlon
Co-stars: Jurgen Arndt Norbert Wartha Wolf Euba

1977 STROSZEK
Director: Werner Herzog
Co-stars: Bruno S. Clemens Scheitz

PAM MATTESON

1987 PUNCHLINE
Director: David Seltzer
Co-stars: Sally Field Tom Hanks John Goodman

CARMEN MATTHEWS

1971 THEY CALL IT MURDER
Director: Walter Grauman
Co-stars: Jim Hutton Lloyd Bochner Jessica Walter

1972 SOUNDER
Director: Martin Ritt
Co-stars: Paul Winfield Cicely Tyson James Best

1990 THE LAST BEST YEAR
Director: John Erman
Co-stars: Mary Tyler Moore Bernadette Peters Dorothy McGuire

CAROLE MATTHEWS

1951 THE MAN WITH MY FACE
Director: Edward Montagne
Co-stars: Barry Nelson Lynn Ainley Jack Warden

1953 MEET ME AT THE FAIR
Director: Douglas Sirk
Co-stars: Diana Lynn Dan Dailey Chet Allen

1953 CITY OF BAD MEN
Director: Harmon Jones
Co-stars: Dale Robertson Jeanne Crain Richard Boone

1956 ASSIGNMENT REDHEAD
Director: MacLean Rogers
Co-stars: Richard Denning Brian Worth Hugh Moxey

DOROTHY MATTHEWS

1928 A GIRL IN EVERY PORT
Director: Howard Hawks
Co-stars: Victor McLaglen Robert Armstrong Louise Brooks

1930 DOORWAY TO HELL
Director: Archie Mayo
Co-stars: Lew Ayres James Cagney Charles Judels

JESSIE MATTHEWS

1931 OUT OF THE BLUE
Director: Gene Gerard
Co-stars: Gene Gerard Kay Hammond Binnie Barnes

1932 THE MIDSHIPMAID
Director: Albert De Courville
Co-stars: Frederick Kerr Nigel Bruce John Mills

1932 THE GOOD COMPANIONS
Director: Victor Saville
Co-stars: John Gielgud Edmund Gwenn Max Miller

1933 WALTZES FROM VIENNA
Director: Alfred Hitchcock
Co-stars: Esmond Knight Edmund Gwenn Fay Compton

1933 FRIDAY THE THIRTEENTH
Director: Victor Saville
Co-stars: Sonnie Hale Edmund Gwenn Max Miller

1934 EVERGREEN
Director: Victor Saville
Co-stars: Sonnie Hale Barry MacKay Betty Balfour

1935 FIRST A GIRL
Director: Victor Saville
Co-stars: Sonnie Hale Griffith Jones Anna Lee

1936 IT'S LOVE AGAIN
Director: Victor Saville
Co-stars: Sonnie Hale Robert Young Robb Wilton

1937 HEAD OVER HEELS
Director: Sonnie Hale
Co-stars: Robert Flemyng Louis Borell Romney Brent

1937 GANGWAY
Director: Sonnie Hale
Co-stars: Barry MacKay Nat Pendleton Alastair Sim

1938 SAILING ALONG
Director: Sonnie Hale
Co-stars: Roland Young Barry MacKay Noel Madison

1938 CLIMBING HIGH
Director: Carol Reed
Co-stars: Michael Redgrave Noel Madison Mary Clare

1943 FOREVER AND A DAY
Director: Victor Saville
Co-stars: Charles Laughton Buster Keaton Edmund Gwenn

1944 CANDLES AT NINE
Director: John Harlow
Co-stars: John Stuart Beatrix Lehman Winifred Shotter

1958 TOM THUMB
Director: George Pal
Co-stars: Russ Tamblyn Peter Sellers Terry-Thomas Alan Young

1977 THE HOUND OF THE BASKERVILLES
Director: Peter Morrissey
Co-stars: Peter Cook Dudley Moore Denholm Elliott

JOYCE MATHEWS

1939 BOY TROUBLE
Director: George Archainbaud
Co-stars: Charles Ruggles Mary Boland Donald O'Connor

LIESEL MATTHEWS *(Child)*

1996 A LITTLE PRINCESS
Director: Alfonso Cuaron
Co-stars: Eleanor Bron Liam Cunningham Vanessa Lee Chester

1997 AIR FORCE ONE
Director: Wolfgang Petersen
Co-stars: Harrison Ford Glenn Close Gary Oldman

MANDY MATTHEWS

1989 DREAM BABY
Director: Angela Pope
Co-stars: Jenny McCrindle Kevin McNally Peter Capaldi

MARTHA MATTOX

1925 THE TORRENT
Director: Monta Bell
Co-stars: Richardo Cortez Greta Garbo Gertrude Olmsted

1932 THE MONSTER WALKS
Director: Frank Strayer
Co-stars: Sheldon Lewis Mischa Auer Rex Lease

MARIA MAUBAN

1949 CAIRO ROAD
Director: David MacDonald
Co-stars: Eric Portman Laurence Harvey Harold Lang

1950 CAGE OF GOLD
Director: Basil Dearden
Co-stars: Jean Simmons David Farrar James Donald

1953 VOYAGE TO ITALY
Director: Roberto Rossellini
Co-stars: Ingrid Bergman George Sanders Paul Muller

JOAN MAUDE

1933 THE WANDERING JEW
Director: Maurice Elvy
Co-stars: Conrad Veidt Maria Ney Peggy Ashcroft

1935 TURN OF THE TIDE
Director: Norman Walker
Co-stars: John Garrick Geraldine Fitzgerald Niall McGinnis

MARY MAUDE

1971 CRUCIBLE OF TERROR
Director: Ted Hooker
Co-stars: Mike Raven James Bolam Ronald Lacey

MONICA MAUGHAN

1990 GOLDEN BRAID
Director: Paul Cox
Co-stars: Chris Haywood Gosia Dobrowolska Norman Kaye

SUSAN MAUGHAN

1963 WHAT A CRAZY WORLD
Director: Michael Carreras
Co-stars: Joe Brown Marty Wilde Harry H.Corbett

CARMEN MAURA

1980 PEPI, LUCY, BOM AND ALL THE OTHER GIRLS
Director: Pedro Almodovar
Co-stars: Eva Siva Olivida Gara

1984 DARK HABITS
Director: Pedro Almodovar
Co-stars: Cristina Pascual Marisa Parides Mari Carrillo

1984 WHAT HAVE I DONE TO DESERVE THIS?
Director: Pedro Almodovar
Co-stars: Luis Hostalot Gonzalo Suarez

1986 MATADOR
Director: Pedro Almodovar
Co-stars: Antonio Banderas Assumpta Serna

1987 LAW OF DESIRE
Director: Pedro Almodovar
Co-stars: Antonio Banderas Bibi Andersson Miguel Molina

1988 WOMEN ON THE VERGE OF A NERVOUS BREAKDOWN
Director: Pedro Almodovar
Co-stars: Antonio Banderas Julietta Serrano

1990 AY! CARMELA!
Director: Carlos Saura
Co-stars: Andres Pajares Gabino Diego

1991 HOW TO BE A WOMAN AND NOT DIE IN THE ATTEMPT
Director: Ana Belen
Co-stars: Antonio Resines Carmen Conesa

1996 LE BONHEUR
Director: Etienne Chatiliez
Co-stars: Michel Serrault Sabine Azema Eric Cantona

MOLLY MAUREEN

1970 THE PRIVATE LIFE OF SHERLOCK HOLMES
Director: Billy Wilder
Co-stars: Robert Stephens Colin Blakely

1987 OUR LADY BLUE
Ûdirector Robin Midgeley
Co-stars: Patricia Hayes Doreen Mantle Eva Griffith

PEGGY MAURER

1957 I BURY THE LIVING
Director: Albert Band
Co-stars: Richard Boone Theodore Bikel Herbert Anderson

NICOLE MAUREY

1951 DIARY OF A COUNTRY PRIEST
Director: Robert Bresson
Co-stars: Claude Laydu Nicole Ladmirale

1953 LITTLE BOY LOST
Director: George Seaton
Co-stars: Bing Crosby Claude Dauphin

1954 SECRET OF THE INCAS
Director: Jerry Hopper
Co-stars: Charlton Heston Yma Sumac Robert Young

1955 THE CONSTANT HUSBAND
Director: Sidney Gilliat
Co-stars: Rex Harrison Kay Kendall Margaret Leighton

1956 THE BOLD AND THE BRAVE
Director: Lewis Foster
Co-stars: Mickey Rooney Wendell Corey

1956 THE WEAPON
Director: Val Guest
Co-stars: Lisabeth Scott Steve Cochran George Cole

1957 ROGUE'S YARN
Director: Vernon Sewell
Co-stars: Derek Bond Hugh Latimer Elwyn Brook-Jones

1958 ME AND THE COLONEL
Director: Peter Glenville
Co-stars: Danny Kaye Curt Jurgens Akim Tamiroff

1959 HOUSE OF THE SEVEN HAWKS
Director: Richard Thorpe
Co-stars: Robert Taylor Linda Christian Donald Wolfit

1959 THE SCAPEGOAT
Director: Robert Hamer
Co-stars: Alec Guinness Bette Davis Irene Worth

1959 THE JAYHAWKERS
Director: Melvyn Frank
Co-stars: Fess Parker Jeff Chandler Henry Silva

1960 HIGH TIME
Director: Blake Edwards
Co-stars: Bing Crosby Tuesday Weld Fabian

1960 THE SIEGE OF SIDNEY STREET
Director: Monty Berman
Co-stars: Donald Sinden Peter Wyngarde Kieron Moore

1960 HIS AND HERS
Director: Brian Desmond Hurst
Co-stars: Terry-Thomas Janette Scott Oliver Reed

1961 DON'T BOTHER TO KNOCK
Director: Cyril Frankel
Co-stars: Richard Todd Elke Sommer Judith Anderson

1962 THE DAY OF THE TRIFFIDS
Director: Steve Sekely
Co-stars: Howard Keel Kieron Moore Janette Scott

1963 THE VERY EDGE
Director: Cyril Frankel
Co-stars: Richard Todd Ann Heywood Jeremy Brett

CLAIRE MAURIER

1959 LES QUATRE CENT COUPS
Director: Francois Truffaut
Co-stars: Jean-Pierre Leaud Albert Remy

1978 LA CAGE AUX FOLLES
Director: Edouard Molinaro
Co-stars: Ugo Tognazzi Michel Serrault Michel Galabru

SARAH MAUR-THORP

1989 EDGE OF SANITY
Director: Gerard Kikoine
Co-stars: Anthony Perkins Glynis Barber David Lodge

1989 RIVER OF DEATH
Director: Steve Carver
Co-stars: Michael Dudikoff Donald Pleasence Herbert Lom

1989 TEN LITTLE INDIANS
Director: Alan Birkinshaw
Co-stars: Donald Pleasence Brenda Vaccaro Frank Stallone

GERDA MAURUS

1928 SPIONE
Director: Fritz Lang
Co-stars: Rudolph Klein-Rogge Willy Fritsch Lupu Pick

1929 WOMAN IN THE MOON
Director: Fritz Lang
Co-stars: Willy Fritsch Gusti Stark-Gattenbaur

JANET MAW

1978 THE MAYOR OF CASTERBRIDGE
Director: David Glies
Co-stars: Alan Bates Anne Stallybrass Anna Massey

**1991 INSPECTOR WEXFORD:
PUT ON BY CUNNING**
Director: Sandy Johnson
Co-stars: George Baker Rossano Brazzi

ANGELA MAWBY

1930 THE MAN FROM BLANKLEY'S
Director: Alfred Green
Co-stars: John Barrymore Loretta Young William Austin

ELSA MAXWELL

1940 PUBLIC DEB NUMBER ONE
Director: Gregory Ratoff
Co-stars: Brenda Joyce George Murphy Ralph Bellamy

JENNY MAXWELL

1961 BLUE HAWAII
Director: Norman Taurog
Co-stars: Elvis Presley Joan Blackman Angela Lansbury

LOIS MAXWELL

1947 THAT HAGEN GIRL
Director: Peter Godfrey
Co-stars: Shirley Temple Ronald Reagan Rory Calhoun

1948 THE BIG PUNCH
Director: Sherry Shourds
Co-stars: Gordon MacRae Wayne Morris Mary Stewart

1948 THE DARK PAST
Director: Rudolph Mate
Co-stars: William Holden Nina Foch Lee J.Cobb

1949 CRIME DOCTOR'S DIARY
Director: Seymour Friedman
Co-stars: Warner Baxter Adele Jergens

1950 DOMANI I TROPPO TARDI
Director: Leonide Moguy
Co-stars: Vittorio De Sica Gabrielle Dorziat

1952 THE WOMAN'S ANGLE
Director: Leslie Arliss
Co-stars: Edward Underdown Cathy O'Donnell Peter Reynolds

1952 WOMEN OF TWILIGHT
Director: Gordon Parry
Co-stars: Freda Jackson Rene Ray Joan Dowling

1953 MANTRAP
Director: Terence Fisher
Co-stars: Paul Henreid Kieron Moore Kay Kendall

1953 AIDA
Director: Clemente Fracassi
Co-stars: Sophia Loren Luciano Della Marra

1956 THE HIGH TERRACE
Director: Henry Cass
Co-stars: Dale Robertson Derek Bond Lionel Jeffries

1956 PASSPORT TO TREASON
Director: Robert Baker
Co-stars: Rod Cameron Clifford Evans Douglas Wilmer

1956 SATELLITE IN THE SKY
Director: Paul Dickson
Co-stars: Kieron Moore Donald Wolfit Jimmy Hanley

1957 TIME WITHOUT PITY
Director: Joseph Losey
Co-stars: Michael Redgrave Leo McKern Ann Todd

1957 KILL ME TOMORROW
Director: Terence Fisher
Co-stars: Pat O'Brien George Coulouris Tommy Steele

1961 LOLITA
Director: Stanley Kubrick
Co-stars: Sue Lyon James Mason Shelley Winters

1962 DR. NO
Director: Terence Young
Co-stars: Sean Connery Ursula Andress Jack Lord

1963 FROM RUSSIA WITH LOVE
Director: Terence Young
Co-stars: Sean Connery Robert Shaw Daniella Bianchi

1963 THE HAUNTING
Director: Robert Wise
Co-stars: Richard Johnson Claire Bloom Russ Tamblyn

1964 GOLDFINGER
Director: Guy Hamilton
Co-stars: Sean Connery Honor Blackman Gert Frobe

1965 THUNDERBALL
Director: Terence Young
Co-stars: Sean Connery Adolfo Celi Claudine Auger

1967 YOU ONLY LIVE TWICE
Director: Lewis Gilbert
Co-stars: Sean Connery Charles Gray Donald Pleasence

1967 OPERATION KID BROTHER
Director: Alberto De Martino
Co-stars: Neil Connery Daniela Bianchi

1969 ON HER MAJESTY'S SECRET SERVICE
Director: Peter Hunt
Co-stars: George Lazenby Diana Rigg Telly Savalas

1971 ENDLESS NIGHT
Director: Sidney Gilliat
Co-stars: Hayley Mills Hywel Bennett George Sanders

1971 DIAMONDS ARE FOREVER
Director: Guy Hamilton
Co-stars: Sean Connery Jill St. John Charles Gray

1973 LIVE AND LET DIE
Director: Guy Hamilton
Co-stars: Roger Moore Jane Seymour Yaphet Kotto

1974 THE MAN WITH THE GOLDEN GUN
Director: Guy Hamilton
Co-stars: Roger Moore Maud Adams Christopher Lee

1977 THE SPY WHO LOVED ME
Director: Lewis Gilbert
Co-stars: Roger Moore Barbara Bach Curt Jurgens

1977 THE AGE OF INNOCENCE
Director: Alan Bridges
Co-stars: David Warner Honor Blackman Cec Linder

1979 MOONRAKER
Director: Lewis Gilbert
Co-stars: Roger Moore Lois Chiles Richard Kiel

1981 FOR YOUR EYES ONLY
Director: John Glen
Co-stars: Roger Moore Topol Julian Glover Carole Bucquet

1983 OCTOPUSSY
Director: John Glen
Co-stars: Roger Moore Maud Adams Louis Jourdan

1985 A VIEW TO A KILL
Director: John Glen
Co-stars: Roger Moore Tanya Roberts Grace Jones

MARILYN MAXWELL

1943 DR. GILLESPIE'S CRIMINAL CASE
Director: Willis Goldbeck
Co-stars: Lionel Barrymore Margaret O'Brien

1943 STAND BY FOR ACTION
Director: Robert Z. Leonard
Co-stars: Robert Taylor Charles Laughton Brian Donlevy

1943 SALUTE TO THE MARINES
Director: S.Sylvan Simon
Co-stars: Wallace Beery Fay Bainter William Lundigan

1944 SWING FEVER
Director: Tim Whelan
Co-stars: Kay Kyser Lena Horne Nat Pendleton William Gargan

1944 THREE MEN IN WHITE

1944 LOST IN A HAREM
Director: Charles Reisner
Co-stars: Bud Abbott Lou Costello Douglass Dumbrille

1944 BETWEEN TWO WOMEN
Director: Willis Goldbeck
Co-stars: Lionel Barrymore Van Johnson Gloria Dehaven

1946 THE SHOW-OFF
Co-stars: Red Skelton

1947 CHAMPION
Director: Mark Robson
Co-stars: Kirk Douglas Arthur Kennedy Ruth Roman

1947 HIGH BARBAREE
Director: Jack Conway
Co-stars: Van Johnson June Allyson Thomas Mitchell

1948 RACE STREET
Director: Edwin Marin
Co-stars: George Raft William Bendix Henry Morgan

1948 SUMMER HOLIDAY
Director: Rouben Mahmoulian
Co-stars: Walter Huston Mickey Rooney Frank Morgan

1950 KEY TO THE CITY
Director: George Sidney
Co-stars: Clark Gable Loeretta Young Frank Morgan

1951 THE LEMON DROP KID
Director: Sidney Lanfield
Co-stars: Bob Hope Lloyd Nolan Jane Darwell

1952 MILITARY POLICEMAN
Director: George Marshall
Co-stars: Bob Hope Mickey Rooney Marvin Miller

1952 NEW MEXICO
Director: Irving Reis
Co-stars: Lew Ayres Robert Hutton Andy Devine

1953 PARIS MODEL
Director: Alfred Green
Co-stars: Paulette Goddard Eva Gabor Tom Conway

1953 EAST OF SUMATRA
Co-stars: Budd Boetticher
Co-stars: Jeff Chandler Anthony Quinn John Sutton

1955 NEW YORK CONFIDENTIAL
Director: Russel Rouse
Co-stars: Broderick Crawford Anne Bancroft Richard Conte

1958 ROCK-A-BYE-BABY
Director: Frank Tashlin
Co-stars: Jerry Lewis Reginald Gardner Isabel Elsom

1963 CRITIC'S CHOICE
Director: Don Weis
Co-stars: Bob Hope Lucille Ball Rip Torn John Dehner

1964 STAGE TO THUNDER ROCK
Director: William Claxton
Co-stars: Barry Sullivan Scott Brady Allan Jones

1968 ARIZONA BUSHWACKERS
Director: Lesley Selander
Co-stars: Howard Keel Yvonne De Carlo Brian Donlevy

1970 WILD WOMEN
Director: Don Taylor
Co-stars: Hugh O'Brian Anne Francis Marie Windsor

ROBERTA MAXWELL

1986 PSYCHO III
Director: Anthony Perkins
Co-stars: Anthony Perkins Diana Scarwid Jeff Fahey Hugh Gillin

1997 WHEN INNOCENCE IS LOST
Co-star: Keri Russell

DEBORAH MAY

1983 RAGE OF ANGELS
Director: Buzz Kulik
Co-stars: Jaclyn Smith Ken Howard Armand Assante

1992 SEXUAL ADVANCES
Director: Donna Deitch
Co-stars: Stephanie Zimbalist William Russ Terry O'Quinn

1992 O-PIONEERS !
Director: Glenn Jordan
Co-stars: Jessice Lange David Strathairn Anne Heche

1995 THE OTHER MOTHER
Director: Bethany Booney
Co-stars: Frances Fisher Connie Clark

ELAINE MAY *(Mother Of Jeannie Berlin)*

1967 ENTER LAUGHING
Director: Carl Reiner
Co-stars: Reni Santoni Jose Ferrer Shelley Winters

1967 LUV
Director: Clive Donner
Co-stars: Jack Lemmon Peter Falk Eddie Mayehoff

1970 A NEW LEAF
Director: Elaine May
Co-stars: Walter Matthau Jack Weston James Coco

1978 CALIFORNIA SUITE
Director: Herbert Ross
Co-stars: Walter Matthau Jane Fonda Maggie Smith

1990 IN THE SPIRIT
Director: Sandra Seacat
Co-stars: Marlo Thomas Jeannie Berlin Melanie Griffith

JODHI MAY (Child) (Sister Of Tat Whalley)

1987 A WORLD APART
Director: Chris Menges
Co-stars: Barbara Hershey Jeroen Krabbe David Suchet

1990 MAX AND HELEN
Director: Philip Saville
Co-stars: Alice Krige Treat Williams Martin Landau

1990 THE GIFT
Director: Red Saunders
Co-star: Tat Whalley

1992 THE LAST OF THE MOHICANS
Director: Michael Mann
Co-stars: Daniel Day-Lewis Madeleine Stowe Russell Means

1995 SISTER, MY SISTER
Director: Nancy Meckler
Co-stars: Joely Richardson Julie Walters

1997 THE GAMBLER
Director: Karoly Makk
Co-stars: Michael Hambon Luise Rainer

1998 THE WOODLANDERS
Director: Phil Agland
Co-stars: Rufus Sewell Polly Walker Emily Woof

JULIE MAY

1968 HOT MILLIONS
Director: Eric Till
Co-stars: Peter Ustinov Maggie Smith Karl Malden

MATHILDA MAY

1985 LIFE FORCE
Director: Tobe Hooper
Co-stars: Peter Firth Frank Finlay Steve Railsback

1987 THE CROSSING
Director: Jean-Claude Sussfeld
Co-star: Pierre Arditi

1990 NAKED TANGO
Director: Leonard Schrader
Co-stars: Vincent D'Onofrio Fernando Rey Josh Mostel

1991 SCREAM OF STONE
Director: Werner Herzog
Co-stars: Vittorio Mezzogiorno Stefan Glowacz Brad Dourif

1992 BECOMING COLETTE
Director: Danny Huston
Co-stars: Klaus Maria Brandauer Virginia Madsen Paul Rhys

1994 THE WHIPPING BOY
Director: Syd McCarthy
Co-stars: George C.Scott Vincent Schiavelli

MELINDA MAY

1968 HOT MILLIONS
Director: Eric Till
Co-stars: Peter Ustinov Maggie Smith Karl Malden

CLARA MAYER

1969 STEREO
Director: David Cronenberg
Co-stars: Ron Mlodzik Jack Messinger Iain Ewing

MITZI MAYFAIR

1944 FOUR JILLS IN A JEEP
Director: William Seiter
Co-stars: Kay Francis Martha Raye Carole Landis

BELINDA MAYNE

1983 DON'T OPEN TILL CHRISTMAS
Director: Edmund Purdom
Co-stars: Alan Lake Mark Jones Edmund Purdon

PHILIPPA MAYNE

1985 TRIAL RUN
Director: Melanie Read
Co-stars: Annie Whittle Judith Gibson Lee Grant

JULIETTE MAYNIEL

1958 LES COUSINS
Director: Claude Chabrol
Co-stars: Jean-Claude Brialy Gerard Blain Claude Cerval

1959 EYES WITHOUT A FACE
Director: Georges Fanju
Co-stars: Pierre Brasseur Alida Valli Edith Scob

1961 THE TROJAN WAR
Director: Giorgio Ferroni
Co-stars: Steve Reeves John Drew Barrymore Hedy Vessel

VIRGINIA MAYO

1943 JACK LONDON
Director: Alfred Santell
Co-stars: Michael O'Shea Susan Hayward Osa Massen

1944 SEVEN DAYS ASHORE
Co-stars: Gordon Oliver Elaine Shepard Alan Dinehart

1944 UP IN ARMS
Director: Elliott Nugent
Co-stars: Danny Kaye Dinah Shore Dana Andrews

1944 THE PRINCESS AND THE PIRATE
Director: David Butler
Co-stars: Bob Hope Victor McLaglen Hugo Haas

1945 WONDER MAN
Director: Bruce Humberstone
Co-stars: Danny Kaye Vera-Ellen S.Z.Sakall

1946 THE KID FROM BROOKLYN
Director: Norman Z. McLeod
Co-stars: Danny Kaye Vera-Ellen Steve Cochran

1946 THE BEST YEARS OF OUR LIVES
Director: William Wyler
Co-stars: Fredric March Myrna Loy Dana Andrews

1947 THE SECRET LIFE OF WALTER MITTY
Director: Norman Z. McLeod
Co-stars: Danny Kaye Boris Karlof Florence Bates

1947 OUT OF THE BLUE
Director: Leigh Jason
Co-stars: George Brent Carole Landis Ann Dvorak

1948 A SONG IS BORN
Director: Howard Hawkes
Co-stars: Danny Kaye Steve Cochran Louis Armstrong

1948 SMART GIRLS DON'T TALK
Director: Richard Bare
Co-stars: Bruce Bennett Robert Hutton

1948 FLAXY MARTIN
Director: Richard Bare
Co-stars: Zachary Scott Dorothy Malone Elisha Cook

1949 THE GIRL FROM JONES BEACH
Director: Peter Godfrey
Co-stars: Ronald Reagan Eddie Bracken

1949	**BACKFIRE**
Director:	Vincent Sherman
Co-stars:	Gordon MacRae Edmond O'Brien

1949 ALWAYS LEAVE THEM LAUGHING
Director: Roy Del Ruth
Co-stars: Milton Berle Bert Lahr Ruth Roman

1949 COLORADO TERRITORY
Director: Raoul Walsh
Co-stars: Joel McCrea Dorothy Malone Henry Hull

1949 RED LIGHT
Director: Roy Del Ruth
Co-stars: George Raft Raymond Burr Gene Lockhart

1949 WHITE HEAT
Director: Raoul Walsh
Co-stars: James Cagney Edmond O'Brien Steve Cochran

1950 FINE AND DANDY
Director: Roy Del Ruth
Co-stars: James Cagney Doris Day Gordon MacRae

1950 THE FLAME AND THE ARROW
Director: Jacques Tourneur
Co-stars: Burt Lancaster Nick Cravat

1950 ALONG THE GREAT DIVIDE
Director: Raoul Walsh
Co-stars: Kirk Douglas Walter Brennan John Agar

1951 CAPTAIN HORATIO HORNBLOWER RN
Director: Raoul Walsh
Co-stars: Gregory Peck Robert Beatty

1951 PAINTING THE CLOUDS WITH SUNSHINE
Director: David Butler
Co-stars: Dennis Morgan Gene Nelson

1951 STARLIFT
Director: Roy Del Ruth
Co-stars: Doris Day Gordon MacRae Gene Nelson

1952 SHE'S WORKING HER WAY THROUGH COLLEGE
Director: Bruce Humberstone
Co-star: Ronald Reagan Gene Nelson Patrick Wymore

1952 THE IRON MISTRESS
Director: Gordon Douglas
Co-stars: Alan Ladd Joseph Callelia Phyllis Kirk

1953 SHE'S BACK ON BROADWAY

1953 DEVIL'S CANYON
Director: Alfred Werker
Co-stars: Dale Robertson Stephen McNally Robert Keith

1954 KING RICHARD AND THE CRUSADERS
Director: David Butler
Co-stars: Rex Harrison Laurence Harvey

1954 THE SILVER CHALICE
Director: Victor Saville
Co-stars: Paul Newman Pier Angeli Jack Palance

1953 SOUTH SEA WOMAN
Director: Arthur Lubin
Co-stars: Burt Lancaster Chuck Connors Arthur Shields

1955 PEARL OF THE SOUTH PACIFIC
Director: Allan Dwan
Co-stars: Dennis Morgan David Farrar Murvyn Vye

1956 THE PROUD ONES
Director: Robert Webb
Co-stars: Robert Ryan Jeffrey Hunter Robert Middleton

1956 GREAT DAY IN THE MORNING
Director: Jacques Tourneur
Co-stars: Robert Stack Ruth Roman Alex Nicol

1956 CONGO CROSSING
Director: Joseph Pevney
Co-stars: George Nader Peter Lorre Rex Ingram

1957 THE BIG LAND
Director: Gordon Douglas
Co-stars: Alan Ladd Edmond O'Brien Julie Bishop

1957 THE STORY OF MANKIND
Director: Irwin Allen
Co-stars: Ronald Coleman Vincent Price Marx Brothers

1957 THE TALL STRANGER
Director: Thomas Carr
Co-stars: Joel McCrea Barry Kelly Michael Ansara

1958 FORT DOBBS
Director: Gordon Douglas
Co-stars: Clint Walker Brian Keith Richard Eyer

1958 JET OVER THE ATLANTIC
Director: Byron Haskin
Co-stars: Guy Madison George Raft Ilona Massey

1959 WESTBOUND
Director: Budd Boetticher
Co-stars: Randolph Scott Karen Steele

1966 CASTLE OF EVIL
Director: Francis Lyon
Co-stars: Scott Brady David Brian Hugh Marlowe

1967 FORT UTAH
Director: Lesley Selander
Co-stars: John Ireland Scott Brady James Craig

1976 WON, TON TON, THE DOG WHO SAVED HOLLYWOOD
Director: Michael Winner
Co-stars: Madeline Kahn Art Carney

KAREN MAYO-CHANDLER

1988 OUT OF THE DARK
Director: Michael Schroeder
Co-stars: Karen Black Cameron Dye Tab Hunter

YELENA MAYOROVA

1992 LOST IN SIBERIA
Director: Alexander Mitta
Co-stars: Anthony Andrews Vladimir Ilyin Ira Mikhalyova

GALE MAYRON

1988 HEART OF MIDNIGHT
Director: Matthew Chapman
Co-stars: Jennifer Jason Leigh Peter Coyote Sam Schacht

MELANIE MAYRON

1974 HARRY AND TONTO
Director: Paul Mazursky
Co-stars: Art Carney Ellen Burstyn Geraldine Fitzgerald

1976 THE GREAT SMOKEY ROADBLOCK
Director: John Leone
Co-stars: Henry Fonda Eileen Brennan Susan Sarandon

1976 GABLE AND LOMBARD
Director: Sidney Furie
Co-stars: James Brolin Jill Clayburgh Red Buttons

1977 YOU LIGHT UP MY LIFE
Director: Joseph Brooks
Co-stars: Didi Conn Joe Silver Michael Zaslow

1978 GIRLFRIENDS
Director: Claudia Weill
Co-stars: Eli Wallach Anita Skinner Bob Balaban

1980 PLAYING FOR TIME
Director: Daniel Mann
Co-stars: Vanessa Redgrave Jane Alexander Maud Adams

1982 MISSING
Director: Costa-Gavras
Co-stars: Jack Lemmon Sissy Spacek John Shea

1985 WALLENBERG: A HERO'S STORY
Director: Lamont Johnson
Co-stars: Richard Chamberlain Alice Krige Stuart Wilson

1988 STICKY FINGERS
Director: Catlin Adams
Co-stars: Helen Slater Eileen Brennan Carol Kane

1988 CHECKING OUT
Director: David Leland
Co-stars: Jeff Daniels Michael Tucker Ann Magnuson

1990 MY BLUE HEAVEN
Director: Herbert Ross
Co-stars: Steve Martin Rick Moranis Joan Cusack

1993 OTHER WOMEN'S CHILDREN
Director: Anne Wheeler
Co-stars: Geraint Wyn Davies

CECEILE MAZAN

1989 WORLD WITHOUT PLAY
Director: Eric Rochant
Co-stars: Hippolyte Girardot Mireille Perrier Yvan Attal

DEBI MAZAR

1991 JUNGLE FEVER
Director: Spike Lee
Co-stars: Wesley Snipes Annabella Sciorra Anthony Quinn

1992 MALCOLM X
Director: Spike Lee
Co-stars: Denzel Washington Spike Lee Angela Bassett

1993 MONEY FOR NOTHING
Director: Ramon Menendez
Co-stars: John Cusack Michael Madsen Maury Chaykin

1993 BEETHOVEN'S 2ND.
Director: Rod Daniel
Co-stars: Charles Grodin Bonnie Hunt Christopher Castle

1997 SPACE TRUCKERS
Co-stars: Dennis Hopper Charles Dance Shane Rimmer

MELONIE MAZMAN

1986 ALEX: THE LIFE OF A CHILD
Director: Robert Markowitz
Co-stars: Bonnie Bedelia Craig T. Nelson

1991 JUNGLE FEVER
Director: Spike Lee
Co-stars: Wesley Snipes Annabella Sciorra Anthony Quinn

ERNESTINE MAZUROWNA

1986 JEAN DE FLORETTE
Director: Claude Berri
Co-stars: Yves Montand Gerard Depardieu Daniel Auteuil

MEG MAZURSKY *(Daughter Of Paul Mazursky)(Child)*

1970 ALEX IN WONDERLAND
Director: Paul Mazursky
Co-stars: Donald Sutherland Ellen Burstyn Jeanne Moreau

ROSY MAZZACURATI

1960 LA NOTTE
Director: Michaelangelo Antonioni
Co-stars: Marcello Mastroianni Jeanne Moreau Monica Vitti

KATHLEEN ROWE McALLEN

1981 FEAR NO EVIL
Director: Frank LaLoggia
Co-stars: Elizabeth Hoffman Frank Birney Daniel Eden

JENNIFER McALLISTER

1980 SERIAL
Director: Bill Persky
Co-stars: Martin Mull Tuesday Weld Sally Kellerman

MARIANNE McANDREW

1969 HELLO DOLLY
Director: Gene Kelly
Co-stars: Barbra Streisand Walter Matthau Michael Crawford

ANDREA McARDLE

1978 RAINBOW
Director: Jackie Cooper
Co-stars: Don Murray Michael Parks Piper Laurie

MAY McAVOY

1923 HOLLYWOOD
Director: James Cruze
Co-stars: Hope Drown Luke Cosgrave Eleanor Lawson

1924 THREE WOMEN
Director: Ernst Lubitsch
Co-stars: Lew Cody Pauline Frederick Marie Prevost

1925 LADY WINDERMERE'S FAN
Director: Ernst Lubitsch
Co-stars: Ronald Colman Irene Rich Bert Lytell

1926 BEN HUR
Director: Fred Niblo
Co-stars: Ramon Navarro Carmel Myers Francis X.Bushman

1927 THE JAZZ SINGER
Director: Alan Crosland
Co-stars: Al Jolson Warner Oland Eugenie Besserer

1928 THE TERROR
Director: Roy Del Ruth
Co-stars: Edward Everett Horton Louise Fazenda John Miljan

DIANE McBAIN

1960 ICE PALACE
Director: Vincent Sherman
Co-stars: Richard Burton Robert Ryan Martha Hyer

1961 CLAUDELLE INGLISH
Director: Gordon Douglas
Co-stars: Arthur Kennedy Constance Ford Chad Everett

1961 PARRISH
Director: Delmer Daves
Co-stars: Troy Donohue Claudette Colbert Karl Malden

1963 MARY MARY
Director: Mervyn Le Roy
Co-stars: Debbie Reynolds Barry Nelson Michael Rennie

1963 BLACK GOLD
Director: Leslie Martinson
Co-stars: Philip Carey Claude Akins James Best

1963 THE CARETAKERS
Director: Hall Bartlett
Co-stars: Polly Bergen Joan Crawford Robert Stack

1964 A DISTANT TRUMPET
Director: Raoul Walsh
Co-stars: Troy Donohue Suzanne Pleshette James Gregory

1966 SPINOUT
Director: Norman Taurog
Co-stars: Elvis Presley Shelley Fabares Cecil Kellaway

MARCIA McBROOM

1970 BEYOND THE VALLEY OF THE DOLLS
Director: Russ Meyer
Co-stars: Dolly Read Cynthia Myers John La Zar

RUTH McCABE

1989 MY LEFT FOOT
Director: Jim Sheridan
Co-stars: Daniel-Day Lewis Ray McAnally Brenda Fricker

1993 THE SNAPPER
Director: Stephen Frears
Co-stars: Tina Kellegher Colm Meaney Peter Rowan

1995 CIRCLE OF FRIENDS
Director: Pat O'Connor
Co-stars: Minnie Driver Chris O'Donnell Colin Firth

DEE McCAFFERTY

1988 SHORT CURCUIT 2
Director: Kenneth Johnson
Co-stars: Fisher Stevens Cynthia Gibb Jack Weston

FRANCES LEE McCAIN

1982 TWO OF A KIND
Director: Roger Young
Co-stars: George Burns Robbie Benson Barbara Barrie

1984 SINGLE BARS, SINGLE WOMEN
Director: Harry Winer
Co-stars: Tony Danza Shelley Hack Christine Lahti

1985 THE RAPE OF RICHARD BECK
Director: Karen Arthur
Co-stars: Richard Crenna Pat Hingle Meredith Baxter

1985 FIRST STEPS
Director: Sheldon Larry
Co-stars: Judd Hirsch Amy Steel Kim Darby

1986 CAN YOU FEEL ME DANCING?
Director: Michael Miller
Co-stars: Justine Bateman Jason Bateman Max Gail

1988 LEAP OF FAITH
Director: Stephen Gyllenhall
Co-stars: Anne Archer Sam Neill James Tolkin

1988 SCANDAL IN SMALL TOWN
Director: Anthony Page
Co-stars: Raquel Welch Christa Denton Ronny Cox

1993 DYING TO LOVE YOU
Director: Robert Iscove
Co-stars: Tim Matheson Tracey Pollan Lee Garlington

JOAN McCALL

1976 GRIZZLY
Director: William Girdler
Co-stars: Christopher George Andrew Prine Richard Jaeckel

JOANNA McCALLUM

1989 THE GINGER TREE
Director: Anthony Garner
Co-stars: Samantha Bond Daisuke Ryu Adrian Rawlins

MERCEDES McCAMBRIDGE
Oscar For Best Supporting Actress in 1949 For "All The King's Men" And
Nominated for Best Supporting Actress in 1956 for "Giant"

1949 ALL THE KING'S MEN
Director: Robert Rossen
Co-stars: Broderick Crawford John Ireland Joanne Dru

1951 LIGHTNING STRIKES TWICE
Director: King Vidor
Co-stars: Richard Todd Ruth Roman Zachary Scott

1951 INSIDE STRAIGHT
Director: Gerald Mayer
Co-stars: David Brian Arlene Dahl Barry Sullivan

1951 THE SCARF
Director: E.A.Dupont
Co-stars: John Ireland Emlyn Williams James Barton

1953 JOHNNY GUITAR
Director: Nicholas Ray
Co-stars: Joan Crawford Sterling Hayden Ernest Borgnine

1956 GIANT
Director: George Stevens
Co-stars: Rock Hudson Elizabeth Taylor James Dean

1957 A FAREWELL TO ARMS
Director: Charles Vidor
Co-stars: Rock Hudson Jennifer Jones Vittorio De Sica

1959 SUDDENLY LAST SUMMER
Director: Joseph Mankiewicz
Co-stars: Katherine Hepburn Elizabeth Taylor Montgomery Clift

1960 CIMARRON
Director: Anthony Mann
Co-stars: Glenn Ford Maria Schell Anne Baxter

1960 ANGEL BABY
Director: Paul Wendkos
Co-stars: Salome Jens George Hamilton Joan Blondell

1971 THE PRESIDENT'S PLANE IS MISSING
Director: Daryl Duke
Co-stars: Buddy Ebsen Arthur Kennedy Rip Torn

1973 THE EXORCIST *(Voice)*
Director: William Friedkin
Co-stars: Ellen Burnstyn Max Von Sydow Linda Blair

1975 WHO IS THE BLACK DAHLIA?
Director: Joseph Pevney
Co-stars: Efrem Zimbzlist Jnr. Ronny Cox Tom Bosley

1979 AIRPORT 80: THE CONCORDE
Director: David Lowell Rich
Co-stars: Alain Delon George Kennedy Eddie Albert

MARIAN McCARGO

1969 THE UNDEFEATED
Director: Andrew McLaglen
Co-stars: John Wayne Rock Hudson Lee Meriwether

MOLLY McCART

1955 TEENAGE CRIME WAVE
Director: Fred Sears
Co-stars: Tommy Cook Sue English James Bell

ANNETTE McCARTHY

1981 CRAZY TIMES
Director: Lee Phillips
Co-stars: Michael Pare Ray Liotta David Caruso

HELENA McCARTHY

1989 ICE DANCE
Director: Alan Dossor
Co-stars: Andrew Fletcher Amanda Worthington Warren Clarke

JULIANNA McCARTHY

1990 THE FIRST POWER
Director: Robert Resnikoff
Co-stars: Lou Diamond Phillips Tracey Griffith

MOLLY McCARTHY

1984 THE FLAMINGO KID
Director: Garry Marshall
Co-stars: Matt Dillon Richard Crenna Jessica Walter

NOBU McCARTHY

1958 THE GEISHA BOY
Director: Frank Tashlin
Co-stars: Jerry Lewis Marie MacDonald Barton MacLane

1960 WALK LIKE A DRAGON
Director: James Clavell
Co-stars: Jack Lord Dan Mainwaring Mel Torme

1960 WAKE ME WHEN IT'S OVER
Director: Mervyn LeRoy
Co-stars: Dick Shawn Ernie Kovacs Jack Warden

1961 TWO LOVES
Director: Charles Walters
Co-stars: Shirley MacLaine Laurence Harvey Jack Hawkins

NYLA McCARTHY

1985 MALA NOCHE
Director: Gus Van Sant
Co-stars: Tim Strecter Doug Cooeyate Ray Monge

SHEILA McCARTHY

1987 I'VE HEARD THE MERMAIDS SINGING
Director: Patricia Rozema
Co-stars: Paule Baillargeon John Evans

1990 BRIGHT ANGEL
Director: Michael Fields
Co-stars: Dermot Mulroney Lili Taylor Sam Shepard

1990 DIE HARD 2
Director: Renny Harlin
Co-stars: Bruce Willis Bonnie Bedelia Franco Nero

1990 WHITE ROOM
Director: Patricia Rozema
Co-stars: Kate Nelligan Margot Kidder Maurice Godin

1991 STEPPING OUT
Director: Lewis Gilbert
Co-stars: Liza Minnelli Shelley Winters Julie Walters

1991 PARADISE
Director: Mary Agnes Donoghue
Co-stars: Melanie Griffith Elijah Wood Thora Birch

1992 BEAUTIFUL DREAMERS
Director: John Kent Harrison
Co-stars: Colm Feore Rip Torn Wendel Meldrum

AINE McCARTNEY

1987 THE VENUS DE MILO INSTEAD
Director: Danny Boyle
Co-stars: Jeananne Crowley Ann Hasson Trudy Kelly

LINDA McCARTNEY

1984 GIVE MY REGARDS TO BROAD STREET
Director: Peter Webb
Co-stars: Paul McCartney Bryan Brown Ringo Star

MARY McCARTY

1955 THE FRENCH LINE
Director: Lloyd Bacon
Co-stars: Jane Russell Gilbert Roland Arthur Hunnicutt

CONSTANCE McCASHIN

1984 OBSESSIVE LOVE
Director: Steven Hillard Stern
Co-stars: Yvette Mimieux Simon MacCorkindale Lainie Kazan

1985 LOVE ON THE RUN
Director: Gus Trikonis
Co-stars: Stephanie Zimbalist Alec Baldwin Howard Duff

1988 NIGHTMARE AT BITTER CREEK
Director: Tim Burstall
Co-stars: Lindsay Wagner Tom Skerritt Joanna Cassidy

1991 NAKED TANGO
Director: Leonard Schrader
Co-stars: Vincent D'Onoforio Mathilda May Fernado Rey

SAUNDRA McCLAIN

1990 CRIMINAL JUSTICE
Director: Andy Wolk
Co-stars: Forest Whittaker Jennifer Grey Rosie Perez

RUE McCLANAHAN

1972 THEY MIGHT BE GIANTS
Director: Anthony Harvey
Co-stars: George C.Scott Joanne Woodward

1978 RAINBOW
Director: Jackie Cooper
Co-stars: Andrea McArdle Don Murray Piper Laurie

1989 TAKE MY DAUGHTERS. PLEASE
Director: Larry Elikann
Co-stars: Kim Delaney Deirdre Hall Susan Ruttan

1990 CHILDREN OF THE BRIDE
Director: Jonathan Sanger
Co-star: Patrick Duffy

1990 MODERN LOVE
Director: Robby Benson
Co-stars: Robby Benson Karla De Vito Burt Reynolds Louise Lasser

1991 BABY OF THE BRIDE
Director: Bill Bixby
Co-stars: Kristy McNichol Ted Shackleford

1991 TO MY DAUGHTER
Director: Larry Shaw

1993 MOTHER OF THE BRIDE
Director: Charles Correll
Co-stars: Paul Dooley Kristy McNichol

CATHERINE McCLEMENTS

1990 WEEKEND WITH KATE
Director: Arch Nicholson
Co-stars: Colin Friels Jerome Ehlers Helen Mutkins

1992 REDHEADS
Director: Danny Vendramini
Co-stars: Claudia Karvan Sally McKenzie Alexander Petersons

LIBBY McCLINTOCK

1964 THE LUCK OF GINGER COFFEY
Director: Irving Kerschner
Co-stars: Robert Shaw Mary Ure Liam Redmond

JACQUELINE ALLAN McCLIVE

1973 ISN'T IT SHOCKING
Director: John Badham
Co-stars: Alan Alda Louise Lasser Edmond O'Brien

SUSAN McCLUNG

1977 BIRCH INTERVAL
Director: Delbert Mann
Co-stars: Eddie Albert Rip Torn Ann Wedgeworth

EDIE MCCLURG

1986 FERRIS BUELLER'S DAY OFF
Director: John Hughes
Co-stars: Matthew Broderick Alan Ruck Mia Sara

1989 ELVIRA, MISTRESS OF THE DARK
Director: James Signorelli
Co-stars: Cassandra Peterson Susan Kellerman

1989 THE LITTLE MERMAID (Voice)
Director: John Musker
Co-stars: Rene Auberjonois Buddy Hackett Jodi Benson

1991 CURLY SUE
Director: John Hughes
Co-stars: Kelly Lynch Alisan Porter James Belushi

1992 A RIVER RUNS THROUGH IT
Director: Robert Redford
Co-stars: Brad Pitt Craig Sheffer Emily Lloyd

JOYCE McCLUSKY

1955 THE NIGHT HOLDS TERROR
Director: Andrew Stone
Co-stars: Jack Kelly John Cassavetes Hildy Parks

HEATHER McCOMB

1989 NEW YORK STORIES
Director: Martin Scorsese
Co-stars: Nick Nolte Rosanna Arquette Mia Farrow

1992 STAY TUNED
Director: Peter Hyams
Co-stars: John Ritter Pam Dawber Jeffrey Jones

JUDY McCONNELL

1970 THE BROTHERHOOD OF SATAN
Director: Bernard McEveety
Co-stars: Strother Martin Alvy Moore Anna Capri

CATHERINE McCORMACK

1995 BRAVEHEART
Director: Mel Gibson
Co-star: Mel Gibson Patrick McGoohan Sophie Marceau

1996 DEACON BRODIE
Co-star: Billy Connolly

1996 LOADED
Director: Anna Campion

1996 THE HONEST COURTESAN
Director: Marshall Herskovitz
Co-stars: Rufus Sewell Jacqueline Bisset

1997 LAND GIRLS
Director: David Leland
Co-stars: Anna Friel Steven MacKintosh Rachel Weisz

MARY McCORMACK

1997 PRIVATE PARTS
Co-star: Howard Stern

PATTY McCORMACK (Child)

Nominated For Best Supporting Actress In 1956 For "The Bad Seed"

1956 THE BAD SEED
Director: Mervyn LeRoy
Co-stars: Nancy Kelly Eileen Heckart Henry Jones

1956 THE DAY THEY GAVE BABIES AWAY
Director: Allen Reisner
Co-stars: Glynis Johns Cameron Mitchell Hope Emerson

1958 KATHY O
Director: Jack Sher
Co-stars: Dan Duryea Jan Sterling Sam Levene

1960 THE ADVENTURES OF HUCKLEBERRY FINN
Director: Michael Curtiz
Co-stars: Eddie Hodges Archie Moore

1975 BUG
Director: Jeannot Szwarc
Co-stars: Bradford Dillman Joanna Miles Alan Fudge

PATRICIA McCORMACK

1983 NIGHT PARTNERS
Director: Noel Nosseck
Co-stars: Yvette Mimieux Diana Canova M.Emmet Walsh

1984 INVITATION TO HELL
Director: Wes Craven
Co-stars: Robert Urich Joanna Cassidy Susan Lucci

CAROLYN McCORMICK

1985 ENEMY MINE
Director: Wolfgang Petersen
Co-stars: Dennis Quaid Lou Gossett Jnr. Brian James

MEGAN McCORMICK

1968 GREETINGS
Director: Brian De Palma
Co-stars: Robert De Niro Jonathan Warden Gerrit Graham

EMER McCOURT

1990 RIFF-RAFF
Director: Ken Loach
Co-stars: Robert Carlyle Jimmy Coleman George Moss

1991 LONDON KILLS ME
Director: Hanif Kureishi
Co-stars: Justin Chadwick Fiona Shaw Brad Dourif

1996 BOSTON KICKOUT
Director: Paul Hill

JOAN McCRACKEN

1947 GOOD NEWS
Director: Charles Walters
Co-stars: June Allyson Peter Lawford Mel Torme

MARGIE McCRAE

1979 ALISON'S BIRTHDAY
Director: Ian Coughlan
Co-stars: Joanne Samuel Lou Brown Vincent Ball

JENNY McCRINDLE

1987 DOWN WHERE THE BUFFALO ROAM
Director: Ian Knox
Co-stars: Harvey Keitel Andrew Byatt Stella Gonet

1989 DREAM BABY
Director: Angela Pope
Co-stars: Kevin McNally Peter Capaldi Mandy Matthews

1991 JUTE CITY
Director: Stuart Orme
Co-stars: David O'Hara Joanna Roth John Sessions

HELEN McCRORY

1998 DAD SAVAGE
Director: Betsan Morris Evans
Co-star: Patrick Stewart

1998 THE JAMES GANG
Director: Mike Barker
Co-stars: John Hannah Jason Flemyng

JILL McCULLOUGH

1990 MY KINGDOM FOR A HORSE
Director: Barbara Rennie
Co-stars: Sean Bean Sheila Hancock Bryan Pringle

JULIE McCULLOUGH

1987 BIG BAD MAMA II
Director: Jim Wynorski
Co-stars: Angie Dickinson Robert Culp Bruce Glover

KIMBERLEY McCULLOUGH

1991   BUGSY
Director: Barry Levinson
Co-stars: Warren Beaty Annette Bening Harvey Keitel

1992   CONSENTING ADULTS
Director: Alan J.Pakula
Co-stars: Kevin Kline Mary Elizabeth Mastrantonio Kevin Spacey

MARY McCUSKER

1991   DREAMING
Director: Mike Alexander
Co-stars: Ewen Bremner Michael Carter Shirley Henderson

STELLA McCUSKER

1990   DEAR SARAH
Director: Frank Cvitanovich
Co-star: Barry McGovern Simon Chandler

DONNA McDANIEL

1984   HOLLYWOOD HOT TUBS
Director: Chuck Vincent
Co-stars: Michael Andrew Edy Williams Paul Gunning

ETTA McDANIEL

1936   THE LONELY TRAIL
Co-star: Ann Rutherford

1942   THE GREAT MAN'S LADY
Director: William Wellman
Co-stars: Barbara Stanwyck Joel McCrea Brian Donlevy

HATTIE McDANIEL
Oscar For Best Supporting Actress In 1939 For "Gone With The Wind"

1935   ALICE ADAMS
Director: George Stevens
Co-stars: Katharine Hepburn Fred MacMurray Charlie Grapewin

1935   CHINA SEAS
Director: Tay Garnett
Co-stars: Clark Gable Jean Harlow Wallace Beery

1935   THE LITTLE COLONEL
Director: David Butler
Co-stars: Shirley Temple Lionel Barrymore Bill Robinson

1935   MUSIC IS MAGIC
Director: George Marshall
Co-stars: Alice Faye Bebe Daniels Ray Walker

1936   SHOWBOAT
Director: James Whale
Co-stars: Irene Dunne Allan Jones Helen Morgan Paul Robeson

1936   THE BRIDE WALKS OUT
Director: Edward Small
Co-stars: Barbara Stanwyck Gene Raymond Robert Young

1936   CAN THIS BE DIXIE
Director: George Marshall
Co-stars: Jane Withers Slim Summerville Helen Wood

1937   NOTHING SACRED
Director: William Wellman
Co-stars: Carole Lombard Fredric March Walter Connolly

1938   BATTLE OF BROADWAY
Director: George Marshall
Co-stars: Victor McLaglen Brian Donlevy Gypsy Rose Lee

1938   CAREFREE
Director: Mark Sandrich
Co-stars: Fred Astaire Ginger Rogers Ralph Bellamy

1938   VIVACIOUS LADY
Director: George Stevens
Co-stars: James Stewart Ginger Rogers Charles Coburn

1938   THE MAD MISS MANTON
Director: Leigh Jason
Co-stars: Barbara Stanwyck Henry Fonda Sam Levene

1938   QUICK MONEY
Co-star: Fred Stone

1938   THE SHOPWORN ANGEL
Director: H.C.Potter
Co-stars: Margaret Sullavan James Stewart Walter Pidgeon

1939   ZENOBIA
Director: Gordon Douglas
Co-stars: Oliver Hardy Harry Langdon Jean Parker

1939   GONE WITH THE WIND
Director: Victor Fleming
Co-stars: Clark Gable Vivien Leigh Leslie Howard

1940   MARYLAND
Director: Henry King
Co-stars: John Payne Brenda Joyce Walter Brennan Fay Bainter

1941   THE GREAT LIE
Director: Edmund Goulding
Co-stars: Bette Davis George Brent Mary Astor

1941   AFFECTIONATELY YOURS
Director: Lloyd Bacon
Co-stars: Merle Oberon Dennis Morgan Rita Hayworth

1942   GEORGE WASHINGTON SLEPT HERE
Director: William Keighley
Co-stars: Jack Benny Ann Sheridan

1942   IN THIS OUR LIFE
Director: John Huston
Co-stars: Bette Davis George Brent Dennis Morgan

1942   THE MALE ANIMAL
Director: Elliott Nugent
Co-stars: Henry Fonda Olivia De Havilland Jack Carson

1943   JOHNNY COME LATELY
Director: William Howard
Co-stars: James Cagney Grace George Marjorie Main

1943   THANK YOUR LUCKY STARS
Director: David Butler
Co-stars: Eddie Cantor Bette Davis Dennis Morgan

1944   JANIE
Director: Michael Curtiz
Co-stars: Joyce Reynolds Robert Hutton Ann Harding

1944   SINCE YOU WENT AWAY
Director: John Cromwell
Co-stars: Claudette Colbert Jennifer Jones Robert Walker

1944   THREE IS A FAMILY
Director: Edward Ludwig
Co-stars: Charles Ruggles Fay Bainter Helen Broderick

1946   MARGIE
Director: Henry King
Co-stars: Jeanne Crain Glenn Langan Alan Young

1946   SONG OF THE SOUTH
Director: Harve Foster
Co-stars: Bobby Driscoll James Baskett Ruth Warwick

1946   JANIE GETS MARRIED
Director: Michael Curtiz
Co-stars: Joan Leslie Robert Hutton Edward Arnold

1947   THE FLAME
Director: John Auer
Co-stars: Vera Ralston John Carroll Broderick Crawford

1949   FAMILY HONEYMOON
Director: Claude Binyon
Co-stars: Claudette Colbert Fred MacMurray Gigi Perreau

FAITH McDEVITT

1992   CLAIRE OF THE MOON
Director: Nicole Conn
Co-stars: Trisha Todd Sheila Dickinson

RUTH McDEVITT

1961   THE PARENT TRAP
Director: David Swift
Co-stars: Hayley Mills Maureen O'Hara Brian Keith

1962   LOVE IS A BALL
Director: David Swift
Co-stars: Glenn Ford Charles Boyer Hope Lange

1964   DEAR HEART
Director: Delbert Mann
Co-stars: Glenn Ford Geraldine Page Angela Lansbury

1967   THE SHAKIEST GUN IN THE WEST
Director: Alan Rafkin
Co-stars: Don Knotts Barbara Rhodes Jackie Coogan

ANN-MARIE McDONALD

1987   I'VE HEARD THE MERMAIDS SINGING
Director: Particia Rozema
Co-stars: Sheila McCarthy Paule Baillargeon

DENISE McDONALD

1989   GOVAN GHOST STORY
Director: David Hayman
Co-stars: Tom Watson Fletcher Mathers Julia Wallace

DOLETTE McDONALD

1985   BRING ON THE NIGHT
Director: Michael Apted
Co-stars: Sting Omar Hakim Darryl Jones

JULIE McDONALD

1991   DECEMBER BRIDE
Director: Thaddeus O'Sullivan
Co-stars: Donal McCann Saskia Reeves Brenda Bruce

KIM McDONALD

1971   THE JOHNSTOWN MONSTER
Director: Olaf Pooley
Co-stars: Connor Brennan Simon Tully Rory Bailey

MARIE McDONALD

1942   LUCKY JORDAN
Director: Frank Tuttle
Co-stars: Alan Ladd Helen Walker Sheldon Leonard

1943   A SCREAM IN THE DARK
Director: George Sherman
Co-stars: Robert Lowery Wally Vernon Jack La Rue

1944   GUEST IN THE HOUSE
Director: John Brahm
Co-stars: Anne Baxter Ralph Bellamy Aline MacMahon

1945   GETTING GERTIE'S GARTER
Director: Allan Dwan
Co-stars: Dennis O'Keefe Binnie Barnes Barry Sullivan

1945   IT'S A PLEASURE
Director: William Seiter
Co-stars: Sonja Henie Michael O'Shea Bill Johnson

1947   LIVING IN A BIG WAY
Director: Gregory La Cava
Co-stars: Gene Kelly Charles Winninger Phyllis Thaxter

1949   TELL IT TO THE JUDGE
Director: Norman Foster
Co-stars: Rosalind Russell Robert Cummings Gig Young

1952   THE STOOGE
Director: Norman Taurog
Co-stars: Dean Martin Jerry Lewis Polly Bergen

1958   THE GEISHA BOY
Director: Frank Tashlin
Co-stars: Jerry Lewis Barton MacLane Suzanne Pleshette

MARY McDONNELL
Nominated For Best Supporting Actress In 1990 For "Dances With Wolves". Nominated For Best Actress In 1993 For "Passion Fish"

1984   GARBO TALKS
Director: Sidney Lumet
Co-stars: Anne Bancroft Ron Silver Carrie Fisher

1987   MATEWAN
Director: John Sayles
Co-stars: Chris Cooper Will Oldham James Earl Jones

1988   TIGER WARSAW
Director: Amin Chaudhri
Co-stars: Patrick Swayze Barbara Williams Piper Laurie

1990   DANCES WITH WOLVES
Director: Kevin Costner
Co-stars: Kevin Costner Graham Greene Maury Chaykin

1991   GRAND CANYON
Director: Lawrence Kasdan
Co-stars: Kevin Kline Danny Glover Steve Martin

1992   SNEAKERS
Director: Phil Alden Robinson
Co-stars: Robert Redford Ben Kingsley Sidney Poitier

1993   ARTHUR MILLER'S AMERICAN CLOCK
Director: Bob Clark
Co-stars: Darren McGavin Kelly Preston Eddie Bracken

1993   PASSION FISH
Director: John Sayles
Co-stars: Alfre Woodard David Strathairn Angela Bassett

1994   BLUE CHIPS
Director: William Friedkin
Co-stars: Nick Nolte J.T.Walsh Ed O'Neill

1995   WOMAN UNDONE
Director: Evelyn Purcell
Co-stars: Randy Quaid Sam Elliott

1996   INDEPENDANCE DAY
Director: Roland Emmerich
Co-stars: Bill Pullman Jeff Goldblum Randy Quaid

MARY BETH McDONOUGH

1971   THE HOMECOMING: A CHRISTMAS STORY
Director: Fielder Cook
Co-stars: Richard Thomas Andrew Duggan Patricia Neal

1982   MOTHER'S DAY ON WALTON'S MOUNTAIN
Director: Gwen Arner
Co-stars: Ralph Waite Michael Learned Eric Scott

1982   A WEDDING ON WALTON'S MOUNTAIN
Director: Lee Phillips
Co-stars: Ralph Waite Jon Walmsley Eric Scott

1982   A DAY FOR THANKS ON WALTON'S MOUNTAIN
Director: Harry Harris
Co-stars: Ralph Waite Ellen Corby Judy Norton-Taylor

FRANCES McDORMAND *(Married Joel Cohen)*
Nominated For Best Supporting Actress In 1988 For "Mississippi Burning". Oscar For Best Actress In 1996 For "Fargo"

1983 BLOOD SIMPLE
Director: Joel Cohen
Co-stars: John Getz Tommy Rettig Dan Hedaya

1985 SCANDAL SHEET
Director: David Lowell Rich
Co-stars: Burt Lancaster Pamela Reed Robert Urich

1987 RAISING ARIZONA
Director: Joel Cohen
Co-stars: Holly Hunter Nicolas Cage John Goodman

1988 MISSISSIPPI BURNING
Director: Alan Parker
Co-stars: Gene Hackman Willem Dafoe Brad Dourif

1990 MILLER'S CROSSING
Director: Joel Cohen
Co-stars: Albert Finney Gabriel Byrne Marcia Gay Harden

1990 HIDDEN AGENDA
Director: Ken Loach
Co-stars: Brian Cox Brad Dourif Mai Zetterling

1990 DARKMAN
Director: Sam Raimi
Co-stars: Liam Neesen Colin Friels Larry Drake

1990 CHATTAHOOCHEE
Director: Mick Jackson
Co-stars: Gary Oldman Dennis Hopper Pamela Reed

1991 THE BUTCHER'S WIFE
Director: Terry Hughes
Co-stars: Demi Moore George Dzundza Jeff Daniels

1992 CRAZY IN LOVE
Director: Martha Coolidge
Co-stars: Holly Hunter Bill Pullman Julian Sands

1993 SHORT CUTS
Director: Robert Altman
Co-stars: Matthew Modine Anne Archer Andie MacDowell

1995 BEYOND RANGOON
Director: John Boorman
Co-stars: Patricia Arquette Spalding Gray

1996 LONE STAR
Director: John Sayles
Co-stars: Kris Kristofferson Elizabeth Pena Chris Cooper

1996 FARGO
Director: Joel Cohen
Co-stars: William H.Macy Steve Buscemi Harve Presnell

1997 PARADISE ROAD
Director: Bruce Beresford
Co-stars: Glenn Close Pauline Collins Jennifer Ehle

1997 PALOOKAVILLE
Director: Alan Taylor
Co-stars: Vincent Gallo William Forsythe

VIRGINIA McDOWALL

1949 THE FAN
Director: Otto Preminger
Co-stars: Jeanne Crain Madeleine Carroll George Sanders

BETTY McDOWELL

1957 TIME LOCK
Director: Gerald Thomas
Co-stars: Robert Beatty Lee Patterson Vincent Winter

1958 JACK THE RIPPER
Director: Monty Berman
Co-stars: Ewen Solon Lee Patterson Eddie Byrne

1960 DEAD LUCKY
Director: Montgomery Tully
Co-stars: Vincent Ball Alfred Burke Sam Kydd

1961 SPARE THE ROD
Director: Leslie Norman
Co-stars: Max Bygraves Gregory Keen Donald Pleasence

1963 ECHO OF DIANA
Director: Ernest Morris
Co-stars: Vincent Ball Geoffrey Toone Clare Owen

1964 FIRST MEN IN THE MOON
Director: Nathan Juran
Co-stars: Lionel Jeffries Edward Judd Martha Hyer

1964 BALLAD IN BLUE
Director: Paul Henreid
Co-stars: Ray Charles Mary Peach Dawn Addams

CLAIRE McDOWELL

1925 THE TOWER OF LIES
Director: Victor Seastrom
Co-stars: Norma Shearer Lon Chaney Ian Keith

1925 THE BIG PARADE
Director: King Vidor
Co-stars: John Gilbert Renee Adoree Claire Adams

1926 BEN HUR
Director: Fred Niblo
Co-stars: Ramon Navarro Carmel Myers May McAvoy

1930 THE SECOND FLOOR MYSTERY
Director: Roy Del Ruth
Co-stars: Loretta Young Grant Withers John Loder

1930 BROTHERS
Co-star: Bert Lytell

1931 AN AMERICAN TRAGEDY
Director: Josef Von Sternberg
Co-stars: Phillips Holmes Sylvia Sidney Frances Dee

ELLEN McELDUFF

1986 MAXIMUM OVERDRIVE
Director: Stephen King
Co-stars: Emilio Estevez Pat Hingle Laura Harrington

1986 WORKING GIRLS
Director: Lizzie Borden
Co-stars: Louise Smith Amanda Goodwin Janne Peters

NATASCHA McELHONE

1996 SURVIVING PICASSO
Director: James Ivory
Co-stars: Anthony Hopkins Julianne Moore

1996 MRS. DALLOWAY
Director: Meleen Goris
Co-stars: Vanessa Redgrave Rupert Graves

1997 THE DEVIL'S OWN
Director: Alan J.Pakula
Co-stars: Brad Pitt Harrison Ford Margaret Colin

ANNIE McENROE

1981 BATTLETRUCK
Director: Harley Cokliss
Co-stars: Michael Beck James Wainwright John Bach

1981 THE HAND
Director: Oliver Stone
Co-stars: Michael Caine Andrea Marcovici Viveca Lindfors

1983 THE SURVIVORS
Director: Michael Ritchie
Co-stars: Walter Matthau Robin Williams Jerry Reed

1985 HOWLING II: YOUR SISTER IS A WEREWOLF
Director: Philippe Mora
Co-stars: Christopher Lee Ferdy Mayne

1986 TRUE STORIES: A FILM ABOUT A GROUP OF PEOPLE IN VIRGIL, TEXAS
Director: David Byrne
Co-stars: David Byrne Alix Elias John Goodman

REBA McENTIRE

1990 TREMORS
Director: Ron Underwood
Co-stars: Kevin Bacon Fred Ward Finn Carter

1991 THE GAMBLER RETURNS: THE LUCK OF THE DRAW
Director: Dick Lowry
Co-stars: Kenny Rogers Mickey Rooney

1995 BUFFALO GIRLS
Co-stars: Angelica Huston Melanie Griffith Gabriel Byrne

GERALDINE McEWAN

1969 THE DANCE OF DEATH
Director: David Giles
Co-stars: Laurence Olivier Robert Lang Carolyn Jones

1976 ESCAPE FROM THE DARK
Director: Charles Jarrott
Co-stars: Alastair Sim Prunella Scales Leslie Sands

1976 THE BAWDY ADVENTURES OF TOM JONES
Director: Cliff Owen
Co-stars: Nicky Henson Trevor Howard Joan Collins

1986 FOREIGN BODY
Director: Ronald Neame
Co-stars: Victor Banerjee Warren Mitchell Anna Massey

1989 HENRY V
Director: Kenneth Branagh
Co-stars: Derek Jacobi Judi Dench Simon Shepherd

1989 ORANGES ARE NOT THE ONLY FRUIT
Director: Beeban Kidron
Co-stars: Emily Aston Charlotte Coleman

1991 ROBIN HOOD, PRINCE OF THIEVES
Director: Kevin Reynolds
Co-stars: Kevin Costner Morgan Freeman Alan Rickman

1992 CONTINENTAL DRIFT
Director: Andrei Nekrasov
Co-stars: Christopher Eccleston Adie Allen

STEPHANIE McFADDEN (child)

1992 LOVE FIELD
Director: Jonathan Kaplan
Co-stars: Michelle Pfeiffer Dennis Haysbert Brian Kerwin

VONETTA McGEE

1967 THE BIG SILENCE
Director: Sergio Corbucci
Co-stars: Jean-Louis Trintignant Klaus Kinski

1972 BLACKULA
Director: William Crain
Co-stars: William Marshall Denise Nicholas Gordon Pinsent

1973 SHAFT IN AFRICA
Director: John Guillermin
Co-stars: Richard Roundtree Frank Finlay Cy Grant

1975 THE EIGER SANCTION
Director: Clint Eastwood
Co-stars: Clint Eastwood George Kennedy Jack Cassidy Heide Bruhl

1977 BROTHERS
Director: Arthur Barron
Co-stars: Bernie Casey Ron O'Neal Renny Roker

1984 REPO MAN
Director: Alex Cox
Co-stars: Harry Dean Stanton Emilio Estevez Olivia Barash

1990 TO SLEEP WITH ANGER
Co-stars: Charles Burnett
Co-stars: Danny Glover Paul Butler Mary Alice

1996 THE MAN NEXT DOOR
Director: Lamont Johnson
Co-stars: Michael Ontkean Pamela Reed Annette O'Toole

BETH McGEE-RUSSELL

1990 THE LADY IN WAITING
Director: Christian Taylor
Co-stars: Virginia McKenna Rodney Hudson Emma Wilson

GLORIA McGILL

1956 THE BOSS
Director: Byron Haskin
Co-stars: John Payne William Bishop Doe Avedon

CAROLE McGILL

1984 CITY GIRL
Director: Martha Coolridge
Co-stars: Laura Harrington Joe Mastroianni Peter Riegert

MOYNA McGILL

1944 FRENCHMAN'S CREEK
Director: Mitchell Leisen
Co-stars: Joan Fontaine Arturo De Cordova Basil Rathbone

1949 PRIVATE ANGELO
Director: Peter Ustinov
Co-stars: Peter Ustinov Godfrey Tearle Robin Bailey

KELLY McGILLIS

1982 REUBEN, REUBEN
Director: Robert Ellis Miller
Co-stars: Tom Conti Roberts Blossom

1985 WITNESS
Director: Peter Weir
Co-stars: Harrison Ford Lukas Haas Josef Sommer

1985 PRIVATE SESSIONS
Director: Michael Pressman
Co-stars: Mike Farrell Maureen Stapleton Hope Lange

1986 TOP GUN
Director: Tony Scott
Co-stars: Tom Cruise Val Kilmer Tom Skerritt

1987 MADE IN HEAVEN
Director: Alan Rudolph
Co-stars: Timothy Hutton Don Murray Debra Winger

1988 THE HOUSE ON CARROLL STREET
Director: Peter Yates
Co-stars: Jeff Daniels Mandy Patinkin Jessica Tandy

1988 ACCUSED
Director: Jonathan Kaplan
Co-stars: Jodie Foster Bernie Coulson

1989 CAT CHASER
Director: Abel Ferrara
Co-stars: Peter Weller Frederic Forrest Phil Leeds

1989 WINTER PEOPLE
Director: Ted Kotcheff
Co-stars: Kurt Russell Lloyd Bridges Mitchell Ryan

1991 GRAND ISLE
Director: Mary Lambert
Co-stars: Adrian Pasdar Ellen Burstyn Glenne Headley

1995 REMEMBER ME
Director: Michael Switzer

CAROL McGINNIS

1976 GABLE AND LOMBARD
Director: Sidney Furie
Co-stars: James Brolin Jill Clayburgh Allen Garfield

CHARLOTTE McGINNIS

1986 REFORM SCHOOL GIRLS
Director: Tom De Simone
Co-stars: Linda Carol Sybil Danning Pat Ast

MAURA McGIVENEY

1965 DO NOT DISTURB
Director: Ralph Levy
Co-stars: Doris Day Rod Taylor Reginald Gardiner

ELIZABETH McGOVERN

1980 ORDINARY PEOPLE
Director: Robert Redford
Co-stars: Donald Sutherland Mary Tyler Moore Judd Hirsch

1981 RAGTIME
Director: Milos Forman
Co-stars: James Cagney Pat O'Brien Mary Steenburgen

1983 LOVESICK
Director: Marshall Brickman
Co-stars: Dudley Moore Alec Guinness John Huston

1984 ONCE UPON A TIME IN AMERICA
Director: Sergio Leone
Co-stars: Robert De Niro James Woods Tuesday Weld

1984 RACING WITH THE MOON
Director: Richard Benjamin
Co-stars: Sean Penn Nicolas Cage Rutanya Alda

1986 NATIVE SON
Director: Jerrold Freedman
Co-stars: Carroll Baker Matt Dillon Geraldine Page

1986 THE BEDROOM WINDOW
Director: Curtis Hanson
Co-stars: Steve Guttenburg Isabelle Huppert Paul Shenar

1988 SHE'S HAVING A BABY
Director: John Hughes
Co-stars: Kevin Bacon Alec Baldwin William Windom

1989 JOHNNY HANDSOME
Director: Walter Hill
Co-stars: Mickey Rourke Ellen Barkin Morgan Freeman

1990 THE HANDMAID'S TALE
Director: Volker Schlondorff
Co-stars: Natasha Richardson Robert Duvall Faye Dunaway

1990 A SHOCK TO THE SYSTEM
Director: Jan Egleson
Co-stars: Michael Caine Swoosie Kurtz Will Patton

1990 WOMEN AND MEN: STORIES OF SEDUCTION
Director: Tony Richardson
Co-stars: Molly Ringwald Beau Bridges James Woods

1990 AUNT JULIA AND THE SCRIPTWRITER
Director: Jon Amiel
Co-stars: Barbara Hershey Keanu Reeves Peter Falk

1993 KING OF THE HILL
Director: Steven Soderberg
Co-stars: Jesse Bradford Jeroen Krabbe Lisa Eichhorn

1994 THE FAVOR
Director: Donald Petrie
Co-stars: Bill Pullman Harley Jane Kozac

ROSE McGOWAN

1998 NOWHERE
Director: Gregg Araki
Co-stars: Shannen Doherty Traci Lords

ERIN McGRANE

1993 DETOUR
Director: Wade Williams
Co-stars: Tom Neal Jnr. Lea Lavish Susanna Foster

LEUEEN McGRATH

1938 PYGMALION
Director: Anthony Asquith
Co-stars: Leslie Howard Wendy Hiller Wilfrid Lawson

1940 THE SAINT'S VACATION
Director: Leslie Fenton
Co-stars: Hugh Sinclair Sally Gray Cecil Parker

1949 EDWARD MY SON
Director: George Cukor
Co-stars: Spencer Tracy Deborah Kerr Ian Hunter

1954 THREE CASES OF MURDER
Director: Wendy Toye
Co-stars: Alan Badel Orson Welles Elizabeth Sellars

MARGARET McGRATH

1943 SCHWEIK'S NEW ADVENTURES
Director: Karel Lamac
Co-stars: Lloyd Pearson George Carney Richard Attenborough

RUTH McGUIGAN

1987 THE VENUS DE MILO INSTEAD
Director: Danny Boyle
Co-stars: Jeananne Crowley Ann Hasson Trudy Kelly

DOROTHY McGUIRE
Nominated For Best Actress In 1947 For "Gentleman's Agreement"

1943 CLAUDIA
Director: Edmound Goulding
Co-stars: Robert Young Ina Clare Reginald Gardiner

1945 THE ENCHANTED COTTAGE
Director: John Cromwell
Co-stars: Robert Young Herbert Marshall Mildred Natwick

1945 A TREE GROWS IN BROOKLYN
Director: Elia Kazan
Co-stars: Peggy Ann Garner James Dunn Joan Blondell

1946 CLAUDIA AND DAVID
Director: Walter Lang
Co-stars: Robert Young Mary Astor John Sutton

1946 TILL THE END OF TIME
Director: Edward Dmytryk
Co-stars: Guy Maddison Robert Mitchum Bill Williams

1946 THE SPIRAL STAIRCASE
Director: Robert Siodmak
Co-stars: George Brent Ethel Barrymore Kent Smith

1947 A GENTLEMAN'S AGREEMENT
Director: Elia Kazan
Co-stars: Gregory Peck John Garfield Celeste Holm

1950 MOTHER DIDN'T TELL ME
Director: Claude Binyon
Co-stars: William Lundigan June Havoc Gary Merrill

1950 **MISTER 880**
Director: Edmund Goulding
Co-stars: Edmund Gwenn Burt Lancaster Millard Mitchell

1951 **I WANT YOU**
Director: Mark Robson
Co-stars: Dana Andrews Farley Granger Peggy Dow

1951 **CALLAWAY WENT THATAWAY**
Director: Melvyn Frank
Co-stars: Howard Keal Fred MacMurray Jesse White

1952 **INVITATION**
Director: Gottfried Reinhardt
Co-stars: Van Johnson Louis Calhern Ruth Roman

1954 **MAKE HASTE TO LIVE**
Director: William Seiter
Co-stars: Stephen McNally Mary Murphy John Howard

1954 **THREE COINS IN THE FOUNTAIN**
Director: Jean Negulesco
Co-stars: Clifton Webb Jean Peters Louis Jourdan

1955 **TRIAL**
Director: Mark Robson
Co-stars: Glenn Ford Arthur Kennedy John Hodiak

1956 **FRIENDLY PERSUASION**
Director: William Wyler
Co-stars: Gary Cooper Anthony Perkins Marjorie Main

1957 **OLD YELLER**
Director: Robert Stevenson
Co-stars: Fess Parker Tommy Kirk Chuck Connors

1959 **THE REMARKABLE MR. PENNYPACKER**
Director: Henry Levin
Co-stars: Clifton Webb Charles Coburn Jill St. John

1959 **A SUMMER PLACE**
Director: Delmer Daves
Co-stars: Richard Egan Sandra Dee Arthur Kennedy

1959 **THIS EARTH IS MINE**
Director: Henry King
Co-stars: Jean Simmons Rock Hudson Claude Rains

1960 **THE SWISS FAMILY ROBINSON**
Director: Ken Annakin
Co-stars: John Mills Tommy Kirk Janet Munro

1960 **THE DARK AT THE TOP OF THE STAIRS**
Director: Delbert Mann
Co-stars: Robert Preston Shirley Knight

1961 **SUSAN SLADE**
Director: Delmer Daves
Co-stars: Connie Stevens Troy Donahue Brain Aherne

1963 **SUMMER MAGIC**
Director: James Neilson
Co-stars: Hayley Mills Burl Ives Darren McGavin

1965 **THE GREATEST STORY EVER TOLD**
Director: George Stevens
Co-stars: Max Von Sydow Charlton Heston

1971 **FLIGHT OF THE DOVES**
Director: Ralph Nelson
Co-stars: Jack Wild Helen Raye Ron Moody

1973 **JONATHAN LIVINGSTON SEAGULL** (*Voice*)
Director: Hall Bartlett
Co-stars: Richard Crenna Kelly Harmon James Franciscus

1975 **THE RUNAWAYS**
Director: Harry Harris
Co-stars: Van Williams John Randolph Neva Patterson

1978 **LITTLE WOMEN**
Director: David Lowell
Co-stars: Greer Garson Robert Young Susan Dey

1983 **GHOST DANCING**
Director: David Greene
Co-stars: Bruce Davison Bo Hopkins Richard Farnsworth

1985 **AMOS**
Director: Michael Tuchner
Co-stars: Kirk Douglas Elizabeth Montgomery

1990 **THE LAST BEST YEAR**
Director: John Erman
Co-stars: Mary Tyler Moore Bernadette Peters Kate Reid

1990 **CAROLINE ?**
Director: Joseph Sargent
Co-stars: Stephanie Zimbalist Pamela Reed Patricia Neal

KATHRYN McGUIRE

1924 **SHERLOCK JUNIOR**
Director: Buster Keaton
Co-stars: Buster Keaton Ward Crane Joseph Keaton

1924 **THE NAVIGATOR**
Director: Donald Crisp
Co-star: Buster Keaton

1960 **THE SIEGE OF SIDNEY STREET**
Director: Monty Berman
Co-stars: Donald Sinden Peter Wyngarde Kieron Moore

MARCY McGUIRE

1942 **SEVEN DAYS LEAVE**
Director: Tim Whelan
Co-stars: Lucille Ball Victor Mature Ginny Sims

1943 **HIGHER AND HIGHER**
Director: Tim Whelan
Co-stars: Michele Morgan Frank Sinatra Jack Haley

1947 **IT HAPPENED IN BROOKLYN**
Director: Richard Whorf
Co-stars: Frank Sinatra Kathryn Grayson Peter Lawford

AISLIN McGUCKIN

1997 **TROJAN EDDIE**
Director: Gilles MacKinnon
Co-stars: Stephen Rea Richard Harris Stuart Townsend

ROSEMARY McHALE

1988 **THE RETURN OF SHERLOCK HOLMES: THE HOUND OF THE BASKERVILLES**
Director: Brian Mills
Co-star: Jeremy Brett Edward Hardwicke

1991 **A TIME TO DANCE**
Director: Kevin Billington
Co-stars: Ronald Pickup Dervla Kirwan Annie Raitt

LIZZIE McINNERNY

1994 **AN EVENING WITH GARY LINEKER**
Director: Andy Wilson
Co-stars: Caroline Quentin Clive Owen Paul Merton

1987 **ROWING WITH THE WIND**
Director: Gonzalo Suarez
Co-stars: Hugh Grant Elizabeth Hurley Valentine Pelka

MARY McINNES

1987 **THE SHUTTER FALLS**
Director: Peter Barber-Fleming
Co-stars: Anthony Higgins Emer Gillespie Stella Gonet

ELLEN McINTOSH

1963 **THE GIRL ON APPROVAL**
Director: Charles Frend
Co-stars: Rachel Roberts James Maxwell Annette Whitley

1964 THE SILENT PLAYGROUND
Director: Stanley Goulder
Co-stars: Roland Curram Bernard Archard Jean Anderson

JUDY McINTOSH

1989 THE GRASSCUTTER
Director: Ian Mune
Co-stars: Ian McElhinney Frances Barber Martin Maguire

1994 EBB TIDE

ARLENE McINTYRE *(Child)*

1983 MAN, WOMAN AND CHILD
Director: Dick Richards
Co-stars: Martin Sheen Blythe Danner David Hemmings

CHRISTINE McINTYRE

1938 THE RANGERS ROUNDUP
Co-stars: Fred Scott Al St. John

1938 SONGS AND BULLETS
Co-star: Fred Scott

1941 THE GUNMAN FROM BODIE
Co-stars: Buck Jones Dave O'Brien

1944 WEST OF THE RIO GRANDE
Co-stars: Johnny Mack Brown Raymond Hatton

LEILA McINTYRE

1939 THE HOUSEKEEPER'S DAUGHTER
Director: Hal Roach
Co-stars: Joan Bennett John Hubbard Adolphe Menjou

PEGGY McINTRYE

1948 I REMEMBER MAMA
Director: George Stevens
Co-stars: Irene Dunne Barbara Bel Geddes Oscar Homolka

GLENDA McKAY

1989 THE RAINBOW
Director: Ken Russell
Co-stars: Sammi Davis Amanda Donohue Paul McGann

WANDA McKAY

1942 BOWERY AT MIDNIGHT
Director: Wallace Fox
Co-stars: Bela Lugosi John Archer Tom Neal

1944 THE MONSTER MAKER
Director: Sam Newfield
Co-stars: Ralph Morgan J.Carrol Naish Glenn Strange

1944 VOODOO MAN
Director: William Beaudine
Co-stars: Bela Lugosi John Carradine George Zucco

1945 THERE GOES KELLY
Co-stars: Jackie Moran Sidney Miller

1945 HOLLYWOOD AND VINE
Director: Alexis Thurn-Taxis
Co-stars: James Ellison June Clyde Ralph Morgan

1947 KILROY WAS HERE
Director: Phil Karlson
Co-stars: Jackie Cooper Jackie Googan Frank Jenks

1948 CHARLIE CHAN AND THE GOLDEN EYE
Director: William Beaudine
Co-stars: Roland Winters Tim Ryan Evelyn Brent

GINA McKEE

1988 THE LAIR OF THE WHITE WORM
Director: Ken Russell
Co-stars: Amanda Donohue Hugh Grant Sammi Davis

1990 HE'S ASKING FOR ME
Director: Vitold Starecki
Co-stars: Maggie O'Neill David Threlfall Marian McLoughlin

1996 ELEMENT OF DOUBT
Director: Christopher Morahan
Co-star: Nigel Havers

1997 MOTHERTIME
Director: Matthew Jacobs
Co-stars: Kate Maberley Imogen Stubbs Anthony Andrews

LONETTE McKEE

1985 BREWSTER'S MILLIONS
Director: Walter Hill
Co-stars: Richard Pryor John Candy Pat Hingle

1986 ROUND MIDNIGHT
Director: Bertrand Tavernier
Co-stars: Dexter Gordon Francois Cluzet Martin Scorsese

1991 JUNGLE FEVER
Director: Spike Lee
Co-stars: Spike Lee Wesley Snipes Annabella Sciorra Ruby Dee

1992 MALCOLM X
Director: Spike Lee
Co-stars: Denzel Washington Spike Lee Angela Bassett

DOROTHY McKEGG

1979 MIDDLE AGE SPREAD
Director: John Reid
Co-stars: Grant Tlly Donna Akersten Bridget Armstrong

DANICAR McKELLAR

1993 SIDEKICKS
Director: Aaron Norris
Co-stars: Chuck Norris Beau Bridges Julia Nickson-Soul

1994 CRADLE OF CONSPIRACY
Director: Gabrielle Beaumont
Co-stars: Dee Wallace Stone

MAXINE McKENDRY

1974 ANDY WARHOL'S DRACULA
Director: Paul Morrissey
Co-stars: Udo Kier Joe Dallesandro Vittoria De Sica

ALEX McKENNA

1996 THE STUPIDS
Director: John Landis
Co-stars: Tom Arnold Bug Hall

BREFFNI McKENNA

1989 CHINESE WHISPERS
Director: Stuart Burge
Co-stars: Niall Buggy Gary Waldhorn Annette Badland

1991 MURDER IN EDEN
Director: Nicholas Renton
Co-stars: Peter Firth Tony Doyle Alun Armstrong

SIOBHAN McKENNA

1946 HUNGRY HILL
Director: Brian Desmond Hurst
Co-stars: Margaret Lockwood Dennis Price Michael Dennison

1948 DAUGHTER OF DARKNESS
Director: Lance Comfort
Co-stars: Anne Crawford Maxwell Reed Honor Blackman

1949 THE LOST PEOPLE
Director: Bernard Knowles
Co-stars: Richard Attenborough Mai Zetterling Dennis Price

1952	**THE ADVENTURERS**	
Director:	David MacDonald	
Co-stars:	Dennis Price Jack Hawkins Peter Hammond	

1952   **THE ADVENTURERS**
Director: David MacDonald
Co-stars: Dennis Price Jack Hawkins Peter Hammond

1961   **KING OF KINGS**
Director: Nicholas Ray
Co-stars: Jefffrey Hunter Robert Ryan Rita Gam

1964   **OF HUMAN BONDAGE**
Director: Henry Hathaway
Co-stars: Kim Novak Laurence Harvey Nanette Newman

1965   **DOCTOR ZHIVAGO**
Director: David Lean
Co-stars: Omar Sharif Julie Christie Rod Steiger

1984   **MEMED MY HAWK**
Director: Peter Ustinov
Co-stars: Peter Ustinov Herbert Lom Dennis Quilley

VIRGINIA McKENNA *(Married Bill Travers)*

1952   **THE ORACLE**
Director: C..M.Pennington-Richards
Co-stars: Robert Beatty Mervyn Johns

1952   **THE SECOND MRS. TANQUERAY**
Director: Dallas Bower
Co-stars: Pamela Brown Hugh Sinclair Ronald Ward

1953   **THE CRUEL SEA**
Director: Charles Frend
Co-stars: Jack Hawkins Donald Sinden Stanley Baker

1955   **THE SHIP THAT DIED OF SHAME**
Director: Basil Dearden
Co-stars: Richard Attenborough George Baker

1955   **SIMBA**
Director: Brian Desmond Hurst
Co-stars: Dirk Bogarde Donald Sinden Stanley Baker

1956   **A TOWN LIKE ALICE**
Director: Jack Lee
Co-stars: Peter Finch Maureen Swanson Jean Anderson

1957   **THE BARRETTS OF WIMPOLE STREET**
Director: Sidney Franklin
Co-stars: Jennifer Jones Bill Travers

1957   **THE SMALLEST SHOW ON EARTH**
Director: Basil Dearden
Co-stars: Bill Travers Peter Sellers Bernard Miles

1958   **PASSIONATE SUMMER**
Director: Rudolph Cartier
Co-stars: Bill Travers Yvonne Mitchell Alexander Knox

1958   **CARVE HER NAME WITH PRIDE**
Director: Lewis Gilbert
Co-stars: Paul Scofield Jack Warner Sidney Tafler

1959   **THE WRECK OF THE MARY DEARE**
Director: Michael Anderson
Co-stars: Gary Cooper Charlton Heston Alexander Knox

1965   **BORN FREE**
Director: James Hill
Co-stars: Bill Travers Geoffrey Keen

1969   **RING OF BRIGHT WATER**
Director: Jack Couffer
Co-stars: Bill Travers Peter Jefffrey Roddy McMillan

1971   **WATERLOO**
Director: Sergei Bondarchuk
Co-stars: Rod Steiger Christopher Plummer Orson Welles

1974   **SWALLOWS AND AMAZONS**
Director: Claude Whatham
Co-stars: Ronald Fraser Simon West

1977   **HOLOCAUST 2000**
Director: Alberto De Martino
Co-stars: Kirk Douglas Simon Ward Anthony Quayle

1977   **THE DISAPPEARANCE**
Director: Stuart Cooper
Co-stars: Donald Sutherland David Hemmings David Warner

1990   **THE LADY IN WAITING**
Director: Christian Taylor
Co-stars: Rodney Hudson Beth McGee-Russell

1991   **THE CAMOMILE LAWN**
Director: Peter Hall
Co-stars: Jennifer Ehle Tara Fitzgerald Oliver Cotton

1994   **STAGGERED**
Director: Martin Clunes
Co-stars: Martin Clunes Michael Praed Griff Rhys Jones Sylvia Syms

FAY McKENZIE

1940   **DEATH RIDES THE RANGE**
Co-stars: Ken Maynard Charles King

1941   **SIERRA SUE**
Co-stars: Gene Autry Smiley Burnette

1941   **DOWN MEXICO WAY**
Director: Joseph Santley
Co-stars: Gene Autry Smiley Burnette Harold Huber

1942   **COWBOY SERENADE**
Co-stars: Gene Autry Smiley Burnette Cecil Cunningham

1944   **THE SINGING SHERIFF**
Co-stars: Bob Crosby Andrew Tombes

1968   **THE PARTY**
Director: Blake Edwards
Co-stars: Peter Sellers Claudine Longet Marge Champion

JACQUELINE McKENZIE

1992   **ROMPER STOMPER**
Director: Geoffrey Wright
Co-stars: Russell Crowe Daniel Pollack

1996   **MR. RELIABLE**
Director: Nadia Tass
Co-stars: Colin Friels Paul Sonkkila

JOYCE McKENZIE

1953   **TARZAN AND THE SHE-DEVIL**
Director: Kurt Neuman
Co-stars: Lex Barker Raymond Burr Tom Conway

JULIA McKENZIE

1986   **HOTEL DU LAC**
Director: Giles Foster
Co-stars: Anna Massey Denhholm Elliott Googie Withers

1991   **ADAM BEDE**
Director: Giles Foster
Co-stars: Patsy Kensit Iain Glenn Susannah Harker

1994   **THE OLD CURIOSITY SHOP**
Co-stars: Peter Ustinov James Fox Sally Walsh

KATE McKENZIE

1991   **GOODBYE CRUEL WORLD**
Director: Adrian Shergold
Co-stars: Alun Armstrong Sue Johnston Brenda Bruce

SALLY MCKENZIE

1992   **REDHEADS**
Director: Danny Vendramini
Co-stars: Catherine McClements Claudia Karvan

SARAH McKENZIE

1977   **CATHY'S CHILD**
Director: Donald Crombie
Co-stars: Michelle Fawdon Alan Cassell Bob Hughes

NANCY McKEON

1983   **HIGH SCHOOL U.S.A.**
Director: Rod Amateau
Co-stars: Michael J.Fox Bob Denver Todd Bridges

1984   **POISON IVY**
Director: Larry Elikann
Co-stars: Michael J.Fox Robert Klein Adam Baldwin

1985   **THIS CHILD IS MINE**
Director: David Greene
Co-stars: Lindsay Wagner Chris Sarandon Michael Lerner

1987   **STRANGE VOICES**
Director: Arthur Seidelman
Co-stars: Valerie Harper Stephen Macht Millie Perkins

1990   **A MOTHER'S GIFT**

1995   **THE WRONG WOMAN**
Director: Douglas Jackson

RAINA McKEON

1982   **FAR EAST**
Director: John Duigan
Co-stars: Bryan Brown Helen Morse John Bell

FLORINNE McKINNEY

1932   **HORSE FEATHERS**
Director: Norman Z.McLeod
Co-stars: Marx Brothers Thelma Todd Nat Pendleton

1933   **BEAUTY FOR SALE**
Director: Richard Boleslawsky
Co-stars: Madge Evans Alice Brady Una Merkel

1934   **DAVID COPPERFIELD**
Director: George Cukor
Co-stars: Freddie Bartholomew W.C.Fields Roland Young

1935   **THE NIGHT LIFE OF THE GODS**
Director: Lowell Sherman
Co-stars: Alan Mowbray Richard Carle Peggy Shannon

1935   **SUPERSEED**
Co-stars: Mary Carlisle Norman Foster

1935   **CAPPY RICKS RETURNS**
Co-star: Ray Walker

JENNIFER McKINNEY

1981   **SILENCE OF THE NORTH**
Director: Allan Winton King
Co-stars: Ellen Burstyn Tom Skerritt Gordon Pinsent

NINA MAE McKINNEY

1929   **HALLELUJAH!**
Director: King Vidor
Co-stars: Daniel L.Haynes William Fountaine Harry Gray

1935   **RECKLESS**
Director: Victor Fleming
Co-stars: Jean Harlow William Powell Franchot Tone

1935   **SANDERS OF THE RIVER**
Director: Zoltan Korda
Co-stars: Leslie Banks Paul Robeson Robert Cochran

1949   **PINKY**
Director: Elia Kazan
Co-stars: Jeanne Crain Ethel Barrymore Ethel Walters

MONA McKINNON

1956   **PLAN 9 FROM OUTER SPACE**
Director: Edward Wood
Co-stars: Bela Lugosi Tor Johnson Lyle Talbot

MARY McLAIN

1990   **ALLIGATOR EYES**
Director: John Feldman
Co-stars: Annabella Larsen Roger Kabler John MacKay

HOLLIS McLAREN

1976   **PARTNERS**
Director: Dan Owen
Co-stars: Denholm Elliott Michael Margotta Lee Broker

1977   **OUTRAGEOUS!**
Director: Richard Benner
Co-stars: Craig Russell Allan Moyle Helen Shaver

SHEILA McLAUGHLIN

185   **SEDUCTION: THE CRUEL WOMAN**
Director: Monika Treut
Co-stars: Mechthild Grossman Udo Kier Georgette Dee

PHEONA McLELLAN

1978   **A HITCH IN TIME**
Director: Jan Darnley Smith
Co-stars: Michael McVey Patrick Troughton Jeff Rawle

CATHERINE McLEOD

1946   **I'VE ALWAYS LOVED YOU**
Director: Frank Borzage
Co-stars: Philip Dorn Felix Bressart Vanessa Brown

1946   **THAT'S MY MAN**
Director: Frank Borzage
Co-stars: Don Ameche Roscoe Karns John Ridgely

1947   **THE FABULOUS TEXAN**
Director: Edward Ludwig
Co-stars: William Elliott John Carroll Andy Devine

1948   **OLD LOS ANGELES**
Co-stars: William Elliott Joseph Schildkraut Tito Renaldo

1952   **MY WIFE'S BEST FRIEND**
Director: Richard Sale
Co-stars: Anne Baxter MacDonald Carey Casey Adams

1953   **SWORD OF VENUS**
Director: Harold Daniels
Co-stars: Robert Clarke Dan O'Herlihy William Schallert

1953   **A BLUEPRINT FOR MURDER**
Director: Andrew Stone
Co-stars: Jean Peters Joseph Cotten Gary Merrill

1954   **THE OUTCAST**
Director: William Witney
Co-stars: John Derek Joan Evans Jim Davis

MARY McLEOD

1945   **A GUY, A GAL AND A PAL**
Co-stars: Ross Hunter Lynn Merrick Ted Donaldson

RONA McLEOD

1982   **THE CLINIC**
Director: David Stevens
Co-stars: Chris Haywood Simon Burke Gerda Nicolson

SHELAGH McLEOD

1989   **COLD FRONT**
Director: Paul Bnarbic
Co-stars: Martin Sheen Beverley D'Angelo Michael Ontkean

ALLYN McLERIE

1948   **WORDS AND MUSIC**
Director: Norman Taurog
Co-stars: Mickey Rooney Tom Drake Gene Kelly

1952   **WHERE'S CHARLEY**
Director: David Butler
Co-stars: Ray Bolger Mary Germaine Robert Shackleton

1953   **THE DESERT SONG**
Director: Bruce Humberstone
Co-stars: Gordon MacRae Kathryn Grayson Steve Cochran

1953   **CALAMITY JANE**
Director: David Butler
Co-stars: Doris Day Howard Keel Phil Carey

1954   **PHANTOM OF THE RUE MORGUE**
Director: Roy Del Ruth
Co-stars: Karl Malden Steve Forrest Patricia Medina

ALLYN ANN McLERIE

1972   **JEREMIAH JOHNSON**
Director: Sydney Pollack
Co-stars: Robert Redford Will Geer Josh Albee

1972   **THE COWBOYS**
Director: Mark Rydell
Co-stars: John Wayne Bruce Dern Colleen Dewhurst

1973   **THE WAY WE WERE**
Director: Sydney Pollack
Co-stars: Barbra Streisand Robert Redford Viveca Lindfors

1974   **CINDERELLA LIBERTY**
Director: Mark Rydell
Co-stars: James Caan Marsha Mason Eli Wallach

1979   **AND BABY MAKES SIX**
Director: Waris Hussein
Co-stars: Colleen Dewhurst Warren Oates Timothy Hutton

1979   **A SHINING SEASON**
Director: Stuart Margolin
Co-stars: Timothy Bottoms Ed Begley Jnr. Rip Torn

1982   **RASCALS AND ROBBERS - THE SECRET ADVENTURES OF TOM SAWYER AND HUCK FINN**
Director: Dick Lowry
Co-stars: Patrick Creadon Anthony Michael Hall Ed Begley Jnr.

1986   **STRANGER IN MY BED**
Director: Larry Elikann
Co-stars: Lindsay Wagner Armand Assante Doug Sheehan

RACHEL McLISH

1992   **IRON EAGLE III**
Director: John Glen
Co-stars: Lou Gossett Jnr. Christopher Cazenove Horst Buchholz

MARIANNE McLOUGHLIN

1988   **ARIA**
Director: Robert Altman
Co-stars: Theresa Russell Elizabeth Hurley Bridget Fonda

1990   **HE'S ASKING FOR ME**
Director: Vitold Starecki
Co-stars: Maggie O'Neill David Threlfall Gina McKee

1991   **THE GRASS ARENA**
Director: Gilles MacKinnon
Co-stars: Mark Rylance Lynsey Baxter Peter Postlethwaite

JUDY McLUSKY

1978   **SPAWN OF THE SLITHIS**
Director: Stephen Traxler
Co-star: Alan Blanchard

SHARON McMANUS

1945   **ANCHORS AWEIGH**
Director: George Sidney
Co-stars: Frank Sinatra Gene Kelly Kathryn Grayson

T. WENDY McMILLAN

1993   **GO FISH**
Director: Rose Troche
Co-stars: Guinevere Turner Anastaia Sharp V.S.Brodie

JOAN McMURTREY

1985   **THIS CHILD IS MINE**
Director: David Greene
Co-stars: Lindsay Wagner Chris Sarandon Nancy McKeon

1990   **WELCOME HOME, ROXY CARMICHAEL**
Director: Jim Abrahams
Co-stars: Winona Ryder Jeff Daniels Laila Robins

PAMELA McMYLER

1970   **CHISUM**
Director: Andrew McLaglen
Co-stars: John Wayne Forrest Tucker Ben Johnson

1977   **THE STICK-UP**
Director: Jeffrey Bloom
Co-stars: David Soul Johnny Wade Michael Balfour

BARBARA McNAIR

1969   **STILETTO**
Director: Bernard Kowalski
Co-stars: Alex Cord Britt Ekland Joseph Wiseman

1969   **THE LONELY PROFESSION**
Director: Douglas Heyes
Co-stars: Harry Guardino Dean Jagger Joseph Cotten

1969   **CHANGE OF HABIT**
Director: William Graham
Co-stars: Elvis Presley Mary Tyler Moore Ed Asner

1970   **THEY CALL ME MISTER TIBBS**
Director: Gordon Douglas
Co-stars: Sidney Poitier Martin Landau Ed Asner

1971   **THE ORGANIZATION**
Director: Don Medford
Co-stars: Sidney Poitier Sheree North Gerald O'Loughlin

MAUREEN McNALLEY

1969   **SWEET HUNTERS**
Director: Ruy Guerra
Co-stars: Sterling Hayden Stuart Whitman Susan Strasberg

MAGGIE McNAMARA

Nominated For Best Actress In 1953 For "The Moon Is Blue"

1953   **THE MOON IS BLUE**
Director: Otto Preminger
Co-stars: David Niven William Holden Dawn Addams

1954   **THREE COINS IN THE FOUNTAIN**
Director: Jean Negulesco
Co-stars: Dorothy McGuire Jean Peters Clifton Webb

1955   **PRINCE OF PLAYERS**
Director: Philip Dunne
Co-stars: Richard Burton John Derek Raymond Massey

1963   **THE CARDINAL**
Director: Otto Preminger
Director: Tom Tyron Carol Lynley Dorothy Gish

JULIA McNEAL

1989   **THE UNBELIEVABLE TRUTH**
Director: Hal Hartley
Co-stars: Adrienne Shelly Robert Burke Mark Bailey

CLAUDIA McNEIL

1961   A RAISIN IN THE SUN
Director: Daniel Petrie
Co-stars: Sidney Poitier Ruby Dee Diana Sands

1970   INCIDENT IN SAN FRANCISCO
Director: Don Medford
Co-stars: Richard Kiley Chris Connelly Ruth Roman

KATE McNEIL

1986   AMAZING STORIES 6
Director: Martin Scorsese
Co-stars: Sam Waterston Max Gail Sid Caesar

1986   VITAL SIGNS
Director: Stuart Millar
Co-stars: Ed Asner Gary Cole Barbara Barrie

1988   MONKEY SHINES: AN EXPERIMENT IN FEAR
Director: George Romero
Co-stars: Jason Beghe John Pankow

1989   THE LADY FORGETS
Director: Bradford May
Co-stars: Donna Mills Greg Evigan Roy Dotrice

KATHY McNEIL

1982   HOUSE OF EVIL
Director: Mark Rosman
Co-stars: Eileen Davidson Christopher Lawrence Janis Zido

1982   BEACH HOUSE
Director: John Gallagher
Co-stars: Richard Duggan John Cosola Ileana Seidel

RITA McNEIL

1987   CANDY MOUNTAIN
Director: Robert Frank
Co-stars: Kevin J.O'Connor Harris Yulin Tom Waits

JENNIE McNEILL

1965   FISTS IN THE POCKET
Director: Marco Bellocchio
Co-stars: Lou Castel Paola Pitagora Marino Mase

KRISTY McNICHOL

1978   LIKE MOM, LIKE ME
Director: Michael Pressman
Co-stars: Linda Lavin Patrick O'Neal Max Gail

1978   SUMMER OF MY GERMAN SOLDIER
Director: Michael Tuchner
Co-stars: Bruce Davison Esther Rolle Barbara Barrie

1980   LITTLE DARLINGS
Director: Ronald Maxwell
Co-stars: Tatum O'Neal Matt Dillon Armand Assante

1981   IT HURTS ONLY WHEN I LAUGH
Director: Glenn Jordan
Co-stars: Marsha Mason James Coco Joan Hackett

1981   THE NIGHT THE LIGHTS WENT OUT IN GEORGIA
Director: Ronald Maxwell
Co-stars: Dennis Quaid Don Stroud

1982   THE PIRATE MOVIE
Director: Ken Annakin
Co-stars: Christopher Atkins Ted Hamilton Bill Kerr

1982   WHITE DOG
Director: Samuel Fuller
Co-stars: Paul Winfield Burl Ives Jameson Parker

1984   JUST THE WAY YOU ARE
Director: Eduoard Molinaro
Co-stars: Michael Ontkean Kaki Hunter Robert Carradine

1985   LOVE, MARY
Director: Robert Day
Co-stars: Matt Clark Rachel Ticotin Piper Laurie

1986   DREAM LOVER
Co-stars: Alan J.Pakula
Co-stars: Ben Masters Paul Shenar Gayle Hunnicutt

1986   WOMEN OF VALOR
Director: Buzz Kulik
Co-stars: Susan Sarandon Alberta Watson Suzanne Lederer

1988   TWO-MOON JUNCTION
Director: Zalman King
Co-stars: Sherilyn Fenn Burl Ives Louise Fletcher

1991   BABY OF THE BRIDE
Director: Bill Bixby
Co-stars: Rue McClanahan Ted Shackleford

1993   MOTHER OF THE BRIDE
Director: Charles Correll
Co-stars: Rue McClanahan Paul Dooley

DOROTHY McNULTY

1930   GOOD NEWS
Director: Nick Grinde
Co-stars: Bessie Love Stanley Smith Lola Lane

MAGGIE McOMIE

1971   THX 1138
Director: George Lucas
Co-stars: Robert Duvall Donald Pleasence Ian Wolfe

ARLENE McQUADE

1951   MOLLY
Co-stars: Larry Robinson Gertrude Berg Philip Loeb

ARMELIA McQUEEN

1990   GHOST
Director: Jerry Zucker
Co-stars: Patrick Swayze Demi Moore Whoopi Goldberg

BUTTERFLY McQUEEN

1939   GONE WITH THE WIND
Director: Victor Fleming
Co-stars: Clark Gable Vivien Leigh Leslie Howard

1946   DUEL IN THE SUN
Director: King Vidor
Co-stars: Gregory Peck Jennifer Jones Joseph Cotten

1986   MOSQUITO COAST
Director: Peter Weir
Co-stars: Harrison Ford Helen Mirren River Phoenix

1989   POLLY
Director: Debbie Allen
Co-stars: Keshia Knight Pulliam Celeste Holm Brock Peters

1990   POLLY, COMIN' HOME
Director: Debbie Allen
Co-stars: Keshia Knight Pulliam Phylicia Rashad Celeste Holm

HEATHER McRAE

1973   THE CONNECTION
Director: Tom Gries
Co-stars: Charles Durning Ronny Cox Zohra Lampert

MAUREEN McRAE

1987 HEAVEN ON EARTH
Director: Allan Kroeker
Co-stars: R.H.Thomson Amos Crawley Cedric Smith

KITTY McSHANE *(Married Arthur Lucan)*

1936 STARS ON PARADE
Director: Oswald Mitchell
Co-stars: Albert Whelan Jimmy James Robb Wilton

1937 OLD MOTHER RILEY
Director: Oswald Mitchell
Co-stars: Arthur Lucan Barbara Everest Patrick Ludlow

1938 OLD MOTHER RILEY IN PARIS
Director: Oswald Mitchell
Co-stars: Arthur Lucan Jerry Verno Magda Kun

1938 OLD MOTHER RILEY M.P.
Director: Oswald Mitchell
Co-stars: Arthur Lucan Barbara Everest Edith Sharpe

1939 OLD MOTHER RILEY JOINS UP
Director: MacLean Rogers
Co-stars: Arthur Lucan Bruce Seton Martita Hunt

1940 OLD MOTHER RILEY IN BUSINESS
Director: John Baxter
Co-stars: Arthur Lucan Charles Victor Edie Martin

1941 OLD MOTHER RILEY IN SOCIETY
Director: John Baxter
Co-stars: Arthur Lucan John Stuart Dennis Wyndham

1941 OLD MOTHER RILEY'S GHOSTS
Director: John Baxter
Co-stars: Arthur Lucan John Stuart Bromley Davenport

1941 OLD MOTHER RILEY'S CIRCUS
Director: Thomas Bentley
Co-stars: Arthur Lucan John Longden Roy Emerton

1943 OLD MOTHER RILEY OVERSEAS
Director: Oswald Mitchell
Co-stars: Arthur Lucan Morris Harvey Ferdy Mayne

1943 OLD MOTHER RILEY, DETECTIVE
Director: Lance Comfort
Co-stars: Arthur Lucan Marjorie Rhodes Peggy Cummins

1945 OLD MOTHER RILEY AT HOME
Director: Oswald Mitchell
Co-stars: Arthur Lucan Wally Patch

1949 OLD MOTHER RILEY'S NEW VENTURE
Director: John Harlow
Co-stars: Arthur Lucan Chili Bouchier John Le Mesurier

1950 OLD MOTHER RILEY, HEADMISTRESS
Director: John Harlow
Co-stars: Arthur Lucan Cyril Smith

1951 OLD MOTHER RILEY'S JUNGLE TREASURE
Director: MacLean Rogers
Co-stars: Arthur Lucan Sebastian Cabot

1952 OLD MOTHER RILEY MEETS THE VAMPIRE
Director: John Gilling
Co-stars: Arthur Lucan Bela Lugosi Dora Bryan

CARMEL McSHARRY

1967 THE WITCHES
Director: Cryil Frankel
Co-stars: Joan Fontaine Kay Walsh Michele Dotrice

1972 ALL COPPERS ARE ...
Director: Sidney Hayers
Co-stars: Nicky Henson Julia Foster Ian Hendry

**1987 INSPECTOR WEXFORD:
        WOLF TO THE SLUGHTER**
Director: John Davies
Co-stars: George Baker Kim Thomson

JANET McTEER

1988 HAWKS
Director: Robert Ellis
Co-stars: Timothy Dalton Anthony Edwards Jill Bennett

1988 PRECIOUS BANE
Director: Christopher Menaul
Co-stars: John Bowe Clive Owen Emily Morgan

1990 YELLOWBACKS
Director: Roy Battersby
Co-stars: Roy Marsden Bill Patterson Imelda Staunton

1990 SWEET NOTHING
Director: Tony Smith
Co-stars: Lee Ross Charlotte Coleman Victor Maddern

1990 PORTRAIT OF A MARRIAGE
Director: Stephen Whittaker
Co-stars: David Haig Cathryn Harrison Peter Birch

1991 PRINCE
Director: David Wheatley
Co-stars: Sean Bean Celia Montague Jackie McGuire

1991 102, BOULEVARD HAUSSMAN
Director: Udayan Prasad
Co-stars: Alan Bates Paul Rhys Jonathan Coy

1991 THE BLACK VELVET GOWN
Director: Norman Stone
Co-stars: Bob Peck Jean Anderson Geraldine Somerville

1992 DEAD ROMANTIC
Director: Partick Lau
Co-stars: Clive Wood Elspet Gray Jonny Lee Miller

1992 WUTHERING HEIGHTS
Director: Peter Kominsky
Co-stars: Juliette Binoche Ralph Fiennes Sophie Ward

1992 A MASCULINE ENDING
Director: Stuart Orme
Co-stars: Imelda Staunton

1993 DON'T LEAVE ME THIS WAY
Director: Stuart Orme
Co-stars: Imelda Staunton Moira Williams Ian McNeice

MARGARET McWADE

1936 MR. DEEDS GOES TO TOWN
Director: Frank Capra
Co-stars: Gary Cooper Jean Arthur Raymond Walburn

1936 THEODORA GOES WILD
Director: Richard Boleslawski
Co-stars: Irene Dunne Melvyn Douglas Thomas Mitchell

JILLIAN McWHIRTER

1989 AFTER MIDNIGHT
Director: Jim Wheat
Co-stars: Pamela Segall Ramy Zade Marc McClurte

CAROLINE McWILLIAMS

1980 THE ALIENS ARE COMING
Director: Harvey Hart
Co-stars: Tom Mason Melinda Fee Ed Harris

1985 INTO THIN AIR
Director: Roger Young
Co-stars: Ellen Burstyn Robert Prosky Sam Robards

1986   **SWORN TO SILENCE**
Director: Peter Levin
Co-stars: Peter Coyote Dabney Coleman Liam Neeson

1990   **MERMAIDS**
Director: Richard Benjamin
Co-stars: Cher Winona Ryder Christina Ricci Bob Hoskins

ANNE MEACHAM

1964   **LILITH**
Director: Robert Rossen
Co-stars: Warren Beatty Jean Seberg Peter Fonda

JULIA MEADE

1959   **PILLOW TALK**
Director: Michael Gordon
Co-stars: Doris Day Rock Hudson Thelma Ritter

1961   **TAMMY TELL ME TRUE**
Director: Henry Keller
Co-stars: Sandra Dee John Gavin Charles Drake

MARY MEADE

1947   **T-MEN**
Director: Anthony Mann
Co-stars: Dennis O'Keefe Wallace Ford June Lockhart

AUDREY MEADOWS

1962   **THAT TOUCH OF MINK**
Director: Delbert Mann
Co-stars: Cary Grant Doris Day Gig Young

1963   **TAKE HER, SHE'S MINE**
Director: Henry Koster
Co-stars: James Stewart Sandra Dee Robert Morley

1967   **ROSIE!**
Director: David Lowell Rich
Co-stars: Rosalind Russell Brain Aherne Sandra Dee

BUNTY MEADOWS

1943   **HAPPIDROME**
Director: Phil Brandon
Co-stars: Harry Korris Robbie Vincent Cecil Frederick

JAYNE MEADOWS

1946   **THE LADY IN THE LAKE**
Director: Robert Montgomery
Co-stars: Robert Montgomery Audrey Totter Leon Ames

1946   **UNDERCURRENT**
Director: Vincente Minnelli
Co-stars: Katherine Hepburn Robert Taylor Robert Mitchum

1947   **SONG OF THE THIN MAN**
Director: Edward Buzzell
Co-stars: William Powell Myrna Loy Dean Stockwell

1947   **DARK DELUSION**
Director: Willis Goldbeck
Co-stars: Lionel Barrymore James Craig Lucille Bremer

1947   **THE LUCK OF THE IRISH**
Director: Henry Koster
Co-stars: Tyrone Power Anne Baxter Cecil Kellaway

1948   **ENCHANTMENT**
Director: Irving Reis
Co-stars: David Niven Teresa Wright Farley Granger

1950   **THE FAT MAN**
Director: William Castle
Co-stars: J.Scott Smart Rock Hudson Julie London

1951   **DAVID AND BATHSHEBA**
Director: Henry King
Co-stars: Gregory Peck Susan Hayward Raymond Massey

1960   **COLLEGE CONFIDENTAIL**
Director: Albert Zugsmith
Co-stars: Steve Allen Mamie Van Doren Herbert Marshall

1982   **MISS ALL-AMERICAN BEAUTY**
Director: Gus Trikonis
Co-stars: Diane Lane Cloris Leachman

1984   **THE RATINGS GAME**
Director: Danny De Vito
Co-stars: Danny De Vito Rhea Perlman Gerrit Graham Steve Allen

1989   **PARENT TRAP III**
Director: Mollie Miller
Co-stars: Hayley Mills Barry Bostwick John M.Jackson

JOYCE MEADOWS

1958   **THE BRAIN FROM PLANET AROUS**
Director: Nathan Hertz
Co-stars: John Agar Robert Fuller Thomas B.Henry

1965   **ZEBRA IN THE KITCHEN**
Director: Ivan Tors
Co-stars: Jay North Martin Milner Andy Devine

1991   **TRUE IDENTITY**
Director: Charles Lane
Co-stars: Lenny Henry Frank Langella J.T. Walsh

JILL MEAGER

1991   **SHUTTLECOCK**
Director: Andrew Piddington
Co-stars: Alan Bates Lambert Wilson Tisha Campbell

ANNE MEARA

1970   **LOVERS AND OTHER STRANGERS**
Director: Cy Howard
Co-stars: Gig Young Bonnie Bedelia Diane Keaton

1970   **THE OUT-OF-TOWNERS**
Director: Arthur Hiller
Co-stars: Jack Lemmon Sandy Dennis Sandy Baron

1976   **NASTY HABITS**
Director: Michael Lindsay-Hogg
Co-stars: Glenda Jackson Melina Mercouri Geraldine Page

1978   **THE BOYS FROM BRAZIL**
Director: Franklin Schaffner
Co-stars: Gregory Peck Laurence Olivier James Mason

1980   **FAME**
Director: Alan Parker
Co-stars: Irene Cara Laura Dean Lee Curreri

1986   **THE LONG SHOT**
Director: Paul Bartel
Co-stars: Tim Conway Jack Weston Harvey Korman

1986   **MY LITTLE GIRL**
Director: Connie Kaiserman
Co-stars: Mary Stuart Masterson Geraldine Page James Earl Jones

1987   **ALF**
Director: Tom Patchett
Co-stars: Max Wright Ann Schedeen Andrea Elson

1990   **AWAKENINGS**
Director: Penny Marshall
Co-stars: Robert De Niro Robin Williams Julie Kavner

DeANN MEARS

1976   **THE LONELIEST RUNNER**
Director: Michael Landon
Co-stars: Michael Landon Lance Kerwin Brian Keith

SYLVIE MEDA

1982   **THE RETURN OF MARTIN GUERRE**
Director: Daniel Vigne
Co-stars: Gerard Depardieu Nathalie Baye

KAY MEDFORD

1960   THE RAT RACE
Director: Robert Mulligan
Co-stars: Tony Curtis Debbie Reynolds Jack Oakie

1960   GIRL OF THE NIGHT
Director: Joseph Cates
Co-stars: Anne Francis Lloyd Nolan John Kerr

1960   BUTTERFIELD 8
Director: Daniel Mann
Co-stars: Elizabeth Taylor Laurence Harvey Eddie Fisher

1964   ENSIGN PULVER
Director: Joshua Logan
Co-stars: Robert Walker Burl Ives Walter Matthau

1966   THE BUSY BODY
Director: William Castle
Co-stars: Robert Ryan Richard Pryor Anne Baxter

1968   FUNNY GIRL
Director: William Wyler
Co-stars: Barbra Streisand Omar Sharif Anne Francis

1969   ANGEL IN MY POCKET
Director: Alan Rafkin
Co-stars: Andy Griffith Edgar Buchanan Margaret Hamilton

1977   FIRE SALE
Director: Alan Arkin
Co-stars: Alan Arkin Vincent Gardenia Sid Caesar Rob Reiner

HAZEL MEDINA

1972   LIMBO
Director: Mark Robson
Co-stars: Kate Jackson Katharine Justice Stuart Margolin

OFELIA MEDINA

1978   THE BIG FIX
Director: Jeremy Paul Kagan
Co-stars: Richard Dreyfuss Susan Anspach Bonnie Bedelia

PATRICIA MEDINA

1942   THE DAY WILL DAWN
Director: Harold French
Co-stars: Hugh Williams Deborah Kerr Ralph Richardson

1944   DON'T TAKE IT TO HEART
Director: Jeffrey Dell
Co-stars: Richard Greene Edward Rigby Alfred Drayton

1945   WALTZ TIME
Director: Paul Stein
Co-stars: Carol Raye Peter Graves Richard Tauber

1946   THE SECRET HEART
Director: Robert Z. Leonard
Co-stars: Claudette Colbert Walter Pidgeon June Allyson

1947   THE FOXES OF HARROW
Director: John Stahl
Co-stars: Rex Harrison Maureen O'Hara Victor McLaglen

1947   MOSS ROSE
Director: Gregory Ratoff
Co-stars: Victor Mature Peggy Cummings Ethel Barrymore

1949   THE FIGHTING O'FLYNN
Director: Arthur Pierson
Co-stars: Douglas Fairbanks Richard Greene

1950   FORTUNES OF CAPTAIN BLOOD
Director: Gordon Douglas
Co-stars: Louis Haywood Dona Drake George Macready

1950   THE JACKPOT
Director: Walter Lang
Co-stars: James Stewart Barbara Hale Natalie Wood

1950   FRANCIS
Director: Arthur Lubin
Co-stars: Donald O'Connor Zasu Pitts John McIntyre Tony Curtis

1950   ABBOTT & COSTELLO IN THE FOREIGN LEGION
Director: Charles Lamont
Co-stars: Bud Abbott Lou Costello Walter Slezak

1951   THE LADY AND THE BANDIT
Director: Ralph Murphy
Co-stars: Louis Hayward Tom Tully John Williams

1951   THE MAGIC CARPET
Director: Lew Landers
Co-stars: Lucille Ball Raymond Burr John Agar

1951   VALENTINO
Director: Lewis Allen
Co-stars: Anthony Dexter Eleanor Parker Dona Drake

1952   DESPERATE SEARCH
Director: Joseph Lewis
Co-stars: Howard Keel Jane Greer Keenan Wynn

1952   CAPTAIN PIRATE
Director: Ralph Murphy
Co-stars: Louis Hayward John Sutton George Givot

1952   BOTANY BAY
Director: John Farrow
Co-stars: Alan Ladd James Mason Cedric Hardwicke

1953   PLUNDER OF THE SUN
Director: John Farrow
Co-stars: Glenn Ford Diana Lynn Douglass Dumbrille

1953   SANGAREE
Director: Edward Ludwig
Co-stars: Fernando Lamas Arlene Dahl Charles Korvin

1953   SIREN OF BAGDAD
Director: Richard Quine
Co-stars: Paul Henreid Hans Conried Charlie Lung

1954   PHANTOM OF THE RUE MORGUE
Director: Roy Del Ruth
Co-stars: Karl Malden Claude Dauphin Steve Forrest

1954   DRUMS OF TAHITI
Director: William Castle
Co-stars: Dennis O'Keefe Sylvia Lewis Francis L.Sullivan

1954   THE BLACK KNIGHT
Director: Tay Garnett
Co-stars: Alan Ladd Peter Cushing Harry Andrews

1955   DUEL ON THE MISSISSIPPI
Director: William Castle
Co-stars: Lex Barker Craig Stevens Warren Stevens

1955   MR. ARKADIN
Director: Orson Welles
Co-stars: Orson Welles Michael Redgrave Akim Tamiroff

1955   PIRATES OF TRIPOLI
Director: Felix Feist
Co-stars: Paul Henreid John Miljan Lillian Bond

1956   STRANGER AT MY DOOR
Director: William Witney
Co-stars: MacDonald Carey Skip Homeier

1956   MIAMI EXPOSE
Director: Fred Sears
Co-stars: Lee J.Cobb Edward Arnold

1956   THE BEAST OF HOLLOW MOUNTAIN
Director: Edward Nassour
Co-stars: Guy Maddison Carlos Rivas

1958   THE BATTLE OF THE VI
Director: Vernon Sewell
Co-stars: Michael Rennie Christopher Lee

1959 COUNT YOUR BLESSINGS
Director: Jean Negulesco
Co-stars: Deborah Kerr Rossano Brazzi Maurice Chevalier

1961 SNOW WHITE AND THE THREE STOOGES
Director: Walter Lang
Co-stars: Carol Heiss Three Stooges

1969 THE KILLING OF SISTER GEORGE
Director: Robert Aldrich
Co-stars: Beryl Reid Susannah York Coral Brown

VICTORIA MEDLIN

1971 VANISHING POINT
Director: Richard Sarafian
Co-stars: Barry Newman Cleavon Little Dean Jagger

EDITH MEEKS

1990 POISON
Director: Todd Haynes
Co-stars: Millie White James Lyons Larry Maxwell

KAY MEERSMAN

1961 THE YOUNG ONE
Director: Luis Bunuel
Co-stars: Zachary Scott Bernie Hamilton Claudio Brook

DEBBIE MEGOWAN

1962 DAYS OF WINE AND ROSES
Director: Blake Edwards
Co-stars: Jack Lemmon Lee Remick Charles Bickford

EVA MARIE MEINECKE

1966 YESTERDAY GIRL
Director: Alexander Kluge
Co-stars: Alexander Kluge Gunther Mack Hans Korte

FREDERIQUE MEININGER

1992 THE LOVER
Director: Jean-Jacques Annaud
Co-stars: Jane March Tony Leung Lisa Faulkner

EDITH MEISER

1952 IT GROWS ON TREES
Director: Arthur Lubin
Co-stars: Irene Dunne Dean Jagger Joan Evans

KATHRYN MEISLE

1990 BASKET CASE 2
Director: Frank Helenlotter
Co-stars: Kevin Van Hentenryck Judy Grafe Annie Ross

ISABELLE MEJIAS

1984 THE BAD BOY
Director: Daniel Petrie
Co-stars: Kiefer Sutherland Liv Ullman Peter Donat

1984 UNFINISHED BUSINESS
Director: Don Owen
Co-stars: Peter Spense Leslie Toth Julie Biggs

1991 SCANNERS 2: THE NEW ORDER
Director: Christian Duguey
Co-stars: David Hewlett Deborah Raffin Tom Butler

1994 MEATBALLS 3
Director: George Mendeluk
Co-stars: Sally Kellermen Patrick Dempsey Al Waxman

MONIQUE MELINAND

1974 THE MOUTH AGAPE
Director: Maurice Pialat
Co-stars: Hubert Deschamps Nathalie Baye Philippe Leotard

1977 LA MACHINE
Director: Paul Vecchiali
Co-stars: Jean-Christophe Bouvet Sonia Saviange

MARIANGELA MELATO

1975 MOSES
Director: Gianfranco De Bosio
Co-stars: Burt Lancaster Anthony Quayle Ingrid Thulin

1981 SO FINE
Director: Andrew Bergman
Co-stars: Ryan O'Neal Jack Warden Richard Kiel

MARIA MELENDEZ

1979 AND BABY MAKES SIX
Director: Waris Hussein
Co-stars: Colleen Dewhurst Warren Oates Timothy Hutton

1980 BABY COMES HOME
Director: Waris Hussein
Co-stars: Colleen Dewhurst Warren Oates Mildred Dunnock

MIGDALIA MELENDEZ

1993 GO FISH
Director: Rose Troche
Co-stars: V.S.Brodie Guinevere Turner Anastasia Sharp

JILL MELFORD

1963 A STITCH IN TIME
Director: Robert Asher
Co-stars: Norman Wisdom Edward Chapman Jerry Desmond

1968 THE VENGEANCE OF SHE
Director: Cliff Owen
Co-stars: John Richardson Olinka Berova Edward Judd

MARISA MELINI

1953 BREAD, LOVE AND DREAMS
Director: Luigi Comencini
Co-stars: Vittorio De Sica Gina Lollobrigida

MARISA MELL

1963 FRENCH DRESSING
Director: Ken Russell
Co-stars: James Booth Roy Kinnear Bryan Pringle

1965 MASQUERADE
Director: Basil Dearden
Co-stars: Cliff Robertson Jack Hawkins Charles Gray

1966 CITY OF FEAR
Director: Peter Bezencenet
Co-stars: Paul Maxwell Terry Moore Albert Lieven

1967 DANGER: DIABOLIK
Director: Mario Bava
Co-stars: John Phillip Law Michel Piccoli Terry-Thomas

1975 MAHOGANY
Director: Berry Gordy
Co-stars: Diana Ross Billy Dee Williams Anthony Perkins

LEONIE MELLINGER *(Child)*

1981 MEMOIRS OF A SURVIVOR
Director: David Gladwell
Co-stars: Julie Christie Christopher Guard

1990 CHILDREN CROSSING
Director: Angela Pope
Co-stars: Peter Firth Saskia Reeves Bob Peck

1994 GHOST DANCE
Director: Ken McCullen
Co-star: Pascale Ogier

MARTHE MELLOT

1934 LE DERNIER MILLIARDAIRE
Director: Rene Clair
Co-stars: Max Dearly Renee Saint-Cyr Raymond Cordy

ANDREE MELLY

1960 BRIDES OF DRACULA
Director: Terence Fisher
Co-stars: Peter Cushing Freda Jackson Martita Hunt

AMY MELHSUISH

1989 BALL TRAP ON THE COTE SAUVAGE
Director: Jack Gold
Co-stars: Jack Shepherd Miranda Richardson

ASHIA MENINA

1993 HOUSE OF CARDS
Director: Michael Lessac
Co-stars: Kathleen Turner Tommy Lee Jones Park Overall

HEATHER MENZIES *(Child)*

1965 THE SOUND OF MUSIC
Director: Robert Wise
Co-stars: Julie Andrews Christopher Plummer Peggy Wood

1973 Ssssss
Director: Bernard Kowalski
Co-stars: Strother Martin Dirk Benedict

1978 PIRANHA
Director: Joe Dante
Co-stars: Bradford Dillman Kevin McCarthy Keenan Wynn

BERYL MERCER

1929 THREE LIVE GHOSTS
Co-stars: Robert Montgomery Claude Allister Hilda Vaughn

1930 ALL QUIET ON THE WESTERN FRONT
Director: Lewis Milestone
Co-stars: Lew Ayres Louis Wolheim John Wray

1930 OUTWARD BOUND
Director: Robert Milton
Co-stars: Leslie Howard Helen Chandler Douglas Fairbanks Jnr.

1930 COMMON CLAY
Director: Victor Fleming
Co-stars: Lew Ayres Constance Bennett Tully Marshall

1930 DUMBBELLS IN ERMINE
Co-stars: Barbara Kent Arthur Hoyt Julia Swayne-Gordon

1930 INSPIRATION
Director: Clarence Brown
Co-stars: Greta Garbo Robert Montgomery Lewis Stone

1930 SEVEN DAYS' LEAVE
Director: Richard Wallace
Co-stars: Gary Cooper Daisy Belmore Nora Cecil

1931 EAST LYNNE
Director: Frank Lloyd
Co-stars: Ann Harding Clive Brook Conrad Nagel

1931 THE MAN IN POSSESSION
Director: Sam Wood
Co-stars: Robert Montgomery Irene Purcell Charlotte Greenwood

1931 MERELY MARY ANN
Director: Henry King
Co-stars: Janet Gaynor Charles Farrell G.P.Huntley

1931 THE PUBLIC ENEMY
Director: William Wellman
Co-stars: James Cagney Jean Harlow Joan Blondell

1932 SMILIN' THROUGH
Director: Irving Thalberg
Co-stars: Norma Shearer Leslie Howard Fredric March

1932 THE DEVIL'S LOTTERY
Co-star: Victor McLaglen

1932 YOUNG AMERICA
Director: Frank Borzage
Co-stars: Spencer Tracy Doris Kenyon Ralph Bellamy

1932 THE MIRACLE WOMAN
Director: Frank Capra
Co-stars: Barbara Stanwyck Sam Hardy David Manners

1933 CAVALCADE
Director: Frank Lloyd
Co-stars: Diana Wynyard Clive Brook Ursula Jeans

1933 BERKELEY SQUARE
Director: Frank Lloyd
Co-stars: Leslie Howard Heather Angel Valerie Taylor

1934 JANE EYRE
Director: Christy Cabanne
Co-stars: Virginia Bruce Colin Clive Jameson Thomas

1934 THE LITTLE MINISTER
Director: Richard Wallace
Co-stars: Katherine Hepburn John Beal Donald Crisp

1934 THE RICHEST GIRL IN THE WORLD
Director: William Seiter
Co-stars: Miriam Hopkins Joel McCrea Fay Wray

1935 HITCH-HIKE LADY
Director: Aubrey Scotto
Co-stars: Alison Skipworth Arthur Treacher Mae Clarke

1936 MY MARRIAGE
Director: George Archainbaud
Co-stars: Claire Trevor Kent Taylor Pauline Frederick

1937 CALL IT A DAY
Director: Archie Mayo
Co-stars: Olivia De Havilland Ian Hunter Anita Louise

1939 THE LITTLE PRINCESS
Director: Walter Lang
Co-stars: Shirley Temple Ian Hunter Richard Greene

1939 THE HOUND OF THE BASKERVILLES
Director: Sidney Lanfield
Co-stars: Basil Rathbone Nigel Bruce Wendy Barrie

FRANCES MERCER

1938 VIVACIOUS LADY
Director: George Stevens
Co-stars: Ginger Rogers James Stewart Charles Coburn

1938 THE MAD MISS MANTON
Director: Leigh Jason
Co-stars: Barbara Stanwyck Henry Fonda Sam Levene

1938 CRIME RING
Co-star: Alan Lane

1946 PICCADILLY INCIDENT
Director: Herbert Wilcox
Co-stars: Anna Neagle Michael Wilding Coral Browne

MAE MERCER

1971 DIRTY HARRY
Director: Don Siegel
Co-stars: Clint Eastwood Harry Guardino

1971 THE BEGUILED
Director: Don Seigel
Co-stars: Clint Eastwood Geraldine Page Elizabeth Hartman

1978   **PRETTY BABY**
Director: Louis Malle
Co-stars: Keith Carradine Susan Sarandon Brooke Shields

MARIAN MERCER

1980   **NINE TO FIVE**
Director: Colin Higgins
Co-stars: Jane Fonda Lily Tomlin Dolly Parton

1982   **LIFE OF THE PARTY:**
        THE STORY OF BEATRICE

1992   **OUT ON A LIMB**
Director: Francis Veber
Co-stars: Matthew Broderick Jeffrey Jones Heidi Kling

VIVIEN MERCHANT *(Married Harold Pinter)*
Nominated For Best Supporting Actress in 1966 for "Alfie"

1966   **ALFIE**
Director: Lewis Gilbert
Co-stars: Michael Caine Shelley Winters Jane Asher

1967   **ACCIDENT**
Director: Joseph Losey
Co-stars: Dirk Bogarde Stanley Baker Harold Pinter

1971   **UNDER MILK WOOD**
Director: Andrew Sinclair
Co-stars: Richard Burton Elizabeth Taylor Glynis Johns

1972   **THE OFFENCE**
Director: Sidney Lumet
Co-stars: Sean Connery Trevor Howard Ian Bannen

1972   **FRENZY**
Director: Alfred Hitchcock
Co-stars: Jon Finch Alex McCowen Barry Foster

1973   **THE HOMECOMING**
Director: Pater Hall
Co-stars: Michael Jayston Cyril Cusack Ian Holm

1974   **THE MAIDS**
Director: Christopher Miles
Co-stars: Susannah York Glenda Jackson Mark Burns

1976   **THE MAN IN THE IRON MASK**
Director: Mike Newell
Co-stars: Richard Chamberlain Louis Jourdan Jenny Agutter

MICHELE MERCIER

1960   **SHOOT THE PIANIST**
Director: Francois Trauffaut
Co-stars: Charles Azanour Nicole Berger Marie Dubois

1960   **FURY AT SMUGGLERS' BAY**
Director: John Gilling
Co-stars: Peter Cushing John Fraser June Thorburn

1961   **THE WONDERS OF ALADDIN**
Director: Mario Bava
Co-stars: Donald O'Connor Vittorio De Sica Aldo Fabrizi

1963   **A GLOBAL AFFAIR**
Director: Jack Arnold
Co-stars: Bob Hope Lilo Pulver Yvonne De Carlo

1963   **BLACK SABBATH**
Director: Mario Bava
Co-stars: Boris Karloff Mark Damon Jacqueline Pierreux

1964   **ANGELIQUE**
Director: Bernard Borderie
Co-stars: Robert Hossein Jean Rochefort Francois Maistre

1967   **THE OLDEST PROFESSION**
Director: Jean-Luc Godard
Co-stars: Elsa Martinelli Jeanne Moreau Raquel Welch

1970   **YOU CAN'T WIN 'EM ALL**
Director: Peter Collinson
Co-stars: Tony Curtis Charles Bronson Gregoire Aslan

1972   **CALL OF THE WILD**
Director: Ken Annakin
Co-stars: Charlton Heston George Eastman Maria Rohm

MELINA MERCOURI *(Married Jules Dassin)*
Nominated For Best Actress In 1960 For "Never On Sunday"

1957   **HE WHO MUST DIE**
Director: Jules Dassin
Co-stars: Jean Servais Carl Mohner Pierre Vaneck

1958   **THE GYPSY AND THE GENTLEMAN**
Director: Joseph Losey
Co-stars: Keith Michell Patrick McGoohan

1959   **NEVER ON SUNDAY**
Director: Jules Dassin
Co-stars: Jules Dassin Georges Foundas Tito Vandis

1962   **PHAEDRA**
Director: Jules Dassin
Co-star: Anthony Perkins

1963   **THE VICTORS**
Director: Carl Foreman
Co-stars: George Peppard George Hamilton Albert Finney

1964   **TOPKAPI**
Director: Jules Dassin
Co-stars: Peter Ustinov Maxmilan Schell Robert Morley

1966   **10.30 P.M. SUMMER**
Director: Jules Dassin
Co-stars: Peter Finch Romy Schneider Julian Mateos

1966   **A MAN COULD GET KILLED**
Director: Ronald Neame
Co-stars: James Garner Sandra Dee Tony Franciosa

1969   **GAILY, GAILY**
Director: Norman Jewison
Co-stars: Beau Bridges Brian Keith George Kennedy

1970   **PROMISE AT DAWN**
Director: Jules Dassin
Co-star: Assef Dayan

1975   **ONCE IS NOT ENOUGH**
Director: Guy Green
Co-star: Kirk Douglass Alexis Smith David Janssen

1976   **NASTY HABITS**
Director: Michael Lindsay-Hogg
Co-stars: Glenda Jackson Geraldine Page Sandy Dennis

1978   **A DREAM OF PASSION**
Director: Jules Dassin
Co-stars: Ellen Burstyn Andreas Voutsinas

MONIQUE MERCURE

1991   **THE NAKED LUNCH**
Director: David Cronenberg
Co-stars: Peter Weller Judy Davis Ian Holm

NICOLE MERCURIO

1992   **SHADES OF GREY**
Director: Kevin James Dobson
Co-stars: Valerie Bertinelli George Dzundza

1993   **WRESTLING ERNEST HEMINGWAY**
Director: Randa Haines
Co-stars: Robert Duvall Richard Harris Shirley MacLaine

1994   **THE CLIENT**
Director: Joel Schumacher
Co-stars: Susan Sarandon Mary Louise Parker Brad Renfro

IRIS MEREDITH

1937 THE MYSTERY OF THE HOODED HORSEMAN
Co-stars: Tex Ritter Horace Murphy

1937 TRAIL OF VENGEANCE
Co-stars: Johnny Mack Brown

1939 OUTPOST OF THE MOUNTIES
Co-star: Charles Starrett

1939 WESTERN CARAVANS
Co-stars: Charles Starrett Charles Brinley Dick Curtis

1939 RIDERS OF BLACK RIVER
Co-stars: Charles Starrett Edmund Cobb

1939 THOSE GREY WALLS
Director: Charles Vidor
Co-stars: Walter Connolly Onslow Stevens Paul Fix

JUDI MEREDITH

1961 JACK THE GIANT KILLER
Director: Nathan Juran
Co-stars: Kerwin Matthews Torin Thatcher Don Beddoe

1964 THE NIGHT WALKER
Director: William Castle
Co-stars: Robert Taylor Barbara Stanwyck Rochelle Hudson

LISA MEREDITH

1987 LOVEBIRDS
Director: Stephen Whittaker
Co-stars: Stephen Bent Paul Bhattacharjee Jane Gurnett

MADGE MEREDITH

1946 THE FALCON'S ADVENTURE
Director: William Berke
Co-stars: Robert Warwick Edward Brophy Tom Conway

1946 CHILD OF DIVORCE
Director: Richard Fleischer
Co-stars: Sharyn Moffet Regis Toomey Una O'Connor

MARTI MERIKA *(Child)*

1964 ONE POTATO, TWO POTATO
Director: Larry Peerce
Co-stars: Barbara Barrie Bernie Hamilton Richard Mulligan

EDA REISS MERIN

1991 DON'T TELL MOM THE BABYSITTER'S DEAD
Director: Stephen Herek
Co-stars: Christina Applegate Joanna Cassidy

YVONNE MERIN

1950 COUNCIL OF THE GODS
Director: Kurt Maetzig
Co-stars: Paul Bildt Agnes Windeck Fritz Tillman

LEE MERIWETHER

1963 THE COURTSHIP OF EDDIE'S FATHER
Director: Vincente Minnelli
Co-stars: Glenn Ford Ronny Howard Shirley Jones

1966 BATMAN
Director: Leslie Martinson
Co-stars: Adam West Burt Ward Cesar Romero

1969 THE UNDEFEATED
Co-stars: Andrew McLaglen
Co-stars: John Wayne Rock Hudson Ben Johnson

MACHA MERIL

1963 WHO'S BEEN SLEEPING IN MY BED?
Director: Daniel Mann
Co-stars: Dean Martin Elizabeth Montgomery Jill St .John

1964 A MARRIED WOMAN
Director: Jean-Luc Godard
Co-stars: Bernard Noel Roger Leenhardt

UNA MERKEL
Nominated For Best Supporting Actress In 1961 For "Summer And Smoke"

1930 ABRAHAM LINCOLN
Director: D.W.Griffith
Co-stars: Walter Huston Edgar Dearing Russell Simpson

1930 THE BAT WHISPERS
Director: Roland West
Co-stars: Chester Morris Maude Eburne Spencer Charters

1931 WICKED
Director: Allan Dwan
Co-stars: Elissa Landi Victor McLaglen Alan Dinehart Oscar Apfel

1931 THE MALTESE FALCON
Director: Roy Del Ruth
Co-stars: Ricardo Cortez Bebe Daniels Thelma Todd

1931 PRIVATE LIVES
Director: Sidney Franklin
Co-stars: Robert Montgomery Norma Shearer Reginald Denny

1931 DADDY LONG LEGS
Director: Alfred Santell
Co-stars: Janet Gaynor Warner Baxter Elizabeth Patterson

1932 RED-HEADED WOMAN
Director: Jack Conway
Co-stars: Jean Harlow Chester Morris Lewis Stone Leila Hyams

1932 WHISTLING IN THE DARK
Co-stars: Edward Arnold John Miljan Ernest Truex

1932 SHE WANTED A MILLIONAIRE
Director: John Blystone
Co-stars: Joan Bennett Spencer Tracy James Kirkwood

1932 THEY CALL IT SIN
Director: Thornton Freeland
Co-stars: Loretta Young George Brent Louis Calhern

1932 HUDDLE
Director: Sam Wood
Co-stars: Ramon Navarro Madge Evans Conrad Nagle Arthur Byron

1932 THE IMPATIENT MAIDEN
Director: James Whale
Co-stars: Mae Clarke Lew Ayres John Halliday

1932 MAN WANTED
Director: William Dieterle
Co-stars: Kay Francis David Manners Andy Devine

1933 MIDNIGHT MARY
Director: William Wellman
Co-stars: Loretta Young Ricardo Cortez Franchot Tone

1933 THIS SIDE OF HEAVEN
Director: William Howard
Co-stars: Lionel Barrymore Fay Bainter Mae Clarke

1933 FORTY-SECOND STREET
Director: Lloyd Bacon
Co-stars: Warner Baxter Ruby Keeler Dick Powell

1933 BROADWAY TO HOLLYWOOD
Director: Willard Mack
Co-stars: Frank Morgan Jimmy Durante Mickey Rooney

1933 THE SECRET OF MADAME BLANCHE
Director: Charles Brabin
Co-stars: Irene Dunne Phillips Holmes Lionel Atwill

1933	**DAY OF RECKONING**	**1937**	**THE GOOD OLD SOAK**
Co-stars:	Stuart Irwin James Gleason	Director:	Walter Ruben
		Co-stars:	Wallace Beery Eric Linden Betty Furness
1933	**REUNION IN VIENNA**		
Director:	Sidney Franklin	**1937**	**SARATOGA**
Co-stars:	John Barrymore Diana Wynard Frank Morgan	Director:	Jack Conway
		Co-stars:	Clark Gable Jean Harlow Lionel Barrymore Frank Morgan
1933	**CLEAR ALL WIRES**		
Co-star:	Lee Tracy	**1937**	**TRUE CONFESSION**
		Director:	Wesley Ruggles
1933	**BOMBSHELL**	Co-stars:	Carole Lombard Fred MacMurray John Barrymore
Director:	Victor Fleming		
Co-stars:	Jean Harlow Lee Tracy Franchot Tone Pat O'Brien	**1938**	**FOUR GIRLS IN WHITE**
		Director:	S.Sylvan Simon
1933	**BEAUTY FOR SALE**	Co-stars:	Florence Rice Ann Rutherford Buddy Ebsen
Director:	Richard Boleslawsky		
Co-stars:	Madge Evans Alice Brady Otto Kruger	**1939**	**ON BORROWED TIME**
		Director:	Harold Bucquet
1934	**EVELYN PRENTICE**	Co-stars:	Lionel Barrymore Beulah Bondi Cedric Hardwicke
Director:	William Howard		
Co-stars:	William Powell Myrna Loy Rosalind Russell	**1939**	**SOME LIKE IT HOT**
		Director:	George Archainbaud
1934	**HAVE A HEART**	Co-stars:	Bob Hope Shirley Ross Richard Denning
Director:	David Butler		
Co-stars:	Jean Parker James Dunn Stuart Erwin	**1940**	**THE BANK DICK**
		Director:	Eddie Cline
1934	**BULLDOG DRUMMOND STRIKES BACK**	Co-stars:	W.C.Fields Cora Witherspoon Franklin Pangborn
Director:	Roy Del Ruth		
Co-stars:	Ronald Colman Loretta Young Warner Oland	**1940**	**SANDY GETS HER MAN**
		Director:	Otis Garrett
1934	**MURDER IN THE PRIVATE CAR**	Co-stars:	Baby Sandy Stuart Erwin Edgar Kennedy
Director:	Harry Beaumont		
Co-stars:	Charles Ruggles Russell Hardie	**1941**	**ROAD TO ZANZIBAR**
		Director:	Victor Schertzinger
1934	**THE NIGHT IS YOUNG**	Co-stars:	Bob Hope Bing Crosby Dorothy Lamour
Director:	Dudley Murphy		
Co-stars:	Evelyn Laye Ramon Navarro Rosalind Russell	**1941**	**DOUBLE DATE**
		Co-stars:	Edmund Lowe Peggy Moran Rand Brooks
1934	**THE MERRY WIDOW**		
Director:	Ernst Lubitsch	**1942**	**TWIN BEDS**
Co-stars:	Maurice Chevalier Jeanette MacDonald George Barbier	Director:	Tim Whelan
		Co-stars:	George Brent Joan Bennett Glenda Farrell
1934	**PARIS INTERLUDE**		
Director:	Edwin Marin	**1942**	**THE MAD DOCTOR OF MARKET STREET**
Co-stars:	Madge Evans Robert Young Otto Kruger Ted Healey	Director:	Joseph Lewis
		Co-stars:	Lionel Atwill Nat Pendleton Claire Dodd
1935	**ONE NEW YORK NIGHT**		
Director:	Jack Conway	**1943**	**THIS IS THE ARMY**
Co-stars:	Franchot Tone Steffi Duna Charles Starrett	Director:	Michael Curtiz
		Co-stars:	George Murphy Ronald Reagan Joan Leslie
1935	**BABY FACE HARRINGTON**		
Director:	Raoul Walsh	**1948**	**THE BRIDE GOES WILD**
Co-stars:	Charles Butterworth Eugene Pallette Nat Pendleton	Director:	Norman Taurog
		Co-stars:	Van Johnson June Allyson Hume Cronyn
1935	**BIOGRAPHY OF A BACHELOR GIRL**		
Director:	Edward Griffith	**1950**	**KILL THE UMPIRE**
Co-stars:	Ann Harding Robert Montgomery	Director:	Lloyd Bacon
		Co-stars:	William Bendix Ray Collins Gloria Henry
1935	**BROADWAY MELODY OF 1936**		
Director:	Roy Del Ruth	**1950**	**MY BLUE HEAVEN**
Co-stars:	Robert Taylor Eleanor Powell Buddy Ebsen	Director:	Henry Koster
		Co-stars:	Betty Grable Dan Dailey Mitzi Gaynor David Wayne
1935	**MURDER IN THE FLEET**		
Director:	Edward Sedgewick	**1951**	**GOLDEN GIRL**
Co-stars:	Robert Taylor Jean Parker Jean Hersholt	Director:	Lloyd Bacon
		Co-stars:	Mitzi Gaynor Dale Robertson James Barton Dennis Day
1935	**RIFF RAFF**		
Director:	Walter Ruben	**1952**	**WITH A SONG IN MY HEART**
Co-stars:	Jean Harlow Spencer Tracy Mickey Rooney	Director:	Walter Lang
		Co-stars:	Susan Hayward David Wayne Thelma Ritter
1936	**THE CAT'S PAW**		
Director:	Sam Taylor	**1952**	**THE MERRY WIDOW**
Co-stars:	Harold Lloyd George Barbier Nat Pendleton	Director:	Curtis Bernhardt
		Co-stars:	Fernando Lamas Lana Turner Richard Haydn
1936	**WE WENT TO COLLEGE**		
Co-stars:	Walter Abel Charles Butterworth Edith Atwater	**1953**	**I LOVE MELVYN**
		Director:	Don Weis
1936	**BORN TO DANCE**	Co-stars:	Donald O'Connor Debbie Reynolds Allyn Joslyn
Director:	Roy Del Ruth		
Co-stars:	James Stewart Eleanor Powell Buddy Ebsen	**1955**	**THE KENTUCKIAN**
		Director:	Burt Lancaster
1937	**CHECKERS**	Co-stars:	Burt Lancaster Dianne Foster Walter Matthau
Director:	Bruce Humberstone		
Co-stars:	Jane Withers Stuart Erwin Marvin Stephens		

1956 BUNDLE OF JOY
Director: Norman Taurog
Co-stars: Debbie Reynolds Eddie Fisher Adolphe Menjou

1957 THE FUZZY PINK NIGHTGOWN
Director: Norman Taurog
Co-stars: Jane Russell Ralph Meeker Keenan Wynn

1958 THE GIRL MOST LIKELY
Director: Mitchell Leisen
Co-stars: Jane Powell Cliff Robertson Keith Andes

1959 THE MATING GAME
Director: George Marshall
Co-stars: Debbie Reynolds Tony Randall Paul Douglas

1961 THE PARENT TRAP
Director: David Swift
Co-stars: Hayley Millls Maureen O'Hara Brian Keith

1961 SUMMER AND SMOKE
Director: Peter Glenville
Co-stars: Geraldine Page Laurence Harvey Rita Moreno

1963 SUMMER MAGIC
Director: James Neilson
Co-stars: Hayley Mills Burl Ives Dorothy McGuire

1963 A TIGER WALKS
Director: Norman Tokar
Co-stars: Sabu Brian Keith Vera Miles Pamela Franklin

1966 SPINOUT
Director: Norman Taurog
Co-stars: Elvis Presley Shelley Fabares Cecil Kellaway

JOANNA MERLIN

1956 THE TEN COMMANDMENTS
Director: Cecil B.DeMille
Co-stars: Charlton Heston Yul Brynner Anne Baxter

1982 BABY, IT'S YOU
Director: John Sayles
Co-stars: Rosanna Arquette Vincent Spano Jack Davidson

1982 LOVE CHILD
Director: Larry Peerce
Co-stars: Amy Madigan Beau Bridges Albert Salmi

1988 MYSTIC PIZZA
Director: Donald Petrie
Co-stars: Julia Roberts Lili Taylor Annabeth Gish

1991 CLASS ACTION
Director: Michael Apted
Co-stars: Gene Hackman Mary Elizabeth Mastrantonio Colin Friels

MARISA MERLINI

1970 JELALOUSY, ITALIAN STYLE
Director: Ettore Scola
Co-stars: Marcello Mastroianni Monica Vitti

1984 AURORA
Director: Maurizio Ponzi
Co-stars: Sophia Loren Daniel J.Travanti Edoardo Ponti

ETHEL MERMAN

1930 FOLLOW THE LEADER
Director: Norman Taurog
Co-stars: Ed Winn Ginger Rogers Stanley Smith

1935 KID MILLIONS
Director: Roy Del Ruth
Ûco-Stars Eddie Cantor Ann Sothern George Murphy Lucille Ball

1934 WE'RE NOT DRESSING
Director: Norman Taurog
Co-stars: Bing Crosby Carole Lombard George Burns Gracie Allen

1935 STRIKE ME PINK
Director: Norman Taurog
Co-stars: Eddie Cantor Sally Eilers Parkyakarkus

1935 THE BIG BROADCAST OF 1936
Director: Norman Taurog
Co-stars: Bing Crosby George Burns Gracie Allen

1936 ANYTHING GOES
Director: Lewis Milestone
Co-stars: Bing Crosby Charles Ruggles Ida Lupino

1938 ALEXANDER'S RAGTIME BAND
Director: Henry King
Co-stars: Tyrone Power Alice Faye Don Ameche

1938 HAPPY LANDING
Director: Roy Del Ruth
Co-stars: Sonja Henie Don Ameche Cesar Romero

1938 STRAIGHT, PLACE AND SHOW
Director: David Butler
Co-stars: Ritz Bros Richard Arlen Phyllis Brooks

1943 STAGE DOOR CANTEEN
Director: Frank Borzage
Co-stars: Cheryl Walker Lon McCallister Judith Anderson

1953 CALL ME MADAM
Director: Walter Lang
Co-stars: Donald O'Connor Vera-Ellen George Sanders

1954 THERE'S NO BUSINESS
LIKE SHOW BUSINESS
Director: Walter Lang
Co-stars: Dan Dailey Donald O'Connor Mitzi Gaynor

1963 ITS A MAD, MAD, MAD, MAD WORLD
Director: Stanley Kramer
Co-stars: Spencer Tracy Mickey Rooney Jimmy Durante

1965 THE ART OF LOVE
Director: Norman Jewison
Co-stars: James Garner Dick Van Dyke Angie Dickenson

1974 JOURNEY BACK TO OZ *(Voice)*
Director: Hal Sutherland
Co-stars: Liza Minnelli Mickey Rooney

1976 WON TON TON, THE DOG
WHO SAVED HOLLYWOOD
Director: Michael Winner
Co-stars: Madeline Kahn Art Carney Bruce Dern

1980 AIRPLANE!
Director: Jerry Zucker
Co-stars: Robert Stack Lloyd Bridges Leslie Neilsen

MARY MERRALL

1940 DR O'DOWD
Director: Herbert Mason
Co-stars: Shaun Glenville Peggy Cummins Patricia Roc

1941 LOVE ON THE DOLE
Director: John Baxter
Co-stars: Deborah Kerr Clifford Evans Joyce Howard

1945 DEAD OF THE NIGHT
Director: Charles Crichton
Co-stars: Mervyn Johns Googie Withers Michael Redgrave

1947 THEY MADE ME A FUGITIVE
Director: Alberto Cavalcanti
Co-stars: Trevor Howard Sally Gray Rene Ray

1947 NICHOLAS NICKLEBY
Director: Alberto Cavalcanti
Co-stars: Derek Bond Cedric Hardwicke Sally Ann Howes

1948 THE THREE WEIRD SISTERS
Director: Dan Birt
Co-stars: Nancy Price Mary Clare Nova Pilbeam

1951   THE LATE EDWINA BLACK
Director: Maurice Elvey
Co-stars: Geraldine Fitzgerald David Farrar Jean Cadell

1954   THE BELLES OF ST. TRINIANS
Director: Frank Launder
Co-stars: Alastair Sim George Cole Joyce Grenfell

1958   R.X.MURDER
Director: Derek Twist
Co-stars: Marius Goring Rick Jason Lisa Gastoni

1961   SPARE THE ROD
Director: Leslie Norman
Co-stars: Max Bygraves Geoffrey Keen Richard O'Sullivan

CHARLOTTE MERRIAM

1931   NIGHT NURSE
Director: William Wellman
Co-stars: Barbara Stanwyck Clark Gable Joan Blondell

DORIS MERRICK

1944   THE BIG NOISE
Director: Mal St.Clair
Co-stars: Stan Laurel Oliver Hardy Jack Norton

1945   HIT THE HAY
Co-stars: Ross Hunter Judy Canova Fortunio Bonanova

1946   SENSATION HUNTERS
Co-stars: Robert Lowery Constance Worth

1947   I LOVE TROUBLE
Director: S.Sylvan Simon
Co-stars: Franchot Tone Janet Blair Glenda Farrell

1948   THE COUNTERFEITERS
Director: Peter Stewart
Co-stars: John Sutton Hugh Beaumont Lon Chaney

1953   THE NEANDERTHAL MAN
Director: E.A.Dupont
Co-stars: Robert Shayne Richard Crane Joyce Terry

LYNN MERRICK

1941   THE APACHE KID
Co-star: Don Barry

1942   JESSE JAMES JR.
Co-star: Don Barry

1942   ARIZONA TERROR
Co-star: Don Barry Al "Fuzzy' St.John

1942   STAGECOACH EXPRESS
Co-star: Don Barry Al "Fuzzy' St.John Robert Kent

1943   CRIME DOCTOR'S STRANGEST CASE
Director: Eugene Forde
Co-stars: Warner Baxter Lloyd Bridges Rose Hobart

1944   NINE GIRLS
Director: Leigh Jason
Co-stars: Ann Harding Evelyn Keyes Anita Louise

1945   BOSTON BLACKIE BOOKED ON SUSPICION
Co-stars: Chester Morris George E.Stone Richard Lane

1945   A GUY, A GAL AND A PAL
Co-stars: Ross Hunter Mary McLeod Ted Donaldson

1945   BLONDE FROM BROOKLYN
Director: Robert Stanton Thurston Hall

DINA MERRIL

1957   THE DESK SET
Director: Walter Lang
Co-stars: Spencer Tracy Katherine Hepburn Gig Young

1958   A NICE LITTLE BANK THAT SHOULD BE ROBBED
Director: Henry Levin
Co-stars: Mickey Rooney Tom Ewell

1959   OPERATION PETTICOAT
Director: Blake Edwards
Co-stars: Cary Grant Tony Curtis Joan O'Brien

1959   DON'T GIVE UP THE SHIP
Director: Norman Taurog
Co-stars: Jerry Lewis Mickey Shaugnessy

1960   BUTTERFIELD 8
Director: Daniel Mann
Co-stars: Elizabeth Taylor Laurence Harvey Eddie Fisher

1960   THE SUNDOWNERS
Director: Fred Zinnemann
Co-stars: Robert Mitchum Deborah Kerr Peter Ustinov

1961   THE YOUNG SAVAGES
Director: John Frankenheimer
Co-stars: Burt Lancaster Shelley Winters Telly Savalas

1963   THE COURTSHIP OF EDDIE'S FATHER
Director: Vincente Minnelli
Co-stars: Glenn Ford Shirley Jones

1965   I'LL TAKE SWEDEN
Director: Frederick De Cordova
Co-stars: Bob Hope Tuesday Weld Frankie Avalon

1969   THE LONELY PROFESSION
Director: Douglas Heyes
Co-stars: Harry Guardino Dean Jagger Joseph Cotten

1972   FAMILY FLIGHT
Director: Marvin Chomsky
Co-stars: Rod Taylor Kristoffer Tabori Janet Margolin

1977   THE GREATEST
Director: Tom Gries
Co-stars: Mohammed Ali Ernest Borgnine Robert Duvall

1978   A WEDDING
Director: Robert Altman
Co-stars: Mia Farrow Lillian Gish Howard Duff

1980   JUST TELL ME WHAT YOU WANT
Director: Sidney Lumet
Co-stars: Ali MacGraw Alan King Myrna Loy

1983   ANNA TO THE INFINITE POWER
Director: Robert Wiemer
Co-stars: Marsha Byrne Mark Patton Jack Gilford

1988   CADDYSHACK II
Director: Alan Arkush
Co-stars: Jackie Mason Dyan Cannon Robert Stack

1989   FEAR
Director: Rockne O'Bannon
Co-stars: Ally Sheedy Lauren Hutton John Agar

1989   TURN BLACK THE CLOCK
Director: Larry Elikann
Co-stars: Connie Sellecca Jere Burns Gene Barry

1991   TRUE COLORS
Director: Herbert Ross
Co-stars: John Cusack James Spader Richard Widmark

1992   THE PLAYER
Director: Robert Altman
Co-stars: Tim Robbins Greta Scacchi Whoopi Goldberg

1993   SUTURE
Director: David Siegel
Co-stars: Dennis Haysbert Mel Harris Michael Harris

BARBARA MERRILL
(Daughter Of Bette Davis And Gary Merrill)

1951   PAYMENT ON DEMAND
Director: Curtis Bernhardt
Co-stars: Bette Davis Barry Sullivan Jane Cowl

JOAN MERRILL

1942   THE MAYOR OF 44TH. STREET
Director: Alfred Green
Co-stars: George Murphy Anne Shirley William Gargan

THERESA MERRITT

1977   THE GOODBYE GIRL
Director: Herbert Ross
Co-stars: Richard Dreyfuss Marsha Mason Quinn Cummings

1978   THE WIZ
Director: Sidney Lumet
Co-stars: Diana Ross Michael Jackson Lena Horne

1979   THE GREAT SANTINI
Director: Lewis John Carlino
Co-stars: Robert Duvall Blythe Danner Michael O'Keefe

1982   THE BEST LITTLE WHOREHOUSE IN TEXAS
Co-stars: Burt Reynolds Dolly Parton Charles Durning

1988   THE SERPENT AND THE RAINBOW
Director: Wes Craven
Co-stars: Bill Pullman Cathy Tyson Paul Winfield

JANE MERROW

1964   THE SYSTEM
Director: Michael Winner
Co-stars: Oliver Reed Barbara Ferris Julia Foster

1964   CATACOMBS
Director: Gordon Hessler
Co-stars: Gary Merrill Neil McCallum Georgina Cookson

1967   NIGHT OF THE BIG HEAT
Director: Terence Fisher
Co-stars: Christopher Lee Peter Cushing Sarah Lawson

1968   THE LION IN WINTER
Director: Anthony Harvey
Co-stars: Katherine Hepburn Peter O'Toole Anthony Hopkins

1970   ADAM'S WOMAN
Director: Philip Leacock
Co-stars: Beau Bridges James Booth John Mills

1971   HAND'S OF THE RIPPER
Director: Peter Sasdy
Co-stars: Angharad Rees Eric Porter Dora Bryan

1974   DIAGNOSIS: MURDER
Director: Sidney Hayers
Co-stars: Christopher Lee Judy Geeson Jon Finch

ARLETTE MERRY

1946   LA FERME DU PENDU
Director: Jean Dreville
Co-stars: Alfred Adam Charles Vanel

ZIENIA MERTON

1969   THE CHAIRMAN
Director: J.Lee-Thompson
Co-stars: Gregory Peck Anne Heywood Arthur Hill

DOLORES MESSINA

1982   BABY, IT'S YOU
Director: John Sayles
Co-stars: Rosanna Arquette Vincent Spano Joanna Merlin

ISABEL MESTRES

1978   CHINA 9, LIBERTY 37
Director: Monte Hellman
Co-stars: Fabio Testi Jenny Agutter Warren Oates

LAURIE METCALF

1985   DESPERATELY SEEKING SUSAN
Director: Susan Seidelman
Co-stars: Rosanna Arquettte Madonna Aidan Quinn

1987   CANDY MOUNTAIN
Director: Robert Frank
Co-stars: Kevin J.O'Connor Harris Yulin Tom Waits

1987   MAKING MR. RIGHT
Director: Susan Seidelman
Co-stars: Ann Magnuson John Malkovich Polly Bergen

1988   STARS AND BARS
Director: Pat O'Connor
Co-stars: Daniel Day-Lewis Harry Dean Stanton Joan Cusack

1989   UNCLE BUCK
Director: John Hughes
Co-stars: John Candy Amy Madigan Macauley Culkin

1990   PACIFIC HEIGHTS
Director: John Schlesinger
Co-stars: Melanie Griffith Matthew Modine Michael Keaton

1990   INTERNAL AFFAIRS
Director: Mike Figgis
Co-stars: Richard Gere Andy Garcia Nancy Travis

1992   J.F.K.
Director: Oliver Stone
Co-stars: Kevin Costner Joe Pesci Gary Oldman

1993   A DANGEROUS WOMAN
Director: Stephen Gyllenhaal
Co-stars: Debra Winger Barbara Hershey Gabriel Byrne

1994   BLINK
Director: Michael Apted
Co-stars: Madeleine Stowe Aidan Quinn Peter Friedman

ELEANOR METHVREN

1989   THE HEN HOUSE
Director: Danny Boyle
Co-stars: Sinead Cusack Tony Boyle Barry Birch

MAYO METHOT *(Married Humphrey Bogart)*

1932   NIGHT CLUB LADY
Director: Irving Cummings
Co-stars: Adolphe Menjou Skeets Gallagher Nat Pendleton

1932   VIRTUE
Director: Eddie Buzzell
Co-stars: Carole Lombard Pat O'Brien Jack La Rue

1933   THE MIND READER
Director: Roy Del Ruth
Co-stars: Warren William Constance Cummings Allen Jenkins

1933   COUNSELLOR-AT-LAW
Director: William Wyler
Co-stars: John Barrymore Bebe Daniels Melvyn Douglas

1934   JIMMY THE GENT
Director: Michael Curtis
Co-stars: James Cagney Bette Davis Alice White

1934   MILLS OF THE GODS
Director: Roy William Neill
Co-stars: May Robson Fay Wray Victor Jory

1935   DR. SOCRATES
Director: William Dieterle
Co-stars: Paul Muni Ann Dvorak Barton MacLane

1937 MARKED WOMAN
Director: Lloyd Bacon
Co-stars: Bette Davis Humphrey Bogart Jane Bryan

1939 UNEXPECTED FATHER
Director: Charles Lamont
Co-stars: Baby Sandy Dennis O'Keefe Shirley Ross

NANCY METTE

1987 MATEWAN
Director: John Sayles
Co-stars: Chris Cooper Mary McDonad Will Oldham

ANNE-LAURE MEURY

1987 MY GIRLFRIEND'S BOYFRIEND
Director: Eric Rohmer
Co-stars: Emmanuelle Chaulet Sophie Renoir Eric Veillard

ANITA MEY

1955 HEIDI AND PETER
Director: Franz Schnyder
Co-stars: Heinrich Gretler Elsbeth Sigmund Thomas Klameth

BESS MEYER

1990 UNSPEAKABLE ACTS
Director: Linda Otto
Co-stars: Brad Davis Bebe Neuwirth

1991 THE INNER CIRCLE
Director: Andrei Konchalovsky
Co-stars: Tom Hulce Lolita Davidovich Bob Hoskins

1993 NECRONOMINON
Director: Brian Yuzna
Co-stars: Bruce Payne Jeffrey Combs David Warner

DINA MEYER

1996 DRAGONHEART !
Co-stars: Dennis Quaid David Thewlis Pete Postlethwaite

1998 STARSHIP TROOPERS
Director: Paul Verhoeven
Co-stars: Casper Van Dien Patrick Muldoon Denise Richards

GRETA MEYER

1937 WHEN LOVE IS YOUNG
Director: Hal Mohr
Co-stars: Virginia Bruce Kent Taylor Walter Brennan

ARI MEYERS *(Child)*

1984 LICENSE TO KILL
Director: Jud Taylor
Co-stars: James Farentino Penny Fuller Don Murray

1988 WINDMILLS OF THE GODS
Director: Lee Philips
Co-stars: Jaclyn Smith Christopher Cazenove Susan Tyrrell

1990 THINK BIG
Director: Jon Turteltaub
Co-stars: Peter Paul David Paul David Carradine

1994 CONFESSIONS:TWO FACES OF EVIL
Director: Gilbert Cates
Co-stars: James Earl Jones Jason Bateman James Wilder

1996 THE KILLING SECRET
Director: Noel Nosseck
Co-star: Soleil Moon Frye

PAULINE MEYERS

1980 ANGEL CITY
Director: Philip Leacock
Co-stars: Ralph Waite Jennifer Jason Leigh Paul Winfield

1992 MY COUSIN VINNY
Director: Jonathan Lynn
Co-stars: Joe Pesci Marisa Tomei Fred Gwynne

MICHELLE MEYRINK

1983 VALLEY GIRL
Director: Martha Coolridge
Co-stars: Nicolas Cage Deborah Foreman Elizabeth Daily

1984 THE JOY OF SEX
Director: Martha Coolridge
Co-stars: Cameron Dye Lisa Langlois Colleen Camp

1985 REAL GENIUS
Director: Martha Coolridge
Co-stars: Val Kilmer Gabe Jarret William Atherton

1987 NICE GIRLS DON'T EXPLODE
Director: Chuck Martinez
Co-stars: Barbara Harris William O'Leary Wallace Shawn

1988 PERMANENT RECORD
Director: Marisa Silver
Co-stars: Alan Boyce Keanu Reeves Jennifer Rubin

MYRIAM MEZIERES

1987 A FLAME IN MY HEART

1992 THE DIARY OF LADY M
Director: Alain Tanner
Co-stars: Juanjo Puigcorbe Felicite Wouassi Nanou

CORA MIAO

1985 DIM SUM: A LITTLE BIT OF HEART
Director: Wayne Wang
Co-stars: Lauren Chew Kim Chew Victor Wong

1989 EAT A BOWL OF TEA
Director: Wayne Wang
Co-stars: Russell Wong Victor Wong Eric Tsang

**1990 LIFE IS SWEET....
        BUT TOILET PAPER IS EXPENSIVE**

NORA MIAO

1972 FIST OF FURY
Director: Lo Wei
Co-stars: Bruce Lee Maria Yi James Tien

1972 THE WAY OF THE DRAGON
Director: Bruce Lee
Co-stars: Bruce Lee Chuck Norris Marisa Longo Robert Wall

GERTRUDE MICHAEL

1933 I'M NO ANGEL
Director: Wesley Ruggles
Co-stars: Mae West Cary Grant Edward Arnold

1933 CRADLE SONG
Director: Mitchell Leisen
Co-stars: Dorothea Wieck Evelyn Venable Kent Taylor

1934 BOLERO
Director: Wesley Ruggles
Co-stars: George Raft Carole Lombard Sally Rand

1934 GEORGE WHITE'S SCANDALS
Director: Harry Lachman
Co-stars: Rudy Vallee Alice Faye Jimmy Durante

1934 I BELIEVED IN YOU
Director: Irving Cummings
Co-stars: Rosemary Ames Victor Jory John Boles

1934 MURDER AT THE VANITIES
Director: Mitchell Leisen
Co-stars: Jack Oakie Victor McLaglen Jesse Ralph

1934   **MURDER ON THE BLACKBOARD**
Director: George Archainbaud
Co-stars: Edna May Oliver James Gleason

1934   **SEARCH FOR BEAUTY**
Director: Erle Kenton
Co-stars: Buster Crabbe Ida Lupino Toby Wing

1934   **THE NOTORIOUS SOPHIE LANG**
Director: Ralph Murphy
Co-stars: Paul Cavanagh Arthur Byron Leon Errol

1934   **MENANCE**
Director: Ralph Murphy
Co-stars: Paul Cavanagh Ray Milland Halliwell Hobbs

1934   **CLEOPATRA**
Director: Cecil B.DeMille
Co-stars: Claudette Colbert Henry Wilcoxon Warren William

1935   **FATHER BROWN, DETECTIVE**
Director: Edward Sedgwick
Co-stars: Walter Connolly Paul Lukas

1935   **FOUR HOURS TO KILL**
Director: Mitchell Leisen
Co-stars: Richard Barthelmess Ray Milland Helen Mack

1935   **THE LAST OUTPOST**
Director: Charles Barton
Co-stars: Cary Grant Claude Rains Akim Tamiroff

1936   **MAKE WAY FOR A LADY**
Director: David Burton
Co-stars: Herbert Marshall Ann Shirley Margot Grahame

1936   **REUNION**
Director: Norman Taurog
Co-star: Herbert Marshall

1936   **TILL WE MEET AGAIN**
Director: Robert Florey
Co-stars: Herbert Marshall Lionel Atwill

1936   **WOMAN TRAP**
Co-stars: George Murphy Roscoe Karns

1936   **FORGOTTEN FACES**
Director: E.A.Dupont
Co-stars: Herbert Marshall Robert Cummings James Burke

1936   **SECOND WIFE**
Co-stars: Walter Abel Erik Rhodes

1937   **MR. DODD TAKES THE AIR**
Director: Alfred Green
Co-stars: Kenny Baker Jane Wyman Alice Brady

1937   **SOPHIE LANG GOES WEST**
Co-stars: Jed Prouty Sandra Storme C.Henry Gordon

1939   **HIDDEN POWER**
Co-star: Jack Holt

1940   **THE FARMER'S DAUGHTER**
Director: James Hogan
Co-stars: Martha Raye Charles Ruggles Richard Denning

1943   **BEHIND PRISON WALLS**
Director: Steve Sekeley
Co-stars: Alan Baxter Tully Marshall Edwin Maxwell

1943   **WHERE ARE YOUR CHILDREN?**
Director: William Nigh
Co-stars: Jackie Cooper Gale Storm John Litel

1943   **WOMEN IN BONDAGE**
Director: Steve Sekeley
Co-stars: Gail Patrick Nancy Kelly Anne Nagel

1949   **FLAMINGO ROAD**
Director: Michael Curtiz
Co-stars: Joan Crawford Zachary Scott Sydney Greenstreet

1950   **CAGED**
Director: John Cromwell
Co-stars: Eleanor Parker Agnes Moorehead Jan Sterling

1951   **DARLING, HOW COULD YOU**
Director: Mitchell Leisen
Co-stars: Joan Fontaine John Lund Mona Freeman

OLIVE MICHAEL

1986   **COMING UP ROSES**
Director: Stephen Bayley
Co-stars: Dafydd Hywel Iola Gregory Mari Emlyn

ATHENA MICHAELIDOU

1957   **A MATTER OF DIGNITY**
Director: Michael Cacoyannis
Co-stars: Ellie Lambetti Georges Pappas

BEVERLY MICHAELS

1951   **PICKUP**
Director: Hugo Haas
Co-stars: Hugo Haas Allan Nixon Howard Chamberlin

1955   **CRASHOUT**
Director: Lewis Foster
Co-stars: William Bendix Arthur Kennedy Luther Adler

1956   **WOMEN WITHOUT MEN**
Director: Elmo Williams
Co-stars: Joan Rice Avril Angers Thora Hird

DOLORES MICHAELS

1957   **APRIL LOVE**
Director: Henry Levin
Co-stars: Pat Boone Shirley Jones Arthur O'Connell

1957   **TIME LIMIT**
Director: Karl Malden
Co-stars: Richard Widmark Richard Basehart June Lockhart

1957   **THE WAYWARD BUS**
Director: Victor Vicas
Co-stars: Dan Dailey Jayne Mansfield Joan Collins

1958   **FRAULEIN**
Director: Henry Koster
Co-stars: Dana Wynter Mel Ferrer Helmut Dantine

1958   **THE FIEND WHO WALKED THE WEST**
Director: Gordon Douglas
Co-stars: Robert Evans Hugh O'Brian Stephen McNally

1958   **FIVE GATES TO HELL**
Director: James Clavell
Co-stars: Patricia Owens Neville Brand Nancy Kulp

1959   **WARLOCK**
Director: Edward Dmytryk
Co-stars: Henry Fonda Richard Widmark Anthony Quinn

1960   **ONE FOOT IN HELL**
Director: James Clark
Co-stars: Alan Ladd Dan O'Herlihy Don Murray

1961   **THE BATTLE AT BLOODY BEACH**
Director: Herbert Coleman
Co-stars: Audie Murphy Gary Crosby

JULIE MICHAELS

1989   **ROAD HOUSE**
Director: Rowdy Herrington
Co-stars: Patrick Swayze Kelly Lynch Ben Gazzara

1991   **POINT BREAK**
Director: Kathryn Bigelow
Co-stars: Keanu Reeves Patrick Swayze Gary Busey

MERLE MICHAELS

1981   AFTERNOON DELIGHTS
Director: Warren Evans
Co-stars: Eric Edwards Veronica Hart Samantha Fox

TOBY MICHAELS

1961   LOVE IN A GOLDFISH BOWL
Director: Jack Sher
Co-stars: Tommy Sands Jan Sterling Fabian

KARI MICHAELSEN

1983   KID WITH THE 200 I.Q.
Director: Leslie Martinson
Co-stars: Gary Coleman Robert Guillaume Dean Butler

MELISSA MICHAELSEN *(Child)*

1979   GOLDIE AND THE BOXER
Director: David Miller
Co-stars: O.J.Simpson Phil Silvers Madlyn Rhue

**1981   GOLDIE AND THE BOXER
GO TO HOLLYWOOD**
Director: David Miller
Co-stars: O.J.Simpson Stubby Kaye Jack Gilford

1981   BROKEN PROMISE
Director: Don Taylor
Co-stars: Chris Sarandon George Coe McKee Anderson

1984   NO MAN'S LAND
Director: Rod Holcomb
Co-stars: Stella Stevens Terri Garber Estelle Getty

DOMINIQUE MICHEL

1986   DECLINE OF THE ROMAN EMPIRE
Director: Denys Arcand
Co-stars: Dorothee Berryman Louise Portal

FRANNIE MICHEL

1970   DIARY OF A MAD HOUSEWIFE
Director: Frank Perry
Co-stars: Carrie Snodgress Richard Benjamin Frank Langella

LORA LEE MICHEL

1949   TOKYO JOE
Director: Stuart Heisler
Co-stars: Humphrey Bogart Florence Marly Alexander Knox

ODILE MICHEL

1977   PEPPERMINT SODA
Director: Diane Kurys
Co-stars: Eleanore Klarwein Anouk Ferjac Yves Renier

MARCELLA MICHELANGELI

1977   PADRE PADRONE
Director: Paolo Taviani
Co-stars: Fabrizio Forte Omero Antonutti Saveirio Marconi

HELENA MICHELL

1988   NUMBER 27
Director: Tristram Powell
Co-stars: Joyce Carey Nigel Planer Alun Armstrong

1988   THE DECEIVERS
Director: Ismail Merchant
Co-stars: Pierce Brosnan Saeed Jaffrey Shashi Kapoor

**1990   THE NEVERENDING STORY II:
THE NEXT CHAPTER**
Director: George Miler
Co-stars: Jonathan Brandis Kenny Morrison

VICKI MICHELLE

1975   ALFIE DARLING
Director: Ken Hughes
Co-stars: Alan Price Jill Townsend Joan Collins

SIMONE MICHELS

1948   CLOCHMERLE
Director: Pierre Chenal
Co-stars: Brochard Jane Marken Paul Demange

MARIA MICHI

1945   ROME OPEN CITY
Director: Roberto Rossellini
Co-stars: Aldo Fabrizi Anna Magnani Marcel Pagliero

1946   PAISA
Director: Roberto Rossellini
Co-stars: William Tubbs Gar Moore Harriet White

1972   LAST TANGO IN PARIS
Director: Bernardo Bertolucci
Co-stars: Marlon Brando Maria Schneider

MICHOU

1973   LA BONNE ANNEE
Director: Claude Lelouche
Co-stars: Lino Ventura Francoise Fabian Mireille Mathieu

DENISE B. MICKLEBURY

1986   A TIME TO TRIUMPH
Director: Noel Black
Co-stars: Patty Duke Joseph Bologna Julie Bovasso

FRAN MIDDLETON

1978   MARTIN
Director: George Romero
Co-stars: John Amplas Lincoln Maazel Christine Forrest

NOELLE MIDDLETON

1954   HAPPY EVER AFTER
Director: Mario Zampi
Co-stars: David Niven Yvonne De Carlo George Cole

1954   CARRINGTON V.C.
Director: Anthony Asquith
Co-stars: David Niven Margaret Leighton Clive Morton

1955   A YANK IN ERMINE
Director: Gordon Parry
Co-stars: Peter Thompson Diana Decker Jon Pertwee

1956   THE IRON PETTICOAT
Director: Ralph Thomas
Co-stars: Bob Hope Katharine Hepburn Robert Helpman

1957   THE VICIOUS CIRCLE
Director: Gerald Thomas
Co-stars: John Mills Derek Farr Roland Culver

FLORENCE MIDGELELY

1928   SADIE THOMPSON
Director: Raoul Walsh
Co-stars: Gloria Swanson Lionel Barrymore Blanche Frederici

BETTE MIDLER
(Married Martin Van Haselberg)
**Nominated For Best Actress In 1979 For "The Rose"
And In 1991 For "For The Boys"**

1966   HAWAII
Director: George Roy Hill
Co-stars: Max Von Sydow Julie Andrews Richard Harris

1979 **THE ROSE**
Director: Mark Rydell
Co-stars: Alan Bates Frederick Forrest Harry Dean Stanton

1980 **DIVINE MADNESS**
Director: Michael Ritchie
Co-stars: The Harlettes (Diva Grey Ula Hedwig Jocelyn Brown)

1982 **JINXED!**
Director: Don Siegel
Co-stars: Ken Wahl Rip Torn Val Avery Jack Elam

1985 **DOWN AND OUT IN BEVERLY HILLS**
Director: Paul Mazursky
Co-stars: Nick Nolte Richard Dreyfuss

1986 **OUTRAGEOUS FORTUNE**
Director: Arthur Hiller
Co-stars: Shelley Long Peter Coyote Robert Prosky

1986 **RUTHLESS PEOPLE**
Director: Jerry Zucker
Co-stars: Danny DeVito Judge Reinhold Helen Slater

1988 **BEACHES**
Director: Garry Marshall
Co-stars: Barbara Hershey John Heard Spalding Gray

1988 **BIG BUSINESS**
Director: Jim Abrahams
Co-stars: Lily Tomlin Fred Ward Edward Herrman

1989 **OLIVER AND COMPANY** *(Voice)*
Director: George Scribner
Co-stars: Billy Joel Joey Lawrence Dom DeLuise

1990 **STELLA**
Director: John Erman
Co-stars: John Goodman Marsha Mason Trini Alvarado

1991 **SCENES FROM A MALL**
Director: Paul Mazursky
Co-stars: Woody Allen Bill Irwin Rebecca Nickels

1991 **FOR THE BOYS**
Director: Mark Rydell
Co-stars: James Caan George Segal Patrick O'Neal

1993 **HOCUS POCUS**
Director: Kenny Ortega
Co-stars: Sarah Jessica Parker Kathy Najimy Vinessa Shaw

1993 **GYPSY**
Director: Emile Ardolino
Co-stars: Cynthia Gibb Peter Riegert Ed Asner

1996 **THE FIRST WIVES CLUB**
Director: Hugh Wilson
Co-stars: Goldie Hawn Diane Keaton Sara Jessica Parker

1996 **THAT OLD FEELING**
Co-stars: Dennis Farina Paula Marshall

JULIA MIGENES-JOHNSON

1984 **CARMEN**
Director: Francesco Rosi
Co-stars: Placido Domingo Ruggero Raimondi Faith Esham

LUDMILA MIKAEL

1968 **THE SERGEANT**
Director: John Flynn
Co-stars: Rod Steiger John Phillip Law Frank Latimore

1989 **NOCHE BLANCHE**
Director: Jean-Claude Brisseau
Co-stars: Vanessa Paradis Bruno Cremer Francois Negret

IRA MIKHALYOVA

1992 **LOST IN SIBERIA**
Director: Alexander Mitta
Co-stars: Anthony Andrews Yelena Mayorova Vladimir Ilyin

LITA MILAN

1957 **THE RIDE BACK**
Director: Allen Miner
Co-stars: Anthony Quinn William Conrad George Trevino

1958 **NEVER LOVE A STRANGER**
Director: Robert Stevens
Co-stars: John Drew Barrymore Steve McQueen Robert Bray

1958 **I, MOBSTER**
Director: Roger Corman
Co-stars: Steve Cochran Robert Strauss Celia Lovsky

1958 **THE LEFT-HANDED GUN**
Director: Arthur Penn
Co-stars: Paul Newman Hurd Hatfield John Dehner

ALYSSA MILANO

1985 **COMMANDO**
Director: Mark Lester
Co-stars: Arnold Schwarzenegger Rae Dawn Chong Dan Hedaya

1988 **DANCE 'TIL DAWN**
Director: Paul Schneider
Co-stars: Tracey Gold Brian Bloom Chris Young

1993 **CASUALTIES OF LOVE:
THE LONG ISLAND LOLITA STORY**
Director: John Herzfeld
Co-stars: Jack Scalia Lawrence Tilly Anne De Salvo

1994 **CONFESSIONS OF A SORORITY GIRL**

1995 **THE SURROGATE**
Director: Jan Egleson
Co-stars: Connie Selleca David Dukes

1996 **DEADLY SINS**
Director: Michael Robinson
Co-star: David Keith

OLIVE MILBOURNE

1955 **ONE WAY OUT**
Director: Francis Searle
Co-stars: Jill Adams Eddie Byrne Lyndon Brook

BETTY MILES

1941 **LONE STAR LAW MEN**
Co-stars: Tom Keene Sugar Dawn Frank Yaconelli

JOANNA MILES

1973 **THE GLASS MENAGERIE**
Director: Anthony Harvey
Co-stars: Katherine Hepburn Sam Waterston Michael Moriarty

1974 **THE ULTIMATE WARRIOR**
Director: Robert Clouse
Co-stars: Yul Brynner Max Von Sydow

1975 **BUG**
Director: Jeannot Szwarc
Co-stars: Bradford Dillman Alan Fudge Patty McCormack

1977 **DELATA COUNTY U.S.A.**
Director: Glen Jordan
Co-stars: Jim Antonio Peter Donat Morgan Brittany

1978 **A FIRE IN THE SKY**
Director: Jerry Jameson
Co-stars: Richard Crenna Elizabeth Ashley David Dukes

1988 **RIGHT TO DIE**
Director: Paul Wendkos
Co-stars: Raquel Welch Michael Gross Bonnie Bartlett

1988 **THE ATTIC**
Director: Doug Adams
Co-stars: Carol Lynley Gail O'Grady Joseph Gian

1990	**ROSENGRANTZ AND GUILDENSTERN ARE DEAD**		1985	**STEAMING**
Director:	Tom Stoppard		*Director:*	Joseph Losey
Co-stars:	Gary Oldman Tim Roth Iain Glen		*Co-stars:*	Vanessa Redgrave Diana Dors Brenda Bruce

1990 ROSENGRANTZ AND GUILDENSTERN ARE DEAD
Director: Tom Stoppard
Co-stars: Gary Oldman Tim Roth Iain Glen

1992 THE HEART OF JUSTICE
Director: Bruno Barreto
Co-stars: Eric Stoltz Dermot Mulroney Vincent Price

LILLIAN MILES

1932 MAN AGAINST WOMAN
Co-star: Jack Holt

1934 THE GAY DIVORCEE
Director: Mark Sandrich
Co-stars: Fred Astaire Ginger Rogers Edward Everett Horton

1936 REEFER MADNESS
Director: Louis Gasnier
Co-stars: Dave O'Brien Dorothy Short Carleton Young

SARAH MILES *(Married Robert Bolt)*
Nominated For Best Actress In 1970 For "Ryan's Daughter"

1962 TERM OF TRIAL
Director: Peter Glenville
Co-stars: Laurence Olivier Simone Signoret Hugh Griffith

1963 THE SERVANT
Director: Joseph Losey
Co-stars: Dirk Bogarde James Fox Wendy Craig

1963 THE CEREMONY
Director: Laurence Harvey
Co-stars: Laurence Harvey Robert Walker John Ireland

1965 I WAS HAPPY HERE
Director: Desmond Davis
Co-stars: Cyril Cusack Julian Glover Sean Caffrey

1965 THOSE MAGNIFICENT MEN IN THEIR FLYING MACHINES
Director: Ken Annakin
Co-stars: Stuart Whitman Benny Hill Terry-Thomas

1966 BLOWUP
Director: Michaelangelo Antonioni
Co-stars: David Hemmings Vanessa Redgrave Peter Bowles

1970 RYAN'S DAUGHTER
Director: David Lean
Co-stars: Robert Mitchum John Mills Chris Jones Trevor Howard

1972 LADY CAROLINE LAMB
Director: Robert Bolt
Co-stars: Jon Finch Richard Chamberlain Ralph Richardson

1973 THE HIRELING
Director: Alan Bridges
Co-stars: Robert Shaw Peter Egan Elizabeth Sellars

1973 THE MAN WHO LOVED CAT DANCING
Director: Richard Sarafian
Co-stars: Burt Reynolds Jack Warden

1974 GREAT EXPECTATIONS
Director: Joseph Hardy
Co-stars: Michael York James Mason Margaret Leighton

1976 THE SAILOR WHO FELL FROM GRACE WITH THE SEA
Director: Lewis John Carlino
Co-star: Kris Kristofferson Jonathon Kahn

1978 THE BIG SLEEP
Director: Michael Winner
Co-stars: Robert Mitchum Richard Boone James Stewart

1981 VENOM
Director: Piers Hagard
Co-stars: Sterling Hayden Klaus Kinski Oliver Reed Susan George

1985 STEAMING
Director: Joseph Losey
Co-stars: Vanessa Redgrave Diana Dors Brenda Bruce

1985 ORDEAL BY INNOCENCE
Director: Desmond Davis
Co-stars: Donald Sutherland Christopher Plummer

1986 HAREM
Director: Billy Hale
Co-stars: Nancy Travis Omar Sharif Ava Gardner

1987 HOPE AND GLORY
Director: John Boorman
Co-stars: Susan Wooldridge Ian Bannen David Hayman

1987 WHITE MISCHIELF
Director: Michael Radford
Co-stars: Charles Dance Greta Scacchi Joss Ackland

1990 A GHOST IN MONTE CARLO
Director: John Hough
Co-stars: Oliver Reed Lysette Anthony

1992 THE SILENT TOUCH
Director: Krzysztof Zanussi
Co-stars: Max Von Sydow Lothaire Bluteau Sofie Grabol

SYLVIA MILES
Nominated For Best Supporting Actress In 1969 For "Midnight Cowboy" And In 1975 For "Farewell My Lovely"

1964 PSYCHOMANIA
Director: Richard Hilliard
Co-stars: Lee Phillips Shepperd Strudwick James Farentino

1969 MIDNIGHT COWBOY
Director: John Schlesinger
Co-stars: Jon Voight Dustin Hoffman Brenda Vaccaro

1971 WHO KILLED MARY WHAT'S HER NAME?
Director: Ernest Pintoff
Co-stars: Red Buttons Sam Waterston

1976 THE GREAT SCOUT AND CATHOUSE THURSDAY
Director: Don Taylor
Co-stars: Lee Marvin Oliver Reed Robert Culp

1975 FAREWELL MY LOVELY
Director: Dick Richards
Co-stars: Robert Mitchum Charlotte Rampling John Ireland

1976 THE SENTINEL
Director: Michael Winner
Co-stars: Christina Raines Chris Sarandon Jose Ferrer

1981 THE FUNHOUSE
Director: Tobe Hunter
Co-stars: Elizabeth Berridge Cooper Huckabee Kevin Conway

1982 EVIL UNDER THE SUN
Director: Guy Hamilton
Co-stars: Peter Ustinov James Mason Diana Rigg

1983 NO BIG DEAL
Director: Robert Carlton
Co-stars: Kevin Dillon Mary Joan Negro

1986 CRITICAL CONDITON
Director: Michael Apted
Co-stars: Richard Pryor Rachel Ticotin

1988 CROSSING DELANCY
Director: Joan Micklin Silver
Co-stars: Amy Irving Peter Riegart

1989 SHE-DEVIL
Director: Susan Seidelman
Co-stars: Meryl Streep Roseanne Barr Ed Begley Jnr.

VERA MILES

1952 FOR MEN ONLY
Director: Paul Henreid
Co-stars: Paul Henreid Robert Sherman Russell Johnson

1953 THE CHARGE AT FEATHER RIVER
Director: Gordon Douglas
Co-stars: Guy Maddison Frank Lovejoy

1955 TARZAN'S HIDDEN JUNGLE
Director: Harold Schuster
Co-stars: Gordon Scott Jack Elam Rex Ingram

1955 WICHITA
Director: Jacques Tourneur
Co-stars: Joel McCrea Lloyd Bridges Edgar Buchanan

1956 23 PACES TO BAKER STREET
Director: Henry Hathaway
Co-stars: Van Johnson Cecil Parker Maurice Denham

1956 THE SEARCHERS
Director: John Ford
Co-stars: John Wayne Jeffrey Hunter Natalie Wood

1956 AUTUMN LEAVES
Director: Robert Aldrich
Co-stars: Joan Crawford Cliff Robertson Lorne Greene

1957 BEAU JAMES
Director: Melville Shavelson
Co-stars: Bob Hope Paul Douglas Alexis Smith

1957 THE WRONG MAN
Director: Alfred Hitchcock
Co-stars: Henry Fonda Anthony Quayle

1959 A TOUCH OF LARCENCY
Director: Guy Hamilton
Co-stars: James Mason George Sanders Rhonda Fleming

1959 THE F.B.I. STORY
Director: Mervyn LeRoy
Co-stars: James Stewart Murray Hamilton Nick Adams

1959 BEYOND THIS PLACE
Director: Jack Cardiff
Co-stars: Van Johnson Emlyn Williams Jean Kent

1960 FIVE BRANDED WOMEN
Director: Martin Ritt
Co-stars: Van Heflin Silvana Mangano Jeanne Moreau

1960 PSYCHO
Director: Alfred Hitchcock
Co-stars: Anthony Perkins Janet Leigh John Gavin

1961 BACK STREET
Director: David Miller
Co-stars: Susan Hayward John Gavin Charles Drake

1962 THE MAN WHO SHOT LIBERTY VALANCE
Director: John Ford
Co-stars: James Stewart John Wayne Lee Marvin

1963 A TIGER WALKS
Director: Norman Tokar
Co-stars: Sabu Brian Keith Pamela Franklin Una Merkel

1964 THOSE CALLOWAYS
Director: Norman Tokar
Co-stars: Brian Keith Brandon De Wilde Walter Brennan

1966 FOLLOW ME, BOYS!
Director: Norman Tokar
Co-stars: Fred MacMurray Lillian Gish Kurt Russell

1967 THE GENTLE GIANT
Director: James Neilson
Co-stars: Dennis Weaver Clint Howard Ralph Meeker

1967 THE SPIRIT IS WILLING
Director: William Castle
Co-stars: Sid Caesar John McGiver Cass Daley

1969 HELLFIGHTERS
Director: Andrew McLaglen
Co-stars: John Wayne Jim Hutton Katharine Ross

1970 CANNON
Director: George McCowan
Co-stars: William Conrad Earl Holliman J.D.Cannon

1970 THE WILD COUNTRY
Director: Robert Totten
Co-stars: Steve Forrest Jack Elam Ronny Howard

1972 MOLLY AND LAWLESS JOHN
Director: Gary Nelson
Co-stars: Clu Gulager Sam Elliott John Anderson

1973 RUNAWAY!
Director: David Lowell Rich
Co-stars: Ben Johnson Ben Murphy Ed Nelson

1973 ONE LITTLE INDIAN
Director: Bernard McEveety
Co-stars: James Garner Pat Hingle Morgan Woodward

1974 THE STRANGE AND DEADLY OCCURENCE
Director: Charles Frend
Co-stars: Robert Stack L.Q.Jones Dena Dietrich

1974 THE CASTAWAY COWBOY
Director: Vincent McEveety
Co-stars: James Garner Robert Culp Eric Shea

1976 JUDGE HORTON AND THE SCOTSBORO BOYS
Director: Fielder Cook
Co-stars: Arthur Hill Ken Kercheval

1977 FIRE

1978 THE GREAT BALLOON ADVENTURE
Director: Richard Colla
Co-stars: Katharine Hepburn George Kennedy

1978 AND I ALONE SURVIVED
Director: William Graham
Co-stars: Blair Brown David Ackroyd G.D.Spradlin

1982 BRAINWAVES
Director: Ulli Lommel
Co-stars: Tony Curtis Keir Dullea Suzanne Love

1983 PSYCHO II
Director: Richard Franklin
Co-stars: Anthony Perkins Meg Tilly Robert Loggia

1985 INTO THE NIGHT
Director: John Landis
Co-stars: Jeff Goldblum Michelle Pfeiffer David Bowie

1988 THE HIJACKING OF THE ACHILLE LAURO
Director: Robert Collins
Co-stars: Karl Malden Lee Grant

KIM MILFORD

1979 CORVETTE SUMMER
Director: Matthew Robbins
Co-stars: Mark Hamill Annie Potts Eugene Roche

NANCY MILFORD

1988 ACT OF PIRACY
Director: John Cardos
Co-stars: Gary Busey Belinda Bauer Ray Sharkey

PENELOPE MILFORD
Nominated For Best Supporting Actress In 1978 For "Coming Home"

1978 COMING HOME
Director: Hal Ashby
Co-stars: Jane Fonda Jon Voight Bruce Dern

1981 **TAKE THIS JOB AND SHOVE IT**
Director: Gus Trikonis
Co-stars: Robert Hays Art Carney Barbara Hershey

1983 **THE GOLDEN SEAL**
Director: Frank Zuniga
Co-stars: Steve Railsback Michael Beck Torquil Campbell

1985 **THE BURNING BED**
Director: Robert Greenwald
Co-stars: Farrah Fawcett Paul Le Mat Richard Masur

1989 **HEATHERS**
Director: Michael Lehman
Co-stars: Winona Ryder Christian Slater Shannen Doherty

LYNN MILGRIM

1983 **ENORMOUS CHANGES AT THE LAST MINUTE**
Director: Mirra Bank
Co-stars: Ellem Barkin Kevin Bacon Maria Tucci

IMOGEN MILLAIS-SCOTT

1988 **SALOME'S LAST DANCE**
Director: Ken Russell
Co-stars: Glenda Jackson Stratford Johns Nikolas Grace

LYNN MILLAND

1948 **CANON CITY**
Director: Crane Wilbur
Co-stars: Scott Brady Jeff Corey Whit Bissell

MARJIE MILLAR

1954 **ABOUT MRS. LESLIE**
Director: Daniel Mann
Co-stars: Shirley Booth Robert Ryan Alex Nicol

1954 **MONEY FROM HOME**
Director: George Marshall
Co-stars: Dean Martin Jerry Lewis Pat Crowley

HELENE MILLARD

1930 **THE DIVORCEE**
Director: Robert Z.Leonard
Co-stars: Norma Shearer Chester Morris Robert Montgomery

1940 **THE BISCUIT EATER**
Director: Stuart Heisler
Co-stars: Billy Lee Cordell Hickman Richard Lane

DIANA MILLAY

1967 **TARZAN AND THE GREAT RIVER**
Director: Robert Day
Co-stars: Mike Henry Jan Murray Rafer Johnson

ANN MILLER

1937 **NEW FACES OF 1937**
Director: Leigh Jason
Co-stars: Milton Berle Parkyakarkus Joe Penner

1937 **LIFE OF THE PARTY**
Director: William Seiter
Co-stars: Gene Raymond Harriet Hilliard Joe Penner

1937 **STAGE DOOR**
Director: Gregory La Cava
Co-stars: Katharine Hepburn Ginger Rogers Eve Arden

1938 **TARNISHED ANGEL**
Co-stars: Sally Eilers Paul Guilfoyle

1938 **RADIO CITY REVELS**
Director: Ben Stoloff
Co-stars: Bob Burns Jack Oakie Kenny Baker Victor Moore

1938 **YOU CAN'T TAKE IT WITH YOU**
Director: Frank Capra
Co-stars: Jean Arthur James Stewart Edward Arnold

1938 **ROOM SERVICE**
Director: William Seiter
Co-stars: Marx Brothers Lucille Ball Frank Albertson

1940 **MELODY RANCH**
Co-stars: Gene Autry Jimmy Durante George 'Gabby' Hayes

1940 **TOO MANY GIRLS**
Director: George Abbott
Co-stars: Lucille Ball Desi Arnaz Eddie Bracken

1940 **GO WEST YOUNG LADY**
Director: Frank Strayer
Co-stars: Glenn Ford Penny Singleton

1941 **NEVER GIVE A SUCKER AN EVEN BREAK**
Director: Edward Cline
Co-stars: W.C.Fields Gloria Jean Leon Errol

1941 **HIT PARADE OF 1941**
Director: John Auer
Co-stars: Kenny Baker Frances Langford Phil Silvers

1942 **PRIORITIES ON PARADE**
Director: Albert Rogell
Co-stars: Johnnie Johnston Jerry Colonna

1943 **WHAT'S BUZZIN' COUSIN**
Director: Charles Barton
Co-stars: John Hubbard Eddie Anderson

1943 **REVEILLE WITH BEVERLEY**
Director: Charles Barton
Co-stars: William Wright Larry Parks Tim Ryan

1944 **JAM SESSION**
Director: Charles Barton
Co-star: Jess Barker

1944 **HEY, ROOKIE**
Director: Charles Barton
Co-stars: Joe Besser Larry Parks Joe Sawyer

1944 **CAROLINA BLUES**
Director: Leigh Jason
Co-stars: Kay Kyser Victor Moore

1945 **EVE KNEW HER APPLES**
Director: Will Jason
Co-stars: Robert Williams William Wright Ray Walker

1945 **EADIE WAS A LADY**
Director: Arthur Dreifuss
Co-stars: Joe Besser William Wright Jeff Donnell

1946 **THE THRILL OF BRAZIL**
Director: S.Sylvan Simon
Co-stars: Evelyn Ankers Keenan Wynn Allyn Joslyn

1948 **EASTER PARADE**
Director: Charles Walters
Co-stars: Fred Astaire Judy Garland Peter Lawford

1948 **THE KISSING BANDIT**
Director: Laslo Benedek
Co-stars: Frank Sinatra Kathryn Grayson Billy Gilbert

1949 **ON THE TOWN**
Director: Stanley Donen
Co-stars: Gene Kelly Frank Sinatra Vera-Ellen

1950 **WATCH THE BIRDIE**
Director: Jack Donaghue
Co-stars: Red Skelton Arlene Dahl Leon Ames

1951 **TEXAS CARNIVAL**
Director: Charles Walters
Co-stars: Esther Williams Howard Keel Red Skelton

1952 LOVELY TO LOOK AT
Director: Mervyn LeRoy
Co-stars: Kathryn Grayson Howard Keel Red Skelton

1953 SMALL TOWN GIRL
Director: Leslie Kardos
Co-stars: Jane Powell Farley Granger Bobby Van Fay Wray

1953 KISS ME KATE
Director: George Sidney
Co-stars: Howard Keel Kathryn Grayson Keenan Wynn

1954 DEEP IN MY HEART
Director: Stanley Donen
Co-stars: Jose Ferrer Merle Oberon Gene Kelly

1955 HIT THE DECK
Director: Roy Rowland
Co-stars: Tony Martin Jane Powell Debbie Reynolds

1956 THE OPPOSITE SEX
Director: David Miller
Co-stars: June Allyson Dolores Gray Joan Collins

1956 THE GREAT AMERICAN PASTIME
Director: Herman Hoffman
Co-stars: Tom Ewell Anne Francis Dean Jones

**1976 WON TON TON, THE DOG
WHO SAVED HOLLYWOOD**
Director: Michael Winner
Co-stars: Madeline Kahn Art Carney Bruce Dern

CHERYL MILLER (U.S.A.)

1965 CLARENCE THE CROSS-EYED LION
Director: Andrew Marton
Co-stars: Marshall Thompson Betsy Drake Richard Haydn

1976 MOUNTAIN MAN
Director: David O'Malley
Co-stars: Denver Pyle John Dehner Ken Berry

CHERYL MILLER (U.K.) *(Child)*

1988 THE DIARY OF RITA PATEL
Director: Michael Jackley
Co-stars: Tony Wredden Indira Joshi Ian Arthur

COLLEEN MILLER

1952 THE LAS VEGAS STORY
Director: Robert Stevenson
Co-stars: Jane Russell Victor Mature Vincent Price

1954 FOUR GUNS TO THE BORDER
Director: Richard Carlson
Co-stars: Rory Calhoun Walter Brennan George Nader

1954 PLAYGIRL
Director: Joseph Pevney
Co-stars: Shelley Winters Barry Sullivan Kent Taylor

1955 THE PURPLE MASK
Director: Bruce Humberstone
Co-stars: Tony Curtis Dan O'Herlihy Gene Barry

1957 MAN IN THE SHADOW
Director: Jack Arnold
Co-stars: Jeff Chandler Orson Welles John Larch

1957 HOT SUMMER NIGHT
Director: David Friedkin
Co-stars: Leslie Nielsen Edward Andrews James Best

1959 STEP DOWN TO TERROR
Director: Harry Keller
Co-stars: Charles Drake Rod Taylor Jocelyn Brando

1964 GUNFIGHT AT COMANCHE CREEK
Director: Frank McDonald
Co-stars: Audie Murphy Ben Cooper John Hubbard

EVE MILLER

1952 APRIL IN PARIS
Director: David Butler
Co-stars: Doris Day Ray Bolger Claude Dauphin

1952 THE BIG TREES
Director: Felix Feist
Co-stars: Kirk Douglas Patrice Wymore Edgar Buchanan

1952 THE WINNING TEAM
Director: Lewis Seiler
Co-stars: Doris Day Ronald Reagan Russ Tamblyn

GERI MILLER

1970 TRASH
Director: Paul Morrissey
Co-stars: Joe Dallesandro Holly Woodlawn Jane Forth

JENNIFER MILLER

1992 HIT THE DUTCHMAN
Director: Menahem Golan
Co-stars: Bruce Nozick Will Kempe Sally Kirkland

JOAN MILLER

1947 THE WOMAN IN THE HALL
Director: Jack Lee
Co-stars: Ursula Jeans Cecil Parker Jean Simmons

1950 CAGED
Director: John Cromwell
Co-stars: Eleanor Parker Agnes Moorehead Jan Sterling

1959 NO TREES IN THE STREET
Director: J.Lee-Thompson
Co-stars: Sylvia Syms Herbert Lom Stanley Holloway

1959 TOO YOUNG TO LOVE
Director: Muriel Box
Co-stars: Thomas Mitchell Pauline Hahn Jess Conrad

KRISTINE MILLER

1947 I WALK ALONE
Director: Byron Haskin
Co-stars: Burt Lancaster Kirk Douglas Lizabeth Scott

1947 DESERT FURY
Director: Lewis Allen
Co-stars: Burt Lancaster Lizabeth Scott John Hodiak

1949 TOO LATE FOR TEARS
Director: Byron Haskin
Co-stars: Lizabeth Scott Don Defore Arthur Kennedy

1949 SHADOW ON THE WALL
Director: Pat Jackson
Co-stars: Ann Sothern Zachary Scot Gigi Perreau

1950 HIGH LONESOME
Director: Alan Le May
Co-stars: John Barrymore Jnr. Chill Wills Lois Butler

LINDA MILLER

1978 AN UNMARRIED WOMAN
Director: Paul Mazursky
Co-stars: Jill Clayburgh Alan Bates Michael Murphy

LORRAINE MILLER

1945 BORDER BADMEN
Co-stars: Larry Crabbe Al 'Fuzzy' St.John

MANDY MILLER *(Child)*

1952 MANDY
Director: Alexander MacKendrick ✳
Co-stars: Jack Hawkins Phyllis Calvert Terence Morgan

1951 MAN IN THE WHITE SUIT
✳ ALEC GUINNESS JOAN GREENWOOD

1953   **BACKGROUND**
Director: Daniel Birt
Co-stars: Valerie Hobson Philip Friend Janette Scott

1954   **DANCE LITTLE LADY**
Director: Val Guest
Co-stars: Mai Zetterling Terence Morgan Guy Rolfe

1955   **RAISING A RIOT**
Director: Wendy Toye
Co-stars: Kenneth More Ronald Squire Shelagh Fraser

1956   **THE FEMININE TOUCH**
Director: Pat Jackson
Co-stars: George Baker Belinda Lee Adrienne Corri

1956   **CHILD IN THE HOUSE**
Director: Raker Endfield
Co-stars: Eric Portman Phyllis Calvert Stanley Baker

1958   **THE SNORKEL**
Director: Guy Green
Co-stars: Peter Van Eyck Betta St.John William Franklyn

MARIAN MILLER

1946   **JUST BEFORE DAWN**
Director: William Castle
Co-stars: Warner Baxter Adelle Roberts Mona Barrie

MARILYN MILLER

1930   **SALLY**
Director: John Francis Dillon
Co-stars: Joe E.Brown Alexander Grey T.Roy Barnes

1930   **SUNNY**
Director: William Seiter
Co-stars: Jack Donahue Lawrence Grey MacKenzie Ward

1931   **HER MAJESTY, LOVE**
Director: William Dieterle
Co-stars: Ben Lyon W.C.Fields Leon Errol

MARY MILLER

1986   **AFTER PILKINGTON**
Director: Christopher Morahan
Co-stars: Bob Peck Miranda Richardson Barry Foster

MAXINE MILLER

1986   **THE CARE BEARS MOVIE II:**
         A NEW GENERATION
Director: Dale Schott
Co-stars: Pam Myatt Hadley Kay

1994   **MY NAME IS KATE**
Director: Rod Hardy
Co-stars: Daniel J. Travanti Eileen Brennan Linda Darlow

PAMELA MILLER

1971   **200 MOTELS**
Director: Frank Zappa
Co-stars: Tony Palmer Theodore Bikel Ringo Star

PATSY RUTH MILLER

1921   **CAMILLE**
Director: Ray Smallwood
Co-stars: Nazimova Rudolph Valentino Arthur Hoyt

1923   **THE HUNCHBACK OF NOTRE DAME**
Director: Wallace Worsley
Co-stars: Lon Chaney Ernest Torrence Kate Lester

1926   **SO THIS IS PARIS**
Director: Ernst Lubitsch
Co-stars: Monte Blue Lilyan Tashman Myrna Loy

1929   **THE HOTTENTOT**
Director: Roy Del Ruth
Co-stars: Edward Everett Horton Douglas Gerrard

1929   **SHOW OF SHOWS**
Director: John Adolphi
Co-stars: Frank Fay Monte Blue Lupino Lane

1930   **THE AVIATOR**
Director: Roy Del Ruth
Co-stars: Edward Everett Horton Johnny Arthur Lee Moran

1930   **THE LAST OF THE LONE WOLF**
Co-star: Bert Lytell

PENELOPE ANN MILLER

1987   **ADVENTURES IN BABYSITTING**
Director: Chris Columbus
Co-stars: Elizabeth Shue Maia Brewton Keith Coogan

1988   **BIG TOP PEE-WEE**
Director: Randal Kleiser
Co-stars: Pee-Wee Herman Kris Kristofferson Susan Tyrrell

1988   **BILOXI BLUES**
Director: Mike Nichols
Co-stars: Matthew Broderick Christopher Walken Matt Mulhern

1988   **MILES FROM HOME**
Director: Gary Sinese
Co-stars: Richard Gere Kevin Anderson John Malkovich

1990   **KINDERGARTEN COP**
Director: Ivan Reitman
Co-stars: Arnold Schwarzenegger Pamela Reed Linda Hunt

1990   **DOWNTOWN**
Director: Richard Benjamin
Co-stars: Anthony Edwards Forest Whitaker Joe Pantoliano

1990   **AWAKENINGS**
Director: Penny Marshall
Co-stars: Robert De Niro Robin Williams Julie Kavner

1991   **OTHER PEOPLE'S MONEY**
Director: Norman Jewison
Co-stars: Gregory Peck Danny DeVito Piper Laurie

1990   **THE FRESHMAN**
Director: Andrew Bergman
Co-stars: Marlon Brando Matthew Broderick Maxmillian Schell

1992   **THE GUN IN BETTY LOU'S HANDBAG**
Director: Allan Moyle
Co-stars: Alfre Woodard Julianne Moore Eric Thal

1992   **YEAR OF THE COMET**
Director: Peter Yates
Co-stars: Tim Daly Louis Jourdan Ian Richardson

1993   **CARLITO'S WAY**
Director: Brian De Palma
Co-stars: Al Pacino Sean Penn Viggo Mortensen

1994   **THE SHADOW**
Director: Russell Mulcahy
Co-stars: Alec Baldwin John Lone Peter Boyle

1997   **THE RELIC**
Co-stars: Tom Sizemore Audra Lindley

1997   **THE HIRED HEART**
Co-star: Brett Cullen

REBECCA MILLER *(Daughter Of Arthur Miller)*

1988   **THE MURDER OF MARY PHAGAN**
Director: Billy Hale
Co-stars: Jack Lemmon Peter Gallagher Richard Jordan

1991   **REGARDING HENRY**
Director: Mike Nichols
Co-stars: Harrison Ford Annette Bening Bill Nunn

1992 CONSENTING ADULTS
Director: Alan J.Pakula
Co-stars: Kevin Kline Mary Elizabeth Mastrantonio Kevin Spacey

1993 WIND
Director: Carroll Ballard
Co-stars: Matthew Modine Jennifer Grey Cliff Robertson

ROBYN MILLER

1975 LIVE A LITTLE, STEAL A LOT
Director: Marvin Chomsky
Co-stars: Robert Conrad Don Stroud Donna Mills

ROSEMARY MILLER

1959 LIFE IN EMERGENCY WARD 10
Director: Robert Day
Co-stars: Michael Craig Dorothy Alison Glyn Owen

RUBY MILLER

1959 ANNA KARENINA
Director: Julien Duvivier
Co-stars: Vivien Leigh Kieron Moore Ralph Richardson

CHRISTINE MILLET

1984 NOVEMBER MOON
Director: Alexandra Von Grote
Co-stars: Gabrile Osburg Daniele Delorme Bruno Pradal

ANDRA MILLIAN

1984 WINNING STREAK
Director: Jim Wilson
Co-star: Kevin Costner

ANGIE MILLIKEN

1991 ACT OF NECESSITY
Director: Ian Munro
Co-stars: Mark Owen-Taylor Stephen Grives

1994 ROUGH DIAMONDS
Co-stars: Jason Donovan

ALLEY MILLS

1994 CAUGHT IN THE CROSSFIRE
Director: Chuck Brown
Co-stars: Dennis Franz Daniel Roebuck

DONNA MILLS

1971 PLAY MISTY FOR ME
Director: Clint Eastwood
Co-stars: Clint Eastwood Jessica Walter John Larch Irene Hervey

1972 NIGHT OF TERROR
Director: Jeannot Szwarc
Co-stars: Martin Balsam Chuck Connors Catherine Burns

1972 HAUNTS OF THE VERY RICH
Director: Paul Wendkos
Co-stars: Lloyd Bridges Cloris Leachman Anne Francis

1973 THE BAIT
Director: Leonard Horn
Co-stars: Michael Constantine William Devane June Lockhart

1975 BEYOND THE BERMUDA TRIANGLE
Director: William Graham
Co-stars: Fred MacMurray Sam Groom Dana Plato

1975 LIVE A LITTLE, STEAL A LOT
Director: Marvin Chomsky
Co-stars: Robert Conrad Don Stroud Robyn Miller

1975 WHO IS THE BLACK DAHLIA?
Director: Joseph Pevney
Co-stars: Efrem Zimbalist Jnr. Lucie Arnaz Ronny Cox

1978 DOCTORS' PRIVATE LIVES
Director: Steven Hillard Stern
Co-stars: Ed Nelson John Gavin Barbara Anderson

1984 HE'S NOT YOUR SON
Director: Don Taylor
Co-stars: Ken Howard Ann Dusenberry George Coe

1988 OUTBACK BOUND
Director: John Llewellyn Moxey
Co-stars: Andrew Clarke John Meillon Nina Foch

1989 THE LADY FORGETS
Director: Bradford May
Co-stars: Greg Evigan Roy Dotrice Andrew Robinson

1990 THE WORLD'S OLDEST LIVING BRIDESMAID
Director: Joseph L. Scanlan
Co-stars: Brian Wimmer Beverley Garland Art Hindle

1992 IN MY DAUGHTER'S NAME
Director: Jud Taylor
Co-stars: John Getz Lee Grant Ari Meyers

1994 MY NAME IS KATE
Director: Rod Hardy
Co-stars: Daniel J. Travanti Eileen Brennan Linda Darlow

1994 DANGEROUS INTENTIONS
Director: Michael Uno
Co-stars: Corbin Bernsen Allison Hossack

HAYLEY MILLS
(Daughter Of John Mills And Mary Hayley Bell, Sister Of Juliette Mills) Special Award 1960

1959 TIGER BAY
Director: J. Lee Thompson
Co-stars: John Mills Horst Buchholz Yvonne Mitchell

1960 POLLYANNA
Director: David Swift
Co-stars: Jane Wyman Karl Malden Nancy Olson

1961 WHISTLE DOWN THE WIND
Director: Bryan Forbes
Co-stars: Alan Bates Bernard Lee Norman Bird

1961 THE PARENT TRAP
Director: David Swift
Co-stars: Maureen O'Hara Brian Keith Charles Ruggles

1961 IN SEARCH OF THE CASTAWAYS
Director: Robert Stevenson
Co-stars: Maurice Chevalier George Sanders

1963 SUMMER MAGIC
Director: James Neilson
Co-stars: Burl Ives Dorothy McGuire Una Merkel

1964 THE MOON SPINNERS
Director: James Neilson
Co-stars: Peter McEnery Eli Wallach Joan Greenwood

1964 THE CHALK GARDEN
Director: Ronald Neame
Co-stars: Edith Evans Deborah Kerr John Mills

1965 SKY WEST AND CROOKED
Director: John Mills
Co-stars: Ian McShane Laurence Naismith Annette Crosbie

1965 THAT DARN CAT
Director: Robert Stevenson
Co-stars: Dean Jones Dorothy Provine Ed Wynn

1965 THE TRUTH ABOUT SPRING
Director: Richard Thorpe
Co-stars: James MacArthur John Mills David Tomlinson

1966　**THE TROUBLE WITH ANGELS**
Director:　Ida Lupino
Co-stars:　Rosalind Russell Binnie Barnes Gypsy Rose Lee

1966　**THE FAMILY WAY**
Director:　Roy Boutling
Co-stars:　John Mills Marjorie Rhodes Hywel Bennett

1967　**AFRICA: TEXAS STYLE**
Director:　Andrew Martin
Co-stars:　John Mills Hugh O'Brian Nigel Green

1967　**PRETTY POLLY**
Director:　Guy Green
Co-stars:　Trevor Howard Brenda De Banzie Shashi Kapoor

1968　**TWISTED NERVE**
Director:　Roy Boutling
Co-stars:　Hywel Bennett Phyllis Calvert Billie Whitelaw

1970　**TAKE A GIRL LIKE YOU**
Director:　Jonathan Miller
Co-stars:　Oliver Reed Noel Harrison Sheila Hancock

1971　**MR. FORBUSH AND THE PENGUINS**
Director:　Roy Boutling
Co-stars:　John Hurt Tony Britton Sally Geeson

1971　**ENDLESS NIGHT**
Director:　Sidney Gilliat
Co-stars:　Hywel Bennett George Sanders Britt Ekland

1974　**DEADLY STRANGERS**
Director:　Sidney Hayers
Co-stars:　Simon Ward Sterling Hayden Peter Jeffrey

1975　**WHAT CHANGED CHARLEY FARTHING?**
Director:　Sidney Hayers
Co-stars:　Doug McClure Lionel Jeffries

1986　**AMAZING STORIES 3**
Director:　Joe Dante
Co-stars:　Stephen Geoffreys Jon Cryer Dennis Lipscomb

1986　**THE PARENT TRAP II**
Director:　Ronald Maxwell
Co-stars:　Tom Skerritt Bridgette Anderson

1988　**APPOINTMENT WITH DEATH**
Director:　Michael Winner
Co-stars:　Peter Ustinov Lauren Bacall David Soul

1989　**BACK HOME**
Director:　Piers Haggard
Co-stars:　Hayley Carr Brenda Bruce Jean Anderson

1989　**THE PARENT TRAP III**
Director:　Mollie Miller
Co-stars:　Barry Bostwick Leanne Creel Monica Creel Joy Creel

1989　**THE PARENT TRAP: HAWAIIAN HONEYMOON**
Director:　Mollie Miller
Co-stars:　Barry Bostwick Leanne Creel Monica Creel Joy Creel

JULIETTE MILLS (Daughter Of John Mills And Mary Hayley Bell Sister Of Hayley Mills)

1961　**NO MY DARLING DAUGHTER**
Director:　Ralph Thomas
Co-stars:　Michael Redgrave Michael Craig Roger Livesey

1962　**TWICE AROUND THE DAFFODILS**
Director:　Gerald Thomas
Co-stars:　Donald Sinden Jill Ireland Andrew Ray

1963　**CARRY ON JACK**
Director:　Gerald Thomas
Co-stars:　Kenneth Williams Bernard Cribbins Donald Houston

1963　**NURSE ON WHEELS**
Director:　Gerald Thomas
Co-stars:　Ronald Lewis Joan Sims Athene Seyler

1966　**THE RARE BREED**
Director:　Andrew McLaglen
Co-stars:　James Stewart Maureen O'Hara Brian Keith

1972　**AVANTI**
Director:　Billy Wilder
Co-stars:　Jack Lemmon Clive Revill Edward Andrews

1975　**BEYOND THE DOOR**
Director:　Oliver Hellman
Co-stars:　Richard Johnson Elizabeth Turner David Colin

1977　**BARNABY AND ME**
Director:　Norman Panama
Co-stars:　Sid Caesar Sally Boyden John Newcombe

1990　**NIGHT OF THE FOX**
Director:　Charles Jarrott
Co-stars:　George Peppard Deborah Raffin John Mills

KIRI MILLS

1993　**DESPERATE REMEDIES**
Director:　Peter Wells
Co-stars:　Jennifer Ward-Lealand Kevin Smith Cliff Curtis

SHIRLEY MILLS

1940　**THE GRAPES OF WRATH**
Director:　John Ford
Co-stars:　Henry Fonda Jane Darwell John Carradine

JUNO MILLS-COCKELL

1989　**PARENTS**
Director:　Bob Balaban
Co-stars:　Randy Quaid Mary Beth Hurt Sandy Dennis

CAROLINE MILMOE

1986　**BRICK IS BEAUTIFUL**
Director:　David Wheatley
Co-stars:　Christopher Wild Ian Mercer Paul Oldham

MEGAN MILNER (child)

1990　**LOOK WHO'S TALKING TOO**
Director:　Amy Heckerling
Co-stars:　John Travolta Kirstie Alley Elias Koteas

SANDRA MILO

1959　**IL GENERALE DELLA ROVERE**
Director:　Roberto Rossellini
Co-stars:　Vittorio De Sica Anne Vernon Hanner Messemer

1960　**ADUA E LA COMPAGNE**
Director:　Antonio Pietrangeli
Co-stars:　Simone Signoret Gina Rovere

1963　**EIGHT AND A HALF**
Director:　Federico Fellini
Co-stars:　Marcello Mastroianni Claudia Cardinale Anouk Aimee

1965　**JULIET OF THE SPIRITS**
Director:　Federico Fellini
Co-stars:　Giulietta Masina Mario Pisu

YVETTE MIMIEUX

1955　**JOY IN THE MORNING**
Director:　Alex Segal
Co-stars:　Richard Chamberlain Arthur Kennedy Oscar Homolka

1960　**PLATINUM HIGH SCHOOL**
Director:　Charles Haas
Co-stars:　Mickey Rooney Dan Duryea Terry Moore

1960　**THE TIME MACHINE**
Director:　George Pal
Co-stars:　Rod Taylor Alan Young Sebastian Cabot

1960	**WHERE THE BOYS ARE**
Director:	Henry Levin
Co-stars:	George Hamilton Dolores Hart Jim Hutton

1961	**THE FOUR HORSEMEN OF THE APOCALYPSE**
Director:	Vincente Minnelli
Co-stars:	Glenn Ford Charles Boyer

1962	**DIAMOND HEAD**
Director:	Guy Green
Co-stars:	Charlton Heston James Darren France Nuyen

1962	**THE WONDERFUL WORLD OF THE BROTHERS GRIMM**
Director:	Henry Levin
Co-stars:	Laurence Harvey Karl Boehm Claire Bloom

1962	**LIGHT IN THE PIAZZA**
Director:	Guy Green
Co-stars:	Olivia De Havilland Rossano Brazzi George Hamilton

1963	**TOYS IN THE ATTIC**
Director:	George Roy Hill
Co-stars:	Geraldine Page Wendy Hiller Dean Martin

1966	**MONKEYS, GO HOME**
Director:	Andrew McLaglen
Co-stars:	Maurice Chevalier Dean Jones Jules Munshin

1966	**THE CAPER OF THE GOLDEN BULLS**
Director:	Russel Rouse
Co-stars:	Stephen Boyd Walter Slezak

1968	**THE MERCENARIES**
Director:	Jack Cardiff
Co-stars:	Rod Taylor Jim Brown Kenneth More

1968	**THREE IN THE ATTIC**
Director:	Richard Wilson
Co-stars:	Chris Jones Judy Pace Maggie Turett

1972	**SKY JACKED**
Director:	John Guillermin
Co-stars:	Charlton Heston James Brolin Jeanne Crain

1973	**THE NEPTUNE FACTOR**
Director:	Daniel Petrie
Co-stars:	Ben Gazzara Walter Pidgeon Ernest Borgnine

1975	**BURN OUT**
Director:	Daniel Mann
Co-stars:	Lindsay Wagner Sam Waterston Zero Mostel

1976	**JACKSON COUNTRY JAIL**
Director:	Michael Miller
Co-stars:	Tommy Lee Jones Robert Carradine Severn Darden

1979	**THE BLACK HOLE**
Director:	Gary Nelson
Co-stars:	Maximilian Schell Anthony Perkins Ernest Borgnine

1983	**NIGHT PARTNERS**
Director:	Noel Nosseck
Co-stars:	Diana Canova M.Emmet Walsh Patricia McCormack

1984	**OBSESSIVE LOVE**
Director:	Steven Hilliard Stern
Co-stars:	Simon MacCorkindale Kin Shriner Allan Miller

1990	**PERRY MASON: THE CASE OF THE DESPERATE DECEPTION**
Director:	Christian Nyby
Co-stars:	Ian McShane Ian Bannen Raymond Burr

ESTER MINCIOTTI

1949	**HOUSE OF STRANGERS**
Director:	Joseph Mankiewicz
Co-stars:	Edward G.Robinson Susan Hayward Luther Adler

1949	**SHOCKPROOF**
Director:	Douglas Sirk
Co-stars:	Cornel Wilde Patricia Knight John Baragrey

1949	**UNDERCOVER MAN**
Director:	Joseph Lewis
Co-stars:	Glenn Ford Nina Foch James Whitmore

1951	**STRICTLY DISHONORABLE**
Director:	Norman Panama
Co-stars:	Ezio Pinza Janet Leigh Millard Mitchell

1955	**MARTY**
Director:	Delbert Mann
Co-stars:	Ernest Borgnine Betsy Blair Joe Mantell

1956	**FULL OF LIFE**
Director:	Richard Quine
Co-stars:	Judy Holliday Richard Conte Salvatore Baccaloni

1957	**THE WRONG MAN**
Director:	Alfred Hitchcock
Co-stars:	Henry Fonda Vera Miles Anthony Quayle

JAN MINER

1974	**LENNY**
Director:	Bob Fosse
Co-stars:	Dustin Hoffman Valerie Perrine Stanley Beck

1990	**MERMAIDS**
Director:	Richard Benjamin
Co-stars:	Cher Bob Hoskins Winona Ryder

MINNA

1992	**AMAZON**
Director:	Mika Kaurismaki
Co-stars:	Kari Vaananen Robert Davi Rae Dawn Chong

LIZA MINNELLI *(Child)*
(Daughter Of Judy Garland And Vincente Minnelli)
Oscar For Best Actress In 1972 For "Cabaret". Nominated For Best Actress In 1969 For "The Sterile Cuckoo"

1949	**IN THE GOOD OLD SUMMERTIME**
Director:	Robert Z. Leonard
Co-stars:	Judy Garland Van Johnson S.Z.Sakall

1968	**CHARLIE BUBBLES**
Director:	Albert Finney
Co-stars:	Albert Finney Billie Whitelaw Colin Blakely

1969	**THE STERILE CUCKOO**
Director:	Alan J. Pakula
Co-stars:	Wendell Burton Tim McIntyre Austin Green

1970	**TELL ME THAT YOU LOVE ME, JUNIE MOON**
Director:	Otto Preminger
Co-stars:	Ken Howard Robert Moore

1972	**CABARET**
Director:	Bob Fosse
Co-stars:	Joel Grey Michael York Helmut Griem Marisa Berenson

1974	**JOURNEY BACK TO OZ** *(Voice)*
Director:	Hal Sutherland
Co-stars:	Mickey Rooney Ethel Merman

1975	**LUCKY LADY**
Director:	Stanley Donen
Co-stars:	Gene Hackman Burt Reynolds Michael Hordern

1976	**A MATTER OF TIME**
Director:	Vincente Minnelli
Co-stars:	Ingrid Bergman Charles Boyer Isabella Rossellini

1976	**SILENT MOVIE**
Director:	Mel Brooks
Co-stars:	Marty Feldman Dom DeLuise Sid Caesar Marcelle Marceau

1977	**NEW YORK, NEW YORK**
Director:	Martin Scorsese
Co-stars:	Robert De Niro Lionel Stander Barry Primus

1981 ARTHUR
Director: Steve Gordon
Co-stars: Dudley Moore John Gielgud Geraldine Fitzgerald

1983 THE KING OF COMEDY
Director: Martin Scorsese
Co-stars: Jerry Lewis Robert De Niro Diahnne Abbot

1984 THE MUPPETS TAKE MANHATTAN
Director: Frank Oz
Co-stars: Art Carney Brooke Shields Joan Rivers

1985 THAT'S DANCING
Director: Jack Haley Jnr.
Co-stars: Gene Kelly Fred Astaire Ray Bolger Sammy Davis

1985 A TIME TO LIVE
Director: Rick Wallace
Co-stars: Jeffrey DeMunn Swoozie Kirtz Corey Haim

1988 RENT-A-COP
Director: Jerry London
Co-stars: Burt Reynolds Robby Benson Dionne Warwick

1988 ARTHUR II: ON THE ROCKS
Director: Bud Yorkin
Co-stars: Dudley Moore John Gielgud Kathy Bates

1991 STEPPING OUT
Director: Lewis Gilbert
Co-stars: Shelley Winters Julie Walters Bill Irwin

1994 PARALLEL LIVES
Director: Linda Yellen
Co-stars: James Belushi JoBeth Williams Dudley Moore

1995 THE WEST SIDE WALTZ
Director: Ernest Thompson
Co-stars: Shirley MacLaine Jennifer Grey

DANNII MINOGUE *(Sister Of Kylie Minogue)*

1992 SECRETS
Director: Michael Pattinson
Co-stars: Beth Champion Malcolm Kennard

KYLIE MINOGUE *(Sister Of Dannii Minogue)*

1989 THE DELINQUENTS
Director: Chris Thomson
Co-stars: Charlie Schlatter Angela Punch-McGregor Todd Boyce

1994 STREETFIGHTER
Director: Steven De Souza
Co-stars: Jean-Claude Van Damme Raul Julia

1995 BIO-DOME
Co-stars: Stephen Baldwin Pauly Shore

QUONA MINSTER

1989 CLOWNS
Director: David Mahoney
Co-stars: Harry Andrews Angela Down Stephen Moore

KELLY JO MINTER

1986 CHARLIE HANNAH
Director: Peter Hunt
Co-stars: Robert Conrad Shane Conrad Christian Conrad

1989 CAT CHASER
Director: Abel Ferrara
Co-stars: Peter Weller Kelly McGillis Charles Durning

1989 A NIGHTMARE ON ELM STREET 5: THE DREAM CHILD
Director: Stephen Hopkins
Co-stars: Robert Englund Lisa Wilcox

1989 DOC HOLLYWOOD
Director: Michael Caton-Jones
Co-stars: Michael J Fox Julie Warner Bridget Fonda

1989 NEW JACK CITY
Director: Mario Van Peebles
Co-stars: Wesley Snipes Bill Nunn Judd Nelson

MARY MILES MINTER

1921 MOONSHINE AND HONEYSUCKLE

YVONNE MINTON

1982 PARSIFAL
Director: Hand Jurgen Syberberg
Co-stars: Michael Kutter Karin Krick Edith Clever

MIOU-MIOU

1973 BURNT BARNS
Director: Jean Chapot
Co-stars: Alain Delon Simone Signoret Paul Grauchet

1974 LES VALSEUSES
Director: Bertrand Blier
Co-stars: Gerard Depardieu Jeanne Moreau Isabelle Huppert

1976 JONAH - WHO WILL BE 25 IN THE YEAR 2000
Director: Alain Tanner
Co-stars: Jean-Luc Bideau Myriam Boyer

1983 DOG DAY
Director: Yves Boisset
Co-stars: Lee Marvin Jean Carmet Victor Lamoux Tina Louise

1983 COUP DE FOUDRE
Director: Diane Kurys
Co-stars: Isabelle Huppert Guy Marchand Jean-Pierre Bacri

1986 TENUE DE SOIREE
Director: Bertrand Blier
Co-stars: Gerard Depardieu Michel Blanc

1988 LA LECTRICE
Director: Michel Deville
Co-stars: Regis Royer Christian Ruche Marianne Denicourt

1988 REVOLVING DOORS
Director: Francis Mankiewcz
Co-stars: Monique Spaziani Gabriel Arcand

1989 MILOU IN MAY
Director: Louis Malle
Co-stars: Michel Piccoli Michel Duchassoy Harriet Walter

1993 TANGO
Director: Patrice Leconte
Co-stars: Thierry L'Hermitte Philippe Noiret Richard Bohringer

1993 GERMINAL
Director: Claude Berri
Co-stars: Gerard Depardieu Renaud Judith Henry Jean Carmen

JOELLE MIQUEL

1986 FOUR ADVENTURES OF REINETTE AND MIRABELLE
Director: Eric Rohmer
Co-stars: Jessica Forde Marie Riviere

BRIGITTE MIRA

1973 FEAR EATS THE SOUL
Director: Rainer Werner Fassbinder
Co-stars: Rainer Werner Fassbinder El Hedi Ben Salem

1973 TENDERNESS OF WOLVES
Director: Ulli Lommel
Co-stars: Kurt Raab Jeff Roden Wolfgang Schenk

1976 CHINESE ROULETTE
Director: Rainer Werner Fassbinder
Co-stars: Margit Carstensen Anna Karina Andrea Schober

IRENE MIRACLE

1978   MIDNIGHT EXPRESS
Director: Alan Parker
Co-stars: Brad Davis Randy Quaid John Hurt

1980   INFERNO
Director: Dario Argento
Co-stars: Leigh McCloskey Eleanora Giorgi

1989   PUPPET MASTER
Director: Davis Schmoller
Co-stars: Paul LeMat Robin Frates William Hickey

AURORA MIRANDA *(Sister Of Carmen Miranda)*

1944   PHANTOM LADY
Director: Robert Siodmak
Co-stars: Franchot Tone Ella Raines Thomas Gomez

1944   THE THREE CABALLEROS
Director: Norman Ferguson
Co-stars: Carmen Molina Dora Luz

CARMEN MIRANDA

1940   DOWN ARGENTINE WAY
Director: Irving Cummings
Co-stars: Betty Grable Don Ameche Charlotte Greenwood

1941   THAT NIGHT IN RIO
Director: Irving Cummings
Co-stars: Don Ameche Alice Faye S.Z.Sakall

1941   WEKEND IN HAVANA
Director: Walter Lang
Co-stars: Alice Faye John Payne Cesar Romero

1942   SPRINGTIME IN THE ROCKIES
Director: Irving Cummings
Co-stars: Betty Grable John Payne Cesar Romero

1943   THE GANG'S ALL HERE
Director: Busby Berkeley
Co-stars: Alice Faye James Ellison Charlotte Greenwood

1944   SOMETHING FOR THE BOYS
Director: Lewis Seiler
Co-stars: Vivian Blaine Michael O'Shea Phil Silvers

1944   FOUR JILLS IN A JEEP
Director: William Seiter
Co-stars: Kay Francis Martha Raye Carole Landis

1944   GREENWICH VILLAGE
Director: Walter Lang
Co-stars: Vivian Blaine Don Ameche William Bendix

1945   DOLL FACE
Director: Lewis Seiler
Co-stars: Vivian Blaine Perry Como Dennis O'Keefe

1946   IF I'M LUCKY
Director: Lewis Seiler
Co-stars: Vivian Blaine Perry Como Harry James

1947   COPACABANA
Director: Alfred Green
Co-stars: Groucho Marx Steve Cochran Gloria Jean

1948   A DATE WITH JUDY
Director: Richard Thorpe
Co-stars: Jane Powell Elizabeth Taylor Wallace Beery

1950   NANCY GOES TO RIO
Director: Robert Z. Leonard
Co-stars: Jane Powell Ann Sothern Barry Sullivan

1953   SCARED STIFF
Director: George Marshall
Co-stars: Dean Martin Jerry Lewis Lisabeth Scott

ISA MIRANDA

1939   HOTEL IMPERIAL
Director: Robert Florey
Co-stars: Ray Milland Reginald Owen Gene Lockhart

1940   ADVENTURES IN DIAMONDS
Director: George Fitzmaurice
Co-stars: George Brent John Loder Nigel Bruce

1949   BEYOND THE GATES
Director: Rene Clement
Co-stars: Jean Gabin Vera Talchi Andrea Checci

1950   LA RONDE
Director: Max Ophuls
Co-stars: Anton Walbrook Simone Signoret Simone Simon

1952   THE SEVEN DEADLY SINS
Director: Roberto Rossellini
Co-stars: Gerard Philipe Henri Vidal Michele Morgan

1955   SUMMER MADNESS
Director: David Lean
Co-stars: Katharine Hepburn Rossano Brazzi Mari Aldon

1964   THE EMPTY CANVAS
Director: Daminio Damiani
Co-stars: Horst Buchholz Catherine Spaak Bette Davis

1967   THE GREAT BRITISH TRAIN ROBBERY
Director: John Olden
Co-stars: Claus Peter Witt Horst Tappert

1971   LAST HOUSE ON THE LEFT PART 2
Director: Mario Bava
Co-stars: Claudine Auger Claudio Volante

1973   THE NIGHT PORTER
Director: Liliana Cavani
Co-stars: Dirk Bogarde Charlotte Rampling Gabriele Ferzetti

SOLEDAD MIRANDA

1969   100 RIFLES
Director: Tom Gries
Co-stars: Jim Brown Raquel Welch Burt Reynolds

1970   COUNT DRACULA
Director: Jess Franco
Co-stars: Christopher Lee Herbert Lom Klaus Kinski

SUSANA MIRANDA

1970   ONE HOUR TO DOOMSDAY
Director: Irwin Allen
Co-stars: Stuart Whitman Robert Wagner Richard Basehart

MIRANDY

1940   COMIN' ROUND THE MOUNTAIN
Co-stars: Bob Burns Una Merkel

MIROSLAVA

1951   THE BRAVE BULLS
Director: Robert Rossen
Co-stars: Mel Ferrer Anthony Quinn Eugene Iglesias

HELEN MIRREN
Nominated For Best Supporting Actress In 1994 For "The Madness Of King George"

1969   AGE OF CONSENT
Director: Michael Powell
Co-stars: James Mason Jack McGowran Neva Carr-Glynn

1972   SAVAGE MESSIAH
Director: Ken Russell
Co-stars: Dorothy Tutin Scott Anthony John Justin

1972   MISS JULIE
Director: Robin Phillips
Co-star: Donal McGann

1973   O LUCKY MAN!
Director: Lindsay Anderson
Co-stars: Malcolm McDowell Arthur Lowe Rachel Roberts

1979   HUSSY
Director: Matthew Chapman
Co-stars: John Shea Jenny Runacre Patti Boulaye

1980   THE FIENDISH PLOT OF DR. FU MANCHU
Director: Piers Haggard
Co-stars: Peter Sellers Simon Williams

1980   CALIGULA
Director: Tinto Brass
Co-stars: Malcolm McDowell John Gielgud Peter O'Toole

1980   THE LONG GOOD FRIDAY
Director: John MacKenzie
Co-stars: Bob Hoskins Dave King Eddie Constantine

1981   EXCALIBUR
Director: John Boorman
Co-stars: Nigel Terry Nicol Williamson Cheri Lunghi

1984   CAL
Director: Pat O'Connor
Co-stars: John Lynch Donal McGann Ray McAnally

1985   WHITE NIGHTS
Director: Taylor Hackford
Co-stars: Mikhail Baryshnikov Jerzy Skolimowsky

1986   MOSQUITO COAST
Director: Peter Weir
Co-stars: Harrison Ford River Phoenix Martha Plimpton

1988   PASCALI'S ISLAND
Director: James Dearden
Co-stars: Ben Kingsley Charles Dance Nadim Sawalha

1989   WHEN THE WHALES CAME
Director: Clive Rees
Co-stars: Paul Scofield David Threlfall David Suchet

**1989   THE COOK, THE THIEF,
HIS WIFE AND HER LOVER**
Director: Peter Greenaway
Co-stars: Michael Gambon Tim Roth

1990   BETHUNE THE MAKING OF A HERO
Director: Phillip Borsos
Co-stars: Donald Sutherland Anouk Aimee

1991   COMFORT OF STRANGERS
Director: Paul Schrader
Co-stars: Christopher Walken Natasha Richardson

1991   WHERE ANGELS FEAR TO TREAD
Director: Charles Sturridge
Co-stars: Rupert Graves Judy Davis

1991   PRIME SUSPECT
Director: Christopher Menhaul
Co-stars: Tom Bell John Benfield Zoe Wanamaker

1992   PRIME SUSPECT 2
Director: John Strickland
Co-stars: Colin Salmon John Benfield Philip Wright

1993   PRIME SUSPECT 3
Director: David Drury
Co-stars: Tom Bell Peter Capaldi David Thewlis

1993   THE HAWK
Director: David Hayman
Co-stars: George Costigan Rosemary Leach John Duttine

1995   THE MADNESS OF KING GEORGE
Director: Nicholas Hytner
Co-stars: Nigel Hawthorne Ian Holm Amanda Donohue

1996   SOME MOTHER'S SON
Director: Terry George
Co-star: Fionnula Flanagan John Lynch Tom Hollander

1996   LOSING CHASE
Director: Kevin Bacon
Co-stars: Kevin Bacon Beau Bridges Kyra Sedgwick

KIKA MIRYLESS

1987   UNREPORTED INCIDENT
Director: Christopher Baker
Co-stars: T.P.McKenna Maurice Roeves Marsha Hunt

CARRIE MITCHAM
(Granddaughter of Robert Mitcham)

1991   DEAD SILENCE
Director: Peter O'Fallon
Co-stars: Steven Brill Renee Estevez Lisanne Falk

ANN MITCHELL

1981   LADY CHATTERLEY'S LOVER
Director: Just Jaeckin
Co-stars: Sylvia Kristel Nicholas Clay Elizabeth Spriggs

BARBARA MITCHELL

1972   FOR THE LOVE OF ADA
Director: Ronnie Baxter
Co-stars: Irene Handl Wilfred Pickles Jack Smethurst

1975   THE TWELVE TASKS OF ASTERIX (Voice)
Director: Rene Goscinny
Co-stars: George Baker Sean Barrett

CAMILLE MITCHELL

1980   WARP SPEED
Director: Allan Sandler
Co-stars: Adam West David Chandler Joanne Nail

CAROLYN MITCHELL

1958   THE CRY BABY KILLER
Director: Justus Addis
Co-stars: Jack Nicholson Harry Lauter Brett Halsey

CHARLOTTE MITCHELL

1951   LADY GODIVA RIDES AGAIN
Director: Frank Launder
Co-stars: Pauline Stroud Dennis Price Diana Dors

1952   CURTAIN UP
Director: Ralph Smart
Co-stars: Margaret Rutherford Robert Morley Kay Kendall

1960   VILLAGE OF THE DAMNED
Director: Wolf Rilla
Co-stars: George Sanders Barbara Shelley Jenny Laird

1970   BLOOD ON SATAN'S CLAW
Director: Piers Haggard
Co-stars: Patrick Wymark Linda Hayden Michele Dotrice

1981   THE FRENCH LIEUTENANT'S WOMAN
Director: Karel Reisz
Co-stars: Jeremy Irons Meryl Streep Leo McKern

DONNA MITCHELL

1979   THE BELL JAR
Director: Larry Peerce
Co-stars: Marilyn Hassett Julie Harris Anne Jackson

1983   ANNA TO THE INFINITE POWER
Director: Robert Wiemer
Co-stars: Dina Merril Marsha Byrne Jack Gilford

1990 PYSCHO IV: THE BEGINNING
Director: Mick Garris
Co-stars: Anthony Perkins Henry Thomas Olivia Hussey

1990 THE ROOKIE
Director: Clint Eastwood
Co-stars: Clint Eastwood Charlie Sheen Raul Julia

GENEVA MITCHELL

1930 SON OF THE GODS
Director: Frank Lloyd
Co-stars: Richard Barthelmess Constance Bennett

1935 AIR FURY
Co-star: Ralph Bellamy

1935 LAWLESS RIDERS
Co-star: Ken Maynard

1935 WESTERN COURAGE
Co-star: Ken Maynard

GWEN MITCHELL

1971 SHAFT
Director: Gordon Parks
Co-stars: Richard Roundtree Moses Gunn Charles Cioffi

1974 CHOSEN SURVIVORS
Director: Sutton Roley
Co-stars: Jackie Cooper Alex Cord Diana Muldaur

HEATHER MITCHELL

1991 PROOF
Director: Jocelyn Moorhouse
Co-stars: Hugo Weaving Genevieve Picot Russell Crowe

JONI MITCHELL

1971 CELEBRATION AT BIG SUR
Director: Baird Bryant
Co-stars: Joan Baez John Sebastian

LISA MITCHELL

1956 THE TEN COMMANDMENTS
Director: Cecil B. DeMille
Co-stars: Charlton Heston Yul Brynner Anne Baxter

MARY MITCHELL

1961 TWIST AROUND THE CLOCK
Director: Oscar Rudolph
Co-stars: Chubby Checker Dion John Cronin

1962 PANIC IN THE YEAR ZERO
Director: Ray Milland
Co-stars: Ray Milland Jean Hagen Frankie Avalon Joan Freeman

1963 DEMENTIA 13
Director: Francis Coppola
Co-stars: Luana Anders William Campbell Patrick Magee

RUTH MITCHELL

1990 THE FOOL
Director: Christine Edzard
Co-stars: Derek Jacobi Cyril Cusack

1996 MOLL FLANDERS
Director: David Attwood
Co-stars: Alex Kingston Ronald Fraser James Fleet

SHAREEN MITCHELL

1991 OUT FOR JUSTICE
Director: John Flynn
Co-stars: Steven Seagal William Forsyth Jerry Orbach

YVONNE MITCHELL

1948 THE QUEEN OF SPADES
Director: Thorold Dickinson
Co-stars: Anton Walbrook Edith Evans Ronald Howard

1953 TURN THE KEY SOFTLY
Director: Jack Lee
Co-stars: Terence Morgan Joan Collins Thora Hird

1954 THE DIVIDED HEART
Director: Charles Crighton
Co-stars: Cornell Borchers Alexander Knox Armin Dahlen

1955 ESCAPADE
Director: Philip Leacock
Co-stars: John Mills Alastair Sim Marie Lohr

1956 YIELD TO THE NIGHT
Director: J.Lee Thompson
Co-stars: Diana Dors Michael Craig Athene Seyler

1957 WOMAN IN A DRESSING GOWN
Director: J.Lee Thompson
Co-stars: Anthony Quayle Sylvia Syms Andrew Ray

1958 PASSIONATE SUMMER
Director: Rudolph Cartier
Co-stars: Bill Travers Virginia McKenna Ellen Barrie

1959 SAPPHIRE
Director: Basil Dearden
Co-stars: Nigel Patrick Michael Craig Bernard Miles

1959 TIGER BAY
Director: J.Lee Thompson
Co-stars: Hayley Mills John Mills Horst Buchholz

1960 THE TRIALS OF OSCAR WILDE
Director: Ken Hughes
Co-stars: Peter Finch John Fraser Nigel Patrick

1960 CONSPIRACY OF HEARTS
Director: Ralph Thomas
Co-stars: Lilli Palmer Sylvia Syms Ronald Lewis

1960 JOHNNY NOBODY
Director: Nigel Patrick
Co-stars: Nigel Patrick Aldo Ray William Bendix Bernie Winters

1962 THE MAIN ATTRACTION
Director: Daniel Petrie
Co-stars: Pat Boone Mai Zetterling Nancy Kwan

1964 GENGHIS KHAN
Director: Henry Levin
Co-stars: Omar Sharif Stephen Boyd James Mason

1971 DEMONS OF THE MIND
Director: Peter Sykes
Co-stars: Paul Jones Gillian Hills Robert Hardy

1972 THE GREAT WALTZ
Director: Andrew Stone
Co-stars: Horst Buchholz Mary Costa Rossano Brazzi

1976 THE INCREDIBLE SARAH
Director: Richard Fleischer
Co-stars: Glenda Jackson Daniel Massey Simon Williams

CAROL MITCHELL-LEON

1993 GETTING OUT
Director: John Korty
Co-stars: Rebecca De Mornay Robert Knepper

RUTH MIX

1931 RED FORK RANGE
Co-stars: Cliff Lyons Jim Corey Al Ferguson

Lana Turner

Jean Simmons

Ingrid Bergman

Jane Russell

KIM MIYORI

1988 **THE BIG PICTURE**
Director: Christopher Guest
Co-stars: Kevin Bacon Jennifer Jason Leigh Teri Hatcher

1989 **THE PUNISHER**
Director: Mark Goldblatt
Co-stars: Dolph Lundgren Louis Gossett Jnr. Jeroen Krabbe

MILADA MLADOVA

1948 **THE SIREN OF ATLANTIS**

ARLENE MLODZIK

1969 **STEREO**
Director: David Cronenberg
Co-stars: Ron Mlodzik Jack Messinger Clara Mayer

GENEVIEVE MNICH

1984 **SUNDAY IN THE COUNTRY**
Director: Bertrand Tavernier
Co-stars: Louis Ducreux Sabine Azema Michel Aumont

MARY ANN MOBLEY

1964 **YOUNG DILLINGER**
Director: Terry Morse
Co-stars: Nick Adams Robert Conrad Victor Buono

1965 **HARUM SCARUM**
Director: Gene Nelson
Co-stars: Elvis Presley Fran Jeffries Michael Ansara

1966 **THREE ON A COUCH**
Director: Jerry Lewis
Co-stars: Jerry Lewis Janet Leigh James Best Leslie Parrish

1974 **THE GIRL ON THE LATE, LATE SHOE**
Director: Gary Nelson
Co-stars: Don Murray Gloria Grahame Van Johnson

MARGARET MODLIN

1973 **LOVE AND PAIN**
        (AND THE WHOLE DAMN THING)
Director: Alan J.Pakula
Co-stars: Maggie Smith Timothy Botoms

ENRICA MARIA MODUGNO

1984 **KAOS**
Director: Paolo Taviani
Co-stars: Margarita Lozano Claudio Bigagli Franco Franchi

MARIA MOERNO

1992 **THE QUINCE TREE SUN**
Director: Victor Erice
Co-stars: Antonio Lopez Enrique Gran

KATHARINE MOFFAT

1986 **PRINCE OF BEL-AIR**
Director: Charles Braverman
Co-stars: Mark Harmon Kirstie Alley Robert Vaughn

KITTY MOFFAT

1982 **THE BEAST WITHIN**
Director: Philippe Mora
Co-stars: Ronny Cox Bibi Besch Paul Clemens

SHANNON MOFFETT

1990 **MEN DON'T LEAVE**
Director: Paul Brickman
Co-stars: Jessica Lange Arliss Howard Joan Cusack

SHARYN MOFFETT *(Child)*

1945 **THE FALCON IN SAN FRANCISCO**
Director: William Clemens
Co-stars: Tom Conway Rita Corday

1946 **CHILD OF DIVORCE**
Director: Richard Fleischer
Co-stars: Regis Toomey Madge Meredith Una O'Connor

1946 **THE LOCKET**
Director: John Brahm
Co-stars: Laraine Day Robert Mitchum Brian Aherne

1947 **THE JUDGE STEPS OUT**
Director: Boris Ingster
Co-stars: Alexander Knox Ann Sothern George Tobias

1947 **BANJO**
Co-stars: George McDonald Jean Moorhead Robbin Winan

1951 **HER FIRST ROMANCE**
Director: Symour Friedman
Co-stars: Margaret O'Brien Allen Martin Jimmy Hunt

NATALIA MOGULICH

1989 **OUT ON THE EDGE**
Director: John Pasquin
Co-stars: Rick Schroder Richard Jenkins Mary Kay Place

ALISON MOIR

1992 **JOHNNY SUEDE**
Director: Tom DiCillo
Co-stars: Brad Pitt Calvin Levels Tina Louise

GRETCHEN MOL

1997 **THE FUNERAL**
Director: Abel Ferrara
Co-stars: Christopher Walken Annabella Sciorra Vincent Gallo

KARIN MOLANDER

1920 **EROTIKON**
Director: Mauritz Stiller
Co-stars: Lars Hanson Tora Teje Anders De Wahl

JULIETTE MOLE

1989 **PIED PIPER**
Director: Norman Stone
Co-stars: Peter O'Toole Mare Winningham Susan Wooldridge

ANGELA MOLINA

1977 **THAT OBSCURE OBJECT OF DESIRE**
Director: Luis Bunuel
Co-stars: Fernando Rey Carole Bouquet

1982 **THE EYES, THE MOUTH**
Director: Marco Bellochio
Co-stars: Lou Castel Emmanuelle Riva Michel Piccoli

1986 **STREETS OF GOLD**
Director: Joe Roth
Co-stars: Klaus Maria Brandauer Adrian Pasdar Wesley Snipes

1992 **1492: CONQUEST OF PARADISE**
Director: Ridley Scott
Co-stars: Gerard Depardieu Sigourney Weaver Loren Dean

CARMEN MOLINA

1945 **THE THREE CABALLEROS**
Director: Norman Ferguson
Co-stars: Aurora Miranda Dora Luz

MONICA MOLINA

1989 **BRAVE LITTLE TAILOR**
Director: Dusan Trancik
Co-stars: Miro Hoga Gunter Mack

GIORGIA MOLL

1958 THE QUIET AMERICAN
Director: Joseph Mankiewicz
Co-stars: Audie Murphy Michael Redgrave Bruce Cabot

1963 ISLAND OF LOVE
Director: Morton Da Costa
Co-stars: Robert Preston Walter Matthau Tony Randall

1963 LE MERRIS

HEIDI MOLLENHAUER

1996 THE HUNCHBACK OF NOTRE DAME *(Voice)*
Director: Kirk Wise
Co-stars: Tom Hulce Demi Moore

DOLLY MOLLINGER

1938 VESSEL OF WRATH
Director: Erich Pommer
Co-stars: Charles Laughton Elsa Lanchester Robert Newton

DEARBHLA MOLLOY

1983 EDUCATING RITA
Director: Lewis Gilbert
Co-stars: Julie Walters Michael Caine Michael Williams

1991 THE PIRATE PRINCE
Director: Alan Horrox
Co-stars: James Hazeldine Beck Newton

LILY MOLNAR

1948 NO ORCHIDS FOR MISS BLANDISH
Director: St. John Clownes
Co-stars: Jack La Rue Linden Travers Zoe Gail

DEBI MONAHAN

1991 SHATTERED
Director: Wolfgang Petersen
Co-stars: Tom Berenger Bob Hoskins Greta Scacchi

1993 SOLDIER OF FORTUNE
Director: Beau Davis
Co-stars: Brandon Lee Ernest Borgnine Werner Pocatin

ANDREA MONET

1965 BE MY GUEST
Director: Lance Comfort
Co-stars: David Hemmings Avril Angers Joyce Blair

PHYLLIS MONKMAN

1929 THE CO-OPTIMISTS
Director: Laddie Cliff
Co-stars: Laddie Cliff Stanley Holloway Davy Burnaby Betty Chester

1935 THE KING OF PARIS
Director: Jack Raymond
Co-stars: Cedric Hardwicke Marie Glory Ralph Richardson

1949 DIAMOND CITY
Director: David MacDonald
Co-stars: David Farrar Honor Blackman Diana Dors

YVONNE MONLAUR

1960 BRIDES OF DRACULA
Director: Terence Fisher
Co-stars: Peter Cushing David Peel Freda Jackson

1960 CIRCUS OF HORRORS
Director: Sidney Hayers
Co-stars: Anton Diffring Erika Remberg Donald Pleasence

1960 INN FOR TROUBLE
Director: C.M.Pennington-Richards
Co-stars: Peggy Mount David Kossoff Leslie Phillips

1961 THE TERROR OF THE TONGS
Director: Anthony Bushell
Co-stars: Geoffrey Toone Christopher Lee Brian Worth

MARILYN MONROE *(Married Joe Dimaggio, Arthur Miller) (Norma Jean Mortensen Baker)*

1948 LADIES OF THE CHORUS
Director: Phil Karlson
Co-stars: Adele Jergens Rand Brooks

1948 SCUDDA HOO, SCUDDA HEY
Director: F.Hugh Herbert
Co-stars: June Haver Walter Brennan Natalie Wood

1949 LOVE HAPPY
Director: David Miller
Co-stars: Marx Brothers Vera-Ellen

1950 THE FIREBALL
Director: Tay Garnett
Co-stars: Mickey Rooney Pat O'Brien Beverley Tyler

1950 RIGHT CROSS
Director: John Sturges
Co-stars: Dick Powell June Allyson Ricardo Montalban

1950 A TICKET TO TOMAHAWK
Director: Richard Sale
Co-stars: Anne Baxter Dan Dailey Walter Brennan

1950 ALL ABOUT EVE
Director: Joseph Mankiewicz
Co-stars: Bette Davis George Sanders Anne Baxter

1950 THE ASPHALT JUNGLE
Director: John Huston
Co-stars: Louis Calhern Sam Jaffe Sterling Hayden

1951 AS YOUNG AS YOU FEEL
Director: Harmon Jones
Co-stars: Monty Wooley David Wayne Jean Peters

1951 LET'S MAKE IT LEGAL
Director: Richard Sale
Co-stars: Claudette Colbert MacDonald Carey

1951 LOVE NEST
Director: Joseph Newman
Co-stars: June Haver William Lundigan

1952 O. HENRY'S FULL HOUSE
Director: Henry King
Co-stars: Charles Laughton David Wayne Jean Peters

1952 CLASH BY NIGHT
Director: Fritz Lang
Co-stars: Robert Ryan Paul Douglas Barbara Stanwyck

1952 MONKEY BUSINESS
Director: Howard Hawks
Co-stars: Cary Grant Ginger Rogers Charles Coburn

1952 WE'RE NOT MARRIED
Director: Edmund Goulding
Co-stars: Ginger Rogers David Wayne Paul Douglas

1952 DON'T BOTHER TO KNOCK
Director: Roy Baker
Co-stars: Richard Widmark Ann Bancroft Jim Backus

1952 NIAGARA
Director: Henry Hathaway
Co-stars: Joseph Cotten Jean Peters Casey Adams

1953 GENTLEMEN PREFER BLONDES
Director: Howard Hawks
Co-stars: Jane Russell Charles Coburn Tommy Noonan

1953 HOW TO MARY A MILLIONAIRE
Director: Jean Negulesco
Co-stars: Betty Grable Lauren Bacall David Wayne

1954 RIVER OF NO RETURN
Director: Otto Preminger
Co-stars: Robert Mitchum Rory Calhoun Tommy Rettig

1954 THERE'S NO BUSINESS LIKE SHOW BUSINESS
Director: Walter Lang
Co-stars: Ethel Merman Dan Dailey Donald O'Connor Mitzi Gaynor

1955 THE SEVEN YEAR ITCH
Director: Billy Wilder
Co-stars: Tom Ewell Evelyn Keyes Sonny Tufts

1956 BUS STOP
Director: Joshua Logan
Co-stars: Don Murray Betty Field Hope Lange

1957 THE PRINCE AND THE SHOWGIRL
Director: Laurence Olivier
Co-stars: Laurence Olivier Jeremy Spenser

1959 SOME LIKE IT HOT
Director: Billy Wilder
Co-stars: Tony Curtis Jack Lemmon

1960 LET'S MAKE LOVE
Director: George Cukor
Co-stars: Yves Montand Tony Randall Frankie Vaughan

1961 THE MISFITS
Director: John Huston
Co-stars: Clark Gable Montgomery Clift Eli Wallach

1962 SOMETHING'S GOT TO GIVE *(Unfinished)*

CELIA MONTAGUE

1991 PRINCE
Director: David Wheatley
Co-stars: Sean Bean Janet McTeer Jackie McGuire

1992 RESNICK: LONELY HEARTS
Director: Bruce MacDonald
Co-stars: Tom Wilkinson Kate Eaton Neil Dudgeon

CELIA MONTALVAN

1934 TONI
Director: Jean Renoir
Co-star: Edward Delmont

KARLA MONTANA

1988 STAND AND DELIVER
Director: Ramon Menendez
Co-stars: Edward James Olmos Lou Diamond Phillips

ANNA MARIA MONTICELLI

1985 NOMADS
Director: John McTiernan
Co-stars: Pierce Brosnan Lesley-Anne Down Adam Ant

LISA MONTELL

1956 TEN THOUSAND BEDROOMS
Director: Richard Thorpe
Co-stars: Dean Martin Eva Bartok Paul Henreid

CONCHITA MONTENEGRO

1931 THE CISCO KID
Director: Irving Cumming
Co-stars: Warner Baxter Edmund Lowe

1931 NEVER THE TWAIN SHALL MEET
Director: W.S.Van Dyke
Co-stars: Leslie Howard Karen Morley C.Aubrey Smith

1932 THE GAY CABALLERO
Co-star: George O'Brien

1934 HANDY ANDY
Director: David Butler
Co-stars: Will Rogers Peggy Wood Robert Taylor

1934 HELL IN THE HEAVENS
Director: John Blystone
Co-stars: Warner Baxter Herbert Mundin Andy Devine

1934 CARAVAN
Director: Erik Charrell
Co-stars: Charles Boyer Annabella

ROSENDA MONTEROS

1956 BATTLE SHOCK
Director: Paul Henreid
Co-stars: Paul Henreid Ralph Meeker Janice Rule

1960 THE MAGNIFICENT SEVEN
Director: John Sturges
Co-stars: Yul Brynner Steve McQueen Charles Bronson

1962 TIARA TAHITI
Director: Ted Kotcheff
Co-stars: James Mason John Mills Claude Dauphin

1965 SHE
Director: Robert Day
Co-stars: Peter Cushing Ursula Andress John Richardson

1967 SAVAGE PAMPAS
Director: Hugo Fregonese
Co-stars: Robert Taylor Ron Randell Ty Hardin

ELISA MONTES

1966 MUTINY AT FORT SHARP
Director: Fernando Cercio
Co-stars: Broderick Crawford Mario Valdermain

1966 RETURN OF THE SEVEN
Director: Burt Kennedy
Co-stars: Yul Brynner Robert Fuller Warren Oates

LILLIANE MONTEVECCHI

1955 MOONFLEET
Director: Fritz Lang
Co-stars: Stewart Granger George Sanders Joan Greenwood

1956 MEET ME IN LAS VEGAS
Director: Roy Rowland
Co-stars: Dan Dailey Cyd Charisse Agnes Moorehead

1956 THE LIVING IDOL
Director: Albert Lewin
Co-stars: James Robertson Justice Steve Forrest

1957 THE SAD SACK
Director: George Marshall
Co-stars: Jerry Lewis David Wayne Phyllis Kirk

1958 ME AND THE COLONEL
Director: Peter Glenville
Co-stars: Danny Kaye Curt Jurgens Nicole Maurey

1958 THE YOUNG LIONS
Director: Edward Dmytryk
Co-stars: Marlon Brando Montgomery Clift Dean Martin

MARIA MONTEZ

1940 BOSS OF BULLION CITY

1941 THAT NIGHT IN RIO
Director: Irving Cummings
Co-stars: Don Ameche Alice Faye Carmen Miranda

1941 BOMBAY CLIPPER
Director: John Rawlins
Co-stars: William Gargan Irene Hervey Turhan Bey

1941   **THE INVISIBLE WOMAN**
Director: Edward Sutherland
Co-stars: John Barrymore Charles Ruggles Virginia Bruce

1941   **SOUTH OF TAHITI**
Director: George Waggner
Co-stars: Brian Donlevy Broderick Crawford Andy Devine

1942   **THE MYSTERY OF MARIE ROGET**
Director: Phil Rosen
Co-stars: Patric Knowles Maria Ouspenskaya John Litel

1942   **ARABIAN NIGHTS**
Director: John Rawlins
Co-stars: Jon Hall Sabu Turhan Bey Billy Gilbert

1943   **WHITE SAVAGE**
Director: Arthur Lubin
Co-stars: Jon Hall Sabu Thomas Gomez Sidney Toler

1944   **GYPSY WILDCAT**
Director: Roy William Neill
Co-stars: Jon Hall Leo Carrillo Gale Sondergaard

1944   **COBRA WOMAN**
Director: Robert Siodmak
Co-stars: Jon Hall Sabu Lon Chaney Mary Nash

1944   **ALI BABA AND THE FORTY THIEVES**
Director: Arthur Lubin
Co-stars: Jon Hall Turhan Bey Scotty Beckett

1944   **BOWERY TO BROADWAY**
Director: Charles Lamont
Co-stars: Jack Oakie Turhan Bey Susanna Foster

1945   **SUDAN**
Co-stars: Jon Hall Turhan Bey George Zucco

1946   **TANGIER**
Director: George Waggner
Co-stars: Sabu Kent Taylor Robert Paige Preston Foster

1947   **PIRATES OF MONTEREY**
Director: Alfred Werker
Co-stars: Rod Cameron Philip Reed Gilbert Roland

1947   **THE EXILE**
Director: Max Ophuls
Co-stars: Douglas Fairbanks Paula Corday Robert Coote

MAGDALENA MONTEZUMA

1981   **TAXI ZUM KLO**
Director: Frank Ripploh
Co-stars: Frank Ripploh Bernd Broaderup Gitte Lederer

BELINDA MONTGOMERY

1970   **THE TODD KILLINGS**
Director: Barry Shear
Co-stars: Robert F.Lyons Richard Thomas Gloria Grahame

1972   **WOMEN IN CHAINS**
Director: Bernard Kowalski
Co-stars: Ida Lupino Lois Nettleton Penny Fuller

1972   **THE DEVIL'S DAUGHTER**
Director: Jeannot Szwarc
Co-stars: Shelley Winters Robert Foxworth Joseph Cotten

1975   **THE OTHER SIDE OF THE MOUNTAIN**
Director: Larry Peerce
Co-stars: Marilyn Hassett Beau Bridges Nan Martin

1976   **BREAKING POINT**
Director: Bob Clark
Co-stars: Bo Svenson Robert Culp John Colicos

1977   **THE OTHER SIDE OF THE MOUNTAIN PART 2**
Director: Larry Peerce
Co-stars: Marilyn Hassett Timothy Bottoms

1980   **STONE COLD DEAD**
Director: George Mendeluk
Co-stars: Richard Crenna Paul Williams

1980   **CONSPIRACY TO KILL**
Director: Paul Krasny
Co-stars: Robert Conrad William Conrad Don Stroud

1983   **UNCOMMON VALOR**
Director: Rod Amateau
Co-stars: Mitchell Ryan Ben Murphy Barbara Parkins

1986   **ADAM: HIS SONG CONTINUES**
Director: Robert Markowitz
Co-stars: Daniel J.Travanti JoBeth Williams

ELIZABETH MONTGOMERY (Married Robert Foxworth, Daughter of Robert Montgomery)

1955   **THE COURT-MARTIAL OF BILLY MITCHELL**
Director: Otto Preminger
Co-stars: Gary Cooper Rod Steiger

1963   **JOHNNY COOL**
Director: William Asher
Co-stars: Henry Silva Marc Lawrence Jim Backus

1963   **WHO'S BEEN SLEEPING IN MY BED?**
Director: Daniel Mann
Co-stars: Dean Martin Jill St. John Carol Burnett

1972   **THE VICTIM**
Director: Herschel Daugherty
Co-stars: George Maharis Eileen Heckhart Sue Ann Langton

1975   **THE LEGEND OF LIZZIE BORDEN**
Director: Paul Wendkos
Co-stars: Ed Flanders Katherine Helmond John Beal

1976   **DARK VICTORY**
Director: Robert Butler
Co-stars: Anthony Hopkins Michele Lee Michael Lerner

1979   **ACT OF VIOLENCE**
Director: Paul Wendkos
Co-stars: James Sloyan Biff McGuire Sean Frye

1983   **MISSING PIECES**
Director: Mike Hodges
Co-stars: Louanne John Reilly Robin Gammell

1983   **THE BLACK WIDOW MURDERS: THE BLANCHE TAYLOR MOORE STORY**

1985   **AMOS**
Director: Michael Tuchner
Co-stars: Kirk Douglas Dorothy McGuire Ray Walston

1991   **SINS OF THE MOTHER**
Director: John Patterson
Co-stars: Dale Midkiff Heather Fairfield Talia Balsam

1992   **WITH SAVAGE INTENT**
Director: Michael Tuchner
Co-star: Robert Foxworth

JULIA MONTGOMERY

1984   **REVENGE OF THE NERDS**
Director: Jeff Kanew
Co-stars: Robert Carradine Anthony Andrews Bernie Casey

1989   **COLUMBO: SEX AND THE MARRIED DETECTIVE**
Director: James Frawley
Co-stars: Peter Falk Lindsay Crouse

MARIA MONTI

1972   **A FISTFUL OF DYNAMITE**
Director: Sergio Leone
Co-stars: Rod Steiger James Coburn Romolo Valli

ANNA MARIA MONTICELLI

1985 THE EMPTY BEACH
Director: Chris Thomson
Co-stars: Bryan Brown Ray Barrett John Wood

SARITA MONTIEL

1953 VERA CRUZ
Director: Robert Aldrich
Co-stars: Gary Cooper Burt Lancaster Denise Darcel

1956 SERENADE
Director: Anthony Mann
Co-stars: Mario Lanza Joan Fontaine Vincent Price

1957 RUN OF THE ARROW
Director: Samuel Fuller
Co-stars: Rod Steiger Charles B Ronson Ralph Meeker

ELIZABETH MOODY

1992 BRAIN DEAD
Director: Peter Jackson
Co-stars: Timothy Balme Diana Penalver Ian Watkin

JEANNE MOODY

1963 A MATTER OF CHOICE
Director: Vernon Sewell
Co-stars: Anthony Steel Ballard Berkeley Penny Morrell

LYNNE MOODY

1978 THE EVIL
Director: Gus Trikonis
Co-stars: Richard Crenna Joanna Pettet Andrew Prine

1982 SOME KIND OF HERO
Director: Michael Pressman
Co-stars: Richard Pryor Margot Kidder Ray Sharkey

1982 WHITE DOG
Director: Samuel Fuller
Co-stars: Kristy McNichol Paul Winfield Burl Ives

1985 LOST IN LONDON
Director: Robert Lewis
Co-stars: Emmanuel Lewis Ben Vereen Freddie Jones

1985 THE ATLANTA CHILD MURDERS
Director: John Erman
Co-stars: Jason Robards James Earl Jones Rip Torn

LYNNE SUE MOON

1960 55 DAYS AT PEKING
Director: Nicholas Ray
Co-stars: Charlton Heston Ava Gardner David Niven

DEBRA MOONEY

1979 CHAPTER TWO
Director: Robert Moore
Co-stars: James Caan Marsha Mason Valerie Harper

LAURA MOONEY

1989 SHE'S OUT OF CONTROL
Director: Stan Dragoti
Co-stars: Tony Danza Catherine Hicks Ami Dolenz

ALICE MOORE

1934 DOWN TO THEIR LAST YACHT
Co-stars: Marie Wilson Lorimer Johnson

BARBARA MOORE

1967 THE HELICOPTER SPIES
Director: Sam Rolfe
Co-stars: Robert Vaughn David McCallum Carol Lynley

CLEO MOORE

1951 ON DANGEROUS GROUND
Director: Nicholas Ray
Co-stars: Ida Lupino Robert Ryan Ed Begley

1954 BAIT
Director: Hugo Haas
Co-stars: Hugo Haas John Agar Emmett Lynn

1956 HOLD BACK TOMORROW
Director: Hugo Haas
Co-stars: John Agar Frank De Kova Dalla Boyd

COLLEEN MOORE

1925 SALLY
Co-star: Leon Errol

1925 SO BIG

1926 IRENE

1928 LILAC TIME
Director: George Fitzmaurice
Co-stars: Gary Cooper Eugenie Besserer Arthur Lake

1933 THE POWER AND THE GLORY
Director: William Howard
Co-stars: Spencer Tracy Helen Vinson Ralph Morgan

1934 THE SCARLET LETTER
Director: Robert Vignola
Co-stars: Hardie Albright William Farnum Alan Hale

1934 SUCCESS AT ANY PRICE
Director: Walter Ruben
Co-stars: Douglas Fairbanks Jnr. Genevieve Tobin Frank Morgan

1934 SOCIAL REGISTER
Director: Marshall Neilan
Co-stars: Charles Winninger Pauline Frederick

CONSTANCE MOORE

1938 WIVES UNDER SUSPICION
Director: James Whale
Co-stars: Warren William Gail Patrick Ralph Morgan

1938 STATE POLICE
Co-star: William Lundigan

1939 CHARLIE McCARTHY, DETECTIVE
Director: Frank Tuttle
Co-stars: Edgar Bergen Robert Cummings John Sutton

1939 EX-CHAMP
Director: Phil Rosen
Co-stars: Victor McLaglen Tom Brown Nan Grey

1939 YOU CAN'T CHEAT AN HONEST MAN
Director: George Marshall
Co-stars: W.C.Fields Edgar Bergen

1939 HAWAIIAN NIGHTS
Co-star: Johnny Downs

1940 FRAMED
Co-stars: Frank Albertson Jerome Cowan

1940 LA CONGA NIGHTS
Co-stars: Dennis O'Keefe Ferike Boros

1940 ARGENTINE NIGHTS
Director: Albert Rogell
Co-stars: Ritz Brothers Andrews Sisters Peggy Moran

1941 BUY ME THAT TOWN
Director: Eugene Ford
Co-stars: Lloyd Nolan Albert Dekker Vera Vague

1941 I WANTED WINGS
Director: Mitchell Leisen
Co-stars: Ray Milland William Holden Veronica Holden

1941   TAKE A LETTER DARLING
Director: Mitchell Leisen
Co-stars: Rosalind Russell Fred MacMurray

1944   SHOW BUSINESS
Director: Edwin Marin
Co-stars: Eddie Cantor Joan Davis George Murphy

1944   ATLANTIC CITY
Director: Ray McCarey
Co-stars: Brad Taylor Jerry Colonna Dorothy Dandridge

1945   DELIGHTFULLY DANGEROUS
Director: Arthur Lubin
Co-stars: Jane Powell Ralph Bellamy Arthur Treacher

1945   MEXICANA
Director: Alfred Santell
Co-stars: Tito Guizar Leo Carrillo Steve Geray

1945   EARL CARROLL VANITIES
Director: Joseph Santley
Co-stars: Dennis O'Keefe Eve Arden Otto Kruger

1947   HIT PARADE OF 1947
Director: Frank McDonald
Co-stars: Eddie Albert Joan Edwards Roy Rogers

DEBORAH MARIA MOORE
(Daughter Of Roger Moore)

1992   INTO THE SUN
Director: Fritz Kiersch
Co-stars: Anthony Michael Hall Michael Pare Terry Kiser

DEMI MOORE (Demetria Guynes)
(Married Freddy Moore, Bruce Willis)

1981   CHOICES
Director: Silvio Narizzano
Co-stars: Paul Carafotes Victor French

1982   YOUNG DOCTORS IN LOVE
Director: Garry Marshall
Co-stars: Michael McKean Sean Young Harry Dean Stanton

1982   PARASITE
Director: Charles Band
Co-stars: Robert Glaudini Luca Bercovici Vivian Blaine

1984   BLAME IT ON RIO
Director: Stanley Donen
Co-stars: Michael Caine Michelle Johnson Joseph Bologna

1984   NO SMALL AFFAIR
Director: Jerry Schatzberg
Co-stars: Jon Cryer George Wendt Elizabeth Daily

1985   ST. ELMO'S FIRE
Director: Joel Schumacher
Co-stars: Rob Lowe Ally Sheedy Andie MacDowell

1986   ABOUT LAST NIGHT
Director: Edward Zwick
Co-stars: Rob Lowe James Belushi Elizabeth Perkins

1989   WE'RE NO ANGELS
Director: Neil Jordan
Co-stars: Robert De Niro Sean Penn Ray McAnally

1990   GHOST
Director: Jerry Zucker
Co-stars: Patrick Swayze Whoopi Goldberg Tony Goldwyn

1991   THE BUTCHER'S WIFE
Director: Terry Hughes
Co-stars: Jeff Daniels Mary Steenburgen George Dzundza

1991   MORTAL THOUGHTS
Director: Alan Rudolph
Co-stars: Bruce Willis Harvey Keitel Glenne Headly

1991   NOTHING BUT TROUBLE
Director: Dan Aykroyd
Co-stars: Dan Aykroyd Chevy Chase John Candy Taylor Negron

1992   A FEW GOOD MEN
Director: Rob Reiner
Co-stars: Tom Cruise Jack Nicholson Kiefer Sutherland

1993   INDECENT PROPOSAL
Director: Adrian Lyne
Co-stars: Robert Redford Woody Harrelson Seymour Cassel

1995   DISCLOSURE
Director: Michael Crighton
Co-stars: Michael Douglas Roma Maffia Caroline Goodall

1995   THE SCARLET LETTER
Director: Roland Joffe
Co-stars: Gary Oldman Robert Duvall

1996   NOW AND THEN
Co-stars: Melanie Grifith Christina Ricci Thora Birch

1996   THE JUROR
Director: Brian Gibson
Co-stars: Alec Baldwin Lindsay Crouse James Gandolfini

1996   STRIPTEASE
Director: Andrew Bergman
Co-stars: Robert Patrick Burt Reynolds Rumer Willis

1996   THE HUNCHBACK OF NOTRE DAME *(Voice)*
Director: Kirk Wise
Co-stars: Tom Hulce Heidi Mollenhauer

1996   IF THESE WALLS COULD TALK
Co-stars: Sissy Spacek Cher

1997   G.I.JANE
Director: Ridley Scott
Co-stars: Viggo Mortensen Anne Bancroft

1998   DECONSTRUCTING HARRY
Director: Woody Allen
Co-stars: Woody Allen Robin Williams Kirstie Alley

DENNIE MOORE

1936   SYLVIA SCARLETT
Director: George Cukor
Co-stars: Katharine Hepburn Cary Grant Edmund Gwenn

1938   BOYS MEET GIRL
Director: Lloyd Bacon
Co-stars: James Cagney Pat O'Brien Marie Wilson

DOROTHY MOORE

1937   THE BIG SHOT
Co-stars: Guy Kibbee Cora Witherspoon

1938   BLONDIE
Director: Frank Strayer
Co-stars: Penny Singleton Arthur Lake Larry Simms

1938   BLONDIE MEETS THE BOSS
Director: Frank Strayer
Co-stars: Penny Singleton Arthur Lake Jonathan Hale

EILEEN MOORE

1952   THE HAPPY FAMILY
Director: Muriel Box
Co-stars: Stanley Holloway Kathleen Harrison Naunton Wayne

1954   AN INSPECTOR CALLS
Director: Guy Hamilton
Co-stars: Alastair Sims Brian Worth Bryan Forbes

1954   MEN OF SHERWOOD FOREST
Director: Val Guest
Co-stars: Don Taylor Patrick Holt Reginald Beckwith

EVA MOORE

1932 THE OLD DARK HOUSE
Director: James Whale
Co-stars: Melvyn Douglas Charles Laughton Raymond Massey

1934 A CUP OF KINDNESS
Director: Tom Walls
Co-stars: Tom Walls Ralph Lynn Robertson Hare Claude Hulbert

1935 VINTAGE WINE
Director: Henry Edwards
Co-stars: Seymour Hicks Claire Luce Judy Gunn

1938 OLD IRON
Director: Tom Walls
Co-stars: Tom Walls Cecil Parker Richard Ainley David Tree

GRACE MOORE
Nominated For Best Actress In 1934 For "One Night Of Love"

1930 A LADY'S MORALS
Director: Sidney Franklin
Co-stars: Reginald Denny Wallace Beery Jobyna Howland

1931 NEW MOON
Co-star: Lawrence Tibbett

1934 ONE NIGHT OF LOVE
Director: Victor Schertzinger
Co-stars: Tullio Carminati Lyle Talbot Mona Barrie

1935 LOVE ME FOREVER
Director: Victor Schertzinger
Co-stars: Leo Carrillo Robert Allan Spring Byington

1936 THE KING STEPS OUT
Director: Joseph Von Sternberg
Co-stars: Franchot Tone Walter Connolly Victor Jory

1937 I'LL TAKE ROMANCE
Director: Edward Griffith
Co-stars: Melvyn Douglas Helen Westley Stuart Erwin

1937 WHEN YOUR IN LOVE
Director: Robert Riskin
Co-stars: Cary Grant Aline MacMahon Thomas Mitchell

IDA MOORE

1947 THE EGG AND I
Director: Chester Erskine
Co-stars: Claudette Colbert Fred MacMurray Marjorie Main

1952 RAINBOW ROUND MY SHOULDER
Director: Richard Quine
Co-stars: Frankie Laine Billy Daniels Arthur Franz

ISA MOORE

1958 ROCK-A-BYE-BABY
Director: Frank Tashlin
Co-stars: Jerry Lewis Marilyn Maxwell Reginald Gardiner

JOANNA MOORE *(Married Ryan O'Neal)*

1957 APPOINTMENT WITH A SHADOW
Director: Richard Carlson
Co-stars: George Nader Brian Keith Virginia Field

1958 TOUCH OF EVIL
Director: Orson Welles
Co-stars: Orson Welles Charlton Heston Janet Leigh Akim Tamiroff

1958 FLOODTIDE

1958 RIDE A CROOKED TRAIL
Director: Jessie Hibbs
Co-stars: Audie Murphy Gia Scala Walter Matthau

1958 MONSTER ON THE CAMPUS
Director: Jack Arnold
Co-stars: Arthur Franz Whit Bissell Troy Donahue

1962 A WALK ON THE WILD SIDE
Director: Edward Dmytryk
Co-stars: Jane Fonda Barbara Stanwyck Capucine

1962 FOLLOW THAT DREAM
Director: Gordon Douglas
Co-stars: Elvis Presley Arthur O'Connell Anne Helm

1967 COUNTDOWN
Director: Robert Altman
Co-stars: James Caan Robert Duvall Barbara Baxley

1968 NEVER A DULL MOMENT
Director: Jerry Paris
Co-stars: Dick Van Dyke Edward G.Robinson Dorothy Provine

JUANITA MOORE
Nominated For Best Supporting Actress In 1959 For "Imitation Of Life"

1956 THE GIRL CAN'T HELP IT
Director: Frank Tashlin
Co-stars: Jayne Mansfield Tom Ewell Edmond O'Brien

1959 IMITATION OF LIFE
Director: Douglas Sirk
Co-stars: Lana Turner John Gavin Susan Kohner

1963 PAPA'S DELICATE CONDITON
Director: George Marshall
Co-stars: Jackie Gleason Glynis Johns Charles Ruggles

1965 THE SINGING NUN
Director: Henry Koster
Co-stars: Debbie Reynolds Ricardo Montablan

1967 ROSIE!
Director: David Lowell Rich
Co-stars: Rosalind Russell Brian Aherne Sandra Dee

1968 UP TIGHT
Director: Jules Dassin
Co-stars: Raymond St.Jacques Ruby Dee Julian Mayfield

1981 PATERNITY
Director: David Steinberg
Co-stars: Burt Reynolds Beverly D'Angelo Norman Fell

1988 TWO-MOON JUNCTION
Director: Zalman King
Co-stars: Sherilyn Fenn Richard Tyson Burl Ives

JULIANNE MOORE

1991 TALES FROM THE DARKSIDE: THE MOVIE
Director: John Harrison
Co-stars: Deborah Harry Christian Slater Alice Drummond

1992 THE HAND THAT ROCKS THE CRADLE
Director: Curtis Hanson
Co-stars: Rebecca De Mornay Anabella Sciorra

1992 BODY OF EVIDENCE
Director: Uli Edel
Co-stars: Madonna Willem Dafoe Anne Archer

1992 THE GUN IN BETTY LOU'S HANDBAG
Director: Allan Moyle
Co-stars: Penelope Ann Miller Eric Thal Alfre Woodard

1993 BENNY AND JOON
Director: Jeremiah Chetchik
Co-stars: Johnny Depp Mary Stuart Masterson

1993 THE FUGITIVE
Director: Andrew Davies
Co-stars: Harrison Ford Tommy Lee Jones Sela Ward

1993 SHORT CUTS
Director: Robert Altman
Co-stars: Matthew Modine Andie MacDowell Jennifer Jason Leigh

1994 VANYA ON 42ND STREET
Director: Louis Malle
Co-stars: Wallace Shawn Brooke Smith

1995 NINE MONTHS
Director: Chris Columbus
Co-stars: Jeff Goldblum Hugh Grant Robin Williams

1995 ASSASSIN
Director: Richard Donner
Co-stars: Sylvester Stallone Antonio Banderas

1996 SURVIVING PICASSO
Director: James Ivory
Co-stars: Anthony Hopkins Natascha McElhone

1996 SAFE
Director: Todd Haynes

1997 THE LOST WORLD: JURASSIC PARK
Director: Steven Spielberg
Co-stars: Jeff Goldblum Richard Attenborough

KAYCEE MOORE

1991 DAUGHTERS OF THE DUST
Director: Julie Dash
Co-stars: Cora Lee Day Alva Rogers Barbara-O

MARGO MOORE

1960 WAKE ME WHEN IT'S OVER
Director: Mervyn Le Roy
Co-stars: Dick Shawn Ernie Kovacs Jack Warden

MARY TYLER MOORE
Nominated For Best Actress In 1980 For "Ordinary People"

1965 WHAT'S SO BAD AOUT FEELING GOOD?
Director: George Seaton
Co-stars: George Peppard Dom DeLuise

1967 THROUGHLY MODERN MILLIE
Director: George Roy Hill
Co-stars: Julie Andrews John Gavin James Fox

1968 DON'T JUST STAND THERE
Director: Ron Winston
Co-stars: Robert Wagner Glynis Johns Barbara Rhoades

1969 CHANGE OF HABIT
Director: William Graham
Co-stars: Elvis Presley Ed Asner Barbara McNair

1980 ORDINARY PEOPLE
Director: Robert Redford
Co-stars: Donald Sutherland Timothy Hutton Judd Hirsch

1982 SIX WEEKS
Director: Tony Bill
Co-stars: Dudley Moore Katherine Healy Shannon Wilcox

1984 HEARTSOUNDS
Director: Glenn Jordan
Co-stars: James Garner Sam Wanamaker Wendy Crewson

1986 JUST BETWEEN FRIENDS
Director: Allan Burns
Co-stars: Ted Danson Christine Lahti Sam Waterston

1990 THE LAST BEST YEAR
Director: John Erman
Co-stars: Bernadette Peters Dorothy McGuire Brian Bedford

1993 STOLEN BABIES
Director: Eric Laneuville
Co-stars: Lea Thompson Kathleen Quinlan

1995 FORBIDDEN MEMORIES
Director: Bob Clark
Co-stars: Shirley Knight Linda Lavin

1996 FLIRTING WITH DISASTER
Director: David Russell
Co-stars: Alan Alda Lily Tomlin Patricia Arquette

1997 KEYS TO TULSA
Co-stars: Eric Stoltz James Spader Deborah Unger

1997 PAYBACK
Director: Ken Cameron
Co-star: Edward Asner

MELBA MOORE

1989 LETHAL ERROR
Director: Susan Rohrer
Co-stars: Jose Ferrer Denise Nichols Art Hindle

1989 ALL DOGS GO TO HEAVEN (Voice)
Director: Gary Goldman
Co-stars: Burt Reynolds Judith Barsi Dom DeLuise

1992 DEF BY TEMPTATION
Director: James Bond III
Co-stars: Cynthia Bond Samuel L. Jackson

NORMA MOORE

1957 FEAR STRIKES OUT
Director: Robert Mulligan
Co-stars: Anthony Perkins Karl Malden Perry Wilson

PAIGE MOORE

1988 THE WIZARD OF SPEED AND TIME
Director: Mike Jittlov
Co-stars: Mike Jittlov Richard Kaye Steve Brodie David Conrad

PAULA MOORE

1975 UNE PARTIE DE PLAISIR
Director: Claude Chabrol
Co-stars: Paul Gegaufff Danielle Gegauff Michel Valette

PAULINE MOORE

1937 WILD AND WOOLLY
Director: Alfred Werker
Co-stars: Jane Withers Walter Brennan Alfalfa Switzer

1937 HEIDI
Director: Allan Dwan
Co-stars: Shirley Temple Jean Hersholt Arthur Treacher

1937 CHARLIE CHAN AT THE OLYMPICS
Director: Bruce Humberstone
Co-stars: Warner Oland Keye Luke Allan Lane

1938 THREE BLIND MICE
Director: William Seiter
Co-stars: Loretta Young Joel McCrea Marjorie Weaver

1939 THE THREE MUSKETEERS
Director: Allan Dwan
Co-stars: Don Ameche Binnie Barnes Ritz Brothers

1939 CHARLIE CHAN IN RENO
Director: Norman Foster
Co-stars: Sidney Toler Ricardo Cortez Phyllis Brooks

1939 CHARLIE CHAN AT TREASURE ISLAND
Director: Norman Foster
Co-stars: Sidney Toler Cesar Romero Sen Yung

1940 ARKANSAS JUDGE
Co-star: Roy Rogers

SHEILA MOORE

1990 THE REFLECTING SKIN
Director: Phillip Ridley
Co-stars: Viggo Mortensen Lindsay Duncan Jeremy Cooper

TERRY MOORE

Nominated For Best Supporting Actress In 1952 For "Come Back Little Sheba"

1944 GASLIGHT
Director: George Cukor
Co-stars: Charles Boyer Ingrid Bergman Joseph Cotten

1948 THE RETURN OF OCTOBER
Director: Joseph Lewis
Co-stars: Glenn Ford May Whitty James Gleason

1949 MIGHTY JOE YOUNG
Director: Ernest Schoedsack
Co-stars: Ben Johnson Robert Armstrong Frank McHugh

1950 THE GREAT RUPERT
Director: Irving Pichel
Co-stars: Jimmy Durante Tom Drake Sara Haden

1950 HE'S A COCKEYED WONDER
Director: Peter Godfrey
Co-stars: Mickey Rooney William Demarest

1951 GAMBLING HOUSE
Director: Ted Tetzlaff
Co-stars: Victor Mature William Bendix Basil Ruysdael

1951 THE BAREFOOT MAILMAN
Director: Earl McEvoy
Co-stars: Robert Cummings Jerome Courtland Will Greer

1951 TWO OF A KIND
Director: Henry Levin
Co-stars: Edmond O'Brien Lisabeth Scott Alexander Knox

1952 COME BACK LITTLE SHEBA
Director: Daniel Mann
Co-stars: Burt Lancaster Shirley Booth Richard Jaeckel

1953 BENEATH THE 12 MILE REEF
Director: Robert Webb
Co-stars: Robert Wagner Gilbert Roland Richard Boone

1953 MAN ON A TIGHTROPE
Director: Elia Kazan
Co-stars: Fredric March Cameron Mitchell Adolphe Menjou

1954 KING OF THE KYBER RIFLES
Director: Henry King
Co-stars: Tyrone Power Michael Rennie John Justin

1955 SHACK OUT ON 101
Director: Ed Dein
Co-stars: Frank Lovejoy Lee Marvin Keenan Wynn

1955 PORTRAIT OF ALISON
Director: Guy Green
Co-stars: Robert Beatty William Sylvester Geoffrey Keen

1955 DADDY LONG LEGS
Director: Jean Negulesco
Co-stars: Fred Astaire Leslie Caron Thelma Ritter

1956 BETWEEN HEAVEN AND HELL
Director: Richard Fleischer
Co-stars: Robert Wagner Broderick Crawford

1957 PEYTON PLACE
Director: Mark Robson
Co-stars: Lana Turner Arthur Kennedy Hope Lange

1957 BERNADINE
Director: Henry Levin
Co-stars: Pat Boone Janet Gaynor Richard Sargent

1959 HOUND-DOG MAN
Director: Don Siegel
Co-stars: Fabian Carol Lynley Stuart Whitman Arthur O'Connell

1959 A PRIVATE'S AFFAIR
Director: Raoul Walsh
Co-stars: Sal Mineo Barry Coe Cary Crosby

1959 CAST A LONG SHADOW
Director: Thomas Carr
Co-stars: Audie Murphy John Dehner James Best

1960 PLATINUM HIGH SCHOOL
Director: Charles Haas
Co-stars: Mickey Rooney Dan Duryea Yvette Mimieux

1966 WACO
Director: R.G.Springsteen
Co-stars: Howard Keel Jane Russell Brian Donlevy

1966 CITY OF FEAR
Director: Peter Bezencenet
Co-stars: Paul Maxwell Marissa Mell Albert Lieven

1991 MARILYN AND ME
Director: John Patterson
Co-stars: Jesse Dabson Joel Grey

AGNES MOOREHEAD

Nominated For Best Supporting Actress In 1944 For "Mrs Parkington", In 1942 For "The Magnificent Ambersons", In 1948 For "Johnny Belinda" And In 1964 For "Hush...Hush Sweet Charlotte"

1941 CITIZEN KANE
Director: Orson Welles
Co-stars: Orson Welles Joseph Cotten Everett Sloane Paul Stewart

1942 THE MAGNIFICENT AMBERSONS
Director: Orson Welles
Co-stars: Orson Welles Joseph Cotten Tim Holt Anne Baxter

1942 JOURNEY INTO FEAR
Director: Orson Welles
Co-stars: Orson Welles Joseph Cotten Dolores Del Rio

1942 THE BIG STREET
Director: Irving Reis
Co-stars: Henry Fonda Lucille Ball Barton MacLane

1943 JANE EYRE
Director: Robert Stevenson
Co-stars: Orson Welles Joan Fontaine Margaret O'Brien

1943 GOVERNMENT GIRL
Director: Dudley Nichols
Co-stars: Olivia De Havilland Sonny Tufts Anne Shirley

1943 THE YOUNGEST PROFESSION
Director: Ed Buzzell
Co-stars: Virginia Weidler Jean Porter Edward Arnold

1944 MRS. PARKINGTON
Director: Tay Garnett
Co-stars: Greer Garson Walter Pidgeon Edward Arnold

1944 TOMORROW THE WORLD
Director: Leslie Fenton
Co-stars: Skip Homeier Fredric March Betty Field

1944 SINCE YOU WENT AWAY
Director: John Cromwell
Co-stars: Claudette Colbert Jennifer Jones Joseph Cotten

1944 DRAGON SEED
Director: Jack Conway
Co-stars: Katharine Hepburn Walter Huston Turhan Bey

1944 THE SEVENTH CROSS
Director: Fred Zinnemann
Co-stars: Spencer Tracy Signe Hasso Jessica Tandy

1945 HER HIGHNESS AND THE BELLBOY
Director: Richard Thorpe
Co-stars: Hedy Lamarr Robert Walker June Allyson

1945 KEEP YOUR POWDER DRY
Director: Ed Buzzell
Co-stars: Lana Turner Laraine Day Susan Peters

1945	**OUR VINES HAVE TENDER GRAPES**		**1955**	**ALL THAT HEAVEN ALLOWS**

1945 **OUR VINES HAVE TENDER GRAPES**
Director: Roy Rowland
Co-stars: Edward G.Robinson Margaret O'Brien

1947 **THE LOST MOMENT**
Director: Martin Gabel
Co-stars: Robert Cummings Susan Hayward Eduardo Cianelli

1947 **DARK PASSAGE**
Director: Delmer Daves
Co-stars: Humphrey Bogart Lauren Bacall Bruce Bennett

1948 **STATION WEST**
Director: Sidney Lanfield
Co-stars: Dick Powell Jane Greer Burl Ives

1948 **JOHNNY BELINDA**
Director: Jean Negulesco
Co-stars: Jane Wyman Lew Ayres Charles Bickford

1948 **SUMMER HOLIDAY**
Director: Rouben Mamoulian
Co-stars: Walter Huston Mickey Rooney Frank Morgan

1948 **THE WOMAN IN WHITE**
Director: Peter Godfrey
Co-stars: Gig Young Eleanor Parker Sydney Greenstreet

1949 **THE GREAT SINNER**
Director: Robert Siodmak
Co-stars: Gregory Peck Ava Gardner Walter Huston

1949 **THE STRATTON STORY**
Director: Sam Wood
Co-stars: James Stewart June Allyson Frank Morgan

1950 **CAGED**
Director: John Cromwell
Co-stars: Eleanor Parker Ellen Corby Jan Sterling

1951 **THE ADVENTURES OF CAPTAIN FABIAN**
Director: William Marshall
Co-stars: Errol Flynn Vincent Price Micheline Presle

1951 **THE BLUE VEIL**
Director: Curtis Bernhardt
Co-stars: Charles Laughton Jane Wyman Joan Blondell

1951 **FOURTEEN HOURS**
Director: Henry Hathaway
Co-stars: Richard Basehart Paul Douglas Barbara Bel Geddes

1951 **SHOW BOAT**
Director: George Sidney
Co-stars: Howard Keel Kathryn Grayson Joe E.Brown Ava Gardner

1952 **CAPTAIN BLACK JACK**
Director: Julien Duvivier
Co-stars: George Sanders Herbert Marshall Patricia Roc

1952 **THE BLAZING FOREST**
Director: Edward Ludwig
Co-stars: John Payne Susan Morrow William Demarest

1953 **THE MAIN STREET TO BROADWAY**
Director: Tay Garnett
Co-stars: Tom Morton Mary Murphy Ethel Barrymore

1953 **THE STORY OF THREE LOVES**
Director: Vincent Minnelli
Co-stars: Ethel Barrymore James Mason Leslie Caron

1953 **SCANDAL AT SCOURIE**
Director: Jean Negulesco
Co-stars: Greer Garson Walter Pidgeon Donna Corcoran

1954 **MAGNIFICENT OBSESSION**
Director: Douglas Sirk
Co-stars: Jane Wyman Rock Hudson Barbara Rush

1955 **THE LEFT HAND OF GOD**
Director: Edward Dmytryk
Co-stars: Humphrey Bogart Gene Tierney Lee J.Cobb

1955 **ALL THAT HEAVEN ALLOWS**
Director: Douglas Sirk
Co-stars: Jane Wyman Rock Hudson Conrad Nagel

1955 **UNTAMED**
Director: Henry King
Co-stars: Tyrone Power Susan Hayward Richard Egan John Justin

1955 **THE CONQUEROR**
Director: Dick Powell
Co-stars: John Wayne Susan Hayward Pedro Armendariz

1956 **MEET ME IN LAS VEGAS**
Director: Roy Rowland
Co-stars: Dan Dailey Cyd Charisse Paul Henreid

1956 **THE OPPOSITE SEX**
Director: David Miller
Co-stars: June Allyson Dolores Gray Joan Collins

1956 **PARDNERS**
Director: Norman Taurog
Co-stars: Dean Martin Jerry Lewis Lori Nelson Jeff Morrow

1956 **THE REVOLT OF MAMIE STOVER**
Director: Raoul Walsh
Co-stars: Jane Russell Richard Egan Joan Leslie

1956 **THE SWAN**
Director: Charles Vidor
Co-stars: Grace Kelly Alec Guinness Louis Jourdan

1956 **THE TRUE STORY OF JESSE JAMES**
Director: Nicholas Ray
Co-stars: Robert Wagner Jeffrey Hunter Hope Lange

1957 **THE RAINTREE COUNTY**
Director: Edward Dmytryk
Co-stars: Elizabeth Taylor Montgomery Clift Lee Marvin

1957 **THE STORY OF MANKIND**
Director: Irwin Allen
Co-stars: Ronald Colman Marx Bros. Hedy Lamarr

1957 **JEANNE EAGELS**
Director: George Sidney
Co-stars: Kim Novak Jeff Chandler Charles Drake

1958 **TEMPEST**
Director: Alberto Lattuada
Co-stars: Van Heflin Silvano Mangano Oscar Homolka

1959 **THE BAT**
Director: Crane Wilbur
Co-stars: Vincent Price Gavin Gordon John Sutton

1960 **POLLYANNA**
Director: David Swift
Co-stars: Hayley Mills Jane Wyman Richard Egan Karl Malden

1961 **BACHELOR IN PARADISE**
Director: Jack Arnold
Co-stars: Bob Hope Lana Turner Paula Prentiss Jim Hutton

1962 **JESSICA**
Director: Jean Negulesco
Co-stars: Angie Dickinson Maurice Chevalier Noel-Noel

1963 **HOW THE WEST WAS WON**
Director: John Ford
Co-stars: Debbie Reynolds Carroll Baker Henry Fonda

1963 **WHO'S MINDING THE STORE?**
Director: Frank Tashlin
Co-stars: Jerry Lewis Jill St. John Ray Walston

1964 **HUSH...HUSH SWEET CHARLOTTE**
Director: Robert Aldrich
Co-stars: Bette Davis Olivia De Havilland Joseph Cotten

1966 **THE SINGING NUN**
Director: Henry Koster
Co-stars: Debbie Reynolds Greer Garson Ricardo Montalban

1971 WHAT'S THE MATTER WITH HELEN
Director: Curtis Harrington
Co-stars: Debbie Reynolds Shelley Winters

1972 CHARLOTTE'S WEB *(Voice)*
Director: Charles Nichols
Co-stars: Debbie Reynolds Martha Scott

1972 NIGHT OF TERROR
Director: Jeannot Szwarc
Co-stars: Donna Mills Martin Balsam Chuck Connors

ELIZABETH MOOREHEAD

1991 WHORE
Director: Ken Russell
Co-stars: Theresa Russell Benjamin Moulton Antonio Fargas

JEAN MOORHEAD *(Child)*

1947 BANJO
Co-stars: Sharyn Moffett George MacDonald Robbin Winan

NATALIE MOORHEAD

1929 THE UNHOLY NIGHT
Director: Lionel Barrymore
Co-stars: Lionel Barrymore Roland Young Boris Karloff John Loder

1930 HOOK, LINE AND SINKER
Director: Eddie Cline
Co-stars: Bert Wheeler Robert Woolsey Dorothy Lee

1930 MANSLAUGHTER
Director: George Abbott
Co-stars: Claudette Colbert Fredric March Emma Dunn

1930 THE BENSON MURDER CASE
Co-star: William Powell

1932 THE MENACE
Director: Roy William Neill
Co-stars: Walter Byron Bette Davis H. B. Warner

1932 THREE WISE GIRLS
Director: William Beaudine
Co-stars: Jean Harlow Mae Clark Marie Prevost

1933 FORGOTTEN
Co-stars: Leon Ames Selmer Jackson

1934 CURTAIN AT EIGHT
Co-star: Paul Cavanagh

TRUDY MOORS *(Child)*

1964 DAYLIGHT ROBBERY
Director: Michael Truman
Co-stars: Gordon Jackson Janet Hannington Kirk Martin

BETTY MORAN

1939 ALL WOMEN HAVE SECRETS
Co-star: Matty Kemp

1939 RANGE WAR
Co-star: William Boyd Russell Hayden Pedro De Cordoba

DOLORES MORAN *(Married Benedict Bogeaus)*

1943 OLD ACQUAINTANCE
Director: Vincent Sherman
Co-stars: Bette Davis Miriam Hopkins Gig Young

1945 TO HAVE AND HAVE NOT
Director: Howard Hawks
Co-stars: Humphrey Bogart Lauren Bacall Walter Brennan

1945 THE HORN BLOWS AT MIDNIGHT
Director: Raoul Walsh
Co-stars: Jack Benny Alexis Smith Guy Kibbee

1946 THE MAN I LOVE
Director: Raoul Walsh
Co-stars: Ida Lupino Robert Alda Martha Vickers

1950 JOHNNY ONE-EYE
Director: Robert Florey
Co-stars: Pat O'Brien Wayne Morris Gayle Reed

1952 COUNT THE HOURS
Director: Don Siegel
Co-stars: Teresa Wright MacDonald Carey Adele Mara

1954 SILVER LODE
Director: Allan Dwan
Co-stars: John Payne Dan Duryea Lizabeth Scott

LOIS MORAN

1925 STELLA DALLAS
Director: Henry King
Co-stars: Belle Bennett Ronald Colman Douglas Fairbanks Jnr

1926 THE ROAD TO MANDALAY
Director: Tod Browning
Co-stars: Lon Chaney Owen Moore Henry B.Walthall

1929 BEHIND THAT CURTAIN
Director: Irving Cummings
Co-stars: Warner Baxter Boris Karloff E.L.Park

1930 THE DANCERS
Co-star: Walter Byron

1930 NOT DAMAGED
Co-star: Walter Byron

1930 MAMMY
Director: Michael Curtiz
Co-stars: Al Jolson Louise Dresser Lowell Sherman

1931 THE SPIDER
Director: Kenneth MacKenna
Co-stars: Edmund Lowe George E.Stone El Brendel

1931 TRANSATLANTIC
Director: William Howard
Co-stars: Edmund Lowe John Halliday Myrna Loy

1932 WEST OF BROADWAY
Director: Harry Beaumont
Co-stars: John Gilbert El Brendel Madge Evans

PATSY MORAN

1948 SONG OF THE DRIFTER
Co-stars: Jimmy Wakely Mildred Coles

PAULINE MORAN

1989 THE WOMAN IN BLACK
Director: Herbert Wise
Co-stars: Adrian Rawlins Bernard Hepton Clare Holman

PEGGY MORAN

1938 GIRL'S SCHOOL
Co-stars: Martha O'Driscoll Marjorie Deane Kenneth Howell

1938 RHYTHM OF THE SADDLE
Co-stars: Gene Autry Smiley Burnette Pert Kelton

1939 LITTLE ACCIDENT
Director: Charles Lamont
Co-stars: Baby Sandy Richard Carlson Florence Rice

1939 THE BIG GUY
Director: Arthur Lubin
Co-stars: Jackie Cooper Victor McLaglen Ona Munson

1940 ALIAS THE DEACON
Director: Christy Cabanne
Co-stars: Bob Burns Dennis O'Keefe Jack Carson

1940 ARGENTINE NIGHTS
Director: Albert Rogell
Co-stars: Andrews Sisters Ritz Brothers Constance Moore

1940 ONE NIGHT IN THE TROPICS
Director: Edward Sutherland
Co-stars: Allan Jones Bud Abbott Lou Costello

1940 THE MUMMY'S HAND
Director: Christy Cabanne
Co-stars: Dick Foran Wallace Ford Cecil Kellaway

1940 TRAIL OF THE VIGILLANTES
Director: Allan Dwan
Co-stars: Franchot Tone Warren William Broderick Crawford

1940 OH, JOHNNY, HOW YOU CAN LOVE
Co-stars: Tom Brown Juanita Quigley

1940 SPRING PARADE
Director: Henry Koster
Co-stars: Deana Durbin Robert Cummings S.Z.Sakall

1941 HORROR ISLAND
Director: George Waggner
Co-stars: Dick Foran Leo Carrillo John Eldredge

1941 FLYING CADETS
Co-stars: Edmund Lowe William Gargan Frank Albertson

1941 DOUBLE DATE
Co-stars: Edmund Lowe Una Merkel Rand Brooks

1942 SEVEN SWEETHEARTS
Director: Frank Borzage
Co-stars: Kathryn Grayson Marsha Hunt Van Heflin

POLLY MORAN

1927 LONDON AFTER MIDNIGHT
Director: Tod Browning
Co-stars: Lon Chaney Marceline Day Conrad Nagel

1927 THE DIVINE WOMAN
Director: Victor Sjostrom
Co-stars: Greta Garbo Lars Hanson Lowell Sherman

1928 BRINGING UP FATHER
Director: Jack Conway
Co-stars: J.Farrell MacDonald Marie Dressler Grant Withers

1929 CHASING RAINBOWS
Director: Charles Reisner
Co-stars: Bessie Love Marie Dressler Jack Benny

1929 THE HOLLYWOOD REVUE
Director: Charles Reisner
Co-stars: Marie Dresler Joan Crawford Buster Keaton

1929 DANGEROUS FEMALES
Director: Charles Reisner
Co-stars: Marie Dressler

1930 CAUGHT SHORT
Director: Charles Reisner
Co-stars: Marie Dressler Charles Morton Anita Page

1930 WAY FOR A SAILOR
Director: Sam Wood
Co-stars: John Gilbert Wallace Beery Leila Hyams

1931 REDUCING
Director: Charles Reisner
Co-stars: Marie Dresler Sally Eilers Anita Page

1931 PAID
Director: Sam Wood
Co-stars: Joan Crawford Kent Douglass Marie Prevost

1931 POLITICS
Director: Charles Reisner
Co-stars: Marie Dressler Roscoe Ates Karen Morley

1931 IT'S A WISE CHILD
Director: Robert Z.Leonard
Co-stars: Marion Davies Sidney Blackmer Marie Prevost

1931 GUILTY HANDS
Director: W.S.Van Dyke
Co-stars: Lionel Barrymore Kay Francis Madge Evans

1932 PROSPERITY
Director: Sam Wood
Co-stars: Marie Dresler Anita Page Norman Foster

1932 THE PASSIONATE PLUMBER
Director: Edward Sedgewick
Co-stars: Buster Keaton Jimmy Durante Gilbert Roland

1934 HOLLYWOOD PARTY
Director: Allan Dwan
Co-stars: Stan Laurel Oliver Hardy Lupe Velez

1940 TOM BROWN'S SCHOOLDAYS
Director: Robert Stevenson
Co-stars: Jimmy Lydon Cedric Hardwicke

ANGELA MORANT

**1991 INSPECTOR MORSE:
SERVICE OF ALL THE DEAD**
Co-stars: John Thaw Kevin Whately John Normington

LAURA MORANTE

1981 THE TRAGEDY OF A RIDICULOUS MAN
Director: Bernardo Bertolucci
Co-stars: Ugo Tognazzi Anouk Aimee

1982 BLOW TO THE HEART
Director: Gianni Amelio
Co-stars: Jean-Louis Trintignant Fausto Rossi Laura Nucci

1987 MAN OF FIRE
Director: Elie Chouraqui
Co-stars: Scott Glenn Joe Pesci Brooke Adams

STELLA MORAY

1972 THE LOVERS
Director: Herbert Wise
Co-stars: Richard Beckinsale Paula Wilcox Joan Scott

MANDY MORE

1990 HAPPY FEET
Director: Mike Bradwell
Co-stars: Phyllis Logan Stephen Hancock Marjie Lawrence

JEANNE MOREAU

1950 MEURTRES
Director: Richard Pottier
Co-stars: Fernandel Raymond Souplex Jacques Varennes

1953 TOUCHEZ PAS AU GRISBI
Director: Jacques Becker
Co-stars: Jean Gabin Lio Ventura Gaby Basset

1957 LIFT TO THE SCAFFOLD
Director: Louis Malle
Co-stars: Maurice Ronet Lino Ventura Georges Poujouly

1958 THE LOVERS
Director: Louis Malle
Co-stars: Alain Cuny Jean-Marc Bory

1959 LES LIASIONS DANGEREUSES
Director: Roger Vadim
Co-stars: Gerard Philipe Jean-Louis Trintignant

1960 LA NOTTE
Director: Michaelangelo Antonioni
Co-stars: Marcello Mastroianni Monica Vitti

1960   **FIVE BRANDED WOMEN**
Director: Martin Ritt
Co-stars: Van Heflin Silvana Mangano Barbara Bel Geddes

1961   **UNE FEMME EST UNE FEMME**
Director: Jean-Luc Godard
Co-stars: Jean-Paul Belmondo Anna Karina

1962   **BAY OF ANGELS**
Director: Jacques Demy
Co-stars: Claude Mann Paul Guers Henri Nassiet

1962   **EVA**
Director: Joseph Losey
Co-stars: Stanley Baker Virna Lisi James Villiers

1962   **JULES AND JIM**
Director: Francois Truffaut
Co-stars: Oskar Werner Henri Serre Marie Dubois

1962   **THE TRIAL**
Director: Orson Welles
Co-stars: Orson Welles Anthony Perkins Elsa Martinelli

1963   **THE VICTORS**
Director: Carl Foreman
Co-stars: Albert Finney George Peppard Elke Sommer

1963   **LE FEU FOLLET**
Director: Louis Malle
Co-stars: Maurice Ronet Lena Skerla Hubert Deschamps

1964   **THE DIARY OF A CHAMBERMAID**
Director: Luis Bunuel
Co-stars: Michel Piccoli Georges Geret

1964   **MATA HARI, AGENT H21**
Director: Jean-Louis Richard
Co-stars: Jean-Louis Trintignant Claude Rich

1964   **THE TRAIN**
Director: John Frankenheimer
Co-stars: Burt Lancaster Paul Scofield Suzanne Flon

1964   **THE YELLOW ROLLS ROYCE**
Director: Anthony Asquith
Co-stars: Rex Harrison Ingrid Bergman Omar Sharif

1965   **VIVA MARIA!**
Director: Louis Malle
Co-stars: Brigitte Bardot George Hamilton Paulette Dubost

1966   **CHIMES AT MIDNIGHT**
Director: Orson Welles
Co-stars: Orson Welles John Gielgud Keith Baxter

1967   **THE BRIDE WORE BLACK**
Director: Francois Truffaut
Co-stars: Jean-Claude Brialy Claude Rich

1967   **MADEMOISELLE**
Director: Tony Richardson
Co-stars: Etorre Manni Keith Skinner Jeanne Beretta

1967   **THE OLDEST PROFESSION**
Director: Jean-Luc Godard
Co-stars: Raquel Welch Elsa Lanchester Anna Karina

1967   **THE SAILOR FROM GIBRALTAR**
Director: Tony Richardson
Co-stars: Ian Bannen Vanessa Redgrave Orson Welles

1968   **THE IMMORTAL STORY**
Director: Orson Welles
Co-stars: Orson Welles Roger Coggio Norman Eshley

1968   **GREAT CATHERINE**
Director: Gordon Flemyng
Co-stars: Peter O'Toole Zero Mostel Jack Hawkins

1970   **ALEX IN WONDERLAND**
Director: Paul Mazursky
Co-stars: Donald Sutherland Ellen Burstyn Federico Fellini

1970   **MONTE WALSH**
Director: William Fraker
Co-stars: Jack Palance Lee Marvin Jim Davis

1972   **LOUISE**
Director: Philippe De Broca
Co-stars: Julian Negulesco Didi Perego Pippo Starnazza

1974   **LES VALSEUSES**
Director: Bertrand Blier
Co-stars: Gerard Depardieu Patrick Deweare Miou-Miou

1976   **MR KLEIN**
Director: Joseph Losey
Co-stars: Alain Delon Suzanne Flon Michael Lonsdale

1976   **LUMIERE**
Director: Jeanne Moreau
Co-stars: Francine Racette Lucia Bose Bruno Ganz

1976   **THE LAST TYCOON**
Director: Elia Kazan
Co-stars: Robert De Niro Robert Mitchum Tony Curtis

1982   **QUERRELLE**
Director: Rainer Werner Fassbinder
Co-stars: Brad Davis Franco Nero Laurent Malet

1990   **NIKITA**
Director: Luc Besson
Co-stars: Anne Parillaud Jean-Hughes Anglade Jean Reno

1991   **UNTIL THE END OF THE WORLD**
Director: Wim Wenders
Co-stars: William Hurt Solveig Dommartin Sam Neill

1992   **THE CLOTHES IN THE WARDROBE**
Director: Waris Hussein
Co-stars: Joan Plowright Julie Walters David Threlfall

1992   **THE LOVER** *(Voice)*
Director: Jean-Jacques Annaud
Co-stars: Jane March Tony Leung Lisa Faulkner

1993   **THE OLD WOMAN WHO WALKED IN THE SEA**
Co-stars: Michel Serrault Luc Thullier

1993   **MAP OF THE HUMAN HEART**
Director: Vincent Ward
Co-stars: Jason Scott Lee Anne Parillaud Patrick Bergin

1997   **THE PROPRIETOR**
Director: Ismael Merchant
Co-stars: Josh Hamilton Sean Young

GAEL MOREL

1994   **THE WILD REEDS**
Director: Andre Techine
Co-star: Frederic Gorny

SHERRY MORELAND

1951   **FURY OF THE CONGO**
Director: William Berke
Co-stars: Johnny Weismuller William Henry Lyle Talbot

RINA MORELLI

1953   **SENSO**
Director: Luchino Visconti
Co-stars: Alida Valli Farley Granger Massimo Girotti

1963   **THE LEOPARD**
Director: Luchino Visconti
Co-stars: Burt Lancaster Claudia Cardinale Alain Delon

BELITA MORENO

1979   **A PERFECT COUPLE**
Director: Robert Altman
Co-stars: Paul Dooley Marta Heflin Titos Vandis

1981 A GUN IN THE HOUSE
Director: Ivan Nagy
Co-stars: Sally Struthers David Ackroyd Millie Perkins

1990 MEN DON'T LEAVE
Director: Paul Brickman
Co-stars: Jessica Lange Arliss Howard Joan Cusack

CHRISTINA MORENO

1974 CHOSEN SURVIVORS
Director: Sutton Roley
Co-stars: Jackie Cooper Alex Cord Richard Jaeckel

MARGUERITE MORENO

1933 LES MISERABLES
Director: Raymond Bernard
Co-stars: Harry Bauer Charles Vanel Florelle

1936 LE ROMAN D'UN TRICHEUR
Director: Sacha Guitry
Co-stars: Sacha Guitry Serge Grave

1937 HARVEST
Director: Marcel Pagnol
Co-stars: Gabriel Gabrio Orane Demazis Fernandel

1943 DOUCE
Director: Claude Autant-Lara
Co-stars: Odette Joyeux Madeleine Robinson Jean Debucourt

1947 LES JEUX SONT FAIT
Director: Jean Delannoy
Co-stars: Micheline Presle Marcel Pagliero Charles Dullin

RITA MORENO *(Rosita Dolores Alverio)*
Oscar for Best Supporting Actress in 1961 For "West Side Story"

1950 PAGAN LOVE SONG
Director: Robert Alton
Co-stars: Esther Williams Howard Keel Minna Gombell

1952 THE RING
Director: Kurt Neuman
Co-stars: Gerald Mohr Lalo Rios Robert Arthur Jack Elam

1952 SINGIN' IN THE RAIN
Director: Gene Kelly
Co-stars: Gene Kelly Donald O'Connor Debbie Reynolds

1952 CATTLE TOWN
Director: Noel Smith
Co-stars: Dennis Morgan Amanda Blake Ray Teal Phil Carey

1953 FORT VENGEANCE
Director: Lesley Slander
Co-stars: James Craig Keith Larsen Reginald Denny

1953 LATIN LOVERS
Director: Mervyn LeRoy
Co-stars: Lana Turner Ricardo Montalban John Lund Jean Hagen

1955 THE LIEUTENANT WORE SKIRTS
Director: Frank Tashlin
Co-stars: Tom Ewell Sheree North Rick Jason

1955 SEVEN CITIES OF GOLD
Director: Robert Webb
Co-stars: Michael Rennie Richard Egan Anthony Quinn

1955 UNTAMED
Director: Henry King
Co-stars: Tyrone Power Susan Hayward Richard Egan John Justin

1956 THE VAGABOND KING
Director: Michael Curtiz
Co-stars: Oreste Kathryn Grayson Cedric Hardwicke

1956 THE KING AND I
Director: Walter Lang
Co-stars: Deborah Kerr Yul Brynner Martin Benson

1961 WEST SIDE STORY
Director: Robert Wise
Co-stars: Natalie Wood Richard Beymer Russ Tamblyn

1962 SUMMER AND SMOKE
Director: Peter Glenville
Co-stars: Geraldine Page Laurence Harvey Una Merkel

1969 THE NIGHT OF THE FOLLOWING DAY
Director: Hubert Cornfield
Co-stars: Marlon Brando Pamela Franklin

1969 POPI
Director: Arthur Hiller
Co-stars: Alan Arkin Miguel Alejandro John Harkins

1969 MARLOWE
Director: Paul Bogart
Co-stars: James Garner Bruce Lee Sharon Farrell Gayle Hunnicutt

1971 CARNAL KNOWLEDGE
Director: Mike Nichols
Co-stars: Jack Nicholson Art Garfunkel Candice Bergen

1976 THE RITZ
Director: Richard Lester
Co-stars: Jack Weston Kaye Ballard Bessie Love

1979 ANATOMY OF A SEDUCTION
Director: Steven Hilliard Stern
Co-stars: Susan Flannery Jameson Parker Ed Nelson

1981 THE FOUR SEASONS
Director: Alan Alda
Co-stars: Alan Alda Carol Burnett Len Cariou Sandy Dennis

1982 PORTRAIT OF A SHOWGIRL
Director: Steven A.Stern
Co-stars: Tony Curtis Lesley Ann Warren

1989 B.L.STRYKER
Director: William Fraker
Co-stars: Burt Reynolds Helen Shaver Ossie Davis

1994 I LIKE IT LIKE THAT
Director: Darnell Martin
Co-stars: Lauren Velez Jon Seda Griffin Dunne

ROSITA MORENO

1931 STAMBOUL
Co-star: Garry Marsh

1934 LADIES SHOULD LISTEN
Director: Frank Tuttle
Co-stars: Cary Grant Frances Drake Edward Everett Horton

CINDY MORGAN

1980 CADDYSHACK
Director: Harold Ramis
Co-stars: Chevy Chase Rodney Dangerfield Bill Murray

1982 TRON
Director: Steven Lisberger
Co-stars: Jeff Bridges Bruce Boxleitner David Warner

EMILY MORGAN

1988 PRECIOUS BANE
Director: Christopher Menaul
Co-stars: Janet McTeer John Bowe Clive Owen

1991 THEY NEVER SLEPT
Director: Udayan Prasad
Co-stars: Edward Fox James Fleet Harriet Walter

GLADYS MORGAN

1965 THE WILD AFFAIR
Director: John Krish
Co-stars: Nancy Kwan Terry-Thomas Bud Flanagan

HELEN MORGAN

1929   **APPLAUSE**
Director: Rouben Mamoulian
Co-stars: Joan Peers Henry Wadsworth Dorothy Cumming

1929   **GLORIFYING THE AMERICAN GIRL**
Director: Millard Webb
Co-stars: Mary Eaton Eddie Cantor Rudy Vallee

1930   **ROADHOUSE NIGHTS**
Director: Hobart Henley
Co-stars: Charles Ruggles Jimmy Durante Fred Kohler

1934   **YOU BELONG TO ME**
Director: Alfred Werker
Co-stars: Lee Tracy Helen Mack Lynne Overman

1934   **MARIE GALANTE**
Director: Henry King
Co-stars: Spencer Tracy Ketti Gallian Ned Sparks

1935   **GO INTO YOUR DANCE**
Director: Archie Mayo
Co-stars: Al Jolson Ruby Keeler Glenda Farrell

1935   **SWEET MUSIC**
Co-stars: Rudy Vallee Ann Dvorak Ned Sparks

1936   **SHOW BOAT**
Director: James Whale
Co-stars: Allan Jones Irene Dunne Paul Robeson

JANE MORGAN

1955   **OUR MISS BROOKS**
Director: Al Lewis
Co-stars: Eve Arden Gale Gordon Robert Rockwell

JANET MORGAN

1935   **THE COWBOY AND THE BANDIT**
Co-stars: Rex Lease Alphonse Martel Benny Corbett

KRISTEN MORGAN *(Child)*

1947   **MY WILD IRISH ROSE**
Director: David Butler
Co-stars: Dennis Morgan Arlene Dahl Andrea King

MICHELLE MORGAN

1937   **GRIBOUILLE**
Director: Marc Allegret
Co-stars: Raimu Jeanne Provost Gilbert Gilles Carette

1938   **QUAI DES BRUMES**
Director: Marcel Carne
Co-stars: Jean Gabin Michel Simon Pierre Brasseur

1940   **HEART OF A NATION**
Director: Julien Duvivier
Co-stars: Louis Jouvet Raimu Suzy Prim Lucien Nat

1942   **JOAN OF PARIS**
Director: Robert Stevenson
Co-stars: Paul Henreid Thomas Mitchell Laird Cregar

1943   **HIGHER AND HIGHER**
Director: Tim Whelan
Co-stars: Frank Sinatra Jack Haley Leon Errol Mel Torme

1943   **TWO TICKETS TO LONDON**
Director: Edwin Marin
Co-stars: Alan Curtis Barry Fitzgerald Dooley Wilson

1944   **PASSAGE TO MARSEILLES**
Director: Michael Curtiz
Co-stars: Humphrey Bogart Claude Rains Peter Lorre

1945   **THE CHASE**
Director: Arthur Ripley
Co-stars: Robert Cummings Steve Cochran Peter Lorre

1946   **LA SYMPHONIE PASTORALE**
Director: Jean Delanoy
Co-stars: Pierre Blanchar Jean Desailly Line Noro

1948   **THE FALLEN IDOL**
Director: Carol Reed
Co-stars: Ralph Richardson Bobby Henry Sonia Dresdel

1951   **FABIOLA**
Co-stars: Henri Vidal Massimo Girotti

1952   **THE SEVEN DEADLY SINS**
Director: Carlo Rim
Co-stars: Gerard Philipe Isa Miranda Noel-Noel

1953   **THE PROUD AND THE BEAUTIFUL**
Director: Yves Allegret
Co-stars: Gerard Philipe Victor Manuel Mendosa

1953   **LOVE, SOLDIERS AND WOMEN**
Director: Jean Delannoy
Co-stars: Claudette Colbert Martine Carol

1955   **MARGUERITE DE LA NUIT**
Director: Claude Autant-Lara
Co-stars: Yves Montand Jean-Francoise Calve

1955   **LES GRANDES MONOEUVERES**
Director: Rene Clair
Co-stars: Gerard Philipe Brigitte Bardot Pierre Dux

1956   **OASIS**
Director: Yves Allegret
Co-stars: Pierre Brasseur Cornell Borchers Gregoire Aslan

1957   **THE VINTAGE**
Director: Jeffrey Hayden
Co-stars: Mel Ferrer John Kerr Pier Angeli

1966   **THE LOST COMMAND**
Co-stars: Mark Robson
Co-stars: Anthony Quinn Alain Delon George Segal

1966   **BENJAMIN**
Director: Michel Deville
Co-stars: Pierre Clementi Catherine Deneuve Michel Piccoli

1990   **EVERYBODY'S FINE**
Director: Guiseppe Tornatore
Co-stars: Marcello Mastroianni Marino Cenna

NANCY MORGAN

1977   **GRAND THEFT AUTO**
Director: Ron Howard
Co-stars: Ron Howard Marion Ross Barry Cahill Hoke Howell

1979   **AMERICATHON**
Director: Neil Israel
Co-stars: Harvey Korman John Ritter Peter Riegart

PATTI MORGAN

1957   **BOOBY TRAP**
Director: Henry Cass
Co-stars: Sydney Tafler Harry Fowler Richard Shaw

PRISCILLA MORGAN

1980   **PRIDE AND PREJUDICE**
Director: Cyril Coke
Co-stars: Elizabeth Garvie Daivd Rintoul Judy Parfitt

SHARON MORGAN

1993   **LEAVING LENIN**
Director: Endaf Emlyn
Co-stars: Ifan Huw Daffyd Shelley Rees Richard Harrington

WENDY MORGAN

1979   **THE BIRTH OF THE BEATLES**
Director: Richard Marquand
Co-stars: Stephen MacKenna John Altman Nigel Havers

1979 YANKS
Director: John Schlesinger
Co-stars: Richard Gere Lisa Eichhorn Vanessa Redgrave

1991 OUT OF THE BLUE
Director: Nick Haam
Co-stars: Catherine Zeta Jones Cathy Tyson Colin Firth

CLAUDIA MORI

1962 SODOM AND GOMORRAH
Director: Robert Aldrich
Co-stars: Stewart Granger Stanley Baker Pier Angeli

PAOLA MORI *(Married Orson Welles)*

1954 CROSSED SWORDS
Director: Milton Krims
Co-stars: Errol Flynn Gina Lollobrigida Nadia Gray

1955 MR. ARKADIN
Director: Orson Welles
Co-stars: Orson Welles Michael Redgrave Katina Paxinou

TOSHIA MORI

1933 THE BITTER TEA OF GENERAL YEN
Director: Frank Capra
Co-stars: Barbara Stanwyck Nils Asther Gavin Gordon

CATHY MORIARTY
Nominated for Best Supporting Actress in 1980 For "Raging Bull"

1980 RAGING BULL
Director: Martin Scorsese
Co-stars: Robert De Niro Joe Pesci Frank Vincent

1981 NEIGHBORS
Director: John Avildsen
Co-stars: John Belushi Dan Aykroyd Kathryn Walker

1987 WHITE OF THE EYE
Director: Donald Cammell
Co-stars: David Keith Art Evans Alberta Watson

1991 SOAPDISH
Director: Michael Hoffman
Co-stars: Sally Field Kevin Kline Robert Downey Jnr.

1992 THE MAMBO KINGS
Director: Arne Glimcher
Co-stars: Armand Assante Antonio Banderas Maruschka Detmers

1992 THE GUN IN BETTY LOU'S HANDBAG
Director: Allan Moyle
Co-stars: Penelope Ann Miller Julianne Moore

1993 MATINEE
Director: Joe Dante
Co-stars: John Goodman Simon Fenton Lisa Jakub

1993 ANOTHER STAKEOUT
Director: John Badham
Co-stars: Richard Dreyfuss Emilio Estevez Rosie O'Donnell

1994 ME AND THE KID
Director: Dan Curtis
Co-stars: Danny Aiello Joe Pantoliano

1996 CASPER
Director: Brad Silverling
Co-stars: Christina Ricci Bill Pullman Eric Idle

TARA MORICE

1992 STRICTLY BALLROOM
Director: Baz Luhrmann
Co-stars: Paul Mercurio Bill Hunter Gia Carides

PATRICIA MORISON

1939 I'M FROM MISSOURI
Director: Theodore Reed
Co-stars: Bob Burns Gladys George Gene Lockhart

1939 THE MAGNIFICENT FRAUD
Director: Robert Florey
Co-stars: Akim Tamiroff Lloyd Nolan Mary Boland

1939 PERSONS IN HIDING
Director: Louis King
Co-stars: Lynne Overman Helen Twelvetrees

1940 UNTAMED
Director: George Archainbaud
Co-stars: Ray Milland Akim Tamiroff Jane Darwell

1940 RANGERS OF FORTUNE
Director: Sam Wood
Co-stars: Fred MacMurray Albert Dekker Gilbert Roland

1941 ONE NIGHT IN LISBON
Director: Edward Griffith
Co-stars: Fred MacMurray Madeleine Carroll

1941 THE ROUND-UP

1942 SILVER SKATES
Director: Leslie Goodwins
Co-stars: Belita Kenny Baker

1942 A NIGHT IN NEW ORLEANS
Director: William Clemens
Co-stars: Preston Foster Albert Dekker

1942 BEYOND THE BLUE HORIZON
Director: Alfred Santell
Co-stars: Dorothy Lamour Richard Denning

1942 ARE HUSBANDS NECESSARY?
Director: Noramn Taurog
Co-stars: Ray Milland Betty Field Cecil Kellaway

1943 CALLING DOCTOR DEATH
Director: Reginald Le Borg
Co-stars: Lon Chaney David Bruce Fay Helm

1943 THE SONG OF BERNADETTE
Director: Henry King
Co-stars: Jennifer Jones Charles Bickford Vincent Price

1943 THE FALLEN SPARROW
Director: Richard Wallace
Co-stars: John Garfield Maureen O'Hara Walter Slezak

1943 HITLER'S MADMAN
Director: Douglas Sirk
Co-stars: John Carradine Alan Curtis Ralph Morgan

1943 WHERE ARE YOUR CHILDREN?
Director: William Nigh
Co-stars: Jackie Cooper Gale Storm John Litel

1945 WITHOUT LOVE
Director: Harold Bucquet
Co-stars: Spencer Tracy Katharine Hepburn Keenan Wynn

1945 LADY ON A TRAIN
Director: Charles David
Co-stars: Deanna Durbin Ralph Bellamy David Bruce

1946 SHERLOCK HOLMES AND THE SECRET CODE
Director: Roy William Neill
Co-stars: Basil Rathbone Nigel Bruce

1947 TARZAN AND THE HUNTRESS
Director: Kurt Neuman
Co-stars: Johnny Weismuller Brenda Joyce

1947 SONG OF THE THIN MAN
Director: Edward Buzzell
Co-stars: William Powell Myrna Loy Dean Stockwell

1948 THE PRINCE OF THIEVES
Director: Howard Bretherton
Co-stars: Jon Hall Alan Mowbray Adele Jergens

1960   SONG WITHOUT END
Director: George Cukor
Co-stars: Dirk Bogarde Capucine Genevieve Page

1985   MIRRORS
Director: Mary Winer
Co-stars: Anthony Hamilton Keenan Wynn Signe Hasso

LOUISA MORITZ

1975   DEATH RACE 2000
Director: Paul Bartel
Co-stars: David Carradine Sylvester Stallone Simone Griffeth

GABY MORLAY

1939   DERRIERE LA FACADE
Director: George Lacombe
Co-stars: Jules Berry Michel Simon Betty Stockfield

1939   ENTENTE CORDIALE
Director: Marcel L'Herbier
Co-stars: Victor Francen Jean Perier Andre Lefaur

1948   GIGI
Director: Jacqueline Audry
Co-stars: Daniele Delorme Frank Villard Yvonne De Bray

1951   ANNA
Director: Alberto Lattuada
Co-stars: Silvana Mangano Raf Vallone Vittorio Gassman

1952   LE PLAISIR
Director: Max Ophuls
Co-stars: Claude Dauphin Danielle Darrieux Simone Simon

KAREN MORLEY *(Mildred Linton)*
(Married Charles Vidor)

1930   INSPIRATION
Director: Clarence Brown
Co-stars: Greta Garbo Robert Montgomery Lewis Stone

1931   POLITICS
Director: Charles Reisner
Co-stars: Marie Dressler Polly Moran Roscoe Ates

1931   NEVER THE TWAIN SHALL MEET
Director: W.S.Van Dyke
Co-stars: Leslie Howard Conchita Montenegro

1931   THE SIN OF MADELEINE CLAUDET
Director: Edgar Selwyn
Co-stars: Helen Hayes Robert Young Neil Hamilton

1931   MATA HARI
Director: George Fitzmaurice
Co-stars: Greta Garbo Ramon Navarro Lionel Barrymore

1931   DAYBREAK
Director: Jacques Feyder
Co-stars: Ramon Navarro Helen Chandler Jean Hersholt

1931   CUBAN LOVE SONG
Director: W.S.Van Dyke
Co-stars: Lawrence Tibbett Lupe Velez Jimmy Durante

1932   ARE YOU LISTENING?
Director: Harry Beaumont
Co-stars: William Haines Madge Evans Neil Hamilton

1932   ARSENE LUPIN
Director: Jack Conway
Co-stars: John Barrymore Lionel Barrymore Tully Marshall

1932   FLESH
Director: John Ford
Co-stars: Wallace Beery Ricardo Cortez Jean Hersholt

1932   MAN ABOUT TOWN
Director: John Francis Dillon
Co-stars: Warner Baxter Conway Tearle Leni Stengel

1932   THE MASK OF FU MANCHU
Director: Charles Brabin
Co-stars: Boris Karloff Lewis Stone Charles Starrett

1932   PHANTOM OF CRESTWOOD
Director: Walter Ruben
Co-stars: Ricardo Cortez Anita Louise Pauline Frederick

1932   SCARFACE
Director: Howard Hawks
Co-stars: Paul Muni Ann Dvorak George Raft Boris Karloff

1932   WASHINGTON MASQUERADE
Director: Charles Brabin
Co-stars: Lionel Barrymore Nils Asther C.Henry Gordon

1933   DINNER AT EIGHT
Director: George Cukor
Co-stars: Lionel Barrymore Jean Harlow Marie Dressler

1933   GABRIEL OVER THE WHITE HOUSE
Director: Gregory La Cava
Co-stars: Walter Huston Franchot Tone

1934   THE CRIME DOCTOR
Director: John Robertson
Co-stars: Otto Kruger Nils Asther Donald Crisp

1934   WEDNESDAY'S CHILD
Co-star: David Durrand

1934   OUR DAILY BREAD
Director: King Vidor
Co-stars: Tom Keene John Qualen Barbara Pepper

1935   THUNDER IN THE NIGHT
Director: George Archainbaud
Co-stars: Edmund Lowe Paul Cavanagh Una O'Connor

1935   10 DOLLAR RAISE
Co-stars: Edward Everet T Horton

1935   THE LITTLEST REBEL
Director: David Butler
Co-stars: Shirley Temple John Boles Jack Holt

1935   BLACK FURY
Director: Michael Curtiz
Co-stars: Paul Muni William Gargan Barton MacLane

1936   BELOVED ENEMY
Director: H.C.Potter
Co-stars: Brian Aherne Merle Oberon David Niven

1937   THE GIRL FROM SCOTLAND YARD
Director: Robert Vignola
Co-stars: Robert Baldwin Eduardo Cianneli

1937   THE LAST TRAIN FROM MADRID
Director: James Hogan
Co-stars: Dorothy Lamour Lew Ayres Helen Mack

1937   ON SUCH A NIGHT
Director: Emmanuel Cohen
Co-stars: Grant Richards Roscoe Karns Eduardo Cianneli

1938   KENTUCKY
Director: David Butler
Co-stars: Loretta Young Richard Greene Walter Brennan

1940   PRIDE AND PREJUDICE
Director: Robert Z. Leonard
Co-stars: Laurence Olivier Greer Garson Edmund Gwenn

1945   JEALOUSY
Director: Gustav Machaty
Co-stars: Nils Asther John Loder Jane Randolph

1946   THE UNKNOWN
Director: Henry Levin
Co-stars: Jeff Donnell Jim Bannon

1951   M
Director: Joseph Losey
Co-stars: David Wayne Howard Da Silva Luther Adler

PENNY MORRELL

1963   A MATTER OF CHOICE
Director: Vernon Sewell
Co-stars: Anthony Steel Jeanne Moody Ballard Berkeley

ANDREA MORRICONE

1989   CINEMA PARADISO
Director: Guiseepe Tornatore
Co-stars: Philippe Noiret Salvatore Cascio Agnese Nano

PRISCILLA MORRILL

1983   RIGHT OF WAY
Director: George Schaeffer
Co-stars: Bette Davis James Stewart Melinda Dillon

ANITA MORRIS

1984   MARIA'S LOVERS
Director: Andrei Konchalovsky
Co-stars: Nastassja Kinski John Savage Robert Mitchum

1984   THE HOTEL NEW HAMPSHIRE
Director: Tony Richardson
Co-stars: Rob Lowe Jodie Foster Beau Bridges

1986   ABSOLUTE BEGINNERS
Director: Julien Temple
Co-stars: Patsy Kensit Eddie O'Connell David Bowie

1986   RUTHLESS PEOPLE
Director: David Zucker
Co-stars: Danny DeVito Bette Midler Judge Reinhold

1987   ARIA
Director: Robert Altman
Co-stars: Theresa Russell Bridget Fonda Elizabeth Hurley

1988   18 AGAIN
Director: Paul Flaherty
Co-stars: George Burns Charlie Schlatter Tony Roberts

1989   BLOODHOUNDS OF BROADWAY
Director: Howard Brookner
Co-stars: Madonna Jennifer Grey Rutger Hauer

1992   OFF AND RUNNING
Director: Edward Bianchi
Co-stars: Cyndi Lauper David Keith Johnny Pinto

1994   RADIOLAND MURDERS
Director: Mel Smith
Co-stars: Mary Stuart Masterson Brian Benben Ned Beatty

BARBOURA MORRIS

1960   A BUCKET OF BLOOD
Director: Roger Corman
Co-stars: Dick Miller Anthony Carbone Ed Nelson

BETH MORRIS

1971   CRUCIBLE OF TERROR
Director: Ted Hooker
Co-stars: Mike Raven James Bolam Ronald Lacey

DOROTHY MORRIS

1944   NONE SHALL ESCAPE
Director: Andre De Toth
Co-stars: Alexander Knox Marsha Hunt Henry Travers

1946   LITTLE MISS BIG
Co-stars: Beverley Simmons Fay Holden Frank McHugh

JANE MORRIS (Child)

1986   GOOD AS GOLD
Director: John Glenister
Co-stars: David Calder Richard Moore Jane Wood

1991   FRANKIE AND JOHNNY
Director: Garry Marshall
Co-stars: Al Pacino Michelle Pfeiffer Kate Nelligan

JUDY MORRIS

1977   THE PICTURE SHOW MAN
Director: John Power
Co-stars: John Meillon Rod Taylor Patrick Cargill

1983   PHAR LAP
Director: Simon Wincer
Co-stars: Tom Burlinson Martin Vaughn Vincent Ball

1984   RAZORBACK
Director: Russell Mulcahy
Co-stars: Gregory Harrison Bill Kerr Chris Haywood

1986   LAST FRONTIER
Director: Simon Wincer
Co-stars: Linda Evans Jack Thompson Jason Robards

1986   THE MORE THINGS CHANGE
Director: Robyn Nevin
Co-stars: Barry Otto Victoria Longley

1991   THE OTHER SIDE OF PARADISE
Director: Renny Rye
Co-stars: Jason Connery Richard Wilson Hywel Bennett

KATHY MORRIS

1994   RISE AND WALK:
        THE DENNIS BYRD STORY
Director: Michael Dinner
Co-stars: Peter Berg Johann Carlo

LANA MORRIS

1948   SPRING IN THE PARK
Director: Herbert Wilcox
Co-stars: Anna Neagle Michael Wilding Tom Walls

1948   THE WEAKER SEX
Director: Roy Baker
Co-stars: Ursula Jeans Cecil Parker Joan Hopkins

1949   THE WOMAN IN QUESTION
Director: Anthony Asquith
Co-stars: Jean Kent Dirk Bogarde Susan Shaw

1949   TROTTIE TRUE
Director: Brian Desmond Hurst
Co-stars: Jean Kent James Donald Bill Owen

1950   GUILT IS MY SHADOW
Director: Roy Kellino
Co-stars: Patrick Holt Elizabeth Sellars Peter Reynolds

1950   THE RELUCTANT WIDOW
Director: Bernard Knowles
Co-stars: Jean Kent Guy Rolfe Kathleen Byron

1950   MORNING DEPARTURE
Director: Roy Baker
Co-stars: John Mills Richard Attenborough Nigel Patrick

1951   A TALE OF FIVE CITIES
Director: Montgomery Tully
Co-stars: Bonar Colleano Gina Lollobrigida

1953   THE RED BERET
Director: Terence Young
Co-stars: Alan Ladd Susan Stephen Leo Genn

1953   TROUBLE IN STORE
Director: John Paddy Carstairs
Co-stars: Norman Wisdom Margaret Rutherford Moira Lister

1954   RADIO CAB MURDER
Director: Vernon Sewell
Co-stars: Jimmy Hanley Sonia Holm Sam Kydd

1955   MAN OF THE MOMENT
Director: John Paddy Carstairs
Co-stars: Norman Wisdom Belinda Lee Jerry Desmonde

1956   HOME AND AWAY
Director: Vernon Sewell
Co-stars: Jack Warner Kathleen Harrison Charles Victor

1959   PASSPORT TO SHAME
Director: Alvin Rakoff
Co-stars: Eddie Constantine Diana Dors Odile Versois

1959   OCTOBER MOTH
Director: John Kruse
Co-stars: Lee Patterson Peter Dyneley Robert Cawdron

1959   NO TREES IN THE STREET
Director: J.Lee Thompson
Co-stars: Sylvia Syms Herbert Lom Melvyn Hayes

1969   I START COUNTING
Director: David Greene
Co-stars: Jenny Agutter Brian Marshall Simon Ward

LIBBY MORRIS

1968   THE ADDING MACHINE
Director: Jerome Epstein
Co-stars: Phyllis Diller Milo O'Shea Billie Whitelaw

LILY MORRIS

1930   ELSTREE CALLING
Director: Arian Brunel
Co-stars: Tommy Handley Jack Hulbert Gordon Harker

1934   RADIO PARADE OF 1935
Director: Arthur Woods
Co-stars: Will Hay Ted Ray Helen Chandler

1941   I THANK YOU
Director: Marcel Varnel
Co-stars: Arthur Askey Richard Murdoch Moore Marriott

MARGARET MORRIS

1936   DESERT GUNS
Co-star: Conway Tearle

MARY MORRIS (U.S.A.)

1934   DOUBLE DOOR
Director: Charles Vidor
Co-stars: Evelyn Venable Kent Taylor Anne Revere

MARY MORRIS (U.K.)

1937   VICTORIA THE GREAT
Director: Herbert Wilcox
Co-stars: Anna Neagle Anton Walbrook H.B.Warner

1938   PRISON WITHOUT BARS
Director: Brian Desmond Hurst
Co-stars: Edna Best Barry K.Barnes Corinne Luchaire

1939   THE SPY IN BLACK
Director: Michael Powell
Co-stars: Conrad Veidt Valerie Hobson Marius Goring

1940   THE THEIF OF BAGDAD
Director: Michael Powell
Co-stars: John Justin Conrad Veidt Sabu

1941   PIMPERNEL SMITH
Director: Leslie Howard
Co-stars: Leslie Howard Francis L.Sullivan David Tomlinson

1943   UNDERCOVER
Director: Sergei Nolbandov
Co-stars: Tom Walls Michael Wilding John Clements

1944   THE AGITATOR
Director: John Harlow
Co-stars: William Hartnell John Laurie Edward Rigby

1945   THE MAN FROM MOROCCO
Director: Max Greene
Co-stars: Anton Walbrook Margaretta Scott Reginald Tate

1949   TRAIN OF EVENTS
Director: Basil Dearden
Co-stars: Valerie Hobson John Clements Susan Shaw

1951   HIGH TREASON
Director: Roy Boulting
Co-stars: Liam Redmond Andre Morell Patric Doonan

1976   FULL CIRCLE
Director: Richard Loncraine
Co-stars: Mia Farrow Keir Dullea Tom Conti

1978   ANNA KARENINA
Director: Basil Coleman
Co-stars: Nicola Pagett Eric Porter Stuart Wilson

1990   SOMETIME IN AUGUST
Director: John Glenister
Co-stars: Craig Lorimer Tom Wilkinson Paul Witherspoon

MAUREEN MORRIS

1989   THE CRONICLES OF NARNIA: THE LION, THE WITCH AND THE WARDROBE
Director: Marilyn Fox
Co-stars: Richard Dempsey Sophie Cook Michael Aldridge

1989   THE CRONICLES OF NARNIA: PRINCE CASPIAN
Director: Marilyn Fox
Co-stars: Richard Dempsey Sophie Cook

1989   THE CRONICLES OF NARNIA: VOYAGE OF THE DAWN TREADER
Director: Alex Kirkby
Co-stars: Richard Dempsey Sophie Cook

PHYLLIS MORRIS

1950   THREE CAME HOME
Director: Jean Negulesco
Co-stars: Claudette Colbert Patric Knowles Florence Desmond

JENNY MORRISON (*Child*)

1994   INTERSECTION
Director: Mark Rydell
Co-stars: Richard Gere Sharon Stone Lolita Davidovich

SHELLEY MORRISON

1969   THREE'S A CROWD
Director: Harry Falk
Co-stars: Larry Hagman Jessica Walter Harvey Korman

1973   BREEZY
Director: Clint Eastwood
Co-stars: William Holden Kay Lenz Joan Hotchkis

ANN MORRISS

1938   THE CHASER
Director: Edwin Marin
Co-stars: Dennis O'Keefe Lewis Stone Nat Pendleton

1940   CRIME DOES NOT PAY: JACKPOT
Director: Roy Rowland
Co-star: Tom Neal

DORETTA MORROW

1952   BECAUSE YOU'RE MINE
Director: Alexander Hall
Co-stars: Mario Lanza James Whitmore

JO MORROW

1959 GIDGET
Director: Paul Wendkos
Co-stars: Sandra Dee Cliff Robertson James Darren

1959 THE LEGEND OF TOM DOOLEY
Director: Ted Post
Co-stars: Michael Landon Richard Rust

1959 OUR MAN IN HAVANA
Director: Carol Reed
Co-stars: Alec Guinness Noel Coward Maureen O'Hara

1959 THE THREE WORLDS OF GULLIVER
Director: Jack Sher
Co-stars: Kerwin Matthews Basil Sydney June Thorburn

1960 13 GHOSTS
Director: William Castle
Co-stars: Charles Herbert Martin Milner Rosemary De Camp

1963 SUNDAY IN NEW YORK
Director: Peter Tewkesbruy
Co-stars: Cliff Robertson Rod Taylor Jane Fonda

1964 HE RIDES TALL
Director: R.G.Springsteen
Co-stars: Tony Young Dan Duryea Madlyn Rhue

SUSAN MORROW

1951 GASOLINE ALLEY
Director: Edward Bernds
Co-stars: Scotty Beckett Jimmy Lydon Don Beddoe

1952 CORKY OF GASOLINE ALLEY
Director: Edward Bernds
Co-stars: Scotty Beckett Jimmy Lydon

1952 THE BLAZING FOREST
Director: Edward Ludwig
Co-stars: John Payne Agnes Moorehead William Demarest

1952 THE SAVAGE
Director: George Marshall
Co-stars: Charlton Heston Joan Taylor Peter Hanson

1953 CAT-WOMEN OF THE MOON
Director: Arthur Hilton
Co-stars: Sonny Tufts Marie Windsor Victor Jory

HELEN MORSE

1975 PICNIC AT HANGING ROCK
Director: Peter Weir
Co-stars: Rachel Roberts Dominic Guard Jacki Weaver

1978 CADDIE
Director: Doanld Crombie
Co-stars: Takis Emmanuel Jacki Weaver Jack Thompson

1979 AGATHA
Director: Michael Apted
Co-stars: Vanessa Redgrave Dustin Hoffman Timothy Dalton

1982 FAR EAST
Director: John Duigan
Co-stars: Bryan Brown John Bell Bill Hunter

**1983 SHERLOCK HOLMES:
THE BASKERVILLE CURSE**
Director: Alex Nicholas
Co-stars: Peter O'Toole Ron Haddrick

LAILA MORSE

1997 NIL BY MOUTH
Director: Gary Oldman
Co-stars: Ray Winstone Kathy Burke Charlie Creed-Miles

NATALIE MORSE

1993 ANCHORESS
Director: Chris Newby
Co-stars: Toyah Wilcox Pete Postlethwaite Eugene Bervoefs

AMY MORTEN

1993 ROOKIE OF THE YEAR
Director: Daniel Stern
Co-stars: Thomas Ian Nicholas Gary Busey Eddie Bracken

ELIZABETH MORTENSEN

1984 PAPER BIRD
Director: Anja Breien
Co-stars: Bjorn Floberg Per Sunderland Bente Borsun

CAROLINE MORTIMER

1969 A PLACE FOR LOVERS
Director: Vittorio De Sica
Co-stars: Faye Dunaway Marcello Mastroianni Karin Engh

1970 THE MACKENZIE BREAK
Director: Lamont Johnson
Co-stars: Brian Keith Ian Hendry Jack Watson

1973 THE HIRELING
Director: Alan Bridges
Co-stars: Robert Shaw Sarah Miles Peter Egan

EMILY MORTIMER

1996 THE LAST OF THE HIGH KINGS
Director: David Keating
Co-stars: Jared Leto Christina Ricci Gabriel Byrne

JOAN MORTIMER

1943 HENRY ALDRICH HAUNTS A HOUSE
Director: Hugh Bennett
Co-stars: Jimmy Lydon Charles Smith Mike Mazurki

1944 HENRY ALDRICH, BOY SCOUT
Director: Hugh Bennett
Co-stars: Jimmy Lydon Charles Smith John Litel

AMY MORTON

1992 STRAIGHT TALK
Director: Barnet Kelman
Co-stars: Dolly Parton James Woods Griffin Dunne

SAMANTHA MORTON

1988 THIS IS THE SEA
Director: Mary McGukian
Co-stars: Richard Harris Gabriel Byrne

1996 EMMA
Director: Andrew Davis
Co-stars: Kate Beckinsale Mark Strong Prunella Scales

EDDA MOSER

1979 DON GIOVANNI
Director: Joseph Losey
Co-stars: Ruggero Raimondi Kiri Te Kanawa John Macurdy

MARIAN MOSES

1966 DEAD HEAT ON A MERRY-GO-ROUND
Director: Bernard Girard
Co-stars: James Coburn Camilla Sparv Aldo Ray

1968 BUONA SERA MRS. CAMPBELL
Director: Melvin Frank
Co-stars: Gina Lollobrigida Telly Savalas Phil Silvers

GRETE MOSHEIM

1935 CAR OF DREAMS
Director: Austin Melford
Co-stars: John Mills Mark Lester Robertson Hare

MARIA LUISA MOSQUERA

1987 MACU, THE POLICEMAN'S WIFE
Director: Solveig Hoogesteijn
Co-stars: Daniel Alvarado Tito Aponti

MARIE MOSQUINI

1927 SEVENTH HEAVEN
Director: Frank Borzage
Co-stars: Janet Gaynor Charles Farrell David Butler

JENNIFER MOSS

1963 LIVE IT UP
Director: Lance Comfort
Co-stars: David Hemmings Joan Newell Veronica Hurst

KATE MOSS

1996 UNZIPPED
Director: Douglas Keeve
Co-stars: Sandra Bernhard Naomi Campbell Cindy Crawford

MYRIAM MOSZKO

1990 SWEET REVENGE
Director: Charlotte Brandstrom
Co-stars: Rosanna Arquette Carrie Fisher John Sessions

EVA MOTLEY

1982 SCRUBBERS
Director: Mai Zetterling
Co-stars: Amanda York Chrissie Cotterill Kate Ingram

BESS MOTTA

1987 YOU TALKIN' TO ME?
Director: Charles Winkler
Co-stars: Jim Young Faith Ford James Noble

EMILY MOULTRIE

1985 STORMIN' HOME
Director: Jerry Jameson
Co-stars: Gil Gerard Lisa Blount Geoffrey Lewis

PEGGY MOUNT

1954 THE EMBEZZLER
Director: John Gilling
Co-stars: Charles Victor Zena Marshall Avice Landon

1956 SAILOR BEWARE
Director: Gordon Parry
Co-stars: Shirley Eaton Ronald Lewis Esma Cannon

1956 DRY ROT
Director: Maurice Elvy
Co-stars: Ronald Shiner Brian Rix Sid James Heather Sears

1957 THE NAKED TRUTH
Director: Mario Zampi
Co-stars: Peter Sellers Terry-Thomas Dennis Price

1960 INN FOR TROUBLE
Director: C.Pennington-Richards
Co-stars: David Kossoff Leslie Phillips Glyn Owen

1963 LADIES WHO DO
Director: C.Pennington-Richards
Co-stars: Robert Morley Miriam Karlin Dandy Nichols

1964 ONE WAY PENDULUM
Director: Peter Yates
Co-stars: Eric Sykes George Cole Julia Foster

1966 FINDERS KEEPERS
Director: Richard Lester
Co-stars: Cliff Richards Robert Morley The Shadows

1966 HOTEL PARADISO
Director: Peter Glenville
Co-stars: Alec Guinness Gina Lollobrigida Robert Morley

1968 OLIVER!
Director: Carol Reed
Co-stars: Mark Lester Ron Moody Oliver Reed Harry Secombe

1992 THE PRINCESS AND THE GOBLIN (Voice)
Director: Jozsef Gemes
Co-stars: Joss Ackland Claire Bloom

NADIA MOUROUZI

1986 THE BEEKEEPER
Director: Theo Angelopoulos
Co-stars: Marcello Mastroianni Serge Reggiani

PRISCILLA MOUZAKIOTIS

1988 THE KISS
Director: Pen Densham
Co-stars: Joanna Pacula Nicholas Kilbertus Meredith Salenger

MOVITA

1935 MUTINY ON THE BOUNTY
Director: Frank Lloyd
Co-stars: Charles Laughton Clark Gable Franchot Tone

1937 PARADISE ISLE
Co-star: Warren Hull

1939 THE GIRL FROM RIO
Co-star: Warren Hull

1941 THE TOWER OF TERROR
Director: Lawrence Huntingdon
Co-stars: Wilfrid Lawson Michael Rennie

1977 PANIC IN ECHO PARK
Director: John Llewellyn Moxey
Co-stars: Dorian Harewood Robin Gammell Tamu

HELEN MOWERY

1946 AVALANCHE
Co-stars: Bruce Cabot Roscoe Karns John Good

1950 ALL ABOUT EVE
Director: Joseph Mankiewicz
Co-stars: Bette Davis George Sanders Anne Baxter

ANTOINETTE MOYA

1992 PETAIN
Director: Jean Marboeuf
Co-stars: Jacques Dufilho Jean Yanne Jean-Pierre Cassel

STELLA MOYA

1937 UNDERNEATH THE ARCHES
Director: Redd David
Co-stars: Bud Flanagan Chesney Allen Enid Stamp-Taylor

ELIZABETH MUELLER

1956 THE POWER AND THE PRIZE
Director: Henry Kostner
Co-stars: Robert Taylor Mary Astor Burl Ives

1959 THE ANGRY HILLS
Director: Robert Aldrich
Co-stars: Robert Mitchum Gia Scala Stanley Baker

ESTHER MUIR

1933   SWEEPINGS
Co-star: Lionel Barrymore

1937   ON AGAIN, OFF AGAIN
Co-stars: Bert Wheeler Robert Woolsey

1937   I'LL TAKE ROMANCE
Director: Edward Griffith
Co-stars: Grace Moore Melvyn Douglas Helen Westley

1937   A DAY AT THE RACES
Director: Sam Wood
Co-stars: Marx Brothers Allan Jones Maureen O'Sullivan

1937   CITY GIRL
Director: Alfred Werker
Co-stars: Phyllis Brooks Ricardo Cortez Robert Wilcox

GERALDINE MUIR (Child)

1987   HOPE AND GLORY
Director: John Boorman
Co-stars: Sarah Miles Suan Wooldridge Ian Bannen

JEAN MUIR

1933   SON OF A SAILOR
Co-star: Johnny Mack Brown

1933   THE WORLD CHANGES
Director: Mervyn LeRoy
Co-stars: Paul Muni Aline McMahon Mary Astor

1934   A MODEN HERO
Director: G.W.Pabst
Co-stars: Richard Barthelmess Marjorie Rambeau Verree Teasdale

1934   BEDSIDE
Co-stars: Warren William Kathryn Sergavia

1934   GENTLEMEN ARE BORN
Director: Alfred Green
Co-stars: Franchot Tone Ross Alexander Dick Foran

1934   DR. MONICA
Director: William Keighley
Co-stars: Kay Francis Warren William Verree Teasdale

1934   DESIRABLE
Director: Archie Mayo
Co-stars: Verree Teasdale George Brent John Halliday

1934   AS THE EARTH TURNS
Director: Alfred Green
Co-stars: Donald Woods Emily Lowry Dorothy Petersen

1935   A MIDSUMMER NIGHT'S DREAM
Director: William Dieterle
Co-stars: Mickey Rooney James Cagney Dick Powell

1935   OIL FOR THE LAMPS OF CHINA
Director: Mervyn LeRoy
Co-stars: Pat O'Brien Josephine Hutchinson

1935   ORCHIDS TO YOU
Director: William Seiter
Co-stars: John Boles Charles Butterworth Spring Byington

1935   STARS OVER BROADWAY
Director: William Keighley
Co-stars: Jane Froman James Melton Pat O'Brien

1935   THE WHITE COCKATOO
Director: Alan Crosland
Co-stars: Ricardo Cortez Ruth Donnelly Minna Gombell

1936   WHITE FANG
Co-star: Michael Whalen

1937   THE OUTCASTS OF POKER FLATS
Director: Christy Cabanne
Co-stars: Preston Foster Van Heflin

1937   WHITE BONDAGE
Co-star: Gordon Oliver

1937   DRAEGERMAN COURAGE
Director: Louis King
Co-stars: Barton MacLane Henry O'Neill Robert Barrat

1938   JANE STEPS OUT
Co-star: Diana Churchill

1940   AND ONE WAS BEAUTIFUL
Director: Robert Sinclair
Co-stars: Robert Cummings Laraine Day Billie Burke

1940   LONE WOLF MEETS A LADY
Director: Sidney Salkow
Co-stars: Warren William Eric Blore Victor Jory

1943   THE CONSTANT NYMPH
Director: Edmund Goulding
Co-stars: Charles Boyer Joan Fontaine Alexis Smith

DIANA MULDAUR

1968   THE SWIMMER
Director: Sydney Pollack
Co-stars: Burt Lancaster Marge Champion Kim Hunter

1969   NUMBER ONE
Director: Tom Gries
Co-stars: Charlton Heston Jessica Walter Bruce Dern

1969   McCLOUD: WHO KILLED MISS U.S.A.?
Director: Richard Colla
Co-stars: Dennis Weaver Craig Stevens Raul Julia

1970   THE LAWYER
Director: Sidney Furie
Co-stars: Barry Newman Harold Gould Kathleen Crowley

1971   ONE MORE TRAIN TO ROB
Director: Andrew McLaglen
Co-stars: George Peppard John Vernon France Nuyen

1972   THE OTHER
Director: Robert Mulligan
Co-stars: Uta Hagen Chris Connelly Victor French

1974   CHOSEN SURVIVORS
Director: Sutton Roley
Co-stars: Jackie Cooper Alex Cord Bradford Dillman

1974   McQ
Director: John Sturges
Co-stars: John Wayne Eddie Albert Colleen Dewhurst

1974   PLANET EARTH
Director: Marc Daniels
Co-stars: John Saxon Ted Cassidy Janet Margolin

KATE MULGREW

1981   A STRANGER IS WATCHING
Director: Roy Rowland
Co-stars: Rip Torn James Naughton Shawn Van Schreiber

1985   REMO: UNARMED AND DANGEROUS
Director: Guy Hamilton
Co-stars: Fred Ward Joel Grey Wilford Brimley

1987   THROW MOMMA FROM THE TRAIN
Director: Danny DeVito
Co-stars: Danny DeVito Billy Crystal Anne Ramsey Kim Griest

1993   FOR LOVE AND GLORY
Director: Roger Young
Co-stars: Robert Foxworth Zach Galligan Olivia D'Abo

DONNA MULLANE

1973   THE OPTIMISTS OF NINE ELMS
Director: Anthony Simmons
Co-stars: Peter Sellers John Chaffey David Daker

BARBARA MULLEN

1941 JEANNIE
Director: Harold French
Co-stars: Michael Redgrave Albert Lieven Wilfrid Lawson

1942 THUNDER ROCK
Director: Roy Boulting
Co-stars: Michael Redgrave Lilli Palmer James Mason

1944 WELCOME MR. WASHINGTON
Director: Leslie Hiscott
Co-stars: Donald Stewart Peggy Cummings Martita Hunt

1944 A PLACE OF ONE'S OWN
Director: Bernard Knowles
Co-stars: James Mason Margaret Lockwood Dennis Price

1948 CORRIDOR OF MIRRORS
Director: Terence Young
Co-stars: Eric Portman Edana Romney Hugh Sinclair

1952 THE GENTLE GUNMAN
Director: Basil Dearden
Co-stars: John Mills Dirk Bogarde Elizabeth Sellers

1952 SO LITTLE TIME
Director: Compton Bennett
Co-stars: Maria Schell Marius Goring Gabrielle Dorziat

1958 INNOCENT SINNERS
Director: Philip Leacock
Co-stars: Flora Robson Catherine Lacy David Kossoff

1960 THE CHALLENGE
Director: John Gilling
Co-stars: Jayne Mansfield Anthony Quayle Peter Reynolds

1963 THE VERY EDGE
Director: Cyril Frankel
Co-stars: Richard Todd Ann Heywood Jeremy Brett

1966 MISS MacTAGGART WON'T LIE DOWN
Director: Francis Searle
Co-stars: Eric Woodburn Jack Lambert

KATHRYN MULLEN

1982 DARK CRYSTAL (Voice)
Director: Jim Henson
Co-stars: Jim Henson Frank Oz Dave Goelz Kiran Shah

PATTY MULLEN

1990 FRANKENHOOKER
Director: Frank Hennenlotter
Co-stars: James Lorinz Shirley Stoller Louise Lasser

GISELA MULLER

1992 THE SECOND HEIMAT
Director: Edgar Reitz
Co-stars: Henry Arnold Salome Kammer Noemi Steuer

RENATE MULLER

1931 SUNSHINE SUSIE
Director: Victor Saville
Co-stars: Jack Hulbert Owen Nares Morris Harvey

1933 VIKTOR UND VIKTORIA
Director: Reinhold Schunzel
Co-stars: Hermann Thimig Adolf Wohlbruck

MICHELLE MULVANEY

1984 KNOCKBACK
Director: Piers Haggard
Co-stars: Pauline Collins Derrick O'Connor Peggy Atchison

HILDA MUNDY

1945 I DIDN'T DO IT
Director: George Formby
Co-stars: George Formby Carl Jaffe Wally Patch

CAROLINE MUNRO

1973 THE GOLDEN VOYAGE OF SINBAD
Director: Gordon Hesler
Co-stars: John Philip Law Tom Baker Douglas Wilmer

1973 CAPTAIN KRONOS, VAMPIRE HUNTER
Director: Brian Clemens
Co-stars: Horst Janson John Carson

1975 I DON'T WANT TO BE BORN
Director: Peter Sasdy
Co-stars: Joan Collins Ralph Bates Eileen Atkins

1976 AT THE EARTH'S CORE
Director: Kevin Connor
Co-stars: Doug McClure Peter Cushing Keith Barron

JANET MUNRO

1957 SMALL HOTEL
Director: David MacDonald
Co-stars: Gordon Harker Irene Handl Billie Whitelaw

1958 THE TROLLENBERG TERROR
Director: Quentin Lawrence
Co-stars: Forrest Tucker Laurence Payne Warren Mitchell

1958 TOMMY THE TOREADOR
Director: John Paddy Carstairs
Co-stars: Tommy Steel Sid James

1959 THIRD MAN ON THE MOUNTAIN
Director: Ken Annakin
Co-stars: James MacArthur Michael Rennie Herbert Lom

1959 DARBY O'GILL AND THE LITTLE PEOPLE
Director: Robert Stevenson
Co-stars: Albert Sharpe Sean Connery

1960 THE SWISS FAMILY ROBERTSON
Director: Ken Annakin
Co-stars: John Mills Dorothy McGuire Tommy Kirk

1961 THE DAY THE EARTH CAUGHT FIRE
Director: Val Guest
Co-stars: Edward Judd Leo McKern Bernard Braden

1962 LIFE FOR RUTH
Director: Basil Dearden
Co-stars: Michael Craig Patrick McGoohan Megs Jenkins

1963 HIDE AND SEEK
Director: Cy Endfield
Co-stars: Ian Carmichael Curt Jurgens Hugh Griffith

1963 BITTER HARVEST
Director: Peter Graham Scott
Co-stars: John Stride Alan Badel Anne Cunningham

1964 A JOLLY BAD FELLOW
Director: Don Chaffey
Co-stars: Leo McKern Dennis Price Miles Malleson

1968 SEBASTIAN
Director: David Greene
Co-stars: Dirk Bogarde John Gielgud Lilli Palmer

NAN MUNRO

1966 MORGAN - A SUITABLE CASE FOR TREATMENT
Director: Karel Reisz
Co-stars: David Warner Vanessa Regrave

1989 GETTING IT RIGHT
Director: Randal Kleiser
Co-stars: Jesse Birdsall Jane Horrocks Lynn Redgrave

PAULINE MUNRO

1968   TELL ME LIES
Director: Peter Brook
Co-stars: Glenda Jackson Paul Scofield Kingsley Amis

PATRICE MUNSEL

1953   MELBA
Director: Lewis Milestone
Co-stars: Robert Morley Martita Hunt Sybil Thorndike

ONA MUNSON

1931   FIVE STAR FINAL
Director: Mervyn LeRoy
Co-stars: Edward G.Robinson Marian Marsh H.B.Warner

1931   BROADMINDED
Director: Mervyn LeRoy
Co-stars: Joe E.Brown Thelma Todd Bela Lugosi

1931   GOING WILD
Co-stars: Joe E.Brown Frank McHugh Laura Lee

1939   GONE WITH THE WIND
Director: Victor Fleming
Co-stars: Clark Gable Vivien Leigh Leslie Howard

1939   THE BIG GUY
Director: Arthur Lubin
Co-stars: Jackie Cooper Victor McLaglen Peggy Moran

1939   SCANDAL SHEET
Director: Nick Grinde
Co-stars: Otto Kruger Edward Norris

1941   WILD GEESE CALLING
Director: John Brahm
Co-stars: Joan Bennett Henry Fonda Warren William

1941   LADY FROM LOUISIANA
Director: Bernard Vorhaus
Co-stars: John Wayne Henry Stephenson Dorothy Dandridge

1942   THE SHANGHAI GESTURE
Director: Josef Von Sternberg
Co-stars: Walter Huston Gene Tierney Victor Mature

1945   THE CHEATERS
Director: Joseph Kane
Co-stars: Joseph Schildkraut Billie Burke Eugene Pallette

1947   THE RED HOUSE
Director: Delmer Daves
Co-stars: Edward G.Robinson Julie London Rory Calhoun

CORINNA MURA

1942   CALL OUT THE MARINES
Director: Frank Ryan
Co-stars: Edmund Lowe Victor McLaglen Binnie Barnes

KARMIN MURCELLO

1985   SEDUCED
Director: Jerrold Freedman
Co-stars: Gregory Harrison Cybill Shepherd Jose Ferrer

VICKY MURDOCK

1987   CHRISTINE
Director: Alan Clarke
Co-stars: Kelly George Joanne Mapp Mark Harvey

BRITTANY MURPHY

1995   CLUELESS
Director: Amy Heckerling
Co-stars: Alicia Silverstone Paul Rudd Stacey Dash

EDNA MURPHY

1928   MY MAN
Director: Archie Mayo
Co-stars: Fanny Brice Guinn Williams Andre De Segurola

1929   LITTLE JOHNNY JONES
Director: Mervyn LeRoy
Co-stars: Eddie Buzzell Alice Day Robert Edeson

FIDELMA MURPHY

1963   NEVER PUT IT IN WRITING
Director: Andrew Stone
Co-stars: Pat Boone Reginald Beckwith Colin Blakely

1968   SINFUL DAVEY
Director: John Huston
Co-stars: John Hurt Pamela Franklin Anjelica Huston

KATY MURPHY

1987   NORMAL SERVICE
Director: Garth Tucker
Co-stars: Kenneth Cranham Richard Wilson Tony Roper

MARY MURPHY

1952   CARRIE
Director: William Wyler
Co-stars: Laurence Oliver Jennifer Jones Miriam Hopkins

1953   BEACHHEAD
Director: Stuart Heisler
Co-stars: Tony Curtis Frank Lovejoy Eduard Franz

1953   MAIN STREET TO BROADWAY
Director: Tay Garnett
Co-stars: Tom Morton Ethel Barrymore Shirley Booth

1954   THE MAD MAGICIAN
Director: John Brahm
Co-stars: Vincent Price Eva Gabor John Emery

1954   MAKE HASTE TO LIVE
Director: William Seiter
Co-stars: Dorothy McGuire Stephen McNally John Howard

1954   SITTING BULL
Director: Sidney Salkow
Co-stars: Dale Robertson J. Carrol Naish John Litel

1954   THE WILD ONE
Director: Laslo Benedek
Co-stars: Marlon Brando Lee Marvin Robert Keith

1955   A MAN ALONE
Director: Ray Milland
Co-stars: Ray Milland Ward Bond Raymond Burr Lee Van Cleef

1955   THE MAVERICK QUEEN
Director: Joe Kane
Co-stars: Barbara Stanwyck Barry Sullivan Scott Brady

1955   THE DESPERATE HOURS
Director: William Wyler
Co-stars: Fredric March Humphrey Bogart Martha Scott

1955   HELL'S ISLAND
Director: Phil Karlson
Co-stars: John Payne Francis L.Sullivan Arnold Moss

1956   THE INTIMATE STRANGER
Director: Joseph Losey
Co-stars: Richard Basehart Mervyn Johns Roger Livesey

1957   THE ESCAPEMENT
Director: Montgomery Tully
Co-stars: Rod Cameron Meredith Edwards Peter Illing

1958   CRIME AND PUNISHMENT U.S.A.
Director: Denis Sanders
Co-stars: George Hamilton Frank Silvera

1972 JUNIOR BONNER
Director: Sam Peckinpah
Co-stars: Steve McQueen Ida Lupino Robert Preston

ROSEANNE MURPHY

1943 HAPPY LAND
Director: Irving Pichel
Co-stars: Don Ameche Frances Dee Ann Rutherford

1945 WONDER MAN
Director: Bruce Humberstone
Co-stars: Danny Kaye Virginia Mayo Vera-Ellen

ROSEMARY MURPHY

1961 YOUNG DOCTORS
Director: Phil Karlson
Co-stars: Fredric March Ben Gazzara Eddie Albert

1962 TO KILL A MOCKINGBIRD
Director: Robert Mulligan
Co-stars: Gregory Peck Mary Badham Philip Alford

1966 ANY WEDNESDAY
Director: Robert Ellis Miller
Co-stars: Jane Fonda Dean Jones Jason Robards

1972 BEN
Director: Phil Karson
Co-stars: Lee Harcourt Montgomery Arthur O'Connell

1972 YOU'LL LIKE MY MOTHER
Director: Lamont Johnson
Co-stars: Patty Duke Richard Thomas Sian-Barbara Allen

1973 ACE ELI AND RODGER OF THE SKIES
Director: John Erman
Co-stars: Cliff Robertson Pamela Franklin

1973 WALKING TALL
Director: Phil Karlson
Co-stars: Joe Don Baker Elizabeth Hartman Gene Evans

1973 FORTY CARATS
Director: Milton Katselas
Co-stars: Liv Ullman Edward Albert Gene Kelly

1977 JULIA
Director: Fred Zinnemann
Co-stars: Jane Fonda Vanessa Redgrave Jason Robards

1979 THE ATTIC
Director: George Edwards
Co-stars: Ray Milland Carrie Snodgress Ruth Cox

1981 THE HAND
Director: Oliver Stone
Co-stars: Michael Caine Andrea Marcovicci Viveca Lindfors

1992 FOR THE BOYS
Director: Mark Rydell
Co-stars: Bette Midler James Caan George Segal

SALLY MURPHY

1992 SCENT OF A WOMAN
Director: Martin Brest
Co-stars: Al Pacino Chris O'Donnell Gabrielle Anwar

ALENA MURRAY

1957 THE THREE FACES OF EVE
Director: Nunnally Johnson
Co-stars: Joanne Woodward David Wayne Lee J.Cobb

1958 THE HUNTERS
Director: Dick Powell
Co-stars: Robert Mitchum Robert Wagner Mai Britt

BARBARA MURRAY

1949 BOYS IN BROWN
Director: Montgomery Tully
Co-stars: Jack Warner Dirk Bogarde Michael Medwin

1949 POET'S PUB
Director: Frederick Wilson
Co-stars: Derek Bond Rona Anderson Joyce Grenfell

1949 PASSPORT TO PIMLICO
Director: Henry Cornelius
Co-stars: Margaret Rutherford Basil Radford Naunton Wayne

1950 TONY DRAWS A HORSE
Director: John Paddy Carstairs
Co-stars: Cecil Parker Anne Crawford Derek Bond

1950 THE DARK MAN
Director: Jeffrey Dell
Co-stars: Maxwell Reed Edward Underdown Natasha Parry

1951 MYSTERY JUNCTION
Co-stars: Michael McCarthy
Co-stars: Sidney Tafler Pat Owens Martin Benson

1952 THE FRIGHTENED MAN
Director: John Gilling
Co-stars: Dermot Walsh Charles Victor John Blythe

1953 MEET MR. LUCIFER
Director: Anthony Pelissier
Co-stars: Stanley Holloway Peggy Cumings Kay Kendall

1953 STREET CORNER
Director: Muriel Box
Co-stars: Rosamund John Anne Crawford Terence Morgan

1957 CAMPBELL'S KINGDOM
Director: Ralph Thomas
Co-stars: Dirk Bogarde Michael Craig Stanley Baker

1957 DOCTOR AT LARGE
Director: Ralph Thomas
Co-stars: Dirk Bogarde Muriel Pavlow Donald Sinden

1958 A CRY FROM THE STREETS
Director: Lewis Gilbert
Co-stars: Max Bygraves Colin Petersen Kathleen Harrison

1959 OPERATION BULLSHINE
Director: Gilbert Gunn
Co-stars: Donald Sinden Carole Lesley Ronald Shiner

1963 THE PUNCH AND JUDY MAN
Director: Jeremy Summers
Co-stars: Tony Hancock Sylvia Syms Ronald Fraser

1970 SOME WILL, SOME WON'T
Director: Duncan Wood
Co-stars: Ronnie Corbett Thora Hird Leslie Phillips

1971 UP POMPEII
Director: Bob Kellett
Co-stars: Frankie Howerd Patrick Gargill Michael Hordern

1972 TALES FROM THE CRYPT
Director: Freddie Francis
Co-stars: Ralph Richardson Joan Collins Geoffrey Bayldon

JAN MURRAY

1967 TARZAN AND THE GREAT RIVER
Director: Robert Day
Co-stars: Mike Henry Diana Millay Rafer Johnson

1969 THE ANGRY BREED
Director: David Commons
Co-stars: Jan Sterling James MacArthur William Windom

1970 WHICH WAY TO THE FRONT?
Director: Jerry Lewis
Co-stars: Jerry Lewis John Wood Kaye Ballard Robert Middleton

1973 DAY OF THE WOLVES
Director: Ferde Grofe
Co-stars: Richard Egan Martha Hyer Rick Jason

MAE MURRAY

1924 CIRCE

1925 THE MERRY WIDOW
Director: Erich Von Stroheim
Co-stars: John Gilbert Tully Marshall Roy D'Arcy

1931 BACHELOR APARTMENT
Director: Lowell Sherman
Co-stars: Lowell Sherman Irene Dunne Norman Kerry

1931 HIGH STAKES
Director: Lowell Sherman
Co-stars: Lowell Sherman Edward Martindell Ethel Levey

PAULINE MURRAY

1963 IT HAPPENED HERE
Director: Kevin Brownloe
Co-stars: Sebastian Shaw Fiona Lekland Honor Fehrson

RITA MURRAY

1970 ANGELS DIE HARD
Director: Richard Compton
Co-stars: Tom Baker William Smith Dan Haggerty

RUBY MURRAY

1956 A TOUCH OF THE SUN
Director: Gordon Parry
Co-stars: Frankie Howerd Dorothy Bromily Gordon Harker

MUSIDORA

1916 JUDEX
Director: Louis Feuillade
Co-stars: Rene Creste Gaston Michel Edouard Mathe

JANE MUSKY

1996 CITY HALL
Director: Harold Becker
Co-stars: John Cusack Al Pacino Bridget Fonda

MARJORIE ANN MUTCHIE

1943 FOOTLIGHT GLAMOUR
Director: Frank Strayer
Co-stars: Penny Singleton Arthur Lake Ann Savage

1945 LEAVE IT TO BLONDIE
Director: Abby Berlin
Co-stars: Penny Singleton Arthur Lake Chick Chandler

ORNELLA MUTI

1979 THEY MADE HIM A CRIMINAL
Director: Giancarlo Giannini
Co-stars: Nicolai Dupak Stefano Nadia

1980 LOVE AND MONEY
Director: James Toback
Co-stars: Ray Sharkey Klaus Kinski Armand Assante

1980 FLASH GORDON
Director: Michael Hodges
Co-stars: Sam J.Jones Melody Anderson Max Von Sydow

1981 TALES OF ORDINARY MADNESS
Director: Marco Ferreri
Co-stars: Ben Gazzara Susan Tyrrell Tanya Lopert

1983 SWANN IN LOVE
Director: Volker Schlondorff
Co-stars: Jeremy Irons Alain Delon Fanny Ardant

1983 THE GIRL FROM TRIESTE
Director: Pasquale Festa
Co-stars: Campanile Ben Gazzara Mimsi Farmer

1987 CHRONICLE OF A DEATH FORTOLD
Director: Francesco Rosi
Co-stars: Rupert Everett Irene Papas

1991 ONCE UPON A CRIME
Director: Eugene Levy
Co-stars: John Candy James Belushi Cybill Shepherd

1991 OSCAR
Director: John Landis
Co-stars: Sylvester Stallone Kirk Douglas Vincent Spano

HELEN MUTKINS

1990 WEEKEND WITH KATE
Director: Colin Friels
Co-stars: Catherine McClements Jerome Ehlers

LINDA MVUSI

1987 A WORLD APART
Director: Chris Menges
Co-stars: Barbara Hershey Jodhi May Jeroen Krabbe

CARMEL MYERS

1918 ALL NIGHT
Director: Paul Powell
Co-stars: Rudolph Valentino Charles Dorian Mary Warren

1918 A SOCIETY SENSATION
Co-star: Rudolph Valentino

1924 BEAU BRUMMELL
Director: Harry Beaumont
Co-stars: John Barymore Mary Astor Irene Rich

1926 BEN HUR
Director: Fred Niblo
Co-stars: Ramon Navarro Francis X.Bushman May McAvoy

1926 TELL IT TO THE MARINES
Director: George Hill
Co-stars: Lon Chaney Eleanor Boardman Warner Oland

1930 A LADY SURRENDERS
Director: John Stahl
Co-stars: Conrad Nagel Genevieve Tobin Basil Rathbone

1931 SVENGALI
Director: Archie Mayo
Co-stars: John Barrymore Marian Marsh Donald Crisp

1931 MAD GENIUS
Co-star: John Barrymore

CYNTHIA MYERS

1970 BEYOND THE VALLEY OF THE DOLLS
Director: Russ Meyer
Co-stars: Dolly Read Marcia McBroom Edy Williams

KATHLEEN MYERS

1925 GO WEST
Director: Buster Keaton
Co-stars: Buster Keaton Howard Truesdall

KIM MYERS

1985 A NIGHTMARE ON ELM STREET II: FREDDY'S REVENGE
Director: Jack Sholder
Co-stars: Robert Englund Mark Patton

1988 ILLEGALLY YOURS
Director: Peter Bogdanovich
Co-stars: Rob Lowe Colleen Camp Kenneth Mars

1989 WHEN HE'S NOT A STRANGER
Director: John Gray
Co-stars: Annabeth Gish Kevin Dillon John Terlesky

1992   FATAL LOVE
Director: Tom Mcloughlin
Co-stars: Molly Ringwald Perry King Lee Grant

KAREN-LISE MYNSTER

1992   SOFIE
Director: Liv Ullmann
Co-stars: Erland Josephson Gita Norby Torben Zeller

ODETTE MYRTIL

1936   DODSWORTH
Director: William Wyler
Co-stars: Walter Huston Mary Astor David Niven

ELYANE NADEAU

1978   MARTIN
Director: George Romero
Co-stars: John Amplas Christine Forrest Tom Savine

LYCIA NAFF

1990   CHOPPER CHICKS IN ZOMBIETOWN
Director: Dan Hoskins
Co-stars: Jamie Rose Catherine Carlen Vicki Frederick

ANNE NAGEL

1936   HOT MONEY
Co-star: Ross Alexander

1937   THE CASE OF THE STUTTERING BISHOP
Director: William Clemens
Co-stars: Donald Woods Ann Dvorak

1937   HOOSIER SCHOOLBOY
Director: William Nigh
Co-stars: Mickey Rooney Frank Shields

1937   THE DEVIL'S SADDLE LEGION
Director: Dick Foran

1938   SALESLADY
Co-star: Weldon Heyburn

1938   GANG BULLETS
Co-stars: Robert Kent Charles Trowbridge

1939   LEGION OF LOST FLYERS
Co-stars: Jack Carson Andy Devine Theodore Von Eltz

1939   CALL A MESSINGER
Director: Arthur Lubin
Co-stars: Billy Halop Robert Armstrong Buster Crabbe

1940   ARGENTINE NIGHTS
Director: Albert Rogell
Co-stars: Ritz Brothers Andrews Sisters Constance Moore

1940   BLACK FRIDAY
Director: Arthur Lubin
Co-stars: Boris Karloff Bella Lugosi Stanley Ridges

1940   DIAMOND FRONTIER
Director: Harold Schuster
Co-stars: Victor McLaglen John Loder Philip Dorn

1940   MAN MADE MONSTER
Director: George Waggner
Co-stars: Lon Chaney Lionel Atwill Frank Albertson

1941   SEALED LIPS
Co-stars: William Gargan John Litel Elliott Sullivan

1941   MUTINY IN THE ARTIC
Co-stars: Richard Arlen Andy Devine

1941   MEET THE CHUMP
Co-star: Hugh Herbert

1941   NEVER GIVE A SUCKER AN EVEN BREAK
Director: Edward Cline
Co-stars: W.C.Fields Gloria Jean Ann Miller

1942   THE MAD MONSTER
Director: Sam Newfield
Co-stars: George Zucco Johnny Downs Glenn Strange

1943   WOMEN IN BONDAGE
Director: Steve Sekely
Co-stars: Gail Patrick Nancy Kelly William Henry

1947   THE TRAP
Director: Howard Bretherton
Co-stars: Sidney Toler Victor Sen Yung Rita Quigley

LEELA NAIDU

1991   ELECTRIC MOON
Director: Pradip Krishen
Co-stars: Roshan Seth Naseeruddin Shah Alice Spivak

JOANNE NAIL

1976   THE GUMBALL RALLY
Director: Chuck Bail
Co-stars: Michael Sarazin Gary Busey Susan Flannery

1979   THE VISITOR
Director: Giulio Paradiso
Co-stars: Glenn Ford Mel Ferrer Shelley Winters

1980   WARP SPEED
Director: Allan Sandler
Co-stars: Adam West Camille Mitchell David Chandler

KATHY NAJIMY

1991   THE FISHER KING
Director: Terry Gilliam
Co-stars: Jeff Bridges Robin Williams Mercedes Ruehl

1991   SOAPDISH
Director: Michael Hoffman
Co-stars: Sally Field Kevin Kline Cathy Moriarty

1991   THE HARD WAY
Director: John Badham
Co-stars: Michael J. Fox James Woods Annabella Sciorra

1992   SISTER ACT
Director: Emile Ardolino
Co-stars: Whoopie Goldberg Maggie Smith Harvey Keitel

1993   SISTER ACT 2: BACK IN THE HABIT
Director: Bill Duke
Co-stars: Whoopie Goldberg Mary Wickes James Coburn

1993   HOCUS POCUS
Director: Kenny Ortega
Co-stars: Bette Midler Sarah Jessica Parker Thora Birch

NITA NALDI

1920   DR. JEKYLL AND MR. HYDE
Director: John Robertson
Co-stars: John Barrymore Martha Mansfield

1922   BLOOD AND SAND
Director: Fred Niblo
Co-stars: Rudolph Valentino Lila Lee George Field

1923   THE TEN COMMANDMENTS
Director: Cecil B. DeMille
Co-stars: Theodore Roberts Richard Dix Leatrice Joy

1923   HOLLYWOOD
Director: James Cruze
Co-stars: Hope Drown Luke Cosgrave Eleanor Lawson

1925   COBRA
Director: Joseph Henabery
Co-stars: Rudolph Valentino Casson Ferguson Getrude Olmstead

1926   THE MOUNTAIN EAGLE
Director: Alfred Hitchcock
Co-stars: Bernard Goetzke Malcolm Keen

ELAINE NALEE

1981 KELLY
Director: Christopher Chapman
Co-stars: Robert Logan Twyla-Dawn Vokins George Clutesi

SHA NA NA

1978 GREASE
Director: Randal Kleiser
Co-stars: John Travolta Olivia Newton-John Stockard Channing

AGNESE NANO

1989 CINEMA PARADISO
Director: Giuseppe Tornatore
Co-stars: Philippe Noiret Salvatore Cascio Jacques Perrin

ISABELLE NANTY

1985 ROUGE BAISER
Director: Vera Belmont
Co-stars: Charlotte Valandray Marthe Keller Lambert Wilson

1991 TATIE DANIELLE
Director: Etienne Chatiliez
Co-stars: Tsilla Chelton Catherine Jacob Eric Prat

DIANA NAPIER

1932 STRANGE EVIDENCE
Director: Robert Milton
Co-stars: Leslie Banks Carol Goodner George Curzon

1932 HER FIRST AFFAIRE
Co-stars: Ida Lupino Arnold Riches

1934 THE PRIVATE LIFE OF DON JUAN
Director: Alexander Korda
Co-stars: Douglas Fairbanks Merle Oberon

1934 CATHERINE THE GREAT
Director: Paul Czinner
Co-stars: Elizabeth Bergner Douglas Fairbanks Jnr.

1935 HEART'S DESIRE
Director: Paul Stein
Co-stars: Richard Tauber Leonora Corbett Frank Vosper

1936 LAND WITHOUT MUSIC
Director: Walter Forde
Co-stars: Richard Tauber Jimmy Durante June Clyde

1936 PAGLIACCI
Director: Karl Grune
Co-stars: Richard Tauber Steffi Duna Edmond Knight

1935 MIMI
Director: Paul Stein
Co-stars: Gertrude Lawrence Douglas Fairbanks Jnr. Harold Warrender

EVE NAPIER

1986 CRAZY MOON
Director: Allan Eastman
Co-stars: Kiefer Sutherland Peter Spence Vanessa Vaugan

PATRICIA NAPIER

1983 BIDDY
Director: Christine Edzard
Co-stars: Celia Bannerman Sam Ghazoros John Dalby

TONI NAPLES

1987 DEATHSTALKER 2: DUEL OF THE TITANS
Director: Jim Wynorski
Co-stars: John Terlesky Monique Gabrielle

KATHARINE NARDUCCI

1993 A BRONX TALE
Director: Robert De Niro
Co-stars: Robert De Niro Chazz Palminteri Lillo Brancato Joe Pesci

JENNIFER NASH

1993 INVISIBLE: THE CRONICLES OF BENJAMIN KNIGHT
Director: Jack Ersgard
Co-star: Brian Cousins

MARILYN NASH

1947 MONSIEUR VERDOUX
Director: Charles Chaplin
Co-stars: Charles Chaplin Martha Raye Isobel Elsom

MARY NASH

1934 UNCERTAIN LADY
Director: Karl Freund
Co-stars: Edward Everett Horton Genevieve Tobin Renee Gadd

1935 COLLEGE SCANDAL
Director: Elliott Nugent
Co-stars: Arline Judge Kent Taylor Wendy Barrie

1937 EASY LIVING
Director: Mitchell Leisen
Co-stars: Jean Arthur Ray Milland Edward Arnold

1937 HEIDI
Director: Allan Dwan
Co-stars: Shirley Temple Jean Hersholt Arthur Treacher

1937 THE KING AND THE CHORUS GIRL
Director: Mervyn LeRoy
Co-stars: Joan Blondell Fernand Gravet Jane Wyman

1937 WELLS FARGO
Director: Frank Lloyd
Co-stars: Joel McCrea Frances Dee Lloyd Nolan

1939 THE RAINS CAME
Director: Clarence Brown
Co-stars: Tyrone Power Myrna Loy George Brent

1939 THE LITTLE PRINCESS
Director: Walter Lang
Co-stars: Shirley Temple Richard Greene Anita Louise

1940 GOLD RUSH MAISIE
Director: Edwin Marin
Co-stars: Ann Sothern Lee Bowman Virginia Weidler

1940 CHARLIE CHAN IN PANAMA
Director: Norman Foster
Co-stars: Sidney Toler Jean Rogers Lionel Atwill

1940 THE PHILADELPHIA STORY
Director: George Cukor
Co-stars: Katherine Hepburn Cary Grant James Stewart

1941 MEN OF BOYS' TOWN
Director: Norman Taurog
Co-stars: Spencer Tracy Mickey Rooney Bobs Watson

1942 CALLING DR. GILLESPIE
Director: Harold Bucquet
Co-stars: Lionel Barrymore Philip Dorn Donna Reed

1944 COBRA WOMAN
Director: Robert Siodmak
Co-stars: Maria Montez Jon Hall Sabu Lon Chaney

1944 IN THE MEANTIME, DARLING
Director: Otto Preminger
Co-stars: Jeanne Crain Frank Latimore Gale Robbins

1944 THE LADY AND THE MONSTER
Director: George Sherman
Co-stars: Erich Von Stroheim Richard Arlen Vera Ralston

1945 YOLANDA AND THE THIEF
Director: Vincente Minnelli
Co-stars: Fred Astaire Lucille Bremer Frank Morgan

1946 TILL THE CLOUDS ROLL BY
Director: Richard Whorf
Co-stars: Robert Walker Van Heflin Judy Garland

1946 MONSIEUR BEAUCAIRE
Director: George Marshall
Co-stars: Bob Hope Joan Caulfield Marjorie Reynolds

MAYBELLE NASH

1961 THE SAND CASTLE
Director: Jerome Hill
Co-stars: Barrie Cardwell Laurie Cardwell George Dunham

NOREEN NASH

1947 THE TENDER YEARS
Director: Harold Schuster
Co-stars: Joe E.Brown Richard Lyon Charles Drake

1947 THE RED STALLION
Co-stars: Robert Paige Ted Donaldson Jane Darwell

1948 THE CHECKERED COAT
Director: Edward Cahn
Co-stars: Tom Conway Hurd Hatfield James Seay

1950 STORM OVER WYOMING
Director: Lesley Selander
Co-stars: Tim Holt Richard Martin Betty Underwood

MARIE-JOSE NAT

1960 LA VERITEE
Director: Henri-Georges Clouzot
Co-stars: Brigitte Bardot Charles Vanel Sami Frey

1961 THE SEVEN DEADLY SINS
Director: Jean-Luc Godard
Co-stars: Claude Brasseur Georges Wilson

ZOE NATHENSON

1986 MONA LISA
Director: Neil Jordan
Co-stars: Bob Hoskins Cathy Tyson Michael Caine

1987 THE RAGGEDY RAWNEY
Director: Bob Hoskins
Co-stars: Bob Hoskins Dexter Fletcher Zoe Wannamaker David Hill

NATHALIE NATTIER

1946 LES PORTES DE LA NUIT
Director: Pierre Brasseur
Co-stars: Yves Montand Serge Reggiani

MILDRED NATWICK

Nominated for Best Supporting Actress in 1967 For "Barefoot in the Park"

1940 THE LONG VOYAGE HOME
Director: John Ford
Co-stars: John Wayne Thomas Mitchell Ian Hunter

1945 THE ENCHANTED COTTAGE
Director: John Cromwell
Co-stars: Robert Young Dorothy McGuire Herbert Marshall

1945 YOLANDA AND THE THIEF
Director: Vincent Minnelli
Co-stars: Fred Astaire Lucille Bremer Frank Morgan

1948 A WOMAN'S VENGEANCE
Director: Zoltan Korda
Co-stars: Charles Boyer Jessica Tandy Ann Blyth

1948 THE KISSING BANDIT
Director: Laslo Benedek
Co-stars: Frank Sinatra Kathryn Grayson Billy Gilbert

1949 SHE WORE A YELLOW RIBBON
Director: John Ford
Co-stars: John Wayne Joanne Dru Victor McLaglen

1950 CHEAPER BY THE DOZEN
Director: Walter Lang
Co-stars: Myrna Loy Clifton Webb Jeanne Crain

1952 AGAINST ALL FLAGS
Director: George Sherman
Co-stars: Errol Flynn Maureen O'Hara Anthony Quine

1952 THE QUIET MAN
Director: John Ford
Co-stars: John Wayne Maureen O'Hara Victor McLaglen

1955 THE TROUBLE WITH HARRY
Director: Alfred Hitchcock
Co-stars: Edmund Gwenn Shirley Maclaine

1955 THE COURT JESTER
Director: Melvyn Frank
Co-stars: Danny Kaye Glynis Johns Basil Rathbone

1956 TEENAGE REBEL
Director: Edmund Goulding
Co-stars: Ginger Rogers Michael Rennie Betty Lou Keim

1967 BAREFOOT IN THE PARK
Director: Gene Saks
Co-stars: Robert Redford Jane Fonda Charles Boyer

1969 IF IT'S TUESDAY, THIS MUST BE BELGIUM
Director: Mel Stuart
Co-stars: Suzanne Pleshette Ian McShane

1969 THE MALTESE BIPPY
Director: Norman Panama
Co-stars: Dan Rowan Dick Martin Carol Lynley Julie Newmar

1971 DO NOT FOLD, SPINDLE OR MUTILATE
Director: Ted Post
Co-stars: Helen Hayes Myrna Loy Sylvia Sydney

1974 DAISY MILLER
Director: Peter Bogdanovich
Co-stars: Cybill Shepherd Cloris Leachman Barry Brown

1975 AT LONG LAST LOVE
Director: Peter Bogdanovich
Co-stars: Cybill Shepherd Burt Reynolds Eileen Brennan

1982 MAID IN AMERICA
Director: Paul Aaron
Co-stars: Susan Clark Alex Karras Fritz Weaver

1982 KISS ME GOODBYE
Director: Robert Mulligan
Co-stars: Sally Field Jeff Bridges Claire Trevor

1987 DEADLY DECEPTION
Director: John Llewellyn Moxey
Co-stars: Matt Salinger Lisa Eilbacher James Noble

1988 DANGEROUS LIAISONS
Director: Stephen Frears
Co-stars: Glenn Close John Malkovich Michelle Pfeiffer

MELINDA NAUD

1982 A DAY FOR THANKS ON WALTONS' MOUNTAIN
Director: Harry Harris
Co-stars: Ralph Waite Ellen Corby Eric Scott

ALITA NAUGHTON

1963 FRENCH DRESSING
Director: Ken Russell
Co-stars: Marisa Mell James Booth Roy Kinnear

MING NA-WEN

1993 THE JOY LUCK CLUB
Director: Wayne Wang
Co-stars: Kieu Ching Tsai Chin France Nuyen

DAPHNE NAYAR

1994 INTIMATE WITH A STRANGER
Director: Mel Woods
Co-stars: Roderick Mangin-Turner Janis Lee Amy Tolsky

ALLA NAZIMOVA

1921 CAMILLE
Director: Ray Smallwood
Co-stars: Rudolph Valentino Arthur Hoyt Zeffie Tilsbury

1922 A DOLL'S HOUSE
Co-star: Alan Hale

1922 SALOME
Director: Charles Bryant
Co-stars: Rose Dione Mitchell Lewis Nigel De Brulier

1940 ESCAPE
Director: Mervyn LeRoy
Co-stars: Norma Shearer Robert Taylor Conrad Veidt

1941 BLOOD AND SAND
Director: Rouben Mamoulian
Co-stars: Tyrone Power Linda Darnell Rita Hayworth

1944 THE BRIDGE OF SAN LUIS REY
Director: Rowland Lee
Co-stars: Lynn Bari Akim Tamiroff Louis Calhern

1944 IN OUR TIME
Director: Vincent Sherman
Co-stars: Ida Lupino Paul Henreid Nancy Coleman

1944 SINCE YOU WENT AWAY
Director: John Cromwell
Co-stars: Claudette Colbert Jennifer Jones Shirley Temple

ANNA NEAGLE *(Marjorie Robertson)*
(Married Herbert Wilcox)

1928 DAWN
Director: Herbert Wilcox
Co-stars: Sybil Thorndyke Marie Ault Haddon Mason

1932 THE FLAG LIEUTENANT
Director: Henry Edwards
Co-stars: Henry Edwards Joyce Bland Abraham Sofaer

1932 GOODNIGHT VIENNA
Director: Herbert Wilcox
Co-stars: Jack Buchanan Gina Malo William Kendall

1933 BITTER SWEET
Director: Herbert Wilcox
Co-stars: Fernand Gravet Hugh Williams Ray Hammond

1933 THE LITTLE DAMOZEL
Director: Herbert Wilcox
Co-stars: James Rennie Benita Hume Alfred Drayton

1934 NELL GWYN
Director: Herbert Wilcox
Co-stars: Cedric Hardwicke Jeanne De Casalai

1935 PEG OF OLD DRURY
Director: Herbert Wilcox
Co-stars: Cedric Hardwicke Jack Hawkins Margaretta Scott

1935 LIMELIGHT
Director: Herbert Wilcox
Co-stars: Arthur Tracy Ellis Jeffreys Tilly Losch

1937 THE THREE MAXIMS
Director: Herbert Wilcox
Co-stars: Tullio Carminati Leslie Banks Horace Hodges

1937 VICTORIA THE GREAT
Director: Herbert Wilcox
Co-stars: Anton Walbrook H.B.Warner Walter Rilla

1938 SIXTY GLORIOUS YEARS
Director: Herbert Wilcox
Co-stars: Anton Walbrook C.Aubrey Smith Felix Aylmer

1938 LONDON MELODY
Director: Herbert Wilcox
Co-stars: Tullio Carminati Robert Douglas Horace Hodges

1939 NURSE EDITH CAVELL
Director: Herbert Wilcox
Co-stars: George Sanders Edna May Oliver May Robson

1940 NO, NO NANETTE
Director: Herbert Wilcox
Co-stars: Richard Carlson Victor Mature Roland Young

1940 IRENE
Director: Herbert Wilcox
Co-stars: Ray Milland Roland Young Alan Marshall

1941 SUNNY
Director: Herbert Wilcox
Co-stars: Ray Bolger John Caroll Frieda Inescort

1941 THEY FLEW ALONE
Director: Herbert Wilcox
Co-stars: Robert Newton Edward Chapman Charles Carson

1943 THE YELLOW CANARY
Director: Herbert Wilcox
Co-stars: Richard Greene Nova Pilbeam Cyril Fletcher

1943 FOREVER AND A DAY
Director: Rene Clair
Co-stars: Ray Milland Claude Rains Charles Laughton

1945 I LIVE IN GROVESNOR SQUARE
Director: Herbert Wilcox
Co-stars: Rex Harrison Dean Jagger Robert Morley

1946 PICCADILLY INCIDENT
Director: Herbert Wilcox
Co-stars: Michael Wilding Coral Browne A.E.Matthews

1947 THE COURTNEYS OF CURZON STREET
Director: Herbert Wilcox
Co-stars: Michael Wilding Coral Browne

1948 SPRING IN PARK LANE
Director: Herbert Wilcox
Co-stars: Michael Wilding Tom Walls Peter Graves

1948 ELIZABETH OF LADYMEAD
Director: Herbert Wilcox
Co-stars: Hugh Williams Bernard Lee Isobel Jeans

1949 MAYTIME IN MAYFAIR
Director: Herbert Wilcox
Co-stars: Michael Wilding Tom Walls Peter Graves

1950 ODETTE
Director: Herbert Wilcox
Co-stars: Trevor Howard Peter Ustinov Marius Goring

1951 THE LADY WITH A LAMP
Director: Herbert Wilcox
Co-stars: Michael Wilding Gladys Young Peter Graves

1952 DERBY DAY
Director: Herbert Wilcox
Co-stars: Michael Wilding Googie Withers Gordon Harker

1954 LILACS IN THE SPRING
Director: Herbert Wilcox
Co-stars: Errol Flynn David Farrar Peter Graves

1955 KING'S RHAPSODY
Director: Herbert Wilcox
Co-stars: Errol Flynn Patrice Wymore Martita Hunt

1956 MY TEENAGE DAUGHTER
Director: Herbert Wilcox
Co-stars: Sylvia Syms Kenneth Haig Julia Lockwood

1957 NO TIME FOR TEARS
Director: Cyril Frankel
Co-stars: Anthony Quayle Sylvia Syms Flora Robson

1958 THE MAN WHO WOULDN'T TALK
Director: Herbert Wilcox
Co-stars: Anthony Quayle Zsa Zsa Gabor Dora Byran

1959 THE LADY IS A SQUARE
Director: Herbert Wilcox
Co-stars: Frankie Vaughan Anhtony Newley Janette Scott

BILLIE NEAL

1991 MORTAL THOUGHTS
Director: Alan Rudolph
Co-stars: Demi Moore Bruce Willis Glenne Headley

1992 CONSENTING ADULTS
Director: Alan J.Pakula
Co-stars: Kevin Kline Kevin Spacey Rebecca Miller

FRANCES NEAL

1941 LADY SCARFACE
Director: Frank Woodruff
Co-stars: Judith Anderson Dennis O'Keefe Eric Blore

PATRICIA NEAL
(Married Roald Dahl Mother Of Tessa Dahl)
**Oscar For Best Actress In 1963 For "Hud". Nominated For Best Actress
In 1968 For "The Subject Was Roses"**

1949 JOHN LOVES MARY
Director: David Butler
Co-stars: Ronald Reagan Jack Carson Virginia Field

1949 THE FOUNTAINHEAD
Director: King Vidor
Co-stars: Gary Cooper Raymond Massey Henry Hull

1949 THE HASTY HEART
Director: Vincent Sherman
Co-stars: Richard Todd Ronald Reagan Orlando Martins

1949 IT'S A GREAT FEELING
Director: David Butler
Co-stars: Doris Day Dennis Morgan Jack Carson

1950 OPERATION PACIFIC
Director: George Waggner
Co-stars: John Wayne Ward Bond Scott Forbes

1950 THREE SECRETS
Director: Robert Wise
Co-stars: Eleanor Parker Ruth Roman Frank Lovejoy

1950 BRIGHT LEAF
Director: Michael Curtiz
Co-stars: Gary Cooper Lauren Bacall Jack Carson

1950 THE BREAKING POINT
Director: Michael Curtiz
Co-stars: John Garfield Phyllis Thaxter

1951 THE DAY THE EARTH STOOD STILL
Director: Robert Wise
Co-stars: Michael Rennie Hugh Marlowe Sam Jaffe

1951 RATON PASS
Director: Edwin Marin
Co-stars: Dennis Morgan Steve Cochran Dorothy Hart

1951 WEEKEND WITH FATHER
Director: Douglas Sirk
Co-stars: Van Heflin Gigi Perreau Virginia Field

1952 DIPLOMATIC COURIER
Director: Henry Hathaway
Co-stars: Tyrone Power Hildegarde Neff Karl Malden

1952 SOMETHING FOR THE BIRDS
Director: Robert Wise
Co-stars: Edmund Gwenn Victor Mature Larry Keating

1952 WASHINGTON STORY
Director: Robert Pirosh
Co-stars: Van Johnson Louis Calhern Sidney Blackmer

1954 STANGER FROM VENUS
Director: Burt Balaban
Co-stars: Helmut Dantine Derek Bond

1955 A FACE IN THE CROWD
Director: Elia Kazan
Co-stars: Andy Griffith Walter Matthau Lee Remick

1961 BREAKFAST AT TIFFANY'S
Director: Blake Edwards
Co-stars: Audrey Hepburn George Peppard Mickey Rooney

1963 HUD
Director: Martin Ritt
Co-stars: Paul Newman Melvyn Douglas Brandon De Wilde

1964 PSYCHE 59
Director: Alexander Singer
Co-stars: Curt Jurgens Samanatha Eggar Ian Bannen

1965 IN HARM'S WAY
Director: Arthur Hiller
Co-stars: John Wayne Kirk Douglas Henry Fonda

1968 THE SUBJECT WAS ROSES
Director: Ula Grosbard
Co-stars: Jack Albertson Martin Sheen Elaine Williams

1971 THE NIGHT DIGGER
Director: Alastair Reid
Co-stars: Nicholas Clay Pamela Browne Yootha Joyce

1971 THE HOMECOMING: A CHRISTMAS STORY
Director: Fielder Cook
Co-stars: Richard Thomas Andrew Duggan Ellen Corby

1972 BAXTER
Director: Lionel Jeffries
Co-stars: Scott Jacoby Britt Ekland Paul Eddington

1975 ERIC
Director: James Goldstone
Co-stars: John Savage Claude Akins Mark Hamil

1978 THE PASSAGE
Director: J.Lee-Thompson
Co-stars: Anthony Quinn James Mason Kay Lenz

1979 ALL QUIET ON THE WESTERN FRONT
Director: Delbert Mann
Co-stars: Richard Thomas Ernest Borgnine Ian Holm

1981 GHOST STORY
Director: John Irvin
Co-stars: Fred Astaire Melvyn Douglas Douglas Fairbanks

1990 CAROLINE?
Director: Joseph Sargent
Co-stars: Stephanie Zimbalist Pamela Reed Dorothy Maguire

1992 SHATTERED SILENCE

SIRI NEAL

1990 THE CHILDREN
Director: Tony Palmer
Co-stars: Ben Kingsley Kim Novak Geraldine Chaplin

LESLIE NEALE

1992 HONEY, I BLEW UP THE KIDS
Director: Randal Reiser
Co-stars: Rick Moranis Marcia Strassman John Shea

HOLLY NEAR

1969   ANGEL, ANGEL, DOWN WE GO
Director: Robert Thom
Co-stars: Jennifer Jones Roddy McDowall Lou Rawls

1991   DOGFIGHT
Director: Nancy Savoca
Co-stars: River Phoenix Lili Taylor Anthony Clark

LAUREL NEAR

1976   ERASERHEAD
Director: David Lynch
Co-stars: John Nance Charlotte Stewart Allen Joseph

CLAIRE NEBOUT

1986   SCENE OF THE CRIME
Director: Andre Techine
Co-stars: Catherine Deneuve Danielle Darrieux

TRACEY NEEDHAM

1992   BONNIE AND CLYDE: THE TRUE STORY
Director: Gary Hofman
Co-stars: Dana Ashbrook Doug Savant

1993   PROPHET OF EVIL
Director: Jud Taylor
Co-stars: Brian Dennehy William Devane Lucy Butler

1994   LUSH LIFE
Director: Michael Elias
Co-stars: Jeff Goldblum Forest Whitaker Kathy Baker

GAIL NEELY

1987   SURF NAZIS MUST DIE
Director: Peter George
Co-stars: Barry Brenner Dawn Wildsmith Bobbie Bresee

JULIE NEESAM

1975   OVERLORD
Director: Stuart Cooper
Co-stars: Brian Stirner Nicholas Ball Davyd Harries

HILDEGARD NEFF
(Hildegard Knef In Continental Films)

1946   DIE MOERDER SIND UNTER UNS
Director: Wolfgang Staudte
Co-stars: Wilheim Borchert Arno Paulsen

1947   FILM OHNE TITEL
Director: Rudolf Jugert
Co-stars: Hans Sohnker Willy Fritsch Fritz Odemar

1951   DECISION BEFORE DAWN
Director: Anatole Litvak
Co-stars: Richard Basehart Gary Merrill Oskar Werner

1952   DIPLOMATIC COURIER
Director: Henry Hathaway
Co-stars: Tyrone Power Patricia Neal Karl Malden

1952   NIGHT WITHOUT SLEEP
Director: Roy Baker
Co-stars: Gary Merrill Linda Darnell Mae Marsh

1952   THE SNOWS OF KILIMANJARO
Director: Henry King
Co-stars: Gregory Peck Susan Hayward Ava Gardner

1952   LA FETE A HENRIETTE
Director: Julien Duvivier
Co-stars: Dany Robin Michel Auclair Michel Roux

1953   THE MAN BETWEEN
Director: Carol Reed
Co-stars: James Mason Claire Bloom Geoffrey Toone

1954   SVENGALI
Director: Noel Langley
Co-stars: Donald Wolfit Terence Morgan Harry Secombe

1959   SUBWAY IN THE SKY
Director: Muriel Box
Co-stars: Van Johnson Katherine Kath Albert Lieven

1962   LANDRU
Director: Claude Chabrol
Co-stars: Charles Denner Michele Morgan Danielle Darrieux

1968   THE LOST CONTINENT
Director: Michael Carreras
Co-stars: Eric Porter Suzanna Leigh Nigel Stock

1978   FEDORA
Director: Bily Wilder
Co-stars: William Holden Henry Fonda Marthe Keller

NATALYA NEGODA

1992   BACK IN THE USSR
Director: Deran Sarafian
Co-stars: Frank Whalley Roman Polanski Brian Blessed

MIREILLE NEGRE

1964   FIFI LA PLUME
Director: Albert Lamorisse
Co-stars: Philippe Avron Henri Lambert Raoul Delfosse

POLA NEGRI

1919   MADAME DUBARRY
Director: Ernst Lubitsch
Co-stars: Emil Jannings Harry Liedtke Reinhold Schunzel

1923   THE CHEAT

1924   FORBIDDEN PARADISE
Director: Ernst Lubitsch
Co-stars: Adolphe Menjou Rod La Rocque Pauline Starke

1932   HOLLYWOOD
Director: James Cruze
Co-stars: Hope Drown Luke Cosgrove Eleanor Lawson

1927   HOTEL IMPERIAL

1932   A WOMAN COMMANDS
Director: Paul Stein
Co-stars: Basil Rathbone Roland Young H.B.Warner

1943   HI DIDDLE DIDDLE
Director: Andrew Stone
Co-stars: Adolphe Menjou Dennis O'Keefe Billie Burke

1964   THE MOON SPINNERS
Director: Roy Ward Baker
Co-stars: Hayley Mills Peter McEnery Eli Wallach

MARY JOAN NEGRO

1983   NO BIG DEAL
Director: Robert Charlton
Co-stars: Kevin Dillion Sylvia Miles

1989   THE LITTLEST VICTIMS
Director: Peter Levin
Co-stars: Tim Matheson Mary Ann Plunkett Lewis Arlit

VYA NEGROMONTE

1989   LAMBADA
Director: Giandomenica Guri
Co-stars: Andrew J.Forest Mary Sellers

CAROLA NEHER

1931   DIE DREIGROSCHENOPER
Director: G.W.Pabst
Co-stars: Rudolph Forster Lotte Lenya Ernst Busch

HILDEGARDE NEIL

1970 THE MAN WHO HAUNTED HIMSELF
Director: Basil Dearden
Co-stars: Roger Moore Anton Rogers Freddie Jones

1972 ENGLAND MADE ME
Director: Peter Duffell
Co-stars: Peter Finch Michael York Michael Hordern

1973 ANTHONY AND CLEOPATRA
Director: Charlton Heston
Co-stars: Charlton Heston Eric Porter John Castle Freddie Jones

1973 A TOUCH OF CLASS
Co-stars: Melvin Frank
Co-stars: Glenda Jackson George Segal Paul Sorvino

1979 THE LEGACY
Director: Richard Marquand
Co-stars: Katharine Ross Sam Elliott Roger Daltrey

1996 MACBETH
Co-stars: Jason Connery Brian Blessed Helen Baxendale

NOEL NEIL

1947 VACATION DAYS
Co-stars: Freddie Stewart Warren Mills

1948 CAMPUS SLEUTH
Co-stars: Freddie Stewart Warren Mills June Preisser

AGNES NEILSEN

1917 THE BUTCHER BOY
Director: Roscoe "Fatty" Arbuckle
Co-stars: Roscoe "Fatty" Arbuckle Arthur Earle Buster Keaton

CATHERINE NEILSON

1988 CODENAME: KYRIL
Director: Ian Sharp
Co-stars: Edward Woodward Denholm Elliott Ian Charleson

1990 SMALL ZONES
Director: Michael Whyte
Co-stars: Sean Bean Suzanna Hamilton Stephanie Turner

1992 THE TRIAL
Director: David Jones
Co-stars: Kyle MacLachlan Anthony Hopkins Juliet Stevenson

PERLITA NEILSON

1958 SHE DIDN'T SAY NO!
Director: Cyril Frankel
Co-stars: Eileen Herlie Jack MacGowran Ian Bannen

PHYLLIS NEILSON-TERRY

1958 RX MURDER
Director: Derek Twist
Co-stars: Marius Goring Rick Jason Lisa Gastoni

1959 LOOK BACK IN ANGER
Director: Tony Richardson
Co-stars: Richard Burton Claire Bloom Mary Ure

1960 CONSPIRACY OF HEARTS
Director: Ralph Thomas
Co-stars: Lilli Palmer Sylvia Syms Yvonne Mitchell

STACEY NELKIN

1983 HALLOWEEN 3: SEASON OF THE WITCH
Director: Tommy Lee Wallace
Co-stars: Tom Atkins Dan O'Herlihy

NATHALIE NELL

1982 MAN, WOMAN OR CHILD
Director: Dick Richards
Co-stars: Martin Sheen Blythe Danner David Hemmings

KATE NELLIGAN

Nominated For Best Supporting Actress In 1991 For "The Prince Of Tides"

1975 THE ROMANTIC ENGLISHWOMAN
Director: Joseph Losey
Co-stars: Glenda Jackson Michael Caine Helmut Berger

1975 THE COUNT OF MONTE CRISTO
Director: David Greene
Co-stars: Richard Chamberlain Louis Jourdan

1979 DRACULA
Director: John Badham
Co-stars: Frank Langella Laurence Oliver Donald Pleasence

1981 THE EYE OF THE NEEDLE
Director: Richard Marquand
Co-stars: Donald Sutherland Christopher Cazenove

1983 WITHOUT A TRACE
Director: Stanley Jaffe
Co-stars: Judd Hirsch David Dukes Stockard Channing

1985 ELENI
Director: Peter Yates
Co-stars: John Malkovich Linda Hunt Ronald Pickup

1987 KOJAK: THE PRICE OF JUSTICE
Director: Alan Metzger
Co-stars: Telly Savalas Pat Hingle Jack Thompson

1989 LOVE AND HATE
Director: Francis Mankievicz
Co-stars: Kenneth Welsh John Colicos Vicki Wauchope

1990 WHITE ROOM
Director: Patricia Rozema
Co-stars: Margot Kidder Maurice Godin Sheila McCarthy

1991 FRANKIE AND JOHNNY
Director: Gary Marshall
Co-stars: Al Pacino Michelle Pfeiffer Hector Elizondo

1991 THE PRINCE OF TIDES
Director: Barbra Streisand
Co-stars: Barbra Streisand Nick Nolte Blythe Danner Melinda Dillon

1993 SPOILS OF WAR
Director: David Greene
Co-stars: John Heard Tobey Maguire

1993 FATAL INSTINCT
Director: Carl Reiner
Co-stars: Armand Assante Sherilyn Fenn Sean Young

1994 WOLF
Director: Mike Nichols
Co-stars: Jack Nicholson James Spader Michellle Pfeiffer

1996 HOW TO MAKE AN AMERICAN QUILT
Director: Jocelyn Moorhouse
Co-stars: Winona Ryder Anne Bancroft Jean Simmons

1996 CAPTIVE HEART: THE JAMES MINK STORY
Director: Bruce Pittman
Co-stars: Lou Gossett Jnr. Peter Outerbridge Rachel Crawford

1997 MARGARET'S MUSEUM
Co-stars: Helen Bonham-Carter Clive Russel

1998 U.S. MARSHALLS
Director: Stuart Baird
Co-stars: Tommy Lee Jones Wesley Snipes Robert Downey Jnr

CONNIE NELSON
1970   ANGELS DIE HARD
Director: Richard Compton
Co-stars: Tom Baker William Smith Rita Murray

GAY NELSON
1948   BLONDIE'S REWARD
Director: Abby Singer
Co-stars: Penny Singleton Arthur Lake Larry Simms

GWEN NELSON
1962   DON'T TALK TO STRANGE MEN
Director: Pat Jackson
Co-stars: Christine Gregg Cyril Raymond Janina Faye

1962   A KIND OF LOVING
Director: John Schlesinger
Co-stars: Alan Bates June Ritchie Thora Hird

1969   THE RECKONING
Director: Jack Gold
Co-stars: Nicol Williamson Rachel Roberts Ann Bell

HARRIET NELSON
1979   DEATH CAR ON THE FREEWAY
Director: Hal Needham
Co-stars: Shelley Hack George Hamilton Barbara Rush

1983   KID WITH THE 200 IQ
Director: Leslie Martinson
Co-stars: Gary Coleman Robert Guillaume Dean Butler

JESSICA NELSON
1986   ASSASSIN
Director: Sandor Stern
Co-stars: Robert Conrad Karen Austin Robert Webber

LORI NELSON
1952   WHERE THE RIVER BENDS
Director: Anthony Mann
Co-stars: James Stewart Arthur Kennedy Rock Hudson

1953   WALKING MY BABY BACK HOME
Director: Lloyd Bacon
Co-stars: Donald O'Connor Janet Leigh Buddy Hackett

1953   ALL I DESIRE
Director: Douglas Sirk
Co-stars: Barbara Stanwyck Richard Carlson Maureen O'Sullivan

1953   THE ALL-AMERICAN
Director: Jesse Hibbs
Co-stars: Tony Curtis Mamie Van Doren Richard Long

1954   DESTRY
Director: George Marshall
Co-stars: Audie Murphy Mari Blanchard Thomas Mitchell

1955   I DIED A THOUSAND TIMES
Director: Stuart Heisler
Co-stars: Jack Palance Shelley Winters Lee Marvin

1955   REVENGE OF THE CREATURE
Director: Jack Arnold
Co-stars: John Agar John Bromfield Nestor Paiva

1955   UNDERWATER
Director: John Sturges
Co-stars: Jane Russell Gilbert Roland Richard Egan

1956   PARDNERS
Director: Norman Taurog
Co-stars: Dean Martin Jerry Lewis Agnes Moorehead

1956   MOHAWK
Director: Kurt Neumann
Co-stars: Scot Brady Rita Gam Neville Brand

1956   THE DAY THE WORLD ENDED
Director: Roger Corman
Co-stars: Richard Denning Adele Jergens Mike Connors

MARGARET NELSON
1975   PICNIC AT HANGING ROCK
Director: Peter Weir
Co-stars: Rachel Roberts Dominic Guard Helen Morse

MERRITT NELSON
1991   TRUST
Director: Hal Hartley
Co-stars: Adrienne Shelley Martin Donovan Eddie Falco

MIMI NELSON
1948   PORT OF CALL
Director: Ingmar Bergman
Co-stars: Nine-Christine Jonsson Bengt Eklund

NAN-LYNN NELSON
1989   THE LITTLEST VICTIMS
Director: Peter Levin
Co-stars: Tim Matheson Mary Joan Negro Ann Plunkett

NORMA NELSON
1940   SEVENTEEN
Director: Louis King
Co-stars: Jackie Cooper Betty Field Otto Kruger

PORTIA NELSON
1965   THE SOUND OF MUSIC
Director: Robert Wise
Co-stars: Julie Andrews Christopher Plummer Peggy Wood

RUTH NELSON
1944   WILSON
Director: Henry King
Co-stars: Alexander Knox Charles Coburn Geraldine Fitzgerald

1944   THE EVE OF ST. MARK
Director: John Stahl
Co-stars: William Eythe Anne Baxter Michael O'Shea

1945   A TREE GROWS IN BROOKLYN
Director: Elia Kazan
Co-stars: Peggy Ann Garner James Dunn Dorothy Mcguire

1946   TILL THE END OF TIME
Director: Edward Dmytryk
Co-stars: Dorothy McGuire Guy Madison Robert Mitchum

1947   THE SEA OF GRASS
Director: Elia Kazan
Co-stars: Spencer Tracy Katherine Hepburn Robert Walker

1947   MOTHER WORE TIGHTS
Director: Walter Lang
Co-stars: Betty Grable Dan Dailey Mona Freeman

1947   HUMORESQUE
Director: Jean Negulesco
Co-stars: Joan Crawford John Garfield Oscar Levant

1977   THE LATE SHOW
Director: Robert Benton
Co-stars: Art Carney Lily Tomlin Joanna Cassidy

1977   THREE WOMEN
Director: Robert Altman
Co-stars: Shelley Duvall Sissy Spacek Janice Rule

1983   THE HAUNTING PASSION
Director: John Korty
Co-stars: Jane Seymour Gerald McRaney Millie Perkins

1990   AWAKENINGS
Director: Penny Marshall
Co-stars: Robert De Niro Robin Williams Julie Kavner

SANDRA NELSON

1994   TRUST IN ME
Director: Bill Corcoran
Co-stars: Stacy Keach Currie Graham

TRACY NELSON

1984   MARIA'S LOVERS
Director: Andrei Konchalovsky
Co-stars: Nastassja Kinski John Savage Robert Mitchum

1986   KATE'S SECRET
Director: Arthur Allan Seidelman
Co-stars: Meredith Baxter Birney Ed Asner Ben Masters

1993   NO CHILD OF MINE
Director: Michael Katleman
Co-stars: Patty Duke G.W.Bailey

CATHLEEN NESBITT

1930   CANARIES SOMETIMES SING
Director: Tom Walls
Co-stars: Tom Walls Yvonne Arnaud

1932   THE FRIGHTENED LADY
Director: Hayes Hunter
Co-stars: Emlyn Williams Gordon Harker Norman McKinnel

1936   THE BELOVED VAGABOND
Director: Ludovici Toeplitz
Co-stars: Maurice Chevalier Margaret Lockwood Betty Stockfield

1936   THE PASSING OF THE THIRD FLOOR BACK
Director: Berthold Viertel
Co-stars: Conrad Veidt Rene Ray Anna Lee

1940   THE DOOR WITH SEVEN LOCKS
Director: Norman Lee
Co-stars: Leslie Banks Lili Palmer Gina Malo

1943   THE LAMP STILL BURNS
Director: Maurice Elvy
Co-stars: Rosamund John Stewart Granger Godfrey Tearle

1944   FANNY BY GASLIGHT
Director: Anthony Asquith
Co-stars: James Mason Phyllis Calvert Stewart Granger

1944   THE AGITATOR
Director: John Harlow
Co-stars: William Hartnell Mary Morris John Laurie Edward Rigby

1946   CARNIVAL
Director: Stanley Haynes
Co-stars: Sally Gray Michael Wilding Bernard Miles Jean Kent

1946   MEN OF TWO WORLDS
Director: Thorold Dickinson
Co-stars: Eric Portman Phyllis Calvert Robert Adams

1947   JASSY
Director: Bernard Knowles
Co-stars: Margaret Lockwood Patricia Roc Dennis Price

1949   MADNESS OF THE HEART
Director: Charles Bennett
Co-stars: Margaret Lockwood Paul Dupuis Kathleen Byron

1950   SO LONG AT THE FAIR
Director: Terence Fisher
Co-stars: Jean Simmons Dirk Bogarde David Tomlinson

1954   DESIREE
Director: Henry Koster
Co-stars: Jean Simmons Marlon Brando Merle Oberon

1954   THREE COINS IN THE FOUNTAIN
Director: Jean Negulesco
Co-stars: Clifton Webb Dorothy McGuire Louis Jourdan

1954   BLACK WIDOW
Director: Nunnally Johnson
Co-stars: Ginger Rogers Van Heflin George Raft

1957   AN AFFAIR TO REMEMBER
Director: Leo McCarey
Co-stars: Cary Grant Deborah Kerr Richard Denning

1958   SEPARATE TABLES
Director: Delbert Mann
Co-stars: Burt Lancaster David Niven Rita Hayworth

1961   THE PARENT TRAP
Director: David Swift
Co-stars: Hayley Mills Maureen O'Hara Brian Keith

1966   PROMISE HER ANYTHING
Director: Arthur Hiller
Co-stars: Warren Beatty Leslie Caron Robert Cummings

1966   THE TRYGON FACTOR
Director: Cyril Frankel
Co-stars: Stewart Granger Susan Hampshire Robert Morley

1969   STAIRCASE
Director: Stanley Donen
Co-stars: Richard Burton Rex Harrison Beatrix Lehman

1971   VILLAIN
Director: Michael Tuchner
Co-stars: Richard Burton Ian McShane Nigel Davenport

1975   FRENCH CONNECTION II
Director: Jon Frankenheimer
Co-stars: Gene Hackman Fernando Rey Charles Millot

1976   FULL CIRCLE
Director: Richard Loncraine
Co-stars: Mia Farrow Keir Dullea Tom Conti

1976   FAMILY PLOT
Director: Alfred Hitchcock
Co-stars: Karen Black Bruce Dern Barbara Harris

1977   JULIA
Director: Fred Zinnemann
Co-stars: Jane Fonda Vanessa Redgrave Jason Robards

OTTOLA NESMITH

1938   FOOLS FOR SCANDAL
Director: Mervyn LeRoy
Co-stars: Carole Lombard Fernand Gravet Ralph Bellamy

1943   RETURN OF THE VAMPIRE
Director: Lew Landers
Co-stars: Bela Lugosi Nina Foch Frieda Inescort

LOIS NETTLETON

1962   COME FLY WITH ME
Director: Henry Levin
Co-stars: Karl Malden Dolores Hart Hugh O'Brian

1962   PERIOD OF ADJUSTMENT
Director: George Roy Hill
Co-stars: Tony Franciosa Jane Fonda Jim Hutton

1963   MAIL ORDER BRIDE
Director: Burt Kennedy
Co-stars: Buddy Ebsen Keir Dullea Warren Oates

1967   VALLEY OF MYSTERY
Director: Josef Leytes
Co-stars: Richard Egan Peter Graves Fernando Lamas

1969   THE GOOD GUYS AND THE BAD GUYS
Director: Burt Kennedy
Co-stars: Robert Mitchum George Kennedy

1970 DIRTY DINGUS MAGEE
Director: Burt Kennedy
Co-stars: Frank Sinatra George Kennedy Jack Elam

1970 WEEKEND OF TERROR
Director: Jud Taylor
Co-stars: Robert Conrad Lee Majors Carol Lynley

1971 TERROR IN THE SKY
Director: Bernard Kowalski
Co-stars: Leif Ericson Doug McClure Keenan Wynn

1971 THE HONKERS
Director: Steve Ihnat
Co-stars: James Coburn Slim Pickens Richard Anderson

1972 WOMEN IN CHAINS
Director: Bernard Kowalski
Co-stars: Ida Lupino Belinda Montgomery

1975 ECHOES OF A SUMMER
Director: Don Taylor
Co-stars: Jodie Foster Richard Harris Brad Savage

1981 DEADLY BLESSING
Director: Wes Craven
Co-stars: Ernest Borgnine Maren Jensen Jeff East

1981 BUTTERFLY
Director: Matt Cimber
Co-stars: Pia Zadora Stacy Keach Orson Welles

1982 THE BEST LITTLE WHOREHOUSE IN TEXAS
Director: Colin Higgins
Co-stars: Burt Reynolds Dolly Parton

DOROTHY NEUMAN

1953 LATIN LOVERS
Director: Mervyn LeRoy
Co-stars: Lana Turner Ricardo Montalban John Lund

1963 THE TERROR
Director: Monte Hellman
Co-stars: Boris Karloff Jack Nicholson Sandra Knight

JENNY NEUMANN

1981 HELL NIGHT
Director: Tom DeSimone
Co-stars: Linda Blair Peter Barton Vincent Van Patten

BEBE NEUWIRTH

1989 SAY ANYTHING
Director: Cameron Crowe
Co-stars: John Cusack Ione Skye Lili Taylor

1990 UNSPEAKABLE ACTS
Director: Linda Otto
Co-stars: Brad Davis Jill Clayburgh Bess Meyers

1991 GREEN CARD
Director: Peter Weir
Co-stars: Gerard Depardieu Andie MacDowell Robert Prosky

1991 BUGSY
Director: Barry Levinson
Co-stars: Warren Beatty Annette Bening Harvey Keitel

1992 PAINTED HEART
Director: Michael Taav
Co-stars: Will Patton Robert Pastorelli Mark Boone

SUZANNE NEVE

1968 MOSQUITO SQUADRON
Director: Boris Sagal
Co-stars: David Buck Dinsdale Landen David McCallum

SARAH NEVILLE

1988 A PERFECT SPY
Director: Peter Smith
Co-stars: Alec Guinness Peggy Ashcroft Peter Egan

1992 CAREFUL
Director: Guy Maddin
Co-stars: Gosia Dobrowolska Brent Neal Paul Cox

SOPHIE NEVILLE (Child)

1974 SWALLOWS AND AMAZONS
Director: Claude Whatham
Co-stars: Virginia McKenna Ronald Fraser Simon West

1976 THE COPTER KIDS
Director: Ronnie Spender
Co-stars: Sophie Ward Kate Dorning Paul Chambers

ROBYN NEVIN

1983 CAREFUL, HE MIGHT HEAR YOU
Director: Carl Schultz
Co-stars: Wendy Hughes Nicholas Gledhill

1984 THE GOLD AND GLORY
Director: Igor Auzins
Co-stars: Joss McWilliam Nick Tate Colin Friels

SARAH NEVIN

1983 HAPPY ENDINGS
Director: Jerry Thorpe
Co-stars: Lee Montgomery Jill Schoelen Laura Dern

CLAUDETTE NEVINS

1977 THE POSSESSED
Director: Jerry Thorpe
Co-stars: James Farentino Joan Hackett Harrison Ford

1982 TAKE YOUR BEST SHOT
Director: David Greene
Co-stars: Robert Urich Meredith Baxter Birney

1985 TUFF TURF
Director: Fritz Kiersch
Co-stars: James Spader Kim Richards Robert Downey Jnr.

1991 SLEEPING WITH THE ENEMY
Director: Joseph Ruben
Co-stars: Julia Roberts Patrick Bergin Kyle Secor

1991 DEAD SILENCE
Director: Peter O'Fallon
Co-stars: Steve Brill Renee Estevez Carrie Mitchum

1995 ABANDONED AND DECEIVED
Director: Joseph Ruben
Co-stars: Lori Loughlin Brian Kerwin Rosemary Forsythe

NANCY NEVINSON

1963 RING OF SPIES
Director: Robert Tronson
Co-stars: Bernard Lee Margaret Tyzack David Kossoff

NANCY NEW

1984 THE BOSTONIANS
Director: James Ivory
Co-stars: Christopher Reeve Vanessa Redgrave Jessica Tandy

FLORA NEWBIGIN

1997 THE BORROWERS
Director: Peter Hewitt
Co-stars: John Goodman Jim Broadbent Celia Imrie

SARAH NEWBOLD

1988 PAPERHOUSE
Director: Bernard Rose
Co-stars: Charlotte Burke Ben Cross Glenne Headley

TRISHA NEWBY

1978 CARRY ON EMMANUELLE
Director: Gerald Thomas
Co-stars: Kenneth Williams Suzanne Danielle Joan Sims

CAROLE IRENE NEWELL

1977 THE ALPHA INCIDENT
Director: Bill Rebane
Co-stars: Ralph Meeker John Goff Staffford Morgan

JOAN NEWELL

1963 LIVE IT UP
Director: Lance Comfort
Co-stars: David Hemmings Veronica Hurst Jennifer Moss

MARY NEWLAND

1934 DEATH AT BROADCASTING HOUSE
Director: Reginald Denham
Co-stars: Ian Hunter Jack Hawkins Donald Wolfit

1935 THE SILENT PASSENGER
Director: Reginald Denham
Co-stars: Peter Haddon John Loder Donald Wolfit

ANNE NEWMAN

1980 ANGEL ON MY SHOUDER
Director: John Berry
Co-stars: Peter Strauss Barbara Hershey Richard Kiley

JOAN NEWMAN

1977 ANNIE HALL
Director: Woody Allen
Co-stars: Woody Allen Diane Keaton Tony Roberts Carol Kane

LARAINE NEWMAN

1985 PERFECT
Director: James Bridges
Co-stars: John Travolta Jaimie Lee Curtis Marilu Henner

1985 THIS WIFE FOR HIRE
Director: James Drake
Co-stars: Pam Dawber Robert Klein Ann Jillian

1986 INVADERS FROM MARS
Director: Tobe Hunter
Co-stars: Karen Black Hunter Carson Timothy Bottoms

1991 PROBLEM CHILD 2
Director: Brian Levant
Co-stars: John Ritter Michael Oliver Jack Warden

1993 CONEHEADS
Director: Steve Barron
Co-stars: Dan Aykroyd Jane Curtin Michelle Burke

1995 ALONE IN THE WOODS
Director: John Putch
Co-stars: Chick Vennera

LIZ NEWMAN

1985 ROBBERY UNDER ARMS
Director: Donald Crombie
Co-stars: Sam Neill Steven Vidler Ed Devereux

MELISSA NEWMAN

1969 THE UNDEFEATED
Director: Andrew McLaglen
Co-stars: John Wayne Rock Hudson Ben Johnson

NANETTE NEWMAN (*Married Bryan Forbes*)

1960 FACES IN THE DARK
Director: David Eady
Co-stars: John Gregson Mai Zetterling John Ireland

1960 THE LEAGUE OF GENTLEMEN
Director: Basil Dearden
Co-stars: Jack Hawkins Nigel Patrick Roger Livesey

1960 THE REBEL
Director: Robert Day
Co-stars: Tony Hancock George Sanders Margit Saad Dennis Price

1961 HOUSE OF MYSTERY
Director: Vernon Sewell
Co-stars: Peter Dyneley Jane Hylton Maurice Kaufman

1961 PIT OF DARKNESS
Director: Lance Comfort
Co-stars: William Franklyn Moira Redmond Nigel Green

1962 THE PAINTED SMILE
Director: Lance Comfort
Co-stars: Liz Fraser Kenneth Griffiths Craig Douglas

1962 TWICE AROUND THE DAFFODILS
Director: Gerald Thomas
Co-stars: Juliet Mills Donald Sinden Jill Ireland

1962 THE WRONG ARM OF THE LAW
Director: Cliff Owen
Co-stars: Peter Sellers Lionel Jeffries Davy Kaye

1964 SEANCE ON A WET AFTERNOON
Director: Bryan Forbes
Co-stars: Kim Stanley Richard Attenborough Patrick Magee

1964 OF HUMAN BONDAGE
Director: Henry Hathaway
Co-stars: Kim Novak Laurence Harvey Roger Livesey

1966 THE WHISPERERS
Director: Bryan Forbes
Co-stars: Edith Evans Eric Portman Ronald Fraser

1966 THE WRONG BOX
Director: Bryan Forbes
Co-stars: John Mills Michael Caine Peter Sellers

1968 DEADFALL
Director: Bryan Forbes
Co-stars: Michael Caine Eric Portman Giovanna Ralli David Buck

1969 CAPTAIN NEMO AND THE UNDERWATER CITY
Director: James Hill
Co-stars: Robert Ryan John Turner Bill Fraser

1969 THE MADWOMAN OF CHAILLOT
Director: Bryan Forbes
Co-stars: Kathleen Hepburn Danny Kaye Yul Brynner

1970 THE RAGING MOON
Director: Bryan Forbes
Co-stars: Malcolm McDowell Georgia Brown Bernard Lee

1973 MAN AT THE TOP
Director: Mike Vardy
Co-stars: Kenneth Haigh Harry Andrews Charlie Williams

1973 IT'S A 2'6" ABOVE THE GROUND WORLD
Director: Ralph Thomas
Co-stars: Hywel Bennett Milo O'shea

1974 THE STEPFORD WIVES
Director: Bryan Forbes
Co-stars: Katharine Ross Paula Prentiss Tina Louise

1978 INTERNATIONAL VELVET
Director: Bryan Forbes
Co-stars: Tatum O'Neal Anthony Hopkins Christopher Plummer

1993 THE MYSTERY OF EDWIN DROOD
Director: Timothy Forder
Co-stars: Robert Powell Gemma Craven Finty Williams

PHYLLIS NEWMAN

1968 BYE BYE BRAVERMAN
Director: Sidney Lumet
Co-stars: George Segal Jack Warden Joseph Wiseman

1972 TO FIND A MAN
Director: Buzz Kulik
Co-stars: Pamela Martin Lloyd Bridges Tom Ewell

SUSAN KENDALL NEWMAN

1978 I WANNA HOLD YOUR HAND
Director: Robert Zemekis
Co-stars: Nancy Allen Bobby DiCicco Will Jordan

JULIE NEWMAR

1953 SERPENT OF THE NILE
Director: William Castle
Co-stars: Rhonda Fleming William Lundigan Raymond Burr

1954 SEVEN BRIDES FOR SEVEN BROTHERS
Director: Stanley Donen
Co-stars: Jane Powell Howard Keel Russ Tamblyn

1959 LI'L ABNER
Director: Norman Panama
Co-stars: Peter Palmer Leslie Parrish Stubby Kaye

1961 THE MARRIAGE-GO-ROUND
Director: Walter Lang
Co-stars: James Mason Susan Hayward Robert Paige

1963 FOR LOVE OR MONEY
Director: Michael Gordon
Co-stars: Kirk Douglas Thelma Ritter Mitzi Gaynor

1968 MACKENNA'S GOLD
Director: J.Lee Thompson
Co-stars: Gregory Peck Omar Sharif Telly Savalas

1969 THE MALTESE BIPPY
Director: Norman Panama
Co-stars: Dan Rowan Dick Martin Carol Lynley

1969 McCLOUD: WHO KILLED MISS U.S.A.
Director: Richard Colla
Co-stars: Dennis Weaver Craig Stevens Raul Julia

1972 A VERY MISING PERSON
Director: Russ Mayberry
Co-stars: Eve Arden James Gregory Ray Danton

1983 HYSTERICAL
Director: Chris Bearde
Co-stars: William Hudson Cindy Pickett Richard Kiel

1990 GHOSTS CAN'T DO IT
Director: John Derek
Co-stars: Bo Derek Anthony Quinn Don Murray

BECKY NEWTON

1991 THE PIRATE PRINCE
Director: Alan Horrox
Co-stars: James Hazeldine Dearbhla Molloy

JOAN NEWTON

1946 RIVERBOAT RHYTHM
Director: Leslie Goodwins
Co-stars: Leon Errol Walter Catlett Jonathan Hale

MADELAINE NEWTON (*Married Kevin Whateley*)

1990 INSPECTOR MORSE: MASONIC MYSTERIES
Director: Danny Boyle
Co-stars: John Thaw Kevin Whateley Diane Fletcher

SALLY ANNE NEWTON

1974 ZARDOS
Director: John Boorman
Co-stars: Sean Connery Charlotte Rampling John Alderton

THANDIE NEWTON

1991 PIRATE PRINCE
Director: Alan Horrox
Co-stars: James Hazeldine

1991 FLIRTING
Director: John Duigan
Co-stars: Noah Taylor Nicole Kidman Kiri Paramore

1993 THE YOUNG AMERICANS
Director: Danny Cannon
Co-stars: Harvey Keitel Iain Glenn Terence Rigby

1997 THE LEADING MAN
Director: John Duigan
Co-stars: Jon Bon Jovi Anna Galiena Patricia Hodge

1997 GRIDLOCK'D
Director: Vandi Curtis Hall
Co-stars: Vandi Curtis Hall Tim Roth Tupac Shakur

OLIVIA NEWTON-JOHN

1978 GREASE
Director: Randall Kleiser
Co-stars: John Travolta Stockard Channing Joan Blondell

1980 XANADU
Director: Robert Greenwald
Co-stars: Gene Kelly Michael Beck

1983 TWO OF A KIND
Director: John Herzfeld
Co-stars: John Travolta Charles Durning Oliver Reed

1990 A MOM FOR CHRISTMAS
Director: George Miller

1991 IN BED WITH MADONNA
Director: Alek Keshishian
Co-star: Madonna Warren Beatty Sandra Bernard

1994 A CHRISTMAS ROMANCE
Director: Sheldon Larry
Co-star: Gregory Harrison

1995 IT'S MY PARTY
Co-stars: Eric Roberts George Segal Marlee Matlin

MARIE NEY

1933 THE WANDERING JEW
Director: Maurice Elvy
Co-stars: Conrad Veidt Anne Grey Dennis Hoey

1935 SCROOGE
Director: Henry Edwards
Co-stars: Seymour Hicks Donald Calthrop Athene Seyler

1939 JAMAICA INN
Director: Alfred Hitchcock
Co-stars: Charles Laughton Maureen O'Hara Robert Newton

1950 SEVEN DAYS TO NOON
Director: John Boutling
Co-stars: Barry Jones Olive Sloane Andre Morell

1955 SIMBA
Director: Brain Desmond Hurst
Co-stars: Dirk Bogarde Donald Sinden Virginia Mckenna

1956 YIELD TO THE NIGHT
Director: J.Lee Thompson
Co-stars: Diana Dors Yvonne Mitchell Michael Craig

1964   WITCHCRAFT
Director: Don Sharp
Co-stars: Jack Hedley Lon Chaney Jill Dixon

ANNE NEYLAND

1957   HIDDEN FEAR
Director: Andre De Toth
Co-stars: John Payne Alexander Knox Conrad Nagel

KIEN CHINH NGUYEN

1989   WELCOME HOME
Director: Franklin Schaffner
Co-stars: Kris Kristofferson JoBeth Williams Sam Waterston

MICHELLE NICASTRO

1986   BAD GUYS
Director: Joel Silberg
Co-stars: Adam Baldwin Mike Jolly James Booth

PENELOPE NICE

1985   SHE'LL BE WEARING PINK PAJAMAS
Director: John Goldschmidt
Co-stars: Julie Walters Anthony Higgins

DENISE NICHOLAS

1972   BLACULA
Director: William Crain
Co-stars: William Marshall Vonetta McGee Gordon Pinsent

1975   MR. RICCO
Director: Paul Bogart
Co-stars: Dean Martin Cindy Williams Geraldine Brooks

1977   A PIECE OF THE ACTION
Director: Sidney Poitier
Co-stars: Sidney Poitier Bill Cosby James Earl Jones Tracy Reed

1984   GHOST DAD
Director: Sidney Poitier
Co-stars: Bill Cosby Kimberly Russell Ian Bannen

1989   LETHAL ERROR
Director: Susan Rohrer
Co-stars: Jose Ferrer Bernie Casey Art Hindle

BARBARA NICHOLS

1956   BEYOND A REASONABLE DOUBT
Director: Fritz Lang
Co-stars: Dana Andrews Joan Fontaine

1957   THE PAJAMA GAME
Director: Stanley Donen
Co-stars: Doris Day John Raitt Carol Haney

1957   PAL JOEY
Director: George Sidney
Co-stars: Frank Sinatra Rita Hayworth Kim Novak

1957   SWEET SMELL OF SUCCESS
Director: Alexander MacKendrick
Co-stars: Burt Lancaster Tony Curtis Sam Levene

1958   THE NAKED AND THE DEAD
Director: Raoul Walsh
Co-stars: Aldo Ray Cliff Robertson Raymond Masey

1958   THE SCARFACE MOB
Director: Phil Karlson
Co-stars: Robert Stack Neville Brand Keenan Wynn

1959   WOMAN OBSESSED
Director: Henry Hathaway
Co-stars: Susan Hayward Stephen Boyd Dennis Holmes

1959   THAT KIND OF WOMAN
Director: Sidney Lumet
Co-stars: Sophia Loren Tab Hunter George Sanders

1960   WHERE THE BOYS ARE
Director: Henry Levin
Co-stars: George Hamilton Dolores Hart Connie Francis

1960   WHO WAS THAT LADY?
Director: George Sidney
Co-stars: Tony Curtis Dean Martin Janet Leigh

1961   THE GEORGE RAFT STORY
Director: Joseph Newman
Co-stars: Ray Danton Julie London Jayne Mansfield

1962   HOUSE OF WOMEN
Director: Walter Doniger
Co-stars: Shirley Knight Andrew Duggan Constance Ford

1964   DEAR HEART
Director: Delbert Mann
Co-stars: Glenn Ford Geraldine Page Angela Lansbury

1964   LOOKING FOR LOVE
Director: Don Weis
Co-stars: Connie Francis Jim Hutton Susan Oliver

1968   THE POWER
Director: Byron Haskin
Co-stars: Michael Rennie George Hamilton Suzanne Pleshette

1973   CHARLEY AND THE ANGEL
Director: Vincent McEveety
Co-stars: Fred MacMurray Henry Morgan Kurt Russell

BRITT NICHOLS

1972   DRACULA, PRISONER OF FRANKENSTEIN
Director: Jesus Franco
Co-stars: Dennis Price Howard Vernon

DANDY NICHOLS

1948   THE FALLEN IDOL
Director: Carol Reed
Co-stars: Ralph Richardson Michele Morgan Bobby Henry

1952   THE HAPPY FAMILY
Director: Muriel Box
Co-stars: Stanley Holloway Kathleen Harrison George Cole

1953   THE WEDDING OF LILLI MARLENE
Director: Arthur Crabtree
Co-stars: Lisa Daniely Hugh McDermott Sid James

1955   WHERE THERE'S A WILL
Director: Vernon Sewell
Co-stars: Kathleen Harrison George Cole

1955   THE DEEP BLUE SEA
Director: Anatole Litvak
Co-stars: Vivien Leigh Kenneth More Moira Lister

1962   DON'T TALK TO STRANGE MEN
Director: Pat Jackson
Co-stars: Christine Gregg Cyril Raymond Janina Faye

1963   LADIES WHO DO
Director: C.M.Pennington-Richards
Co-stars: Peggy Mount Miriam Karlin Robert Morley

1964   ACT OF MURDER
Director: Alan Bridges
Co-stars: John Carson Anthony Bate Justine Lord

1965   THE EARLY BIRD
Director: Robert Asher
Co-stars: Norman Wisdom Edward Chapman Jerry Wisdom

1966   GEORGY GIRL
Director: Silvio Narizzano
Co-stars: James Mason Lynn Redgrave Charlotte Rampling

1968   CARRY ON DOCTOR
Director: Gerald Thomas
Co-stars: Frankie Howerd Jim Dale Barbara Windsor

1968   **THE BIRTHDAY PARTY**
Director: William Freidkin
Co-stars: Robert Shaw Patrick McGee Sidney Tafler

1968   **TILL DEATH DO US PART**
Director: Norman Cohen
Co-stars: Warren Mitchell Una Stubbs Anthony Booth

1972   **THE ALF GARNETT SAGA**
Director: Bob Kellett
Co-stars: Warren Mitchell Adrienne Posta Roy Kinnear

1973   **O LUCKY MAN!**
Director: Lindsay Anderson
Co-stars: Malcolm McDowell Arthur Lowe Ralph Richardson

1974   **CONFESSIONS OF A WINDOW CLEANER**
Director: Val Guest
Co-stars: Robin Askwith Anthony Booth Sheila White

JENNY NICHOLS

1989   **CRIMES AND MISDEMEANORS**
Director: Woody Allen
Co-stars: Woody Allen Mia Farrow Anjelica Huston Claire Bloom

KYRA NICHOLS

1993   **THE NUTCRACKER**
Director: Emile Ardolino
Co-stars: Darci Kister Macauley Culkin Damian Woetzel

NICHELLE NICHOLS

1970   **TARZAN'S DEADLY SILENCE**
Director: Robert Friend
Co-stars: Ron Ely Jock Mahoney Woody Strode

1979   **STAR TREK: THE MOTION PICTURE**
Director: Robert Wise
Co-stars: William Shatner Leonard Nimoy

1982   **STAR TREK II: THE WRATH OF KHAN**
Director: Nicholas Meyer
Co-stars: DeForest Kelly Walter Koenig

1984   **STAR TREK III: THE SEARCH FOR SPOCK**
Director: Leonard Nimoy
Co-stars: Leonard Nimoy James Doohan George Takei

1984   **STAR TREK IV: THE JOURNEY HOME**
Director: Leonard Nimoy
Co-stars: Leonard Nimoy William Shatner DeForest Kelly

1989   **STAR TREK V: THE FINAL FRONTIER**
Director: William Shatner
Co-stars: William Shatner Leonard Nimoy Walter Koenig

1991   **STAR TREK VI: THE UNDISCOVERED COUNTRY**
Director: Nicholas Meyer
Co-stars: Christopher Plummer David Warner

PATTI NICHOLLS

1986   **RITA, SUE AND BOB TOO**
Director: Alan Clarke
Co-stars: Michelle Holmes George Costigan Siobhan Finneran

PHOEBE NICHOLLS

1983   **THE MISSIONARY**
Director: Richard Loncraine
Co-stars: Michael Palin Maggie Smith Trevor Howard

1983   **PARTY PARTY**
Director: Terry Windsor
Co-stars: Daniel Peacock Perry Fenwick Caroline Quentin

1984   **POPPYLAND**
Director: John Madden
Co-stars: Alan Howard Richard Wilson Isla Blair

1985   **ORDEAL BY INNOCENCE**
Director: Desmond Davis
Co-stars: Donald Sutherland Christopher Plummer Sarah Miles

1987   **MAURICE**
Director: James Ivory
Co-stars: James Wilby Hugh Grant Rupert Graves

1990   **DROWNING IN THE SHALLOW END**
Director: Colin Gregg
Co-stars: Paul McGann Adrian Dunbar Alfred Molina

1998   **FAIRYTALE: A TRUE STORY**
Director: Charles Sturridge
Co-stars: Paul McGann Peter O'Toole Harvey Keitel

CAROLYN NICHOLSON

1983   **LOOKS AND SMILES**
Director: Ken Loach
Co-stars: Graham Green Tony Pitts Cilla Mason

DENISE NICHOLSON

1975   **LETS DO IT AGAIN**
Director: Sidney Poitier
Co-stars: Sidney Poitier Bill Cosby Calvin Lockhart John Amos

NORA NICHOLSON

1955   **THE HORNET'S NEST**
Director: Charles Saunders
Co-stars: Paul Carpenter June Thorburn Marla Landi

1956   **A TOWN LIKE ALICE**
Director: Jack Lee
Co-stars: Virginia McKenna Peter Finch Maureen Swanson

1959   **UPSTAIRS AND DOWNSTAIRS**
Director: Ralph Thomas
Co-stars: Michael Craig Anne Heywood Mylene Demongeot

1961   **DANGEROUS AFTERNOON**
Director: Charles Saunders
Co-stars: Ruth Dunning Joanna Dunham Howard Pays

1964   **DEVIL DOLL**
Director: Lindsay Shonteff
Co-stars: Bryant Halliday Sandra Dorne William Sylvester

1968   **DIAMONDS FOR BREAKFAST**
Director: Christopher Morahan
Co-stars: Marcello Mastroianni Rita Tushingham

REBECCA NICKELS

1991   **SCENES FROM A MALL**
Director: Paul Mazursky
Co-stars: Bette Midler Woody Allen Bill Irwin

JULIA NICKSON *(From 1990 Julia Nickson-Soul)*

1985   **RAMBO: FIRST BLOOD PART II**
Director: George Pan Cosmatos
Co-stars: Sylvester Stallone Richard Crenna

1988   **AROUND THE WORLD IN EIGHTY DAYS**
Director: Buzz Kulik
Co-stars: Pierce Brosnan Peter Ustinov Eric Idle

1990   **CHINA CRY**
Director: James F. Collier
Co-stars: Russell Wong James Shigeta France Nuyen

1990   **VICTIM OF INNOCENCE**
Director: Mel Damski
Co-stars: Cheryl Ladd Joe Spano Melissa Chan

1991   **K2**
Director: Franc Roddam
Co-stars: Michael Biehn Matt Craven Patricia Charbonneau

1992 AMITYVILLE A NEW GENERATION
Director: John Murlowski
Co-stars: Ross Partridge Lala Sloatman

1993 SIDEKICKS
Director: Aaron Norris
Co-stars: Chick Norris Beau Bridges Jonathan Brandis

MYLENE NICOLE

1956 IT'S A WONDERFUL WORLD
Director: Val Guest
Co-stars: Terence Morgan George Cole Kathleen Harrison

DARIA NICOLODI

1979 BEYOND THE DOOR 2
Director: Mario Bava
Co-stars: John Steiner David Colin Ivan Rassimov

1982 TENEBRAE
Director: Dario Argento
Co-stars: Anthony Franciosa John Saxon John Steiner

1985 MACARONI
Director: Ettore Scolla
Co-stars: Marcello Mastroianni Jack Lemmon Isa Danieli

GERDA NICHOLSON

1982 NEXT OF KIN
Director: Tony Williams
Co-stars: Jackie Kerin John Jarratt Alex Scott

1982 THE CLINIC
Director: David Stevens
Co-stars: Chris Haywood Simon Burke Rona McLeod

ASTA NIELSEN

1925 JOYLESS STREET
Director: G.W.Pabst
Co-stars: Werner Krauss Greta Garbo Valeska Gert

BRIGITTE NIELSEN

1985 RED SONJA
Director: Richard Fleischer
Co-stars: Arnold Schwarzenneger Sandahl Bergman Ronald Lacey

1985 ROCKY IV
Director: Sylvester Stallone
Co-stars: Sylvester Stallone Dolph Lundgren Talia Shire Burt Young

1986 COBRA
Director: George Pan Cosmatos
Co-stars: Sylvester Stallone Reni Santoni Andrew Robinson

1987 BEVERLEY HILLS COP II
Director: Tony Scott
Co-stars: Eddie Murphy Judge Reinhold Dean Stockwell

1989 MURDER ON THE MOON
Director: Michael Lindsay-Hogg
Co-stars: Julian Sands Jane Lapotaire Brian Cox

CONNIE NIELSEN

1993 THE VOYAGE
Director: John MacKenzie
Co-stars: Eric Roberts Karen Allen Rutger Hauer

NORMA NIELSON

1953 THE ACTRESS
Director: George Cukor
Co-stars: Jean Simmons Spencer Tracy Teresa Wright

GERTRUDE NIESEN

1937 TOP OF THE TOWN
Director: Ralph Murphy
Co-stars: George Murphy Doris Nolan Ella Logan

1943 THUMBS UP
Director: Joseph Santly
Co-stars: Brenda Joyce Richard Fraser Elsa Lanchester

1943 THIS IS THE ARMY
Director: Michael Curtiz
Co-stars: George Murphy Joan Leslie Ronald Reagan

JANE NIGH

1949 FIGHTING MAN OF THE PLAINS
Director: Edwin Marin
Co-stars: Randolph Scott Bill Williams Victor Jory

1950 CAPTAIN CAREY U.S.A.
Director: Mitchell Leisen
Co-stars: Alan Ladd Wanda Hendrix Francis Lederer

LESLEY NIGHTINGALE

1989 ONE WAY OUT
Director: Robert Young
Co-stars: Bob Peck Denis Lawson Samantha Bond

JUDY NIHEI

1981 CHAN IS MISSING
Director: Wayne Wang
Co-stars: Wood Moy Lauren Chew Peter Wang

JULIE NIHILL

1985 REBEL
Director: Michael Jenkins
Co-stars: Matt Dillon Debbie Byrne Bryan Brown

1986 KANGAROO
Director: Tim Burstall
Co-stars: Colin Friels Judy Davis John Walton

1988 BOUNDARIES OF THE HEART
Director: Lex Marinos
Co-stars: John Hargreaves Wendy Hughes Norman Kaye

ANNA Q. NILSSON

1921 WITHOUT LIMIT

1923 HOLLYWOOD
Director: James Cruze
Co-stars: Hope Drown Luke Cosgrave Eleanor Lawson

1933 THE WORLD CHANGES
Director: Mervyn LeRoy
Co-stars: Paul Muni Aline MacMahon Mary Astor

1938 PRISON FARM
Director: Louis King
Co-stars: Lloyd Nolan Shirley Ross J.Carrol Naish

1950 SUNSET BOULEVARD
Director: Billy Wilder
Co-stars: Gloria Swanson William Holden Erich Von Stroheim

HELENA NILSSON

1964 DEAR JOHN
Director: Lars Magnus Lindgren
Co-stars: Jarl Kulle Christina Schollin Morgan Anderson

CAROLE NIMMONS

1992 RUNNING LATE
Director: Udayan Prasad
Co-stars: Peter Bowles Renee Asherson Ian McNeice

ANAIS NIN

**1954 KENNETH ANGER, VOL. 2:
INAUGURATION OF THE PLEASURE DOME**
Director: Kenneth Anger
Co-star: Marjorie Cameron

MARINA NINCHI

1971   JUSTE AVANT LA NUIT
Director: Claude Chabrol
Co-stars: Stephane Audran Michel Bouquet Anna Douking

NATASA NINKOVIC

1998   SAVIOR
Director: Peter Antonijevic
Co-stars: Dennis Quaid Nastassja Kinski

YVETTE NIPAR

1986   TERMINAL ENTRY
Director: John Kincade
Co-stars: Paul Smith Yaphet Kotto Edward Albert

1989   SKI PATROL
Director: Richard Correll
Co-stars: Roger Rose Cory Timbrook Ray Walston

1995   ROLLING THUNDER
Director: P. J. Pesce
Co-stars: Stephen Shellen

GRETA NISSEN

1931   AMBASSADOR BILL
Director: Sam Taylor
Co-stars: Will Rogers Margueritte Churchill Ray Milland

1931   TRANSATLANTIC
Director: William Howard
Co-stars: Edmund Lowe Lois Moran Myrna Loy

1931   WOMEN OF ALL NATIONS
Director: Raoul Walsh
Co-stars: Edmund Lowe Victor McLaglen Humphrey Bogart

1932   SILENT WITNESS
Director: Marcel Varnell
Co-stars: Lionel Atwill Helen Mack Alan Mowbray

1932   RACKETY RAX
Director: Alfred Werker
Co-stars: Victor McLaglen Nell O'Day Alan Dinehart

1933   RED WAGON
Director: Paul Stein
Co-stars: Charles Bickford Raquel Torres Jimmy Hanley

1933   MELODY CRUISE
Director: Mark Sandrich
Co-stars: Phil Harris Charles Ruggles Helen Mack

1933   THE CIRCUS QUEEN MURDER
Director: Roy William Neill
Co-stars: Adolphe Menjou Ruthelma Stevens

1933   LIFE IN THE RAW
Co-star: George O'Brien

1936   CAFE COLETTE
Director: Paul Stein
Co-stars: Paul Cavanagh Sally Gray Bruce Seton

CYNTHIA NIXON

**1982   RASCALS AND ROBBERS -
THE SECRET ADVENTURES OF
TOM SAWYER AND HUCK FINN**
Director: Dick Lowry
Co-stars: Patrick Creadon Anthony Michael Hall Ed Begley Jnr.

1986   THE MANHATTAN PROJECT
Director: Marshall Brickman
Co-stars: John Lithgow Jill Eikenberry Sully Boyar

1994   BABY'S DAY OUT
Director: Patrick Read Johnson
Co-stars: Joe Mantegna Joe Pantoliano Baby Bink

MARIAN NIXON

1926   HANDS UP
Director: Clarence Badger
Co-stars: Raymond Griffith Mack Swain Mantagu Love

1929   SAY IT WITH SONGS
Director: Lloyd Bacon
Co-stars: Al Jolson Davey Lee Fred Kohler

1929   SHOW OF SHOWS
Director: John Adolfi
Co-stars: Frank Fay Monte Blue Douglas Fairbanks Jnr.

1930   THE LASH
Director: Frank Lloyd
Co-stars: Richard Barthelmess Mary Astor James Rennie

1930   GENERAL CRACK
Director: Alan Crossland
Co-stars: John Barrymore Hobart Bosworth Armida

1930   EX-FLAME
Director: Victor Halperin
Co-stars: Neil Hamilton Norman Kerry Roland Drew

1930   COURAGE
Director: Archie Mayo
Co-stars: Belle Bennett Rex Bell Leon Janney

1930   THE PAT OFF
Co-star: William Janney

1932   CHARLIE CHAN'S CHANCE
Director: John Blystone
Co-stars: Warner Oland Ralph Morgan H.B.Warner

1932   AMATEUR DADDY
Director: John Blystone
Co-stars: Warner Baxter Rita LeRoy William Pawley

1932   AFTER TOMORROW
Director: Frank Borzage
Co-stars: Charles Farrell Minna Gombell Josephine Hull

1932   REBECCA OF SUNNYBROOK FARM
Director: Alfred Santell
Co-stars: Ralph Bellamy Mae Marsh Alan Hale

1932   TOO BUSY TO WORK
Director: John Blystone
Co-stars: Will Rogers Dick Powell Louise Beavers

1932   WINNER TAKE ALL
Director: Roy Del Ruth
Co-stars: James Cagney Guy Kibbee Virginia Bruce

1933   PILGRIMAGE
Director: John Ford
Co-stars: Henrietta Crossman Heather Angel Norman Foster

1933   FACE IN THE SKY
Director: Harry Lachman
Co-stars: Spencer Tracy Stuart Erwin Lila Lee

1933   DR. BULL
Director: John Ford
Co-stars: Will Rogers Louise Dresser Andy Devine

1933   CHANCE AT HEAVEN
Co-star: Joel McCrea

1933   BEST OF ENEMIES
Co-star: Buddy Rogers

1934   ONCE TO EVERY BACHELOR
Co-star: Neil Hamilton

1934   BY YOUR LEAVE
Director: Lloyd Corrigan
Co-stars: Frank Morgan Genevieve Tobin Neil Hamilton

1935   EMBARRASSING MOMENTS
Co-star: Chester Morris

1936   TANGO

MARNI NIXON

1956 THE KING AND I *(Voice)*
Director: Walter Lang
Co-stars: Yul Brynner Deborah Kerr Rita Moreno

1965 THE SOUND OF MUSIC
Director: Robert Wise
Co-stars: Julie Andrews Christopher Plummer Peggy Wood

AMANDA NOAR

1989 I BOUGHT A VAMPIRE MOTORCYCLE
Director: Dirk Campbell
Co-stars: Neil Morrissey Michael Elphick

KERRY NOBLE

1994 SKALLAGRIGG
Director: Richard Spence
Co-stars: Bernard Hill Richard Briers Billie Whitelaw

TRISHA NOBLE

1968 CARRY ON CAMPING
Director: Gerald Thomas
Co-stars: Sid James Barbara Windsor Kenneth Williams

LUISA DELLA NOCE

1965 JULIET OF THE SPIRITS
Director: Federico Fellini
Co-stars: Giulietta Masina Mario Pisu Sylva Koscina

MAGALI NOEL

1955 RIFIFI
Director: Jules Dassin
Co-stars: Jean Servais Carl Mohner Robert Manuel

1956 ELEANA AND THE MEN
Director: Jean Renoir
Co-stars: Ingrid Bergman Jean Marais Mel Ferrer

1960 LA DOLCE VITA
Director: Federico Fellini
Co-stars: Marcello Mastroianni Anita Ekberg Anouk Aimee

1969 SATYRICON
Director: Federico Fellini
Co-stars: Martin Potter Hiram Keller Capucine

1973 AMARCORD
Director: Federico Fellini
Co-stars: Pupella Maggio Armando Brancia Luigi Rossi

NATALIA NOGULICH

1990 THE GUARDIAN
Director: William Friedkin
Co-stars: Jenny Seagrove Carey Lowell Dwier Brown

1991 HOMICIDE
Director: David Mamet
Co-stars: Joe Mantegna William H.Macy Rebecca Pidgeon

DORIS NOLAN

1936 THE MAN I MARRY
Co-stars: Michael Whalen Skeets Gallagher Cliff Edwards

1937 AS GOOD AS MARRIED
Co-star: John Boles

1937 TOP OF THE TOWN
Director: Ralph Murphy
Co-stars: George Murphy Hugh Herbert Ella Logan

1938 HOLIDAY
Director: George Cukor
Co-stars: Katherine Hepburn Cary Grant Lew Ayres

1940 MOON OVER BURMA
Director: Louis King
Co-stars: Dorothy Lamour Robert Preston Preston Foster

1943 FOLLIES GIRL
Director: William Rowland
Co-stars: Wendy Barrie Gordon Oliver Anne Barrett

JEANNETTE NOLAN

1948 MACBETH
Director: Orson Welles
Co-stars: Orson Welles Dan O'Herlihy Roddy McDowall

1950 SADDLE TRAMP
Director: Hugo Fregonese
Co-stars: Joel McCrea Wanda Hendrix John Russell

1951 THE SECRET OF CONVICT LAKE
Director: Michael Gordon
Co-stars: Glenn Ford Gene Tierney Ethel Barrymore

1952 THE HAPPY TIME
Director: Richard Fleischer
Co-stars: Charles Boyer Louis Jourdan Marsha Hunt

1952 HANGMAN'S KNOT
Director: Roy Huggins
Co-stars: Randolph Scott Donna Reed Glenn Langan

1953 THE BIG HEAT
Director: Fritz Lang
Co-stars: Glenn Ford Gloria Grahame Lee Marvin

1955 A LAWLESS STREET
Director: Joseph Lewis
Co-stars: Randolph Scott Angela Lansbury Jean Parker

1956 7TH. CAVALRY
Director: Joseph Lewis
Co-stars: Randolph Scott Barbara Hale Frank Faylen

1956 TRIBUTE TO A BAD MAN
Director: Robert Wise
Co-stars: James Cagney Irene Papas Pete Duel

1957 APRIL LOVE
Director: Henry Levin
Co-stars: Pat Boone Shirley Jones Arthur O'Connell

1958 THE DEEP SIX
Director: Rudolph Mate
Co-stars: Alan Ladd William Bendix Diane Foster

1959 THE RABBIT TRAP
Director: Philip Leacock
Co-stars: Ernest Borgnine Bethel Leslie David Brian

1962 THE MAN WHO SHOT LIBERTY VALANCE
Director: John Ford
Co-stars: James Stewart John Wayne Vera Miles

1963 TWILIGHT OF HONOR
Director: Boris Sagal
Co-stars: Richard Chamberlain Claude Rains Joey Heatherton

1965 MY BLOOD RUNS COLD
Director: William Conrad
Co-stars: Troy Donohue Joey Heatherton Barry Sullivan

1966 CHAMBER OF HORRORS
Director: Hy Averbach
Co-stars: Patrick O'Neal Patrice Wymore Cesare Danova

1967 DID YOU HEAR THE ONE ABOUT THE TRAVELLING SALESLADY?
Director: Don Weis
Co-star: Phyllis Diller Bob Denver Joe Flynn

1967 THE RELUCTANT ASTRONAUT
Director: Edward Montague
Co-stars: Don Knotts Leslie Nielsen Arthur O'Connell

1978 LASSIE: THE NEW BEGINNING
Director: Don Chaffey
Co-stars: John McIntyre David Wayne Gene Evans

1978 AVALANCHE
Director: Corey Allen
Co-stars: Rock Hudson Mia Farrow Robert Forster Barry Primus

1981 GOLIATH AWAITS
Director: Kevin Connor
Co-stars: Mark Harmon Christopher Lee Eddie Albert

KATHLEEN NOLAN

1972 LIMBO
Director: Mark Robson
Co-stars: Kate Jackson Katherine Justice Stuart Margolin

1981 AMY
Director: Vincent McEveety
Co-stars: Jenny Agutter Barry Newman Margaret O'Brien

KIRRILY NOLAN

1978 CADDIE
Director: Donald Crombie
Co-stars: Helen Morse Jack Thompson Jacki Weaver

MARGARET NOLAN

1971 CARRY ON AT YOUR CONVENIENCE
Director: Gerald Thomas
Co-stars: Sid James Joan Sims Hattie Jacques

1973 CARRY ON GIRLS
Director: Gerald Thomas
Co-stars: Sid James Barbara Windsor Kenneth Connor

1974 CARRY ON DICK
Director: Gerald Thomas
Co-stars: Sid James Kenneth Williams Bernard Bresslaw

MARY NOLAN

1928 WEST OF ZANZIBAR
Director: Tod Browning
Co-stars: Lon Chaney Lionel Barrymore Jacqueline Gadsen

1929 CHARMING SINNERS
Director: Robert Milton
Co-stars: Ruth Chatterton Clive Brook William Powell

1930 OUTSIDE THE LAW
Director: Tod Browning
Co-stars: Edward G.Robinson Owen Moore Wynne Gibson

ANN NOLAND

1975 BEST FRIENDS
Director: Noel Nosseck
Co-stars: Richard Hatch Doug Chapin Susanne Benton

MARIA NOLGARD

1971 THE TOUCH
Director: Ingmar Bergman
Co-stars: Bibi Andersson Elliott Gould Max Von Sydow

AURELIA NOLIN

1996 A SUMMER'S TALE
Director: Eric Rohmer
Co-stars: Melvil Poupand Amanda Langlet Gwenaelle Simons

CLAUDE NOLLIER

1952 MOULIN ROUGE
Director: John Houston
Co-stars: Jose Ferrer Zsa Zsa Gabor Colette Marchand

1961 THE GREENGAGE SUMMER
Director: Lewis Gilbert
Co-stars: Susannah York Kenneth More Danielle Darrieux

CHRISTINE NOONAN

1968 IF...
Director: Lindsay Anderson
Co-stars: Malcolm McDowell Peter Jeffrey Graham Crowden

KATHLEEN NOONE

1996 HEARTS ADRIFT
Director: Vic Sarin
Co-stars: Sydney Penny Scott Reeves

GHITA NORBY

1992 BEST INTENTIONS
Director: Billie August
Co-stars: Samuel Froler Perilla August Max Von Sydow

1992 SOPHIE

CHRISTINE NORDEN

1947 MINE OWN EXECUTIONER
Director: Anthony Kimmins
Co-stars: Burgess Meredith Dulcie Gray Kieron Moore

1948 AN IDEAL HUSBAND
Director: Alexander Korda
Co-stars: Paulette Goddard Hugh Williams Glynis Johns

1948 IDOL OF PARIS
Director: Leslie Arliss
Co-stars: Beryl Baxter Michael Rennie Margaretta Scott

1948 NIGHT BEAT
Director: Harold Huth
Co-stars: Anne Crawford Maxwell Reed Ronald Howard

1948 SAINTS AND SINNERS
Director: Leslie Arliss
Co-stars: Kieron Moore Shelia Manahan Maire O'Neill

1949 THE INTERUPTED JOURNEY
Director: Daniel Birt
Co-stars: Richard Todd Valerie Hobson Tom Walls

1950 A CASE FOR P.C.49
Director: Francis Searle
Co-stars: Brian Reece Joy Shelton Leslie Bradley

1951 BLACK WIDOW
Director: Vernon Sewell
Co-stars: Robert Ayres Anthony Forwood John Longden

1951 RELUCTANT HEROES
Director: Jack Raymond
Co-stars: Brian Rix Ronald Shiner Derek Farr

BIRGIT NORDIN

1975 THE MAGIC FLUTE
Director: Ingmar Bergman
Co-stars: Ulric Cold Erik Saeden Irma Urrila

INGRID NORDINE

1959 LUNCH ON THE GRASS
Director: Jean Renoir
Co-stars: Paul Meurisse Catherine Rouvel Fernand Sardou

EVY NORLUND

1959 THE FLYING FONTAINES
Director: George Sherman
Co-stars: Michael Callan Joan Evans Joe Desantis

LUCILLE NORMAN

1951 PAINTING THE CLOUDS WITH SUNSHINE
Director: David Butler
Co-stars: Virginia Mayo Dennis Morgan Gene Nelson

1952 CARSON CITY
Director: Andre De Toth
Co-stars: Randolph Scott Raymond Massey Richard Webb

SUSAN NORMAN
1990 POISON
Director: Todd Haynes
Co-stars: Edith Meeks Millie White James Lyons

BEATRICE NORMAND
1975 THE ROMANTIC ENGLISHWOMAN
Director: Joseph Losey
Co-stars: Glenda Jackson Michael Caine Helmut Berger

MABEL NORMAND
1916 HE DID AND HE DIDN'T
Co-star: Roscoe "Fatty" Arbuckle

1923 THE EXTRA GIRL
Director: Mack Sennett
Co-stars: Max Davidson Ralph Graves George Nicholls

HEATHER NORTH
1970 THE BAREFOOT EXECUTIVE
Director: Robert Butler
Co-stars: Kurt Russell Harry Morgan Joe Flynn

SHEREE NORTH
1954 LIVING IT UP
Director: Norman Taurog
Co-stars: Dean Martin Jerry Lewis Janet Leigh Edward Arnold

1955 THE LIEUTENANT WORE SKIRTS
Director: Frank Tashlin
Co-stars: Tom Ewell Rita Moreno Rick Jason

1955 HOW TO BE VERY POPULAR
Director: Nunnally Johnson
Co-stars: Betty Grable Robert Cummings

1956 THE BEST THINGS IN LIFE ARE FREE
Director: Michael Curtiz
Co-stars: Dan Dailey Gordon MacRae Ernest Borgnine

1957 NO DOWN PAYMENT
Director: Martin Ritt
Co-stars: Joanne Woodward Tony Randall Jeffrey Hunter

1957 THE WAY TO THE GOLD
Director: Robert Webb
Co-stars: Jeffrey Hunter Walter Brennan Barry Sullivan

1958 MARDI GRAS
Director: Edmund Goulding
Co-stars: Pat Boone Christine Carere Tommy Sands

1958 IN LOVE AND WAR
Director: Phillip Dunne
Co-stars: Jeffrey Hunter Robert Wagner Hope Lange

1968 MADIGAN
Director: Don Siegel
Co-stars: Richard Widmark Henry Fonda Inger Stevens

1969 THE TROUBLE WITH GIRLS
Director: Peter Tewksbury
Co-stars: Elvis Presley Edward Andrews Vincent Price

1969 THE GYPSY MOTHS
Director: John Frankenheimer
Co-stars: Burt Lancaster Deborah Kerr Gene Hackman

1970 LAWMAN
Director: Michael Winner
Co-stars: Burt Lancaster Robert Ryan Robert Duvall

1971 THE ORGANISATION
Director: Don Medford
Co-stars: Sidney Poitier Barbara McNair Gerald S.O'Loughlin

1973 SNATCHED
Director: Sutton Roley
Co-stars: Howard Duff Leslie Nielsen Barbara Parkins

1973 CHARLEY VARRICK
Director: Don Seigel
Co-stars: Walter Matthau Joe Don Baker Felicia Farr

1974 THE OUTFIT
Director: John Flynn
Co-stars: Robert Duvall Karen Black Robert Ryan Jane Greer

1975 BREAKOUT
Director: Tom Gries
Co-stars: Charles Bronson Robert Duvall John Huston

1976 THE SHOOTIST
Director: Don Seigel
Co-stars: John Wayne Lauren Bacall James Stewart Ron Howard

1977 THE NIGHT THEY TOOK MISS BEAUTIFUL
Director: Robert Michael Lewis
Co-stars: Chuck Connors Phil Silvers

1977 TELEFON
Director: Don Seigel
Co-stars: Charles Bronson Lee Remick Tyne Daly Donald Pleasence

1978 A REAL AMERICAN HERO
Director: Lou Antonio
Co-stars: Brian Dennehy Forrest Tucker Brian Kerwin

1980 MARILYN: THE UNTOLD STORY
Director: John Flynn
Co-stars: Catharine Hicks Richard Basehart

1983 LEGS
Director: Jerrold Freedman
Co-stars: Gwen Verdon John Heard Shanna Reed

1988 MANIAC COP
Director: William Lustig
Co-stars: Tom Atkins Bruce Campbell Richard Roundtree

1989 COLD DOG SOUP
Director: Alan Metter
Co-stars: Randy Quaid Frank Whaley Christine Harnos

1992 DEFENSELESS
Director: Martin Campbell
Co-stars: Barbara Hershey Sam Shepard J.T.Walsh

VIRGINIA NORTH
1967 THE LONG DUEL
Director: Ken Annakin
Co-stars: Trevor Howard Yul Brynner Charlotte Rampling

1971 THE ABOMINABLE DR. PHIBES
Director: Robert Fuest
Co-stars: Vincent Price Joseph Cotten Hugh Griffith

NADINE NORTIMER *(Child)*
1967 MOUCHETTE
Director: Robert Bresson
Co-stars: Jean-Claude Guilbert Maria Cardinal Paul Herbert

DEBORAH NORTON
1981 COUNTRY
Director: Richard Eyre
Co-stars: Leo McKern Wendy Hiller James Fox

DEEDEE NORTON
1988 DAKOTA
Director: Fred Holmed
Co-stars: Lou Diamond Phillips Eli Cummins Steve Ruge

JUDY NORTON-TAYLOR

1971 THE HOMECOMING: A CHRISTMAS STORY
Director: Fielder Cook
Co-stars: Richard Thomas Andrew Duggan Patricia Neal

1982 MOTHER'S DAY ON WALTON'S MOUNTAIN
Director: Gwen Arner
Co-stars: Ralph Waite Michael Learned

1982 A WEDDING ON WALTON'S MOUNTAIN
Director: Lee Philips
Co-stars: Ralph Waite Jon Walmsley Eric Scott

1982 A DAY FOR THANKS ON WALTON'S MOUNTAIN
Director: Harry Harris
Co-stars: Ralph Waite Ellen Corby

NATALIE NORWICK

1957 HIDDEN FEAR
Director: Andre De Toth
Co-stars: John Payne Anne Neyland Alexander Knox

SHELLEY NOVACK

1969 TELL THEM WILLIE BOY IS HERE
Director: Abraham Polonsky
Co-stars: Robert Redford Robert Blake Katherine Ross

1969 McCLOUD: WHO KILLED MISS U.S.A.
Director: Richard Colla
Co-stars: Dennis Weaver Craig Stevens Raul Julia

BLAINE NOVAK

1992 THEY ALL LAUGHED
Director: Peter Bogdanovich
Co-stars: Audrey Hepburn Ben Gazzara John Ritter

EVA NOVAK

1945 THE BELLS OF ST. MARY'S
Director: Leo McCarey
Co-stars: Bing Crosby Ingrid Bergman Henry Travers

1965 WILD SEED
Director: Brian Hutton
Co-stars: Michael Parks Celia Kaye Ross Elliott

JANE NOVAK

1936 HOLLYWOOD BOULEVARD
Director: Robert Florey
Co-stars: John Halliday Marsha Hunt Robert Cummings

KIM NOVAK

1954 THE FRENCH LINE (*Marilyn Novak*)
Director: Lloyd Bacon
Co-stars: Jane Russell Gilbert Roland

1954 PHFFFT!
Director: Mark Robson
Co-stars: Jack Lemmon Judy Holiday Jack Carson

1954 PUSHOVER
Director: Richard Quine
Co-stars: Fred MacMurray Phil Carey E.G.Marshall

1955 FIVE AGAINST THE HOUSE
Director: Phil Karlson
Co-stars: Guy Madison Brian Keith Kerwin Matthew

1955 PICNIC
Director: Joshua Logan
Co-stars: William Holden Rosalind Russell

1956 THE EDDY DUCHIN STORY
Director: George Sidney
Co-stars: Tyrone Power Victoria Shaw

1957 JEANNE EAGELS
Director: George Sidney
Co-stars: Jeff Chandler Agnes Moorehead

1957 PAL JOEY
Director: George Sidney
Co-stars: Frank Sinatra Rita Hayworth

1958 THE MAN WITH THE GOLDEN ARM
Director: Otto Preminger
Co-stars: Frank Sinatra Eleanor Parker

1958 BELL, BOOK AND CANDLE
Director: Richard Quine
Co-stars: James Stewart Jack Lemmon Janice Rule

1958 VERTIGO
Director: Alfred Hitchcock
Co-stars: James Stewart Barbara Bel Geddes

1959 MIDDLE OF THE NIGHT
Director: Delbert Mann
Co-stars: Glenda Farrell Lee Grant Jan Norris

1960 STRANGERS WHEN WE MEET
Director: Richard Quine
Co-stars: Kirk Douglas Walter Matthau

1962 THE NOTORIOUS LANDLADY
Director: Richard Quine
Co-stars: Jack Lemmon Fred Astaire Maxwell Reed

1962 BOYS' NIGHT OUT
Director: Michael Gordon
Co-stars: James Garner Tony Randall Howard Duff

1964 KISS ME, STUPID
Director: Billy Wilder
Co-stars: Dean Martin Ray Walston Felicia Farr

1964 OF HUMAN BONDAGE
Director: Ken Hughes
Co-stars: Laurence Harvey Nanette Newman Roger Livesey

1965 THE AMOROUS ADVENTURES OF MOLL FLANDERS
Director: Terence Young
Co-stars: Richard Johnson George Sanders

1967 EYE OF THE DEVIL
(*Injured While Filming, Replaced By Deborah Kerr*)
Co-stars: David Niven Flora Robson

1968 THE LEGEND OF LYLAH CLARE
Director: Robert Aldrich
Co-stars: Peter Finch Ernest Borgnine

1969 THE GREAT BANK ROBBERY
Director: Hy Averback
Co-stars: Zero Mostel Clint Walker Akim Tamiroff

1973 TALES THAT WITNESS MADNESS
Director: Freddie Francis
Co-stars: Jack Hawkins Joan Collins

1975 SATAN'S TRIANGLE
Director: Sutton Rolley
Co-stars: Doug McClure Jim Davis Alejandro Rey

1977 THE WHITE BUFFALO
Director: J.Lee Thompson
Co-stars: Charles Bronson Clint Walker

1978 JUST A GIGOLO
Director: David Hemmings
Co-stars: David Bowie Marlene Dietrich

1981 THE MIRROR CRACKED
Director: Guy Hamilton
Co-stars: Angela Lansbury Elizabeth Taylor

1990 THE CHILDREN
Director: Tony Palmer
Co-stars: Ben Kingsley Geraldine Chaplin

1991   LIEBESTRAUM
Director: Mike Figgis
Co-stars: Kevin Anderson Pamela Gidley Bill Pullman

PEGGY NOVAK

1942   WOMEN AREN'T ANGELS
Director: Laurence Huntington
Co-stars: Robertson Hare Alfred Drayton Polly Ward

JULIETA NOVIS

1940   MUSIC IN MY HEART
Director: Joseph Santley
Co-stars: Rita Hayworth Tony Martin Edith Fellows

JARMILA NOVOTNA

1948   THE SEARCH
Director: Fred Zinnemann
Co-stars: Montgomery Clift Aline MacMahon Ivan Jandl

LAURA NUCCI

1982   BLOW TO THE HEART
Director: Gianni Amelio
Co-stars: Jean-Louis Trintignant Laura Morante Fausto Rossi

JUDY NUGENT

1956   NAVY WIFE
Director: Edward Bernds
Co-stars: Joan Benett Gary Merrill Shirley Yagamuchi

JUDY NUNN

1983   HOSTAGE
Director: Frank Shields
Co-stars: Ralph Schicha Clare Binney

LOREDANA NUSCIAK

1964   GLADIATORS 7
Director: Pedro Lazaga
Co-stars: Richard Harrison Gerard Tichy Joseph Marco

1965   DJANGO
Director: Sergio Corbucci
Co-stars: Franco Nero Angel Alvarez Jose Bodalo

FRANCE NUYEN

1958   IN LOVE AND WAR
Director: Philip Dunne
Co-stars: Jeffrey Hunter Robert Wagner Dana Wynter

1958   SOUTH PACIFIC
Director: Joshua Logan
Co-stars: Mitzi Gaynor Rossano Brazzi John Kerr

1961   THE LAST TIME I SAW ARCHIE
Director: Jack Webb
Co-stars: Jack Webb Robert Mitchum Martha Hyer Richard Arlen

1962   A GIRL NAMED TAMIKO
Director: John Sturges
Co-stars: Laurence Harvey Martha Hyer Michael Wilding

1962   SATAN NEVER SLEEPS
Director: Leo McCarey
Co-stars: William Holden Clifton Webb Athene Seyler

1962   DIAMOND HEAD
Director: Guy Green
Co-stars: Charlton Heston Yvette Mimieux James Darren

1964   THE MAN IN THE MIDDLE
Director: Guy Hamilton
Co-stars: Robert Mitchum Trevor Howard Barry Sullivan

1966   DIMENSION 5
Director: Franklin Adreon
Co-stars: Jeffrey Hunter Donald Woods Harold Sakata

1971   ONE MORE TRAIN TO ROB
Director: Andrew McLaglen
Co-stars: George Peppard Diana Muldaur John Vernon

1972   HORROR AT 37,000 FEET
Director: David Lowell Rich
Co-stars: William Shatner Roy Thinnes Buddy Ebsen

1984   JEALOUSY
Director: Jeffrey Bloom
Co-stars: Angie Dickenson David Carradine Bo Svenson

1990   CHINA CRY
Director: James F Collier
Co-stars: Russell Wong James Shigeta Julia Nickson-Soul

1993   THE JOY LUCK CLUB
Director: Wayne Wang
Co-stars: Kieu Ching Tsai Chin Andrew McCarthy

CARRIE NYE

1979   THE SEDUCTION OF JOE TYNAN
Director: Jerry Schatzberg
Co-stars: Alan Alda Barbara Harris Meryl Streep

1982   CREEPSHOW
Director: George Romero
Co-stars: Viveca Lindfors Stephen King Leslie Nielsen

LENA NYMAN

1978   AUTUMN SONATA
Director: Ingmar Bergman
Co-stars: Ingrid Bergman Liv Ullmann Halvar Bjork

BARBARA O

1991 DAUGHTERS OF THE DUST
Director: Julie Dash
Co-stars: Cora Lee Day Alva Rogers Kaycee Moore

VIVIEN OAKLAND

1928 WE FAW DOWN
Director: Leo McCarey
Co-stars: Stan Laurel Oliver Hardy Bess Flowers

1929 THAT'S MY WIFE
Director: Lloyd French
Co-stars: Stan Laurel Oliver Hardy William Courtright

1931 A HOUSE DIVIDED
Director: William Wyler
Co-stars: Walter Huston Kent Douglass Helen Chandler

1932 SCRAM!
Director: Ray McCarey
Co-stars: Stan Laurel Oliver Hardy Arthur Housman

MARCIA OAKLEY

1990 THE BIG BANG
Director: James Toback
Co-stars: Emma Astner Polly Frost Sheila Kennedy

CLAIRE OBERMAN

1980 GOODBYE PORK PIE
Director: Geoff Murphy
Co-stars: Tony Barry Kelly Johnson Bruno Lawrence

ELAN OBERON

1994 MOTORCYCLE GANG
Director: John Milius
Co-stars: Gerard McRaney Carla Gugino Jake Busey

MERLE OBERON
(Estelle Thompson) (Married Robert Wolders)
Nominated For Best Actress In 1935For "The Dark Angel"

1932 MEN OF TOMORROW
Director: Zoltan Korda
Co-stars: Emlyn Williams Robert Donat

1932 SERVICE FOR LADIES
Director: Alexander Korda
Co-stars: Leslie Howard Elizabeth Allan

1932 WEDDING REHEARSAL
Director: Alexander Korda
Co-stars: Roland Young George Crossmith

1933 THE PRIVATE LIFE OF HENRY VIII
Director: Alexander Korda
Co-stars: Charles Laughton Robert Donat

1934 THE PRIVATE LIFE OF DON JUAN
Director: Alexander Korda
Co-stars: Douglas Fairbanks Joan Gardner

1934 THE SCARLET PIMPERNEL
Director: Harold Young
Co-stars: Leslie Howard Raymond Massey Nigel Bruce

1934 BROKEN MELODY
Director: James Murray

1934 THE BATTLE
Director: Leon Garganoff
Co-stars: Charles Boyer John Loder Betty Stockfield

1935 FOLIES BERGERE
Director: Roy Del Ruth
Co-stars: Maurice Chevalier Ann Sothern Eric Blore

1935 THE DARK ANGEL
Director: Sidney Franklin
Co-stars: Frederic March Herbert Marshall

1936 BELOVED ENEMY
Director: H.C. Potter
Co-stars: Brian Aherne David Niven Karen Morley

1936 THESE THREE
Director: William Wyler
Co-stars: Miriam Hopkins Joel McCrea

1937 OVER THE MOON
Director: Thornton Freedland
Co-stars: Rex Harrison Ursula Jeans

1938 THE DIVORCE OF LADY X
Director: Tim Whelan
Co-stars: Laurence Olivier Ralph Richardson

1938 THE COWBOY AND THE LADY
Director: H.C. Potter
Co-stars: Gary Cooper Walter Brennan Patsy Kelly

1939 THE LION HAS WINGS
Director: Michael Powell
Co-stars: Ralph Richardson June Duprez

1939 WUTHERING HEIGHTS
Director: William Wyler
Co-stars: Laurence Olivier David Niven

1940 TILL WE MEET AGAIN
Director: Edmund Goulding
Co-stars: George Brent Frank McHugh Pat O'Brien

1941 THAT UNCERTAIN FEELING
Director: Ernst Lubitsch
Co-stars: Melvyn Douglas Burgess Meredith Eve Arden

1941 LYDIA
Director: Julien Duvivier
Co-stars: Alan Marshall Joseph Cotten Edna May Oliver

1941 AFFECTIONATELY YOURS
Director: Lloyd Bacon
Co-stars: Dennis Morgan Rita Hayworth James Gleason

1943 FIRST COMES COURAGE
Director: Dorothy Arzner
Co-stars: Brian Aherne Carl Esmond Erik Rolf

1943 STAGE DOOR CANTEEN
Director: Frank Borzage
Co-stars: Cheryl Walker Lon McCallister Judith Anderson

1943 FOREVER AND A DAY
Director: Rene Clair
Co-stars: Anna Neagle Ray Milland Charles Laughton

1944 THE LODGER
Director: John Brahm
Co-stars: Laird Cregar George Sanders Cedric Hardwicke

1944 DARK WATERS
Director: Andre De Toth
Co-stars: Franchot Tone Thomas Mitchell Fay Bainter

1944 A SONG TO REMEMBER
Director: Charles Vidor
Co-stars: Paul Muni Cornel Wilde Sig Arno

1945 THIS LOVE OF OURS
Director: William Dieterle
Co-stars: Claude Rains Charles Korvin

1946 TEMPTATION
Director: Irving Pichel
Co-stars: George Brent Charles Korvin Paul Lukas

1946 A NIGHT IN PARADISE
Director: Arthur Lubin
Co-stars: Turhan Bey Gale Sondergaard Thomas Gomez

1947 NIGHT SONG
Director: John Cromwell
Co-stars: Dana Andrews Hoagy Carmichael

1948 BERLIN EXPRESS
Director: Jaques Tourneur
Co-stars: Robert Ryan Charles Korvin Paul Lukas

1952 24 HOURS OF A WOMAN'S LIFE
Director: Victor Saville
Co-stars: Richard Todd Leo Genn Stephen Murray

1954 DEEP IN MY HEART
Director: Stanley Donen
Co-stars: Jose Ferrer Paul Henreid Walter Pidgeon

1954 DESIREE
Director: Henry Koster
Co-stars: Marlon Brando Jean Simmons Michael Rennie

1956 THE PRICE OF FEAR
Director: Abner Biberman
Co-stars: Lex Barker Charles Drake Gia Scala

1963 OF LOVE AND DESIRE
Director: Richard Rush
Co-stars: Steve Cochrane Curt Jurgens John Agar

1966 THE OSCAR
Director: Russel Rouse
Co-stars: Stephen Boyd Eleanor Parker Tony Bennett

1967 HOTEL
Director: Richard Quine
Co-stars: Rod Taylor Karl Malden Melvyn Douglas

ANA OBREGON

1984 BOLERO
Director: Claude Lelouch
Co-stars: James Caan Geraldine Chaplin Robert Hossein

1986 KILLING MACHINE
Director: Antonia De La Loma
Co-stars: Jorge Rivero Margaux Hemingway Lee Van Cleef

EILEEN O'BRIEN

1983 RUNNERS
Director: Charles Sturridge
Co-stars: James Fox Jane Asher Kate Hardie

ERIN O'BRIEN

1958 GIRL ON THE RUN
Director: Richard Bare
Co-stars: Efrem Zimbalist Jnr

1958 ONIONHEAD
Director: Norman Taurog
Co-stars: Andie Griffith Feliciar Farr Walter Matthau

1959 JOHN PAUL JONES
Director: John Farrow
Co-stars: Robert Stack Bette Davies Charles Coburn

JOAN O'BRIEN

1958 HANDLE WITH CARE
Director: David Friedkin
Co-stars: Dean Jones Thomas Mitchell Walter Abel

1959 OPERATION PETTICOAT
Director: Blake Edwards
Co-stars: Cary Grant Tony Curtis Dina Merril

1960 THE ALAMO
Director: John Wayne
Co-stars: Richard Widmark Laurence Harvey John Wayne

1962 IT HAPPENED AT THE WORLD'S FAIR
Director: Norman Taurog
Co-stars: Elvis Presley Gary Lockwood Ginny Tiu

1962 IT'S ONLY MONEY
Director: Frank Tashlin
Co-stars: Jerry Lewis Zachary Scott Jack Weston

1962 SIX BLACK HORSES
Director: Harry Keller
Co-stars: Audie Murphy Dan Duryea George Wallace

1962 WE JOINED THE NAVY
Director: Wendy Toye
Co-stars: Kenneth More Lloyd Nolan Mischa Auer

JOCELYN O'BRIEN

1991 OSCAR
Director: John Landis
Co-stars: Slyvester Stallone Kirk Douglas Ornella Muti

**1992 DELIVER THEM FROM EVIL
THE TAKING OF ALTA VIEW**
Director: Peter Lavin
Co-stars: Harry Hamlin Teri Garr

LAURIE O'BRIEN

1986 THE DEFIANT ONES
Director: David Lowell Rich
Co-stars: Robert Urich Carl Weathers

MARGARET O'BRIEN (Child)

1942 JOURNEY FOR MARGARET
Director: W.S. Van Dyke
Co-stars: Robert Young Laraine Day Fay Bainter

1943 DR GILLESPIE'S CRIMINAL CASE
Director: Willis Goldbeck
Co-stars: Lionel Barrymore Donna Reed Keye Luke

1943 MADAME CURRIE
Director: Mervyn LeRoy
Co-stars: Greer Garson Walter Pidgeon Robert Walker

1943 THOUSANDS CHEER
Director: George Sidney
Co-stars: Gene Kelly Kathryn Grayson Jose Iturbi

1943 LOST ANGEL
Director: Roy Rowland
Co-stars: James Craig Marsha Hunt Keenan Wynn

1943 JANE EYRE
Director: Robert Stevenson
Co-stars: Joan Fontaine Orson Welles John Sutton

1944 MUSIC FOR MILLIONS
Director: Henry Koster
Co-stars: June Allyson Jose Iturbi Jimmy Durante

1944 THE CANTERVILLE GHOST
Director: Jules Dassin
Co-stars: Charles Laughton Robert Young Peter Lawford

1944   **MEET ME IN ST. LOUIS**
Director: Vincente Minnelli
Co-stars: Judy Garland Tom Drake Mary Astor

1945   **OUR VINES HAVE TENDER GRAPES**
Director: Roy Rowland
Co-stars: Edward G Robinson James Craig Butch Jenkins

1946   **BAD BASCOM**
Director: S. Sylvan Simon
Co-stars: Wallace Beery Marjorie Main J. Carrol Naish

1947   **THE UNFINISHED DANCE**
Director: Henry Koster
Co-stars: Cyd Charisse Danny Thomas Karin Booth

1948   **THE BIG CITY**
Director: Norman Taurog
Co-stars: Robert Preston Danny Thomas George Murphy

1948   **TENTH AVENUE ANGEL**
Director: Roy Rowland
Co-stars: George Murphy Angela Lansbury Phyllis Thaxter

1948   **THREE WISE FOOLS**
Director: Edward Buzzell
Co-stars: Lionel Barrymore Thomas Mitchell Edward Arnold

1949   **THE SECRET GARDEN**
Director: Fred Wilcox
Co-stars: Herbert Marshall Dean Stockwell Gladys Cooper

1949   **LITTLE WOMEN**
Director: Mervyn LeRoy
Co-stars: Elizabeth Taylor June Allyson Janet Leigh

1951   **HER FIRST ROMANCE**
Director: Seymour Friedman
Co-stars: Allen Martin Jimmy Hunt

1955   **GLORY**
Director: David Butler
Co-stars: Walter Brennan Charlotte Greenwood

1960   **HELLER IN PINK TIGHTS**
Director: George Cukor
Co-stars: Sophia Loren Anthony Quinn Ramon Navarro

1981   **AMY**
Director: Vincent McEveety
Co-stars: Jenny Agutter Barry Newman Nanette Fabray

MARIA O'BRIEN

1983   **TABLE FOR FIVE**
Director: Robert Lieberman
Co-stars: Jon Voight Richard Crenna Millie Perkins

1988   **PROMISED A MIRACLE**
Director: Steven Gyllenhaal
Co-stars: Judge Reinhold Tom Bower Rosanna Arquette

MARIE O'BRIEN

1975   **SHELL GAME**
Director: Glenn Jordan
Co-stars: John Davidson Tommy Atkins Signe Hasso

MAUREEN O'BRIEN

1997   **LAND GIRLS**
Director: David Leland
Co-stars: Catherine McCormack Anna Friel Rachel Weisz

VIRGINIA O'BRIEN

1941   **RINGSIDE MAISIE**
Director: Edwin Marin
Co-stars: Ann Sothern George Murphy Robert Sterling

1941   **THE BIG STORE**
Director: Charles Reisner
Co-stars: Marx Brothers Tony Martin Virginia Grey

1941   **LADY BE GOOD**
Director: Norman Z McLeod
Co-stars: Eleanor Powell Robert Young Red Skelton

1942   **SHIP AHOY**
Director: Eddie Buzzell
Co-stars: Eleanor Powell Red Skelton Bert Lahr

1942   **PANAMA HATTIE**
Director: Norman Z McLeod
Co-stars: Ann Sothern Dan Dailey Red Skelton

1943   **DUBARRY WAS A LADY**
Director: Roy Del Ruth
Co-stars: Lucille Ball Gene Kelly Red Skelton

1944   **TWO GIRLS AND A SAILOR**
Director: Richard Thorpe
Co-stars: June Allyson Gloria DeHaven Van Johnson

1944   **MEET THE PEOPLE**
Director: Charles Reisner
Co-stars: Lucille Ball Dick Powell June Allyson

1946   **THE HARVEY GIRLS**
Director: George Sidney
Co-stars: Judy Garland Ray Bolger John Hodiak

1946   **TILL THE CLOUDS ROLL BY**
Director: Richard Whorf
Co-stars: Robert Walker Van Heflin Lucille Bremer

1947   **MERTON OF THE MOVIES**
Director: Robert Alton
Co-stars: Red Skelton Gloria Grahame Leon Ames

ERIN O'BRIEN-MOORE

1934   **DANGEROUS CORNER**
Director: Phil Rosen
Co-stars: Melvyn Douglas Conrad Nagel Virginia Bruce

1934   **HIS GREATEST GAMBLE**
Co-stars: Richard Dix Dorothy Wilson

1935   **LITTLE MEN**
Director: Phil Rosen
Co-stars: Ralph Morgan Junior Durkin Frankie Darro

1935   **OUR LITTLE GIRL**
Director: John Robertson
Co-stars: Shirley Temple Joel McCrea Rosemary Ames

1935   **THE LEAVENWORTH CASE**
Co-stars: Norman Foster Donald Cook Warren Hymer

1936   **BLACK LEGION**
Director: Archie Mayo
Co-stars: Humphrey Bogart Dick Foran Ann Sheridan

1937   **THE LIFE OF EMIL ZOLA**
Director: William Dieterle
Co-stars: Paul Muni Gale Sondergaard Gloria Holden

1951   **THE FAMILY SECRET**
Director: Henry Levin
Co-stars: John Derek Lee J. Cobb Jody Lawrance

CINDY O'CALLAGHAN *(Child)*

1971   **BEDKNOBS AND BROOMSTICKS**
Director: Robert Stevenson
Co-stars: Angela Lansbury David Tomlinson Sam Jaffe

ANDREA OCCHIPINTI

1984   **BOLERO**
Director: John Derek
Co-stars: Bo Derek George Kennedy Ana Obregon

1990   **NIGHT OF THE FOX**
Director: Charles Jarrott
Co-stars: George Peppard Deborah Raffin John Mills

DEIRDRE O'CONNELL

1991 FALLING FROM GRACE
Director: John Mellencamp
Co-stars: Mariel Hemingway Kay Lenz Claude Akins

1992 STRAIGHT TALK
Director: Barnet Kellman
Co-stars: Dolly Parton James Woods Griffin Dunne

1992 COOL WORLD
Director: Ralph Bakshi
Co-stars: Kim Basinger Gabriel Byrne Brad Pitt

1993 FEARLESS
Director: Peter Weir
Co-stars: Jeff Bridges Isabella Rossellini Rosie Perez

DENISE O'CONNELL

1981 SCARECROW
Director: Sam Pilsbury
Co-stars: John Carradine Tracy Mann Jonathan Smith

SUSAN O'CONNELL

1970 THE BALLAD OF CABLE HOGUE
Director: Sam Peckinpah
Co-stars: Jason Robards David Warner Strother Martin

FRANCES O'CONNOR

1996 LOVE AND OTHER CATASTROPHIES
Director: Emma-Kate Croghan
Co-stars: Alice Garner Matthew Dyktynski

GLYNNIS O'CONNOR

1973 JEREMY
Director: Arthur Barron
Co-stars: Robby Benson Len Bari Leonard Cimino

1976 BABY BLUE MARINE
Director: John Hancock
Co-stars: Jan-Michael Vincent Katherine Helmond Richard Gere

1976 ODE TO BILLY JOE
Director: Max Baer
Co-stars: Robby Benson Joan Hotchkis Sandy McPeak

1981 THE WHITE LIONS
Director: Mel Stuart
Co-stars: Michael York Donald Moffat Roger Mosley

1982 NIGHT CROSSING
Director: Delbert Mann
Co-stars: Jane Alxander Beau Bridges Doug McKeon

1984 JOHNNY DANGEROUSLY
Director: Amy Heckerling
Co-stars: Michael Keaton Marilu Henner Maureen Stapleton

1986 THE DELIBERATE STRANGER
Director: Marvin Chomsky
Co-stars: Mark Harmon Frederic Forrest Ben Masters

1988 POLICE STORY: COP KILLER
Director: Larry Shaw
Co-stars: Ken Olin Joseph Bottoms Patricia Wettig

1988 TO HEAL A NATION
Director: Michael Pressman
Co-stars: Eric Roberts Marshall Colt Scott Paulin

1988 TOO GOOD TO BE TRUE
Director: Christian Nyby
Co-stars: Loni Anderson Patrick Duffy Julie Harris

1992 NIGHTMARE IN THE DAYLIGHT
Director: Lou Antonio
Co-stars: Jaclyn Smith Christopher Reeve Eric Bell

1995 DEATH IN SMALL DOSES
Director: Sondra Locke
Co-stars: Richard Thomas Tess Harper Shawn Elliott

HAZEL O'CONNOR

1980 BREAKING GLASS
Director: Brian Gibson
Co-stars: Phil Daniels Jon Finch Jonathan Pryce

HELEN O'CONNOR

1992 FRAUDS
Director: Stephen Elliott
Co-stars: Phil Collins Hugo Weaving Josephine Byrnes

LOYOLO O'CONNOR

1919 TRUE HEART SUSIE
Director: D.W. Griffiths
Co-stars: Lillian Gish Robert Harron Clarine Seymour

MAUREEN O'CONNOR

1937 I PROMISE TO PAY
Director: Ross Lederman
Co-stars: Chester Morris Helen Mack Thomas Mitchell

1937 BOY OF THE STREETS
Director: William Nigh
Co-stars: Jackie Cooper Kathleen Burke Marjorie Main

PATSY O'CONNOR

1943 IT AIN'T HAY
Director: Erle Kenton
Co-stars: Bud Abbott Lou Costello Grace McDonald

1943 YOU'RE A LUCKY FELLOW, MR SMITH
Director: Felix Feist
Co-stars: Allan Jones Evelyn Ankers Billie Burke

1944 PARDON MY RHYTHM
Director: Felix Feist
Co-stars: Mel Torme Gloria Jean Patric Knowles

RENNEE O'CONNOR

1991 DANIELLE STEEL'S CHANGES
Director: Charles Jarrott
Co-stars: Michael Nouri Cheryl Ladd Randee Heller

SINEAD O'CONNOR

1990 HUSH-A-BYE-BABY
Director: Margo Harker
Co-stars: Emer McCourt Michael Liebman Cathy Casey

1998 THE BUTCHER BOY
Director: Neil Jordan
Co-stars: Fiona Shaw Eamonn Owens Andrew Fullerton

UNA O'CONNOR

1933 THE INVISIBLE MAN
Director: James Whale
Co-stars: Claude Rains Gloria Stuart Henry Travers

1933 MARY STEVENS M.D.
Director: Lloyd Bacon
Co-stars: Kay Francis Lyle Talbot Glenda Farrell

1933 CALVACADE
Director: Frank Lloyd
Co-stars: Clive Brook Diana Wynyard Herbert Mundin

1934 THE BARRETTS OF WIMPOLE STREET
Director: Sidney Franklin
Co-stars: Charles Laughton Norma Shearer

1934 **CHAINED**
Director: Clarence Brown
Co-stars: Joan Crawford Clark Gable Otto Kruger

1934 **DAVID COPPERFIELD**
Director: George Cukor
Co-stars: Freddie Bartholomew W.C. Fields Madge Evans

1934 **ORIENT EXPRESS**
Director: Paul Martin
Co-stars: Heather Angel Ralph Morgan Herbert Mundin

1934 **STINGAREE**
Director: William Wellman
Co-stars: Irene Dunne Richard Dix Mary Boland

1935 **THE INFORMER**
Director: John Ford
Co-stars: Victor McLaglen Heather Angel Preston Foster

1935 **FATHER BROWN, DETECTIVE**
Director: Edward Sedgewich
Co-stars: Walter Connolly Paul Lukas

1935 **THE BRIDE OF FRANKENSTEIN**
Director: James Whale
Co-stars: Boris Karloff Elsa Lanchester Colin Clive

1935 **THUNDER IN THE NIGHT**
Director: George Archainbaud
Co-stars: Edmund Lowe Karen Morley Gene Lockhart

1936 **THE PLOUGH AND THE STARS**
Director: John Ford
Co-stars: Barbara Stanwyck Preston Foster Barry Fitzgerald

1936 **LITTLE LORD FAUNTLEROY**
Director: John Cromwell
Co-stars: Freddie Bartholomew Mickey Rooney Dolores Costello

1936 **ROSE MARIE**
Director: W.S. Van Dyke
Co-stars: Jeanette McDonald Nelson Eddy James Stewart

1936 **LLOYDS OF LONDON**
Director: Henry King
Co-stars: Tyrone Power Madeleine Carroll George Sanders

1937 **PERSONAL PROPERTY**
Director: W.S. Van Dyke
Co-stars: Jean Harlow Robert Taylor Reginald Owen

1937 **CALL IT A DAY**
Director: Archie Mayo
Co-stars: Olivia De Havilland Ian Hunter Roland Young

1938 **THE RETURN OF THE FROG**
Director: Maurice Elvy
Co-stars: Gordon Harker Rene Ray Hartley Power

1938 **THE ADVENTURES OF ROBIN HOOD**
Director: Michael Curtiz
Co-stars: Errol Flynn Olivia De Havilland Alan Hale

1939 **WE ARE NOT ALONE**
Director: Edmund Goulding
Co-stars: Paul Muni Jane Bryan Flora Robson

1940 **THE SEA HAWK**
Director: Michael Curtiz
Co-stars: Errol Flynn Flora Robson Brenda Marshall

1940 **LILLIAN RUSSELL**
Director: Irving Cummings
Co-stars: Alice Faye Don Ameche Henry Fonda

1940 **IT ALL CAME TRUE**
Director: Lewis Seiler
Co-stars: Humphrey Bogart Ann Sheridan Jeffrey Lynn

1940 **HE STAYED FOR BREAKFAST**
Director: Alexander Hall
Co-stars: Melvyn Douglas Loretta Young

1941 **HER FIRST BEAU**
Director: Theodore Reed
Co-stars: Jane Withers Jackie Cooper Edith Fellows

1941 **THE STRAWBERRY BLONDE**
Director: Raoul Walsh
Co-stars: James Cagney Olivia De Havilland Rita Hayworth

1942 **ALWAYS IN MY HEART**
Director: Joe Graham
Co-stars: Walter Huston Kay Francis Gloria Warren

1942 **THREE GIRLS ABOUT TOWN**
Director: Leigh Jason
Co-stars: Joan Blondell Janet Blair Binnie Barnes

1943 **THE CANTERVILLE GHOST**
Director: Jules Dassin
Co-stars: Charles Laughton Margaret O'Brien Robert Young

1943 **FOREVER AND A DAY**
Director: Rene Clair
Co-stars: Charles Laughton Buster Keaton Anna Neagle

1943 **GOVERNMENT GIRL**
Director: Dudley Nichols
Co-stars: Olivia De Havilland Sonny Tufts Ann Shirley

1943 **HOLY MATRIMONY**
Director: John Stahl
Co-stars: Monty Woolley Gracie Fields Laird Cregar

1943 **THIS LAND IS MINE**
Director: Jean Renoir
Co-stars: Charles Laughton Maureen O'Hara George Sanders

1945 **THE BELL'S OF ST. MARY'S**
Director: Leo McCarey
Co-stars: Bing Crosby Ingrid Bergman Henry Travers

1945 **CHRISTMAS IN CONNECTICUT**
Director: Peter Godfrey
Co-stars: Barbara Stanwyck Dennis Morgan

1946 **CHILD OF DIVORCE**
Director: Richard Fleischer
Co-stars: Sharon Moffet Regis Toomey Madge Meredith

1946 **CLUNY BROWN**
Director: Ernst Lubitsch
Co-stars: Jennifer Jones Charles Boyer Richard Haydn

1946 **THE RETURN OF MONTE CRISTO**
Director: Henry Levin
Co-stars: Louis Hayward Barbara Britton

1947 **IVY**
Director: Sam Wood
Co-stars: Joan Fontaine Herbert Marshall Patric Knowles

1947 **THE CORPSE CAME C.O.D.**
Director: Henry Levin
Co-stars: George Brent Joan Blondell Adele Jergens

1948 **THE ADVENTURES OF DON JUAN**
Director: Vincent Sherman
Co-stars: Errol Flynn Viveca Lindfors Alan Hale

1948 **FIGHTING FATHER DUNNE**
Director: Ted Tetzlaff
Co-stars: Pat O'Brien Darryl Hickman Charles Kemper

1957 **WITNESS FOR THE PROSECUTION**
Director: Billy Wilder
Co-stars: Charles Laughton Tyrone Power Marlene Dietrich

ANITA O'DAY

1959 **THE GENE KRUPA STORY**
Director: Don Weis
Co-stars: Sal Mineo Susan Kohner James Darren

1959 JAZZ ON A SUMMER'S DAY
Director: Bert Stern
Co-stars: Louis Armstrong Chuck Berry Dinah Washington

MOLLY O'DAY

1932 DEVIL ON DECK
Co-star: Reed Howes

1935 LAWLESS BORDERS
Co-star: Bill Cody

NELL O'DAY

1932 RACKETY RAX
Director: Alfred Werker
Co-stars: Victor McLaglen Greta Nissen Alan Dinehart

1940 SON OF ROARING DAN
Co-stars: Lafe McKee Dick Alexander

1941 ARIZONA CYCLONE
Co-stars: Johnny Mack Brown Fuzzy Knight Dick Curtis

1942 THE MYSTERY OF MARIE ROGET
Director: Phil Rosen
Co-stars: Maria Montez Patric Knowles John Litel

JUDITH O'DEA

1968 NIGHT OF THE LIVING DEAD
Director: George Romero
Co-stars: Duane Jones Karl Hardman Keith Wayne

SUNNY O'DEA

1936 SHOW BOAT
Director: James Whale
Co-stars: Allan Jones Irene Dunne Paul Robeson

ODETTA

1961 SANCTUARY
Director: Tony Richardson
Co-stars: Lee Remick Yves Montand Bradford Dillman

CATHY O'DONNELL

1946 THE BEST YEARS OF OUR LIVES
Director: William Wyler
Co-stars: Fredric March Myrna Loy Dana Andrews

1947 BURY ME DEAD
Director: Bernard Vorhaus
Co-stars: June Lockhart Hugh Beaumont Mark Daniels

1948 THE SPIRITUALIST
Director: Bernard Vorhaus
Co-stars: Turhan Bey Lynn Bari Richard Carlson

1948 THEY LIVE BY NIGHT
Director: Nicholas Ray
Co-stars: Farley Granger Howard Da Silva Helen Graig

1949 SIDE STREET
Director: Anthony Mann
Co-stars: Farley Granger James Craig Jean Hagan

1950 THE MINIVER STORY
Director: H.C. Potter
Co-stars: Greer Garson Walter Pidgeon John Hodiak

1952 THE WOMAN'S ANGLE
Director: Leslie Arliss
Co-stars: Edward Underdown Lois Maxwell Marjorie Fielding

1953 EIGHT O'CLOCK WALK
Director: Lance Comfort
Co-stars: Richard Attenborough Derek Farr Ian Hunter

1955 THE MAN FROM LARAMIE
Director: Anthony Mann
Co-stars: James Stewart Arthur Kennedy Donald Crisp

1958 TERROR IN THE HAUNTED HOUSE
Director: Harold Daniels
Co-stars: Gerald Mohr John Qualen William Ching

1958 BEN-HUR
Director: William Wyler
Co-stars: Charlton Heston Stephen Boyd Hugh Griffith

ROSIE O'DONNELL

1992 A LEAGUE OF THEIR OWN
Director: Penny Marshall
Co-stars: Geena Davis Tom Hanks Madonna

1993 EXIT TO EDEN
Director: Garry Marshall
Co-stars: Dana Delany Paul Mercurio

1993 ANOTHER STAKEOUT
Director: John Badham
Co-stars: Richard Dreyfuss Emilio Estevez Cathy Moriarty

1993 SLEEPLESS IN SEATTLE
Director: Nora Ephron
Co-stars: Tom Hanks Meg Ryan Ross Malinger

1994 THE FLINTSTONES
Director: Brian Levant
Co-stars: John Goodman Rick Moranis Elizabeth Perkins

1996 NOW AND THEN
Co-stars: Demi Moore Melanie Griffith Christina Ricci

MARTHA O'DRISCOLL

1938 GIRLS SCHOOL
Co-stars: Kenneth Howell Peggy Moran Marjorie Dean

1940 WAGON TRAIN
Director: Edward Killy
Co-stars: Tim Holt Ray Whitley Emmett Lynn

1941 THE LADY EVE
Director: Preston Sturges
Co-stars: Barbara Stanwyck Henry Fonda Charles Coburn

1942 MY HEART BELONGS TO DADDY
Director: Robert Siodmak
Co-stars: Richard Carlson Cecil Kellaway

1942 REAP THE WILD WIND
Director: Cecil B. DeMille
Co-stars: John Wayne Ray Milland Paulette Goddard

1942 PACIFIC BLACKOUT
Director: Ralph Murphy
Co-stars: Robert Preston Eva Gabor Philip Merivale

1942 YOUNG AND WILLING
Director: Edward Griffith
Co-stars: William Holden Susan Hayward Eddie Bracken

1943 WE'VE NEVER BEEN LICKED
Director: John Rawlins
Co-stars: Richard Quine Ann Gwynne Harry Davenport

1943 THE FALLEN SPARROW
Director: Richard Wallace
Co-stars: John Garfield Maureen O'Hara Walter Slezak

1943 CRAZY HOUSE
Director: Edward Cline
Co-stars: Olsen & Johnson Patric Knowles Percy Kilbride

1944 WEEKEND PASS
Co-stars: Noah Beery Jnr.

1944 THE GHOST CATCHERS
Director: Edward Cline
Co-stars: Olsen & Johnson Gloria Jean Leo Carrillo

1945 THE DALTONS RIDE AGAIN
Director: Ray Taylor
Co-stars: Alan Taylor Lon Chaney Noah Beery

1945 HERE COME THE CO-EDS
Director: Jean Yarborough
Co-stars: Bud Abbott Lou Costello Peggy Ryan

1945 HER LUCKY NIGHT

1945 HOUSE OF DRACULA
Director: Earl Kenton
Co-stars: Onslow Stevens John Carradine Lon Chaney

1945 UNDER WESTERN SKIES
Director: Jean Yarborough
Co-star: Leon Errol

1945 SHADY LADY
Director: George Waggner
Co-stars: Charles Coburn Ginny Simms Robert Paige

1946 BLONDE ALIBI
Co-star: Peter Whitney

1946 CRIMINAL COURT
Director: Robert Wise
Co-stars: Tom Conway Robert Armstrong Steve Brodie

1947 CARNEGIE HALL
Director: Edgar Ulmer
Co-stars: Marsha Hunt William Prince Frank McHugh

CHERYL O'DWYER

1993 HENRI
Director: Simon Shore
Co-stars: Kara Bowman John Hewitt Joe McPartland

RITA OEHMEN

1938 GUN LAW
Co-stars: George O'Brien Robert Glecker

BERNADETTE O'FARRELL

1950 THE HAPPIEST DAYS OF YOUR LIFE
Director: Frank Launder
Co-stars: Alastair Sim Margaret Rutherford

1951 LADY GODIVA RIDES AGAIN
Director: Frank Launder
Co-stars: Pauline Stroud Dennis Price Diana Dors

1959 THE BRIDAL PATH
Director: Frank Launder
Co-stars: Bill Travers Patricia Bredin George Cole

LUCY OFFERALL

1971 200 MOTELS
Director: Frank Zappa
Co-stars: Tony Palmer Theodore Bikel Ringo Starr

DEBORAH OFFNER

1988 CROSSING DELANCEY
Director: Joan Micklin Silver
Co-stars: Amy Irving Peter Riegert Jeroen Krabbe

1992 UNLAWFUL ENTRY
Director: Jonathan Kaplan
Co-stars: Kurt Russell Madeleine Stowe Ray Liotta

PASCALE OGIER *(Daughter Of Bulle Ogier)*

1984 FULL MOON IN PARIS
Director: Eric Rohmer
Co-stars: Tcheky Karyo Fabrice Luchini Christian Vadim

1994 GHOST DANCE
Director: Ken McCullen
Co-star: Leonie Mellinger

GAIL O'GRADY

1988 THE ATTIC
Director: Doug Adams
Co-stars: Carol Lynley Joseph Gian Joanna Miles

1990 PARKER KANE
Director: Steve Perry
Co-stars: Jeff Fahey Marisa Tomei Amanda Pays

1995 SHE STOOD ALONE :
THE TAILHOOK SCANDAL
Director: Larry Shaw
Co-star: Bess Armstrong

1997 TWO SMALL VOICES
Director: Peter Levin
Co-star: Mary McDonnell

OYAFUNMIKA OGUNIANO

1993 SANKOFA
Director: Haile Gerima
Co-stars: Kofi Ghanaba Alexandra Duah Nick Medley

CLAUDIA OHANA

1982 ERENDIRA
Director: Ruy Guerra
Co-stars: Irene Papas Oliver Wehe Michel Lonsdale

1988 FABLE OF THE BEAUTIFUL PIGEON FANCIER
Director: Ruy Guerra
Co-stars: Ney Lotorraco Tonia Carrero

CATHERINE O'HARA

1985 AFTER HOURS
Director: Martin Scorsese
Co-stars: Griffin Dunne Rosanna Arquette Teri Garr

1986 HEARTBURN
Director: Mike Nichols
Co-stars: Meryl Streep Jack Nicholson Jeff Daniels

1988 BEETLEJUICE
Director: Tim Burton
Co-stars: Alec Baldwin Michael Keaton Geena Davis

1990 BETSEY'S WEDDING
Director: Alan Alda
Co-stars: Molly Ringwald Madeline Kahn Joey Bishop

1990 HOME ALONE
Director: Chris Columbus
Co-stars: Macauley Culkin Joe Pesci Daniel Stern

1992 HOME ALONE 2
Director: Chris Columbus
Co-stars: Macauley Culkin Joe Pesci John Heard

1994 THE PAPER
Director: Ron Howard
Co-stars: Michael Keaton Marisa Tomei Robert Duvall

JENNY O'HARA

1976 BRINKS : THE GREAT ROBBERY
Director: Martin Chomsky
Co-stars: Carl Betz Stephen Collins Leslie Nielsen

1977 GOOD AGAINST EVIL
Director: Paul Wendkos
Co-stars: Dack Rambo Dan O'Herlihy Elyssa Davalos

1988 THE SECRET LIFE OF KATHY McCORMICK
Director: Robert Lewis
Co-stars: Barbara Eden Josh Taylor Judy Geeson

1991 CAREER OPPORTUNITIES
Director: Bryan Gordon
Co-stars: Frank Whaley Jennifer Connelly

1994 ANGIE
Director: Martha Coolidge
Co-stars: Geena Davis Stephen Rea James Gandolfini

KAREEN O'HARA

1967 ANY GUN CAN PLAY
Director: Enzo Castellari
Co-stars: Gilbert Roland Edd Byrnes George Hilton

MAUREEN O'HARA

1939 MY IRISH MOLLY
Co-star: Binkie Stuart

1939 JAMAICA INN
Director: Alfred Hitchcock
Co-stars: Charles Laughton Robert Newton

1939 THE HUNCHBACK OF NOTRE DAME
Director: William Dieterle
Co-stars: Charles Laughton Edmond O'Brien

1940 DANCE, GIRL, DANCE
Director: Dorothy Arzner
Co-stars: Louis Hayward Lucille Ball Mary Carlisle

1940 A BILL OF DIVORCEMENT
Director: John Farrow
Co-stars: Adolphe Menjou Patric Knowles Herbert Marshall

1941 THEY MET IN ARGENTINA
Director: Jack Hively
Co-stars: James Ellison Buddy Ebsen Alberto Vila

1941 HOW GREEN WAS MY VALLEY
Director: John Ford
Co-stars: Walter Pidgeon Roddy McDowall Donald Crisp

1942 TEN GENTLEMEN FROM WEST POINT
Director: Henry Hathaway
Co-stars: George Montgomery John Sutton

1942 TO THE SHORES OF TRIPOLI
Director: Bruce Humberstone
Co-stars: John Payne Randolph Scott Nancy Kelly

1942 THE BLACK SWAN
Director: Henry King
Co-stars: Tyrone Power George Sanders Laird Cregar

1943 THE IMMORTAL SERGEANT
Director: John Stahl
Co-stars: Henry Fonda Thomas Mitchell Allyn Joslyn

1943 THE FALLEN SPARROW
Director: Richard Wallace
Co-stars: John Garfield Walter Slezak John Banner

1943 THIS LAND IS MINE
Director: Jean Renoir
Co-stars: Charles Laughton George Sanders Walter Slezak

1944 BUFFALO BILL
Director: William Wellman
Co-stars: Joel McCrea Linda Darnell Thomas Mitchell

1945 THE SPANISH MAIN
Director: Frank Borzage
Co-stars: Paul Henreid Binnie Barnes Walter Slezak

1946 SENTIMENTAL JOURNEY
Director: Walter Lang
Co-stars: John Payne William Bendix Cedric Hardwicke

1946 DO YOU LOVE ME ?
Director: Gregory Ratoff
Co-stars: Dick Haymes Harry James Reginald Gardiner

1947 THE FOXES OF HARROW
Director: John Stahl
Co-stars: Rex Harrison Richard Haydn Victor McLaglen

1947 THE HOMESTRETCH
Director: Bruce Humberstone
Co-stars: Cornel Wilde Glenn Langan Helen Walker

1947 MIRACLE ON 34TH STREET
Director: George Seaton
Co-stars: Edmund Gwenn John Payne Natalie Wood

1947 SINBAD THE SAILOR
Director: Richard Wallace
Co-stars: Douglas Fairbanks Walter Slezak

1948 SITTING PRETTY
Director: Walter Lang
Co-stars: Clifton Webb Robert Young Richard Haydn

1948 BRITANNIA MEWS
Director: Jean Negulesco
Co-stars: Dana Andrews Sybil Thorndyke Fay Compton

1949 BAGDAD
Director: Charles Lamont
Co-stars: Vincent Price Paul Christian John Sutton

1949 FATHER WAS A FULLBACK
Director: John Stahl
Co-stars: Fred McMurray Natalie Wood Rudy Vallee

1949 A WOMAN'S SECRET
Director: Nicholas Ray
Co-stars: Gloria Grahame Melvyn Douglas Victor Jory

1950 COMANCHE TERRITORY
Director: George Sherman
Co-stars: MacDonald Carey Will Geer Charles Drake

1950 TRIPOLI
Director: Will Price
Co-stars: John Payne Howard Da Silva

1950 RIO GRANDE
Director: John Ford
Co-stars: John Wayne Ben Johnson Victor McLaglen

1951 FLAME OF ARABY
Director: Charles Lamont
Co-stars: Jeff Chandler Richard Egan Susan Cabot

1952 KANGAROO
Director: Lewis Milestone
Co-stars: Peter Lawford Richard Boone Finley Currie

1952 AGAINST ALL FLAGS
Director: George Sherman
Co-stars: Errol Flynn Anthony Quinn Mildred Natwick

1952 SONS OF THE MUSKETEERS
Director: Lewis Allen
Co-stars: Cornel Wilde Dan O'Herlihy Alan Hale Jnr.

1952 THE QUIET MAN
Director: John Ford
Co-stars: John Wayne Victor McLaglen Barry Fitzgerald

1953 THE REDHEAD FROM WYOMING
Director: Lee Sholem

1954 MALAGA
Director: Richard Sale
Co-stars: MacDonald Carey Binnie Barnes Guy Middleton

1955 THE MAGNIFICENT MATADOR
Director: Budd Boeticher
Co-stars: Anthony Quinn Richard Denning

1955 LADY GODIVA
Director: Arthur Lubin
Co-stars: George Nader Victor McLaglen Torin Thatcher

1955 THE LONG GRAY LINE
Director: John Ford
Co-stars: Tyrone Power Ward Bond Donald Crisp

1956 EVERYTHING BUT THE TRUTH
Director: Jerry Hopper
Co-stars: John Forsythe Frank Faylen Tim Hovey

1956 LISBON
Director: Ray Milland
Co-stars: Claude Rains Ray Milland Francis Lederer

1957 THE WINGS OF EAGLES
Director: John Ford
Co-stars: John Wayne Ward Bond Dan Dailey

1959 OUR MAN IN HAVANA
Director: Carol Reed
Co-stars: Alec Guinness Noel Coward Burl Ives

1961 THE PARENT TRAP
Director: David Swift
Co-stars: Hayley Mills Brian Keith Charles Ruggles

1961 THE DEADLY COMPANIONS
Director: Sam Peckinpah
Co-stars: Brian Keith Chill Wills Steve Cochran

1962 MR HOBBS TAKES A VACATION
Director: Henry Koster
Co-stars: James Stewart John Saxon Marie Wilson

1963 McLINTOCK !
Director: Andrew McLaglen
Co-stars: John Wayne Yvonne De Carlo Chill Wills

1963 SPENCER'S MOUNTAIN
Director: Delmer Daves
Co-stars: Henry Fonda Donald Crisp James MacArthur

1964 THE BATTLE OF THE VILLA FIORITA
Director: Delmer Daves
Co-stars: Rossano Brazzi Richard Todd

1966 THE RARE BREED
Director: Andrew McLaglen
Co-stars: James Stewart Brian Keith Juliette Mills

1970 HOW DO I LOVE THEE
Director: Michael Gordon
Co-stars: Jackie Gleason Shelley Winters Rick Lenz

1971 BIG JAKE
Director: George Sherman
Co-stars: John Wayne Richard Boone Bruce Cabot

1973 THE RED PONY
Director: Robert Totten
Co-stars: Henry Fonda Ben Johnson Richard Jaeckel

1991 ONLY THE LONELY
Director: Chris Columbus
Co-stars: John Candy Anthony Quinn Ally Sheedy

PAIGE O'HARA

1992 BEAUTY AND THE BEAST *(Voice)*
Director: Kirk Wise
Co-stars: Robby Benson Jerry Orbach Angela Lansbury

SHIRLEY O'HARA

1929 THE WILD PARTY
Director: Dorothy Arzner
Co-stars: Clara Bow Fredric March Marceline Day

1945 TARZAN AND THE AMAZONS
Director: Kurt Newman
Co-stars: Johnny Weismuller Brenda Joyce Johnny Sheffield

CAITLIN O'HEANEY

1980 HE KNOWS YOU'RE ALONE
Director: Armand Mastroianni
Co-stars: Don Scardino Tom Hanks Elizabeth Kemp

1987 ENIGMA
Director: Lucio Fulci
Co-stars: Jared Martin Susan Kendall

EILEEN O'HEARN

1941 RICHEST MAN IN TOWN
Director: Charles Barton
Co-stars: Frank Craven Edgar Buchanan Roger Pryor

CAROL OHMART

1955 THE SCARLET HOUR
Director: Michael Curtiz
Co-stars: Tom Tyron Jody Lawrance Elaine Strich

1956 THE WILD PARTY
Director: Harry Horner
Co-stars: Anthony Quinn Jay Robinson Arthur Franz

1958 HOUSE ON HAUNTED HILL
Director: William Castle
Co-stars: Vincent Price Richard Long Alan Marshall

1959 BORN RECKLESS
Director: Howard Koch
Co-stars: Mamie Van Doren Jeff Richards Arthur Hunnicutt

1964 ONE MAN'S WAY
Director: Denis Sanders
Co-stars: Don Murray Diana Hyland William Windom

ANITA OLANICK

1989 A WINTER TAN
Director: Bashar Shbib
Co-stars: Daphna Kastner David Duchovny

1991 JULIA HAS TWO LOVERS
Director: Jackie Burroughs
Co-stars: Erando Gonzales Javier Torres Zarragoza

LENA OLIN
Nominated For Best Supporting Actress In 1989 For "Enemies: A Love Story"

1984 AFTER THE REHEARSAL
Director: Ingmar Bergman
Co-stars: Erland Josephson Ingrid Thulin

1988 THE UNBEARABLE LIGHTNESS OF BEING
Director: Philip Kaufman
Co-stars: Daniel Day-Lewis Juliette Binoche

1989 ENEMIES : A LOVE STORY
Director: Paul Mazursky
Co-stars: Ron Silver Anjelica Huston

1990 HAVANA
Director: Sydney Pollack
Co-stars: Robert Redford Alan Arkin Raul Julia

1993 ROMEO IS BLEEDING
Director: Peter Medak
Co-stars: Gary Oldman Annabella Sciorra Juliette Lewis

1994 MR JONES
Director: Mike Figgis
Co-stars: Richard Gere Anne Bancroft Tom Irwin

INGRID OLIU

1988 STAND AND DELIVER
Director: Ramon Menendez
Co-stars: Edward James Olmos Lou Diamond Phillips Andy Garcia

DEANNA OLIVER

1987 THE BRAVE LITTLE TOASTER *(Voice)*
Director: Jerry Rees
Co-stars: Jon Levitz Tim Stack Phil Hartman

EDNA MAY OLIVER
Nominated For Best Supporting Actress In 1939 For "Drums Along The Mohawk"

1930   HALF SHOT AT SUNRISE
Director: Paul Sloane
Co-stars: Bert Wheeler & Robert Woolsey Dorothy Lee

1931   CRACKED NUTS
Director: Edward Cline
Co-stars: Bert Wheeler & Robert Woolsey Ben Turpin Dorothy Lee

1931   LAUGH AND GET RICH
Director: Gregory La Cava
Co-stars: Hugh Herbert Dorothy Lee Emmett Keane

1931   CIMARRON
Director: Wesley Ruggles
Co-stars: Richard Dix Irene Dunne Estelle Taylor

1931   FANNY FOLEY HERSELF
Director: Melville Brown
Co-stars: Helen Chandler Rochelle Hudson John Darrow

1932   PENGUIN POOL MURDER
Director: George Archainbaud
Co-stars: James Gleason Mae Clark Donald Cook

1932   LADIES OF THE JURY
Director: Lowell Sherman
Co-stars: Ken Murray Roscoe Ates Guinn Williams

1932   THE CONQUERORS
Director: William Wellman
Co-stars: Richard Dix Ann Harding Guy Kibbee

1932   HOLD 'EM JAIL
Director: Edward Cline
Co-stars: Bert Wheeler & Robert Woolsey Edgar Kennedy Betty Grable

1933   ALICE IN WONDERLAND
Director: Norman Z. McLeod
Co-stars: Cary Grant Gary Cooper W.C. Fields

1933   ANN VICKERS
Director: John Cromwell
Co-stars: Irene Dunne Walter Huston Bruce Cabot

1933   LITTLE WOMEN
Director: George Cukor
Co-stars: Katherine Hepburn Joan Bennett Jean Parker

1933   MEET THE BARON
Director: Walter Lang
Co-stars: Jack Pearl Jimmy Durrante Zasu Pitts

1933   ONLY YESTERDAY
Director: John Stahl
Co-stars: Margaret Sullavan John Boles Billie Burke

1934   MURDER ON THE BLACKBOARD
Director: George Archainbaud
Co-stars: James Gleason Regis Toomey

1934   THE POOR RICH
Co-star: Edward Everett Horton

1934   THE LAST GENTLEMAN
Director: Sidney Lanfield
Co-stars: George Arliss Ralph Morgan Janet Beecher

1935   NO MORE LADIES
Director: George Cukor
Co-stars: Joan Crawford Robert Montgomery Gail Patrick

1935   DAVID COPPERFIELD
Director: George Cukor
Co-stars: Freddie Bartholomew W.C. Fields Madge Evans

1935   A TALE OF TWO CITIES
Director: Jack Conway
Co-stars: Ronald Colman Elizabeth Allan Basil Rathbone

1935   MURDER ON A HONEYMOON
Director: George Archainbaud
Co-stars: James Gleason Lola Lane

1936   ROMEO AND JULIET
Director: George Cukor
Co-stars: Leslie Howard Norma Shearer John Barrymore

1937   ROSALIE
Director: W.S. Van Dyke
Co-stars: Nelson Eddy Eleanor Powell Ray Bolger

1937   PARNELL
Director: John Stahl
Co-stars: Clark Gable Myrna Loy Edmund Gwenn

1937   PARADISE FOR 3
Director: Edward Buzzell
Co-stars: Robert Young Frank Morgan Mary Astor

1937   MY DEAR MISS ALDRICH
Director: George Seitz
Co-stars: Maureen O'Sullivan Walter Pidgeon

1938   LITTLE MISS BROADWAY
Director: Irving Cummings
Co-stars: Shirley Temple George Murphy Jane Darwell

1939   THE STORY OF VERNON AND IRENE CASTLE
Director: H.C. Potter
Co-stars: Fred Astaire Ginger Rogers

1939   SECOND FIDDLE
Director: Sidney Lanfield
Co-stars: Tyrone Power Sonja Henie Rudy Vallee

1939   NURSE EDITH CAVELL
Director: Herbert Wilcox
Co-stars: Anna Neagle George Sanders May Robson

1939   DRUMS ALONG THE MOHAWK
Director: John Ford
Co-stars: Henry Fonda Claudette Colbert Ward Bond

1940   PRIDE AND PREJUDICE
Director: Robert Z. Leonard
Co-stars: Laurence Olivier Greer Garson Edmund Gwenn

1941   LYDIA
Director: Julien Duvivier
Co-stars: Merle Oberon Alan Marshall Joseph Cotten

NANCY OLIVER

1982   AMERCIAN NIGHTMARE
Director: Don McBrearty
Co-stars: Lawrence S. Day Lora Stanley Lenore Zann

SUSAN OLIVER

1959   THE GENE KRUPA STORY
Director: Don Weis
Co-stars: Sal Mineo Susan Kohner James Darren

1960   BUTTERFIELD 8
Director: Daniel Mann
Co-stars: Elizabeth Taylor Laurence Harvey Eddie Fisher

1963   GUNS OF DIABLO
Director: Boris Sagal
Co-stars: Charles Bronson Kurt Russell Jan Merlin

1964   THE DISORDERLY ORDERLY
Director: Frank Tashlin
Co-stars: Jerry Lewis Glenda Farrell Everett Sloane

1964   YOUR CHEATIN' HEART
Director: Gene Nelson
Co-star: George Hamilton

1964   LOOKING FOR LOVE
Director: Don Weis
Co-stars: Connie Francis Jim Hutton Barbara Nichols

1969   **A MAN CALLED GANNON**
Director: James Goldstone
Co-stars: Tony Franciosa Michael Sarrazin Judi West

1969   **CHANGE OF MIND**
Director: Robert Stevens
Co-stars: Raymond St. Jacques Leslie Nielsen Janet McLachlan

THELMA OLIVER

1965   **THE PAWNBROKER**
Director: Sidney Lumet
Co-stars: Rod Steiger Geraldine Fitzgerald Brock Peters

MARIE-CLAIRE OLIVIA

1951   **L'AUBERGE ROUGE**
Director: Claude Autant-Lara
Co-stars: Fernandel Francoise Rosay Gregoire Aslan

MAGGIE OLLERENSHAW

1988   **THE BELL RUN**
Director: Alan Dosser
Co-stars: Amanda Hillwood Bruce Payne Abigail Cruttenden

GERTRUDE OLMSTED

1925   **COBRA**
Director: Joseph Henabery
Co-stars: Rudolph Valentino Nita Naldi Casson Ferguson

1925   **THE MONSTER**
Director: Roland West
Co-stars: Lon Chaney Hallam Cooley Walter James

1925   **THE TORRENT**
Director: Monta Bell
Co-stars: Greta Garbo Ricardo Cortez Edward Connelly

1928   **BRINGING UP FATHER**
Director: Jack Conway
Co-stars: J. Farrell MacDonald Marie Dressler Polly Moran

APRIL OLRICH

1956   **THE BATTLE OF RIVER PLATE**
Director: Michael Powell
Co-stars: Anthony Quayle John Gregson Peter Finch

1965   **THE INTELLIGENCE MEN**
Director: Robert Asher
Co-stars: Eric Morecambe Ernie Wise William Franklyn

MARY-KATE OLSEN

1993   **HOW THE WEST WAS FUN**
Director: Stuart Margolin
Co-star: Ashley Olsen

1993   **DOUBLE, DOUBLE, TOIL AND TROUBLE**
Director: Stuart Margolin
Co-star: Ashley Olsen Chris Leachman

NANCY OLSON

Nominated For Best Supporting Actress In 1950 For "Sunset Boulevard"

1949   **CANADIAN PACIFIC**
Director: Edwin Marin
Co-stars: Randolph Scott Jane Wyatt Victor Jory

1950   **MR MUSIC**
Director: Richard Haydn
Co-stars: Bing Crosby Marge Champion Gower Champion

1950   **SUNSET BOULEVARD**
Director: Billy Wilder
Co-stars: Gloria Swanson William Holden Erich Von Stroheim

1950   **UNION STATION**
Director: Rudolph Mate
Co-stars: William Holden Barry Fitzgerald Lyle Bettger

1951   **FORCE OF ARMS**
Director: Michael Curtiz
Co-stars: William Holden Frank Lovejoy Gene Evans

1951   **SUBMARINE COMMAND**
Director: John Farrow
Co-stars: William Holden Don Taylor William Bendix

1952   **BIG JIM McLAIN**
Director: Edward Ludwig
Co-stars: John Wayne James Arness Veda Ann Borg

1953   **SO BIG**
Director: Robert Wise
Co-stars: Jane Wyman Sterling Hayden Richard Beymer

1954   **THE BOY FROM OKLAHOMA**
Director: Michael Curtiz
Co-stars: Will Rogers Jnr. Lon Chaney Merv Griffin

1955   **BATTLE CRY**
Director: Raoul Walsh
Co-stars: Van Heflin Aldo Ray Mona Freeman

1960   **THE ABSENT-MINDED PROFESSOR**
Director: Robert Stevenson
Co-stars: Fred MacMurray Keenan Wynn Ed Wynn

1972   **SNOWBALL EXPRESS**
Director: Norman Tolkar
Co-stars: Dean Jones Henry Morgan Mary Wickes

1974   **AIRPORT '75**
Director: Jack Smight
Co-stars: Charlton Heston Karen Black Helen Reddy

1982   **MAKING LOVE**
Director: Arthur Hiller
Co-stars: Michael Ontkean Kate Jackson Harry Hamlin

KATARINA OLSSON

1989   **THE WOMEN ON THE ROOF**
Director: Carl-Gustav Nykvist
Co-stars: Amanda Ooms Helena Bergstrom

KATE O'MARA

1967   **CORRUPTION**
Director: Robert Hartford Davis
Co-stars: Peter Cushing Sue Lloyd David Lodge

1968   **THE DESPERADOES**
Director: Henry Levin
Co-stars: Jack Palance Vince Edwards Sylvia Syms

1970   **THE HORROR OF FRANKENSTEIN**
Director: Jimmy Sangster
Co-stars: Ralph Bates Dennis Price Joan Rice

1970   **THE VAMPIRE LOVERS**
Director: Roy Ward Baker
Co-stars: Ingrid Pitt Peter Cushing Pippa Steele

MUTIA OMOOLU

1930   **TRADER HORN**
Director: W.S. Van Dyke
Co-stars: Harry Carey Edwina Booth Duncan Renaldo

ANNIE ONDRA

1929   **THE MANXMAN**
Director: Alfred Hitchcock
Co-stars: Carl Brisson Malcolm Keen Clare Greet

1929   **BLACKMAIL**
Director: Alfred Hitchcock
Co-stars: Sara Allgood John Longden Donald Calthrop

ANN O'NEAL

1949   **NOT WANTED**
Director: Elmer Clifton
Co-stars: Sally Forrest Keefe Brasselle Leo Penn

CYNTHIA O'NEAL

1971 CARNAL KNOWLEDGE
Director: Mike Nichols
Co-stars: Jack Nicholson Art Garfunkel Candice Bergen

TATUM O'NEAL *(Child) (Daughter Of Ryan O'Neal & Joanna Moore) (Married John McEnroe)*
Best Supporting Actress In 1973 For "Paper Moon"

1973 PAPER MOON
Director: Peter Bogdanovich
Co-stars: Ryan O'Neal Madeline Kahn

1976 NICKELODEON
Director: Peter Bogdanovich
Co-stars: Ryan O'Neal Burt Reynolds Stella Stevens

1976 THE BAD NEWS BEAR
Director: Michael Ritchie
Co-stars: Walter Matthau Vic Morrow

1978 INTERNATIONAL VELVET
Director: Bryan Forbes
Co-stars: Nanette Newman Anthony Hopkins Christopher Plummer

1980 CIRCLE OF TWO
Director: Jules Dassin
Co-stars: Richard Burton Nuala Fitzgerald Kate Reid

1980 LITTLE DARLINGS
Director: Ronald Maxwell
Co-stars: Kristy McNichol Matt Dillon

1985 GOLDILOCKS
Director: Gilbert Cates
Co-stars: Hoyt Axton John Lithgow

ZELMA O'NEAL

1930 FOLLOW THRU
Director: Lloyd Corrigan
Co-stars: Charles Rogers Nancy Carroll Jack Haley

1930 PARAMOUNT ON PARADE
Director: Dorothy Arzner
Co-stars: Clara Bow Gary Cooper Fay Wray

1930 DAMES AHOY
Co-star: Glenn Tryon

1934 GIVE HER A RING
Director: Arthur Woods
Co-stars: Clifford Mollison Wendy Barrie Stewart Granger

AMY O'NEIL

1989 DESPERATE FOR LOVE
Director: Michael Tuchner
Co-stars: Christian Slater Veronica Cartwright Brian Bloom

1989 HONEY, I SHRUNK THE KIDS
Director: Joe Johnston
Co-stars: Rick Moranis Matt Frewer Marcia Strassman

1992 HONEY, I BLEW UP THE KIDS
Director: Randal Reiser
Co-stars: Rick Moranis Marcia Strassman John Shea

BARBARA O'NEIL
Nominated For Best Supporting Actress In 1940 For "All This And Heaven Too"

1937 STELLA DALLAS
Director: King Vidor
Co-stars: Barbara Stanwyck John Boles Anne Shirley

1938 THE TOY WIFE
Director: Richard Thorpe
Co-stars: Luise Rainer Melvyn Douglas Robert Young

1938 I AM THE LAW
Director: Alexander Hall
Co-stars: Edward G. Robinson Otto Kruger John Beal

1939 GONE WITH THE WIND
Director: Victor Fleming
Co-stars: Clark Gable Vivien Leigh Leslie Howard

1939 THE SUN NEVER SETS
Director: Rowland Lee
Co-stars: Basil Rathbone Douglas Fairbanks Jnr. Virginia Field

1939 TOWER OF LONDON
Director: Rowland Lee
Co-stars: Basil Rathbone Boris Karloff Ian Hunter

1939 WHEN TOMORROW COMES
Director: John Stahl
Co-stars: Charles Boyer Irene Dunne Nydia Westman

1940 ALL THIS AND HEAVEN TOO
Director: Anatole Litvak
Co-stars: Charles Boyer Bette Davis Jeffrey Lynn

1941 SHINING VICTORY
Director: Irving Rapper
Co-stars: James Stephenson Geraldine Fitzgerald Donald Crisp

1948 SECRET BEYOND THE DOOR
Director: Fritz Lang
Co-stars: Joan Bennett Michael Redgrave Anne Revere

1948 I REMEMBER MAMA
Director: George Stevens
Co-stars: Irene Dunne Barbara Bel Geddes Oscar Homolka

1950 WHIRLPOOL
Director: Otto Preminger
Co-stars: Gene Tierney Jose Ferrer Richard Conte

1952 ANGEL FACE
Director: Otto Preminger
Co-stars: Jean Simmons Robert Mitchum Herbert Marshall

1955 FLAME OF THE ISLANDS
Director: Edward Ludwig
Co-stars: Yvonne De Carlo Howard Duff Zachary Scott

COLETTE O'NEIL

1989 WILD FLOWERS
Director: Robert Smith
Co-stars: Alan Bates Beatie Edney Sheila Keith

JENNIFER O'NEIL

1970 RIO LOBO
Director: Howard Hawks
Co-stars: John Wayne Jorge Rivero Jack Elam

1971 SUMMER OF '42
Director: Robert Mulligan
Co-stars: Gary Grimes Jerry Houser Lou Frizell

1971 SUCH GOOD FRIENDS
Director: Otto Preminger
Co-stars: Dyan Cannon James Coco Nini Foch

1972 THE CAREY TREATMENT
Director: Blake Edwards
Co-stars: James Coburn Pat Hingle Dan O'Herlihy

1973 LADY ICE
Director: Tom Gries
Co-stars: Donald Sutherland Robert Duvall Patrick Magee

1974 THE REINCARNATION OF PETER PROUD
Director: J. Lee-Thompson
Co-stars: Michael Sarrazin Margot Kidder

1975 W.H.I.F.F.S.
Director: Ted Post
Co-stars: Elliott Gould Eddie Albert Harry Guardino

1976 THE INNOCENT
Director: Luchino Visconti
Co-stars: Giancarlo Giannini Laura Antonelli Marc Porel

1977 CLOUD DANCER
Director: Barry Brown
Co-stars: David Carradine Joseph Bottoms Salome Jens

1978 CARAVANS
Director: James Fargo
Co-stars: Anthony Quinn Michael Sarrazin Joseph Cotten

1979 STEEL
Director: Steve Carver
Co-stars: Lee Majors Art Carney George Kennedy

1980 SCANNERS
Director: David Cronenberg
Co-stars: Patrick McGoohan Stephen Lack Michael Ironside

1985 CHASE
Director: Rod Holcomb
Co-stars: Michael Parks Richard Farnsworth Robert S. Woods

1988 GLORY DAYS
Director: Robert Conrad
Co-stars: Shane Conrad Stacy Edwards Ed O'Ross

1988 THE RED SPIDER
Director: Jerry Jameson
Co-stars: James Farentino Amy Steel Philip Casnof

1989 FULL EXPOSURE: THE SEX TALES SCANDAL
Director: Noel Nosseck
Co-stars: Lisa Hartman Vanessa Williams

1995 SILVER STRAND
Director: George Miller
Co-stars: Nicolette Sheridan Gil Bellows Tony Plana

NANCE O'NEIL

1929 HIS GLORIOUS NIGHT
Director: Lionel Barrymore
Co-stars: John Gilbert Catherine Dale Owen Hedda Hopper

1930 LADY OF SCANDAL
Director: Sidney Franklin
Co-stars: Ruth Chatterton Basil Rathbone Ralph Forbes

1930 CALL OF THE FLESH
Director: Charles Brabin
Co-stars: Ramon Navarro Dorothy Jordan Renee Adoree

1930 LADIES OF LEISURE
Director: Frank Capra
Co-stars: Barbara Stanwyck Ralph Graves Marie Prevost

1930 THE ROGUE SONG
Director: Lionel Barrymore
Co-stars: Laurence Tibbett Stan Laurel Oliver Hardy

1931 TRANSGRESSION
Director: Herbert Brenon
Co-stars: Kay Francis Ricardo Cortez Paul Cavanagh

1931 ROYAL BED
Director: Lowell Sherman
Co-stars: Mary Astor Anthony Bushell Robert Warwick

1931 RESURRECTION
Director: Edwin Carewe
Co-stars: Lupe Velez John Boles William Keighley

1931 CIMARRON
Director: Wesley Ruggles
Co-stars: Richard Dix Irene Dunne Estelle Taylor

NANCY O'NEIL

1934 JACK AHOY !
Director: Walter Forde
Co-stars: Jack Hulbert Alfred Drayton Tamara Desni

1934 THE SECRET OF THE LOCK
Director: Milton Rosmer
Co-stars: Seymour Hicks Gibson Gowland Rosamond John

1935 BREWSTER'S MILLIONS
Director: Thornton Freeland
Co-stars: Jack Buchanan Lili Damita Fred Emney

1936 EDUCATED EVANS
Director: William Beaudine
Co-stars: Max Miller Clarice Mayne Albert Whelan

1936 TWELVE GOOD MEN
Director: Ralph Ince
Co-stars: Henry Kendall Joyce Kennedy Percy Parsons

PADDIE O'NEIL

1965 THE EARLY BIRD
Director: Robert Asher
Co-stars: Norman Wisdom Edward Chapman Jerry Desmonde

1983 FANNY HILL
Director: Gerry O'Hara
Co-stars: Lisa Raines Oliver Reed Shelley Winters

REMY O'NEIL

1990 HOLLYWOOD HOT TUBS 2: EDUCATING CRYSTAL
Director: Ken Raich
Co-stars: Jewel Shepard Patrick Day

TRICIA O'NEIL

1977 MARY JANE HARPER CRIED LAST NIGHT
Director: Allen Reisner
Co-stars: Susan Dey Bernie Casey John Vernon

1981 PIRANHA II: THE SPAWNING
Director: James Cameron
Co-stars: Steve Marachuk Lance Henriksen

MAGGIE O'NEILL

1988 GORILLAS IN THE MIST
Director: Michael Apted
Co-stars: Sigourney Weaver Bryan Brown Julie Harris

1988 DEFROSTING THE FRIDGE
Director: Sandy Johnson
Co-stars: Joe Don Baker Phyllis Logan Emma Wray

1989 BLORE M.P.
Director: Robert Young
Co-stars: Timothy West Jill Baker Stephen Moore

1989 TAKE ME HOME
Director: Jane Howell
Co-stars: Keith Barron Annette Crosbie Reece Dinsdale

1990 HE'S ASKING FOR ME
Director: Vitold Starecki
Co-stars: David Threfall Gina McKee Marian McLoughlin

1991 UNDER SUSPICION
Director: Simon Moore
Co-stars: Liam Neesen Kenneth Cranham Laura San Giacomo

1992 FRIDAY ON MY MIND
Director: Marc Evans
Co-stars: Christopher Eccleston David Calder Deborah Poplett

1997 THE FIX
Director: Paul Greengrass
Co-stars: Paul McGann Steve Coogan Michael Elphick

MARIE O'NEILL

1930 JUNO AND THE PAYCOCK
Director: Alfred Hitchcock
Co-stars: Sara Allgood Edward Chapman John Laurie

1938 PENNY PARADISE
Director: Carol Reed
Co-stars: Edmund Gwenn Betty Driver Jimmy O'Dea

1941 THOSE KIDS FROM TOWN
Director: Lance Comfort
Co-stars: Shirley Lenner Percy Marmont George Cole

1941 LOVE ON THE DOLE
Director: John Baxter
Co-stars: Deborah Kerr Clifford Evans Geoffrey Hibbert

1945 GREAT DAY
Director: Lance Comfort
Co-stars: Flora Robson Eric Portman Sheila Sim

1948 SAINTS AND SINNERS
Director: Leslie Arliss
Co-stars: Kieron Moore Christine Norden Sheila Manahan

1951 JUDGEMENT DEFERRED
Director: John Baxter
Co-stars: Hugh Sinclair Helen Shingler Joan Collins

MARY ELLEN O'NEILL

1980 THE BIG BRAWL
Director: Robert Clouse
Co-stars: Jackie Chan Jose Ferrer Mako

SALLY O'NEILL

1925 SALLY, IRENE AND MARY
Director: Edmund Goulding
Co-stars: Constance Bennett Joan Crawford William Haines

1926 BATTLING BUTLER
Director: Buster Keaton
Co-stars: Buster Keaton Snitz Edwards Francis McDonald

1929 ON WITH THE SHOW
Director: Alan Crosland
Co-stars: Betty Compson Joe E. Brown Louise Fazenda

1929 SHOW OF SHOWS
Director: John Adolfi
Co-stars: Frank Fay Lupino Lane Douglas Fairbanks Jnr.

1930 HOLD EVERYTHING
Director: Roy Del Ruth
Co-stars: Joe E. Brown Winnie Lightner Georges Carpentier

1930 GIRL OF THE PORT
Co-stars: Reginald Sharland Mitchell Lewis

1931 BRAT !
Co-stars: Frank Albertson Alan Dinehart

1931 SALVATION NELL
Director: James Cruze
Co-stars: Helen Chandler Ralph Graves Jason Robards

1933 BY APPOINTMENT ONLY
Co-star: Lew Cody

1935 TOO TOUGH TO KILL
Co-stars: Victor Jory James Millican

YOKO ONO (Married John Lennon)

1970 LET IT BE
Director: Michael Lindsay-Hogg
Co-stars: John Lennon Paul McCartney George Harrison

1988 IMAGINE: JOHN LENNON
Director: Andrew Solt
Co-stars: John Lennon George Harrison

AMANDA OOMS

1989 THE WOMEN ON THE ROOF
Director: Carl-Gustav Nykvist
Co-stars: Helena Bergstrom Percy Brandt Beryl Orde

1934 RADIO PARADE OF 1935
Director: Arthur Woods
Co-stars: Will Hay Helen Chandler Ted Ray

1943 THE DUMMY TALKS
Director: Oswald Mitchell
Co-stars: Jack Warner Claude Hulbert Ivy Benson

KATHLEEN O'REGAN

1930 JUNO AND THE PAYCOCK
Director: Alfred Hitchcock
Co-stars: Sara Allwood Edward Chapman Maire O'Neill

1943 THURSDAY'S CHILD
Director: Rodney Ackland
Co-stars: Sally Ann Howes Wilfrid Lawson Stewart Granger

ERIN O'REILLY

1971 T.R. BASKIN
Director: Herbert Rose
Co-stars: Candice Bergen Peter Boyle James Caan

1973 BUSTING
Director: Peter Hyams
Co-stars: Elliott Gould Robert Blake Allen Garfield

MOIRA ORFEI

1963 FIRE OVER ROME
Director: Guido Malatesta
Co-stars: Lang Jeffries Cristina Gaioni Mario Feliciani

1963 THE HERO OF BABYLON
Director: Gordon Scott
Co-stars: Genevieve Grad Andrea Scotti

LISA ORGOLINI

1986 TRICK OR TREAT
Director: Charles Martin Smith
Co-stars: Marc Price Tony Fields Ozzy Osbourne

FELICE ORLANDI

1978 THE DRIVER
Director: Walter Hill
Co-stars: Ryan O'Neal Bruce Dern Isabelle Adjani

LUBOV ORLOVA (Married Grigori Alexandrov)

1934 JAZZ COMEDY
Director: Grigori Alexandrov
Co-stars: Leonid Utyosov Maria Strelkova

JULIA ORMOND

1990 INSPECTOR WEXFORD : THE BEST MAN TO DIE
Director: Herbert Wise
Co-stars: George Baker Diane Keen

1993 THE BABY OF MACON
Director: Peter Greenaway
Co-stars: Ralph Fiennes Philip Stone Celia Gregory

1993 NOSTRADAMUS
Director: Roger Christian
Co-stars: Tcheky Karyo Amanda Plummer Anthony Higgins

1994 CAPTIVES
Director: Angela Pope
Co-stars: Tim Roth Keith Allen Peter Capaldi

1995 LEGENDS OF THE FALL
Director: Edward Zwick
Co-stars: Anthony Hopkins Brad Pitt Aidan Quinn

1995 FIRST KNIGHT
Director: Jerry Zucker
Co-stars: Richard Gere Sean Connery

1996 SABRINA
Director: Sidney Pollack
Co-stars: Harrison Ford John Wood Fanny Ardant

1997 SMILLA'S FEELING FOR SNOW
Director: Bille August
Co-stars: Gabriel Byrne Clipper Miano Richard Harris

HEATHER O'ROURKE *(Child)*
(Died At The Age Of Twelve)

1982 POLTERGEIST
Director: Tobe Hooper
Co-stars: JoBeth Williams Craig T. Nelson Beatrice Straight

1985 SURVIVING
Director: Waris Hussein
Co-stars: Ellen Burstyn Marsha Mason River Phoenix

1986 POLTERGEIST II
Director: Brian Gibson
Co-stars: JoBeth Willams Craig T. Nelson Zelda Rubinstein

1988 POLTERGEIST III
Director: Gary Sherman
Co-stars: Tom Skerritt Nancy Allen Lara Flynn Boyle

CAIT O'RIORDAN

1988 THE COURIER
Director: Joe Lee
Co-stars: Gabriel Byrne Ian Bannen Padraig O'Loingsigh

PATRICIA O'ROURKE

1942 THE JUNGLE BOOK
Director: Zoltan Korda
Co-stars: Sabu Rosemary De Camp Joseph Calleia

ANGELYN ORR

1946 BLONDIE'S LUCKY DAY
Director: Abby Berlin
Co-stars: Penny Singleton Arthur Lake Larry Simms

LEIGH ANN ORSI

1994 PET SHOP
Director: Hope Perello
Co-stars: Spencer Vrooman Joanne Baron

MARINA ORSINI

1988 THE TADPOLE AND THE WHALE
Director: Jean-Claude Lord
Co-stars: Fanny Lauzier Denis Forest

1989 EDDIE AND THE CRUISERS II:EDDIE LIVES
Director: Jean-Claude Lord
Co-stars: Michael Pare Bernie Coulson

ANGIE ORTAGO

1971 THE HOSPITAL
Director: Arthur Hiller
Co-stars: George C. Scott Diana Rigg Nancy Marchand

APRIL ORTIZ

1992 FATHER OF THE BRIDE
Director: Charles Shyer
Co-stars: Steve Martin Diane Keaton Kimberley Williams

VIVIENNE OSBOURNE

1931 HUSBAND'S HOLIDAY
Director: Robert Milton
Co-stars: Clive Brook Charles Ruggles Charles Winninger

1931 THE BELOVED BACHELOR
Director: Lloyd Corrigan
Co-stars: Paul Lukas Dorothy Jordan Charles Ruggles

1932 THE DARK HORSE
Director: Alfred Green
Co-stars: Guy Kibbee Bette Davis Warren William

1932 LIFE BEGINS
Director: James Flood
Co-stars: Elliott Nugent Loretta Young Glenda Farrell

1932 TWO SECONDS
Director: Mervyn LeRoy
Co-stars: Edward G. Robinson Preston Foster J. Carrol Naish

1932 WEEKEND MARRIAGE
Director: Thornton Freeland
Co-stars: Loretta Young Norman Foster George Brent

1933 SUPERNATURAL
Director: Victor Halperin
Co-stars: Carole Lombard Randolph Scott H.B. Warner

1933 SAILOR BE GOOD
Co-star: Jack Oakie

1933 MEN ARE SUCH FOOLS
Co-stars: Leo Carrillo Earle Foxe

1933 LUXURY LINER
Director: Lothar Mendes
Co-stars: George Brent Zita Johnson Alice White

1933 THE DEVIL'S IN LOVE
Director: William Dieterle
Co-stars: Loretta Young Victor Jory David Manners

1937 CHAMPAGNE WALTZ
Director: Edward Sutherland
Co-stars: Fred MacMurray Gladys Swarthout Jack Oakie

1937 SINNER TAKE ALL
Director: Errol Taggart
Co-stars: Bruce Cabot Margaret Lindsay Joseph Calleia

GABRILE OSBURG

1984 NOVEMBER MOON
Director: Alexandra Von Grote
Co-stars: Christine Millet Daniele Delorme Bruno Pradal

ETHEL O'SHEA

1953 RECOIL
Director: John Gilling
Co-stars: Kieron Moore Elizabeth Sellars Edward Underdown

TESSIE O'SHEA

1946 LONDON TOWN
Director: Wesley Ruggles
Co-stars: Sid Field Greta Gynt Kay Kendall

1949 THE BLUE LAMP
Director: Basil Dearden
Co-stars: Jack Warner Jimmy Hanley Dirk Bogarde

1957 THE SHIRALEE
Director: Leslie Norman
Co-stars: Peter Finch Elizabeth Sellars Dana Wilson

1966 THE RUSSIANS ARE COMING:
THE RUSSIANS ARE COMING !
Director: Norman Jewison
Co-stars: Carl Reiner Alan Arkin Eva Marie Saint

1971 BEDKNOBS AND BROOMSTICKS
Director: Robert Stevenson
Co-stars: Angela Lansbury David Tomlinson

GRACE OSHITA

1983 REVENGE OF THE NINJA
Director: Sam Firstenberg
Co-stars: Sho Kosugi Keith Vitali Virgil Frye

K.T. OSLIN

1993 MURDER SO SWEET
Director: Larry Peerce
Co-stars: Harry Hamlin Helen Shaver Terence Knox

MARIE OSMOND *(Sister Of Donny Osmond)*

1982 SIDE BY SIDE
Director: Russ Mayberry
Co-star: Joseph Bottoms

1983 I MARRIED WYATT EARP
Director: Michael O'Herlihy
Co-stars: Bruce Boxleitner Ross Martin Jeffrey DeMunn

BIBI OSTERWALD

1974 BANK SHOT
Director: Gower Champion
Co-stars: George C. Scott Joanna Cassidy Sorrell Booke

1983 HAPPY ENDINGS
Director: Noel Black
Co-stars: John Schneider Catherine Hicks Ana Alicia

PAMELA OSTRER

1934 JEW SUSS
Director: Lothar Mendes
Co-stars: Conrad Veidt Cedric Hardwicke Benita Hume

MAUREEN O'SULLIVAN *(Married John Farrow – Mother Of Mia & Tisa Farrow)*

1930 SONG O' MY HEART
Director: Frank Borzage
Co-stars: John McCormack John Garrick Alice Joyce

1930 JUST IMAGINE
Director: David Butler
Co-stars: El Brendel John Garrick Mischa Auer

1931 A CONNECTICUT YANKEE
Director: David Butler
Co-stars: Will Rogers Myrna Loy William Farnum

1932 PAYMENT DEFERRED
Director: Lothar Mendes
Co-stars: Charles Laughton Ray Milland Verree Teasdale

1932 THE SILVER LINING
Co-star: William Gargan

1932 OKAY AMERICA
Director: Tay Garnett
Co-stars: Lew Ayres Louis Calhern Edward Arnold

1932 SKYSCRAPER SOULS
Director: Edgar Selwyn
Co-stars: Warren William Gregory Ratoff Jean Hersholt

1932 STRANGE INTERLUDE
Director: Robert Z. Leonard
Co-stars: Norma Shearer Clark Gable Robert Young

1932 TARZAN THE APE MAN
Director: W.S. Van Dyke
Co-stars: Johnny Weismuller Neil Hamilton C. Aubrey Smith

1933 THE COHENS AND THE KELLYS IN TROUBLE
Director: Harry Pollard
Co-stars: George Sidney Charles Murray

1933 STAGE MOTHER
Director: Charles Brabin
Co-stars: Alice Brady Franchot Tone Phillips Holmes

1933 TUGBOAT ANNIE
Director: Mervyn LeRoy
Co-stars: Marie Dressler Wallace Beery Robert Young

1934 THE BARRETTS OF WIMPOLE STREET
Director: Sidney Franklin
Co-stars: Charles Laughton Norma Shearer

1934 HIDE-OUT
Director: W.S. Van Dyke
Co-stars: Robert Montgomery Mickey Rooney Edward Arnold

1934 TARZAN AND HIS MATE
Director: Jack Conway
Co-stars: Johnny Weismuller Neil Hamilton Paul Cavanagh

1934 THE THIN MAN
Director: W.S. Van Dyke
Co-stars: William Powell Myrna Loy Nat Pendleton

1935 WEST POINT OF THE AIR
Director: Richard Rossen
Co-stars: Wallace Beery Robert Young Lewis Stone

1935 WOMAN WANTED
Director: George Seitz
Co-stars: Joel McCrea Lewis Stone Louis Calhern

1935 THE FLAME WITHIN
Director: Edmund Goulding
Co-stars: Ann Harding Louis Hayward Herbert Marshall

1935 DAVID COPPERFIELD
Director: George Cukor
Co-stars: Freddie Bartholomew W.C. Fields Roland Young

1935 CARDINAL RICHELIEU
Director: Rowland Lee
Co-stars: George Arliss Edward Arnold Cesar Romero

1935 THE BISHOP MISBEHAVES
Director: E.A. Dupont
Co-stars: Edmund Gwenn Lucile Watson Reginald Owen

1935 ANNA KARENINA
Director: Clarence Brown
Co-stars: Greta Garbo Fredric March Basil Rathbone

1936 THE DEVIL-DOLL
Director: Tod Browning
Co-stars: Lionel Barrymore Frank Lawton Grace Ford

1936 TARZAN ESCAPES
Director: Richard Thorpe
Co-stars: Johnny Weismuller Benita Hume Herbert Mundin

1936 THE VOICE OF BUGLE ANN
Director: Richard Thorpe
Co-stars: Lionel Barrymore Eric Linden Dudley Digges

1937 MY DEAR MISS ALDRICH
Director: George Seitz
Co-stars: Walter Pidgeon Edna May Oliver Rita Johnson

1937 LET US LIVE
Director: John Brahm
Co-stars: Henry Fonda Ralph Bellamy

1937 THE EMPEROR'S CANDLESTICKS
Director: George Fitzmaurice
Co-stars: William Powell Luise Rainer

1937 A DAY AT THE RACES
Director: Sam Wood
Co-stars: Marx Bros. Allan Jones Margaret Dumont

1937 BETWEEN TWO WOMEN
Director: George Seitz
Co-stars: Franchot Tone Virginia Bruce Edward Norris

1938 THE CROWD ROARS
Director: Richard Thorpe
Co-stars: Robert Taylor Edward Arnold Frank Morgan

1938 HOLD THAT KISS
Director: Edwin Marin
Co-stars: Dennis O'Keefe Mickey Rooney George Barbier

1938   **PORT OF SEVEN SEAS**
Director: James Whale
Co-stars: Wallace Beery Frank Morgan John Beal

1938   **SPRING MADNESS**
Director: S. Sylvan Simon
Co-stars: Lew Ayres Ruth Hussey Burgess Meredith

1938   **A YANK AT OXFORD**
Director: Jack Conway
Co-stars: Robert Taylor Vivien Leigh Griffith Jones

1939   **TARZAN FINDS A SON**
Director: Richard Thorpe
Co-stars: Johnny Weismuller Johnny Sheffield Laraine Day

1940   **MAISIE WAS A LADY**
Director: Edwin Marin
Co-stars: Ann Sothern Lew Ayres C. Aubrey Smith

1941   **TARZAN'S SECRET TREASURE**
Director: Richard Thorpe
Co-stars: Barry Fitzgerald Tom Conway Reginald Owen

1940   **PRIDE AND PREJUDICE**
Director: Robert Z. Leonard
Co-stars: Laurence Olivier Greer Garson Edmund Gwenn

1942   **TARZAN'S NEW YORK ADVENTURE**
Director: Richard Thorpe
Co-stars: Johnny Weismuller Charles Bickford Paul Kelly

1948   **THE BIG CLOCK**
Director: John Farrow
Co-stars: Charles Laughton Ray Milland Rita Johnson

1950   **WHERE DANGER LIVES**
Director: John Farrow
Co-stars: Robert Mitchum Faith Domergue Claude Rains

1952   **BONZO GOES TO COLLEGE**
Director: Frederick De Cordova
Co-stars: Charles Drake Edmund Gwenn

1953   **ALL I DESIRE**
Director: Douglas Sirk
Co-stars: Barbara Stanwyck Richard Carlson Lyle Bettger

1953   **DUFFY OF SAN QUENTIN**
Director: Walter Donniger
Co-stars: Louis Hayward Paul Kelly Joanne Dru

1957   **THE TALL T**
Director: Budd Boeticher
Co-stars: Randolph Scott Richard Boone

1965   **NEVER TOO LATE**
Director: Bud Yorkin
Co-stars: Paul Ford Connie Stevens Jim Hutton

1986   **PEGGY SUE GOT MARRIED**
Director: Francis Coppola
Co-stars: Kathleen Turner Nicolas Cage Leon Ames

1986   **HANNAH AND HER SISTERS**
Director: Woody Allen
Co-stars: Mia Farrow Dianne Wiest Michael Caine

1992   **THE HABITATION OF DRAGONS**
Director: Michael Lindsay-Hogg
Co-stars: Brad Davis Lucinda Jenney

MOYA O'SULLIVAN

1982   **GREAT EXPECTATIONS** *(Voice)*
Director: Jean Tych
Co-stars: Bill Kerr Philip Hinton Simon Hinton

1983   **SHERLOCK HOLMES:**
           THE BASKERVILLE CURSE *(Voice)*
Director: Alex Nicholas
Co-stars: Peter O'Toole Helen Morse

CARRE OTIS

1989   **WILD ORCHID**
Director: Zalman King
Co-stars: Jacqueline Bissett Mickey Rourke Assumpta Serna

ANNETTE O'TOOLE

1974   **SMILE**
Director: Michael Ritchie
Co-stars: Bruce Dern Barbara Felden Melanie Griffith

1975   **THE ENTERTAINER**
Director: Donald Wrye
Co-stars: Jack Lemmon Ray Bolger Sada Thompson

1977   **ONE ON ONE**
Director: Lamont Johnson
Co-stars: Robby Benson Gail Strickland

1978   **KING OF THE GYPSIES**
Director: Frank Pierson
Co-stars: Sterling Hayden Shelley Winters Eric Roberts

1980   **FOOLIN' AROUND**
Director: Richard Heffron
Co-stars: Gary Busey Eddie Albert Cloris Leachman

1981   **STAND BY YOUR MAN**
Director: Jerry Jameson
Co-stars: Tim McIntyre Cooper Huckabee James Hampton

1982   **CAT PEOPLE**
Director: Paul Schrader
Co-stars: Nastassja Kinski Malcolm McDowell Ruby Dee

1982   **48 HOURS**
Director: Walter Hill
Co-stars: Nick Nolte Eddie Murphy Frank McRae

1983   **SUPERMAN III**
Director: Richard Lester
Co-stars: Christopher Reeve Richard Pryor Jackie Cooper

1985   **COPACABANA**
Director: Waris Hussein
Co-stars: Barry Manilow Joseph Bologna Estelle Getty

1987   **BROKEN VOWS**
Director: Jud Taylor
Co-stars: Tommy Lee Jones Milo O'Shea M. Emmet Walsh

1987   **CROSS MY HEART**
Director: Armyan Bernstein
Co-stars: Martin Short Paul Reiser Joanna Kerns

1990   **IT**
Director: Tommy Lee Wallace
Co-stars: Tim Curry John Ritter Olivia Hussey

1990   **LOVE AT LARGE**
Director: Alan Rudolph
Co-stars: Tom Berenger Elizabeth Perkins Anne Archer

1992   **DANIELLE STEEL'S JEWELS**
Director: Roger Young
Co-stars: Anthony Andrews Jurgen Prochnow Sheila Gish

1993   **DESPERATE JUSTICE**
Director: Armand Mastroianni
Co-stars: Leslie Ann Warren Bruce Davison

1994   **MY BROTHER'S KEEPER**
Director: Glenn Jordan
Co-stars: John Lithgow Veronica Cartwright

1996   **THE MAN NEXT DOOR**
Director: Lamont Johnson
Co-stars: Michael Ontkean Pamela Reed Vonetta McKee

KATE O'TOOLE

1969   **LAUGHTER IN THE DARK**
Director: Tony Richardson
Co-stars: Nicol Williamson Anna Karina Sian Phillips

RAFAELA OTTIANO

1932 GRAND HOTEL
Director: Edmund Goulding
Co-stars: Greta Garbo John Barrymore Wallace Beery

1932 AS YOU DESIRE ME
Director: George Fitzmaurice
Co-stars: Greta Garbo Melvyn Douglas Owen Moore

1933 SHE DONE HIM WRONG
Director: Lowell Sherman
Co-stars: Mae West Cary Grant Gilbert Roland

1934 GREAT EXPECTATIONS
Director: Stuart Walker
Co-stars: Phillips Holmes Jane Wyatt Henry Hull

1935 CURLY TOP
Director: Irving Cummings
Co-stars: Shirley Temple John Boles Rochelle Hudson

1935 ONE FRIGHTENED NIGHT
Director: Christy Cabanne
Co-stars: Charles Grapewin Mary Carlisle Arthur Hohl

1936 THE DEVIL-DOLL
Director: Tod Browning
Co-stars: Lionel Barrymore Maureen O'Sullivan Frank Lawton

1937 MAYTIME
Director: Robert Z. Leonard
Co-stars: Jeanette MacDonald Nelson Eddy John Barrymore

1938 SUEZ
Director: Allan Dwan
Co-stars: Tyrone Power Loretta Young Annabella

1940 VICTORY
Director: John Cromwell
Co-stars: Fredric March Betty Field Cedric Hardwicke

MIRANDA OTTO

1988 THE THIRTEENTH FLOOR
Director: Chris Roach
Co-stars: Lisa Hemsley Tim McKenzie

1990 THE LAST DAYS OF CHEZ NOUS
Director: Gillian Armstrong
Co-stars: Lisa Harrow Bruno Ganz Kerry Fox

1991 DAYDREAM BELIEVER
Director: Kathy Mueller
Co-stars: Martin Kemp Anne Looby Gia Carides

1996 LOVE SERENADE
Director: Shirley Barrett
Co-star: Rebecca Frith

VICTORIA OTTO

1992 WITH A VENGEANCE
Director: Michael Switzer
Co-stars: Melissa Gilbert Jack Scalia Michael Gross

MIEKO OUCHI

1996 THE WAR BETWEEN US
Director: Anne Wheeler
Co-stars: Shannon Lawson Robert Wisden

DANIELE OUIMET

1971 DAUGHTERS OF DARKNESS
Director: Harry Kumel
Co-stars: Delphine Seyrig John Karlen Paul Esser

MARIA OUSPENSKAYA
Nominated For Best Supporting Actress In 1936 For Dodsworth & In 1939 For Love Affair

1936 DODSWORTH
Director: William Wyler
Co-stars: Walter Huston Mary Astor Ruth Chatterton

1939 LOVE AFFAIR
Director: Leo McCarey
Co-stars: Irene Dunne Charles Boyer Lee Bowman

1939 JUDGE HARDY AND SON
Director: George Seitz
Co-stars: Mickey Rooney Lewis Stone Fay Holden

1939 THE RAINS CAME
Director: Clarence Brown
Co-stars: Tyrone Power Myrna Loy Brenda Joyce

1940 WATERLOO BRIDGE
Director: Mervyn LeRoy
Co-stars: Robert Taylor Vivien Leigh Virginia Field

1940 THE MORTAL STORM
Director: Frank Borzage
Co-stars: James Stewart Margaret Sullavan Frank Morgan

1940 THE MAN I MARRIED
Director: Irving Pichel
Co-stars: Joan Bennett Francis Lederer Anna Sten

1940 DR EHRLICH'S MAGIC BULLET
Director: William Dieterle
Co-stars: Edward G. Robinson Ruth Gordon

1940 DANCE, GIRL, DANCE
Director: Dorothy Arzner
Co-stars: Maureen O'Hara Louis Hayward Lucille Ball

1940 THE WOLF MAN
Director: George Waggner
Co-stars: Lon Chaney Claude Rains Bela Lugosi

1941 THE SHANGHAI GESTURE
Director: Josef Von Sternberg
Co-stars: Ona Munsen Victor Mature Walter Huston

1942 KING'S ROW
Director: Sam Wood
Co-stars: Robert Cummings Ronald Reagan Ann Sheridan

1942 THE MYSTERY OF MARIE ROGET
Director: Phil Rosen
Co-stars: Maria Montez Patric Knowles John Litel

1943 FRANKENSTEIN MEETS THE WOLFMAN
Director: Roy William Neill
Co-stars: Lon Chaney Bela Lugosi Ilona Massey

1945 TARZAN AND THE AMAZONS
Director: Kurt Neuman
Co-stars: Johnny Weismuller Johnny Sheffield Brenda Joyce

1946 I'VE ALWAYS LOVED YOU
Director: Frank Borzage
Co-stars: Philip Dorn Catherine McLeod Felix Bressart

1949 A KISS IN THE DARK
Director: Delmer Daves
Co-stars: David Niven Jane Wyman Broderick Crawford

PARK OVERALL *(Child)*

1993 HOUSE OF CARDS
Director: Michael Lessac
Co-stars: Kathleen Turner Shiloh Strong Tommy Lee Jones

1993 PRECIOUS VICTIMS
Director: Peter Levin
Co-stars: Richard Thomas Robby Benson

KELLIE OVERBEY

1991 DEFENSELESS
Director: Martin Campbell
Co-stars: Barbara Hershey Sam Shepard Sheree North

CATHERINE DALE OWEN

1929   **HIS GLORIOUS NIGHT**
Director: Lionel Barrymore
Co-stars: John Gilbert Hedda Hopper Nance O'Neill

1930   **BORN RECKLESS**
Director: John Ford
Co-stars: Edmund Lowe Lee Tracy Marguerite Churchill

1930   **SUCH MEN ARE DANGEROUS**
Director: Kenneth Hawks
Co-stars: Warner Baxter Hedda Hopper

1930   **THE ROGUE SONG**
Director: Lionel Barrymore
Co-stars: Laurence Tibbett Stan Laurel Oliver Hardy

CLARE OWEN

1963   **SHADOW OF FEAR**
Director: Ernest Morris
Co-stars: Paul Maxwell Anita West Alan Tilvern

1963   **ECHO OF DIANA**
Director: Ernest Morris
Co-stars: Vincent Ball Betty McDowall Geoffrey Toone

GILLIAN OWEN

1958   **A LADY MISLAID**
Director: David MacDonald
Co-stars: Phyllis Calvert Alan White Thorley Walters

MEG WYNN OWEN

1973   **BLUE BLOOD**
Director: Andrew Sinclair
Co-stars: Oliver Reed Derek Jacobi Anna Gael

1987   **WHITE LADY**
Director: David Rudkin
Co-stars: Cornelius Garrett Sophie Thompson Jessica Martin

NANCY LEA OWEN

1984   **THE RIVER RAT**
Director: Tom Rickman
Co-stars: Tommy Lee Jones Brian Dennehy Martha Plimpton

RENA OWEN

1994   **ONCE WERE WARRIORS**
Director: Lee Tamahori
Co-star: Temuera Morrison

SEENA OWEN

1919   **THE FALL OF BABYLON**
Director: D.W. Griffith
Co-stars: Tully Marshall Constance Talmadge Elmer Clifton

1929   **QUEEN KELLY**
Director: Erich Von Stroheim
Co-stars: Gloria Swanson Walter Byron Madge Hunt

VIRGINIA OWEN

1947   **THUNDER MOUNTAIN**
Co-star: Jason Robards

YVONNE OWEN

1945   **THE SEVENTH VEIL**
Director: Compton Bennett
Co-stars: James Mason Ann Todd Herbert Lom

1946   **A GIRL IN A MILLION**
Director: Francis Searle
Co-stars: Joan Greenwood Hugh Williams Basil Radford

1947   **HOLIDAY CAMP**
Director: Ken Annakin
Co-stars: Jack Warner Kathleen Harrison Hazel Court

1948   **MY BROTHER'S KEEPER**
Director: Roy Rich
Co-stars: Jack Warner George Cole Jane Hylton

1949   **THIRD TIME LUCKY**
Director: Gordon Parry
Co-stars: Glynis Johns Dermot Walsh Charles Goldner

1950   **SOMEONE AT THE DOOR**
Director: Francis Searle
Co-stars: Michael Medwin Garry Marsh

AYSE OWENS

1992   **THE LONG DAY CLOSES**
Director: Terence Davies
Co-stars: Marjorie Yates Leigh McCormack Tina Malone

PAT OWENS

1951   **MYSTERY JUNCTION**
Director: Michael McCarthy
Co-stars: Sidney Tafler Barbara Murray Martin Benson

PATRICIA OWENS

1957   **SAYONARA**
Director: Joshua Logan
Co-stars: Marlon Brando Miyoshi Umeka Red Buttons

1957   **ISLAND IN THE SUN**
Director: Robert Rossen
Co-stars: James Mason Harry Belafonte Dorothy Dandridge

1957   **NO DOWN PAYMENT**
Director: Martin Ritt
Co-stars: Joanne Woodward Tony Randall Sheree North

1958   **THE LAW AND JAKE WADE**
Director: John Sturges
Co-stars: Robert Taylor Richard Widmark Henry Silva

1958   **THE GUN RUNNERS**
Director: Don Siegel
Co-stars: Audie Murphy Eddie Albert Everett Sloane

1958   **THE FLY**
Director: Kurt Neumann
Co-stars: David Hedison Herbert Marshall Vincent Price

1958   **THESE THOUSAND HILLS**
Director: Richard Fleischer
Co-stars: Don Murray Lee Remick Stuart Whitman

1959   **FIVE GATES TO HELL**
Director: James Clavell
Co-stars: Dolores Michaels Neville Brand Kevin Scott

1960   **HELL TO ETERNITY**
Director: Phil Carson
Co-stars: Jeffrey Hunter David Janssen Vic Damone

CATHERINE OXENBURG

1987   **STILL CRAZY LIKE A FOX**
Director: Paul Krasny
Co-stars: Jack Warden John Rubenstein Robbie Kiger

1988   **THE LAIR OF THE WHITE WORM**
Director: Ken Russell
Co-stars: Amanda Donohoe Hugh Grant

1989   **SWIMSUIT**
Director: Chris Thomson
Co-stars: William Katt Cyd Charisse Nia Peeples

1989   **TRENCHCOAT IN PARADISE**
Director: Martha Coolidge
Co-stars: Dirk Benedict Bruce Dern Michelle Phillips

1993 RUBDOWN
Director: Stuart Cooper
Co-stars: Jack Coleman Michelle Phillips William Devane

1994 TREACHEROUS BEAUTIES
Director: Charles Jarrot
Co-stars: Emma Samms Bruce Greenwood Mark Humphreys

DAPHNE OXENFORD

1974 ALL CREATURES GREAT AND SMALL
Director: Claude Whatham
Co-stars: Simon Ward Anthony Hopkins Lisa Harrow

1980 SWEET WILLIAM
Director: Claude Whatham
Co-stars: Sam Waterston Jenny Agutter Anna Massey

MADELEINE OZERAY

1935 CRIME AND PUNISHMENT
Director: Pierre Chenal
Co-stars: Pierre Blanchar Harry Baur Marcelle Geniat

1939 LA FIN DU JOUR
Director: Julien Duvivier
Co-stars: Victor Francen Louis Jouvet Michel Simon

JUDY PACE

1968 THREE IN THE ATTIC
Director: Richard Wilson
Co-stars: Chris Jones Yvette Mimieux Maggie Turett

1968 THE THOMAS CROWN AFFAIR
Director: Norman Jewison
Co-stars: Steve McQueen Faye Dunaway Paul Burke

1970 UP IN THE CELLAR
Director: Theodore Flicker
Co-stars: Wes Stern Joan Collins Larry Hagman

1970 COTTON COMES TO HARLEM
Director: Ossie Davis
Co-stars: Godfrey Cambridge Raymond St. Jacques Redd Foxx

1971 BRIAN'S SONG
Director: Buzz Kulik
Co-stars: Billy Dee Williams James Caan Jack Warden

1972 COOL BREEZE
Director: Barry Pollack
Co-stars: Thalmus Rasulala Raymond St. Jacques Jim Watkins

1972 FROGS
Director: George McCowan
Co-stars: Ray Milland Joan Van Ark Sam Elliott

STEPHANIE PACK

1992 THE HOURS AND THE TIMES
Director: Christopher Munch
Co-stars: Ian Hart David Angus

JOANNA PACULA

1983 GORKY PARK
Director: Michael Apted
Co-stars: William Hurt Lee Marvin Brian Dennehy

1985 NOT QUITE JERUSALEM
Director: Lewis Gilbert
Co-stars: Sam Robards Kevin McNally Selina Cadell

1987 DEATH BEFORE DISHONOR
Director: Terry Leonard
Co-stars: Fred Dryer Brian Keith Paul Winfield

1988 THE KISS
Director: Pen Densham
Co-stars: Nicholas Kilbertus Meredith Salenger Mimi Kusyk

1989 BREAKING POINT
Director: Peter Markle
Co-stars: Corbin Bernsen John Glover David Marshall

1990 MARKED FOR DEATH
Director: Dwight Little
Co-stars: Steven Seagal Keith David Tom Wright

1992 A PASSION FOR MURDER
Director: Neill Fearnley
Co-stars: Michael Nouri Michael Ironside Victor Cowie

1993 UNDER INVESTIGATION
Director: Kevin Meyer
Co-stars: Harry Hamlin Ed Lauter

1993 WARLOCK: THE ARMAGEDDON
Director: Anthony Hickox
Co-stars: Julian Sands Chris Young Paula Marshall

1994 LAST GASP
Director: Scott McGinnis
Co-stars: Robert Patrick Mimi Craven

DEBBIE PADBURY

1979 ELECTRIC ESKIMO
Director: Frank Godwin
Co-stars: Kris Emmerson Ian Sears

WENDY PADBURY

1970 BLOOD ON SATAN'S CLAW
Director: Piers Haggard
Co-stars: Patrick Wymark Linda Hayden Simon Williams

SARA PADDEN

1931 THE YELLOW TICKET
Director: Raoul Walsh
Co-stars: Elissa Landi Laurence Olivier Lionel Barrymore

1932 YOUNG AMERICA
Director: Frank Borzage
Co-stars: Spencer Tracy Doris Kenyon Ralph Bellamy

1941 MURDER BY INVITATION
Co-star: Wallace Ford

1943 ASSIGNMENT IN BRITTANY
Director: Jack Conway
Co-stars: Jean-Pierre Aumont Signe Hasso Susan Peters

1946 WILD WEST
Co-stars: Al "Lash" Larue Louise Currie Roscoe Ates

DAPHNE PADEL

1950 THE TWENTY QUESTIONS MURDER MYSTERY
Director: Paul Stein
Co-stars: Robert Beatty Rona Anderson

MARIA PADILHA

1988 LAND
Director: David Wheatley
Co-stars: John Terry Bebeto Baia Rui Polanah

LEA PADOVANI

1947 CALL OF THE BLOOD
Director: John Clements
Co-stars: Kay Hammond John Justin Robert Rietti

1949 GIVE US THIS DAY
Director: Edward Dmytryk
Co-stars: Sam Wanamaker Kathleen Ryan Bonar Colleano

1951 HONEYMOON DEFERRED
Director: Mario Camerini
Co-stars: Griffith Jones Sally Ann Howes Kieron Moore

1956 AN EYE FOR AN EYE
Director: Andre Cayatte
Co-stars: Curt Jurgens Folco Lulli

1959 THE NAKED MAJA
Director: Henry Koster
Co-stars: Anthony Franciosa Ava Gardner Gino Cervi

1964 THE EMPTY CANVAS
Director: Damiano Damiani
Co-stars: Bette Davis Horst Buchholz Catherine Spaak

ANA PADRAO

1989   1871
Director: Ken McMullen
Co-stars: Roshan Seth John Lynch Timothy Spall

1993   THE EDGE OF THE HORIZON
Director: Fernando Lopes
Co-stars: Claude Brasseur Andre Ferreol

DIRA PAES

1988   LAND
Director: David Wheatley
Co-stars: John Terry Bebeto Baia Maria Padilha

GIULIA PAGANO

1981   THE ANTAGONISTS
Director: Boris Sagal
Co-stars: Peter O'Toole Peter Strauss Barbara Carrera

ANITA PAGE

1928   OUR DANCING DAUGHTERS
Director: Harry Beaumont
Co-stars: Joan Crawford Johnny Mack Brown Nils Asther

1929   OUR MODERN MAIDENS
Co-stars: Joan Crawford Douglas Fairbanks Jnr Rod La Rocque

1929   BROADWAY MELODY
Director: Harry Beaumont
Co-stars: Bessie Love Charles King Jed Prouty

1930   OUR BLUSHING BRIDES
Co-stars: Joan Crawford Robert Montgomery Dorothy Sebastian

1930   CAUGHT SHORT
Director: Charles Reisner
Co-stars: Marie Dressler Polly Moran Charles Morton

1930   FREE AND EASY
Director: Edward Sedgewick
Co-stars: Buster Keaton Robert Montgomery Trixie Friganza

1930   LITTLE ACCIDENT
Director: William James Craft
Co-stars: Douglas Fairbanks Sally Blane Zasu Pitts

1931   THE EASIEST WAY
Director: Jack Conway
Co-stars: Constance Bennett Robert Montgomery Clark Gable

1931   GENTLEMAN'S FATE
Director: Mervyn LeRoy
Co-stars: John Gilbert Leila Hyams Louis Wolheim

1931   REDUCING
Director: Charles Reisner
Co-stars: Marie Dressler Polly Moran Sally Eilers

1931   SIDEWALKS OF NEW YORK
Director: Jules White
Co-stars: Buster Keaton Cliff Edwards Frank Rowan

1932   SKYSCRAPER SOULS
Director: Edgar Selwyn
Co-stars: Warren William Maureen O'Sullivan Jean Hersholt

1932   PROSPERITY
Director: Sam Wood
Co-stars: Marie Dressler Polly Moran Norman Foster

1932   NIGHT COURT
Director: W.S. Van Dyke
Co-stars: Walter Huston Lewis Stone Jean Hersholt

1932   ARE YOU LISTENING ?
Director: Harry Beaumont
Co-stars: William Haines Karen Morley Madge Evans

1933   THE BIG CAGE
Director: Kurt Neuman
Co-stars: Clyde Beatty Mickey Rooney Andy Devine

1933   JUNGLE BRIDE
Co-star: Charles Starrett

DOROTHY PAGE

1935   KING SOLOMON OF BROADWAY
Director: Alan Crosland
Co-stars: Edmund Lowe Pinky Tomlin Louise Henry

1938   WATER RUSTLERS
Co-star: Dave O'Brien

GALE PAGE

1938   CRIME SCHOOL
Director: Lewis Seiler
Co-stars: Humphrey Bogart Dead End Kids Billy Halop

1938   HEART OF THE NORTH
Director: Lewis Seiler
Co-stars: Dick Foran Gloria Dickson Allen Jenkins

1938   THE AMAZING DR CLITTERHOUSE
Director: Anatole Litvak
Co-stars: Edward G. Robinson Claire Trevor Humphrey Bogart

1938   FOUR DAUGHTERS
Director: Michael Curtiz
Co-stars: Priscilla Rosemary Lola Lane Claude Rains

1939   DAUGHTERS COURAGEOUS
Director: Michael Curtiz
Co-stars: Lola Lane John Garfield Jeffrey Lynn

1939   FOUR WIVES
Director: Michael Curtiz
Co-stars: Lola Lane May Robson Eddie Albert

1939   A CHILD IS BORN
Director: Lloyd Bacon
Co-stars: Geraldine Fitzgerald Jeffrey Lynn Gladys George

1939   INDIANAPOLIS SPEEDWAY
Director: Lloyd Bacon
Co-stars: Pat O'Brien John Payne Ann Sheridan

1939   NAUGHTY BUT NICE
Director: Ray Enright
Co-stars: Dick Powell Ann Sheridan Ronald Reagan

1939   YOU CAN'T GET AWAY WITH MURDER
Director: Lewis Seiler
Co-stars: Humphrey Bogart Bally Halop Henry Travers

1940   THEY DRIVE BY NIGHT
Director: Raoul Walsh
Co-stars: George Raft Humphrey Bogart Ida Lupino

1940   KNUTE ROCKNE, ALL AMERICAN
Director: Lloyd Bacon
Co-stars: Pat O'Brien Ronald Reagan Donald Crisp

1941   FOUR MOTHERS
Director: William Keighley
Co-stars: Lola Lane Claude Rains Dick Foran

1948   THE TIME OF YOUR LIFE
Director: H.C. Potter
Co-stars: James Cagney William Bendix Wayne Morris

1949   ANNA LUCASTA
Director: Irving Rapper
Co-stars: Paulette Goddard Oscar Homolka Broderick Crawford

GENEVIEVE PAGE

1951   FANFAN LA TULIPE
Director: Christian-Jacque
Co-stars: Gerard Philipe Gina Lollobrigida

1956   **FOREIGN INTRIQUE**
Director: Sheldon Reynolds
Co-stars: Robert Mitchum Ingrid Thulin Eugene Deckers

1956   **THE SILKEN AFFAIR**
Director: Roy Kelling
Co-stars: David Niven Ronald Squire Beatrice Straight

1960   **SONG WITHOUT END**
Director: George Cukor
Co-stars: Dirk Bogarde Capucine Patricia Morison

1961   **EL CID**
Director: Anthony Mann
Co-stars: Charlton Heston Sophia Loren Raf Vallone

1964   **TODAY WE LIVE**
Co-star: Simone Signoret

1964   **YOUNGBLOOD HAWKE**
Director: Delmer Daves
Co-stars: James Franciscus Suzanne Pleshette Eva Gabor

1966   **GRAND PRIX**
Director: John Frankenheimer
Co-stars: James Garner Eva Marie Saint Yves Montand

1967   **BELLE DE JOUR**
Director: Luis Bunuel
Co-stars: Catherine Deneuve Jean Sorel Michel Piccoli

1968   **MAYERLING**
Director: Terence Young
Co-stars: Catherine Deneuve Omar Sharif James Mason

1968   **DECLINE AND FALL**
Director: John Frish
Co-stars: Robin Phillips Donald Wolfit Leo McKern

1969   **A TALENT FOR LOVING**
Director: Richard Quine
Co-stars: Richard Widmark Cesar Romero Topol

1970   **THE PRIVATE LIFE OF SHERLOCK HOLMES**
Director: Billy Wilder
Co-stars: Robert Stephens Colin Blakely

1979   **BUFFET FROID**
Director: Bertrand Blier
Co-stars: Gerard Depardieu Bernard Blier Jean Carmet

1983   **DEADLY RUN**
Director: Claude Miller
Co-stars: Isabelle Adjani Michel Serrault Guy Marchand

1986   **BEYOND THERAPY**
Director: Robert Altman
Co-stars: Glenda Jackson Tom Conti Jeff Goldblum

GERALDINE PAGE

Best Actress In 1985 For "The Trip To Bountiful". Nominated For Best Actress In 1961 For "Summer And Smoke", In 1962 For "Sweet Bird Of Youth" And In 1978 For "Interiors". Nominated For Best Supporting Actress In 1954 For "Hondo", In 1967 For "You're A Big Boy Now", In 1972 For "Pete 'N' Tillie", In 1984 For "The Pope Of Greenwich Village"

1954   **HONDO**
Director: John Farrow
Co-stars: John Wayne Ward Bond Michael Pate

1961   **SUMMER AND SMOKE**
Director: Peter Glenville
Co-stars: Laurence Harvey Una Merkel Rita Moreno

1962   **SWEET BIRD OF YOUTH**
Director: Richard Brooks
Co-stars: Paul Newman Ed Begley Rip Torn

1963   **TOYS IN THE ATTIC**
Director: George Roy Hill
Co-stars: Wendy Hiller Dean Martin Gene Tierney

1964   **DEAR HEART**
Director: Delbert Mann
Co-stars: Glenn Ford Angela Lansbury Charles Drake

1967   **THE HAPPIEST MILLIONAIRE**
Director: Norman Tokar
Co-stars: Fred MacMurray Tommy Steele Greer Garson

1967   **YOU'RE A BIG BOY NOW**
Director: Francis Ford Coppola
Co-stars: Peter Kastner Elizabeth Hartman

1969   **WHATEVER HAPPENED TO AUNT ALICE ?**
Director: Lee Katzin
Co-stars: Ruth Gordon Rosemary Forsyth

1971   **J.W. COOP**
Director: Cliff Robertson
Co-stars: Christina Ferrare R.G. Armstrong

1971   **THE BEGUILED**
Director: Don Siegel
Co-stars: Clint Eastwood Elizabeth Hartman Jo Ann Harris

1972   **PETE 'N' TILLIE**
Director: Martin Ritt
Co-stars: Walter Matthau Carol Burnett Rene Auberjonois

1975   **DAY OF THE LOCUST**
Director: John Schlesinger
Co-stars: William Atherton Karen Black Donald Sutherland

1976   **NASTY HABITS**
Director: Michael Lindsay-Hogg
Co-stars: Glenda Jackson Edith Evans Sandy Dennis

1977   **THE RESCUERS (VOICE)**
Director: Art Stevens
Co-stars: Bob Newhart Eva Gabor John McIntyre

1978   **INTERIORS**
Director: Woody Allen
Co-stars: Richard Jordan Diane Keaton Maureen Stapleton

1981   **HONKY TONK FREEWAY**
Director: John Schlesinger
Co-stars: William Devane Beau Bridges Teri Garr

1982   **I'M DANCING AS FAST AS I CAN**
Director: Jack Hofsiss
Co-stars: Jill Clayburgh Nicol Williamson

1983   **LOVING**
Director: Michael Lindsay-Hogg
Co-star: Lloyd Bridges

1984   **THE DOLLMAKER**
Director: Daniel Petrie
Co-stars: Jane Fonda Levon Helm Susan Kingsley

1984   **THE PARADE**
Director: Peter Hunt
Co-stars: Frederic Forrest Michael Learned Rosanna Arquette

1984   **THE POPE OF GREENWICH VILLAGE**
Director: Stuart Rosenberg
Co-stars: Eric Roberts Mickey Rourke

1985   **THE BRIDE**
Director: Franc Roddam
Co-stars: Sting Jennifer Beals David Rappaport

1985   **WHITE NIGHTS**
Director: Taylor Hackford
Co-stars: Mikhail Baryshnikov Gregory Hines Helen Mirren

1985   **THE TRIP TO BOUNTIFUL**
Director: Peter Masterson
Co-stars: Rebecca De Mornay John Heard

1985 WALLS OF GLASS
Director: Scott Goldstein
Co-stars: Philip Bosco Olympia Dukakis Linda Thorson

1986 NATIVE SON
Director: Jerrold Freedman
Co-stars: Carroll Baker Matt Dillon Art Evans

1986 MY LITTLE GIRL
Director: Connie Kaiserman
Co-stars: James Earl Jones Mary Stuart Masterson

IDA PAGE

1974 AKENFIELD
Director: Peter Hall
Co-stars: Garrow Shand Peggy Cole Barbara Tilney

JOANNE PAGE

1948 MAN-EATER OF KUMAON
Director: Byron Haskin
Co-stars: Sabu Wendell Corey Morris Carnovsky

JOY PAGE

1950 THE BULLFIGHTER AND THE LADY
Director: Budd Boetticher
Co-stars: Robert Stack Gilbert Roland Katy Jurado

1953 FIGHTER ATTACK
Director: Lesley Selander
Co-stars: Sterling Hayden Kenneth Tobey J. Carrol Naish

1953 CONQUEST OF COCHISE
Director: William Castle
Co-stars: Robert Stack John Hodiak

1955 THE SHRIKE
Director: Jose Ferrer
Co-stars: June Allyson Jacqueline De Wit Kendall Clark

JOY ANN PAGE

1944 KISMET
Director: William Dieterle
Co-stars: Ronald Colman Marlene Dietrich James Craig

KATHERINE PAGE

1966 MISS MacTAGGART WON'T LIE DOWN
Director: Francis Searle
Co-stars: Barbara Mullen Eric Woodburn

LAWANDA PAGE

1983 MAUSOLEUM
Director: Michael Dugan
Co-stars: Bobbie Bresee Marjoe Gortner Norman Burton

PATTI PAGE

1960 ELMER GANTRY
Director: Richard Brooks
Co-stars: Burt Lancaster Jean Simmons Shirley Jones

1960 DONDI
Director: Albert Zugsmith
Co-stars: David Janssen Mickey Shaughnessy Robert Strauss

1962 BOYS' NIGHT OUT
Director: Michael Gordon
Co-stars: James Garner Kim Novak Howard Duff

REBECCA PAGE

1979 DANNY
Director: Gene Feldman
Co-stars: Janet Zarish Gloria Maddox

DEBRA PAGET

1948 CRY OF THE CITY
Director: Robert Siodmak
Co-stars: Victor Mature Richard Conte Shelley Winters

1948 HOUSE OF STRANGERS
Director: Jospeh Mankiewicz
Co-stars: Edward G. Robinson Susan Hayward Richard Conte

1950 BROKEN ARROW
Director: Delmer Daves
Co-stars: James Stewart Jeff Chandler Arthur Hunnicutt

1951 ANNE OF THE INDIES
Director: Jacques Tourneur
Co-stars: Jean Peters Louis Jourdan Thomas Gomez

1951 BIRD OF PARADISE
Director: Delmer Daves
Co-stars: Louis Jourdan Jeff Chandler Everett Sloane

1951 FOURTEEN HOURS
Director: Henry Hathaway
Co-stars: Richard Basehart Paul Douglas Grace Kelly

1951 BELLES ON THEIR TOES
Director: Henry Levin
Co-stars: Myrna Loy Jeanne Crain Hoagy Carmichael

1952 LES MISERABLES
Director: Lewis Milestone
Co-stars: Michael Rennie Robert Newton Sylvia Sidney

1952 STARS AND STRIPES FOREVER
Director: Henry Koster
Co-stars: Clifton Webb Ruth Hussey Robert Wagner

1954 SEVEN ANGRY MEN
Director: Charles Marquis Warren
Co-stars: Raymond Massey Jeffrey Hunter John Smith

1954 PRINCESS OF THE NILE
Director: Harmon Jones
Co-stars: Michael Rennie Jeffrey Hunter Dona Drake

1954 PRINCE VALIANT
Director: Henry Hathaway
Co-stars: Robert Wagner James Mason Janet Leigh

1954 THE GAMBLER FROM NATCHEZ
Director: Henry Levin
Co-stars: Dale Robertson Thomas Gomez Woody Strode

1954 DEMETRIUS AND THE GLADIATORS
Director: Delmer Daves
Co-stars: Victor Mature Susan Hayward Michael Rennie

1955 WHITE FEATHER
Director: Robert Webb
Co-stars: Robert Wagner Jeffrey Hunter John Lund

1956 THE TEN COMMANDMENTS
Director: Cecil B. DeMille
Co-stars: Charlton Heston Yvonne De Carlo Yul Brynner

1956 THE RIVER'S EDGE
Director: Allan Dwan
Co-stars: Ray Milland Anthony Quinn Harry Carey

1956 LOVE ME TENDER
Director: Robert Webb
Co-stars: Elvis Presley Richard Egan William Campbell

1956 THE LAST HUNT
Director: Richard Brooks
Co-stars: Robert Taylor Stewart Granger Russ Tamblyn

1957 OMAR KHAYYAM
Director: William Dieterle
Co-stars: Cornel Wilde Michael Rennie Raymond Massey

1958 **FROM THE EARTH TO THE MOON**
Director: Byron Haskin
Co-stars: Joseph Cotten George Sanders

1962 **TALES OF TERROR**
Director: Roger Corman
Co-stars: Vincent Price Peter Lorre Basil Rathbone

1963 **THE HAUNTED PALACE**
Director: Roger Corman
Co-stars: Vincent Price Lon Chaney Leo Gordon

TINA PAGET-BROWN

1968 **THE GREAT PONY RAID**
Director: Frederick Goode
Co-stars: Edward Underdown Patrick Barr Michael Brennan

NICOLA PAGETT

1967 **THE VIKING QUEEN**
Director: Don Chaffey
Co-stars: Don Murray Donald Houston Andrew Keir

1975 **OPERATION DAYBREAK**
Director: Lewis Gilbert
Co-stars: Timothy Bottoms Martin Shaw Joss Ackland

1978 **OLIVER'S STORY**
Director: John Korty
Co-stars: Ryan O'Neal Candice Bergen Ray Milland

1982 **PRIVATES ON PARADE**
Director: Michael Blakemore
Co-stars: John Cleese Dennis Quilley Michael Elphick

1987 **SCOOP**
Director: Gavin Miller
Co-stars: Michael Maloney Donald Pleasence Denholm Elliott

1987 **VISITORS**
Director: Piers Haggard
Co-stars: Michael Brandon John Standing Glynis Barber

JACQUELINE PAGNOL
(Married Marcel Pagnol)

1986 **MANON DES SOURCES**
Director: Marcel Pagnol
Co-stars: Raymond Pellegrin Henri Vibert Henri Poupon

SUZEE PAI

1986 **BIG TROUBLE IN LITTLE CHINA**
Director: John Carpenter
Co-stars: Kurt Russell Kim Cattrall James Hong

ELAINE PAGE

1978 **ADVENTURES OF A PLUMBER'S MATE**
Director: Stanley Long
Co-stars: Christopher Neil Arther Mullard

1989 **UNEXPLAINED LAUGHTER**
Director: Gareth Davies
Co-stars: Diana Rigg Joanna David Jon Finch

1989 **A VIEW OF HARRY CLARK**
Director: Alastair Reid
Co-stars: Griff Rhys Jones Charlotte Coleman Ian Hart

JANIS PAIGE

1944 **HOLLYWOOD CANTEEN**
Director: Delmer Daves
Co-stars: Joan Leslie Robert Hutton Dane Clark

1946 **OF HUMAN BONDAGE**
Director: Edmund Goulding
Co-stars: Paul Henreid Eleanor Parker Alexis Smith

1946 **TWO GUYS FROM MILWAUKIE**
Director: David Butler
Co-stars: Dennis Morgan Jack Carson Joan Leslie

1946 **THE TIME, THE PLACE AND THE GIRL**
Director: David Butler
Co-stars: Dennis Morgan Jack Carson

1946 **HER KIND OF MAN**
Director: Frederick De Cordova
Co-stars: Dane Clark Zachary Scot George Tobias

1947 **LOVE AND LEARN**
Director: Frederick De Cordova
Co-stars: Jack Carson Robert Hutton

1947 **CHEYENNE**
Director: Raoul Walsh
Co-stars: Dennis Morgan Jane Wyman Arthur Kennedy

1948 **ONE SUNDAY AFTERNOON**
Director: Raoul Walsh
Co-stars: Dennis Morgan Dorothy Malone Don Defore

1948 **ROMANCE ON THE HIGH SEAS**
Director: Michael Curtiz
Co-stars: Doris Day Jack Carson Oscar Levant

1948 **WALLFLOWER**
Director: Frederick De Cordova
Co-stars: Joyce Reynolds Robert Hutton

1948 **WINTER MEETING**
Director: Bretaigne Windust
Co-stars: Bette Davis Jim Davis Florence Bates

1949 **THE YOUNGER BROTHERS**
Director: Edwin Marin
Co-stars: Wayne Morris Bruce Bennett Robert Hutton

1949 **THE HOUSE ACROSS THE STREET**
Director: Richard Bare
Co-stars: Wayne Morris James Mitchell Alan Hale

1951 **MR UNIVERSE**
Director: Joseph Lerner
Co-stars: Bert Lahr Jack Carson Robert Alda

1957 **SILK STOCKINGS**
Director: Rouben Mamoulian
Co-stars: Fred Astaire Cyd Charisse Peter Lorre

1960 **PLEASE DON'T EAT THE DAISIES**
Director: Charles Walters
Co-stars: Doris Day David Niven Patsy Kelly

1961 **BACHELOR IN PARADISE**
Director: Jack Arnold
Co-stars: Bob Hope Lana Turner Paula Prentiss

1963 **THE CARETAKERS**
Director: Hall Bartlett
Co-stars: Polly Bergen Joan Crawford Robert Stack

1963 **FOLLOW THE BOYS**
Director: Richard Thorpe
Co-stars: Connie Francis Paula Prentiss Russ Tamblyn

1967 **WELCOME TO HARD TIMES**
Director: Burt Kennedy
Co-stars: Henry Fonda Janice Rule Warren Oates

1980 **ANGEL ON MY SHOULDER**
Director: John Berry
Co-stars: Peter Strauss Richard Kiley Barbara Hershey

1984 **NO MAN'S LAND**
Director: Rod Holcomb
Co-stars: Stella Stevens Terri Garber Robert Webber

MABEL PAIGE

1942 YOUNG AND WILLING
Director: Edward Griffith
Co-stars: William Holden Susan Hayward Eddie Bracken

1942 HAPPY GO LUCKY
Director: Curtis Bernhardt
Co-stars: Mary Martin Dick Powell Betty Hutton

1942 LUCKY JORDAN
Director: Frank Tuttle
Co-stars: Alan Ladd Helen Walker Marie McDonald

1943 THE GOOD FELLOWS
Director: Jo Graham
Co-stars: Cecil Kellaway Helen Walker James Brown

1943 TRUE TO LIFE
Director: George Marshall
Co-stars: Mary Martin Dick Powell Franchot Tone

1944 YOU CAN'T RATION LOVE
Director: Lester Fuller
Co-stars: Betty Jane Rhodes Johnnie Johnston Marie Wilson

1945 MURDER HE SAYS
Director: George Marshall
Co-stars: Fred MacMurray Marjorie Main Helen Walker

1945 DANGEROUS PARTNERS
Director: Edward Cahn
Co-stars: James Craig Signe Hasso Edmund Gwenn

1946 NOCTURNE
Director: Edwin Marin
Co-stars: George Raft Lynn Bari Virginia Huston

1947 HER HUSBAND'S AFFAIRS
Director: S. Sylvan Simon
Co-stars: Lucille Ball Franchot Tone Gene Lockhart

1948 JOHNNY BELINDA
Director: Jean Negulesco
Co-stars: Jane Wyman Lew Ayres Charles Bickford

1948 THE SCAR
Director: Steve Sekely
Co-stars: Joan Bennett Paul Henreid Eduard Franz

1950 EDGE OF DOOM
Director: Mark Robson
Co-stars: Dana Andrews Farley Granger Joan Evans

PATSY PAIGE

1930 LILIES OF THE FIELD
Director: Alexander Korda
Co-stars: Corinne Griffith Ralph Forbes John Loder

CHRISTINE PAK

1987 90 DAYS
Director: Giles Walker
Co-stars: Stefan Wodoslawsky Sam Grana Farnanda Tavares

HOLLY PALANCE

1985 THE BEST OF TIMES
Director: Roger Spottiswoode
Co-stars: Robin Williams Kurt Russell Pamela Reed

NATALIE PALIE

1935 SYLVIA SCARLETT
Director: George Cukor
Co-stars: Katherine Hepburn Cary Grant Edmund Gwenn

GERALDINE PALIHAS

1992 IP5
Director: Jean-Jacques Beineix
Co-stars: Yves Montand Olivier Martinez Sekkou Sall

OLGA PALINKAS

1973 F FOR FAKE
Director: Orson Welles
Co-stars: Joseph Cotten Francois Reichenbach Orson Welles

ANNA PALK

1966 THE FROZEN DEAD
Director: Herbert Leder
Co-stars: Dana Andrews Philip Gilbert Kathleen Breck

1972 TOWER OF EVIL
Director: Jim O'Connolly
Co-stars: Bryant Halliday Jill Haworth William Lucas

ANITA PALLENBERG

1967 BARBARELLA
Director: Roger Vadim
Co-stars: Jane Fonda John Phillip Law David Hemmings

1970 PERFORMANCE
Director: Nicolas Roeg
Co-stars: James Fox Mick Jagger Michele Breton

GABRIELLA PALLOTTA

1957 IL GRIDO
Director: Michelangelo Antonioni
Co-stars: Steve Cochran Alida Valli Betsy Blair

1962 THE PIGEON THAT TOOK ROME
Director: Melville Shavelson
Co-stars: Charlton Heston Elsa Martinelli

1964 ARM OF FIRE
Director: Richard McNamara
Co-stars: Gordon Scott Massimo Serato

1974 FOOTBALL CRAZY
Director: Luigi Filipo D'Amico
Co-stars: Lando Buzzanca Joan Collins Daniele Vargas

BETSY PALMER

1955 THE LONG GRAY LINE
Director: John Ford
Co-stars: Tyrone Power Maureen O'Hara Donald Crisp

1955 MISTER ROBERTS
Director: Mervyn LeRoy
Co-stars: Henry Fonda James Cagney William Powell

1955 QUEEN BEE
Director: Ranald MacDougall
Co-stars: Joan Crawford Barry Sullivan John Ireland

1957 THE TIN STAR
Director: Anthony Mann
Co-stars: Henry Fonda Anthony Perkins Neville Brand

1959 THE LAST ANGRY MAN
Director: Daniel Mann
Co-stars: Paul Muni David Wayne Luther Adler

1980 FRIDAY THE 13TH
Director: Sean Cunningham
Co-stars: Adrienne King Jeannine Taylor Kevin Bacon

1981 ISABEL'S CHOICE
Director: Guy Green
Co-stars: Jean Stapleton Richard Kiley Peter Coyote

1984 THE ADVENTURES OF SHERLOCK HOLMES: THE DANCING MAN
Director: John Bruce
Co-stars: Jeremy Brett David Burke

EFFIE PALMER

1931   WAY BACK HOME
Director: William Seiter
Co-stars: Phillips Lord Bette Davis Frank Albertson

GRETCHEN PALMER

1990   CHOPPER CHICKS IN ZOMBIETOWN
Director: Dan Hoskins
Co-stars: Jamie Rose Catherine Carlen Lycia Naff

LILLI PALMER *(Married Rex Harrison)*

1936   SECRET AGENT
Director: Alfred Hitchcock
Co-stars: John Gielgud Madeleine Carroll

1936   WHERE THERE'S A WILL
Director: William Beaudine
Co-stars: Will Hay Graham Moffatt Hartley Power

1937   GOOD MORNING BOYS
Director: Marcel Varnel
Co-stars: Will Hay Graham Moffatt Charles Hawtrey

1937   THE GREAT BARRIER
Director: Milton Rosmer
Co-stars: Richard Arlen Barry Mackay Roy Emerton

1937   COMMAND PERFORMANCE
Director: Sinclair Hill
Co-stars: Arthur Tracy Finlay Currie Mark Daly

1938   CRACKERJACK
Director: Albert De Courville
Co-stars: Tom Walls Noel Madison Leon Lion

1939   A GIRL MUST LIVE
Director: Carol Reed
Co-stars: Margaret Lockwood Rennee Houston Hugh Sinclair

1937   SUNSET IN VIENNA
Director: Norman Walker
Co-stars: Tullio Carminati John Garrick

1940   THE DOOR WITH SEVEN LOCKS
Director: Norman Lee
Co-stars: Leslie Banks Gina Malo Cathleen Nesbitt

1942   THUNDER ROCK
Director: Roy Boulting
Co-stars: Michael Redgrave James Mason Barbara Mullen

1943   THE GENTLE SEX
Director: Leslie Howard
Co-stars: Joan Gates Rosamund John Joan Greenwood

1944   ENGLISH WITHOUT TEARS
Director: Harold French
Co-stars: Michael Wilding Margaret Rutherford Roland Culver

1945   THE RAKE'S PROGRESS
Director: Sidney Gilliat
Co-stars: Rex Harrison Margaret Johnston Guy Middleton

1946   CLOAK AND DAGGER
Director: Fritz Lang
Co-stars: Gary Cooper Robert Alda Vladimir Sokoloff

1946   BEWARE OF PITY
Director: Maurice Elvey
Co-stars: Albert Lieven Cedric Hardwicke Gladys Cooper

1947   BODY AND SOUL
Director: Robert Rossen
Co-stars: John Garfield Anne Revere Canada Lee

1948   MY GIRL TISA
Director: Elliott Nugent
Co-stars: Sam Wanamaker Akim Tamiroff Alan Hale

1948   NO MINOR VICES
Director: Lewis Milestone
Co-stars: Dana Andrews Louis Jordan Jane Wyatt

1951   THE LONG DARK HALL
Director: Reginald Beck
Co-stars: Rex Harrison Patricia Wayne Brenda De Banzie

1952   THE FOUR POSTER
Director: Irving Reis
Co-star: Rex Harrison

1953   MAIN STREET TO BROADWAY
Director: Tay Garnett
Co-stars: Tom Morton Mary Murphy Rex Harrison

1958   MONTPARNASSE 19
Director: Jacques Becker
Co-stars: Gerard Philipe Anouk Aimee Lino Ventura

1958   MADCHEN IN UNIFORM
Director: Geza Radvanyl
Co-stars: Romy Schneider Christine Kaufman

1959   BUT NOT FOR ME
Director: Walter Lang
Co-stars: Clark Gable Carroll Baker Lee J. Cobb

1960   CONSPIRACY OF HEARTS
Director: Ralph Thomas
Co-stars: Sylvia Sims Yvonne Mitchell Ronald Lewis

1961   THE PLEASURE OF HIS COMPANY
Director: George Seaton
Co-stars: Fred Astaire Debbie Reynolds

1962   THE COUNTERFEIT TRAITOR
Director: George Seaton
Co-stars: William Holden Hugh Griffith

1962   ADORABLE JULIA
Director: Alfred Weidenmann
Co-stars: Charles Boyer Jean Sorel Jeanne Valeri

1963   THE MIRACLE OF THE WHITE STALLIONS
Director: Arthur Hiller
Co-stars: Robert Taylor Eddie Albert

1965   OPERATION CROSSBOW
Director: Michael Anderson
Co-stars: George Peppard Tom Courtenay John Mills

**1965   THE AMOROUS ADVENTURES
OF MOLL FLANDERS**
Director: Terence Young
Co-stars: Kim Novak Richard Johnson George Sanders

1967   JACK OF DIAMONDS
Director: Don Taylor
Co-stars: Joseph Cotten George Hamilton Carroll Baker

1968   NOBODY RUNS FOREVER
Director: Ralph Thomas
Co-stars: Rod Taylor Christopher Plummer Franchot Tone

1968   OEDIPUS THE KING
Director: Philip Saville
Co-stars: Christopher Plummer Richard Johnson Orson Welles

1968   SEBASTIAN
Director: David Greene
Co-stars: Dirk Bogarde John Gielgud Susannah York

1969   HARD CONTRACT
Director: Lee Pogostin
Co-stars: James Coburn Lee Remick Burgess Meredith

1969   DE SADE
Director: Cy Endfield
Co-stars: Keir Dullea John Huston Senta Berger

1971 MURDERS IN THE RUE MORGUE
Director: Gordon Hessler
Co-stars: Jason Robards Herbert Lom Michael Dunn

1971 NIGHT HAIR CHILD
Director: James Kelly
Co-stars: Mark Lester Britt Ekland Harry Andrews

1978 THE BOYS FROM BRAZIL
Director: Franklin Schaffner
Co-stars: Laurence Olivier Gregory Peck James Mason

1985 THE HOLCROFT CONVENANT
Director: John Frankenheimer
Co-stars: Michael Caine Anthony Andrews Victoria Tennant

MARIA PALMER

1943 MISSION TO MOSCOW
Director: Michael Curtiz
Co-stars: Walter Huston Ann Harding Oscar Homoika

1944 DAYS OF GLORY
Director: Jacques Tourneur
Co-stars: Tamara Toumanova Gregory Peck Hugo Haas

1946 RENDEZVOUS 24
Director: James Tinling
Co-stars: William Gargan Pat O'Moore Herman Bing

1947 THE WEB
Director: Michael Gordon
Co-stars: Edmond O'Brien Vincent Price Ella Raines

1947 THE OTHER LOVE
Director: Andre De Toth
Co-stars: Barbara Stanwyck David Niven Richard Conte

1951 STRICTLY DISHONORABLE
Director: Norman Panama
Co-stars: Ezio Pinza Janet Leigh Millard Mitchell

GWYNETH PALTROW

1993 MALICE
Director: Harold Becker
Co-stars: Nicole Kidman Alec Baldwin Bill Pullman

1993 FLESH AND BONE
Director: Steve Kloves
Co-stars: Dennis Quaid Meg Ryan James Caan

1995 SEVEN
Director: David Fincher
Co-stars: Brad Pitt Morgan Freeman

1996 MOONLIGHT AND VALENTINO
Director: David Anspaugh
Co-stars: Elizabeth Perkins Kathleen Turner Jon Bon Jovi

1996 EMMA
Director: Douglas McGrath
Co-stars: Greta Scacchi Ewan McGregor Juliet Stevenson

1997 SLIDING DOORS
Director: Peter Howitt
Co-stars: John Hannah John Lynch Jeanne Tripplehorn

1997 HARD EIGHT
Director: Paul Thomas Anderson
Co-stars: Philip Baker Hall John C Reilly

1998 GREAT EXPECTATIONS
Director: Alfonso Cuaron
Co-stars: Ethan Hawke Robert De Niro Anne Bancroft

LUCIANA PALUZZI

1958 NO TIME TO DIE
Director: Terence Young
Co-stars: Victor Mature Leo Genn Anthony Newley

1958 SEA FURY
Director: Cy Endfield
Co-stars: Stanley Baker Victor McLaglen Robert Shaw

1959 CARLTON-BROWNE OF THE F.O.
Director: Roy Boulting
Co-stars: Terry-Thomas Peter Sellers Ian Bannen

1961 RETURN TO PEYTON PLACE
Director: Jose Ferrer
Co-stars: Jeff Chandler Carol Lynley Eleanor Parker

1964 MUSCLE BEACH PARTY
Director: William Asher
Co-stars: Frankie Avalon Annette Funicello Don Rickles

1965 THUNDERBALL
Director: Terence Young
Co-stars: Sean Connery Adolfo Celi Claudine Auger

1965 TO TRAP A SPY
Director: Don Medford
Co-stars: Robert Vaughn Patricia Crowley David McCallum

1966 THE VENETIAN AFFAIR
Director: Jerry Thorpe
Co-stars: Robert Vaughn Elke Sommer Felicia Farr

1967 CHUKA
Director: Gordon Douglas
Co-stars: Rod Taylor Ernest Borgnine John Mills

1969 A BLACK VEIL FOR LISA
Director: Massimo Dallamano
Co-stars: John Mills Robert Hoffman Renate Kasche

1969 CAPTAIN NEMO AND THE UNDERWATER CITY
Director: James Hill
Co-stars: Robert Ryan Chuck Connors

1969 THE GREEN SLIME
Director: Kinji Fukasaki
Co-stars: Robert Horton Richard Jaeckel

1970 POWDERKEG
Director: Douglas Heyes
Co-stars: Rod Taylor Dennis Cole Fernando Lamas

1974 THE KLANSMAN
Director: Terence Young
Co-stars: Lee Marvin Richard Burton Cameron Mitchell

CECILE PAOLI

1989 THE GINGER TREE
Director: Anthony Garner
Co-stars: Samantha Bond Daisuke Ryu Joanna McCallum

IRENE PAPAS

1955 ATTILA THE HUN
Director: Pietro Francisci
Co-stars: Anthony Quinn Sophia Loren Henri Vidal

1956 TRIBUTE TO A BAD MAN
Director: Robert Wise
Co-stars: James Cagney Don Dubbins Stephen McNally

1961 THE GUNS OF NAVARONE
Director: J Lee-Thompson
Co-stars: Gregory Peck David Niven Anthony Quinn

1964 THE MOON SPINNERS
Director: James Nielson
Co-stars: Hayley Mills Peter McEnery Eli Wallach

1964 ZORBA THE GREEK
Director: Michael Cacoyannis
Co-stars: Anthony Quinn Alan Bates Lila Kedrova

1968   Z
Director: Costa-Gavras
Co-stars: Jean-Louis Trintignant Yves Montand Jacques Perrin

1968   THE BROTHERHOOD
Director: Martin Ritt
Co-stars: Kirk Douglas Alex Cord Susan Strasberg

1969   ANNE OF A THOUSAND DAYS
Director: Charles Jarrott
Co-stars: Richard Burton Genevieve Bujold Anthony Quayle

1969   A DREAM OF KINGS
Director: Daniel Mann
Co-stars: Anthony Quinn Inger Stevens Sam Levene

1975   MOSES
Director: Gianfranco De Basio
Co-stars: Burt Lancaster Anthony Quayle Ingrid Thulin

1976   MOHAMMED, MESSENGER OF GOD
Director: Moustapha Akkad
Co-stars: Anthony Quinn Michael Ansara

1979   CHRIST STOPPED AT EBOLI
Director: Francesco Rosi
Co-stars: Gian-Maria Volonte Alain Cuny

1979   BLOODLINE
Director: Terence Young
Co-stars: Audrey Hepburn Ben Gazzara James Mason

1980   LION OF THE DESERT
Director: Moustapha Akkad
Co-stars: Anthony Quinn Rod Steiger Oliver Reed

1982   ERENDIRA
Director: Ruy Gerra
Co-stars: Oliver Wehe Michel Lonsdale

1985   THE ASSISI UNDERGROUND
Director: Guiseppe Ramati
Co-stars: Ben Cross James Mason Edmund Purdom

1985   INTO THE NIGHT
Director: John Landis
Co-stars: Jeff Goldblum Michelle Pfeiffer David Bowie

1987   HIGH SEASON
Director: Clare Peplow
Co-stars: Jacqueline Bisset James Fox Kenneth Branagh

1987   CHRONICLE OF A DEATH FORTOLD
Director: Francesco Rosi
Co-stars: Rupert Everett Ornella Muti

1989   ISLAND
Director: Paul Cox
Co-star: Norman Kaye

ANNA PAQUIN (Child)
Won Oscar For Best Supporting Actress In 1993 For "The Piano"

1993   THE PIANO
Director: Jane Campion
Co-stars: Holly Hunter Sam Neill Harvey Keitel

1996   JANE EYRE
Director: Franco Zefferelli
Co-stars: Charlotte Gainsbourg William Hurt Samuel West

1997   FLY AWAY HOME
Director: Carroll Ballard
Co-stars: Jeff Daniels Dana Delaney

VANESSA PARADIS

1989   NOCE BLANCHE
Director: Jean-Claude Brisseau
Co-stars: Bruno Cremer Ludmilla Mikael Francois Negret

1995   ELISA
Director: Jean Becker
Co-star: Gerard Depardieu

MARISA PAREDES

1984   DARK HABITS
Director: Pedro Almodovar
Co-stars: Christina Pascual Carmen Maura Mari Carillo

1991   HIGH HEELS
Director: Pedro Almodovar
Co-stars: Victoria Abril Miguel Bose

1996   THE FLOWER OF MY SECRET
Director: Pedro Almodovar
Co-stars: Chus Lampreave

MILA PARELY

1939   CIRCONSTANCES ATTENUANTES
Director: Jean Boyer
Co-stars: Arletty Michel Simon Suzanne Dantes

1939   LA REGLE DU JEU
Director: Jean Renoir
Co-stars: Marcel Dalio Nora Gregor Gaston Modot

1943   LES ANGES DU PECHE
Director: Robert Bresson
Co-stars: Renee Faure Jany Holt Sylvie

1946   LA BELLE ET LA BETE
Director: Jean Cocteau
Co-stars: Jean Marais Josette Day Marcel Andre

1948   SNOWBOUND
Director: David MacDonald
Co-stars: Robert Newton Dennis Price Herbert Lom

JUDY PARFITT

1969   HAMLET
Director: Tony Richardson
Co-stars: Nicol Williamson Gordon Jackson Anthony Hopkins

1975   GALILEO
Director: Joseph Losey
Co-stars: Topol Edward Fox Tom Conti

1980   PRIDE AND PREJUDICE
Director: Cyril Coke
Co-stars: Elizabeth Garvie David Rintoul Barbara Shelley

1983   CHAMPIONS
Director: John Irvin
Co-stars: John Hurt Edward Woodward Jan Francis

1984   THE CHAIN
Director: Jack Gold
Co-stars: Denis Lawson Billie Whitelaw Nigel Hawthorne

1987   MAURICE
Director: James Ivory
Co-stars: James Wilby Hugh Grant Denholm Elliott

1989   DIAMOND SKULLS
Director: Nicholas Broomfield
Co-stars: Gabriel Byrne Amanda Donohue Sadie Frost

1989   GETTING IT RIGHT
Director: Randal Kleiser
Co-stars: Jesse Birdsall Jane Horrocks Lynn Redgrave

1990   THE GRAVY TRAIN
Director: David Tucker
Co-stars: Ian Richardson Christophe Waltz Alexei Sayle

ANNE PARILLAUD

1980   THREE MEN TO KILL
Director: Alain Delon
Co-stars: Michel Auclair Daniel Ceccadi

1990　NIKITA
Director:　Luc Besson
Co-stars:　Jean-Hughes Anglade Jeanne Moreau Tcheky Karyo

1992　MAP OF THE HUMAN HEART
Director:　Vincent Ward
Co-stars:　Jason Scott Lee Patrick Bergin

1993　INNOCENT BLOOD
Director:　John Landis
Co-stars:　Robert Loggia Anthony LaPaglia Don Rickles

1998　THE MAN IN THE IRON MASK
Director:　Randall Wallace
Co-stars:　Leonardo DiCaprio Jeremy Irons John Malkovich

JUDITH PARIS

1988　THE RAINBOW
Director:　Ken Russell
Co-stars:　Sammi Davis Amanda Donohue Paul McGann

ANDREA PARKER

1994　XXXS AND OOOS
Director:　Alan Arkush
Co-stars:　Debrah Farentino Nia Peeples

1996　ED McBAIN'S 87TH PRECINCT:ICE
Director:　Bradford May
Co-stars:　Dale Midkiff Joe Pantoliano Andrea Ferrell

BROOK PARKER

1992　THE SILENCER
Director:　Amy Goldstein
Co-stars:　Lynette Walden Chris Mulkey Paul Ganus

CECILIA PARKER *(Julia Parker)*

1933　RIDERS OF DESTINY
Co-star:　John Wayne

1934　THE TRAIL DRIVE
Co-star:　Ken Maynard

1935　NAUGHTY MARIETTA
Director:　W.S. Van Dyke
Co-stars:　Jeanette MacDonald Nelson Eddy Frank Morgan

1936　OLD HUTCH
Director:　Walter Ruben
Co-stars:　Wallace Beery Elizabeth Patterson Eric Linden

1936　BELOW THE DEALINE
Co-star:　Russell Hopton

1936　IN HIS STEPS

1937　SWEETHEART OF THE NAVY

1937　GIRL LOVES BOY
Co-star:　Eric Linden

1937　DAMAGED LIVES
Director:　Edgar Ulmer
Co-stars:　Diane Sinclair Lyman Williams Jason Robards

1937　A FAMILY AFFAIR
Director:　George Seitz
Co-stars:　Lionel Barrymore Spring Byington Mickey Rooney

1938　BURN 'EM UP O'CONNOR
Director:　Edward Sedgwick
Co-stars:　Dennis O'Keefe Harry Carey Nat Pendleton

1938　YOU'RE ONLY YOUNG ONCE
Director:　George Seitz
Co-stars:　Mickey Rooney Lewis Stone Fay Holden

1938　JUDGE HARRY'S CHILDREN
Director:　George Seitz
Co-stars:　Mickey Rooney Lewis Stone Fay Holden

1938　OUT WEST WITH THE HARDIES
Director:　George Seitz
Co-stars:　Mickey Rooney Lewis Stone Fay Holden

1938　LOVE FINDS ANDY HARDY
Director:　George Seitz
Co-stars:　Mickey Rooney Judy Garland Lana Turner

1939　THE HARDYS RIDE HIGH
Director:　George Seitz
Co-stars:　Mickey Rooney Lewis Stone Sara Haden

1939　JUDGE HARDY AND SON
Director:　George Seitz
Co-stars:　Mickey Rooney June Preisser Maria Ouspenskaya

1939　ANDY HARDY GETS SPRING FEVER
Director:　W.S. Van Dyke
Co-stars:　Mickey Rooney Ann Rutherford Lewis Stone

1940　ANDY HARDY MEETS A DEBUTANTE
Director:　George Seitz
Co-stars:　Mickey Rooney Judy Garland Diana Lewis

1941　LIFE BEGINS FOR ANDY HARDY
Director:　George Seitz
Co-stars:　Mickey Rooney Judy Garland Lewis Stone

1941　ANDY HARDY'S PRIVATE SECRETARY
Director:　George Seitz
Co-stars:　Mickey Rooney Kathryn Grayson Fay Holden

1942　ANDY HARDY'S DOUBLE LIFE
Director:　George Seitz
Co-stars:　Mickey Rooney Esther Williams Susan Peters

1942　THE COURTSHIP OF ANDY HARDY
Director:　George Seitz
Co-stars:　Mickey Rooney Fay Holden Sara Haden

1942　GRAND CENTRAL MURDER
Director:　S. Sylvan Simon
Co-stars:　Van Heflin Sam Levene Tom Conway

1942　SEVEN SWEETHEARTS
Director:　Frank Borzage
Co-stars:　Kathryn Grayson Marsha Hunt Van Heflin

1944　ANDY HARDY'S BLONDE TROUBLE
Director:　George Seitz
Co-stars:　Mickey Rooney Bonita Granville Jean Porter

1946　LOVE LAUGHS AT ANDY HARDY
Director:　George Seitz
Co-stars:　Mickey Rooney Lewis Stone Lina Romey

1958　ANDY HARDY COMES HOME
Director:　Howard Koch
Co-stars:　Mickey Rooney Fay Holden Patricia Breslin

ELEANOR PARKER
Nominated For Best Actress In 1950 For "Caged" And In 1951 For "Detective Story"

1942　BUSES ROAR
Director:　Ross Lederman
Co-stars:　Richard Travis Julie Bishop Charles Drake

1943　MISSION TO MOSCOW
Director:　Michael Curtiz
Co-stars:　Walter Huston Ann Harding Oscar Homolka

1943　THE MYSTERIOUS DOCTOR
Director:　Ben Stolof
Co-stars:　John Loder Bruce Lester Forrester Harvey

1944　THE VERY THOUGHT OF YOU
Director:　Delmer Daves
Co-stars:　Dennis Morgan Dane Clark Beulah Bondi

1944　CRIME BY NIGHT
Director:　William Clemens
Co-stars:　Jerome Cowan Jane Wyman Faye Emerson

1944	**BETWEEN TWO WORLDS**	
Director:	Edward Blatt	
Co-stars:	John Garfield Edmund Gwenn Sydney Greenstreet	

1944 **BETWEEN TWO WORLDS**
Director: Edward Blatt
Co-stars: John Garfield Edmund Gwenn Sydney Greenstreet

1945 **PRIDE OF THE MARINES**
Director: Delmer Daves
Co-stars: John Garfield Dane Clark Ann Doran

1946 **NEVER SAY GOODBYE**
Director: James Kern
Co-stars: Errol Flynn Lucile Watson S.Z. Sakall

1946 **OF HUMAN BONDAGE**
Director: Edmund Goulding
Co-stars: Paul Henreid Alexis Smith Edmund Gwenn

1947 **ESCAPE ME NEVER**
Director: Peter Godfrey
Co-stars: Errol Flynn Ida Lupino Gig Young

1947 **THE VOICE OF THE TURTLE**
Director: Irving Rapper
Co-stars: Ronald Reagan Eve Arden Wayne Morris

1948 **THE WOMAN IN WHITE**
Director: Peter Godfrey
Co-stars: Gig Young Sydney Greenstreet Agnes Moorehead

1949 **IT'S A GREAT FEELING**
Director: David Butler
Co-stars: Doris Day Jack Carson Dennis Morgan

1950 **CAGED**
Director: John Cromwell
Co-stars: Agnes Moorehead Jan Sterling Ellen Corby

1950 **CHAIN LIGHTNING**
Director: Stuart Heisler
Co-stars: Humphrey Bogart Raymond Massey Richard Whorf

1950 **THREE SECRETS**
Director: Robert Wise
Co-stars: Patricia Neal Ruth Roman Frank Lovejoy

1951 **A MILLIONAIRE FOR CHRISTY**
Director: George Marshall
Co-stars: Fred MacMurray Richard Carlson

1951 **DETECTIVE STORY**
Director: William Wyler
Co-stars: Kirk Douglas Lee Grant William Bendix

1951 **VALENTINO**
Director: Lewis Allen
Co-stars: Anthony Dexter Richard Carlson Dona Drake

1952 **SCARAMOUCHE**
Director: George Sidney
Co-stars: Stewart Granger Mel Ferrer Janet Leigh

1952 **ABOVE AND BEYOND**
Director: Melvin Frank
Co-stars: Robert Taylor James Whitmore Larry Keating

1953 **ESCAPE FROM FORT BRAVO**
Director: John Sturges
Co-stars: William Holden John Forsythe William Demarest

1954 **VALLEY OF THE KINGS**
Director: Robert Pirosh
Co-stars: Robert Taylor Carlos Thompson Kurt Kasznar

1954 **THE NAKED JUNGLE**
Director: Byron Haskin
Co-stars: Charlton Heston William Conrad Abraham Sofaer

1955 **MANY RIVERS TO CROSS**
Director: Roy Rowland
Co-stars: Robert Taylor Victor McLaglen Russ Tamblyn

1955 **INTERRUPTED MELODY**
Director: Curtis Bernhardt
Co-stars: Glenn Ford Cecil Kellaway Roger Moore

1956 **KING AND FOUR QUEENS**
Director: Raoul Walsh
Co-stars: Clark Gable Jo Van Fleet Barbara Nicholls

1957 **LIZZIE**
Director: Hugo Haas
Co-stars: Richard Boone Joan Blondell Hugo Haas

1957 **THE SEVENTH SIN**
Director: Ronald Neame
Co-stars: Bill Travers George Sanders Jean-Pierre Aumont

1958 **THE MAN WITH THE GOLDEN ARM**
Director: Otto Preminger
Co-stars: Frank Sinatra Kim Novak Darren McGavin

1959 **HOLE IN THE HEAD**
Director: Frank Capra
Co-stars: Frank Sinatra Edward G. Robinson Carolyn Jones

1959 **HOME FROM THE HILL**
Director: Vincente Minnelli
Co-stars: Robert Mitchum George Peppard George Hamilton

1961 **RETURN TO PEYTON PLACE**
Director: Jose Ferrer
Co-stars: Jeff Chandler Carol Lynley Mary Astor

1962 **MADISON AVENUE**
Director: Bruce Humberstone
Co-stars: Dana Andrews Jeanne Crain Eddie Albert

1964 **PANIC BUTTON**
Director: George Sherman
Co-stars: Maurice Chevalier Jayne Mansfield Akim Tamirof

1965 **THE SOUND OF MUSIC**
Director: Robert Wise
Co-stars: Julie Andrews Christopher Plummer Richard Haydn

1966 **THE OSCAR**
Director: Russel Rouse
Co-stars: Stephen Boyd Elke Sommer Tony Bennett

1966 **AN AMERICAN DREAM**
Director: Robert Gist
Co-stars: Stuart Whitman Janet Leigh Lloyd Nolan

1967 **THE TIGER AND THE PUSSYCAT**
Director: Dino Riss
Co-stars: Vittorio Gassman Ann-Margaret

1967 **WARNING SHOT**
Director: Buzz Kulick
Co-stars: David Janssen Lillian Gish Sam Wanamaker

1969 **EYE OF THE CAT**
Director: David Lowell Rich
Co-stars: Michael Sarrazin Gayle Hunnicutt Tim Henry

1979 **SHE'S DRESSED TO KILL**
Director: Gus Trikonis
Co-stars: Jessica Walter John Rubinstein Clive Revill

1979 **SUNBURN**
Director: Richard Sarafian
Co-stars: Farrah Fawcett Charles Grodin Art Carney

1980 **ONCE UPON A SPY**
Director: Ivan Nagy
Co-stars: Ted Danson Christopher Lee Mary Louise Weller

JEAN PARKER

1932 **STORM AT DAYBREAK**
Director: Richard Boleslawski
Co-stars: Walter Huston Kay Francis Nils Asther

1932 **RASPUTIN AND THE EMPRESS**
Director: Richard Boleslawski
Co-stars: Ethel John Lionel Barrymore Diana Wynyard

1932 **A DIVORCE IN THE FAMILY**
Director: Charles Reisner
Co-stars: Jackie Cooper Lewis Stone Conrad Nagel

1933 **LADY FOR A DAY**
Director: Frank Capra
Co-stars: May Robson Glenda Farrell Warren William

1933 **LITTLE WOMEN**
Director: George Cukor
Co-stars: Katherine Hepburn Joan Bennett Paul Lukas

1933 **THE SECRET OF MADAME BLANCHE**
Director: Charles Brabin
Co-stars: Irene Dunne Phillips Holmes Lionel Atwill

1934 **A WICKED WOMAN**
Director: Charles Brabin
Co-stars: Mady Christians Charles Bickford Robert Taylor

1934 **YOU CAN'T BUY EVERYTHING**
Director: Charles Reisner
Co-stars: May Robson Lewis Stone Mary Forbes

1934 **TWO ALONE**
Director: Elliott Nugent
Co-stars: Tom Brown Zasu Pitts Beulah Bondi

1934 **SEQUOIA**
Director: Chester Franklin
Co-stars: Russell Hardie Samuel S. Hinds

1934 **LIMEHOUSE BLUES**
Director: Alexander Hall
Co-stars: George Raft Anna May Wong Eric Blore

1934 **LAZY RIVER**
Director: George Seitz
Co-stars: Robert Young Ted Healy Nat Pendleton

1934 **HAVE A HEART**
Director: David Butler
Co-stars: James Dunn Una Merkel Stuart Erwin

1934 **CARAVAN**
Director: Eric Charrell
Co-stars: Loretta Young Charles Boyer Phillips Holmes

1934 **OPERATOR 13**
Director: Richard Boleslawski
Co-stars: Marion Davies Gary Cooper Ted Healy

1935 **PRINCESS O'HARA**
Director: David Burton
Co-stars: Chester Morris Leon Errol Henry Armetta

1935 **MURDER IN THE FLEET**
Director: Edward Sedgwick
Co-stars: Robert Taylor Jean Hersholt Una Merkel

1936 **THE GHOST GOES WEST**
Director: Rene Clair
Co-stars: Robert Donat Eugene Pallette Elsa Lanchester

1936 **THE FARMER IN THE DELL**
Co-stars: Frank Albertson Moroni Olsen Fred Stone

1936 **THE TEXAS RANGERS**
Director: King Vidor
Co-stars: Fred MacMurray Jack Oakie Lloyd Nolan

1937 **THE BARRIER**
Director: Lesley Selander
Co-stars: Leo Carrilio James Ellison Otto Kruger

1938 **THE ARKANSAS TRAVELLER**
Director: Alfred Santell
Co-stars: Bob Burns Fay Bainter Irvin Cobb

1938 **PENITENTIARY**
Director: John Brahm
Co-stars: John Howard Walter Connolly Robert Barrat

1939 **ZENOBIA**
Director: Gordon Douglas
Co-stars: Oliver Hardy Harry Langdon Billie Burke

1939 **THE FLYING DEUCES**
Director: Edward Sutherland
Co-stars: Stan Laurel Oliver Hardy James Finlayson

1939 **ROMANCE OF THE REDWOODS**
Co-stars: Charles Bickford Gordon Oliver Al Bridge

1939 **SHE MARRIED A COP**
Co-star: Phil Regan

1940 **BEYOND TOMORROW**
Director: Edward Sutherland
Co-stars: Richard Carlson Charles Winninger

1941 **NO HANDS ON THE CLOCK**
Director: Frank McDonald
Co-stars: Chester Morris Rose Hobart Rod Cameron

1941 **THE PITTSBURGH KID**
Co-stars: John Kelly Billy Conn

1941 **POWER DIVE**
Co-star: Richard Arlen

1943 **HIGH EXPLOSIVE**
Co-stars: Barry Sullivan Rand Brooks

1943 **MINESWEEPER**
Co-star: Russel Hayden

1943 **ALASKA HIGHWAY**
Director: Frank McDonald
Co-stars: Richard Arlen Bill Henry Ralph Sanford

1944 **ADVENTURES OF KITTY O'DAY**
Director: William Beaudine
Co-stars: Peter Cookson Tim Ryan Ralph Sanford

1944 **BLUEBEARD**
Director: Edgar Ulmer
Co-stars: John Carradine Nils Asther Iris Adrian

1944 **DEAD MAN'S EYES**
Director: Reginald LeBorg
Co-stars: Lon Chaney Paul Kelly Acquanetta

1944 **ONE BODY TOO MANY**
Director: Frank McDonald
Co-stars: Jack Haley Bela Lugosi Lyle Talbot

1944 **OH! WHAT A NIGHT**
Co-stars: Marjorie Rambeau Claire Dubrey

1944 **THE NAVY WAY**
Co-stars: Robert Lowery Bill Henry

1944 **LADY IN THE DEATH HOUSE**

1950 **THE GUNFIGHTER**
Director: Henry King
Co-stars: Gregory Peck Karl Malden Skip Homeier

1952 **TOUGHEST MAN IN ARIZONA**
Director: R. G. Springsteen
Co-stars: Vaughan Monroe Joan Leslie Victor Jory

1954 **BLACK TUESDAY**
Director: Hugo Fregonese
Co-stars: Edward G. Robinson Peter Graves Jack Kelly

1955 **A LAWLESS STREET**
Director: Joseph Lewis
Co-stars: Randolph Scott Warner Anderson Angela Lansbury

JESSICA PARKER

1941 **BULLETS FOR O'HARA**
Director: William Howard
Co-stars: Roger Pryor Anthony Quinn Joan Perry

KELLIE PARKER

1988   **MOONWALKER**
Director: Colin Chilvers
Co-stars: Michael Jackson Joe Pesci Sean Lennon

KIM PARKER

1958   **FIEND WITHOUT A FACE**
Director: Arthur Crabtree
Co-stars: Kynaston Reeves Marshall Thompson

LARA PARKER

1969   **HI, MOM!**
Director: Brian De Palma
Co-stars: Robert De Niro Allen Garfield Charles Durnham

1971   **NIGHT OF DARK SHADOWS**
Director: Dan Curtis
Co-star: David Selby

1975   **RACE WITH THE DEVIL**
Director: Jack Starrett
Co-stars: Peter Fonda Warren Oates Loretta Swit

LINDSAY PARKER (*Child*)

1987   **FLOWERS IN THE ATTIC**
Director: Jeffrey Bloom
Co-stars: Louise Fletcher Victoria Tennant Ben Ganger

1988   **CRITTERS 2**
Director: Mick Garris
Co-stars: Scott Grimes Barry Corbin Liane Curtis

MARY PARKER

1957   **THE HOSTAGE**
Director: Harold Huth
Co-stars: Ron Randell Carl Jaffe Margaret Diamond

MARY-LOUISE PARKER

1990   **LONGTIME COMPANION**
Director: Norman Rene
Co-stars: Stephen Caffrey Patrick Cassidy Bruce Davison

1991   **GRAND CANYON**
Director: Lawrence Kasdan
Co-stars: Danny Glover Kevin Kline Mary McDonnell

1991   **FRIED GREEN TOMATOES AT THE WHISTLE STOP CAFÉ**
Director: John Avnet
Co-stars: Jessica Tandy Kathy Bates

1993   **MR WONDERFUL**
Director: Anthony Minghella
Co-stars: Matt Dillon Annabelle Sciorra William Hurt

1993   **A PLACE FOR ANNIE**
Director: John Grey
Co-stars: Sissy Spacek Joan Plowright

1994   **THE CLIENT**
Director: Joel Schumacher
Co-stars: Susan Sarandon Brad Renfro Tommy Lee Jones

1995   **NAKED IN NEW YORK**
Director: Don Algrant
Co-stars: Eric Stoltz Kathleen Turner Timothy Dalton

1995   **BOYS ON THE SIDE**
Director: Herbert Ross
Co-stars: Drew Barrymore Whoopi Goldberg Estelle Parsons

1996   **THE PORTRAIT OF A LADY**
Director: Jane Campion
Co-stars: Nicole Kidman Barbara Hershey John Malkovich

MELANIE PARKER

1988   **MONKEY SHINES**
Director: George Romero
Co-stars: Jason Beghe John Pankow Kate McNeil

MOLLY PARKER

1988   **KISSED**
Director: Lynne Stopkewich
Co-star: Peter Outerbridge

MONICA PARKER

1981   **IMPROPER CHANNELS**
Director: Eric Till
Co-stars: Alan Arkin Mariette Hartley Sarah Stevens

NOELLE PARKER (*Child*)

1988   **ERNEST SAVES CHRISTMAS**
Director: John R Cherry
Co-stars: Jim Varney Douglas Seale Oliver Clark

1992   **LETHAL LOLITA**
Director: Bradford May
Co-stars: Ed Marinaro Lawrence Dane Kate Lynch

SACHI PARKER

1991   **WELCOME HOME, ROXY CARMICHAEL**
Director: Jim Abrahams
Co-stars: Winona Ryder Jeff Daniels Dinah Manoff

SAGE PARKER

1986   **THE DIRT BIKE KID**
Director: Hoite Caston
Co-stars: Peter Billingsley Stuart Pankin Anne Bloom

SARAH JESSICA PARKER

1983   **SOMEWHERE TOMORROW**
Director: Robert Wiemer
Co-stars: Nancy Addison Tom Shea Rick Weber

1984   **FIRSTBORN**
Director: Michael Apted
Co-stars: Teri Garr Peter Weller Corey Haim

1984   **FOOTLOOSE**
Director: Herbert Ross
Co-stars: Kevin Bacon Lori Singer John Lithgow

1985   **GOING FOR GOLD: THE BILL JOHNSON STORY**
Director: Don Taylor
Co-stars: Anthony Edwards Dennis Weaver

1985   **GIRLS JUST WANT TO HAVE FUN**
Director: Alan Metter
Co-stars: Helen Hunt Lee Montgomery

1986   **FLIGHT OF THE NAVIGATOR**
Director: Randal Kleiser
Co-stars: Joey Cramer Veronica Cartwright Matt Adler

1987   **THE ROOM UPSTAIRS**
Director: Stuart Margolin
Co-stars: Stockard Channing Sam Waterston Linda Hunt

1988   **THE RYAN WHITE STORY**
Director: John Herzfeld
Co-stars: Lukas Haas Judith Light George C. Scott

1991   **L.A. STORY**
Director: Mick Jackson
Co-stars: Steve Martin Victoria Tennant Marilu Henner

1992   **IN THE BEST INTEREST OF THE CHILDREN**
Director: Michael Ray Rhodes
Co-stars: Sally Struthers Elizabeth Ashley

1992 HONEYMOON IN VEGAS
Director: Andrew Bergman
Co-stars: James Caan Nicolas Cage Anne Bancroft

1993 STRIKING DISTANCE
Director: Rowdy Herrington
Co-stars: Bruce Willis Dennis Farina Tom Sizemore

1993 HOCUS POCUS
Director: Kenny Ortega
Co-stars: Bette Midler Kathy Najimy Thora Birch

1994 ED WOOD
Director: Tim Burton
Co-stars: Johnny Depp Martin Landau

1995 MIAMI RHAPSODY
Director: David Frankel
Co-stars: Antonio Banderas Mia Farrow

1996 EXTREME MEASURES
Director: Michael Apted
Co-stars: Hugh Grant Gene Hackman

1996 THE FIRST WIVES' CLUB
Director: Hugh Wilson
Co-stars: Goldie Hawn Diane Keaton Bette Midler

1997 MARS ATTACKS !
Director: Tim Burton
Co-stars: Jack Nicholson Annette Bening Glenn Close

1997 'TIL THERE WAS YOU
Co-stars: Jeanne Triplehorn Dylan McDermott Jennifer Aniston

SUZY PARKER

1957 FUNNY FACE
Director: Stanley Donen
Co-stars: Fred Astaire Audrey Hepburn Kay Thompson

1957 KISS THEM FOR ME
Director: Stanley Donen
Co-stars: Cary Grant Jayne Mansfield Ray Walston

1958 TEN NORTH FREDERICK
Director: Philip Dunne
Co-stars: Gary Cooper Geraldine Fitzgerald Diane Varsi

1959 THE BEST OF EVERYTHING
Director: Jean Negulesco
Co-stars: Joan Crawford Hope Lange Louis Jourdan

1960 A CIRCLE OF DECEPTION
Director: Jack Lee
Co-stars: Bradford Dillman Harry Andrews Robert Stephens

1962 THE INTERNS
Director: David Swift
Co-stars: Cliff Robertson James MacArthur Nick Adams

1963 FLIGHT FROM ASHIYA
Director: Michael Anderson
Co-stars: Yul Brynner Richard Widmark Shirley Knight

1966 CHAMBER OF HORRORS
Director: Hy Averback
Co-stars: Patrick O'Neal Cesare Danova Patrice Wymore

BARBARA PARKINS

1967 VALLEY OF THE DOLLS
Director: Mark Robson
Co-stars: Patty Duke Susan Hayward Sharon Tate

1970 THE KREMLIN LETTER
Director: John Huston
Co-stars: Richard Boone Orson Welles Bibi Andersson

1971 THE DEADLY TRAP
Director: Rene Clement
Co-stars: Faye Dunaway Frank Langella

1971 THE MEPHISTO WALTZ
Director: Paul Wendkos
Co-stars: Alan Alda Jacqueline Bisset Curt Jurgens

1971 PUPPET ON A CHAIN
Director: Geoffrey Reeve
Co-stars: Sven-Bertil Taube Alexander Knox Patrick Allen

1971 A TASTE OF EVIL
Director: John Llewellyn Moxey
Co-stars: Barbara Stanwyck Roddy McDowall Dawn Frame

1972 ASYLUM
Director: Roy Ward Baker
Co-stars: Robert Powell Richard Todd Charlotte Rampling

1973 SNATCHED
Director: Sutton Roley
Co-stars: Howard Duff Leslie Nielsen Sheree North

1974 CHRISTINA
Director: Paul Krasny
Co-stars: Peter Haskell Marlyn Mason Barbara Gordon

1976 SHOUT AT THE DEVIL
Director: Peter Hunt
Co-stars: Lee Marvin Roger Moore Ian Holm

1979 BEAR ISLAND
Director: Don Sharp
Co-stars: Vanessa Redgrave Donald Sutherland Richard Widmark

1982 BREAKFAST IN PARIS
Director: John Lamond
Co-stars: Rod Mullinar Jack Lenoir Jeremy Higgins

1983 UNCOMMON VALOR
Director: Rod Amateau
Co-stars: Mitchell Ryan Ben Murphy Salome Jens

1984 TO CATCH A KING
Director: Clive Donner
Co-stars: Robert Wagner Teri Garr John Standing

1984 THE CALENDAR GIRL MURDERS
Director: William Graham
Co-stars: Tom Skerritt Sharon Stone Robert Morse

CATHERINE PARKS

1982 FRIDAY 13TH PART III
Director: Steve Miner
Co-stars: Dana Kimmell Richard Brooker Paul Kratka

1989 WEEKEND AT BERNIE'S
Director: Ted Kotchoff
Co-stars: Andrew McCarthy Jonathan Silverman Terry Kiser

1933 WEEKEND AT BERNIE'S II
Director: Robert Klane
Co-stars: Andrew McCarthy Jonathan Silverman Don Caffa

HILDY PARKS

1955 THE NIGHT HOLDS TERROR
Director: Andrew Stone
Co-stars: Jack Kelly John Cassavetes David Cross

NANETTA PARKS

1945 SNAFU
Director: Jack Moss
Co-stars: Robert Benchley Vera Vague Conrad Janus

DITA PARLO

1934 L'ATALANTE
Director: Jean Vigo
Co-stars: Jean Daste Michel Simon Giles Margarites

1937 LA GRANDE ILLUSION
Director: Jean Renoir
Co-stars: Pierre Fresnay Jean Gabin Erich Von Stroheim

1937 MADEMOISELLE DOCTEUR
Director: Edmond Greville
Co-stars: John Loder Erich Von Stroheim Claire Luce

JACQUELINE PARON

1984 ALICE

1986 ANTOINETTE
Co-stars: Francois Marthouret Laurent Ternois

KATE PARR

1977 ALIEN ENCOUNTERS
Director: Ed Hunt
Co-stars: Robert Vaughn Helen Shaver Christopher Lee

HELEN PARRISH

1930 THE BIG TRAIL
Director: Raoul Walsh
Co-stars: John Wayne Marguerite Churchill El Brendel

1938 LITTLE TOUGH GUY
Director: Harold Young
Co-stars: Billy Halop Marjorie Main Huntz Hall

1938 LITTLE TOUGH GUYS IN SOCIETY
Director: Erle Kenton
Co-stars: Mary Boland Jackie Searle Mischa Auer

1938 MAD ABOUT MUSIC
Director: Norman Taurog
Co-stars: Deanna Durbin Herbert Marshall Gail Patrick

1939 FIRST LOVE
Director: Henry Koster
Co-stars: Deanna Durbin Robert Stack Eugene Pallette

1939 THREE SMART GIRLS GROW UP
Director: Henry Koster
Co-stars: Deanna Durbin Nan Grey Charles Winninger

1939 WINTER CARNIVAL
Director: Charles Riesner
Co-stars: Ann Sheridan Richard Carlson Virginia Gilmore

1940 YOU'LL FIND OUT
Director: David Butler
Co-stars: Kay Kyser Dennis O'Keefe Ginny Simms

1941 TOO MANY BLONDES
Co-stars: Rudy Vallee Jerome Cowan

1941 SIX LESSONS FROM MADAME LA ZONGA
Director: John Rawlins
Co-stars: Lupe Velez Leon Errol Charles Lang

1942 THEY ALL KISSED THE BRIDE
Director: Alexander Hall
Co-stars: Joan Crawford Melvyn Douglas Mary Treen

1942 IN OLD CALIFORNIA
Director: William McGann
Co-stars: John Wayne Binnie Barnes Albert Dekker

1942 SUNSET SERENADE
Co-stars: Roy Rogers Jack Rockwell

1943 THE MYSTERY OF THE 13TH GUEST
Director: William Beaudine
Co-stars: Dick Purcell Tim Ryan Frank Faylen

JULIE PARRISH

1972 THE DOBERMAN GANG
Director: Byron Chudnow
Co-stars: Simmy Bow Hal Reed Byron Mabe

LESLIE PARRISH

1959 LI'L ABNER
Director: Norman Panama
Co-stars: Peter Palmer Stubby Kaye Julie Newman

1961 PORTRAIT OF A MOBSTER
Director: Joseph Pevney
Co-stars: Vic Morrow Ray Danton Peter Breck

1962 THE MANCHURIAN CANDIDATE
Director: John Frankenheimer
Co-stars: Frank Sinatra Laurence Harvey Janet Leigh

1963 FOR LOVE OR MONEY
Director: Michael Gordon
Co-stars: Kirk Douglas Mitzi Gaynor Thelma Ritter

1966 THREE ON A COUCH
Director: Jerry Lewis
Co-stars: Janet Leigh James Best Jerry Lewis

1968 THE CANDY MAN
Director: Herbert Leder
Co-stars: George Sanders Gina Roman Manolo Fabregas

1968 THE DEVIL'S EIGHT
Director: Burt Topper
Co-stars: Christopher George Ralph Meeker Fabian

1975 THE GIANT SPIDER INVASION
Director: Bill Rebane
Co-stars: Barbara Hale Steve Brodie Alan Hale Jnr.

1977 CRASH !
Director: Charles Band
Co-stars: Jose Ferrer Sue Lyon John Ericson

PAT PARRISH

1944 THEY LIVE IN FEAR
Co-stars: Otto Kruger Clifford Severn

1945 LET'S GO STEADY
Co-stars: Mel Torme June Preisser Jimmy Lloyd

LORETTA PARRY *(Child)*

1960 HAND IN HAND
Director: Philip Leacock
Co-stars: Philip Needs Miriam Karlin John Gregson

NATASHA PARRY

1950 MIDNIGHT EPISODE
Director: Gordon Parry
Co-stars: Stanley Holloway Leslie Dwyer Meredith Edwards

1950 DANCE HALL
Director: Charles Crighton
Co-stars: Petula Clark Bonar Colleano Diana Dors

1950 THE DARK MAN
Director: Jeffrey Dell
Co-stars: Maxwell Reed Edward Underdown Barbara Murray

1954 KNAVE OF HEARTS
Director: Rene Clement
Co-stars: Gerard Philippe Margaret Johnston Joan Greenwood

1957 WINDOM'S WAY
Director: Ronald Neame
Co-stars: Peter Finch Mary Ure Robert Flemyng

1959 THE ROUGH AND THE SMOOTH
Director: Robert Siodmak
Co-stars: Tony Britton William Bendix Nadja Tiller

1960 MIDNIGHT LACE
Director: David Miller
Co-stars: Doris Day Rex Harrison Myrna Loy

1963 GIRL IN THE HEADLINES
Director: Michael Truman
Co-stars: Ian Hendry Ronald Fraser Margaret Johnston

1968 ROMEO AND JULIET
Director: Franco Zefferelli
Co-stars: Olivia Hussey Leonard Whiting

ESTELLE PARSONS
Best Supporting Actress In 1967For "Bonnie And Clyde".
Nominated For Best Supporting Actress In 1968 For "Rachel, Rachel"

1967   BONNIE AND CLYDE
Director: Arthur Penn
Co-stars: Warren Beatty Faye Dunaway Gene Hackman

1968   RACHEL, RACHEL
Director: Paul Newman
Co-stars: Joanne Woodward James Olson Don Moffat

1969   I NEVER SANG FOR MY FATHER
Director: Gilbert Cates
Co-stars: Melvyn Douglas Gene Hackman Dorothy Stickney

1969   DON'T DRINK THE WATER
Director: Howard Morris
Co-stars: Jackie Gleason Ted Bessell

1970   I WALK THE LINE
Director: John Frankenheimer
Co-stars: Gregory Peck Tuesday Weld Ralph Meeker

1970   WATERMELON MAN
Director: Melvin Van Peebles
Co-stars: Godfrey Cambridge Howard Caine Manton Moreland

1973   TWO PEOPLE
Director: Robert Wise
Co-stars: Peter Fonda Lindsay Wagner Alan Fudge

1974   FOR PETE'S SAKE
Director: Peter Yates
Co-stars: Barbra Streisand Michael Sarazin Molly Picon

1990   THE LEMON SISTERS
Director: Joyce Chopra
Co-stars: Diane Keaton Carol Kane Elliott Gould

1992   A PRIVATE MATTER
Director: Joan Micklin Silver
Co-stars: Sissy Spacek Aidan Quinn

1995   BOYS ON THE SIDE
Director: Herbert Ross
Co-stars: Whoopi Goldberg Mary Louise Parker Drew Barrymore

1997   LOOKING FOR RICHARD
Director: Al Pacino
Co-stars: Aidan Quinn Winona Ryder Kevin Spacey

JULIE PARSONS

1979   HOMETOWN U.S.A.
Director: Max Baer
Co-stars: Gary Springer David Wilson Sally Kirkland

LOUELLA PARSONS

1937   HOLLYWOOD HOTEL
Director: Busby Berkeley
Co-stars: Dick Powell Rosemary Lane Lola Lane

1946   WITHOUT RESERVATIONS
Director: Mervyn LeRoy
Co-stars: Claudette Colbert John Wayne Don Defore

1951   STARLIFT
Director: Roy Del Ruth
Co-stars: Janice Rule Dick Wesson Doris Day

NANCY PARSONS

1980   MOTEL HELL
Director: Kevin Connor
Co-stars: Rory Calhoun Paul Linke Nina Axelrod

1981   PORKY'S
Director: Bob Clark
Co-stars: Dan Monahan Mark Herrier Kim Cattrall

1992   LADYBUGS
Director: Sidney Furie
Co-stars: Rodney Dangerfield Vinessa Shaw Tom Parks

1992   THE DOCTOR
Director: Randa Haines
Co-stars: William Hurt Christine Lahti Elizabeth Perkins

DOLLY PARTON

1980   NINE TO FIVE
Director: Colin Higgins
Co-stars: Jane Fonda Lily Tomlin Sterling Hayden

1982   THE BEST LITTLE WHOREHOUSE IN TEXAS
Director: Colin Higgins
Co-stars: Burt Reynolds Dom DeLuise

1984   RHINESTONE
Director: Bob Clark
Co-stars: Sylvester Stallone Richard Farnsworth Ron Leibman

1986   SMOKY MOUNTAIN CHRISTMAS
Director: Henry Winkler
Co-stars: Lee Majors

1989   STEEL MAGNOLIAS
Director: Herbert Ross
Co-stars: Sally Field Shirley MacLaine Julia Roberts

1991   WILD TEXAS WIND
Director: Joan Tewkesbury
Co-stars: Gary Busey Ray Benson

1992   STRAIGHT TALK
Director: Barnett Kelman
Co-stars: James Woods Griffin Dunne Michael Madsen

1994   THE BEVERLEY HILLBILLIES
Director: Penelope Spheeris
Co-stars: Jim Varney Dabney Coleman Lily Tomlin

1996   UNLIKELY ANGEL

KIMBERLEY PARTRIDGE *(Child)*

1982   BETTER LATE THAN NEVER
Director: Bryan Forbes
Co-stars: David Niven Art Carney Maggie Smith

CHRISTINE PASCAL

1973   THE WATCHMAKER OF ST. PAUL
Director: Bertrand Tavernier
Co-stars: Philippe Noiret Jean Rochefort

1986   ROUND MIDNIGHT
Director: Bertrand Tavernier
Co-stars: Dexter Gordon Francois Cluzet Martin Scorsese

1988   LE GRAND CHEMIN
Director: Jean-Loup Hubert
Co-stars: Anemone Richard Bohringer Antoine Hubert

OLIVIA PASCAL

1980   BURNING RUBBER
Director: Norman Cohen
Co-stars: Alan Longmuir Sascha Hehn Stuart Wood

NATHALIE PASCAUD

1953   MONSIEUR HULOT'S HOLIDAY
Director: Jacques Tati
Co-stars: Jacques Tati Michele Rolla Valentine Camax

ISABELLE PASCO

1989   ROSELYN AND THE LIONS
Director: Jean-Jacques Beineix
Co-stars: Gerard Sandoz Phillippe Clevenot

1991 PROSPERO'S BOOKS
Director: Peter Greenaway
Co-stars: John Gielgud Michel Blanc Tom Bell

CRISTINA S. PASCUAL

1984 DARK HABITS
Director: Pedro Almodovar
Co-stars: Marisa Paredes Carmen Maura Mari Carrillo

ENCARNA PASO

1982 BEGIN THE BEGUINE
Director: Jose Luis Garci
Co-stars: Antonio Ferrandis Jose Bodalo Pablo Hoyo

SUSANNA PASOLINI

(Mother Of Pier Paolo Pasolini)

1964 THE GOSPEL ACCORDING TO MATTHEW
Director: Pier Paolo Pasolini
Co-stars: Enrique Irazoqui Mario Socrate

FRANCA PASUT

1961 ACCATONE
Director: Pier Paolo Pasolini
Co-stars: Franco Citti Silvana Corsini Paolo Guidi

CLARA PASTOR

1988 ANGUISH
Director: Bigas Luna
Co-stars: Zelda Rubinstein Talia Paul Michael Lerner

ROSANA PASTOR

1995 LAND AND FREEDOM
Director: Ken Loach
Co-star: Ian Hart

PATACHOU

1955 FRENCH CAN-CAN
Director: Jean Renoir
Co-stars: Jean Gabin Maria Felix Edith Piaf

1988 THE MAN WHO LIVED AT THE RITZ
Director: Desmond Davis
Co-stars: Perry King Leslie Caron Cherie Lunghi

1993 WILD TARGET
Director: Pierre Salvadori
Co-stars: Jean Rochefort Marie Trintignant

SOPHIE PATEL

1992 BITTER MOON
Director: Roman Polanski
Co-stars: Hugh Grant Kristin Scott-Thomas Peter Coyote

DANIELLE PATELLA

1972 ALFREDO, ALFREDO
Director: Pietro Germi
Co-stars: Dustin Hoffman Stefania Sandrelli Carla Gravina

CAROLINE PATERSON

1989 VENUS PETER
Director: Ian Sellar
Co-stars: Ray McAnally David Hayman Sinead Cusack

PAT PATERSON

1930 LOTTERY LOVER
Director: William Thiele
Co-stars: Lew Ayres Reginald Denny Sterling Holloway

1933 BITTER SWEET
Director: Herbert Wilcox
Co-stars: Anna Neagle Fernand Gravet Ivy St. Helier

1934 BOTTOMS UP
Director: David Butler
Co-stars: Spencer Tracy John Boles Sid Silvers

1934 CALL IT LUCK
Co-star: Charles Starrett

1934 LOVE TIME
Director: James Tinling
Co-stars: Nils Asther Herbert Mundin Harry Green

1935 CHARLIE CHAN IN EGYPT
Director: Louis King
Co-stars: Warner Oland Rita Hayworth Thomas Beck

1936 SPENDTHRIFT
Director: Raoul Walsh
Co-stars: Henry Fonda Mary Brian George Barbier

1938 IDIOT'S DELIGHT
Director: Clarence Brown
Co-stars: Clark Gable Norma Shearer Edward Arnold

LAURIE PATON

1993 THE AMY FISHER STORY
Director: Andy Tennant
Co-stars: Drew Barrymore Anthony John Dennison Harley Jane Kozak

ANNA PATRICK

1995 OTHELLO
Director: Oliver Parker
Co-stars: Laurence Fishburne Kenneth Branagh Irene Jacob

CYNTHIA PATRICK

1956 THE MOLE PEOPLE
Director: Virgil Vogel
Co-stars: John Agar Hugh Beaumont Alan Napier

DOROTHY PATRICK

1946 THE MIGHTY McGURK
Director: John Waters
Co-stars: Wallace Beery Dean Stockwell Edward Arnold

1946 TILL THE CLOUDS ROLL BY
Director: Richard Whorf
Co-stars: Robert Walker Van Heflin Lucille Bremer

1946 BOYS' RANCH
Director: Roy Rowland
Co-stars: James Craig Butch Jenkins Skip Homeier

1947 HIGH WALL
Director: Curtis Bernhardt
Co-stars: Robert Taylor Herbert Marshall Audrey Totter

1947 NEW ORLEANS
Director: Arthur Lubin
Co-stars: Louis Armstrong Arturo De Cordova Billie Holliday

1949 FOLLOW ME QUIETLY
Director: Richard Fleischer
Co-stars: William Lundigan Jeff Corey Paul Guilfoyle

1949 COME TO THE STABLE
Director: Henry Koster
Co-stars: Loretta Young Celeste Holm Hugh Marlowe

1950 HOUSE BY THE RIVER
Director: Fritz Lang
Co-stars: Louis Hayward Jane Wyatt Lee Bowman

1950 711 OCEAN DRIVE
Director: Joseph Newman
Co-stars: Edmond O'Brien Joanne Dru Otto Kruger

1953 TORCH SONG
Director: Charles Walters
Co-stars: Joan Crawford Michael Wilding Gig Young

GAIL PATRICK

1933 THE PHANTOM BROADCAST
Co-star: Ralph Forbes

1933 MURDERS IN THE ZOO
Director: Edward Sutherland
Co-stars: Lionel Atwill Charles Ruggles Randolph Scott

1934 MURDER AT THE VANITIES
Director: Mitchell Leisen
Co-stars: Jack Oakie Victor McLaglen Carl Brissen

1934 DEATH TAKES A HOLIDAY
Director: Mitchell Leisen
Co-stars: Fredric March Evelyn Venable

1934 TAKE THE STAND

1934 WAGON WHEELS
Co-star: Russell Hopton

1935 DOUBTING THOMAS
Director: David Butler
Co-stars: Will Rogers Billie Burke Alison Skipworth

1935 THE LONE WOLF RETURNS
Director: Roy William Neill
Co-stars: Melvyn Douglas Tala Birell

1935 MISSISSIPPI
Director: Edward Sutherland
Co-stars: Bing Crosby W.C. Fields Joan Bennett

1935 BIG BROADCAST OF 1936
Director: Ben Glazer
Co-stars: Bing Crosby Gracie Allen Jack Oakie

1935 NO MORE LADIES
Director: George Cukor
Co-stars: Joan Crawford Franchot Tone Robert Montgomery

1935 RUMBA
Director: Marion Gering
Co-stars: Carole Lombard George Raft Lynne Overman

1935 SMART GIRL
Director: Aubrey Scotto
Co-stars: Ida Lupino Kent Taylor Pinky Tomlin

1935 TWO FISTED
Director: James Cruze
Co-stars: Lee Tracy Roscoe Karns Kent Taylor

1936 TWO IN THE DARK
Director: Ben Stoloff
Co-stars: Walter Abel Margot Grahame Wallace Ford

1936 EARLY TO BED
Co-stars: Charles Ruggles Mary Boland

1936 MY MAN GODFREY
Director: Gregory La Cava
Co-stars: Carole Lombard William Powell Alice Brady

1936 WHITE HUNTER
Director: Irving Cummings
Co-stars: Warner Baxter Wilfrid Lawson June Lang

1937 STAGE DOOR
Director: Gregory La Cava
Co-stars: Katharine Hepburn Ginger Rogers Lucille Ball

1937 JOHN MEADE'S WOMEN
Director: Richard Wallace
Co-stars: Edward Arnold Francine Larrimore

1937 HER HUSBAND LIES
Director: Edward Ludwig
Co-stars: Ricardo Cortez Akim Tamiroff Louis Calhern

1937 ARTISTS AND MODELS
Director: Raoul Walsh
Co-stars: Jack Benny Ida Lupino Richard Arlen

1938 DANGEROUS TO KNOW
Director: Robert Florey
Co-stars: Akim Tamiroff Anna May Wong Lloyd Nolan

1938 DISBARRED
Director: Robert Florey
Co-stars: Otto Kruger Robert Preston Sidney Toler

1938 KING OF ALCATRAZ
Director: Robert Florey
Co-stars: Lloyd Nolan Robert Preston Dennis Morgan

1938 MAD ABOUT MUSIC
Director: Norman Taurog
Co-stars: Deanna Durbin Herbert Marshall Arthur Treacher

1938 WIVES UNDER SUSPICION
Director: James Whale
Co-stars: Warren William Ralph Morgan Constance Moore

1939 RENO
Director: John Farrow
Co-stars: Richard Dix Anita Louise Hobart Cavanagh

1939 GRAND JURY SECRETS
Co-star: John Howard

1939 MAN OF CONQUEST
Director: George Nicholls
Co-stars: Richard Dix Joan Fontaine Edward Ellis

1940 GALLANT SONS
Director: George Seitz
Co-stars: Jackie Cooper Bonita Granville Gene Reynolds

1940 MY FAVORITE WIFE
Director: Garson Kanin
Co-stars: Irene Dunne Cary Grant Randolph Scott

1941 KATHLEEN
Director: Harold Bucquet
Co-stars: Shirley Temple Herbert Marshall Laraine Day

1941 LOVE CRAZY
Director: Jack Conway
Co-stars: William Powell Myrna Loy Jack Carson

1942 WE WERE DANCING
Director: Robert Z. Leonard
Co-stars: Norma Shearer Melvyn Douglas Lee Bowman

1942 TALES OF MANHATTAN
Director: Julien Duvivier
Co-stars: Charles Boyer Rita Hayworth Henry Fonda

1943 STAGE DOOR CANTEEN
Director: Frank Borzage
Co-stars: Cheryl Walker Lon McCallister Judith Anderson

1943 QUIET PLEASE, MURDER
Director: John Larkin
Co-stars: George Sanders Kurt Katch Richard Denning

1943 HIT PARADE OF 1943
Director: Albert Rogell
Co-stars: John Carroll Susan Hayward Dorothy Dandridge

1943 WOMEN IN BONDAGE
Director: Steve Sekeley
Co-stars: Nancy Kelly Gertrude Michael Tala Birell

1944 UP IN MABEL'S ROOM
Director: Allan Dwan
Co-stars: Dennis O'Keefe Mischa Auer Marjorie Reynolds

1945 BREWSTER'S MILLIONS
Director: Allan Dwan
Co-stars: Dennis O'Keefe Mischa Auer Eddie Anderson

1945 TWICE BLESSED
Director: Harry Beaumont
Co-stars: Lee & Lyn Wilde Preston Foster Richard Gaines

1946 **THE PLAINSMAN AND THE LADY**
Director: Joseph Kane
Co-stars: William Elliott Vera Ralston

1946 **THE MADONNA'S SECRET**
Director: William Thiele
Co-stars: Francis Lederer Ann Rutherford John Litel

1946 **CLAUDIA AND DAVID**
Director: Walter Lang
Co-stars: Dorothy McGuire Robert Young John Sutton

1947 **CALENDAR GIRL**
Director: Allan Dawn
Co-stars: Irene Rich Victor McLaglen Jane Frazee

1948 **THE INSIDE STORY**
Director: Allan Dwan
Co-stars: Marsha Hunt Charles Winninger William Lundigan

LEE PATRICK

1937 **MUSIC FOR MADAME**
Director: John Blystone
Co-stars: Nino Martini Joan Fontaine Alan Mowbray

1938 **LAW OF THE UNDERWORLD**
Director: Lew Landers
Co-stars: Chester Morris Ann Shirley Eduardo Ciannelli

1938 **THE SISTERS**
Director: Anatole Litvak
Co-stars: Bette Davis Errol Flynn Ian Hunter

1938 **CRASHING HOLLYWOOD**
Director: Lew Landers
Co-stars: Lee Tracy Joan Woodbury Jack Carson

1938 **CONDEMNED WOMAN**
Director: Lew Landers
Co-stars: Sally Eilers Ann Shirley Louis Hayward

1939 **FISHERMAN'S WHARF**
Director: Bernard Vorhaus
Co-stars: Bobby Breen Leo Carrillo Henry Armetta

1940 **MONEY AND THE WOMAN**
Director: William Howard
Co-stars: Jeffrey Lynn Brenda Marshall John Litel

1940 **SATURDAY'S CHILDREN**
Director: Vincent Sherman
Co-stars: John Garfield Claude Rains Ann Shirley

1940 **CITY FOR CONQUEST**
Director: Anatole Litvak
Co-stars: James Cagney Ann Sheridan Donald Crisp

1940 **SOUTH OF THE SUEZ**
Director: Lewis Seiler
Co-stars: George Brent Brenda Marshall George Tobias

1940 **INVISIBLE STRIPES**
Director: Lloyd Bacon
Co-stars: George Raft Humphrey Bogart Flora Robson

1940 **THE NURSE'S SECRET**
Director: Noel Smith
Co-stars: Regis Toomey Julie Bishop Charles Trowbridge

1941 **MILLION DOLLAR BABY**
Director: Curtis Bernhardt
Co-stars: Priscilla Lane Jeffrey Lynn Ronald Reagan

1941 **THE MALTESE FALCON**
Director: John Huston
Co-stars: Humphrey Bogart Peter Lorre Sydney Greenstreet

1941 **HONEYMOON FOR THREE**
Director: Lloyd Bacon
Co-stars: George Brent Ann Sheridan Osa Massen

1941 **FOOTSTEPS IN THE DARK**
Director: Lloyd Bacon
Co-stars: Errol Flynn Brenda Marshall Ralph Bellamy

1941 **DANGEROUSLY THEY LIVE**
Director: Robert Florey
Co-stars: John Garfield Raymond Massey Moroni Olsen

1942 **GEORGE WASHINGTON SLEPT HERE**
Director: William Keighley
Co-stars: Jack Benny Ann Sheridan William Tracy

1942 **IN THIS OUR LIFE**
Director: John Huston
Co-stars: Bette Davis Olivia De Havilland Charles Coburn

1942 **SOMEWHERE I'LL FIND YOU**
Director: Wesley Ruggles
Co-stars: Clark Gable Lana Turner Robert Sterling

1942 **NOW VOYAGER**
Director: Iring Rapper
Co-stars: Bette Davis Paul Henreid Claude Rains

1943 **A NIGHT TO REMEMBER**
Director: Richard Wallace
Co-stars: Loretta Young Brian Aherne Jeff Donnell

1943 **JITTERBUGS**
Director: Mal St. Clair
Co-stars: Stan Laurel Oliver Hardy Vivian Blaine

1945 **KEEP YOUR POWDER DRY**
Director: Edward Buzzell
Co-stars: Lana Turner Laraine Day Susan Peters

1945 **OVER 21**
Director: Alexander Hall
Co-stars: Irene Dunne Alexander Knox Charles Coburn

1946 **THE WALLS CAME TUMBLING DOWN**
Director: Lothar Mendes
Co-stars: Lee Bowman Marguerite Chapman

1946 **WAKE UP AND DREAM**
Director: Lloyd Bacon
Co-stars: June Haver John Payne Connie Marshall

1947 **MOTHER WORE TIGHTS**
Director: Walter Lang
Co-stars: Betty Grable Dan Dailey Mona Freeman

1948 **THE SNAKE PIT**
Director: Anatole Litvak
Co-stars: Olivia De Havilland Leo Genn Mark Stevens

1950 **CAGED**
Director: John Cromwell
Co-stars: Eleanor Parker Agnes Moorehead Ellen Corby

1950 **THE FULLER BRUSH GIRL**
Director: Lloyd Bacon
Co-stars: Lucille Ball Eddie Albert Jeff Donnell

1950 **THE LAWLESS**
Director: Joseph Losey
Co-stars: MacDonald Cary Gail Russell John Hoyt

1953 **TAKE ME TO TOWN**
Director: Douglas Sirk
Co-stars: Ann Sheridan Sterling Hayden Philip Reed

1958 **AUNTIE MAME**
Director: Morton DeCosta
Co-stars: Rosalind Russell Forrest Tucker Coral Browne

1959 **PILLOW TALK**
Director: Michael Gordon
Co-stars: Doris Day Rock Hudson Tony Randall

1960 **VISIT TO A SMALL PLANET**
Director: Norman Taurog
Co-stars: Jerry Lewis Joan Blackman John Williams

1961 **SUMMER AND SMOKE**
Director: Peter Glenville
Co-stars: Geraldine Page Laurence Harvey Una Merkel

1964 **7 FACES OF DR LAO**
Director: George Pal
Co-stars: Tony Randall Barbara Eden Arthur O'Connell

1964 **THE NEW INTERNS**
Director: John Rich
Co-stars: George Segal Telly Savalas Dean Jones

1975 **THE BLACK BIRD**
Director: David Giler
Co-stars: George Segal Stephane Audran Elisha Cook

LUANA PATTEN (*Child*)

1946 **SONG OF THE SOUTH**
Director: Wilfred Jackson
Co-stars: James Baskett Ruth Warrick Bobby Driscoll

1946 **LITTLE MR JIM**
Director: Fred Zinnemann
Co-stars: Butch Jenkins James Craig Frances Gifford

1948 **SO DEAR TO MY HEART**
Director: Harold Schuster
Co-stars: Burl Ives Bobby Driscoll Beulah Bondi

1956 **ROCK, PRETTY BABY**
Director: Richard Bartlett
Co-stars: Sal Mineo John Saxon Fay Wray

1957 **JOHNNY TREMAIN**
Director: Robert Stevenson
Co-stars: Hal Stalmaster Jeff York Richard Beymer

1957 **JOE DAKOTA**
Director: Richard Bartlett
Co-stars: Jock Mahoney Charles McGraw Barbara Lawrence

1959 **HOME FROM THE HILL**
Director: Vincente Minnelli
Co-stars: Robert Mitchum George Peppard George Hamilton

1959 **THE RESTLESS YEARS**
Director: Helmut Kautner
Co-stars: Sandra Dee John Saxon Teresa Wright

1960 **GO NAKED IN THE WORLD**
Director: Ranald MacDougall
Co-stars: Gina Lollobrigida Tony Franciosa

1961 **A THUNDER OF DRUMS**
Director: Joseph Newman
Co-stars: Richard Boone George Hamilton Charles Bronson

1961 **THE LITTLE SHEPHERD
OF KINGDOM COME**
Director: Andrew McLaglen
Co-star: Jimmie Rodgers

1966 **FOLLOW ME, BOYS!**
Director: Norman Tokar
Co-stars: Fred MacMurray Vera Miles Kurt Russell

ELIZABETH PATTERSON

1931 **HEAVEN ON EARTH**
Director: Russell Mack
Co-stars: Lew Ayres Anita Louise John Carradine

1931 **DADDY LONG LEGS**
Director: Alfred Santell
Co-stars: Janet Gaynor Warner Baxter Una Merkel

1931 **HUSBAND'S HOLIDAY**
Director: Robert Milton
Co-stars: Clive Brook Vivienne Osbourne Charles Winninger

1931 **THE SMILING LIEUTENANT**
Director: Ernst Lubitsch
Co-stars: Maurice Chevalier Claudette Colbert

1931 **TARNISHED LADY**
Director: George Cukor
Co-stars: Tallulah Bankhead Clive Brook Phoebe Foster

1932 **MISS PINKERTON**
Director: Lloyd Bacon
Co-stars: Joan Blondell George Brent Mae Madison

1932 **LOVE ME TONIGHT**
Director: Rouben Mamoulian
Co-stars: Maurice Chevalier Jeanette MacDonald

1932 **A BILL OF DIVORCEMENT**
Director: David O. Selznick
Co-stars: John Barrymore Katherine Hepburn

1932 **NEW MORALS FOR OLD**
Director: Charles Brabin
Co-stars: Robert Young Myrna Loy Jean Hersholt

1932 **NO MAN OF HER OWN**
Director: Wesley Ruggles
Co-stars: Clark Gable Carole Lombard Dorothy Mackail

1932 **LIFE BEGINS**
Director: James Flood
Co-stars: Elliott Nugent Loretta Young Glenda Farrell

1933 **DINNER AT EIGHT**
Director: George Cukor
Co-stars: Marie Dressler Jean Harlow Lionel Barrymore

1933 **THE STORY OF TEMPLE DRAKE**
Director: Stephen Roberts
Co-stars: Miriam Hopkins Jack La Rue William Gargan

1934 **HIDE-OUT**
Director: W.S. Van Dyke
Co-stars: Robert Montgomery Maureen O'Sullivan Mickey Rooney

1935 **SO RED THE ROSE**
Director: King Vidor
Co-stars: Margaret Sullavan Randolph Scott Robert Cummings

1935 **CHASING YESTERDAY**
Director: George Nicholls
Co-stars: O.P. Heggie Ann Shirley Helen Westley

1936 **GO WEST, YOUNG MAN**
Director: Henry Hathaway
Co-stars: Mae West Randolph Scott Warren William

1936 **HER MASTER'S VOICE**
Director: Joseph Santley
Co-stars: Edward Everett Horton Peggy Conklin

1936 **OLD HUTCH**
Director: Walter Ruben
Co-stars: Wallace Beery Eric Linden Cecilia Parker

1936 **SMALL TOWN GIRL**
Director: William Wellman
Co-stars: Janet Gaynor Robert Taylor James Stewart

1937 **SCANDAL SHEET**
Director: James Hogan
Co-stars: Lew Ayres Louise Campbell Virginia Weidler

1937 **NIGHT CLUB SCANDAL**
Director: Ralph Murphy
Co-stars: John Barrymore Charles Bickford Evelyn Brent

1937 **HIGH, WIDE AND HANDSOME**
Director: Rouben Mamoulian
Co-stars: Irene Dunne Dorothy Lamour Randolph Scott

1938 **BLUEBEARD'S EIGHTH WIFE**
Director: Ernst Lubitsch
Co-stars: Gary Cooper Claudette Colbert

1938 **SING YOU SINNERS**
Director: Wesley Ruggles
Co-stars: Bing Crosby Fred MacMurray Donald O'Connor

1939   **THE CAT AND THE CANARY**
Director: Elliott Nugent
Co-stars: Bob Hope Paulette Goddard Gale Sondergaard

1939   **OUR LEADING CITIZEN**
Director: Alfred Santell
Co-stars: Bob Burns Susan Hayward Charles Bickford

1940   **ADVENTURE IN DIAMONDS**
Director: George Fitzmaurice
Co-stars: George Brent Isa Miranda Nigel Bruce

1940   **MICHAEL SHAYNE, PRIVATE DETECTIVE**
Director: Eugene Forde
Co-stars: Lloyd Nolan Marjorie Weaver

1940   **REMEMBER THE NIGHT**
Director: Mitchell Leisen
Co-stars: Barbara Stanwyck Fred MacMurray Beulah Bondi

1941   **THE VANISHING VIRGINIAN**
Director: Frank Borzage
Co-stars: Frank Morgan Kathryn Grayson

1941   **BELLE STAR**
Director: Kenneth MacGowan
Co-stars: Gene Tierney Randolph Scott Dana Andrews

1941   **TOBACCO ROAD**
Director: John Ford
Co-stars: Gene Tierney Charley Grapewin Dana Andrews

1941   **KISS THE BOYS GOODBYE**
Director: Victor Schertzinger
Co-stars: Don Ameche Mary Martin Oscar Levant

1942   **MY SISTER EILEEN**
Director: Alexander Hall
Co-stars: Rosalind Russell Janet Blair Brian Aherne

1942   **I MARRIED A WITCH**
Director: Rene Clair
Co-stars: Fredric March Veronica Lake Cecil Kellaway

1942   **BEYOND THE BLUE HORIZON**
Director: Alfred Santell
Co-stars: Dorothy Lamour Richard Denning

1942   **HER CARDBOARD LOVER**
Director: George Cukor
Co-stars: Norma Shearer Robert Taylor George Sanders

1943   **THE SKY'S THE LIMIT**
Director: Edward Griffith
Co-stars: Fred Astaire Joan Leslie Robert Benchley

1944   **TOGETHER AGAIN**
Director: Charles Vidor
Co-stars: Irene Dunne Charles Boyer Charles Coburn

1944   **HAIL THE CONQUERING HERO**
Director: Preston Sturges
Co-stars: Eddie Bracken Ella Raines William Demarest

1944   **FOLLOW THE BOYS**
Director: Edward Sutherland
Co-stars: Jeanette MacDonald Dinah Shore George Raft

1945   **COLONEL EFFINGHAM'S RAID**
Director: Irving Pichel
Co-stars: Charles Coburn Joan Bennett William Eythe

1946   **THE SHOCKING PILGRIM**
Director: George Seaton
Co-stars: Betty Grable Dick Haymes Anne Revere

1946   **THE SECRET HEART**
Director: Robert Z. Leonard
Co-stars: Claudette Colbert Walter Pidgeon June Allyson

1947   **WELCOME STRANGER**
Director: Elliott Nugent
Co-stars: Bing Crosby Joan Caulfield Barry Fitzgerald

1947   **OUT OF THE BLUE**
Director: Leigh Jason
Co-stars: George Brent Carole Landis Virginia Mayo

1948   **MISS TATLOCK'S MILLIONS**
Director: Richard Haydn
Co-stars: Wanda Hendrix John Lund Monty Woolley

1949   **SONG OF SURRENDER**
Director: Mitchell Leisen
Co-stars: Wanda Hendrix Claude Rains MacDonald Carey

1949   **LITTLE WOMEN**
Director: Mervyn LeRoy
Co-stars: June Allyson Elizabeth Taylor Margaret O'Brien

1949   **INTRUDER IN THE DUST**
Director: Clarence Brown
Co-stars: Juano Hernandez Claude Jarman Jnr.

1950   **BRIGHT LEAF**
Director: Michael Curtiz
Co-stars: Gary Cooper Lauren Bacall Patricia Neal

1951   **KATIE DID IT**
Director: Frederick De Cordova
Co-stars: Ann Blyth Mark Stevens Cecil Kellaway

1952   **WASHINGTON STORY**
Director: Robert Pirosh
Co-stars: Van Johnson Patricia Neal Louis Calhern

1957   **PAL JOEY**
Director: George Sidney
Co-stars: Frank Sinatra Rita Hayworth Kim Novak

1959   **THE OREGON TRAIL**
Director: Gene Fowler
Co-stars: Fred MacMurray William Bishop Nina Shipman

1960   **TALL STORY**
Director: Joshua Logan
Co-stars: Anthony Perkins Jane Fonda Ray Walston

LORNA PATTERSON

1980   **AIRPLANE !**
Director: Jerry Zucker
Co-stars: Robert Stack Lloyd Bridges Ethel Merman

MELODY PATTERSON

1969   **THE ANGRY BREED**
Director: David Commons
Co-stars: Jan Sterling James MacArthur William Windom

NEVA PATTERSON

1952   **TAXI**
Director: Gregory Ratoff
Co-stars: Dan Dailey Constance Smith Blanche Yurka

1956   **THE SOLID GOLD CADILLAC**
Director: Richard Quine
Co-stars: Judy Holliday Paul Douglas John Williams

1957   **THE DESK SET**
Director: Walter Lang
Co-stars: Spencer Tracy Katherine Hepburn Gig Young

1957   **AN AFFAIR TO REMEMBER**
Director: Leo McCarey
Co-stars: Cary Grant Deborah Kerr Cathleen Nesbitt

1958   **TOO MUCH, TOO SOON**
Director: Art Napoleon
Co-stars: Dorothy Malone Errol Flynn Ray Danton

1962   **THE SPIRAL ROAD**
Director: Robert Mulligan
Co-stars: Rock Hudson Burl Ives Gena Rowlands

1962 DAVID AND LISA
Director: Frank Perry
Co-stars: Keir Dullea Janet Margolin Howard Da Silva

1964 DEAR HEART
Director: Delbert Mann
Co-stars: Glenn Ford Geraldine Page Angela Lansbury

1971 THE SKIN GAME
Director: Paul Bogart
Co-stars: James Garner Lou Gossett Susan Clark

1975 THE RUNAWAYS
Director: Harry Harris
Co-stars: Dorothy McGuire Van Williams John Randolph

1977 THE DOMINO KILLINGS
Director: Stanley Kramer
Co-stars: Gene Hackman Richard Widmark Mickey Rooney

1983 V
Director: Kenneth Johnson
Co-stars: Marc Singer Faye Grant Michael Durrell

SARAH PATTERSON

1984 THE COMPANY OF WOLVES
Director: Neil Jordan
Co-stars: Angela Lansbury David Warner Brian Glover

SHIRLEY PATTERSON

1944 RIDING WEST
Co-stars: Charles Starrett Steve Clark

VIRGINIA PATTON

1947 THE BURNING CROSS
Director: Walter Colmes
Co-stars: Hank Daniels Raymond Bond

ALEXANDRA PAUL

1983 CHRISTINE
Director: John Carpenter
Co-stars: Keith Gordon John Stockwell Harry Dean Stanton

1984 GETTING PHYSICAL
Director: Steven Hilliard Stern
Co-stars: Sandahl Bergman Robert Webber John Aprea

1985 AMERICAN FLYERS
Director: John Badham
Co-stars: Kevin Costner Rae Dawn Chong Jennifer Grey

1986 8 MILLION WAYS TO DIE
Director: Hal Ashby
Co-stars: Jeff Bridges Rosanna Arquette Randy Brooks

1987 DRAGNET
Director: Tom Mankiewicz
Co-stars: Dan Aykroyd Tom Hanks Christopher Plummer

1987 THE PASSAGE
Director: Harry Thompson
Co-stars: Brian Keith Ned Beatty Barbara Barrie

**1989 PERRY MASON:
THE CASE OF THE MUSICAL MURDER**
Director: Christian Nyby
Co-stars: Raymond Burr Debbie Reynolds

**1989 PERRY MASON:
THE CASE OF THE ALL-STAR ASSASSIN**
Director: Christian Nyby
Co-stars: Raymond Burr Barbara Hale

1991 PREY OF THE CHAMELION
Director: Tex Fuller
Co-stars: Daphne Zuniga James Wilder Don Harvey

1993 DEATH TRAIN
Director: David S. Jackson
Co-stars: Pierce Brosnan Patrick Stewart Christopher Lee

GLORIA PAUL

1970 DARLING LILI
Director: Blake Edwards
Co-stars: Julie Andrews Rock Hudson Jeremy Kemp

NANCY PAUL

1991 VI WARSHAWSKI
Director: Jeff Kanew
Co-stars: Kathleen Turner Charles Durning Angela Goethals

TALIA PAUL

1988 ANGUISH
Director: Biggas Luna
Co-stars: Zelda Rubinstein Michael Lerner Clara Pastor

PAMELA PAULSON

1953 ROBOT MONSTER
Director: Phil Tucker
Co-stars: George Nader Claudia Barrett Selena Royle

REBECCA PAULY

1982 THE STATE OF THINGS
Director: Wim Wenders
Co-stars: Isabelle Weingarten Patrick Bauchau Paul Getty

RITA PAUNCEFORT

1939 MR CHEDWORTH STEPS OUT
Director: Ken Hall
Co-stars: Cecil Kellaway Jean Hatton Peter Finch

MARISA PAVAN
Nominated For Best Supporting Actress In 1955 For "The Rose Tattoo"

1952 WHAT PRICE GLORY ?
Director: John Ford
Co-stars: James Cagney Dan Dailey Corinne Calvet

1954 DOWN THREE DARK STREETS
Director: Arnold Laven
Co-stars: Broderick Crawford Ruth Roman Martha Hyer

1954 DRUM BEAT
Director: Delmer Daves
Co-stars: Alan Ladd Audrey Dalton Robert Keith

1955 DIANE
Director: David Miller
Co-stars: Lana Turner Roger Moore Pedro Armendariz

1955 THE ROSE TATTOO
Director: Daniel Mann
Co-stars: Anna Magnani Burt Lancaster Jo Van Fleet

1956 THE MAN IN THE GRAY FLANNEL SUIT
Director: Nunnally Johnson
Co-stars: Gregory Peck Jennifer Jones

1959 JOHN PAUL JONES
Director: John Farrow
Co-stars: Robert Stack Charles Coburn Bette Davis

1959 SOLOMON AND SHEBA
Director: King Vidor
Co-stars: Yul Brynner Gina Lollobrigida George Sanders

MURIEL PAVLOW

1945 NIGHT BOAT TO DUBLIN
Director: Lawrence Huntington
Co-stars: Robert Newton Raymond Lovell Herbert Lom

1946 **THE SHOP AT SLY CORNER**
Director: George King
Co-stars: Oscar Homolka Derek Farr Kenneth Griffith

1952 **IT STARTED IN PARADISE**
Director: Compton Bennett
Co-stars: Jane Hylton Ian Hunter Terence Morgan

1953 **THE MALTA STORY**
Director: Brian Desmond Hurst
Co-stars: Alec Guinness Anthony Steel Jack Hawkins

1953 **CONFLICT OF WINGS**
Director: John Eldridge
Co-stars: John Gregson Kieron Moore Sheila Sweet

1953 **THE NET**
Director: Anthony Asquith
Co-stars: Phyllis Calvert James Donald Herbert Lom

1954 **DOCTOR IN THE HOUSE**
Director: Ralph Thomas
Co-stars: Dirk Bogarde Kenneth More Donald Sinden

1955 **SIMON AND LAURA**
Director: Muriel Box
Co-stars: Peter Finch Kay Kendall Ian Carmichael

1956 **TIGER IN THE SMOKE**
Director: Roy Baker
Co-stars: Tony Wright Donald Sinden Alec Clunes

1956 **REACH FOR THE SKY**
Director: Lewis Gilbert
Co-stars: Kenneth More Lyndon Brook Lee Patterson

1956 **EYEWITNESS**
Director: Muriel Box
Co-stars: Donald Sinden Belinda Lee Michael Craig

1957 **DOCTOR AT LARGE**
Director: Ralph Thomas
Co-stars: Dirk Bogarde Donald Sinden Shirley Eaton

1958 **ROONEY**
Director: George Pollock
Co-stars: John Gregson Barry Fitzgerald June Thorburn

1959 **WHIRLPOOL**
Director: Lewis Allen
Co-stars: Juliette Greco William Sylvester Marius Goring

1961 **MURDER, SHE SAID**
Director: George Pollock
Co-stars: Margaret Rutherford Stringer Davis Arthur Kennedy

KATINA PAXINOU
Won Oscar For Best Supporting Actress In 1943 For "Whom The Bell Tolls"

1943 **FOR WHOM THE BELL TOLLS**
Director: Sam Wood
Co-stars: Gary Cooper Ingrid Bergman Akim Tamiroff

1943 **HOSTAGES**
Director: Frank Tuttle
Co-stars: Luise Rainer Paul Lukas William Bendix

1945 **CONFIDENTIAL AGENT**
Director: Herman Shumlin
Co-stars: Charles Boyer Lauren Bacall Wanda Hendrix

1947 **UNCLE SILAS**
Director: Charles Frank
Co-stars: Jean Simmons Derrick De Marney Esmond Knight

1947 **MOURNING BECOMES ELECTRA**
Director: Dudley Nicholls
Co-stars: Michael Redgrave Rosalind Russell

1949 **PRINCE OF FOXES**
Director: Henry King
Co-stars: Tyrone Power Orson Welles Wanda Hendrix

1955 **MR ARKADIN**
Director: Orson Welles
Co-stars: Michael Redgrave Akim Tamiroff Patricia Medina

1959 **THE MIRACLE**
Director: Irving Rapper
Co-stars: Carroll Baker Roger Moore Walter Slezak

1960 **ROCCO AND HIS BROTHERS**
Director: Luchino Visconti
Co-stars: Alain Delon Renato Salvatori

SALLY PAYNE

1941 **SHERIFF OF TOMBSTONE**
Co-stars: Roy Rogers Elyse Knox

1941 **ROBIN HOOD OF THE PECOS**
Co-stars: Roy Rogers Marjorie Reynolds

1941 **JESSE JAMES AT BAY**
Co-stars: Roy Rogers Gale Storm Gabby Hayes

1942 **ROMANCE ON THE RANGE**
Co-stars: Roy Rogers Gabby Hayes Bob Nolan

SUSAN PAYNE

1968 **HEADLINE HUNTERS**
Director: Jonathan Ingrams
Co-stars: Leonard Brockwell Bill Owen Reginald Marsh

AMANDA PAYS *(Married Corbin Bernson)*

1984 **OXFORD BLUES**
Director: Robert Boris
Co-stars: Rob Lowe Ally Sheedy Alan Howard

1984 **THE COLD ROOM**
Director: James Dearden
Co-stars: George Segal Renee Soutendjik Warren Clarke

1988 **SAIGON**
Director: Christopher Crowe
Co-stars: Willem Dafoe Gregory Hines Scott Glenn

1989 **LEVIATHAN**
Director: George Pan Cosmatos
Co-stars: Peter Weller Daniel Stern Meg Foster

1990 **PARKER KANE**
Director: Steve Perry
Co-stars: Jeff Fahey Marisa Tomei Drew Snydes

1991 **HIGH ART**

1994 **WEB OF DECEIT**
Director: Bill Corcorran
Co-stars: Corbin Bernsen Don Enright Mimi Kuzyk

1994 **SOLITAIRE FOR 2**
Director: Gary Sinyor
Co-star: Mark Frankel

SHERRI PAYSINGER

1991 **WEDLOCK**
Director: Lewis Teague
Co-stars: Rutger Hauer Mimi Rogers Joan Chen

BLANCHE PAYSON

1932 **HELPMATES**
Director: James Parrott
Co-stars: Stan Laurel Oliver Hardy Robert Callahan

BARBARA PAYTON

1950 **DALLAS**
Director: Stuart Heisler
Co-stars: Gary Cooper Ruth Roman Raymond Massey

1950 ONLY THE VALIANT
Director: Gordon Douglas
Co-stars: Gregory Peck Gig Young Ward Bond

1950 KISS TOMORROW GOODBYE
Director: Gordon Douglas
Co-stars: James Cagney Luther Adler Ward Bond

1951 DRUMS IN THE DEEP SOUTH
Director: William Cameron Menzies
Co-stars: James Craig Guy Madison

1951 BRIDE OF THE GORILLA
Director: Curt Siodmak
Co-stars: Lon Chaney Raymond Burr Tom Conway

1953 FOUR-SIDED TRIANGLE
Director: Terence Fisher
Co-stars: Stephen Murray James Hayter Percy Marmont

1953 THE FLANAGAN BOY
Director: Reginald LeBorg
Co-stars: Tony Wright Sid James John Slater

1953 THE GREAT JESSE JAMES RAID
Director: Reginald Leborg
Co-stars: Willard Parker Tom Neal Wallace Ford

PAMELA PAYTON-WRIGHT

1990 THE FRESHMAN
Director: Andrew Bergman
Co-stars: Marlon Brando Matthew Broderick Maximilian Schell

MARY PEACH

1958 ROOM AT THE TOP
Director: Jack Clayton
Co-stars: Laurence Harvey Simone Signoret Heather Sears

1960 NO LOVE FOR JOHNNIE
Director: Ralph Thomas
Co-stars: Peter Finch Stanley Holloway Billie Whitelaw

1962 A PAIR OF BRIEFS
Director: Ralph Thomas
Co-stars: Michael Craig Brenda De Banzie Liz Fraser

1963 A GATHERING OF EAGLES
Director: Delbert Mann
Co-stars: Rock Hudson Rod Taylor Barry Sullivan

1964 BALLAD IN BLUE
Director: Paul Henreid
Co-stars: Ray Charles Dawn Addams Tom Bell

1966 THE PROJECTED MAN
Director: Ian Curteis
Co-stars: Bryant Halliday Norman Wooland Derek Farr

CHIARA PEACOCK

1988 FRESH HORSES
Director: David Anspaugh
Co-stars: Molly Ringwald Andrew McCarthy Patti D'Arbanville

KIM PEACOCK

1936 MIDNIGHT AT MADAME TUSSAUD'S
Director: George Pearson
Co-stars: Lucille Lisle James Caren Bernard Miles

TRACY PEACOCK

1988 JOYRIDERS
Director: Aisling Walsh
Co-stars: Patricia Kerrigan Andrew Connolly Billie Whitelaw

TESSA PEAKE-JONES

1987 QUARTERMAINE'S TERMS
Director: Bill Hays
Co-stars: Edward Fox Eleanor Bron John Gielgud

E.J. PEAKER

1969 HELLO DOLLY
Director: Gene Kelly
Co-stars: Barbra Streisand Walter Matthau Michael Crawford

1969 THREE'S A CROWD
Director: Harry Falk
Co-stars: Larry Hagman Jessica Walter Harvey Korman

1971 GETTING AWAY FROM IT ALL
Director: Lee Philips
Co-stars: Gary Collins Barbara Feldon Larry Hagman

ADELE PEARCE

1938 UTAH TRAIL
Co-star: Tex Ritter

1940 POP ALWAYS PAYS
Director: Leslie Goodwins
Co-stars: Leon Errol Dennis O'Keefe Marjorie Gateson

ALICE PEARCE

1949 ON THE TOWN
Director: Gene Kelly
Co-stars: Frank Sinatra Ann Miller Vera-Ellen

1952 THE BELLE OF NEW YORK
Director: Charles Walters
Co-stars: Fred Astaire Vera-Ellen Marjorie Main

1956 THE OPPOSITE SEX
Director: David Miller
Co-stars: June Allyson Ann Miller Dolores Gray

1964 THE DISORDERLY ORDERLY
Director: Frank Tashlin
Co-stars: Jerry Lewis Glenda Farrell Karen Sharpe

1964 DEAR HEART
Director: Delbert Mann
Co-stars: Glenn Ford Geraldine Page Angela Lansbury

1965 DEAR BRIGITTE
Director: Henry Koster
Co-stars: James Stewart Glynis Johns Fabian

HELEN PEARCE

1989 WHEN THE WHALES CAME
Director: Clive Rees
Co-stars: Paul Scofield David Threlfall Helen Mirren

JACQUELINE PEARCE

1965 THE PLAGUE OF THE ZOMBIES
Director: John Gilling
Co-stars: Andre Morrell John Carson Diane Clare

1966 THE REPTILE
Director: John Gilling
Co-stars: Noel Willman Jennifer Daniel Ray Barrett

1968 DON'T RAISE THE BRIDGE, LOWER THE RIVER
Director: Jerry Paris
Co-stars: Jerry Lewis Terry Thomas

1989 HOW TO GET AHEAD IN ADVERTISING
Director: Bruce Robinson
Co-stars: Richard E. Grant Rachel Ward Richard Wilson

JOANNE PEARCE

1984 MORONS FROM OUTER SPACE
Director: Mike Hodges
Co-stars: Mel Smith Griff Rhys Jones Jimmy Nail

1989   **JUMPING THE QUEUE**
Director: Claude Whatham
Co-stars: Sheila Hancock David Threlfall John Stride

1990   **MURDER EAST, MURDER WEST**
Director: Peter Smith
Co-stars: Jeroen Krabbe Suzanna Hamilton Kevin Elyot

1991   **FOR THE GREATER GOOD**
Director: Danny Boyle
Co-stars: Martin Shaw Fiona Shaw Roy Dotrice

MARY VIVIAN PEARCE

1969   **MONDO TRASHO**
Director: John Waters
Co-stars: Divine Mink Stole David Lochary

1973   **PINK FLAMINGOES**
Director: John Waters
Co-stars: Divine Mink Stole David Lochary

1975   **FEMALE TROUBLE**
Director: John Waters
Co-stars: Divine Mink Stole David Lochary

VERA PEARCE

1933   **THAT'S A GOOD GIRL**
Director: Jack Buchanan
Co-stars: Elsie Randolph Dorothy Hyson Jack Buchanan

1933   **YES MR BROWN**
Director: Jack Buchanan
Co-stars: Elsie Randolph Hartley Power Jack Buchanan

1937   **PLEASE TEACHER**
Director: Stafford Dickens
Co-stars: Bobby Howes Rene Ray Wylie Watson

1938   **YES MADAM**
Director: Norman Lee
Co-stars: Bobby Howes Diana Churchill Fred Emney

1947   **NICHOLAS NICKLEBY**
Director: Alberto Cavalcanti
Co-stars: Derek Bond Cedric Hardwicke Sally Ann Howes

1951   **ONE WILD OAT**
Director: Charles Saunders
Co-stars: Robertson Hare Stanley Holloway Sam Costa

1961   **NOTHING BARRED**
Director: Darcey Conyers
Co-stars: Brian Rix Leo Franklyn Naunton Wayne

PATRICIA PEARCEY

1976   **SQUIRM**
Director: Jeff Lieberman
Co-stars: John Scardino Jean Sullivan Fran Higgins

PRINCESS PEARL

1936   **EVERYTHING IS RHYTHM**
Director: Alfred Goulding
Co-stars: Harry Roy Ivor Moreton Dave Kaye

BEATRICE PEARSON

1948   **FORCE OF EVIL**
Director: Abraham Polonsky
Co-stars: John Garfield Thomas Gomez Marie Windsor

1949   **LOST BOUNDARIES**
Director: Alfred Werker
Co-stars: Mel Ferrer Susan Douglas Canada Lee

KAREN PEARSON

1973   **TOM SAWYER**
Director: James Neilson
Co-stars: Josh Albee Jane Wyatt Buddy Ebsen

PATSY PEASE

1983   **SPACE RAIDERS**
Director: Howard Cohen
Co-stars: Vince Edwards David Mendenhall

JULIE PEASGOOD

1983   **HOUSE OF THE LONG SHADOWS**
Director: Pete Walker
Co-stars: Christopher Lee Vincent Price Richard Todd

CECILIA PECK

1991   **AMBITION**
Director: Scott Goldstein
Co-stars: Lou Diamond Phillips Clancy Brown Richard Bradford

ALISON PEEBLES

1991   **THE ADVOCATES**
Director: Peter Barber-Fleming
Co-stars: Isla Blair Stella Gonet Hugh Ross

1992   **THE ADVOCATES: ABOVE THE LAW**
Director: Peter Barber-Fleming
Co-stars: Isla Blair Ewan Stewart Michael Kitchen

EDNA PEEL

1937   **SPORTING LOVE**
Director: Elder Wills
Co-stars: Stanley Lupino Laddie Cliff Henry Carlisle

EILEEN PEEL

1932   **AFTER OFFICE HOURS**
Director: Thomas Bentley
Co-stars: Frank Lawton Heather Angel Garry Marsh

TRACY PEEL (Child)

1975   **HIJACK !**
Director: Michael Forlong
Co-stars: Richard Morant James Forlong Sally Forlong

NIA PEEPLES

1987   **NORTH SHORE**
Director: William Phelps
Co-stars: Matt Adler John Philbin Cristina Raines

1989   **SWIMSUIT**
Director: Chris Thomson
Co-stars: William Katt Catherine Oxenberg Cyd Charisse

1989   **DEEPSTAR SIX**
Director: Sean Cunningham
Co-stars: Taurean Blacque Nancy Everhard Miguel Ferrer

1992   **I DON'T BUY KISSES ANYMORE**
Director: Robert Marcarelli
Co-stars: Jason Alexander Lainie Kazan Eileen Brennan

1994   **XXXS AND OOOS**
Director: Allan Arkush
Co-stars: Debrah Farentino Andrea Parker

1994   **MY NAME IS KATE**
Director: Rod Hardy
Co-stars: Donna Mills Daniel J. Travanti Eileen Brennan

1995   **DEADLOCKED: ESCAPE FROM ZONE 14**
Director: Graeme Campbell
Co-stars: Esai Morales Stephen McHattie

JOAN PEERS

1929   **APPLAUSE**
Director: Rouben Mamoulian
Co-stars: Helen Morgan Henry Wadsworth Dorothy Cumming

1930 RAIN OR SHINE
Director: Frank Capra
Co-stars: Joe Cook Louise Fazenda Dave Chasen

1930 PARAMOUNT ON PARADE
Director: Dorothy Arzner
Co-stars: Jean Arthur Gary Cooper Clara Bow

1930 TOL'ABLE DAVID
Director: John Blystone
Co-stars: Richard Cromwell Noah Beery Henry B. Walthall

LISA PEERS

1979 ALISON'S BIRTHDAY
Director: Ian Coughlan
Co-stars: Joanne Samuel Lou Brown Vinent Ball

YAKIRA PEGUEIRO

1996 KIDS
Director: Larry Clark
Co-stars: Leo Fitzpatrick Chloe Sivigny Justin Pierce

SARAH PEIRSE

1994 HEAVENLY CREATURES
Director: Peter Jackson
Co-stars: Kate Winslet Melanie Lynskey

LISA PELIKAN

1978 PERFECT GENTLEMEN
Director: Jackie Cooper
Co-stars: Lauren Bacall Ruth Gordon Sandy Dennis

1985 GHOULIES
Director: Luca Bercovici
Co-Stars: Peter Liapis Jack Nance Michael Des Barres

1990 A.W.O.L.
Director: Sheldon Lettich
Co-stars: Jean-Claude Van Damme Harrison Page Deborah Rennard

1991 RETURN TO THE BLUE LAGOON
Director: William Graham
Co-stars: Brian Krause Milla Jovovich

1991 INTO THE BADLANDS
Director: Sam Pillsbury
Co-stars: Bruce Dern Mariel Hemingway Dylan McDermott

CLARA PELLER

1985 MOVING VIOLATIONS
Director: Neal Israel
Co-stars: Stephen McHattie Jennifer Tilly Sally Kellerman

ANDREE PELLETIER

1984 WALLS
Director: Thomas Shandell
Co-stars: Winston Rekert Alan Scarfe

YVONNE PELLETIER

1931 RIDERS OF THE PURPLE SAGE
Director: Hamilton McFadden
Co-stars: George O'Brien Marguerite Churchill

PINA PELLICER

1961 ONE-EYED JACKS
Director: Marlon Brando
Co-stars: Karl Malden Katy Jurado Marlon Brando

STELITA PELUFFE

1938 OUTLAWS OF SONORA
Co-stars: Bob Livingstone Ray Corrigan Max Terhune

ANTONIA PEMBERTON

1984 A PASSAGE TO INDIA
Director: David Lean
Co-stars: Judy Davis Alec Guinness Peggy Ashcroft

1989 BEHAVING BADLY
Director: David Tucker
Co-stars: Judi Dench Ronald Pickup Frances Barber

ELIZABETH PENA

1985 DOWN AND OUT IN BEVERLY HILLS
Director: Paul Mazursky
Co-stars: Nick Nolte Richard Dreyfuss Bette Midler

1985 CROSSOVER DREAMS
Director: Leon Ichaso
Co-stars: Ruben Blades Shawn Elliott Joel Diamond

1987 BATTERIES NOT INCLUDED
Director: Matthew Robbins
Co-stars: Hume Cronyn Jessica Tandy Frank McRae

1987 LA BAMBA
Director: Luis Valdez
Co-stars: Lou Diamond Phillips Rosana De Soto Joe Pantoliano

1989 SHANNON'S DEAL
Director: Lewis Teague
Co-stars: Jamey Sheridan Alberta Watson Miguel Ferrer

1990 JACOB'S LADDER
Director: Adrian Lyne
Co-stars: Tim Robbins Danny Aiello Matt Craven

1990 BLUE STEEL
Director: Kathryn Bigelow
Co-stars: Jaime Lee Curtis Ron Silver Clancy Brown

1991 THE WATERDANCE
Director: Neal Jimenez
Co-stars: Eric Stoltz Wesley Snipes William Forsythe

1994 ROOMMATES
Director: Alan Metzger
Co-stars: Randy Quaid Eric Stoltz Charles Durning

1996 LONE STAR
Director: John Sayles
Co-stars: Kris Kristofferson Chris Cooper Frances McDormand

VICTORIA PENA (Vicky)

1981 THE HOUSE OF BERNARDA ALBA
Director: Mario Camus
Co-stars: Irene Gutierrez Caba Ana Belin Florinda Chico

1986 DRAGON RAPIDE
Director: Jaime Camino
Co-stars: Juan Diego Manuel De Blas Saturnino Cerra

DIANA PENALVER

1992 BRAIN DEAD
Director: Peter Jackson
Co-stars: Timothy Balme Elizabeth Moody Ian Watkin

JANICE PENDARVIS

1985 BRING ON THE NIGHT
Director: Michael Apted
Co-stars: Sting Omar Hakin Kenny Kirkland

SUSAN PENHALIGON

1973 NO SEX PLEASE WE'RE BRITISH
Director: Cliff Owen
Co-stars: Ronnie Corbett Arthur Lowe Beryl Reid

1974 THE LAND THAT TIME FORGOT
Director: Kevin Connor
Co-stars: Doug McClure John McEnery Keith Barron

1976 NASTY HABITS
Director: Michael Lindsay-Hogg
Co-stars: Glenda Jackson Melina Mercouri Edith Evans

1977 COUNT DRACULA
Director: Philip Saville
Co-stars: Louis Jourdan Frank Finlay Judi Bowker

1977 LEOPARD IN THE SNOW
Director: Gerry O'Hara
Co-stars: Keir Dullea Kenneth More Billie Whitelaw

1977 THE UNCANNY
Director: Denis Heroux
Co-stars: Peter Cushing Ray Milland Joan Greenwood

1978 PATRICK
Director: Richard Franklin
Co-stars: Robert Helpman Julia Blake Bruce Barry

1979 SOLDIER OF ORANGE
Director: Paul Verhoeven
Co-stars: Rutger Hauer Jeroen Krabbe Derek De Lint

LEA PENMAN

1950 FANCY PANTS
Director: George Marshall
Co-stars: Bob Hope Lucille Ball Bruce Cabot

DENA PENN (Child)

1944 DAYS OF GLORY
Director: Jacques Tourneur
Co-stars: Tamara Toumanova Gregory Peck Hugo Haas

ANN PENNINGTON

1929 GOLD DIGGERS OF BROADWAY
Director: Roy Del Ruth
Co-stars: Nancy Welford Conway Tearle Winnie Lightner

1929 IS EVERYBODY HAPPY ?
Director: Archie Mayo
Co-stars: Ted Lewis Alice Day Lawrence Grant

PAT PENNY

1947 BUSH CHRISTMAS
Director: Ralph Smart
Co-stars: Chips Rafferty John McCallum John Fernside

SYDNEY PENNY (Child)

1985 PALE RIDER
Director: Clint Eastwood
Co-stars: Michael Moriarty Carrie Snodgress Clint Eastwood

1996 HEARTS ADRIFT
Director: Vic Sarin
Co-stars: Scott Reeves Kathleen Noone

BARBARA PEPPER

1934 OUR DAILY BREAD
Director: King Vidor
Co-stars: Karen Morley Tom Keene John Qualen

1935 SAGEBRUSH TROUBADOUR
Co-star: Gene Autry

1935 FORCED LANDING
Co-stars: Onslow Stevens Toby Wing

1936 MUMMY'S BOYS
Director: Fred Guiol
Co-stars: Bert Wheeler Robert Woolsey Willie Best

1937 PORTIA ON TRIAL
Director: George Nichols
Co-stars: Frieda Inescort Walter Abel Heather Angel

1937 FORTY NAUGHTY GIRLS
Co-stars: Marjorie Lord George Shelley

1937 TOO MANY WIVES
Co-star: John Morley

1938 LADY IN THE MORGUE
Director: Otis Garrett
Co-stars: Preston Foster Patricia Ellis Frank Jenks

1940 FOREIGN CORRESPONDENT
Director: Alfred Hitchcock
Co-stars: Joel McCrea Laraine Day Edmund Gwenn

1940 THE RETURN OF FRANK JAMES
Director: Fritz Lane
Co-stars: Henry Fonda Gene Tierney Henry Hull

1943 LET'S FACE IT
Director: Sidney Lanfield
Co-stars: Bob Hope Betty Hutton Dona Drake

1944 HENRY ALDRICH PLAYS CUPID
Director: Hugh Bennett
Co-stars: Jimmy Lydon Diana Lynn Vera Vague

1947 THE MILLERSON CASE
Director: George Archainbaud
Co-stars: Warner Baxter Nancy Saunders Clem Bevans

1964 KISS ME, STUPID
Director: Billy Wilder
Co-stars: Dean Martin Kim Novak Ray Walston

MARILIA PERA

1981 PIXOTE
Director: Hector Babenco
Co-stars: Fernando Ramos Da Silva Jorge Juliao Gilberto Moura

1984 MIXED BLOOD
Director: Paul Morrissey
Co-stars: Richard Ulacia Linda Kerridge Angel David

SUSAN PERETZ

1975 DOG DAY AFTERNOON
Director: Sidney Lumet
Co-stars: Al Pacino Charles Durning Chris Sarandon

1982 TAKE YOUR BEST SHOT
Director: David Greene
Co-stars: Robert Urich Meredith Baxter Birney Jack Bannon

BARBARA PEREZ

1962 NO MAN IS AN ISLAND
Director: Richard Goldstone
Co-stars: Jeffrey Hunter Marshall Thompson

ROSIE PEREZ
Nominated For Best Supporting Actress In 1993 For "Fearless"

1989 DO THE RIGHT THING
Director: Spike Lee
Co-stars: Danny Aiello Ossie Davis Ruby Dee

1990 CRIMINAL JUSTICE
Director: Andy Wolk
Co-stars: Forest Whitaker Jennifer Grey Tony Todd

1991 NIGHT ON EARTH
Director: Jim Jarmusch
Co-stars: Winona Ryder Gena Rowlands Beatrice Dalle

1992 WHITE MEN CAN'T JUMP
Director: Ron Shelton
Co-stars: Wesley Snipes Woody Harrelson Tyra Ferrell

1993 UNTAMED HEART
Director: Tony Bill
Co-stars: Christian Slater Marisa Tomei Kyle Secor

1993 FEARLESS
Director: Peter Weir
Co-stars: Jeff Bridges Isabella Rossellini Tom Hulce

1995 IT COULD HAPPEN TO YOU
Director: Andrew Bergman
Co-stars: Nicolas Cage Bridget Fonda Isaac Hayes

CECILIA PEREZ-CERVERA

1990 MIAMI BLUES
Director: George Armitage
Co-stars: Fred Ward Alec Baldwin Jennifer Jason Leigh

BEATRIZ PEREZ-PORRO

1983 SKYLINE
Director: Fernando Colomo
Co-stars: Antonio Resines Jaime Noz Roy Hoffman

CLARE PERKINS

1991 HALLELUJAH ANYHOW
Director: Matthew Jacobs
Co-stars: Dona Croll Keith David George Harris

1994 LADYBIRD LADYBIRD

ELIZABETH PERKINS

1986 ABOUT LAST NIGHT
Director: Edward Zwick
Co-stars: Rob Lowe Demi Moore James Belushi

1987 FROM THE HIP
Director: Bob Clark
Co-stars: Judd Nelson John Hurt Ray Walston

1988 BIG
Director: Penny Marshall
Co-stars: Tom Hanks John Heard Robert Loggia

1988 SWEET HEARTS DANCE
Director: Robert Greenwald
Co-stars: Don Johnson Susan Sarandon Jeff Daniels

1989 OVER HER DEAD BODY
Director: Maurice Phillips
Co-stars: Judge Reinhold Jeffrey Jones Rhea Perlman

1990 AVALON
Director: Harry Levinson
Co-stars: Aidan Quinn Joan Plowright Armin Mueller-Stahl

1990 LOVE AT LARGE
Director: Alan Rudolph
Co-stars: Tom Berenger Anne Archer Kate Capshaw

1991 HE SAID, SHE SAID
Director: Marisa Silver
Co-stars: Kevin Bacon Anthony LaPaglia Sharon Stone

1992 THE DOCTOR
Director: Randa Haines
Co-stars: William Hurt Christine Lahti Mandy Patinkin

1993 INDIAN SUMMER
Director: Mike Binder
Co-stars: Alan Arkin Matt Craven

1994 MIRACLE ON 34TH STREET
Director: Lee Mayfield
Co-stars: Richard Attenborough Mara Wilson

1994 THE FLINTSTONES
Director: Brian Levant
Co-stars: John Goodman Rick Moranis Rosie O'Donnell

1996 MOONLIGHT AND VALENTINO
Director: David Anspaugh
Co-stars: Jon Bon Jovi Kathleen Turner Whoopi Goldberg

EMILY PERKINS

1989 SMALL SACRIFICES
Director: David Greene
Co-stars: Farrah Fawcett Ryan O'Neal John Shea

MILLE PERKINS

1959 THE DIARY OF ANNE FRANK
Director: George Stevens
Co-stars: Joseph Schildkraut Shelley Winters

1961 WILD IN THE COUNTRY
Director: Philip Dunne
Co-stars: Elvis Presley Hope Lange Tuesday Weld

1964 ENSIGN PULVER
Director: Joshua Logan
Co-stars: Robert Walker Burl Ives Walter Matthau

1965 RIDE IN THE WHIRLWIND
Director: Monte Hellman
Co-stars: Cameron Mitchell Jack Nicholson Tom Filer

1966 THE SHOOTING
Director: Monte Hellman
Co-stars: Warren Oates Jack Nicholson Will Hutchins

1968 WILD IN THE STREETS
Director: Barry Shear
Co-stars: Chris Jones Shelley Winters Diane Varsi

1981 A GUN IN THE HOUSE
Director: Ivan Nagy
Co-stars: Sally Struthers David Ackroyd Joel Bailey

1983 TABLE FOR FIVE
Director: Robert Lieberman
Co-stars: Jon Voight Richard Crenna Roxana Zal

1983 THE HAUNTING PASSION
Director: John Korty
Co-stars: Jane Seymour Gerald McRaney Ruth Nelson

1984 ANATOMY OF AN ILLNESS
Director: Richard Heffron
Co-stars: Ed Asner Eli Wallach Lelia Goldoni

1984 LICENCE TO KILL
Director: Jud Taylor
Co-stars: Penny Fuller Don Murray James Farentino

1986 AT CLOSE RANGE
Director: James Foley
Co-stars: Sean Penn Christopher Penn Mary Stuart Masterson

1987 SLAMDANCE
Director: Wayne Wang
Co-stars: Tom Hulce Virginia Madsen Mary Elizabeth Mastrantonio

1987 STRANGE VOICES
Director: Arthur Seidelman
Co-stars: Valerie Harper Nancy McKeon Stephen Macht

1988 BROKEN ANGEL
Director: Richard Heffron
Co-stars: William Shatner Susan Blakely Roxann Biggs

1996 NECRONOMICON
Director: Brian Yuzna
Co-stars: Jeffrey Combs Bruce Payne David Warner

REBECCA PERLE

1984 TIGHTROPE
Director: Richard Tuggle
Co-stars: Clint Eastwood Genevieve Bujold Dan Hedaya

RHEA PERLMAN *(Married Danny DeVito)*

1982 DROP-OUT FATHER
Director: Don Taylor
Co-stars: Dick Van Dyke Mariette Hartley George Coe

1984 **THE RATINGS GAME**
Director: Danny DeVito
Co-stars: Kevin McCarthy Huntz Hall Gerrit Graham

1985 **AMAZING STORIES 2**
Director: Steven Spielberg
Co-stars: Danny DeVito Lukas Haas Gregory Hines

1986 **MY LITTLE PONY** *(Voice)*
Director: Michael Joens
Co-stars: Danny DeVito Madeline Kahn Tony Randall

1989 **OVER HER DEAD BODY**
Director: Maurice Phillips
Co-stars: Elizabeth Perkins

1993 **SHATTERED FAMILY**
Director: Sandy Smolan
Co-stars: Richard Crenna Linda Kelsey Tom Guiry

1994 **CANADIAN BACON**
Director: Michael Moore
Co-stars: John Candy Alan Alda

1995 **COACH**

1996 **ROALD DAHL'S MATILDA**
Director: Danny DeVito
Co-stars: Mara Wilson Pam Ferris Elizabeth Davidtz Danny DeVito

FLORENCE PERNELL

1993 **THREE COLOURS:BLUE**
Director: Krzysztof Kieslowski
Co-stars: Juliette Binoche Benoit Regent

1993 **THREE COLOURS:WHITE**
Director: Krzysztof Kieslowski
Co-stars: Zbigniew Zamachowski Julie Delpy

GIGI PERREAU *(Child)*

1944 **THE MASTER RACE**
Director: Herbert Biberman
Co-stars: George Coulouris Osa Massen Lloyd Bridges

1947 **SONG OF LOVE**
Director: Clarence Brown
Co-stars: Katharine Hepburn Paul Henreid Robert Walker

1947 **GREEN DOLPHIN STREET**
Director: Victor Saville
Co-stars: Lana Turner Van Heflin Edmund Gwenn

1949 **FAMILY HONEYMOON**
Director: Claude Binyon
Co-stars: Claudette Colbert Fred MacMurray Rita Johnson

1949 **MY FOOLISH HEART**
Director: Mark Robson
Co-stars: Susan Hayward Dana Andrews Kent Smith

1949 **SHADOW ON THE WALL**
Director: Pat Jackson
Co-stars: Ann Sothern Zachary Scott Nancy Davis

1949 **ROSEANNA McCOY**
Director: Irving Reis
Co-stars: Joan Evans Farley Granger Charles Bickford

1950 **NEVER A DULL MOMENT**
Director: George Marshall
Co-stars: Irene Dunne Fred MacMurray William Demarest

1950 **FOR HEAVEN'S SAKE**
Director: George Seaton
Co-stars: Clifton Webb Edmund Gwenn Joan Bennett

1951 **THE LADY PAYS OFF**
Director: Douglas Sirk
Co-stars: Linda Darnell Stephen McNally Virginia Field

1951 **WEEKEND WITH FATHER**
Director: Douglas Sirk
Co-stars: Van Heflin Patricia Neal Virginia Field

1952 **HAS ANYBODY SEEN MY GAL ?**
Director: Douglas Sirk
Co-stars: Piper Laurie Rock Hudson Charles Coburn

1952 **BONZO GOES TO COLLEGE**
Director: Frederick De Cordova
Co-stars: Maureen O'Sullivan Edmund Gwenn

1956 **THE MAN IN THE GRAY FLANNEL SUIT**
Director: Nunnally Johnson
Co-stars: Gregory Peck Fredric March Jennifer Jones

1956 **DANCE WITH ME HENRY**
Director: Charles Barton
Co-stars: Abbott & Costello Rusty Hamer

1958 **THE COOL AND THE CRAZY**
Director: William Whitney
Co-stars: Scott Marlow Dick Bakalyan Dick Jones

1961 **LOOK IN ANY WINDOW**
Director: William Alland
Co-stars: Paul Anka Ruth Roman Alex Nicol

1967 **TIME WARP**
Director: David Hewitt
Co-stars: Scott Brady Anthony Eisley Abrham Sofaer

MIREILLE PERREY

1964 **LES PARAPLUIES DE CHERBOURG**
Director: Jacques Demy
Co-stars: Catherine Deneuve Anne Vernon Marc Michel

LYNNE PERRIE

1969 **KES**
Director: Ken Loach
Co-stars: Colin Welland Brian Glover David Bradley

MIREILLE PERRIER

1989 **WORLD WITHOUT PITY**
Director: Eric Rochant
Co-stars: Hippolyte Girardot Yvan Attal Cecile Mazan

1989 **TOTO THE HERO**
Director: Jaco Van Dormael
Co-stars: Michel Bouquet Thomas Godet

VALERIE PERRINE
Nominated For Best Actress In 1974 For "Lenny"

1972 **SLAUGHTERHOUSE FIVE**
Director: George Roy Hill
Co-stars: Michael Sacks Sharon Gans Ron Leibman

1973 **THE LAST AMERICAN HERO**
Director: Lamont Johnson
Co-stars: Jeff Bridges Geraldine Fitzgerald Ned Beatty

1974 **LENNY**
Director: Bob Fosse
Co-stars: Dustin Hoffman Jan Miner Stanley Beck

1976 **W.C. FIELDS AND ME**
Director: Arthur Hiller
Co-stars: Rod Steiger John Marley Jack Cassidy

1977 **MR BILLION**
Director: Jonathan Kaplan
Co-stars: Terence Hill Jackie Gleason Slim Pickens

1978 **SUPERMAN**
Director: Richard Donner
Co-stars: Christopher Reeve Marlon Brando Margot Kidder

1979   **THE MAGICIAN OF LUBLIN**
Director: Menahem Golan
Co-stars: Alan Arkin Louise Fletcher Shelley Winters

1979   **THE ELECTRIC HORSEMAN**
Director: Sydney Pollack
Co-stars: Robert Redford Jane Fonda Willie Nelson

1980   **SUPERMAN II**
Director: Richard Lester
Co-stars: Christopher Reeve Gene Hackman Susannah York

1980   **CAN'T STOP THE MUSIC**
Director: Nancy Walker
Co-stars: Village People Steve Guttenberg June Havoc

1981   **AGENCY**
Director: George Kaczender
Co-stars: Robert Mitchum Lee Majors Alexandra Stewart

1982   **THE BORDER**
Director: Tony Richardson
Co-stars: Jack Nicholson Harvey Keitel Warren Oates

1985   **WATER**
Director: Dick Clement
Co-stars: Michael Caine Brenda Vaccaro Leonard Rossiter

1987   **MAID TO ORDER**
Director: Amy Jones
Co-stars: Ally Sheedy Michael Ontkean Dick Shawn

1990   **BRIGHT ANGEL**
Director: Michael Fields
Co-stars: Dermot Mulrony Lili Taylor Sam Shepard

1989   **SWEET BIRD OF YOUTH**
Director: Nicolas Roeg
Co-stars: Elizabeth Taylor Mark Harmon Rip Torn

1993   **BOILING POINT**
Director: James B. Harris
Co-stars: Wesley Snipes Dennis Hopper Lolita Davidovich

JOAN PERRY

1935   **CASE OF THE MISSING MAN**
Co-stars: Roger Pryor Paul Guilfoyle Tom Dugan

1936   **THE MYSTERIOUS AVENGER**
Co-star: Charles Starrett

1936   **MEET NERO WOLFE**
Director: Herbert Biberman
Co-stars: Edward Arnold Lionel Stander Rita Hayworth

1937   **THE DEVIL IS DRIVING**
Co-stars: Richard Dix James Millican

1937   **COUNTERFEIT LADY**
Co-star: Ralph Bellamy

1938   **START CHEERING**
Director: Albert Rogell
Co-stars: Jummy Durante Walter Connolly Charles Starrett

1939   **GOOD GIRLS GO TO PARIS**
Director: Alexander Hall
Co-stars: Melvyn Douglas Joan Blondell Alan Curtis

1940   **MAISIE WAS A LADY**
Director: Edwin Marin
Co-stars: Ann Sothern Lew Ayres Maureen O'Sullivan

1940   **THE LONE WOLF STRIKES**
Director: Sidney Salkow
Co-stars: Warren William Eric Blore Astrid Allwyn

1941   **STRANGE ALIBI**
Director: Ross Lederman
Co-stars: Arthur Kennedy Howard Da Silva Florence Bates

LINDA PERRY

1936   **TWO AGAINST THE WORLD**
Director: William McGann
Co-stars: Humphrey Bogart Beverley Roberts Henry O'Neill

1937   **THEY WON'T FORGET**
Director: Mervyn LeRoy
Co-stars: Claude Rains Lana Turner Otto Kruger

1937   **THE CASE OF THE STUTTERING BISHOP**
Director: William Clemens
Co-stars: Donald Woods Ann Dvorak Anne Nagel

SUSAN PERRY

1949   **KNOCK ON ANY DOOR**
Director: Nicholas Ray
Co-stars: Humphrey Bogart John Derek George Macready

MARIA PERSCHY

1962   **THE PASSWORD IS COURAGE**
Director: Andrew Stone
Co-stars: Dirk Bogarde Alfred Lynch Nigel Stock

1964   **633 SQUADRON**
Director: Walter Grauman
Co-stars: Cliff Robertson George Chakiris Harry Andrews

1964   **BANDITS OF THE RIO GRANDE**
Co-stars: Harald Leipnitz Wolfgang Kieling

1964   **MAN'S FAVORITE SPORT**
Director: Howard Hawks
Co-stars: Rock Hudson Paula Prentiss John McGiver

1967   **THE CASTLE OF FU MANCHU**
Director: Jesus Franco
Co-stars: Christopher Lee Richard Greene Gunther Stoll

1977   **BATTLE FLAG**

LISA JANE PERSKY

1979   **THE GREAT SANTINI**
Director: Lewis John Carlino
Co-stars: Robert Duvall Blythe Danner Michael O'Keefe

1985   **THE SURE THING**
Director: Rob Reiner
Co-stars: John Cusack Daphne Zuniga Tim Robbins

1986   **THE BIG EASY**
Director: Jim McBride
Co-stars: Dennis Quaid Ellen Barkin Ned Beatty

1988   **SHARING RICHARD**
Director: Peter Bonerz
Co-stars: Ed Marinaro Eileen Davidson Nancy Frangione

1989   **WHEN HARRY MET SALLY**
Director: Rob Reiner
Co-stars: Billy Crystal Meg Ryan Carrie Fisher

1990   **BLUE HEAT**
Director: John McKenzie
Co-stars: Brian Dennehy Joe Pantoliano Jeff Fahey

1993   **CONEHEADS**
Director: Steve Barron
Co-stars: Dan Aykroyd Jane Curtin Michelle Burke

ESSY PERSSON

1970   **CRY OF THE BANSHEE**
Director: Gordon Hessler
Co-stars: Vincent Price Elisabeth Bergner Patrick Mower

DONNA PESCOW

1977   **SATURDAY NIGHT FEVER**
Director: John Badham
Co-stars: John Travolta Karen Lynn Gorney Barry Miller

1978 RAINBOW
Director: Jackie Cooper
Co-stars: Andrea McArdle Don Murry Piper Laurie

1986 JAKE SPEED
Director: Andrew Lane
Co-stars: Wayne Crawford John Hurt Leon Ames

BERNADETTE PETERS

1973 ACE ELI AND RODGER OF THE SKIES
Director: John Erman
Co-stars: Cliff Robertson Pamela Franklin

1974 THE MEAN MACHINE
Director: Robert Aldrich
Co-stars: Burt Reynolds Eddie Albert Ed Lauter

1976 SILENT MOVIE
Director: Mel Brooks
Co-stars: Marty Feldman Dom DeLuise Sid Ceasar

1976 W.C. FIELDS AND ME
Director: Arthur Hiller
Co-stars: Rod Steiger Valerie Perrine Paul Stewart

1979 THE JERK
Director: Carl Reiner
Co-stars: Steve Martin Catlin Adams Bill Macy

1982 ANNIE
Director: John Huston
Co-stars: Albert Finney Aileen Quinn Carol Burnett

1982 PENNIES FROM HEAVEN
Director: Herbert Ross
Co-stars: Steve Martin Christopher Walker Tommy Rall

1986 SUNDAY IN THE PARK WITH GEORGE
Director: James Lapine
Co-star: Mandy Patinkin

1989 SLAVES OF NEW YORK
Director: James Ivory
Co-stars: Madeleine Potter Nick Corri Chris Sarandon

1989 THE PINK CADILLAC
Director: Buddy Van Horn
Co-stars: Clint Eastwood Timothy Carhart Geoffrey Lewis

1989 IMPROMPTU
Director: James Lapine
Co-stars: Judy Davis Hugh Grant Mandy Patinkin

1990 ALICE
Director: Woody Allen
Co-stars: Mia Farrow Joe Mantegna Alec Baldwin

1990 FALL FROM GRACE
Director: Karen Arthur
Co-stars: Kevin Spacey Beth Grant Travis Swords

1990 THE LAST BEST YEAR
Director: John Erman
Co-stars: Mary Tyler Moore Brian Bedford Kate Reid

1998 ANASTASIA *(Voice)*
Co-stars: Meg Ryan John Cusack Christopher Lloyd

ELIZABETH PETERS

1989 SHE-DEVIL
Director: Susan Seidelman
Co-stars: Meryl Streep Roseanne Barr Linda Hunt

JEAN PETERS *(Married Howard Hughes)* (1957)

1947 CAPTAIN FROM CASTILE
Director: Henry King
Co-stars: Tyrone Power Lee J. Cobb Cesar Romero

1948 DEEP WATERS
Director: Henry King
Co-stars: Dana Andrews Dean Stockwell Cesar Romero

1949 IT HAPPENS EVERY SPRING
Director: Lloyd Bacon
Co-stars: Ray Milland Paul Douglas Ed Begley

1950 LOVE THAT BRUTE
Director: Alexander Hall
Co-stars: Paul Douglas Cesar Romero Keenan Wynn

1951 TAKE GIRL OF MY LITTLE GIRL
Director: Jean Negulesco
Co-stars: Jeanne Crain Mitzi Gaynor Jeffrey Hunter

1951 AS YOUNG AS YOU FEEL
Director: Harmon Jones
Co-stars: Monty Woolley Thelma Ritter David Wayne

1951 ANNE OF THE INDIES
Director: Jacques Tourneur
Co-stars: Louis Jourdan Debra Paget Herbert Marshall

1952 LURE OF THE WILDERNESS
Director: Jean Negulesco
Co-stars: Jeffrey Hunter Walter Brennan Jack Elam

1952 O. HENRY'S FULL HOUSE
Director: Henry King
Co-stars: Charles Laughton David Wayne Marilyn Monroe

1952 VIVA ZAPATA !
Director: Elia Kazan
Co-stars: Marlon Brando Anthony Quinn Joseph Wiseman

1952 WAIT TIL THE SUN SHINES NELLIE
Director: Henry King
Co-stars: David Wayne Hugh Marlowe Alan Hale

1953 VICKI
Director: Harry Horner
Co-stars: Jeanne Crain Richard Boone Casey Adams

1953 PICKUP ON SOUTH STREET
Director: Samuel Fuller
Co-stars: Richard Widmark Thelma Ritter Richard Kiley

1953 NIAGARA
Director: Henry Hathaway
Co-stars: Marilyn Monroe Joseph Cotten Casey Adams

1953 A BLUEPRINT FOR MURDER
Director: Andrew Stone
Co-stars: Joseph Cotten Gary Merrill Jack Kruschen

1954 APACHE
Director: Robert Aldrich
Co-stars: Burt Lancaster John McIntrye Charles Bronson

1954 THREE COINS IN THE FOUNTAIN
Director: Jean Negulesco
Co-stars: Clifton Webb Dorothy McGuire Rossano Brazzi

1954 BROKEN LANCE
Director: Edward Dmytryk
Co-stars: Spencer Tracey Richard Widmark Katy Jurado

1955 A MAN CALLED PETER
Director: Henry Koster
Co-stars: Richard Todd Marjorie Rambeau Jill Esmond

1975 THE GREAT WALDO PEPPER
Director: George Roy Hill
Co-stars: Robert Redford Susan Sarandon Bo Svenson

KELLY JEAN PETERS

1970 LITTLE BIG MAN
Director: Arthur Penn
Co-stars: Dustin Hoffman Martin Balsam Faye Dunaway

1972 POCKET MONEY
Director: Stuart Rosenberg
Co-stars: Paul Newman Lee Marvin Strother Martin

LAURI PETERS

1962 MR HOBBS TAKES A VACATION
Director: Henry Koster
Co-stars: James Stewart Maureen O'Hara Fabian

1962 SUMMER HOLIDAY
Director: Peter Yates
Co-stars: Cliff Richards Una Stubbs Melvyn Hayes

1968 FOR LOVE OF IVY
Director: Daniel Mann
Co-stars: Sidney Poitier Abby Lincoln Beau Bridges

LORRAINE PETERS

1984 THE ADVENTURES OF SHERLOCK HOLMES : THE DANCING MAN
Director: John Bruce
Co-stars: Jeremy Brett David Burke

ROBERTA PETERS

1953 TONIGHT WE SING
Director: Mitchell Leisen
Co-stars: David Wayne Anne Bancroft Ezio Pinza

SUSAN PETERS

(Married Richard Quine) (Hurt In Hunting Accident)
Nominated For Best Supporting Actress In 1942 For "Random Harvest"

1942 ANDY HARDY'S DOUBLE LIFE
Director: George Seitz
Co-stars: Mickey Rooney Lewis Stone Esther Williams

1942 DR GILLESPIE'S NEW ASSISTANT
Director: Willis Goldbeck
Co-stars: Lionel Barrymore Van Johnson Keye Luke

1942 THE BIG SHOT
Director: Lewis Seiler
Co-stars: Humphrey Bogart Irene Manning Donald Crisp

1942 RANDOM HARVEST
Director: Mervyn LeRoy
Co-stars: Ronald Colman Greer Garson Philip Dorn

1942 TISH
Director: S. Sylvan Simon
Co-stars: Marjorie Main Zasu Pitts Aline McMahon

1943 YOUNG IDEAS
Director: Jules Dassin
Co-stars: Mary Astor Herbert Marshall Elliott Reid

1943 ASSIGNMENT IN BRITTANY
Director: Jack Conway
Co-stars: Jean-Pierre Aumont Signe Hasso Richard Whorf

1944 SONG OF RUSSIA
Director: Gregory Ratoff
Co-stars: Robert Taylor Robert Benchley John Hodiak

1945 KEEP YOUR POWDER DRY
Director: Edward Buzzell
Co-stars: Lana Turner Laraine Day Agnes Moorehead

1948 SIGN OF THE RAM (Wheelchair)
Director: John Sturges
Co-stars: Alexander Knox Peggy Ann Garner May Whitty

AMANDA PETERSON

1985 EXPLORERS
Director: Joe Dante
Co-stars: Ethan Hawke River Phoenix Jason Presson

1987 CAN'T BUY ME LOVE
Director: Steve Rash
Co-stars: Patrick Dempsey Seth Green Tina Caspary

1991 HELL HATH NO FURY
Director: Thomas Wright
Co-stars: Barbara Eden Loretta Swit David Ackroyd

1991 I POSED FOR PLAYBOY
Director: Stephen Stafford
Co-stars: Lynda Carter Michelle Greene

CASSANDRA PETERSON

1986 ALLAN QUARTERMAIN AND THE LOST CITY OF GOD
Director: Gary Nelson
Co-stars: Richard Chamberlain Sharon Stone

1989 ELVIRA, MISTRESS OF THE DARK
Director: James Signorelli
Co-stars: Daniel Greene Susan Kellerman

DOROTHY PETERSON

1931 TRAVELLING HUSBANDS
Co-stars: Constance Cummings Stanley Fields Frank McHugh

1931 BUSINESS AND PLEASURE
Director: David Butler
Co-stars: Will Rogers Jetta Goudal Joel McCrea

1931 FORBIDDEN
Director: Frank Capra
Co-stars: Barbara Stanwyck Adolphe Menjou Ralph Bellamy

1931 RICH MAN'S FOLLY
Director: John Cromwell
Co-stars: George Bancroft Frances Dee Robert Ames

1931 BOUGHT
Director: Archie Mayo
Co-stars: Constance Bennett Ben Lyon Ray Milland

1932 ATTORNEY FOR THE DEFENSE
Director: Irving Cummings
Co-stars: Edmund Lowe Evelyn Brent

1932 PAYMENT DEFERRED
Director: Lothar Mendes
Co-stars: Charles Laughton Ray Milland Maureen O'Sullivan

1932 WAY BACK HOME
Co-star: Frankie Darro

1932 SHE WANTED A MILLIONAIRE
Director: John Blystone
Co-stars: Joan Bennett Spencer Tracey Una Merkel

1933 BIG EXECUTIVE
Director: Erle Kenton
Co-stars: Ricardo Cortez Richard Bennett Elizabeth Young

1933 BELOVED
Director: Victor Schertzinger
Co-stars: John Boles Gloria Stuart Albert Conti

1934 AS THE EARTH TURNS
Director: Alfred Green
Co-stars: Jean Muir Donald Woods Emily Lowry

1934 PECK'S BAD BOY
Director: Edward Cline
Co-stars: Jackie Cooper Jackie Searle Thomas Meighan

1935 PURSUIT
Director: Edwin Marin
Co-stars: Chester Morris Sally Eilers Scotty Beckett

1935 MAN OF IRON
Director: William McGann
Co-stars: Barton MacLane Mary Astor John Eldredge

1936 THE COUNTRY DOCTOR
Director: Henry King
Co-stars: Jean Hesholt Dione Quins Slim Summerville

1936 THE DEVIL IS A SISSY
Director: W.S. Van Dyke
Co-stars: Freddie Bartholomew Mickey Rooney Jackie Cooper

1937 CONFESSION
Director: Joe May
Co-stars: Kay Francis Basil Rathbone Ian Hunter

1938 BREAKING THE ICE
Director: Edward Cline
Co-stars: Bobby Breen Charles Ruggles Dolores Costello

1938 HUNTED MEN
Director: Louis King
Co-stars: Lloyd Nolan Lynne Overman Mary Carlisle

1939 DARK VICTORY
Director: Edmund Goulding
Co-stars: Bette Davis George Brent Humphrey Bogart

1939 TWO BRIGHT BOYS
Director: Joseph Santley
Co-stars: Jackie Cooper Freddie Bartholomew Alan Dinehart

1940 TOO MANY HUSBANDS
Director: Wesley Ruggles
Co-stars: Jean Arthur Melvyn Douglas Fred MacMurray

1940 LILLIAN RUSSELL
Director: Irving Cummings
Co-stars: Alice Faye Don Ameche Henry Fonda

1942 SABOTEUR
Director: Alfred Hitchcock
Co-stars: Robert Cummings Priscilla Lane Otto Kruger

1942 WOMEN IN WAR
Director: John Auer
Co-stars: Elsie Janis Wendy Barrie Mae Clarke

1943 THE MOON IS DOWN
Director: Irving Pichel
Co-stars: Cedric Hardwicke Henry Travers Margaret Wycherley

1943 THIS IS THE LIFE
Director: Felix Feist
Co-stars: Donald O'Connor Peggy Ryan Susannah Foster

1944 WHEN THE LIGHTS GO ON AGAIN
Director: William Howard
Co-stars: James Lydon Barbara Belden Grant Mitchell

1944 THE WOMAN IN THE WINDOW
Director: Fritz Lang
Co-stars: Edward G. Robinson Joan Bennett Raymond Massey

1946 SISTER KENNY
Director: Dudley Nichols
Co-stars: Rosalind Russell Alexander Knox Dean Jagger

1947 THAT HAGEN GIRL
Director: Peter Godfrey
Co-stars: Shirley Temple Ronald Reagan Rory Calhoun

LENKA PETERSON

1955 THE PHENIX CITY STORY
Director: Phil Karlson
Co-stars: Richard Kiley Edward Andrews John McIntyre

1975 THE RUNAWAYS
Director: Harry Harris
Co-stars: Dorothy McGuire Van Williams John Randolph

MARION PETERSON

1988 ARIA
Director: Robert Altman
Co-stars: Bridget Fonda Elizabeth Hurley John Hurt

1992 LAPSE OF MEMORY
Director: Patrick DeWolf
Co-stars: John Hurt Marthe Keller Matthew MacKay

RUTH PETERSON

1935 CHARLIE CHAN IN PARIS
Director: Lewis Seiler
Co-stars: Warner Oland Mary Brian Thomas Beck

HORTENSE PETRA

1965 WHEN THE BOYS MEET THE GIRLS
Director: Alvin Ganzer
Co-stars: Connie Francis Louis Armstrong Harve Presnell

POLINA PETRENKO

1987 THE BURGLAR
Director: Valery Ogorodnikov
Co-stars: Oleg Olykomov Konstantine Kerchev Svetlana Gaitan

DORIS PETRIE

1989 LOVE AND HATE
Director: Francis Mankiewicz
Co-stars: Kenneth Welsh Kate Nelligan John Colicos

SUSAN PETRIE

1975 SHIVERS
Director: David Cronenberg
Co-stars: Paul Hampton Joe Silver Lynn Lowry

NINA PETRONZIO

1990 VINCENT AND ME
Director: Michael Rubbo

BRIGITTA PETTERSSON

1959 THE VIRGIN SPRING
Director: Ingmar Bergman
Co-stars: Max Von Sydow Brigitta Valberg Gunnel Lindblom

JOANNA PETTET

1966 THE GROUP
Director: Sidney Lumet
Co-stars: Candice Bergen Joan Hackett Shirley Knight

1967 THE NIGHT OF THE GENERALS
Director: Anatole Litvak
Co-stars: Peter O'Toole Omar Sharif Charles Gray

1967 ROBBERY
Director: Peter Yates
Co-stars: Stanley Baker James Booth Frank Finlay

1967 CASINO ROYALE
Director: Val Guest
Co-stars: David Niven Orson Welles Deborah Kerr

1968 THE BEST HOUSE IN LONDON
Director: Philip Saville
Co-stars: David Hemmings George Sanders Dany Robin

1968 BLUE
Director: Silvio Narizzano
Co-stars: Terence Stamp Karl Malden Ricardo Montalban

1973 WELCOME TO ARROW BEACH
Director: Laurence Harvey
Co-stars: John Ireland Meg Foster Stuart Whitman

1974 A CRY IN THE WILDERNESS
Director: Gordon Hessler
Co-stars: George Kennedy Lee H. Montgomery

1978 THE EVIL
Director: Gus Trikonis
Co-stars: Richard Crenna Andrew Prine Victor Buono

1979 CRY OF THE INNOCENT
Director: Michael O'Herlihy
Co-stars: Rod Taylor Nigel Davenport Cyril Cusack

1979 FOR HEAVEN'S SAKE
Director: Jerry Thorpe
Co-stars: Ray Bolger Kent McCord Kenneth Mars

LORI PETTY

1987 BATES MOTEL
Director: Richard Rothstein
Co-stars: Bud Cort Jason Bateman Gregg Henry

1990 CADILLAC MAN
Director: Roger Donaldson
Co-stars: Robin Williams Tim Robbins Pamela Reed

1992 A LEAGUE OF THEIR OWN
Director: Penny Marshall
Co-stars: Geena Davis Tom Hanks Madonna

1993 FREE WILLY
Director: Simon Wincer
Co-stars: Jason James Richter Jayne Atkinson Michael Madsen

1993 THE GLASS SHIELD
Director: Charles Burnett
Co-stars: Michael Boatman Richard Anderson

1995 TANK GIRL
Co-stars: Malcolm McDowell Ice-T.

PENNY PEYSER

1979 THE IN-LAWS
Director: Arthur Hiller
Co-stars: Peter Falk Alan Arkin Richard Libertini

DEDEE PFEIFFER *(Sister Of Michelle Pfeiffer)*

1986 VAMP
Director: Richard Wenk
Co-stars: Chris Makepeace Sandy Baron Grace Jones

1987 THE ALLNIGHTER
Director: Tamar Simon Hoffs
Co-stars: Susannah Hoffs Joan Cusack Michael Ontkean

1989 THE HORROW SHOW
Director: James Isaac
Co-stars: Lance Henriksen Brion James Rita Taggart

1991 AUNT JULIA AND THE SCRIPTWRITER
Director: Jon Amiel
Co-stars: Barbara Hershey Keanu Reeves Peter Falk

1993 RUNNING COOL
Director: Beverley Sebastian
Co-stars: Andrew Divoff Tracy Sebastian

MICHELLE PFEIFFER

(Married Peter Horton & David Kelley)
**Nominated For Best Actress In 1989 For "The Fabulous Baker Boys" and
In 1992 For "Love Field. Nominated For Best Supporting Actress In 1988
For "Dangerous Liaisons"**

1980 FALLING IN LOVE AGAIN
Director: Steven Paul
Co-stars: Elliott Gould Susannah York Kaye Ballard

**1980 CHARLIE CHAN AND THE
CURSE OF THE DRAGON QUEEN**
Director: Clive Donner
Co-stars: Peter Ustinov Angie Dickinson

1981 CALLIE AND SON
Director: Waris Hussein
Co-stars: Lindsay Wagner Jameson Parker

1982 GREASE 2
Director: Patricia Birch
Co-stars: Maxwell Caulfield Lorna Luft Eve Arden

1983 SCARFACE
Director: Brian De Palma
Co-stars: Al Pacino Steven Bauer Robert Loggia

1985 LADYHAWKE
Director: Richard Donner
Co-stars: Matthew Broderick Rutger Hauer Leo McKern

1985 INTO THE NIGHT
Director: John Landis
Co-stars: Jeff Goldblum Richard Farnsworth Irene Papas

1986 SWEET LIBERTY
Director: Alan Alda
Co-stars: Michael Caine Bob Hoskins Lillian Gish

1987 THE WITCHES OF EASTWICK
Director: George Miller
Co-stars: Susan Sarandon Jack Nicholson Cher

1987 AMAZON WOMEN ON THE MOON
Director: John Landis
Co-stars: Rosanna Arquette Carrie Fisher Griffin Dunne

1988 DANGEROUS LIAISONS
Director: Stephen Frears
Co-stars: John Malkovich Glenn Close Una Thurman

1988 MARRIED TO THE MOB
Director: Jonathan Demme
Co-stars: Matthew Modine Dean Stockwell Alec Baldwin

1988 TEQUILA SUNRISE
Director: Robert Towne
Co-stars: Mel Gibson Kurt Russell Raul Julia

1989 THE FABULOUS BAKER BOYS
Director: Steve Kloves
Co-stars: Jeff Bridges Beau Bridges Jennifer Tilly

1990 THE RUSSIA HOUSE
Director: Fred Schepisi
Co-stars: Sean Connery Roy Scheider James Fox

1991 FRANKIE AND JOHNNY
Director: Garry Marshall
Co-stars: Al Pacino Hector Elizondo Kate Nelligan

1992 LOVE FIELD
Director: Jonathan Caplan
Co-stars: Dennis Haysbert Stephanie McFadden Louise Latham

1992 BATMAN RETURNS
Director: Tim Burton
Co-stars: Michael Keaton Danny DeVito Michael Gough

1993 THE AGE OF INNOCENCE
Director: Martin Scorsese
Co-stars: Daniel Day-Lewis Winona Ryder Miriam Margoyles

1994 WOLF
Director: Mike Nichols
Co-stars: Jack Nicholson James Spader Kate Nelligan

1996 DANGEROUS MINDS
Director: John N. Smith
Co-stars: George Dzundza

1996 UP CLOSE AND PERSONAL
Director: Jon Avnet
Co-stars: Robert Redford Stockard Channing

1997 ONE FINE DAY
Director: Michael Hoffman
Co-stars: George Clooney Mae Whitman Alex D. Linz

1998 A THOUSAND ACRES
Director: Jocelyn Moorhouse
Co-stars: Jennifer Jason Leigh Jessica Lange Jason Robards

JO ANN PFLUG

1970 M*A*S*H
Director: Robert Altman
Co-stars: Donald Sutherland Elliott Gould Sally Kellerman

1971 THEY CALL IT MURDER
Director: Walter Grauman
Co-stars: Jim Hutton Jessica Walter Lloyd Bochner

1971 WHERE DOES IT HURT ?
Director: Rod Amateau
Co-stars: Peter Sellers Rick Lenz Eve Druce

1971 CATLOW
Director: Sam Wanamaker
Co-stars: Yul Brynner Leonard Nimoy Richard Crenna

1972 THE NIGHT STRANGLER
Director: Dan Curtis
Co-stars: Darren McGavin Simon Oakland John Carradine

LINH DAN PHAM

1991 INDOCHINE
Director: Regis Wargnier
Co-stars: Catherine Deneuve Vincent Perez Jean Yanne

LUCIE PHAN

1992 LE PETIT PRINCE A DIT
Director: Christine Pascal
Co-stars: Richard Berry Marie Kleiber Anemone

MARY PHILBIN

1925 PHANTON OF THE OPERA
Director: Rupert Julian
Co-stars: Lon Chaney Norman Kerry Gibson Gowland

BRITTA PHILLIPS

1988 SATISFACTION
Director: Joan Freeman
Co-stars: Justine Bateman Liam Neeson Trini Alvarado

CHYNNA PHILLIPS

1988 MOVING TARGET
Director: Chris Thomson
Co-stars: Jason Bateman Richard Dysart Tom Skerritt

1988 THE INVISIBLE KID
Director: Avery Crounse
Co-stars: Jay Underwood Karen Black Wally Ward

1989 ROXANNE:THE PRIZE PULITZER
Director: Richard Colla
Co-stars: Perry King Courteney Cox Betsy Russell

1989 SAY ANYTHING
Director: Cameron Crowe
Co-stars: John Cusack Ione Skye Lili Taylor

JEAN PHILLIPS

1942 DR BROADWAY
Director: Anthony Mann
Co-stars: MacDonald Carey J. Carrol Naish Richard Lane

JULIANNE PHILLIPS

1984 HIS MISTRESS
Director: David Lowell Rich
Co-stars: Robert Urich Cynthia Silkes Linda Kelsey

1989 FLETCH LIVES
Director: Michael Ritchie
Co-stars: Chevy Chase Hal Holbrook Cleavon Little

1989 SKIN DEEP
Director: Blake Edwards
Co-stars: John Ritter Vincent Gardenia Alyson Reed

1993 THE ONLY WAY OUT
Director: Rod Hardy
Co-stars: John Ritter Henry Winkler Stephanie Faracy

1994 A VOW TO KILL
Director: Harry S. Longstreet
Co-stars: Richard Grieco Gordon Pinsent

MACKENZIE PHILLIPS

1973 AMERICAN GRAFFITI
Director: George Lucas
Co-stars: Richard Dreyfuss Ron Howard Cindy Williams

1982 LOVE CHILD
Director: Larry Peerce
Co-stars: Amy Madigan Beau Bridges Joanna Merlin

MARY PHILLIPS

1932 A FAREWELL TO ARMS
Director: Frank Borzage
Co-stars: Gary Cooper Helen Hayes Adolphe Menjou

1937 MANNEQUIN
Director: Frank Borzage
Co-stars: Joan Crawford Spencer Tracy Alan Curtis

1937 THAT CERTAIN WOMAN
Director: Edmund Goulding
Co-stars: Bette Davis Henry Fonda Ian Hunter

1937 THE BRIDE WORE RED
Director: Dorothy Arzner
Co-stars: Joan Crawford Robert Young Franchot Tone

1944 LADY IN THE DARK
Director: Mitchell Leisen
Co-stars: Ginger Rogers Warner Baxter Ray Milland

1945 CAPTAIN EDDIE
Director: Lloyd Bacon
Co-stars: Fred MacMurray Lynn Bari Thomas Mitchell

1945 INCENDIARY BLONDE
Director: George Marshall
Co-stars: Betty Hutton Arturo De Cordova Charles Ruggles

1945 LEAVE HER TO HEAVEN
Director: John Stahl
Co-stars: Gene Tierney Cornel Wilde Jeanne Crain

1947 DEAR RUTH
Director: William Russell
Co-stars: Joan Caulfield William Holden Mona Freeman

1949 A WOMAN'S SECRET
Director: Nicholas Ray
Co-stars: Maureen O'Hara Gloria Grahame Melvyn Douglas

MEREDITH PHILLIPS

1986 SKY PIRATES
Director: Colin Eggleston
Co-stars: John Hargreaves Max Phipps Bill Hunter

MICHELLE PHILLIPS

1973 DILLINGER
Director: John Millius
Co-stars: Warren Oates Ben Johnson Richard Dreyfuss

1974 THE CALIFORNIA KID
Director: Richard Heffron
Co-stars: Martin Sheen Vic Morrow Nick Nolte

1977 VALENTINO
Director: Ken Russell
Co-stars: Rudolf Nureyev Leslie Caron Felicity Kendall

1980 THE MAN WITH BOGART'S FACE
Director: Robert Day
Co-stars: Robert Sacchi Misty Rowe Franco Nero

1984 SECRETS OF A MARRIED MAN
Director: William Graham
Co-stars: William Shatner Cybill Shepherd

1986   STARK:MIRROR IMAGE
Director: Noel Nosseck
Co-stars: Nicolas Surovy Kirstie Alley Ben Murphy

1986   AMERICAN ANTHEM
Director: Albert Magnoli
Co-stars: Mitch Gaylord Janet Jones Patrice Donnelly

1987   ASSAULT AND MATRIMONY
Director: James Frawley
Co-stars: Jill Eikenberry Michael Tucker Joseph Cortese

**1989   MICKEY SPILLANE'S MIKE HAMMER:
             MURDER TAKES ALL**
Director: John Nicolella
Co-stars: Stacy Keach Don Stroud

1989   LET IT RIDE
Director: Joe Pykta
Co-stars: Richard Dreyfuss Teri Garr Jennifer Tilly

1989   TRENCHCOAT IN PARADISE
Director: Martha Coolidge
Co-stars: Dirk Benedict Bruce Dern Sydney Walsh

1991   SCISSORS
Director: Frank De Felitta
Co-stars: Sharon Stone Steve Railsback Ronny Cox

1993   THE JOSHUA TREE
Director: Vic Armstrong
Co-stars: Dolph Lundgren George Segal Kristian Alfonso

1993   RUBDOWN
Director: Stuart Cooper
Co-stars: Jack Coleman William Devane Catherine Oxenberg

NANCIE PHILLIPS

1970   LOVING
Director: Irvin Kershner
Co-stars: George Segal Eva Marie Saint Sterling Hayden

PATRICIA PHILLIPS

1990   LOOKING FOR MIRACLES
Director: Kevin Sullivan
Co-stars: Greg Spottiswood Zachary Bennett Joe Flaherty

1990   JANE OF LANTERN HILL
Director: Kevin Sullivan
Co-stars: Sam Waterston Marion Bennett

SAMANTHA PHILLIPS

1988   PHANTASM 2
Director: Don Cascorelli
Co-stars: James Le Gros Reggie Bannister Paula Irvine

SIAN PHILLIPS *(Married Peter O'Toole)*

1964   BECKETT
Director: Peter Glenville
Co-stars: Peter O'Toole Richard Burton John Gielgud

1964   YOUNG CASSIDY
Director: Jack Cardiff
Co-stars: Rod Taylor Maggie Smith Edith Evans

1969   GOODBYE, MR CHIPS
Director: Herbert Ross
Co-stars: Peter O'Toole Petula Clark Michael Bryant

1969   LAUGHTER IN THE DARK
Director: Tony Richardson
Co-stars: Nicol Williamson Jean-Claude Drouot

1971   MURPHY'S WAR
Director: Peter Yates
Co-stars: Peter O'Toole Philippe Noiret Horst Janson

1971   UNDER MILK WOOD
Director: Andrew Sinclair
Co-stars: Richard Burton Elizabeth Taylor Peter O'Toole

1979   TINKER, TAILOR, SOLDIER, SPY
Director: John Irvin
Co-stars: Alec Guinness Bernard Hepton Terence Rigby

1981   CLASH OF THE TITANS
Director: Desmond Davis
Co-stars: Laurence Olivier Claire Bloom Maggie Smith

1984   DUNE
Director: David Lynch
Co-stars: Francesca Annis Jose Ferrer Brad Dourif

1985   THE DOCTOR AND THE DEVILS
Director: Freddie Francis
Co-stars: Timothy Dalton Jonathan Pryce Twiggy

1989   VALMONT
Director: Milos Forman
Co-stars: Colin Firth Annette Bening Meg Tilly

1991   THE BLACK CANDLE
Director: Roy Battersby
Co-stars: Samantha Bond Denholm Elliott Tara Fitzgerald

1993   THE AGE OF INNOCENCE
Director: Martin Scorsese
Co-stars: Michelle Pfeiffer Daniel Day-Lewis Winona Ryder

1997   HOUSE OF AMERICA
Director: Marc Evans
Co-star: Steven MacKintosh

WENDY PHILLIPS

1991   BUGSY
Director: Barry Levinson
Co-stars: Warren Beatty Annette Bening Harvey Keitel

1994   MacSHAYNE:WINNER TAKES ALL
Director: E.W. Swackhamer
Co-stars: Kenny Rogers Terry O'Quinn

AMBROSINE PHILLPOTTS

1950   HAPPY GO LOVELY
Director: Bruce Humberstone
Co-stars: David Niven Vera-Ellen Cesar Romero

1956   UP IN THE WORLD
Director: John Paddy Carstairs
Co-stars: Norman Wisdom Maureen Swanson Colin Gordon

1958   ROOM AT THE TOP
Director: Jack Clayton
Co-stars: Laurence Harvey Simone Signoret Heather Sears

1959   EXPRESSO BONGO
Director: Val Guest
Co-stars: Laurence Harvey Sylvia Syms Cliff Richard

1961   TWO AND TWO MAKE SIX
Director: Freddie Francis
Co-stars: George Chakiris Janette Scott Alfred Lynch

1963   CARRY ON CABBY
Director: Gerald Thomas
Co-stars: Sid James Hattie Jacques Liz Fraser

1980   THE WILDCATS OF ST. TRINIAN'S
Director: Frank Launder
Co-stars: Sheila Hancock Michael Hordern Joe Melia

GEMMA PHOENIX

1993   RAINING STONES
Director: Ken Loach
Co-stars: Bruce Jones Julie Brown Ricky Tomlinson

PATRICIA PHOENIX *(Married Anthony Booth)*

1962 THE L-SHAPED ROOM
Director: Bryan Forbes
Co-stars: Leslie Caron Tom Bell Brock Peters

RAIN PHOENIX

1992 MY OWN PRIVATE IDAHO
Director: Gus Van Sant
Co-stars: River Phoenix Keanu Reeves James Russo

1994 EVEN COWGIRLS GET THE BLUES
Director: Gus Van Sant
Co-stars: Uma Thurman John Hurt Keanu Reeves

EDITH PIAF

1955 FRENCH CAN-CAN
Director: Jean Renoir
Co-stars: Jean Gabin Francoise Arnoul Maria Felix

TINA PICA

1963 YESTERDAY, TODAY AND TOMORROW
Director: Vittorio De Sica
Co-stars: Sophia Loren Marcello Mastroianni

PALOMA PICASSO

1974 IMMORAL TALES
Director: Walerian Borowczyk
Co-stars: Lise Danvers Charlotte Alexandra Fabrice Luchini

ANNA MARIA PICCHIO

1985 TANGOS, THE EXILE OF GARDEL
Director: Fernando Solanas
Co-stars: Marie Laforet Philippe Leotard

OTTAVIA PICCOLO

1973 ZORRO
Director: Duccio Tessari
Co-stars: Alain Delon Frank Latimore Stanley Baker

LUPU PICK

1928 SPIONE
Director: Fritz Lang
Co-stars: Rudolph Klein-Rogge Gerda Maurus Willy Fritsch

HELENA PICKARD

1944 THE LODGER
Director: John Brahm
Co-stars: Laird Cregar Merle Oberon George Sanders

1947 THE TURNERS OF PROSPECT ROAD
Director: Maurice Wilson
Co-stars: Wilfrid Lawson Jeanne De Casalis

1949 MISS PILGRIM'S PROGRESS
Director: Val Guest
Co-stars: Yolande Donlan Michael Rennie Garry Marsh

1951 THE LADY WITH A LAMP
Director: Herbert Wilcox
Co-stars: Anna Neagle Michael Wilding Feliz Aylmer

SARAH PICKERING

1987 LITTLE DORRIT
Director: Christine Edzard
Co-stars: Derek Jacobi Alec Guinness Max Wall

CINDY PICKETT

1980 NIGHT GAMES
Director: Roger Vadim
Co-stars: Joanna Cassidy Barry Primus

1983 HYSTERICAL
Director: Chris Bearde
Co-stars: William Hudson Mark Hudson Brett Hudson

1986 FERRIS BUELLER'S DAY OFF
Director: John Hughes
Co-stars: Matthew Broderick Mia Sara Jennifer Grey

1987 AMERIKA
Director: Donald Wyre
Co-stars: Kris Kristofferson Sam Neill Mariel Hemingway

1987 INTO THE HOMELAND
Director: Lesli Linka Glatter
Co-stars: Powers Boothe Paul LeMat David Caruso

1988 HOT TO TROT
Director: Michael Dinner
Co-stars: Bob Goldthwait Virginia Madsen Dabney Coleman

1989 I KNOW MY FIRST NAME IS STEVEN
Director: Larry Elikann
Co-stars: John Ashton Corin Nemec Ray Walston

1989 DEEPSTAR SIX
Director: Sean Cunningham
Co-stars: Taurean Blacque Nancy Everhard Miguel Ferrer

1991 CROOKED HEARTS
Director: Michael Bortman
Co-stars: Peter Coyote Vincent D'Onofrio Jennifer Jason Leigh

1992 STEPHEN KING'S SLEEPWALKERS
Director: Mick Garris
Co-stars: Brian Krause Madchen Amick

1993 SON IN LAW
Director: Steve Rash
Co-stars: Pauly Shore Carla Gugino Lane Smith

MARY PICKFORD *(Gladys Smith)*
(Married Charles Rogers/Douglas Fairbanks)
Oscar For Best Actress In 1929 For "Coquette"
Honorary Award Presented In 1975

1912 THE NEW YORK HAT
Director: D.W. Griffith
Co-stars: Lionel Barrymore Lillian Gish Dorothy Gish

1914 TESS OF THE STORM COUNTRY
Director: Edwin Porter
Co-stars: Harold Lockwood Olive Fuller Golden

1915 MADAME BUTTERFLY

1917 REBECCA OF SUNNYBROOK FARM
Director: Marshall Neilan
Co-stars: Eugene O'Brien Helen Jerome Eddy

1918 M'LISS

1918 STELLA MARIS
Director: Marshall Neilan
Co-stars: Conway Tearle Ida Waterman Camille Ankewich

1919 DADDY LONG LEGS

1920 POLLYANNA

1921 LITTLE LORD FAUNTLEROY
Director: Jack Pickford
Co-stars: Claude Gillingwater Rose Dionne

1922 TESS OF THE STORM COUNTRY
Director: John Robertson
Co-stars: Lloyd Hughes Jean Hersholt Gloria Hope

1923 HOLLYWOOD
Director: James Cruze
Co-stars: Hope Drown Luke Cosgrove Ruby Lafayette

1925 LITTLE ANNIE ROONEY
Director: William Beaudine
Co-stars: William Haines Walter James Gordon Griffith

1927 THE GAUCHO
Director: Richard Jones
Co-stars: Douglas Fairbanks Lupe Velez Gustav Von Seyffertitz

1927 MY BEST GIRL
Director: Sam Taylor
Co-stars: Charles Rogers Sunshine Hart Carmelita Gerraghty

1929 COQUETTE
Director: Sam Taylor
Co-stars: Johnny Mack Brown Matt Moore William Janney

1929 THE TAMING OF THE SHREW
Director: Sam Taylor
Co-stars: Douglas Fairbanks Joseph Cawthorn Clyde Cook

1931 KIKI
Director: Sam Taylor
Co-stars: Reginald Denny Joseph Cawthorn Margaret Livingston

1933 SECRETS
Director: Frank Borzage
Co-stars: Leslie Howard Blanche Frederici C. Aubrey Smith

CAROLYN PICKLES

1979 TESS
Director: Roman Polanski
Co-stars: Nastassja Kinski Leigh Lawson Peter Firth

CHRISTINA PICKLES

1987 MASTERS OF THE UNIVERSE
Director: Gary Goddard
Co-stars: Dolph Lundgrew Frank Langella Meg Foster

1988 THE HIJACKING OF THE ACHILLE LAURO
Director: Robert Collins
Co-stars: Karl Malden Lee Grant Vera Miles

1992 A NIGHTMARE IN THE DAYLIGHT
Director: Lou Antonio
Co-stars: Jaclyn Smith Christopher Reeve

1994 LEGENDS OF THE FALL
Director: Edward Zwick
Co-stars: Brad Pitt Anthony Hopkins Julia Ormond

VIVIAN PICKLES

1966 ISADORA
Director: Ken Russell

1971 HAROLD AND MAUDE
Director: Hal Ashby
Co-stars: Ruth Gordon Bud Cort Cyril Cusack

1971 SUNDAY, BLOODY SUNDAY
Director: John Schlesinger
Co-stars: Glenda Jackson Peter Finch Murray Head

1977 CANDLESHOE
Director: Norman Tokar
Co-stars: David Niven Helen Hayes Jodie Foster

MOLLY PICON

1962 COME BLOW YOUR HORN
Director: Bud Yorkin
Co-stars: Frank Sinatra Tony Bill Lee J. Cobb

1971 FIDDLER ON THE ROOF
Director: Norman Jewison
Co-stars: Topol Norma Crane Leonard Frey

1974 FOR PETE'S SAKE
Director: Peter Yates
Co-stars: Barbra Streisand Michael Sarrazin Estelle Parsons

1981 THE CANNONBALL RUN
Director: Hal Needham
Co-stars: Burt Reynolds Roger Moore Dean Martin

GENEVIEVE PICOT

1991 PROOF
Director: Jocelyn Moorhouse
Co-stars: Hugo Weaving Russell Crowe Heather Mitchell

REBECCA PIDGEON

1988 THE DAWNING
Director: Robert Knights
Co-stars: Anthony Hopkins Trevor Howard Hugh Grant

1989 SHE'S BEEN AWAY
Director: Peter Hall
Co-stars: Peggy Ashcroft Geraldine James James Fox

1991 HOMICIDE
Director: David Mamet
Co-stars: Joe Mantegna William H. Macy Ving Rhames

BETTY PIERCE

1930 ALIAS FRENCH GERTIE
Director: George Archainbaud
Co-stars: Bebe Daniels Ben Lyon

LINDA PIERCE

1989 BLACK RAINBOW
Director: Mike Hodges
Co-stars: Rosanna Arquette Jason Robards Tom Hulce

1991 VICTIM OF BEAUTY
Director: Roger Young
Co-stars: William Devane Jerilynn Ryan Michele Abrams

MAGGIE PIERCE

1967 THE FASTEST GUITAR ALIVE
Director: Michael Moore
Co-stars: Roy Orbison Sammy Jackson Joan Freeman

JENNIFER PIERCEY

1981 FRIEND OR FOE
Director: John Krish
Co-stars: Mark Luxford John Holmes Stacey Trendetter

1983 ANOTHER TIME, ANOTHER PLACE
Director: Michael Radford
Co-stars: Phyllis Logan Giovanni Mauriello

1987 THE DUNROAMIN' RISING
Director: Moira Armstrong
Co-stars: Russell Hunter Elizabeth Sellars Hugh Lloyd

JACQUELINE PIERREUX

1963 BLACK SABBATH
Director: Mario Bava
Co-stars: Boris Karloff Michele Mercier Mark Damon

MAREILLE PIERREY

1953 MADAME DE ...
Director: Max Ophuls
Co-stars: Charles Boyer Danielle Darrieux Vittorio De Sica

SARAH PIERSE

1989 THE NAVIGATOR: A MEDIEVAL ODYSSEY
Director: Vincent Ward
Co-stars: Bruce Lyons Chris Haywood

ALEXANDRA PIGG

1985 LETTER TO BREZHNEV
Director: Chris Bernard
Co-stars: Margi Clarke Peter Firth Alfred Molina

1986 SMART MONEY
Director: Bernard Rose
Co-stars: Bruce Payne Spencer Leigh Iain Cuthbertson

1988 A CHORUS OF DISAPPROVAL
Director: Michael Winner
Co-stars: Anthony Hopkins Jeremy Irons Patsy Kensit

1990 CHICAGO JOE AND THE SHOWGIRL
Director: Berbard Rose
Co-stars: Emily Lloyd Kiefer Sutherland

1990 BULLSEYE !
Director: Michael Winner
Co-stars: Michael Caine Roger Moore Sally Kirkland

1990 MURDER EAST, MURDER WEST
Director: Peter West
Co-stars: Jeroen Krabbe Suzzana Hamilton Joanne Pearce

NOVA PILBEAM

1933 THE MAN WHO KNEW TOO MUCH
Director: Alfred Hitchcock
Co-stars: Leslie Banks Edna Best Peter Lorre

1934 THE LITTLE FRIEND
Director: Berthold Viertel
Co-stars: Matheson Lang Lydia Sherwood

1936 TUDOR ROSE
Director: Robert Stevenson
Co-stars: Cedric Hardwicke John Mills Miles Malleson

1937 YOUNG AND INNOCENT
Director: Alfred Hitchcock
Co-stars: Derrick De Marney Mary Clare Basil Radford

1939 CHEER BOYS CHEER
Director: Walter Forde
Co-stars: Edmund Gwenn Jimmy O'Dea Moore Marriott

1940 PASTOR HALL
Director: Roy Boulting
Co-stars: Wilfrid Lawson Seymour Hicks Marius Goring

1940 SPRING MEETING
Director: Walter Mycroft
Co-stars: Basil Sidney Sarah Churchill Michael Wilding

1941 BANANA RIDGE
Director: Walter Mycroft
Co-stars: Robertson Hare Alfred Drayton Isabel Jeans

1942 NEXT OF KIN
Director: Thorold Dickinson
Co-stars: Mervyn Johns Basil Radford Naunton Wayne

1943 THE YELLOW CANARY
Director: Herbert Wilcox
Co-stars: Anna Neagle Richard Greene Cyril Fletcher

1946 THIS MAN IS MINE
Director: Marcel Varnel
Co-stars: Tom Wall Glynis Johns Jeanne De Casalais

1946 GREEN FINGERS
Director: John Harlow
Co-stars: Robert Beatty Carol Raye Moore Marriott

1948 COUNTERBLAST
Director: Paul Stein
Co-stars: Robert Beatty Mervyn Johns Margaretta Scott

1948 THE THREE WEIRD SISTERS
Director: Dan Birt
Co-stars: Nancy Price Mary Clare Raymond Lovell

LORRAINE PILKINGTON

1991 THE MIRACLE
Director: Neil Jordan
Co-stars: Niall Byrne Donal McCann Beverly D'angelo

1996 THE LAST OF THE HIGH KINGS
Director: David Keating
Co-stars: Gabriel Byrne Catherine O'Hara

SILVIA PINAL

1961 VIRIDIANA
Director: Luis Bunuel
Co-stars: Francisco Rabal Fernando Rey Teresa Rabal

1962 THE EXTERMINATING ANGEL
Director: Luis Bunuel
Co-stars: Enrique Rambal Jacqueline Andere Jose Baveira

1965 SIMON OF THE DESERT
Director: Luis Bunuel
Co-stars: Claudio Brock Jesus Fernandez

1967 GUNS FOR SAN SEBASTIAN
Director: Henri Verneuil
Co-stars: Anthony Quinn Charles Bronson Sam Jaffe

1969 SHARK
Director: Samuel Fuller
Co-stars: Burt Reynolds Barry Sullivan Enrique Lucero

ROSAMOND PINCHOT

1935 THE THREE MUSKETEERS
Director: Rowland Lee
Co-stars: Walter Abel Paul Lukas Heather Angel

JADA PINKETT

1993 JASON'S LYRIC
Director: Doug McHenry
Co-stars: Allen Payne Forest Whitaker

1993 MENACE 11 SOCIETY
Director: Albert Hughes
Co-stars: Tyrin Turner Larenz Tate Bill Duke

1994 A LOW DOWN DIRTY SHAME
Director: Keenan Ivory Wayans
Co-star: Charles S. Dutton Keenan Ivory Wayans

1994 NO ORDINARY SUMMER
Director: Matty Rich
Co-stars: Larenz Tate Joe Morton

1996 THE NUTTY PROFESSOR
Director: Tom Shadyac
Co-stars: Eddie Murphy Dave Chappelle

1997 SET IF OFF
Director: F. Gary Grey
Co-stars: Viveca A. Fox Queen Latifah Kimberley Elise

COLLEAN ZENK PINTER

1993 WOMAN ON THE LEDGE
Director: Chris Thomson
Co-stars: Deidre Hall Leslie Charleson Josh Taylor

EMMA PIPER

1983 AGATHA CHRISTIE:IN A GLASS DARKLY
Director: Desmond Davis
Co-stars: Nicholas Clay Elspet Gray

JACKI PIPER

1970 CARRY ON UP THE JUNGLE
Director: Gerald Thomas
Co-stars: Sid James Kenneth Connor Frankie Howard

1970 CARRY ON LOVING
Director: Gerald Thomas
Co-stars: Sid James Hattie Jacques Terry Scott

1971 CARRY ON AT YOUR CONVENIENCE
Director: Gerald Thomas
Co-stars: Sid James Kenneth Williams Joan Sims

ANNE-MARIE PISANI

1991 DELICATESSEN
Director: Marc Caro
Co-stars: Dominique Pinon Jean-Claude Dreyfus Karin Viard

MARIE-FRANCE PISIER

1963 LOVE AT TWENTY
Director: Francois Truffaut
Co-stars: Jean-Pierre Leaud Cristina Gajoni

1974 CELINE AND JULIE GO BOATING
Director: Jacques Rivette
Co-stars: Juliet Berto Dominique Labourier

1975 COUSIN COUSINE
Director: Jean-Charles Tachella
Co-stars: Victor Lanoux Marie-Christine Barault

1977 THE OTHER SIDE OF MIDNIGHT
Director: Charles Jarrott
Co-stars: John Beck Susan Sarandon Raf Vallone

1979 LOVE ON THE RUN
Director: Francois Truffaut
Co-stars: Jean-Pierre Leaud Claude Jade Dorothee

1982 BOULEVARD OF ASSASSINS
Director: Boramy Tioulong
Co-stars: Jean-Louis Trintignant Victor Lanoux

1983 THE PRIZE OF PERIL
Director: Yves Boisset
Co-stars: Michel Piccoli Gerard Lanvin Bruno Cremer

KIMBERLEY PISTONE

1986 BLUE DE VILLE
Director: Jim Johnston
Co-stars: Jennifer Runyon Mark Thomas Miller Alan Autry

PAOLA PITAGORA

1965 FISTS IN THE POCKET
Director: Marco Bellocchio
Co-stars: Lou Castel Liliona Gerace Marino Mase

1969 IN SEARCH OF GREGORY
Director: Peter Wood
Co-stars: Julie Christie Michael Sarrazin John Hurt

1977 THE DEVIL'S ADVOCATE
Director: Guy Green
Co-stars: John Mills Stephane Audran Timothy West

MARIA PITILLO

1994 ESCAPE FROM TERROR: THE TERESA STAMPER STORY
Director: Michael Scott
Co-stars: Adam Storke Brad Douriff

1994 BETWEEN LOVE AND HONOR
Director: Sam Pillsbury
Co-star: Grant Show

1998 SOMETHING TO BELIEVE IN
Director: John Hough
Co-star: William McNamara

ANNE PITONIAK

1985 AGNES OF GOD
Director: Norman Jewison
Co-stars: Jane Fonda Ann Bancroft Meg Tilly

1987 HOUSEKEEPING
Director: Bill Forsyth
Co-stars: Christine Lahti Sara Walker Andrea Burchill

1989 OLD GRINGO
Director: Luis Puenzo
Co-stars: Jane Fonda Gregory Peck Jimmy Smits

1991 VI WARSHAWSKI
Director: Jeff Kanew
Co-stars: Kathleen Turner Charles Durning Angela Goethals

1993 HOUSE OF CARDS
Director: Michael Lessac
Co-stars: Kathleen Turner Park Overall Tommy Lee Jones

INGRID PITT

1970 THE VAMPIRE LOVERS
Director: Roy Ward Baker
Co-stars: Peter Cushing Madeleine Smith Dawn Addams

1970 THE HOUSE THAT DRIPPED BLOOD
Director: Peter Duffell
Co-stars: John Bennett Christopher Lee Jon Pertwee

1971 COUNTESS DRACULA
Director: Peter Sasdy
Co-stars: Nigel Green Sandor Eles Peter Jeffrey

1973 THE WICKER MAN
Director: Robin Hardy
Co-stars: Edward Woodward Britt Ekland Diane Cilento

1982 WHO DARES WINS
Director: Ian Sharp
Co-stars: Lewis Collins Judy Davis Richard Widmark

1985 UNDERWORLD
Director: George Pavlou
Co-stars: Denholm Elliott Miranda Richardson Larry Lamb

1988 HANNA'S WAR
Director: Menahem Golan
Co-stars: Maruschka Detmers Ellen Burstyn Anthony Andrews

ZASU PITTS

1923 GREED
Director: Erich Von Stroheim
Co-stars: Gibson Gowland Jean Hersholt Chester Conklin

1925 PRETTY LADIES
Director: Monta Bell
Co-stars: Norma Shearer Lilyan Tashman Conrad Nagle

1928 THE WEDDING MARCH
Director: Erich Von Stroheim
Co-stars: Fay Wray Matthew Betz Erich Von Strohiem

1929 THE LOCKED DOOR
Director: George Fitzmaurice
Co-stars: Barbara Stanwyck Rod La Rocque William Boyd

1929 THE SQUALL
Director: Alexander Korda
Co-stars: Myrna Loy Alice Joyce Loretta Young

1929 ALL QUIET ON THE WESTERN FRONT
Replaced By Beryl Mercer

1930 THE LOTTERY BRIDE
Director: Paul Stein
Co-stars: Jeanette MacDonald John Garrick Joe E. Brown

1930 MONTE CARLO
Director: Ernst Lubitsch
Co-stars: Jeanette MacDonald Jack Buchanan Claud Allister

1930 NO, NO NANETTE
Director: Clarence Badger
Co-stars: Bernice Claire Lucien Littlefield Lilyan Tashman

1930 RIVER'S END
Director: Michael Curtiz
Co-stars: Charles Bickford Evalyn Knapp J. Farrell MacDonald

1930 DEVIL'S HOLIDAY
Director: Edmund Goulding
Co-stars: Nancy Carroll Phillips Holmes Paul Lukas

1930 FINN AND HATTIE
Director: Norman Taurog
Co-stars: Leon Errol Mitzi Green Jackie Searle

1930 HONEY
Director: Wesley Ruggles
Co-stars: Nancy Carroll Stanley Smith Lillian Roth

1930 LITTLE ACCIDENT
Director: William James Craft
Co-stars: Douglas Fairbanks Anita Page Sally Blane

1931 BAD SISTER
Director: Hobart Henlet
Co-stars: Conrad Nagel Sidney Fox Bette Davis

1931 A WOMAN OF EXPERIENCE
Co-stars: William Bakewell Helen Twelvetrees Franklyn Pangborn

1931 SEED
Director: John Stahl
Co-stars: John Boles Genevieve Tobin Lois Wilson

1931 THE GUARDSMAN
Director: Sidney Franklin
Co-stars: Alfred Lunt Lynn Fontanne Roland Young

1932 BLONDIE OF THE FOLLIES
Director: Edmund Goulding
Co-stars: Marion Davies Jimmy Durante Robert Montgomery

1932 BROKEN LULLABY
Director: Ernst Lubitsch
Co-stars: Lionel Barrymore Nancy Carroll Phillips Holmes

1932 MAKE ME A STAR
Director: William Beaudine
Co-stars: Stuart Erwin Joan Blondell Ben Turpin

1932 BACK STREET
Director: John Stahl
Co-stars: Irene Dunne John Boles June Clyde

1932 ROAR OF THE DRAGON
Director: Wesley Ruggles
Co-stars: Richard Dix Gwili Andre Arline Judge

1932 SHOPWORN
Director: Nick Grinde
Co-stars: Barbara Stanwyck Regis Toomey Lucien Littlefield

1932 THE TRIAL OF VIVIENNE WARE
Director: William Howard
Co-stars: Joan Bennett Donald Cook Lillian Bond

1932 WESTWARD PASSAGE
Director: Robert Milton
Co-stars: Ann Harding Laurence Olivier Irving Pichel

1933 PROFESSIONAL SWEETHEART
Director: William Seiter
Co-stars: Ginger Rogers Gregory Ratoff Betty Furness

1933 HER FIRST MATE
Co-star: Slim Summerville

1933 ONCE IN A LIFETIME
Director: Russell Mack
Co-stars: Jack Oakie Sidney Fox Aline MacMahon

1933 MR SKITCH
Director: James Cruze
Co-stars: Will Rogers Florence Desmond Rochelle Hudson

1933 MEET THE BARON
Director: Walter Lang
Co-stars: Jack Pearl Jimmy Durante Ted Healy

1933 HELLO SISTER
Director: Erich Von Stroheim
Co-stars: James Dunn Boots Mallory Minna Gombell

1933 AGGIE APPLEBY, MAKER OF MEN
Director: Mark Sandrich
Co-stars: Wynne Gibson Charles Farrell Betty Furness

1933 THEY JUST HAD TO GET MARRIED
Director: Edward Ludwig
Co-stars: Slim Summerville Roland Young

1934 TWO ALONE
Director: Elliott Nugent
Co-stars: Jean Parker Tom Brown Beulah Bondi

1934 THEIR BIG MOMENT
Director: James Cruze
Co-stars: Slim Summerville William Gaxton Ralph Morgan

1934 MRS WIGGS OF THE CABBAGE PATCH
Director: Norman Taurog
Co-stars: Pauline Lord W.C. Fields

1934 THE GAY BRIDE
Director: Jack Conway
Co-stars: Carole Lombard Chester Morris Nat Pendleton

1934 DAMES
Director: Ray Enright
Co-stars: Joan Blondell Dick Powell Ruby Keeler

1935 GOING HIGHBROW
Director: Robert Florey
Co-stars: Guy Kibbee Ross Alexander Judy Canova

1935 HOT TIP
Co-star: Margaret Calahan

1935 RUGGLES OF RED GAP
Director: Leo McCarey
Co-stars: Charles Laughton Charles Ruggles Mary Boland

1935 SPRING TONIC
Director: S. Sylvan Simon
Co-stars: Lew Ayres Claire Trevor Jack Haley

1936 13 HOURS BY AIR
Director: Mitchell Leisen
Co-stars: Fred MacMurrey Joan Bennett Brian Donlevy

1936 SING ME A LOVE SONG
Director: Ray Enright
Co-stars: James Melton Patricia Ellis Hugh Herbert

1936 THE PLOT THICKENS
Director: Ben Holmes
Co-stars: James Gleason Owen Davis Jnr. Louise Latimer

1936 MAD HOLIDAY
Director: George Seitz
Co-stars: Edmund Lowe Elissa Landi Edmund Gwenn

1937 MERRY COMES TO TOWN
Director: George King
Co-stars: Guy Newall Betty Ann Davies Hermione Gingold

1937 52ND STREET
Director: Harold Young
Co-stars: Kenny Baker Ella Logan Ian Hunter

1937 FORTY NAUGHTY GIRLS
Director: Edward Cline
Co-stars: James Gleason Marjorie Lord Joan Woodbury

1939 NAUGHTY BUT NICE
Director: Ray Enright
Co-stars: Dick Powell Ann Sheridan Ronald Reagan

1939 ETERNALLY YOURS
Director: Tay Garnett
Co-stars: Loretta Young David Niven Broderick Crawford

1939 THE LADY'S FROM KENTUCKY
Director: Alexander Hall
Co-stars: George Raft Ellen Drew Hugh Herbert

1940 **NO, NO NANETTE**
Director: Herbert Wilcox
Co-stars: Anna Neagle Richard Carlson Victor Mature

1940 **IT ALL CAME TRUE**
Director: Lewis Seiler
Co-stars: Humphrey Bogart Ann Sheridan Jeffrey Lynn

1941 **MEXICAN SPITFIRE'S BABY**
Director: Leslie Goodwins
Co-stars: Lupe Velez Leon Errol Charles Rogers

1941 **MEXICAN SPITFIRE AT SEA**
Director: Leslie Goodwins
Co-stars: Lupe Velez Marion Martin Florence Bates

1941 **WEEKEND FOR THREE**
Director: Irving Reis
Co-stars: Dennis O'Keefe Jane Wyatt Philip Reed

1941 **NIAGARA FALLS**
Director: Gordon Douglas
Co-stars: Slim Summerville Tom Brown Marjorie Woodworth

1941 **BROADWAY LIMITED**
Director: Gordon Douglas
Co-stars: Marjorie Woodworth Leonid Kinsky Victor McLaglen

1942 **TISH**
Director: S. Sylvan Simon
Co-stars: Marjorie Main Aline MacMahon Susan Peters

1943 **LET'S FACE IT**
Director: Sidney Lanfield
Co-stars: Bob Hope Betty Hutton Eve Arden

1945 **BREAKFAST IN HOLLYWOOD**
Director: Harold Schuster
Co-stars: Tom Breneman Bonita Granville Beulah Bondi

1946 **THE PERFECT MARRIAGE**
Director: Lewis Allen
Co-stars: David Niven Loretta Young Eddie Albert

1947 **LIFE WITH FATHER**
Director: Michael Curtiz
Co-stars: William Powell Irene Dunne Elizabeth Taylor

1950 **FRANCIS**
Director: Arthur Lubin
Co-stars: Donald O'Connor Patricia Medina Ray Collins

1952 **DENVER AND RIO GRANDE**
Director: Byron Haskin
Co-stars: Edmond O'Brien Sterling Hayden Dean Jagger

1957 **THIS COULD BE THE NIGHT**
Director: Robert Wise
Co-stars: Jean Simmons Paul Douglas Joan Blondell

1959 **THE GAZEBO**
Director: George Marshall
Co-stars: Glenn Ford Debbie Reynolds Carl Reiner

1963 **IT'S A MAD, MAD, MAD, MAD WORLD**
Director: Stanley Kramer
Co-stars: Spencer Tracy Jimmy Durante Ethel Merman

1963 **THE THRILL OF IT ALL**
Director: Norman Jewison
Co-stars: Doris Day James Garner Edward Andrews

MARY KAY PLACE

1972 **KANSAS CITY BOMBER**
Director: Jerrold Freedman
Co-stars: Raquel Welch Kevin McCarthy Jodie Foster

1977 **NEW YORK, NEW YORK**
Director: Martin Scorsese
Co-stars: Liza Minnelli Robert De Niro Lionel Stander

1980 **PRIVATE BENJAMIN**
Director: Howard Zieff
Co-stars: Goldie Hawn Eileen Brennan Sam Wanamaker

1983 **THE BIG CHILL**
Director: Lawrence Kasdan
Co-stars: Tom Berenger Glenn Close William Hurt

1985 **SMOOTH TALK**
Director: Joyce Chopra
Co-stars: Treat Williams Laura Dern Levon Helm

1988 **A NEW LIFE**
Director: Alan Alda
Co-stars: Ann-Margret Hal Linden Alan Alda

1989 **OUT ON THE EDGE**
Director: John Pasquin
Co-stars: Rick Schroder Richard Jenkins Natalia Mogulich

1992 **CAPTAIN RON**
Director: Thom Eberhardt
Co-stars: Kurt Russell Martin Short Paul Anka

1994 **THE PRICE OF VENGEANCE**
Director: Dick Lowry
Co-stars: Dean Stockwell Michael Gross Kathleen Robertson

1998 **THE RAINMAKER**
Director: Francis Coppolo
Co-stars: Matt Damon Jon Voight Danny DeVito

MICHELE PLACIDO

1988 **BIG BUSINESS**
Director: Jim Abrahams
Co-stars: Bette Midler Lily Tomlin Fred Ward

1991 **FOREVER MARY**
Director: Marco Risi
Co-stars: Claudio Amendola Francesco Benigno

SUZIE PLAKSON

1989 **LITTLE WHITE LIES**
Director: Ansom Williams
Co-stars: Ann Jillian Tim Matheson Amy Yasbeck

1994 **DISCLOSURE**
Director: Barry Levinson
Co-stars: Michael Douglas Demi Moore Donald Sutherland

CHERYL PLATT

1991 **LANA IN LOVE**
Director: Bashar Shbib
Co-stars: Daphna Kastner Clark Gregg Michael Gillis

LOUISE PLATT

1937 **I MET MY LOVE AGAIN**
Director: Joshua Logan
Co-stars: Henry Fonda Joan Bennett Alan Marshall

1938 **SPAWN OF THE NORTH**
Director: Henry Hathaway
Co-stars: Henry Fonda George Raft Dorothy Lamour

1939 **STAGECOACH**
Director: John Ford
Co-stars: John Wayne Claire Trevor Thomas Mitchell

1939 **TELL NO TALES**
Director: Leslie Fenton
Co-stars: Melvyn Douglas Gene Lockhart Zeffie Tilbury

1940 **FORGOTTEN GIRLS**
Director: Phil Rosen
Co-stars: Donald Woods Wynne Gibson Robert Armstrong

1940 **CAPTAIN CAUTION**
Director: Richard Wallace
Co-stars: Victor Mature Bruce Cabot Alan Ladd

1942 STREET OF CHANCE
Director: Jack Hively
Co-stars: Burgess Meredith Claire Trevor Jerome Cowan

SUSAN PLAYER-JARREAU

1978 MALIBU BEACH
Director: Robert Rosenthal
Co-stars: Kim Lankford James Draughton Stephen Oliver

WENDY PLAYFAIR

1978 SHIMMERING LIGHT
Director: Don Chaffey
Co-stars: Beau Bridges Lloyd Bridges Victoria Shaw

ALICE PLAYTEN

1971 WHO KILLED MARY WHAT'S HER NAME ?
Director: Ernest Pintoff
Co-stars: Red Buttons Sylvia Miles Sam Waterston

1985 LEGEND
Director: Ridley Scott
Co-stars: Tom Cruise Tim Curry Mia Sara

ANGELA PLEASENCE

1970 THE SIX WIVES OF HENRY VIII
Director: John Glenister
Co-stars: Keith Michell Annette Crosbie Elvi Hale

1984 A CHRISTMAS CAROL
Director: Clive Donner
Co-stars: George C. Scott Frank Finlay David Warner

1985 SILAS MARNER
Director: Giles Foster
Co-stars: Ben Kingsley Jenny Agutter Patsy Kensit

1986 MANSFIELD PARK
Director: David Giles
Co-stars: Sylvestra Le Touzel Anna Massey Bernard Hepton

**1992 THE FAVOUR, THE WATCH AND
THE VERY BIG FISH**
Director: Ben Lewin
Co-stars: Bob Hoskins Jeff Goldblum Natasha Richardson

SUZANNE PLESHETTE (*Married Troy Donahue*)

1958 THE GEISHA BOY
Director: Frank Tashlin
Co-stars: Jerry Lewis Marie MacDonald Sessue Hayakawa

1962 ROME ADVENTURE
Director: Delmer Daves
Co-stars: Troy Donahue Angie Dickinson Rossano Brazzi

1963 WALL OF NOISE
Director: Richard Wilson
Co-stars: Ty Hardin Dorothy Provine Ralph Meeker

1963 FORTY POUNDS OF TROUBLE
Director: Norman Jewison
Co-stars: Tony Curtis Phil Silvers Claire Wilcox

1963 THE BIRDS
Director: Alfred Hitchcock
Co-stars: Tippi Hedren Rod Taylor Jessica Tandy

1964 A DISTANT TRUMPET
Director: Raoul Walsh
Co-stars: Troy Donahue James Gregory Diane McBain

1964 FATE IS THE HUNTER
Director: Ralph Nelson
Co-stars: Glenn Ford Rod Taylor Nancy Kwan

1964 YOUNGBLOOD HAWKE
Director: Delmer Daves
Co-stars: James Franciscus Genevieve Page Mary Astor

1965 A RAGE TO LIVE
Director: Walter Grauman
Co-stars: Bradford Dillman Ben Gazzara Peter Graves

1966 THE UGLY DACHSHUND
Director: Norman Tokar
Co-stars: Dean Jones Charles Ruggles Parley Baer

1966 NEVADA SMITH
Director: Henry Hathaway
Co-stars: Steve McQueen Karl Malden Arthur Kennedy

1966 MISTER BUDDWING
Director: Delbert Mann
Co-stars: James Garner Jean Simmons Angela Lansbury

1966 THE ADVENTURES OF BULLWHIP GRIFFIN
Director: James Neilson
Co-stars: Roddy McDowall Karl Malden

1968 BLACKBEARD'S GHOST
Director: Robert Stevenson
Co-stars: Peter Ustinov Dean Jones Elsa Lanchester

1968 THE POWER
Director: Byron Haskin
Co-stars: Michael Rennie George Hamilton Yvonne De Carlo

1968 TARGET HARRY
Director: Roger Corman
Co-stars: Vic Morrow Cesar Romero Stanley Holloway

**1969 SUPPOSE THEY GAVE A WAR
AND NOBODY CAME**
Director: Hy Averback
Co-stars: Tony Curtis Tom Ewell Brian Keith

1969 IF IT'S TUESDAY, THIS MUST BE BELGIUM
Director: Mel Stuart
Co-stars: Ian McShane Mildred Natwick

1970 HUNTERS ARE FOR KILLING
Director: Bernard Kowalski
Co-stars: Burt Reynolds Melvyn Douglas Martin Balsam

1971 IN BROAD DAYLIGHT
Director: Robert Day
Co-stars: Richard Boone Stella Stevens Whit Bissell

1971 SUPPORT YOUR LOCAL GUNFIGHTER
Director: Burt Kennedy
Co-stars: James Garner Joan Blondell Harry Morgan

1976 THE SHAGGY D.A.
Director: Robert Stevenson
Co-stars: Dean Jones Tim Conway Keenan Wynn

1979 HOT STUFF
Director: Dom DeLuise
Co-stars: Ossie Davis Jerry Reed Luis Avalos

1980 IF THINGS WERE DIFFERENT
Director: Robert Michael Lewis
Co-stars: Tony Roberts Arte Johnson Chuck McCann

1980 OH GOD ! BOOK II
Director: Gilbert Cates
Co-stars: George Burns Louanne Howard Duff

1983 DIXIE: CHANGING HABITS
Director: George Englund
Co-stars: Cloris Leachman Geraldine Fitzgerald Judith Ivey

1987 A STRANGER WAITS
Director: Robert Lewis
Co-stars: Tom Atkins Paul Benjamin Ann Wedgeworth

1990 THE QUEEN OF MEAN
Director: Richard Michaels
Co-stars: Lloyd Bridges Joe Regalbuto Raymond Singer

1991 BATTLING FOR BABY
Director: Art Wolff
Co-stars: Debbie Reynolds John Terlesky

1993   **A TWIST OF THE KNIFE**
Director: Jerry London
Co-stars: Dick Van Dyke Cynthia Gibb

MARTHA PLIMPTON *(Child)*

1984   **THE RIVER RAT**
Director: Tom Rickman
Co-stars: Tommy Lee Jones Nancy Lea Owen Brian Dennehy

1985   **THE GOONIES**
Director: Richard Donner
Co-stars: Sean Astin Corey Feldman Josh Brolin

1986   **MOSQUITO COAST**
Director: Peter Weir
Co-stars: Harrison Ford Helen Mirren River Phoenix

1987   **SHY PEOPLE**
Director: Andrei Konchalovsky
Co-stars: Jill Clayburgh Barbara Hershey John Philbin

1988   **STARS AND BARS**
Director: Pat O'Connor
Co-stars: Daniel Day-Lewis Harry Dean Stanton Joan Cusack

1988   **RUNNING ON EMPTY**
Director: Sidney Lumet
Co-stars: Christine Lahti River Phoenix Judd Hirsch

1988   **ANOTHER WOMAN**
Director: Woody Allen
Co-stars: Gena Rowlands Mia Farrow Gene Hackman

1989   **PARENTHOOD**
Director: Ron Howard
Co-stars: Steve Martin Tom Hulce Keanu Reeves

1989   **SILENCE LIKE GRASS**
Director: Carl Schenkel
Co-stars: Jami Gertz George Peppard Rip Torn

1989   **STANLEY AND IRIS**
Director: Martin Ritt
Co-stars: Jane Fonda Robert De Niro Swoosie Kurtz

1993   **JOSH AND S.A.M.**
Director: Billy Weber
Co-stars: Jacob Tierney Joan Allen Chris Penn

1994   **FORBIDDEN CHOICES**
Director: Jennifer Warren
Co-stars: Kelly Lynch Rutger Hauer

JOAN PLOWRIGHT *(Married Laurence Olivier)*
Nominated For Best Supporting Actress In 1992 For "Enchanted April"

1957   **TIME WITHOUT PITY**
Director: Joseph Losey
Co-stars: Michael Redgrave Alex McCowan Leo McKern

1960   **THE ENTERTAINER**
Director: Tony Richardson
Co-stars: Laurence Olivier Alan Bates Albert Finney

1970   **THE THREE SISTERS**
Director: Laurence Olivier
Co-stars: Jeanne Watts Derek Jacobi Alan Bates

1977   **EQUUS**
Director: Sidney Lumet
Co-stars: Richard Burton Peter Firth Colin Blakely

1982   **BRIMSTONE AND TREACLE**
Director: Richard Loncraine
Co-stars: Sting Denholm Elliott Dudley Sutton

1982   **BRITANNIA HOSPITAL**
Director: Lindsay Anderson
Co-stars: Malcolm McDowell Arthur Lowe Leonard Rossiter

1986   **REVOLUTION**
Director: Hugh Hudson
Co-stars: Al Pacino Nastassja Kinski Donald Sutherland

1988   **THE DRESSMAKER**
Director: Jim O'Brien
Co-stars: Billie Whitelaw Jane Horrocks Tim Ransom

1988   **DROWNING BY NUMBERS**
Director: Peter Greenaway
Co-stars: Bernard Hill Juliet Stevenson John Richardson

1989   **AND A NIGHTINGALE SANG**
Director: Robert Knights
Co-stars: Phyllis Logan Tom Watt Pippa Hinchley

1990   **AVALON**
Director: Barry Levinson
Co-stars: Elizabeth Perkins Aidan Quinn Armin Mueller-Stahl

1990   **I LOVE YOU TO DEATH**
Director: Lawrence Kasdan
Co-stars: Kevin Kline Tracy Ullman River Phoenix

1991   **ENCHANTED APRIL**
Director: Mike Newell
Co-stars: Miranda Richardson Josie Lawrence Polly Walker

1993   **A PLACE FOR ANNIE**
Director: John Grey
Co-stars: Sissy Spacek Mary-Louise Parker

1992   **THE CLOTHES IN THE WARDROBE**
Director: Waris Hussein
Co-stars: Jeanne Moreau Julie Walters

1993   **DENNIS**
Director: Nick Castle
Co-stars: Walter Matthau Christopher Lloyd Lea Thompson

1993   **THE LAST ACTION HERO**
Director: John McTiernan
Co-stars: Arnold Schwarzenneger Austin O'Brien

1994   **WIDOWS'S PEAK**
Director: John Irvin
Co-stars: Mia Farrow Natasha Richardson Jim Broadbent

1996   **SURVIVING PICASSO**
Director: James Ivory
Co-stars: Anthony Hopkins Natasha McElhone Julianne Moore

1996   **101 DALMATIONS**
Director: Stephen Herek
Co-stars: Glenn Close Hugh Laurie Joely Richardson

1996   **JANE EYRE**
Director: Franco Zefferelli
Co-stars: Charlotte Gainsbourg William Hurt Fiona Shaw

LOUISE PLOWRIGHT

1990   **PALMER**
Director: Keith Washington
Co-stars: Ray Winstone Dora Bryan Gerard Moran

ERIKA PLUHAR

1978   **JUST A GIGOLO**
Director: David Hemmings
Co-stars: David Bowie Kim Novak Marlene Dietrich

EVE PLUMB

1976   **DAWN: PORTRAIT OF A RUNAWAY TEENAGER**
Director: Randal Kleiser
Co-stars: Bo Bopkins Lynn Carlin

1977   **ALEXANDER:THE OTHER SIDE OF DAWN**
Director: Randal Kleiser
Co-star: Leigh J. McCloskey

1978   **LITTLE WOMEN**
Director: David Lowell
Co-stars: Meredith Baxter Susan Dey Dorothy McGuire

AMANDA PLUMMER

1981 CATTLE ANNIE AND LITTLE BRITCHES
Director: Lamont Johnson
Co-stars: Burt Lancaster Diane Lane Rod Steiger

1984 THE DOLLMAKER
Director: Daniel Petrie
Co-stars: Jane Fonda Susan Kingsley Geraldine Page

1987 MADE IN HEAVEN
Director: Alan Rudolph
Co-stars: Timothy Hutton Kelly McGillis Maureen Stapleton

1990 JOE VERSUS THE VOLCANO
Director: John Patrick Shanley
Co-stars: Tom Hanks Meg Ryan Lloyd Bridges

1991 THE FISHER KING
Director: Terry Gilliam
Co-stars: Robin Williams Jeff Bridges Mercedes Ruehl

1992 FREEJACK
Director: Geoff Murphy
Co-stars: Emilio Estevez Mick Jagger Rene Russo

1993 SO I MARRIED AN AXE MURDERER
Director: Thomas Schlamme
Co-stars: Mike Myers Nancy Travis Brenda Fricker

1993 NEEDFUL THINGS
Director: Fraser Heston
Co-stars: Max Von Sydow Ed Harris Bonnie Bedelia

1993 NOSTRADAMUS
Director: Roger Christian
Co-stars: Tcheky Karyo Julia Ormond Rutger Hauer

1993 LAST LIGHT
Director: Kiefer Sutherland
Co-star: Forest Whitaker Keifer Sutherland

1993 WHOSE CHILD IS THIS
Director: John Kent Harrison
Co-stars: Susan Dey Michael Ontkean David Keith

1994 PULP FICTION
Director: Quentin Tarantino
Co-stars: John Travolta Bruce Willis Harvey Keitel

1995 UNDER THE PIANO
Director: Stefan Scaini
Co-stars: Teresa Stratus Megan Follows

MARY ANN PLUNKETT

1989 THE LITTLEST VICTIMS
Director: Peter Levin
Co-stars: Tim Matheson Mary Joan Negro Nan-Lynn Nelson

PATRICIA PLUNKETT

1947 IT ALWAYS RAINS ON SUNDAY
Director: Robert Hamer
Co-stars: Googie Withers John McCallum Jack Warner

1948 FOR THEM THAT TRESPASS
Director: Alberto Cavalcanti
Co-stars: Richard Todd Stephen Murray Joan Dowling

1948 BOND STREET
Director: Gordon Parry
Co-stars: Roland Young Jean Kent Hazel Court

1949 LANDFALL
Director: Ken Annakin
Co-stars: Michael Dennison David Tomlinson Joan Dowling

1950 MURDER WITHOUT CRIME
Director: J. Lee-Thompson
Co-stars: Dennis Price Derek Farr Joan Dowling

MICI PLWM

1992 THE CORMORANT
Director: Peter Markham
Co-stars: Ralph Fiennes Helen Schlesinger Thomas Williams

MARIE-SOPHIE POCHAT

1986 A MAN AND A WOMAN:20 YEARS LATER
Director: Claude Lelouch
Co-stars: Anouk Aimee Jean-Louis Trintignant

ALEJANDRA PODESTA

1993 WE DON'T WANT TO TALK ABOUT IT
Director: Maria Luisa Bemberg
Co-stars: Marcello Mastroianni Luisina Brando

ROSANNA PODESTA

1954 ULYSSES
Director: Mario Camerini
Co-stars: Kirk Douglas Silvana Mangano Anthony Quinn

1955 HELEN OF TROY
Director: Robert Wise
Co-stars: Jacques Sernas Stanley Baker Brigitte Bardot

1956 SANTIAGO
Director: Gordon Douglas
Co-stars: Alan Ladd Lloyd Nolan Chill Wills

1958 RAW WIND IN EDEN
Director: Richard Wilson
Co-stars: Esther Williams Jeff Chandler Carlos Thompson

1962 SODOM AND GOMORRAH
Director: Robert Aldrich
Co-stars: Stewart Granger Stanley Baker Pier Angeli

1965 SEVEN GOLDEN MEN
Director: Marco Vicario
Co-stars: Philippe Leroy Gastone Moschin Gabriele Tinti

1983 HERCULES
Director: Luigi Cozzi
Co-stars: Lou Ferrigno Mirella D'Angelo Sybil Danning

CATHY PODEWELL

1991 EARTH ANGEL
Director: Joe Napolitano
Co-stars: Mark Hamill Roddy McDowall

LISA ANNE POGGI

1992 OBSESSED
Director: Jonathan Sanger
Co-stars: William Devane Shannen Doherty Lois Chiles

KATHRYN POGSON

1984 THE COMPANY OF WOLVES
Director: Neil Jordan
Co-stars: Angela Lansbury David Warner Brian Glover

1987 THE HAPPY VALLEY
Director: Ross Devenish
Co-stars: Denholm Elliott Holly Aird Amanda Hillwood

PRISCILLA POINTER

1976 CARRIE
Director: Brian De Palma
Co-stars: Sissy Spacek Piper Laurie Amy Irving

1977 LOOKING FOR MR GOODBAR
Director: Richard Brooks
Co-stars: Diane Keaton Tuesday Weld Richard Gere

1977 MARY JANE HARPER CRIED LAST NIGHT
Director: Allen Reisner
Co-stars: Susan Dey John Vernon Bernie Casey

1979 THE ONION FIELD
Director: Harold Becker
Co-stars: John Savage James Woods Ted Danson

1981 THE ARCHER AND THE SORCERESS
Director: Nick Corea
Co-stars: Belinda Bauer Lane Caudell Kabir Bedi

1987 A NIGHTMARE ON ELM STREET III: DREAM WARRIORS
Director: Chuck Russell
Co-stars: Patricia Arquette John Saxon

1992 UNBECOMING AGE
Director: Alfredo Ringel
Co-stars: Diane Salinger John Calvin George Clooney

ARLETTE POIRIER

1952 COIFFEUR POUR DAMES
Director: Jean Boyer
Co-stars: Fernandel Blanchette Crunoy Renee Devillers

TALITHA POL

1965 RETURN FROM THE ASHES
Director: J.lee-Thompson
Co-stars: Maximillian Schell Samantha Eggar Ingrid Thulin

LINDA POLAN

1987 CARIANI AND THE COURTESANS
Director: Leslie Megahey
Co-stars: Paul McGann Lucy Hancock Diana Quick

HAYDEE POLITOFF

1967 LA COLLECTIONNEUSE
Director: Eric Rohmer
Co-star: Patrick Bauchan

CHERYL POLLACK

1988 PERFECT PEOPLE
Director: Bruce Seth Green
Co-stars: Lauren Hutton Perry King June Lockhart

1990 PUMP UP THE VOLUME
Director: Allan Moyle
Co-stars: Christian Slater Samantha Mathis Annie Ross

TRACY POLLAN (*Married Michael J. Fox*)

1984 A GOOD SPORT
Director: Lou Antonio
Co-stars: Lee Remick Ralph Waite Dan Frazer

1988 BRIGHT LIGHTS, BIG CITY
Director: James Bridges
Co-stars: Michael J. Fox Phoebe Cates Dianne Wiest

1988 PROMISED LAND
Director: Michael Hoffman
Co-stars: Kiefer Sutherland Meg Ryan Jason Gedrick

1992 CLOSE TO EDEN
Director: Sidney Lumet
Co-stars: Melanie Griffith Eric Thal Mia Sara

1993 DYING TO LOVE YOU
Director: Robert Iscove
Co-stars: Tim Matheson Christine Ebersole Lee Garlington

1994 CHILDREN OF THE DARK
Director: Michael Switzer
Co-star: Peter Horton

DAPHNE POLLARD

1930 LOOSE ANKLES
Director: Ted Wilde
Co-stars: Loretta Young Douglas Fairbanks Jnr. Louise Fazenda

1935 THICKER THAN WATER
Director: James Horne
Co-stars: Stan Laurel Oliver Hardy James Finlayson

1936 OUR RELATIONS
Director: Harry Lachman
Co-stars: Stan Laurel Oliver Hardy Sidney Toler

SARAH POLLEY

1989 THE ADVENTURES OF BARON MUNCHAUSEN
Director: Terry Gilliam
Co-stars: John Neville Eric Idle Oliver Reed

1997 THE SWEET HEREAFTER
Director: Atom Egoyan
Co-star: Ian Holm

EILEEN POLLOCK

1990 DEAR SARAH
Director: Frank Cvitanovich
Co-stars: Barry McGovern Simon Chandler Stella McCusker

1992 FAR AND AWAY
Director: Ron Howard
Co-stars: Tom Cruise Nicole Kidman Barbara Babcock

ELLEN POLLOCK

1939 SONS OF THE SEA
Director: Maurice Elvy
Co-stars: Leslie Banks Kay Walsh Cecil Parker

1951 TO HAVE AND TO HOLD
Director: Godfrey Grayson
Co-stars: Avis Scott Patrick Barr Robert Ayres

1973 HORROR HOSPITAL

NANCY POLLOCK

1959 THE LAST ANGRY MAN
Director: Daniel Mann
Co-stars: Paul Muni David Wayne Betsy Palmer

TERI POLO

1990 THE PHANTOM OF THE OPERA
Director: Tony Richardson
Co-stars: Charles Dance Burt Lancaster Andrea Ferreol

1993 CROSSFIRE
Director: Rick King
Co-stars: Jeff Fahey Robert Davi Tia Carrere

1993 THE HOUSE OF THE SPIRITS
Director: Bille August
Co-stars: Jeremy Irons Meryl Streep Glenn Close

1993 ASPEN EXTREME
Director: Patrick Hasburgh
Co-stars: Paul Gross Peter Berg Finola Hughes

1994 THE GOLDEN GATE
Director: John Madden
Co-stars: Matt Dillon Joan Chen Bruno Kirby

ANNA POLONY

1982 DIARY FOR MY CHILDREN
Director: Marta Meszaros
Co-stars: Zsuzsa Czinkoczi Jan Nowicki Pal Zolnay

1987 DIARY FOR MY LOVES
Director: Marta Meszaros
Co-stars: Zsuzsa Czinkoczi Jan Nowicki Laszlo Szabo

LILY PONS

1935 I DREAM TOO MUCH
Director: John Cromwell
Co-stars: Henry Fonda Eric Blore Lucille Ball

1936 THAT GIRL FROM PARIS
Director: Leigh Jason
Co-stars: Gene Raymond Jack Oakie Herman Bing

1937 HITTING A NEW HIGH
Director: Raoul Walsh
Co-stars: Jack Oakie Eric Blore Lucille Ball

1947 CARNEGIE HALL
Director: Edgar Ulmer
Co-stars: Marsha Hunt William Prince Frank McHugh

JOAN PONSFORD

1937 NIGHT RIDE
Director: John Paddy Carstairs
Co-stars: Julian Vedey Jimmy Hanley Wally Patch

DEBORAH POPLETT

1989 INSPECTOR WEXFORD: THE VEILED ONE
Director: Mary McMurray
Co-stars: George Baker Louie Ramsey

1992 FRIDAY ON MY MIND
Director: Marc Evans
Co-stars: Maggie O'Neill Christopher Eccleston David Calder

PAULINA PORIZKOVA

1987 ANNA
Director: Yurek Bogayevicz
Co-stars: Sally Kirkland Robert Fields

1989 HER ALIBI
Director: Bruce Beresford
Co-stars: Tom Selleck James Farentino Hurd Hatfield

1992 ARIZONA DREAM
Director: Emir Kusturica
Co-stars: Johnny Depp Jerry Lewis Faye Dunaway

GABRIELE PORKS

1960 THE MAGNIFICENT REBEL
Director: Georg Tressler
Co-stars: Karl Boehm Ernst Nadhering Ivan Desny

ANGIE PORRES

1988 STONES FOR IBARRA
Director: Jack Gold
Co-stars: Glenn Close Keith Carradine Alfonso Arau

LOUISE PORTAL

1986 DECLINE OF THE AMERICAN EMPIRE
Director: Denys Arcand
Co-stars: Dominique Michel Dorothee Berryman

ALISAN PORTER *(Child)*

1991 CURLY SUE
Director: John Hughes
Co-stars: James Belushi Kelly Lynch John Getz

JEAN PORTER

1943 THE YOUNGEST PROFESSION
Director: Edward Buzzell
Co-stars: Virginia Weidler Edward Arnold John Carroll

1943 THAT NAZTY NUISANCE
Director:
Co-stars: Frank Faylen Ian Keith Bobby Watson

1944 ANDY HARDY'S BLONDE TROUBLE
Director: George Seitz
Co-stars: Mickey Rooney Lewis Stone Fay Holden

1944 BATHING BEAUTY
Director: George Sidney
Co-stars: Esther Williams Red Skelton Basil Rathbone

1945 ABBOTT AND COSTELLO IN HOLLYWOOD
Director: S. Sylvan Simon
Co-stars: Bud Abbott Lou Costello Dean Stockwell

1947 LITTLE MISS BROADWAY
Co-star: Jerry Wald

1951 CRY DANGER
Director: Robert Parrish
Co-stars: Dick Powell Rhonda Fleming Richard Erdman

NYREE DAWN PORTER

1961 PART TIME WIFE
Director: Max Varnel
Co-stars: Anton Rogers Kenneth J. Warren Susan Richards

1963 TWO LEFT FEET
Director: Roy Baker
Co-stars: Michael Crawford Julia Foster Dilys Watling

1963 THE CRACKSMAN
Director: Peter Graham Scott
Co-stars: Charlie Drake George Sanders Dennis Price

1970 THE HOUSE THAT DRIPPED BLOOD
Director: Peter Duffell
Co-stars: John Bennett Denholm Elliott Christopher Lee

1971 JANE EYRE
Director: Delbert Mann
Co-stars: George C. Scott Susannah York Ian Bannen

1973 FROM BEYOND THE GRAVE
Director: Kevin Connor
Co-stars: Peter Cushing David Warner Diana Dors

SUSIE PORTER

1997 IDIOT BOX
Director: David Caesar
Co-stars: Ben Mendelson Jeremy Sims Robyn Loau

ROSE PORTILLO

1985 THE MEAN SEASON
Director: Philip Borsos
Co-stars: Kurt Russell Mariel Hemingway Richard Jordan

NATALIE PORTMAN *(Child)*

1994 LEON
Director: Luc Besson
Co-stars: Jean Reno Gary Oldman

1996 BEAUTIFUL GIRLS
Director: Ted Demme
Co-stars: Uma Thurman Mira Sorvino Timothy Hutton

1996 MARS ATTACKS !
Director: Tim Burton
Co-stars: Jack Nicholson Annette Bening Glenn Close

MARKIE POST

1982 NOT JUST ANOTHER AFFAIR
Director: Steven Hilliard Stern
Co-stars: Victoria Principal Gil Gerard

1988 TRICKS OF THE TRADE
Director: Jack Bender
Co-stars: Cindy Williams Scott Paulin

1988 GLITZ
Director: Sandor Stern
Co-stars: Jimmy Smits John Diehl Madison Mason

1994 SOMEONE SHE KNOWS
Director: Eric Laneauville
Co-stars: Gerald McRaney Sharon Lawrence

SASKIA POST

1984　ONE NIGHT STAND
Director:　John Duigan
Co-stars:　Tyler Coppin Cassandra Delaney Jay Hackett

1986　DOGS IN SPACE
Director:　Richard Lowenstein
Co-stars:　Michael Hutchence Nique Needles Chris Haywood

1991　PROOF
Director:　Jocelyn Moorhouse
Co-stars:　Hugo Weaving Genevieve Picot Russell Crowe

ADRIENNE POSTA

1967　UP THE JUNCTION
Director:　Peter Collinson
Co-stars:　Suzy Kendall Dennis Waterman Liz Fraser

1967　HERE WE GO ROUND THE MULBERRY BUSH
Director:　Clive Donner
Co-stars:　Judy Geeson Moyra Fraser Barry Evans

1969　SOME GIRLS DO
Director:　Ralph Thomas
Co-stars:　Richard Johnson Daliah Lavi Sydne Rome

1970　PERCY
Director:　Ralph Thomas
Co-stars:　Hywel Bennett Denholm Elliott Elke Sommer

1970　SPRING AND PORT WINE
Director:　Peter Hammond
Co-stars:　James Mason Susan George Diana Coupland

1970　ALL THE WAY UP
Director:　James McTaggart
Co-stars:　Warren Mitchell Kenneth Cranham Pat Heywood

1971　UP POMPEII
Director:　Bob Kellett
Co-stars:　Frankie Howerd Patrick Cargill Barbara Murray

1972　THE ALF GARNETT SAGA
Director:　Bob Kellett
Co-stars:　Warren Mitchell Dandy Nichols Mike Angelis

1974　PERCY'S PROGRESS
Director:　Ralph Thomas
Co-stars:　Leigh Lawson Elke Sommer Denholm Elliott

1975　CARRY ON BEHIND
Director:　Gerald Thomas
Co-stars:　Elke Sommer Jack Douglas Kenneth Williams

1976　ADVENTURES OF A TAXI DRIVER
Director:　Stanley Long
Co-stars:　Barry Evans Judy Geeson Liz Fraser

1977　ADVENTURES OF A PRIVATE EYE
Director:　Stanley Long
Co-stars:　Christopher Neil Suzy Kendall Liz Fraser

BETTY POTTER

1946　A MATTER OF LIFE AND DEATH
Director:　Michael Powell
Co-stars:　David Niven Roger Livesey Kim Hunter

CAROL POTTER

**1992　BEVERLY HILLS 90210:
WALSH FAMILY CHRISTMAS**
Director:　Aaron Spelling
Co-stars:　Jason Priestly Luke Perry

MADELEINE POTTER

1984　THE BOSTONIANS
Director:　James Ivory
Co-stars:　Christopher Reeve Vanessa Redgrave Jessica Tandy

1989　BLOODHOUNDS OF BROADWAY
Director:　Howard Brookner
Co-stars:　Madonna Jennifer Grey Rutger Hauer

1989　SLAVES OF NEW YORK
Director:　James Ivory
Co-stars:　Bernadette Peters Nick Corri Chris Sarandon

1990　TWO EVIL EYES
Director:　Dario Argento
Co-stars:　Harvey Keitel Sally Kirkland John Amos

MAUREEN POTTER

1967　ULYSSES
Director:　Joseph Strick
Co-stars:　Maurise Roeves Milo O'Shea Barbara Jefford

MONICA POTTER

**1998　MARTHA-MEET FRANK,
DANIEL AND LAURENCE**
Director:　Nick Hamm
Co-stars:　Joseph Fiennes Ray Winstone Rufus Sewell

SALLY POTTER

1997　THE TANGO LESSON
Director:　Sally Potter
Co-star:　Pablo Veron

ANNIE POTTS

1979　CORVETTE SUMMER
Director:　Matthew Robbins
Co-stars:　Mark Hamill Eugene Roche Kim Milford

1981　HEARTACHES
Director:　Donald Shebib
Co-stars:　Margot Kidder Robert Carradine Winston Rekert

1983　COWBOY
Director:　Jerry Jameson
Co-stars:　James Brolin Randy Quaid Ted Danson

1984　CRIMES OF PASSION
Director:　Ken Russell
Co-stars:　Kathleen Turner Anthony Perkins Bruce Davison

1984　GHOSTBUSTERS
Director:　Ivan Reitman
Co-stars:　Bill Murray Dan Aykroyd Sigourney Weaver

1986　JUMPIN' JACK FLASH
Director:　Penny Marshall
Co-stars:　Whoopi Goldberg Stephen Collins Carol Kane

1986　PRETTY IN PINK
Director:　Howard Deutch
Co-stars:　Molly Ringwald Andrew McCarthy Jon Cryer

1989　WHO'S HARRY CRUMB?
Director:　Paul Flaherty
Co-stars:　John Candy Jeffrey Jones Barry Corbin

1989　GHOSTBUSTERS II
Director:　Ivan Reitman
Co-stars:　Bill Murray Harold Ramis Rick Moranis

1990　TEXASVILLE
Director:　Peter Bogdanovich
Co-stars:　Jeff Bridges Cybil Shepherd Timothy Bottoms

NELL POTTS
(Daughter Of Joanne Woodward And Paul Newman)

**1972　THE EFFECT OF GAMMA RAYS ON
MAN IN THE MOON MARIGOLDS**
Director:　Paul Newman
Co-stars:　Joanne Woodward Roberta Wallach

ELY POUGET

1989 L.A. TAKEDOWN
Director: Michael Mann
Co-stars: Scott Plank Laura Harrington

KAREN POULSEN

1946 DITTE, CHILD OF MAN
Director: Astrid Henning-Jensen
Co-stars: Tove Maes Rasmus Ottesen

MABEL POULTON

1928 THE CONSTANT NYMPH
Director: Adrian Brunel
Co-stars: Ivor Novello George Heinrich Dorothy Boyd

1930 ESCAPE
Director: Basil Dean
Co-stars: Gerald Du Maurier Edna Best Madeleine Carroll

C.C.H. POUNDER

1987 BAGDAD CAFÉ
Director: Percy Adlon
Co-stars: Marianne Sagebright Jack Palance Christine Kaufman

1990 POSTCARDS FROM THE EDGE
Director: Mike Nichols
Co-stars: Meryl Streep Shirley MacLaine Gene Hackman

1993 LIFEPOD
Director: Ron Silver
Co-stars: Robert Loggia Stan Shaw Jessica Tuck

1993 SLITHER
Director: Phillip Noyce
Co-stars: Sharon Stone William Baldwin Tom Berenger

1993 BENNY AND JOON
Director: Jeremiah Chechik
Co-stars: Mary Stuart Masterson Johnny Depp Aidan Quinn

PHYLLIS POVAH

1939 THE WOMEN
Director: George Cukor
Co-stars: Norma Shearer Joan Crawford Rosalind Russell

1943 LET'S FACE IT
Director: Sidney Lanfield
Co-stars: Bob Hope Betty Hutton Eve Arden

1952 PAT AND MIKE
Director: George Cukor
Co-stars: Spencer Tracy Kathleen Hepburn Aldo Ray

1959 HAPPY ANNIVERSARY
Director: David Miller
Co-stars: David Niven Mitzi Gaynor Patty Duke

ELEANOR POWELL (*Married Glenn Ford*)

1935 GEORGE WHITE'S 1935 SCANDALS
Director: George White
Co-stars: Alice Faye James Dunn Ned Sparks

1935 BROADWAY MELODY OF 1936
Director: Roy Del Ruth
Co-stars: Robert Taylor Jack Benny Buddy Ebsen

1936 BORN TO DANCE
Director: Roy Del Ruth
Co-stars: James Stewart Buddy Ebsen Frances Langford

1937 BROADWAY MELODY OF 1938
Director: Roy Del Ruth
Co-stars: Robert Taylor Judy Garland Sophie Tucker

1937 ROSALIE
Director: W.S. Van Dyke
Co-stars: Nelson Eddy Ray Bolger Ilona Massey

1938 HONOLULU
Director: Edward Buzzell
Co-stars: Robert Young George Burns Gracie Allen

1939 BROADWAY MELODY OF 1940
Director: Norman Taurog
Co-stars: Fred Astaire George Murphy Frank Morgan

1941 LADY BE GOOD
Director: Norman Z. McLeod
Co-stars: Robert Young Red Skelton Dan Dailey

1942 SHIP AHOY
Director: Edward Buzzell
Co-stars: Red Skelton Bert Lahr Virginia O'Brien

1943 THOUSANDS CHEER
Director: George Sidney
Co-stars: Kathryn Grayson Gene Kelly John Boles

1943 I DOOD IT
Director: Vincente Minnelli
Co-stars: Red Skelton John Hodiak Lena Horne

1944 SENSATIONS OF 1945
Director: Andrew Stone
Co-stars: W.C. Fields Dennis O'Keefe Sophie Tucker

1950 DUCHESS OF IDAHO
Director: Robert Z. Leonard
Co-stars: Esther Williams Van Johnson Mel Torme

JANE POWELL

1944 SONG OF THE OPEN ROAD
Director: S. Sylvan Simon
Co-stars: Bonita Granville W.C. Fields Edgar Bergen

1945 DELIGHTFULLY DANGEROUS
Director: Arthur Lubin
Co-stars: Constance Moore Ralph Bellamy

1946 HOLIDAY IN MEXICO
Director: George Sidney
Co-stars: Walter Pidgeon Ilona Massey Jose Iturbi

1948 LUXURY LINER
Director: Richard Whorf
Co-stars: George Brent Lauritz Melchior

1948 THREE DARING DAUGHTERS
Director: Fred Wilcox
Co-stars: Jeanette MacDonald Jose Iturbi Ann Todd

1949 A DATE WITH JUDY
Director: Richard Thorpe
Co-stars: Elizabeth Taylor Robert Stack Leon Ames

1950 NANCY GOES TO RIO
Director: Robert Z. Leonard
Co-stars: Ann Sothern Carmen Miranda

1950 TWO WEEKS WITH LOVE
Director: Roy Rowland
Co-stars: Ricardo Montalban Louis Calhern

1950 ROYAL WEDDING
Director: Stanley Donen
Co-stars: Fred Astaire Peter Lawford Keenan Wynn

1951 RICH, YOUNG AND PRETTY
Director: Norman Taurog
Co-stars: Danielle Darrieux Vic Damone

1953 SMALL TOWN GIRL
Director: Leslie Kardos
Co-stars: Farley Granger Ann Miller Bobby Van

1953 THREE SAILORS AND A GIRL
Director: Roy Del Ruth
Co-stars: Gordon MacRae Gene Nelson Sam Levene

1954 ATHENA
Director: Richard Thorpe
Co-stars: Edmund Purdom Debbie Reynolds

1954 DEEP IN MY HEART
Director: Stanley Donen
Co-stars: Jose Ferrer Merle Oberon Paul Henreid

1954 SEVEN BRIDES FOR SEVEN BROTHERS
Director: Stanley Donen
Co-stars: Howard Keel Russ Tamblyn

1955 HIT THE DECK
Director: Roy Rowland
Co-stars: Ann Miller Debbie Reynolds Tony Martin

1958 THE GIRL MOST LIKELY
Director: Mitchell Leisen
Co-stars: Cliff Robertson Keith Andes Una Merkel

1958 ENCHANTED ISLAND
Director: Allan Dwan
Co-stars: Dana Andrews Arthur Shields

1976 MAYDAY AT 40,000 FEET
Director: Robert Butler
Co-stars: David Janssen Ray Milland Don Meredith

1977 TUBBY THE TUBA (VOICE)
Director: Alexander Schure
Co-stars: Dick Van Dyke Pearl Bailey

LOVELADY POWELL

1975 THE HAPPY HOOKER
Director: Nicholas Sgarro
Co-stars: Lynn Redgrave Jean-Pierre Aumont Tom Poston

CAMILLA POWER

1990 THE CHRONICLES OF NARNIA:
THE SILVER CHAIR
Director: Alex Kirby
Co-stars: David Thwaites Tom Baker

SHARON POWER

1991 BLONDE FIST
Director: Frank Clarke
Co-stars: Margi Clarke Carroll Baker Ken Hutchison

TARYN POWER *(Daughter Of Tyrone Power)*

1975 THE COUNT OF MONTE CRISTO
Director: David Greene
Co-stars: Richard Chamberlain Tony Curtis Trevor Howard

1977 TRACKS
Director: Henry Jaglom
Co-stars: Dennis Hopper Dean Stockwell Michael Emil

1977 SINBAD AND THE EYE OF THE TIGER
Director: Sam Wanamaker
Co-stars: Patrick Wayne Jane Seymour

LUCILLE POWERS

1931 MAN TO MAN
Co-star: Phillips Holmes

1932 THE TEXAS BAD MAN
Co-star: Tom Mix

MALA POWERS

1950 EDGE OF DOOM
Director: Mark Robson
Co-stars: Dana Andrews Farley Granger Joan Evans

1950 OUTRAGE
Director: Ida Lupino
Co-stars: Tod Andrews Robert Clarke Lilian Hamilton

1950 CYRANO DE BERGERAC
Director: Michael Gordon
Co-stars: Jose Ferrer William Prince Morris Carnowsky

1952 ROSE OF CIMARRON
Director: Harry Keller
Co-stars: Jack Buetel Bill Williams Jim Davis

1953 THE CITY THAT NEVER SLEEPS
Director: John Auer
Co-stars: Gig Young Edward Arnold William Talman

1953 CITY BENEATH THE SEA
Director: Budd Boetticher
Co-stars: Robert Ryan Anthony Quinn Suzan Ball

1954 THE YELLOW MOUNTAIN
Director: Jesse Hibbs
Co-stars: Lex Barker Howard Duff William Demarest

1955 RAGE AT DAWN
Director: Tim Whelan
Co-stars: Randolph Scott Forrest Tucker Edgar Buchanan

1955 BENGAZI
Director: John Brahm
Co-stars: Victor McLaglen Richard Conte Richard Carlson

1957 DEATH IN SMALL DOSES
Director: Joseph Newman
Co-stars: Peter Graves Chuck Connors Merry Anders

1957 TAMMY AND THE BACHELOR
Director: Joseph Pevney
Co-stars: Debbie Reynolds Walter Brennan Leslie Nielsen

1958 THE COLOSSUS OF NEW YORK
Director: Eugene Lourie
Co-stars: Otto Kruger Ross Martin Robert Hutton

1969 DADDY'S GONE A-HUNTING
Director: Mark Robson
Co-stars: Carol White Paul Burke Scott Hylands

MARIE POWERS

1951 THE MEDIUM
Director: Gian-Carlo Manotti
Co-stars: Anna Maria Alberghetti Leo Coleman

STEPHANIE POWERS MARRIED WILLIAM HOLDEN

1962 IF A MAN ANSWERS
Director: Henry Levin
Co-stars: Sandra Dee Bobby Darin Cesar Romero

1962 EXPERIMENT IN TERROR
Director: Blake Edwards
Co-stars: Glenn Ford Lee Remick Ross Martin

1962 THE INTERNS
Director: David Swift
Co-stars: Cliff Robertson James MacArthur Suzy Parker

1963 McLINTOCK !
Director: Andrew McLaglen
Co-stars: John Wayne Maureen O'Hara Yvonne De Carlo

1963 PALM SPRINGS WEEKEND
Director: Norman Taurog
Co-stars: Troy Donahue Ty Hardin Connie Stevens

1964 THE NEW INTERNS
Director: John Rich
Co-stars: George Segal Telly Savalas Dean Jones

1964 LOVE HAS MANY FACES
Director: Alexander Singer
Co-stars: Cliff Robertson Hugh O'Brian

1964 FANATIC
Director: Silvio Narizzano
Co-stars: Tallulah Bankhead Peter Vaughan Yootha Joyce

1966 STAGECOACH
Director: Gordon Douglas
Co-stars: Alex Cord Ann-Margret Bing Crosby

1967 WARNING SHOT
Director: Buzz Kulik
Co-stars: David Janssen Lillian Gish Sam Wanamaker

1969 CRESCENDO
Director: Alan Gibson
Co-stars: James Olson Margaretta Scott Jane Laportaire

1970 THE BOATNIKS
Director: Norman Tokar
Co-stars: Phil Silvers Norman Fell Robert Morse

1971 ELLERY QUEEN:DON'T LOOK BEHIND YOU
Director: Barry Shear
Co-stars: Peter Lawford Harry Morgan

1972 THE MAGNIFICENT SEVEN RIDE !
Director: George McCowan
Co-stars: Lee Van Cleef Pedro Armendariz Jnr.

1974 HERBIE RIDES AGAIN
Director: Robert Stevenson
Co-stars: Helen Hayes Ken Berry Keenan Wynn

1974 NIGHT GAMES
Director: Don Taylor
Co-stars: Barry Newman Susan Howard Albert Salmi

1974 SKYWAY TO DEATH
Director: Gordon Hessler
Co-stars: Ross Martin Bobby Sherman Tige Andrews

1975 SKY HEIST
Director: Lee Katzin
Co-stars: Frank Gorshin Don Meredith Joseph Campanella

1978 A DEATH IN CANAAN
Director: Tony Richardson
Co-stars: Paul Clemens Tom Atkins Brian Dennehy

1979 ESCAPE TO ATHENA
Director: George Pan Cosmatos
Co-stars: Roger Moore David Niven Sonny Bono

1979 HART TO HART
Director: Tom Mankiewicz
Co-stars: Robert Wagner Lionel Stander Roddy McDowall

1984 FAMILY SECRETS
Director: Jack Hoffsiss
Co-stars: Maureen Stapleton Melissa Gilbert James Spader

1985 DECEPTIONS
Director: Melville Shavelson
Co-stars: Barry Bostwick Sam Wanamaker Gina Lollobrigida

1987 AT MOTHER'S REQUEST
Director: Michael Tuchner
Co-stars: E.G. Marshall Frances Sternhagen Penny Fuller

1990 THROW-AWAY WIVES
Director: Richard Michaels
Co-star: David Birney

1992 NIGHT HUNT
Director: Bill Corcoran
Co-stars: Helen Shaver Kathleen Robertson

JANNINA POYNTER

1988 ANGEL OF VENGEANCE
Director: Ted Mikels
Co-stars: David O'Hara Macka Foley Carl Irwin

MARISA PRADO

1953 THE BANDIT
Director: Lima Berreto
Co-stars: Milton Ribeiro Alberto Ruschel Vanjo Orico

EDITH PRAGER

1955 HERR PUNTILA AND HIS SERVANT MATTI
Director: Alberto Cavalcanti
Co-stars: Curt Bois Maria Emo

SALLY PRAGER (Child)

1973 THE HIDEAWAYS
Director: Fielder Cook
Co-stars: Ingrid Bergman Johnny Duran Madeline Kahn

JOAN PRATHER

**1976 DAWN: PORTRAIT OF A
RUNAWAY TEENAGER**
Director: Randall Kleiser
Co-stars: Eve Plumb Bo Hopkins Lynn Carlin

TERRY SUE PRATT

1986 BRICK IS BEAUTIFUL
Director: David Wheatley
Co-stars: Christopher Wild Caroline Milmoe Ian Mercer

HANNA-MARIA PRAVDA

1970 AND SOON THE DARKNESS
Director: Robert Fuest
Co-stars: Pamela Franklin Michele Dotrice Sandor Eles

JUNE PREISSER

1939 BABES IN ARMS
Director: Busby Berkeley
Co-stars: Judy Garland Mickey Rooney Charles Winninger

1939 DANCING CO-ED
Director: S. Sylvan Simon
Co-stars: Lana Turner Richard Carlson Artie Shaw

1939 JUDGE HARDY AND SON
Director: George Seitz
Co-stars: Mickey Rooney Lewis Stone Fay Holden

1940 STRIKE UP THE BAND
Director: Busby Berkeley
Co-stars: Judy Garland Mickey Rooney Paul Whiteman

1940 GALLANT SONS
Director: George Sietz
Co-stars: Jackie Cooper Bonita Granville Gene Reynolds

1942 SWEATER GIRL
Co-star: Eddie Bracken

1944 MURDER IN THE BLUE ROOM
Director: Leslie Goodwins
Co-stars: Anne Gwynne Donald Cook Grace McDonald

1945 I'LL TELL THE WORLD
Director: Leslie Goodwins
Co-stars: Lee Tracy Brenda Joyce Raymond Walburn

1945 LET'S GO STEADY
Co-stars: Mel Torme Jimmy Lloyd Pat Parrish

1946 FREDDIE STEPS OUT
Co-stars: Warren Mills Freddie Stewart

1946 JUNIOR PROM
Co-stars: Warren Mills Freddie Stewart

1948 CAMPUS SLEUTH
Co-stars: Warren Mills Freddie Stewart Noel Neill

TESSA PRENDERGAST

1954 HIS MAJESTY O'KEEFE
Director: Byron Haskin
Co-stars: Burt Lancaster Joan Rice Andre Morrell

ANN PRENTISS

1966 ANY WEDNESDAY
Director: Robert Ellis Miller
Co-stars: Jane Fonda Dean Jones Jason Robards

1970 THE OUT-OF-TOWNERS
Director: Arthur Hiller
Co-stars: Jack Lemmon Sandy Dennis Anne Meara

1974 CALIFORNIA SPLIT
Director: Robert Altman
Co-stars: Elliott Gould George Segal Gwen Welles

1988 MY STEPMOTHER IS AN ALIAN (VOICE)
Director: Richard Benjamin
Co-stars: Dan Aykroyd Kim Basinger

PAULA PRENTISS *(Married Richard Benjamin)*

1960 WHERE THE BOYS ARE
Director: Henry Levin
Co-stars: George Hamilton Jim Hutton Connie Francis

1961 BACHELOR IN PARADISE
Director: Jack Arnold
Co-stars: Bob Hope Lana Turner Janis Paige

1961 THE HONEYMOON MACHINE
Director: Richard Thorpe
Co-stars: Steve McQueen Jim Hutton Dean Jagger

1962 THE HORIZONTAL LIEUTENANT
Director: Richard Thorpe
Co-stars: Jim Hutton Jim Backus Jack Carter

1963 FOLLOW THE BOYS
Director: Richard Thorpe
Co-stars: Connie Francis Janis Paige Russ Tamblyn

1964 MAN'S FAVOURITE SPORT
Director: Howard Hawks
Co-stars: Rock Hudson Maria Perschy Charlene Holt

1964 THE WORLD OF HENRY ORIENT
Director: George Roy Hill
Co-stars: Peter Sellers Angela Lansbury

1965 WHAT'S NEW PUSSYCAT
Director: Clive Donner
Co-stars: Peter Sellers Peter O'Toole Woody Allen

1965 IN HARM'S WAY
Director: Arthur Hiller
Co-stars: John Wayne Kirk Douglas Tom Tyron

1970 MOVE
Director: Stuart Rosenberg
Co-stars: Elliott Gould John Larch Joe Silver

1970 CATCH 22
Director: Mike Nichols
Co-stars: Alan Arkin Jon Voight Martin Balsam

1971 BORN TO WIN
Director: Ivan Passer
Co-stars: George Segal Karen Black Robert De Niro

1972 LAST OF THE RED HOT LOVERS
Director: Gene Saks
Co-stars: Alan Arkin Sally Kellerman Renee Taylor

1973 CRAZY JOE
Director: Carlo Litzanni
Co-stars: Peter Boyle Eli Wallach Rip Torn

1974 THE STEPFORD WIVES
Director: Bryan Forbes
Co-stars: Katharine Ross Nanette Newman

1974 THE PARALLAX VIEW
Director: Alan J. Pakula
Co-stars: Warren Beatty Hume Cronyn

1978 NO ROOM TO RUN
Director: Robert Michael Lewis
Co-stars: Richard Benjamin Barry Sullivan

1980 THE BLACK MARBLE
Director: Robert Foxworth
Co-stars: Robert Foxworth James Woods

1981 BUDDY, BUDDY
Director: Billy Wilder
Co-stars: Walter Matthau Jack Lemon Klaus Kinski

1983 PACKIN' IT IN
Director: Jud Taylor
Co-stars: Richard Benjamin Molly Ringwald Mari Gorman

SHANNON PRESBY

1983 TRACKDOWN:
FINDING THE GOODBAR KILLER
Director: Bill Persky
Co-stars: George Segal Alan North

MICHELINE PRESLE

1947 LES JEUX SONT FAITS
Director: Jean Delannoy
Co-stars: Marcel Pagliero Margueritte Moreno

1947 LE DIABLE AU CORPS
Director: Claude Autant Lara
Co-stars: Gerard Philipe Jacques Tati Denise Grey

1948 FOOLISH HUSBAND
Director: Fernand Gravet

1950 I SHALL RETURN
Director: Fritz Lang
Co-stars: Tyrone Power Tom Ewell Robert Barrat

1950 UNDER MY SKIN
Director: Jean Negulesco
Co-stars: John Garfield Luther Adler Orley Lindgren

1951 THE ADVENTURES OF CAPTAIN FABIAN
Director: William Marshall
Co-stars: Errol Flynn Vincent Price

1958 THE BRIDE IS TOO BEAUTIFUL
Director: Fred Surin
Co-stars: Brigitte Bardot Louis Jourdan Marcel Amont

1959 BLIND DATE
Director: Joseph Losey
Co-stars: Hardy Kruger Stanley Baker Robert Flemying

1961 THE ASSASSIN
Director: Elio Petrie
Co-stars: Marcello Mastroianni Salvo Randone Andrea Checci

1962 IF A MAN ANSWERS
Director: Henry Levin
Co-stars: Sandra Dee Bobby Darin John Lund

1963 THE PRIZE
Director: Mark Robson
Co-stars: Paul Newman Elke Sommer Edward G. Robinson

1965 LA RELIGIEUSE
Director: Jacques Rivette
Co-stars: Anna Karina Liselotte Pulver

1966 KING OF HEARTS
Director: Phillippe De Broca
Co-stars: Alan Bates Pierre Brasseur Genevieve Bujold

1989 I WANT TO GO HOME
Director: Alain Renais
Co-stars: Gerard Depardieu Adolph Green Linda Lavin

PRISCILLA PRESLEY *(Married Elvis Presley)*

1988 **THE NAKED GUN:**
        FROM THE FILES OF POLICE SQUAD
Director: David Zucker
Co-stars: Leslie Nielsen O.J. Simpson

1990 **THE ADVENTURES OF FORD FAIRLANE**
Director: Renny Harlin
Co-stars: Andrew Dice Clay Wayne Newton

1991 **THE NAKED GUN 2: THE SMELL OF FEAR**
Director: David Zucker
Co-stars: Leslie Nielsen George Kennedy

1993 **NAKED GUN 33^1/$_3$: THE FINAL INSULT**
Director: Peter Segal
Co-stars: Leslie Nielsen O.J. Simpson Fred Ward

FIONA PRESS

1990 **WAITING**
Director: Jackie McKimmie
Co-stars: Noni Hazlehurst Deborra-Lee Furness Helen Jones

SANTHA PRESS

1990 **IN TOO DEEP**
Director: Colin South
Co-stars: Hugo Race Rebekah Elmaloglou John Flaus

CYNDY PRESTON

1986 **MILES TO GO**
Director: David Greene
Co-stars: Jill Clayburgh Tom Skerritt Mimi Kuzyk

1991 **TEEN AGENT**
Director: William Dear
Co-stars: Richard Griego Linda Hunt Roger Rees

KELLY PRESTON *(Married John Travolta)*

1985 **MISCHIEF**
Director: Mel Damski
Co-stars: Doug McKeon Chris Nash Catherine Mary Stewart

1986 **SPACECAMP**
Director: Harry Winer
Co-stars: Kate Capshaw Lea Thompson Leaf Phoenix

1986 **52 PICK-UP**
Director: John Frankenheimer
Co-stars: Roy Scheider Ann-Margret John Glover

1987 **THE EXPERTS**
Director: Dave Thomas
Co-stars: John Travolta Ayre Gross Deborah Foreman

1987 **A TIGER'S TALE**
Director: Peter Douglas
Co-stars: Ann-Margret C. Thomas Howell Charles Durning

1988 **TWINS**
Director: Ivan Reitman
Co-stars: Arnold Schwarzenegger Danny DeVito Chloe Webb

1992 **ONLY YOU**
Director: Betty Thomas
Co-stars: Andrew McCarthy Helen Hunt Daniel Roebuck

1993 **ARTHUR MILLER'S AMERICAN CLOCK**
Director: Bob Clark
Co-stars: Mary McDonnell David Strathairn Tony Roberts

1994 **DOUBLE CROSS**
Director: Michael Keusch
Co-stars: Patrick Bergin Jennifer Tilly

1994 **CHEYENNE WARRIOR**
Director: Mark Griffith
Co-star: Pato Hoffman

1997 **ADDICTED TO LOVE**
Director: Griffin Dunne
Co-stars: Matthew Broderick Meg Ryan Tcheky Karyo

1997 **JERRY MAGUIRE**
Co-stars: Tom Cruise Cuba Golding Jnr. Renee Zellweger

GISELE PREVILLE

1950 **THE DANCING YEARS**
Director: Harold French
Co-stars: Dennis Price Patricia Dainton

FRANCOISE PREVOST

1960 **PARIS NOUS APPARTIENT**
Director: Jacques Rivette
Co-stars: Betty Schneider Gianni Esposito

1960 **THE ENEMY GENERAL**
Director: George Sherman
Co-stars: Van Johnson Jean-Pierre Aumont Dany Carrel

1961 **PAYROLL**
Director: Sidney Hayers
Co-stars: Billie Whitelaw Michael Craig Tom Bell

1962 **THE CONDEMNED OF ALTONA**
Director: Vittorio De Sica
Co-stars: Sophia Loren Fredric March Maximillian Schell

MARIE PREVOST *(Mary Bickford Dunn)*

1924 **THREE WOMEN**
Director: Ernst Lubitsch
Co-stars: Pauline Frederick May McAvoy Lew Cody

1924 **THE MARRIAGE CIRCLE**
Director: Ernst Lubitsch
Co-stars: Monte Blue Florence Vidor Adolphe Menjou

1925 **KISS ME AGAIN**
Director: Ernst Lubitsch
Co-stars: Monte Blue John Roche Clara Bow

1926 **THE CAVE MAN**
Director: Lewis Milestone
Co-stars: Matt Moore Myrna Loy Hedda Hopper

1928 **THE RACKET**
Director: Lewis Milestone
Co-stars: Thomas Meighan Louis Wolheim George Stone

1930 **LADIES OF LEISURE**
Director: Frank Capra
Co-stars: Barbara Stanwyck Lowell Sherman Ralph Graves

1930 **PARTY GIRL**
Co-star: Jeanette Loff

1931 **IT'S A WISE CHILD**
Director: Robert Z. Leonard
Co-stars: Marion Davies Sidney Blackmer James Gleason

1931 **HELL DIVERS**
Director: George Hill
Co-stars: Wallace Beery Clark Gable Dorothy Jordon

1931 **GENTLEMAN'S FATE**
Director: Mervyn LeRoy
Co-stars: John Gilbert Louis Wolheim Leila Hyams

1931 **PAID**
Director: Sam Wood
Co-stars: Joan Crawford Kent Douglass Robert Armstrong

1931 **THE SIN OF MADELON CLAUDET**
Director: Edgar Selwyn
Co-stars: Helen Hayes Robert Young Lewis Stone

1932 **THREE WISE GIRLS**
Director: William Beaudine
Co-stars: Jean Harlow Mae Clarke Walter Byron

1935 HANDS ACROSS THE TABLE
Director: Mitchell Leisen
Co-stars: Carole Lombard Fred MacMurray Ralph Bellamy

ANNABELLA PRICE

1990 GOOD NIGHT SWEET WIFE
Director: Jerrold Freedman
Co-stars: Ken Olin Margaret Colin B.D. Wong

KATE PRICE

1921 LITTLE LORD FAUNTLEROY
Director: Alfred Green
Co-stars: Mary Pickford Claude Gillingwater Rose Dione

1926 THE COHENS AND THE KELLYS
Director: Harry Pollard
Co-stars: George Sidney Charles Murray Vera Gordon

1927 THE COHENS AND THE KELLYS IN NEW YORK
Co-stars: George Sidney Charles Murray Vera Gordon

1928 THE COHENS AND THE KELLYS IN PARIS
Director: William Beaudine
Co-stars: George Sidney Charles Murray

1929 THE COHENS AND THE KELLYS IN ATLANTIC CITY
Co-stars: George Sidney Charles Murray

1930 THE COHENS AND THE KELLYS IN AFRICA
Co-stars: George Sidney Charles Murray Vera Gordon

1930 THE COHENS AND THE KELLYS IN SCOTLAND
Director: William James Craft
Co-stars: George Sidney Vera Gordon

1930 DANCING SWEETIES
Co-stars: Grant Withers Sue Carol

1932 THE COHENS AND THE KELLYS IN HOLLYWOOD
Co-stars: George Sidney Lew Ayres Sidney Fox

1933 THE COHENS AND THE KELLYS IN TROUBLE
Co-stars: George Sidney Maureen O'Sullivan

MOLLY PRICE

1992 JERSEY GIRL
Director: David Burton Morris
Co-stars: Jami Gertz Dylan McDermot Joseph Bologna

NANCY PRICE

1930 GIRL IN THE SNOW
Co-stars: Jed Prouty Bessie Love Raymond Hackett

1931 THE SPECKLED BAND
Director: Jack Raymond
Co-stars: Raymond Massey Athole Stewart Angela Baddeley

1939 THE STARS LOOK DOWN
Director: Carol Reed
Co-stars: Michael Redgrave Margaret Lockwood Emlyn Williams

1939 DEAD MAN'S SHOES
Director: Thomas Bentley
Co-stars: Leslie Banks Joan Marion Wilfrid Lawson

1942 SECRET MISSION
Director: Harold French
Co-stars: Hugh Williams Carla Lehman James Mason

1944 MADONNA OF THE SEVEN MOONS
Director: Arthur Crabtree
Co-stars: Phyllis Calvert Stewart Granger Jean Kent

1945 I KNOW WHERE I'M GOING
Director: Michael Powell
Co-stars: Wendy Hiller Roger Livesey

1945 I LIVE IN GROSVENOR SQUARE
Director: Herbert Wilcox
Co-stars: Anna Neagle Rex Harrison Dean Jagger

1946 CARNIVAL
Director: Stanley Haynes
Co-stars: Sally Gray Michael Wilding Bernard Miles

1947 MASTER OF BANKDAM
Director: Walter Forde
Co-stars: Tom Walls Anne Crawford Dennis Price

1948 THE THREE WEIRD SISTERS
Director: Dan Birt
Co-stars: Mary Clare Mary Merrall Nova Pilbeam

1952 MANDY
Director: Alexander MacKendrick
Co-stars: Terence Morgan Phyllis Calvert Mandy Miller

AURORE PRIETO

1990 DR PETIOT
Director: Christian De Chalonge
Co-stars: Michel Serrault Pierre Romans Andre Chaumeau

SUZY PRIM *(Suzanne Arduini)*

1935 MAYERLING
Director: Anatole Litvak
Co-stars: Charles Boyer Danielle Darrieux Marthe Regnier

1936 TARAKANOVA

1940 HEART OF A NATION
Director: Julien Duvivier
Co-stars: Louis Jouvet Michele Morgan Raimu

1947 AU BONHEUR DES DAMES
Director: Andre Cayatte

1949 AU ROYAUME DES CIEUX
Director: Julien Duvivier

1955 CAN-CAN
Director: Jean Renoir

FAITH PRINCE

1985 THE LAST DRAGON
Director: Michael Schulz
Co-stars: Vanity Chris Murney Keshia Knight

1993 DAVE
Director: Ivan Britman
Co-stars: Kevin Kline Sigourney Weaver Frank Langella

1994 MY FATHER, THE HERO
Director: Steve Miner
Co-stars: Gerard Depardieu Lauren Hutton Emma Thompson

VICTORIA PRINCIPAL

1972 THE LIFE AND TIMES OF JUDGE ROY BEAN
Director: John Huston
Co-stars: Paul Newman Anthony Perkins

1974 EARTHQUAKE
Director: Mark Robson
Co-stars: Charlton Heston Ava Gardner George Kennedy

1975 I WILL...I WILL...FOR NOW
Director: Norman Panama
Co-stars: Elliott Gould Diane Keaton Paul Sorvino

1982 NOT JUST ANOTHER AFFAIR
Director: Steven Hilliard Stern
Co-stars: Gil Gerard Robert Webber Ed Begley Jnr.

1987 MISTRESS
Director: Michael Tuchner

1989 NAKED LIE
Director: Richard Colla
Co-stars: James Farentino Glenn Withrow William Lucking

1989 BLIND WITNESS
Director: Richard Colla
Co-stars: Paul Le Mat Stephen Macht Matt Clark

1990 THE PRICE OF PASSION
Director: Richard Colla
Co-stars: Ted Wass Hector Elizondo Elaine Stritch

1991 NIGHTMARE
Director: John Pasquin
Co-star: Paul Sorvino

1993 BEYOND OBSESSION
Director: David Greene
Co-stars: Donelly Rhodes Emily Warfield

1995 DANCING IN THE DARK
Director: Bill Corcoran
Co-stars: Robert Vaughn Nicholas Campbell

AILEEN PRINGLE

1930 PRINCE OF DIAMONDS
Co-stars: Ian Keith Claude King

1934 JANE EYRE
Director: Christy Cabanne
Co-stars: Virginia Bruce Colin Clive Beryl Mercer

ANNA PROCLEMER

1953 VOYAGE TO ITALY
Director: Roberto Rossellini
Co-stars: Ingrid Bergman George Sanders Paul Muller

MELISSA PROPHET

1979 VAN NUYS BOULEVARD
Director: William Sachs
Co-stars: Bill Adler Cynthia Wood Dennis Bowen

1985 INVASION, U.S.A.
Director: Joseph Zito
Co-stars: Chuck Norris Richard Lynch Alexander Zale

DOROTHY PROVINE

1958 THE BONNIE PARKER STORY
Director: William Witney
Co-stars: Jack Hogan Richard Bakalyan

1963 WALL OF NOISE
Director: Richard Wilson
Co-stars: Suzanne Pleshette Ty Hardin Ralph Meeker

1963 IT'S A MAD, MAD, MAD, MAD WORLD
Director: Stanley Kramer
Co-stars: Spencer Tracy Terry-Thomas Ben Blue

1964 GOOD NEIGHBOUR SAM
Director: David Swift
Co-stars: Jack Lemmon Romy Schneider Edward G. Robinson

1965 THAT DARN CAT !
Director: Robert Stevenson
Co-stars: Hayley Mills Dean Jones Roddy McDowall

1965 THE GREAT RACE
Director: Blake Edwards
Co-stars: Jack Lemmon Tony Curtis Natalie Wood

1966 ONE SPY TOO MANY
Director: Joseph Sargent
Co-stars: Robert Vaughn David McCallum Rip Torn

1966 KISS THE GIRLS AND MAKE THEM DIE
Director: Henry Levin
Co-stars: Michael Connors Raf Vallone Terry-Thomas

1967 WHO'S MINDING THE MINT ?
Director: Howard Morris
Co-stars: Jim Hutton Milton Berle Walter Brennan

1968 NEVER A DULL MOMENT
Director: Jerry Paris
Co-stars: Dick Van Dyke Edward G. Robinson Tony Bill

JEANNE PROVOST

1937 GRIBOUILLE
Director: Marc Allegret
Co-stars: Raimu Michele Morgan Gilbert Gilles

JULIET PROWSE

1960 G.I. BLUES
Director: Norman Taurog
Co-stars: Elvis Presley Robert Ivers Leticia Roman

1960 CAN CAN
Director: Walter Lang
Co-stars: Frank Sinatra Shirley MacLaine Maurice Chevalier

1961 THE FIERCEST HEART
Director: George Sherman
Co-stars: Stuart Whitman Raymond Massey Ken Scott

1961 THE RIGHT APPROACH
Director: David Butler
Co-stars: Frankie Vaughan Martha Hyer Gary Crosby

1961 SECOND TIME AROUND
Director: Vincent Sherman
Co-stars: Debbie Reynolds Andy Griffith Thelma Ritter

1965 DINGAKA
Director: Jaimie Uys
Co-stars: Stanley Baker Ken Gampu Paul Makgoba

ANNA PRUCHNAL

1974 SWEET MOVIE
Director: Dusan Makevejev
Co-stars: Carole Laure Pierre Clementi Sami Frey

1980 CITY OF WOMEN
Director: Federico Fellini
Co-stars: Marcello Mastroianni Bernice Stegers Ettore Manni

MAUREEN PRYOR

1962 LIFE FOR RUTH
Director: Basil Dearden
Co-stars: Michael Craig Patrick McGoohan Janet Munro

1970 THE MUSIC LOVERS
Director: Ken Russell
Co-stars: Richard Chamberlain Christopher Gable Glenda Jackson

KESHIA KNIGHT PULLIAM *(Child)*

1989 POLLY
Director: Debbie Allen
Co-stars: Phylicia Rashad Celeste Holm Butterfly McQueen

1990 POLLY, COMIN' HOME
Director: Debbie Allen
Co-stars: Phylicia Rashad Celeste Holm Brock Peters

LILO PULVER

1958 A TIME TO LOVE AND A TIME TO DIE
Director: Douglas Sirk
Co-stars: John Gabin Kennan Wynn Jock Mahoney

1963 A GLOBAL AFFAIR
Director: Jack Arnold
Co-stars: Bob Hope Michele Mercier Yvonne De Carlo

LISELOTTE PULVER

1956 THE ADVENTURES OF ARSENE LUPIN
Director: Jacques Becker
Co-stars: Robert Lamoureux Otto Hasse

1965 LA RELIGIEUSE
Director: Jacques Rivette
Co-stars: Anna Karina Micheline Presle Christine Lenier

ANGELA PUNCH-MCGREGOR

1978 THE CHANT OF JIMMIE BLACKSMITH
Director: Fred Schepisi
Co-stars: Tommy Lewis Jack Thompson Ray Barrett

1979 NEWSFRONT
Director: Phillip Noyce
Co-stars: Bill Hunter Wendy Hughes Chris Hayward

1980 THE SURVIVOR
Director: David Hemmings
Co-stars: Robert Powell Jenny Agutter Joseph Cotten

1980 THE ISLAND
Director: Michael Ritchie
Co-stars: Michael Caine David Warner Frank Middlemass

1981 DOUBLE DEAL
Director: Brian Kavanagh
Co-stars: Louis Jourdan Diane Craig Warwick Comber

1981 THE BEST OF FRIENDS
Director: Michael Robertson
Co-star: Graeme Blundell

1982 WE OF THE NEVER NEVER
Director: Igor Auzins
Co-stars: Arthur Dignam Tony Barry Martin Vaughan

1989 THE DELINQUENTS
Director: Chris Thomson
Co-stars: Kylie Minogue Charlie Schlatter Bruno Lawrence

IRENE PURCELL

1931 JUST A GIGOLO
Director: William Haines
Co-stars: Lillian Bond C. Aubrey Smith

1931 THE MAN IN POSSESSION
Director: Sam Wood
Co-stars: Robert Montgomery Charlotte Greenwood Beryl Mercer

1932 THE CROOKED CIRCLE
Co-stars: Ben Lyon C. Henry Gordon

1932 THE PASSIONATE PLUMBER
Director: Edward Sedgwick
Co-stars: Buster Keaton Jimmy Durante Polly Moran

LEE PURCELL

1970 ADAM AT 6 A.M.
Director: Robert Scheerer
Co-stars: Michael Douglas Joe Don Baker Meg Foster

1972 DIRTY LITTLE BILLY
Director: Stan Dragoti
Co-stars: Michael J. Pollard Richard Evans Charles Aidman

1973 KID BLUE
Director: James Frawley
Co-stars: Dennis Hopper Warren Oates Ben Johnson

1973 NECROMANCY
Director: Bert Gordon
Co-stars: Orson Welles Pamela Franklin Michael Ontkean

1974 MR MAJESTYK
Director: Richard Fleischer
Co-stars: Charles Bronson Al Lettieri Linda Cristal

1977 THE AMAZING HOWARD HUGHES
Director: William Graham
Co-stars: Tommy Lee Jones Ed Flanders Ed Harris

1978 BIG WEDNESDAY
Director: John Milius
Co-stars: Jan-Michael Vincent William Katt Gary Busey

1981 KILLER AT HELL'S GATE
Director: Jerry Jameson
Co-stars: Robert Urich Deborah Raffin

1983 EDDIE MACON'S RUN
Director: Jeff Kanen
Co-stars: Kirk Douglas John Schneider Leah Ayres

**1985 MY WICKED WICKED WAYS:
THE LEGEND OF ERROL FLYNN**
Director: Don Taylor
Co-stars: Duncan Regehr Barbara Hershey

1988 THE HEAL A NATION
Director: Michael Pressman
Co-stars: Eric Roberts Glynnis O'Connor

1991 THE LONG ROAD HOME
Director: John Korty
Co-stars: Mark Harmon Morgan Weisser Leon Russon

1993 SECRET SINS OF THE FATHER
Director: Beau Bridges
Co-star: Lloyd Bridges

LINDA PURL

1975 CRAZY MAMA
Director: Jonatham Demme
Co-stars: Cloris Leachman Ann Sothern Stuart Whitman

1979 THE FLAME IS LOVE
Director: Michael O'Herlihy
Co-stars: Shane Briant Timothy Dalton Richard Johnson

1981 THE ADVENTURES OF NELLIE BLY
Director: Henning Schellerup
Co-stars: Gene Barry John Randolph

1981 THE HIGH COUNTRY
Director: Harvey Hart
Co-stars: Timothy Bottoms George Sims Jim Lawrence

1981 VISITING HOURS
Director: Jean Claude Lord
Co-stars: Lee Remick Michael Ironside William Shatner

1986 OUTRAGE
Director: Walter Grauman
Co-stars: Robert Preston Burgess Meredith Beau Bridges

1987 HOLLOW POINT
Director: Bruce Seth Green
Co-star: Yaphet Kotto

1988 ADDICTED TO HIS LOVE
Director: Arthur Allan Seidelman
Co-stars: Barry Bostwick Polly Bergen Erin Gray

1988 SPIES, LIES AND NAKED THIGHS
Director: James Frawley
Co-stars: Harry Anderson Ed Begley Jnr. Wendy Crewson

1988 VIPER
Director: Peter Maris
Co-stars: James Tolkan Chris Robinson Jeff Kober

1992 DANIELLE STEEL'S SECRETS
Director: Peter Hunt
Co-stars: Stephanie Beacham Christopher Plummer

1992 BODY LANGUAGE
Director: Arthur Allan Seidelman
Co-stars: Heather Locklear Edward Albert Gary Bisig

1993 ACCIDENTAL MEETING
Director: Michael Zinberg
Co-stars: Linda Gray Leigh J. McCloskey

1994 NATURAL CAUSES
Director: James Becket
Co-star: Cary Tagawa

LOUISE PURNELL

1970 THE THREE SISTERS
Director: Laurence Olivier
Co-stars: Joan Plowright Alan Bates Laurence Olivier

EDNA PURVIANCE

1915 THE TRAMP
Director: Charles Chaplin
Co-stars: Charles Chaplin Bud Jamison Leo White

1917 EASY STREET
Director: Charles Chaplin
Co-stars: Charles Chaplin Albert Austin Eric Campbell

1917 THE ADVENTURER
Director: Charles Chaplin
Co-stars: Charles Chaplin Eric Campbell Henry Bergman

1917 THE CURE
Director: Charles Chaplin
Co-stars: Charles Chaplin Eric Campbell Henry Bergman

1917 THE IMMIGRANT
Director: Charles Chaplin
Co-stars: Charles Chaplin Albert Austin Henry Bergman

1918 SHOULDER ARMS
Director: Charles Chaplin
Co-stars: Charles Chaplin Sydney Chaplin Henry Bergman

1919 A DAY'S PLEASURE
Director: Charles Chaplin
Co-stars: Charles Chaplin Jackie Coogan Henry Bergman

1919 SUNNYSIDE
Director: Charles Chaplin
Co-stars: Charles Chaplin Tom Wilson Albert Austin

1921 THE KID
Director: Charles Chaplin
Co-star: Charles Chaplin Jackie Coogan

1922 THE IDLE CLASS
Director: Charles Chaplin
Co-star: Charles Chaplin Mack Swain

1923 THE PILGRIM
Director: Charles Chaplin
Co-stars: Charles Chaplin Mack Swain Kitty Bradbury

1923 A WOMAN OF PARIS
Director: Charles Chaplin
Co-stars: Adolphe Menjou Carl Miller Lydia Knott

1925 A DOG'S LIFE
Director: Charles Chaplin
Co-stars: Charles Chaplin Chuck Riesner Henry Bergman

JESSICA PUSCAS

1988 ANDY COLBY'S INCREDIBLE ADVENTURE
Director: Deborah Brock
Co-stars: Randy Josselyn Vince Edwards

CINDY PUTNAM *(Child)*

**1966 THE RUSSIANS ARE COMING !
THE RUSSIANS ARE COMING !**
Director: Norman Jewison
Co-stars: Eva Marie Saint Carl Reiner Alan Arkin

NATASHA PYNE

1964 THE DEVIL-SHIP PIRATES
Director: Don Sharp
Co-stars: Christopher Lee Andrew Keir John Cairney

1966 THE IDOL
Director: Daniel Petrie
Co-stars: Jennifer Jones Michael Parks John Leyton

1967 THE TAMING OF THE SHREW
Director: Franco Zeffirelli
Co-stars: Richard Burton Elizabeth Taylor Michael York

1973 MADHOUSE
Director: Jim Clark
Co-stars: Vincent Price Peter Cushing Adrienne Corri

KE HUY QUAN

**1984 INDIANA JONES AND
THE TEMPLE OF DOOM**
Director: Steven Spielberg
Co-stars: Harrison Ford Kate Capshaw Philip Stone

STELLA QUAN

1984 EL NORTE
Director: Gregory Nava
Co-stars: Zaide Silvia Gutierrez David Villapando Alicia Del Lago

NENA QUARTARO

1931 BACHELOR FATHER
Director: Robert Z. Leonard
Co-stars: Marion Davies C. Aubrey Smith Ray Milland

1937 LEFT-HANDED LAW
Co-stars: Buck Jones George Regas

ANNA QUAYLE

1966 DROP DEAD DARLING
Director: Ken Hughes
Co-stars: Tony Curtis Rosanna Schiaffino Zsa Zsa Gabor

1967 SMASHING TIME
Director: Desmond Davis
Co-stars: Rita Tushingham Lynn Redgrave Ian Carmichael

1968 CHITTY CHITTY BANG BANG
Director: Ken Hughes
Co-stars: Dick Van Dyke Sally Ann Howes Lionel Jeffries

1971 UP THE CHASTITY BELT
Director: Bob Kellett
Co-stars: Frankie Howerd Graham Crowden Roy Hudd

1977 ADVENTURES OF A PRIVATE EYE
Director: Stanley Long
Co-stars: Christopher Neil Suzy Kendall Liz Fraser

1978 ADVENTURES OF A PLUMBER'S MATE
Director: Stanley Long
Co-stars: Christopher Neil Arthur Mullard

VALERIE QUENNESSEN

1982 CONAN THE BARBARIAN
Director: John Milius
Co-stars: Arnold Schwarzenegger James Earl Jones Mako

1982 SUMMER LOVERS
Director: Randal Kleiser
Co-stars: Peter Gallacher Daryl Hannah

CAROLINE QUENTIN

1983 PARTY PARTY
Director: Terry Winsor
Co-stars: Daniel Peacock Perry Fenwick Phoebe Nicholls

1994 AN EVENING WITH GARY LINEKER
Director: Andy Wilson
Co-stars: Paul Merton Clive Owen Martin Clunes

1996 MEN BEHAVING BADLY
Co-stars: Martin Clunes Neil Morrissey Leslie Ash

MAE QUESTEL

1961 A MAJORITY OF ONE
Director: Mervyn LeRoy
Co-stars: Rosalind Russell Alec Guinness Madlyn Rhue

1989 NEW YORK STORIES
Director: Woody Allen
Co-stars: Mia Farrow Marvin Chatinover Woody Allen

DIANA QUICK

1977 THE THREE HOSTAGES
Director: Clive Donner
Co-stars: Barry Foster John Castle Peter Blyth

1978 THE ODD JOB
Director: Peter Medak
Co-stars: Graham Chapman David Jason Simon Williams

1981 BRIDESHEAD REVISITED
Director: Charles Sturridge
Co-stars: Jeremy Irons Anthony Andrews Claire Bloom

1985 19/19
Director: Hugh Brody
Co-stars: Paul Scofield Maria Schell Colin Firth

1985 ORDEAL BY INNOCENCE
Director: Desmond David
Co-stars: Donald Sutherland Christopher Plummer Sarah Miles

1986 MAX, MON AMOUR
Director: Nagisha Oshima
Co-stars: Charlotte Rampling Victoria Abril Anthony Higgins

1987 CARIANI AND THE COURTESANS
Director: Lesley Megahey
Co-stars: Paul McGann Lucy Hancock Michael Gough

**1988 MINDER: AN OFFICER AND
A CAR SALESMAN**
Director: Roy Ward Baker
Co-stars: George Cole Richard Briers

1989 THE JUSTICE GAME
Director: Norman Stone
Co-stars: Denis Lawson Michael Kitchen Joss Ackland

1989 WILT
Director: Michael Tuchner
Co-stars: Griff Rhys Jones Mel Smith Alison Steadman

1990 THE ORCHID HOUSE
Director: Horace Ove
Co-stars: Frances Barber Kate Buffery Elizabeth Hurley

1991 CLARISSA
Director: Robert Bierman
Co-stars: Saskia Wickham Sean Bean Cathryn Harrison

**1992 INSPECTOR MORSE:
ABSOLUTE CONVICTION**
Director: Antonia Bird
Co-stars: Sean Bean Jim Broadbent Richard Wilson

1993 NOSTRADAMUS
Director: Roger Christian
Co-stars: Tcheky Karyo Amanda Plummer Julia Ormond

1997 BURNING UP
Director: Julian Temple
Co-stars: James Frain Romagne Bohringer Jim Carter

1997 EVENT HORIZON
Director: Paul Anderson
Co-stars: Laurence Fishburne Sean Pertwee

1997 THE LEADING MAN
Director: John Duigan
Co-stars: Jon Bon Jovi Anna Galiena Lambert Wilson

JUANITA QUIGLEY (Child)

1934 THE MAN WHO RECLAIMED HIS HEAD
Director: Edward Ludwig
Co-stars: Claude Rains Joan Bennett Henry O'Neill

1936 RIFFRAFF
Director: J. Walter Ruben
Co-stars: Jean Harlow Spencer Tracey Mickey Rooney

1938 THAT CERTAIN AGE
Director: Edward Ludwig
Co-stars: Deanna Durbin Melvyn Douglas Irene Rich

1940 OH JOHNNY, HOW YOU CAN LOVE
Co-stars: Tom Brown Peggy Moran

LINNEA QUIGLEY

1984 SAVAGE STREETS
Director: Danny Steinmann
Co-stars: Linda Blair John Vernon Robert Dryer

1988 HOLLYWOOD CHAINSAW HOOKERS
Director: Fred Olen Ray
Co-stars: Gunnar Hansen Michelle Bauer Jay Richardson

RITA QUIGLEY

1940 SUSAN AND GOD
Director: George Cukor
Co-stars: Joan Crawford Fredric March Ruth Hussey

1943 ISLE OF FORGOTTEN SINS
Director: Edgar Ulmer
Co-stars: John Carradine Gale Sondergaard Sidney Toler

1947 THE TRAP
Director: Howard Bretherton
Co-stars: Sidney Toler Manton Moreland Victor Sen Yung

VERONICA QUILLIGAN

1973 MALACHI'S COVE
Director: Henry Herbert
Co-stars: Donald Pleasence Arthur English Dai Bradley

1975 LISZTOMANIA
Director: Ken Russell
Co-stars: Roger Daltrey Paul Nicholas Sara Kestelman

1977 CANDLESHOE
Director: Norman Tokar
Co-stars: David Niven Helen Hayes Jodie Foster

1982 ANGEL
Director: Neil Jordon
Co-stars: Stephen Rea Alan Devlin Peter Caffrey

1990 CENTREPOINT
Director: Piers Haggard
Co-stars: Jonathan Firth Murray Head Cheryl Campbell

MARGARET QUIMBY

1929 LUCKY BOY
Director: Norman Taurog
Co-stars: George Jessel Rosa Rosanova William K. Strauss

1930 LADIES LOVE BRUTES
Director: Rowland Lee
Co-stars: George Bancroft Mary Astor Fredric March

KATHLEEN QUINLAN

1973 AMERICAN GRAFFITI
Director: George Lucas
Co-stars: Richard Dreyfuss Ron Howard Paul LeMat

1976 LIFEGUARD
Director: Daniel Petrie
Co-stars: Sam Elliott Anne Archer Parker Stevenson

1977 AIRPORT 77
Director: Jerry Jameson
Co-stars: Jack Lemmon James Stewart Brenda Vacarro

1977 I NEVER PROMISED YOU A ROSE GARDEN
Director: Anthony Page
Co-stars: Bibi Andersson Sylvia Sidney

1979 THE PROMISE
Director: Gilbert Cates
Co-stars: Stephen Collins William Prince Beatrice Straight

1979 THE RUNNER STUMBLES
Director: Stanley Kramer
Co-stars: Dick Van Dyke Ray Bolger Beau Bridges

1981 SHE'S IN THE ARMY NOW
Director: Hy Averbach
Co-stars: Jamie Lee Curtis Melanie Griffith Susan Blanchard

1982 HANKY PANKY
Director: Sidney Poitier
Co-stars: Gene Wilder Richard Widmark Gilda Radner

1983 INDEPENDENCE DAY
Director: Robert Mandel
Co-stars: David Keith Dianne Wiest Cliff DeYoung

1983 THE LAST WINTER
Director: Riki Shelach Missimoff
Co-stars: Yona Elian Stephen Macht Zippora Peled

1983 TWILIGHT ZONE:THE MOVIE
Director: John Landis
Co-stars: Dan Aykroyd Vic Morrow Kevin McCarthy

1985 WARNING SIGN
Director: Hal Barwood
Co-stars: Sam Waterston Yaphet Kotto Richard Dysart

1985 BLACKOUT
Director: Douglas Hickox
Co-stars: Richard Widmark Keith Carradine Michael Beck

1988 SUNSET
Director: Blake Edwards
Co-stars: Bruce Willis James Garner Mariel Hemingway

1988 CLARA'S HEART
Director: Robert Mulligan
Co-stars: Whoopi Goldberg Neil Patrick Harris Spalding Grey

1989 TRAPPED
Director: Fred Walton
Co-stars: Bruce Abbot Ben Loggins Tyress Allen

1990 THE OPERATION
Director: Thomas Wright
Co-stars: Joe Penny Lisa Hartman Dori Brenner

1991 THE DOORS
Director: Oliver Stone
Co-stars: Val Kilmer Meg Ryan Kyle MacLachlan

1992 AFTER THE GLORY
Director: John Grey
Co-stars: Brad Johnson Tom Sizemore Josef Sommer

1993 STOLEN BABIES
Director: Eric Laneuville
Co-stars: Lea Thompson Mary Tyler Moore Mary Nell Santacroce

1996   IN THE LAKE OF THE WOODS
Director: Carl Schenkel
Co-star: Peter Strauss

1997   LAWN DOGS
Director: John Duigan
Co-stars: Sam Rockwell Christopher McDonald Mischa Barton

1998   BREAKDOWN
Director: Jonathan Mastow
Co-stars: Kurt Russell J.T. Walsh

AILEEN QUINN

1982   ANNIE
Director: John Huston
Co-stars: Albert Finney Carol Burnett Ann Reinking

PAT QUINN

1969   ALICE'S RESTAURANT
Director: Arthur Penn
Co-stars: Arlo Guthrie James Broderick Tina Chen

1971   SHOOTOUT
Director: Henry Hathaway
Co-stars: Gregory Peck James Gregory Susan Tyrrell

1971   ZACHARIAH
Co-star: John Rubinstein

1975   THE ROCKY HORROR SHOW
Director: Jim Sharman
Co-stars: Tim Curry Susan Sarandon Koo Stark

1978   AN UNMARRIED WOMAN
Director: Paul Mazursky
Co-stars: Jill Clayburgh Alan Bates Michael Murphy

1979   THE OUTSIDER
Director: Tony Luraschi
Co-stars: Craig Wasson Sterling Hayden Ray McAnally

1981   SHOCK TREATMENT
Director: Jim Sharman
Co-stars: Jessica Harper Cliff De Young Richard O'Brien

BEULAH QUO

1979   SAMURAI
Director: Lee Katzin
Co-stars: Joe Penny James Shigeta Morgan Brittany

1980   THE CHILDREN OF AN LAC
Director: John Llewellyn Moxey
Co-stars: Shirley Jones Ina Balin Alan Fudge

MARIANNE QUON

1944   CHARLIE CHAN IN THE SECRET SERVICE
Director: Phil Rosen
Co-stars: Sidney Toler Manton Moreland Benson Fong

ELIE RAAB *(Child)*

1989 THE FABULOUS BAKER BOYS
Director: Steve Kloves
Co-stars: Jeff Bridges Beau Bridges Michelle Pfeiffer

1992 ROADSIDE PROPHETS
Director: Abbe Wool
Co-stars: John Doe Adam Horowitz John Cusack

TERESA RABAL

1961 VIRIDIANS
Director: Luis Bunuel
Co-stars: Silvia Pinal Francisco Rabal Fernando Rey

PAMELA RABE

1994 SIRENS
Director: John Duigan
Co-stars: Hugh Grant Tara Fitzgerald Sam Neill

CATHERINE RABETT

1989 CONFESSIONAL
Director: Gordon Flemyng
Co-stars: Robert Lindsay Keith Carradine Anthony Quayle

1990 FRANKENSTEIN UNBOUND
Director: Roger Corman
Co-stars: John Hurt Raul Julia Bridget Fonda

FRANCINE RACETTE

1976 LUMIERE
Director: Jeanne Moreau
Co-stars: Lucia Bose Bruno Ganz Caroline Lartier

1977 THE DISAPPEARANCE
Director: Stuart Cooper
Co-stars: Donald Sutherland David Hemmings John Hurt

1987 AU REVOIR LES ENFANTS
Director: Louis Malle
Co-stars: Gaspard Manesse Raphael Fejto Peter Fitz

VICTORIA RACIMO

1979 THE PROPHECY
Director: John Frankenheimer
Co-stars: Talia Shire Robert Foxworth Armand Assante

1980 THE MOUNTAIN MEN
Director: Richard Lang
Co-stars: Charlton Heston Brian Keith Seymour Cassel

1981 THE VIOLATION OF SARAH McDAVID
Director: John Llewellyn Moxey
Co-stars: Patty Duke Ned Beatty Ally Sheedy

1983 GHOST DANCING
Director: David Greene
Co-stars: Dorothy McGuire Bruce Davison Bo Hopkins

1986 ON DANGEROUS GROUND
Director: Chuck Bail
Co-stars: Stephen Collins Bo Svenson Nicholas Pryor

1987 ERNEST GOES TO CAMP
Director: John R. Cherry
Co-stars: Jim Varney John Vernon Iron Eyes Cody

1994 WHITE FANG 2: MYTH OF THE WHITE WOLF
Director: Ken Olin
Co-stars: Scott Bairstow Charmaine Craig

PORSCHA RADCLIFFE

1988 MYSTIC PIZZA
Director: Donald Petrie
Co-stars: Julia Roberts Annabeth Gish Lili Taylor

ROSEMARY RADCLIFFE

1985 ANNE OF GREEN GABLES
Director: Kevin Sullivan
Co-stars: Megan Follows Colleen Dewhurst Charmion King

LYNNE RADFORD

1985 WINGS OF DEATH
Director: Nicholas Bruce
Co-stars: Dexter Fletcher Kate Hardie Tony Haygarth

RADHA

1951 THE RIVER
Director: Jean Renoir
Co-stars: Nora Swinburne Esmond Knight Adrienne Corri

GILDA RADNER

1982 HANKY PANKY
Director: Sidney Poitier
Co-stars: Gene Wilder Richard Widmark Kathleen Quinlan

1984 THE WOMAN IN RED
Director: Gene Wilder
Co-stars: Kelly LeBrock Charles Grodin Joseph Bologna

1985 MOVERS AND SHAKERS
Director: William Asher
Co-stars: Walter Matthau Charles Grodin Tyne Daly

1986 HAUNTED HONEYMOON
Director: Gene Wilder
Co-stars: Dom DeLuise Jonathan Pryce Gene Wilder

BARBRA RAE

1980 HIDE IN PLAIN SIGHT
Director: James Caan
Co-stars: Jill Eikenberry Danny Aiello Kenneth McMillan James Caan

CHARLOTTE RAE

1975 QUEEN OF THE STARDUST BALLROOM
Director: Sam O'Steen
Co-stars: Maureen Stapleton Charles Durning

1986 WORDS BY HEART
Director: Robert Thompson
Co-stars: Rob Hooks Alfre Woodard

1988 SAVE THE DOG !
Director: Paul Aaron
Co-stars: Cindy Williams Tony Randall Tom Poston

FRANCES RAFFERTY

1942 THE WAR AGAINST MRS HADLEY
Director: Harold Bucquet
Co-stars: Fay Bainter Edward Arnold Jean Rogers

1944 MRS PARKINGTON
Director: Tay Garnett
Co-stars: Greer Garson Walter Pidgeon Edward Arnold

1944 DRAGON SEED
Director: Harold Bucquet
Co-stars: Katherine Hepburn Walter Huston Turhan Bey

1944   BARBARY COAST GENT
Director: Roy Del Ruth
Co-stars: Wallace Beery Binnie Barnes Chill Wills

1945   THE HIDDEN EYE
Director: Richard Whorf
Co-stars: Edward Arnold William Phillips Ray Collins

1945   ABBOTT AND COSTELLO IN HOLLYWOOD
Director: S. Sylvan Simon
Co-stars: Bud Abbott Lou Costello Jean Porter

1946   BAD BASCOMB
Director: S. Sylvan Simon
Co-stars: Wallace Beery Margaret O'Brien Marjorie Main

**1947   THE ADVENTURES OF CURLEY
          AND HIS GANG**
Director: Bernard Carr
Co-stars: Larry Olsen Eileen Janssen

DEBORAH RAFFIN *(Married Michael Viner)*

1973   FORTY CARATS
Director: Milton Katselas
Co-stars: Liv Ullman Edward Albert Gene Kelly

1974   THE DOVE
Director: Charles Jarrott
Co-stars: Joseph Bottoms John McLiam Dabney Coleman

1975   ONCE IS NOT ENOUGH
Director: Guy Green
Co-stars: Kirk Douglas Alexis Smith Melina Mercouri

1976   THE SENTINEL
Director: Michael Winner
Co-stars: Cristina Raines Chris Sarandon Ava Gardner

1976   GOD TOLD ME TO
Director: Larry Cohen
Co-stars: Tony LoBianco Sandy Dennis Sylvia Sydney

1979   MIND OVER MURDER
Director: Ivan Nagy
Co-stars: David Ackroyd Bruce Davison Andrew Prine

1980   FOR THE LOVE OF IT
Director: Hal Kanter
Co-stars: Jeff Conaway Barbi Benton Don Rickles

1980   TOUCHED BY LOVE
Director: Gus Trikonis
Co-stars: Diane Ladd Michael Learned Cristina Raines

1981   KILLER AT HELL'S GATE
Director: Jerry Jameson
Co-stars: Robert Urich Lee Purcell Joel Higgins

1983   AGATHA CHRISTIE'S SPARKLING CYANIDE
Director: Robert Lewis
Co-stars: Anthony Andrews Harry Morgan

1983   RUNNING OUT
Director: Robert Day
Co-stars: Tony Bill Toni Kalem Ari Meyers

1984   THREESOME
Director: Lou Antonio
Co-stars: Stephen Collins Joel Higgins Susan Hess

1985   DEATH WISH 3
Director: Michael Winner
Co-stars: Charles Bronson Ed Lauter Martin Balsam

1990   NIGHT OF THE FOX
Director: Charles Jarrott
Co-stars: George Peppard Michael York John Mills

1991   SCANNERS 2:THE NEW ORDER
Director: Christian Duguay
Co-stars: David Hewlett Yvan Ponton

1993   MORNING GLORY
Director: Steven Stern
Co-stars: Christopher Reeve Nina Foch Helen Shaver

GILLIAN RAINE

1987   SWEET AS YOU ARE
Director: Angela Pope
Co-stars: Miranda Richardson Liam Neeson Alex Pakenham

1990   FRANKENSTEIN'S BABY
Director: Robert Bierman
Co-stars: Kate Buffery Nigel Planer William Armstrong

1990   CHILDREN CROSSING
Director: Angela Pope
Co-stars: Peter Firth Saskia Reeves Bob Peck

1992   SUDDENLY, LAST SUMMER
Director: Richard Eyre
Co-stars: Maggie Smith Natasha Richardson Rob Lowe

LUISE RAINER *(Married Clifford Odets)*
Won Oscar For Best Actress In 1936 For "The Great Ziegfeld" And In 1937 For "The Good Earth"

1935   ESCAPADE
Director: Robert Z. Leonard
Co-stars: William Powell Virginia Bruce Frank Morgan

1936   THE GREAT ZIEGFELD
Director: Robert Z. Leonard
Co-stars: William Powell Myrna Loy Frank Morgan

1937   THE GOOD EARTH
Director: Sidney Franklin
Co-stars: Paul Muni Walter Connolly Tillie Losch

1937   THE BIG CITY
Director: Frank Borzage
Co-stars: Spencer Tracy Charley Grapewin William Demarest

1937   THE EMPEROR'S CANDLESTICK
Director: George Fitzmaurice
Co-stars: William Powell Frank Morgan

1938   THE GREAT WALTZ
Director: Julien Duvivier
Co-stars: Fernand Gravet Miliza Korjus Lionel Atwill

1938   DRAMATIC SCHOOL
Director: Robert Sinclair
Co-stars: Paulette Goddard Lana Turner Alan Marshall

1938   THE TOY WIFE
Director: Richard Thorpe
Co-stars: Melvyn Douglas Robert Young H.B. Warner

1943   HOSTAGES
Director: Frank Tuttle
Co-stars: Paul Lukas William Bendix Oscar Homolka

1997   THE GAMBLER
Director: Karoly Makk
Co-stars: Michael Gambon Jodhi May

BETH RAINES

1978   FOREVER
Director: John Korty
Co-stars: Stephanie Zimbalist Dean Butler Diana Scarwid

CRISTINA RAINES

1975   RUSSIAN ROULETTE
Director: Lou Lombardo
Co-stars: George Segal Gordon Jackson Denholm Elliott

1976   THE SENTINEL
Director: Michael Winner
Co-stars: Chris Sarandon Ava Gardner John Carradine

1977 THE DUELLISTS
Director: Ridley Scott
Co-stars: Keith Carradine Harvey Keitel Albert Finney

1980 SILVER DREAM RACER
Director: David Wickes
Co-stars: David Essex Beau Bridges Harry H. Corbett

1980 TOUCHED BY LOVE
Director: Gus Trikonis
Co-stars: Deborah Raffin Diane Lane Michael Learned

1983 NIGHTMARES
Director: Joseph Sargent
Co-stars: Emilio Estevez Veronica Cartwright Richard Masur

1983 REAL LIFE
Director: Francis Megahy
Co-stars: Rupert Everett Warren Clarke Isla Blair

1987 NORTH SHORE
Director: William Phelps
Co-stars: Matt Adler Nia Peeples John Philbin

ELLA RAINES

1943 CRY HAVOC
Director: Richard Thorpe
Co-stars: Margaret Sullavan Joan Blondell Ann Sothern

1943 CORVETTE K225
Director: Richard Rosson
Co-stars: Randolph Scott Barry Fitzgerald Andy Devine

1944 ENTER ARSENE LUPIN
Director: Ford Beebe
Co-stars: Charles Korvin J. Carrol Naish Gale Sondergaard

1944 HAIL THE CONQUERING HERO
Director: Preston Sturges
Co-stars: Eddie Bracken William Demarest

1944 PHANTOM LADY
Director: Robert Siodmak
Co-stars: Franchot Tone Alan Curtis Aurora Miranda

1944 THE SUSPECT
Director: Robert Siodmak
Co-stars: Charles Laughton Henry Daniell Dean Harens

1944 TALL IN THE SADDLE
Director: Edwin Marin
Co-stars: John Wayne Ward Bond George "Gabby" Hayes

1945 THE STRANGE AFFAIR OF UNCLE HARRY
Director: Robert Siodmak
Co-stars: George Sanders Geraldine Fitzgerald

1946 THE RUNAROUND
Director: Charles Lamont
Co-stars: Broderick Crawford Rod Cameron Frank McHugh

1946 WHITE TIE AND TALES
Director: Charles Barton
Co-stars: Dan Duryea William Bendix Frank Jenks

1947 BRUTE FORCE
Director: Jules Dassin
Co-stars: Burt Lancaster Hume Cronyn Yvonne De Carlo

1947 TIME OUT OF MIND
Director: Robert Siodmak
Co-stars: Phyllis Calvert Robert Hutton Eddie Albert

1947 THE SENATOR WAS INDISCREET
Director: George Kauffman
Co-stars: William Powell Arleen Whelan

1947 THE WEB
Director: Michael Gordon
Co-stars: Edmond O'Brien Vincent Price William Bendix

1949 THE WALKING HILLS
Director: John Sturges
Co-stars: Randolph Scott Arthur Kennedy

1949 IMPACT
Director: Arthur Lubin
Co-stars: Brian Donlevy Charles Coburn Helen Walker

1949 A DANGEROUS PROFESSION
Director: Ted Tetzlaff
Co-stars: Pat O'Brien George Raft Bill Williams

1952 RIDE THE MAN DOWN
Director: Joe Kane
Co-stars: Brian Donlevy Rod Cameron Forrest Tucker

1957 THE MAN IN THE ROAD
Director: Lance Comfort
Co-stars: Derek Farr Donald Wolfit Lisa Daniely

LISA RAINES

1983 FANNY HILL
Director: Gerry O'Hara
Co-stars: Oliver Reed Shelley Winters Alfred Marks

RACHEL RAINS

1990 RETURN HOME
Director: Ray Argall
Co-stars: Dennis Coard Ben Mendelson

KATE RAISON

1994 EBBTIDE

ANNE RAITT

1971 BLEAK MOMENTS
Director: Mike Leigh
Co-stars: Sarah Stephenson Eric Allan Liz Smith

1991 A TIME TO DANCE
Director: Kevin Billington
Co-stars: Ronald Pickup Dervla Kirwan Rosemary McHale

BONNIE RAITT

1980 URBAN COWBOY
Director: James Bridges
Co-stars: John Travolta Debra Winger

LAYA RAKI

1954 THE SEEKERS
Director: Ken Annakin
Co-stars: Jack Hawkins Glynis Johns Noel Purcell

1955 THE ADVENTURES OF QUENTIN DURWARD
Director: Richard Thorpe
Co-stars: Robert Taylor Kay Kendall

GIOVANNA RALLI

1956 THE BIGAMIST
Director: Luciano Emmer
Co-stars: Marcello Mastroianni Vittorio De Sica Franca Valeri

1959 IL GENERALE DELLA ROVERE
Director: Roberto Rossellini
Co-stars: Vittorio De Sica Sandra Milo Anne Vernon

1966 THE CAPER OF THE GOLDEN BULLS
Director: Russel Rouse
Co-stars: Stephen Boyd Yvette Mimieux

1966 WHAT DID YOU DO IN THE WAR DADDY ?
Director: Blake Edwards
Co-stars: James Coburn Dick Shawn Aldo Ray

1968 DEADFALL
Director: Bryan Forbes
Co-stars: Michael Caine Eric Portman Nanette Newman

1970 CANNON FOR CORDOBA
Director: Paul Wendkos
Co-stars: George Peppard Pete Duel Raf Vallone

ANNA RALPH

1980 MANGANINNIE
Director: John Honey
Co-stars: Mawuyul Yanthalawuy Phillip Hinton Reg Evans

HANNA RALPH

1924 THE NIBERLUNGEN
Director: Fritz Lang
Co-stars: Paul Richter Margarete Schon Theodore Loos

JESSIE RALPH

1933 ELMER THE GREAT
Director: Mervyn LeRoy
Co-stars: Joe E. Brown Patricia Ellis Frank McHugh

1934 THE AFFAIRS OF CELLINI
Director: Gregory La Cava
Co-stars: Fredric March Constance Bennett Frank Morgan

1934 NANA
Director: Dorothy Arzner
Co-stars: Anna Sten Lionel Atwill Phillips Holmes

1934 MURDER AT THE VANITIES
Director: Mitchell Leisen
Co-stars: Jack Oakie Carl Brisson Victor McLaglen

1934 WE LIVE AGAIN
Director: Rouben Mamoulian
Co-stars: Fredric March Anna Sten Sam Jaffe

1934 ONE NIGHT OF LOVE
Director: Victor Schertzinger
Co-stars: Grace Moore Tullio Carminati Wendy Barrie

1935 LES MISERABLES
Director: Richard Boleslawski
Co-stars: Fredric March Charles Laughton Rochelle Hudson

1935 VANESSA, HER LOVE STORY
Director: William Howard
Co-stars: Helen Hayes Robert Montgomery May Robson

1935 JALNA
Director: John Cromwell
Co-stars: Kay Johnson Ian Hunter Nigel Bruce

1935 I LIVE MY LIFE
Director: W.S. Van Dyke
Co-stars: Joan Crawford Brian Aherne Frank Morgan

1935 I FOUND STELLA PARISH
Director: Mervyn LeRoy
Co-stars: Kay Francis Paul Lukas Sybil Jason

1935 MARK OF THE VAMPIRE
Director: Ted Browning
Co-stars: Lionel Barrymore Jean Hersholt Elizabeth Allan

1935 ENCHANTED APRIL
Director: Harry Beaumont
Co-stars: Ann Harding Frank Morgan Jane Baxter

1936 AFTER THE THIN MAN
Director: W.S. Van Dyke
Co-stars: William Powell Myrna Loy James Stewart

1936 BUNKER BEAN
Director: Edward Killy
Co-stars: Owen Davis Lucille Ball Louise Latimer

1936 THE GOOD EARTH
Director: Sidney Franklin
Co-stars: Paul Muni Luise Rainer Walter Connolly

1936 LITTLE LORD FAUNTLEROY
Director: John Cromwell
Co-stars: Freddie Bartholomew Mickey Rooney

1936 SAN FRANCISCO
Director: W.S. Van Dyke
Co-stars: Clark Gable Jeanette MacDonald Spencer Tracy

1936 THE UNGUARDED HOUR
Director: Sam Wood
Co-stars: Franchot Tone Loretta Young Roland Young

1937 THE LAST OF MRS CHEYNEY
Director: Richard Boleslawski
Co-stars: Joan Crawford Robert Montgomery

1937 DOUBLE WEDDING
Director: Richard Thorpe
Co-stars: William Powell Myrna Loy Florence Rice

1938 FOUR GIRLS IN WHITE
Director: S. Sylvan Simon
Co-stars: Florence Rice Una Merkel Mary Howard

1938 HOLD THAT KISS
Director: Edwin Marin
Co-stars: Maureen O'Sullivan Dennis O'Keefe Mickey Rooney

1938 LOVE IS A HEADACHE
Director: Richard Thorpe
Co-stars: Franchot Tone Gladys George Mickey Rooney

1938 PORT OF SEVEN SEAS
Director: James Whale
Co-stars: Maureen O'Sullivan Wallace Beery Frank Morgan

1939 DRUMS ALONG THE MOHAWK
Director: John Ford
Co-stars: Henry Fonda Claudette Colbert Ward Bond

1939 ST. LOUIS BLUES
Director: Raoul Walsh
Co-stars: Dorothy Lamour Lloyd Nolan Tito Guizar

1940 STAR DUST
Director: Walter Lang
Co-stars: Linda Darner John Payne Charlotte Greenwood

1940 I WANT A DIVORCE
Director: Ralph Murphy
Co-stars: Dick Powell Joan Blondell Gloria Dickson

1940 THE BANK DICK
Director: Eddie Cline
Co-stars: W.C. Fields Franklin Pangborn

1940 THE GIRL FROM AVENUE A
Director: Otto Brower
Co-stars: Jane Withers Kent Taylor Elyse Knox

1940 THE BLUE BIRD
Director: Walter Lang
Co-stars: Shirley Temple Johnny Russell Nigel Bruce

1941 THE LADY FROM CHEYENNE
Director: Frank Lloyd
Co-stars: Loretta Young Robert Preston Edward Arnold

1941 THEY MET IN BOMBAY
Director: Clarence Brown
Co-stars: Clark Gable Rosalind Russell Peter Lorre

SHERYL LEE RALPH

1989 THE MIGHTY QUINN
Director: Carl Shenkel
Co-stars: Denzel Washington James Fox Mimi Rogers

1990 TO SLEEP WITH ANGER
Director: Charles Burnett
Co-stars: Danny Glover Paul Butler Mary Alice

1990 OLIVER AND COMPANY *(Voice)*
Director: George Scribner
Co-stars: Billy Joel Bette Midler Joey Lawrence

1992 THE DISTINGUISHED GENTLEMAN
Director: Jonathan Lynn
Co-stars: Eddie Murphy Lane Smith Joe Don Baker

1993 SISTER ACT 2: BACK IN THE HABIT
Director: Bill Duke
Co-stars: Whoopi Goldberg Kathy Najimy Maggie Smith

ESTHER RALSTON

1928 PETER PAN

1930 THE MIGHTY
Co-star: George Bancroft

1931 THE PRODIGAL
Director: Harry Pollard
Co-stars: Lawrence Tibbett Roland Young Hedda Hopper

1932 ROME EXPRESS
Director: Walter Forde
Co-stars: Conrad Veidt Gordon Harker Cedric Hardwicke

1932 AFTER THE BALL
Co-star: Marie Burke

1933 BY CANDLELIGHT
Director: James Whale
Co-stars: Elissa Landi Paul Lukas Nils Asther

1934 SADIE McKEE
Director: Clarence Brown
Co-stars: Joan Crawford Franchot Tone Gene Raymond

1935 MR DYNAMITE
Co-stars: Edmund Lowe Jean Dixon

1940 TIN PAN ALLEY
Director: Walter Lang
Co-stars: Alice Faye Betty Grable John Payne

1950 THE EAGLE AND THE HAWK
Director: Lewis Foster
Co-stars: John Payne Dennis O'Keefe Rhonda Fleming

JOBYNA RALSTON *(Married Richard Arlen)*

1923 WHY WORRY ?
Director: Sam Taylor
Co-stars: Harold Lloyd Leo White

1924 HOT WATER
Director: Sam Taylor
Co-stars: Harold Lloyd Josephine Crowell

1925 THE FRESHMAN
Director: Sam Taylor
Co-stars: Harold Lloyd Brooks Benedict

1926 FOR HEAVEN'S SAKE
Director: Sam Taylor
Co-stars: Harold Lloyd Noah Young Paul Weigel

1927 THE KID BROTHER
Director: Ted Wilde
Co-stars: Harold Lloyd Walter James Leo Willis

1927 WINGS
Director: William Wellman
Co-stars: Clara Bow Charles Rogers Richard Arlen

1928 POWER OF THE PRESS
Director: Frank Capra
Co-stars: Douglas Fairbanks Jnr. Robert Edeson Mildred Harris

MARCIA RALSTON

1937 SH ! THE OCTOPUS
Director: William McGann
Co-stars: Hugh Herbert Allen Jenkins John Eldredge

1939 GOLD IS WHERE YOU FIND IT
Director: Michael Curtiz
Co-stars: George Brent Olivia De Havilland

VERA HRUBA RALSTON

1942 ICE-CAPADES REVUE
Director: Bernard Vorhaus
Co-stars: Ellen Drew Richard Denning Jerry Colonna

1944 LAKE PLACID SERENADE
Director: Steve Sekely
Co-stars: Robert Livingston Vera Vague Eugene Pallette

1944 THE LADY AND THE MONSTER
Director: George Sherman
Co-stars: Erich Von Stroheim Richard Arlen

1944 STORM OVER LISBON
Director: George Sherman
Co-stars: Erich Von Stroheim Richard Arlen Otto Kruger

1945 DAKOTA
Director: Joseph Kane
Co-stars: John Wayne Walter Brennan Ward Bond

1946 MURDER IN THE MUSIC HALL
Director: John English
Co-stars: Helen Walker Nancy Kelly William Gargan

1946 THE PLAINSMAN AND THE LADY
Director: Joseph Kane
Co-stars: William Elliott Gail Patrick

1947 WYOMING
Director: Joseph Kane
Co-stars: William Elliott John Carroll Albert Dekker

1947 THE FLAME
Director: John Auer
Co-stars: John Carroll Robert Paige Broderick Crawford

1948 ANGEL ON THE AMAZON
Director: John Auer
Co-stars: George Brent Constance Bennett Brian Aherne

1948 I, JANE DOE
Director: John Auer
Co-stars: John Carroll Ruth Hussey Gene Lockhart

1949 THE FIGHTING KENTUCKIAN
Director: George Waggner
Co-stars: John Wayne Oliver Hardy Philip Dorn

1951 BELLE LE GRAND
Director: Allan Dwan
Co-stars: John Carroll Hope Emerson William Ching

1952 HOODLUM EMPIRE
Director: Joseph Kane
Co-stars: Brian Donlevy Forrest Tucker Claire Trevor

1952 PERILOUS JOURNEY
Director: R.G. Springsteen
Co-stars: David Brian Charles Winninger Scott Brady

1952 THE WILD BLUE YONDER
Director: Allan Dwan
Co-stars: Wendell Corey Forrest Tucker Walter Brennan

1953 FAIR WIND TO JAVA
Director: Joseph Kane
Co-stars: Fred MacMurray Victor McLaglen Robert Douglas

1954 JUBILEE TRAIL
Director: Joseph Kane
Co-stars: Pat O'Brien Forrest Tucker Joan Leslie

1954 TIMBERJACK
Director: Joseph Kane
Co-stars: Sterling Hayden Hoagy Carmichael Adolphe Menjou

1956   **ACCUSED OF MURDER**
Director: Joseph Kane
Co-stars: David Brian Virginia Grey Lee Van Cleef

1958   **THE MAN WHO DIED TWICE**
Director: Joseph Kane
Co-stars: Rod Cameron Mike Mazurki Gerald Milton

MARJORIE RAMBEAU
Nominated For Best Supporting Actress In 1940 For the "Primrose Path" And In 1953 For "Torch Song"

1930   **MIN AND BILL**
Director: George Hill
Co-stars: Marie Dressler Wallace Beery Dorothy Jordan

1930   **INSPIRATION**
Director: Clarence Brown
Co-stars: Greta Garbo Robert Montgomery Lewis Stone

1930   **HER MAN**
Director: Tay Garnett
Co-stars: Helen Twelvetrees Ricardo Cortez James Gleason

1931   **THE EASIEST WAY**
Director: Jack Conway
Co-stars: Constance Bennett Robert Montgomery Adolphe Menjou

1931   **HELL DIVERS**
Director: George Hill
Co-stars: Wallace Beery Clark Gable Dorothy Jordan

1931   **LAUGHING SINNERS**
Director: Harry Beaumont
Co-stars: Joan Crawford Clark Gable Neil Hamilton

1931   **SILENCE**
Co-stars: Clive Brook

1931   **THE SECRET SIX**
Director: George Hill
Co-stars: Wallace Beery Clark Gable Jean Harlow

1931   **STRANGERS MAY KISS**
Director: George Fitzmaurice
Co-stars: Norma Shearer Robert Montgomery Irene Rich

1933   **THE WARRIOR'S HUSBAND**
Director: Walter Lang
Co-stars: Elissa Landi Ernest Truex David Manners

1933   **STRICTLY PERSONAL**
Co-stars: Hugh Herbert Eddie Quillan

1933   **A MAN'S CASTLE**
Director: Frank Borzage
Co-stars: Spencer Tracy Loretta Young Glenda Farrell

1934   **GRAND CANARY**
Director: Irving Cummings
Co-stars: Warner Baxter Madge Evans Juliette Compton

1934   **A MODERN HERO**
Director: G.W. Pabst
Co-stars: Richard Barthelmess Jean Muir Verree Teasdale

1937   **FIRST LADY**
Director: Stanley Logan
Co-stars: Kay Francis Preston Foster Anita Louise

1938   **MERRILY WE LIVE**
Director: Norman Z. McLeod
Co-stars: Constance Bennett Brian Aherne Billie Burke

1939   **HEAVEN WITH A BARBED WIRE FENCE**
Director: Ricardo Cortez
Co-stars: Glenn Ford Jean Rogers

1939   **THE RAINS CAME**
Director: Clarence Brown
Co-stars: Tyrone Power Myrna Loy George Brent

1940   **EAST OF THE RIVER**
Director: Alfred Green
Co-stars: John Garfield William Lundigan Brenda Marshall

1940   **PRIMROSE PATH**
Director: Gregory La Cava
Co-stars: Ginger Rogers Joel McCrea Henry Travers

1940   **TUGBOAT ANNIE SAILS AGAIN**
Director: Lewis Seiler
Co-stars: Jane Wyman Ronald Reagan Alan Hale

1940   **20 MULE TEAM**
Director: Richard Thorpe
Co-stars: Wallace Beery Leo Carrillo Anne Baxter

1941   **TOBACCO ROAD**
Director: John Ford
Co-stars: Gene Tierney Dana Andrews Charley Grapewin

1942   **BROADWAY**
Director: William Seiter
Co-stars: George Raft Pat O'Brien Broderick Crawford

1943   **WAR OF THE WILDCATS**
Director: Albert Rogell
Co-stars: John Wayne Martha Scott Albert Dekker

1944   **OH, WHAT A NIGHT !**
Co-stars: Jean Parker Claire Dubrey

1945   **SALOME, WHERE SHE DANCED**
Director: Charles Lamont
Co-stars: Yvonne De Carlo Rod Cameron Albert Dekker

1948   **THE WALLS OF JERICHO**
Director: John Stahl
Co-stars: Cornel Wilde Linda Darnell Anne Baxter

1949   **ANY NUMBER CAN PLAY**
Director: Mervyn LeRoy
Co-stars: Clark Gable Alexis Smith Frank Morgan

1953   **TORCH SONG**
Director: Charles Walters
Co-stars: Joan Crawford Michael Wilding Gig Young

1954   **BAD FOR EACH OTHER**
Director: Irving Rapper
Co-stars: Charlton Heston Lisbeth Scott

1955   **THE VIEW FROM POMPEY'S HEAD**
Director: Philip Dunne
Co-stars: Richard Egan Dana Wynter Cameron Mitchell

1955   **A MAN CALLED PETER**
Director: Henry Koster
Co-stars: Richard Todd Jean Peters Jill Esmond

1956   **SLANDER**
Director: Roy Rowland
Co-stars: Van Johnson Ann Blyth Steve Cochran

1957   **MAN OF A THOUSAND FACES**
Director: Joseph Pevney
Co-stars: James Cagney Dorothy Malone Robert Evans

SUNIL Y RAMJITSINGH *(Child)*
1992   **THE HUMMINGBIRD TREE**
Director: Noella Smith
Co-stars: Patrick Bergin Susan Wooldridge Tom Beasley

RAMONA
1935   **THANKS A MILLION**
Director: Roy Del Ruth
Co-stars: Dick Powell Ann Dvorak Fred Allen

CHARLOTTE RAMPLING
1965   **ROTTEN TO THE CORE**
Director: John Boulting
Co-stars: Anton Rodgers Eric Sykes Ian Bannen

1966	**GEORGY GIRL**
Director:	Silvio Narizzano
Co-stars:	Lynn Redgrave James Mason Alan Bates

1967	**THE LONG DUEL**
Director:	Ken Annakin
Co-stars:	Trevor Howard Yul Brynner Harry Andrews

1968	**TARGET HARRY**
Director:	Roger Corman
Co-stars:	Vic Morrow Suzanne Pleshette Victor Buono

1969	**THE DAMNED**
Director:	Joseph Losey
Co-stars:	Dirk Bogarde Ingrid Thulin Helmut Berger

1969	**THREE**
Director:	James Salter
Co-stars:	Sam Waterston Robie Porter Pascale Roberts

1971	**CORKY**
Director:	Leonard Horn
Co-stars:	Robert Blake Patrick O'Neal Christopher Connolly

1971	**VANISHING POINT**
Director:	Richard Sarafian
Co-stars:	Barry Newman Dean Jagger Cleavon Little

1972	**ASYLUM**
Director:	Roy Ward Baker
Co-stars:	Patrick Magee Robert Powell Barbara Parkins

1972	**HENRY VIII AND HIS SIX WIVES**
Director:	Warris Hussein
Co-stars:	Keith Michell Jane Asher Frances Cuka

1973	**THE NIGHT PORTER**
Director:	Liliana Cavani
Co-stars:	Dirk Bogarde Isa Miranda Philippe Leroy

1974	**THE FLESH OF THE ORCHID**
Director:	Patrice Cherreau
Co-stars:	Edwige Feuillere Simone Signoret Valli

1974	**CARAVAN TO VACCARES**
Director:	Geoffrey Reeve
Co-stars:	David Birney Michael Bryant

1974	**ZARDOS**
Director:	John Boorman
Co-stars:	Sean Connery John Alderton Sara Kestelman

1975	**FAREWELL MY LOVELY**
Director:	Dick Richards
Co-stars:	Robert Mitchum John Ireland Sylvia Miles

1976	**SHERLOCK HOLMES IN NEW YORK**
Director:	Boris Sagal
Co-stars:	Roger Moore John Huston Gig Young

1977	**ORCA-KILLER WHALE**
Director:	Michael Anderson
Co-stars:	Richard Harris Keenan Wynn Will Sampson

1977	**FOXTROT**
Director:	Arturo Ripstein
Co-stars:	Peter O'Toole Max Von Sydow Jorge Luke

1980	**STARDUST MEMORIES**
Director:	Woody Allen
Co-stars:	Tony Roberts Jessica Harper Amy Wright

1982	**THE VERDICT**
Director:	Sidney Lumet
Co-stars:	Paul Newman James Mason Jack Warden

1986	**MAX, MON AMOUR**
Director:	Nagisa Oshima
Co-stars:	Anthony Higgins Bernard-Pierre Donnadieu

1987	**ANGEL HEART**
Director:	Alan Parker
Co-stars:	Mickey Rourke Robert De Niro Lisa Bonet

1988	**D.O.A.**
Director:	Rocky Morton
Co-stars:	Dennis Quaid Meg Ryan Daniel Stern

1988	**PARIS BY NIGHT**
Director:	David Hare
Co-stars:	Michael Gambon Robert Hardy Jane Asher

1998	**WINGS OF THE DOVE**
Director:	Iain Softly
Co-stars:	Helena Bonham-Carter Linus Roache Alison Eliott

LOUIE RAMSAY

1988	**INSPECTOR WEXFORD: A GUILTY THING SURPRISED**
Director:	Mary McMurray
Co-stars:	George Baker Nigel Terry

1988	**INSPECTOR WEXFORD: NO CRYING SHE MAKES**
Director:	Mary McMurray
Co-stars:	George Baker Jane Horrocks

1988	**INSPECTOR WEXFORD: SHAKE HANDS FOREVER**
Director:	Don Leaver
Co-stars:	George Baker Tom Wilkinson

1989	**INSPECTOR WEXFORD: THE VEILED ONE**
Director:	Mary McMurray
Co-stars:	George Baker Paolo Dionisotti

1990	**INSPECTOR WEXFORD: SOME LIE AND SOME DIE**
Director:	Sandy Johnson
Co-stars:	George Baker Gemma Jones

1990	**INSPECTOR WEXFORD: THE BEST MAN TO DIE**
Director:	Herbert Wise
Co-stars:	George Baker Julia Ormond

1991	**INSPECTOR WEXFORD: FROM DOON WITH DEATH**
Director:	Mary McMurray
Co-stars:	George Baker Amanda Redman

1991	**INSPECTOR WEXFORD: MURDER BEING ONCE DONE**
Director:	John Gorrie
Co-stars:	George Baker Diane Keen

1991	**INSPECTOR WEXFORD: MEANS OF EVIL**
Director:	Sarah Hellings
Co-stars:	George Baker Cheryl Campbell

1991	**INSPECTOR WEXFORD: PUT ON BY CUNNING**
Director:	Sandy Johnson
Co-stars:	George Baker Rossano Brazzi

1991	**INSPECTOR WEXFORD: AN UNKINDNESS OF RAVENS**
Director:	John Gorrie
Co-stars:	George Baker Norma West

ANNE RAMSEY
Nominated For Best Supporting Actress In 1987 For "Throw Momma From The Train"

1976	**DAWN: PROTRAIT OF A RUNAWAY TEENAGER**
Director:	Randal Kleiser
Co-stars:	Eve Plumb Lynn Carlin Bo Hopkins

1978 GOIN' SOUTH
Director: Jack Nicholson
Co-stars: Mary Steenburgen Danny DeVito Jack Nicholson

1980 ANY WHICH WAY YOU CAN
Director: Buddy Van Horn
Co-stars: Clint Eastwood Ruth Gordon Sondra Locke

1980 THE BLACK MARBLE
Director: Harold Becker
Co-stars: Robert Foxworth Paula Prentiss Harry Dean Stanton

1980 MARILYN: THE UNTOLD STORY
Director: Jack Arnold
Co-stars: Catherine Hicks Richard Basehart Sheree North

1980 WHITE MAMA
Director: Jackie Cooper
Co-stars: Bette Davis Ernest Harden Eileen Heckart

1981 A SMALL KILLING
Director: Steven Hilliard Stern
Co-stars: Edward Asner Jean Simmons Sylvia Sidney

1981 THE KILLING OF RANDY WEBSTER
Director: Sam Wanamaker
Co-stars: Hal Holbrook Sean Penn James Whitmore

1983 ANOTHER CHANCE
Director: Jesse Vint
Co-stars: Bruce Greenwood Vanessa Angle Jeff East

1985 THE GOONIES
Director: Richard Donner
Co-stars: Sean Astin Corey Feldman Martha Plimpton

1986 DEADLY FRIEND
Director: Wes Craven
Co-stars: Matthew Laborteaux Kristy Swanson Anne Twomey

1987 THROW MOMMA FROM THE TRAIN
Director: Danny DeVito
Co-stars: Billy Crystal Kim Greist Danny DeVito

ANNE ELIZABETH RAMSEY

1992 A LEAGUE OF THEIR OWN
Director: Penny Marshall
Co-stars: Geena Davis Tom Hanks Madonna

MARION RAMSEY

1985 POLICE ACADEMY 2:
THEIR FIRST ASSIGNMENT
Director: Jerry Paris
Co-stars: Steve Guttenberg Bubba Smith

1986 POLICE ACADEMY 3: BACK IN TRAINING
Director: Jerry Paris
Co-stars: Steve Guttenberg Michael Winslow

1989 POLICE ACADEMY 6: CITY UNDER SIEGE
Director: Peter Bonerz
Co-stars: Bubba Smith Leslie Easterbrook

SALLY RAND

1928 A GIRL IN EVERY PORT
Director: Howard Hawks
Co-stars: Victor McLaglen Robert Armstrong Louise Brooks

1934 BOLERO
Director: Wesley Ruggles
Co-stars: George Raft Carole Lombard Ray Milland

ANNE RANDALL

1969 A TIME FOR DYING
Director: Budd Boetticher
Co-stars: Audie Murphy Richard Lapp Victor Jory

LEXI RANDALL (Child)

1991 SARAH, PLAIN AND TALL
Director: Glenn Jordan
Co-stars: Glenn Close Christopher Walken Jon DeVries

1992 IN THE BEST INTEREST OF THE CHILDREN
Director: Michael Ray Rhodes
Co-stars: Sarah Jessica Parker Elizabeth Ashley

1993 SKYLARK
Director: Joseph Sargent
Co-stars: Glenn Close Christopher Walken Christopher Bell

1996 THE WAR
Director: Roger Avnet
Co-stars: Kevin Costner Elijah Wood

MEG RANDALL

1948 THE LIFE OF RILEY
Director: Irving Brecher
Co-stars: William Bendix James Gleason Rosemary De Camp

1949 MA AND PA KETTLE
Director: Charles Lamont
Co-stars: Marjorie Main Percy Kilbride Richard Long

1952 WITHOUT WARNING
Director: Arnold Laven
Co-stars: Adam Williams Edward Binns

1957 LAST OF THE BADMEN
Director: Paul Landres
Co-stars: George Montgomery James Best Michael Ansara

STACIE RANDALL

1993 GHOULIES 4
Director: Jim Wynorski
Co-stars: Pete Liapis Raquel Krelle Bobby Di Cicco

1993 TRANCERS 4: JACK OF SWORDS
Director: David Nutter
Co-stars: Tim Thomerson Ty Miller

SUE RANDALL

1957 THE DESK SET
Director: Walter Lang
Co-stars: Spencer Tracy Katharine Hepburn Gig Young

THERESA RANDALL

1992 MALCOLM X
Director: Spike Lee
Co-stars: Denzel Washington Christopher Plummer Angela Bassett

1992 THE FIVE HEARTBEATS
Director: Robert Townsend
Co-stars: Robert Townsend Michael Wright Diahann Carroll

1993 SUGAR HILL
Director: Leon Ichaso
Co-stars: Wesley Snipes Michael Wright Abe Vigoda

1994 BEVERLY HILLS COP 3
Director: John Landis
Co-stars: Eddie Murphy Hector Elizondo Judge Reinhold

1996 GIRL 6
Director: Spike Lee
Co-star: Quentin Tarantino

MARY JO RANDLE

1990 INSPECTOR MORSE:
DRIVEN TO DISTRACTION
Director: Sandy Johnson
Co-stars: John Thaw Kevin Whately

1992 BAD BEHAVIOUR
Director: Les Blair
Co-stars: Stephen Rea Sinead Cusack Clare Higgins

BELLA RANDLES
1966 THE NAKED PREY
Director: Cornel Wilde
Co-stars: Cornel Wilde Gert Van Den Berg Ken Gampu

BEVERLEY RANDOLPH
1985 RETURN OF THE LIVING DEAD
Director: Dan O'Bannon
Co-stars: Clu Gulager James Karen Don Calfa

ELSIE RANDOLPH (*Married Jack Buchanan*)
1933 YES MR BROWN
Director: Herbert Wilcox
Co-stars: Jack Buchanan Hartley Power Clifford Heatherley

1933 THAT'S A GOOD GIRL
Director: Jack Buchanan
Co-stars: Jack Buchanan Dorothy Hyson Garry Marsh Vera Pearce

1936 THIS'LL MAKE YOU WHISTLE
Director: Herbert Wilcox
Co-stars: Jack Buchanan Jean Gillie William Kendall

1937 SMASH AND GRAB
Director: Tim Whelan
Co-stars: Jack Buchanan Zoe Wynn Arthur Margetson

ISABEL RANDOLPH
1944 PRACTICALLY YOURS
Director: Mitchell Leisen
Co-stars: Claudette Colbert Fred MacMurray Gil Lamb

1945 THE MISSING CORPSE
Director: Albert Herman
Co-stars: J. Edward Bromberg Ben Welden Frank Jenks

1945 TELL IT TO A STAR
Director: Frank McDonald
Co-stars: Ruth Terry Robert Livingston Alan Mowbray

JANE RANDOLPH
1942 CAT PEOPLE
Director: Jacques Tourneur
Co-stars: Simone Simon Kent Smith Tom Conway

1942 THE FALCON'S BROTHER
Director: Stanley Logan
Co-stars: George Sanders Tom Conway Keye Luke

1942 HIGHWAYS BY NIGHT
Director: Peter Godfrey
Co-stars: Richard Carlson Jane Darwell Barton Maclane

1944 THE CURSE OF THE CAT PEOPLE
Director: Robert Wise
Co-stars: Simone Simon Kent Smith Ann Carter

1945 JEALOUSY
Director: Gustav Muchaty
Co-stars: Nils Asther John Loder Karen Morley

1945 A SPORTING CHANCE
Co-star: Edward Gargan

1947 RAILROADED
Director: Anthony Mann
Co-stars: John Ireland Sheila Ryan Hugh Beaumont

**1948 ABBOTT AND COSTELLO
MEET FRANKENSTEIN**
Director: Charles Barton
Co-stars: Bud Abbott Lou Costello Bela Lugosi

LILLIAN RANDOLPH
1946 CHILD OF DIVORCE
Director: Richard Fleischer
Co-stars: Sharyn Moffet Regis Toomey Madge Meredith

PRUNELLA RANSOME
1967 FAR FROM THE MADDING CROWD
Director: John Schlesinger
Co-stars: Julie Christie Terence Stamp Alan Bates

1969 ALFRED THE GREAT
Director: Clive Donner
Co-stars: David Hemmings Michael York Colin Blakely

1971 MAN IN THE WILDERNESS
Director: Richard Sarafian
Co-stars: Richard Harris John Huston Henry Wilcoxon

STEPHANIE RASCOE
1987 POSITIVE ID
Director: Andy Anderson
Co-stars: John Davies Laura Lane Steve Fromholtz

KARIN RASENACH
1984 HEIMAT
Director: Edgar Reitz
Co-stars: Marita Breuer Dieter Schaad Michael Lesch

PHYLICIA RASHAD
1987 UNCLE TOM'S CABIN
Director: Stan Lathan
Co-stars: Bruce Dern Edward Woodward Kate Burton

1989 POLLY
Director: Debbie Allan
Co-stars: Keshie Knight Pulliam Celeste Holm Brock Peters

1990 POLLY, COMIN' HOME
Director: Debbie Allan
Co-stars: Keshie Knight Pulliam Celeste Holm Brock Peters

1989 FALSE WITNESS
Director: Arthur Allan Seidelman
Co-star: Philip Michael Thomas George Grizzard

1994 DAVID'S MOTHER
Director: Robert Allan Ackerman
Co-stars: Kirstie Alley Sam Waterston Stockard Channing

1996 THE BABYSITTER'S SEDUCTION
Director: David Burton Morris
Co-stars: Keri Russell Stephen Collins

SANDY RATCLIFFE
1971 FAMILY LIFE
Director: Ken Loach
Co-stars: Bill Dean Grace Cave Malcolm Tierney

1979 HUSSY
Director: Matthew Chapman
Co-stars: Helen Mirren John Shea Jenny Runacre

1994 MEN OF THE MONTH
Director: Jean Stuart
Co-stars: Douglas Hodge Alexander Morton Clare Higgins

DOLLY RATHEBE
1993 FRIENDS
Director: Elaine Proctor
Co-stars: Kerry Fox Dambisa Kente Michelle Birgers

HEATHER RATTRAY
1975 ADVENTURES OF THE WILDERNESS FAMILY
Director: Stuart Raffill
Co-stars: Robert Logan Ham Larsen

1977 ACROSS THE GREAT DIVIDE
Director: Stuart Raffill
Co-stars: Robert Logan George Flower

1978 SHIPWRECK !
Director: Stuart Raffill
Co-stars: Robert Logan Mikki Jamison-Olsen Sharron Naylor

1979 MOUNTAIN FAMILY ROBINSON
Director: John Cotter
Co-stars: Robert Logan Susan Damante Shaw Ham Larsen

1990 BASKET CASE 2
Director: Frank Hennenlotter
Co-stars: Kevin Van Hentenryck Judy Grafe Annie Ross

ANDREA RAU

1971 DAUGHTERS OF DARKNESS
Director: Harry Kumel
Co-stars: Delphine Seyrig John Karlen Paul Esser

SYBILLE RAUCH

1985 ALPHA CITY
Co-stars: Claude-Olivier Rudolph Al Corley

GINA RAVERA

1998 SOUL FOOD
Director: George Tillman Jnr.
Co-stars: Vanessa Williams Nia Long Vivica Fox

ELSA RAVEN

1988 THE MODERNS
Director: Alan Rudolph
Co-stars: Keith Carradine Linda Fiorentino John Lone

1990 DESCENDING ANGEL
Director: Jeremy Paul Kagan
Co-stars: Eric Roberts Diane Lane George C. Scott

THYRZA RAVESTEIJN

1996 ANTONIA'S LINE
Director: Marleen Gorris
Co-star: Willeke Van Ammerlrooy

LOUISE RAWLINGS

1958 MISTER SKEETER
Director: Colin Finbow
Co-stars: Peter Bayliss Orlando Wells Susannah York

MARGARET RAWLINGS

1953 ROMAN HOLIDAY
Director: William Wyler
Co-stars: Gregory Peck Audrey Hepburn Eddie Albert

1954 BEAUTIFUL STRANGER
Director: David Miller
Co-stars: Ginger Rogers Stanley Baker Herbert Lom

JACQUELINE RAY

1981 BEYOND THE UNIVERSE
Director: Allan Sandler
Co-stars: David Ladd Christopher Gary

LEAH RAY

1937 SING AND BE HAPPY
Co-stars: Tony Martin Dixie Dunbar

1937 THE HOLY TERROR
Director: James Tinling
Co-stars: Jane Withers Tony Martin Joan Davis

NATALIA RAY

1953 VOYAGE TO ITALY
Director: Roberto Rossellini
Co-stars: Ingrid Bergman George Sanders Paul Muller

RENE RAY

1935 THE PASSING OF THE THIRD FLOOR BACK
Director: Berthold Viertel
Co-stars: Conrad Veidt Anna Lee Mary Clare

1936 CRIME OVER LONDON
Director: Alfred Zeisler
Co-stars: Margot Grahame Paul Cavanagh Basil Sydney

1936 HIS LORDSHIP
Director: Herbert Mason
Co-stars: George Arliss Romilly Lunge Jessie Winter

1937 FAREWELL AGAIN
Director: Tim Whelan
Co-stars: Flora Robson Leslie Banks Robert Newton

1937 THE GREEN COCKATOO
Director: William Menzies
Co-stars: John Mills Robert Newton Bruce Seton

1937 PLEASE TEACHER
Director: Stafford Dickens
Co-stars: Bobby Howes Vera Pearce Wylie Watson

1937 THE RAT
Director: Jack Raymond
Co-stars: Anton Walbrook Ruth Chatterton Felix Aylmer

1938 THE RETURN OF THE FROG
Director: Maurice Elvey
Co-stars: Gordon Harker Una O'Connor Hartley Power

1938 BANK HOLIDAY
Director: Carol Reed
Co-stars: Margaret Lockwood Hugh Williams Linden Travers

1938 HOUSEMASTER
Director: Herbert Brenon
Co-stars: Otto Kruger Diana Churchill Phillips Holmes

1940 OLD BILL AND SON
Director: Ian Dalrymple
Co-stars: John Mills Morland Graham Mary Clare

1947 THEY MADE ME A FUGITIVE
Director: Alberto Cavalcanti
Co-stars: Trevor Howard Griffith Jones

1951 GALLOPING MAJOR
Director: Henry Cornelius
Co-stars: Basil Radford Janette Scott Hugh Griffith

1952 WOMEN OF TWILIGHT
Director: Gordon Parry
Co-stars: Freda Jackson Joan Dowling Laurence Harvey

1954 THE GOOD DIE YOUNG
Director: Lewis Gilbert
Co-stars: Laurence Harvey Gloria Grahame Joan Collins

1957 THE VICIOUS CIRCLE
Director: Gerald Thomas
Co-stars: John Mills Derek Farr Noelle Middleton

CAROL RAYE

1944 STRAWBERRY ROAN
Director: Maurice Elvey
Co-stars: William Hartnell Sophie Stewart Petula Clark

1945 WALTZ TIME
Director: Paul Stein
Co-stars: Peter Graves Richard Tauber Patricia Medina

1946 SPRING SONG
Co-star: Peter Graves

1946 GREEN FINGERS
Director: John Harlow
Co-stars: Robert Beatty Nova Pilbeam Felix Aylmer

1947 WHILE I LIVE
Director: John Harlow
Co-stars: Tom Walls Sonia Dresdel Clifford Evans

HELEN RAYE (Child)

1971 FLIGHT OF THE DOVES
Director: Ralph Nelson
Co-stars: Ron Moody Dorothy McGuire Jack Wild

MARTHA RAYE

1936 RHYTHM ON THE RANGE
Director: Norman Taurog
Co-stars: Bing Crosby Frances Farmer Bob Burns

1936 COLLEGE HOLIDAY
Director: Frank Tuttle
Co-stars: George Burns Gracie Allen Jack Benny

1936 THE BIG BROADCAST OF 1937
Director: Mitchell Leisen
Co-stars: George Burns Gracie Allen Jack Benny

1937 ARTISTS AND MODELS
Director: Raoul Walsh
Co-stars: Jack Benny Ida Lupino Ben Blue

1937 DOUBLE OR NOTHING
Director: Theodore Reed
Co-stars: Bing Crosby Andy Devine Mary Carlisle

1937 HIDEAWAY GIRL
Director: George Archainbaud
Co-stars: Shirley Ross Robert Cummings

1937 MOUNTAIN MUSIC
Director: Robert Florey
Co-stars: Bob Burns John Howard Fuzzy Knight

1937 WAIKIKI WEDDING
Director: Frank Tuttle
Co-stars: Bing Crosby Shirley Ross Bob Burns

1938 THE BIG BROADCAST OF 1938
Director: Mitchell Leisen
Co-stars: W.C. Fields Bob Hope Shirley Ross

1938 GIVE ME A SAILOR
Director: Elliott Nugent
Co-stars: Bob Hope Betty Grable Jack Whiting

1938 COLLEGE SWING
Director: Raoul Walsh
Co-stars: Bob Hope George Burns Gracie Allen

1939 NEVER SAY DIE
Director: Elliott Nugent
Co-stars: Bob Hope Andy Devine Monty Woolley

1939 TROPIC HOLIDAY
Director: Theodore Reed
Co-stars: Dorothy Lamour Ray Milland Bob Burns

1940 THE FARMER'S DAUGHTER
Director: James Hogan
Co-stars: Charles Ruggles Richard Denning

1940 THE BOYS FROM SYRACUSE
Director: Edward Sutherland
Co-stars: Allan Jones Joe Penner Rosemary Lane

1941 KEEP 'EM FLYING
Director: Arthur Lubin
Co-stars: Bud Abbott Lou Costello Dick Foran

1941 NAVY BLUES
Director: Lloyd Bacon
Co-stars: Jack Oakie Ann Sheridan Jack Haley

1942 HELLZAPOPPIN
Director: H.C. Potter
Co-stars: Ole Olsen Chic Johnson Robert Paige

1944 FOUR JILLS IN A JEEP
Director: William Seiter
Co-stars: Kay Francis Carole Landis Dick Haymes

1944 PIN UP GIRL
Director: Bruce Humberstone
Co-stars: Betty Grable John Harvey Joe E. Brown

1947 MONSIEUR VERDOUX
Director: Charles Chaplin
Co-star: Charles Chaplin Isabel Elsom

1962 JUMBO
Director: Charles Walters
Co-stars: Doris Day Jimmy Durante Stephen Boyd

1970 PUFNSTUF
Director: Hollingsworth Morse
Co-stars: Jack Wild Billie Hayes Mama Cass

1979 AIRPORT '80:THE CONCORDE
Director: David Lowell Rich
Co-stars: Alain Delon Susan Blakely Sylvia Kristel

CANDY RAYMOND

1978 MONEY MOVERS
Director: Bruce Beresford
Co-stars: Terence Donovan Bryan Brown Ed Devereaux

1983 MONKEY GRIP
Director: Ken Cameron
Co-stars: Noni Hazlehurst Colin Friels Alice Garner

JILL RAYMOND

1947 THE WOMAN IN THE HALL
Director: Jack Lee
Co-stars: Ursula Jeans Cecil Parker Jean Simmons

PAULA RAYMOND

1949 CHALLENGE OF THE RANGE
Co-star: Charles Starrett

1950 DEVIL'S DOORWAY
Director: Anthony Mann
Co-stars: Robert Taylor Louis Calhern Edgar Buchanan

1950 CRISIS
Director: Richard Brooks
Co-stars: Cary Grant Jose Ferrer Signe Hasso

1950 GROUNDS FOR MARRIAGE
Director: Robert Z. Leonard
Co-stars: Van Johnson Kathryn Grayson Lewis Stone

1950 DUCHESS OF IDAHO
Director: Robert Z. Leonard
Co-stars: Van Johnson Esther Williams Eleanor Powell

1951 TEXAS CARNIVAL
Director: Charles Walters
Co-stars: Esther Williams Howard Keel Red Skelton

1951 THE TALL TARGET
Director: Anthony Mann
Co-stars: Dick Powell Adolphe Menjou Marshall Thompson

1951 THE SELLOUT
Director: Gerald Meyer
Co-stars: Walter Pidgeon John Hodiak Audrey Totter

1951 INSIDE STRAIGHT
Director: Gerald Meyer
Co-stars: David Brian Arlene Dahl Barry Sullivan

1951 THE BANDITS OF CORSICA
Director: Ray Nazzaro
Co-stars: Richard Greene Raymond Burr Dona Drake

1953 THE BEAST FROM 20,000 FATHOMS
Director: Eugene Lourie
Co-stars: Paul Christian Cecil Kellaway

1953 THE CITY THAT NEVER SLEEPS
Director: John Auer
Co-stars: Gig Young Mala Powers Chill Wills

1954 THE HUMAN JUNGLE
Director: Joseph Newman
Co-stars: Gary Merrill Jan Sterling Regis Toomey

1961 THE FLIGHT THAT DISAPPEARED
Director: Reginald Le Borg
Co-stars: Addison Richards Gregory Morton Craig Hill

ROBIN RAYMOND

1944 LADIES OF WASHINGTON
Co-stars: Anthony Quinn Sheila Ryan

MINNIE RAYNER

1930 I LIVED WITH YOU
Director: Maurice Elvey
Co-stars: Ivor Novello Ursula Jeans Ida Lupino

1933 THIS WEEK OF GRACE
Director: Maurice Elvey
Co-stars: Gracie Fields Frank Pettingell Henry Kendall

DIANA RAYWORTH

1984 KNOCKBACK
Director: Piers Haggard
Co-stars: Pauline Collins Derrick O'Connor Peggy Atchison

1985 INSURANCE MAN
Director: Richard Eyre
Co-stars: Trevor Peacock Alan MacNaughton Daniel Day-Lewis

1990 HAPPY FEET
Director: Mike Bradwell
Co-stars: Phyllis Logan Stephen Hancock Derrick O'Connor

PEGGY REA

1990 ANGEL OF DEATH
Director: Bill Norton
Co-stars: Jane Seymour Gregory Harrison Ray Walston

1992 LOVE FIELD
Director: Jonathan Kaplan
Co-stars: Michelle Pfeiffer Dennis Haysbert Louise Latham

BARBARA READ

1936 THREE SMART GIRLS
Director: Henry Koster
Co-stars: Deanna Durbin Nan Grey Charles Winninger

1937 THE ROAD BACK
Director: James Whale
Co-stars: Richard Cromwell Slim Summerville Andy Devine

1937 THE MAN WHO CRIED WOLF
Director: Lewis Foster
Co-stars: Lewis Stone Tom Brown Marjorie Main

1937 MAKE WAY FOR TOMORROW
Director: Leo McCarey
Co-stars: Victor Moore Beulah Bondi Thomas Mitchell

1937 THE MIGHTY TREVE
Co-stars: Noah Beery Jnr. Samuel S. Hinds

1938 THE CRIME OF DR HALLET
Director: S. Sylvan Simon
Co-stars: Ralph Bellamy Josephine Hutchinson

1939 THE SPELLBINDER
Director: Jack Hively
Co-stars: Lee Tracy Patric Knowles Allan Lane

1940 CURTAIN CALL
Director: Frank Woodruff
Co-stars: Alan Mowbray Donald MacBride Helen Vinson

1946 THE SHADOW RETURNS
Co-stars: Kane Richmond Tom Dugan

1948 CORONER CREEK
Director: Ray Enright
Co-stars: Randolph Scott Marguerite Chapman George Macready

DOLLY READ

1970 BEYOND THE VALLEY OF THE DOLLS
Director: Russ Meyer
Co-stars: Cynthia Myers Marcia McBroom John Lazar

BEATRICE READING

1983 THE MOON IN THE GUTTER
Director: Jean-Jacques Beineix
Co-stars: Gerard Depardieu Nastassja Kinski

DONNA READING

1976 THE AMOROUS MILKMAN
Director: Derren Nesbitt
Co-stars: Julie Ege Diana Dors Brendan Price

SANDRA REAVES-PHILLIPS

1986 ROUND MIDNIGHT
Director: Bertrand Tavernier
Co-stars: Dexter Gordon Francois Cluzet Martin Scorsese

MARY-ROBIN REDD

1966 THE GROUP
Director: Sidney Lumet
Co-stars: Candice Bergen Joan Hackett Shirley Knight

HELEN REDDY

1974 AIRPORT '75
Director: Jack Smight
Co-stars: Charlton Heston Karen Black George Kennedy

1977 PETE'S DRAGON
Director: Don Chaffey
Co-stars: Sean Marshall Mickey Rooney Shelley Winters

LOIS RED ELK

1978 ISHI:THE LAST OF HIS TRIBE
Director: Robert Ellis Miller
Co-stars: Dennis Weaver Joseph Running-Fox

JEMMA REDGRAVE
(Daughter Of Corin Redgrave, Grand-Daughter Of Michael Redgrave, Niece Of Vanessa Redgrave)

1988 DREAM DEMON
Director: Harley Cockliss
Co-star: Mark Greenstreet

1989 THE REAL CHARLOTTE
Director: Tony Barry
Co-stars: Jeananne Crowley Patrick Bergin Joanna Roth

1992 HOWARDS END
Director: James Ivory
Co-stars: Anthony Hopkins Vanessa Redgrave Emma Thompson

LYNN REDGRAVE (*Sister Of Vanessa Redgrave*)
(Daughter Of Michael Redgrave & Rachel Kempson)
Nominated For Best Actress In 1966 For "Georgy Girl"

1963 TOM JONES
Director: Tony Richardson
Co-stars: Albert Finney Susannah York Hugh Griffith

1963 GIRL WITH GREEN EYES
Director: Desmond Davis
Co-stars: Rita Tushingham Peter Finch

1966 THE DEADLY AFFAIR
Director: Sidney Lumet
Co-stars: James Mason Simone Signoret Kenneth Haigh

1966 GEORGY GIRL
Director: Silvio Narizzano
Co-stars: James Mason Charlotte Rampling Alan Bates

1967 SMASHING TIME
Director: Desmond Davis
Co-stars: Rita Tushingham Ian Carmichael Michael York

1969 THE VIRGIN SOLDIERS
Director: John Dexter
Co-stars: Hywel Bennett Nigel Patrick Nigel Davenport

1972 EVERY LITTLE CROOK AND NANNY
Director: Cy Howard
Co-stars: Victor Mature Dom DeLuise Paul Sand

1972 EVERYTHING YOU ALWAYS WANTED TO KNOW ABOUT SEX ETC.
Director: Woody Allen
Co-star: Anthony Quayle Woody Allen Louise Lasser

1973 THE NATIONAL HEALTH
Director: Jack Gold
Co-stars: Jim Dale Eleanor Bron Donald Sinden

1975 THE HAPPY HOOKER
Director: Nicholas Sgarro
Co-stars: Jean-Pierre Aumont Lovelady Powell

1976 THE BIG BUS
Director: James Frawley
Co-stars: Joseph Bologna Jose Ferrer Ruth Gordon

1982 REHEARSAL FOR MURDER
Director: David Greene
Co-stars: Robert Preston Patrick MacNee Madolyn Smith

1984 THE SEDUCTION OF MISS LEONA
Director: Joseph Hardy
Co-stars: Anthony Zerbe Brian Dennehy

1988 A WOMAN ALONE
Director: Sharon Miller
Co-stars: Nicholas Teare Anthony Best

1988 DEATH OF A SON
Director: Ross Devenish
Co-stars: Malcolm Storry Jay Simpson Frederick Treves

1989 GETTING IT RIGHT
Director: Randal Kleiser
Co-stars: Jesse Birdsall Jane Horrocks Peter Cook

1991 WHATEVER HAPPENED TO BABY JANE ?
Director: David Greene
Co-stars: Vanessa Redgrave John Glover

1996 SHINE
Director: Scott Hick
Co-stars: Noah Taylor Geoffrey Rush Googie Withers

VANESSA REDGRAVE
(Daughter Of Michael Redgrave And Rachel Kempson, Sister Of Lynn Redgrave And Corin Redgrave, Married Tony Richardson, Mother Of Natasha, Miranda And Joely Richardson)
Oscar For Best Supporting Actress In 1977 For "Julia"
Nominated For Best Actress In 1966 For "Morgan - A Suitable Case For Treatment", In 1968 For "Isadora", In 1971 For "Mary Queen Of Scots" And In 1984 For "The Bostonians". Nominated For Best Supporting Actress In 1992 For "Howards End"

1958 BEHIND THE MASK
Director: Brian Desmond Hurst
Co-stars: Michael Redgrave Tony Britton Brenda Bruce

1966 BLOWUP
Director: Michaelangelo Antonioni
Co-stars: David Hemmings Sarah Miles Jane Birkin

1966 MORGAN - A SUITABLE CASE FOR TREATMENT
Director: Karel Reisz
Co-stars: David Warner Robert Stephens

1967 CAMELOT
Director: Joshua Logan
Co-stars: Richard Harris David Hemmings Franco Nero

1968 THE CHARGE OF THE LIGHT BRIGADE
Director: Tony Richardson
Co-stars: David Hemmings Trevor Howard

1968 OH! WHAT A LOVELY WAR
Director: Richard Attenborough
Co-stars: John Gielgud Laurence Olivier

1968 THE SEAGULL
Director: Sidney Lumet
Co-stars: James Mason Simone Signoret David Warner

1968 ISADORA
Director: Karel Reisz
Co-stars: Jason Robards James Fox John Fraser

1971 THE DEVIL
Director: Ken Russell
Co-stars: Oliver Reed Gemma Jones Dudley Sutton

1971 MARY QUEEN OF SCOTS
Director: Charles Jarrott
Co-stars: Glenda Jackson Trevor Howard Patrick McGoohan

1971 THE TROJAN WOMEN
Director: Michael Cacoyanis
Co-stars: Katherine Hepburn Irene Papas

1974 MURDER ON THE ORIENT EXPRESS
Director: Sidney Lumet
Co-stars: Albert Finney Ingrid Bergman Sean Connery

1975 OUT OF SEASON
Director: Alan Bridges
Co-stars: Cliff Robertson Susan George Edward Evans

1976 THE SEVEN PERCENT SOLUTION
Director: Herbert Ross
Co-stars: Nicol Williamson Robert Duvall

1977 JULIA
Director: Fred Zinnemann
Co-stars: Jane Fonda Jason Robards Hal Holbook

1979 AGATHA
Director: Michael Apted
Co-stars: Dustin Hoffman Timothy Dalton Timothy West

1979 BEAR ISLAND
Director: Don Sharp
Co-stars: Donald Sutherland Richard Widmark Christopher Lee

1979 YANKS
Director: John Schlesinger
Co-stars: Richard Gere Lisa Eichhorn William Devane

1980 PLAYING FOR TIME
Director: Daniel Mann
Co-stars: Jane Alexander Maud Adams Christine Baranski

1982 MY BODY, MY CHILD
Director: Marvin Chomsky
Co-stars: Jack Albertson Joseph Campanella Gail Strickland

1983 WAGNER
Director: Tony Palmer
Co-stars: Richard Burton Gemma Craven Marthe Keller

1984 THE BOSTONIANS
Director: James Ivory
Co-stars: Christopher Reeve Jessica Tandy Linda Hunt

1985 STEAMING
Director: Joseph Losey
Co-stars: Sarah Miles Diana Dors Patti Love

1985 WETHERBY
Director: David Hare
Co-stars: Ian Holm Judi Dench Stuart Wilson

1986 COMRADES
Director: Bill Douglas
Co-stars: James Fox Freddie Jones Imelda Staunton

1986 SECOND SERVE
Director: Anthony Page
Co-stars: Martin Balsam Alice Krige Louise Fletcher

1987 PRICK UP YOUR EARS
Director: Stephen Frears
Co-stars: Gary Oldman Alfred Molina Julie Walters

1988 A MAN FOR ALL SEASONS
Director: Charlton Heston
Co-stars: John Gielgud Richard Johnson Roy Kinnear

1988 CONSUMING PASSIONS
Director: Giles Foster
Co-stars: Jonathan Pryce Freddie Jones Sami Davis

1990 ORPHEUS DESCENDING
Director: Peter Hall
Co-stars: Kevin Anderson Ann Twomey Miriam Margoyles

1991 THE BALLAD OF THE SAD CAFÉ
Director: Simon Callow
Co-stars: Keith Carradine Rod Steiger Beth Dixon

1991 WHATEVER HAPPENED TO BABY JANE ?
Director: David Greene
Co-stars: Lynn Redgrave John Glover

1992 HOWARDS END
Director: James Ivory
Co-stars: Anthony Hopkins Emma Thompson Jemma Redgrave

1993 THE HOUSE OF THE SPIRITS
Director: Bille August
Co-stars: Jeremy Irons Glenn Close Meryl Streep

1993 THEY WATCH
Director: John Korty
Co-stars: Patrick Bergin Valerie Mahaffey

1993 MOTHER'S BOYS
Director: Yves Simoneau
Co-stars: Jamie Lee Curtis Joanne Whalley Peter Gallagher

1994 LITTLE ODESSA
Director: James Gray
Co-stars: Tim Roth Edward Furlong Maximilian Schell

1995 SPARROW
Director: Franco Zefferelli
Co-stars: Angela Bettis Jonathan Schaech

1996 MRS DALLOWAY
Director: Melee Gorris
Co-stars: Rupert Graves Natascha McElhone

1996 MISSION IMPOSSIBLE
Director: Brian De Palma
Co-stars: Tom Cruise Kristin Scott-Thomas Jon Voight

1996 A MONTH BY THE LAKE
Director: John Irvin
Co-stars: Edward Fox Uma Thurman Alessandro Gassman

1997 SMILLA'S FEELING FOR SNOW
Director: Bille August
Co-stars: Julia Ormond Gabriel Byrne Richard Harris

1997 WILDE
Director: Brian Gilbert
Co-stars: Stephen Fry Jude Law Jennifer Ehle

1998 DEEP IMPACT
Director: Mimi Leder
Co-stars: Tea Leoni Robert Duvall Morgan Freeman

1998 BELLA MAFIA
Co-stars: Nastassja Kinski Jennifer Tilly Ileana Douglas

AMANDA REDMAN

1980 RICHARD'S THINGS
Director: Anthony Harvey
Co-stars: Liv Ullman Tim Pigott-Smith Elizabeth Spriggs

1988 FOR QUEEN AND COUNTRY
Director: Martin Stellman
Co-stars: Denzel Washington George Baker

1990 THE LORELEI
Director: Terry Johnson
Co-stars: Michael Malony John Nettleton Iola Gregory

**1991 INSPECTOR WEXFORD:
FROM DOON WITH DEATH**
Director: Mary McMurray
Co-stars: George Baker Diane Keen

JOYCE REDMAN
Nominated For Best Supporting Actress In 1963 For "Tom Jones" And In 1965 For "Othello"

1941 ONE OF OUR AIRCRAFT IS MISSING
Director: Michael Powell
Co-stars: Godfrey Tearle Eric Portman Hugh Williams

1963 TOM JONES
Director: Tony Richardson
Co-stars: Albert Finney Susannah York Hugh Griffith

1965 OTHELLO
Director: Stuart Burge
Co-stars: Laurence Olivier Frank Finlay Maggie Smith

1969 PRUDENCE AND THE PILL
Director: Fielder Cook
Co-stars: David Niven Deborah Kerr Judy Geeson

1978 LES MISERABLES
Director: Glenn Jordan
Co-stars: Richard Jordan Anthony Perkins Flora Robson

MARGE REDMOND

1966 THE TROUBLE WITH ANGELS
Director: Ida Lupino
Co-stars: Rosalind Russell Hayley Mills June Harding

1973 A BRAND NEW LIFE
Director: Sam O'Steen
Co-stars: Cloris Leachman Martin Balsam Gene Nelson

MOIRA REDMOND

1961 PIT OF DARKNESS
Director: Lance Comfort
Co-stars: William Franklyn Leonard Sachs Nanette Newman

1962 KILL OR CURE
Director: George Pollock
Co-stars: Terry-Thomas Eric Sykes Dennis Price

1964 NIGHTMARE
Director: Freddie Francis
Co-stars: David Knight Brenda Bruce Jennie Linden

1992 SUDDENLY, LAST SUMMER
Director: Richard Eyre
Co-stars: Maggie Smith Natasha Richardson Rob Lowe

SIOBHAN REDMOND

1987 THE DUNROAMIN' RISING
Director: Moira Armstrong
Co-stars: Russell Hunter Elizabeth Sellars Hugh Lloyd

1992 THE ADVOCATES:ABOVE THE LAW
Director: Peter Barber-Fleming
Co-stars: Isla Blair Ewan Stewart Hugh Ross

1994 CAPTIVES
Director: Angela Pope
Co-stars: Tim Roth Julia Ormond Keith Allen

ALYSON REED

1985 A CHORUS LINE
Director: Richard Attenborough
Co-stars: Michael Douglas Terence Mann Vicki Frederick

1989 SKIN DEEP
Director: Blake Edwards
Co-stars: John Ritter Vincent Gardenia Chelsea Field

DONNA REED
Oscar For Best Supporting Actress In 1953For "From Here To Eternity"

1941 THE GETAWAY
Director: Edward Buzzell
Co-stars: Robert Sterling Dan Dailey

1941 THE BUGLE SOUNDS
Director: S. Sylvan Simon
Co-stars: Wallace Beery Marjorie Main William Lundigan

1941 SHADOW OF THE THIN MAN
Director: W.S. Van Dyke
Co-stars: William Powell Myrna Loy Barry Nelson

1942 EYES IN THE NIGHT
Director: Fred Zinnemann
Co-stars: Edward Arnold Ann Harding Allen Jenkins

1942 THE COURTSHIP OF ANDY HARDY
Director: George Seitz
Co-stars: Mickey Rooney Lewis Stone William Lundigan

1942 CALLING DR GILLESPIE
Director: Harold Bucquet
Co-stars: Lionel Barrymore Philip Dorn Nat Pendleton

1942 APACHE TRAIL
Director: Richard Thorpe
Co-stars: Lloyd Nolan William Lundigan

1943 DR GILLESPIE'S CRIMINAL CASE
Director: Willis Goldbeck
Co-stars: Lionel Barrymore Margaret O'Brien

1943 THE HUMAN COMEDY
Director: Clarence Brown
Co-stars: Mickey Rooney Frank Morgan James Craig

1943 THE MAN FROM DOWN UNDER
Director: Robert Z. Leonard
Co-stars: Charles Laughton Binnie Barnes Richard Carlson

1944 SEE HERE PRIVATE HARGROVE
Director: Wesley Ruggles
Co-stars: Robert Walker Robert Benchley Keenan Wynn

1944 GENTLE ANNIE
Director: Andrew Marton
Co-stars: Marjorie Main James Craig Henry Morgan

1945 WHAT NEXT CORPORAL HARGROVE
Co-stars: Robert Walker Chill Wills Paul Langton

1944 THE PICTURE OF DORIAN GRAY
Director: Albert Lewin
Co-stars: Hurd Hatfield George Sanders Angela Lansbury

1945 THEY WERE EXPENDABLE
Director: John Ford
Co-stars: John Wayne Robert Montgomery Jack Holt

1946 IT'S A WONDERFUL LIFE
Director: Frank Capra
Co-stars: James Stewart Henry Travers Thomas Mitchell

1946 FAITHFUL IN MY FASHION
Director: Sidney Salkow
Co-stars: Tom Drake Spring Byington Sig Ruman

1947 GREEN DOLPHIN STREET
Director: Victor Saville
Co-stars: Lana Turner Van Heflin Edmund Gwenn

1948 BEYOND GLORY
Director: John Farrow
Co-stars: Alan Ladd Audie Murphy George Coulouris

1949 CHICAGO DEADLINE
Director: Lewis Allen
Co-stars: Alan Ladd June Havoc Arthur Kennedy

1951 SATURDAY'S HERO
Director: David Miller
Co-stars: John Derek Sidney Blackmer Alexander Knox

1952 SCANDAL SHEET
Director: Phil Karlson
Co-stars: John Derek Broderick Crawford Rosemary DeCamp

1952 HANGMAN'S KNOT
Director: Roy Huggins
Co-stars: Randolph Scott Claude Jarman Lee Marvin

1953 GUN FURY
Director: Raoul Walsh
Co-stars: Rock Hudson Lee Marvin Phil Carey

1953 FROM HERE TO ETERNITY
Director: Fred Zinnemann
Co-stars: Burt Lancaster Frank Sinatra Deborah Kerr

1953 THE CADDY
Director: Norman Taurog
Co-stars: Dean Martin Jerry Lewis Barbara Bates

1953 TROUBLE ALONG THE WAY
Director: Michael Curtiz
Co-stars: John Wayne Charles Coburn Tom Tully

1954 THE LAST TIME I SAW PARIS
Director: Richard Brooks
Co-stars: Elizabeth Taylor Van Johnson Eva Gabor

1954 THREE HOURS TO KILL
Director: Alfred Werker
Co-stars: Dana Andrews Dianne Foster Stephen Elliott

1954 THEY RODE WEST
Director: Phil Karlson
Co-stars: Phil Carey Jack Kelly May Wynn

1955 THE FAR HORIZONS
Director: Rudolph Mate
Co-stars: Fred MacMurray Charlton Heston Barbara Hale

1955 BEYOND MOMBASSA
Director: George Marshall
Co-stars: Cornel Wilde Ron Randell Leo Genn

1955 THE BENNY GOODMAN STORY
Director: Valentine Davies
Co-stars: Steve Allen Sammy Davis. Harry James

1956 RANSOM
Director: Alex Segal
Co-stars: Glenn Ford Leslie Nielsen Robert Keith

1958 THE WHOLE TRUTH
Director: John Guillermin
Co-stars: Stewart Granger George Sanders

1983 DEADLY LESSONS
Director: William Wiard
Co-stars: Larry Wilcox Ally Sheedy David Ackroyd

FLORENCE REED

1934 GREAT EXPECTATIONS
Director: Stuart Walker
Co-stars: Phillips Holmes Jane Wyatt Henry Hull

GAYLE REED

1950 JOHNNY ONE-EYE
Director: Robert Florey
Co-stars: Pat O'Brien Wayne Morris Dolores Moran

LYDIA REED *(Child)*

1955 SEVEN LITTLE FOYS
Director: Melville Shavelson
Co-stars: Bob Hope Milly Vitale George Tobias

1956 HIGH SOCIETY
Director: Charles Walters
Co-stars: Bing Crosby Grace Kelly Frank Sinatra

1957 THE VAMPIRE
Director: Paul Landres
Co-stars: John Beal Coleen Gray Raymond Greenleaf

MIRIAM REED

1992 RUBY CAIRO
Director: Graeme Clifford
Co-stars: Andie MacDowell Liam Neesen Viggo Mortensen

PAMELA REED

1980 MELVIN AND HOWARD
Director: Jonathan Demme
Co-stars: Paul LeMat Jason Robards Mary Steenburgen

1980 THE LONG RIDERS
Director: Walter Hill
Co-stars: David Carradine Keith Carradine Dennis Quaid

1981 EYE WITNESS
Director: Peter Yates
Co-stars: William Hurt Christopher Plummer Sigourney Weaver

1983 I WANT TO LIVE
Director: David Lowell Rich
Co-stars: Lindsay Wagner Martin Balsam Seymour Cassel

1983 THE RIGHT STUFF
Director: Philip Kaufman
Co-stars: Sam Shepard Scott Glenn Ed Harris

1984 THE GOODBYE PEOPLE
Director: Herb Gardner
Co-stars: Martin Balsam Judd Hirsch Ron Silver

1985 CLAN OF THE CAVE BEAR
Director: Michael Chapman
Co-stars: Daryl Hannah James Remar Thomas G. Waites

1985 THE BEST OF TIMES
Director: Roger Spottiswoode
Co-stars: Robin Williams Kurt Russell Holly Palance

1985 SCANDAL SHEET
Director: David Lowell Rich
Co-stars: Burt Lancaster Robert Urich Lauren Hutton

1987 RACHEL RIVER
Director: Sandy Smolan
Co-stars: Zeljko Ivanek James Olson Viveca Lindfors

1990 CAROLINE ?
Dire2ctor Joseph Sargent
Co-stars: Stephanie Zimbalist Patricia Neal Dorothy McGuire

1990 KINDERGARTEN COP
Director: Ivan Reitman
Co-stars: Arnold Schwarzenegger Linda Hunt Carroll Baker

1990 CHATTAHOOCHEE
Director: Mick Jackson
Co-stars: Gary Oldman Dennis Hopper Frances McDormand

1990 CADILLAC MAN
Director: Roger Donaldson
Co-stars: Robin Williams Tim Robbins Zack Norman

1992 PASSED AWAY
Director: Charlie Peters
Co-stars: Bob Hoskins Jack Warden Maureen Stapleton

1993 BORN TOO SOON
Director: Noel Hossek
Co-star: Michael Moriarty

1994 DEADLY WHISPERS
Director: Bill Norton
Co-stars: Tony Danza Ving Rhames

1995 THE MAN NEXT DOOR
Director: Lamont Johnson
Co-star: Michael Ontkean

SHANNA REED

1983 LEGS
Director: Jerrold Freedman
Co-stars: Gwen Verdon John Heard Sheree North

1985 MIRRORS
Director: Harry Winer
Co-stars: Timothy Daly Anthony Hamilton Signe Hasso

1990 COINS IN THE FOUNTAIN
Director: Tony Wharmby
Co-stars: Loni Anderson Stepfanie Kramer Anthony Newley

1993 MOMENT OF TRUTH:STALKING BACK
Director: Corey Allen

1994 SEEDS OF DECEPTION
Director: Arlene Sanford
Co-stars: Melissa Gilbert Tom Verica

1994 DON'T TALK TO STRANGERS
Director: Robert Lewis
Co-stars: Pierce Brosnan Terry O'Quinn

1996 UNLIKELY SUSPECTS
Director: Joseph L. Scanlan

1996 RATTLED
Director: Tony Randell
Co-stars: William Katt Ed Lauter

SUZANNE REED

1975 BEYOND THE BERMUDA TRIANGLE
Director: William Graham
Co-stars: Fred MacMurray Donna Mills

TRACY REED

1963 **DR STRANGELOVE**
Director: Stanley Kubrick
Co-stars: Peter Sellers George C. Scott Sterling Hayden

1964 **DEVILS OF DARKNESS**
Director: Lance Comfort
Co-stars: William Sylvester Diana Decker Rona Anderson

1964 **A SHOT IN THE DARK**
Director: Blake Edwards
Co-stars: Peter Sellers Elke Sommer George Sanders

1967 **MAROC 7**
Director: Gerry O'Hara
Co-stars: Gene Barry Elsa Martinelli Cyd Charisse

1976 **CAR WASH**
Director: Michael Schultz
Co-stars: Franklyn Ajaye Sully Boyar Richard Pryor

1977 **A PIECE OF THE ACTION**
Director: Sidney Poitier
Co-stars: Sidney Poitier James Earl Jones Bill Cosby Hope Clarke

1978 **SAMMY'S SUPER T-SHIRT**
Director: Jeremy Summers
Co-stars: Reggie Winch Richard Vernon Patsy Rowlands

1981 **THE CALIFORNIA DOLLS**
Director: Robert Aldrich
Co-stars: Peter Falk Vicki Frederick Burt Young

1984 **SINS OF THE PAST**
Director: Peter Hunt
Co-stars: Barbara Carrera Kim Cattrall Kirstie Alley

1986 **RUNNING SCARED**
Director: Peter Hyams
Co-stars: Gregory Hines Billy Crystal Steven Bauer

ANGHARAD REES

1971 **UNDER MILK WOOD**
Director: Andrew Sinclair
Co-stars: Richard Burton Elizabeth Taylor Peter O'Toole

1971 **HANDS OF THE RIPPER**
Director: Peter Sasdy
Co-stars: Eric Porter Dora Bryan Jane Merrow

1973 **IT'S A 2' 6" ABOVE THE GROUND WORLD**
Director: Ralph Thomas
Co-stars: Nanette Newman Hywel Bennett

1988 **THE TEMPTATION OF EILEEN HUGHES**
Director: Tristram Powell
Co-stars: Jim Norton Ethna Roddy John Pine

BETTY ANNE REES

1972 **THE UNHOLY ROLLERS**
Director: Vernon Zimmerman
Co-stars: Claudia Jennings Louis Quinn Roberta Collins

DONOGH REES

1984 **CONSTANCE**
Director: Bruce Morrison
Co-stars: Shane Briant Judie Douglass Martin Vaughan

1992 **CRUSH**
Director: Alison Maclean
Co-stars: Marcia Gay Harden William Zappa Caitlin Bossley

JOAN REES

1944 **LOVE STORY**
Director: Leslie Arliss
Co-stars: Margaret Lockwood Stewart Granger Patricia Roc

SHELLEY REES

1993 **LEAVING LENIN**
Director: Endaf Emlyn
Co-stars: Sharon Morgan Richard Harrington Catrin Mai

YVETTE REES

1965 **CURSE OF THE FLY**
Director: Don Sharp
Co-stars: Brian Donlevy George Baker Carole Gray

BARBARA REESE

1987 **HOUSEKEEPING**
Director: Bill Forsyth
Co-stars: Christine Lahti Sara Walker Anne Pitoniak

DELLA REESE

1989 **HARLEM NIGHTS**
Director: Eddie Murphy
Co-stars: Richard Pryor Danny Aiello Eddie Murphy

ADA REEVE

1944 **THEY CAME TO A CITY**
Director: Basil Dearden
Co-stars: Googie Withers John Clements Raymond Huntley

1952 **I BELIEVE IN YOU**
Director: Basil Dearden
Co-stars: Celia Johnson Cecil Parker Joan Collins

1956 **EYEWITNESS**
Director: Muriel Box
Co-stars: Donald Sinden Muriel Pavlow Belinda Lee

LISA REEVES

1977 **THE CHICKEN CHRONICLES**
Director: Francis Simon
Co-stars: Phil Silvers Steve Guttenberg Ed Lauter

SASKIA REEVES

1990 **ANTONIA AND JANE: A DEFINITIVE REPORT**
Director: Beeban Kidron
Co-stars: Imelda Staunton Brenda Bruce

1990 **THE BRIDGE**
Director: Syd Macartney
Co-stars: David O'Hara Joss Ackland Geraldine James

1990 **CHILDREN CROSSING**
Director: Angela Pope
Co-stars: Peter Firth Bob Peck Richard Hope

1991 **CLOSE MY EYES**
Director: Stephen Polliakoff
Co-stars: Clive Owen Alan Rickman

1991 **DECEMBER BRIDE**
Director: Thadeus O'Sullivan
Co-stars: Donal McCann Frank Echlin Brenda Bruce

1995 **BUTTERFLY KISS**

JAYNE REGAN

1938 **BOOLOO**
Co-star: Colin Tapley

LINDA REGAN

1975 **CONFESSIONS OF A POP PERFORMER**
Director: Norman Cohen
Co-stars: Robin Askwith Anthony Booth

RIFF REGAN

1991 **MURDER IN NEW HAMPSHIRE**
Director: Joyce Chopra
Co-stars: Helen Hunt Chad Allen Ken Howard

NADJA REGIN

1957 THE MAN WITHOUT A BODY
Director: Charles Saunders
Co-stars: George Coulouris Robert Hutton Julia Arnall

1959 DON'T PANIC CHAPS !
Director: George Pollock
Co-stars: Dennis Price George Cole Harry Fowler

1963 FROM RUSSIA WITH LOVE
Director: Terence Young
Co-stars: Sean Connery Robert Shaw Lotte Lenya

CAROLA REGNIER

1985 SEDUCTION: THE CRUEL WOMAN
Director: Monika Treut
Co-stars: Mechthild Grossman Udo Lier Peter Weibel

1988 FURTHER AND PARTICULAR
Director: Steve Dwoskin
Co-stars: Richard Butler Irene Marot Jean Fennell

MARTHE REGNIER

1935 MAYERLING
Director: Anatole Litvak
Co-stars: Charles Boyer Danielle Darrieux Suzy Prim

BERYL REID

1954 THE BELLES OF ST. TRINIAN'S
Director: Frank Launder
Co-stars: Alastair Sim George Cole Joyce Grenfell

1956 THE EXTRA DAY
Director: William Fairchild
Co-stars: Richard Basehart Simone Simon George Baker

1960 TWO-WAY STRETCH
Director: Robert Day
Co-stars: Peter Sellers Lionel Jeffries Liz Fraser

1962 THE DOCK BRIEF
Director: James Hill
Co-stars: Peter Sellers Richard Attenborough Frank Pettingell

1968 THE ASSASSINATION BUREAU
Director: Basil Dearden
Co-stars: Oliver Reed Diana Rigg Telly Savalas

1968 INSPECTOR CLOUSEAU
Director: Bud Yorkin
Co-stars: Alan Arkin Delia Boccardo Frank Finlay

1968 STAR !
Director: Robert Wise
Co-stars: Julie Andrews Daniel Massey Michael Craig

1969 THE KILLING OF SISTER GEORGE
Director: Robert Aldrich
Co-stars: Susannah York Coral Browne

1969 ENTERTAINING MR SLOANE
Director: Douglas Hickox
Co-stars: Harry Andrews Peter McEnery Alan Webb

1970 THE BEAST IN THE CELLAR
Director: James Kelly
Co-stars: Flora Robson Tessa Wyatt T.P. McKenna

1972 DR PHIBES RISES AGAIN
Director: Robert Fuest
Co-stars: Vincent Price Valli Kemp Fiona Lewis

1973 FATHER DEAR FATHER
Director: William Stewart
Co-stars: Patrick Cargill Donald Sinden

1973 NO SEX PLEASE WE'RE BRITISH
Director: Cliff Owen
Co-stars: Ronnie Corbett Arthur Lowe David Swift

1973 PSYCHOMANIA
Director: Don Sharp
Co-stars: George Sanders Nicky Henson Robert Hardy

1977 JOSEPH ANDREWS
Director: Tony Richardson
Co-stars: Peter Firth Ann-Margret Hugh Griffith

1978 CARRY ON EMMANUELLE
Director: Gerald Thomas
Co-stars: Suzanne Danielle Kenneth Williams Kenneth Connor

1979 TINKER, TAILOR, SOLDIER, SPY
Director: John Irvin
Co-stars: Alec Guinness Bernard Hepton Terence Rigby

FIONA REID

1983 ACCIDENT AT MEMORIAL STATION
Director: Donald Brittain
Co-stars: Terence Kelly Frank Perry

FRANCES REID

1973 THE AFFAIR
Director: Gilbert Cates
Co-stars: Natalie Wood Robert Wagner Bruce Davison

1988 MERCY OR MURDER ?
Director: Steve Gethers
Co-stars: Robert Young Michael Learned Eddie Albert

KATE REID

1966 THIS PROPERTY IS CONDEMNED
Director: Sydney Pollack
Co-stars: Natalie Wood Robert Redford Charles Bronson

1970 THE ANDROMEDA STRAIN
Director: Robert Wise
Co-stars: Arthur Hill David Wayne James Olson

1973 A DELICATE BALANCE
Director: Tony Richardson
Co-stars: Katherine Hepburn Paul Scofield Lee Remick

1973 HAWKINS ON MURDER
Director: Jud Taylor
Co-stars: James Stewart Bonnie Bedelia Strother Martin

1973 SHE CRIED MURDER
Director: Herschel Daughterty
Co-stars: Telly Savalas Lynda Day George Jeff Toner

1977 EQUUS
Director: Sidney Lumet
Co-stars: Richard Burton Peter Firth Jenny Agutter

1980 DOUBLE NEGATIVE
Director: George Bloomfield
Co-stars: Michael Sarrazin Susan Clark Anthony Perkins

1980 DEATH SHIP
Director: Alvin Rakoff
Co-stars: George Kennedy Richard Crenna Sally Ann Howes

1980 CIRCLE OF TWO
Director: Jules Dassin
Co-stars: Richard Burton Tatum O'Neal Nuala Fitzgerald

1981 ATLANTIC CITY
Director: Louis Malle
Co-stars: Burt Lancaster Susan Sarandon Michel Piccoli

1984 HIGHPOINT
Director: Peter Carter
Co-stars: Richard Harris Christopher Plummer Beverly D'Angelo

1985 CATHOLIC BOYS
Director: Michael Dinner
Co-stars: Donald Sutherland Andrew McCarthy John Heard

1985 DEATH OF A SALESMAN
Director: Volker Schlondorff
Co-stars: Dustin Hoffman John Malkovich Stephen Lang

1986 FIRE WITH FIRE
Director: Duncan Gibbins
Co-stars: Virginia Madsen Craig Sheffer Jon Polito

1988 SWEET HEARTS DANCE
Director: Robert Greenwald
Co-stars: Don Johnson Susan Sarandon Jeff Daniels

1990 THE LAST BEST YEAR
Director: John Erman
Co-stars: Mary Tyler Moore Bernadette Peters Dorothy McGuire

1992 DECEIVED
Director: Damian Harris
Co-stars: Goldie Hawn John Heard Beatrice Straight

SHEILA REID

1971 THE TOUCH
Director: Ingmar Bergman
Co-stars: Bibi Andersson Elliott Gould Max Von Sydow

1988 RASPBERRY RIPPLE
Director: Nigel Finch
Co-stars: John Gordon Sinclair Faye Dunaway Rosie Kerslake

GABRIELLE REIDY

1983 EDUCATING RITA
Director: Lewis Gilbert
Co-stars: Julie Walters Michael Caine Michael Williams

1991 ROBIN HOOD
Director: John Irvin
Co-stars: Patrick Bergin Uma Thurman Edward Fox

1991 DECEMBER BRIDE
Director: Thaddeus O'Sullivan
Co-stars: Donal McCann Saskia Reeves Brenda Bruce

1993 THE BABY OF MACON
Director: Peter Greenaway
Co-stars: Julia Ormond Ralph Fiennes Philip Stone

1994 ALL THINGS BRIGHT AND BEAUTIFUL
Director: Barry Devlin
Co-stars: Ciaran Fitzgerald Tom Wilkinson

MAXINE REINER

1936 CHARLIE CHAN AT THE CIRCUS
Director: Harry Lachman
Co-stars: Warner Oland Keye Luke J. Carrol Naish

TRACY REINER

1991 NEW YEARS DAY
Director: Henry Jaglom
Co-stars: Maggie Jakobson Gwen Welles David Duchovny

1992 A LEAGUE OF THEIR OWN
Director: Penny Marshall
Co-stars: Geena Davis Madonna Tom Hanks

ANNA REINKING

1979 ALL THAT JAZZ
Director: Bob Fosse
Co-stars: Roy Scheider Jessica Lange Ben Vereen

1982 ANNIE
Director: John Huston
Co-stars: Albert Finney Carol Burnett Aileen Quinn

1984 MICKI AND MAUDE
Director: Blake Edwards
Co-stars: Dudley Moore Amy Irving Richard Mulligan

DIANA REIS

1986 APOLOGY FOR MURDER
Director: Robert Bierman
Co-stars: Lesley Ann Warren Peter Weller John Glover

WHITNEY REIS

1990 CHOPPER CHICKS IN ZOMBIETOWN
Director: Dan Hoskins
Co-stars: Jamie Rose Vicki Frederick Lycia Naff

SYLVIA REIZE

1984 IN THE BELLY OF THE WHALE
Director: Doris Dorrie
Co-stars: Janna Marangosoff Eisi Gulp Peter Saltman

MARIE-THERESE RELIN

1984 SECRET PLACES
Director: Zelda Baron
Co-stars: Tara MacGowran Jenny Agutter Claudine Auger

ERIKA REMBERG

1960 CIRCUS OF HORRORS
Director: Sidney Hayers
Co-stars: Anton Diffring Yvonne Monlaur Donald Pleasance

1963 SATURDAY NIGHT OUT
Director: Robert Hartford-Davis
Co-stars: Bernard Lee Heather Sears Nigel Green

LEE REMICK
Nominated For Best Actress In 1962 For "Days Of Wine And Roses"

1955 A FACE IN THE CROWD
Director: Elia Kazan
Co-stars: Andy Griffith Patricia Neal Walter Matthau

1958 THESE THOUSAND HILLS
Director: Richard Fleischer
Co-stars: Don Murray Richard Egan Stuart Whitman

1958 THE LONG HOT SUMMER
Director: Martin Ritt
Co-stars: Paul Newman Orson Welles Joanne Woodward

1959 ANATOMY OF A MURDER
Director: Otto Preminger
Co-stars: James Stewart Arthur O'Conell Ben Gazzara

1960 WILD RIVER
Director: Elia Kazan
Co-stars: Montgomery Clift Jo Van Fleet Bruce Dern

1961 SANCTUARY
Director: Tony Richardson
Co-stars: Bradford Dillman Yves Montand Odetta

1962 EXPERIMENT IN TERROR
Director: Blake Edwards
Co-stars: Glenn Ford Stephanie Powers Ross Martin

1962 DAYS OF WINE AND ROSES
Director: Blake Edwards
Co-stars: Jack Lemmon Charles Bickford Jack Klugman

1963 THE RUNNING MAN
Director: Carol Reed
Co-stars: Laurence Harvey Alan Bates Felix Aylmer

1963 SEPARATE BEDS
Director: Arther Hiller
Co-stars: James Garner Phil Harris Chill Wills

1964 BABY THE RAIN MUST FALL
Director: Robert Mulligan
Co-stars: Steve McQueen Don Murray Paul Fix

1965 THE HALLELUJAH TRAIL
Director: John Sturges
Co-stars: Burt Lancaster Brian Keith Donald Pleasence

1968 NO WAY TO TREAT A LADY
Director: Jack Smight
Co-stars: Rod Steiger George Segal Michael Dunn

1968 THE DETECTIVE
Director: Gordon Douglas
Co-stars: Frank Sinatra Jacqueline Bisset Ralph Meeker

1970 LOOT
Director: Silvio Narizzano
Co-stars: Richard Attenborough Hywel Bennett Dick Emery

1970 HARD CONTRACT
Director: Lee Pogostin
Co-stars: James Coburn Lilli Palmer Burgess Meredith

1970 A SEVERED HEAD
Director: Dick Clement
Co-stars: Ian Holm Claire Bloom Jennie Linden

1971 NEVER GIVE AN INCH
Director: Paul Newman
Co-stars: Henry Fonda Michael Sarrazin Paul Newman

1973 A DELICATE BALANCE
Director: Tony Richardson
Co-stars: Katharine Hepburn Paul Scofield Joseph Cotten

1973 THE BLUE KNIGHT
Director: Robert Butler
Co-stars: William Holden Joe Santos Sam Elliott

1975 HENNESSY
Director: Don Sharp
Co-stars: Rod Steiger Richard Johnson Trevor Howard

1975 A GIRL NAMED SOONER
Director: Delbert Mann

1976 THE HUNTED

1976 THE OMEN
Director: Richard Donner
Co-stars: Gregory Peck David Warner Billie Whitelaw

1977 TELEFON
Director: Don Siegel
Co-stars: Charles Bronson Alan Badel Sheree North

1978 THE MEDUSA TOUCH
Director: Jack Gold
Co-stars: Richard Burton Lino Ventura Alan Badel

1978 BREAKING UP
Director: Delbert Mann

1979 TORN BETWEEN TWO LOVERS
Director: Delbert Mann
Co-stars: George Peppard Joseph Bologna Molly Cheek

1980 THE COMPETITION
Director: Joel Oliansky
Co-stars: Richard Dreyfuss Amy Irving Sam Wanamaker

1981 TRIBUTE
Director: Bob Clarke
Co-stars: Jack Lemmon Bobby Benson Colleen Dewhurst

1981 VISITING HOURS
Director: Jean-Claude Lord
Co-stars: Michael Ironside Linda Purl William Shatner

1979 THE EUROPEANS
Director: James Ivory
Co-stars: Robin Ellis Tim Woodward Lisa Eichhorn

1982 THE LETTER
Director: John Erman
Co-stars: Ronald Pickup Ian McShane Jack Thompson

1984 A GOOD SPORT
Director: Lou Antonio
Co-stars: Ralph Waite Sam Gray Antonio Fargas

1986 OF PURE BLOOD
Director: Joseph Sargent
Co-stars: Patrick McGoohan Gottfreid John

1987 THE VISION
Director: Norman Stone
Co-stars: Dirk Bogarde Eileen Atkins Lynda Bellingham

1988 JESSE
Director: Glenn Jordan
Co-stars: Scott Wilson Richard Marcus Albert Salmi

1988 AROUND THE WORLD IN EIGHTY DAYS
Director: Buzz Kulik
Co-stars: Pierce Brosnan Eric Idle Peter Ustinov

1988 BRIDGE TO SILENCE

1989 PASSPORT TO TERROR
Director: Lou Antonio
Co-stars: Norma Aleando Tony Goldwyn Roy Thinnes

COLETTE RENARD

1992 IP5
Director: Jean-Jacques Beiniex
Co-stars: Yves Montand Olivier Martinez Sekkou Sall

MADELEINE RENAUD

1932 LA MATERNELLE
Director: Marie Epstein
Co-stars: Paulette Elambert Alice Tissot Mady Berry

1935 MARIA CHAPDELAINE
Director: Julien Duvivier
Co-stars: Jean Gabin Suzanne Despres Jean-Pierre Aumont

1941 STORMY WATERS
Director: Jean Gremillon
Co-stars: Jean Gabin Michele Morgan Jean Marchat

1943 LUMIERE D'ETE
Director: Jean Gremillon
Co-stars: Pierre Brasseur Madeleine Robinson Jane Marken

1952 LE PLAISIR
Director: Max Ophuls
Co-stars: Claude Dauphin Danielle Darrieux Simone Simon

SIMONE RENAULT

1965 BEDEVILLED
Director: Mitchell Leisen
Co-stars: Anne Baxter Steve Forrest Joseph Tomelty

DOROTHY RENIER

1930 A LADY TO LOVE
Director: Victor Seastrom
Co-stars: Edward G. Robinson Vilma Banky Robert Ames

KATHARINA RENN

1966 THE RISE TO POWER OF LOUIS XIV
Director: Roberto Rossellini
Co-stars: Jean-Marie Patte Raymond Jourdan

SIMONE RENNANT

1947 QUAI DES OFREVRES
Director: Henri-Georges Clouzot
Co-stars: Louis Jouvet Bernard Blier Suzy Delair

1964 THAT MAN FROM RIO
Director: Philippe De Broca
Co-stars: Jean-Paul Belmondo Jean Servais Adolfo Celi

DEBORAH RENNARD

1990   AWOL
Director: Sheldon Lettich
Co-stars: Jean-Claude Van Damme Harrison Page Lisa Pelikan

LINDA RENNHOFER

1977   ALIEN ENCOUNTERS
Director: Ed Hunt
Co-stars: Robert Vaughn Christopher Lee Helen Shaver

GINETTE RENO

1992   LEOLO
Director: Jean-Claude Lauzon
Co-stars: Maxime Collin Julien Guiomar Pierre Bourgault

SOPHIE RENOIR

1987   MY GIRLFRIEND'S BOYFRIEND
Director: Eric Rohmer
Co-stars: Emmanuelle Chaulet Anne-Laure MeuryEric Vieillard

EVA RENZI

**1967   THE AMOROUS ADVENTURES OF
          A YOUNG POSTMAN**
Director: Anthony Baker
Co-star: Richard Jordan

1967   FUNERAL IN BERLIN
Director: Guy Hamilton
Co-stars: Michael Caine Hugh Burden Oscar Homolka

1968   THE PINK JUNGLE
Director: Delbert Mann
Co-stars: James Garner George Kennedy Nigel Green

1968   A TASTE OF EXCITEMENT
Director: Don Sharp
Co-stars: David Buck Peter Vaughan Sophie Hardy

1969   THE BIRD WITH THE CRYSTAL PLUMAGE
Director: Dario Argento
Co-stars: Tony Musante Suzy Kendall

MAGGIE RENZI

1984   THE BROTHER FROM ANOTHER PLANET
Director: John Sayles
Co-stars: Joe Morton Tom Wright Caroline Aaron

1991   CITY OF HOPE
Director: John Sayles
Co-stars: Vincent Spano Todd Graff Tony LoBianco

ELLA RETFORD

1942   VARIETY JUBILEE
Director: Maclean Rogers
Co-stars: George Robey Slim Rhyder Lesley Brook

CATHERINE RETORE

1977   MESSIDOR
Director: Alain Tanner
Co-stars: Clementine Amouroux Gerald Battiaz

MARA REVEL

1961   IL POSTO
Director: Ermanno Olmi
Co-stars: Sandro Panzeri Loredana Detto

ANNE REVERE

**Oscar For Best Supporting Actress In 1944 For "National Velvet"
Nominated For Best Supporting Actress In 1943 For "The Song Of
Bernadette" And In 1947 For "Gentleman's Agreement"**

1934   DOUBLE DOOR
Director: Charles Vidor
Co-stars: Mary Morris Kent Taylor Evelyn Venable

1941   THE DEVIL COMMANDS
Director: Edward Dmytryk
Co-stars: Boris Karloff Amanda Duff Richard Fiske

1941   MEN OF BOYS' TOWN
Director: Norman Taurog
Co-stars: Spencer Tracy Mickey Rooney Bobs Watson

1941   THE FLAME OF NEW ORLEANS
Director: Rene Clair
Co-stars: Marlene Dietrich Bruce Cabot Roland Young

1941   REMEMBER THE DAY
Director: Henry King
Co-stars: Claudette Colbert John Payne Shepperd Strudwick

1942   STAR SPANGLED RHYTHM
Director: George Marshall
Co-stars: Victor Moore Betty Hutton Eddie Bracken

1943   OLD ACQUAINTANCE
Director: Vincent Sherman
Co-stars: Bette Davis Miriam Hopkins Gig Young

1943   THE MEANEST MAN IN THE WORLD
Director: Sidney Lanfield
Co-stars: Jack Benny Rochester Priscilla Lane

1943   THE SONG OF BERNADETTE
Director: Henry King
Co-stars: Jennifer Jones Charles Bickford Vincent Price

1944   KEYS OF THE KINGDOM
Director: John Stahl
Co-stars: Gregory Peck Thomas Mitchell Edmund Gwenn

1944   NATIONAL VELVET
Director: Clarence Brown
Co-stars: Elizabeth Taylor Mickey Rooney Donald Crisp

1944   RAINBOW ISLAND
Director: Ralph Murphy
Co-stars: Dorothy Lamour Eddie Bracken Barry Sullivan

1944   SUNDAY DINNER FOR A SOLDIER
Director: Lloyd Bacon
Co-stars: Anne Baxter John Hodiak Charles Winninger

1944   STANDING ROOM ONLY
Director: Sidney Lanfield
Co-stars: Paulette Goddard Fred MacMurray Edward Arnold

1944   THE THIN MAN GOES HOME
Director: Richard Thorpe
Co-stars: William Powell Myrna Loy Gloria De Haven

1945   FALLEN ANGEL
Director: Otto Preminger
Co-stars: Alice Faye Dana Andrews Linda Darnell

1945   DON JUAN QUILLIGAN
Director: Frank Tuttle
Co-stars: William Bendix Joan Blondell Mary Treen

1946   DRAGONWYCK
Director: Joseph Mankiewicz
Co-stars: Gene Tierney Vincent Price Walter Huston

1947   THE SHOCKING MISS PILGRIM
Director: George Seaton
Co-stars: Betty Grable Dick Haymes Allyn Joslyn

1947   GENTLEMAN'S AGREEMENT
Director: Elia Kazan
Co-stars: Gregory Peck Dorothy McGuire John Garfield

1947   FOREVER AMBER
Director: Otto Preminger
Co-stars: Linda Darnell Cornel Wilde George Sanders

1947   BODY AND SOUL
Director: Robert Rossen
Co-stars: John Garfield Lilli Palmer Hazel Brooks

1948	**DEEP WATERS**
Director:	Henry King
Co-stars:	Dean Stockwell Jean Peters Dana Andrews

1948	**SCUDDA HOO, SCUDDA HEY**
Director:	Hugh Herbert
Co-stars:	June Haver Lon McCallister Walter Brennan

1948	**SECRET BEYOND THE DOOR**
Director:	Fritz Lang
Co-stars:	Joan Bennett Michael Redgrave Barbara O'Neill

1949	**YOU'RE MY EVERYTHING**
Director:	Walter Lang
Co-stars:	Dan Dailey Anne Baxter Stanley Ridges

1950	**THE GREAT MISSOURI RAID**
Director:	Gordon Douglas
Co-stars:	MacDonald Carey Wendell Corey Ellen Drew

1951	**A PLACE IN THE SUN**
Director:	George Stevens
Co-stars:	Montgomery Clift Elizabeth Taylor Shelley Winters

DOROTHY REVIER

1930	**CALL OF THE WEST**
Director:	Albert Ray
Co-star:	Matt Moore

1930	**THE WAY OF ALL MEN**
Co-star:	Douglas Fairbanks Jnr.

1931	**THE AVENGER**
Co-star:	Buck Jones

1931	**THE BLACK CAMEL**
Director:	Hamilton McFadden
Co-stars:	Warner Oland Bela Lugosi Sally Eilers

1932	**NIGHT WORLD**
Director:	Hobart Henley
Co-stars:	Lew Ayres Boris Karloff George Raft

1933	**THE THRILL HUNTER**
Director:	George Seitz
Co-stars:	Buck Jones Arthur Rankin

1934	**THE FIGHTING RANGER**
Co-stars:	Buck Jones Ward Bond

1934	**WHEN A MAN SEES RED**
Co-star:	Buck Jones

ROSAURA REVUULTAS

1953	**SALT OF THE EARTH**
Director:	Herbert Biberman
Co-stars:	Juan Chacon Will Geer Mervin Williams

ANTONIA REY

1991	**I WAS ON MARS**
Director:	Dani Levy
Co-stars:	Maria Schrader Penny Arcade Mario Giacalone

1991	**JACOB'S LADDER**
Director:	Adrian Lynne
Co-stars:	Tim Robbins Danny Aiello Elizabeth Pena

DEBBIE REYNOLDS (*Mary Frances Reynolds*)
(*Married Eddie Fisher, Mother Of Carrie Fisher*)
Nominated For Best Actress In 1964 For "The Unsinkable Molly Brown"

1948	**JUNE BRIDE**
Director:	Bretaigne Windust
Co-stars:	Bette Davis Robert Montgomery

1950	**THE DAUGHTER OF ROSIE O'GRADY**
Director:	David Butler
Co-stars:	June Haver Gordon MacRae

1950	**THREE LITTLE WORDS**
Director:	Richard Thorpe
Co-stars:	Fred Astaire Red Skelton Vera-Ellen

1950	**TWO WEEKS WITH LOVE**
Director:	Roy Rowland
Co-stars:	Jane Powell Carleton Carpenter Ann Harding

1951	**YOU BELONG TO MY HEART**
Director:	Don Hartman
Co-stars:	Ezio Pinza Lana Turner Marjorie Main

1952	**SKIRTS AHOY**
Director:	Sidney Lanfield
Co-stars:	Esther Williams Vivian Blaine Joan Evans

1952	**SINGIN' IN THE RAIN**
Director:	Stanley Donen
Co-stars:	Gene Kelly Donald O'Connor Jean Hagen

1953	**GIVE A GIRL A BREAK**
Director:	Stanlen Donen
Co-stars:	Marge Champion Gower Champion Bob Fosse

1953	**THE AFFAIRS OF DOBIE GILLES**
Director:	Don Weis
Co-stars:	Bobby Van Bob Fosse Barbara Ruick

1953	**I LOVE MELVYN**
Director:	Don Weis
Co-stars:	Donald O'Connor Una Merkel Allyn Joslyn

1954	**ATHENA**
Director:	Richard Thorpe
Co-stars:	Jane Powell Edmund Purdom Vic Damone

1954	**SUSAN SLEPT HERE**
Director:	Frank Tashlin
Co-stars:	Dick Powell Ann Francis Glenda Farrell

1955	**THE TENDER TRAP**
Director:	Charles Walters
Co-stars:	Frank Sinatra David Wayne Celeste Holm

1955	**HIT THE DECK**
Director:	Roy Rowland
Co-stars:	Jane Powell Tony Martin Ann Miller

1956	**BUNDLE OF JOY**
Director:	Norman Taurog
Co-stars:	Eddie Fisher Adolphe Menjou Tommy Noonan

1956	**THE CATERED AFFAIR**
Director:	Richard Brooks
Co-stars:	Bette Davis Ernest Borgnine Rod Taylor

1957	**TAMMY AND THE BACHELOR**
Director:	Joseph Pevney
Co-stars:	Walter Brennan Leslie Nielsen Fay Wray

1958	**THIS HAPPY FEELING**
Director:	Blake Edwards
Co-stars:	Curt Jurgens Alexis Smith Mary Astor

1959	**THE MATING GAME**
Director:	George Marshall
Co-stars:	Tony Randall Paul Douglas Fred Clark

1959	**IT STARTED WITH A KISS**
Director:	George Marshall
Co-stars:	Glenn Ford Edgar Buchanan Fred Clark

1959	**THE GAZEBO**
Director:	George Marshall
Co-stars:	Glenn Ford Carl Reiner Zasu Pitts

1959	**SAY ONE FOR ME**
Director:	Frank Tashlin
Co-stars:	Bing Crosby Robert Wagner Ray Walston

1961	**THE SECOND TIME AROUND**
Director:	Vincent Sherman
Co-stars:	Steve Forrest Andy Griffith Ken Scott

1961 THE PLEASURE OF HIS COMPANY
Director: George Seaton
Co-stars: Fred Astaire Lilli Palmer

1962 HOW THE WEST WAS WON
Director: John Ford
Co-stars: Carroll Baker George Peppard James Stewart

1963 MARY MARY
Director: Mervyn Le Roy
Co-stars: Barry Nelson Michael Rennie

1963 MY SIX LOVES
Director: Gower Champion
Co-stars: David Jansson Cliff Robertson

1964 THE UNSINKABLE MOLLY BROWN
Director: Charles Walters
Co-stars: Harve Presnell Ed Begley Audrey Christie

1964 GOODBYE CHARLIE
Director: Vincente Minnelli
Co-stars: Tony Curtis Walter Matthau Pat Boone

1966 THE SINGING NUN
Director: Henry Koster
Co-stars: Greer Garson Ricardo Montalban

1967 DIVORCE AMERICAN STYLE
Director: Bud Yorkin
Co-stars: Dick Van Dyke Jean Simmons Van Johnson

1968 HOW SWEET IT IS
Director: Jerry Paris
Co-stars: James Garner Terry-Thomas Maurice Ronet

1971 WHAT'S THE MATTER WITH HELEN
Director: Curtis Harrington
Co-stars: Shelley Winters Agnes Moorhead

1972 CHARLOTTE'S WEB *(Voice)*
Director: Charles Nichols
Co-stars: Martha Scott Agnes Moorhead

1989 PERRY MASON:
THE CASE OF THE MUSICAL MURDER
Director: Christian Nyby
Co-star: Raymond Burr

1991 BATTLING FOR BABY
Director: Art Wolff
Co-stars: Suzanne Pleshettte John Terwesky

1993 HEAVEN AND EARTH
Director: Oliver Stone
Co-stars: Tommy Lee Jones Hiep Thi Le Joan Chen

1998 IN AND OUT
Director: Frank Oz
Co-stars: Kevin Kline Joan Cusack Matt Dillion

HELEN REYNOLDS

1942 MOONTIDE
Director: Archie Mayo
Co-stars: Jean Gabin Ida Lupino Claude Rains

1944 THE BERMUDA MYSTERY
Director: Ben Stoloff
Co-stars: Preston Foster Ann Rutherford Jean Howard

HILARY REYNOLDS

1983 EDUCATING RITA
Director: Lewis Gilbert
Co-stars: Julie Walters Michael Caine Michael Williams

1987 THE ROCKINGHAM SHOOT
Director: Kieran Hickey
Co-stars: Bosco Hogan Niall Tobin Tony Rohr

JOYCE REYNOLDS

1943 THE CONSTANT NYMPH
Director: Edmund Goulding
Co-stars: Charles Boyer Joan Fontaine Alexis Smith

1944 JANIE
Director: Michael Curtiz
Co-stars: Robert Hutton Ann Harding Edward Arnold

1947 ALWAYS TOGETHER
Director: Frederick De Cordova
Co-stars: Robert Hutton Cecil Kellaway Ernest Truex

1948 WALLFLOWER
Director: Frederick De Cordova
Co-stars: Robert Hutton Janis Paige Edward Arnold

JULIE MARIE REYNOLDS

1990 HUSH-A-BYE-BABY
Director: Margo Harker
Co-stars: Emer McCourt Sinead O'Connor Cathy Casey

KAY REYNOLDS

1967 HOW TO SUCCEED IN BUSINESS
WITHOUT REALLY TRYING
Director: David Swift
Co-star: Robert Morse Rudy Vallee Michele Lee

MARJORIE REYNOLDS

1938 WESTERN TRAILS
Director: Bob Baker

1939 ROCKETEERS OF THE RANGE
Co-stars: George O'Brien Gay Seabrook

1941 ROBIN HOOD OF THE PECOS
Co-stars: Roy Rogers Sally Payne

1941 CYCLONE ON HORSEBACK
Co-star: Tim Holt

1942 HOLIDAY INN
Director: Mark Sandrich
Co-stars: Bing Crosby Fred Astaire Walter Abel

1943 DIXIE
Director: Edward Sutherland
Co-stars: Bing Crosby Dorothy Lamour Billy De Wolfe

1944 MINISTRY OF FEAR
Director: Fritz Lang
Co-stars: Ray Milland Hilary Brooke Dan Duryea

1944 THREE IS A FAMILY
Director: Edward Ludwig
Co-stars: Charles Ruggles Fay Bainter Helen Broderick

1944 UP IN MABEL'S ROOM
Director: Allan Dwan
Co-stars: Dennis O'Keeve Mischa Auer Charlotte Greenwood

1945 DUFFY'S TAVERN
Director: Hal Walker
Co-stars: Victor Moore Bing Crosby Bob Hope

1945 BRING ON THE GIRLS
Director: Sidney Lanfield
Co-stars: Veronica Lake Eddie Bracken Sonny Tufts

1946 MEET ME ON BROADWAY
Director: Leigh Jason
Co-stars: Fred Brady Jinx Falkenburg Gene Lockhart

1946 MONSIEUR BEAUCAIRE
Director: George Marshall
Co-stars: Bob Hope Joan Caulfield Patric Knowles

1946 THE TIME OF THEIR LIVES
Director: Charles Barton
Co-stars: Bud Abbott Lou Costello Gale Sondergaard

1947 HEAVEN ONLY KNOWS
Director: Albert Rogell
Co-stars: Robert Cummings Brian Donlevy Stuart Erwin

1949 THE BAD MEN OF TOMBSTONE
Director: Kurt Neuman
Co-stars: Broderick Crawford Barry Sullivan Julie Gibson

1949 THAT MIDNIGHT KISS
Director: Norman Taurog
Co-stars: Mario Lanza Ethel Barrymore Kathryn Grayson

1950 THE GREAT JEWEL ROBBER
Director: Peter Godfrey
Co-stars: David Brian John Archer Jacqueline De Wit

1951 HIS KIND OF WOMAN
Director: John Farrow
Co-stars: Robert Mitchum Jane Russell Vincent Price

VERA REYNOLDS

1930 LONE RIDER
Co-star: Buck Jones

1932 THE MONSTER WALKS
Director: Frank Strayer
Co-stars: Sheldon Lewis Mischa Auer Rex Lease

ASHLEY RHEA

1993 PRELUDE TO LOVE
Director: Ralph Portillo

ALICIA RHETT

1939 GONE WITH THE WIND
Director: Victor Fleming
Co-stars: Clark Gable Vivien Leigh Leslie Howard

STELLA RHO

1936 SWEENEY TODD, THE DEMON BARBER OF FLEET STREET
Director: George King
Co-stars: Tod Slaughter Bruce Seton

BARBARA RHOADES

1967 THE SHAKIEST GUN IN THE WEST
Director: Alan Rafkin
Co-stars: Don Knotts Jackie Coogan Don Barry

1968 DON'T JUST STAND THERE
Director: Ron Winston
Co-stars: Mary Tyler Moore Robert Wagner Glynis Johns

1977 THE GOODBYE GIRL
Director: Herbert Ross
Co-stars: Richard Dreyfuss Marsha Mason Quinn Cummings

1985 PICKING UP THE PIECES
Director: Paul Wendkos
Co-stars: Margot Kidder David Ackroyd James Farentino

1987 DOUBLE SWITCH
Director: David Greenwalt
Co-stars: George Newbern Elizabeth Shue John Lawlor

SYBIL RHODA

1927 DOWNHILL
Director: Alfred Hitchcock
Co-stars: Ivor Novello Ben Webster Ian Hunter

BETTY JANE RHODES

1941 ALONG THE RIO GRANDE
Co-star: Tim Holt

1942 THE FLEET'S IN
Director: Victor Schertzinger
Co-stars: Dorothy Lamour William Holden Betty Hutton

1942 PRIORITIES ON PARADE
Director: Albert Rogell
Co-stars: Ann Miller Johnnie Johnston Jerry Colonna

1943 SALUTE FOR THREE
Director: Ralph Murphy
Co-stars: MacDonald Carey Dona Drake Marty May

1944 YOU CAN'T RATION LOVE
Director: Lester Fuller
Co-stars: Johnnie Johnston Marjorie Weaver Marie Wilson

CYNTHIA RHODES

1983 STAYING ALIVE
Director: Sylvester Stallone
Co-stars: John Travolta Finola Hughes Julie Bovasso

1984 RUNAWAY
Director: Michael Crichton
Co-stars: Tom Selleck Kirstie Alley Stan Shaw

1987 DIRTY DANCING
Director: Emile Ardolino
Co-stars: Patrick Swayze Jennifer Grey Jerry Orbach

ILA RHODES

1939 SECRET SERVICE OF THE AIR
Director: Noel Smith
Co-stars: Ronald Reagan Eddie Foy Jnr. John Litel

MARJORIE RHODES

1941 LOVE ON THE DOLE
Director: John Baxter
Co-stars: Deborah Kerr Clifford Evans Joyce Howard

1942 WHEN WE ARE MARRIED
Director: Herbert Mason
Co-stars: Raymond Huntley Sydney Howard Olga Lindo

1943 THEATRE ROYAL
Director: John Baxter
Co-stars: Flanagan & Allen Horace Kenny Peggy Dexter

1943 OLD MOTHER RILEY, DETECTIVE
Director: Lance Comfort
Co-stars: Arthur Lucan Kitty McShane Peggy Cummins

1944 TAWNY PIPIT
Director: Bernard Miles
Co-stars: Rosamund Johns Jean Gillie Lucie Mannheim

1944 IT HAPPENED ONE SUNDAY
Director: Karel Lamac
Co-stars: Robert Beatty Barbara White Ernest Butcher

1945 GREAT DAY
Director: Lance Comfort
Co-stars: Eric Portman Flora Robson Sheila Sim

1946 SCHOOL FOR SECRETS
Director: Peter Ustinov
Co-stars: Ralph Richardson Raymond Huntley John Laurie

1947 UNCLE SILAS
Director: Charles Frank
Co-stars: Jean Simmons Derrick De Marney Katina Paxinou

1948 THIS WAS A WOMAN
Director: Tim Whelan
Co-stars: Sonia Dresdel Barbara White Walter Fitzgerald

1949 PRIVATE ANGELO
Director: Peter Ustinov
Co-stars: Peter Ustinov Godfrey Tearle Robin Bailey Maria Denis

1949 THE CURE FOR LOVE
Director: Robert Donat
Co-stars: Renee Asherson Dora Bryan Charles Victor

1952 **TIME GENTLEMEN PLEASE !**
Director: Lewis Gilbert
Co-stars: Eddie Byrne Dora Bryan Thora Hird

1953 **THOSE PEOPLE NEXT DOOR**
Director: John Harlow
Co-stars: Jack Warner Charles Victor Jimmy James

1954 **CHILDREN GALORE**
Director: Terence Fisher
Co-stars: Eddie Byrne June Thorburn Betty Ann Davies

1955 **FOOTSTEPS IN THE FOG**
Director: Arthur Lubin
Co-stars: Stewart Granger Jean Simmons Bill Travers

1955 **LOST**
Director: Guy Green
Co-stars: David Farrar Julia Arnall Eleanor Summerfield

1956 **THE PASSIONATE STRANGER**
Director: Muriel Box
Co-stars: Ralph Richardson Margaret Leighton

1957 **THERE'S ALWAYS THURSDAY**
Director: Charles Saunders
Co-stars: Charles Victor Jill Ireland Patrick Holt

1961 **WATCH IT SAILOR !**
Director: Wolf Rilla
Co-stars: Dennis Price Irene Handl Liz Fraser

1966 **THE FAMILY WAY**
Director: Roy Boulting
Co-stars: John Mills Hayley Mills Hywel Bennett

1968 **MRS BROWN YOU'VE GOT
A LOVELY DAUGHTER**
Director: Saul Swimmer
Co-stars: Herman's Hermits Stanley Holloway

MADLYN RHUE

1961 **A MAJORITY OF ONE**
Director: Mervyn LeRoy
Co-stars: Rosalind Russell Alec Guinness Ray Danton

1962 **ESCAPE FROM ZAHRAIN**
Director: Ronald Neame
Co-stars: Yul Brynner Sal Mineo Jack Warden

1964 **HE RIDES TALL**
Director: R.G. Springsteen
Co-stars: Tony Young Dan Duryea Jo Morrow

1971 **STAND UP AND BE COUNTED**
Director: Jackie Cooper
Co-stars: Jacqueline Bisset Stella Stevens Loretta Swit

1979 **GOLDIE AND THE BOXER**
Director: David Miller
Co-stars: O.J. Simpson Melissa Michaelson

CANDICE RIALSON

1976 **HOLLYWOOD BOULEVARD**
Director: Joe Dante
Co-stars: Mary Woronov Rita George Jeffrey Kramer

RENIE RIANO

1939 **NANCY DREW, REPORTER**
Director: William Clemens
Co-stars: Bonita Granville Frankie Thomas John Litel

1941 **ZIEGFIELD GIRL**
Director: Robert Z. Leonard
Co-stars: Judy Garland Lana Turner Hedy Lamarr

1942 **BLONDIE FOR VICTORY**
Director: Frank Strayer
Co-stars: Penny Singleton Arthur Lake Larry Simms

1946 **BRINGING UP FATHER**
Co-star: Joe Yule

1946 **CLUB HAVANA**
Director: Edgar Ulmer
Co-stars: Tom Neal Margaret Lindsay Ernest Truex

1946 **SO GOES MY LOVE**
Director: Frank Ryan
Co-stars: Myrna Loy Don Ameche Bobby Driscoll

CATHERINE RIBERO

1963 **LES CARABINIERS**
Director: Jean-Luc Godard
Co-stars: Marino Mase Albert Juross Genevieve Galea

MARISSA RIBISI

1993 **DAZED AND CONFUSED**
Director: Richard Linklater
Co-stars: Jason London Wiley Wiggins Milla Jovovich

CHRISTINA RICCI *(Child)*

1990 **MERMAIDS**
Director: Richard Benjamin
Co-stars: Cher Winona Ryder Bob Hoskins

1991 **THE HARD WAY**
Director: John Badham
Co-stars: Michael J. Fox James Woods Annabella Sciorra

1991 **THE ADDAMS FAMILY**
Director: Barry Sonnenfeld
Co-stars: Anjelica Huston Raul Julia Christopher Lloyd

1993 **THE ADDAMS FAMILY VALUES**
Director: Barry Sonnenfeld
Co-stars: Anjelica Huston Joan Cusack Carol Kane

1995 **CASPER**
Director: Brad Silberling
Co-star: Bill Pullman

1996 **THE LAST OF THE HIGH KINGS**
Director: David Keating
Co-stars: Jared Leto Catherine O'Hara Gabriel Byrne

1996 **NOW AND THEN**
Co-stars: Demi Moore Melanie Griffith Thora Birch

1998 **THE ICE STORM**
Director: Ang Lee
Co-stars: Kevin Kline Sigourney Weaver Joan Allen

NORA RICCI

1972 **LUDWIG**
Director: Luchino Visconti
Co-stars: Helmut Berger Romy Schneider Trevor Howard

KATIA RICCIARELLI

1986 **OTELLO**
Director: Franco Zefferelli
Co-stars: Placido Domingo Justino Diaz Petra Malakova

FLORENCE RICE

1934 **FUGITIVE LADY**
Co-star: Neil Hamilton

1934 **THE BEST MAN WINS**
Director: Erle Kenton
Co-stars: Jack Holt Edmund Lowe Bela Lugosi

1935 **UNDER PRESSURE**
Co-stars: Victor McLaglen Edmund Lowe Charles Bickford

1935 **CARNIVAL**
Director: Walter Lang
Co-stars: Lee Tracy Jimmy Durante Sally Eilers

1935 **DEATH FLIES EAST**
Co-star: Conrad Nagel

1936 **THE BLACKMAILER**
Co-star: William Gargan

1937 **DOUBLE WEDDING**
Director: Richard Thorpe
Co-stars: William Powell Myrna Loy Jessie Ralph

1937 **MAN OF THE PEOPLE**
Director: Edwin Marin
Co-stars: Joseph Calleia Thomas Mitchell Catharine Doucet

1937 **BEG, BORROW OR STEAL**
Co-star: John Beal

1937 **MARRIED BEFORE BREAKFAST**
Director: Edwin Marin
Co-stars: Robert Young June Clayworth Warren Hymer

1937 **RIDIN' ON AIR**
Co-star: Joe E. Brown

1937 **NAVY BLUE AND GOLD**
Director: Sam Wood
Co-stars: Robert Young James Stewart Lionel Barrymore

1937 **PARADISE FOR 3**
Director: Edward Buzzell
Co-stars: Robert Young Frank Morgan Mary Astor

1937 **UNDER COVER OF NIGHT**
Director: George Seitz
Co-stars: Edmund Lowe Henry Daniell Dean Jagger

1938 **SWEETHEARTS**
Director: W.S. Van Dyke
Co-stars: Jeanette MacDonald Nelson Eddy Ray Bolger

1938 **STAND UP AND FIGHT**
Director: W.S. Van Dyke
Co-stars: Wallace Beery Robert Taylor Charles Bickford

1938 **FOUR GIRLS IN WHITE**
Director: S. Sylvan Simon
Co-stars: Ann Rutherford Una Merkel Mary Howard

1938 **FAST COMPANY**
Director: Edward Buzzell
Co-stars: Melvyn Douglas Louis Calhern Clare Dodd

1939 **AT THE CIRCUS**
Director: Edward Buzzell
Co-stars: Marx Bros. Margaret Dumont Eve Arden

1939 **LITTLE ACCIDENT**
Director: Charles Lamont
Co-stars: Baby Sandy Hugh Herbert Richard Carlson

1939 **MIRACLES FOR SALE**
Director: Tod Browning
Co-stars: Robert Young Henry Hull Lee Bowman

1940 **BROADWAY MELODY OF 1940**
Director: Norman Taurog
Co-stars: Fred Astaire Eleanor Powell George Murphy

1940 **CHEROKEE STRIP**
Director: Lesley Selander
Co-stars: Richard Dix William Henry Victor Jory

1941 **FATHER TAKES A WIFE**
Director: Jack Hively
Co-stars: Gloria Swanson Adolphe Menjou Helen Broderick

1941 **DOCTORS DON'T TELL**
Co-stars: John Beal Edward Morris

1941 **MR DISTRICT ATTORNEY**
Director: William Morgan
Co-stars: Dennis O'Keefe Peter Lorre Stanley Ridge

1941 **THE BLONDE FROM SINGAPORE**
Co-stars: Leif Erickson Gordon Jones

1942 **TRAMP, TRAMP, TRAMP**
Co-star: Jackie Gleason

1942 **LET'S GET TOUGH**
Co-star: Tom Brown

1943 **THE GHOST AND THE GUEST**
Director: William Nigh
Co-stars: James Dunn Mabel Todd Sam McDaniel

JOAN RICE

1950 **BLACKMAILED**
Director: Marc Allegret
Co-stars: Dirk Bogarde Mai Zetterling Fay Compton

1952 **CURTAIN UP**
Director: Ralph Smart
Co-stars: Margaret Rutherford Robert Morley Kay Kendall

1952 **THE GIFT HORSE**
Director: Compton Bennett
Co-stars: Trevor Howard Sonny Tufts Hugh Williams

1952 **THE STORY OF ROBIN HOOD
AND HIS MERRIE MEN**
Director: Ken Annakin
Co-stars: Richard Todd Peter Finch

1953 **THE STEEL KEY**
Director: Robert Baker
Co-stars: Terence Morgan Dianne Foster Esmond Knight

1953 **A DAY TO REMEMBER**
Director: Ralph Thomas
Co-stars: Donald Sinden Odile Versois Bill Owen

1954 **THE CROWDED DAY**
Director: John Guillermin
Co-stars: John Gregson Rachel Roberts Sid James

1954 **ONE GOOD TURN**
Director: John Paddy Carstairs
Co-stars: Norman Wisdom Shirley Abicair Thora Hird

1954 **HIS MAJESTY O'KEEFE**
Director: Byron Haskin
Co-stars: Burt Lancaster Andre Morrell Abraham Sofaer

1955 **POLICE DOG**
Director: Derek Twist
Co-stars: Tim Turner Sandra Dorne Christopher Lee

1956 **WOMEN WITHOUT MEN**
Director: Elmo Williams
Co-stars: Beverley Michaels Gordon Jackson Thora Hird

1961 **PAYROLL**
Director: Sidney Hayers
Co-stars: Michael Craig Billie Whitelaw Tom Bell

1970 **THE HORROR OF FRANKENSTEIN**
Director: Jimmy Sangster
Co-stars: Ralph Bates Kate O'Mara Dennis Price

MARY ALICE RICE

1936 **LOVE LETTERS OF A STAR**
Director: Lewis Foster
Co-stars: Henry Hunter Polly Rowles C. Henry Gordon

MANDY RICE-DAVIES

1986 **ABSOLUTE BEGINNERS**
Director: Julien Temple
Co-stars: Patsy Kensit Eddie O'Connell

IRENE RICH

1924　BEAU BRUMMELL
Director:　Harry Beaumont
Co-stars:　John Barrymore Mary Astor Carmel Myers

1925　LADY WINDERMERE'S FAN
Director:　Ernst Lubitsch
Co-stars:　Ronald Colman May McAvoy Bert Lytell

1925　THE PLEASURE BUYERS
Co-star:　Clive Brook

1930　CHECK AND DOUBLE CHECK
Director:　Melville Brown
Co-stars:　Freeman Gosden (Amos) Charles Correll (Andy)

1930　FATHER'S SON
Co-stars:　Lewis Stone Leon Janney

1931　THE MAD PARADE
Director:　William Beaudine
Co-stars:　Evelyn Brent Louise Fazenda Lilyan Tashman

1931　FIVE AND TEN
Director:　Robert Z. Leonard
Co-stars:　Leslie Howard Marion Davies Kent Douglass

1931　THE CHAMP
Director:　King Vidor
Co-stars:　Wallace Beery Jackie Cooper Roscoe Ates

1931　BEAU IDEAL
Director:　Herbert Brenon
Co-stars:　Ralph Forbes Loretta Young Lester Vail

1931　STRANGERS MAY KISS
Director:　George Fitzmaurice
Co-stars:　Norma Shearer Robert Montgomery Neil Hamilton

1932　DOWN TO EARTH
Director:　David Butler
Co-stars:　Will Rogers Dorothy Jordan Mary Carlisle

1932　MANHATTAN TOWER
Co-star:　Nydia Westman

1938　THAT CERTAIN AGE
Director:　Edward Ludwig
Co-stars:　Deanna Durbin Melvyn Douglas Jackie Cooper

1940　THE MORTAL STORM
Director:　Frank Borzage
Co-stars:　Margaret Sullavan James Stewart Robert Young

1940　KEEPING COMPANY
Director:　S. Sylvan Simon
Co-stars:　Frank Morgan Ann Rutherford Dan Dailey

1940　THE LADY IN QUESTION
Director:　Charles Vidor
Co-stars:　Brian Aherne Rita Hayworth Glenn Ford

1941　THE WILD MAN OF BORNEO
Director:　Robert Sinclair
Co-stars:　Frank Morgan Mary Howard Dan Dailey

1947　CALENDAR GIRL
Director:　Allan Dwan
Co-stars:　Jane Frazee Gail Patrick Kenny Baker

1947　ANGEL AND THE BADMAN
Director:　James Edward Grant
Co-stars:　John Wayne Gail Russell Bruce Cabot

1948　FORT APACHE
Director:　John Ford
Co-stars:　John Wayne Henry Fonda Shirley Temple

LILLIAN RICH

1925　THE GOLDEN BED
Co-star:　Warner Baxter

DAWN RICHARD

1957　I WAS A TEENAGE WEREWOLF
Director:　Gene Fowler
Co-stars:　Michael Landon Whit Bissell Yvonne Lime

FIRNINE RICHARD

1989　ROMUALD AND JULIETTE
Director:　Coline Serreau
Co-stars:　Daniel Auteuil Pierre Vernier Maxime Lerous

IRENE RICHARD

1980　SENSE AND SENSIBILITY
Director:　Rodney Bennett
Co-stars:　Tracey Childs Diana Fairfax

VIOLA RICHARD

1927　FLYING ELEPHANTS
Director:　Frank Butler
Co-stars:　Stan Laurel Oliver Hardy James Finlayson

ANGELA RICHARDS

1988　ACROSS THE LAKE
Director:　Tony Maylam
Co-stars:　Anthony Hopkins Rosemary Leach Dexter Fletcher

ANN RICHARDS

1944　AN AMERICAN ROMANCE
Director:　King Vidor
Co-stars:　Brian Donlevy John Quayle Walter Abel

1945　LOVE LETTERS
Director:　William Dieterle
Co-stars:　Jennifer Jones Joseph Cotten Gladys Cooper

1946　THE SEARCHING WIND
Director:　William Dieterle
Co-stars:　Robert Young Sylvia Sidney Douglas Dick

1946　BADMAN'S TERRITORY
Director:　Tim Whelan
Co-stars:　Randolph Scott Steve Brodie Lawrence Tierney

1947　LOST HONEYMOON
Director:　Leigh Jason
Co-stars:　Franchot Tone Tom Conway Clarence Kolb

1947　LOVE FROM A STRANGER
Director:　Richard Whorf
Co-stars:　Sylvia Sidney John Hodiak John Howard

1948　SORRY, WRONG NUMBER
Director:　Anatole Litvak
Co-stars:　Barbara Stanwyck Burt Lancaster Ed Begley

ARIANA RICHARDS (Child)

1989　SPACED INVADERS
Director:　Patrick Read Johnson
Co-stars:　Douglas Barr Royal Dano Gregg Berger

1989　PRANCER
Director:　John Hancock
Co-stars:　Sam Elliott Rebecca Harrell Cloris Leachman

1990　TREMORS
Director:　Ron Underwood
Co-stars:　Kevin Bacon Fred Ward Finn Carter

1993　JURASSIC PARK
Director:　Steven Spielberg
Co-stars:　Sam Neill Laura Dern Jeff Goldblum

BEAH RICHARDS

1962　THE MIRACLE WORKER
Director:　Arthur Penn
Co-stars:　Anne Bancroft Patty Duke Victor Jory

1967 HURRY SUNDOWN
Director: Otto Preminger
Co-stars: Jane Fonda Michael Caine Rex Ingram

1967 GUESS WHO'S COMING TO DINNER
Director: Stanley Kramer
Co-stars: Spencer Tracy Katherine Hepburn

1970 THE GREAT WHITE HOPE
Director: Martin Ritt
Co-stars: James Earl Jones Jane Alexander Hal Holbrook

1972 THE BISCUIT EATER
Director: Vincent McEveety
Co-stars: Earl Holliman Lew Ayres Godfrey Cambridge

1975 MAHOGANY
Director: Berry Gordy
Co-stars: Diana Ross Anthony Perkins Billy Dee Williams

1986 ACCEPTABLE RISKS
Director: Rick Wallace
Co-stars: Brian Dennehy Christine Ebersole Cicely Tyson

1986 AS SUMMER DIES
Director: Jean-Claude Tramont
Co-stars: Scott Glenn Bette Davis Jaimie Lee Curtis

1989 HOMER AND EDDIE
Director: Andrei Konchalovsky
Co-stars: James Belushi Whoopi Goldberg Karen Black

1993 OUT OF DARKNESS
Director: Larry Elikann
Co-stars: Diana Ross Lindsay Crouse Ann Weldon

DENISE RICHARDS

1998 STARSHIP TROOPERS
Director: Paul Verhoeven
Co-stars: Patrick Muldoon Michael Ironside Casper Van Dien

KIM RICHARDS (Child)

1974 ESCAPE TO WITCH MOUNTAIN
Director: John Hough
Co-stars: Ray Milland Eddie Albert Ike Eisenmann

1976 ASSAULT ON PRECINCT 13
Director: John Carpenter
Co-stars: Austin Stoker Laurie Zimmer Nancy Loomis

1976 NO DEPOSIT, NO RETURN
Director: Norman Tokar
Co-stars: David Niven Darren McGavin Don Knotts

1978 RETURN FROM WITCH MOUNTAIN
Director: John Hough
Co-stars: Bette Davis Christopher Lee Ike Eisenmann

1984 MEATBALLS 2
Director: Ken Wiederhorn
Co-stars: Richard Mulligan John Mengatti Tammy Taylor

1985 TUFF TURF
Director: Fritz Kiersch
Co-stars: James Spader Paul Mones Robert Downey Jnr.

LISA RICHARDS

1977 ROLLING THUNDER
Director: John Flynn
Co-stars: William Devane Linda Haynes Tommy Lee Jones

1977 THE PRINCE OF CENTRAL PARK
Director: Harvey Hart
Co-stars: Ruth Gordon T.J. Hargrave

1990 EATING
Director: Henry Jaglom
Co-stars: Mary Crosby Gwen Welles Frances Bergen

MICHELE LAMAR RICHARDS

1992 THE BODYGUARD
Director: Mick Jackson
Co-stars: Kevin Costner Whitney Houston Gary Kemp

SUSAN RICHARDS

1961 PART TIME WIFE
Director: Max Varnel
Co-stars: Anton Rodgers Nyree Dawn Porter

VALERIE RICHARDS

1988 APPOINTMENT WITH DEATH
Director: Michael Winner
Co-stars: Peter Ustinov Lauren Bacall Carrie Fisher

WENDY RICHARDS

1970 NO BLADE OF GRASS
Director: Cornel Wilde
Co-stars: Nigel Davenport Jean Wallace Patrick Holt

1972 CARRY ON MATRON
Director: Gerald Thomas
Co-stars: Sid James Kenneth Williams Barbara Windsor

1977 ARE YOU BEING SERVED
Director: Bob Kellett
Co-stars: Mollie Sugden John Inman Frank Thornton

JOELY RICHARDSON
(Daughter Of Vanessa Redgrave And Tony Richardson / Sister Of Natasha And Miranda Richardson)

1985 WETHERBY
Director: David Hare
Co-stars: Vanessa Redgrave Ian Holm Judi Dench

1988 DROWNING BY NUMBERS
Director: Peter Greenaway
Co-stars: Bernard Hill Joan Plowright Juliet Stevenson

1989 BEHAVING BADLY
Director: David Tucker
Co-stars: Judi Dench Ronald Pickup Francer Barber

1990 AVAILABLE LIGHT
Director: Bob Bently
Co-stars: Tom Bell David Morrissey Tiga Adams

1991 HEADING HOME
Director: David Hare
Co-stars: Gary Oldman Stella Gonet Michael Bryant

1991 REBECCA'S DAUGHTERS
Director: Karl Francis
Co-stars: Peter O'Toole Paul Rhys Keith Allen

1992 SHINING THROUGH
Director: David Seltzer
Co-stars: Michael Douglas Melanie Griffith Liam Neesen

1994 I'LL DO ANYTHING
Director: James Brooks
Co-stars: Nick Nolte Albert Brooks Whittni Wright

1994 LADY CHATTERLEY
Director: Ken Russell
Co-stars: Sean Bean James Wilby Shirley Anne Field

1995 SISTER, MY SISTER

1996 LOCH NESS
Director: John Henderson
Co-stars: Ted Danson Ian Holm Keith Allen

1996 HOLLOW REED
Director: Angela Pope
Co-stars: Martin Donovan Jason Flemyng Sam Bould

1996   101 DALMATIONS
Director: Stephen Herek
Co-stars: Glenn Close Jeff Daniels Hugh Laurie

1997   EVENT HORIZON
Director: Paul Anderson
Co-stars: Sam Neill Laurence Fishburne Sean Pertwee

MIRANDA RICHARDSON

*(Daughter Of Vanessa Redgrave And Tony
Richardson, Sister Of Natasha And Joely Richardson)*
**Nominated For Best Supporting Actress In 1992 For "Damage" And
Nominated For Best Actress In 1994 For Tom & Viv**

1985   THE INNOCENT
Director: John Mackenzie
Co-stars: Andrew Hawley Kika Markham Tom Bell

1985   UNDERWORLD
Director: George Pavlou
Co-stars: Denholm Elliott Steven Berkoff Larry Lamb

1985   DANCE WITH A STRANGER
Director: Mike Newell
Co-stars: Rupert Everett Ian Holm Joanne Whalley

1986   AFTER PILKINGTON
Director: Christopher Morahan
Co-stars: Bob Peck Barry Foster Gary Waldhorn

1987   EMPIRE OF THE SUN
Director: Steven Spielberg
Co-stars: Christian Bale John Malkovich Nigel Havers

1987   SWEET AS YOU ARE
Director: Angela Pope
Co-stars: Liam Neeson Alex Pakenham Gillian Raine

1989   BALL TRAP ON THE COTE SAUVAGE
Director: Jack Gold
Co-stars: Jack Shepherd Zoe Wanamaker Michael Kitchen

1991   REDEMPTION
Director: Malcolm McKay
Co-stars: Tom Courtenay Lindsay Duncan Nick Moran

1991   ENCHANTED APRIL
Director: Mike Newell
Co-stars: Josie Lawrence Joan Plowright Polly Walker

1992   MR WAKEFIELD'S CRUSADE
Director: Angela Pope
Co-stars: Peter Capaldi Pam Ferris Richard Griffiths

1992   DAMAGE
Director: Louis Malle
Co-stars: Jeremy Irons Juliette Binoche Leslie Caron

1992   THE CRYING GAME
Director: Neil Jordan
Co-stars: Forest Whitaker Stephen Rea Jaye Davison

1993   CENTURY
Director: Stephen Poliakoff
Co-stars: Charles Dance Clive Owens Robert Stephens

1993   TOM AND VIV
Director: Brian Gilbert
Co-stars: Willem Dafoe Rosemary Harris Tim Dutton

1994   FATHERLAND
Director: Christopher Menaul
Co-stars: Rutger Hauer Jean Marsh Peter Vaughan

1996   KANSAS CITY
Director: Robert Altman
Co-stars: Jennifer Jason Leigh Dermot Mulhoney Harry Belafonte

1997   EVENING STAR
Co-star: Shirley Maclaine

1998   THE APOSTLE
Director: Robert Duvall
Co-stars: Farrah Fawcett Billy Bob Thornton Robert Duvall

NATASHA RICHARDSON

*(Married Liam Neeson, Daughter Of Vanessa
Redgrave And Tony Richardson, Sister Of Miranda
And Joely Richardson)*

1985   IN THE SECRET STATE
Director: Christopher Morahan
Co-stars: Frank Finlay Matthew Marsh Ronald Fraser

**1985   THE ADVENTURES OF SHERLOCK
HOLMES: THE COPPER BEACHES**
Director: Paul Annett
Co-stars: Jeremy Brett David Burke

1986   GOTHIC
Director: Ken Russell
Co-stars: Gabriel Byrne Julian Sands Timothy Spall

1987   A MONTH IN THE COUNTRY
Director: Pat O'Connor
Co-stars: Colin Firth Kenneth Branagh Patrick Malahide

1988   PATTY HEARST
Director: Paul Schrader
Co-stars: William Forsythe Frances Fisher Ving Rhames

1989   SHADOW MAKERS
Director: Roland Joffe
Co-stars: Paul Newman Dwight Schulz Bonnie Bedelia

1990   THE HANDMAID'S TALE
Director: Volker Schlondorff
Co-stars: Robert Duvall Faye Dunaway Anthony Quinn

1991   COMFORT OF STRANGERS
Director: Paul Schrader
Co-stars: Rupert Everett Christopher Walker Helen Mirren

**1992   THE FAVOUR, THE WATCH AND
THE VERY BIG FISH**
Director: Ben Lewin
Co-stars: Bob Hoskins Jeff Goldblum

1992   HOSTAGES
Director: David Wheatley
Co-stars: Kathy Bates Colin Firth Ciaran Hinds

1992   SUDDENLY, LAST SUMMER
Director: Richard Byre
Co-stars: Maggie Smith Rob Lowe Richard E. Grant

1994   WIDOW'S PEAK
Director: John Irvin
Co-stars: Mia Farrow Joan Plowright Adrian Dunbar

1994   NELL
Director: Michael Apted
Co-stars: Jodie Foster Liam Neeson

PATRICIA RICHARDSON

1989   THE ROAD HOME
Director: Hugh Hudson
Co-stars: Donald Sutherland Adam Horovitz Amy Locane

REGINA RICHARDSON

1985   NINE DEATHS OF THE NINJA
Director: Emmett Alston
Co-stars: Sho Kusugi Brent Huff Blackie Dammett

CAROLE RICHERT

1992   TOUS LES MATINS DU MONDE
Director: Alain Corneau
Co-stars: Gerard Depardieu Anne Brochet

FIONA RICHMOND

1987   EAT THE RICH
Director: Peter Richardson
Co-stars: Nosher Powell Lanah Pellay Ronald Allen

IRENE RICHMOND

1964 NIGHTMARE
Director: Freddie Francis
Co-stars: Moira Redmond David Knight Brenda Bruce

DEBORAH RICHTER

1987 SQUARE DANCE
Director: Daniel Petrie
Co-stars: Jason Robards Jane Alexander Rob Lowe

1989 CYBORG
Director: Albert Pym
Co-stars: Jean-Claude Van Damme Vincent Klyn Rolf Muller

MARIA RICHWINE

1978 THE BUDDY HOLLY STORY
Director: Steve Rash
Co-stars: Gary Busey Don Stroud Charles Martin

MARGARET RICKETTS

1988 CELIA
Director: Ann Turner
Co-stars: Rebecca Smart Nicholas Eadie Victoria Longley

SHIRLEY RICKETTS

1934 'NEATH ARIZONA SKIES
Director: Harry Fraser
Co-stars: John Wayne Sheila Terry George Hayes

JILL RIDDICK

1971 HOVERBUG
Director: Jan Darley-Smith
Co-stars: John Trayhorn Arthur Howard Cardew Robinson

LINDA RIDGEWAY

1972 THE MECHANIC
Director: Michael Winner
Co-stars: Charles Bronson Jan-Michael Vincent Jill Ireland

LENI RIEFENSTAHL

1933 SOS ICEBERG
Director: Tay Garnett
Co-stars: Rod LaRocque Sepp Rist Gibson Gowland

KATJA RIEMANN

1992 MAKING UP
Director: Katja Von Garnier
Co-stars: Nina Kronjaear Gedeon Burkhard

DIANA RIGG

1968 THE ASSASSINATION BUREAU
Director: Basil Dearden
Co-stars: Oliver Reed Telly Savalas Curt Jurgens

1969 JULIUS CAESAR
Director: Stuart Burge
Co-stars: Richard Johnson Charlton Heston John Gielgud

1969 ON HER MAJESTY'S SECRET SERVICE
Director: Peter Hunt
Co-stars: George Lazenby Telly Savalas Bernard Lee

1973 THEATRE OF BLOOD
Director: Douglas Hickox
Co-stars: Vincent Price Ian Hendry Coral Browne

1975 IN THIS HOUSE OF BREDE
Director: George Schaefer
Co-stars: Judi Bowker Pamela Brown Dennis Quilley

1977 A LITTLE NIGHT MUSIC
Director: Hal Prince
Co-stars: Elizabeth Taylor Len Cariou Hermione Gingold

1981 THE GREAT MUPPET CAPER
Director: Jim Henson
Co-stars: John Cleese Trevor Howard Peter Ustinov

1982 EVIL UNDER THE SUN
Director: Guy Hamilton
Co-stars: Peter Ustinov James Mason Maggie Smith

1983 KING LEAR
Director: Michael Elliott
Co-stars: Laurence Olivier Dorothy Tutin

1987 A HAZARD OF HEARTS
Director: John Hough
Co-stars: Edward Fox Helena Bonham-Carter Fiona Fullerton

1989 MOTHER LOVE
Director: Simon Langton
Co-stars: James Wilby David McCallum Isla Blair

1989 UNEXPLAINED LAUGHTER
Director: Gareth Davies
Co-stars: Elaine Paige Joanna David Jon Finch

1992 MRS 'ARRIS GOES TO PARIS
Director: Anthony Shaw
Co-stars: Angela Lansbury Omar Sharif John Savident

1994 GENGHIS COHN
Director: Elijah Moshinsky
Co-stars: Anthony Sher Robert Lindsay John Wells

1996 REBECCA
Co-stars: Charles Dance Elicia Fox

REBECCA RIGG

1991 SPOTSWOOD
Director: Mark Joffe
Co-stars: Anthony Hopkins Ben Mendelsohn Toni Collette

**1993 MERCY MISSION:
THE RESCUE OF FLIGHT 771**
Director: Roger Young
Co-stars: Robert Loggia Scott Bakula

JULIA RIGHTON

1988 FURTHER AND PARTICULAR
Director: Steve Dwoskin
Co-stars: Richard Butler Irene Marot Carola Regnier

ROBIN RIKER

1980 ALLIGATOR
Director: Lewis Teague
Co-stars: Robert Forster Dean Jagger Henry Silva

ELAINE RILEY

1945 WHAT A BLONDE
Co-stars: Veda Ann Borg Michael St. Angel

1946 THE DEVIL'S PLAYGROUND

1948 FALSE PARADISE
Director: George Archainbaud
Co-stars: William Boyd Andy Clyde Rand Brooks

1948 SINISTER JOURNEY
Co-stars: William Boyd Andy Clyde Rand Brooks

JEANINE RILEY

1973 ELECTRA GLIDE IN BLUE
Director: James William Guercio
Co-stars: Robert Blake Billy Green Bush

SUSAN RINELL

1986 ONE TERRIFIC GUY
Director: Lou Antonio
Co-stars: Mariette Hartley Wayne Rogers Brian Robbins

1987   PALS
Director: Lou Antonio
Co-stars: George C. Scott Don Ameche Sylvia Sidney

BLANCHE RING

1940   IF I HAD MY WAY
Director: David Butler
Co-stars: Bing Crosby Charles Winninger Gloria Jean

MOLLY RINGWALD

1983   PACKIN' IT IN
Director: Jud Taylor
Co-stars: Richard Benjamin Paula Prentiss Tony Roberts

**1983   SPACEHUNTER: ADVENTURES IN
         THE FORBIDDEN ZONE**
Director: Lamont Johnson
Co-star: Peter Strauss

1984   SIXTEEN CANDLES
Director: John Hughes
Co-stars: Justin Henry Michael Schoeffling Gedde Watanabe

1985   THE BREAKFAST CLUB
Director: John Hughes
Co-stars: Emilio Estevez Judd Nelson Anthony Michael Hall

1985   SURVIVING
Director: Waris Hussein
Co-stars: Ellen Burstyn Len Cariou River Phoenix

1986   PRETTY IN PINK
Director: Howard Deutch
Co-stars: Harry Dean Stanton Andrew McCarthy Jon Cryer

1987   THE PICK-UP ARTIST
Director: James Toback
Co-stars: Robert Downey Jnr. Dennis Hopper Danny Aiello

1987   KING LEAR
Director: Jean-Luc Godard
Co-stars: Burgess Meredith Peter Sellers Woody Allen

1988   FRESH HORSE
Director: David Anspaugh
Co-stars: Andrew McCarthy Patti D'Arbanville Ben Stiller

1988   MAYBE BABY
Director: John Avildsen
Co-stars: Randall Batinkoff Kenneth Mars Conchata Ferrell

**1990   WOMEN AND MEN:
         STORIES OF SEDUCTION**
Director: Tony Richardson
Co-stars: Melanie Griffith Beau Bridges James Woods

1990   BETSY'S WEDDING
Director: Alan Alda
Co-stars: Madeline Kahn Joe Pesci Ally Sheedy

1990   STRIKE IT RICH
Director: James Scott
Co-stars: Robert Lindsay John Gielgud Max Wall

1992   FATAL LOVE
Director: Tom McLoughlin
Co-stars: Lee Grant Perry King Martin Landau

MARJORIE RIORDAN

1943   STAGE DOOR CANTEEN
Director: Frank Borzage
Co-stars: Cheryl Walker Lon McCallister Judith Anderson

1944   MR SKEFFINGTON
Director: Vincent Sherman
Co-stars: Bette Davis Claude Rains Walter Abel

1945   PURSUIT TO ALGIERS
Director: Roy William Neill
Co-stars: Basil Rathbone Nigel Bruce Rosalind Ivan

1946   THREE STRANGERS
Director: Jean Negulesco
Co-stars: Sydney Greenstreet Peter Lorre Geraldine Fitzgerald

GENEVIEVE RIOUX

1986   DECLINE OF THE AMERICAN EMPIRE
Director: Denys Arcand
Co-stars: Dominique Michel Dorothee Berryman

ELIZABETH RISDON

1916   THE MANXMAN
Co-star: Henry Ainley

1931   GUILTY HANDS
Director: W.S. Van Dyke
Co-stars: Lionel Barrymore Kay Francis Madge Evans

1935   CRIME AND PUNISHMENT
Director: Josef Von Sternberg
Co-stars: Peter Lorre Edward Arnold Tala Birrell

1936   CRAIG'S WIFE
Director: Dorothy Arzner
Co-stars: Rosalind Russell John Boles Billie Burke

1936   THE KING STEPS OUT
Director: Josef Von Sternberg
Co-stars: Grace Moore Franchot Tone Victor Jory

1936   LADY OF SECRETS
Director: Marion Gering
Co-stars: Ruth Chatterton Otto Kruger Lionel Atwill

1937   THE WOMAN BETWEEN
Director: Anatole Litvak
Co-stars: Paul Muni Miriam Hopkins Louis Hayward

1937   THEY WON'T FORGET
Director: Mervyn LeRoy
Co-stars: Claude Rains Gloria Dickson Lana Turner

1937   MANNEQUIN
Director: Frank Borzage
Co-stars: Joan Crawford Spencer Tracy Alan Curtis

1937   MAKE WAY FOR TOMORROW
Director: Leo McCarey
Co-stars: Victor Moore Beulah Bondi Thomas Mitchell

1938   THE AFFAIRS OF ANNABEL
Director: Lew Landers
Co-stars: Lucille Ball Jack Oakie Ruth Donnelly

1938   GIRLS ON PROBATION
Director: William McGann
Co-stars: Jane Bryan Ronald Reagan Sheila Bromley

1938   TOM SAWYER, DETECTIVE
Director: Louis King
Co-stars: Billy Cook Donald O'Connor Porter Hall

1939   MEXICAN SPITFIRE
Director: Leslie Goodwins
Co-stars: Lupe Velez Leon Errol Donald Woods

1939   I AM NOT AFRAID
Director: Crane Wilbur
Co-stars: Charley Grapewin Jane Bryan Henry O'Neill

1939   THE ROARING TWENTIES
Director: Raoul Walsh
Co-stars: James Cagney Humphrey Bogart Priscilla Lane

1939   THE FORGOTTEN WOMAN
Director: Harold Young
Co-stars: Sigrid Gurie Eve Arden William Lundigan

1939   FIVE CAME BACK
Director: John Farrow
Co-stars: Chester Morris Lucille Ball Patric Knowles

1939 DISPUTED PASSAGE
Director: Frank Borzage
Co-stars: Dorothy Lamour John Howard Akim Tamiroff

1940 HONEYMOON DEFERRED
Director: Lew Landers
Co-stars: Edmund Lowe Margaret Lindsay Joyce Compton

1940 THE HOWARDS OF VIRGINIA
Director: Frank Lloyd
Co-stars: Cary Grant Martha Scott Alan Marshall

1940 LET'S MAKE MUSIC
Director: Leslie Goodwins
Co-stars: Bob Crosby Jean Rogers Joseph Buloff

1940 SATURDAY'S CHILDREN
Director: Vincent Sherman
Co-stars: John Garfield Anne Shirley Claude Rains

1941 MR DYNAMITE
Director: John Rawlins
Co-stars: Lloyd Nolan Robert Armstrong Irene Hervey

1941 MEXICAN SPITFIRE'S BABY
Director: Leslie Goodwins
Co-stars: Lupe Velez Leon Errol Marion Martin

1941 MEXICAN SPITFIRE AT SEA
Director: Leslie Goodwins
Co-stars: Lupe Velez Leon Errol Charles Rogers

1942 MEXICAN SPITFIRE SEES A GHOST
Director: Leslie Goodwins
Co-stars: Lupe Velez Leon Errol Donald MacBride

1942 JAIL HOUSE BLUES
Co-stars: Robert Paige Nat Pendleton

1942 MEXICAN SPITFIRE'S ELEPHANT
Director: Leslie Goodwins
Co-stars: Lupe Velez Leon Errol Lyle Talbot

1942 ARE HUSBANDS NECESSARY
Director: Norman Taurog
Co-stars: Ray Milland Betty Field Patricia Morison

1943 HIGHER AND HIGHER
Director: Tim Whelan
Co-stars: Frank Sinatra Michele Morgan Jack Haley

1944 TALL IN THE SADDLE
Director: Edwin Marin
Co-stars: John Wayne Ella Raines Ward Bond

1944 WEIRD WOMAN
Director: Reginald LeBorg
Co-stars: Lon Chaney Evelyn Ankers Anne Gwynne

1945 MAMA LOVES PAPA
Director: Frank Strayer
Co-stars: Leon Errol Lawrence Tierney Edwin Maxwell

1945 GRISSLY'S MILLIONS
Director: John English
Co-stars: Paul Kelly Virginia Grey Robert Barret

1946 THE SHOCKING MISS PILGRIM
Director: George Seaton
Co-stars: Betty Grable Dick Haymes Ann Revere

1946 THE WALLS CAME TUMBLING DOWN
Director: Lothar Mendes
Co-stars: Lee Bowman Marguerite Chapman Lee Patrick

1947 LIFE WITH FATHER
Director: Michael Curtiz
Co-stars: William Powell Irene Dunn Elizabeth Taylor

1948 EVERY GIRL SHOULD BE MARRIED
Director: Don Hartman
Co-stars: Cary Grant Betsy Drake Franchot Tone

1950 GUILTY OF TREASON
Director: Felix Feist
Co-stars: Charles Bickford Paul Kelly Bonita Granville

1950 THE SECRET FURY
Director: Mel Ferrer
Co-stars: Claudette Colbert Robert Ryan Jane Cowl

1950 BUNCO SQUAD
Director: Norman Taurog
Co-stars: Robert Sterling Ricardo Cortez Joan Dixon

1951 BANNERLINE
Director: Henry Berman
Co-stars: Lionel Barrymore Sally Forrest Keefe Brasselle

MIRIAM RISELLE

1939 TEVYA THE MILKMAN
Director: Maurice Schwarz
Co-stars: Rebecca Weintraub Paula Lubelska

GIUDITTA RISSONE

1942 FOUR STEPS IN THE CLOUDS
Director: Alessandro Blasetti
Co-stars: Gino Cervi Adriana Benetti

JUNE RITCHIE

1962 A KIND OF LOVING
Director: John Schlesinger
Co-stars: Alan Bates Thora Hird Gwen Nelson

1962 LIVE NOW - PAY LATER
Director: Jay Lewis
Co-stars: Ian Hendry John Gregson Liz Fraser

1963 THIS IS MY STREET
Director: Sidney Hayers
Co-stars: Ian Hendry Avice Landon John Hurt

1963 THE WORLD TEN TIMES OVER
Director: Wolf Rilla
Co-stars: Sylvia Syms Edward Judd William Hartnell

THELMA RITTER
Nominated For Best Supporting Actress Is 1951 For "The Mating Season",
In 1952 For "With A Song In My Heart", In 1953 For "Pickup On South
Street", In 1959 For "Pillow Talk" And In 1961 For "Birdman Of Alcatraz"

1947 MIRACLE ON 34TH STREET
Director: George Seaton
Co-stars: Edmund Gwenn Maureen O'Hara John Payne

1949 CITY ACROSS THE RIVER
Director: Maxwell Shane
Co-stars: Stephen McNally Tony Curtis Jeff Corey

1949 A LETTER TO THREE WIVES
Director: Joseph Mankiewicz
Co-stars: Jeanne Crain Linda Darnell Ann Sothern

1950 I'LL GET BY
Director: Richard Sale
Co-stars: June Haver Gloria De Haven William Lundigan

1950 PERFECT STRANGERS
Director: Bretaigne Windust
Co-stars: Ginger Rogers Dennis Morgan

1950 ALL ABOUT EVE
Director: Joseph Mankiewicz
Co-stars: Bette Davis George Sanders Anne Baxter

1951 THE MATING SEASON
Director: Mitchell Leisen
Co-stars: Gene Tierney John Lund Jan Sterling

1951 THE MODEL AND THE MARRIAGE BROKER
Director: George Cukor
Co-stars: Jeanne Crain Scott Brady Zero Mostel

1951 AS YOUNG AS YOU FEEL
Director: Harmon Jones
Co-stars: Monty Woolley David Wayne Jean Peters

1952 WITH A SONG IN MY HEART
Director: Walter Lang
Co-stars: Susan Hayward David Wayne Rory Calhoun

1953 TITANIC
Director: Jean Negulesco
Co-stars: Clifton Webb Barbara Stanwyck Robert Wagner

1953 PICKUP ON SOUTH STREET
Director: Samuel Fuller
Co-stars: Richard Widmark Jean Peters Richard Kiley

1953 THE FARMER TAKES A WIFE
Director: Henry Levin
Co-stars: Betty Grable Dale Robertson John Carroll

1954 REAR WINDOW
Director: Alfred Hitchcock
Co-stars: James Stewart Grace Kelly Raymond Burr

1955 LUCY GALLANT
Director: Robert Parrish
Co-stars: Jane Wyman Charlton Heston Claire Trevor

1955 DADDY LONG LEGS
Director: Jean Negulesco
Co-stars: Fred Astaire Leslie Caron Terry Moore

1956 THE PROUD AND PROFANE
Director: George Seaton
Co-stars: William Holden Deborah Kerr Dean Martin

1959 PILLOW TALK
Director: Michael Gordon
Co-stars: Doris Day Rock Hudson Tony Randall

1959 HOLE IN THE HEAD
Director: Frank Capra
Co-stars: Frank Sinatra Edward G. Robinson Eleanor Parker

1961 SECOND TIME AROUND
Director: Vincent Sherman
Co-stars: Debbie Reynolds Steve Forrest Andy Griffith

1961 THE MISFITS
Director: John Huston
Co-stars: Clark Gable Marilyn Monroe Montgomery Clift

1961 BIRDMAN OF ALCATRAZ
Director: John Frankenheimer
Co-stars: Burt Lancaster Karl Malden Betty Field

1962 HOW THE WEST WAS WON
Director: John Ford
Co-stars: Debbie Reynolds Carroll Baker George Peppard

1963 FOR LOVE OR MONEY
Director: Michael Gordon
Co-stars: Kirk Douglas Mitzi Gaynor Julie Newman

1963 MOVE OVER DARLING
Director: Michael Gordon
Co-stars: Doris Day James Garner Polly Bergen

1963 A NEW KIND OF LOVE
Director: Melville Shavelson
Co-stars: Paul Newman Joanne Woodward

1965 BOEING BOEING
Director: John Rich
Co-stars: Tony Curtis Jerry Lewis Dany Saval

1967 THE INCIDENT
Director: Larry Peerce
Co-stars: Martin Sheen Tony Musante Beau Bridges

EMMANUELE RIVA

1959 HIROSHIMA MON AMOUR
Director: Alain Resnais
Co-stars: Eiji Okada Stella Dassas Pierre Barbaud

1960 KAPO
Director: Gillo Pontecorvo
Co-stars: Susan Strasberg Laurent Terzieff

1960 ADUA E LE COMPAGNE
Director: Antonio Pietrangeli
Co-stars: Simone Signoret Marcello Mastroianni

1961 LEON MARIN, PRIEST
Director: Jean-Pierre Melville
Co-stars: Jean-Paul Belmondo Irene Tunc

1965 THOMAS L'IMPOSTEUR
Director: Georges Franjou
Co-stars: Frabrice Rouleau Jean Servais Edith Scob

1982 THE EYES, THE MOUTH
Director: Marco Bellochio
Co-stars: Lou Castel Angela Molina Michel Piccoli

1993 THREE COLOURS:BLUE
Director: Krzysztof Kieslowski
Co-stars: Juliette Binoche Benoit Regent

LUISA RIVELLI

1966 THE BIG GUNDOWN
Director: Sergio Sellima
Co-stars: Lee Van Cleef Tomas Milian Walter Barnes

CECILIA RIVERA

1972 AGUIRRE, WRATH OF GOD
Director: Werner Herzog
Co-stars: Klaus Kinski Ruy Guerra Helena Rojo

CHITA RIVERA

1969 SWEET CHARITY
Director: Robert Fosse
Co-stars: Shirley Maclaine Ricardo Montalban Stubby Kaye

1973 THE MARCUS-NELSON MURDERS
Director: Joseph Sargent
Co-stars: Telly Savalas Marjoe Gortner Jose Ferrer

1987 MAYFLOWER MADAM
Director: Lou Antonio
Co-stars: Candice Bergen Chris Sarandon Caitlin Clarke

JOAN RIVERS

1968 THE SWIMMER
Director: Sydney Pollack
Co-stars: Burt Lancaster Janice Rule Kim Hunter

1984 THE MUPPETS TAKE MANHATTAN
Director: Frank Oz
Co-stars: Art Carney Liza Minnelli Brooke Shields

1987 SPACEBALLS
Director: Mel Brooks
Co-stars: John Candy Rick Moranis Bill Pullman

1990 HOW TO MURDER A MILLIONAIRE
Director: Paul Schneider
Co-stars: Alex Rocca Morgan Fairchild David Ogden Stiers

1994 STARTING AGAIN
Director: Oz Scott
Co-stars: Melissa Rivers Mark Kelly

MELISSA RIVERS

1994 STARTING AGAIN
Director: Oz Scott
Co-stars: Mark Kelly Joan Rivers

MARIE RIVIERE

1986 FOUR ADVENTURES OF REINETTE AND MIRABELLE
Director: Eric Rohmer
Co-stars: Joelle Miquel Jessica Forde

1986 THE GREEN RAY
Director: Eric Rohmer
Co-stars: Lisa Heredia Vincent Gautier Eric Hamm

ELENA RIZZIERI

1949 THE GLASS MOUNTAIN (Voice)
Director: Henry Cass
Co-stars: Michael Dennison Dulcie Gray Valentina Cortesa

LESLEY ROACH (Child)

1971 MR HORATIO KNIBBLES
Director: Robert Hird
Co-stars: Gary Smith Rachel Brennock John Ash

VIOLA ROCHE

1950 ROYAL WEDDING
Director: Stanley Donen
Co-stars: Fred Astaire Jane Powell Peter Lawford

AMY ROBBINS

1997 UP ON THE ROOF
Director: Simon Moore
Co-star: Adrian Lester

BARBARA ROBBINS

1934 HAT, COAT AND GLOVES
Director: Worthington Miner
Co-stars: Ricardo Cortez John Beal Margaret Hamilton

CAROL ROBBINS

1986 'NIGHT MOTHER
Director: Tom Moore
Co-stars: Anne Bancroft Sissy Spacek Ed Berke

GALE ROBBINS

1944 IN THE MEANTIME, DARLING
Director: Otto Preminger
Co-stars: Jeanne Crain Frank Latimore Mary Nash

1948 RACE STREET
Director: Edwin Marin
Co-stars: George Raft Marilyn Maxwell William Bendix

1949 THE BARKLEYS OF BROADWAY
Director: Charles Walters
Co-stars: Fred Astaire Ginger Rogers Oscar Levant

1950 BETWEEN MIDNIGHT AND DAWN
Director: Gordon Douglas
Co-stars: Mark Stevens Edmond O'Brien Gale Storm

1950 THE FULLER BRUSH GIRL
Director: Lloyd Bacon
Co-stars: Lucille Ball Eddie Albert Jeff Donnell

1950 THREE LITTLE WORDS
Director: Richard Thorpe
Co-stars: Fred Astaire Red Skelton Vera-Ellen

1951 STRICTLY DISHONORABLE
Director: Norman Panama
Co-stars: Ezio Pinza Janet Leigh Maria Palmer

1952 THE BRIGAND
Director: Phil Karlson
Co-stars: Anthony Dexter Anthony Quinn Jody Lawrance

1952 THE BELLE OF NEW YORK
Director: Charles Walters
Co-stars: Fred Astaire Vera-Ellen Marjorie Main

1953 CALAMITY JANE
Director: David Butler
Co-stars: Doris Day Howard Keel Philip Carey

1958 QUANTRILL'S RAIDERS
Director: Edward Bernds
Co-stars: Steve Cochran Diane Brewster Leo Gordon

HELENE ROBERT

1939 FRIC-FRAC
Director: Maurice Lehmann
Co-stars: Michel Simon Fernandel Arletty

LYDA ROBERTI

1932 THE KID FROM SPAIN
Director: Leo McCarey
Co-stars: Eddie Cantor Robert Young Ruth Hall

1932 MILLION DOLLAR LEGS
Director: Edward Cline
Co-stars: W.C. Fields Jack Oakie Hugh Herbert

1932 DANCERS IN THE DARK
Director: David Burton
Co-stars: Mirian Hopkins Jack Oakie George Raft

1933 THREE-CORNERED MOON
Director: Elliott Nugent
Co-stars: Claudette Colbert Mary Bolland Richard Arlen

1933 TORCH SINGER
Director: Alexander Hall
Co-stars: Claudette Colbert Ricardo Cortez David Manners

1934 COLLEGE RHYTHM
Director: Norman Taurog
Co-stars: Jack Oakie Joe Penner Mary Brian

1935 GEORGE WHITE'S 1935 SCANDALS
Director: George White
Co-stars: Alice Faye James Dunn Eleanor Powell

1935 THE BIG BROADCAST OF 1936
Director: Norman Taurog
Co-stars: Jack Oakie Bing Crosby Ethel Merman

1937 NOBODY'S BABY
Director: Gus Meins
Co-stars: Patsy Kelly Lynne Overman Robert Armstrong

1937 PICK A STAR
Director: Edward Sedgwick
Co-stars: Jack Haley Patsy Kelly Rosina Lawrence

1938 WIDE OPEN FACES
Director: Kurt Neuman
Co-stars: Joe E. Brown Jane Wyman Alison Skipworth

ADELE ROBERTS

1946 THE NOTORIOUS LONE WOLF
Director: Ross Lederman
Co-stars: Gerald Mohr Janis Carter Eric Blore

1946 JUST BEFORE DAWN
Director: William Castle
Co-stars: Warner Baxter Martin Kosleck Mona Barrie

ALICE ROBERTS

1929 PANDORA'S BOX
Director: G.W. Pabst
Co-stars: Louise Brooks Fritz Kortner Franz Lederer

ALLENE ROBERTS

1947   **THE RED HOUSE**
Director: Delmer Daves
Co-stars: Edward G. Robinson Rory Calhoun Lon McCallister

1948   **SIGN OF THE RAM**
Director: John Sturges
Co-stars: Susan Peters Alexander Knox Peggy Ann Garner

1949   **KNOCK ON ANY DOOR**
Director: Nicholas Ray
Co-stars: Humphrey Bogart John Derek George Macready

1950   **UNION STATION**
Director: Rudolph Mate
Co-stars: William Holden Barry Fitzgerald Nancy Olson

1951   **THE HOODLUM**
Director: Max Nosseck
Co-stars: Lawrence Tierney Liza Golm Edward Tierney

BEATRICE ROBERTS

1937   **LOVE TAKES FLIGHT**
Co-star: Bruce Cabot

1938   **THE DEVIL'S PARTY**
Co-star: Victor McLaglen

BEVERLY ROBERTS

1936   **CHINA CLIPPER**
Director: Ray Enright
Co-stars: Pat O'Brien Humphrey Bogart Ross Alexander

1936   **THE SINGING KID**
Director: William Keighley
Co-stars: Al Jolson Sybil Jason Allen Jenkins

1936   **TWO AGAINST THE WORLD**
Director: William McGann
Co-stars: Humphrey Bogart Henry O'Neill Linda Perry

1937   **WEST OF SHANGHAI**
Director: John Farrow
Co-stars: Boris Karloff Ricardo Cortez Gordon Oliver

1937   **THE PERFECT SPECIMEN**
Director: Michael Curtiz
Co-stars: Errol Flynn May Robson Joan Blondell

1937   **HER HUSBAND'S SECRETARY**
Co-star: Warren Hull

1937   **GOD'S COUNTRY AND THE WOMAN**
Director: William Keighley
Co-stars: George Brent Barton Maclane Alan Hale

1937   **EXPENSIVE HUSBANDS**
Co-star: Patric Knowles

1938   **FLIRTING WITH FATE**
Director: Frank McDonald
Co-stars: Joe E. Brown Wynne Gibson Steffi Duna

1938   **MAKING THE HEADLINES**
Co-stars: Jack Holt Marjorie Gateson Tom Kennedy

1938   **CALL OF THE YUKON**
Co-stars: Richard Arlen Lyle Talbot

1938   **THE DAREDEVIL DRIVERS**
Director: Dick Purcell

1939   **TROPIC FURY**
Co-stars: Richard Arlen Andy Devine

1939   **FIRST OFFENDERS**
Co-stars: Walter Abel John Hamilton

DORIS ROBERTS

1970   **THE HONEYMOON KILLERS**
Director: Leonard Kastle
Co-stars: Shirley Stoler Tony LoBianco Kip McArdle

1974   **HESTER STREET**
Director: Joan Micklin Silver
Co-stars: Steven Keats Carol Kane Mel Howard

1983   **A LETTER TO THREE WIVES**
Director: Larry Elikann
Co-stars: Loni Anderson Michele Lee Ben Gazzara

1983   **ANOTHER WOMAN'S CHILD**
Director: John Erman
Co-stars: Linda Lavin Tony LoBianco Joyce Van Patton

1987   **NUMBER ONE WITH A BULLET**
Director: Jack Smight
Co-stars: Robert Carradine Billy Dee Williams

1989   **NATIONAL LAMPOON'S CHRISTMAS VACATION**
Director: Jermiah Chechik
Co-stars: Chevy Chase Beverly D'Angelo

FLORENCE ROBERTS

1932   **WESTWARD PASSAGE**
Director: Robert Milton
Co-stars: Ann Harding Laurence Olivier Zasu Pitts

1932   **MAKE ME A STAR**
Director: William Beaudine
Co-stars: Stuart Erwin Joan Blondell Zasu Pitts

1933   **TORCH SINGER**
Director: Alexander Hall
Co-stars: Claudette Colbert Baby Leroy Ricardo Cortez

1933   **DANGEROUSLY YOURS**
Director: Frank Tuttle
Co-stars: Warner Baxter Miriam Jordan Herbert Mundin

1934   **BABES IN TOYLAND**
Director: Gus Meins
Co-stars: Stan Laurel Oliver Hardy Charlotte Henry

1936   **EVERY SATURDAY NIGHT**
Director: Frank Strayer
Co-stars: Jed Prouty Spring Byington June Carlson

1936   **EDUCATING FATHER**
Director: Frank Strayer
Co-stars: Jed Prouty Spring Byington George Ernest

1936   **BACK TO NATURE**
Director: Frank Strayer
Co-stars: Jed Prouty Spring Byington Kenneth Lake

1937   **BIG BUSINESS**
Director: Frank Strayer
Co-stars: Jed Prouty Spring Byington June Lang

1937   **OFF TO THE RACES**
Director: Frank Strayer
Co-stars: Jed Prouty Spring Byington June Carlson

1937   **BORROWING TROUBLE**
Director: Frank Strayer
Co-stars: Jed Prouty Spring Byington George Ernest

1937   **HOT WATER**
Director: Frank Strayer
Co-stars: Jed Prouty Spring Byington Kenneth Lake

1937   **LOVE ON A BUDGET**
Director: Frank Strayer
Co-stars: Jed Prouty Spring Byington June Lang

1938   **TRIP TO PARIS**
Director: Frank Strayer
Co-stars: Jed Prouty Spring Byington June Carlson

1938　SAFETY IN NUMBERS
Director:　Frank Strayer
Co-stars:　Jed Prouty Spring Byington George Ernest

1938　DOWN ON THE FARM
Director:　Frank Strayer
Co-stars:　Jed Prouty Spring Byington George Ernest

1939　EVERYBODY'S BABY
Director:　Frank Strayer
Co-stars:　Jed Prouty Spring Byington June Carlson

1939　QUICK MILLIONS
Director:　Frank Strayer
Co-stars:　Jed Prouty Spring Byington June Lang

1939　THE JONES FAMILY IN HOLLYWOOD
Director:　Frank Strayer
Co-stars:　Jed Prouty Kenneth Lake June Lang

1939　TOO BUSY TO WORK
Director:　Frank Strayer
Co-stars:　Jed Prouty Spring Byington Billy Mahan

1940　ON THEIR OWN
Director:　Frank Strayer
Co-stars:　Jed Prouty Spring Byington June Carlson

GENE ROBERTS

1948　STORK BITES MAN
Director:　Cyril Endfield
Co-stars:　Jackie Cooper Gus Schilling Emory Parnell

JUDITH ROBERTS

1971　MINNIE AND MOSKOWITZ
Director:　John Cassavetes
Co-stars:　Gena Rowlands Seymour Cassel Val Avery

1976　ERASERHEAD
Director:　David Lynch
Co-stars:　John Nance Charlotte Stewart Allen Joseph

JULIA ROBERTS
(Sister Of Eric Roberts / Married Lyle Lovett)
Nominated For Best Actress In 1990 For "Pretty Woman"
Nominated For Best Supporting Actress In 1989 For "Steel Magnolias"

1988　BLOOD RED
Director:　Peter Masterson
Co-stars:　Eric Roberts Dennis Hopper Burt Young

1988　SATISFACTION
Director:　Joan Freeman
Co-stars:　Justine Bateman Liam Neeson Trini Alvarado

1988　MYSTIC PIZZA
Director:　Donald Petrie
Co-stars:　Annabeth Gish Lili Taylor Conchata Ferrell

1989　STEEL MAGNOLIAS
Director:　Herbert Ross
Co-stars:　Sally Field Shirley Maclaine Dolly Parton

1990　FLATLINERS
Director:　Joel Schumacher
Co-stars:　Kiefer Sutherland Kevin Bacon

1990　PRETTY WOMAN
Director:　Gary Marshall
Co-stars:　Richard Gere Ralph Bellamy Laura San Giacomo

1991　DYING YOUNG
Director:　Joel Schumacher
Co-stars:　Campbell Scott Colleen Dewhurst Ellen Burstyn

1991　HOOK
Director:　Steven Spielberg
Co-stars:　Robin Williams Dustin Hoffman Bob Hoskins

1991　SLEEPING WITH THE ENEMY
Director:　Joseph Ruben
Co-stars:　Patrick Bergin Kevin Anderson Kyle Secor

1992　THE PLAYER
Director:　Robert Altman
Co-stars:　Tim Robbins Greta Scacchi Whoopi Goldberg

1993　THE PELICAN BRIEF
Director:　Alan J. Pakula
Co-stars:　Denzel Washington Sam Shepard Robert Culp

1994　I LOVE TROUBLE
Director:　Charles Shyer
Co-stars:　Nick Nolte Robert Loggia Olympia Dukakis

1994　PRET-A-PORTER
Director:　Robert Altman
Co-stars:　Kim Basinger Sophia Loren Tim Robbins

1995　MARY REILLY
Director:　Stephen Frears
Co-stars:　Glenn Close John Malkovich

1996　SOMETHING TO TALK ABOUT
Director:　Lasse Hallstrom
Co-stars:　Robert Duvall Dennis Quaid Gena Rowlands

1996　MICHAEL COLLINS
Director:　Neil Jordan
Co-stars:　Stephen Rea Liam Neeson Alan Rickman

1996　EVERYBODY SAYS I LOVE YOU
Director:　Woody Allen
Co-stars:　Goldie Hawn Drew Barrymore Edward Norton

1997　MY BEST FRIEND'S WEDDING
Director:　P.J. Hogan
Co-stars:　Dermot Mulroney Cameron Diaz Rupert Everett

1997　THE CONSPIRACY THEORY
Director:　Richard Donner
Co-stars:　Mel Gibson Patrick Stewart

LEONA ROBERTS

1939　GONE WITH THE WIND
Director:　Victor Fleming
Co-stars:　Clark Gable Vivien Leigh Leslie Howard

LYNNE ROBERTS

1937　MAMA RUNS WILD
Co-star:　William Henry

1937　HEART OF THE ROCKIES
Co-stars:　Ray Corrigan Max Terhune

1938　THE HIGGINS FAMILY
Director:　Gus Meins
Co-stars:　James Gleason Lucile Gleason Russell Gleason

1938　BILLY THE KID RETURNS
Co-star:　Roy Rogers

1938　DICK TRACY RETURNS
Director:　William Witney
Co-stars:　Ralph Byrd Charles Middleton Jerry Tucker

1941　THE BRIDE WORE CRUTCHES
Director:　Shepherd Traube
Co-stars:　Ted North Edgar Kennedy Lionel Stander

1941　LAST OF THE DUANES
Co-star:　George Montgomery

1941　ROMANCE OF THE RIO GRANDE
Director:　Herbert Leeds
Co-stars:　Cesar Romero Patricia Morison

1942　DR RENAULT'S SECRET
Director:　Harry Lachman
Co-stars:　George Zucco J. Carrol Naish John Shepperd

1943   **THE GHOST THAT WALKS ALONE**
Director: Lew Landers
Co-stars: Arthur Lake Janis Carter Frank Sully

1943   **QUIET PLEASE, MURDER**
Director: John Larkin
Co-stars: George Sanders Gail Patrick Richard Denning

1944   **MY BUDDY**
Director: Steve Sekely
Co-stars: Don Barry Ruth Terry Emma Dunn

1945   **THE BIG BONANZA**
Co-stars: Richard Arlen George Hayes

1945   **THE PHANTOM SPEAKS**
Co-stars: Richard Arlen Jonathan Hale

1947   **SADDLE PALS**
Co-star: Gene Autry

1947   **ROBIN HOOD OF TEXAS**
Co-star: Gene Autry

1947   **THAT'S MY GIRL**
Co-stars: Don Barry Paul Stanton

1948   **LIGHTNIN' IN THE FOREST**
Co-star: Warren Douglas

1952   **THE BLAZING FOREST**
Director: Edward Ludwig
Co-stars: John Payne Susan Morrow Agnes Moorehead

1952   **BECAUSE OF YOU**
Director: Joseph Pevney
Co-stars: Loretta Young Jeff Chandler Alex Nicol

NANCY ROBERTS

1956   **IT'S A GREAT DAY**
Director: John Warrington
Co-stars: Ruth Dunning Edward Evans Christopher Beeny

RACHEL ROBERTS *(Married Rex Harrison)*
Nominated For Best Supporting Actress In 1963 For This Sporting Life

1953   **VALLEY OF SONG**
Director: Gilbert Gunn
Co-stars: Mervyn Jones Clifford Evans Maureen Swanson

1953   **THE WEAK AND THE WICKED**
Director: J. Lee-Thompson
Co-stars: Glynis Johns Diana Dors John Gregson

1954   **THE CROWDED DAY**
Director: John Guillermin
Co-stars: Joan Rice John Gregson Freda Jackson

1957   **THE GOOD COMPANIONS**
Director: J. Lee-Thompson
Co-stars: Eric Portman Celia Johnson Janette Scot

1960   **SATURDAY NIGHT AND SUNDAY MORNING**
Director: Karel Reisz
Co-stars: Albert Finney Hylda Baker

1963   **THIS SPORTING LIFE**
Director: Lindsay Anderson
Co-stars: Richard Harris Alan Badel William Hartnell

1963   **THE GIRL ON APPROVAL**
Director: Charles Frend
Co-stars: James Maxwell Annette Whitley John Dare

1968   **A FLEA IN HER EAR**
Director: Jacques Charon
Co-stars: Rex Harrison Rosemary Harris Louis Jourdan

1969   **THE RECKONING**
Director: Jack Gold
Co-stars: Nicol Williamson Ann Bell Zena Walker

1970   **DOCTORS' WIVES**
Director: George Schaefer
Co-stars: Richard Crenna Gene Hackman Janice Rule

1971   **WILD ROVERS**
Director: Blake Edwards
Co-stars: William Holden Ryan O'Neal Karl Malden

1973   **O LUCKY MAN !**
Director: Lindsay Anderson
Co-stars: Malcolm McDowell Arthur Lowe Helen Mirren

1973   **ALPHA BETA**
Director: Anthony Page
Co-star: Albert Finney

1973   **THE BELSTONE FOX**
Director: James Hill
Co-stars: Eric Porter Jeremy Kemp Bill Travers

1974   **GREAT EXPECTATIONS**
Director: Joseph Hardy
Co-stars: Michael York Sarah Miles James Mason

1974   **MURDER ON THE ORIENT EXPRESS**
Director: Sidney Lumet
Co-stars: Albert Finney Ingrid Bergman Lauren Bacall

1975   **PICNIC AT HANGING ROCK**
Director: Peter Weir
Co-stars: Dominic Guard Helen Morse Kirsty Child

1978   **FOUL PLAY**
Director: Colin Higgins
Co-stars: Goldie Hawn Chevy Chase Burgess Meredith

1979   **WHEN A STRANGER CALLS**
Director: Fred Walton
Co-stars: Charles Durning Carol Kane Tony Beckley

1979   **YANKS**
Director: John Schlesinger
Co-stars: Richard Gere Vanessa Redgrave Lisa Eichhorn

1980   **CHARLIE CHAN AND THE CURSE OF THE DRAGON QUEEN**
Director: Clive Donner
Co-stars: Peter Ustinov Brian Keith

ROWENA ROBERTS

1988   **WORDS OF LOVE**
Director: Charlie Creed-Miles
Co-stars: Tom Bell Liz Smith

TANYA ROBERTS

1977   **FINGERS**
Director: James Toback
Co-stars: Harvey Keitel Tisa Farrow Jim Brown

1982   **THE BEASTMASTER**
Director: Don Coscarelli
Co-stars: Marc Singer Rip Torn John Amos

1983   **MURDER ME, MURDER YOU**
Director: Gary Nelson
Co-stars: Stacy Keach Don Stroud Delta Burke

1984   **SHEENA QUEEN OF THE JUNGLE**
Director: John Guillermin
Co-stars: Ted Wass Donovan Scott

1985   **A VIEW TO A KILL**
Director: John Glen
Co-stars: Roger Moore Christopher Walken Grace Jones

1990   **NIGHT EYES**
Director: Jag Mundrha
Co-star: Andrew Stevens

TRACEY ROBERTS

1952 ACTORS AND SIN
Director: Ben Hecht
Co-stars: Edward G. Robinson Marsha Hunt Eddie Albert

1952 FORT DEFIANCE
Director: John Rawlins
Co-stars: Dane Clark Ben Johnson Peter Graves

JENNY ROBERTSON

1988 BULL DURHAM
Director: Ron Sheldon
Co-stars: Kevin Costner Susan Sarandon Tim Robbins

1989 UNCONQUERED
Director: Dick Lowry
Co-stars: Peter Coyote Dermot Mulroney Tess Harper

1992 THE DANGER OF LOVE
Director: Joyce Chopra
Co-stars: Joseph Bologna Joe Penny

KATHLEEN ROBERTSON

1992 LAPSE OF MEMORY
Director: Patrick DeWolf
Co-stars: John Hurt Marthe Keller Matthew MacKay

1992 NIGHT HUNT
Director: Bill Corcoran
Co-stars: Stefanie Powers Helen Shaver

1994 THE PRICE OF VENGEANCE
Director: Dick Lowry
Co-stars: Dean Stockwell Michael Gross Mary Kay Place

RACHEL ROBERTSON

1990 THE WRECK ON THE HIGHWAY
Director: Sandy Johnson
Co-stars: Tam White Lynn Anderson Ryan Quinn

WENDY ROBIE

1991 THE PEOPLE UNDER THE STAIRS
Director: Wes Craven
Co-stars: Brandon Adams Everett McGill Ving Rhames

DANY ROBIN

1947 LE SILENCE EST D'OR
Director: Rene Clair
Co-stars: Maurice Chevalier Francois Perier Marcelle Derrien

1951 HISTOIRE D'AMOUR
Director: Robert Clavel
Co-stars: Louis Jouvet Daniel Gelin

1952 LA FETE A HENRIETTE
Director: Julien Duvivier
Co-stars: Michel Auclair Hildegard Knef Michel Roux

1954 ACT OF LOVE
Director: Anatole Litvak
Co-stars: Kirk Douglas Barbara Laage Brigitte Bardot

1962 WALTZ OF THE TOREADORS
Director: John Guillermin
Co-stars: Peter Sellers Margaret Leighton John Fraser

1963 FOLLOW THE BOYS
Director: Richard Thorpe
Co-stars: Connie Francis Paula Prentiss Russ Tamblyn

1966 CARRY ON DON'T LOSE YOUR HEAD
Director: Gerald Thomas
Co-stars: Sid James Kenneth Williams Joan Sims

1968 THE BEST HOUSE IN LONDON
Director: Philip Saville
Co-stars: David Hemmings George Sanders John Cleese

1969 TOPAZ
Director: Alfred Hitchcock
Co-stars: John Forsythe John Vernon Karin Dor

MARY ROBIN-REDD

1973 LINDA
Director: Jack Smight
Co-stars: Stella Stevens Ed Nelson John Saxon

JESSIE ROBINS

1967 THE FEARLESS VAMPIRE KILLERS
Director: Roman Polanski
Co-stars: Sharon Tate Jack MacGowran Alfie Bass

LAILA ROBINS

1987 PLANES, TRAINS AND AUTOMOBILES
Director: John Hughes
Co-stars: Steve Martin John Candy Kevin Bacon

1989 AN INNOCENT MAN
Director: Peter Yates
Co-stars: Tom Selleck F. Murray Abraham David Rasche

1990 WELCOME HOME, ROXY CARMICHAEL
Director: Jim Abrahams
Co-stars: Winona Ryder Jeff Daniels Dinah Manoff

PHYLLIS ROBINS

1947 THEY MADE ME A FUGITIVE
Director: Alberto Cavalcanti
Co-stars: Trevor Howard Sally Gray Rene Ray

AEMELIA ROBINS *(Child)*

1995 THE HAUNTING OF LISA
Director: Don McBrearty
Co-stars: Cheryl Ladd Duncan Regehr

AMY ROBINSON

1973 MEAN STREETS
Director: Martin Scorsese
Co-stars: Harvey Keitel Robert De Niro David Carradine

ANGELA ROBINSON

1988 OUT OF THE DARK
Director: Michael Schroeder
Co-stars: Karen Black Cameron Dye Tab Hunter

ANN ROBINSON

1953 WAR OF THE WORLDS
Director: Byron Haskin
Co-stars: Gene Barry Les Tremayne Sandra Giglio

1954 DRAGNET
Director: Jack Webb
Co-stars: Richard Boone Ben Alexander Jack Webb

1959 IMITATION OF LIFE
Director: Douglas Sirk
Co-stars: Lana Turner Juanita Moore John Gavin

CLAUDIA ROBINSON

1987 THE UNHOLY
Director: Camilio Vilo
Co-stars: Trevor Howard Ben Cross Hal Halbrook

1992 WIDE SARGASSO SEA
Director: John Duigan
Co-stars: Karina Lombard Rachel Ward Michael York

FRANCES ROBINSON

1938 FORBIDDEN VALLEY
Co-stars: Noah Beery Jnr. Samuel S. Hinds

1939 DESPERATE TRAILS
Co-stars: Johnny Mack Brown Bob Baker

1939 LITTLE ACCIDENT
Director: Charles Lamont
Co-stars: Baby Sandy Richard Carlson Florence Rice

1941 SMILIN' THROUGH
Director: Frank Borzage
Co-stars: Jeanette MacDonald Gene Raymond Brian Aherne

1941 THE LONE WOLF KEEPS A DATE
Director: Sidney Salkow
Co-stars: Warren William Bruce Bennett Eric Blore

HARRIET ROBINSON

1993 WHITE ANGEL
Director: Chris Jones
Co-stars: Peter Firth Don Henderson Anne Catherine Arton

JO-ANN ROBINSON

1970 THE CROSS AND THE SWITCHBLADE
Director: Don Murray
Co-stars: Pat Boone Erik Estrada Jackie Giroux

JULIA ANNE ROBINSON

1972 THE KING OF MARVIN GARDENS
Director: Bob Rafelson
Co-stars: Jack Nicholson Bruce Dern Ellen Burstyn

JULIE ROBINSON

1956 LUST FOR LIFE
Director: Vincent Minnelli
Co-stars: Kirk Douglas Anthony Quinn Pamela Brown

LAURA ROBINSON

1983 THRILLKILL
Director: Anthony D'Andrea
Co-stars: Robin Ward Gina Massey Eugene Clerk

MADELEINE ROBINSON

1943 DOUCE
Director: Claude Autant-Lara
Co-stars: Odette Joyeux Jean Debucourt Marguerite Moreno

1943 LUMIERE D'ETE
Director: Jean Gremillion
Co-stars: Madeleine Renaud Pierre Brasseur Jane Marken

1948 SUCH A PRETTY LITTLE BEACH
Director: Yves Allegret
Co-stars: Gerard Philipe Jean Servais Jane Marken

1948 ENTRE ONZE HEURES ET MINUIT
Director: Henri Decoin
Co-stars: Lois Jouvet Robert Arnoux

1950 DIEU A BESOIN DES HOMMES
Director: Jean Delannoy
Co-stars: Pierre Fresnay Daniel Gelin Sylvie

1959 A DOUBLE TOUR
Director: Claude Chabrol
Co-stars: Antonella Lualdi Jacques Dacqmine Bernadette Lafont

1962 THE TRIAL
Director: Orson Welles
Co-stars: Jeanne Moreau Anthony Perkins Elsa Martinelli

SHARI ROBINSON

1949 YOU'RE MY EVERYTHING
Director: Walter Lang
Co-stars: Anne Baxter Dan Dailey Anne Revere

SUSAN ROBINSON

1972 THE GREAT WALTZ
Director: Andrew Stone
Co-stars: Horst Buchholz Nigel Patrick Mary Costa

FLORA ROBSON
Nominated For Best Supporting Actress In 1943 For "Saratoga Trunk"

1934 CATHERINE THE GREAT
Director: Paul Czinner
Co-stars: Elizabeth Bergner Douglas Fairbanks

1937 FIRE OVER ENGLAND
Director: William Howard
Co-stars: Laurence Olivier Raymond Massey Vivien Leigh

1937 FAREWELL AGAIN
Director: Tim Whelan
Co-stars: Leslie Banks Robert Newton Rene Ray

1939 INVISIBLE STRIPES
Director: Lloyd Bacon
Co-stars: George Raft Humphrey Bogart William Holden

1939 POISON PEN
Director: Paul Stein
Co-stars: Robert Newton Ann Todd Reginald Tate

1939 WE ARE NOT ALONE
Director: Edmund Goulding
Co-stars: Paul Muni Jane Bryan Una O'Connor

1939 WUTHERING HEIGHTS
Director: William Wyler
Co-stars: Laurence Olivier Merle Oberon David Niven

1940 THE SEA HAWK
Director: Michael Curtiz
Co-stars: Errol Flynn Brenda Marshall Claude Rains

1941 BAHAMA PASSAGE
Director: Edward Griffith
Co-stars: Madeleine Carroll Sterling Hayden

1943 SARATOGA TRUNK
Director: Sam Wood
Co-stars: Gary Cooper Ingrid Bergman Florence Bates

1944 TWO THOUSAND WOMEN
Director: Frank Launder
Co-stars: Phyllis Calvert Patricia Roc Anne Crawford

1945 GREAT DAY
Director: Lance Comfort
Co-stars: Eric Portman Sheila Sim Philip Friend

1945 CAESAR AND CLEOPATRA
Director: Gabriel Pascal
Co-stars: Claude Rains Vivien Leigh Stewart Granger

1946 THE YEARS BETWEEN
Director: Compton Bennett
Co-stars: Michael Redgrave Valerie Hobson Dulcie Gray

1947 HOLIDAY CAMP
Director: Ken Annakin
Co-stars: Jack Warner Kathleen Harrison Dennis Price

1947 BLACK NARCISSUS
Director: Michael Powell
Co-stars: Deborah Kerr David Farrar Sabu

1948 FRIEDA
Director: Basil Dearden
Co-stars: Mai Zetterling David Farrar Glynis Johns

1948 SARABAND FOR DEAD LOVERS
Director: Michael Relph
Co-stars: Stewart Granger Joan Greenwood

1950 GOOD TIME GIRL
Director: David MacDonald
Co-stars: Jean Kent Dennis Price Bonar Colleano

1952 THE TALL HEADLINES
Director: Terence Young
Co-stars: Michael Dennison Mai Zetterling Dennis Price

1953 THE MALTA STORY
Director: Brian Desmond Hurst
Co-stars: Alec Guinness Anthony Steel Jack Hawkins

1954 ROMEO AND JULIET
Director: Renato Castellani
Co-stars: Laurence Harvey Susan Shentall Mervyn Johns

1957 NO TIME FOR TEARS
Director: Cyril Frankel
Co-stars: Anna Neagle Anthony Quayle Sylvia Sims

1957 HIGH TIDE AT NOON
Director: Philip Leacock
Co-stars: Betta St. John Michael Craig Patrick McGoohan

1958 INNOCENT SINNERS
Director: Philip Leacock
Co-stars: Catherine Lacey David Kossoff Barbara Mullen

1958 THE GYPSY AND THE GENTLEMAN
Director: Joseph Losey
Co-stars: Melina Mercouri Keith Michel Helen Haye

1962 55 DAYS AT PEKING
Director: Nicholas Ray
Co-stars: Charlton Heston Ava Gardner David Niven

1963 MURDER AT THE GALLUP
Director: George Pollock
Co-stars: Margaret Rutherford Robert Morley Finlay Currie

1964 YOUNG CASSIDY
Director: John Ford
Co-stars: Rod Taylor Maggie Smith Edith Evans

1964 GUNS AT BATASI
Director: John Guillermin
Co-stars: Richard Attenborough Mia Farrow Jack Hawkins

1965 THOSE MAGNIFICENT MEN IN THEIR FLYING MACHINES
Director: Ken Annakin
Co-stars: Terry-Thomas Sarah Miles Tony Hancock

1966 SEVEN WOMEN
Director: John Ford
Co-stars: Anne Bancroft Sue Lyon Anna Lee

1966 EYE OF THE DEVIL
Director: J. Lee-Thompson
Co-stars: David Niven Deborah Kerr Emlyn Williams

1967 THE SHUTTERED ROOM
Director: David Greene
Co-stars: Gig Young Carol Lynley Oliver Reed

1970 FRAGMENT OF FEAR
Director: Richard Sarafian
Co-stars: David Hemmings Gayle Hunnicutt

1970 THE BEAST IN THE CELLAR
Director: James Kelly
Co-stars: Beryl Reid Tessa Wyatt T.P. McKenna

1972 ALICE'S ADVENTURES IN WONDERLAND
Director: William Sterling
Co-stars: Fiona Fullerton Peter Sellers

1978 DOMINIQUE
Director: Michael Anderson
Co-stars: Jean Simmons Cliff Robertson

1978 LES MISERABLES
Director: Glenn Jordan
Co-stars: Richard Jordan Anthony Perkins John Gielgud

1981 CLASH OF THE TITANS
Director: Desmond Davis
Co-stars: Laurence Olivier Harry Hamlin Judy Bowker

GREER ROBSON

1981 SMASH PALACE
Director: Roger Donaldson
Co-stars: Bruno Lawrence Anna Jemison Keith Aberdein

1987 STARLIGHT HOTEL
Director: Sam Pillsbury
Co-stars: Peter Phelps Marshall Napier Alice Fraser

LINDA ROBSON

1973 ANOOP AND THE ELEPHANT
Director: David Eady
Co-stars: Anoop Singh Jimmy Edwards Julian Orchard

MAY ROBSON
Nominated For Best Actress In 1933 For "Lady For A Day"

1931 THE SHE-WOLF
Director: James Flood
Co-stars: James Hall Lawrene Gray Frances Dade

1932 STRANGE INTERLUDE
Director: Robert Z. Leonard
Co-stars: Norma Shearer Clark Gable Robert Young

1932 LITTLE ORPHAN ANNIE
Director: John Robertson
Co-stars: Mitzi Green Edgar Kennedy Buster Phelps

1932 READ HEADED WOMAN
Director: Jack Conway
Co-stars: Jean Harlow Chester Morris Lewis Stone

1932 LETTY LYNTON
Director: Clarence Brown
Co-stars: Joan Crawford Robert Montgomery Nils Asther

1932 IF I HAD A MILLION
Director: Ernst Lubitsch
Co-stars: Charles Laughton Gary Cooper George Raft

1933 ALICE IN WONDERLAND
Director: Norman Z. McLeod
Co-stars: W.C. Fields Cary Grant Gary Cooper

1933 BROADWAY TO HOLLYWOOD
Director: Willard Mack
Co-stars: Jimmy Durante Mickey Rooney Frank Morgan

1933 DINNER AT EIGHT
Director: George Cukor
Co-stars: Lionel Barrymore Wallace Beery Jean Harlow

1933 DANCING LADY
Director: Robert Z. Leonard
Co-stars: Joan Crawford Clark Gable Fred Astaire

1933 ONE MAN'S JOURNEY
Director: John Robertson
Co-stars: Lionel Barrymore Dorothy Jordan Joel McCrea

1933 LADY FOR A DAY
Director: Frank Capra
Co-stars: Warren William Guy Kibbee Glenda Farrell

1933 REUNION IN VIENNA
Director: Sidney Franklin
Co-stars: John Barrymore Diana Wynyard Frank Morgan

1933 THE SOLITAIRE MAN
Director: Jack Conway
Co-stars: Herbert Marshall Elizabeth Allan Mary Bolland

1933 THE WHITE SISTER
Director: Victor Fleming
Co-stars: Helen Hayes Clark Gable Lewis Stone

1934 YOU CAN'T BUY EVERYTHING
Director: Charles Reisner
Co-stars: Jean Parker Lewis Stone Mary Forbes

1934 MILLS OF THE GODS
Director: Roy William Neill
Co-stars: Fay Wray Victor Jory Mayo Methot

1934 LADY BY CHOICE
Director: David Burton
Co-stars: Carole Lombard Walter Connolly Roger Pryor

1935 THREE KIDS AND A QUEEN
Director: Edward Ludwig
Co-stars: Frankie Darro Charlotte Henry Billy Benedict

1935 AGE OF INDISCRETION
Director: Edward Ludwig
Co-stars: Helen Vinson Madge Evans Paul Lukas

1935 GRAND OLD GIRL

1935 ANNA KARENINA
Director: Clarence Brown
Co-stars: Greta Garbo Fredric March Basil Rathbone

1935 VANESSA, HER LOVE STORY
Director: William Howard
Co-stars: Helen Hayes Robert Montgomery Otto Kruger

1935 RECKLESS
Director: Victor Fleming
Co-stars: Jean Harlow William Powell Franchot Tone

1936 RAINBOW ON THE RIVER
Director: Kurt Neuman
Co-stars: Bobby Breen Louise Beavers Charles Butterworth

1936 WIFE VS SECRETARY
Director: Clarence Brown
Co-stars: Clark Gable Myrna Loy Jean Harlow

1936 THE CAPTAIN'S KID
Director: Nick Grinde
Co-stars: Guy Kibbee Sybil Jason Jane Bryan

1937 THE PERFECT SPECIMEN
Director: Michael Curtiz
Co-stars: Errol Flynn Joan Blondell Dick Foran

1937 A STAR IS BORN
Director: William Wellman
Co-stars: Janet Gaynor Fredric March Adolphe Menjou

1938 THE TEXANS
Director: James Hogan
Co-stars: Joan Bennett Randolph Scott Robert Cummings

1938 FOUR DAUGHTERS
Director: Michael Curtiz
Co-stars: Claude Rains John Garfield Lola Lane

1938 BRINGING UP BABY
Director: Howard Hawks
Co-stars: Cary Grant Katharine Hepburn Charles Ruggles

1938 THE ADVENTURES OF TOM SAWYER
Director: Norman Taurog
Co-stars: Tommy Kelly Walter Brennan Victor Jory

1939 DAUGHTERS COURAGEOUS
Director: Michael Curtiz
Co-stars: Fay Bainter Donald Crisp Priscilla Lane

1939 FOUR WIVES
Director: Michael Curtiz
Co-stars: Claude Rains Eddie Albert Gale Page

1939 GRANNY GET YOUR GUN
Director: George Amy
Co-stars: Harry Davenport Margot Stevenson Hardie Albright

1939 THE KID FROM KOKOMO
Director: Lewis Seiler
Co-stars: Pat O'Brien Wayne Morris Joan Blondell

1939 NURSE EDITH CAVELL
Director: Herbert Wilcox
Co-stars: Anna Neagle George Sanders Alan Marshall

1939 THAT'S RIGHT, YOU'RE WRONG
Director: David Butler
Co-stars: Kay Kyser Adolphe Menjou Lucille Ball

1939 THEY MADE ME A CRIMINAL
Director: Busby Berkeley
Co-stars: John Garfield Claude Rains Dead End Kids

1939 YES, MY DARLING DAUGHTER
Director: William Keighley
Co-stars: Priscilla Lane Jeffrey Lynn Fay Bainter

1940 TEXAS RANGERS RIDE AGAIN
Director: James Hogan
Co-stars: John Howard Ellen Drew Akim Tamiroff

1940 IRENE
Director: Herbert Wilcox
Co-stars: Anna Neagle Ray Milland Roland Young

1941 MILLION DOLLAR BABY
Director: Curtis Bernhardt
Co-stars: Priscilla Lane Jeffrey Lynn Ronald Reagan

1941 PLAYMATES
Director: David Butler
Co-stars: Kay Kyser John Barrymore Lupe Velez

1942 JOAN OF PARIS
Director: Robert Stevenson
Co-stars: Michele Morgan Paul Henreid Thomas Mitchell

PATRICIA ROC

1938 THE GAUNT STRANGER
Director: Walter Forde
Co-stars: Sonnie Hale Wilfrid Lawson Alexander Knox

1939 REBEL SON
Director: Adrian Brunel
Co-stars: Harry Baur Roger Livesey Anthony Bushell

1939 A WINDOW IN LONDON
Director: Herbert Mason
Co-stars: Michael Redgrave Sally Gray Paul Lukas

1940 THE FARMER'S WIFE
Director: Norman Lee
Co-stars: Basil Sydney Wilfrid Lawson Nora Swinburne

1940 DR O'DOWD
Director: Herbert Mason
Co-stars: Shaun Glenville Peggy Cummins Mary Merrall

1942 LET THE PEOPLE SING
Director: John Baxter
Co-stars: Alastair Sim Fred Emney Edward Rigby

1942 WE'LL MEET AGAIN
Director: Phil Brandon
Co-stars: Vera Lynn Ronald Ward Donald Gray

1943 SUSPECTED PERSON
Director: Lawrence Huntingdon
Co-stars: Clifford Evans Robert Beatty David Farrar

1943 MILLIONS LIKE US
Director: Frank Launder
Co-stars: Gordon Jackson Basil Radford Naunton Wayne

1944 MADONNA OF THE SEVEN MOONS
Director: Arthur Crabtree
Co-stars: Phyllis Calvert Stewart Granger

1944 LOVE STORY
Director: Leslie Arliss
Co-stars: Margaret Lockwood Stewart Granger Tom Walls

1944 TWO THOUSAND WOMEN
Director: Frank Launder
Co-stars: Phyllis Calvert Flora Robson Jean Kent

1945 THE WICKED LADY
Director: Leslie Arliss
Co-stars: Margaret Lockwood James Mason Griffith Jones

1945 JOHNNY FRENCHMAN
Director: Charles Frend
Co-stars: Francoise Rosay Tom Walls Paul Dupuis

1946 CANYON PASSAGE
Director: Jacques Tourneur
Co-stars: Dana Andrews Hoagy Carmichael Susan Hayward

1947 THE BROTHERS
Director: David MacDonald
Co-stars: Maxwell Reed Duncan Macrae Finlay Currie

1947 JASSY
Director: Bernard Knowles
Co-stars: Margaret Lockwood Dennis Price Basil Sydney

1947 SO WELL REMEMBERED
Director: Edward Dmytryk
Co-stars: John Mills Martha Scott Trevor Howard

1947 WHEN THE BOUGH BREAKS
Director: Lawrence Huntingdon
Co-stars: Bill Owen Rosamund John Patrick Holt

1948 ONE NIGHT WITH YOU
Director: Terence Young
Co-stars: Nino Martini Bonar Colleano Guy Middleton

1949 THE MAN ON THE EIFFEL TOWER
Director: Burgess Meredith
Co-stars: Charles Laughton Jean Wallace

1949 THE PERFECT WOMAN
Director: Bernard Knowles
Co-stars: Nigel Patrick Miles Malleson Stanley Holloway

1951 CIRCLE OF DANGER
Director: Jacques Tourneur
Co-stars: Ray Milland Marius Goring Hugh Sinclair

1952 CAPTAIN BLACK JACK
Director: Julien Duvivier
Co-stars: George Sanders Herbert Marshall Agnes Moorehead

1952 SOMETHING MONEY CAN'T BUY
Director: Pat Jackson
Co-stars: Anthony Steel Moira Lister Diane Hart

1954 CARTOUCHE
Director: Steve Sekely
Co-stars: Richard Basehart Akim Tamiroff Massimo Serato

1957 HOUSE IN THE WOODS
Director: Maxwell Munden
Co-stars: Ronald Howard Michael Gough

1960 BLUEBEARD'S TEN HONEYMOONS
Director: Lee Wilder
Co-stars: George Sanders Corinne Calvet Jean Kent

PASCALE ROCARD

1985 POLICE
Director: Maurice Pialat
Co-stars: Gerard Depardieu Sophie Marceau Sandrine Bonnaire

DANIELLA ROCCA

1961 DIVORCE ITALIAN STYLE
Director: Pietro Germi
Co-stars: Marcello Mastroianni Stefania Sandrelli

1963 CAPTIVE CITY
Director: Joseph Anthony
Co-stars: David Niven Lea Massari Ben Gazzara

1964 BEHOLD A PALE HORSE
Director: Fred Zinnemann
Co-stars: Gregory Peck Anthony Quinn Omar Sharif

MARY ROCHE

1943 THE HEAT'S ON
Director: Gregory Ratoff
Co-stars: Mae West Victor Moore William Gaxton

SUZZY ROCHE

1988 CROSSING DELANCEY
Director: Joan Micklin Silver
Co-stars: Amy Irving Peter Riegert Jeroen Krabbe

ROSINE ROCHETTE

1973 L'INVITATION
Director: Claude Goretta
Co-stars: Jean-Luc Bideau Jean Champion Corinne Coderay

LELA ROCHON

1996 WAITING TO EXHALE
Director: Forest Whitaker
Co-stars: Whitney Houston Angela Bassett Loretta Devine

CRISSY ROCK

1994 LADYBIRD LADYBIRD
Director: Ken Loach
Co-stars: Vladimir Vega Ray Winstone Sandie Lavelle

1996 BRAZEN HUSSIES
Director: Elijah Moshinsky
Co-stars: Julie Walters Robert Lindsay Alun Armstrong

MARCIA RODD

1971 LITTLE MURDERS
Director: Alan Arkin
Co-stars: Elliott Gould Donald Sutherland Vincent Gardenia

1971 T.R. BASKIN
Director: Herbert Ross
Co-stars: Candice Bergen James Caan Peter Boyle

1977 CITIZENS' BAND
Director: Jonathan Demme
Co-stars: Paul LeMat Candy Clark Ann Wedgeworth

1979 LAST EMBRACE
Director: Jonathan Demme
Co-stars: Roy Scheider Janet Margolin Sam Levene

ETHNA RODDY

1988 THE TEMPATATION OF EILEEN HUGHES
Director: Tristram Powell
Co-stars: Jim Norton Angharad Rees

1989 HOME RUN
Director: Nicholas Renton
Co-stars: Michael Kitchen Keith Barron Corinne Dacla

1989 THE ATTRACTIONS
Director: Anthony Garner
Co-stars: Benjamin Whitrow Reece Dinsdale

NINA PENS RODE

1966 GERTRUD
Director: Carl Theodor Dreyer
Co-stars: Bendt Ebbe Rode Axel Strobye

SUE RODERICK

1992 HEDD WYN: THE ARMAGEDDON POET
Director: Paul Turner
Co-stars: Huw Garmon Carin Fychan Gwen Ellis

1992 REBECCA'S DAUGHTERS
Director: Karl Francis
Co-stars: Peter O'Toole Paul Rhys Joely Richardson

1992   LOSING TRACK
Director: Jim Lee
Co-stars: Alan Bates Geraldine James Ben Holden

KATE RODGER
1996   MIND BREAKERS
Director: Fred Gallo
Co-stars: Adam Baldwin Robert Englund

ILONA RODGERS
1968   SALT AND PEPPER
Director: Richard Donner
Co-stars: Sammy Davis Jnr. Peter Lawford Michael Bates
1983   UTU
Director: Geoff Murphy
Co-stars: Anzac Wallace Bruno Lawrence Tim Elliott

OLGA RODINA
1994   ZINKY BOYS GO UNDERGROUND
Director: Paul Tickell
Co-stars: Dmitri Shevchenko Natasha Bain

ESTELITA RODRIGUEZ
1945   MEXICANA
Director: Alfred Santell
Co-stars: Tito Guizar Constance Moore Leo Carrillo
1945   ALONG THE NAVAJO TRAIL
Co-star: Roy Rogers

GABRIELA ROEL
1988   EL DORADO
Director: Carlos Saura
Co-stars: Omero Antonutti Lambert Wilson Jose Sancho
1989   OLD GRINGO
Director: Luis Puenzo
Co-stars: Jane Fonda Gregory Peck Jimmy Smits

GINGER ROGERS
(Virginia Rogers) (Married Lew Ayres & Jacques Bergerac, Cousin Of Rita Hayworth)
Oscar For Best Actress In 1940 For "Kitty Foyle"
1930   YOUNG MAN OF MANHATTAN
1930   MANHATTAN MARY
Co-stars: Ed Wynn Lou Holtz
1930   FOLLOW THE LEADER
Director: Norman Taurog
Co-stars: Ed Wynn Ethel Merman Stanley Smith
1930   QUEEN HIGH
Co-stars: Frank Morgan Charles Ruggles
1930   THE SAP FROM SYRACUSE
Co-star: Jack Oakie
1931   HONOR AMONG LOVERS
Director: Dorothy Arzner
Co-stars: Fredric March Claudette Colbert
1931   THE TENDERFOOT
Director: Ray Enright
Co-stars: Joe E. Brown Lew Cody Robert Greig
1932   YOU SAID A MOUTHFUL
Director: Lloyd Bacon
Co-stars: Joe E. Brown Sheila Terry Guinn Williams
1932   THE 13TH GUEST
Director: Albert Ray
Co-stars: Lyle Talbot James Eagles Eddie Phillips

1932   HAT CHECK GIRL
Co-stars: Sally Eilers Monroe Owsley
1933   GOLD DIGGERS OF 1933
Director: Mervyn LeRoy
Co-stars: Joan Blondell Ruby Keeler Warren William
1933   BROADWAY BAD
Director: Sidney Lanfield
Co-stars: Joan Blondell Ricardo Cortez Donald Crisp
1933   DON'T BET ON LOVE
Co-Strar Lew Ayres
1933   THE SHREIK IN THE NIGHT
1933   PROFESSIONAL SWEETHEART
Director: William Seiter
Co-stars: Gregory Ratoff Frank McHugh Zasu Pitts
1933   SITTING PRETTY
Director: Harry Joe Brown
Co-stars: Jack Oakie Jack Haley Thelma Todd
1933   FORTY-SECOND STREET
Director: Lloyd Bacon
Co-stars: Warner Baxter Ruby Keeler George Brent
1933   FLYING DOWN TO RIO
Director: Thornton Freeland
Co-stars: Fred Astaire Dolores Del Rio Gary Raymond
1934   THE GAY DIVORCEE
Director: Mark Sandrich
Co-stars: Fred Astaire Eric Blore Betty Grable
1934   FINISHING SCHOOL
Director: George Nicholls
Co-stars: Francis Dee Bruce Cabot Billie Burke
1934   CHANGE OF HEART
Director: John Blystone
Co-stars: Janet Gaynor Charles Farrell Shirley Temple
1934   ROMANCE IN MANHATTAN
Director: Stephen Roberts
Co-stars: Francis Lederer Arthur Hohl Donald Meek
1934   TWENTY MILLION SWEETHEARTS
Director: Ray Enright
Co-stars: Dick Powell Pat O'Brien Mills Bros.
1934   UPPERWORLD
Director: Roy Del Ruth
Co-stars: Warren William Mary Astor Mickey Rooney
1935   ROBERTA
Director: William Seiter
Co-stars: Fred Astaire Irene Dunne Randolph Scott
1937   TOP HAT
Director: Mark Sandrich
Co-stars: Fred Astaire Helen Broderick Eric Blore
1935   STAR OF MIDNIGHT
Director: Stephen Roberts
Co-stars: William Powell Paul Kelly Ralph Morgan
1935   IN PERSON
Director: William Seiter
Co-stars: George Brent Alan Mowbray Grant Mitchell
1936   FOLLOW THE FLEET
Director: Mark Sandrich
Co-stars: Fred Astaire Randolph Scott Tony Martin
1936   SWING TIME
Director: George Stevens
Co-stars: Fred Astaire Victor Moore Eric Blore
1937   SHALL WE DANCE
Director: Mark Sandrich
Co-stars: Fred Astaire Eric Blore Edward Everett Horton

1937 STAGE DOOR
Director: Gregory La Cava
Co-stars: Katharine Hepburn Lucille Ball Ann Miller

1938 HAVING WONDERFUL TIME
Director: Alfred Santell
Co-stars: Douglas Fairbanks Lucille Ball Red Skelton

1938 CAREFREE
Director: Mark Sandrich
Co-stars: Fred Astaire Ralph Bellamy Jack Carson

1938 VIVACIOUS LADY
Director: George Stevens
Co-stars: James Stewart Charles Coburn Beulah Bondi

**1939 THE STORY OF VERNON
AND IRENE CASTLE**
Director: H.C. Potter
Co-stars: Fred Astaire Walter Brennan

1939 FIFTH AVENUE GIRL
Director: Gregory La Cava
Co-stars: Walter Connolly Tim Holt James Ellison

1939 BACHELOR MOTHER
Director: Garson Kanin
Co-stars: David Niven Charles Coburn Frank Albertson

1940 KITTY FOYLE
Director: Sam Wood
Co-stars: Dennis Morgan James Craig Gladys Cooper

1940 LUCKY PARTNERS
Director: Lewis Milestone
Co-stars: Ronald Colman Jack Carson Spring Byington

1940 PRIMROSE PATH
Director: Gregory La Cava
Co-stars: Joel McCrea Marjorie Rambeau Henry Travers

1941 TOM, DICK AND HARRY
Director: Garson Kanin
Co-stars: George Murphy Burgess Meredith Phil Silvers

1942 TALES OF MANHATTAN
Director: Julien Duvivier
Co-stars: Henry Fonda Charles Laughton Paul Robeson

1942 ROXIE HART
Director: William Wellman
Co-stars: George Montgomery Adolphe Menjou Nigel Bruce

1942 THE MAJOR AND THE MINOR
Director: Billy Wilder
Co-stars: Ray Milland Rita Johnson Diana Lynn

1942 ONCE UPON A HONEYMOON
Director: Leo McCarey
Co-stars: Cary Grant Walter Slezak Albert Dekker

1943 STAGE DOOR CANTEEN
Director: Frank Borzage
Co-stars: Lon McCallister Judith Anderson Paul Muni

1943 TENDER COMRADE
Director: Edward Dmytryk
Co-stars: Robert Ryan Ruth Hussey Kim Hunter

1944 LADY IN THE DARK
Director: Mitchell Leisin
Co-stars: Warner Baxter Ray Milland Jon Hall

1944 I'LL BE SEEING YOU
Director: William Dieterle
Co-stars: Joseph Cotten Shirley Temple Chill Wills

1945 WEEKEND AT THE WALDORF
Director: Robert Z. Leonard
Co-stars: Walter Pidgeon Van Johnson Lana Turner

1946 HEARTBEAT
Director: Sam Wood
Co-stars: Jean-Pierre Aumont Adolphe Menjou Basil Rathbone

1946 MAGNIFICENT DOLL
Director: Frank Borzage
Co-stars: David Niven Burgess Meredith Stephen McNally

1947 IT HAD TO BE YOU
Director: Rudolph Mate
Co-stars: Cornel Wilde Spring Byington Ron Randell

1949 THE BARKLEYS OF BROADWAY
Director: Charles Walters
Co-stars: Fred Astaire Oscar Levant Billie Burke

1950 PERFECT STRANGERS
Director: Bretagne Windust
Co-stars: Dennis Morgan Thelma Ritter

1950 STORM WARNING
Director: Stuart Heisler
Co-stars: Doris Day Steve Cochran Ronald Reagan

1951 THE GROOM WORE SPURS
Director: Richard Whorf
Co-stars: Jack Carson Joan Davis Stanley Ridges

1952 DREAMBOAT
Director: Claude Binyon
Co-stars: Clifton Webb Anne Francis Elsa Lanchester

1952 MONKEY BUSINESS
Director: Howard Hawks
Co-stars: Cary Grant Charles Coburn Marilyn Monroe

1952 WE'RE NOT MARRIED
Director: Edmund Goulding
Co-stars: Marilyn Monroe David Wayne Fred Allen

1953 FOREVER FEMALE
Director: Irving Rapper
Co-stars: William Holden Paul Douglas James Gleason

1954 BEAUTIFUL STRANGER
Director: David Miller
Co-stars: Stanley Baker Herbert Lom Coral Browne

1954 BLACK WIDOW
Director: Nunnally Johnson
Co-stars: Van Heflin George Raft Gene Tierney

1955 TIGHT SPOT
Director: Phil Karlson
Co-stars: Edward G. Robinson Brian Keith Lorne Greene

1956 TEENAGE REBEL
Director: Edmund Goulding
Co-stars: Michael Rennie Mildred Natwick Irene Hervey

1956 THE FIRST TRAVELLING SALESLADY
Director: Arthur Lubin
Co-stars: Carol Channing Barry Nelson David Brian

1957 OH MEN ! OH WOMEN !
Director: Nunnally Johnson
Co-stars: David Niven Dan Dailey Barbara Rush

1964 CINDERELLA
Director: Charles Dubin
Co-stars: Walter Pidgeon Celeste Holm

1964 QUICK, LET'S GET MARRIED
Director: William Dieterle
Co-stars: Ray Milland Barbara Eden Elliott Gould

1965 HARLOW
Director: Alex Segal
Co-stars: Carol Lynley Efrem Zimbalist Jnr Barry Sullivan

**1984 GEORGE STEVENS -
A FILM-MAKER'S JOURNEY**
Director: George Stevens
Co-stars: Cary Grant Joel McCrea

INGRID ROGERS

1993 **CARLITO'S WAY**
Director: Brian De Palma
Co-stars: Al Pacino Penelope Ann Miller Sean Penn

JEAN ROGERS

1935 **STORMY**
Co-stars: Noah Beery Jnr. Fred Kohler

1936 **CONFLICT**
Co-stars: John Wayne

1937 **NIGHT KEY**
Director: Lloyd Corrigan
Co-stars: Boris Karloff Warren Hull Ward Bond

1937 **THE WILDCATTER**
Co-stars: Scott Colton

1937 **REPORTED MISSING**
Co-star: William Gargan

1938 **ALWAYS IN TROUBLE**
Co-stars: Jane Withers Eddie Collins

1939 **HEAVEN WITH A BARBED WIRE FENCE**
Director: Ricardo Cortez
Co-stars: Glenn Ford Richard Conte Ward Bond

1940 **CHARLIE CHAN IN PANAMA**
Director: Norman Foster
Co-stars: Sidney Toler Lionel Atwill Mary Nash

1940 **LET'S MAKE MUSIC**
Director: Leslie Goodwins
Co-stars: Bob Crosby Elisabeth Risdon Joseph Buloff

1940 **THE MAN WHO WOULDN'T TALK**
Director: David Burton
Co-stars: Lloyd Nolan Eric Blore Mae Marsh

1940 **VIVA CISCO KID**
Director: Norman Foster
Co-stars: Cesar Romero Chris-Pin Martin Stanley Fields

1941 **DESIGN FOR SCANDAL**
Director: Norman Taurog
Co-stars: Rosalind Russell Walter Pidgeon Edward Arnold

1942 **PACIFIC RENDEZVOUS**
Director: George Sidney
Co-stars: Lee Bowman Mona Maris Carl Esmond

1942 **THE WAR AGAINST MRS HADLEY**
Director: Harold Bucquet
Co-stars: Fay Bainter Edward Arnold Richard Ney

1943 **WHISTLING IN BROOKLYN**
Director: S. Sylvan Simon
Co-stars: Red Skelton Ann Rutherford Rags Ragland

1943 **SWING-SHIFT MAISIE**
Director: Norman Z. McLeod
Co-stars: Ann Sothern James Craig Connie Gilchrist

1943 **A STRANGER IN TOWN**
Director: Roy Rowland
Co-stars: Frank Morgan Richard Carlson Porter Hall

1945 **THE STRANGE MR GREGORY**
Director: Phil Rosen
Co-stars: Edmund Lowe Don Douglas Frank Reicher

1945 **ROUGH, TOUGH AND READY**
Director: Del Lord
Co-stars: Victor McLaglen Chester Morris Veda Ann Borg

1946 **HOT CARGO**
Co-stars: Philip Reed William Gargan

MARIANNE ROGERS

1991 **THE GAMBLER RETURNS:**
        THE LUCK OF THE DRAW
Director: Dick Lowry
Co-stars: Kenny Rogers Reba McEntyre

MIMI ROGERS *(Married Tom Cruise)*

1985 **EMBASSY**
Director: Robert Lewis
Co-stars: Nick Mancuso Richard Masur Sam Wanamaker

1986 **GUNG HO !**
Director: Ron Howard
Co-stars: Michael Keaton Gedde Watanabe George Wendt

1987 **STREET SMART**
Director: Jerry Schattzberg
Co-stars: Christopher Reeve Kathy Baker Morgan Freeman

1987 **SOMEONE TO WATCH OVER ME**
Director: Ridley Scott
Co-stars: Tom Berenger Lorraine Bracco Jerry Orbach

1987 **YOU RUINED MY LIFE**
Director: David Ashwell
Co-stars: Paul Reiser Soleil Moon Frye

1989 **THE MIGHTY QUINN**
Director: Carl Shenkel
Co-stars: Denzel Washington James Fox M.Emmet Walsh

1990 **DESPERATE HOURS**
Director: Michael Cimino
Co-stars: Mickey Rourke Anthony Hopkins Lindsay Crouse

1991 **HIDER IN THE HOUSE**
Director: Matthew Patrick
Co-stars: Gary Busey Michael McKee

1991 **THE RAPTURE**
Director: Michael Tolkin
Co-stars: David Duchovny Patrick Bauchau Kimberly Cullum

1991 **WEDLOCK**
Director: Lewis Teague
Co-stars: Rutger Hauer Joan Chen James Remar

1992 **WHITE SANDS**
Director: Roger Donaldson
Co-stars: Willem Dafoe Mary Elizabeth Mastrantonio Mickey Rourke

1992 **LADYKILLER**
Director: Michael Scott
Co-stars: John Shea Alice Krige Tom Irwin

1993 **THOSE BEDROOM EYES**
Director: Leon Ichaso
Co-stars: Tim Matheson William Forsythe Carroll Baker

1994 **MONKEY TROUBLE**
Director: Franco Amurri
Co-stars: Harvey Keitel Thora Birch

1994 **FAR FROM HOME: THE ADVENTURES**
        OF A YELLOW DOG
Director: Phillip Borsos
Co-stars: Bruce Davison Jesse Bradford

1994 **REFLECTIONS ON A CRIME**
Director: Jon Purdy
Co-stars: Billy Zane John Terry

1994 **KILLER**
Director: Mark Malone
Co-stars: Anthony LaPaglia Matt Craven Peter Boyle

1997 **THE MIRROR HAS TWO FACES**
Director: Barbra Streisand
Co-stars: Jeff Bridges Lauren Bacall George Segal

1997 TREES LOUNGE
Director: Steve Buscemi
Co-star: Samuel L. Jackson Steve Buscemi

MITZI ROGERS

1962 THE NIGHT OF THE PROWLER
Director: Francis Searle
Co-stars: Patrick Holt Benny Lee Anthony Wager

MARCELLE ROGEZ

1937 BIG FELLA
Director: J. Elder Wills
Co-stars: Paul Robeson Elizabeth Welch Roy Emerton

MARIA ROHM

1970 COUNT DRACULA
Director: Jess Franco
Co-stars: Christopher Lee Herbert Lom Klaus Kinski

1971 BLACK BEAUTY
Director: James Hill
Co-stars: Mark Lester Walter Slezak Patrick Mower

1972 CALL OF THE WILD
Director: Ken Annakin
Co-stars: Charlton Heston Michele Mercier

1974 AND THEN THERE WERE NONE
Director: Peter Collinson
Co-stars: Oliver Reed Elke Sommer Herbert Lom

HELENA ROJO

1972 AGUIRRE, WRATH OF GOD
Director: Werner Herzog
Co-stars: Klaus Kinski Ruy Guerra Cecilia Rivera

1977 FOXTROT
Director: Arturo Ripstein
Co-stars: Peter O'Toole Charlotte Rampling Max Von Sydow

MARIA ROJO

1988 BREAK OF DAWN

1991 DANZON
Director: Maria Novaro
Co-stars: Carmen Salinas Blanca Guerra Margarita Isabel

JEANNE ROLAND

1964 CURSE OF THE MUMMY'S TOMB
Director: Michael Carreras
Co-stars: Ronald Howard Terence Morgan Fred Clark

TUTTA ROLF

1935 SWEDENHIELMS
Director: Gustaf Mollander
Co-stars: Ingrid Bergman Gosta Ekman

1935 DRESSED TO THRILL
Co-stars: Clive Brook Nydia Westman

1938 DOLLAR
Director: Gustaf Mollander
Co-stars: Ingrid Bergman Georg Rydeberg Kotti Chave

MICHELE ROLLA

1953 MONSIEUR HULOT'S HOLIDAY
Director: Jacques Tati
Co-stars: Jacques Tati Nathalie Pascaud Valentine Camax

ESTHER ROLLE

1973 DON'T PLAY US CHEAP
Director: Melvin Van Peebles
Co-stars: Avon Long Rhetta Hughes George McCurn

1978 SUMMER OF MY GERMAN SOLDIER
Director: Michael Tuchner
Co-stars: Kristy McNichol Bruce Davison

1989 THE MIGHTY QUINN
Director: Carl Shenkel
Co-stars: Denzel Washington James Fox Mimi Rogers

1989 DRIVING MISS DAISY
Director: Bruce Beresford
Co-stars: Jessica Tandy Morgan Freeman Dan Aykroyd

1993 HOUSE OF CARDS
Director: Michael Lessac
Co-stars: Kathleen Turner Tommy Lee Jones Park Overall

1993 TO DANCE WITH THE WHITE DOG
Director: Glenn Jordan
Co-stars: Hume Cronyn Jessica Tandy

YVONNE ROMAIN

1961 THE CURSE OF THE WEREWOLF
Director: Terence Fisher
Co-stars: Oliver Reed Clifford Evans Warren Mitchell

1962 FRIGHTENED CITY
Director: John Lemont
Co-stars: Herbert Lom Sean Connery John Gregson

1963 THE DEVIL DOLL
Director: Lindsay Shonteff
Co-stars: Bryant Halliday William Sylvester

1964 SMOKESCREEN
Director: Jim O'Connolly
Co-stars: Peter Vaughan John Carson Gerald Flood

1965 THE BRIGAND OF KANDAHAR
Director: John Gilling
Co-stars: Oliver Reed Ronald Lewis Duncan Lamont

1966 THE SWINGER
Director: George Sidney
Co-stars: Ann-Margret Tony Franciosa Robert Coote

1967 DOUBLE TROUBLE
Director: Norman Taurog
Co-stars: Elvis Presley Annette Day John Williams

CANDICE ROMAN

1972 THE UNHOLY ROLLERS
Director: Vernon Zimmerman
Co-stars: Claudia Jennings Louis Quinn Alan Vint

GINA ROMAN

1968 THE CANDY MAN
Director: Herbert Leder
Co-stars: George Sanders Leslie Parrish Manolo Fabregas

LETICIA ROMAN

1960 G.I. BLUES
Director: Norman Taurog
Co-stars: Elvis Presley Juliet Prowse Robert Ivers

1961 GOLD OF THE SEVEN SAINTS
Director: Gordon Douglas
Co-stars: Clint Walker Roger Moore Chill Wills

1961 PIRATES OF TORTUGA
Director: Robert Webb
Co-stars: Ken Scott Dave King Robert Stephens

1962 PONTIUS PILATE
Director: Irving Rapper
Co-stars: Jean Marais Jeanne Crain Basil Rathbone

1965 FANNY HILL
Director: Russ Meyer
Co-stars: Miriam Hopkins Walter Giller Helmut Weiss

1966 THE SPY IN THE GREEN HAT
Director: Joseph Sargent
Co-stars: Robert Vaughn David McCallum Janet Leigh

RUTH ROMAN

1948 GOOD SAM
Director: Leo McCarey
Co-stars: Gary Cooper Ann Sheridan Edmund Lowe

1948 BELLE STARR'S DAUGHTER
Co-stars: George Montgomery Rod Cameron Jack Lambert

1949 ALWAYS LEAVE THEM LAUGHING
Director: Roy Del Ruth
Co-stars: Milton Berle Bert Lahr Virginia Mayo

1949 CHAMPION
Director: Mark Robson
Co-stars: Kirk Douglas Arthur Kennedy Marilyn Maxwell

1949 BARRICADE
Director: Peter Godfrey
Co-stars: Raymond Massey Dane Clark

1949 BEYOND THE FOREST
Director: King Vidor
Co-stars: Bette Davis Joseph Cotten David Brian

1949 THE WINDOW
Director: Ted Tetzlaff
Co-stars: Bobby Driscoll Barbara Hale Arthur Kennedy

1950 THREE SECRETS
Director: Robert Wise
Co-stars: Eleanor Parker Patricia Neal Frank Lovejoy

1950 DALLAS
Director: Stuart Heissler
Co-stars: Gary Cooper Raymond Massey Steve Cochran

1950 COLT 45
Director: Edwin Marin
Co-stars: Randolph Scott Zachary Scott Lloyd Bridges

1951 LIGHTNING STRIKES TWICE
Director: King Vidor
Co-stars: Richard Todd Mercedes McCambridge Zachary Scott

1951 STRANGERS ON A TRAIN
Director: Alfred Hitchcock
Co-stars: Robert Walker Farley Granger

1951 TOMORROW IS ANOTHER DAY
Director: Felix Feist
Co-stars: Steve Cochran Ray Teal Lurene Tuttle

1951 STARLIFT
Director: Roy Del Ruth
Co-stars: Janice Rule Dick Wesson Doris Day

1952 YOUNG MAN WITH IDEAS
Director: Mitchell Leisen
Co-stars: Glenn Ford Nina Foch Denise Darcel

1952 INVITATION
Director: Gottfreid Reinhardt
Co-stars: Dorothy McGuire Van Johnson Louis Calhern

1952 MARU MARU
Director: Gordon Douglas
Co-stars: Errol Flynn Raymond Burr Paul Picerni

1953 BLOWING WILD
Director: Hugo Fregonese
Co-stars: Gary Cooper Barbara Stanwyck Anthony Quinn

1954 TANGANYIKA
Director: Andre De Toth
Co-stars: Van Heflin Howard Duff Jeff Morrow

1954 THE FAR COUNTRY
Director: Anthony Mann
Co-stars: James Stewart Walter Brennan Corinne Calvet

1954 DOWN THREE DARK STREETS
Director: Arnold Laven
Co-stars: Broderick Crawford Martha Hyer Marisa Pavan

1955 JOE MACBETH
Director: Ken Hughes
Co-stars: Paul Douglas Bonar Colleano Gregoire Aslan

1956 FIVE STEPS TO DANGER
Director: Henry Kesler
Co-stars: Sterling Hayden Werner Klemperer Richard Gaines

1956 GREAT DAY IN THE MORNING
Director: Jacques Tourneur
Co-stars: Robert Stack Virginia Mayo Alex Nicol

1956 THE BOTTOM OF THE BOTTLE
Director: Henry Hathaway
Co-stars: Van Johnson Joseph Cotten Jack Carson

1956 REBEL IN TOWN
Director: Alfred Werker
Co-stars: John Payne John Smith J. Carrol Naish

1957 BITTER VICTORY
Director: Nicholas Ray
Co-stars: Richard Burton Curt Jurgens Nigel Green

1961 LOOK IN ANY WINDOW
Director: William Alland
Co-stars: Paul Anka Alex Nichol Gigi Perreau

1964 LOVE HAS MANY FACES
Director: Alexander Singer
Co-stars: Lana Turner Cliff Robertson Hugh O'Brian

1970 INCIDENT IN SAN FRANCISCO
Director: Don Medford
Co-stars: Richard Kiley Leslie Nielsen Phyllis Thaxter

1970 THE OLD MAN WHO CRIED
Director: Walter Grauman
Co-stars: Edward G. Robinson Sam Jaffe Martin Balsam

1973 THE BABY
Director: Ted Post
Co-stars: Anjanette Comer Marianna Hill

1976 DAY OF THE ANIMALS
Director: William Girdler
Co-stars: Christopher George Leslie Nielsen Richard Jaeckel

SUSAN ROMAN

1977 RABID
Director: David Cronenberg
Co-stars: Marilyn Chambers Frank Moore Joe Silver

VIVIANE ROMANCE *(Pauline Ortman)*

1935 LA BANDERA
Director: Julien Duvivier

1936 LA BELLE EQUIPE
Director: Julien Duvivier
Co-stars: Jean Gabin Charles Vanel Raymond Aimes

1937 LE PURITAN
Director: Jeff Musso
Co-stars: Jean-Louis Berrault Pierre Fresnay Mady Berry

1946 PANIQUE
Director: Julien Duvivier
Co-stars: Michel Simon Paul Bernard

1946 CARMEN

1952 THE SEVEN DEADLY SINS
Director: Roberto Rossellini
Co-stars: Isa Miranda Michele Morgan Gerard Philip

1963 MELODIE EN SOUS-SOL
Director: Henri Verneuil

1964 NADA
Director: Claude Chabrol

BEATRICE ROMAND

1970 CLAIRE'S KNEE
Director: Eric Rohmer
Co-stars: Jean-Claude Brialy Aurora Cornu Laurence De Monaghan

1983 HOUSE OF THE YELLOW CARPET
Director: Carlo Lizzani
Co-stars: Erland Josephson Milena Vukotic

1986 FOUR ADVENTURES OF REINETTE AND MIRABELLE
Director: Eric Rohmer
Co-stars: Joelle Miquel Jessica Forde

1986 THE GREEN RAY
Director: Eric Rohmer
Co-stars: Marie Riviere Lisa Heredia Vincent Gautier

CARLA ROMANELLI

1974 STEPPENWOLF
Director: Fred Haines
Co-stars: Max Von Sydow Dominique Sanda Pierre Clementi

LINA ROMAY

1944 TWO GIRLS AND A SAILOR
Director: Richard Thorpe
Co-stars: June Allyson Gloria DeHaven Van Johnson

1946 LOVE LAUGHS AT ANDY HARDY
Director: George Seitz
Co-stars: Mickey Rooney Lewis Stone Fay Holden

1947 HONEYMOON
Director: William Keighley
Co-stars: Shirley Temple Franchot Tone Guy Madison

1952 THE MAN BEHIND THE GUN
Director: Felix Feist
Co-stars: Randolph Scott Patrice Wymore Dick Wesson

SYDNE ROME

1969 SOME GIRLS DO
Director: Ralph Thomas
Co-stars: Richard Johnson Dahlia Lavi Robert Morley

1975 THAT LUCKY TOUCH
Director: Christopher Miles
Co-stars: Roger Moore Susannah York Shelley Winters

1978 JUST A GIGOLO
Director: David Hemmings
Co-stars: David Bowie Kim Novak Marlene Dietrich

TARA ROMER

1988 LA VIE EST UNE LONG FLEUVE TRANQUILLE
Director: Etienne Chatilliez
Co-stars: Benott Magimel Valerie Lalande

JOANELLE NADINE ROMERO

1988 POWWOW HIGHWAY
Director: Jonathan Wacks
Co-stars: Gary Farmer A. Martinez Amanda Wyss

EDANA ROMNEY

1940 EAST OF PICCADILY
Director: Harold Huth
Co-stars: Sebastian Shaw Judy Campbell Martita Hunt

1942 ALIBI
Director: Brian Desmond Hurst
Co-stars: Margaret Lockwood Hugh Sinclair James Mason

1948 CORRIDOR OF MIRRORS
Director: Terence Young
Co-stars: Eric Portman Barbara Mullen Hugh Sinclair

CLELIA RONDINELLI

1984 WHERE'S PICONE ?
Director: Nanni Loy
Co-stars: Giancarlo Gianinni Lina Sastri Carlo Croccolo

EDINA RONAY

1966 SLAVE GIRLS
Director: Michael Carreras
Co-stars: Michael Latimer Martine Beswick Carol White

LINDA RONSTADT

1978 FM
Director: John Alonzo
Co-stars: Michael Brandon Eileen Brennan Cassie Yates

1983 THE PIRATES OF PENZANCE
Director: Wilford Leach
Co-stars: Douglas Slocombe Kevin Kline Angela Lansbury

1987 HAIL ! HAIL ! ROCK 'N' ROLL
Director: Taylor Hackford
Co-stars: Chuck Berry Keith Richards

JEAN RONVEROL

1935 THE LEAVENWORTH CASE
Director: Lewis Collins
Co-stars: Donald Cook Norman Foster Maude Eburne

1938 ANNABEL TAKES A TOUR
Director: Lew Landers
Co-stars: Lucille Ball Jack Oakie Ruth Donnelly

ANNE ROONEY

1944 SLIGHTLY TERRIFIC
Co-star: Eddie Quillan

AMANDA ROOT

1990 BFG (Voice)
Director: Brian Cosgrove
Co-stars: David Jason Angela Thorne Michael Knowles

1995 PERSUASION
Director: Roger Michell
Co-stars: Ciaran Hands Corin Redgrave Sophie Thompson

1996 JANE EYRE
Director: Franco Zeffirelli
Co-stars: Charlotte Gainsbourg Anna Paquin William Hurt

ROSSANA RORY

1957 THE BIG BOODLE
Director: Richard Wilson
Co-stars: Errol Flynn Gia Scala Pedro Armendariz

1958 I SOLITI IGNOTI
Director: Mario Monicelli
Co-stars: Vittorio Gassman Renato Salvatori Marcello Mastroianni

1961 COME SEPTEMBER
Director: Robert Mulligan
Co-stars: Rock Hudson Gina Lollobrigida

1962 THE ECLIPSE
Director: Michaelangelo Antonioni
Co-stars: Monica Vitti Alain Delon Francisco Rabal

SIMONE DALLA ROSA

1987 LONG LIVE THE LADY !
Director: Ermanno Olmi
Co-stars: Marco Esposito Simona Brandalise Tarcisio Tosi

ROSA ROSANOVA

1929   LUCKY BOY
Director: Norman Taurog
Co-stars: George Jessel William K. Strauss Margaret Quimby

FRANCOISE ROSAY *(Married Jacques Feyder)*

1922   CRAINQUEBILLE
Director: Jacques Feyder
Co-stars: Maurice De Feraudy Felix Oudart

1934   LE GRAND JEU
Director: Jacques Feyder
Co-stars: Pierre-Richard Willm Marie Bell Charles Vanel

1935   LA KERMESSE HEROIQUE
Director: Jacques Feyder
Co-stars: Louis Jouvet Jean Murat Alfred Adam

1937   DROLE DE DRAME
Director: Marcel Carne
Co-stars: Michel Simon Louis Jouvet Jean-Pierre Aumont

1937   UN CARNET DE BAL
Director: Julien Duvivier
Co-stars: Marie Bell Louis Jouvet Raimu Fernandel

1938   MATERNITÉ

1938   LES GENS DU VOYAGE
Director: Jacques Feyder
Co-stars: Andre Brule Fabien Loris Mary Glory

1944   UNE FEMME DISPARAIT
Director: Jacques Feyder
Co-stars: Henri Guisol Jean Nohain Claire Gerard

1944   THE HALFWAY HOUSE
Director: Basil Dearden
Co-stars: Mervyn Johns Glynis Johns Tom Walls

1945   JOHNNY FRENCHMAN
Director: Charles Frend
Co-stars: Tom Walls Paul Dupuis Patricia Roc

1948   SARABAND FOR DEAD LOVERS
Director: Basil Dearden
Co-stars: Stewart Granger Joan Greenwood Flora Robson

1950   SEPTEMBER AFFAIR
Director: William Dieterle
Co-stars: Joseph Cotten Joan Fontaine Jessica Tandy

1951   THE 13TH LETTER
Director: Otto Preminger
Co-stars: Charles Boyer Linda Darnell Constance Smith

1952   THE SEVEN DEADLY SINS
Director: Carlo Rim
Co-stars: Gerard Philipe Isa Miranda Michele Morgan

1952   L'AUBERGE ROUGE
Director: Claude Autant-Lara
Co-stars: Fernandel Julien Carette Gregoire Aslan

1955   THAT LADY
Director: Terence Young
Co-stars: Olivia De Havilland Paul Scofield Gilbert Roland

1957   THE SEVENTH SIN
Director: Ronald Neame
Co-stars: Eleanor Parker Bill Travers George Sanders

1957   INTERLUDE
Director: Douglar Sirk
Co-stars: Rossano Brazzi June Allyson Keith Andes

1958   ME AND THE COLONEL
Director: Peter Glenville
Co-stars: Danny Kaye Curt Jurgens Nicole Maurey

1959   THE SOUND AND THE FURY
Director: Martin Ritt
Co-stars: Yul Brynner Joanne Woodward Margaret Leighton

1960   THE FULL TREATMENT
Director: Val Guest
Co-stars: Ronald Lewis Diane Cilento Bernard Braden

1965   UP FROM THE BEACH
Director: Robert Parrish
Co-stars: Cliff Robertson Red Buttons Marius Goring

BIANCA ROSE

1987   EYE ON THE SPARROW
Director: John Korty
Co-stars: Mare Winningham Keith Carradine Conchata Ferrell

CHRISTINE ROSE

1986   FATHERLAND
Director: Kenneth Loach
Co-stars: Gerulf Pannach Fabienne Babe Sigfrit Steiner

1991   AIMEE
Director: Pedr James
Co-stars: Donald Sumpter Juliet Stevenson Simon Chandler

GABRIELLE ROSE

1988   FAMILY VIEWING
Director: Atom Egoyan
Co-stars: David Hemblem Aiden Tierney Silma Kelikian

1989   SPEAKING PARTS
Director: Atom Egoyan
Co-stars: Michael McManus Arsinee Khanjia David Hemblem

1991   THE ADJUSTOR
Director: Atom Egoyan
Co-stars: Elias Koteas Arsinee Khanjia Maury Chaykin

JAIMIE ROSE

1989   SHATTERED
Director: Lamont Johnson
Co-stars: Shelley Long Tom Conti Alan Fudge

1990   CHOPPER CHICKS IN ZOMBIETOWN
Director: Dan Hoskins
Co-stars: Catherine Carlen Vicki Frederick

JANE ROSE

1957   THE MONTE CARLO STORY
Director: Samuel Taylor
Co-stars: Marlene Dietrich Vittorio De Seca

1963   FLIPPER
Director: James Clark
Co-stars: Chuck Connors Luke Halpin Kathleen Maguire

SHERRIE ROSE

1992   DOUBLE THREAT
Director: David Prior
Co-stars: Sally Kirkland Andrew Stevens Anthony Franciosa

VERONICA ROSE

1933   A CUCKOO IN THE NEST
Director: Tom Walls
Co-stars: Ralph Lynn Yvonne Arnaud Mary Brough

1937   FOR VALOUR
Director: Tom Walls
Co-stars: Ralph Lynn Joan Marion Tom Walls

1938   SECOND BEST BED
Director: Tom Walls
Co-stars: Jane Baxter Carl Jaffe Greta Gynt

1947   DEATH IN HIGH HEELS
Director: Lionel Tomlinson
Co-stars: Don Stannard Bill Hodge Patricia Laffan

SHEILA ROSENTHAL

1991 NOT WITHOUT MY DAUGHTER
Director: Brian Gilbert
Co-stars: Sally Field Alfred Molina Sarah Badel

ROSETTE

1992 A WINTER'S TALE
Director: Eric Rohmer
Co-stars: Charlotte Very Michel Voletti Herve Furic

CATHY ROSIER

1967 THE SAMURAI
Director: Jean-Pierre Melville
Co-stars: Alain Delon Francois Perier Nathalie Delon

ANNIE ROSS

1972 STRAIGHT ON TILL MORNING
Director: Peter Collinson
Co-stars: Rita Tushingham Shane Briant Tom Bell

1975 ALFIE DARLING
Director: Ken Hughes
Co-stars: Alan Price Jill Townsend Joan Collins

1979 YANKS
Director: John Schlesinger
Co-stars: Vanessa Redgrave Richard Gere Lisa Eichhorn

1983 SUPERMAN III
Director: Richard Lester
Co-stars: Christopher Reeve Richard Pryor Jackie Cooper

1983 FUNNY MONEY
Director: James Kenhelm Clarke
Co-stars: Elizabeth Dailey Gregg Henry Gareth Hunt

1987 THROW MOMMA FROM THE TRAIN
Director: Danny DeVito
Co-stars: Billy Crystal Anne Ramsey Kim Greist

1990 PUMP UP THE VOLUME
Director: Allan Moyle
Co-stars: Christian Slater Samantha Mathis Ellen Greene

1990 BASKET CASE 2
Director: Frank Hennenlotter
Co-stars: Kevin Van Hentenryck Heather Rattray Ted Sorel

1991 BASKET CASE 3
Director: Frank Hennenlotter
Co-stars: Kevin Van Hentenryck Dan Biggers Gil Roper

1993 SHORT CUTS
Director: Robert Altman
Co-stars: Matthew Modine Anne Archer Andie MacDowell

BETSY KING ROSS *(Child)*

1933 SMOKE LIGHTNING
Co-star: George O'Brien

CHARLOTTE ROSS

1991 SHE SAYS SHE'S INNOCENT
Director: Charles Correll
Co-stars: Katey Sagal Jameson Parker Alan Rachins

DIANA ROSS
Nominated For Best Actress In 1972 For "Lady Sings The Blues"

1972 LADY SINGS THE BLUES
Director: Sidney Furie
Co-stars: Billy Dee Williams Richard Pryor

1975 MAHOGANY
Director: Berry Gordy
Co-stars: Billy Dee Williams Anthony Perkins Jean-Pierre Aumont

1978 THE WIZ
Director: Sidney Lumet
Co-stars: Michael Jackson Richard Pryor Lena Horne

1993 OUT OF DARKNESS
Director: Larry Elikann
Co-stars: Lindsay Crouse Ann Weldon Beah Richards

KATHERINE ROSS
Nominated For Best Supporting Actress In 1967 For "The Graduate"

1965 SHENANDOAH
Director: Andrew McLaglen
Co-stars: James Stewart Doug McClure Rosemary Forsyth

1966 MISTER BUDDWING
Director: Delbert Mann
Co-stars: James Garner Jean Simmons Angela Lansbury

1966 THE SINGING NUN
Director: Henry Koster
Co-stars: Debbie Reynolds Greer Garson Ricardo Montalban

1967 THE GRADUATE
Director: Mike Nichols
Co-stars: Dustin Hoffman Anne Bancroft Murray Hamilton

1967 GAMES
Director: Curtis Harrington
Co-stars: Simone Signoret James Caan Don Stroud

1969 HELLFIGHTERS
Director: Andrew McLaglen
Co-stars: John Wayne Jim Hutton Vera Miles

1969 BUTCH CASSIDY AND THE SUNDANCE KID
Director: George Roy Hill
Co-stars: Paul Newman Robert Redford

1969 TELL THEM WILLIE BOY IS HERE
Director: Abraham Polonsky
Co-stars: Robert Redford Robert Blake Susan Clark

1970 FOOLS
Director: Tom Gries
Co-stars: Jason Robards Scott Hylands

1972 THEY ONLY KILL THEIR MASTERS
Director: James Goldstone
Co-stars: James Garner June Allyson Tom Ewell

1974 THE STEPFORD WIVES
Director: Bryan Forbes
Co-stars: Paula Prentiss Nanette Newman Tina Louise

1976 VOYAGE OF THE DAMNED
Director: Stuart Rosenberg
Co-stars: Oscar Werner Wendy Hiller James Mason

1977 THE BETSY
Director: Daniel Petrie
Co-stars: Laurence Olivier Robert Duvall Tommy Lee Jones

1978 THE SWARM
Director: Irwin Allen
Co-stars: Michael Caine Richard Widmark Olivia De Havilland

1979 THE LEGACY
Director: Richard Marquand
Co-stars: Sam Elliott Roger Daltrey Charles Gray

1980 THE FINAL COUNTDOWN
Director: Don Taylor
Co-stars: Kirk Douglas Martin Sheen James Farentino

1982 THE MAN WITH THE DEADLY LENS
Director: Richard Brooks
Co-stars: Sean Connery George Grizzard

1982 THE SHADOW RIDERS
Director: Andrew McLaglen
Co-stars: Tom Selleck Sam Elliott Ben Johnson

1991 CONAGHER
Director: Bey Villa Lobos
Co-stars: Sam Elliott Barry Corbin

LIZ ROSS

1977 THE END OF THE WORLD
Director: John Hayes
Co-stars: Christopher Lee Sue Lyon Lew Ayres

MARGERY ROSS

1991 THE NAKED GUN 2: THE SMELL OF FEAR
Director: David Zucker
Co-stars: Leslie Nielsen Priscilla Presley

MARION ROSS

1953 THE GLENN MILLER STORY
Director: Anthony Mann
Co-stars: James Stewart June Allyson Henry Morgan

1956 THE PROUD AND PROFANE
Director: George Seaton
Co-stars: William Holden Deborah Kerr Thelma Ritter

1957 GOD IS MY PARTNER
Director: William Claxton
Co-stars: Walter Brennan John Hoyt Jesse White

1960 BLUEPRINT FOR ROBBERY
Director: Jerry Hopper
Co-stars: J. Pat O'Malley Robert Gist Tom Dugan

1977 GRAND THEFT AUTO
Director: Ron Howard
Co-stars: Nancy Morgan Barry Cahill Ron Howard

1979 SURVIVAL OF DANA
Director: Jack Starrett
Co-stars: Melissa Sue Anderson Robert Carradine Talia Balsam

MARY ELLA ROSS

1992 BOUND AND GAGGED
Director: Daniel Appleby
Co-stars: Chris Denton Elizabeth Saltorrelli Karen Black

MERRIE LYNN ROSS

1981 CLASS OF 1984
Director: Mark Lester
Co-stars: Perry King Timothy Van Patten Roddy McDowell

SHERRI ROSS

1977 ALIEN ENCOUNTERS
Director: Ed Hunt
Co-stars: Robert Vaughn Christopher Lee Helen Shaver

SHIRLEY ROSS

1934 MANHATTAN MELODRAMA
Director: W.S. Van Dyke
Co-stars: Clark Gable William Powell Myrna Loy

1934 THE MERRY WIDOW
Director: Ernst Lubitsch
Co-stars: Maurice Chevalier Jeanette MacDonald Una Merkel

1936 SAN FRANCISCO
Director: W.S. Van Dyke
Co-stars: Clark Gable Jeanette MacDonald Spencer Tracy

1936 THE BIG BROADCAST OF 1937
Director: Mitchell Leisen
Co-stars: Jack Benny George Burns Gracie Allen

1937 WAIKIKI WEDDING
Director: Frank Tuttle
Co-stars: Bing Crosby Bob Burns Martha Raye

1937 BLOSSOMS ON BROADWAY
Director: Richard Wallace
Co-stars: Edward Arnold John Trent Frank Craven

1938 PARIS HONEYMOON
Director: Frank Tuttle
Co-stars: Bing Crosby Franciska Gaal Akim Tamiroff

1938 PRISON FARM
Director: Louis King
Co-stars: Lloyd Nolan John Howard Porter Hall

1938 BIG BROADCAST OF 1938
Director: Mitchell Leisen
Co-stars: Bob Hope W.C. Fields Tito Guizar

1938 THANKS FOR THE MEMORY
Director: George Archainbaud
Co-star: Bob Hope

1939 UNEXPECTED FATHER
Director: Charles Lamont
Co-stars: Baby Sandy Mischa Auer Dennis O'Keefe

1939 SOME LIKE IT HOT
Director: George Archainbaud
Co-stars: Bob Hope Una Merkel Richard Denning

1939 CAFÉ SOCIETY
Director: Edward Griffith
Co-stars: Madeleine Carroll Fred MacMurray

1941 KISSES FOR BREAKFAST
Co-star: Dennis Morgan

TERRY ANN ROSS

1958 CRY TERROR
Director: Andrew Stone
Co-stars: James Mason Rod Steiger Inger Stevens

ISABELLA ROSSELLINI
(Daughter Of Ingrid Bergman & Roberto Rossellini)

1976 A MATTER OF TIME
Director: Vincente Minnelli
Co-stars: Liza Minnelli Ingrid Bergman Charles Boyer

1985 WHITE NIGHTS
Director: Taylord Hackford
Co-stars: Mikhail Baryshnikov Helen Mirren Gregory Hines

1986 BLUE VELVET
Director: David Lynch
Co-stars: Kyle Maclachlan Dennis Hopper Laura Dern

1987 TOUGH GUYS DON'T DANCE
Director: Norman Mailer
Co-stars: Ryan O'Neal Debra Sandlund Wings Hauser

1987 SIESTA
Director: Mary Lambert
Co-stars: Ellen Barkin Gabriel Byrne Jodie Foster

1988 ZELLY AND ME
Director: Tina Rathbone
Co-stars: Glynis Johns David Lynch Joe Morton

1989 COUSINS
Director: Joel Schumacher
Co-stars: Ted Danson Sean Young Lloyd Bridges

1990 WILD AT HEART
Director: David Lynch
Co-stars: Nicolas Cage Laura Dern Diane Ladd

1990 THE LAST ELEPHANT
Director: Joseph Sargent
Co-stars: John Lithgow James Earl Jones Olek Krupa

1991 LIES OF THE TWINS
Director: Tim Hunter
Co-stars: Aidan Quinn Claudia Christian Iman

1992 DEATH BECOMES HER
Director: Robert Zemeckis
Co-stars: Meryl Streep Goldie Hawn Bruce Willis

1993 FEARLESS
Director: Peter Weir
Co-stars: Jeff Bridges Rosie Perez John Turturro

1994 IMMORTAL BELOVED
Director: Bernard Rose
Co-stars: Gary Oldman Jeroen Krabbe

1994 THE INNOCENT
Director: John Schlesinger
Co-stars: Anthony Hopkins Campbell Scott Hart Bochner

1996 CRIME OF THE CENTURY
Director: Mark Rydell
Co-star: Stephen Rea

1997 THE FUNERAL
Director: Abel Ferrara
Co-stars: Christopher Walken Christopher Penn Annabella Sciorra

1997 BIG NIGHT
Co-stars: Minnie Driver Stanley Tucci Allison Janney

CAROL ROSSEN

1969 THE ARRANGEMENT
Director: Elia Kazan
Co-stars: Kirk Douglas Faye Dunaway Deborah Kerr

1974 THE STEPFORD WIVES
Director: Bryan Forbes
Co-stars: Katherine Ross Paula Prentiss Nanette Newman

1978 THE FURY
Director: Brian De Palma
Co-stars: Kirk Douglas John Cassavetes Carrie Snodgress

1981 A QUESTION OF HONOUR
Director: Jud Taylor
Co-stars: Ben Gazzara Paul Sorvino Danny Aiello

1982 NOT IN FRONT OF THE CHILDREN
Director: Joseph Hardy
Co-stars: Linda Gray John Getz John Lithgow

KATHRYN ROSSETTER

1988 BLUE JEAN COP
Director: James Glickenhaus
Co-stars: Peter Weller Sam Elliott Patricia Charbonneau

LUISA ROSSI

1945 THE LAST CHANCE
Director: Leopold Lindtberg
Co-stars: E.G. Morrison Ray Reagan John Hoy

MICHELLE ROSSIGNOL

1977 ANGELA
Director: Boris Sagal
Co-stars: Sophia Loren John Vernon John Huston

MAGGIE ROSWELL

1985 LOST IN AMERICA
Director: Albert Brooks
Co-stars: Julie Hagerty Michael Greene Albert Brooks

CELIA ROTH

1982 LABYRINTH OF PASSION
Director: Pedro Almodovar
Co-stars: Imanol Arias Helga Line Antonio Banderas

JOANNA ROTH

1989 THE REAL CHARLOTTE
Director: Tony Barry
Co-stars: Jeanette Crowley Patrick Bergin Jemma Redgrave

1990 ROSENCRANTZ AND GUILDENSTERN ARE DEAD
Director: Tom Stoppard
Co-stars: Gary Oldman Tim Roth Iain Glen

1990 VAN GOGH
Director: Anna Benson Gyles
Co-stars: Linus Roache Jack Shepherd Anna Cropper

1991 JUTE CITY
Director: Stuart Orme
Co-stars: David O'Hara John Sessions Annette Crosbie

LILLIAN ROTH

1929 THE LOVE PARADE
Director: Ernst Lubitsch
Co-stars: Maurice Chevalier Jeanette MacDonald Lupino Lane

1930 MADAME SATAN
Director: Cecil B. DeMille
Co-stars: Kay Johnson Reginald Denny Roland Young

1930 HONEY
Director: Wesley Ruggles
Co-stars: Nancy Carroll Mitzi Green Zasu Pitts

1930 ANIMAL CRACKERS
Director: Victor Heerman
Co-stars: Marx Brothers Margaret Dumont Margaret Irving

1930 THE VAGABOND KING
Director: Ludwig Berger
Co-stars: Dennis King Jeanette MacDonald Warner Oland

1933 LADIES THEY TALK ABOUT
Director: William Keighley
Co-stars: Barbara Stanwyck Preston Foster Maude Eburne

1933 TAKE A CHANCE
Co-stars: Charles Rogers James Dunn Cliff Edwards

MARTA ROTH

1956 MASSACRE
Director: Louis King
Co-stars: Dane Clark James Craig Jaime Fernandez

WANDA ROTHA

1953 SAADIA
Director: Albert Lewin
Co-stars: Cornel Wilde Mel Ferrer Rita Gam

1964 THE MAGNIFICENT SHOWMAN
Director: Henry Hathaway
Co-stars: John Wayne Rita Hayworth Claudia Cardinale

CYNTHIA ROTHROCK

1993 IRRESISTABLE FORCE
Director: Kevin Hooks
Co-stars: Stacy Keach Paul Winfield

1995 CITY COPS

BRIGITTE ROUAN

1991 OLIVIER, OLIVIER
Director: Agniewzka Holland
Co-stars: Francois Cluzet Jean-Francois Stevenin

CECILIA ROUAUD

1990 CROSS MY HEART
Director: Jacques Fansten
Co-stars: Sylvain Copans Nicolas Parodi Lucie Blossier

ALIDA ROUFFE

1932 FANNY
Director: Marc Allegret
Co-stars: Raimu Pierre Fresnay Orane Demazis

JENNY ROUSSEA

1986 THE BEEKEEPER
Director: Theo Angelopoulos
Co-stars: Marcello Mastroianni Nadia Mourouzi

MARIE-ISABELLE ROUSSEAU

1993 LE JEUNE WERTHER
Director: Jacques Doillon
Co-stars: Ismael Jole Thomas Bremond

ANNE ROUSSEL

1988 THE MUSIC TEACHER
Director: Gerard Corbiau
Co-stars: Jose Van Dam Philippe Volter Sylvie Fennec

NATHALIE ROUSSELL

1990 LE CHATEAU DE MA MERE
Director: Yves Robert
Co-stars: Julien Ciamaca Julie Timmerman Joris Molinas

1991 LA GLOIRE DE MON PERE
Director: Yves Robert
Co-stars: Julien Ciamaca Therese Liotard Didier Pain

MADELEINE ROUSSET

1948 GIGI
Director: Jacqueline Audry
Co-stars: Daniele Delorme Gaby Morlay Frank Villard

ALISON ROUTLEDGE

1985 THE QUIET EARTH
Director: Geoff Murphy
Co-stars: Bruno Lawrence Peter Smith

PATRICIA ROUTLEDGE

1967 TO SIR WITH LOVE
Director: James Clavell
Co-stars: Sidney Poitier Judy Geeson Suzy Kendall

1967 30 IS A DANGEROUS AGE, CYNTHIA
Director: Joe McGrath
Co-stars: Dudley Moore Suzy Kendall

1967 PRETTY POLLY
Director: Guy Green
Co-stars: Hayley Mills Trevor Howard Brenda De Banzie

1968 THE BLISS OF MRS BLOSSOM
Director: Josef Shaftel
Co-stars: Richard Attenborough Shirley Maclaine James Booth

1968 DON'T RAISE THE BRIDGE, LOWER THE RIVER
Director: Jerry Paris
Co-stars: Jerry Lewis Terry-Thomas

1969 IF IT'S TUESDAY, THIS MUST BE BELGIUM
Director: Mel Stuart
Co-stars: Ian McShane Suzanne Pleshette Mildred Natwick

1971 GIRL STROKE BOY
Director: Bob Kellett
Co-stars: Joan Greenwood Michael Hordern Clive Francis

1989 FIRST AND LAST
Director: Alan Dosser
Co-stars: Joss Ackland Pat Heywood Lionel Jeffries

1990 MISSING PERSONS
Director: Derek Bennett
Co-stars: Jimmy Jewel Jean Heywood Jean Kent

CATHERINE ROUVEL

1959 LUNCH ON THE GRASS
Director: Jean Renoir
Co-stars: Paul Meurisse Fernand Sardou Ingrid Nordine

1962 LANDRU
Director: Claude Chabrol
Co-stars: Charles Denner Michele Morgan Danielle Darrieux

1970 BORSALINO
Director: Jacques Deray
Co-stars: Jean-Paul Belmondo Alain Delon Michel Bouquet

1974 BORSALINO AND CO.
Director: Jacques Deray
Co-stars: Alain Delon Riccardo Cucciolla Daniel Ivernal

1976 BLACK AND WHITE IN COLOUR
Director: Jean-Jacques Annaud
Co-stars: Jean Carmet Jacques Dufilho Dora Doll

MARCELLA ROVENA

1954 LA STRADA
Director: Federico Fellini
Co-stars: Giulietta Masina Anthony Quinn Richard Basehart

GINA ROVERE

1957 HERCULES
Director: Pietro Francisci
Co-stars: Steve Reeves Sylva Koscina Fabrizio Mione

1960 ADUA E LE COMPAGNE
Director: Antonio Pietrangeli
Co-stars: Simone Signoret Marcello Mastroianni

DIANA ROWAN

1980 BEYOND REASONABLE DOUBT
Director: John Laing
Co-stars: David Hemmings John Hargreaves Tony Barry

FRANCES ROWE

1944 THEY CAME TO A CITY
Director: Basil Dearden
Co-stars: Googie Withers John Clements Raymond Huntley

MISTY ROWE

1976 GOODBYE, NORMA JEAN
Director: Larry Buchanan
Co-stars: Terrence Locke Preston Hanson Marty Zagon

1980 THE MAN WITH BOGART'S FACE
Director: Robert Day
Co-stars: Robert Sacchi Franco Nero Olivia Hussey

MYRTLE ROWE

1955 NO SMOKING
Director: Henry Cass
Co-stars: Reg Dixon Belinda Lee Lionel Jeffries

VICTORIA ROWELL

1992 THE DISTINGUISHED GENTLEMAN
Director: Jonathan Lynn
Co-stars: Eddie Murphy Lane Smith Joe Don Baker

1994 DUMB AND DUMBER
Director: Peter Farrelly
Co-stars: Jim Carrey Jeff Daniels Lauren Holly

LEESA ROWLAND

1991 CLASS OF NUKE 'EM HIGH PART II: SCHUMANOID MELTDOWN
Director: Eric Louzil
Co-stars: Brick Bronsky Lisa Gaye

GENA ROWLANDS
(Married John Cassavetes, Son Nick Cassavetes)
Nominated For Best Actress In 1974 For "A Woman Under The Influence" And In 1980 For "Gloria"

1958   **THE HIGH COST OF LOVING**
Director: Jose Ferrer
Co-stars: Joanne Gilbert Jim Backus Bobby Troup

1962   **LONELY ARE THE BRAVE**
Director: David Miller
Co-stars: Kirk Douglas Walter Matthau Carroll O'Connor

1962   **THE SPIRAL ROAD**
Director: Robert Mulligan
Co-stars: Rock Hudson Burl Ives Geoffrey Keen

1963   **A CHILD IS WAITING**
Director: John Cassavetes
Co-stars: Judy Garland Burt Lancaster Bruce Ritchie

1967   **TONY ROME**
Director: Gordon Douglas
Co-stars: Frank Sinatra Jill St. John Richard Conte

1969   **FACES**
Director: John Cassavetes
Co-stars: John Marley Lynn Carlin Seymour Cassel

1970   **MACHINE GUN McCAIN**
Director: Guillano Montaldo
Co-stars: John Cassavetes Peter Falk Britt Ekland

1971   **MINNIE AND MOSKOWITZ**
Director: John Cassavetes
Co-stars: Seymour Cassel Katherine Cassavetes

1974   **A WOMAN UNDER THE INFLUENCE**
Director: John Cassavetes
Co-stars: Peter Falk Katherine Cassavetes

1976   **TWO-MINUTE WARNING**
Director: Larry Peerce
Co-stars: Charlton Heston Beau Bridges John Cassavetes

1978   **A QUESTION OF LOVE**
Director: Jerry Thorpe
Co-stars: Jane Alexander Ned Beatty Clu Gulager

1978   **OPENING NIGHT**
Director: John Cassavetes
Co-stars: Ben Gazzara Joan Blondell Paul Stewart

1978   **THE BRINK'S JOB**
Director: William Friedkin
Co-stars: Peter Falk Warren Oates Peter Boyle

1980   **GLORIA**
Director: John Cassavetes
Co-stars: John Adames Buck Henry Julie Carmen

1983   **THURSDAY'S CHILD**
Director: David Lowell Rich
Co-stars: Don Murray Rob Lowe Jessica Walter

1984   **LOVE STREAMS**
Director: John Cassavetes
Co-stars: John Cassavetes Dianne Abbott Seymour Cassel

1985   **AN EARLY FROST**
Director: John Erman
Co-stars: Ben Gazzara Sylvia Sidney Aidan Quinn

1987   **THE BETTY FORD STORY**
Director: David Greene
Co-stars: Josef Sommer Nan Woods Concetta Tomei

1987   **LIGHT OF DAY**
Director: Paul Schrader
Co-stars: Michael J. Fox Joan Jett Michael McKean

1988   **ANOTHER WOMAN**
Director: Woody Allen
Co-stars: Mia Farrow Ian Holm Blythe Danner

1991   **ONCE AROUND**
Director: Lasse Hallstrom
Co-stars: Holly Hunter Richard Dreyfuss Danny Aiello

1991   **NIGHT ON EARTH**
Director: Jim Jarmusch
Co-stars: Winona Ryder Beatrice Dalle Rosie Perez

1992   **CRAZY IN LOVE**
Director: Martha Coolidge
Co-stars: Holly Hunter Bill Pullman Julian Sands

1994   **PARALLEL LIVES**
Director: Linda Yellen
Co-stars: Liza Minnelli Helen Slater Ben Gazzara

1995   **THE NEON BIBLE**
Director: Terence Davies
Co-stars: Diana Scarwid Denis Leary Jacob Tierney

1996   **SOMETHING TO TALK ABOUT**
Director: Lasse Hallstrom
Co-stars: Julia Roberts Robert Duvall Dennis Quaid

1997   **UNHOOK THE STARS**
Director: Nick Cassavetes
Co-stars: Gerard Depardieu Marisa Tomei

LADY ROWLANDS

1974   **A WOMAN UNDER THE INFLUENCE**
Director: John Cassavetes
Co-stars: Gena Rowlands Peter Falk Katherine Cassavetes

PATSY ROWLANDS

1965   **DATELINE DIAMONDS**
Director: Jeremy Summers
Co-stars: William Lucas Kenneth Cope Conrad Phillips

1969   **CARRY ON AGAIN DOCTOR**
Director: Gerald Thomas
Co-stars: Sid James Kenneth Williams Jim Dale

1971   **CARRY ON AT YOUR CONVENIENCE**
Director: Gerald Thomas
Co-stars: Sid James Charles Hawtrey Joan Sims

1971   **PLEASE SIR !**
Director: Mark Stuart
Co-stars: John Alderton Derek Guyler Joan Sanderson

1973   **CARRY ON GIRLS**
Director: Gerald Thomas
Co-stars: Sid James Barbara Windsor Sally Geeson

1974   **CARRY ON DICK**
Director: Gerald Thomas
Co-stars: Sid James Bernard Bresslaw Bill Maynard

1975   **CARRY ON BEHIND**
Director: Gerald Thomas
Co-stars: Elke Sommer Kenneth Williams Liz Fraser

1992   **FEMME FATALE**
Director: Udayan Prasad
Co-stars: Simon Callow Colin Welland Sophia Diaz

POLLY ROWLES

1936   **LOVE LETTERS OF A STAR**
Director: Lewis Foster
Co-stars: Henry Hunter Walter Coy C. Henry Gordon

1937   **WESTBOUND LIMITED**
Co-star: Lyle Talbot

1937   **SPRINGTIME IN THE ROCKIES**
Co-stars: Gene Autry Smiley Burnette

GLORIA ROY

1936   **CHARLIE CHAN AT THE RACETRACK**
Director: Bruce Humberstone
Co-stars: Warner Oland Keye Luke Gavin Muir

1937   **FAIR WARNING**
Director: Norman Foster
Co-stars: J. Edward Bromberg Betty Furness John Payne

SUZANNE ROYLANCE

1982   **THE CLINIC**
Director: David Stevens
Co-stars: Chris Haywood Simon Burke Gerda Nicolson

CAROL ROYLE

1984   **AND THE WALL CAME TUMBLING DOWN**
Director: Paul Annett
Co-stars: Peter Wyngarde Gareth Hunt Brian Deacon

1989   **BLACKEYES**
Director: Dennis Potter
Co-stars: Michael Gough Nigel Planer Gina Bellman

SELENA ROYLE

1944   **MRS PARKINGTON**
Director: Tay Garnett
Co-stars: Greer Garson Walter Pidgeon Edward Arnold

1944   **THE FIGHTING SULLIVANS**
Director: Lloyd Bacon
Co-stars: Anne Baxter Thomas Mitchell James Cardwell

1944   **MAIN STREET AFTER DARK**
Director: Edward Cahn
Co-stars: Edward Arnold Audrey Totter Dan Duryea

1945   **THIS MAN'S NAVY**
Director: William Wellman
Co-stars: Wallace Beery James Gleason Tom Drake

1946   **THE HARVEY GIRLS**
Director: George Sidney
Co-stars: Judy Garland Ray Bolger John Hodiak

1946   **THE GREEN YEARS**
Director: Victor Saville
Co-stars: Charles Coburn Hume Cronyn Dean Stockwell

1946   **THE COURAGE OF LASSIE**
Director: Fred Wilcox
Co-stars: Elizabeth Taylor Frank Morgan Tom Drake

1947   **CASS TIMBERLANE**
Director: George Sidney
Co-stars: Spencer Tracy Lana Turner Zachary Scott

1947   **THE ROMANCE OF ROSY RIDGE**
Director: Roy Rowland
Co-stars: Van Johnson Thomas Mitchell Janet Leigh

1948   **SUMMER HOLIDAY**
Director: Rouben Mamoulian
Co-stars: Walter Huston Mickey Rooney Frank Morgan

1948   **YOU WERE MEANT FOR ME**
Director: Lloyd Bacon
Co-stars: Jeanne Crain Dan Dailey Oscar Levant

1949   **THE HEIRESS**
Director: William Wyler
Co-stars: Olivia De Havilland Montgomery Clift Ralph Richardson

1948   **A DATE WITH JUDY**
Director: Richard Thorpe
Co-stars: Jane Powell Elizabeth Taylor Wallace Beery

1949   **YOU'RE MY EVERYTHING**
Director: Walter Lang
Co-stars: Dan Dailey Anne Baxter Alan Mowbray

1950   **BRANDED**
Director: Rudolph Mate
Co-stars: Alan Ladd Mona Freeman Charles Bickford

1950   **THE BIG HANGOVER**
Director: Norman Krasna
Co-stars: Van Johnson Elizabeth Taylor Leon Ames

1950   **THE DAMNED DON'T CRY**
Director: Vincent Sherman
Co-stars: Joan Crawford Kent Smith David Brian

1951   **COME FILL THE CUP**
Director: Gordon Douglas
Co-stars: James Cagney Gig Young Raymond Massey

1953   **ROBOT MONSTER**
Director: Phil Tucker
Co-stars: George Nader Claudia Barrett Pamela Paulson

LITA ROZA

1978   **THE BILL DOUGLAS TRILOGY: MY WAY HOME**
Director: Bill Douglas
Co-stars: Stephen Archibald Paul Kermack

SHEYLA ROZIN

1968   **VENGEANCE**
Director: Anthony Dawson
Co-stars: Richard Harrison Claudio Camaso Allan Collins

MARIA RUBELL

1988   **976-EVIL**
Director: Robert Englund
Co-stars: Stephen Geoffreys Sandy Dennis Patrick O'Bryan

ALMA RUBENS

1916   **THE AMERICANO**
Director: John Emerson
Co-stars: Douglas Fairbanks Lillian Langdon

1925   **EAST LYNNE**

JENNIFER RUBIN

1988   **BLUEBERRY HILL**
Director: Strathford Hamilton
Co-stars: Carrie Snodgress Margaret Avery Matt Lattanzi

1988   **PERMANENT RECORD**
Director: Marisa Silver
Co-stars: Alan Boyce Keanu Reeves Michelle Meyrink

1990   **DELUSION**
Director: Carl Colpaert
Co-stars: Jim Metzler Kyle Secor

1991   **VICTIM OF BEAUTY**
Director: Paul Lynch
Co-stars: Sally Kellerman Peter Outerbridge Michael Ironside

1993   **THE CRUSH**
Director: Alan Shapiro
Co-stars: Cary Elwes Alicia Silverstone Amber Benson

1993   **BITTER HARVEST**
Director: Duane Clark
Co-stars: Patsy Kensit Stephen Baldwin

1994   **PLAYMAKER**
Director: Yuri Zeltser
Co-stars: Colin Firth John Getz

1994   **SCREAMERS**
Director: Christian Duguay
Co-stars: Peter Weller Roy Dupuis

1994   **EDGE OF DECEPTION**
Director: George Mihalka
Co-stars: Mariel Hemingway Stephen Shellen

GUILIA RUBINI

1959 GOLIATH AND THE BARBARIANS
Director: Carlo Campogalliani
Co-stars: Steve Reeves Bruce Cabot

1966 RINGO AND HIS GOLDEN PISTOL
Director: Sergio Corbucci
Co-stars: Mark Damon Valeria Fabrizi

ZELDA RUBINSTEIN

1982 POLTERGEIST
Director: Tobe Hooper
Co-stars: JoBeth Williams Craig T. Nelson Heather O'Rourke

1986 POLTERGEIST II
Director: Brian Gibson
Co-stars: JoBeth Williams Craig T. Nelson Heather O'Rourke

1988 POLTERGEIST III
Director: Gary Sherman
Co-stars: Tom Skerritt Nancy Allen Heather O'Rourke

1988 ANGUISH
Director: Biggas Luna
Co-stars: Talia Paul Michael Lerner Clara Pastor

THELMA RUBY

1955 WHERE THERE'S A WILL
Director: Vernon Sewell
Co-stars: Kathleen Harrison George Cole Leslie Dwyer

EDITH RUDDICK

1987 THE DARK ROOM
Director: Guy Slater
Co-stars: Susan Wooldridge Philip Jackson Julie Graham

EVELYN RUDIE *(Child)*

1958 THE GIFT OF LOVE
Director: Jean Negulesco
Co-stars: Lauren Bacall Robert Stack Lorne Greene

RITA RUDNER

1992 PETER'S FRIENDS
Director: Kenneth Branagh
Co-stars: Emma Thompson Stephen Fry Hugh Laurie

VERENICE RUDOLPH

1981 THE GERMAN SISTERS
Director: Margarethe Von Trotta
Co-stars: Jutte Lampa Barbara Sukowa Doris Schade

KRISTIN RUDRUD

1997 FARGO
Co-stars: Frances McDormand William H. Macey

MERCEDES RUEHL
Oscar For Best Supporting Actress In 1991 For "The Fisher King"

1979 THE WARRIORS
Director: Walter Hill
Co-stars: Michael Beck James Remar Thomas Waites

1986 84, CHARING CROSS ROAD
Director: David Jones
Co-stars: Anne Bancroft Anthony Hopkins Judi Dench

1988 MARRIED TO THE MOB
Director: Jonathan Demme
Co-stars: Michelle Pfeiffer Matthew Modine Dean Stockwell

1990 CRAZY PEOPLE
Director: Tony Bill
Co-stars: Dudley Moore Daryl Hannah Paul Reiser

1991 ANOTHER YOU
Director: Maurice Phillips
Co-stars: Richard Pryor Gene Wilder Vanessa Williams

1991 THE FISHER KING
Director: Terry Gilliam
Co-stars: Robin Williams Jeff Bridges Amanda Plummer

1993 THE LAST ACTION HERO
Director: John McTiernan
Co-stars: Arnold Schwarzenegger Charles Dance Anthony Quinn

1993 LOST IN YONKERS
Director: Martha Coolidge
Co-stars: Richard Dreyfuss Irene Worth Brad Stoll

1997 ROSEANNA'S GRAVE
Director: Paul Weiland
Co-stars: Jean Reno Luigi Diberti

ELEANORA RUFFO

1953 I VITELLONI
Director: Federico Fellini
Co-stars: Franco Fabrizi Franco Interlenghi Alberto Sordi

BARBARA RUICK

1953 THE AFFAIRS OF DOBIE GILLES
Director: Don Weis
Co-stars: Bobby Van Debbie Reynolds Bob Fosse

1956 CAROUSEL
Director: Henry King
Co-stars: Gordon MacRae Shirley Jones Cameron Mitchell

1974 CALIFORNIA SPLIT *(Died While Filming)*
Director: Robert Altman
Co-stars: George Segal Elliott Gould Gwen Welles

ELISA RUIS

1938 LA MARSEILLAISE
Director: Jean Renoir
Co-stars: Pierre Renoir Lise Delamere Louis Jouvet

CHELA RUIZ

1985 THE OFFICIAL VERSION
Director: Luis Puenzo
Co-stars: Norma Aleandro Hector Alterio

MERCEDES RUIZ

1965 DOCTOR ZHIVAGO
Director: David Lean
Co-stars: Omar Sharif Julie Christie Alec Guinness

JANICE RULE

1951 STARLIFT
Director: Roy Del Ruth
Co-stars: Dick Wesson Doris Day Gordon MacRae

1951 GOODBYE MY FANCY
Director: Vincent Sherman
Co-stars: Joan Crawford Robert Young Frank Lovejoy

1952 HOLIDAY FOR SINNERS
Director: Gerald Mayer
Co-stars: Gig Young Keenan Wynn William Campbell

1953 ROGUE'S MARCH
Director: Allan Davis
Co-stars: Peter Lawford Richard Greene John Abbott

1956 BATTLE SHOCK
Director: Paul Henreid
Co-stars: Ralph Meeker Rosenda Monteros Paul Henreid

1956 GUN FOR A COWARD
Director: Abner Biberman
Co-stars: Fred MacMurray Jeffrey Hunter Dean Stockwell

1958 BELL, BOOK AND CANDLE
Director: Richard Quine
Co-stars: James Stewart Kim Novak Jack Lemmon

1960 THE SUBTERRANEANS
Director: Ranald MacDougall
Co-stars: George Peppard Leslie Caron Roddy McDowall

1964 INVITATION TO A GUNFIGHTER
Director: Richard Wilson
Co-stars: Yul Brynner George Segal Pat Hingle

1966 ALVAREZ KELLY
Director: Edward Dmytryk
Co-stars: William Holden Richard Widmark Patrick O'Neal

1966 THE CHASE
Director: Arthur Penn
Co-stars: Marlon Brando Robert Redford Jane Fonda

1967 WELCOME TO HARD TIMES
Director: Burt Kennedy
Co-stars: Henry Fonda Janis Paige Warren Oates

1967 THE AMBUSHERS
Director: Henry Levin
Co-stars: Dean Martin Senta Berger Kurt Kasznar

1968 THE SWIMMER
Director: Sidney Pollack
Co-stars: Burt Lancaster Kim Hunter Marge Champion

1970 DOCTORS' WIVES
Director: George Schaefer
Co-stars: Richard Crenna Gene Hackman Dyan Cannon

1971 GUMSHOE
Director: Stephen Frears
Co-stars: Albert Finney Billie Whitelaw Frank Finlay

1971 KID BLUE
Director: James Frawley
Co-stars: Dennis Hopper Warren Oates Ben Johnson

1977 3 WOMEN
Director: Robert Altman
Co-stars: Sissy Spacek Shelley Duvall Robert Fortier

1985 AMERICAN FLYERS
Director: John Badham
Co-stars: Kevin Costner David Grant Rae Dawn Chong

JENNY RUNACRE

1970 HUSBANDS
Director: John Cassavetes
Co-stars: Peter Falk Ben Gazzara Jenny Lee Wright

1971 THE CANTERBURY TALES
Director: Pier Paolo Pasolini
Co-stars: Franco Citti Hugh Griffith Tom Baker

1973 THE FINAL PROGRAMME
Director: Robert Fuest
Co-stars: Jon Finch Hugh Griffith Sterling Hayden

1974 ALL CREATURES GREAT AND SMALL
Director: Claude Whatham
Co-stars: Simon Ward Anthony Hopkins Lisa Harrow

1975 PROFESSION:REPORTER
Director: Michaelangelo Antonioni
Co-stars: Jack Nicholson Maria Schneider

1978 JUBILEE
Director: Derek Jarman
Co-stars: Toyah Wilcox Ian Charleson Adam Ant

1979 HUSSY
Director: Matthew Chapman
Co-stars: Helen Mirren John Shea Patti Boulaye

KICKI RUNDGREN

1985 MY LIFE AS A DOG
Director: Lasse Hallstrom
Co-stars: Anton Glanzelius Anki Liden Leif Erickson

JENNIFER RUNYON

1986 BLUE DE VILLE
Director: Jim Johnston
Co-stars: Kimberley Pistone Alan Autry Mark Thomas Miller

1988 18 AGAIN !
Director: Paul Flaherty
Co-stars: George Burns Charlie Schlatter Tony Roberts

1989 QUANTUM LEAP
Co-stars: Scott Bakula Dean Stockwell

1993 CARNOSAUR
Director: Adam Simon
Co-stars: Diane Ladd Raphael Sbarge

KATJA RUPE

1984 FAVOURITES OF THE MOON
Director: Otar Iosseliani
Co-stars: Christiane Bailly Jean-Pierre Beauviala

ELIZABETH RUSCIO

1987 BURGLAR
Director: Hugh Wilson
Co-stars: Whoopi Goldberg Bob Goldthwait Lesley Ann Warren

1988 LEAP OF FAITH
Director: Stephen Gyllenhaal
Co-stars: Anne Archer Sam Neill James Tolkin

1993 THE POSITIVELY TRUE ADVENTURES OF THE ALLEGED TEXAS CHEERLEADER MURDERING MOM
Director: Michael Ritchie
Co-stars: Holly Hunter Beau Bridges

BARBARA RUSH

1951 QUEBEC
Director: George Templeton
Co-stars: Corinne Calvet John Barrymore Jnr.

1951 WHEN WORLDS COLLIDE
Director: Rudolph Mate
Co-stars: Richard Derr Larry Keating Peter Hanson

1951 FLAMING FEATHER
Director: Ray Enright
Co-stars: Sterling Hayden Forrest Tucker Victor Jory

1951 THE FIRST LEGION
Director: Douglas Sirk
Co-stars: Charles Boyer William Demarest Lyle Bettger

1953 IT CAME FROM OUTER SPACE
Director: Jack Arnold
Co-stars: Richard Carlson Charles Drake

1953 PRINCE OF PIRATES
Director: Sidney Salkow
Co-stars: John Derek Carla Balenda Edgar Barrier

1954 TAZA, SON OF COCHISE
Director: Douglas Sirk
Co-stars: Rock Hudson Jeff Chandler Bart Roberts

1954 MAGNIFICENT OBSESSION
Director: Douglas Sirk
Co-stars: Rock Hudson Jane Wyman Agnes Moorehead

1955 CAPTAIN LIGHTFOOT
Director: Douglas Sirk
Co-stars: Rock Hudson Kathleen Ryan Finlay Currie

1955   **WORLD IN MY CORNER**
Director: Jesse Hibbs
Co-stars: Audie Murphy Jeff Morrow Tommy Rall

1956   **FLIGHT TO HONG KONG**
Director: Joseph Newman
Co-stars: Rory Calhoun Douglas Donlon Pat Conway

1956   **BIGGER THAN LIFE**
Director: Nicholas Ray
Co-stars: James Mason Walter Matthau Robert Simon

1957   **NO DOWN PAYMENT**
Director: Martin Ritt
Co-stars: Joanne Woodward Tony Randall Sheree North

1957   **OH MEN ! OH WOMEN !**
Director: Nunnally Johnson
Co-stars: David Niven Ginger Rogers Dan Dailey

1958   **THE YOUNG LIONS**
Director: Edward Dmytryk
Co-stars: Marlon Brando Dean Martin Mongomery Clift

1958   **HARRY BLACK AND THE TIGER**
Director: Hugo Fregonese
Co-stars: Stewart Granger Anthony Steel

1959   **THE YOUNG PHILADEPHIANS**
Director: Vincent Sherman
Co-stars: Paul Newman Alexis Smith John Williams

1960   **STRANGERS WHEN WE MEET**
Director: Richard Quine
Co-stars: Kirk Douglas Kim Novak Ernie Kovacs

1960   **THE BRAMBLE BUSH**
Director: Daniel Petrie
Co-stars: Richard Burton Angie Dickinson Jack Carson

1962   **COME BLOW YOUR HORN**
Director: Bud Yorkin
Co-stars: Frank Sinatra Tony Bill Jill St. John

1964   **ROBIN AND THE SEVEN HOODS**
Director: Gordon Douglas
Co-stars: Frank Sinatra Dean Martin Bing Crosby

1972   **MOON OF THE WOLF**
Director: Daniel Petrie
Co-stars: David Janssen Bradford Dillman Royal Dano

1972   **THE MAN**
Director: Joseph Sargent
Co-stars: James Earl Jones Martin Balsam Lew Ayres

1972   **THE EYES OF CHARLES SAND**
Director: Reza Badiyi
Co-stars: Peter Haskell Joan Bennett Bradford Dillman

1973   **CRIME CLUB**
Director: David Lowell Rich
Co-stars: Lloyd Bridges Martin Sheen Victor Buono

1973   **A SUMMER WITHOUT BOYS**
Director: Jeannot Szwarc
Co-stars: Kay Lenz Michael Moriarty Mildred Dunnock

1974   **SUPERDAD**
Director: Vincent McEveety
Co-stars: Bob Crane Kurt Russell Kathleen Cody

1979   **DEATH CAR ON THE FREEWAY**
Director: Hal Needham
Co-stars: Shelley Hack George Hamilton Dinah Shore

1980   **CAN'T STOP THE MUSIC**
Director: Nancy Walker
Co-stars: Valerie Perrine June Havoc Steve Guttenberg

DEBORAH RUSH

1981   **HONKY TONK FREEWAY**
Director: John Schlesinger
Co-stars: William Devane Beau Bridges Teri Garr

1988   **PARENTS**
Director: Bob Balaban
Co-stars: Mary Beth Hurt Randy Quaid Sandy Dennis

1990   **MY BLUE HEAVEN**
Director: Herbert Ross
Co-stars: Steve Martin Rick Moranis Joan Cusack

LOUISE RUSH

1975   **CONFESSIONS OF A SEX MANIAC**
Director: Alan Birkinshaw
Co-stars: Roger Lloyd-Pack Vicki Hodge

CLAIRE RUSHBROOK

1996   **SECRET AND LIES**
Director: Mike Leigh
Co-stars: Timothy Spall Brenda Blethyn Phyllis Logan

RITA RUSIC

1987   **RUSSICUM**
Director: Pasquale Squitieri
Co-stars: F. Murray Abraham Treat Williams Danny Aiello

SHEILA RUSKIN

1992   **BORN KICKING**
Director: Mandie Fletcher
Co-stars: Eve Barker Denis Lawson Carole Hayman

ESMERALDA RUSPOLI

1968   **ROMEO AND JULIET**
Director: Franco Zefferelli
Co-stars: Olivia Hussey Leonard Whiting Michael York

BETSY RUSSELL

1989   **ROXANNE: THE PRIZE PULITZER**
Director: Richard Colla
Co-stars: Perry King Chynna Phillips Courteney Cox

CATHERINE RUSSELL

1987   **AIRBASE**
Director: David Attwood
Co-stars: Anton Lesser Clive Mantle Norman Beaton

1992   **SOFT TOP, HARD SHOULDER**
Director: Stefan Schwartz
Co-stars: Peter Capaldi Elaine Collins Frances Barber

1994   **CLOCKWORK MICE**
Director: Vadim Jean
Co-stars: Ian Hart John Alderton

CONNIE RUSSELL

1956   **NIGHTMARE**
Director: Maxwell Shane
Co-stars: Edward G. Robinson Kevin McCarthy Virginia Christine

ELIZABETH RUSSELL

1942   **THE CORPSE VANISHES**
Director: Wallace Fox
Co-stars: Bela Lugosi Minerva Urecal Luana Walters

1944   **THE CURSE OF THE CAT PEOPLE**
Director: Robert Wise
Co-stars: Simone Simon Kent Smith Jane Randolph

GAIL RUSSELL

1944　**THE UNINVITED**
Director:　Lewis Allen
Co-stars:　Ray Milland Ruth Hussey Donald Crisp

1944　**OUR HEARTS WERE YOUNG AND GAY**
Director:　Lewis Allen
Co-stars:　Diana Lynn Beulah Bondi

1945　**OUR HEARTS WERE GROWING UP**
Director:　William Russell
Co-stars:　Diana Lynn Brian Donlevy

1945　**SALTY O'ROURKE**
Director:　Raoul Walsh
Co-stars:　Alan Ladd William Demarest

1945　**THE UNSEEN**
Director:　Lewis Allen
Co-stars:　Joel McCrea Herbert Marshall

1946　**BACHELOR GIRLS**
Director:　Andrew Stone
Co-stars:　Adolphe Menjou Claire Trevor Jane Wyatt

1947　**ANGEL AND THE BADMAN**
Director:　James Edward Grant
Co-stars:　John Wayne Bruce Cabot

1947　**VARIETY GIRL**
Director:　George Marshall
Co-stars:　Mary Hatcher Olga San Juan Glenn Tryon

1947　**CALCUTTA**
Director:　John Farrow
Co-stars:　Alan Ladd William Bendix June Duprez

1948　**MOONRISE**
Director:　Frank Borzage
Co-stars:　Dane Clark Ethel Barrymore Rex Ingram

1948　**NIGHT HAS A THOUSAND EYES**
Director:　John Farrow
Co-stars:　Edward G. Robinson John Lund

1948　**WAKE OF THE RED WITCH**
Director:　Edward Ludwig
Co-stars:　John Wayne Luther Adler Gig Young

1949　**SONG OF INDIA**
Director:　Albert Rogell
Co-stars:　Sabu Turhan Bey Anthony Caruso

1949　**THE GREAT DAN PATCH**
Director:　Joseph Newman
Co-stars:　Dennis O'Keefe Ruth Warwick Henry Hull

1949　**EL PASO**
Director:　Lewis Foster
Co-stars:　John Payne Sterling Hayden Dick Foran

1949　**CAPTAIN CHINA**
Director:　Lewis Foster
Co-stars:　John Payne Jeffrey Lynn Lon Chaney

1950　**THE LAWLESS**
Director:　Joseph Losey
Co-stars:　MacDonald Carey Lee Patrick

1951　**AIR CADET**
Director:　Joseph Pevney
Co-stars:　Stephen McNally Rock Hudson

1956　**SEVEN MEN FROM NOW**
Director:　Budd Boetticher
Co-stars:　Randolph Scott Lee Marvin Don Barry

1957　**THE TATTERED DRESS**
Director:　Jack Arnold
Co-stars:　Jeff Chandler Jack Carson Jeanne Crain

HARRIET RUSSELL

1935　**THE CRIME OF DR CRESPI**
Director:　John Auer
Co-stars:　Erich Von Stroheim Dwight Frye Paul Guilfoyle

JACKIE RUSSELL

1967　**A GUIDE FOR THE MARRIED MAN**
Director:　Gene Kelly
Co-stars:　Walter Matthau Robert Morse Inger Stevens

1970　**THE CHEYENNE SOCIAL CLUB**
Director:　Gene Kelly
Co-stars:　James Stewart Henry Fonda Shirley Jones

JANE RUSSELL

1943　**THE OUTLAW**
Director:　Howard Hughes
Co-stars:　Thomas Mitchell Walter Huston Jack Buetel

1946　**THE YOUNG WIDOW**
Director:　Edwin Marin
Co-stars:　Louis Hayward Faith Domergue Marie Wilson

1948　**THE PALEFACE**
Director:　Norman Z. McLeod
Co-stars:　Bob Hope Robert Armstrong

1951　**DOUBLE DYNAMITE**
Director:　Irving Cummings
Co-stars:　Frank Sinatra Groucho Marx Don McGuire

1951　**HIS KIND OF WOMAN**
Director:　John Farrow
Co-stars:　Robert Mitchum Vincent Price Raymond Burr

1952　**THE LAS VEGAS STORY**
Director:　Robert Stevenson
Co-stars:　Victor Mature Hoagy Carmichael

1952　**MACAO**
Director:　Nicholas Ray
Co-stars:　Robert Mitchum Gloria Grahame Thomas Gomez

1952　**ROAD TO BALI**
Director:　Hal Walker
Co-stars:　Bing Crosby Bob Hope Dorothy Lamour

1952　**SON OF PALEFACE**
Director:　Frank Tashlin
Co-stars:　Bob Hope Roy Rogers Bill Williams

1953　**GENTLEMEN PREFER BLONDES**
Director:　Howard Hawks
Co-stars:　Marilyn Monroe Charles Coburn Tommy Noonan

1954　**UNDERWATER**
Director:　John Sturges
Co-stars:　Gilbert Roland Richard Egan Lori Nelson

1955　**THE FRENCH LINE**
Director:　Lloyd Bacon
Co-stars:　Gilbert Roland Arthur Hunnicutt Mary McCarty

1955　**GENTLEMEN MARRY BRUNETTES**
Director:　Richard Sale
Co-stars:　Jeanne Crain Alan Young Rudy Vallee

1955　**HOT BLOOD**
Director:　Nicholas Ray
Co-stars:　Cornel Wilde Joseph Calleia

1955　**FOXFIRE**
Director:　Joseph Pevney
Co-stars:　Jeff Chandler Dan Duryea

1955　**THE TALL MEN**
Director:　Raoul Walsh
Co-stars:　Clark Gable Robert Ryan Cameron Mitchell

1956 THE REVOLT OF MAMIE STOVER
Director: Raoul Walsh
Co-stars: Agnes Moorehead Richard Egan Joan Leslie

1957 THE FUZZY PINK NIGHTGOWN
Director: Norman Taurog
Co-stars: Ralph Meeker Keenan Wynn Adolphe Menjou

1964 FATE IS THE HUNTER
Director: Ralph Nelson
Co-stars: Glenn Ford Rod Taylor Suzanne Pleshette

1966 WACO
Director: R.G. Springsteen
Co-stars: Howard Keel John Smith Terry Moore

1967 BORN LOSERS
Director: Tom Laughlin
Co-stars: Elizabeth James Tom Laughlin Jeremy Slate

1970 DARKER THAN AMBER
Director: Robert Clouse
Co-stars: Rod Taylor Suzy Kendall James Booth

JASMINE RUSSELL

1996 GUILTRIP
Director: Gerard Stembridge
Co-star: Andrew Connolly

KERI RUSSELL

1992 HONEY, I BLEW UP THE KIDS
Director: Randal Reiser
Co-stars: Rick Moranis Marcia Strassman Lloyd Bridges

1996 THE BABYSITTER'S SEDUCTION
Director: David Burton Morris
Co-stars: Stephen Collins Phylicia Rashad

1996 EIGHT DAYS A WEEK
Director: Michael Davis
Co-stars: Joshua Schaefer

1997 WHEN INNOCENCE IS LOST
Co-star: Roberta Maxwell

KIMBERLEY RUSSELL

1984 GHOST DAD
Director: Sidney Poitier
Co-stars: Bill Cosby Denise Nicholas Ian Bannen

1991 HANGIN' WITH THE HOMEBOYS
Director: Joseph Vasquez
Co-stars: Doug E. Doug Mario Joyner Nestor Serrano

MARY RUSSELL

1938 EXTORTION
Co-stars: Gene Morgan Ann Doran J. Farrell MacDonald

ROSALIND RUSSELL

Nominated For Best Actress In 1943 For "My Sister Eileen", In 1946 For "Sister Kenny", In 1947 For "Mourning Becomes Electra" And In 1958 For "Auntie Mame"

1934 THE PRESIDENT VANISHES
Director: William Wellman
Co-stars: Arthur Byron Janet Beecher Paul Kelly

1934 THE NIGHT IS YOUNG
Director: Dudley Murphy
Co-stars: Evelyn Laye Ramon Navarro Una Merkel

1934 FORSAKING ALL OTHERS
Director: W.S. Van Dyke
Co-stars: Clark Gable Joan Crawford Robert Montgomery

1934 EVELYN PRENTICE
Director: William Howard
Co-stars: Myrna Loy William Powell Una Merkel

1935 CHINA SEAS
Director: Tay Garnett
Co-stars: Clark Gable Jean Harlow Wallace Beery

1935 THE CASINO MURDER CASE
Director: Edwin Marin
Co-stars: Paul Lukas Eric Blore Louise Fazenda

1935 RECKLESS
Director: Victor Fleming
Co-stars: Jean Harlow William Powell Allan Jones

1935 RENDEZVOUS
Director: William Howard
Co-stars: William Powell Binnie Barnes Cesar Romero

1935 WEST POINT OF THE AIR
Director: Richard Rossen
Co-stars: Wallace Beery Robert Young Maureen O'Sullivan

1936 UNDER TWO FLAGS
Director: Frank Lloyd
Co-stars: Ronald Colman Claudette Colbert Victor McLaglen

1936 TROUBLE FOR TWO
Director: Walter Rubin
Co-stars: Robert Montgomery Frank Morgan Louis Hayward

1936 IT HAD TO HAPPEN
Director: Roy Del Ruth
Co-stars: George Raft Leo Carrillo Alan Dinehart

1936 CRAIG'S WIFE
Director: Dorothy Arzner
Co-stars: John Boles Billie Burke Thomas Mitchell

1937 LIVE, LOVE AND LEARN
Director: George Fitzmaurice
Co-stars: Robert Montgomery Mickey Rooney

1937 NIGHT MUST FALL
Director: Richard Thorpe
Co-stars: Robert Montgomery May Whitty Alan Marshall

1938 MAN-PROOF
Director: Richard Thorpe
Co-stars: Myrna Loy Franchot Tone Walter Pidgeon

1938 FOUR'S A CROWD
Director: Michael Curtiz
Co-stars: Errol Flynn Olivia De Havilland

1938 THE CITADEL
Director: King Vidor
Co-stars: Robert Donat Rex Harrison Ralph Richardson

1939 FAST AND LOOSE
Director: Edwin Marin
Co-stars: Robert Montgomery Ralph Morgan Reginald Owen

1938 THE WOMEN
Director: George Cukor
Co-stars: Norma Shearer Joan Crawford Paulette Goddard

1940 NO TIME FOR COMEDY
Director: William Keighley
Co-stars: James Stewart Charles Ruggles Genevieve Tobin

1940 HIS GIRL FRIDAY
Director: Howard Hawks
Co-stars: Cary Grant Ralph Bellamy Gene Lockhart

1940 HIRED WIFE
Director: William Seiter
Co-stars: Brian Aherne Virginia Bruce John Carroll

1941 THE FEMININE TOUCH
Director: W.S. Van Dyke
Co-stars: Don Ameche Kay Francis Van Heflin

1941 THIS THING CALLED LOVE
Director: Alexander Hall
Co-stars: Melvyn Douglas Binnie Barnes Lee J. Cobb

1941   **THEY MET IN BOMBAY**
Director: Clarence Brown
Co-stars: Clark Gable Peter Lorre Reginald Owen

1941   **DESIGN FOR SCANDAL**
Director: Norman Taurog
Co-stars: Walter Pidgeon Edward Arnold Lee Bowman

1943   **MY SISTER EILEEN**
Director: Alexander Hall
Co-stars: Janet Blair Brian Aherne June Havoc

1942   **TAKE A LETTER, DARLING**
Director: Mitchell Leisen
Co-stars: Fred MacMurray Constance Moore

1943   **WHAT A WOMAN**
Director: Irving Cummings
Co-stars: Brian Aherne Willard Parker Alan Dinehard

1943   **FLIGHT FOR FREEDOM**
Director: Lothar Mendes
Co-stars: Fred MacMurray Herbert Marshall Eduardo Ciannelli

1945   **ROUGHLY SPEAKING**
Director: Michael Curtiz
Co-stars: Jack Carson Robert Hutton Donald Woods

1946   **SHE WOULDN'T SAY YES**
Director: Alexander Hall
Co-stars: Lee Bowman Charles Winninger Adele Jergens

1946   **SISTER KENNY**
Director: Dudley Nichols
Co-stars: Alexander Knox Dean Jagger Beulah Bondi

1947   **MOURNING BECOMES ELECTRA**
Director: Dudley Nichols
Co-stars: Michael Redgrave Kirk Douglas Katina Paxinou

1947   **THE GUILT OF JANET AMES**
Director: Henry Levin
Co-stars: Melvyn Douglas Sid Caesar Betsy Blair

1948   **THE VELVET TOUCH**
Director: John Gage
Co-stars: Leo Genn Sydney Greenstreet Claire Trevor

1949   **TELL IT TO THE JUDGE**
Director: Norman Foster
Co-stars: Robert Cummings Gig Young Marie McDonald

1952   **NEVER WAVE AT A WAC**
Director: Norman Z. McLeod
Co-stars: Paul Douglas Marie Wilson Leif Erikson

1955   **PICNIC**
Director: Joshua Logan
Co-stars: William Holden Kim Novak Susan Strasberg

1955   **THE GIRL RUSH**
Director: Robert Pirosh
Co-stars: Fernando Lamas Gloria DeHaven Eddie Albert

1958   **AUNTIE MAME**
Director: Morton DaCosta
Co-stars: Forrest Tucker Coral Browne Peggy Cass

1961   **A MAJORITY OF ONE**
Director: Mervyn LeRoy
Co-stars: Alec Guinness Ray Danton Madlyn Rhue

1962   **FIVE FINGER EXERCISE**
Director: Daniel Mann
Co-stars: Jack Hawkins Richard Beymer Maria Schell

1962   **GYPSY**
Director: Mervyn LeRoy
Co-stars: Natalie Wood Karl Malden Ann Jillian

1966   **THE TROUBLE WITH ANGELS**
Director: Ida Lupino
Co-stars: Hayley Mills June Harding Louise Horvick

1967   **ROSIE!**
Director: David Lowell Rich
Co-stars: Brian Aherne Sandra Dee Juanita Moore

1967   **OH DAD, POOR DAD, MAMA'S HUNG YOU IN THE CLOSET AND I'M FEELING SO SAD**
Director: Richard Quine
Co-star: Robert Morse Hugh Griffith Lionel Jeffries

1968   **WHERE ANGELS GO, TROUBLE FOLLOWS**
Director: James Neilson
Co-stars: Stella Stevens Van Johnson

1970   **MRS POLLIFAX SPY**
Director: Leslie Martinson
Co-star: Darren McGavin

THERESA RUSSELL (*Married Nicolas Roeg*)

1976   **THE LAST TYCOON**
Director: Elia Kazan
Co-stars: Robert De Niro Tony Curtis Robert Mitchum

1978   **STRAIGHT TIME**
Director: Ulu Grosbard
Co-stars: Dustin Hoffman Gary Busey Harry Dean Stanton

1980   **BAD TIMING**
Director: Nicolas Roeg
Co-stars: Art Garfunkel Harvey Keitel Denholm Elliott

1982   **EUREKA**
Director: Nicolas Roeg
Co-stars: Gene Hackman Rutger Hauer Jane Lapotaire

1984   **THE RAZOR'S EDGE**
Director: John Byrum
Co-stars: Bill Murray Denholm Elliott Catherine Hicks

1985   **INSIGNIFICANCE**
Director: Nicolas Roeg
Co-stars: Tony Curtis Gary Busey Michael Emil

1986   **BLACK WIDOW**
Director: Bob Rafelson
Co-stars: Debra Winger Sami Frey Dennis Hopper

1987   **TRACK 29**
Director: Nicolas Roeg
Co-stars: Gary Oldman Christopher Lloyd Sarah Bernhard

1988   **ARIA**
Director: Nicolas Roeg
Co-stars: Julie Hagerty Bridget Fonda Sophie Ward

1989   **PHYSICAL EVIDENCE**
Director: Michael Crichton
Co-stars: Burt Reynolds Ned Beatty Kay Lenz

1990   **IMPULSE**
Director: Sondra Locke
Co-stars: Jeff Fahey George Dzundza Shaun Elliott

1991   **KAFKA**
Director: Steven Soderbergh
Co-stars: Jeremy Irons Joel Grey Alec Guinness

1992   **COLD HEAVEN**
Director: Nicolas Roeg
Co-stars: Mark Harmon James Russo Talia Shire

1994   **WHORE**
Director: Ken Russell
Co-stars: Benjamin Moulton Antonio Fargas Elizabeth Moorehead

1994   **A YOUNG CONNECTICUT YANKEE IN KING ARTHUR'S COURT**
Director: R.G. Thomas
Co-star: Michael York

1995   **THE GROTESQUE**
Co-stars: Alan Bates Sting Trudie Styler

1996 THE PROPOSITION
Co-star: Patrick Bergin

PENELOPE RUSSIANOFF

1978 AN UNMARRIED WOMAN
Director: Paul Mazursky
Co-stars: Jill Clayburgh Alan Bates Michael Murphy

ISABEL RUSSINOVA

1989 MY FIRST 40 YEARS
Director: Carlo Vanzina
Co-stars: Carol Alt Elliott Gould Jean Rochefort

FILUMINA RUSSO

1952 DUE SOLDI DI SPERANZA
Director: Renato Casellani
Co-stars: Vincenzo Musolino Maria Fiore Luigi Astarita

RENE RUSSO

1989 MAJOR LEAGUE
Director: David Ward
Co-stars: Charles Sheen Tom Berenger Corbin Bernsen

1990 MR DESTINY
Director: James Orr
Co-stars: James Belushi Michael Caine Linda Hamilton

1991 ONE GOOD COP
Director: Ralf Bode
Co-stars: Michael Keaton Anthony LaPaglia Rachel Ticotin

1992 LETHAL WEAPON 3
Director: Richard Donner
Co-stars: Mel Gibson Danny Glover Joe Pesci

1992 FREEJACK
Director: Geoff Murphy
Co-stars: Emilio Estevez Mick Jagger Anthony Hopkins

1993 IN THE LINE OF FIRE
Director: Wolfgang Petersen
Co-stars: Clint Eastwood John Malkovich Gary Cole

1994 OUTBREAK
Co-stars: Dustin Hoffman Donald Sutherland Kevin Spacey

1996 GET SHORTY
Director: Barry Sonnenfeld
Co-stars: John Travolta Gene Hackman Bette Midler

1996 TIN CUP
Director: Ron Shelton
Co-stars: Kevin Costner Don Johnson

1996 RANSOM
Director: Ron Howard
Co-stars: Mel Gibson Gary Sinise Lily Taylor

1996 BUDDY
Director: Caroline Thompson
Co-star: Robbie Coltrane

ISABEL RUTH

1989 BEARSKIN
Director: Ann Guedes
Co-stars: Tom Waits Damon Lowry Charlotte Coleman

PHYLLIS RUTH

1943 LET'S FACE IT
Director: Sidney Lanfield
Co-stars: Bob Hope Betty Hutton Eve Arden

ANN RUTHERFORD

1936 COMIN' ROUND THE MOUNTAIN
Co-stars: Gene Autry Smiley Burnett

1936 DOWN TO THE SEA
Co-stars: Ben Lyon Russell Hardy

1936 THE LONELY TRAIL
Co-star: Hetty McDaniel

1936 THE LAWLESS NINETIES
Co-star: John Wayne

1937 A FAMILY AFFAIR
Director: George Seitz
Co-stars: Mickey Rooney Lionel Barrymore Spring Byington

1938 YOU'RE ONLY YOUNG ONCE
Director: George Seitz
Co-stars: Mickey Rooney Lewis Stone Fay Holden

1938 JUDGE HARDY'S CHILDREN
Director: George Seitz
Co-stars: Mickey Rooney Lewis Stone Fay Holden

1938 OUT WEST WITH THE HARDIES
Director: George Seitz
Co-stars: Mickey Rooney Sarah Haden Cecilia Parker

1938 LOVE FINDS ANDY HARDY
Director: George Seitz
Co-stars: Mickey Rooney Lewis Stone Cecilia Parker

1938 OF HUMAN HEARTS
Director: Clarence Brown
Co-stars: Walter Huston James Stewart Beulah Bondi

1938 DRAMATIC SCHOOL
Director: Robert Sinclair
Co-stars: Luise Rainer Alan Marshall Lana Turner

1938 A CHRISTMAS CAROL
Director: Edwin Marin
Co-stars: Reginald Owen Terry Kilburn Gene Lockhart

1939 ANDY HARDY GETS SPRING FEVER
Director: W.S. Van Dyke
Co-stars: Mickey Rooney Terry Kilburn Fay Holden

1939 DANCING CO-ED
Director: S. Sylvan Simon
Co-stars: Lana Turner Richard Carlson Monty Woolley

1939 THOSE GLAMOROUS GIRLS
Director: S. Sylvan Simon
Co-stars: Lana Turner Richard Carlson Lew Ayres

1939 FOUR GIRLS IN WHITE
Co-stars: Una Merkel Florence Rice Mary Howard

1939 GONE WITH THE WIND
Director: Victor Fleming
Co-stars: Clark Gable Vivien Leigh Leslie Howard

1939 THE HARDYS RIDE HIGH
Director: George Seitz
Co-stars: Mickey Rooney Cecilia Parker Sara Haden

1940 THE GHOST COMES HOME
Director: William Thiele
Co-stars: Frank Morgan Billie Burke Reginald Owen

1940 KEEPING COMPANY
Director: S. Sylvan Simon
Co-stars: Frank Morgan Irene Rich Dan Dailey

1940 WYOMING
Director: Richard Thorpe
Co-stars: Wallace Beery Leo Carrillo Marjorie Main

1940 PRIDE AND PREJUDICE
Director: Robert Z. Leonard
Co-stars: Laurence Olivier Greer Garson Edmund Gwenn

1940 ANDY HARDY MEETS A DEBUTANTE
Director: George Seitz
Co-stars: Mickey Rooney Judy Garland Tom Neal

1941   **BADLANDS OF DAKOTA**
Director: Alfred Green
Co-stars: Robert Stack Broderick Crawford Frances Farmer

1941   **THE COURTSHIP OF ANDY HARDY**
Director: George Seitz
Co-stars: Mickey Rooney Lewis Stone Sara Haden

1941   **WHISTLING IN THE DARK**
Director: S. Sylvan Simon
Co-stars: Red Skelton Conrad Veidt Eve Arden

1942   **WHISTLING IN DIXIE**
Director: S. Sylvan Simon
Co-stars: Red Skelton George Bancroft Guy Kibbee

1942   **THE COURTSHIP OF ANDY HARDY**
Director: George Seitz
Co-stars: Mickey Rooney Donna Reed William Lundigan

1942   **ANDY HARDY'S DOUBLE LIFE**
Director: George Seitz
Co-stars: Mickey Rooney Esther Williams Susan Peters

1942   **THIS TIME FOR KEEPS**
Co-star: Robert Sterling

1942   **ORCHESTRA WIVES**
Director: Archie Mayo
Co-stars: George Montgomery Cesar Romero Lynn Bari

1943   **HAPPY LAND**
Director: Irving Pichel
Co-stars: Don Ameche Harry Carey Frances Dee

1943   **WHISTLING IN BROOKLYN**
Director: S. Sylvan Simon
Co-stars: Red Skelton Jean Rogers Rags Ragland

1943   **LIFE BEGINS FOR ANDY HARDY**
Director: George Seitz
Co-stars: Mickey Rooney Lewis Stone Fay Holden

1944   **ANDY HARDY'S BLONDE TROUBLE**
Director: George Seitz
Co-stars: Mickey Rooney Bonita Granville Keye Luke

1944   **THE BERMUDA MYSTERY**
Director: Ben Stoloff
Co-stars: Preston Foster Charles Butterworth

1945   **BEDSIDE MANNER**
Director: Andrew Stone
Co-stars: Ruth Hussey John Carroll Charles Ruggles

1945   **TWO O'CLOCK COURAGE**
Director: Anthony Mann
Co-stars: Tom Conway Richard Lane Jane Greer

1946   **THE MADONNA'S SECRET**
Director: William Thiele
Co-stars: Francis Lederer Gail Patrick John Litel

1946   **INSIDE JOB**
Co-stars: Alan Curtis Joe Sawyer Jimmie Moss

1946   **MURDER IN THE MUSIC HALL**
Director: John English
Co-stars: Vera Ralston Helen Walker Nancy Kelly

1947   **THE SECRET LIFE OF WALTER MITTY**
Director: Norman Z. McLeod
Co-stars: Danny Kaye Virginia Mayo Fay Bainter

1948   **THE ADVENTURES OF DON JUAN**
Director: Vincent Sherman
Co-stars: Errol Flynn Viveca Lindfors Alan Hale

1972   **THEY ONLY KILL THEIR MASTERS**
Director: James Goldstone
Co-stars: James Garner June Allyson Tom Ewell

KELLY RUTHERFORD

1996   **DANIELLE STEEL'S NO GREATER LOVE**
Director: Richard Heffron
Co-stars: Chris Sarandon Simon MacCorkindale

MARGARET RUTHERFORD
Oscar For Best Supporting Actress In 1963 For "The V.I.P.S"

1938   **DUSTY ERMINE**
Director: Bernard Vorhaus
Co-stars: Jane Baxter Anthony Bushell Ronald Squire

1940   **SPRING MEETING**
Director: Walter Mycroft
Co-stars: Nova Pilbeam Basil Sidney Sarah Churchill

1943   **THE YELLOW CANARY**
Director: Buzz Kulik
Co-stars: Anna Neagle Richard Greene Nova Pilbeam

1943   **THE DEMI-PARADISE**
Director: Anthony Asquith
Co-stars: Laurence Olivier Guy Middleton Joyce Grenfell

1944   **ENGLISH WITHOUT TEARS**
Director: Harold French
Co-stars: Lilli Palmer Michael Wilding Penelope Dudley Ward

1945   **BLITHE SPIRIT**
Director: David Lean
Co-stars: Rex Harrison Constance Cummings Kay Hammond

1946   **MEET ME AT DAWN**
Director: Thornton Freeland
Co-stars: Hazel Court William Eythe Basil Sidney

1946   **WHILE THE SUN SHINES**
Director: Anthony Asquith
Co-stars: Brenda Bruce Ronald Howard Bonar Colleano

1947   **MIRANDA**
Director: Ken Annakin
Co-stars: Glynis Johns Griffith Jones David Tomlinson

1949   **PASSPORT TO PIMLICO**
Director: Henry Cornelius
Co-stars: Basil Radford Naunton Wayne Stanley Holloway

1950   **THE HAPPIEST DAYS OF YOUR LIFE**
Director: Frank Launder
Co-stars: Alastair Sim Joyce Grenfell

1950   **HER FAVOURITE HUSBAND**
Director: Mario Soldati
Co-stars: Jean Kent Robert Beatty Gordon Harker

1951   **THE MAGIC BOX**
Director: John Boulting
Co-stars: Robert Donat Margaret Johnston Maria Schell

1952   **MISS ROBIN HOOD**
Director: John Guillermin
Co-stars: Sid James Reg Varney Richard Hearne

1952   **THE IMPORTANCE OF BEING ERNEST**
Director: Anthony Asquith
Co-stars: Michael Redgrave Edith Evans

1952   **CURTAIN UP**
Director: Ralph Smart
Co-stars: Robert Morley Joan Rice Kay Kendall

1952   **CASTLE IN THE AIR**
Director: Henry Cass
Co-stars: David Tomlinson Helen Cherry Barbara Kelly

1953   **INNOCENTS IN PARIS**
Director: Gordon Parry
Co-stars: Alastair Sim Claire Bloom Laurence Harvey

1953   **TROUBLE IN STORE**
Director: John Paddy Carstairs
Co-stars: Norman Wisdom Lana Morris Moira Lister

1954   THE RUNAWAY BUS
Director: Val Guest
Co-stars: Frankie Howerd Petula Clark George Coulouris

1954   MAD ABOUT MEN
Director: Ralph Thomas
Co-stars: Glynis Johns Donald Sinden Anne Crawford

1954   AUNT CLARA
Director: Anthony Kimmins
Co-stars: Ronald Shiner A.E. Matthews Jill Bennett

1955   AN ALLIGATOR NAMED DAISY
Director: J. Lee Thompson
Co-stars: Donald Sinden Diana Dors Jean Carson

1957   JUST MY LUCK
Director: John Paddy Carstairs
Co-stars: Norman Wisdom Jill Dixon Leslie Phillips

1957   THE SMALLEST SHOW ON EARTH
Director: Basil Dearden
Co-stars: Virginia McKenna Bill Travers Peter Sellers

1959   I'M ALL RIGHT JACK
Director: John Boulting
Co-stars: Peter Sellers Ian Carmichael Terry-Thomas

1961   ON THE DOUBLE
Director: Melville Shavelson
Co-stars: Danny Kaye Dana Wynter Diana Dors

1961   MURDER, SHE SAID
Director: George Pollock
Co-stars: Stringer Davis Charles Tingwall Arthur Kennedy

1963   THE MOUSE ON THE MOON
Director: Richard Lester
Co-stars: Ron Moody Bernard Cribbins Michael Crawford

1963   THE V.I.P.S
Director: Anthony Asquith
Co-stars: Richard Burton Elizabeth Taylor Maggie Smith

1963   MURDER AT THE GALLUP
Director: George Pollock
Co-stars: Stringer Davis Flora Robson Robert Morley

1964   MURDER AHOY
Director: George Pollock
Co-stars: Stringer Davis Lionel Jeffries Derek Nimmo

1964   MURDER MOST FOUL
Director: George Pollock
Co-stars: Stringer Davis Ron Moody Megs Jenkins

1966   CHIMES AT MIDNIGHT
Director: Orson Welles
Co-stars: John Gielgud Jeanne Moreau Orson Welles

1967   A COUNTESS FROM HONG KONG
Director: Charles Chaplin
Co-stars: Marlon Brando Sophia Loren Sidney Chaplin

1969   ARABELLA
Director: Mauro Blognini
Co-stars: Virna Lisi James Fox Terry-Thomas

1977   TO SEE SUCH FUN
Director: Jon Scoffield
Co-stars: Gracie Fields Norman Wisdom Spike Milligan

ALLISON RUTLEDGE-PARISI

1989   METROPOLITAN
Director: Whit Stillman
Co-stars: Carolyn Farina Edward Clementes Taylor Nichols

SUSAN RUTTAN

1985   DO YOU REMEMBER LOVE ?
Director: Jeff Bleckner
Co-stars: Joanne Woodward Richard Kiley Jim Metzler

1987   BAY COVEN
Director: Carl Schenkel
Co-stars: Pamela Sue Martin Tim Matheson Woody Harrelson

1989   CHANCES ARE
Director: Emile Ardolino
Co-stars: Cybill Shepherd Robert Downey Jnr. Ryan O'Neal

1989   TAKE MY DAUGHTERS, PLEASE
Director: Larry Elikann
Co-stars: Rue McClanahan Kim Delaney Deidre Hall

1990   A PERFECT LITTLE MURDER
Director: Anson Williams
Co-stars: Teri Garr Robert Urich Tom Poston

1990   FUNNY ABOUT LOVE
Director: Leonard Nimoy
Co-stars: Gene Wilder Christine Lahti Mary Stuart Masterson

1995   JACK REED:A SEARCH FOR JUSTICE
Director: Brian Dennehy
Co-star: Charles S. Dutton Brian Dennehy

BARBARA RUTTING

1953   THE LAST BRIDGE
Director: Helmut Kautner
Co-stars: Maria Schell Bernard Wicki Carl Mohner

ANNE RYAN

1987   THREE O'CLOCK HIGH
Director: Phil Joanou
Co-stars: Casey Siemaszko Richard Tyson

EILEEN RYAN

1986   AT CLOSE RANGE
Director: James Foley
Co-stars: Sean Penn Christopher Walken Mary Stuart Masterson

1989   WINTER PEOPLE
Director: Ted Kotcheff
Co-stars: Kurt Russell Kelly McGillis Lloyd Bridges

1991   THE INDIAN RUNNER
Director: Sean Penn
Co-stars: David Morse Viggo Mortensen Charles Bronson

FRAN RYAN

1973   AMERICANA
Director: David Carradine
Co-stars: Barbara Hershey Michael Greene David Carradine

1987   GUNSMOKE:RETURN TO DODGE
Director: Vincent McEveety
Co-stars: James Arness Amanda Blake Earl Holliman

HELEN RYAN

1980   THE ELEPHANT MAN
Director: David Lynch
Co-stars: John Hurt Anthony Hopkins Anne Bancroft

1985   THE ADVENTURES OF SHERLOCK HOLMES:THE NORWOOD BUILDER
Director: Ken Grieve
Co-star: Jeremy Brett David Burke

1993   THE HAWK
Director: David Hayman
Co-stars: Helen Mirren George Costigan Rosemary Leach

HILARY RYAN

1977   THE GETTING OF WISDOM
Director: Bruce Beresford
Co-stars: Susannah Fowle Sheila Helpman John Waters

IRENE RYAN

1944   **SAN DIEGO, I LOVE YOU**
Director: Reginald LeBorg
Co-stars: Louise Allbritton Jon Hall Buster Keaton

1944   **HOT RHYTHM**
Co-star: Tim Ryan

1945   **THAT NIGHT WITH YOU**
Director: William Seiter
Co-stars: Franchot Tone Susanna Foster David Bruce

1946   **THE DIARY OF A CHAMBERMAID**
Director: Jean Renoir
Co-stars: Paulette Goddard Burgess Meredith Hurd Hatfield

1951   **HALF ANGEL**
Director: Richard Sale
Co-stars: Loretta Young Joseph Cotten Cecil Kellaway

1951   **MEET ME AFTER THE SHOW**
Director: Richard Sale
Co-stars: Betty Grable MacDonald Carey Eddie Albert

1952   **BONZO GOES TO COLLEGE**
Director: Frederick De Cordova
Co-stars: Maureen O'Sullivan Charles Drake

1952   **BLACKBEARD THE PIRATE**
Director: Raoul Walsh
Co-stars: Robert Newton Linda Darnell William Bendix

1956   **SPRING REUNION**
Director: Robert Pirosh
Co-stars: Betty Hutton Dana Andrews Jean Hagen

JACQUELINE RYAN *(Child)*

1956   **JACQUELINE**
Director: Roy Baker
Co-stars: John Gregson Kathleen Ryan Noel Purcell

JERILYN RYAN

1991   **VICTIM OF BEAUTY**
Director: Roger Young
Co-stars: William Devane Michele Abrams Linda Pierce

1992   **OVEREXPOSED**
Director: Robert Markovitch
Co-stars: Marcy Walker Dan Lauria Terence Knox

KATHLEEN RYAN

1946   **ODD MAN OUT**
Director: Carol Reed
Co-stars: James Mason Robert Newton Cyril Cusack

1947   **CAPTAIN BOYCOTT**
Director: Frank Launder
Co-stars: Stewart Granger Alastair Sim Cecil Parker

1947   **ESTHER WATERS**
Director: Peter Proud
Co-stars: Dirk Bogarde Cyril Cusack Fay Compton

1949   **GIVE US THIS DAY**
Director: Edward Dmytryk
Co-stars: Sam Wanamaker Lea Padovani Bonar Colleano

1949   **CHRISTOPHER COLUMBUS**
Director: David MacDonald
Co-stars: Fredric March Florence Eldridge Derek Bond

1950   **PRELUDE TO FAME**
Director: Fergus McDoneld
Co-stars: Jeremy Spenser Guy Rolfe Kathleen Byron

1951   **TRY AND GET ME**
Director: Cyril Endfield
Co-stars: Frank Lovejoy Lloyd Bridges Richard Carlson

1952   **THE YELLOW BALLOON**
Director: J. Lee-Thompson
Co-stars: Kenneth More William Sylvester Andrew Ray

1952   **LAXDALE HALL**
Director: John Eldridge
Co-stars: Raymond Huntley Ronald Squire Fulton Mackay

1955   **CAPTAIN LIGHTFOOT**
Director: Douglas Sirk
Co-stars: Rock Hudson Barbara Rush Jeff Morrow

1956   **JACQUELINE**
Director: Roy Baker
Co-stars: John Gregson Jacqueline Ryan Noel Purcell

MADGE RYAN

1962   **SUMMER HOLIDAY**
Director: Peter Yates
Co-stars: Cliff Richard Lauri Peters Una Stubbs

1963   **THIS IS MY STREET**
Director: Sidney Hayers
Co-stars: June Ritchie Ian Hendry John Hurt

1978   **WHO IS KILLING THE GREAT CHEFS OF EUROPE ?**
Director: Ted Kotcheff
Co-stars: George Segal Jacqueline Bisset

MEG RYAN *(Margaret Mary Emily Anne Hyra)* *(Married Dennis Quaid)*

1981   **RICH AND FAMOUS**
Director: George Cukor
Co-stars: Candice Bergen Jacqueline Bisset David Selby

1984   **AMITYVILLE 3D**
Director: Richard Fleischer
Co-stars: Tony Roberts Tess Harper Candy Clark

1985   **ARMED AND DANGEROUS**
Director: Mark Lester
Co-stars: John Candy Eugene Levy Robert Loggia

1986   **TOP GUN**
Director: Tony Scott
Co-stars: Tom Cruise Kelly McGillis Val Kilmer

1987   **INNERSPACE**
Director: Joe Dante
Co-stars: Dennis Quaid Martin Short Fiona Lewis

1988   **PROMISED LAND**
Director: Michael Hoffman
Co-stars: Kiefer Sutherland Jason Gedrick Tracy Pollan

1988   **D.O.A.**
Director: Rocky Morton
Co-stars: Dennis Quaid Charlotte Rampling Daniel Stern

1988   **THE PRESIDIO**
Director: Peter Hyams
Co-stars: Sean Connery Mark Harmon Jack Warden

1989   **WHEN HARRY MET SALLY**
Director: Rob Reiner
Co-stars: Billy Crystal Carrie Fisher Bruno Kirby

1990   **JOE AND THE VOLCANO**
Director: John Patrick Shanley
Co-stars: Tom Hanks Lloyd Bridges Robert Stack

1991   **THE DOORS**
Director: Oliver Stone
Co-stars: Val Kilmer Kyle MacLachlan Kevin Dillon

1992   **PRELUDE TO A KISS**
Director: Norman Rene
Co-stars: Alec Baldwin Sydney Walker Patty Duke

1993 **FLESH AND BONE**
Director: Steve Cloves
Co-stars: Dennis Quaid James Caan Gwyneth Paltrow

1993 **SLEEPLESS IN SEATTLE**
Director: Nora Ephron
Co-stars: Tom Hanks Ross Malinger Bill Pullman

1994 **I.Q.**
Director: Fred Schepisi
Co-stars: Tim Robbins Walter Matthau

1994 **WHEN A MAN LOVES A WOMAN**
Director: Luis Mandoki
Co-stars: Andy Garcia Ellen Burstyn Gail Strickland

1995 **FRENCH KISS**
Director: Lawrence Kasdan
Co-stars: Kevin Kline Timothy Hutton

1996 **RESTORATION**
Director: Michael Hoffman
Co-stars: Robert Downey Jnr. Polly Walker Sam Neill

1996 **COURAGE UNDER FIRE**
Director: Edward Zwick
Co-stars: Denzel Washington Lou Diamond Phillips Scott Glenn

1997 **ADDICTED TO LOVE**
Director: Griffin Dunne
Co-stars: Matthew Broderick Kelly Preston Tcheky Karyo

1998 **ANASTASIA** *(Voice)*
Co-stars: John Cusack Angela LansburyChristopher Lloyd

1998 **CITY OF ANGELS**
Director: Brad Silberling
Co-stars: Nicolas Cage Dennis Franz Andre Brauger

NATASHA RYAN

1979 **THE AMITYVILLE HORROR**
Director: Stuart Rosenberg
Co-stars: James Brolin Margot Kidder Rod Steiger

PEGGY RYAN

1942 **WHEN JOHNNY COMES MARCHING HOME**
Director: Charles Lamont
Co-stars: Allan Jones Jane Frazer Donald O'Connor

1942 **MISS ANNIE ROONEY**
Director: Edwin Marin
Co-stars: Shirley Temple William Gargan Guy Kibbee

1942 **PRIVATE BUCKAROO**
Director: Edward Cline
Co-stars: Andrews Sisters Harry James Donald O'Connor

1942 **GIVE OUT SISTERS**
Director: Edward Cline
Co-stars: Andrews Sisters Dan Dailey Grace McDonald

1942 **GET HEP TO LOVE**
Director: Charles Lamont
Co-stars: Donald O'Connor Gloria Jean Jane Frazer

1943 **MR BIG**
Director: Charles Lamont
Co-stars: Donald O'Connor Gloria Jean Robert Paige

1943 **THIS IS THE LIFE**
Director: Felix Feist
Co-stars: Donald O'Connor Susanna Foster Patric Knowles

1943 **TOP MAN**
Director: Charles Lamont
Co-stars: Richard Dix Donald O'Connor Susanna Foster

1944 **PATRICK THE GREAT**
Director: Frank Ryan
Co-stars: Donald O'Connor Frances Dee Eve Arden

1944 **THE MERRY MONAHANS**
Director: Charles Lamont
Co-stars: Donald O'Connor Jack Oakie Ann Blyth

1944 **BOWERY TO BROADWAY**
Director: Charles Lamont
Co-stars: Donald O'Connor Maria Montez Turhan Bey

1944 **FOLLOW THE BOYS**
Director: Edward Sutherland
Co-stars: George Raft Donald O'Connor Orson Welles

1944 **CHIP OFF THE OLD BLOCK**
Director: Charles Lamont
Co-stars: Donald O'Connor Ann Blyth Patric Knowles

1945 **HERE COMES THE CO-EDS**
Director: Jean Yarbrough
Co-stars: Bud Abbott Lou Costello Lon Chaney

1945 **MEN IN HER DIARY**
Director: Charles Barton
Co-stars: Jon Hall Louise Allbritton William Terry

1945 **ON STAGE EVERYBODY**
Director: Jean Yarbrough
Co-stars: Jack Oakie Johnny Coy Julie London

1949 **THERE'S A GIRL IN MY HEART**
Director: Arthur Dreifuss
Co-stars: Lee Bowman Elyse Knox Lon Chaney

1949 **SHAMROCK HILL**
Co-star: Ray MacDonald

1952 **ALL ASHORE**
Director: Richard Quine
Co-stars: Mickey Rooney Dick Haymes Ray MacDonald

SHEILA RYAN

1940 **THE GAY CABALLERO**
Director: Otto Brower
Co-stars: Cesar Romero Robert Sterling Chris-Pin Martin

1941 **GREAT GUNS**
Director: Monty Banks
Co-stars: Stan Laurel Oliver Hardy Dick Nelson

1941 **DEAD MEN TELL**
Director: Harry Lachman
Co-stars: Sidney Toler Sen Yung Robert Weldon

1942 **A-HAUNTING WE WILL GO**
Director: Alfred Werker
Co-stars: Stan Laurel Oliver Hardy Elisha Cook Jnr.

1942 **CAREFUL, SOFT SHOULDER**
Director: Walter Morosco
Co-stars: Virginia Bruce James Ellison Ralph Byrd

1943 **THE GANG'S ALL HERE**
Director: Busby Berkeley
Co-stars: Alice Faye Carmen Miranda James Ellison

1943 **SONG OF TEXAS**
Co-stars: Roy Rogers Arline Judge

1944 **SOMETHING FOR THE BOYS**
Director: Lewis Seiler
Co-stars: Carmen Miranda Vivian Blaine Michael O'Shea

1944 **LADIES OF WASHINGTON**
Co-stars: Anthony Quinn Robin Raymond

1945 **THE CARIBBEAN MYSTERY**
Director: Robert Webb
Co-stars: James Dunn Edward Ryan Reed Hadley

1945 **GETTING GERTIE'S GARTER**
Director: Allan Dwan
Co-stars: Dennis O'Keefe Marie McDonald Barry Sullivan

1946	**DEADLINE FOR MURDER**	**1994**	**REALITY BITES**

1946 **DEADLINE FOR MURDER**
Director: James Tinling
Co-stars: Paul Kelly Kent Taylor Jerome Cowan

1947 **THE LONE WOLF IN MEXICO**
Director: Ross Lederman
Co-stars: Gerald Mohr Jacqueline De Wit Eric Blore

1947 **RAILROADED**
Director: Anthony Mann
Co-stars: John Ireland Hugh Beaumont Jane Randolph

1947 **PHILO VANCE'S SECRET MISSION**
Co-star: Alan Curtis

1947 **HEARTACHES**
Co-stars: Edward Norris Chill Wills Ken Farrell

1948 **THE COBRA STRIKES**
Co-star: Richard Fraser

1947 **CAGED FURY**
Co-stars: Richard Denning Buster Crabbe Mary Beth Hughes

1953 **ON TOP OF OLD SMOKEY**
Director: George Archainbaud
Co-stars: Gene Autry Smiley Burnette Gail Davis

WINONA RYDER

(Winona Laura Harowitz, Partner Johnny Depp)

Nominated For Best Supporting Actress In 1993 For "The Age Of Innocence". Nominated For Best Actress In 1994 For "Little Women"

1986 **LUCAS**
Director: David Seltzer
Co-stars: Corey Haim Kerri Green Charlie Sheen

1987 **SQUARE DANCE**
Director: Daniel Petrie
Co-stars: Jason Robards Jane Alexander Rob Lowe

1988 **1969**
Director: Ernest Thompson
Co-stars: Robert Downey Jnr. Kiefer Sutherland Joanna Cassidy

1988 **BEETLEJUICE**
Director: Tim Burton
Co-stars: Michael Keaton Alec Baldwin Geena Davis

1989 **GREAT BALLS OF FIRE !**
Director: Jim McBride
Co-stars: Dennis Quaid Alec Baldwin Joe Bob Briggs

1989 **HEATHERS**
Director: Michael Lehman
Co-stars: Christian Slater Shannen Doherty Lisanna Falk

1990 **WELCOME HOME, ROXY CARMICHAEL**
Director: Jim Abrahams
Co-stars: Jeff Daniels Laila Robins Dinah Manoff

1990 **MERMAIDS**
Director: Richard Benjamin
Co-stars: Cher Bob Hoskins Christina Ricci

1990 **EDWARD SCISSORHANDS**
Director: Tim Burton
Co-stars: Johnny Depp Diane Wiest Alan Arkin

1991 **NIGHT ON EARTH**
Director: Jim Jarmusch
Co-stars: Gena Rowlands Beatrice Dalle Giancarlo Espositos

1992 **BRAM STOKER'S DRACULA**
Director: Frances Coppola
Co-stars: Gary Oldman Anthony Hopkins Keanu Reeves

1993 **THE HOUSE OF THE SPIRITS**
Director: Bille August
Co-stars: Jeremy Irons Meryl Streep Glenn Close

1993 **THE AGE OF INNOCENCE**
Director: Martin Scorsese
Co-stars: Daniel Day-Lewis Michelle Pfeiffer

1994 **REALITY BITES**
Director: Ben Stiller
Co-stars: Ethan Hawke Swoosie Kurtz Joe Don Baker

1994 **LITTLE WOMEN**
Director: Gillian Armstrong
Co-star: Susan Sarandon Gabriel Byrne Lukas Haas

1995 **BOYS**
Co-star: Lukas Haas

1996 **THE CRUCIBLE**
Director: Nicholas Hynter
Co-stars: Daniel Day-Lewis Peter Vaughan

1996 **HOW TO MAKE AN AMERICAN QUILT**
Director: Jocelyn Moorhouse
Co-stars: Anne Bancroft Ellen Burstyn Jean Simmons

1997 **LOOKING FOR RICHARD**
Director: Al Pacino
Co-stars: Alec Baldwin Aidan Quinn Estelle Parsons

1997 **ALIEN RESURRECTION**
Director: Jean-Pierre Jeunet
Co-star: Sigourney Weaver

MARGIT SAAD

1960　THE CRIMINAL
Director: Joseph Losey
Co-stars: Stanley Baker Sam Wanamaker Patrick Magee

1960　THE REBEL
Director: Robert Day
Co-stars: Tony Hancock George Sanders Paul Massie

1967　THE MAGNIFICENT TWO
Director: Cliff Owen
Co-stars: Eric Morecambe Ernie Wise Cecil Parker

MARIE SABOURET

1955　RIFIFI
Director: Jules Dassin
Co-stars: Jean Servais Carl Mohner Robert Manuel

SABRINA

1957　BLUE MURDER AT ST. TRINIANS
Director: Frank Launder
Co-stars: Terry-Thomas George Cole Joyce Grenfell

SALLI SACHSE

1967　THE TRIP
Director: Roger Corman
Co-stars: Peter Fonda Susan Strasberg Bruce Dern

SADE

1986　ABSOLUTE BEGINNERS
Director: Julien Temple
Co-stars: Patsy Kensit Eddie O'Connell David Bowie

AVRIL SADLER

1966　THE HAND OF NIGHT
Director: Frederick Goode
Co-stars: William Sylvester Diane Clare Alizia Gur

LAURA SADLER

1997　INTIMATE RELATIONS
Director: Philip Goodhew
Co-stars: Julie Walters Rupert Graves Matthew Walker

ANDRINE SAETHER

1998　JUNK MAIL
Co-star: Robert Skjaerstad

KATEY SAGAL

1988　THE PRICE OF PASSION
Director: Leonard Nimoy
Co-stars: Diane Keaton Liam Neeson Jason Robards

1991　SHE SAYS SHE'S INNOCENT
Director: Charles Correll
Co-stars: Jameson Parker Charlotte Ross Alan Rachins

1995　TRAIL OF TEARS
Director: Donald Wrye
Co-stars: Pam Dawber William Russ

MARIANNE SAGEBRECHT

1988　BAGDAD CAFÉ
Director: Percy Adlon
Co-stars: Jack Palance Christine Kaufman Monica Calhoun

1988　MOON OVER PARADOR
Director: Paul Mazursky
Co-stars: Richard Dreyfuss Raul Julia Sonia Bragg

1989　ROSALIE GOES SHOPPING
Director: Percy Adlon
Co-stars: Brad Davis Judge Reinhold Erika Blumberger

1989　THE WAR OF THE ROSES
Director: Danny De Vito
Co-stars: Danny De Vito Michael Douglas Kathleen Turner

SUSAN SAIGER

1982　EATING RAOUL
Director: Paul Bartel
Co-stars: Paul Bartel Mary Woronov Robert Beltran

EVA MARIE SAINT

Oscar For Best Supporting Actress In 1954 For "On The Waterfront"

1954　ON THE WATERFRONT
Director: Elia Kazan
Co-stars: Marlon Brando Karl Malden Rod Steiger

1956　THAT CERTAIN FEELING
Director: Melvyn Frank
Co-stars: Bob Hope George Sanders Pearl Bailey

1957　A HATFUL OF RAIN
Director: Fred Zinnemann
Co-stars: Don Murray Anthony Franciosa Lloyd Nolan

1957　RAINTREE COUNTY
Director: Edward Dmytryk
Co-stars: Elizabeth Taylor Montgomery Clift Lee Marvin

1959　NORTH BY NORTHWEST
Director: Alfred Hitchcock
Co-stars: Cary Grant James Mason Martin Landau

1960　EXODUS
Director: Otto Preminger
Co-stars: Paul Newman Sal Mineo John Derek

1962　ALL FALL DOWN
Director: John Frankenheimer
Co-stars: Warren Beatty Brandon De Wilde Karl Malden

1964　36 HOURS
Director: George Seaton
Co-stars: James Garner Rod Taylor Werner Peters

1965　THE SANDPIPER
Director: Vincente Minnelli
Co-stars: Elizabeth Taylor Richard Burton Charles Bronson

**1966　THE RUSSIANS ARE COMING!
THE RUSSIANS ARE COMING!**
Director: Norman Jewison
Co-stars: Alan Arkin Carl Reiner Tessie O'Shea

1966　GRAND PRIX
Director: John Frankenheimer
Co-stars: James Garner Yves Montand Jessica Walter

1968　THE STALKING MOON
Director: Robert Mulligan
Co-stars: Gregory Peck Robert Forster Noland Clay

1970　LOVING
Director: Irving Kershner
Co-stars: George Segal Sterling Hayden Keenan Wynn

1972   **CANCEL MY RESERVATION**
Director: Paul Bogart
Co-stars: Bob Hope Ralph Bellamy Anne Archer

1986   **NOTHING IN COMMON**
Director: Gary Marshall
Co-stars: Jackie Gleason Tom Hanks Hector Elizondo

1987   **BREAKING HOME TIES**

1988   **I'LL BE HOME FOR CHRISTMAS**
Director: Marvin Chomsky
Co-stars: Hal Halbrook Courteney Cox Nancy Travis

1990   **VOYAGE OF TERROR**
Director: Alberto Negrin
Co-stars: Burt Lancaster Rebecca Schaeffer Robert Culp

1991   **DANIELLE STEEL'S PALOMINO**
Director: Michael Miller
Co-stars: Lindsay Frost Lee Horsley Rod Taylor

1995   **MY ANTONIA**
Director: Joseph Sargent
Co-stars: Jason Robards Neil Patrick Harris

SUSAN SAINT JAMES

1965   **WHAT'S SO BAD ABOUT FEELING GOOD**
Director: George Seaton
Co-stars: George Peppard Mary Tyler Moore

1967   **NEW FACE IN HELL**
Director: John Guillermin
Co-stars: George Peppard Gayle Hunnicutt Coleen Gray

1968   **WHERE ANGELS GO, TROUBLE FOLLOWS**
Director: James Neilson
Co-stars: Rosalind Russell Stella Stevens

1977   **OUTLAW BLUES**
Director: Richard Heffron
Co-stars: Peter Fonda John Crawford Michael Lerner

1979   **LOVE AT FIRST BITE**
Director: Stan Dragoti
Co-stars: George Hamilton Richard Benjamin Dick Shawn

1980   **HOW TO BEAT THE HIGH COST OF LIVING**
Director: Robert Scheerer
Co-stars: Jane Curtin Jessica Lange

1981   **CARBON COPY**
Director: Michael Schultz
Co-stars: George Segal Denzel Washington Jack Warden

RENEE SAINT-CYR

1934   **LE DERNIER MILLIARDAIRE**
Director: Rene Clare
Co-stars: Max Dearly Marthe Mellot Raymond Cordy

1938   **STRANGE BOARDERS**
Director: Herbert Mason
Co-stars: Tom Walls Googie Withers Irene Handl

1946   **SYMPHONIE FANTASTIQUE**
Director: Christian Jacque
Co-stars: Jean-Louis Barrault Jules Berry Bernard Blier

LUCILLE SAINT-PETER

1988   **BRAIN DAMAGE**
Director: Frank Henenlotter
Co-stars: Rick Herbst Jennifer Lowry Theo Barnes

LUCILE SAINT-SIMON

1960   **LES BONNES FEMMES**
Director: Claude Chabrol
Co-stars: Stephane Audran Bernadette Lafont Claude Berri

MARIN SAIS

1938   **PHANTOM GOLD**
Co-stars: Jack Ludin Beth Marion Jimmy Robinson

TATJANA SAIS

1948   **BERLINER BALLADE**
Director: Robert Stemmle
Co-stars: Gert Frobe Anton Zeithammer O.E. Hasse

CHLOE SALAMAN

1981   **DRAGONSLAYER**
Director: Matthew Robbins
Co-stars: Peter MacNichol Caitlin Clarke Ralph Richardson

1989   **THESE FOOLISH THINGS**
Director: Charles Gormley
Co-stars: James Fox Lindsay Duncan Ciaran Madden

CLARA SALAMAN

1992   **A FATAL DIVERSION**
Director: Tim Pywell
Co-stars: Douglas Hodge Jeremy Northam Saira Todd

JOANAISE SALAMONE

1976   **THE WHITE DAWN**
Director: Philip Kaufman
Co-stars: Warren Oates Timothy Bottoms Lou Gossett

LAURA SALARI

1953   **ROMAN HOLIDAY**
Director: William Wyler
Co-stars: Gregory Peck Audrey Hepburn Eddie Albert

THERESA SALDANA

1980   **SOPHIA LOREN: HER OWN STORY**
Director: Mel Stuart
Co-stars: Sophia Loren John Gavin Rip Torn

1980   **RAGING BULL**
Director: Martin Scorsese
Co-stars: Robert De Niro Cathy Moriarty Joe Pesci

1980   **DEFIANCE**
Director: John Flynn
Co-stars: Jan Michael-Vincent Art Carney Danny Aiello

1984   **THE EVIL THAT MEN DO**
Director: J. Lee-Thompson
Co-stars: Charles Bronson Joseph Maher Jose Ferrer

VIRGINIA SALE

1930   **EMBARRASSING MOMENTS**
Co-star: Reginald Denny

1935   **IT'S A SMALL WORLD**
Director: Irving Cummings
Co-stars: Spencer Tracy Wendy Barrie Raymond Walburn

PAMELA SALEM

1983   **NEVER SAY NEVER AGAIN**
Director: Irving Kerschner
Co-stars: Sean Connery Barbara Carrera Kim Basinger

1985   **AFTER DARKNESS**
Director: Sergio Guerrez
Co-stars: John Hurt Julian Sands Victoria Abril

MEREDITH SALENGER

1985   **THE JOURNEY OF NATTY GANN**
Director: Jeremy Kagan
Co-stars: John Cusack Ray Wise Lainie Kazan

1988 THE KISS
Director: Pen Densham
Co-stars: Nicholas Kilbertus Joanna Pacula Mimi Kuzyk

1988 A NIGHT IN THE LIFE OF JIMMY REARDON
Director: William Richert
Co-stars: River Phoenix Ann Magnuson

1989 DREAM A LITTLE DREAM
Director: Marc Rocco
Co-stars: Corey Feldman Jason Robards Piper Laurie

SARA SALBY

1962 TOWER OF LONDON
Director: Roger Corman
Co-stars: Vincent Price Michael Pate Joan Freeman

CARMEN SALINAS

1991 DANZON
Director: Maria Novaro
Co-stars: Maria Rojo Blanca Guerra Tito Vasconcelos

DIANE SALINGER

1985 PEE-WEE'S BIG ADVENTURE
Director: Tim Burton
Co-stars: Paul Reubens Elizabeth Daily Tony Bill

1986 THE MORNING AFTER
Director: Sidney Lumet
Co-stars: Jane Fonda Jeff Bridges Raul Julia

1991 ALICE
Director: Woody Allen
Co-stars: Mia Farrow Alec Baldwin William Hurt

1992 BATMAN RETURNS
Director: Tim Burton
Co-stars: Michael Keaton Danny DeVito Michelle Pfeiffer

1992 UNBECOMING AGE
Director: Alfredo Ringel
Co-stars: John Calvin Priscilla Pointer George Clooney

EMMANUELLE SALLET

1986 UNDER THE CHERRY MOON
Director: Prince
Co-stars: Prince Kristin Scott-Thomas Jerome Benton Lea Salonga

1992 ALADDIN *(Voice)*
Director: Ron Clements
Co-stars: Brad Kane Jonathan Freeman Robin Williams

JENNIFER SALT

1969 HI, MOM!
Director: Brian De Palma
Co-stars: Robert De Niro Charles Durnham Allen Garfield

1970 THE REVOLUTIONARY
Director: Paul Williams
Co-stars: Jon Voight Robert Duvall

1972 PLAY IT AGAIN SAM
Director: Herbert Ross
Co-stars: Woody Allen Diane Keaton Susan Anspach

1973 SISTERS
Director: Brian De Palma
Co-stars: Margot Kidder Charles Durning Bill Finley

1986 OUT OF THE DARKNESS
Director: Jud Taylor
Co-stars: Martin Sheen Hector Elizondo Matt Clark

THELMA SALTER

1917 SLUMBERLAND
Co-star: Laura Sears

ELIZABETH SALTORRELLI

1992 BOUND AND GAGGED
Director: Daniel Appleby
Co-stars: Chris Denton Ginger Lynn Allen Chris Mulkey

BARBARA SAMMETH

1969 THE MAD ROOM
Director: Bernard Girard
Co-stars: Stella Stevens Shelley Winters Carol Cole

EMMA SAMMS

1979 ARABIAN ADVENTURE
Director: Kevin Connor
Co-stars: Christopher Lee Oliver Tobias Mickey Rooney

1981 GOLIATH AWAITS
Director: Kevin Connor
Co-stars: Mark Harmon Christopher Lee Eddie Albert

1986 AGATHA CHRISTIE'S MURDER IN THREE ACTS
Director: Gary Nelson
Co-stars: Peter Ustinov Tony Curtis

1988 THE LADY AND THE HIGHWAYMAN
Director: John Hough
Co-stars: Oliver Reed Claire Bloom Lysette Anthony

1989 A CONNECTICUT YANKEE IN KING ARTHUR'S COURT
Director: Mel Damski
Co-stars: Keshia Knight Pulliam Jean Marsh

1990 BEJEWELLED
Director: Terry Marcel

1991 DELIRIOUS
Director: Tom Mankiewicz
Co-stars: John Candy Mariel Hemingway Raymond Burr

1992 SHADOW OF A STRANGER
Director: Richard Friedman
Co-star: Parker Stevenson

1993 HARMFUL INTENT
Director: John Patterson
Co-stars: Tim Matheson Robert Pastorelli

1994 TREACHEROUS BEAUTIES
Director: Charles Jarrot
Co-stars: Catherine Oxenberg Bruce Greenwood

TATIANA SAMOILOVA

1957 THE CRANES ARE FLYING
Director: Mikhail Kalatozov
Co-stars: Alexei Batalov Vasili Merkuriev

JOANNE SAMUEL

1979 ALISON'S BIRTHDAY
Director: Ian Coughlan
Co-stars: Lou Brown Bunny Brooke Vincent Ball

1979 MAD MAX
Director: George Miller
Co-stars: Mel Gibson Steve Bisley Hugh Keays-Bryne

NANCY SAMUELS

1980 PROSTITUTE
Director: Tay Garnett
Co-stars: Eleanor Forsythe Kate Crutchley Kim Lockett

HELEN SANBORN

1936 THE CHARGE OF THE LIGHT BRIGADE
Director: Michael Curtiz
Co-stars: Errol Flynn Olivia De Havilland

HERMINA SANCHEZ

1990   **HELLO HEMINGWAY**
Director: Fernando Perez
Co-stars: Laura De La Uz Raul Paz Enrique Molina

AITANA SANCHEZ-GIJON

1996   **A WALK IN THE CLOUDS**
Co-stars: Keanu Reeves Anthony Quinn

DOMINIQUE SANDA

1970   **THE GARDEN OF FINZI-CONTINIS**
Director: Vittoria De Sica
Co-stars: Lino Capolicchio Helmut Berger

1971   **THE CONFORMIST**
Director: Bernardo Bertolucci
Co-stars: Jean-Louis Trintignant Stefania Sandrelli

1973   **IMPOSSIBLE OBJECT**
Director: John Frankenheimer
Co-stars: Alan Bates Lea Massari Michel Auclair

1973   **THE MACKINTOSH MAN**
Director: John Huston
Co-stars: Paul Newman James Mason Nigel Patrick

1974   **STEPPENWOLF**
Director: Fred Haines
Co-stars: Max Von Sydow Pierre Clementi Roy Bosier

1974   **CONVERSATION PIECE**
Director: Luchino Visconti
Co-stars: Burt Lancaster Helmut Berger Silvana Mangano

1976   **THE INHERITANCE**
Director: Mauro Bolognini
Co-stars: Anthony Quinn Fabio Testi Adriana Asti

1976   **1900**
Director: Bernardo Bertolucci
Co-stars: Burt Lancaster Robert De Niro Gerard Depardieu

1977   **DAMNATION ALLEY**
Director: Jack Smight
Co-stars: Jan-Michael Vincent George Peppard Paul Winfield

1981   **CABOBLANCO**
Director: J. Lee-Thompson
Co-stars: Charles Bronson Jason Robards Camilla Sparv

1990   **VOYAGE OF TERROR**
Director: Alberto Negrin
Co-stars: Burt Lancaster Eve Marie Saint Robert Culp

1990   **I, THE WORST OF ALL**
Director: Maria Luisa Bemberg
Co-stars: Assumpta Serna Hector Alterio

CLARE SANDARS *(Child)*

1942   **MRS MINIVER**
Director: William Wyler
Co-stars: Greer Garson Walter Pidgeon Teresa Wright

ANN D. SANDERS

1991   **STRAIGHT OUT OF BROOKLYN**
Director: Matty Rich
Co-stars: George T. Odom Lawrence Gilliard Barbara Sanon

BARBARA ANN SANDERS

1953   **BRIGHT ROAD**
Director: Gerald Mayer
Co-stars: Dorothy Dandridge Harry Belafonte Robert Horton

FLORENCE SANDERS

1923   **THE WANDERING JEW**
Director: Maurice Elvey
Co-stars: Matheson Lang Hutin Britton Isobel Elsom

LORI SANDERS

1980   **CAPTIVE**
Director: Allan Sandler
Co-stars: David Ladd Cameron Mitchell Donald Bishop

JEAN SANDERSON

1971   **THE NIGHT DIGGER**
Director: Alastair Read
Co-stars: Patricia Neal Nicholas Clay Pamela Browne

JOAN SANDERSON

1971   **PLEASE SIR!**
Director: Mark Stuart
Co-stars: John Alderton Derek Guyler Noel Howlett

CATHY SANDFORD

1988   **HOME FRONT**
Director: Penny Cherns
Co-stars: Stephen McGann Jason Cunliffe Simon Vaughan

1991   **THE BLACK CANDLE**
Director: Roy Battersby
Co-stars: Samantha Bond Denholm Elliott Tara Fitzgerald

ISABELLE SANDFORD

1967   **GUESS WHO'S COMING TO DINNER**
Director: Stanley Kramer
Co-stars: Spencer Tracy Katherine Hepburn Sidney Poitier

DEBRA SANDLUND

1987   **TOUGH GUYS DON'T DANCE**
Director: Norman Mailer
Co-stars: Ryan O'Neal Isabella Rossellini Wings Hauser

STEFANIA SANDRELLI

1961   **DIVORCE ITALIAN STYLE**
Director: Pietro Germi
Co-stars: Marcello Mastroianni Daniella Rocca

1971   **THE CONFORMIST**
Director: Bernard Bertolucci
Co-stars: Jean-Louis Trintignent Dominique Sanda

1972   **ALFREDO, ALFREDO**
Director: Pietro Germi
Co-stars: Dustin Hoffman Carla Gravina Clara Colosimo

1974   **SOMEWHERE BEYOND LOVE**
Director: Luigi Comencini
Co-stars: Giuliano Gemma Emilio Bonucci Antonio Judice

1975   **POLICE PYTHON 357**
Director: Alain Corneau
Co-stars: Yves Montand Simone Signoret Francois Perrier

1976   **1900**
Director: Bernardo Bertolucci
Co-stars: Burt Lancaster Robert De Niro Gerard Depardieu

1988   **MIGNON HAS LEFT**
Director: Francesca Archibugi
Co-stars: Celine Beauvallet Jean-Pierre Duriez

1992   **JAMON, JAMON**
Director: Bigas Luna
Co-stars: Penelope Cruz Anna Galiena Javier Bardem

1996   **STEALING BEAUTY**
Director: Bernardo Bertolucci
Co-stars: Liv Tyler Roberto Zebetti Sinead Cusack

ANNA MARIA SANDRI

1956   **THE BLACK TENT**
Director: Brian Desmond Hurst
Co-stars: Anthony Steel Donald Sinden Andre Morrell

DIANA SANDS

1961 A RAISIN IN THE SUN
Director: Daniel Petrie
Co-stars: Sidney Poitier Claudia McNeil Ruby Dee

1970 THE LANDLORD
Director: Hal Ashby
Co-stars: Beau Bridges Lee Grant Pearl Bailey

1970 DOCTORS' WIVES
Director: George Schaefer
Co-stars: Richard Crenna Janice Rule Gene Hackman

ELLEN SANDWEISS

1982 THE EVIL DEAD
Director: Sam Raimi
Co-stars: Bruce Campbell Betsy Baker Hall Delrich

LAURA SAN GIACOMO

1989 SEX, LIES AND VIDEOTAPE
Director: Steve Soderbergh
Co-stars: James Spader Andie MacDowell Peter Gallagher

1990 VITAL SIGNS
Director: Marisa Silver
Co-stars: Adrian Pasdar Diane Lane Jimmy Smits

1990 QUIGLEY DOWN UNDER
Director: Simon Wincer
Co-stars: Tom Selleck Alan Rickman Chris Haywood

1990 PRETTY WOMAN
Director: Garry Marshall
Co-stars: Richard Gere Julia Roberts Ralph Bellamy

1991 ONCE AROUND
Director: Lasse Hellstrom
Co-stars: Holly Hunter Richard Dreyfuss Danny Aiello

1991 UNDER SUSPICION
Director: Simon Moore
Co-stars: Liam Neeson Kenneth Cranham Maggie O'Neill

1992 WHERE THE DAY TAKES YOU
Director: Marc Rocco
Co-stars: Dermot Mulroney Sean Astin Lara Flynn Boyle

MARIA LUISA SANIELLA

1985 MACARONI
Director: Ettore Scolla
Co-stars: Jack Lemmon Marcello Mastroianni Daria Nicolodi

OLGA SAN JUAN

1946 BLUE SKIES
Director: Stuart Heisler
Co-stars: Fred Astaire Bing Crosby Joan Caulfirld

1947 VARIETY GIRL
Director: George Marshall
Co-stars: Mary Hatchet DeForrest Kelly Glenn Tryon

1948 ARE YOU WITH IT ?
Director: Jack Hively
Co-stars: Donald O'Connor Martha Stewart Lew Parker

1948 THE COUNTESS OF MONTE CRISTO
Director: Frederick De Cordova
Co-stars: Sonja Henie Dorothy Hart

1948 ONE TOUCH OF VENUS
Director: William Seiter
Co-stars: Ava Gardner Robert Walker Dick Haymes

1949 THE BEAUTIFUL BLONDE FROM BASHFUL BEND
Director: Preston Sturges
Co-stars: Betty Grable Cesar Romero

BARBARA SANON

1991 STRAIGHT OUT OF BROOKLYN
Director: Matty Rich
Co-stars: George T. Odom Ann D. Sanders Lawrence Gilliard

MARY NELL SANTACROCE

1993 STOLEN BABIES
Director: Eric Laneuville
Co-stars: Lea Thompson Kathleen Quinlan Mary Tyler Moore

PENNY SANTON

1979 AND YOUR NAME IS JONAH
Director: Richard Michaels
Co-stars: Sally Struthers James Woods Randee Heller

ALICE SAPRICH

1971 DELUSIONS OF GRANDEUR
Director: Gerard Oury
Co-stars: Yves Montand Louis De Funes Paul Preboist

MIA SARA *(Married Jason Connery)*

1985 LEGEND
Director: Ridley Scott
Co-stars: Tom Cruise Tim Curry David Bennent

1986 FERRIS BUELLER'S DAY OFF
Director: John Hughes
Co-stars: Matthew Broderick Alan Ruck Jennifer Gray

1987 APPRENTICE TO MURDER
Director: R.L. Thomas
Co-stars: Chad Lowe Donald Sutherland Rutanya Alda

1990 DAUGHTER OF DARKNESS
Director: Stuart Gordon
Co-stars: Anthony Perkins Jack Coleman Robert Reynolds

1992 CLOSE TO EDEN
Director: Sidney Lumet
Co-stars: Melanie Griffith Eric Thal John Pankow

1992 BY THE SWORD
Director: Jeremy Paul Kagan
Co-stars: F. Murray Abraham Eric Roberts Chris Rydell

1993 SOMEONE'S WATCHING
Director: Scott McGinnis
Co-stars: Tim Daly Paul LeMat

1993 CALL OF THE WILD
Director: Michael Uno
Co-star: Ricky Schroeder

1993 BLINDSIDED
Director: Tom Donnelly
Co-star: Jeff Fahey

1994 TIMECOP
Director: Peter Hyams
Co-stars: Jean-Claude Van Damme Ron Silver Bruce McGill

1994 BY THE SWORD
Director: Jeremy Paul Kagan
Co-stars: F. Murray Abraham Eric Roberts Elaine Kagan

SUSAN SARANDON
(Married Chris Sarandon, Tim Robbins)

Oscar For Best Actress In 1995 For "Dead Man Walking". Nominated For Best Actress In 1981 For "Atlantic City" And In 1994 For "The Client"

1970 JOE
Director: John Avildsen
Co-stars: Dennis Patrick Peter Boyle Patrick McDermott

1973   **LOVIN' MOLLY**
Director: Sidney Lumet
Co-stars: Anthony Perkins Beau Bridges Blythe Danner

1974   **FRONT PAGE**
Director: Billy Wilder
Co-stars: Walter Matthau Jack Lemmon David Wayne

1974   **F. SCOTT FITZGERALD AND "THE LAST OF THE BELLES"**
Director: George Schaefer
Co-stars: Blythe Danner Richard Chamberlain

1975   **THE GREAT WALDO PEPPER**
Director: George Roy Hill
Co-stars: Robert Redford Bo Svenson Bo Brundin

1975   **THE ROCKY HORROR PICTURE SHOW**
Director: Jim Sharman
Co-stars: Tim Curry Barry Bostwick Koo Stark

1976   **ONE SUMMER LOVE**
Director: Gilbert Cates
Co-stars: Beau Bridges Mildred Dunnock Michael B. Miller

1976   **THE GREAT SMOKEY ROADBLOCK**
Director: John Leone
Co-stars: Henry Fonda Eileen Brennan John Byner

1977   **THE OTHER SIDE OF MIDNIGHT**
Director: Charles Jarrott
Co-stars: John Beck Marie-France Pisier Raf Vallone

1978   **PRETTY BABY**
Director: Louis Malle
Co-stars: Brooke Shields Keith Carradine Antonio Fargas

1978   **KING OF THE GYPSIES**
Director: Frank Pierson
Co-stars: Sterling Hayden Eric Roberts Brooke Shields

1980   **LOVING COUPLES**
Director: Jack Smight
Co-stars: Shirley MacLaine James Coburn Stephen Collins

1981   **ATLANTIC CITY**
Director: Louis Malle
Co-stars: Burt Lancaster Kate Reid Michel Piccoli

1983   **THE HUNGER**
Director: Tony Scott
Co-stars: Catherine Deneuvre David Bowie Willem Dafoe

1984   **THE BUDDY SYSTEM**
Director: Glenn Jordan
Co-stars: Richard Dreyfuss Nancy Allen

1985   **COMPROMISING POSITIONS**
Director: Frank Perry
Co-stars: Raul Julia Edward Herrman Judith Ivey

1986   **WOMEN OF VALOR**
Director: Buzz Kulik
Co-stars: Kirsty McNichol Alberta Watson Suzanne Lederer

1987   **THE WITCHES OF EASTWICK**
Director: George Miller
Co-stars: Michelle Pfeiffer Jack Nicholson Cher

1988   **SWEET HEARTS DANCE**
Director: Robert Greenwald
Co-stars: Don Johnson Jeff Daniels Kate Reid

1988   **BULL DURHAM**
Director: Ron Sheldon
Co-stars: Kevin Costner Tim Robbins Trey Wilson

1989   **A DRY WHITE SEASON**
Director: Euzhan Palcy
Co-stars: Donald Sutherland Janet Suzman Marlon Brando

1989   **THE JANUARY MAN**
Director: Pat O'Connor
Co-stars: Kevin Kline Harvey Keitel Rod Steiger

1990   **WHITE PALACE**
Director: Luis Mondoki
Co-stars: James Spader Kathy Bates Eileen Brennan

1991   **THELMA AND LOUISE**
Director: Ridley Scott
Co-stars: Genna Davis Harvey Keitel Brad Pitt

1991   **LIGHT SLEEPER**
Director: Paul Schrader
Co-stars: Willem Dafoe Dana Delany David Glennon

1992   **BOB ROBERTS**
Director: Tim Robbins
Co-stars: Tim Robbins Gore Vidal Ray Wise

1992   **LORENZO'S OIL**
Director: George Miller
Co-stars: Nick Nolte Peter Ustinov Kathleen Wilhoite

1992   **THE PLAYER**
Director: Robert Altman
Co-stars: Tim Robbins Greta Scacchi Whoopi Goldberg

1994   **THE CLIENT**
Director: Joel Schumacher
Co-stars: Brad Renfro Tommy Lee Jones Anthony LePaglia

1994   **LITTLE WOMEN**
Director: Gillian Armstrong
Co-stars: Winona Ryder Gabriel Byrne Samantha Mathis

1995   **SAFE PASSAGE**
Co-star: Sam Shepard

1995   **DEAD MAN WALKING**
Director: Tim Robbins
Co-stars: Sean Penn Robert Prosky Scott Wilson

1996   **JAMES AND THE GIANT PEACH** *(Voice)*
Director: Henry Selig
Co-stars: Paul Terry Joanna Lumley Simon Callow

LEILANI SARELLE

1992   **BASIC INSTINCT**
Director: Paul Verhoeven
Co-stars: Michael Douglas Sharon Stone George Dzundza

1992   **THE HARVEST**
Director: David Marconi
Co-stars: Miguel Ferrer Harvey Fierstein Henry Silva

JACQUELINE SASSARD

1967   **ACCIDENT**
Director: Joseph Losey
Co-stars: Dirk Bogarde Stanley Baker Michael York

1968   **LES BICHES**
Director: Claude Chabrol
Co-stars: Stephane Audran Jean-Louis Trintignant

CATYA SASSOON

1985   **TUFF TURF**
Director: Fritz Kiersch
Co-stars: James Spader Kim Richards Robert Downey Jnr.

LINA SASTRI

1984   **WHERE'S PICONE ?**
Director: Nanni Loy
Co-stars: Giancarlo Giannini Aldo Giuffre Carlo Croccolo

MARI SATO

1988 CAPTIVE HEARTS
Director: Paul Almond
Co-stars: Pat Morita Chris Makepeace Michael Sarrazin

JEANNE SATTERFIELD

1983 BORN IN FLAMES
Director: Lizzie Borden
Co-stars: Honey Adele Bertei Kathryn Bigelow

BRENDA SAUNDERS

1990 CIRCLES OF DECEIT
Director: Stuart Burge
Co-stars: Edward Fox Jane Lapotaire Brenda Bruce

JENNIFER SAUNDERS

1985 THE SUPERGRASS
Director: Peter Richardson
Co-stars: Peter Richardson Adrian Edmondson Dawn French

1987 EAT THE RICH
Director: Peter Richardson
Co-stars: Peter Richardson Nosher Powell Fiona Richmond

1988 THE STRIKE
Director: Peter Richardson
Co-stars: Peter Richardson Alexei Sayle Robbie Coltrane

1995 IN THE BLEAK MIDWINTER
Director: Kenneth Branagh
Co-stars: Michael Maloney Julia Sawalha Celia Imrie

1996 MUPPET TREASURE ISLAND
Co-star: Tim Curry

1996 ABSOLUTELY FABULOUS
Co-stars: Joanne Lumley Julia Sawalha Jane Horrocks

1997 SPICEWORLD - THE MOVIE
Co-stars: Spice Girls Richard E. Grant Roger Moore

KIM SAUNDERS

1983 GETTING IT ON
Director: William Olsen
Co-stars: Martin Yost Heather Kennedy Jeff Edmond

MADGE SAUNDERS

1930 TONS OF MONEY
Director: Tom Walls
Co-stars: Ralph Lynn Yvonne Arnaud Robertson Hare

MARY JANE SAUNDERS

1949 SORROWFUL JONES
Director: Sidney Lanfield
Co-stars: Bob Hope Lucille Ball William Demarest

1950 A WOMAN OF DISTINCTION
Director: Edward Buzzell
Co-stars: Rosalind Russell Ray Milland Edmund Gwenn

1953 THE GIRL NEXT DOOR
Director: Richard Sale
Co-stars: Dan Dailey June Haver Billy Gray

NANCY SAUNDERS

1947 THE LONE WOLF IN LONDON
Director: Leslie Goodwins
Co-stars: Gerald Mohr Eric Blore Evelyn Ankers

1947 THE MILLERSON CASE
Director: George Archainbaud
Co-stars: Warner Baxter Barbara Pepper Clem Bevans

TERRY SAUNDERS

1956 THE KING AND I
Director: Walter Lang
Co-stars: Yul Brynner Deborah Kerr Rita Moreno

ANN SAVAGE

1941 MEET BOSTON BLACKIE
Director: Lew Landers
Co-stars: Chester Morris George E. Stone Richard Lane

1941 CONFESSIONS OF BOSTON BLACKIE
Director: Lew Landers
Co-stars: Chester Morris Richard Lane

1942 ALIAS BOSTON BLACKIE
Director: Lew Landers
Co-stars: Chester Morris George E. Stone Walter Sande

1942 BOSTON BLACKIE GOES TO HOLLYWOOD
Director: Lew Landers
Co-stars: Chester Morris George E. Stone

1943 AFTER MIDNIGHT WITH BOSTON BLACKIE
Director: Lew Landers
Co-stars: Chester Morris Walter Sande

1943 ONE DANGEROUS NIGHT
Director: Michael Gordon
Co-stars: Warren Williams Marguerite Chapman Eric Blore

1943 TWO SENORITAS FROM CHICAGO
Co-stars: Joan Davis Jinx Falkenberg Bob Haymes

1943 FOOTLIGHT GLAMOUR
Director: Frank Strayer
Co-stars: Penny Singleton Arthur Lake Larry Simms

1943 WHAT A WOMAN
Director: Irving Cummings
Co-stars: Rosalind Russell Brian Aherne Willard Parker

1943 KLONDYKE KATE
Co-star: Tom Neal

1944 EVER SINCE VENUS
Director: Arthur Dreifuss
Co-stars: Hugh Herbert Glenda Farrell Billy Gilbert

1944 TWO-MAN SUBMARINE
Co-stars: Tom Neal Abner Biberman

1945 DETOUR
Director: Edgar Ulmer
Co-stars: Tom Neal Claudia Drake Tim Ryan

1945 SCARED STIFF
Director: Frank McDonald
Co-stars: Jack Haley Barton MacLane Veda Ann Borg

1945 MIDNIGHT MANHUNT
Co-star: William Gargan

1946 THE DARK HORSE
Co-stars: Philip Terry Allen Jenkins

1986 FIRE WITH FIRE
Director: Duncan Gibbings
Co-stars: Virginia Madsen Craig Sheffer Kate Reid

NELLY SAVAGE

1929 THE HOLE IN THE WALL
Director: Robert Florey
Co-stars: Edward G. Robinson Claudette Colbert David Newell

TRACIE SAVAGE

1982 FRIDAY THE 13TH, PART III
Director: Steve Miner
Co-stars: Dana Kimmell Richard Brooker Catherine Parks

DANY SAVAL

1962 MOON PILOT
Director: James Neilson
Co-stars: Tom Tryon Brian Keith Edmond O'Brien

1965 BOEING BOEING
Director: John Rich
Co-stars: Tony Curtis Jerry Lewis Thelma Ritter

SONIA SAVIANGE

1977 LA MACHINE
Director: Paul Vecchiali
Co-stars: Jean-Christophe Bouvet Monique Melinaud Philippe Chemin

1981 LOIN DE MANHATTAN
Director: Jean-Claude Biette
Co-stars: Jean-Christophe Bouvet Laura Betti Howard Vernon

JENNIFER SAVIDGE

1988 SHOOTDOWN
Director: Michael Pressman
Co-stars: Angela Lansbury George Coe Kyle Secor

ANDRIA SAVIO

1983 STRYKER
Director: Cirio H. Santiago
Co-stars: Steve Sandor William Ostrander

TERESA ANN SAVOY

1980 CALIGULA
Director: Tinto Brass
Co-stars: Malcolm McDowell John Gielgud Peter O'Toole

JULIA SAWALHA

1995 IN THE BLEAK MIDWINTER
Director: Kenneth Branagh
Co-stars: Michael Maloney John Sessions Richard Briers

1996 ABSOLUTELY FABULOUS
Co-stars: Jennifer Saunders Joanna Lumley Jane Horrocks

1996 PRIDE AND PREJUDICE
Co-stars: Colin Firth Alison Steadman Benjamin Whitrow

SARAH SAWATSKY

1991 THE GIRL FROM MARS
Director: Neill Fernley
Co-stars: Edward Albert Eddie Albert

JACKIE SAWIRIS

1998 THE BIG SWAP
Director: Niall Johnson
Co-star: Mark Adams

MARIE SAXON

1930 THE BROADWAY HOOVER
Co-star: Jack Egan

DIANE SAYER

1963 THE STRANGLER
Director: Burt Topper
Co-stars: Victor Buono David McLean Ellen Corby

JO ANN SAYERS

1939 CRIMES DOES NOT PAY: DRUNK DRIVING
Director: David Miller
Co-star: Dick Purcell

1939 CRIME DOES NOT PAY: HELP WANTED
Director: Fred Zinnemann
Co-star: Tom Neal

1940 THE MAN WITH NINE LIVES
Director: Nick Grinde
Co-stars: Boris Karloff Byron Foulger Roger Pryor

LORETTA SAYERS

1932 HIGH SPEED
Co-stars: Buck Jones Wallace MacDonald

KATIE SAYLOR

1974 MEN OF THE DRAGON
Director: Harry Falk
Co-stars: Jared Martin Joseph Wiseman Robert Ito

SHARRON SAYLOR

1978 SHIPWRECK
Director: Stewart Raffill
Co-stars: Robert L. Logan Heather Rattray Mikki Jamison-Olsen

CARMELA SAZIO

1946 PAISA
Director: Roberto Rossellini
Co-stars: William Tubbs Gar Moore Maria Michi

GRETA SCACCHI

1982 HEAT AND DUST
Director: James Ivory
Co-stars: Julie Christie Christopher Cazenove Julian Glover

1983 DR FISCHER OF GENEVA
Director: Michael Lindsay-Hogg
Co-stars: James Mason Alan Bates Clarissa Kaye

1985 DEFENCE OF THE REALM
Director: David Drury
Co-stars: Gabriel Byrne Denholm Elliott Ian Bannen

1985 THE COCA-COLA KID
Director: Dusan Makavejev
Co-stars: Eric Roberts Bill Kerr Max Cillies

1985 BURKE AND WILLS
Director: Graeme Clifford
Co-stars: Jack Thompson Nigel Havers Matthew Fargher

1987 GOOD MORNING BABYLON
Director: Paolo Taviani
Co-stars: Vincent Spano Charles Dance Joaquim De Almeida

1987 A MAN IN LOVE
Director: Diane Kurys
Co-stars: Peter Coyote Claudia Cardinale Jaimie Lee Curtis

1987 THREE SISTERS
Director: Margarethe Von Trotta
Co-stars: Fanny Ardant Valeria Golino Peter Simonisch

1987 WHITE MISCHIEF
Director: Michael Radford
Co-stars: Charles Dance Joss Ackland Sarah Miles

1990 PRESUMED INNOCENT
Director: Alan Pakula
Co-stars: Harrison Ford Bonnie Bedelia Brian Dennehy

1991 SHATTERED
Director: Wolfgang Petersen
Co-stars: Tom Berenger Bob Hoskins Joanne Whalley

1991 TURTLE BEACH
Director: Stephen Wallace
Co-stars: Joan Chen Jack Thompson Art Malik

1991 FIRES WITHIN
Director: Gillian Armstrong
Co-stars: Jimmy Smits Vincent D'Onofrio Brit Hathaway

1992   **THE PLAYER**
Director: Robert Altman
Co-stars: Tim Robbins Fred Ward Whoopi Goldberg

1993   **SALT ON OUR SKIN**
Director: Andrew Birkin
Co-stars: Vincent D'Onofrio Claudine Auger Petra Berndt

1994   **THE BROWNING VERSION**
Director: Mike Figgis
Co-stars: Albert Finney Matthew Modine Julian Sands

1995   **THE SERPENT'S KISS**
Co-star: Ewan McGregor

1995   **JEFFERSON IN PARIS**
Director: James Ivory
Co-stars: Nick Nolte Jean-Pierre Aumont

1996   **EMMA**
Director: Douglas McGrath
Co-stars: Gwyneth Paltrow Jeremy Northam Juliet Stevenson

GIA SCALA

1958   **THE PRICE OF FEAR**
Director: Abner Biberman
Co-stars: Merle Oberon Lex Barker Charles Drake

1956   **FOUR GIRLS IN TOWN**
Director: Jack Sher
Co-stars: George Nader Julie Adams Elsa Martinelli

1957   **DON'T GO NEAR THE WATER**
Director: Charles Walters
Co-stars: Glenn Ford Fred Clark Russ Tamblyn

1957   **THE BIG BOODLE**
Director: Richard Wilson
Co-stars: Errol Flynn Pedro Armendariz Rossana Rory

1957   **TIP ON A DEAD JOCKEY**
Director: Richard Thorpe
Co-stars: Robert Taylor Dorothy Malone Jack Lord

1957   **THE GARMENT JUNGLE**
Director: Robert Aldrich
Co-stars: Lee J. Cobb Kerwin Matthews Richard Boone

1958   **RIDE A CROOKED TRAIL**
Director: Jesse Hibbs
Co-stars: Audie Murphy Walter Matthau Henry Silva

1958   **THE TUNNEL OF LOVE**
Director: Gene Kelly
Co-stars: Doris Day Richard Widmark Gig Young

1958   **THE TWO-HEADED SPY**
Director: Andre De Toth
Co-stars: Jack Hawkins Alexander Knox Donald Pleasence

1959   **BATTLE OF THE CORAL SEA**
Director: Paul Wendkos
Co-stars: Cliff Robertson Patricia Cutts

1959   **THE ANGRY HILLS**
Director: Robert Aldrich
Co-stars: Robert Mitchum Elizabeth Mueller Stanley Baker

1960   **I AIM AT THE STARS**
Director: J. Lee-Thompson
Co-stars: Curt Jurgens Herbert Lom Victoria Shaw

1961   **THE GUNS OF NAVARONE**
Director: J. Lee-Thompson
Co-stars: Gregory Peck David Niven Stanley Baker

MICHELLE SCARABELLI

1986   **AIRWOLF: THE STAVOGRAD INCIDENT**
Director: Ken Jubenvill
Co-stars: Barry Von Dyke Anthony Sherwood

1991   **A MONTH OF SUNDAYS**
Director: Allan Kroeker
Co-stars: Hume Cronyn Vincent Gardenia Tandy Cronyn

1992   **DEADBOLT**
Director: Douglas Jackson
Co-stars: Justine Bateman Adam Baldwin

1995   **ALIEN NATION: DARK HORIZON**
Director: Kenneth Johnson
Co-stars: Gary Graham Eric Pierpoint

PRUNELLA SCALES

1953   **HOBSON'S CHOICE**
Director: David Lean
Co-stars: Charles Laughton John Mills Brenda De Banzie

1962   **WALTZ OF THE TOREADORS**
Director: John Guillermin
Co-stars: Peter Sellers Margaret Leighton Dany Robin

1976   **ESCAPE FROM THE DARK**
Director: Charles Jarrott
Co-stars: Alastair Sim Peter Barkworth Leslie Sands

1977   **THE HOUND OF THE BASKERVILLES**
Director: Paul Morrissey
Co-stars: Peter Cook Dudley Moore Max Wall

1978   **THE BOYS FROM BRAZIL**
Director: Franklin Schaffner
Co-stars: Gregory Peck Laurence Olivier James Mason

1983   **THE WICKED LADY**
Director: Michael Winner
Co-stars: Faye Dunaway Alan Bates John Gielgud

1987   **THE LONELY PASSION OF JUDITH HEARNE**
Director: Jack Clayton
Co-stars: Maggie Smith Bob Hoskins Wendy Hiller

1988   **CONSUMING PASSIONS**
Director: Giles Foster
Co-stars: Vanessa Redgrave Jonathan Pryce Sammi Davis

1988   **A CHORUS OF DISAPPROVAL**
Director: Michael Winner
Co-stars: Anthony Hopkins Jeremy Irons Patsy Kensit

1989   **BEYOND THE PALE**
Director: Diarmuid Lawrence
Co-stars: Annette Crosbie Ronald Hines Jeff Rawle

1991   **A QUESTION OF ATTRIBUTION**
Director: John Schlessinger
Co-stars: James Fox Geoffrey Palmer David Calder

1992   **HOWARDS END**
Director: James Ivory
Co-stars: Anthony Hopkins Vanessa Redgrave Helena Bonham-Carter

1992   **FREDDIE AS FRO7** *(Voice)*
Director: Jon Acevski
Co-stars: Ben Kingsley Jenny Agutter Brian Blessed

1996   **PERIOD**
Director: Gary Sinyor
Co-stars: Sam West Georgina Cates Peter Ustinov

1996   **EMMA**
Co-stars: Kate Beckinsale Mark Strong Samantha Bond

1998   **STIFF UPPER LIPS**
Director: Gary Sinyor
Co-stars: Sam West Georgina Cates Robert Portal

CAROL SCANLAN

1988   **REEFER AND THE MODEL**
Director: Joe Comerford
Co-stars: Ian McElhinney Eve Watkinson Birdy Sweeney

CARMEN SCARPITTA

1976 CASANOVA
Director: Federico Fellini
Co-stars: Donald Sutherland Tina Aumont Cicely Browne

DIANA SCARWID

Nominated For Best Supporting Actress In 1980 For "Inside Moves"

1977 THE POSSESSED
Director: Jerry Thorpe
Co-stars: James Farantino Joan Hackett Harrison Ford

1978 PRETTY BABY
Director: Louis Malle
Co-stars: Keith Carradine Susan Sarandon Brooke Shields

1978 FOREVER
Director: John Korty
Co-stars: Stephanie Zimbalist Dean Butler Beth Raines

1980 INSIDE MOVES
Director: Richard Donner
Co-stars: John Savage David Morse Harold Russell

1981 MOMMIE DEAREST
Director: Frank Perry
Co-stars: Faye Dunaway Steve Forrest Howard Da Silva

1982 THOU SHALT NOT KILL
Director: I.C. Rappaport
Co-stars: Lee Grant Robert Culp Gary Graham

1983 STRANGE INVADERS
Director: Michael Laughlin
Co-stars: Paul LeMat Nancy Alen Michael Lerner

1983 SILKWOOD
Director: Mike Nichols
Co-stars: Meryl Streep Kurt Russell Cher

1983 RUMBLE FISH
Director: Francis Coppola
Co-stars: Matt Dillon Mickey Rourke Diane Lane

1986 PSYCHO III
Director: Anthony Perkins
Co-stars: Anthony Perkins Jeff Fahey Roberta Maxwell

1986 EXTREMITIES
Director: Robert Young
Co-stars: Farrah Fawcett James Russo Alfre Woodard

1987 AFTER THE PROMISE
Director: David Greene
Co-stars: Mark Harmon Rosemary Dunsmore Mark Hildreth

1987 HEAT
Director: R.M. Richards
Co-stars: Burt Reynolds Karen Young Peter MacNicol

1995 THE NEON BIBLE
Director: Terence Davies
Co-stars: Gena Rowlands Denis Leary Jacob Tierney

1996 THE CURE
Director: Peter Horton
Co-stars: Brad Renfro Annabella Sciorra Joseph Mazello

KATRIN SCHAAKE

1975 THE BITTER TEARS OF PETRA VON KANT
Director: Rainer Werner Fassbinder
Co-stars: Margit Carstensen Hanna Schygulla

WENDY SCHAAL

1984 WHERE THE BOYS ARE
Director: Hy Averbach
Co-stars: Lisa Hartman Lorna Luft Russel Todd

1989 THE BURBS
Director: Joe Dante
Co-stars: Tom Hanks Bruce Dern Carrie Fisher

1990 GOING UNDER
Director: Mark Travis
Co-stars: Bill Pullman Ned Beatty

DORIS SCHADE

1981 THE GERMAN SISTERS
Director: Margarethe Von Trotta
Co-stars: Jutte Lampe Barbara Sukowa Rudiger Vogler

1982 VERONIKA VOSS
Director: Rainer Werner Fassbinder
Co-stars: Rosel Zech Hilmar Thate Annemarie Duringer

REBECCA SCHAEFFER

1990 VOYAGE OF TERROR
Director: Alberto Negrin
Co-stars: Burt Lancaster Eva Marie Saint Robert Culp

NATALIE SCHAFER

1944 MARRIAGE IS A PRIVATE AFFAIR
Director: Robert Z. Leonard
Co-stars: Lana Turner James Craig John Hodiak

1945 MASQUERADE IN MEXICO
Director: Mitchell Leisen
Co-stars: Dorothy Lamour Arturo De Cordova Ann Dvorak

1945 WONDER MAN
Director: Bruce Humberstone
Co-stars: Danny Kaye Vera-Ellen Virginia Mayo

1945 MOLLY AND ME
Director: Lewis Seiler
Co-stars: Gracie Fields Monty Woolley Roddy McDowall

1945 KEEP YOUR POWDER DRY
Director: Edward Buzzell
Co-stars: Lana Turner Laraine Day Susan Peters

1948 SECRET BEYOND THE DOOR
Director: Fritz Lang
Co-stars: Joan Bennett Michael Redgrave Barbara O'Neil

1948 THE SNAKE PIT
Director: Anatole Litvak
Co-stars: Olivia De Havilland Leo Genn Mark Stevens

1948 THE TIME OF YOUR LIFE
Director: H.C. Potter
Co-stars: James Cagney Wayne Morris William Bendix

1949 CAUGHT
Director: Max Ophuls
Co-stars: James Mason Robert Ryan Barbara Bel Geddes

1951 CALLAWAY WENT THATAWAY
Director: Melvin Frank
Co-stars: Dorothy McGuire Fred MacMurray Howard Keel

1952 JUST ACROSS THE STREET
Director: Joseph Pevney
Co-stars: Ann Sheridan John Lund Robert Keith

1953 THE GIRL NEXT DOOR
Director: Richard Sale
Co-stars: Dan Dailey June Haver Billy Gray

1955 FEMALE ON THE BEACH
Director: Joseph Pevney
Co-stars: Joan Crawford Jeff Chandler Jan Sterling

1957 BERNADINE
Director: Henry Levin
Co-stars: Pat Boone Terry Moore Janet Gaynor

1961 SUSAN SLADE
Director: Delmer Daves
Co-stars: Connie Stevens Troy Donahue Dorothy McGuire

1973 FORTY CARATS
Director: Milton Katselas
Co-stars: Liv Ullmann Edward Albert Gene Kelly

1990 I'M DANGEROUS TONIGHT
Director: Tobe Hooper
Co-stars: Madchen Amick Anthony Perkins Daisy Hall

TANARA SCHANZARA

1973 TENDERNESS OF WOLVES
Director: Ulli Lommel
Co-stars: Kurt Raab Jeff Roden Margit Carstensen

SABRINA SCHARF

1967 HELL'S ANGELS OF WHEELS
Director: Richard Rush
Co-stars: Adam Roarke Jack Nicholson Jana Taylor

SARAH SCHAUB

1991 IN YOUR WILDEST DREAM
Director: Bruce Neibaur
Co-stars: Trevor Black Lisa Williams

1993 A HOME OF OUR OWN
Director: Tony Bill
Co-stars: Kathy Bates Edward Furlong Clarissa Lassig

ANNE SCHEDEEN

1976 EMBRYO
Director: Ralph Nelson
Co-stars: Rock Hudson Diane Ladd Barbara Carrera

1977 THE EXO-MAN
Director: Richard Irving
Co-stars: David Ackroyd Jose Ferrer Harry Morgan

1982 SECOND THOUGHTS
Director: Lawrence Turman
Co-stars: Lucie Arnaz Craig Wasson Ken Howard

1987 ALF
Director: Tom Patchett
Co-stars: Max Wright Liz Sheridan Anne Meara

1993 PRAYING MANTIS
Director: James Keach
Co-stars: Jane Seymour Barry Bostwick Daphne Zuniga

CATHERINE SCHELL

1965 TRAITOR'S GATE
Director: Freddie Francis
Co-stars: Albert Lieven Gary Raymond Klaus Kinski

1968 AMSTERDAM AFFAIR
Director: Gerry O'Hara
Co-stars: Wolfgang Kieling William Marlowe Pamela Ann Davy

1974 CALLAN
Director: Don Sharp
Co-stars: Edward Woodward Eric Porter Russell Hunter

1974 THE RETURN OF THE PINK PANTHER
Director: Blake Edwards
Co-stars: Peter Sellers Herbert Lom Peter Arne

1976 GULLIVER'S TRAVELS
Director: Peter Hunt
Co-stars: Richard Harris Norman Shelley Meredith Edwards

1979 THE PRISONER OF ZENDA
Director: Richard Quine
Co-stars: Peter Sellers Lynne Frederick Lionel Jeffries

1987 BORDER
Director: Misha Williams
Co-stars: Shaun Scott Edita Brychta Daniel Hill

1969 MOON ZERO TWO
Director: Roy Ward Baker
Co-stars: James Olson Warren Mitchell Adrienne Corri

MARIA SCHELL

1949 THE ANGEL WITH THE TRUMPET
Director: Anthony Bushell
Co-stars: Anthony Bushell Eileen Herlie Basil Sydney

1951 THE MAGIC BOX
Director: John Boulting
Co-stars: Robert Donat Margaret Johnston Robert Beatty

1952 SO LITTLE TIME
Director: Compton Bennett
Co-stars: Marius Goring Barbara Mullen Gabrielle Dorziat

1953 THE DIARY OF A MARRIED WOMAN
Director: Josef Von Baky
Co-stars: O.W. Fischer Franco Andrei

1953 THE HEART OF THE MATTER
Director: George More O'Ferrall
Co-stars: Trevor Howard Elizabeth Allan Peter Finch

1953 THE LAST BRIDGE
Director: Helmut Kautner
Co-stars: Bernhard Wicki Barbara Rutting Carl Mohner

1956 GERVAIS
Director: Rene Clement
Co-stars: Francois Perier Suzy Delair Mathilde Casadeus

1957 THE BROTHERS KARAMAZOV
Director: Richard Brooks
Co-stars: Yul Brynner Richard Basehart Claire Bloom

1957 THE HANGING TREE
Director: Delmer Daves
Co-stars: Gary Cooper Karl Malden George C. Scott

1960 CIMARRON
Director: Anthony Mann
Co-stars: Glenn Ford Anne Baxter Russ Tamblyn

1961 THE MARK
Director: Guy Green
Co-stars: Stuart Whitman Rod Steiger Brenda De Banzie

1974 THE ODESSA FILE
Director: Ronald Neame
Co-stars: Jon Voight Maximilian Schell Mary Tamm

1976 VOYAGE OF THE DAMNED
Director: Stuart Rosenberg
Co-stars: Faye Dunaway Oskar Werner Orson Welles

1978 JUST A GIGOLO
Director: David Hemmings
Co-stars: David Hemmings Kim Novak David Bowie

1985 19/19
Director: Hugh Brody
Co-stars: Paul Scofield Colin Firth Diana Quick

LEILA SCHENNA

1970 RAMPARTS OF CLAY
Director: Jean-Louis Bertucelli

ROSANNA SCHIAFFINO

1962 TWO WEEKS IN ANOTHER TOWN
Director: Vincente Minnelli
Co-stars: Kirk Douglas Edward G. Robinson Daliah Lavi

1963 THE VICTORS
Director: Carl Foreman
Co-stars: George Peppard Albert Finney George Hamilton

THE LONG SHIPS

1964   **THE LONG SHIPS**
Director: Jack Cardiff
Co-stars: Richard Widmark Sidney Poitier Russ Tamblyn

1964   **EL GRECO**
Director: Luciano Salce
Co-stars: Mel Ferrer Adolfo Celi Angel Aranda

1965   **THE CAVERN**
Director: Edgar Ulmer
Co-stars: John Saxon Briah Aherne Larry Hagman

1966   **DROP DEAD DARLING**
Director: Ken Hughes
Co-stars: Tony Curtis Zsa Zsa Gabor Nancy Kwan

1973   **THE MAN CALLED NOON**
Director: Peter Collinson
Co-stars: Richard Crenna Stephen Boyd Farley Granger

CLAUDIA SCHIFFER

1998   **THE BLACKOUT**
Director: Abel Ferrara
Co-stars: Matthew Modine Dennis Hopper

MARGARETE SCHLEGEL

1931   **BERLIN ALEXANDERPLATZ**
Director: Phil Jutzi
Co-stars: Heinrich George Bernhard Minetti Albert Florath

HELEN SCHLESINGER

1992   **THE CORMORANT**
Director: Peter Markham
Co-stars: Ralph Fiennes Thomas Williams Karl Francis

KATHERINE SCHLESINGER

1987   **NORTHANGER ABBEY**
Director: Giles Foster
Co-stars: Googie Withers Robert Hardy Peter Firth

HEDWIG SCHLICHTER

1931   **MADCHEN IN UNIFORM**
Director: Leontine Sagan
Co-stars: Emelia Unda Dorothea Wieck Hertha Thiele

ANJA SCHMIDT

1971   **THE BALLAD OF JOE HILL**
Director: Bo Widerberg
Co-stars: Thommy Berggren Evert Anderson Cathy Smith

CHRISTIANE SCHMIDTMER

1965   **BOEING BOEING**
Director: John Rich
Co-stars: Tony Curtis Jerry Lewis Thelma Ritter

SYBILE SCHMITZ

1932   **VAMPYR**
Director: Carl Theodore Dreyer
Co-stars: Julian West Maurice Schutz Jan Hieron Imko

MONIKA SCHNARRE

1994   **KILLER**
Director: Mark Malone
Co-stars: Anthony LaPaglia Mimi Rogers Peter Boyle

BETTY SCHNEIDER

1958   **MON ONCLE**
Director: Jacques Tati
Co-stars: Jacques Tati Jean-Pierre Zola Yvonne Arnaud

1960   **PARIS NOUS APPARTIENT**
Director: Jacques Rivette
Co-stars: Gianni Esposito Francoise Prevost Daniel Crohem

EDITH SCHNEIDER

1986   **OF PURE BLOOD**
Director: Joseph Sargent
Co-stars: Lee Remick Patrick McGoohan Richard Munch

HELEN SCHNEIDER

1983   **EDDIE AND THE CRUISERS**
Director: Martin Davidson
Co-stars: Tom Berenger Michael Pare Ellen Barkin

MAGDA SCHNEIDER
(Mother Of Romy Schneider)

1932   **LIEBELEI**
Director: Max Ophuls
Co-stars: Wolfgang Liebeneiner Luise Ullrich Willy Eichberger

1932   **TELL ME TONIGHT**
Director: Anatole Litvak
Co-stars: Jan Kiepura Sonnie Hale Edmund Gwenn

MARIA SCHNEIDER

1972   **LAST TANGO IN PARIS**
Director: Bernardo Bertolucci
Co-stars: Marlon Brando Jean-Pierre Leaud Maria Michi

1975   **PROFESSION: REPORTER**
Director: Michaelangelo Antonioni
Co-stars: Jack Nicholson Jenny Runacre Ian Hendry

1985   **A SONG FOR EUROPE**
Director: John Goldschmidt
Co-stars: David Suchet Ernst Schroeder Robert Freitag

1998   **SOMETHING TO BELIEVE IN**
Director: John Hough
Co-stars: Maria Pitillo William McNamara Tom Conti

ROMY SCHNEIDER
(Daughter Of Magda Schneider)

1958   **MADCHEN IN UNIFORM**
Director: Geza Radvanyl
Co-stars: Lilli Palmer Christine Kaufman Therese Gierse

1962   **BOCCACCIO 70**
Director: Vittorio De Sica
Co-stars: Sophia Loren Anita Ekberg Peppino De Filippo

1962   **THE TRIAL**
Director: Orson Welles
Co-stars: Orson Welles Jeanne Moreau Anthony Perkins

1963   **THE VICTORS**
Director: Carl Foreman
Co-stars: George Peppard Eli Wallach Melina Mercouri

1963   **THE CARDINAL**
Director: Otto Preminger
Co-stars: Tom Tyron Carol Lynley John Huston

1964   **GOOD NEIGHBOUR SAM**
Director: David Swift
Co-stars: Jack Lemmon Dorothy Provine Senta Berger

1965   **WHAT'S NEW PUSSYCAT ?**
Director: Clive Donner
Co-stars: Peter O'Toole Woody Allen Capucine

1966   **10.30 P.M. SUMMER**
Director: Jules Dassin
Co-stars: Peter Finch Melina Mercouri Julian Mateos

1967   **TRIPLE CROSS**
Director: Terence Young
Co-stars: Christopher Plummer Yul Brynner Trevor Howard

1968   **OTLEY**
Director: Dick Clement
Co-stars: Tom Courtenay Alan Badel Leonard Rossiter

1968   **CHRISTINE**
Co-star: Alain Delon

1969   **THE THINGS OF LIFE**
Director: Claude Sautet
Co-stars: Michel Piccoli Lea Massari Jean Bouise

1969   **BLOOMFIELD**
Director: Richard Harris
Co-stars: Richard Harris Kim Burfield Maurice Kaufman

1969   **THE SWIMMING POOL**
Director: Jacques Deray
Co-stars: Alain Delon Maurice Ronet Jane Birkin

1972   **LE TRAIN**
Director: Pierre Gramier-Deferre
Co-stars: Jean-Louis Trintignant Anne Wiazemsky

1972   **LUDWIG**
Director: Luchino Visconti
Co-stars: Helmut Berger Trevor Howard Silvana Mangano

1972   **THE ASSASSINATION OF TROTSKY**
Director: Joseph Losey
Co-stars: Richard Burton Alain Delon

1972   **CESAR AND ROSALIE**
Director: Claude Sautet
Co-stars: Yves Montand Sami Frey Umberto Orsini

1973   **LOVING IN THE RAIN**
Director: Jean-Claude Brialy
Co-stars: Nino Castelnuovo Suzanne Flon Mehdi

1979   **BLOODLINE**
Director: Terence Young
Co-stars: Audrey Hepburn Ben Gazzara James Mason

1980   **DEATH WATCH**
Director: Bertrand Tavernier
Co-stars: Harvey Keitel Harry Dean Stanton Max Von Sydow

1981   **GARDE A VUE**
Director: Claude Miller
Co-stars: Lino Ventura Michel Serrault Guy Marchand

ANDREA SCHOBER

1971   **THE MERCHANT OF FOUR SEASONS**
Director: Rainer Werner Fassbinder
Co-stars: Hans Hirschmuller Hanna Schygulla

1976   **CHINESE ROULETTE**
Director: Rainer Werner Fassbinder
Co-stars: Marget Carstensen Ulli Lommel Anna Karina

BARBARA SCHOCK

1989   **FROM HOLLYWOOD TO DEADWOOD**
Director: Rex Pickett
Co-stars: Scott Paulin Jim Haynie Jurgen Doeres

JILL SCHOELEN

1983   **HAPPY ENDINGS**
Director: Jerry Thorpe
Co-stars: Sarah Nevin Laura Dern Lee Montgomery

1985   **THAT WAS THEN...THIS IS NOW**
Director: Christopher Cain
Co-stars: Emilio Estevez Craig Sheffer Kim Delaney

1986   **SHATTERED SPIRITS**
Director: Robert Greenwald
Co-stars: Martin Sheen Melinda Dillon Lukas Haas

1986   **THE STEPFATHER**
Director: Joseph Ruben
Co-stars: Terry O'Quinn Shelley Hack Charles Lanyer

1986   **BABES IN TOYLAND**
Director: Clive Donner
Co-stars: Drew Barrymore Eileen Brennan Keanu Reeves

1989   **PHANTOM OF THE OPERA**
Director: Dwight Little
Co-stars: Robert Englund Bill Nighy Stephanie Lawrence

1993   **WHEN A STRANGER CALLS BACK**
Director: Fred Walton
Co-stars: Charles Durning Carol Kane

MARGARETHE SCHOEN

1924   **NIBELUNGEN, DIE KRIEMHILDS RACHE**
Director: Fritz Lang
Co-stars: Rudolph Klein Rogge Rudolph Rittner

1924   **NIBELUNGEN, DIE SIEGFRIEDS TOT**
Director: Fritz Lang
Co-stars: Paul Richter Hanna Ralph Theodor Loos

KATHERINE SCHOFIELD

1975   **THE NAKED CIVIL SERVANT**
Director: Jack Gold
Co-stars: John Hurt Patricia Hodge Quentin Crisp

1987   **THE LION OF AFRICA**
Director: Kevin Connor
Co-stars: Brian Dennehy Brooke Adams Don Warrington

NELL SCHOFIELD

1981   **PUBERTY BLUES**
Director: Bruce Beresford
Co-stars: Tony Hughes Jad Capelja Geoff Rhoe

CHRISTINA SCHOLLIN

1964   **DEAR JOHN**
Director: Lars Magnus Lindgren
Co-stars: Jarl Kulle Helena Nilsson Morgan Anderson

1970   **SONG OF NORWAY**
Director: Andrew Stone
Co-stars: Toralv Maurstad Harry Secombe Edward G. Robinson

1982   **FANNY AND ALEXANDER**
Director: Ingmar Bergman
Co-stars: Gunn Wallgren Ewa Frohling Allan Edwall

MARIA SCHRADER

1991   **I WAS ON MARS**
Director: Dani Levy
Co-stars: Dani Levy Mario Giacalone Antonia Rey

1997   **FLIRT**
Director: Hal Hartley

LISA SCHRAGE

1989   **FOOD OF THE GODS II**
Director: Damian Lee
Co-stars: Paul Coufos Jackie Borroughs Colin Fox

GRETA SCHROEDER-MATRAY

1921   **NOSFERATU**
Director: F.W. Murnau
Co-stars: Max Schreck Alexander Granach Ruth Landshoff

REBECCA SCHULL

1993   **MY LIFE**
Director: Bruce Joel Rubin
Co-stars: Michael Keaton Nicole Kidman Haing S. Ngor

MME. SCHUMANN-HEINK

1935   **HERE'S TO ROMANCE**
Director: Alfred Greene
Co-stars: Nino Martini Genevieve Tobin Reginald Denny

IDA SCHUSTER

1991 AND THE COW JUMPED OVER THE MOON
Director: Penny Cherns
Co-stars: Phyllis Logan Elaine Collins Anne Downie

LANA SCHWAB

1990 REPOSSESSED
Director: Bob Logan
Co-stars: Linda Blair Ned Beatty Leslie Neilsen

IVYANN SCHWAN *(Child)*

1989 PARENTHOOD
Director: Ron Howard
Co-stars: Steve Martin Tom Hulce Dianne Wiest

1991 PROBLEM CHILD 2
Director: Brian Levant
Co-stars: John Ritter Jack Warden Amy Yasbeck

ELLEN SCHWANNECKE

1931 MADCHEN IN UNIFORM
Director: Leontine Sagan
Co-stars: Emilia Unda Dorothea Wieck Herthe Thiele

HANNA SCHYGULLA

1971 THE MERCHANT OF FOUR SEASONS
Director: Rainer Werner Fassbinder
Co-star: Hans Hirschmuller Irm Herrmann

1974 EFFIE BRIEST
Director: Rainer Werner Fassbinder
Co-stars: Wolfgang Schenk Ulli Lommel Ursula Stratz

1975 THE BITTER TEARS OF PETRA VON KANT
Director: Rainer Werner Fassbinder
Co-stars: Margit Carstensen Irm Herrmann

1979 BERLIN ALEXANDERPLATZ
Director: Rainer Werner Fassbinder
Co-stars: Gunter Lamprecht Gottfried John Barbara Sukowa

1980 LILI MARLEEN
Director: Rainer Werner Fassbinder
Co-stars: Giancarlo Giannini Mel Ferrer Karl Heinz

1981 CIRCLE OF DECEIT
Director: Volker Schlondorff
Co-stars: Bruno Ganz Jerry Skolimowski

1982 THAT NIGHT IN VARENNES
Director: Ettore Scola
Co-stars: Jean-Louis Barrault Marcello Mastroianni

1987 FOREVER LULU
Director: Amos Kollek
Co-stars: Alec Baldwin Deborah Harry

1988 THE SUMMER OF MISS FORBES
Director: Jaime Humberto Hermosillo
Co-star: Alexis Castanares Victor Cesar

1991 DEAD AGAIN
Director: Kenneth Branagh
Co-stars: Kenneth Branagh Emma Thompson Andy Garcia

ANNABELLA SCIORRA

1989 TRUE LOVE
Director: Nancy Savoca
Co-stars: Ron Eldard Star Jasper Aida Turturro

1990 CADILLAC MAN
Director: Roger Donaldson
Co-stars: Robin Williams Tim Robbins Pamela Reed

1990 REVERSAL OF FORTUNE
Director: Barbet Schroeder
Co-stars: Glenn Close Jeremy Irons Ron Silver

1990 INTERNAL AFFAIRS
Director: Mike Figgis
Co-stars: Richard Gere Andy Garcia Nancy Travis

1991 THE HARD WAY
Director: John Badham
Co-stars: Michael J. Fox James Woods Penny Marshall

1991 JUNGLE FEVER
Director: Spike Lee
Co-stars: Spike Lee Wesley Snipes Ruby Dee

1991 PRISON STORIES: WOMEN ON THE INSIDE
Director: Donna Deitch
Co-stars: Rae Dawn Chong Lolita Davidovich

1992 WHISPERS IN THE DARK
Director: Christopher Crowe
Co-stars: Jamey Sheridan Alan Alda Jill Clayburgh

1992 THE HAND THAT ROCKS THE CRADLE
Director: Curtis Hanson
Co-stars: Rebecca De Mornay Matt McCoy Julianne Moore

1993 MR WONDERFUL
Director: Anthony Minghella
Co-stars: Matt Dillon Mary-Louise Parker William Hurt

1993 THE NIGHT WE NEVER MET
Director: Warren Leight
Co-stars: Matthew Broderick Kevin Anderson Justine Bateman

1993 ROMEO IS BLEEDING
Director: Peter Medak
Co-stars: Gary Oldman Lena Olin Juliette Lewis

1996 THE INNOCENT SLEEP
Director: Scott Michell
Co-stars: Rupert Graves Michael Gambon Franco Nero

1996 THE CURE
Director: Peter Horton
Co-stars: Brad Renfro Diana Scarwid Joseph Mazello

1997 COPLAND
Director: James Mangold
Co-stars: Sylvester Stallone Harvey Keitel Robert De Niro

1997 THE FUNERAL
Director: Abel Ferrara
Co-stars: Christopher Walken Christopher Penn Isabella Rossellini

EDITH SCOB

1959 EYES WITHOUT A FACE
Director: Georges Franju
Co-stars: Pierre Brasseur Alida Valli Francois Guerin

1963 JUDEX
Director: Georges Franju
Co-stars: Channing Pollock Francine Berge Sylva Koscina

1965 THOMAS L'IMPOSTEUR
Director: George Franju
Co-stars: Emmanuelle Riva Fabrice Rouleau Jean Servais

1968 THE MILKY WAY
Director: Luis Bunuel
Co-stars: Laurent Terzieff Delphine Seyrig Paul Frankeur

TRACY SCOGGINS

1990 WATCHERS 2
Director: Thierry Notz
Co-stars: Marc Singer Tom Poster Jonathan Farwell

1990 THE GUMSHOE KID
Director: Joseph Manduke
Co-stars: Jay Underwood Vince Edwards Pamela Springstein

CATHY SCORSESE

1982 KING OF COMEDY
Director: Martin Scorsese
Co-stars: Robert De Niro Jerry Lewis Diahnne Abbott

CATHERINE SCORSESE
(Mother of Martin Scorsese)

1982 KING OF COMEDY
Director: Martin Scorsese
Co-stars: Robert De Niro Jerry Lewis Diahnne Abbott

1990 GOODFELLAS
Director: Martin Scorsese
Co-stars: Robert De Niro Ray Liotta Lorraine Bracco

1992 CAPE FEAR
Director: Martin Scorsese
Co-stars: Nick Nolte Robert De Niro Jessica Lange

DOMENICA SCORSESE

1992 CAPE FEAR
Director: Martin Scorsese
Co-stars: Nick Nolte Robert De Niro Jessica Lange

NICOLETTE SCORSESE

1993 BOXING HELENA
Director: Jennifer Chambers Lynch
Co-stars: Julian Sands Sherilyn Fenn Bill Paxton

1993 ASPEN EXTREME
Director: Patrick Hasburgh
Co-stars: Paul Gross Peter Berg Teri Polo

1994 GIRLS IN PRISON
Director: John McNaughton
Co-stars: Missy Crider Ione Skye Anne Heche

IZABELLA SCORUPCO

1995 GOLDENEYE
Director: Martin Campbell
Co-stars: Pierce Brosnan Robbie Coltrane Minnie Driver

ADRIENNE SCOTT

1953 FORCES' SWEETHEART
Director: MacLean Rogers
Co-stars: Hy Hazell Harry Secombe Michael Bentine

1953 FLANNELFOOT
Director: MacLean Rogers
Co-stars: Ronald Howard Mary Germaine Jack Watling

AMBER SCOTT

1991 HOOK
Director: Steven Spielberg
Co-stars: Dustin Hoffman Robin Williams Julia Roberts

ANN SCOTT

1983 THE PLOUGHMAN'S LUNCH
Director: Richard Eyre
Co-stars: Jonathan Pryce Tim Curry Frank Finlay

AVIS SCOTT

1950 WATERFRONT
Director: Michael Anderson
Co-stars: Robert Newton Richard Burton Susan Shaw

1951 TO HAVE AND TO HOLD
Director: Godfrey Grayson
Co-stars: Patrick Barr Eunice Gayson Robert Ayres

BRENDA SCOTT

1966 JOHNNY TIGER
Director: Paul Wendkos
Co-stars: Robert Taylor Geraldine Brooks Chad Everett

1966 JOURNEY TO SHILOH
Director: William Hale
Co-stars: James Caan Michael Sarrazin Harrison Ford

CONNIE SCOTT

1963 FLIPPER
Director: James Clark
Co-stars: Chuck Connors Luke Halpin Kathleen Maguire

DEBRA LEE SCOTT

1973 A SUMMER WITHOUT BOYS
Director: Jeannot Szwarc
Co-stars: Barbara Rush Kay Lenz Michael Moriarty

EVELYN SCOTT

1985 PEYTON PLACE: THE NEXT GENERATION
Director: Larry Elikann
Co-stars: Dorothy Malone Barbara Parkins Ed Nelson

HAZEL SCOTT

1943 I DOOD IT!
Director: Vincente Minnelli
Co-stars: Red Skelton Eleanor Powell John Hodiak

1943 THE HEAT'S ON
Director: Gregory Ratoff
Co-stars: Mae West Victor Moore William Gaxton

1945 RHAPSODY IN BLUE
Director: Irving Rapper
Co-stars: Robert Alda Joan Leslie Alexis Smith

JACQUELINE SCOTT

1958 MACABRE
Director: William Castle
Director: William Prince Jim Backus Ellen Corby

1971 DUEL
Director: Steven Spielberg
Co-stars: Dennis Weaver Eddie Firestone Lou Frizzell

1977 EMPIRE OF THE ANTS
Director: Bert Gordon
Co-stars: Joan Collins Robert Lansing Albert Salmi

JANETTE SCOTT *(Child) (Daughter Of Thora Hird)*

1949 NO PLACE FOR JENNIFER
Director: Henry Cass
Co-stars: Leo Genn Rosamund John Beatrice Campbell

1951 NO HIGHWAY
Director: Henry Koster
Co-stars: James Stewart Marlene Dietrich Glynis Johns

1951 GALLOPING MAJOR
Director: Henry Cornelius
Co-stars: Basil Radford Hugh Griffith Jimmy Hanley

1953 BACKGROUND
Director: Daniel Birt
Co-stars: Valerie Hobson Philip Friend Mandy Miller

1955 AS LONG AS THEY'RE HAPPY
Director: J. Lee-Thompson
Co-stars: Jack Buchanan Jean Carson Diana Dors

1955 HELEN OF TROY
Director: Robert Wise
Co-stars: Rosanna Podesta Jacques Sernas Brigitte Bardot

1955   **NOW AND FOREVER**
Director: Mario Zampi
Co-stars: Vernon Gray Jack Warner Pamela Brown

1957   **HAPPY IS THE BRIDE**
Director: Roy Boulting
Co-stars: Ian Carmichael Cecil Parker Joyce Grenfell

1957   **THE GOOD COMPANIONS**
Director: J. Lee-Thompson
Co-stars: Eric Portman Celia Johnson Rachel Roberts

1959   **THE LADY IS A SQUARE**
Director: Herbert Wilcox
Co-stars: Anna Neagle Frankie Vaughan Anthony Newley

1959   **THE DEVIL'S DISCIPLE**
Director: Guy Hamilton
Co-stars: Burt Lancaster Kirk Douglas Laurence Olivier

1960   **HIS AND HERS**
Director: Brian Desmond Hurst
Co-stars: Terry-Thomas Nicole Maurey Oliver Reed

1960   **SCHOOL FOR SCOUNDRELS**
Director: Robert Hamer
Co-stars: Terry-Thomas Alastair Sim Ian Carmichael

1961   **TWO AND TWO MAKE SIX**
Director: Freddie Francis
Co-stars: George Chakaris Jackie Lane

1961   **DOUBLE BUNK**
Director: C. Pennington-Richards
Co-stars: Ian Carmichael Liz Fraser Sid James

1962   **THE DAY OF THE TRIFFIDS**
Director: Steve Sekely
Co-stars: Howard Keel Nicole Maurey Kieron Moore

1962   **THE OLD DARK HOUSE**
Director: William Castle
Co-stars: Tom Poston Robert Morley Joyce Grenfell

1963   **THE SIEGE OF THE SAXONS**
Director: Nathan Juran
Co-stars: Ronald Lewis Ronald Howard John Laurie

1963   **PARANOIAC**
Director: Freddie Francis
Co-stars: Oliver Reed Alexander Davion Maurice Denham

1964   **THE BEAUTY JUNGLE**
Director: Val Guest
Co-stars: Ian Hendry Ronald Fraser Edmund Purdom

1965   **CRACK IN THE WORLD**
Director: Andrew Marton
Co-stars: Dana Andrews Kieron Moore Alexander Knox

JOAN SCOTT

1972   **THE LOVERS**
Director: Herbert Wise
Co-stars: Richard Beckinsale Paula Wilcox John Comer

1987   **THE SHUTTER FALLS**
Director: Peter Barber-Fleming
Co-stars: Anthony Higgins Emer Gillespie Stella Gonet

JUDITH SCOTT

1990   **NEWS HOUNDS**
Director: Les Blair
Co-stars: Adrian Edmondson Alison Steadman Linda Bassett

1991   **TELL ME THAT YOU LOVE ME**
Director: Bruce MacDonald
Co-stars: Sean Bean James Wilby Rowena Cooper

1994   **A LANDING IN THE SUN**
Director: Nicholas Renton
Co-stars: Robert Glenister Susan Fleetwood Roger Allam

KAY SCOTT

1947   **FEAR IN THE NIGHT**
Director: Maxwell Shane
Co-stars: Paul Kelly DeForrest Kelly Ann Doran

KIMBERLEY SCOTT

1989   **THE ABYSS**
Director: James Cameron
Co-stars: Mary Elizabeth Mastrantonio Ed Harris Michael Biehn

1990   **DOWNTOWN**
Director: Richard Benjamin
Co-stars: Anthony Edwards Forest Whitaker Penelope Ann Miller

1990   **FLATLINERS**
Director: Joel Schumacher
Co-stars: Kiefer Sutherland Julia Roberts Kevin Bacon

1994   **THE CLIENT**
Director: Joel Schumacher
Co-stars: Susan Sarandon Brad Renfro Tommy Lee Jones

KATHRYN LEIGH SCOTT

1986   **ASSASSINATION**
Director: Peter Hunt
Co-stars: Charles Bronson Jill Ireland Randy Brooks

1986   **MURROW**
Director: Jack Gold
Co-stars: Daniel J. Travanti Dabney Coleman David Suchet

1989   **VOICE OF THE HEART**
Director: Tony Wharmby
Co-stars: Lindsay Wagner Victoria Tennant James Brolin

LISABETH SCOTT

1945   **YOU CAME ALONG**
Director: John Farrow
Co-stars: Robert Cummings Don Defore Kim Hunter

1946   **THE STRANGE LOVE OF MARTHA IVERS**
Director: Lewis Milestone
Co-stars: Barbara Stanwyck Van Heflin

1947   **DESERT FURY**
Director: Lewis Allen
Co-stars: Burt Lancaster John Hodiak Wendell Corey

1947   **I WALK ALONE**
Director: Byron Haskin
Co-stars: Burt Lancaster Kirk Douglas Wendell Corey

1947   **VARIETY GIRL**
Director: George Marshall
Co-stars: Mary Hatcher Olga San Juan Glenn Tryon

1947   **DEAD RECKONING**
Director: John Cromwell
Co-stars: Humphrey Bogart Morris Carnovsky

1948   **THE PITFALL**
Director: Andre De Toth
Co-stars: Dick Powell Jane Wyatt Raymond Burr

1949   **EASY LIVING**
Director: Jacques Tourneur
Co-stars: Victor Mature Lucille Ball Sonny Tufts

1949   **TOO LATE FOR TEARS**
Director: Byron Haskin
Co-stars: Don Defore Arthur Kennedy Dan Duryea

1950   **PAID IN FULL**
Director: William Dieterle
Co-stars: Robert Cummings Diana Lynn Eve Arden

1950   **DARK CITY**
Director: William Dieterle
Co-stars: Charlton Heston Dean Jagger Jack Webb

1950 THE COMPANY SHE KEEPS
Director: John Cromwell
Co-stars: Dennis O'Keefe Jane Greer John Hoyt

1951 THE RACKET
Director: John Cromwell
Co-stars: Robert Mitchum Robert Ryan Ray Collins

1951 TWO OF A KIND
Director: Henry Levin
Co-stars: Edmond O'Brien Terry Moore Alexander Knox

1952 A STOLEN FACE
Director: Terence Fisher
Co-stars: Paul Henreid Andre Morrell Susan Stephens

1952 RED MOUNTAIN
Director: William Dieterle
Co-stars: Alan Ladd Arthur Kennedy John Ireland

1953 SCARED STIFF
Director: George Marshall
Co-stars: Dean Martin Jerry Lewis Carmen Miranda

1954 SILVER LODE
Director: Allan Dwan
Co-stars: John Payne Dan Duryea Dolores Moran

1954 BAD FOR EACH OTHER
Director: Irving Rapper
Co-stars: Charlton Heston Marjorie Rambeau

1956 THE WEAPON
Director: Val Guest
Co-stars: George Cole Herbert Marshall Jon Whiteley

1957 LOVING YOU
Director: Hal Kanter
Co-stars: Elvis Presley Wendell Corey Dolores Hart

1972 PULP
Director: Mike Hodges
Co-stars: Mickey Rooney Michael Caine Lionel Stander

MARGARETTA SCOTT

1934 DIRTY WORK
Director: Tom Walls
Co-stars: Ralph Lynn Gordon Harker Robertson Hare

1935 PEG OF OLD DRURY
Director: Herbert Wilcox
Co-stars: Anna Neagle Cedric Hardwicke Jack Hawkins

1936 THINGS TO COME
Director: William Menzies
Co-stars: Raymond Massey Cedric Hardwicke

1937 RETURN OF THE SCARLET PIMPERNEL
Director: Hans Schwarz
Co-stars: Barry K. Barnes James Mason

1937 ACTION FOR SLANDER
Director: Tim Whelan
Co-stars: Clive Brook Ann Todd Ronald Squire

1940 THE GIRL IN THE NEWS
Director: Carol Reed
Co-stars: Margaret Lockwood Barry K. Barnes Emlyn Williams

1941 ATLANTIC FERRY
Director: Walter Forde
Co-stars: Michael Redgrave Valerie Hobson Griffith Jones

1941 QUIET WEDDING
Director: Anthony Asquith
Co-stars: Margaret Lockwood Derek Farr Bernard Miles

1944 FANNY BY GASLIGHT
Director: Anthony Asquith
Co-stars: James Mason Phyllis Calvert Stewart Granger

1945 THE MAN FROM MOROCCO
Director: Max Greene
Co-stars: Anton Walbrook Mary Morris Peter Sinclair

1947 MRS FITZHERBERT
Director: Montgomery Tully
Co-stars: Peter Graves Joyce Howard Leslie Banks

1948 THE STORY OF SHIRLEY YORKE
Director: MacClean Rogers
Co-stars: Derek Farr Dinah Sheridan

1948 IDOL OF PARIS
Director: Leslie Arliss
Co-stars: Beryl Baxter Christine Norden Michael Rennie

1948 THE FIRST GENTLEMEN
Director: Cavalcanti
Co-stars: Cecil Parker Joan Hopkins Jean-Pierre Aumont

1948 COUNTERBLAST
Director: Paul Stein
Co-stars: Robert Beatty Mervyn Johns Nova Pilbeam

1949 LANDFALL
Director: Ken Annakin
Co-stars: Michael Dennison Patricia Plunkett Laurence Harvey

1952 WHERE'S CHARLEY ?
Director: David Butler
Co-stars: Ray Bolger Mary Germaine Robert Shackleton

1956 THE LAST MAN TO HANG ?
Director: Terence Fisher
Co-stars: Tom Conway Elizabeth Sellars Eunice Gayson

1956 TOWN ON TRIAL
Director: John Guillermin
Co-stars: John Mills Charles Coburn Barbara Bates

1957 THE SCAMP
Director: Wolf Rilla
Co-stars: Richard Attenborough Dorothy Alison Colin Petersen

1959 AN HONOURABLE MURDER
Director: Godfrey Grayson
Co-stars: Norman Wooland Lisa Daniely

1969 CRESCENDO
Director: Alan Gibson
Co-stars: Stefanie Powers James Olson Jane Lapotaire

1970 PERCY
Director: Ralph Thomas
Co-stars: Hywel Bennett Denholm Elliott Cyd Hayman

MARTHA SCOTT

Nominated For Best Actress In 1940 For Our Town

1940 OUR TOWN
Director: Sam Wood
Co-stars: Frank Craven William Holden Thomas Mitchell

1940 THE HOWARDS OF VIRGINIA
Director: Frank Lloyd
Co-stars: Cary Grant Cedric Hardwicke Paul Kelly

1941 ONE FOOT IN HEAVEN
Director: Irving Rapper
Co-stars: Fredric March Beulah Bondi Gene Lockhart

1941 THEY DARE NOT LOVE
Director: James Whale
Co-stars: George Brent Paul Lukas Lloyd Bridges

1941 CHEERS FOR MISS BISHOP
Director: Tay Garnett
Co-stars: William Gargan Edmund Gwenn Sidney Blackmer

1943 HI DIDDLE DIDDLE
Director: Andrew Stone
Co-stars: Adolphe Menjou Dennis O'Keefe Pola Negri

1943 WAR OF THE WILDCATS
Director: Albert Rogell
Co-stars: John Wayne Albert Dekker Dale Evans

1947 SO WELL REMEMBERED
Director: Edward Dmytryk
Co-stars: John Mills Trevor Howard Patricia Roc

1949 STRANGE BARGAIN
Director: Will Price
Co-stars: Jeffrey Lynn Henry Morgan Henry O'Neill

1951 WHEN I GROW UP
Director: Michael Kanin
Co-stars: Robert Preston Bobby Driscoll Charley Grapewin

1955 THE DESPERATE HOURS
Director: William Wyler
Co-stars: Fredric March Humphrey Bogart Gig Young

1956 THE TEN COMMANDMENTS
Director: Cecil B. DeMille
Co-stars: Charlton Heston John Derek Nina Foch

1957 SAYONARA
Director: Joshua Logan
Co-stars: Marlon Brando Miiko Taka Red Buttons

1958 BEN HUR
Director: William Wyler
Co-stars: Charlton Heston Stephen Boyd Hugh Griffith

1972 CHARLOTTE'S WEB (Voice)
Director: Iwao Takamoto
Co-stars: Debbie Reynolds Agnes Moorehead

1974 AIRPORT '75
Director: Jack Smight
Co-stars: Charlton Heston Karen Black Myrna Loy

1974 THURSDAY'S GAME
Director: Robert Moore
Co-stars: Gene Wilder Bob Newhart Ellen Burstyn

1977 THE TURNING POINT
Director: Herbert Ross
Co-stars: Anne Bancroft Shirley MacLaine Mikhail Baryshnikov

1983 ADAM
Director: Michael Tuchner
Co-stars: Daniel J. Travanti JoBeth Williams Richard Masur

1986 ADAM: HIS SONG CONTINUES
Director: Robert Markowitz
Co-stars: Daniel J. Travanti Belinda Montgomery Paul Regina

PATRICIA SCOTT

1935 KENTUCKY BLUE STREAK
Co-star: Edward Nugent

PIPPA SCOTT

1958 AUNTIE MAME
Director: Morton DaCosta
Co-stars: Rosalind Russell Forrest Tucker Peggy Cass

1968 PETULIA
Director: Richard Lester
Co-stars: Julie Christie George C.Scott Shirley Knight

1971 COLD TURKEY
Director: Norman Lear
Co-stars: Dick Van Dyke Tom Poston Edward Everett Horton

RACHEL SCOTT

1990 DAKOTA ROAD
Director: Nick Ward
Co-stars: Charlotte Chatton Jason Carter Amelda Brown

SANDRA SCOTT

1963 THE INCREDIBLE JOURNEY
Director: Fletcher Markle
Co-stars: Emile Genest Tommy Tweed John Drainie

KRISTIN SCOTT-THOMAS

1986 UNDER THE CHERRY MOON
Director: Prince
Co-stars: Prince Jerome Benton Steven Berkoff

1988 THE TENTH MAN
Director: Jack Gold
Co-stars: Anthony Hopkins Derek Jacobi Cyril Cusack

1988 A HANDFUL OF DUST
Director: Charles Sturridge
Co-stars: James Wilby Rupert Graves Alec Guinness

1989 FORCE MAJEURE
Director: Pierre Jolivet
Co-stars: Alan Bates Patrick Buel Francois Cluzet

**1990 SPYMAKER:
THE SECRET LIFE OF IAN FLEMING**
Director: Ferdinand Fairfax
Co-stars: Jason Connery Patricia Hodge

1990 FRAMED
Director: Dean Parisot
Co-stars: Jeff Goldblum Michael Lerner Todd Graff

1991 TITMUSS REGAINED
Director: Martyn Friend
Co-stars: David Threlfall Peter Capaldi Jane Booker

1992 BITTER MOON
Director: Roman Polanski
Co-stars: Hugh Grant Emmanuelle Seigner Peter Coyote

1992 AUTOBUS - AUX YEUX DU MONDE
Director: Eric Rochantay
Co-stars: Yvan Attal Charlotte Gainsbourg Marc Berman

1993 WEEP NO MORE MY LADY
Director: Michael Andrieu
Co-stars: Shelley Winters Daniel J. Travanti

1994 FOUR WEDDINGS AND A FUNERAL
Director: Mike Newell
Co-stars: Hugh Grant Andie MacDowell Simon Callow

1996 RICHARD III
Director: Ian McKellen
Co-stars: Ian McKellen Maggie Smith Nigel Hawthorne

1996 MISSION IMPOSSIBLE
Director: Brian De Palma
Co-stars: Tom Cruise Emmanuelle Beart Jon Voight

1997 THE ENGLISH PATIENT
Director: Anthony Minghella
Co-stars: Ralph Fiennes Juliette Binoche

SERENA SCOTT-THOMAS

1991 LET HIM HAVE IT
Director: Peter Medak
Co-stars: Christopher Eccleston Paul Reynolds Tom Bell

1992 HARNESSING PEACOCKS
Director: James Cellan Jones
Co-stars: Tom Beasley John Mills Renee Asherson

1992 BERMUDA GRACE
Director: Mark Sobel
Co-stars: William Sadler David Harewood Leslie Phillips

1994 SHERWOOD'S TRAVELS
Director: Steve Miner
Co-stars: Jamey Sheridan Edward Fox

ANDREA SCOTTI

1963 THE HERO OF BABYLON
Director: Siro Marcellini
Co-stars: Gordon Scott Moira Orfei Genevieve Grad

SHEILA SCOTT-WILKINSON

1973 THE NATIONAL HEALTH
Director: Jack Gold
Co-stars: Jim Dale Lynn Redgrave Donald Sinden

ANGELAR SCOULAR

1967 HERE WE GO ROUND THE MULBERRY BUSH
Director: Clive Donner
Co-stars: Barry Evans Judy Geeson Denholm Elliott

1969 ON HER MAJESTY'S SECRET SERVICE
Director: Peter Hunt
Co-stars: George Lazenby Diana Rigg Telly Savalas

1970 DOCTOR IN TROUBLE
Director: Ralph Thomas
Co-stars: Leslie Phillips Harry Secombe Robert Morley

1976 ADVENTURES OF A TAXI DRIVER
Director: Stanley Long
Co-stars: Barry Evans Judy Geeson Liz Fraser

SUSAN SEAFORTH

1963 CALIFORNIA
Director: James West
Co-stars: Jock Mahoney Faith Domergue Michael Pate

1965 BILLIE
Director: Don Weis
Co-stars: Patty Duke Jim Backus Jane Greer

OBA SEAGRAVE

1994 O MARY THIS LONDON
Director: Suri Krishnamma
Co-stars: Jason Barry Dylan Tighe Leslie Manville

JENNY SEAGROVE

1983 LOCAL HERO
Director: Bill Forsyth
Co-stars: Burt Lancaster Peter Riegert Denis Lawson

1983 SAVAGE ISLANDS
Director: Ferdinando Fairfax
Co-stars: Tommy Lee Jones Michael O'Keefe Grant Tilly

1984 MARK OF THE DEVIL
Director: Val Guest
Co-stars: Dirk Benedict George Sewell

1987 THE ADVENTURES OF SHERLOCK HOLMES: THE SIGN OF FOUR
Director: Peter Hammond
Co-stars: Jeremy Brett John Thaw

1988 A CHORUS OF DISAPPROVAL
Director: Michael Winner
Co-stars: Jeremy Irons Anthony Hopkins Prunella Scales

1990 THE GUARDIAN
Director: William Friedkin
Co-stars: Dwier Brown Carey Lowell Miguel Ferrer

1990 MAGIC MOMENTS
Director: Lawrence Gordon Clark
Co-stars: John Shea Paul Freeman Deborah Weston

1991 SOME OTHER SPRING
Director: Peter Duffell
Co-stars: Dinsdale Landen Jean-Claude Dauphin

BARBARA SEAGULL *(See Barbara Hershey)*

ELIZABETH SEAL

1954 RADIO CAB MURDER
Director: Vernon Sewell
Co-stars: Jimmy Hanley Lana Morris Sonia Holm

1956 TOWN ON TRIAL
Director: John Guillermin
Co-stars: John Mills Charles Coburn Barbara Bates

1960 CONE OF SILENCE
Director: Charles Frend
Co-stars: Michael Craig George Sanders Bernard Lee

1971 VAMPIRE CIRCUS
Director: Robert Young
Co-stars: Adrienne Corri Laurence Payne Lynne Frederick

ANN SEARS

1958 CAT AND MOUSE
Director: Paul Rotha
Co-stars: Lee Patterson Victor Maddern George Rose

DJANET SEARS

1994 APRIL ONE
Director: Murray Battle
Co-stars: Stephen Shellen David Strathairn

HEATHER SEARS

1956 DRY ROT
Director: Maurice Elvy
Co-stars: Ronald Shiner Brian Rix Sid James

1957 THE STORY OF ESTHER COSTELLO
Director: David Miller
Co-stars: Joan Crawford Rossano Brazzi Ron Randell

1958 ROOM AT THE TOP
Director: Jack Clayton
Co-stars: Laurence Harvey Simone Signoret Donald Wolfit

1959 THE SIEGE OF PINCHGUT
Director: Harry Watt
Co-stars: Aldo Ray Neil McCallum Victor Maddern

1960 SONS AND LOVERS
Director: Jack Cardiff
Co-stars: Dean Stockwell Trevor Howard Wendy Hiller

1962 PHANTOM OF THE OPERA
Director: Terence Fisher
Co-stars: Herbert Lom Edward De Souza Michael Gough

1963 SATURDAY NIGHT OUT
Director: Robert Hartford-Davis
Co-stars: Bernard Lee Francesca Annis Nigel Green

1964 THE BLACK TORMENT
Director: Robert Hartford-Davis
Co-stars: John Tirner Ann Lynn Peter Arne

LAURA SEARS *(Child)*

1917 SLUMBERLAND
Co-star: Thelma Salter

DOROTHY SEBASTIAN

1926 BLUEBEARD'S SEVEN WIVES
Director: Alfred Santell
Co-stars: Lois Wilson Ben Lyon Blanche Sweet

1928 OUR DANCING DAUGHTERS
Director: Harry Beaumont
Co-stars: Joan Crawford Johnny Mack Brown Anita Page

1929 THE SINGLE STANDARD
Director: John Robertson
Co-stars: Greta Garbo Nils Asther Johnny Mack Brown

1929   **SPITE MARRIAGE**
Director: Edward Sedgwick
Co-stars: Buster Keaton Leila Hyams Edward Earle

1929   **A WOMAN OF AFFAIRS**
Director: Clarence Brown
Co-stars: Greta Garbo Lewis Stone John Gilbert

1930   **OUR BLUSHING BRIDES**
Director: Harry Beaumont
Co-stars: Joan Crawford Robert Montgomery Anita Page

1930   **HIS FIRST COMMAND**
Co-star: William Boyd

1930   **HELL'S ISLAND**
Co-stars: Ralph Graves Jack Holt

1931   **THE BIG GAMBLE**
Co-star: Warner Oland

1931   **THE LIGHTNING FLYER**
Co-star: James Hall

1931   **THE DECEIVER**
Co-star: Lloyd Hughes

1933   **SHIP OF WANTED MEN**
Co-star: Leon Waycoff

TRACY SEBASTIAN

1993   **RUNNING COOL**
Director: Beverley Sebastian
Co-stars: Andrew Divoff Dedee Pfeiffer

JEAN SEBERG

1957   **SAINT JOAN**
Director: Otto Preminger
Co-stars: Richard Widmark Anton Walbrook John Gielgud

1957   **BONJOUR TRISTESSE**
Director: Otto Preminger
Co-stars: David Niven Deborah Kerr Juliette Greco

1959   **THE MOUSE THAT ROARED**
Director: Jack Arnold
Co-stars: Peter Sellers David Kossoff Leo McKern

1960   **BREATHLESS**
Director: Jean-Luc Godard
Co-stars: Jean-Luc Godard Jean-Paul Belmondo Daniel Boulanger

1960   **LET NO MAN WRITE MY EPITAPH**
Director: Phillip Leacock
Co-stars: James Darren Shelley Winters

1962   **IN THE FRENCH STYLE**
Director: Robert Parrish
Co-stars: Stanley Baker Philippe Fouquet

1964   **LILITH**
Director: Robert Rossen
Co-stars: Warren Beatty Peter Fonda Kim Hunter

1964   **BACKFIRE**
Director: Jean Becker
Co-stars: Jean-Paul Belmondo Gert Frobe

1966   **A FINE MADNESS**
Director: Irvin Kershner
Co-stars: Sean Connery Joanne Woodward Patrick O'Neal

1966   **MOMENT TO MOMENT**
Director: Mervyn LeRoy
Co-stars: Honor Blackman Sean Garrison Gregore Aslan

1966   **THE LOOTERS**

1968   **BIRDS COME TO DIE IN PERU**
Director: Romain Gary
Co-stars: Maurice Ronet Danielle Darrieux Pierre Brasseur

1969   **PENDULUM**
Director: George Schaeffer
Co-stars: George Peppard Richard Kiley Charles McGraw

1969   **PAINT YOUR WAGON**
Director: Joshua Logan
Co-stars: Clint Eastwood Lee Marvin Ray Walston

1970   **AIRPORT**
Director: George Seaton
Co-stars: Burt Lancaster Dean Martin Helen Hayes

1970   **MACHO CALLAHAN**
Director: Bernard Kowalski
Co-stars: David Janssen David Carradine James Booth

1971   **KILL!**
Director: Romain Gary
Co-stars: James Mason Stephen Boyd Curt Jurgens

MARGARET SEDDON

1933   **THE WORST WOMAN IN PARIS**
Director: Monta Bell
Co-stars: Benita Hume Adolphe Menjou Helen Chandler

1936   **THE BIG GAME**
Co-star: Guinn Williams

EDIE SEDGWICK

1973   **CIAO MANHATTAN**
Director: John Palmer
Co-stars: Wesley Hayes Isabel Jewell Geoffrey Briggs

KYRA SEDGWICK *(Married Kevin Bacon)*

1987   **THE MAN WHO BROKE 1000CHAINS**
Director: Daniel Man
Co-stars: Val Kilmer Charles Durning Sonia Braga

1988   **KANSAS**
Director: David Stevens
Co-stars: Andrew McCarthy Matt Dillon Leslie Hope

1989   **BORN ON THE FOURTH OF JULY**
Director: Oliver Stone
Co-stars: Tom Cruise Bryan Larkin Willem Dafoe

1990   **MR AND MRS BRIDGE**
Director: James Ivory
Co-stars: Paul Newman Joanne Woodward Blythe Danner

1991   **PYRATES**
Director: Noah Stern
Co-stars: Kevin Bacon Kristin Dattilo Buckley Norris

1991   **WOMEN AND MEN:**
        IN LOVE THERE ARE NO RULES
Director: Mike Figgis
Co-stars: Scott Glen Matt Dillon Ray Liotta

1992   **SINGLES**
Director: Cameron Crowe
Co-stars: Bridget Fonda Matt Dillon Campbell Scott

1993   **FAMILY PICTURES**
Director: Phillip Saville
Co-stars: Angelica Huston Sam Neill Dermot Mulroney

1993   **HEART AND SOULS**
Director: Ron Underwood
Co-stars: Robert Downey Jnr. Charles Grodin Alfre Woodard

1996   **SOMETHING TO TALK ABOUT**
Director: Lasse Hallstrom
Co-stars: Julia Roberts Robert Duvall Gena Rowlands

1996   **PHENOMENON**
Director: Jon Turteltaub
Co-stars: John Travolta Robert Duvall Forest Whitaker

1996 LOOSING CHASE
Director: Kevin Bacon
Co-stars: Helen Mirren Beau Bridges Kevin Bacon

MIRIAM SEEGAR

1929 SEVEN KEYS TO BALDPATE
Co-stars: Richard Dix Nella Walker Joseph Allen

1930 MOVIETONE FOLLIES OF 1930
Director: Ben Stoloff
Co-stars: El Brendel Marjorie White Frank Richardson

1930 THE DAWN TRAIL
Co-star: Buck Jones

BLOSSOM SEELEY

1933 BLOOD MONEY
Director: Rowland Brown
Co-stars: George Bancroft Frances Dee Judith Anderson

1933 BROADWAY THRU A KEYHOLE
Director: Lowell Sherman
Co-stars: Constance Cummings Russ Columbo Paul Kelly

WENDY SEELY

1988 STARLINGS
Director: David Wheatley
Co-stars: Michael Maloney Lynsey Baxter Jane Downs

DOROTHY SEESE (Child)

**1939 FIVE LITTLE PEPPERS AND
HOW THEY GREW**
Director: Charles Barton
Co-stars: Edith Fellows Clarence Kolb

1939 FIVE LITTLE PEPPERS AT HOME
Director: Charles Barton
Co-stars: Tommy Bond Ronald Sinclair Charles Peck

1939 OUT WEST WITH THE PEPPERS
Director: Charles Barton
Co-stars: Edith Fellows Jimmy Leake Clarence Kolb

1940 FIVE LITTLE PEPPERS IN TROUBLE
Director: Charles Barton
Co-stars: Edith Fellows Tommy Bond Ronald Sinclair

1943 LET'S HAVE FUN
Co-stars: Margaret Lindsay John Beal Bert Gordon

VIVIENNE SEGAL

1930 GOLDEN DAWN
Director: Ray Enright
Co-stars: Walter Woolf Noah Beery Lupino Lane

1930 BRIDE OF THE REGIMENT
Director: John Francis Dillon
Co-stars: Allan Prior Walter Pidgeon Louise Fazenda

1930 SONG OF THE WEST
Co-star: John Boles

1933 THE CAT AND THE FIDDLE
Director: William Howard
Co-stars: Jeanette MacDonald Ramon Navarro Frank Morgan

SOPHIE SEGALEN

1988 THE LEGEND OF THE HOLY DRINKER
Director: Ermanno Olmi
Co-stars: Rutger Hauer Anthony Quayle Sandrine Dumas

PAMELA SEGALL (Child)

1986 THE LEFTOVERS
Director: Paul Schneider
Co-stars: John Denver Cindy Williams George Wyner

1986 WILLY/MILLY
Director: Paul Schneider
Co-stars: Patty Duke John Glover Eric Gurry

1989 SAY ANYTHING
Director: Cameron Crowe
Co-stars: John Cusack Ione Skye Lili Taylor

1989 AFTER MIDNIGHT
Director: Ken Wheat
Co-stars: Jillian McWhirter Ramy Zade Marc McClure

ILEANA SEIDEL

1982 BEACH HOUSE
Director: John Gallagher
Co-stars: Kathy McNeil Richard Duggan John Cosola

SILVIA SEIDEL

1987 ANNA - THE MOVIE
Co-stars: Patrick Bacj Jon Peterson

EMMANUELLE SEIGNER
(Married Roman Polanski)

1988 FRANTIC
Director: Roman Polanski
Co-stars: Harrison Ford Betty Buckley Alexandra Stewart

1992 BITTER MOON
Director: Roman Polanski
Co-stars: Hugh Grant Kristin Scott-Thomas Peter Coyote

FRANCOISE SEIGNER

1969 L'ENFANT SAUVAGE
Director: Francois Truffaut
Co-stars: Francois Truffaut Jean-Pierre Cargol Jean Daste

MICHELE SEIPP

1988 THE BLUE IGUANA
Director: John Lafia
Co-stars: Dylan McDermott Jessica Harper Dean Stockwell

EDDA SEIPPEL

1976 DIE MARQUISE VON O
Director: Eric Rohmer
Co-stars: Edith Clever Bruno Ganz Peter Luhr

MARIAN SELDES

1958 CRIME AND PUNISHMENT U.S.A.
Director: Denis Sanders
Co-stars: George Hamilton Frank Silvera Mary Murphy

1965 THE GREATEST STORY EVER TOLD
Director: George Stevens
Co-stars: Max Von Sydow Dorothy McGuire Claude Rains

1977 FINGERS
Director: James Toback
Co-stars: Harvey Keitel Tisa Farrow Jim Brown

CONNIE SELLECCA

1979 SHE'S DRESSED TO KILL
Director: Gus Trikonis
Co-stars: Eleanor Parker John Rubinstein Jessica Walter

1983 HOTEL
Director: Jerry London
Co-stars: Bette Davis James Brolin Shirley Jones

1987 DOWNPAYMENT ON MURDER
Director: Waris Hussein
Co-stars: Ben Gazzara David Morse John Karlen

1987 THE LAST FLING
Director: Corey Allen
Co-stars: John Ritter Randee Heller Scott Bakula

1988	**MIRACLE LANDING**
Director:	Dick Lowry
Co-stars:	Wayne Rogers Nancy Kwan Ana Alicia

1989	**TURN BACK THE CLOCK**
Director:	Larry Elikann
Co-stars:	Wendy Kilbourne Dina Merril Gene Barry

1992	**A HOUSE OF SECRETS AND LIES**
Director:	Paul Schneider
Co-stars:	Kevin Dobson Grace Zabriskie

1993	**PASSPORT TO MURDER**
Director:	David Hemmings
Co-star:	Peter Bowles

1994	**A DANGEROUS AFFAIR**
Director:	Alan Metzger
Co-star:	Gregory Harrison

1995	**SHE LED TWO LIVES**
Director:	Bil Corcoran
Co-stars:	Perry King A. Martinez

ELIZABETH SELLERS

1949	**FLOODTIDE**
Director:	Frederick Wilson
Co-stars:	Gordon Jackson Rona Anderson Jack Lambert

1949	**MADELEINE**
Director:	David Lean
Co-stars:	Ann Todd Leslie Banks Ivor Barnard

1950	**GUILT IS MY SHADOW**
Director:	Roy Kellino
Co-stars:	Patrick Holt Peter Reynolds Lana Morris

1951	**CLOUDBURST**
Director:	Francis Searle
Co-stars:	Robert Preston Colin Tapley Harold Lang

1952	**THE GENTLE GUNMAN**
Director:	Basil Dearden
Co-stars:	John Mills Dirk Bogarde Barbara Mullen

1952	**HUNTED**
Director:	Charles Crichton
Co-stars:	Dirk Bogarde Jon Whiteley Kay Walsh

1952	**THE LONG MEMORY**
Director:	Robert Hamer
Co-stars:	John Mills John McCallum Geoffrey Keen

1953	**RECOIL**
Director:	John Gilling
Co-stars:	Kieron Moore Edward Underdown Ian Fleming

1954	**THREE CASES OF MURDER**
Director:	Wendy Toye
Co-stars:	Orson Welles Alan Badel John Gregson

1954	**FORBIDDEN CARGO**
Director:	Harold French
Co-stars:	Nigel Patrick Terence Morgan Jack Warner

1954	**DESIREE**
Director:	Henry Koster
Co-stars:	Jean Simmons Marlon Brando Merle Oberon

1954	**THE BAREFOOT CONTESSA**
Director:	Joseph Mankiewicz
Co-stars:	Humphrey Bogart Ava Gardner Edmond O'Brien

1955	**PRINCE OF PLAYERS**
Director:	Philip Dunne
Co-stars:	Richard Burton Maggie McNamara Raymond Massey

1956	**THE MAN IN THE SKY**
Director:	Charles Crichton
Co-stars:	Jack Hawkins Walter Fitzgerald Eddie Byrne

1956	**THE LAST MAN TO HANG ?**
Director:	Terence Fisher
Co-stars:	Tom Conway Eunice Gayson Anthony Newley

1957	**THE SHIRALEE**
Director:	Leslie Norman
Co-stars:	Peter Finch Dana Wilson Tessie O'Shea

1958	**LAW AND DISORDER**
Director:	Charles Crichton
Co-stars:	Michael Redgrave Robert Morley Lionel Jeffries

1960	**NEVER LET GO**
Director:	John Guillermin
Co-stars:	Richard Todd Peter Sellers Adam Faith

1960	**THE DAY THEY ROBBED THE BANK OF ENGLAND**
Director:	John Guillermin
Co-stars:	Peter O'Toole Hugh Griffith

1962	**THE WEBSTER BOY**
Director:	Don Chaffey
Co-stars:	Richard O'Sullivan John Cassavetes David Farrar

1964	**THE CHALK GARDEN**
Director:	Ronald Neame
Co-stars:	Edith Evans Deborah Kerr John Mills

1967	**THE MUMMY'S SHROUD**
Director:	John Gilling
Co-stars:	Andre Morell Catharine Lacey

1973	**THE HIRELING**
Director:	Alan Bridges
Co-stars:	Robert Shaw Sarah Miles Peter Egan

1987	**THE DUNROAMIN' RISING**
Director:	Moira Armstrong
Co-stars:	Russell Hunter Thorley Walters Hugh Lloyd

MARY SELLERS

1989	**LAMBADA**
Director:	Giandomenica Guri
Co-stars:	Andrew J. Forest Uya Negromonte

SABINA SELMAN

1960	**THE KING AVENGER**
Director:	Andre Hunebelle
Co-stars:	Jean Marias Jean Le Poulain Bourvil

ANNE SEMLER

1978	**MAGEE AND THE LADY**
Director:	Gene Levitt
Co-stars:	Tony LoBianco Sally Kellerman Rod Mullinar

SUSAN SENNETT

1974	**BIG BAD MAMA**
Director:	Steve Carver
Co-stars:	Angie Dickinson William Shatner Tom Skerritt

GIANNA SERA

1968	**THE GLASS SPHINX**
Director:	Fulvio Lucisano
Co-stars:	Robert Taylor Anita Ekberg Jack Stuart

SERENA

1978	**THE ABDUCTION OF LORELEI**
Director:	Richard Rank
Co-stars:	John Galt Charles Neal Jenny Gillian

1981	**AFTERNOON DELIGHTS**
Director:	Warren Evans
Co-stars:	Eric Edwards Merle Michaels Samantha Fox

KATHLEEN SERGAVA

1934 BEDSIDE
Co-stars: Warren William Jean Muir

1935 EIGHTEEN MINUTES
Co-stars: John Loder Benita Hume Hugh Wakefield

GLENNA SERGENT (Child)

1970 ALEX IN WONDERLAND
Director: Paul Mazursky
Co-stars: Donald Sutherland Jeanne Moreau Ellen Burstyn

ASSUMPTA SERNA

1986 MATADOR
Director: Pedro Almodovar
Co-stars: Antonio Banderas Carmen Maura Hacho Martinez

1989 WILD ORCHID
Director: Zalman King
Co-stars: Jacqueline Bissett Mickey Rourke Carre Otis

1990 I, THE WORST OF ALL
Director: Maria Luisa Bemberg
Co-stars: Dominique Sanda Hector Alterio

1992 THE FENCING MASTER
Director: Pedro Olea
Co-stars: Omero Antonutti Joaquim De Almeida Miguel Rellan

1992 CHAIN OF DESIRE
Director: Temistocles Lopez
Co-stars: Linda Fiorentino Elias Koteas Grace Zabriskie

1993 NOSTRADAMUS
Director: Roger Christian
Co-stars: Tcheky Karyo Amanda Plummer Julia Ormond

1993 SHARPE'S RIFLES
Director: Tom Clegg
Co-stars: Sean Bean Brian Cox David Troughton

1993 SHARPE'S EAGLES
Director: Tom Clegg
Co-stars: Sean Bean Brian Cox Daragh O'Malley

1994 DAY OF RECKONING
Director: Brian Grant
Co-star: Fred Dryer

JULIETTA SERRANO

**1988 WOMEN ON THE VERGE
OF A NERVOUS BREAKDWON**
Director: Pedro Almodovar
Co-stars: Carmen Maura Antonio Banderas

1989 TIE ME UP! TIE ME DOWN!
Director: Pedro Almodovar
Co-stars: Antonio Banderas Victoria Abril

1991 MATADOR
Director: Pedro Almodovar
Co-stars: Antonio Banderas Assumpta Serna

ADRIENNE SERVATIE

1958 MON ONCLE
Director: Jacques Tati
Co-stars: Jacques Tati Jean-Pierre Zola Alain Becourt

SABINA SESSELMAN

1961 INFORMATION RECEIVED
Director: Robert Lynn
Co-stars: William Sylvester Hermione Baddeley Edward Underdown

1962 THE DOOR WITH SEVEN LOCKS
Director: Alfred Vohrer
Co-stars: Eddie Arent Klaus Kinski Heinz Drache

ALMIRA SESSIONS

1943 THE HEAT'S ON
Director: Gregory Ratoff
Co-stars: Mae West Victor Moore William Gaxton

1946 THE DIARY OF A CHAMBERMAID
Director: Jean Renoir
Co-stars: Paulette Goddard Burgess Meredith Hurd Hatfield

ROSHAN SETH

1985 MY BEAUTIFUL LAUNDERETTE
Director: Stephen Frears
Co-stars: Daniel Day-Lewis Saeed Jaffrey Gordon Warnecke

CAROLYN SETMORE

1994 REFORM SCHOOL GIRL
Director: Jonathan Kaplan
Co-stars: Aimee Graham Matt LeBlanc

JOAN SEVERANCE

1989 SEE NO EVIL - HEAR NO EVIL
Director: Arthur Hiller
Co-stars: Richard Pryor Gene Wilder Kevin Spacey

1989 NO HOLDS BARRED
Director: Thomas Wright
Co-stars: Hulk Hogan Kurt Fuller Tiny Lister

1990 BIRD ON A WIRE
Director: John Badham
Co-stars: Mel Gibson Goldie Hawn David Carradine

1992 LAKE CONSEQUENCE
Director: Rafael Eisenman
Co-stars: Billy Zane May Karasun Whip Hubley

1992 THE RUNESTONE
Director: Willard Carroll
Co-stars: Peter Riegert William Hickey Lawrence Tierney

1994 DANGEROUS INDISCRETION
Director: Richard Kletter
Co-stars: C. Thomas Howell Malcolm McDowell

1994 HARD EVIDENCE
Director: Michael Kennedy
Co-stars: Gregory Harrison Cali Timmons

1995 BLACK SCORPION

1996 BLACK SCORPION: GROUND ZERO
Director: Jonathan Winfrey

SUSAN SEVEREIDI

1988 HOWLING IV: THE ORIGINAL NIGHTMARE
Director: John Hough
Co-stars: Romy Windsor Anthony Hamilton

CHLOE SEVIGNY

1996 KIDS
Director: Larry Clark
Co-stars: Leo Fitzpatrick Justin Pierce Sarah Henderson

CARMEN SEVILLA

1958 THE SPANISH AFFAIR
Director: Don Siegel
Co-stars: Richard Kiley Jose Guardiola

BILLY SEWARD

1934 AMONG THE MISSING
Co-stars: Richard Cromwell Henrietta Crosman Paul Hurst

1935 LAW BEYOND THE RANGE
Co-star: Tim McCoy

1935 RIDING WILD
Co-star: Tim McCoy

ATHENE SEYLER

1932 TELL ME TONIGHT
Director: Anatole Litvak
Co-stars: Jan Kiepura Sonnie Hale Magda Schneider

1934 BLOSSOM TIME
Director: Paul Stein
Co-stars: Richard Tauber Jane Baxter Carl Esmond

1935 DRAKE OF ENGLAND
Director: Arthur Woods
Co-stars: Matheson Lang Jane Baxter Donald Wolfit

1935 MOSCOW NIGHTS
Director: Anthony Asquith
Co-stars: Laurence Olivier Penelope Dudley Ward

1935 SCROOGE
Director: Henry Edwards
Co-stars: Seymour Hicks Donald Calthrop Barbara Everest

1936 SENSATION
Director: Brian Desmond Hurst
Co-stars: John Lodge Diana Churchill Francis Lister

1936 IT'S LOVE AGAIN
Director: Victor Saville
Co-stars: Jessie Matthews Robert Young Sonnie Hale

1937 THE LILAC DOMINO
Director: Fred Zelnik
Co-stars: June Knight Michael Bartlett Fred Emney

1937 THE MILL ON THE FLOSS
Director: Tim Whelan
Co-stars: Geraldine Fitzgerald Frank Lawton James Mason

1937 NON-STOP NEW YORK
Director: Robert Stevenson
Co-stars: John Loder Anna Lee Frank Cellier

1938 THE WARE CASE
Director: Robert Stevenson
Co-stars: Clive Brook Jane Baxter Barry K. Barnes

1938 SAILING ALONG
Director: Sonnie Hale
Co-stars: Jessie Matthews Roland Young Barry Mackay

1939 THE SAINT IN LONDON
Director: John Paddy Carstairs
Co-stars: George Sanders Sally Gray David Burns

1940 TILLY OF BLOOMSBURY
Director: Lesley Hiscott
Co-stars: Sidney Howard Jean Gillie Michael Wilding

1941 QUIET WEDDING
Director: Anthony Asquith
Co-stars: Margaret Lockwood Derek Farr Peggy Ashcroft

1943 DEAR OCTOPUS
Director: Harold French
Co-stars: Margaret Lockwood Michael Wilding Celia Johnson

1948 THE FIRST GENTLEMAN
Director: Cavalcanti
Co-stars: Cecil Parker Jean-Pierre Aumont Joan Hopkins

1948 THE QUEEN OF SPADES
Director: Thorold Dickinson
Co-stars: Edith Evans Anton Walbrook Ronald Howard

1951 YOUNG WIVES' TALE
Director: Henry Cass
Co-stars: Joan Greenwood Nigel Patrick Derek Farr

1952 TREASURE HUNT
Director: John Paddy Carstairs
Co-stars: Jimmy Edwards Martita Hunt Naunton Wayne

1952 SECRET PEOPLE
Director: Thorold Dickinson
Co-stars: Valentina Cortesa Serge Reggiani Audrey Hepburn

1952 MADE IN HEAVEN
Director: John Paddy Carstairs
Co-stars: David Tomlinson Petula Clark Sonja Zieman

1952 THE BEGGAR'S OPERA
Director: Peter Brook
Co-stars: Laurence Olivier Dorothy Tutin Stanley Holloway

1953 THE WEAK AND THE WICKED
Director: J. Lee-Thompson
Co-stars: Glynis Johns John Gregson Diana Dors

1954 FOR BETTER FOR WORSE
Director: J. Lee-Thompson
Co-stars: Dirk Bogarde Susan Stephen Dennis Price

1955 AS LONG AS THEY'RE HAPPY
Director: J. Lee-Thompson
Co-stars: Jack Buchanan Jean Carson Diana Dors

1956 YIELD TO THE NIGHT
Director: J. Lee-Thompson
Co-stars: Diana Dors Yvonne Mitchell Michael Craig

1957 NIGHT OF THE DEMON
Director: Jacques Tourneur
Co-stars: Dana Andrews Peggy Cummins Brian Wilde

1957 HOW TO MURDER A RICH UNCLE
Director: Nigel Patrick
Co-stars: Nigel Patrick Charles Coburn Katie Johnson

1957 HAPPY IS THE BRIDE
Director: Roy Boulting
Co-stars: Ian Carmichael Janette Scott Cecil Parker

1957 DOCTOR AT LARGE
Director: Ralph Thomas
Co-stars: Dirk Bogarde Muriel Pavlow Donald Sinden

1957 CAMPBELL'S KINGDOM
Director: Ralph Thomas
Co-stars: Dirk Bogarde Michael Craig Barbara Murray

1958 THE INN OF THE SIXTH HAPPINESS
Director: Mark Robson
Co-stars: Ingrid Bergman Curt Jurgens Robert Donat

1958 A TALE OF TWO CITIES
Director: Ralph Thomas
Co-stars: Dirk Bogarde Dorothy Tutin Christopher Lee

1960 MAKE MINE MINK
Director: Robert Asher
Co-stars: Terry-Thomas Hattie Jacques Billie Whitelaw

1960 TWO AND TWO MAKE SIX
Director: Freddie Francis
Co-stars: George Chakiris Janette Scott Alfred Lynch

1960 A FRENCH MISTRESS
Director: Roy Boulting
Co-stars: Agnes Laurent Cecil Parker Ian Bannen

1961 FRANCIS OF ASSISI
Director: Michael Curtiz
Co-stars: Bradford Dillman Doloris Hart Stuart Whitman

1962 THE GIRL ON THE BOAT
Director: Henry Kaplan
Co-stars: Norman Wisdom Richard Briers Millicent Martin

1962 I THANK A FOOL
Director: Robert Stevens
Co-stars: Peter Finch Susan Hayward Diane Cilento

1962 SATAN NEVER SLEEPS
Director: Leo McCarey
Co-stars: Clifton Webb William Holden France Nuyen

1963 NURSE OF WHEELS
Director: Gerald Thomas
Co-stars: Juliette Mills Ronald Lewis Joan Sims

ANNE SEYMOUR

1949 ALL THE KING'S MEN
Director: Robert Rossen
Co-stars: Broderick Crawford Mercedes McCambridge John Ireland

1958 DESIRE UNDER THE ELMS
Director: Delbert Mann
Co-stars: Sophia Loren Burl Ives Anthony Perkins

1960 THE SUBTERRANEANS
Director: Ranald MacDougall
Co-stars: George Peppard Leslie Caron Roddy McDowell

1960 ALL THE FINE YOUNG CANNIBALS
Director: Michael Anderson
Co-stars: Natalie Wood Robert Wagner Pearl Bailey

1961 MISTY
Director: James Clark
Co-stars: Arthur O'Connell David Ladd Pam Smith

1964 STAGE TO THUNDER ROCK
Director: William Claxton
Co-stars: Barry Sullivan Marilyn Maxwell Allan Jones

1967 FITZWILLY
Director: Delbert Mann
Co-stars: Dick Van Dyke Edith Evans Barbara Feldon

1976 DAWN: PORTRAIT OF A RUNAWAY TEENAGER
Director: Randal Kleiser
Co-stars: Eve Plumb Bo Hopkins Lynn Carlin

1980 ANGEL ON MY SHOULDER
Director: John Berry
Co-stars: Peter Strauss Barbara Hershey Richard Kiley

1984 FUTURE COP
Director: Jud Taylor
Co-stars: Tim Thomerson Ernest Borgnine Helen Hunt

1985 TRANCERS
Director: Charles Band
Co-stars: Tim Thomerson Helen Hunt Biff Manard

1986 THE LEFTOVERS
Director: Paul Schneider
Co-stars: John Denver Cindy Williams Pamela Segall

CAROLYN SEYMOUR

1971 UNMAN, WITTERING AND ZIGO
Director: John MacKenzie
Co-stars: David Hemmings Douglas Wilmer Michael Kitchen

1971 GUMSHOE
Director: Stephen Frears
Co-stars: Albert Finney Billie Whitelaw Frank Finlay

1972 THE RULING CLASS
Director: Peter Medak
Co-stars: Peter O'Toole Alastair Sim Coral Browne

1972 STEPTOE AND SON
Director: Cliff Owen
Co-stars: Harry H. Corbett Wilfred Brambell Victor Maddern

1973 YELLOW DOG
Director: Terence Donovan
Co-stars: Robert Hardy Jiro Tamiya Joseph O'Connor

1975 THE SURVIVORS
Director: Pennant Roberts
Co-stars: Lucy Fleming Peter Copley

1977 THE ASSIGNMENT
Director: George Bisset
Co-stars: Christopher Plummer Fernando Rey Thomas Hellberg

1979 THE BITCH
Director: Gerry O'Hara
Co-stars: Joan Collins Kenneth Haigh Ian Hendry

1981 MISTRESS OF PARADISE
Director: Peter Medak
Co-stars: Genevieve Bujold Chad Everett Anthony Andrews

1983 DEATH RIDE TO OSAKA
Director: Jonathan Kaplan
Co-stars: Jennifer Jason Leigh Ann Jillian Mako

1983 THE LAST NINJA
Director: William Graham
Co-stars: Michael Beck Nancy Kwan Mako

CLARINE SEYMOUR

1919 TRUE HEART SUSIE
Director: D.W. Griffith
Co-stars: Lillian Gish Robert Harron Loyola O'Connor

JANE SEYMOUR

1972 YOUNG WINSTON
Director: Richard Attenborough
Co-stars: Simon Ward Robert Shaw Anne Bancroft

1973 LIVE AND LET DIE
Director: Guy Hamilton
Co-stars: Roger Moore Yaphet Kotto David Hedison

1976 THE FOUR FEATHERS
Director: Don Sharp
Co-stars: Beau Bridges Robert Powell Simon Ward

1977 KILLER ON BOARD
Director: Philip Leacock
Co-stars: Claude Akins Beatrice Straight Patty Duke Astin

1977 SINBAD AND THE EYE OF THE TIGER
Director: Sam Wanamaker
Co-stars: Patrick Wayne Taryn Power

1978 BATTLESTAR: GALACTICA
Director: Richard Colla
Co-stars: Lorne Greene Ray Milland Lew Ayres

1980 OH HEAVENLY DOG
Director: Joe Camp
Co-stars: Chevy Chase Omar Sharif Robert Morley

1980 SOMEWHERE IN TIME
Director: Jeannot Szwarc
Co-stars: Christopher Reeve Christopher Plummer Teresa Wright

1982 THE SCARLET PIMPERNEL
Director: Clive Donner
Co-stars: Anthony Andrews Ian McKellen James Villiers

1983 THE HAUNTING PASSION
Director: John Korty
Co-stars: Gerald McRaney Millie Perkins Paul Rossilli

1984 DARK MIRROR
Director: Richard Lng
Co-stars: Stephen Collins Vincent Gardenia Hank Brandt

1984 LASSITER
Director: Roger Young
Co-stars: Tom Selleck Lauren Hutton Bob Hoskins

1985 THE SUN ALSO RISES
Director: James Goldstone
Co-stars: Hart Bochner Robert Carradine Leonard Nimoy

1986 THE ONLY WAY
Director: Bent Christensen
Co-stars: Ove Sprogoe Martin Potter Ebbe Rude

1988 ONASSIS: THE RICHEST MAN IN THE WORLD
Director: Waris Hussein
Co-stars: Raul Julia Anthony Quinn

1988 JACK THE RIPPER
Director: David Wickes
Co-stars: Michael Caine Armand Assante Ray McAnally

1992 SUNSTROKE
Director: James Keach
Co-stars: Stephen Meadows Don Ameche Ray Wise

1993 PRAYING MANTIS
Director: James Keach
Co-stars: Barry Bostwick Frances Fisher Ann Schedeen

1993 QUEST FOR JUSTICE
Director: James Keach
Co-stars: Richard Kiley D.W. Moffett

JANE SEYMOUR (U.S.A.)

1941 TOM, DICK AND HARRY
Director: Garson Kanin
Co-stars: Ginger Rogers Burgess Meredith George Murphy

1941 REMEMBER THE DAY
Director: Henry King
Co-stars: Claudette Colbert John Payne Shepperd Strudwick

LYNN SEYMOUR

1987 DANCERS
Director: Herbert Ross
Co-stars: Mikhail Baryshnikov Leslie Browne Alessandra Ferri

DELPHINE SEYRIG

1961 LAST YEAR IN MARIENBAD
Director: Alain Resnais
Co-stars: Giorgio Albertazzi Sacha Pitoeff

1963 MURIEL
Director: Alain Resnais
Co-stars: Jean-Pierre Kerien Nita Klein Claude Sainval

1967 ACCIDENT
Director: Joseph Losey
Co-stars: Dirk Bogarde Stanley Baker Jacqueline Sassard

1968 THE MILKY WAY
Director: Luis Bunuel
Co-stars: Laurent Terzieff Paul Frankeur Alain Cuny

1968 STOLEN KISSES
Director: Francois Truffaut
Co-stars: Jean-Pierre Leaud Michel Lonsdale Claude Jade

1971 DAUGHTERS OF DARKNESS
Director: Harry Kumel
Co-stars: Daniele Ouimet John Karlen Andrea Rau

1972 THE DISCREET CHARM OF THE BOURGEOISIE
Director: Luis Bunuel
Co-stars: Fernando Rey Stephane Audran

1973 THE DAY OF THE JACKAL
Director: Fred Zinnemann
Co-stars: Edward Fox Alan Badel Tony Britton

1973 A DOLL'S HOUSE
Director: Joseph Losey
Co-stars: Jane Fonda David Warner Trevor Howard

1974 THE BLACK WINDMILL
Director: Don Siegel
Co-stars: Michael Caine Donald Pleasence Clive Revill

VICTORIA SHALET

1989 TESTIMONY OF A CHILD
Director: Peter Smith
Co-stars: Jill Baker John Bowe Paul Copley

1992 SHINING THROUGH
Director: David Sheltzer
Co-stars: Melanie Griffith Michael Douglas Joely Richardson

SHEILA SHAND-GIBBS

1952 THE GREAT GAME
Director: Maurice Elvy
Co-stars: James Hayter Diana Dors Glyn Huston

1958 A LADY MISLAID
Director: David MacDonald
Co-stars: Phyllis Calvert Alan White Thorley Walters

1966 THE SPECIALIST
Director: James Hill
Co-stars: Bernard Miles Colin Ellis Jimmy Gardner

KITTY SHANE

1981 AMERICAN PIE
Director: Jeffrey Fairbanks
Co-stars: Arcadia Lake Lysa Thatcher

LINDA SHANE

1983 SCREWBALLS
Director: Rafal Zielinski
Co-stars: Peter Keleghan Kent Deuters Jason Warren

SARA SHANE

1954 MAGNIFICENT OBSESSION
Director: Douglas Sirk
Co-stars: Jane Wyman Rock Hudson Barbara Rush

1959 TARZAN'S GREATEST ADVENTURE
Director: John Guillermin
Co-stars: Gordon Scott Anthony Quayle Sean Connery

AMELIA SHANKLEY

1985 DREAMCHILD
Director: Gavin Miller
Co-stars: Coral Browne Peter Gallagher Jane Asher

EFFIE SHANNON

1925 SALLY OF THE SAWDUST
Director: D.W. Griffith
Co-stars: W.C. Fields Carol Dempster Alfred Lunt

PEGGY SHANNON

1931 THE ROAD TO RENO
Co-star: Irving Pichel

1931 THE SECRET CALL
Co-star: Richard Arlen

1932 SOCIETY GIRL
Director: Sidney Lanfield
Co-stars: James Dunn Spencer Tracy Marjorie Gateson

1932 PAINTED WOMAN
Director: John Blystone
Co-stars: Spencer Tracy Irving Pichel Raul Roulien

1932 THIS RECKLESS AGE
Director: Frank Tuttle
Co-stars: Charles Rogers Charles Ruggles Frances Dee

1933 TURN BACK THE CLOCK
Director: Edgar Selwyn
Co-stars: Lee Tracy Otto Kruger Mae Clarke

1934 FURY OF THE JUNGLE
Co-star: Harold Huber

1935 THE NIGHT LIFE OF THE GODS
Director: Lowell Sherman
Co-stars: Alan Mowbray Florine McKinney Richard Carle

1939 FIXER DUGGAN
Co-star: Lee Tracy

ANASTASIA SHARP

1993 GO FISH
Director: Rose Troche
Co-stars: V.S. Brodie Guinevere Turner Migdalia Melendez

LESLEY SHARP

1986 RITA, SUE AND BOB TOO
Director: Alan Clarke
Co-stars: Michelle Holmes Siobhan Finneran George Costigan

1987 ROAD
Director: Alan Clarke
Co-stars: Jane Horrocks Neil Dudgeon Mossie Smith

1989 THE RACHEL PAPERS
Director: Damian Harris
Co-stars: Dexter Fletcher Ione Skye James Spader

1990 NIGHT VOICE
Director: Richard Spence
Co-stars: Alexei Sayle Kevin Whately Ruth Sheen

1991 CLOSE MY EYES
Director: Stephen Poliakoff
Co-stars: Saskia Reeves Clive Owen Alan Rickman

1993 NAKED
Director: Mike Leigh
Co-stars: David Thewlis Katrin Cartlidge Claire Skinner

1994 PRIEST
Director: Antonia Bird
Co-stars: Linus Roache Tom Wilkinson

SALLY SHARP

1981 THE END OF AUGUST
Director: Bob Graham
Co-stars: Lilia Skala Kathleen Widdows Paul Shenar

VANESSA SHARP

1986 NUTCRACKER - THE MOTION PICTURE
Director: Carroll Ballard
Co-stars: Hugh Bigny Patricia Barker Wade Walthall

ANNE SHARPE

1958 BLIND SPOT
Director: Peter Maxwell
Co-stars: Robert MacKenzie Michael Caine John Le Mesurier

CORNELIA SHARPE

1973 SERPICO
Director: Sidney Lumet
Co-stars: Al Pacino John Randolph Jack Kehoe

1974 THE REINCARNATION OF PETER PROUD
Director: J. Lee-Thompson
Co-stars: Michael Sarrazin Jennifer O'Neill

1974 OPEN SEASON
Director: Peter Collinson
Co-stars: Peter Fonda William Holden John Philip Law

1976 THE NEXT MAN
Director: Richard Sarafian
Co-stars: Sean Connery Albert Paulsen Adolfo Celi

1981 VENOM
Director: Piers Haggard
Co-stars: Sterling Hayden Klaus Kinski Oliver Reed

EDITH SHARPE

1938 OLD MOTHER RILEY M.P.
Director: Oswald Mitchell
Co-stars: Arthur Lucan Kitty McShane Barbara Everest

1957 HAPPY IS THE BRIDE
Director: Roy Boulting
Co-stars: Ian Carmichael Janette Scott Cecil Parker

1960 A FRENCH MISTRESS
Director: Roy Boulting
Co-stars: Agnes Laurent James Robertson Justice Ian Bannen

1961 CASH ON DEMAND
Director: Quentin Lawrence
Co-stars: Peter Cushing Andre Morell Richard Vernon

KAREN SHARPE

1953 MEXICAN MANHUNT
Director: Rex Bailey
Co-stars: George Brent Hillary Brooke Marjorie Lord

1955 THE MAN WITH THE GUN
Director: Richard Wilson
Co-stars: Robert Mitchum Jan Sterling Henry Hull

1964 THE DISORDERLY ORDERLY
Director: Frank Tashlin
Co-stars: Jerry Lewis Glenda Farrell Susan Oliver

MELANIE SHATNER
(Daughter Of William Shatner)

1989 STAR TREK V: THE FINAL FRONTIER
Director: William Shatner
Co-stars: William Shatner Leonard Nimoy Deforest Kelley

1996 ALIEN WITHIN
Co-stars: Roddy McDowall Alex Hyde-White

SHARI SHATTUCK

1994 DEADLY GROUND
Director: Steven Seagal
Co-stars: Michael Caine Joan Chen Steven Seagal

HELEN SHAVER

1977 OUTRAGEOUS!
Director: Richard Benner
Co-stars: Craig Russell Hollis McLaren Richard Easley

1977 ALIEN ENCOUNTERS
Director: Ed Hunt
Co-stars: Robert Vaughn Christopher Lee Kate Parr

1978 HIGH-BALLIN'
Director: Peter Carter
Co-stars: Peter Fonda Jerry Reed Chris Wiggins

1978 IN PRAISE OF OLDER WOMEN
Director: George Kaczender
Co-stars: Tom Berenger Karen Black Susan Strasberg

1979 THE AMITYVILLE HORROR
Director: Stuart Rosenberg
Co-stars: James Brolin Margot Kidder Rod Steiger

1982 HARRY TRACY, DEAD OR ALIVE
Director: William Graham
Co-stars: Bruce Dern Gordon Lightfoot

1983 THE OSTERMAN WEEKEND
Director: Sam Peckinpah
Co-stars: Rutger Hauer John Hurt Burt Lancaster

1984 BEST DEFENSE
Director: Willard Huyck
Co-stars: Dudley Moore Eddie Murphy Kate Capshaw

1985	**DESERT HEARTS**	
Director:	Donna Deitch	
Co-stars:	Patricia Charbonneau Audra Lindley Andra Akers	

1985 DESERT HEARTS
Director: Donna Deitch
Co-stars: Patricia Charbonneau Audra Lindley Andra Akers

1985 THE PARK IS MINE
Director: Steven Hillard Stern
Co-stars: Tommy Lee Jones Yaphet Kotto Lawrence Dane

1986 THE COLOR OF MONEY
Director: Martin Scorsese
Co-stars: Paul Newman Tom Cruise Mary Elizabeth Mastrantonio

1987 THE BELIEVERS
Director: John Schlesinger
Co-stars: Martin Sheen Robert Loggia Harley Cross

1988 THE LAND BEFORE TIME *(Voice)*
Director: Don Bluth
Co-stars: Gabriel Damon Bill Erwin Pat Hingle

1988 TREE OF HANDS
Director: Giles Foster
Co-stars: Lauren Bacall Peter Firth Paul McGann

1989 B.L. STRYKER
Director: William Fraker
Co-stars: Burt Reynolds Rita Moreno Ossie Davis

1990 BETHUNE THE MAKING OF A HERO
Director: Phillip Borsos
Co-stars: Donald Sutherland Helen Mirren Anouk Aimee

1992 FATAL MEMORIES
Director: Daryl Duke
Co-stars: Shelley Long Dean Stockwell

1992 NIGHT HUNT
Director: Bill Corcoran
Co-stars: Stefanie Powers Kathleen Robertson

1992 ZEBRAHEAD
Director: Anthony Drazan
Co-stars: Michael Rappaport Ray Sharkey DeShonn Castle

1992 THAT NIGHT
Director: Craig Bolotin
Co-stars: C. Thomas Howell Eliza Dushku Juliette Lewis

1993 MURDER SO SWEET
Director: Larry Peerce
Co-stars: Harry Hamlin K.T. Oslin Terence Knox

1993 MORNING GLORY
Director: Steven Stern
Co-stars: Christopher Reeve Deborah Raffin Nina Foch

1994 ROADRACERS
Director: Robert Rodriguez
Co-stars: David Arquette Jason Wiles

1994 TRAPPED AND DECEIVED
Director: Robert Iscove
Co-stars: Jennie Garth Jill Eikenberry Paul Sorvino

ALONNA SHAW

1991 DOUBLE IMPACT
Director: Sheldon Lettich
Co-stars: Jean-Claude Van Damme Geoffrey Lewis Alan Scarfe

ANABEL SHAW

1944 HERE COME THE WAVES
Director: Mark Sandrich
Co-stars: Bing Crosby Betty Hutton Sonny Tufts

1946 SHOCK
Director: Alfred Werker
Co-stars: Vincent Price Lynn Bari Frank Latimore

1946 STRANGE TRIANGLE
Co-stars: Preston Foster Signe Hasso John Shepperd

1949 GUN CRAZY
Director: Joseph Lewis
Co-stars: John Dall Peggy Cummins Morris Carnovsky

FIONA SHAW

1989 MY LEFT FOOT
Director: Jim Sheridan
Co-stars: Daniel Day Lewis Ray McAnally Brenda Fricker

1989 MOUNTAINS OF THE MOON
Director: Bob Rafelson
Co-stars: Patrick Bergin Iain Glen Richard E. Grant

1990 THREE MEN AND A LITTLE LADY
Director: Emile Ardolino
Co-stars: Tom Selleck Ted Danson

1991 FOR THE GREATER GOOD
Director: Danny Boyle
Co-stars: Martin Shaw Roy Dotrice Joanna Pearce

1991 LONDON KILLS ME
Director: Hanif Kureishi
Co-stars: Justin Chadwick Steven MacKintosh Brad Dourif

1992 MARIA'S CHILD
Director: Malcolm McKay
Co-stars: Yolanda Vasquez David O'Hara Alec McCowen

1993 UNDERCOVER BLUES
Director: Herbert Ross
Co-stars: Kathleen Turner Dennis Quaid Stanley Tucci

1993 SUPER MARIO BROTHERS
Director: Rocky Morton
Co-stars: Bob Hoskins John Leguizamo Dennis Hopper

1996 JANE EYRE
Director: Franco Zefferelli
Co-stars: Charlotte Gainsbourg William Hurt Joan Plowright

1998 THE BUTCHER BOY
Director: Neil Jordan
Co-stars: Eamonn Owens Sinead O'Connor Andrew Fullerton

JANET SHAW

1945 THE SCARLET CLUE
Director: Phil Rosen
Co-stars: Sidney Toler Benson Fong Manton Moreland

LYNN SHAW

1957 IL GRIDO
Director: Michaelangelo Antonioni
Co-stars: Steve Cochran Alida Valli Betsy Blair

PAULA SHAW

1979 AND YOUR NAME IS JONAH
Director: Richard Michaels
Co-stars: Sally Struthers James Woods Robert Davi

RETA SHAW

1955 PICNIC
Director: Joshua Logan
Co-stars: William Holden Kim Novak Rosalind Russell

1957 THE PAJAMA GAME
Director: Stanley Donen
Co-stars: Doris Day John Raitt Carol Haney

1960 POLLYANNA
Director: David Swift
Co-stars: Hayley Mills Jane Wyman Karl Malden

1961 SANCTUARY
Director: Tony Richardson
Co-stars: Lee Remick Yves Montand Bradford Dillman

1961　BACHELOR IN PARADISE
Director:　Jack Arnold
Co-stars:　Bob Hope Lana Turner Janis Paige

1965　THE GHOST AND MR CHICKEN
Director:　Alan Rafkin
Co-stars:　Don Knotts Skip Homeier Joan Staley

1974　ESCAPE TO WITCH MOUNTAIN
Director:　John Hough
Co-stars:　Ray Milland Eddie Albert Donald Pleasence

SUSAN SHAW

1947　HOLIDAY CAMP
Director:　Ken Annakin
Co-stars:　Jack Warner Kathleen Harrison Flora Robson

1947　IT ALWAYS RAINS ON SUNDAY
Director:　Robert Hamer
Co-stars:　Googie Withers John McCallum Jack Warner

1948　IT'S NOT CRICKET
Director:　Alfred Roome
Co-stars:　Basil Radford Naunton Wayne Maurice Denham

1948　QUARTET
Director:　Arthur Crabtree
Co-stars:　George Cole Hermione Baddeley Mervyn Johns

1948　LONDON BELONGS TO ME
Director:　Sidney Gilliat
Co-stars:　Alastair Sim Stephen Murray Fay Compton

1948　THE WOMAN IN QUESTION
Director:　Anthony Asquith
Co-stars:　Jean Kent Dirk Bogarde John McCallum

1948　HERE COME THE HUGGETTS
Director:　Ken Annakin
Co-stars:　Jack Warner Jane Hylton Petula Clark

1949　THE HUGGETTS ABROAD
Director:　Ken Annakin
Co-stars:　Dinah Sheridan Jimmy Hanley Peter Hammond

1949　VOTE FOR HUGGETT
Director:　Ken Annakin
Co-stars:　David Tomlinson Diana Dors Anthony Newley

1949　TRAIN OF EVENTS
Director:　Basil Dearden
Co-stars:　Valerie Hobson John Clements Peter Finch

1949　MARRY ME
Director:　Terence Fisher
Co-stars:　Derek Bond Patrick Holt Carol Marsh

1950　POOL OF LONDON
Director:　Basil Dearden
Co-stars:　Bonar Colleano Renee Asherson Earl Cameron

1950　WATERFRONT
Director:　Michael Anderson
Co-stars:　Robert Newton Richard Burton Kathleen Harrison

1951　WALL OF DEATH
Director:　Lewis Gilbert
Co-stars:　Maxwell Reed Laurence Harvey

1951　THERE IS ANOTHER SUN
Director:　Lewis Gilbert
Co-stars:　Maxwell Reed Laurence Harvey Leslie Dwyer

1955　STOCK CAR
Director:　Wolf Rilla
Co-stars:　Paul Carpenter Rona Anderson

1956　FIRE MAIDENS FROM OUTER SPACE
Director:　Cy Roth
Co-stars:　Anthony Dexter Harry Fowler Sidney Tafler

1957　DAVY
Director:　Michael Relph
Co-stars:　Harry Secombe Ron Randell Alexander Knox

1958　THE DIPLOMATIC CORPSE
Director:　Montgomery Tully
Co-stars:　Robin Bailey Harry Fowler Liam Redmond

SUSAN DAMANTE SHAW

**1975　THE ADVENTURES OF
　　　　THE WILDERNESS FAMILY**
Director:　Stewart Rafill
Co-stars:　Robert Logan Heather Rattray

**1978　THE ADVENTURES OF
　　　　THE WILDERNESS FAMILY: PART 2**
Director:　Frank Zuniga
Co-stars:　Robert Logan Ham Larsen

1979　MOUNTAIN FAMILY ROBINSON
Director:　John Cotter
Co-stars:　Robert Logan Heather Rattray William Bryant

VICTORIA SHAW

1956　THE EDDY DUCHIN STORY
Director:　George Sidney
Co-stars:　Tyrone Power Kim Novak James Whitmore

1959　THE CRIMSON KIMONO
Director:　Samuel Fuller
Co-stars:　Glenn Corbett James Shigeta Anna Lee

1959　EDGE OF ETERNITY
Director:　Don Siegel
Co-stars:　Cornel Wilde Edgar Buchanan Mickey Shaughnessy

1960　BECAUSE THEY'RE YOUNG
Director:　Jerry Bressler
Co-stars:　Michael Callan Tuesday Weld Doug McClure

1960　I AIM AT THE STARS
Director:　J. Lee-Thompson
Co-stars:　Curt Jurgens Herbert Lom Gia Scala

1966　ALVAREZ KELLY
Director:　Edward Dmytryk
Co-stars:　William Holden Richard Widmark Janice Rule

1973　WESTWORLD
Director:　Michael Crichton
Co-stars:　Yul Brynner Richard Benjamin James Brolin

1978　SHIMMERING LIGHT
Director:　Don Chaffey
Co-stars:　Beau Bridges Lloyd Bridges John Meillon

VINESSA SHAW

1992　LADYBIRDS
Director:　Sidney Furie
Co-stars:　Rodney Dangerfield Jonathan Brandis Tom Parks

1993　HOCUS POCUS
Director:　Kenny Ortega
Co-stars:　Bette Midler Kathy Najimy Sarah Jessica Parker

1996　COYOTE SUMMER
Director:　Matias Alvarez
Co-star:　Adam Beach

WINI SHAW

1934　MILLION DOLLAR RANSOM
Director:　Murray Roth
Co-stars:　Edward Arnold Phillips Holmes Mary Carlisle

1934　GOLD DIGGERS OF 1935
Director:　Busby Berkeley
Co-stars:　Dick Powell Adolphe Menjou Gloria Stuart

1935 IN CALIENTE
Director: Lloyd Bacon
Co-stars: Dolores Del Rio Pat O'Brien Edward Everett Horton

1935 FRONT PAGE WOMAN
Director: Michael Curtiz
Co-stars: Bette Davis George Brent J.Carrol Naish

1935 THE CASE OF THE CURIOUS BRIDE
Director: Michael Curtiz
Co-stars: Warren William Margaret Lindsay Errol Flynn

1935 BROADWAY HOSTESS
Director: Frank McDonald
Co-stars: Genevieve Tobin Lyle Talbot Allen Jenkins

1935 SWEET ADELINE
Director: Mervyn LeRoy
Co-stars: Irene Dunne Donald Woods Hugh Herbert

1936 SONS O' GUNS
Director: Lloyd Bacon
Co-stars: Joe E. Brown Joan Blondell Eric Blore

1936 THE SINGING KID
Director: William Keighley
Co-stars: Al Jolson Sybil Jason Allen Jenkins

1936 SATAN MET A LADY
Director: William Dieterle
Co-stars: Bette Davis Warren William Alison Skipworth

1936 SMART BLONDE
Director: Frank McDonald
Co-stars: Glenda Farrell Barton MacLane Jane Wyman

1936 THE CASE OF THE VELVET CLAWS
Director: William Clemens
Co-stars: Warren William Claire Dodd Eddie Acuff

1937 MELODY FOR TWO
Director: Louis King
Co-stars: James Melton Patricia Ellis Marie Wilson

1937 READY, WILLING AND ABLE
Director: Ray Enright
Co-stars: Ruby Keeler Ross Alexander Jane Wyman

JOAN SHAWLEE

1946 BUCK PRIVATES COME HOME
Director: Charles Barton
Co-stars: Bud Abbott Lou Costello Beverly Simmons

1959 SOME LIKE IT HOT
Director: Billy Wilder
Co-stars: Jack Lemmon Tony Curtis Marilyn Monroe

1960 THE APARTMENT
Director: Billy Wilder
Co-stars: Jack Lemmon Shirley MacLaine Fred MacMurray

1963 IRMA LA DOUCE
Director: Billy Wilder
Co-stars: Jack Lemmon Shirley MacLaine Lou Jacobi

1981 BUDDY, BUDDY
Director: Billy Wilder
Co-stars: Jack Lemmon Walter Matthau Paula Prentiss

TAMARA SHAYNE

1946 THE JOLSON STORY
Director: Alfred Green
Co-stars: Larry Parks Evelyn Keyes William Demarest

1949 JOLSON SINGS AGAIN
Director: Henry Levin
Co-stars: Larry Parks Barbara Hale William Demarest

1961 ROMANOFF AND JULIET
Director: Peter Ustinov
Co-stars: Peter Ustinov Sandra Dee John Gavin

ANN SHEA

1992 12-01
Director: Jack Sholder
Co-stars: Jonathan Silverman Helen Slater Martin Landau

GLORIA SHEA

1934 MONEY MEANS NOTHING
Co-star: Wallace Ford

1935 THE LAST DAYS OF POMPEII
Director: Merian Cooper
Co-stars: Preston Foster Basil Rathbone Dorothy Wilson

1936 DANGEROUS INTRIQUE
Co-stars: Ralph Bellamy Fred Kohler Georgie Bellings

PEARL SHEAR

1966 THE PAD AND HOW TO USE IT
Director: Brian Hutton
Co-stars: Brian Bedford Julie Sommars James Farentino

MOIRA SHEARER *(Married Ludovic Kennedy)*

1948 THE RED SHOES
Director: Michael Powell
Co-stars: Anton Walbrook Marius Goring Robert Helpman

1951 THE TALES OF HOFFMAN
Director: Michael Powell
Co-stars: Robert Helpman Leonide Massine Richard Rounseville

1953 THE STORY OF THREE LOVES
Director: Vincente Minnelli
Co-stars: James Mason Kirk Douglas Leslie Caron

1954 THE MAN WHO LOVED REDHEADS
Director: Harold French
Co-stars: John Justin Roland Culver Gladys Cooper

1960 PEEPING TOM
Director: Michael Powell
Co-stars: Michael Powell Carl Boehm Anna Massey

NORMA SHEARER *(Married Irving Thalberg)*
Oscar For Best Actress In 1930 For "The Divorcee". Nominated For Best Actress In 1931 For "A Free Sou"l, In 1934 For "The Barretts Of Wimpole Street", In 1936 For "Romeo And Juliet" & In 1938 For "Marie Antoinette"

1924 HE WHO GETS SLAPPED
Director: Victor Sjostrom
Co-stars: Lon Chaney John Gilbert Tully Marshall

1925 THE TOWER OF LIES
Director: Victor Sjostrom
Co-stars: Lon Chaney Ian Keith Claire McDowell

1925 PRETTY LADIES
Director: Monta Bell
Co-stars: Zasu Pitts Tom Moore Joan Crawford

1927 THE STUDENT PRINCE
Director: Ernst Lubitsch
Co-stars: Ramon Navarro Jean Hersholt Philippe De Lacy

1928 THE ACTRESS
Director: Sidney Franklin
Co-stars: Ralph Forbes Owen Moore O.P. Heggie

1929 THE LAST OF MRS CHEYNEY
Director: Sidney Franklin
Co-stars: Basil Rathbone Hedda Hopper Moon Carroll

1929 THE TRIAL OF MARY DUGGAN

1929 THE HOLLYWOOD REVUE OF 1929
Director: Charles Reisner
Co-stars: Joan Crawford Jack Benny Buster Keaton

1930 THE DIVORCEE
Director: Robert Z. Leonard
Co-stars: Chester Morris Florence Eldridge Conrad Nagel

1930 THEIR OWN DESIRE

1930 LET US BE GAY
Director: Robert Z. Leonard
Co-stars: Rod La Rocque Marie Dressler Sally Eilers

1931 STRANGERS MAY KISS
Director: George Fitzmaurice
Co-stars: Robert Montgomery Neil Hamilton

1931 PRIVATE LIVES
Director: Sidney Franklin
Co-stars: Robert Montgomery Reginald Denny Una Merkel

1931 A FREE SOUL
Director: Clarence Brown
Co-stars: Lionel Barrymore Leslie Howard Clark Gable

1932 SMILIN' THROUGH
Director: Sidney Franklin
Co-stars: Leslie Howard Fredric March Ralph Forbes

1932 STRANGE INTERLUDE
Director: Robert Z. Leonard
Co-stars: Clark Gable Robert Young Maureen O'Sullivan

1934 RIPTIDE
Director: Edmund Goulding
Co-stars: Robert Montgomery Herbert Marshall

1934 THE BARRETTS OF WIMPOLE STREET
Director: Sidney Franklin
Co-stars: Charles Laughton Fredric March

1936 ROMEO AND JULIET
Director: George Cukor
Co-stars: Leslie Howard John Barrymore Basil Rathbone

1938 MARIE ANTOINETTE
Director: W.S. Van Dyke
Co-stars: Tyrone Power Robert Morley John Barrymore

1938 IDIOT'S DELIGHT
Director: Clarence Brown
Co-stars: Clark Gable Edward Arnold Charles Coburn

1939 THE WOMEN
Director: George Cukor
Co-stars: Joan Crawford Mary Boland Paulette Goddard

1940 ESCAPE
Director: Mervyn LeRoy
Co-stars: Robert Taylor Conrad Veidt Nazimova

1942 WE WERE DANCING
Director: Robert Z. Leonard
Co-stars: Melvyn Douglas Gail Patrick Ava Gardner

1942 HER CARDBOARD LOVER
Director: George Cukor
Co-stars: Robert Taylor George Sanders Frank McHugh

ALICE SHEED

1986 MOSQUITO COAST
Director: Peter Weir
Co-stars: Harrison Ford Helen Mirren River Phoenix

ALLY SHEEDY

1981 THE DAY THE LOVING STOPPED
Director: Daniel Mann
Co-stars: Dennis Weaver Valerie Harper Dominique Dunne

1981 THE VIOLATION OF SARAH McDAVID
Director: John Llewellyn Moxey
Co-stars: Patty Duke Astin Ned Beatty

1983 BAD BOYS
Director: Rick Rosenthal
Co-stars: Sean Penn Reni Santoni Jim Moody

1983 WAR GAMES
Director: John Badham
Co-stars: Matthew Broderick Dabney Coleman John Wood

1983 DEADLY LESSONS
Director: William Wiard
Co-stars: Donna Reed Larry Wilcox David Ackroyd

1984 OXFORD BLUES
Director: Robert Boris
Co-stars: Rob Lowe Alan Howard Amanda Pays

1985 ST. ELMO'S FIRE
Director: Joel Schumacher
Co-stars: Rob Lowe Demi Moore Andrew McCarthy

1985 TWICE IN A LIFETIME
Director: Bud Yorkin
Co-stars: Gene Hackman Ellen Burstyn Ann-Margret

1985 THE BREAKFAST CLUB
Director: John Hughes
Co-stars: Emilio Estevez Judd Nelson Molly Ringwald

1986 BLUE CITY
Director: Michelle Manning
Co-stars: Judd Nelson David Caruso Paul Winfield

1986 SHORT CIRCUIT
Director: John Badham
Co-stars: Steve Guttenberg Fisher Stevens Austin Pendleton

1987 MAID TO ORDER
Director: Amy Jones
Co-stars: Michael Ontkean Beverly D'Angelo Valerie Perrine

1989 FEAR
Director: Rockne O'Bannon
Co-stars: Pruitt Taylor Vince Lauren Hutton Michael O'Keefe

1990 BETSY'S WEDDING
Director: Alan Alda
Co-stars: Alan Alda Molly Ringwald Madeline Kahn

1991 ONLY THE LONELY
Director: Chris Columbus
Co-stars: Maureen O'Hara John Candy Anthony Quinn

1993 MAN'S BEST FRIEND
Director: John Lafia
Co-stars: Lance Hendriksen Robert Costanzo John Cassini

1994 THE HAUNTING OF SEACLIFF INN
Director: Walter Klenhard
Co-stars: William R. Moses Lucinda West

1995 BEFORE THE NIGHT
Director: Talia Shire
Co-stars: A. Martinez Frederic Forrest

1997 JAILBREAK
Director: Victoria Muspratt
Co-star: David Carradine

CAROLE SHEELY

1968 THE ODD COUPLE
Director: Gene Saks
Co-stars: Jack Lemmon Walter Matthau John Fiedler

LUCY SHEEN

1986 PING PONG
Director: Po Chih Leong
Co-stars: David Yip Robert Lee Victor Kan

RUTH SHEEN

1988 HIGH HOPES
Director: Mike Leigh
Co-stars: Philip Davis Edna Dore Lesley Manville

1990 NIGHT VOICE
Director: Richard Spence
Co-stars: Alexei Sayle Kevin Whately Sam Kelly

1991 CLUBLAND
Director: Laura Sims
Co-stars: Paul Bhattacharjee David Morrissey Daniel Webb

1996 SECRETS AND LIES
Director: Mike Leigh
Co-stars: Brenda Blethyn Timothy Spall Phyllis Logan

FLORA SHEFFIELD

1931 EAST LYNNE
Director: Frank Lloyd
Co-stars: Ann Harding Clive Brook Beryl Mercer

LaRITA SHELBY

1992 SOUTH CENTRAL
Director: Steve Anderson
Co-stars: Glenn Plummer Carl Lumbly Byron Keith Minns

JANA SHELDEN

1992 SMALL METAL JACKET
Director: Steve Hilliker
Co-stars: Debora Weston Marie Theodore Tracy Thorne

BARBARA SHELDON

1933 THE LUCKY TEXAN
Director: Robert Bradbury
Co-stars: John Wayne George Hayes Yakima Canutt

LORI SHELLE

1969 GOODBYE, COLUMBUS
Director: Larry Peerce
Co-stars: Richard Benjamin Ali MacGraw Jack Klugman

ADRIENNE SHELLEY

1989 THE UNBELIEVABLE TRUTH
Director: Hal Hartley
Co-stars: Robert Burke Christopher Cooke Julia McNeal

1991 TRUST
Director: Hal Hartley
Co-stars: Martin Donovan Merritt Nelson Eddie Falco

1992 STEPKIDS
Director: Joan Micklin Silver
Co-stars: Griffin Dunne Patricia Kalember Jenny Lewis

1993 HEXED
Director: Alan Spencer
Co-stars: Ayre Gross Claudia Christian Ray Baker

1994 SLEEPING WITH STRANGERS
Director: William Bolson
Co-stars: Neil Duncan Kymberley Huffman

BARBARA SHEELEY

1958 THE CAMP ON BLOOD ISLAND
Director: Val Guest
Co-stars: Andre Morrell Carl Mohner Edward Underdown

1958 BLOOD OF THE VAMPIRE
Director: Henry Cass
Co-stars: Donald Wolfit Vincent Ball Victor Maddern

1959 BOBBIKINS
Director: Robert Day
Co-stars: Max Bygraves Shirley Jones Billie Whitelaw

1960 VILLAGE OF THE DAMNED
Director: Wolf Rilla
Co-stars: George Sanders Laurence Naismith Michael Gwynn

1961 SHADOW OF THE CAT
Director: John Gilling
Co-stars: Andre Morrell William Lucas Conrad Phillips

1961 POSTMAN'S KNOCK
Director: Robert Lynn
Co-stars: Spike Milligan Wilfrid Lawson Miles Malleson

1963 BLIND CORNER
Director: Lance Comfort
Co-stars: William Sylvester Elizabeth Shepherd

1964 THE GORGON
Director: Terence Fisher
Co-stars: Peter Cushing Richard Pasco Patrick Troughton

1964 THE SECRET OF BLOOD ISLAND
Director: Quentin Lawrence
Co-stars: Jack Hedley Bill Owen Lee Montague

1966 RASPUTIN THE MAD MONK
Director: Don Sharp
Co-stars: Christopher Lee Richard Pasco Renee Asherson

1966 DRACULA, PRINCE OF DARKNESS
Director: Terence Fisher
Co-stars: Christopher Lee Philip Latham

1967 QUATERMASS AND THE PIT
Director: Roy Ward Baker
Co-stars: Andrew Keir James Donald Julian Glover

1969 THE SPY KILLER
Director: Roy Baker
Co-stars: Robert Horton Jill St. John Sebastian Cabot

1975 GHOST STORY
Director: Stephen Weeks
Co-stars: Murray Melvin Marianne Faithfull Leigh Lawson

1980 PRIDE AND PREJUDICE
Director: Cyril Coke
Co-stars: Elizabeth Garvie David Rintoul Judy Parfitt

1988 THE DARK ANGEL
Director: Peter Hammond
Co-stars: Peter O'Toole Jane Lapotaire Beatie Edney

CAROLE SHELLEY

1991 THE SUPER
Director: Rod Daniel
Co-stars: Joe Pesci Vincent Gardenia Madolyn Smith

RACHEL SHELLEY

1998 PHOTOGRAPHING FAIRIES
Director: Nick Willing
Co-stars: Frances Barber Ben Kingsley Emily Woof

ANNE SHELTON

1942 KING ARTHUR WAS A GENTLEMAN
Director: Marcel Varnel
Co-stars: Arthur Askey Evelyn Dall Max Bacon

1943 BEES IN PARADISE
Director: Val Guest
Co-stars: Arthur Askey Peter Graves Jean Kent

1943 MISS LONDON LTD.
Director: Val Guest
Co-stars: Arthur Askey Evelyn Dall Richard Hearne

DEBORAH SHELTON

1984 BODY DOUBLE
Director: Brian De Palma
Co-stars: Craig Wasson Melanie Griffith Gregg Henry

1992 BLIND DATE
Director: Shuki Levy
Co-stars: Lenny Van Donlen Louise Fletcher Ned Beatty

JOY SHELTON

1943 MILLIONS LIKE US
Director: Frank Launder
Co-stars: Patricia Roc Gordon Jackson Anne Crawford

1945 WATERLOO ROAD
Director: Sidney Gilliat
Co-stars: John Mills Stewart Granger Alastair Sim

1948 UNEASY TERMS
Director: Vernon Sewell
Co-stars: Michael Rennie Moira Lister Nigel Patrick

1948 NO ROOM AT THE INN
Director: Dan Birt
Co-stars: Freda Jackson Hermione Baddeley Joan Dowling

1950 ONCE A SINNER
Director: Lewis Gilbert
Co-stars: Pat Kirkwood Jack Watling Sidney Tafler

1950 MIDNIGHT EPISODE
Director: Gordon Parry
Co-stars: Stanley Holloway Natasha Parry Leslie Dwyer

1950 A CASE FOR P.C. 49
Director: Francis Searle
Co-stars: Brian Reece Christine Norden Leslie Bradley

1952 EMERGENCY CALL
Director: Lewis Gilbert
Co-stars: Jack Warner Anthony Steel Freddie Mills

MARLA SHELTON

1937 STAND-IN
Director: Tay Garnett
Co-stars: Leslie Howard Joan Blondell Humphrey Bogart

MARLEE SHELTON

1992 GRAND CANYON
Director: Lawrence Kasdan
Co-stars: Kevin Kline Danny Glover Mary McDonnell

1993 AMBUSH IN WACO
Director: Dick Lowry
Co-stars: Timothy Daly Dan Lauria

1997 TROJAN WAR
Co-star: Will Friedle

SUSAN SHENTALL

1954 ROMEO AND JULIET
Director: Renato Castellani
Co-stars: Laurence Harvey Flora Robson Mervyn Johns

ELAINE SHEPARD

1943 THE FALCON IN DANGER
Director: William Clemens
Co-stars: Tom Conway Jean Brooks Amelita Ward

1944 SEVEN DAYS ASHORE
Co-stars: Virginia Mayo Alan Dinehart Marjorie Gateson

JEWEL SHEPARD

1984 HOLLYWOOD HOT TUBS
Director: Chuck Vincent
Co-stars: Donna McDaniel Edy Williams Michael Andrew

1990 HOLLYWOOD HOT TUBS 2: EDUCATING CRYSTAL
Director: Ken Raich
Co-stars: Patrick Day David Tiefen Remy O'Neil

PATTY SHEPARD

1974 BLOOD MONEY
Director: Anthony Dawson
Co-stars: Lee Van Cleef Lo Lieh Karen Yeh

HILARY SHEPHARD

1990 PEACEMAKER
Director: Kevin Tenney
Co-stars: Robert Forster Lance Edwards Robert Davi

AMANDA SHEPHERD

1993 HOCUS POCUS
Director: Kenny Ortega
Co-stars: Bette Midler Sarah Jessica Parker Kathy Najimy

CYBIL SHEPHERD

1971 THE LAST PICTURE SHOW
Director: Peter Bogdanovich
Co-stars: Jeff Bridges Timothy Bottoms

1972 THE HEARTBREAK KID
Director: Elaine May
Co-stars: Charles Grodin Jeannie Berlin Eddie Albert

1974 DAISY MILLER
Director: Peter Bogdanovich
Co-stars: Barry Brown Cloris Leachman Eileen Brennan

1975 AT LONG LAST LOVE
Director: Peter Bogdanovich
Co-stars: Burt Reynolds Madeline Kahn Mildred Natwick

1976 SPECIAL DELIVERY
Director: Paul Wendkos
Co-stars: Bo Svenson Michael C. Gwynne Jeff Goldblum

1976 TAXI DRIVER
Director: Martin Scorsese
Co-stars: Robert De Niro Jodie Foster Harvey Keitel

1977 SILVER BEARS
Director: Ivan Passer
Co-stars: Michael Caine Louis Jourdan David Warner

1979 THE LADY VANISHES
Director: Anthony Page
Co-stars: Elliott Gould Angela Lansbury Ian Carmichael

1984 SECRETS OF A MARRIED MAN
Director: William Graham
Co-stars: William Shatner Michelle Philips

1985 SEDUCED
Director: Jerrold Freedman
Co-stars: Gregory Harrison Mel Ferrer Michael C. Gwynne

1985 THE LONG HOT SUMMER
Director: Stuart Cooper
Co-stars: Ava Gardner Judith Ivey Don Johnson

1989 CHANCES ARE
Director: Emile Ardolino
Co-stars: Robert Downey Ryan O'Neal Mary Stuart Masterson

1990 ALICE
Director: Woody Allen
Co-stars: Mia Farrow Joe Mantegna Alec Baldwin

1990 TEXASVILLE
Director: Peter Bogdanovich
Co-stars: Jeff Bridges Annie Potts Cloris Leachman

1991 ONCE UPON A CRIME
Director: Eugene Levy
Co-stars: John Candy James Belushi Sean Young

1992 STORMY WEATHERS
Director: Will Mackenzie

1993 MARRIED TO IT
Director: Arthur Hiller
Co-stars: Beau Bridges Stockard Channing Mary Stuart Masterson

ELIZABETH SHEPHERD

1961 THE QUEEN'S GUARDS
Director: Michael Powell
Co-stars: Raymond Massey Daniel Massey Robert Stephens

1963 BLIND CORNER
Director: Lance Comfort
Co-stars: William Sylvester Barbara Shelley

1964 THE TOMB OF LIGEIA
Director: Roger Corman
Co-stars: Vincent Price Derek Francis Richard Vernon

1970 HELL BOATS
Director: Paul Wendkos
Co-stars: James Franciscus Ronald Allen Inigo Jackson

1978 DAMIEN: OMEN II
Director: Don Taylor
Co-stars: William Holden Lee Grant Robert Foxworth

1985 INVITATION TO THE WEDDING
Director: Joseph Brooks
Co-stars: Ralph Richardson Paul Nicholas

1989 CRIMINAL LAW
Director: Martin Campbell
Co-stars: Gary Oldman Kevin Bacon Karen Young

FREDA SHEPHERD

1970 BRONCO BULLFROG
Director: Del Walker
Co-stars: Anne Gooding Sam Shepherd

PAULA SHEPPARD

1982 LIQUID SKY
Director: Slava Tsukerman
Co-stars: Anne Carlisle Susan Doukas Bob Brady

ANN SHERIDAN (*Married George Brent*)

1934 BEHOLD MY WIFE
Director: B.P. Shulberg
Co-stars: Sylvia Sidney Gene Raymond Juliette Compton

1934 LIMEHOUSE BLUES
Director: Alexander Hall
Co-stars: George Raft Jean Parker Anna May Wong

1934 MURDER AT THE VANITIES
Co-stars: Jack Oakie Victor McLaglen

1935 FIGHTING YOUTH
Co-star: Charles Farrell

1935 ROCKY MOUNTAIN MYSTERY
Director: Charles Barton
Co-stars: Randolph Scott Kathleen Burke

1935 CAR 99
Director: Charles Barton
Co-stars: Fred MacMurray Sir Guy Standing

1936 BLACK LEGION
Director: Archie Mayo
Co-stars: Humphrey Bogart Dick Foran Robert Barrat

1937 THE GREAT O'MALLEY
Director: William Dieterle
Co-stars: Humphrey Bogart Pat O'Brien Donald Crisp

1937 SAN QUENTIN
Director: Lloyd Bacon
Co-stars: Humphrey Bogart Pat O'Brien Barton McLane

1937 THE FOOTLOOSE HEIRESS
Co-stars: William Hopper Frank Orth

1938 MYSTERY HOUSE
Co-star: Dick Purcell

1938 SHE LOVED A FIREMAN
Co-stars: Robert Armstrong Dick Foran

1938 LETTER OF INTRODUCTION
Director: John Stahl
Co-stars: Adolphe Menjou Andrea Leeds George Murphy

1938 COWBOY FROM BROOKLYN
Director: Lloyd Bacon
Co-stars: Dick Powell Pat O'Brien Ronald Reagan

1938 BROADWAY MUSKETEERS
Director: John Farrow
Co-stars: Marie Wilson Margaret Lindsay Dick Purcell

1938 ANGELS WITH DIRTY FACES
Director: Michael Curtiz
Co-stars: James Cagney Humphrey Bogart Leo Gorcey

1938 ALCATRAZ ISLAND
Director: William McGann
Co-stars: John Litel Dick Purcell Mary Maguire

1939 ANGELS WASH THEIR FACES
Director: Ray Enright
Co-stars: Ronald Reagan Frankie Thomas Leo Gorcey

1939 INDIANAPOLIS SPEEDWAY
Director: Lloyd Bacon
Co-stars: Pat O'Brien John Payne Gale Page

1939 NAUGHTY BUT NICE
Director: Ray Enright
Co-stars: Dick Powell Ronald Reagan Jerry Colonna

1939 THEY MADE ME A CRIMINAL
Director: Busby Berkeley
Co-stars: John Garfield Claude Rains Billy Halop

1939 WINTER CARNIVAL
Director: Charles Riesner
Co-stars: Richard Carlson Robert Walker Helen Parrish

1939 DODGE CITY
Director: Michael Curtiz
Co-stars: Errol Flynn Olivia De Havilland Alan Hale

1940 CASTLE ON THE HUDSON
Director: Anatole Litvak
Co-stars: John Garfield Pat O'Brien Burgess Meredith

1940 CITY FOR CONQUEST
Director: Anatole Litvak
Co-stars: James Cagney Donald Crisp Arthur Kennedy

1940 IT ALL CAME TRUE
Director: Lewis Seiler
Co-stars: Humphrey Bogart Jeffrey Lynn Zasu Pitts

1940 THEY DRIVE BY NIGHT
Director: Raoul Walsh
Co-stars: Humphrey Bogart George Raft Ida Lupino

1940 TORRID ZONE
Director: William Keighley
Co-stars: James Cagney Pat O'Brien George Tobias

1941 NAVY BLUES
Director: Lloyd Bacon
Co-stars: Jack Oakie Jack Carson Jack Haley

1941 HONEYMOON FOR THREE
Director: Lloyd Bacon
Co-stars: George Brent Osa Massen Charles Ruggles

1941 THE MAN WHO CAME TO DINNER
Director: William Keighley
Co-stars: Monty Woolley Bette Davis Billie Burke

1942   **KING'S ROW**
Director: Sam Wood
Co-stars: Ronald Reagan Robert Cummings Betty Field

1942   **JUKE GIRL**
Director: Curtis Bernhardt
Co-stars: Ronald Reagan Richard Whorf Alan Hale

1942   **WINGS FOR THE EAGLE**
Director: Lloyd Bacon
Co-stars: Dennis Morgan Jack Carson George Tobias

1942   **GEORGE WASHINGTON SLEPT HERE**
Director: William Keighley
Co-stars: Jack Benny Charles Coburn

1943   **EDGE OF DARKNESS**
Director: Lewis Milestone
Co-stars: Errol Flynn Walter Huston Ruth Gordon

1943   **THANK YOUR LUCKY STARS**
Director: David Butler
Co-stars: Eddie Cantor Dennis Morgan Joan Leslie

1944   **SHINE ON HARVEST MOON**
Director: David Butler
Co-stars: Dennis Morgan Jack Carson Irene Manning

1944   **THE DOUGHGIRLS**
Co-stars: Jack Carson Jane Wyman Alexis Smith

1946   **ONE MORE TOMORROW**
Director: Peter Godfrey
Co-stars: Dennis Morgan Jack Carson Alexis Smith

1947   **THE UNFAITHFUL**
Director: Vincent Sherman
Co-stars: Zachary Scott Lew Ayres Eve Arden

1947   **NORA PRENTISS**
Director: Vincent Sherman
Co-stars: Kent Smith Robert Alda Bruce Bennett

1948   **SILVER RIVER**
Director: Raoul Walsh
Co-stars: Errol Flynn Thomas Mitchell Bruce Bennett

1948   **GOOD SAM**
Director: Leo McCarey
Co-stars: Gary Cooper Ray Collins Edmund Lowe

1949   **YOU CAN'T SLEEP HERE**
Director: Howard Hawks
Co-stars: Cary Grant Marion Marshall Randy Stuart

1950   **STELLA**
Director: Claude Binyon
Co-stars: Victor Mature Frank Fontaine

1950   **WOMAN ON THE RUN**
Director: Norman Foster
Co-stars: Dennis O'Keefe Robert Keith Ross Elliott

1952   **STEEL TOWN**
Director: George Sherman
Co-stars: John Lund Howard Duff James Best

1952   **JUST ACROSS THE STREET**
Director: Joseph Pevney
Co-stars: John Lund Robert Keith Cecil Kellaway

1953   **APPOINTMENT IN HONDURAS**
Director: Jacques Tourneur
Co-stars: Glenn Ford Zachary Scott Jack Elam

1953   **TAKE ME TO TOWN**
Director: Douglas Sirk
Co-stars: Sterling Hayden Philip Reed Lee Patrick

1955   **COME NEXT SPRING**
Director: R.G. Springsteen
Co-stars: Steve Cochran Walter Brennan Mae Clarke

1956   **THE OPPOSITE SEX**
Director: David Miller
Co-stars: June Allyson Dolores Gray Joan Collins

1957   **THE WOMAN AND THE HUNTER**
Director: George Breakston
Co-stars: David Farrar John Loder

DINAH SHERIDAN *(Married Jimmy Hanley, Mother Of Jenny Hanley And Jeremy Hanley)*

1942   **SALUTE JOJN CITIZEN**
Director: Maurice Elvy
Co-stars: Edward Rigby Stanley Holloway George Robey

1943   **GET CRACKING**
Director: Marcel Varnel
Co-stars: George Formby Edward Rigby Frank Pettingell

1945   **FOR YOU ALONE**
Director: Geoffrey Faithfull
Co-stars: Lesley Brook Jimmy Hanley Irene Handl

1945   **29, ACACIA AVENUE**
Director: Henry Cass
Co-stars: Gordon Harker Betty Balfour Jimmy Hanley

1945   **MURDER IN REVERSE**
Director: Montgomery Tully
Co-stars: William Hartnell Jimmy Hanley Chili Bouchier

1948   **THE STORY OF SHIRLEY YORKE**
Director: MacLean Rogers
Co-stars: Derek Farr Margaretta Scott Valentine Dyall

1949   **THE HUGGETTS ABROAD**
Director: Ken Annakin
Co-stars: Jack Warner Jimmy Hanley Kathleen Harrison

1950   **BLACKOUT**
Director: Monty Berman
Co-stars: Maxwell Reed Patrick Doonan Eric Pohlman

1950   **NO TRACE**
Director: John Gilling
Co-stars: Hugh Sinclair John Laurie Dora Bryan

1951   **WHERE NO VULTURES FLY**
Director: Harry Watt
Co-stars: Anthony Steel Harold Warrender Meredith Edwards

1952   **THE SOUND BARRIER**
Director: David Lean
Co-stars: Nigel Patrick Ralph Richardson Ann Todd

1952   **APPOINTMENT IN LONDON**
Director: Philip Leacock
Co-stars: Dirk Bogarde Ian Hunter Bill Kerr

1953   **THE STORY OF GILBERT AND SULLIVAN**
Director: Sidney Gilliat
Co-stars: Robert Morley Maurice Evans Peter Finch

1953   **GENEVIEVE**
Director: Henry Cornelius
Co-stars: Kay Kendall John Gregson Kenneth More

1970   **THE RAILWAY CHILDREN**
Director: Lionel Jeffries
Co-stars: Jenny Agutter Garry Warren Sally Thomsett

GAIL SHERIDAN

1936   **HOPALONG CASSIDY RETURNS**
Director: Howard Bretherton
Co-stars: Bill Boyd George Hayes Irving Bacon

LIZ SHERIDAN

1987   **ALF**
Director: Tom Patchett
Co-stars: Max Wright Ann Schedeen Anne Meara

MARGARET SHERIDAN

1951 THE THING FROM ANOTHER WORLD
Director: Christian Nyby
Co-stars: Kenneth Tobey James Arness

1952 ONE MINUTE TO ZERO
Director: Tay Garnett
Co-stars: Robert Mitchum Ann Blyth William Talman

1954 THE DIAMOND
Director: Montgomery Tully
Co-stars: Dennis O'Keefe Philip Friend Alan Wheatley

NICOLLETTE SHERIDAN

1985 THE SURE THING
Director: Rob Reiner
Co-stars: John Cusack Daphne Zuniga Tim Robbins

1986 DEAD MAN'S FOLLY
Director: Clive Donner
Co-stars: Peter Ustinov Constance Cummings Jean Stapleton

1990 DECEPTIONS
Director: Ruben Preuss
Co-stars: Harry Hamlin Robert Davi Kevin King

1992 SOMEBODY'S DAUGHTER
Director: Joseph Sargent
Co-stars: Nick Mancuso Elliott Gould

1994 A TIME TO HEAL
Director: Michael Uno
Co-stars: Gary Cole Mara Wilson

1994 THE DEVIL'S BED
Director: Sam Pillsbury
Co-stars: Joe Lando Adrian Pasdar

1995 ROBIN COOK'S FORMULA FOR DEATH
Director: Armand Mastroianni
Co-star: William Devane

1995 SILVER STRAND
Director: George Miller
Co-stars: Gil Bellows Jennifer O'Neill Tony Plana

GERALDINE SHERMAN

1967 POOR COW
Director: Ken Loach
Co-stars: Carol White Terence Stamp Kate Williams

HAZEL SHERMET

1954 A STAR IS BORN
Director: George Cukor
Co-stars: Judy Garland James Mason Charles Bickford

MARTHA SHERRILL

1949 CALL OF THE FOREST
Co-star: Robert Lowery

DIANNE SHERVILLE

1978 SMOKEY AND THE GOOD-TIME OUTLAWS
Director: Alex Grashoff
Co-stars: Jesse Turner Slim Pickens Sully Boyer

LYDIA SHERWOOD

1933 DON QUIXOTE
Director: G.W. Pabst
Co-stars: Feodor Chaliapin George Robey Sidney Fox

1934 THE LITTLE FRIEND
Director: Berthold Viertel
Co-stars: Nova Pilbeam Matheson Lang Arthur Margetson

1936 MIDNIGHT AT MADAME TUSSAUD'S
Director: George Pearson
Co-stars: Lucille Lisle Patrick Barr Bernard Miles

1939 THE FOUR JUST MEN
Director: Walter Forde
Co-stars: Hugh Sinclair Griffith Jones Anna Lee

1943 THEATRE ROYAL
Director: John Baxter
Co-stars: Bud Flanagan Chesney Allen Horace Kenny

1954 ROMEO AND JULIET
Director: Renata Castellani
Co-stars: Laurence Harvey Susan Shentall Flora Robson

1960 THE LEAGUE OF GENTLEMEN
Director: Basil Dearden
Co-stars: Jack Hawkins Nigel Patrick Roger Livesey

MADELEINE SHERWOOD

1958 CAT ON A HOT TIN ROOF
Director: Richard Brooks
Co-stars: Paul Newman Elizabeth Taylor Burl Ives

1962 SWEET BIRD OF YOUTH
Director: Richard Brooks
Co-stars: Paul Newman Geraldine Brooks Ed Begley

1967 HURRY SUNDOWN
Director: Otto Preminger
Co-stars: Jane Fonda Michael Caine Rex Ingram

1969 PENDULUM
Director: George Schaefer
Co-stars: George Peppard Jean Seberg Richard Kiley

1987 BROKEN VOWS
Director: Jud Taylor
Co-stars: Tommy Lee Jones Annette O'Toole Milo O'Shea

ROBERTA SHERWOOD

1963 THE COURTSHIP OF EDDIE'S FATHER
Director: Vincente Minnelli
Co-stars: Glenn Ford Shirley Jones Ron Howard

BROOKE SHIELDS *(Child)*

1978 PRETTY BABY
Director: Louis Malle
Co-stars: Keith Carradine Susan Sarandon Antonio Fargas

1978 KING OF THE GYPSIES
Director: Frank Pierson
Co-stars: Sterling Hayden Shelley Winters Eric Roberts

1979 JUST YOU AND ME KID
Director: Leonard Stern
Co-stars: George Burns Burl Ives Ray Bolger

1979 WANDA NEVADA
Director: Peter Fonda
Co-stars: Peter Fonda Fiona Lewis Luke Askew

1979 TILT
Director: Rudy Durand
Co-stars: Ken Marshall Charles Durning Geoffrey Lewis

1980 THE BLUE LAGOON
Director: Randal Kleiser
Co-stars: Christopher Atkins Leo McKern William Daniels

1981 ENDLESS LOVE
Director: Franco Zefferelli
Co-stars: Martin Hewitt Shirley Knight Don Murray

1984 THE MUPPETS TAKE MANHATTAN
Director: Frank Oz
Co-stars: Art Carney Liza Minnelli Elliott Gould

1984 SAHARA
Director: Andrew McLaglen
Co-stars: Lambert Wilson Horst Buchholz John Mills

1984 WET GOLD
Director: Dick Lowry
Co-stars: Burgess Meredith Tom Byrd Brian Kerwin

1990 BACKSTREET DREAMS
Director: Jason O'Malley
Co-star: Jason O'Malley Sherilyn Fenn

1993 FREAKED
Director: Tom Stern
Co-stars: Alex Winter Megan Ward Randy Quaid

MIRIAM SHILLER

1946 SPECTRE OF THE ROSE
Director: Ben Hecht
Co-stars: Viola Essen Ivan Kirov Michael Chekhov

MARION SHILLING

1935 CAPTURED IN CHINATOWN
Director: Charles Delaney
Co-star: Bobby Nelson

1935 STONE OF SILVER CREEK
Co-stars: Buck Jones Niles Welch

1936 IDAHO KID
Co-stars: Rex Bell Lafe McKee Charles King

1936 ROMANCE RIDES THE RANGE
Co-star: Fred Scott

YOKO SHIMADA

1981 SHOGUN
Director: Jerry London
Co-stars: Richard Chamberlain Alan Badel Toshiro Mifune

JOANNA SHIMKUS

1968 HO!
Director: Robert Enrico
Co-stars: Jean-Pierre Belmondo Sydney Chaplin

1968 BOOM!
Director: Joseph Losey
Co-stars: Elizabeth Taylor Richard Burton Noel Coward

1969 THE LOST MAN
Director: Robert Alan Arthur
Co-stars: Sidney Poitier Al Freeman Richard Dysart

1970 THE VIRGIN AND THE GYPSY
Director: Christopher Miles
Co-stars: Franco Nero Honor Blackman Kay Walsh

1971 A TIME FOR LOVING
Director: Christopher Miles
Co-stars: Mel Ferrer Britt Ekland Lila Kedrova

1971 THE MARRIAGE OF A YOUNG STOCKBROKER
Director: Lawrence Turman
Co-stars: Richard Benjamin Elizabeth Ashley

HELEN SHINGLER

1946 QUIET WEEKEND
Director: Harold French
Co-stars: Derek Farr Marjorie Fielding Edward Rigby

1947 THE SILVER DARLINGS
Director: Clifford Evans
Co-stars: Clifford Evans Carl Bernard Norman Shelley

1950 THE ROSSITER CASE
Director: Francis Searle
Co-stars: Clement McCallin Sheila Burrell Frederick Leister

1951 JUDGEMENT DEFERRED
Director: John Baxter
Co-stars: Hugh Sinclair Leslie Dwyer Joan Collins

GWYNE SHIPMAN

1936 TRAIL DUST
Co-stars: William Boyd James Ellison George Hayes

HELEN SHIPMAN

1933 CHRISTOPER BEAN
Director: Sam Wood
Co-stars: Marie Dressler Lionel Barrymore Beulah Bondi

NINA SHIPMAN

1958 THE HUNTERS
Director: Dick Powell
Co-stars: Robert Mitchum Robert Wagner May Britt

1959 BLUE DENIM
Director: Philip Dunne
Co-stars: Carol Lynley Brandon De Wilde Marsha Hunt

1959 THE OREGON TRAIL
Director: Gene Fowler
Co-stars: Fred MacMurray William Bishop Gloria Talbot

MARY SHIPP

1953 JENNIFER
Director: Joel Newton
Co-stars: Ida Lupino Howard Duff Robert Nicholas

TALIA SHIRE *(Sister Of Francis Ford Coppola)*
Nominated For Best Actress In 1976 For "Rocky". Nominated For Best Supporting Actress In 1974 For "The Godfather: Part II"

1970 THE DUNWICH HORROR
Director: Daniel Haller
Co-stars: Dean Stockwell Sandra Dee Ed Begley

1970 GAS! OR IT MAY BECOME NECESSARY TO DESTROY THE WORLD IN ORDER TO SAVE IT
Director: Roger Corman
Co-stars: Robert Corff Ben Vereen Bud Cort

1972 THE GODFATHER
Director: Francis Ford Coppola
Co-stars: Marlon Brando Al Pacino Robert Duvall

1974 THE GODFATHER PART II
Director: Francis Ford Coppola
Co-stars: Al Pacino Robert De Niro Diane Keaton

1976 ROCKY
Director: John Avildsen
Co-stars: Sylvester Stallone Burgess Meredith Burt Young

1977 KILL ME IF YOU CAN
Director: Buzz Kulik
Co-stars: Alan Alda John Hillerman Barnard Hughes

1978 OLD BOYFRIENDS
Director: Joan Tewkesbury
Co-stars: Richard Jordan John Belushi Keith Carradine

1979 PROPHECT
Director: John Frankenheimer
Co-stars: Robert Foxworth Armand Assante Richard Dysart

1979 ROCKY II
Director: Sylvester Stallone
Co-stars: Sylvester Stallone Burgess Meredith Burt Young

1980 WINDOWS
Director: Gordon Willis
Co-stars: Elizabeth Ashley Joseph Cortese

1982 ROCKY III
Director: Sylvester Stallone
Co-stars: Sylvester Stallone Burgess Meredith Burt Young

1985 ROCKY IV
Director: Sylvester Stallone
Co-stars: Sylvester Stallone Dolph Lundgren Brigitte Nielson

1987 BLOOD VOWS
Director: Paul Wendkos
Co-stars: Melissa Gilbert Joe Penny Eileen Brennan

1989 NEW YORK STORIES
Director: Martin Scorsese
Co-stars: Nick Nolte Rosanna Arquette Mia Farrow

1990 ROCKY V
Director: John Avildsen
Co-stars: Sylvester Stallone Burt Young Burgess Meredith

1990 THE GODFATHER PART III
Director: Francis Ford Coppola
Co-stars: Al Pacino Andy Garcia Eli Wallach

1992 COLD HEAVEN
Director: Nicholas Roeg
Co-stars: Theresa Russell Mark Harmon Will Patton

1992 BED AND BREAKFAST
Director: Robert Ellis Miller
Co-stars: Roger Moore Colleen Dewhurst Ford Rainey

1992 FATHER, SON AND THE MISTRESS
Director: Jay Sandrich
Co-star: Jack Lemmon Madeline Kahn Joanna Gleason

ANN SHIRLEY (Dawn O'Day In First Four Films)
Nominated For Best Supporting Actress In 1937 For "Stella Dallas"

1924 THE MAN WHO FIGHTS ALONE
Co-stars: William Farnum Lois Wilson

1930 LILIOM
Director: Frank Borzage
Co-stars: Charles Farrell Rose Hobart Lee Tracy

1930 CITY GIRL
Director: F.W. Murna
Co-stars: Charles Farrell Mary Duncan Edith Yorke

1932 RASPUTIN AND THE EMPRESS
Director: Richard Boleslawski
Co-stars: Ethel Barrymore John Barrymore Diana Wynyard

1934 ANNE OF GREEN GABLES
Director: George Nicholls
Co-stars: Tom Brown O.P. Heggie Helen Westley

1935 CHASING YESTERDAY
Director: George Nicholls
Co-stars: John Qualen O.P. Heggie Helen Westley

1935 CHATTERBOX
Director: George Nicholls
Co-stars: Phillips Holmes Edward Ellis Erik Rhodes

1935 STEAMBOAT ROUND THE BEND
Director: John Ford
Co-stars: Will Rogers Eugene Pallette Berton Churchill

1936 M'LISS
Director: George Nicholls
Co-stars: Guy Kibbee John Beal Moroni Olsen

1936 MAKE WAY FOR A LADY
Director: David Burton
Co-stars: Herbert Marshall Gertrude Michael Margot Grahame

1937 MEET THE MISSUS
Director: Joseph Santley
Co-stars: Victor Moore Helen Broderick Willie Best

1937 STELLA DALLAS
Director: King Vidor
Co-stars: Barbara Stanwyck John Boles Tim Holt

1938 MOTHER CAREY'S CHICKENS
Director: Rowland Lee
Co-stars: Ruby Keeler Fay Bainter Walter Brennan

1938 LAW OF THE UNDERWORLD
Director: Lew Landers
Co-stars: Chester Morris Eduardo Ciannelli Walter Abel

1938 CONDEMNED WOMAN
Director: Lew Landers
Co-stars: Sally Eilers Louis Hayward Lee Patrick

1938 A MAN TO REMEMBER
Director: Garson Kanin
Co-stars: Edward Ellis Lee Bowman William Henry

1939 CAREER
Director: Leigh Jason
Co-stars: Edward Ellis Samuel S. Hinds Leon Errol

1939 BOY SLAVES
Director: P.J. Wolfson
Co-stars: Roger Daniel James McCallion Alan Baxter

1940 SATURDAY'S CHILDREN
Director: Vincent Sherman
Co-stars: John Garfield Claude Rains Lee Patrick

1940 ANNE OF WINDY POPLARS
Director: Jack Hively

1940 VIGIL IN THE NIGHT
Director: George Stevens
Co-stars: Carole Lombard Brian Aherne Alfred Newman

1941 UNEXPECTED UNCLE
Director: Peter Godfrey
Co-stars: Charles Coburn James Craig Ernest Truex

1941 ALL THAT MONEY CAN BUY
Director: William Dieterle
Co-stars: Walter Huston Edward Arnold Simone Simon

1942 FOUR JACKS AND A JILL
Director: Jack Hively
Co-stars: Ray Bolger Desi Arnaz June Havoc

1942 THE MAYOR OF 44TH STREET
Director: Alfred Green
Co-stars: George Murphy Richard Barthelmess William Gargan

1942 THE POWERS GIRL
Director: Norman Z. McLeod
Co-stars: George Murphy Carole Landis Benny Goodman

1943 GOVERNMENT GIRL
Director: Dudley Nichols
Co-stars: Olivia De Havilland Sonny Tufts James Dunn

1944 MUSIC IN MANHATTAN
Director: Phillip Terry

1943 BOMBARDIER
Director: Richard Wallace
Co-stars: Pat O'Brien Randolph Scott Eddie Albert

1944 MAN FROM FRISCO
Co-star: Michael O'Shea

1945 FAREWELL, MY LOVELY
Director: Edward Dmytryk
Co-stars: Dick Powell Claire Trevor Otto Kruger

STEPHANIE SHOCKLEY

1989 HOWLING V: THE REBIRTH
Director: Neal Sundstrom
Co-stars: Victoria Catlin Elizabeth Silverstein Mark Faulkner

SHOPE SHODEINDE

1978 THE SAILOR'S RETURN
Director: Jack Gold
Co-stars: Tom Bell George Costigan Clive Swift

ANN SHOEMAKER

1934 CHEATING CHEATERS
Director: Richard Thorpe
Co-stars: Fay Wray Cesar Romero Minna Gombell

1935 ALICE ADAMS
Director: George Stevens
Co-stars: Katherine Hepburn Fred MacMurray Evelyn Venable

1937 SHALL WE DANCE ?
Director: Mark Sandrich
Co-stars: Fred Astaire Ginger Rogers Eric Blore

1939 ROMANCE OF THE REDWOODS
Co-stars: Jean Parker Charles Bickford Al Bridge

1940 STRIKE UP THE BAND
Director: Busby Berkeley
Co-stars: Judy Garland Mickey Rooney Paul Whiteman

1940 SEVENTEEN
Director: Louis King
Co-stars: Jackie Cooper Betty Field Otto Kruger

1940 MY FAVORITE WIFE
Director: Garson Kanin
Co-stars: Irene Dunne Cary Grant Randolph Scott

1940 THE GIRL FROM AVENUE A
Director: Otto Brower
Co-stars: Jane Withers Kent Taylor Elyse Knox

1945 CONFLICT
Director: Curtis Bernhardt
Co-stars: Humphrey Bogart Alexis Smith Rose Hobart

1945 CRIME DOES NOT PAY: PHANTOMS INC.
Director: Harold Young
Co-star: Frank Reicher

1947 MAGIC TOWN
Director: William Wellman
Co-stars: James Stewart Jane Wyman Regis Toomey

1950 HOUSE BY THE RIVER
Director: Fritz Lang
Co-stars: Louis Hayward Jane Wyatt Lee Bowman

1960 SUNRISE AT CAMPOBELLO
Director: Vincent Donehue
Co-stars: Ralph Bellamy Greer Garson Hume Cronyn

PAMELA SHOOP

1977 EMPIRE OF THE ANTS
Director: Bert Gordon
Co-stars: Joan Collins Robert Lansing Albert Salmi

DINAH SHORE

1943 THANK YOUR LUCKY STARS
Director: David Butler
Co-stars: Eddie Cantor Dennis Morgan Joan Leslie

1944 UP IN ARMS
Director: Elliott Nugent
Co-stars: Danny Kaye Constance Dowling Dana Andrews

1944 FOLLOW THE BOYS
Director: Edward Sutherland
Co-stars: Orson Welles George Raft Marlene Dietrich

1945 BELLE OF THE YUKON
Director: William Seiter
Co-stars: Randolph Scott Gypsy Rose Lee Charles Winninger

1946 TILL THE CLOUDS ROLL BY
Director: Richard Whorf
Co-stars: Robert Walker Van Heflin Lucille Bremer

1946 MAKE MINE MUSIC *(Voice)*
Director: Walt Disney
Co-stars: Nelson Eddy Benny Goodman Andrews Sisters

1952 AARON SLICK FROM PUNKIN CRICK
Director: Claude Binyon
Co-stars: Alan Young Adele Jergens Guy Mitchell

1977 OH GOD!
Director: Carl Reiner
Co-stars: George Burns John Denver Ralph Bellamy

1979 DEATH CAR ON THE FREEWAY
Director: Hal Needham
Co-stars: Shelley Hack George Hamilton Barbara Rush

DOROTHY SHORT

1935 ASSASSIN OF YOUTH
Director: Elmer Clifton
Co-stars: Luanna Walters Arthur Gardner Earl Dwire

1936 REEFER MADNESS
Director: Louis Gasnier
Co-stars: Dave O'Brien Lillian Miles Carleton Young

JEAN SHORT

1948 THE RED SHOES
Director: Michael Powell
Co-stars: Moira Shearer Anton Walbrook Marius Goring

1948 THE FATAL NIGHT
Director: Mario Zampi
Co-stars: Lester Ferguson Leslie Armstrong Patrick McNee

CONSTANCE SHOTTER

1935 OFF THE DOLE
Director: Arthur Mertz
Co-stars: George Formby Beryl Formby Dan Young

WINIFRED SHOTTER

1930 PLUNDER
Director: Tom Walls
Co-stars: Tom Walls Ralph Lynn Robertson Hare

1930 ROOKERY NOOK
Director: Tom Walls
Co-stars: Tom Walls Ralph Lynn Robertson Hare

1932 A NIGHT LIKE THIS
Director: Tom Walls
Co-stars: Tom Walls Ralph Lynn Robertson Hare

1932 JACK'S THE BOY
Director: Walter Forde
Co-stars: Jack Hulbert Cicely Courtneidge Francis Lister

1933 NIGHT OF THE GARTER
Director: Jack Raymond
Co-stars: Sydney Howard Elsie Randolph Austin Melford

1933 SORRELL AND SON
Director: Jack Raymond
Co-stars: H.B. Warner Hugh Williams Margot Grahame

1936 PETTICOAT FEVER
Director: George Fitzmaurice
Co-stars: Robert Montgomery Myrna Loy Reginald Owen

1944 CANDLES AT NINE
Director: John Harlow
Co-stars: Jessie Matthews John Stuart Beatrix Lehman

MELOVA SHOUVER

1992 SPLIT INFINITY
Director: Stan Ferguson
Co-stars: Trevor Black H.E.D. Redford

JEAN SHRIMPTON

1967 PRIVILEGE
Director: Peter Watkins
Co-stars: Paul Jones Mark London Max Bacon

KIM SHRINER

1988 ANGEL: THE FINAL CHAPTER
Director: Tom De Simone
Co-stars: Mitzi Kapture Maud Adams Richard Roundtree

NANCY SHUBERT

1933 SAGEBRUSH TRAIL
Director: Armand Schaefer
Co-stars: John Wayne Lane Chandler Yakima Canutt

ELIZABETH SHUE

1984 THE KARATE KID
Director: John Avildsen
Co-stars: Ralph Macchio Pat Morita Randee Heller

1986 LINK
Director: Richard Franklin
Co-stars: Terence Stamp Steven Pinner Richard Garnett

1987 DOUBLE SWITCH
Director: David Greenwalt
Co-stars: George Newbern Mariclare Costello Barbara Rhoades

1987 ADVENTURES IN BABYSITTING
Director: Chris Columbus
Co-stars: Maia Brewton Penelope Ann Miller Keith Coogan

1989 BACK TO THE FUTURE II
Director: Robert Zemeckis
Co-stars: Michael J. Fox Christopher Lloyd Lea Thompson

1990 BACK TO THE FUTURE III
Director: Robert Zemeckis
Co-stars: Michael J. Fox Mary Steenburgen Lea Thompson

1991 SOAPDISH
Director: Michael Hoffman
Co-stars: Sally Field Kevin Kline Robert Downey Jnr.

1991 TOO HOT TO HANDLE
Director: Jerry Rees
Co-stars: Kim Basinger Alec Baldwin Robert Loggia

1993 TWENTY BUCKS
Director: Keva Rosenfeld
Co-stars: Brendan Fraser Linda Hunt

1993 HEART AND SOULS
Director: Ron Underwood
Co-stars: Robert Downey Jnr. Charles Grodin Alfre Woodard

1994 BLIND JUSTICE
Director: Richard Spence
Co-stars: Armand Assante Robert Davi

1996 COUSIN BETTE
Director: Des McAnuff
Co-stars: Jessica Lange Bob Hoskins Kelly MacDonald

1996 LEAVING LAS VEGAS
Director: Mike Figgis
Co-stars: Nicolas Cage Julian Sands

1998 THE SAINT
Co-star: Val Kilmer

1998 DECONSTRUCTING HARRY
Director: Woody Allen
Co-stars: Robin Williams Kirstie Alley

1998 PALMETTO
Director: Volker Schlondorff
Co-star: Woody Harrelson

JAN SHUTAN

1977 DRACULA'S DOG
Director: Albert Band
Co-stars: Jose Ferrer Michael Pataki Libbie Chase

ETHEL SHUTTA

1930 WHOOPEE
Director: Thornton Freeland
Co-stars: Eddie Cantor Eleanor Hunt Paul Gregory

SABRINA SIANA

1982 ATOR, THE FIGHTING EAGLE
Director: David Hills
Co-stars: Miles O'Keefe Edmund Purdom Ritza Brown

NADIA SIBIRSKAIA

1924 MENILMONTANT
Director: Dimitri Kisanov
Co-stars: Yolande Beaulieu Guy Belmont Jean Pasquier

ANN SIDNEY

1970 PERFORMANCE
Director: Nicolas Roeg
Co-stars: James Fox Mick Jagger Anita Pallenberg

SYLVIA SIDNEY (*Sophia Kosow*)

Nominated For Best Supporting Actress In 1973 For "Summer Wishes,
Winter Dreams"

1931 STREET SCENE
Director: King Vidor
Co-stars: William Collier Max Mantor Russell Hopton

1931 CONFESSIONS OF A CO-ED
Co-stars: Phillips Holmes Norman Foster

1931 AN AMERICAN TRAGEDY
Director: Josef Von Sternberg
Co-stars: Phillips Holmes Irving Pichel

1931 LADIES OF THE BIG HOUSE
Director: Marion Gering
Co-stars: Gene Raymond Wynne Gibson Earle Foxe

1932 MADAME BUTTERFLY
Director: Marion Gering
Co-stars: Cary Grant Charles Ruggles Irving Pichel

1932 THE MIRACLE MAN
Director: Norman Z. McLeod
Co-stars: Chester Morris John Wray Ned Sparks

1932 MERRILY WE GO TO HELL
Director: Dorothy Arzner
Co-stars: Fredric March Adrienne Allen Cary Grant

1932 MAKE ME A STAR
Director: William Beaudine
Co-stars: Stuart Erwin Joan Blondell Zasu Pitts

1933 PICK-UP
Director: Marion Gering
Co-stars: George Raft William Harrigan

1933 JENNIE GERHARDT
Director: Marion Gering
Co-stars: Donald Cook Mary Astor Edward Arnold

1934 GOOD DAME
Director: Marion Gering
Co-stars: Fredric March Jack La Rue Noel Francis

1934 30 DAY PRINCESS
Director: Marion Gering
Co-stars: Cary Grant Edward Arnold Henry Stephenson

1935 MARY BURNS FUGITIVE
Director: William Howard
Co-stars: Melvyn Douglas Brian Donlevy Wallace Ford

1935 BEHOLD MY WIFE
Director: Mitchell Leisen
Co-stars: Gene Raymond Juliette Compton

1935 **ACCENT ON YOUTH**
Co-stars: Herbert Marshall Phillips Holmes

1936 **FURY**
Director: Fritz Lang
Co-stars: Spencer Tracy Walter Brennan Walter Abel

1936 **THE TRAIL OF THE LONESOME PINE**
Director: Henry Hathaway
Co-stars: Henry Fonda Fred MacMurray

1937 **YOU ONLY LIVE ONCE**
Director: Fritz Lang
Co-stars: Henry Fonda Barton MacLane William Gargan

1937 **DEAD END**
Director: William Wyler
Co-stars: Joel McCrea Humphrey Bogart Ward Bond

1938 **YOU AND ME**
Director: Fritz Lang
Co-stars: George Raft Harry Carey Warren Hymer

1939 **ONE-THIRD OF A NATION**
Director: Dudley Murphy
Co-stars: Leif Erickson Myron McCormick Sidney Lumet

1941 **THE WAGONS ROLL AT NIGHT**
Director: Ray Enright
Co-stars: Humphrey Bogart Eddie Albert Joan Leslie

1945 **BLOOD ON THE SUN**
Director: Frank Lloyd
Co-stars: James Cagney Wallace Ford Robert Armstrong

1946 **MR ACE**
Director: Edwin Marin
Co-stars: George Raft Stanley Ridges Sara Haden

1946 **THE SEARCHING WIND**
Director: William Dieterle
Co-stars: Robert Young Ann Richards

1947 **LOVE FROM A STRANGER**
Director: Richard Whorf
Co-stars: John Hodiak Ann Richards John Howard

1952 **LES MISERABLES**
Director: Lewis Milestone
Co-stars: Michael Rennie Robert Newton Debra Paget

1955 **VIOLENT SATURDAY**
Director: Richard Fleischer
Co-stars: Richard Egan Victor Mature Lee Marvin

1956 **BEHIND THE HIGH WALL**
Director: Abner Biberman
Co-stars: Tom Tully John Gavin Betty Lynn

1973 **SUMMER WISHES, WINTER DREAMS**
Director: Gilbert Cates
Co-stars: Joanne Woodward Martin Balsam

1975 **WINNER TAKE ALL**
Director: Paul Bogart
Co-stars: Shirley Jones Joan Blondell Sam Groom

1976 **GOD TOLD ME TO**
Director: Larry Cohen
Co-stars: Tony LoBianco Deborah Raffin Sandy Dennis

1977 **I NEVER PROMISED YOU A ROSE GARDEN**
Director: Anthony Page
Co-stars: Kathleen Quinlan Bibi Andersson

1978 **DAMIEN: OMEN II**
Director: Don Taylor
Co-stars: William Holden Lee Grant Lew Ayres

1981 **A SMALL KILLING**
Director: Steven Hillard Stern
Co-stars: Jean Simmons Edward Asner

1982 **HAMMETT**
Director: Wim Wenders
Co-stars: Fredric Forrest Peter Boyle Roy Kinnear

1983 **ORDER OF DEATH**
Director: Roberto Faenza
Co-stars: Harvey Keitel John Lydon Nicole Garcia

1985 **AN EARLY FROST**
Director: John Erman
Co-stars: Gena Rowlands Ben Gazarra Aidan Quinn

1987 **PALS**
Director: Lou Antonio
Co-stars: Don Ameche George C. Scott Susan Rinell

1988 **BEETLEJUICE**
Director: Tim Burton
Co-stars: Alec Baldwin Geena Davis Winona Ryder

1992 **USED PEOPLE**
Director: Beebon Kidron
Co-stars: Shirley MacLaine Kathy Bates Jessica Tandy

1997 **MARS ATTACKS!**
Director: Tim Burton
Co-stars: Jack Nicholson Glenn Close Rod Steiger

MARIA SIEBER

1934 **THE SCARLET EMPRESS**
Director: Josef Von Sternberg
Co-stars: Marlene Dietrich John Lodge Sam Jaffe

CASEY SIEMASZKO

1992 **PAINTED HEART**
Director: Michael Taav
Co-stars: Will Patton Robert Pastorelli Bebe Neuwirth

NINA SIEMASZKO

1988 **LICENCE TO DRIVE**
Director: Greg Beeman
Co-stars: Corey Haim Corey Feldman Carol Kane

1992 **BED AND BREAKFAST**
Director: Robert Ellis Miller
Co-stars: Roger Moore Talia Shire Colleen Dewhurst

1993 **THE SAINT OF FORT WASHINGTON**
Director: Tim Hunter
Co-stars: Matt Dillon Danny Glover Rick Aviles

1996 **RUNAWAY CAR**
Director: Jack Sholder
Co-star: Judge Reinhold

ELSBETH SIGMUND (Child)

1952 **HEIDI**
Director: Luigi Comencini
Co-stars: Heinrich Gretler Thomas Klameth Elsie Attenoff

1955 **HEIDI AND PETER**
Director: Frank Schnyder
Co-stars: Heinrich Gretler Thomas Klameth Anita Mey

SIMONE SIGNORET (Married Yves Montand)
Oscar For Best Actress In 1959 For "Room At The Top". Nominated For Best Actress In 1965 For "Ship Of Fools"

1947 **AGAINST THE WIND**
Director: Charles Crighton
Co-stars: Robert Beatty Jack Warner Paul Dupuis

1948 **DEDEE D'ANVERS**
Director: Yves Allegret
Co-stars: Marcel Pagliero Bernard Blier

1950 **MANEGES**
Director: Yves Allegret
Co-stars: Bernard Blier Jane Marken Frank Villard

1950   **LA RONDE**
Director: Max Ophuls
Co-stars: Anton Walbrook Danielle Darrieux Simone Simon

1952   **LA CASQUE D'OR**
Director: Jacques Becker
Co-stars: Serge Reggiani Claude Dauphin

1954   **LES DIABOLIQUES**
Director: Henri-Georges Clouzot
Co-stars: Vera Clouzot Paul Meurisse

1956   **EVIL EDEN**
Director: Luis Bunuel
Co-stars: Georges Marchal Charles Vanel Tito Junco

1957   **THE WITCHES OF SALEM**
Director: Raymond Rouleau
Co-stars: Yves Montand Mylene Demongeot

1958   **ROOM AT THE TOP**
Director: Jack Clayton
Co-stars: Laurence Harvey Heather Sears

1960   **ADUA ET LE COMPAGNE**
Director: Antonio Pietrangeli
Co-stars: Marcello Mastroianni Sandra Mico

1962   **TERM OF TRIAL**
Director: Peter Glenville
Co-stars: Laurence Olivier Sarah Miles

1964   **TODAY WE LIVE**
Co-star: Genevieve Page

1965   **IS PARIS BURNING ?**
Director: Rene Clement
Co-stars: Leslie Caron Charles Boyer

1965   **THE SLEEPING CAR MURDERS**
Director: Costa-Gavras
Co-stars: Yves Montand Jean-Louis Trintignant

1965   **SHIP OF FOOLS**
Director: Stanley Kramer
Co-stars: Vivien Leigh Jose Ferrer Lee Marvin

1966   **THE DEADLY AFFAIR**
Director: Sidney Lumet
Co-stars: James Mason Harry Andrews Lynn Redgrave

1967   **GAMES**
Director: Curtis Harrington
Co-stars: James Caan Katherine Ross Don Stroud

1968   **THE SEA GULL**
Director: Sidney Lumet
Co-stars: James Mason Vanessa Redgrave Ronald Radd

1969   **THE ARMY IN THE SHADOWS**
Director: Jean-Pierre Melville
Co-stars: Lino Ventura Jean-Pierre Cassel

1970   **THE CONFESSION**
Director: Costa-Gavras
Co-stars: Yves Montand Gabriele Ferzetti

1971   **LE CHAT**
Director: Pierre Granier-Deferre
Co-stars: Jean Gabin Annie Cordy

1972   **THE WIDOW COUDERC**
Director: Pierre Granier-Deferre

1973   **BURNT BARNS**
Director: Jean Chapot
Co-stars: Alain Delon Miou-Miou Catherine Allegret

1975   **POLICE PYTHON 357**
Director: Alain Corneau
Co-stars: Yves Montand Francois Perrier

1974   **THE FLESH OF THE ORCHID**
Director: Patrice Chereau
Co-stars: Charlotte Rampling Edwige Feuillere

1977   **MADAME ROSA**
Director: Moshe Mizrahi
Co-stars: Claude Dauphin Samy Ben Youb

1982   **L'ETOILE DU NORD**
Director: Pierre Granier-Deferre
Co-stars: Phillippe Noiret Fanny Cottencon

CAROLINE SIHOL

1983   **FINALLY, SUNDAY**
Director: Francois Truffaut
Co-stars: Fanny Ardant Jean-Louis Trintignant

1986   **AUTHOR'S DISAPPOINTMENT**
Director: Roger Pigaut
Co-stars: Jacques Debasy Marc Eyraud Frederic Lambre

1992   **TOUS LES MATINS DU MONDE**
Director: Alain Corneau
Co-stars: Gerard Depardieu Anne Brochet Guillaume Depardieu

CYNTHIA SIKES

1983   **THE MAN WHO LOVED WOMEN**
Director: Blake Edwards
Co-stars: Burt Reynolds Julie Andrews Kim Basinger

1984   **HIS MISTRESS**
Director: David Lowell Rich
Co-stars: Robert Urich Julianne Phillips Linda Kelsey

1988   **ARTHUR II: ON THE ROCKS**
Director: Bud Yorkin
Co-stars: Dudley Moore Liza Minnelli John Gielgud

1990   **LOVE HURTS**
Director: Bud Yorkin
Co-stars: Jeff Daniels Judith Ivey John Mahoney

1990   **IN DEFENSE OF A MARRIED MAN**
Director: Joel Oliansky
Co-stars: Judith Light Michael Ontkean Jerry Orbach

KAREN SILLAS

1992   **SIMPLE MEN**
Director: Hal Hartley
Co-stars: Robert Burke William Sage Martin Donovan

1994   **WHAT HAPPENED WAS**
Director: Tom Noonan
Co-star: Tom Noonan

SIMONE SILVA

1951   **LADY GODIVA RIDES AGAIN**
Director: Frank Launder
Co-stars: Pauline Stroud Dennis Price Diana Dors

1952   **SOUTH OF ALGIERS**
Director: Jack Lee
Co-stars: Van Heflin Wanda Hendrix Eric Portman

1953   **ESCAPE BY NIGHT**
Director: John Gilling
Co-stars: Bonar Colleano Andrew Ray Ted Ray

1955   **THIRD PARTY RISK**
Director: Daniel Birt
Co-stars: Lloyd Bridges Maureen Swanson Finlay Currie

LEONORE SILVEIRA

1993   **ABRAHAM VALLEY**
Director: Manoel De Oliviera
Co-stars: Luis Miguel Cintra Cecile Sanz De Alba

CHRISTINE SILVER

1950   **ROOM TO LET**
Director: Godfrey Grayson
Co-stars: Jimmy Hanley Valentine Dyall Constance Smith

1955   THE HORNET'S NEST
Director: Charles Saunders
Co-stars: Paul Carpenter June Thorburn Marla Landi

VERONIQUE SILVER

1981   THE WOMAN NEXT DOOR
Director: Francois Truffaut
Co-stars: Gerard Depardieu Fanny Ardant Henri Garcin

ELIZABETH SILVERSTEIN

1989   HOWLING V: THE REBIRTH
Director: Neal Sundstrom
Co-stars: Victoria Catlin Mark Faulkner Stephanie Shockley

ALICIA SILVERSTONE

1993   THE CRUSH
Director: Alan Shapiro
Co-stars: Cary Elwes Jennifer Rubin Amber Benson

1994   THE COOL AND THE CRAZY
Director: Ralph Bakshi
Co-stars: Jared Leto Jennifer Blanc Matthew Flint

1995   CLUELESS
Director: Amy Heckerling
Co-stars: Stacey Dash Paul Rudd

1996   BATMAN AND ROBIN
Director: Joel Schumacher
Co-stars: George Clooney Chris O'Donnell Arnold Schwarzenegger

ZANDE SILVIA

1992   DEATH AND THE COMPASS
Director: Alex Cox
Co-stars: Peter Boyle Christopher Eccleston Pedro Armendariz

SHEILA SIM *(Married Richard Attenborough)*

1944   A CANTERBURY TALE
Director: Michael Powell
Co-stars: Eric Portman Dennis Price Esmond Knight

1945   GREAT DAY
Director: Lance Comfort
Co-stars: Eric Portman Flora Robson Isabel Jeans

1947   DANCING WITH CRIME
Director: John Paddy Carstairs
Co-stars: Richard Attenborough Barry K. Barnes Barry Jones

1948   THE GUINEA PIG
Director: Roy Boulting
Co-stars: Richard Attenborough Robert Flemyng Bernard Miles

1949   DEAR MR PROHACK
Director: Thornton Freeland
Co-stars: Cecil Parker Dirk Bogarde Glynis Johns

1951   PANDORA AND THE FLYING DUTCHMAN
Director: Albert Lewin
Co-stars: James Mason Ava Gardner Nigel Patrick

1954   THE NIGHT MY NUMBER CAME UP
Director: Leslie Norman
Co-stars: Michael Redgrave Alexander Knox Bill Kerr

1954   WEST OF ZANZIBAR
Director: Harry Watt
Co-stars: Anthony Steel Orlando Martins Martin Benson

ANNETTE SIMMONDS

1949   THE ADVENTURES OF P.C. 49
Director: Godfrey Grayson
Co-stars: Hugh Latimer John Penrose Patricia Cutts

BEVERLEY SIMMONS *(Child)*

1945   FRONTIER GAL
Director: Charles Lamont
Co-stars: Yvonne De Carlo Rod Cameron Sheldon Leonard

1946   BUCK PRIVATES COME HOME
Director: Charles Barton
Co-stars: Bud Abbot Lou Costello Tom Brown

1946   CUBAN PETE
Director: Jean Yarbrough
Co-stars: Desi Arnaz Joan Fulton Don Porter

1946   LITTLE MISS BIG
Co-stars: Fay Holden Fred Brady Frank McHugh

GRACE SIMMONS

1986   ASSASSIN
Director: Sandor Stern
Co-stars: Robert Conrad Karen Austin Robert Webber

JEAN SIMMONS *(Child)*
(Married Stewart Granger, Richard Brooks)
Nominated For Best Actress In 1969 For "The Happy Ending"
Nominated For Best Supporting Actress In 1948 For "Hamlet"

1944   GIVE US THE MOON
Director: Val Guest
Co-stars: Margaret Lockwood Vic Oliver Peter Graves

1945   THE WAY TO THE STARS
Director: Anthony Asquith
Co-stars: John Mills Michael Redgrave Rosamund John

1945   CAESAR AND CLEOPATRA
Director: Gabriel Pascal
Co-stars: Claude Rains Vivien Leigh Stewart Granger

1946   GREAT EXPECTATIONS
Director: David Lean
Co-stars: John Mills Alec Guinness Martita Hunt

1946   HUNGRY HILL
Director: Brian Desmond Hurst
Co-stars: Margaret Lockwood Dennis Price Dermot Walsh

1947   UNCLE SILAS
Director: Charles Frank
Co-stars: Derrick De Marney Katina Paxinou Derek Bond

1947   THE WOMAN IN THE HALL
Director: Jack Lee
Co-stars: Ursula Jeans Cecil Parker Edward Underdown

1947   BLACK NARCISSUS
Director: Michael Powell
Co-stars: Deborah Kerr David Farrar Sabu

1948   HAMLET
Director: Laurence Olivier
Co-stars: Laurence Olivier Eileen Herlie Basil Sydney

1949   THE BLUE LAGOON
Director: Frank Launder
Co-stars: Donald Houston Noel Purcell Peter Jones

1949   ADAM AND EVELYNE
Director: Harold French
Co-stars: Stewart Granger Helen Cherry Beatrice Varley

1950   CAGE OF GOLD
Director: Basil Dearden
Co-stars: David Farrar James Donald Herbert Lom

1950   THE CLOUDED YELLOW
Director: Ralph Thomas
Co-stars: Trevor Howard Barry Jones Kenneth More

1950   SO LONG AT THE FAIR
Director: Terence Fisher
Co-stars: Dirk Bogarde David Tomlinson Honor Blackman

1950	**TRIO**
Director:	Harold French
Co-stars:	Michael Rennie Nigel Patrick James Hayter

1952	**ANDROCLES AND THE LION**
Director:	Chester Erskine
Co-stars:	Alan Young Robert Newton Victor Mature

1952	**ANGEL FACE** ✓
Director:	Otto Preminger
Co-stars:	Robert Mitchum Herbert Marshall Barbara O'Neil

1952	**BEAUTIFUL BUT DANGEROUS**
Director:	Lloyd Bacon
Co-stars:	Robert Mitchum Arthur Hunnicutt Wallace Ford

1953	**THE ACTRESS**
Director:	George Cukor
Co-stars:	Spencer Tracy Teresa Wright Anthony Perkins

1953	**AFFAIR WITH A STRANGER**
Director:	Roy Rowland
Co-stars:	Victor Mature Jane Darwell Mary Jo Torola

1953	**THE ROBE**
Director:	Henry Koster
Co-stars:	Richard Burton Victor Mature Michael Rennie

1953	**YOUNG BESS**
Director:	George Sidney
Co-stars:	Stewart Granger Charles Laughton Deborah Kerr

1954	**THE EGYPTIAN**
Director:	Michael Curtiz
Co-stars:	Edmund Purdom Victor Mature Peter Ustinov

1954	**DESIREE**
Director:	Henry Koster
Co-stars:	Marlon Brando Merle Oberon Michael Rennie

1954	**A BULLET IS WAITING**
Director:	John Farrow
Co-stars:	Rory Calhoun Stephen McNally Brian Aherne

1955	**FOOTSTEPS IN THE FOG**
Director:	Arthur Lubin
Co-stars:	Stewart Granger Bill Travers Finlay Currie

1955	**GUYS AND DOLLS**
Director:	Joseph Mankiewicz
Co-stars:	Marlon Brando Frank Sinatra Vivian Blaine

1956	**HILDA CRANE**
Director:	Phillip Dunne
Co-stars:	Guy Madison Jean-Pierre Aumont Judith Evelyn

1957	**THIS COULD BE THE NIGHT**
Director:	Robert Wise
Co-stars:	Paul Douglas Tony Franciosa Joan Blondell

1957	**UNTIL THEY SAIL**
Director:	Robert Wise
Co-stars:	Paul Newman Joan Fontaine Piper Laurie

1958	**HOME BEFORE DARK**
Director:	Mervyn LeRoy
Co-stars:	Dan O'Herlihy Rhonda Fleming Efrem Zimbalist Jnr.

1958	**THE BIG COUNTRY**
Director:	William Wyler
Co-stars:	Gregory Peck Charlton Heston Burl Ives

1959	**THIS EARTH IS MINE**
Director:	Henry King
Co-stars:	Claude Rains Rock Hudson Dorothy McGuire

1960	**SPARTACUS**
Director:	Stanley Kubrick
Co-stars:	Kirk Douglas Tony Curtis Charles Laughton

1960	**THE GRASS IS GREENER**
Director:	Stanley Donen
Co-stars:	Cary Grant Deborah Kerr Robert Mitchum

1960	**ELMER GANTRY**
Director:	Richard Brooks
Co-stars:	Burt Lancaster Shirley Jones Arthur Kennedy

1963	**ALL THE WAY HOME**
Director:	Alex Segal
Co-stars:	Robert Preston Aline MacMahon Pat Hingle

1965	**LIFE AT THE TOP**
Director:	Ted Kotchoff
Co-stars:	Laurence Harvey Donald Wolfit Honor Blackman

1966	**MISTER BUDDWING**
Director:	Delbert Mann
Co-stars:	James Garner Angela Lansbury Katharine Ross

1967	**DIVORCE AMERICAN STYLE**
Director:	Bud Yorkin
Co-stars:	Dick Van Dyke Debbie Reynolds Jason Robards

1967	**ROUGH NIGHT IN JERICO**
Director:	Arnold Laven
Co-stars:	George Peppard Dean Martin John McIntyre

1968	**HEIDI**
Director:	Delbert Mann
Co-stars:	Jennifer Edwards Maximilian Schell Michael Redgrave

1969	**THE HAPPY ENDING**
Director:	Richard Brooks
Co-stars:	John Forsythe Shirley Jones Bobby Darin

1970	**SAY HELLO TO YESTERDAY**
Director:	Alvin Rakoff
Co-stars:	Leonard Whiting Evelyn Laye John Lee

1978	**DOMINIQUE**
Director:	Michael Anderson
Co-stars:	Cliff Robertson Jenny Agutter Judy Geeson

1981	**GOLDEN GATE**
Director:	Paul Wendkos
Co-stars:	Richard Kiley Perry King Melanie Griffith

1981	**A SMALL KILLING**
Director:	Steven Hillard Stern
Co-stars:	Ed Asner Sylvia Sidney Andrew Prine

1984	**GOING UNDERCOVER**
Director:	James Kenelm Clarke
Co-stars:	Lea Thompson Chris Lemmon Viveca Lindfors

1987	**PERRY MASON:** **THE CASE OF THE LOST LOVE**
Co-stars:	Raymond Burr Barbara Hale Gene Barry

1988	**INHERIT THE WIND**
Director:	David Greene
Co-stars:	Kirk Douglas Jason Robards Darren McGavin

1988	**THE DAWNING**
Director:	Robert Knights
Co-stars:	Anthony Hopkins Rebecca Pidgeon Trevor Howard

1991	**MISS MARPLE: THEY DO IT BY MIRRORS**
Director:	Norman Stone
Co-stars:	Joan Hickson Joss Ackland Faith Brook

1996	**HOW TO MAKE AN AMERICAN QUILT**
Director:	Jocelyn Moorhouse
Co-stars:	Winona Ryder Anne Bancroft Ellen Burstyn

1998	**DAISIES IN DECEMBER**
Director:	Mark Haber
Co-stars:	Joss Ackland Pippa Guard Muriel Pavlow

ROBYN SIMMONS

1989	**LEAVING NORMAL**
Director:	Edward Zwick
Co-stars:	Christine Lahti Meg Tilly Maury Chaykin

ROS SIMMONS

1984 THE ADVENTURES OF SHERLOCK HOLMES: THE BLUE CARBUNCLE
Director: David Carson
Co-stars: Jeremy Brett David Burke

GINNY SIMMS

1939 THAT'S RIGHT, YOU'RE WRONG
Director: David Butler
Co-stars: Kay Kyser Adolphe Menjou Lucille Ball

1940 YOU'LL FIND OUT
Director: David Butler
Co-stars: Kay Kyser Dennis O'Keefe Boris Karloff

1941 PLAYMATES
Director: David Butler
Co-stars: Kay Kyser John Barrymore Lupe Velez

1941 LOOK WHO'S LAUGHING
Director: Allan Dwan
Co-stars: Lucille Ball Edgar Bergen Charlie McCarthy

1942 SEVEN DAYS LEAVE
Director: Tim Whelan
Co-stars: Lucille Ball Victor Mature Marcy McGuire

1942 HERE WE GO AGAIN
Director: Allan Dwan
Co-stars: Jim Jordan Marion Jordan Edgar Bergen

1943 HIT THE ICE
Director: Charles Lamont
Co-stars: Bud Abbott Lou Costello Patric Knowles

1943 AROUND THE WORLD
Director: Allan Dwan
Co-stars: Kay Kyser Joan Davis Ish Kabibble

1944 BROADWAY RHYTHM
Director: Roy Del Ruth
Co-stars: George Murphy Charles Winninger Gloria De Haven

1945 SHADY LADY
Director: George Waggner
Co-stars: Charles Coburn Robert Paige Martha O'Driscoll

1946 NIGHT AND DAY
Director: Michael Curtiz
Co-stars: Cary Grant Alexis Smith Monty Woolley

HILDA SIMMS

1953 THE JOE LOUIS STORY
Director: Robert Gordon
Co-stars: Coley Wallace Paul Stewart James Edwards

1954 BLACK WIDOW
Director: Nunnally Johnson
Co-stars: Ginger Rogers Van Heflin George Raft

CARLY SIMON

1971 TAKING OFF
Director: Milos Forman
Co-stars: Lynn Carlin Buck Henry Linnea Heacock

JOSETTE SIMON

1989 HERE IS THE NEWS
Director: Udayan Prasad
Co-stars: Richard E. Grant Gary Love Alan MacNaughton

1992 BITTER HARVEST
Director: Simon Cellan Jones
Co-stars: Sue Johnston Rudolph Walker Tomas Milian

1992 SEEKERS
Director: Peter Barber-Fleming
Co-stars: Brenda Fricker Michael Carter Harry Jones

MAE SIMON

1931 MY-YIDDISHE-MAMA
Co-star: Seymour Rechzeit

SIMONE SIMON

1936 GIRL'S DORMITORY
Director: Irving Cummings
Co-stars: Herbert Marshall Tyrone Power

1936 LADIES IN LOVE
Director: Edward Griffith
Co-stars: Janet Gaynor Loretta Young Tyrone Power

1937 LOVE AND HISSES
Director: Sidney Lanfield
Co-stars: Walter Winchell Bert Lahr Joan Davis

1937 SEVENTH HEAVEN
Director: Henry King
Co-stars: James Stewart Jean Hersholt J. Edward Bromberg

1938 JOSETTE
Director: Allan Dwan
Co-stars: Don Ameche Robert Young Joan Davis

1938 LA BETE HUMANE
Director: Jean Renoir
Co-stars: Jean Gabin Fernand Ledoux Jean Renoir

1941 ALL THAT MONEY CAN BUY
Director: William Dieterle
Co-stars: Walter Huston Edward Arnold James Craig

1942 CAT PEOPLE
Director: Jacques Tourneur
Co-stars: Kent Smith Tom Conway Jane Randolph

1943 TAHITI HONEY
Co-star: Dennis O'Keefe

1944 THE CURSE OF THE CAT PEOPLE
Director: Robert Wise
Co-stars: Kent Smith Jane Randolph Ann Carter

1944 JOHNNY DOESN'T LIVE HERE ANYMORE
Director: Joe May
Co-stars: James Ellison Robert Mitchum

1944 MADEMOISELLE FIFI
Director: Robert Wise
Co-stars: Kurt Kreuger John Emery Jason Robards Snr.

1947 TEMPTATION HARBOUR
Director: Lance Comfort
Co-stars: Robert Newton William Hartnell Marcel Dalio

1950 LA RONDE
Director: Max Ophuls
Co-stars: Anton Walbrook Danielle Darrieux Simone Signoret

1952 LE PLAISIR
Director: Max Ophuls
Co-stars: Claude Dauphin Jean Gabin Danielle Darrieux

1956 THE EXTRA DAY
Director: William Fairchild
Co-stars: Richard Basehart Sid James Beryl Reid

LISA SIMONE

1959 THE GIANT GILA MONSTER
Director: Ray Kellogg
Co-stars: Don Sullivan Shug Fisher

MICHELE SIMONNET

1988 BERNADETTE
Director: Jean Delannoy
Co-stars: Sydney Penny Jean-Marc Bory Roland Lesaffre

GWENAELLE SIMONS

1996 A SUMMER'S TALE
Director: Eric Rohmer
Co-stars: Melvil Poupaud Amanda Langlet Aurelia Nolin

JULIETTE SIMPSON

1985 HAREM
Director: Arthur Joffe
Co-stars: Nastassja Kinski Ben Kingsley Dennis Goldson

JOAN SIMS

1953 WILL ANY GENTLEMAN ?
Director: Michael Anderson
Co-stars: George Cole Alan Badel Veronica Hurst

1953 TROUBLE IN STORE
Director: John Paddy Carstairs
Co-stars: Norman Wisdom Lana Morris Margaret Rutherford

1954 THE BELLES OF ST. TRINIAN'S
Director: Frank Launder
Co-stars: Alastair Sim George Cole Joyce Grenfell

1955 AS LONG AS THEY'RE HAPPY
Director: J. Lee-Thompson
Co-stars: Jack Buchanan Jean Carson Diana Dors

1955 LOST
Director: Guy Green
Co-stars: David Farrar Julia Arnall Eleanor Summerfield

1956 DRY ROT
Director: Maurice Elvey
Co-stars: Ronald Shiner Brian Rix Sid James

1957 DAVY
Director: Michael Relph
Co-stars: Harry Secombe Ron Randell Susan Shaw

1957 CARRY ON ADMIRAL
Director: Val Guest
Co-stars: David Tomlinson Peggy Cummins Eunice Gayson

1958 THE CAPTAIN'S TABLE
Director: Jack Lee
Co-stars: John Gregson Peggy Cummins Donald Sinden

1959 LIFE IN EMERGENCY WARD 10
Director: Robert Day
Co-stars: Michael Craig Dorothy Alison Glyn Owen

1959 PASSPORT TO SHAME
Director: Alvin Rakoff
Co-stars: Eddie Constantine Diana Dors Odile Versois

1959 PLEASE TURN OVER
Director: Gerald Thomas
Co-stars: Ted Ray Jean Kent Leslie Phillips

1959 UPSTAIRS AND DOWNSTAIRS
Director: Ralph Thomas
Co-stars: Michael Craig Anne Heywood Sid James

1959 CARRY ON NURSE
Director: Gerald Thomas
Co-stars: Shirley Eaton Bill Owen June Whitfield

1959 CARRY ON TEACHER
Director: Gerald Thomas
Co-stars: Ted Ray Kenneth Williams Leslie Phillips

1960 CARRY ON CONSTABLE
Director: Gerald Thomas
Co-stars: Sid James Eric Barker Shirley Eaton

1960 DOCTOR IN LOVE
Director: Ralph Thomas
Co-stars: Michael Craig Leslie Phillips Virginia Maskell

1960 HIS AND HERS
Director: Brian Desmond Hurst
Co-stars: Terry-Thomas Janette Scott Oliver Reed

1961 MR TOPAZE
Director: Peter Sellers
Co-stars: Peter Sellers Herbert Lom Leo McKern

1961 WATCH YOUR STERN
Director: Gerald Thomas
Co-stars: Kenneth Connor Eric Barker Noel Purcell

1961 A PAIR OF BRIEFS
Director: Ralph Thomas
Co-stars: Michael Craig Mary Peach Liz Fraser

1961 CARRY ON REGARDLESS
Director: Gerald Thomas
Co-stars: Liz Fraser Stanley Unwin Bill Owen

1962 TWICE ROUND THE DAFFODILS
Director: Gerald Thomas
Co-stars: Juliette Mills Andrew Ray Jill Ireland

1963 NURSE ON WHEELS
Director: Gerald Thomas
Co-stars: Juliette Mills Athene Seyler Ronald Lewis

1965 THE BIG JOB
Director: Gerald Thomas
Co-stars: Sid James Dick Emery Sylvia Syms

1965 CARRY ON CLEO
Director: Gerald Thomas
Co-stars: Amanda Barrie Kenneth Williams Sid James

1965 CARRY ON COWBOY
Director: Gerald Thomas
Co-stars: Jim Dale Angela Douglas Sid James

1966 CARRY ON: DON'T LOSE YOUR HEAD
Director: Gerald Thomas
Co-stars: Dany Robin Peter Gilmore Peter Butterworth

1966 DOCTOR IN CLOVER
Director: Ralph Thomas
Co-stars: Leslie Phillips Arthur Haynes Fenella Fielding

1967 CARRY ON, FOLLOW THAT CAMEL
Director: Gerald Thomas
Co-stars: Phil Silvers Anita Harris Jim Dale

1968 CARRY ON DOCTOR
Director: Gerald Thomas
Co-stars: Jim Dale Anita Harris Frankie Howerd

1968 CARRY ON UP THE KHYBER
Director: Gerald Thomas
Co-stars: Roy Castle Terry Scott Bernard Bresslaw

1969 CARRY ON CAMPING
Director: Gerald Thomas
Co-stars: Barbara Windsor Dilys Lane Charles Hawtrey

1969 CARRY ON AGAIN DOCTOR
Director: Gerald Thomas
Co-stars: Sid James Hattie Jacques Barbara Windsor

1970 CARRY ON HENRY
Director: Gerald Thomas
Co-stars: Sid James Kenneth Williams Charles Hawtrey

1970 CARRY ON LOVING
Director: Gerald Thomas
Co-stars: Sid James Hattie Jacques Terry Scott

1970 CARRY ON UP THE JUNGLE
Director: Gerald Thomas
Co-stars: Frankie Howerd Terry Scott Kenneth Connor

1970 DOCTOR IN TROUBLE
Director: Ralph Thomas
Co-stars: Leslie Phillips Harry Secombe Angela Scoular

1971 CARRY ON AT YOUR CONVENIENCE
Director: Gerald Thomas
Co-stars: Kenneth Cope Kenneth Williams Patsy Rowlands

1971 THE MAGNIFICENT SEVEN DEADLY SINS
Director: Graham Stark
Co-stars: Roy Hudd Julie Ege Spike Milligan

1972 CARRY ON ABROAD
Director: Gerald Thomas
Co-stars: Charles Hawtrey Peter Butterworth Sally Geeson

1972 CARRY ON MATRON
Director: Gerald Thomas
Co-stars: Sid James Kenneth Cope Terry Scott

1972 DON'T JUST LIE THERE, SAY SOMETHING
Director: Bob Kellett
Co-stars: Joanna Lumley Brian Rix Leslie Phillips

1972 THE ALF GARNETT SAGA
Director: Bob Kellett
Co-stars: Warren Mitchell Dandy Nichols

1972 NOT NOW DARLING
Director: Ray Cooney
Co-stars: Ray Cooney Leslie Phillips Moira Lister

1974 CARRY ON DICK
Director: Gerald Thomas
Co-stars: Sid James Hattie Jacques Barbara Windsor

1975 CARRY ON BEHIND
Director: Gerald Thomas
Co-stars: Elke Sommer Jack Douglas Windsor Davies

1975 ONE OF OUR DINOSAURS IS MISSING
Director: Robert Stevenson
Co-stars: Helen Hayes Peter Ustinov

1976 CARRY ON ENGLAND
Director: Gerald Thomas
Co-stars: Patrick Mower Judy Geeson Diane Langton

1978 CARRY ON EMMANUELLE
Director: Gerald Thomas
Co-stars: Suzanne Danielle Beryl Reid Jack Douglas

1985 DECEPTIONS
Director: Melville Shavelson
Co-stars: Stefanie Powers Barry Bostwick Jeremy Brett

1993 TENDER LOVING CARE
Director: Dewi Humphreys
Co-stars: Dawn French Rosemary Leach Peter Jones

NANCY SINATRA *(Daughter Of Frank Sinatra)*

1964 FOR THOSE WHO THINK YOUNG
Director: Leslie Martinson
Co-stars: James Darren Pamela Tiffin George Raft

1965 MARRIAGE ON THE ROCKS
Director: Jack Donohue
Co-stars: Frank Sinatra Dean Martin Deborah Kerr

1966 THE LAST OF THE SECRET AGENTS ?
Director: Norman Abbott
Co-stars: Marty Allen John Williams

1966 THE WILD ANGELS
Director: Roger Corman
Co-stars: Peter Fonda Bruce Dern Michael J. Pollard

DIANE SINCLAIR

1932 WASHINGTON MASQUERADE
Co-stars: Lionel Barrymore Henry Kolker

1933 FIGHTING CODE
Co-stars: Buck Jones Ward Bond

1933 DAMAGED LIVES *(Released 1937)*
Director: Edgar Ulmer
Co-stars: Lyman Williams Cecilia Parker George Irving

MADGE SINCLAIR

1974 CONRACK
Director: Martin Ritt
Co-stars: Jon Voight Paul Winfield Hume Cronyn

1975 I WILL...I WILL...FOR NOW
Director: Norman Panama
Co-stars: Elliott Gould Diane Keaton Victoria Principal

1978 CONVOY
Director: Sam Peckinpah
Co-stars: Kris Kristofferson Ali MacGraw Ernest Borgnine

1988 COMING TO AMERICA
Director: John Landis
Co-stars: Eddie Murphy Arsinio Hall James Earl Jones

1990 THE ORCHID HOUSE
Director: Horace Ove
Co-stars: Diana Quick Frances Barber Kate Buffery

1994 THE LION KING *(Voice)*
Director: Rob Minkoff
Co-stars: Matthew Broderick James Earl Jones Jeremy Irons

MARY SINCLAIR

1953 ARROWHEAD
Director: Charles Marquis Warren
Co-stars: Charlton Heston Jack Palance Katy Jurado

LORI SINGER

1984 FOOTLOOSE
Director: Herbert Ross
Co-stars: Kevin Bacon John Lithgow Diane Wiest

1985 THE FALCON AND THE SNOWMAN
Director: John Schlesinger
Co-stars: Timothy Hutton Sean Penn David Suchet

1985 THE MAN WITH ONE RED SHOE
Director: Stan Dragoti
Co-stars: Tom Hanks James Belushi Carrie Fisher

1985 TROUBLE IN MIND
Director: Alan Rudolph
Co-stars: Kris Kristofferson Keith Carradine Genevieve Bujold

1989 WARLOCK
Director: Steve Miner
Co-stars: Richard E. Grant Julian Sands Mary Woronov

1990 STORM AND SORROW
Director: Richard A. Colla
Co-star: Todd Allen

1992 EQUINOX
Director: Alan Rudolph
Co-stars: Matthew Modine Lara Flynn Boyle Marisa Tomei

1993 SHORT CUTS
Director: Robert Altman
Co-stars: Matthew Modine Andie MacDowall Jennifer Jason Leigh

EVA MARIE SINGHAMMER *(Child)*

1965 HEIDI
Director: Werner Jacobs
Co-stars: Gertraud Mittermayr Gustav Knuth Lotte Ledi

PENNY SINGLETON

1930 GOOD NEWS
Director: Nick Grinde
Co-stars: Bessie Love Stanley Smith Lola Lane

1937 SWING YOUR LADY
Director: Ray Enright
Co-stars: Humphrey Bogart Louise Fazenda Nat Pendleton

1937 VOGUES OF 1938
Director: Irving Cummings
Co-stars: Joan Bennett Warner Baxter Helen Vinson

1938 SECRETS OF AN ACTRESS
Director: William Keighley
Co-stars: Kay Francis George Brent Ian Hunter

1938 RACKET BUSTERS
Director: Lloyd Bacon
Co-stars: George Brent Humphrey Bogart Gloria Dickson

1938 BOY MEETS GIRL
Director: Lloyd Bacon
Co-stars: James Cagney Pat O'Brien Marie Wilson

1938 MEN ARE SUCH FOOLS
Director: Busby Berkeley
Co-stars: Humphrey Bogart Wayne Morris Priscilla Lane

1938 HARD TO GET
Director: Ray Enright
Co-stars: Dick Powell Olivia De Havilland Charles Winninger

1938 GARDEN OF THE MOON
Director: Busby Berkeley
Co-stars: Pat O'Brien John Payne Margaret Lindsay

1938 BLONDIE
Director: Frank Strayer
Co-stars: Arthur Lake Larry Simms Gene Lockhart

1939 BLONDIE BRINGS UP BABY
Director: Frank Strayer
Co-stars: Arthur Lake Danny Mummert Peggy Ann Garner

1939 BLONDIE MEETS THE BOSS
Director: Frank Strayer
Co-stars: Arthur Lake Dorothy Moore Don Beddoe

1939 BLONDIE TAKES A VACATION
Director: Frank Strayer
Co-stars: Arthur Lake Donald MacBride Elizabeth Dunne

1940 GO WEST YOUNG LADY
Director: Frank Strayer
Co-stars: Glenn Ford Ann Miller Charles Ruggles

1940 BLONDIE HAS SERVANT TROUBLE
Director: Frank Strayer
Co-stars: Arthur Lake Arthur Hohl Esther Dale

1940 BLONDIE ON A BUDGET
Director: Frank Strayer
Co-stars: Arthur Lake Rita Hayworth John Qualen

1940 BLONDIE PLAYS CUPID
Director: Frank Strayer
Co-stars: Arthur Lake Glenn Ford Luana Walters

1941 BLONDIE GOES LATIN
Director: Frank Strayer
Co-stars: Arthur Lake Tito Guizar Ruth Terry

1941 BLONDIE IN SOCIETY
Director: Frank Strayer
Co-stars: Arthur Lake William Frawley Edgar Kennedy

1942 BLONDIE FOR VICTORY
Director: Frank Strayer
Co-stars: Arthur Lake Stuart Erwin Majelle White

1942 BLONDIE GOES TO COLLEGE
Director: Frank Strayer
Co-stars: Arthur Lake Larry Parks Janet Blair

1942 BLONDIE'S BLESSED EVENT
Director: Frank Strayer
Co-stars: Arthur Lake Hans Conreid Mary Wickes

1943 FOOTLIGHT GLAMOUR
Director: Frank Strayer
Co-stars: Arthur Lake Ann Savage Thurston Hall

1943 IT'S A GREAT LIFE
Director: Frank Strayer
Co-stars: Arthur Lake Larry Simms Hugh Herbert

1945 LEAVE IT TO BLONDIE
Director: Abby Berlin
Co-stars: Arthur Lake Jonathen Hale Marjorie Ann Mutchie

1946 THE YOUNG WIDOW
Director: Edwin Marin
Co-stars: Jane Russell Louis Hayward Faith Domergue

1946 LIFE WITH BLONDIE
Director: Abby Berlin
Co-stars: Arthur Lake Ernest Truex Marc Lawrence

1946 BLONDIE KNOWS BEST
Director: Abby Berlin
Co-stars: Arthur Lake Steven Geray Jerome Cowan

1946 BLONDIE'S LUCKY DAY
Director: Abby Berlin
Co-stars: Arthur Lake Robert Stanton Frank Jenks

1947 BLONDIE'S BIG MOMENT
Director: Abby Berlin
Co-stars: Arthur Lake Marjorie Kent Anita Louise

1947 BLONDIE'S HOLIDAY
Director: Abby Berlin
Co-stars: Arthur Lake Grant Mitchell Eddie Acuff

1947 BLONDIE IN THE DOUGH
Director: Abby Berlin
Co-stars: Arthur Lake Hugh Herbert Clarence Kolb

1947 BLONDIE'S ANNIVERSARY
Director: Abby Berlin
Co-stars: Arthur Lake Adele Jergens Jerome Cowan

1948 BLONDIE'S REWARD
Director: Abby Singer
Co-stars: Arthur Lake Gay Nelson Ross Ford

1949 BLONDIE'S SECRET
Director: Edward Bernds
Co-stars: Arthur Lake Thurston Hall Jack Rice

1949 BLONDIE HITS THE JACKPOT
Director: Edward Bernds
Co-stars: Arthur Lake Lloyd Corrigan Ann Carter

1949 BLONDIE'S BIG DEAL
Director: Edward Bernds
Co-stars: Arthur Lake Colette Lyons Ray Walker

1950 BLONDIE'S HERO
Director: Edward Bernds
Co-stars: Arthur Lake Joe Sawyer Iris Adrian

1950 BEWARE OF BLONDIE
Director: Edward Bernds
Co-stars: Arthur Lake Adele Jergens Dick Wessel

1990 JETSONS: THE MOVIE (Voice)
Director: Hanna-Barbera
Co-stars: Mel Blanc George O'Hanlon Tiffany

MARINA SIRTIS

1987 STAR TREK THE NEXT GENERATION
Director: Rob Bowman
Co-stars: Patrick Stewart Jonathan Frakes Brent Spiner

1990 ONE LAST CHANCE
Director: Gabrielle Beaumont
Co-stars: George Jackos Mark Jefferis Timothy Morand

MEADOW SISTO

1992　CAPTAIN RON
Director: Thom Eberhardt
Co-stars: Kurt Russell Martin Short Paul Anka

EVA SITTA

1989　ISLAND
Director: Paul Cox
Co-stars: Irene Papas Chris Haywood Norman Kaye

1992　THE NUN AND THE BANDIT
Director: Paul Cox
Co-stars: Gosia Dobrowolska Chris Haywood Victoria Eagger

EVA SIVA

1980　PEPI, LUCY, BOM AND ALL THE OTHER GIRLS
Director: Pedro Almodovar
Co-stars: Carmen Maura Olvida Gara

EVA SIX

1963　BEACH PARTY
Director: William Asher
Co-stars: Robert Cummings Annette Funicello Frankie Avalon

DEE SJENDERY

1971　BURKE AND HARE
Director: Vernon Sewell
Co-stars: Harry Andrews Derren Nesbitt Glynn Edwards

LILIA SKALA

Nominated For Best Supporting Actress In 1963 For "Lilies Of The Field"

1963　LILIES OF THE FIELD
Director: Ralph Nelson
Co-stars: Sidney Poitier Dan Fraser Lisa Mann

1965　SHIP OF FOOLS
Director: Stanley Kramer
Co-stars: Vivien Leigh Simone Signoret Oskar Werner

1967　CAPRICE
Director: Frank Tashlin
Co-stars: Doris Day Richard Harris Ray Walston

1968　CHARLY
Director: Ralph Nelson
Co-stars: Cliff Robertson Claire Bloom Leon Janney

1977　ROSELAND
Director: James Ivory
Co-stars: Geraldine Chaplin Teresa Wright Joan Copeland

1979　HEARTLAND
Director: Richard Pearce
Co-stars: Rip Torn Conchata Ferrell Barry Primus

1981　THE END OF AUGUST
Director: Bob Graham
Co-stars: Sally Sharp Kathleen Widdoes Paul Shenar

1983　FLASHDANCE
Director: Adrian Lyne
Co-stars: Jennifer Beals Michael Nouri Sunny Johnson

1983　TESTAMENT
Director: Lynne Littman
Co-stars: Jane Alexander William Devane Lukas Haas

1987　HOUSE OF GAMES
Director: David Mamet
Co-stars: Lindsay Crouse Joe Mantegna Mike Nussbaum

1991　MEN OF RESPECT
Director: William Reilly
Co-stars: John Turturro Rod Steiger Katherine Borowitz

LENA SKERLA

1963　LE FEU FOLLET
Director: Louis Malle
Co-stars: Maurice Ronet Jeanne Moreau Yvonne Clech

ALISON SKILBECK

1984　THE ADVENTURES OF SHERLOCK HOLMES: THE NAVAL TREATY
Director: Alan Grint
Co-stars: Jeremy Brett David Burke

ANITA SKINNER

1978　GIRLFRIENDS
Director: Claudia Weill
Co-stars: Melanie Mayron Eli Wallach Bob Balaban

CLAIRE SKINNER

1990　LIFE IS SWEET
Director: Mike Leigh
Co-stars: Alison Steadman Jim Broadbent Jane Horrocks

1993　NAKED
Director: Mike Leigh
Co-stars: David Thewlis Lesley Sharp Katrin Cartlidge

CORNELIA OTIS SKINNER

1943　STAGE DOOR CANTEEN
Director: Frank Borzage
Co-stars: Cheryl Walker Lon McCallister Judith Anderson

1944　THE UNINVITED
Director: Lewis Allen
Co-stars: Ray Milland Ruth Hussey Gail Russell

1955　THE GIRL IN THE RED VELVET SWING
Director: Richard Fleischer
Co-stars: Joan Collins Ray Milland Farley Granger

1968　THE SWIMMER
Director: Frank Perry
Co-stars: Burt Lancaster Janice Rule Kim Hunter

EDNA SKINNER

1953　EASY TO LOVE
Director: Charles Walters
Co-stars: Esther Williams Van Johnson Tony Martin

ALISON SKIPWORTH

1930　DUBARRY, WOMAN OF PASSION
Director: Sam Taylor
Co-stars: Norma Talmadge William Farnum Conrad Nagel

1930　RAFFLES
Director: Harry D'Arrast
Co-stars: Ronald Colman Kay Frances Frances Dade

1930　OUTWARD BOUND
Director: Robert Milton
Co-stars: Leslie Howard Douglas Fairbanks Helen Chandler

1931　THE NIGHT ANGEL
Director: Edmund Goulding
Co-stars: Fredric March Nancy Carroll Alan Hale

1931　TONIGHT OR NEVER
Director: Mervyn LeRoy
Co-stars: Gloria Swanson Melvyn Douglas Boris Karloff

1932　TONIGHT IS OURS
Director: Stuart Walker
Co-stars: Fredric March Claudette Colbert Paul Cavanagh

1932　SINNERS IN THE SUN
Director: Alexander Hall
Co-stars: Carole Lombard Chester Morris Cary Grant

1932	**NIGHT AFTER NIGHT**
Director:	Archie Mayo
Co-stars:	George Raft Constance Cummings Mae West
1932	**MADAME RACKETEER**
Director:	Alexander Hall
Co-stars:	Richard Bennett George Raft Evelyn Knapp
1932	**IF I HAD A MILLION**
Director:	Ernst Lubitsch
Co-stars:	Charles Laughton Gary Cooper George Raft
1933	**ALICE IN WONDERLAND**
Director:	Norman Z. McLeod
Co-stars:	Charlotte Henry Cary Grant Gary Cooper
1933	**A LADY'S PROFESSION**
Director:	Norman Z. McLeod
Co-stars:	Roland Young Kent Taylor Sari Maritza
1933	**HE LEARNED ABOUT WOMEN**
Co-stars:	Stuart Erwin Susan Fleming
1933	**MIDNIGHT CLUB**
Director:	Alexander Hall
Co-stars:	Clive Brook George Raft Helen Vinson
1933	**SONG OF SONGS**
Director:	Rouben Mamoulian
Co-stars:	Marlene Dietrich Brian Aherne Lionel Atwill
1933	**TILLIE AND GUS**
Director:	Francis Martin
Co-stars:	W.C. Fields Baby LeRoy Edgar Kennedy
1934	**WHARF ANGEL**
Director:	William Cameron Menzies
Co-stars:	Victor McLaglen Preston Foster Dorothy Dell
1934	**SIX OF A KIND**
Director:	Leo McCarey
Co-stars:	Charles Ruggles Mary Boland W.C. Fields
1934	**SHOOT THE WORKS**
Director:	Wesley Ruggles
Co-stars:	Jack Oakie Dorothy Dell Ben Bernie
1934	**THE NOTORIOUS SOPHIE LANG**
Director:	Ralph Murphy
Co-stars:	Gertrude Michael Paul Cavanagh
1934	**HERE IS MY HEART**
Director:	Frank Tuttle
Co-stars:	Bing Crosby Kitty Carlisle Roland Young
1934	**THE CAPTAIN HATES THE SEA**
Director:	Lewis Milestone
Co-stars:	John Gilbert Victor McLaglen
1935	**DANGEROUS**
Director:	Alfred Green
Co-stars:	Bette Davis Franchot Tone Margaret Lindsay
1935	**BECKY SHARP**
Director:	Kenneth MacGowan
Co-stars:	Miriam Hopkins Cedric Hardwicke Francis Dee
1935	**THE DEVIL IS A WOMAN**
Director:	Josef Von Sternberg
Co-stars:	Marlene Dietrich Lionel Atwill
1935	**DOUBTING THOMAS**
Director:	David Butler
Co-stars:	Will Rogers Billie Burke Gail Patrick
1935	**THE CASINO MURDER CASE**
Director:	Edwin Marin
Co-stars:	Paul Lukas Rosalind Russell Eric Blore
1935	**THE GIRL FROM 10ᵀᴴ AVENUE**
Director:	Alfred Green
Co-stars:	Bette Davis Ian Hunter Colin Clive

1935	**HITCH-HIKE LADY**
Director:	Aubrey Scotto
Co-stars:	Arthur Treacher Mae Clarke James Ellison
1935	**SHANGHAI**
Director:	James Flood
Co-stars:	Loretta Young Charles Boyer Warner Oland
1936	**WHITE HUNTER**
Director:	Irving Cummings
Co-stars:	Warner Baxter Wilfrid Lawson June Lang
1936	**SATAN MET A LADY**
Director:	William Dieterle
Co-stars:	Bette Davis Warren William Arthur Treacher
1936	**THE PRINCESS COMES ACROSS**
Director:	William Howard
Co-stars:	Fred MacMurray Carole Lombard
1936	**THE GORGEOUS HUSSY**
Director:	Clarence Brown
Co-stars:	Joan Crawford Robert Taylor James Stewart
1937	**STOLEN HOLIDAY**
Director:	Michael Curtiz
Co-stars:	Claude Rains Kay Francis Ian Hunter
1938	**WIDE OPEN FACES**
Director:	Kurt Neuman
Co-stars:	Joe E. Brown Jane Wyman Lyda Roberti

BIBI SKOGLUND

1948	**MUSIC IS MY FUTURE**
Director:	Ingmar Bergman
Co-stars:	Mai Zetterling Birger Malmsten Naima Wifstrand

IONE SKYE

1986	**RIVER'S EDGE**
Director:	Tim Hunter
Co-stars:	Crispin Glover Keanu Reeves Dennis Hopper
1988	**A NIGHT IN THE LIFE OF JIMMY REARDON**
Director:	William Richert
Co-stars:	River Phoenix Ann Magnuson
1989	**THE RACHEL PAPERS**
Director:	Damian Harris
Co-stars:	Dexter Fletcher James Spader Jonathan Pryce
1989	**SAY ANYTHING**
Director:	Cameron Crowe
Co-stars:	John Cusack John Mahoney Lili Taylor
1991	**GAS, FOOD, LODGING**
Director:	Allison Anders
Co-stars:	Brooke Adams Fairuza Balk James Brolin
1992	**GUNCRAZY**
Director:	Tamra Davis
Co-stars:	Drew Barrymore James LeGros Joe Dallesandro
1992	**WAYNE'S WORLD**
Director:	Penelope Spheeris
Co-stars:	Mike Myers Dana Carvey Rob Lowe
1994	**GIRLS IN PRISON**
Director:	John McNaughton
Co-stars:	Missy Crider Anne Heche Nicolette Scorsese
1995	**FOUR ROOMS**
Director:	Allison Anders
Co-stars:	Tim Roth Antonio Banderas Jennifer Beals

DAPHNE SLATER

1947	**THE COURTNEYS OF CURZON STREET**
Director:	Herbert Wilcox
Co-stars:	Anna Neagle Michael Wilding Coral Browne

HELEN SLATER

1984 SUPERGIRL
Director: Jeannot Szwarc
Co-stars: Faye Dunaway Peter O'Toole Mia Farrow

1985 THE LEGEND OF BILLIE JEAN
Director: Matthew Robbins
Co-stars: Keith Gordon Richard Bradford

1986 RUTHLESS PEOPLE
Director: David Zucker
Co-stars: Danny DeVito Bette Midler Judge Reinhold

1987 THE SECRET OF MY SUCCESS
Director: Herbert Ross
Co-stars: Michael J. Fox Richard Jordan John Pankow

1988 STICKY FINGERS
Director: Catlin Adams
Co-stars: Melanie Mayron Carol Kane Eileen Brennan

1989 HAPPY TOGETHER
Director: Mel Damski
Co-stars: Patrick Dempsey Barbara Babcock Brad Pitt

1991 CITY SLICKERS
Director: Ron Underwood
Co-stars: Billy Crystal Jack Palance Daniel Stern

1993 12-01
Director: Jack Sholder
Co-stars: Jonathan Silverman Martin Landau Ann Shea

1994 LASSIE
Director: Daniel Petrie
Co-stars: Thomas Guiry Jon Tenney

1994 PARALLEL LIVES
Director: Linda Yellen
Co-stars: Liza Minnelli Ben Gazzara Gena Rowlands

1995 THE STEAL
Director: John Hay
Co-star: Alfred Molina

MARTHA SLEEPER

1933 PENTHOUSE
Director: Warner Baxter

1934 SPITFIRE
Director: John Cromwell
Co-stars: Katharine Hepburn Robert Young Ralph Bellamy

1934 WEST OF PECOS
Co-star: Richard Dix

1935 TWO SINNERS
Director: Arthur Lubin
Co-stars: Otto Kruger Minna Gombell Cora Sue Collins

1935 THE SCOUNDREL
Director: Ben Hecht
Co-stars: Noel Coward Alexander Woollcott Julie Haydon

1945 THE BELLS OF ST. MARY'S
Director: Leo McCarey
Co-stars: Bing Crosby Ingrid Bergman Henry Travers

OLIVE SLOANE

1938 CONSIDER YOUR VERDICT
Director: Roy Boulting
Co-stars: Marius Goring Manning Whiley Hay Petrie

1939 INQUEST
Director: Roy Boulting
Co-stars: Elizabeth Allan Herbert Lom Barbara Everest

1942 LET THE PEOPLE SING
Director: John Baxter
Co-stars: Alastair Sim Fred Emney Patricia Roc

1945 THEY KNEW MR KNIGHT
Director: Norman Walker
Co-stars: Mervyn Johns Alfred Drayton Joan Greenwood

1950 SEVEN DAYS TO NOON
Director: John Boulting
Co-stars: Barry Jones Andre Morrell Joan Hickson

1950 WATERFRONT
Director: Michael Anderson
Co-stars: Robert Newton Kathleen Harrison Richard Burton

1952 CURTAIN UP
Director: Ralph Smart
Co-stars: Margaret Rutherford Robert Morley Kay Kendall

1953 THE WEAK AND THE WICKED
Director: J. Lee-Thompson
Co-stars: Glynis Johns Diana Dors John Gregson

1957 BROTHERS IN LAW
Director: Roy Boulting
Co-stars: Ian Carmichael Terry-Thomas Miles Malleson

LALA SLOATMAN

1991 PUMP UP THE VOLUME
Director: Allan Moyle
Co-stars: Christian Slater Samantha Mathis Annie Ross

1992 AMITYVILLE A NEW GENERATION
Director: John Murlowski
Co-stars: Ross Partridge Julia Nickson-Soul Terry O'Quinn

GEORGIA SLOWE

1984 THE COMPANY OF WOLVES
Director: Neil Jordan
Co-stars: Angela Lansbury David Warner Brian Glover

1985 BLACK ARROW
Director: John Hough
Co-stars: Oliver Reed Stephan Chase Donald Pleasence

1992 WITCHCRAFT
Director: Peter Sasdy
Co-stars: Peter McEnery Lisa Harrow Alan Howard

MARYA SMALL

1982 NATIONAL LAMPOON'S CLASS REUNION
Director: Michael Miller
Co-stars: Gerrit Graham Michael Lerner

1983 FADE TO BLACK
Director: Vernon Zimmerman
Co-stars: Dennis Christopher Linda Kerridge Mickey Rourke

NEVA SMALL

1971 FIDDLER ON THE ROOF
Director: Norman Jewison
Co-stars: Topol Norma Crane Molly Picon

DEE SMART

1996 BACK OF BEYOND
Director: Michael Robertson
Co-stars: Paul Mercurio Colin Friels John Polson

JEAN SMART

1986 FIRE WITH FIRE
Director: Duncan Gibbins
Co-stars: Virginia Madsen Craig Sheffer Kate Reid

1987 PROJECT X
Director: Jonathan Kaplan
Co-stars: Christopher George Matthew Broderick Helen Hunt

1991 BLIND JUDGEMENT
Director: George Kaczender
Co-stars: Lesley Ann Warren Peter Coyote Matt Clark

1992 OVERKILL: THE AILEEN WUORNOS STORY
Director: Peter Levin
Co-star: Brion James

1993 HOMEWARD BOUND: THE INCREDIBLE JOURNEY
Director: DuWayne Dunham
Co-stars: Robert Hayes Kim Griest Benj Thall

REBECCA SMART *(Child)*

1988 CELIA
Director: Ann Turner
Co-stars: Nicholas Eadie Victoria Longley Mary-Anne Fahey

DENA SMILES

1996 SMALLTIME
Director: Shane Meadows
Co-stars: Shane Meadows Mat Hand Gena Kawecka

ALEXIS SMITH

1941 STEEL AGAINST THE SKY
Director: Lloyd Nolan Gene Lockhart

1941 THE SMILING GHOST
Director: Lewis Seiler
Co-stars: Wayne Morris Brenda Marshall Alan Hale

1941 DIVE BOMBER
Director: Michael Curtiz
Co-stars: Errol Flynn Fred MacMurray Ralph Bellamy

1942 GENTLEMAN JIM
Director: Raoul Walsh
Co-stars: Errol Flynn Jack Carson Alan Hale

1943 THANK YOUR LUCKY STARS
Director: David Butler
Co-stars: Eddie Cantor Dennis Morgan Joan Leslie

1944 THE DOUGHGIRLS
Co-stars: Jane Wyman Jack Carson Ann Sheridan

1944 THE ADVENTURES OF MARK TWAIN
Director: Irving Rapper
Co-stars: Fredric March Donald Crisp

1944 HOLLYWOOD CANTEEN
Director: Delmer Daves
Co-stars: Joan Leslie Robert Hutton Dane Clark

1945 CONFLICT
Director: Curtis Bernhardt
Co-stars: Humphrey Bogart Sydney Greenstreet

1945 SAN ANTONIO
Director: David Butler
Co-stars: Errol Flynn Paul Kelly S.Z. Sakall

1945 RHAPSODY IN BLUE
Director: Irving Rapper
Co-stars: Robert Alda Joan Leslie Oscar Levant

1946 NIGHT AND DAY
Director: Michael Curtiz
Co-stars: Cary Grant Monty Wooley Mary Martin

1946 ONE MORE TOMORROW
Director: Peter Godfrey
Co-stars: Ann Sheridan Dennis Morgan Jack Carson

1946 OF HUMAN BONDAGE
Director: Edmund Goulding
Co-stars: Paul Henreid Eleanor Parker Edmund Gwenn

1947 STALLION ROAD
Director: James Kern
Co-stars: Ronald Reagan Zachary Scott Peggy Knudsen

1947 THE TWO MRS CARROLLS
Director: Peter Godfrey
Co-stars: Humphrey Bogart Barbara Stanwyck Nigel Bruce

1945 THE HORN BLOWS AT MIDNIGHT
Co-stars: Jack Benny Dolores Moran

1947 ONE LAST FLING

1948 WHIPLASH
Director: Lewis Seiler
Co-stars: Dane Clark Zachary Scott S.Z. Sakall

1948 THE WOMAN IN WHITE
Director: Peter Godfrey
Co-stars: Eleanor Parker Gig Young Sydney Greenstreet

1948 THE DECISION OF CHRISTOPHER BLAKE
Director: Peter Godfrey
Co-stars: Robert Douglas Cecil Kellaway

1949 ANY NUMBER CAN PLAY
Director: Mervyn LeRoy
Co-stars: Clark Gable Mary Astor Frank Morgan

1949 SOUTH OF ST. LOUIS
Director: Ray Enright
Co-stars: Joel McCrea Zachary Scott Dorothy Malone

1950 UNDERCOVER GIRL
Director: Joseph Pevney
Co-stars: Scott Brady Richard Egan Gladys George

1950 WYOMING MAIL
Director: Reginald LeBorg
Co-stars: Stephen McNally Howard Da Silva Ed Begley

1950 MONTANA
Director: Ray Enright
Co-stars: Errol Flynn Douglas Kennedy S.Z. Sakall

1951 CAVE OF OUTLAWS
Director: William Castle
Co-stars: MacDonald Carey Edgar Buchanan Hugh O'Brian

1951 HERE COMES THE GROOM
Director: Frank Capra
Co-stars: Bing Crosby Jane Wyman Franchot Tone

1952 THE TURNING POINT
Director: William Dieterle
Co-stars: William Holden Edmond O'Brien

1953 SPLIT SECOND
Director: Dick Powell
Co-stars: Stephen McNally Jan Sterling Keith Andes

1954 THE SLEEPING TIGER
Director: Joseph Losey
Co-stars: Dirk Bogarde Alexander Knox Hugh Griffith

1955 THE ETERNAL SEA
Director: John Auer
Co-stars: Sterling Hayden Dean Jagger Virginia Grey

1957 BEAU JAMES
Director: Melville Shavelson
Co-stars: Bob Hope Paul Douglas Vera Miles

1958 THIS HAPPY FEELING
Director: Blake Edwards
Co-stars: Curt Jurgens Debbie Reynolds John Saxon

1959 THE YOUNG PHILADELPHIANS
Director: Vincent Sherman
Co-stars: Paul Newman Barbara Rush Brian Keith

1975 ONCE IS NOT ENOUGH
Director: Guy Green
Co-stars: Kirk Douglas David Janssen Brenda Vacarro

1976 THE LITTLE GIRL WHO LIVES DOWN THE LANE
Director: Zev Braun
Co-stars: Jodie Foster Martin Sheen

1978 CASEY'S SHADOW
Director: Martin Ritt
Co-stars: Walter Matthau Robert Webber

1985   A DEATH IN CALFORNIA
Director: Delbert Mann
Co-stars: Cheryl Ladd Sam Elliott Fritz Weaver

1986   TOUGH GUYS
Director: Jeff Kanew
Co-stars: Burt Lancaster Kirk Douglas Eli Wallach

1993   THE AGE OF INNOCENCE
Director: Martin Scorsese
Co-stars: Daniel Day-Lewis Michelle Pfeiffer Winona Ryder

ALISON SMITH

1991   WILDFLOWER
Director: Diane Keaton
Co-stars: Patricia Arquette Beau Bridges Reese Witherspoon

1993   JASON GOES TO HELL: THE FINAL FRIDAY
Director: Adam Marcus
Co-stars: Steve Williams Kari Keegan Erin Gray

1995   YOUNG INDIANA JONES AND THE HOLLYWOOD FOLLIES
Director: Michael Schultz
Co-stars: Sean Patrick Flanery Bill Cusack

BROOKE SMITH

1991   THE SILENCE OF THE LAMBS
Director: Jonathan Demme
Co-stars: Jody Foster Anthony Hopkins Scott Glenn

1994   VANYA ON 42ND STREET
Director: Louis Malle
Co-stars: Wallace Shawn Julianne Moore Larry Pine

CATHY SMITH

1971   THE BALLAD OF JOE HILL
Director: Bo Widerberg
Co-stars: Thommy Berggren Anja Schmidt Evert Anderson

CONSTANCE SMITH

1950   THE MUDLARK
Director: Jean Negulesco
Co-stars: Alec Guinness Irene Dunne Andrew Ray

1950   ROOM TO LET
Director: Godfrey Grayson
Co-stars: Jimmy Hanley Valentine Dyall Christine Silver

1951   THE 13TH LETTER
Director: Otto Preminger
Co-stars: Charles Boyer Linda Darnell Michael Rennie

1952   RED SKIES OF MONTANA
Director: Joseph Newman
Co-stars: Richard Widmark Jeffrey Hunter Richard Boone

1952   TAXI
Director: Gregory Ratoff
Co-stars: Dan Dailey Neva Patterson Blanche Yurka

1952   TREASURE OF THE GOLDEN CONDOR
Director: Delmer Daves
Co-stars: Cornel Wilde Finlay Currie Fay Wray

1952   LURE OF THE WILDERNESS
Director: Jean Negulesco
Co-stars: Jeffrey Hunter Jean Peters Walter Brennan

1953   THE MAN IN THE ATTIC
Director: Hugo Fregonese
Co-stars: Jack Palance Frances Bavier Rhys Williams

1955   TIGER BY THE TAIL
Director: John Gilling
Co-stars: Larry Parks Lisa Daniely Thora Hird

1955   THE BIG TIP OFF
Director: Frank McDonald
Co-stars: Richard Conte Bruce Bennett Cathy Downs

CYNTHIA SMITH

1974   BENJI
Director: Joe Camp
Co-stars: Peter Breck Edgar Buchanan Christopher Connelly

1977   FOR THE LOVE OF BENJI
Director: Joe Camp
Co-stars: Patsy Garrett Peter Bowles Ed Nelson

DESIREE SMITH

1989   THE DELINQUENTS
Director: Chris Thomson
Co-stars: Kylie Minogue Charlie Schlatter Bruno Lawrence

1991   WENDY CRACKS A WALNUT
Director: Michael Pattinson
Co-stars: Rosanna Arquette Bruce Spence Hugo Weaving

EBBE ROE SMITH

1986   THE BIG EASY
Director: Jim McBride
Co-stars: Dennis Quaid Ellen Barkin Ned Beatty

EMMA SMITH

1990   INSPECTOR WEXFORD: SOME LIE AND SOME DIE
Director: Sandy Johnson
Co-stars: George Baker Diane Keen Gemma Jones

ETHEL SMITH

1944   BATHING BEAUTY
Director: George Sidney
Co-stars: Esther Williams Red Skelton Basil Rathbone

1945   GEORGE WHITE'S SCANDALS
Director: Felix Feist
Co-stars: Joan Davis Jack Haley Jane Greer

1946   EASY TO WED
Director: Edward Buzzell
Co-stars: Esther Williams Van Johnson Lucille Ball

GERALDINE SMITH

1969   FLESH
Director: Paul Morrissey
Co-stars: Joe Dallesandro John Christian Candy Darling

1984   MIXED BLOOD
Director: Paul Morrissey
Co-stars: Marilia Pera Linda Kerridge Richard Ulacia

HILLARY BAILEY SMITH

1988   SHAPING RICHARD
Director: Peter Bonertz
Co-stars: Ed Marinaro Eileen Davidson Nancy Frangione

JACLYN SMITH *(Married Anthony Richmond)*

1970   THE ADVENTURERS
Director: Lewis Gilbert
Co-stars: Alan Badel Candice Bergen Bekim Fehmiu

1977   ESCAPE FROM BOGEN COUNTY
Director: Steven Hilliard Stern
Co-stars: Mitchell Ryan Michael Parks

1981   JACQUELINE BOUVIER KENNEDY
Director: Stephen Gethers

1983   RAGE OF ANGELS
Director: Buzz Kulik
Co-stars: Ken Howard Joseph Wiseman Armand Assante

1984 SENTIMENTAL JOURNEY
Director: James Goldstone
Co-stars: David Dukes Maureen Stapleton

1984 THE NIGHT THEY SAVED CHRISTMAS
Director: Jackie Cooper
Co-stars: Art Carney Paul LeMat Paul Williams

1985 DÉJÀ VU
Director: Anthony Richmond
Co-stars: Nigel Terry Claire Bloom Shelley Winters

1988 WINDMILLS OF THE GODS
Director: Lee Philips
Co-stars: Christopher Cazenove John Standing Avi Meyers

1989 SETTLE THE SCORE
Director: Edwin Sherin
Co-stars: Jeffrey DeMunn Louise Latham Howard Duff

1990 DANIELLE STEEL'S KALEIDASCOPE
Director: Jud Taylor
Co-stars: Perry King Donald Moffat Colleen Dewhurst

1991 LIES BEFORE KISSES
Director: Lou Antonio

1992 LOVE CAN BE MURDER
Director: Jack Bender
Co-stars: Corbin Bernsen Cliff De Young Anne Francis

1992 A NIGHTMARE IN THE DAYLIGHT
Director: Lou Antonio
Co-stars: Christopher Reeve Eric Bell Tom Mason

1994 VICTIM OF RAGE
Director: Armand Mastroianni
Co-star: Brad Johnson

1996 MY VERY BEST FRIEND
Co-star: Jill Eikenberry

JEAN TAYLOR SMITH

1956 IT'S NEVER TOO LATE
Director: Michael McCarthy
Co-stars: Phyllis Calvert Patrick Barr Guy Rolfe

1972 THE BILL DOUGLAS TRILOGY: MY CHILDHOOD
Director: Bill Douglas
Co-stars: Stephen Archibald Hughie Restorick

1974 THE BILL DOUGLAS TRILOGY: MY AIN FOLK
Director: Bill Douglas
Co-stars: Stephen Archibald Paul Kermack

JEANNE SMITH

1989 FUN DOWN THERE
Director: Roger Stigliano
Co-stars: Michael Waite Martin Goldin Elizabeth Waite

JOANNE SMITH

1950 NO WAY OUT
Director: Joseph Mankiewicz
Co-stars: Richard Widmark Sidney Poitier Linda Darnell

KATE SMITH

1932 HELLO EVERYBODY
Director: William Seiter
Co-stars: Randolph Scott Sally Blane Jerry Tucker

1932 THE BIG BROADCAST
Director: Frank Tuttle
Co-stars: Bing Crosby George Burns Gracie Allen

1943 THIS IS THE ARMY
Director: Michael Curtiz
Co-stars: George Murphy Joan Leslie Irving Berlin

KEELEY SMITH

1958 THUNDER ROAD
Director: Arthur Ripley
Co-stars: Robert Mitchum Gene Barry James Mitchum

LIZ SMITH

1971 BLEAK MOMENTS
Director: Mike Leigh
Co-stars: Anne Raitt Sarah Stephenson Eric Allan

1983 SEPARATE TABLES
Director: John Schlesinger
Co-stars: Alan Bates Julie Christie Claire Boom

1984 A PRIVATE FUNCTION
Director: Malcolm Mowbray
Co-stars: Michael Palin Maggie Smith Denholm Elliott

1988 WE THINK THE WORLD OF YOU
Director: Colin Gregg
Co-stars: Alan Bates Max Wall Frances Barber

1988 WORDS OF LOVE
Director: Colin Nutley
Co-stars: Charlie Creed-Miles Tom Bell Rowena Roberts

1988 HIGH SPIRITS
Director: Neil Jordan
Co-stars: Peter O'Toole Daryl Hannah Steve Guttenberg

1988 APARTMENT ZERO
Director: Martin Donovan
Co-stars: Colin Firth Hart Bochner Dora Bryan

1989 THE COOK, THE THIEF, HIS WIFE AND HER LOVER
Director: Peter Greenaway
Co-stars: Michael Gambon Helen Mirren

1996 SECRETS AND LIES
Director: Mike Leigh
Co-stars: Brenda Blethyn Timothy Spall Phyllis Logan

1997 KEEP THE ASPIDISTRA FLYING
Director: Robert Bierman
Co-stars: Helena Bonham-Carter Richard E. Grant

LOIS SMITH

1955 EAST OF EDEN
Director: Elia Kazan
Co-stars: James Dean Julie Harris Raymond Massey

1955 STRANGE LADY IN TOWN
Director: Mervyn LeRoy
Co-stars: Greer Garson Dana Andrews Cameron Mitchell

1970 FIVE EASY PIECES
Director: Bob Rafelson
Co-stars: Jack Nicholson Susan Anspach Karen Black

1975 NEXT STOP, GREENWICH VILLAGE
Director: Paul Mazursky
Co-stars: Lenny Baker Shelley Winters Ellen Greene

1986 BLACK WIDOW
Director: Bob Rafelson
Co-stars: Debra Winger Theresa Russell Dennis Hopper

1987 FATAL ATTRACTION
Director: Adrian Lyne
Co-stars: Michael Douglas Glenn Close Anne Archer

1991 FRIED GREEN TOMATOES
Director: Jon Avnet
Co-stars: Jessica Tandy Mary-Louise Parker Mary Stuart Masterson

1991 GREEN CARD
Director: Peter Weir
Co-stars: Gerard Depardieu Andie MacDowall Bebe Neuwirth

1992 FALLING DOWN
Director: Joel Schumacher
Co-stars: Michael Douglas Robert Duvall Barbara Hershey

1994 HOLY MATRIMONY
Director: Leonard Nimoy
Co-stars: Patricia Arquette Tate Donovan Joseph Gordon-Levitt

1996 HOW TO MAKE AN AMERICAN QUILT
Director: Jocelyn Moorhouse
Co-stars: Winona Ryder Anne Bancroft Jean Simmons

MADELEINE SMITH

1970 THE VAMPIRE LOVERS
Director: Roy Ward Baker
Co-stars: Ingrid Pitt Peter Cushing Pippa Steele

1971 UP POMPEII
Director: Bob Kellett
Co-stars: Frankie Howerd Patrick Cargill Barbara Murray

1972 UP THE FRONT
Director: Bob Kellett
Co-stars: Frankie Howerd Bill Fraser Zsa Zsa Gabor

1972 THE AMAZING MR BLUNDEN
Director: Lionel Jeffries
Co-stars: Laurence Naismith Lynne Frederick Diana Dors

1973 FRANKENSTEIN AND THE MONSTER FROM HELL
Director: Terence Fisher
Co-stars: Peter Cushing Shane Briant

MADOLYN SMITH (Madolyn Smith-Osborne

From "The Rose And The Jackal")

1980 URBAN COWBOY
Director: James Bridges
Co-stars: John Travolta Debra Winger Scott Glenn

1982 REHEARSAL FOR MURDER
Director: David Greene
Co-stars: Robert Preston Lynn Redgrave Patrick MacNee

1984 ALL OF ME
Director: Carl Reiner
Co-stars: Steve Martin Lily Tomlin Victoria Tennant

1985 DEADLY INTENTIONS
Director: Noel Black
Co-stars: Michael Biehn Morgana King Cloris Leachman

1986 IF TOMORROW COMES
Director: Jerry London
Co-stars: Tom Berenger David Keith Richard Kiley

1988 FUNNY FARM
Director: George Roy Hill
Co-stars: Chevy Chase Joseph Maher Jack Gilpin

1990 THE PLOT TO KILL HITLER
Director: Lawrence Schiller
Co-stars: Brad Davis Ian Richardson Michael Byrne

1990 THE ROSE AND THE JACKAL
Director: Jack Gold
Co-stars: Christopher Reeve Carrie Snodgress Kevin McCarthy

1991 THE SUPER
Director: Rod Daniel
Co-stars: Joe Pesci Vincent Gardenia Ruben Blades

MAGGIE SMITH (Married Robert Stephens)

Oscar For Best Actress In 1969 For "The Prime Of Miss Jean Brodie".
Oscar For Best Supporting Actress In 1978 For "California Suite".
Nominated For Best Actress In 1972 For "Travels With My Aunt"
Nominated For Best Supporting Actress In 1965 For "Othello" And In
1985 For "A Room With A View"

1958 NOWHERE TO GO
Director: Seth Holt
Co-stars: George Nader Bernard Lee Bessie Love

1961 GO TO BLAZES
Director: Michael Truman
Co-stars: Daniel Massey Dave King Robert Morley

1963 THE VIPS
Director: Anthony Asquith
Co-stars: Richard Burton Elizabeth Taylor Margaret Rutherford

1964 THE PUMPKIN EATER
Director: Jack Clayton
Co-stars: Anne Bancroft Peter Finch James Mason

1964 YOUNG CASSIDY
Director: John Ford
Co-stars: Rod Taylor Edith Evans Flora Robson

1965 OTHELLO
Director: Stuart Burge
Co-stars: Laurence Olivier Frank Finlay Joyce Redman

1967 THE HONEY POT
Director: Joseph Mankiewicz
Co-stars: Rex Harrison Capucine Susan Hayward

1968 HOT MILLIONS
Director: Eric Till
Co-stars: Peter Ustinov Karl Malden Bob Newhart

1968 OH! WHAT A LOVELY WAR
Director: Richard Attenborough
Co-stars: John Mills Kenneth More Laurence Olivier

1969 THE PRIME OF MISS JEAN BRODIE
Director: Ronald Neame
Co-stars: Robert Stephens Celia Johnson Pamela Franklyn

1972 TRAVELS WITH MY AUNT
Director: George Cukor
Co-stars: Alex McCowen Robert Stephens Lou Gossett

1973 LOVE AND PAIN (AND THE WHOLE DAMN THING)
Director: Alan J. Pakula
Co-star: Timothy Bottoms

1976 MURDER BY DEATH
Director: Robert Moore
Co-stars: David Niven Peter Falk Alec Guinness

1978 DEATH ON THE NILE
Director: John Guillermin
Co-stars: Peter Ustinov David Niven Bette Davis

1978 CALIFORNIA SUITE
Director: Herbert Ross
Co-stars: Michael Caine Walter Matthau Jane Fonda

1981 CLASH OF THE TITANS
Director: Desmond Davis
Co-stars: Laurence Olivier Harry Hamlin Judy Bowker

1981 QUARTET
Director: James Ivory
Co-stars: Alan Bates Isabel Adjani Anthony Higgins

1982 BETTER LATE THAN NEVER
Director: Bryan Forbes
Co-stars: David Niven Art Carney Lionel Jeffries

1982 EVIL UNDER THE SUN
Director: Guy Hamilton
Co-stars: Peter Ustinov Diana Rigg James Mason

1983 THE MISSIONARY
Director: Richard Loncraine
Co-stars: Michael Palin Michael Hordern Trevor Howard

1984 A PRIVATE FUNCTION
Director: Malcolm Mowbray
Co-stars: Michael Palin Liz Smith Denholm Elliott

1985 **A ROOM WITH A VIEW**
Director: James Ivory
Co-stars: Helena Bonham Carter Denholm Elliott Judi Dench

1985 **LILY IN LOVE**
Director: Karoly Makk
Co-stars: Christopher Plummer Elke Sommer Adolph Green

1987 **THE LONELY PASSION OF JUDITH HEARNE**
Director: Jack Clayton
Co-stars: Bob Hoskins Wendy Hiller

1991 **HOOK**
Director: Steven Spielberg
Co-stars: Robin Williams Dustin Hoffman Julia Roberts

1992 **SUDDENLY, LAST SUMMER**
Director: Richard Eyre
Co-stars: Natasha Richardson Rob Lowe Richard E. Grant

1992 **MEMENTO MORI**
Director: Jack Clayton
Co-stars: Michael Hordern Renee Asherson

1992 **SISTER ACT**
Director: Emile Ardolino
Co-stars: Whoopi Goldberg Harvey Keitel Bill Nunn

1993 **SISTER ACT 2: BACK IN THE HABIT**
Director: Bill Duke
Co-stars: Whoopi Goldberg James Coburn Kathy Najimy

1993 **THE SECRET GARDEN**
Director: Agnieszka Holland
Co-stars: Kate Maberley Haydon Prowse John Lynch

1996 **RICHARD III**
Co-stars: Ian McKellen Annette Bening Patrick Stewart

1998 **WASHINGTON SQUARE**
Director: Agnieszka Holland
Co-stars: Albert Finney Ben Chaplin

MARIA SMITH

1974 **THE LORDS OF FLATBUSH**
Director: Martin Davidson
Co-stars: Perry King Henry Winkler Sylvester Stallone

1981 **THE INCREDIBLE SHRINKING WOMAN**
Director: Joel Schumacher
Co-stars: Lily Tomlin Charles Grodin Ned Beatty

MAUDIE SMITH

1987 **OUR LADY BLUE**
Director: Robin Midgeley
Co-stars: Patricia Hayes Doreen Mantle Eva Griffith

MELANIE SMITH

1992 **TRANCERS: DETH LIVES**
Director: Courtney Joyner
Co-stars: Tim Thomerson Andrew Robinson Helen Hunt

PAM SMITH

1961 **MISTY**
Director: David Ladd
Co-stars: Arthur O'Connell Anne Seymour

PATRICIA SMITH

1957 **THE SPIRIT OF ST. LOUIS**
Director: Billy Wilder
Co-stars: James Stewart Murray Hamilton Marc Connelly

1957 **THE BACHELOR PARTY**
Director: Delbert Mann
Co-stars: Don Murray Jack Warden Carolyn Jones

1973 **SAVE THE TIGER**
Director: John Avildsen
Co-stars: Jack Lemmon Jack Gilford Laurie Heineman

1983 **WHO WILL LOVE MY CHILDREN ?**
Director: John Erman
Co-stars: Ann-Margret Frederic Forrest Donald Moffat

PRISCILLA CAROLINE SMITH

1988 **HOSTAGE**
Director: Peter Levin
Co-stars: Carol Burnett Carrie Hamilton Annette Bening

QUEENIE SMITH

1935 **MISSISSIPPI**
Director: Edward Sutherland
Co-stars: Bing Crosby W.C. Fields Joan Bennett

1936 **SHOW BOAT**
Director: James Whale
Co-stars: Irene Dunne Allan Jones Paul Robeson

1947 **THE LONG NIGHT**
Director: Anatole Litvak
Co-stars: Henry Fonda Barbara Bel Geddes Vincent Price

1950 **THE GREAT RUPERT**
Director: Irving Pichel
Co-stars: Jimmy Durante Terry Moore Tom Drake

RAINBEAUX SMITH

1974 **CAGED HEAT**
Director: Jonathan Demme
Co-stars: Juanita Brown Erica Gavin Barbara Steele

ROBERTA SMITH

1944 **BLOCK BUSTERS**
Director: Wallace Fox
Co-stars: Leo Gorcey Huntz Hall Gabriel Dell

SALLY SMITH

1960 **TROUBLE WITH EVE**
Director: Francis Searle
Co-stars: Robert Urquhart Hy Hazell Garry Marsh

1963 **FATHER CAME TOO**
Director: Peter Graham Scott
Co-stars: James Robertson Justice Stanley Baxter Leslie Phillips

SHAWNEE SMITH

1985 **CRIME OF INNOCENCE**
Director: Michael Miller
Co-stars: Andy Griffith Diane Ladd Ralph Waite

1986 **EASY PREY**
Director: Sandor Stern
Co-stars: Gerald McRaney Sean McCann Susan Hogan

1987 **SUMMER SCHOOL**
Director: Carl Reiner
Co-stars: Mark Harmon Kirstie Alley Robin Thomas

1988 **THE BLOB**
Director: Chuck Russell
Co-stars: Kevin Dillon Candy Clark Donovan Leitch

1989 **BRAND NEW LIFE**
Director: Eric Laneuville
Co-stars: Barbara Eden Don Murray Jenny Garth

1989 **WHO'S HARRY CRUMB ?**
Director: Paul Flaherty
Co-stars: John Candy Jeffrey Jones Annie Potts

1990 **DESPERATE HOURS**
Director: Michael Cimino
Co-stars: Mickey Rourke Anthony Hopkins Mimi Rogers

1996 **FACE OF EVIL**
Director: Mary Lambert
Co-stars: Tracey Gold Perry King

TERRI SUSAN SMITH

1982 BASKET CASE
Director: Frank Hennenlotter
Co-stars: Kevin Van Hentenryck Beverley Bonner Robert Vogel

TRACY N. SMITH

1984 HOT DOG...THE MOVIE
Director: Peter Markle
Co-stars: David Naughton Patrick Hauser

JAN SMITHERS

1974 WHERE THE LILIES BLOOM
Director: William A. Graham
Co-stars: Julie Gholson Harry Dean Stanton

LAURA SMITHSON

1936 MEN ARE NOT GOD
Director: Walter Reisch
Co-stars: Miriam Hopkins Rex Harrison Gertrude Lawrence

SONJA SMITS

1983 VIDEODROME
Director: David Cronenberg
Co-stars: James Woods Deborah Harry Peter Dvorsky

TRACI LORDS SMITS

1992 STEPHEN KING'S THE TOMMYKNOCKERS
Director: John Power
Co-stars: Marg Helgenberger Robert Carradine E.G. Marshall

JOSEPHINE SMULDERS

1984 THE GOLD AND THE GLORY
Director: Igor Auzins
Co-stars: Joss McWilliam Nick Tate

VICTORIA SMURFIT

1996 THE RUN OF THE COUNTRY
Director: Peter Yates
Co-stars: Albert Finney Anthony Brophy Matt Keeslar

SARAH SMUTS-KENNEDY

1990 AN ANGEL AT MY TABLE
Director: Jane Campion
Co-stars: Kerry Fox Alexia Keogh Karen Fergusson

1992 JACK BE NIMBLE
Director: Garth Maxwell
Co-stars: Alexis Arquette Bruno Lawrence Tony Berry

CARRIE SNODGRESS

Nominated For Best Actress In 1970 For "Diary Of A Mad Housewife"

1969 SILENT NIGHT, LONELY NIGHT
Director: Daniel Petrie
Co-stars: Lloyd Bridges Shirley Jones Lynn Carlin

1970 RABBIT, RUN
Director: Jack Smight
Co-stars: James Caan Anjanette Comer Arthur Hill

1970 DIARY OF A MAD HOUSEWIFE
Director: Frank Perry
Co-stars: Richard Benjamin Frank Langella Lorraine Cullen

1978 THE FURY
Director: Brian De Palma
Co-stars: Kirk Douglas John Cassavetes Amy Irving

1979 THE ATTIC
Director: George Edwards
Co-stars: Ray Milland Ruth Cox Rosemary Murphy

1985 PALE RIDER
Director: Clint Eastwood
Co-stars: Clint Eastwood Michael Moriarty Christopher Penn

1986 MURPHY'S LAW
Director: J. Lee-Thompson
Co-stars: Charles Bronson Kathleen Wilhoite Richard Romanus

1988 BLUEBERRY HILL
Director: Strathford Hamilton
Co-stars: Jennifer Rubin Margaret Avery Matt Lattanzi

1990 THE ROSE AND THE JACKAL
Director: Jack Gold
Co-stars: Christopher Reeve Madolyn Smith Osborne Kevin McCarthy

1993 THE BALLAD OF LITTLE JOE
Director: Maggie Greenwald
Co-stars: Suzy Amis Bo Hopkins Ian McKellen

1994 8 SECONDS
Director: John Avildsen
Co-stars: Luke Perry Stephen Baldwin James Rebhorn

1994 RISE AND WALK: THE DENNIS BYRD STORY
Director: Michael Dinner
Co-stars: Peter Berg Kathy Morris Johann Carlo

VICTORIA SNOW

1989 GETTING MARRIED IN BUFFALO JUNCTION
Director: Eric Till
Co-stars: Wendy Crewson Paul Gross Marion Gilsenan

JANE SNOWDEN

1985 THE FROG PRINCE
Director: Brian Gilbert
Co-stars: Jean Herviale Francoise Brion Pierre Vernier

SUZANNE SNYDER

1985 WEIRD SCIENCE
Director: John Hughes
Co-stars: Anthony Michael Hall Kelly LeBrock Bill Paxton

1987 THE RETURN OF THE LIVING DEAD: PART 2
Director: Ken Widerhorn
Co-stars: James Karen Thom Matthews

1988 RETRIBUTION
Director: Guy Magar
Co-stars: Dennis Lipscomb Leslie Wing Jeff Pomerantz

1991 FEMME FATALE
Director: Andre Guttfreund
Co-stars: Colin Firth Liza Zane Billy Zane

JEANNE SOBKOWSKI

1989 FUN DOWN THERE
Director: Roger Stigliano
Co-stars: Michael Waite Martin Goldin Elizabeth Waite

MARIA SOCAS

1987 DEATHSTALKER 2: DUEL OF THE TITANS
Director: Jim Wynorski
Co-stars: John Terlesky Monique Gabrielle

KRISTINA SODERBAUM

1940 JEW SUSS
Director: Veit Harlan
Co-stars: Ferdinand Marian Werner Krauss Heinrich George

ELENA SOFONOVA

1987 BLACK EYES
Director: Nikita Mikhalkov
Co-stars: Marcello Mastroianni Silvana Mangano Marthe Kelle

1992 L'ACCOMPAGNATRICE
Director: Claude Miller
Co-stars: Romane Bohringer Richard Bohringer

MARILYN SOKOL

1977 THE GOODBYE GIRL
Director: Herbert Ross
Co-stars: Richard Dreyfuss Marsha Mason Quinn Cummings

1978 FOUL PLAY
Director: Colin Higgins
Co-stars: Goldie Hawn Chevy Chase Rachel Roberts

1979 THE LAST MARRIED COUPLE IN AMERICA
Director: Gilbert Cates
Co-stars: Natalie Wood George Segal Richard Benjamin

ETHEL SOKOLOW

1969 TAKE THE MONEY AND RUN
Director: Woody Allen
Co-stars: Janet Margolin Lonny Chapman Louise Lasser

TANYA SOLER

1992 CAPTAIN RON
Director: Thom Eberhardt
Co-stars: Kurt Russell Martin Short Paul Anka

MADELEINE SOLOGNE

1943 LOVE ETERNAL
Director: Jean Delannoy
Co-stars: Jean Marais Jean Murat Yvonne De Bray

CLAIRE SOMBERT

1956 INVITATION TO THE DANCE
Director: Gene Kelly
Co-stars: Tommy Rall Tamara Toumanova Belita

SUZANNE SOMERS

1973 AMERICAN GRAFFITI
Director: George Lucas
Co-stars: Richard Dreyfuss Ronny Howard Paul LeMat

1977 IT HAPPENED AT LAKEWOOD MANOR
Director: Robert Sheerer
Co-stars: Robert Foxworth Myrna Loy Lynda Day George

1979 YESTERDAY'S HERO
Director: Neil Leifer
Co-stars: Ian McShane Adam Faith Paul Nicholas

1980 NOTHING PERSONAL
Director: George Bloomfield
Co-stars: Laurence Dane Roscoe Lee Browne Donald Sutherland

1994 SEDUCED BY EVIL
Director: Tony Wharmby
Co-star: James B. Sikking

1994 SERIAL MOM
Director: John Waters
Co-stars: Kathleen Turner Sam Waterston Ricki Lake

GERALDINE SOMERVILLE

1991 THE BLACK VELVET GOWN
Director: Norman Stone
Co-stars: Janet McTeer Bob Peck Jean Anderson

1996 TRUE BLUE
Director: Ferdinand Fairfax
Co-stars: Dominic West Johan Leyson Dylan Baker

GRETCHEN SOMERVILLE

1989 FUN DOWN THERE
Director: Roger Stigliano
Co-stars: Michael Waite Martin Goldin Elizabeth Waite

JULIE SOMMARS

1965 THE GREAT SIOUX MASSACRE
Director: Sidney Salkow
Co-stars: Joseph Cotten Darren McGavin Phil Carey

1966 THE PAD AND HOW TO USE IT
Director: Brian Hutton
Co-stars: Brian Redford James Farantino Edy Williams

1977 HERBIE GOES TO MONTE CARLO
Director: Vincent McEveety
Co-stars: Dean Jones Don Knotts Roy Kinnear

ELKE SOMMER

1961 DON'T BOTHER TO KNOCK
Director: Cyril Frankel
Co-stars: Richard Todd Judith Anderson June Thorburn

1963 THE PRIZE
Director: Mark Robson
Co-stars: Paul Newman Edward G. Robinson Diane Baker

1963 THE VICTORS
Director: Carl Foreman
Co-stars: George Peppard Albert Finney Eli Wallach

1964 A SHOT IN THE DARK
Director: Blake Edwards
Co-stars: Peter Sellers Herbert Lom George Sanders

1965 THE ART OF LOVE
Director: Norman Jewison
Co-stars: James Garner Dick Van Dyke Angie Dickenson

1966 BOY, DID I GET A WRONG NUMBER!
Director: George Marshall
Co-stars: Bob Hope Phyllis Diller Benny Baker

1966 THE CORRUPT ONES
Director: James Hill
Co-stars: Robert Stack Nancy Kwan Christian Marquand

1966 THE MONEY TRAP
Director: Burt Kennedy
Co-stars: Glenn Ford Rita Hayworth Ricardo Montalban

1966 THE OSCAR
Director: Russel Rouse
Co-stars: Stephen Boyd Tony Bennett Eleanor Parker

1966 THE VENETIAN AFFAIR
Director: Jerry Thorpe
Co-stars: Robert Vaughn Felicia Farr Karl Boehm

1967 DEADLIER THAN THE MALE
Director: Ralph Thomas
Co-stars: Richard Johnson Sylva Koscina Nigel Green

1968 THE WRECKING CREW
Director: Phil Karlson
Co-stars: Dean Martin Sharon Tate Nigel Green

1969 THEY CAME TO ROB LAS VEGAS
Director: Antonio Isasi
Co-stars: Jack Palance Lee J. Cobb Gary Lockwood

1970 PERCY
Director: Ralph Thomas
Co-stars: Hywel Bennett Denholm Elliott Britt Ekland

1971 ZEPPELIN
Director: Etienne Perrier
Co-stars: Michael York Marius Goring Rupert Davies

1972 LISA AND THE DEVIL
Director: Mario Bava
Co-stars: Telly Savalas Sylva Koscina Robert Alda

1974 AND THEN THERE WERE NONE
Director: Peter Collinson
Co-stars: Oliver Reed Herbert Lom Charles Aznavor

1974	**PERCY'S PROGRESS**	**1940**	**THE LETTER**
Director:	Ralph Thomas	*Director:*	William Wyler
Co-stars:	Leigh Lawson Denholm Elliott Judy Geeson	*Co-stars:*	Bette Davis Herbert Marshall James Stephenson

1974 **PERCY'S PROGRESS**
Director: Ralph Thomas
Co-stars: Leigh Lawson Denholm Elliott Judy Geeson

1975 **THE SWISS CONSPIRACY**
Director: Jack Arnold
Co-stars: David Janssen Senta Berger John Ireland

1975 **CARRY ON BEHIND**
Director: Gerald Thomas
Co-stars: Kenneth Williams Liz Fraser Joan Sims

1977 **THE TREASURE SEEKERS**
Director: Henry Levin
Co-stars: Rod Taylor Stuart Whitman Keenan Wynn

1979 **THE DOUBLE McGUFFIN**
Director: Joe Camp
Co-stars: Ernest Borgnine George Kennedy Vincent Spano

1979 **THE PRISONER OF ZENDA**
Director: Richard Quine
Co-stars: Peter Sellers Lynne Frederick Stuart Wilson

1979 **A NIGHTINGALE SANG IN BERKELEY SQUARE**
Director: Ralph Thomas
Co-stars: Richard Jordan David Niven Gloria Grahame

1985 **LILY IN LOVE**
Director: Karoly Makk
Co-stars: Christopher Plummer Maggie Smith Adolph Green

1986 **ANASTASIA: THE MYSTERY OF ANNA**
Director: Marvin Chomsky
Co-stars: Amy Irving Olivia De Havilland Omar Sharif

1992 **SEVERED TIES**
Director: Damon Santostefano
Co-stars: Billy Morrisette Garrett Morris

GALE SONDERGAARD
(Married Herbert Biberman)

Oscar For Best Supporting Actress In 1936 For "Anthony Adverse". Nominated For Best Supporting Actress In 1946 For "Anna And The King Of Siam"

1936 **ANTHONY ADVERSE**
Director: Mervyn LeRoy
Co-stars: Fredric March Olivia De Havilland Edmund Gwenn

1937 **THE LIFE OF EMIL ZOLA**
Director: William Dieterle
Co-stars: Paul Muni Joseph Schildkraut Donald Crisp

1937 **MAID OF SALEM**
Director: Frank Lloyd
Co-stars: Claudette Colbert Fred MacMurray Bonita Granville

1937 **SEVENTH HEAVEN**
Director: Henry King
Co-stars: James Stewart Simone Simon Jean Hersholt

1938 **LORD JEFF**
Director: Sam Wood
Co-stars: Freddie Bartholomew Mickey Rooney Charles Coburn

1938 **DRAMATIC SCHOOL**
Director: Robert Sinclair
Co-stars: Luise Rainer Paulette Goddard Lana Turner

1939 **THE CAT AND THE CANARY**
Director: Elliott Nugent
Co-stars: Bob Hope Paulette Goddard George Zucco

1939 **JUAREZ**
Director: William Dieterle
Co-stars: Paul Muni Bette Davis Brian Aherne

1939 **NEVER SAY DIE**
Director: Elliott Nugent
Co-stars: Bob Hope Martha Raye Andy Devine

1940 **THE LETTER**
Director: William Wyler
Co-stars: Bette Davis Herbert Marshall James Stephenson

1940 **THE BLUE BIRD**
Director: Walter Lang
Co-stars: Shirley Temple Johnny Russell Nigel Bruce

1941 **THE BLACK CAT**
Director: Albert Rogell
Co-stars: Basil Rathbone Gladys Cooper Broderick Crawford

1941 **PARIS CALLING**
Director: Edwin Marin
Co-stars: Elisabeth Bergner Basil Rathbone Randolph Scott

1942 **MY FAVOURITE BLONDE**
Director: Sidney Lanfield
Co-stars: Bob Hope Madeleine Carroll George Zucco

1942 **ENEMY AGENTS MEET ELLERY QUEEN**
Director: James Hogan
Co-stars: William Gargan Margaret Lindsay

1943 **APPOINTMENT IN BERLIN**
Director: Alfred Green
Co-stars: George Sanders Marguerite Chapman

1943 **ISLE OF FORGOTTEN SINS**
Director: Edgar Ulmer
Co-stars: John Carradine Sidney Toler Veda Ann Borg

1943 **A NIGHT TO REMEMBER**
Director: Richard Wallace
Co-stars: Loretta Young Brian Aherne Sidney Toler

1943 **THE STRANGE DEATH OF ADOLF HITLER**
Director: James Hogan
Co-stars: Ludwig Donath Fritz Kortner

1944 **THE INVISIBLE MAN'S REVENGE**
Director: Ford Beebe
Co-stars: Jon Hall Leon Errol John Carradine

1944 **GYPSY WILDCAT**
Director: Roy William Neill
Co-stars: Maria Montez Jon Hall Leo Carrillo

1944 **ENTER ARSENE LUPIN**
Director: Ford Beebe
Co-stars: Charles Korvin Ella Raines George Dolenz

1944 **THE CLIMAX**
Director: George Waggner
Co-stars: Boris Karloff Susanna Foster Turhan Bey

1944 **SHERLOCK HOLMES AND THE SPIDER WOMAN**
Director: Roy William Neill
Co-stars: Basil Rathbone Nigel Bruce Dennis Hoey

1944 **CHRISTMAS HOLIDAY**
Director: Robert Siodmak
Co-stars: Gene Kelly Deanna Durbin Gladys George

1946 **ANNA AND THE KING OF SIAM**
Director: John Cromwell
Co-stars: Rex Harrison Irene Dunne Linda Darnell

1946 **A NIGHT IN PARADISE**
Director: Arthur Lubin
Co-stars: Merle Oberon Turhan Bey George Dolenz

1946 **THE SPIDER WOMAN STRIKES BACK**
Director: Arthur Lubin
Co-stars: Brenda Joyce Rondo Hatton

1946 **THE TIME OF THEIR LIVES**
Director: Charles Barton
Co-stars: Bud Abbott Lou Costello Marjorie Reynolds

1947 **ROAD TO RIO**
Director: Norman Z. McLeod
Co-stars: Bob Hope Bing Crosby Dorothy Lamour

1947 PIRATES OF MONTERAY
Director: Alfred Werker
Co-stars: Maria Montez Rod Cameron Gilbert Roland

1949 EAST SIDE, WEST SIDE
Director: Mervyn LeRoy
Co-stars: James Mason Barbara Stanwyck Van Heflin

1969 SLAVES
Director: Herbert Biberman
Co-stars: Stephen Boyd Ossie Davis

1973 THE CAT CREATURE
Director: Curtis Harrington
Co-stars: Meredith Baxter David Hedison Stuart Whitman

1976 THE RETURN OF A MAN CALLED HORSE
Director: Irvin Kershner
Co-stars: Richard Harris Geoffrey Lewis

JOHANNA SONNEX

1979 STORIES FROM A FLYING TRUNK
Director: Christine Edzard
Co-stars: Murray Melvin Ann Firbank Tasneem Maqsood

AGNES SORAL

1987 THREE SISTERS
Director: Margarethe Von Trotta
Co-stars: Greta Scacchi Fanny Ardant Valeria Golino

1989 AUSTRALIA
Director: Jean-Jacques Andrien
Co-stars: Jeremy Irons Fanny Ardant Tcheky Karyo

JULIET SORCEY

1989 TAKEN AWAY
Director: John Patterson
Co-stars: Valerie Bertinelli Kevin Dunn Nada Despotovich

ANN SOREEN

1937 THE BLACK TULIP
Director: Alex Bryce
Co-stars: Patrick Waddington Bernard Lee Ronald Shiner

LOUISE SOREL

1963 THE PARTY'S OVER
Director: Guy Hamilton
Co-stars: Oliver Reed Eddie Albert Ann Lynn

1970 B.S. I LOVE YOU
Director: Steven Hillard Stern
Co-stars: Peter Kastner Joanna Cameron Joanna Barnes

1971 PLAZA SUITE
Director: Arthur Hiller
Co-stars: Walter Matthau Maureen Stapleton Lee Grant

1971 THE PRESIDENT'S PLANE IS MISSING
Director: Daryl Duke
Co-stars: Buddy Ebsen Arthur Kennedy Rip Torn

1976 PERILOUS VOYAGE
Director: William Graham
Co-stars: Michael Parks Lee Grant William Shatner

1978 WHEN EVERY DAY WAS THE FOURTH OF JULY
Director: Dan Curtis
Co-stars: Dean Jones Chris Peterson Harris Yulin

1983 SUNSET LIMOUSINE
Director: Terry Hughes
Co-stars: John Ritter Susan Dey Lainie Kazan

LINDA SORENSON

1980 STONE COLD DEAD
Director: George Mendeluk
Co-stars: Richard Crenna Paul Williams Belinda Montgomery

1980 KAVIK, THE WOLF DOG
Director: Peter Carter
Co-stars: Ronny Cox John Ireland John Candy

ALEXANDRA SORINA

1925 HANDS OF ORLAC
Director: Robert Wiene
Co-stars: Conrad Veidt Fritz Strassny Fritz Kortner

MIRA SORVINO

1994 PARALLEL LIVES
Director: Linda Yellen
Co-stars: Liza Minnelli Ben Gazzara Gena Rowlands

1994 BARCELONA
Director: Whit Stillman
Co-stars: Taylor Nichols Chris Eigeman Tushka Bergen

1996 BEAUTIFUL GIRLS
Director: Ted Demme
Co-stars: Uma Thurman Natalie Portman Timothy Hutton

1996 MIGHTY APHRODITE
Director: Woody Allen
Co-stars: Woody Allen Helena Bonham-Carter F. Murray Abraham

1997 ROMY AND MICHELE'S HIGH SCHOOL REUNION
Co-star: Lisa Kudrow

1998 THE REPLACEMENT KILLERS
Co-star: Chow Yun-Fat

1998 MIMIC
Director: Giovanni Del Toro
Co-star: Jeremy Northam

GEOANN SOSA

1975 THE MASTER GUNFIGHTER
Director: Tom Loughlin
Co-stars: Tom Loughlin Ron O'Neal Barbara Carrera

ANN SOTHERN

Nominated For Best Supporting Actress In 1987 For "The Whales Of August"

1934 MELODY IN SPRING
Director: Norman Z. McLeod
Co-stars: Lanny Ross Charles Ruggles Mary Boland

1934 LET'S FALL IN LOVE
Director: David Burton
Co-stars: Edmund Lowe Gregory Ratoff Miriam Jordan

1934 BLIND DATE
Director: Roy William Neill
Co-stars: Paul Kelly Neil Hamilton Mickey Rooney

1934 THE PARTY'S OVER
Co-stars: Stuart Erwin William Bakewell Arline Judge

1934 THE HELLCAT
Co-star: Robert Armstrong

1935 EIGHT BELLS
Co-stars: Ralph Bellamy John Buckler

1935 FOLIES BERGERE
Director: Roy Del Ruth
Co-stars: Maurice Chevalier Merle Oberon Eric Blore

1935 THE GIRL FRIEND
Director: Eddie Buzzell
Co-stars: Jack Haley Roger Pryor Victor Kilian

1935 HOORAY FOR LOVE
Director: Walter Lang
Co-stars: Gene Raymond Lionel Stander Bill Robinson

1935   **KID MILLIONS**
Director: Roy Del Ruth
Co-stars: Eddie Cantor Ethel Merman George Murphy

1935   **GRAND EXIT**
Director: Erle Kenton
Co-stars: Edmund Lowe Onslow Stevens Selmer Jackson

1936   **YOU MAY BE NEXT**
Co-stars: Lloyd Nolan Douglass Dumbrille

1936   **WALKING ON AIR**
Co-stars: Henry Stephenson Jessie Ralph

1936   **SMARTEST GIRL IN TOWN**
Co-stars: Gene Raymond Eric Blore

1936   **DON'T GAMBLE WITH LOVE**

1937   **THERE GOES MY GIRL**
Co-star: Gene Raymond

1937   **DANGEROUS NUMBER**
Director: Richard Thorpe
Co-stars: Robert Young Reginald Owen Cora Witherspoon

1937   **DANGER - LOVE AT WORK**
Director: Otto Preminger
Co-stars: Jack Haley Mary Boland John Carradine

1937   **FIFTY ROADS TO TOWN**
Director: Norman Taurog
Co-stars: Don Ameche Slim Summerville John Qualen

1937   **SUPER SLEUTH**
Director: Ben Stoloff
Co-stars: Jack Oakie Edgar Kennedy Eduardo Ciannelli

1937   **THERE GOES THE GROOM**
Director: Joseph Santly
Co-stars: Burgess Meredith Mary Boland Onslow Stevens

1938   **SHE'S GOT EVERYTHING**
Director: Joseph Santly
Co-stars: Gene Raymond Victor Moore Helen Broderick

1938   **TRADE WINDS**
Director: Tay Garnett
Co-stars: Fredric March Joan Bennett Ralph Bellamy

1939   **HOTEL FOR WOMEN**
Director: Gregory Ratoff
Co-stars: Elsa Maxwell Linda Darnell James Ellison

1939   **FAST AND FURIOUS**
Director: Busby Berkeley
Co-star: Franchot Tone

1939   **MAISIE**
Director: Edwin Marin
Co-stars: Robert Young Ian Hunter Ruth Hussey

1940   **BROTHER ORCHID**
Director: Lloyd Bacon
Co-stars: Edward G. Robinson Humphrey Bogart Donald Crisp

1940   **CONGO MAISIE**
Director: H.C. Potter
Co-stars: John Carroll Rita Johnson Shepperd Strudwick

1940   **GOLD RUSH MAISIE**
Director: Edwin Marin
Co-stars: Lee Bowman Slim Summerville Virginia Weidler

1941   **LADY BE GOOD**
Director: Norman Z. McLeod
Co-stars: Eleanor Powell Robert Young Dan Dailey

1941   **MAISIE WAS A LADY**
Director: Edwin Marin
Co-stars: Lew Ayres Maureen O'Sullivan C. Aubrey Smith

1941   **RINGSIDE MAISIE**
Director: Edwin Marin
Co-stars: George Murphy Robert Sterling Virginia O'Brien

1942   **MAISIE GETS HER MAN**
Director: Roy Del Ruth
Co-stars: Red Skelton Leo Gorcey Allen Jenkins

1942   **PANAMA HATTIE**
Director: Norman Z. McLeod
Co-stars: Red Skelton Dan Dailey Marsha Hunt

1943   **SWING-SHIFT MAISIE**
Director: Norman Z. McLeod
Co-stars: James Craig Jean Rogers John Qualen

1943   **THREE HEARTS FOR JULIA**
Director: Richard Thorpe
Co-stars: Melvyn Douglas Lee Bowman Felix Bressart

1943   **CRY HAVOC**
Director: Richard Thorpe
Co-stars: Margaret Sullavan Joan Blondell Ella Raines

1944   **MAISIE GOES TO RENO**
Director: Harry Beaumont
Co-stars: John Hodiak Ava Gardner Tom Drake

1946   **UP GOES MAISIE**
Co-star: George Murphy

1947   **UNDERCOVER MAISIE**
Director: Harry Beaumont
Co-stars: Barry Nelson Leon Ames Clinton Sundberg

1947   **THE JUDGE STEPS OUT**
Director: Boris Ingster
Co-stars: Alexander Knox George Tobias Sharyn Moffett

1948   **A LETTER TO THREE WIVES**
Director: Joseph Mankiewicz
Co-stars: Jeanne Crain Linda Darnell Kirk Douglas

1948   **WORDS AND MUSIC**
Director: Norman Taurog
Co-stars: Tom Drake Mickey Rooney Gene Kelly

1948   **APRIL SHOWERS**
Director: James Kern
Co-stars: Jack Carson Robert Alda S.Z. Sakall

1949   **SHADOW ON THE WALL**
Director: Pat Jackson
Co-stars: Zachary Scott Gigi Perreau Nancy Davis

1950   **NANCY GOES TO RIO**
Director: Robert Z. Leonard
Co-stars: Jane Powell Carmen Miranda Barry Sullivan

1953   **THE BLUE GARDENIA**
Director: Fritz Lang
Co-stars: Anne Baxter Richard Conte Raymond Burr

1964   **THE BEST MAN**
Director: Franklin Schaffner
Co-stars: Henry Fonda Cliff Robertson Lee Tracy

1964   **LADY IN A CAGE**
Director: Walter Grauman
Co-stars: Olivia De Havilland James Caan Jeff Corey

1965   **SYLVIA**
Director: Gordon Douglas
Co-stars: Carroll Baker George Maharis Vivecca Lindfors

1967   **THE OUTSIDER**
Director: Michael Ritchie
Co-stars: Darren McGavin Anna Hagan Edmond O'Brien

1967   **CHUBASCO**
Director: Allen Miner
Co-stars: Chris Jones Richard Egan Susan Strasberg

1974   **GOLDEN NEEDLES**
Director: Robert Clouse
Co-stars: Joe Don Baker Elizabeth Ashley Burgess Meredith

Kay Kendall

Giulietta Masina

Leslie Caron

Susannah York

1975	**CRAZY MAMA**	
Director:	Jonathan Demme	
Co-stars:	Cloris Leachman Linda Purl Stuart Whitman	

1975 **CRAZY MAMA**
Director: Jonathan Demme
Co-stars: Cloris Leachman Linda Purl Stuart Whitman

1978 **MANITOU**
Director: William Girdler
Co-stars: Tony Curtis Susan Strasberg Burgess Meredith

1983 **A LETTER TO THREE WIVES**
Director: Larry Elikann
Co-stars: Loni Anderson Stephanie Zimbalist Michele Lee

1987 **THE WHALES OF AUGUST**
Director: Lindsay Anderson
Co-stars: Bette Davis Lillian Gish Vincent Price

TALISA SOTO

1989 **LICENCE TO KILL**
Director: John Glen
Co-stars: Timothy Dalton Carey Lowell Robert Davi

1991 **PRISON STORIES: WOMEN ON THE INSIDE**
Director: Donna Deitch
Co-stars: Rae Dawn Chong Lolita Davidovich

1992 **HOSTAGE**
Director: Robert Young
Co-stars: Sam Neill James Fox Michael Kitchen

1992 **THE MAMBO KING**
Director: Arne Glimcher
Co-stars: Antonio Banderas Armand Assante Cathy Moriarty

1995 **DON JUAN DeMARCO**
Director: Jeremy Leven
Co-stars: Johnny Depp Marlon Brando Faye Dunaway

RENEE SOUTENDIJK

1980 **SPETTERS**
Director: Paul Verhoeven
Co-stars: Jeroen Krabbe Rutger Hauer Toon Agterberg

1983 **THE FOURTH MAN**
Director: Paul Verhoeven
Co-stars: Jeroen Krabbe Thom Hoffman Dolf De Vries

1984 **THE COLD ROOM**
Director: James Dearden
Co-stars: George Segal Amanda Pays Warren Clarke

1987 **SCOOP**
Director: Gavin Miller
Co-stars: Michael Maloney Denholm Elliott Nicola Pagett

EVE SOUTHERN

1930 **MOROCCO**
Director: Josef Von Sternberg
Co-stars: Marlene Dietrich Gary Cooper Adolphe Menjou

TAMMARA SOUZA

1988 **ASSAULT OF THE KILLER BIMBOS**
Director: Anita Rosenberg
Co-stars: Christina Whitaker Nick Cassavetes Griffin O'Neal

CATHARINE SPAAK

1964 **THE EMPTY CANVAS**
Director: Damiano Damiani
Co-stars: Bette Davis Horst Buchholz Isa Miranda

1964 **LA RONDE**
Director: Roger Vadim
Co-stars: Marie Dubois Anna Karina Jane Fonda

1966 **ADULTERY ITALIAN STYLE**
Director: Pasquale Festa Campanile
Co-stars: Nino Manfredi Vittorio Caprioli

1967 **HOTEL**
Director: Richard Quine
Co-stars: Rod Taylor Karl Malden Merle Oberon

1971 **CAT O' NINE TAILS**
Director: Dario Argento
Co-stars: Karl Malden James Franciscus

1975 **TAKE A HARD RIDE**
Director: Anthony Dawson
Co-stars: Jim Brown Lee Van Cleef Dana Andrews

SISSY SPACEK

(Married Jack Fisk / Cousin Of Rip Torn)
Oscar For Best Actress In 1980 For "Coal Miner's Daughter". Nominated For Best Actress In 1976 For "Carrie", In 1982 For "Missing" And In 1984 For "The River"

1972 **PRIME CUT**
Director: Michael Ritchie
Co-stars: Gene Hackman Lee Marvin Angel Tompkins

1973 **BADLANDS**
Director: Terrence Malick
Co-stars: Martin Sheen Warren Oates Ramon Bieri

1974 **THE MIGRANTS**
Director: Tom Gries
Co-stars: Cloris Leachman Ron Howard Cindy Williams

1976 **WELCOME TO L.A.**
Director: Alan Rudolph
Co-stars: Keith Carradine Sally Kellerman Harvey Keitel

1976 **CARRIE**
Director: Brian De Palma
Co-stars: Piper Laurie Amy Irvine William Katt

1977 **3 WOMEN**
Director: Robert Altman
Co-stars: Shelley Duvall Janice Rule Ruth Nelson

1979 **HEART BEAT**
Director: John Byrum
Co-stars: Nick Nolte John Heard Ray Sharkey

1980 **COAL MINER'S DAUGHTER**
Director: Michael Apted
Co-stars: Tommy Lee Jones Beverly D'Angelo Levon Helm

1981 **RAGGEDY MAN**
Director: Jack Fisk
Co-stars: Eric Roberts Sam Shepard R.G. Armstrong

1982 **MISSING**
Director: Costa-Gavras
Co-stars: Jack Lemmon Melanie Mayron John Shea

1983 **THE MAN WITH TWO BRAINS** *(Voice)*
Director: Carl Reiner
Co-stars: Steve Martin Kathleen Turner David Warner

1984 **THE RIVER**
Director: Mark Rydell
Co-stars: Mel Gibson Scott Glenn Shane Bailey

1985 **MARIE**
Director: Roger Donaldson
Co-stars: Jeff Daniels Morgan Freeman Lisa Baines

1986 **'NIGHT MOTHER**
Director: Tom Moore
Co-stars: Anne Bancroft Ed Burke Carol Robbins

1986 **VIOLETS ARE BLUE**
Director: Jack Fisk
Co-stars: Kevin Kline Bonnie Bedelia Jack Kellogg

1986 **CRIMES OF THE HEART**
Director: Bruce Beresford
Co-stars: Diane Keaton Jessica Lange Sam Shepard

1990 THE LONG WALK HOME
Director: Richard Peerce
Co-stars: Whoopi Goldberg Ving Rhames Dwight Schultz

1991 J.F.K.
Director: Oliver Stone
Co-stars: Kevin Costner Joe Pesci Tommy Lee Jones

1991 HARD PROMISES
Director: Martin Davidson
Co-stars: William Petersen Brian Kerwin Mare Winningham

1992 A PRIVATE MATTER
Director: Joan Micklin Silver
Co-stars: Aidan Quinn Estelle Parsons

1993 A PLACE FOR ANNIE
Director: John Grey
Co-stars: Joan Plowright Mary-Louise Parker

1994 THE MOMMY MARKET
Director: Tia Brellis
Co-stars: Anna Chlumsky Aaron Michael Asher Metchick

1996 IF THESE WALLS COULD TALK
Co-stars: Cher Demi Moore

1998 THE GRASS HARP
Director: Charles Matthau
Co-stars: Edward Furlong Piper Laurie Walter Matthau

MERRI SPAETH

1964 THE WORLD OF HENRY ORIENT
Director: George Roy Hill
Co-stars: Peter Sellers Tippy Walker Paula Prentiss

FAY SPAIN

1957 DRAGSTRIP GIRL
Director: Edward Cahn
Co-stars: John Ashley Steve Terrell Frank Gorshin

1957 THE ABDUCTORS
Director: Andrew McLaglen
Co-stars: Victor McLaglen Gavin Muir George Macready

1957 GOD'S LITTLE ACRE
Director: Anthony Mann
Co-stars: Robert Ryan Aldo Ray Tina Louise

1959 THE BEAT GENERATION
Director: Charles Haas
Co-stars: Ray Danton Steve Cochran Jackie Coogan

1959 AL CAPONE
Director: Richard Wilson
Co-stars: Rod Steiger Murvin Vye Martin Balsam

1967 WELCOME TO HARD TIMES
Director: Burt Kennedy
Co-stars: Henry Fonda Janice Rule Keenan Wynn

LOURETTE SPANG

1978 BATTLESHIP: GALACTICA
Director: Richard Colla
Co-stars: Lorne Green Ray Milland Dirk Benedict

PIP SPARKE

1964 FATHER GOOSE
Director: Ralph Nelson
Co-stars: Cary Grant Leslie Caron Trevor Howard

CAMILLA SPARV

1966 THE TROUBLE WITH ANGELS
Director: Ida Lupino
Co-stars: Rosalind Russell Hayley Mills June Harding

1966 MURDERER'S ROW
Director: Henry Levin
Co-stars: Dean Martin Ann-Margret Karl Malden

1966 DEAD HEAT ON A MERRY-GO-ROUND
Director: Bernard Girard
Co-stars: James Coburn Aldo Ray Robert Webber

1968 ASSIGNMENT K
Director: Val Guest
Co-stars: Stephen Boyd Michael Redgrave Leo McKern

1968 NOBODY RUNS FOREVER
Director: Ralph Thomas
Co-stars: Rod Taylor Christopher Plummer Lilli Palmer

1969 MacKENNA'S GOLD
Director: J. Lee-Thompson
Co-stars: Gregory Peck Omar Sharif Telly Savalas

1969 DOWNHILL RACER
Director: Michael Ritchie
Co-stars: Robert Redford Gene Hackman Dabney Coleman

1978 THE GREEK TYCOON
Director: J. Lee-Thompson
Co-stars: Anthony Quinn Jacqueline Bisset Raf Vallone

1981 CABOBLANCO
Director: J. Lee-Thompson
Co-stars: Charles Bronson Jason RobardsDominique Sanda

MONIQUE SPAZIANI

1988 REVOLVING DOORS
Director: Francis Mankiewicz
Co-stars: Gabriel Arcand Miou-Miou Francois Methe

1994 APRIL ONE
Director: Murray Battle
Co-stars: Stephen Shellen Djanet Sears David Strathairn

HAZEL SPEARS

1979 PENITENTIARY
Director: Jamaa Fanaka
Co-stars: Leon Isaac Kennedy Thommy Pollard Gloria Delaney

LYNDA SPECIALE

1983 SCREWBALLS
Director: Rafal Zielinski
Co-stars: Peter Keleghan Kent Deuters Linda Shane

JUTTA SPEIDEL

1988 JUDGEMENT IN BERLIN
Director: Leo Penn
Co-stars: Martin Sheen Sam Wanamaker Sean Penn

DONA SPEIR

1987 HARD TICKET TO HAWAII
Director: Andy Sidaris
Co-stars: Hope Maris Carlton Ronn Moss Harold Diamond

ROSALIND SPEIRS

1979 ALISON'S BIRTHDAY
Director: Ian Coughlan
Co-stars: Lou Brown Bunny Brooke Vincent Ball

WANDA SPELL (Child)

1970 THEY CALL ME MISTER TIBBS!
Director: Gordon Douglas
Co-stars: Sidney Poitier Martin Landau Barbara McNair

TORI SPELLING

1995 AWAKE TO DANGER
Director: Michael Tuchner
Co-stars: Michael Gross John Getz

1996 DEADLY PURSUITS
Director: Felix Enriques Alcala
Co-stars: Patrick Muldoon Richard Belzer

1996 CO-ED CALL GIRL
Director: Michael Ray Rhodes
Co-stars: Susan Blakely Scott Plank Charles Grant

SHARON SPELLMAN

1977 DEADLY GAME
Director: Lane Slate
Co-stars: Andy Griffith Mitzi Koag Dan O'Herlihy

DANIELLE SPENCER

1990 THE CROSSING
Director: George Ogilvie
Co-stars: Russell Crowe Robert Mammone

DIANA SPENCER

1959 DON'T GIVE UP THE SHIP
Director: Norman Taurog
Co-stars: Jerry Lewis Dina Merril Robert Middleton

LEE SPENCER

1994 TAKING LIBERTY
Director: Stuart Gillard
Co-stars: David Warner Kenneth Jones

MARIAN SPENCER

1942 LET THE PEOPLE SING
Director: John Baxter
Co-stars: Alastair Sim Fred Emney Patricia Roc

1943 WHEN WE ARE MARRIED
Director: Lance Comfort
Co-stars: Raymond Huntley Olga Lindo Sydney Howard

1944 FLIGHT FROM FOLLY
Director: Herbert Mason
Co-stars: Pat Kirkwood Hugh Sinclair Sydney Howard

1953 INTIMATE RELATIONS
Director: Charles Frank
Co-stars: Ruth Dunning Harold Warrender Russell Enoch

1958 CORRIDORS OF BLOOD
Director: Robert Day
Co-stars: Boris Karloff Christopher Lee Betta St. John

1959 THE THREE WORLDS OF GULLIVER
Director: Jack Sher
Co-stars: Kerwin Matthews Basil Sydney June Thorburn

WENDIE JO SPERBER

1980 USED CARS
Director: Robert Zemeckis
Co-stars: Kurt Russell Jack Warden Gerrit Graham

1983 THE FIRST TIME
Director: Charlie Loventhal
Co-stars: Tim Choate Krista Errickson Wendy Fulton

1985 MOVING VIOLATIONS
Director: Neal Israel
Co-stars: Stephen McHattie Jennifer Tilly Sally Kellerman

ERICA SPEYER

1961 THE SAND CASTLE
Director: Jerome Hill
Co-stars: Barrie Cardwell Laurie Cardwell George Dunham

ROS SPIERS

1975 THE MAN FROM HONG KONG
Director: Brian Trenchard-Smith
Co-stars: George Lazenby Jimmy Wang Yu Rebecca Gilling

FANNY SPIES

1980 FRIENDLY FIRE
Director: David Greene
Co-stars: Carol Burnett Ned Beatty Sam Waterston

GRAZIA MARIA SPINA

1962 TIGER OF THE SEVEN SEAS
Director: Luigi Capuano
Co-stars: Gianna Maria Canale Anthony Steel Ernesto Calindri

CAROLL SPINNEY

1985 FOLLOW THAT BIRD
Director: Ken Kwapis
Co-stars: Jim Henson Frank Oz John Candy

ALICE SPIVAK

1991 ELECTRIC MOON
Director: Pradip Krishen
Co-stars: Roshan Seth Leela Naidu Naseeruddin Shah

VICTORIA SPIVEY

1929 HALLELUJAH!
Director: King Vidor
Co-stars: Daniel L. Haynes Nina Mae McKinney Harry Gray

MADAME SPIVY

1962 REQUIEM FOR A HEAVYWEIGHT
Director: Ralph Nelson
Co-stars: Anthony Quinn Mickey Rooney Julie Harris

VIOLA SPOLIN

1970 ALEX IN WONDERLAND
Director: Paul Mazursky
Co-stars: Donald Sutherland Jeanne Moreau Ellen Burstyn

ELIZABETH SPRIGGS

1968 WORK IS A FOUR-LETTER WORD
Director: Peter Hall
Co-stars: David Warner Cilla Black Joe Gladwin

1980 RICHARD'S THINGS
Director: Anthony Harvey
Co-stars: Liv Ullman Amanda Redman Tim Pigott-Smith

1981 LADY CHATTERLEY'S LOVER
Director: Just Jaeckin
Co-stars: Sylvia Kristel Nicholas Clay Shane Briant

1982 AN UNSUITABLE JOB FOR A WOMAN
Director: Christopher Petit
Co-stars: Pippa Guard Billie Whitelaw Dominic Guard

1989 ORANGES ARE NOT THE ONLY FRUIT
Director: Beeban Kidron
Co-stars: Geraldine McEwan Charlotte Coleman Kenneth Cranham

1990 SURVIVAL OF THE FITTEST
Director: Martyn Friend
Co-stars: Jean Anderson Timothy West Nerys Hughes

1991 THE OLD DEVILS
Director: Tristram Powell
Co-stars: John Stride Ray Smith Anna Cropper

1992 ANGLO-SAXON ATTITUDES
Director: Diarmuid Lawrence
Co-stars: Richard Johnson Dorothy Tutin Tara Fitzgerald

1993 THE HOUR OF THE PIG
Director: Leslie Megahey
Co-stars: Colin Firth Lysette Anthony Ian Holm

1996 SENSE AND SENSIBILITY
Director: Ang Lee
Co-stars: Emma Thompson Hugh Grant Kate Winslet

1997 PARADISE ROAD
Director: Bruce Beresford
Co-stars: Pauline Collins Jennifer Ehle Glenn Close

HELEN SPRING

1948 COVER-UP
Director: Alfred Green
Co-stars: Dennis O'Keefe William Bendix Barbara Britton

PAMELA SPRINGSTEIN

1990 THE GUMSHOE KID
Director: Joseph Manduke
Co-stars: Jay Underwood Tracy Scoggins Vince Edwards

SANDRA SPURR

1961 HUNTED IN HOLLAND
Director: Derek Williams
Co-stars: Sean Scully Jacques Verbrugge Thom Kelling

LINDA SPURRIER

1978 JUBILEE
Director: Derek Jarman
Co-stars: Jenny Runacre Toyah Wilcox Ian Charleson

DINA SPYBEY

1997 SUBURBIA
Director: Richard Linklater

KATHERINE SQUIRE

1965 RIDE IN THE WHIRLWIND
Director: Monte Hellman
Co-stars: Cameron Mitchell Jack Nicholson Millie Perkins

1973 THE LOLLY MADONNA WAR
Director: Richard Sarafian
Co-stars: Rod Steiger Robert Ryan Scott Wilson

SHEILA STAEFEL

1968 BABY LOVE
Director: Alastair Reid
Co-stars: Linda Hayden Ann Lynn Keith Barron

1970 SOME WILL, SOME WON'T
Director: Duncan Wood
Co-stars: Thora Hird Ronnie Corbett Leslie Phillips

1970 PERCY
Director: Ralph Thomas
Co-stars: Hywel Bennett Denholm Elliott Cyd Hayman

1971 MELODY
Director: Waris Hussein
Co-stars: Jack Wild Mark Lester Tracy Hyde

1975 NEVER TOO YOUNG TO ROCK
Director: Dennis Abey
Co-stars: Peter Denyer Peter Noone Freddie Jones

1977 ARE YOU BEING SERVED ?
Director: Bob Kellett
Co-stars: John Inman Frank Thornton Mollie Sugden

1983 BLOODBATH AT THE HOUSE OF DEATH
Director: Ray Cameron
Co-stars: Kenny Everett Pamela Stephenson Vincent Price

KATHY STAFF

1983 SEPARATE TABLES
Director: John Schlesinger
Co-stars: Alan Bates Julie Christie Claire Bloom

NANCY STAFFORD

1993 A CHILD TOO MANY
Director: Jorge Montesi
Co-stars: Michelle Greene Connor O'Farrell

1995 DEADLY INVASION
Director: Rockne S. O'Bannon
Co-stars: Robert Hays Gregory Gordon

TAMARA STAFFORD

1985 THE HILLS HAVE EYES, PART II
Director: Wes Craven
Co-stars: Michael Berryman Kevin Blair John Bloom

JOAN STALEY

1965 THE GHOST AND MR CHICKEN
Director: Alan Rafkin
Co-stars: Don Knots Skip Homeier Reta Shaw

1966 GUNPOINT
Director: Earl Bellamy
Co-stars: Audie Murphy Edgar Buchanan Denver Pyle

ANNE STALLYBRASS

1970 THE SIX WIVES OF HENRY VIII
Director: John Glenister
Co-stars: Keith Michell Annette Crosby Dorothy Tutin

1978 THE MAYOR OF CASTERBRIDGE
Director: David Giles
Co-stars: Alan Bates Anna Massey Janet Maw

1991 THE OLD DEVILS
Director: Tristram Powell
Co-stars: John Stride James Grant Sheila Allen

ENID STAMP-TAYLOR

1935 WHILE PARENTS SLEEP
Co-stars: Jean Gillie MacKenzie Ward

1936 QUEEN OF HEARTS
Director: Monty Banks
Co-stars: Gracie Fields John Loder Edward Rigby

1936 HOUSE BROKEN
Director: Michael Hankinson
Co-stars: Mary Lawson Jack Lambert Louis Borell

1936 BLIND MAN'S BUFF
Director: Albert Parker
Co-stars: Basil Sydney James Mason Barbara Greene

1937 FEATHER YOUR NEST
Director: William Beaudine
Co-stars: George Formby Polly Ward Davy Burnabe

1937 OKAY FOR SOUND
Director: Marcel Varnel
Co-stars: Bud Flanagan Chesney Allen Graham Moffat

1937 UNDERNEATH THE ARCHES
Director: Redd David
Co-stars: Bud Flanagan Chesney Allen Lyn Harding

1938 OLD IRON
Director: Tom Walls
Co-stars: Tom Walls Eva Moore Cecil Parker

1938 CLIMBING HIGH
Director: Carol Reed
Co-stars: Jessie Matthews Michael Redgrave Alastair Sim

1938 BLONDES FOR DANGER
Director: Jack Raymond
Co-stars: Gordon Harker Ivan Brandt

1939 THE LAMBETH WALK
Director: Albert De Courville
Co-stars: Lupino Lane Sally Gray Seymour Hicks

1940   **SPRING MEETING**
Director: Walter Mycroft
Co-stars: Nova Pilbeam Basil Sydney Michael Wilding

1941   **SOUTH AMERICAN GEORGE**
Director: Marcel Varnel
Co-stars: George Formby Linden Travers Jacques Brown

1941   **HATTER'S CASTLE**
Director: Lance Comfort
Co-stars: Robert Newton Deborah Kerr James Mason

1942   **ALIBI**
Director: Brian Desmond Hurst
Co-stars: Margaret Lockwood Hugh Sinclair James Mason

1943   **CANDLELIGHT IN ALGERIA**
Director: George King
Co-stars: Carla Lehman James Mason Walter Rilla

1945   **THE WICKED LADY**
Director: Leslie Arliss
Co-stars: Margaret Lockwood James Mason Griffith Jones

1947   **CARAVAN**
Director: Arthur Crabtree
Co-stars: Stewart Granger Jean Kent Anne Crawford

FLORENCE STANLEY

1975   **THE PRISONER OF SECOND AVENUE**
Director: Melvin Frank
Co-stars: Jack Lemmon Anne Bancroft Gene Saks

1975   **THE FORTUNE**
Director: Mike Nichols
Co-stars: Jack Nicholson Warren Beatty Stockard Channing

HELENE STANLEY

1952   **DREAMBOAT**
Director: Claude Binyon
Co-stars: Clifton Webb Ginger Rogers Anne Francis

1952   **WAIT TIL THE SUN SHINES NELLIE**
Director: Henry King
Co-stars: David Wayne Jean Peters Hugh Marlowe

JILL STANLEY

1988   **TOMMY TRICKER AND THE STAMP TRAVELLER**
Director: Michael Rubbo
Co-stars: Lucas Evans Anthony Rogers

KIM STANLEY

Nominated For Best Actress In 1964 For "Séance On A Wet Afternoon"

1958   **THE GODDESS**
Director: John Cromwell
Co-stars: Lloyd Bridges Steven Hill Patty Duke

1964   **SÉANCE ON A WET AFTERNOON**
Director: Bryan Forbes
Co-stars: Richard Attenborough Nanette Newman Patrick Magee

1982   **FRANCES**
Director: Graeme Clifford
Co-stars: Jessica Lange Sam Shepard Jeffrey DeMunn

1983   **THE RIGHT STUFF**
Director: Philip Kaufman
Co-stars: Sam Shepard Scott Glen Dennis Quaid

1984   **CAT ON A HOT TIN ROOF**
Director: Jack Hofsiss
Co-stars: Jessica Lange Tommy Lee Jones Rip Torn

LAUREN STANLEY

1988   **MAC AND ME**
Director: Stewart Raffill
Co-stars: Christine Ebersole Jonathan Ward Tina Caspary

LORA STANLEY

1982   **AMERICAN NIGHTMARE**
Director: Don McBrearty
Co-stars: Lawrence S. Day Lenore Zann Paul Bradley

LOUISE STANLEY

1937   **SING COWBOY SING**
Co-star: Tex Ritter

MARTINA STANLEY

1990   **AUGUST SATURDAY**
Director: Diarmuid Lawrence
Co-stars: Sorcha Cusack Tim McInnerny Barry McGovern

PHYLLIS STANLEY

1939   **THERE AIN'T NO JUSTICE**
Director: Pen Tennyson
Co-stars: Jimmy Hanley Edward Rigby Mary Clare

1943   **THEY MET IN THE DARK**
Director: Karel Lamac
Co-stars: Tom Walls Joyce Howard James Mason

1948   **LOOK BEFORE YOU LOVE**
Director: Harold Huth
Co-stars: Margaret Lockwood Griffith Jones Norman Wooland

1953   **TAKE ME TO TOWN**
Director: Douglas Sirk
Co-stars: Ann Sheridan Sterling Hayden Philip Reed

CLAIRE STANSFIELD

1994   **DROP ZONE**
Director: John Badham
Co-stars: Wesley Snipes Yancy Butler Gary Busey

1995   **WES CRAVEN PRESENTS MIND RIPER**
Director: Joe Gayton
Co-stars: Lance Henriksen Natasha Wagner

BARBARA STANWYCK *(Ruby Stevens)*
(Married Frank Fay, Robert Taylor)

Nominated For Best Actress In 1937 For "Stella Dallas", In 1941 For "Ball Of Fire", In 1944 For "Double Indemnity" And In 1948 For "Sorry, Wrong Number" (Honorary Award 1981)

1929   **THE LOCKED DOOR**
Director: George Fitzmaurice
Co-stars: Rod La Rocque William Boyd Zasu Pitts

1930   **LADIES OF LEISURE**
Director: Frank Capra
Co-stars: Lowell Sherman Ralph Graves Marie Prevost

1931   **ILLICIT**
Director: Archie Mayo
Co-stars: Ricardo Cortez Joan Blondell James Rennie

1931   **NIGHT NURSE**
Director: William Wellman
Co-stars: Ben Lyon Joan Blondell Clark Gable

1931   **TEN CENTS A DANCE**
Director: Lionel Barrymore
Co-stars: Monroe Owsley Ricardo Cortez

1932   **THE MIRACLE WOMAN**
Director: Frank Capra
Co-stars: Sam Hardy David Manners Beryl Mercer

1932   **SO BIG**
Director: William Wellman
Co-stars: George Brent Bette Davis Dickie Moore

1932   **SHOPWORN**
Director: Nick Grinde
Co-stars: Regis Toomey Zasu Pitts Clara Blandick

1932 **FORBIDDEN**	**1938** **THE MAD MISS MANTON**
Director: Frank Capra	*Director:* Leigh Jason
Co-stars: Adolphe Menjou Ralph Bellamy	*Co-stars:* Henry Fonda Sam Levene Vicki Lester
1932 **PURCHASE PRICE**	**1939** **GOLDEN BOY**
Co-stars: George Brent Lyle Talbot	*Director:* Rouben Mamoulian
	Co-stars: William Holden Adolphe Menjou
1933 **BABY FACE**	**1938** **ALWAYS GOODBYE**
Director: Alfred Green	*Director:* Sidney Lanfield
Co-stars: George Brent John Wayne Margaret Lindsay	*Co-stars:* Herbert Marshall Ian Hunter Cesar Romero
1933 **THE BITTER TEA OF GENERAL YEN**	**1939** **UNION PACIFIC**
Director: Frank Capra	*Director:* Cecil B. DeMille
Co-stars: Nils Aster Walter Connolly	*Co-stars:* Joel McCrea Robert Preston Anthony Quinn
1933 **EVER IN MY HEART**	**1940** **REMEMBER THE NIGHT**
Director: Archie Mayo	*Director:* Mitchell Leisen
Co-stars: Otto Kruger Ralph Bellamy Ruth Donnelly	*Co-stars:* Fred MacMurray Beulah Bondi
1933 **LADIES THEY TALK ABOUT**	**1941** **THE LADY EVE**
Director: William Keighley	*Director:* Preston Sturges
Co-stars: Preston Foster Lyle Talbot	*Co-stars:* Henry Fonda Charles Coburn Eric Blore
1934 **A LOST LADY**	**1941** **YOU BELONG TO ME**
Director: Alfred Green	*Director:* Wesley Ruggles
Co-stars: Frank Morgan Ricardo Cortez Lyle Talbot	*Co-stars:* Henry Fonda Edgar Buchanan Ruth Donnelly
1934 **GAMBLING LADY**	**1941** **MEET JOHN DOE**
Director: Archie Mayo	*Director:* Frank Capra
Co-stars: Joel McCrea Pat O'Brien Philip Reed	*Co-stars:* Gary Cooper Edward Arnold Walter Brennan
1935 **ANNIE OAKLEY**	**1941** **BALL OF FIRE**
Director: George Stevens	*Director:* Howard Hawks
Co-stars: Preston Foster Melvyn Douglas Pert Kelton	*Co-stars:* Gary Cooper Oscar Homolka S.Z. Sakall
1935 **RED SALUTE**	**1942** **THE GAY SISTERS**
Director: Sidney Lanfield	*Director:* Irving Rapper
Co-stars: Robert Young Hardie Albright Ruth Donnelly	*Co-stars:* George Brent Geraldine Fitzgerald Donald Crisp
1935 **THE SECRET BRIDE**	**1942** **THE GREAT MAN'S LADY**
Director: William Dieterle	*Director:* William Wellman
Co-stars: Warren William Glenda Farrell	*Co-stars:* Joel McCrea Brian Donlevy Lloyd Corrigan
1935 **THE WOMAN IN RED**	**1943** **LADY OF BURLESQUE**
Director: Robert Florey	*Director:* William Wellman
Co-stars: Genevieve Tobin Gene Raymond Philip Reed	*Co-stars:* Michael O'Shea Iris Adrian J. Edward Bromberg
1936 **THE PLOUGH AND THE STARS**	**1943** **FLESH AND FANTASY**
Director: John Ford	*Director:* Julien Duvivier
Co-stars: Preston Foster Barry Fitzgerald Arthur Shields	*Co-stars:* Charles Boyer Edward G. Robinson Betty Field
1936 **A MESSAGE TO GARCIA**	**1944** **HOLLYWOOD CANTEEN**
Director: George Marshall	*Director:* Delmer Daves
Co-stars: Wallace Beery John Boles Herbert Mundin	*Co-stars:* Robert Hutton Joan Leslie Janis Paige
1936 **HIS BROTHER'S WIFE**	**1944** **DOUBLE INDEMNITY**
Director: W.S. Van Dyke	*Director:* Billy Wilder
Co-stars: Robert Taylor John Eldridge Joseph Calleia	*Co-stars:* Fred MacMurray Edward G. Robinson
1936 **THE BRIDE WALKS OUT**	**1945** **CHRISTMAS IN CONNECTICUT**
Director: Leigh Jason	*Director:* Peter Godfrey
Co-stars: Gene Raymond Robert Young Helen Broderick	*Co-stars:* Dennis Morgan Sydney Greenstreet Una O'Connor
1936 **BANJO ON MY KNEE**	**1946** **THE BRIDE WORE BOOTS**
Director: John Cromwell	*Director:* Irving Pichel
Co-stars: Joel McCrea Walter Brennan Buddy Ebsen	*Co-stars:* Robert Cummings Diana Lynn Natalie Wood
1937 **BREAKFAST FOR TWO**	**1946** **CALIFORNIA**
Director: Alfred Santell	*Director:* John Farrow
Co-stars: Herbert Marshall Glenda Farrell Donald Meek	*Co-stars:* Ray Milland Barry Fitzgerald Anthony Quinn
1937 **INTERNES CAN'T TAKE MONEY**	**1946** **MY REPUTATION**
Director: Alfred Santell	*Director:* Curtis Bernhardt
Co-stars: Joel McCrea Lloyd Nolan Lee Bowman	*Co-stars:* George Brent Warner Anderson Eve Arden
1937 **STELLA DALLAS**	**1946** **THE STRANGE LOVE OF MARTHA IVERS**
Director: King Vidor	*Director:* Lewis Milestone
Co-stars: John Boles Ann Shirley Tim Holt	*Co-stars:* Kirk Douglas Van Heflin
1937 **THIS IS MY AFFAIR**	**1947** **THE TWO MRS CARROLLS**
Director: William Seiter	*Director:* Peter Godfrey
Co-stars: Robert Taylor Victor McLaglen Brian Donlevy	*Co-stars:* Humphrey Bogart Alexis Smith Nigel Bruce

1947	**VARIETY GIRL**		1955	**ESCAPE TO BURMA**
Director:	George Marshall		*Director:*	Allan Dwan
Co-stars:	Mary Hatcher Olga San Juan Glenn Tryon		*Co-stars:*	Robert Ryan David Farrar Reginald Denny

1947 VARIETY GIRL
Director: George Marshall
Co-stars: Mary Hatcher Olga San Juan Glenn Tryon

1947 THE OTHER LOVE
Director: Andre De Toth
Co-stars: David Niven Richard Conte Gilbert Roland

1947 CRY WOLF
Director: Peter Godfrey
Co-stars: Errol Flynn Geraldine Brooks Richard Basehart

1948 B.F.'S DAUGHTER
Director: Robert Z. Leonard
Co-stars: Van Heflin Charles Coburn Margaret Lindsay

1948 SORRY, WRONG NUMBER
Director: Anatole Litvak
Co-stars: Burt Lancaster Wendell Corey Ed Begley

1949 NO MAN OF HER OWN
Director: Mitchell Leisen
Co-stars: John Lund Lyle Bettger Jane Cowl

1949 THE LADY GAMBLES
Director: Michael Gordon
Co-stars: Robert Preston Stephen McNally John Hoyt

1949 EAST SIDE, WEST SIDE
Director: Mervyn LeRoy
Co-stars: James Mason Ava Gardner Van Heflin

1949 THE FILE ON THELMA JORDAN
Director: Robert Siodmak
Co-stars: Wendell Corey Paul Kelly Stanley Ridges

1950 TO PLEASE A LADY
Director: Clarence Brown
Co-stars: Clark Gable Adolphe Menjou Will Geer

1951 THE MAN WITH A CLOAK
Director: Fletcher Markle
Co-stars: Joseph Cotten Louis Calhern Leslie Caron

1951 THE FURIES
Director: Anthony Mann
Co-stars: Walter Huston Wendell Corey Beulah Bondi

1952 CATTLE QUEEN OF MONTANA
Director: Allan Dwan
Co-stars: Ronald Reagan Gene Evans Lance Fuller

1952 CLASH BY NIGHT
Director: Fritz Lang
Co-stars: Robert Ryan Paul Douglas Marilyn Monroe

1953 BLOWING WILD
Director: Hugo Fregonese
Co-stars: Gary Cooper Anthony Quinn Ruth Roman

1953 ALL I DESIRE
Director: Douglas Sirk
Co-stars: Richard Carlson Maureen O'Sullivan Lori Nelson

1953 JEOPARDY
Director: John Sturges
Co-stars: Barry Sullivan Ralph Meeker

1953 THE MOONLIGHTER
Director: Roy Rowland
Co-stars: Fred MacMurray Ward Bond John Dierkes

1953 TITANIC
Director: Jean Negulesco
Co-stars: Clifton Webb Robert Wagner Thelma Ritter

1954 WITNESS TO MURDER
Director: Roy Rowland
Co-stars: George Sanders Gary Merrill Harry Shannon

1954 EXECUTIVE SUITE
Director: Robert Wise
Co-stars: Fredric March William Holden June Allyson

1955 ESCAPE TO BURMA
Director: Allan Dwan
Co-stars: Robert Ryan David Farrar Reginald Denny

1955 THE MAVERICK QUEEN
Director: Joe Kane
Co-stars: Barry Sullivan Scott Brady Wallace Ford

1955 THE VIOLENT MEN
Director: Rudolph Mate
Co-stars: Edward G. Robinson Glenn Ford Brian Keith

1956 THERE'S ALWAYS TOMORROW
Director: Douglas Sirk
Co-stars: Fred MacMurray Joan Bennett

1956 THESE WILDER YEARS
Director: Roy Rowland
Co-stars: James Cagney Walter Pidgeon Edward Andrews

1957 TROOPER HOOK
Director: Charles Marquis Warren
Co-stars: Joel McCrea John Dehner Edward Andrews

1957 FORTY GUNS
Director: Samuel Fuller
Co-stars: Barry Sullivan Dean Jagger John Erikson

1957 CRIME OF PASSION
Director: Gerd Oswald
Co-stars: Sterling Hayden Raymond Burr Fay Wray

1962 A WALK ON THE WILD SIDE
Director: Edward Dmytryk
Co-stars: Jane Fonda Capucine Laurence Harvey

1964 ROUSTABOUT
Director: John Rich
Co-stars: Elvis Presley Leif Erikson Raquel Welch

1964 THE NIGHT WALKER
Director: William Castle
Co-stars: Robert Taylor Rochelle Hudson Lloyd Bochner

1970 THE HOUSE THAT WOULD NOT DIE
Director: John Llewellyn Moxey
Co-stars: Michael Anderson Richard Egan

1971 A TASTE OF EVIL
Director: John Llewellyn Moxey
Co-stars: Barbara Parkins Roddy McDowall

JEAN STAPLETON

1960 BELLS ARE RINGING
Director: Vincent Minnelli
Co-stars: Judy Holiday Dean Martin Fred Clark

1961 SOMETHING WILD
Director: Jack Garfein
Co-stars: Carroll Baker Ralph Meeker Mildred Dunnock

1971 COLD TURKEY
Director: Norman Lear
Co-stars: Dick Van Dyke Pippa Scott Tom Poston

1975 UP THE DOWN STAIRCASE
Director: Robert Mulligan
Co-stars: Sandy Dennis Patrick Bedford Eileen Heckart

1981 ISABEL'S CHOICE
Director: Guy Green
Co-stars: Richard Kiley Peter Coyote Betsy Palmer

1984 THE BUDDY SYSTEM
Director: Glen Jordan
Co-stars: Richard Dreyfuss Susan Sarandon Nancy Allen

1986 DEAD MAN'S FOLLY
Director: Clive Donner
Co-stars: Peter Ustinov Constance Cummings Jonathan Cecil

1992 **THE HABITATION OF DRAGONS**
Director: Michael Lindsay-Hogg
Co-stars: Brad Davis Lucinda Jenney Pat Hingle

1993 **THE TRIAL**
Director: David Jones
Co-stars: Kyle MacLachlan Anthony Hopkins Jason Robards

1993 **BURY ME IN NIAGARA**
Director: Dave Thomas

MAUREEN STAPLETON

Oscar For Best Supporting Actress In 1981 For "Reds". Nominated For Best Supporting Actress In 1958 For "Lonelyhearts", In 1970 For "Airport" And In 1978 For "Interiors"

1958 **LONELYHEARTS**
Director: Vincent Donahue
Co-stars: Montgomery Clift Robert Ryan Myrna Loy

1960 **THE FUGITIVE KIND**
Director: Sidney Lumet
Co-stars: Marlon Brando Anna Magnani Joanne Woodward

1961 **A VIEW FROM THE BRIDGE**
Director: Sidney Lumet
Co-stars: Raf Vallone Carol Lawrence Jean Sorel

1963 **BYE BYE BIRDIE**
Director: George Sidney
Co-stars: Dick Van Dyke Ann-Margret Janet Leigh

1970 **AIRPORT**
Director: George Seaton
Co-stars: Burt Lancaster Dean Martin Helen Hayes

1971 **PLAZA SUITE**
Director: Arthur Hiller
Co-stars: Walter Matthau Barbara Harris Lee Grant

1975 **QUEEN OF THE STARDUST BALLROOM**
Director: Sam O'Stern
Co-stars: Charles Durning Michael Brandon

1978 **INTERIORS**
Director: Woody Allen
Co-stars: Marybeth Hurt Richard Jordan Diane Keaton

1979 **LOST AND FOUND**
Director: Melvyn Frank
Co-stars: Glenda Jackson George Segal Paul Sorvino

1979 **THE RUNNER STUMBLES**
Director: Stanley Kramer
Co-stars: Dick Van Dyke Kathleen Quinlan Ray Bolger

1981 **REDS**
Director: Warren Beatty
Co-stars: Warren Beatty Diane Keaton Edward Herrman

1981 **ON THE RIGHT TRACK**
Director: Lee Phillips
Co-stars: Gary Coleman Lisa Eilbacher

1981 **THE FAN**
Director: Edward Bianchi
Co-stars: Lauren Bacall James Garner Michael Biehn

1984 **FAMILY SECRETS**
Director: Jack Hofsiss
Co-stars: Stefanie Powers Melissa Gilbert James Spader

1984 **SENTIMENTAL JOURNEY**
Director: James Goldstone
Co-stars: Jaclyn Smith David Dukes Jessica Rene Carrol

1984 **JOHNNY DANGEROUSLY**
Director: Amy Heckerling
Co-stars: Michael Keaton Griffin Dunne Marilu Henner

1985 **PRIVATE SESSIONS**
Director: Michael Pressman
Co-stars: Mike Farrell Kelly McGillis Hope Lange

1985 **COCOON**
Director: Ron Howard
Co-stars: Don Ameche Wilford Brimley Jessica Tandy

1986 **THE MONEY PIT**
Director: Richard Benjamin
Co-stars: Shelly Long Tom Hanks Joe Montegna

1986 **HEARTBURN**
Director: Mike Nichols
Co-stars: Meryl Streep Jack Nicholson Jeff Daniels

1987 **MADE IN HEAVEN**
Director: Alan Rudolph
Co-stars: Timothy Hutton Kelly McGillis Don Murray

1987 **NUTS**
Director: Martin Ritt
Co-stars: Barbra Streisand Richard Dreyfuss Karl Malden

1987 **SWEET LORRAINE**
Director: Steve Gomer
Co-stars: Trini Alvarado Lee Richardson John Bedford

1988 **COCOON: THE RETURN**
Director: Daniel Petrie
Co-stars: Jack Gilford Steve Guttenberg Elaine Strich

CECILIA STARK

1984 **STRANGER THAN PARADISE**
Director: Jim Jarmusch
Co-stars: John Lurie Richard Edson Eszter Balint

KATHERINE STARK

1987 **DOWN WHERE THE BUFFALO ROAM**
Director: Ian Knox
Co-stars: Harvey Keitel Stella Gonet Andrew Byatt

KOO STARK

1975 **THE ROCKY HORROR PICTURE SHOW**
Director: Jim Sharman
Co-stars: Tim Curry Susan Sarandon Barry Bostwick

PAULINE STARKE

1924 **FORBIDDEN PARADISE**
Director: Ernst Lubitsch
Co-stars: Pola Negri Adolphe Menjou Rod La Rocque

CAROL STARKS

1992 **THE GUILTY**
Director: Colin Gregg
Co-stars: Michael Kitchen Sean Gallagher Caroline Catz

FRANCES STARR

1931 **THE STAR WITNESS**
Director: William Wellman
Co-stars: Walter Huston Chic Sale Sally Blane

1932 **THIS RECKLESS AGE**
Director: Frank Tuttle
Co-stars: Charles Rogers Charles Ruggles Frances Dee

SALLY STARR

1930 **FOR THE LOVE O' LIL**
Co-stars: Elliott Nugent Jack Mulhall

MARION STATENS

1991 **LES AMANTS DU PONT NEUF**
Director: Leos Carax
Co-stars: Juliette Binoche Denis Lavant Daniel Buain

IMELDA STAUNTON

1986   **COMRADES**
Director: Bill Douglas
Co-stars: Vanessa Redgrave James Fox Freddie Jones

1989   **THE HEAT OF THE DAY**
Director: Christopher Morahan
Co-stars: Michael Gambon Patricia Hodge

1989   **INSPECTOR WEXFORD: A SLEEPING LIFE**
Director: Bill Hats
Co-stars: George Baker Christopher Ravenscroft

1990   **YELLOWBACKS**
Director: Roy Battersby
Co-stars: Janet McTeer Roy Marsden Bill Patterson

1990   **THE ENGLISHMAN'S WIFE**
Director: Robert Cooper
Co-stars: Adrian Dunbar Laura Hill Trevor Moore

1990   **ANTONIA AND JANE: A DEFINITIVE REPORT**
Director: Beeban Kidron
Co-stars: Saskia Reeves Brenda Bruce

1992   **PETER'S FRIENDS**
Director: Kenneth Branagh
Co-stars: Kenneth Branagh Hugh Laurie Stephen Fry

1992   **A MASCULINE ENDING**
Director: Stuart Orme
Co-star: Janet McTeer

1993   **MUCH ADO ABOUT NOTHING**
Director: Kenneth Branagh
Co-stars: Kenneth Branagh Emma Thompson Richard Briers

1993   **DON'T LEAVE ME THIS WAY**
Director: Stuart Orme
Co-stars: Janet McTeer Moira Williams

1994   **DEADLY AFFAIR**
Director: Mandie Fletcher
Co-stars: Jane Horrocks Brenda Fricker Jonathan Pryce

1996   **SENSE AND SENSIBILITY**
Director: Ang Lee
Co-stars: Emma Thompson Hugh Grant Kate Winslet

1996   **TWELTH NIGHT**
Director: Trevor Nunn
Co-stars: Helena Bonham Carter Imogen Stubbs Nigel Hawthorne

1996   **REMEMBER ME ?**
Director: Nick Hurran
Co-stars: Robert Lindsay Rik Mayall Brenda Blethyn

MARY STAVIN

1985   **A VIEW TO A KILL**
Director: John Glen
Co-stars: Roger Moore Tanya Roberts Grace Jones

1986   **HOUSE**
Director: Steve Miner
Co-stars: William Katt George Wendt Kay Lenz

ALISON STEADMAN *(Married Mike Leigh)*

1976   **NUTS IN MAY**
Director: Mike Leigh
Co-stars: Roger Sloman Anthony O'Donnell

1977   **ABIGAIL'S PARTY**
Director: Mike Leigh
Co-stars: Tim Stern John Salthouse

1982   **P'TANG YANG KIPPERBANG**
Director: Michael Apted
Co-stars: Garry Cooper Abigail Cruttenden

1984   **NUMBER ONE**
Director: Les Blair
Co-stars: Bob Geldof Mel Smith Alfred Molina

1984   **A PRIVATE FUNCTION**
Director: Malcolm Mowbray
Co-stars: Michael Palin Maggie Smith Denholm Elliott

1986   **CLOCKWISE**
Director: Christopher Morahan
Co-stars: John Cleese Penelope Wilton Stephen Moore

1989   **THE ADVENTURES OF BARON MUNCHAUSEN**
Director: Terry Gilliam
Co-stars: John Neville Eric Idle

1989   **SHIRLEY VALENTINE**
Director: Lewis Gilbert
Co-stars: Pauline Collins Tom Conti Bernard Hill

1989   **A SMALL MOURNING**
Director: Chris Bernard
Co-stars: Stratford Johns Ian Deam Pauline Yates

1989   **STORMY MONDAY**
Director: Mike Figgis
Co-stars: Melanie Griffith Sean Bean Tommy Lee Jones

1989   **VIRTUOSO**
Director: Tony Smith
Co-stars: John Heard Jane Booker Alfred Molina

1989   **WILT**
Director: Michael Tuchner
Co-stars: Griff Rhys Jones Mel Smith Diana Quick

1990   **NEWS HOUNDS**
Director: Les Blair
Co-stars: Adrian Edmondson Linda Bassett Paul Kember

1990   **LIFE IS SWEET**
Director: Mike Leigh
Co-stars: Jim Broadbent Jane Horrocks Timothy Spall

1991   **BLAME IT ON THE BELLBOY**
Director: Mark Herman
Co-stars: Dudley Moore Patsy Kensit Bryan Brown

1996   **SECRETS AND LIES**
Director: Mike Leigh
Co-stars: Brenda Blethyn Timothy Spall Phyllis Logan

LYNDA STEADMAN

1991   **CHILDREN OF THE NORTH**
Director: David Drury
Co-stars: Michael Gough Tony Doyle Patrick Malahide

1997   **CAREER GIRLS**
Director: Mike Leigh
Co-stars: Katrin Cartlidge Mark Benton

MAGGIE STEED

1990   **BLOOD RIGHTS**
Director: Lesley Manning
Co-stars: Brian Bovell Robert Glenister Sam Kelly

1992   **THE CLOTHES IN THE WARDROBE**
Director: Waris Hussein
Co-stars: Jeanne Moreau Joan Plowright Julie Walters

LYDIA ST.CLAIR

1945   **THE HOUSE ON 92ND STREET**
Director: Henry Hathaway
Co-stars: William Eythe Lloyd Nolan Signe Hasso

MONIQUE ST. CLAIR

1965   **ADIOS GRINGOS**
Director: George Finlay
Co-stars: Montgomery Wood Evelyn Stewart Peter Cross

LILI ST. CYR

1955 SON OF SINBAD
Director: Ted Tetzlaff
Co-stars: Dale Robertson Vincent Price Sally Forrest

1958 THE NAKED AND THE DEAD
Director: Raoul Walsh
Co-stars: Aldo Ray Dale Robertson Raymond Massey

1958 I, MOBSTER
Director: Roger Corman
Co-stars: Steve Cochran Lita Milan Robert Strauss

MYRTLE STEDMAN

1930 LUMMOX
Co-star: Winifred Westover

AMY STEEL

1982 FRIDAY THE 13TH, PART II
Director: Steve Miner
Co-stars: John Furey Adrienne King Warrington Gillette

1985 FIRST STEPS
Director: Sheldon Larry
Co-stars: Judd Hirsch Kim Darby John Pankow

1986 APRIL FOOL'S DAY
Director: Fred Walton
Co-stars: Deborah Foreman Griffin O'Neal Deborah Goodrich

1988 THE RED SPIDER
Director: Jerry Jameson
Co-stars: James Farantino Jennifer O'Neill Philip Casnoff

1991 WHATEVER HAPPENED TO BABY JANE ?
Director: David Greene
Co-stars: Vanessa Redgrave Lynn Redgrave John Glover

1995 ABANDONED AND DECEIVED
Director: Joseph Dougherty
Co-stars: Lori Loughlin Brian Kerwin Bibi Besch

CYNTHIA STEEL

1994 INDECENT BEHAVIOUR II
Director: Carlo Gustav
Co-stars: James Brolin Shannon Tweed

JANET STEEL

1989 SEEING IN THE DARK
Director: Gareth Jones
Co-stars: David Threlfall Sylvestra Le Touzel Greg Hicks

AGNES STEEL

1928 YOU'RE DARN TOOTIN'
Director: Edgar Kennedy
Co-stars: Stan Laurel Oliver Hardy

BARBARA STEELE

1958 BACHELOR OF HEARTS
Director: Wolf Rilla
Co-stars: Hardy Kruger Sylvia Syms Ronald Lewis

1960 BLACK SUNDAY
Director: Mario Bava
Co-stars: John Richardson Ivo Garrani

1961 PIT AND THE PENDULUM
Director: Roger Corman
Co-stars: Vincent Price John Kerr Luana Anders

1963 EIGHT AND A HALF
Director: Federico Fellini
Co-stars: Marcello Mastroianni Claudia Cardinale Anouk Aimee

1964 THE LONG HAIR OF DEATH
Director: Anthony Dawson
Co-stars: Giorgio Ardisson Halina Zalewska

1966 YOUNG TORLESS
Director: Volker Schlondorff
Co-stars: Matthieu Carriere Bernd Fischer Alfred Dietz

1968 CURSE OF THE CRIMSON ALTAR
Director: Vernon Sewell
Co-stars: Boris Karloff Christopher Lee Rupert Davies

1974 CAGED HEAT
Director: Jonathan Demme
Co-stars: Juanita Brown Erica Gavin Rainbeaux Smith

1975 SHIVERS
Director: David Cronenberg
Co-stars: Paul Hampton Joe Silver Lynn Lowry

1978 PIRANHA
Director: Joe Dante
Co-stars: Bradford Dillman Heather Menzies Keenan Wynn

1978 PRETTY BABY
Director: Louis Malle
Co-stars: Keith Carradine Susan Sarandon Brooke Shields

KAREN STEELE

1955 MARTY
Director: Delbert Mann
Co-stars: Ernest Borgnine Betsy Balir Esther Minciotti

1956 TOWARD THE UNKNOWN
Director: Mervyn LeRoy
Co-stars: William Holden Lloyd Nolan Virginia Leith

1957 DECISION AT SUNDOWN
Director: Budd Boetticher
Co-stars: Randolph Scott John Carroll Valerie French

1957 BAIL OUT AT 43,000 FEET
Director: Francis Lyon
Co-stars: John Payne Paul Kelly Richard Eyer

1959 RIDE LONESOME
Director: Budd Boetticher
Co-stars: Randolph Scott Pernell Roberts James Coburn

1959 THE SHARKFIGHTERS
Director: Jerry Hopper
Co-stars: Victor Mature James Olson Claude Akins

1959 WEST BOUND
Director: Budd Boetticher
Co-stars: Randolph Scott Virginia Mayo Andrew Duggan

1960 THE RISE AND FALL OF LEGS DIAMOND
Director: Budd Boetticher
Co-stars: Ray Danton Elaine Stewart Warren Oates

MARGARET STEELE

1952 THE BRIDE COMES TO YELLOW SKY
Director: Bretaigne Windust
Co-stars: Robert Preston Minor Watson

MARY STEELE

1958 THE GOLDEN DISC
Director: Don Sharp
Co-stars: Lee Patterson Terry Dene

PIPPA STEELE

1970 THE VAMPIRE LOVERS
Director: Roy Ward Baker
Co-stars: Ingrid Pitt Peter Cushing Madeleine Smith

TAMARA STEELE

1986 FRANKIE AND JOHNNIE
Director: Martin Campbell
Co-stars: Hywel Bennett Samuel West Sam Kelly

JESSICA STEEN

1989 SING
Director: Richard Baskin
Co-stars: Lorraine Bracco Peter Dobson Louise Lasser

1991 THE GREAT PRETENDER
Director: Gus Trikonis
Co-stars: Bruce Greenwood Gregg Henry Donald Moffat

MARY STEENBURGEN
(Married Malcolm McDowall, Ted Danson)
Oscar For Best Supporting Actress In 1980 For "Melvyn And Howard"

1978 GOIN' SOUTH
Director: Jack Nicholson
Co-stars: Jack Nicholson Christopher Lloyd Danny DeVito

1979 TIME AFTER TIME
Director: Nicholas Meyer
Co-stars: Malcolm McDowall David Warner

1980 MELVYN AND HOWARD
Director: Jonathan Demme
Co-stars: Paul Le Mat Jason Robards Gloria Grahame

1981 RAGTIME
Director: Milos Forman
Co-stars: James Cagney Pat O'Brien James Olson

1982 A MIDSUMMER NIGHT'S SEX COMEDY
Director: Woody Allen
Co-stars: Woody Allen Mia Farrow Jose Ferrer

1983 CROSS CREEK
Director: Martin Ritt
Co-stars: Rip Torn Peter Coyote Malcolm McDowall

1983 ROMANTIC COMEDY
Director: Arthur Hiller
Co-stars: Dudley Moore Frances Sternhagen Janet Eilber

1985 ONE MAGIC CHRISTMAS
Director: Philip Borsos
Co-stars: Gary Basaraba Harry Dean Stanton Arthur Hill

1986 DEAD OF WINTER
Director: Arthur Penn
Co-stars: Roddy McDowall Jan Rubes William Russ

1989 MISS FIRECRACKER
Director: Thomas Schlamme
Co-stars: Holly Hunter Tim Robbins Scott Glenn

1989 PARENTHOOD
Director: Ron Howard
Co-stars: Steve Martin Jason Robards Dianne Wiest

1990 BACK TO THE FUTURE III
Director: Robert Zemeckis
Co-stars: Michael J. Fox Christopher Lloyd

1991 THE BUTCHER'S WIFE
Director: Terry Hughes
Co-stars: Demi Moore Jeff Daniels George Dzundza

1993 PHILADELPHIA
Director: Jonathan Demme
Co-stars: Tom Hanks Denzel Washington Antonio Banderas

1993 WHAT'S EATING GILBERT GRAPE
Director: Lasse Hallstrom
Co-stars: Johnny Depp Leonardo Di Caprio Juliette Lewis

1994 PONTIAC MOON
Director: Peter Medak
Co-stars: Ted Danson Ryan Todd

1994 CLIFFORD
Director: Paul Flaherty
Co-stars: Charles Grodin Martin Short

1995 NIXON
Director: Oliver Stone
Co-stars: Anthony Hopkins Joan Allen Ed Harris

1996 GULLIVER'S TRAVELS
Co-stars: Ted Danson Geraldine Chaplin Omar Sharif

1997 POWDER
Director: Victor Salva
Co-stars: Sean Patrick Flanery Jeff Goldblum

ROBYN STEFAN

1994 INTERSECTION
Director: Mark Rydell
Co-stars: Richard Gere Sharon Stone Lolita Davidovich

PEGGY STEFFANS

1963 HALLELUJAH THE HILLS
Director: Adolfas Mekas
Co-stars: Peter H. Beard Martin Greenbaum Sheila Finn

VALERIE STEFFEN

1986 SKY BANDITS
Director: Zoran Perisic
Co-stars: Scott McGinnis Ronald Lacey Miles Anderson

BERNICE STEGERS

1980 CITY OF WOMEN
Director: Federico Fellini
Co-stars: Marcello Mastroianni Anna Prucnal Etorre Manni

1992 DEAD ROMANTIC
Director: Patrick Lau
Co-stars: Janet McTeer Clive Wood Elspet Gray

1993 TO PLAY THE KING
Director: Paul Seed
Co-stars: Ian Richardson Michael Kitchen Kitty Aldridge

ANDREA STEIN

1993 SHELF LIFE
Director: Paul Bartel
Co-stars: Paul Bartel O-Lan Jones Jim Turner

MARGARET SOPHIE STEIN

1989 ENEMIES: A LOVE STORY
Director: Paul Mazursky
Co-stars: Angelica Huston Ron Silver Lena Olin

1991 SARAH, PLAIN AND TALL
Director: Glenn Jordan
Co-stars: Glenn Close Christopher Walken Jon De Vries

1993 SKY LARK
Director: Joseph Sargent
Co-stars: Glenn Close Christopher Walken Lexi Randall

SHIRLEY STELFOX

1987 PERSONAL SERVICES
Director: Terry Jones
Co-stars: Julie Walters Alex McCowan Tim Woodward

ANNA STEN

1932 THE YELLOW TICKET

1932 THE BROTHERS KARAMAZOV

1932 TEMPEST

1934 NANA
Director: Dorothy Arzner
Co-stars: Phillips Holmes Lionel Atwill Richard Bennett

1934 WE LIVE AGAIN
Director: Rouben Mamoulian
Co-stars: Fredric March Jane Baxter Sam Jaffe

1935 THE WEDDING NIGHT
Director: King Vidor
Co-stars: Gary Cooper Sig Ruman Helen Vinson

1936 A WOMAN ALONE
Director: Eugene Frenke
Co-stars: Henry Wilcoxon Viola Keats John Garrick

1939 EXILE EXPRESS
Director: Otis Garrett
Co-stars: Alan Marshall Jerome Cowan Jed Prouty

1940 THE MAN I MARRIED
Director: Irving Pichel
Co-stars: Joan Bennett Francis Lederer Lloyd Nolan

1941 SO ENDS OUR NIGHT
Director: John Cromwell
Co-stars: Fredric March Margaret Sullavan Glenn Ford

1943 THREE RUSSIAN GIRLS
Director: Henry Kasler
Co-stars: Kent Smith Mimi Forsythe Kathy Frye

1943 CHETNIKS-THE FIGHTING GUERRILLAS
Director: Louis King
Co-stars: Philip Dorn John Shepperd Virginia Gilmore

1943 THEY CAME TO BLOW UP AMERICA
Director: Edward Ludwig
Co-stars: George Sanders Ward Bond Sig Roman

1948 LET'S LIVE A LITTLE
Director: Richard Wallace
Co-stars: Hedy Lamarr Robert Cummings Robert Shayne

1955 SOLDIER OF FORTUNE
Director: Edward Dmytryk
Co-stars: Clark Gable Susan Hayward Gene Barry

1962 THE NUN AND THE SERGEANT
Director: Franklin Adreon
Co-stars: Robert Webber Leo Gordon Hari Rhodes

HELEN STENBORG

1987 A HOBO'S CHRISTMAS
Director: Will MacKenzie
Co-stars: Barnard Hughes Gerald McRaney Wendy Crewson

YUTTE STANSGAARD

1970 LUST FOR A VAMPIRE
Director: Jimmy Sangster
Co-stars: Ralph Bates Barbara Jefford Suzanna Leigh

NICOLE STEPHANE

1950 LES ENFANTS TERRIBLES
Director: Jean-Pierre Melville
Co-stars: Edouard Dermithe Renee Cosima Jacques Bernard

1953 LE DEFROQUE
Director: Leo Joannon
Co-stars: Pierre Fresnay Pierre Trabaud Rene Blancard

1958 CARVE HER NAME WITH PRIDE
Director: Lewis Gilbert
Co-stars: Virginia McKenna Paul Scofield Jack Warner

SUSAN STEPHEN

1951 HIS EXCELLENCY
Director: Robert Hamer
Co-stars: Cecil Parker Eric Portman Helen Cherry

1952 FATHER'S DOING FINE
Director: Henry Cass
Co-stars: Heather Thatcher Richard Attenborough Noel Purcell

1952 A STOLEN FACE
Director: Terence Fisher
Co-stars: Paul Henreid Lizabeth Scott Andre Morrell

1952 TREASURE HUNT
Director: John Paddy Carstairs
Co-stars: Jimmy Edwards Martita Hunt Naunton Wayne

1953 THE RED BERET
Director: Terence Fisher
Co-stars: Alan Ladd Leo Genn Harry Andrews

1954 FOR BETTER FOR WORSE
Director: J. Lee-Thompson
Co-stars: Dirk Bogarde Dennis Price Sid James

1955 AS LONG AS THEY'RE HAPPY
Director: J. Lee-Thompson
Co-stars: Jack Buchanan Jean Carson Janette Scott

1955 VALUE FOR MONEY
Director: Ken Annakin
Co-stars: John Gregson Diana Dors Derek Farr

1956 PACIFIC DESTINY
Director: Wolf Rilla
Co-stars: Denholm Elliott Michael Hordern Gordon Jackson

1956 IT'S NEVER TOO LATE
Director: Michael McCarthy
Co-stars: Phyllis Calvert Guy Rolfe Sarah Lawson

1960 CARRY ON NURSE
Director: Gerald Thomas
Co-stars: Shirley Eaton Kenneth Connor Kenneth Williams

ANN STEPHENS

1943 DEAR OCTOPUS
Director: Harold French
Co-stars: Margaret Lockwood Michael Wilding Celia Johnson

1947 THE UPTURNED GLASS
Director: Lawrence Huntington
Co-stars: James Mason Pamela Kellino Rosamund John

1950 THE FRANCHISE AFFAIR
Director: Lawrence Huntington
Co-stars: Michael Dennison Dulcie Gray Hy Hazell

BARBARA STEPHENS

1978 BECAUSE HE'S MY FRIEND
Director: Ralph Nelson
Co-stars: Karen Black Keir Dullea Jack Thompson

LARAINE STEPHENS

1967 FORTY GUNS TO APACHE PASS
Director: William Witney
Co-stars: Audie Murphy Michael Burns Kenneth Tobey

1969 THE ONE THOUSAND PLANE RAID
Director: Boris Sagal
Co-stars: Christopher George Ben Murphy J.D. Cannon

1974 THE GIRL ON THE LATE LATE SHOW
Director: Gary Nelson
Co-stars: Don Murray Yvonne De Carlo Gloria Grahame

1975 MATT HELM
Director: Buzz Kulik
Co-stars: Anthony Franciosa Ann Turkel Patrick MacNee

DENISE STEPHENSON

1988 THE DEAD CAN'T LIE
Director: Lloyd Fonvielle
Co-stars: Tommy Lee Jones Virginia Madsen Frederic Forrest

JODY STEPHENSON

1977 CATHY'S CHILD
Director: Donald Crombie
Co-stars: Michelle Fawdon Alan Cassell Harry Michael

PAMELA STEPHENSON

1978 THE COMEBACK
Director: Peter Walker
Co-stars: Jack Jones Sheila Keith Bill Owen

1983 BLOODBATH AT THE HOUSE OF DEATH
Director: Ray Cameron
Co-stars: Kenny Everett Vincent Price

1983 SUPERMAN III
Director: Richard Lester
Co-stars: Christopher Reeve Margot Kidder Richard Pryor

1984 SCANDALOUS!
Director: Rob Cohen
Co-stars: Robert Hays John Gielgud Jim Dale

1987 LES PATTERSON SAVES THE WORLD
Director: George Miller
Co-stars: Barry Humphries Andrew Clarke

1987 THOSE DEAR DEPARTED
Director: Ted Robinson
Co-stars: Garry McDonald Su Cruikshank

SARAH STEPHENSON

1971 BLEAK MOMENTS
Director: Mike Leigh
Co-stars: Anne Raitt Eric Allan Liz Smith

ILSE STEPPAT

1969 ON HER MAJESTY'S SECRET SERVICE
Director: Peter Hunt
Co-stars: George Lazenby Diana Rigg Telly Savalas

JEANETTE STERKE

1955 THE PRISONER
Director: Peter Glenville
Co-stars: Alec Guinness Jack Hawkins Wilfrid Lawson

1958 SAFECRACKER
Director: Ray Milland
Co-stars: Ray Milland Barry Jones Victor Maddern

1963 A STITCH IN TIME
Director: Robert Asher
Co-stars: Norman Wisdom Edward Chapman Jill Melford

1975 MOMENTS
Director: Peter Crane
Co-stars: Keith Michell Angharad Rees Bill Fraser

ALISON STERLING

1990 MAGIC MOMENTS
Director: Lawrence Gordon Clark
Co-stars: John Shea Jenny Seagrove Paul Freeman

ANNE STERLING

1944 BOWERY CHAMPS
Director: William Beaudine
Co-stars: Leo Gorcey Huntz Hall Evelyn Brent

JAN STERLING *(Married Paul Douglas)*

**Nominated For Best Supporting Actress In 1954 For
"The High And The Mighty"**

1948 JOHNNY BELINDA
Director: Jean Negulesco
Co-stars: Jane Wyman Lew Ayres Stephen McNally

1949 APPOINTMENT WITH DANGER
Director: Lewis Allen
Co-stars: Alan Ladd Phyllis Calvert Jack Webb

1950 UNION STATION
Director: Rudolph Mate
Co-stars: William Holden Nancy Olsen Barry Fitzgerald

1950 MYSTERY STREET
Director: John Sturges
Co-stars: Ricardo Montalban Sally Forrest Elsa Lanchester

1950 CAGED
Director: John Cromwell
Co-stars: Eleanor Parker Agnes Moorehead Ellen Corby

1951 THE MATING SEASON
Director: Mitchell Leisen
Co-stars: Gene Tierney John Lund Thelma Ritter

1951 RHUBARB
Director: Arthur Lubin
Co-stars: Ray Milland Gene Lockhart William Frawley

1951 ACE IN THE HOLE
Director: Billy Wilder
Co-stars: Kirk Douglas Porter Hall Bob Arthur

1952 FLESH AND FURY
Director: Joseph Pevney
Co-stars: Tony Curtis Mona Freeman Wallace Ford

1952 SKY FULL OF MOON
Director: Norman Foster
Co-stars: Carleton Carpenter Keenan Wynn

1953 THE VANQUISHED
Director: Edward Ludwig
Co-stars: John Payne Colleen Gray Lyle Bettger

1953 SPLIT SECOND
Director: Dick Powell
Co-stars: Stephen McNally Alexis Smith Arthur Hunnicutt

1953 PONY EXPRESS
Director: Jerry Hopper
Co-stars: Charlton Heston Forrest Tucker

1953 ALASKA SEAS
Director: Jerry Hopper
Co-stars: Robert Ryan Gene Barry Brian Keith

1954 THE HIGH AND THE MIGHTY
Director: William Wellman
Co-stars: John Wayne Robert Stack Robert Newton

1954 THE HUMAN JUNGLE
Director: Joseph Newman
Co-stars: Gary Merrill Paula Raymond Regis Toomey

1955 FEMALE ON THE BEACH
Director: Joseph Pevney
Co-stars: Joan Crawford Jeff Chandler Cecil Kellaway

1955 THE MAN WITH THE GUN
Director: Richard Wilson
Co-stars: Robert Mitchum Karen Sharpe Henry Hull

1956 1984
Director: Michael Anderson
Co-stars: Michael Redgrave Edmond O'Brien

1956 THE HARDER THEY FALL
Director: Mark Robson
Co-stars: Humphrey Bogart Rod Steiger Mark Lane

1957 THE FEMALE ANIMAL
Director: Harry Keller
Co-stars: Hedy Lamarr Jane Powell George Nader

1957 SLAUGHTER ON TENTH AVENUE
Director: Arnold Laven
Co-stars: Richard Egan Dan Duryea Walter Matthau

1958 KATHY O
Director: Jack Sher
Co-stars: Patty McCormack Dan Duryea Sam Levene

1961 LOVE IN A GOLDFISH BOWL
Director: Jack Sher
Co-stars: Tommy Sands Fabian Toby Michaels

1969   THE ANGRY BREED
Director: David Commons
Co-stars: James MacArthur William Windom Jan Murray

1981   FIRST MONDAY IN OCTOBER
Director: Ronald Neame
Co-stars: Jill Clayburgh Walter Matthau

TISHA STERLING

1968   COOGAN'S BLUFF
Director: Don Siegel
Co-stars: Clint Eastwood Lee J. Cobb Don Stroud

1968   NORWOOD
Director: Jack Haley Jnr.
Co-stars: Glen Campbell Kim Darby Carol Lynley

1975   CRAZY MAMA
Director: Jonathan Demme
Co-stars: Ann Sothern Cloris Leachman Linda Purl

FRANCES STERNHAGEN

1973   TWO PEOPLE
Director: Robert Wise
Co-stars: Peter Fonda Lindsay Wagner Estelle Parsons

1978   FEDORA
Director: Billy Wilder
Co-stars: William Holden Marthe Keller Jose Ferrer

1983   INDEPENDENCE DAY
Director: Robert Mandel
Co-stars: Kathleen Quinlan David Keith Dianne Wiest

1983   PROTOTYPE
Director: David Greene
Co-stars: Christopher Plummer David Morse Stephen Elliott

1984   ROMANTIC COMEDY
Director: Arthur Hiller
Co-stars: Dudley Moore Mary Steenburgen Janet Eilber

1986   RESTING PLACE
Director: John Korty
Co-stars: John Lithgow Richard Bradford Morgan Freeman

1987   AT MOTHER'S REQUEST
Director: Michael Tuchner
Co-stars: Stefanie Powers E.G. Marshall Penny Fuller

1988   BRIGHT LIGHTS, BIG CITY
Director: James Bridges
Co-stars: Michael J. Fox Kiefer Sutherland Phoebe Cates

1990   COMMUNION
Director: Philippe Mora
Co-stars: Christopher Walken Lindsay Crouse Joel Carlson

1990   MISERY
Director: Rob Reiner
Co-stars: James Caan Kathy Bates Richard Farnsworth

1990   SIBLING RIVALRY
Director: Carl Reiner
Co-stars: Kirstie Alley Bill Pullman Carrie Fisher

1991   DOC HOLLYWOOD
Director: Michael Caton-Jones
Co-stars: Michael J. Fox Julie Warner Bridget Fonda

NOEMI STEUER

1992   THE SECOND HEIMAT
Director: Edgar Reitz
Co-stars: Henry Arnold Salome Kammer Gisela Muller

ROBYN STEVAN

1989   BYE BYE BLUES
Director: Anne Wheeler
Co-stars: Michael Ontkean Rebecca Jenkins Stuart Margolin

1991   STEPPING OUT
Director: Lewis Gilbert
Co-stars: Liza Minnelli Shelley Winters Julie Walters

1991   SYLVAN LAKE SUMMER
Director: Peter Campbell

1994   WHILE JUSTICE SLEEPS
Director: Alan Smithee
Co-stars: Cybill Shepherd Tim Matheson Dion Anderson

ANGELA STEVENS

1952   JACK McCALL DESPERADO
Director: Sidney Salkow
Co-stars: George Montgomery Douglas Kennedy Jay Silverheels

1955   THE CREATURE WITH THE ATOM BRAIN
Director: Edward Cahn
Co-stars: Richard Denning Gregory Gaye Tristram Coffin

1956   BLACKJACK, KETCHUM, DESPERADO

CONNIE STEVENS

1958   ROCK-A-BYE-BABY
Director: Frank Tashlin
Co-stars: Jerry Lewis Marilyn Maxwell Reginald Gardiner

1961   SUSAN SLADE
Director: Delmer Daves
Co-stars: Troy Donahue Dorothy McGuire Brian Aherne

1961   PARRISH
Director: Delmer Daves
Co-stars: Troy Donahue Claudette Colbert Karl Malden

1963   PALM SPRINGS WEEKEND
Director: Norman Taurog
Co-stars: Troy Donahue Ty Hardin Stefanie Powers

1965   NEVER TOO LATE
Director: Bud Yorkin
Co-stars: Maureen O'Sullivan Paul Ford Jim Hutton

1965   TWO ON A GUILLOTINE
Director: William Conrad
Co-stars: Dean Jones Cesar Romero Virginia Gregg

1966   WAY…WAY OUT
Director: Gordon Douglas
Co-stars: Jerry Lewis Robert Morley Anita Ekberg

1971   THE GRISSOM GANG
Director: Robert Aldrich
Co-stars: Kim Darby Scott Wilson Tony Musante

1982   GREASE 2
Director: Patricia Birch
Co-stars: Maxwell Caulfield Michelle Pfeiffer Lorna Luft

1987   BACK TO THE BEACH
Director: Lyndall Hobbs
Co-stars: Annette Funicello Frankie Avalon Lori Loughlin

DORINDA STEVENS

1960   THE GENTLE TRAP
Director: Charles Saunders
Co-stars: Spencer Teakle Felicity Young Martin Benson

INGER STEVENS

1957   MAN ON FIRE
Director: Ranald MacDougall
Co-stars: Bing Crosby Mary Fickett E.G. Marshall

1958   CRY TERROR
Director: Andrew Stone
Co-stars: James Mason Rod Steiger Angie Dickenson

1958   THE BUCCANEER
Director: Anthony Quinn
Co-stars: Yul Brynner Claire Bloom Charles Boyer

1959   **THE WORLD, THE FLESH AND THE DEVIL**
Director: Ranald MacDougall
Co-stars: Harry Belafonte Mel Ferrer

1964   **THE NEW INTERNS**
Director: John Rich
Co-stars: George Segal Telly Savalas Dean Jones

1967   **HANG 'EM HIGH**
Director: Ted Post
Co-stars: Clint Eastwood Ed Begley Pat Hingle

1967   **A TIME FOR KILLING**
Director: Phil Karlson
Co-stars: Glenn Ford George Hamilton Harrison Ford

1967   **A GUIDE FOR THE MARRIED MAN**
Director: Gene Kelly
Co-stars: Walter Matthau Lucille Ball Jack Benny

1968   **FIVE CARD STUD**
Director: Henry Hathaway
Co-stars: Dean Martin Robert Mitchum Roddy McDowall

1968   **FIRECREEK**
Director: Bernard McEveety
Co-stars: James Stewart Henry Fonda Dean Jagger

1968   **HOUSE OF CARDS**
Director: John Guillermin
Co-stars: George Peppard Orson Welles Keith Michell

1968   **MADIGAN**
Director: Don Siegel
Co-stars: Richard Widmark Henry Fonda Michael Dunn

1969   **A DREAM OF KINGS**
Director: Daniel Mann
Co-stars: Anthony Quinn Irene Papas Sam Levene

1970   **RUN, SIMON, RUN**
Director: George McCowan
Co-stars: Burt Reynolds James Best Royal Dano

JEAN STEVENS

1944   **THE MISSING JUROR**
Director: Budd Boetticher
Co-stars: Jim Bannon Janis Carter George Macready

JOSEPHINE STEVENS

1917   **THE BUTCHER BOY**
Director: Roscoe "Fatty" Arbuckle
Co-stars: Roscoe "Fatty" Arbuckle Arthur Earle Buster Keaton

JULIE STEVENS

1965   **CARRY ON CLEO**
Director: Gerald Thomas
Co-stars: Sid James Amanda Barrie Kenneth Williams

KATHERINE STEVENS

1941   **THE GREAT MAN'S LADY**
Director: William Wellman
Co-stars: Barbara Stanwyck Joel McCrea Brian Donlevy

K.T. STEVENS

1949   **PORT OF NEW YORK**
Director: Laslo Benedek
Co-stars: Scott Brady Richard Rober Yul Brynner

1950   **HARRIET CRAIG**
Director: Vincent Sherman
Co-stars: Joan Crawford Wendell Corey Allyn Joslyn

1953   **VICE SQUAD**
Director: Arnold Laven
Co-stars: Edward G. Robinson Paulette Goddard Lee Van Cleef

1959   **MISSILE TO THE MOON**
Director: Richard Cunha
Co-stars: Cathy Downs Richard Travis

MARTI STEVENS

1961   **ALL NIGHT LONG**
Director: Basil Dearden
Co-stars: Patrick McGoohan Richard Attenborough Betsy Blair

NAOMI STEVENS

1958   **THE BLACK ORCHID**
Director: Martin Ritt
Co-stars: Sophia Loren Anthony Quinn Ina Balin

RISÉ STEVENS

1941   **THE CHOCOLATE SOLDIER**
Director: Roy Del Ruth
Co-stars: Nelson Eddy Nigel Bruce Florence Bates

1944   **GOING MY WAY**
Director: Leo McCarey
Co-stars: Bing Crosby Barry Fitzgerald Frank McHugh

1947   **CARNEGIE HALL**
Director: Edgar Ulmer
Co-stars: Marsha Hunt William Prince Frank McHugh

RUTHELMA STEVENS

1933   **THE CIRCUS QUEEN MURDER**
Director: Roy William Neill
Co-stars: Adolphe Menjou Greta Nissen Donald Cook

1934   **THE SCARLET EMPRESS**
Director: Josef Von Sternberg
Co-stars: Marlene Dietrich John Lodge Sam Jaffe

SARAH STEVENS

1981   **IMPROPER CHANNELS**
Director: Eric Till
Co-stars: Alan Arkin Mariette Hartley Monica Parker

STELLA STEVENS

1959   **LI'L ABNER**
Director: Melvin Frank
Co-stars: Peter Palmer Leslie Parrish Stubby Kaye

1961   **MAN-TRAP**
Director: Edmond O'Brien
Co-stars: Jeffrey Hunter David Janssen Hugh Sanders

1962   **TOO LATE BLUES**
Director: John Cassavetes
Co-stars: Bobby Darin Everett Chambers Marilyn Clark

1962   **GIRLS! GIRLS! GIRLS!**
Director: Norman Taurog
Co-stars: Elvis Presley Laurel Goodwin Jeremy Slate

1963   **THE COURTSHIP OF EDDIE'S FATHER**
Director: Vincente Minnelli
Co-stars: Glenn Ford Ronny Howard

1963   **THE NUTTY PROFESSOR**
Director: Jerry Lewis
Co-stars: Jerry Lewis Howard Morris Kathleen Freeman

1964   **ADVANCE TO THE REAR**
Director: George Marshall
Co-stars: Glenn Ford Melvyn Douglas Joan Blondell

1965   **THE SECRET OF MY SUCCESS**
Director: Andrew Stone
Co-stars: James Booth Lionel Jeffries Shirley Jones

1965   **SYNANON**
Director: Richard Quine
Co-stars: Edmond O'Brien Chuck Connors Alex Cord

1966	**THE SILENCERS**	
Director:	Phil Karlson	
Co-stars:	Dean Martin Daliah Lavi Cyd Charisse	

1966 THE SILENCERS
Director: Phil Karlson
Co-stars: Dean Martin Daliah Lavi Cyd Charisse

1966 RAGE
Director: Gilberto Gazcon
Co-stars: Glenn Ford David Reynoso Armando Silvestre

1968 WHERE ANGELS GO, TROUBLE FOLLOWS
Director: James Neilson
Co-stars: Rosalind Russell Binnie Barnes

1968 HOW TO SAVE A MARRIAGE.. AND RUIN YOUR LIFE
Director: Fielder Cook
Co-stars: Dean Martin Betty Field

1968 SOL MADRID
Director: Brian Hutton
Co-stars: David McCallum Telly Savalas Rip Torn

1969 THE MAD ROOM
Director: Bernard Girard
Co-stars: Shelley Winters Carol Cole Skip Ward

1970 THE BALLAD OF CABLE HOGUE
Director: Sam Peckinpah
Co-stars: Jason Robards David Warner Strother Martin

1971 IN BROAD DAYLIGHT
Director: Robert Day
Co-stars: Richard Boone Suzanne Pleshette Fred Beir

1971 STAND UP AND BE COUNTED
Director: Jackie Cooper
Co-stars: Jacqueline Bisset Loretta Swit

1971 A TOWN CALLED BASTARD
Director: Robert Parrish
Co-stars: Robert Shaw Telly Savalas Michael Craig

1972 THE POSEIDON ADVENTURE
Director: Ronald Neame
Co-stars: Gene Hackman Shelley Winters Ernest Borgnine

1973 LINDA
Director: Jack Smight
Co-stars: Ed Nelson John Saxon John McIntyre

1973 ARNOLD
Director: Georg Fenady
Co-stars: Roddy McDowall Elsa Lanchester Shani Wallis

1974 THE DAY THE EARTH MOVED
Director: Robert Michael Lewis
Co-stars: Jackie Cooper Cleavon Little

1975 THE NEW ORIGINAL WONDER WOMAN
Director: Leonard Horn
Co-stars: Lynda Carter Lyle Waggoner

1976 NICKELODEON
Director: Peter Bogdanovich
Co-stars: Ryan O'Neal Tatum O'Neal Burt Reynolds

1977 THE NIGHT THEY TOOK MISS BEAUTIFUL
Director: Robert Michael Lewis
Co-stars: Chuck Connors Phil Silvers

1978 THE MANITOU
Director: William Girdler
Co-stars: Tony Curtis Susan Strasberg Ann Sothern

1979 HART TO HART
Director: Tom Mankiewicz
Co-stars: Robert Wagner Stefanie Powers Lionel Stander

1981 WACKO
Director: Greydon Clark
Co-stars: Joe Don Baker George Kennedy Jeff Altman

1983 CHAINED HEAT
Director: Paul Nicolas
Co-stars: Linda Blair John Vernon Sybil Danning

1984 NO MAN'S LAND
Director: Rod Holcomb
Co-stars: Terri Garber Estelle Getty Janis Paige

1984 AMAZONS
Director: Paul Michael Glaser
Co-stars: Jack Scalia Madeleine Stowe Tamara Dobson

1986 THE LONGSHOT
Director: Paul Bartel
Co-stars: Tim Conway Jack Weston Harvey Korman

1986 A MASTERPIECE OF MURDER
Co-stars: Bob Hope Don Ameche Yvonne De Carlo

CYNTHIA STEVENSON

1992 THE PLAYER
Director: Robert Altman
Co-stars: Tim Robbins Greta Scacchi Whoopi Goldberg

1993 WATCH IT
Director: Tom Flynn
Co-stars: Peter Gallagher Suzy Amis John Tenney

1995 FORGET PARIS
Director: Billy Crystal
Co-stars: Billy Crystal Debra Winger Joe Mantegna

1996 HOME FOR THE HOLIDAYS
Director: Jodie Foster
Co-stars: Holly Hunter Anne Bancroft Robert Downey Jnr.

GERDA STEVENSON

1992 BLUE BLACK PERMANENT
Director: Margaret Tait
Co-stars: Celia Imrie Jack Shepherd James Fleet

1995 BRAVEHEART
Director: Mel Gibson
Co-stars: Mel Gibson Sophie Marceau Patrick McGoohan

JULIET STEVENSON

1987 STANLEY
Director: Anna Benson Gyles
Co-stars: Anton Lesser Sarah Berger Lesley Dunlop

1988 OUT OF LOVE
Director: Michael Houldey
Co-stars: Dafydd Hywel Emrys James Cadfan Roberts

1988 LADDER OF SWORDS
Director: Norman Hull
Co-stars: Martin Shaw Eleanor David Bob Peck

1988 DROWNING BY NUMBERS
Director: Peter Greenaway
Co-stars: Bernard Hill Joan Plowright Joely Richardson

1991 AIMEE
Director: Pedr James
Co-stars: Donald Sumpter Simon Chandler Christine Rose

1991 TRULY, MADLY, DEEPLY
Director: Anthony Minghella
Co-stars: Alan Rickman Bill Paterson Michael Maloney

1992 THE TRIAL
Director: David Jones
Co-stars: Kyle MacLachlan Anthony Hopkins Jason Robards

1994 THE SECRET RAPTURE
Director: Howard Davies
Co-stars: Penelope Wilton Joanne Whalley Alan Howard

1996 STONES, SCISSORS AND PAPER
Director: Richard Cameron
Co-star: Ken Stott

MARGOT STEVENSON

1939 CALLING PHILO VANCE
Director: William Clemens
Co-stars: James Stephenson Henry O'Neill Ralph Forbes

1939 GRANNY GET YOUR GUN
Director: George Amy
Co-stars: May Robson Harry Davenport Hardie Albright

VENETIA STEVENSON

1957 DARBY'S RANGERS
Director: William Wellman
Co-stars: James Garner Jack Warden Stuart Whitman

1958 DAY OF THE OUTLAW
Director: Andre De Toth
Co-stars: Robert Ryan Burl Ives Tina Louise

1958 ISLAND OF LOST WOMEN
Director: Frank Tuttle
Co-stars: Jeff Richards John Smith Alan Napier

1958 JET OVER THE ATLANTIC
Director: Byron Haskin
Co-stars: Guy Madison Virginia Mayo George Raft

1960 CITY OF THE DEAD
Director: John Moxey
Co-stars: Patricia Jessel Betta St. John Christopher Lee

1960 SEVEN WAYS FROM SUNDOWN
Director: Harry Keller
Co-stars: Audie Murphy Barry Sullivan John McIntyre

1960 STUDS LONIGAN
Director: Irving Lerner
Co-stars: Christopher Knight Jack Nicholson Frank Gorshin

ALEXANDRA STEWART

1960 TARZAN THE MAGNIFICENT
Director: Robert Day
Co-stars: Gordon Scott Betta St. John Jock Mahoney

1960 EXODUS
Director: Otto Preminger
Co-stars: Paul Newman Eva Marie Saint John Derek

1965 MICKEY ONE
Director: Arthur Penn
Co-stars: Warren Beatty Hurd Hatfield Franchot Tone

1967 MAROC 7
Director: Gerry O'Hara
Co-stars: Gene Barry Elsa Martinelli Cyd Charisse

1968 ONLY WHEN I LARF
Director: Basil Dearden
Co-stars: Richard Attenborough David Hemmings Melissa Stribling

1970 THE MAN WHO HAD POWER OVER WOMEN
Director: John Krish
Co-stars: Rod Taylor Carol White James Booth

1971 ZEPPELIN
Director: Etienne Perier
Co-stars: Michael York Elke Sommer Marius Goring

1973 DAY FOR NIGHT
Director: Francois Truffaut
Co-stars: Jacqueline Bisset Valentina Cortese Jean-Pierre Aumont

1974 THE MARSEILLES CONTRACT
Director: Robert Parrish
Co-stars: Michael Caine Anthony Quinn James Mason

1977 THE UNCANNY
Director: Denis Heroux
Co-stars: Peter Cushing Ray Milland Susan Penhaligon

1978 IN PRAISE OF OLDER WOMEN
Director: George Kaczender
Co-stars: Tom Berenger Karen Black Susan Strasberg

1980 PHOBIA
Director: John Huston
Co-stars: Paul Michael Glaser John Colicos Susan Hogan

1986 UNDER THE CHERRY MOON
Director: Prince
Co-stars: Kristin Scott-Thomas Jerome Benton Steven Berkoff

1988 FRANTIC
Director: Roman Polanski
Co-stars: Harrison Ford Betty Buckley Emmanuelle Seigneur

BLANCE STEWART

1940 NIGHT AT EARL CARROLL'S
Director: Kurt Neumann
Co-stars: J. Carrol Naish Lilian Cornell

CATHERINE MARY STEWART

1980 THE APPLE
Director: Menahem Golan
Co-stars: Allan Love Grace Kennedy Joss Ackland

1984 THE LAST STARFIGHTER
Director: Nick Castle
Co-stars: Lance Guest Dan O'Herlihy Robert Preston

1984 NIGHT OF THE COMET
Director: Tom Eberhardt
Co-stars: Kelli Maroney Geoffrey Lewis Mary Woronov

1985 MISCHIEF
Director: Mel Damski
Co-stars: Doug McKeon Kelly Preston Chris Nash

1986 MURDER BY THE BOOK
Director: Mel Damski
Co-star: Robert Hays

1986 THE ANNIHILATOR
Director: Michael Chapman
Co-stars: Mark Lindsay Chapman Susan Blakely Lisa Blount

1987 DUDES
Director: Penelope Spheeris
Co-stars: Jon Cryer Daniel Roebuck Lee Ving

1989 WEEKEND AT BERNIE'S
Director: Ted Kotcheff
Co-stars: Andrew McCarthy Jonathan Silverman Terry Kiser

1993 SAMURAI COWBOY
Director: Michael Keusch
Co-star: Hiromi Go

1993 WEEKEND AT BERNIE'S II
Director: Robert Klane
Co-stars: Andrew McCarthy Barry Bostwick Terry Kiser

1994 OUT OF ANNIE'S PAST
Director: Stuart Cooper
Co-star: Denis Farina

CHARLOTTE STEWART

1976 ERASERHEAD
Director: David Lynch
Co-stars: John Nance Allen Joseph Jeanne Bates

1990 TREMORS
Director: Roy Underwood
Co-stars: Kevin Bacon Fred Ward Finn Carter

ELAINE STEWART

1952 A SLIGHT CASE OF LARCENY
Director: Don Weis
Co-stars: Mickey Rooney Eddie Bracken Marilyn Erskine

1952 YOU FOR ME
Director: Don Weis
Co-stars: Peter Lawford Jane Greer Gig Young

1953 YOUNG BESS
Director: George Sidney
Co-stars: Jean Simmons Stewart Granger Charles Laughton

1953 TAKE THE HIGH GROUND
Director: Richard Brooks
Co-stars: Richard Widmark Karl Malden Carleton Carpenter

1953 CODE TWO
Director: Fred Wilcox
Co-stars: Ralph Meeker Sally Forrest Keenan Wynn

1954 BRIGADOON
Director: Vincente Minnelli
Co-stars: Gene Kelly Cyd Charisse Van Johnson

1954 THE ADVENTURES OF HAJJI BABA
Director: Don Weis
Co-stars: John Derek Thomas Gomez Amanda Blake

1957 NIGHT PASSAGE
Director: James Neilson
Co-stars: James Stewart Audie Murphy Dan Duryea

1958 HIGH HILL
Director: Burt Balaban
Co-stars: John Derek Rodney Burke

1959 ESCORT WEST
Director: Francis Lyon
Co-stars: Victor Mature Faith Domergue Rex Ingram

1960 THE RISE AND FALL OF LEGS DIAMOND
Director: Budd Boetticher
Co-stars: Ray Danton Karen Steele Warren Oates

ELEANOR STEWART

1938 STAGECOACH DAYS
Co-star: Jack Luden

1938 ROLLING CARAVANS
Co-stars: Jack Luden Lafe McKee

EVELYN STEWART

1965 ADIOS GRINGOS
Director: George Finlay
Co-stars: Montgomery Wood Peter Cross Grant Laramy

KATE McGREGOR STEWART

1992 FATHER OF THE BRIDE
Director: Charles Shyer
Co-stars: Steve Martin Diane Keaton Kimberley Williams

MARGIE STEWART

1943 GILDERSLEEVE'S BAD DAY
Co-stars: Richard Le Grand Freddie Mercer

MARTHA STEWART

1945 DOLL FACE
Director: Lewis Seiler
Co-stars: Vivian Blaine Carmen Miranda Perry Como

1946 JOHNNY COMES FLYING HOME

1947 I WONDER WHO'S KISSING HER NOW
Director: Lloyd Bacon
Co-stars: Mark Stevens June Haver Reginald Gardiner

1947 DAISY KENYON
Director: Otto Preminger
Co-stars: Joan Crawford Henry Fonda Dana Andrews

1948 ARE YOU WITH IT ?
Director: Jack Hively
Co-stars: Donald O'Connor Olga San Juan Lew Parker

1950 IN A LONELY PLACE
Director: Nicholas Ray
Co-stars: Humphrey Bogart Gloria Grahame Frank Lovejoy

MARY STEWART

1948 THE BIG PUNCH
Director: Sherry Shourds
Co-stars: Gordon MacRae Wayne Morris Lois Maxwell

1948 HENRY THE RAINMAKER
Director: Jean Yarbrough
Co-stars: Raymond Walburn William Tracy Walter Catlett

PEGGY STEWART

1937 WELLS FARGO
Director: Frank Lloyd
Co-stars: Joel McCrea Frances Dee Lloyd Nolan

1944 SILVER CITY KID
Co-star: Allan Lane

1945 OREGON TRAIL
Co-star: Sunset Carson

1945 THE VAMPIRE'S GHOST
Director: Lesley Selander
Co-stars: John Abbott Charles Gordon Grant Withers

1946 ALIAS BILLY THE KID
Co-star: Sunset Carson

1946 DAYS OF BUFFALO BILL
Co-stars: Sunset Carson Tom London Eddie Parker

PENELOPE STEWART

1984 VIGIL
Director: Vincent Ward
Co-stars: Bill Kerr Fiona Kay Gordon Shields

SOPHIE STEWART

1935 MARIA MARTEN OR THE MURDER IN THE RED BARN
Director: George King
Co-stars: Tod Slaughter Eric Portman

1935 THE CITY OF BEAUTIFUL NONSENSE
Director: Adrian Brunel
Co-stars: Emlyn Williams Eve Lister George Carney

1936 AS YOU LIKE IT
Director: Paul Czinner
Co-stars: Elisabeth Bergner Laurence Olivier Felix Aylmer

1936 THE MAN WHO COULD WORK MIRACLES
Director: Lothar Mendes
Co-stars: Roland Young Ralph Richardson Joan Gardner

1936 THINGS TO COME
Director: William Cameron Menzies
Co-stars: Raymond Massey Cedric Hardwicke

1937 UNDER THE RED ROBE
Director: Victor Sjostrom
Co-stars: Conrad Viedt Raymond Massey Annabella

1937 RETURN OF THE SCARLET PIMPERNEL
Director: Hans Schwarz
Co-stars: Barry K. Barnes Margaretta Scott James Mason

1943 THE LAMP STILL BURNS
Director: Maurice Elvy
Co-stars: Rosamund John Stewart Granger Godfrey Tearle

1944 STRAWBERRY ROAN
Director: Maurice Elvy
Co-stars: William Hartnell Carol Raye Petula Clark

1947 UNCLE SILAS
Director: Charles Frank
Co-stars: Jean Simmons Derrick De Marney Derek Bond

1952   **MADE IN HEAVEN**
Director: John Paddy Carstairs
Co-stars: David Tomlinson Petula Clark Sonja Ziemann

1954   **DEVIL GIRL FROM MARS**
Director: David MacDonald
Co-stars: Patricia Laffan Hugh McDermott Adrienne Corri

1957   **NO TIME FOR TEARS**
Director: Cyril Frankel
Co-stars: Anna Neagle Anthony Quayle Sylvia Sims

1957   **YANGTSE INCIDENT**
Director: Michael Anderson
Co-stars: Richard Todd William Hartnell Akim Tamiroff

TRISH STEWART

1979   **SALVAGE**
Director: Lee Phillips
Co-stars: Andy Griffith Joel Higgins Richard Jaeckel

IVY ST. HELIER

1933   **BITTER SWEET**
Director: Herbert Wilcox
Co-stars: Anna Neagle Fernand Gravet Hugh Williams

1946   **HENRY V**
Director: Laurence Olivier
Co-stars: Laurence Olivier Robert Newton Renee Asherson

1948   **LONDON BELONGS TO ME**
Director: Sidney Gilliat
Co-stars: Alastair Sim Stephen Murray Richard Attenborough

1955   **THE GOLD EXPRESS**
Director: Guy Fergusson
Co-stars: Vernon Gray Ann Walford Delphi Lawrence

DOROTHY STICKNEY

1932   **WAYWARD**
Co-stars: Richard Arlen Nancy Carroll

1934   **THE LITTLE MINISTER**
Director: Richard Wallace
Co-stars: Katherine Hepburn John Beal Donald Crisp

1934   **MURDER AT THE VANITIES**
Director: Mitchell Leisen
Co-stars: Jack Oakie Victor McLaglen Kitty Carlisle

1936   **AND SO THEY WERE MARRIED**
Director: Elliott Nugent
Co-stars: Melvyn Douglas Mary Astor Edith Fellows

1936   **THE MOON'S OUR HOME**
Director: William Seiter
Co-stars: Margaret Sullavan Henry Fonda Beulah Bondi

1937   **I MET MY LOVE AGAIN**
Director: Joshua Logan
Co-stars: Henry Fonda Joan Bennett Alan Marshall

1944   **THE UNINVITED**
Director: Lewis Allen
Co-stars: Ray Milland Ruth Hussey Gail Russell

1948   **MISS TATLOCK'S MILLIONS**
Director: Richard Haydn
Co-stars: John Lund Wanda Hendrix Monty Woolley

1956   **THE CATERED AFFAIR**
Director: Richard Brooks
Co-stars: Bette Davis Ernest Borgnine Debbie Reynolds

1969   **I NEVER SANG FOR MY FATHER**
Director: Gilbert Cates
Co-stars: Melvyn Douglas Gene Hackman Estelle Parsons

1971   **THE HOMECOMING: A CHRISTMAS STORY**
Director: Fielder Cook
Co-stars: Patricia Neal Richard Thomas Ellen Corby

VIOLA KATE STIMPSON

1985   **THE ALCHEMIST**
Director: James Amante
Co-stars: Robert Ginty Lucinda Dooling Robert Glaudini

SARA STIMSON *(Child)*

1980   **LITTLE MISS MARKER**
Director: Walter Bernstein
Co-stars: Walter Matthau Julie Andrews Tony Curtis

LINDA STIRLING

1945   **THE SHERIFF OF CIMARRON**
Co-star: Sunset Carson

1946   **THE MADONNA'S SECRET**
Director: William Thiele
Co-stars: Francis Lederer Gail Patrick Ann Rutherford

PAMELA STIRLING

1945   **THE ECHO MURDERS**
Director: John Harlow
Co-stars: David Farrar Dennis Price Julian Mitchell

BETTA ST. JOHN

1953   **ALL THE BROTHERS WERE VALIANT**
Director: Richard Thorpe
Co-stars: Stewart Granger Robert Taylor Ann Blyth

1953   **DREAM WIFE**
Director: Sidney Sheldon
Co-stars: Cary Grant Deborah Kerr Walter Pidgeon

1953   **THE ROBE**
Director: Henry Koster
Co-stars: Richard Burton Jean Simmons Victor Mature

1954   **THE SARACEN BLADE**
Director: William Castle
Co-stars: Ricardo Montalban Rick Jason Carolyn Jones

1954   **THE STUDENT PRINCE**
Director: Richard Thorpe
Co-stars: Edmund Purdom Ann Blyth Edmund Gwenn

1954   **THE LAW VERSUS BILLY THE KID**
Director: William Castle
Co-stars: Scott Brady James Griffith Alan Hale Jnr.

1954   **DANGEROUS MISSION**
Director: Louis King
Co-stars: Victor Mature Piper Laurie Vincent Price

1956   **ALIAS JOHN PRESTON**
Director: David MacDonald
Co-stars: Christopher Lee Alexander Knox Patrick Holt

1956   **THE NAKED DAWN**
Director: Edgar Ulmer
Co-stars: Arthur Kennedy Eugene Iglesias

1957   **HIGH TIDE AT NOON**
Director: Philip Leacock
Co-stars: Michael Craig Patrick McGoohan Flora Robson

1957   **TARZAN AND THE LOST SAFARI**
Director: Bruce Humberstone
Co-stars: Gordon Scott Yolande Donlan Robert Beatty

1958   **THE SNORKEL**
Director: Guy Green
Co-stars: Peter Van Eyck Mandy Miller William Franklyn

1958   **CORRIDORS OF BLOOD**
Director: Robert Day
Co-stars: Boris Karloff Christopher Lee Finlay Currie

1960   **CITY OF THE DEAD**
Director: John Moxey
Co-stars: Patricia Jessel Christopher Lee Dennis Lotis

1960 TARZAN THE MAGNIFICENT
Director: Robert Day
Co-stars: Gordon Scott Jock Mahoney John Carradine

JILL ST. JOHN

1959 HOLIDAY FOR LOVERS
Director: Henry Levin
Co-stars: Clifton Webb Jane Wyman Carol Lynley

1959 THE REMARKABLE MR PENNYPACKER
Director: Henry Levin
Co-stars: Clifton Webb Dorothy McGuire Ron Ely

1960 THE LOST WORLD
Director: Irwin Allen
Co-stars: Claude Rains Michael Rennie Fernando Lamas

1962 TENDER IS THE NIGHT
Director: Henry King
Co-stars: Jennifer Jones Jason Robards Joan Fontaine

1962 THE ROMAN SPRING OF MRS STONE
Director: Jose Quintero
Co-stars: Vivien Leigh Warren Beatty Lotte Lenya

1962 COME BLOW YOUR HORN
Director: Bud Yorkin
Co-stars: Frank Sinatra Tony Bill Barbara Rush

1963 WHO'S BEEN SLEEPING IN MY BED ?
Director: Daniel Mann
Co-stars: Dean Martin Richard Conte

1963 WHO'S MINDING THE STORE ?
Director: Frank Tashlin
Co-stars: Jerry Lewis Ray Walston Agnes Moorehead

1964 HONEYMOON HOTEL
Director: Henry Levin
Co-stars: Nancy Kwan Robert Goulet Elsa Lanchester

1965 THE LIQUIDATOR
Director: Jack Cardiff
Co-stars: Rod Taylor Trevor Howard David Tomlinson

1966 EIGHT ON THE LAM
Director: George Marshall
Co-stars: Bob Hope Phyllis Diller Shirley Eaton

1966 THE OSCAR
Director: Russel Rouse
Co-stars: Stephen Boyd Elke Sommer Joseph Cotten

1967 HOW I SPENT MY SUMMER VACATION
Director: William Hale
Co-stars: Robert Wagner Peter Lawford Lola Albright

1967 BANNING
Director: Ron Winston
Co-stars: Robert Wagner Guy Stockwell James Farentino

1967 THE KING'S PIRATE
Director: Don Weiss
Co-stars: Doug McClure Guy Stockwell Kurt Kasznar

1967 TONY ROME
Director: Gordon Douglas
Co-stars: Frank Sinatra Gena Rowlands Sue Lyon

1969 THE SPY KILLER
Director: Roy Baker
Co-stars: Robert Horton Sebastian Cabot Barbara Shelley

1969 FOREIGN EXCHANGE
Director: Roy Baker
Co-stars: Robert Horton Sebastian Cabot Dudley Foster

1971 DIAMONDS ARE FOREVER
Director: Guy Hamilton
Co-stars: Sean Connery Charles Gray Lana Wood

1972 SITTING TARGET
Director: Douglas Hickox
Co-stars: Oliver Reed Ian McShane Edward Woodward

1979 HART TO HART
Director: Tom Mankiewicz
Co-stars: Robert Wagner Stefanie Powers Lionel Stander

1981 MATT HOUSTON
Director: Richard Lang
Co-stars: Lee Horsley Barbara Carrera Dale Robertson

1982 THE ACT
Director: Sig Shore
Co-stars: Eddie Albert Robert Ginty

1988 AROUND THE WORLD IN EIGHTY DAYS
Director: Buzz Kulik
Co-stars: Pierce Brosnan Eric Idle John Mills

KATHLEEN ST. JOHN

1986 PAST CARING
Director: Richard Eyre
Co-stars: Denholm Elliott Emlyn Williams Joan Greenwood

MARGO ST. JOHN

1984 TIGHTROPE
Director: Richard Tuggle
Co-stars: Clint Eastwood Genevieve Bujold Dan Hedaya

MICHELLE ST. JOHN

1989 WHERE THE SPIRIT LIVES
Director: Bruce Pittman
Co-star: Graham Greene

BARBARA STOCK

1985 SPENSER: FOR HIRE
Director: Lee Katzin
Co-stars: Robert Urich Chuck Connors Geoffrey Lewis

1986 LONG TIME GONE
Director: Robert Butler
Co-stars: Paul LeMat Wil Wheaton Ann Dusenberry

AMY STOCK-POINTON

1991 BILL AND TED'S BOGUS JOURNEY
Director: Pete Hewitt
Co-stars: Alex Winter Keanu Reeves Jeff Miller

SARA STOCKBRIDGE

1992 SPLIT SECOND
Director: Tony Maylam
Co-stars: Rutger Hauer Kim Cattrall Neil Duncan

1993 U.F.O.: THE MOVIE
Director: Tony Dow
Co-stars: Roy "Chubby" Brown Roger Lloyd Pack

BETTY STOCKFIELD

1934 THE MAN WHO CHANGED HIS NAME
Director: Henry Edwards
Co-stars: Lyn Harding Leslie Perrins Ben Welden

1934 THE BATTLE
Director: Nicolas Farkas
Co-stars: Charles Boyer Merle Oberon John Loder

1935 THE LAD
Director: Henry Edwards
Co-stars: Gordon Harker Jane Carr Michael Shepley

1936 DISHONOUR BRIGHT
Director: Tom Walls
Co-stars: Tom Walls Eugene Pallette Diana Churchill

1936 THE BELOVED VAGABOND
Director: Curtis Bernhardt
Co-stars: Maurice Chevalier Margaret Lockwood Austin Trevor

1938 I SEE ICE
Director: Anthony Kimmins
Co-stars: George Formby Kay Walsh Garry Marsh

1939 DERRIERE LA FAÇADE
Director: Georges Lacombe
Co-stars: Lucien Baroux Jules Berry Gaby Morlay

1942 FLYING FORTRESS
Director: Walter Forde
Co-stars: Richard Greene Carla Lehmann Donald Stewart

1942 HARD STEEL
Director: Norman Walker
Co-stars: Wilfrid Lawson John Stuart George Carney

1950 THE GIRL WHO COULDN'T QUITE
Director: Norman Lee
Co-stars: Bill Owen Iris Hoey Elizabeth Henson

1951 EDOUARD ET CAROLINE
Director: Jacques Becker
Co-stars: Daniel Gelin Anne Vernon William Tubbs

1956 GUILTY ?
Director: Edmond Greville
Co-stars: John Justin Barbara Laage Donald Wolfit

MINK STOLE

1969 MONDO TRASHO
Director: John Waters
Co-stars: Divine David Lochary Mary Vivian Pearce

1973 PINK FLAMINGOES
Director: John Waters
Co-stars: Divine David Lochary Mary Vivian Pearce

1975 FEMALE TROUBLE
Director: John Waters
Co-stars: Divine David Lochary Mary Vivian Pearce

1994 SERIAL MOM
Director: John Waters
Co-stars: Kathleen Turner Sam Waterston Ricki Lake

SHIRLEY STOLER

1970 THE HONEYMOON KILLERS
Director: Leonard Kastle
Co-stars: Tony LoBianco Doris Roberts Kip McArdle

1975 SEVEN BEAUTIES
Director: Lina Wertmuller
Co-stars: Giancarlo Giannini Fernando Rey Piero Di Iorio

1978 THE DEER HUNTER
Director: Michael Cimino
Co-stars: Robert De Niro John Savage Meryl Streep

1990 FRANKENHOOKER
Director: Frank Henenlotter
Co-stars: James Lorinz Patty Mullen Louise Lasser

1990 MIAMI BLUES
Director: George Armitage
Co-stars: Alec Baldwin Jennifer Jason Leigh Fred Ward

CAROL STONE

1935 FRECKLES
Director: William Hamilton
Co-stars: Tom Brown Virginia Weidler James Bush

MARIANNE STONE

1957 WOMAN IN A DRESSING GOWN
Director: J. Lee-Thompson
Co-stars: Yvonne Mitchell Anthony Quayle Sylvia Sims

1961 LOLITA
Director: Stanley Kubrick
Co-stars: James Mason Sue Lyon Shelley Winters

1972 CARRY ON MATRON
Director: Gerald Thomas
Co-stars: Sid James Kenneth Williams Hattie Jacques

PAULA STONE

1935 HOPALONG CASSIDY
Co-stars: William Boyd James Ellison Robert Warwick

SHARON STONE

1981 DEADLY BLESSING
Director: Wes Craven
Co-stars: Ernest Borgnine Maren Jensen Jeff East

1984 THE CALENDAR GIRL MURDERS
Director: William A. Graham
Co-stars: Tom Skerritt Robert Morse Robert Culp

1984 THE IRRECONCILABLE DIFFERENCES
Director: Charles Shyer
Co-stars: Ryan O'Neal Shelley Long Sam Wanamaker

1985 KING SOLOMON'S MINES
Director: J. Lee-Thompson
Co-stars: Richard Chamberlain Herbert Lom John Rhys-Davies

1987 ALLAN QUARTERMAIN AND THE LOST CITY OF GOLD
Director: Gary Nelson
Co-stars: Richard Chamberlain Henry Silva

1987 POLICE ACADEMY 4: CITIZENS ON PATROL
Director: Jim Drake
Co-stars: Steve Guttenberg Bubba Smith

1988 ACTION JACKSON
Director: Craig Baxley
Co-stars: Carl Weathers Craig T. Nelson Bill Duke

1988 TEARS IN THE RAIN

1988 ABOVE THE LAW
Director: Andrew Davis
Co-stars: Steven Seagal Pam Grier Henry Silva

1989 BEYOND THE STARS
Director: David Saperstein
Co-stars: Christian Slater Martin Sheen Olivia D'Abo

1990 TOTAL RECALL
Director: Paul Verhoeven
Co-stars: Arnold Schwarzenegger Rachel Ticotin Ronny Cox

1991 HE SAID, SHE SAID
Director: Marisa Silver
Co-stars: Kevin Bacon Elizabeth Perkins Nathan Lane

1991 SCISSORS
Director: Frank De Felitta
Co-stars: Steve Railsback Michelle Philips Ronny Cox

1991 WHERE SLEEPING DOGS LIE
Director: Charles Finch
Co-stars: Dylan McDermott Tom Sizemore

1992 YEAR OF THE GUN
Director: John Frankenheimer
Co-stars: Andrew McCarthy Valeria Golino John Pankow

1992 BASIC INSTINCT
Director: Paul Verhoeven
Co-stars: Michael Douglas George Dzundza Jeanne Triplehorn

1992 DIARY OF A HIT MAN
Director: Roy London
Co-stars: Forest Whitaker Sherilyn Fenn Seymour Cassel

1993 SLIVER
Director: Phillip Noyce
Co-stars: William Baldwin Tom Berenger Martin Landau

1993 INTERSECTION
Director: Mark Rydell
Co-stars: Richard Gere Lolita Davidovich Martin Landau

1994 THE SPECIALIST
Director: Luis Llosa
Co-stars: Sylvester Stallone James Woods Rod Steiger

1995 THE QUICK AND THE DEAD
Director: Sam Raimi
Co-stars: Gene Hackman Gary Sinise Leonardo Di Caprio

1996 THE LADY TAKES AN ACE
Co-star: John Travolta

1996 CASINO
Director: Martin Scorsese
Co-stars: Robert De Niro Joe Pesci James Woods

1996 DIABOLIQUE
Director: Jeremiah Chechik
Co-stars: Isabelle Adjani Chazz Palminterri

1996 LAST DANCE
Director: Bruce Beresford
Co-stars: Peter Gallagher Rob Morrow Randy Quaid

1998 SPHERE
Director: Barry Levinson
Co-stars: Dustin Hoffman Samuel L. Jackson Peter Coyote

SHERRI STONER

1986 REFORM SCHOOL GIRLS
Director: Tom De Simone
Co-stars: Linda Carol Pat Ast Sybil Danning

JUNE STOREY

1938 IN OLD CHICAGO
Director: Henry King
Co-stars: Tyrone Power Alice Faye Don Ameche

1939 SOUTH OF THE BORDER
Director: George Sherman
Co-stars: Gene Autry Smiley Burnette Duncan Renaldo

1939 BLUE MONTANA SKIES
Co-stars: Gene Autry Smiley Burnette

1939 IN OLD MONTEREY
Co-stars: Gene Autry Smiley Burnette

1946 THE STRANGE WOMAN
Director: Edgar Ulmer
Co-stars: Hedy Lamar George Sanders Louis Hayward

1949 MISS MINK OF 1949
Co-stars: Richard Lane Lois Collier Don Kohler

RUTH STOREY

1960 BELLS ARE RINGING
Director: Vincent Minnelli
Co-stars: Judy Holiday Dean Martin Jean Stapleton

DEBI STORM

1970 THE BROTHERHOOD OF SATAN
Director: Bernard McEveety
Co-stars: Strother Martin Alvy Moore Anna Capri

EMY STORM

1963 RAVEN'S END
Director: Bo Widerberg
Co-stars: Thommy Berggren Keve Hjelm Christina Framback

GALE STORM

1940 TOM BROWN'S SCHOOLDAYS
Director: Robert Stevenson
Co-stars: Freddie Bartholomew Cedric Hardwicke Jimmy Lydon

1941 JESSE JAMES AT BAY
Co-stars: Roy Rogers George Hayes Sally Payne

1942 RHYTHM PARADE
Co-star: Chick Chandler

1943 WHERE ARE YOUR CHILDREN ?
Director: William Nigh
Co-stars: Jackie Cooper Patricia Morison John Litel

1943 REVENGE OF THE ZOMBIES
Director: Steve Sekeley
Co-stars: John Carradine Robert Lowery Veda Ann Borg

1945 G.I. HONEYMOON
Co-stars: Peter Cookson Jerome Cowan

1945 FOREVER YOURS
Co-stars: Johnny Downs Frank Craven C. Aubrey Smith

1945 SUNBONNET SUE
Director: Ralph Murphy
Co-stars: Phil Regan Minna Gombell Alan Mowbray

1946 SWING PARADE OF 1946
Co-stars: Phil Regan John Eldredge

1947 IT HAPPENED ON 5TH AVENUE
Director: Roy Del Ruth
Co-stars: Ann Harding Victor Moore Charles Ruggles

1948 THE DUDE GOES WEST
Co-star: Eddie Albert

1949 CURTAIN CALL AT CACTUS CREEK
Director: Charles Lamont
Co-stars: Donald O'Connor Walter Brennan Eve Arden

1949 ABANDONED
Director: Joseph Newman
Co-stars: Dennis O'Keefe Raymond Burr Jeff Chandler

1950 AL JENNINGS OF OKLAHOMA
Director: Ray Nazarro
Co-stars: Dan Duryea Dick Foran Gloria Henry

1950 BETWEEN MIDNIGHT AND DAWN
Director: Gordon Douglas
Co-stars: Mark Stevens Edmond O'Brien Donald Buka

1950 THE KID FROM TEXAS
Director: Kurt Neuman
Co-stars: Audie Murphy Albert Dekker Will Geer

1950 THE UNDERWORLD STORY
Director: Cy Endfield
Co-stars: Dan Duryea Herbert Marshall Michael O'Shea

1951 THE TEXAS RANGERS
Director: Phil Karlson
Co-stars: George Montgomery Jerome Courtland Noah Beery Jnr.

1952 WOMAN OF THE NORTH COUNTRY
Director: Joseph Kane
Co-stars: Ruth Hussey Rod Cameron John Agar

SANDRA STORME

1937 SOPHIE LANG GOES WEST
Co-stars: Jed Prouty C. Henry Gordon

JUDITH STOTT

1961 THE QUEEN'S GUARDS
Director: Michael Powell
Co-stars: Raymond Massey Daniel Massey Robert Stephens

MADELEINE STOWE

1984 AMAZONS
Director: Paul Michael Glaser
Co-stars: Tamara Dobson Jennifer Warren Stella Stevens

1986 BLOOD AND ORCHIDS
Director: Jerry Thorpe
Co-stars: Kris Kristofferson Jane Alexander Sean Young

1987 STAKEOUT
Director: John Badham
Co-stars: Richard Dreyfuss Emilio Estevez Aidan Quinn

1989 REVENGEE
Director: Tony Scott
Co-stars: Kevin Costner Anthony Quinn Tom Milian

1990 THE TWO JAKES
Director: Jack Nicholson
Co-stars: Jack Nicholson Harvey Keitel Meg Tilly

1990 WORTH WINNING
Director: Will MacKenzie
Co-stars: Mark Harmon Lesley Ann Warren

1992 UNLAWFUL ENTRY
Director: Jonathan Kaplan
Co-stars: Kurt Russell Ray Liotta Ken Lerner

1992 THE LAST OF THE MOHICANS
Director: Michael Mann
Co-stars: Daniel Day-Lewis Russell Means Jodhi May

1993 SHORT CUTS
Director: Robert Altman
Co-stars: Matthew Modine Andie MacDowall Anne Archer

1993 ANOTHER STAKEOUT
Director: John Badham
Co-stars: Richard Dreyfuss Emilio Estevez Rosie O'Donnell

1994 BAD GIRLS
Director: Jonathan Kaplan
Co-stars: Mary Stuart Masterson Andie MacDowall Drew Barrymore

1994 BLINK
Director: Michael Apted
Co-stars: Aidan Quinn Laurie Metcalf James Remar

1994 CHINA MOON
Director: John Bailey
Co-stars: Ed Harris Charles Dance Patricia Healy

1991 CLOSET LAND
Director: Radha Bharadwaj
Co-star: Alan Rickman

1996 TWELVE MONKIES
Director: Terry Gilliam
Co-stars: Brad Pitt Bruce Willis Christopher Plummer

ROSE STRADNER

1937 THE LAST GANGSTER
Director: Edward Ludwig
Co-stars: Edward G. Robinson James Stewart Lionel Stander

1939 BLIND ALLEY
Director: Charles Vidor
Co-stars: Chester Morris Ralph Bellamy Ann Dvorak

1944 KEYS OF THE KINGDOM
Director: John Stahl
Co-stars: Gregory Peck Thomas Mitchell Edmund Gwenn

BEATRICE STRAIGHT
Oscar For Best Supporting Actress In 1976 For "Network"

1956 PATTERNS
Director: Fielder Cook
Co-stars: Van Heflin Everett Sloane Ed Begley

1956 THE SILKEN AFFAIR
Director: Roy Kellino
Co-stars: David Niven Genevieve Page Wilfrid Hyde White

1959 THE NUN'S STORY
Director: Fred Zinnemann
Co-stars: Audrey Hepburn Peter Finch Edith Evans

1976 NETWORK
Director: Sidney Lumet
Co-stars: Faye Dunaway William Holden Peter Finch

1977 KILLER ON BOARD
Director: Philip Leacock
Co-stars: Claude Akins George Hamilton Patty Duke

1979 THE PROMISE
Director: Gilbert Cates
Co-stars: Kathleen Quinlan Stephen Collins William Prince

1980 THE FORMULA
Director: John Avildsen
Co-stars: George C. Scott Marlon Brando John Gielgud

1981 ENDLESS LOVE
Director: Franco Zefferelli
Co-stars: Brooke Shields Martin Hewitt Shirley Knight

1982 POLTERGEIST
Director: Tobe Hooper
Co-stars: JoBeth Williams Craig T. Nelson Heather O'Rourke

1983 TWO OF A KIND
Director: John Herzfield
Co-stars: John Travolta Olivia Newton-John Oliver Reed

1985 POWER
Director: Sidney Lumet
Co-stars: Richard Gere Julie Christie Gene Hackman

1985 CHILLER
Director: Wes Craven
Co-stars: Michael Beck Paul Sorvino Laura Johnson

1992 DECEIVED
Director: Damian Harris
Co-stars: Goldie Hawn John Heard Robin Bartlett

JULIE STRAIN

1993 MIDNIGHT CONFESSIONS
Director: Allan Shusstak
Co-stars: Carol Hoyt David Milbern

1995 VIRTUAL DESIRE
Director: Noble Henri

SUSAN STRANKS *(Child)*

1949 THE BLUE LAGOON
Director: Frank Launder
Co-stars: Jean Simmons Donald Houston Noel Purcell

ANNA STRASBERG

1984 AURORA
Director: Maurizio Ponzi
Co-stars: Sophia Loren Daniel J. Travanti Edoardo Ponti

SUSAN STRASBERG *(Daughter Of Steven Strasberg, Married Chris Jones)*

1955 THE COBWEB
Director: Vincent Minnelli
Co-stars: Richard Widmark Lauren Bacall Charles Boyer

1955 PICNIC
Director: Joshua Logan
Co-stars: William Holden Kim Novak Rosalind Russell

1957 STAGE STRUCK
Director: Sidney Lumet
Co-stars: Henry Fonda Herbert Marshall Joan Greenwood

1960 **KAPO**
Director: Gillo Pontecorvo
Co-stars: Laurent Terzieff Emmanuelle Riva

1961 **SCREAM OF FEAR**
Director: Seth Holt
Co-stars: Ann Todd Christopher Lee Ronald Lewis

1962 **ADVENTURES OF A YOUNG MAN**
Director: Martin Ritt
Co-stars: Richard Beymer Diane Baker Paul Newman

1965 **THE HIGH BRIGHT SUN**
Director: Ralph Thomas
Co-stars: Dirk Bogarde Denholm Elliott George Chakiris

1967 **CHUBASCO**
Director: Allen Miner
Co-stars: Chris Jones Richard Egan Ann Sothern

1967 **THE TRIP**
Director: Roger Corman
Co-stars: Peter Fonda Bruce Dern Dennis Hopper

1968 **PSYCH-OUT**
Director: Richard Rush
Co-stars: Dean Stockwell Jack Nicholson Bruce Dern

1968 **THE BROTHERHOOD**
Director: Martin Ritt
Co-stars: Kirk Douglas Alex Cord Irene Papas

1969 **SWEET HUNTERS**
Director: Riy Guerra
Co-stars: Sterling Hayden Maureen McNally Stuart Whitman

1974 **AND MILLIONS WILL DIE**
Director: Leslie Martinson
Co-stars: Richard Basehart Leslie Nielsen Tony Wager

1977 **ROLLERCOASTER**
Director: James Goldstone
Co-stars: George Segal Timothy Bottoms Henry Fonda

1978 **THE MANITOU**
Director: William Girdler
Co-stars: Tony Curtis Stella Stevens Burgess Meredith

1978 **IN PRAISE OF OLDER WOMEN**
Director: George Kaczender
Co-stars: Tom Berenger Karen Black Helen Shaver

1990 **OUT OF DARKNESS**
Director: Gray Hoffmeyr
Co-stars: Malcolm McDowell Andrew Davis

ROBIN STRASSEN

1988 **GLITZ**
Director: Sandor Stern
Co-stars: Jimmy Smits Markie Post John Diehl

MARCIA STRASSMAN

1985 **THE AVIATOR**
Director: George Miller
Co-stars: Christopher Reeve Rosanna Arquette Tyne Daly

1989 **HONEY, I SHRUNK THE KIDS**
Director: Joe Johnston
Co-stars: Rick Moranis Matt Frewer Kristine Sutherland

1992 **HONEY, I BLEW UP THE KIDS**
Director: Randal Reiser
Co-stars: Rick Moranis Robert Oliveri Lloyd Bridges

1993 **ANOTHER STAKEOUT**
Director: John Badham
Co-stars: Richard Dreyfuss Emilio Estevez Madeleine Stowe

DOROTHY R. STRATTEN (*Murdered By Ex-Husband On Night Galaxina Was Premiered*)

1980 **GALAXINA**
Director: William Sachs
Co-stars: Stephen Macht Avery Schreiber James David Hinton

1982 **THEY ALL LAUGHED**
Director: Peter Bogdanovich
Co-stars: Audrey Hepburn Ben Gazzara John Ritter

INGER STRATTON

1967 **THE NAKED RUNNER**
Director: Sidney Furie
Co-stars: Frank Sinatra Peter Vaughan Nadia Gray

TERESA STRATAS

1961 **THE CANADIANS**
Director: Burt Kennedy
Co-stars: Robert Ryan John Dehner Torin Thatcher

1982 **LA TRAVIATA**
Director: Franco Zefferelli
Co-stars: Placido Domingo Allan Monk Cornell MacNeil

1995 **UNDER THE PIANO**
Director: Stefan Scaini
Co-stars: Megan Follows Amanda Plummer

URSULA STRATZ

1974 **EFFI BRIEST**
Director: Rainer Werner Fassbinder
Co-stars: Hanna Schygulla Wolfgang Schenck Ulli Lommel

MERYL STREEP

Oscar For Best Actress In 1982 For" Sophie's Choice". Oscar For Best Supporting Actress In 1979 For "Kramer Vs Kramer". Nominated For Best Actress In 1981 For "The French Lieutenant's Woman", In 1983 For "Silkwood, In 1985 "For Out Of Africa", In 1987 For "Ironweed", In 1995 For "The Bridges of Madison County" And In 1990 For "Postcards From The Edge". Nominated For Best Supporting Actress In 1978 For "The Deer Hunter"

1977 **JULIA**
Director: Fred Zinnemann
Co-stars: Jane Fonda Vanessa Redgrave Jason Robards

1978 **THE DEER HUNTER**
Director: Michael Cimino
Co-stars: Robert De Niro Christopher Walken John Savage

1979 **THE SEDUCTION OF JOE TYNAN**
Director: Jerry Schatzberg
Co-stars: Alan Alda Barbara Harris Rip Torn

1979 **MANHATTAN**
Director: Woody Allen
Co-stars: Woody Allen Diane Keaton Mariel Hemingway

1979 **KRAMER VS KRAMER**
Director: Robert Benton
Co-stars: Dustin Hoffman Justin Henry Howard Duff

1981 **THE FRENCH LIEUTENANT'S WOMAN**
Director: Karel Reisz
Co-stars: Jeremy Irons Leo McKern Patience Collier

1982 **SOPHIE'S CHOICE**
Director: Alan J. Pakula
Co-stars: Kevin Kline Peter MacNicol Rita Karin

1982 **STILL OF THE NIGHT**
Director: Robert Benton
Co-stars: Roy Scheider Jessica Tandy Sara Botsford

1983 **SILKWOOD**
Director: Mike Nichols
Co-stars: Cher Kurt Russell Craig T. Nelson

1984	**FALLING IN LOVE**
Director:	Ulu Grosbard
Co-stars:	Robert De Niro Harvey Keitel George Martin

1985	**OUT OF AFRICA**
Director:	Sydney Pollack
Co-stars:	Robert Redford Michael Kitchen Michael Gough

1985	**PLENTY**
Director:	Fred Schepisi
Co-stars:	Charles Dance John Gielgud Sting

1986	**HEARTBURN**
Director:	Mike Nichols
Co-stars:	Jack Nicholson Jeff Daniels Maureen Stapleton

1987	**IRONWEED**
Director:	Hector Babenco
Co-stars:	Jack Nicholson Carroll Baker Michael O'Keefe

1988	**A CRY IN THE DARK**
Director:	Fred Schepisi
Co-stars:	Sam Neill Dale Reeves Dorothy Alison

1989	**SHE-DEVIL**
Director:	Susan Seidelman
Co-stars:	Roseanne Barr Ed Begley Jnr. Sylvia Miles

1990	**POSTCARDS FROM THE EDGE**
Director:	Mike Nichols
Co-stars:	Shirley MacLaine Dennis Quaid Annette Bening

1991	**DEFENDING YOUR LIFE**
Director:	Albert Brooks
Co-stars:	Albert Brooks Rip Torn Lee Grant

1992	**DEATH BECOMES HER**
Director:	Robert Zemeckis
Co-stars:	Goldie Hawn Bruce Willis Isabella Rosselini

1993	**THE HOUSE OF THE SPIRITS**
Director:	Bille August
Co-stars:	Jeremy Irons Glenn Close Vanessa Redgrave

1994	**THE RIVER WILD**
Director:	Curtis Hanson
Co-stars:	Kevin Bacon David Strathairn Joseph Mazzello

1995	**THE BRIDGES OF MADISON COUNTY**
Director:	Clint Eastwood
Co-star:	Clint Eastwood

1996	**BEFORE AND AFTER**
Director:	Barbet Schroeder
Co-stars:	Liam Neeson Edward Furlong Alfred Molina

1997	**MARVIN'S ROOM**
Director:	Jerry Zaks
Co-stars:	Diane Keaton Hume Cronyn Leonardo Di Caprio

| 1997 | **FIRST DO NO HARM** |

WENDY STREHLOW

1991	**ACT OF NECESSITY**
Director:	Ian Munro
Co-stars:	Angie Milliken Mark Owen-Taylor Stephen Grives

BARBRA STREISAND *(Married Elliott Gould, James Brolin, Mother of Jason Gould)*

Oscar For Best Actress In 1968 For "Funny Girl". Nominated For Best Actress In 1973 For "The Way We Were"

1968	**FUNNY GIRL**
Director:	William Wyler
Co-stars:	Omar Sharif Anne Francis Walter Pidgeon

1969	**HELLO DOLLY**
Director:	Gene Kelly
Co-stars:	Walter Matthau Michael Crawford Louis Armstrong

1970	**ON A CLEAR DAY YOU CAN SEE FOREVER**
Director:	Vincente Minnelli
Co-stars:	Yves Montano Bob Newman

1970	**THE OWL AND THE PUSSYCAT**
Director:	Herbert Ross
Co-stars:	George Segal Robert Klein Allen Garfield

1972	**UP THE SANDBOX**
Director:	Irwin Kershner
Co-stars:	David Selby Ariane Heller Jane Hoffman

1972	**WHAT'S UP DOC ?**
Director:	Peter Bogdanovich
Co-stars:	Ryan O'Neal Kenneth Mars Madeline Kahn

1973	**THE WAY WE WERE**
Director:	Sydney Pollack
Co-stars:	Robert Redford Patrick O'Neal Lois Chiles

1974	**FOR PETE'S SAKE**
Director:	Peter Yates
Co-stars:	Michael Sarazin Estelle Parsons Molly Picon

1975	**FUNNY LADY**
Director:	Herbert Ross
Co-stars:	James Caan Omar Sharif Roddy McDowall

1976	**A STAR IS BORN**
Director:	Frank Pierson
Co-stars:	Kris Kristofferson Paul Mazursky Gary Busey

1979	**THE MAIN EVENT**
Director:	Howard Zieff
Co-stars:	Ryan O'Neal Paul Sand Patti D'Arbanville

1981	**ALL NIGHT LONG**
Director:	Jean Claude Tramont
Co-stars:	Gene Hackman Diane Ladd Dennis Quaid

1983	**YENTL**
Director:	Barbra Streisand
Co-stars:	Mandy Patinkin Amy Irving Steven Hill

1987	**NUTS**
Director:	Martin Ritt
Co-stars:	Richard Dreyfuss Karl Malden Eli Wallach

| 1990 | **LISTEN UP: THE LIVES OF QUINCY JONES** |
| *Director:* | Ellen Weissbrod (Documentary) |

1991	**THE PRINCE OF TIDES**
Director:	Barbra Streisand
Co-stars:	Nick Nolte Blythe Danner Melinda Dillon

1997	**THE MIRROR HAS TWO FACES**
Director:	Barbra Streisand
Co-stars:	Jeff Bridges Mimi Rogers Pierce Brosnan

MARIA STRELKOVA

1934	**JAZZ COMEDY**
Director:	Grigori Alexandrov
Co-stars:	Lubov Orlova Leonid Utyosov

MELISSA STRIBLING

1958	**DRACULA**
Director:	Terence Fisher
Co-stars:	Peter Cushing Christopher Lee Carol Marsh

1958	**SAFECRACKER**
Director:	Ray Milland
Co-stars:	Ray Milland Barry Jones Jeanette Sterke

1960	**THE LEAGUE OF GENTLEMEN**
Director:	Basil Dearden
Co-stars:	Jack Hawkins Nigel Patrick Roger Livesey

1961	**THE SECRET PARTNER**
Director:	Basil Dearden
Co-stars:	Stewart Granger Haya Harareet Bernard Lee

1968   **ONLY WHEN I LARF**
Director: Basil Dearden
Co-stars: Richard Attenborough David Hemmings Alexandra Stewart

1971   **CRUCIBLE OF TERROR**
Director: Ted Hooker
Co-stars: Mike Raven James Bolam Ronald Lacey

1974   **CONFESSIONS OF A WINDOW CLEANER**
Director: Val Guest
Co-stars: Robin Askwith Anthony Booth Bill Maynard

ELAINE STRICH

1955   **THE SCARLET HOUR**
Director: Michael Curtiz
Co-stars: Carol Ohmart Tom Tyron Jody Lawrance

1956   **THREE VIOLENT PEOPLE**
Director: Rudolph Mate
Co-stars: Charlton Heston Anne Baxter Tom Tyron

1957   **A FAREWELL TO ARMS**
Director: Charles Vidor
Co-stars: Jennifer Jones Rock Hudson Vittorio De Sica

1958   **THE PERFECT FURLOUGH**
Director: Blake Edwards
Co-stars: Tony Curtis Janet Leigh Keenan Wynn

1975   **THE SPIRAL STAIRCASE**
Director: Peter Collinson
Co-stars: Jacqueline Bisset Christopher Plummer

1977   **PROVIDENCE**
Director: Alain Resnais
Co-stars: John Gielgud Dirk Bogarde Ellen Burstyn

1987   **SEPTEMBER**
Director: Woody Allen
Co-stars: Mia Farrow Denholm Elliott Dianne Wiest

1988   **COCOON: THE RETURN**
Director: Daniel Petrie
Co-stars: Don Ameche Hume Cronyn Jessica Tandy

1990   **THE PRICE OF PASSION**
Director: Richard Colla
Co-stars: Victoria Principal Ted Wass Ralph Waite

1990   **RUNAWAY HEART**
Director: James Frawley
Co-stars: Jill Eikenberry Michael Tucker Ray Wise

GAIL STRICKLAND

1975   **THE DROWNING POOL**
Director: Stuart Rosenberg
Co-stars: Paul Newman Joanne Woodward Melanie Griffith

1976   **BOUND FOR GLORY**
Director: Hal Ashby
Co-stars: David Carradine Ronny Cox Melinda Dillon

1977   **ONE ON ONE**
Director: Lamont Johnson
Co-stars: Robby Benson Annette O'Toole

1978   **WHO'LL STOP THE RAIN**
Director: Karel Reisz
Co-stars: Nick Nolte Michael Moriarty Tuesday Weld

1979   **NORMA RAE**
Director: Martin Ritt
Co-stars: Sally Field Beau Bridges Ron Leibman

1980   **KING CRAB**
Director: Marvin Chomsky
Co-stars: Barry Newman Julie Bovasso Jeffrey DeMunn

1982   **MY BODY, MY CHILD**
Director: Marvin Chomsky
Co-stars: Vanessa Redgrave Joseph Campanella Stephen Elliott

1983   **STARFLIGHT: THE PLANE THAT COULDN'T LAND**
Director: Jerry Jameson
Co-stars: Lee Majors Lauren Hutton Ray Milland

1984   **PROTOCOL**
Director: Herbert Ross
Co-stars: Goldie Hawn Chris Sarandon Cliff De Young

1984   **OXFORD BLUES**
Director: Robert Boris
Co-stars: Rob Lowe Ally Sheedy Julian Sands

1991   **THE MAN IN THE MOON**
Director: Robert Mulligan
Co-stars: Sam Waterston Tess Harper Reese Witherspoon

1993   **THREE OF HEARTS**
Director: Yurek Bogayevicz
Co-stars: Kelly Lynch Sherilyn Fenn William Baldwin

1994   **WHEN A MAN LOVES A WOMAN**
Director: Luis Mandoki
Co-stars: Andy Garcia Meg Ryan Ellen Burstyn

EWA STROEMBERG

1970   **THE DEVIL CAME FROM ARKANSAS**
Director: Jesus Franco
Co-stars: Fred Williams Susann Korda Horst Tappert

KANDICE STROH

1980   **FOXES**
Director: Adrian Lyne
Co-stars: Jodie Foster Sally Kellerman Adam Faith

TARA STROHMEIER

1976   **THE GREAT TEXAS DYNAMITE CHASE**
Director: Michael Pressman
Co-stars: Claudia Jennings Jocelyn Jones Johnny Crawford

1976   **HOLLYWOOD BOULEVARD**
Director: Joe Dante
Co-stars: Candice Rialson Mary Woronov Rita George

ULLA STROMSTEDT

1970   **TARZAN'S JUNGLE REBELLION**
Director: William Whitney
Co-stars: Ron Ely Sam Jaffe William Marshall

TAMI STRONACH

1984   **THE NEVERENDING STORY**
Director: Wolfgang Petersen
Co-stars: Barret Oliver Gerald McRaney Patricia Hayes

BRENDA STRONG

1993   **ISLAND CITY**
Director: Jorge Montesi
Co-stars: Kevin Conroy Eric McCormack Pete Koch

GWYNETH STRONG

1972   **NOTHING BUT THE NIGHT**
Director: Peter Sasdy
Co-stars: Christopher Lee Peter Cushing Diana Dors

1980   **DARK WATER**
Director: Andrew Bogle
Co-stars: Phil Davis David Beames

1997   **A TOUCH OF FROST: TRUE CONFESSIONS**
Director: Sandy Johnson
Co-stars: David Jason Isla Blair Kenneth Cope

PAULINE STROUD

1951   **LADY GODIVA RIDES AGAIN**
Director: Frank Launder
Co-stars: Dennis Price Diana Dors Kay Kendall

SALLY ANN STROUD

1974 FOXY BROWN
Director: Jack Hill
Co-stars: Pam Grier Antonio Fargas Peter Brown

KAY STROZZI

1931 CAPTAIN APPLEJACK
Director: Hobart Henley
Co-stars: John Halliday Mary Brian Louise Closser Hale

SALLY STRUTHERS

1970 FIVE EASY PIECES
Director: Bob Rafelson
Co-stars: Jack Nicholson Karen Black Susan Anspach

1972 THE GETAWAY
Director: Sam Peckinpah
Co-stars: Steve McQueen Ali MacGraw Ben Johnson

1974 ALOHA MEANS GOODBYE
Director: David Lowell Rich

1975 HEY, I'M ALIVE!
Director: Lawrence Schiller
Co-star: Ed Asher

1979 AND YOUR NAME IS JONAH
Director: Richard Michaels
Co-stars: James Woods Randee Heller Robert Davi

1981 A GUN IN THE HOUSE
Director: Ivan Nagy
Co-stars: David Ackroyd Millie Perkins Jeffrey Tambor

1989 A DEADLY SILENCE
Director: John Patterson
Co-stars: Mike Farrell Bruce Weitz Heather Fairfield

1992 IN THE BEST INTEREST OF THE CHILDREN
Director: Michael Ray Rhodes
Co-stars: Sarah Jessica Parker Elizabeth Ashley

AMY STRYKER

1978 A WEDDING
Director: Robert Altman
Co-stars: Carol Burnett Paul Dooley Mia Farrow

1984 IMPULSE
Director: Graham Baker
Co-stars: Tim Matheson Meg Tilly Hume Cronyn

BARBARA STUART

1969 HELLFIGHTERS
Director: Andrew McLaglen
Co-stars: John Wayne Jim Hutton Katherine Ross

1984 BACHELOR PARTY
Director: Neal Israel
Co-stars: Tom Hanks Tawny Kitaen George Grizzard

BINKI STUART (Child)

1936 KEEP YOUR SEATS PLEASE
Director: Monty Banks
Co-stars: George Formby Florence Desmond Alastair Sim

1937 MOONLIGHT SONATA
Director: Lothar Mendes
Co-stars: Ignace Paderewski Eric Portman Marie Tempest

1937 OUR FIGHTING NAVY
Director: Norman Walker
Co-stars: Robert Douglas Noah Beery H.B. Warner

1937 SPLINTERS IN THE AIR
Director: Jack Raymond
Co-star: Sidney Howard

1938 SEEING STARS
Co-star: Laurence Olivier

1938 ROSE OF TRALEE

1938 LITTLE MISS SOMEBODY

1938 LITTLY DOLLY DAYDREAMS

1939 MY IRISH MOLLY

CASSIE STUART

1984 SECRET PLACES
Director: Zelda Baron
Co-stars: Marie-Therese Relin Tara MacGowran Jenny Agutter

1987 HIDDEN CITY
Director: Stephen Poliakoff
Co-stars: Charles Dance Bill Paterson Richard E. Grant

1988 THE PICNIC
Director: Paul Seed
Co-stars: Billie Whitelaw Iain Glen Brenda Fricker

1988 STEALING HEAVEN
Director: Clive Donner
Co-stars: Derek De Lint Kim Thompson Denholm Elliott

GLORIA STUART
(Gloria Von Dietrich Stuart Finch)
Nominated For Best Supporting Actress In 1998 For "Titanic"

1932 THE OLD DARK HOUSE
Director: James Whale
Co-stars: Charles Laughton Melvyn Douglas Raymond Massey

1932 STREET OF WOMEN
Director: Archie Mayo
Co-stars: Kay Francis Alan Dinehart Roland Young

1932 LAUGHTER IN HELL
Co-star: Pat O'Brien

1932 THE ALL-AMERICAN
Director: Russell Mack
Co-stars: Richard Arlen Andy Devine Preston Foster

1932 AIR MAIL
Director: John Ford
Co-stars: Pat O'Brien Ralph Bellamy Russell Hopton

1933 BELOVED
Director: Victor Schertzinger
Co-stars: John Boles Albert Conti Dorothy Peterson

1933 THE GIRL IN 419
Co-star: James Dunn

1933 THE INVISIBLE MAN
Director: James Whale
Co-stars: Claude Rains Henry Travers Una O'Connor

1933 ROMAN SCANDALS
Director: Frank Tuttle
Co-stars: Eddie Cantor Ruth Etting Edward Arnold

1933 THE SECRET OF THE BLUE ROOM
Director: Kurt Neuman
Co-stars: Lionel Atwill Paul Lukas Edward Arnold

1934 HERE COMES THE NAVY
Director: Lloyd Bacon
Co-stars: James Cagney Pat O'Brien Frank McHugh

1934 THE GIFT OF GAB
Director: Karl Freund
Co-stars: Edmund Lowe Ruth Etting Ethel Waters

1935 MAYBE IT'S LOVE
Co-stars: Ruth Donnelly Henry Travers Frank McHugh

1935 GOLD DIGGERS OF 1935
Director: Bushby Berkeley
Co-stars: Dick Powell Adolphe Menjou Alice Brady

1935 SECRETS OF CHINA TOWN

1936 THE CRIME OF DR FORBES
Director: George Marshall
Co-stars: Robert Kent J. Edward Bromberg Sara Haden

1936 THE GIRL ON THE FRONT PAGE
Director: Harry Beaumont
Co-stars: Edmund Lowe Spring Byington Richard Owen

1936 POOR LITTLE RICH GIRL
Director: Irving Cummings
Co-stars: Shirley Temple Jack Haley Alice Faye

1936 THE PRISONER OF SHARK ISLAND
Director: John Ford
Co-stars: Warner Baxter Harry Carey John Carradine

1936 PROFESSIONAL SOLDIER
Director: Tay Garnett
Co-stars: Victor McLaglen Freddie Bartholomew Constance Collier

1936 WANTED: JANE TURNER
Director: Edward Killy
Co-stars: Lee Tracy Judith Blake John McGuire

1937 LIFE BEGINS IN COLLEGE
Director: William Seiter
Co-stars: Joan Davis Tony Martin Ritz Bros.

1937 GIRL OVERBOARD
Co-star: Walter Pidgeon

1938 KEEP SMILING
Director: John Stone
Co-stars: Jane Withers Henry Wilcoxon Helen Westley

1938 CHANGE OF HEART
Director: James Tinling
Co-stars: Michael Whalen Lyle Talbot Jane Darwell

1938 REBECCA OF SUNNYBROOK FARM
Director: Allan Dwan
Co-stars: Shirley Temple Randolph Scott Jack Haley

1939 THE THREE MUSKETEERS
Director: Allan Dwan
Co-stars: Don Ameche Ritz Bros. Pauline Moore

1939 IT COULD HAPPEN TO YOU
Director: Alfred Werker
Co-stars: Stuart Erwin Raymond Walburn Douglas Fowley

1946 SHE WROTE THE BOOK
Director: Charles Lamont
Co-stars: Joan Davis Mischa Auer Jack Oakie

1998 TITANIC
Director: James Cameron
Co-stars: Kate Winslet Leonardo Di Caprio Billy Zane

JEANNE STUART

1935 DEATH ON THE SET
Director: Leslie Hiscott
Co-stars: Henry Kendall Eve Gray Garry Marsh

JOSEPHINE STUART

1947 MY BROTHER JONATHAN
Director: Harold French
Co-stars: Michael Dennison Dulcie Gray Ronald Howard

1947 THE LOVES OF JOANNA GODDEN
Director: Charles Frend
Co-stars: Googie Withers John McCallum Jean Kent

MAXINE STUART

1975 THE PRISONER OF SECOND AVENUE
Director: Melvin Frank
Co-stars: Jack Lemmon Anne Bancroft Gene Saks

1980 COAST TO COAST
Director: Joseph Sargent
Co-stars: Dyan Cannon Robert Blake Michael Lerner

1993 THE HAUNTING OF SEACLIFF INN
Director: Walter Klenhard
Co-stars: Ally Sheedy William R. Moses Louise Fletcher

RANDY STUART (Child)

1948 APARTMENT FOR PEGGY
Director: George Seaton
Co-stars: Jeanne Crain William Holden Edmund Gwenn

1948 SITTING PRETTY
Director: Walter Lang
Co-stars: Clifton Webb Robert Young Maureen O'Hara

1949 DANCING IN THE DARK
Director: Irving Reis
Co-stars: William Powell Betsy Drake Mark Stevens

1949 I WAS A MALE WAR BRIDE
Director: Howard Hawks
Co-stars: Cary Grant Ann Sheridan Marion Marshall

1950 ALL ABOUT EVE
Director: Joseph Mankiewicz
Co-stars: Bette Davies Anne Baxter George Sanders

1951 I CAN GET IT FOR YOU WHOLESALE
Director: Michael Gordon
Co-stars: Susan Hayward Dan Dailey George Sanders

1952 ROOM FOR ONE MORE
Director: Norman Taurog
Co-stars: Cary Grant Betsy Drake George Winslow

1957 THE INCREDIBLE SHRINKING MAN
Director: Jack Arnold
Co-stars: Grant Williams April Kent Paul Langton

IMOGEN STUBBS (Partner Trevor Nunn)

1988 A SUMMER STORY
Director: Piers Haggard
Co-stars: James Wilby Ken Colley Susannah York

1988 DEADLINE
Director: Richard Stroud
Co-stars: John Hurt Robert McBain Julian Curry

1989 ERIK THE VIKING
Director: Terry Jones
Co-stars: Terry Jones Tim Robbins Mickey Rooney

1989 FELLOW TRAVELLER
Director: Philip Saville
Co-stars: Ron Silver Hart Bochner Daniel J. Travanti

1991 TRUE COLOURS
Director: Herbert Ross
Co-stars: John Cusack James Spader Mandy Patinkin

1993 ANNA LEE: HEADCASE
Director: Colin Bucksey
Co-stars: Alan Howard Michael Bryant Brian Glover

1994 A PIN FOR THE BUTTERFLY
Director: Hannah Kodichek
Co-stars: Hugh Laurie Ian Bannen Joan Plowright

1996 SENSE AND SENSIBILITY
Director: Ang Lee
Co-stars: Emma Thompson Hugh Grant Kate Winslet

1996 TWELTH NIGHT
Director: Trevor Nunn
Co-stars: Ben Kingsley Nigel Hawthorne Richard E. Grant

1997 MOTHERTIME
Director: Matthew Jacobs
Co-stars: Gina McKee Kate Maberley Anthony Andrews

UNA STUBBS

1962 SUMMER HOLIDAY
Director: Peter Yates
Co-stars: Cliff Richards Lauri Peters Ron Moody

1964 WONDERFUL LIFE
Director: Sidney Furie
Co-stars: Cliff Richards Susan Hampshire Walter Slezak

1965 THREE HATS FOR LISA
Director: Sidney Hayers
Co-stars: Joe Brown Sid James Sophie Hardy

1968 TILL DEATH US DO PART
Director: Norman Cohen
Co-stars: Warren Mitchell Dandy Nicholls Tony Booth

1973 PENNY GOLD
Director: Jack Cardiff
Co-stars: James Booth Francesca Annis

VICTORIA STUDD

1982 PRIVILEGED
Director: Michael Hoffman
Co-stars: Robert Woolley Hugh Grant James Wilby

OLIVE STURGESS

1963 THE RAVEN
Director: Roger Corman
Co-stars: Vincent Price Peter Lorre Boris Karloff

ANGELIKA STUTE

1983 MISCHIEF
Director: Peter Fleischmann
Co-stars: Peter Fleischmann Isolde Barth Baldwin Baas

DARLENE STUTO

1981 MS. 45
Director: Abel Ferrara
Co-stars: Zoe Tamerlis Steve Singer Peter Yellen

TRUDIE STYLER *(Married Sting)*

1985 BRING ON THE NIGHT
Director: Michael Apted
Co-stars: Sting Omar Hakim Miles Copeland

1989 FAIR GAME
Director: Mario Orfini
Co-stars: Gregg Henry Bill Moseley

1996 THE GROTESQUE
Co-stars: Sting Alan Bates Theresa Russell

AMBER STYLES

1991 DREAM ON
Director: Kitty Fitzgerald
Co-stars: Maureen Harold Anna-Maria Gascoigne Ray Stubbs

HERKIE STYLES

1960 THE BELLBOY
Director: Jerry Lewis
Co-stars: Jerry Leiws Milton Berle Alex Gerry

MARINA SUDINA

1996 MUTE WITNESS
Director: Anthony Waller

MOLLIE SUGDEN

1977 ARE YOU BEING SERVED ?
Director: Bob Kellett
Co-stars: John Inman Frank Thornton Wendy Richards

1992 THE PRINCESS AND THE GOBLIN *(Voice)*
Director: Jozsef Gemes
Co-stars: Joss Ackland Claire Bloom Roy Kinnear

BARBARA SUKOWA

1979 BERLIN ALEXANDERPLATZ
Director: Rainer Werner Fassbinder
Co-stars: Gunter Lamprecht Hanna Schygulla

1981 THE GERMAN SISTERS
Director: Margarethe Von Trotta
Co-stars: Jutte Lampe Rudiger Vogler Doris Schade

1982 DEADLY GAME
Director: Karoly Makk
Co-stars: Helmut Berger Mel Ferrer

1982 LOLA
Director: Rainer Werner Fassbinder
Co-stars: Mario Adorf Armin Muller-Stahl Ivan Desny

1987 THE SICILIAN
Director: Michael Cimino
Co-stars: Christopher Lambert Terence Stamp Joss Ackland

1991 VOYAGER
Director: Volker Schlondorff
Co-stars: Sam Shepard Julie Delpy Traci Lind

1992 EUROPA
Director: Lars Von Trier
Co-stars: Jean-Marc Barr Udo Kier Eddie Constantine

1993 M BUTTERFLY
Director: David Cronenberg
Co-stars: Jeremy Irons John Lone Ian Richardson

ANIA SULI

1994 FUN
Director: Rafal Zielinski
Co-stars: Alicia Witt Renee Humphrey Leslie Hope

MARGARET SULLAVAN
(Married Henry Fonda, Leland Hayward)
Nominated For Best Actress In 1938 For "Three Comrades"

1933 ONLY YESTERDAY
Director: John Stahl
Co-stars: John Boles Billie Burke Reginald Denny

1934 LITTLE MAN, WHAT NOW?
Director: Frank Borzage
Co-stars: Douglass Montgomery Alan Hale Mae Marsh

1934 THE GOOD FAIRY
Director: William Wyler
Co-stars: Frank Morgan Herbert Marshall Beulah Bondi

1935 SO RED THE ROSE
Director: King Vidor
Co-stars: Randolph Scott Walter Connelly Robert Cummings

1936 THE NEXT TIME WE LOVE
Director: Edward Griffith
Co-stars: James Stewart Ray Milland Grant Mitchell

1936 THE MOON'S OUR HOME
Director: William Seiter
Co-stars: Henry Fonda Beulah Bondi Charles Butterworth

1938 THREE COMRADES
Director: Frank Borzage
Co-stars: Robert Taylor Robert Young Franchot Tone

1938 THE SHINING HOUR
Director: Frank Borzage
Co-stars: Joan Crawford Melvyn Douglas Robert Young

1938 THE SHOPWORN ANGEL
Director: H.C. Potter
Co-stars: James Stewart Walter Pidgeon Hattie McDaniel

1940 THE SHOP AROUND THE CORNER
Director: Ernst Lubitsch
Co-stars: James Stewart Frank Morgan Sara Haden

1940 THE MORTAL STORM
Director: Frank Borzage
Co-stars: Frank Morgan James Stewart Robert Young

1941 SO ENDS OUR NIGHT
Director: John Cromwell
Co-stars: Fredric March Glenn Ford Erich Von Stroheim

1941 BACK STREET
Director: Robert Stevenson
Co-stars: Charles Boyer Richard Carlson Tim Holt

1941 APPOINTMENT FOR LOVE
Director: William Seiter
Co-stars: Charles Boyer Eugene Pallette Rita Johnson

1943 CRY HAVOC
Director: Richard Thorpe
Co-stars: Joan Blondell Ann Sothern Marsha Hunt

1950 NO SAD SONGS FOR ME
Director: Rudolph Mate
Co-stars: Wendell Corey Natalie Wood Viveca Lindfors

DAIL SULLIVAN

1993 CENTURY
Director: Stephen Poliakoff
Co-stars: Charles Dance Clive Owen Miranda Richardson

JEAN SULLIVAN

1944 UNCERTAIN GLORY
Director: Raoul Walsh
Co-stars: Errol Flynn Paul Lukas Lucile Watson

1945 ROUGHLY SPEAKING
Director: Michael Curtiz
Co-stars: Rosalind Russell Jack Carson Robert Hutton

1945 ESCAPE IN THE DESERT
Director: Edward Blatt
Co-stars: Philip Dorn Helmut Dantine Irene Manning

1976 SQUIRM
Director: Jeff Lieberman
Co-stars: John Scardino Patricia Pearcey Fran Higgins

JENNY SULLIVAN

1971 PLAZA SUITE
Director: Arthur Hiller
Co-stars: Walter Matthau Maureen Stapleton Lee Grant

SUSAN SULLIVAN

1977 THE INCREDIBLE HULK
Director: Kenneth Johnson
Co-stars: Bill Bixby Lou Ferrigno Jack Colvin

1978 THE NEW MAVERICK
Director: Hy Averback
Co-stars: Charles Frank James Garner Jack Kelly

YMA SUMAC

1954 SECRET OF THE INCAS
Director: Jerry Hopper
Co-stars: Charlton Heston Robert Young Nicole Maurey

1956 OMAR KHAYAM
Director: William Dieterle
Co-stars: Cornel Wilde Michael Rennie Debra Paget

DONNA SUMMER

1978 THANK GOD IT'S FRIDAY
Director: Robert Klane
Co-stars: Valerie Landsburg Terri Nunn Chick Vennera

ELEANOR SUMMERFIELD

1948 LONDON BELONGS TO ME
Director: Sidney Gilliat
Co-stars: Alastair Sim Stephen Murray Richard Attenborough

1949 NO WAY BACK
Co-stars: Terence De Marney Jack Raine

1952 THE LAST PAGE
Director: Terence Fisher
Co-stars: George Brent Marguerite Chapman Diana Dors

1952 ISN'T LIFE WONDERFUL ?
Director: Harold French
Co-stars: Donald Wolfit Eileen Herlie Cecil Parker

1953 STREET CORNER
Director: Muriel Box
Co-stars: Rosamund John Anne Crawford Peggy Cummins

1954 FACE THE MUSIC
Director: Terence Fisher
Co-stars: Alex Nicol Paul Carpenter Geoffrey Keen

1955 LOST
Director: Guy Green
Co-stars: David Knight Julia Arnall David Farrarr

1956 ODONGO
Director: John Gilling
Co-stars: MacDonald Carey Rhonda Fleming Earl Cameron

1956 IT'S GREAT TO BE YOUNG
Director: Cyril Frankel
Co-stars: John Mills Cecil Parker Jeremy Spenser

1958 A CRY FROM THE STREETS
Director: Lewis Gilbert
Co-stars: Max Bygraves Barbara Murray Colin Petersen

1961 DON'T BOTHER TO KNOCK
Director: Cyril Frankel
Co-stars: Richard Todd Elke Sommer June Thorburn

1961 ON THE FIDDLE
Director: Cyril Frankel
Co-stars: Alfred Lynch Sean Connery Cecil Parker

1961 PETTICOAT PIRATES
Director: David MacDonald
Co-stars: Charlie Drake Cecil Parker Anne Heywood

1961 SPARE THE ROD
Director: Leslie Norman
Co-stars: Max Bygraves Geoffrey Keen Richard O'Sullivan

1962 ON THE BEAT
Director: Robert Asher
Co-stars: Norman Wisdom Jennifer Jayne Raymond Huntley

1963 THE RUNNING MAN
Director: Carol Reed
Co-stars: Laurence Harvey Alan Bates Lee Remick

1962 GUNS OF DARKNESS
Director: Anthony Asquith
Co-stars: David Niven Leslie Caron James Robertson Justice

1969 THE SPY KILLER
Director: Roy Baker
Co-stars: Robert Horton Sebastian Cabot Jill St. John

1970 SOME WILL, SOME WON'T
Director: Duncan Wood
Co-stars: Ronnie Corbett Thora Hird Leslie Phillips

DOROTHY SUMMERS

1943 IT'S THAT MAN AGAIN
Director: Walter Forde
Co-stars: Tommy Handley Jack Train Greta Gynt

JOANIE SUMMERS
1961 EVERYTHING'S DUCKIE
Director: Don Taylor
Co-stars: Mickey Rooney Buddy Hackett Jackie Cooper

IRENE SUNTERS
1987 THE DARK ROOM
Director: Guy Slater
Co-stars: Susan Wooldridge Philip Jackson Julie Graham

CONCHITA SUPERVIA
1934 EVENSONG
Director: Victor Saville
Co-stars: Evelyn Laye Fritz Kortner Emlyn Williams

HELENE SURGERE
1975 SALO OR THE 120 DAYS OF SODOM
Director: Pier Paolo Pasolini
Co-stars: Paolo Bonacelli Giorgio Cataldi

1977 LA MACHINE
Director: Paul Vecchiali
Co-stars: Jean-Christophe Bouvet Sonia Saviange Monique Melinaud

1989 AUSTRALIA
Director: Jean-Jacques Andrien
Co-stars: Jeremy Irons Fanny Ardant Agnes Soral

CAROL-ANN SUSI
1987 THE SECRET OF MY SUCCESS
Director: Herbert Ross
Co-stars: Michael J. Fox Helen Slater Richard Jordan

MARIE SUSINI
1967 MOUCHETTE
Director: Robert Bresson
Co-stars: Nadine Nortier Jean-Claude Guilbert Maria Cardinal

CLARE SUTCLIFFE
1969 I START COUNTING
Director: David Greene
Co-stars: Jenny Agutter Brian Marshall Simon Ward

ANN SUTHERLAND
1931 MY SIN
Director: George Abbott
Co-stars: Tallulah Bankhead Fredric March Harry Davenport

KRISTINE SUTHERLAND
1989 HONEY, I SHRUNK THE KIDS
Director: Joe Johnston
Co-stars: Rick Moranis Marcia Strasman Matt Frewer

DOLORES SUTTON
1976 F. SCOTT FITZGERALD IN HOLLYWOOD
Director: Anthony Page
Co-stars: Jason Miller Tuesday Weld Julia Foster

1991 TALES FROM THE DARKSIDE: THE MOVIE
Director: John Harrison
Co-stars: Deborah Harry Christian Slater Steve Buscemi

KAY SUTTON
1938 THE SAINT IN NEW YORK
Director: Ben Holmes
Co-stars: Louis Hayward Sig Ruman Jack Carson

LISA SUTTON
1984 RAW COURAGE
Director: Robert Rosen
Co-stars: Ronny Cox Lois Chiles Art Hindle

JANET SUZMAN
Nominated For Best Actress In 1971 For "Nicholas And Alexandra"
1971 NICHOLAS AND ALEXANDRA
Director: Franklin Schaffner
Co-stars: Michael Jayston Lynne Frederick

1971 A DAY IN THE DEATH OF JOE EGG
Director: Peter Medak
Co-stars: Alan Bates Peter Bowles Sheila Gish

1974 THE BLACK WINDMILL
Director: Don Siegel
Co-stars: Michael Caine Joseph O'Connor Delphine Seyrig

1976 VOYAGE OF THE DAMNED
Director: Stuart Rosenberg
Co-stars: Oskar Werner Faye Dunaway Max Von Sydow

1980 NIJINSKY
Director: Herbert Ross
Co-stars: Alan Bates George De La Pena Alan Badel

1981 PRIEST OF LOVE
Director: Christopher Miles
Co-stars: Ian McKellen Ava Gardner Penelope Keith

1983 THE DRAUGHTMAN'S CONTRACT
Director: Peter Greenaway
Co-stars: Anthony Higgins Anne Louise Lambert

1983 AND THE SHIP SAILS ON
Director: Federico Fellini
Co-stars: Freddie Jones Barbara Jefford

1984 THE ZANY ADVENTURES OF ROBIN HOOD
Director: Ray Austin
Co-stars: George Segal Morgan Fairchild

1989 A DRY WHITE SEASON
Director: Euzhan Palcy
Co-stars: Donald Sutherland Susan Sarandon Marlon Brando

1990 NUNS ON THE RUN
Director: Jonathan Lynn
Co-stars: Eric Idle Robbie Coltrane Camille Coduri

1993 INSPECTOR MORSE: DEADLY SLUMBER
Director: Stuart Orme
Co-stars: John Thaw Kevin Whately Brian Cox

INGER SVENSON
1962 ADVISE AND CONSENT
Director: Otto Preminger
Co-stars: Don Murray Charles Laughton Henry Fonda

DORIS SVETLUND
1949 THE DEVIL'S WANTON
Director: Ingmar Bergman
Co-stars: Birger Malmsten Eva Henning Hasse Ekman

DOMINIQUE SWAIN
1998 LOLITA
Co-stars: Jeremy Irons Melanie Griffith

NICOLA SWAIN
1988 ARIA
Director: Nicolas Roeg
Co-stars: John Hurt Elizabeth Hurley Bridget Fonda

HARDA SWANHILDE
1945 CAESAR AND CLEOPATRA
Director: Gabriel Pascal
Co-stars: Claude Rains Vivien Leigh Stewart Granger

HILARY SWANK

1994 THE NEXT KARATE KID
Director: Christopher Cain
Co-stars: Pat Morita Michael Ironside

1996 SLEEPWALKER
Director: John Cosgrove
Co-stars: Jeffrey Nordling Charles Esten

ALISON SWANN

1992 A LITTLE BIT OF LIPPY
Director: Chris Bernard
Co-stars: Kenneth Cranham Rachel Davies Tina Earl

GLORIA SWANSON

Nominated For Best Actress In 1929 For "The Trespasser" And In 1950 For "Sunset Boulevard"

1919 MALE AND FEMALE
Director: Cecil B. DeMille
Co-stars: Bebe Daniels Thomas Meighan Lila Lee

1921 THE AFFAIRS OF ANATOLE
Director: Cecil B. DeMille
Co-stars: Wallace Reid Bebe Daniels Monte Blue

1924 MANHANDLED
Director: Allan Dwan
Co-stars: Tom Moore Frank Morgan Lilyan Tashman

1925 MADAME SANS-GENE
Director: Leonce Perret
Co-stars: Charles De Roche Emile Drain

1925 STAGE STRUCK
Director: Allan Dwan
Co-stars: Lawrence Gray Gertrude Astor Ford Sterling

1927 THE LOVES OF SUNYA
Director: Albert Parker
Co-stars: John Boles Flobelle Fairbanks Hugh Miller

1927 COAST OF FOLLY

1928 QUEEN KELLY
Director: Eric Von Stroheim
Co-stars: Walter Byron Seena Owen Madge Hunt

1928 SADIE THOMPSON
Director: Raoul Walsh
Co-stars: Charles Lane Lionel Barrymore Blanche Federici

1929 THE TRESPASSER
Director: Edmund Goulding
Co-stars: Robert Ames Purnell Pratt William Holden

1930 WHAT A WIDOW!
Co-star: Owen Moore

1931 TONIGHT OR NEVER
Director: Mervyn LeRoy
Co-stars: Melvyn Douglas Alison Skipworth Boris Karloff

1931 INDISCREET
Director: Leo McCarey
Co-stars: Ben Lyon Monroe Owsley Barbara Kent

1933 PERFECT UNDERSTANDING
Director: Cyril Gardner
Co-stars: Laurence Olivier John Halliday Nigel Playfair

1934 MUSIC IN THE AIR
Director: Joe May
Co-stars: John Boles Douglass Montgomery Reginald Owen

1941 FATHER TAKES A WIFE
Director: Jack Hively
Co-stars: Adolphe Menjou Desi Arnaz John Howard

1950 SUNSET BOULEVARD
Director: Billy Wilder
Co-stars: William Holden Erich Von Stroheim

1952 THREE FOR BEDROOM C
Director: Milton Bren
Co-stars: Fred Clark Steve Brodie Margaret Dumont

1959 WHEN COMEDY WAS KING
Director: Robert Youngston
Co-stars: Stan Laurel Oliver Hardy Charlie Chaplin

1974 AIRPORT '75
Director: Jack Smight
Co-stars: Charlton Heston Myrna Loy Helen Reddy

1974 KILLER BEES
Director: Curtis Harrington
Co-star: Edward Albert

KRISTY SWANSON

1986 DEADLY FRIEND
Director: Wes Craven
Co-stars: Matthew Laborteaux Anne Twomey Anne Ramsey

1987 FLOWERS IN THE ATTIC
Director: Jeffrey Bloom
Co-stars: Louise Fletcher Victoria Tennant Jeb Stuart

1991 HOT SHOTS!
Director: Jim Abrahams
Co-stars: Charlie Sheen Cary Elwes Valeria Golino

1991 MANNEQUIN TWO: ON THE MOVE
Director: Stewart Raffill
Co-stars: William Ragsdale Terry Kizer Stuart Pankin

1992 BUFFY THE VAMPIRE SLAYER
Director: Fran Rubel Kuzui
Co-stars: Donald Sutherland Rutger Hauer Luke Perry

1993 THE PROGRAM
Director: David Ward
Co-stars: James Caan Halle Berry Craig Sheffer

1994 THE CHASE
Director: Adam Rifkin
Co-stars: Charlie Sheen Henry Rollins Josh Mostel

1995 HIGHER LEARNING
Director: John Singleton
Co-stars: Omar Epps Laurence Fishburne Michael Rapaport

1997 THE PHANTOM
Co-stars: Billy Zane Treat Williams Catherine Zeta Jones

1997 EIGHT HEADS IN A DUFFEL BAG
Co-stars: Joe Pesci Dyan Cannon Andy Comeau

LAURA SWANSON

1986 DOGS IN SPACE
Director: Richard Lowenstein
Co-stars: Michael Hutchence Saskia Post Nique Needles

MAUREEN SWANSON

1953 VALLEY OF SONG
Director: Gilbert Gunn
Co-stars: Mervyn Johns Clifford Evans Rachel Roberts

1954 KNIGHTS OF THE ROUND TABLE
Director: Richard Thorpe
Co-stars: Robert Taylor Mel Ferrer Ava Gardner

1955 THIRD PARTY RISK
Director: Daniel Birt
Co-stars: Lloyd Bridges Finlay Currie Simone Silva

1956 UP IN THE WORLD
Director: John Paddy Carstairs
Co-stars: Norman Wisdom Jerry Desmonde Colin Gordon

1956 A TOWN LIKE ALICE
Director: Jack Lee
Co-stars: Virginia McKenna Peter Finch Jean Anderson

1956   **THE SPANISH GARDENER**
Director: Phillip Leacock
Co-stars: Dirk Bogarde Michael Hordern Jon Whiteley

1957   **ROBBERY UNDER ARMS**
Director: Jack Lee
Co-stars: Peter Finch David McCallum Jill Ireland

GLADYS SWARTHOUT

1935   **ROSE OF THE RANCHO**
Director: Marion Gering
Co-stars: John Boles Charles Bickford H.B. Warner

1936   **GIVE US THIS NIGHT**
Co-stars: Jan Kiepura Philip Merivale

1937   **CHAMPAGNE WALTZ**
Director: Edward Sutherland
Co-stars: Fred MacMurray Jack Oakie Fritz Leiber

1938   **AMBUSH**
Director: Kurt Neuman
Co-stars: Lloyd Nolan Ernest Truex Broderick Crawford

1938   **ROMANCE IN THE DARK**
Director: H.C. Potter
Co-stars: John Boles John Barrymore Claire Dodd

JULIA SWAYNE-GORDON

1923   **SCARAMOUCHE**
Director: Rex Ingram
Co-stars: Ramon Novarro Lewis Stone Alice Terry

1930   **DUMBBELLS IN ERMINE**
Co-stars: Beryl Mercer Arthur Hoyt Barbara Kent

JULIA SWEENEY

1994   **IT'S PAT**
Director: Adam Bernstein
Co-star: David Foley

GAIL SWEENY

1983   **FAST TALKING**
Director: Ken Cameron
Co-stars: Rod Zuanic Toni Allaylis Chris Truswell

BLANCHE SWEET

1913   **JUDITH OF BETHULIA**
Director: D.W. Griffith
Co-stars: Henry B. Walthall Lionel Barrymore Lillian Gish

1914   **HOME SWEET HOME**
Director: D.W. Griffith
Co-stars: Henry B. Walthall Lillian Gish Dorothy Gish

1923   **ANNA CHRISTIE**
Director: John Griffith Wray
Co-stars: William Russell Eugenie Besserer George F. Marion

1926   **BLUEBEARD'S SEVEN WIVES**
Director: Alfred Santell
Co-stars: Ben Lyon Lois Wilson Dorothy Sebastian

1930   **SHOWGIRL IN HOLLYWOOD**
Director: Mervyn LeRoy
Co-stars: Alice White Jack Mulhall Ford Sterling

1930   **THE WOMAN RACKET**
Co-star: Tom Moore

SHEILA SWEET

1953   **CONFLICT OF WINGS**
Director: John Eldridge
Co-stars: John Gregson Muriel Pavlow Kieron Moore

1954   **THE ANGEL WHO PAWNED HER HARP**
Director: Alan Bromly
Co-stars: Diane Cilento Felix Aylmer Alfie Bass

1956   **IT'S A GREAT DAY**
Director: John Warrington
Co-stars: Ruth Dunning Edward Evans Christopher Beeney

1959   **LIFE IN EMERGENCY WARD 10**
Director: Robert Day
Co-stars: Michael Craig Dorothy Alison Glyn Owen

INGA SWENSON

1962   **ADVISE AND CONSENT**
Director: Otto Preminger
Co-stars: Don Murray Charles Laughton Henry Fonda

1962   **THE MIRACLE-WORKER**
Director: Arthur Penn
Co-stars: Anne Bancroft Patty Duke Victory Jory

SUSAN SWIFT (Child)

1977   **AUDREY ROSE**
Director: Robert Wise
Co-stars: Anthony Hopkins Marsha Mason John Beck

NORA SWINBURNE

1933   **PERFECT UNDERSTANDING**
Director: Cyril Gardner
Co-stars: Gloria Swanson Laurence Olivier Genevieve Tobin

1935   **JURY'S EVIDENCE**
Director: Ralph Ince
Co-stars: Margaret Lockwood Hartley Power Sebastian Shaw

1937   **DINNER AT THE RITZ**
Director: Harold Schuster
Co-stars: Annabella Paul Lukas David Niven

1940   **THE FARMER'S WIFE**
Director: Leslie Arliss
Co-stars: Basil Sydney Wilfrid Lawson Patricia Roc

1941   **THEY FLEW ALONE**
Director: Herbert Wilcox
Co-stars: Anna Neagle Robert Newton Edward Chapman

1943   **THE MAN IN GREY**
Director: Leslie Arliss
Co-stars: James Mason Margaret Lockwood Stewart Granger

1943   **DEAR OCTOPUS**
Director: Harold French
Co-stars: Margaret Lockwood Michael Wilding Celia Johnson

1944   **FANNY BY GASLIGHT**
Director: Anthony Asquith
Co-stars: Phyllis Calvert James Mason Stewart Granger

1945   **THEY KNEW MR KNIGHT**
Director: Norman Walker
Co-stars: Mervyn Johns Alfred Drayton Joan Greenwood

1947   **JASSY**
Director: Bernard Knowles
Co-stars: Margaret Lockwood Patricia Roc Dennis Price

1948   **THE BLIND GODDESS**
Director: Harold French
Co-stars: Eric Portman Anne Crawford Michael Dennison

1948   **QUARTET**
Director: Ken Annakin
Co-stars: Mai Zetterling Dirk Bogarde George Cole

1948   **THE BAD LORD BYRON**
Director: David MacDonald
Co-stars: Dennis Price Mai Zetterling Joan Greenwood

1949   **MARRY ME**
Director: Terence Fisher
Co-stars: Derek Bond Susan Shaw Patrick Holt

| | | | |

1949   **FOOLS RUSH IN**
Director: John Paddy Carstairs
Co-stars: Sally Ann Howes Guy Rolfe Raymond Lovell

1950   **MY DAUGHTER JOY**
Director: Gregory Ratoff
Co-stars: Edward G. Robinson Peggy Cummins Richard Greene

1951   **THE RIVER**
Director: Jean Renoir
Co-stars: Adrienne Corri Esmond Knight Arthur Shields

1951   **QUO VADIS**
Director: Mervyn LeRoy
Co-stars: Robert Taylor Deborah Kerr Peter Ustinov

1954   **THE END OF THE AFFAIR**
Director: Edward Dmytryk
Co-stars: Deborah Kerr Van Johnson John Mills

1954   **BETRAYED**
Director: Gottfried Reinhardt
Co-stars: Clark Gable Lana Turner Victor Mature

1959   **THIRD MAN ON THE MOUNTAIN**
Director: Ken Annakin
Co-stars: James MacArthur Michael Rennie Janet Munro

1960   **CONSPIRACY OF HEARTS**
Director: Ralph Thomas
Co-stars: Lilli Palmer Sylvia Syms Yvonne Mitchell

1968   **INTERLUDE**
Director: Kevin Billington
Co-stars: Oskar Werner Barbara Ferris Virginia Maskell

1969   **ANNE OF A THOUSAND DAYS**
Director: Charles Jarrott
Co-stars: Richard Burton Genevieve Bujold

TILDA SWINTON

1986   **CARAVAGGIO**
Director: Derek Jarman
Co-stars: Nigel Terry Sean Bean Robbie Coltrane

1988   **WAR REQUIEM**
Director: Derek Jarman
Co-stars: Nathaniel Parker Laurence Olivier Nigel Terry

1988   **ARIA**
Director: Derek Jarman
Co-stars: Amy Johnson John Hurt Bridget Fonda

1989   **PLAY ME SOMETHING**
Director: Timothy Neat
Co-stars: Lucia Lanzarini Charlie Barron John Berger

1990   **THE GARDEN**
Director: Derek Jarman
Co-stars: Kevin Collins Roger Cook Jody Graber

1991   **EDWARD II**
Director: Derek Jarman
Co-stars: Steven Waddington Kevin Collins Dudley Sutton

1991   **LIES BEFORE KISSES**
Director: Lou Antonio

1992   **MAN TO MAN**
Director: John Maybury

1992   **ORLANDO**
Director: Sally Potter
Co-stars: Billy Zane John Wood Dudley Sutton

1993   **WITTGENSTEIN**
Director: Derek Jarman
Co-stars: Karl Johnson Michael Gough Kevin Collins

1994   **VICTIM OF RAGE**
Director: Armand Mastroianni
Co-star: Brad Johnson

1997   **FEMALE PERVERSIONS**
Co-star: Amy Madigan

LORETTA SWIT

1971   **STAND UP AND BE COUNTED**
Director: Jackie Cooper
Co-stars: Jacqueline Bisset Stella Stevens

1973   **SHIRTS/SKINS**
Director: William Graham
Co-stars: Bill Bixby Doug McClure Rene Auberjonois

1974   **FREEBIE AND THE BEAN**
Director: Richard Rush
Co-stars: James Caan Alan Arkin Jack Kruschen

1975   **THE LAST DAY**
Director: Vincent McEveety
Co-stars: Richard Widmark Richard Jaeckel Gene Evans

1975   **RACE WITH THE DEVIL**
Director: Jack Starrett
Co-stars: Peter Fonda Warren Oates Lara Parker

1981   **S.O.B.**
Director: Blake Edwards
Co-stars: Julie Andrews William Holden Robert Preston

1981   **CAGNEY AND LACEY**
Director: Ted Post
Co-stars: Tyne Daly Al Waxman Joan Copeland

1983   **FIRST AFFAIR**
Director: Gus Trikonis
Co-stars: Melissa Sue Anderson Joel Higgins Robin Morse

1985   **THE EXECUTION**
Director: Paul Wendkos
Co-stars: Rip Torn Sandy Dennis Jessica Walter

1985   **BEER**
Director: Patrick Kelly
Co-stars: Rip Torn Kenneth Mars David Alan Grier

1986   **DREAMS OF GOLD:**
           THE MEL FISHER STORY
Director: James Goldstone
Co-stars: Cliff Robertson Scott Paulin

1986   **WHOOPS APOCALYPSE!**
Director: Tom Bussman
Co-stars: Peter Cook Rik Mayall Richard Wilson

1988   **14 GOING ON 30**
Director: Paul Schneider
Co-stars: Steve Eckholt Patrick Duffy Harry Morgan

1991   **HELL HATH NO FURY**
Director: Thomas Wright
Co-stars: Barbara Eden David Ackroyd Amanda Petersen

TRACY BROOKS SWOPE

1986   **HAPPY NEW YEAR**
Director: John Avildsen
Co-stars: Peter Falk Charles Durning Wendy Hughes

1991   **TOY SOLDIERS**
Director: Daniel Petrie Jnr.
Co-stars: Sean Astin Wil Wheaton Keith Coogan

AMELIE SYBERBERG

1977   **HITLER, A FILM FROM GERMANY**
Director: Hans Jurgen Syberberg
Co-stars: Heinz Schubert Andre Heller Harry Baer

BRENDA SYKES

1971   **THE SKIN GAME**
Director: Paul Bogart
Co-stars: James Garner Lou Gossett Susan Clark

1973 CLEOPATRA JONES
Director: Jack Starrett
Co-stars: Tamara Dobson Shelley Winters Bernie Casey

1975 MANDINGO
Director: Richard Fleischer
Co-stars: James Mason Susan George Ken Norton

REBECCA SYKES

1990 CAPTAIN JOHNNO
Director: Mario Andreacchio
Co-stars: John Waters Damien Walters

SUZAN SYLVESTER

1991 MISTERIOSO
Director: John Glenister
Co-stars: Jack Shepherd Sharon Duce Angela Douglas

GABY SYLVIA

1954 HUIS CLOS
Director: Jacqueline Audry
Co-stars: Arletty Frank Villard

SYLVIE

1938 ENTRÉE DES ARTISTES
Director: Marc Allegret
Co-stars: Louis Jouvet Odette Joyeux Claude Dauphin

1939 LA FIN DU JOUR
Director: Julien Duvivier
Co-stars: Victor Francen Louis Jouvet Michel Simon

1943 LES ANGES DU PECHE
Director: Robert Bresson
Co-stars: Renee Faure Jany Holt Mila Parely

1950 DIEU A BESOIN DES HOMMES
Director: Jean Delannoy
Co-stars: Pierre Fresnay Madeleine Robinson Daniel Gelin

1952 LE FRUIT DEFENDU
Director: Henri Verneuil
Co-stars: Fernandel Francoise Arnoul Claude Nollier

1952 THE LITTLE WORLD OF DON CAMILLO
Director: Julien Duvivier
Co-stars: Fernandel Gino Cervi Vera Talqui

KARI SYLVAN

1976 FACE TO FACE
Director: Ingmar Bergman
Co-stars: Liv Ullmann Erland Josephson Gunnar Bjornstrand

SYLVIA SYMS

1956 MY TEENAGE DAUGHTER
Director: Herbert Wilcox
Co-stars: Anna Neagle Kenneth Haigh Julia Lockwood

1957 NO TIME FOR TEARS
Director: Cyril Frankel
Co-stars: Anna Neagle Anthony Quayle Flora Robson

1957 WOMAN IN A DRESSING GOWN
Director: J. Lee-Thompson
Co-stars: Yvonne Mitchell Anthony Quayle Anthony Ray

1957 THE BIRTHDAY PRESENT
Director: Pat Jackson
Co-stars: Tony Britton Jack Watling Walter Fitzgerald

1958 BACHELOR OF HEARTS
Director: Wolf Rilla
Co-stars: Hardy Kruger Ronald Lewis Eric Barker

1958 FERRY TO HONG KONG
Director: Lewis Gilbert
Co-stars: Curt Jurgens Orson Welles Jeremy Spencer

1958 ICE COLD IN ALEX
Director: J. Lee-Thompson
Co-stars: John Mills Anthony Quayle Harry Andrews

1958 THE MOONRAKER
Director: David MacDonald
Co-stars: George Baker Marius Goring Gary Raymond

1959 NO TREES IN THE STREET
Director: J. Lee-Thompson
Co-stars: Herbert Lom Melvyn Hayes Stanley Holloway

1959 EXPRESSO BONGO
Director: Val Guest
Co-stars: Laurence Harvey Cliff Richard Yolande Donlon

1960 CONSPIRACY OF HEARTS
Director: Ralph Thomas
Co-stars: Lilli Palmer Yvonne Mitchell Ronald Lewis

1960 THE WORLD OF SUZIE WONG
Director: Richard Quine
Co-stars: William Holden Nancy Kwan Michael Wilding

1961 FLAME IN THE STREETS
Director: Roy Ward Baker
Co-stars: John Mills Brenda De Banzie Johnny Sekka

1961 VICTIM
Director: Basil Dearden
Co-stars: Dirk Bogarde Peter McEnery Dennis Price

1963 THE WORLD TEN TIMES OVER
Director: Wolf Rilla
Co-stars: June Ritchie Edward Judd William Hartnell

1963 THE QUARE FELLOW
Director: Arthur Dreifuss
Co-stars: Patrick McGoohan Dermot Kelly Walter Macken

1963 THE PUNCH AND JUDY MAN
Director: Jeremy Summers
Co-stars: Tony Hancock Ronald Fraser Hugh Lloyd

1964 EAST OF SUDAN
Director: Nathan Juran
Co-stars: Anthony Quayle Jenny Agutter

1965 OPERATION CROSSBOW
Director: Michael Anderson
Co-stars: George Peppard Tom Courtenay Sophia Loren

1967 THE FICTION MAKERS
Director: Roy Ward Baker
Co-star: Roger Moore

1967 DANGER ROUTE
Director: Seth Holt
Co-stars: Richard Johnson Diana Dors Carol Lynley

1968 THE DESPERADOES
Director: Henry Levin
Co-stars: Jack Palance Vince Edwards George Maharis

1969 RUN WILD, RUN FREE
Director: Richard Sarafian
Co-stars: John Mills Mark Lester Bernard Miles

1972 ASYLUM
Director: Roy Ward Baker
Co-stars: Barbara Parkins Richard Todd Charlotte Rampling

1974 THE TAMARIND SEED
Director: Blake Edwards
Co-stars: Julie Andrews Omar Sharif Anthony Quayle

1980 THERE GOES THE BRIDE
Director: Terence Marcel
Co-stars: Twiggy Tom Smothers Phil Silvers

1989 SHIRLEY VALENTINE
Director: Lewis Gilbert
Co-stars: Pauline Collins Tom Conti Julia McKenzie

1989   **A CHORUS OF DISAPPROVAL**
Director: Michael Winner
Co-stars: Jeremy Irons Anthony Hopkins Patsy Kensit

1989   **INSPECTOR WEXFORD: A SLEEPING LIFE**
Director: Bill Hays
Co-stars: George Baker Imelda Staunton

1991   **THE LAUGHTER OF GOD**
Director: Tony Bicat
Co-stars: Peter Firth Amanda Donohue Sharon Cheyne

1992   **SHINING THROUGH**
Director: David Seltzer
Co-stars: Michael Douglas Melanie Griffith

1993   **DIRTY WEEKEND**
Director: Michael Winner
Co-stars: Lia Williams Rufus Sewell David McCallum

1994   **STAGGERED**
Director: Martin Clunes
Co-stars: Martin Clunes Michael Praed Griff Rhys-Jones

JOANNA SZCZERBIC

1984   **SUCCESS IS THE BEST REVENGE**
Director: Jerzy Skolimovski
Co-stars: Michael York Michael Lyndon Anouk Aimee

MAGDA SZUBANSKI

1995   **BABE**
Director: Chris Noonan
Co-stars: James Cromwell Miriam Margoyles

UTA TAEGER

1967   LIVE FOR LIFE
Director: Claude Lelouch
Co-stars: Yves Montand Candice Bergen Annie Girardot

SARA TAFT

1951   YOU NEVER CAN TELL
Director: Lou Breslow
Co-stars: Dick Powell Peggy Dow Charles Drake

RITA TAGGART

1978   STRAIGHT TIME
Director: Ulu Grosbard
Co-stars: Dustin Hoffman Theresa Russell Gary Busey

1984   TORCHLIGHT
Director: Tom Wright
Co-stars: Pamela Sue Martin Steve Railsback Ian McShane

1988   SPLASH TOO
Director: Greg Antonacci
Co-stars: Todd Waring Amy Yasbeck Donovan Scott

1989   THE HORROR SHOW
Director: James Isaac
Co-stars: Lance Henriksen Brion James Dedee Pfeiffer

1990   COUPE DE VILLE
Director: Joe Roth
Co-stars: Patrick Dempsey Arye Gross Daniel Stern

SHARMILA TAGORE

1991   MISSISSIPPI MASALA
Director: Mira Nair
Co-stars: Denzel Washington Roshan Seth Sarita Choudhury

MIIKO TAKA

1957   SAYONARA
Director: Joshua Logan
Co-stars: Marlon Brando Miyoshi Umeka Red Buttons

1961   CRY FOR HAPPY
Director: George Marshall
Co-stars: Glenn Ford Donald O'Connor James Shigeta

1966   WALK DON'T RUN
Director: Charles Walters
Co-stars: Cary Grant Samantha Eggar Jim Hutton

1968   THE POWER
Director: Byron Haskin
Co-stars: Michael Rennie George Hamilton Suzanne Pleshette

1975   PAPER TIGER
Director: Ken Annakin
Co-stars: David Niven Toshiro Mifune Hardy Kruger

AYA TAKANASHI

1992   MR BASEBALL
Director: Fred Schepisi
Co-stars: Tom Selleck Dennis Haysbert Ken Takakura

ODETTE TALAZAC

1931   LE MILLION
Director: Rene Clair
Co-stars: Annabella Rene Lefevre Paul Oliver

1931   THE BLOOD OF A POET
Director: Jean Cocteau
Co-stars: Lee Miller Enrique Rivero Pauline Carton

GLORIA TALBOTT

1951   CATTLE EMPIRE
Director: Charles Marquis Warren
Co-stars: Joel McCrea Don Haggerty Phyllis Coates

1955   ALL THAT HEAVEN ALLOWS
Director: Douglas Sirk
Co-stars: Jane Wyman Rock Hudson Agnes Moorehead

1956   THE CYCLOPS
Director: Bert Gordon
Co-stars: James Craig Lon Chaney Tom Drake

1956   THE OKLAHOMAN
Director: Francis Lyon
Co-stars: Joel McCrea Barbara Hale Brad Dexter

1957   DAUGHTER OF DR JEKYLL
Director: Edgar Ulmer
Co-stars: Arthur Shields Joan Agar John Dierkes

1958   I MARRIED A MONSTER FROM OUTER SPACE
Director: Gene Fowler
Co-stars: Tom Tyron Robert Ivers Jean Carson

1959   THE OREGON TRAIL
Director: Gene Fowler
Co-stars: Fred MacMurray William Bishop Henry Hull

1965   ARIZONA RAIDERS
Director: William Witney
Co-stars: Audie Murphy Michael Dante Buster Crabbe

NITA TALBOT

1956   I MARRIED A WOMAN
Director: Hal Kanter
Co-stars: George Gobel Diana Dors Adolphe Menjou

1956   BUNDLE OF JOY
Director: Norman Taurog
Co-stars: Debbie Reynolds Eddie Fisher Adolphe Menjou

1958   ONCE UPON A HORSE
Director: Hal Kanter
Co-stars: Dan Rowan Dick Martin Martha Hyer

1962   WHO'S GOT THE ACTION
Director: Daniel Mann
Co-stars: Dean Martin Lana Turner Eddie Albert

1965   A VERY SPECIAL FAVOR
Director: Michael Gordon
Co-stars: Rock Hudson Charles Boyer Leslie Caron

1965   THAT FUNNY FEELING
Director: Richard Thorpe
Co-stars: Sandra Dee Bobby Darin Donald O'Connor

1965   GIRL HAPPY
Director: Boris Sagal
Co-stars: Elvis Presley Shelley Fabares Gary Crosby

1967   THE COOL ONES
Director: Gene Nelson
Co-stars: Roddy McDowell Robert Coote Phil Harris

1971   BUCK AND THE PREACHER
Director: Sidney Poitier
Co-stars: Sidney Poitier Harry Belafonte Ruby Dee

1971 THEY CALL IT MURDER
Director: Walter Grauman
Co-stars: Jim Hutton Jessica Walter Leslie Nielsen

1974 THE ROCKFORD FILES
Director: Richard Heffron
Co-stars: James Garner Lindsay Wagner William Smith

1980 SERIAL
Director: Bill Persky
Co-stars: Martin Mull Tuesday Weld Sally Kellerman

1985 MOVERS AND SHAKERS
Director: William Asher
Co-stars: Walter Matthau Charles Grodin Tyne Daly

VERA TALCHI

1949 AU-DELA DES GRILLES
Director: Rene Clement
Co-stars: Jean Gabin Isa Miranda Andrea Checci

MARIA TALLCHIEF

1952 MILLION DOLLAR MERMAID
Director: Mervyn LeRoy
Co-stars: Esther Williams Victor Mature Walter Pidgeon

MARGARET TALLICHET

1938 GIRL'S SCHOOL
Co-stars: Kenneth Howell Martha O'Driscoll Peggy Moran

1940 STRANGER ON THE THIRD FLOOR
Director: Boris Ingster
Co-stars: Peter Lorre Elisha Cook Jnr. John McGuire

1941 IT STARTED WITH EVE
Director: Henry Koster
Co-stars: Deanna Durbin Charles Laughton Robert Cummings

NADINE TALLIER

1959 TREASURE OF SAN TERESA
Director: Alvin Rakoff
Co-stars: Eddie Constantine Dawn Addams Marius Goring

PATRICIA TALLMAN

1990 NIGHT OF THE LIVING DEAD
Director: Tom Savini
Co-stars: Tony Wood Tom Towles William Butler

CONSTANCE TALMADGE

1916 INTOLERANCE
Director: D.W. Griffith
Co-stars: Mae Marsh Lillian Gish Elmo Lincoln

1919 THE FALL OF BABYLON
Director: D.W. Griffith
Co-stars: Tully Marshall Elmer Clifton Seena Owen

NATALIE TALMADGE (Married Buster Keaton)

1923 OUR HOSPITALITY
Director: Jack Blystone
Co-stars: Buster Keaton Joe Keaton Kittie Bradbury

NORMA TALMADGE

1922 SMILIN' THROUGH
Director: Sidney Franklin

1927 CAMILLE
Director: Fred Niblo
Co-stars: Gilbert Roland Lilyann Tashman Maurice Costello

1929 NEW YORK NIGHTS
Director: Lewis Milestone
Co-stars: Gilbert Roland Lilyann Tashman John Wray

1930 DUBARRY, WOMAN OF PASSION
Director: Sam Taylor
Co-stars: William Farnum Conrad Nagel Alison Skipworth

VERA TALQUI

1952 THE LITTLE WORLD OF DON CAMILLO
Director: Julien Duvivier
Co-stars: Fernandel Gino Cervi Sylvie

ALIX TALTON

1957 THE DEADLY MANTIS
Director: Nathan Juran
Co-stars: Craig Stevens William Hopper

ZOE TAMERLIS

1981 MS. 45
Director: Abel Ferrara
Co-stars: Steve Singer Darlene Stuto Peter Yellen

MARY TAMM

1973 TALES THAT WITNESS MADNESS
Director: Freddie Francis
Co-stars: Jack Hawkins Georgia Brown Kim Novak

1974 THE ODESSA FILE
Director: Ronald Neame
Co-stars: Jon Voight Maria Schell Maximilian Schell

1976 THE LIKELY LADS
Director: Michael Tuchner
Co-stars: Rodney Bewes James Bolam Brigit Forsyth

1984 THE ASSASSINATION RUN
Director: Ken Hannam
Co-stars: Malcolm Stoddard Sandor Eles

EMMA TAMMI

1992 USED PEOPLE
Director: Beeban Kidron
Co-stars: Shirley MacLaine Marcello Mastroianni Jessica Tandy

TAMU

1974 CLAUDINE
Director: John Berry
Co-stars: Diahann Carroll James Earl Jones Lawrence Hinton

VIVIEN TAN

1991 THE OTHER SIDE OF PARADISE
Director: Renny Rye
Co-stars: Jason Connery Richard Wilson Hywel Bennett

JESSICA TANDY (Married Jack Hawkins, Hume Cronyn, Mother Of Tandy Cronyn)

Oscar For Best Actress In 1989 For "Driving Miss Daisy".
Nominated For Best Supporting Actress In 1991 For "Fried Green Tomatoes At The Whistle-Stop Café"

1938 MURDER IN THE FAMILY
Director: Al Parker
Co-stars: Barry Jones Roddy McDowall Glynis Johns

1944 THE SEVENTH CROSS
Director: Fred Zinnemann
Co-stars: Spencer Tracy Signe Hasso Hume Cronyn

1945 THE VALLEY OF DECISION
Director: Tay Garnett
Co-stars: Greer Garson Gregory Peck Lionel Barrymore

1946 THE GREEN YEARS
Director: Victor Saville
Co-stars: Charles Coburn Dean Stockwell Hume Cronyn

1946	**DRAGONWYCK**
Director:	Joseph Mankiewicz
Co-stars:	Gene Tierney Vincent Price Ann Revere

1947	**FOREVER AMBER**
Director:	Otto Preminger
Co-stars:	Linda Darnell Cornel Wilde George Sanders

1948	**A WOMAN'S VENGEANCE**
Director:	Zoltan Korda
Co-stars:	Charles Boyer Ann Blyth Cedric Hardwicke

1950	**SEPTEMBER AFFAIR**
Director:	William Dieterle
Co-stars:	Joseph Cotten Joan Fontaine

1951	**THE DESERT FOX**
Director:	Henry Hathaway
Co-stars:	James Mason Cedric Hardwicke Luther Adler

1958	**THE LIGHT IN THE FOREST**
Director:	Herschel Daugherty
Co-stars:	James MacArthur Carol Lynley

1962	**HEMINGWAY'S ADVENTURES OF A YOUNG MAN**
Director:	Martin Ritt
Co-stars:	Richard Beymer Paul Newman Dan Dailey

1963	**THE BIRDS**
Director:	Alfred Hitchcock
Co-stars:	Tippi Hedren Rod Taylor Suzanne Pleshette

1973	**BUTLEY**
Director:	Harold Pinter
Co-stars:	Alan Bates Richard O'Callaghan Susan Engel

1981	**HONKY TONK FREEWAY**
Director:	John Schlesinger
Co-stars:	William Devane Beau Bridges Teri Garr

1982	**BEST FRIENDS**
Director:	Norman Jewison
Co-stars:	Burt Reynolds Goldie Hawn Keenan Wynn

1982	**STILL OF THE NIGHT**
Director:	Robert Benton
Co-stars:	Roy Scheider Meryl Streep Josef Somner

1982	**THE WORLD ACCORDING TO GARP**
Director:	George Roy Hill
Co-stars:	Robin Williams Glenn Close

1984	**THE BOSTONIANS**
Director:	James Ivory
Co-stars:	Christopher Reeve Vanessa Redgrave Linda Hunt

1985	**COCOON**
Director:	Ron Howard
Co-stars:	Dom Ameche Hume Cronyn Wilford Brimley

1987	**FOXFIRE**
Director:	Jud Taylor
Co-stars:	Hume Cronyn John Denver Harriet Hall

1987	**BATTERIES NOT INCLUDED**
Director:	Matthew Robbins
Co-stars:	Hume Cronyn Frank McRae Elizabeth Pena

1988	**COCOON: THE RETURN**
Director:	Daniel Petrie
Co-stars:	Don Ameche Hume Cronyn Gwen Verdon

1988	**THE HOUSE ON CARROLL STREET**
Director:	Peter Yates
Co-stars:	Kelly McGillis Jeff Daniels Mandy Patinkin

1989	**DRIVING MISS DAISY**
Director:	Bruce Beresford
Co-stars:	Morgan Freeman Dan Aykroyd Patti Lupone

1990	**THE STORY LADY**
Director:	Larry Elikann
Co-stars:	Tandy Cronyn Ed Begley Jnr Charles Durning

1991	**FRIED GREEN TOMATOES AT THE WHISTLE-STOP CAFÉ**
Director:	Jon Avnet
Co-stars:	Kathy Bates Cicely Tyson Mary Stuart Masterson

1992	**USED PEOPLE**
Director:	Beeban Kidron
Co-stars:	Shirley MacLaine Marcello Mastroianni

1993	**TO DANCE WITH THE WHITE DOG**
Director:	Glenn Jordan
Co-stars:	Hume Cronyn Esther Rolle

1994	**CAMILLA**
Director:	Deepa Mehta
Co-stars:	Bridget Fonda Maury Chaykin

YOKO TANI

1958	**THE WIND CANNOT READ**
Director:	Ralph Thomas
Co-stars:	Dirk Bogarde Ronald Lewis John Fraser

1960	**THE SAVAGE INNOCENTS**
Director:	Nicholas Ray
Co-stars:	Anthony Quinn Peter O'Toole Anna May Wong

1960	**PICCADILLY THIRD STOP**
Director:	Wolf Rilla
Co-stars:	Terence Morgan Mai Zetterling William Hartnell

1962	**MY GEISHA**
Director:	Jack Cardiff
Co-stars:	Shirley MacLaine Yves Montand Edward G. Robinson

1963	**WHO'S BEEN SLEEPING IN MY BED**
Director:	Daniel Mann
Co-stars:	Dean Martin Elizabeth Montgomery Jill St. John

1965	**INVASION**
Director:	Alan Bridges
Co-stars:	Edward Judd Valerie Gearon Tsai Chin

MARY TANNER

1986	**WILLY/MILLY**
Director:	Paul Schneider
Co-stars:	Pamela Segall Eric Gurry Patty Duke

TAPIA

1989	**SANTA SANGRE**
Director:	Alejandro Jodorowsky
Co-stars:	Axel Jodorowsky Blanca Guerra Guy Stockwell

ROSE TAPLEY

1931	**RESURRECTION**
Director:	Edwin Carewe
Co-stars:	Lupe Velez John Boles Nance O'Neil

BARBARA TARBUCK

1990	**THE DEATH OF THE INCREDIBLE HULK**
Director:	Bill Bixby
Co-stars:	Bill Bixby Lou Ferrigno Elizabeth Gracen

1991	**CURLY SUE**
Director:	John Hughes
Co-stars:	Kelly Lynch James Belushi Alisan Porter

TARITA *(Taritatumi Teriipaia)*

1962	**MUTINY ON THE BOUNTY**
Director:	Lewis Milestone
Co-stars:	Trevor Howard Marlon Brando Richard Harris

MARY JO TAROLA

1953   AFFAIR WITH A STRANGER
Director: Roy Rowland
Co-stars: Jean Simmons Victor Mature Jane Darwell

LILYANN TASHMAN

1924   MANHANDLED
Director: Allan Dwan
Co-stars: Gloria Swanson Tom Moore Frank Morgan

1925   PRETTY LADIES
Director: Monta Bell
Co-stars: Zasu Pitts Norma Shearer Joan Crawford

1926   SO THIS IS PARIS
Director: Ernst Lubitsch
Co-stars: Monte Blue Myrna Loy Patsy Ruth Miller

1927   CAMILLE
Director: Fred Niblo
Co-stars: Norma Talmadge Gilbert Roland Maurice Costello

1929   NEW YORKS NIGHTS
Director: Lewis Milestone
Co-stars: Norma Talmadge Gilbert Roland John Wray

1929   BULLDOG DRUMMOND
Director: Richard Jones
Co-stars: Ronald Colman Joan Bennett Claude Allister

1929   GOLD DIGGERS OF BROADWAY
Director: Roy Del Ruth
Co-stars: Nancy Welford Winnie Lightner Conway Tearle

1929   THE MARRIAGE PLAYGROUND
Director: Lothar Mendes
Co-stars: Fredric March Kay Francis Mary Brian

1930   FINN AND HATTIE
Director: Norman Taurog
Co-stars: Zasu Pitts Leon Errol Mitzi Green

1930   LEATHERNECKING
Director: Edward Cline
Co-stars: Irene Dunne Ken Murray Louise Fazenda

1930   NO, NO, NANETTE
Director: Clarence Badger
Co-stars: Bernice Claire Lucien Littlefield Zasu Pitts

1930   ONE HEAVENLY NIGHT
Director: George Fitzmaurice
Co-stars: Evelyn Laye John Boles Leon Errol

1930   PUTTIN' ON THE RITZ
Director: Edward Sloman
Co-stars: Harry Richman Joan Bennett James Gleason

1931   UP POPS THE DEVIL
Director: Edward Sutherland
Co-stars: Carole Lombard Norman Foster Stuart Erwin

1931   MURDER BY THE CLOCK
Director: Edward Sloman
Co-stars: William Boyd Regis Toomey Irving Pichel

1931   THE MAD PARADE
Director: William Beaudine
Co-stars: Evelyn Brent Irene Rich Louise Fazenda

1931   GIRLS ABOUT TOWN
Director: George Cukor
Co-stars: Kay Francis Joel McCrea Eugene Pallette

1932   SCARLET DAWN
Director: William Dieterle
Co-stars: Douglas Fairbanks Jnr. Nancy Carroll Guy Kibbee

1932   THE WISER SEX
Director: Berthold Viertel
Co-stars: Claudette Colbert Melvyn Douglas William Boyd

1933   TOO MUCH HARMONY
Director: Edward Sutherland
Co-stars: Bing Crosby Jack Oakie Skeets Gallagher

1933   MAMA LOVES PAPA
Director: Norman Z. McLeod
Co-stars: Charles Ruggles Mary Boland George Barbier

1934   RIPTIDE
Director: Edmund Goulding
Co-stars: Norma Shearer Robert Montgomery Herbert Marshall

LAURA TATE

1991   SUBSPECIES
Director: Ted Nicolaou
Co-stars: Michael Watson Anders Hove

SHARON TATE
(Married Roman Polanski, Murdered In 1969)

1966   EYE OF THE DEVIL
Director: J. Lee-Thompson
Co-stars: David Niven Deborah Kerr Flora Robson

1967   DON'T MAKE WAVES
Director: Alexander MacKendrick
Co-stars: Tony Curtis Claudia Cardinale Jim Backus

1967   THE FEARLESS VAMPIRE KILLERS
Director: Roman Polanski
Co-stars: Roman Polanski Jack MacGowran Alfie Bass

1967   VALLEY OF THE DOLLS
Director: Mark Robson
Co-stars: Barbara Parkins Patty Duke Susan Hayward

1968   THE WRECKING CREW
Director: Phil Karlson
Co-stars: Dean Martin Elke Sommer Nancy Kwan

1970   TWELVE PLUS ONE
Director: Nicholas Gessner
Co-stars: Vittorio Gassman Orson Welles Terry-Thomas

VIVA TATTERSHALL

1933   CYNARA
Director: King Vidor
Co-stars: Ronald Colman Kay Francis Phyllis Barry

JEANNE TATUM

1958   THE ASTOUNDING SHE-MONSTER
Director: Ronnie Ashcroft
Co-stars: Robert Clarke Ken Duncan Marilyn Harvey

TIFFANY TAUBMAN

1992   NOWHERE TO RUN
Director: Robert Harmon
Co-stars: Jean Claude Van Damme Rosanna Arquette Kieran Culkin

1995   SEE JANE RUN
Director: John Patterson
Co-stars: Joanna Kerns John Shea Katy Boyer

FARNANDA TAVERES

1987   90 DAYS
Director: Giles Walker
Co-stars: Stefan Wodoslawsky Sam Grana Christine Pak

ALMA TAYLOR

1919   THE NATURE OF THE BEAST
Director: Cecil Hepworth
Co-stars: Gerald Ames James Carew Mary Dibley

1923   COMIN' THRO' THE RYE
Director: Cecil Hepworth
Co-stars: Shayle Gardner Eileen Dennes Ralph Forbes

AVONNE TAYLOR

1931   **HONOR AMONG LOVERS**
Director: Dorothy Arzner
Co-stars: Claudette Colbert Fredric March Ginger Rogers

CLARICE TAYLOR

1971   **PLAY MISTY FOR ME**
Director: Clint Eastwood
Co-stars: Clint Eastwood Jessica Walter Donna Mills

1993   **SOMMERSBY**
Director: Jon Amiel
Co-stars: Richard Gere Jodie Foster Bill Pullman

DELORES TAYLOR

1971   **BILLY JACK**
Director: Tom Laughlin
Co-stars: Tom Laughlin Bert Freed Clark Howatt

1974   **THE TRIAL OF BILLY JACK**
Director: Tom Laughlin
Co-stars: Tom Laughlin Victor Izay Teresa Laughlin

1977   **BILLY JACK GOES TO WASHINGTON**
Director: Tom Laughlin
Co-stars: Tom Laughlin E.G. Marshall Sam Wanamaker

ELAINE TAYLOR

1967   **HALF A SIXPENCE**
Director: George Sidney
Co-stars: Tommy Steele Julia Foster Penelope Horner

1968   **DIAMONDS FOR BREAKFAST**
Director: Christopher Morahan
Co-stars: Marcello Mastroianni Rita Tushingham

1968   **THE ANNIVERSARY**
Director: Roy Ward Baker
Co-stars: Bette Davis Jack Hedley Sheila Hancock

1969   **LOCK UP YOUR DAUGHTERS**
Director: Peter Coe
Co-stars: Christopher Plummer Susannah York Glynis Johns

1970   **THE GAMES**
Director: Michael Winner
Co-stars: Stanley Baker Michael Crawford Ryan O'Neal

1970   **ALL THE WAY UP**
Director: James McTaggart
Co-stars: Warren Mitchell Kenneth Cranham Pat Heywood

ELIZABETH TAYLOR *(Child)*

(Married Conrad Hilton, Michael Wilding, Michael Todd, Eddie Fisher & Richard Burton)

Oscar For Best Actress In 1960 For "Butterfield 8" And In 1966 For "Who's Afraid Of Virginia Woolf". Nominated For Best Actress In 1957 For "Raintree County", In 1958 For "Cat On A Hot Tin Roof" And In 1959 For "Suddenly Last Summer"

1943   **LASSIE COME HOME**
Director: Fred Wilcox
Co-stars: Donald Crisp Roddy McDowall Edmund Gwenn

1944   **THE WHITE CLIFFS OF DOVER**
Director: Clarence Brown
Co-stars: Peter Lawford Irene Dunne Roddy McDowall

1944   **JANE EYRE**
Director: Robert Stevenson
Co-stars: Joan Fontaine Orson Welles Margaret O'Brien

1944   **NATIONAL VELVET**
Director: Clarence Brown
Co-stars: Mickey Rooney Anne Revere Donald Crisp

1946   **THE COURAGE OF LASSIE**
Director: Fred Wilcox
Co-stars: Frank Morgan Tom Drake Selena Royle

1947   **CYNTHIA**
Director: Robert Z. Leonard
Co-stars: Mary Astor George Murphy S.Z. Sakall

1947   **LIFE WITH FATHER**
Director: Michael Curtiz
Co-stars: Irene Dunne William Powell

1948   **JULIA MISBEHAVES**
Director: Jack Conway
Co-stars: Greer Garson Walter Pidgeon Peter Lawford

1948   **A DATE WITH JUDY**
Director: Richard Thorpe
Co-stars: Jane Powell Wallace Beery Robert Stack

1949   **LITTLE WOMEN**
Director: Mervyn LeRoy
Co-stars: June Allyson Peter Lawford Margaret O'Brien

1949   **CONSPIRATOR**
Director: Victor Saville
Co-stars: Robert Taylor Harold Warrender

1950   **THE BIG HANGOVER**
Director: Norman Krasna
Co-stars: Van Johnson Leon Ames Edgar Buchanan

1950   **FATHER OF THE BRIDE**
Director: Vincente Minnelli
Co-stars: Spencer Tracy Joan Bennett

1951   **FATHER'S LITTLE DIVIDEND**
Director: Vincente Minnelli
Co-stars: Spencer Tracy Joan Bennett

1951   **LOVE IS BETTER THAN EVER**
Director: Stanley Donen
Co-stars: Larry Parks Josephine Hutchinson

1951   **A PLACE IN THE SUN**
Director: George Stevens
Co-stars: Montgomery Clift Shelley Winters

1952   **IVANHOE**
Director: Richard Thorpe
Co-stars: Robert Taylor Joan Fontaine George Sanders

1953   **THE GIRL WHO HAD EVERYTHING**
Director: Richard Thorpe
Co-stars: William Powell Fernando Lamas

1954   **BEAU BRUMMEL**
Director: Curtis Bernhardt
Co-stars: Stewart Granger Peter Ustinov

1954   **ELEPHANT WALK**
Director: William Dieterle
Co-stars: Peter Finch Dana Andrews

1954   **THE LAST TIME I SAW PARIS**
Director: Richard Brooks
Co-stars: Van Johnson Walter Pidgeon Donna Reed

1954   **RHAPSODY**
Director: Charles Vidor
Co-stars: Vittorio Gassman Louis Calhern

1956   **GIANT**
Director: George Stevens
Co-stars: Rock Hudson James Dean Carroll Baker

1957   **RAINTREE COUNTY**
Director: Edward Dmytryk
Co-stars: Montgomery Clift Lee Marvin

1958   **CAT ON A HOT TIN ROOF**
Director: Richard Brooks
Co-stars: Paul Newman Burl Ives Jack Carson

1959   **SUDDENLY LAST SUMMER**
Director: Joseph L. Mankiewicz
Co-stars: Katherine Hepburn Montgomery Clift

1959   **SCENT OF MYSTERY**
Director: Jack Cardiff
Co-stars: Denholm Elliott Peter Lorre

1960   **BUTTERFIELD 8**
Director: Daniel Mann
Co-stars: Laurence Harvey Eddie Fisher Betty Field

1963   **CLEOPATRA**
Director: Joseph L. Mankiewicz
Co-stars: Richard Burton Rex Harrison

1963   **THE V.I.P.S**
Director: Anthony Asquith
Co-stars: Richard Burton Maggie Smith

1965   **THE SANDPIPER**
Director: Vincente Minnelli
Co-stars: Richard Burton Eva Marie Saint

1966   **WHO'S AFRAID OF VIRGINIA WOOLF**
Director: Mike Nichols
Co-stars: Richard Burton Sandy Dennis George Segal

1967   **DR FAUSTUS**
Director: Richard Burton
Co-stars: Richard Burton Andreas Teuber

1967   **THE COMEDIANS**
Director: Peter Glenville
Co-stars: Richard Burton Peter Ustinov

1967   **REFLECTIONS IN A GOLDEN EYE**
Director: John Huston
Co-stars: Marlon Brando Julie Harris Brian Keith

1967   **THE TAMING OF THE SHREW**
Director: Franco Zefferelli
Co-stars: Richard Burton Michael York

1968   **BOOM**
Director: Joseph Losey
Co-stars: Richard Burton Noel Coward

1969   **SECRET CEREMONY**
Director: Joseph Losey
Co-stars: Robert Mitchum Mia Farrow

1969   **THE ONLY GAME IN TOWN**
Director: George Stevens
Co-stars: Warren Beatty Charles Braswell

1971   **UNDER MILK WOOD**
Director: Andrew Sinclair
Co-stars: Richard Burton Peter O'Toole

1971   **ZEE AND CO.**
Director: Brian Hutton
Co-stars: Michael Caine Susannah York

1972   **HAMMERSMITH IS OUT**
Director: Peter Ustinov
Co-stars: Richard Burton Beau Bridges

1973   **ASH WEDNESDAY**
Director: Larry Peerce
Co-stars: Henry Fonda Helmut Berger

1973   **NIGHT WATCH**
Director: Brian Hutton
Co-stars: Laurence Harvey Billie Whitelaw

1975   **JAMES DEAN -**
         THE FIRST AMERICAN TEENAGER
Director: Ray Connolly
Co-stars: Rock Hudson Leslie Caron

1976   **THE BLUE BIRD**
Director: George Cukor
Co-stars: Ava Gardner Patsy Kensit Jane Fonda

1977   **A LITTLE NIGHT MUSIC**
Director: Hal Prince
Co-stars: Diana Rigg Hermione Gingold

1979   **WINTER KILLS**
Director: William Richert
Co-stars: Jeff Bridges John Huston Anthony Perkins

1980   **THE MIRROR CRACK'D**
Director: Guy Hamilton
Co-stars: Angela Lansbury Kim Novak Tony Curtis

1983   **BETWEEN FRIENDS**
Director: Lou Antonio
Co-stars: Carol Burnett Barbara Bush Stephen Young

1985   **MALICE IN WONDERLAND**
Director: Gus Trikonis
Co-stars: Jane Alexander Richard Dysart

1986   **THERE MUST BE A PONY**
Director: Joseph Sargent
Co-stars: Robert Wagner Mickey Rooney

1987   **POKER ALICE**
Director: Arthur Seidelman
Co-stars: George Hamilton David Wayne

1989   **SWEET BIRD OF YOUTH**
Director: Nicholas Roeg
Co-stars: Mark Harmon Michael Wilding Jnr.

1994   **THE FLINTSTONES**
Director: Brian Levant
Co-stars: John Goodman Elizabeth Perkins Rick Moranis

ESTELLE TAYLOR

1923   **THE TEN COMMANDMENTS**
Director: Cecil B. DeMille
Co-stars: Theodore Roberts Richard Dix Nita Naldi

1926   **DON JUAN**
Director: Alan Crosland
Co-stars: John Barrymore Mary Astor Myrna Loy

1930   **LILIOM**
Director: Frank Borzage
Co-stars: Charles Farrell Rose Hobart Lee Tracy

1931   **CIMARRON**
Director: Wesley Ruggles
Co-stars: Richard Dix Irene Dunne Nance O'Neil

1931   **STREET SCENE**
Director: King Vidor
Co-stars: Sylvia Sidney William Collier Jnr. Max Mantor

1931   **THE UNHOLY GARDEN**
Director: George Fitzmaurice
Co-stars: Ronald Colman Fay Wray Tully Marshall

1932   **CALL HER SAVAGE**
Director: John Francis Dillon
Co-stars: Clara Bow Gilbert Roland Thelma Todd

GWEN TAYLOR

1979   **MONTY PYTHON'S LIFE OF BRIAN**
Director: Terry Jones
Co-stars: Terry Jones Graham Chapman Michael Palin

1989   **INSPECTOR MORSE: HAPPY FAMILIES**
Director: Adrian Shergold
Co-stars: John Thaw Kevin Whately Anna Massey

1990   **KEEPING TOM NICE**
Director: Louise Panton
Co-stars: John Alderton Linus Roache Henrietta Bass

JANA TAYLOR

1967   HELL'S ANGELS ON WHEELS
Director: Richard Rush
Co-stars: Adam Roarke Jack Nicholson Sabrina Scharf

JANET TAYLOR

1985   SKY HIGH
Director: Nico Mastorakis
Co-stars: Daniel Hirsch Clayton Norcross Frank Schultz

JEANNINE TAYLOR

1980   FRIDAY THE 13TH
Director: Sean Cunningham
Co-stars: Betsy Palmer Adrienne King Kevin Bacon

JENNIFER TAYLOR

1995   THE CRUDE OASIS
Director: Alex Graves
Co-star: Aaron Shields

JOAN TAYLOR

1952   THE SAVAGE
Director: George Marshall
Co-stars: Charlton Heston Susan Morrow Peter Hanson

1955   FORT YUMA
Director: Lesley Selander
Co-stars: Peter Graves Joan Vohs John Hudson

1955   APACHE WOMAN
Director: Roger Corman
Co-stars: Lloyd Bridges Lance Fuller Paul Birch

1956   EARTH VERSUS THE FLYING SAUCERS
Director: Fred Sears
Co-stars: Hugh Marlowe Donald Curtis Morris Ankrum

1957   20 MILLION MILES TO EARTH
Director: Nathan Juran
Co-stars: William Hopper Frank Puglia Thomas B. Henry

JOYCE TAYLOR

1961   RING OF FIRE
Director: Andrew Stone
Co-stars: David Janssen Frank Gorshin Joel Marston

1961   ATLANTIS, THE LOST CONTINENT
Director: George Pal
Co-stars: Anthony Hall John Dall Edward Platt

LAUREN TAYLOR

1985   SKY HIGH
Director: Nico Mastorakis
Co-stars: Daniel Hirsch Clayton Norcross Frank Schultz

LAURETTE TAYLOR

1923   PEG O' MY HEART
Director: King Vidor
Co-stars: Mahlon Hamilton Russell Simpson Nigel Barrie

LILI TAYLOR

1988   MYSTIC PIZZA
Director: Donald Petrie
Co-stars: Annabeth Gish Julia Roberts Conchata Ferrell

1989   SAY ANYTHING
Director: Cameron Crowe
Co-stars: John Cusack Ione Skye John Mahoney

1990   BRIGHT ANGEL
Director: Michael Fields
Co-stars: Dermot Mulroney Sam Shepard Valerie Perrine

1991   DOGFIGHT
Director: Nancy Savoca
Co-stars: River Phoenix Anthony Clark Holly Near

1992   ARIZONA DREAM
Director: Emir Kusturica
Co-stars: Johnny Depp Jerry Lewis Faye Dunaway

1993   WATCH IT
Director: Tom Flynn
Co-stars: Peter Gallagher Suzy Amis Cynthia Stevenson

1993   SHORT CUTS
Director: Robert Altman
Co-stars: Matthew Modine Andie MacDowall Anne Archer

1995   FOUR ROOMS
Director: Allison Anders
Co-stars: Madonna Jennifer Beals Antonio Banderas

1996   I SHOT ANDY WARHOL
Director: Mary Harron

1997   RANSOM
Director: Ron Howard
Co-stars: Mel Gibson Rene Russo Gary Sinise

LYNNE TAYLOR

1962   LIFE FOR RUTH
Director: Basil Dearden
Co-stars: Michael Craig Janet Munro Patrick McGoohan

MARJORIE TAYLOR

1937   THE TICKET OF LEAVE MAN
Director: George King
Co-stars: Tod Slaughter John Warwick Robert Adair

1939   THE FACE AT THE WINDOW
Director: George King
Co-stars: Tod Slaughter John Warwick Aubrey Mallalieu

1936   THE CRIMES OF STEPHEN HAWKE
Director: George King
Co-stars: Tod Slaughter Eric Portman Gerald Barry

1937   IT'S NEVER TOO LATE TO MEND
Director: David MacDonald
Co-stars: Tod Slaughter Jack Livesey Lawrence Hanray

MARY TAYLOR

1935   SOAK THE RICH
Director: Ben Hecht
Co-stars: Walter Connolly John Howard Lionel Stander

RENEE TAYLOR *(Married Joe Bologna)*

1968   THE PRODUCERS
Director: Mel Brooks
Co-stars: Zero Mostel Gene Wilder Estelle Winwood

1971   MADE FOR EACH OTHER
Director: Robert Bean
Co-star: Joe Bologna

1971   JENNIFER ON MY MIND
Director: Noel Black
Co-stars: Michael Brandon Tippy Walker Lou Gilbert

1972   LAST OF THE RED HOT LOVERS
Director: Gene Saks
Co-stars: Alan Arkin Sally Kellerman Paula Prentiss

1983   LOVESICK
Director: Marshall Brickman
Co-stars: Dudley Moore Elizabeth McGovern Alec Guinness

SHARON TAYLOR

1978   ATTACK OF THE KILLER TOMATOES
Director: John De Bello
Co-stars: David Miller George Wilson Jack Riley

SUE TAYLOR

1973   THE AFFAIR
Director: Gilbert Cates
Co-stars: Natalie Wood Robert Wagner Bruce Davison

TAMMY TAYLOR

1984   MEATBALLS 2
Director: Ken Wiederhorn
Co-stars: Richard Mulligan Kim Richards John Mengatti

VALERIE TAYLOR

1933   BERKELEY SQUARE
Director: Frank Lloyd
Co-stars: Leslie Howard Heather Angel Beryl Mercer

1942   WENT THE DAY WELL
Director: Alberto Cavalcanti
Co-stars: Leslie Banks Elizabeth Allan Frank Lawton

1961   WHAT A CARVE UP !
Director: Pat Jackson
Co-stars: Sid James Kenneth Connor Shirley Eaton

JEAN TAYLOR-SMITH

1969   RING OF BRIGHT WATER
Director: Jack Couffer
Co-stars: Bill Travers Virginia McKenna Peter Jeffrey

LEIGH TAYLOR-YOUNG

1968   I LOVE YOU, ALICE B. TOKLAS
Director: Hy Averback
Co-stars: Peter Sellers Jo Van Fleet Joyce Van Patten

1969   THE BIG BOUNCE
Director: Alex March
Co-stars: Ryan O'Neal Van Heflin Lee Grant

1970   THE BUTTERCUP CHAIN
Director: Robert Ellis Miller
Co-stars: Hywel Bennett Jane Asher Roy Dotrice

1970   THE ADVENTURERS
Director: Lewis Gilbert
Co-stars: Bekim Fehmiu Candice Bergen Olivia De Havilland

1970   THE HORSEMEN
Director: John Frankenheimer
Co-stars: Omar Sharif Jack Palance Peter Jeffrey

**1971   THE GANG THAT COULDN'T
         SHOOT STRAIGHT**
Director: James Goldstone
Co-stars: Jerry Orbach Jo Van Fleet Robert De Niro

1973   SOYLENT GREEN
Director: Richard Fleischer
Co-stars: Charlton Heston Edward G. Robinson Joseph Cotten

1980   CAN'T STOP THE MUSIC
Director: Nancy Walker
Co-stars: The Village People Valerie Perrine Steve Guttenberg

1981   LOOKER
Director: Michael Crichton
Co-stars: Albert Finney James Coburn Susan Dey

1985   JAGGED EDGE
Director: Richard Marquand
Co-stars: Jeff Bridges Glenn Close Peter Coyote

**1987   PERRY MASON:
         THE CASE OF THE SINISTER SPIRIT**
Director: Richard Lang
Co-stars: Raymond Burr Barbara Hale

1994   MURDER OR MEMORY ?
Director: Christopher Leitch
Co-star: Michael Brandon

TAMARA TAXMAN

1985   THE HOUR OF THE STAR
Director: Suzana Amaral
Co-stars: Marcelia Cartaxo Jose Dumont Umberto Magnani

OLGA TCHEKOVA

1927   AN ITALIAN STRAW HAT
Director: Rene Clair
Co-stars: Albert Prejean Marisse Maia

1930   DREI VON DER TANKSTELLE
Director: William Thiele
Co-stars: Willy Fritsch Lilian Harvey Oskar Karlweis

LUDMILLA TCHERINA

1948   THE RED SHOES
Director: Michael Powell
Co-stars: Moira Shearer Anton Walbrook Robert Helpman

1951   THE TALES OF HOFFMAN
Director: Michael Powell
Co-stars: Moira Shearer Robert Rounsville Pamela Brown

1954   SIGN OF THE PAGAN
Director: Douglas Sirk
Co-stars: Jeff Chandler Jack Palance Rita Gam

1955   OH ROSALINDA !
Director: Michael Powell
Co-stars: Anton Walbrook Michael Redgrave Mel Ferrer

1959   HONEYMOON
Director: Michael Powell
Co-stars: Anthony Steel Leonine Massine Antonio

1962   LOVERS OF TERUEL
Director: Raymond Rouleau
Co-stars: Milko Sparemblek Milenko Banovitch

VERREE TEASDALE

1932   PAYMENT DEFERRED
Director: Lothar Mendes
Co-stars: Charles Laughton Maureen O'Sullivan Ray Milland

1932   SKYSCRAPER SOULS
Director: Edgar Selwyn
Co-stars: Warren William Maureen O'Sullivan Jean Hersholt

1933   THEY JUST HAD TO GET MARRIED
Director: Edward Ludwig
Co-stars: Zasu Pitts Slim Summerville

1933   TERROR ABROAD
Director: Paul Sloane
Co-stars: Charles Ruggles John Halliday

1933   ROMAN SCANDALS
Director: Frank Tuttle
Co-stars: Eddie Cantor Gloria Stuart Ruth Etting

1933   LUXURY LINER
Director: Lothar Mendes
Co-stars: George Brent Alice White Frank Morgan

1934   MADAME DUBARRY
Director: William Dieterle
Co-stars: Dolores Del Rio Reginald Owen Victor Jory

1934   **GOODBYE LOVE**
Co-stars: Charles Ruggles Sidney Blackmer

1934   **THE FIREBIRD**
Director: William Dieterle
Co-stars: Ricardo Cortez Lionel Atwill

1934   **FASHIONS OF 1934**
Director: William Dieterle
Co-stars: Bette Davis William Powell Frank McHugh

1934   **DR MONICA**
Director: William Keighley
Co-stars: Kay Francis Warren William Jean Muir

1934   **DESIRABLE**
Director: Archie Mayo
Co-stars: Jean Muir George Brent John Halliday

1934   **A MODERN HERO**
Director: G.W. Pabst
Co-stars: Richard Attenborough Jean Muir Florence Eldridge

1935   **A MIDSUMMER NIGHT'S DREAM**
Director: William Dieterle
Co-stars: James Cagney Dick Powell Mickey Rooney

1936   **THE MILKY WAY**
Director: Leo McCarey
Co-stars: Harold Lloyd Helen Mack Adolphe Menjou

1937   **FIRST LADY**
Director: Stanley Logan
Co-stars: Kay Francis Preston Foster Anita Louise

1938   **TOPPER TAKES A TRIP**
Director: Norman Z. McLeod
Co-stars: Roland Young Constance Bennett Billie Burke

1939   **I TAKE THIS WOMAN**
Director: W.S. Van Dyke
Co-stars: Spencer Tracy Hedy Lamar Laraine Day

1939   **FIFTH AVENUE GIRL**
Director: Gregory La Cava
Co-stars: Ginger Rogers Walter Connolly Tim Holt

1940   **LOVE THY NEIGHBOUR**
Director: Mark Sandrich
Co-stars: Jack Benny Fred Allen Mary Martin

1940   **TURNABOUT**
Director: Hal Roach
Co-stars: Adolphe Menjou John Hubbard Carole Landis

1941   **COME LIVE WITH ME**
Director: Clarence Brown
Co-stars: James Stewart Hedy Lamar Ian Hunter

SUSAN TEBBS

1976   **ESCAPE FROM THE DARK**
Director: Charles Jarrott
Co-stars: Alastair Sim Prunella Scales Leslie Sands

IRENE TEDROW

1984   **FAMILY SECRETS**
Director: Jack Hofsiss
Co-stars: Maureen Stapleton Stefanie Powers Melissa Gilbert

ELSA TEE

1947   **DEATH IN HIGH HEELS**
Director: Lionel Tomlinson
Co-stars: Don Stannard Veronica Rose Patricia Laffan

JILL TEED

1994   **ROOMMATES**
Director: Alan Metzger
Co-stars: Randy Quaid Charles Durning Elizabeth Pena

MAUREEN TEEFY

1983   **LEGS**
Director: Jerrold Freedman
Co-stars: Gwen Verdon John Heard Sheree North

LOTTE TEIG

1976   **EDVARD MUNCH**
Director: Peter Watkins
Co-stars: Geir Westby Gro Fraas Johan Halsborg

TORA TEJE

1920   **EROTIKON**
Director: Mauritz Stiller
Co-stars: Lars Hanson Karin Molander Anders De Wahl

ISABELLA TELEZYNSKA

1970   **THE MUSIC LOVERS**
Director: Ken Russell
Co-stars: Richard Chamberlain Christopher Gable Glenda Jackson

OLIVE TELL

1929   **THE VERY IDEA**
Co-stars: Frank Craven Doris Eaton Allen Kearns

1931   **LADIES' MAN**
Director: Lothar Mendes
Co-stars: William Powell Kay Francis Carole Lombard

1934   **THE SCARLET EMPRESS**
Director: Josef Von Sternberg
Co-stars: Marlene Dietrich John Lodge Sam Jaffe

ISABEL TELLARIA

1972   **THE SPIRIT OF THE BEEHIVE**
Director: Victor Erice
Co-stars: Fernando Fernan Gomez Teresa Gimpera Ana Torrent

ALBERTINA TEMBA

1952   **CRY THE BELOVED COUNTRY**
Director: Zoltan Korda
Co-stars: Canada Lee Sidney Poitier Charles Carson

MARIE TEMPEST

1937   **MOONLIGHT SONATA**
Director: Lothar Mendes
Co-stars: Ignace Paderewski Eric Portman Charles Farrell

1938   **YELLOW SANDS**
Director: Herbert Brenon
Co-stars: Wilfrid Lawson Robert Newton Belle Chrystall

SHIRLEY TEMPLE *(Married John Agar)*
Received A Special Award in 1934

1932   **GLAD RAGS TO RICHES**
Director: Eugene Butler

1934   **MANDALAY**
Director: Michael Curtiz
Co-stars: Kay Francis Ricardo Cortez Lyle Talbot

1934   **CHANGE OF HEART**
Director: John Blystone
Co-stars: Janet Gaynor Charles Farrell Ginger Rogers

1934   **STAND UP AND CHEER**
Director: Hamilton McFadden
Co-stars: Warner Baxter Madge Evans Nigel Bruce

1934   **BRIGHT EYES**
Director: David Butler
Co-stars: Jane Withers James Dunn Lois Wilson

1934 BABY TAKE A BOW
Director: Harry Lachman
Co-stars: Claire Trevor James Dunn Alan Dinehart

1934 NOW I'LL TELL
Director: Edwin Burke
Co-stars: Spencer Tracy Helen Twelvetrees Alice Faye

1934 NOW AND FOREVER
Director: Henry Hathaway
Co-stars: Gary Cooper Carole Lombard

1934 LITTLE MISS MARKER
Director: Alexander Hall
Co-stars: Adolphe Menjou Charles Bickford

1935 THE LITTLE COLONEL
Director: David Butler
Co-stars: Lionel Barrymore Bill Robinson John Lodge

1935 THE LITTLEST REBEL
Director: David Butler
Co-stars: John Boles Karen Morley Bill Robinson

1935 OUR LITTLE GIRL
Director: John Robertson
Co-stars: Joel McCrea Rosemary Ames Lyle Talbot

1935 CURLY TOP
Director: Irving Cummings
Co-stars: John Boles Rochelle Hudson Jane Darwell

1936 CAPTAIN JANUARY
Director: David Butler
Co-stars: Guy Kibbee Buddy Ebsen June Lang

1936 DIMPLES
Director: William Seiter
Co-stars: Frank Morgan Helen Westley Robert Kent

1936 POOR LITTLE RICH GIRL
Director: Irving Cummings
Co-stars: Jack Haley Alice Faye Gloria Stuart

1936 STOWAWAY
Director: William Seiter
Co-stars: Robert Young Alice Faye Eugene Pallette

1937 WEE WILLIE WINKIE
Director: John Ford
Co-stars: Victor McLaglen June Lang Cesar Romero

1937 HEIDI
Director: Allan Dwan
Co-stars: Jean Hersholt Arthur Treacher Helen Westley

1938 JUST AROUND THE CORNER
Director: Irving Cummings
Co-stars: Charles Farrell Bill Robinson Bert Lahr

1938 LITTLE MISS BROADWAY
Director: Irving Cummings
Co-stars: George Murphy Jimmy Durante Donald Meek

1938 REBECCA OF SUNNYBROOK FARM
Director: Allan Dwan
Co-stars: Randolph Scott Jack Haley Bill Robinson

1939 THE LITTLE PRINCESS
Director: Walter Lang
Co-stars: Richard Greene Anita Louise Ian Hunter

1939 SUSANNAH OF THE MOUNTIES
Director: William Seiter
Co-stars: Randolph Scott Margaret Lockwood

1940 YOUNG PEOPLE
Director: Allan Dwan
Co-stars: Jack Oakie Charlotte Greenwood Arleen Whelan

1940 THE BLUE BIRD
Director: George Cukor
Co-stars: Johnny Russell Gale Sondergaard Nigel Bruce

1941 KATHLEEN
Director: Harold Bucquet
Co-stars: Herbert Marshall Laraine Day Gail Patrick

1942 MISS ANNIE ROONEY
Director: Edwin Marin
Co-stars: William Gargan Guy Kibbee Peggy Ryan

1944 TAKE IT OR LEAVE IT
Director: Ben Stoloff
Co-stars: Phil Baker Phil Silvers Betty Grable

1944 I'LL BE SEEING YOU
Director: William Dieterle
Co-stars: Ginger Rogers Joseph Cotten Chill Wills

1944 SINCE YOU WENT AWAY
Director: John Cromwell
Co-stars: Claudette Colbert Jennifer Jones Robert Walker

1945 KISS AND TELL
Director: Richard Wallace
Co-stars: Walter Abel Darryl Hickman Porter Hall

1947 THAT HAGEN GIRL
Director: Peter Godfrey
Co-stars: Ronald Reagan Rory Calhoun Lois Maxwell

1947 HONEYMOON
Director: William Keighley
Co-stars: Franchot Tone Guy Madison Gene Lockhart

1947 BACHELOR KNIGHT
Director: Irving Reis
Co-stars: Cary Grant Myrna Loy Rudy Vallee

1948 FORT APACHE
Director: John Ford
Co-stars: John Wayne Henry Fonda John Agar

1949 THE STORY OF SEABISCUIT
Director: David Butler
Co-stars: Barry Fitzgerald Lon McCallister

1949 MR BELVEDERE GOES TO COLLEGE
Director: Elliott Nugent
Co-stars: Clifton Webb Alan Young Tom Drake

1949 A KISS FOR CORLISS
Director: Richard Wallace
Co-stars: David Niven Darryl Hickman Tom Tully

1949 ADVENTURE IN BALTIMORE
Director: Richard Wallace
Co-stars: Robert Young John Agar Albert Sharpe

STACEY TENDETER

1971 ANNE AND MURIEL
Director: Francois Truffaut
Co-stars: Jean-Pierre Leaud Kika Markham Sylvia Marriott

1981 FRIEND OR FOE
Director: John Krish
Co-stars: Mark Luxford John Holmes Valerie Lush

1988 RUN FOR THE LIFEBOAT
Director: Douglas Livingstone
Co-stars: David Burke Jeff Rawle Tenniel Evans

VICTORIA TENNANT *(Married Steve Martin)*

1972 THE RAGMAN'S DAUGHTER
Director: Harold Becker
Co-stars: Simon Rouse Leslie Sands Brian Murphy

1983 DEMPSEY
Director: Gus Trikonis
Co-stars: Treat Williams Sam Waterston Sally Kellerman

1983 STRANGER'S KISS
Director: Matthew Chapman
Co-stars: Peter Coyote Blaine Novak Richard Romanus

1984   ALL OF ME
Director: Carl Reiner
Co-stars: Steve Martin Lily Tomlin Madolyn Smith

1985   THE HOLCROFT COVENANT
Director: John Frankenheimer
Co-stars: Michael Caine Anthony Andrews Lilli Palmer

1987   BEST SELLER
Director: John Flynn
Co-stars: James Woods Brian Dennehy George Coe

1987   FLOWERS IN THE ATTIC
Director: Jeffrey Bloom
Co-stars: Louise Fletcher Jeb Stuart

1989   ACT OF WILL
Director: Don Sharp
Co-stars: Elizabeth Hurley Peter Coyote Jean Marsh

1989   VOICE OF THE HEART
Director: Tony Wharmby
Co-stars: Lindsay Wagner James Brolin Richard Johnson

1990   THE HANDMAID'S TALE
Director: Volker Schlondorff
Co-stars: Natasha Richardson Robert Duvall

1991   L.A. STORY
Director: Mick Jackson
Co-stars: Steve Martin Richard E. Grant Marilu Henner

AMY TERELINCK

1993   NO WORRIES
Director: David Elfick
Co-stars: Geoff Morrell Susan Lyons Geraldine James

NORMA TERRIS

1929   MARRIED IN HOLLYWOOD
Co-star: J. Harold Murray

1930   CAMEO KIRBY
Co-star: J. Harold Murray

ELLALINE TERRISS

1935   THE IRON DUKE
Director: Victor Saville
Co-stars: George Arliss Gladys Cooper Emlyn Williams

1939   THE FOUR JUST MEN
Director: Walter Forde
Co-stars: Hugh Sinclair Griffith Jones Frank Lawton

ALICE TERRY *(Married Rex Ingram)*

1921   THE FOUR HORSEMEN
OF THE APOCALYPSE
Director: Rex Ingram
Co-stars: Rudolph Valentino Wallace Beery

1922   THE PRISONER OF ZENDA
Director: Rex Ingram

1923   SCARAMOUCHE
Director: Rex Ingram
Co-star: Ramon Navarro

1924   THE ARAB
Director: Rex Ingram

1925   MARE NOSTRUM
Director: Rex Ingram
Co-stars: Antonio Moreno Alex Nova

1926   THE MAGICIAN
Director: Rex Ingram
Co-stars: Paul Wegener Ivan Petrovitch

1927   THE GARDEN OF ALLAH
Director: Rex Ingram

HAZEL TERRY

1937   OUR FIGHTING NAVY
Director: Norman Walker
Co-stars: Robert Douglas Richard Cromwell H.B. Warner

JOYCE TERRY

1953   THE NEANDERTHAL MAN
Director: E.A. Dupont
Co-stars: Robert Shayne Richard Crane Doris Merrick

LINDA TERRY

1938   CRIME DOES NOT PAY:
THE WRONG WAY OUT
Director: Gustav Machaty
Co-star: Kenneth Howell

RUTH TERRY

1937   LOVE AND HISSES
Director: Sidney Lanfield
Co-stars: Joan Davis Bert Lahr Simone Simon

1938   INTERNATIONAL SETTLEMENT
Director: Eugene Forde
Co-stars: George Sanders Dolores Del Rio June Lang

1938   HOLD THAT CO-ED
Director: George Marshall
Co-stars: John Barrymore Joan Davis George Murphy

1940   SLIGHTLY HONOURABLE
Director: Tay Garnett
Co-stars: Pat O'Brien Broderick Crawford Edward Arnold

1941   BLONDIE GOES LATIN
Director: Frank Strayer
Co-stars: Penny Singleton Arthur Lake Tito Guizar

1941   APPOINTMENT FOR LOVE
Director: William Seiter
Co-stars: Charles Boyer Margaret Sullavan Rita Johnson

1941   ROOKIES ON PARADE
Co-star: Marie Wilson

1942   CALL OF THE CANYON
Co-stars: Gene Autry Bob Nolan Hugh Farr

1943   HANDS ACROSS THE BORDER
Co-star: Roy Rogers

1943   MYSTERY BROADCAST
Director: George Sherman
Co-stars: Frank Albertson Nils Asther Wynne Gibson

1944   MY BUDDY
Director: Steve Sekely
Co-stars: Don Barry Lynne Roberts Emma Dunn

1945   STEPPIN' IN SOCIETY
Director: Alexandre Esway
Co-stars: Edward Everett Horton Gladys George Jack La Rue

1945   TELL IT TO A STAR
Director: Frank McDonald
Co-stars: Robert Livingston Alan Mowbray Franklin Pangborn

1945   THE CHEATERS
Director: Joseph Kane
Co-stars: Joseph Schildkraut Billie Burke Eugene Pallette

SHEILA TERRY

1932   SCARLET DAWN
Director: William Dieterle
Co-stars: Douglas Fairbanks Jnr. Nancy Carroll Lilyann Tashman

1932   YOU SAID A MOUTHFUL
Director: Lloyd Bacon
Co-stars: Joe E. Brown Ginger Rogers Guinn Williams

1933 20,000 YEARS IN SING SING
Director: Michael Curtiz
Co-stars: Spencer Tracy Bette Davis Louis Calhern

1933 THE SPHINX
Director: Phil Rosen
Co-stars: Lionel Atwill Paul Hurst Luis Alberni

1934 'NEATH ARIZONA SKIES
Director: Harry Fraser
Co-stars: John Wayne George Hayes Yakima Canutt

1934 ROCKY RHOADES
Co-star: Buck Jones

1935 THE LAWLESS FRONTIER
Co-stars: John Wayne George Hayes Yakima Canutt

1935 BARS OF HATE
Co-star: Regis Toomey

1936 SPECIAL INVESTIGATOR
Co-stars: Richard Dix Erik Rhodes

MABEL TERRY-LEWIS

1939 A STOLEN LIFE
Director: Paul Czinner
Co-stars: Elisabeth Bergner Michael Redgrave Wilfrid Lawson

1944 THEY CAME TO A CITY
Director: Basil Dearden
Co-stars: Googie Withers John Clements Raymond Huntley

JOHANNA TER STEEGE

1990 VINCENT AND THEO
Director: Robert Altman
Co-stars: Tim Roth Paul Rhys Anne Canovas

1991 MEETING VENUS
Director: Istvan Szabo
Co-stars: Glenn Close Niels Arestrup Erland Josephson

1994 IMMORTAL BELOVED
Director: Bernard Rose
Co-stars: Gary Oldman Jeroen Krabbe Isabella Rossellini

1997 PARADISE ROAD
Director: Bruce Beresford
Co-stars: Glenn Close Pauline Collins Jennifer Ehle

JOAN TETZEL (*Married Oscar Homolka*)

1946 DUEL IN THE SUN
Director: King Vidor
Co-stars: Gregory Peck Jennifer Jones Joseph Cotten

1947 THE PARADINE CASE
Director: Alfred Hitchcock
Co-stars: Gregory Peck Alida Valli Ann Todd

1949 THE FILE ON THELMA JORDAN
Director: Robert Siodmak
Co-stars: Barbara Stanwyck Wendell Corey Paul Kelly

1954 HELL BELOW ZERO
Director: Mark Robson
Co-stars: Alan Ladd Stanley Baker Jill Bennett

1965 JOY IN THE MORNING
Director: Alex Segal
Co-stars: Richard Chamberlain Yvette Mimieux Oscar Homolka

VIRGINIA TEXERA

1960 THE BOY WHO STOLE A MILLION
Director: Charles Crichton
Co-stars: Maurice Reyna Harold Kasket Bill Nagy

ANNE TEYSSEDRA

1989 A TALE OF SPRINGTIME
Director: Eric Rohmer
Co-stars: Hugues Questell Florence Darel

KATHARINA THALBACH

1979 DIE BLECHTROMMEL
Director: Volker Schloendorff
Co-stars: David Bennett Mario Adorf Angela Winkler

1988 WELCOME TO GERMANY
Director: Thomas Brasch
Co-stars: Tony Curtis Matthias Habiac

TILDA THAMER

1954 THE MASTER PLAN
Director: Hugh Raker
Co-stars: Wayne Morris Norman Wooland Arnold Bell

1957 THE FANATICS
Director: Alex Joffe
Co-stars: Pierre Fresnay Michel Auclair Gregoire Aslan

WIN MIN THAN

1954 THE PURPLE PLAIN
Director: Robert Parrish
Co-stars: Gregory Peck Maurice Denham Lyndon Brook

HEATHER THATCHER

1932 BUT THE FLESH IS WEAK
Director: Jack Conway
Co-stars: Robert Montgomery C. Aubrey Smith Nils Asther

1933 IT'S A BOY
Director: Tim Whelan
Co-stars: Edward Everett Horton Leslie Henson Alfred Drayton

1933 LOYALTIES
Director: Basil Dean
Co-stars: Basil Rathbone Miles Mander Joan Wyndham

1938 IF I WERE KING
Director: Frank Lloyd
Co-stars: Ronald Colman Basil Rathbone Frances Dee

1939 BEAU GESTE
Director: William Wellman
Co-stars: Gary Cooper Ray Milland Robert Preston

1941 MAN HUNT
Director: Fritz Lang
Co-stars: Walter Pidgeon Joan Bennett George Sanders

1942 WE WERE DANCING
Director: Robert Z. Leonard
Co-stars: Norma Shearer Melvyn Douglas Gail Patrick

1943 UNDYING MONSTER
Director: John Brahm
Co-stars: James Ellison John Howard Heather Angel

1943 THE MOON AND SIXPENCE
Director: Albert Lewin
Co-stars: George Sanders Herbert Marshall Steve Geray

1944 GASLIGHT
Director: George Cukor
Co-stars: Charles Boyer Ingrid Bergman Joseph Cotten

1948 ANNA KARENINA
Director: Julien Duvivier
Co-stars: Vivien Leigh Kieron Moore Ralph Richardson

1949 DEAR MR PROHACK
Director: Thornton Freeland
Co-stars: Cecil Parker Dirk Bogarde Glynis Johns

1952   **THE HOUR OF THIRTEEN**
Director: Harold French
Co-stars: Peter Lawford Dawn Addams Roland Culver

1952   **FATHER'S DOING FINE**
Director: Henry Cass
Co-stars: Richard Attenborough Susan Stephen Noel Purcell

1953   **WILL ANY GENTLEMAN ?**
Director: Michael Anderson
Co-stars: George Cole Alan Badel Veronica Hurst

1955   **JOSEPHINE AND MEN**
Director: Ray Boulting
Co-stars: Glynis Johns Jack Buchanan Donald Sinden

LYSA THATCHER

1981   **AMERICAN PIE**
Director: Jeffrey Fairbanks
Co-stars: Arcadia Lake Kitty Shane Eric Edwards

PHYLLIS THAXTER

1944   **THIRTY SECONDS OVER TOKYO**
Director: Mervyn LeRoy
Co-stars: Spencer Tracy Van Johnson Robert Walker

1945   **WEEKEND AT THE WALDORF**
Director: Robert Z. Leonard
Co-stars: Ginger Rogers Walter Pidgeon Van Johnson

1947   **THE SEA OF GRASS**
Director: Elia Kazan
Co-stars: Spencer Tracy Katherine Hepburn Robert Walker

1947   **LIVING IN A BIG WAY**
Director: Gregory La Cava
Co-stars: Gene Kelly Marie McDonald Charles Winninger

1948   **BLOOD ON THE MOON**
Director: Robert Wise
Co-stars: Robert Mitchum Robert Preston Barbara Bel Geddes

1948   **ACT OF VIOLENCE**
Director: Fred Zinnemann
Co-stars: Van Heflin Robert Ryan Janet Leigh

1948   **TENTH AVENUE ANGEL**
Director: Roy Rowland
Co-stars: Margaret O'Brien Angela Lansbury George Murphy

1949   **NO MAN OF HER OWN**
Director: Mitchell Leisen
Co-stars: Barbara Stanwyck John Lund Lyle Bettger

1950   **THE BREAKING POINT**
Director: Michael Curtiz
Co-stars: John Garfield Patricia Neal Juano Hernandez

1951   **COME FILL THE CUP**
Director: Gordon Douglas
Co-stars: James Cagney Gig Young Raymond Massey

1951   **FORT WORTH**
Director: Edwin Marin
Co-stars: Randolph Scott David Brian Paul Picerni

1951   **JIM THORPE, ALL AMERICAN**
Director: Michael Curtiz
Co-stars: Burt Lancaster Charles Bickford Steve Cochran

1952   **SPRINGFIELD RIFLE**
Director: Andre De Toth
Co-stars: Gary Cooper David Brian Paul Kelly

1952   **SHE'S WORKING HER WAY THROUGH COLLEGE**
Director: Bruce Humberstone
Co-stars: Virginia Mayo Ronald Reagan Gene Nelson

1957   **MAN AFRAID**
Director: Harry Keller
Co-stars: George Nader Tim Hovey Eduard Franz

1964   **THE WORLD OF HENRY ORIENT**
Director: George Roy Hill
Co-stars: Peter Sellers Tippy Walker Merri Spaeth

1970   **INCIDENT IN SAN FRANCISCO**
Director: Don Medford
Co-stars: Richard Kiley Chris Connelly Ruth Roman

1978   **SUPERMAN**
Director: Richard Donner
Co-stars: Christopher Reeve Marlon Brando Margot Kidder

JULIA THAYER

1937   **GUNSMOKE RANCH**
Co-stars: Bob Livingstone Ray Corrigan Max Terhune

LORNA THAYER

1955   **THE BEAST WITH A MILLION EYES**
Director: David Karminsky
Co-stars: Paul Burch Dick Sargent Chester Conklin

TINA THAYER

1942   **SECRETS OF A CO-ED**
Co-star: Rick Vallin

1942   **A YANK AT ETON**
Director: Norman Taurog
Co-stars: Mickey Rooney Freddie Bartholomew Edmund Gwenn

1943   **THE PAYOFF**
Director: Arthur Dreifuss
Co-stars: Lee Tracy Tom Brown Evelyn Brent

ROSEMARY THEBY

1933   **THE FATAL GLASS OF BEER**
Director: Clyde Bruckman
Co-stars: W.C. Fields Richard Cramer George Chandler

NINA THEILADE

1935   **A MIDSUMMER NIGHT'S DREAM**
Director: William Dieterle
Co-stars: James Cagney Dick Powell Mickey Rooney

JODI THELEN

1981   **FOUR FRIENDS**
Director: Arthur Penn
Co-stars: Craig Wasson Michael Huddleston Jim Metzler

1983   **THE BLACK STALLION RETURNS**
Director: Robert Dalva
Co-stars: Kelly Reno Ferdy Mayne Woody Strode

GENEVIEVE THENIER

1969   **THE LAST SHOT**
Director: Sergio Gobbi
Co-stars: Robert Hossein Charles Aznavour Virna Lisi

MARIE THEODORE

1992   **SMALL METAL JACKET**
Director: Steve Hilliker
Co-stars: Debora Watson Toshie Ogura Jana Sheldon

SONDRA THEODORE

1978   **ABIGAIL WANTED**
Director: Richard Taylor
Co-stars: Sherry Jackson Christopher Mitchum Bill Watson

CHARLIZE THERON

1997   **TRIAL AND ERROR**
Director: Jonathan Lynn
Co-stars: Jeff Daniels Michael Richards

VIRGINIA THEVENET

1984 FULL MOON IN PARIS
Director: Eric Rohmer
Co-stars: Pascale Ogier Tcheky Karyo Fabrice Luchini

OLIVETTE THIBAULT

1971 MON ONCLE ANTOINE
Director: Claude Jutra
Co-stars: Jean Duceppe Jacques Gagnon Lyne Champagne

HERTHA THIELE

1931 MADCHEN IN UNIFORM
Director: Leontine Sagan
Co-stars: Emilia Unda Dorothea Wieck Hedwig Schlichter

URSULA THIESS

1952 MONSOON

1954 THE IRON GLOVE
Director: William Castle
Co-stars: Robert Stack Richard Stapley Alan Hale Jnr.

1954 BENGAL RIFLES
Director: Laslo Benedek
Co-stars: Rock Hudson Arlene Dahl Dan O'Herlihy

1955 THE AMERICANO
Director: William Castle
Co-stars: Glenn Ford Cesar Romero Abbe Lane

1956 BANDIDO
Director: Richard Fleischer
Co-stars: Robert Mitchum Gilbert Roland Zachary Scott

TIFFANI-AMBER THIESSEN

1995 SHE FOUGHT ALONE
Director: Christopher Leitch
Co-stars: Brian Austin Green Isabella Hoffman

LYNNE THIGPEN

1973 GODSPELL
Director: David Greene
Co-stars: Victor Garber David Haskell Katie Hanley

1989 FEAR STALK
Director: Larry Shaw
Co-stars: Jill Clayburgh Stephen Macht Lorna Luft

1991 SEPARATE BUT EQUAL
Director: George Stevens Jnr.
Co-stars: Sidney Poitier Burt Lancaster Richard Kiley

HELENE THIMIG

1943 EDGE OF DARKNESS
Director: Lewis Milestone
Co-stars: Errol Flynn Ann Sheridan Walter Huston

1944 THE HITLER GANG
Director: John Farrow
Co-stars: Robert Watson Martin Kosleck Victor Varconi

1944 NONE BUT THE LONELY HEART
Director: Clifford Odets
Co-stars: Cary Grant Ethel Barrymore June Duprez

1945 HOTEL BERLIN
Director: Peter Godfrey
Co-stars: Raymond Massey Peter Lorre Faye Emerson

1946 ISLE OF THE DEAD
Director: Mark Robson
Co-stars: Boris Karloff Ellen Drew Katherine Emery

1946 CLOAK AND DAGGER
Director: Fritz Lang
Co-stars: Gary Cooper Lilli Palmer Robert Alda

1947 CRY WOLF
Director: Peter Godfrey
Co-stars: Barbara Stanwyck Errol Flynn Geraldine Brooks

1947 ESCAPE ME NEVER
Director: Peter Godfrey
Co-stars: Errol Flynn Ida Lupino Gig Young

VICTOIRE THIVISOL

1998 PONETTE

BETTY THOMAS

1987 PRISON FOR CHILDREN
Director: Larry Peerce
Co-stars: Kenny Ransom Josh Brolin John Ritter

1989 TROOP BEVERLY HILLS
Director: Jeff Kanew
Co-stars: Shelley Long Craig T. Nelson Stephanie Beacham

HEATHER THOMAS

1988 DIRTY DOZEN: THE FATAL MISSION
Director: Lee Katzin
Co-stars: Telly Savalas Ernest Borgnine Alex Cord

JUDY THOMAS

1969 THE WEDDING PARTY
Director: Cynthia Munroe
Co-stars: Jill Clayburgh Ray McNally Robert De Niro

MADOLINE THOMAS

1986 PAST CARING
Director: Richard Eyre
Co-stars: Denholm Elliott Emlyn Williams Joan Greenwood

MARLO THOMAS

1984 ACT OF PASSION
Director: Simon Langton
Co-stars: Kris Kristofferson George Dzundza Linda Thorsen

1986 NOBODY'S CHILD
Director: Lee Grant
Co-stars: Ray Baker Kathy Baker Caroline Kava

1990 IN THE SPIRIT
Director: Sandra Seacat
Co-stars: Elaine May Peter Falk Jeannie Berlin

1993 REUNION
Director: Lee Grant
Co-star: Peter Strauss

1993 ULTIMATE BETRAYAL
Director: Donald Wrye
Co-star: Mel Harris

MARY THOMAS (Child)

1942 MRS WIGGS OF THE CABBAGE PATCH
Director: Ralph Murphy
Co-stars: Fay Bainter Hugh Herbert Vera Vague

MELODY THOMAS

1977 SECRETS
Director: Paul Wendkos
Co-stars: Susan Blakely Roy Thinnes John Randolph

1978 PIRANHA
Director: Joe Dante
Co-stars: Bradford Dillman Heather Menzies Keenan Wynn

NINA THOMAS

1974 DEAD CERT
Director: Tony Richardson
Co-stars: Scott Anthony Judi Dench Michael Williams

PAMELA THOMAS

1956 THE CASE OF THE MUKKINESE BATTLEHORN
Director: Joseph Sterling
Co-stars: Peter Sellers Spike Milligan

RACHEL THOMAS

1939 THE PROUD VALLEY
Director: Pen Tennyson
Co-stars: Paul Robeson Edward Chapman Edward Rigby

1943 UNDERCOVER
Director: Sergei Nolbandov
Co-stars: Tom Walls Michael Wilding John Clements

1953 VALLEY OF SONG
Director: Gilbert Gunn
Co-stars: Mervyn Johns Maureen Swanson Rachel Roberts

1964 CATACOMBS
Director: Gordon Hessler
Co-stars: Gary Merrill Neil McCallum Jane Merrow

1971 UNDER MILK WOOD
Director: Andrew Sinclair
Co-stars: Richard Burton Elizabeth Taylor Glynis Johns

SIAN THOMAS

1990 FRANKENSTEIN'S BABY
Director: Robert Bierman
Co-stars: Kate Buffery Nigel Planer Yvonne Bryceland

1991 STANLEY AND THE WOMEN
Director: David Tucker
Co-stars: John Thaw Geraldine James Sheila Gish

1993 WIDE EYED AND LEGLESS
Director: Richard Loncraine
Co-stars: Julie Walters Jim Broadbent Thora Hird

VIRGINIA THOMAS

1929 THE WILD PARTY
Director: Dorothy Arzner
Co-stars: Clara Bow Fredric March Shirley O'Hara

BEATRICE THOMPSON

1934 THE OLD CURIOSITY SHOP
Director: Thomas Bentley
Co-stars: Hay Petrie Ben Webster Elaine Benson

EMMA THOMPSON *(Daughter Of Phyllida Law)*

Oscar For Best Actress In 1992 For "Howards End". Nominated For Best Actress In 1993 For "The Remains Of The Day" And In 1996 For "Sense And Sensibility". Nominated For Best Supporting Actress In 1993 For "In The Name Of The Father"

1989 IMPROMPTU
Director: James Lapine
Co-stars: Judy Davis Hugh Grant Mandy Patinkin

1989 THE TALL GUY
Director: Mel Smith
Co-stars: Jeff Goldblum Geraldine James Anna Massey

1989 HENRY V
Director: Kenneth Branagh
Co-stars: Kenneth Branagh Derek Jacobi Simon Shepherd

1991 DEAD AGAIN
Director: Kenneth Branagh
Co-stars: Andy Garcia Lois Hall Richard Easton

1992 PETER'S FRIENDS
Director: Kenneth Branagh
Co-stars: Imelda Staunton Hugh Laurie Stephen Fry

1992 HOWARDS END
Director: James Ivory
Co-stars: Anthony Hopkins Vanessa Redgrave James Wilby

1993 MUCH ADO ABOUT NOTHING
Director: Kenneth Branagh
Co-stars: Kenneth Branagh Richard Briers Michael Keaton

1993 THE REMAINS OF THE DAY
Director: James Ivory
Co-stars: Anthony Hopkins Christopher Reeves Hugh Grant

1993 IN THE NAME OF THE FATHER
Director: Jim Sheridan
Co-stars: Daniel Day-Lewis Peter Postlethwaite John Lynch

1994 MY FATHER, THE HERO
Director: Steve Miner
Co-stars: Gerard Depardieu Katherine Heigl Dalton James

1995 CARRINGTON
Director: Christopher Hampton
Co-stars: Jonathan Pryce Rufus Sewell Samuel West

1995 JUNIOR
Co-stars: Arnold Schwarzenegger Danny De Vito

1996 SENSE AND SENSIBILITY
Director: Ang Lee
Co-stars: Hugh Grant Kate Winslet James Fleet

1997 PRIMARY COLORS
Director: Mike Nichols
Co-stars: John Travolta Kathy Bates

1998 THE WINTER GUEST
Director: Alan Rickman
Co-star: Phyllida Law

HILARIE THOMPSON

1968 HOW SWEET IT IS !
Director: Jerry Paris
Co-stars: James Garner Debbie Reynolds Maurice Ronet

1980 THE FALLS
Director: Peter Greenaway
Co-stars: Colin Cantlie Sheila Canfield Adam Leys

1981 NIGHT HAWKS
Director: Bruce Malmuth
Co-stars: Sylvester Stallone Billy Dee Williams Lindsay Wagner

KAY THOMPSON

1957 FUNNY FACE
Director: Stanley Donen
Co-stars: Fred Astaire Audrey Hepburn Robert Flemyng

1970 TELL ME THAT YOU LOVE ME, JUNIE MOON
Director: Otto Preminger
Co-stars: Liza Minnelli Ken Howard Robert Moore

LEA THOMPSON

1983 JAWS 3
Director: Joe Alves
Co-stars: Dennis Quaid Bess Armstrong Simon MacCorkindale

1983 ALL THE RIGHT MOVES
Director: Michael Chapman
Co-stars: Tom Cruise Craig T. Nelson Christopher Penn

1984 GOING UNDERCOVER
Director: James Kennedy Clarke
Co-stars: Chris Lemmon Jean Simmons Viveca Lindfors

1985 BACK TO THE FUTURE
Director: Robert Zemeckis
Co-stars: Michael J. Fox Christopher Lloyd Crispin Clover

1986 HOWARD THE DUCK
Director: Willard Huyck

Co-stars: Tim Robbins Jeffrey Jones Paul Guilfoyle

1986 SPACECAMP
Director: Harry Winer
Co-stars: Kate Capshaw Leaf Phoenix Tom Skerritt

1987 SOME KIND OF WONDERFUL
Director: Howard Deutch
Co-stars: Eric Stoltz Mary Stuart Masterson Craig Sheffer

1988 THE WIZARD OF LONELINESS
Director: Jenny Bowen
Co-stars: Lukas Haas Lance Guest John Randolph

1988 CASUAL SEX ?
Director: Genevieve Robert
Co-stars: Victoria Jackson Stephen Shellen Jerry Levine

1989 NIGHTBREAKER
Director: Peter Markle
Co-stars: Martin Sheen Emilio Estevez Melinda Dillon

1989 BACK TO THE FUTURE II
Director: Robert Zemeckis
Co-stars: Michael J. Fox Christopher Lloyd Joe Flaherty

1990 BACK TO THE FUTURE III
Director: Robert Zemeckis
Co-stars: Michael J. Fox Mary Steenburgen Matt Clark

1992 ARTICLE 99
Director: Howard Deutch
Co-stars: Ray Liotta Kiefer Sutherland Eli Wallach

1993 DENNIS
Director: Nick Castle
Co-stars: Walter Matthau Christopher Lloyd Mason Gamble

1993 STOLEN BABIES
Director: Eric Laneuville
Co-stars: Mary Tyler Moore Kathleen Quinlan Mary Nell Santacroce

1994 THE BEVERLY HILLBILLIES
Director: Penelope Spheeris
Co-stars: Jim Varney Dabney Coleman Lily Tomlin

1994 THE SUBSTITUTE WIFE
Director: Peter Werner
Co-stars: Farrah Fawcett Peter Weller Karis Bryant

1995 UNSPOKEN TRUTH
Director: Peter Werner
Co-stars: Patricia Kalember Robert Englund

NATALIE THOMPSON

1941 RINGSIDE MAISIE
Director: Edwin Marin
Co-stars: Ann Sothern George Murphy Virginia O'Brien

SADA THOMPSON

1971 DESPERATE CHARACTERS
Director: Frank Gilroy
Co-stars: Shirley MacLaine Kenneth Mars Gerald S. O'Loghlin

1975 THE ENTERTAINER
Director: Donald Wrye
Co-stars: Jack Lemmon Ray Bolger Tyne Daly

1989 FEAR STALK
Director: Larry Shaw
Co-stars: Jill Clayburgh Stephen Macht Lorna Luft

1989 HOME FIRES BURNING
Director: Glenn Jordan
Co-stars: Barnard Hughes Robert Prosky Bill Pullman

1990 ANDRE'S MOTHER
Director: Deborah Reinisch
Co-star: Richard Thomas

SHELLEY THOMPSON

1986 LABYRINTH
Director: Jim Henson
Co-stars: David Bowie Jennifer Connelly Toby Froud

1992 JUST LIKE A WOMAN
Director: Christopher Monger
Co-stars: Julie Walters Adrian Pasdar Susan Wooldridge

SOPHIE THOMPSON
(Sister Of Emma Thompson)

1987 WHITE LADY
Director: David Rudkin
Co-stars: Cornelius Garrett Jessica Martin Meg Wynn Owen

1991 TWENTY-ONE
Director: Don Boyd
Co-stars: Patsy Kensit Jack Shepherd Patrick Ryecart

1995 PERSUASION
Director: Roger Michell
Co-stars: Ciaran Hands Corin Redgrave Amanda Root

1996 EMMA
Director: Douglas McGrath
Co-stars: Gwyneth Paltrow Greta Scacchi Ewan McGregor

SUSANNA THOMPSON

1994 LITTLE GIANTS
Director: Duwayne Dunham
Co-stars: Rick Moranis Ed O'Neill Mary Ellen Trainor

1995 BERMUDA TRIANGLE
Director: Ian Toynton
Co-stars: Sam Behens Lisa Jakub

SALLY THOMSETT

1970 THE RAILWAY CHILDREN
Director: Lionel Jeffries
Co-stars: Jenny Agutter Dinah Sheridan Bernard Cribbins

1972 BAXTER
Director: Lionel Jeffries
Co-stars: Patricia Neal Scott Jacoby Britt Ekland

1974 A MAN ABOUT THE HOUSE
Director: John Robins
Co-stars: Richard O'Sullivan Paula Wilcox Yootha Joyce

BEATRIX THOMSON

1931 DREYFUSS
Director: Milton Rosmer
Co-stars: Cedric Hardwicke George Merritt Charles Carson

KIM THOMSON

**1987 INSPECTOR WEXFORD:
WOLF TO THE SLAUGHTER**
Director: John Davies
Co-stars: George Baker Christopher Ravenscroft

1988 STEALING HEAVEN
Director: Clive Donner
Co-stars: Derek De Lint Denholm Elliott Kenneth Cranham

1989 THE TALL GUY
Director: Mel Smith
Co-stars: Jeff Goldblum Emma Thompson Geraldine James

**1990 PERRY MASON: THE CASE OF THE
DESPERATE DECEPTION**
Director: Christian Nyby
Co-stars: Raymond Burr Ian McShane

1990 JEKYLL AND HYDE
Director: David Wickes
Co-stars: Michael Caine Joss Ackland Ronald Pickup

1990 INSPECTOR MORSE: SINS OF THE FATHER
Director: Peter Hammond
Co-stars: John Thaw Kevin Whately Lisa Harrow

1990 HANDS OF A MURDERER
Director: Stuart Orme
Co-stars: Edward Woodward Anthony Andrews Warren Clark

MARJORIE THOMSON

1950 THE GORBALS STORY
Director: David MacKane
Co-stars: Howard Connell Betty Henderson Russell Hunter

JUNE THORBURN

1953 THE CRUEL SEA
Director: Charles Frend
Co-stars: Jack Hawkins Donald Sinden Denholm Elliott

1954 ORDERS ARE ORDERS
Director: David Paltenghi
Co-stars: Peter Sellers Sid James Tony Hancock

1954 FAST AND LOOSE
Director: Gordon Parry
Co-stars: Brian Reece Stanley Holloway Kay Kendall

1954 DELAYED ACTION
Director: John Harlow
Co-stars: Robert Ayres Alan Wheatley Bruce Seton

1954 CHILDREN GALORE
Director: Terence Fisher
Co-stars: Eddie Byrne Marjorie Rhodes Betty Ann Davies

1955 THE HORNET'S NEST
Director: Charles Saunders
Co-stars: Paul Carpenter Marla Landi Nora Nicholson

1955 TOUCH AND GO
Director: Michael Truman
Co-stars: Jack Hawkins Margaret Johnston Roland Culver

1957 TRUE AS A TURTLE
Director: Wendy Toye
Co-stars: John Gregson Cecil Parker Keith Michell

1958 TOM THUMB
Director: George Pal
Co-stars: Russ Tamblyn Jessie Matthews Peter Sellers

1958 ROONEY
Director: George Pollock
Co-stars: John Gregson Barry Fitzgerald Muriel Pavlow

1958 BROTH OF A BOY
Director: George Pollock
Co-stars: Barry Fitzgerald Tony Wright Marie Keen

1959 THE THREE WORLDS OF GULLIVER
Director: Jack Sher
Co-stars: Kerwin Matthews Basil Sydney Mary Ellis

1960 FURY AT SMUGGLER'S BAY
Director: John Gilling
Co-stars: Peter Cushing John Fraser William Franklyn

1961 DON'T BOTHER TO KNOCK
Director: Cyril Frankel
Co-stars: Richard Todd Elke Sommer Nicole Maurey

1963 MASTER SPY
Director: Montgomery Tully
Co-stars: Stephen Murray Alan Wheatley John Carson

1963 THE SCARLET BLADE
Director: John Gilling
Co-stars: Oliver Reed Lionel Jeffries Jack Hedley

KELLY THORDSEN

1966 THE UGLY DACHSHUND
Director: Norman Tokar
Co-stars: Dean Jones Suzanne Pleshette Charles Ruggles

1966 BOY, DID I GET A WRONG NUMBER !
Director: George Marshall
Co-stars: Bob Hope Elke Sommer Phyllis Diller

1974 THE PARALLAX VIEW
Director: Alan J. Pakula
Co-stars: Warren Beatty Paula Prentiss Hume Cronyn

SYBIL THORNDYKE

1928 DAWN
Director: Herbert Wilcox
Co-stars: Marie Ault Mary Brough Haddon Mason

1931 THE GENTLEMAN OF PARIS
Director: Sinclair Hill
Co-stars: Arthur Wontner Hugh Williams

1936 TUDOR ROSE
Director: Robert Stevenson
Co-stars: Cedric Hardwicke Nova Pilbeam John Mills

1941 MAJOR BARBARA
Director: David Lean
Co-stars: Wendy Hiller Rex Harrison Deborah Kerr

1947 NICHOLAS NICKLEBY
Director: Alberto Cavalcanti
Co-stars: Derek Bond Bernard Miles James Hayter

1948 BRITANNIA MEWS
Director: Jean Negulesco
Co-stars: Maureen O'Hara Dana Andrews Fay Compton

1950 GONE TO EARTH
Director: Michael Powell
Co-stars: Jennifer Jones David Farrar Cyril Cusack

1950 STAGE FRIGHT
Director: Alfred Hitchcock
Co-stars: Marlene Dietrich Jane Wyman Richard Todd

1951 THE MAGIC BOX
Director: John Boulting
Co-stars: Robert Donat Maria Schell Margaret Johnston

1953 MELBA
Director: Lewis Milestone
Co-stars: Patrice Munsel Robert Morley

1953 THE WEAK AND THE WICKED
Director: J. Lee-Thompson
Co-stars: Glynis Johns Diana Dors John Gregson

1957 THE PRINCE AND THE SHOWGIRL
Director: Laurence Olivier
Co-stars: Laurence Olivier Marilyn Monroe Jeremy Spencer

1958 SMILEY GETS A GUN
Director: Anthony Kimmins
Co-stars: Chips Rafferty Keith Calvert

1958 ALIVE AND KICKING
Director: Cyril Frankel
Co-stars: Kathleen Harrison Estelle Winwood

1959 JET STORM
Director: Cy Endfield
Co-stars: Stanley Baker Diane Cilento Harry Secombe

1959 SHAKE HANDS WITH THE DEVIL
Director: Michael Anderson
Co-stars: James Cagney Don Murray Dana Wynter

1960 HAND IN HAND
Director: Philip Leacock
Co-stars: John Gregson Loretta Parry Philip Needs

1960   THE BIG GAMBLE
Director: Richard Fleischer
Co-stars: Stephen Boyd Juliette Greco David Wayne

ANGELA THORNE

1982   ANYONE FOR DENIS?
Director: Dick Clement
Co-star: John Wells

1983   BULLSHOT
Director: Dick Clement
Co-stars: Alan Shearman Frances Tomelty Michael Aldridge

1990   B.F.G. (VOICE)
Director: Brian Cosgrove
Co-stars: David Jason Amanda Root Michael Knowles

TRACY THORNE

1992   SMALL METAL JACKET
Director: Steve Hilliker
Co-stars: Debora Weston Marie Theodore Jana Sheldon

SIGRID THORNTON

1982   THE MAN FROM SNOWY RIVER
Director: George Miller
Co-stars: Kirk Douglas Jack Thompson Terence Donovan

1987   SLATE, WYN & ME
Director: Don McLennan
Co-stars: Simon Burke Martin Sacks Tommy Lewis

1992   OVER THE HILL
Director: George Miller
Co-stars: Olympia Dukakis Derek Fowlds Bill Kerr

1994   TRAPPED IN SPACE
Director: Arthur Allan Seidelman
Co-stars: Jack Wagner Jack Coleman Kay Lenz

LINDA THORSON

1984   ACT OF PASSION
Director: Simon Langton
Co-stars: Kris Kristofferson Marlo Thomas George Dzundza

1985   WALLS OF GLASS
Director: Scott Goldstein
Co-stars: Philip Bosco Geraldine Page Olympia Dukakis

1985   JOEY
Director: Joseph Ellison
Co-stars: Neil Barry James Quinn Elisa Heinsohn

ELIZABETH THREATT

1952   THE BIG SKY
Director: Howard Hawks
Co-stars: Kirk Douglas Arthur Hunnicutt Dewey Martin

INGRID THULIN

1956   FOREIGN INTRIGUE
Director: Sheldon Reynolds
Co-stars: Robert Mitchum Genevieve Page Eugene Deckers

1957   WILD STRAWBERRIES
Director: Ingmar Bergman
Co-stars: Victor Sjostrom Bibi Andersson Naima Wifstrand

1958   THE FACE
Director: Ingmar Bergman
Co-stars: Max Von Sydow Gunnar Bjornstrand Naima Wifstrand

1961   THE FOUR HORSEMEN OF THE APOCALYPSE
Director: Vincente Minnelli
Co-stars: Glenn Ford Charles Boyer Lee J. Cobb

1962   WINTER LIGHT
Director: Ingmar Bergman
Co-stars: Max Von Sydow Gunnar Bjornstrand Gunnel Lindblom

1963   THE SILENCE
Director: Ingmar Bergman
Co-stars: Gunnel Lindblom Haken Jahnherb Birger Malmsten

1965   RETURN FROM THE ASHES
Director: J. Lee-Thompson
Co-stars: Maximilian Schell Samantha Eggar Herbert Lom

1966   NIGHT GAMES
Director: Mai Zetterling
Co-stars: Keve Hjelm Lena Brundin Naima Wifstrand

1966   LA GUERRE EST FINIE
Director: Alain Resnais
Co-stars: Yves Montand Genevieve Bujold Michel Piccoli

1969   THE DAMNED
Director: Luchino Visconti
Co-stars: Dirk Bogarde Helmut Berger Helmut Griem

1969   THE RITE
Director: Ingmar Bergman
Co-stars: Anders Ek Gunnar Bjornstrand Erik Hell

1972   CRIES AND WHISPERS
Director: Ingmar Bergman
Co-stars: Harriet Andersson Kari Sylwan Liv Ullman

1975   MOSES
Director: Gianfranco De Bosio
Co-stars: Burt Lancaster Anthony Quayle Irene Papas

1976   THE CASSANDRA CROSSING
Director: Brian De Palma
Co-stars: Sophia Loren Burt Lancaster Ava Gardner

1984   AFTER THE REHEARSAL
Director: Ingmar Bergman
Co-stars: Erland Josephson Lena Olin

UMA THURMAN
(Married Gary Oldman, Partner Of Ethan Hawke)
Nominated For Best Supporting Actress In 1994 For "Pulp Fiction"

1988   DANGEROUS LIAISONS
Director: Stephen Frears
Co-stars: Glenn Close John Malkovich Michelle Pfeiffer

1989   THE ADVENTURES OF BARON MUNCHAUSEN
Director: Terry Gilliam
Co-stars: John Neville Oliver Reed Eric Idle

1990   HENRY AND JUNE
Director: Philip Kaufman
Co-stars: Fred Ward Maria De Mederios Richard E. Grant

1990   WHERE THE HEART IS
Director: John Boorman
Co-stars: Dabney Coleman Joanna Cassidy Suzy Amis

1991   ROBIN HOOD
Director: John Irvin
Co-stars: Patrick Bergin Jurgen Prochnow Edward Fox

1992   MAD DOG AND GLORY
Director: John McNaughton
Co-stars: Robert De Niro Bill Murray David Caruso

1992   JENNIFER EIGHT
Director: Bruce Robinson
Co-stars: Andy Garcia John Malkovich Kathy Baker

1992   FINAL ANALYSIS
Director: Phil Joanou
Co-stars: Richard Gere Kim Basinger Eric Roberts

1993   EVEN COWGIRLS GET THE BLUES
Director: Gus Van Sant
Co-stars: John Hurt Rain Phoenix Pat Morita

1994   PULP FICTION
Director: Quentin Tarantino
Co-stars: John Travolta Bruce Willis Samuel L. Jackson

1996   THE TRUTH ABOUT CATS AND DOGS
Director: Michael Lehman
Co-stars: Ben Chaplin Janeane Garofalo

1996   A MONTH BY THE LAKE
Director: John Irvin
Co-stars: Vanessa Redgrave Edward Fox Allesandro Gassman

1996   BEAUTIFUL GIRLS
Director: Ted Demme
Co-stars: Timothy Hutton Mira Sorvino Natalie Portman

1997   THE EIGHTH DAY
Director: Jaco Van Dormael
Co-stars: Jude Law Daniel Auteuil Pascal Duquenne

1997   BATMAN AND ROBIN
Director: Joel Schumacher
Co-stars: George Clooney Arnold Schwarzenegger Alicia Silverstone

1998   GATTACA
Director: Andrew Niccol
Co-stars: Ethan Hawke Alan Arkin Loren Dean

SOPHIE THURSFIELD

1995   SISTER, MY SISTER
Director: Nancy Meckler
Co-stars: Joely Richardson Julie Walters Jodhi May

CAROL THURSTON

1944   THE STORY OF DR WASSELL
Director: Cecil B. DeMille
Co-stars: Gary Cooper Laraine Day Signe Hasso

1944   THE CONSPIRATORS
Director: Jean Negulesco
Co-stars: Hedy Lamarr Paul Henreid Sydney Greenstreet

1945   CHINA SKY
Director: Ray Enright
Co-stars: Randolph Scott Ellen Drew Ruth Warrick

1946   SWAMP FIRE
Director: William Pine
Co-stars: Johnny Weismuller Buster Crabbe Virginia Grey

1947   THE LAST ROUND-UP
Co-stars: Gene Autry Bobby Blake

ARABELLA TJYE

1993   JILLY COOPER'S RIDERS
Director: Gabrielle Beaumont
Co-stars: Marcus Gilbert Michael Praed Caroline Harker

RACHEL TICOTIN

1981   FORT APACHE, THE BRONX
Director: Daniel Petrie
Co-stars: Paul Newman Ed Asner Danny Aiello

1985   LOVE, MARY
Director: Robert Day
Co-stars: Kristy McNichol Piper Laurie David Paymer

1986   CRITICAL CONDITION
Director: Michael Apted
Co-stars: Richard Pryor Joe Mantegna Sylvia Miles

1986   ROCKABYE
Director: Richard Michaels
Co-stars: Valerie Bertinelli Jason Alexander Jo Henderson

1986   WHEN THE BOUGH BREAKS
Director: Waris Hussein
Co-stars: Ted Danson Richard Masur David Huddleston

1990   TOTAL RECALL
Director: Paul Verhoeven
Co-stars: Arnold Schwarzenegger Sharon Stone Ronny Cox

1991   PRISON STORIES: WOMEN ON THE INSIDE
Director: Donna Deitch
Co-stars: Lolita Davidovich Rae Dawn Chong

1991   ONE GOOD COP
Director: Ralph Bode
Co-stars: Michael Keaton Rene Russo Anthony LaPaglia

1991   F/X2
Director: Richard Franklin
Co-stars: Bryan Brown Brian Dennehy Joanna Gleason

1992   FALLING DOWN
Director: Joel Schumacher
Co-stars: Michael Douglas Robert Duvall Barbara Hershey

1995   DON JUAN DeMARCO
Director: Jeremy Leven
Co-stars: Johnny Depp Marlon Brando Faye Dunaway

1995   THE WHARF RAT
Director: Jimmy Huston
Co-stars: Judge Reinhold Lou Diamond Phillips Rita Moreno

1996   STEAL BIG, STEAL LITTLE
Director: Andrew Davis
Co-stars: Andy Garcia Alan Arkin

1997   TURBULENCE
Co-stars: Lauren Holly Ray Liotta Ben Cross

INGA TIDBLAD

1936   INTERMEZZO
Director: Gustav Molander
Co-stars: Gosta Ekman Ingrid Bergman Bulleb Berglund

KERSTIN TIDELIUS

1969   ADALEN 31
Director: Bo Widerberg
Co-stars: Peter Schildt Roland Hedlund Anita Bjork

FRIEDERIKE TIEFENBACHER

1989   THREE WOMEN IN LOVE
Director: Rudolf Thome
Co-stars: Johannes Herrschmann Adrianna Altaras Jurgen Wink

HANNELORE TIEFENBRUNNER

1973   TENDERNESS OF WOLVES
Director: Ulli Lommel
Co-stars: Kurt Raab Jeff Roden Margit Carstensen

GENE TIERNEY

Nominated For Best Actress In 1945 For Leave Her To Heaven

1940   THE RETURN OF FRANK JAMES
Director: Fritz Lang
Co-stars: Henry Fonda Jackie Cooper Henry Hull

1940   HUDSON'S BAY
Director: Irving Pichel
Co-stars: Paul Muni Laird Cregar John Sutton

1941   SUNDOWN
Director: Henry Hathaway
Co-stars: Bruce Cabot George Sanders Harry Carey

1941   THE SHANGHAI GESTURE
Director: Josef Von Sternberg
Co-stars: Victor Mature Walter Huston Ona Munson

1941 TOBACCO ROAD
Director: John Ford
Co-stars: Charley Grapewin Elizabeth Patterson Dana Andrews

1941 BELLE STARR
Director: Irving Cummings
Co-stars: Randolph Scott Dana Andrews Chill Wills

1942 RINGS ON HER FINGERS
Director: Rouben Mamoulian
Co-stars: Henry Fonda Laird Cregar Spring Byington

1942 SON OF FURY
Director: John Cromwell
Co-stars: Tyrone Power George Sanders Frances Farmer

1942 THUNDERBIRDS
Director: William Wellman
Co-stars: Preston Foster John Sutton May Whitty

1942 CHINA GIRL
Director: Henry Hathaway
Co-stars: George Montgomery Lynn Bari Victor McLaglen

1943 HEAVEN CAN WAIT
Director: Ernst Lubitsch
Co-stars: Don Ameche Laird Cregar Charles Coburn

1944 LAURA
Director: Otto Preminger
Co-stars: Dana Andrews Clifton Webb Vincent Price

1945 LEAVE HER TO HEAVEN
Director: John Stahl
Co-stars: Cornel Wilde Jeanne Crain Vincent Price

1945 A BELL FOR ADANO
Director: Henry King
Co-stars: John Hodiak William Bendix Richard Conte

1946 DRAGONWYCK
Director: Joseph Mankiewicz
Co-stars: Vincent Price Glenn Langan Walter Huston

1946 THE RAZOR'S EDGE
Director: Edmund Goulding
Co-stars: Tyrone Power Anne Baxter Clifton Webb

1947 THE GHOST AND MRS MUIR
Director: Joseph Mankiewicz
Co-stars: Rex Harrison George Sanders Edna Best

1948 THE IRON CURTAIN
Director: William Wellman
Co-stars: Dana Andrews Edna Best Barry Kroeger

1948 THAT WONDERFUL URGE
Director: Robert Sinclair
Co-stars: Tyrone Power Reginald Gardiner Gene Lockhart

1950 WHERE THE SIDEWALK ENDS
Director: Otto Preminger
Co-stars: Dana Andrews Gary Merrill Karl Malden

1950 WHIRLPOOL
Director: Otto Preminger
Co-stars: Jose Ferrer Richard Conte Charles Bickford

1950 NIGHT AND THE CITY
Director: Jules Dassin
Co-stars: Richard Widmark Googie Withers Herbert Lom

1951 THE SECRET OF CONVICT LAKE
Director: Michael Gordon
Co-stars: Glenn Ford Ann Dvorak Ethel Barrymore

1951 ON THE RIVIERA
Director: Walter Lang
Co-stars: Danny Kaye Corinne Calvet Marcel Dalio

1951 THE MATING SEASON
Director: Mitchell Leisen
Co-stars: John Lund Thelma Ritter Jan Sterling

1951 CLOSE TO MY HEART
Director: William Keighley
Co-stars: Ray Milland Fay Bainter Howard St. John

1952 PLYMOUTH ADVENTURE
Director: Clarence Brown
Co-stars: Spencer Tracy Van Johnson Dawn Addams

1952 WAY OF A GAUCHO
Director: Jacques Tourneur
Co-stars: Rory Calhoun Richard Boone Hugh Marlowe

1953 PERSONAL AFFAIR
Director: Anthony Pellissier
Co-stars: Leo Genn Glynis Johns Pamela Brown

1953 NEVER LET ME GO
Director: Delmer Daves
Co-stars: Clark Gable Richard Hayden Keneth More

1954 THE EGYPTIAN
Director: Michael Curtiz
Co-stars: Edmund Purdom Victor Mature Peter Ustinov

1954 BLACK WIDOW
Director: Nunnally Johnson
Co-stars: Ginger Rogers Van Heflin George Raft

1955 THE LEFT HAND OF GOD
Director: Edward Dmytryk
Co-stars: Humphrey Bogart Lee J. Cobb Agnes Moorehead

1962 ADVISE AND CONSENT
Director: Otto Preminger
Co-stars: Don Murray Charles Laughton Henry Fonda

1963 TOYS IN THE ATTIC
Director: George Roy Hill
Co-stars: Geraldine Page Wendy Hiller Dean Martin

1964 THE PLEASURE SEEKERS
Director: Jean Negulesco
Co-stars: Ann-Margret Carol Lynley Pamela Tiffin

MAURA TIERNEY

1988 CROSSING THE MOB
Director: Steven Hillard Stern
Co-stars: Jason Bateman Patti D'Arbanville Frank Stallone

1992 WHITE SANDS
Director: Roger Donaldson
Co-stars: Willem Dafoe Samuel L. Jackson Mickey Rourke

1997 LIAR LIAR
Director: Tom Shadyac
Co-stars: Jim Carrey Amanda Donohue Justin Cooper

TIFFANY

1990 JETSONS: THE MOVIE (Voice)
Director: William Hanna
Co-stars: George O'Hanlon Penny Singleton Mel Blanc

PAMELA TIFFIN

1961 ONE, TWO, THREE
Director: Billy Wilder
Co-stars: James Cagney Horst Bushholz Arlene Francis

1962 SUMMER AND SMOKE
Director: Peter Glenville
Co-stars: Geraldine Page Laurence Harvey Una Merkel

1962 STATE FAIR
Director: Jose Ferrer
Co-stars: Pat Boone Alice Faye Tom Ewell

1962 COME FLY WITH ME
Director: Henry Levin
Co-stars: Hugh O'Brian Dolores Hart Karl Malden

1964   FOR THOSE WHO THINK YOUNG
Director: Leslie Martinson
Co-stars: James Darren Nancy Sinatra Tina Louise

1964   THE PLEASURE SEEKERS
Director: Jean Negulesco
Co-stars: Ann-Margret Tony Franciosa Carol Lynley

1965   THE HALLELUJAH TRAIL
Director: John Sturges
Co-stars: Burt Lancaster Lee Remick Brian Keith

1966   THE MOVING TARGET
Director: Jack Smight
Co-stars: Paul Newman Lauren Bacall Shelley Winters

1969   VIVA MAX
Director: Jerry Paris
Co-stars: Peter Ustinov John Astin Keenan Wynn

1973   DEAF SMITH AND JOHNNY EARS
Director: Paolo Cavara
Co-stars: Anthony Quinn Franco Nero

PAULA TILBROOK

1990   EFFIE'S BURNING
Director: Nigel Evans
Co-stars: Phyllis Logan Gordon Jackson Ian Sexton

ZEFFIE TILBURY

1921   CAMILLE
Director: Ray Smallwood
Co-stars: Nazimova Rudolph Valentino Arthur Hoyt

1935   WEREWOLF IN LONDON
Director: Stuart Walker
Co-stars: Henry Hull Warner Oland Valerie Hobson

1936   DESIRE
Director: Frank Borzage
Co-stars: Marlene Dietrich Gary Cooper John Halliday

1936   THE BOHEMIAN GIRL
Director: James Horne
Co-stars: Stan Laurel Oliver Hardy Mae Busch

1939   TELL NO TALES
Director: Leslie Fenton
Co-stars: Melvyn Douglas Louise Platt Gene Lockhart

1940   THE GRAPES OF WRATH
Director: John Ford
Co-stars: Henry Fonda Jane Darwell John Carradine

1941   TOBACCO ROAD
Director: John Ford
Co-stars: Gene Tierney Dana Andrews Elizabeth Patterson

JENNY TILL

1966   THEATRE OF DEATH
Director: Sam Gallu
Co-stars: Christopher Lee Lelia Goldoni Julian Glover

1967   A CHALLENGE FOR ROBIN HOOD
Director: C.M. Pennington-Richards
Co-stars: Barrie Ingham James Hayter Gay Hamilton

NADJA TILLER

1958   THE GIRL ROSEMARIE
Director: Rolf Thiele
Co-stars: Peter Van Eck Gert Frobe Carl Raddatz

1959   THE ROUGH AND THE SMOOTH
Director: Robert Siodmak
Co-stars: Tony Britton William Bendix Natasha Parry

1962   NO ORCHIDS FOR LULU

JENNIFER TILLY *(Sister Of Meg Tilly)*
Nominated For Best Supporting Actress In 1994 For "Bullets Over Broadway"

1985   MOVING VIOLATIONS
Director: Neal Israel
Co-stars: Stephen McHattie James Keach Sally Kellerman

1989   LET IT RIDE
Director: Joe Pykta
Co-stars: Richard Dreyfuss Teri Garr Allen Garfield

1989   THE FABULOUS BAKER BOYS
Director: Steve Kloves
Co-stars: Jeff Bridges Beau Bridges Michelle Pfeiffer

1991   SCORCHERS
Director: David Beard
Co-stars: Faye Dunaway Denholm Elliott Emily Lloyd

1993   MADE IN AMERICA
Director: Richard Benjamin
Co-stars: Whoopi Goldberg Ted Danson Nia Long

1993   SHADOW OF THE WOLF
Director: Jacques Dorfman
Co-stars: Lou Diamond Phillips Donald Sutherland

1994   THE GETAWAY
Director: Roger Donaldson
Co-stars: Alec Baldwin Kim Basinger Michael Madsen

1994   BULLETS OVER BROADWAY
Director: Woody Allen
Co-stars: John Cusack Dianne Wiest

1994   HEADS
Director: Paul Shapiro
Co-stars: Jon Cryer Edward Asner Roddy McDowall

1996   BOUND
Director: Andy Wachowski
Co-stars: Gina Gershon Joe Pantoliano

1997   LIAR LIAR
Director: Tom Shadyac
Co-stars: Jim Carrey Amanda Donohue Justin Cooper

1998   BELLA MAFIA
Co-stars: Vanessa Redgrave Nastassja Kinski Ileana Douglas

MEG TILLY *(Sister Of Jennifer Tilly)*
Nominated For Best Supporting Actress In 1985 For "Agnes Of God"

1982   TEX
Director: Tim Hunter
Co-stars: Matt Dillon Jim Metzler Ben Johnson

1983   PSYCHO II
Director: Richard Franklin
Co-stars: Anthony Perkins Vera Miles Robert Loggia

1983   THE BIG CHILL
Director: Lawrence Kasdan
Co-stars: Tom Berenger Glenn Close Kevin Kline

1984   IMPULSE
Director: Graham Baker
Co-stars: Tim Matheson Hume Cronyn John Karlen

1985   AGNES OF GOD
Director: Norman Jewison
Co-stars: Jane Fonda Anne Bancroft Anne Pitoniak

1986   OFF BEAT
Director: Michael Dinner
Co-stars: Judge Reinhold Joe Mantegna Cleavant Derricks

1988   MASQUERADE
Director: Bob Swaim
Co-stars: Rob Lowe Kim Cattrall John Glover

1988 **THE GIRL IN THE SWING**
Director: Gordon Hessler
Co-stars: Rupert Fraser Lynsey Baxter

1989 **VALMONT**
Director: Milos Foreman
Co-stars: Colin Firth Annette Bening Fairusa Balk

1989 **IN THE BEST INTEREST OF THE CHILD**
Director: David Greene
Co-stars: Michael O'Keefe Ed Begley Jnr.

1990 **THE TWO JAKES**
Director: Jack Nicholson
Co-stars: Jack Nicholson Harvey Keitel Madeleine Stowe

1993 **BODY SNATCHERS**
Director: Abel Ferarra
Co-stars: Gabrielle Anwar Billy Wirth Terry Kinney

1994 **SLEEP WITH ME**
Director: Rory Kelly
Co-stars: Eric Stoltz Craig Sheffer

BARBARA TILNEY

1974 **AKENFIELD**
Director: Peter Hall
Co-stars: Garrow Shand Peggy Cole Ida Page

CHARLENE TILTON

1976 **FREAKY FRIDAY**
Director: Gary Nelson
Co-stars: Jodie Foster Barbara Harris John Astin

1990 **BORDER SHOOT-OUT**
Director: Chris McIntyre
Co-stars: Glenn Ford Cody Glenn Michael Ansara

1996 **SILENCE OF THE HAMS**
Director: Ezio Greggio

JULIE TIMMERMAN

1990 **LE CHATEAU DE MA MERE**
Director: Yves Robert
Co-stars: Philippe Caubere Nathalie Roussell Didier Pain

CALI TIMMONS

1994 **HARD EVIDENCE**
Director: Michael Kennedy
Co-stars: Gregory Harrison Joan Severance

ANNE MARIE TIMONEY

1992 **THE LONG ROADS**
Director: Tristram Powell
Co-stars: Edith MacArthur Robert Urquhart Michelle Fairley

FAY TINCHER

1914 **THE BATTLE OF THE SEXES**
Director: D.W. Griffith
Co-stars: Donald Crisp Lillian Gish Robert Harron

GABRIELE TINTI

1965 **SEVEN GOLDEN MEN**
Director: Marco Vicario
Co-stars: Rossana Podesta Philippe Leroy Gastone Moschin

1968 **THE LEGEND OF LYLAH CLARE**
Director: Robert Aldrich
Co-stars: Kim Novak Peter Finch Ernest Borgnine

1970 **RIDER ON THE RAIN**
Director: Rene Clement
Co-stars: Charles Bronson Marlene Jobert Jill Ireland

1972 **LISA AND THE DEVIL**
Director: Mario Bava
Co-stars: Elke Sommer Telly Savalas Alida Valli

ALICE TISSOT

1927 **AN ITALIAN STRAW HAT**
Director: Rene Clair
Co-stars: Albert Prejean Olga Tschechowa Marise Maia

1932 **LA MATERNELLE**
Director: Marie Epstein
Co-stars: Madeleine Renaud Paulette Elambert Mady Berry

GINNY TIU

1962 **IT HAPPENED AT THE WORLD'S FAIR**
Director: Norman Taurog
Co-stars: Elvis Presley Gary Lockwood Joan O'Brien

THELMA TIXOU

1989 **SANTA SANGRE**
Director: Alejandro Jodorowsky
Co-stars: Axel Jodorowsky Blanca Guerra Guy Stockwell

HEATHER TOBIAS

1988 **HIGH HOPES**
Director: Mike Leigh
Co-stars: Ruth Sheen Lesley Manville David Bamber

1989 **TESTIMONY OF A CHILD**
Director: Peter Smith
Co-stars: Jill Baker John Bowe Jonathan Leigh

GENEVIEVE TOBIN

1930 **FREE LOVE**
Co-stars: Conrad Nagel Reginald Pasch Bertha Mann

1930 **A LADY SURRENDERS**
Director: John Stahl
Co-stars: Conrad Nagel Basil Rathbone Rose Hobart

1931 **THE GAY DIPLOMAT**
Director: Richard Boleslawski
Co-stars: Ivan Lebedeff Ilka Chase Betty Compson

1931 **SEED**
Director: John Stahl
Co-stars: John Boles Lois Wilson Bette Davis

1932 **ONE HOUR WITH YOU**
Director: Ernst Lubitsch
Co-stars: Maurice Chevalier Jeanette MacDonald

1932 **THE COHENS AND THE KELLYS IN HOLLYWOOD**
Director: Harry Pollard
Co-stars: George Sidney Charles Murray Sydney Fox

1932 **HOLLYWOOD SPEAKS**
Director: Eddie Buzzell
Co-stars: Pat O'Brien Lucien Prival Rita Leroy

1933 **GOLDEN HARVEST**
Co-star: Chester Morris

1933 **EASY TO LOVE**
Director: William Keighley
Co-stars: Adolphe Menjou Mary Astor Guy Kibbee

1933 **PLEASURE CRUISE**
Co-stars: Ralph Forbes Roland Young

1933 **GOODBYE AGAIN**
Director: Michael Curtiz
Co-stars: Warren William Joan Blondell Hugh Herbert

1933 **INFERNAL MACHINE**
Co-star: Chester Morris

1933 I LOVED A WOMAN
Director: Alfred Green
Co-stars: Edward G. Robinson Kay Francis Henry Kolker

1933 PERFECT UNDERSTANDING
Director: Cyril Gardner
Co-stars: Gloria Swanson Laurence Olivier Nora Swinburne

1934 UNCERTAIN LADY
Director: Karl Freund
Co-stars: Edward Everett Horton Rennee Gadd Paul Cavanagh

1934 DARK HAZARD
Director: Alfred Green
Co-stars: Edward G. Robinson Glenda Farrell Robert Barrat

1934 SUCCESS AT ANY PRICE
Director: Walter Ruben
Co-stars: Douglas Fairbanks Frank Morgan Colleen Moore

1934 THE NINTH GUEST
Director: Roy William Neil
Co-stars: Donald Cook Hardie Albright Edward Ellis

1934 KISS AND MAKE UP
Director: Harlan Thompson
Co-stars: Cary Grant Helen Mack Mona Maris

1934 BY YOUR LEAVE
Director: Lloyd Corrigan
Co-stars: Frank Morgan Neil Hamilton Marian Nixon

1935 THE GOOSE AND THE GANDER
Co-stars: Ralph Forbes Frank Orth Charles Coleman

1935 THE WOMAN IN RED
Director: Robert Florey
Co-stars: Barbara Stanwyck John Eldredge Gene Raymond

1935 HERE'S TO ROMANCE
Director: Alfred Green
Co-stars: Nino Martini Reginald Denny Anita Louise

1935 BROADWAY HOSTESS
Director: Frank McDonald
Co-stars: Wini Shaw Lyle Talbot Allen Jenkins

1936 THE MAN IN THE MIRROR
Director: Maurice Elvey
Co-stars: Edward Everett Horton Garry Marsh Ursula Jeans

1936 SNOWED UNDER
Co-stars: George Brent Patricia Ellis Glenda Farrell

1936 THE PETRIFIED FOREST
Director: Archie Mayo
Co-stars: Leslie Howard Bette Davis Humphrey Bogart

1937 THE GREAT GAMBINI
Director: Charles Vidor
Co-stars: Akim Tamiroff Marian Marsh William Demarest

1938 THE CASE OF THE LUCKY LEGS
Director: Archie Mayo
Co-stars: Warren William Allen Jenkins Patricia Ellis

1938 DRAMATIC SCHOOL
Director: Robert Sinclair
Co-stars: Luise Rainer Paulette Goddard Lana Turner

1938 KATE PLUS TEN
Director: Reginald Denham
Co-stars: Jack Hulbert Noel Maddison Googie Withers

1938 ZAZA
Director: George Cukor
Co-stars: Claudette Colbert Herbert Marshall Bert Lahr

1939 YES, MY DARLING DAUGHTER
Director: William Keighley
Co-stars: Priscilla Lane Jeffrey Lynn May Robson

1939 OUR NEIGHBOURS THE CARTERS
Director: Ralph Murray
Co-stars: Fay Bainter Frank Craven Edmund Lowe

1940 NO TIME FOR COMEDY
Director: William Keighley
Co-stars: James Stewart Rosalind Russell Charles Ruggles

VIVIAN TOBIN

1932 THE SIGN OF THE CROSS
Director: Cecil B. DeMille
Co-stars: Fredric March Claudette Colbert Charles Laughton

ANN TODD *(Married David Lean)*

1931 THE GHOST TRAIN
Director: Walter Forde
Co-stars: Jack Hulbert Cicely Courtneidge Angela Baddeley

1931 KEEPERS OF YOUTH
Director: Thomas Bentley
Co-stars: Garry Marsh Robin Irvine Mary Clare

1931 THESE CHARMING PEOPLE

1932 THE WATER GYPSIES
Director: Maurice Elvey
Co-stars: Sari Maritza Richard Bird Ian Hunter

1934 THE RETURN OF BULLDOG DRUMMOND
Director: Walter Summers
Co-stars: Ralph Richardson Claud Allister

1936 THINGS TO COME
Co-stars: Raymond Massey Margaretta Scott

1937 THE SQUEAKER
Director: William Howard
Co-stars: Edmund Lowe Sebastian Shaw Robert Newton

1937 SOUTH RIDING
Director: Victor Saville
Co-stars: Ralph Richardson Edna Best Glynis Johns

1937 ACTION FOR SLANDER
Director: Tim Whelan
Co-stars: Clive Brook Margaretta Scott Ronald Squire

1939 POISON PEN
Director: Paul Stein
Co-stars: Flora Robson Robert Newton Reginald Tate

1941 SHIPS WITH WINGS
Director: Sergei Nolbandov
Co-stars: John Clements Leslie Banks Hugh Williams

1941 DANNY BOY
Director: Oswald Mitchell
Co-stars: Wilfrid Lawson David Farrar Grant Tyler

1945 PERFECT STRANGERS
Director: Alexander Korda
Co-stars: Robert Donat Deborah Kerr Glynis Johns

1945 THE SEVENTH VEIL
Director: Compton Bennett
Co-stars: James Mason Herbert Lom Yvonne Owen

1946 GAIETY GEORGE
Director: George King
Co-stars: Richard Greene Peter Graves Hazel Court

1946 DAYBREAK
Director: Compton Bennett
Co-stars: Eric Portman Maxwell Reed Bill Owen

1947 THE PARADINE CASE
Director: Alfred Hitchcock
Co-stars: Gregory Peck Charles Laughton Valli

1948 SO EVIL MY LOVE
Director: Lewis Allen
Co-stars: Ray Milland Geraldine Fitzgerald Moira Lister

1949 THE PASSIONATE FRIENDS
Director: David Lean
Co-stars: Claude Rains Trevor Howard Isabel Dean

1949   MADELEINE
Director: David Lean
Co-stars: Leslie Banks Elizabeth Sellars Edward Chapman

1952   THE SOUND BARRIER
Director: David Lean
Co-stars: Ralph Richardson Nigel Patrick John Justin

1954   THE GREEN SCARF
Director: George More O'Ferrall
Co-stars: Michael Redgrave Leo Genn Kieron Moore

1957   TIME WITHOUT PITY
Director: Josey Losey
Co-stars: Michael Redgrave Alex McCowan Leo McKern

1961   SCREAM OF FEAR
Director: Seth Holt
Co-stars: Susan Strasberg Ronald Lewis Christopher Lee

1962   SON OF CAPTAIN BLOOD
Co-stars: Sean Flynn Jose Nieto John Kitzmiller

1979   THE HUMAN FACTOR
Director: Otto Preminger
Co-stars: Nicol Williamson Richard Attenborough

ANN E. TODD (Child)

1940   ALL THIS AND HEAVEN TOO
Director: Anatole Litvak
Co-stars: Charles Boyer Bette Davis Barbara O'Neil

1941   THE MEN IN HER LIFE
Director: Gregory Ratoff
Co-stars: Loretta Young Conrad Veidt Dean Jagger

1941   HOW GREEN WAS MY VALLEY
Director: John Ford
Co-stars: Walter Pidgeon Maureen O'Hara Roddy McDowall

1946   MARGIE
Director: Henry King
Co-stars: Jeanne Crain Glenn Langan Alan Young

1948   THREE DARING DAUGHTERS
Director: Fred Wilcox
Co-stars: Jeanette MacDonald Jane Powell Jose Iturbi

1948   COVER-UP
Director: Alfred Green
Co-stars: Dennis O'Keefe William Bendix Barbara Britton

1951   BOMBA AND THE ELEPHANT STAMPEDE
Director: Ford Beebe
Co-star: Johnny Sheffield

BEVERLY TODD

1970   BROTHER JOHN
Director: James Goldstone
Co-stars: Sidney Poitier Bradford Dillman Will Geer

1978   THE GHOST OF FLIGHT 401
Director: Steven Hillard Stern
Co-stars: Ernest Borgnine Gary Lockwood Tina Chen

1987   A DIFFERENT AFFAIR
Director: Noel Masseck
Co-stars: Anne Archer Tony Roberts Bobby Jacoby

1988   CLARA'S HEART
Director: Robert Mulligan
Co-stars: Whoopi Goldberg Michael Ontkean Neil Patrick Harris

1988   MOVING
Director: Allan Metter
Co-stars: Richard Pryor Randy Quaid Dave Thomas

DIANE TODD

1958   6:5 SPECIAL
Director: Alfred Shaughnessy
Co-stars: Pete Murray Josephine Douglas Petula Clark

MABEL TODD

1938   THE COWBOY AND THE LADY
Director: H.C. Potter
Co-stars: Gary Cooper Merle Oberon Walter Brennan

1943   THE GHOST AND THE GUEST
Director: William Nigh
Co-stars: James Dunn Florence Rice Sam McDaniel

SAIRA TODD

1992   BAD BEHAVIOUR
Director: Les Blair
Co-stars: Stephen Rea Sinead Cusack Philip Jackson

1992   A FATAL INVERSION
Director: Tim Fywell
Co-stars: Douglas Hodge Julia Ford Jeremy Northam

SONIA TODD

1996   SHINE
Director: Scott Hicks
Co-stars: Geoffrey Rush Lynn Redgrave John Gielgud

THELMA TODD (Found Dead In Garage After Dispute With Lucky Luciano)

1929   SEVEN FOOTSTEPS TO SATAN
Director: Benjamin Christensen
Co-stars: Sheldon Lewis Ivan Christie

1929   UNACCUSTOMED AS WE ARE
Director: Lewis Foster
Co-stars: Stan Laurel Oliver Hardy Edgar Kennedy

1930   ANOTHER FINE MESS
Director: James Parrott
Co-stars: Stan Laurel Oliver Hardy James Finlayson

1930   FOLLOW THRU
Director: Lloyd Corrigan
Co-stars: Charles Rogers Nancy Carroll Jack Haley

1931   CHICKENS COME HOME
Director: James Horne
Co-stars: Stan Laurel Oliver Hardy James Finlayson

1931   BROADMINDED
Director: Mervyn LeRoy
Co-stars: Joe E. Brown Ona Munson Bela Lugesi

1931   THE MALTESE FALCON
Director: Roy Del Ruth
Co-stars: Ricardo Cortez Bebe Daniels Dudley Digges

1931   MONKEY BUSINESS
Director: Norman Z. McLeod
Co-stars: Marx Brothers Ruth Hall Harry Woods

1932   THIS IS THE NIGHT
Director: Frank Tuttle
Co-stars: Lili Damita Charles Ruggles Cary Grant

1932   HORSE FEATHERS
Director: Norman Z. McLeod
Co-stars: Marx Brothers David Landau Nat Pendleton

1932   SPEAK EASILY
Director: Edward Sedgwick
Co-stars: Buster Keaton Jimmy Durante Hedda Hopper

1932   CALL HER SAVAGE
Director: John Francis Dillon
Co-stars: Clara Bow Gilbert Roland Monroe Owsley

1933   COUNSELLOR-AT-LAW
Director: William Wyler
Co-stars: John Barrymore Bebe Daniels Melvyn Douglas

1933   FRA DIAVOLO
Director: Hal Roach
Co-stars: Stan Laurel Oliver Hardy Dennis King

1933 MARY STEVENS M.D.
Director: Lloyd Bacon
Co-stars: Kay Francis Lyle Talbot Glenda Farrell

1933 SITTING PRETTY
Director: Harry Joe Brown
Co-stars: Jack Oakie Jack Haley Ginger Rogers

1934 YOU MADE ME LOVE YOU
Director: Monty Banks
Co-stars: Stanley Lupino John Loder James Carew

1934 BOTTOMS UP
Director: David Butler
Co-stars: Spencer Tracy John Boles Pat Patterson

1934 HIPS, HIPS HOORAY
Director: Mark Sandrich
Co-stars: Bert Wheeler Robert Woolsey Ruth Etting

1934 COCKEYED CAVALIERS
Director: Mark Sandrich
Co-stars: Bert Wheeler Robert Woolsey Noah Berry

1935 TWO FOR TONIGHT
Director: Frank Tuttle
Co-stars: Bing Crosby Joan Bennett Lynne Overman

1936 THE BOHEMIAN GIRL
Director: Charles Rogers
Co-stars: Stan Laurel Oliver Hardy Mae Busch

TRISHA TODD

1992 CLAIRE OF THE MOON
Director: Nicole Conn
Co-stars: Faith McDevitt Sheila Dickinson

BORA TODOROVIC

1981 MONTENEGRO
Director: Dusan Makavejev
Co-stars: Susan Anspach Erland Josephson Per Oscarsson

MARILYN TOKUDA

1989 FAREWELL TO THE KING
Director: John Milius
Co-stars: Nick Nolte Nigel Havers James Fox

BERLINDA TOLBERT

1989 HARLEM NIGHTS
Director: Eddie Murphy
Co-stars: Eddie Murphy Richard Pryor Danny Aiello

KAREN TOLIN

1993 PRIME SUSPECT 3
Director: David Drury
Co-stars: Helen Mirren Tom Bell Peter Capaldi

MARILU TOLO

1972 BLUEBEARD
Director: Edward Dmytryk
Co-stars: Richard Burton Raquel Welch Virna Lisi

AMY TOLSKY

1994 INTIMATE WITH A STRANGER
Director: Mel Woods
Co-stars: Roderick Mangin-Turner Daphne Nayar Janis Lee

HEATHER TOM

1995 DEADLY WHISPERS
Director: Bill Norton
Co-stars: Tony Danza Pamela Reed Ving Rhames

LAUREN TOM

1984 NOTHING LASTS FOREVER
Director: Tom Schiller
Co-stars: Zach Galligan Dan Aykroyd Imogene Coca

1994 IN THE LINE OF DUTY: KIDNAPPED
Director: Bobby Roth
Co-stars: Dabney Coleman Tim Busfield

1994 WHEN A MAN LOVES A WOMAN
Director: Luis Mandoki
Co-stars: Andy Garcia Meg Ryan Ellen Burstyn

NICHOLLE TOM *(Child)*

1992 BEETHOVEN
Director: Brian Levant
Co-stars: Charles Grodin Bonnie Hunt Dean Jones

1993 BEETHOVEN'S 2ND
Director: Rod Daniel
Co-stars: Charles Grodin Bonnie Hunt Debi Mazar

DARA TOMANOVICH

1995 BIO-DOME
Co-stars: Stephen Baldwin Pauly Shore Kylie Minogue

CONCETTA TOMEI

1986 MURDER IN THREE ACTS
Director: Gary Nelson
Co-stars: Peter Ustinov Tony Curtis Emma Samms

1987 THE BETTY FORD STORY
Director: David Greene
Co-stars: Gena Rowlands Josef Sommer Nan Woods

1991 DON'T TELL MOM THE BABYSITTER'S DEAD
Director: Stephen Herek
Co-stars: Christina Applegate Joanna Cassidy John Getz

MARISA TOMEI

Oscar For Best Supporting Actress In 1992 For "My Cousin Vinny"

1990 PARKER KANE
Director: Steve Perry
Co-stars: Jeff Fahey Drew Snyder Amanda Pays

1991 OSCAR
Director: John Landis
Co-stars: Sylvester Stallone Kirk Douglas Tim Curry

1992 EQUINOX
Director: Alan Rudolph
Co-stars: Matthew Modine Fred Ward Tyra Ferrell

1992 MY COUSIN VINNY
Director: Jonathan Lynn
Co-stars: Joe Pesci Ralph Macchio Fred Gwynne

1993 UNTAMED HEART
Director: Tony Bill
Co-stars: Christian Slater Rosie Perez Kyle Secor

1994 THE PAPER
Director: Ron Howard
Co-stars: Michael Keaton Robert Duvall Glenn Close

1994 ONLY YOU
Director: Norman Jewison
Co-stars: Robert Downey Jnr. Bonnie Hunt

1995 FOUR ROOMS
Director: Quentin Tarantino
Co-stars: Tim Roth Antonio Banderas Sammi Davis

1996 THE PEREZ FAMILY
Director: Mira Nair
Co-stars: Alfred Molina Anjelica Huston Chazz Palminteri

1997 UNHOOK THE STARS
Director: Nick Cassavetes
Co-stars: Gena Rowlands Gerard Depardieu

FRANCES TOMELTY

1983 BULLSHOT
Director: Dick Clement
Co-stars: Alan Shearman Michael Aldridge Diz White

1986 LAMB
Director: Colin Gregg
Co-stars: Liam Neeson Harry Towb Ian Bannen

1987 BELLMAN AND TRUE
Director: Richard Loncraine
Co-stars: Bernard Hill Derek Newark Richard Hope

1989 STAR TRAP
Director: Tony Bicat
Co-stars: Nicky Henson Jeananne Crowley Jim Carter

1990 THE FIELD
Director: Jim Sheridan
Co-stars: Richard Harris John Hurt Sean Bean

1993 HIGH BOOT BENNY
Director: Joe Comerford
Co-stars: Marc O'Shea Alan Devlin

TAMLYN TOMITA

1986 THE KARATE KID, PART II
Director: John Avildsen
Co-stars: Ralph Macchio Pat Morita Nobu McCarthy

1990 COME SEE THE PARADISE
Director: Alan Parker
Co-stars: Dennis Quaid Sab Shimono Stan Egi

1990 VIETNAM, TEXAS
Director: Robert Ginty
Co-stars: Robert Ginty Haing S. Ngor Tim Thomerson

1993 THE JOY LUCK CLUB
Director: Wayne Wang
Co-stars: Kieu Chinh Tsai Chin France Nuyen

1993 BABYLON 5
Director: Richard Compton
Co-stars: Michael O'Hare Jerry Doyle Mira Furlan

1995 FOUR ROOMS
Director: Allison Anders
Co-stars: Tim Roth Antonio Banderas Ione Skye

1996 THE KILLING JAR
Director: Evan Cooke
Co-stars: Brett Cullen M. Emmet Walsh

LILY TOMLIN
Nominated For Best Supporting Actress In 1975 For "Nashville"

1975 NASHVILLE
Director: Robert Altman
Co-stars: Keith Carradine Karen Black Geraldine Chaplin

1977 THE LATE SHOW
Director: Robert Benton
Co-stars: Art Carney Bill Macy Howard Duff

1979 MOMENT BY MOMENT
Director: Jane Wagner
Co-stars: John Travolta Andra Akers Bert Kramer

1980 NINE TO FIVE
Director: Colin Higgins
Co-stars: Jane Fonda Dolly Parton Sterling Hayden

1981 THE INCREDIBLE SHRINKING WOMAN
Director: Joel Schumacher
Co-stars: Charles Grodin Ned Beatty Maria Smith

1984 ALL OF ME
Director: Carl Reiner
Co-stars: Steve Martin Victoria Tennant Madolyn Smith

1988 BIG BUSINESS
Director: Jim Abrahams
Co-stars: Bette Midler Fred Ward Edward Herrman

1991 SHADOWS AND FOG
Director: Woody Allen
Co-stars: Woody Allen Kathy Bates Jodie Foster

1991 THE PLAYER
Director: Robert Altman
Co-stars: Tim Robbins Greta Scacchi Whoopi Goldberg

1993 SHORT CUTS
Director: Robert Altman
Co-stars: Matthew Modine Andie McDowell Anne Archer

1993 AND THE BAND PLAYED ON
Director: Roger Spottiswoode
Co-stars: Matthew Modine Alan Alda Phil Collins

1994 THE BEVERLY HILLBILLIES
Director: Penelope Speeris
Co-stars: Jim Varney Dabney Coleman Cloris Leachman

1996 FLIRTING WITH DISASTER
Director: David Russell
Co-stars: Mary Tyler Moore Alan Alda Patricia Arquette

1996 BLUE IN THE FACE
Co-stars: Madonna Harvey Keitel Roseanne Barr

ANGEL TOMPKINS

1970 I LOVE MY WIFE
Director: Mel Stuart
Co-stars: Elliott Gould Brenda Vaccaro Dabney Coleman

1972 PRIME CUT
Director: Michael Ritchie
Co-stars: Gene Hackman Lee Marvin Sissy Spacek

1973 THE DON IS DEAD
Director: Richard Fleischer
Co-stars: Anthony Quinn Fredric Forrest Robert Forster

1986 MURPHY'S LAW
Director: J. Lee-Thompson
Co-stars: Charles Bronson Carrie Snodgress Kathleen Wilhoite

DARLENE TOMPKINS

1959 BEYOND THE TIME BARRIER
Director: Edgar Ulmer
Co-stars: Robert Clarke Arianne Arden Vladimif Sokoloff

JACQUELINE TONG

1989 HOW TO GET AHEAD IN ADVERTISING
Director: Bruce Robinson
Co-stars: Richard E. Grant Rachel Ward Richard Wilson

1992 FEMME FATALE
Director: Udayan Prasad
Co-stars: Simon Callow Colin Welland James Fleet

PETA TOPPANO

1987 SHADOWS OF THE PEACOCK
Director: Philip Noyce
Co-stars: Wendy Hughes John Lone Gillian Jones

MARTA TOREN

1948 CASBAH
Director: John Berry
Co-stars: Tony Martin Yvonne De Carlo Peter Lorre

1948 ROGUE'S REGIMENT
Director: Robert Florey
Co-stars: Dick Powell Vincent Price Stephen McNally

1949 ILLEGAL ENTRY
Director: Frederick De Cordova
Co-stars: Howard Duff George Brent Tom Tully

1949 SWORD IN THE DESERT
Director: George Sherman
Co-stars: Dana Andrews Jeff Chandler Stephen McNally

1950 ONE WAY STREET
Director: Hugo Fregonese
Co-stars: James Mason Dan Duryea William Conrad

1950 SPY HUNT
Director: George Sherman
Co-stars: Howard Duff Philip Friend Robert Douglas

1951 SIROCCO
Director: Curtis Bernhardt
Co-stars: Humphrey Bogart Lee J. Cobb Everett Sloane

1952 THE MAN WHO WATCHED TRAINS GO BY
Director: Harold French
Co-stars: Claude Rains Marius Goring Anouk Aimee

1952 ASSIGNMENT - PARIS
Director: Robert Parrish
Co-stars: George Sanders Dana Andrews Audrey Totter

SARAH TORGOV

1988 AMERICAN GOTHIC
Director: John Hough
Co-stars: Rod Steiger Yvonne De Carlo Michael J. Pollard

CAPRICE TORIEL

1958 MURDER BY CONTRACT
Director: Irving Lerner
Co-stars: Vince Edwards Philip Pine Herschel Bernardi

KAY TORNBORG

1974 WHO ?
Director: Jack Gold
Co-stars: Trevor Howard Elliott Gould Lyndon Brook

REGINA TORNE

1992 LIKE WATER FOR CHOCOLATE
Director: Alfonso Arau
Co-stars: Lumi Cavazos Marco Leonardi Claudette Maille

KRISTINA TORNQUIST

1987 PELLE THE CONQUEROR
Director: Bille August
Co-stars: Max Von Sydow Pelle Hvenegaard Erik Paaske

MARI TOROCSIK

1989 MUSIC BOX
Director: Costa-Gavras
Co-stars: Jessice Lange Frederic Forrest Armin Mueller-Stahl

ANA TORRENT (Child)

1973 THE SPIRIT OF THE BEEHIVE
Director: Victor Erice
Co-stars: Fernando Fernan Gomez Teresa Gimpera

1992 VACAS
Director: Julio Medem
Co-stars: Emma Suarez Carmelo Gomez Klara Badiola

RAQUEL TORRES (Raquel Von Osterman)

1927 WHITE SHADOWS IN THE SOUTH SEAS
Director: W.S. Van Dyke
Co-star: Monte Blue

1930 UNDER A TEXAS MOON
Director: Michael Curtiz
Co-stars: Frank Fay Myrna Loy Noah Beery

1930 THE SEA BAT
Director: Wesley Ruggles
Co-stars: Charles Bickford Nils Asther Boris Karloff

1933 RED WAGON
Director: Paul Stein
Co-stars: Charles Bickford Greta Nissen Jimmy Hanley

1933 DUCK SOUP
Director: Leo McCarey
Co-stars: Marx Brothers Margaret Dumont Louis Calhern

1933 SO THIS IS AFRICA
Co-stars: Bert Wheeler Robert Woolsey

CARLINA TORTA

1989 THE ICICLE THIEF
Director: Maurizio Nichetti
Co-stars: Maurizio Nichetti Federico Rizzo Renato Scarpa

MERLE TOTTENHAM

1933 CAVALCADE
Director: Frank Lloyd
Co-stars: Clive Brook Diana Wynyard Ursula Jeans

1937 NIGHT MUST FALL
Director: Richard Thorpe
Co-stars: Robert Montgomery Rosalind Russell May Whitty

1938 BANK HOLIDAY
Director: Carol Reed
Co-stars: Margaret Lockwood Hugh Williams Kathleen Harrison

1958 ROOM TO LET
Director: Godfrey Grayson
Co-stars: Jimmy Hanley Valentine Dyall Charles Hawtrey

AUDREY TOTTER

1944 MAIN STREET AFTER DARK
Director: Edward Cahn
Co-stars: Edward Arnold Selena Royle Dan Duryea

1945 BEWITCHED (Voice)
Director: Arch Obeler
Co-stars: Phyllis Thaxter Edmund Gwenn Addison Richards

1945 DANGEROUS PARTNERS
Director: Edward Cahn
Co-stars: James Craig Signe Hasso Edmund Gwenn

1946 THE COCKEYED MIRACLE
Director: S. Sylvan Simon
Co-stars: Frank Morgan Keenan Wynn Cecil Kellaway

1946 THE SAILOR TAKES A WIFE
Director: Richard Whorf
Co-stars: Robert Walker June Allyson Hume Cronyn

1946 THE POSTMAN ALWAYS RINGS TWICE
Director: Tay Garnett
Co-stars: Lana Turner John Garfield Cecil Kellaway

1946 THE LADY IN THE LAKE
Director: Robert Montgomery
Co-stars: Robert Montgomery Lloyd Nolan

1947 HIGH WALL
Director: Curtis Bernhardt
Co-stars: Robert Taylor Herbert Marshall

1947 THE BEGINNING OR THE END
Director: Norman Taurog
Co-stars: Robert Walker Brian Donlevy Tom Drake

1947 THE UNSUSPECTED
Director: Michael Curtiz
Co-stars: Claude Rains Joan Caulfield

1948 THE SAXON CHARM
Director: Claude Binyon
Co-stars: Robert Montgomery John Payne

1948	**TENTH AVENUE ANGEL**	
Director:	Roy Rowland	
Co-stars:	Margaret O'Brien George Murphy	

1948 **TENTH AVENUE ANGEL**
Director: Roy Rowland
Co-stars: Margaret O'Brien George Murphy

1949 **ALIAS NICK BEAL**
Director: John Farrow
Co-stars: Ray Milland Thomas Mitchell

1949 **THE SET-UP**
Director: Robert Wise
Co-stars: Robert Ryan George Tobias Wallace Ford

1949 **ANY NUMBER CAN PLAY**
Director: Mervyn LeRoy
Co-stars: Clark Gable Alexis Smith Mary Astor

1950 **TENSION**
Director: John Berry
Co-stars: Richard Basehart Barry Sullivan

1951 **THE BLUE VEIL**
Director: Curtis Bernhardt
Co-stars: Jane Wyman Charles Laughton

1951 **THE SELLOUT**
Director: Gerald Mayer
Co-stars: Walter Pidgeon John Hodiak Karl Malden

1952 **MY PAL GUS**
Director: Robert Parrish
Co-stars: Richard Widmark Joanne Dru Regis Toomey

1952 **THE WOMAN THEY ALMOST LYNCHED**
Director: Allan Dwan
Co-stars: Joan Leslie John Lund Brian Donlevy

1952 **ASSIGNMENT - PARIS**
Director: Robert Parrish
Co-stars: George Sanders Dana Andrews

1953 **CRUISIN' DOWN THE RIVER**
Director: Richard Quine
Co-stars: Dick Haymes Cecil Kellaway

1953 **THE MAN IN THE DARK**
Director: Lew Landers
Co-stars: Edmond O'Brien Ted De Corsia

1955 **A BULLET FOR JOEY**
Director: Lewis Allen
Co-stars: Edward G. Robinson George Raft

1964 **THE CARPETBAGGERS**
Director: Edward Dmytryk
Co-stars: George Peppard Carroll Baker Alan Ladd

1967 **THE OUTSIDER**
Director: Michael Ritchie
Co-stars: Darren McGavin Edmond O'Brien

1979 **THE APPLE DUMPLING GANG RIDES AGAIN**
Director: Vincent McEveety
Co-stars: Tim Conway Don Knotts Harry Morgan

ELISA TOUATI

1992 **GOLDEN BALLS**
Director: Bigas Luna
Co-stars: Javier Bardem Maribel Verdu Rachel Bianca

TAMARA TOUMANOVA

1944 **DAYS OF GLORY**
Director: Jacques Tourneur
Co-stars: Gregory Peck Alan Reed Hugo Haas

1953 **TONIGHT WE SING**
Director: Mitchell Leisen
Co-stars: David Wayne Anne Bancroft Ezio Pinza

1954 **DEEP IN MY HEART**
Director: Stanley Donen
Co-stars: Jose Ferrer Merle Oberon Paul Henreid

1956 **INVITATION TO THE DANCE**
Director: Gene Kelly
Co-stars: Gene Kelly Tommy Rall Carol Haney

1966 **TORN CURTAIN**
Director: Alfred Hitchcock
Co-stars: Paul Newman Julie Andrews Lila Kedrova

1970 **THE PRIVATE LIFE OF SHERLOCK HOLMES**
Director: Billy Wilder
Co-stars: Robert Stephens Colin Blakely Irene Handl

SHEILA TOUSEY

1992 **THUNDERHEART**
Director: Michael Apted
Co-stars: Val Kilmer Sam Shepard Graham Greene

1993 **SILENT TONGUE**
Director: Sam Shepard
Co-stars: Alan Bates Richard Harris River Phoenix

1993 **MEDICINE RIVER**
Director: Stuart Margolin
Co-stars: Graham Greene Janet-Laine Green

BETH TOUSSAINT

1994 **BREACH OF CONDUCT**
Director: Tim Matheson
Co-stars: Peter Coyote Tom Verica Courtney Thorne-Smith

LORRAINE TOUSSAINT

1986 **A CASE OF DEADLY FORCE**
Director: Michael Miller
Co-stars: Richard Crenna John Shea Tate Donovan

1989 **BREAKING IN**
Director: Bill Forsyth
Co-stars: Burt Reynolds Casey Siemaszko Sheila Kelley

1991 **HUDSON HAWK**
Director: Michael Lehman
Co-stars: Bruce Willis Danny Aiello Andie MacDowell

1993 **LOVE, LIES AND LULLABIES**
Director: Rod Hardy
Co-stars: Susan Dey Piper Laurie Andy Romano

CORINNE TOUZET

1991 **RED FOX**
Director: Ian Toynton
Co-stars: John Hurt Brian Cox Jane Birkin

1992 **DANIELLE STEEL'S JEWELS**
Director: Roger Young
Co-stars: Annette O'Toole Anthony Andrews Sheila Gish

LUPITA TOVAR

1939 **THE FIGHTING GRINGO**
Director: David Howard
Co-stars: George O'Brien Glenn Strange Lucie Villegas

1945 **CRIME DOCTOR'S COURAGE**
Director: George Sherman
Co-stars: Warner Baxter Hillary Brooke Jerome Cowan

ROBERTA TOVEY

1965 **DR WHO AND THE DALEKS**
Director: Gordon Flemyng
Co-stars: Peter Cushing Roy Castle Jennie Linden

1966 **DALEKS - INVASION EARTH 2150**
Director: Gordon Flemyng
Co-stars: Peter Cushing Roy Castle Jennie Linden

CONSTANCE TOWERS

1955 BRING YOUR SMILE ALONG
Director: Blake Edwards
Co-stars: Frankie Laine Keefe Brasselle

1959 THE HORSE SOLDIERS
Director: John Ford
Co-stars: John Wayne William Holden Anna Lee

1960 SERGEANT RUTLEDGE
Director: John Ford
Co-stars: Jeffrey Hunter Woody Strode Billie Burke

1963 SHOCK CORRIDOR
Director: Samuel Fuller
Co-stars: Peter Breck Gene Evans James Best

1964 THE NAKED KISS
Director: Samuel Fuller
Co-stars: Anthony Eisley Michael Dante Virginia Grey

1985 SYLVESTER
Director: Tim Hunter
Co-stars: Richard Farnsworth Melissa Gilbert Michael Schoeffling

ALINE TOWNE

1952 THE STEEL TRAP
Director: Andrew Stone
Co-stars: Joseph Cotten Teresa Wright Jonathan Hale

ROSELLA TOWNE

1939 CODE OF THE SECRET SERVICE
Director: Noel Smith
Co-stars: Ronald Reagan Moroni Olsen Eddie Foy Jnr.

1939 THE ADVENTURES OF JANE ARDEN
Co-star: William Gargan

BARBARA TOWNSEND

1986 THE ANNIHILATOR
Director: Michael Chapman
Co-stars: Mark Lindsay Chapman Susan Blakely Lisa Blount

COLLEEN TOWNSEND

1948 THE WALLS OF JERICHO
Director: John Stahl
Co-stars: Cornel Wilde Linda Darnell Anne Baxter

1949 CHICKEN EVERY SUNDAY
Director: George Seaton
Co-stars: Dan Dailey Celeste Holm Natalie Wood

1950 WHEN WILLIE COMES MARCHING HOME
Director: John Ford
Co-stars: Dan Dailey Corinne Calvet William Demarest

JILL TOWNSEND

1975 ALFIE DARLING
Director: Ken Hughes
Co-stars: Alan Price Joan Collins Annie Ross

1980 THE AWAKENING
Director: Mike Newell
Co-stars: Charlton Heston Susannah York Stephanie Zimbalist

PATRICE TOWNSEND

1978 SITTING DUCKS
Director: Henry Jaglom
Co-stars: Michael Emil Zack Norman Irene Forrest

1985 ALWAYS
Director: Henry Jaglom
Co-stars: Henry Jaglom Joanna Frank Allan Rachins

MARY ELLEN TRAINOR

1988 ACTION JACKSON
Director: Craig Baxley
Co-stars: Carl Weathers Sharon Stone Robert Davi

1991 RICOCHET
Director: Russell Mulcahy
Co-stars: Denzel Washington John Lithgow Lindsay Wagner

1992 GRAND CANYON
Director: Lawrence Kasdan
Co-stars: Kevin Kline Danny Glover Mary McDonnell

1992 KUFFS
Director: Bruce A. Evans
Co-stars: Christian Slater Milla Jovovich Tony Goldwyn

1995 SEDUCED AND BETRAYED
Director: Felix Enriques Alcala
Co-stars: Susan Lucci Peter Donat David Charvet

CORDULA TRANTOW

1960 THE CROSSING OF THE RHINE
Director: Andre Cayatte
Co-stars: Charles Aznavour Nicole Courcel Georges Riviere

1969 THE CASTLE
Director: Rudolf Noelte
Co-stars: Maximilian Schell Trudik Daniel Franz Misar

MONICA TRAPAGA

1987 HIGH TIDE
Director: Gillian Armstrong
Co-stars: Judy Davis Jan Adele Colin Friels

BARBARA TRAUB

1970 THE BIG BANG
Director: James Toback
Co-stars: Emma Astner Polly Frost Missy Boyd

HELEN TRAUBEL

1954 DEEP IN MY HEART
Director: Stanley Donen
Co-stars: Jose Ferrer Merle Oberon Walter Pidgeon

1961 LADIES' MAN
Director: Jerry Lewis
Co-stars: Jerry Lewis Gloria Jean George Raft

1967 GUNN
Director: Blake Edwards
Co-stars: Craig Stevens Laura Devon Ed Asner

LINDEN TRAVERS

1937 THE LAST ADVENTURERS
Director: Roy Kellino
Co-stars: Niall MacGinnis Kay Walsh Katie Johnson

1938 THE LADY VANISHES
Director: Alfred Hitchcock
Co-stars: Margaret Lockwood Michael Redgrave May Whitty

1938 THE TERROR
Director: Richard Bird
Co-stars: Wilfrid Lawson Arthur Wontner Alastair Sim

1938 BANK HOLIDAY
Director: Carol Reed
Co-stars: Margaret Lockwood Hugh Williams Rene Ray

1939 THE STARS LOOK DOWN
Director: Carol Reed
Co-stars: Michael Redgrave Margaret Lockwood Emlyn Williams

1939 INSPECTOR HORNLEIGH ON HOLIDAY
Director: Walter Forde
Co-stars: Gordon Harker Alastair Sim Edward Chapman

1941 THE GHOST TRAIN
Director: Walter Forde
Co-stars: Arthur Askey Richard Murdoch Katherine Harrison

1941 THE SEVENTH SURVIVOR
Director: Leslie Hiscott
Co-stars: Austin Trevor Martita Hunt Jane Carr

1941 SOUTH AMERICAN GEORGE
Director: Marcel Varnel
Co-stars: George Formby Enid Stamp-Taylor Jacques Brown

1946 BEWARE OF PITY
Director: W.P. Lipscomb
Co-stars: Lilli Palmer Albert Lieven Cedric Hardwicke

1947 JASSY
Director: Bernard Knowles
Co-stars: Margaret Lockwood Dennis Price Patricia Roc

1947 MASTER OF BANKDAM
Director: Walter Forde
Co-stars: Tom Walls Anne Crawford Dennis Price

1948 NO ORCHIDS FOR MISS BLANDISH
Director: St. John Clowes
Co-stars: Jack La Rue Hugh McDermott Zoe Gail

1948 THE BAD LORD BYRON
Director: David MacDonald
Co-stars: Dennis Price Mai Zetterling Sonia Holm

1948 QUARTET
Director: Ken Annakin
Co-stars: Nora Swinburne Felix Aylmer Cecil Parker

1949 DON'T EVER LEAVE ME
Director: Arthur Crabtree
Co-stars: Jimmy Hanley Petula Clark Anthony Newley

1949 CHRISTOPHER COLUMBUS
Director: David MacDonald
Co-stars: Fredric March Florence Eldridge Francis L. Sullivan

SUSAN TRAVERS

1971 THE ABOMINABLE DR PHIBES
Director: Robert Fuest
Co-stars: Vincent Price Joseph Cotten Hugh Griffiths

JUNE TRAVIS

1930 OVER THE WALL
Director: Frank MacDonald
Co-stars: Dick Foran John Litel Dick Purcell

1936 CEILING ZERO
Director: Howard Hawks
Co-stars: James Cagney Pat O'Brien Stuart Erwin

1936 THE CASE OF THE BLACK CAT
Director: William McGann
Co-stars: Ricardo Cortez Harry Davenport Jane Bryan

1936 EARTHWORM TRACTORS
Director: Ray Enright
Co-stars: Joe E. Brown Guy Kibbee Dick Foran

1936 JAILBREAK
Co-stars: Craig Reynolds Eddie Acuff

1937 LOVE IS ON THE AIR
Co-star: Ronald Reagan

1937 OVER THE GOAL
Co-star: William Hopper

1937 EXILED TO SHANGHAI
Co-stars: James Dunn William Bakewell

1937 THE KID COMES BACK
Director: Reeves Easton
Co-stars: Wayne Morris Barton MacLane Maxie Rosenbloom

1938 GO CHASE YOURSELF
Director: Edward Cline
Co-stars: Joe Penner Lucille Ball Richard Lane

1938 THE GLADIATOR
Director: Edward Sedgwick
Co-stars: Joe E. Brown Dickie Moore Man Mountain Dean

1952 THE STAR
Director: Stuart Heisler
Co-stars: Bette Davis Sterling Hayden Natalie Wood

NANCY TRAVIS

1986 HAREM
Director: Billy Hale
Co-stars: Art Malik Omar Sharif Ava Gardner

1987 THREE MEN AND A BABY
Director: Leonard Nimoy
Co-stars: Tom Selleck Ted Danson Steven Guttenberg

1988 I'LL BE HOME FOR CHRISTMAS
Director: Marvin Chomsky
Co-stars: Eva Marie Saint Hal Holbrook

1989 LOOSE CANNONS
Director: Bob Clark
Co-stars: Gene Hackman Dan Aykroyd Dom DeLuise

1990 INTERNAL AFFAIRS
Director: Mike Figgis
Co-stars: Richard Gere Andy Garcia Laurie Metcalf

1990 THREE MEN AND A LITTLE LADY
Director: Emile Ardolino
Co-stars: Christopher Casenove Sheila Hancock

1990 AIR AMERICA
Director: Roger Spottiswode
Co-stars: Mel Gibson Robert Downey Ken Jenkins

1992 PASSED AWAY
Director: Charlie Peters
Co-stars: Bob Hoskins Jack Warden Maureen Stapleton

1993 THE VANISHING
Director: George Sluizer
Co-stars: Jeff Bridges Kiefer Sutherland Sandra Bullock

1993 SO I MARRIED AN AXE MURDERER
Director: Thomas Schlamme
Co-stars: Mike Myers Brenda Fricker Amanda Plummer

1994 GREEDY
Director: Jonathan Lynn
Co-stars: Olivia D'Abo Kirk Douglas Michael J. Fox

1995 FLUKE
Director: Carlo Carlei
Co-stars: Matthew Modine Eric Stoltz Max Pomeranc

STACEY TRAVIS

1990 HARDWARE
Director: Richard Stanley
Co-stars: Dylan McDermott John Lynch William Hootkins

1991 THE SUPER
Director: Rod Daniel
Co-stars: Joe Pesci Vincent Gardenia Ruben Blades

1993 DRACULA RISING
Director: Fred Gallo
Co-stars: Christopher Atkins Doug Wert

1993 ONLY THE STRONG
Director: Sheldon Lettich
Co-stars: Mark Dacascos Todd Susman

LIZ TREADWELL

1975   ADIOS AMIGO
Director: Fred Williamson
Co-stars: Fred Williamson Richard Pryor James Brown

TERRI TREAS

1989   DEATHSTALKER 3
Director: Alfonso Corona
Co-stars: John Allen Nelson Carla Herd Aaron Hernan

1992   HOUSE IV: THE REPOSSESSION
Director: Lewis Abernathy
Co-stars: William Katt Denny Dillon Melissa Clayton

DOROTHY TREE

1932   LIFE BEGINS
Director: James Flood
Co-stars: Elliott Nugent Loretta Young Glenda Farrell

1934   THE FIREBIRD
Director: William Dieterle
Co-stars: Verree Teasdale Ricardo Cortez Anita Louise

1934   HERE COMES THE NAVY
Director: Lloyd Bacon
Co-stars: James Cagney Pat O'Brien Gloria Stuart

1935   FOUR HOURS TO KILL
Director: Mitchell Leisen
Co-stars: Richard Bathelmess Ray Milland Gertrude Michael

1937   THE GREAT GARRICK
Director: James Whale
Co-stars: Brian Aherne Olivia De Havilland Lana Turner

1939   CONFESSIONS OF A NAZI SPY
Director: Anatole Litvak
Co-stars: Edward G. Robinson Paul Lukas George Sanders

1939   CHARLIE CHAN IN CITY OF DARKNESS
Director: Herbert Leeds
Co-stars: Sidney Toler Lynn Bari Noel Madison

1940   SPIRIT OF THE PEOPLE
Director: John Cromwell
Co-stars: Raymond Massey Ruth Gordon Gene Lockhart

1942   NAZI AGENT
Director: Jules Dassin
Co-stars: Conrad Veidt Ann Ayars Frank Reicher

1942   HITLER: DEAD OR ALIVE
Director: Nick Grinde
Co-stars: Ward Bond Warren Hymer Bobby Watson

1950   THE MEN
Director: Fred Zinnemann
Co-stars: Marlon Brando Teresa Wright Jack Webb

1950   THE ASPHALT JUNGLE
Director: John Huston
Co-stars: Sterling Hayden Louis Calhern Marilyn Monroe

LADY TREE

1932   WEDDING REHEARSAL
Director: Alexander Korda
Co-stars: Roland Young Wendy Barrie Merle Oberon

1933   THE PRIVATE LIFE OF HENRY VIII
Director: Alexander Korda
Co-stars: Charles Laughton Robert Donat Merle Oberon

1933   THE GIRL FROM MAXIM'S
Director: Alexander Korda
Co-stars: Leslie Henson Frances Day

MARY TREEN

1937   EVER SINCE EVE
Director: Lloyd Bacon
Co-stars: Marion Davies Robert Montgomery Patsy Kelly

1937   THEY GAVE HIM A GUN
Director: W.S. Van Dyke
Co-stars: Spencer Tracy Gladys George Franchot Tone

1940   KITTY FOYLE
Director: Sam Wood
Co-stars: Ginger Rogers Dennis Morgan Gladys Cooper

1942   THE POWERS GIRL
Director: Norman Z. McLeod
Co-stars: George Murphy Anne Shirley Carole Landis

1942   THEY ALL KISSED THE BRIDE
Director: Alexander Hall
Co-stars: Joan Crawford Melvyn Douglas Roland Young

1942   IT'S A WONDERFUL LIFE
Director: Frank Capra
Co-stars: James Stewart Donna Reed Thomas Mitchell

1944   I LOVE A SOLDIER
Director: Mark Sandrich
Co-stars: Paulette Goddard Sonny Tufts Beulah Bondi

1944   CASANOVA BROWN
Director: Sam Wood
Co-stars: Gary Cooper Teresa Wright Frank Morgan

1945   DON JUAN QUILLIGAN
Director: Frank Tuttle
Co-stars: William Bendix Joan Blondell Phil Silvers

1946   FROM THIS DAY FORWARD
Director: John Berry
Co-stars: Joan Fontaine Mark Stevens Henry Morgan

1948   LET'S LIVE A LITTLE
Director: Richard Wallace
Co-stars: Hedy Lamar Robert Cummings Anna Sten

JEANETTE TREGARTHEN

1947   HOLIDAY CAMP
Director: Ken Annakin
Co-stars: Jack Warner Kathleen Harrison Flora Robson

JOHANNE-MARIE TREMBLAY

1989   JESUS OF MONTREAL
Director: Denys Arcand
Co-stars: Lothaire Bluteau Catherine Wilkening Remy Girard

HELEN TRENHOLME

1934   THE CASE OF THE HOWLING DOG
Director: Alan Crosland
Co-stars: Warren William Mary Astor Allen Jenkins

JOANNA TREPECHINSKA

1993   PAPER MARRIAGE
Director: Krzysztof Lang
Co-stars: Gary Kemp Rita Tushingham David Horovitch

ANNIKA TRETOW

1953   SAWDUST AND TINSEL
Director: Ingmar Bergman
Co-stars: Harriet Andersson Ake Gronberg Hasse Ekman

CLAIRE TREVOR

Oscar For Best Supporting Actress In 1948 For "Key Largo". Nominated For Best Supporting Actress In 1937 For "Dead End" And In 1954 For "The High And The Mighty"

1933	**THE MAD GAME**
Director:	Irving Cummings
Co-stars:	Spencer Tracy Ralph Morgan J. Carrol Naish

1933	**JIMMY AND SALLY**
Co-stars:	James Dunn Matt McHugh

1934	**WILD GOLD**
Co-star:	Monroe Owsley

1934	**HOLD THAT GIRL**
Co-star:	James Dunn Effie Elsier

1934	**BABY TAKE A BOW**
Director:	Harry Lachman
Co-stars:	Shirley Temple James Dunn Alan Dinehart

1935	**ELINOR NORTON**
Director:	Hamilton McFadden
Co-stars:	Gilbert Roland Hugh Williams Norman Foster

1935	**BLACK SHEEP**
Director:	Allan Dwan
Co-stars:	Edmund Lowe Tom Brown Adrienne Ames

1935	**DANTE'S INFERNO**
Director:	Harry Lachman
Co-stars:	Spencer Tracy Scotty Beckett Rita Hayworth

1935	**NAVY WIFE**
Director:	Allan Dwan
Co-stars:	Ralph Bellamy Ben Lyon Jane Darwell

1935	**SPRING TONIC**
Director:	S. Sylvan Simon
Co-stars:	Lew Ayres Jack Haley Zasu Pitts

1935	**HUMAN CARGO**
Co-star:	Brian Donlevy

1935	**MY MARRIAGE**
Director:	George Archainbaud
Co-stars:	Kent Taylor Pauline Frederick Paul Kelly

1936	**15, MAIDEN LANE**
Co-stars:	Cesar Romero Douglas Fowley

1936	**THE SONG AND DANCE MAN**
Director:	Allan Dwan
Co-stars:	Paul Kelly Michael Whalen Ruth Donnelly

1936	**HUMAN CARGO**
Director:	Allan Dwan
Co-stars:	Brian Donlevy Ralph Morgan Rita Hayworth

1936	**TO MARY - WITH LOVE**
Director:	John Cromwell
Co-stars:	Warner Baxter Myrna Loy Ian Hunter

1936	**CAREER WOMAN**
Director:	Lewis Seiler
Co-stars:	Michael Whalen Eric Linden Isabel Jewel

1937	**BIG TOWN GIRL**
Director:	Alfred Werker
Co-stars:	Donald Wood Alan Dinehart Alan Baxter

1937	**KING OF GAMBLERS**
Director:	Robert Florey
Co-stars:	Akim Tamiroff Lloyd Nolan Porter Hall

1937	**ONE MILE FROM HEAVEN**
Director:	Allan Dwan
Co-stars:	Sally Blane Douglas Fowley Bill Robinson

1937	**TIME OUT FOR ROMANCE**
Director:	Malcolm St.Clair
Co-stars:	Michael Whalen Joan Davis William Demarest

1937	**SECOND HONEYMOON**
Director:	Walter Lang
Co-stars:	Tyrone Power Loretta Young Stuart Erwin

1937	**DEAD END**
Director:	William Wyler
Co-stars:	Joel McCrea Sylvia Sidney Humphrey Bogart

1938	**WALKING DOWN BROADWAY**
Co-star:	Michael Whalen

1938	**THE AMAZING DR CLITTERHOUSE**
Director:	Anatole Litvak
Co-stars:	Edward G. Robinson Humphrey Bogart

1938	**FIVE OF A KIND**
Director:	Herbert Leeds
Co-stars:	Dionne Quins Jean Hersholt Cesar Romero

1938	**VALLEY OF THE GIANTS**
Director:	William Keighley
Co-stars:	Wayne Morris Frank McHugh Alan Hale

1939	**I STOLE A MILLION**
Director:	Frank Tuttle
Co-stars:	George Raft Dick Foran Victor Jory

1939	**STAGECOACH**
Director:	John Ford
Co-stars:	John Wayne Thomas Mitchell Tim Holt

1939	**THE FIRST REBEL**
Director:	William Seiter
Co-stars:	John Wayne Brian Donlevy George Sanders

1940	**THE DARK COMMAND**
Director:	Raoul Walsh
Co-stars:	John Wayne Walter Pidgeon Roy Rogers

1941	**TEXAS**
Director:	George Marshall
Co-stars:	William Holden Glenn Ford George Bancroft

1941	**HONKY TONK**
Director:	Jack Conway
Co-stars:	Clark Gable Lana Turner Frank Morgan

1942	**STREET OF CHANCE**
Director:	Jack Hively
Co-stars:	Burgess Meredith Sheldon Leonard Jerome Cowan

1942	**CROSSROADS**
Director:	Jack Conway
Co-stars:	William Powell Hedy Lamarr Basil Rathbone

1943	**THE DESPERADOES**
Co-stars:	Glenn Ford Randolph Scott

1942	**THE ADVENTURES OF MARTIN EDEN**
Director:	Sidney Salkow
Co-stars:	Glenn Ford Evelyn Keyes Stuart Erwin

1943	**GOOD LUCK MR YATES**
Co-stars:	Jess Barker Frank Sulley

1943	**THE WOMAN OF THE TOWN**
Director:	George Archainbaud
Co-stars:	Albert Dekker Barry Sullivan Henry Hull

1944	**FAREWELL MY LOVELY**
Director:	Edward Dmytryk
Co-stars:	Dick Powell Ann Shirley Mike Mazurki

1945	**JOHNNY ANGEL**
Director:	Edwin Marin
Co-stars:	George Raft Signe Hasso Hoagy Carmichael

1946	**CRACK-UP**
Director:	Irving Reis
Co-stars:	Pat O'Brien Herbert Marshall Ray Collins

1946	**THE BACHELOR'S DAUGHTERS**
Director:	Andrew Stone
Co-stars:	Adolphe Menjou Gail Russell Ann Dvorak

1947	**LADY OF DECEIT**
Director:	Robert Wise
Co-stars:	Lawrence Tierney Walter Slezak Audrey Long

1948   **THE LUCKY STIFF**
Director: Lewis Foster
Co-stars: Dorothy Lamour Brian Donlevy Irene Hervey

1948   **THE VELVET TOUCH**
Director: John Gage
Co-stars: Rosalind Russell Leo Genn Sydney Greenstreet

1948   **RAW DEAL**
Director: Anthony Mann
Co-stars: Dennis O'Keefe Marsha Hunt Raymond Burr

1948   **THE BABE RUTH STORY**
Director: Roy Del Ruth
Co-stars: William Bendix Charles Bickford

1948   **KEY LARGO**
Director: John Huston
Co-stars: Humphrey Bogart Edward G. Robinson Lauren Bacall

1950   **BORDERLINE**
Director: William Seiter
Co-stars: Fred MacMurray Raymond Burr Roy Roberts

1951   **BEST OF THE BADMEN**
Director: William Russell
Co-stars: Robert Ryan Robert Preston Walter Brennan

1951   **HARD, FAST AND BEAUTIFUL**
Director: Ida Lupino
Co-stars: Ida Lupino Sally Forrest Carleton Young

1952   **HOODLUM EMPIRE**
Director: Joseph Kane
Co-stars: Brian Donlevy Forrest Tucker Vera Ralston

1952   **MY MAN AND I**
Director: William Wellman
Co-stars: Ricardo Montalban Shelley Winters Wendell Corey

1953   **STRANGER WORE A GUN**
Director: Andre De Toth
Co-stars: Randolph Scott Lee Marvin Ernest Borgnine

1953   **STOP YOU'RE KILLING ME**
Director: Roy Del Ruth
Co-stars: Broderick Crawford Sheldon Leonard

1954   **THE HIGH AND THE MIGHTY**
Director: William Wellman
Co-stars: John Wayne Robert Stack Robert Newton

1955   **LUCY GALLANT**
Director: Robert Parrish
Co-stars: Jane Wyman Charlton Heston Thelma Ritter

1955   **MAN WITHOUT A STAR**
Director: King Vidor
Co-stars: Kirk Douglas Jeanne Crain Richard Boone

1956   **THE MOUNTAIN**
Director: Edward Dmytryk
Co-stars: Robert Wagner Spencer Tracy William Demarest

1958   **MARJORIE MORNINGSTAR**
Director: Irving Rapper
Co-stars: Natalie Wood Gene Kelly Carolyn Jones

1962   **TWO WEEKS IN ANOTHER TOWN**
Director: Vincente Minnelli
Co-stars: Kirk Douglas Edward G. Robinson

1964   **HOW TO MURDER YOUR WIFE**
Director: Richard Quine
Co-stars: Jack Lemmon Virna Lisi Terry-Thomas

1963   **THE STRIPPER**
Director: Franklin Schaffner
Co-stars: Joanne Woodward Richard Beymer Carol Lynley

1967   **CAPETOWN AFFAIR**
Director: Robert Webb
Co-stars: James Brolin Jacqueline Bisset Jon Whiteley

1982   **KISS ME GOODBYE**
Director: Robert Mulligan
Co-stars: Sally Field James Caan Jeff Bridges

1987   **BREAKING HOME TIES**

SARAH TRIGGER

1990   **KID**
Director: John Mark Robinson
Co-stars: C. Thomas Howell Dale Dye R. Lee Ermey

1991   **THE LAST TO GO**
Director: John Erman
Co-stars: Tyne Daly Terry O'Quinn Annabeth Gish

1991   **PARADISE**
Director: Mary Agness Donaghue
Co-stars: Elijah Wood Thora Birch Melanie Griffith

1991   **BILL AND TED'S BOGUS JOURNEY**
Director: Pete Hewitt
Co-stars: Keanu Reeves Alex Winter Jeff Miller

1992   **GRAND CANYON**
Director: Lawrence Kasdan
Co-stars: Kevin Kline Danny Glover Mary McDonnell

1994   **P.C.U.**
Director: Hart Bochner
Co-stars: Chris Young David Spade Jeremy Piven

ZOE TRILLING

1993   **TOBE HOOPER'S NIGHT TERRORS**
Director: Tobe Hooper
Co-stars: Robert Englund William Finley

MARIE TRINTIGNANT
(Daughter Of Nadine And Jean-Louis Trintignant)

1973   **FORBIDDEN TO KNOW**
Director: Nadine Trintignant
Co-stars: Jean-Louis Trintignant Michel Bouqet Charles Denner

1990   **WINGS OF FAME**
Director: Otakar Votocek
Co-stars: Peter O'Toole Colin Firth Andrea Ferreol

1993   **WILD TARGET**
Director: Pierre Salvadori
Co-stars: Jean Rochefort Guillaume Depardieu

ANN TRIOLA

1946   **WITHOUT RESERVATIONS**
Director: Mervyn LeRoy
Co-stars: Claudette Colbert John Wayne Don Defore

1951   **LULLABY OF BROADWAY**
Director: David Butler
Co-stars: Doris Day Gene Nelson Gladys George

JEANNE TRIPPLEHORN

1992   **BASIC INSTINCT**
Director: Paul Verhoeven
Co-stars: Michael Douglas Sharon Stone George Dzundza

1993   **THE FIRM**
Director: Sydney Pollack
Co-stars: Tom Cruise Gene Hackman Holly Hunter

1993   **THE NIGHT WE NEVER MET**
Director: Warren Leight
Co-stars: Matthew Broderick Annabella Sciorra Kevin Anderson

1995   **WATERWORLD**
Director: Kevin Reynolds
Co-stars: Kevin Costner Dennis Hopper

1997   'TIL THERE WAS YOU
Co-stars: Dylan McDermott Sarah Jessica Parker

1998   SLIDING DOORS
Director: Peter Howitt
Co-stars: Gwyneth Paltrow John Lynch John Hannah

ELISABETH TRISSENAAR

1977   THE STATIONMASTER'S WIFE
Director: Rainer Werner Fassbinder
Co-stars: Kurt Raab Bernhard Helfrich Udo Kier

1978   IN A YEAR WITH 13   MOONS
Director: Rainer Werner Fassbinder
Co-stars: Volker Spencer Ingrid Caven Eve Mattes

DOROTHY TRISTAN

1971   KLUTE
Director: Alan J. Pakula
Co-stars: Jane Fonda Donald Sutherland Rita Gam

1973   ISN'T IT SHOCKING ?
Director: John Badham
Co-stars: Alan Alda Louise Lasser Edmond O'Brien

1973   SCARECROW
Director: Jerry Schatzberg
Co-stars: Gene Hackman Al Pacino Eileen Brennan

1975   MAN ON A SWING
Director: Frank Perry
Co-stars: Cliff Robertson Joel Grey Peter Masterson

MARGOT TROOGER

1965   TRAITOR'S GATE
Director: Freddie Francis
Co-stars: Albert Lieven Gary Raymond Klaus Kinski

KATE TROTTER

1990   CLARENCE
Director: Eric Till
Co-star: Robert Carradine

RUTH TROUNCER

1955   NO SMOKING
Director: Henry Cass
Co-stars: Reg Dixon Belinda Lee Lionel Jeffries

ANDREA TROWBRIDGE

1957   HOUSE IN THE WOODS
Director: Maxwell Munden
Co-stars: Ronald Howard Patricia Roc Michael Gough

HELEN TROY

1936   HUMAN CARGO
Director: Allan Dwan
Co-stars: Claire Trevor Brian Donlevy Rita Hayworth

PAULA TRUEMAN

1934   CRIME WITHOUT PASSION
Director: Ben Hecht
Co-stars: Claude Rains Whitney Bourne Margo

1974   THE STEPFORD WIVES
Director: Bryan Forbes
Co-stars: Katherine Ross Paula Prentiss Nanette Newman

1976   THE OUTLAW JOSEY WALES
Director: Clint Eastwood
Co-stars: Clint Eastwood Chief Dan George Sondra Locke

1986   CLASSIFIED LOVE
Director: Don Taylor
Co-stars: Michael McKean Stephanie Feracy Dinah Manoff

TOTTI TRUMAN-TAYLOR

1967   OUCH !
Director: Gerard Bryant
Co-stars: Peter Butterworth Dilys Watling Johnny Wade

MARLA MAPLES TRUMP

1996   EXECUTIVE DECISIONS
Director: Stuart Baird
Co-stars: Kurt Russell Halle Berry Steven Seagal

NATALIE TRUNDY

1957   THE CARELESS YEARS
Director: Arthur Hiller
Co-stars: Dean Stockwell John Larch

1957   THE MONTE CARLO STORY
Director: Samuel Taylor
Co-stars: Marlene Dietrich Vittorio De Sica Arthur O'Connell

1969   BENEATH THE PLANET OF THE APES
Director: Ted Post
Co-stars: James Franciscus Charlton Heston Kim Hunter

1971   ESCAPE FROM THE PLANET OF THE APES
Director: Don Taylor
Co-stars: Roddy McDowall Kim Hunter Sal Mineo

1972   CONQUEST OF THE PLANET OF THE APES
Director: J. Lee-Thompson
Co-stars: Roddy McDowall Ricardo Montalban

1973   BATTLE FOR THE PLANET OF THE APES
Director: J. Lee-Thompson
Co-stars: Roddy McDowall John Huston Lew Ayres

1974   HUCKLEBERRY FINN
Director: J. Lee-Thompson
Co-stars: Jeff East Paul Winfield David Wayne

IRENE TSU

1965   PARADISE HAWAIIAN STYLE
Director: Michael Moore
Co-stars: Elvis Presley Suzanna Leigh James Shigeta

1966   SEVEN WOMEN
Director: John Ford
Co-stars: Anne Bancroft Flora Robson Margaret Leighton

1967   CAPRICE
Director: Frank Tashlin
Co-stars: Doris Day Richard Harris Ray Walston

1968   THE GREEN BERETS
Director: John Wayne
Co-stars: John Wayne David Janssen Jim Hutton

1975   PAPER TIGER
Director: Ken Annakin
Co-stars: David Niven Hardy Kruger Toshiro Mifune

JEANETTE LIN TSUI

1991   IRON & SILK
Director: Shirley Sun
Co-stars: Mark Salzman Vivian Wu Pan Quingfu

FRANCESCA TU

1968   DIAMONDS FOR BREAKFAST
Director: Christopher Morahan
Co-stars: Marcello Mastroianni Rita Tushingham

MARIA TUCCI

1983   ENORMOUS CHANGES AT
THE LAST MINUTE
Director: Mirra Bank
Co-stars: Ellen Barkin Kevin Bacon Sudie Bond

1986 TOUCH AND GO
Director: Robert Mandel
Co-stars: Michael Keaton Max Wright Maria Conchita Alonso

JESSICA TUCK

1993 LIFEPOD
Director: Ron Silver
Co-stars: Robert Loggia Stan Shaw Kelli Williams

1995 THE O.J. SIMPSON STORY
Director: Jerrold Freeman
Co-stars: Bobby Hosea Bruce Weitz

ALLISON TUCKER

1978 THE END OF THE WORLD
Director: Lina Wertmuller
Co-stars: Candice Bergen Giancarlo Giannini Jill Eikenberry

1990 RUNAWAY HEART
Director: James Frawley
Co-stars: Jill Eikenberry Michael Tucker Ray Wise

SOPHIE TUCKER

1929 HONKY TONK
Director: Lloyd Bacon
Co-stars: Lila Lee Audrey Ferris George Duryea

1937 BROADWAY MELODY OF 1938
Director: Roy Del Ruth
Co-stars: Robert Taylor Eleanor Powell Judy Garland

1944 SENSATIONS OF 1945
Director: Andrew Stone
Co-stars: Eleanor Powell W.C. Fields Dennis O'Keefe

TANYA TUCKER

1981 HARD COUNTRY
Director: David Greene
Co-stars: Jan-Michael Vincent Kim Basinger Michael Parks

VICTORIA TUCKER

1984 THE CALENDAR GIRL MURDERS
Director: William Graham
Co-stars: Tom Skerritt Sharon Stone Robert Morse

MANDY TULLOCH

1975 ROBIN HOOD JUNIOR
Director: Matt McCarthy
Co-stars: Keith Chegwin Maurice Kaufman Andrew Sachs

AMANDA JANE TULLY

1971 THE JOHNSTOWN MONSTER
Director: Olaf Pooley
Co-stars: Connor Brennan Simon Tully Kim McDonald

IRENE TUNC

1961 LEON MARIN, PRIEST
Director: Jean-Pierre Melville
Co-stars: Jean-Paul Belmondo Emmanuele Riva Marielle Gozzi

1967 LIVE FOR LIFE
Director: Claude Lelouch
Co-stars: Yves Montand Candice Bergen Annie Girardot

1971 ANNE AND MURIEL
Director: Francois Truffaut
Co-stars: Jean-Pierre Leaud Kika Markham Stacey Tendetter

ROBIN TUNNEY

1996 THE CRAFT
Director: Andrew Fleming
Co-stars: Fairuza Balk Neve Campbell

MAGGIE TURETT

1968 THREE IN THE ATTIC
Director: Richard Wilson
Co-stars: Chris Jones Yvette Mimieux Judy Pace

ANN TURKEL

1974 99 AND 44/100% DEAD
Director: John Frankenheimer
Co-stars: Richard Harris Edmond O'Brien Bradford Dillman

1975 MATT HELM
Director: Buzz Kulik
Co-stars: Anthony Franciosa Laraine Stephens Patrick McNee

1976 THE CASSANDRA CROSSING
Director: Brian De Palma
Co-stars: Sophia Loren Richard Harris Ava Gardner

1977 GOLDEN RENDEZVOUS
Director: Ashley Lazarus
Co-stars: Richard Harris David Janssen Burgess Meredith

1977 PORTRAIT OF A HITMAN
Director: Allan Buckhantz
Co-stars: Jack Palance Rod Steiger Richard Roundtree

1980 HUMANOIDS FROM THE DEEP
Director: Barbara Peeters
Co-stars: Vic Morrow Doug McClure Denis Galek

VERONICA TURLEIGH

1952 THE CARD
Director: Ronald Neame
Co-stars: Alec Guinness Glynis Johns Petula Clark

1958 THE HORSE'S MOUTH
Director: Ronald Neame
Co-stars: Alec Guinness Kay Walsh Renee Houston

CHRISTY TURLINGTON

1996 UNZIPPED
Director: Douglas Keeve
Co-stars: Naomi Campbell Cindy Crawford Kate Moss

BARBARA TURNER *(Married Vic Morrow, Mother Of Jennifer Jason Leigh)*

1957 MONSTER FROM GREEN HELL
Director: Kenneth Crane
Co-stars: Jim Davis Eduardo Ciannelli Vladimir Sokoloff

CLARA MAE TURNER

1956 CAROUSEL
Director: Henry King
Co-stars: Gordon MacRae Shirley Jones Barbara Ruick

DEBBIE TURNER

1965 THE SOUND OF MUSIC
Director: Robert Wise
Co-stars: Julie Andrews Christopher Plummer Richard Haydn

ELIZABETH TURNER

1975 BEYOND THE DOOR
Director: Oliver Hellman
Co-stars: Juliet Mills Richard Johnson David Colin

FLORENCE TURNER

1927 COLLEGE
Director: James Horne
Co-stars: Buster Keaton Ann Cornwall Snitz Edwards

GERALDINE TURNER

1977 SUMMERFIELD
Director: Ken Hannam
Co-stars: Nick Tate John Walters Elizabeth Alexander

1983 CAREFUL HE MIGHT HEAR YOU
Director: Carl Schultz
Co-stars: Wendy Hughes Robyn Nevin Nicholas Gledhill

GUINEVERE TURNER

1993 GO FISH
Director: Rose Troche
Co-stars: V.S. Brodie Anastasia Sharp T. Wendy McMillan

JANINE TURNER

1993 CLIFFHANGER
Director: Renny Harlin
Co-stars: Sylvester Stallone John Lithgow Michael Rooker

KATHLEEN TURNER
Nominated For Best Actress In 1986 For "Peggy Sue Got Married"

1981 BODY HEAT
Director: Lawrence Kasdan
Co-stars: William Hurt Richard Crenna Mickey Rourke

1983 THE MAN WITH TWO BRAINS
Director: Carl Reiner
Co-stars: Steve Martin David Warner Paul Benedict

1984 A BREED APART
Director: Philippe Mora
Co-stars: Rutger Hauer Powers Booth Donald Pleasence

1984 CRIMES OF PASSION
Director: Ken Russell
Co-stars: Anthony Perkins Annie Potts John Laughlin

1984 ROMANCING THE STONE
Director: Robert Zemeckis
Co-stars: Michael Douglas Danny De Vito Zack Norman

1985 PRIZZI'S HONOR
Director: John Huston
Co-stars: Jack Nicholson Anjelica Huston William Hickey

1985 THE JEWEL OF THE NILE
Director: Lewis Teague
Co-stars: Michael Douglas Danny De Vito Spiros Focas

1986 PEGGY SUE GOT MARRIED
Director: Francis Coppola
Co-stars: Nicolas Cage Maureen O'Sullivan Helen Hunt

**1987 DEAR AMERICA:
LETTERS HOME FROM VIETNAM**
Director: Bill Couturie
Co-stars: Robert De Niro Willem Dafoe

1988 THE ACCIDENTAL TOURIST
Director: Lawrence Kasdan
Co-stars: William Hurt Geena Davis Bill Pullman

1988 SWITCHING CHANNELS
Director: Ted Kotcheff
Co-stars: Burt Reynolds Christopher Reeves Ned Beatty

1988 WHO FRAMED ROGER RABBIT ? *(Voice)*
Director: Robert Zemeckis
Co-stars: Bob Hoskins Stubby Kaye Joanna Cassidy

1989 THE WAR OF THE ROSES
Director: Danny De Vito
Co-stars: Danny De Vito Michael Douglas Marianne Sagebrecht

1991 V.I. WARSHAWSKI
Director: Jeff Kanew
Co-stars: Jay O. Saunders Charles Durning Nancy Paul

1993 HOUSE OF CARDS
Director: Michael Lessac
Co-stars: Tommy Lee Jones Park Overall Anne Pitoniak

1993 UNDERCOVER BLUES
Director: Herbert Ross
Co-stars: Dennis Quaid Fiona Shaw Larry Miller

1994 SERIAL MOM
Director: John Waters
Co-stars: Sam Waterston Ricki Lake Matthew Lillard

1995 NAKED IN NEW YORK
Director: Don Algrant
Co-stars: Eric Stoltz Mary-Louise Parker Timothy Dalton

1996 MOONLIGHT AND VALENTINO
Director: David Anspach
Co-stars: Elizabeth Perkins Gwyneth Paltrow Whoopi Goldberg

1998 THE REAL BLONDE
Director: Tom DiCillo
Co-stars: Matthew Modine Elizabeth Berkley Buck Henry

LANA TURNER
Nominated For Best Actress In 1957 For "Peyton Place"

1937 THEY WON'T FORGET
Director: Mervyn LeRoy
Co-stars: Claude Rains Gloria Dickson Otto Kruger

1937 A STAR IS BORN
Director: William Wellman
Co-stars: Janet Gaynor Fredric March Adolphe Menjou

1937 THE GREAT GARRICK
Director: James Whale
Co-stars: Brian Aherne Olivia De Havilland Lionel Atwill

1938 THE ADVENTURES OF MARCO POLO
Director: Archie Mayo
Co-stars: Gary Cooper Sigrid Gurie Binnie Barnes

1938 DRAMATIC SCHOOL
Director: Robert Sinclair
Co-stars: Luise Rainer Paulette Goddard Alan Marshall

1938 RICH MAN, POOR GIRL
Director: Rheinhold Schunzel
Co-stars: Lew Ayres Ruth Hussey Robert Young

1938 LOVE FINDS ANDY HARDY
Director: George Seitz
Co-stars: Mickey Rooney Judy Garland Lewis Stone

1939 THOSE GLAMOROUS GIRLS
Director: S. Sylvan Simon
Co-stars: Lew Ayres Tom Brown Jane Bryan

1939 DANCING CO-ED
Director: S. Sylvan Simon
Co-stars: Richard Carlson Leon Errol Monty Woolley

1939 CALLING DR KILDARE
Director: Harold Bucquet
Co-stars: Lew Ayres Lionel Barrymore Laraine Day

1940 TWO GIRLS ON BROADWAY
Director: S. Sylvan Simon
Co-stars: George Murphy Joan Blondell Kent Taylor

1941 ZIEGFELD GIRL
Director: Robert Z. Leonard
Co-stars: Judy Garland Hedy Lamarr James Stewart

1942 JOHNNY EAGAR
Director: Mervyn LeRoy
Co-stars: Robert Taylor Van Heflin Edward Arnold

1941 HONKY TONK
Director: Jack Conway
Co-stars: Clark Gable Frank Morgan Marjorie Main

1941 DR JEKYLL AND MR HYDE
Director: Victor Fleming
Co-stars: Spencer Tracy Ingrid Bergman Ian Hunter

1942 SOMEWHERE I'LL FIND YOU
Director: Wesley Ruggles
Co-stars: Clark Gable Robert Sterling Lee Patrick

1943 SLIGHTLY DANGEROUS
Director: Wesley Ruggles
Co-stars: Robert Young Walter Brennan May Whitty

1943 THE YOUNGEST PROFESSION
Director: Edward Buzzell
Co-stars: Virginia Weidler Jean Porter Edward Arnold

1944 MARRIAGE IS A PRIVATE AFFAIR
Director: Robert Z.Leonard
Co-stars: James Craig John Hodiak Keenan Wynn

1945 KEEP YOUR POWDER DRY
Director: Edward Buzzell
Co-stars: Laraine Day Susan Peters Bill Johnson

1945 WEEKEND AT THE WALDORF
Director: Robert Z. Leonard
Co-stars: Ginger Rogers Walter Pidgeon Van Johnson

1946 THE POSTMAN ALWAYS RINGS TWICE
Director: Tay Garnett
Co-stars: John Garfield Cecil Kellaway Leon Ames

1947 GREEN DOLPHIN STREET
Director: Victor Saville
Co-stars: Van Heflin Donna Reed Edmund Gwenn

1947 CASS TIMBERLANE
Director: George Sidney
Co-stars: Spencer Tracy Zachary Scott Mary Astor

1948 HOMECOMING
Director: Mervyn LeRoy
Co-stars: Clark Gable Anne Baxter John Hodiak

1948 THE THREE MUSKETEERS
Director: George Sidney
Co-stars: Gene Kelly Van Heflin June Allyson

1950 A LIFE OF HER OWN
Director: George Cukor
Co-stars: Ray Milland Tom Ewell Ann Dvorak

1951 YOU BELONG TO MY HEART
Director: Don Hartman
Co-stars: Ezio Pinza Marjorie Main Debbie Reynolds

1952 THE MERRY WIDOW
Director: Curtis Bernhardt
Co-stars: Fernando Lamas Richard Haydn Una Merkel

1952 THE BAD AND THE BEAUTIFUL
Director: Vincente Minnelli
Co-stars: Kirk Douglas Gloria Grahame Dick Powell

1953 LATIN LOVERS
Director: Mervyn LeRoy
Co-stars: Ricardo Montalban Barry Sullivan John Lund

1954 THE FLAME AND THE FLESH
Director: Richard Brooks
Co-stars: Carlos Thompson Bonar Colleano Pier Angeli

1954 BETRAYED
Director: Gottfried Reinhardt
Co-stars: Clark Gable Victor Mature Louis Calhern

1955 DIANE
Director: David Miller
Co-stars: Roger Moore Pedro Armendariz Cedric Hardwicke

1955 THE PRODIGAL
Director: Richard Thorpe
Co-stars: Edmund Purdom Louis Calhern Joseph Wiseman

1955 THE RAINS OF RANCHIPUR
Director: Jean Negulesco
Co-stars: Richard Burton Fred MacMurray Joan Caulfield

1955 THE SEA CHASE
Director: John Farrow
Co-stars: John Wayne James Arness David Farrar

1957 PEYTON PLACE
Director: Mark Robson
Co-stars: Hope Lange Lloyd Nolan Russ Tamblyn

1958 THE LADY TAKES A FLYER
Director: Jack Arnold
Co-stars: Jeff Chandler Richard Denning Chuck Connors

1958 ANOTHER TIME, ANOTHER PLACE
Director: Lewis Allen
Co-stars: Sean Connery Glynis Johns Barry Sullivan

1959 IMITATION OF LIFE
Director: Douglas Sirk
Co-stars: Juanita Moore Susan Kohner Sandra Dee

1960 PORTRAIT IN BLACK
Director: Michael Gordon
Co-stars: Anthony Quinn Richard Basehart Anna May Wong

1961 BY LOVE POSSESSED
Director: John Sturges
Co-stars: Efrem Zimbalist Jason Robards Barbara Bel Geddes

1961 BACHELOR IN PARADISE
Director: Jack Arnold
Co-stars: Bob Hope Janis Page Paula Prentiss

1962 WHO'S GOT THE ACTION
Director: Daniel Mann
Co-stars: Dean Martin Eddie Albert Walter Matthau

1964 LOVE HAS MANY FACES
Director: Alexander Singer
Co-stars: Cliff Robertson Hugh O'Brian Ruth Roman

1965 MADAME X
Director: David Lowell Rich
Co-stars: John Forsythe Ricardo Montalban Burgess Meredith

1969 THE BIG CUBE
Director: Tito Davison
Co-stars: George Chakiris Dan O'Herlihy Richard Egan

1974 PERSECUTION
Director: Don Chaffey
Co-stars: Ralph Bates Trevor Howard Ronald Howard

1976 BITTERSWEET LOVE
Director: David Miller
Co-stars: Robert Alda Celeste Holm Scott Hylands

STEPHANIE TURNER

1990 SMALL ZONES
Director: Michael Whyte
Co-stars: Catherine Neilson Suzanna Hamilton Sean Bean

TINA TURNER *(Anna Mae Bullock)*

1971 TAKING OFF
Director: Milos Forman
Co-stars: Lynn Carlin Buck Henry Ike Turner

1975 TOMMY
Director: Ken Russell
Co-stars: Ann-Margret Oliver Reed Roger Daltrey

1985 MAD MAX BEYOND THUNDERDOME
Director: George Miller
Co-stars: Mel Gibson Angelo Rossito Helen Buday

VICKERY TURNER

1969 PRUDENCE AND THE PILL
Director: Fielder Cook
Co-stars: David Niven Deborah Kerr Judy Geeson

1970 THE MIND OF MR SOAMES
Director: Alan Cooke
Co-stars: Terence Stamp Robert Vaughn Nigel Davenport

1981 THE GOOD SOLDIER
Director: Kevin Billington
Co-stars: Jeremy Brett Susan Fleetwood Robin Ellis

WINKI TURNER

1940 SOMEWHERE IN ENGLAND
Director: John Blakeley
Co-stars: Frank Randle Harry Korris Robbie Vincent

YOLANDE TURNER

1962 FIVE MILES TO MIDNIGHT
Director: Anatole Litvak
Co-stars: Sophia Loren Anthony Perkins Gig Young

BAHNI TURPIN

1994 GIRLS IN PRISON
Director: John McNaughton
Co-stars: Missy Crider Ione Skye Anne Heche

AIDA TURTURRO

1989 TRUE LOVE
Director: Nancy Savoca
Co-stars: Annabella Sciorra Ron Eldard Star Jasper

1991 WHAT ABOUT BOB ?
Director: Frank Oz
Co-stars: Richard Dreyfuss Bill Murray Julie Hagerty

1992 JERSEY GIRL
Director: David Burton Morris
Co-stars: Jamie Gertz Dylan McDermott Joseph Bologna

1994 ANGIE
Director: Martha Coolidge
Co-stars: Geena Davis Stephen Rea Philip Bosco

RITA TUSHINGHAM

1961 A TASTE OF HONEY
Director: Tony Richardson
Co-stars: Dora Bryan Robert Stephens Murray Melvin

1963 THE LEATHER BOYS
Director: Sidney Furie
Co-stars: Colin Campbell Dudley Sutton Gladys Henson

1963 GIRL WITH GREEN EYES
Director: Desmond Davis
Co-stars: Peter Finch Lynn Redgrave

1963 A PLACE TO GO
Director: Basil Dearden
Co-stars: Mike Sarne Doris Hare John Slater

1965 DOCTOR ZHIVAGO
Director: David Lean
Co-stars: Julie Christie Omar Sharif Alec Guinness

1965 THE KNACK, AND HOW TO GET IT
Director: Richard Lester
Co-stars: Michael Crawford Ray Brooks

1966 THE TRAP
Director: Sidney Hayers
Co-stars: Oliver Reed Barbara Chilcott

1967 SMASHING TIME
Director: Desmond Davis
Co-stars: Lynn Redgrave Ian Carmichael Michael York

1968 DIAMONDS FOR BREAKFAST
Director: Christopher Morahan
Co-stars: Marcello Mastroianni Warren Mitchell

1969 THE BED SITTING ROOM
Director: Richard Lester
Co-stars: Ralph Richardson Dudley Moore Spike Milligan

1969 THE GURU
Director: James Ivory
Co-stars: Michael York Barry Foster Utpall Dutt

1972 STRAIGHT ON TILL MORNING
Director: Peter Collinson
Co-stars: Shane Briant Tom Bell James Bolam

1975 THE HUMAN FACTOR
Director: Edward Dmytryk
Co-stars: George Kennedy John Mills Raf Vallone

1986 A JUDGEMENT IN STONE

1989 RESURRECTED
Director: Paul Greengrass
Co-stars: David Thewlis Tom Bell Michael Pollitt

1993 PAPER MARRIAGE
Director: Krzysztof Lang
Co-stars: Gary Kemp Joanne Trepechinska David Horovich

DOROTHY TUTIN

1952 THE BEGGAR'S OPERA
Director: Peter Brook
Co-stars: Laurence Olivier Stanley Holloway Hugh Griffith

1952 THE IMPORTANCE OF BEING ERNEST
Director: Anthony Asquith
Co-stars: Michael Redgrave Michael Dennison

1958 A TALE OF TWO CITIES
Director: Ralph Thomas
Co-stars: Dirk Bogarde Christopher Lee Ian Bannen

1970 CROMWELL
Director: Ken Hughes
Co-stars: Richard Harris Alec Guinness Robert Morley

1970 THE SIX WIVES OF HENRY VIII
Director: John Glenister
Co-stars: Keith Michell Annette Crosbie

1972 SAVAGE MESSIAH
Director: Ken Russell
Co-stars: Scott Anthony Helen Mirren John Justin

1983 KING LEAR
Director: Michael Elliott
Co-stars: Laurence Olivier Diana Rigg

1984 THE SHOOTING PARTY
Director: Alan Bridges
Co-stars: James Mason Edward Fox Gordon Jackson

1985 MURDER WITH MIRRORS
Director: Dick Lowry
Co-stars: Helen Hayes Bette Davis John Mills

**1991 INSPECTOR WEXFORD:
A NEW LEASE OF LIFE**
Director: Herbert Wise
Co-stars: George Baker Diane Keen

1992 ANGLO-SAXON ATTITUDES
Director: Diarmuid Lawrence
Co-stars: Richard Johnson Elizabeth Spriggs

1996 ALIVE AND KICKING
Director: Nancy Meckler
Co-stars: Jason Flemyng Anthony Sher

LURENE TUTTLE

1951 TOMORROW IS ANOTHER DAY
Director: Felix Feist
Co-stars: Steve Cochran Ruth Roman Ray Teal

1952 ROOM FOR ONE MORE
Director: Norman Taurog
Co-stars: Cary Grant Betsy Drake Randy Stuart

1952 NIAGARA
Director: Henry Hathaway
Co-stars: Marilyn Monroe Joseph Cotten Jean Peters

1952 DON'T BOTHER TO KNOCK
Director: Roy Baker
Co-stars: Marilyn Monroe Richard Widmark Anne Bancroft

1966 THE FORTUNE COOKIE
Director: Billy Wilder
Co-stars: Jack Lemmon Walter Matthau Ron Rich

1977 FINAL CHAPTER: WALKING TALL
Director: Jack Starrett
Co-stars: Bo Svenson Margaret Blye Libby Boone

1980 WHITE MAMA
Director: Jackie Cooper
Co-stars: Bette Davis Ernest Harden Jnr. Eileen Heckart

1981 THE ADVENTURES OF HUCKLEBERRY FINN
Director: Jack Hively
Co-stars: Kurt Ida Brock Peters Forrest Tucker

SHANNON TWEED

1991 NIGHT EYES II
Director: Rodney MacDonald
Co-star: Andrew Stevens

1993 INDECENT BEHAVIOUR
Director: Lawrence Lanoff
Co-star: Jan-Michael Vincent

1994 MEATBALLS 3
Director: George Mendeluk
Co-stars: Sally Kellerman Patrick Dempsey Al Waxman

1994 INDECENT BEHAVIOUR II
Director: Carlo Gustav
Co-stars: James Brolin Cynthia Steel

1994 NO CONTEST
Director: Paul Lynch
Co-stars: Andrew "Dice" Clay Robert Davi

1995 BODY CHEMISTRY 4: FULL EXPOSURE
Director: Jim Wynorski

HELEN TWELVETREES *(Helen Jurgens)*

1930 THE CAT CREEPS
Director: Rupert Julian
Co-stars: Raymond Hackett Neil Hamilton Jean Hersholt

1930 HER MAN
Director: Tay Garnett
Co-stars: Ricardo Cortez Marjorie Rambeau James Gleason

1930 SWING HIGH
Co-star: Fred Scott

1931 MILLIE
Co-star: John Halliday

1931 A WOMAN OF EXPERIENCE
Co-stars: William Bakewell Zasu Pitts Franklin Pangborn

1931 BAD COMPANY
Director: Tay Garnett
Co-stars: Ricardo Cortez Frank Conroy John Garrick

1931 THE PAINTED DESERT
Director: Howard Higgins
Co-stars: William Boyd Clark Gable William Farnum

1932 STATE'S ATTORNEY
Director: George Archainbaud
Co-stars: John Barrymore Jill Esmond William Boyd

1932 PANAMA FLO
Co-star: Charles Bickford

1932 UNASHAMED
Co-stars: Robert Young Robert Warwick

1933 MY WOMAN
Co-star: Victor Jory

1933 DISGRACED
Co-star: Bruce Cabot

1933 KING FOR A NIGHT
Director: Kurt Neuman
Co-stars: Chester Morris Grant Mitchell Alice White

1933 A BEDTIME STORY
Director: Norman Taurog
Co-stars: Maurice Chevalier Baby LeRoy Edward Everett Horton

1934 ALL MEN ARE ENEMIES
Director: George Fitzmaurice
Co-stars: Hugh Williams Mona Barrie Herbert Mundin

1934 THE CASE OF THE HOWLING DOG
Director: Alan Crosland
Co-stars: Warren William Mary Astor Allen Jenkins

1934 NOW I'LL TELL
Director: Edwin Burke
Co-stars: Spencer Tracy Alice Faye Shirley Temple

1934 SHE WAS A LADY
Co-star: Donald Woods

1935 ONE HOUR LATE
Co-star: Joe Morrison

1935 FRISCO WATERFRONT
Co-stars: Ben Lyon Rod La Rocque

1935 TIMES SQUARE LADY
Director: George Seitz
Co-stars: Robert Taylor Virginia Bruce Nat Pendleton

1935 THE SPANISH CAPE MYSTERY
Director: Lewis Collins
Co-stars: Donald Cook Berton Churchill

1937 HOLLYWOOD ROUND-UP
Co-stars: Buck Jones Dickie Jones

1939 PERSONS IN HIDING
Director: Louis King
Co-stars: Patricia Morison J. Carrol Naish Lynne Overman

1939 UNMARRIED
Director: Kurt Neuman
Co-stars: Buck Jones Donald O'Connor

TWIGGY *(Leslie Hornby)*

1971 THE BOY FRIEND
Director: Ken Russell
Co-stars: Christopher Gable Tommy Tune Barbara Windsor

1973 W
Director: Richard Quine
Co-stars: Michael Witney Dirk Benedict John Vernon

1980 THERE GOES THE BRIDE
Director: Terence Marcel
Co-stars: Tom Smothers Sylvia Syms Phil Silvers

1980 THE BLUES BROTHERS
Director: John Landis
Co-stars: John Belushi Dan Aykroyd Kathleen Freeman

1985 THE DOCTOR AND THE DEVILS
Director: Freddie Francis
Co-stars: Timothy Dalton Jonathan Pryce Sian Phillips

1986 CLUB PARADISE
Director: Harold Ramis
Co-stars: Robin Williams Peter O'Toole Rick Moranis

1988 MADAME SOUSATZKA
Director: John Schlesinger
Co-stars: Shirley MacLaine Peggy Ashcroft Leigh Lawson

1989 ISTANBUL
Director: Mats Arehn
Co-stars: Timothy Bottoms Robert Morley Emme Kilberg

ANNE TWOMEY

1985 92, GROSVENOR STREET
Director: Sheldon Larry
Co-stars: Hal Holbrook David McCallum Maryam D'Abo

1986 DEADLY FRIEND
Director: Wes Craven
Co-stars: Matthew Laborteaux Kirsty Swanson Anne Ramsey

1988 LAST RITES
Director: Donald Bellisario
Co-stars: Tom Berenger Daphne Zuniga Dane Clark

1990 ORPHEUS DESCENDING
Director: Peter Hall
Co-stars: Vanessa Redgrave Kevin Anderson Miriam Margoyles

1991 BUMP IN THE NIGHT
Director: Karen Arthur
Co-stars: Meredith Baxter-Birney Christopher Reeve Shirley Knight

BEVERLY TYLER

1946 THE GREEN YEARS
Director: Victor Saville
Co-stars: Charles Coburn Dean Stockwell Tom Drake

1946 MY BROTHER TALKS TO HORSES
Director: Fred Zinnemann
Co-stars: Butch Jenkins Peter Lawford Charles Ruggles

1947 THE BEGINNING OR THE END
Director: Norman Taurog
Co-stars: Brian Donlevy Robert Walker Hume Cronyn

1950 THE FIREBALL
Director: Tay Garnett
Co-stars: Mickey Rooney Pat O'Brien Marilyn Monroe

1951 THE CIMARRON KID
Director: Budd Boetticher
Co-stars: Audie Murphy James Best Hugh O'Brian

JUDY TYLER (Killed In A Car Crash In 1957)

1957 BOP GIRL GOES CALYPSO
Director: Howard Koch
Co-stars: Bobby Troup Margo Woode Lucien Littlefield

1957 JAILHOUSE ROCK
Director: Richard Thorpe
Co-stars: Elvis Presley Mickey Shaughnessy Dean Jones

LIV TYLER

1995 SILENT FALL
Director: Bruce Beresford
Co-stars: Richard Dreyfuss Linda Hamilton

1995 HEAVY
Director: James Mangold
Co-stars: Pruitt Taylor Vince Shelley Winters Deborah Harry

1996 STEALING BEAUTY
Director: Bernardo Bertolucci
Co-stars: Roberto Zebetti Jeremy Irons Sinead Cusack

1996 THAT THING YOU DO
Director: Tom Hanks
Co-stars: Tom Hanks Jonathan Schaech Tom Everett Scott

1996 EMPIRE RECORDS
Director: Allan Moyle
Co-star: Anthony LaPaglia

1997 INVENTING THE ABBOTTS
Director: Pat O'Connor
Co-stars: Jennifer Connelly Joaquin Phoenix Kathy Baker

ANN TYRRELL

1953 JULIUS CAESAR
Director: Joseph Mankiewicz
Co-stars: John Gielgud James Mason Marlon Brando

SUSAN TYRRELL

Nominated For Best Supporting Actress In 1972 For "Fat City"

1971 SHOOTOUT
Director: Henry Hathaway
Co-stars: Gregory Peck Pat Quinn Rita Gam

1972 FAT CITY
Director: John Huston
Co-stars: Jeff Bridges Stacy Keach Candy Clark

1974 ZANDY'S BRIDE
Director: Jan Troell
Co-stars: Gene Hackman Liv Ullmann Eileen Heckart

1976 ISLANDS IN THE STREAM
Director: Franklin Schaffnel
Co-stars: George C. Scott David Hemmings Claire Bloom

1977 ANOTHER MAN, ANOTHER CHANCE
Director: Claude Lelouch
Co-stars: James Caan Genevieve Bujold Francis Huster

1977 ANDY WARHOL'S BAD
Director: Jed Johnson
Co-stars: Carroll Baker Perry King Stefania Cassini

1977 SEPTEMBER 30TH 1955
Director: James Bridges
Co-stars: Richard Thomas Deborah Benson Lisa Blount

1981 TALES OF ORDINARY MADNESS
Director: Marco Ferreri
Co-stars: Ben Gazzara Ornella Muti Tanja Lopert

1981 LIAR'S MOON
Director: David Fisher
Co-stars: Matt Dillon Cindy Fisher Yvonne De Carlo

1982 FAST WALKING
Director: James Harris
Co-stars: James Woods Kay Lenz Robert Hooks

1983 NIGHT WARNING
Director: William Asher
Co-stars: Jimmy McNichol Bo Svenson Marcia Lewis

1984 ANGEL
Director: Robert Vincent O'Neil
Co-stars: Cliff Gorman Donna Wilkes Rory Calhoun

1985 AVENGING ANGEL
Director: Robert Vincent O'Neil
Co-stars: Rory Calhoun Ossie Davis Betsy Russell

1985 FLESH AND BLOOD
Director: Paul Verhoeven
Co-stars: Rutger Hauer Jennifer Jason Leigh Ronald Lacey

1987 POKER ALICE
Director: Arthur Seidelman
Co-stars: Elizabeth Taylor George Hamilton Tom Skerritt

1988 BIG TOP PEE-WEE
Director: Randal Kleiser
Co-stars: Pee-Wee Herman Penelope Ann Miller Kris Kristofferson

1988 WINDMILLS OF THE GODS
Director: Lee Philips
Co-stars: Jaclyn Smith Christopher Cazenove John Standing

1990 CRY-BABY
Director: John Waters
Co-stars: Johnny Depp Amy Locane Polly Bergen

1993 MOTORAMA
Director: Barry Shils
Co-stars: Drew Barrymore Jordan Michael

MARGARET TYSACK

1963 RING OF SPIES
Director: Robert Tronson
Co-stars: Bernard Lee David Kossoff William Sylvester

1966 THE WHISPERERS
Director: Bryan Forbes
Co-stars: Edith Evans Eric Portman Nanette Newman

1968 2001: A SPACE ODYSSEY
Director: Stanley Kubrick
Co-stars: Keir Dullea Gary Lockwood Leonard Rossiter

1979 THE LEGACY
Director: Richard Marquand
Co-stars: Katharine Ross Sam Elliott Roger Daltrey

1985 THE CORSICAN BROTHERS
Director: Ian Sharp
Co-stars: Trevor Eve Geraldine Chaplin Olivia Hussey

1986 MR LOVE
Director: Roy Battersby
Co-stars: Barry Jackson Maurice Denham Linda Marlowe

1990 THE KING'S WHORE
Director: Alex Corti
Co-stars: Timothy Dalton Valeria Golino Robin Renucci

CATHY TYSON

1986 MONA LISA
Director: Neil Jordan
Co-stars: Bob Hoskins Michael Caine Sammi Davis

1987 ON THE PALM
Director: Michael White
Co-stars: Peter Martin Philip Jackson Bert Parnaby

1987 BUSINESS AS USUAL
Director: Lezli-An Barrett
Co-stars: Glenda Jackson John Thaw Mark McGann

1988 THE SERPENT AND THE RAINBOW
Director: Wes Craven
Co-stars: Bill Pullman Paul Winfield Zakes Mokae

1991 OUT OF THE BLUE
Director: Nick Hamm
Co-stars: Colin Firth Catherine Zeta Jones John Lynch

1991 THE LOST LANGUAGE OF CRANES
Director: Nigel Finch
Co-stars: Brian Cox Eileen Atkins Angus MacFayden

1991 THE GOLDEN YEARS
Director: Paul Bryers
Co-stars: Ronald Pickup Robert Powell John Bennett

1992 ANGELS
Director: Philip Saville
Co-stars: Tom Bell Alfred Molina Warren Clarke

CICELY TYSON

Nominated For Best Actress In 1972 For "Sounder"

1967 THE COMEDIANS
Director: Peter Glenville
Co-stars: Richard Burton Elizabeth Taylor Alec Guinness

1968 THE HEART IS A LONELY HUNTER
Director: Robert Ellis Miller
Co-stars: Alan Arkin Sondra Locke Stacy Keach

1972 SOUNDER
Director: Martin Ritt
Co-stars: Paul Winfield Kevin Hooks James Best

1976 THE BLUE BIRD
Director: George Cukor
Co-stars: Elizabeth Taylor Ava Gardner Patsy Kensit

1977 A HERO AIN'T NOTHING BUT A SANDWICH
Director: Ralph Nelson
Co-stars: Paul Winfield Helen Martin Larry B. Scott

1979 AIRPORT '80: THE CONCORDE
Director: David Lowell Rich
Co-stars: Alain Delon Susan Blakely Sylvia Kristel

1982 BENNY'S PLACE
Director: Michael Schultz
Co-stars: Lou Gossett Jnr. David Harris Anna Maria Horsford

1985 PLAYING WITH FIRE
Director: Ivan Nagy
Co-stars: Gary Coleman Yaphet Kotto

1986 ACCEPTABLE RISKS
Director: Rick Wallace
Co-stars: Brian Dennehy Kenneth McMillan Christine Ebersole

1990 HEAT WAVE
Director: Kevin Hooks
Co-stars: Blair Underwood James Earl Jones Sally Kirkland

1991 FRIED GREEN TOMATOES AT THE WHISTLE STOP CAFÉ
Director: Jon Avnet
Co-stars: Jessica Tandy Kathy Bates Mary Stuart Masterson

ALANNA UBACH

1994 RENAISSANCE MAN
Director: Penny Marshall
Co-stars: Danny De Vito Gregory Hines Cliff Robertson

FABIANA UDENIO

1990 RE-ANIMATOR 2
Director: Brian Yuzna
Co-stars: Bruce Abbott David Gale Jeffrey Combs

1991 BRIDE OF RE-ANIMATOR
Director: Brian Yuzna
Co-stars: Jeffrey Combs Bruce Abbott Kathleen Kinmont

1991 DIPLOMATIC IMMUNITY
Director: Peter Maris
Co-stars: Bruce Boxleitner Billy Drago Meg Foster

LESLIE UDWIN

1989 SITTING TARGETS
Director: Jenny Wilkes
Co-stars: Phyllis Logan Jonathan Hyde Mary Wimbush

CLAUDIA UDY

1982 AMERICAN NIGHTMARE
Director: Don McBrearty
Co-stars: Lora Stanley Lawrence S. Day Lenore Zann

LIV ULLMAN

Nominated for Best Actress In 1972 For "The Emigrants" And In 1976 for "Face to Face"

1966 PERSONA
Director: Ingmar Bergman
Co-stars: Bibi Andersson Gunnar Bjornstrand

1970 THE NIGHT VISITOR
Director: Laslo Benedek
Co-stars: Max Von Sydow Trevor Howard Andrew Keir

1970 THE EMIGRANTS
Director: Jan Troeli
Co-stars: Max Von Sydow Eddie Axberg Svenolof Bern

1971 COLD SWEAT
Director: Terence Young
Co-stars: Charles Bronson James Mason Jill Ireland

1972 POPE JOAN
Director: Michael Anderson
Co-stars: Trevor Howard Olivia De Havilland

1972 CRIES AND WHISPERS
Director: Ingmar Bergman
Co-stars: Harriet Andersson Ingrid Thulin

1972 LOST HORIZON
Director: Charles Jarrott
Co-stars: Peter Finch Michael York Bobby Van

1973 FORTY CARATS
Director: Milton Katselas
Co-stars: Edward Albert Gene Kelly Nancy Walker

1974 THE ABDICATION
Director: Anthony Harvey
Co-stars: Peter Finch Cyril Cusack Michael Dunn

1974 SCENES FROM A MARRIAGE
Director: Ingmar Bergman
Co-stars: Erland Josephson Jan Malmsjo

1974 ZANDY'S BRIDE
Director: Joan Troel
Co-stars: Gene Hackman Eileen Heckart Joe Santos

1976 FACE TO FACE
Director: Ingmar Bergman
Co-stars: Erland Josephson Gunnar Bjornstrand

1977 THE SERPENT'S EGG
Director: Ingmar Bergman
Co-stars: David Carradine James Whitmore

1977 A BRIDGE TOO FAR
Director: Richard Attenborough
Co-stars: Michael Caine Sean Connery James Caan

1978 AUTUMN SONATA
Director: Ingmar Bergman
Co-stars: Ingrid Bergman Halvar Bjork

1980 RICHARD'S THINGS
Director: Anthony Harvey
Co-stars: Amanda Redman Tim Pigott-Smith

1983 THE WILD DUCK
Director: Henri Safran
Co-stars: Jeremy Irons Lucinda Jones John Meillon

1983 PRISONER WITHOUT A NAME, CELL WITHOUT A NUMBER
Director: Linda Yellen
Co-star: Roy Scheider Sam Robards Davis Cryer

1983 DANGEROUS MOVES
Director: Richard Dembo
Co-stars: Leslie Caron Michel Piccoli

1984 THE BAY BOY
Director: Daniel Petrie
Co-stars: Keifer Sutherland Peter Donat Allan Scarfe

1987 GARY - A TRUE STORY
Director: Luis Mandoki
Co-stars: Robert Loggia Rachel Levin

1988 THE GIRLFRIEND
Director: Jeanine Meerapfel
Co-stars: Cipe Lincovsky Frederico Luppi

1992 THE OX
Director: Sven Nykist
Co-stars: Stellan Skarsgard Max Von Sydow

1992 THE LONG SHADOW
Director: Vilmos Zsigmond
Co-stars: Michael York Oded Teomi Ava Haddad

TRACEY ULLMAN

1984 GIVE MY REGARDS TO BROAD STREET
Director: Peter Webb
Co-stars: Paul McCartney Ringo Starr Bryan Brown

1985 PLENTY
Director: Fred Schepesi
Co-stars: Meryl Streep Charles Dance John Gielgud

1986 JUMPING JACK FLASH
Director: Penny Marshall
Co-stars: Whoopi Goldberg Stephen Collins Carol Kane

1990 I LOVE YOU TO DEATH
Director: Lawrence Kasdan
Co-stars: Kevin Kline Joan Plowright River Phoenix

1990 **HAPPILY EVER AFTER** *(Voice)*
Director: John Howley
Co-stars: Malcolm McDowell Phyllis Diller Ed Asner

1993 **ROBIN HOOD:MEN IN TIGHTS**
Director: Mel Brooks
Co-stars: Mel Brooks Cary Elwes Roger Rees

1994 **I'LL DO ANYTHING**
Director: James L. Brooks
Co-stars: Nick Nolte Joely Richardson Albert Brooks

LUISE ULLRICH

1932 **LIEBELEI**
Director: Max Ophuls
Co-stars: Magda Schneider Wolfgang Liebeneiner Willy Eichberger

LENORE ULRIC

1929 **FROZEN JUSTICE**
Co-stars: Robert Fraser Louis Wolheim

1937 **CAMILLE**
Director: George Cukor
Co-stars: Greta Garbo Robert Taylor Lionel Barrymore

1946 **TEMPTATION**
Director: Irving Pichel
Co-stars: Merle Oberon George Brent Charles Korvin

JOLANTA UMECKA

1962 **KNIFE IN THE WATER**
Director: Roman Polanski
Co-stars: Leon Niemczyk Zygmunt Malanowicz

MIYOSHI UMEKI
Oscar For Best Supporting Actress In 1957 For "Sayonara"

1957 **SAYONARA**
Director: Joshua Logan
Co-stars: Marlon Brando Red Buttons Miiko Taka

1961 **FLOWER DRUM SONG**
Director: Henry Koster
Co-stars: Nancy Kwan James Shigeta Juanita Hall

1961 **CRY FOR HAPPY**
Director: Daryl Duke
Co-stars: Glenn Ford Donald O'Connor Miiko Taka

1962 **A GIRL NAMED TAMIKO**
Director: John Sturges
Co-stars: Laurence Harvey France Nuyen Martha Hyer

1962 **THE HORIZONTAL LIEUTENANT**
Director: Richard Thorpe
Co-stars: Jum Hutton Paula Prentiss Jim Backus

ELLEN UMLAUF

1984 **FLIGHT TO BERLIN**
Director: Christopher Petit
Co-stars: Tusse Silberg Lisa Kreuzer Paul Freeman

GRACE UNA

1996 **LOVE AND BETRAYAL**
Co-stars: Patsy Kensit Dennis Boutsikaris

EMILIA UNDA

1931 **MADCHEN IN UNIFORM**
Director: Leontine Sagan
Co-stars: Dorothea Wieck Hedwig Schlichter Hertha Thiele

BETTY UNDERWOOD

1949 **A DANGEROUS PROFESSION**
Director: Ted Tetzlaff
Co-stars: Pat O'Brien George Raft Ella Rains

1950 **STORM OVER WYOMING**
Director: Lesley Selander
Co-stars: Tim Holt Richard Martin Noreen Nash

DEBORAH UNGER

1990 **BLOOD OATH**
Director: Stephen Wallace
Co-stars: Bryan Brown George Takei Terry O'Quinn

1991 **TILL THERE WAS YOU**
Director: John Seale
Co-stars: Mark Harmon Jeroen Krabbe Shane Briant

1992 **WHISPERS IN THE DARK**
Director: Christopher Crowe
Co-stars: Annabella Sciorra Jamey Sheridan Alan Alda

1995 **HIGHLANDER III:THE SORCERER**
Director: Andy Morahan
Co-stars: Christopher Lambert Mario Van Peebles Mako

1997 **KEYS TO TULSA**
Co-stars: Eric Stoltz James Spader Mary Tyler Moore

1997 **THE GAME**
Director: David Fincher
Co-stars: Michael Douglas Sean Penn

SUE UPTON

1977 **CONFESSIONS FROM A HOLIDAY CAMP**
Director: Norman Cohen
Co-stars: Robin Askwith Anthony Booth Bill Maynard

MARYANN URBANO

1990 **LASERMAN**
Director: Peter Wang
Co-stars: Peter Wang Marc Hayashi Tony Leung

VANNA URBINO

1962 **JULES AND JIM**
Director: Francois Truffaut
Co-stars: Jeanne Moreau Oskar Werner Henri Serre

MARY URE *(Married Robert Shaw)*
Nominated For Best Supporting Actress In 1960 For "Sons And Lovers"

1955 **STORM OVER THE NILE**
Director: Terence Young
Co-stars: Anthony Steel Laurence Harvey

1957 **WINDOM'S WAY**
Director: Ronald Neame
Co-stars: Peter Finch Natasha Parry Michael Hordern

1959 **LOOK BACK IN ANGER**
Director: Tony Richardson
Co-stars: Richard Burton Claire Bloom Edith Evans

1960 **SONS AND LOVERS**
Director: Jack Cardiff
Co-stars: Dean Stockwell Trevor Howard Wendy Hiller

1962 **THE MIND BENDERS**
Director: Basil Dearden
Co-stars: Dirk Bogarde John Clements Michael Bryant

1964 **THE LUCK OF GINGER COFFEY**
Director: Irvin Kerschner
Co-stars: Robert Shaw Liam Redmond Tom Harvey

1967 **CUSTER OF THE WEST**
Director: Robert Siodmak
Co-stars: Robert Shaw Robert Ryan Ty Hardin

1969 **WHERE EAGLES DARE**
Director: Brian Hutton
Co-stars: Richard Burton Clint Eastwood Patrick Wymark

1971   **A REFLECTION OF FEAR**
Director: William Fraker
Co-stars: Robert Shaw Signe Hasso Sondra Locke

MINERVA URECAL

1941   **ACCENT ON LOVE**
Director: Ray McCarey
Co-stars: George Montgomery Osa Massen J. Carrol Naish

1942   **THE CORPSE VANISHES**
Director: Wallace Fox
Co-stars: Bela Lugosi Luana Walters Elizabeth Russell

1943   **THE APE MAN**
Director: William Beaudine
Co-stars: Bela Lugosi Wallace Ford Louise Currie

1944   **BLOCK BUSTERS**
Director: Wallace Fox
Co-stars: Leo Gorcey Huntz Hall Gabriel Dell

1944   **LOUISIANA HAYRIDE**
Co-stars: Judy Canova Matt Willis

1949   **THE LOVEABLE CHEAT**
Co-star: Charles Ruggles

1952   **AARON SLICK FROM PUNKIN CREEK**
Director: Claude Binyon
Co-stars: Alan Young Dinah Shore Adele Jergens

1964   **7 FACES OF DR LAO**
Director: George Pal
Co-stars: Tony Randall Barbara Eden Arthur O'Connell

IRMA URRILA

1975   **THE MAGIC FLUTE**
Director: Ingmar Bergman
Co-stars: Ulric Cold Josel Kostlinger Birgit Nordin

SUSAN URSITTI

1985   **TEEN WOLF**
Director: Rod Daniel
Co-stars: Michael J. Fox James Hampton Scott Paulin

PAULA USTINOV *(Daughter Of Peter Ustinov, Sister Of Tamara Ustinov)*

1978   **THE THIEF OF BAGHDAD**
Director: Clive Donner
Co-stars: Roddy McDowall Peter Ustinov Terence Stamp

TAMARA USTINOV
(Daughter Of Peter Ustinov, Sister Of Paula Ustinov)

1970   **BLOOD ON SATAN'S CLAW**
Director: Piers Haggard
Co-stars: Patrick Wymark Linda Hayden Michele Dotrice

1971   **BLOOD FROM THE MUMMY'S TOMB**
Director: Seth Holt
Co-stars: Andrew Kier Valerie Leon James Villiers

BRENDA VACCARO
Nominated For Best Supporting Actress In 1975 For "Once Is Not Enough"

1969 WHERE IT'S AT
Director: Garson Kanin
Co-stars: David Janssen Rosemary Forsyth Robert Drivas

1969 MIDNIGHT COWBOY
Director: John Schlesinger
Co-stars: Jon Voight Dustin Hoffman Sylvia Miles

1970 I LOVE MY WIFE
Director: Mel Stuart
Co-stars: Elliott Gould Angel Tompkins Dabney Coleman

1971 GOING HOME
Director: Herbert Leonard
Co-stars: Robert Mitchum Jan-Michael Vincent

1971 WHAT'S A NICE GIRL LIKE YOU...?
Director: Jerry Paris
Co-stars: Jack Warden Vincent Price Edmond O'Brien

1971 SUMMERTREE
Director: Anthony Newley
Co-stars: Michael Douglas Barbara Bel Geddes

1971 TRAVIS LOGAN D.A.
Director: Paul Wendkos
Co-stars: Vic Morrow Chris Robinson Hal Holbrook

1975 ONCE IS NOT ENOUGH
Director: Guy Green
Co-stars: Kirk Douglas Alexis Smith David Janssen

1976 DEATH WEEKEND
Director: William Fruet
Co-stars: Don Stroud Chuck Shamata Kyle Edwards

1977 AIRPORT 77
Director: Jerry Jameson
Co-stars: Jack Lemmon James Stewart Joseph Cotten

1978 CAPRICORN ONE
Director: Peter Hyams
Co-stars: Elliott Gould James Brolin Telly Savalas

1979 FAST CHARLIE - THE MOONBEAM RIDER
Director: Steve Carver
Co-stars: David Carradine Jesse Vint

1980 THE FIRST DEADLY SIN
Director: Brian Hutton
Co-stars: Frank Sinatra Faye Dunaway James Whitmore

1981 ZORRO, THE GAY BLADE
Director: Peter Medak
Co-stars: George Hamilton Lauren Hutton James Booth

1984 SUPERGIRL
Director: Jeannot Szwarc
Co-stars: Helen Slater Peter O'Toole Mia Farrow

1985 WATER
Director: Dick Clement
Co-stars: Michael Caine Leonard Rossiter

1985 DECEPTIONS
Director: Melville Shavelson
Co-stars: Stefanie Powers Gina Lollobrigida

1988 HEART OF MIDNIGHT
Director: Matthew Chapman
Co-stars: Jennifer Jason Leigh Peter Coyote Frank Stallone

1989 COOKIE
Director: Susan Seidelman
Co-stars: Emily Lloyd Peter Falk Dianne Wiest

1989 TEN LITTLE INDIANS
Director: Alan Birkinshaw
Co-stars: Donald Pleasence Herbert Lom

1990 I WANT HIM BACK
Director: Catlin Adams
Co-stars: Valerie Harper Elliott Gould Bruce Davison

1994 FOLLOWING HER HEART
Director: Lee Grant
Co-stars: Ann-Margret George Segal

1997 THE MIRROR HAS TWO FACES
Director: Barbra Streisand
Co-stars: Barbra Streisand Jeff Bridges Mimi Rogers

IRIS VADELEUR

1941 GERT AND DAISY'S WEEKEND
Director: Maclean Rogers
Co-stars: Elsie Waters Doris Waters John Slater

1942 GERT AND DAISY CLEAN UP
Director: Maclean Rogers
Co-stars: Elsie Waters Doris Waters Joss Ambler

ANNETTE VADIM

1959 LES LIAISONS DANGEREUSES
Director: Roger Vadim
Co-stars: Gerard Philipe Jeanne Moreau Simone Renant

1960 BLOOD AND ROSES
Director: Roger Vadim
Co-stars: Mel Ferrer Elsa Martinelli Marc Allegret

VERA VAGUE *(Also Acted As Barbara Jo Allen)*

1941 BUY ME THAT TOWN
Director: Eugene Forde
Co-stars: Lloyd Nolan Constance Moore Albert Dekker

1942 MRS WIGGS OF THE CABBAGE PATCH
Director: Ralph Murphy
Co-stars: Fay Bainter Hugh Herbert Carl Switzer

1942 LARCENCY INC.
Director: Lloyd Bacon
Co-stars: Edward G. Robinson Broderick Crawford Jane Wyman

1942 PRIORITIES ON PARADE
Director: Albert Rogell
Co-stars: Ann Miller Johnnie Johnston Jerry Colonna

1943 SWING YOUR PARTNER
Co-stars: Scotty And Lulubelle

1944 ROSIE THE RIVETER
Director: Joseph Santley
Co-stars: Jane Frazee Frank Albertson Maude Eburne

1944 LAKE PLACID SERENADE
Director: Steve Sekely
Co-stars: Vera Ralston Robert Livingston Eugene Pallette

1944 HENRY ALDRICH PLAYS CUPID
Director: Hugh Bennett
Co-stars: Jimmy Lydon Diana Lynn John Litel

1944 MOON OVER LAS VEGAS
Co-stars: David Bruce Ann Gwynne Alan Dinehart

1945   SNAFU
Director: Jack Moss
Co-stars: Robert Benchley Conrad Janus Nanette Parks

1956   MOHAWK
Director: Kurt Neuman
Co-stars: Scott Brady Rita Gam Lori Nelson

MYRTLE VAIL

1960   THE LITTLE SHOP OF HORRORS
Director: Roger Corman
Co-stars: Jonathan Haze Mel Welles Jack Nicholson

VAJIRA

1976   EAST OF ELEPHANT ROCK
Director: Don Boyd
Co-stars: Judi Bowker Jeremy Kemp John Hurt

CHARLOTTE VALANDREY

1985   ROUGE BAISER
Director: Vera Belmont
Co-stars: Lambert Wilson Marthe Keller Isabelle Nanty

1992   ORLANDO
Director: Sally Potter
Co-stars: Tilda Swinton Billy Zane John Wood

BRIGITTA VALBERG

1959   THE VIRGIN SPRING
Director: Ingmar Bergman
Co-stars: Max Von Sydow Gunnel Lindblom Brigitta Pettersson

SIGRID VALDIS

1966   OUR MAN FLINT
Director: Daniel Mann
Co-stars: James Coburn Lee J. Cobb Gila Golan

NINA VALE

1945   CORNERED
Director: Edward Dmytryk
Co-stars: Dick Powell Micheline Cheirel Walter Slezak

1946   THE MYSTERIOUS INTRUDER
Director: William Castle
Co-stars: Richard Dix Barton MacLane Regis Toomey

RITA VALE

1952   THE THIEF
Director: Russel Rouse
Co-stars: Ray Milland Rita Gam Martin Gabel

VIRGINIA VALE

1939   THREE SONS
Co-stars: Kent Taylor Robert Stanton Edward Ellis

1939   THE MARSHALL OF MESA CITY
Director: David Howard
Co-stars: George O'Brien Leon Ames Henry Brandon

1941   BLONDE COMET
Co-star: Robert Kent

NANCY VALEN

1989   LOVERBOY
Director: Joan Micklin Silver
Co-stars: Patrick Dempsey Kate Jackson Kirstie Alley

PAULA VALENSKA

1948   BOND STREET
Director: Gordon Parry
Co-stars: Roland Young Jean Kent Hazel Court

1952   GOLDEN ARROW
Director: Gordon Parry
Co-stars: Jean-Pierre Aumont Burgess Meredith Richard Murdoch

BARBARA VALENTIN

1973   FEAR EATS THE SOUL
Director: Rainer Werner Fassbinder
Co-stars: Rainer Werner Fassbinder Brigitte Mira El Hedi Ben Salem

KAREN VALENTINE

1973   COFFEE, TEA OR ME ?
Director: Norman Panama
Co-stars: John Davidson Louise Lasser Lou Jacobi

1977   MURDER AT THE WORLD SERIES
Director: Andrew McLaglen
Co-stars: Lynda Day Geoge Murray Hamilton Janet Leigh

1979   THE NORTH AVENUE IRREGULARS
Director: Bruce Bilson
Co-stars: Edward Herrman Barbara Harris

1982   STREET COP
Director: Sandor Stern
Co-stars: John Getz Anne De Salvo Vincent Gardenia

1983   A DEADLY PUZZLE
Director: Walter Grauman

1984   HE'S FIRED, SHE'S HIRED
Director: Marc Daniels
Co-stars: Wayne Rogers Elizabeth Ashley

1986   A FIGHTING CHOICE
Director: Ferdinand Fairfax
Co-stars: Beau Bridges Patrick Dempsey

1988   PERFECT PEOPLE
Director: Bruce Seth Green
Co-stars: Lauren Hutton Perry King Cheryl Pollack

1994   THE POWER WITHIN
Co-star: Ted Jan Roberts

NANCY VALENTINE

1959   -30-
Director: Jack Webb
Co-stars: Jack Webb William Conrad David Nelson

1960   TESS OF THE STORM COUNTRY
Director: Paul Guilfoyle
Co-stars: Diane Baker Jack Ging Lee Philips

MARIELLA VALENTINI

1991   VOLERE VOLARE
Director: Guido Manuli
Co-stars: Maurizio Nichetti Angela Finocchiaro Remo Remotti

LILY VALENTY

1957   WILD IS THE WIND
Director: George Cukor
Co-stars: Anna Magnani Anthony Quinn Tony Franciosa

1970   THE BABY MAKER
Director: James Bridges
Co-stars: Barbara Hershey Scott Glenn Jeannie Berlin

1980   TELL ME A RIDDLE
Director: Lee Grant
Co-stars: Lila Kedrova Melvyn Douglas Brooke Adams

SIMONE VALERE

1949   LA BEAUTE DU DIABLE
Director: Rene Clair
Co-stars: Michel Simon Gerard Philipe Raymond Cordy

1972 DIRTY MONEY
Director: Jean-Pierre Melville
Co-stars: Alain Delon Richard Crenna Catherine Deneuvre

FRANCA VALERI

1956 THE BIGAMIST
Director: Luciano Emmer
Co-stars: Marcello Mastroianni Vittorio De Sica Giovanna Ralli

JOAN VALERIE

1940 CHARLIE CHAN AT THE WAX MUSEUM
Director: Lynn Shores
Co-stars: Sidney Toler Sen Yung Marguerite Chapman

1940 MICHAEL SHAYNE, PRIVATE DETECTIVE
Director: Eugene Forde
Co-stars: Lloyd Nolan Walter Able Marjorie Weaver

ROSA VALETTI

1930 THE BLUE ANGEL
Director: Joseph Von Sternberg
Co-stars: Marlene Dietrich Emil Jannings Kurt Gerron

HELEN VALKIS

1938 THE OLD BARN DANCE
Co-stars: Gene Autry Smiley Burnette

LOUISE VALLANCE

1982 THE ROBBERS OF THE SACRED MOUNTAIN
Director: Bob Schulz
Co-stars: Simon MacCorkindale John Marley

1993 THE ONLY WAY OUT
Director: Rod Hardy
Co-stars: John Ritter Henry Winkler Stephanie Feracy

ALIDA VALLI

1942 WE THE LIVING
Director: Goffredo Alessandrini
Co-stars: Rossano Brazzi Fosco Giachetti

1942 THE MIRACLE OF THE BELLS
Director: Irving Pichel
Co-stars: Fred MacMurray Frank Sinatra Lee J. Cobb

1947 THE PARADINE CASE
Director: Alfred Hitchcock
Co-stars: Gregory Peck Ann Todd Louis Jourdan

1949 THE THIRD MAN
Director: Carol Reed
Co-stars: Joseph Cotten Trevor Howard Orson Welles

1950 WALK SOFTLY STRANGER
Director: Robert Stevenson
Co-stars: Joseph Cotten Paul Stewart

1950 THE WHITE TOWER
Director: Ted Tetzlaff
Co-stars: Glenn Ford Claude Rains Lloyd Bridges

1952 THE LOVERS OF TOLEDO
Director: Henri Decoin
Co-stars: Pedro Armendariz Gerard Landry Francoise Arnoul

1953 THE STRANGER'S HAND
Director: Mario Soldati
Co-stars: Trevor Howard Richard O'Sullivan

1953 SENSO
Director: Luchino Visconti
Co-stars: Farley Granger Christian Marquand

1957 IL GRIDO
Director: Michaelangelo Antonioni
Co-stars: Steve Cochran Betsy Blair

1958 HEAVEN FELL THAT NIGHT
Director: Roger Vadim
Co-stars: Brigitte Bardot Stephen Boyd Pepe Nieto

1959 EYES WITHOUT A FACE
Director: Georges Franju
Co-stars: Pierre Brasseur Edith Scob Francois Guerin

1961 THE LONG ABSENCE
Director: Henri Colpi
Co-stars: George Wilson Jacques Harden

1962 THE HAPPY THIEVES
Director: George Marshall
Co-stars: Rex Harrison Rita Hayworth Joseph Wiseman

1967 OEDIPUS REX
Director: Pier Paulo Pasolini
Co-stars: Franco Citti Sylvana Mangano

1970 FUNGUS
Director: Marc Simenon
Co-stars: Mylene Demongeot Jean-Claude Bouillon

1970 THE SPIDER'S STRATAGEM
Director: Bernado Bertolucci
Co-stars: Giullo Brogi Tino Scotti Pino Campanini

1972 LISA AND THE DEVIL
Director: Mario Bava
Co-stars: Elke Sommer Telly Savalas Sylva Koscina

1974 THE FLESH OF THE ORCHID
Director: Patrice Chereau
Co-stars: Charlotte Rampling Simone Signoret

1976 THE CASSANDRA CROSSING
Director: Brian De Palma
Co-stars: Sophia Loren Richard Harris Ava Gardner

1976 SUSPIRIA
Director: Dario Argento
Co-stars: Jessica Harper Joan Bennett Stefania Casini

1976 LUMIERE
Director: Jeanne Moreau
Co-stars: Francine Racette Lucia Boce Jeanne Moreau

1981 ASPERN
Director: Eduardo De Grigorio
Co-stars: Jean Sorel Bulle Ogier Ana Marta

VIRGINIA VALLI

1925 THE PLEASURE GARDEN
Director: Alfred Hitchcock
Co-stars: John Stuart Miles Mander Carmelita Geraghty

ELEANORA VALLONE

1981 A TALE OF AFRICA
Director: Susumo Hani
Co-stars: James Stewart Philip Sayer Heekura Simba

LUCY VALNOR

1946 L'HOMME AU CHAPEAU ROND
Director: Pierre Billon
Co-stars: Raimu Aime Clariond

VALERIE VALOIS

1992 SCANNERS 3: THE TAKEOVER
Director: Christian Duguay
Co-stars: Steve Parrish Colin Fox Daniel Pilon

INDIRA VAMA

1997 KAMA SUTRA
Director: Mira Nair
Co-star: Navern Andrews

VAMPIRA

1956   **PLAN 9 FROM OUTER SPACE**
Director: Edward Wood
Co-stars: Bela Lugosi Tor Johnson Lyle Talbot

BETTY VAN ALLEN

1931   **THE BELOVED BACHELOR**
Director: Lloyd Corrigan
Co-stars: Paul Lukas Dorothy Jordon Charles Ruggles

WILLEKE VAN AMMERLROOY

1996   **ANTONIA'S LINE**
Director: Marleen Gorris
Co-star: Thyrza Ravesteijn

JOAN VAN ARK

1972   **FROGS**
Director: George McCowan
Co-stars: Ray Milland Sam Elliott Judy Pace

1975   **SHELL GAME**
Director: Glenn Jordan
Co-stars: John Davidson Tommy Atkins Signe Hasso

1977   **THE LAST DINOSAUR**
Director: Tom Kotani
Co-stars: Richard Boone Steven Keats

1981   **RED FLAG:THE ULTIMATE GAME**
Director: Don Taylor
Co-stars: Barry Bostwick William Devane Debra Feuer

1988   **MY FIRST LOVE**
Director: Gilbert Cates
Co-stars: Beatrice Arthur Richard Kiley Anne Francis

1992   **TERROR ON TRACK NINE**
Director: Robert Iscove
Co-stars: Richard Crenna Cliff Gorman Swoosie Kurtz

1994   **CULT RESCUE**
Director: Chuck Bowman
Co-stars: Stephen Macht Tom Kurlander

INGRID VAN BERGEN

1962   **ESCAPE FROM EAST BERLIN**
Director: Robert Siodmak
Co-stars: Don Murray Christine Kaufman Werner Klemperer

IRENE VANBRUGH

1934   **CATHERINE THE GREAT**
Director: Paul Czinner
Co-stars: Elisabeth Bergner Douglas Fairbanks Jnr. Flora Robson

1935   **ESCAPE ME NEVER**
Director: Paul Czinner
Co-stars: Elisabeth Bergner Hugh Sinclair Griffith Jones

1937   **KNIGHT WITHOUT ARMOUR**
Director: Jacques Feyder
Co-stars: Robert Donat Marlene Dietrich Herbert Lom

1937   **WINGS OF THE MORNING**
Director: Harold Schuster
Co-stars: Henry Fonda Annabella Leslie Banks

1944   **IT HAPPENED ONE SUNDAY**
Director: Karel Lamac
Co-stars: Robert Beatty Barbara White Judy Kelly

VIOLET VANBRUGH

1938   **PYGMALION**
Director: Anthony Asquith
Co-stars: Leslie Howard Wendy Hiller Wilfrid Lawson

DANITRA VANCE

1988   **STICKY FINGERS**
Director: Catlin Adams
Co-stars: Helen Slater Melanie Mayron Carol Kane

1989   **LIMIT UP**
Director: Richard Martini
Co-stars: Nancy Allen Dean Stockwell Brad Hall

1992   **LITTLE MAN TATE**
Director: Jodie Foster
Co-stars: Jodie Foster Dianne Wiest Adam Hann-Byrd

VIVIAN VANCE

1965   **THE GREAT RACE**
Director: Blake Edwards
Co-stars: Jack Lemmon Tony Curtis Natalie Wood

1971   **GETTING AWAY FROM IT ALL**
Director: Lee Philips
Co-stars: Gary Collins Barbara Feldon Larry Hagman

JOYCE VANDERVEEN

1956   **THE TEN COMMANDMENTS**
Director: Cecil B. DeMille
Co-stars: Charlton Heston Anne Baxter John Derek

NADINE VAN DER VELDE

1986   **CRITTERS**
Director: Stephen Herek
Co-stars: Dee Wallace M. Emmet Walsh Billy Zane

1989   **AFTER MIDNIGHT**
Director: Jim Wheat
Co-stars: Jillian McWhirter Pamela Segall Marc McClure

DIANE VAN DER VLIS

1963   **THE MAN WITH X-RAY EYES**
Director: Roger Corman
Co-stars: Ray Milland Don Rickles John Hoyt

1967   **THE INCIDENT**
Director: Larry Peerce
Co-stars: Tony Musante Martin Sheen Beau Bridges

1968   **THE SWIMMER**
Director: Frank Perry
Co-stars: Burt Lancaster Janice Rule Marge Champion

TRISH VAN DEVERE

1970   **WHERE'S POPPA ?**
Director: Carl Reiner
Co-stars: George Segal Ruth Gordon Ron Leibman

1971   **THE LAST RUN**
Director: Richard Fleischer
Co-stars: George C. Scott Tony Musante Colleen Dewhurst

1972   **ONE IS A LONELY NUMBER**
Director: Mel Stuart
Co-stars: Monte Markham Melvyn Douglas Janet Leigh

1973   **HARRY IN YOUR POCKET**
Director: Bruce Geller
Co-stars: James Coburn Michael Sarrazin Walter Pidgeon

1973   **THE DAY OF THE DOLPHIN**
Director: Mike Nichols
Co-stars: George C. Scott Paul Sorvino Fritz Weaver

1978   **MOVIE MOVIE**
Director: Stanley Donen
Co-stars: George C. Scott Red Buttons Eli Wallach

1979   **THE CHANGELING**
Director: Peter Medak
Co-stars: George C. Scott Melvyn Douglas Jean Marsh

1980   **THE HEARSE**
Director: George Bowers
Co-stars: Joseph Cotten David Gautreaux Donald Petrie

1980   **ALL GOD'S CHILDREN**
Director: Jerry Thorpe
Co-stars: Richard Widmark Ned Beatty Ruby Dee

1984   **HAUNTED**
Director: Michael Roemer
Co-stars: Brooke Adams John Devries Ari Meyers

1985   **UPHILL ALL THE WAY**
Director: Frank Dobbs
Co-stars: Roy Clark Mel Tillis Burl Ives

MAMIE VAN DOREN MARRIED: RAY ANTHONY

1953   **THE ALL-AMERICAN**
Director: Jesse Hibbs
Co-stars: Tony Curtis Lori Nelson Gregg Palmer

1954   **YANKEE PASHA**
Director: Joseph Pevney
Co-stars: Jeff Chandler Rhonda Fleming Lee J. Cobb

1955   **THE SECOND GREATEST SEX**
Director: George Marshall
Co-stars: Jeanne Crain George Nader Bert Lahr

1955   **AIN'T MISBEHAVIN'**
Director: Edward Buzzell
Co-stars: Rory Calhoun Piper Laurie Jack Carson

1957   **THE GIRL IN BLACK STOCKINGS**
Director: Howard Koch
Co-stars: Anne Bancroft Lex Barker Marie Windsor

1958   **TEACHER'S PET**
Director: George Seaton
Co-stars: Clark Gable Doris Day Gig Young

1959   **BORN RECKLESS**
Director: Howard Koch
Co-stars: Jeff Richards Arthur Hunnicutt Carol Ohmart

1959   **THE BIG OPERATOR**
Director: Charles Haas
Co-stars: Mickey Rooney Steve Cochran Mel Torme

1959   **THE BEAT GENERATION**
Director: Charles Haas
Co-stars: Ray Danton Steve Cochran Fay Spain

1960   **COLLEGE CONFIDENTIAL**
Director: Albert Zugsmith
Co-stars: Steve Allen Jayne Meadows Herbert Marshall

CONNY VAN DYKE

1974   **FRAMED**
Director: Phil Karlson
Co-stars: Joe Don Baker Gabriel Dell Brock Peters

MARCIA VAN DYKE

1949   **IN THE GOOD OLD SUMMERTIME**
Director: Robert Z. Leonard
Co-stars: Judy Garland Van Johnson Buster Keaton

JO VAN FLEET
Oscar For Best Supporting Actress In 1955 For "East Of Eden"

1955   **THE ROSE TATTOO**
Director: Daniel Mann
Co-stars: Anna Magnani Burt Lancaster Marisa Pavan

1955   **I'LL CRY TOMORROW**
Director: Daniel Mann
Co-stars: Susan Hayward Richard Conte Eddie Albert

1955   **EAST OF EDEN**
Director: Elia Kazan
Co-stars: James Dean Raymond Massey Julie Harris

1956   **KING AND FOUR QUEENS**
Director: Raoul Walsh
Co-stars: Clark Gable Eleanor Parker Jean Willes

1957   **GUNFIGHT AT THE O.K. CORAL**
Director: John Sturges
Co-stars: Burt Lancaster Kirk Douglas Rhonda Fleming

1960   **WILD RIVER**
Director: Elia Kazan
Co-stars: Montgomery Clift Lee Remick Bruce Dern

1964   **CINDERELLA**
Director: Charles Dubin
Co-stars: Ginger Rogers Celeste Holm Walter Pidgeon

1967   **COOL HAND LUKE**
Director: Stuart Rosenberg
Co-stars: Paul Newman George Kennedy Lou Antonio

1968   **I LOVE YOU, ALICE B. TOKLAS**
Director: Hy Averback
Co-stars: Peter Sellers Joyce Van Patten David Arkin

1971   **THE GANG THAT COULDN'T SHOOT STRAIGHT**
Director: James Goldstone
Co-stars: Jerry Orbach Leigh Taylor-Young

1972   **THE FAMILY RICO**
Director: Paul Wendkos
Co-stars: Ben Gazzara Sal Mineo James Farantino

1976   **THE TENANT**
Director: Roman Polanski
Co-stars: Roman Polanski Melvyn Douglas Isabelle Adjani

1986   **SEIZE THE DAY**
Director: Fielder Cook
Co-stars: Robin Williams Joseph Wiseman Glenne Headley

RENATA VANNI

1960   **PAY OR DIE**
Director: Richard Wilson
Co-stars: Ernest Borgnine Alan Austin Zohra Lampert

1989   **THE LADY IN WHITE**
Director: Frank La Loggia
Co-stars: Lukas Haas Len Cariou Alex Rocco

JOANNE VANNICOLA

1989   **BETRAYAL OF SILENCE**
Director: Jeffrey Woolnough
Co-stars: Meg Foster Alex Carter

1993   **LOVE AND HUMAN REMAINS**
Director: Denys Arcand
Co-stars: Thomas Gibson Ruth Marshall Mia Kirshner

1995   **DERBY**
Director: Bob Clark

NINA VAN PALLANDT *(Found Fame As Member Of Singing Duo, Nina And Frederick)*

1973   **THE LONG GOODBYE**
Director: Robert Altman
Co-stars: Elliott Gould Sterling Hayden Mark Rydell

1978   **A WEDDING**
Director: Robert Altman
Co-stars: Carol Burnett Mia Farrow Howard Duff

1979   **QUINTET**
Director: Robert Altman
Co-stars: Paul Newman Vittorio Gassman Brigitte Fossey

1980 AMERICAN GIGOLO
Director: Paul Schrader
Co-stars: Richard Gere Lauren Hutton Bill Duke

1981 CUTTER'S WAY
Director: Ivan Passer
Co-stars: Jeff Bridges John Heard Lisa Eichhorn

1982 THE SWORD AND THE SORCERER
Director: Albert Pyun
Co-stars: Lee Horsley Kathleen Beller Simon MacCorkindale

JOYCE VAN PATTEN

1968 I LOVE YOU, ALICE B. TOKLAS
Director: Hy Averbach
Co-stars: Peter Sellers Jo Van Fleet

1969 THE TROUBLE WITH GIRLS
Director: Peter Tewkesbury
Co-stars: Elvis Presley Marilyn Mason Sheree North

1974 MAME
Director: Gene Saks
Co-stars: Lucille Ball Beatrice Arthur Robert Preston

1974 THE STRANGER WITHIN
Director: Lee Phillips
Co-stars: Barbara Eden George Grizzard Nehemiah Persoff

1975 WINNER TAKES ALL
Director: Paul Bogart
Co-stars: Shirley Jones Joan Blondell Sylvia Sidney

1976 MIKEY AND NICKY
Director: Elaine May
Co-stars: Peter Falk John Cassavetes Ned Beatty

1976 THE BAD NEWS BEAR
Director: Michael Ritchie
Co-stars: Walter Matthau Tatum O'neal Vic Morrow

1983 ANOTHER WOMAN'S CHILD
Director: John Erman
Co-stars: Linda Lavin Tony LoBianca Doris Roberts

1983 IN DEFENSE OF KIDS
Director: Gene Reynolds
Co-stars: Blythe Danner Sam Waterston Beth Ehlers

1985 MALICE IN WONDERLAND
Director: Gus Trikonis
Co-stars: Elizabeth Taylor Jane Alexander Richard Dysart

1985 ST. ELMO'S FIRE
Director: Joel Schumacher
Co-stars: Rob Lowe Demi Moore Ally Sheedy

1985 PICKING UP THE PIECES
Director: Paul Wendkos
Co-stars: Margot Kidder David Ackroyd James Farantino

1986 UNDER THE INFLUENCE
Director: Thomas Carter
Co-stars: Andy Griffith Season Hubley Keanu Reeves

1986 BILLY GALVIN
Director: John Gray
Co-stars: Karl Malden Lenny Van Dohlen Toni Kalem

**1988 MONKEY SHINES:
AN EXPERIMENT IN FEAR**
Director: George Romero
Co-stars: Jason Beghe John Pankow

1991 THE HAUNTED
Director: Robert Mandel
Co-stars: Sally Kirkland Jeffrey DeMunn Louise Latham

1994 THE GIFT OF LOVE
Director: Paul Bogart
Co-stars: Andy Griffith Blair Brown Will Friedle

1994 BREATHING LESSONS
Director: John Erman
Co-stars: James Garner Joanne Woodward Kathryn Erbe

WENDY VAN RIESEN

1995 THE MAN WHO WOULDN'T DIE
Director: Bill Condon
Co-stars: Roger Moore Malcolm McDowell

DEBORAH VAN VALKENBURGH

1979 THE WARRIORS
Director: Walter Hill
Co-stars: Michael Beck James Remar Mercedes Ruehl

1985 STREETS OF FIRE
Director: Walter Hill
Co-stars: Michael Pare Diane Lane Willem Dafoe

**1985 GOING FOR THE GOLD:
THE BILL JOHNSON STORY**
Director: Don Taylor
Co-stars: Anthony Edwards Dennis Weaver

1987 RAMPAGE
Director: William Friedkin
Co-stars: Michael Biehn Alex McArthur Nicholas Campbell

BABETTE VAN VEEN

1989 BLUEBERRY HILL
Director: Robbe De Hert
Co-star: Michael Pas

MONIQUE VAN VOOREN

1953 TARZAN AND THE SHE-DEVIL
Director: Kurt Neuman
Co-stars: Lex Barker Raymond Burr Tom Conway

1974 FLESH FOR FRANKENSTEIN
Director: Paul Morrissey
Co-stars: Joe Dallesandro Udo Kier Arno Juerging

EVELYN VARDEN

1949 PINKY
Director: Elia Kazan
Co-stars: Jeanne Crain Ethel Barrymore Ethel Waters

1950 WHEN WILLIE COMES MARCHING HOME
Director: John Ford
Co-stars: Dan Dailey Corinne Calvet William Demarest

1951 ELOPEMENT
Director: Henry Koster
Co-stars: Clifton Webb Anne Francis Charles Bickford

1952 PHONE CALL FROM A STRANGER
Director: Jean Negulesco
Co-stars: Bette Davis Gary Merrill Michael Rennie

1954 ATHENA
Director: Richard Thorpe
Co-stars: Edmund Purdom Jane Powell Debbie Reynolds

1954 THE STUDENT PRINCE
Director: Richard Thorpe
Co-stars: Edmund Purdom Ann Blyth Edmund Gwenn

1955 THE NIGHT OF THE HUNTER
Director: Charles Laughton
Co-stars: Robert Mitchum Shelley Winters Lillian Gish

1956 HILDA CRANE
Director: Philip Dunne
Co-stars: Jean Simmons Guy Madison Jean-Pierre Aumont

1956 THE BAD SEED
Director: Mervyn LeRoy
Co-stars: Nancy Kelly Patty McCormack Eileen Heckart

NORMA VARDEN

1935 GET OFF MY FOOT
Director: William Beaudine
Co-stars: Max Miller Chilli Bouchier Jane Carr

1935 FOREIGN AFFAIRS
Director: Tom Walls
Co-stars: Tom Walls Roy Kellino Robertson Hare

1935 BOYS WILL BE BOYS
Director: William Beaudine
Co-stars: Will Hay Gordon Harker Jimmy Hanley

1936 WHERE THERE'S A WILL
Director: William Beaudine
Co-stars: Will Hay Graham Moffatt Lilli Palmer

1936 WINDBAG THE SAILOR
Director: William Beaudine
Co-stars: Will Hay Moore Marriott Graham Moffatt

1940 SHIPYARD SALLY
Director: Monty Banks
Co-stars: Gracie Fields Sydney Howard Oliver Wafefield

1941 SCOTLAND YARD
Director: Norman Foster
Co-stars: Nancy Kelly Edmund Gwenn Henry Wilcoxon

1942 THE MAJOR AND THE MINOR
Director: Billy Wilder
Co-stars: Ginger Rogers Ray Milland Robert Benchley

1944 NATIONAL VELVET
Director: Clarence Brown
Co-stars: Elizabeth Taylor Mickey Rooney Anne Revere

1944 MADEMOISELLE FIFI
Director: Robert Wise
Co-stars: Simone Simon Kurt Kreuger John Emery

1945 HOLD THAT BLONDE
Director: George Marshall
Co-stars: Eddie Bracken Veronica Lake Albert Dekker

1945 GIRLS OF THE BIG HOUSE
Co-star: Richard Powers

1947 IVY
Director: Sam Wood
Co-stars: Joan Fontaine Herbert Marshall Patric Knowles

1947 THE TROUBLE WITH WOMEN
Director: Sidney Lanfield
Co-stars: Ray Milland Teresa Wright Brian Donlevy

1949 ADVENTURE IN BALTIMORE
Director: Richard Wallace
Co-stars: Shirley Temple Robert Young John Agar

1950 FANCY PANTS
Director: George Marshall
Co-stars: Bob Hope Lucille Ball Bruce Cabot

1957 WITNESS FOR THE PROSECUTION
Director: Billy Wilder
Co-stars: Marlene Dietrich Tyrone Power Charles Laughton

1965 THE SOUND OF MUSIC
Director: Robert Wise
Co-stars: Julie Andrews Christopher Plummer Eleanor Parker

MARIA VARGA

1989 A HUNGARIAN FAIRY TALE
Director: Gyula Gazdag
Co-stars: David Vermes Frantisek Husak

DANIELE VARGAS

1974 FOOTBALL CRAZY
Director: Luigi Filipo D'Amico
Co-stars: Lando Buzzanca Joan Collins Gabriella Pallotta

VALENTINA VARGAS

1986 THE NAME OF THE ROSE
Director: Jean-Jacques Annaud
Co-stars: Sean Connery Christian Slater William Hickey

ZSUZSANNA VARKONYI

1991 FORGET ABOUT ME
Director: Michael Winterbottom
Co-stars: Ewen Bremner Brian McCardie Katalin Pataki

BEATRICE VARLEY

1941 HATTER'S CASTLE
Director: Lance Comfort
Co-stars: Robert Newton Deborah Kerr James Mason

1941 KIPPS
Director: Carol Reed
Co-stars: Michael Redgrave Phyllis Calvert Diana Wynyard

1942 SQUADRON LEADER X
Director: Lance Comfort
Co-stars: Eric Portman Ann Dvorak Walter Fitzgerald

1943 THE BELLS GO DOWN
Director: Basil Dearden
Co-stars: Tommy Trinder James Mason Mervyn Johns

1945 GREAT DAY
Director: Lance Comfort
Co-stars: Eric Portman Flora Robson Sheila Sim

1945 WATERLOO ROAD
Director: Sidney Gilliat
Co-stars: John Mills Stewart Granger Joy Shelton

1947 MASTER OF BANKDAM
Director: Walter Forde
Co-stars: Tom Walls Anne Crawford Dennis Price

1948 MY BROTHER'S KEEPER
Director: Alfred Roome
Co-stars: Jack Warner George Cole Jane Hylton

1950 GONE TO EARTH
Director: Michael Powell
Co-stars: Jennifer Jones Cyril Cusack David Farrar

1950 SHE SHALL HAVE MURDER
Director: Daniel Birt
Co-stars: Rosamund John Derrick De Marney Mary Jerrold

1954 THE BLACK RIDER
Director: Wolf Rilla
Co-stars: Jimmy Hanley Rona Anderson Lionel Jeffries

1956 TIGER IN THE SMOKE
Director: Roy Baker
Co-stars: Tony Wright Muriel Pavlow Donald Sinden

SARAH JANE VARLEY

1975 MR QUILP
Director: Michael Tuchner
Co-stars: Anthony Newley David Hemmings David Warner

1991 DOUBLE IMPACT
Director: Sheldon Lettich
Co-stars: Jean-Claude Van Damme Geoffrey Lewis Alan Scarfe

DIANE VARSI

Nominated For Best Supporting Actress In 1957 For "Peyton Place"

1957 PEYTON PLACE
Director: Mark Robson
Co-stars: Lana Turner Hope Lange Arthur Kennedy

1958 TEN NORTH FREDERICK
Director: Philip Dunne
Co-stars: Gary Cooper Geraldine Fitzgerald Stuart Whitman

1958   **FROM HELL TO TEXAS**
Director: Henry Hathaway
Co-stars: Don Murray Chill Wills Dennis Hopper

1959   **COMPULSION**
Director: Richard Fleischer
Co-stars: Dean Stockwell Bradford Dillman Orson Welles

1968   **WILD IN THE STREETS**
Director: Barry Shear
Co-stars: Chris Jones Shelley Winters Millie Perkins

1969   **BLOODY MAMA**
Director: Roger Corman
Co-stars: Shelley Winters Bruce Dern Robert De Niro

1971   **JOHNNY GOT HIS GUN**
Director: Dalton Trumbo
Co-stars: Timothy Bottoms Jason Robards Marsha Hunt

ROSY VARTE

1979   **LOVE ON THE RUN**
Director: Francois Truffaut
Co-stars: Jean-Pierre Leaud Claude Jade Marie-France Pisier

YOLANDA VAQUEZ

1986   **SHIFT WORK**
Director: Angela Pope
Co-stars: Maureen Lipman Stephen Dillon Tony Alleff

1992   **MARIA'S CHILD**
Director: Malcolm McKay
Co-stars: David O'Hara Fiona Shaw Alec McCowen

1994   **THE AIR UP THERE**
Director: Paul-Michael Glaser
Co-stars: Kevin Bacon Charles Gitonga Maina Sean McCann

QUEENIE VASSAR

1940   **PRIMROSE PATH**
Director: Gregory La Cava
Co-stars: Ginger Rogers Joel McCrea Henry Travers

CECILE VASSORT

1973   **L'INVITATION**
Director: Claude Goretta
Co-stars: Jean-Luc Bideau Jean Champion Corinne Coderey

SARAH VAUGHAN

1960   **MURDER INC.**
Director: Stuart Rosenberg
Co-stars: Stuart Whitman Mai Britt Henry Morgan

VANESSA VAUGHAN

1986   **CRAZY MOON**
Director: Allan Eastman
Co-stars: Kiefer Sutherland Peter Spence Eve Napier

ALBERTA VAUGHN

1929   **NOISY NEIGHBORS**

1932   **DARING DANGER**
Director: Ross Lederman
Co-stars: Tim McCoy Wallace MacDonald

1934   **RANDY RIDES ALONE**
Director: Henry Frazer
Co-stars: John Wayne George Hayes Yakima Canutt

HILDA VAUGHN

1929   **THREE LIVE GHOSTS**
Co-stars: Robert Montgomery Beryl Mercer Claude Allister

1940   **CHARLIE CHAN AT THE WAX MUSEUM**
Director: Lynn Shores
Co-stars: Sidney Toler Sen Yung Marc Lawrence

SELMA VAZ DIAZ

1960   **BLUEBEARD'S TEN HONEYMOONS**
Director: Lee Wilder
Co-stars: George Sanders Corinne Calvet Jean Kent

ISELA VEGA

1974   **BRING ME THE HEAD OF ALFREDO GARCIA**
Director: Sam Peckinpah
Co-stars: Warren Oates Gig Young Robert Webber

1976   **DRUM**
Director: Steve Carver
Co-stars: Warren Oates Ken Norton Yaphet Kotto

1976   **THE BLACK RIDER**
Director: Larry Spangler
Co-stars: Fred Williamson Brenda Venus Stacy Newton

1982   **BARBAROSA**
Director: Fred Schepisi
Co-stars: Willy Nelson Gary Busey Gilbert Roland

1987   **THE ALAMO:THIRTEEN DAYS TO GLORY**
Director: Burt Kennedy
Co-stars: James Arness Brian Keith Lorne Greene

ISIDRA VEGA

1998   **HURRICANE STREETS**
Director: Morgan J. Freeman
Co-star: Brendan Sexton III

MARIA VELASCO

1961   **ALL NIGHT LONG**
Director: Basil Dearden
Co-stars: Patrick McGoohan Richard Attenborough Betsy Blair

LAUREN VELEZ

1994   **I LIKE IT LIKE THAT**
Director: Darnell Martin
Co-stars: Jon Seda Lisa Vidal Rita Moreno

LUPE VELEZ *(Married Johnny Weissmulller)*

1928   **THE GAUCHO**
Director: Lotta Woods
Co-stars: Douglas Fairbanks Geraine Greear Gustav Von Seyffertitz

1929   **WOLF SONG**
Co-star: Gary Cooper

1929   **LADY OF THE PAVEMENTS**
Director: D.W. Griffith
Co-stars: William Boyd Albert Conti Jetta Goudal

1930   **HELL HARBOUR**
Director: Henry King
Co-stars: Jean Hersholt Gibson Gowland John Holland

1930   **EAST IS WEST**
Director: Monta Bell
Co-stars: Edward G. Robinson Lew Ayres Mary Forbes

1930   **THE STORM**
Director: William Wyler
Co-stars: Paul Cavanagh William Boyd

1931   **THE SQUAW MAN**
Director: Cecil B. DeMille
Co-stars: Warner Baxter Charles Bickford Eleanor Boardman

1931   **RESURRECTION**
Director: Edwin Carewe
Co-stars: John Boles Nance O'Neil Rose Tapley

1931 CUBAN LOVE SONG
Director: W.S. Van Dyke
Co-stars: Lawrence Tibbett Jimmy Durante Karen Morley

1932 THE BROKEN WING
Director: Lloyd Corrigan
Co-stars: Melvyn Douglas Leo Carrillo George Barbier

1932 THE HALF-NAKED TRUTH
Director: Gregory La Cava
Co-stars: Lee Tracy Eugene Pallette Frank Morgan

1932 KONGO
Director: William Cowen
Co-stars: Walter Huston Virginia Bruce Conrad Nagel

1933 HOT PEPPER
Director: John Blystone
Co-stars: Edmund Lowe Victor McLaglen Lillian Bond

1934 LAUGHING BOY
Director: W.S. Van Dyke
Co-stars: Ramon Novarro William Davidson Chief Thundercloud

1934 PALOOKA
Co-stars: Jimmy Durante Stuart Erwin

1934 STRICTLY DYNAMITE
Co-stars: Jimmy Durante Stanley Fields

1934 HOLLYWOOD PARTY
Director: Allan Dwan
Co-stars: Stan Laurel Oliver Hardy Jimmy Durante

1936 THE MORALS OF MARCUS
Director: Miles Mander
Co-stars: Ian Hunter Noel Madison Adrienne Allen

1937 HIGH FLYERS
Director: Edward Cline
Co-stars: Bert Wheeler Robert Woolsey Jack Carson

1939 THE GIRL FROM MEXICO
Director: Leslie Goodwins
Co-stars: Donald Woods Leon Errol Linda Hayes

1939 MEXICAN SPITFIRE
Director: Leslie Goodwins
Co-stars: Donald Woods Leon Errol Cecil Kellaway

1940 MEXICAN SPITFIRE OUT WEST
Director: Leslie Goodwins
Co-stars: Donald Woods Leon Errol

1941 MEXICAN SPITFIRE'S BABY
Director: Leslie Goodwins
Co-stars: Leon Errol Charles Rogers Marion Martin

1941 MEXICAN SPITFIRE AT SEA
Director: Leslie Goodwins
Co-stars: Leon Errol Charles Rogers Elisabeth Risdon

1941 SIX LESSONS FROM MADAME LA ZONGA
Director: John Rawlins
Co-stars: Leon Errol William Frawley Helen Parrish

1941 PLAYMATES
Director: David Butler
Co-stars: Kay Kyser John Barrymore Ginny Simms

1941 HONOLULU LU
Co-stars: Leo Carrillo Lloyd Bridges Larry Parks

1942 MEXICAN SPITFIRE SEES A GHOST
Director: Leslie Goodwins
Co-stars: Leon Errol Charles Rogers Donald MacBride

1942 MEXICAN SPITFIRE'S ELEPHANT
Director: Leslie Goodwins
Co-stars: Leon Errol Walter Reed Marion Martin

1943 MEXICAN SPITFIRE'S BLESSED EVENT
Director: Leslie Goodwins
Co-stars: Leon Errol Donald Woods

1943 REDHEAD FROM MANHATTAN
Co-star: Michael Duane

EVELYN VENABLE

1933 CRADLE SONG
Director: Mitchell Leisen
Co-stars: Dorothea Wieck Louise Dresser Kent Taylor

1934 DAVID HARUM
Director: James Cruze
Co-stars: Will Rogers Kent Taylor Louise Dresser

1934 DOUBLE DOOR
Director: Charles Vidor
Co-stars: Mary Morris Kent Taylor Anne Revere

1934 DEATH TAKES A HOLIDAY
Director: Mitchell Leisen
Co-stars: Fredric March Guy Standing Gail Patrick

1934 THE COUNTY CHAIRMAN
Director: John Blystone
Co-stars: Will Rogers Kent Taylor Mickey Rooney

1934 MRS WIGGS OF THE CABBAGE PATCH
Director: Norman Taurog
Co-stars: Pauline Lord Zasu Pitts W.C. Fields

1935 THE LITTLE COLONEL
Director: David Butler
Co-stars: Shirley Temple Lionel Barrymore Bill Robinson

1935 ALICE ADAMS
Director: George Stevens
Co-stars: Katherine Hepburn Fred MacMurray Hattie McDaniel

1935 STREAMLINE EXPRESS
Co-stars: Ralph Forbes Victor Jory

1935 HARMONY LANE
Director: Joseph Santly
Co-stars: Douglass Montgomery Adrienne Ames Joseph Cawthorn

1935 VAGABOND LADY
Director: Sam Taylor
Co-stars: Robert Young Reginald Denny Frank Craven

1936 STAR FOR A NIGHT
Co-stars: J. Edward Bromberg Jane Darwell

1937 HAPPY GO LUCKY
Director: Aubrey Scotto
Co-stars: Phil Regan Jed Prouty William Newell

1938 MY OLD KENTUCKY HOME
Co-star: Grant Richards

1938 FEMALE FUGITIVE
Co-star: Craig Reynolds

1939 HERITAGE OF THE DESERT
Co-stars: Donald Woods C. Henry Gordon

1940 PINOCCHIO (Voice)
Director: Ben Sharpsteen
Co-stars: Dickie Jones Christian Rub Walter Catlett

SARAH VENABLE

1978 MARTIN
Director: George Romero
Co-stars: John Amplas Christine Forrest Tom Savine

MAGALI VENDEUIL

1952 LES BELLES DE NUIT
Director: Rene Clair
Co-stars: Gerard Philipe Gina Lollobrigida Martine Carol

AMY VENESS

1931 MY WIFE'S FAMILY
Director: Monty Banks
Co-stars: Gene Gerrard Muriel Angelus Jimmy Godden

1934 LORNA DOONE
Director: Basil Dean
Co-stars: Victoria Hopper Margaret Lockwood John Loder

1935 DRAKE OF ENGLAND
Director: Arthur Woods
Co-stars: Matheson Lang Athene Seyler Jane Baxter

1937 THE SHOW GOES ON
Director: Basil Dean
Co-stars: Gracie Fields Owen Nares Edward Rigby

1939 FLYING FIFTY-FIVE
Director: Reginald Denham
Co-stars: Derrick De Marney Marius Goring Ronald Shiner

1944 DON'T TAKE IT TO HEART
Director: Jeffrey Dell
Co-stars: Richard Greene Edward Rigby Patricia Medina

1944 THIS HAPPY BREED
Director: David Lean
Co-stars: Robert Newton Celia Johnson Stanley Holloway

1948 BLANCHE FURY
Director: Marc Allegret
Co-stars: Valerie Hobson Stewart Granger Walter Fitzgerald

1948 MY BROTHER'S KEEPER
Director: Roy Rich
Co-stars: Jack Warner George Cole Jane Hylton

1949 THE HUGGETTS ABROAD
Director: Ken Annakin
Co-stars: Jack Warner Katherine Harrison Susan Shaw

1951 TOM BROWN'S SCHOOLDAYS
Director: Gordon Parry
Co-stars: John Howard Davies Robert Newton Diana Wynward

INGRID VENIGAR

1993 HUSH LITTLE BABY
Director: Jorge Montesi
Co-stars: Diane Ladd Wendel Meldrum Norma Edwards

DIANE VENORA

1981 WOLFEN
Director: Michael Wadleigh
Co-stars: Albert Finney Gregory Hines Tom Noonan

1984 THE COTTON CLUB
Director: Francis Coppola
Co-stars: Richard Gere Gregory Hines Nicolas Cage

1986 F/X - MURDER BY ILLUSION
Director: Robert Mandel
Co-stars: Bryan Brown Brian Dennehy Jerry Orbach

1987 IRONWEED
Director: Hector Babenco
Co-stars: Jack Nicholson Meryl Streep Carroll Baker

1988 BIRD
Director: Clint Eastwood
Co-stars: Forest Whitaker Michael Zelnikar Michael McGuire

1996 HEAT
Director: Michael Mann
Co-stars: Robert De Niro Val Kilmer Al Pacino

1997 WILLIAM SHAKESPEAR'S ROMEO AND JULIET
Director: Baz Luhrman
Co-stars: Leanardo DiCaprio Claire Danes

1998 THE JACKAL
Director: Michael Caton-Jones
Co-stars: Bruce Willis Richard Gere

WANDA VENTHAM

1967 THE BLOOD BEAST TERROR
Director: Vernon Sewell
Co-stars: Robert Flemyng Peter Cushing Roy Hudd

1967 MISTER TEN PER CENT
Director: Peter Graham Scott
Co-stars: Charlie Drake Derek Nimmo

1973 CAPTAIN KRONOS, VAMPIRE HUNTER
Director: Brian Clemens
Co-stars: Horst Janson John Carson Caroline Munro

VIVIANNE VENTURA

1966 FINDERS KEEPERS
Director: Sidney Hayers
Co-stars: Cliff Richard Robert Morley Peggy Mount

1968 BATTLE BENEATH THE EARTH
Director: Montgomery Tully
Co-stars: Kerwin Matthews Robert Ayres Peter Arne

LIDIA VENTURINI

1954 LA STRADA
Director: Federico Fellini
Co-stars: Giulietta Masina Anthony Quinn Richard Basehart

BRENDA VENUS

1976 THE BLACK RIDER
Director: Larry Spangler
Co-stars: Fred Williamson Isela Vega Stacy Newton

VERA-ELLEN

1945 WONDER MAN
Director: Bruce Humberstone
Co-stars: Danny Kaye Virginia Mayo Steve Cochran

1946 THE KID FROM BROOKLYN
Director: Norman Z. Mcleod
Co-stars: Danny Kaye Virginia Mayo Eve Arden

1946 THREE LITTLE GIRLS IN BLUE
Director: Bruce Humberstone
Co-stars: June Haver Vivian Blaine Celeste Holm

1947 CARNIVAL IN COSTA RICA
Director: Gregory Ratoff
Co-stars: Dick Haymes Celeste Holm Cesar Romero

1948 WORDS AND MUSIC
Director: Norman Taurog
Co-stars: Mickey Rooney Tom Drake Perry Como

1949 ON THE TOWN
Director: Gene Kelly
Co-stars: Frank Sinatra Ann Miller Betty Garrett

1949 LOVE HAPPY
Director: David Miller
Co-stars: Marx Bros. Ilona Massey Marilyn Monroe

1950 THREE LITTLE WORDS
Director: Richard Thorpe
Co-stars: Fred Astaire Red Skelton Arlene Dahl

1951 HAPPY GO LOVELY
Director: Bruce Humberstone
Co-stars: David Niven Cesar Romero Bobby Howes

1952 THE BELLE OF NEW YORK
Director: Charles Walters
Co-stars: Fred Astaire Marjorie Main Keenan Wynn

1953 BIG LEAGUER
Director: Robert Aldrich
Co-stars: Edward G. Robinson Jeff Richards William Campbell

1953 CALL ME MADAM
Director: Walter Lang
Co-stars: Ethel Merman Donald O'Connor George Sanders

1954 WHITE CHRISTMAS
Director: Michael Curtiz
Co-stars: Bing Crosby Danny Kaye Rosemary Clooney

1957 LET'S BE HAPPY
Director: Henry Levin
Co-stars: Tony Martin Robert Flemyng Zena Marshall

GWEN VERDON (Married Bob Fosse)

1951 MEET ME AFTER THE SNOW
Director: Richard Sale
Co-stars: Betty Grable Macdonald Carey Eddie Albert

1958 DAMN YANKEES
Director: George Abbott
Co-stars: Tab Hunter Ray Walston Russ Brown

1983 LEGS
Director: Jerrold Freedman
Co-stars: John Heard Sheree North Shanna Reed

1984 THE COTTON CLUB
Director: Francis Coppola
Co-stars: Richard Gere Bob Hoskins Diane Lane

1985 COCOON
Director: Ron Howard
Co-stars: Don Ameche Hume Cronyn Maureen Stapleton

1987 NADINE
Director: Robert Benton
Co-stars: Jeff Bridges Kim Basinger Rip Torn

1988 COCOON: THE RETURN
Director: Daniel Petrie
Co-stars: Don Ameche Courtenay Cox Steve Guttenberg

1990 ALICE
Director: Woody Allen
Co-stars: Mia Farrow William Hurt Alec Baldwin

1996 MARVIN'S ROOM
Co-stars: Diane Keaton Meryl Streep Leonardo DiCaprio

MARIBEL VERDU

1991 LOVERS
Director: Vincente Aranda
Co-stars: Victoria Abril Jorge Sanz

1992 BELLE EPOQUE
Director: Fernando Trueba
Co-stars: Jorge Sanz Penelope Cruz Ariadne Gil

1992 GOLDEN BALLS
Director: Bigas Luna
Co-stars: Javier Bardem Elisa Touati Maria De Medeiros

ELENA VERDUGO

1943 THE MOON AND SIXPENCE
Director: Albert Lewin
Co-stars: George Sanders Herbert Marshall Steve Geray

1945 HOUSE OF FRANKENSTEIN
Director: Erle Kenton
Co-stars: Boris Karloff John Carradine J. Carrol Naish

1945 THE FROZEN GHOST
Director: Harold Young
Co-stars: Lon Chaney Evelyn Ankers Tala Birell

1946 LITTLE GIANT
Director: William Seiter
Co-stars: Bud Abbott Lou Costello Brenda Joyce

1949 THE SKY DRAGON
Director: Lesley Selander
Co-stars: Roland Winters Keye Luke Iris Adrian

1950 CYRANO DE BERGERAC
Director: Michael Gordon
Co-stars: Jose Ferrer Mala Powers William Prince

1952 THIEF OF DAMASCUS
Director: Will Jason
Co-stars: Paul Henreid Jeff Donnell Lon Chaney

LISETTE VEREA

1946 A NIGHT IN CASABLANCA
Director: Archie Mayo
Co-stars: Marx Bros. Sig Ruman Charles Drake

FRANCOISE VERLEY

1972 LOVE IN THE AFTERNOON
Director: Eric Rohmer
Co-stars: Zouzou Bernard Verley

KAREN VERNE (Ingabor Katrine Klinckerfuss)

1938 TEN DAYS IN PARIS
Director: Tim Whelan
Co-stars: Rex Harrison Leo Genn Joan Marion

1940 SKY MURDER
Director: George Seitz
Co-stars: Walter Pidgeon Donald Meek Tom Conway

1941 UNDERGROUND
Director: Vincent Sherman
Co-stars: Jeffrey Lynn Philip Dorn Mona Maris

1942 KING'S ROW
Director: Sam Wood
Co-stars: Ann Sheridan Robert Cummings Ronald Reagan

1942 ALL THROUGH THE NIGHT
Director: Vincent Sherman
Co-stars: Humphrey Bogart Conrad Veidt Peter Lorre

1942 SHERLOCK HOLMES AND THE SECRET WEAPON
Director: Roy William Neill
Co-stars: Basil Rathbone Nigel Bruce

1942 THE GREAT IMPERSONATION
Director: John Rawlins
Co-stars: Ralph Bellamy Evelyn Ankers Edward Norris

1965 SHIP OF FOOLS
Director: Stanley Kramer
Co-stars: Vivien Leigh Simone Signoret Oskar Werner

ANNE VERNON

1948 WARNING TO WANTONS
Director: Donald Wilson
Co-stars: Harold Warrender David Tomlinson Sonia Holm

1950 SHAKEDOWN
Director: Joseph Pevney
Co-stars: Howard Duff Brian Donlevy Peggy Dow

1951 A TALE OF FIVE CITIES
Director: Montgomery Tully
Co-stars: Bonar Colleano Gina Lollobrigida Lana Morris

1951 EDOUARD ET CAROLINE
Director: Jacques Becker
Co-stars: Daniel Gelin William Tubbs Jean Galland

1952 TIME BOMB
Director: Ted Tatzlaff
Co-stars: Glenn Ford Maurice Denham Harold Warrender

1953 THE LOVE LOTTERY
Director: Charles Crichton
Co-stars: David Niven Peggy Cummins Herbert Lom

1953 RUE DE L'ESTRAPADE
Director: Jacques Becker
Co-stars: Louis Jourdan Daniel Gelin Jean Servais

1959 IL GENERALE DELLA ROVERE
Director: Roberto Rossellini
Co-stars: Vittorio De Sica Sandra Milo

1964 LES PARAPLUIES DE CHERBOURG
Director: Jacques Demy
Co-stars: Catherine Deneuvre Marc Michel Ellen Farmer

KATE VERNON

1984 ROADHOUSE 66
Director: John Mark Robinson
Co-stars: Willem Dafoe Judge Reinhold Stephen Elliott

1984 ALPHABET CITY
Director: Amos Poe
Co-stars: Vincent Spano Michael Winslow Zohra Lampert

1992 MALCOLM X
Director: Spike Lee
Co-stars: Spike Lee Denzel Washington Angela Bassett

1993 DANGEROUS TOUCH
Director: Lou Diamond Phillips
Co-star: Lou Diamond Phillips

1994 HOUSE OF SECRETS
Director: Mimi Leder
Co-stars: Melissa Gilbert Bruce Boxleitner

1994 SOFT DECEIT
Director: Jorge Montesi
Co-star: Patrick Bergin

1995 BLOODKNOT
Director: Jorge Montesi
Co-stars: Patrick Dempsey Margot Kidder Craig Sheffer

LYNNE VERRALL

1987 LILY MY LOVE
Director: Adrian Shergold
Co-stars: Bill Paterson Cindy Holden Ian Sharp

MARIE VERSINI

1958 A TALE OF TWO CITIES
Director: Ralph Thomas
Co-stars: Dirk Bogarde Dorothy Tutin Christopher Lee

1965 APACHE GOLD
Director: Harald Reini
Co-stars: Lex Barker Mario Adorf Pierre Brice

ODILLE VERSOIS

1948 LES DERNIERES VACANCES
Director: Roger Leenhardt
Co-stars: Michel Francois Renee Devillers Pierre Dux

1951 INTO THE BLUE
Director: Herbert Wilcox
Co-stars: Michael Wilding Jack Hulbert Constance Cummings

1953 A DAY TO REMEMBER
Director: Ralph Thomas
Co-stars: Stanley Holloway Donald Sinden Joan Rice

1954 TO PARIS WITH LOVE
Director: Robert Hamer
Co-stars: Alec Guinness Vernon Gray Claude Romain

1954 THE YOUNG LOVERS
Director: Anthony Asquith
Co-stars: David Knight David Kossoff Jill Adams

1956 CHECKPOINT
Director: Ralph Thomas
Co-stars: Anthony Steel Stanley Baker Michael Medwin

1959 PASSPORT TO SHAME
Director: Alvin Rakoff
Co-stars: Eddie Constantine Brenda De Banzie Herbert Lom

1961 CARTOUCHE
Director: Philippe De Broca
Co-stars: Jean-Paul Belmondo Claudia Cardinale Marcel Dalio

1966 BENJAMIN
Director: Michel Deville
Co-stars: Pierre Clementi Michele Morgan Catherine Deneuve

CHARLOTTE VERY

1992 A WINTER'S TALE
Director: Eric Rohmer
Co-stars: Michel Voletti Herve Furic Christiane Desbois

1993 THREE COLOURS:BLUE
Director: Krzysztof Kieslowski
Co-stars: Juliette Binoche Benoit Regent Florence Pernel

HEDY VESSEL

1961 THE TROJAN WAR
Director: Giorgio Ferroni
Co-stars: Steeve Reeves John Drew Barrymore Juliette Mayniel

VICTORIA VETRI

1970 NIGHT CHASE
Director: Jack Starrett
Co-stars: David Janssen Yaphet Kotto Elisha Cook Jnr.

HENRIQUE VIANA

1988 HARD TIMES
Director: Joao Botelho
Co-stars: Luis Estrela Julia Britton Isabel De Castro

MARTHA VICKERS

1943 CAPTIVE WILD WOMAN
Director: Edward Dmytryk
Co-stars: Evelyn Ankers John Carradine Acuanetta

1946 THE BIG SLEEP
Director: Howard Hawks
Co-stars: Humphrey Bogart Lauren Bacall Dorothy Malone

1946 THE MAN I LOVE
Director: Raoul Walsh
Co-stars: Ida Lupino Robert Alda Andrea King

1946 THE TIME, THE PLACE AND THE GIRL
Director: David Butler
Co-stars: Dennis Morgan Jack Carson Janis Paige

1947 THAT WAY WITH WOMEN
Director: Frederick De Cordova
Co-stars: Sydney Greenstreet Dane Clark Alan Hale

1947 LOVE AND LEARN
Director: Frederick De Cordova
Co-stars: Jack Carson Robert Hutton Janis Paige

1948 RUTHLESS
Director: Edgar Ulmer
Co-stars: Zachary Scott Sydney Greenstreet Diana Lynn

1949 BAD BOY
Co-stars: Audie Murphy Lloyd Nolan Jane Wyatt

1949 DAUGHTER OF THE WEST
Co-stars: Philip Reed Donald Woods James Griffith

1957 THE BURGLAR
Director: Paul Wendkos
Co-stars: Dan Duryea Jayne Mansfield Phoebe Mackay

YVETTE VICKERS

1958 **ATTACK OF THE 50FT WOMAN**
Director: Nathan Hertz
Co-stars: Allison Hayes William Hudson Roy Gordon

1959 **ATTACK OF THE GIANT LEECHES**
Director: Bernard Kowalski
Co-stars: Ken Clark Michael Emmet Bruno De Sota

1963 **HUD**
Director: Martin Ritt
Co-stars: Paul Newman Patricia Neal Melvyn Douglas

FIONA VICTORY

1992 **RESNICK: LONELY HEARTS**
Director: Bruce MacDonald
Co-stars: Tom Wilkinson David Neilson Neil Dudgeon

CHRISTINA VIDAL *(Child)*

1993 **GIVE ME A BREAK**
Director: James Lapine
Co-stars: Michael J. Fox Nathan Lane Cyndi Lauper

LISA VIDAL

1994 **I LIKE IT LIKE THAT**
Director: Darnell Martin
Co-stars: Lauren Velez Jon Seda Rita Moreno

SUSAN VIDLER

1993 **NAKED**
Director: Mike Leigh
Co-stars: David Thewliss Lesley Sharp Claire Skinner

FLORENCE VIDOR

1924 **THE MARRIAGE CIRCLE**
Director: Ernst Lubitsch
Co-stars: Monte Blue Marie Prevost Adolphe Menjou

1928 **THE PATRIOT**
Director: Ernst Lubitsch
Co-stars: Emil Jannings Lewis Stone Neil Hamilton

ASIA VIEIRA *(Child)*

1988 **THE PRICE OF PASSION**
Director: Leonard Nimoy
Co-stars: Diane Keaton Liam Neeson Ralph Bellamy

1991 **OMEN IV: THE AWAKENING**
Director: Jorge Montesi
Co-stars: Faye Grant Michael Woods Michael Lerner

1992 **USED PEOPLE**
Director: Beeban Kidron
Co-stars: Shirley MacLaine Marcello Mastroianni Jessica Tandy

KRISTEN VIGARD

1979 **THE BLACK STALLION**
Director: Caroll Ballard
Co-stars: Mickey Rooney Kelly Reno Teri Garr

1983 **THE SURVIVORS**
Director: Michael Ritchie
Co-stars: Walter Matthau Robin Williams Jerry Reed

PASCALE VIGNAL

1989 **LIFE AND NOTHING BUT**
Director: Bertrand Tavernier
Co-stars: Philippe Noiret Sabine Azema Maurice Barrier

CHUNCHUNA VILLAFANE

1985 **THE OFFICIAL VERSION**
Director: Luis Puenzo
Co-stars: Norma Aleandro Hector Alterior Chela Ruiz

MARTHE VILLALONGA

1985 **THREE MEN AND A CRADLE**
Director: Coline Serreau
Co-stars: Roland Giraud Michel Bonjenah Andre Dussollier

1993 **MA SAISON PREFEREE**
Director: Andre Techine
Co-stars: Catherine Deneuvre Daniel Auteuil

MAVIS VILLIERS

1939 **AN ENGLISHMAN'S HOME**
Director: Albert Rodney
Co-stars: Edmund Gwenn Mary Maguire Paul Henreid

1940 **SALOON BAR**
Director: Walter Forde
Co-stars: Gordon Harker Elizabeth Allan Mervyn Johns

PAMELA VILLORESI

1989 **SPLENDOR**
Director: Ettote Scola
Co-stars: Marcello Mastroianni Marina Vlady Massimo Troisi

HELENE VINCENT

1991 **J'EMBARASSE PAS**
Director: Andre Techine
Co-stars: Manuel Blanc Philippe Noiret Emmanuelle Beart

1993 **THREE COLOURS:BLUE**
Director: Krzysztof Kieslowski
Co-stars: Juliette Binoche Benoit Regent Florence Pernel

JUNE VINCENT

1944 **SING A JINGLE**
Co-stars: Allan Jones Dicky Love

1945 **HERE COME THE CO-EDS**
Director: Jean Yarbrough
Co-stars: Bud Abbott Lou Costello Peggy Ryan

1946 **BLACK ANGEL**
Director: Roy William Neill
Co-stars: Dan Duryea Peter Lorre Constance Dowling

1948 **THE CHALLENGE**
Director: Jean Yarbrough
Co-stars: Tom Conway Richard Stapley

1948 **THE CREEPER**
Director: Jean Yarbrough
Co-stars: Ralph Morgan Onslow Stevens Richard Lane

1949 **THE LONE WOLF AND HIS LADY**
Director: John Hoffman
Co-stars: Ron Randell Alan Mowbray William Frawley

VIRGINIA VINCENT

1958 **I WANT TO LIVE**
Director: Robert Wise
Co-stars: Susan Hayward Simon Oakland Theodore Bikel

1958 **THE RETURN OF DRACULA**
Director: Paul Landers
Co-stars: Francis Lederer Norma Eberhardt Jimmie Baird

1958 **THE BLACK ORCHID**
Director: Martin Ritt
Co-stars: Sophia Loren Anthony Quinn Ina Balin

1978 **THE HILLS HAVE EYES**
Director: Wes Craven
Co-stars: Susan Lanier Robert Houston Dee Wallace

FANNY VINER

1986 **THE GOOD FATHER**
Director: Mike Newell
Co-stars: Anthony Hopkins Harriet Walter Jim Broadbent

MARGARET VINES

1934 OPEN ALL NIGHT
Director: George Pearson
Co-stars: Frank Vosper Gillian Lind Leslie Perrins

HELEN VINSON

1932 JEWEL ROBBERY
Director: William Dieterle
Co-stars: William Powell Kay Francis Alan Mowbray

1932 I AM A FUGITIVE FROM A CHAIN GANG
Director: Mervyn LeRoy
Co-stars: Paul Muni Glenda Farrell

1932 LAWYER MAN
Director: William Dieterle
Co-stars: William Powell Joan Blondell Allen Jenkins

1932 TWO AGAINST THE WORLD
Director: Archie Mayo
Co-stars: Constance Bennett Oscar Apfel Neil Hamilton

1933 THE POWER AND THE GLORY
Director: William Howard
Co-stars: Spencer Tracy Colleen Moore Ralph Morgan

1933 MIDNIGHT CLUB
Director: Alexander Hall
Co-stars: George Raft Clive Brook Alison Skipworth

1933 THE LITTLE GIANT
Director: Roy Del Ruth
Co-stars: Edward G. Robinson Mary Astor Russell Hopton

1933 THE KENNEL MURDER CASE
Director: Michael Curtiz
Co-stars: William Powell Mary Astor Ralph Morgan

1933 GRAND SLAM
Director: William Dieterle
Co-stars: Paul Lukas Loretta Young Frank McHugh

1934 AS HUSBANDS GO
Director: Hamilton McFadden
Co-stars: Warner Baxter Warner Oland G.P. Huntley Jnr.

1934 BROADWAY BILL
Director: Frank Capra
Co-stars: Warner Baxter Walter Connolly Myrna Loy

1934 THE CAPTAIN HATES THE SEA
Director: Lewis Milestone
Co-stars: John Gilbert Walter Connolly

1934 LET'S TRY AGAIN
Director: Worthington Miner
Co-stars: Diana Wynyard Clive Brook Irene Hervey

1934 THE LIFE OF VERGIE WINTERS
Director: Alfred Santell
Co-stars: Ann Harding John Boles Donald Crisp

1935 THE WEDDING NIGHT
Director: King Vidor
Co-stars: Gary Cooper Anna Sten Ralph Bellamy

1935 THE TUNNEL
Director: Maurice Elvey
Co-stars: Richard Dix Leslie Banks Madge Evans

1935 PRIVATE WORLDS
Director: Gregory La Cava
Co-stars: Claudette Colbert Charles Boyer

1935 A NOTORIOUS GENTLEMAN
Director: Edward Laemmie
Co-stars: Charles Bickford Onslow Stevens Sidney Blackmer

1935 KING OF THE DAMNED
Director: Walter Forde
Co-stars: Conrad Veidt Noah Beery Raymond Lovell

1935 AGE OF INDISCRETION
Director: Edward Ludwig
Co-stars: Paul Lukas May Robson Madge Evans

1936 LOVE IN EXILE
Director: Alfred Werker
Co-stars: Clive Brook Mary Carlisle Will Fyffe

1936 REUNION
Director: Norman Taurog
Co-stars: Jean Hersholt Rochelle Hudson Sara Haden

1937 VOGUES OF 1938
Director: Irving Cummings
Co-stars: Joan Bennett Warner Baxter Mischa Auer

1937 LIVE, LOVE AND LEARN
Director: George Fitzmaurice
Co-stars: Robert Montgomery Rosalind Russell

1939 IN NAME ONLY
Director: John Cromwell
Co-stars: Cary Grant Carole Lombard Kay Francis

1940 BEYOND TOMORROW
Director: Edward Sutherland
Co-stars: Charles Winninger Jean Parker Harry Carey

1940 CURTAIN CALL
Director: Frank Woodruff
Co-stars: Alan Mowbray Donald MacBride John Archer

1940 TORRID ZONE
Director: William Keighley
Co-stars: James Cagney Pat O'Brien Ann Sheridan

1941 NOTHING BUT THE TRUTH
Director: Elliott Nugent
Co-stars: Bob Hope Paulette Goddard Edward Arnold

1944 THE LADY AND THE MONSTER
Director: George Sherman
Co-stars: Erich Von Stroheim Vera Ralston

1944 CHIP OFF THE OLD BLOCK
Director: Charles Lamont
Co-stars: Donald O'Connor Peggy Ryan Ann Blyth

1944 ARE THESE OUR PARENTS?
Director: William Nigh
Co-stars: Lyle Talbot Ivan Lebedeff Ann Richards

ANN VIRELA

1958 TERROR IN A TEXAS TOWN
Director: Joseph Lewis
Co-stars: Sterling Hayden Sebastian Cabot Carol Kelly

MILLY VITALE

1953 THE JUNGLE
Director: Edward Dmytryk
Co-stars: Kirk Douglas Paul Stewart Joey Walsh

1955 SEVEN LITTLE FOYS
Director: Melville Shavelson
Co-stars: Bob Hope George Tobias James Cagney

1956 WAR AND PEACE
Director: King Vidor
Co-stars: Audrey Hepburn Henry Fonda Mel Ferrer

1957 THE FLESH IS WEAK
Director: Don Chaffey
Co-stars: John Derek William Franklyn Freda Jackson

1958 THE BATTLE OF THE VI
Director: Vernon Sewell
Co-stars: Michael Rennie Patricia Medina Esmond Knight

1960 A BREATH OF SCANDAL
Director: Michael Curtiz
Co-stars: Sophia Loren Maurice Chevalier John Gavin

1960 HANNIBAL
Director: Edgar Ulmer
Co-stars: Victor Mature Rita Gam Gabriele Ferzetti

JUDITH VITTET

1995 THE CITY OF LOST CHILDREN
Director: Jean-Pierre Jeunet
Co-stars: Ron Perlman Daniel Emilfork

MONICA VITTI

1956 MODESTY BLAISE
Director: Joseph Losey
Co-stars: Dirk Bogarde Terence Stamp Michael Craig

1960 LA NOTTE
Director: Michaelangelo Antoniono
Co-stars: Marcello Mastroianni Jeanne Moreau Bernhard Wicki

1960 L'AVENTURA
Director: Michaelangelo Antoniono
Co-stars: Gabriele Ferzetti Lea Massari James Addams

1962 THE ECLIPSE
Director: Michaelangelo Antoniono
Co-stars: Alain Delon Francisco Rabal Rossana Rory

1964 THE RED DESERT
Director: Michaelangelo Antoniono
Co-stars: Richard Harris Carlos Chionetti

1967 THE CHASTITY BELT
Director: Pasquale Festa Campanile
Co-stars: Tony Curtis Hugh Griffith John Richardson

1970 JEALOUSY, ITALIAN STYLE
Director: Ettore Scola
Co-stars: Marcello Mastroianni Giancarlo Gianinni Marisa Merlini

1979 AN ALMOST PERFECT AFFAIR
Director: Michael Ritchie
Co-stars: Keith Carradine Raf Vallone

VIVA

1969 LIONS LOVE
Director: Agnes Varda
Co-stars: Gerome Ragni James Rado Shirley Clarke

1971 CICCO PIKE

1972 PLAY IT AGAIN SAM
Director: Herbert Ross
Co-stars: Woody Allen Diane Keaton Jerry Lacey

1993 THE MAN WITHOUT A FACE
Director: Mel Gibson
Co-stars: Mel Gibson Margaret Whitton Geoffrey Lewis

RUTH VIVIAN

1941 THE MAN WHO CAME TO DINNER
Director: William Keighley
Co-stars: Monty Woolley Bette Davis Ann Sheridan

MARINA VLADY

1966 CHIMES AT MIDNIGHT
Director: Orson Welles
Co-stars: Orson Welles John Gielgud Margaret Rutherford

1978 THE THIEF OF BAGHDAD
Director: Clive Donner
Co-stars: Roddy McDowall Peter Ustinov Frank Finlay

1985 TANGOS, THE EXILE OF GARDEL
Director: Fernando Solanas
Co-stars: Marie Laforet Philippe Leotard

1989 SPLENDOR
Director: Ettore Scola
Co-stars: Marcello Mastroianni Massimo Troisi Paolo Panelli

SANDRA VOE

1988 COPPERS
Director: Ted Clisby
Co-stars: Tim Roth Reece Dinsdale Marion Bailey

JOAN VOHS

1953 FORT TI
Director: William Castle
Co-stars: George Montgomery Irving Bacon James Seay

1953 VICE SQUAD
Director: Arnold Laven
Co-stars: Edward G. Robinson Paulette Goddard K.T. Stevens

1954 SABRINA
Director: Billy Wilder
Co-stars: Audrey Hepburn Humphrey Bogart William Holden

1954 CRY VENGEANCE
Director: Mark Stevens
Co-stars: Mark Stevens Martha Hyer Skip Homeier

1955 FORT YUMA
Director: Lesley Selander
Co-stars: Peter Graves John Hudson Joan Taylor

MAY VOKES

1924 JANICE MEREDITH
Director: Mason Hopper
Co-stars: Marion Davies Harrison Ford W.C. Fields

TWYLA-DAWN VOKINS

1981 KELLY
Director: Christopher Chapman
Co-stars: Robert Logan Elaine Nalee George Clutesi

NEDRA VOLZ

1985 MOVING VIOLATIONS
Director: Neal Israel
Co-stars: Stephen McHattie Jennifer Tilly John Murray

JOHANNA VON KOSZIAN

1959 FOR THE FIRST TIME
Director: Rudolph Mate
Co-stars: Mario Lanza Kurt Kasznar Zsa Zsa Gabor

IRENE VON MEYENDORFF

1947 FILM OHNE TITEL
Director: Rudolf Jugert
Co-stars: Hans Sohnker Hildegard Knef Willy Fritsch

VEOLO VONN

1954 PHANTOM OF THE RUE MORGUE
Director: Roy Del Ruth
Co-stars: Karl Malden Claude Dauphin Patricia Medina

JENNA VON OY

1989 BORN ON THE FOURTH OF JULY
Director: Oliver Stone
Co-stars: Tom Cruise Bryan Larkin Willem Dafoe

HEIDI VON PALLESKE

1988 DEAD RINGERS
Director: David Cronenberg
Co-stars: Jeremy Irons Genevieve Bujold Barbara Gordon

1991 DECEIVED
Director: Damian Harris
Co-stars: Goldie Hawn John Heard Ashley Peldon

GILA VON WEITERSHAUSEN

1983   TRENCHCOAT
Director: Michael Tuchner
Co-stars: Margot Kidder Robert Hays David Suchet

DANIELLE VON ZERNECK

1985   MY SCIENCE PROJECT
Director: Jonathan Beteul
Co-stars: John Stockwell Dennis Hopper Fisher Stevens

1987   LA BAMBA
Director: Luis Valdez
Co-stars: Lou Diamond Phillips Esai Morales Elizabeth Pena

1992   SURVIVE THE SAVAGE SEA
Director: Kevin James Dobson
Co-stars: Ali MacGraw Robert Urich

TILLY VOSBURGH

1987   WILL YOU LOVE ME TOMORROW ?
Director: Adrian Shergold
Co-stars: Joanne Whalley Iain Glen Phil Daniels

JUDITH VOSELLI

1930   THE ROGUE SONG
Director: Lionel Barrymore
Co-stars: Laurence Tibbett Stan Laurel Oliver Hardy

1930   INSPIRATION
Director: Clarence Brown
Co-stars: Greta Garbo Robert Montgomery Lewis Stone

LORINNE VOZOFF

1984   IMPULSE
Director: Graham Baker
Co-stars: Tim Matheson Meg Tilly Hume Cronyn

SANNA VRAA

1994   IVANA TRUMP'S FOR LOVE ALONE
Director: Michael Lindsay Hogg
Co-stars: Stephen Collins Trevor Eve

MILENA VUKOTIC

1974   BLOOD FOR DRACULA
Director: Paul Morrissey
Co-stars: Udo Kier Joe Dallesandro Vittorio De Sica

1977   THAT OBSCURE OBJECT OF DESIRE
Director: Luis Bunuel
Co-stars: Fernando Rey Carole Bouquet Angela Molina

1983   HOUSE OF THE YELLOW CARPET
Director: Carlo Lizzani
Co-stars: Erland Josephson Beatrise Romand

1983   THE MOON IN THE GUTTER
Director: Jean-Jacques Beineix
Co-stars: Gerard Depardieu Nastassja Kinski Victoria Abril

MARGARET VYNER

1936   SENSATION
Director: Brian Desmond Hurst
Co-stars: John Lodge Diana Churchill Athene Seyler

1937   THE VICAR OF BRAY
Director: Henry Edwards
Co-stars: Stanley Holloway Felix Aylmer Esmond Knight

1938   CLIMBING HIGH
Director: Carol Reed
Co-stars: Jessie Matthews Michael Redgrave Noel Madison

1941   THIS MAN IS DANGEROUS
Director: Lawrence Huntington
Co-stars: James Mason Mary Clare Frederick Valk

1943   THE LAMP STILL BURNS
Director: Maurice Elvey
Co-stars: Rosamund John Stewart Granger Godfrey Tearle

LINDSAY WAGNER

1973 THE PAPER CHASE
Director: James Bridges
Co-star: Timothy Bottoms John Houseman Edward Herrman

1973 TWO PEOPLE
Director: Robert Wise
Co-star: Peter Fonda Estelle Parsons Alan Fudge

1974 THE ROCKFORD FILES
Director: Richard Heffron
Co-stars: James Garner William Smith Nita Talbot

1975 BURN OUT
Director: Daniel Mann
Co-stars: Shelley Winters Ian McShane Sam Waterson

1979 THE TWO WORLDS OF JENNY LOGAN
Director: Frank De Felitta
Co-stars: Marc Singer Linda Gray Henry Wilcoxon

1981 NIGHTHAWKS
Director: Bruce Malmuth
Co-stars: Sylvester Stallone Nigel Davenport Rutger Hauer

1981 HIGH RISK
Director: Stewart Raffill
Co-stars: James Brolin Ernest Borgnine James Coburn

1981 CALLIE AND SON
Director: Waris Hussein
Co-stars: Jameson Parker Dabney Coleman Michelle Pfeiffer

1983 I WANT TO LIVE
Director: David Lowell Rich
Co-stars: Martin Balsam Harry Dean Stanton Pamela Reed

1983 TWO KINDS OF LOVE
Director: Jack Bender
Co-stars: Ricky Schroder Peter Weller Sydney Penny

1985 THIS CHILD IS MINE
Director: David Greene
Co-stars: Chris Sarandon Nancy McKeon Michael Lerner

1985 MARTIN'S DAY
Director: Alan Gibson
Co-stars: Richard Harris James Coburn Justin Henry

1986 CONVICTED
Director: David Lowell Rich
Co-star: John Larroquette

1986 STRANGER IN MY BED
Director: Larry Elikann
Co-stars: Armand Assante Doug Sheehan Allyn Ann McLerie

1987 STUDENT EXCHANGE
Director: Mollie Miller
Co-stars: Lisa Hartman O.J. Simpson

1988 EVIL IN CLEAR RIVER
Director: Karen Arthur
Co-stars: Randy Quaid Michael Flynn Stephanie Dees

1989 VOICE OF THE HEART
Director: Tony Wharmby
Co-stars: Victoria Tennant James Brolin Honor Blackman

1989 BIONIC SHOWDOWN: THE SIX MILLION DOLLAR MAN AND THE BIONIC WOMAN
Director: Alan Levi
Co-stars: Lee Majors Sandra Bullock

1990 SHATTERED DREAMS
Director: Robert Iscove
Co-star: Michael Nouri

1991 TO BE THE BEST
Director: Tony Wharmby
Co-stars: Anthony Hopkins Stephanie Beacham Stuart Wilson

1991 RICHOCHET
Director: Russell Mulcahy
Co-stars: Denzel Washington John Lithgow Kevin Pollack

1992 SHE WOKE UP
Director: Waris Hussein

1992 A MESSAGE FROM HOLLY
Director: Rod Holcomb
Co-star: Shelley Long

1993 NURSES ON THE LINE
Director: Larry Shaw
Co-stars: Robert Loggia David Clennon

1994 FIGHTING FOR MY DAUGHTER
Director: Peter Levin
Co-stars: Piper Laurie Chad Lowe

1997 SECOND CHANCE

NATASHA GREGSON WAGNER
(Daughter Of Natalie Wood)

1993 THE SUBSTITUTE
Director: Martin Donovan
Co-stars: Amanda Donohue Dalton James Marky Mark

1994 DRAGSTRIP GIRL
Director: Mary Lambert
Co-stars: Mark Dacaslos Traci Lords

1995 WES CRAVEN PRESENTS MIND RIPPER
Director: Joe Gayton
Co-stars: Lance Henriksen Claire Stansfield

WENDE WAGNER

1964 RIO CONCHOS
Director: Gordon Douglas
Co-stars: Richard Boone Edmond O'Brien Stuart Whitman

ELSIE WAGSTAFFE

1949 CELIA
Director: Francis Searle
Co-stars: Hy Hazell Bruce Lister John Bailey

1961 WHISTLE DOWN THE WIND
Director: Bryan Forbes
Co-stars: Hayley Mills Alan Bates Bernard Lee

NANCIE WAIT

1976 THE AMOROUS MILKMAN
Director: Derren Nesbitt
Co-stars: Julie Ege Diana Dors Roy Kinnear

ELIZABETH WAITE

1989 FUN DOWN THERE
Director: Roger Stigliano
Co-stars: Michael Waite Martin Goldin Jeanne Smith

GENEVIEVE WAITE

1968 JOANNA
Director: Michael Sarne
Co-stars: Christian Doermer Calvin Lockhart Donald Sutherland

1970 MOVE
Director: Stuart Rosenberg
Co-stars: Elliott Gould Paula Prentiss John Larch

DEBORAH WAKEHAM

1980 MIDDLE AGE CRAZY
Director: John Trent
Co-stars: Bruce Dern Ann-Margret Graham Jarvis

1986 NORTHSTAR
Director: Peter Levin
Co-stars: Greg Evigan Mitchell Ryan David Hayward

1989 STRANDED
Director: Paul Tucker
Co-star: Ryan Michael

LYNETTE WALDEN

1992 THE SILENCER
Director: Amy Goldstein
Co-stars: Chris Culkey Paul Ganus Brook Parker

MARIAN WALDMAN

1974 BLACK CHRISTMAS
Director: Robert Clark
Co-stars: Olivia Hussey Keir Dullea Margot Kidder

JANET WALDO

1938 TOM SAWYER, DETECTIVE
Director: Louis King
Co-stars: Billy Cook Donald O'Connor Porter Hall

1939 THE STAR MAKER
Director: Roy Del Ruth
Co-stars: Bing Crosby Linda Ware Ned Sparks

1980 YOGI'S FIRST CHRISTMAS *(Voice)*
Director: Ray Patterson
Co-stars: Daws Butler Don Messick Hal Smith

SHAWNA WALDRON

1994 LITTLE GIANTS
Director: Duwayne Dunham
Co-stars: Rick Moranis Ed O'Neill Mary Ellen Trainor

ETHEL WALES

1923 THE COVERED WAGON
Director: James Cruze
Co-stars: Ernest Torrence Tully Marshall Lois Wilson

1930 TOM SAWYER
Director: John Cromwell
Co-stars: Jackie Coogan Junior Durkin Mitzi Green

1933 THE FIGHTING PARSON
Co-stars: Marceline Day Hoot Gibson Bill Robbins

1934 CRIME DOCTOR
Co-star: Otto Kruger

1938 THE GLADIATOR
Director: Edward Sedgwick
Co-stars: Joe E. Brown Dickie Moore Lucien Littlefield

ANN WALFORD

1955 THE GOLD EXPRESS
Director: Guy Fergusson
Co-stars: Vernon Gray May Hallatt Delphi Lawrence

ALLY WALKER

1992 UNIVERSAL SOLDIER
Director: Roland Emmerich
Co-stars: Jean-Claude Van Damme Dolph Lundgren Jerry Orbach

1993 WHEN THE BOUGH BREAKS
Director: Michael Cohn
Co-stars: Martin Sheen Ron Perlman

1995 SOMEONE TO DIE FOR
Director: Clay Borris
Co-stars: Corbin Bernsen Shell Danielson

AMANDA WALKER

1985 A ROOM WITH A VIEW
Director: James Ivory
Co-stars: Maggie Smith Denholm Elliott Helena Bonham Carter

1990 THE BIG MAN
Director: David Leland
Co-stars: Liam Neeson Joanne Whalley Billy Connolly

ARNETIA WALKER

1989 SCENES FROM THE CLASS STRUGGLE IN BEVERLEY HILLS
Director: Paul Bartel
Co-stars: Paul Bartel Jacqueline Bissett Ray Sharkey

1992 LOVE CRIMES
Director: Lizzie Borden
Co-stars: Sean Young Patrick Bergin Ron Orbach

AURORA WALKER

1952 EL
Director: Luis Bunuel
Co-stars: Arturo De Cordova Delia Garces Luis Beristain

CHARLOTTE WALKER

1916 THE TRAIL OF THE LONESOME PINE
Director: Cecil B. DeMille
Co-stars: Theodore Roberts Earle Fox Thomas Meighan

CHERYL WALKER

1943 STAGE DOOR CANTEEN
Director: Frank Borzage
Co-stars: Lon McCallister Judith Anderson Tallulah Bankhead

1945 IDENTITY UNKNOWN
Director: Walter Colmes
Co-stars: Richard Arlen Bobby Driscoll Lola Lane

FIONA WALKER

1967 FAR FROM THE MADDING CROWD
Director: John Schlesinger
Co-stars: Julie Christie Peter Finch Alan Bates

1973 THE ASPHYX
Director: Peter Newbrook
Co-stars: Robert Stephens Robert Powell Jane Lapotaire

1993 CENTURY
Director: Stephen Poliakoff
Co-stars: Charles Dance Clive Owen Miranda Richardson

GLORIA WALKER

1976 ADVENTURES OF A TAXI DRIVER
Director: Stanley Long
Co-stars: Barry Evans Judy Geeson Liz Fraser

HELEN WALKER

1942 LUCKY JORDAN
Director: Frank Tuttle
Co-stars: Alan Ladd Sheldon Leonard Marie McDonald

1943 **THE GOOD FELLOWS**
Director: Jo Graham
Co-stars: Cecil Kellaway James Brown Mabel Paige

1944 **ABROAD WITH TWO YANKS**
Director: Allan Dwan
Co-stars: Dennis O'Keefe William Bendix John Loder

1944 **THE MAN IN HALF-MOON STREET**
Director: Ralph Murphy
Co-stars: Nils Asther Brandon Hurst

1945 **HER ADVENTUROUS NIGHT**
Director: John Rawlins
Co-stars: Dennis O'Keefe Tom Powers Fuzzy Knight

1945 **BREWSTER'S MILLIONS**
Director: Allan Dwan
Co-stars: Dennis O'Keefe Eddie Anderson Gail Patrick

1945 **MURDER HE SAY**
Director: George Marshall
Co-stars: Fred MacMurray Marjorie Main Peter Whitney

1946 **MURDER IN THE MUSIC HALL**
Director: John English
Co-stars: Vera Ralston Nancy Kelly William Gargan

1946 **CLUNY BROWN**
Director: Ernst Lubitsch
Co-stars: Jennifer Jones Charles Boyer Richard Haydn

1946 **PEOPLE ARE FUNNY**
Co-stars: Jack Haley Rudy Vallee Philip Reed

1947 **THE HOMESTRETCH**
Director: Bruce Humberstone
Co-stars: Cornel Wilde Maureen O'Hara Glenn Langan

1947 **NIGHTMARE ALLEY**
Director: Edmund Goulding
Co-stars: Tyrone Power Coleen Gray Joan Blondell

1948 **MY DEAR SECRETARY**
Director: Charles Martin
Co-stars: Kirk Douglas Laraine Day Rudy Vallee

1948 **CALL NORTHSIDE 777**
Director: Henry Hathaway
Co-stars: James Stewart Lee J. Cobb Richard Conte

1949 **IMPACT**
Director: Arthur Lubin
Co-stars: Brian Donlevy Ella Raines Charles Coburn

1955 **THE BIG COMBO**
Director: Joseph Lewis
Co-stars: Cornel Wilde Jean Wallace Richard Conte

JENNIE WALKER

1989 **CRIMINAL LAW**
Director: Martin Campbell
Co-stars: Gary Oldman Kevin Bacon Karen Young

JESSICA WALKER

1972 **WOMEN IN CHAINS**
Director: Bernard Kowalski
Co-stars: Ida Lupino Lois Nettleton Penny Fuller

JUNE WALKER

1930 **WAR NURSE**
Co-star: Robert Montgomery

1960 **THE UNFORGIVEN**
Director: John Huston
Co-stars: Burt Lancaster Audrey Hepburn Audie Murphy

KATHRYN WALKER

1979 **RICH KIDS**
Director: Robert M. Young
Co-stars: Trini Alvarado Jeremy Levy John Lithgow

1981 **NEIGHBORS**
Director: John Avildsen
Co-stars: John Belushi Dan Aykroyd Cathy Moriarty

1981 **FAMILY REUNION**
Director: Fielder Cook
Co-stars: Bette Davis John Shea Roy Dotrice

1982 **TOO FAR TO GO**
Director: Fielder Cook
Co-stars: Michael Moriarty Blythe Danner Glenn Close

1985 **D.A.R.Y.L.**
Director: Simon Wincer
Co-stars: Mary Beth Hurt Michael McKean Colleen Camp

1986 **MRS DELAFIELD WANTS TO MARRY**
Director: George Shaefer
Co-stars: Katherine Hepburn Harold Gould Bibi Besch

1987 **UNCLE TOM'S CABIN**
Director: Stan Lathan
Co-stars: Avery Brooks Kate Burton Bruce Dern

1988 **THE MURDER OF MARY PHAGAN**
Director: Billy Hale
Co-stars: Jack Lemmon Peter Gallagher Richard Jordan

KERRY WALKER

1978 **THE NIGHT PROWLER**
Director: Jim Sharman
Co-stars: Ruth Cracknell John Frawley John Derum

1981 **DOUBLE DEAL**
Director: Brian Kavanagh
Co-stars: Louis Jourdan Angela Punch McGregor Diane Craig

1990 **THE LAST CROP**
Director: Sue Clayton
Co-stars: Noah Taylor Sarah Hooper Les Foxcroft

1991 **WENDY CRACKS A WALNUT**
Director: Michael Pattison
Co-stars: Rosanna Arquette Bruce Spence Hugo Weaving

1993 **THE PIANO**
Director: Jane Campion
Co-stars: Holly Hunter Sam Neill Harvey Keitel

KIM WALKER

1989 **HEATHERS**
Director: Michael Lehman
Co-stars: Winona Ryder Christian Slater Shannen Doherty

LIZA WALKER

1991 **REDEMPTION**
Director: Malcolm McKay
Co-stars: Tom Courtenay Miranda Richardson Lindsay Duncan

1993 **INSPECTOR MORSE:**
 CHERUBIM AND SERAPHIM
Director: Danny Boyle
Co-stars: John Thaw Kevin Whately Isla Blair

1993 **CENTURY**
Director: Stephen Poliakoff
Co-stars: Charles Dance Clive Owen Miranda Richardson

MARCY WALKER

1988 **THE RETURN OF DESPERADO**
Director: E.W. Swackhamer
Co-stars: Alex McArthur Robert Foxworth Billy Dee Williams

1992 OVEREXPOSED
Director: Robert Markovitch
Co-stars: Dan Lauria Jerilyn Ryan Terence Knox

1992 MIDNIGHT'S CHILD
Director: Colin Bucksey
Co-stars: Olivia D'Abo Cotter Smith

1995 TERROR IN THE SHADOWS
Director: William Graham
Co-stars: Genie Francis Leigh J. McCloskey

NANCY WALKER

1943 GIRL CRAZY
Director: Norman Taurog
Co-stars: Judy Garland Mickey Rooney June Allyson

1943 BEST FOOT FORWARD
Director: Edward Buzzell
Co-stars: Lucille Ball Harry James Chill Wills

1954 LUCKY ME
Director: Jack Donohue
Co-stars: Doris Day Robert Cummings Phil Silvers

1973 FORTY CARATS
Director: Milton Katselas
Co-stars: Liv Ullman Gene Kelly Edward Albert

1974 THURSDAY'S GAME
Director: Robert Moore
Co-stars: Gene Wilder Cloris Leachman Ellen Burstyn

1976 MURDER BY DEATH
Director: Robert Moore
Co-stars: Peter Sellers David Niven Maggie Smith

NELLA WALKER

1929 SEVEN KEYS TO BALDPATE
Co-stars: Richard Dix Miriam Seegar Joseph Allen

1932 LADY WITH A PAST
Director: Edward Griffith
Co-stars: Constance Bennett Ben Lyon David Manners

1934 FOUR FRIGHTENED PEOPLE
Director: Cecil B. DeMille
Co-stars: Claudette Colbert Herbert Marshall Mary Boland

1934 ALL OF ME
Director: James Flood
Co-stars: Fredric March Miriam Hopkins George Raft

1934 ELMER AND ELSIE
Director: Gilbert Pratt
Co-stars: George Bancroft Frances Fuller Roscoe Karns

1939 THREE SMART GIRLS GROW UP
Director: Henry Koster
Co-stars: Deanna Durbin Nan Grey Charles Winninger

1941 KATHLEEN
Director: Harold Bucquet
Co-stars: Shirley Temple Herbert Marshall Laraine Day

1942 HELLZAPOPPIN
Director: H.C. Potter
Co-stars: Ole Olsen Chic Johnson Jane Frazee

1943 AIR RAID WARDENS
Director: Edward Sedgwick
Co-stars: Stan Laurel Oliver Hardy Edgar Kennedy

1943 HERS TO HOLD
Director: Frank Ryan
Co-stars: Deanna Durbin Joseph Cotten Charles Winninger

1944 IN SOCIETY
Director: Jean Yarborough
Co-stars: Bud Abbott Lou Costello Marion Hutton

1944 MURDER IN THE BLUE ROOM
Director: Leslie Goodwins
Co-stars: Anne Gwynne Donald Cook Grace McDonald

1954 SABRINA
Director: Billy Wilder
Co-stars: Audrey Hepburn Humphrey Bogart William Holden

POLLY WALKER (U.S.A.)

1930 HIT THE DECK
Director: Luther Reed
Co-stars: Jack Oakie Roger Gray Harry Sweet

POLLY WALKER (U.K.)

1990 LORNA DOONE
Director: Andrew Grieve
Co-stars: Clive Owen Sean Bean Billie Whitelaw

1990 KREMLIN FAREWELL
Director: Tristram Powell
Co-stars: Freddie Jones Richard Wilson Kenneth Colley

1991 ENCHANTED APRIL
Director: Mike Newell
Co-stars: Miranda Richardson Josie Lawrence Joan Plowright

1992 PATRIOT GAMES
Director: Philip Noyce
Co-stars: Harrison Ford Patrick Bergin Sean Bean

1992 THE TRIAL
Director: David Jones
Co-stars: Kyle McLachlan Anthony Hopkins Juliet Stevenson

1993 SLIVER
Director: Philip Noyce
Co-stars: Sharon Stone William Baldwin Tom Beringer

1996 RESTORATION
Director: Michael Hoffman
Co-stars: Robert Downey Jnr. Sam Neill Meg Ryan

1996 EMMA
Director: Douglas McGrath
Co-stars: Gwyneth Paltrow Greta Scacchi Toni Colette

1996 THE WOODLANDERS
Director: Phil Agland
Co-stars: Rufus Sewell Jodhi May Emily Woof

1997 THE GAMBLER
Director: Karoly Makk
Co-stars: Michael Gambon Jodhi May Dominic West

RITA WALKER

1987 CRY FROM THE MOUNTAIN
Director: J.F. Collier
Co-stars: Wes Parker Chris Kidd Billy Graham

SARA WALKER

1987 HOUSEKEEPING
Director: Bill Forsyth
Co-stars: Christine Lahti Andrea Burchill Anne Pitoniak

SARAH WALKER

1983 MAN OF FLOWERS
Director: Paul Cox
Co-stars: Norman Kaye Alison Best Chris Haywood

TERRY WALKER

1937 BLONDE TROUBLE
Co-star: Benny Baker

1937 23 HOURS LEAVE
Co-star: James Ellison

TIPPY WALKER

1964 THE WORLD OF HENRY ORIENT
Director: George Roy Hill
Co-stars: Peter Sellers Merri Spaeth Paula Prentiss

1971 JENNIFER ON MY MIND
Director: Noel Black
Co-stars: Michael Brandon Lou Gilbert Renee Taylor

TRACEY WALKER

1981 RAGGEDY MAN
Director: Jack Fisk
Co-stars: Sissy Spacek Eric Roberts Sam Shepard

WENDY JANE WALKER

1984 THE ADVENTURES OF SHERLOCK HOLMES: THE DANCING MAN
Director: John Bruce
Co-stars: Jeremy Brett David Burke

ZENA WALKER

1961 HELLIONS
Director: Ken Annakin
Co-stars: Richard Todd Lionel Jeffries Anne Aubrey

1962 THE TRAITORS
Director: Robert Tronson
Co-stars: Patrick Allen James Maxwell Ewan Roberts

1963 THE MARKED ONE
Director: Francis Searle
Co-stars: William Lucas Patrick Jordan Laurie Leigh

1963 SAMMY GOING SOUTH
Director: Alexander MacKendrick
Co-stars: Fergus McClelland Edward G. Robinson

1969 THE RECKONING
Director: Jack Gold
Co-stars: Nicol Williamson Rachel Roberts Ann Bell

1970 THE LAST SHOT YOU HEAR
Director: Gordon Hessler
Co-stars: Hugh Marlowe Patricia Haines Thorley Walters

1976 THE LIKELY LADS
Director: Michael Tuchner
Co-stars: Rodney Bewes James Bolam Brigit Forsyth

1983 THE DRESSER
Director: Peter Yates
Co-stars: Albert Finney Tom Courtenay Edward Fox

DEE WALLACE *(Dee Wallace-Stone From 1985)*

1978 THE HILLS HAVE EYES
Director: Wes Craven
Co-stars: Susan Lanier Robert Houston Virginia Vincent

1979 10
Director: Blake Edwards
Co-stars: Dudley Moore Julie Andrews Bo Derek

1981 THE HOWLING
Director: Joe Dante
Co-stars: Patrick MacNee Kevin McCarthy John Carradine

1981 THE FIVE OF ME
Director: Paul Wendkos
Co-stars: David Birney Mitchell Ryan John McLiam

1982 E.T. THE EXTRA-TERRESTRIAL
Director: Steven Spielberg
Co-stars: Henry Thomas Peter Coyote Drew Barrymore

1982 JIMMY THE KID
Director: Gary Nelson
Co-stars: Gary Coleman Paul LeMat Walter Olkevicz

1983 CUJO
Director: Lewis Teague
Co-stars: Daniel-Hugh Kelly Ed Lauter Christopher Stone

1985 LEGEND OF THE WHITE HORSE
Director: Jerzy Domaradski
Co-stars: Christopher Lloyd Allison Balson

1986 SIN OF INNOCENCE
Director: Arthur Allan Seidelman
Co-star: Bill Bixby

1986 CRITTERS
Director: Stephen Herek
Co-stars: M. Emmet Walsh Billy Green Bush Billy Zane

1988 ADDICTED TO HIS LOVE
Director: Arthur Allan Seidelman
Co-stars: Barry Bostwick Polly Bergen Erin Gray

1988 STRANGER ON MY LAND
Director: Larry Elikann
Co-stars: Tommy Lee Jones Ben Johnson Pat Hingle

1990 I'M DANGEROUS TONIGHT
Director: Tobe Hooper
Co-stars: Madchen Amick Anthony Perkins Daisy Hall

1993 PROPHET OF EVIL
Director: Jud Taylor
Co-stars: Brian Dennehy Tracy Needham William Devane

1994 CRADLE OF CONSPIRACY
Director: Gabrielle Beaumont
Co-star: Danica McKellar

1994 RUNAWAY DAUGHTERS
Director: Joe Dante
Co-stars: Holly Fields Julie Bowen Jenny Lewis

1994 PHOENIX AND THE MAGIC CARPET
Co-stars: Timothy Hegeman Nick Klein

JEAN WALLACE *(Married Cornel Wilde)*

1948 WHEN MY BABY SMILES AT ME
Director: Walter Lang
Co-stars: Betty Grable Dan Dailey Jack Oakie

1949 JIGSAW
Director: Fletcher Markle
Co-stars: Franchot Tone Marlene Dietrich Henry Fonda

1949 THE MAN ON THE EIFFEL TOWER
Director: Burgess Meredith
Co-stars: Burgess Meredith Charles Laughton Franchot Tone

1954 STAR OF INDIA
Director: Arthur Lubin
Co-stars: Cornel Wilde Herbert Lom Basil Sydney

1955 STORM FEAR
Director: Cornel Wilde
Co-stars: Cornel Wilde Dan Duryea Lee Grant

1955 THE BIG COMBO
Director: Joseph Lewis
Co-stars: Cornel Wilde Richard Conte Brian Donlevy

1957 THE DEVIL'S HAIRPIN
Director: Cornel Wilde
Co-stars: Cornel Wilde Mary Astor Arthur Franz

1958 MARACAIBO
Director: Cornel Wilde
Co-stars: Cornel Wilde Abbe Lane Francis Lederer

1962 LANCELOT AND GUINEVERE
Director: Cornel Wilde
Co-stars: Cornel Wilde Brian Aherne George Baker

1967 BEACH RED
Director: Cornel Wilde
Co-stars: Cornel Wilde Rip Torn Burr De Benning

1970 NO BLADE OF GRASS
Director: Cornel Wilde
Co-stars: Nigel Davenport Patrick Holt John Hamill

JULIA WALLACE

1989 GOVAN GHOST STORY
Director: David Hayman
Co-stars: Tom Watson Fletcher Mathers Denise McDonald

JULIE T. WALLACE

1988 HAWKS
Director: Robert Ellis
Co-stars: Timothy Dalton Anthony Edwards Janet McTeer

1992 THE LUNATIC
Director: Lol Crème
Co-stars: Paul Campbell Reggie Carter Carl Bradshaw

MAY WALLACE

1932 COUNTY HOSPITAL
Director: James Parrott
Co-stars: Stan Laurel Oliver Hardy Billy Gilbert

NELLIE WALLACE

1934 RADIO PARADE OF 1935
Director: Arthur Woods
Co-stars: Will Hay Helen Chandler Ted Ray

ROWENA WALLACE

1986 RELATIVES
Director: Anthony Bowman
Co-stars: Bill Kerr Ray Barrett Norman Kaye

1989 CAPPUCCINO
Director: Anthony Bowman
Co-stars: John Clayton Cristina Parker

ROBERTA WALLACH *(Daughter Of Eli Wallach)*

1972 THE EFFECT OF GAMMA RAYS ON MAN IN THE MOON MARIGOLDS
Director: Paul Newman
Co-stars: Joanne Woodward Nell Potts

1981 FAMILY REUNION
Director: Fielder Cook
Co-stars: Bette Davis John Shea Roy Dotrice

DEBORAH WALLEY

1962 BON VOYAGE !
Director: James Neilson
Co-stars: Fred MacMurray Jane Wyman Tommy Kirk

1963 SUMMER MAGIC
Director: James Neilson
Co-stars: Hayley Mills Burl Ives Dorothy McGuire

1964 THE YOUNG LOVERS
Director: Samuel Goldwyn Jnr.
Co-stars: Peter Fonda Sharon Hugueny Nick Adams

1965 SERGEANT DEADHEAD
Director: Norman Taurog
Co-stars: Frankie Avalon Cesar Romero Eve Arden

1966 SPINOUT
Director: Norman Taurog
Co-stars: Elvis Presley Shelley Fabares Cecil Kellaway

1966 THE GHOST IN THE INVISIBLE BIKINI
Director: Don Weis
Co-stars: Boris Karloff Basil Rathbone Tommy Kirk

GUNN WALLGREN

1982 FANNY AND ALEXANDER
Director: Ingmar Bergman
Co-stars: Ewa Frohling Allan Edwall Pernilla Allwin

SHANI WALLIS

1956 THE EXTRA DAY
Director: William Fairchild
Co-stars: Richard Basehart Simone Simon George Baker

1968 OLIVER !
Director: Carol Reed
Co-stars: Ron Moody Oliver Reed Mark Lester

1973 TERROR IN THE WAX MUSEUM
Director: George Fenady
Co-stars: Ray Milland Broderick Crawford Louis Hayward

1973 ARNOLD
Director: George Fenady
Co-stars: Stella Stevens Elsa Lanchester Farley Granger

ANGELA WALSH

1988 DISTANT VOICES, STILL LIVES
Director: Terence Davies
Co-stars: Freda Dowie Peter Postlethwaite Dean Williams

1990 I HIRED A CONTRACT KILLER
Director: Aki Kaurismaki
Co-stars: Jean-Pierre Leaud Margi Clarke Kenneth Colley

1990 SMALL ZONES
Director: Michael Whyte
Co-stars: Catherine Neilson Sean Bean Suzanna Hamilton

1991 TRUE LOVE
Director: Nancy Savoca
Co-stars: Annabella Sciorra Ron Eldard Aida Turturro

GWYNETH WALSH

1988 THE RETURN OF BEN CASEY
Director: Joseph Scanlan
Co-stars: Vince Edwards Al Waxman Harry Landers

1991 THE GIRL FROM MARS
Director: Neill Fernley
Co-stars: Edward Albert Eddie Albert Sarah Sawatsky

1993 THE CRUSH
Director: Alan Shapiro
Co-stars: Cary Elwes Alicia Silverstone Jennifer Rubin

1993 FALSELY ACCUSED
Director: Noel Nosseck
Co-stars: Lisa Hartman Christopher Meloni Cloris Leachman

JANE WALSH

1931 THE SLEEPING CARDINAL
Director: Leslie Hiscott
Co-stars: Arthur Wontner Ian Fleming Norman McKinnel

1937 THE MAN WHO FOUND HIMSELF
Director: Lew Landers
Co-stars: Joan Fontaine John Beal Philip Huston

KATHERINE WALSH

1967 THE TRIP
Director: Roger Corman
Co-stars: Peter Fonda Susan Strasberg Bruce Dern

KAY WALSH

1936 THE SECRET OF STAMBOUL
Director: Andrew Marton
Co-stars: Valerie Hobson James Mason

1937   **THE LAST ADVENTURERS**
Director: Roy Kellino
Co-stars: Niall McGinnis Linden Travers Katie Johnson

1937   **KEEP FIT**
Director: Anthony Kimmins
Co-stars: George Formby Guy Middleton George Benson

1938   **I SEE ICE**
Director: Anthony Kimmins
Co-stars: George Formby Cyril Ritchard Betty Stockfield

1938   **MEET MR PENNY**
Director: David MacDonald
Co-stars: Richard Goolden Vic Oliver Hermione Gingold

1939   **THE MIDDLE WATCH**
Director: Thomas Bentley
Co-stars: Jack Buchanan Fred Emney Greta Gynt

1939   **THE MIND OF MR REEDER**
Director: Jack Raymond
Co-stars: Will Fyffe Chili Bouchier George Curzon

1939   **SONS OF THE SEA**
Director: Maurice Elvey
Co-stars: Leslie Banks Cecil Parker Nigel Stock

1939   **THE CHINESE BUNGALOW**
Director: George King
Co-stars: Paul Lukas Jane Baxter Robert Douglas

1942   **IN WHICH WE SERVE**
Director: David Lean
Co-stars: Noel Coward Bernard Miles John Mills

1944   **THIS HAPPY BREED**
Director: David Lean
Co-stars: Robert Newton Celia Johnson Stanley Holloway

1947   **VICE VERSA**
Director: Peter Ustinov
Co-stars: Roger Livesey Anthony Newley Petula Clark

1947   **THE OCTOBER MAN**
Director: Roy Baker
Co-stars: John Mills Joan Greenwood Edward Chapman

1948   **OLIVER TWIST**
Director: David Lean
Co-stars: Alec Guinness Robert Newton Anthony Newley

1950   **STAGE FRIGHT**
Director: Alfred Hitchcock
Co-stars: Marlene Dietrich Jane Wyman Richard Todd

1950   **THE MAGNET**
Director: Charles Frend
Co-stars: James Fox Stephen Murray Meredith Edwards

1950   **LAST HOLIDAY**
Director: Henry Cass
Co-stars: Alec Guinness Beatrice Campbell Bernard Lee

1951   **ENCORE**
Director: Pat Jackson
Co-stars: Nigel Patrick Roland Culver Glynis Johns

1952   **HUNTED**
Director: Charles Crichton
Co-stars: Dirk Bogarde Jon Whitely Elizabeth Sellars

1952   **MEET ME TONIGHT**
Director: Anthony Pelisier
Co-stars: Ted Ray Stanley Holloway Nigel Patrick

1953   **YOUNG BESS**
Director: George Sidney
Co-stars: Jean Simmons Stewart Granger Charles Laughton

1954   **THE RAINBOW JACKET**
Director: Basil Dearden
Co-stars: Bill Owen Edward Underdown Robert Morley

1954   **LEASE OF LIFE**
Director: Charles Frend
Co-stars: Robert Donat Adrienne Corri Denholm Elliott

1955   **NOW AND FOREVER**
Director: Mario Zampi
Co-stars: Janette Scott Vernon Gray Jack Warner

1955   **CAST A DARK SHADOW**
Director: Lewis Gilbert
Co-stars: Dirk Bogarde Margaret Lockwood Robert Flemyng

1958   **THE HORSE'S MOUTH**
Director: Ronald Neame
Co-stars: Alec Guinness Renee Houston Robert Coote

1960   **TUNES OF GLORY**
Director: Ronald Neame
Co-stars: Alec Guinness John Mills Susannah York

1960   **GREYFRIARS BOBBY**
Director: Don Chaffey
Co-stars: Donald Crisp Laurence Naismith Andrew Cruikshank

1962   **REACH FOR GLORY**
Director: Philip Leacock
Co-stars: Harry Andrews Alexis Kanner Michael Anderson

1962   **LUNCH HOUR**
Director: James Hill
Co-stars: Shirley Anne Field Robert Stephens Nigel Davenport

1963   **DR SYN ALIAS THE SCARECROW**
Director: James Neilson
Co-stars: Patrick McGoohan George Cole

1963   **EIGHTY THOUSAND SUSPECTS**
Director: Val Guest
Co-stars: Claire Bloom Richard Johnson Yolande Donlon

1964   **THE BEAUTY JUNGLE**
Director: Val Guest
Co-stars: Janette Scott Ian Hendry Edmund Purdom

1964   **THE MAGNIFICENT SHOWMAN**
Director: Henry Hathaway
Co-stars: John Wayne Rita Hayworth Claudia Cardinale

1965   **HE WHO RIDES A TIGER**
Director: Charles Crichton
Co-stars: Tom Bell Judi Dench Paul Rogers

1965   **A STUDY IN TERROR**
Director: James Hill
Co-stars: John Neville Donald Houston Robert Morley

1966   **THE WITCHES**
Director: Cyril Frankel
Co-stars: Joan Fontaine Alex McCowen Leonard Rossiter

1968   **A TASTE OF EXCITEMENT**
Director: Don Sharp
Co-stars: Eva Renzi David Buck Peter Vaughan

1969   **CONNECTING ROOMS**
Director: Franklin Gollings
Co-stars: Bette Davis Michael Redgrave Alexis Kanner

1970   **THE VIRGIN AND THE GYPSY**
Director: Christopher Miles
Co-stars: Joanna Shimkus Franco Nero

1970   **SCROOGE**
Director: Ronald Neame
Co-stars: Albert Finney Michael Medwin Alec Guinness

1972   **THE RULING CLASS**
Director: Peter Medak
Co-stars: Peter O'Toole Alastair Sim Coral Browne

1981   **NIGHT CROSSING**
Director: Delbert Mann
Co-stars: John Hurt Jane Alexander Beau Bridges

MARGARET WALSH

1990 MR AND MRS BRIDGE
Director: James Ivory
Co-stars: Paul Newman Joanne Woodward Blythe Danner

SALLY WALSH *(Child)*

1994 THE OLD CURIOSITY SHOP
Co-stars: Peter Ustinov James Fox Julia McKenzie

HARRIET WALTER

1980 THE IMITATION GAME
Director: Richard Eyre

1984 THE AMY JOHNSON STORY
Director: Nat Crosby
Co-stars: Clive Francis Patrick Troughton

1985 TURTLE DIARY
Director: John Irvin
Co-stars: Glenda Jackson Ben Kingsley Richard Johnson

1986 THE GOOD FATHER
Director: Mike Newell
Co-stars: Anthony Hopkins Jim Broadbent Simon Callow

1989 MILOU IN MAY
Director: Louis Malle
Co-stars: Michel Piccoli Miou Miou Dominique Blanc

1991 THEY NEVER SLEPT
Director: Udayan Prasad
Co-stars: Edward Fox Emily Morgan James Fleet

1993 THE HOUR OF THE PIG
Director: Leslie Megahey
Co-stars: Colin Firth Amina Annabi Ian Holm

1993 INSPECTOR MORSE:
THE DAY OF THE DEVIL
Director: Stephen Whittaker
Co-stars: John Thaw Kevin Whately

1995 THE MEN'S ROOM
Co-star: Bill Nighy

1996 SENSE AND SENSIBILITY
Director: Ang Lee
Co-stars: Emma Thompson Kate Winslet Hugh Grant

1997 THE LEADING MAN
Director: John Duigan
Co-stars: Jon Bon Jovi Patricia Hodge Anna Galiena

1997 KEEP THE ASPIDISTRA FLYING
Director: Robert Bierman
Co-stars: Helena Bonham-Carter Richard E. Grant Liz Smith

JESSICA WALTER

1964 LILITH
Director: Robert Rossen
Co-stars: Warren Beatty Jean Seberg Peter Fonda

1966 THE GROUP
Director: Sidney Lumet
Co-stars: Candice Bergen Joan Hackett Shirley Knight

1966 GRAND PRIX
Director: John Frankenheimer
Co-stars: James Garner Eva Marie Saint Yves Montand

1968 BYE BYE BRAVERMAN
Director: Sidney Lumet
Co-stars: George Segal Jack Warden Joseph Wiseman

1969 NUMBER ONE
Director: Tom Gries
Co-stars: Charlton Heston Bruce Dern John Randolph

1969 THREE'S A CROWD
Director: Harry Falk
Co-stars: Larry Hagman E.J. Peaker Harvey Korman

1971 THEY CALL IT MURDER
Director: Walter Grauman
Co-stars: Jim Hutton Lloyd Bochner Jo Ann Pflug

1971 PLAY MISTY FOR ME
Director: Clint Eastwood
Co-stars: Clint Eastwood Donna Mills Irene Hervey

1979 SHE'S DRESSED TO KILL
Director: Gus Trikonis
Co-stars: Eleanor Parker Clive Revell John Rubinstein

1983 THURSDAY'S CHILD
Director: David Lowell Rich
Co-stars: Gena Rowlands Don Murray Rob Lowe

1984 THE FLAMINGO KID
Director: Garry Marshall
Co-stars: Matt Dillon Richard Crenna Hector Elizondo

1985 THE EXECUTION
Director: Paul Wendkos
Co-stars: Loretta Swit Rip Torn Sandy Dennis

1994 P.C.U.
Director: Hart Bochner
Co-stars: Jeremy Piven Chris Young Sarah Trigger

TRACEY WALTER

1984 REPO MAN
Director: Alex Cox
Co-stars: Emilio Estevez Harry Dean Stanton Vonetta McGee

1986 AT CLOSE RANGE
Director: James Foley
Co-stars: Sean Penn Christopher Walken Mary Stewart Masterson

1991 CITY SLICKERS
Director: Ron Underwood
Co-stars: Billy Crystal Daniel Stern Bruno Kirby

JULIE WALTERS
Nominated For Best Actress In 1983 For "Educating Rita"

1981 DAYS AT THE BEACH
Director: Malcolm Mowbray
Co-stars: Sam Kelly Stephen Bill Mark Aspinall

1982 INTENSIVE CARE
Director: Gavin Millar
Co-stars: Alan Bennett Thora Hird Helen Fraser

1983 EDUCATING RITA
Director: Lewis Gilbert
Co-stars: Michael Caine Michael Williams Maureen Lipman

1984 UNFAIR EXCHANGES
Director: Gavin Millar
Co-stars: David Rappaport Robert Kingswell Bert Parnaby

1985 SHE'LL BE WEARING PINK PYJAMAS
Director: John Goldschmidt
Co-stars: Anthony Higgins Jane Evers Paula Jacobs

1986 CAR TROUBLE
Director: David Green
Co-stars: Ian Charleson Stratford Johns Vincenzo Ricotta

1987 PERSONAL SERVICES
Director: Terry Jones
Co-stars: Alec McCowan Shirley Stelfox Tim Woodward

1987 PRICK UP YOUR EARS
Director: Stephen Frears
Co-stars: Gary Oldman Alfred Molina Vanessa Redgrave

1988   **BUSTER**
Director: David Green
Co-stars: Phil Collins Larry Lamb Martin Jarvis

1989   **KILLING DAD**
Director: Michael Austin
Co-stars: Denholm Elliott Richard E. Grant Anna Massey

1991   **STEPPING OUT**
Director: Lewis Gilbert
Co-stars: Liza Minnelli Shelley Winters Ellen Greene

1992   **JUST LIKE A WOMAN**
Director: Christopher Monger
Co-stars: Adrian Pasdar Susan Wooldridge Gordon Kennedy

1992   **THE CLOTHES IN THE WARDROBE**
Director: Waris Hussein
Co-stars: Jeanne Moreau Joan Plowright David Threlfall

1993   **WIDE EYED AND LEGLESS**
Director: Richard Loncraine
Co-stars: Jim Broadbent Thora Hird Sian Thomas

1994   **BAMBINO MIO**
Director: Edward Bennett
Co-stars: Georges Corraface John McArdle

1995   **SISTER, MY SISTER**
Director: Nancy Mecklar
Co-stars: Joely Richardson Jodhi May Sophie Thursfield

1996   **BRAZEN HUSSIES**
Director: Elijah Majinsky
Co-stars: Alun Armstrong Robert Lindsay Crissy Rock

1997   **INTIMATE RELATIONS**
Director: Philip Goodhale
Co-stars: Rupert Graves Laura Sadler Matthew Walker

1998   **GIRLS' NIGHT**
Co-stars: Brenda Blethyn Kris Kristofferson

LUANA WALTERS

1933   **END OF THE TRAIL**
Director: Ross Lederman
Co-stars: Tim McCoy Wheeler Oakman

1935   **ASSASSIN OF YOUTH**
Director: Elmer Clifton
Co-stars: Arthur Gardner Dorothy Short Fern Emmett

1937   **SOULS AT SEA**
Director: Henry Hathaway
Co-stars: Gary Cooper George Raft Frances Day

1940   **BLONDIE PLAYS CUPID**
Director: Frank Strayer
Co-stars: Penny Singleton Arthur Lake Glenn Ford

1941   **ROAD AGENT**
Co-stars: Leo Carrillo Anne Gwynne Andy Devine

1942   **THUNDERING HOOFS**
Director: Lesley Selander
Co-stars: Tim Holt Archie Twitchell Ray Whitley

1942   **THE CORPSE VANISHES**
Director: Wallace Fox
Co-stars: Bela Lugosi Minerva Urecal Elizabeth Russell

MELANIE WALTERS

1988   **RUN FOR THE LIFEBOAT**
Director: Douglas Livingstone
Co-stars: Stacey Tendetter David Burke Jeff Rawle

MELORA WALTERS

1994   **MIDNIGHT RUN FOR YOUR LIFE**
Director: Daniel Sackheim
Co-stars: Ed O'Ross Christopher McDonald

1994   **CABIN BOY**
Director: Adam Resnick
Co-stars: Chris Elliott James Gammon Russ Tamblyn

NANCY WALTERS

1961   **BLUE HAWAII**
Director: Norman Taurog
Co-stars: Elvis Presley Joan Blackman Angela Lansbury

1961   **THE GREEN HELMET**
Director: Michael Forlong
Co-stars: Bill Travers Ed Begley Sid James

PATRICIA WALTERS

1951   **THE RIVER**
Director: Jean Renoir
Co-stars: Nora Swinburne Esmond Knight Adrienne Corri

POLLY WALTERS

1931   **BLONDE CRAZY**
Director: Roy Del Ruth
Co-stars: James Cagney Joan Blondell Ray Milland

SUSAN WALTERS

1987   **RUSSKIES**
Director: Rick Rosenthal
Co-stars: Whip Hubley Susan Blanchard Summer Phoenix

1990   **A COP FOR THE KILLING**
Director: Dick Lowry
Co-stars: James Farentino Steven Weber Charles Haid

1990   **GRAND SLAM**
Director: Bill Norton
Co-stars: John Schneider Paul Rodriguez Joan Fernandez

LISA WALTZ

1986   **BRIGHTON BEACH MEMOIRS**
Director: Gene Saks
Co-stars: Blythe Danner Bob Dishy Judith Ivey

1991   **PET SEMATARY TWO**
Director: Mary Lambert
Co-stars: Edward Furlong Anthony Edwards Clancy Brown

1994   **ROSWELL**
Director: Jeremy Kagan
Co-stars: Kyle MacLachlan Martin Sheen Kim Greist

ZOE WANAMAKER
(Daughter Of Sam Wanamaker)

1987   **THE RAGGEDY RAWNEY**
Director: Bob Hoskins
Co-stars: Bob Hoskins Dexter Fletcher David Hill

1988   **THE DOG IT WAS THAT DIED**
Director: Peter Wood
Co-stars: Alan Bates Alan Howard Simon Cadell

1989   **BALL TRAP ON THE COTE SAUVAGE**
Director: Jack Gold
Co-stars: Miranda Richardson Jack Shepherd Edward Holmes

1991   **PRIME SUSPECT**
Director: Christopher Menaul
Co-stars: Helen Mirren Tom Bell John Bowe

1997   **WILDE**
Director: Brian Gilbert
Co-stars: Stephen Fry Jude Law Vanessa Redgrave

1998   **AMY FOSTER**
Director: Beeban Kidron
Co-stars: Rachel Weisz Vincent Perez

DOREEN WARBURTON

1985 ARCHER'S ADVENTURE
Director: Denny Lawrence
Co-stars: Brett Climo Robert Coleby Ned Lander

1991 WENDY CRACKS A WALNUT
Director: Michael Pattison
Co-stars: Rosanna Arquette Bruce Spence Kerry Walker

AMELITA WARD

1943 THE FALCON IN DANGER
Director: William Clemens
Co-stars: Tom Conway Jean Brooks Ed Gargan

1943 CLANCY STREET BOYS
Director: William Beaudine
Co-stars: Leo Gorcy Huntz Hall Bobby Jordan

1943 AERIAL GUNNER
Director: William Pine
Co-stars: Richard Arlen Chester Morris Jimmy Lydon

1943 GANGWAY FOR TOMORROW
Director: John Auer
Co-stars: Robert Ryan John Carradine Margo

1944 SEVEN DAYS ASHORE
Co-stars: Virginia Mayo Gordon Oliver Alan Dinehart

1945 JUNGLE CAPTIVE
Director: Harold Young
Co-stars: Otto Kruger Rondo Hatton Jerome Cowan

FANNY WARD

1915 THE CHEAT
Director: Cecil B. DeMille
Co-stars: Sessue Hayakawa Jack Dean James Neill

JANET WARD

1974 DR MAX
Director: James Goldstone
Co-stars: Lee J. Cobb Robert Lipton Katherine Helmond

JOANNA WARD

1997 THE GIRL WITH BRAINS IN HER FEET
Co-star: John Thomson

LOTTIE WARD

1985 THE ADVENTURES OF SHERLOCK HOLMES: THE COPPER BEACHES
Director: Paul Annett
Co-stars: Jeremy Brett Natasha Richardson

MARY B. WARD

1991 HANGIN' WITH THE HOMEBOYS
Director: Joseph Vasquez
Co-stars: Mario Joyner Kimberly Russell Nestor Serrano

MEGAN WARD

1991 TRANCERS 2: THE RETURN OF JACK DETH
Director: Charles Band
Co-stars: Tim Thomerson Helen Hunt Martine Beswick

1992 TRANCERS 3: DETH LIVES
Director: Courtney Joyner
Co-stars: Tim Thomerson Melanie Smith Helen Hunt

1992 AMITYVILLE 1992: IT'S ABOUT TIME
Director: Tony Randel
Co-stars: Stephen Macht Shawn Weatherly Damon Martin

1992 CALIFORNIA MAN
Director: Les Mayfield
Co-stars: Sean Astin Pauly Shore Brendan Fraser

1993 FREAKED
Director: Tom Stern
Co-stars: Alex Winter Randy Quaid Brooke Shields

1996 JOE'S APARTMENT
Director: John Payson
Co-stars: Jerry O'Connell Robert Vaughn

POLLY WARD

1930 HARMONY HEAVEN
Director: Thomas Bentley
Co-stars: Stuart Hall Trilby Clark Jack Raine

1934 THE OLD CURIOSITY SHOP
Director: Thomas Bentley
Co-stars: Hay Petrie Elaine Benson Ben Webster

1937 FEATHER YOUR NEST
Director: William Beaudine
Co-stars: George Formby Enid Stamp-Taylor Val Rosing

1938 HOLD MY HAND
Director: Thornton Freeland
Co-stars: Stanley Lupino Fred Emney Sally Gray

1938 IT'S IN THE AIR
Director: Anthony Kimmins
Co-stars: George Formby Garry Marsh Hal Gordon

1942 WOMEN AREN'T ANGELS
Director: Laurence Huntington
Co-stars: Robertson Hare Alfred Drayton Joyce Heron

RACHEL WARD
(Daughter Of Simon Ward, Sister Of Sophie Ward)

1981 SHARKY'S MACHINE
Director: Burt Reynolds
Co-stars: Burt Reynolds Vittorio Gassman Brian Keith

1982 DEAD MEN DON'T WEAR PLAID
Director: Carl Reiner
Co-stars: Carl Reiner Steve Martin Reni Santoni

1983 CAMPSITE MASSACRE
Director: Andrew Davis
Co-stars: Daryl Hannah John Friedich Adrian Zmed

1984 AGAINST ALL ODDS
Director: Taylor Hackford
Co-stars: Jeff Bridges James Woods Jane Greer

1986 THE GOOD WIFE
Director: Ken Cameron
Co-stars: Bryan Brown Sam Neill Steven Vidler

1989 HOW TO GET AHEAD IN ADVERTISING
Director: Bruce Robinson
Co-stars: Richard E. Grant Richard Wilson

1990 AFTER DARK, MY SWEET
Director: James Foley
Co-stars: Jason Patric Bruce Dern James Cotton

1992 CHRISTOPHER COLUMBUS: THE DISCOVERY
Director: John Glenn
Co-stars: George Corraface Marlon Brando

1992 WIDE SARGASSO SEA
Director: John Duigan
Co-stars: Michael York Karina Lombard Nathaniel Parker

1992 BLACK MAGIC
Director: Daniel Taplitz
Co-stars: Judge Reinhold Brion James Anthony LaPaglia

1992 DOUBLE JEOPARDY
Director: Lawrence Schiller
Co-stars: Bruce Boxleitner Sela Ward Sally Kirkland

SELA WARD

1985 RUSTLERS' RHAPSODY
Director: Hugh Wilson
Co-stars: Tom Berenger Marilu Henner Andy Griffith

1989 BRIDESMAIDS
Director: Lila Garrett
Co-stars: Shelley Hack Audra Lindley Brooke Adams

1992 DOUBLE JEOPARDY
Director: Lawrence Schiller
Co-stars: Rachel Ward Bruce Boxleitner Sally Kirkland

1993 THE FUGITIVE
Director: Andrew Davies
Co-stars: Harrison Ford Tommy Lee Jones Julianne Moore

1993 KILLER RULES
Director: Robert Ellis Miller
Co-stars: Jamey Sheridan Peter Dobson Sam Wanamaker

SOPHIE WARD
(Daughter Of Simon Ward, Sister Of Rachel Ward)

1976 THE COPTER KIDS
Director: Ronnie Spender
Co-stars: Sophie Neville Kate Dorning

1985 YOUNG SHERLOCK HOLMES
Director: Barry Levinson
Co-stars: Nicholas Rowe Alan Cox Freddie Jones

1988 A SUMMER STORY
Director: Piers Haggard
Co-stars: James Wilby Imogen Stubbs Susannah York

1988 ARIA
Director: Nicholas Roeg
Co-stars: Theresa Russell Bridget Fonda John Hurt

1991 EVENTS AT DRIMAGHLEEN
Director: Robert Cooper
Co-stars: T.P. McKenna Hugh Fraser Nick Dunning

1992 WUTHERING HEIGHTS
Director: Peter Kominsky
Co-stars: Juliette Binoche Ralph Fiennes

1994 A DARK ADAPTED EYE
Director: Tim Fywell
Co-stars: Helena Bonham Carter Celia Imrie Robin Ellis

JENNIFER WARD-LEALAND

1993 DESPERATE REMEDIES
Director: Peter Wells
Co-stars: Kevin Smith Lisa Chappell Cliff Curtis

HELEN WARE

1929 THE VIRGINIAN
Director: Victor Fleming
Co-stars: Gary Cooper Walter Huston Mary Brian

1930 SLIGHTLY SCARLET
Director: Louis Gasnier
Co-stars: Clive Brook Evelyn Brent Paul Lukas

1931 I TAKE THIS WOMAN
Director: Marion Gehring
Co-stars: Gary Cooper Carole Lombard Lester Vail

1933 THE WARRIOR'S HUSBAND
Director: Walter Lang
Co-stars: Elissa Landi Marjorie Rambeau David Manners

HERTA WARE

1988 CRITTERS 2: THE MAIN COURSE
Director: Mick Garris
Co-stars: Scott Grimes Liane Curtis Don Opper

1991 SOAPDISH
Director: Michael Hoffman
Co-stars: Sally Field Kevin Kline Whoopi Goldberg

1992 CRAZY IN LOVE
Director: Martha Coolidge
Co-stars: Holly Hunter Bill Pullman Julian Sands

IRENE WARE

1932 SIX HOURS TO LIVE
Director: William Dieterle
Co-stars: Warner Baxter John Boles Miriam Jordan

1932 CHANDU THE MAGICIAN
Director: Marcel Varnel
Co-stars: Edmund Lowe Bela Lugosi Herbert Mundin

1934 ORIENT EXPRESS
Director: Paul Martin
Co-stars: Heather Angel Ralph Morgan Norman Foster

1935 THE RAVEN
Director: Lew Landers
Co-stars: Bela Lugosi Boris Karloff Samuel S. Hinds

1935 RENDEZVOUS AT MIDNIGHT
Director: Christy Cabanne
Co-stars: Ralph Bellamy Valerie Hobson Catherine Doucet

1935 WHISPERING SMITH SPEAKS
Co-star: George O'Brien

1935 THE CHEERS OF THE CROWD
Co-star: Russell Hopton

1938 NO PARKING
Director: Jack Raymond
Co-stars: Gordon Harker Leslie Perrins Cyril Smith

1940 OUTSIDE THE 3-MILE LIMIT
Co-star: Donald Briggs

LINDA WARE *(Child)*

1939 THE STAR MAKER
Director: Roy Del Ruth
Co-stars: Bing Crosby Louise Campbell Ned Sparks

1941 PAPER BULLETS
Director: Phil Rosen
Co-stars: Joan Woodbury Jack La Rue Alan Ladd

EMILY WARFIELD

1991 THE MAN IN THE MOON
Director: Robert Mulligan
Co-stars: Sam Waterston Tess Harper Gail Strickland

1993 BEYOND OBSESSION
Director: David Greene
Co-stars: Victoria Principal Donelly Rhodes

BARBARA WARING

1943 THE GENTLE SEX
Director: Leslie Howard
Co-stars: Joan Gates Rosamund John Joan Greenwood

LESLEY WARING

1935 FIGHTING STOCK
Director: Tom Walls
Co-stars: Tom Walls Ralph Lynn Robertson Hare

MARCIAN WARMAN

1988 A FATHER'S HOMECOMING
Director: Rick Wallace
Co-stars: Michael McKean Jonathan Ward Brandon Douglas

JULIE WARNER

1990 I WANT HIM BACK
Director: Catlin Adams
Co-stars: Valerie Harper Elliott Gould Brenda Vaccaro

1991 DOC HOLLYWOOD
Director: Michael Caton-Jones
Co-stars: Michael J. Fox Bridget Fonda Barnard Hughes

1992 MR SATURDAY NIGHT
Director: Billy Crystal
Co-stars: Billy Crystal David Paymer Helen Hunt

1993 INDIAN SUMMER
Director: Mike Binder
Co-stars: Alan Arkin Elizabeth Perkins Matt Craven

BETTY WARREN

1942 VARIETY JUBILEE
Director: Maclean Rogers
Co-stars: Lesley Brook George Robey Ellis Irving

1944 CHAMPAGNE CHARLIE
Director: Alberto Cavalcanti
Co-stars: Tommy Trinder Stanley Holloway Jean Kent

1949 PASSPORT TO PIMLICO
Director: Henry Cornelius
Co-stars: Stanley Holloway Margaret Rutherford Basil Radford

1950 SO LONG AT THE FAIR
Director: Terence Fisher
Co-stars: Jean Simmons Dirk Bogarde David Tomlinson

FRAN WARREN

**1952 ABBOTT AND COSTELLO
MEET CAPTAIN KIDD**
Director: Charles Lamont
Co-stars: Bud Abbott Lou Costello Charles Laughton

GLORIA WARREN

1942 ALWAYS IN MY HEART
Director: Joe Graham
Co-stars: Walter Huston Kay Francis Sidney Blackmer

1943 CINDERELLA SWINGS IT
Co-star: Leonid Kinskey

1946 DANGEROUS MONEY
Director: Terry Morse
Co-stars: Sidney Toler Rick Vallin Willie Best

JANET WARREN

1945 THE JADE MASK
Director: Phil Rosen
Co-stars: Sidney Toler Manton Moreland Hardie Albright

JENNIFER WARREN

1975 NIGHT MOVES
Director: Arthur Penn
Co-stars: Gene Hackman Melanie Griffith Edward Binns

1977 SLAPSHOT
Director: George Roy Hill
Co-stars: Paul Newman Michael Ontkean Lindsay Crouse

1977 ANOTHER MAN, ANOTHER CHANCE
Director: Claude Lelouch
Co-stars: James Caan Genevieve Bujold Susan Tyrrell

1978 STEEL COWBOY
Director: Harvey Laidman
Co-stars: James Brolin Rip Torn Melanie Griffith

1978 ICE CASTLES
Director: Donald Wrye
Co-stars: Robby Benson Lynn-Holly Johnson Colleen Dewhurst

1980 ANGEL CITY
Director: Philip Leacock
Co-stars: Ralph Waite Paul Winfield Jennifer Jason Leigh

1983 CONFESSIONS OF A MARRIED MAN
Director: Charles Pratt
Co-stars: Robert Conrad Mary Crosby Ann Dusenberry

1984 AMAZONS
Director: Paul Michael Glaser
Co-stars: Madeleine Stowe Tamara Dobson Stella Stevens

1987 FATAL BEAUTY
Director: Tom Holland
Co-stars: Whoopi Goldberg Sam Elliott Ruben Blades

KATHERINE WARREN

1951 FORCE OF ARMS
Director: Michael Curtiz
Co-stars: William Holden Nancy Olson Frank Lovejoy

1951 THE PROWLER
Director: Joseph Losey
Co-stars: Van Heflin Evelyn Keyes John Maxwell

LESLEY ANN WARREN

Nominated For Best Supporting Actress In 1982 For "Victor/Victoria"

1964 CINDERELLA
Director: Charles Dubin
Co-stars: Ginger Rogers Walter Pidgeon Celeste Holm

1967 THE HAPPIEST MILLIONAIRE
Director: Norman Tokar
Co-stars: Fred MacMurray Tommy Steele Greer Garson

**1968 THE ONE AND ONLY GENUINE
ORIGINAL FAMILY BAND**
Director: Michael O'Harlihy
Co-stars: Walter Brennan Buddy Ebsen Kurt Russell

1972 PICKUP ON 101
Director: John Florea
Co-stars: Jack Albertson Martin Sheen Michael Ontkean

1972 ASSIGNMENT MUNICH
Director: David Lowell Rich
Co-stars: Roy Scheider Richard Basehart Pernell Roberts

1976 HARRY AND WALTER GO TO NEW YORK
Director: Mark Rydell
Co-stars: James Caan Elliott Gould Michael Caine

1981 TREASURE OF THE YANKEE ZEPHYR
Director: David Hemmings
Co-stars: Ken Wahl George Peppard Donald Pleasence

1982 VICTOR/VICTORIA
Director: Blake Edwards
Co-stars: Julie Andrews Robert Preston James Garner

1984 SONGWRITER
Director: Alan Rudolph
Co-stars: Willie Nelson Kris Kristofferson Melinda Dillon

1984 CHOOSE ME
Director: Alan Rudolph
Co-stars: Genevieve Bujold Keith Carradine Rae Dawn Chong

1985 CLUE
Director: Jonathan Lynn
Co-stars: Eileen Brennan Tim Curry Madeline Kahn

1986 APOLOGY FOR MURDER
Director: Robert Bierman
Co-stars: Peter Weller George Loros John Glover

1987 BURGLAR
Director: Hugh Wilson
Co-stars: Whoopi Goldberg Bob Goldthwaite James Handy

1988 COP
Director: James Harris
Co-stars: James Woods Charles Durning

1990 FAMILY OF SPIES
Director: Stephen Gyllenthal
Co-stars: Powers Boothe Graham Beckel Jeroen Krabbe

1990 WORTH WINNING
Director: Will MacKenzie
Co-stars: Mark Harmon Madeleine Stowe

1991 LIFE STINKS
Director: Mel Brooks
Co-stars: Mel Brooks Jeffrey Tambor Stuart Pankin

1991 BLIND JUDGEMENT
Director: George Kaczender
Co-stars: Peter Coyote Jean Smart Matt Clark

1992 PURE COUNTRY
Director: Christopher Cain
Co-star: George Strait

1992 HEARTS ON FIRE
Director: Jeff Bleckner
Co-stars: Tom Skerritt Marg Helgenberger

1993 DESPERATE JUSTICE
Director: Armand Mastroianni
Co-stars: Bruce Davison Annette O'Toole

1995 JOSEPH IN EGYPT
Director: Roger Young
Co-stars: Paul Mercurio Ben Kingsley Alice Krige

MARY WARREN

1918 ALL NIGHT
Director: Paul Powell
Co-stars: Rudolph Valentino Carmel Myers Charles Dorian

NICOLA WARREN

1988 FURTHER AND PARTICULAR
Director: Steve Dwoskin
Co-stars: Richard Butler Irene Marot Carola Regnier

RUTH WARRICK

1941 THE OBLIGING YOUNG LADY
Director: Richard Wallace
Co-stars: Joan Carroll Edmond O'Brien Eve Arden

1941 CITIZEN KANE
Director: Orson Welles
Co-stars: Orson Welles Joseph Cotten Dorothy Comingore

1942 JOURNEY INTO FEAR
Director: Orson Welles
Co-stars: Orson Welles Joseph Cotten Dolores Del Rio

1942 THE CORSICAN BROTHERS
Director: Gregory Ratoff
Co-stars: Douglas Fairbanks Akim Tamiroff J. Carrol Naish

1943 FOREVER AND A DAY
Director: Rene Clair
Co-stars: Charles Laughton Ray Milland Anna Neagle

1943 THE IRON MAJOR
Director: Ray Enright
Co-stars: Pat O'Brien Robert Ryan Leon Ames

1944 MR WINKLE GOES TO WAR
Director: Alfred Green
Co-stars: Edward G. Robinson Robert Armstrong

1944 SECRET COMMAND
Director: Edward Sutherland
Co-stars: Pat O'Brien Carole Landis Chester Morris

1944 GUEST IN THE HOUSE
Director: John Brahm
Co-stars: Anne Baxter Ralph Bellamy Aline MacMahon

1945 CHINA SKY
Director: Ray Enright
Co-stars: Randolph Scott Ellen Drew Anthony Quinn

1946 PERILOUS HOLIDAY
Director: Edward Griffith
Co-stars: Pat O'Brien Alan Hale Minna Gombell

1946 SWELL GUY
Co-star: Sonny Tufts

1946 SONG OF THE SOUTH
Director: Harve Foster
Co-stars: James Baskett Bobby Driscoll Luana Patten

1947 DRIFTWOOD
Director: Allan Dwan
Co-stars: Natalie Wood Walter Brennan Dean Jagger

1947 DAISY KENYON
Director: Otto Preminger
Co-stars: Joan Crawford Henry Fonda Dana Andrews

1948 ARCH OF TRIUMPH
Director: Lewis Milestone
Co-stars: Charles Boyer Ingrid Bergman Charles Laughton

1949 THE GREAT DAN PATCH
Director: Joseph Newman
Co-stars: Dennis O'Keefe Gail Russell Charlotte Greenwood

1950 LET'S DANCE
Director: Norman Z. McLeod
Co-stars: Fred Astaire Betty Hutton Roland Young

1950 THREE HUSBANDS
Director: Irving Reis
Co-stars: Emlyn Williams Eve Arden Vanessa Brown

1966 RIDE BEYOND VENGEANCE
Director: Bernard McEveety
Co-stars: Chuck Connors Michael Rennie Gloria Grahame

1969 THE GREAT BANK ROBBERY
Director: Hy Averback
Co-stars: Kim Novak Clint Walker Zero Mostel

1985 PEYTON PLACE: THE NEXT GENERATION
Director: Larry Elikann
Co-stars: Dorothy Malone Barbara Parkins

RUTH WARSHAWSKY

1977 DEATH GAME
Director: Peter Traynor
Co-stars: Sondra Locke Colleen Camp Seymour Cassel

1990 ALMOST AN ANGEL
Director: John Cornell
Co-stars: Paul Hogan Elias Koteas Linda Kozlowski

DIONNE WARWICK

1967 VALLEY OF THE DOLLS *(Voice)*
Director: Mark Robson
Co-stars: Barbara Parkins Patty Duke Susan Hayward

1969 SLAVES
Director: Herbert Biberman
Co-stars: Stephen Boyd Ossie Davis Gale Sondergaard

1988 RENT-A-COP
Director: Jerry London
Co-stars: Burt Reynolds Liza Minnelli Robby Benson

MONA WASHBOURNE

1954 CHILD'S PLAY
Director: Margaret Thomson
Co-stars: Peter Martin Dorothy Alison Ingeborg Wells

1955 CAST A DARK SHADOW
Director: Lewis Gilbert
Co-stars: Dirk Bogarde Margaret Lockwood Kay Walsh

1958 A CRY FROM THE STREETS
Director: Lewis Gilbert
Co-stars: Max Bygraves Barbara Murray Colin Petersen

1959 COUNT YOUR BLESSINGS
Director: Jean Negulesco
Co-stars: Deborah Kerr Maurice Chevalier Rossano Brazzi

1960 BRIDES OF DRACULA
Director: Anthony Hinds
Co-stars: David Peel Peter Cushing Martita Hunt

1963 BILLY LIAR
Director: John Schlesinger
Co-stars: Tom Courtenay Julie Christie Helen Fraser

1964 MY FAIR LADY
Director: George Cukor
Co-stars: Rex Harrison Audrey Hepburn Stanley Holloway

1964 NIGHT MUST FALL
Director: Karel Reisz
Co-stars: Albert Finney Susan Hampshire Sheila Hancock

1965 THE THIRD DAY
Director: Jack Smight
Co-stars: George Peppard Elizabeth Ashley Roddy Mcdowall

1965 ONE WAY PENDULUM
Director: Peter Yates
Co-stars: Eric Sykes George Cole Julia Foster

1965 THE COLLECTOR
Director: William Wyler
Co-stars: Samantha Eggar Terence Stamp

1968 IF
Director: Lindsay Anderson
Co-stars: Malcolm McDowell Peter Jeffrey Arthur Lowe

**1968 MRS BROWN, YOU'VE GOT
A LOVELY DAUGHTER**
Director: Saul Swimmer
Co-stars: Herman's Hermits Stanley Holloway

1969 THE BED SITTING ROOM
Director: Richard Lester
Co-stars: Ralph Richardson Rita Tushingham Peter Cook

1970 THE GAMES
Director: Michael Winner
Co-stars: Stanley Baker Michael Crawford Ryan O'Neal

1970 FRAGMENT OF FEAR
Director: Richard Sarafian
Co-stars: David Hemmings Gayle Hunnicutt Flora Robson

1971 WHAT BECAME OF JACK AND JILL ?
Director: Bill Bain
Co-stars: Vanessa Howard Paul Nicholas Peter Jeffrey

1973 O LUCKY MAN !
Director: Lindsay Anderson
Co-stars: Malcolm McDowell Arthur Lowe Rachel Roberts

1978 STEVIE
Director: Robert Enders
Co-stars: Glenda Jackson Trevor Howard Alex McCowen

1979 THE LONDON CONNECTION
Director: Robert Clouse
Co-stars: Jeffrey Byron Larry Cedar Roy Kinnear

1981 BRIDESHEAD REVISITED
Director: Charles Sturridge
Co-stars: Jeremy Irons Anthony Andrews Diana Quick

DINAH WASHINGTON

1959 JAZZ ON A SUMMER'S DAY
Director: Bert Stern
Co-stars: Louis Armstrong Chuck Berry Mahalia Jackson

FREDI WASHINGTON

1934 IMITATION OF LIFE
Director: John Stahl
Co-stars: Claudette Colbert Louise Beavers Warren William

1937 ONE MILE FROM HEAVEN
Director: Allan Dwan
Co-stars: Claire Trevor Sally Blane Douglas Fowley

IDA WATERMAN

1918 STELLA MARIS
Director: Marshall Neilan
Co-stars: Mary Pickford Conway Tearle Herbert Standing

FELICITY WATERMAN

1994 UNLAWFUL PASSAGE
Director: Camilo Vila
Co-stars: Lee Horsley William Zabka

JUANITA WATERMAN

1987 CRY FREEDOM
Director: Richard Attenborough
Co-stars: Kevin Kline Penelope Wilton Denzel Washington

CHERYL WATERS

1973 MACON COUNTY LINE
Director: Richard Compton
Co-stars: Alan Vint Geoffrey Lewis Joan Blackman

ELSIE AND DORIS WATERS
(Sisters Of Jack Warner)

1941 GERT AND DAISY'S WEEKEND
Director: Maclean Rogers
Co-stars: John Slater Iris Vandeleur Wally Patch

1942 GERT AND DAISY CLEAN UP
Director: Maclean Rogers
Co-stars: Iris Vandeleur Elizabeth Hunt Ralph Michael

ETHEL WATERS
Nominated For Best Supporting Actress In 1949 For Pinky

1929 ON WITH THE SHOW
Director: Alan Crosland
Co-stars: Betty Compson Louise Fazenda Joe E. Brown

1934 THE GIFT OF THE GAB
Director: Karl Freund
Co-stars: Edmund Lowe Gloria Stuart Ruth Etting

1942 CAIRO
Director: W.S. Van Dyke
Co-stars: Jeanette McDonald Robert Young Mona Barrie

1942 TALES OF MANHATTAN
Director: Julien Duvivier
Co-stars: Henry Fonda Charles Laughton Ginger Rogers

1943 STAGE DOOR CANTEEN
Director: Frank Borzage
Co-stars: Cheryl Walker Lon McCallister Judith Anderson

1943 CABIN IN THE SKY
Director: Vincente Minnelli
Co-stars: Eddie Anderson Lena Horne Louis Armstrong

1949 PINKY
Director: Elia Kazan
Co-stars: Jeanne Crain Ethel Barrymore William Lundigan

1952 THE MEMBER OF THE WEDDING
Director: Fred Zinnemann
Co-stars: Julie Harris Brandon De Wilde Nancy Gates

1959 THE SOUND AND THE FURY
Director: Martin Ritt
Co-stars: Yul Brynner Joanne Woodward Margaret Lockwood

MIRA WATERS

1969 THE LEARNING TREE
Director: Gordon Parks
Co-stars: Kyle Johnson Alex Clarke Estelle Evans

GWEN WATFORD

1950 THE FALL OF THE HOUSE OF USHER
Director: Ivan Barnett
Co-stars: Kay Tendeter Irving Steen

1960 NEVER TAKE SWEETS FROM A STRANGER
Director: Cyril Frankel
Co-stars: Patrick Allen Felix Aylmer Janina Faye

1970 TASTE THE BLOOD OF DRACULA
Director: Peter Sasdy
Co-stars: Christopher Lee Geoffrey Keen Peter Sallis

1975 IN THIS HOUSE OF BREDE
Director: George Schaefer
Co-stars: Diana Rigg Judi Bowker Pamela Brown

1975 THE GHOUL
Director: Freddie Francis
Co-stars: Peter Cushing Alexandra Bastedo John Hurt

1982 THE CASE OF THE MIDDLE-AGED WIFE

1989 BEHAVING BADLY
Director: David Tucker
Co-stars: Judi Dench Ronald Pickup Frances Barber

1992 MISS MARPLE: THE MIRROR CRACK'D SIDE TO SIDE
Director: Norman Stone
Co-stars: Joan Hickson Claire Bloom

CARLINE WATKINS

1983 TOUGH ENOUGH
Director: Richard Fleischer
Co-stars: Dennis Quaid Stan Shaw Pam Grier

LINDA WATKINS

1957 FROM HELL IT CAME
Director: Dan Milner
Co-stars: Tod Andrews Tina Carver

EVE WATKINSON

1988 REEFER AND THE MODEL
Director: Joe Comerford
Co-stars: Ian McElhinney Carol Scanlan Sean Lawlor

DEBBIE WATLING
(Daughter Of Jack Watling, Sister Of Dilys Watling)

1973 THAT'LL BE THE DAY
Director: Claude Whatham
Co-stars: David Essex Ringo Starr Rosemary Leach

1973 TAKE ME HIGH
Director: David Askey
Co-stars: Cliff Richard Hugh Griffith Anthony Andrews

DILYS WATLING *(Daughter Of Jack Watling, Sister Of Debbie Watling)*

1963 TWO LEFT FEET
Director: Roy Baker
Co-stars: Michael Crawford Julia Foster David Hemmings

1963 CALCULATED RISK
Director: Norman Harrison
Co-stars: William Lucas John Rutland Warren Mitchell

1967 OUCH !
Director: Gerard Bryant
Co-stars: Peter Butterworth Johnny Wade Garry Marsh

ALBERTA WATSON

1983 THE KEEP
Director: Michael Mann
Co-stars: Scott Glenn Jurgen Prochnow Gabriel Byrne

1986 WHITE OF THE EYE
Director: Donald Cammell
Co-stars: David Keith Cathy Moriarty Art Evans

1986 WOMEN OF VALOR
Director: Buzz Kulik
Co-stars: Susan Sarandon Kristy McNichol Suzanne Lederer

1989 SHANNON'S DEAL
Director: Lewis Teague
Co-stars: Jamey Sheridan Elizabeth Pena Jenny Lewis

1991 THE HITMAN
Director: Aaron Norris
Co-stars: Chuck Norris Michael Parks Al Waxman

1993 MIND OF A KILLER
Director: John Patterson
Co-stars: Tim Matheson Claudia Christian

DEBBIE WATSON

1967 THE COOL ONES
Director: Gene Nelson
Co-stars: Roddy McDowall Robert Coote Phil Harris

1967 TAMMY AND THE MILLIONAIRE
Director: Sidney Miller
Co-stars: Donald Woods Denver Pyle Dorothy Green

EMILY WATSON
Nominated For Best Supporting Actress In 1996 For "Breaking the Waves"

1996 BREAKING THE WAVES
Director: Lars Von Trier
Co-stars: Katrin Cartlidge Stellan Skarsgard

1997 THE MILL ON THE FLOSS
Director: Hugh Stoddart
Co-star: James Frain

1998 THE BOXER
Director: Jim Sheridan
Co-stars: Daniel Day-Lewis Brian Cox Ken Stott

JULIA WATSON

1991 THE YELLOW WALLPAPER
Director: John Clive

LUCILE WATSON
Nominated For Best Supporting Actress In 1943 For "Watch On The Rhine"

1934 WHAT EVERY WOMAN KNOWS
Director: Gregory La Cava
Co-stars: Helen Hayes Brian Aherne Madge Evans

1935 THE BISHOP MISBEHAVES
Director: E.A. Dupont
Co-stars: Edmund Gwenn Maureen O'Sullivan Reginald Owen

1936   A WOMAN REBELS
Director: Mark Sandrich
Co-stars: Katherine Hepburn Herbert Marshall Elizabeth Allan

1936   RHYTHM ON THE RANGE
Director: Norman Taurog
Co-stars: Bing Crosby Martha Raye Francer Farmer

1938   SWEETHEARTS
Director: W.S. Van Dyke
Co-stars: Jeanette MacDonald Nelson Eddy Ray Bolger

1938   MADE FOR EACH OTHER
Director: John Cromwell
Co-stars: Carole Lombard James Stewart Charles Coburn

1939   THE WOMEN
Director: George Cukor
Co-stars: Norma Shearer Joan Crawford Rosalind Russell

1940   WATERLOO BRIDGE
Director: Mervyn LeRoy
Co-stars: Vivien Leigh Robert Taylor Virginia Field

1940   FLORIAN
Director: Edwin Marin
Co-stars: Robert Young Helen Gilbert Charles Coburn

1941   FOOTSTEPS IN THE DARK
Director: Lloyd Bacon
Co-stars: Errol Flynn Brenda Marshall Ralph Bellamy

1941   THE GREAT LIE
Director: Edmund Goulding
Co-stars: Bette Davis Mary Astor George Brent

1941   MR AND MRS SMITH
Director: Alfred Hitchcock
Co-stars: Carole Lombard Robert Montgomery Jack Carson

1941   RAGE IN HEAVEN
Director: W.S. Van Dyke
Co-stars: Robert Montgomery Ingrid Bergman George Sanders

1943   WATCH ON THE RHINE
Director: Herman Shumlin
Co-stars: Bette Davis Paul Lukas Geraldine Fitzgerald

1944   UNCERTAIN GLORY
Director: Raoul Walsh
Co-stars: Errol Flynn Paul Lukas Jean Sullivan

1944   THE THIN MAN GOES HOME
Director: Richard Thorpe
Co-stars: William Powell Myrna Loy Gloria De Haven

1944   TILL WE MEET AGAIN
Director: Frank Borzage
Co-stars: Ray Milland Barbara Britton Mona Freeman

1945   TOMORROW IS FOREVER
Director: Irving Pichel
Co-stars: Orson Welles Claudette Colbert Natalie Wood

1946   SONG OF THE SOUTH
Director: Wilfred Jackson
Co-stars: James Baskett Bobby Driscoll Luana Patten

1946   THE RAZOR'S EDGE
Director: Edmund Goulding
Co-stars: Tyrone Power Gene Tierney Anne Baxter

1946   NEVER SAY GOODBYE
Director: James Kern
Co-stars: Errol Flynn Eleanor Parker S.Z. Sakall

1946   MY REPUTATION
Director: Curtis Bernhardt
Co-stars: Barbara Stanwyck George Brent Eve Arden

1947   IVY
Director: Sam Wood
Co-stars: Joan Fontaine Herbert Marshall Patric Knowles

1948   JULIA MISBEHAVES
Director: Jack Conway
Co-stars: Greer Garson Walter Pidgeon Elizabeth Taylor

1948   THE EMPEROR WALTZ
Director: Billy Wilder
Co-stars: Bing Crosby Joan Fontaine Richard Haydn

1948   THAT WONDERFUL URGE
Director: Robert Sinclair
Co-stars: Tyrone Power Gene Tierney Reginald Gardiner

1949   EVERYBODY DOES IT
Director: Edmund Goulding
Co-stars: Paul Douglas Linda Darnell Celeste Holm

1950   HARRIET CRAIG
Director: Vincent Sherman
Co-stars: Joan Crawford Wendell Cory Allyn Joslyn

1950   LET'S DANCE
Director: Norman Z. McLeod
Co-stars: Fred Astaire Betty Hutton Roland Young

1951   MY FORBIDDEN PAST
Director: Robert Stevenson
Co-stars: Ava Gardner Robert Mitchum Melvyn Douglas

VERNEE WATSON

1981   THE VIOLATION OF SARAH McDAVID
Director: John Llewellyn Moxey
Co-stars: Patty Duke Ned Beatty Ally Sheedy

DODO WATTS

1930   THE MIDDLE WATCH
Director: Norman Walker
Co-stars: Owen Nares Jacqueline Logan Jack Raine

JEANNE WATTS

1970   THE THREE SISTERS
Director: Laurence Olivier
Co-stars: Laurence Olivier Joan Plowright Alan Bates

NAOMI WATTS

1991   FLIRTING
Director: John Duigan
Co-stars: Noah Taylor Thandie Newton Nicole Kidman

1997   PERSONS UNKNOWN
Director: George Hickenlooper
Co-stars: Joe Mantegna Kelly Lynch J.T. Walsh

QUEENIE WATTS

1967   POOR COW
Director: Ken Loach
Co-stars: Carol White Terence Stamp Kate Williams

1972   ALL COPPERS ARE
Director: Sidney Hayers
Co-stars: Nicky Henson Julia Foster Martin Potter

VICKIE WAUCHOPE (Victoria)

1987   BLUFFING IT
Director: James Sadwith
Co-stars: Dennis Weaver Janet Carroll Michelle Little

1987   LENA: MY 100 CHILDREN
Director: Ed Sherin
Co-stars: Linda Lavin Leonore Harris Cynthia Wilde

1989   LOVE AND HATE
Director: Francis Mankiewicz
Co-stars: Kenneth Welsh Kate Nelligan John Colicos

EILEEN WAY

1958 THE VIKINGS
Director: Richard Fleischer
Co-stars: Kirk Douglas Tony Curtis Ernest Borgnine

1986 NAMING THE NAMES
Director: Stuart Burge
Co-stars: Sylvestra Le Touzel Michael Maloney James Ellis

1989 QUEEN OF HEARTS
Director: Jon Amiel
Co-stars: Vittorio Duse Joseph Long Anita Zagaria

RUBY WAX

1981 CHARIOTS OF FIRE
Director: Hugh Hudson
Co-stars: Ben Cross Ian Charleson Nigel Havers

1981 SHOCK TREATMENT
Director: Jim Sharman
Co-stars: Jessica Harper Cliff De Young Richard O'Brien

1985 ROMANCE ON THE ORIENT EXPRESS
Director: Lawrence Gordon Clark
Co-stars: Cheryl Ladd Stuart Wilson

1987 THE SECRET POLICEMAN'S THIRD BALL
Director: Ken O'Neill
Co-stars: Lenny Henry Robbie Coltrane

1996 THE BORROWERS
Co-stars: John Goodman Jim Broadbent Celia Imrie

KRISTINA WAYBORN

1983 OCTOPUSSY
Director: John Glen
Co-stars: Roger Moore Maud Adams Louis Jourdan

ALISSA WAYNE *(Daughter Of John Wayne)*

1960 THE ALAMO
Director: John Wayne
Co-stars: John Wayne Richard Widmark Laurence Harvey

CAROL WAYNE

1984 HEARTBREAKERS
Director: Bobby Roth
Co-stars: Peter Coyote Nick Mancuso Carol Laure

NINA WAYNE

1966 DEAD HEAT ON A MERRY-GO-ROUND
Director: Bernard Girard
Co-stars: James Coburn Camilla Sparv Aldo Ray

1967 LUV
Director: Clive Donner
Co-stars: Jack Lemmon Peter Falk Elaine May

NORMA JEAN WAYNE

1942 BLONDIE'S BLESSED HEART
Director: Frank Strayer
Co-stars: Penny Singleton Arthur Lake Mary Wickes

PATRICIA WAYNE

1951 THE LONG DARK HALL
Director: Anthony Bushell
Co-stars: Rex Harrison Lilli Palmer Raymond Huntley

DOODLES WEAVER

1961 LADIES' MAN
Director: Jerry Lewis
Co-stars: Jerry Lewis Helen Traubel Gloria Jean

JACKI WEAVER

1973 ALVIN PURPLE
Director: Tim Burstall
Co-stars: Graeme Blundell Lynette Curran Dina Mann

1974 PETERSEN
Director: Tim Burstall
Co-stars: Jack Thompson Amanda Hunt George Mallaby

1975 PICNIC AT HANGING ROCK
Director: Peter Weir
Co-stars: Rachel Roberts Dominic Guard Helen Morse

1978 CADDIE
Director: Donald Crombie
Co-stars: Helen Morse Jack Thompson Takis Emmanuel

1986 THE PERFECTIONIST
Director: Chris Thomson
Co-stars: John Waters Noel Ferrier

MARJORIE WEAVER

1937 SECOND HONEYMOON
Director: Walter Lang
Co-stars: Tyrone Power Loretta Young Claire Trevor

1937 THIS IS MY AFFAIR
Director: William Seiter
Co-stars: Robert Taylor Barbara Stanwyck Victor McLaglen

1937 THE CALIFORNIANS
Co-star: Ricardo Cortez

1938 THREE BLIND MICE
Director: William Seiter
Co-stars: Loretta Young Joel McCrea Binnie Barnes

1938 SALLY, IRENE AND MARY
Director: William Seiter
Co-stars: Alice Faye Tony Martin Joan Davis

1938 KENTUCKY MOONSHINE
Director: David Butler
Co-stars: Ritz Brothers Tony Martin John Carradine

1938 I'LL GIVE A MILLION
Director: Walter Lang
Co-stars: Warner Baxter Peter Lorre John Carradine

1938 HOLD THAT CO-ED
Director: George Marshall
Co-stars: John Barrymore Jack Haley Joan Davis

1939 THE CHICKEN WAGON FAMILY
Director: Herbert Leeds
Co-stars: Jane Withers Leo Carrillo Spring Byington

1939 YOUNG MR LINCOLN
Director: John Ford
Co-stars: Henry Fonda Alice Brady Arleen Whelan

1939 THE HONEYMOON'S OVER
Co-star: Stuart Erwin

1940 MICHAEL SHAYNE, PRIVATE DETECTIVE
Director: Eugene Forde
Co-stars: Lloyd Nolan Walter Abel Donald McBride

1940 MURDER OVER NEW YORK
Director: Harry Lachman
Co-stars: Sidney Toler Robert Lowry Ricardo Cortez

1941 MURDER AMONG FRIENDS
Director: Ray McCarey
Co-stars: John Hubbard Mona Barrie Cobina Wright Jnr.

1941 MAN AT LARGE
Co-star: George Reeves

1941 DRESSED TO KILL
Director: Eugene Forde
Co-star: Lloyd Nolan

1941	**BLUE, WHITE AND PERFECT**
Director:	Herberts Leeds
Co-star:	Lloyd Nolan

1941	**SLEEPERS WEST**
Director:	Eugene Forde
Co-star:	Lloyd Nolan

1942	**JUST OFF BROADWAY**
Director:	Herbert Leeds
Co-stars:	Lloyd Nolan Phil Silvers Janis Carter

1942	**TIME TO KILL**
Director:	Herbert Leeds
Co-star:	Lloyd Nolan

1942	**THE MAN WHO WOULDN'T DIE**
Director:	Herbert Leeds
Co-star:	Lloyd Nolan

1944	**YOU CAN'T RATION LOVE**
Director:	Lester Fuller
Co-stars:	Betty Jane Rhodes Johnnie Johnston Marie Wilson

1944	**PARDON MY RHYTHM**
Director:	Felix Feist
Co-stars:	Gloria Jean Mel Torme Evelyn Ankers

1944	**SHADOW OF SUSPICION**
Co-star:	Peter Cookson

SIGOURNEY WEAVER (*Susan Weaver*)

Nominated For Best Actress In 1986 For "Aliens" And In 1988 For "Gorillas In The Mist". Nominated For Best Supporting Actress In 1988 For "Working Girl"

1977	**ANNIE HALL**
Director:	Woody Allen
Co-stars:	Woody Allen Diane Keaton Tony Roberts

1979	**ALIEN**
Director:	Ridley Scott
Co-stars:	John Hurt Tom Skerritt Harry Dean Stanton

1981	**EYEWITNESS**
Director:	Peter Yates
Co-stars:	William Hurt Christopher Plummer James Woods

1982	**THE YEAR OF LIVING DANGEROUSLY**
Director:	Peter Weir
Co-stars:	Mel Gibson Linda Hunt Bill Kerr

1983	**DEAL OF THE CENTURY**
Director:	William Friedkin
Co-stars:	Chevy Chase Gregory Hines Vince Edwards

1984	**GHOSTBUSTERS**
Director:	Ivan Reitman
Co-stars:	Bill Murray Dan Aykroyd Rick Moranis

1985	**UNE FEMME OU DEUX**
Director:	Daniel Vigne
Co-stars:	Gerard Depardieu Dr Ruth Westheimer Zabou

1986	**ALIENS**
Director:	James Cameron
Co-stars:	Carrie Henn Michael Biehn Bill Paxton

1986	**HALF MOON STREET**
Director:	Bob Swaim
Co-stars:	Michael Caine Patrick Cavanaugh Keith Buckley

1988	**GORILLAS IN THE MIST**
Director:	Michael Apted
Co-stars:	Bryan Brown Julie Harris Ian Cuthbertson

1988	**WORKING GIRL**
Director:	Mike Nichols
Co-stars:	Melanie Griffith Harrison Ford Alec Baldwin

1989	**GHOSTBUSTERS II**
Director:	Ivan Reitman
Co-stars:	Bill Murray Dan Aykroyd Annie Potts

1992	**ALIEN 3**
Director:	David Fincher
Co-stars:	Charles Dance Brian Glover Paul McGann

1992	**1492: CONQUEST OF PARADISE**
Director:	Ridley Scott
Co-stars:	Gerard Depardieu Fernando Rey Armand Assante

1993	**DAVE**
Director:	Ivan Reitman
Co-stars:	Kevin Kline Frank Langella Ben Kingsley

1994	**DEATH AND THE MAIDEN**
Director:	Roman Polanski
Co-stars:	Ben Kingsley Stuart Wilson

1995	**JEFFREY**
Co-stars:	Steven Webber Michael T. Weiss Patrick Stewart

1996	**COPYCAT**
Director:	Jon Amiel
Co-stars:	Holly Hunter Harry Connick Jnr. Will Paton

1997	**SNOW WHITE: A TALE OF TERROR**
Director:	Michael Cohn
Co-star:	Monica Keena

1997	**ALIEN RESURRECTION**
Director:	Jean-Pierre Jeunet
Co-star:	Winona Ryder

1998	**THE ICE STORM**
Director:	Ang Lee
Co-stars:	Kevin Kline Christina Ricci Joan Allen

CHLOE WEBB

1986	**SID AND NANCY**
Director:	Alex Cox
Co-stars:	Gary Oldman David Hayman Debby Bishop

1987	**THE BELLY OF AN ARCHITECT**
Director:	Peter Greenaway
Co-stars:	Brian Dennehy Lambert Wilson

1988	**TWINS**
Director:	Ivan Reitman
Co-stars:	Arnold Schwarzenegger Danny De Vito Kelly Preston

1990	**HEART CONDITION**
Director:	James Parriott
Co-stars:	Bob Hoskins Denzel Washington Jeffrey Meek

1993	**A DANGEROUS WOMAN**
Director:	Stephen Gyllenhaal
Co-stars:	Debra Winger Gabriel Byrne Barbara Hershey

JANET WEBB

1976	**THE AMOROUS MILKMAN**
Director:	Derren Nesbitt
Co-stars:	Brendan Price Julie Ege Diana Dors

JULIE WEBB

1971	**BILLY JACK**
Director:	Tom Laughlin
Co-stars:	Tom Laughlin Delores Taylor Bert Freed

RITA WEBB

1959	**THE BOY AND THE BRIDGE**
Director:	Kevin McGlory
Co-stars:	Ian MacLaine Liam Redmond James Hayter

1970	**UP POMPEII**
Director:	Bob Kellett
Co-stars:	Frankie Howerd Patrick Cargill Barbara Murray

1970	**PERCY**
Director:	Ralph Thomas
Co-stars:	Hywel Bennett Denholm Elliott Cyd Hayman

SARAH WEBB

1975 MR QUILP
Director: Michael Tuchner
Co-stars: Anthony Newley David Hemmings Jill Bennett

PEGGY WEBBER

1948 MACBETH
Director: Orson Welles
Co-stars: Orson Welles Jeanette Nolan Dan O'Herlihy

1951 SUBMARINE COMMAND
Director: John Farrow
Co-stars: William Holden Nancy Olsen Don Taylor

1958 THE SPACE CHILDREN
Director: Jack Arnold
Co-stars: Adam Williams Michel Ray Jackie Coogan

SABINE WEBER

1990 THE GRAVY TRAIN
Director: David Tucker
Co-stars: Ian Richardson Christoph Waltz Judy Parfitt

SUZANNE WEBER

1982 COLD RIVER
Director: Fred Sullivan
Co-star: Pat Petersen

JOY WEBSTER

1961 DURING ONE NIGHT
Director: Sidney Furie
Co-stars: Susan Hampshire Don Borisenko Sean Sullivan

LEILA WEBSTER

1986 NAMING THE NAMES
Director: Stuart Burge
Co-stars: Sylvestra La Touzel Michael Maloney James Ellis

MARY WEBSTER

1957 THE TIN STAR
Director: Anthony Mann
Co-stars: Henry Fonda Anthony Perkins Betsy Palmer

1961 MASTER OF THE WORLD
Director: William Witney
Co-stars: Vincent Price Charles Bronson Henry Hull

ANN WEDGEWORTH

1973 SCARECROW
Director: Jerry Schatzberg
Co-stars: Gene Hackman Al Pacino Eileen Brennan

1973 BANG THE DRUM SLOWLY
Director: John Hancock
Co-stars: Michael Moriarty Robert De Niro Vincent Gardenia

1974 LAW AND DISORDER
Director: Ivan Passer
Co-stars: Ernest Borgnine Carroll O'Connor Karen Black

1977 CITIZENS' BAND
Director: Jonathan Demme
Co-stars: Paul LeMat Candy Clark Marcia Rodd

1977 BIRCH INTERVAL
Director: Delbert Mann
Co-stars: Eddie Albert Rip Torn Susan McClung

1980 BOGIE
Director: Vincent Sherman
Co-stars: Kevin O'Connor Kathryn Harrold Drew Barrymore

1984 NO SMALL AFFAIR
Director: Jerry Schatzberg
Co-stars: Jon Cryer Demi Moore George Wendt

1985 RIGHT TO KILL?
Director: John Erman
Co-stars: Frederic Forrest Christopher Collet Justine Bateman

1985 SWEET DREAMS
Director: Karel Reisz
Co-stars: Jessica Lange Ed Harris David Clennon

1987 A STRANGER WAITS
Director: Robert Lewis
Co-stars: Suzanne Pleshette Tom Atkins Paul Benjamin

1987 MADE IN HEAVEN
Director: Alan Rudolph
Co-stars: Timothy Hutton Kelly McGillis

1987 A TIGER'S TALE
Director: Peter Douglas
Co-stars: Ann-Margret C. Thomas Howell Kelly Preston

1988 FAR NORTH
Director: Sam Shepard
Co-stars: Jessica Lange Tess Harper Charles Durning

1989 MISS FIRECRACKER
Director: Thomas Schlamme
Co-stars: Holly Hunter Mary Steenburgen Tim Robbins

1989 STEEL MAGNOLIAS
Director: Herbert Ross
Co-stars: Sally Field Julia Roberts Dolly Parton

1991 HARD PROMISES
Director: Martin Davidson
Co-stars: Sissy Spacek William Petersen Mare Winningham

BARBARA WEEKS

1931 PALMY DAYS
Director: Edward Sutherland
Co-stars: Eddie Cantor Charlotte Greenwood George Raft

1932 BY WHOSE HAND ?
Director: Ben Stoloff
Co-stars: Ben Lyon Kenneth Thomson Tom Dugan

ANOJA WEERASINGHE

1989 ISLAND
Director: Paul Cox
Co-stars: Irene Papas Eva Sitta Chris Haywood

VIRGINIA WEIDLER *(Child)*

1934 MRS WIGGS OF THE CABBAGE PATCH
Director: Norman Taurog
Co-stars: Pauline Lord Zasu Pitts

1935 PETER IBBETSON
Director: Henry Hathaway
Co-stars: Gary Cooper Ann Harding John Halliday

1935 THE BIG BROADCAST OF 1936
Director: Ben Glazer
Co-stars: Bing Crosby Ethel Merman George Burns

1935 FRECKLES
Director: Edward Killy
Co-stars: Tom Brown Carol Stone Lunsden Hare

1936 GIRL OF THE OZARKS
Co-star: Leif Erikson

1937 SOULS AT SEA
Director: Henry Hathaway
Co-stars: Gary Cooper George Raft Frances Dee

1937 SCANDAL SHEET
Director: James Hogan
Co-stars: Lew Ayres Louise Campbell Roscoe Karns

1938 MOTHER CAREY'S CHICKENS
Director: Rowland Lee
Co-stars: Anne Shirley Ruby Keeler Walter Brennan

1938   TOO HOT TO HANDLE
Director: Jack Conway
Co-stars: Clark Gable Myrna Loy Walter Pidgeon

1938   LOVE IS A HEADACHE
Director: Richard Thorpe
Co-stars: Franchot Tone Gladys George Mickey Rooney

1938   MEN WITH WINGS
Director: William Wellman
Co-stars: Fred MacMurray Ray Milland Louise Campbell

1938   THE GREAT MAN VOTES
Director: Garson Kanin
Co-stars: John Barrymore William Demarest Donald MacBride

1939   BAD LITTLE ANGEL
Director: William Thiele
Co-stars: Guy Kibbee Gene Reynolds Ian Hunter

1939   THE WOMEN
Director: George Cukor
Co-stars: Norma Shearer Joan Crawford Rosalind Russell

1939   THE LONE WOLF SPY HUNT
Director: Peter Godfrey
Co-stars: Warren William Ida Lupino Rita Hayworth

1939   THE UNDERPUP
Director: Richard Wallace
Co-stars: Gloria Jean Robert Cummings Nan Grey

1940   YOUNG TOM EDISON
Director: Norman Taurog
Co-stars: Mickey Rooney Eugene Pallette George Bancroft

1940   THE PHILADELPHIA STORY
Director: George Cukor
Co-stars: Katherine Hepburn Cary Grant James Stewart

1940   KEEPING COMPANY
Director: S. Sylvan Simon
Co-stars: Frank Morgan Irene Rich Dan Dailey

1940   GOLD RUSH MAISIE
Director: Edwin Marin
Co-stars: Ann Sothern Lee Bowman Slim Summerville

1940   ALL THIS AND HEAVEN TOO
Director: Anatole Litvak
Co-stars: Charles Boyer Bette Davis Barbara O'Neill

1941   BABES ON BROADWAY
Director: Busby Berkeley
Co-stars: Judy Garland Mickey Rooney Ray MacDonald

1941   BARNACLE BILL
Director: Richard Thorpe
Co-stars: Wallace Beery Marjorie Main Leo Carrillo

1941   BORN TO SING
Director: Edward Ludwig
Co-stars: Larry Nunn Leo Gorcey Ray MacDonald

1942   THE AFFAIRS OF MARTHA
Director: Jules Dassin
Co-stars: Marsha Hunt Richard Carlson Spring Byington

1942   THE BIG STREET
Director: Irving Reis
Co-stars: Henry Fonda Lucille Ball Eugene Pallette

1943   THE YOUNGEST PROFESSION
Director: Edward Buzzell
Co-stars: Jean Porter Edward Arnold John Carroll

ISABELLE WEINGARTEN

1982   THE STATE OF THINGS
Director: Wim Wenders
Co-stars: Rebecca Pauly Patrick Bauchau Samuel Fuller

CINDY WEINTRAUB

1980   HUMANOIDS FROM THE DEEP
Director: Barbara Peeters
Co-stars: Vic Morrow Doug McClure Ann Turkel

REBECCA WEINTRAUB

1939   TEVYA THE MILKMAN
Director: Maurice Schwarz
Co-stars: Maurice Schwarz Miriam Riselle Paula Lubelski

ARABELLA WEIR

1985   BLOOD HUNT
Director: Peter Barber-Fleming
Co-stars: Andrew Keir Iain Glen Nigel Stock

1986   HONEST, DECENT AND TRUE
Director: Les Blair
Co-stars: Derrick O'Connor Yvonne French Richard E. Grant

MOLLY WEIR

1953   FORCES' SWEETHEART
Director: Maclean Rogers
Co-stars: Hy Hazell Harry Secombe Michael Bentine

1954   LIFE WITH THE LYONS
Director: Val Guest
Co-stars: Bebe Daniels Ben Lyon Barbara Lyon

1959   THE BRIDAL PATH
Director: Frank Launder
Co-stars: Bill Travers George Cole Patricia Bredin

1973   ASSASSIN
Director: Peter Crane
Co-stars: Ian Hendry Edward Judd Ray Brooks

HEIDELINDE WEIS

1970   SOMETHING FOR EVERYONE
Director: Harold Prince
Co-stars: Angela Lansbury Michael York Anthony Corlan

ROBIN WEISMAN (Child)

1990   THREE MEN AND A LITTLE LADY
Director: Emile Ardolino
Co-stars: Tom Selleck Steve Guttenberg Ted Danson

ROBERTA WEISS

1985   ABDUCTED
Director: Boon Collins
Co-stars: Dan Haggerty William Nunn Steven Miller

RACHEL WEISZ

1992   THE ADVOCATES: ABOVE THE LAW
Director: Peter Barber-Fleming
Co-stars: Isla Blair Ewan Stewart Michael Kitchen

1996   STEALING BEAUTY
Director: Bernardo Bertolucci
Co-stars: Liv Tyler Sinead Cusack Jeffrey Irons

1996   CHAIN REACTION
Co-stars: Keanu Reeves Morgan Freeman Brian Cox

1997   LAND GIRLS
Director: David Leland
Co-stars: Catherine McCormack Anna Friel Steven MacKintosh

1998   GOING ALL THE WAY
Co-stars: Ben Affleck Jeremy Davies

1998   AMY FOSTER
Director: Beeban Kidron
Co-stars: Vincent Perez Zoe Wanamaker

ELIZABETH WELCH

1936   SONG OF FREEDOM
Director: J. Elder Wills
Co-stars: Paul Robeson George Mosart Esme Percy

1937   BIG FELLA
Director: J. Elder Wills
Co-stars: Paul Robeson Roy Emerton Marcelle Rogez

1942   ALIBI
Director: Brian Desmond Hurst
Co-stars: Margaret Lockwood Hugh Sinclair James Mason

1944   FIDDLERS THREE
Director: Harry Watt
Co-stars: Tommy Trinder Sonnie Hale Diana Decker

1945   DEAD OF NIGHT
Director: Alberto Cavalcanti
Co-stars: Mervyn Johns Googie Withers Sally Ann Howes

1971   GIRL STROKE BOY
Director: Bob Kellett
Co-stars: Joan Greenwood Michael Hordern Patricia Routledge

1979   ARABIAN ADVENTURE
Director: Kevin Connor
Co-stars: Christopher Lee Oliver Tobias Mickey Rooney

1980   THE TEMPEST
Director: Derek Jarman
Co-stars: Heathcote Williams Toyah Wilcox Karl Johnson

JOAN KEMP WELCH

1942   HARD STEEL
Director: Norman Walker
Co-stars: Wilfrid Lawson Betty Stockfield John Stuart

MARY WELCH

1952   PARK ROW
Director: Samuel Fuller
Co-stars: Gene Evans Herbert Hayes Forrest Taylor

PHYLLIS WELCH

1939   PROFESSOR BEWARE
Director: Elliott Nugent
Co-stars: Harold Lloyd Raymond Walburn Lionel Stander

RAQUEL WELCH

1964   ROUSTABOUT
Director: John Rich
Co-stars: Elvis Presley Barbara Stanwyck

1964   A HOUSE IS NOT A HOME
Director: Russel Rouse
Co-stars: Shelley Winters Robert Taylor Cesar Romero

1966   ONE MILLION YEARS B.C.
Director: Don Chaffey
Co-stars: John Richardson Robert Brown Martine Beswick

1966   FANTASTIC VOYAGE
Director: Richard Fleischer
Co-stars: Stephen Boyd Edmond O'Brien

1967   FATHOM
Director: Leslie Martinson
Co-stars: Tony Franciosa Clive Revell Greta Chi

1967   THE BIGGEST BUNDLE OF THEM ALL
Director: Ken Annakin
Co-stars: Edward G. Robinson Robert Wagner

1967   BEDAZZLED
Director: Stanley Donen
Co-stars: Peter Cook Dudley Moore Barry Humphries

1967   THE OLDEST PROFESSION
Director: Jean-Luc Godard
Co-stars: Elsa Martinelli Jeanne Moreau Anna Karen

1968   LADY IN CEMENT
Director: Gordon Douglas
Co-stars: Frank Sinatra Richard Conte Dan Blocker

1968   BANDOLERO
Director: Andrew McLaglen
Co-stars: James Stewart Dean Martin George Kennedy

1969   FLARE UP
Director: James Neilson
Co-stars: James Stacy Luke Askew Don Chastain

1969   THE MAGIC CHRISTIAN
Director: Joseph McGrath
Co-stars: Peter Sellers Ringo Starr Laurence Harvey

1969   ONE HUNDRED RIFLES
Director: Tom Gries
Co-stars: Jim Brown Burt Reynolds Fernando Lamas

1970   MYRA BRECKINRIDGE
Director: Mike Sarne
Co-stars: Mae West John Huston Jim Backus

1971   HANNIE CAULDER
Director: Burt Kennedy
Co-stars: Robert Culp Ernest Borgnine Diana Dors

1972   KANSAS CITY BOMBER
Director: Jerold Freedman
Co-stars: Kevin McCarthy Norman Alden Jody Foster

1972   SIN
Co-star: Richard Johnson

1972   FUZZ
Director: Richard Colla
Co-stars: Burt Reynolds Jack Weston Tom Skerritt

1972   BLUEBEARD
Director: Edward Dmytryk
Co-stars: Richard Burton Joey Heatherton Virna Lisi

1973   THE LAST OF SHEILA
Director: Herbert Ross
Co-stars: Richard Benjamin James Coburn Dyan Cannon

**1973   THE THREE MUSKETEERS:
THE QUEEN'S DIAMONDS**
Director: Richard Lester
Co-stars: Oliver Reed Michael York Frank Finlay

1974   THE FOUR MUSKETEERS
Director: Richard Lester
Co-stars: Richard Chamberlain Frank Finlay Simon Ward

1975   THE WILD PARTY
Director: James Ivory
Co-stars: James Coco Perry King Tiffany Bolling

1976   MOTHER, JUGS AND SPEED
Director: Peter Yates
Co-stars: Bill Cosby Harvey Keitel Larry Hagman

1978   THE PRINCE AND THE PAUPER
Director: Richard Fleischer
Co-stars: Mark Lester Oliver Reed Rex Harrison

1982   THE LEGEND OF WALKS FAR WOMAN
Director: Mel Damski
Co-stars: Bradford Dillman George Clutesi Nick Ramos

1988   RIGHT TO DIE
Director: Paul Wendkos
Co-stars: Michael Gross Bonnie Bartlett Joanna Miles

1988   SCANDAL IN A SMALL TOWN
Director: Anthony Page
Co-stars: Christa Denton Francis Lee McCain

1989	**TROUBLE IN PARADISE**
1992	**TAINTED BLUE**
1993	**NAKED GUN 33 1/3: THE FINAL INSULT**

Director: Peter Segal
Co-stars: Leslie Nielsen Priscilla Presley O.J. Simpson

| 1993 | **TORCH SONG** |

Director: Michael Miller

TAHNEE WELCH *(Daughter Of Raquel Welch)*

| 1985 | **COCOON** |

Director: Ron Howard
Co-stars: Don Ameche Hume Cronyn Steven Guttenberg

GERTRUDE WELCKER

| 1922 | **DOCTOR MABUSE THE GAMBLER** |

Director: Fritz Lang
Co-stars: Rudolph Klein-Roger Alfred Abel Lil Dagover

JOSEPHINE WELCOME

| 1990 | **AMONGST BARBARIANS** |

Director: Jane Howell
Co-stars: David Jason Rowena Cooper Kathy Burke

TUESDAY WELD *(Child)*

Nominated For Best Supporting Actress In 1977 For "Looking For Mr Goodbar"

| 1956 | **ROCK, ROCK, ROCK !** |

Director: Will Price
Co-stars: Terry Randazzo Alan Freed Chuck Berry

| 1958 | **RALLY ROUND THE FLAG BOYS** |

Director: Leo McCarey
Co-stars: Paul Newman Joanne Woodward Joan Collins

| 1959 | **THE FIVE PENNIES** |

Director: Melville Shavelson
Co-stars: Danny Kaye Barbara Bel Geddes

| 1960 | **BECAUSE THEY'RE YOUNG** |

Director: Paul Wendkos
Co-stars: Dick Clark Doug McClure James Darren

| 1960 | **HIGH TIME** |

Director: Blake Edwards
Co-stars: Bing Crosby Fabian Richard Beymer

| 1961 | **BACHELOR FLAT** |

Director: Frank Tashlin
Co-stars: Terry-Thomas Richard Beymer Celeste Holm

| 1961 | **RETURN TO PEYTON PLACE** |

Director: Jose Ferrer
Co-stars: Jeff Chandler Carol Lynley Eleanor Parker

| 1961 | **WILD IN THE COUNTRY** |

Director: Philip Dunne
Co-stars: Elvis Presley Hope Lange Millie Perkins

| 1963 | **SOLDIER IN THE RAIN** |

Director: Ralph Nelson
Co-stars: Jackie Gleason Steve McQueen Tony Bill

| 1965 | **I'LL TAKE SWEDEN** |

Director: Frederick De Cordova
Co-stars: Bob Hope Frankie Avalon Dina Merril

| 1965 | **THE CINCINNATI KID** |

Director: Norman Jewison
Co-stars: Steve McQueen Edward G. Robinson Karl Malden

| 1966 | **LORD LUV A DUCK** |

Director: George Axelrod
Co-stars: Roddy McDowall Lola Albright Ruth Gordon

| 1968 | **PRETTY POISON** |

Director: Noel Black
Co-stars: Anthony Perkins Beverley Garland John Randolph

| 1970 | **I WALK THE LINE** |

Director: John Frankenheimer
Co-stars: Gregory Peck Johnny Cash Ralph Meeker

| 1971 | **A SAFE PLACE** |

Director: Henry Jaglom
Co-stars: Orson Welles Gwen Welles Jack Nicholson

| 1972 | **PLAY IT AS IT LAYS** |

Director: Frank Perry
Co-stars: Anthony Perkins Tammy Grimes Ruth Ford

| 1976 | **F. SCOTT FITZGERALD IN HOLLYWOOD** |

Director: Anthony Page
Co-stars: Jason Miller Julia Foster Michael Learner

| 1977 | **LOOKING FOR MR GOODBAR** |

Director: Richard Brooks
Co-stars: Diane Keaton William Atherton Richard Gere

| 1978 | **DOG SOLDIERS** |

Director: Karel Reisz
Co-stars: Nick Nolte Michael Moriarty Anthony Zerbe

| 1980 | **SERIAL** |

Director: Bill Persky
Co-stars: Martin Mull Sally Kellerman Christopher Lee

| 1981 | **THIEF** |

Director: Michael Mann
Co-stars: James Caan Willie Nelson James Belushi

| 1981 | **LADY X** |

| 1982 | **AUTHOR! AUTHOR!** |

Director: Arthur Hiller
Co-stars: Al Pacino Dyan Cannon Bob Dishey

| 1984 | **ONCE UPON A TIME IN AMERICA** |

Director: Sergio Leone
Co-stars: Robert De Niro James Woods Joe Pesci

| 1988 | **HEARTBREAK HOTEL** |

Director: Chris Columbus
Co-stars: David Keith Charlie Schlatter

| 1992 | **FALLING DOWN** |

Director: Joel Schumacher
Co-stars: Michael Douglas Robert Duvall Barbara Hershey

ANN WELDON

| 1993 | **OUT OF DARKNESS** |

Director: Larry Elikann
Co-stars: Diana Ross Lindsay Crouse Beah Richards

JOAN WELDON

| 1953 | **THE SYSTEM** |

Director: Lewis Seiler
Co-stars: Frank Lovejoy Bob Arthur Don Beddoe

| 1953 | **STRANGER WORE A GUN** |

Director: Andre De Toth
Co-stars: Randolph Scott Claire Trevor George Macready

| 1953 | **SO THIS IS LOVE** |

Director: Gordon Douglas
Co-stars: Kathryn Grayson Merv Griffin Walter Abel

| 1954 | **THEM !** |

Director: Gordon Douglas
Co-stars: James Whitmore Edmund Gwenn James Arness

| 1954 | **RIDING SHOTGUN** |

Director: Andre De Toth
Co-stars: Randolph Scott Wayne Morris Charles Bronson

| 1954 | **DEEP IN MY HEART** |

Director: Stanley Donen
Co-stars: Jose Ferrer Merle Oberon Paul Henreid

1954 **THE COMMAND**
Director: David Butler
Co-stars: Guy Madison James Whitmore Ray Teal

1957 **DAY OF THE BADMEN**
Director: Harry Keller
Co-stars: Fred MacMurray John Ericson Marie Windsor

MARION WELDON

1937 **DODGE CITY TRAIL**
Co-star: Charles Starrett

1937 **KNIGHT OF THE PLAINS**
Co-star: Fred Scott

NANCY WELFORD

1929 **GOLD DIGGERS OF BROADWAY**
Director: Roy Del Ruth
Co-stars: Conway Tearle Winnie Lightner Lilyan Tashman

MARY LOUISE WELLER

1978 **HUNTERS OF THE REEF**
Director: Alex Singer
Co-stars: Michael Parks William Windom Steve Macht

1978 **NATIONAL LAMPOON'S ANIMAL HOUSE**
Director: John Landis
Co-stars: John Belushi Tim Matheson Tom Hulce

1980 **ONCE UPON A SPY**
Director: Ivan Nagy
Co-stars: Ted Danson Christopher Lee Eleanor Parker

GWEN WELLES

1971 **A SAFE PLACE**
Director: Henry Jaglom
Co-stars: Tuesday Weld Orson Welles Jack Nicholson

1973 **HIT !**
Director: Sidney Furie
Co-stars: Billy Dee Williams Richard Pryor Paul Hampton

1974 **CALIFORNIA SPLIT**
Director: Robert Altman
Co-stars: Elliott Gould George Segal Barbara Ruick

1975 **NASHVILLE**
Director: Robert Altman
Co-stars: Keith Carradine Lily Tomlin Shelley Duvall

1977 **BETWEEN THE LINES**
Director: Joan Micklin Silver
Co-stars: John Heard Lindsay Crouse Jeff Goldblum

1985 **DESERT HEARTS**
Director: Donna Deitch
Co-stars: Helen Shaver Patricia Charbonneau Audra Lindley

1986 **NOBODY'S FOOL**
Director: Evelyn Purcell
Co-stars: Rosanna Arquette Eric Roberts Mare Winningham

1988 **STICKY FINGERS**
Director: Catlin Adams
Co-star: Eileen Brennan

1989 **NEW YEAR'S DAY**
Director: Henry Jaglom
Co-stars: Henry Jaglom Maggie Jakobson Melanie Winter

1990 **EATING**
Director: Henry Jaglom
Co-stars: Lisa Richards Mary Crosby Nelly Alard

REBECCA WELLES

1958 **DESIRE UNDER THE ELMS**
Director: Delbert Mann
Co-stars: Sophia Loren Anthony Perkins Burl Ives

VIRGINIA WELLES

1945 **KISS AND TELL**
Director: Richard Wallace
Co-stars: Shirley Temple Walter Abel Jerome Courtland

1946 **TO EACH HIS OWN**
Director: Mitchell Leisen
Co-stars: Olivia De Havilland John Lund Roland Culver

1947 **LADIES' MAN**
Director: William Russell
Co-stars: Eddie Bracken Cass Daley Spike Jones

1947 **DEAR RUTH**
Director: William Russell
Co-stars: Joan Caulfield William Holden Mona Freeman

HELEN WELLINGTON-LLOYD

1978 **JUBILEE**
Director: Derek Jarman
Co-stars: Jenny Runacre Toyah Wilcox Ian Charleson

ANNIKA WELLS

1962 **SOME PEOPLE**
Director: Clive Donner
Co-stars: Kenneth More Ray Brooks Angela Douglas

CAROLE WELLS

1973 **THE HOUSE OF SEVEN CORPSES**
Director: Paul Harrison
Co-stars: John Ireland Faith Domergue John Carradine

1975 **FUNNY LADY**
Director: Herbert Ross
Co-stars: Barbra Streisand James Caan Omar Sharif

CLAUDIA WELLS

1985 **BACK TO THE FUTURE**
Director: Robert Zemeckis
Co-stars: Michael J. Fox Christopher Lloyd Lea Thompson

DAWN WELLS

1977 **RETURN TO BOGGY CREEK**
Director: Tom Moore
Co-star: Dana Plato

INGEBORG WELLS

1954 **CHILD'S PLAY**
Director: Margaret Thompson
Co-stars: Mona Washbourne Dorothy Alison Peter Martyn

1954 **DOUBLE EXPOSURE**
Director: John Gilling
Co-stars: John Bentley Rona Anderson Garry Marsh

JACQUELINE WELLS

1933 **TILLIE AND GUS**
Director: Francis Martin
Co-stars: W.C. Fields Alison Skipworth Baby Leroy

1933 **TARZAN THE FEARLESS**
Director: Robert Hill
Co-stars: Buster Crabbe Edward Woods Mischa Auer

1934 **THE BLACK CAT**
Director: Edgar Ulmer
Co-stars: Boris Karloff Bela Lugosi Julie Bishop

1936 **THE BOHEMIAN GIRL**
Director: James Horne
Co-stars: Stan Laurel Oliver Hardy Mae Busch

1937 **COUNSEL FOR CRIME**
Director: John Brahm
Co-stars: Otto Kruger Douglass Montgomery Nana Bryant

1938 SPRING MADNESS
Director: S. Sylvan Simon
Co-stars: Maureen O'Sullivan Lew Ayres Ruth Hussey

1938 ALL AMERICAN SWEETHEART
Co-stars: Allen Brook Patricia Farr Scott Colton

1938 MAIN EVENT
Co-stars: Robert Paige Oscar O'Shea Arthur Loft

1939 BEHIND PRISON GATES
Director: Charles Barton
Co-stars: Brian Donlevy Paul Fix Joseph Crehan

1941 BACK IN THE SADDLE
Co-stars: Gene Autry Smiley Burnette

JOAN WELLS

1946 TILL THE CLOUDS ROLL BY
Director: Richard Whorf
Co-stars: Robert Walker Van Heflin Lucille Bremer

ARIADNA WELTER

1955 THE CRIMINAL LIFE OF ARCHIBALDO DE LA CRUZ
Director: Luis Bunuel
Co-stars: Ernesto Alonso Rita Macedo

1966 RAGE
Director: Gilberto Gascon
Co-stars: Glenn Ford Stella Stevens David Reynoso

JANE WELSH

1931 THE BELLS
Director: Oscar Werndorff
Co-stars: Donald Calthrop Edward Sinclair

1932 CONDEMNED TO DEATH
Director: Walter Forde
Co-stars: Arthur Wontner Edmund Gwenn Gordon Harker

MAGGIE WELSH

1992 AMERICAN HEART
Director: Martin Bell
Co-stars: Jeff Bridges Edward Furlong Lucinda Jenney

ELIZABETH WENDT

1931 KAMERADSCHAFT
Director: G.W. Pabst
Co-stars: Ernst Busch Alexander Granach Fritz Kampers

MING-NA WENG

1997 ONE NIGHT STAND
Director: Mike Figgis
Co-stars: Wesley Snipes Nastassja Kinski Robert Downey Jnr.

JANE WENHAM

1954 AN INSPECTOR CALLS
Director: Guy Hamilton
Co-stars: Alastair Sim Brian Worth Bryan Forbes

JOANNA WENT

1992 THE LIVING END
Director: Gregg Araki
Co-stars: Mike Dytri Craig Bilmore Mark Finch

MARTHA WENTWORTH

1943 CLANCY STREET BOYS
Director: William Beaudine
Co-stars: Leo Gorcy Huntz Hall Bobby Jordan

GISELA WERBISECK

1945 WONDER MAN
Director: Bruce Humberstone
Co-stars: Danny Kaye Vera-Ellen Virginia Mayo

BARBARA WERLE

1965 BATTLE OF THE BULGE
Director: Ken Annakin
Co-stars: Henry Fonda Robert Shaw Robert Ryan

1968 KRAKATOA, EAST OF JAVA
Director: Bernard Kowalski
Co-stars: Maximilian Schell Diane Baker Brian Keith

1969 CHARRO !
Director: Charles Marquis Warren
Co-stars: Elvis Presley Ina Balin Lynn Kellogg

KASSIE WESLEY

1987 EVIL DEAD 2
Director: Sam Raimi
Co-stars: Bruce Campbell Sarah Berry Dan Hicks

MICHELLE WESSON

1992 GHOSTWATCH
Director: Lesley Manning
Co-stars: Michael Parkinson Sarah Greene Mike Smith

ANITA WEST

1963 SHADOW OF FEAR
Director: Ernest Morris
Co-stars: Paul Maxwell Clare Owen Alan Tilvern

CHANDRA WEST

1993 PUPPET MASTER 4
Director: Jeff Burr
Co-stars: Guy Rolfe Gordon Currie Jason Adams

1997 RUNNING WILD
Director: Chuck Bowan
Co-stars: Morgan Fairchild Michael Woods

JUDI WEST

1966 THE FORTUNE COOKIE
Director: Billy Wilder
Co-stars: Jack Lemmon Walter Matthau Ron Rich

1969 A MAN CALLED GANNON
Director: James Goldstone
Co-stars: Tony Franciosa Michael Sarrazin Susan Oliver

LUCINDA WEST

1994 THE HAUNTING OF SEACLIFF INN
Director: Walter Klenhard
Co-stars: Ally Sheedy William R. Moses

MAE WEST

1932 NIGHT AFTER NIGHT
Director: Archie Mayo
Co-stars: George Raft Constance Cummings Wynne Gibson

1933 SHE DONE HIM WRONG
Director: Lowell Sherman
Co-stars: Cary Grant Gilbert Roland Owen Moore

1933 I'M NO ANGEL
Director: Wesley Ruggles
Co-stars: Cary Grant Edward Arnold Kent Taylor

1934 IT AIN'T NO SIN
Co-star: Johnny Mack Brown

1934   **BELLE OF THE NINETIES**
Director: Leo McCarey
Co-stars: Roger Pryor Johnny Mack Brown Katherine DeMille

1935   **GOIN' TO TOWN**
Director: Alexander Hall
Co-stars: Paul Cavanagh Tito Coral Fred Kohler

1936   **GO WEST, YOUNG MAN**
Director: Henry Hathaway
Co-stars: Randolph Scott Warren William Alice Brady

1936   **KLONDIKE ANNIE**
Director: Raoul Walsh
Co-stars: Victor McLaglen Philip Reed Harold Huber

1937   **EVERY DAY'S A HOLIDAY**
Director: Edward Sutherland
Co-stars: Edmund Lowe Charles Winninger

1940   **MY LITTLE CHICKADEE**
Director: Edward Cline
Co-stars: W.C. Fields Joseph Calleia Dick Foran

1943   **THE HEAT'S ON**
Director: Gregory Ratoff
Co-stars: Victor Moore William Gaxton Lloyd Bridges

1970   **MYRA BRECKINRIDGE**
Director: Mike Sarne
Co-stars: Raquel Welch John Huston Jim Backus

1978   **SEXTETTE**
Director: Ken Hughes
Co-stars: Tony Curtis Ringo Starr Timothy Dalton

NORMA WEST

1983   **AND THE SHIP SAILS ON**
Director: Federico Fellini
Co-stars: Freddie Jones Barbara Jefford Janet Suzman

1991   **INSPECTOR WEXFORD:**
         AN UNKINDNESS OF RAVENS
Director: John Gorrie
Co-stars: George Baker Diane Keen Louie Ramsey

TAMSIN WEST

1985   **JENNY KISSED ME**
Director: Brian Trenchard-Smith
Co-stars: Deborra-Lee Furness Ivar Kants Paula Duncan

HELEN WESTCOTT

1949   **HOMICIDE**
Director: Felix Jacoves
Co-stars: Robert Douglas Robert Alda

1950   **THE GUNFIGHTER**
Director: Henry King
Co-stars: Gregory Peck Millard Mitchell Karl Malden

1952   **LOAN SHARK**
Director: Seymour Friedman
Co-stars: George Raft Dorothy Hart Paul Stewart

1952   **WITH A SONG IN MY HEART**
Director: Walter Lang
Co-stars: Susan Hayward David Wayne Thelma Ritter

1953   **CHARGE AT FEATHER RIVER**
Director: Gordon Douglas
Co-stars: Guy Madison Frank Lovejoy Vera Miles

1953   **BATTLES OF CHIEF PONTIAC**
Director: Felix Feist
Co-stars: Lon Chaney Lex Barker Roy Roberts

1955   **HOT BLOOD**
Director: Nicholas Ray
Co-stars: Cornel Wilde Jane Russell Joseph Calleia

1957   **GOD'S LITTLE ACRE**
Director: Anthony Mann
Co-stars: Robert Ryan Aldo Ray Tina Louise

1958   **DAY OF THE OUTLAW**
Director: Andre De Toth
Co-stars: Robert Ryan Burl Ives Tina Louise

1960   **STUDS LONIGAN**
Director: Irving Lerner
Co-stars: Christopher Knight Jack Nicholson Frank Gorshin

ELLEN WESTERFJELL

1981   **LITTLE IDA**
Director: Laila Mikkelsen
Co-stars: Sunniva Lindekleiv Howard Halvorsen Lise Fjeldstad

DR RUTH WESTHEIMER

1985   **UNE FEMME OU DEUX**
Director: Daniel Vigne
Co-stars: Gerard Depardieu Sigourney Weaver Michel Aumont

HILARY WESTLAKE

1964   **THE BLACK TORMENT**
Director: Robert Hartford-Davis
Co-stars: John Turner Heather Sears Ann Lynn

1983   **THE GOLD DIGGERS**
Director: Sally Potter
Co-stars: Julie Christie Colette Lafont David Gale

HELEN WESTLEY

1934   **AGE OF INNOCENCE**
Director: Philip Moeller
Co-stars: Irene Dunne John Boles Lionel Atwill

1934   **ANNE OF GREEN GABLES**
Director: George Nicholls
Co-stars: Ann Shirley Tom Brown Charley Grapewin

1934   **DEATH TAKES A HOLIDAY**
Director: Mitchell Leisen
Co-stars: Fredric March Evelyn Venable

1934   **THE HOUSE OF ROTHSCHILD**
Director: Alfred Werker
Co-stars: George Arliss Loretta Young Robert Young

1934   **MOULIN ROUGE**
Director: Sidney Lanfield
Co-stars: Constance Bennett Franchot Tone

1935   **ROBERTA**
Director: William Seiter
Co-stars: Irene Dunne Fred Astaire Ginger Rogers

1935   **SPLENDOR**
Director: Elliott Nugent
Co-stars: Joel McCrea Miriam Hopkins David Niven

1935   **CHASING YESTERDAY**
Director: George Nicholls
Co-stars: O.P. Heggie Ann Shirley John Qualen

1935   **THE MELODY LINGERS ON**
Co-star: Josephine Hutchinson

1935   **CAPTAIN HURRICANE**
Director: John Robertson
Co-stars: James Barton Helen Mack Gene Lockhart

1936   **DIMPLES**
Director: William Seiter
Co-stars: Shirley Temple Frank Morgan Robert Kent

1936   **SHOWBOAT**
Director: James Whale
Co-stars: Allan Jones Irene Dunne Helen Morgan

1936 STOWAWAY
Director: William Seiter
Co-stars: Shirley Temple Robert Young Alice Faye

1936 BANJO ON MY KNEE
Director: John Cromwell
Co-stars: Joel McCrea Barbara Stanwyck Walter Brennan

1937 HEIDI
Director: Allan Dwan
Co-stars: Shirley Temple Jean Hersholt Arthur Treacher

1937 CAFÉ METROPOLE
Director: Edward Griffith
Co-stars: Loretta Young Tyrone Power Adolphe Menjou

1937 I'LL TAKE ROMANCE
Director: Edward Griffith
Co-stars: Grace Moore Melvyn Douglas Stuart Erwin

1938 KEEP SMILING
Co-stars: Jane Withers Henry Wilcoxon Gloria Stuart

1938 REBECCA OF SUNNYBROOK FARM
Director: Allan Dwan
Co-stars: Shirley Temple Randolph Scott Jack Haley

1938 ZAZA
Director: George Cukor
Co-stars: Claudette Colbert Herbert Marshall

1938 THE BARONESS AND THE BUTLER
Director: Walter Lang
Co-stars: William Powell Annabella Nigel Bruce

1939 WIFE, HUSBAND AND FRIEND
Director: Gregory Ratoff
Co-stars: Loretta Young Warner Baxter Cesar Romero

1940 ALL THIS AND HEAVEN TOO
Director: Anatole Litvak
Co-stars: Charles Boyer Bette Davis Henry Daniell

1940 THE CAPTAIN IS A LADY
Director: Robert Sinclair
Co-stars: Dan Dailey Billie Burke Charles Coburn

1940 THE LADY WITH RED HAIR
Director: Curtis Bernhardt
Co-stars: Miriam Hopkins Claude Rains Victor Jory

1940 LILLIAN RUSSELL
Director: Irving Cummings
Co-stars: Alice Faye Don Ameche Henry Fonda

1941 MILLION DOLLAR BABY
Director: Curtis Bernhardt
Co-stars: Priscilla Lane Ronald Reagan Jeffrey Lynn

1941 LADY FROM LOUISIANA
Director: Bernard Vorhaus
Co-stars: John Wayne Ona Munson Dorothy Dandridge

1941 BEDTIME STORY
Director: Alexander Hall
Co-stars: Loretta Young Fredric March Eve Arden

NYDIA WESTMAN

1932 MANHATTAN TOWER
Co-star: Irene Rich

1933 LITTLE WOMEN
Director: George Cukor
Co-stars: Katherine Hepburn Joan Bennett Frances Dee

1933 THE WAY TO LOVE
Director: Norman Taurog
Co-stars: Maurice Chevalier Ann Dvorak Edward Everett Horton

1934 TWO ALONE
Director: Elliott Nugent
Co-stars: Jean Parker Tom Brown Zasu Pitts

1934 THE TRUMPET BLOWS
Director: Stephen Roberts
Co-stars: George Raft Adolphe Menjou Frances Drake

1934 SUCCESS AT ANY PRICE
Director: Walter Ruben
Co-stars: Douglas Fairbanks Jnr. Genevieve Tobin Frank Morgan

1934 ONE NIGHT OF LOVE
Director: Victor Schertzinger
Co-stars: Grace Moore Tullio Carminati Mona Barrie

1934 LADIES SHOULD LISTEN
Director: Frank Tuttle
Co-stars: Cary Grant Frances Drake Rosita Moreno

1935 A FEATHER IN HER HAT
Director: Alfred Santell
Co-stars: Pauline Lord Basil Rathbone Louis Hayward

1935 DRESSED TO THRILL
Co-stars: Clive Brook Tutta Rolf

1935 SWEET ADELINE
Director: Mervyn LeRoy
Co-stars: Irene Dunne Donald Woods Hugh Herbert

1936 THE INVISIBLE RAY
Director: Lambert Hillyer
Co-stars: Boris Karloff Bela Lugosi Frances Drake

1938 THE GOLDWYN FOLLIES
Director: George Marshall
Co-stars: Kenny Baker Vera Zorina Ritz Brothers

1938 THE FIRST HUNDRED YEARS
Director: Richard Thorpe
Co-stars: Robert Montgomery Virginia Bruce Binnie Barnes

1939 THE CAT AND THE CANARY
Director: Elliott Nugent
Co-stars: Bob Hope Paulette Goddard Douglass Montgomery

1939 WHEN TOMMOROW COMES
Director: John Stahl
Co-stars: Charles Boyer Irene Dunne Barbara O'Neil

1940 HULLABALOO
Director: Edwin Marin
Co-stars: Frank Morgan Dan Dailey Virginia Grey

1940 FORTY LITTLE MOTHERS
Director: Busby Berkeley
Co-stars: Eddie Cantor Judith Anderson Bonita Granville

1942 THE REMARKABLE ANDREW
Director: Stuart Heisler
Co-stars: William Holden Brian Donlevy Ellen Drew

1947 THE LATE GEORGE APLEY
Director: Joseph Mankiewicz
Co-stars: Ronald Colman Edna Best Vanessa Brown

1966 THE SWINGER
Director: George Sidney
Co-stars: Ann-Margret Tony Franciosa Robert Coote

1969 SILENT NIGHT, LONELY NIGHT
Director: Daniel Petrie
Co-stars: Lloyd Nolan Shirley Jones Lynn Carlin

LUCY WESTMORE

1965 DR ZHIVAGO
Director: David Lean
Co-stars: Omar Sharif Julie Christie Tom Courtenay

CELIA WESTON

1989 THE ROAD HOME
Director: Hugh Hudson
Co-stars: Donald Sutherland Adam Horovitz Amy Locane

1991 LITTLE MAN TATE
Director: Jodie Foster
Co-stars: Jodie Foster Dianne Wiest Adam Hann-Byrd

DEBORAH WESTON

1990 MAGIC MOMENTS
Director: Lawrence Gordon Clark
Co-stars: John Shea Jenny Seagrove Paul Freeman

DORIS WESTON

1937 SUBMARINE D1
Director: Lloyd Bacon
Co-stars: Pat O'Brien George Brent Wayne Morris

1937 THE SINGING MARINE
Director: Ray Enright
Co-stars: Dick Powell Jane Darwell Larry Adler

1940 CHIP OF THE FLYING U
Co-stars: Johnny Mack Brown Forrest Taylor

RUTH WESTON

1935 SPLENDOR
Director: Eliott Nugent
Co-stars: Joel McCrea Miriam Hopkins David Niven

WINIFRED WESTOVER

1930 LUMMOX
Co-star: Myrtle Stedman

VIRGINIA WETHERELL

1968 CURSE OF THE CRIMSON ALTAR
Director: Vernon Sewell
Co-stars: Boris Karloff Mark Eden

PATRICIA WETTIG *(Married Ken Olin)*

1988 POLICE STORY: COP KILLER
Director: Larry Shaw
Co-stars: Ken Olin Joseph Bottoms Glynnis O'Connor

1991 SILENT MOTIVE
Director: Lee Phillips
Co-stars: Mike Farrell Ed Asner David Packer

1991 GUILTY BY SUSPICION
Director: Irving Winkler
Co-stars: Robert De Niro Annette Bening Sam Wanamaker

1991 CITY SLICKERS
Director: Ron Underwood
Co-stars: Billy Crystal Daniel Stern Helen Slater

**1994 CITY SLICKERS 2:
THE LEGEND OF CURLY'S GOLD**
Director: Paul Weiland
Co-stars: Billy Crystal Jack Palance Daniel Stern

RUTH WEYHER

1926 SECRETS OF A SOUL
Director: G.W. Pabst
Co-stars: Werner Krauss Jack Trevor Pawel Pawlow

SAMANTHA WEYSON

1981 THE APPOINTMENT
Director: Lindsey Vickey
Co-stars: Edward Woodward John Judd

JOANNE WHALLEY *(Married Val Kilmer)*
(Whalley-Kilmer From Scandal To The Secret Rapture)

1985 DANCE WITH A STRANGER
Director: Mike Newell
Co-stars: Miranda Richardson Rupert Everett Ian Holm

1986 THE GOOD FATHER
Director: Mike Newell
Co-stars: Anthony Hopkins Jim Broadbent Simon Callow

1987 WILL YOU LOVE ME TOMORROW ?
Director: Adrian Shergold
Co-stars: Tilly Vosburgh Iain Glen Phil Daniels

1988 TO KILL A PRIEST
Director: Agnieszka Holland
Co-stars: Christopher Lambert Ed Harris David Suchet

1988 WILLOW
Director: Ron Howard
Co-stars: Val Kilmer Jean Marsh Patricia Hayes

1988 SCANDAL
Director: Michael Caton-Jones
Co-stars: John Hurt Bridget Fonda Britt Ekland

1989 KILL ME AGAIN
Director: John Dahl
Co-stars: Val Kilmer Michael Madsen Nick Dimitri

1990 NAVY SEALS
Director: Lewis Teague
Co-stars: Charlie Sheen Michael Biehn Bill Paxton

1990 THE BIG MAN
Director: David Leland
Co-stars: Liam Neesen Ian Bannen Billy Connolly

1991 SHATTERED
Director: Wolfgang Petersen
Co-stars: Tom Berenger Greta Scacchi Corbin Bernsen

1992 STORYVILLE
Director: Mark Frost
Co-stars: James Spader Jason Robards Charlotte Lewis

1993 MOTHER'S BOYS
Director: Yves Simoneau
Co-stars: Jamie Leigh Curtis Vanessa Redgrave Peter Gallagher

1994 THE SECRET RAPTURE
Director: Howard Davies
Co-stars: Juliet Stevenson Penelope Wilton Alan Howard

1997 WATCH THAT MAN
Director: Jon Amiel
Co-stars: Bill Murray Alfred Molina Richard Wilson

LEANNE WHALLEY

1994 CRIMINAL
Director: Corin Campbell-Hill
Co-stars: Paul Popplewell Cheryl Godber Nicky Evans

LOIS WHEELER

1949 MY FOOLISH HEART
Director: Mark Robson
Co-stars: Susan Hayward Dana Andrews Gigi Perreau

DANA WHEELER-NICHOLSON

1985 FLETCH
Director: Michael Ritchie
Co-stars: Chevy Chase Tim Matheson Geena Davis

1995 DENISE CALLS UP
Director: Hal Salwen
Co-stars: Timothy Daly Caroleen Feeney

1996 NICK AND JANE
Co-star: James McCaffrey

ALISON WHELAN

1989 MY LEFT FOOT
Director: Jim Sheridan
Co-stars: Daniel Day-Lewis Brenda Fricker Ray McAnally

ARLEN WHELAN

1938 THANKS FOR EVERYTHING
Director: William Seiter
Co-stars: Adolphe Menjou Jack Oakie Jack Haley

1938 KIDNAPPED
Director: Alfred Werker
Co-stars: Warner Baxter Freddie Bartholomew John Carradine

1938 GATEWAY
Director: Alfred Werker
Co-stars: Don Ameche Gregory Ratoff Raymond Walburn

1939 YOUNG MR LINCOLN
Director: John Ford
Co-stars: Alice Brady Marjorie Weaver Richard Cromwell

1940 YOUNG PEOPLE
Director: Allan Dwan
Co-stars: Shirley Temple Jack Oakie George Montgomery

1941 CHARLEY'S AUNT
Director: Archie Mayo
Co-stars: Jack Benny Kay Francis Anne Baxter

1942 CASTLE IN THE DESERT
Director: Harry Lachman
Co-stars: Sidney Toler Sen Yung Henry Daniell

1947 RAMROD
Director: Andre De Toth
Co-stars: Veronica Lake Joel McCrea Preston Foster

1947 THE SENATOR WAS INDISCREET
Director: George Kaufman
Co-stars: William Powell Ella Raines Hans Conried

1947 SUDDENLY IT'S SPRING
Director: Mitchell Leisen
Co-stars: Paulette Goddard Fred MacMurray

1948 THAT WONDERFUL URGE
Director: Robert Sinclair
Co-stars: Tyrone Power Gene Tierney Reginald Gardiner

1951 PASSAGE WEST
Director: Lewis Foster
Co-stars: John Payne Dennis O'Keefe Peter Hanson

1952 NEVER WAVE AT A WAC
Director: Norman Z. Mcleod
Co-stars: Rosalind Russell Paul Douglas Marie Wilson

1952 SAN ANTONE
Director: Joe Kane
Co-stars: Rod Cameron Forrest Tucker Katy Jurado

1952 THE SUN SHINES BRIGHT
Director: John Ford
Co-stars: Charles Winninger John Russell Russell Simpson

1957 THE BADGE OF MARSHALL BRENNAN
Director: Albert Gannoway
Co-stars: Jim Davis Louis Jean Heydt

CHRISTINA WHITAKER

1988 ASSAULT OF THE KILLER BIMBOS
Director: Anita Rosenberg
Co-stars: Elizabeth Kaitan Nick Cassavetes Griffin O'Neal

ALICE WHITE

1927 THE SEA TIGER

1927 THE PRIVATE LIFE OF HELEN OF TROY
Director: Alexander Korda
Co-stars: Maria Corda Lewis Stone Ricardo Cortez

1929 SHOW OF SHOWS
Director: John Adolfi
Co-stars: Frank Fay Douglas Fairbanks Jnr. John Barrymore

1930 THE WIDOW FROM CHICAGO
Director: Edward Cline
Co-stars: Edward G. Robinson Neil Hamilton Frank McHugh

1930 SHOWGIRL IN HOLLYWOOD
Director: Mervyn LeRoy
Co-stars: Jack Mulhall Blanche Sweet Ford Sterling

1933 THE PICTURE SNATCHER
Director: Lloyd Bacon
Co-stars: James Cagney Ralph Bellamy Patricia Ellis

1933 KING FOR A NIGHT
Director: Kurt Neuman
Co-stars: Chester Morris Helen Twelvetrees Grant Mitchell

1933 LUXURY LINER
Director: Lothar Mendes
Co-stars: George Brent Zita Johanne Frank Morgan

1933 EMPLOYEES' ENTRANCE
Director: Roy Del Ruth
Co-stars: Warren William Loretta Young Wallace Ford

1934 THE GIFT OF GAB
Director: Karl Freund
Co-stars: Edmund Lowe Gloria Stuart Ruth Etting

1934 JIMMY THE GENT
Director: Michael Curtiz
Co-stars: James Cagney Bette Davis Mayo Methot

1934 A VERY HONORABLE GUY
Co-stars: Joe E. Brown Hobart Cavanaugh

1935 CORONADO
Director: Norman Z. McLeod
Co-stars: Jack Haley Johnny Downs Betty Burgess

BARBARA WHITE

1944 IT HAPPENED ONE SUNDAY
Director: Karel Lamac
Co-stars: Robert Beatty Marjorie Rhodes Judy Kelly

1946 WHILE THE SUN SHINES
Director: Anthony Asquith
Co-stars: Brenda Bruce Ronald Howard Bonar Colleano

1947 MINE OWN EXECUTIONER
Director: Anthony Kimmins
Co-stars: Burgess Meredith Kieron Moore Dulcie Gray

1948 THIS WAS A WOMAN
Director: Tim Whelan
Co-stars: Sonia Dresdel Walter Fitzgerald Cyril Raymond

1950 ALL ABOUT EVE
Director: Joseph Mankiewicz
Co-stars: Bette Davis George Sanders Anne Baxter

BETTY WHITE

1991 CHANCE OF A LIFETIME
Director: Jonathan Sanger
Co-stars: Ed Begley Jnr. Leslie Nielsen William Windom

BRITTANY WHITE *(Child)*
(Sister Of Courtney White)

1983 MR MOM
Director: Stan Dragoti
Co-stars: Michael Keaton Teri Garr Ann Jillian

CAROL WHITE

1956 CIRCUS FRIENDS
Director: Gerald Thomas
Co-stars: Meredith Edwards Alan Coleshill Sam Kydd

1959 CARRY ON TEACHER
Director: Gerald Thomas
Co-stars: Ted Ray Charles Hawtrey Leslie Philips

1960   **NEVER LET GO**
Director: John Guillermin
Co-stars: Richard Todd Peter Sellers Adam Faith

1960   **LINDA**

1961   **THE MAN IN THE BACK SEAT**
Director: Vernon Sewell
Co-stars: Derren Nesbitt Keith Faulkner Harry Locke

1961   **A MATTER OF W.H.O.**
Director: Don Chaffey
Co-stars: Terry-Thomas Sonja Ziemann Alex Nicol

1961   **VILLAGE OF DAUGHTERS**
Director: George Pollock
Co-stars: Eric Sykes Warren Mitchell Scilla Gabel

1962   **GAOLBREAK**
Director: Francis Searle
Co-stars: Peter Reynolds Avice Landon David Kernan

1963   **LADIES WHO DO**
Director: C. Pennington-Richards
Co-stars: Peggy Mount Miriam Karlin Dandy Nichols

1966   **SLAVE GIRLS**
Director: Michael Carreras
Co-stars: Martine Beswick Michael Latimer Edina Ronay

1966   **CATHY COME HOME**
Director: Ken Loach
Co-star: Ray Brooks

1967   **POOR COW**
Director: Ken Loach
Co-stars: Terence Stamp John Bindon Kate Williams

1967   **I'LL NEVER FORGET WHAT'S 'IS NAME**
Director: Michael Winner
Co-stars: Oliver Reed Orson Welles Wendy Craig

1968   **THE FIXER**
Director: John Frankenheimer
Co-stars: Alan Bates Dirk Bogarde Georgia Brown

1969   **DADDY'S GONE A-HUNTING**
Director: Mark Robson
Co-stars: Paul Burke Scott Hylands Mala Powers

1970   **THE MAN WHO HAD POWER OVER WOMEN**
Director: John Krish
Co-stars: Rod Taylor James Booth Keith Barron

1971   **DULCIMA**
Director: Frank Nesbitt
Co-stars: John Mills Stuart Wilson Bernard Lee

1971   **SOMETHING BIG**
Director: Andrew McLaglen
Co-stars: Dean Martin Brian Keith Honor Blackman

1972   **MADE**
Director: John MacKenzie
Co-stars: John Castle Margery Mason Roy Harper

1973   **SOME CALL IT LOVING**
Director: James Harris
Co-stars: Zalman King Tisa Farrow Richard Pryor

1977   **THE SQUEEZE**
Director: Michael Apted
Co-stars: Stacy Keach Freddie Starr Edward Fox

1979   **THE SPACEMAN AND KING ARTHUR**
Director: Russ Mayberry
Co-stars: Jim Dale Kenneth More Ron Moody

1982   **NUTCRACKER**
Director: Anwar Kawadri
Co-stars: Joan Collins Paul Nicholas Finola Hughes

COURTNEY WHITE (Child)
(Sister Of Brittany White)

1983   **MR MOM**
Director: Stan Dragoti
Co-stars: Michael Keaton Teri Garr Ann Jillian

DEBORAH WHITE

1976   **THE VAN**
Director: Sam Grossman
Co-stars: Stuart Getz Danny De Vito Harry Moses

HARRIET WHITE

1946   **PAISA**
Director: Roberto Rossellini
Co-stars: William Tubbs Gar Moore Maria Michi

JACQUELINE WHITE

1943   **AIR RAID WARDENS**
Director: Edward Sedgwick
Co-stars: Stan Laurel Oliver Hardy Edgar Kennedy

1944   **THIRTY SECONDS OVER TOKYO**
Director: Mervyn LeRoy
Co-stars: Spencer Tracy Van Johnson Robert Walker

1947   **SEVEN KEYS TO BALDPATE**
Co-stars: Phillip Terry Eduardo Ciannelli

1947   **CROSSFIRED**
Director: Edward Dmytryk
Co-stars: Robert Young Robert Mitchum Robert Ryan

1948   **MYSTERY IN MEXICO**
Director: Robert Wise
Co-stars: William Lundigan Ricardo Cortez Tony Barrett

1948   **RETURN OF THE BAD MEN**
Director: Ray Enright
Co-stars: Randolph Scott Robert Ryan Anne Jeffreys

1950   **THE CAPTURE**
Director: John Sturges
Co-stars: Lew Ayres Teresa Wright Victor Jory

1952   **THE NARROW MARGIN**
Director: Richard Fleischer
Co-stars: Charles McGraw Marie Windsor Don Beddoe

LOUISE WHITE

1970   **QUIET DAYS IN CLICHY**
Director: Jens-Jorgen Thorsen
Co-stars: Paul Valjean Susanne Krage Ulla Lemvigh-Muller

LYNNE WHITE (Child)

1974   **WHAT NEXT ?**
Director: Peter Smith
Co-stars: Peter Robinson Perry Benson James Cossins

MAJELLE WHITE

1942   **BLONDIE FOR VICTORY**
Director: Frank Strayer
Co-stars: Penny Singleton Arthur Lake Stuart Erwin

MARJORIE WHITE

1930   **HAPPY DAYS**
Director: Benjamin Stoloff
Co-stars: Janet Gaynor Charles Farrell Will Rogers

1930   **JUST IMAGINE**
Director: David Butler
Co-stars: El Brendel Maureen O'Sullivan Frank Albertson

1930   **MOVIETONE FOLLIES OF 1930**
Director: Ben Stoloff
Co-stars: El Brendel Miriam Seegar William Collier Jnr.

1930 THE GOLDEN CALF
Co-stars: El Brendel Sue Carol Jack Mulhall

1931 BROADMINDED
Director: Mervyn LeRoy
Co-stars: Joe E. Brown Ona Munson Bela Lugosi

1931 POSSESSED
Director: Clarence Brown
Co-stars: Joan Crawford Clark Gable Wallace Ford

1931 CHARLIE CHAN CARRIES ON
Director: Hamilton McFadden
Co-stars: Warner Oland Marguerite Churchill George Brent

1933 DIPLOMANIACS
Director: William Seiter
Co-stars: Bert Wheeler Robert Wolsey Hugh Herbert

MILLIE WHITE

1990 POISON
Director: Todd Haynes
Co-stars: Edith Meeks Scott Renderer James Lyons

PEARL WHITE

1912 THE PERILS OF PAULINE

1914 THE EXPLOITS OF ELAINE

1915 THE NEW EXPLOITS OF ELAINE

1915 THE ROMANCE OF ELAINE

1961 THE DAYS OF THRILLS AND LAUGHTER
Director: Robert Youngson
Co-stars: Douglas Fairbanks Ben Turpin Houdini

RHONDA STUBBINS WHITE

1993 OUT OF DARKNESS
Director: Larry Elikann
Co-stars: Diana Ross Lindsay Crouse Ann Weldon

RUTH WHITE

1957 EDGE OF THE CITY
Director: Martin Ritt
Co-stars: Sidney Poitier John Cassavetes Ruby Dee

1962 TO KILL A MOCKINGBIRD
Director: Robert Mulligan
Co-stars: Gregory Peck Mary Badham Philip Alford

1964 BABY THE RAIN MUST FALL
Director: Robert Mulligan
Co-stars: Steve McQueen Lee Remick Don Murray

1965 A RAGE TO LIVE
Director: Walter Grauman
Co-stars: Suzanne Pleshette Bradford Dillman Ben Gazzara

1967 THE TIGER MAKES OUT
Director: Arthur Hiller
Co-stars: Eli Wallach Anne Jackson Bob Dishy

1970 THE PURSUIT OF HAPPINESS
Director: Robert Mulligan
Co-stars: Michael Sarrazin Barbara Hershey Arthur Hill

1975 UP THE DOWN STAIRCASE
Director: Robert Mulligan
Co-stars: Sandy Dennis Patrick Bedford Eileen Heckart

SHEILA WHITE

1967 HERE WE GO ROUND THE MULBERRY BUSH
Director: Clive Donner
Co-stars: Barry Evans Judy Geeson Angela Scoular

1974 CONFESSIONS OF A WINDOW CLEANER
Director: Val Guest
Co-stars: Robin Askwith Anthony Booth Dandy Nichols

1975 CONFESSIONS OF A POP PERFORMER
Director: Norman Cohen
Co-stars: Robin Askwith Anthony Booth Bill Maynard

1975 ALFIE DARLING
Director: Ken Hughes
Co-stars: Alan Price Joan Collins Annie Ross

1976 CONFESSIONS OF A DRIVING INSTRUCTOR
Director: Norman Cohen
Co-stars: Robin Askwith Liz Fraser Doris Hare

1977 CONFESSIONS FROM A HOLIDAY CAMP
Director: Norman Cohen
Co-stars: Robin Askwith Anthony Booth Bill Maynard

1979 THE SPACEMAN AND KING ARTHUR
Director: Russ Mayberry
Co-stars: Jim Dale Ron Moody Kenneth More

THELMA WHITE

1936 REEFER MADNESS
Director: Louis Gasnier
Co-stars: Dave O'Brien Dorothy Short Lillian Miles

1943 SPY TRAIN
Co-stars: Richard Travis Catherine Craig Bill Hunter

VALERIE WHITE

1946 HUE AND CRY
Director: Charles Crichton
Co-stars: Alastair Sim Jack Warner Harry Fowler

RUTH WHITEHEAD

1988 ANGEL VOICES
Director: Michael Darlow
Co-stars: Michael Williams Stephen Bird Kevin Scot

BILLIE WHITELAW

1953 THE FAKE
Director: Godfrey Grayson
Co-stars: Dennis O'Keefe Coleen Gray Hugh Williams

1954 THE SLEEPING TIGER
Director: Joseph Losey
Co-stars: Dirk Bogarde Alexis Smith Alexander Knox

1957 SMALL HOTEL
Director: David MacDonald
Co-stars: Gordon Harker Marie Lohr Irene Handl

1957 MIRACLE IN SOHO
Director: Julian Amyes
Co-stars: John Gregson Belinda Lee Cyril Cusack

1958 CARVE HER NAME WITH PRIDE
Director: Lewis Gilbert
Co-stars: Virginia McKenna Paul Scofield Bill Owen

1959 BOBBIKINS
Director: Robert Day
Co-stars: Max Bygraves Shirley Jones Barbara Shelley

1959 THE FLESH AND THE FIENDS
Director: John Gilling
Co-stars: Peter Cushing Donald Pleasence June Laverick

1959 HELL IS A CITY
Director: Val Guest
Co-stars: Stanley Baker Donald Pleasence Maxine Audley

1960 NO LOVE FOR JOHNNY
Director: Ralph Thomas
Co-stars: Peter Finch Mary Peach Stanley Holloway

1960	**MAKE MINE MINK**	
Director:	Robert Asher	
Co-stars:	Terry-Thomas Athene Seyler Jack Hedley	

1960 **MAKE MINE MINK**
Director: Robert Asher
Co-stars: Terry-Thomas Athene Seyler Jack Hedley

1961 **PAYROLL**
Director: Sidney Hayers
Co-stars: Michael Craig Tom Bell Kenneth Griffith

1961 **MR TOPAZE**
Director: Peter Sellers
Co-stars: Peter Sellers Herbert Lom Leo McKern

1962 **THE DEVIL'S AGENT**
Director: John Paddy Carstairs
Co-stars: Peter Van Eyck Marianne Koch Macdonald Carey

1964 **THE COMEDY MAN**
Director: Alvin Rakoff
Co-stars: Kenneth More Angela Douglas Cecil Parker

1968 **THE ADDING MACHINE**
Director: Jerome Epstein
Co-stars: Milo O'Shea Phyllis Diller Sydney Chaplin

1969 **TWISTED NERVE**
Director: Roy Boulting
Co-stars: Hayley Mills Hywell Bennett Phyllis Calvert

1968 **CHARLIE BUBBLES**
Director: Albert Finney
Co-stars: Albert Finney Liza Minnelli Colin Blakeley

1969 **START THE REVOLUTION WITHOUT ME**
Director: Bud Yorkin
Co-stars: Donald Sutherland Gene Wilder

1970 **LEO THE LAST**
Director: John Boorman
Co-stars: Marcello Mastroianni Calvin Lockhart

1970 **EAGLE IN A CAGE**
Director: Fielder Cook
Co-stars: Kenneth Haigh John Gielgud Ralph Richardson

1971 **GUMSHOE**
Director: Stephen Frears
Co-stars: Albert Finney Fulton MacKay Frank Finlay

1972 **FRENZY**
Director: Alfred Hitchcock
Co-stars: Jon Finch Barry Foster Alex McCowen

1973 **NIGHT WATCH**
Director: Brian Hutton
Co-stars: Elizabeth Taylor Laurence Harvey Tony Britton

1976 **THE OMEN**
Director: Richard Donner
Co-stars: Gregory Peck Lee Remick David Warner

1977 **LEOPARD IN THE SNOW**
Director: Gerry O'Hara
Co-stars: Keir Dullea Susan Penhaligon Kenneth More

1978 **THE WATER BABIES**
Director: Lionel Jeffries
Co-stars: James Mason David Tomlinson Bernard Cribbins

1982 **AN UNSUITABLE JOB FOR A WOMAN**
Director: Christopher Petit
Co-stars: Pippa Guard Dominic Guard

1983 **SLAYGROUND**
Director: Terry Bedford
Co-stars: Peter Coyote Mel Smith Philip Sayer

1984 **THE CHAIN**
Director: Jack Gold
Co-stars: Denis Lawson Maurice Denham Nigel Hawthorne

1985 **SHADEY**
Director: Philip Saville
Co-stars: Anthony Sher Patrick MacNee Leslie Ash

1987 **MAURICE**
Director: James Ivory
Co-stars: James Wilby Hugh Grant Rupert Graves

1988 **JOYRIDERS**
Director: Aisling Walsh
Co-stars: Patricia Kerrigan Andrew Connolly David Kelly

1988 **THE PICNIC**
Director: Paul Seed
Co-stars: Iain Glenn Cassie Stuart Brenda Fricker

1988 **THE DRESSMAKER**
Director: Jim O'Brien
Co-stars: Joan Plowright Jane Horrocks Peter Postlethwaite

1989 **THE FIFTEEN STREETS**
Director: David Wheatley
Co-stars: Owen Teale Sean Bean Ian Bannen

1990 **THE KRAYS**
Director: Peter Medak
Co-stars: Gary Kemp Martin Kemp Susan Fleetwood

1990 **LORNA DOONE**
Director: Andrew Grieve
Co-stars: Clive Owen Sean Bean Kenneth Haigh

1991 **A MURDER OF QUALITY**
Director: Gavin Miller
Co-stars: Denholm Elliott Glenda Jackson Joss Ackland

1992 **FREDDIE AS FRO7** *(Voice)*
Director: Jon Acevski
Co-stars: Ben Kingsley Jenny Agutter Phyllis Logan

1994 **SKALLAGRIGG**
Director: Richard Spence
Co-stars: Bernard Hill Ian Drury Richard Briers

1994 **DEADLY ADVICE**
Director: Mandie Fletcher
Co-stars: Jane Horrocks Imelda Staunton Brenda Fricker

ANNETTE WHITELEY

1963 **THE GIRL ON APPROVAL**
Director: Charles Frend
Co-stars: Rachel Roberts James Maxwell John Dare

1964 **THE DEVIL-SHIP PIRATES**
Director: Don Sharp
Co-stars: Christopher Lee Andrew Keir John Cairney

THELMA WHITELEY

1985 **THE BURSTON REBELLION**
Director: Norman Stone
Co-stars: Eileen Atkins Bernard Hill John Shrapnel

JUNE WHITFIELD

1959 **CARRY ON NURSE**
Director: Gerald Thomas
Co-stars: Shirly Eaton Kenneth Connor Charles Hawtrey

1966 **THE SPY WITH A COLD NOSE**
Director: Daniel Petrie
Co-stars: Lionel Jeffries Laurence Harvey Eric Sykes

1972 **BLESS THIS HOUSE**
Director: Gerald Thomas
Co-stars: Sid James Diana Coupland Terry Scott

1972 **CARRY ON ABROAD**
Director: Gerald Thomas
Co-stars: Sid James Barbara Windsor Kenneth Williams

1973 **CARRY ON GIRLS**
Director: Gerald Thomas
Co-stars: Sid James Joan Sims Sally Geeson

1992   CARRY ON COLUMBUS
Director: Gerald Thomas
Co-stars: Jim Dale Leslie Phillips Bernard Cribbins

1996   JUDE
Director: Michael Winterbottom
Co-stars: Christopher Eccleston Kate Winslet Rachel Griffiths

LYNN WHITFIELD

1986   THE GEORGE McKENNA STORY
Director: Eric Laneuville
Co-stars: Denzel Washington Richard Masur Virginia Capers

1986   JOHNNIE MAE GIBSON: F.B.I.

1991   THE JOSEPHINE BAKER STORY
Director: Brian Gibson
Co-stars: Ruben Blades David Dukes Craig T. Nelson

1992   TAKING THE HEAT
Director: Tom Mankiewicz
Co-stars: Tony Goldwyn George Segal Alan Arkin

1996   A THIN LINE BETWEEN LOVE AND HATE
Co-star: Martin Laurence

BARBARA WHITING

1945   JUNIOR MISS
Director: George Seaton
Co-stars: Peggy Ann Garner Allyn Joslyn Mona Freeman

1946   HOME SWEET HOMICIDE
Director: Lloyd Bacon
Co-stars: Lynn Bari Randolph Scott Dean Stockwell

1946   CENTENNIAL SUMMER
Director: Otto Preminger
Co-stars: Jeanne Crain Cornel Wilde Linda Darnell

1949   CITY ACROSS THE RIVER
Director: Maxwell Shane
Co-stars: Stephen McNally Al Ramsen Tony Curtis

1952   BEWARE MY LOVELY
Director: Harry Horner
Co-stars: Ida Lupino Robert Ryan Taylor Holmes

1953   DANGEROUS WHEN WET
Director: Charles Walters
Co-stars: Esther Williams Charlotte Greenwood Jack Carson

MARGARET WHITING

1963   THE INFORMERS
Director: Ken Annakin
Co-stars: Nigel Patrick Harry Andrews Frank Finlay

1977   SINBAD AND THE EYE OF THE TIGER
Director: Sam Wanamaker
Co-stars: Patrick Wayne Taryn Power Jane Seymour

JILL WHITLOW

1986   THUNDER ROW
Director: Gary Hudson
Co-stars: Forrest Tucker John Ireland John Shepherd

1986   NIGHT OF THE CREEPS
Director: Fred Dekker
Co-stars: Jason Lively Steve Marshall Tom Atkins

1989   GHOST CHASE
Director: Roland Emmerich
Co-stars: Jason Lively Tim McDaniel Paul Gleason

MAE WHITMAN

1994   WHEN A MAN LOVES A WOMAN
Director: Luis Mandoki
Co-stars: Andy Garcia Meg Ryan Lauren Tom

1997   ONE FINE DAY
Director: Michael Hoffman
Co-stars: George Clooney Michelle Pfeiffer Alex D. Linz

BEVERLY WHITNEY

1944   IRISH EYES ARE SMILING
Director: Gregory Ratoff
Co-stars: Dick Haymes June Haver Monty Woolley

ELEANOR WHITNEY

1935   MILLIONS IN THE AIR
Director: Ray McCarey
Co-stars: Willie Howard Wendy Barrie Robert Cummings

1936   COLLEGE HOLIDAY
Director: Frank Tuttle
Co-stars: Jack Benny George Burns Gracie Allen

1936   ROSE BOWL
Co-star: Tom Brown

1936   THREE CHEERS FOR LOVE
Co-star: Robert Cummings

1936   THE BIG BROADCAST OF 1937
Director: Mitchell Leisen
Co-stars: George Burns Gracie Allen Shirley Ross

1937   THRILL OF A LIFETIME
Director: George Archainbaud
Co-stars: Judy Canova Betty Grable Ben Blue

1937   TURN OFF THE MOON
Director: Lewis Seiler
Co-stars: Charles Ruggles Johnny Downs Kenny Baker

1937   CLARENCE
Co-stars: Johnny Downs Roscoe Karns

GRACE LEE WHITNEY

**1991   STAR TREK VI:
         THE UNDISCOVERED COUNTRY**
Director: Nicholas Meyer
Co-stars: William Shatner Leonard Nimoy

HELENE WHITNEY

1940   THE SAINT'S DOUBLE TROUBLE
Director: Jack Hively
Co-stars: George Sanders Bela Lugosi Jonathan Hale

ANNIE WHITTLE

1985   TRIAL RUN
Director: Melanie Read
Co-stars: Judith Gibson Christopher Brown Lee Grant

MARGARET WHITTON

1982   LOVE CHILD
Director: Larry Peerce
Co-stars: Amy Madigan Beau Bridges Joanna Merlin

1986   NINE AND HALF WEEKS
Director: Adrian Lyne
Co-stars: Mickey Rourke Kim Basinger Karen Young

1987   THE SECRET OF MY SUCCESS
Director: Herbert Ross
Co-stars: Michael J. Fox Helen Slater Richard Jordan

1989   MAJOR LEAGUE
Director: David Ward
Co-stars: Charlie Sheen Tom Berenger Rene Russo

1989   LITTLE MONSTERS
Director: Richard Alan Greenberg
Co-stars: Fred Savage Howie Mandel Daniel Stern

1992	**STEPKIDS**
Director:	Joan Micklin Silver
Co-stars:	Griffin Dunne Patricia Kalember Jenny Lewis

1993	**THE MAN WITHOUT A FACE**
Director:	Mel Gibson
Co-stars:	Mel Gibson Nick Stahl Geoffrey Lewis

1994	**MAJOR LEAGUE II**
Director:	David Ward
Co-stars:	Charlie Sheen Corbin Bernsen

DAME MAY WHITTY

**Nominated For Best Supporting Actress In 1937 For "Night Must Fall"
And In 1942 For "Mrs Miniver"**

1937	**CONQUEST**
Director:	Clarence Brown
Co-stars:	Greta Garbo Charles Boyer Reginald Owen

1937	**I MET MY LOVE AGAIN**
Director:	Joshua Logan
Co-stars:	Henry Fonda Joan Bennett Alan Marshall

1937	**NIGHT MUST FALL**
Director:	Richard Thorpe
Co-stars:	Robert Montgomery Rosalind Russell Alan Marshall

1938	**THE LADY VANISHES**
Director:	Alfred Hitchcock
Co-stars:	Margaret Lockwood Michael Redgrave Basil Radford

1939	**RAFFLES**
Director:	Sam Wood
Co-stars:	David Niven Olivia De Havilland Dudley Digges

1940	**RETURN TO YESTERDAY**
Director:	Robert Stevenson
Co-stars:	Clive Brook Anna Lee Hartley Power

1940	**A BILL OF DIVORCEMENT**
Director:	John Farrow
Co-stars:	Maureen O'Hara Adolphe Menjou Patric Knowles

1941	**ONE NIGHT IN LISBON**
Director:	Edward Griffith
Co-stars:	Madeleine Carroll Fred MacMurray Edmund Gwenn

1941	**SUSPICION**
Director:	Alfred Hitchcock
Co-stars:	Joan Fontaine Cary Grant Nigel Bruce

1942	**THUNDERBIRDS**
Director:	William Wellman
Co-stars:	Gene Tierney Preston Foster John Sutton

1942	**MRS MINIVER**
Director:	William Wyler
Co-stars:	Greer Garson Walter Pidgeon Teresa Wright

1943	**STAGE DOOR CANTEEN**
Director:	Frank Borzage
Co-stars:	Cheryl Walker Lon McCallister Judith Anderson

1943	**SLIGHTLY DANGEROUS**
Director:	Wesley Ruggles
Co-stars:	Lana Turner Robert Young Walter Brennan

1943	**MADAME CURRIE**
Director:	Mervyn LeRoy
Co-stars:	Greer Garson Walter Pidgeon Henry Travers

1943	**LASSIE COME HOME**
Director:	Fred Wilcox
Co-stars:	Roddy McDowall Elizabeth Taylor Donald Crisp

1943	**FOREVER AND A DAY**
Director:	Rene Clair
Co-stars:	Anna Neagle Ray Milland Charles Laughton

1943	**CRASH DIVE**
Director:	Archie Mayo
Co-stars:	Tyrone Power Anne Baxter Dana Andrews

1943	**THE CONSTANT NYMPH**
Director:	Edmund Goulding
Co-stars:	Charles Boyer Joan Fontaine Alexis Smith

1943	**FLESH AND FANTASY**
Director:	Julien Duvivier
Co-stars:	Edward G. Robinson Barbara Stanwyck Charles Boyer

1944	**GASLIGHT**
Director:	George Cukor
Co-stars:	Charles Boyer Ingrid Bergman Joseph Cotten

1944	**THE WHITE CLIFFS OF DOVER**
Director:	Clarence Brown
Co-stars:	Irene Dunne Alan Marshall Frank Morgan

1945	**MY NAME IS JULIA ROSS**
Director:	Joseph Lewis
Co-stars:	Nina Foch George Macready Doris Lloyd

1948	**THE RETURN OF OCTOBER**
Director:	Joseph Lewis
Co-stars:	Glenn Ford Terry Moore James Gleason

1948	**SIGN OF THE RAM**
Director:	John Sturges
Co-stars:	Susan Peters Alexander Knox Peggy Ann Garner

1948	**IF WINTER COMES**
Director:	Victor Saville
Co-stars:	Walter Pidgeon Deborah Kerr Janet Leigh

ANNE WIAZEMSKY

1967	**WEEKEND**
Director:	Jean-Luc Godard
Co-stars:	Mireille Darc Jean Yanne Jean-Pierre Leaud

1968	**THEOREM**
Director:	Pier Paolo Pasolini
Co-stars:	Terence Stamp Silvana Mangano Laura Betti

1972	**TOUT VA BIEN**
Director:	Jean-Luc Godard
Co-stars:	Jane Fonda Yves Montand Jean Pignol

1972	**LE TRAIN**
Director:	Pierre Gramier-Deferre
Co-stars:	Jean-Louis Trintignant Romy Schneider

MARY WICKES

1941	**THE MAN WHO CAME TO DINNER**
Director:	William Keighley
Co-stars:	Monty Woolley Bette Davis Billie Burke

1942	**THE MAYOR OF 44TH STREET**
Director:	Alfred Green
Co-stars:	George Murphy Anne Shirley William Gargan

1942	**BLONDIE'S BLESSED EVENT**
Director:	Frank Strayer
Co-stars:	Penny Singleton Arthur Lake Larry Simms

1942	**WHO DONE IT ?**
Director:	Erle Kenton
Co-stars:	Bud Abbott Lou Costello William Bendix

1943	**HIGHER AND HIGHER**
Director:	Tim Whelan
Co-stars:	Frank Sinatra Michelle Morgan Jack Haley

1943	**RHYTHM OF THE ISLANDS**
Director:	Roy William Neill
Co-stars:	Allan Jones Jane Frazee Andy Devine

1948	**THE DECISION OF CHRISTOPHER BLAKE**
Director:	Peter Godfrey
Co-stars:	Alexis Smith Robert Douglas John Hoyt

1948	**JUNE BRIDE**
Director:	Bretagne Windust
Co-stars:	Bette Davis Robert Montgomery Debbie Reynolds

1949 ANNA LUCASTA
Director: Irving Rapper
Co-stars: Paulette Goddard Oscar Homolka Broderick Crawford

1950 THE PETTY GIRL
Director: Henry Levin
Co-stars: Joan Caulfield Robert Cummings Elsa Lanchester

1951 I'LL SEE YOU IN MY DREAMS
Director: Michael Curtiz
Co-stars: Doris Day Danny Thomas Patrice Wymore

1951 ON MOONLIGHT BAY
Director: Roy Del Ruth
Co-stars: Doris Day Gordon MacRae Leon Ames

1952 YOUNG MAN WITH IDEAS
Director: Mitchell Leisen
Co-stars: Glenn Ford Ruth Roman Denise Darcel

1952 BLOODHOUNDS OF BROADWAY
Director: Harmon Jones
Co-stars: Mitzi Gaynor Scott Brady Mitzi Green

1953 THE ACTRESS
Director: George Cukor
Co-stars: Jean Simmons Spencer Tracy Teresa Wright

1953 HALF A HERO
Director: Don Weis
Co-stars: Red Skelton Jean Hagen Polly Bergin

1953 BY THE LIGHT OF THE SILVERY MOON
Director: David Butler
Co-stars: Doris Day Gordon MacRae Rosemary DeCamp

1954 DESTRY
Director: George Marshall
Co-stars: Audie Murphy Mari Blanchard Edgar Buchanan

1954 WHITE CHRISTMAS
Director: Michael Curtiz
Co-stars: Bing Crosby Danny Kaye Vera-Ellen

1955 GOOD MORNING MISS DOVE
Director: Henry Koster
Co-stars: Jennifer Jones Robert Stack Robert Douglas

1957 DON'T GO NEAR THE WATER
Director: Charles Walters
Co-stars: Glenn Ford Gia Scala Anne Francis

1960 THE SINS OF RACHEL CADE
Director: Gordon Douglas
Co-stars: Angie Dickinson Peter Finch Roger Moore

1961 CIMARRON
Director: Anthony Mann
Co-stars: Glenn Ford Anne Baxter Maria Schell

1964 DEAR HEART
Director: Delbert Mann
Co-stars: Glenn Ford Geraldine Page Angela Lansbury

1967 THE SPIRIT IS WILLING
Director: William Castle
Co-stars: Sid Ceasar Vera Miles Cass Daley

1968 WHERE ANGELS GO, TROUBLE FOLLOWS
Director: James Neilson
Co-stars: Rosalind Russell Stella Stevens Binnie Barnes

1972 SNOWBALL EXPRESS
Director: Norman Tokar
Co-stars: Dean Jones Nancy Olson Henry Morgan

1980 TOUCHED BY LOVE
Director: Gus Trikonis
Co-stars: Deborah Raffin Diane Lane Cristina Raines

1986 THE CHRISTMAS GIFT
Director: Michael Pressman
Co-stars: John Denver Jane Kaczmarek Gennie James

1990 POSTCARDS FROM THE EDGE
Director: Mike Nichols
Co-stars: Meryl Streep Shirley MacLaine Dennis Quaid

1992 SISTER ACT
Director: Emile Ardolino
Co-stars: Whoopi Goldberg Maggie Smith Harvey Keitel

1993 SISTER ACT 2: BACK IN THE HABIT
Director: Bill Duke
Co-stars: Whoopi Goldberg Maggie Smith James Coburn

1995 LITTLE WOMEN
Director: Gillian Armstrong
Co-stars: Susan Sarandon Winona Ryder Samantha Mathis

SASKIA WICKHAM

1991 CLARISSA
Director: Robert Bierman
Co-stars: Sean Bean Cathryn Harrison Lynsey Baxter

KATHLEEN WIDDOES

1966 THE GROUP
Director: Sidney Lumet
Co-stars: Candice Bergen Joan Hackett Shirley Knight

1968 PETULIA
Director: Richard Lester
Co-stars: Julie Christie George C.Scott Richard Chamberlain

1968 THE SEA GULL
Director: Sidney Lumet
Co-stars: James Mason Simone Signoret Vanessa Redgrave

1981 THE END OF AUGUST
Director: Bob Graham
Co-stars: Sally Sharp Lilian Skala Paul Shenar

1983 WITHOUT A TRACE
Director: Stanley Jaffe
Co-stars: Kate Nelligan Judd Hirsch David Dukes

NINA WIDERBERG

1967 ELVIRA MADIGAN
Director: Bo Widerberg
Co-stars: Pia Degermark Thommy Berggren Cleo Jensen

DOROTHEA WIECK

1931 MADCHEN IN UNIFORM
Director: Leontine Sagan
Co-stars: Emilia Unda Hedwig Schlichter Hertha Thiele

1933 CRADLE SONG
Director: Mitchell Leisen
Co-stars: Evelyn Venable Louise Dresser Sir Guy Standing

1933 MISS FANE'S BABY IS STOLEN
Director: Alexander Hall
Co-stars: Alice Brady William Frawley Baby LeRoy

1953 MAN ON A TIGHTROPE
Director: Elia Kazan
Co-stars: Fredric March Adolphe Menjou Gloria Grahame

1958 A TIME TO LOVE AND A TIME TO DIE
Director: Douglas Sirk
Co-stars: John Gavin Lilo Pulver Keenan Wynn

DIANNE WIEST
Oscar For Best Supporting Actress In 1986 For "Hannah And Her Sisters". Nominated For Best Supporting Actress In 1989 For "Parenthood"

1982 I'M DANCING AS FAST AS I CAN
Director: Jack Hofsiss
Co-stars: Jill Clayburgh Nicol Williamson

1983 INDEPENDENCE DAY
Director: Robert Mandel
Co-stars: Kathleen Quinlan David Keith Cliff DeYoung

1984 FALLING IN LOVE
Director: Ulu Grosbard
Co-stars: Robert De Niro Meryl Streep Harvey Keitel

1984 FOOTLOOSE
Director: Herbert Ross
Co-stars: Kevin Bacon Lori Singer John Lithgow

1985 THE PURPLE ROSE OF CAIRO
Director: Woody Allen
Co-stars: Mia Farrow Jeff Daniels Van Johnson

1986 HANNAH AND HER SISTERS
Director: Woody Allen
Co-stars: Woody Allen Mia Farrow Michael Caine

1987 RADIO DAYS
Director: Woody Allen
Co-stars: Woody Allen Mia Farrow Seth Green

1987 SEPTEMBER
Director: Woody Allen
Co-stars: Mia Farrow Denholm Elliott Sam Waterston

1987 THE LOST BOYS
Director: Joel Schumacher
Co-stars: Jason Patric Kiefer Sutherland Jami Gertz

1988 BRIGHT LIGHTS, BIG CITY
Director: James Bridges
Co-stars: Michael J. Fox Kiefer Sutherland Phoebe Cates

1989 COOKIE
Director: Susan Seidelman
Co-stars: Peter Falk Emily Lloyd Brenda Vaccaro

1989 PARENTHOOD
Director: Ron Howard
Co-stars: Steve Martin Jason Robards Keanu Reeves

1990 EDWARD SCISSORHANDS
Director: Tim Burton
Co-stars: Johnny Depp Winona Ryder Vincent Price

1991 LITTLE MAN TATE
Director: Jody Foster
Co-stars: Jody Foster Harry Connick Jnr. David Pierce

1994 COPS AND ROBBERSONS
Director: Michael Ritchie
Co-stars: Chevy Chase Jack Palance Robert Davi

1994 BULLETS OVER BROADWAY
Director: Woody Allen
Co-stars: John Cusack Jennifer Tilly

1994 THE SCOUT
Director: Michael Ritchie
Co-stars: Albert Brooks Brendan Fraser

1996 THE BIRDCAGE
Director: Mike Nichols
Co-stars: Robin Williams Nathan Lane Gene Hackman

1996 THE ASSOCIATE
Co-stars: Whoopi Goldberg Eli Wallach

MOGENS WIETH

1951 THE TALES OF HOFFMAN
Director: Michael Powell
Co-stars: Moira Shearer Robert Rounseville Robert Helpman

1956 THE MAN WHO KNEW TOO MUCH
Director: Alfred Hitchcock
Co-stars: James Stewart Doris Day Bernard Miles

1962 PRIVATE POTTER
Director: Caspar Wrede
Co-stars: Tom Courtenay Ronald Fraser James Maxwell

NAIMA WIFSTRAND

1948 MUSIC IS MY FUTURE
Director: Ingmar Bergman
Co-stars: Mai Zetterling Birger Malmsten Douglas Hage

1954 JOURNEY INTO AUTUMN
Director: Ingmar Bergman
Co-stars: Eva Dahlbeck Harriet Andersson Gunnar Bjornstrand

1955 SMILES OF A SUMMER NIGHT
Director: Ingmar Bergman
Co-stars: Gunnar Bjornstrand Eva Dahlbeck Ulla Jacobsson

1957 WILD STRAWBERRIES
Director: Ingmar Bergman
Co-stars: Victor Sjostrom Ingrid Thulin Bibi Andersson

1958 THE FACE
Director: Ingmar Bergman
Co-stars: Max Von Sydow Ingrid Thulin Gunnar Bjornstrand

1966 NIGHT GAMES
Director: Mai Zetterling
Co-stars: Ingrid Thulin Keve Hjelm Lena Brundin

CLAIRE WILCOX *(Child)*

1963 WIVES AND LOVERS
Director: John Rich
Co-stars: Van Johnson Shelley Winters Janet Leigh

1963 FORTY POUNDS OF TROUBLE
Director: Norman Jewison
Co-stars: Tony Curtis Suzanne Pleshette Phil Silvers

LISA WILCOX

1988 A NIGHTMARE ON ELM STREET IV
Director: Renny Harlin
Co-stars: Robert Englund Rodney Eastman Tuesday Knight

1989 A NIGHTMARE ON ELM STREET V
Director: Stephen Hopkins
Co-stars: Robert Englund Kelly Jo Minter Nick Mele

PAULA WILCOX

1972 THE LOVERS
Director: Herbert Wise
Co-stars: Richard Beckinsdale Joan Scott John Comer

1974 A MAN ABOUT THE HOUSE
Director: John Robins
Co-stars: Richard O'Sullivan Sally Thomsett Yootha Joyce

SHANNON WILCOX

1982 THE BORDER
Director: Tony Richardson
Co-stars: Jack Nicholson Harvey Keitel Valerie Perrine

1982 SIX WEEKS
Director: Tony Bill
Co-stars: Dudley Moore Mary Tyler Moore Katherine Healy

1990 83 HOURS TILL DAWN
Director: Donald Wrye
Co-stars: Peter Strauss Robert Urich Samantha Mathis

1992 FOR THE BOYS
Director: Mark Rydell
Co-stars: Bette Midler James Caan George Segal

SOPHIE WILCOX

1989 THE CHRONICLES OF NARNIA: THE LION, THE WITCH AND THE WARDROBE
Director: Marilyn Fox
Co-star: Richard Dempsey Sophie Cook

1989 **THE CHRONICLES OF NARNIA:
PRINCE CASPIAN**
Director: Marilyn Fox
Co-stars: Sophie Cook Jonathan Scott

1989 **THE CHRONICLES OF NARNIA:
VOYAGE OF THE DAWN TREADER**
Director: Alex Kirby
Co-stars: Michael Aldridge Jeffrey Perry

TOYAH WILCOX

1978 **JUBILEE**
Director: Derek Jarman
Co-stars: Jenny Runacre Ian Charleson Adam Ant

1979 **QUADROPHENIA**
Director: Frank Roddam
Co-stars: Phil Daniels Leslie Ash Sting

1980 **THE TEMPEST**
Director: Derek Jarman
Co-stars: Heathcote Williams Karl Johnson Elizabeth Welch

1993 **ANCHORESS**
Director: Chris Newby
Co-stars: Natalie Morse Peter Postlethwaite Christopher Eccleston

COLLIN WILCOX-HORNE

1970 **THE BABY MAKER**
Director: James Bridges
Co-stars: Barbara Hershey Sam Groom Scott Glenn

KATY WILD

1964 **THE EVIL OF FRANKENSTEIN**
Director: Freddie Francis
Co-stars: Peter Cushing Sandor Eles Peter Woodthorpe

1982 **THE SETTLEMENT**
Director: Howard Rubie
Co-stars: Bill Kerr John Jarrett Lorna Lesley

BARBIE WILDE

1988 **HELLBOUND: HELLRAISER II**
Director: Tony Randel
Co-stars: Clare Higgins Ashley Laurence Kenneth Cranham

COLETTE WILDE

1962 **THE NIGHT OF THE PROWLER**
Director: Francis Searle
Co-stars: Patrick Holt Benny Lee Anthony Wager

CYNTHIA WILDE

1987 **LENA: MY 100 CHILDREN**
Director: Ed Sherin
Co-stars: Linda Lavin Leonore Harris Sam Malkin

LEE AND LYN WILDE *(Wilde Twins)*

1944 **ANDY HARDY'S BLONDE TROUBLE**
Director: George Seitz
Co-stars: Mickey Rooney Lewis Stone Fay Holden

1945 **TWICE BLESSED**
Director: Harry Beaumont
Co-stars: Preston Foster Gail Patrick Richard Gaines

LOIS WILDE

1936 **THE SINGING COWBOY**
Co-stars: Gene Autry Smiley Burnette

1938 **CARYL OF THE MOUNTAINS**
Co-stars: Francis X. Bushman Rin Tin Tin

SONYA WILDE

1960 **I PASSED FOR WHITE**
Director: Fred Wilcox
Co-stars: James Franciscus Pat Michon Elizabeth Council

PATRICIA WILDER

1936 **SPEED**
Co-stars: James Stewart Ted Healy

YVONNE WILDER

1971 **THE RETURN OF COUNT YORGA**
Director: Bob Kelljan
Co-stars: Robert Quarry Mariette Hartley George Macready

1974 **DEATH SENTENCE**
Director: E.W. Swackhamer
Co-stars: Cloris Leachman Laurence Luckinbill Nick Nolte

1978 **BLOODBROTHERS**
Director: Robert Mulligan
Co-stars: Paul Sorvino Tony LoBianco Richard Gere

DAWN WILDSMITH

1987 **SURF NAZIS MUST DIE**
Director: Peter George
Co-stars: Barry Brenner Gail Neely Michael Sonye

1988 **HOLLYWOOD CHAINSAW HOOKERS**
Director: Fred Olen Ray
Co-stars: Gunnar Hansen Linnea Quigley Jay Richardson

1988 **B.O.R.N.**

1989 **THE ALIENATOR**
Director: Fred Olen Ray
Co-stars: Jan-Michael Vincent John Phillip Law Ross Hagen

JAN WILEY

1942 **THE LIVING GHOST**
Co-stars: James Dunn George Eldredge Edna Johnson

1942 **CITY OF SILENT MEN**
Director: William Nigh
Co-stars: Frank Albertson June Lang Richard Clarke

KATHLEEN WILHOITE

1984 **FLIGHT 90: DISASTER ON THE POTOMAC**
Director: Robert Lewis
Co-stars: Richard Masur Stephen Macht Ken Olin

1986 **THE MORNING AFTER**
Director: Sidney Lumet
Co-stars: Jane Fonda Jeff Bridges Raul Julia

1986 **MURPHY'S LAW**
Director: J. Lee-Thompson
Co-stars: Charles Bronson Carrie Snodgress Robert F. Lyons

1987 **UNDER COVER**
Director: John Stockwell
Co-stars: David Neidorf Jennifer Jason Leigh Barry Corbin

1987 **CAMPUS MAN**
Director: Ron Casden
Co-stars: John Dye Steve Lyon Morgan Fairchild

1987 **ANGEL HEART**
Director: Alan Parker
Co-stars: Mickey Rourke Robert De Niro Lisa Bonet

1988 **CROSSING DELANCEY**
Director: Joan Micklin Silver
Co-stars: Amy Irving Peter Riegert Jeroen Krabbe

1990 **BAD INFLUENCE**
Director: Curtis Hanson
Co-stars: Rob Lowe James Spader Lisa Zane

1990 EVERYBODY WINS
Director: Karel Weisz
Co-stars: Debra Winger Nick Nolte Will Paton

1992 LORENZO'S OIL
Director: George Miller
Co-stars: Nick Nolte Susan Sarandon Peter Ustinov

1992 LIVE: FROM DEATH ROW
Director: Petrick Duncan
Co-stars: Bruce Davison Joanna Cassidy Jason Tomlins

1994 GETTING EVEN WITH DAD
Director: Howard Deutsch
Co-stars: Macaulay Culkin Ted Danson Glenne Headley

CATHERINE WILKENING

1989 JESUS OF MONTREAL
Director: Denys Arcand
Co-stars: Lothaire Bluteau Remy Girard Robert Lepage

DONNA WILKES

1984 ANGEL
Director: Robert Vincent O'Neil
Co-stars: Cliff Gorman Rory Calhoun Susan Tyrrell

ELAINE WILKES

1984 THE ROOMMATE
Director: Nell Cox
Co-stars: Lance Guest Barry Miller Melissa Ford

ELLEN WILKIE

1988 RASPBERRY RIPPLE
Director: Nigel Finch
Co-stars: Faye Dunaway John Gordon Sinclair Rosie Kerslake

AMBER WILKINSON

1986 COMRADES
Director: Bill Douglas
Co-stars: Vanessa Redgrave James Fox Freddie Jones

ELLENOR WILKINSON

1994 INTIMATE WITH A STRANGER
Director: Mel Woods
Co-stars: Roderick Mangin-Turner Daphne Nayar Janis Lee

JUNE WILKINSON

1959 THE CAREER GIRL
Director: Harold David
Co-stars: Charles Robert Keane Lisa Barrie Joe Sullivan

RACHEL WILKINSON

1992 SEEKERS
Director: Peter Barber-Fleming
Co-stars: Brenda Fricker Josette Simon Michael Carter

JEAN WILLES

1949 CHINATOWN AT MIDNIGHT
Director: Seymour Friedman
Co-stars: Hurd Hatfield Tom Powers Ray Walker

1955 FIVE AGAINST THE HOUSE
Director: Phil Karlson
Co-stars: Guy Madison Kim Novak Brian Keith

1955 MASTERSON OF KANSAS
Director: William Castle
Co-stars: George Montgomery Nancy Gates James Griffith

1956 KING AND FOUR QUEENS
Director: Raoul Walsh
Co-stars: Clark Gable Eleanor Parker Jo Van Fleet

1957 HEAR ME GOOD
Director: Don McGuire
Co-stars: Hal March Joe E. Ross Merry Anders

BARBARA WILLIAMS

1984 THIEF OF HEARTS
Director: Douglas Day Stewart
Co-stars: Steven Bauer John Getz David Caruso

1988 TIGER WARSAW
Director: Amin Chaudhri
Co-stars: Patrick Swayze Piper Laurie Lee Richardson

1989 PETER GUNN
Director: Blake Edwards
Co-stars: Peter Strauss Pearl Bailey Jennifer Edwards

1991 CITY OF HOPE
Director: John Sayles
Co-stars: Vincent Spano Joe Morton Tony LoBianco

1992 BLACK DEATH
Director: Sheldon Larry
Co-stars: Kate Jackson Jerry Orbach Al Waxman

1992 INDECENCY
Director: Marisa Silver
Co-stars: Jennifer Beals Sammi Davis James Remar

1992 OH! WHAT A NIGHT
Director: Eric Till
Co-stars: Corey Haim Robbie Coltrane

1993 DIGGER
Director: Robert Turner
Co-stars: Adam Hann-Byrd Joshua Jackson

1993 SPENSER: PALE KINGS AND PRINCES
Director: Vic Jarin
Co-stars: Robert Urich Avery Brooks

1992 SPENSER: CEREMONY
Director: Andrew Wild
Co-stars: Robert Urich Avery Brooks

CARA WILLIAMS
Nominated For Best Supporting Actress In 1958 For "The Defiant Ones"

1943 HAPPY LAND
Director: Irving Pichel
Co-stars: Don Ameche Frances Dee Natalie Wood

1944 SOMETHING FOR THE BOYS
Director: Lewis Seiler
Co-stars: Carmen Miranda Vivian Blaine Michael O'Shea

1947 BOOMERANG
Director: Elia Kazan
Co-stars: Dana Andrews Jane Wyatt Lee J. Cobb

1948 THE SAXON CHARM
Director: Claude Binyon
Co-stars: Robert Montgomery Susan Hayward John Payne

1953 THE GIRL NEXT DOOR
Director: Richard Sale
Co-stars: Dan Dailey June Haver Billy Gray

1954 THE GREAT DIAMOND ROBBERY
Director: Robert Z. Leonard
Co-stars: Red Skelton James Whitmore Kurt Kasznar

1956 MEET ME IN LAS VEGAS
Director: Roy Rowland
Co-stars: Dan Dailey Cyd Charisse Paul Henreid

1957 THE HELEN MORGAN STORY
Director: Michael Curtiz
Co-stars: Ann Blyth Paul Newman Richard Carlson

1958 NEVER STEAL ANYTHING SMALL
Director: Charles Lederer
Co-stars: James Cagney Shirley Jones Roger Smith

1958   **THE DEFIANT ONES**
Director: Stanley Kramer
Co-stars: Tony Curtis Sidney Poitier Theodore Bikel

1963   **THE MAN FROM THE DINER'S CLUB**
Director: Frank Tashlin
Co-stars: Danny Kaye Telly Savalas Martha Hyer

1970   **DOCTORS' WIVES**
Director: George Schaefer
Co-stars: Richard Crenna Janice Rule Gene Hackman

1977   **THE WHITE BUFFALO**
Director: J. Lee-Thompson
Co-stars: Charles Bronson Jack Warden Kim Novak

CAROLINE WILLIAMS

1986   **THE TEXAS CHAINSAW MASSACRE II**
Director: Tobe Hooper
Co-stars: Dennis Hopper Bill Johnson

1989   **STEPFATHER II: MAKE ROOM FOR DADDY**
Director: Jeff Burr
Co-stars: Terry O'Quinn Meg Foster Jonathan Brandis

1990   **TRUE BETRAYAL**
Director: Roger Young
Co-stars: Mark Winningham Peter Gallagher M. Emmet Walsh

1990   **DAYS OF THUNDER**
Director: Tony Scott
Co-stars: Tom Cruise Robert Duvall Nicole Kidman

CINDY WILLIAMS

1970   **GAS-S-S-S !**
Director: Roger Corman
Co-stars: Robert Corff Elaine Giftos Ben Vereen

1972   **TRAVELS WITH MY AUNT**
Director: George Cukor
Co-stars: Maggie Smith Alex McCowen Robert Stephens

1973   **AMERICAN GRAFFITI**
Director: George Lucas
Co-stars: Richard Dreyfuss Ron Howard Paul LeMat

1974   **THE CONVERSATION**
Director: Francis Coppola
Co-stars: Gene Hackman Allen Garfield Frederic Forrest

1974   **THE MIGRANTS**
Director: Tom Gries
Co-stars: Cloris Leachman Ron Howard Sissy Spacek

1975   **MR RICCO**
Director: Paul Bogart
Co-stars: Dean Martin Eugene Roche Geraldine Brooks

1976   **THE FIRST NUDIE MUSICAL**
Director: Mark Haggard
Co-stars: Bruce Kimmel Stephen Nathan Diana Canova

1979   **MORE AMERICAN GRAFFITI**
Director: B.W.L. Norton
Co-stars: Candy Clark Ron Howard Paul LeMat

1980   **U.F.ORIA**
Director: John Bender
Co-star: Harry Dean Stanton

1985   **WHEN DREAMS COME TRUE**
Director: John Llewellyn Moxey
Co-stars: David Morse Lee Horsley Jessica Harper

1986   **THE LEFTOVERS**
Director: Paul Schneider
Co-stars: John Denver Pamela Segall Anne Seymour

1988   **SAVE THE DOG !**
Director: Paul Aaron
Co-stars: Tony Randall Katherine Helmond Tom Poston

1988   **TRICKS OF THE TRADE**
Director: Jack Bender
Co-stars: Scott Paulin Markie Post

1989   **RUDE AWAKENING**
Director: Aaron Russo
Co-stars: Cheech Marin Eric Robert Julie Hagerty

1989   **PERRY MASON:**
         THE CASE OF THE POISONED PEN
Director: Christian Nyby
Co-stars: Raymond Burr Barbara Hale

1991   **BINGO**
Director: Matthew Robbins
Co-stars: David Rasche Robert J. Steinmiller David French

1995   **ESCAPE FROM TERROR**
Director: Michael Scott
Co-stars: Adam Storke Maria Pitillo Brad Dourif

CYNDA WILLIAMS

1990   **MO' BETTER BLUES**
Director: Spike Lee
Co-stars: Spike Lee Denzel Washington Wesley Snipes

1991   **ONE FALSE MOVE**
Director: Carl Franklin
Co-stars: Bill Paxton Jim Metzler Michael Beach

EDY WILLIAMS

1966   **THE PAD AND HOW TO USE IT**
Director: Brian Hutton
Co-stars: Brian Bedford Julie Sommars James Farentino

1968   **THE SECRET LIFE OF AN AMERICAN WIFE**
Director: George Axelrod
Co-stars: Walter Matthau Anne Jackson

1970   **BEYOND THE VALLEY OF THE DOLLS**
Director: Russ Meyer
Co-stars: Dolly Read Cynthia Myers Marcia McBroom

1971   **THE SEVEN MINUTES**
Director: Russ Meyer
Co-stars: Yvonne De Carlo Phil Carey John Carradine

1984   **HOLLYWOOD HOT TUBS**
Director: Chuck Vincent
Co-stars: Donna McDaniel Michael Andrew Paul Gunning

ELAINE WILLIAMS

1968   **THE SUBJECT WAS ROSES**
Director: Ulu Grosbard
Co-stars: Patricia Neal Jack Albertson Martin Sheen

ESTHER WILLIAMS

1942   **ANDY HARDY'S DOUBLE LIFE**
Director: George Seitz
Co-stars: Mickey Rooney Lewis Stone Bonita Granville

1943   **A GUY NAMED JOE**
Director: Victor Fleming
Co-stars: Spencer Tracy Irene Dunne Van Johnson

1944   **BATHING BEAUTY**
Director: George Sidney
Co-stars: Red Skelton Basil Rathbone Keenan Wynn

1945   **THRILL OF A ROMANCE**
Director: Richard Thorpe
Co-stars: Van Johnson Lauritz Melchior Frances Gifford

1945   **ZIEGFELD FOLLIES**
Director: Vincente Minnelli
Co-stars: William Powell Fred Astaire Judy Garland

1946 EASY TO WED
Director: Edward Buzzell
Co-stars: Van Johnson Lucille Ball Keenan Wynn

1946 THE HOODLUM SAINT
Director: Norman Taurog
Co-stars: William Powell Angela Lansbury James Gleason

1947 THIS TIME FOR KEEPS
Director: Richard Thorpe
Co-stars: Lauritz Melchior Jimmy Durante Johnnie Johnston

1947 FIESTA
Director: Richard Thorpe
Co-stars: Ricardo Montalban Cyd Charisse Mary Astor

1948 ON AN ISLAND WITH YOU
Director: Richard Thorpe
Co-stars: Peter Lawford Ricardo Montalban Jimmy Durante

1949 TAKE ME OUT TO THE BALL GAME
Director: Busby Berkeley
Co-stars: Gene Kelly Frank Sinatra Betty Garrett

1949 NEPTUNE'S DAUGHTER
Director: Edward Buzzell
Co-stars: Red Skelton Betty Garrett Keenan Wynn

1950 PAGAN LOVE SONG
Director: Robert Alton
Co-stars: Howard Keel Rita Moreno Minna Gombell

1950 DUCHESS OF IDAHO
Director: Robert Z. Leonard
Co-stars: Van Johnson John Lund Eleanor Powell

1951 TEXAS CARNIVAL
Director: Charles Walters
Co-stars: Howard Keel Red Skelton Ann Miller

1952 SKIRTS AHOY
Director: Sidney Lanfield
Co-stars: Vivian Blaine Joan Evans Debbie Reynolds

1952 MILLION DOLLAR MERMAID
Director: Mervyn LeRoy
Co-stars: Victor Mature Walter Pidgeon David Brian

1953 EASY TO LOVE
Director: Charles Walters
Co-stars: Van Johnson Tony Martin Carroll Baker

1953 DANGEROUS WHEN WET
Director: Charles Walters
Co-stars: William Demarest Charlotte Greenwood Fernando Lamas

1954 JUPITER'S DARLING
Director: George Sidney
Co-stars: Howard Keel Marge Champion Gower Champion

1956 THE UNGUARDED MOMENT
Director: Harry Keller
Co-stars: George Nader John Saxon Edward Andrews

1958 RAW WIND IN EDEN
Director: Richard Wilson
Co-stars: Jeff Chandler Carlos Thompson Rossana Podesta

1961 THE BIG SHOW
Director: James Clark
Co-stars: Cliff Robertson Robert Vaughn Nehemiah Persoff

FINTY WILLIAMS
(Daughter Of Judi Dench And Michael Williams)

1993 THE MYSTERY OF EDWIN DROOD
Director: Timothy Forder
Co-stars: Robert Powell Nanette Newman Gemma Craven

1997 MRS BROWN
Director: John Madden
Co-stars: Judi Dench Billy Connolly Geoffrey Palmer

HOPE WILLIAMS

1935 THE SCOUNDREL
Director: Ben Hecht
Co-stars: Noel Coward Alexander Woolcott Julie Haydon

JoBETH WILLIAMS

1979 KRAMER Vs KRAMER
Director: Robert Benton
Co-stars: Dustin Hoffman Meryl Streep Justin Henry

1980 THE DOGS OF WAR
Director: John Irvin
Co-stars: Christopher Walken Tom Berenger Colin Blakely

1980 STIR CRAZY
Director: Sidney Poitier
Co-stars: Gene Wilder Richard Pryor George Stanford Brown

1981 JOE DANCER:THE BIG BLACK PILL
Director: Reza S. Badiyi
Co-stars: Robert Blake Neva Patterson Veronica Cartwright

1982 POLTERGEIST
Director: Tobe Hooper
Co-stars: Craig T. Nelson Heather O'Rourke Beatrice Straight

1982 ENDANGERED SPECIES
Director: Alan Rudolph
Co-stars: Robert Urich Paul Dooley Peter Coyote

1983 THE BIG CHILL
Director: Lawrence Kasdan
Co-stars: Tom Berenger Glenn Close William Hurt

1983 ADAM
Director: Michael Tuchner
Co-stars: Daniel J. Travanti Martha Scott Richard Masur

1984 AMERICAN DREAMER
Director: Rick Rosenthal
Co-stars: Tom Conti Giancarlo Giannini Coral Browne

1984 TEACHERS
Director: Arthur Hiller
Co-stars: Nick Nolte Judd Hirsch Laura Dern

1986 POLTERGEIST II
Director: Brian Gibson
Co-stars: Craig T. Nelson Heather O'Rourke Oliver Robins

1986 DESERT BLOOM
Director: Eugene Corr
Co-stars: Jon Voight Annabeth Gish Ellen Barkin

1988 MEMORIES OF ME
Director: Henry Winkler
Co-stars: Billy Crystal Alan King Sean Connery

1988 BABY M
Director: James Steven Sadwith
Co-stars: John Shea Dabney Coleman Anne Jackson

1989 WELCOME HOME
Director: Franklin J. Schaffner
Co-stars: Kris Kristofferson Brian Keith Sam Waterston

1990 CHILD IN THE NIGHT
Director: Mike Robe
Co-star: Elijah Wood

1991 SWITCH
Director: Blake Edwards
Co-stars: Ellen Barkin Jimmy Smits Lorraine Bracco

1991 DUTCH
Director: Peter Faiman
Co-stars: Ed O'Neill Ethan Randall Christopher McDonald

1991 VICTIM OF LOVE
Director: Jerry London
Co-stars: Pierce Brosnan Virginia Madsen Georgia Brown

1992 **STOP ! OR MY MOM WILL SHOOT**
Director: Roger Spottiswoode
Co-stars: Sylvester Stallone Estelle Getty Roger Rees

1993 **SEX, LOVE AND COLD HARD CASH**
Director: Harry Longstreet
Co-stars: Robert Forster Anthony John Denison

1994 **SILHOUETTE**
Director: Eric Till
Co-stars: Corbin Bernsen Stephanie Zimbalist

KATE WILLIAMS

1967 **POOR COW**
Director: Ken Loach
Co-stars: Carol White Terence Stamp John Bindon

1973 **LOVE THY NEIGHBOUR**
Director: John Robins
Co-stars: Jack Smethurst Rudolph Walker Nina Baden-Semper

KATHLYN WILLIAMS

1928 **OUR DANCING DAUGHTERS**
Director: Harry Beaumont
Co-stars: Joan Crawford Johnny Mack Brown Anita Page

KAY WILLIAMS

1953 **THE ACTRESS**
Director: George Cukor
Co-stars: Jean Simmons Spencer Tracy Teresa Wright

KELLI WILLIAMS

1990 **ZAPPED AGAIN**
Director: Douglas Campbell
Co-stars: Todd Eric Andrews Linda Blair Karen Black

1992 **A WOMAN DECEIVED**
Director: Dick Lowry
Co-stars: Meredith Baxter Judith Ivey Ray Baker

1993 **LIFEPOD**
Director: Ron Silver
Co-stars: Ron Silver Robert Loggia Stan Shaw

1993 **SNOWBOUND**
Director: Christian Duguay
Co-stars: Neil Patrick Harris Susan Clark Michael Gross

1994 **THERE GOES MY BABY**
Director: Floyd Mutrux
Co-stars: Dermot Mulroney Rick Schroder

KIMBERLEY WILLIAMS

1992 **FATHER OF THE BRIDE**
Director: Charles Shyer
Co-stars: Steve Martin Diane Keaton Martin Short

1993 **INDIAN SUMMER**
Director: Mike Binder
Co-stars: Alan Arkin Elizabeth Perkins Vincent Spano

LAURA WILLIAMS

1984 **THE BOY WHO HAD EVERYTHING**
Director: Stephen Wallace
Co-stars: Jason Connery Diane Cilento Ian Gilmour

LIA WILLIAMS

1991 **THE YOB**
Director: Ian Emes
Co-stars: Keith Allen Gary Olsen Linda Henry

1993 **DIRTY WEEKEND**
Director: Michael Winner
Co-stars: Rufus Sewell Sylvia Syms David McCallum

LISA WILLIAMS

1991 **IN YOUR WILDEST DREAMS**
Director: Bruce Neibaur
Co-stars: Trevor Black Sarah Schaub

MOIRA WILLIAMS

1993 **DON'T LEAVE ME THIS WAY**
Director: Stuart Orme
Co-stars: Janet McTeer Imelda Staunton Bill Nighy

NOELLE WILLIAMS

1956 **THE TEN COMMANDMENTS**
Director: Cecil B. DeMille
Co-stars: Charlton Heston Yul Brynner Anne Baxter

PAT WILLIAMS

1981 **BURNING AN ILLUSION**
Director: Menelik Shabazz
Co-stars: Victor Romero Beverley Martin Angela Wynter

ROSALIE WILLIAMS

1984 **THE ADVENTURES OF SHERLOCK HOLMES: THE SPECKLED BAND**
Director: John Bruce
Co-stars: Jeremy Brett Jeremy Kemp

1984 **THE ADVENTURES OF SHERLOCK HOLMES: A SCANDAL IN BOHEMIA**
Director: Paul Annett
Co-stars: Jeremy Brett Gayle Hunnicutt

1985 **THE ADVENTURES OF SHERLOCK HOLMES: THE FINAL PROBLEM**
Director: Alan Grint
Co-star: Jeremy Brett

1987 **THE RETURN OF SHERLOCK HOLMES: THE SIGN OF FOUR**
Co-stars: Jeremy Brett Edward Hardwicke

SYLVIA WILLIAMS

1976 **OBSESSION**
Director: Brian De Palma
Co-stars: Cliff Robertson Genevieve Bujold John Lithgow

VANESSA WILLIAMS

1989 **FULL EXPOSURE: THE SEX TAPE SCANDAL**
Director: Noel Nosseck
Co-stars: Lisa Hartman Jennifer O'Neil Anthony Denison

1991 **NEW JACK CITY**
Director: Mario Van Peebles
Co-stars: Wesley Snipes Judd Nelson Bill Nunn

1991 **HARLEY DAVIDSON AND THE MARLBORO MAN**
Director: Simon Wincer
Co-stars: Mickey Rourke Don Johnson

1991 **ANOTHER YOU**
Director: Maurice Phillips
Co-stars: Richard Pryor Gene Wilder Mercedes Ruehl

1992 **CANDYMAN**
Director: Bernard Rose
Co-stars: Virginia Madsen Tony Todd Kasi Lemmons

1996 **ERASER**
Director: Charles Russell
Co-stars: Arnold Schwarzenegger James Caan Robert Pastorelli

1998 **SOUL FOOD**
Director: George Tillman Jnr.
Co-stars: Nia Long Vivica Fox Brandon Hammond

WENDY O. WILLIAMS

1986 REFORM SCHOOL GIRLS
Director: Tom De Simone
Co-stars: Linda Carol Pat Ast Sybil Danning

KATE WILLIAMSON

1984 RACING WITH THE MOON
Director: Richard Benjamin
Co-stars: Sean Penn Nicolas Cage Elizabeth McGovern

1993 DREAM LOVER
Director: Nicholas Kazan
Co-stars: James Spader Madchen Amick Bess Armstrong

PEGGY WILLIAMSON

1986 PASSION FLOWER
Director: Joseph Sargent
Co-stars: Bruce Boxleitner Barbara Hershey Nicol Williamson

CONSTANCE WILLIS

1939 THE MIKADO
Director: Victor Schertzinger
Co-stars: Martyn Green Kenny Baker John Barclay

RUMER WILLIS (Child)

1996 STRIPTEASE
Director: Andrew Bergman
Co-stars: Demi Moore Burt Reynolds Robert Patrick

SUSAN WILLIS

1991 WHAT ABOUT BOB ?
Director: Frank Oz
Co-stars: Bill Murray Richard Dreyfuss Julie Hagerty

MARGARET WILLOCK

1974 THE STRANGE AND DEADLY OCCURRENCE
Director: John Llewellyn Moxey
Co-stars: Robert Stack Vera Miles

LISA WILLS

1983 YOUNG GIANTS
Director: Terrill Tannen
Co-stars: Peter Fox John Huston Severn Darden

BARBARA WILSHIRE

**1984 THE ADVENTURES OF SHERLOCK HOLMES:
THE SOLITARY CYCLIST**
Director: Paul Annett
Co-stars: Jeremy Brett David Burke

BARBARA WILSON

1962 INVASION OF THE ANIMAL PEOPLE
Director: Virgel Voegel
Co-stars: John Carradine Jerry Warren

BRIDGETTE WILSON

1998 THE REAL BLONDE
Director: Tom DiCillo
Co-stars: Matthew Modine Daryl Hannah Kathleen Turner

DANA WILSON (Child)

1957 THE SHIRALEE
Director: Leslie Norman
Co-stars: Peter Finch Elizabeth Sellars Tessie O'Shea

1958 A CRY FROM THE STREETS
Director: Lewis Gilbert
Co-stars: Max Bygraves Barbara Murray Colin Petersen

DOROTHY WILSON

1931 ARE THESE OUR CHILDREN ?

1932 AGE OF CONSENT
Director: Gregory La Cava
Co-stars: Richard Cromwell Eric Linden John Halliday

1933 BEFORE DAWN
Director: Irving Pichel
Co-stars: Warner Oland Stuart Erwin Dudley Digges

1933 LUCKY DEVILS
Director: Ralph Ince
Co-stars: William Boyd William Gargan Roscoe Ates

1934 EIGHT GIRLS IN A BOAT
Co-star: Douglass Montgomery

1934 THE WHITE PARADE
Director: Irving Cummings
Co-stars: Loretta Young John Boles Sara Haden

1934 HIS GREATEST GAMBLE
Co-stars: Richard Dix Erin O'Brien Moore

1935 IN OLD KENTUCKY
Director: George Marshall
Co-stars: Will Rogers Bill Robinson Russell Hardie

1935 THE LAST DAYS OF POMPEII
Director: Merian Cooper
Co-stars: Preston Foster Basil Rathbone Alan Hale

1935 WHEN A MAN'S A MAN
Co-stars: George O'Brien Harry Woods

1936 CRAIG'S WIFE
Director: Dorothy Arzner
Co-stars: Rosalind Russell John Boles Billie Burke

ELIZABETH WILSON

1956 PATTERNS
Director: Fielder Cook
Co-stars: Van Heflin Everett Sloane Ed Begley

1958 THE TUNNEL OF LOVE
Director: Gene Kelly
Co-stars: Doris Day Richard Widmark Gig Young

1967 THE GRADUATE
Director: Mike Nichols
Co-stars: Dustin Hoffman Anne Bancroft Katherine Ross

1971 LITTLE MURDERS
Director: Alan Arkin
Co-stars: Alan Arkin Elliott Gould Marcia Rodd

1975 THE HAPPY HOOKER
Director: Nicholas Sgarro
Co-stars: Lynn Redgrave Jean-Pierre Aumont Tom Poston

1975 THE PRISONER OF SECOND AVENUE
Director: Melvin Frank
Co-stars: Jack Lemmon Anne Bancroft Gene Saks

1980 NINE TO FIVE
Director: Colin Higgins
Co-stars: Jane Fonda Lily Tomlin Dolly Parton

1984 GRACE QUIGLEY
Director: Anthony Harvey
Co-stars: Katherine Hepburn Nick Nolte Walter Abel

1987 CONSPIRACY OF LOVE
Director: Noel Black
Co-stars: Robert Young Drew Barrymore

1987 THE BELIEVERS
Director: John Schlesinger
Co-stars: Martin Sheen Helen Shaver Robert Loggia

1991　THE ADDAMS FAMILY
Director:　Barry Sonnenfield
Co-stars:　Anjelica Huston Raul Julia Christopher Lloyd

1991　REGARDING HENRY
Director:　Mike Nichols
Co-stars:　Harrison Ford Annette Bening Bill Nunn

1994　QUIZ SHOW
Director:　Robert Redford
Co-stars:　John Turturro Ralph Fiennes Paul Scofield

EMMA WILSON

1990　THE LADY IN WAITING
Director:　Christian Taylor
Co-stars:　Virginia McKenna Rodney Hudson Beth McGee-Russell

JANIS WILSON

1943　WATCH ON THE RHINE
Director:　Herman Shumlin
Co-stars:　Bette Davis Paul Lukas Lucile Watson

JOSEPHINE WILSON

1943　WE DIVE AT DAWN
Director:　Anthony Asquith
Co-stars:　John Mills Eric Portman Jack Watling

1943　THE DARK TOWER
Director:　John Harlow
Co-stars:　Ben Lyon Anne Crawford David Farrar

JULIE WILSON

1957　THIS COULD BE THE NIGHT
Director:　Robert Wise
Co-stars:　Jean Simmons Paul Douglas Joan Blondell

KRISTEN WILSON

1995　TYSON
Director:　Uli Edel
Co-stars:　George C. Scott Paul Winfield Michael Jai White

KYM WILSON

1991　FLIRTING
Director:　John Duigan
Co-stars:　Noah Taylor Thandie Newton Nicole Kidman

LOIS WILSON

1922　MANSLAUGHTER
Director:　Cecil B. DeMille
Co-stars:　Leatrice Joy Thomas Meighan John Miltern

1923　RUGGLES OF RED GAP
Director:　James Cruze
Co-stars:　Edward Everett Horton Ernest Torrence Louise Dresser

1923　THE COVERED WAGON
Director:　James Cruze
Co-stars:　J. Warren Kerrigan Ernest Torrence Alan Hale

1923　HOLLYWOOD
Director:　James Cruze
Co-stars:　Hope Drown Luke Cosgrove Eleanor Lawson

1925　THE THUNDERING HERD
Director:　William Howard
Co-stars:　Jack Holt Noah Beery Tim McCoy

1926　BLUEBEARD'S SEVEN WIVES
Director:　Alfred Santell
Co-stars:　Ben Lyon Blanche Sweet Dorothy Sebastian

1928　ON TRIAL
Co-stars:　Jason Robards Bert Lytell

1931　THE AGE FOR LOVE
Director:　Frank Lloyd
Co-stars:　Billie Dove Adrian Morris Charles Starrett

1931　SEED
Director:　John Stahl
Co-stars:　John Boles Genevieve Tobin Bette Davis

1932　A DIVORCE IN THE FAMILY
Director:　Charles Reisner
Co-stars:　Jackie Cooper Conrad Nagel Lewis Stone

1932　DRIFTING SOULS
Co-star:　Theodore Von Eltz

1932　THE EXPERT
Co-stars:　Dickie Moore Charles Sale

1933　OBEY THE LAW
Co-star:　Leo Carrillo

1934　LIFE RETURNS
Director:　Eugene Frenke
Co-stars:　Onslow Stevens Valerie Hobson George Breakston

1934　BRIGHT EYES
Director:　David Butler
Co-stars:　Shirley Temple Jane Withers James Dunn

1934　THERE'S ALWAYS TOMORROW
Director:　Edward Sloman
Co-stars:　Frank Morgan Binnie Barnes Robert Taylor

1937　LAUGHING AT TROUBLE
Director:　Frank Strayer
Co-stars:　Jane Darwell Sara Haden Allan Lane

MARA WILSON (Child)

1993　MRS DOUBTFIRE
Director:　Chris Columbus
Co-stars:　Robin Williams Sally Field Pierce Brosnan

1994　A TIME TO HEAL
Director:　Michael Toshiyuki
Co-stars:　Nicolette Sheridan Gary Cole

1995　MIRACLE OF 34TH STREET
Director:　Les Mayfield
Co-stars:　Richard Attenborough Elizabeth Perkins

1996　ROALD DAHL'S MATILDA
Director:　Danny De Vito
Co-stars:　Danny De Vito Rhea Perlman Pam Ferris

1997　A SIMPLE WISH
Co-stars:　Kathleen Turner Martin Short Robert Pastorelli

MARIE WILSON

1934　DOWN TO THEIR LAST YACHT
Co-stars:　Lorimer Johnson Alice Moore

1934　BABES IN TOYLAND
Director:　Gus Meins
Co-stars:　Stan Laurel Oliver Hardy Charlotte Henry

1934　MY GIRL SALLY
Co-star:　Sterling Holloway

1935　STARS OVER BROADWAY
Director:　William Keighley
Co-stars:　James Melton Jane Froman Pat O'Brien

1936　SATAN MET A LADY
Director:　William Dieterle
Co-stars:　Bette Davis Warren William Arthur Treacher

1936　COLLEEN
Director:　Alfred Green
Co-stars:　Dick Powell Ruby Keeler Louise Fazenda

1936　CHINA CLIPPER
Director:　Ray Enright
Co-stars:　Pat O'Brien Beverley Roberts Humphrey Bogart

1937 **THE GREAT GARRICK**
Director: James Whale
Co-stars: Brian Aherne Olivia De Havilland Lana Turner

1937 **MELODY FOR TWO**
Director: Louis King
Co-stars: James Melton Patricia Ellis Wini Shaw

1938 **THE INVISIBLE MENACE**
Director: John Farrow
Co-stars: Boris Karloff Regis Toomey Henry Kolker

1938 **FOOLS FOR SCANDAL**
Director: Mervyn LeRoy
Co-stars: Carole Lombard Fernand Gravet Ralph Bellamy

1938 **BROADWAY MUSKETEERS**
Director: John Farrow
Co-stars: Ann Sheridan Margaret Lindsay Dick Purcell

1939 **SWEEPSTAKE WINNER**
Co-star: Johnnie Davis

1938 **BOY MEETS GIRL**
Director: Lloyd Bacon
Co-stars: James Cagney Pat O'Brien Ralph Bellamy

1939 **THE COWBOY QUARTERBACK**
Co-stars: Bert Wheeler Robert Woolsey

1940 **VIRGINIA**
Director: Edward Griffith
Co-stars: Madeleine Carroll Fred MacMurray Sterling Hayden

1941 **ROOKIES ON PARADE**
Co-star: Ruth Terry

1944 **YOU CAN'T RATION LOVE**
Director: Lester Fuller
Co-stars: Betty Jane Rhodes Johnnie Johnston

1942 **BROADWAY**
Director: William Seiter
Co-stars: George Raft Pat O'Brien Broderick Crawford

1944 **SHINE ON HARVEST MOON**
Director: David Butler
Co-stars: Ann Sheridan Dennis Morgan Jack Carson

1946 **THE YOUNG WIDOW**
Director: Edwin Marin
Co-stars: Jane Russell Louis Hayward Faith Domergue

1946 **NO LEAVE, NO LOVE**
Director: Charles Martin
Co-stars: Van Johnson Pat Kirkwood Keenan Wynn

1947 **THE PRIVATE AFFAIRS OF BEL AMI**
Director: Albert Lewin
Co-stars: George Sanders Angela Lansbury Frances Dee

1949 **MY FRIEND IRMA**
Director: George Marshall
Co-stars: John Lund Dean Martin Jerry Lewis

1950 **MY FRIEND IRMA GOES WEST**
Director: Hal Walker
Co-stars: Dean Martin Jerry Lewis John Lund

1952 **NEVER WAVE AT A WAC**
Director: Norman Z. McLeod
Co-stars: Rosalind Russell Paul Douglas Leif Erikson

1952 **A GIRL IN EVERY PORT**
Director: Chester Erskine
Co-stars: Groucho Marx William Bendix Don Defore

1953 **MARRY ME AGAIN**
Director: Frank Tashlin
Co-stars: Robert Cummings Ray Walker Mary Costa

1962 **MR. HOBBS TAKES A VACATION**
Director: Henry Koster
Co-stars: James Stewart Maureen O'Hara Fabian

MARY LOUISE WILSON

1983 **ZELIG**
Director: Woody Allen
Co-stars: Woody Allen Mia Farrow Stephanie Farrow

1991 **GREEN CARD**
Director: Peter Weir
Co-stars: Gerard Depardieu Andie MacDowell Bebe Neuwirth

MELISSA WILSON

1988 **THE DIARY OF RITA PATEL**
Director: Michael Jackley
Co-stars: Cheryl Miller Tony Wreddin Indira Joshi

RITA WILSON *(Married Tom Hanks)*

1985 **VOLUNTEERS**
Director: Nicholas Meyer
Co-stars: Tom Hanks John Candy Tim Thomerson

1993 **SLEEPLESS IN SEATTLE**
Director: Nora Ephron
Co-stars: Tom Hanks Meg Ryan Ross Malinger

1996 **NOW AND THEN**
Co-stars: Demi Moore Melanie Griffith Thora Birch

1996 **JINGLE ALL THE WAY**
Director: Brian Levant
Co-stars: Arnold Schwarzenegger Jake Lloyd Phil Hartman

1996 **THAT THING YOU DO**
Director: Tom Hanks
Co-stars: Tom Hanks Liv Tyler Tom Everett Scott

SHEREE J. WILSON

1985 **CRIMEWAVE**
Director: Sam Raimi
Co-stars: Louise Lasser Brion James Paul L. Smith

PENELOPE WILTON
(Married Daniel Massey, Ian Holm)

1984 **LAUGHTERHOUSE**
Director: Richard Eyre
Co-stars: Ian Holm Bill Owen Stephen Moore

1986 **CLOCKWISE**
Director: Christopher Morahan
Co-stars: John Cleese Alison Steadman Stephen Moore

1991 **BLAME IT ON THE BELLBOY**
Director: Mark Herman
Co-stars: Dudley Moore Patsy Kensit Bryan Brown

1994 **THE SECRET RAPTURE**
Director: Howard Davies
Co-stars: Juliet Stevenson Joanne Whalley Alan Howard

MARY WIMBUSH

1989 **SITTING TARGETS**
Director: Jenny Wilkes
Co-stars: Leslee Udwin Phyllis Logan John Bowe

1990 **NEVER COME BACK**
Director: Ben Bolt
Co-stars: Nathaniel Parker James Fox Suzanna Hamilton

AGNES WINDECK

1950 **COUNCIL OF THE GODS**
Director: Kurt Maetzig
Co-stars: Paul Bildt Yvonne Merin Fritz Tilman

1958 **A TIME TO LOVE AND A TIME TO DIE**
Director: Douglas Sirk
Co-stars: John Gavin Lilo Pulver Keenan Wynn

ILKA WINDISH

1951 THE MAGIC FACE
Director: Frank Tuttle
Co-stars: Luther Adler Patricia Knight William Shirer

1962 TARAS BULBA
Director: J. Lee-Thompson
Co-stars: Tony Curtis Yul Brynner Christine Kaufman

BARBARA WINDSOR

1962 SPARROWS CAN'T SING
Director: Joan Littlewood
Co-stars: James Booth Roy Kinnear Barbara Ferris

1963 CROOKS IN CLOISTERS
Director: Jeremy Summers
Co-stars: Ronald Fraser Bernard Cribbins Davy Kaye

1965 A STUDY IN TERROR
Director: James Hill
Co-stars: John Neville Donald Houston Robert Morley

1965 CARRY ON SPYING
Director: Gerald Thomas
Co-stars: Kenneth Williams Bernard Cribbins Eric Barker

1968 CARRY ON DOCTOR
Director: Gerald Thomas
Co-stars: Frankie Howerd Jim Dale Sid James

1969 CARRY ON AGAIN DOCTOR
Director: Gerald Thomas
Co-stars: Sid James Charles Hawtrey Joan Sims

1969 CARRY ON CAMPING
Director: Gerald Thomas
Co-stars: Kenneth Williams Terry Scott Dilys Laye

1970 CARRY ON HENRY
Director: Gerald Thomas
Co-stars: Sid James Kenneth Williams Joan Sims

1971 THE BOY FRIEND
Director: Ken Russell
Co-stars: Twiggy Christopher Gable Tommy Tune

1972 NOT NOW DARLING
Director: Ray Cooney
Co-stars: Ray Cooney Leslie Phillips Moira Lister

1972 CARRY ON ABROAD
Director: Gerald Thomas
Co-stars: Sid James Kenneth Connor Sally Geeson

1972 CARRY ON MATRON
Director: Gerald Thomas
Co-stars: Hattie Jacques Kenneth Williams Joan Sims

1973 CARRY ON GIRLS
Director: Gerald Thomas
Co-stars: Sid James June Whitfield Bernard Bresslaw

1974 CARRY ON DICK
Director: Gerald Thomas
Co-stars: Sid James Peter Butterworth Jack Douglas

CLAIRE WINDSOR

1929 CAPTAIN LASH
Director: John Blystone
Co-stars: Victor McLaglen Arthur Stone Albert Conti

MARIE WINDSOR

1948 FORCE OF EVIL
Director: Abraham Polonsky
Co-stars: John Garfield Thomas Gomez Beatrice Pearson

1949 OUTPOST IN MOROCCO
Director: Robert Florey
Co-stars: George Raft Akim Tamiroff Eduard Franz

1949 THE FIGHTING KENTUCKIAN
Director: George Waggner
Co-stars: John Wayne Vera Ralston Oliver Hardy

1950 FRENCHIE
Director: Louis King
Co-stars: Shelley Winters Joel McCrea Elsa Lanchester

1950 DAKOTA LIL
Director: Lesley Selander
Co-stars: George Montgomery Rod Cameron John Emery

1950 THE SHOWDOWN
Director: Stuart McGowan
Co-stars: Wild Bill Elliott Walter Brennan Henry Morgan

1951 LITTLE BIG HORN
Director: Charles Marquis Warren
Co-stars: Lloyd Bridges John McIntyre Hugh O'Brian

1951 HURRICANE ISLAND
Director: Lew Landers
Co-stars: Jon Hall Edgar Barrier Jo Gilbert

1952 JAPANESE WAR BRIDE
Director: King Vidor
Co-stars: Shirley Yamaguchi Don Taylor Cameron Mitchell

1952 THE NARROW MARGIN
Director: Richard Fleischer
Co-stars: Charles McGraw Jacqueline White Queenie Leonard

1952 THE SNIPER
Director: Edward Dmytryk
Co-stars: Adolphe Menjou Arthur Franz Gerald Mohr

1953 TROUBLE ALONG THE WAY
Director: Michael Curtiz
Co-stars: John Wayne Donna Reed Charles Coburn

1953 CITY THAT NEVER SLEEPS
Director: John Auer
Co-stars: Gig Young Mala Powers William Talman

1953 CAT WOMEN OF THE MOON
Director: Arthur Hilton
Co-stars: Sonny Tufts Victor Jory Douglas Fowley

1954 THE BOUNTY HUNTER
Director: Andre De Toth
Co-stars: Randolph Scott Ernest Borgnine Dolores Dorn

1955 ABBOTT & COSTELLO MEET THE MUMMY
Director: Charles Lamont
Co-stars: Bud Abbott Lou Costello Michael Ansara

1956 THE KILLING
Director: Stanley Kubrick
Co-stars: Sterling Hayden Elisha Cook Coleen Gray

1957 THE UNHOLY WIFE
Director: John Farrow
Co-stars: Diana Dors Rod Steiger Beulah Bondi

1957 THE GIRL IN BLACK STOCKINGS
Director: Howard Koch
Co-stars: Anne Bancroft Lex Barker John Dehner

1957 DAY OF THE BADMAN
Director: Harry Keller
Co-stars: Fred MacMurray Skip Homeier Joan Weldon

1962 THE DAY MARS INVADED EARTH
Director: Maury Dexter
Co-stars: Kent Taylor William Mims

1963 CRITIC'S CHOICE
Director: Don Weis
Co-stars: Bob Hope Lucille Ball Marilyn Maxwell

1963 MAIL ORDER BRIDE
Director: Burt Kennedy
Co-stars: Buddy Ebsen Lois Nettleton Keir Dullea

1964   **BEDTIME STORY**
Director: Ralph Levy
Co-stars: Marlon Brando David Niven Shirley Jones

1969   **THE GOOD GUYS AND THE BAD GUYS**
Director: Burt Kennedy
Co-stars: Robert Mitchum George Kennedy

1970   **WILD WOMEN**
Director: Don Taylor
Co-stars: Hugh O'Brian Marilyn Maxwell Anne Francis

1971   **SUPPORT YOUR LOCAL GUNFIGHTER**
Director: Burt Kennedy
Co-stars: James Garner Suzanne Pleshette Jack Elam

1973   **CAHILL, U.S. MARSHALL**
Director: Andrew McLaglen
Co-stars: John Wayne George Kennedy Neville Brand

1974   **THE OUTFIT**
Director: John Flynn
Co-stars: Robert Duvall Karen Black Robert Ryan

1976   **FREAKY FRIDAY**
Director: Gary Nelson
Co-stars: Jodie Foster Barbara Harris Patsy Kelly

ROMY WINDSOR

1988   **HOWLING IV: THE ORIGINAL NIGHTMARE**
Director: Michael T. Weiss
Co-stars: Anthony Hamilton Susanne Severeid

PENELOPE WINDUST

1983   **V**
Director: Kenneth Johnson
Co-stars: Marc Singer Faye Grant Robert Englund

1988   **GHOST TOWN**
Director: Richard Govenor
Co-stars: Franc Luz Catherine Hickland Bruce Glover

1992   **THE NIGHTMAN**
Director: Charles Haid
Co-stars: Joanna Kerns Ted Marcoux Lou Walker

1994   **IRON WILL**
Director: Charles Haid
Co-stars: MacKenzie Astin Kevin Spacey Brian Cox

JOAN WINFIELD

1943   **MURDER ON THE WATERFRONT**
Co-stars: John Loder James Flavin William Davidson

OPRAH WINFREY
Nominated For Best Supporting Actress In 1985 For "The Color Purple"

1985   **THE COLOR PURPLE**
Director: Steven Spielberg
Co-stars: Whoopi Goldberg Danny Glover Margaret Avery

1987   **THROW MOMMA FROM THE TRAIN**
Director: Danny DeVito
Co-stars: Danny DeVito Billy Crystal Anne Ramsey

1989   **WOMEN OF BREWSTER PLACE**
Director: Donna Deitch
Co-stars: Mary Alice Olivia Cole

1993   **THERE ARE NO CHILDREN HERE**
Director: Anita Addison
Co-stars: Norman Golden Mark Lane

ANNA WING

1973   **A DOLL'S HOUSE**
Director: Joseph Losey
Co-stars: Jane Fonda David Warner Trevor Howard

1977   **PROVIDENCE**
Director: Alain Resnais
Co-stars: John Gielgud Dirk Bogarde Ellen Burstyn

TOBY WING

1932   **IF I HAD A MILLION**
Director: James Cruze
Co-stars: Charles Laughton Gary Cooper W.C. Fields

1934   **SEARCH FOR BEAUTY**
Director: Erle Kenton
Co-stars: Buster Crabbe Ida Lupino James Gleason

1934   **COME ON MARINES**
Co-stars: Ida Lupino Richard Arlen

1935   **FORCED LANDING**
Co-stars: Onslow Stevens Barbara Pepper

1937   **SING WHILE YOU'RE ABLE**

1938   **SILKS AND SADDLES**
Co-star: Herman Brix

DEBRA WINGER *(Married Timothy Hutton)*
Nominated For Best Actress In 1982,For "An Officer And A Gentleman",
In 1983 For "Terms Of Endearment" And In 1993 For "Shadowlands"

1978   **THANK GOD IT'S FRIDAY**
Director: Robert Klane
Co-stars: Valerie Landsberg Donna Summer Chick Vennera

1980   **URBAN COWBOY**
Director: James Bridges
Co-stars: John Travolta Scott Glenn Madolyn Smith

1982   **AN OFFICER AND A GENTLEMAN**
Director: Taylor Hackford
Co-stars: Richard Gere Louis Gossett Jnr.

1982   **CANNERY ROW**
Director: David Ward
Co-stars: Nick Nolte Audra Lindley John Huston

1983   **TERMS OF ENDEARMENT**
Director: James Brooks
Co-stars: Shirley MacLaine Jack Nicholson Danny De Vito

1984   **MIKE'S MURDER**
Director: James Bridges
Co-stars: Mark Keyloun Paul Winfield Darrell Larson

1985   **LEGAL EAGLES**
Director: Ivan Reitman
Co-stars: Robert Redford Daryl Hannah Terence Stamp

1986   **BLACK WIDOW**
Director: Bob Rafelson
Co-stars: Theresa Russell Dennis Hopper Nicol Williamson

1987   **MADE IN HEAVEN**
Director: Alan Rudolph
Co-stars: Timothy Hutton Kelly McGillis Don Murray

1988   **BETRAYED**
Director: Constantin Costa-Gavras
Co-stars: Tom Berenger John Heard Betsy Blair

1990   **EVERYBODY WINS**
Director: Karel Reisz
Co-stars: Nick Nolte Jack Warden Judith Ivey

1990   **THE SHELTERING SKY**
Director: Bernardo Bertolucci
Co-stars: John Malkovich Timothy Spall Campbell Scott

1992   **LEAP OF FAITH**
Director: Richard Pearce
Co-stars: Steve Martin Lolita Davidovich Lukas Haas

1993   **WILDER NAPALM**
Director: Gwenn Gordon Caron
Co-stars: Dennis Quaid Arliss Howard M. Emmett Walsh

1993 A DANGEROUS WOMAN
Director: Stephen Gyllenhaal
Co-stars: Barbara Hershey Gabriel Byrne Laurie Metcalf

1993 SHADOWLANDS
Director: Richard Attenborough
Co-stars: Anthony Hopkins Joseph Mazzello Edward Hardwicke

1995 FORGET PARIS
Director: Billy Crystal
Co-stars: Billy Crystal Joe Mantegna Julie Kavner

ANGELA WINKLER

1979 THE TIN DRUM
Director: Volker Schlondorff
Co-stars: Mario Adorf David Bennent Katharina Thalbach

1980 THE GIRL FROM LORRAINE
Director: Claude Goretta
Co-stars: Nathalie Baye Bruno Ganz Pierre Vernier

1982 DANTON
Director: Andrzej Wajda
Co-stars: Gerard Depardieu Patrice Chereau Roland Blanche

1992 BENNY'S VIDEO
Director: Michael Hanneke
Co-star: Arno Frisch

SARAH WINMAN

1994 STAGGERED
Director: Martin Clunes
Co-stars: Martin Clunes Michael Praed Sylvia Syms

KITTY WINN (Katherine)

1970 THE HOUSE THAT WOULD NOT DIE
Director: John Llewellyn Moxey
Co-stars: Barbara Stanwyck Michael Anderson

1971 MAN ON A STRING
Director: Joseph Sargent
Co-stars: Christopher George Joel Grey Jack Warden

1971 THE PANIC IN NEEDLE PARK
Director: Jerry Schatzberg
Co-stars: Al Pacino Adam Vint Richard Bright

1973 THE EXORCIST
Director: William Friedkin
Co-stars: Ellen Burstyn Max Von Sydow Linda Blair

1975 PEEPER
Director: Peter Hyams
Co-stars: Michael Caine Natalie Wood Liam Dunn

1977 EXORCIST II: THE HERETIC
Director: John Boorman
Co-stars: Richard Burton Linda Blair Louise Fletcher

MARE WINNINGHAM

Nominated For Best Supporting Actress In 1995 For "Georgia"

1980 AMBER WAVES
Director: Joseph Sargent
Co-stars: Dennis Weaver Kurt Russell Penny Fuller

1981 THRESHOLD
Director: Richard Pearce
Co-stars: Donald Sutherland Jeff Goldblum Michael Lerner

1985 ST. ELMO'S FIRE
Director: Joel Schumacher
Co-stars: Rob Lowe Demi Moore Ally Sheedy

1985 LOVE IS NEVER SILENT
Director: Joseph Sargent
Co-stars: Phyllis Frelich Ed Waterstreet Cloris Leachman

1986 NOBODY'S FOOL
Director: Evelyn Purcell
Co-stars: Rosanna Arquette Eric Roberts Louise Fletcher

1986 WHO IS JULIA ?
Director: Walter Grauman
Co-stars: Jameson Parker Jeffry DeMunn Jonathan Banks

1987 SHY PEOPLE
Director: Andrei Konchalovsky
Co-stars: Jill Clayburgh Barbara Hershey Martha Plimpton

1987 MADE IN HEAVEN
Director: Alan Rudolph
Co-stars: Timothy Hutton Kelly McGillis Don Murray

1987 EYE ON THE SPARROW
Director: John Korty
Co-stars: Keith Carradine Conchata Ferrell Bianca Rose

1988 GOD BLESS THE CHILD
Director: Larry Elikann
Co-stars: Grace Johnston Dorian Harewood Charlaine Woodard

1989 MIRACLE MILE
Director: Steve De Jarnatt
Co-stars: Anthony Edwards John Agar Lou Hancock

1989 PIED PIPER
Director: Norman Stone
Co-stars: Peter O'Toole Susan Wooldridge Michael Kitchen

1989 TURNER & HOOCH
Director: Roger Spottiswoode
Co-stars: Tom Hanks Craig T. Nelson Scott Paulin

1991 HARD PROMISES
Director: Martin Davidson
Co-stars: Sissy Spacek William Petersen Rip Torn

1991 THOSE SECRETS
Director: David Manson
Co-stars: Blair Brown Arliss Howard

1993 BETRAYED BY LOVE
Director: John Power
Co-stars: Steven Weber Patricia Arquette

1995 GEORGIA

BERNADETTE WINSHIP

1975 AVALANCHE
Director: Frederic Goode
Co-stars: Michael Portman David Ponder Ann Mannion

KATE WINSLET

1995 HEAVENLY CREATURES
Director: Peter Jackson
Co-star: Melanie Lynskey

1996 JUDE
Director: Michael Winterbottom
Co-stars: Christopher Eccleston Rachel Griffiths

1996 SENSE AND SENSIBILITY
Director: Ang Lee
Co-stars: Emma Thompson Hugh Grant James Fleet

1997 HAMLET
Director: Kenneth Branagh
Co-stars: Kenneth Branagh Julie Christie Richard Briers

1998 TITANIC
Director: James Cameron
Co-stars: Leonardo DiCaprio Billy Zane Gloria Stuart

PAULA WINSLOWE

1942 BAMBI (Voice)
Director: David Hand
Co-star: Peter Behn

HATTIE WINSTON

1986 GOOD TO GO
Director: Blaine Novak
Co-stars: Art Garfunkel Robert Doqui Harris Yulin

1988 CLARA'S HEART
Director: Robert Mulligan
Co-stars: Whoopi Goldberg Michael Ontkean Neil Patrick Harris

HELENE WINSTON

1970 THE BROTHERHOOD OF SATAN
Director: Bernard McEveety
Co-stars: Strother Martin Alvy Moore Anna Capri

JESSIE WINTER

1936 HIS LORDSHIP
Director: Herbert Mason
Co-stars: George Arliss Rene Ray Allan Jeayes

JUDY WINTER

1983 THE BEAUTIFUL END OF THIS WORLD
Director: Rainer Erler
Co-stars: Robert Atzorn Claire Oberman Gotz George

MELANIE WINTER

1989 NEW YEAR'S DAY
Director: Henry Jaglom
Co-stars: Henry Jaglom Maggie Jakobson Gwen Welles

DEBORAH WINTERS

1981 KOTCH
Director: Jack Lemmon
Co-stars: Walter Matthau Felicia Farr Charles Aidman

1973 CLASS OF 44
Director: Paul Bogart
Co-stars: Gary Grimes Jerry Houser William Atherton

LINDA WINTERS

1939 BLONDIE MEETS THE BOSS
Director: Frank Strayer
Co-stars: Penny Singleton Arthur Lake Jonathan Hale

SHELLEY WINTERS *(Shelley Winter)*
Oscar For Best Supporting Actress In 1959 For "The Diary Of Ann Frank" And In 1965 For "A Patch Of Blue". Nominated For Best Actress In 1951 For "A Place In The Sun". Nominated For Best Supporting Actress In 1972 For "The Poseidon Adventure"

1944 KNICKERBOCKER HOLIDAY
Director: Harry Joe Brown
Co-stars: Nelson Eddy Charles Coburn Constance Dowling

1945 1001 NIGHTS
Director: Alfred Green
Co-stars: Cornel Wilde Evelyn Keyes Phil Silvers

1945 TONIGHT AND EVERY NIGHT
Director: Victor Saville
Co-stars: Rita Hayworth Lee Bowman Janet Blair

1947 A DOUBLE LIFE
Director: George Cukor
Co-stars: Ronald Colman Edmond O'Brien Signe Hasso

1947 NEW ORLEANS
Director: Arthur Lubin
Co-stars: Louis Armstrong Arturo De Cordova Dorothy Patrick

1948 CRY OF THE CITY
Director: Robert Siodmak
Co-stars: Victor Mature Richard Conte Mimi Aguglia

1948 LARCENCY
Director: George Sherman
Co-stars: John Payne Joan Caulfield Dan Duryea

1949 JOHNNY STOOL PIGEON
Director: William Castle
Co-stars: Howard Duff Dan Duryea Tony Curtis

1949 THE GREAT GATSBY
Director: Elliott Nugent
Co-stars: Alan Ladd Betty Field Howard Da Silva

1949 SOUTH SEA SINNER
Director: Bruce Humberstone
Co-stars: Macdonald Carey Luther Adler Liberace

1949 TAKE ONE FALSE STEP
Director: Chester Erskine
Co-stars: William Powell Marsha Hunt Dorothy Hart

1950 WINCHESTER 73
Director: Anthony Mann
Co-stars: James Stewart Dan Duryea Stephen McNally

1950 FRENCHIE
Director: Louis King
Co-stars: Joel McCrea Paul Kelly Elsa Lanchester

1951 BEHAVE YOURSELF
Director: George Beck
Co-stars: Farley Granger William Demarest Allen Jenkins

1951 A PLACE IN THE SUN
Director: George Stevens
Co-stars: Montgomery Clift Elizabeth Taylor

1951 THE RAGING TIDE
Director: George Sherman
Co-stars: Richard Conte Charles Bickford Alex Nicol

1951 MEET DANNY WILSON
Director: Joseph Pevney
Co-stars: Frank Sinatra Alex Nicol Raymond Burr

1952 UNTAMED FRONTIER
Director: Hugo Fregonese
Co-stars: Joseph Cotten Scott Brady Suzan Ball

1952 MY MAN AND I
Director: William Wellman
Co-stars: Ricardo Montalban Claire Trevor Wendell Corey

1952 PHONE CALL FROM A STRANGER
Director: Jean Negulesco
Co-stars: Gary Merrill Bette Davis Michael Rennie

1954 SASKATCHEWAN
Director: Raoul Walsh
Co-stars: Alan Ladd J. Carrol Naish Hugh O'Brian

1954 TENNESSEE CHAMP
Director: Fred Wilcox
Co-stars: Earl Holliman Dewey Martin Keenan Wynn

1954 PLAYGIRL
Director: Joseph Pevney
Co-stars: Barry Sullivan Colleen Miller Kent Taylor

1954 EXECUTIVE SUITE
Director: Robert Wise
Co-stars: Fredric March Barbara Stanwyck Dean Jagger

1954 MAMBO
Director: Robert Rossen
Co-stars: Silvana Mangano Michael Rennie

1955 THE NIGHT OF THE HUNTER
Director: Charles Laughton
Co-stars: Robert Mitchum Lillian Gish Don Beddoe

1955 THE TREASURE OF PANCHO VILLA
Director: George Sherman
Co-stars: Rory Calhoun Gilbert Roland

1955	**I AM A CAMERA**	**1969**	**BLOODY MAMA**

1955   **I AM A CAMERA**
Director: Henry Cornelius
Co-stars: Julie Harris Laurence Harvey Ron Randell

1955   **THE BIG KNIFE**
Director: Robert Aldrich
Co-stars: Jack Palance Ida Lupino Rod Steiger

1955   **I DIED A THOUSAND TIMES**
Director: Stuart Heisler
Co-stars: Jack Palance Lori Nelson Lee Marvin

1959   **THE DIARY OF ANN FRANK**
Director: George Stevens
Co-stars: Millie Perkins Joseph Schildkraut Ed Wynn

1959   **ODDS AGAINST TOMORROW**
Director: Robert Wise
Co-stars: Robert Ryan Harry Bellafonte Gloria Grahame

1960   **LET NO MAN WRITE MY EPITAPH**
Director: Philip Leacock
Co-stars: James Darren Burl Ives Jean Seberg

1961   **THE YOUNG SAVAGES**
Director: John Frankenheimer
Co-stars: Burt Lancaster Dina Merril Telly Savalas

1962   **LOLITA**
Director: Stanley Kubrick
Co-stars: James Mason Sue Lyon Peter Sellers

1962   **THE CHAPMAN REPORT**
Director: George Cukor
Co-stars: Claire Bloom Glynis Johns Jane Fonda

1963   **THE BALCONY**
Director: Joseph Strick
Co-stars: Lee Grant Peter Falk Kent Smith

1963   **WIVES AND LOVERS**
Director: John Rich
Co-stars: Van Johnson Janet Leigh Martha Hyer

1964   **A HOUSE IS NOT A HOME**
Director: Russel Rouse
Co-stars: Robert Taylor Cesar Romero Broderick Crawford

1965   **THE GREATEST STORY EVER TOLD**
Director: George Stevens
Co-stars: Max Von Sydow Dorothy McGuire Ed Wynn

1965   **A PATCH OF BLUE**
Director: Guy Green
Co-stars: Sidney Poitier Elizabeth Hartman Wallace Ford

1966   **THE MOVING TARGET**
Director: Jack Smight
Co-stars: Paul Newman Lauren Bacall Janet Leigh

1966   **ALFIE**
Director: Lewis Gilbert
Co-stars: Michael Caine Jane Asher Julia Foster

1967   **ENTER LAUGHING**
Director: Carl Reiner
Co-stars: Reni Santoni Jose Ferrer Elaine May

1968   **WILD IN THE STREETS**
Director: Barry Shear
Co-stars: Chris Jones Millie Perkins Diane Varsi

1968   **THE SCALPHUNTERS**
Director: Sydney Pollack
Co-stars: Burt Lancaster Ossie Davis Telly Savalas

1968   **BUONA SERA MRS CAMPBELL**
Director: Melvin Frank
Co-stars: Gina Lollobrigida Telly Savalas Phil Silvers

1969   **THE MAD ROOM**
Director: Bernard Girard
Co-stars: Stella Stevens Skip Ward Carole Cole

1969   **BLOODY MAMA**
Director: Roger Corman
Co-stars: Pat Hingle Don Stroud Diane Varsi

1970   **HOW DO I LOVE THEE ?**
Director: Michael Gordon
Co-stars: Jackie Gleason Maureen O'Hara Rick Lenz

1970   **FLAP**
Director: Carol Reed
Co-stars: Anthony Quinn Claude Akins Tony Bill

1971   **SOMETHING TO HIDE**
Co-stars: Peter Finch Linda Hayden John Stride

1971   **WHAT'S THE MATTER WITH HELEN ?**
Director: Curtis Harrington
Co-stars: Debbie Reynolds Dennis Weaver

1971   **WHOEVER SLEW AUNTIE ROO ?**
Director: Curtis Harrington
Co-stars: Ralph Richardson Mark Lester

1972   **THE POSEIDON ADVENTURE**
Director: Ronald Neame
Co-stars: Gene Hackman Ernest Borgnine Stella Stevens

1972   **THE DEVIL'S DAUGHTER**
Director: Jeannot Szwarc
Co-stars: Belinda Montgomery Robert Foxworth

1973   **CLEOPATRA JONES**
Director: Jack Starrett
Co-stars: Tamara Dobson Bernie Casey Brenda Sykes

1973   **BLUME IN LOVE**
Director: Paul Mazursky
Co-stars: George Segal Susan Anspach Marsha Mason

1975   **BURN OUT**
Director: Daniel Mann
Co-stars: Lindsay Wagner Sam Waterston Zero Mostel

1975   **DIAMONDS**
Director: Menaham Golan
Co-stars: Robert Shaw Richard Roundtree Barbara Seagull

1975   **NEXT STOP, GREENWICH VILLAGE**
Director: Paul Mazursky
Co-stars: Lenny Baker Lois Smith Ellen Greene

1975   **THAT LUCKY TOUCH**
Director: Christopher Miles
Co-stars: Roger Moore Susannah York Lee J. Cobb

1976   **THE TENANT**
Director: Roman Polanski
Co-stars: Roman Polanski Melvyn Douglas Isabelle Adjani

1977   **TENTACLES**
Director: Oliver Hellman
Co-stars: Henry Fonda John Huston Bo Hopkins

1977   **PETE'S DRAGON**
Director: Don Chaffey
Co-stars: Sean Marshall Mickey Rooney Helen Reddy

1978   **KING OF THE GYPSIES**
Director: Frank Pierson
Co-stars: Sterling Hayden Susan Sarandon Eric Roberts

1978   **THE INITIATION OF SARAH**
Director: Robert Day
Co-stars: Kay Lenz Kathryn Crosby Tony Bill

1979   **CITY ON FIRE**
Director: Alvin Rakoff
Co-stars: Barry Newman Susan Clark Henry Fonda

1979   **ELVIS**
Director: John Carpenter
Co-stars: Kurt Russell Pat Hingle Ed Begley Jnr.

1979	**THE MAGICIAN OF LUBLIN**
Director:	Menahem Golan
Co-stars:	Alan Arkin Louise Fletcher Valerie Perrine

1980	**THE VISITOR**
Director:	Giulio Paradisi
Co-stars:	Mel Ferrer Glenn Ford Sam Peckinpah

1981	**S.O.B.**
Director:	Blake Edwards
Co-stars:	Julie Andrews Robert Preston Loretta Swit

1983	**FANNY HILL**
Director:	Gerry O'Hara
Co-stars:	Lisa Raines Oliver Reed Alfred Marks

1983	**OVER THE BROOKLYN BRIDGE**
Director:	Menahem Golan
Co-stars:	Elliott Gould Margaux Hemingway Carol Kane

1985	**ALICE IN WONDERLAND**
Director:	Harry Harris
Co-stars:	Lloyd Bridges Ringo Starr Patrick Duffy

1985	**DÉJÀ VU**
Director:	Anthony Richmond
Co-stars:	Jaclyn Smith Nigel Terry Claire Bloom

1988	**THE PURPLE PEOPLE EATER**

1991	**STEPPING OUT**
Director:	Lewis Gilbert
Co-stars:	Liza Minnelli Julie Walters Bill Irwin

1992	**WEEP NO MORE MY LADY**
Director:	Michael Andriev
Co-stars:	Kristin Scott-Thomas Daniel J. Travanti

1993	**THE PICKLE**
Director:	Paul Mazursky
Co-stars:	Danny Aiello Dyan Cannon Barry Miller

1996	**THE PORTRAIT OF A LADY**
Director:	Jane Campion
Co-stars:	Nicole Kidman John Malkovich Barbara Hershey

COLLEEN WINTON

1991	**YES VIRGINIA, THERE IS A SANTA CLAUS**
Director:	Charles Jarrett
Co-stars:	Charles Bronson Richard Thomas

JANE WINTON

1927	**THE PATSY**
Director:	King Vidor
Co-stars:	Marion Davies Marie Dressler Del Henderson

SHEREE WINTON

1959	**THE DEVIL'S DISCIPLE**
Director:	Guy Hamilton
Co-stars:	Burt Lancaster Kirk Douglas Laurence Olivier

ESTELLE WINWOOD

1937	**QUALITY STREET**
Director:	George Stevens
Co-stars:	Katherine Hepburn Franchot Tone Fay Bainter

1954	**THE GLASS SLIPPER**
Director:	Charles Walters
Co-stars:	Leslie Caron Michael Wilding Elsa Lanchester

1956	**THE SWAN**
Director:	Charles Vidor
Co-stars:	Grace Kelly Alec Guinness Louis Jourdan

1956	**23 PACES TO BAKER STREET**
Director:	Henry Hathaway
Co-stars:	Van Johnson Vera Miles Cecil Parker

1958	**ALIVE AND KICKING**
Director:	Cyril Frankel
Co-stars:	Sybil Thorndike Kathleen Harrison Joyce Carey

1958	**THIS HAPPY FEELING**
Director:	Blake Edwards
Co-stars:	Debbie Reynolds Curt Jurgens Alexis Smith

1959	**DARBY O'GILL AND THE LITTLE PEOPLE**
Director:	Robert Stevenson
Co-stars:	Albert Sharpe Sean Connery Janet Munro

1961	**THE MISFITS**
Director:	John Huston
Co-stars:	Clark Gable Marilyn Monroe Montgomery Clift

1962	**THE NOTORIOUS LANDLADY**
Director:	Richard Quine
Co-stars:	Kim Novak Jack Lemmon Fred Astaire

1962	**THE MAGIC SWORD**
Director:	Bert Gordon
Co-stars:	Basil Rathbone Gary Lockwood Anne Helm

1964	**DEAD RINGER**
Director:	Paul Henreid
Co-stars:	Bette Davis Karl Malden Peter Lawford

1967	**CAMELOT**
Director:	Joshua Logan
Co-stars:	Richard Harris Vanessa Redgrave David Hemmings

1967	**GAMES**
Director:	Curtis Harrington
Co-stars:	Simone Signoret James Caan Katherine Ross

1968	**THE PRODUCERS**
Director:	Mel Brooks
Co-stars:	Zero Mostel Gene Wilder Kenneth Mars

1976	**MURDER BY DEATH**
Director:	Robert Moore
Co-stars:	Peter Falk Alec Guinness Peter Sellers

GOOGIE WITHERS *(Married John Mccallum)*

1935	**THE LOVE TEST**
Director:	Michael Powell
Co-stars:	Louis Hayward Judy Gunn David Hutcheson

1936	**CRIME OVER LONDON**
Director:	Alfred Zeisler
Co-stars:	Margot Grahame Paul Cavanagh Joseph Cawthorn

1936	**ACCUSED**
Director:	Thornton Freeland
Co-stars:	Douglas Fairbanks Dolores Del Rio

1937	**PARADISE FOR 2**
Director:	Thornton Freeland
Co-stars:	Jack Hulbert Patricia Ellis

1938	**STRANGE BOARDERS**
Director:	Herbert Mason
Co-stars:	Tom Walls Renee Saint-Cyr Irene Handl

1938	**THE LADY VANISHES**
Director:	Alfred Hitchcock
Co-stars:	Margaret Lockwood Michael Redgrave

1938	**KATE PLUS TEN**
Director:	Reginald Denham
Co-stars:	Jack Hulbert Genevieve Tobin

1938	**CONVICT 99**
Director:	Marcel Varnel
Co-stars:	Will Hay Moore Marriott Graham Moffatt

1939	**THE GANGS ALL HERE**
Director:	Thornton Freeland
Co-stars:	Jack Buchanan Otto Kruger Edward Everett Horton

1939	**TROUBLE BREWING**
Director:	Anthony Kimmins
Co-stars:	George Formby Martita Hunt Ronald Shiner

1940 **BUSMAN'S HONEYMOON**
Director: Arthur Woods
Co-stars: Robert Montgomery Constance Cummings Leslie Banks

1941 **JEANNIE**
Director: Harold French
Co-stars: Barbara Mullen Michael Redgrave Albert Lieven

1941 **ONE OF OUR AIRCRAFT IS MISSING**
Director: Michael Powell
Co-stars: Eric Portman Hugh Williams Bernard Miles

1942 **BACK ROOM BOY**
Director: Herbert Mason
Co-stars: Arthur Askey Moore Marriott Graham Moffatt

1943 **SILVER FLEET**
Director: Vernon Sewell
Co-stars: Ralph Richardson Esmond Knight Kathleen Byron

1944 **THEY CAME TO A CITY**
Director: Basil Dearden
Co-stars: John Clements Raymond Huntley Ada Reeve

1944 **ON APPROVAL**
Director: Clive Brook
Co-stars: Clive Brook Beatrice Lillie Roland Culver

1945 **PINK STRING AND SEALING WAX**
Director: Robert Hamer
Co-stars: Mervyn Johns Gordon Jackson Garry Marsh

1947 **ONCE UPON A DREAM**
Director: Ralph Thomas
Co-stars: Griffith Jones Guy Middleton Hubert Gregg

1947 **MIRANDA**
Director: Ken Annakin
Co-stars: Glynis Johns Griffith Jones John McCallum

1947 **THE LOVES OF JOANNA GODDEN**
Director: Charles Frend
Co-stars: John McCallum Jean Kent Derek Bond

1947 **IT ALWAYS RAINS ON SUNDAY**
Director: Robert Hamer
Co-stars: John McCallum Jack Warner Susan Shaw

1949 **TRAVELLER'S JOY**
Director: Ralph Thomas
Co-stars: John McCallum Yolande Donlan Maurice Denham

1950 **NIGHT AND THE CITY**
Director: Jules Dassin
Co-stars: Richard Widmark Gene Tierney Hugh Marlowe

1951 **THE MAGIC BOX**
Director: John Boulting
Co-stars: Robert Donat Margaret Johnston Maria Schell

1951 **LADY GODIVA RIDES AGAIN**
Director: Frank Launder
Co-stars: Pauline Stroud John McCallum Dennis Price

1951 **WHITE CORRIDORS**
Director: Pat Jackson
Co-stars: James Donald Petula Clark Jack Watling

1952 **DERBY DAY**
Director: Herbert Wilcox
Co-stars: Anna Neagle John McCallum Michael Wilding

1954 **DEVIL ON HORSEBACK**
Director: Cyril Frankel
Co-stars: John McCallum Jeremy Spencer Sam Kydd

1971 **THE NICKEL QUEEN**
Director: John McCallum
Co-stars: John McCallum John Laws Ed Devereaux

1985 **TIME AFTER TIME**
Director: Bill Hays
Co-stars: John Gielgud Helen Cherry Trevor Howard

1986 **HOTEL DU LAC**
Director: Giles Foster
Co-stars: Anna Massey Denholm Elliott Patricia Hodge

1987 **NORTHANGER ABBEY**
Director: Giles Foster
Co-stars: Katharine Schlesinger Peter Firth Robert Hardy

1990 **ENDING UP**
Director: Peter Sasdy
Co-stars: Wendy Hiller John Mills Michael Hordern

1996 **SHINE**
Director: Scott Hick
Co-stars: Lynn Redgrave Noah Taylor Geoffrey Rush

ISABEL WITHERS

1950 **BEWARE OF BLONDIE**
Director: Edward Bernds
Co-stars: Penny Singleton Arthur Lake Adele Jergens

JANE WITHERS

1934 **BRIGHT EYES**
Director: David Butler
Co-stars: Shirley Temple James Dunn Lois Wilson

1935 **GINGER**

1935 **THE FARMER TAKES A WIFE**
Director: Victor Fleming
Co-stars: Janet Gaynor Henry Fonda Charles Bickford

1935 **PADDY O'DAY**
Director: Lewis Seiler
Co-stars: Rita Hayworth Pinky Tomlin Jane Darwell

1935 **THIS IS THE LIFE**
Co-star: John McGuire

1936 **CAN THIS BE DIXIE ?**
Director: George Marshall
Co-stars: Slim Summerville Claude Gillingwater Helen Wood

1936 **PEPPER**
Co-star: Irwin S. Cobb

1936 **GENTLE JULIA**
Co-star: Jackie Searle

1937 **ANGEL'S HOLIDAY**
Director: James Tinling
Co-stars: Robert Kent Joan Davis Sally Blane

1937 **CHECKERS**
Director: Bruce Humberstone
Co-stars: Stuart Erwin Una Merkel Minor Watson

1937 **FORTY FIVE FATHERS**
Director: James Tinling
Co-stars: Thomas Beck Grace Hartman Paul Hartman

1937 **THE HOLY TERROR**
Director: James Tinling
Co-stars: Tony Martin Joan Davis El Brendel

1937 **WILD AND WOOLLEY**
Director: Alfred Werker
Co-stars: Walter Brennan Alfafa Switzer Pauline Moore

1938 **RASCALS**
Director: Bruce Humberstone
Co-stars: Rochelle Hudson Borrah Minevitch Steffi Duna

1938 **ALWAYS IN TROUBLE**
Co-stars: Jean Rogers Eddie Collins

1938 **KEEP SMILING**
Co-stars: Henry Wilcoxon Gloria Stuart Helen Westley

1939 **PACK UP YOUR TROUBLES**
Director: Bruce Humberstone
Co-stars: Ritz Brothers Joseph Schildkraut Lynn Bari

1939	**BOY FRIEND**

1939	**THE CHICKEN WAGON FAMILY**
Director:	Herbert Leeds
Co-stars:	Leo Carrillo Marjorie Weaver Spring Byington

1940	**HIGH SCHOOL**
Co-star:	Joe Brown Jnr.

1940	**THE GIRL FROM AVENUE A**
Director:	Otto Brower
Co-stars:	Kent Taylor Jesse Ralph Elyse Knox

1941	**HER FIRST BEAU**
Director:	Theodore Reed
Co-stars:	Jackie Cooper Edith Fellows William Tracy

1941	**SMALL TOWN DEB**
Co-stars:	Jackie Searle Jane Darwell

1941	**A VERY YOUNG LADY**
Director:	Harold Schuster
Co-stars:	John Sutton Nancy Kelly Cecil Kellaway

1942	**YOUNG AMERICA**
Co-stars:	Robert Wilde Irving Bacon Ben Carter

1942	**JOHNNY DOUGHBOY**
Co-stars:	Bobby Breen Patrick Brook

1943	**NORTH STAR**
Director:	Lewis Milestone
Co-stars:	Anne Baxter Farley Granger Dana Andrews

1946	**SHOOTING HIGH**
Co-star:	Gene Autry

1947	**DANGER STREET**
Co-stars:	Robert Lowery Charles Coleman

1956	**GIANT**
Director:	George Stevens
Co-stars:	Elizabeth Taylor Rock Hudson James Dean

1963	**CAPTAIN NEWMAN MUS.**
Director:	David Miller
Co-stars:	Gregory Peck Tony Curtis Angie Dickinson

MARGARET WITHERS

1946	**DAYBREAK**
Director:	Compton Bennett
Co-stars:	Eric Portman Ann Todd Maxwell Reed

1952	**HOME AT SEVEN**
Director:	Ralph Richardson
Co-stars:	Ralph Richardson Margaret Leighton Jack Hawkins

1957	**THE FLYING SCOTT**
Director:	Compton Bennett
Co-stars:	Lee Patterson Kay Callard Alan Gifford

1957	**THAT WOMAN OPPOSITE**
Director:	Compton Bennett
Co-stars:	Phyllis Kirk Dan O'Herlihy Petula Clark

1958	**FERRY TO HONG KONG**
Director:	Lewis Gilbert
Co-stars:	Orson Welles Curt Jurgens Sylvia Syms

CORA WITHERSPOON

1931	**PEACH O'RENO**
Director:	William Seiter
Co-stars:	Bert Wheeler Robert Woolsey Dorothy Lee

1932	**LADIES OF THE JURY**
Director:	Lowell Sherman
Co-stars:	Edna May Oliver Ken Murray Kitty Kelly

1934	**MIDNIGHT**
Director:	Chester Erskine
Co-stars:	Sidney Fox Henry Hull Humphrey Bogart

1936	**PICCADILLY JIM**
Director:	Robert Z. Leonard
Co-stars:	Robert Montgomery Madge Evans Frank Morgan

1936	**LIBELLED LADY**
Director:	Jack Conway
Co-stars:	Spencer Tracy William Powell Jean Harlow

1937	**QUALITY STREET**
Director:	George Stevens
Co-stars:	Katherine Hepburn Franchot Tone Fay Bainter

1937	**THE BIG SHOT**
Co-stars:	Guy Kibbee Dorothy Moore

1937	**DANGEROUS NUMBER**
Director:	Richard Thorpe
Co-stars:	Robert Young Ann Sothern Dean Jagger

1937	**PERSONAL PROPERTY**
Director:	W.S. Van Dyke
Co-stars:	Jean Harlow Robert Taylor Reginald Owen

1938	**JUST AROUND THE CORNER**
Director:	Irving Cummings
Co-stars:	Shirley Temple Bert Lahr Bill Robinson

1938	**HE COULDN'T SAY NO**
Co-stars:	Jane Wyman Frank McHugh Berton Churchill

1938	**PORT OF SEVEN SEAS**
Director:	James Whale
Co-stars:	Wallace Beery Maureen O'Sullivan Frank Morgan

1938	**MARIE ANTOINETTE**
Director:	W.S. Van Dyke
Co-stars:	Norma Shearer Tyrone Power John Barrymore

1938	**PROFESSOR BEWARE**
Director:	Elliott Nugent
Co-stars:	Harold Lloyd Phyllis Welch Lionel Stander

1938	**THREE LOVES HAS NANCY**
Director:	Richard Thorpe
Co-stars:	Janet Gaynor Robert Montgomery Franchot Tone

1939	**WOMAN DOCTOR**
Director:	Sidney Salkow
Co-stars:	Frieda Inescort Henry Wilcoxon Claire Dodd

1939	**THE WOMEN**
Director:	George Cukor
Co-stars:	Norma Shearer Joan Crawford Rosalind Russell

1939	**DARK VICTORY**
Director:	Edmund Goulding
Co-stars:	Bette Davis George Brent Humphrey Bogart

1940	**THE BANK DICK**
Director:	Eddie Cline
Co-stars:	W.C. Fields Franklin Pangborn Shemp Howard

1940	**CHARLIE CHAN'S MURDER CRUISE**
Director:	Eugene Forde
Co-stars:	Sidney Toler Sen Yung Lionel Atwill

1940	**I WAS AN ADVENTURESS**
Director:	Gregory Ratoff
Co-stars:	Vera Zorina Erich Von Stroheim Peter Lorre

1943	**FOLLIES GIRL**
Director:	William Rowland
Co-stars:	Wendy Barrie Gordon Oliver Doris Nolan

1945	**COLONEL EFFINGHAM'S RAID**
Director:	Irving Pichel
Co-stars:	Charles Coburn Joan Bennett William Eythe

1945	**OVER 21**
Director:	Alexander Hall
Co-stars:	Irene Dunne Alexander Knox Charles Coburn

1946	**THE YOUNG WIDOW**
Director:	Edwin Marin
Co-stars:	Jane Russell Faith Domergue Louis Hayward

1952 JUST FOR YOU
Director: Elliott Nugent
Co-stars: Bing Crosby Jane Wyman Natalie Wood

REESE WITHERSPOON *(Child)*

1991 WILDFLOWER
Director: Diane Keaton
Co-stars: Patricia Arquette Beau Bridges

1991 THE MAN IN THE MOON
Director: Robert Mulligan
Co-stars: Sam Waterston Tess Harper Gail Strickland

1993 A FAR-OFF PLACE
Director: Mikael Saloman
Co-star: Ethan Randall

1996 FEAR
Director: James Foley
Co-stars: Mark Wahlberg William Petersen

ALICIA WITT

1993 BODIES, REST AND MOTION
Director: Michael Steinberg
Co-stars: Bridget Fonda Phoebe Cates Tim Roth

1994 FUN
Director: Rafal Zielinski
Co-stars: Renee Humphrey Leslie Hope Ania Suli

1994 THE DISAPPEARANCE OF VONNIE
Director: Graeme Campbell
Co-stars: Ann Jillian Joe Penny Kim Zimmer

KAREN WITTER

1988 OUT OF THE DARK
Director: Michael Schroeder
Co-stars: Karen Black Cameron Dye Bud Cort

ABIGAIL WOLCOTT

1988 HELLGATE
Director: William Levy
Co-star: Ron Palillo

HILARY WOLF

1992 STEPKIDS
Director: Joan Micklin Silver
Co-stars: Margaret Whitton David Strathairn Griffin Dunne

1992 HOME ALONE 2
Director: Chris Columbus
Co-stars: Macauley Culkin Joe Pesci Brenda Fricker

KELLY WOLF

1989 TRIUMPH OF THE SPIRIT
Director: Robert Young
Co-stars: Willem Dafoe Robert Loggia Wendy Gazelle

1990 GRAVEYARD SHIFT
Director: Ralph Singleton
Co-stars: David Andrews Stephen Macht Brad Dourif

1991 A DAY IN OCTOBER
Director: Kenneth Madsen
Co-stars: D.B. Sweeney Daniel Banzali Tove Feldshuh

RITA WOLF

1985 MY BEAUTIFUL LAUNDERETTE
Director: Stephen Frears
Co-stars: Saeed Jaffrey Roshan Seth Daniel Day-Lewis

TRACIE WOLFE

1987 LETHAL WEAPON
Director: Richard Donner
Co-stars: Mel Gibson Danny Glover Gary Busey

1989 LETHAL WEAPON 2
Director: Richard Donner
Co-stars: Mel Gibson Danny Glover Patsy Kensit

1992 LETHAL WEAPON 3
Director: Richard Donner
Co-stars: Mel Gibson Danny Glover Rene Russo

EDNA MAY WONACOTT *(Child)*

1943 SHADOW OF A DOUBT
Director: Alfred Hitchcock
Co-stars: Joseph Cotten Teresa Wright Hume Cronyn

ANNA MAY WONG

1923 THE THIEF OF BAGDAD
Director: Raoul Walsh
Co-stars: Douglas Fairbanks Snitz Edwards Etta Lee

1927 MR WU
Director: William Nigh
Co-stars: Lon Chaney Louise Dresser Ralph Forbes

1929 PICCADILLY
Director: E.A. Dupont
Co-stars: Gilda Gray Jameson Thomas Charles Laughton

1931 DAUGHTER OF THE DRAGON
Director: Lloyd Corrigan
Co-stars: Warner Oland Sessue Hayakawa

1932 SHANGHAI EXPRESS
Director: Josef Von Sternberg
Co-stars: Marlene Dietrich Clive Brook Warner Oland

1933 A STUDY IN SCARLET
Director: Edwin Marin
Co-stars: Reginald Owen Warburton Gamble Alan Dinehart

1934 LIMEHOUSE BLUES
Director: Alexander Hall
Co-stars: George Raft Jean Parker Ann Sheridan

1934 CHU CHIN CHOW
Director: Walter Forde
Co-stars: George Robey Fritz Kortner Dennis Hoey

1935 JAVA HEAD
Director: Walter Ruben
Co-stars: John Loder Elizabeth Allan Edmund Gwenn

1937 DAUGHTER OF SHANGHAI
Director: Robert Florey
Co-stars: Charles Bickford Buster Crabbe Anthony Quinn

1938 DANGEROUS TO KNOW
Director: Robert Florey
Co-stars: Akim Tamiroff Gail Patrick Lloyd Nolan

1939 ISLAND OF LOST MEN
Director: Kurt Neuman
Co-stars: Broderick Crawford Anthony Quinn J. Carrol Naish

1939 KING OF CHINATOWN
Director: Nick Grinde
Co-stars: Akim Tamiroff Sidney Toler J. Carrol Naish

1941 ELLERY QUEEN'S PENTHOUSE MYSTERY
Director: James Hogan
Co-stars: Ralph Bellamy Margaret Lindsay

1942 BOMBS OVER BURMA
Director: Joseph Lewis
Co-stars: Noel Madison Leslie Denison Nedrick Young

1960 PORTRAIT IN BLACK
Director: Michael Gordon
Co-stars: Lana Turner Anthony Quinn Richard Basehart

1960 THE SAVAGE INNOCENTS
Director: Nicholas Ray
Co-stars: Anthony Quinn Yoko Tani Peter O'Toole

IRIS WONG

1943 CHINA
Director: John Farrow
Co-stars: Alan Ladd Loretta Young William Bendix

JANET WONG

1981 BUSTIN' LOOSE
Director: Oz Scott
Co-stars: Richard Pryor Cicely Tyson Angel Ramirez

VIVIAN WOO

1993 TEENAGE MUTANT NINJA TURTLES 3
Director: Stuard Gillard
Co-stars: Elias Koteas Paige Turco Stuart Wilson

CINDI WOOD

1961 THE HOODLUM PRIEST
Director: Irvin Kershner
Co-stars: Don Murray Keir Dullea Larry Gates

CYNTHIA WOOD

1979 VAN NUYS BOULEVARD
Director: William Sachs
Co-stars: Bill Adler Dennis Bowen Melissa Prophet

EDNA WOOD

1946 WANTED FOR MURDER
Director: Lawrence Huntington
Co-stars: Eric Portman Dulcie Gray Derek Farr

FLORENCE WOOD

1934 THE PRIVATE LIFE OF DON JUAN
Director: Alexander Korda
Co-stars: Douglas Fairbanks Merle Oberon Binnie Barnes

HARLENE WOOD

1937 THE FEUD OF THE TRAIL
Co-star: Tom Tyler

HELEN WOOD

1936 CAN THIS BE DIXIE ?
Director: George Marshall
Co-stars: Jane Withers Slim Summerville Hattie McDaniel

1936 CHARLIE CHAN AT THE RACE TRACK
Director: Bruce Humberstone
Co-stars: Warner Oland Keye Luke Thomas Beck

1936 HIGH TENSION
Director: Allan Dwan
Co-stars: Brian Donlevy Norman Foster Glenda Farrell

1936 CRACK-UP
Director: Mal St. Clair
Co-stars: Peter Lorre Brian Donlevy Ralph Morgan

1936 CHAMPAGNE CHARLIE
Co-stars: Paul Cavanagh Minna Gombell

JANE WOOD

1985 THE RUSSIAN SOLDIER
Director: Gavin Millar
Co-stars: Warren Clarke Patrick Malahide Jerome Flynn

1986 GOOD AS GOLD
Director: John Glenister
Co-stars: David Calder Jane Morris Richard Moore

1988 PRECIOUS BANE
Director: Christopher Menaul
Co-stars: Janet McTeer John Bowe Clive Owen

JUDITH WOOD

1934 THE CRIME DOCTOR
Director: John Robertson
Co-stars: Otto Kruger Karen Morley Nils Asther

LANA WOOD *(Sister Of Natalie Wood)*

1962 FIVE FINGER EXERCISE
Director: Daniel Mann
Co-stars: Rosalind Russell Jack Hawkins Maximilian Schell

1971 DIAMONDS ARE FOREVER
Director: Guy Hamilton
Co-stars: Sean Connery Jill St. John Charles Gray

1977 GRAYEAGLE
Director: Charles Pierce
Co-stars: Ben Johnson Jack Elam Paul Fix

MARY LAURA WOOD

1951 VALLEY OF EAGLES
Director: Terence Young
Co-stars: Jack Warner John McCallum Nadia Gray

1953 BLACK ORCHID
Director: Charles Saunders
Co-stars: Ronald Howard Olga Edwardes John Bentley

1956 THE HIGH TERRACE
Director: Henry Cass
Co-stars: Lois Maxwell Dale Robertson Derek Bond

1957 HOUR OF DECISION
Director: C. Pennington-Richards
Co-stars: Jeff Morrow Hazel Court Lionel Jeffries

NANCY WOOD

1984 SCANDALOUS !
Director: Rob Cohen
Co-stars: Robert Hays John Gielgud Jim Dale

NATALIE WOOD *(Child)*

(Married Robert Wagner, Richard Gregson, Robert Wagner, Sister Of Lana Wood, Mother Of Natasha Gregson Wagner) (Natasha Nikolaeuna)
Nominated For Best Actress In 1961 For "Splendor In The Grass" And In 1963 For "Love With The Proper Stranger". Nominated For Best Supporting Actress In 1955 For "Rebel Without A Cause"

1943 HAPPY LAND
Director: Irving Pichel
Co-stars: Don Ameche Frances Dee Henry Morgan

1945 TOMORROW IS FOREVER
Director: Irving Pichel
Co-stars: Orson Welles Claudette Colbert George Brent

1946 THE BRIDE WORE BOOTS
Director: Irving Pichel
Co-stars: Barbara Stanwyck Robert Cummings

1947 THE GHOST AND MRS MUIR
Director: Joseph Mankiewicz
Co-stars: Rex Harrison Gene Tierney Edna Best

1947 MIRACLE OF 34TH STREET
Director: George Seaton
Co-stars: Edmund Gwenn Maureen O'Hara John Payne

1947 DRIFTWOOD
Director: Allan Dwan
Co-stars: Dean Jagger Walter Brennan Ruth Warrick

1948 SUMMER LIGHTNING
Director: Hugh Herbert
Co-stars: June Haver Walter Brennan Lon McCallister

1949	**FATHER WAS A FULLBACK**
Director:	John Stahl
Co-stars:	Fred MacMurray Maureen O'Hara Rudy Vallee

1949	**GREEN PROMISE**
Director:	William Russell
Co-stars:	Walter Brennan Marguerite Chapman Robert Paige

1949	**CHICKEN EVERY SUNDAY**
Director:	George Seaton
Co-stars:	Dan Dailey Celeste Holm Colleen Townsend

1950	**THE JACKPOT**
Director:	Walter Lang
Co-stars:	James Stewart Barbara Hale James Gleason

1950	**NO SAD SONGS FOR ME**
Director:	Rudolph Mate
Co-stars:	Margaret Sullavan Wendell Corey

1950	**NEVER A DULL MOMENT**
Director:	George Marshall
Co-stars:	Irene Dunne Fred MacMurray Gigi Perreau

1950	**OUR VERY OWN**
Director:	David Miller
Co-stars:	Ann Blyth Farley Granger Joan Evans

1951	**THE BLUE VEIL**
Director:	Norman Krasma
Co-stars:	Jane Wyman Charles Laughton Joan Blondell

1952	**THE STAR**
Director:	Stuart Heisler
Co-stars:	Bette Davis Sterling Hayden Minor Watson

1952	**JUST FOR YOU**
Director:	Elliott Nugent
Co-stars:	Bing Crosby Jane Wyman Bob Arthur

1954	**THE SILVER CHALICE**
Director:	Victor Saville
Co-stars:	Paul Newman Pier Angeli Virginia Mayo

1955	**REBEL WITHOUT A CAUSE**
Director:	Nicholas Ray
Co-stars:	James Dean Sal Mineo Dennis Hopper

1956	**ONE DESIRE**
Director:	Jerry Hopper
Co-stars:	Anne Baxter Rock Hudson Julie Adams

1956	**THE SEARCHERS**
Director:	John Ford
Co-stars:	John Wayne Jeffrey Hunter Vera Miles

1956	**THE GIRL HE LEFT BEHIND**
Director:	David Butler
Co-stars:	Tab Hunter Jim Backus Alan King

1956	**A CRY IN THE NIGHT**
Director:	Frank Tuttle
Co-stars:	Raymond Burr Edmond O'Brien Brian Donlevy

1956	**THE BURNING HILLS**
Director:	Stuart Heisler
Co-stars:	Tab Hunter Eduard Franz Earl Holliman

1957	**NO SLEEP TILL DAWN**
Director:	Gordon Douglas
Co-stars:	Karl Malden Marsha Hunt Efrem Zimbalist

1958	**MARJORIE MORNINGSTAR**
Director:	Irving Rapper
Co-stars:	Gene Kelly Ed Wynn Claire Trevor

1958	**KINGS GO FORTH**
Director:	Delmer Daves
Co-stars:	Frank Sinatra Tony Curtis Leora Dana

1960	**CASH MCCALL**
Director:	Joseph Pevney
Co-stars:	James Garner Nina Foch Dean Jagger

1960	**ALL THE FINE YOUNG CANNIBALS**
Director:	Michael Anderson
Co-stars:	Robert Wagner Pearl Bailey

1961	**SPLENDOR IN THE GRASS**
Director:	Elia Kazan
Co-stars:	Warren Beatty Pat Hingle Sandy Dennis

1961	**WEST SIDE STORY**
Director:	Robert Wise
Co-stars:	Richard Beymer Russ Tamblyn Rita Moreno

1962	**GYPSY**
Director:	Mervyn LeRoy
Co-stars:	Rosalind Russell Karl Malden Ann Jillian

1963	**LOVE WITH THE PROPER STRANGER**
Director:	Robert Mulligan
Co-stars:	Steve McQueen Edie Adams

1964	**SEX AND THE SINGLE GIRL**
Director:	Richard Quine
Co-stars:	Henry Fonda Tony Curtis Lauren Bacall

1965	**INSIDE DAISY CLOVER**
Director:	Robert Mulligan
Co-stars:	Robert Redford Ruth Gordon Christopher Plummer

1965	**THE GREAT RACE**
Director:	Blake Edwards
Co-stars:	Tony Curtis Jack Lemmon Peter Falk

1966	**PENELOPE**
Director:	Arthur Hiller
Co-stars:	Ian Bannen Dick Shawn Jonathan Winters

1966	**THIS PROPERTY IS CONDEMNED**
Director:	Sydney Pollack
Co-stars:	Robert Redford Charles Bronson

1969	**BOB AND CAROL AND TED AND ALICE**
Director:	Paul Mazursky
Co-stars:	Dyan Cannon Robert Culp Elliott Gould

1973	**THE AFFAIR**
Director:	Gilbert Cates
Co-stars:	Robert Wagner Bruce Davison Kent Smith

1975	**JAMES DEAN:** **THE FIRST AMERICAN TEENAGER**
Director:	Ray Connolly
Co-stars:	Rock Hudson Julie Harris

1975	**PEEPER**
Director:	Peter Hyams
Co-stars:	Michael Caine Kitty Winn Thayer David

1976	**CAT ON A HOT TIN ROOF**
Director:	Robert Moore
Co-star:	Laurence Olivier

1979	**THE CRACKER FACTORY**

1979	**THE LAST MARRIED COUPLE IN AMERICA**
Director:	Gilbert Cates
Co-stars:	George Segal Richard Benjamin

1979	**METEOR**
Director:	Ronald Neame
Co-stars:	Sean Connery Henry Fonda Trevor Howard

1980	**THE MEMORY OF EVA RYKER**
Director:	Walter Grauman
Co-stars:	Robert Foxworth Ralph Bellamy Mel Ferrer

1980	**WILLIE AND PHIL**
Director:	Paul Mazursky
Co-stars:	Michael Ontkean Ray Sharkey Margot Kidder

1983	**BRAINSTORM**
Director:	Douglas Trumball
Co-stars:	Christopher Walken Louise Fletcher

PEGGY WOOD
Nominated For Best Supporting Actress In 1965 For "The Sound Of Music"

1934 HANDY ANDY
Director: David Butler
Co-stars: Will Rogers Conchita Montenegro Mary Carlisle

1935 JALNA
Director: John Cromwell
Co-stars: Kay Johnson Ian Hunter Nigel Bruce

1935 RIGHT TO LIVE
Director: William Keighley
Co-stars: George Brent Colin Clive Josephine Hutchinson

1937 CALL IT A DAY
Director: Archie Mayo
Co-stars: Olivia De Havilland Ian Hunter Anita Louise

1939 THE HOUSEKEEPER'S DAUGHTER
Director: Hal Roach
Co-stars: Joan Bennett John Hubbard Adolphe Menjou

1946 THE BRIDE WORE BOOTS
Director: Irving Pichel
Co-stars: Barbara Stanwyck Robert Cummings Natalie Wood

1946 MAGNIFICENT DOLL
Director: Frank Borzage
Co-stars: Ginger Rogers David Niven Burgess Meredith

1947 DREAM GIRL
Director: Mitchell Leisen
Co-stars: Betty Hutton Macdonald Carey Walter Abel

1960 THE STORY OF RUTH
Director: Henry Koster
Co-stars: Elana Eden Viveca Lindfors Stuart Whitman

1965 THE SOUND OF MUSIC
Director: Robert Wise
Co-stars: Julie Andrews Christopher Plummer Eleanor Parker

VICTORIA WOOD

1982 THE SECRET POLICEMAN'S OTHER BALL
Director: Roger Graef
Co-stars: Peter Cook John Cleese Michael Palin

1996 THE WIND IN THE WILLOWS
Director: Terry Jones
Co-stars: Terry Jones Eric Idle Steve Coogan

ALFRE WOODARD
Nominated For Best Supporting Actress In 1983 For Cross Creek

1978 REMEMBER MY NAME
Director: Alan Rudolph
Co-stars: Geraldine Chaplin Anthony Perkins Jeff Goldblum

1982 THE AMBUSH MURDERS
Director: Steven Hillard Stern
Co-stars: James Brolin Dorian Harewood Amy Madigan

1983 CROSS CREEK
Director: Martin Ritt
Co-stars: Mary Steenburgen Rip Torn Peter Coyote

1984 THE KILLING FLOOR
Director: William Duke
Co-stars: Damien Leake Moses Gunn Clarence Felder

1986 EXTREMITIES
Director: Robert M. Young
Co-stars: Farrah Fawcett James Russo Diana Scarwid

1986 UNNATURAL CAUSES
Director: Lamont Johnson
Co-stars: John Ritter Patti LaBelle John Sayles

1986 WORDS BY HEART
Director: Robert Thompson
Co-stars: Rob Hooks Charlotte Rae

1988 THE CHILD SAVER
Director: Stan Lathan
Co-stars: Michael Warren Deon Richmond Martin Balsam

1989 MISS FIRECRACKER
Director: Thomas Schlamme
Co-stars: Holly Hunter Mary Steenburgen Tim Robbins

**1989 MOTHER'S COURAGE:
THE MARY THOMAS STORY**
Director: John Patterson
Co-stars: A.J. Johnson Chick Vennera

1990 BLUE BAYOU
Director: Karen Arthur
Co-stars: Mario Van Peebles Elizabeth Ashley Roy Thinnes

1991 GRAND CANYON
Director: Lawrence Kasdan
Co-stars: Danny Glover Kevin Kline Steve Martin

1992 THE GUN IN BETTY LOU'S HANDBAG
Director: Allan Moyle
Co-stars: Penelope Ann Miller Eric Thal Julianne Moore

1992 PASSION FISH
Director: John Sayles
Co-stars: Mary McDonnell David Strathairn Nora Dunn

1993 BOPHA !
Director: Morgan Freeman
Co-stars: Danny Glover Malcolm McDowell Marius Weyers

1993 HEART AND SOULS
Director: Ron Underwood
Co-stars: Robert Downey Jnr. Charles Grodin Kyra Sedgwick

1994 CROOKLYN
Director: Spike Lee
Co-stars: Delroy Lindo Zelda Harris Carlton Williams

1994 BLUE CHIPS
Director: William Friedkin
Co-stars: Nick Nolte Mary McDonnell J.T. Walsh

1996 PRIMAL FEAR
Director: Gregory Hoblit
Co-stars: Richard Gere Laura Linney Edward Norton

1996 HOW TO MAKE AN AMERICAN QUILT
Director: Jocelyn Moorhouse
Co-stars: Winona Ryder Anne Bancroft Jean Simmons

CHARLAYNE WOODARD

1988 GOD BLESS THE CHILD
Director: Larry Elikann
Co-stars: Mare Winningham Grace Johnston Dorian Harewood

1991 ONE GOOD COP
Director: Ralf Bode
Co-stars: Michael Keaton Rene Russo Rachel Ticotin

1991 HE SAID, SHE SAID
Director: Marisa Silver
Co-stars: Kevin Bacon Elizabeth Perkins Sharon Stone

JOAN WOODBURY

1935 THE EAGLE'S BROOD
Co-stars: Bill Boyd George Hayes

1936 THE ROGUE'S TAVERN
Co-star: Jack Mulhall

1936 THE LION'S DEN
Co-star: Tim McCoy

1937 FORTY NAUGHTY GIRLS
Director: Edward Cline
Co-stars: Zasu Pitts James Gleason Marjorie Lord

1937 SUPER SLEUTH
Director: Ben Stoloff
Co-stars: Jack Oakie Ann Sothern Edgar Kennedy

1937 CHARLIE CHAN ON BROADWAY
Director: Eugene Forde
Co-stars: Warner Oland Keye Luke Leon Ames

1938 CRASHING HOLLYWOOD
Director: Lew Landers
Co-stars: Lee Tracy Paul Guilfoyle Jack Carson

1941 PAPER BULLETS
Director: Phil Rosen
Co-stars: Jack La Rue Alan Ladd Linda Ware

1941 I KILLED THAT MAN
Co-star: Ricardo Cortez

1941 IN OLD CHEYENNE
Co-star: Roy Rogers

1942 PHANTON KILLER
Director: William Beaudine
Co-stars: Dick Purcell John Hamilton Warren Hymer

1944 THE CHINESE CAT
Director: Phil Rosen
Co-stars: Sidney Toler Benson Fong Ian Keith

1956 THE TEN COMMANDMENTS
Director: Cecil B. DeMille
Co-stars: Charlton Heston Yul Brynner Anne Baxter

1964 THE TIME TRAVELLERS
Director: Ib Melchior
Co-stars: Preston Foster Phil Carey Merry Anders

MARGO WOODE

1945 THE BULLFIGHTERS
Director: Mal St. Clair
Co-stars: Stan Laurel Oliver Hardy Richard Lane

1946 IT SHOULDN'T HAPPEN TO A DOG
Director: Herbert Leeds
Co-stars: Allyn Joslyn Carole Landis Henry Morgan

1947 MOSS ROSE
Director: Gregory Ratoff
Co-stars: Peggy Cummins Victor Mature Ethel Barrymore

1957 BOP GIRL GOES CALYPSO
Director: Howard Koch
Co-stars: Judy Tyler Bobby Troup Lucien Littlefield

HOLLY WOODLAWN

1970 TRASH
Director: Paul Morrissey
Co-stars: Joe Dallesandro Geri Miller Jane Forth

BARBARA ALYN WOODS

1993 GHOULIES 4
Director: Jim Wynorski
Co-stars: Pete Liapis Stacie Randall Raquel Krelle

CAROL WOODS

1991 STEPPING OUT
Director: Lewis Gilbert
Co-stars: Liza Minnelli Shelley Winters Julie Walters

ILENE WOODS

1950 CINDERELLA (Voice)
Director: Clyde Geronimi
Co-stars: William Phipps Eleanor Audley

MAXINE WOODS

1969 THE PLOT AGAINST HARRY
Director: Robert Young
Co-stars: Martin Priest Ben Lang Henry Nemo

MYRTLE WOODS

1991 A WOMAN'S TALE
Director: Paul Cox
Co-stars: Sheila Florance Gosia Dobrowolska Norman Kaye

NAN WOODS

1987 THE BETTY FORD STORY
Director: David Greene
Co-stars: Gena Rowlands Josef Sommer Concetta Tomei

CATHERINE WOODVILLE

1962 THE WILD AND THE WILLING
Director: Ralph Thomas
Co-stars: Virginia Maskell Paul Rogers Ian McShane

1963 THE INFORMERS
Director: Ken Annakin
Co-stars: Nigel Patrick Colin Blakeley Frank Finlay

1964 THE CROOKED ROAD
Director: Don Chaffey
Co-stars: Robert Ryan Stewart Granger Nadia Gray

1964 THE PARTY'S OVER
Director: Guy Hamilton
Co-stars: Oliver Reed Eddie Albert Ann Lynn

KATE WOODVILLE

1975 POSSE
Director: Kirk Douglas
Co-stars: Kirk Douglas Bruce Dern Bo Hopkins

1977 WHERE'S WILLIE ?
Director: John Florea
Co-stars: Guy Madison Henry Darrow Marc Gilpin

CHARLAINE WOODWARD

1982 HARD FEELINGS
Director: Daryl Duke
Co-stars: Carl Marotte Vincent Bufano Lisa Langlois

JOANNE WOODWARD
(Married Paul Newman, Mother Of Nell Potts)
Oscar For Best Actress In 1957 For "The Three Face Of Eve". Nominated For Best Actress In 1968 For "Rachel, Rachel", In 1973 For "Summer Wishes, Winter Dreams" And In 1990 For "Mr And Mrs Bridge"

1955 COUNT THREE AND PRAY
Director: George Sherman
Co-stars: Van Heflin Phil Carey Raymond Burr

1956 A KISS BEFORE DYING
Director: Gerd Oswald
Co-stars: Robert Wagner Jeffrey Hunter Mary Astor

1957 NO DOWN PAYMENT
Director: Martin Ritt
Co-stars: Tony Randall Sheree North Jeffrey Hunter

1957 THE THREE FACES OF EVE
Director: Nunnally Johnson
Co-stars: David Wayne Lee J. Cobb Nancy Kulp

1958 RALLY ROUND THE FLAG BOYS
Director: Leo McCarey
Co-stars: Paul Newman Joan Collins Jack Carson

1958 THE LONG HOT SUMMER
Director: Martin Ritt
Co-stars: Paul Newman Orson Welles Tony Franciosa

1959 THE SOUND AND THE FURY
Director: Martin Ritt
Co-stars: Yul Brynner Margaret Leighton Stuart Whitman

1960 **THE FUGITIVE KIND**
Director: Sidney Lumet
Co-stars: Marlon Brando Anna Magnani Maureen Stapleton

1960 **FROM THE TERRACE**
Director: Mark Robson
Co-stars: Paul Newman Myrna Loy Leon Ames

1961 **PARIS BLUES**
Director: Martin Ritt
Co-stars: Paul Newman Sidney Poitier Diahann Carroll

1963 **A NEW KIND OF LOVE**
Director: Melville Shavelson
Co-stars: Paul Newman Maurice Chevalier

1963 **THE STRIPPER**
Director: Franklin Schaffner
Co-stars: Richard Beymer Claire Trevor Carol Lynley

1964 **SIGNPOST TO MURDER**
Director: George Englund
Co-stars: Stuart Whitman Alan Napier Edward Mulhare

1966 **A FINE MADNESS**
Director: Irvin Kershner
Co-stars: Sean Connery Jean Seberg Patrick O'Neal

1966 **BIG DEAL AT DODGE CITY**
Director: Fielder Cook
Co-stars: Henry Fonda Jason Robards Charles Bickford

1968 **RACHEL, RACHEL**
Director: Paul Newman
Co-stars: Estelle Parsons James Olson Kate Harrington

1969 **WINNING**
Director: James Goldstone
Co-stars: Paul Newman Robert Wagner Richard Thomas

1970 **W.U.S.A.**
Director: Stuart Rosenberg
Co-stars: Paul Newman Anthony Perkins Laurence Harvey

1971 **THEY MIGHT BE GIANTS**
Director: Anthony Harvey
Co-stars: George C. Scott Jack Gilford Lester Rawlins

1972 **THE EFFECT OF GAMMA RAYS ON MAN IN THE MOON MARIGOLDS**
Director: Paul Newman
Co-star: Nell Potts Roberta Wallach

1973 **SUMMER WISHES, WINTER DREAMS**
Director: Gilbert Cates
Co-stars: Martin Balsam Sylvia Sidney

1975 **THE DROWNING POOL**
Director: Stuart Rosenberg
Co-stars: Paul Newman Melanie Griffith Coral Browne

1978 **THE END**
Director: Burt Reynolds
Co-stars: Burt Reynolds Dom DeLuise Sally Field

1980 **THE SHADOW BOX**

1984 **PASSIONS**

1984 **HARRY AND SON**
Director: Paul Newman
Co-stars: Paul Newman Robby Benson Ellen Barkin

1985 **DO YOU REMEMBER LOVE ?**
Director: Jeff Bleckner
Co-stars: Richard Kiley Geraldine Fitzgerald Susan Ruttan

1987 **THE GLASS MENAGERIE**
Director: Paul Newman
Co-stars: John Malkovich Karen Allen James Naughton

1990 **MR AND MRS BRIDGE**
Director: James Ivory
Co-stars: Paul Newman Blythe Danner Simon Callow

1992 **FOREIGN AFFAIRS**

1993 **PHILADELPHIA**
Director: Jonathan Demme
Co-stars: Tom Hanks Denzel Washington Antonio Banderas

1993 **BLIND SPOT**
Director: Michael Uno
Co-stars: Laura Linney Reed Diamond Fritz Weaver

1993 **THE AGE OF INNOCENCE (Voice)**
Director: Martin Scorsese
Co-stars: Cecil Day-Lewis Winona Ryder Michelle Pfeiffer

1993 **BREATHING LESSONS**
Director: John Erman
Co-star: James Garner Joyce Van Patten

MARJORIE WOODWORTH

1941 **NIAGRA FALLS**
Director: Gordon Douglas
Co-stars: Zasu Pitts Slim Summerville Tom Brown

1941 **BROADWAY LIMITED**
Director: Gordon Douglas
Co-stars: Leonid Kinskey Victor McLaglen Dennis O'Keefe

1942 **THE DEVIL WITH HITLER**
Director: Gordon Douglas
Co-stars: Alan Mowbray Bobby Watson George E. Stone

1943 **FALL IN**
Director: Kurt Neuman
Co-stars: William Tracy Joe Sawyer Jean Porter

EMILY WOOF (Child)

1997 **PHOTOGRAPHING FAIRIES**
Director: Nick Willing
Co-stars: Frances Barber Ben Kingsley Toby Stephens

1998 **THE WOODLANDERS**
Director: Phil Agland
Co-stars: Polly Walker Rufus Sewell Jodhi May

SUSAN WOOLDRIDGE

1986 **DEAD MAN'S FOLLY**
Director: Clive Donner
Co-stars: Peter Ustinov Jonathan Cecil Jean Stapleton

1987 **THE DARK ROOM**
Director: Guy Slater
Co-stars: Philip Jackson Julie Graham Edith Ruddick

1987 **HOPE AND GLORY**
Director: John Boorman
Co-stars: Sarah Miles Ian Bannen David Hayman

1989 **HOW TO GET AHEAD IN ADVERTISING**
Director: Bruce Robinson
Co-stars: Richard E. Grant Richard Wilson Rachel Ward

1989 **PIED PIPER**
Director: Norman Stone
Co-stars: Peter O'Toole Mare Winningham Michael Kitchen

1990 **CHANGING STEP**
Director: Richard Wilson
Co-stars: James Convey Eleanor Bron Anthony Sher

1991 **BROKE**
Director: Alan Dosser
Co-stars: Timothy Spall Larry Lamb Sheila Kelley

1991 **TWENTY-ONE**
Director: Don Boyd
Co-stars: Patsy Kensit Jack Shepherd Patrick Ryecart

1992 **THE HUMMINGBIRD TREE**
Director: Noella Smith
Co-stars: Patrick Bergin Tim Beasley Sunil Y Ramjitsingh

1992 AFRAID OF THE DARK
Director: Mark Peploe
Co-stars: James Fox Fanny Ardant Paul McGann

1992 JUST LIKE A WOMAN
Director: Christopher Monger
Co-stars: Adrian Pasdar Julie Walters Gordon Kennedy

1993 BAD COMPANY
Director: David Drury
Co-stars: Jonny Lee Miller Ken Stott Brian McGrath

LOUISA WOOLF

1990 AVAILABLE LIGHT
Director: Bob Bentley
Co-stars: Tom Bell Joely Richardson David Morrissey

VICKI WOOLF

1972 THE GREAT WALTZ
Director: Andrew Stone
Co-stars: Horst Buchholz Nigel Patrick Rossano Brazzi

KAREN WOOLRIDGE

1989 CRIMINAL LAW
Director: Martin Campbell
Co-stars: Gary Oldman Kevin Bacon Karen Young

SARITA WOOTEN (Child)

1939 WUTHERING HEIGHTS
Director: William Wyler
Co-stars: Laurence Olivier Merle Oberon David Niven

JO ANNE WORLEY

1976 THE SHAGGY D.A.
Director: Robert Stevenson
Co-stars: Dean Jones Tim Conway Suzanne Pleshette

MARY WORONOV

1975 DEATH RACE 2000
Director: Paul Bartel
Co-stars: David Carradine Simone Griffith Sylvester Stallone

1976 HOLLYWOOD BOULEVARD
Director: Joe Dante
Co-stars: Candice Rialson Rita George Dick Miller

1981 ANGEL OF HEAT
Director: Meryl Schreibman
Co-stars: Marilyn Chambers Stephen Johnson Dan Jesse

1982 EATING RAOUL
Director: Paul Bartel
Co-stars: Paul Bartel Robert Beltran Susan Saiger

1984 NIGHT OF THE COMET
Director: Tom Eberhardt
Co-stars: Catherine Mary Stewart Kelli Maroney Robert Beltran

1988 WARLOCK
Director: Steve Miner
Co-stars: Richard E. Grant Julian Sands Lori Singer

1989 SCENES FROM THE CLASS STRUGGLE IN BEVERLY HILLS
Director: Paul Bartel
Co-stars: Paul Bartel Jacqueline Bisset Ray Sharkey

1989 LET IT RIDE
Director: Joe Pykta
Co-stars: Richard Dreyfuss Teri Garr Jennifer Tilly

1991 WHERE SLEEPING DOGS LIE
Director: Charles Finch
Co-stars: Sharon Stone Dylan McDermott Tom Sizemore

CONSTANCE WORTH

1937 CHINA PASSAGE
Co-star: Vinton Hayworth

1943 SHE HAS WHAT IT TAKES
Director: Charles Barton
Co-stars: Jinx Falkenberg Tom Neal Joe King

1946 SENSATION HUNTERS
Co-stars: Robert Lowery Doris Merrick

IRENE WORTH

1948 ANOTHER SHORE
Director: Charles Crichton
Co-stars: Robert Beatty Stanley Holloway Moira Lister

1948 ONE NIGHT WITH YOU
Director: Terence Young
Co-stars: Nino Martini Patricia Roc Bonar Colleano

1951 THE SECRET PEOPLE
Director: Thorold Dickinson
Co-stars: Valentina Cortese Audrey Hepburn Charles Goldner

1958 ORDERS TO KILL
Director: Anthony Asquith
Co-stars: Paul Massie Eddie Albert Lillian Gish

1959 THE SCAPEGOAT
Director: Robert Hamer
Co-stars: Alec Guinness Bette Davis Nicole Maurey

1962 SEVEN SEAS TO CALAIS
Director: Rudolph Mate
Co-stars: Rod Taylor Keith Michell Basil Dignam

1971 NICHOLAS AND ALEXANDRA
Director: Franklin Schaffner
Co-stars: Michael Jayston Janet Suzman Tom Baker

1971 KING LEAR
Director: Peter Brook
Co-stars: Paul Scofield Cyril Cusack Alan Webb

1981 EYEWITNESS
Director: Peter Yates
Co-stars: William Hurt Christopher Plummer Sigourney Weaver

1982 DEATHTRAP
Director: Sidney Lumet
Co-stars: Michael Caine Christopher Reeve Dyan Cannon

1983 SEPARATE TABLES
Director: John Schlesinger
Co-stars: Alan Bates Julie Christie Claire Bloom

1993 LOST IN YONKERS
Director: Martha Coolidge
Co-stars: Richard Dreyfuss Mercedes Ruehl Brad Stoll

LILLIAN WORTH

1929 TARZAN THE TIGER
Director: Henry McRae
Co-stars: Frank Merrill Natalie Kingston

ANNE WORTHINGTON

1989 ICE DANCE
Director: Alan Dossor
Co-stars: Andrew Fletcher Warren Clarke Helena McCarthy

FELICITE WOUASSI

1992 THE DIARY OF LADY M
Director: Alain Tanner
Co-stars: Myriam Mezieres Juanjo Puigcorbe Nanou

1994 LE CRI DU COEUR
Director: Idrissa Ouedraogo
Co-stars: Richard Bohringer Said Diarra Clementine Celarie

SUZANNE WOUK
1989 PASSPORT TO TERROR
Director: Lou Antonio
Co-stars: Lee Remick Norma Aleandro Roy Thinnes

MARY WOYONOV
1992 THE LIVING END
Director: Gregg Araki
Co-stars: Mike Dytri Craig Bilmore Mark Finch

EMMA WRAY
1988 DEFROSTING THE FRIDGE
Director: Sandy Johnson
Co-stars: Joe Don Baker Phyllis Logan Maggie O'Neill

1995 THE BIG GAME
Director: Bob Keen
Co-stars: Gary Webster Chris Jury

FAY WRAY
1926 THE WEDDING MARCH
Director: Erich Von Stroheim
Co-stars: Erich Von Stroheim Zasu Pitts Matthew Betz

1928 THE HONEYMOON
Director: Erich Von Stroheim
Co-stars: Erich Von Stroheim Zasu Pitts Maude George

1929 THUNDERBOLT
Director: Josef Von Sternberg
Co-stars: George Bancroft Richard Arlen

1929 POINTED HEELS
Director: Edward Sutherland
Co-stars: William Powell Phillips Holmes

1929 THE FOUR FEATHERS
Director: Lothar Mendes
Co-stars: Richard Arlen William Powell

1930 BEHIND THE MAKE-UP
Director: Robert Milton
Co-stars: William Powell Hal Skelly Kay Francis

1930 PARAMOUNT ON PARADE
Director: Lothar Mendes
Co-stars: Jean Arthur Clara Bow Fredric March

1930 THE SEA GOD
Co-star: Richard Arlen

1930 THE TEXAN
Director: John Cromwell
Co-stars: Gary Cooper Emma Dunn Oscar Apfel

1931 THE CONQUERING HERO
Co-star: Richard Arlen

1931 THE UNHOLY GARDEN
Director: George Fitzmaurice
Co-stars: Ronald Colman Tully Marshall

1931 DIRIGIBLE
Director: Frank Capra
Co-stars: Jack Holt Ralph Graves Roscoe Karns

1931 CAPTAIN THUNDER

1932 DOCTOR X
Director: Michael Curtiz
Co-stars: Lee Tracy Preston Foster Lionel Atwill

1932 THE FINGER POINTS
Director: John Francis Dillon
Co-stars: Clark Gable Richard Barthelmess

1932 THE MOST DANGEROUS GAME
Director: Irving Pichel
Co-stars: Joel McCrea Leslie Banks Robert Armstrong

1933 THE MYSTERY OF THE WAX MUSEUM
Director: Michael Curtiz
Co-stars: Lionel Atwill Glenda Farrell

1933 ONE SUNDAY AFTERNOON
Director: Stephen Roberts
Co-stars: Gary Cooper Frances Fuller Roscoe Karns

1933 SHANGHAI EXPRESS
Director: John Blystone
Co-stars: Spencer Tracy Ralph Morgan Eugene Pallette

1933 THE VAMPIRE BAT
Director: Frank Strayer
Co-stars: Lionel Atwill Melvyn Douglas George E. Stone

1933 THE WOMAN I STOLE
Co-star: Jack Holt

1933 THE BIG BRAIN

1933 ANN CARVER'S PROFESSION
Co-star: Arthur Pierson

1933 THE BOWERY
Director: Raoul Walsh
Co-stars: Wallace Beery George Raft Pert Kelton

1933 BELOW THE SEA
Co-star: Paul Page

1933 MASTER OF MEN
Co-star: Jack Holt

1933 KING KONG
Director: Ernest Schoedsack
Co-stars: Robert Armstrong Bruce Cabot

1933 THE COUNTESS OF MONTE CRISTO
Director: Karl Freund
Co-stars: Paul Lukas Patsy Kelly Reginald Owen

1934 THE CLAIRVOYANT
Director: Maurice Elvey
Co-stars: Claude Rains Jane Baxter Mary Clare

1934 CHEATING CHEATERS
Director: Richard Thorpe
Co-stars: Cesar Romero Frances L. Sullivan

1934 MADAME SPY
Co-star: Nils Asther

1934 BLACK MOON
Co-star: Jack Holt Sig Ruman

1934 WHITE LIES
Co-stars: Victor Jory William Demarest Walter Connolly

1934 ONCE TO EVERY WOMAN
Director: Lambert Hillyer
Co-stars: Ralph Bellamy Walter Connolly

1934 VIVA VILLA
Director: Jack Conway
Co-stars: Wallace Beery Leo Carillo Stuart Erwin

1934 THE RICHEST GIRL IN THE WORLD
Director: William Seiter
Co-stars: Miriam Hopkins Joel McCrea

1934 THE AFFAIRS OF CELLINI
Director: Gregory La Cava
Co-stars: Fredric March Constance Bennett Frank Morgan

1934 MILLS OF THE GODS
Director: Roy William Neill
Co-stars: May Robson Victor Jory Mayo Methot

1935 WOMAN IN THE DARK
Director: Phil Rossen
Co-stars: Melvyn Douglas Ralph Bellamy Roscoe Ates

1935 COME OUT OF THE PANTRY
Director: Jack Raymond
Co-stars: Jack Buchanan Ronald Squire Fred Emney

1935 BULLDOG JACK
Director: Walter Forde
Co-stars: Jack Hulbert Claude Hulbert Ralph Richardson

1936 WHEN KNIGHTS WERE BOLD
Director: Jack Raymond
Co-stars: Jack Buchanan Garry Marsh

1936 ROAMING LADY
Co-star: Ralph Bellamy

1936 THEY MET IN A TAXI
Co-star: Chester Morris

1937 THE JURY'S SECRET
Director: Edward Sloman
Co-stars: Kent Taylor Jane Darwell Nan Grey

1937 IT HAPPENED IN HOLLYWOOD
Director: Harry Lachman
Co-stars: Richard Dix Victor Kilian

1939 SMASHING THE SPY RING
Co-star: Ralph Bellamy

1941 ADAM HAD FOUR SONS
Director: Gregory Ratoff
Co-stars: Ingrid Bergman Warner Baxter

1941 MELODY FOR THREE
Co-stars: Jean Hersholt Walter Woolf King

1952 TREASURE ON THE GOLDEN CONDOR
Director: Delmer Daves
Co-stars: Cornel Wilde Constance Smith Finlay Currie

1953 SMALL TOWN GIRL
Director: Leslie Kardos
Co-stars: Jane Powell Ann Miller Farley Granger

1955 QUEEN BEE
Director: Ranald MacDougall
Co-stars: Joan Crawford Barry Sullivan

1955 HELL ON FRISCO BAY
Director: Frank Tuttle
Co-stars: Alan Ladd Edward G. Robinson Joanne Dru

1956 CRIME OF PASSION
Director: Gerd Oswald
Co-stars: Barbara Stanwyck Sterling Hayden Raymond Burr

1956 ROCK PRETTY BABY
Director: Richard Bartlett
Co-stars: John Saxon Luana Patten Sal Mineo

1957 TAMMY AND THE BACHELOR
Director: Joseph Pevney
Co-stars: Debbie Reynolds Walter Brennan Leslie Nielsen

CLARE WREN

1988 AN AMERICAN MURDER
Director: Doug Campbell
Co-stars: Michael Bowen Ray Wise Michael J. Pollard

AMY WRIGHT

1979 HEARTLAND
Director: Richard Pearce
Co-stars: Rip Torn Conchata Ferrell Barry Primus

1979 WISE BLOOD
Director: John Huston
Co-stars: John Huston Brad Dourif Ned Beatty

1980 INSIDE MOVES
Director: Richard Donner
Co-stars: John Savage David Morse Diana Scarwid

1980 STARDUST MEMORIES
Director: Woody Allen
Co-stars: Woody Allen Charlotte Rampling Jessica Harper

1986 TRAPPED IN SILENCE
Director: Michael Tuchner
Co-stars: Marsha Mason Kiefer Sutherland John Mahoney

1988 THE ACCIDENTAL TOURIST
Director: Lawrence Kasdan
Co-stars: William Hurt Kathleen Turner Geena Davis

1989 MISS FIRECRACKER
Director: Thomas Schlamme
Co-stars: Holly Hunter Mary Steenburgen Tim Robbins

1989 SETTLE THE SCORE
Director: Edwin Sherrin
Co-stars: Jaclyn Smith Jeffrey DeMunn Howard Duff

1990 DADDY'S DYIN': WHO'S GOT THE WILL
Director: Jack Fisk
Co-stars: Beau Bridges Beverly D'Angelo Tess Harper

1990 LOVE HURTS
Director: Bud Yorkin
Co-stars: Jeff Daniels Judith Ivey John Mahoney

1991 DECEIVED
Director: Damian Harris
Co-stars: Goldie Hawn John Heard Robin Bartlett

1993 GOLD DIGGER
Director: Mark Richardson
Co-stars: Joe Pantoliano John Rhys-Davies

CATHERINE WRIGHT

1988 TOMMY TRICKER AND THE STAMP TRAVELLER
Director: Michael Rubbo
Co-stars: Lucas Evans Anthony Rogers

COBINA WRIGHT JNR.

1941 MURDER AMONG FRIENDS
Director: Ray McCarey
Co-stars: John Hubbard Marjorie Weaver Mona Barrie

1941 CHARLIE CHAN IN RIO
Director: Harry Lachman
Co-stars: Sidney Toler Victor Jory Mary Beth Hughes

1941 ACCENT ON LOVE
Director: Ray McCarey
Co-stars: George Montgomery Osa Massen J. Carrol Naish

1941 MOON OVER MIAMI
Director: Walter Lang
Co-stars: Don Ameche Betty Grable Carole Landis

1941 WEEKEND IN HAVANA
Director: Walter Lang
Co-stars: Alice Faye John Payne Carmen Miranda

1942 FOOTLIGHT SERENADE
Director: Gregory Ratoff
Co-stars: Betty Grable John Payne Victor Mature

HEATHER WRIGHT

1973 THE BELSTONE FOX
Director: James Hill
Co-stars: Eric Porter Rachel Roberts Jeremy Kemp

JENNY WRIGHT

1985 ST. ELMO'S FIRE
Director: Joel Schumacher
Co-stars: Rob Lowe Demi Moore Ally Sheedy

1986 OUT OF BOUNDS
Director: Richard Tuggle
Co-stars: Anthony Michael Hall Jeff Kober Glynn Turman

1987 NEAR DARK
Director: Kathryn Bigelow
Co-stars: Adrian Pasdar Lance Henriksen Bill Paxton

1988 TWISTER
Director: Michael Almereyda
Co-stars: Harry Dean Stanton Suzy Amis Crispin Glover

1990 A SHOCK TO THE SYSTEM
Director: Jan Egleson
Co-stars: Michael Caine Elizabeth McGovern Peter Riegert

1992 LAWNMOWER MAN
Director: Brett Leonard
Co-stars: Jeff Fahey Pierce Brosnan Geoffrey Lewis

JENNY LEE WRIGHT

1970 HUSBANDS
Director: John Cassavetes
Co-stars: John Cassavetes Ben Gazzara Peter Falk

1972 TRIPLE ECHO
Director: Michael Apted
Co-stars: Glenda Jackson Oliver Reed Brian Deacon

MAGGIE WRIGHT

1969 ONE MORE TIME
Director: Jerry Lewis
Co-stars: Sammy Davis Jnr. Peter Lawford Esther Anderson

N'BUSHE WRIGHT

1992 ZEBRAHEAD
Director: Anthony Drazan
Co-stars: Michael Rapaport Helen Shaver Ray Sharkey

1994 FRESH
Director: Boaz Yakin
Co-stars: Sean Nelson Giancarlo Esposito Samuel L. Jackson

PAMELA PAYTON WRIGHT

1986 MY LITTLE GIRL
Director: Connie Kaiserman
Co-stars: Mary Stuart Masterson James Earl Jones Anne Meara

ROBIN WRIGHT *(Married Sean Penn)*

1987 THE PRINCESS BRIDE
Director: Rob Reiner
Co-stars: Cary Elwes Mandy Patinkin Chris Sarandon

1990 STATE OF GRACE
Director: Phil Joanou
Co-stars: Sean Penn Gary Oldman Ed Harris

1992 TOYS
Director: Barry Levinson
Co-stars: Robin Williams Michael Gambon Joan Cusack

1992 THE PLAYBOYS
Director: Gilles MacKinnon
Co-stars: Albert Finney Aidan Quinn Milo O'Shea

1994 FORREST GUMP
Director: Robert Zemeckis
Co-stars: Tom Hanks Gary Sinise Sally Field

1996 THE CROSSING GUARD
Director: Sean Penn
Co-stars: Jack Nicholson David Morse Anjelica Huston

1997 MOLL FLANDERS
Director: Pen Densham
Co-stars: Stockard Channing Morgan Freeman John Lynch

TERESA WRIGHT *(Married Niven Busch)*
Oscar For Best Supporting Actress In 1942 For "Mrs Miniver"
Nominated For Best Actress In 1942 For "The Pride Of The Yankees"
Nominated For Best Supporting Actress In 1941 For "The Little Foxes"

1941 THE LITTLE FOXES
Director: William Wyler
Co-stars: Bette Davis Herbert Marshall Dan Duryea

1942 MRS MINIVER
Director: William Wyler
Co-stars: Greer Garson Walter Pidgeon Richard Ney

1942 THE PRIDE OF THE YANKEES
Director: Sam Wood
Co-stars: Gary Cooper Walter Brennan Dan Duryea

1943 SHADOW OF A DOUBT
Director: Alfred Hitchcock
Co-stars: Joseph Cotten Henry Travers Hume Cronyn

1944 CASANOVA BROWN
Director: Sam Wood
Co-stars: Gary Cooper Frank Morgan Anita Louise

1946 THE BEST YEARS OF OUR LIVES
Director: William Wyler
Co-stars: Fredric March Myrna Loy Dana Andrews

1946 THE IMPERFECT LADY
Director: Lewis Allen
Co-stars: Ray Milland Cedric Hardwicke Anthony Quinn

1947 PURSUED
Director: Raoul Walsh
Co-stars: Robert Mitchum Judith Anderson Dean Jagger

1947 THE TROUBLE WITH WOMEN
Director: Sidney Lanfield
Co-stars: Ray Milland Brian Donlevy Lloyd Bridges

1946 ENCHANTMENT
Director: Irving Reis
Co-stars: David Niven Farley Granger Evelyn Keyes

1950 THE CAPTURE
Director: John Sturges
Co-stars: Lew Ayres Victor Jory Duncan Renaldo

1950 THE MEN
Director: Fred Zinnemann
Co-stars: Marlon Brando Everett Sloane Jack Webb

1952 CALIFORNIA CONQUEST
Director: Lew Landers
Co-stars: Cornel Wilde Alfonso Bedova John Dehner

1952 COUNT THE HOURS
Director: Don Siegel
Co-stars: Macdonald Carey Adele Mara Dolores Moran

1952 SOMETHING TO LIVE FOR
Director: George Stevens
Co-stars: Ray Milland Joan Fontaine

1952 THE STEEL TRAP
Director: Andrew Stone
Co-stars: Joseph Cotten Jonathan Hale Walter Sande

1953 THE ACTRESS
Director: George Cukor
Co-stars: Jean Simmons Spencer Tracy Anthony Perkins

1954 TRACK OF THE CAT
Director: William Wellman
Co-stars: Robert Mitchum Diana Lynn Beulah Bondi

1956 SEARCH FOR BRIDEY MURPHY
Director: Noel Langley
Co-stars: Louis Hayward Nancy Gates

1957 ESCAPADE IN JAPAN
Director: Arthur Lubin
Co-stars: Cameron Mitchell Jon Prevost Clint Eastwood

1959 THE RESTLESS YEARS
Director: Helmut Kautner
Co-stars: John Saxon Sandra Dee Margaret Lindsay

1969 THE HAPPY ENDING
Director: Richard Brooks
Co-stars: Jean Simmons John Forsythe Shirley Jones

1976   **FLOOD**
Director: Earl Bellamy
Co-stars: Robert Culp Barbara Hershey Richard Basehart

1977   **ROSELAND**
Director: James Ivory
Co-stars: Geraldine Chaplin Christopher Walken

1980   **SOMEWHERE IN TIME**
Director: Jeannot Szwarc
Co-stars: Christopher Reeve Christopher Plummer

1988   **THE PRICE OF PASSION**
Director: Leonard Nimoy
Co-stars: Diane Keaton Liam Neeson Jason Robards

WHITTNI WRIGHT *(Child)*

1994   **I'LL DO ANYTHING**
Director: James Brooks
Co-stars: Nick Nolte Albert Brooks Joely Richardson

MARIS WRIXON

1940   **BRITISH INTELLIGENCE**
Director: Terry Morse
Co-stars: Margaret Lindsay Boris Karloff Bruce Lester

1940   **THE APE**
Director: William Nigh
Co-stars: Boris Karloff Gertrude Hoffman Henry Hall

1941   **BULLETS FOR O'HARA**
Director: William Howard
Co-stars: Roger Pryor Anthony Quinn Joan Perry

1941   **THE CASE OF THE BLACK PARROT**
Director: Noel Smith
Co-stars: William Lundigan Paul Cavanagh Eddie Foy Jnr.

1941   **SUNSET IN WYOMING**
Co-stars: Gene Autry Smiley Burnette

1944   **WATERFRONT**
Co-stars: John Carradine Olga Fabian

1946   **THE FACE OF MARBLE**
Co-stars: John Carradine Robert Shayne Claudia Drake

VIVIAN WU

1991   **IRON & SILK**
Director: Shirley Sun
Co-stars: Mark Salzman Pan Quingfu Jeanette Lin Tsui

1996   **PILLOW BOOK**
Director: Peter Greenaway
Co-stars: Ewan McGregor Yoshi Oida Ken Ogata

KARI WUHRER

1991   **BEASTMASTER 2:**
       THROUGH THE PORTALS OF TIME
Director: Sylvio Tabet
Co-stars: Marc Singer Wings Hauser Sarah Douglas

1997   **KOLYA**
Co-stars: Zdenek Sverak Andrej Chalimon

JANE WYATT

1934   **ONE MORE RIVER**
Director: James Whale
Co-stars: Colin Clive Diana Wynyard C. Aubrey Smith

1934   **GREAT EXPECTATIONS**
Director: Stuart Walker
Co-stars: Phillips Holmes Henry Hull Alan Hale

1936   **THE LUCKIEST GIRL IN THE WORLD**
Director: Eddie Buzzell
Co-stars: Louis Hayward Eugene Pallette

1936   **WE'RE ONLY HUMAN**
Director: James Flood
Co-stars: Preston Foster James Gleason Jane Darwell

1937   **LOST HORIZON**
Director: Frank Capra
Co-stars: Ronald Colman Thomas Mitchell Margo

1941   **WEEKEND FOR THREE**
Director: Irving Reis
Co-stars: Dennis O'Keefe Philip Reed Zasu Pitts

1942   **ARMY SURGEON**
Co-stars: James Ellison Kent Taylor

1942   **THE NAVY COMES THROUGH**
Director: Edward Sutherland
Co-stars: Pat O'Brien George Murphy Max Baer

1943   **THE KANSAN**
Director: George Archinbaud
Co-stars: Richard Dix Albert Dekker Victor Jory

1943   **BUCKSKIN FRONTIER**
Director: Lesley Selander
Co-stars: Richard Dix Albert Dekker Lee J. Cobb

1944   **NONE BUT THE LONELY HEART**
Director: Clifford Odets
Co-stars: Cary Grant Ethel Barrymore Dan Duryea

1946   **BACHELOR GIRLS**
Director: Andrew Stone
Co-stars: Adolphe Menjou Gail Russell Claire Trevor

1947   **BOOMERANG**
Director: Elia Kazan
Co-stars: Dana Andrews Lee J. Cobb Arthur Kennedy

1948   **THE PITFALL**
Director: Andre De Toth
Co-stars: Dick Powell Lizabeth Scott Raymond Burr

1948   **NO MINOR VICES**
Director: Lewis Milestone
Co-stars: Dana Andrews Lilli Palmer Louis Jourdan

1949   **TASK FORCE**
Director: Delmer Daves
Co-stars: Gary Cooper Walter Brennan Jack Holt

1949   **CANADIAN PACIFIC**
Director: Edwin Marin
Co-stars: Randolph Scott Nancy Olson J. Carrol Naish

1949   **BAD BOY**
Co-stars: Lloyd Nolan Martha Vickers Rhys Williams

1950   **HOUSE BY THE RIVER**
Director: Fritz Lang
Co-stars: Louis Hayward Lee Bowman Ann Shoemaker

1950   **THE MAN WHO CHEATED HIMSELF**
Director: Felix Feist
Co-stars: Lee J. Cobb John Dall Terry Frost

1950   **MY BLUE HEAVEN**
Director: Henry Koster
Co-stars: Betty Grable Dan Dailey Mitzi Gaynor

1950   **OUR VERY OWN**
Director: David Miller
Co-stars: Ann Blyth Farley Granger Natalie Wood

1957   **INTERLUDE**
Director: Douglas Sirk
Co-stars: Rossano Brazzi June Allyson Keith Andes

1965   **NEVER TOO LATE**
Director: Bud Yorkin
Co-stars: Maureen O'Sullivan Paul Ford Jim Hutton

1970 WEEKEND OF TERROR
Director: Jud Taylor
Co-stars: Robert Conrad Lee Majors Carol Lynley

1973 TOM SAWYER
Director: James Neilson
Co-stars: Josh Albee Buddy Ebsen Vic Morrow

1976 TREASURE OF MATECHUMBA
Director: Vincente McEveety
Co-stars: Robert Foxworth Peter Ustinov

1989 AMITYVILLE 4: THE EVIL ESCAPES
Director: Sandor Stern
Co-stars: Patty Duke Norman Lloyd

TESSA WYATT

1970 THE BEAST IN THE CELLAR
Director: James Kelly
Co-stars: Flora Robson Beryl Reid John Hamill

1972 ENGLAND MADE ME
Director: Peter Duffell
Co-stars: Peter Finch Michael York Hildegarde Neil

MARGARET WYCHERLY
Nominated For Best Supporting Actress In 1941 For "Sergeant York"

1929 THE 13TH CHAIR
Director: Tod Browning
Co-stars: Bela Lugosi Conrad Nagel Leila Hyams

1934 MIDNIGHT
Director: Chester Erskine
Co-stars: Humphrey Bogart Sidney Fox Henry Hull

1940 VICTORY
Director: John Cromwell
Co-stars: Fredric March Betty Field Cedric Hardwicke

1941 SERGEANT YORK
Director: Howard Hawks
Co-stars: Gary Cooper Joan Leslie Walter Brennan

1942 RANDOM HARVEST
Director: Mervyn LeRoy
Co-stars: Ronald Colman Greer Garson Susan Peters

1942 KEEPER OF THE FLAME
Director: George Cukor
Co-stars: Spencer Tracy Katherine Hepburn Richard Whorf

1942 CROSSROADS
Director: Jack Conway
Co-stars: William Powell Hedy Lamarr Basil Rathbone

1943 ASSIGNMENT IN BRITTANY
Director: Jack Conway
Co-stars: Jean-Pierre Aumont Signe Hasso Susan Peters

1943 HANGMEN ALSO DIE
Director: Fritz Lang
Co-stars: Brian Donlevy Walter Brennan Anna Lee

1943 THE MOON IS DOWN
Director: Irving Pichel
Co-stars: Henry Travers Cedric Hardwicke Lee J. Cobb

1944 EXPERIMENT PERILOUS
Director: Jacques Tourneur
Co-stars: Hedy Lamarr Paul Lukas George Brent

1945 JOHNNY ANGEL
Director: Edwin Marin
Co-stars: George Raft Claire Trevor Signe Hasso

1946 THE YEARLING
Director: Clarence Brown
Co-stars: Gregory Peck Jane Wyman Claude Jarman Jnr

1947 FOREVER AMBER
Director: Otto Preminger
Co-stars: Linda Darnell Cornel Wilde George Sanders

1948 THE LOVES OF CARMEN
Director: Charles Vidor
Co-stars: Rita Hayworth Glenn Ford Victor Jory

1949 WHITE HEAT
Director: Raoul Walsh
Co-stars: James Cagney Edmond O'Brien Virginia Mayo

1951 THE MAN WITH A CLOAK
Director: Fletcher Markle
Co-stars: Joseph Cotten Barbara Stanwyck Leslie Caron

KATYA WYETH

1971 TWINS OF EVIL
Director: John Hough
Co-stars: Madeleine Collinson Mary Collinson Peter Cushing

1974 CONFESSIONS OF A WINDOW CLEANER
Director: Val Guest
Co-stars: Robin Askwith Anthony Booth Bill Maynard

JANE WYMAN *(Married Ronald Reagan)*
Oscar For Best Actress In 1948 For "Johnny Belinda". Nominated For Best Actress In 1946 For "The Yearling," In 1951 For "The Blue Veil" And In 1954 For "Magnificent Obsession"

1936 SMART BLONDE
Director: Frank McDonald
Co-stars: Glenda Farrell Barton MacLane

1937 SLIM
Director: Ray Enright
Co-stars: Pat O'Brien Henry Fonda Margaret Lindsay

1937 READY, WILLING AND ABLE
Director: Ray Enright
Co-stars: Ruby Keeler Ross Alexander Lee Dixon

1937 PUBLIC WEDDING
Co-star: William Hopper

1937 THE KING AND THE CHORUS GIRL
Director: Mervyn LeRoy
Co-stars: Joan Blondell Fernand Gravet

1937 MR DODD TAKES THE AIR
Director: Alfred Green
Co-stars: Kenny Baker Alice Brady Frank McHugh

1938 WIDE OPEN FACES
Director: Kurt Neuman
Co-stars: Joe E. Brown Alison Skipworth

1938 THE CROWD ROARS
Director: Richard Thorpe
Co-stars: Robert Taylor Frank Morgan Maureen O'Sullivan

1938 HE COULDN'T SAY NO
Co-stars: Frank McHugh Cora Witherspoon

1938 THE SPY RING
Co-stars: Robert Warwick William Hall

1938 BROTHER RAT
Director: William Keighley
Co-stars: Ronald Reagan Wayne Morris

1939 BROTHER RAT AND A BABY
Director: Ray Enright
Co-stars: Ronald Reagan Wayne Morris Eddie Albert

1939 TORCHY PLAYS WITH DYNAMITE
Director: William Beaudine
Co-star: Allen Jenkins

1939 KID NIGHTINGALE
Director: George Amy
Co-stars: John Payne Walter Catlett Ed Brophy

1939 TAIL SPIN
Director: Roy Del Ruth
Co-stars: Alice Faye Constance Bennett Nancy Kelly

1939	**PRIVATE DETECTIVE**
1940	**TUGBOAT ANNIE SAILS AGAIN**
Director:	Lewis Seiler
Co-stars:	Marjorie Rambeau Alan Hale

1940 FLIGHT ANGELS
Director: Lewis Seiler
Co-stars: Dennis Morgan Virginia Bruce

1940 THE KID FROM KOKOMO
Director: Lewis Seiler
Co-stars: Pat O'Brien Wayne Morris Joan Blondell

1940 MY LOVE CAME BACK
Director: Curtis Bernhardt
Co-stars: Olivia De Havilland Jeffrey Lynn

1940 GAMBLING ON THE HIGH SEAS
Director: George Amy
Co-stars: Wayne Morris Gilbert Roland John Litel

1941 BAD MEN OF MISSOURI
Director: Ray Enright
Co-stars: Dennis Morgan Wayne Morris Victor Jory

1941 THE BODY DISAPPEARS
Director: Ross Lederman
Co-stars: Edward Everett Horton Jeffrey Lynn

1941 YOU'RE IN THE ARMY NOW
Director: Lewis Seiler
Co-stars: Jimmy Durante Phil Silvers Regis Toomey

1941 HONEYMOON FOR THREE
Director: Lloyd Bacon
Co-stars: George Brent Ann Sheridan Osa Massen

1942 FOOTLIGHT SERENADE
Director: Gregory Ratoff
Co-stars: Betty Grable John Payne Victor Mature

1942 LARCENCY INC.
Director: Lloyd Bacon
Co-stars: Edward G. Robinson Broderick Crawford

1942 MY FAVOURITE SPY
Director: Tay Garnett
Co-stars: Kay Kyser Ginny Sims Ellen Drew

1944 MAKE YOUR OWN BED
Director: Peter Godfrey
Co-stars: Jack Carson Irene Manning Alan Hale

1944 HOLLYWOOD CANTEEN
Director: Delmer Daves
Co-stars: Joan Leslie Janis Paige Robert Hutton

1944 CRIME BY NIGHT
Director: William Clemens
Co-stars: Jerome Cowan Eleanor Parker

1944 THE DOUGHGIRLS
Co-stars: Alexis Smith Ann Sheridan Jack Carson

1943 PRINCESS O'ROURKE
Director: Norman Krasna
Co-stars: Olivia De Havilland Robert Cummings

1945 THE LOST WEEKEND
Director: Billy Wilder
Co-stars: Ray Milland Howard Da Silva

1946 NIGHT AND DAY
Director: Michael Curtiz
Co-stars: Cary Grant Alexis Smith Mary Martin

1946 THE YEARLING
Director: Clarence Brown
Co-stars: Gregory Peck Claude Jarman Chill Wills

1946 ONE MORE TOMORROW
Director: Peter Godfrey
Co-stars: Dennis Morgan Jack Carson Ann Sheridan

1947 THE WYOMING KID
Director: Raoul Walsh
Co-stars: Dennis Morgan Arthur Kennedy

1947 MAGIC TOWN
Director: William Wellman
Co-stars: James Stewart Kent Smith Regis Toomey

1948 JOHNNY BELINDA
Director: Jean Negulesco
Co-stars: Lew Ayres Stephen McNally

1949 A KISS IN THE DARK
Director: Delmer Daves
Co-stars: David Niven Broderick Crawford

1949 IT'S A GREAT FEELING
Director: David Butler
Co-stars: Doris Day Dennis Morgan Jack Carson

1949 THE LADY TAKES A SAILOR
Director: Michael Curtiz
Co-stars: Dennis Morgan Eve Arden Allyn Joslyn

1950 THE GLASS MENAGERIE
Director: Irving Rapper
Co-stars: Gertrude Lawrence Kirk Douglas

1950 STAGE FRIGHT
Director: Alfred Hitchcock
Co-stars: Marlene Dietrich Richard Todd

1950 THE STORY OF WILL ROGERS
Director: Michael Curtiz
Co-stars: Will Rogers Jnr. Eddie Cantor

1951 HERE COMES THE GROOM
Director: Frank Capra
Co-stars: Bing Crosby Franchot Tone Alexis Smith

1951 THREE GUYS NAMED MIKE
Director: Charles Walters
Co-stars: Howard Keel Van Johnson Barry Sullivan

1951 STARLIFT
Director: Roy Del Ruth
Co-stars: Janis Rule Dick Wesson Richard Webb

1951 THE BLUE VEIL
Director: Curtis Bernhardt
Co-stars: Charles Laughton Joan Blondell

1952 JUST FOR YOU
Director: Elliott Nugent
Co-stars: Bing Crosby Natalie Wood

1953 LET'S DO IT AGAIN
Director: Alexander Hall
Co-stars: Ray Milland Aldo Ray Leon Ames

1953 SO BIG
Director: Robert Wise
Co-stars: Sterling Hayden Richard Beymer

1954 MAGNIFICENT OBSESSION
Director: Douglas Sirk
Co-stars: Rock Hudson Agnes Moorehead Barbara Rush

1955 ALL THAT HEAVEN ALLOWS
Director: Douglas Sirk
Co-stars: Rock Hudson Agnes Moorehead Conrad Nagle

1955 LUCY GALLANT
Director: Robert Parrish
Co-stars: Charlton Heston Thelma Ritter

1956 MIRACLE IN THE RAIN
Director: Rudolph Mate
Co-stars: Van Johnson Fred Clark William Gargan

1959 HOLIDAY FOR LOVERS
Director: Henry Levin
Co-stars: Clifton Webb Paul Henreid Carol Lynley

1960   POLLYANNA
Director: David Swift
Co-stars: Hayley Mills Karl Malden

1962   BON VOYAGE
Director: James Neilson
Co-stars: Fred MacMurray Tommy Kirk Ivan Desny

1969   HOW TO COMMIT MARRIAGE
Director: Norman Panama
Co-stars: Bob Hope Jackie Gleason Tina Louise

PATRICE WYMORE

1950   TEA FOR TWO
Director: David Butler
Co-stars: Doris Day Gordon MacRae Gene Nelson

1950   ROCKY MOUNTAIN
Director: William Keighley
Co-stars: Errol Flynn Scott Forbes Guinn Williams

**1952   SHE'S WORKING HER WAY
THROUGH COLLEGE**
Director: Bruce Humberstone
Co-stars: Virginia Mayo Ronald Reagan

1952   THE MAN BEHIND THE GUN
Director: Felix Feist
Co-stars: Randolph Scott Dick Wesson Lina Romay

1960   OCEAN'S ELEVEN
Director: Lewis Milestone
Co-stars: Frank Sinatra Peter Lawford Dean Martin

1966   CHAMBER OF HORRORS
Director: Hy Averback
Co-stars: Patrick O'Neal Laura Devon Wilfrid Hyde White

JOAN WYNDHAM

1931   UP FOR THE CUP
Director: Jack Raymond
Co-stars: Sydney Howard Sam Livesey Moore Marriott

1933   LOYALTIES
Director: Basil Dean
Co-stars: Basil Rathbone Miles Mander Heather Thatcher

1937   JUGGERNAUT
Director: Henry Edwards
Co-stars: Boris Karloff Mona Goya Arthur Margetson

MAY WYNN

1954   THEY RODE WEST
Director: Phil Karlson
Co-stars: Robert Francis Donna Reed Phil Carey

1954   THE CAINE MUTINY
Director: Edward Dmytryk
Co-stars: Humphrey Bogart Jose Ferrer Van Johnson

1955   THE VIOLENT MEN
Director: Rudolph Mate
Co-stars: Edward G. Robinson Barbara Stanwyck Glenn Ford

NAN WYNN

1941   MILLION DOLLAR BABY
Director: Curtis Bernhardt
Co-stars: Priscilla Lane Jeffrey Lynn Ronald Reagan

1941   A SHOT IN THE DARK
Co-star: Donald Douglas

1942   PARDON MY SARONG
Director: Erle Kenton
Co-stars: Bud Abbott Lou Costello Virginia Bruce

PEGGY WYNN

1947   THE WILD COUNTRY
Co-stars: Eddie Dean Roscoe Ates

ZOE WYNN

1937   SMASH AND GRAB
Director: Tim Whelan
Co-stars: Jack Buchanan Elsie Randolph Arthur Margetson

ANGELA WYNTER

1981   BURNING AN ILLUSION
Director: Menelik Shabazz
Co-stars: Victor Romero Beverley Martin Pat Williams

DANA WYNTER

1955   THE VIEW FROM POMPEY'S HEAD
Director: Philip Dunne
Co-stars: Richard Egan Cameron Mitchell Sidney Blackmer

1956   D-DAY, THE SIXTH OF JUNE
Director: Robert Taylor
Co-stars: Richard Todd Edmond O'Brien

1956   INVASION OF THE BODY SNATCHERS
Director: Don Siegel
Co-stars: Kevin McCarthy Larry Gates Carolyn Jones

1957   SOMETHING OF VALUE
Director: Richard Brooks
Co-stars: Rock Hudson Sidney Poitier Wendy Hiller

1958   IN LOVE AND WAR
Director: Philip Dunne
Co-stars: Jeffrey Hunter Bradford Dillman Hope Lange

1958   FRAULEIN
Director: Henry Koster
Co-stars: Mel Ferrer Margaret Hayes Helmut Dantine

1959   SHAKE HANDS WITH THE DEVIL
Director: Michael Anderson
Co-stars: James Cagney Glynis Johns Don Murray

1960   SINK THE BISMARCK !
Director: Lewis Gilbert
Co-stars: Kenneth More Karel Stepanek Geoffrey Keen

1961   ON THE DOUBLE
Director: Melville Shavelson
Co-stars: Danny Kaye Diana Dors Margaret Rutherford

1963   THE LIST OF ADRIAN MESSINGER
Director: John Huston
Co-stars: George C. Scott Clive Brook Herbert Marshall

1973   THE CONNECTION
Director: Tom Gries
Co-stars: Charles Durning Ronny Cox Zohra Lampert

1973   SANTEE
Director: Gary Nelson
Co-stars: Glenn Ford Michael Burns Jay Silverheels

1978   LE SAUVAGE
Director: Jean-Paul Rappeneau
Co-stars: Yves Montand Catherine Deneuve Luigi Vannucchi

CHARLOTTE WYNTERS

1931   THE STRUGGLE
Director: D.W. Griffith
Co-stars: Hal Skelly Zita Johann Jackson Halliday

1936   THE CALLING OF DAN MATTHEWS
Co-stars: Donald Cook Douglas Dumbrille

1938   SINNERS IN PARADISE
Director: James Whale
Co-stars: Madge Evans John Boles Bruce Cabot

DIANA WYNYARD *(Dorothy Cox)*
Nominated For Best Actress In 1933 For "Calvacade"

1932 RASPUTIN AND THE EMPRESS
Director: Richard Boleslawski
Co-stars: John Barrymore Lionel Barrymore Ethel Barrymore

1933 CALVACADE
Director: Frank Lloyd
Co-stars: Clive Brook Ursula Jeans Herbert Mundin

1933 MEN MUST FIGHT
Director: Edgar Selwyn
Co-stars: Robert Young Phillips Holmes Lewis Stone

1933 REUNION IN VIENNA
Director: Sidney Franklin
Co-stars: John Barrymore May Robson Frank Morgan

1934 WHERE SINNERS MEET
Director: J. Walter Ruben
Co-stars: Clive Brook Billie Burke Reginald Owen

1934 ONE MORE RIVER
Director: James Whale
Co-stars: Colin Clive Jane Wyatt Lionel Atwill

1934 LETS TRY AGAIN
Director: Worthington Miner
Co-stars: Clive Brook Irene Hervey Helen Vinson

1938 GASLIGHT
Director: Thorold Dickinson
Co-stars: Anton Walbrook Robert Newton Jimmy Hanley

1939 ON THE NIGHT OF THE FIRE
Director: Brian Desmond Hurst
Co-stars: Ralph Richardson Mary Clare Henry Oscar

1940 THE PRIME MINISTER
Director: Thorold Dickinson
Co-stars: John Gielgud Will Fyffe Stephen Murray

1941 KIPPS
Director: Carol Reed
Co-stars: Michael Redgrave Phyllis Calvert Max Adrian

1941 FREEDOM RADIO
Director: Anthony Asquith
Co-stars: Clive Brook Raymond Huntley Joyce Howard

1948 AN IDEAL HUSBAND
Director: Alexander Korda
Co-stars: Paulette Goddard Hugh Williams Michael Wilding

1951 TOM BROWN'S SCHOOLDAYS
Director: Gordon Parry
Co-stars: Robert Newton John Howard Davies Kathleen Byron

1956 THE FEMININE TOUCH
Director: Pat Jackson
Co-stars: George Baker Belinda Lee Delphi Lawrence

1957 ISLAND IN THE SUN
Director: Robert Rossen
Co-stars: James Mason Joan Fontaine Harry Belafonte

AMANDA WYSS

1984 A NIGHTMARE ON ELM STREET
Director: Wes Craven
Co-stars: Robert Englund John Saxon Ronee Blakley

1984 MY MOTHER'S SECRET LIFE
Director: Robert Markowitz
Co-stars: Loni Anderson Paul Sorvino James Sutorius

1987 INDEPENDENCE
Director: John Patterson
Co-stars: John Bennett Perry Isabella Hofman Sandy McPeak

1988 POWWOW HIGHWAY
Director: Jonathan Wacks
Co-stars: A. Martinez Gary Farmer Geoff Rivas

XOCHITL

1972 APACHE MASSACRE
Director: William Graham
Co-stars: Harry Dean Stanton Cliff Potts Don Wilbanks

VALENTINA YAKUNINA

1989 CONFESSIONAL
Director: Gordon Flemying
Co-stars: Robert Lindsay Keith Carradine Anthony Quayle

SHIRLEY YAMAGUCHI

1952 JAPANESE WAR BRIDE
Director: King Vidor
Co-stars: Don Taylor Cameron Mitchell Marie Windsor

1955 HOUSE OF BAMBOO
Director: Samuel Fuller
Co-stars: Robert Stack Robert Ryan Cameron Mitchell

1956 NAVY WIFE
Director: Edward Bernds
Co-stars: Joan Bennett Gary Merrill Judy Nugent

EMILY YANCY

1970 COTTON COMES TO HARLEM
Director: Ossie Davis
Co-stars: Godfrey Cambridge Raymond St. Jacques Judy Pace

LAURA YANG

1988 AMERICAN COMMANDO NINJA
Co-stars: Patrick L'Argent Daniel Garfield Kelvin Wong

MARIE YANG

1960 THE SAVAGE INNOCENTS
Director: Nicholas Ray
Co-stars: Anthony Quinn Yoko Tani Peter O'Toole

MAWUYUL YANTHALAWUY

1980 MANGANINNIE
Director: John Honey
Co-stars: Anna Ralph Phillip Hinton Reg Evans

LILLIAN YARBO

1938 YOU CAN'T TAKE IT WITH YOU
Director: Frank Capra
Co-stars: Jean Arthur James Stewart Lionel Barrymore

MARGARET YARDE

1935 SQUIBS
Director: Henry Edwards
Co-stars: Betty Balfour Gordon Harker Stanley Holloway

LORENE YARNELL

1987 SPACEBALLS
Director: Mel Brooks
Co-stars: Mel Brooks John Candy Rick Moranis

AMY YASBECK

1987 HOUSE II:THE SECOND STORY
Director: Ethan Wiley
Co-stars: Ayre Gross Jonathan Stark Royal Dano

1988 SPLASH TOO
Director: Greg Antonacci
Co-stars: Todd Waring Donovan Scott Rita Taggart

1989 LITTLE WHITE LIES
Director: Anson Williams
Co-stars: Ann Jillian Tim Matheson Suzie Plakson

1990 PROBLEM CHILD
Director: Dennis Dugan
Co-stars: John Ritter Jack Warden Michael Oliver

1990 PRETTY WOMAN
Director: Garry Marshall
Co-stars: Richard Gere Julia Roberts Ralph Bellamy

1991 PROBLEM CHILD 2
Director: Brian Levant
Co-stars: John Ritter Jack Warden Michael Oliver

1993 ROBIN HOOD:MEN IN TIGHTS
Director: Mel Brooks
Co-stars: Mel Brooks Cary Elwes Roger Rees

1994 THE MASK
Director: Charles Russell
Co-stars: Jim Carrey Cameron Diaz Peter Riegert

PATTI YASUTAKI

1992 STOP! OR MY MUM WILL SHOOT
Director: Roger Spottiswoode
Co-stars: Sylvester Stallone Estelle Getty

1993 BLIND SPOT
Director: Michael Toshiuki
Co-stars: Joanne Woodward Reed Diamond Fritz Weaver

CASSIE YATES

1978 F.I.S.T.
Director: Norman Jewison
Co-stars: Sylvester Stallone Rod Steiger Melinda Dillon

1978 F.M.
Director: John Alonzo
Co-stars: Michael Brandon Eileen Brennan Cleavon Little

1978 CONVOY
Director: Sam Peckinpah
Co-stars: Kris Kristofferson Ali McGraw Ernest Borgnine

1978 THE EVIL
Director: Gus Trikonis
Co-stars: Richard Crenna Joanna Pettet Victor Buono

1981 OF MICE AND MEN
Director: Reza Badiyi
Co-stars: Robert Blake Randy Quaid Lew Ayres

1982 THE GIFT OF LIFE
Director: Jerry London
Co-stars: Susan Dey Paul LeMat Edward Herrman

1983 LISTEN TO YOUR HEART
Director: Don Taylor
Co-stars: Kate Jackson Tim Matheson George Coe

1983 THE OSTERMAN WEEKEND
Director: Sam Peckinpah
Co-stars: Rutger Hauer Burt Lancaster John Hurt

1984 UNFAITHFULLY YOURS
Director: Howard Zieff
Co-stars: Dudley Moore Nastassja Kinski Albert Brooks

1985 PERRY MASON RETURNS
Director: Ron Satlof
Co-stars: Raymond Burr Barbara Hale William Katt

MARJORIE YATES

1973 THE OPTIMISTS OF NINE ELMS
Director: Anthony Kimmins
Co-stars: Peter Sellers Donna Mullane John Chaffey

1975 LEGEND OF THE WEREWOLF
Director: Freddie Francis
Co-stars: Peter Cushing Ron Moody Hugh Griffith

1977 THE BLACK PANTHER
Director: Ian Merrick
Co-stars: Donald Sumpter Debbie Farrington David Swift

1992 THE LONG DAY CLOSES
Director: Terence Davies
Co-stars: Leigh McCormack Ayse Owens Tina Malone

PAULINE YATES

1965 DARLING
Director: John Schlesinger
Co-stars: Julie Christie Dirk Bogarde Laurence Harvey

1989 A SMALL MOURNING
Director: Chris Bernard
Co-stars: Alison Steadman Stratford Johns Ian Deam

KAREN YEH

1974 BLOOD MONEY
Director: Anthony Dawson
Co-stars: Lee Van Cleef Lo Lieh Patty Shepard

SALLY YEH

1990 LASERMAN
Director: Peter Wang
Co-stars: Peter Wang Marc Hayashi Tony Leung

MICHELLE YEOH

1997 TOMORROW NEVER DIES
Co-stars: Pierce Brosnan Teri Hatcher Judi Dench

ERICA YOHN

1979 AND YOUR NAME IS JONAH
Director: Richard Michaels
Co-stars: Sally Struthers James Woods Robert Davi

1984 A STREETCAR NAMED DESIRE
Director: John Erman
Co-stars: Ann-Margret Treat Williams Beverly D'Angelo

**1991 AN AMERICAN TALE:
FIEVEL GOES WEST** *(Voice)*
Director: Simon Wells
Co-stars: James Stewart John Cleese Philip Glasser

AMANDA YORK

1982 SCRUBBERS
Director: Mai Zetterling
Co-stars: Chrissie Cotterill Kate Ingram Honey Bane

FRANCINE YORK

1970 CANNON FOR CORDOBA
Director: Paul Wendkos
Co-stars: George Peppard Raf Vallone Pete Duel

1972 WELCOME HOME, SOLDIER BOYS
Director: Richard Crompton
Co-stars: Joe Don Baker Alan Vint Geoffrey Lewis

KATHLEEN YORK

1985 THIS CHILD IS MINE
Director: David Greene
Co-stars: Lindsay Wagner Chris Sarandon Nancy McKeon

1986 THOMPSON'S LAST RUN
Director: Jerrold Freedman
Co-stars: Robert Mitchum Wilford Brimley Guy Boyd

1987 THE ALAMO: THIRTEEN DAYS TO GLORY
Director: Burt Kennedy
Co-stars: James Arness Brian Keith Alec Baldwin

1989 COLD FEET
Director: Robert Dornheim
Co-stars: Keith Carradine Sally Kirkland Tom Waits

1991 WILD HEARTS CAN'T BE BROKEN
Director: Steve Miner
Co-stars: Gabrielle Anwar Cliff Robertson

1992 SWITCHING PARENTS
Director: Linda Otto
Co-stars: Joseph Gordon-Levitt Daniel DeSanto Brian Cook

1993 LOVE, LIES AND LULLABIES
Director: Rod Hardy
Co-stars: Susan Dey Piper Laurie Andy Romano

1994 DREAM LOVER
Director: Nicholas Kazan
Co-stars: James Spader Madchen Amick Bess Armstrong

SARAH YORK

1983 THE EVIL DEAD
Director: Sam Raimi
Co-stars: Bruce Campbell Ellen Sandweiss Betsy Baker

SUSANNAH YORK

Nominated For Best Supporting Actress In 1969 For "They Shoot Horses, Don't They?"

1958 MISTER SKEETER
Director: Colin Finbow
Co-stars: Peter Bayliss Orlando Wells Rose Hill

1960 TUNES OF GLORY
Director: Ronald Neame
Co-stars: Alec Guinness John Mills Dennis Price

1960 THERE WAS A CROOKED MAN
Director: Stuart Burge
Co-stars: Norman Wisdom Alfred Marks

1961 THE GREENGAGE SUMMER
Director: Lewis Gilbert
Co-stars: Kenneth More Danielle Darrieux

1962 FREUD
Director: John Huston
Co-stars: Montgomery Clift Larry Parks Eileen Herlie

1963 TOM JONES
Director: Tony Richardson
Co-stars: Albert Finney Hugh Griffith Diane Cilento

1964 THE SEVENTH DAWN
Director: Lewis Gilbert
Co-stars: William Holden Capucine Tetsuro Tamba

1965 SANDS OF THE KALAHARI
Director: Cy Endfield
Co-stars: Stanley Baker Stuart Whitman

1966 A MAN FOR ALL SEASONS
Director: Fred Zinnemann
Co-stars: Paul Scofield Wendy Hiller John Hurt

1966 KALEIDOSCOPE
Director: Jack Smight
Co-stars: Warren Beatty Clive Revell Eric Porter

1968 DUFFY
Director: Robert Parrish
Co-stars: James Coburn James Mason James Fox

1968 OH! WHAT A LOVELY WAR
Director: Richard Attenborough
Co-stars: John Gielgud Ralph Richardson

1968 SEBASTIAN
Director: David Greene
Co-stars: Dirk Bogarde Lilli Palmer Janet Munro

1969 THEY SHOOT HORSES, DON'T THEY?
Director: Sydney Pollack
Co-stars: Gig Young Jane Fonda

1969 LOCK UP YOUR DAUGHTERS
Director: Peter Coe
Co-stars: Christopher Plummer Glynis Johns Tom Bell

1969 THE KILLING OF SISTER GEORGE
Director: Robert Aldrich
Co-stars: Beryl Reid Coral Browne

1969 COUNTRY DANCE
Director: J. Lee-Thompson
Co-stars: Peter O'Toole Michael Craig Cyril Cusack

1969 BATTLE OF BRITAIN
Director: Guy Hamilton
Co-stars: Michael Caine Robert Shaw Kenneth More

1971 HAPPY BIRTHDAY, WANDA JUNE
Director: Mark Robson
Co-stars: Rod Steiger Don Murray Steven Paul

1971 JANE EYRE
Director: Delbert Mann
Co-stars: George C. Scott Jack Hawkins Ian Bannen

1971 ZEE AND CO.
Director: Brian Hutton
Co-stars: Elizabeth Taylor Michael Caine

1972 IMAGES
Director: Robert Altman
Co-stars: Rene Auberjonois Marcel Borzuffi

1974 THE MAIDS
Director: Christopher Miles
Co-stars: Glenda Jackson Vivien Merchant

1974 GOLD
Director: Peter Hunt
Co-stars: Roger Moore Ray Milland John Gielgud

1975 CONDUCT UNBECOMING
Director: Michael Anderson
Co-stars: Michael York Stacey Keach Trevor Howard

1975 THAT LUCKY TOUCH
Director: Christopher Miles
Co-stars: Roger Moore Lee J. Cobb Shelley Winters

1976 SKY RIDERS
Director: Douglas Hickox
Co-stars: James Coburn Robert Culp Charles Aznavour

1976 ELIZA FRASER
Director: Tim Burstall
Co-stars: Trevor Howard Noel Ferrier John Waters

1978 THE SHOUT
Director: Jerzy Skolimovski
Co-stars: Alan Bates John Hurt Robert Stephens

1978 THE SILENT PARTNER
Director: Daryl Duke
Co-stars: Christopher Plummer Elliott Gould

1978 SUPERMAN
Director: Richard Donner
Co-stars: Christopher Reeve Margot Kidder

1979 THE GOLDEN GATE MURDERS
Director: Walter Grauman
Co-stars: David Janssen Kim Hunter Tim O'Connor

1980 SUPERMAN II
Director: Richard Lester
Co-stars: Christopher Reeve Gene Hackman

1980 LOOPHOLE
Director: John Quested
Co-stars: Albert Finney Martin Sheen

1980 FALLING IN LOVE AGAIN
Director: Steven Paul
Co-stars: Elliott Gould Kaye Ballard Michelle Pfeiffer

1980 THE AWAKENING
Director: Mike Newell
Co-stars: Charlton Heston Stephanie Zimbalist

1981 ALICE
Director: Jerry Gruza
Co-stars: Jean-Pierre Cassel Sophie Barjac Paul Nicholas

1984 A CHRISTMAS CAROL
Director: Clive Donner
Co-stars: George C. Scott Frank Finlay David Warner

1988 JUST ASK FOR DIAMOND
Director: Stephen Bayly
Co-stars: Dursley McLinden Colin Dale Jimmy Nail

1988 AMERICAN ROULETTE
Director: Maurice Hatton
Co-stars: Andy Garcia Kitty Aldridge

1988 A SUMMER STORY
Director: Piers Haggard
Co-stars: James Wilby Imogen Stubbs Sophie Ward

1989 MELANCHOLIA
Director: Andi Engel
Co-stars: Jeroen Krabbe Jane Gurnett Kate Hardie

1990 THE MAN FROM THE PRU
Director: Rob Rohrer
Co-stars: Jonathan Pryce Anna Massey Richard Pasco

CAROL YORKE

1948 LETTER FROM AN UNKNOWN WOMAN
Director: Max Ophuls
Co-stars: Joan Fontaine Louis Jourdan Mady Christians

1955 THE FLAW
Director: Terence Fisher
Co-stars: John Bentley Donald Houston Rona Anderson

EDITH YORKE

1930 CITY GIRL
Director: F.W. Murnau
Co-stars: Charles Farrell Mary Duncan Dawn O'Day

DORIS YOUNANE

1989 MORTGAGE
Director: Bill Bennett
Co-stars: Brian Vriends Bruce Vanables Andrew Gilbert

1992 DEATH IN BRUNSWICK
Director: John Ruane
Co-stars: Sam Neill Zoe Carides Yvonne Lawley

1993 THE HEARTBREAK KID
Director: Michael Jenkins
Co-stars: Claudia Karvan Alex Dimitriades Steve Bastoni

AUDREY YOUNG

1947 THE WISTFUL WIDOW OF WAGON GAP
Director: Charles Barton
Co-stars: Bud Abbott Lou Costello Marjorie Main

CLARA KIMBELL YOUNG

1931   KEPT HUSBANDS
Co-stars: Joel McCrea Dorothy MacKaill Freeman Wood

1934   ROMANCE IN THE RAIN
Director: Stuart Walker
Co-stars: Roger Pryor Heather Angel Victor Moore

1938   THE FRONTIERSMAN

ELIZABETH YOUNG

1933   BIG EXECUTIVE
Director: Erle Kenton
Co-stars: Ricardo Cortez Richard Bennett Dorothy Peterson

1933   QUEEN CHRISTINA
Director: Rouben Mamoulian
Co-stars: Greta Garbo John Gilbert Lewis Stone

1934   THERE'S ALWAYS TOMORROW
Co-stars: Robert Taylor Frank Morgan Binnie Barnes

1935   EAST OF JAVA
Director: George Melford
Co-stars: Charles Bickford Frank Albertson Sig Ruman

FELICITY YOUNG

1960   COVER GIRL KILLER
Director: Terry Bishop
Co-stars: Harry H. Corbett Victor Brooks Tony Doonan

1960   THE GENTLE TRAP
Director: Charles Saunders
Co-stars: Spencer Teakle Martin Benson Dorinda Stevens

GLADYS YOUNG

1947   THE COURTNEYS OF CURZON STREET
Director: Herbert Wilcox
Co-stars: Anna Neagle Michael Wilding Coral Browne

1951   THE LADY WITH A LAMP
Director: Herbert Wilcox
Co-stars: Anna Neagle Michael Wilding Sybil Thorndyke

JANIS YOUNG

1970   LOVING
Director: Irvin Kershner
Co-stars: George Segal Eva Marie Saint Sterling Hayden

JOAN YOUNG

1947   VICE VERSA
Director: Peter Ustinov
Co-stars: Roger Livesey Anthony Newley Petula Clark

1948   THE SMALL VOICE
Director: Fergus McDonell
Co-stars: James Donald Valerie Hobson Howard Keel

1954   CHILD'S PLAY
Director: Margaret Thomson
Co-stars: Mona Washbourne Dorothy Alison Peter Martyn

KAREN YOUNG

1982   HANDGUN
Director: Tony Garnett
Co-stars: Clayton Day Suzie Humphreys Helena Humann

1984   ALMOST YOU
Director: Adam Brooks
Co-stars: Brooke Adams Griffin Dunne Dana Delany

1984   MARIA'S LOVERS
Director: Andrei Konchalovsky
Co-stars: Nastassja Kinski John Savage Robert Mitchum

1984   BIRDY
Director: Alan Parker
Co-stars: Matthew Modine Nicolas Cage Sandy Baron

1986   THE HIGH PRICE OF PASSION
Director: Larry Elikann
Co-stars: Richard Crenna Sean McCann Terry Tweed

1986   NINE AND A HALF WEEKS
Director: Adrian Lyne
Co-stars: Mickey Rourke Kim Basinger Margaret Whitton

1987   HEAT
Director: R.M. Richards
Co-stars: Burt Reynolds Peter MacNicol Diana Scarwid

1987   JAWS:THE REVENGE
Director: Joseph Sargent
Co-stars: Lorraine Gary Lance Guest Michael Caine

1988   TORCH SONG TRILOGY
Director: Paul Bogart
Co-stars: Harvey Fierstein Anne Bancroft Matthew Broderick

1989   CRIMINAL LAW
Director: Martin Campbell
Co-stars: Gary Oldman Kevin Bacon Tess Harper

LORETTA YOUNG

(Sister of Polly Ann Young and Sally Blane)
Oscar For Best Actress In 1947 For "The Farmer's Daughter".
Nominated For Best Actress In 1949 For "Come To The Stable"

1929   THE SQUALL
Director: Alexander Korda
Co-stars: Myrna Loy Richard Ticker Zasu Pitts

1930   THE SECOND-FLOOR MYSTERY
Director: Roy Del Ruth
Co-stars: Grant Withers H.B. Warner John Loder

1930   THE MAN FROM BLANKLEY'S
Director: Alfred Green
Co-stars: John Barrymore William Austin

1930   LOOSE ANKLES
Director: Ted Wilde
Co-stars: Douglas Fairbanks Jnr. Louise Fazenda Otis Harlan

1930   KISMET
Director: John Francis Dillon
Co-stars: Otis Skinner David Manners

1931   THE DEVIL TO PAY
Director: George Fitzmaurice
Co-stars: Ronald Colman Myrna Loy Frederick Kerr

1931   BEAU IDEAL
Director: Herbert Brenon
Co-stars: Ralph Forbes Lester Vail George Rigas

1931   BIG BUSINESS GIRL
Director: William Seiter
Co-stars: Ricardo Cortez Joan Blondell Jack Albertson

1931   PLATINUM BLONDE
Director: Frank Capra
Co-stars: Jean Harlow Robert Williams Richard Owen

1931   I LIKE YOUR NERVE
Director: William McGann
Co-stars: Douglas Fairbanks Henry Kolker Boris Karloff

1931   TAXI !
Director: Roy Del Ruth
Co-stars: James Cagney George Raft Guy Kibbee

1932   THEY CALL IT SIN
Director: Thornton Freeland
Co-stars: George Brent Louis Calhern David Manners

1932 WEEKEND MARRIAGE
Director: Thornton Freeland
Co-stars: George Brent Norman Foster Aline McMahon

1932 LIFE BEGINS
Director: James Flood
Co-stars: Elliott Nugent Vivienne Osborne Preston Foster

1932 THE HATCHETT MAN
Director: William Wellman
Co-stars: Edward G. Robinson Dudley Digges

1933 SHE HAD TO SAY YES
Co-Star Regis Toomey

1933 EMPLOYEE'S ENTRANCE
Director: Roy Del Ruth
Co-stars: Warren William Alice White Wallace Ford

1933 THE DEVIL'S IN LOVE
Director: William Dieterle
Co-stars: Victor Jory David Manners J. Carrol Naish

1933 GRAND SLAM
Director: William Dieterle
Co-stars: Paul Lukas Frank McHugh Glenda Farrell

1933 HEROES FOR SALE
Director: William Wellman
Co-stars: Richard Barthelmess Aline McMahon

1933 A MAN'S CASTLE
Director: Frank Borzage
Co-stars: Spencer Tracy Glenda Farrell Walter Connolly

1933 THE LIFE OF JIMMY DOLAN
Director: Archie Mayo
Co-stars: Douglas Fairbanks Aline McMahon John Wayne

1933 MIDNIGHT MARY
Director: William Wellman
Co-stars: Ricardo Cortez Franchot Tone Una Merkel

1933 ZOO IN BUDAPEST
Director: Rowland Lee
Co-stars: Gene Raymond O.P. Heggie Wally Albright

1934 THE WHITE PARADE
Director: Irving Cummings
Co-stars: John Boles Dorothy Wilson Sara Haden

1934 THE HOUSE OF ROTHSCHILD
Director: Alfred Werker
Co-stars: George Arliss Robert Young Boris Karloff

1934 CLIVE OF INDIA
Director: Richard Boleslawski
Co-stars: Ronald Colman Colin Clive Mischa Auer

1934 CARAVAN
Director: Erik Charrell
Co-stars: Charles Boyer Jean Parker Phillips Holmes

1934 BORN TO BE BAD
Director: Lowell Sherman
Co-stars: Cary Grant Jackie Kelk Henry Travers

1934 BULLDOG DRUMMOND STRIKES BACK
Director: Roy Del Ruth
Co-stars: Warner Oland Ronald Colman Una Merkel

1935 CALL OF THE WILD
Director: William Wellman
Co-stars: Clark Gable Jack Oakie Reginald Owen

1935 THE CRUSADES
Director: Cecil B. DeMille
Co-stars: Henry Wilcoxon Katherine DeMille

1935 SHANGHAI
Director: James Flood
Co-stars: Charles Boyer Warner Oland Alison Skipworth

1936 THE UNGUARDED HOUR
Director: Sam Wood
Co-stars: Franchot Tone Roland Young Henry Daniell

1936 RAMONA
Director: Henry King
Co-stars: Don Ameche Kent Taylor Katherine DeMille

1936 PRIVATE NUMBER
Director: Roy Del Ruth
Co-stars: Robert Taylor Basil Rathbone Patsy Kelly

1936 LADIES IN LOVE
Director: Edward Griffith
Co-stars: Tyrone Power Don Ameche Simone Simon

1937 CAFÉ METROPOLE
Director: Edward Griffith
Co-stars: Tyrone Power Adolphe Menjou Charles Winninger

1937 LOVE IS NEWS
Director: Tay Garnett
Co-stars: Tyrone Power Don Ameche Jane Darwell

1937 SECOND HONEYMOON
Director: Walter Lang
Co-stars: Tyrone Power Stuart Erwin Claire Trevor

1937 LOVE UNDER FIRE
Director: George Marshall
Co-stars: Don Ameche Frances Drake John Carradine

1937 WIFE, DOCTOR AND NURSE
Director: Walter Lang
Co-stars: Virginia Bruce Warner Baxter Jane Darwell

1938 SUEZ
Director: Allan Dwan
Co-stars: Tyrone Power Annabella Henry Stephenson

1938 THREE BLIND MICE
Director: William Seiter
Co-stars: Joel McCrea Marjorie Weaver David Niven

1938 KENTUCKY
Director: David Butler
Co-stars: Richard Greene Walter Brennan Karen Morley

1938 FOUR MEN AND A PRAYER
Director: John Ford
Co-stars: Richard Greene George Sanders David Niven

1939 ETERNALLY YOURS
Director: Tay Garnett
Co-stars: David Niven Broderick Crawford Eve Arden

1939 THE STORY OF ALEXANDER BELL
Director: Irving Cummings
Co-stars: Don Ameche Henry Fonda Charles Coburn

1939 WIFE, HUSBAND AND FRIEND
Director: Gregory Ratoff
Co-stars: Warner Baxter Binnie Barnes Cesar Romero

1940 HE STAYED FOR BREAKFAST
Director: Alexander Hall
Co-stars: Melvyn Douglas Alan Marshall

1940 THE DOCTOR TAKES A WIFE
Director: Alexander Hall
Co-stars: Ray Milland Edmund Gwenn Reginald Gardner

1941 BEDTIME STORY
Director: Alexander Hall
Co-stars: Fredric March Robert Benchley Eve Arden

1941 THE LADY FROM CHEYENNE
Director: Frank Lloyd
Co-stars: Robert Preston Edward Arnold Gladys George

1941 THE MEN IN HER LIFE
Director: Gregory Ratoff
Co-stars: Conrad Veidt Dean Jagger Otto Kruger

1943 **A NIGHT TO REMEMBER**
Director: Richard Wallace
Co-stars: Brian Aherne Sidney Toler Lee Patrick

1943 **CHINA**
Director: John Farrow
Co-stars: Alan Ladd William Bendix Philip Ahn

1944 **AND NOW TOMORROW**
Director: Irving Pichel
Co-stars: Alan Ladd Susan Hayward Beulah Bondi

1944 **LADIES COURAGEOUS**
Director: John Rawlings
Co-stars: Geraldine Fitzgerald Diana Barrymore

1945 **ALONG CAME JONES**
Director: Stuart Heisler
Co-stars: Gary Cooper William Demarest Dan Duryea

1946 **A PERFECT MARRIAGE**
Director: Lewis Allen
Co-stars: David Niven Eddie Albert Virginia Field

1946 **THE STRANGER**
Director: Orson Welles
Co-stars: Orson Welles Edward G. Robinson Philip Merivale

1947 **THE FARMER'S DAUGHTER**
Director: H.C. Potter
Co-stars: Joseph Cotten Ethel Barrymore Charles Bickford

1947 **THE BISHOP'S WIFE**
Director: Henry Koster
Co-stars: Cary Grant David Niven Monty Woolley

1948 **THE ACCUSED**
Director: William Dieterle
Co-stars: Robert Cummings Wendell Corey

1948 **MOTHER IS A FRESHMAN**
Director: Lloyd Bacon
Co-stars: Van Johnson Rudy Vallee Barbara Lawrence

1948 **RACHEL AND THE STRANGER**
Director: Norman Foster
Co-stars: Robert Mitchum William Holden Tom Tully

1949 **COME TO THE STABLE**
Director: Henry Koster
Co-stars: Celeste Holm Elsa Lanchester Hugh Marlowe

1950 **KEY TO THE CITY**
Director: George Sidney
Co-stars: Clark Gable Frank Morgan Marilyn Maxwell

1951 **HALF ANGEL**
Director: Richard Sale
Co-stars: Joseph Cotten Cecil Kellaway Jim Backus

1951 **CAUSE FOR ALARM**
Director: Tay Garnett
Co-stars: Barry Sullivan Bruce Cowling Irving Bacon

1952 **BECAUSE OF YOU**
Director: Joseph Pevney
Co-stars: Jeff Chandler Alex Nichol

1952 **PAULA**
Director: Rudolph Mate
Co-stars: Kent Smith Tommy Rettig Alexander Knox

1953 **IT HAPPENS EVERY THURSDAY**
Director: Joseph Pevney
Co-stars: John Forsythe Jimmy Conlin Jane Darwell

1989 **LADY IN A CORNER**
Director: Peter Levin

MARY YOUNG

1945 **THE STORK CLUB**
Director: Hal Walker
Co-stars: Betty Hutton Barry Fitzgerald Don Defore

1945 **THE LOST WEEKEND**
Director: Billy Wilder
Co-stars: Ray Milland Jane Wyman Phillip Terry

1947 **A LIKELY STORY**
Director: H.C. Potter
Co-stars: Barbara Hale Bill Williams Sam Levene

POLLY ANN YOUNG
(Sister of Loretta Young and Sally Blane)

1934 **THE MAN FROM UTAH**
Director: Robert Bradbury
Co-stars: John Wayne George Hayes Yakima Canutt

1935 **CRIMSON TRAIL**
Co-Star Buck Jones

SEAN YOUNG

1980 **JANE AUSTIN IN MANHATTAN**
Director: James Ivory
Co-stars: Robert Powell Anne Baxter Michael Wager

1981 **STRIPES**
Director: Ivan Reitman
Co-stars: Bill Murray Harold Ramis Warren Oates

1982 **YOUNG DOCTORS IN LOVE**
Director: Garry Marshall
Co-stars: Michael McKean Harry Dean Stanton Demi Moore

1982 **BLADE RUNNER**
Director: Ridley Scott
Co-stars: Harrison Ford Rutger Hauer Daryl Hannah

1985 **UNDER THE BALTIMORE CLOCK**
Director: Neal Miller
Co-stars: Lenny Von Dohlen Barnard Hughes Mark Hulsey

1985 **BABY..SECRET OF THE LOST LEGEND**
Director: B.W. Norton
Co-stars: William Katt Patrick McGoohan Julian Fellowes

1986 **BLOOD AND ORCHIDS**
Director: Jerry Thorpe
Co-stars: Kris Kristofferson Jane Alexander Jose Ferrer

1987 **NO WAY OUT**
Director: Roger Donaldson
Co-stars: Kevin Costner Gene Hackman Howard Duff

1987 **WALL STREET**
Director: Oliver Stone
Co-stars: Michael Douglas Charlie Sheen Daryl Hannah

1988 **THE BOOST**
Director: Harold Becker
Co-stars: James Woods John Kapelos Steven Hill

1989 **COUSINS**
Director: Joel Schumacher
Co-stars: Ted Danson Isabella Rossellini Lloyd Bridges

1990 **WINGS OF THE APACHE**
Director: David Green
Co-stars: Nicolas Cage Tom Skerritt Tommy Lee Jones

1991 **ONCE UPON A CRIME**
Director: Eugene Levy
Co-stars: John Candy James Belushi Cybil Shepherd

1991 **A KISS BEFORE DYING**
Director: James Dearden
Co-stars: Matt Dillon Max Von Sydow Diane Ladd

1992 **LOVE CRIMES**
Director: Lizzie Borden
Co-stars: Patrick Bergin Arnetia Walker Ron Orbach

1992 **BLUE ICE**
Director: Russell Mulcahy
Co-stars: Michael Caine Alun Armstrong Bob Hoskins

1993 ACE VENTURA, PET DETECTIVE
Director: Tom Shadyac
Co-stars: Jim Carrey Courteney Cox Tone Loc

1993 EVEN COWGIRLS GET THE BLUES
Director: Gus Van Sant
Co-stars: Uma Thurman John Hurt Rain Phoenix

1993 FATAL INSTINCT
Director: Carl Reiner
Co-stars: Armand Assante Sherilyn Fenn Kate Nelligan

1993 WITNESS TO THE EXECUTION
Director: Tommy Lee Wallace
Co-stars: Tim Daly Len Cariou

1995 DR JEKYLL AND M/S HYDE
Co-stars: Tim Daly Lysette Anthony

1997 THE PROPRIETOR
Director: Ismael Merchant
Co-stars: Jeanne Moreau Josh Hamilton

TRUDY YOUNG

1977 AGE OF INNOCENCE
Director: Alan Bridges
Co-stars: David Warner Honor Blackman Cec Linder

GAIL YOUNGS

1984 THE STONE BOY
Director: Christopher Cain
Co-stars: Robert Duvall Jason Presson Glenn Close

1987 TIMESTALKERS
Director: Michael Schultz
Co-stars: William Devane Lauren Hutton Klaus Kinski

ALEXIS YULIN

1988 THE HOUSE ON CARROLL STREET
Director: Peter Yates
Co-stars: Kelly McGillis Jeff Daniels Mandy Patinkin

BLANCHE YURKA

1935 A TALE OF TWO CITIES
Director: Jack Conway
Co-stars: Ronald Colman Elizabeth Allan Basil Rathbone

1940 CITY FOR CONQUEST
Director: Anatole Litvak
Co-stars: James Cagney Ann Sheridan Donald Crisp

1940 QUEEN OF THE MOB
Director: James Hogan
Co-stars: Ralph Bellamy Jack Carson Richard Denning

1941 LADY FOR A NIGHT
Director: Leigh Jason
Co-stars: Joan Blondell John Wayne Ray Middleton

1941 ELLERY QUEEN AND THE MURDER RING
Director: James Hogan
Co-stars: Ralph Bellamy Margaret Lindsay Mona Barrie

1942 PACIFIC RENDEZVOUS
Director: George Sidney
Co-stars: Lee Bowman Jean Rogers Mona Maris

1943 TONIGHT WE RAID CALAIS
Director: John Brahm
Co-stars: John Sutton Lee J. Cobb Annabella

1943 A NIGHT TO REMEMBER
Director: Richard Wallace
Co-stars: Loretta Young Brian Aherne Jeff Donnell

1944 ONE BODY TOO MANY
Director: Frank McDonald
Co-stars: Jack Haley Bela Lugosi Jean Parker

1944 THE BRIDGE OF SAN LUIS REY
Director: Rowland Lee
Co-stars: Lynn Bari Akim Tamiroff Louis Calhern

1945 THE SOUTHERNER
Director: Jean Renoir
Co-stars: Zachary Scott Betty Field Beulah Bondi

1946 13 RUE MADELEINE
Director: Henry Hathaway
Co-stars: James Cagney Richard Conte Annabella

1947 THE FLAME
Director: John Auer
Co-stars: Vera Ralston John Carroll Robert Paige

1951 SONS OF THE MUSKETEERS
Director: Lewis Allen
Co-stars: Cornel Wilde Maureen O'Hara Gladys Cooper

1951 THE FURIES
Director: Anthony Mann
Co-stars: Barbara Stanwyck Walter Huston Gilbert Roland

1952 TAXI
Director: Gregory Ratoff
Co-stars: Dan Dailey Constance Smith Neva Patterson

1958 THUNDER IN THE SUN
Director: Russel Rouse
Co-stars: Susan Hayward Jeff Chandler Jacques Bergerac

ALICE TISSOT YVONNECK

1927 AN ITALIAN STRAW HAT
Director: Rene Clair
Co-stars: Albert Prejean Olga Tschechowa Marise Maias

ZABOU

1985 UNE FEMME OU DEUX
Director: Daniel Vigne
Co-stars: Gerard Depardieu Sigourney Weaver Ruth Westheimer

1990 C'EST LA VIE
Director: Diane Kurys
Co-stars: Nathalie Richard Berry Julie Bataille

GRACE ZABRISKIE

1982 AN OFFICER AND A GENTLEMAN
Director: Taylor Hackford
Co-stars: Richard Gere Debra Winger David Keith

1984 MY MOTHER'S SECRET LIFE
Director: Robert Markowitz
Co-stars: Noni Anderson Paul Sorvino

1985 THE BURNING BED
Director: Robert Greenwald
Co-stars: Farrah Fawcett Paul LeMat Richard Masur

1986 THE BIG EASY
Director: Jim McBride
Co-stars: Dennis Quaid Ellen Barkin Ned Beatty

1988 THE BOOST
Director: Harold Becker
Co-stars: James Woods Sean Young Steven Hill

1988 THE RYAN WHITE STORY
Director: John Herzfield
Co-stars: Lukas Haas George C. Scott Sarah Jessica Parker

1989 MEGAVILLE
Director: Peter Lehner
Co-stars: Daniel J. Travanti Billy Zane Kirsten Cloke

1989 DRUGSTORE COWBOY
Director: Gus Van Sant
Co-stars: Matt Dillon Kelly Lynch James Remar

1990 WILD AT HEART
Director: David Lynch
Co-stars: Nicolas Cage Laura Dern Diane Ladd

1991 CHILD'S PLAY 2
Director: John Lafia
Co-stars: Alex Vincent Jenny Agutter Gerrit Graham

1991 FRIED GREEN TOMATOES
Director: Jon Avnet
Co-stars: Mary Stuart Masterson Jessica Tandy Kathy Bates

1991 THE SERVANTS OF TWILIGHT
Director: Jeffrey Obrow
Co-stars: Bruce Greenwood Belinda Bauer Richard Bradford

1991 AMBITION
Director: Scott Goldstein
Co-stars: Lou Diamond Phillips Clancy Brown Cecilia Peck

1991 PRISON STORIES: WOMEN ON THE INSIDE
Director: Donna Deitch
Co-stars: Rae Dawn Chong Lolita Davidovich

1992 FERN GULLY: THE LAST RAINFOREST
Director: Bill Kroyer
Co-stars: Samantha Mathis Tim Curry Christian Slater

1992 CHAIN OF DESIRE
Director: Temistocles Lopez
Co-stars: Malcolm McDowell Seymour Cassel Linda Fiorentino

1992 A HOUSE OF SECRETS AND LIES
Director: Paul Schneider
Co-stars: Connie Sellecca Kevin Dobson

1992 MY OWN PRIVATE IDAHO
Director: Gus Van Sant
Co-stars: River Phoenix Keanu Reeves James Russo

1993 THE BLACK WIDOW MURDERS: THE BLANCHE TAYLOR MOORE STORY
Director: Alan Metzger
Co-stars: David Glennon Elizabeth Montgomery

1994 DROP ZONE
Director: John Badham
Co-stars: Wesley Snipes Yancy Butler Gary Busey

1994 EVEN COWGIRLS GET THE BLUES
Director: Gus Van Sant
Co-stars: Uma Thurman John Hurt Rain Phoenix

PIA ZADORA

1981 BUTTERFLY
Director: Matt Cimber
Co-stars: Stacy Keach Orson Welles Lois Nettleton

1983 THE LONELY LADY
Director: Peter Sasdy
Co-stars: Lloyd Bochner Bibi Besch Ray Liotta

1988 HAIRSPRAY
Director: John Waters
Co-stars: Sonny Bono Debbie Harry Ricki Lane

1993 NAKED GUN 331/3: THE FINAL INSULT
Director: Peter Segal
Co-stars: Leslie Nielsen Priscilla Presley Fred Ward

ANITA ZAGARIA

1989 QUEEN OF HEARTS
Director: Jon Amiel
Co-stars: Joseph Long Vittorio Duse Ian Hawkes

1990 THE JUSTICE GAME 2: THE LADY FROM ROME
Director: Moira Armstrong
Co-stars: Denis Lawson Barbara Flynn

1990 THE GRAVY TRAIN
Director: David Tucker
Co-stars: Ian Richardson Christoph Waltz Alexei Sayle

1991 THE GRAVY TRAIN GOES EAST
Director: James Cellan Jones
Co-stars: Ian Richardson Francesca Annis Cecil Paoli

1993 KILLER RULES
Director: Robert Ellis Miller
Co-stars: James Sheridan Sela Ward Sam Wanamaker

ROXANA ZAL *(Child)*

1983 TABLE FOR FIVE
Director: Robert Lieberman
Co-stars: Jon Voight Richard Crenna Millie Perkins

1983 TESTAMENT
Director: Lynne Littman
Co-stars: Jane Alexander William Devane Lukas Haas

1986 SHATTERED SPIRITS
Director: Robert Greenwald
Co-stars: Martin Sheen Melinda Dillon Lukas Haas

1988 FAREWELL MISS FREEDOM
Director: George Miller
Co-stars: Louis Gossett Jnr. Chris Sarandon

1989 EVERYBODY'S BABY
Director: Mel Damski
Co-stars: Pat Hingle Patty Duke Beau Bridges

1992 FATAL LOVE
Director: Tom McLoughlin
Co-stars: Molly Ringwald Lee Grant Perry King

HALINA ZALEWSKA

1964 THE LONG HAIR OF DEATH
Director: Anthony Dawson
Co-stars: Barbara Steele Giorgio Ardisson

LISA ZANE *(Sister Of Billy Zane)*

1990 BAD INFLUENCE
Director: Curtis Hanson
Co-stars: Rob Lowe James Spader Kathleen Wilhoite

1991 FEMME FATALE
Director: Andre Guttfreund
Co-stars: Colin Firth Billy Zane Scott Wilson

1991 FREDDY'S DEAD-THE FINAL NIGHTMARE
Director: Rachel Talalay
Co-stars: Robert Englund Lezlie Deane Yaphet Kotto

1994 FLOUNDERING
Director: Peter McCarthy
Co-stars: James Le Gros John Cusack Ethan Hawke

1994 NATURAL SELECTION
Director: Jack Sholder
Co-Star C. Thomas Howell

1995 THE NURSE

NANCY DEE ZANE

1955 THE NIGHT HOLDS TERROR
Director: Andrew Stone
Co-stars: Jack Kelly John Cassavetes Hildy Parks

LENORE ZANN

1981 VISITING HOURS
Director: Jean Claude Lord
Co-stars: Michael Ironside Lee Remick Linda Purl

1982 AMERICAN NIGHTMARE
Director: Don McBrearty
Co-stars: Lawrence S. Day Lora Stanley Paul Bradley

1996 ED McBAIN'S 87TH PRECINCT: ICE
Director: Bradford May
Co-stars: Dale Midkiff Joe Pantoliano Andrea Parker

VANESSA ZAOUI

1992 ALAN AND NAOMI
Director: Sterling Van Wagenen
Co-stars: Lukas Haas Michael Gross

DOMINIQUE ZARDI

1968 LES BICHES
Director: Claude Chabrol
Co-stars: Stephane Audran Jacqueline Sassard Jean-Louis Trintignant

1972 DOCTEUR POPAUL
Director: Claude Chabrol
Co-stars: Jean-Paul Belmondo Mia Farrow Laura Antonelli

ROSEL ZECH

1982 VERONIKA VOSS
Director: Rainer Werner Fassbinder
Co-stars: Hilmar Thate Annemarie Duringer Doris Schade

1991 SALMONBERRIES
Director: Percy Adlon
Co-stars: k.d. lang Chuck Connors Jane Lind

PATRICIA ZEHENTMAYR

1989 ROSALIE GOES SHOPPING
Director: Percy Adlon
Co-stars: Marianne Sagebrecht Brad Davis Judge Reinhold

RENEE ZELWEGGER

1994 LOVE AND A .45
Director: C.M. Talkington
Co-stars: Gil Bellows Rory Cochrane Peter Fonda

1994 SHAKE, RATTLE AND ROCK
Director: Allan Arkush
Co-stars: Howie Mandel Dick Miller

1997 JERRY MAGUIRE
Co-stars: Tom Cruise Cuba Gooding Jnr. Joseph Lipnicki

ELIZABETH ZEMACH

1959 THE SAVAGE EYE
Director: Ben Maddow
Co-stars: Barbara Baxley Jean Hidey Gary Merrill

SUZANNE ZENOR

1972 GET TO KNOW YOUR RABBIT
Director: Brian De Palma
Co-stars: Tom Smothers John Astin Orson Welles

KATE ZENTALL

1979 ACT OF VIOLENCE
Director: Paul Wendkos
Co-stars: Elizabeth Montgomery James Sloyan Sean Frye

DELPHINE ZENTOUT *(Child)*

1988 VIRGIN-36 FILLETTE
Director: Catherine Breillat
Co-stars: Etienne Chicot Oliver Parnere Berta Dominguez

MAI ZETTERLING

1944 FRENZY
Director: Alf Sjoberg
Co-stars: Stig Jarrel Alf Kjellin

1947 FRIEDA
Director: Basil Dearden
Co-stars: David Farrar Flora Robson Glynis Johns

1948 MUSIC IS MY FUTURE
Director: Ingmar Bergman
Co-stars: Birger Malmsten Olaf Winnerstrand

1948 PORTRAIT FROM LIFE
Director: Terence Fisher
Co-stars: Robert Beatty Guy Rolfe Herbert Lom

1948 THE BAD LORD BYRON
Director: David MacDonald
Co-stars: Dennis Price Joan Greenwood Sonia Holm

1949 THE LOST PEOPLE
Director: Bernard Knowles
Co-stars: Richard Attenborough Siobhan McKenna

1949 THE ROMANTIC AGE
Director: Edmond Greville
Co-stars: Hugh Williams Petula Clark Carol Marsh

1950 BLACKMAILED
Director: Marc Allegret
Co-stars: Dirk Bogarde Fay Compton Robert Flemyng

1951 HELL IS SOLD OUT
Director: Michael Anderson
Co-stars: Herbert Lom Richard Attenborough

1952 THE RINGER
Director: Guy Hamilton
Co-stars: Donald Wolfit Herbert Lom Greta Gynt

1952 THE TALL HEADLINES
Director: Terence Young
Co-stars: Flora Robson Michael Dennison Jane Hylton

1953 DESPERATE MOMENT
Director: Compton Bennett
Co-stars: Dirk Bogarde Albert Lieven Philip Friend

1954 DANCE LITTLE LADY
Director: Val Guest
Co-stars: Terence Morgan Mandy Miller Eunice Gayson

1954 KNOCK ON WOOD
Director: Melvin Frank
Co-stars: Danny Kaye Torin Thatcher David Burns

1955 A PRIZE OF GOLD
Director: Mark Robson
Co-stars: Richard Widmark Nigel Patrick George Cole

1956 SEVEN WAVES AWAY
Director: Richard Sale
Co-stars: Tyrone Power Lloyd Nolan Moira Lister

1957 THE TRUTH ABOUT WOMEN
Director: Muriel Box
Co-stars: Laurence Harvey Julie Harris Diane Cilento

1959 JET STORM
Director: Cy Endfield
Co-stars: Richard Attenborough Harry Secombe

1960 FACES IN THE DARK
Director: David Eady
Co-stars: John Gregson Michael Dennison John Ireland

1960 OFFBEAT
Director: Cliff Owen
Co-stars: William Sylvester John Meillon Joseph Furst

1960 PICCADILLY THIRD STOP
Director: Wolf Rilla
Co-stars: Terence Morgan Yoko Tani William Hartnell

1962 THE MAN WHO FINALLY DIED
Director: Quentin Lawrence
Co-stars: Stanley Baker Peter Cushing

1962 ONLY TWO CAN PLAY
Director: Sidney Gilliat
Co-stars: Peter Sellers Virginia Maskell

1962 THE MAIN ATTRACTION
Director: Daniel Petrie
Co-stars: Pat Boone Nancy Kwan Yvonne Mitchell

1963 THE BAY OF ST. MICHEL
Director: John Ainsworth
Co-stars: Keenan Wynn Ronald Howard Rona Anderson

1990 HIDDEN AGENDA
Director: Ken Loach
Co-stars: Brian Cox Frances McDormand Brad Dourif

1990 THE WITNESS
Director: Nicholas Roeg
Co-stars: Anjelica Huston Jason Fisher Jane Horrocks

JANIS ZIDO

1982 HOUSE OF EVIL
Director: Mark Rosman
Co-stars: Kathryn McNeil Eileen Davidson Christopher Lawrence

ANN ZIEGLER *(Singing Partner Of Webster Booth)*

1946 THE LAUGHING LADY
Director: Paul Stein
Co-stars: Webster Booth Peter Graves Paul Dupuis

SONJA ZIEMANN

1952 MADE IN HEAVEN
Director: John Paddy Carstairs
Co-stars: David Tomlinson Petula Clark A.E. Matthews

1961 A MATTER OF WHO
Director: Don Chaffey
Co-stars: Terry-Thomas Alex Nicol Richard Briers

1961 THE SECRET WAYS
Director: Phil Karlson
Co-stars: Richard Widmark Walter Rilla Senta Berger

1969 DE SADE
Director: Cy Endfield
Co-stars: Keir Dullea John Huston Lilli Palmer

YELENA ZIGON

1977 THE PICTURE SHOW MAN
Director: John Power
Co-stars: John Meillon Rod Taylor Judy Morris

MADELINE ZIMA *(Child)*

1992 MR NANNY
Director: Michael Gottlieb
Co-stars: Hulk Hogan Austin Pendleton Robert Gorman

1992 THE HAND THAT ROCKS THE CRADLE
Director: Curtis Hanson
Co-stars: Annabella Sciorra Rebecca De Mornay Matt McCoy

VANESSA ZIMA *(Child)*

1998 ULEE'S GOLD
Director: Victor Nunez
Co-stars: Peter Fonda Tom Wood Jessica Bielin

STEPHANIE ZIMBALIST

1978 THE MAGIC OF LASSIE
Director: Don Chaffey
Co-stars: James Stewart Alice Faye Mickey Rooney

1978 FOREVER
Director: John Korty
Co-stars: Dean Butler John Friedrich Beth Raines

1980 THE AWAKENING
Director: Mike Newell
Co-stars: Charlton Heston Susannah York Jill Townsend

1985 LOVE ON THE RUN
Director: Gus Trikonis
Co-stars: Alec Baldwin Constance McCashin Howard Duff

1988 A LETTER TO THREE WIVES
Director: Larry Elikann
Co-stars: Loni Anderson Michele Lee Ben Gazzara

1990 CAROLINE ?
Director: Joseph Sargent
Co-stars: Pamela Reed Patricia Neal Dorothy McGuire

1991 BREAKING THE SILENCE
Director: Robert Iscove
Co-stars: Gregory Harrison Chris Young

1991 THE STRANGE LADY
Director: Larry Elikann
Co-stars: Jessica Tandy Ed Begley Jnr. Tandy Cronyn

1992 SEXUAL ADVANCES
Director: Donna Deitch
Co-stars: William Russ Terry O'Quinn Deborah May

1993 INCIDENT IN A SMALL TOWN
Director: Delbert Mann
Co-stars: Walter Matthau Harry Morgan

1993 JERICHO FEVER
Director: Sandor Stern
Co-stars: Perry King Alan Scarfe Dan Harvey

1994 SILHOUETTE
Director: Eric Till
Co-stars: JoBeth Williams Corbin Bernsen

1997 PRISON OF SECRETS
Director: Fred Gerber
Co-Star Dan Lauria

KIM ZIMMER

1991 HELL HATH NO FURY
Director: Thomas Wright
Co-stars: Barbara Eden Loretta Swit David Ackroyd

1994 THE DISAPPEARANCE OF VONNIE
Director: Graeme Campbell
Co-stars: Ann Jillian Joe Penny Alicia Witt

SONIA ZIMMER

1981 BY DESIGN
Director: Claude Jutra
Co-stars: Patty Duke Sara Botsford Saul Rubinek

MARYA ZIMMET

1969 THE RAIN PEOPLE
Director: Francis Coppola
Co-stars: James Caan Shirley Knight Robert Duvall

NIETTA ZOCCHI

1954 ROMEO AND JULIET
Director: Renato Castellani
Co-stars: Laurence Harvey Susan Shentall Flora Robson

RITA ZOHAR

1992 FINAL ANALYSIS
Director: Phil Joanou
Co-stars: Richard Gere Kim Basinger Uma Thurman

TANIA ZOLTY

1970 CRIMES OF THE FUTURE
Director: David Cronenberg
Co-stars: Ronald Mlodzik Jon Lidolt Paul Mulholland

VERA ZORINA

1938 THE GOLDWYN FOLLIES
Director: George Marshall
Co-stars: Kenny Baker Adolphe Menjou Ritz Brothers

1939 ON YOUR TOES
Director: Ray Enright
Co-stars: Eddie Albert Alan Hale Donald O'Connor

1940 I WAS AN ADVENTURESS
Director: Gregory Ratoff
Co-stars: Erich Von Stroheim Peter Lorre Richard Greene

1941 LOUISIANA PURCHASE
Director: Irving Cummings
Co-stars: Bob Hope Victor Moore Dona Drake

1942 STAR SPANGLED RHYTHM
Director: George Marshall
Co-stars: Victor Moore Betty Hutton Eddie Bracken

1944 FOLLOW THE BOYS
Director: Edward Sutherland
Co-stars: George Raft Orson Welles Marlene Dietrich

1946 LOVER COME BACK
Director: William Seiter
Co-stars: George Brent Lucille Ball Charles Winninger

ZOUZOU

1972 LOVE IN THE AFTERNOON
Director: Eric Rohmer
Co-stars: Bernard Verley Francoise Verley

1973 S*P*Y*S*
Director: Irwin Kershner
Co-stars: Elliott Gould Donald Sutherland Joss Ackland

1976 SKY RIDERS
Director: Douglas Hickox
Co-stars: James Coburn Susannah York Robert Culp

DAPHNE ZUNIGA

1983 QUARTERBACK PRINCESS
Director: Noel Black
Co-stars: Helen Hunt Don Murray Barbara Babcock

1985 THE SURE THING
Director: Rob Reiner
Co-stars: John Cusack Anthony Edwards Tim Robbins

1987 SPACEBALLS
Director: Mel Brooks
Co-stars: Mel Brooks John Candy Rick Moranis

1988 LAST RITES
Director: Donald Bellisario
Co-stars: Tom Berenger Chick Vennera Dane Clark

1989 GROSS ANATOMY
Director: Thom Eberhardt
Co-stars: Matthew Modine Christine Lahti Todd Field

1989 THE FLY II
Director: Chris Walas
Co-stars: Eric Stoltz Lee Richardson Gary Chalk

1991 PREY OF THE CHAMELEON
Director: Tex Fuller
Co-stars: James Wilder Alexander Paul Don Harvey

1992 MAD AT THE MOON
Director: Martin Donovan
Co-stars: Mary Stuart Masterson Hart Bochner Stephen Blake

1994 JULES VERNE'S 800 LEAGUES DOWN THE AMAZON
Director: Luis Llosa
Co-stars: Adam Baldwin Barry Bostwick

ELSA ZYLBERSTEIN

1992 VAN GOGH
Director: Maurice Pialat
Co-stars: Jacques Dutronc Alexandra London Gerard Sety

1993 MINA TANNENBAUM
Director: Martine Dogowson
Co-Star Romagne Bohringer

1927/28

Best Picture: Wings
Nominations: The Racket, Seventh Heaven

Actor: Emil Jannings
(The Last Command, The Way Of All Flesh)
Nomination: Richard Barthelmess
(The Noose, The Patent Leather Kid)

Actress: Janet Gaynor
(Seventh Heaven, Street Angel, Sunrise)
Nominations: Gloria Swanson (Sadie Thompson)
Louise Dresser (A Ship Comes In)

Dramatic Picture
Director: Frank Borzage (Seventh Heaven)
Nominations: King Vidor (The Crowd)
Herbert Brenon (Sorrell And Son)

Comedy Picture
Director: Lewis Milestone (Two Arabian Knights)
Nomination Ted Wilde (Speedy)

Honorary Award: Charles Chaplin (The Circus)

1928/29

Best Picture: The Broadway Melody
Nominations: Alibi, In Old Arizona, Hollywood Revue,
The Patriot

Actor: Warner Baxter (In Old Arizona)
George Bancroft (Thunderbolt)
Nominations: Chester Morris (Alibi) Lewis Stone (The Patriot)
Paul Muni (The Valiant)

Actress: Mary Pickford (Coquette)
Nominations: Bessie Love (The Broadway Melody)
Ruth Chatterton (Madame X)
Betty Compson (The Barker)
Jeanne Eagels (The Letter)
Corinne Griffith (The Divine Lady)

Director: Frank Lloyd (The Divine Lady)
Nominations: Harry Beaumont (The Broadway Melody)
Ernst Lubitsch (The Patriot)
Lionel Barrymore (Madame X)
Irving Cummings (In Old Arizona)

1929/30

Best Picture: All Quiet On The Western Front
Nominations: The Big House, The Divorcee,
The Love Parade, Disraeli

Actor: George Arliss (Disraeli)
Nominations: Wallace Beery (The Big House)
Ronald Colman
(Bulldog Drummond, Condemned)
Maurice Chevalier
(The Love Parade, The Big Pond)
Lawrence Tippett (Rogue Song)
George Arliss (The Green Goddess)

Actress: Norma Shearer (The Divorcee)
Nominations: Greta Garbo (Anna Christie, Romance)
Norma Shearer (Their Own Desire)
Nancy Carroll (The Devil's Holiday)
Ruth Chatterton (Sarah And Son)
Gloria Swanson (The Trespasser)

Director: Lewis Milestone (All Quiet On The Western Front)
Nominations: Robert Z. Leonard (The Divorcee)
King Vidor (Hallelujah)
Clarence Brown (Anna Christie)
Ernst Lubitsch (The Love Parade)

1930/31

Best Picture: Cimarron
Nominations: The Front Page, Skippy, Trader Horn, East Lynne

Actor: Lionel Barrymore (A Free Soul)
Nominations: Richard Dix (Cimarron)
Adolphe Menjou (The Front Page)
Fredric March (The Royal Family Of Broadway)
Jackie Cooper (Skippy)

Actress: Marie Dressler (Min And Bill)
Nominations: Irene Dunne (Cimarron)
Norma Shearer (A Free Soul)
Marlene Dietrich (Morocco)
Ann Harding (Holiday)

Director: Norman Taurog (Skippy)
Nominations: Wesley Ruggles (Cimarron)
Lewis Milestone (The Front Page)
Josef Von Sternberg (Morocco)
Clarence Brown (A Free Soul)

1931/32

Best Picture: Grand Hotel
Nominations: Arrowsmith, Bad Girl, Five Star Final,
Shanghai Express The Smiling Lieutenant,
One Hour With You, The Champ

Actor: (Tie) Wallace Beery (The Champ)
Fredric March (Dr Jekyll And Mr Hyde)
Nomination: Alfred Lunt (The Guardsman)

Actress: Helen Hayes (The Sin Of Madelon Claudet)
Nominations: Marie Dressler (Emma)
Lynn Fontanne (The Guardsman)

Director: Frank Borzage (Bad Girl)
Nominations: King Vidor (The Champ)
Josef Von Sternberg (Shanghai Express)

Honorary Award: Walt Disney (Mickey Mouse)

1932/33

Best Picture: Cavalcade
Nominations: A Farewell To Arms, Lady For A Day,
She Done Him Wrong, I Am A Fugitive From A
Chain Gang, State Fair, 42nd Street, Smilin'
Through, The Private Life Of Henry VIII,
Little Women

Actor: Charles Laughton (The Private Life Of Henry VIII)
Nominations: Leslie Howard (Berkeley Square)
Paul Muni (I Am A Fugitive From A Chain Gang)

Actress: Katherine Hepburn (Morning Glory)
Nominations: Diana Wynyard (Cavalcade)
May Robson (Lady For A Day)

Director: Frank Lloyd (Cavalcade)
Nominations: Frank Capra (Lady For A Day)
George Cukor (Little Women)

1934

Best Picture: It Happened One Night
Nominations: The Barretts Of Wimpole Street, The Thin Man,
The Gay Divorcee, Imitation Of Life ,Flirtation
Walk, The House Of Rothschild, Here Comes
The Navy, One Night Of Love, The White Parade,
Cleopatra, Viva Villa

Actor: Clark Gable (It Happened One Night)
Nominations: William Powell (The Thin Man)
Frank Morgan (The Affairs Of Cellini)

Actress:	Claudette Colbert (It Happened One Night)
Nominations:	Norma Shearer (The Barretts Of Wimpole Street)
	Grace Moore (One Night Of Love)
	Bette Davis (Of Human Bondage)
Director:	Frank Capra (It Happened One Night)
Nominations:	Victor Schertzinger (One Night Of Love)
	W.S. Van Dyke (The Thin Man)
Special Award:	Shirley Temple
Best Song:	The Continental (The Gay Divorcee)
Nominations:	Carioca (Flying Down To Rio)
	Love In Bloom (She Loves Me Not)

1935

Best Picture:	Mutiny On The Bounty
Nominations:	The Informer, Ruggles Of Red Gap, Broadway Melody Of 1936, A Midsummer Night's Dream, Top Hat, David Copperfield, Alice Adams, The Lives Of A Bengal Lancer, Captain Blood, Naughty Marietta, Les Miserables
Actor:	Victor McLaglen (The Informer)
Nominations:	Clark Gable, Charles Laughton, Franchot Tone (Mutiny On The Bounty)
	Paul Muni (Black Fury)
Actress:	Bette Davis (Dangerous)
Nominations:	Claudette Colbert (Private Worlds)
	Merle Oberon (The Dark Angel)
	Katherine Hepburn (Alice Adams)
	Miriam Hopkins (Becky Sharp)
	Elizabeth Bergner (Escape Me Never)
Director:	John Ford (The Informer)
Nominations:	Henry Hathaway (The Lives Of A Bengal Lancer)
	Frank Lloyd (Mutiny On The Bounty)
	Michael Curtiz (Captain Blood)
Honorary Award:	David Wark Griffiths
Best Song:	Lullaby Of Broadway (Gold Diggers Of 1935)
Nominations:	Cheek To Cheek (Top Hat)
	Lovely To Look At (Roberta)

1936

Best Picture:	The Great Ziegfeld
Nominations:	The Story Of Louis Pasteur, Anthony Adverse, Dodsworth, A Tale Of Two Cities, Romeo And Juliet, Libeled Lady, Three Smart Girls, Mr Deeds Goes To Town, San Francisco
Actor:	Paul Muni (The Story Of Louis Pasteur)
Nominations:	Walter Huston (Dodsworth)
	William Powell (My Man Godfrey)
	Gary Cooper (Mr Deeds Goes To Town)
	Spencer Tracy (San Francisco)
Actress:	Luise Rainer (The Great Ziegfeld)
Nominations:	Carole Lombard (My Man Godfrey)
	Irene Dunne (Theodora Goes Wild)
	Glady George (Valiant Is The Word For Carrie)
	Norma Shearer (Romeo And Juliet)
Director:	Frank Capra (Mr Deeds Goes To Town)
Nominations:	William Wyler (Dodsworth)
	Gregory La Cava (My Man Godfrey)
	Robert Z. Leonard (The Great Ziegfeld)
	W.S. Van Dyke (San Francisco)
Supporting Actor:	Walter Brennan (Come And Get It)
Nominations:	Basil Rathbone (Romeo And Juliet)
	Mischa Auer (My Man Godfrey)
	Akim Tamiroff (The General Died At Dawn)
	Stuart Erwin (Pigskin Parade)

Supporting Actress:	Gale Sondergaard (Anthony Adverse)
Nominations:	Beulah Bondi (The Gorgeous Hussy)
	Alice Brady (My Man Godfrey)
	Maria Ouspenskaya (Dodsworth)
	Bonita Granville (These Three)
Best Song:	The Way You Look Tonight (Swing Time)
Nominations:	I've Got You Under My Skin (Born To Dance)
	Pennies From Heaven (Pennies From Heaven)
	When Did You Leave Heaven ? (Sing, Baby, Sing)
	Did I Remember (Suzy)
	A Melody From The Sky (Trail Of The Lonesome Pine)

1937

Best Picture:	The Life Of Emile Zola
Nominations:	A Star Is Born, The Awful Truth, One Hundred Men And A Girl, Stage Door, In Old Chicago, Captains Courageous, Dead End, The Good Earth, Lost Horizon
Actor:	Spencer Tracy (Captains Courageous)
Nominations:	Charles Boyer (Conquest)
	Paul Muni (The Life Of Emile Zola)
	Fredric March (A Star Is Born)
	Robert Montgomery (Night Must Fall)
Actress:	Luise Rainer (The Good Earth)
Nominations:	Irene Dunne (The Awful Truth)
	Janet Gaynor (A Star Is Born)
	Greta Garbo (Camille)
	Barbara Stanwyck (Stella Dallas)
Director:	Leo McCarey (The Awful Truth)
Nominations:	William A. Wellman (A Star Is Born)
	Gregory La Cava (Stage Door)
	Sidney Franklin (The Good Earth)
	William Dieterle (The Life Of Emile Zola)
Supporting Actor:	Joseph Schildkraut (The Life Of Emile Zola)
Nominations:	Ralph Bellamy (The Awful Truth)
	H.B. Warner (Lost Horizon)
	Thomas Mitchell (The Hurricane)
	Roland Young (Topper)
Supporting Actress:	Alice Brady (In Old Chicago)
Nominations:	Claire Trevor (Dead End)
	Anne Shirley (Stella Dallas)
	Andrea Leeds (Stage Door)
	Dame May Whitty (Night Must Fall)
Honorary Awards:	Mack Sennett, Edgar Bergen
Best Song:	Sweet Leilani (Waikiki Wedding)
Nominations:	Whispers In The Dark (Artists And Models)
	That Old Feeling (Vogue's Of 1938)
	They Can't Take That Away From Me (Shall We Dance)
	Remember Me (Mr Dodd Takes The Air)

1938

Best Picture:	You Can't Take It With You
Nominations:	The Adventures Of Robin Hood, Test Pilot, Pygmalion, Alexander's Rag -Time Band, Boys Town, The Citadel, La Grande Illusion, Four Daughters, Jezebel
Actor:	Spencer Tracy (Boys Town)
Nominations:	Leslie Howard (Pygmalion)
	Robert Donat (The Citadel)
	James Cagney (Angels With Dirty Faces)
	Charles Boyer (Algiers)
Actress:	Bette Davis (Jezebel)
Nominations:	Wendy Hiller (Pygmalion)
	Norma Shearer (Marie Antoinette)
	Margaret Sullavan (Three Comrades)
	Fay Bainter (White Banners)

Director:	Frank Capra (You Can't Take It With You)
Nominations:	Norman Taurog (Boys Town)
	King Vidor (The Citadel)
	Michael Curtiz (Angels With Dirty Faces)
	Michael Curtiz (Four Daughters)

Supporting Actor:	Walter Brennan (Kentucky)
Nominations:	John Garfield (Four Daughters)
	Gene Lockhart (Algiers)
	Robert Morley (Marie Antoinette)
	Basil Rathbone (If I Were King)

Supporting Actress:	Fay Bainter (Jezebel)
Nominations:	Beulah Bondi (Of Human Hearts)
	Miliza Korjus (The Great Waltz)
	Spring Byington (You Can't Take It With You)
	Billie Burke (Merrily We Live)

Honorary Awards:	Walt Disney (Snow White And The Seven Dwarfs),
	Deanna Durbin, Mickey Rooney

Best Song:	Thanks For The Memory
	(Big Broadcast Of 1938)
Nominations:	Now It Can Be Told (Alexander's Rag-Time Band)
	Always And Always (Mannequinn)
	Change Partners (Carefree)
	Dust (Under Western Stars)
	Jeepers Creepers (Going Places)
	Merrily We Live (Merrily We Live)
	A Mist Over The Moon (The Lady Objects)
	My Own (That Certain Age)
	The Cowboy And The Lady
	(The Cowboy And The Lady)

1939

Best Picture:	Gone With The Wind
Nominations:	The Wizard Of Oz, Goodbye Mr Chips,
	Wuthering Heights , Mr Smith Goes To
	Washington, Stagecoach, Ninotchka, Dark
	Victory, Of Mice And Men, Love Affair

Actor:	Robert Donat (Goodbye Mr Chips)
Nominations:	Clark Gable (Gone With The Wind)
	Mickey Rooney (Babes In Arms)
	Laurence Olivier (Wuthering Heights)
	James Stewart (Mr Smith Goes To Washington)

Actress:	Vivien Leigh (Gone With The Wind)
Nominations:	Greer Garson (Goodbye Mr Chips)
	Bette Davis (Dark Victory)
	Greta Garbo (Ninotchka)
	Irene Dunne (Love Affair)

Director:	Victor Fleming (Gone With The Wind)
Nominations:	Sam Wood (Goodbye Mr Chips)
	William Wyler (Wuthering Heights)
	Frank Capra (Mr Smith Goes To Washington)
	John Ford (Stagecoach)

Supporting Actor:	Thomas Mitchell (Stagecoach)
Nominations:	Brian Donlevy (Beau Geste)
	Brian Aherne (Juarez)
	Harry Carey (Mr Smith Goes To Washington)
	Claude Rains (Mr Smith Goes To Washington)

Supporting Actress:	Hattie McDaniel (Gone With The Wind)
Nominations:	Edna May Oliver (Drums Along The Mohawk)
	Maria Ouspenskaya (Love Affair)
	Olivia De Havilland (Gone With The Wind)
	Geraldine Fitzgerald (Wuthering Heights)

Honorary Awards:	Judy Garland, Douglas Fairbanks

Best Song:	Over The Rainbow (Wizard Of Oz)
Nominations:	Faithful Forever (Gulliver's Travels)
	Wishing (Love Affair)
	I Poured My Heart Into A Song (Second Fiddle)

1940

Best Picture:	Rebecca
Nominations:	The Grapes Of Wrath, The Philadelphia Story,
	The Letter, The Great Dictator, The Long
	Voyage Home, Kitty Foyle, Foreign
	Correspondent, Our Town, All This And
	Heaven Too

Actor:	James Stewart (The Philadelphia Story)
Nominations:	Henry Fonda (The Grapes Of Wrath)
	Charles Chaplin (The Great Dictator)
	Laurence Olivier (Rebecca)
	Raymond Massey (Abe Lincoln In Illinois)

Actress:	Ginger Rogers (Kitty Foyle)
Nominations:	Bette Davis (The Letter)
	Katherine Hepburn (The Philadelphia Story)
	Martha Scott (Our Town)
	Joan Fontaine (Rebecca)

Director:	John Ford (The Grapes Of Wrath)
Nominations:	Alfred Hitchcock (Rebecca)
	Sam Wood (Kitty Foyle)
	George Cukor (The Philadelphia Story)
	William Wyler (The Letter)

Supporting Actor:	Walter Brennan (The Westerner)
Nominations:	Jack Oakie (The Great Dictator)
	James Stephenson (The Letter)
	Albert Basserman (Foreign Correspondent)
	William Gargan (They Knew What They Wanted)

Supporting Actress:	Jane Darwell (The Grapes Of Wrath)
Nominations:	Judith Anderson (Rebecca)
	Barbara O'Neil (All This And Heaven Too)
	Ruth Hussey (The Philadelphia Story)
	Marjorie Rambeau (Primrose Path)

Honorary Award:	Bob Hope

Best Song:	When You Wish Upon A Star (Pinocchio)
Nominations:	Our Love Affair (Strike Up The Band)
	Love Of My Life (Second Chorus)
	Only Forever (Rhythm On The River)
	Down Argentine Way (Down Argentine Way)
	I'd Know You Anywhere (You'll Find Out)
	It's A Blue World (Music In My Heart)
	Who Am I ? (Hit Parade Of 1941)
	Waltzing In The Clouds (Spring Parade)

1941

Best Picture:	How Green Was My Valley
Nominations:	Citizen Kane, The Maltese Falcon, Here Comes
	Mr Jordan, Sergeant York, The Little Foxes,
	Blossoms In The Dust, Suspicion, Hold Back
	The Dawn , One Foot In Heaven

Actor:	Gary Cooper (Sergeant York)
Nominations:	Orson Welles (Citizen Kane)
	Robert Montgomery (Here Comes Mr Jordan)
	Cary Grant (Penny Serenade)
	Walter Huston (All That Money Can Buy)

Actress:	Joan Fontainne (Suspicion)
Nominations:	Olivia De Havilland (Hold Back The Dawn)
	Bette Davis (The Little Foxes)
	Greer Garson (Blossoms In The Dust)
	Barbara Stanwyck (Ball Of Fire)

Director:	John Ford (How Green Was My Valley)
Nominations:	Orson Welles (Citizen Kane)
	William Wyler (The Little Foxes)
	Howard Hawks (Sergeant York)
	Alexander Hall (Here Comes Mr Jordan)

Supporting Actor:	Donald Crisp (How Green Was My Valley)
Nominations:	Sydney Greenstreet (The Maltese Falcon)
	Walter Brennan (Sergeant York)
	Charles Coburn (The Devil And Miss Jones)
	James Gleason (Here Comes Mr Jordan)

Supporting Actress: Mary Astor (The Great Lie)
Nominations: Sara Allgood (How Green Was My Valley)
Teresa Wright (The Little Foxes)
Margaret Wycherly (Sergeant York)
Patricia Collinge (The Little Foxes)

Honorary Award: Walt Disney (Fantasia)

Best Song: The Last Time I Saw Paris (Lady Be Good)
Nominations: Blues In The Night (Blues In The Night)
Baby Mine (Dumbo)
Dolores (Las Vegas Nights)
Since I Kissed My Baby Goodbye
    (You'll Never Get Rich)
Out Of The Silence (All American Co-Ed)
Be Honest With Me (Ridin' On A Rainbow)
Chattanooga Choo Choo (Sun Valley Serenade)
Boogie Woogie Bugle Boy Of Company B
    (Buck Privates)

1942

Best Picture: Mrs Miniver
Nominations: Random Harvest, The Pride Of The Yankees,
Yankee Doodle Dandy, The Talk Of The Town,
The Pied Piper, The Magnificent Ambersons
Kings Row, Wake Island, The Invaders

Actor: James Cagney (Yankee Doodle Dandy)
Nominations: Walter Pidgeon (Mrs Miniver)
Gary Cooper (The Pride Of The Yankees)
Monty Woolley (The Pied Piper)
Ronald Colman (Random Harvest)

Actress: Greer Garson (Mrs Miniver)
Nominations: Katherine Hepburn (Woman Of The Year)
Bette Davis (Now Voyager)
Rosalind Russell (My Sister Eileen)
Teresa Wright (The Pride Of The Yankees)

Director: William Wyler (Mrs Miniver)
Nominations: Michael Curtiz (Yankee Doodle Dandy)
Sam Wood (Kings Row)
Mervyn LeRoy (Random Harvest)
John Farrow (Wake Island)

Supporting Actor: Van Heflin (Johnny Eagar)
Nominations: Walter Huston (Yankee Doodle Dandy)
William Bendix (Wake Island)
Henry Travers (Mrs Miniver)
Frank Morgan (Tortilla Flat)

Supporting Actress: Teresa Wright (Mrs Miniver)
Nominations: Gladys Cooper (Now Voyager)
Dame May Whitty (Mrs Miniver)
Agnes Moorehead (The Magnificent Ambersons)
Susan Peters (Random Harvest)

Honorary Awards: Noel Coward, Charles Boyer

Best Song: White Christmas (Holiday Inn)
Nominations: Love Is A Song (Bambi)
How About You (Babes On Broadway)
Pig Foot Pete (Hellzapoppin)
Always In My Heart (Always In My Heart)
I've Got A Gal In Kalamazoo (Orchestra Wives)
Dearly Beloved (You Were Never Lovelier)
It Seems I Heard That Song Before
    (Youth On Parade)
Pennies For Peppino (Flying With Music)
There's A Breeze On Lake Louise
    (The Mayor Of 44th Street)

1943

Best Picture: Casablanca
Nominations: For Whom The Bell Tolls, Watch On The Rhine,
Madame Curie, The Song Of Bernadette, The
Ox-Bow Incident, Heaven Can Wait, The
Human Comedy, The More The Merrier,
In Which We Serve

Actor: Paul Lukas (Watch On The Rhine)
Nominations: Humphrey Bogart (Casablanca)
Gary Cooper (For Whom The Bell Tolls)
Mickey Rooney (The Human Comedy)
Walter Pidgeon (Madame Curie)

Actress: Jennifer Jones (The Song Of Bernadette)
Nominations: Ingrid Bergman (For Whom The Bell Tolls)
Greer Garson (Madame Curie)
Joan Fontaine (The Constant Nymph)
Jean Arthur (The More The Merrier)

Director: Michael Curtiz (Casablanca)
Nominations: Henry King (The Song Of Bernadette)
Ernst Lubitsch (Heaven Can Wait)
Clarence Brown (The Human Comedy)
George Stevens (The More The Merrier)

Supporting Actor: Charles Coburn (The More The Merrier)
Nominations: Claude Rains (Casablanca)
Akim Tamiroff (For Whom The Bell Tolls)
Charles Bickford (The Song Of Bernadette)
J. Carrol Naish (Sahara)

Supporting Actress: Katina Paxinou (For Whom The Bell Tolls)
Nominations: Paulette Goddard (So Proudly We Hail)
Lucile Watson (Watch On The Rhine)
Gladys Cooper (The Song Of Bernadette)
Anne Revere (The Song Of Bernadette)

Best Song: You'll Never Know (Hello, Frisco, Hello)
Nominations: Black Magic (Star Spangled Rhythm)
A Change Of Heart (Hit Parade Of 1943)
Happiness Is A Thing Called Joe
    (Cabin In The Sky)
My Shining Hour (The Sky's The Limit)
Say A Prayer For The Boys Over There
    (Hers To Hold)
Saludos Amigos (Saludos Amigos)
We Mustn't Say Goodbye (Stage Door Canteen)
You'd Be So Nice To Come Home To
    (Something To Shout About)
They're Either Too Young Or Too Old
    (Thank Your Lucky Stars)

1944

Best Picture: Going My Way
Nominations: Since You Went Away, Double Indemnity,
Wilson, Gaslight

Actor: Bing Crosby (Going My Way)
Nominations: Cary Grant (None But The Lonely Heart)
Charles Boyer (Gaslight)
Barry Fitzgerald (Going My Way)
Alexander Knox (Wilson)

Actress: Ingrid Bergman (Gaslight)
Nominations: Claudette Colbert (Since You Went Away)
Bette Davis (Mr Skeffington)
Greer Garson (Mrs Parkington)
Barbara Stanwyck (Double Indemnity)

Director: Leo McCarey (Going My Way)
Nominations: Billy Wilder (Double Indemnity)
Otto Preminger (Laura)
Alfred Hitchcock (Lifeboat)
Henry King (Wilson)

Supporting Actor: Barry Fitzgerald (Going My Way)
Nominations: Monty Woolley (Since You Went Away)
Clifton Webb (Laura)
Hume Cronyn (The Seventh Cross)
Claude Rains (Mr Skeffington)

Supporting Actress: Ethel Barrymore (None But The Lonely Heart)
Nominations: Jennifer Jones (Since You Went Away)
Angela Lansbury (Gaslight)
Aline MacMahon (Dragon Seed)
Agnes Moorehead (Mrs Parkington)

Honorary Award:s Bob Hope, Margaret O'Brien

Best Song:	Swinging On A Star (Going My Way)
Nominations:	Long Ago And Far Away (Cover Girl)
	Rio De Janeiro (Brazil)
	Now I Know (Up In Arms)
	The Trolley Song (Meet Me In St. Louis)
	Remember Me To Carolina (Minstrel Man)
	Sweet Dreams, Sweetheart (Hollywood Canteen)
	I'll Walk Alone (Follow The Boys)
	I Couldn't Sleep A Wink Last Night
	(Higher And Higher)
	I'm Making Believe (Sweet And Low Down)
	Silver Shadows And Golden Dreams
	(Lady Let's Dance)

1945

Best Picture:	The Lost Weekend
Nominations:	The Bells Of St. Mary's, Spellbound, Anchors Aweigh, Mildred Pierce
Actor:	Ray Milland (The Lost Weekend)
Nominations:	Gene Kelly (Anchors Aweigh)
	Cornel Wilde (A Song To Remember)
	Bing Crosby (The Bells Of St. Mary's)
	Gregory Peck (The Keys Of The Kingdom)
Actress:	Joan Crawford (Mildred Pierce)
Nominations:	Jennifer Jones (Love Letters)
	Gene Tierney (Leave Her To Heaven)
	Ingrid Bergman (The Bells Of St. Mary's)
	Greer Garson (The Valley Of Decision)
Director:	Billy Wilder (The Lost Weekend)
Nominations:	Clarence Brown (National Velvet)
	Jean Renoir (The Southerner)
	Alfred Hitchcock (Spellbound)
	Leo McCarey (The Bells Of St. Mary's)
Supporting Actor:	James Dunn (A Tree Grows In Brooklyn)
Nominations:	John Dall (The Corn Is Green)
	Michael Chekhov (Spellbound)
	Robert Mitchum (The Story Of G.I. Joe)
	J. Carroll Naish (A Medal For Benny)
Supporting Actress:	Anne Revere (National Velvet)
Nominations:	Joan Lorring (The Corn Is Green)
	Ann Blyth (Mildred Pierce)
	Angela Lansbury (The Picture Of Dorian Gray)
	Eve Arden (Mildred Pierce)
Honorary Award:	Peggy Ann Garner
Best Song:	It Might As Well Be Spring (State Fair)
Nominations:	I Fall In Love Too Easily (Anchors Aweigh)
	So In Love (Wonder Man)
	Aren't You Glad You're You
	(The Bells Of St. Mary's)
	Anywhere (Tonight And Every Night)
	Accentuate The Positive (Here Come The Waves)
	Endlessly (Earl Carroll Vanities)
	The Cat And The Canary
	(Why Girls Leave Home)
	Linda (G.I. Joe)
	I'll Buy That Dream (Sing Your Way Home)
	Love Letters (Love Letters)
	More And More (Can't Help Singing)
	Sleighride In July (Belle Of The Yukon)
	Some Sunday Morning (San Antonio)

1946

Best Picture:	The Best Years Of Our Lives
Nominations:	It's A Wonderful Life, The Yearling, Henry V, The Razor's Edge
Actor:	Fredric March (The Best Years Of Our Lives)
Nominations:	James Stewart (It's A Wonderful Life)
	Laurence Olivier (Henry V)
	Gregory Peck (The Yearling)
	Larry Parks (The Jolson Story)

Actress:	Olivia De Havilland (To Each His Own)
Nominations:	Jane Wyman (The Yearling)
	Jennifer Jones (Duel In The Sun)
	Celia Johnson (Brief Encounter)
	Rosalind Russell (Sister Kenny)
Director:	William Wyler (The Best Years Of Our Lives)
Nominations:	Frank Capra (It's A Wonderful Life)
	Clarence Brown (The Yearling)
	David Lean (Brief Encounter)
	Robert Siodmak (The Killers)
Supporting Actor:	Harold Russell (The Best Years Of Our Lives)
Nominations:	Clifton Webb (The Razor's Edge)
	Charles Coburn (The Green Years)
	William Demarest (The Jolson Story)
	Claude Rains (Notorious)
Supporting Actress:	Anne Baxter (The Razor's Edge)
Nominations:	Lillian Gish (Duel In The Sun)
	Flora Robson (Saratoga Trunk)
	Gale Sondergaard (Anna And The King Of Siam)
	Ethel Barrymore (The Spiral Staircase)
Honorary Award:s	Laurence Olivier, Claude Jarman Jnr., Harold Russell, Ernst Lubitsch
Best Song:	On The Atchison, Topeka And The Santa Fe (The Harvey Girls)
Nominations:	You Keep Coming Back Like A Song (Blue Skies)
	I Can't Begin To Tell You (The Dolly Sisters)
	All Through The Day (Centennial Summer)
	Old Buttermilk Sky (Canyon Passage)

1947

Best Picture:	Gentleman's Agreement
Nominations:	The Bishop's Wife, Great Expectations, Crossfire, Miracle On 34th Street
Actor:	Ronald Colman (A Double Life)
Nominations:	John Garfield (Body And Soul)
	William Powell (Life With Father)
	Gregory Peck (Gentleman's Agreement)
	Michael Redgrave (Mourning Becomes Electra)
Actress:	Loretta Young (The Farmer's Daughter)
Nominations:	Dorothy McGuire (Gentleman's Agreement)
	Joan Crawford (Possessed)
	Susan Hayward
	(Smash Up:The Story Of A Woman)
	Rosalind Russell (Mourning Becomes Electra)
Director:	Elizan Kazan (Gentleman's Agreement)
Nominations:	David Lean (Great Expectations)
	Henry Koster (The Bishop's Wife)
	Edward Dmytryk (Crossfire)
	George Cukor (A Double Life)
Supporting Actor:	Edmund Gwenn (Miracle On 34th Street)
Nominations:	Charles Bickford (The Farmer's Daughter)
	Robert Ryan (Crossfire)
	Richard Widmark (Kiss Of Death)
	Thomas Gomez (Ride The Pink Horse)
Supporting Actress:	Celeste Holm (Gentleman's Agrement)
Nominations:	Ethel Barrymore (The Paradine Case)
	Gloria Grahame (Crossfire)
	Marjorie Main (The Egg And I)
	Anne Revere (Gentleman's Agreement)
Honorary Award:	James Baskett
Best Song:	Zip-A-Dee-Doo-Dah (Song Of The South)
Nominations:	I Wish I Didn't Love You So (The Perils Of Pauline)
	You Do (Mother Wore Tights)
	A Gal In Calico
	(The Time, The Place And The Girl)
	Pass The Peace Pipe (Good News)

1948

Best Picture: Hamlet
Nominations: The Snake Pit, Johnny Belinda, The Red Shoes
The Treasure Of The Sierre Madre

Actor: Laurence Olivier (Hamlet)
Nominations:
Montgomery Clift (The Search)
Lew Ayres (Johnny Belinda)
Dan Dailey (When My Baby Smiles At Me)
Clifton Webb (Sitting Pretty)

Actress: Jane Wyman (Johnny Belinda)
Nominations:
Barbara Stanwyck (Sorry, Wrong Number)
Irene Dunne (I Remember Mama)
Olivia De Havilland (The Snake Pit)
Ingrid Bergman (Joan Of Arc)

Director: John Huston (The Treasure Of The Sierre Madre)
Nominations:
Laurence Olivier (Hamlet)
Jean Negulesco (Johnny Belinda)
Fred Zinnemann (The Search)
Anatole Litvak (The Snake Pit)

Supporting Actor: Walter Huston (The Treasure Of The Sierre Madre)
Nominations:
Charles Bickford (Johnny Belinda)
Jose Ferrer (Joan Of Arc)
Oscar Homolka (I Remember Mama)
Cecil Kellaway (The Luck Of The Irish)

Supporting Actress: Claire Trevor (Key Largo)
Nominations:
Barbara Bel Geddes (I Remember Mama)
Jean Simmons (Hamlet)
Agnes Moorehead (Johnny Belinda)
Ellen Corby (I Remember Mama)

Honorary Award: Ivan Jandl
Best Foreign Film: Monsieur Vincent (French)

Best Song: Buttons And Bows (The Paleface)
Nominations:
It's Magic (Romance On The High Seas)
For Every Man There's A Woman (Casbah)
This Is The Moment (That Lady In Ermine)
The Woody Woodpecker Song
(Wet Blanket Policy)

1949

Best Picture: All The King's Men
Nominations: The Heiress, Twelve O'clock High, Battleground,
A Letter To Three Wives

Actor: Broderick Crawford (All The King's Men)
Nominations:
Richard Todd (The Hasty Heart)
Gregory Peck (Twelve O'clock High)
Kirk Douglas (Champion)
John Wayne (Sands Of Iwo Jima)

Actress: Olivia De Havilland (The Heiress)
Nominations:
Susan Hayward (My Foolish Heart)
Jeanne Crain (Pinky)
Deborah Kerr (Edward, My Son)
Loretta Young (Come To The Stable)

Director: Joseph L. Mankiewicz (A Letter To Three Wives)
Nominations:
Robert Rossen (All The King's Men)
William A. Wellman (Battleground)
William Wyler (The Heiress)
Carol Reed (The Fallen Idol)

Supporting Actor: Dean Jagger (Twelve O'clock High)
Nominations:
John Ireland (All The King's Men)
Arthur Kennedy (Champion)
Ralph Richardson (The Heiress)
Whitmore (Battleground)

Supporting Actress: Mercedes Mccambridge (All The King's Men)
Nominations:
Ethel Barrymore (Pinky)
Ethel Waters (Pinky)
Celeste Holm (Come To The Stable)
Elsa Lanchester (Come To The Stable)

Honorary Awards: Fred Astaire, Bobby Driscoll, Cecil B. Demille,
Jean Hersholt

Best Foreign Film: Bicycle Thieves (Italian)

Best Song: Baby, It's Cold Outside (Neptune's Daughter)
Nominations:
My Foolish Heart (My Foolish Heart)
Lavender Blue (So Dear To My Heart)
It's A Great Feeling (It's A Great Feeling)
Through A Long And Sleepless Night
(Come To The Stable)

1950

Best Picture: All About Eve
Nominations: Sunset Boulevard, Born Yesterday,
King Solomon's Mines, Father Of The Bride

Actor: Jose Ferrer (Cyrano De Bergerac)
Nominations:
William Holden (Sunset Boulevard)
James Stewart (Harvey)
Spencer Tracy (Father Of The Bride)
Louis Calhern (The Magnificent Yankee)

Actress: Judy Holliday (Born Yesterday)
Nominations:
Gloria Swanson (Sunset Boulevard)
Bette Davis (All About Eve)
Eleanor Parker (Caged)
Anne Baxter (All About Eve)

Director: Joseph L. Mankiewicz (All About Eve)
Nominations:
Billy Wilder (Sunset Boulevard)
Carol Reed (The Third Man)
George Cukor (Born Yesterday)
John Huston (The Asphalt Jungle)

Supporting Actor: George Sanders (All About Eve)
Nominations:
Erich Von Stroheim (Sunset Boulevard)
Sam Jaffe (The Asphalt Jungle)
Jeff Chandler (Broken Arrow)
Edmund Gwenn (Mister 880)

Supporting Actress: Josephine Hull (Harvey)
Nominations:
Nancy Olsen (Sunset Boulevard)
Celeste Holm (All About Eve)
Hope Emerson (Caged)
Thelma Ritter (All About Eve)

Honorary Awards: George Murphy, Louis B. Mayer

Best Foreign Film: The Walls Of Malapaga (French/Italian)

Best Song: Mona Lisa (Captain Carey U.S.A.)
Nominations:
Bibberti-Bobberti-Boo (Cinderella)
Be My Love (The Toast Of New Orleans)
Mule Train (Singing Guns)
Wilhelmina (Wabash Avenue)

1951

Best Picture: An American In Paris
Nominations: A Place In The Sun, Decision Before Dawn,
Quo Vadis, A Streetcar Named Desire

Actor: Humphrey Bogart (The African Queen)
Nominations:
Marlon Brando (A Streetcar Named Desire)
Fredric March (Death Of A Salesman)
Montgomery Clift (A Place In The Sun)
Arthur Kennedy (Bright Victory)

Actress: Vivien Leigh (A Streetcar Named Desire)
Nominations:
Katherine Hepburn (The African Queen)
Jame Wyman (The Blue Veil)
Shelley Winters (A Place In The Sun)
Eleanor Parker (Detective Story)

Director: George Stevens (A Place In The Sun)
Nominations:
John Huston (The African Queen)
William Wyler (Detective Story)
Vincente Minnelli (An American In Paris)
Elia Kazan (A Streetcar Named Desire)

Supporting Actor:	Karl Malden (A Streetcar Named Desire)
Nominations:	Kevin McCarthy (Death Of A Salesman)
	Peter Ustinov (Quo Vadis)
	Leo Genn (Quo Vadis)
	Gig Young (Come Fill The Cup)

Supporting Actress:	Kim Hunter (A Streetcar Named Desire)
Nominations:	Joan Blondell (The Blue Veil)
	Lee Grant (Detective Story)
	Mildred Dunnock (Death Of A Salesman)
	Thelma Ritter (The Mating Season)

Honorary Award: Gene Kelly

Best Foreign Film: Rashomon (Japanese)

Best Song:	In The Cool, Cool, Cool Of The Evening
	(Here Comes The Groom)
Nominations:	Too Late Now (Royal Wedding)
	A Kiss To Build A Dream On (The Strip)
	Never (Golden Girl)
	Wonder Why (Rich, Young And Pretty)

1952

Best Picture:	The Greatest Show On Earth
Nominations:	High Noon, Ivanhoe, The Quiet Man,
	Moulin Rouge

Actor:	Gary Cooper (High Noon)
Nominations:	Jose Ferrer (Moulin Rouge)
	Kirk Douglas (The Bad And The Beautiful)
	Alec Guinness (The Lavender Hill Mob)
	Marlon Brando (Viva Zapata)

Actress:	Shirley Booth (Come Back Little Sheba)
Nominations:	Susan Hayward (With A Song In My Heart)
	Bette Davis (The Star)
	Joan Crawford (Sudden Fear)
	Julie Harris (The Member Of The Wedding)

Director:	John Ford (The Quiet Man)
Nominations:	Cecil B. DeMille (The Greatest Show On Earth)
	John Huston (Moulin Rouge)
	Joseph L. Mankiewicz (Five Fingers)
	Fred Zinnemann (High Noon)

Supporting Actor:	Anthony Quinn (Viva Zapata)
Nominations:	Victor McLaglen (The Quiet Man)
	Richard Burton (My Cousin Rachel)
	Arthur Hunnicutt (The Big Sky)
	Jack Palance (Sudder Fear)

Supporting Actress:	Gloria Grahame (The Bad And The Beautiful)
Nominations:	Thelma Ritter (With A Song In My Heart)
	Colette Marchand (Moulin Rouge)
	Terry Moore (Come Back Little Sheba)
	Jean Hagen (Singing In The Rain)

Honorary Awards: Bob Hope, Harold Lloyd

Best Foreign Film: Forbidden Games (French)

Best Song:	High Noon (High Noon)
Nominations:	Because You're Mine (Because You're Mine)
	Am I In Love ? (Son Of Paleface)
	Thumbelina (Hans Christian Anderson)
	Zing A Little Song (Just For You)

1953

| Best Picture: | From Here To Eternity |
| Nominations: | Shane, Roman Holiday, The Robe, Julius Caesar |

Actor:	William Holden (Stalag 17)
Nominations:	Burt Lancaster (From Here To Eternity)
	Richard Burton (The Robe)
	Montgomery Clift (From Here To Eternity)
	Marlon Brando (Julius Caesar)

Actress:	Audrey Hepburn (Roman Holiday)
Nominations:	Leslie Caron (Lili)
	Deborah Kerr (From Here To Eternity)

| | Ava Gardner (Mogambo) |
| | Maggie Mcnamara (The Moon Is Blue) |

Director:	Fred Zinnemann (From Here To Eternity)
Nominations:	George Stevens (Shane)
	William Wyler (Roman Holiday)
	Charles Walters (Lili)
	Billy Wilder (Stalag 17)

Supporting Actor:	Frank Sinatra (From Here To Eternity)
Nominations:	Eddie Albert (Roman Holiday)
	Robert Strauss (Stalag 17)
	Brandon De Wilde (Shane)
	Jack Palance (Shane)

Supporting Actress:	Donna Reed (From Here To Eternity)
Nominations:	Geraldine Page (Hondo)
	Thelma Ritter (Pick-Up On South Street)
	Grace Kelly (Mogambo)
	Marjorie Rambeau (Torch Song)

Honorary Award: Pete Smith

Best Song:	Secret Love (Calamity Jane)
Nominations:	That's Amore (The Caddy)
	My Flaming Heart (Small Town Girl)
	Blue Pacific Blues (Miss Sadie Thompson)
	The Moon Is Blue (The Moon Is Blue)

1954

Best Picture:	On The Waterfront
Nominations:	Seven Brides For Seven Brothers,
	The Country Girl, Three Coins In A Fountain,
	The Caine Mutiny

Actor:	Marlon Brando (On The Waterfront)
Nominations:	James Mason (A Star Is Born)
	Humphrey Bogary (The Caine Mutiny)
	Bing Crosby (The Country Girl)
	Dan O'Herlihy (Adventures Of Robinson Crusoe)

Actress:	Grace Kelly (The Country Girl)
Nominations:	Judy Garland (A Star Is Born)
	Dorothy Dandridge (Carmen Jones)
	Audrey Hepburn (Sabrina)
	Jane Wyman (Magnificent Obsession)

Director:	Elia Kazan (On The Waterfront)
Nominations:	Alfred Hitchcock (Rear Window)
	George Seaton (The Country Girl)
	Billy Wilder (Sabrina)
	William A. Wellman (The High And The Mighty)

Supporting Actor:	Edmund O'Brien (The Barefoot Contessa)
Nominations:	Karl Malden (On The Waterfront)
	Rod Steiger (On The Waterfront)
	Lee J. Cobb (On The Waterfront)
	Tom Tully (The Caine Mutiny)

Supporting Actress:	Eva Marie Saint (On The Waterfront)
Nominations:	Jan Sterling (The High And The Mighty)
	Katy Jurado (Broken Lance)
	Claire Trevor (The High And The Mighty)
	Nini Foch (Executive Suite)

| Honorary Awards: | Greta Garbo, Danny Kaye, Jon Whiteley, |
| | Vincent Winter |

Best Foreign Film: Gate Of Hell (Japanese)

Best Song:	Three Coins In A Fountain
	(Three Coins In A Fountain)
Nominations:	The High And The Mighty
	(The High And The Mighty)
	The Man That Got Away (A Star Is Born)
	Hold My Hand (Susan Slept Here)
	Count Your Blessings Instead Of Sheep
	(White Christmas)

1955

Best Picture: Marty
Nominations: Love Is A Many-Splendored Thing, Mister Roberts, The Rose Tattoo, Picnic

Actor: Ernest Borgnine (Marty)
Nominations: Frank Sinatra (The Man With The Golden Arm)
James Dean (East Of Eden)
James Cagney (Love Me Or Leave Me)
Spencer Tracy (Bad Day At Black Rock)

Actress: Anna Magnani (The Rose Tattoo)
Nominations: Susan Hayward (I'll Cry Tomorrow)
Katherine Hepburn (Summer Madness)
Jennifer Jones (Love Is A Many-Splendored Thing)
Eleanor Parker (Interrupted Melody)

Director: Delbert Mann (Marty)
Nominations: Elia Kazan (East Of Eden)
David Lean (Summer Madness)
Joshua Logan (Picnic)
John Sturges (Bad Day At Black Rock)

Supporting Actor: Jack Lemmon (Mister Roberts)
Nominations: Sal Mineo (Rebel Without A Cause)
Joe Mantell (Marty)
Arthur Kennedy (Trial)
Arthur O'Connell (Picnic)

Supporting Actress: Jo Van Fleet (East Of Eden)
Nominations: Natalie Wood (Rebel Without A Cause)
Betsy Blair (Marty)
Peggy Lee (Pete Kelly's Blues)
Marisa Pavan (The Rose Tattoo)

Best Foreign Film: Samurai, The Legend Of Musashi (Japanese)

Best Song: Love Is A Many-Splendored Thing (Love Is A Many-Splendored Thing)
Nominations: The Tender Trap (The Tender Trap)
Something's Gotta Give (Daddy Long Legs)
Unchained Melody (Unchained)
I'll Never Stop Loving You (Love Me Or Leave Me)

1956

Best Picture: Around The World In Eighty Days
Nominations: The Ten Commandments, Giant, The King And I, Friendly Persuasion

Actor: Yul Brynner (The King And I)
Nominations: Rock Hudson (Giant)
Kirk Douglas (Lust For Life)
James Dean (Giant)
Laurence Olivier (Richard III)

Actress: Ingrid Bergman (Anastasia)
Nominations: Deborah Kerr (The King And I)
Carroll Baker (Baby Doll)
Katherine Hepburn (The Rainmaker)
Nancy Kelly (The Bad Seed)

Director: George Stevens (Giant)
Nominations: King Vidor (War And Peace)
Walter Lang (The King And I)
Michael Anderson (Friendly Persuasion)

Supporting Actor: Anthony Quinn (Lust For Life)
Nominations: Don Murray (Bus Stop)
Robert Stack (Written On The Wind)
Mickey Rooney (The Bold And The Brave)
Anthony Perkins (Friendly Persuasion)

Supporting Actress: Dorothy Malone (Written On The Wind)
Nominations: Patty McCormack (The Bad Seed)
Mercedes McCambridge (Giant)
Eileen Heckart (The Bad Seed)
Mildred Dunnock (Baby Doll)

Honorary Award: Eddie Cantor

Best Foreign Film: La Strada (Italy)

Best Song: Que Sera, Sera (The Man Who Knew Too Much)
Nominations: Friendly Persuasion (Friendly Persuasion)
True Love (High Society)
Written On The Wind (Written On The Wind)
Julie (Julie)

1957

Best Picture: The Bridge On The River Kwai
Nominations: Twelve Angry Men, Witness For The Prosecution, Peyton Place, Sayonara

Actor: Alec Guinness (The Bridge On The River Kwai)
Nominations: Charles Laughton (Witness For The Prosecution)
Marlon Brando (Sayonara)
Anthony Quinn (Wild Is The Wind)
Anthony Franciosa (A Hatful Of Rain)

Actress: Joanne Woodward (The Three Faces Of Eve)
Nominations: Elizabeth Taylor (Raintree County)
Lana Turner (Peyton Place)
Anna Magnani (Wild Is The Wind)
Deborah Kerr (Heaven Knows, Mr Allison)

Director: David Lean (The Bridge On The River Kwai)
Nominations: Billy Wilder (Witness For The Prosecution)
Joshua Logan (Sayonara)
Sidney Lumet (Twelve Angry Men)
Mark Robson (Peyton Place)

Supporting Actor: Red Buttons (Sayonara)
Nominations: Vittorio De Sica (A Farewell To Arms)
Arthur Kennedy (Peyton Place)
Sessue Hayakawa (The Bridge On The River Kwai)
Russ Tamblyn (Peyton Place)

Supporting Actress: Miyoshi Umeki (Sayonara)
Nominations: Elsa Lanchester (Witness For The Prosecution)
Hope Lange (Peyton Place)
Carolyn Jones (The Bachelor Party)
Diane Varsi (Peyton Place)

Best Foreign Film: The Nights Of Cabiria (Italy)
Best Song: All The Way (The Joker Is Wild)
Nominations: An Affair To Remember (An Affair To Remember)
Wild Is The Wind (Wild Is The Wind)
April Love (April Love)
Tammy (Tammy And The Bachelor)

1958

Best Picture: Gigi
Nominations: Cat On A Hot Tin Roof, The Defiant Ones, Auntie Mame, Separate Tables

Actor: David Niven (Separate Tables)
Nominations: Paul Newman (Cat On A Hot Tin Roof)
Tony Curtis (The Defiant Ones)
Spencer Tracy (The Old Man And The Sea)
Sidney Poitier (The Defiant Ones)

Actress: Susan Hayward (I Want To Live)
Nominations: Elizabeth Taylor (Cat On A Hot Tin Roof)
Rosalind Russell (Auntie Mame)
Deborah Kerr (Separate Tables)
Shirley MacLaine (Some Came Running)

Director: Vincente Minnelli (Gigi)
Nominations: Stanley Kramer (The Defiant Ones)
Richard Brooks (Cat On A Hot Tin Roof)
Mark Robson (The Inn Of The Sixth Happiness)
Robert Wise (I Want To Live !)

Supporting Actor: Burl Ives (The Big Country)
Nominations: Gig Young (Teacher's Pet)
Lee J. Cobb (The Brothers Karamazov)
Theodore Bikel (The Defiant Ones)
Arthur Kennedy (Some Came Running)

Supporting Actress: Wendy Hiller (Separate Tables)
Nominations: Peggy Cass (Auntie Mame)
Cara Williams (The Defiant Ones)

Martha Hyer (Some Came Running)
Maureen Stapleton (Lonely Hearts)

Honorary Award: Maurice Chevalier

Best Foreign Film: Mon Oncle (French)

Best Song: Gigi (Gigi)
Nominations: Almost In Your Arms (Houseboat)
A Very Precious Love (Marjorie Morningstar)
A Certain Smile (A Certain Smile)
To Love And To Be Loved (Some Came Running)

1959

Best Picture: Ben Hur
Nominations: Anatomy Of A Murder, The Diary Of Anne Frank, Room At The Top, The Nun's Story

Actor: Charlton Heston (Ben Hur)
Nominations: Jack Lemmon (Some Like It Hot)
Laurence Harvey (Room At The Top)
James Stewart (Anatomy Of A Murder)
Paul Muni (The Last Angry Man)

Actress: Simone Signoret (Room At The Top)
Nominations: Elizabeth Taylor (Suddenly Last Summer)
Doris Day (Pillow Talk)
Katherine Hepburn (Suddenly Last Summer)
Audrey Hepburn (The Nun's Story)

Director: William Wyler (Ben Hur)
Nominations: Billy Wilder (Some Like It Hot)
Fred Zinnemann (The Nun's Story)
George Stevens (The Diary Of Anne Frank)
Jack Clayton (Room At The Top)

Supporting Actor: Hugh Griffith (Ben Hur)
Nominations: Arthur O'Connell (Anatomy Of A Murder)
Ed Winn (The Diary Of Anne Frank)
George C. Scott (Anatomy Of A Murder)
Robert Vaughn (The Young Philadelphians)

Supporting Actress: Shelley Winters (The Diary Of Anne Frank)
Nominations: Thelma Ritter (Pillow Talk)
Juanita Moore (Imitation Of Life)
Hermione Baddeley (Room At The Top)
Susan Kohner (Imitation Of Life)

Honorary Award: Buster Keaton

Best Foreign Film: Black Orpheus (French)

Best Song: High Hopes (A Hole In The Head)
Nominations: The Hanging Tree (The Hanging Tree)
The Five Pennies (The Five Pennies)
The Best Of Everything (The Best Of Everything)
Strange Are The Ways Of Love (The Young Land)

1960

Best Picture: The Apartment
Nominations: Elmer Gantry, The Alamo, Sons And Lovers, The Sundowners

Actor: Burt Lancaster (Elmer Gantry)
Nominations: Spencer Tracy (Inherit The Wind)
Jack Lemmon (The Apartment)
Trevor Howard (Sons And Lovers)
Laurence Olivier (The Entertainer)

Actress: Elizabeth Taylor (Butterfield 8)
Nominations: Deborah Kerr (The Sundowners)
Shirley MacLaine (The Apartment)
Greer Garson (Sunrise At Campobello)
Melina Mercouri (Never On Sunday)

Director: Billy Wilder (The Apartment)
Nominations: Alfred Hitchcock (Psycho)
Jack Cardiff (Sons And Lovers)
Fred Zinnemann (The Sundowners)
Jules Dassin (Never On Sunday)

Supporting Actor: Peter Ustinov (Spartacus)
Nominations: Sal Mineo (Exodus)
Jack Kruschen (The Apartment)
Chill Wills (The Alamo)
Peter Falk (Murder Inc.)

Supporting Actress: Shirley Jones (Elmer Gantry)
Nominations: Shirley Knight (The Dark At The Top Of The Stairs)
Janet Leigh (Psycho)
Glynis Johns (The Sundowners)
Mary Ure (Sons And Lovers)

Honorary Awards: Hayley Mills, Gary Cooper, Stan Laurel

Best Foreign Film: The Virgin Spring (Swedish)

Best Song: Never On Sunday (Never On Sunday)
Nominations: The Green Leaves Of Summer (The Alamo)
The Facts Of Life (The Facts Of Life)
Faraway Part Of Town (Pepe)
The Second Time Around (High Time)

1961

Best Picture: West Side Story
Nominations: Judgement At Nuremburg, Fanny, The Hustler, The Guns Of Navarone

Actor: Maximillian Schell (Judgement At Nuremburg)
Nominations: Paul Newman (The Hustler)
Spencer Tracy (Judgement At Nuremburg)
Charles Boyer (Fanny)
Stuart Whitman (The Mark)

Actress: Sophia Loren (Two Women)
Nominations: Natalie Wood (Splendor In The Grass)
Audrey Hepburn (Breakfast At Tiffany's)
Geraldine Page (Summer And Smoke)
Piper Laurie (The Hustler)

Director: Jerome Robbins/Robert Wise (West Side Story)
Nominations: Stanley Kramer (Judgement At Nuremburg)
Robert Rossen (The Hustler)
J. Lee-Thompson (The Guns Of Navarone)
Federico Fellini (La Dolce Vita)

Supporting Actor: George Chakiris (West Side Story)
Nominations: Montgomery Clift (Judgement At Nuremburg)
Jackie Gleason (The Hustler)
Peter Falk (Pocketful Of Miracles)
George C. Scott (The Hustler) Refused

Supporting Actress: Rita Moreno (West Side Story)
Nominations: Judy Garland (Judgement At Nuremburg)
Fay Bainter (The Children's Hour)
Una Merkel (Summer And Smoke)
Lotte Lenya (The Roman Spring Of Mrs Stone)

Best Foreign Film: Through A Glass Darkly (Swedish)

Best Song: Moon River (Breakfast At Tiffany's)
Nominations: The Falcon And The Dove (El Cid)
Town Without Pity (Town Without Pity)
Pocketful Of Miracles (Pocketful Of Miracles)
Bachelor In Paradise (Bachelor In Paradise)

1962

Best Picture: Lawrence Of Arabia
Nominations: The Music Man, To Kill A Mockingbird, Mutiny On The Bounty, The Longest Day

Actor: Gregory Peck (To Kill A Mockingbird)
Nominations: Peter O'Toole (Lawrence Of Arabia)
Burt Lancaster (Birdman Of Alcatraz)
Jack Lemmon (Days Of Wine And Roses)
Marcello Mastroianni (Divorce - Italian Style)

Actress: Anne Bancroft (The Miracle Worker)
Nominations: Geraldine Page (Sweet Bird Of Youth)
Lee Remick (Days Of Wine And Roses)
Katherine Hepburn (Long Day's Journey Into Night)
Bette Davis (Whatever Happened To Baby Jane ?)

| Director:
Nominations: | David Lean (Lawrence Of Arabia)
Arthur Penn (The Miracle Worker)
Robert Mulligan (To Kill A Mockingbird)
Frank Perry (David And Lisa)
Pietro Germi (Divorce - Italian Style) | Actress:
Nominations: | Julie Andrews (Mary Poppins)
Anne Bancroft (The Pumpkin Eater)
Kim Stanley (Seance On A Wet Afternoon)
Sophia Loren (Marriage, Italian Style)
Debbie Reynolds (The Unsinkable Molly Brown) |

Supporting Actor:
Nominations: Ed Begley (Sweet Bird Of Youth)
Omar Sharif (Lawrence Of Arabia)
Terence Stamp (Billy Budd)
Telly Savalas (Birdman Of Alcatraz)
Victor Buono (Whatever Happened To Baby Jane?)

Supporting Actress: Patty Duke (The Miracle Worker)
Nominations: Mary Badham (To Kill A Mockingbird)
Shirley Knight (Sweet Bird Of Youth)
Thelma Ritter (Birdman Of Alcatraz)
Angela Lansbury (The Manchunian Candidate)

Best Foreign Film: Sundays And Cybele (French)

Best Song:
Nominations: Days Of Wine And Roses (Days Of Wine And Roses)
Follow Me (Mutiny On The Bounty)
Tender Is The Night (Tender Is The Night)
Walk On The Wild Side (Walk On The Wild Side)
Second Chance (Two For The Seesaw)

1963

Best Picture: Tom Jones
Nominations: Cleopatra, Lilies Of The Field,
How The West Was Won, America, America

Actor: Sidney Poitier (Lilies Of The Field)
Nominations: Albert Finney (Tom Jones)
Richard Harris (This Sporting Life)
Rex Harrison (Cleopatra)
Paul Newman (Hud)

Actress: Patricia Neal (Hud)
Nominations: Natalie Wood (Love With The Proper Stranger)
Leslie Caron (The L-Shaped Room)
Shirley MacLaine (Irma La Douce)
Rachel Roberts (This Sporting Life)

Director: Tony Richardson (Tom Jones)
Nominations: Elia Kazan (America, America)
Otto Preminger (The Cardinal)
Martin Ritt (Hud)
Federico Fellini (8)

Supporting Actor: Melvyn Douglas (Hud)
Nominations: Hugh Griffith (Tom Jones)
Nick Adams (Twilight Of Honor)
John Huston (The Cardinal)
Bobby Darin (Captain Newman M.D.)

Supporting Actress: Margaret Rutherford (The V.I.P.'S)
Nominations: Diane Cilento (Tom Jones)
Lilia Skala (Lilies Of The Field)
Edith Evans (Tom Jones)
Joyce Redman (Tom Jones)

Best Foreign Film: 8 (Italian)

Best Song: Call Me Irresponsible (Papa's Delicate Condition)
Nominations: Charade (Charade)
So Little Time (55 Days At Peking)
More (Mondo Cane)
It's A Mad, Mad, Mad, Mad World
(It's A Mad, Mad, Mad, Mad World)

1964

Best Picture: My Fair Lady
Nominations: Mary Poppins, Zorba The Greek,
Dr Strangelove, Becket

Actor: Rex Harrison (Mr Fair Lady)
Nominations: Anthony Quinn (Zorba The Greek)
Richard Burton (Becket)
Peter Sellers (Dr Strangelove)
Peter O'Toole (Becket)

Director: George Cukor (My Fair Lady)
Nominations: Robert Stevenson (Mary Poppins)
Peter Glenville (Becket)
Michael Cacoyannis (Zorba The Greek)
Stanley Kubrick (Dr Strangelove)

Supporting Actor: Peter Ustinov (Topkapi)
Nominations: Stanley Holloway (My Fair Lady)
John Gielgud (Becket)
Lee Tracy (The Best Man)
Edmond O'Brien (Seven Days In May)

Supporting Actress: Lila Kedrova (Zorba The Greek)
Nominations: Gladys Cooper (My Fair Lady)
Edith Evans (The Chalk Garden)
Grayson Hall (The Night Of The Iguana)
Agnes Moorehead (Hush…Hush, Sweet Charlotte)

Best Foreign Film: Yesterday, Today And Tomorrow (Italian)

Best Song: Chim-Chim-Cher-Ee (Mary Poppins)
Nominations: My Kind Of Town (Robin And The 7 Hoods)
Dear Heart (Dear Heart)
Where Love Has Gone (Where Love Has Gone)
Hush…Hush, Sweet Charlotte
(Hush…Hush, Sweet Charlotte)

1965

Best Picture: The Sound Of Music
Nominations: Doctor Zhivago, Ship Of Fools,
Darling, A Thousand Clowns

Actor: Lee Marvin (Cat Ballou)
Nominations: Rod Steiger (The Pawnbroker)
Oskar Werner (Ship Of Fools)
Richard Burton (The Spy Who Came In From The Cold)
Laurence Olivier (Othello)

Actress: Julie Christie (Darling)
Nominations: Julie Andrews (The Sound Of Music)
Samantha Eggar (The Collector)
Elizabeth Hartman (A Patch Of Blue)
Simone Signoret (Ship Of Fools)

Director: Robert Wise (The Sound Of Music)
Nominations: David Lean (Doctor Zhivago)
William Wyler (The Collector)
John Schlesinger (Darling)
Hiroshi Teshigahara (Woman In The Dunes)

Supporting Actor: Martin Balsam (A Thousand Clowns)
Nominations: Tom Courtenay (Doctor Zhivago)
Ian Bannen (The Flight Of The Phoenix)
Michael Dunn (Ship Of Fools)
Frank Finlay (Othello)

Supporting Actress: Shelley Winters (A Patch Of Blue)
Nominations: Peggy Wood (The Sound Of Music)
Ruth Gordon (Inside Daisy Clover)
Maggie Smith (Othello)
Joyce Redman (Othello)

Honorary Award: Bob Hope

Best Foreign Film: The Shop On Main Street (Czechoslovakian)

Best Song: The Shadow Of Your Smile (The Sandpiper)
Nominations: The Ballad Of Cat Ballou (Cat Ballou)
The Sweetheart Tree (The Great Race)
What's New Pussycat (What's New Pussycat)
I Will Wait For You (The Umbrellas Of Cherbourg)

1966

Best Picture: A Man For All Seasons
Nominations: Alfie, The Sand Pebbles, Who's Afraid Of Virginia Woolf ?, The Russians Are Coming! The Russians Are Coming!

Actor: Paul Scofield (A Man For All Seasons)
Nominations: Steve McQueen (The Sand Pebbles)
Michael Caine (Alfie)
Alan Arkin (The Russians Are Coming ! The Russians Are Coming !)
Richard Burton (Who's Afraid Of Virginia Woolf ?)

Actress: Elizabeth Taylor (Who's Afraid Of Virginia Woolf ?)
Nominations: Vanessa Redgrave (Morgan, A Suitable Case For Treatment)
Lynn Redgrave (Georgy Girl)
Anouk Aimee (A Man And A Woman)
Ida Kaminska (The Shop On Main Street)

Director: Fred Zinnemann (A Man For All Seasons)
Nominations: Michaelangelo Antonioni (Blow Up)
Richard Brooks (The Professionals)
Mike Nichols (Who's Afraid Of Virginia Woolf ?)
Claude Lelouche (A Man And A Woman)

Supporting Actor: Walter Matthau (The Fortune Cookie)
Nominations: James Mason (Georgy Girl)
Robert Shaw (A Man For All Seasons)
Mako (The Sand Pebbles)
George Segal (Who's Afraid Of Virginia Woolf ?)

Supporting Actress: Sandy Dennis (Who's Afraid Of Virginia Woolf ?)
Nominations: Geraldine Page (You're A Big Boy Now)
Jocelyn Lagarde (Hawaii)
Wendy Hiller (A Man For All Seasons)
Vivien Merchant (Alfie)

Honorary Award: Yakima Canutt

Best Foreign Film: A Man And A Woman (French)

Best Song: Born Free (Born Free)
Nominations: Alfie (Alfie)
Georgy Girl (Georgy Girl)
My Wishing Doll (Hawaii)
A Time For Love (An American Dream)

1967

Best Picture: In The Heat Of The Night
Nominations: Bonnie And Clyde, Doctor Doolittle, The Graduate, Guess Who's Coming To Dinner

Actor: Rod Steiger (In The Heat Of The Night)
Nominations: Warren Beatty (Bonnie And Clyde)
Paul Newman (Cool Hand Luke)
Spencer Tracy (Guess Who's Coming To Dinner)
Dustin Hoffman (The Graduate)

Actress: Katherine Hepburn (Guess Who's Coming To Dinner)
Nominations: Faye Dunaway (Bonnie And Clyde)
Edith Evans (The Whisperers)
Anne Bancroft (The Graduate)
Audrey Hepburn (Wait Until Dark)

Director: Mike Nichols (The Graduate)
Nominations: Norman Jewison (In The Heat Of The Night)
Richard Brooks (In Cold Blood)
Stanley Kramer (Guess Who's Coming To Dinner)
Arthur Penn (Bonnie And Clyde)

Supporting Actor: George Kennedy (Cool Hand Luke)
Nominations: Gene Hackman (Bonnie And Clyde)
John Cassavetes (The Dirty Dozen)
Michael J. Pollard (Bonnie And Clyde)
Cecil Kellaway (Guess Who's Coming To Dinner)

Supporting Actress: Estelle Parsons (Bonnie And Clyde)
Nominations: Katherine Ross (The Graduate)
Mildred Natwick (Barefoot In The Park)
Beah Richards (Guess Who's Coming To Dinner)
Carol Channing (Thoroughly Modern Millie)

Honorary Award: Arthur Fred

Best Foreign Film: Closely Watched Trains (Czechoslovakian)

Best Song: Talk To The Animals (Doctor Doolittle)
Nominations: Thoroughly Modern Millie (Thoroughly Modern Millie)
The Look Of Love (Casino Royale)
The Bare Necessities (Jungle Book)
The Eyes Of Love (Banning)

1968

Best Picture: Oliver !
Nominations: Funny Girl, The Lion In Winter, Romeo And Juliet, Rachel, Rachel

Actor: Cliff Robertson (Charly)
Nominations: Ron Moody (Oliver !)
Peter O'Toole (The Lion In Winter)
Alan Arkin (The Heart Is A Lonely Hunter)
Alan Bates (The Fixer)

Actress: (Tie) Katherine Hepburn (The Lion In Winter)
Barbra Streisand (Funny Girl)
Nominations: Patricia Neal (The Subject Was Roses)
Vanessa Redgrave (Isadora)
Joanne Woodward (Rachel, Rachel)

Director: Carol Reed (Oliver !)
Nominations: Franco Zeffirelli (Romeo And Juliet)
Anthony Harvey (The Lion In Winter)
Stanley Kubrick (2001:A Space Odyssey)
Gillo Pontecurvo (The Battle Of Algiers)

Supporting Actor: Jack Albertson (The Subject Was Roses)
Nominations: Jack Wild (Oliver !)
Gene Wilder (The Producers)
Daniel Massey (Star !)
Seymour Cassel (Faces)

Supporting Actress: Ruth Gordon (Rosemary's Baby)
Nominations: Kay Medford (Funny Girl)
Lynn Carlin (Faces)
Sondra Locke (The Heart Is A Lonely Hunter)
Estelle Parsons (Rachel, Rachel)

Best Foreign Film: War And Peace (Russian)

Best Song: The Windmills Of Your Mind (The Thomas Crown Affair)
Nominations: Chitty, Chitty, Bang Bang (Chitty, Chitty, Bang Bang)
Funny Girl (Funny Girl)
Star ! (Star !)
For Love Of Ivy (For Love Of Ivy)

1969

Best Picture: Midnight Cowboy
Nominations: Hello Dolly, Butch Cassidy And The Sundance Kid, Anne Of The Thousand Days, Z

Actor: John Wayne (True Grit)
Nominations: Dustin Hoffman (Midnight Cowboy)
Peter O'Toole (Goodbye Mr Chips)
Jon Voight (Midnight Cowboy)
Richard Burton (Anne Of The Thousand Days)

Actress: Maggie Smith (The Prime Of Miss Jean Brodie)
Nominations: Liza Minnelli (The Sterile Cuckoo)
Jean Simmons (The Happy Ending)
Jane Fonda (They Shoot Horses, Don't They ?)
Genevieve Bujold (Anne Of The Thousand Days)

Director:	John Schlesinger (Midnight Cowboy)
Nominations:	George Roy Hill
	(Butch Cassidy And The Sundance Kid)
	Costa-Gavras (Z)
	Arthur Penn (Alice's Restaurant)
	Sydney Pollack (They Shoot Horses, Don't They?)

Supporting Actor:	Gig Young (They Shoot Horses, Don't They ?)
Nominations:	Anthony Quayle (Anne Of The Thousand Days)
	Rupert Crosse (The Reivers)
	Jack Nicholson (Easy Rider)
	Elliott Gould (Bob And Carol And Ted And Alice)

Supporting Actress:	Goldie Hawn (Cactus Flower)
Nominations:	Susannah York (They Shoot Horses, Don't They?)
	Cathy Burns (Last Summer)
	Dyan Cannon (Bob And Carol And Ted And Alice)
	Sylvia Miles (Midnight Cowboy)

Honorary Award:	Cary Grant
Best Foreign Film:	Z (Algerian)
Best Song:	Raindrops Keep Fallin' On My Head
	(Butch Cassidy And The Sundance Kid)
Nominations:	True Grit (True Grit)
	Come Saturday Morning (The Sterile Cuckoo)
	What Are You Doing The Rest Of Your Life ?
	(The Happy Ending)
	Jean (The Prime Of Miss Jean Brodie)

1970

| Best Picture: | Patton |
| Nominations: | Airport, Love Story, M*A*S*H, Five Easy Pieces |

Actor:	George C. Scott (Patton)
Nominations:	Ryan O'Neal (Love Story)
	James Earl Jones (The Great White Hope)
	Melvyn Douglas (I Never Sang For My Father)
	Jack Nicholson (Five Easy Pieces)

Actress:	Glenda Jackson (Women In Love)
Nominations:	Ali McGraw (Love Story)
	Carrie Snodgress (Diary Of A Mad Housewife)
	Jane Alexander (The Great White Hope)
	Sarah Miles (Ryan's Daughter)

Director:	Franklin J. Schaffner (Patton)
Nominations:	Robert Altman (M*A*S*H)
	Arthur Hiller (Love Story)
	Ken Russell (Women In Love)
	Federico Fellini (Satyricon)

Supporting Actor:	John Mills (Ryan's Daughter)
Nominations:	John Marley (Love Story)
	Chief Dan George (Little Big Man)
	Gene Hackman (I Never Sang For My Father)
	Richard Castellano (Lovers And Other Strangers)

Supporting Actress:	Helen Hayes (Airport)
Nominations:	Lee Grant (The Landlord)
	Maureen Stapleton (Airport)
	Sally Kellerman (M*A*S*H)
	Karen Black (Five Easy Pieces)

Honorary Awards:	Lillian Gish, Orson Welles
Best Foreign Film:	Investigation Of A Citizen Above Suspicion (Italian)
Best Song:	For All We Know (Sons And Lovers)
Nominations:	Whistling Away The Dark (Darling Lili)
	Thank You Very Much (Scrooge)
	Pieces Of Dreams (Pieces Of Dreams)
	Till Love Touches Your Life (Madron)

1971

Best Picture:	The French Connection
Nominations:	The Last Picture Show, Fiddler On The Roof,
	A Clockwork Orange, Nicholas And Alexandra

Actor:	Gene Hackman (The French Connection)
Nominations:	Peter Finch (Sunday, Bloody Sunday)
	Walter Matthau (Kotch)
	Chaim Topol (Fiddler On The Roof)
	George C. Scott (The Hospital)

Actress:	Jane Fonda (Klute)
Nominations:	Vanessa Redgrave (Mary, Queen Of Scots)
	Janet Suzman (Nicholas And Alexandra)
	Julie Christie (Mccabe And Mrs Miller)
	Glenda Jackson (Sunday, Bloody Sunday)

Director:	William Friedkin (The French Connection)
Nominations:	Peter Bogdanovich (The Last Picture Show)
	Stanley Kubrick (A Clockwork Orange)
	John Schlesinger (Sunday, Bloody Sunday)
	Norman Jewison (Fiddler On The Roof)

Supporting Actor:	Ben Johnson (The Last Picture Show)
Nominations:	Jeff Bridges (The Last Picture Show)
	Leonard Frey (Fiddler On The Roof)
	Roy Scheider (The French Connection)
	Richard Jaeckel (Never Give An Inch)

Supporting Actress:	Cloris Leachman (The Last Picture Show)
Nominations:	Margaret Leighton (The Go-Between)
	Ann-Margret (Carnal Knowledge)
	Ellen Burstyn (The Last Picture Show)
	Barbara Harris (Who Is Harry Kellerman And
	Why Is He Saying Those Things About Me ?)

Honorary Award:	Charles Chaplin
Best Foreign Film:	The Garden On The Finzi-Continis (Italian)
Best Song:	Theme From Shaft (Shaft)
Nominations:	Life Is What You Make It (Kotch)
	All His Children (Never Give An Inch)
	The Age Of Not Believing
	(Bedknobs And Broomsticks)
	Bless The Beasts And Children
	(Bless The Beasts And Children)

1972

| Best Picture: | The Godfather |
| Nominations: | Cabaret, Deliverance, Sounder, The Emigrants |

Actor:	Marlon Brando (The Godfather)
Nominations:	Laurence Olivier (Sleuth)
	Paul Winfield (Sounder)
	Michael Caine (Sleuth)
	Peter O'Toole (The Ruling Class)

Actress:	Liza Minnelli (Cabaret)
Nominations:	Maggie Smith (Travels With My Aunt)
	Cicely Tyson (Sounder)
	Diana Ross (Lady Sings The Blues)
	Liv Ullmann (The Emigrants)

Director:	Bob Fosse (Cabaret)
Nominations:	Francis Ford Coppola (The Godfather)
	John Boorman (Deliverance)
	Joseph L. Mankiewicz (Sleuth)
	Jan Troell (The Emigrants)

Supporting Actor:	Joel Gray (Cabaret)
Nominations:	James Caan (The Godfather)
	Robert Duvall (The Godfather)
	Al Pacino (The Godfather)
	Eddie Albert (The Heartbreak Kid)

Supporting Actress:	Eileen Heckart (Butterflies Are Free)
Nominations:	Geraldine Page (Pete 'N' Tillie)
	Susan Tyrrell (Fat City)
	Shelley Winters (The Poseidon Adventure)
	Jeannie Berlin (The Heartbreak Kid)

| Honorary Award: | Edward G. Robinson |
| Best Foreign Film: | The Discreet Charm Of The Bourgeoisie (French) |

Best Song:	The Morning After (The Poseidon Adventure)
Nominations:	Marmalade, Molasses And Honey
	(The Life And Times Of Judge Roy Bean)
	Ben (Ben)
	Come Follow, Follow Me (The Little Ark)
	Strange Are The Ways Of Love (The Stepmother)

1973

Best Picture:	The Sting
Nominations:	American Graffiti, A Touch Of Class,
	The Exorcist, Cries And Whispers
Actor:	Jack Lemmon (Save The Tiger)
Nominations:	Robert Redford (The Sting)
	Marlon Brando (Last Tango In Paris)
	Jack Nicholson (The Last Detail)
	Al Pacino (Serpico)
Actress:	Glenda Jackson (A Touch Of Class)
Nominations:	Barbra Streisand (The Way We Were)
	Ellen Burstyn (The Exorcist)
	Marsha Mason (Cinderella Liberty)
	Joanne Woodward (Summer Wishes, Winter Dreams)
Director:	George Roy Hill (The Sting)
Nominations:	George Lucas (American Graffiti)
	William Friedkin (The Exorcist)
	Bernardo Bertolucci (Last Tango In Paris)
	Ingmar Bergman (Cries And Whispers)
Supporting Actor:	John Houseman (The Paper Chase)
Nominations:	Vincent Gardenia (Bang The Drum Softly)
	Jack Gilford (Save The Tiger)
	Randy Quaid (The Last Detail)
	Jason Miller (The Exorcist)
Supporting Actress:	Tatum O'Neal (Paper Moon)
Nominations:	Sylvia Sidney (Summer Wishes, Winter Dreams)
	Linda Blair (The Exorcist)
	Candy Clark (American Graffiti)
	Madeline Kahn (Paper Moon)
Honorary Award:	Groucho Marx
Best Foreign Film:	Day For Night (French)
Best Song:	The Way We Were (The Way We Were)
Nominations:	Nice To Be Around (Cinderella Liberty)
	Live And Let Die (Live And Let Die)
	All That Love Went To Waste (A Touch Of Class)
	Love (Robin Hood)

1974

Best Picture:	The Godfather Part II
Nominations:	The Towering Inferno, Chinatown,
	The Conversation, Lenny
Actor:	Art Carney (Harry And Tonto)
Nominations:	Jack Nicholson (Chinatown)
	Al Pacino (The Godfather Part Ii)
	Albert Finney (Murder On The Orient Express)
	Dustin Hoffman (Lenny)
Actress:	Ellen Burstyn (Alice Doesn't Live Here Anymore)
Nominations:	Gena Rowlands (A Woman Under The Influence)
	Faye Dunaway (Chinatown)
	Diahann Carroll (Claudine)
	Valerie Perrine (Lenny)
Director:	Francis Ford Coppola (The Godfather Part Ii)
Nominations:	Roman Polanski (Chinatown)
	John Cassavetes (A Woman Under The Influence)
	Bob Fosse (Lenny)
	Francois Truffaut (Day For Night)
Supporting Actor:	Robert De Niro (The Godfather Part II)
Nominations:	Fred Astaire (The Towering Inferno)
	Lee Strasberg (The Godfather Part II)
	Jeff Bridges (Thunderbolt And Lightfoot)
	Michael V. Gazzo (The Godfather Part II)

Supporting Actress:	Ingrid Bergman (Murder On The Orient Express)
Nominations:	Diane Ladd (Alice Doesn't Live Here Anymore)
	Madeline Kahn (Blazing Saddles)
	Talia Shire (The Godfather Part II)
	Valentina Cortese (Day For Night)
Honorary Awards:	Howard Hawks, Jean Renoir
Best Foreign Film:	Amarcord (Italian)
Best Song:	We May Never Love Like This Again
	(The Towering Inferno)
Nominations:	Wherever Love Takes Me (Gold)
	Blazing Saddles (Blazing Saddles)
	I Feel Love (Benji)
	Little Prince (The Little Prince)

1975

Best Picture:	One Flew Over The Cuckoo's Nest
Nominations:	Nashville, Jaws, Barry Lyndon,
	Dog Day Afternoon
Actor:	Jack Nicholson (One Flew Over The Cuckoo's Nest)
Nominations:	Walter Matthau (The Sunshine Boys)
	Al Pacino (Dog Day Afternoon)
	Maximillian Schell (The Man In The Glass Booth)
	James Whitmore (Give 'Em Hell, Harry !)
Actress:	Louise Fletcher
	(One Flew Over The Cuckoo's Nest)
Nominations:	Glenda Jackson (Hedda)
	Ann-Margret (Tommy)
	Carol Kane (Hester Street)
	Isabelle Adjani (The Story Of Adele H.)
Director:	Milos Forman (One Flew Over The Cuckoo's Nest)
Nominations:	Robert Altman (Nashville)
	Stanley Kubrick (Barry Lyndon)
	Sidney Lumet (Dog Day Afternoon)
	Federico Fellini (Amarcord)
Supporting Actor:	George Burns (The Sunshine Boys)
Nominations:	Burgess Meredith (The Day Of The Locust)
	Jack Warden (Shampoo)
	Brad Dourif (One Flew Over The Cuckoo's Nest)
	Chris Sarandan (Dog Day Afternoon)
Supporting Actress:	Lee Grant (Shampoo)
Nominations:	Ronee Blakeley (Nashville)
	Sylvia Miles (Farewell, My Lovely)
	Lily Tomlin (Nashville)
	Brenda Vaccaro (Once Is Not Enough)
Honorary Award:	Mary Pickford
Best Foreign Film:	Dersu Uzala (Russian)
Best Song:	I'm Easy (Nashville)
Nominations:	How Lucky Can You Get ? (Funny Lady)
	Do You Know Where You're Going To (Mahogany)
	Richard's Window
	(The Other Side Of The Mountain)
	Now That We're In Love (Whiffs)

1976

Best Picture:	Rocky
Nominations:	All The President's Men, Network, Taxi Driver,
	Bound For Glory
Actor:	Peter Finch (Network)
Nominations:	Sylvester Stallone (Rocky)
	William Holden (Network)
	Robert De Niro (Taxi Driver)
	Giancarlo Giannini (Seven Beauties)
Actress:	Fay Dunaway (Network)
Nominations:	Sissy Spacek (Carrie)
	Talia Shire (Rocky)
	Liv Ullman (Face To Face)
	Marie Christine Barrault (Cousin, Cousine)

Director:	John G. Avildsen (Rocky)
Nominations:	Sidney Lumet (Network)
	Lina Wertmuller (Seven Beauties)
	Alan J. Pakula (All The President's Men)
	Ingmar Bergman (Face To Face)

Supporting Actor:	Jason Robards (All The President's Men)
Nominations:	Burgess Meredith (Rocky)
	Laurence Olivier (Marathon Man)
	Burt Young (Rocky)
	Ned Beatty (Network)

Supporting Actress:	Beatrice Straight (Network)
Nominations:	Jane Alexander (All The President's Men)
	Jodie Foster (Taxi Driver)
	Lee Grant (Voyage Of The Damned)
	Piper Laurie (Carrie)

Best Foreign Film:	Black And White In Colour (Ivory Coast)

Best Song:	Evergreen (A Star Is Born)
Nominations:	Gonna Fly Now (Rocky)
	Ave Satani (The Omen)
	Come To Me (The Pink Panther Strikes Again)
	A World That Never Was (Half A House)

1977

Best Picture:	Annie Hall
Nominations:	Julia, Star Wars, The Turning Point,
	The Goodbye Girl

Actor:	Richard Dreyfuss (The Goodbye Girl)
Nominations:	Marcello Mastroianni (A Special Day)
	Richard Burton (Equus)
	John Travolta (Saturday Night Fever)
	Woody Allen (Annie Hall)

Actress:	Diane Keaton (Annie Hall)
Nominations:	Anne Bancroft (The Turning Point)
	Marsha Mason (The Goodbye Girl)
	Shirley MacLaine (The Turning Point)
	Jane Fonda (Julia)

Director:	Woody Allen (Annie Hall)
Nominations:	Fred Zinnemann (Julia)
	Herbert Ross (The Turning Point)
	Steven Spielberg
	(Close Encounters Of The Third Kind)
	George Lucas (Star Wars)

Supporting Actor:	Jason Robards (Julia)
Nominations:	Alec Guinness (Star Wars)
	Peter Firth (Equus)
	Mikhail Barishnikov (The Turning Point)
	Maximilian Schell (Julia)

Supporting Actress:	Vanessa Redgrave (Julia)
Nominations:	Quinn Cummings (The Goodbye Girl)
	Tuesday Weld (Looking For Mr Goodbar)
	Melinda Dillon (Close Encounters Of The Third Kind)
	Leslie Browne (The Turning Point)

Best Foreign Film:	Madame Rosa (French)

Best Song:	You Light Up My Life (You Light Up My Life)
Nominations:	Candle On The Water (Pete's Dragon)
	Nobody Does It Better (The Spy Who Loved Me)
	Someone's Waiting For You (The Rescuers)
	He Danced With Me/She Danced With Me
	(The Slipper And The Rose)

1978

Best Foreign	The Deer Hunter
Nominations:	Heaven Can Wait, Midnight Express,
	Coming Home, An Unmarried Woman

Actor:	Jon Voight (Coming Home)
Nominations:	Robert De Niro (The Deer Hunter)
	Warren Beatty (Heaven Can Wait)
	Laurence Olivier (The Boys From Brazil)
	Gary Busey (The Buddy Holly Story)

Actress:	Jane Fonda (Coming Home)
Nominations:	Geraldine Page (Interiors)
	Ellen Burstyn (Same Time, Next Year)
	Ingrid Bergman (Autumn Sonata)
	Jill Clayburgh (An Unmarried Woman)

Director:	Michael Cimino (The Deer Hunter)
Nominations:	Hal Ashby (Coming Home)
	Warren Beatty/Buck Henry (Heaven Can Wait)
	Alan Parker (Midnight Express)
	Woody Allen (Interiors)

Supporting Actor:	Christopher Walken (The Deer Hunter)
Nominations:	John Hurt (Midnight Express)
	Richard Farnsworth (Comes A Horseman)
	Jack Warden (Heaven Can Wait)
	Bruce Dern (Coming Home)

Supporting Actress:	Maggie Smith (California Suite)
Nominations:	Penelope Milford (Coming Home)
	Maureen Stapleton (Interiors)
	Meryl Streep (The Deer Hunter)
	Dyan Cannon (Heaven Can Wait)

Honorary Award:s	Laurence Olivier, King Vidor

Best Foreign Film:	Get Out Your Handkerchiefs (French)

Best Song:	Last Dance (Thank God It's Friday)
Nominations:	Hopelessly Devoted To You (Grease)
	Ready To Take A Chance Again (Foul Play)
	The Last Time I Felt Like This
	(Same Time, Next Year)
	When You're Loved (The Magic Of Lassie)

1979

Best Picture:	Kramer Vs. Kramer
Nominations:	All That Jazz, Breaking Away, Apocalypse Now,
	Norma Rae

Actor:	Dustin Hoffman (Kramer Vs. Kramer)
Nominations:	Roy Scheider (All That Jazz)
	Jack Lemmon (The China Syndrome)
	Peter Sellers (Being There)
	Al Pacino (...And Justice For All)

Actress:	Sally Field (Norma Rae)
Nominations:	Marsha Mason (Chapter Two)
	Jane Fonda (The China Syndrome)
	Bette Midler (The Rose)
	Jill Clayburgh (Starting Over)

Director:	Robert Benton (Kramer Vs. Kramer)
Nominations:	Bob Fosse (All That Jazz)
	Francis Ford Coppola (Apocalypse Now)
	Peter Yates (Breaking Away)
	Edouard Molinaro (La Cage Aux Folles)

Supporting Actor:	Melvyn Douglas (Being There)
Nominations:	Mickey Rooney (The Black Stallion)
	Robert Duvall (Apocalypse Now)
	Justin Henry (Kramer Vs. Kramer)
	Frederic Forrest (The Rose)

Supporting Actress:	Meryl Streep (Kramer Vs. Kramer)
Nominations:	Mariel Hemingway (Manhattan)
	Barbara Barrie (Breaking Away)
	Jane Alexander (Kramer Vs. Kramer)
	Candice Bergen (Starting Over)

Honorary Award:	Alec Guinness

Best Foreign Film:	The Tin Drum (German)

Best Song:	It Goes Like It Goes (Norma Rae)
Nominations:	It's Easy To Say (10)
	The Rainbow Connection (The Muppet Movie)
	Through The Eyes Of Love (Ice Castles)
	I'll Never Say Goodbye (The Promise)

1980

Best Picture:	Ordinary People
Nominations:	Coal Miner's Daughter, Tess, Raging Bull, The Elephant Man
Actor:	Robert De Niro (Raging Bull)
Nominations:	Peter O'Toole (The Stunt Man)
	Jack Lemmon (Tribute)
	John Hurt (The Elephant Man)
	Robert Duvall (The Great Santini)
Actress:	Sissy Spacek (Coal Miner's Daughter)
Nominations:	Goldie Hawn (Private Benjamin)
	Ellen Burstyn (Resurrection)
	Gena Rowlands (Gloria)
	Mary Tyler Moore (Ordinary People)
Director:	Robert Redford (Ordinary People)
Nominations:	Louis Malle (Atlantic City)
	David Lynch (The Elephant Man)
	Martin Scorsese (Raging Bull)
	Richard Rush (The Stunt Man)
	Roman Polanski (Tess)
Supporting Actor:	Timothy Hutton (Ordinary People)
Nominations:	Jason Robards (Melvin And Howard)
	Michael O'Keefe (The Great Santini)
	Joe Pesci (Raging Bull)
	Judd Hirsch (Ordinary People)
Supporting Actress:	Mary Steenburgen (Melvin And Howard)
Nominations:	Eileen Brennan (Private Benjamin)
	Diana Scarwid (Inside Moves)
	Cathy Moriarty (Raging Bull)
	Eva Le Gallienne (Resurrection)
Honorary Award:	Henry Fonda
Best Foreign Film:	Moscow Does Not Believe In Tears (Russian)
Best Song:	Fame (Fame)
Nominations:	Nive To Five (Nine To Five)
	On The Road Again (Honeysuckle Rose)
	People Alone (The Competition)
	Out Here On My Own (Fame)

1981

Best Picture:	Chariots Of Fire
Nominations:	On Golden Pond, Raiders Of The Lost Ark, Reds, Atlantic City
Actor:	Henry Fonda (On Golden Pond)
Nominations:	Paul Newman Absence Of Malice)
	Dudley Moore (Arthur)
	Warren Beatty (Reds)
	Burt Lancaster (Atlantic City)
Actress:	Katherine Hepburn (On Golden Pond)
Nominations:	Meryl Streep (The French Lieutenant's Woman)
	Diane Keaton (Reds)
	Marsha Mason (It Hurts Only When I Laugh)
	Susan Sarandon (Atlantic City)
Director:	Warren Beatty (Reds)
Nominations:	Hugh Hudson (Chariots Of Fire)
	Mark Rydell (On Golden Pond)
	Steven Spielberg (Raiders Of The Lost Ark)
	Louis Malle (Atlantic City)
Supporting Actor:	John Gielgud (Arthur)
Nominations:	Ian Holm (Chariots Of Fire)
	James Coco (It Hurts Only When I Laugh)
	Howard E. Rollins Jnr. (Ragtime)
	Jack Nicholson (Reds)
Supporting Actress:	Maureen Stapleton (Reds)
Nominations:	Jane Fonda (On Golden Pond)
	Melinda Dillon ((Absence Of Malice)
	Joan Hackett (It Hurts Only When I Laugh)
	Elizabeth McGovern (Ragtime)

Honorary Award:	Barbara Stanwyck
Best Foreign Film:	Mephisto (Hungary)
Best Song:	Best That You Can Do (Arthur)
Nominations:	For Your Eyes Only (For Your Eyes Only)
	One More Hour (Ragtime)
	The First Time It Happens (The Great Muppet Caper)
	Endless Love (Endless Love)

1982

Best Picture:	Gandhi
Nominations:	E.T., Missing, Tootsie, The Verdict
Actor:	Ben Kingsley (Gandhi)
Nominations:	Paul Newman (The Verdict)
	Dustin Hoffman (Tootsie)
	Jack Lemmon (Missing)
	Peter O'Toole (My Favorite Year)
Actress:	Meryl Streep (Sophie's Choice)
Nominations:	Jessica Lange (Frances)
	Debra Winger (An Officer And A Gentleman)
	Julie Andrews (Victor/Victoria)
	Sissy Spacek (Missing)
Director:	Richard Attenborough (Gandhi)
Nominations:	Steven Spielberg (E.T.)
	Sydney Pollack (Tootsie)
	Sidney Lumet (The Verdict)
	Wolfgang Petersen (Das Boot)
Supporting Actor:	Louis Gossett Jnr. (An Officer And A Gentleman)
Nominations:	Robert Preston (Victor/Victoria)
	John Lithgow (The World According To Garp)
	James Mason (The Verdict)
	Charles Durning (The Best Little Whorehouse In Texas)
Supporting Actress:	Jessica Lange (Tootsie)
Nominations:	Lesley Ann Warren (Victor/Victoria)
	Teri Garr (Tootsie)
	Glenn Close (The World According To Garp)
	Kim Stanley (Frances)
Honorary Award:	Mickey Rooney
Best Foreign Film:	Volver Empezar (Spanish)
Best Song:	Up Where We Belong (An Officer And A Gentleman)
Nominations:	How Do You Keep The Music Playing? (Best Friends)
	It Might Be You (Tootsie)
	Eye Of The Tiger (Rocky III)
	If We Were In Love (Yes, Giorgio)

1983

Best Picture:	Terms Of Endearment
Nominations:	Tender Mercies, The Dresser, The Big Chill, The Right Stuff
Actor:	Robert Duvall (Tender Mercies)
Nominations:	Albert Finney (The Dresser)
	Michael Caine (Educating Rita)
	Tom Courtenay (The Dresser)
	Tom Conti (Reuben, Reuben)
Actress:	Shirley MacLaine (Terms Of Endearment)
Nominations:	Julie Walters (Educating Rita)
	Meryl Streep (Silkwood)
	Debra Winger (Terms Of Endearment)
	Jane Alexander (Testament)
Director:	James L. Brooks (Terms Of Endearment)
Nominations:	Ingmar Bergman (Fanny And Alexander)
	Peter Yates (The Dresser)
	Mike Nichols (Silkwood)
	Bruce Beresford (Tender Mercies)

Supporting Actor:	Jack Nicholson (Terms Of Endearment)
Nominations:	Rip Torn (Cross Creek)
	Charles Durning (To Be Or Not To Be)
	Sam Shepard (The Right Stuff)
	John Lithgow (Terms Of Endearment)
Supporting Actress:	Linda Hunt (The Year Of Living Dangerously)
Nominations:	Glenn Close (The Big Chill)
	Alfre Woodard (Cross Creek)
	Cher (Silkwood)
	Amy Irving (Yentl)
Honorary Award:	Hal Roach
Best Foreign Film:	Fanny And Alexander (Swedish)
Best Song:	Flashdance, What A Feeling (Flashdance)
Nominations:	Papa, Can You Hear Me ? (Yentl)
	The Way He Makes Me Feel (Yentl)
	Maniac (Flashdance)
	Over You (Tender Mercies)

1984

Best Picture:	Amadeus
Nominations:	Places In The Heart, The Killing Fields,
	A Soldier's Story, Passage To India
Actor:	F. Murray Abraham (Amadeus)
Nominations:	Tom Hulce (Amadeus)
	Sam Waterston (The Killing Fields)
	Albert Finney (Under The Volcano)
	Jeff Bridges (Starman)
Actress:	Sally Field (Places In The Heart)
Nominations:	Jessica Lange (Country)
	Vanessa Redgrave (The Bostonians)
	Judy Davis (A Passage To India)
	Sissy Spacek (The River)
Director:	Milos Forman (Amadeus)
Nominations:	Robert Benton (Places In The Heart)
	Woody Allen (Broadway Danny Rose)
	David Lean (A Passage To India)
	Roland Joffe (The Killing Fields)
Supporting Actor:	Haing S. Ngor (The Killing Fields)
Nominations:	Pat Morita (The Karate Kid)
	Adolph Caesar (A Soldier's Story)
	Ralph Richardson (Greystoke)
	John Malkovich (Places In The Heart)
Supporting Actress:	Peggy Ashcroft (A Passage To India)
Nominations:	Geraldine Page (The Pope Of Greenwich Village)
	Glenn Close (The Natural)
	Lindsay Crouse (Places In The Heart)
	Christine Lahti (Swing Shift)
Honorary Award:	James Stewart
Best Foreign Film:	Dangerous Moves (Swiss)
Best Song:	I Just Called To Say I Love You (The Woman In Red)
Nominations:	Footloose (Footloose)
	Let's Hear It For The Boy (Footloose)
	Take A Look At Me Now (Against All Odds)
	Ghostbusters (Ghostbusters)

1985

Best Picture:	Out Of Africa
Nominations:	The Color Purple, Kiss Of The Spider Woman,
	Witness, Prizzi's Honor
Actor:	William Hurt (Kiss Of The Spider Woman)
Nominations:	Harrison Ford (Witness)
	Jon Voight (Runaway Train)
	James Garner (Murphy's Romance)
	Jack Nicholson (Prizzi's Honor)

Actress:	Geraldine Page (The Trip To Bountiful)
Nominations:	Whoopi Goldberg (The Color Purple)
	Meryl Streep (Out Of Africa)
	Anne Bancroft (Agnes Of God)
	Jessica Lange (Sweet Dreams)
Director:	Sydney Pollack (Out Of Africa)
Nominations:	John Huston (Prizzi's Honor)
	Hector Babenco (Kiss Of The Spider Woman)
	Peter Weir (Witness)
	Akiri Kurosawa (Ran)
Supporting Actor:	Don Ameche (Cocoon)
Nominations:	Klaus Maria Brandauer (Out Of Africa)
	Eric Roberts (Runaway Train)
	Robert Loggia (Jagged Edge)
	William Hickey (Prizzi's Honor)
Supporting Actress:	Anjelica Huston (Prizzi's Honor)
Nominations:	Oprah Winfrey (The Color Purple)
	Meg Tilly (Agnes Of God)
	Margaret Avery (The Color Purple)
	Amy Madigan (Twice In A Lifetime)
Honorary Award:	Paul Newman
Best Foreign Film:	The Official Story (Argentine)
Best Song:	Say You, Say Me (White Nights)
Nominations:	Miss Celie's Blues (The Color Purple)
	Separate Lives (White Nights)
	The Power Of Love (Back To The Future)
	Surprise, Surprise (A Chorus Line)

1986

Best Picture:	Platoon
Nominations:	Children Of A Lesser God, The Mission,
	A Room With A View, Hannah And Her Sisters
Actor:	Paul Newman (The Color Of Money)
Nominations:	Bob Hoskins (Mona Lisa)
	Dexter Gordon ('Round Midnight)
	William Hurt (Children Of A Lesser God)
	James Woods (Salvador)
Actress:	Marlee Matlin (Children Of A Lesser God)
Nominations:	Sigourney Weaver (Aliens)
	Kathleen Turner (Peggy Sue Got Married)
	Sissy Spacek (Crimes Of The Heart)
	Jane Fonda (The Morning After)
Director:	Oliver Stone (Platoon)
Nominations:	James Ivory (A Room With A View)
	David Lynch (Blue Velvet)
	Roland Joffe (The Mission)
	Woody Allen (Hannah And Her Sisters)
Supporting Actor:	Michael Caine (Hannah And Her Sisters)
Nominations:	Denholm Elliott (A Room With A View)
	Tom Berenger (Platoon)
	Dennis Hopper (Hoosiers)
	Willem Dafoe (Platoon)
Supporting Actress:	Dianne Wiest (Hannah And Her Sisters)
Nominations:	Piper Laurie (Children Of A Lesser God)
	Maggie Smith (A Room With A View)
	Mary Elizabeth Mastrantonio (The Color Of Money)
	Tess Harper (Crimes Of The Heart)
Honorary Award:	Ralph Bellamy
Best Foreign Film:	The Assault (Dutch)
Best Song:	Take My Breath Away (Top Gun)
Nominations:	Somewhere Out There (An American Tail)
	Glory Of Love (The Karate Kid II)
	Life In A Looking Glass (That's Life)
	Mean Green Mother From Outer Space
	(Little Shop Of Horror)

1987

Best Picture: The Last Emperor
Nominations: Moonstruck, Hope And Glory, Fatal Attraction, Broadcast News

Actor: Micahel Douglas (Wall Street)
Nominations: William Hurt (Broadcast News)
Robin Williams (Good Morning Vietnam)
Jack Nicholson (Ironweed)
Marcello Mastroianni (Dark Eyes)

Actress: Cher (Moonstruck)
Nominations: Holly Hunter (Broadcast News)
Glenn Close (Fatal Attraction)
Meryl Streep (Ironweed)
Sally Kirkland (Anna)

Director: Bernardo Bertolucci (The Last Emperor)
Nominations: Norman Jewison (Moonstruck)
Adrian Lyne (Fatal Attraction)
John Boorman (Hope And Glory)
Lasse Hallstrom (My Life As A Dog)

Supporting Actor: Sean Connery (The Untouchables)
Nominations: Vincent Gardenia (Moonstruck)
Albert Brooks (Broadcast News)
Morgan Freeman (Street Smart)
Denzel Washington (Cry Freedom)

Supporting Actress: Olympic Dukakis (Moonstruck)
Nominations: Anne Ramsey (Throw Momma From The Train)
Anne Archer (Fatal Attraction)
Ann Sothern (The Whales Of August)
Norma Aleandro (Gaby - A True Story)

Best Foreign Film: Babette's Feast (Danish)

Best Song: The Time Of My Life (Dirty Dancing)
Nominations: Shakedown (Beverly Hills Cop 2)
Nothing's Gonna Stop Us Now (Mannequin)
Cry Freedom (Cry Freedom)
Storybook Love (The Princess Bride)

1988

Best Picture: Rain Man
Nominations: Working Girl, The Accidental Tourist, Dangerous Liaisons Mississippi Burning

Actor: Dustin Hoffman (Rain Man)
Nominations: Tom Hanks (Big)
Edward James Olmos (Stand And Deliver)
Gene Hackman (Mississippi Burning)
Max Von Sydow (Pele The Conqueror)

Actress: Jodie Foster (The Accused)
Nominations: Melanie Griffith (Working Girl)
Sigourney Weaver (Gorillas In The Mist)
Glenn Close (Dangerous Liaisons)
Meryl Streep (A Cry In The Dark)

Director: Berry Levinson (Rain Man)
Nominations: Mike Nichols (Working Girl)
Alan Parker (Mississippi Burning)
Charles Crichton (A Fish Called Wanda)
Martin Scorsese (The Last Temptation Of Christ)

Supporting Actor: Kevin Kline (A Fish Called Wanda)
Nominations: Alec Guinness (Little Dorrit)
Dean Stockwell (Married To The Mob)
Martin Landau (Tucker, The Man And His Dream)
River Phoenix (Running On Empty)

Supporting Actress: Geena Davis (The Accidental Tourist)
Nominations: Sigourney Weaver (Working Girl)
Michelle Pfeiffer (Dangerous Liaisons)
Joan Cusack (Working Girl)
Frances McDormand (Mississippi Burning)

Best Foreign Film: Pele The Conqueror (Danish)

Best Song: Let The River Run (Working Girl)
Nominations: Two Hearts (Buster) Calling You (Bagdad Café)

1989

Best Picture: Driving Miss Daisy
Nominations: My Left Foot, Born On The Fourth Of July, Field Of Dreams, Dead Poets Society

Actor: Daniel Day-Lewis (My Left Foot)
Nominations: Tom Cruise (Born On The Fourth Of July)
Kenneth Branagh (Henry V)
Robin Williams (Dead Poets Society)
Morgan Freeman (Driving Miss Daisy)

Actress: Jessica Tandy (Driving Miss Daisy)
Nominations: Michelle Pfeiffer (The Fabulous Baker Boys)
Jessica Lange (Music Box)
Pauline Collins (Shirley Valentine)
Isabelle Adjani (Camille Claudel)

Director: Oliver Stone (Born On The Fourth Of July)
Nominations: Jim Sheridan (My Left Foot)
Woody Allen (Crimes And Misdemeanours)
Kenneth Branagh (Henry V)
Peter Weir (Dead Poets Society)

Supporting Actor: Denzel Washington (Glory)
Nominations: Danny Aiello (Do The Right Thing)
Martin Landau (Crimes And Misdemeanours)
Marlon Brando (A Dry White Season)
Dan Aykroyd (Driving Miss Daisy)

Supporting Actress: Brenda Fricker (My Left Foot)
Nominations: Julia Roberts (Steel Magnolias)
Anjelica Huston (Enemies, A Love Story)
Dianne Wiest (Parenthood)
Lena Olin (Enemies, A Love Story)

Best Foreign Film: Cinema Paradiso (Italian)

Best Song: Under The Sea (The Little Mermaid)
Nominations: The Girl Who Used To Be Me (Shirley Valentine)
Kiss The Girl (The Little Mermaid)
I Love To See You Smile (Parenthood)
After All (Chances Are)

1990

Best Picture: Dances With Wolves
Nominations: Ghost, Awakenings, The Godfather Part III, Goodfellas

Actor: Jeremy Irons (Reversal Of Fortune)
Nominations: Kevin Costner (Dances With Wolves)
Robert De Niro (Awakenings)
Gerard Depardieu (Cyrano De Bergerac)
Richard Harris (The Field)

Actress: Kathy Bates (Misery)
Nominations: Meryl Streep (Postcards From The Edge)
Julie Roberts (Pretty Woman)
Anjelica Huston (The Grifters)
Joanne Woodward (Mr And Mrs Bridge)

Director: Kevin Costner (Dances With Wolves)
Nominations: Martin Scorsese (Goodfellas)
Frances Ford Coppola (The Godfather Part III)
Stephen Frears (The Grifters)
Barbet Schroeder (Reversal Of Fortune)

Supporting Actor: Joe Pesci (Goodfellas)
Nominations: Graham Greene (Dances With Wolves)
Al Pacino (Dick Tracy)
Bruce Davison (Longtime Companion)
Andy Garcia (The Godfather Part III)

Supporting Actress: Whoopi Goldberg (Ghost)
Nominations: Annette Bening (The Grifters)
Diane Ladd (Wild At Heart)
Lorraine Bracco (Goodfellas)
Mary McDonnell (Dances With Wolves)

*Honorary Award:*s	Sophia Loren, Myrna Loy
Best Foreign Film:	Journey Of Hope (Swiss)
Best Song:	Sooner Or Later (Dick Tracy)
Nominations:	I'm Checking Out (Postcards From The Edge)
	Blaze Of Glory (Young Guns II)
	Promise Me You'll Remember
	(The Godfather Part III)
	Somewhere In My Memory (Home Alone)

1991

Best Picture:	The Silence Of The Lambs
Nominations:	Beauty And The Beast, The Prince Of Tides, Bugsy, J.F.K.
Actor:	Anthony Hopkins (The Silence Of The Lambs)
Nominations:	Nick Nolte (The Prince Of Tides)
	Warren Beatty (Bugsy)
	Robert De Niro (Cape Fear)
	Robin Williams (The Fisher King)
Actress:	Jodie Foster (The Silence Of The Lambs)
Nominations:	Geena Davis (Thelma And Louise)
	Laura Dern (Rambling Rose)
	Susan Sarandon (Thelma And Louise)
	Bette Midler (For The Boys)
Director:	Jonathan Demme (The Silence Of The Lambs)
Nominations:	Ridley Scott (Thelma And Louise)
	Oliver Stone (J.F.K.)
	Barry Levinson (Bugsy)
	John Singleton (Boyz N The Hood)
Supporting Actor:	Jack Palance (City Slickers)
Nominations:	Harvey Keitel (Bugsy)
	Tommy Lee Jones (J.F.K.)
	Ben Kingsley (Bugsy)
	Michael Lerner (Barton Fink)
Supporting Actress:	Mercedes Ruehl (The Fisher King)
Nominations:	Diane Ladd (Rambling Rose)
	Juliette Lewis (Cape Fear)
	Jessica Tandy (Fried Green Tomatoes)
	Kate Nelligan (The Prince Of Tides)
Best Foreign Film:	Mediterraneo (Italian)
Best Song:	Beauty And The Beast (Beauty And The Beast)
Nominations:	Everything I Do; I Do It For You
	(Robin Hood, Prince Of Thieves)
	When You're Alone (Hook)
	Belle (Beauty And The Beast)
	Be Our Guest (Beauty And The Beast)

1992

Best Picture:	Unforgiven
Nominations:	The Crying Game, Scent Of A Woman, A Few Good Men, Howard's End
Actor:	Al Pacino (Scent Of A Woman)
Nominations:	Robert Downey Jnr. (Chaplin)
	Stephen Rea (The Crying Game)
	Clint Eastwood (Unforgiven)
	Denzel Washington (Malcolm X)
Actress:	Emma Thompson (Howard's End)
Nominations:	Michelle Pfeiffer (Love Field)
	Susan Sarandon (Lorenzo's Oil)
	Mary McDonnell (Passion Fish)
	Catherine Deneuve (Indochine)
Director:	Clint Eastwood (Unforgiven)
Nominations:	Robert Altman (The Player)
	Neil Jordan (The Crying Game)
	James Ivory (Howard's End)
	Martin Brest (Scent Of A Woman)

Supporting Actor:	Gene Hackman (Unforgiven)
Nominations:	Al Pacino (Glengarry Glenn Ross)
	Jack Nicholson (A Few Good Men)
	David Paymer (Mr Saturday Night)
	Jaye Davidson (The Crying Game)
Supporting Actress:	Marisa Tomei (My Cousin Vinny)
Nominations:	Miranda Richardson (Damage)
	Vanessa Redgrave (Howard's End)
	Joan Plowright (Enchanted April)
	Judy Davis (Husbands And Wives)
Honorary Award:	Federico Fellini
Best Foreign Film:	Indochine (French)
Best Song:	A Whole New World (Aladdin)
Nominations:	I Have Nothing (The Bodyguard)
	Friends Like Me (Aladdin)
	Run To You (The Bodyguard)
	Beautiful Maria Of My Soul (The Mambo Kings)

1993

Best Picture:	Schindler's List
Nominations:	The Piano, The Fugitive, In The Name Of The Father, The Remains Of The Day
Actor:	Tom Hanks (Philadelphia)
Nominations:	Liam Neeson (Schindler's List)
	Daniel Day-Lewis (In The Name Of The Father)
	Anthony Hopkins (The Remains Of The Day)
	Laurence Fishburne (What's Love Got To Do With It?)
Actress:	Holly Hunter (The Piano)
Nominations:	Emma Thompson (The Remains Of The Day)
	Debra Winger (Shadowlands)
	Angela Bassett (What's Love Got To Do With It?)
	Stockard Channing (Six Degrees Of Separation)
Director:	Steven Spielberg (Schindler's List)
Nominations:	Robert Altman (Short Cuts)
	Jim Sheridan (In The Name Of The Father)
	Jane Campion (The Piano)
	James Ivory (The Remains Of The Day)
Supporting Actor:	Tommy Lee Jones (The Fugitive)
Nominations:	John Malkovich (In The Line Of Fire)
	Ralph Fiennes (Schindler's List)
	Pete Postlethwaite (In The Name Of The Father)
	Leonardo Di Caprio (What's Eating Gilbert Grapes?)
Supporting Actress:	Anna Paquin (The Piano)
Nominations:	Holly Hunter (The Firm)
	Emma Thompson (In The Name Of The Father)
	Rosie Perez (Fearless)
	Winona Ryder (The Age Of Innocence)
Honorary Award:	Deborah Kerr
Best Foreign Film:	Belle Epoque (Spanish)
Best Song:	Streets Of Philadelphia (Philadelphia)
Nominations:	A Wink And A Smile (Sleepless In Seattle)
	Philadelphia (Philadelphia)
	The Day I Fall In Love (Beethoven's Second)
	Again (Poetic Justice)

1994

Best Picture:	Forrest Gump
Nominations:	Four Weddings And A Funeral, Pulp Fiction, Quiz Show, The Shawshank Redemption
Actor:	Tom Hanks (Forrest Gump)
Nominations:	Nigel Hawthorne (The Madness Of King George)
	John Travolta (Pulp Fiction)
	Morgan Freeman (The Shawshank Redemption)
	Paul Newman (Nobody's Fool)
Actress:	Jessica Lange (Blue Sky)
Nominations:	Jodie Foster (Nell)
	Susan Sarandon (The Client)
	Miranda Richardson (Tom & Viv)
	Winona Ryder (Little Women)

Director:	Robert Zemeckis (Forrest Gump)
Nominations:	Woody Allen (Bullets Over Broadway)
	Robert Redford (Quiz Show)
	Quentin Tarantino (Pulp Fiction)
	Krzysztof Kieslowski (Red)

Supporting Actor:	Martin Landau (Ed Wood)
Nominations:	Gary Sinise (Forrest Gump)
	Paul Scofield (Quiz Show)
	Samuel L. Jackson (Pulp Ficition)
	Chazz Palminteri (Bullets Over Broadway)

Supporting Actress:	Dianne Wiest (Bullets Over Broadway)
Nominations:	Uma Thurman (Pulp Fiction)
	Rosemary Harris (Tom & Viv)
	Helen Mirren (The Madness Of King George)
	Jennifer Tilly (Bullets Over Broadway)

| Honorary Award: | Michaelangelo Antonioni |

| Best Foreign Film: | Burnt By The Sun (Russian) |

Best Song:	Can You Feel The Love Tonight (The Lion King)
Nominations:	Circle Of Life (The Lion King)
	Look What Love Has Done (Junior)
	Hakuna Matata (The Lion King)
	Make Up Your Mind (The Paper)

1995

| Best Picture: | Braveheart |
| Nominations: | Apollo 13, Babe, Il Postino, Sense And Sensibility |

Actor:	Nicolas Cage (Leaving Las Vegas)
Nominations:	Anthony Hopkins (Nixon)
	Massimo Troisi (Il Postino)
	Sean Penn (Dead Man Walking)
	Richard Dreyfuss (Mr Holland's Opus)

Actress:	Susan Sarandon (Dead Man Walking)
Nominations:	Emma Thompson (Sense And Sensibility)
	Sharon Stone (Casino)
	Elizabeth Shue (Leaving Las Vegas)
	Meryl Streep (The Bridges Of Madison County)

Director:	Mel Gibson (Braveheart)
Nominations:	Tim Robbins (Dead Man Walking)
	Chris Noonan (Babe)
	Michael Radford (Il Postino)
	Mike Figgis (Leaving Las Vegas)

Supporting Actor:	Kevin Spacey (The Usual Suspects)
Nominations:	Tim Roth (Rob Roy)
	Ed Harris (Apollo 13)
	Brad Pitt (12 Monkeys)
	James Cromwell (Babe)

Supporting Actress:	Mira Sorvino (Mighty Aphrodite)
Nominations:	Kate Winslet (Sense And Sensibility)
	Kathleen Quinlan (Apollo 13)
	Joan Allen (Nixon)
	Mare Winningham (Georgia)

| Honorary Awards: | Kirk Douglas, Chuck Jones |

| Best Foreign Film: | Antonia's Line (Dutch) |

Best Song:	Colors Of The Wind (Pocahontas)
Nominations:	Dead Man Walkin' (Dead Man Walking)
	Moonlight (Sabrina)
	Have You Ever Really Loved A Woman
	(Don Juan Demarco)
	You've Got A Friend In Me (Toy Story)

1996

| Best Picture: | The English Patient |
| Nominations: | Secrets And Lies, Jerry Maguire, Shine, Fargo |

Actor:	Geoffrey Rush (Shine)
Nominations:	Ralph Fiennes (The English Patient)
	Tom Cruise (Jerry Maguire)
	Woody Harrelson (The People Vs. Larry Flynt)
	Billy Bob Thornton (Sling Blade)

Actress:	Frances McDormand (Fargo)
Nominations:	Brenda Blethyn (Secrets And Lies)
	Kristen Scott-Thomas (The English Patient)
	Emily Watson (Breaking The Waves)
	Diane Keaton (Marvin's Room)

Director:	Anthony Minghella (The English Patient)
Nominations:	Joel Coen (Fargo)
	Scott Hicks (Shine)
	Milos Forman (The People Vs. Larry Flynt)
	Mike Leigh (Secrets And Lies)

Supporting Actor:	Cuba Gooding Jnr. (Jerry Maguire)
Nominations:	James Woods (Ghosts Of Mississippi)
	William H. Macy (Fargo)
	Armin Mueller-Stahl (Shine)
	Edward Norton (Primal Fear)

Supporting Actress:	Juliette Binoche (The English Patient)
Nominations:	Marianne Jean-Baptiste (Secrets And Lies)
	Joan Allen (The Crucible)
	Lauren Bacall (The Mirror Has Two Faces)
	Barbara Hershey (The Portrait Of A Lady)

| Honorary Award: | Michael Kidd |

| Best Foreign Film: | Kolya (Czech) |

Best Song:	You Must Love Me (Evita)
Nominations:	Because You Loved Me (Up Close And Personal)
	For The First Time (One Fine Day)
	I Finally Found Someone (The Mirror Has Two Faces)
	That Thing You Do ! (That Thing You Do !)

1997

Best Picture:	Titanic
Nominations:	L.A. Confidential, As Good As It Gets,
	The Full Monty, Good Will Hunting

Actor:	Jack Nicholson (As Good As It Gets)
Nominations:	Matt Damon (Good Will Hunting)
	Robert Duvall (The Apostle)
	Peter Fonda (Ulee's Gold)
	Dustin Hoffman (Wag The Dog)

Actress:	Helen Hunt (As Good As It Gets)
Nominations:	Kate Winslet (Titanic)
	Helena Bonham-Carter (The Wings Of The Dove)
	Julie Christie (Afterglow)
	Judi Dench (Mrs Brown)

Director:	James Cameron (Titanic)
Nominations:	Gus Van Sant (Good Will Hunting)
	Curtis Hanson (L.A. Confidential)
	Atom Egoyan (The Sweet Hereafter)
	Peter Cattaneo (The Full Monty)

Supporting Actor:	Robin Williams (Good Will Hunting)
Nominations:	Robert Forster (Jackie Brown)
	Burt Reynolds (Boogie Nights)
	Anthony Hopkins (Amistad)
	Greg Kinnear (As Good As It Gets)

Supporting Actress:	Kim Basinger (L.A. Confidential)
Nominations:	Minnie Driver (Good Will Hunting)
	Joan Cusack (In And Out)
	Gloria Stuart (Titanic)
	Julianne Moore (Boogie Nights)

| Honorary Award: | Stanley Donen |

| Best Foreign Film: | Character (Dutch) |

Best Song:	My Heart Will Go On (Titanic)
Nominations:	Go The Distance (Hercules)
	How Do I Live (Con Air)
	Journey To The Past (Anastasia)
	Miss Misery (Good Will Hunting)

STUDIOS AND STARS

WARNER BROTHERS

Bette Davis	52 Films	Loretta Young	17 Films
Joan Blondell	43 Films	Doris Day	17 Films
Glenda Farrell	42 Films	Eleanor Parker	16 Films
Jane Wyman	36 Films	Priscilla Lane	16 Films
Ann Sheridan	35 Films	Claire Dodd	15 Films
Margaret Lindsay	28 Films	Joan Leslie	15 Films
Olivia De Havilland	25 Films	Jean Muir	14 Films
Virginia Mayo	24 Films	Jane Bryan	14 Films
Kay Francis	22 Films	Gale Page	13 Films
Alexis Smith	22 Films	Ruth Roman	12 Films
Ruth Donnelly	20 Films	Janis Paige	12 Films
Ann Dvorak	19 Films		

COLUMBIA

Rita Hayworth	22 Films	Janis Carter	14 Films
Jean Arthur	17 Films	Marguerite Chapman	13 Films
Evelyn Keyes	17 Films	Kim Novak	11 Films
Nina Foch	15 Films	Grace Moore	5 Films
Jeff Donnell	15 Films		

METRO-GOLDWYN-MAYER

Joan Crawford	46 Films	Ava Gardner	17 Films
Maureen O'Sullivan	33 Films	Kathryn Grayson	17 Films
Myrna Loy	31 Films	Jeanette MacDonald	17 Films
Lana Turner	31 Films	Rosalind Russell	17 Films
Judy Garland	28 Films	Marion Davies	16 Films
June Allyson	25 Films	Janet Leigh	16 Films
Greta Garbo	24 Films	Margaret O'Brien	16 Films
Elizabeth Taylor	24 Films	Jean Harlow	16 Films
Norma Shearer	23 Films	Marie Dressler	15 Films
Madge Evans	23 Films	Debbie Reynolds	15 Films
Greer Garson	20 Films	Jane Powell	13 Films
Esther Williams	20 Films	Jean Hagan	13 Films
Ann Sothern	19 Films	Gloria De Haven	13 Films
Cecilia Parker	19 Films	Hedy Lamarr	12 Films
Cyd Charisse	18 Films	Katherine Hepburn	11 Films
Laraine Day	18 Films	Leslie Caron	10 Films

REPUBLIC

Vera Ralston	21 Films

PARAMOUNT

Dorothy Lamour	37 Films	Martha Raye	14 Films
Claudette Colbert	32 Films	Sylvia Sidney	13 Films
Carole Lombard	20 Films	Gracie Allen	12 Films
Ellen Drew	17 Films	Frances Dee	11 Films
Nancy Carroll	16 Films	Diana Lynn	11 Films
Betty Hutton	16 Films	Mona Freeman	10 Films
Veronica Lake	16 Films	Mae West	10 Films
Kay Francis	14 Films	Joan Caulfield	10 Films

R.K.O.

Ginger Rogers	25 Films	Katherine Hepburn	14 Films
Lucille Ball	25 Films	Edna May Oliver	12 Films
Ann Shirley	20 Films	Joan Fontaine	10 Films
Irene Dunne	17 Films		

20TH CENTURY FOX

Lynn Bari	33 Films	Jeanne Crain	22 Films
Alice Faye	31 Films	Anne Baxter	21 Films
Linda Darnell	28 Films	Joan Davis	19 Films
Betty Grable	27 Films	Jean Peters	18 Films
Gene Tierney	26 Films	Marilyn Monroe	18 Films
Jane Withers	24 Films	Debra Paget	14 Films
Claire Trevor	23 Films	Sally Eilers	12 Films
Loretta Young	23 Films	Carmen Miranda	10 Films
Shirley Temple	22 Films	Vivian Blaine	10 Films
Janet Gaynor	22 Films	Sonja Henie	9 Films

UNIVERSAL

Ann Gwynne	22 Films	Yvonne De Carlo	15 Films
Evelyn Ankers	21 Films	Maria Montez	15 Films
Deanna Durbin	20 Films	Piper Laurie	12 Films
Ann Blyth	16 Films		

CO-STAR SEQUENCES

Penny Singleton & Arthur Lake ....27 Films	Marjorie Main & Percy Kilbride ....7 Films
Myrna Loy & William Powell....................................14 Films	Claudette Colbert & Fred MacMurray ....7 Films
Gracie Allen & George Burns ....14 Films	Alice Faye & Don Ameche..6 Films
Janet Gaynor & Charles Farrell..................................12 Films	Laraine Day & Lew Ayres...6 Films
Mae Busch & Laurel & Hardy ....11 Films	Sondra Locke & Clint Eastwood................................6 Films
Jill Ireland & Charles Bronson ....11 Films	Maria Montez & Jon Hall ....6 Films
Ginger Rodgers & Fred Astaire ....10 Films	Jessica Tandy & Hume Cronyn..................................6 Films
Dorothy Lamour & Bob Hope ....10 Films	Anna Neagle & Michael Wilding ....6 Films
Peggy Ryan & Donald O'Connor ....10 Films	Maureen O'Sullivan & Johnny Weismuller...................6 Films
Elizabeth Taylor & Richard Burton.............................10 Films	Googie Withers & John McCallum..............................6 Films
Joanne Woodward & Paul Newman ....10 Films	Spring Byington & Jed Prouty ....6 Films
Bette Davie & George Brent.....................................10 Films	Myrna Loy & Clark Gable...6 Films
Judy Garland & Mickey Rooney.................................9 Films	Kay Francis & William Powell ....5 Films
Glenda Farrell & Barton MacLane ....9 Films	Kay Francis & George Brent ....5 Films
Katherine Hepburn & Spencer Tracy ....8 Films	Jean Harlow & Clark Gable.......................................5 Films
Jeanette MacDonald & Nelson Eddy ....8 Films	Kathleen Harrison & Jack Warner ....5 Films
Joan Blondell & Dick Powell ....8 Films	Virginia Mayo & Danny Kaye ....5 Films
Joan Crawford & Clark Gable ....8 Films	Maureen O'Hara & John Wayne.................................5 Films
Cicely Courtneidge & Jack Hulbert ....8 Films	Loretta Young & Tyrone Power ....5 Films
Olivia De Havilland & Errol Flynn ....7 Films	Doris Day & Gordon MacRae ....5 Films
Greer Garson & Walter Pidgeon.................................7 Films	Jane Wyman & Dennis Morgan..................................5 Films
Elsa Lanchester & Charles Laughton ....7 Films	Joan Blondell & James Cagney...................................5 Films

CHILD STARS *(With First Film)*

Jenny Agutter	East Of Sudan
Anna Maria Alberghetti	The Medium
Mikki Allen	Regarding Henry
Genevieve Ambas	The Little Ark
June Archer	Innocent Sinners
Nadene Ashdown	The Bridges At Toko-Ri
Emily Ashton	Oranges Are Not The Only Fruit
Mary Badham	To Kill A Mocking Bird (Nomination)
Fairusa Balk	Return To Oz
Karen Balkin	The Children's Hour
Drew Barrymore	Bogie
Mischa Barton	Lawn Dogs
Kathryn Beaumont	Alice In Wonderland
Linda Bennett	The Seven Little Foys
Mayim Bialik	Beaches
Thora Birch	Paradise
Linda Blair	The Exorcist (Nomination)
Imogen Boorman	Dream Child
Katrine Boorman	Dream One
Kara Bowman	Henri
Sarah Boyd	Old Enough
Joan Breslau	In Person
Betty Brewer	Mrs Wiggs Of The Cabbage Patch
Karis Paige Bryant	While Justice Sleeps
Amelia Burnette	Winter People
Olivia Burnette	Hard Promises
Terry Burnham	Imitation Of Life
Donna Butterworth	The Family Jewels
Adrienne Byrne	Mischief
Marsha Byrne	Anna To The Infinite Power
Laurie Cardwell	The Sand Castle
Joan Carroll	Primrose Path
Ann Carter	North Star
Juliette Caton	Courage Mountain
Joan Chandler	Stallion Road
Anna Chlumsky	My Girl
Petula Clark	Medal For The General
Cora Sue Collins	Two Sinners
Gia Coppola	New York Stories
Sophia Coppola	Peggy Sue Got Married
Donna Corcoran	Million Dollar Mermaid
Jeni Courtney	The Secret Of Roan Innish
Joy Creel	Parent Trap III
Leanna Creel	Parent Trap III
Monica Creel	Parent Trap III
Quinn Cummings	The Goodbye Girl (Nomination)
Cathryn Damon	Not In Front Of The Children
Irene Dare	Everything's On Ice
Gemma Darlington	Loving Hazel
Sugar Dawn	Lone Star Law Men
Catherine Demongeot	Zazie Dans La Metro
Sandy Descher	The Opposite Sex
Mary Elinor Donahue	Three Daring Daughters
Sarah Rowland Doroff	Three Fugitives
Karen Dotrice	The Three Lives Of Thomasina
Joan Dowling	Hue And Cry
Leslie Dudley	John And Julie
Deanna Durbin	Every Sunday
Eliza Dushku	That Night
Jennifer Edwards	Heidi
Rebecca Edwards	God On The Rocks
Paulette Elambert	La Maternelle
Janina Faye	The Adventures Of Hal 5
Edith Fellows	Mrs Wiggs Of The Cabbage Patch
Jan Ford	The Devil On Wheels
Sally Forlong	Hijack !
Brigitte Fossey	Forbidden Games
Jodie Foster	Tom Sawyer
Missy Francis	Man, Woman And Child
Pamela Franklin	The Lion
Shelagh Fraser	Master Of Bankdam
Mona Freeman	Junior Miss
Soleil Moon Frye	You Ruined My Life
Fiona Fullerton	Run Wild, Run Free
Annette Funicello	The Shaggy Dog
Judy Garland	Every Sunday
Peggy Ann Garner	Blondie Brings Up Baby
Sara Gilbert	Sudie And Simpson
Patricia Gozzi	Sundays And Cybele
Bonita Granville	These Three
Kerri Green	The Goonies
Mitzi Green	Finn And Hattie
Nona Griffith	The Unseen
Karolyn Grimes	The Private Affairs Of Bel Ami
Denise Gyngell	The Zoo Robbery
Diana Hale	The Good Fellows
Brit Hathaway	Fires Within
Charlotte Hughes Haywood	The Nun And The Bandit
Elizabeth Harnois	One Magic Christmas
Zelda Harris	Crooklyn
Katherine Healy	Six Weeks
Love Hewitt	Little Miss Millions
Mara Hobel	Mommie Dearest
Gaby Hoffman	Uncle Buck
Sally Ann Howes	Thursday's Child
Sherry Jackson	Trouble Along The Way
Gennie James	Places In The Heart
Eileen Janssen	The Adventures Of Curly And His Gang
Sybil Jason	Little Big Shot
Gloria Jean	The Underpup
Glynis Johns	South Riding
Marcia Mae Jones	These Three
Grace Jones	Beaches
Kym Karath	The Sound Of Music

CHILD STARS (With First Film)

Patsy Kensit	The Blue Bird
Marjorie Kent	Leave It To Blondie
Marie Kleiber	Le Petit Prince A Dit
Marilyn Knowlden	David Copperfield
Vivian Kubrick	2001:A Space Odyssey
Tito Larriva	The Tender
Fanny Lauzier	The Tadpole And The Whale
Carolyn Lee	Mrs Wiggs Of The Cabbage Patch
Marcie Leeds	Beaches
Sunniva Lindekleiv	Little Ida
Cheryl Lynn	The Bridges At Toko-Ri
Diana Lynn (Dolly Loehr)	There's Magic In Music
Kate Maberley	The Secret Garden
Tina Majorino	When A Man Loves A Woman
Sally Anne Marlow	Wreck Raisers
Kellie Martin	Secret Witness
Marie Martin	Little Girl Lost
Johdi May	A World Apart
Meg Mazursky	Alex In Wonderland
Andrea McArdle	Rainbow
Patty McCormack	The Bad Seed (Nomination)
Arleen McIntyre	Man, Woman And Child
Stephanie McFadden	Love Field
Kay Meersman	The Young One
Heather Menzies	The Sound Of Music
Melissa Michaelson	Goldie And The Boxer
Mandy Miller	MAN IN THE WHITE SUIT ...Mandy
Hayley Mills	Tiger Bay
Megan Milner	Look Who's Talking Too
Liza Minnelli	In The Good Old Summertime
Sharyn Moffett	The Falcon In San Francisco
Kristen Morgan	My Wild Irish Rose
Jenny Morrison	Intersection
Kim Myers	A Nightmare On Elm Street II
Portia Nelson	The Sound Of Music
Sophie Neville	Swallows And Amazons
Margaret O'Brien	Journey For Margaret
Cindy O'Callaghan	Bedknobs And Broomsticks
Tatum O'Neal	Paper Moon (Oscar)
Heather O'Rourke	Poltergeist
Park Overall	House Of Cards
Anna Paquin	The Piano (Oscar)
Lindsay Parker	Flowers In The Attic
Noelle Parker	Ernest Saves Christmas
Loretta Parry	Hand In Hand
Kimberly Partridge	Better Late Than Never
Luana Patten	Song Of The South
Tracey Peel	Hijack !
Ashley Peldon	Drop Dead Fred
Dena Penn	Days Of Glory
Sydney Penny	Pale Rider
Gigi Perreau	The Master Race
Martha Plimpton	The River Rat
Alisan Porter	Curly Sue
Nathalie Portman	Leon
Sally Prager	The Hideaways
June Preisser	Babes In Arms
Keshia Knight Pulliam	Polly
Cindy Putnam	The Russians Are Coming ! The Russians Are Coming !
Juanita Quigley	The Man Who Reclaimed His Head
Aileen Quinn	Annie
Elie Raab	The Fabulous Baker Boys
Lexi Randall	Sarah, Plain And Tall
Helen Raye	Flight Of The Doves
Lydia Reed	The Seven Little Foys
Christina Ricci	Mermaids
Ariana Richards	Prancer
Kim Richards	Escape To Witch Mountain
Lesley Roach	Mr Horatio Knibbles
Betsy King Ross	Smoke Lightning
Evelyn Rudie	The Gift Of Love
Jacquelin Ryan	Jacqueline
Clare Sandars	Mrs Miniver
Ivyann Schwan	Parenthood
Janette Scott	No Place For Jennifer
Laura Sears	Slumberland
Dorothy Seese	Five Little Peppers And How They Grew
Pamela Segall	The Leftovers
Glenna Sergent	Alex In Wonderland
Brooke Shields	Pretty Baby
Anne Shirley (Dawn O'Day)	The Man Who Fights Alone
Elsbeth Sigmund	Heidi
Beverley Simmons	Frontier Gal
Jean Simmons	The Way To The Stars
Eva Marie Singhammer	Heidi
Rebecca Smart	Celia
Wanda Spell	They Call Me Mister Tibbs !
Susan Stranks	The Blue Lagoon
Binkie Stuart	Keep Your Seats Please
Randy Stuart	Sitting Pretty
Susan Swift	Audrey Rose
Elizabeth Taylor	Lassie Come Home
Shirley Temple	Stand Up And Cheer
Victoria Thivisol	Ponette
Mary Thomas	Mrs Wiggs Of The Cabbage Patch
Sally Thomsett	The Railway Children
Ann E. Todd	All This And Heaven Too
Nicholle Tom	Beethoven
Ana Torrent	The Spirit Of The Beehive
Christina Vidal	Give Me A Break
Asia Vieira	The Price Of Passion
Sally Walsh	The Old Curiosity Shop
Linda Ware	The Star Maker
Virginia Weidler	Mrs Wiggs Of The Cabbage Patch

CHILD STARS *(With First Film)*

Robin Weisman...Three Men And A Little Lady

Brittany White...Mr Mom

Courtney White..Mr Mom

Lynne White...What Next ?

Claire Wilcox...Forty Pounds Of Trouble

Rumer Willis...Striptease

Dana Wilson...The Shiralee

Mara Wilson...Mrs Doubtfire

Jane Withers...Bright Eyes

Reese Witherspoon..Wildflower

Edna May Wonacott...Shadow Of A Doubt

Natalie Wood...Happy Land

Emily Woof...Photographing Fairies

Sarita Wooten..Wuthering Heights

Whittni Wright..I'll Do Anything

Roxana Zal...Table For Five

Madeline Zima..................................The Hand That Rocks The Cradle

Vanessa Zima..Ulee's Gold

Special Awards Were Given To:

Shirley Temple ....(1934)

Deanna Durbin ....(1938)

Judy Garland ....(1939)

Peggy Ann Garner ....(1945)

Hayley Mills ....(1960)

Margaret O'Brien ....(1944)

ACTRESSES DIRECTED BY HUSBANDS OR PARTNERS

Alice Terry	Rex Ingram	Bo Derek	John Derek
Eleanor Boardman	King Vidor	Nanette Newman	Bryan Forbes
Elizabeth Bergner	Paul Czinner	Brigitte Bardot	Roger Vadim
Gracie Fields	Monty Banks	Jane Fonda	Roger Vadim
Jessie Matthews	Sonnie Hale	Diane Keaton	Woody Allen
Anna Neagle	Herbert Wilcox	Mia Farrow	Woody Allen
Paulette Goddard	Charles Chaplin	Julie Andrews	Blake Edwards
Ann Dvorak	Leslie Fenton	Sharon Tate	Roman Polanski
Maureen O'Sullivan	John Farrow	Joan Plowright	Laurence Olivier
Judy Garland	Vincente Minnelli	Sondra Locke	Clint Eastwood
Ingrid Bergman	Roberto Rossellini	Alison Steadman	Mike Leigh
Gloria Grahame	Nicholas Ray	Jessica Lange	Sam Shepard
Ann Todd	David Lean	Sarah Miles	Robert Bolt
Patricia Knight	Cornel Wilde	Theresa Russell	Nicolas Roeg
Jean Wallace	Cornel Wilde	Kate Capshaw	Steven Spielberg
Francoise Rosay	Jacques Feyder	Jean Simmons	Richard Brooks
Stephane Audran	Claude Chabrol	Karla De Vito	Robby Benson
Giulietta Masina	Federico Fellini	Yolande Donlan	Val Guest
Melina Mercouri	Jules Dassin	Christine Lahti	Thomas Schlamme
Anna Karina	Jean-Luc Godard	Emma Thompson	Kenneth Branagh
Gena Rowlands	John Cassavetes	Geena Davis	Renny Harlin
Anne Bancroft	Mel Brooks	Imogen Stubbs	Trevor Nunn
Ursula Andress	John Derek	Nancy Allen	Brian De Palma

ACTRESSES WITH SPECIAL AFFINITY WITH DIRECTORS

Marlene Dietrich	Josef Von Sternberg	Naima Wifstrand	Ingmar Bergman
Bibi Anderson	Ingmar Bergman	Liv Ullman	Ingmar Bergman
Harriet Andersson	Ingmar Bergman	Sylvia Sidney	Marion Gering
Eva Dahlbeck	Ingmar Bergman	Shelley Duvall	Robert Altman
Ingrid Thulin	Ingmar Bergman	Carmen Maura	Pedro Almodovar

ACTRESSES WHO MARRIED STUDIO HEADS OR EXECUTIVES

Norma Shearer	Irving Thalberg	Vera Ralston	Herbert Yates
Jean Peters	Howard Hughes	Billie Burke	Florenz Ziegfeld
Jennifer Jones	David O. Selznick	Martha Hyer	Hal Wallis

ACTRESSES ACTING WITH HUSBANDS OR PARTNERS

Florence Arliss	George Arliss	Joan Blondell	Dick Powell
Cicely Courtneidge	Jack Hulbert	Pamela Kellino	James Mason
Natalie Talmadge	Buster Keaton	Edna Best	Herbert Marshall
Gracie Allen	George Burns	Vivien Leigh	Laurence Olivier
Elsie Randolph	Jack Buchanan	Joan Plowright	Laurence Olivier
Mary Pickford	Douglas Fairbanks	Helen Cherry	Trevor Howard
Janet Gaynor	Charles Farrell	Dulcie Gray	Michael Dennison
Florence Eldridge	Fredric March	Googie Withers	John McCallum
Elsa Lanchester	Charles Laughton	Betty Grable	Harry James
Ruby Keeler	Al Jolson	Jessica Tandy	Hume Cronyn

ACTRESSES ACTING WITH HUSBANDS OR PARTNERS (Cont)

Lilli Palmer	Rex Harrison
Kay Kendall	Rex Harrison
Rachel Roberts	Rex Harrison
Elizabeth Taylor	Richard Burton
Elizabeth Taylor	Eddie Fisher
Lauren Bacall	Humphrey Bogart
Mayo Methot	Humphrey Bogart
Virginia McKenna	Bill Travers
Ruth Chatterton	Ralph Forbes
Ruth Chatterton	George Brent
Ann Sheridan	George Brent
Betsy Drake	Cary Grant
Frances Dee	Joel McCrea
Marge Champion	Gower Champion
Janet Leigh	Tony Curtis
Christine Kaufman	Tony Curtis
Katherine Hepburn	Spencer Tracy
Bette Davis	Gary Merrill
Margaret Sullavan	Henry Fonda
Annabella	Tyrone Power
Ali MacGraw	Steve McQueen
Carole Lombard	Clark Gable
Joan Collins	Anthony Newley
Audrey Hepburn	Mel Ferrer
Jan Sterling	Paul Douglas
Jean Simmons	Stewart Granger
Wynne Gibson	William Powell
Rita Hayworth	Orson Welles
Claire Bloom	Rod Steiger
Jennifer Jones	Robert Walker
Angela Douglas	Kenneth More
Vera Miles	Gordon Scott
Anne Baxter	John Hodiak
Jill Ireland	Charles Bronson
Joanne Woodward	Paul Newman
Felicia Farr	Jack Lemmon
Lucille Ball	Desi Arnez
Maggie Smith	Robert Stephens
Simone Signoret	Yves Montand
Paulette Goddard	Burgess Meredith
Dinah Sheridan	Jimmy Hanley
Sian Phillips	Peter O'Toole
Kathleen De Mille	Anthony Quinn
Shirley Temple	John Agar
Jane Wyman	Ronald Reagan
Nancy Davis	Ronald Reagan
Madeleine Carroll	Sterling Hayden
Jeanette MacDonald	Gene Raymond
Sheila Sim	Richard Attenborough
Rachel Kempson	Michael Redgrave
Debbie Reynolds	Eddie Fisher
Meriel Forbes	Ralph Richardson
Joan Fontaine	Edmond O'Brien
Ginger Rogers	Lew Ayres
Ilona Massey	Alan Curtis
Barbara Stanwyck	Robert Taylor
Joan Crawford	Douglas Fairbanks Jnr.
Joan Crawford	Franchot Tone
Bebe Daniels	Ben Lyons
Dixie Lee	Bing Crosby
Britt Ekland	Peter Sellers
Lynne Frederick	Peter Sellers
Dianna Douglas	Kirk Douglas
Zsa Zsa Gabor	George Sanders
Phyllis Calvert	Peter Murray-Hill
Natalie Wood	Robert Wagner
Dale Evans	Roy Rogers
Anne Jackson	Eli Wallach
Rhea Perlman	Danny DeVito
Mary Ure	Robert Shaw
Judi Dench	Michael Williams
Diane Ladd	Bruce Dern
Jill Eikenberry	Michael Tucker
Sandra Dee	Bobby Darin
Sinead Cusack	Jeremy Irons
Loni Anderson	Burt Reynolds
Debra Winger	Timothy Hutton
Joanne Whalley	Val Kilmer
Patty Duke	John Astin
Rachel Ward	Bryan Brown
Annette Bening	Warren Beatty
Virginia Bruce	John Gilbert
Cher	Sonny Bono
Dolores Costello	John Barrymore
Connie Booth	John Cleese
Geena Davis	Jeff Goldblum
Greer Garson	Richard Ney
Anjelica Huston	Jack Nicholson
Goldie Hawn	Kurt Russell
Stefanie Powers	William Holden
Natasha Richardson	Liam Neeson
Ellen Barkin	Gabriel Byrne
Nicole Kidman	Tom Cruise
Melanie Griffith	Don Johnson
Meg Ryan	Dennis Quaid
Demi Moore	Bruce Willis
Winona Ryder	Johnny Depp
Victoria Tennant	Steve Martin
Judy Davis	Colin Friels
Mary Steenburgen	Malcolm McDowell
Uma Thurman	Ethan Hawke
Susan Sarandon	Tim Robbins